S0-BFC-577

ELEMENTS OF LITERATURE

ANNOTATED TEACHER'S EDITION

FIFTH COURSE

Literature of the United States

The Authors

Robert Anderson is a playwright, novelist, screenwriter, and teacher. His plays include *Tea and Sympathy; Silent Night, Lonely Night; You Know I Can't Hear You When the Water's Running;* and *I Never Sang for My Father.* His screenplays include *The Nun's Story* and *The Sand Pebbles.* Mr. Anderson has taught at the Writer's Workshop at the University of Iowa, the American Theatre Wing Professional Training Program, and the Salzburg Seminar in American Studies. He is a Past President of the Dramatists' Guild, Vice-President of the Author's League of America, and a member of the Theatre Hall of Fame. He makes his home in Connecticut and New York.

John Malcolm Brinnin, author of six volumes of poetry which have received many prizes and awards, is a member of the American Academy and Institute of Arts and Letters. He is also a critic of poetry and a biographer of poets and was for a number of years Director of New York's famous Poetry Center. His teaching career, begun at Vassar College, included long terms at the University of Connecticut and Boston University, where he succeeded Robert Lowell as Professor of Creative Writing and Contemporary Letters. Mr. Brinnin has written *Dylan Thomas in America: An Intimate Journal* and *Sextet: T. S. Eliot & Truman Capote & Others.* He divides his time between Duxbury, Massachusetts, and Key West, Florida.

John Leggett is a novelist, a biographer, and a teacher who went to the Writer's Workshop at the University of Iowa in the spring of 1969, expecting to put in a single semester. In 1970 he assumed temporary charge of the program and was its Director for the next seventeen years. Mr. Leggett's novels include *Wilder Stone, The Gloucester Branch, Who Took the Gold Away, Gulliver House,* and *Making Believe.* He is also the author of the highly acclaimed biography *Ross and Tom: Two American Tragedies.* His short fiction, articles, and reviews have appeared in *Harper's, Esquire, Mademoiselle, The Ladies Home Journal,* and the *Los Angeles Times.* A native New Yorker, Mr. Leggett now lives in San Francisco.

Gary Q. Arpin received his doctorate from the University of Virginia, where he taught for several years before taking a position with Western Illinois University at Macomb. He has written articles on John Berryman and other American poets, and has published a book, *John Berryman: A Reference Guide.* He currently is an editor at the *Reader's Digest* and lives in Katonah, New York.

Susan Allen Toth has written *Blooming: A Small-Town Girlhood,* about her childhood in Ames, Iowa, and a sequel, *Ivy Days: Making My Way Out East,* about her experiences at Smith College in Northampton, Massachusetts. She studied at the University of California at Berkeley and received her doctorate from the University of Minnesota. She currently teaches at Macalaster College in St. Paul, Minnesota. She contributes articles to many periodicals, including *Harper's, Redbook, McCalls,* and the *New York Times.*

ELEMENTS OF LITERATURE

ANNOTATED TEACHER'S EDITION

FIFTH COURSE

Literature of the United States

Holt, Rinehart and Winston, Inc.

Harcourt Brace Jovanovich, Inc.

Austin • Orlando • San Diego • Chicago • Dallas • Toronto

Sandra Cisneros has served as Consultant for the program. A graduate of the Writer's Workshop at the University of Iowa, she has written two long works of fiction—*The House on Mango Street* and *Woman Hollering Creek*— and several collections of poems, including *My Wicked, Wicked Ways*. She has taught at California State University, Chico, and now makes her home in Texas.

Nancy E. Wiseman Seminoff has served as Consultant in Reading and Questioning Strategies for the program. Dr. Seminoff is Dean, School of Education at the William Paterson College of New Jersey. She has served as a reading consultant at the secondary level and as a classroom teacher. She has published widely in national and state educational periodicals.

Richard Zahner assisted in the planning, development, and writing of the Exercises in Critical Thinking and Writing. He also reviewed critically the essays on The American Language. For many years, Mr. Zahner was Head of the English Department at Bunnell High School in Stratford, Connecticut. He also served as a reader for the Advanced Placement Examinations in English.

Printed in the United States of America

ISBN 0-03-075942-0

2 3 4 5 6 7 8 9 10 036 96 95 94 93 92

Cover: *The Brooklyn Bridge: Variation on an Old Theme* by Joseph Stella (1939). Oil on canvas, 70″ × 42″, Collection of the Whitney Museum of American Art, New York. Purchase 42.15. Photography by Geoffrey Clements, N. Y.

Page A3: *Threshing* (detail) by John Steuart Curry (c. 1935). Oil. Collection of Barbara and Steven Grossman. The Kennedy Galleries, Inc., New York.

Acknowledgments

Grateful acknowledgment is made to the teachers who reviewed materials for the 1989 edition of ELEMENTS OF LITERATURE, in manuscript or in classroom tests:

Jean Gelsinger
Ruskin Senior High School
Kansas City, Missouri

Delores Obermiller
Corpus Christi Independent School District
Corpus Christi, Texas

Geraldine Pelegano
Mountain View School
Bristol, Connecticut

Eva-Lynn Powell
Dade County Schools
Dade County, Florida

Charles I. Schuster
Seattle, Washington

Grateful acknowledgment is also made to the teachers who evaluated materials for the 1993 edition of ELEMENTS OF LITERATURE and who recommended new selections:

Kansas City, Missouri
Dr. Ula Manzo: Coordinator of Language Arts K–12, Kansas City School District; Ann Crockett: Metro Tech High School; Michael Lyons, Patricia Lyons: Southwest High School; Elizabeth M. Smith: Van Horn High School; Linda Watkins: East High School

Reno, Nevada
Joanne Walen: English/Language Arts Program Coordinator K–12; Rita Hambleton: Hug High School; Phil Harriman: Sparks High School; Olivia Martin: Reno High School; Mel Shields: McQueen High School; Beverly Wooster: Reed High School

Killeen, Texas
Phyllis Wheeler: Secondary Language Arts Consultant, Killeen Independent School District; Roberta Brooks, Debbie Prude, Barbara Teer, Veda Kay Waheed: Ellison High School; Paula Brock, Susie DeVault, Glen Martin, Bunnie Montgomery, Mark Noblitt, Debbie Siegman: Killeen High School

For permission to reprint copyrighted material in the Pupil's Edition, grateful acknowledgment is made to the following sources:

Arte Publico Press: From "Ghosts and Voices" and "Notes to a Young(er) Writer" by Sandra Cisneros from *The Americas Review,* Spring 1987. Copyright © 1987 by Sandra Cisneros. "Straw into Gold," first published under the title "A Writer's Voyage" in *The Texas Observer,* September 1987. Copyright © 1987 by Sandra Cisneros. ***Baltimore Evening Sun:*** From review by H. L. Mencken of "The Great Gatsby" from *Baltimore Evening Sun,* 1925. Copyright 1925 by the *Baltimore Evening Sun.* ***Elizabeth Barnett, Literary Executor:*** "Dirge Without Music," "First Fig," and "Recuerdo" from *Collected Poems* by Edna St. Vincent Millay. Copyright © 1922, 1928, 1950, 1955 by Edna St. Vincent Millay and Norma Millay Ellis. Published by Harper & Row Publishers, Inc. Letter 9 from *Letters of Edna St. Vincent Millay.* Copyright © 1952 by Norma Millay Ellis. Published by Harper & Brothers. ***Basic Books, a division of HarperCollins Publishers:*** From *Walt Whitman: The Making of the Poet* by Paul Zweig. Copyright © 1984 by Paul Zweig. ***Beacon Press:*** "Autobiographical Notes" from *Notes of a Native Son* by James Baldwin. Copyright © 1955 and renewed © 1983 by James Baldwin. ***Susan Bergholz Literary Services, New York, N.Y.:*** From *My English* by Julia Alvarez. Copyright © 1989 by Julia Alvarez. ***Book-of-the-Month Club:*** From "*Animal Farm* by George Orwell: A Review" by Christopher Morley from *Book-of-the-Month Club News,* 1946. ***Gwendolyn Brooks:*** From "Of De Witt Williams on His Way to Lincoln Cemetery" from *Blacks* by Gwendolyn Brooks. Copyright © 1987 by Gwendolyn Brooks. ***Cleis Press:*** "Daughter of Invention" by Julia Alvarez from *New Women's Fiction: Unholy Alliances,* edited by Louise Rafkin. Copyright © 1988 by Louise Rafkin. ***Contemporary Books, Inc.:*** From *Growing Up* by Russell Baker. Copyright © 1982 by Russell Baker. ***Delacorte Press/Seymour Lawrence, a division of Bantam Doubleday Dell Publishing Group, Inc.:*** "That Gull" from *Skin Diving in the Virgins and Other Poems* by John Malcolm Brinnin. Copyright © 1970 by John Malcolm Brinnin. "Tamar" from *Ellis Island & Other Stories* by Mark Helprin. Copyright © 1976, 1977, 1979, 1980, 1981 by Mark Helprin. ***Doubleday, a division of Bantam Doubleday Dell Publishing Group, Inc.:*** "Elegy for Jane" and from "Open House" from *The Collected Poems of Theodore Roethke.* Copyright 1941, 1950 by Theodore Roethke. From *Memoirs* by Tennessee Williams. Copyright © 1972, 1975 by Tennessee Williams. From *Inventing America: Jefferson's Declaration of Independence* by Garry Wills. Copyright © 1978 by Garry Wills. ***Dover Publications Inc.:*** From *The World's Great Speeches,* edited by Lewis Copeland and Lawrence W. Lamm. Copyright © 1942, 1973 by Copeland and Lamm, Inc.; copyright renewed © 1969 by Faye Copeland. Copyright © 1958, 1973 by Dover Publications, Inc. ***Farrar, Straus & Giroux, Inc.:*** "Winter Landscape" from *Short Poems* by John Berryman. Copyright 1940 and renewed © 1968 by John Berryman. "First Death in Nova Scotia" and "Little Exercise" from *The Complete Poems 1927–1979* by Elizabeth Bishop. Copyright © 1946, 1955, 1962, 1973 by Elizabeth Bishop; copyright renewed © 1979 by Alice Helen Methfessel. From "John Wayne: A Love Song" from *Slouching Towards Bethlehem* by Joan Didion. Copyright © 1961, 1964, 1965, 1966, 1967, 1968 by Joan Didion. From Introduction and "The Death of the Ball Turret Gunner" from *The Complete Poems* by Randall Jarrell. Copyright © 1945, 1969, 1972 by Mrs. Randall Jarrell. From *A Small Place* by Jamaica Kincaid. Copyright © 1988 by Jamaica Kincaid. "For the Union Dead" and from "Memories of West Street and Lepke" from *Selected Poems* by Robert Lowell. Copyright © 1956, 1959, 1973 by Robert Lowell. "The Magic Barrel" from *The Magic Barrel* by Bernard Malamud. Copyright 1954, © 1982 by Bernard Malamud. From "A View of the Woods" from *The Complete Stories* by Flannery O'Connor. Copyright © 1957, 1968 by the Estate of Mary Flannery O'Connor. From *The Habit of Being* by Flannery O'Connor. Copyright © 1979 by Regina O'Connor. "The Key" from *A Friend of Kafka* by Isaac Bashevis Singer. Copyright © 1970 by Isaac Bashevis Singer. Isaac Bashevis Singer's *Nobel Lecture.* Copyright © 1978 by The Nobel Foundation. English translation copyright © 1979 by Farrar, Straus & Giroux, Inc. ***Freedomways Associates:*** From "Lorraine Hansberry's Children: Black Artists and *A Raisin in the Sun*" by Woodie King, Jr., from *Freedomways* Magazine, vol. 19, no. 4, 1979. Copyright © 1979 by Freedomways Associates, Inc. ***GRM Associates, Inc.:*** "Incident," "Only the Polished Skeleton," and "Tableau" from *On These I Stand* by Countee Cullen. Copyright 1925 by Harper & Brothers; copyright renewed 1953 by Ida M. Cullen. ***Grove Press:*** From "How I Learned to Sweep" from *Homecoming* by Julia Alvarez. Copyright © 1984 by Julia Alvarez. ***Harcourt Brace Jovanovich, Inc.:*** "Argument and Persuasion" from *A Rhetoric Case Book,* Third Edition, by Francis Connolly and Gerald Levin. Copyright © 1969 by Harcourt Brace Jovanovich, Inc. "The Love Song of J. Alfred Prufrock" from *Collected Poems 1909–1962* by T. S. Eliot. Copyright 1936 by Harcourt Brace Jovanovich, Inc.; copyright © 1964, 1963 by T. S. Eliot. From *Babbit* by Sinclair Lewis. Copyright 1922 by Harcourt Brace Jovanovich, Inc.; copyright renewed 1950 by Sinclair Lewis. "The Life You Save May Be Your Own" from *A Good Man Is Hard to Find and Other Stories* by Flannery O'Connor. Copyright 1953 by Flannery O'Connor; copyright renewed © 1981 by Regina O'Connor. "The Jilting of Granny Weatherall" from *Flowering Judas and Other Stories* by Katherine Anne Porter. Copyright 1930 and renewed © 1958 by Katherine Anne Porter. From "Notes for a Preface" from *The Complete Poems of Carl Sandburg.* Copyright 1950 by Carl Sandburg; copyright renewed © 1978 by Margaret Sandburg, Helga Sandburg Crile and Janet Sandburg. "Choice: A Tribute to Martin Luther King, Jr.," from *In Search of Our Mothers' Gardens* by Alice Walker. Copyright © 1983 by Alice Walker. "A Worn Path" from *A Curtain of Green and Other Stories* by Eudora Welty. Copyright 1941 and renewed © 1969 by Eudora Welty. "The Beautiful Changes" from *The Beautiful Changes and Other Poems* by Richard Wilbur. Copyright 1947 and renewed © 1975 by Richard Wilbur. "Year's-End" from *Ceremony and Other Poems* by Richard Wilbur. Copyright 1949 and renewed © 1977 by Richard Wilbur. ***HarperCollins Publishers:*** "Homework" from *Collected Poems 1947–1980* by Allen Ginsberg. Copyright © 1989 by Allen Ginsberg. From *Dust Tracks on a Road* by Zora Neale Hurston. Copyright 1942 by Zora Neale Hurston; copyright renewed © 1970 by John C. Hurston. From "How the Lion Met the King of the World" from *Mules and Men* by Zora Neale Hurston. Copyright 1935 by Zora Neale Hurston; copyright renewed © 1963 by John C. Hurston and Joel Hurston. From "The Rookers" from *Shiloh and Other Stories* by Bobbie Ann Mason. Copyright © 1982 by Bobbie Ann Mason. "Death of a Pig" from *Essays of E. B. White.* Copyright 1947 by E. B. White. "His Father's Earth" from *The Web and the Rock* by Thomas Wolfe. Copyright 1937, 1938, 1939 by Maxwell Perkins as Executor of the Estate of Thomas Wolfe; copyright renewed © 1965 by Paul Gitlin, CTA/Administrator of the Estate of Thomas Wolfe. From *Black Boy* by Richard Wright. Copyright 1937, 1942, 1944, 1945 by Richard Wright. ***Harvard University Press and the Trustees of Amherst College:*** "Because I could not stop for Death," "A Bird came down the Walk," "Heart! We Will Forget him!," "I died for Beauty—but was scarce," "I Heard a Fly Buzz—when I died," "I never saw a Moor," "If you were coming in the Fall," from "Success is counted sweetest,"

"The Soul selects her own Society," and "Tell all the Truth" from *The Poems of Emily Dickinson,* edited by Thomas H. Johnson, Cambridge, Mass.: The Belknap Press of Harvard University Press. Copyright 1951, © 1955, 1979, 1983 by the President and Fellows of Harvard College. ***Hill and Wang, a division of Farrar, Straus and Giroux, Inc.:*** From *Night* by Elie Wiesel, translated by Stella Rodway. English translation copyright © 1960 by MacGibbon and Kee. ***Henry Holt and Company, Inc.:*** From *Israfel: The Life and Times of Edgar Allan Poe* by Hervey Allen. Copyright 1926 by Hervey Allen; copyright renewed 1954 by Ann Andrews Allen. "Indian Boarding School: The Runaways" from *Jacklight: Poems* by Louise Erdrich. Copyright © 1984 by Louise Erdrich. First appeared in *Frontiers* magazine. "The Death of the Hired Man," "Design," "Mending Wall," "Neither Out Far Nor In Deep," "Nothing Gold Can Stay," and "Once by the Pacific" from *The Poetry of Robert Frost,* edited by Edward Connery Lathem. Copyright 1923, 1928, 1930, 1939, © 1969 by Holt, Rinehart and Winston; copyright 1936, 1951, © 1956, 1958 by Robert Frost. From *Across Spoon River: An Autobiography* by Edgar Lee Masters. Copyright 1936 by Edgar Lee Masters. Copyright © 1964 by Ellen Coyne Masters. From *The Bluest Eye* by Toni Morrison. Copyright © 1970 by Toni Morrison. ***Houghton Mifflin Co.:*** "Riding the Elevator into the Sky" from *The Awful Rowing Toward God* by Anne Sexton. Copyright © 1975 by Loring Conant, Jr., Executor of the Estate of Anne Sexton. ***International Creative Management, Inc.:*** "Speaking of Courage" by Tim O'Brien from *The Massachusetts Review,* vol. XVII, no. 2, Summer 1976. Copyright © 1976 by Tim O'Brien. ***Mary Jarrell:*** From "Obscurity of the Poet" from *Poetry and the Age* by Randall Jarrell. Copyright 1951, 1953 by Randall Jarrell. ***Alfred A. Knopf, Inc.:*** From *Dispatches* (Retitled: "The Highlands," "Tell My Folks . . . ," "The Wounded," "The Correspondents," "Back Home," "Remembering the Dead," and "The War Ends") by Michael Herr. Copyright © 1977 by Michael Herr. "A Noiseless Flash" from *Hiroshima* by John Hersey. Copyright renewed 1973 by John Hersey. "Dream Deferred" (Retitled: "Harlem") from *The Panther and the Lash* by Langston Hughes. Copyright 1926 by Alfred A. Knopf, Inc., and renewed 1951 by Langston Hughes. "Harlem," "I, Too," and "The Weary Blues" from *Selected Poems of Langston Hughes.* Copyright 1926, 1948 by Alfred A. Knopf, Inc.; renewed 1954 by Langston Hughes. From "Obscurity of the Poet" from *Poetry and the Age* by Randall Jarrell. Copyright 1951, 1953 by Randall Jarrell. From *An American Procession* by Alfred Kazin. Copyright © 1984 by Alfred Kazin. From *The Woman Warrior* by Maxine Hong Kingston. Copyright © 1975, 1976 by Maxine Hong Kingston. "Spinster" from *The Colossus and Other Poems* by Sylvia Plath. Copyright © 1961 by Sylvia Plath. "Bells for John Whiteside's Daughter" from *Selected Poems, Third Edition, Revised and Enlarged* by John Crowe Ransom. Copyright 1924 by Alfred A. Knopf, Inc., and renewed 1952 by John Crowe Ransom. "Parting Without a Sequel" from *Selected Poems, Third Edition, Revised and Enlarged* by John Crowe Ransom. Copyright 1927 by Alfred A. Knopf, Inc., and renewed 1955 by John Crowe Ransom. "Anecdote of the Jar," "The Death of a Soldier," and "Disillusionment of Ten O'Clock" from *The Collected Poems of Wallace Stevens.* Copyright 1923 and renewed 1951 by Wallace Stevens. From *Letters of Wallace Stevens,* selected and edited by Holly Stevens. Copyright © 1966 by Holly Stevens. From "Of Modern Poetry" from *The Collected Poems of Wallace Stevens.* Copyright 1942 by Wallace Stevens; copyright renewed © 1970 by Holly Stevens. "Son" from *Problems and Other Stories* by John Updike. Copyright © 1973 by John Updike. From "1865: The Better Angels of Our Nature" from *The Civil War: An Illustrated History* by Geoffrey C. Ward, based on a documentary filmscript by Geoffrey C. Ward, Ric Burns, and Ken Burns. Copyright © 1990 by American Documentaries, Inc. ***Rozanne Knudson, Executor of the Literary Estate of May Swenson:*** From the Introduction by May Swenson from *Spoon River Anthology* by Edgar Lee Masters. Published by Macmillan Publishing Company. ***Lescher & Lescher, Ltd.:*** "Huckleberry Finn: The Little Lower Layer" from *Three Bags Full: Essays in American Fiction* by Philip Young. Copyright © 1952, 1972 by Philip Young. ***Little, Brown and Company:*** From *Longfellow: His Life and Work* by Newton Arvin. Copyright © 1963 by Newton Arvin. From "Why I Like Country Music" from *Elbow Room* by James Alan McPherson. Slightly abridged. Copyright © 1974 by James Alan McPherson. From "Out East" from *Ivy Days: Making My Way Out East* by Susan Allen Toth. Copyright © 1984 by Susan Allen Toth. ***Little, Brown and Company, in association with The Atlantic Monthly Press:*** From *Blue Highways: A Journey into America* by William Least Heat Moon. Copyright © 1982 by William Least Heat Moon. ***Liveright Publishing Corporation:*** "what if a much of a which of a wind" and from Introduction to *New Poems* from *Collected Poems, 1913–1962* by E. E. Cummings. Copyright © 1923, 1925, 1931, 1935, 1938, 1939, 1940, 1944, 1945, 1946, 1947, 1948, 1949, 1950, 1951, 1952, 1953, 1954, 1955, 1956, 1957, 1958, 1959, 1960, 1961, 1962 by the Trustees for the E. E. Cummings Trust; copyright © 1961, 1963, 1968 by Marion Morehouse Cummings. "nobody loses all the time" from *IS 5, poems* by E. E. Cummings. Copyright 1926 by Horace Liveright; copyright renewed 1954 by E. E. Cummings. "Summertime and the Living . . ." from *Angle of Ascent, New and Selected Poems* by Robert Hayden. Copyright © 1966, 1970, 1972, 1975 by Robert Hayden. ***Macmillan Publishing Company:*** "Poetry" from *Collected Poems of Marianne Moore.* Copyright 1935 by Marianne Moore; copyright renewed © 1963 by Marianne Moore and T. S. Eliot. ***Robert MacNeil and Reader's Digest:*** From "The Trouble with Television" delivered by Robert MacNeil at The President's Leadership Forum, State University of New York at Purchase, November 13, 1984. Originally appeared in *Reader's Digest,* March 1985. ***Ellen C. Masters:*** "Butch Weldy," "Lucinda Matlock," "Mrs. George Reece," and "Richard Bone" from *Spoon River Anthology* by Edgar Lee Masters. Published by Macmillan Publishing Company. ***McIntosh and Otis, Inc.:*** From John Steinbeck's Acceptance Speech for the Nobel Prize for literature in 1962. Copyright © 1963 by John Steinbeck. Originally published in *Vogue* Magazine, March 1, 1963. ***Merriam-Webster Inc:*** The definition "proud" from *Webster's Third International Dictionary.* Copyright © 1986 by Merriam-Webster Inc., publisher of the Merriam-Webster® dictionaries. ***James Merrill:*** "Kite Poem" from *First Poems* by James Merrill. Copyright 1950 by Alfred A. Knopf, Inc.: copyright renewed © 1978 by James Merrill. ***William Morrow Co.:*** From *Kate Chopin* by Emily Toth. Copyright © 1990 by Emily Toth. ***Ellen Neuwald, Inc.:*** From a quote by David Rabe from *Dispatches* by Michael Herr. ***New Directions Publishing Corporation:*** From "Letters to Francis Scott Fitzgerald" from *The Crack Up* by F. Scott Fitzgerald. Copyright 1945 by New Directions Publishing Corporation. "The Garden," "In a Station of the Metro," "A Pact," and "The River Merchant's Wife" from *Personae* by Ezra Pound. Copyright 1926 by Ezra Pound. "Letter to Harriet Monroe" by Ezra Pound from *Selected Letters 1907–1941.* Copyright 1950 by Ezra Pound. "The Red Wheelbarrow," "Spring and All," and "Tract" by William Carlos Williams. Copyright 1938 by New Directions Publishing Corporation. From *The Autobiography of William Carlos Williams.* Copyright 1951 by William Carlos Williams. "The Great Figure" from *Collected Poems, Volume 1: 1909–1939* by William Carlos Williams. Copyright 1938 by New Directions Publishing Corporation. ***New World Dictionaries, A division of Simon & Schuster, Inc., New York, NY:*** From *Webster's New World Dictionary of the American Language,* Second College Edition. Copyright © 1986 by Simon & Schuster, Inc. ***The New York Times Company:*** "Little Red Riding Hood Revisited" by Russell Baker from *The New York Times,* January 13, 1980. Copyright © 1980 by The New York Times Company. "School vs. Education" by

Russell Baker from *The New York Times,* September 9, 1975. Copyright © 1975 by The New York Times Company. From "Robert Frost Relieves His Mind" by Rose C. Feld, from *The New York Times Book Review,* October 21, 1923. Copyright © 1923 by The New York Times Company. From "Fitzgerald Revisited" by Jay McInerney (review of *The Short Stories of F. Scott Fitzgerald*) from *The New York Times,* Sunday Book Review, August 15, 1991. Copyright © 1991 by The New York Times Company. From "Master Republican" by Alden Todd (review of *James Madison, The Founding Father*) from *The New York Times Book Review,* December 13, 1987. Copyright © 1987 by The New York Times Company. "The Importance of Being Remembered" by Susan Allen Toth from *The New York Times Book Review,* June 28, 1987. Copyright © 1987 by The New York Times Company. ***The New Yorker:*** From "James Thurber" from *The New Yorker,* November 11, 1961. Copyright © 1961 by The New Yorker Magazine, Inc. From "Medicine of Make-Believe" by Brendan Gill from *The New Yorker,* December 12, 1983. Copyright © 1983 by Brendan Gill. ***W. W. Norton:*** "Power" from *The Fact of a Doorframe, Poems Selected and New, 1950–1984* by Adrienne Rich. Copyright © 1975, 1978 by W. W. Norton & Company, Inc.; copyright © 1981, 1984 by Adrienne Rich. Excerpt by Anne Tyler from *The Writer on Her Work,* edited by Janet Sternburg. Copyright © 1980 by Janet Sternburg. ***Harold Ober Associates Incorporated:*** "The Egg" by Sherwood Anderson. Copyright 1921 by B. W. Huebsch, Inc.; copyright renewed 1948 by Eleanor C. Anderson. From *Letters of Sherwood Anderson,* edited by H. M. Jones and Walter Rideout. Copyright 1953 by Eleanor Anderson; copyright renewed © 1981 by Eleanor Copenhaver Anderson. Published by Little, Brown and Company. ***Simon J. Ortiz:*** "Washyuma Motor Hotel" from *Going for the Rain* by Simon J. Ortiz. Copyright © 1976 by Simon J. Ortiz. ***Oxford University Press, Inc.:*** From *The Great War and Modern Memory* by Paul Fussell. Copyright © 1975 by Oxford University Press, Inc. Footnotes omitted. From *The Life of Langston Hughes, Volume I: 1902–1941* by Arnold Rampersad. Copyright © 1986 by Arnold Rampersad. ***Pantheon Books, a division of Random House, Inc.:*** "Grandmother Spider Steals the Sun" from *American Indian Myths and Legends* by Richard Erdoes and Alfonso Ortiz. Copyright © 1984 by Richard Erdoes and Alfonso Ortiz. ***Prentice Hall:*** From *The Scope of Fiction* by Robert Penn Warren and Cleanth Brooks. Copyright © 1960 by Appleton-Century-Crofts, Inc. ***Publisher's Weekly:*** Quote by E. B. White from *Publisher's Weekly,* December 6, 1971. Copyright © 1971 by Xerox Corporation. Published by R. R. Bowker Company, a Xerox company. ***The Putnam Publishing Group:*** From *The Joy Luck Club* by Amy Tan. Copyright © 1989 by Amy Tan. ***Random House, Inc.:*** "The Unknown Citizen" from *W. H. Auden: Collected Poems* by W. H. Auden, edited by Edward Mendelson. Copyright 1940 and renewed © 1968 by W. H. Auden. From "My Man Bovanne" from *Gorilla, My Love* by Toni Cade Bambara. Copyright © 1972 by Toni Cade Bambara. From *The Americans: The National Experience* by Daniel Boorstin. Copyright © 1965 by Daniel Boorstin. "A Rose for Emily" by William Faulkner from *Collected Stories of William Faulkner.* Copyright 1930 and renewed © 1958 by William Faulkner. From "William Faulkner's Speech of Acceptance upon the award of the Nobel Prize for Literature" from *The Faulkner Reader.* Copyright 1954 by William Faulkner. From *A Raisin in the Sun* by Lorraine Hansberry. Copyright © 1958 by Robert Nemiroff, as an unpublished work. Copyright © 1959, 1966, 1984 by Robert Nemiroff. Slightly adapted. "Love the Wild Swan" from *The Selected Poetry of Robinson Jeffers.* Copyright 1935 and renewed © 1963 by Donnan Jeffers and Garth Jeffers. "Shine, Perishing Republic" from *The Selected Poetry of Robinson Jeffers.* Copyright 1925 and renewed 1953 by Robinson Jeffers. From "New African" from *Sarah Phillips* by Andrea Lee. Copyright © 1984 by Andrea Lee. From *Hugging the Shore* by John Updike. Copyright © 1983 by John Updike. "Small Eternity" from *Rumor Verified: Poems 1979–1980* by Robert Penn Warren. Copyright © 1979, 1980, 1981 by Robert Penn Warren. "Is Phoenix Jackson's Grandson Really Dead?" from *The Eye of the Story: Selected Essays and Reviews* by Eudora Welty. Copyright © 1978 by Eudora Welty. From *The Glass Menagerie* by Tennessee Williams. Copyright 1945 by Tennessee Williams and Edwina D. Williams; copyright renewed © 1973 by Tennessee Williams. ***Russell & Volkening as agents for Anne Tyler:*** "Your Place Is Empty" by Anne Tyler. Copyright © 1976 by Anne Tyler. Originally appeared in *The New Yorker,* November 22, 1976. ***St. Martin's Press, Inc.:*** From *American Literature: The Makers and the Making,* Volume II, edited by Cleanth Brooks, R. W. B. Lewis, and Robert Penn Warren. Copyright © 1973 by St. Martin's Press. From "A Rose for Emily (1930)" from *American Literature: The Makers and the Making,* Volume II, edited by Cleanth Brooks, R. W. B. Lewis, and Robert Penn Warren. Copyright © 1973 by St. Martin's Press, Inc. ***The Saturday Evening Post Society:*** From "I Saw Lee Surrender" by Seth M. Flint from *The Saturday Evening Post,* vol. 248, no. 5, July/August 1976. Copyright © 1976 by The Saturday Evening Post Company. ***John Sayles:*** From "I-80 Nebraska M.490-M.205" by John Sayles from *The Atlantic Monthly,* May 1975. Copyright © 1975 by John Sayles. ***Charles Scribner's Sons, an imprint of Macmillan Publishing Company:*** "Winter Dreams" from *All the Sad Young Men* by F. Scott Fitzgerald. Copyright 1922 by Metropolitan Publications, Inc.; copyright renewed 1950 by Frances Scott Fitzgerald Lanahan. "In Another Country" from *Men Without Women* by Ernest Hemingway. Copyright 1927 by Charles Scribner's Sons; copyright renewed © 1955 by Ernest Hemingway. From "Haircut" from *Haircut and Other Stories* by Ring Lardner. Copyright 1925, 1953 by Ellis A. Lardner. ***Simon & Schuster, Inc.:*** From "Catch-22: The Great American Trap" from *Catch-22* by Joseph Heller. Copyright © 1955, 1961 by Joseph Heller. ***Sunstone Press:*** "Breath of Life" by Frank Hamilton Cushing and "Song of the Sky Loom" from *Songs of the Tewa,* translated by Dr. Herbert Joseph Spinden from *Four Winds: Poems from Indian Rituals* by Gene Meany Hodge. Copyright © 1977 by Gene Meany Hodge. ***Joan Chatfield Taylor:*** From "Cosmo Talks to Amy Tan" from *Cosmopolitan,* November 1989, p. 178. Copyright © 1989 by Hearst Corporation. ***Rosemary Thurber:*** "The Secret Life of Walter Mitty" from *My World—And Welcome to It* by James Thurber. Copyright 1942 by James Thurber; copyright © 1970 by Helen W. Thurber and Rosemary T. Sauers. ***Time Warner Inc.:*** From "Book of Changes" by Paul Gray from *Time,* December 6, 1976. Copyright © 1976 by Time Warner Inc. ***Twayne Publishers, a division of G. K. Hall & Co., Boston:*** "America" from *Selected Poems of Claude McKay.* Copyright © 1981 by Twayne Publishers, a division of G. K. Hall & Co. ***Universal Press Syndicate:*** "Coyote Finishes His Work" from *Giving Birth to Thunder, Sleeping with His Daughter: Coyote Builds North America* by Barry Lopez. Copyright © 1977 by Barry Holstun Lopez. ***University of Arizona Press:*** From "Whatever Is Really Yours" from *Survival This Way: Interviews with American Indian Poets* by Joseph Bruchac. Copyright © 1987 by The Arizona Board of Regents. All rights reserved. ***University of New Mexico Press:*** From *The Way to Rainy Mountain* by N. Scott Momaday. Copyright © 1969 by The University of New Mexico Press. First published in *The Reporter,* January 26, 1967. ***Amanda Urban as Agent for Toni Morrison:*** From *The Bluest Eye* by Toni Morrison. Copyright © 1970 by Toni Morrison. ***Viking Penguin, a division of Penguin Books USA Inc.:*** From Introduction from *Penguin Book of Contemporary Essays* by Maureen Howard. Introduction, selection, and compilation copyright © 1984 by Maureen Howard. "Go Down Death—A Funeral Sermon," "Preface" from *God's Trombones* by James Weldon Johnson. Copyright 1927 by The Viking Press, Inc., copyright renewed © 1955 by Grace Nail Johnson. From *Studies in Classic American Literature* by D. H. Lawrence. Copyright

1923 by Thomas Seltzer, Inc.; renewed 1950 by Frieda Lawrence; copyright © 1961 by The Estate of Mrs. Frieda Lawrence. From *Death of a Salesman* by Arthur Miller. Copyright 1949, © 1977 by Arthur Miller. "The Steeple-Jack" from *The Complete Poems of Marianne Moore*. Copyright 1951, © 1970 by Marianne Moore; copyright renewed © 1979 by Lawrence E. Brinn and Louise Cranee, Executors of the Estate of Marianne Moore. "The Leader of the People" from *The Red Pony* by John Steinbeck. Copyright 1933, 1937, 1938, © renewed 1961, 1965, 1966 by John Steinbeck. "Ceti" from *The Lives of a Cell* by Lewis Thomas. Copyright © 1972 by The Massachusetts Medical Society. From *Benjamin Franklin* by Carl Van Doren. Copyright 1938 by Carl Van Doren; renewed © 1966 by Margaret Van Doren Bevans, Anne Van Doren Ross, and Barbara Van Doren Klaw. ***Vintage Press, a division of Random House, Inc.:*** From *The Odyssey* by Homer, translated by Robert Fitzgerald. Copyright © 1963 by Robert Fitzgerald. ***The Washington Post:*** From "Mah-Jongg and the Ladies of the Club" by Susan Dooley from "Book World," page 7, from *The Washington Post*, March 5, 1989. Copyright © 1989 by *The Washington Post*. ***Wesleyan University Press and University Press of New England:*** "Blessing" from *The Branch Will Not Break* by James Wright. Copyright © 1961 by James Wright. "Sled Burial, Dream Ceremony" from *Poems 1957–1967* by James Dickey. Copyright © 1965 by James Dickey. ***Wylie, Aitken & Stone, Inc., as agents for the Estate of Donald Barthelme:*** "Game" from *Unspeakable Practices, Unnatural Acts* by Donald Barthelme. Copyright © 1965, 1968 by Donald Barthelme. Originally published in *The New Yorker*. ***William K. Zinsser:*** From *On Writing Well*, Third Edition, by William Zinsser. Copyright © 1976, 1980, 1985 by William K. Zinsser.

For permission to reprint copyrighted material in the Annotated Teacher's Edition, grateful acknowledgment is made to the following sources:

Columbia University Press: From *James Merrill: An Introduction to the Poetry* by Judith Moffett. Copyright © 1984 by Columbia University Press. ***Doubleday, a division of Bantam Doubleday Dell Publishing Group, Inc.:*** From *Self-Interviews* by James Dickey, recorded and edited by Barbara and James Reiss. Copyright © 1970 by James Dickey. From *Conversations with Isaac Bashevis Singer* by Isaac Bashevis Singer and Richard Burgin. Copyright © 1985 by Isaac Bashevis Singer and Richard Burgin. ***Farrar, Straus and Giroux, Inc.:*** From "The Music of Poetry" from *On Poetry and Poets* by T. S. Eliot. Copyright © 1957 by T. S. Eliot; copyright renewed © 1985 by Valerie Eliot. From "Ezra Pound" from *Poetry LXVIII*, September 1946. Copyright © 1946 by Modern Poetry Association; copyright © 1958 by T. S. Eliot. From "The Three Voices of Poetry" from *On Poetry and Poets* by T. S. Eliot. Copyright © 1957 by T. S. Eliot; copyright renewed © by Valerie Eliot. ***Harcourt Brace Jovanovich, Inc.:*** From "Notes for a Preface" from *Complete Poems* by Carl Sandburg. Copyright © 1950 by Harcourt Brace Jovanovich, Inc. ***HarperCollins Publishers:*** From *American Poetry Since 1945* by Stephen Stepanchev. Copyright © 1965 by Stephen Stepanchev. ***Houghton Mifflin Company:*** From *Name of the Land* by George R. Stewart. Copyright 1945, © 1958, and renewed © 1972 by George Stewart. ***Liveright Publishing Corporation:*** From interview with Robert Hayden from *Interviews with Black Writers*, edited by John O'Brien. Copyright © 1973 by Liveright Publishing Corporation. ***Los Angeles Times Syndicate:*** From "Of Flying Horses, Carpentry and Shakespeare" by Leslie Hanscom from *Newsday*, September 2, 1984. Copyright © 1984 by Los Angeles Times Syndicate. ***Macmillan Publishing Company:*** From *The Magic Maker: E. E. Cummings* by Charles Norman. Copyright © 1958 by Charles Norman. ***James Alan McPherson:*** From "On Becoming an American Writer" by James Alan McPherson from *The Atlantic Monthly*, December 1978. Copyright © 1978 by James Alan McPherson. ***National Geographic Society:*** From "I Am Alive" by N. Scott Momaday from *The World of the American Indian*, edited by Jules B. Billard. Copyright © 1974, 1979 by National Geographic Society, Washington, D.C. ***Princeton University Press:*** From *Wallace Stevens: A Celebration*, edited by Frank Doggett and Robert Buttel. Copyright © 1980 by Princeton University Press. ***The Sewanee Review:*** From "T. S. Eliot: Thinker and Artist" by Cleanth Brooks from *The Sewanee Review*. From "A Personal Memoir" by Robert Giroux from *The Sewanee Review*, 74, Winter 1966. Copyright © 1966 by the University of the South. ***Mark Shechner:*** From "Sad Music" by Mark Shechner. First published in *Partisan Review*. ***Shenandoah: The Washington and Lee University Review:*** From "One Answer to a Question" by John Berryman from *Shenandoah*, XVII, Autumn 1965. ***Southern Illinois University Press:*** From *John Updike: Yea Sayings* by Rachel C. Burchard. Copyright © 1971 by Southern Illinois University Press. ***Twayne Publishers, an imprint of Macmillan Publishing Company:*** From *Chicano Literature* by Charles M. Tatum, edited by Warren French. Copyright © 1982 by G. K. Hall & Co. ***University of California Press and The Regents of the University of California:*** From *Wallace Stevens: A Mythology of Self* by Milton J. Bates. Copyright © 1985 by The Regents of the University of California. ***Viking Penguin, a division of Penguin Books USA Inc.:*** From *The Story of English* by Robert McCrum, William Cran and Robert MacNeil. From *T. S. Eliot* by Stephen Spender. Copyright © 1975 by Stephen Spender.

PICTURE CREDITS Table of Contents credits appear at the end of the PICTURE CREDITS. **Unit 1** p. 3 top rt.: Culver Pictures; p. 3 bottom left: Laurie Platt Winfrey, Inc.; p. 9: The Granger Collection, New York; p. 29: The New York Public Library; p. 33: The Granger Collection, New York; p. 36: The Bettmann Archive; p. 48: Frans Lanting/Photo Researchers, Inc.; p. 55: Rare Books and Manuscripts Division, The New York Public Library, Astor, Lenox and Tilden Foundations. p. 59 top rt.: Sun or Moon symbol courtesy of the Museum of Northern Arizona, Flagstaff. **Unit 2** p. 65: Photo: Schoonover Studios, Ltd.; p. 75: The Granger Collection, New York; p. 89: The Granger Collection, New York; p. 93: The Bettmann Archive; p. 100: Independence National Historic Park; p. 109: The Granger Collection, New York. **Unit 3** p. 118: Laurie Platt Winfrey, Inc.; p. 122 top: The Bettmann Archive; p. 122 bottom: Kaari Ward; p. 124: The Max Polster Archive; p. 138: The National Academy of Design; p. 140: Bill Wilson/Photo Researchers; p. 146: The Bettmann Archive; p. 152: The Granger Collection, New York; p. 155: John Lewis Stage/The Image Bank; p. 156: The Granger Collection, New York; p. 161: The Granger Collection, New York; p. 162: Phillip N. Known/Stock, Boston; p. 165: Scott Camazzine/Photo Researchers; p. 167: The Granger Collection, New York; p. 169: Giraudon/Art Resource, New York; p. 171: Omni International; p. 173: Culver Pictures; p. 175: Murray Belsky. **Unit 4** p. 181: Culver Pictures; p. 183: The Bettmann Archive; p. 184: The Bettmann Archive; p. 185: Rebus, Inc.; p. 186: Rebus, Inc.; p. 189: The Bettmann Archive; p. 192: Art Resource; p. 197: Stuart Cohen/Stock, Boston; p. 198: Michael Gadomski, Bruce Coleman Inc.; p. 201: Margaret Durrance/Photo Researchers; p. 203: David E. Scherman; p. 210: Eliot Porter; p. 226: The Bettmann Archive; p. 229: The Granger Collection, New York; p. 235: New York Public Library, Prints Division; p. 249: Lee Boltin; p. 252: Historic New Orleans Collection; p. 253: Nimatallah/Art Resource, New York; p. 256: Photo: Antonio Frasconi; p. 263: The Bettmann Archive; p. 294: Culver Pictures; p. 295: The Lighthouse Museum, Stonington, Connecticut. **Unit 5** p. 324: Rare Books and Manuscripts Division, The New York Public Library, Astor, Lenox and Tilden

Foundations; p. 325: Culver Pictures; p. 326: The Granger Collection, New York; p. 329: Culver Pictures; p. 341: © Steven Kaufman/Peter Arnold Inc.; p. 349: The Bettmann Archive; p. 352: Culver Pictures; p. 354: Sotheby's; p. 356: Jerry L. Thompson; p. 359: Sotheby's; p. 361: © S. J. Krasemann/Peter Arnold; p. 365: International Museum of Photography at George Eastman House, Rochester, New York; p. 366: Steven J. Krasemann/Photo Researchers; p. 368: Bill Ivey/Photo Researchers; p. 369: Stephen Dalton/Photo Researchers. **Unit 6** p. 376: The New York Public Library, Rare Book Division; p. 378: The National Archives; p. 379: The Library of Congress; p. 380: International Museum of Photography at George Eastman House, Rochester, New York; p. 381: International Museum of Photography at George Eastman House, Rochester, New York; p. 384: Laurie Platt Winfrey, Inc.; p. 385: Collection of Robert Weinstein; p. 393: Culver Pictures; p. 401: Arizona Pioneer Historical Society; p. 402: The Bettmann Archive; p. 430: The Bettmann Archive; p. 439: (left) Samuel Higginbotham Orange; Photo by Larry Sherer; (right) Massachusetts Historical Society; p. 441: Library of Congress; p. 442: (knife) Museum of the Confederacy, from *The Civil War: Confederate Ordeal.* Photo by Larry Scherer. © 1984 Time-Life Books Inc. (sword) Craig Caba. Photo by Larry Sherer. (cap) Craig Nannos, from *The Civil War: Decoying the Yanks.* Photo by Larry Sherer. © 1984 Time-Life Books Inc.; pp. 442–443: (rifle) Mollus, from *The Civil War: Fight for Chattanooga.* Photo by Larry Sherer. © 1985 Time-Life Books Inc.; p. 443: (canteen) Russ A. Pritchard, from *The Civil War: Confederate Ordeal.* Photo by Larry Sherer. © 1984 Time-Life Books Inc. (shoes) Museum of the Confederacy, from *The Civil War: Confederate Ordeal.* Photo by Larry Sherer. © 1984 Time-Life Books Inc. (cap) Museum of the Confederacy, from *The Civil War: Decoying the Yanks.* Photo by Larry Sherer. © 1984 Time-Life Books Inc. (cartridges) Museum of the Confederacy, from *The Civil War: Master Index.* Photo by Larry Sherer. © 1987 Time-Life Books Inc. (purse) Howard Wert Collection, from *The Civil War: Gettysburg.* Photo by Larry Sherer. © 1985 Time-Life Books Inc. (photo, left) Atlanta Historical Society; (photo, right) Eleanor S. Brockenbrough Library, The Museum of the Confederacy, Richmond. Photo by Katherine Wetzel. (postmark) George Fistrovich; p. 445: Library of Congress; p. 446: (center) Chicago Historical Society; (bottom) Library of Congress; p. 447: Massachusetts Commandery Military Order of the Loyal Legion and the U.S. Army Military History Institute; p. 449: (left) Museum of the Confederacy, from *The Civil War: Tenting Tonight.* Photo by Larry Sherer. © 1984 Time-Life Books Inc. (right) George Fistrovich; p. 451: (left) Historical Picture Services; (right) Library of Congress; pp. 452, 452–453 bottom: Library of Congress; p. 453 top: (detail) The Lincoln Museum, Fort Wayne, Indiana, a part of Lincoln National Corporation; p. 454: (top rt.) Library of Congress; (bottom) Appomattox Court House National Historical Park, National Park Service, U.S. Department of the Interior, from *The Civil War: Pursuit to Appomattox.* Photo by Ronald Jennings. © 1987 Time-Life Books Inc.; p. 455: The Bettmann Archive; p. 456: The University of Virginia Library; pp. 458–459: Antietam Battlefield Park, from *The Civil War: Bloodiest Day.* Photo by Larry Sherer. © 1984 Time-Life Books Inc; p. 480: Missouri Historical Society. **Unit 7** p. 494: Culver Pictures; p. 496: Culver Pictures; p. 497: The New York Public Library; p. 498: David E. Scherman; p. 499: Rebus, Inc.; p. 501: Culver Pictures; p. 503: Joseph Martin/Art Resource, New York; p. 510: The Bettmann Archive; p. 513: Photographic Archives, The University of Louisville; p. 517: The Bettmann Archive; p. 525: Culver Pictures; p. 533: The Bettmann Archive; p. 536: Peter Fiore/The Image Bank; p. 543: © Liberty Collection/The Image Bank; p. 549: © Meryl Rosner/The Image Bank; p. 552: Culver Pictures; p. 553: The Granger Collection, New York; p. 559: The Berg Collection/The New York Public Library; p. 561: Doran H. Ross, Los Angeles; p. 564: Culver Pictures; p. 570: The Granger Collection, New York; p. 575: Culver Pictures; p. 576: Culver Pictures; p. 582: Culver Pictures; p. 590: The Granger Collection, New York; p. 602: AP/Wide World Photos; p. 604: Arthur Rothstein; p. 613: UPI/Bettmann Newsphotos; p. 615: Roland Freeman; p. 621: Harbaugh/Rothco Cartoons. **Unit 8** p. 628: Rapho Agence/Photo Researchers; p. 630: The Library of Congress, Manuscript Division; p. 631: © 1987, Donna Van Der Zee; p. 632: Rebus, Inc.; p. 633: The Bettmann Archive; p. 635: Giraudon/Art Resource New York; p. 638: Culver Pictures; p. 641: Christie's; p. 642: Dennis Stock/Magnum; p. 644: The Granger Collection, New York; p. 647: The Bettmann Archive; p. 649: Sotheby's; p. 652: The Bettmann Archive; p. 653: UPI/Bettmann Newsphotos; p. 654: Ross Jacana/The Image Bank; p. 657: Photo courtesy of The Museum of Fine Arts, Boston; p. 661: The New York Public Library; p. 664: Sotheby's; p. 671: D. P. Hershkowitz/Bruce Coleman, Inc.; p. 672: The Granger Collection, New York; p. 674: Private Collection; p. 676: UPI/Bettmann Newsphotos; p. 678: © Horst Schaefer/Peter Arnold Inc.; p. 680: The Granger Collection, New York; p. 682: Studio Museum, Harlem; p. 685: © 1983 Eve Arnold/Magnum; p. 688: UPI/Bettmann Newsphotos; p. 691: Photo: Chris Eden; p. 694: The Granger Collection, New York; p. 699: Fisher/Punch/Rothco Cartoons: p. 700: Rebus, Inc. **Unit 9** p. 707: Culver Pictures; p. 715: The Bettmann Archive; p. 717: Culver Pictures; p. 718: Gordon R. Gainer/The Stock Market; p. 719: Jeffrey Gove/The Image Bank; p. 721: Photo courtesy of Jay Johnson, America's Folk Heritage Gallery, New York; p. 722: Alvis Upitis/The Image Bank; p. 724: The Bettmann Archive; pp. 726–727: Nicholas DeVore III/Bruce Coleman Inc.; p. 729: The Bettmann Archive; p. 730: The Bettmann Archive; p. 735: AP/Wide World; p. 738: Photo: D. James Dee; p. 740: UPI/Bettmann Newsphotos; p. 741: Bob Rubic/Gotham Book Mart; p. 750: The Bettmann Archive, p. 751: Bob Rubic/Gotham Book Mart; p. 753: Judy Lee Wade/Rebus, Inc. **Unit 10** p. 757: The Triton Gallery; p. 759: Philip Prosen/The Image Bank; p. 762: Inge Morath/Magnum; p. 763: PLAYBILL®, Inc. Used by permission; p. 764: PLAYBILL®, Inc. Used by permission; p. 765: Culver Pictures; p. 766: PLAYBILL®, Inc. Used by permission; p. 767: Martha Swope; p. 768: The Bettmann Archive; pp. 769–805: T. Charles Erickson, The Long Wharf Theater, New Haven, Connecticut; p. 812: The Bettmann Archive; pp. 813–863: Billy Rose Theatre Collection, The New York Public Library for the Performing Arts, Astor, Lenox and Tilden Foundations. Photos by Bob Rubic. **Unit 11** p. 870: Culver Pictures; p. 871: Photo courtesy of The Phyllis Kind Gallery, Chicago; p. 886: SCALA/Art Resource, New York; p. 895: SCALA/Art Resource Inc.; p. 896: Santi Visalli/The Image Bank; p. 897: The Granger Collection, New York; p. 899: Joan Liftin/Magnum; p. 902: UPI/Bettmann Newsphotos; p. 911: © 1990 Robert Foothorap; p. 914: (top) Maria Taglienti/The Image Bank; (bottom) Whitney Lane/The Image Bank; p. 924: Culver Pictures; p. 926: N. R. Farbman/Life Picture Service; p. 934: Kelly Wise, Alfred A. Knopf; p. 936: Eric Meola/The Image Bank; p. 941: Bob Gelberg/The Image Bank; p. 942: Wide World Photos; p. 945: Roland Freeman; p. 953: Diana Walker, Alfred A. Knopf; p. 960: Alan Reininger/Contact Stock Images/Woodfin Camp; p. 969: Oliver Rebbot/Woodfin Camp. **Unit 12** p. 983: © David Hockney; p. 994: UPI/Bettmann Newsphotos; p. 998: Beverly Hall; p. 1003: Cornell Capa/Magnum; p. 1004: AP/Wide World Photos; p. 1014: Jim Kalett; p. 1015: Photo by James O. Milmoe; p. 1021: Schomburg Center for Research in Black Culture, The New York Public Library; p. 1025: Floyd K. Takeuchi, Alfred A. Knopf; p. 1028: Eve Arnold/Magnum; p. 1035: Cornell Capa, LIFE Magazine © Time-Warner, Inc.; p. 1039: Melissa Matine; p. 1040: © Jeff Reinking/Picture Group; p. 1044: Rubén Guzmán; p. 1048: The Granger Collection, New York; p. 1049: Culver Pictures; p. 1052: Shunkichi/Kikuchi/Magnum; p. 1058: © 1988 Thomas Victor; p. 1059: Leroy Massie; p. 1064: Sigrid Estrada; p. 1067: Melchior DiGiacomo/The Image Bank; p. 1070: Robert Lindholm; p. 1078: Culver Pictures; p. 1079: Culver Pictures; p. 1080: Culver Pictures; p. 1081: Schwadron/Rothco Cartoons. **Unit 13** p. 1087: Burt Glinn/Magnum; p. 1088: Rollie McKenna; p. 1092: LeRoy Woodson, Jr./Wheeler Pictures; p. 1093: Rollie McKenna; p. 1098: UPI/Bettmann Newsphotos; p. 1100: The Granger Collection, New York; p. 1102: The Bettmann Archive; p. 1103: UPI/Bettmann Newsphotos; p. 1106: R. Avery/Stock, Boston; p. 1108: Clemens Kalischer; p. 1109: © Bill O'Conner/Peter Arnold Inc.; p. 1117: Thomas Victor; p. 1119: © Rollie McKenna; p. 1122: UPI/Bettmann Newsphotos; p. 1124: © Rollie McKenna; p. 1125: SCALA/Art Resource, New York; p. 1130: © Christopher Little/Outline Press, p. 1131: © Bruce Hucko.

Table of Contents p. viii: Collection of Dr. William Greenspon. Photo: Whitney Museum of American Art; p. x: Calouste Gulbenkian Museum, Lisbon, Portugal; p. xi: Chicago Historical Society; p. xiii: Bob Gelberg/The Image Bank; p. xv: © Bruce Hucko; p. xvi: Patti McConville/The Image Bank.

CONTENTS
A Chronological Survey of American Literature

UNIT THREE:
AMERICAN ROMANTICISM

UNIT FOUR:
THE AMERICAN RENAISSANCE — FIVE MAJOR WRITERS

UNIT FIVE: A NEW AMERICAN POETRY — WHITMAN AND DICKINSON

UNIT SIX: THE RISE OF REALISM — THE CIVIL WAR AND POST-WAR PERIOD

UNIT SEVEN: THE MODERNS — THE AMERICAN VOICE IN FICTION

UNIT EIGHT: POETRY — VOICES OF AMERICAN CHARACTER

UNIT NINE: IMAGISM AND SYMBOLISM

Unit Ten: AMERICAN DRAMA

Unit Eleven: FICTION — 1945 TO THE PRESENT

Unit Twelve: MODERN NONFICTION

UNIT THIRTEEN: POETRY IN A TIME OF DIVERSITY

American Flag: A Mosaic of Faces is part of the "Peopling of America" exhibit at the Ellis Island Immigration Museum. From 1891 to 1954 this New York Harbor island was a U.S. immigration station, processing over 16 million immigrants. The island now houses a museum honoring all new arrivals, past and present, to these shores.

CONTENTS
An Organization by Themes

THEME ONE: THE PERILOUS JOURNEY AND THE QUEST

THEME TWO: OH BRAVE NEW WORLD

THEME SIX: THE CLASH OF GENERATIONS

THEME SEVEN: LOSS AND RENEWAL

THEME EIGHT: THE TRIUMPH OF LOVE

THEME NINE: THE ANTI-HERO—LOSS OF THE HEROIC

THEME TEN: THE DESTRUCTION OF INNOCENCE

THEME ELEVEN: FREEDOM VS. BONDAGE

THEME TWELVE: ROGUES VS. CONVENTIONAL TYPES

THEME THIRTEEN: WAR AND DISINTEGRATION

THEME FOURTEEN: THE POWER OF NATURE

THEME FIFTEEN: THE POWER OF THE IMAGINATION

THEME SIXTEEN: SPIRITUALITY AND THE SOUL

INTEGRATING the LANGUAGE ARTS

UNIT 1: The Colonial Period—The Age of Faith

Selection	Literary Elements	WRITING ABOUT LITERATURE: Creative Response	WRITING ABOUT LITERATURE: Critical Response	Language and Style
UNIT INTRODUCTION	Plain Style			
Of Plymouth Plantation William Bradford	Point of View Purpose	Using Another Point of View	Contrasting Two Historical Accounts	Archaic Language
ELEMENTS OF LITERATURE: THE PLAIN STYLE	Plain Style			Diction Archaic Language
A Narrative of Her Captivity Mary Rowlandson	Subjective Reporting Attitude Allegory	Using Another Point of View	Explaining an Allusion	
The Journal of Madam Knight Sarah Kemble Knight	Journal Metaphor Tone	Writing a Journal Entry	Analyzing Character	
Sinners in the Hands of an Angry God Jonathan Edwards	Sermon Purpose Figures of Speech Imagery	Adapting the Sermon Using Another Point of View		
Upon the Burning of Our House Anne Bradstreet	Extended Metaphor Writer's Attitude Meter Couplet Iamb Iambic Tetrameter		Analyzing the Writer's Attitude	The "Poetic" Style *Language Skills:* Sentence Inversion
Upon a Spider Catching a Fly Edward Taylor	Parable Rhyme	Rewriting the Poem	Comparing Spiders	Archaisms
ELEMENTS OF LITERATURE: THE CONCEIT	Conceit Paradox	Writing an Original Conceit		
God's Determinations Edward Taylor	Images Pun Paradox		Comparing the Poem with Job	Imagery: Sights, Sounds, Textures
The History of the Dividing Line William Byrd	Satire Diction		Contrasting Two Histories Analyzing the History	
A Sample of Native American Myths and Ritual Songs	Myths How-and-Why Tales Ritual Songs			*Language Skills:* Plain Style
EXERCISES IN CRITICAL THINKING AND WRITING: DETERMINING THE PRECISE MEANINGS OF WORDS	Precise Meanings Denotation Connotation		Analyzing the Meanings of Two Words or Phrases	Precise Meanings Multiple Meanings Abstract Words Etymology Archaic and Obsolete Words
Word Analogies				*Word Analogies*

All entries refer to the Pupil's Edition features *except* entries in italics, which are located in the Core Components Binder.

UNIT 2: The Revolutionary Period—The Age of Reason

Selection	Literary Elements	WRITING ABOUT LITERATURE: Creative Response	WRITING ABOUT LITERATURE: Critical Response	Language and Style
UNIT INTRODUCTION				
The Autobiography Benjamin Franklin	Character		Comparing and Contrasting Two Writers Responding to Critical Comments	American English
Sayings of Poor Richard Benjamin Franklin	Irony	Analyzing Contemporary Maxims		
The Middle Passage Olaudah Equiano	*Autobiography* *Narrative*			*Language Skills:* Transitional Expressions
Speech to the Virginia Convention Patrick Henry	Main Idea Metaphor Rhetorical Question Allusion	Reporting on the Speech	Comparing and Contrasting Speeches	
ELEMENTS OF LITERATURE: PERSUASION	Persuasion			
The Crisis, No. 1 Thomas Paine	Argument Main Idea Images Metaphor Analogy	Writing a Firsthand Account	Evaluating a Generalization	
The Autobiography: The Declaration of Independence Thomas Jefferson	Parallelism		Analyzing Its Reasoning Responding to a Point of View Responding to Changes in the Document	Precise Meanings Parallel Construction
THE AMERICAN LANGUAGE: "REVOLUTIONARY" ENGLISH				Lost Meanings of Words Americanisms American vs. British Pronunciation
EXERCISES IN CRITICAL THINKING AND WRITING: ANALYZING AND EVALUATING PERSUASION: LOGIC	Persuasion Logic Either-or Fallacy False Analogy Non Sequitur Appeal to Authority		Analyzing and Evaluating Logic	Guidelines for Evaluating an Argument Introduction Thesis Statement Body Conclusion
Word Analogies				*Word Analogies*

All entries refer to the Pupil's Edition features *except* entries in italics, which are located in the Core Components Binder.

UNIT 3: American Romanticism

Selection	Literary Elements	WRITING ABOUT LITERATURE: Creative Response	WRITING ABOUT LITERATURE: Critical Response	Language and Style
UNIT INTRODUCTION				
Rip Van Winkle Washington Irving	Characterization Theme Tone Setting Satire Stereotyped Character The Battle of the Sexes	Writing an Epilogue	Modernizing the Story Explaining a Parallel Analyzing a Conflict	Inflated Language *Language Skills:* Revision
To a Waterfowl William Cullen Bryant	Onomatopoeia Symbolism Theme		Analyzing the Poem	
Thanatopsis William Cullen Bryant	Personification Tone Imagery Metaphor Iambic Pentameter	Writing a Letter	Comparing and Contrasting Poems Analyzing Imagery and Meaning	Inverted Syntax Archaic Language
The Cross of Snow Henry Wadsworth Longfellow	Figurative Language		Responding to the Poem	
ELEMENTS OF LITERATURE: THE SONNET	Sonnet Petrarchan (Italian) Sonnet Elizabethan (Shakespearean) Sonnet			
The Ropewalk Henry Wadsworth Longfellow	Simile Imagery Metaphor Tone	Describing an Idyllic Scene		Trochaic Meter
The Tide Rises, the Tide Falls Henry Wadsworth Longfellow	Onomatopoeia Personification		Comparing and Contrasting Poems	
Snow-Bound: A Winter Idyll John Greenleaf Whittier	Imagery		Analyzing the Poem's Appeal	Allusions
Old Ironsides Oliver Wendell Holmes	Metaphor Irony Symbolism	Applying the Poem to Other Situations	Finding Contemporary Parallels	Connotations
The Chambered Nautilus Oliver Wendell Holmes	Metaphor Imagery Paraphrase	Taking Another Point of View	Responding to a "Message" Analyzing the Poem's Appeal	Archaic Words Inverted Syntax
She Came and Went James Russell Lowell	Simile Imagery Paraphrase Refrain		Comparing Two Poems on the Same Theme	

UNIT 3: American Romanticism (continued)

Selection	Literary Elements	WRITING ABOUT LITERATURE: Creative Response	WRITING ABOUT LITERATURE: Critical Response	Language and Style
A Fable for Critics James Russell Lowell	Incongruity Paradox		Summarizing a Verse	
THE AMERICAN LANGUAGE: "NOAH'S ARK": WEBSTER'S DICTIONARY				Written Grammars Spelling Reform
EXERCISES IN CRITICAL THINKING AND WRITING: RESPONDING TO LITERATURE			Responding to a Poem Planning a Response Essay	
Word Analogies				*Word Analogies*

UNIT 4: The American Renaissance—Five Major Writers

Selection	Literary Elements	Creative Response	Critical Response	Language and Style
UNIT INTRODUCTION	Transcendentalism: American Roots Symbolism			
Nature Ralph Waldo Emerson	Imagery		Comparing Two Descriptions	Paradoxes
Self-Reliance Ralph Waldo Emerson		Writing an Essay	Writing a Response	Figures of Speech Metaphor
Concord Hymn Ralph Waldo Emerson	Apostrophe Hyperbole Figurative Language	Writing a Letter	Paraphrasing the Poem	
The Rhodora Ralph Waldo Emerson	Personification Apostrophe Iambic Pentameter		Analyzing the Poem Comparing Philosophies	Inversions
The Snow-Storm Ralph Waldo Emerson	Personification Figurative Language Sensory Language		Comparing Poems	
Aphorisms Ralph Waldo Emerson				
Walden, or Life in the Woods Henry David Thoreau	Imagery Tone Subject Matter	Writing a Journal Entry Writing from Another Point of View	Developing a Topic Comparing a Poem with *Walden*	Metaphorical Style Metaphor Simile
Resistance to Civil Government Henry David Thoreau	Paradox	Taking Another Point of View	Supporting a Statement Comparing or Contrasting Two Political Statements	Precise Meanings

All entries refer to the Pupil's Edition features *except* entries in italics, which are located in the Core Components Binder.

UNIT 4: The American Renaissance—Five Major Writers (continued)

Selection	Literary Elements	WRITING ABOUT LITERATURE: Creative Response	WRITING ABOUT LITERATURE: Critical Response	Language and Style
The Masque of the Red Death Edgar Allan Poe	Imagery Climax Symbolism Allegory Allusion Theme Psychological Effect	Staging the Story Writing an Opening Sentence	Commenting on a Criticism	Emotional Effects
The Fall of the House of Usher Edgar Allan Poe	Imagery Setting Point of View Allegory	Using Another Point of View	Analyzing the Story's Effect Comparing Two Stories Analyzing the Story's Meaning	Suggestive Words Personification Adjectives and Adverbs
ELEMENTS OF LITERATURE: SYMBOLS	Symbols			
Eldorado Edgar Allan Poe	Meter Connotation Tone Symbolism			
Annabel Lee Edgar Allan Poe	End Rhyme Internal Rhyme Meter Repetition	Imitating the Poem	Comparing Poems	
To Helen Edgar Allan Poe	Simile Alliteration Rhyme Allusion Extended Simile		Analyzing the Poem	
The Raven Edgar Allan Poe	Imagery Tone Symbolism Rhyme Scheme Meter Meaning and Message Speaker Sound Effects	Describing an Alternate Setting Imitating Poe's Technique	Comparing Poems Analyzing the Poem	
ELEMENTS OF LITERATURE: SOUND EFFECTS	Trochee Internal Rhyme Alliteration Onomatopoeia			
The Minister's Black Veil Nathaniel Hawthorne	Characterization Symbolism Tone Theme Parable	Using Another Point of View	Comparing the Story to a Sermon Comparing the Story to an Essay	Archaic and Old-Fashioned Words

UNIT 4: The American Renaissance—Five Major Writers (continued)

Selection	Literary Elements	WRITING ABOUT LITERATURE: Creative Response	WRITING ABOUT LITERATURE: Critical Response	Language and Style
Rappaccini's Daughter Nathaniel Hawthorne	Ambiguity Characterization Climax Setting Irony Moral Foils Symbolic Level	Ending the Story	Analyzing the Story's Romantic Elements Comparing Stories (2) Describing Biblical Parallels	Connotations Figures of Speech
Moby-Dick Herman Melville **"Loomings"**	Point of View Foreshadowing Characterization			
"Ahab"	Figurative Language Simile Characterization			
"The Quarter-Deck"	Point of View Omniscient Point of View Character Metaphor Parody Foreshadowing			
"Moby-Dick"	Personification Imagery Attitude Symbolism	Describing an Event from Another Point of View	Comparing Ahab's Speech with Transcendental Ideas Analyzing a Character Explaining a Symbol	Names and Their Significance
Shiloh Herman Melville	Paraphrasing Irony			
Art Herman Melville			Comparing Poems	
EXERCISES IN CRITICAL THINKING AND WRITING: ANALYZING AND EVALUATING PERSUASIVE WRITING: RHETORIC	Rhetoric Rhetorical Question Hyperbole Ridicule Connotation Rhythm Repetition Parallel Structure Purpose Thesis Statement		Analyzing and Evaluating Emerson's Rhetoric	
Word Analogies				*Word Analogies*

All entries refer to the Pupil's Edition features *except* entries in italics, which are located in the Core Components Binder.

UNIT 5: A New American Poetry—Whitman and Dickinson

Selection	Literary Elements	WRITING ABOUT LITERATURE: Creative Response	WRITING ABOUT LITERATURE: Critical Response	Language and Style
UNIT INTRODUCTION	Cadence Free Verse			
I Hear America Singing Walt Whitman				
I celebrate myself . . . Walt Whitman				
ELEMENTS OF LITERATURE: FREE VERSE	Free Verse Assonance Alliteration Onomatopoeia Parallel Structure Imagery Cadence Trochaic Tetrameter			
Alone far in the wilds . . . Walt Whitman	Sensory Images Cadence Tone Attitude			
Now I will do nothing but listen . . . Walt Whitman	Catalogue Parallelism Onomatopoeia			
I understand the large hearts of heroes . . . Walt Whitman	Sentence Structure Rhythm Sensory Images Tone			
The spotted hawk swoops by . . . Walt Whitman	Purpose	Writing an Essay as a Poem	Comparing Whitman to Emerson Comparing a Poem to a Psalm	
On the Beach at Night Walt Whitman	Symbolism Imagery			
On the Beach at Night Alone Walt Whitman	Catalogue		Comparing the Poem to "Thanatopsis"	
When I Heard the Learned Astronomer Walt Whitman			Comparing Poems	
A Sight in Camp in the Daybreak Gray and Dim Walt Whitman	Setting Cadence Catalogue Tone			

UNIT 5: A New American Poetry—Whitman and Dickinson (continued)

Selection	Literary Elements	WRITING ABOUT LITERATURE		Language and Style
		Creative Response	Critical Response	
THE POEMS AS A WHOLE	Rhythm Diction Catalogue Subject Matter Tone Imagery	Writing a Free-Verse Poem	Analyzing the Ideas in the Poems Explaining the Poet's Statement Contrasting Whitman with a Fireside Poet Comparing Whitman to Taylor and Emerson Analyzing the Prose	
Heart! We will forget him! Emily Dickinson	Tone			
Success is counted sweetest Emily Dickinson	Imagery			*Language Skills:* Revision
The Soul selects her own Society Emily Dickinson	Imagery Metaphor Meter		Evaluating a Title	
ELEMENTS OF LITERATURE: SLANT RHYME	Exact Rhyme Slant Rhyme (Off-Rhyme, Half Rhyme)			
A bird came down the Walk Emily Dickinson	Simile Figures of Speech Imagery			
I died for Beauty—but was scarce Emily Dickinson	Meter Slant Rhyme Metaphor Message			
I heard a Fly buzz—when I died— Emily Dickinson	Irony Tone			
If you were coming in the Fall Emily Dickinson	Simile Tone			
Because I could not stop for Death— Emily Dickinson	Personification Irony Tone		Commenting on a Critic	
I never saw a Moor— Emily Dickinson				
Tell all the Truth Emily Dickinson	Metaphor			

All entries refer to the Pupil's Edition features *except* entries in italics, which are located in the Core Components Binder.

UNIT 5: A New American Poetry—Whitman and Dickinson (continued)

Selection	Literary Elements	WRITING ABOUT LITERATURE		Language and Style
		Creative Response	Critical Response	
Apparently with no surprise Emily Dickinson	Personification Theme Pun			
To make a prairie it takes a clover and one bee Emily Dickinson				
THE POEMS AS A WHOLE	Metaphor Imagery Theme Tone	Writing Quatrains	Analyzing a Poem Analyzing an Edited Version Comparing Poems	Diction Syntax
EXERCISES IN CRITICAL THINKING AND WRITING: COMPARING AND CONTRASTING POEMS	Subject Figurative Language Imagery Sound Effects Form Theme Meter Rhyme Free Verse Thesis Statement		Comparing and Contrasting Two Poems	
Word Analogies				*Word Analogies*

UNIT 6: The Rise of Realism—The Civil War and Post-War Period

Selection	Literary Elements	Creative Response	Critical Response	Language and Style
UNIT INTRODUCTION	Romantic Novel Realism Regionalism Naturalism Ironic View			
The Battle with Mr. Covey Frederick Douglass	Autobiography Personal Characteristics	Applying Meanings	Responding to an Idea	Metaphors
Go Down, Moses **Follow the Drinking Gourd**		Writing a Stanza	Analyzing Allusions Reporting on Other Spirituals Comparing the Spirituals to the Puritans' Writings Analyzing a Code Song	
The Outcasts of Poker Flat Bret Harte	Complications Foreshadowing Theme	Casting a Film	Comparing Depictions of the Frontier	Euphemism Irony *Language Skills:* Fragments and Run-on Sentences

UNIT 6: The Rise of Realism (continued)

Selection	Literary Elements	WRITING ABOUT LITERATURE		Language and Style
		Creative Response	Critical Response	
Life on the Mississippi Mark Twain	Catalogue Imagery Characters Metaphors	Writing an Exaggerated Boast Rewriting Dialect		Dialect Hyperbole Metaphor Incongruity Boast Digression
The Adventures of Huckleberry Finn Mark Twain	Imagery Figures of Speech Characterization Irony Symbolism Comic Tone	Imitating a Writer's Technique Writing a Journal Entry	Responding to a Critic Analyzing the Selection Evaluating "Voice"	Descriptive Language Examples of Poetic Language Use of Imagery
An Occurrence at Owl Creek Bridge Ambrose Bierce	Setting Flashback Point of View Theme	Imitating a Technique	Analyzing Suspense Responding to a Critical Comment	*Language Skills:* Misplaced and Dangling Modifiers
Voices from the Civil War	*Tone* *Style*			*Language Skills:* The Narrative Paragraph
A Mystery of Heroism Stephen Crane	Imagery Motivation Ambiguity Personification		Comparing a Poem and a Story Responding to a Critic	*Language Skills:* Adverb Phrases
The Open Boat Stephen Crane	External Conflict Internal Conflict Complication Suspense Naturalism Symbolism Point of View Omniscient Narrator	Reporting the Facts	Explaining the Theme Comparing the Story with a Poem Contrasting Two Views of Nature	*Language Skills:* Descriptive Paragraph
A Pair of Silk Stockings Kate Chopin	Characterization Motivation Symbolism Conflict	Writing the Next Scene	Comparing Stories	*Language Skills:* Prepositions, Prepositional Phrases
THE AMERICAN LANGUAGE: A PERIOD OF VOCABULARY GROWTH				Vernacular "Stump Style" Newspaper Language Loan Words New Place Names
EXERCISES IN CRITICAL THINKING AND WRITING: MAKING INFERENCES AND ANALYZING POINT OF VIEW	Motivation Character Trait Theme Point of View		Analyzing Point of View	
Word Analogies				*Word Analogies*

All entries refer to the Pupil's Edition features *except* entries in italics, which are located in the Core Components Binder.

UNIT 7: The Moderns—The American Voice in Fiction

Selection	Literary Elements	WRITING ABOUT LITERATURE: Creative Response	WRITING ABOUT LITERATURE: Critical Response	Language and Style
UNIT INTRODUCTION	Modernism Stream of Consciousness			
The Egg Sherwood Anderson	Symbolism Theme	Using Another Point of View	Analyzing Conflict	*Language Skills:* Varying Sentence Length
Babbitt's After-Dinner Speech Sinclair Lewis	Satire Irony	Answering Babbitt Updating Babbitt	Comparing and Contrasting the Speech with "Self-Reliance"	Clichés *Language Skills:* Transitional Expressions
A Wagner Matinée Willa Cather	Flashback Omniscient Narrator Theme Setting Imagery	Describing a Character	Analyzing Imagery Comparing Responses to Nature	Figures of Speech *Language Skills:* Participles and Participial Phrases
His Father's Earth Thomas Wolfe	Onomatopoeia Alliteration Poetic Devices Catalogue Imagery	Using Accumulation of Detail in a Description	Comparing Styles and Techniques	*Language Skills:* Descriptive Paragraph
Winter Dreams F. Scott Fitzgerald	Theme	Using Another Point of View	Analyzing Characterization Responding to a Critic	Paradox
In Another Country Ernest Hemingway	Characters Setting Attitude Theme	Describing a Setting	Responding to Theme	
How the Lion Met the King of the World Zora Neale Hurston	Message Irony Character Types Colloquialism Rhyme Figures of Speech	Writing a Folktale Preparing a Folktale for Performance	Comparing Tall Tales	
The Leader of the People John Steinbeck	Characterization Irony Conflict Theme	Using Another Point of View	Comparing and Contrasting Characters Comparing Themes	Simile Metaphor Personification Oxymoron Hyperbole *Language Skills:* Verbs
The Secret Life of Walter Mitty James Thurber	Setting Free Association Irony Parody Jargon		Analyzing Characters Comparing Stories	
The Jilting of Granny Weatherall Katherine Anne Porter	Epiphany Irony Ambiguity Point of View	Writing a Monologue	Comparing a Story and a Poem	Interior Monologue Stream of Consciousness *Language Skills:* Apostrophe

UNIT 7: The Moderns—The American Voice in Fiction (continued)

Selection	Literary Elements	WRITING ABOUT LITERATURE		Language and Style
		Creative Response	Critical Response	
A Rose for Emily William Faulkner	Foreshadowing Conflict Setting Narrator Symbolism	Writing a Horror Story	Analyzing a Character Analyzing Plot Sequence	*Language Skills:* Appositives, Appositive Phrases
The Life You Save May Be Your Own Flannery O'Connor	Setting Characterization Dialogue Irony Theme Effect Tone	Extending the Story	Expressing an Opinion Analyzing the Story	Connotations Figures of Speech
ELEMENTS OF LITERATURE: THE FOUR "MODES" OF FICTION	Romance Tragedy Irony Comedy			
A Worn Path Eudora Welty	Appearance Speech Behavior Character Irony Setting Theme	Extending the Story	Analyzing the Journey Responding to a Comment Analyzing Character	*Language Skills:* Varying Sentence Beginnings
THE AMERICAN LANGUAGE: AMERICAN SLANG				Slang Nonstandard English Standard English Figures of Speech in Slang Clipped Forms of Words
EXERCISES IN CRITICAL THINKING AND WRITING: MAKING GENERALIZATIONS	Generalization Theme Subject Character Key Passage		Discussing the Theme of a Short Story	
Word Analogies				*Word Analogies*

"Most of the time, we Americans have believed in progress—in the fact that our lives are getting better. We tend to view history as a narrative, with a beginning and an end."

—John Leggett, page 496

All entries refer to the Pupil's Edition features *except* entries in italics, which are located in the Core Components Binder.

UNIT 8: Poetry—Voices of American Character

Selection	Literary Elements	WRITING ABOUT LITERATURE		Language and Style
		Creative Response	Critical Response	
UNIT INTRODUCTION				
Richard Cory Edwin Arlington Robinson	Irony Tone Moral			Connotations
Miniver Cheevy Edwin Arlington Robinson	Personification Tone	Using Another Point of View Answering a Speaker	Responding to the Poems Comparing Characters	
Richard Bone Edgar Lee Masters	Analogy	Inventing Names for Characters		
Lucinda Matlock Edgar Lee Masters	Theme			
"Butch" Weldy Edgar Lee Masters	Simile Irony Tone		Comparing and Contrasting Poems	
The Haunted Oak Paul Laurence Dunbar	Symbolism Meter Rhyme Repetition Tone	Setting the Poem to Music	Analyzing Imagery	Archaic Diction
Recuerdo Edna St. Vincent Millay	Metaphor Meter Rhyme Scheme Mood			Imagery and Feelings Connotations
Dirge Without Music Edna St. Vincent Millay	Tone Rhythm Rhyme	Writing a Conversation	Responding to the Poem Comparing and Contrasting Poems	
Design Robert Frost	Simile Octave Sestet Tone Rhyme Scheme		Responding to a Critic Contrasting Three Selections Comparing Poems	
Neither Out Far nor In Deep Robert Frost	Simile Irony Symbol Tone	Revising the Poem Inventing a Melody	Comparing Literary Works Comparing Poems	
Birches Robert Frost	Metaphor Onomatopoeia Simile Symbol Parable	Reading Nature	Comparing Writings Comparing Attitudes Responding to the Poem	
Mending Wall Robert Frost	Simile Symbol	Changing the Poem's Voice	Comparing Poems	
Once by the Pacific Robert Frost	Personification Title Symbol		Comparing Poems	

UNIT 8: Poetry—Voices of American Character (continued)

Selection	Literary Elements	WRITING ABOUT LITERATURE: Creative Response	WRITING ABOUT LITERATURE: Critical Response	Language and Style
The Death of the Hired Man Robert Frost	Imagery Setting Character Irony Message	Extending the Poem	Analyzing Characters	Blank Verse
Nothing Gold Can Stay Robert Frost	Allusion Symbol Rhyme Rhythm Alliteration Slant Rhyme Sound Echoes Tone	Paraphrasing	Comparing Poems	
Bells for John Whiteside's Daughter John Crowe Ransom	Simile Tone			
Parting, Without a Sequel John Crowe Ransom	Conflict Symbol Rhyme		Comparing Poems (2) Filling In Meanings Responding to a Critic	Multiple Meanings of Words
Shine, Perishing Republic Robinson Jeffers	Implied Metaphor Tone			
Love the Wild Swan Robinson Jeffers	Sestet Symbol Extended Metaphor	Rephrasing a Poem	Responding to the Poem	Exact Rhyme Slant Rhyme
Go Down Death James Weldon Johnson	Simile Symbolism	Extending the Poem	Comparing Sermons Comparing and Contrasting Poems	Free Verse and the Orator's Style
America Claude McKay	Personification Imagery Paradox	Capturing the Poet's Feelings	Comparing and Contrasting Poems	
Harlem Langston Hughes		Writing a News Report	Comparing Poems	
I, Too Langston Hughes	Tone			
The Weary Blues Langston Hughes	Mood Alliteration Onomatopoeia Imagery Simile	Creating Music for a Poem	Comparing the Voices in Two Poems Comparing Poems	
Tableau Countee Cullen	Metaphor			

All entries refer to the Pupil's Edition features *except* entries in italics, which are located in the Core Components Binder.

UNIT 8: Poetry—Voices of American Character (continued)

Selection	Literary Elements	WRITING ABOUT LITERATURE: Creative Response	WRITING ABOUT LITERATURE: Critical Response	Language and Style
Incident Countee Cullen	Ironic Overtones	Writing Dialogue Planning a Screen-play Setting the Poem to Music	Comparing Poems	
THE AMERICAN LANGUAGE: AMERICAN DIALECTS				Dialect Three Major Dialect Regions Dialects and Characterization
EXERCISES IN CRITICAL THINKING AND WRITING: INTERPRETING AND RESPONDING TO A POEM	Connotations Imagery Subject Main Idea Tone Feeling		Interpreting and Responding to a Poem	
Word Analogies				*Word Analogies*

UNIT 9: Imagism and Symbolism

Selection	Literary Elements	Creative Response	Critical Response	Language and Style
UNIT INTRODUCTION	Symbolism Revelation Imagism Haiku Imagery Free Verse			
The River-Merchant's Wife: A Letter Ezra Pound	Imagery Mood			*Language Skills:* Diction
ELEMENTS OF LITERATURE: THE OBJECTIVE CORRELATIVE	Objective Correlative			
The Garden Ezra Pound	Simile Pun	Creating an Image	Explaining Images	
The Red Wheelbarrow William Carlos Williams				
The Great Figure William Carlos Williams	Metaphor Imagery			
Tract William Carlos Williams	Main Idea			

UNIT 9: Imagism and Symbolism (continued)

Selection	Literary Elements	WRITING ABOUT LITERATURE		Language and Style
		Creative Response	**Critical Response**	
Spring and All William Carlos Williams	Imagery Paradox	Retitling Poems	Analyzing a Poem	
The Steeple-Jack Marianne Moore	Syllables Rhyme Scheme Imagery Tone	Imitating the Poet's Technique	Comparing the Poem to a Prose Text	Precise Meanings of Words
Chicago Carl Sandburg	Epithet Imagery Parallelism	Writing an Apostrophe	Comparing and Contrasting Poems	
Limited Carl Sandburg	Paradox Main Idea Irony			
nobody loses all the time E. E. Cummings	Irony Title	Writing in Cummings's Style	Comparing and Contrasting Poems	
what if a much of a which of a wind E. E. Cummings	Imagery Rhyme Scheme Slant Rhyme		Comparing Poems Comparing the Poems to a Statement	Diction
The Love Song of J. Alfred Prufrock T. S. Eliot	Simile Imagery Extended Metaphor Setting Irony Paraphrase	Writing a Dialogue Imitating Eliot's Style	Evaluating a Character Comparing Characters Responding to a Critic Supporting a Premise	Rhythms Rhymes Metaphors Allusions
The Death of a Soldier Wallace Stevens	Symbolism Elegy			
Anecdote of the Jar Wallace Stevens	Symbolism		Comparing Poems Analyzing the Poem's Message	Precise Meanings Diction
EXERCISES IN CRITICAL THINKING AND WRITING: ANALYZING A POEM	Subject Tone Imagery Figures of Speech Symbolism Feelings Rhyme Meter Sound Effects Title		Analyzing a Poem	
Word Analogies				*Word Analogies*

All entries refer to the Pupil's Edition features *except* entries in italics, which are located in the Core Components Binder.

UNIT 10: American Drama

Selection	Literary Elements	WRITING ABOUT LITERATURE		Language and Style
		Creative Response	**Critical Response**	
UNIT INTRODUCTION	Protagonist External Conflict Internal Conflict Exposition Realism Expressionism			
The Glass Menagerie Tennessee Williams **Scenes 1 and 2**	"Theater Poetry"			*Language Skills:* Revision
Scenes 3 and 4	Conflict			
Scenes 5 and 6	Dramatic Situation Surprise Suspense Characterization			
Scene 7	Dramatic Elements Progression			
THE PLAY AS A WHOLE	Symbolism Climax	Extending the Play	Responding to the Play Commenting on "Biographical Criticism" Evaluating Different Versions of the Play Describing the Use of Lights Comparing the Play to the Memoirs	
A Raisin in the Sun Lorraine Hansberry **Act One**	Conflict Characterization			*Language Skills:* Revision
Act Two	Characterization Reversals			
Act Three	Climax Symbol Stage Directions Dynamic Character Static Character Theme Suspense Reversal			
THE PLAY AS A WHOLE		Extending the Play	Responding to the Characters Evaluating the Play	

UNIT 10: American Drama (continued)

Selection	Literary Elements	WRITING ABOUT LITERATURE		Language and Style
		Creative Response	Critical Response	
EXERCISES IN CRITICAL THINKING AND WRITING: EVALUATING A PLAY	Characters Motivation Plot Conflict Suspense Unity Coherence Climax Subplot Theme Setting Mood		Evaluating a Play	
Word Analogies				*Word Analogies*

UNIT 11: Fiction—1945 to the Present

Selection	Literary Elements	Creative Response	Critical Response	Language and Style
UNIT INTRODUCTION				
The Key Isaac Bashevis Singer	Setting Conflict Foreshadowing Figurative Language Comedy Omniscient Narrator Point of View Theme	Adopting Another Point of View	Analyzing the Theme Relating the Speech to the Story Comparing Stories	Imagery *Language Skills:* Active and Passive Voice
The Magic Barrel Bernard Malamud	Paradox Theme Plot	Extending the Story	Comparing Two Stories Responding to a Critic	*Language Skills:* Adjective Clauses
Son John Updike	Theme Tone	Imitating the Story's Structure	Analyzing the Writer's Method	A "Pictorial" Style Simile Personification *Language Skills:* Varying Sentence Structure
Daughter of Invention Julia Alvarez	Aphorism Title Theme Climax Characterization	Writing a Character's Speech	Analyzing Conflict	*Language Skills:* Diction

All entries refer to the Pupil's Edition features *except* entries in italics, which are located in the Core Components Binder.

UNIT 11: Fiction—1945 to the Present (continued)

Selection	Literary Elements	WRITING ABOUT LITERATURE		Language and Style
		Creative Response	Critical Response	
Rules of the Game Amy Tan	Characterization Conflict Motivation Title		Responding to a Critic Putting the Characters in Different Stories	The "Language" of Games *Language Skills:* Irregular Verbs
Game Donald Barthelme	Narrator Setting Conflict Resolution Repetition Theme Title	Writing the Beginning of a Story Extending the Story	Comparing the Story to a Poem	*Language Skills:* Pronoun-Antecedent Agreement
ELEMENTS OF LITERATURE: SATIRE	Satire Irony Hyperbole Incongruity Fantasy			
Tamar Mark Helprin	Paradox	Writing a Journal Entry	Explaining a Statement Responding to a Title	Simile Personification Metaphor Irony *Language Skills:* Adverb Clauses
Speaking of Courage Tim O'Brien	Setting Symbolism Irony Internal Conflict	Inventing an Interview	Comparing Stories	*Language Skills:* Commas
Why I Like Country Music James Alan McPherson	Conflict Comedy Tone	Writing a Characterization	Analyzing a Character Analyzing Humor	*Language Skills:* Noun Clauses
Your Place Is Empty Anne Tyler	Flashback Conflict Tone Theme	Taking Another Point of View	Comparing Two Stories Responding to the Story	*Language Skills:* End Marks
New African Andrea Lee	Setting Resolution Characterization Conflict Title Themes	Imitating the Writer's Style	Analyzing Character Making Generalizations About the Stories	*Language Skills:* Appositives and Appositive Phrases
THE AMERICAN LANGUAGE: EUPHEMISMS				Euphemism Vulgar Speech Latinate Words Anglo-Saxon Words Distortion
EXERCISES IN CRITICAL THINKING AND WRITING: EVALUATING A STORY'S ENDING	Foreshadowing		Analyzing the Ending of a Story	
Word Analogies				*Word Analogies*

UNIT 12: Modern Nonfiction

Selection	Literary Elements	WRITING ABOUT LITERATURE		Language and Style
		Creative Response	Critical Response	
UNIT INTRODUCTION				
Death of a Pig E. B. White	Hyperbole Purpose Theme	Imitating White's Technique	Analyzing Style Describing a Character Explaining Allusion	*Language Skills:* Clauses
Ceti Lewis Thomas		Expressing Your Point of View	Evaluating the Essay	*Language Skills:* Semicolons and Colons
Little Red Riding Hood Revisited Russell Baker	Irony Slang Jargon Pleonasm Euphemism Satire	Imitating Baker's Technique		Jargon Cliché
School vs. Education Russell Baker	Satire Hyperbole Theme	Answering the Writer	Supporting an Assertion with Examples	Irony *Language Skills:* Parallel Structure
Black Boy Richard Wright	Imagery Characterization	Experimenting with Point of View	Comparing and Contrasting Two Writers	Dialogue *Language Skills:* Coordinating Conjunctions
The Way to Rainy Mountain N. Scott Momaday	Imagery Symbol Mood Elegy	Writing a Description	Analyzing Atmosphere Responding to a Statement	Poetic Prose Figures of Speech Imagery Implied Comparison Metaphor Simile Personification *Language Skills:* Adjectives
Autobiographical Notes James Baldwin	Tone	Writing a Response		*Language Skills:* Repetition and Wordiness
The Girl Who Wouldn't Talk, from **The Woman Warrior** Maxine Hong Kingston			Analyzing a Character	Imagery Feelings *Language Skills:* Prepositions and Prepositional Phrases
Out East, from **Ivy Days** Susan Allen Toth	Characterization Stereotypes	Imitating Toth's Technique Changing the Point of View	Developing a Statement Evaluating Objectivity	*Language Skills:* Spelling Demons
Choice: A Tribute to Dr. Martin Luther King, Jr. Alice Walker	Paradox	An Oral Presentation		*Language Skills:* Subordinate Clauses

All entries refer to the Pupil's Edition features *except* entries in italics, which are located in the Core Components Binder.

UNIT 12: Modern Nonfiction (continued)

Selection	Literary Elements	WRITING ABOUT LITERATURE: Creative Response	WRITING ABOUT LITERATURE: Critical Response	Language and Style
Straw into Gold: The Metamorphosis of the Everyday Sandra Cisneros	Imagery Figures of Speech Metaphor Purpose Main Idea		Identifying the Main Idea	*Language Skills:* Weak Words and Clichés
A Noiseless Flash, from **Hiroshima** John Hersey	Imagery Human Interest Characterization Irony Attitude		Analyzing Suspense Classifying a Literary Work Evaluating the Report	Japanese Terms *Language Skills:* Infinitives and Infinitive Phrases
Dispatches Michael Herr		Assessing the Impact of an Essay	Comparing and Contrasting Two Writers Analyzing a Writer's Personality Analyzing Women's Roles	
A Small Place Jamaica Kincaid	Tone Irony Satire Theme	Taking Your Readers on a Tour		*Language Skills:* The Descriptive Paragraph
Blue Highways William Least Heat Moon	Concrete Detail Imagery Expressions Proverbs	Writing an Essay About Place Names	Describing the Writer's Character Comparing and Contrasting Literary Journeys	Metaphor *Language Skills:* Nouns
THE AMERICAN LANGUAGE: HIGH TECH'S INFLUENCE				Railroad Terms Adopting Specialized Vocabulary for General Use Metaphor Modern Terms with Greek Roots Acronyms Aeronautical Terms Space and Computer Jargon
EXERCISES IN CRITICAL THINKING AND WRITING: EVALUATING NONFICTION: FACT AND OPINION	Fact Opinion Purpose Audience Research Evidence Tone Feelings		Distinguishing Between Fact and Opinion Evaluating Nonfiction	
Word Analogies				*Word Analogies*

UNIT 13: Poetry in a Time of Diversity

Selection	Literary Elements	WRITING ABOUT LITERATURE		Language and Style
		Creative Response	Critical Response	
UNIT INTRODUCTION	Modernist Poetry Confessional Poetry			
Elegy for Jane Theodore Roethke	Figures of Speech Tone		Comparing Poems	
"Summertime and the Living . . ." Robert Hayden	Imagery Irony Tone	Giving an Oral Reading	Analyzing the Poem	
First Death in Nova Scotia Elizabeth Bishop	Imagery Rhetorical Question Tone			
Little Exercise Elizabeth Bishop	Simile Personification	Imitating the Writer's Technique	Comparing Poems	Multiple Meanings
The Death of the Ball Turret Gunner Randall Jarrell			Writing from Another Point of View	
Of De Witt Williams on His Way to Lincoln Cemetery Gwendolyn Brooks	Irony Tone	Preparing a Choral Reading		
For the Union Dead Robert Lowell	Imagery Metaphor Tone	Writing a Description	Comparing and Contrasting Poems	
The Beautiful Changes Richard Wilbur	Paraphrase			
Year's End Richard Wilbur	Problem Imagery Paradox		Analyzing the Poems	Sound Effects Rhyme Scheme Internal Rhyme Meter Alliteration Assonance
Sled Burial, Dream Ceremony James Dickey	Metaphor Simile			
Kite Poem James Merrill	Internal Rhyme Alliteration	Taking Another Point of View		
Power Adrienne Rich	Irony		Analyzing the Poem	
Spinster Sylvia Plath	Symbolism Metaphor			Multiple Meanings

All entries refer to the Pupil's Edition features *except* entries in italics, which are located in the Core Components Binder.

UNIT 13: Poetry in a Time of Diversity (continued)

Selection	Literary Elements	WRITING ABOUT LITERATURE		Language and Style
		Creative Response	Critical Response	
Riding the Elevator into the Sky Anne Sexton		Describing Images	Writing a Comparison	
Winter Landscape John Berryman		Imitating the Poet's Technique		
A Blessing James Wright	Anthropomorphism Metamorphosis		Comparing Two Writers	
Indian Boarding School: The Runaways Louise Erdrich	Diction Imagery		Responding to a Remark by the Poet	
How I Learned to Sweep Julia Alvarez	Rhyme Meter		Analyzing an Image Comparing Poems	
Homework Allen Ginsberg	Metaphor Tone Title Main Idea Repetition Rhythm Rhyme Figurative Language	Imitating the Writer's Technique	Evaluating the Poem	
EXERCISES IN CRITICAL THINKING AND WRITING: EVALUATING A POEM	Controlling Idea Imagery Figures of Speech		Analyzing and Evaluating a Poem	
Word Analogies				*Word Analogies*

> **In the decade that witnessed the beginnings of the American civil rights movement, [James] Baldwin's audacious, searing scrutiny of racial injustice played a major role in forcing leaders, black and white, to come to terms with the nation's most anguishing problem: the treatment of black Americans.''**
>
> **—Susan Allen Toth, page 1021**

Literature and Language Exercises

Selection	Literary Elements	WRITING ABOUT LITERATURE		Language and Style
		Creative Response	Critical Response	
Literature and Language: Using Pronouns and Antecedents Correctly (Toni Morrison)		Writing a Response to the Selection		Pronouns Personal Pronouns Possessive Forms Antecedents Vague Use of Pronouns
Literature and Language: Combining Sentences (Arnold Rampersad)		Writing a Biographical Sketch		Combining Sentences Simple Sentences Coordinating Conjunctions Subordinate Clauses Independent Clauses
Literature and Language: Correcting Sentence Fragments (Joan Didion)		Describing a Movie Star or Character		Sentence Sentence Fragments Dependent Clauses
Literature and Language: Using Commas Correctly (Elie Wiesel)		Changing Sentence Style		Commas Independent Clause Comma Splice Nonrestrictive Elements Restrictive Elements Items in a Series
Literature and Language: Using the Descriptive and Narrative Modes (Julia Alvarez)	Description Mood Emotion Tone Narration Chronological Order	Writing a Character Sketch Changing the Tone		Descriptive Words and Phrases
Literature and Language: Using the Expository and Persuasive Aims (Robert MacNeil)	Exposition Persuasion Opinion	Writing a Rebuttal		Facts Examples Opinions
Literature and Language: Using the Persuasive Aim (Tecumseh)	Persuasion Intellectual Argument Emotional Appeal	Persuading Others to Your Way of Thinking Answering Tecumseh		Persuasion
Literature and Language: Using Effective Diction (Robert Penn Warren)		Describing a Feeling Describing Faces		Diction Precise Words Vivid Words Metaphor Connotations Oxymoron

All entries refer to the Pupil's Edition features *except* entries in italics, which are located in the Core Components Binder.

SUPPLEMENTARY SUPPORT MATERIALS: UNIT ONE

1. Unit Introduction Test *(CCB)*
2. Word Analogies Test *(CCB)*
3. Unit Review Test *(CCB)*
4. Critical Thinking and Writing Test *(CCB)*
5. Instructional Overhead Transparencies

A. Discussing the Quotation Students should be encouraged to remember the phrase "city upon a hill," for it illustrates the Puritans' outlook on their coming to the New World. As one would expect, the phrase comes from the Bible, Matthew 5:14, in the Sermon on the Mount—"Ye are the light of the world. A city that is set on a hill cannot be hid."

B. Humanities Connection: Responding to the Fine Art ? This watercolor was painted in the nineteenth century. In what ways might you expect a painting of Christopher Columbus's landing in the "New World" done today to differ? (Answers will vary. This painting is more a patriotic representation of the landing than an attempt to capture real events. A contemporary artist might be more interested in realistic detail.)

THE COLONIAL PERIOD THE AGE OF FAITH

by **Gary Q. Arpin**

A

For we must consider that we shall be as a city upon a hill, the eyes of all people are upon us. So that if we shall deal falsely with our God in this work we have undertaken, and so cause Him to withdraw His present help from us, we shall be made a story and a by-word through the world: we shall open the mouths of enemies to speak evil of the ways of God and all professors for God's sake; we shall shame the faces of many of God's worthy servants, and cause their prayers to be turned into curses upon us, till we be consumed out of the good land whither we are going.

—from a sermon preached on the way to the New World, spring 1630, by John Winthrop

The Europeans Visit the New World

B

Christopher Columbus Landing on the Island of San Salvadore by an unknown artist (19th century). Watercolor.

New York State Historical Association, Cooperstown.

The adventurers came first. They landed their ships on the beaches of the unexplored continent and, sometimes foolheartedly, marched into the wilderness. Some survived to record their adventures. Many never came out alive.

In 1528, only 36 years after Columbus first sighted that flickering fire on the beach of San Salvadore, a Spaniard named Alvar Nuñez Cabeza de Vaca landed with an expedition (he was its treasurer) near the entrance to Tampa Bay, on the west coast of what is now called Florida. (Cabeza De Vaca's curious name, meaning "cow's head," was his mother's. It was bestowed on one of her ancestors by the king of Spain, after the man had guided the king's army through a pass marked with a cow's skull.) De Vaca and others left the ships and marched inland. The fleet waited a year for the expedition to return. When it didn't, the boats turned around and sailed for Mexico, giving the explorers up for dead.

De Vaca and the others were lost in the wilderness, at times held captive by native groups, but they were not dead. De Vaca himself would spend the next eight years walking around what is now Texas, New Mexico, and Arizona, trying to find fellow explorers who might help him get home.

De Vaca's narrative of his incredible hardships is a gripping adventure story; it is also a firsthand account of the habits of the natives of the American wilderness—de Vaca records what the natives ate (very little), how they housed themselves, and what their religious beliefs were. De Vaca also provides the first account of some animals and plants that Europeans had never known existed. The opossum, for example, first enters the historical record with de Vaca's narrative.

Here is part of de Vaca's account of the expedition's experiences with a tribal group in Florida.

THE COLONIAL PERIOD
THE AGE OF FAITH

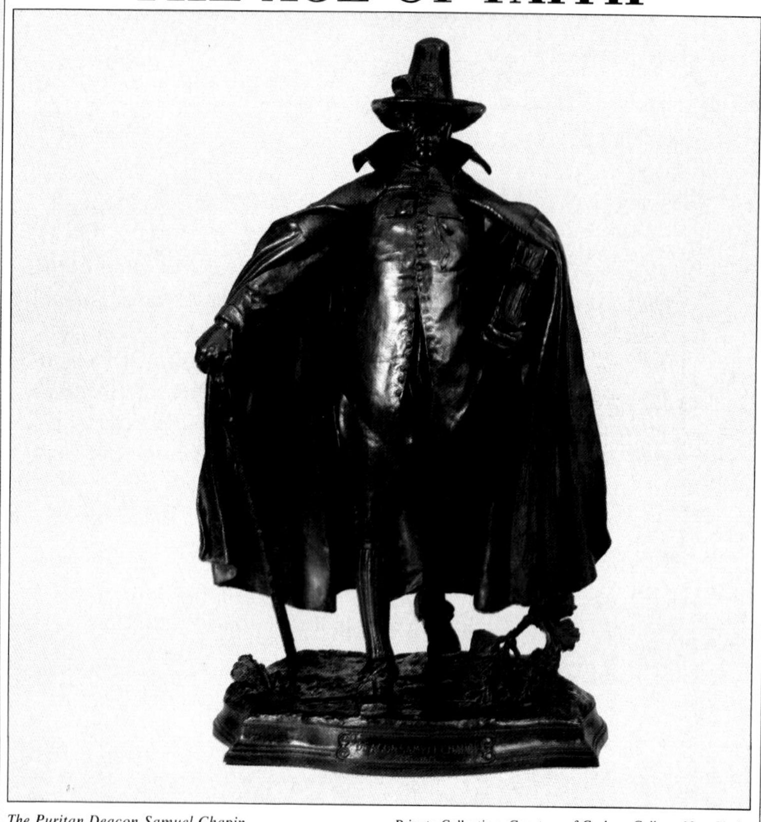

The Puritan Deacon Samuel Chapin by Augustus Saint-Gaudens (1899). Bronze. Private Collection. Courtesy of Graham Gallery, New York.

UNIT ONE

Humanities Connection: Responding To The Fine Art

Augustus Saint-Gaudens (1848–1907), one of America's greatest sculptors, was born in Dublin, Ireland. He trained at the Ecole des Beaux-Arts, Paris, and studied in Italy. Emigrating to the United States, he created the famous statue of Admiral Farragut for Madison Square, New York City, in 1881, and later the General Sherman statue at the entrance to Central Park.

? What generalizations can you make about the Puritan "spirit" from this statue? (Answers will vary. Students might note the dignity and pride reflected in the deacon's bearing. The Puritans' faith is reflected in the massive Bible and steadfast stance.)

Teaching the Colonial Period

Teaching American literature chronologically—beginning at the beginning—presents an obvious challenge. The nation's earliest literature is not the fast-paced prose or engaging poetry of later years. Instead, it consists mainly of serious-minded journals, sermons, personal narratives, religious poetry, and histories, all written in a language that may seem archaic and rather difficult

In spite of these obstacles, the literature of the Colonial period is important to students, for it introduces them to a way of thinking and living—the Puritan ethic—that has shaped many of our values and that continues to affect our lives. With this unit, it is especially important to provide a historical context for the literature. The unit introduction in the student text (pages 2–10) and the background information on the authors and the selections provide students with a much needed overview of Puritan history and beliefs.

This unit concentrates on the Puritans of New England, because the Puritans, inward-looking and industrious, were America's principal writers of the pre-Revolutionary period. Of the seven writers featured in this unit, six are New Englanders, five of whom are deeply religious Puritans who provide us with the subtitle for the unit—the Age of Faith. Well-educated Southern planters, sophisticated though they were, produced little writing of permanent interest. A notable exception was the Virginia planter William Byrd, whose witty and graceful writing closes the unit.

Objectives of the Colonial Period Unit

1. To improve reading proficiency and expand vocabulary
2. To gain exposure to notable colonial writers and their works
3. To define and identify significant literary techniques
4. To define and identify elements of poetry and nonfiction
5. To interpret and respond to poetry and nonfiction, orally and in writing
6. To practice the following critical thinking and writing skills
   a. Analyzing a writer's attitude
   b. Comparing and contrasting historical accounts
   c. Interpreting an allusion
   d. Analyzing character
   e. Comparing and contrasting the use of metaphors
   f. Analyzing the use of imagery and the conceit
   g. Interpreting metaphor

A. Expansion
Students should understand that the text on this page is from the Spaniard Cabeza de Vaca's account of his travels in what is now Florida. De Vaca's adventures preceded John Winthrop's voyage to the New World by more than a century.

Their support is principally roots, of two or three kinds, [A] and they look for them over the face of all the country. The food is poor and gripes the persons who eat it. The roots require roasting two days: many are very bitter, and withal difficult to be dug. They are sought the distance of two or three leagues, and so great is the want these people experience, that they cannot get through the year without them. Occasionally they kill deer, and at times take fish; but the quantity is so small and the famine so great, that they eat spiders and the eggs of ants, worms, lizards, salamanders, snakes, and vipers that kill whom they strike; and they eat earth and wood, and all that there is, the dung of deer, and other things that I omit to mention; and I honestly believe that were there stones in that land they would eat them. They save the bones of the fishes they consume, of snakes and other animals, that they may afterwards beat them together and eat the powder. The men bear no burthens, nor carry anything of weight; such are borne by women and old men who are of the least esteem. . . . The women work very hard, and do a great deal; of the twenty-four hours they have only six of repose; the rest of the night they pass in heating the ovens to bake those roots they eat. At daybreak they begin to dig them, to bring wood and water to their houses and get in readiness other things that may be necessary. . . .

Their houses are of matting, placed upon four hoops. They carry them on the back, and remove every two or three days in search of food. Nothing is planted for support. They are a merry people, considering the hunger they suffer; for they never cease, notwithstanding, to observe their festivities and

B

Earliest picture of an American bison from Gomara's *Historia General de las Indias* (1554). Woodcut.

"I honestly believe that were there stones in the land they would eat them."
—Cabeza de Vaca

C

Spanish Frontier Guard by an unknown artist (17th century). Watercolor.

Archivo de Indias, Seville, Spain.

B. Humanities Connection: Responding to the Fine Art
? How does the earliest drawing of an American bison differ from an actual bison? (The head is too small in proportion to the body. The body is too long. The hump is too far back. The legs are too large. The horns are too close together.)

C. Humanities Connection: Responding to the Fine Art (Challenging)
? What effect did the Spaniards' introduction of the horse have on the lives of Native Americans of the Great Plains? (By making buffalo [bison] hunting possible, it permitted formerly settled tribes to venture farther onto the plains for their livelihood. In the process the tribes became nomadic. The men became skilled horsemen, making them harder for Europeans to subdue.)

A. Humanities Connection: Discussing the Fine Art
If students have never heard of the Florida coachwhip snake, have them check the entry for *racer* in an encyclopedia. The coachwhip is one variety of racer.

William Bartram (1739–1823), a naturalist, is known primarily for his book *Travels,* an illustrated account of his journey in the southeastern United States. His descriptions of the plants and animals of the region influenced the writings of William Wordsworth and Samuel Taylor Coleridge, among others.

B. Responding
De Vaca writes that the Florida natives "appear to have the affliction of holy Lazarus." **?** Who was Lazarus and what was his affliction? (There are two Lazaruses in the Bible. The one de Vaca means was a beggar "full of sores." Luke 16:19–25)

C. Humanities Connection: Discussing the Fine Art
John White (?–1593), an artist, mapmaker, and explorer, accompanied the Roanoke Island expedition. His specific task was to record pictures of the flora and fauna of the New World. Seventy-five of his watercolors survive.

White labeled the painting on this page "Allagatto" and noted, "This being but one moneth old was 3 foote 4 ynches in length and lyue in water." Actually, the animal appears to be a baby crocodile.

A

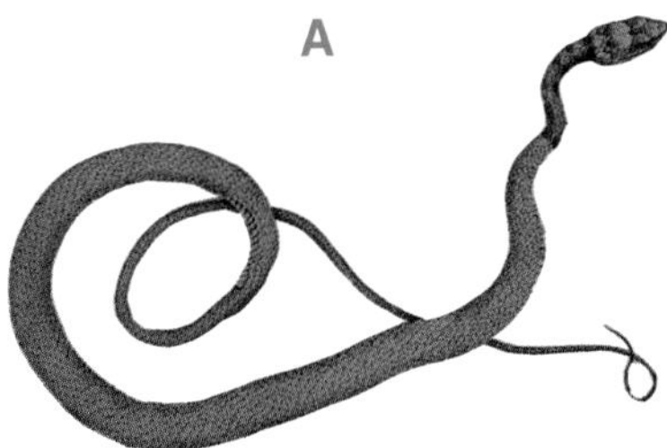

Florida Coachwhip Snake by William Bartram (1769). Watercolor.

Botanical Library, American Museum of Natural History, New York City.

Florida Alligator by John White (1585). Watercolor.

The British Museum, London.

C

areytos [ceremonial songs and dances]. To them the happiest part of the year is the season of eating prickly pears; they have hunger then no longer, pass all the time in dancing, and eat day and night.

It occurred to us many times while we were among this people, and there was no food, to be three or four days without eating, when they . . . would tell us not to be sad, that soon there would be prickly pears when we should eat a plenty and drink of the juice, when our bellies would be very big and we should be content and joyful, having no hunger. From the time they first told us this, to that at which the earliest were ripe enough to be eaten, was an interval of five or six months; so having tarried until the lapse of this period, and the season had come, we went to eat the fruit.

We found mosquitos of three sorts, and all of them abundant in every part of the country. They poison and inflame, and during the greater part of the summer gave us great annoyance. As a protection we made fires, encircling the people with them, burning rotten and wet wood to produce smoke without flame. The remedy brought another trouble, and the night long we did little else than shed tears from the smoke that came into our eyes, besides feeling intense heat from the many fires, and if at any time we went out for repose to the seaside and fell asleep, we were reminded with blows to make up the fires. . . .

They are accustomed also to kill deer by encircling them with fires. The pasturage is taken from the cattle by burning, that necessity may drive them to seek it in places where it is desired they should go. They encamp only where there are wood and water; and sometimes all carry loads of these when they go to hunt deer, which are usually found where neither is to be got. On the day of their arrival, they kill the deer and other animals which they can, and consume all the water and all the wood in cooking and on the fires they make to relieve them of mosquitos. They remain the next day to get something to sustain them on their return; and when they go, such is their state from those insects that they appear to have the affliction of holy Lazarus. In this way do they appease their hunger, two or three times in the year, at the cost I have mentioned. From my own experience, I can state there is no torment known in this world that can equal it. B

—Cabeza de Vaca

Interesting and valuable as these explorers' writings are, they were not as important to the development of the American literary tradition as were the writings of the Puritans of the New England colonies. It was the Puritans who most powerfully influenced the course of American literature and the formation of the American imagination. In fact, much of what we now identify as "American" comes from the moral, ethical, and religious convictions of that small group of early New England settlers who landed, in 1620, on the tip of Cape Cod, just before Christmas.

A. Humanities Connection: Discussing the Fine Art
Students who think of Puritan clothing as being essentially American will observe that Matthew Hopkins, pictured here, is an Englishman. You may want to make the point—however obvious it seems—that Puritans in the New World wore the clothing they had brought with them. Consequently, there is nothing incorrect about using this famous illustration, as publishers sometimes do, in books about American Puritans. It shows the way Puritan men dressed on both sides of the Atlantic.

B. Responding
Separation of church and state is a basic principle of American society. Have students notice that such separation was not the practice in England following King Henry VIII's break with the pope.
? How would the Puritans have viewed separation of church and state? (Since they hated the established church of England, most of them did not want a national church in the New World. But they did believe that government—a necessity—had to follow the law of God. See page 7.)

The Puritans in New England: A Spiritual Journey

Their voyage from Plymouth in southwestern England to Cape Cod in North America lasted more than two months and was fraught with disaster. The Puritans began in two ships, the *Mayflower* and the *Speedwell,* but they were forced twice to turn back. They finally had to abandon the inaptly named *Speedwell,* which was prone to leaks. A hired sailor on the *Mayflower* who had mocked and cursed the Puritan passengers died of a fever early in the voyage—evidence, wrote William Bradford, of "the just hand of God upon him." Halfway across the Atlantic, the main beam of the *Mayflower* buckled in a storm, and the group almost turned back for good. But the Puritans had brought with them a large iron screw—a sort of heavy-duty jack. They straightened the beam with the screw, discussed the practical details with the captain, "committed themselves to the will of God," as Bradford put it, "and resolved to proceed."

Each of these attitudes, actions, and decisions is absolutely characteristic of the Puritans. They were practical, as shown by their repair of the beam. But they were also single-minded visionaries convinced of the rightness of their cause, as shown by Bradford's comments on the sailor's death. Their real commerce was with heaven, but they were competent in the business of the world as well. The founding of the New World was a business venture as well as a spiritual one—and for the Puritans, as we shall see, the everyday world and the spiritual world were closely intertwined.

A

Matthew Hopkins, an English Puritan.

Rare Book Division, The New York Public Library, Astor, Lenox and Tilden Foundations.

Who Were These Puritans?

B

Puritan is a broad term, referring to any of a number of Protestant sects that sought to "purify" the established Church of England. The English Puritans, who were part of a much larger pattern of Protestant reform sweeping Western Europe, wished to return to the simple forms of worship and church organization as described in the New Testament. Because they refused to conform to the state church's beliefs and practices, the Puritans were also called "Nonconformists" or "Dissenters." Since the time of King Henry VIII (who reigned from 1509 to 1547), the English church had been virtually inseparable from the government; the Puritans thus represented a threat to the political stability of the nation. "I will *make* them conform," King James I had said of the Puritans in 1604, "or I will harry them out of the land." As it turned out, it was in the end the Puritans who harried the royal family out of the land: forty-five years later, they beheaded James's son Charles I and forced Charles II into exile in France.

Even so, many Puritans suffered persecution. Some of them left England, at first for Holland. But fearing that they would lose their identity as English Christians, a small advance group of about a hundred Puritans set sail in 1620 for the New World. There they hoped to realize their dream of building a new secular society patterned after God's word. "As one small candle may light a thousand," William Bradford would write later, "so the light kindled here hath shone unto many, yes, in some sort to our whole nation."

A. Responding to the Time Line Students should understand that in the time line two or three entries may appear under a single date heading. At least one of them is an event in the American colonies; the other may be a major event in Europe. Boldface type indicates people and events covered in this unit.

? Which of the events have some sort of causal relationship with the other event or events listed for that date? (For example, 1492–1500: the arrival of Europeans in the New World eventually resulted in a decline in the Indian population; 1619–1620: slavery played a part in the history of this nation from its beginnings; 1635–1636: early respect for learning and literacy in the New World contributed to the growth of a national literature; 1639–1640: printing press resulted in wide distribution of books in New World)

Puritan Beliefs

> **"Strangely enough, at the center of Puritan theology was an uneasy mixture of certainty and doubt."**

What sort of spiritual and intellectual cargo did the Puritans bring with them on the *Mayflower*? They were practical, intensely committed, and convinced of the rightness of their purpose. But strangely enough, at the center of Puritan theology was an uneasy mixture of certainty and doubt. The certainty was that because of Adam and Eve's sin of disobedience, most of humanity would be damned for all eternity. "In Adam's fall," as the Puritan primer taught, "we sinned all." Yet, though Adam's sin was damning, the Puritans were certain that God in His mercy sent His son to earth to allow some to be saved.

Their doubt centered on whether a particular individual was to be one of the saved or one of the damned. In theory, a person's fate was *determined* by God; that is, a person could do nothing to become one of the saved. In practice, though, the Puritans strove intensely for salvation and led very pious lives. This was in part because of the consequences of this question: How did you know if you were saved or damned?

As it turns out, you did not know. A theology that was so clear-cut in its division of the world between saints and sinners (or the "elect" and the "unregenerate") was fuzzy when it came to determining which were which. There were two principal indications of the state of your soul, neither of them completely certain. You were

1492–1500	1503–1513	1517–1521	1528–1531
Christopher Columbus lands on San Salvador, October 11–14, 1492 25 million Indians live in North and South America, 1500	In Italy, Leonardo da Vinci paints *Mona Lisa,* 1503 Juan Ponce de Leon discovers Florida, 1513	Martin Luther begins Protestant Reformation in Europe, 1517 Aztec Empire falls to Spaniards, 1521	Cabeza de Vaca lands in Florida, 1528 Henry VIII replaces the Pope as Supreme Head of the Church of England, 1531
1605–1607	**1611–1612**	**1619–1620**	**1626–1630**
A Shakespeare's *King Lear* and *Macbeth* first performed in London, 1605 Settlement founded at Jamestown, Virginia, 1607	King James version of the Bible completed in England, 1611 **Anne Bradstreet born in England, 1612**	First Africans arrive in the New World, on Dutch slave ships, 1619 *Mayflower* arrives in the New World, November 11, 1620	Peter Minuit buys the island of Manhattan from Native American chiefs for about $24 worth of merchandise, 1626 **William Bradford begins his history, 1630**
1657–1665	**1666**	**1668–1674**	**1675**
William Bradford dies at Plymouth, 1657 The Great Plague kills nearly 70,000 people in London, 1665	**Sarah Kemble Knight born in Boston, 1666** **Anne Bradstreet's house burns in Andover, 1666**	**Edward Taylor arrives in Boston, 1668** **Anne Bradstreet dies in Andover, 1672** **William Byrd born in Virginia, 1674**	Metacomet's war on the colonial settlements in Massachusetts, 1675 **Mary Rowlandson captured by Metacomet's people, 1675**

saved by the grace of God, and you could *feel* this grace arriving, in an intensely emotional fashion. The inner arrival of God's grace was demonstrated by your outward behavior. After receiving grace, you were "reborn" as a member of the community of saints, and you behaved like a saint. People hoping to be among the saved examined their inner lives closely for signs of grace, and they tried to behave in as exemplary a manner as possible. So "idle hands" really were "the devil's playground," and American Puritans came to value the virtues of industriousness, temperance, sobriety, and simplicity. These were, coincidentally, the ideal qualities needed to carve a civilization out of the wilderness.

Religion for the Puritans, then, was first of all a personal, inner experience. They did not believe that the clergy or the Church should or could act as an intermediary between the individual and God. Not all Puritans felt that the state should be distinct from the Church, but most of the New England colonists were strongly against the idea of a national church. Nevertheless, religious attitudes affected the government, for Puritans believed that the sinful state of humanity made governments necessary. They also believed that the foundation of all governmental laws was the inflexible law of God. In the Puritan view, a covenant, or contract, existed between God and humanity. This covenant was a useful model for social organization as well: people should enter freely into agreements concerning their form of political organization. On

A

"American Puritans came to value the virtues of industriousness, temperance, sobriety, and simplicity. These were, coincidentally, the ideal qualities needed to carve a civilization out of the wilderness."

A. Expansion
Questions about the separation of church and state are often in the news. Frequently they involve public and private education. If you think it appropriate, you may wish to discuss some of these current issues in class.

1558–1579	1587–1588	1590–1594	1603
Elizabeth, daughter of Henry VIII, becomes Queen of England, 1558 **John Smith born in England, 1579**	Virginia Dare, first English child born in North America, 1587 The British defeat the Spanish Armada, 1588	**William Bradford born in England, 1590** Shakespeare's *Romeo and Juliet* first performed in London, 1594	Bubonic plague, which would kill 150,000 people, breaks out in London, 1603
1635–1636	**1639–1640**	**1642–1643**	**1649–1650**
First public school in America, 1635 **Mary Rowlandson born in England, 1636** Harvard College founded 1636	First printing press in the New World, 1639 First book published in the New World *(Bay Psalm Book)*, 1640	**Edward Taylor born in England, 1642** English Civil War begins, 1643	King Charles I of England beheaded, 1649 **Anne Bradstreet's first book of poetry published in England, 1650**
1690–1692	**1703–1728**	**1741**	**1740–1745**
Slaves held in all English colonies in North America, 1690 Witch trials held in Salem, Massachusetts, 1692	**Jonathan Edwards born in Connecticut, 1703** **Mrs. Knight travels to New York, 1704** **William Byrd goes on his expedition, 1728**	**Jonathan Edwards preaches "Sinners in the Hands of an Angry God," 1741** Handel's *The Messiah* first performed in Dublin, 1741	The Great Awakening, 1740–1745, is touched off by a traveling English preacher

A. Humanities Connection: Responding to the Fine Art
Sir Christopher Wren (1632–1723) was one of England's great architects. From 1670 to 1711 he designed 52 London churches, most of them still standing. His churches are renowned for their elegance, order, and dignity. Wren greatly influenced church and especially steeple design both in England and abroad.

? Why is this illustration appropriate here? (Answers will vary. The church steeple reflects the religious purposes behind the Pilgrims' voyage to the New World and the religious conviction that so shaped their lives and their literature.)

B. Expansion
The distinction between Pilgrims and Puritans is not always clear. Certainly many, if not most, of the Puritans who came to America thought of themselves as pilgrims. Yet the term Pilgrim (with a capital P) is generally reserved for the small band of English Puritans who founded the colony of Plymouth in 1620—in other words, the people who came over on the *Mayflower.* The many other Puritans who later arrived in the New World are usually just called Puritans.

For Further Reading
For Students
A. L. Rowse, a British writer, presents the story of American Puritanism in historical perspective in "Pilgrims and Puritans," *American Heritage,* October 1959. The article ends with a brief but useful evaluation of Puritan writing.

A

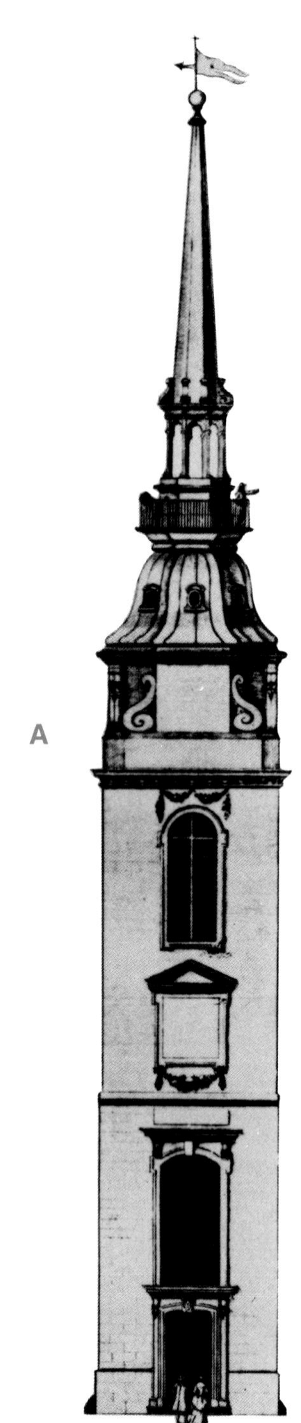

English church steeple designed by Sir Christopher Wren (1666–1718).

The Wren Society Publications, 1932.

the *Mayflower,* for example, the Puritans composed and signed a compact outlining how they would be governed once they landed. In this and other ways, they prepared the ground for the later growth of American democracy.

B The Puritans' Model: The Pilgrim

Every age has at least one figure, or heroic type, that seems to embody its ideas and aspirations. The Puritans who came to America identified so powerfully with one figure that they called themselves by that name: "Pilgrim." A pilgrim is someone who makes a pilgrimage, or journey to a holy place. But for the Puritans, the word *pilgrimage* took on a wider meaning—it was a journey to salvation.

For the Pilgrims, the outward journey of their lives and the specific voyage to America were also inner, spiritual journeys. "A Christian is sailing through this world unto his heavenly country," the poet Anne Bradstreet wrote some years after sailing across the Atlantic to America. "We must, therefore, be here as strangers and pilgrims, that we may plainly declare that we seek a city above." In a way, each Pilgrim was acting out a tale of salvation in which he or she saw outward physical events as having inner, spiritual meaning.

The Pilgrims read their lives the way a literary critic reads a book, examining the significance of each event. John Winthrop, a governor of the Massachusetts Bay Colony, includes an account in his *Diary* of a snake entering the church during a synod, or council meeting. One of the elders "trod upon the head of it," and the snake was killed. It is perhaps not unnatural for a snake to find its way into a country church on a hot August day, but Winthrop saw far more significance in the snake's visit. "The serpent is the devil; the synod, the representative of the churches of Christ in New England. The devil had . . . lately attempted their disturbance, . . . but their faith . . . overcame him and crushed his head."

The Bible in the American Wilderness

The Puritans read the Bible as the story of the creation, fall, wanderings, and rescue of the human race. Within this long and complex narrative, each Puritan could see connections to events in his or her own life or to events in the life of the community. Thus, William Bradford (page 11) compares the experiences of the Pilgrims to the experiences of the Israelites wandering in the wilderness. Mary Rowlandson (page 23) sees countless similarities between her captivity by the Indians and captivities recorded in the Old Testament.

The Puritans believed that the Bible was the literal word of God. Reading the Bible was a necessity for all Puritans, as was the ability to understand closely reasoned theological debates. For these reasons, the Puritans placed great emphasis on education.

But their interest in education was not confined to simple literacy. Many of the New England settlers had enjoyed the benefits of higher education in England, and they wanted the same for their children. Thus, Harvard College was founded in 1636, just six years after the Massachusetts Bay Colony was established and only sixteen years after the first Pilgrims had landed.

Puritan Writings

The Bible was also the foundation upon which Puritan literature was built. In their religious services, Puritans rejected any ceremonies or adornments not mentioned in the Bible—clerical vestments, stained-glass windows, and the use of incense, for example. The same restrictions applied to literature. The Puritans did not object to figures of speech used to drive home a point, but they rejected mere "adornments" such as ornate figures of speech or witty plays on words. The ideal Puritan style was a **plain style**—strong, simple, and logical. It was a literary style that could make explanations of the scriptures accessible to everyone.

Their beliefs required the Puritans to keep a close watch on both the inner and outer events of their lives. This central aspect of the Puritan mind greatly affected their literature. Inner events, such as feelings of despair or great joy, were stages on the road to salvation; external events, like a snake entering a church, con-

John Eliot Preaching to the Indians (19th century). Colored engraving.

A

A. Humanities Connection: Discussing the Fine Art
This colored engraving, *John Eliot Preaching to the Indians,* shows in an idealized way John Eliot's painstaking efforts to convert the Native Americans of Massachusetts to Christianity. Most Puritans thought of the Indians as instruments of Satan. Eliot (1604–1690) did not. He regarded them as the lost tribes of Israel, human beings created by God, with souls to be saved. As part of his missionary efforts, Eliot learned the Mahican dialect of the Algonquian language and translated the Bible into it: *Mamusse Wunneetupanatamwe Up-Biblum God* ("The whole Holy his-Bible God") was the first Bible printed in America (1659).

Reading Check Test

1. Cabeza de Vaca was (a) a Spanish explorer (b) a Mexican adventurer (c) an Italian mapmaker *(a)*
2. The Puritans wanted to "purify" (a) the Roman Catholic Church (b) the New Testament (c) the Church of England *(c)*
3. A Puritan believed that he or she could be saved by (a) prayer (b) good deeds (c) God's grace *(c)*
4. Puritans saw the hand of God in (a) Indian ceremonies (b) stained-glass windows (c) everyday events *(c)*
5. God reveals His purpose through the Bible, the natural world, and (a) poetry (b) miracles (c) direct intervention *(c)*

A. Architecture Connection

? What does this style of building, typical of the Puritans, tell you about Puritan beliefs as they are reflected in their architecture? (The Puritans did not believe in adornment.)

A

Drawing of a Plymouth meeting house (1683).

Pilgrim Society, Plymouth, Massachusetts.

"The Puritans were complex and complete human beings who took great joy in their lives and relationships, while facing hardships difficult to imagine today."

tained messages from God. And so diaries and histories were important forms of Puritan literature, because they were records of the workings of God.

Such concerns determined as well what incidents the Puritans chose to write about. They recorded forms of *revelation*. The Puritans believed that God revealed His purpose to humanity in three principal ways: through the Bible, through the natural world, and through Divine Providence, or God's direct intervention in human affairs. Thus the Puritans wrote on Biblical and devotional topics: the first American bestseller was Michael Wigglesworth's long poem on the Judgment Day, *The Day of Doom* (1662). They wrote about the spiritual truth they discovered in the natural world: Edward Taylor's poems (page 45) are especially good examples, but you will find this theme in diaries and histories as well. And they wrote about moments of special Providence or events that contained great lessons, such as Anne Bradstreet's poem on the destruction of her house by fire (page 43).

The Puritans were not machines programmed for worship and nothing else, however. Although they cannot be separated from their religion, neither can they be fully contained by it. They were complex and complete human beings who took great joy in their lives and relationships, while facing hardships difficult to imagine today. Anne Bradstreet's poem on the burning of her house, for example, does not simply draw a dry lesson from the event. It records her moments of joy in the house and works through her grief to a spiritual solace. If there had been no complexity in her, no conflict between her love of things of this world and her conviction that the ultimate value lay in the spiritual world, the poem would have been very different. At its best, Puritan literature records not merely the moments when the physical and the spiritual worlds cross but rather the moments when they seem to diverge—when love of things of this world threatens to push out love of eternity.

A. Humanities Connection: Discussing the Fine Art
William Bradford's 270-page manuscript, *Of Plymouth Plantation,* was bound in vellum or heavy parchment, originally white, but yellowing, cracked, and scaled by the time of its return to the United States from London in 1897 (see page 12). Bradford's handwriting varies from fine to rather coarse, but it is readable.

A common misconception about the manuscript is that it is the log of the *Mayflower.* Actually, it is neither a log nor a daily journal, but rather a history that Bradford began many years after the arrival of the Pilgrims.

B. Expansion
The information in this (or any) biography of William Bradford comes originally from official documents of the late 1500's and early 1600's or from Bradford's own later writings. No contemporary portrait or written description of William Bradford exists. Ask students to suggest reasons for this lack of attention to the great Puritan leader in his own time. (Puritans did not believe in honoring individuals, only in honoring God. The harsh early years at Plymouth allowed little time for either writing or painting.)

William Bradford (1590–1657)

William Bradford's life displayed a mixture of the commonplace and the extraordinary that was characteristic of the Puritan experience. Bradford was the son of a prosperous farmer in Yorkshire, England. His father died when William was a baby, and the child was raised by his grandparents and uncles. It was assumed that the young man would take over the family holdings when he came of age; in keeping with this expectation, he received no higher education but instead was taught the practical arts of farming. Despite his lack of formal training (or perhaps because of it), Bradford was to become a successful, longstanding Colonial governor in the New World, dealing out justice and settling disputes of all kinds. He would also write the first history that depicts America as a unique social experiment.

Bradford might have become the prosperous Yorkshire farmer he was prepared to become if he had not taken a radical step when he was twelve years old. Inspired by his reading of the Bible and by the sermons of a Puritan minister, he joined a small group of Nonconformists despite the vehement objections of his family and friends. The group could not worship publicly, so they met furtively in a private house in the nearby town of Scrooby. Seven years later, under increasing pressure of persecution and fearful that they would be imprisoned, the Scrooby group crossed the North Sea to Holland. There, Bradford set up a weaving business. He also married Dorothy May, a young woman who was a fellow emigrant from England, and the couple had a child. In 1620, after ten years in Holland, the group was aided by London profiteers and merchants, who lent them a ship and crew as an investment, and the Nonconformists sailed for the New World.

For Bradford, the hardships of the ocean voyage did not end with the landing at Plymouth. In December, while the *Mayflower* was anchored in Provincetown Bay, Bradford and other men took a small boat ashore to scout for a place to land and build shelter. When they returned, Bradford learned that his young wife had fallen or jumped from the ship and was drowned. The act may well have been suicide. Dorothy Bradford had been on the crowded ship for more than two months, and when land was finally sighted, she did not see the hoped-for green hills of an earthly paradise. Beyond the ship lay only the bleak sand dunes of Cape Cod. That bitter winter, half the settlers were to die of cold, disease, and malnutrition.

First page, *Of Plimoth Plantation* by William Bradford.

Pilgrim Society, Plymouth, Massachusetts.

The following year, Bradford was elected governor of the plantation at the age of thirty-one. "Had he not been a person of more than ordinary piety, wisdom, and courage," the Puritan preacher Cotton Mather later recorded, "he must have sunk" under the difficulties of governing such a shaky settlement. But, Mather continued, Bradford had been "laying up a treasure of experience, and he had now occasion to use it." Bradford proved an exemplary leader, and he went on to be elected governor of the Colony no fewer than thirty times.

In 1630, Bradford began to write a history of the Plymouth Colony from its beginning. He continued writing an annual account of the settlement until 1647. His record, *Of Plymouth Plantation,* was not composed for immediate

A. Humanities Connection: Responding to the Fine Art
Born in Kirkdale, England, W(illiam) F(ormby) Halsall (1841–1919) went to sea at the age of twelve in the ship *Ocean Rover* out of Portsmouth, New Hampshire, and served with the United States Navy during part of the Civil War. From that experience came one of his best-known paintings—*First Fight of Ironclads, Monitor and Merrimac*—which is sometimes seen in American history textbooks.

? How does this painting make you feel? Does the artist present a pleasant scene of the *Mayflower* at anchor, or is there a sense of foreboding here? (A sense of foreboding; the ship is dark, and night is coming on.)

? Why might some sense of foreboding be appropriate in a painting depicting the arrival of the Pilgrims in the New World? (From the biography, students know how difficult life was going to be in the New World and that Mrs. Bradford may have committed suicide over the bleak prospect of a Cape Cod winter.)

For Further Reading For Students
Bradford Smith's *Bradford of Plymouth* (J. B. Lippincott, 1951) is an excellent, detailed biography of William Bradford. Highly readable, it is an ideal resource for biographical research on "the greatest of the Pilgrims."

publication or to attract more colonists, like many other early Colonial accounts. It was written for posterity, although by the end of his life Bradford's dreams of that posterity had been shattered.

As the years passed, the plantation at Plymouth prospered economically. Beaver pelts from the Indians brought good money in England, and eventually the plantation managed to pay off its debt. But as the group prospered and grew, it also became more diffuse and less pious. Despite Bradford's efforts to hold it together, the Plymouth Colony gradually disintegrated as a religious community. The ideal of the "city on the hill," the Pilgrims' dream of an ideal society founded on religious principles, gradually gave way to the realities of life in the New World. Bradford's record of this grand experiment ends in disappointment. When more fertile areas for settlement were found and when Boston became a more convenient port to England, Plymouth lost much of its population—especially its young people. "Thus was this poor church left," Bradford wrote in 1644, near the conclusion of his history, "like an ancient mother grown old and forsaken of her children. She that had made so many rich became herself poor."

The first nine chapters of Bradford's history were copied into the Plymouth church records, but the entire manuscript was later lost. Most likely it was carried back to England as a souvenir by a British soldier during the Revolutionary War. The soldier might have sold it for a few cents to a bookseller in London. It was almost a century later that Governor Bradford's vellum-bound volume was discovered in the library of the Bishop of London. *Of Plymouth Plantation* was first published in 1856 by the Massachusetts Historical Society. After long negotiations, the manuscript was finally returned to the United States in 1897. It can be seen today in the Statehouse in Boston.

The Mayflower in Plymouth Harbor by W. F. Halsall (1882). Oil.

A

Pilgrim Society, Plymouth, Massachusetts.

SUPPLEMENTARY SUPPORT MATERIALS
1. Vocabulary Activity Worksheet (*CCB*)
2. Review and Response Worksheet: Archaic Language (*CCB*)
3. Selection Test (*CCB*)

DEVELOPING VOCABULARY
The following words from the history are tested in the Selection Test. (See also Vocabulary Activity Worksheet.)
profane recompense
succor discourse
lee

PREPARATION
1. BUILDING ON PRIOR KNOWLEDGE. Students already know that, in spite of great difficulties, the Pilgrims were successful in their attempts to found a colony. Have students review what they have learned about beliefs and characteristics of the Pilgrims that helped them to succeed. (The Pilgrims were strong in the religious convictions that brought them to the New World. They also believed in the values of industriousness, temperance, and sobriety.)

2. ESTABLISHING A PURPOSE. The strong faith of the Pilgrims included a belief that outward, physical events had an inner, spiritual meaning. As the headnote indicates, have students read to find references to God's role in the voyage and to note how outward events have a spiritual significance.

A. Responding
As many historians have noted, the Pilgrims were at least as practical as they were pious.
? Why is practicality so vital to the Pilgrims' success? (Answers will vary, but students should note that once they reach the New World, the Pilgrims must be entirely self-sufficient. They must build shelter, raise food, take care of the sick, and establish an understanding with the Indians.)

FROM OF PLYMOUTH PLANTATION

The following extracts from Bradford's history describe some celebrated events: the landing at Plymouth, the framing of the Mayflower Compact, the Pilgrims' early encounters with the native inhabitants, and their first Thanksgiving. In the first paragraph, notice how matter-of-fact Bradford is about God's role in their voyage. Look for similar references to Divine Providence in the rest of the history. Note also how outward events contain an inner, spiritual significance. A

Chapter 9

Of Their Voyage, and How They Passed the Sea; and of Their Safe Arrival At Cape Cod

September 6 [1620]. These troubles[1] being blown over, and now all being compact together in one ship, they put to sea again with a prosperous wind, which continued divers [many] days together, which was some encouragement unto them; yet, according to the usual manner, many were afflicted with seasickness. And I may not omit here a special work of God's Providence. There was a proud and very profane young man, one of the seamen, of a lusty [energetic], able body, which made him the more haughty; he would always be condemning the poor people in their sickness and cursing them daily with grievous execrations; and did not let to tell them that he hoped to help to cast half of them overboard before they came to their journey's end, and to make merry with what they had; and if he were by any gently reproved, he would curse and swear most bitterly. But it pleased God before they came half seas over, to smite this young man with a grievous disease, of which he died in a desperate manner, and so was himself the first that was thrown overboard. Thus his curses light on his own head, and it was an astonishment to all his fellows, for they noted it to be the just hand of God upon him.

After they had enjoyed fair winds and weather for a season, they were encountered many times with crosswinds and met with many fierce storms, with which the ship was shroudly[2] shaken and her upper works made very leaky; and one of the main beams in the midships was bowed and cracked, which put them in some fear that the ship could not be able to perform the voyage. So some of the chief of the company, perceiving the mariners to fear the sufficiency of the ship, as appeared by their mutterings, they entered into serious consultation with the master and other officers of the ship, to consider in time of the danger, and rather to return than to cast themselves into a desperate and inevitable peril. And truly there was great distraction and difference of opinion amongst the mariners themselves; fain [gladly] would they do what could be done for their wages' sake (being now near half the seas over), and on the other hand they were loath [reluctant] to hazard their lives too desperately. But in examining all opinions, the master and others affirmed they knew the ship to be strong and firm under water; and for the buckling of the main beam, there was a great iron screw the passengers brought out of Holland, which would raise the beam into his place; the which being done, the carpenter and master affirmed that with a post put under it, set firm in the lower deck, and otherways bound, he would make it sufficient. And as for the decks and upper works, they would caulk them as well as they could, and though with the working of the ship they would not long keep staunch [watertight], yet there would otherwise be no great danger, if they did not overpress her with sails. So they committed themselves to the will of God and resolved to proceed.

1. **troubles:** the return of the *Speedwell* to England and the transfer of her passengers to the *Mayflower*.

2. **shroudly:** shrewdly, used here in its archaic sense of "wickedly."

A. Responding
Perceptive readers will notice that the land the Pilgrims reach "is called Cape Cod." Although the Pilgrims were the first Europeans to settle in the region, they were not the first to arrive there. In 1614 Captain John Smith had mapped the New World's coast from Maine to Cape Cod. Even the name Plymouth, forever associated with the Pilgrims, appeared earlier on Captain Smith's map.
? What might the Pilgrims have called Cape Cod and Plymouth had these places not already been named? (Students are likely to suggest Biblical names, but, in fact, English settlers, including the Pilgrims, tended to choose names from the map of England or the royal family, such as Boston or Cape Anne; or Anglicized Native American names, such as Massachusetts.)

B. Allusions (Challenging)
This reference to "a sea of troubles" echoes William Shakespeare's *Hamlet.* In his famous soliloquy "To be or not to be," Hamlet asks: "Whether 'tis nobler in the mind to suffer/The slings and arrows of outrageous fortune,/ Or to take arms against a sea of troubles. . . ."
? Do you think that Bradford is more likely to have acquired the phrase from Shakespeare or to have coined it himself? (He probably got it, consciously or not, from Shakespeare. *Hamlet* was produced in London in 1600/01, and by the time Bradford wrote his history, the play was widely known.)

In sundry of these storms the winds were so fierce and the seas so high as they could not bear a knot of sail, but were forced to hull[3] for divers days together. And in one of them, as they thus lay at hull in a mighty storm, a lusty young man called John Howland, coming upon some occasion above the gratings, was, with a seele [roll] of the ship, thrown into sea; but it pleased God that he caught hold of the topsail halyards which hung overboard and ran out at length. Yet he held his hold (though he was sundry fathoms under water) till he was hauled up by the same rope to the brim of the water, and then with a boat hook and other means got into the ship again and his life saved. And though he was something ill with it, yet he lived many years after and became a profitable member both in church and commonwealth. In all this voyage there died but one of the passengers, which was William Butten, a youth, servant to Samuel Fuller, when they drew near the coast.

But to omit other things (that I may be brief) A after long beating at sea they fell with that land which is called Cape Cod;[4] the which being made and certainly known to be it, they were not a little joyful. After some deliberation had amongst themselves and with the master of the ship, they tacked about and resolved to stand for the southward (the wind and weather being fair) to find some place about Hudson's River[5] for their habitation. But after they had sailed that course about half the day, they fell amongst dangerous shoals and roaring breakers, and they were so far entangled therewith as they conceived themselves in great danger; and the wind shrinking upon them withal, they resolved to bear up again for the Cape and thought themselves happy to get out of those dangers before night overtook them, as by God's good Providence they did. And the next day[6] they got into the Cape Harbor,[7] where they rid in safety. . . .

Being thus arrived in a good harbor, and brought safe to land, they fell upon their knees and blessed the God of Heaven who had brought them over the vast and furious ocean, and delivered them from all the perils and miseries thereof, again to set their feet on the firm and stable earth, their proper element. . . .

But here I cannot but stay and make a pause, and stand half amazed at this poor people's present condition; and so I think will the reader, too, when he well considers the same. Being thus passed the vast ocean, and a sea of troubles before B in their preparation (as may be remembered by that which went before), they had now no friends to welcome them nor inns to entertain or refresh their weather-beaten bodies; no houses or much less towns to repair to, to seek for succor [aid]. It is recorded in Scripture[8] as a mercy to the Apostle and his shipwrecked company, that the barbarians showed them no small kindness in refreshing them, but these savage barbarians, when they met with them (as after will appear) were readier to fill their sides full of arrows than otherwise. And for the season it was winter, and they that know the winters of that country know them to be sharp and violent, and subject to cruel and fierce storms, dangerous to travel to unknown places, much more to search an unknown coast. Besides, what could they see but a hideous and desolate wilderness, full of wild beasts and wild men—and what multitudes there might be of them they knew not. Neither could they, as it were, go up to the top of Pisgah[9] to view from this wilderness a more goodly country to feed their hopes; for which way soever they turned their eyes (save upward to the heavens) they could have little solace or content in respect of any outward objects. For summer being done, all things stand upon them with a weather-beaten face, and the whole country, full of woods and thickets, represented a wild and savage hue. If they looked behind them, there was the mighty ocean which they had passed and was now as a main bar and gulf to separate them from all the civil parts of the world. . . .

What could now sustain them but the Spirit of God and His grace? May not and ought not the children of these fathers rightly say: "Our fathers

3. **hull:** lay to and drift under short sail.
4. They sighted Cape Cod at daybreak on November 9, 1620.
5. They were trying for Manhattan Island. Henry Hudson had made his voyage in 1609 and had claimed the area for the Dutch, but the English did not recognize the Dutch claim.
6. November 11. The sea voyage from England had taken sixty-five days.
7. Cape Harbor is now Provincetown Harbor.
8. In the Acts of the Apostles (Chapter 28), St. Paul tells how the shipwrecked Christians were helped by the "barbarous people" of Malta.
9. Pisgah was the mountain from which Moses first viewed the Promised Land (Deuteronomy 34:1).

A were Englishmen which came over this great ocean, and were ready to perish in this wilderness; but they cried unto the Lord, and He heard their voice and looked on their adversity,"[10] etc? "Let them therefore praise the Lord, because He is good: and His mercies endure forever." "Yea, let them which have been redeemed of the Lord, shew how He hath delivered them from the hand of the oppressor. When they wandered in the desert wilderness out of the way, and found no city to dwell in, both hungry and thirsty, their soul was overwhelmed in them. Let them confess before the Lord His lovingkindness and His wonderful works before the sons of men."[11]

Chapter 10

Showing How They Sought out a Place of Habitation; and What Befell Them Thereabout

[1620] Being thus arrived at Cape Cod the 11th of November, and necessity calling them to look out a place for habitation (as well as the master's and mariners' importunity); they having brought a large shallop[12] with them out of England, stowed in quarters in the ship, they now got her out and set their carpenters to work to trim her up; but being much bruised and shattered in the ship with foul weather, they saw she would be long in mending. Whereupon a few of them tendered themselves to go by land and discover those nearest places, whilst the shallop was in mending; and the rather because as they went into that harbor there seemed to be an opening some two or three leagues[13] off, which the master judged to be a river. It was conceived there might be some danger in the attempt, yet seeing them resolute, they were permitted to go, being sixteen of them well armed under the conduct of Captain Standish,[14] having such instructions given them as was thought meet.

They set forth the 15th of November; and when they had marched about the space of a mile by the seaside, they espied five or six persons with a dog coming toward them who were savages; but they fled from them and ran up into the woods, and the English followed them, partly to see if they could speak with them and partly to discover if there might not be more of them lying in ambush. But the Indians, seeing themselves thus followed, they again forsook the woods and ran away on the sands as hard as they could, so as they could not come near them but followed them by the track of their feet sundry miles and saw that they had come the same way. So, night coming on, they made their rendezvous and set out their sentinels, and rested in quiet that night; and the next morning followed their track till they had headed a great creek and so left the sands, and turned another way into the woods. But they still followed them by guess, hoping to find their dwellings; but they soon lost both them and themselves, falling into such thickets as were ready to tear their clothes and armor in pieces; but were most distressed for want of drink. But at length they found water and refreshed themselves, being the first New England water they drunk of, and was now in great thirst as pleasant unto them as wine or beer had been in foretimes.

Afterward they directed their course to come to the other shore, for they knew it was a neck of land they were to cross over, and so at length got to the seaside and marched to this supposed river, and by the way found a pond of clear, fresh water, and shortly after a good quantity of clear ground where the Indians had formerly set corn, and some of their graves. And proceeding further they saw new stubble where corn had been set the same year, also they found where lately a house had been, where some planks and a great kettle were remaining, and heaps of sand newly paddled with their hands. Which, they digging up, found in them divers fair Indian baskets filled with corn, and some in ears, fair and good, of divers colors, which seemed to them a very goodly sight (having never seen any such before). This was near the place of that supposed river they came to seek, to which they went and found it to open itself into two arms with a high cliff of sand in the entrance but more like to be creeks of salt water than any fresh, for aught they saw; and that there was good harborage for their shallop, leaving it further to be discovered by their shallop, when she was ready. So, their time limited them being expired, they returned to the ship lest they should be in

10. A quotation from Deuteronomy 26:7.
11. The quotations are from Psalm 107.
12. **shallop:** a small, open boat. This one was fitted with oars and a sail.
13. **leagues:** one league is equivalent to about three miles.
B 14. Myles Standish (1584–1656) was a soldier who had been hired to handle the colonists' military affairs. Not a member of the Puritan congregation, he still became one of their staunchest supporters.

A. Responding
At the end of Chapter 9, you may want to have students reflect on what they have read so far.
? What sort of person do you imagine William Bradford to be? How would you react to being under his leadership, facing a bitter winter, a less-than-friendly native population, and an uncertain future? (Responses will vary and will largely depend on the extent to which students sympathize with—or at least understand—the Puritan world view.)

B. Expansion
You might emphasize to students that not everyone on the *Mayflower* was a Pilgrim. While this fact is implicit in the text and some of the footnotes, it may nonetheless be overlooked. Ask students why there were non-Pilgrims on the ship. (As the footnote says, Miles Standish was there as a military expert. Most of the non-Pilgrims, including the captain of the ship, were sailors who intended to return to England.)

A. Humanities Connection: Responding to the Fine Art
This romanticized scene of the Pilgrims landing at Plymouth Rock, painted nearly two centuries after the event, is the work of Michel Corné (1752–1845), an Italian-born marine and portrait painter. Originally from Elba, the island of Napoleon's exile, Corné emigrated to the United States at the age of 47. Four years later, still a recent immigrant, he painted *Landing of the Pilgrims at Plymouth.* Corné, who reputedly introduced the tomato to the United States as a food plant, spent most of the rest of his long life in Newport, Rhode Island.

? How historically accurate do you think this painting is? (It is highly unlikely that there were Native Americans standing on shore, as depicted here, since the Indians usually ran away from white settlers at first; see page 15. Also, the Pilgrims would probably have been reluctant to land if there were Indians on shore.)

A

Landing of the Pilgrims at Plymouth by Michel Felice Corné (1803). Oil.

fear of their safety; and took with them part of the corn and buried up the rest. . . .

After this, the shallop being got ready, they set out again for the better discovery of this place, and the master of the ship desired to go himself. So there went some thirty men but found it to be no harbor for ships but only for boats. There was also found two of their houses [the Indians'] covered with mats, and sundry of their implements in them, but the people were run away and could not be seen. Also there was found more of their corn and of their beans of various colors; the corn and beans they brought away, purposing to give them full satisfaction when they should meet with any of them, as about some six months afterward they did, to their good content.

And here is to be noted a special Providence of God, and a great mercy to this poor people, that here they got seed to plant them corn the next year, or else they might have starved, for they had

Literature and Language: Shortening Sentences
Read aloud any paragraph from "Of Plymouth Plantation," and ask students what makes this language immediately recognizable as coming from a past century. Students should note examples of archaic vocabulary (*herewith, hence, shallop*) as well as differences in syntax.

Ask students to look closely at one or two of the extraordinarily long sentences, as for example, the sentence that begins, "Being landed, . . . " near the top of the right column below. If this sentence appeared in a student-written essay today, it might be considered a **run-on sentence**—one that meanders endlessly on and on, often without proper punctuation.

Suggest that students work in pairs or groups of three to break a passage of their choice from "Of Plymouth Plantation" into shorter sentences.

Pilgrim Society, Plymouth, Massachusetts.

A none nor any likelihood to get any till the season had been past, as the sequel did manifest. Neither is it likely they had had this if the first voyage had not been made, for the ground was now all covered with snow and hard frozen; but the Lord is never wanting unto His in their greatest needs; let His holy name have all the praise.

The month of November being spent in these affairs, and much foul weather falling in, the 6th of December they sent out their shallop again with ten of their principal men and some seamen, upon further discovery, intending to circulate that deep bay of Cape Cod. The weather was very cold and it froze so hard as the spray of the sea lighting on their coats; they were as if they had been glazed. Yet that night betimes they got down into the bottom of the bay, and as they drew near the shore they saw some ten or twelve Indians very busy about something. They landed about a league or two from them, and had much ado to put ashore anywhere—it lay so full of flats. Being landed, it grew late and they made themselves a barricado with logs and boughs as well as they could in the time, and set out their sentinel and betook them to rest, and saw the smoke of the fire the savages made that night. When morning was come they divided their company, some to coast along the shore in the boat, and the rest marched through the woods to see the land, if any fit place might be for their dwelling. They came also to the place where they saw the Indians the night before, and found they had been cutting up a great fish like a grampus, being some two inches thick of fat like a hog, some pieces whereof they had left by the way. And the shallop found two more of these fishes dead on the sands, a thing usual after storms in that place, by reason of the great flats of sand that lie off. . . .

From hence they departed and coasted all along but discerned no place likely for harbor; and therefore hasted to a place that their pilot (one Mr. Coppin, who had been in the country before) did assure them was a good harbor, which he had been in, and they might fetch it before night; of which they were glad, for it began to be foul weather.

After some hours' sailing, it began to snow and rain, and about the middle of the afternoon the wind increased and the sea became very rough, and they broke their rudder, and it was as much as two men could do to steer her with a couple of oars. But their pilot bade them be of good cheer, for he saw the harbor; but the storm increasing, and night drawing on, they bore what sail they could to get in while they could see. But herewith they broke their mast in three pieces and their sail fell overboard in a very grown sea, so as they had like to have been cast away. Yet by God's mercy they recovered themselves and, having the flood [the tide] with them, struck into the harbor. But when it came to, the pilot was deceived in the place, and said the Lord be merciful unto them, for his eyes never saw that place before; and he

A. Expansion
Have students notice this further tribute to God's benevolence. You might wish to discuss why Bradford, crediting all occurrences to God, gives thanks for the good that the Pilgrims encounter but never complains about the bad.

A. Expansion
Most Americans probably harbor an image of the *Mayflower* arriving at Cape Cod, the Pilgrims coming ashore immediately, and the entire shipboard company establishing Plymouth Colony as quickly as possible. By the end of Chapter 10, your students know better than that. While the *Mayflower* lay at anchor off Cape Cod, volunteers spent a total of five weeks, in a shallop and other smaller boats, exploring the coast for a suitable place to settle. Meanwhile, the other Pilgrims and crew members stayed on the overcrowded *Mayflower.* Whether the Pilgrims should have gone ashore earlier and thus had time to settle in before winter is a subject for speculation. Advise students to keep this point in mind as they read Chapter 11.

and the master's mate would have run her ashore in a cove full of breakers before the wind. But a lusty seaman which steered bade those which rowed, if they were men, about with her or else they were all cast away; the which they did with speed. So he bid them be of good cheer and row lustily, for there was a fair sound before them, and he doubted not but they should find one place or other where they might ride in safety. And though it was very dark and rained sore, yet in the end they got under the lee of a small island and remained there all that night in safety. But they knew not this to be an island till morning, but were divided in their minds; some would keep the boat for fear they might be amongst the Indians; others were so wet and cold they could not endure, but got ashore, and with much ado got fire (all things being so wet); and the rest were glad to come to them, for after midnight the wind shifted to the northwest and it froze hard.

But though this had been a day and night of much trouble and danger unto them, yet God gave them a morning of comfort and refreshing (as usually He doth to His children), for the next day was a fair, sunshining day, and they found themselves to be on an island secure from the Indians, where they might dry their stuff, fix their pieces, and rest themselves; and gave God thanks for His mercies in their manifold deliverances. And this being the last day of the week, they prepared there to keep the Sabbath.

A On Monday they sounded the harbor and found it fit for shipping, and marched into the land and found divers cornfields and little running brooks, a place (as they supposed) fit for situation. At least it was the best they could find, and the season and their present necessity made them glad to accept of it. So they returned to their ship again with this news to the rest of their people, which did much comfort their hearts.

On the 15th of December they weighed anchor to go to the place they had discovered, and came within two leagues of it, but were fain to bear up again; but the 16th day, the wind came fair, and they arrived safe in this harbor. And afterward took better view of the place, and resolved where to pitch their dwelling; and the 25th day began to erect the first house for common use to receive them and their goods.[15]

15. This text is the only account written by a participant of the famous landing at Plymouth Rock on December 11, 1620.

From
Chapter 11
The Starving Time

[1620–1621] But that which was most sad and lamentable was that in two or three months' time half of their company died, especially in January and February, being the depth of winter, and wanting houses and other comforts; being infected with the scurvy and other diseases which this long voyage and their inaccommodate condition had brought upon them. So as there died sometimes two or three of a day in the foresaid time, that of 100 and odd persons, scarce fifty remained. And of these, in the time of most distress, there was but six or seven sound persons who to their great commendations, be it spoken, spared no pains night nor day, but with abundance of toil and hazard of their own health, fetched them wood, made them fires, dressed them meat, made their beds, washed their loathsome clothes, clothed and unclothed them: in a word, did all the homely and necessary offices for them which dainty and queasy stomachs cannot endure to hear named; and all this willingly and cheerfully, without any grudging in the least, showing herein their true love unto their friends and brethren; a rare example and worthy to be remembered. Two of these seven were Mr. William Brewster, their reverend elder, and Myles Standish, their captain and military commander, to whom myself and many others were much beholden in our low and sick condition. And yet the Lord so upheld these persons as in this general calamity they were not at all infected either with sickness or lameness. And what I have said of these I may say of many others who died in this general visitation, and others yet living; that whilst they had health, yea, or any strength continuing, they were not wanting to any that had need of them. And I doubt not but their recompense is with the Lord.

But I may not here pass by another remarkable passage not to be forgotten. As this calamity fell among the passengers that were to be left here to plant, and were hasted ashore and made to drink water that the seamen might have the more beer, and one[16] in his sickness desiring but a small can of beer, it was answered that if he were their own father he should have none. The disease began to

16. This is Bradford himself.

READING CHECK TEST

1. The sailor who condemns the sick Pilgrims (a) has been drinking too much (b) falls overboard during a fight (c) becomes ill and dies (d) is converted to Puritanism *(c)*

2. Expeditions are sent out in a shallop to search for (a) food and water (b) friendly natives (c) a suitable place to make a settlement (d) other English settlers to the south *(c)*

3. In an encounter with the Indians (a) several Pilgrims receive arrow wounds (b) Squanto is taken captive (c) the Pilgrims offer to sign a treaty (d) the Pilgrims follow the "savages" for some distance *(d)*

4. During the first winter (a) half of the settlers die (b) the *Mayflower* sinks (c) gifts of corn from the Indians help (d) the Pilgrims build a church *(a)*

5. The Native American most helpful to the Pilgrims is (a) Samoset (b) Massasoit (c) Squanto (d) Gorges *(c)*

fall amongst them [the seamen] also, so as almost half of their company died before they went away, and many of their officers and lustiest men, as the boatswain, gunner, three quartermasters, the cook, and others. At which the master was something strucken and sent to the sick ashore and told the governor he should send for beer for them that had need of it, though he drank water homeward bound.

A But now amongst his [the ship master's] company there was far another kind of carriage in this misery than amongst the passengers. For they that before had been boon companions in drinking and jollity in the time of their health and welfare began now to desert one another in this calamity, saying they would not hazard their lives for them, they should be infected by coming to help them in their cabins; and so, after they came to lie by it, would do little or nothing for them but, "If they died, let them die." But such of the passengers as were yet aboard showed them what mercy they could, which made some of their hearts relent, as the boatswain (and some others), who was a proud young man and would often curse and scoff at the passengers. But when he grew weak, they had compassion on him and helped him; then he confessed he did not deserve it at their hands, he had abused them in word and deed. "Oh!" (saith he) "you, I now see, show your love like Christians indeed one to another, but we let one another lie and die like dogs." Another lay cursing his wife, saying if it had not been for her he had never come this unlucky voyage, and anon cursing his fellows, saying he had done this and that for some of them; he had spent so much and so much amongst them, and they were now weary of him and did not help him, having need. Another gave his companion all he had, if he died, to help him in his weakness; he went and got a little spice and made him a mess of meat once or twice. And because he died not so soon as he expected, he went among his fellows and swore the rogue would cozen [cheat] him, he would see him choked before he made him any more meat; and yet the poor fellow died before morning.

Indian Relations

All this while the Indians came skulking about them, and would sometimes show themselves aloof off, but when any approached near them, they would run away; and once they stole away their tools where they had been at work and were gone to dinner. But about the 16th of March, a certain Indian came boldly amongst them and spoke to them in broken English, which they could well understand but marveled at it. At length they understood, by discourse with him, that he was not of these parts but belonged to the eastern parts where some English ships came to fish, with whom he was acquainted and could name sundry of them by their names, amongst whom he had got his language. He became profitable to them in acquainting them with many things concerning the state of the country in the east parts where he lived, which was afterward profitable unto them; as also of the people here, of their names, number, and strength, of their situation and distance from this place, and who was chief amongst them. His name was Samoset.[17] He told them also of another Indian whose name was Squanto,[18] a native of this place, who had been in England and could speak better English than himself.

Being, after some time of entertainment and gifts, dismissed, a while after he came again, and five more with him, and they brought again all the tools that were stolen away before, and made way for the coming of their great Sachem, called Massasoit.[19] Who, about four or five days after, came with the chief of his friends and other attendance, with the aforesaid Squanto. With whom, after friendly entertainment and some gifts given him, they made a peace with him (which hath now continued this 24 years)[20] in these terms:

1. That neither he nor any of his should injure or do hurt to any of their people.

2. That if any of his did hurt to any of theirs, he should send the offender, that they might punish him.

3. That if anything were taken away from any of theirs, he should cause it to be restored; and they should do the like to his.

4. If any did unjustly war against him, they would aid him; if any did war against them, he should aid them.

5. He should send to his neighbors confederates

17. Samoset was an Algonquin from Maine.
18. Squanto was the sole survivor of the Pawtuckets.
19. Massasoit was the sachem (chief) of the Wampanoag and presided from a place called Sowams, the present-day site of Barrington, Rhode Island.
20. The treaty was kept faithfully until the reign of Massasoit's son Metacomet, known as King Philip by the colonists. See Mary Rowlandson's narrative on page 24.

A. Responding Chapter 11 provides a fascinating contrast between the actions of the Pilgrims and the sailors in "the starving time," during which half the company and half the sailors died. **?** Describe in general terms the actions of these two groups. Was there any exception to the sailors' mean-spirited viciousness? (Yes. The ship's captain donated beer to sick people ashore even though it meant he and his crew would have to drink water on the return voyage.)

ANALYZING THE HISTORY
Identifying Facts
1. Bradford says that death from God's "just hand" punished the profane young seaman for his curses. Bradford also seems to credit God with the repair of the main beam. He believes that divine intervention saves John Howland's life when the young man catches hold of a halyard upon being swept overboard.

Bradford sees God's hand, too, in the decision to return to Cape Cod when the ship encounters dangerous shoals on the way to Manhattan.

2. They have no friends and no towns or other places of refuge. The season is winter, and travel is dangerous because of fierce storms. They face a desolate wilderness, which they believe to be full of wild men and wild beasts. The ocean bars their escape back to civilization. They can expect no help or supplies from their brethren in Holland or elsewhere.

Bradford says that the Pilgrims need the Spirit of God and His grace.

3. He credits the finding of seed corn to God's Providence. Without the seed planted the following spring, the Pilgrims might not have survived the second winter. Bradford also credits Providence

CLOSURE
You might want students to brainstorm random thoughts of an unspecified Pilgrim, thinking back over the first year of Plymouth Colony.

FOR FURTHER READING
For Students
In *One Small Candle: The Pilgrims' First Year in America* (W. W. Norton, 1964), Thomas J. Fleming gives a vivid detailed account of the first Thanksgiving to which Massasoit brought no fewer than ninety men (compare Brownscombe's painting on this page).

The First Thanksgiving by Jennie Brownscombe (1914). Oil. Pilgrim Society, Plymouth, Massachusetts.

to certify them of this, that they might not wrong them, but might be likewise comprised in the conditions of peace.

6. That when their men came to them, they should leave their bows and arrows behind them.

After these things he returned to his place, called Sowams, some 40 miles from this place, but Squanto continued with them and was their interpreter and was a special instrument sent of God for their good beyond their expectation. He directed them how to set their corn, where to take fish and to procure other commodities, and was also their pilot to bring them to unknown places for their profit, and never left them till he died. He was a native of this place, and scarce any left alive besides himself. He was carried away with divers others by one Hunt, a master of a ship, who thought to sell them for slaves in Spain. But he got away for England and was entertained by a merchant in London, and employed to Newfoundland and other parts, and lastly brought hither into these parts by one Mr. Dermer, a gentleman employed by Sir Ferdinando Gorges and others for discovery and other designs in these parts. . . .

First Thanksgiving

[1621] They began now to gather in the small harvest they had, and to fit up their houses and dwellings against winter, being all well recovered in health and strength and had all things in good plenty. For as some were thus employed in affairs abroad, others were exercised in fishing, about cod and bass and other fish, of which they took good store, of which every family had their portion. All the summer there was no want; and now began to come in store of fowl, as winter approached, of which this place did abound when they came first (but afterward decreased by degrees). And besides waterfowl there was great store of wild turkeys, of which they took many, besides venison, etc. Besides they had about a peck of meal a week to a person, or now since harvest, Indian corn to that proportion. Which made many afterward write so largely of their plenty here to their friends in England, which were not feigned but true reports.

with preserving the company in their boat after the mast and rudder break.
4. Six or seven healthy settlers faithfully attend the sick, who include Bradford himself. The ship's company share their beer with the settlers, even though this means none for them on the return journey. When a young boatswain who had earlier cursed the Pilgrims falls ill, they care for him.

Interpreting Meanings
5. In general, the terms seem favorable to both parties, although students may note that the first three provisions appear to assume that the Indians, not the settlers, are the potential aggressors. Likewise, the last provision requires the Indians to leave their weapons behind when visiting settlers, but contains no such requirement for the settlers visiting Indians. Bradford is very favorable to Squanto, "a special instrument sent of God."
6. Answers will vary. Practical problems among the Pilgrims involve the necessity for mutual confidence, loyalty, hard work, and the ability to endure setbacks. Ethical problems are raised by the behavior of the crew and by the settlers' dealings with the Indians, as when the Pilgrims borrow corn.

Answers will vary. Current events or reading can provide appropriate examples. The Pilgrims' endurance under pressure would be helpful in any pioneering venture, such as space exploration or medical research.
7. Students will probably agree that the inclusion of this event would have made Bradford's history more moving and deeply personal.

Answers will vary. Puritanical acceptance of God's will may have played a part. Or Bradford may have felt that mention of the event would be depressing to his readers, whom he hoped to encourage to emigrate.
8. Answers will vary. Some students may say that the lighting and the poses suggest an idealized event. Encourage students to point out details in the painting to back up their responses.

Responding to the History

Analyzing the History

Identifying Facts

1. Historian Samuel Eliot Morison has said that "Bradford . . . had a constant sense of an unseen hand . . . that seemed to be guiding Puritan policy." What events on the voyage to the New World does Bradford credit to the direct intervention of God?
2. According to the end of Chapter 9, what hardships and dangers still face the settlers after the voyage is over? According to Bradford, what is the one thing that can sustain the group during these trials?
3. The famous entry in Chapter 10 reports in detail on the Pilgrims' first landing in the New World. What events during those first explorations does Bradford credit to God's Providence?
4. Bradford wrote his history of the "Old Comers" in part for the newcomers, the young people who, he hoped, would carry on the Pilgrims' ideals. What acts of charity and kindness during the "Starving Time" (Chapter 11) would remind later Puritans of their uniqueness and their obligations to their community?

Interpreting Meanings

5. Consider the treaty drawn up with Massasoit (page 19), and explain whether or not you feel its terms were equally favorable to both parties. What seems to be Bradford's attitude toward the Indians?
6. There is a certain timelessness in the Pilgrims' story. What practical and ethical problems common to many societies are reflected in their experience? In what ways might this wilderness experience be relevant to contemporary pilgrims or pioneers?
7. One event that Bradford does not describe is the death of his wife, who either fell or jumped overboard in Provincetown Harbor. How would his history have been different if he had included this tragedy? What reasons can you propose for his having omitted it?
8. Using what you have read, comment on the famous painting on page 20. Do you think it is realistic? Or does it idealize the First Thanksgiving?

Writing About the History

A Creative Response

1. **Using Another Point of View.** Retell the events of Chapter 10 from the point of view of one of the Native Americans who came upon the scouts. Narrate only what the observer would see happening and what you imagine he or she might be feeling.

A Critical Response

2. **Contrasting Two Historical Accounts.** Captain John Smith (1579–1631) had led the first permanent English settlement in the New World, at Jamestown, Virginia, in 1607. He hoped to establish another colony in New England, and in order to attract settlers, he wrote a pamphlet. Here is how Smith, somewhat like a contemporary travel agent, attempted to persuade people to join him in the New World:

> Here nature and liberty afford us that freely which in England we want, or it costs us dearly. What pleasure can be more than (being tired with any occasion ashore) in planting vines, fruits, or herbs, in contriving their own grounds, to the pleasure of their own minds, their fields, gardens, orchards, buildings, ships, and other works, etc., to re-create themselves before their own doors, in their own boats upon the sea, where man, woman, and child, with a small hook and line, by angling, may take divers sorts of excellent fish at their pleasures? And is it not pretty sport to pull up two pence, six pence, and twelve pence as fast as you can haul and veer a line? He is a very bad fisher [who] cannot kill in one day with his hook and line one, two, or three hundred cods, which dressed and dried, if they be sold there for ten shillings the hundred [pounds], though in England they will give more than twenty, may not both the servant, the master, and merchant be well content with this gain? If a man work but three days in seven, he may get more than he can spend, unless he will be excessive. . . .
>
> For hunting also, the woods, lakes, and rivers afford not only chase sufficient for any that delight in that kind of toil or pleasure, but such beasts to hunt that besides the delicacy of their bodies for food, their skins are so rich as may well recompense thy daily labor with a captain's pay.
>
> —from "A Description of New England," 1616, John Smith

Write a brief essay in which you contrast John Smith's promises with William Bradford's actual experiences in the New World. Begin by contrasting the **purposes** of the two writers and their intended **audiences.** Then mention at least three idealistic promises Smith makes and contrast these with Bradford's real experiences. You may also want to point out what Smith *omits* from his pamphlet. Finally, describe the different kinds of newcomers each writer was likely to attract, and explain the reasons for your answer.

A. Expansion (Challenging)
Among modern writers, one leading exponent of a "plain style" is E. B. White (see page 987). His book *The Elements of Style,* with co-author William Strunk, Jr. (Macmillan, 1959), offers many pointers on writing simply and lucidly. Your students might discuss the question of whether Strunk and White's book, along with White's crystalline essays, will seem as archaic three hundred years from now as William Bradford's prose seems to today's readers.

Primary Sources
The First Thanksgiving

On December 11, 1621, colonist Edward Winslow sent a letter to a friend in England describing the first Thanksgiving in the Colonies. The letter was reprinted in a book called *A Relation or Journall of the Beginning and Proceedings of the English Plantation settled at Plimouth in New England* (1622). The preface is signed "G. Mourt." Edward Winslow's letter is reprinted as follows. The governor is William Bradford.

"Our harvest being gotten in, our governor sent four men on fowling, that so we might after a more special manner rejoice together, after we had gathered the fruit of our labors. They four in one day killed as much fowl as, with a little help besides, served the company almost a week. At which time, amongst other recreations, we exercised our arms, many of the Indians coming among us, and amongst the rest their greatest king, Massasoit, with some 90 men, whom for three days we entertained and feasted. And they went out and killed five deer which they brought to the plantation and bestowed on our governor and upon the captain and others."

—Edward Winslow

The actual day on which the celebration took place was never recorded.

Elements of Literature

THE PLAIN STYLE

A At the beginning of his history, Bradford says he will try to unfold his story "in a plain style, with singular regard unto the simple truth in all things." He means that he will not imitate the ornate "high style" that was in fashion in England at the time—a style that used classical allusions, Latin quotations, and elaborate figures of speech. In a sense, Bradford's stylistic preference reflected the division between the Puritans and the Anglicans in matters of worship. A plain writing style was in keeping with the Puritans' preference for plainness in all other things, especially in church ritual.

One of the English writers who used a "high style" was John Donne, the poet and Anglican clergyman. This passage in the "high style" is from a sermon he delivered on Christmas Day in 1629:

> First, for the incomprehensibleness of God, the understanding of man hath a limited, a determined latitude; it is an intelligence able to move that sphere which it is fixed to, but could not move a greater: I can comprehend *naturam naturatam,* created nature, but for that *natura naturans,* God himself, the understanding of man cannot comprehend. I can see the sun in a looking glass, but the nature and the whole working of the sun I cannot see in that glass. I can see God in the creature, but the nature, the essence, the secret purposes of God, I cannot see there. There is *defatigatio in intellectualibus,* says the saddest and soundest of the Hebrew Rabbins; the soul may be tired, as well as the body, and the understanding dazzled, as well as the eye.
>
> —John Donne

The Puritans thought that a "plain style" was much more effective in revealing God's truth. The "plain style" imitated the style of the Geneva Bible, published in 1560 and used by the Puritans. (Other English Protestants of the time used the elegant King James translation, published in 1611.)

Bradford's history is plain, but this does not mean it is crude or lacking in art. Biblical quotations and allusions abound in Bradford's story; the Puritans' experiences are continually related to the experiences of the early Israelites or early Christians.

Bradford imitates the Geneva Bible in another one of his favorite stylistic devices. When he wants to be emphatic, he uses curious combinations of words that mean the same or nearly the same thing: "Firm and stable earth" on page 14 is an example.

Bradford's style is difficult to understand today because his syntax and vocabulary are now archaic, or not in common use. Take the passage that opens Chapter 10 and recast it into plain modern prose. In doing this, have you lost the "Biblical" sound?

Mary Rowlandson (c. 1636–c. 1678)

From June 1675 to August 1676, the Wampanoag chief Metacomet, called King Philip by the colonists, carried out a series of bloody raids on Colonial settlements in what is now called King Philip's war. The Puritans thought of the war as a sign of God's punishment for the sins of the younger generation (young people had taken to dancing and wearing their hair long), but such a conflict was probably inevitable. It was the natural result of growing encroachments by the settlers on tribal land and of the conflict between the two cultures. Despite careful attempts by Colonial leaders to regulate the buying of territory, the New England tribes had been forced into ever more restricted areas. And although the natives had sold the land, they rejected the condition that they could no longer hunt on it. To them, "selling" meant selling the right to share the land with the buyers, not selling its exclusive ownership.

Matters came to a head when Metacomet's former assistant, who had given information to the whites, was killed by his own people. His killers were tried and hanged by the Puritans. This was too much for Metacomet to bear, and two weeks later the most severe war in the history of New England began. Its tragic result was the virtual extinction of tribal life in the region.

Among the war's victims was Mary Rowlandson. Mrs. Rowlandson was the wife of the Congregational minister of Lancaster, a frontier town of about fifty families that was located thirty miles west of Boston. On a February morning, she and her three children were carried away by a raiding party that wanted to trade hostages for money. After eleven weeks and five days of captivity, her ransom was paid. She was to survive for only two more years.

Her captors, it is important to remember, were only slightly better off than their prisoners. Virtually without food, they were chased from camp to camp by Colonial soldiers. Their captives, they thought, were the only currency with which to buy supplies and food. In a graphic passage, Rowlandson describes the lengths to which the Indians were driven by their hunger: "They would pick up old bones," she wrote, "and cut them to pieces at the joints, and if they were full of worms and maggots, they would scald them over the fire to make the vermin come out, and then boil them, and drink up the liquor . . . They would eat horses' guts, and ears, and all sorts of wild birds which they could catch: also bear, venison, beaver, tortoise, frogs, squirrels, dogs, skunks, rattlesnakes; yea, the very bark of trees . . . I can but stand in admiration," she concluded, "to see the wonderful power of God, in providing for such a vast number of our enemies in the wilderness, where there was nothing to be seen, but from hand to mouth."

Rowlandson's moving tale of survival shows us the ordinary Puritan mind at work in extraordinary circumstances. Through apt quotations from the Bible, she places her experiences in the context of ancient Biblical captivities, such as the enslavement of Moses and the Israelites by the Egyptians. The Puritans regarded such Biblical captivity narratives as allegories representing the Christian's liberation from sin through the intervention of God's grace. Rowlandson viewed her own experiences as a repetition of the same pattern.

Her narrative, then, not only presents a terrifying and moving tale of frontier life but also provides insight into how the Puritans viewed their lives with a characteristic double vision. For Rowlandson, events had both a physical and a spiritual significance. She did not want merely to record her horrifying experience; she wished to demonstrate how it revealed God's purpose. The full title of her narrative illustrates this intention: *The Sovereignty and Goodness of God, Together with the Faithfulness of His Promises Displayed: Being a Narrative of the Captivity and Restoration of Mrs. Mary Rowlandson.*

Mary Rowlandson's *Narrative* was one of the most widely read prose works of the seventeenth century. It was especially popular in England, [A] where people were eager for lurid tales of the native inhabitants of the New World. The popularity of Rowlandson's story even gave rise to a mass of imitations that were often purely fictional. These "captivity" stories might have been entertaining, but they had a tragic side effect: They contributed to the further deterioration of relations between Native Americans and colonists.

A. Responding Mary Rowlandson's account of her capture and survival went through at least thirty editions. The genre became more sophisticated and literary as time went on, and factual captivity narratives (as opposed to later fictional ones) continued to appear for more than two hundred years after Mrs. Rowlandson's archetypal effort.

? Why do you think that this form of writing had such a long life? (Such stories are exciting. Ann Stanford's "Images of Women in Early American Literature" points out that the "experience itself—capture, adjustment, and escape or redemption—provided a good narrative sequence. To this Mrs. Rowlandson added a simple and direct style with some of the cadence of Biblical narrative. . . .")

SUPPLEMENTARY SUPPORT MATERIALS
1. Vocabulary Activity Worksheet (*CCB*)
2. Review and Response Worksheet: Subjective versus Objective Reporting (*CCB*)
3. Selection Test (*CCB*)

DEVELOPING VOCABULARY
The following words from the narrative are tested in the Selection Test. (See also Vocabulary Activity Worksheet.)

to bereave | sabbath
to entreat | savory
bier

PREPARATION
1. BUILDING ON PRIOR KNOWLEDGE. You may want to discuss with students their own preconceptions of the natives encountered by these early settlers. Once students have read the selection, they can discuss which preconceptions may have been erroneous.

A. Expansion
Students may wonder how twelve people could have been killed and twenty-five taken captive at one house. The answer is that six houses in Lancaster had been designated as garrison houses. In the event of an attack, specified families were to assemble there. Five houses held off the assault, but the sixth, the Rowlandsons', fell.

B. Subjective/Objective Reporting
It has often been remarked that the early accounts of conflict between white settlers and Native Americans were written by whites. Since most of the early colonists saw the Native Americans as heathens at best and instruments of the Devil at worst, it is remarkable that Mrs. Rowlandson's narrative is as objective as it is. Advise students to keep in mind question 5, page 30, as they read the selection.

FROM A NARRATIVE OF HER CAPTIVITY

A **In the opening part of her narrative, Mary Rowlandson describes the attack on Lancaster and the assault on her own house, where twelve people were killed and twenty-five taken captive. The first episode here recounts how her captors took her and her wounded child to Princeton, Massachusetts. Watch for the ways Mary Rowlandson links her sufferings with the sufferings of people in the Bible. Look also for indications of how the writer feels about her captors.**

The Move to Princeton, Massachusetts (February 11)

But now, the next morning, I must turn my back upon the town and travel with them [her captors] into the vast and desolate wilderness, I knew not whither. It is not my tongue, or pen, can express the sorrows of my heart and bitterness of my spirit that I had at this departure; but God was with me in a wonderful manner, carrying me along and bearing up my spirit, that it did not quite fail. One of the Indians carried my poor wounded babe upon a horse; it went moaning all along, "I shall die, I shall die." I went on foot after it, with sorrow that cannot be expressed. At length I took it off the horse and carried it in my arms till my strength failed, and I fell down with it. Then they set me upon a horse with my wounded child in my lap, and there being no furniture upon the horse's back, as we were going down a steep hill we both fell over the horse's head. . . . But the Lord renewed my strength still and carried me along, that I might see more of His power; yea, so much that I could never have thought of had I not experienced it.

After this it quickly began to snow, and when night came on, they stopped, and now down I must sit in the snow, by a little fire, and a few boughs behind me, with my sick child in my lap; and calling much for water, being now (through the wound) fallen into a violent fever. My own wound [was] also growing so stiff that I could scarce sit down or rise up; yet so it must be, that I must sit all this cold winter night upon the cold snowy ground, with my sick child in my arms, looking that every hour would be the last of its life; and having no Christian friend near me, either to comfort or help me. Oh, I may see the wonderful power of God, that my spirit did not utterly sink under my affliction: still the Lord upheld me with His gracious and merciful spirit, and we were both alive to see the light of the next morning.

The Move to an Indian Village on the Ware River, Near Braintree (February 12–27)

The morning being come, they prepared to go on their way. One of the Indians got up upon a horse, and they set me up behind him, with my poor sick babe in my lap. A very wearisome and tedious day I had of it, what with my own wound and my child's being so exceeding sick and in a lamentable condition with her wound. It may be easily judged what a poor feeble condition we were in, there being not the least crumb of refreshing that came within either of our mouths from Wednesday night to Saturday night, except only a little cold water. This day in the afternoon, about an hour by sun, we came to the place where they intended, viz., an Indian town, called Wenimesset, northward of Quabaug. . . . I sat much alone with a poor wounded child in my lap, which moaned night and day, having nothing to revive the body or cheer the spirits of her, but instead of that, sometimes one Indian would come and tell me one hour that "your master will knock your child in the head," and then a second, and then a third, "Your master will quickly knock your child in the head." B

2. Establishing a Purpose. Each part of the narrative details the author's experiences as she is moved to a new location by her captors. You might suggest that students read each part to learn about these experiences as well as the author's means of coping with them both physically and mentally.

Portrait of Ninigret II, Chief of the Niantic Indians. Anonymous (c.1681). Oil.

Museum of Art, Rhode Island School of Design. Gift of Mr. Robert Winthrop.

Humanities Connection: Responding to the Fine Art

This painting of Ninigret II is one of the few portraits of a New England Indian from approximately the time of King Philip's War. There is no authentic portrait of Metacomet (King Philip).

The Niantic Indians, a tribe of the southern Narragansetts, remained friendly to the English and opposed to King Philip throughout the war, which may account for this portrait being painted.

? Do you think that this artist's purpose was to produce a historical record or an artistic work? (The realistic details and relative lack of imagination suggest that his purpose was the former.)

A. Humanities Connection: Discussing the Fine Art
Thomas Davies (1737–1812) was a British army officer stationed in Canada for more than thirty years. His chief duties were surveying and mapping, and in the course of his travels he painted scenes such as *Algonquin Indian Encampment.*

The various tribes involved in King Philip's War—Wampanoag, Narragansett, and Nipmuck—were all Algonquins. *Algonquin* is a broad term covering the tribes that inhabited the forests from Labrador and Quebec south to Virginia. The various tribes, although often at war with one another, shared many characteristics.

B. Allusion
Mrs. Rowlandson identifies her suffering with that of Job in the Bible. Her lament is that of Job 16:11–12: "God hath delivered me over to the ungodly, and turned me into the hands of the wicked. I was at ease, but he hath broken me asunder: he hath also taken me by my neck, and shaken me to pieces, and set me up for his mark." But, like Job, she cannot believe that God is unjust.

A *Algonquin Indian Encampment* by Thomas Davies (1788). Watercolor. The National Gallery of Canada, Ottawa.

B This was the comfort I had from them, miserable comforters are ye all, as he[1] said. Thus nine days I sat upon my knees, with my babe in my lap, till my flesh was raw again; my child being even ready to depart this sorrowful world, they bade me carry it out to another wigwam (I suppose because they would not be troubled with such spectacles), whither I went with a very heavy heart, and down I sat with the picture of death in my lap. About two hours in the night, my sweet babe like a lamb departed this life on February 18, 1675, it being about six years and five months old. It was nine days from the first wounding, in this miserable condition, without any refreshing of one nature or other, except a little cold water. I cannot but take notice how at another time I could not bear to be in the room where any dead person was, but now the case is changed; I must and could lie down by my dead babe, side by side all the night after. I have thought since of the wonderful goodness of God to me in preserving me in the use of my reason and senses in that distressed time, that I did not use wicked and violent means to end my own miserable life. In the morning, when they understood that my child was dead, they sent for me home to my master's wigwam (by my master in this writing must be understood Quanopin, who was a Sagamore,[2] and married King Philip's wife's sister; not that he first took me, but I was sold to him by another Narragansett Indian, who took me when first I came out of the garrison). I went to take up my dead child in my arms to carry it with me, but they bid me let it alone; there was no resisting, but go I must and

1. **he:** the Biblical allusion is to Job 16:2. In the passage cited, Job addresses those who try to console him in his afflictions. God had severely tested Job's faith: He lost his children and his money, and broke out in boils all over his body.

2. **Sagamore:** a subordinate chief in the Algonquin hierarchy.

COMMENT FROM THE WRITER
Mary Rowlandson's constantly repeated praise for God amid accumulating disasters may be hard for students to comprehend. From her viewpoint, however, it made perfect sense, as the following passage from her narrative makes clear.

"Before I knew what affliction meant, I was ready sometimes to wish for it. When I lived in prosperity, having the comforts of the World about me, my Heart chearfull, and taking little care for any thing; and yet seeing many, whom I preferred before my self, under many tryals and afflictions, in sickness, weakness, poverty, losses, crosses, and cares of the World, I should be sometimes jealous least I should have my portion in this life, and that Scripture would come to my mind, Heb. 12.6 *For whom the Lord loveth he chasteneth, and scourageth every Son whom he receiveth.* But now I see the Lord had his time to scourge and chasten me."

leave it. When I had been at my master's wigwam, I took the first opportunity I could get to go look after my dead child. When I came. I asked them what they had done with it; then they told me it was upon the hill. Then they went and showed me where it was, where I saw the ground was newly digged, and there they told me they had buried it. There I left that child in the wilderness, and must commit it, and myself also in this wilderness condition, to Him who is above all. God having taken away this dear child, I went to see my daughter Mary, who was at this same Indian town, at a wigwam not very far off, though we had little liberty or opportunity to see one another. She was about ten years old, and taken from the door at

A first by a Praying Ind. and afterward sold for a gun. When I came in sight, she would fall aweeping; at which they were provoked, and would not let me come near her, but bade me be gone; which was a heart-cutting word to me. I had one child dead, another in the wilderness, I knew not where, the third they would not let me come near to: "Me (as he said) have ye bereaved of my Children, Joseph is not, and Simeon is not, and ye will take Benjamin also, all these things are against me."[3] I could not sit still in this condition, but kept walking from one place to another. And as I was going along, my heart was even overwhelmed with the thoughts of my condition, and that I should have children, and a nation which I knew not ruled over them. Whereupon I earnestly entreated the Lord, that He would consider my low estate and show me a token for good and, if it were His blessed will, some sign and hope of some relief. And indeed quickly the Lord answered, in some measure, my poor prayers; for as I was going up and down mourning and lamenting my condition, my son came to me and asked me how I did. I had not seen him before, since the destruction of the town, and I knew not where he was till I was informed by himself that he was among a smaller parcel of Indians, whose place was about six miles off. With tears in his eyes, he asked me whether his sister Sarah was dead; and told me he had seen his sister Mary; and prayed me that I would not be troubled in reference to himself. . . . I cannot but take notice of the wonderful mercy of God to me in those afflictions, in sending me a Bible. One of the Indians that came from [the] Medfield fight had brought some plunder, came to me and asked me if I would have a Bible, he had got one in his basket. I was glad of it and asked him whether he thought the Indians would let me read. He answered, yes. So I took the Bible, and in that melancholy time, it came into my mind to read first the 28th chapter of Deuteronomy,[4] which I did, and when I had read it, my dark heart wrought on this manner: that there was no mercy for me, that the blessings were gone, and the curses come in their room, and that I had lost my opportunity. But the Lord helped me still to go on reading till I came to Chapter 30, the seven first verses, where I found there was mercy promised again, if we would return to Him by repentance; and though we were scattered from one end of the earth to the other, yet the Lord would gather us together and turn all those curses upon our enemies. I do not desire to live to forget this Scripture, and what comfort it was to me. . . .

Crossing the Bacquaug (now Miller's) River, in Orange, Massachusetts (March 3–5)

The occasion (as I thought) of their moving at this time was the English Army,[5] it being near and following them. For they [the Indians] went as if they had gone for their lives, for some considerable way, and then they made a stop, and chose some of their stoutest men, and sent them back to hold the English Army in play while the rest escaped. And then, like Jehu,[6] they marched on furiously, with their old and with their young: some carried their old decrepit mothers, some carried one, and some another. Four of them carried a great Indian upon a bier; but going through a thick wood with him, they were hindered and could make no haste, whereupon they took him upon their backs and carried him, one at a time,

3. Rowlandson quotes Jacob's lament in Genesis 42:36. All of Jacob's sons had left the country, and he had only the youngest, Benjamin, at home.

4. In Deuteronomy 28, Moses warns that God will bless those who obey Him and curse those who do not.

5. **the English Army:** the Massachusetts and Connecticut forces, led by Thomas Savage.

6. **Jehu:** the Israelite king who led his armies against King Ahab and slew Ahab and all his men (2 Kings 9–10).

A. Responding
When Mrs. Rowlandson refers to a "Praying Ind.," she means an Indian who has been converted to Christianity. Point out to students that while this particular Praying Indian was untrustworthy (as were others), many stayed loyal to the settlers and remained firm in their faith throughout 1675–1676. Yet some Praying Indians were cruelly mistreated by whites during the war for fear that the converted Indians might revert to their "savage ways" when their unconverted brethren went on the warpath.

? Identify another instance in American history in which a group was interned—as some Praying Indians were—out of fear that they might aid the enemy in wartime. (During World War II, Japanese-Americans on the West Coast were interned because of concern for their loyalty.)

Reading Check Test

1. After her capture, Rowlandson is not allowed to see any of her children except Sarah. *False*
2. An Indian who has plundered a Bible gives it to Rowlandson. *True*
3. Despite the constant traveling and the cold weather, the Indians have enough dried fruit and meat with them so that food is not a problem. *False*
4. Rowlandson agrees to smoke a pipe with King Philip (Metacomet) because it is an Indian custom and she hopes not to offend him. *False*
5. Mary Rowlandson interprets her captivity as God's test of her faith. *True*

Closure

You might have students write a brief character sketch of Mary Rowlandson. The sketch should summarize her religious beliefs and personal characteristics as well as her attitudes toward Native Americans.

A. Responding

? When do you suppose that Mrs. Rowlandson wrote her narrative? Is it an actual journal—that is, one written day by day? And, if so, how? We know she carried her knitting, but did she also carry pencil and paper? (The text provides no answer, but most captivity narratives were written soon after the captive's return from the wilderness.)

? Do you find any indication in the text that the narrative is being written after Rowlandson's return? (The fact that Rowlandson has achieved some objectivity indicates some lapse of time between her experiences and the writing of this account.)

till they came to Bacquaug River. Upon a Friday, a little after noon, we came to this river. When all the company was come up and were gathered together, I thought to count the number of them, but they were so many, and being somewhat in A motion, it was beyond my skill. In this travel, because of my wound, I was somewhat favored in my load; I carried only my knitting work and two quarts of parched meal. Being very faint, I asked my mistress to give me one spoonful of the meal, but she would not give me a taste. They quickly fell to cutting dry trees, to make rafts to carry them over the river; and soon my turn came to go over. By the advantage of some brush which they had laid upon the raft to sit upon, I did not wet my foot (which many of themselves at the other end were mid-leg deep), which cannot but be acknowledged as a favor of God to my weakened body, it being a very cold time. I was not before acquainted with such kind of doings or dangers. "When thou passeth through the waters I will be with thee, and through the rivers they shall not overflow thee" (Isaiah 43.2). A certain number of us got over the river that night, but it was the night after the sabbath before all the company was got over. On the Saturday they boiled an old horse's leg which they had got, and so we drank of the broth as soon as they thought it was ready, and when it was almost all gone, they filled it up again.

The first week of my being among them I hardly ate anything; the second week I found my stomach grow very faint for want of something; and yet it was very hard to get down their filthy trash; but the third week, though I could think how formerly my stomach would turn against this or that, and I could starve and die before I could eat such things, yet they were sweet and savory to my taste. . . .

The Move to Coasset, Vermont

. . . We traveled on till night; and in the morning, we must go over the river to Philip's crew. When I was in the canoe, I could not but be amazed at the numerous crew of pagans that were on the bank on the other side. When I came ashore, they gathered all about me, I sitting alone in the midst. I observed they asked one another questions, and laughed, and rejoiced over their gains and victories. Then my heart began to fail; and I fell aweeping, which was the first time to my remembrance that I wept before them. Although I had met with so much affliction, and my heart was many times ready to break, yet could I not shed one tear in their sight; but rather had been all this while in a maze and like one astonished. But now I may say as Psalm 137.1, "By the Rivers of Babylon, there we sate down: yea, we wept when we remembered Zion." There one of them asked me why I wept. I could hardly tell what to say; yet I answered, they would kill me. "No," said he, "none will hurt you." Then came one of them and gave me two spoonfuls of meal to comfort me, and another gave me half a pint of peas; which was more worth than many bushels at another time. Then I went to see King Philip. He bade me come in and sit down, and asked me whether I would smoke it (a usual compliment nowadays among saints and sinners), but this no way suited me. For though I had formerly used tobacco, yet I had left it ever since I was first taken. It seems to be a bait the devil lays to make men lose their precious time. I remember with shame how formerly, when I had taken two or three pipes, I was presently ready for another, such a bewitching thing it is. But I thank God, He has now given me power over it; surely there are many who may be better employed than to lie sucking a stinking tobacco pipe.

Now the Indians gather their forces to go against Northhampton. Over night one went about yelling and hooting to give notice of the design. Whereupon they fell to boiling of groundnuts and parching of corn (as many as had it) for their provision; and in the morning away they went. During my abode in this place, Philip spoke to me to make a shirt for his boy, which I did, for which he gave me a shilling. I offered the money to my master, but he bade me keep it; and with it I bought a piece of horseflesh. Afterward he asked me to make a cap for his boy, for which he invited me to dinner. I went, and he gave me a pancake, about as big as two fingers. It was made of parched wheat, beaten, and fried in bear's grease, but I thought I never tasted pleasanter meat in my life. There was a squaw who spake to me to make a shirt for her *sannup* [husband], for which she gave me a piece of bear. Another asked me to knit a pair of stockings, for which she gave me a quart of peas. I boiled my peas and bear together, and invited my master and mistress to dinner; but the proud gossip [old woman], because I served them both in one dish, would eat nothing, except one bit that he gave her upon the point of his knife. . . .

Analyzing the Journal

Identifying Facts

1. One of the Indians carries her wounded child on a horse, while Rowlandson walks. Later, after carrying Sarah and becoming exhausted, both of them are put on a horse. At nightfall, the Indians stop. Throughout the night Rowlandson shivers in the snow by a fire with her child in her arms.

Rowlandson refers several times to God's presence and to His renewal of her faith.

2. The Indians at one point refuse her a spoonful of meal. Later, they boil an old horse's leg.

3. She makes articles of clothing for her captors.

By the third week, she is so hungry she is ready to eat food she once have considered inedible.

4. Students will find many examples. Rowlandson believes that God saves many of her family from death, preserves her sanity and prevents her from committing suicide, and brings her son, who is held captive by a different group of Indians, to meet her.

(Answers continue on page 30.)

The Move to the Ashuelot Valley, New Hampshire

But instead of going either to Albany or homeward, we must go five miles up the river and then go over it. Here we abode [stayed] awhile. Here lived a sorry Indian, who spoke to me to make him a shirt. When I had done it, he would pay me nothing. But he living by the riverside, where I often went to fetch water, I would often be putting of him in mind and calling for my pay. At last he told me if I would make another shirt, for a papoose not yet born, he would give me a knife, which he did when I had done it. I carried the knife in, and my master asked me to give it him, and I was not a little glad that I had anything that they would accept of and be pleased with. When we were at this place, my master's maid came home; she had been gone three weeks into the Narragansett country to fetch corn, where they had stored up some in the ground. She brought home about a peck and a half of corn. This was about the time that their great captain, Naananto, was killed in the Narragansett country. My son being now about a mile from me, I asked liberty to go and see him; they bade me go, and away I went but quickly lost myself, traveling over hills and through swamps, and could not find the way to him. And I cannot but admire at the wonderful power and goodness of God to me in that, though I was gone from home, and met with all sorts of Indians, and those I had no knowledge of, and there being no Christian soul near me, yet not one of them offered the least imaginable miscarriage to me. I turned homeward again and met with my master. He showed me the way to my son. . . .

But I was fain to go and look after something to satisfy my hunger, and going among the wigwams, I went into one and there found a squaw who showed herself very kind to me and gave me a piece of bear. I put it into my pocket and came home, but could not find an opportunity to broil it, for fear they would get it from me, and there it lay all that day and night in my stinking pocket. In the morning I went to the same squaw, who had a kettle of groundnuts boiling. I asked her to let me boil my piece of bear in her kettle, which she did, and gave me some groundnuts to eat with it; and I cannot but think how pleasant it was to me. I have sometimes seen bear baked very handsomely among the English, and some like it, but the thought that it was bear made me tremble. But now that was savory to me that one would think was enough to turn the stomach of a brute creature.

One bitter cold day I could find no room to sit down before the fire. I went out and could not tell what to do, but I went in to another wigwam, where they were also sitting round the fire, but the squaw laid a skin for me, and bid me sit down, and gave me some groundnuts, and bade me come again; and told me they would buy me, if they were able, and yet these were strangers to me that I never saw before. . . .

A

NARRATIVE

OF THE

CAPTIVITY, SUFFERINGS AND REMOVES

OF

Mrs. *Mary Rowlandſon*,

Who was taken Priſoner by the INDIANS with ſeveral others, and treated in the moſt barbarous and cruel Manner by thoſe vile Savages: With many other remarkable Events during her TRAVELS.

Written by her own Hand, for her private Uſe, and now made public at the earneſt Deſire of ſome Friends, and for the Benefit of the afflicted.

BOSTON

Printed and Sold at JOHN BOYLE's Printing-Office, next Door to the *Three Doves* in Marlborough-Street. 1773.

A. Attitude

Do you find any evidence that the author's attitude toward her captors is changing? Is she, as the illustrated title page states, being "treated in the most barbarous and cruel manner by those vile savages"? See question 6, page 30. (The author's statement that "not one of them offered the least imaginable miscarriage to me" suggests a change in attitude. Although the food was primitive and the travel difficult, Rowlandson was not mistreated by the Indians.)

(Answers begin on page 29.)

Interpreting Meanings

5. Answers will vary. Rowlandson, quoting Job 16:2, calls the Indians "miserable comforters" (page 26) and describes their food as "filthy trash" (page 28).

6. Instances of kindness include the Indians permitting her to ride on a horse with her wounded child on her lap and an Indian giving her a Bible to read.

Throughout the narrative, Rowlandson mentions instances of kindness. Early in the narrative, however, she makes a few barbed comments about the Indians. Yet despite her sufferings, she is not vindictive. Her attitude seems to become more favorable toward the Indians in the later extracts of the journal.

7. Answers will vary. Rowlandson's "miserable comforters" quotation from the Book of Job suggests that the Indian attack on her house is an affliction similar to the one visited on Job—a severe testing by God. Later in her journal, Rowlandson refers to Jacob's lament for his absent children.

(Answers continue in left-hand column.)

(Continued from top.)

Answers will vary. In each Biblical story, severe afflictions threaten to destroy people's faith in God. But that faith, even in the most dire circumstances, is maintained and rewarded.

8. Answers will vary. Students may mention her religious faith, her concern for her family, her courage, and her ability to do useful work.

Answers will vary.

9. Students may mention the suspenseful plot (albeit a true story), the setting (which to the English would have been remote and exotic), and the religious motif (in an era of religious fervor).

Many aspects of the journal might promote such views: for example, the fact that Rowlandson is held in slavery as the consequence of an Indian raid and her depiction of the Indians as savages.

10. The captivity motif appears in many contemporary works of nonfiction about prisoners-of-war, hostages, political prisoners.

Responding to the Journal

Analyzing the Journal

Identifying Facts

1. In the first extract, what does Rowlandson tell us about how she was treated? What details in the narrative reveal how her religious faith helped her survive?
2. Find the details in Rowlandson's later diary entries that reveal that her captors themselves are desperate to find food.
3. What jobs does Rowlandson do to earn her food? How does her attitude toward food change while she is a captive?
4. Identify at least three occasions during her captivity in which Rowlandson is able to see Divine Providence at work.

Interpreting Meanings

5. Despite her efforts to be accurate, Rowlandson's journal is full of **subjective reporting**. Select any extract from the journal and find the words that reveal her **attitude** toward her captors—words that a detached historian would not use.
6. What instances of kindness does Rowlandson mention in her later entries? Does she reveal any conflicting attitudes toward her captors? Do you think her attitude changes? Explain.
7. The Puritans' habit of seeing specific allegorical meaning in their experiences helped them find significance in even very minor events. In an **allegory,** events, characters, and setting possess both a literal and a symbolic meaning. Describe at least two events of Rowlandson's captivity that she sees as allegories of Biblical stories. Identify the specific ways in which each of these Biblical stories resembles Rowlandson's.
8. What personal characteristics do you think helped Rowlandson survive her experience? Do you think personal courage or religious faith was more significant? Explain.
9. This captivity account was enormously popular in England. What reasons can you propose for its popularity? What aspects of Rowlandson's journal would promote stereotyped (and hostile) views toward Native Americans?
10. Are "captivity stories" still popular today? In what ways are contemporary captivity stories different from Rowlandson's? In what ways are they similar to her account?

Writing About the Journal

A Creative Response

1. **Using Another Point of View.** Write a journal entry in which you explain the situation of the Wampanoag people who captured Rowlandson. Try to account for the causes of the attack on the settlement and for the natives' desperate conditions. Use history texts or encyclopedias for your sources. You will find information under "King Philip's War" and "Metacomet." Write your entry from the point of view of a member of the Wampanoag tribe.

A Critical Response

2. **Explaining an Allusion.** On page 28, Mary Rowlandson alludes to Psalm 137, which is a well-known "captivity" psalm. It was composed when the Israelites were held captive in Babylon by King Nebuchadnezzar. Here is the whole psalm:

> By the rivers of Babylon, there we sat down; yea, we wept, when we remembered Zion.
>
> We hanged our harps upon the willows in the midst thereof.
>
> For there they that carried us away captive required of us a song; and they that wasted us required of us mirth, saying, Sing us one of the songs of Zion.
>
> How shall we sing the Lord's song in a strange land?
>
> If I forget thee, O Jerusalem, let my right hand forget her cunning.
>
> If I do not remember thee, let my tongue cleave to the roof of my mouth; if I prefer not Jerusalem above my chief joy.
>
> Remember, O Lord, the children of Edom in the day of Jerusalem; who said, Raze it, raze it, even to the foundation thereof.
>
> O daughter of Babylon, who art to be destroyed; happy shall he be, that rewardeth thee as thou hast served us.
>
> Happy shall he be, that taketh and dasheth thy little ones against the stones.
>
> —Psalm 137

In a brief essay, explain why Rowlandson thought of this psalm at a certain point in her sufferings. What parallel would she see between her experience and that of the psalmist? In her mind, what would "Babylon" be?

A. Expansion
Sarah Kemble Knight is so spirited a traveler that students may get the impression that few obstacles stood in the path of women in colonial America. That is far from the truth. Although churches were accepting women more readily into full participation (though not as ministers), the lives of most women were still circumscribed. You might discuss with your students the rights that women of Knight's time did not have. (They lacked the right to vote. Their property rights were severely limited. They were not yet accepted in the professions.)

Sarah Kemble Knight (1666–1727)

Sarah Kemble Knight's husband, a sea captain and the London representative for an American company, was frequently abroad. In his absence, the capable and energetic Mrs. Knight ran a boardinghouse in Boston. She also taught school (Benjamin Franklin is reputed to have been one of her pupils), gave handwriting lessons, and assisted people with legal matters. It was in this last capacity that she journeyed from Boston to New York in the fall of 1704, to settle a family estate.

A

In Colonial America, it was almost unheard of for a woman to travel such a long distance with only guides as company. Overland travel was unsafe and far from comfortable, as Knight's account makes clear. A trip that today might be made by plane in an hour, or by train in four, took Knight about two weeks on horseback. But those two weeks were hardly wasted time. Knight's shorthand diary of the journey, kept for her own pleasure and not published until the nineteenth century, gives a lively and accurate portrait of life "on the road" in early eighteenth-century America. It also offers a nice secular contrast to the religious tenor of much Colonial writing. At the same time, it puts us in the company of a most interesting traveling companion. Knight's shrewd observations, her personal strength, and her no-nonsense attitude are qualities especially appealing to modern readers. Like many travelers today, she complains about the food: A Frenchman's fricassee was "so contrary" to her notion of cookery that she went to bed supperless. The beds were bad: "my poor bones complained bitterly." And the prices were too high, "as dear as if we had had far better fare." The feisty Sarah Knight has more in common with Ben Franklin than with many early Puritans. Her point of view is practical rather than theological, and she is more apt to allude to classical literature than to the Bible. To this extent, her diary suggests how Puritan culture was changing. Knight looks forward to the country's future rather than backward to its origins.

A few years after Knight's journey, her husband apparently died: After 1706, there is no further reference to him in her diaries. In 1714, she moved to New London, Connecticut, with her married daughter. There she ran a shop and an inn and made a number of investments in property that—as we might expect—were extremely profitable.

B. Humanities Connection: Discussing the Fine Art
Petrus Svinin (1787–1839), a Russian-born landscape and portrait painter, came to America as secretary to the Russian Consul-General. Stationed in Philadelphia, he traveled from Maine to Virginia, painting more than fifty watercolors of American scenes. His stay lasted two years.

Svinin's *Ferry Scene on the Susquehanna at Wright's Ferry, near Havre de Grace* was painted more than a hundred years after Sarah Kemble Knight made her journey.

B

Ferry Scene on the Susquehanna at Wright's Ferry, near Havre de Grace by Petrus Svinin (1811). Watercolor.

The Metropolitan Museum of Art, New York. Rogers Fund, 1942.

SUPPLEMENTARY SUPPORT MATERIALS
1. Vocabulary Activity Worksheet (*CCB*)
2. Review and Response Worksheet: Tone (*CCB*)
3. Selection Test (*CCB*)

DEVELOPING VOCABULARY
The following words from the journal are tested in the Selection Test. (See also Vocabulary Activity Worksheet.)

cloyed	clamor
circumspect	prodigious
formidable	contriving
ravenous	dram
descent	carcass

PREPARATION
1. ESTABLISHING A PURPOSE. As the headnote suggests, have students read to determine the writer's tone toward her material and what this tone reveals about Knight's personality.

A. Expansion
To help students place Knight's trip in historical context, have them look at the time line on page 7. They will notice that the Salem witch trials preceded the trip by only twelve years.

B. Responding
Knight's journal begins with references to "the post." What methods of communication other than the post, or mail, existed between Boston and New York in 1704? (None except personal visits, which was why Knight was making this journey)

FROM THE JOURNAL OF MADAM KNIGHT
A JOURNEY FROM BOSTON TO NEW YORK

As you read Knight's journal, try to form a precise idea of the writer's *tone*, or attitude toward her material. How does this tone contrast with what you might have expected from a Puritan writer? What does the tone reveal about the writer's personality?

A

Tuesday, October 3, 1704

B

About eight in the morning, I with the post proceeded forward without observing anything remarkable; and about two, afternoon, arrived at the post's second stage, where the western post met him and exchanged letters.[1] Here, having called for something to eat, the woman brought in a twisted thing like a cable, but something [somewhat] whiter; and laying it on the board, tugged for life to bring it into a capacity to spread; which having with great pains accomplished, she served in a dish of pork and cabbage, I suppose the remains of dinner. The sauce was of a deep purple, which I thought was boiled in her dye kettle; the bread was Indian, and everything on the table service agreeable to these. I, being hungry, got a little down; but my stomach was soon cloyed [filled], and what cabbage I swallowed served me for a cud the whole day after.

Having here discharged the ordinary[2] for self and guide (as I understood was the custom), about three, afternoon, went on with my [second] guide, who rode very hard; and having crossed Providence ferry, we came to a river which they generally ride through. But I dared not venture; so the post got a lad and canoe to carry me to t'other side, and he rode through and led my horse. The canoe was very small and shallow, so that when we were in, she seemed ready to take in water, which greatly terrified me and caused me to be very circumspect, sitting with my hands fast on each side, my eyes steady, not daring so much as to lodge my tongue a hairbreadth more on one side of my mouth than t'other nor so much as think on Lot's wife,[3] for a wry thought would have overset our wherry [small boat]; but was soon put out of this pain by feeling the canoe on shore, which I as soon almost saluted with my feet; and rewarding my sculler, again mounted and made the best of our way forward. The road here was very even and the day pleasant, it being now near sunset. But the post told me we had near fourteen miles to ride to the next stage (where we were to lodge). I asked him of the rest of the road, foreseeing we must travail in the night. He told me that there was a bad river we were to ride through, which was so very fierce a horse could sometimes hardly stem it; but it was but narrow, and we should soon be over. I cannot express the concern of mind this relation set me in: no thoughts but those of the dangerous river could entertain my imagination, and they were as formidable as various, still tormenting me with blackest ideas of my approaching fate—sometimes seeing myself

1. Knight is traveling on horseback in the company of mail carriers. They have reached a stop where two carriers exchange pouches of mail.
2. **discharged the ordinary:** paid for the meal. "Ordinary" referred both to a meal bought in a public house (as it does here) and to a public house itself (as it does later in Mrs. Knight's account).
3. **Lot's wife:** Lot's wife was turned into a pillar of salt when she turned to look back at Sodom, the city she and her family were fleeing (Genesis 19:28).

2. **Prereading Journal.** As students read, you might have them write about two main problems that they think Knight will encounter on her trip from Boston to New York in 1704. In their journals, students might assume the viewpoint of Knight, thinking ahead to her journey.

A. Humanities Connection: Discussing the Fine Art
Your students are bombarded with four-color photographs, book and periodical illustrations, and video images. This glut is a twentieth-century phenomenon, and students may not realize that as late as the nineteenth century it was a common practice to have black-and-white engravings watercolored by hand to produce a print that could be framed and hung for home decoration. Original art, then as now, was prohibitively expensive, but engravings were moderately priced.

B. Allusion/ Figurative Language
The descriptions here are remarkably literary for a writer who was not anticipating publication. Identify an allusion, a metaphor, and a simile on this page. (Allusion: "the glorious luminary with his swift coursers"; metaphor: "Each lifeless trunk . . . shattered limbs . . . an armed enemy" [there are others]; simile: "every little stump like a ravenous devourer")

A

American Stage Wagon (1798). Colored engraving.

drowning, otherwhiles drowned, and at the best, like a holy sister just come out of a spiritual bath in dripping garments.

B Now was the glorious luminary with his swift coursers arrived at his stage,[4] leaving poor me with the rest of this part of the lower world in darkness, with which we were soon surrounded. The only glimmering we now had was from the spangled skies, whose imperfect reflections rendered every object formidable. Each lifeless trunk, with its shattered limbs, appeared an armed enemy; and every little stump like a ravenous devourer. Nor could I so much as discern my guide, when at any distance, which added to the terror.

Thus, absolutely lost in thought, and dying with the very thoughts of drowning, I come up with the post, who I did not see 'til even with his horse; he told me he stopped for me, and we rode on very deliberately a few paces, when we entered a thicket of trees and shrubs, and I perceived by the horse's going we were on the descent of a hill, which, as we come nearer the bottom, 'twas totally dark with the trees that surrounded it. But I knew by the going of the horse we had entered the water, which my guide told me was the hazardous river he had told me of; and he, riding up close to my side, bid me not fear—we should be over immediately. I now rallied all the courage I was mistress of, knowing that I must either ven-

4. That is, the sun had set. The reference is to Apollo, the sun god in Greek mythology. The Greeks believed that he pulled the sun as he rode across the sky in a chariot drawn by "coursers," or horses.

Closure

To check that students understand the differences in tone between Rowlandson's narrative and this journal, have students rewrite a passage from the captivity narrative as it might have been written by Knight. Or, you might have students rewrite a portion of Knight's journal as Rowlandson might have written it.

Reading Check Test

1. Despite her guide's suggestion that she hire a canoe to take her across the first river, Mrs. Knight insists on riding through it on her horse. *False*
2. Although the beds are often uncomfortable, the post stations on Knight's journey usually provide excellent food. *False*
3. Knight writes her journal entries at night before going to bed. *True*
4. On the night of October 3, two town drunks keep Knight awake until late at night. *True*
5. While crossing a bridge over a swift river, Knight falls into the water. *False*

A. Responding

Knight's evening at Mr. Havens's public house provides insight into Knight's character. **?** How does Knight react to the dispute between the "town topers"? What does this reaction tell us about Knight's character? (Knight "heartily fretted" about being kept awake by the ridiculous argument and composed a humorous verse as a way of coping with the situation. Her reaction indicates that she is capable of dealing with a difficult situation in a positive way.)

ture my fate of drowning or be left like the children in the wood.[5] So, as the post bid me, I gave reins to my nag; and sitting as steady as just before in the canoe, in a few minutes got safe to the other side, which he told me was the Narragansett country. . . .

Being come to Mr. Havens',[6] I was very civilly received, and courteously entertained, in a clean comfortable house; and the good woman was very active in helping off my riding clothes, and then asked what I would eat. I told her I had some chocolate, if she would prepare it; which with the help of some milk, and a little clean brass kettle, she soon effected to my satisfaction. I then betook me to my apartment, which was a little room parted from the kitchen by a single board partition; where, after I had noted the occurrences of the past day, I went to bed, which, though pretty hard, [was] yet neat and handsome. But I could get no sleep, because of the clamor of some of the town topers in next room, who were entered into a strong debate concerning the signification of the name of their country (*viz.*), *Narragansett*. One said it was named so by the Indians, because there grew a brier there of a prodigious height and bigness, the like hardly ever known, called by the Indians narragansett; and quotes an Indian of so barbarous a name for his author that I could not write it. His antagonist replied no—it was from a spring it had its name, which he well knew where it was, which was extreme cold in summer, and as hot as could be imagined in the winter, which was much resorted to by the natives, and by them called Narragansett (hot and cold), and that was the original of their place's name—with a thousand impertinences not worth notice, which he uttered with such a roaring voice and thundering blows with the fist of wickedness on the table that it pierced my very head. I heartily fretted, and wished 'um tongue-tied; but with as little success as a friend of mine once, who was (as she said) kept a whole night awake, on a journey, by a country left, and a sergeant insigne,[7] and a deacon, contriving how to bring a triangle into a square. They kept calling for t'other gill,[8] which while they were swallowing, was some intermission; but presently, like oil to fire, increased the flame. I set my candle on a chest by the bedside, and setting up, fell to my old way of composing my resentments, in the following manner:

I ask thy aid, O potent rum!
To charm these wrangling topers dumb.
Thou hast their giddy brains possessed—
The man confounded with the beast—
And I, poor I, can get no rest.
Intoxicate them with thy fumes:
O still their tongues 'til morning comes!

And I know not but my wishes took effect; for the dispute soon ended with t'other dram. And so good night!

Friday, October 6

I got up very early, in order to hire somebody to go with me to New Haven, being in great perplexity at the thoughts of proceeding alone; which my most hospitable entertainer observing, himself went, and soon returned with a young gentleman of the town, who he could confide in to go with me; and about eight this morning, with Mr. Joshua Wheeler my new guide, taking leave of this worthy gentleman, we advanced on toward Seabrook. The roads all along this way are very bad, encumbered with rocks and mountainous passages, which were very disagreeable to my tired carcass; but we went on with a moderate pace which made the journey more pleasant. But after about eight miles riding, in going over a bridge under which the river run very swift, my horse stumbled and very narrowly escaped falling over into the water; which extremely frightened me. But through God's goodness I met with no harm, and mounting again, in about half a mile's riding, come to an ordinary, were well entertained by a woman of about seventy and vantage [more], but of as sound intellectuals as one of seventeen. She entertained Mr. Wheeler with some passages of a wedding awhile ago at a place hard by, the brides-groom being about her age or something above, saying his children was dreadfully against their father's marrying, which she condemned them extremely for.

From hence we went pretty briskly forward and arrived at Saybrook ferry about two of the clock

5. The phrase "children in the wood," or "babes in the woods," refers to a ballad in which two children are taken out to be murdered and instead are left in the woods, where they die during the night.
6. **Mr. Havens':** the public house where they are to stay.
7. **left . . . insigne:** a lieutenant and an ensign, low-level military officers.
8. **gill:** measure of wine or liquor. A gill is four ounces.

ANALYZING THE JOURNAL
Identifying Facts
1. Traveling conditions were uncomfortable. The food was bad, and the beds in the inns were hard. Other patrons or guests might keep travelers awake with loud conversation. Travel on horseback was difficult.
2. The "twisted thing" seems to be a tablecloth.
3. Answers will vary. Students may mention the placement of the prepositional phrase ("with the post") in the first sentence of the October 3 entry; the word order of the last sentence of this entry: "And I know not but my wishes took effect"; and the idiom in the first sentence of the second paragraph of the October 6 entry: ". . . arrived at Saybrook ferry about two of the clock afternoon."

Interpreting Meanings
4. Answers will vary. Wry humor comes through in her remark that the cabbage she swallowed served for a cud. Kemble makes a comic comparison between herself and Lot's wife—daring not even to *think* of turning her head for fear of upsetting the canoe. Another comic comparison is that between the *Narragansett* topers and the two drunks trying to square a triangle.
5. Knight's metaphor compares the trees in the darkened forest to armed enemies, waiting like "ravenous devourers." This stylistic device, together with the mythological allusion to the sun god and his "swift coursers," would not be typical of the writing of Bradford or Rowlandson.
6. Most will agree that Knight's humor gives her journal a light tone, different from the solemn, pious tones of Bradford and Rowlandson. (Notice that the purposes of the writers are very distinct.)
7. Compare, for example, with John Steinbeck's *Travels with Charley in Search of America* (he also complains about inns or motels) or with Least Heat Moon's *Blue Highways* (see page 1071 of this book).

afternoon; and crossing it, we called at an inn to bait[9] (foreseeing we should not have such another opportunity 'til we come to Killingsworth). Landlady come in, with her hair about her ears and hands at full pay [busily] scratching. She told us she had some mutton which she would broil, which I was glad to hear; but I suppose [she] forgot to wash her scratches; in a little time she brought it in; but it being pickled, and my guide said it smelled strong of head sauce [cheese sauce], we left it, and paid sixpence a piece for our dinners, which was only smell. . . .

9. **bait:** stop for food and rest.

Responding to the Journal

Analyzing the Journal

Identifying Facts

1. Name at least five facts that you learned from Knight's diary about daily life in early eighteenth-century America—facts about food, inns, and travel.
2. Identify the "twisted thing like a cable" that is spread on the table before lunch (page 32).
3. Find at least three details in the journal that indicate that Knight's grammar and syntax were different from today's standard English.

Interpreting Meanings

4. Find at least three details in the entry for October 3 that show Knight's talent for wry humor and comic comparisons.
5. Explain the comparison implied in the **metaphor** describing the sunset on October 3. Is this stylistic device different from what you might have found in William Bradford's or Mary Rowlandson's writings? Explain.
6. How does Knight's journal differ in **tone** from the writings of William Bradford and Mary Rowlandson?
7. What did you like or dislike about Sarah Knight's journal? How does it compare with travel literature written today?

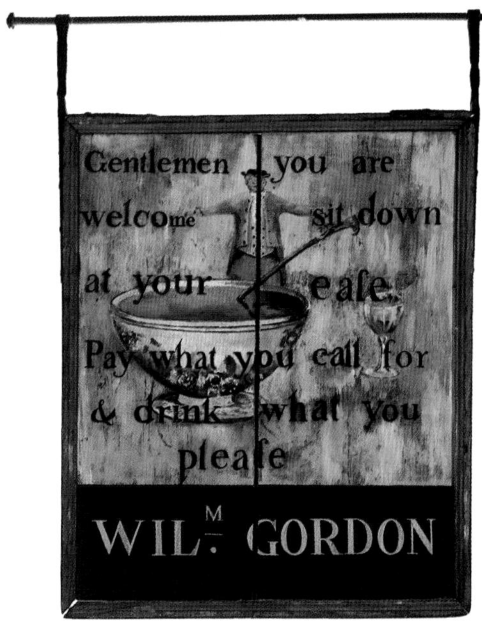

Tavern sign from New London, Connecticut (c. 1750).

Morgan B. Brainard Collection, The Connecticut Historical Society, Hartford, Connecticut.

Writing About the Journal

A Creative Response

1. **Writing a Journal Entry.** Write a journal entry in which you narrate a trip you have taken recently. To dramatize the differences—and the similarities—between travel today and travel in the early eighteenth century, consider these topics: method of travel; length of trip; discomforts or dangers; food; motel or hotel accommodations. Before you write, decide what **tone** you want to take toward the trip: Humorous? Self-mocking? Satirical? Serious?

A Critical Response

2. **Analyzing Character.** You have read selections by two remarkable women who lived in Colonial America. The experiences they describe are vastly different. But can you detect any similarities in their characters or personalities? Write an essay in which you discuss the characters of Mary Rowlandson and Sarah Kemble Knight. In your essay, consider these points: their response to danger; their ability to surmount difficulties, even terrible sufferings; their attitude toward food; what they reveal about their religious convictions. Quote from both journals to support what you say.

A. Responding (Challenging) Jonathan Edwards is often regarded as the last of the great New England Calvinists (Puritans). As such, he believed in predestination—the salvation only of those "elected" by God from the beginning of time. Yet Edwards, by instigating the evangelical revivalism of the Great Awakening, helped bring about the downfall of Calvinism.

? How did the rise of revivalism contribute to the fall of Calvinism with its doctrine of predestination? (Revivalist preachers offered salvation for any repentant person. Puritan-Calvinist doctrine held that to be an impossibility—God had already chosen His elect, and no amount of penitence could change the fate of those already damned.)

B. Humanities Connection: Discussing the Fine Art Point out to students that not only is Jonathan Edwards the first author in the book to be pictured but that the oil painting of him is the work of one of America's earliest and best-known portrait painters.

Charles Willson Peale (1741–1827) was a patriot and naturalist as well as a portraitist. Elected a first lieutenant of militia in Philadelphia, he fought in the Revolutionary War battles of Trenton and Princeton. During the war, he began painting miniature portraits of his fellow officers. After the war, he opened a gallery-museum in Philadelphia. His most famous portraits are those of George Washington, whom he painted sixty times, seven times from life.

Jonathan Edwards (1703–1758)

Jonathan Edwards is known today principally as the author of the great sermon, "Sinners in the Hands of an Angry God." Despite his fire-and-brimstone imagery, Edwards was not merely a stern, zealous preacher. He was a brilliant, thoughtful, and complicated man whose accomplishments and failures deserve our interest and study. Born eighty years after the Puritans landed in New England and only three years before the birth of Benjamin Franklin, Edwards stood between Puritan America and modern America. Tragically, he fit into neither world.

Edwards's grandfather, Solomon Stoddard, was pastor of the Congregational Church in Northampton, Massachusetts. Stoddard was so powerful a figure in religious affairs that he was known as the "Pope of the Connecticut Valley." His grandson's abilities were recognized early; even in his teens Jonathan was being groomed to succeed his grandfather. The boy entered Yale in 1716, when he was only thirteen. A few years after his graduation, he was made senior tutor of the college—a significant achievement for one so young. In 1726, Jonathan became his grandfather's co-pastor. When Stoddard died three years later, his grandson succeeded him.

A Edwards was a strong-willed and charismatic pastor. His formidable presence and brilliant sermons helped to bring about the religious revival known as the "Great Awakening." This revival began in Northampton in the 1730's and during the next fifteen years spread throughout the Eastern Seaboard. The Great Awakening was marked by waves of conversions that spread from congregation to congregation—conversions so intensely emotional as to amount at times to mass hysteria.

The Great Awakening began at a time when enthusiasm for the old Puritan religion was declining. To offset the losses in their congregations, churches had been accepting increasing numbers of "unregenerate" Christians. These were people who accepted church doctrine and lived upright lives but who had not confessed they had been "born again" in God's grace. Thus they were not considered to be saved. In

Jonathan Edwards by Charles Willson Peale. Oil. B

their sermons, Edwards and other pastors strove to make these "sinners" understand the precariousness of their situation by helping them actually to *feel* the horror of their sinful state.

"Sinners in the Hands of an Angry God" is the greatest and best-known example of these sermons. Edwards's methods in the sermon were influenced by the work of the English philosopher John Locke (1632–1704). Locke believed that everything we know comes from experience, and he emphasized that understanding and feeling were two distinct kinds of knowledge. (To Edwards, the difference between these two kinds of knowledge was like the difference between reading the word *fire* and actually being burned.) Edwards preached his famous sermon in Enfield, Massachusetts, in July of 1741. Although he read it in his usual straightforward, unemotional manner, it had such a powerful effect on the congregation that the minister had to pause several times to ask for quiet.

Intellectually, Edwards straddled two ages: the modern, secular world exemplified by such men as Benjamin Franklin, and the religious world of his zealous Puritan ancestors. Edwards

SUPPLEMENTARY SUPPORT MATERIALS

1. Vocabulary Activity Worksheet (*CCB*)
2. Review and Response Worksheet: Figures of Speech (*CCB*)
3. Selection Test (*CCB*)

DEVELOPING VOCABULARY

The following words from the sermon are tested in the Selection Test. (See also Vocabulary Activity Worksheet.)

to abate	salvation
contrivance	vexation
asunder	taciturn

PREPARATION

ESTABLISHING A PURPOSE. As the biography indicates, Edwards's purpose in preaching sermons such as this one was to make sinners feel the horror of their sinful state and thus repent. Have students read to determine what in Edwards's sermon made him so successful in accomplishing this goal.

could draw on the ideas of philosophers such as John Locke, but he used those ideas to achieve a vision compatible with that of older Puritans such as William Bradford. Science, reason, and observation of the physical world only confirmed Edwards's vision of a universe filled with the presence of God. As he explained in his autobiography (see page 41), his sense of God was formed not only by his reading of the Bible but also by his close examination of nature. "God's excellency," he wrote, "seemed to appear in everything: in the sun, moon, and stars; in the clouds and blue sky; in the grass, flowers, and trees; in the water, and all nature."

Edwards became known for his extremism as a pastor. In his sermons, he didn't hesitate to accuse prominent church members, by name, of relapsing into sin. He was also unbending in his refusal to accept the "unregenerate" into his church. Such attitudes eventually lost him the support of his congregation. In 1750, he was voted out of his prestigious position in Northampton and sent to the then remote and raw Mohican Indian community of Stockbridge, Massachusetts. After eight years of missionary work in this lonely exile, Edwards was "rescued" and named president of the College of New Jersey (which later became Princeton University). Three months after assuming his position, he died of a smallpox inoculation—a modern medical procedure that had been promoted by the old-style Puritan Cotton Mather (see page 66).

SINNERS IN THE HANDS OF AN ANGRY GOD

FROM A SERMON DELIVERED ON JULY 8, 1741

The first two paragraphs of Edwards's sermon contain clues about the audience he was especially trying to awaken and persuade: "natural men" (people in the congregation who were not "reborn"); or those who were "out of Christ" (those who had not specifically confessed Christ as their only Savior). Although Edwards's warnings may strike you as harsh, remember that the Puritans had a vivid sense of divine wrath and an unwavering belief in the sinfulness of the human race. As you read, be aware of the vivid imagery and of how it would affect a member of Edwards's congregation.

So that thus it is that natural men are held in the hand of God, over the pit of hell; they have deserved the fiery pit, and are already sentenced to it; and God is dreadfully provoked, his anger is as great toward them as to those that are actually suffering the executions of the fierceness of his wrath in hell, and they have done nothing in the least to appease or abate that anger, neither is God in the least bound by any promise to hold them up one moment; the devil is waiting for them, hell is gaping for them, the flames gather and flash about them, and would fain lay hold on them, and swallow them up; the fire pent up in their own hearts is struggling to break out; and they have no interest in any Mediator, there are no means within reach that can be any security to them. In short, they have no refuge, nothing to take hold of; all that preserves them every moment is the mere arbitrary will, and uncovenanted, unobliged forbearance of an incensed God.

A

The use of this awful subject may be for awakening unconverted persons in this congregation. This that you have heard is the case of every one of you that are out of Christ. That world of misery, that lake of burning brimstone, is extended abroad under you. There is the dreadful pit of the glowing flames of the wrath of God; there is hell's wide

B

A. Parallelism

Point out to students that some of the power of Edwards's sermon derives from his use of parallel constructions: ". . . the devil is waiting for them, hell is gaping for them, the flames gather and flash about them. . . ."

B. Author's Purpose

? Edwards makes a direct statement about what he hopes his sermon will accomplish. What does he say? (He wants to "awaken unconverted persons" in the congregation. See question 1, page 40.)

A. Humanities Connection: Responding to the Illustration

? What do these names mean: *Beelzebub* (the devil; originally, the prince of devils), *Apollyon* (the angel of the bottomless pit in the Book of Revelation), *Lucifer* (the devil; originally, the morning star—a fallen rebel archangel), *Sion* (Zion; heaven; the city of God; in Judaism, the Jewish people or their homeland)?

B. Figurative Language/Simile

? What are the three extended metaphors beginning on this page and continuing onto the next page? (Dammed waters = wrath of God; bow and arrow = God's wrath/justice; spider = human being ["you"] over pit of hell. See question 2, page 40).

You might remind students that figures of speech can occur *within* figures of speech. The entire paragraph beginning with "The wrath of God," for example, is an extended metaphor, an elaborate comparison between dammed waters and the wrath of God.

? The "wrath of God" extended metaphor begins with a straightforward simile. What is the simile? ("The wrath of God is like great waters that are dammed for the present. . . .")

gaping mouth open; and you have nothing to stand upon, nor anything to take hold of; there is nothing between you and hell but the air; it is only the power and mere pleasure of God that holds you up.

You probably are not sensible of this; you find you are kept out of hell, but do not see the hand of God in it; but look at other things, as the good state of your bodily constitution, your care of your own life, and the means you use for your own preservation. But indeed these things are nothing; if God should withdraw his hand, they would avail no more to keep you from falling than the thin air to hold up a person that is suspended in it.

A

The Progress of Sin (1744). Woodcut.

Sinclair Hamilton Collection, Graphic Arts Collection, Princeton University Library.

Your wickedness makes you as it were heavy as lead, and to tend downward with great weight and pressure toward hell; and if God should let you go, you would immediately sink and swiftly descend and plunge into the bottomless gulf, and your healthy constitution, and your own care and prudence, and best contrivance, and all your righteousness, would have no more influence to uphold you and keep you out of hell than a spider's web would have to stop a fallen rock. . . .

The wrath of God is like great waters that are dammed for the present; they increase more and more, and rise higher and higher, till an outlet is given; and the longer the stream is stopped, the more rapid and mighty is its course when once it is let loose. It is true, that judgment against your evil works has not been executed hitherto; the floods of God's vengeance have been withheld; but your guilt in the meantime is constantly increasing, and you are every day treasuring up more wrath; the waters are constantly rising, and waxing more and more mighty; and there is nothing but the mere pleasure of God that holds the waters back, that are unwilling to be stopped, and press hard to go forward. If God should only withdraw his hand from the floodgate, it would immediately fly open, and the fiery floods of the fierceness and wrath of God would rush forth with inconceivable fury, and would come upon you with omnipotent power; and if your strength were ten thousand times greater than it is, yea, ten thousand times greater than the strength of the stoutest, sturdiest devil in hell, it would be nothing to withstand or endure it. B

The bow of God's wrath is bent, and the arrow made ready on the string, and justice bends the arrow at your heart, and strains the bow, and it is nothing but the mere pleasure of God, and that of an angry God, without any promise or obligation at all, that keeps the arrow one moment from being made drunk with your blood. Thus all you that never passed under a great change of heart, by the mighty power of the Spirit of God upon your souls; all you that were never born again, and made new creatures, and raised from being dead in sin, to a state of new, and before altogether unexperienced light and life, are in the hands of an angry God. However you may have reformed your life in many things, and may have had religious affections,[1] and may keep up a form of re-

1. **affections:** feelings.

Reading Check Test

1. Sinners are saved from hell only at the pleasure of ______. *God*
2. God's wrath is held back like the great waters behind a ______. *dam*
3. A sinner is held over the pit of hell much as a ______ might be. *spider*
4. The wrath a sinner will suffer is not momentary but ______. *everlasting*
5. A person who "has not been born again" is in danger of losing his or her ______. *soul*

Closure

Have students prepare a list, individually or in a class brainstorming session, of the rhetorical devices, figures of speech, and imagery that make this a successful sermon.

ligion in your families and closets,[2] and in the house of God, it is nothing but his mere pleasure that keeps you from being this moment swallowed up in everlasting destruction. However unconvinced you may now be of the truth of what you hear, by and by you will be fully convinced of it. Those that are gone from being in the like circumstances with you see that it was so with them; for destruction came suddenly upon most of them; when they expected nothing of it, and while they were saying, Peace and safety: now they see that those things on which they depended for peace and safety were nothing but thin air and empty shadows.

The God that holds you over the pit of hell, much as one holds a spider, or some loathsome insect over the fire, abhors you, and is dreadfully provoked: his wrath toward you burns like fire; he looks upon you as worthy of nothing else but to be cast into the fire; he is of purer eyes than to bear to have you in his sight; you are ten thousand times more abominable in his eyes than the most hateful venomous serpent is in ours. You have offended him infinitely more than ever a stubborn rebel did his prince; and yet it is nothing but his hand that holds you from falling into the fire every moment. It is to be ascribed to nothing else, that you did not go to hell the last night; that you was suffered to awake again in this world, after you closed your eyes to sleep. And there is no other reason to be given why you have not dropped into hell since you arose in the morning, but that God's hand has held you up. There is no other reason to be given why you have not gone to hell, since you have sat here in the house of God, provoking his pure eyes by your sinful wicked manner of attending his solemn worship. Yea, there is nothing else that is to be given as a reason why you do not this very moment drop down into hell!

A O sinner! Consider the fearful danger you are in: it is a great furnace of wrath, a wide and bottomless pit, full of the fire of wrath, that you are held over in the hand of that God, whose wrath is provoked and incensed as much against you as against many of the damned in hell. You hang by a slender thread, with the flames of divine wrath flashing about it, and ready every moment to singe it, and burn it asunder; and you have no interest in any Mediator, and nothing to lay hold of to save
B yourself, nothing to keep off the flames of wrath, nothing of your own, nothing that you ever have done, nothing that you can do, to induce God to spare you one moment. . . .

It is *everlasting* wrath. It would be dreadful to suffer this fierceness and wrath of Almighty God one moment; but you must suffer it to all eternity. There will be no end to this exquisite horrible misery. When you look forward, you shall see a long forever, a boundless duration before you, which will swallow up your thoughts and amaze your soul; and you will absolutely despair of ever having any deliverance, any end, any mitigation, any rest at all. You will know certainly that you must wear out long ages, millions of millions of ages, in wresting and conflicting with this almighty merciless vengeance; and then when you have so done, when so many ages have actually been spent by you in this manner, you will know that all is but a point to what remains. So that your punishment will indeed be infinite. Oh, who can express what the state of a soul in such circumstances is! All that we can possibly say about it gives but a very feeble, faint representation of it; it is inexpressible and inconceivable: For "who knows the power of God's anger?"

How dreadful is the state of those that are daily and hourly in the danger of this great wrath and infinite misery! But this is the dismal case of every soul in this congregation that has not been born again, however moral and strict, sober and religious, they may otherwise be. Oh, that you would consider it, whether you be young or old! There is reason to think, that there are many in this congregation now hearing this discourse that will actually be the subjects of this very misery to all eternity. We know not who they are, or in what seats they sit, or what thoughts they now have. It may be they are now at ease, and hear all these things without much disturbance, and are now flattering themselves that they are not the persons, promising themselves that they shall escape. If we knew that there was one person, and but one, in the whole congregation that was to be the subject of this misery, what an awful thing would it be to think of! If we knew who it was, what an awful sight would it be to see such a person! How might all the rest of the congregation lift up a lamentable and bitter cry over him! But, alas! Instead of one, how many is it likely will remember this discourse in hell? And it would be a wonder if some that are now present should not be in hell in a very short time, even before this year is out. And it would

2. **closets:** rooms for meditation (such as studies).

A. Direct Address/ Apostrophe

? When Edwards says "O sinner!" is he merely addressing his audience, or is he using an apostrophe? (The word *O* often appears in an apostrophe: "O liberty!" "O times! O customs!" But, with an apostrophe, the speaker is usually addressing an absent person or a personified thing. Edwards is addressing an unspecified person in his audience. Thus his "O sinner!" should probably be regarded as direct address.)

B. Repetition

You might want students to identify uses of repetition on this page. (". . . nothing to lay hold of to save yourself, nothing to keep off the flames of wrath, nothing of your own, nothing that you have ever done, nothing that you can do . . ."; ". . . you will absolutely despair of ever having any deliverance, any end, any mitigation, any rest at all.")

ANALYZING THE SERMON
Identifying Facts

1. At the beginning of the second paragraph of the selection, Edwards says that "the use of this awful subject" (namely, the terrible danger of being condemned to the torments of hell) "may be for awakening unconverted persons" in the congregation.

2. All three images relate to the wrath of God. Like waters temporarily blocked by a dam, God's anger is ready to burst forth. His wrath will bend like a bow to send the arrow of retribution into a sinner's heart. His wrath holds humanity like a spider over the fire of the pit of hell.

Edwards extends all three metaphors with powerful rhetoric. He speaks of rising waters and of God's hand on the floodgate. He tells of the mounting tension on the bow, which will inevitably lead to God's letting loose the arrow of vengeance on sinful man. He extends the figure of the spider when he says to the congregation, "You are ten thousand times more abominable in his eyes, than the most hateful, venomous serpent is in ours."

3. Edwards tells his listeners that they must "pass under a great change of

FOR FURTHER READING
For Students

An excellent brief biography of Jonathan Edwards, first published in 1765, is David Levin's *Jonathan Edwards: A Profile* (Hill and Wang, 1969).

be no wonder if some persons that now sit here, in some seats of this meetinghouse, in health, quiet, and secure, should be there before tomorrow morning. Those of you that finally continue in a natural condition, that shall keep out of hell longest, will be there in a little time! Your damnation does not slumber; it will come swiftly and, in all probability, very suddenly upon many of you. You have reason to wonder that you are not already in hell. It is doubtless the case of some whom you have seen and known that never deserved hell more than you, and that heretofore appeared as likely to have been now alive as you. Their case is past all hope; they are crying in extreme misery and perfect despair. But here you are in the land of the living and in the house of God, and have an opportunity to obtain salvation. What would not those poor damned hopeless souls give for one day's opportunity such as you now enjoy!

And now you have an extraordinary opportunity, a day wherein Christ has thrown the door of mercy wide open, and stands in calling and crying with a loud voice to poor sinners; a day wherein many are flocking to him, and pressing into the kingdom of God. Many are daily coming from the east, west, north, and south; many that were very lately in the same miserable condition that you are in are now in a happy state, with their hearts filled with love to him who has loved them and washed them from their sins in his own blood, and rejoicing in hope of the glory of God. How awful is it to be left behind at such a day! To see so many others feasting, while you are pining and perishing! To see so many rejoicing and singing for joy of heart, while you have cause to mourn for sorrow of heart, and howl for vexation of spirit! How can you rest one moment in such a condition? . . .

Responding to the Sermon

Analyzing the Sermon

Identifying Facts

1. Where does Edwards declare his **purpose**?
2. There are three famous **figures of speech** in Edwards's sermon: the images of the dam, the bow and arrow, and the spider. To what does Edwards compare these familiar, ordinary things? In each case, how does Edwards extend the figure of speech?
3. In the sixth paragraph, where does Edwards remind his audience of what action they must take to escape God's wrath? What behavior does he say is useless to prevent their everlasting destruction?

Interpreting Meanings

4. What does Edwards mean when he says at the end of his sermon that the "door of mercy" is wide open? Does he talk of God's mercy elsewhere in the sermon?
5. Edwards is directing his sermon to what he calls "natural men," those members of his congregation who have not been "reborn." He wants to make these people *feel* the truth of his statements, as direct experience. He does not want them simply to understand his sermon abstractly. What **images** in the first four paragraphs do you think helped his listeners to feel the peril of their unregenerate condition?
6. Why does Edwards want his listeners to feel or experience what eternity is? What does he say to help them experience this difficult concept? Did you find his description effective?
7. During Edwards's sermon, some members of the congregation were said to have cried out and fainted in terror. Identify the parts of the sermon that you think would have called forth such emotional responses.
8. Literature offers several examples of "hellfire" sermons. (Another famous one is found in James Joyce's novel *Portrait of the Artist as a Young Man.*) Think of orations you might hear today. Do they exhibit the imagery and emotional appeals of Edwards's sermon?
9. Compare Edwards's idea of God in the sermon with the ideas expressed in his autobiography (page 41).

Writing About the Sermon

A Creative Response

1. **Adapting the Sermon.** Consider the differences between Edwards's audience and present-day Americans. Then select any two paragraphs from the sermon. Rewrite the paragraphs as Edwards might deliver them today.
2. **Using Another Point of View.** Write a paragraph from the point of view of a member of Edwards's congregation, describing the sermon's effect.

heart" and be "born again."

He warns the congregation that it is useless to reform their lives privately, taking refuge in illusions of "peace and safety." He implies that they must publicly profess a lasting conversion to the ways of God.

Interpreting Meanings

4. He means that sinners may return to God with sincere repentance at any time. His references to the "hand of God" holding his listeners up and keeping them out of hell, at least for the moment, might be interpreted as allusions to divine mercy. However, he does not use the word *mercy* until the end of the sermon.

5. Edwards refers to the "fiery pit of hell" in the first paragraph and mentions its "gaping mouth" in the second. In the third paragraph, he speaks of man's falling through thin air if the sustaining hand of God should be withdrawn. In the fourth paragraph, he compares man's weakness to the heaviness of lead, which will draw him down to hell just as surely as a heavy rock will smash a spider's web.

6. Answers will vary. Probably he wants his listeners to comprehend the nature of eternity so that they will understand what they must go through if they fail to repent.

He refers to the "millions and millions of ages" that they will spend suffering "this almighty merciless vengeance." He says it is entirely possible that within a very short time some of his listeners will face the everlasting torment of damnation. In other words, hell is not far off and abstract—it is, or may be, imminent and real.

Answers will vary.

7. Answers will vary. One likely part is near the end where Edwards states that some in the congregation may die soon and suddenly, unrepentant, and have to face eternal damnation.

8. Answers will vary. Students may note that with the increase of liberal churches, this kind of preaching is less frequently found.

9. In the autobiography, the word *sweetness* is often used to describe God. Also, distinct from the sermon, the words *meekness, grace, gentleness,* and *love.*

Primary Sources
Journals

When Jonathan Edwards was twenty years old, he wrote this tribute to Sarah Pierrepont, who was then only thirteen. Jonathan married Sarah four years later.

"They say there is a young lady in [New Haven] who is beloved of that Great Being, who made and rules the world, and that there are certain seasons in which this Great Being, in some way or other invisible, comes to her and fills her mind with exceeding sweet delight, and that she hardly cares for anything, except to meditate on Him—that she expects after a while to be received up where He is, to be raised up out of the world and caught up into heaven; being assured that He loves her too well to let her remain at a distance from Him always. There she is to dwell with Him, and to be ravished with His love and delight forever. Therefore, if you present all the world before her, with the richest of its treasures, she disregards it and cares not for it, and is unmindful of any pain or affliction. She has a strange sweetness in her mind, and singular purity in her affections; is most just and conscientious in all her conduct; and you could not persuade her to do anything wrong or sinful, if you would give her all the world, lest she should offend this Great Being. She is of a wonderful sweetness, calmness, and universal benevolence of mind; especially after this Great God has manifested Himself to her mind. She will sometimes go about from place to place, singing sweetly; and seems to be always full of joy and pleasure; and no one knows for what. She loves to be alone, walking in the fields and groves, and seems to have someone invisible always conversing with her."

—Jonathan Edwards

Edwards began an autobiography but did not write anything after 1740. His contemporary Benjamin Franklin also began an autobiography (page 74), but where Franklin describes his wordly success, Edwards records his spiritual experience. In the following selection he is a young man walking alone after a talk with his father:

". . . And as I was walking there, and looking up on the sky and clouds, there came into my mind so sweet a sense of the glorious *majesty* and *grace* of God, that I know not how to express. I seemed to see them both in a sweet conjunction; majesty and meekness joined together; it was a sweet, and gentle, and holy majesty; and also a majestic meekness; an awful sweetness; a high, and great, and holy gentleness.

"After this my sense of divine things gradually increased, and became more and more lively, and had more of that inward sweetness. The appearance of every thing was altered; there seemed to be, as it were, a calm, sweet cast, or appearance of divine glory, in almost every thing. God's excellency, his wisdom, his purity, and love, seemed to appear in every thing; in the sun, moon, and stars; in the clouds, and blue sky; in the grass, flowers, trees; in the water, and all nature; which used greatly to fix my mind. I often used to sit and view the moon for continuance; and in the day, spent much time in viewing the clouds and sky, to behold the sweet glory of God in these things; in the meantime, singing forth, with a low voice, my contemplations of the Creator and Redeemer. And scarce any thing, among all the works of nature, was so sweet to me as thunder and lightning; formerly, nothing had been so terrible to me. Before, I used to be uncommonly terrified with thunder, and to be struck with terror when I saw a thunderstorm rising; but now, on the contrary, it rejoiced me. I felt God, so to speak, at the first appearance of a thunderstorm; and used to take the opportunity, at such times, to fix myself in order to view the clouds, and see the lightnings play, and hear the majestic and awful voice of God's thunder, which oftentimes was exceedingly entertaining, leading me to sweet contemplations of my great and glorious God."

—Jonathan Edwards

This journal entry was written by Jonathan Edwards's daughter Esther, who died in 1755, when she was only twenty-three years old. Esther's son, Aaron Burr, became the Vice President of the United States.

"*May 1* [1742] I have just come back from a wonderful ride with my honored father, Mr. Edwards, through the spring woods. He usually rides alone. But today he said he had something he wanted to show me. The forests between our house and the full-banked river were very beautiful. The wild cherry and the dogwood were in full bloom. The squirrels were leaping from tree to tree, and the birds were making a various melody. Though father is usually taciturn or preoccupied—my mother will call these large words—even when he takes one of us children with him, today he discoursed to me of the awful sweetness of walking with God in Nature. He seems to feel God in the woods, the sky, and the grand sweep of the river which winds so majestically through the woody silences here."

—Esther Edwards

For Further Reading
For Students
In *An American Triptych: Anne Bradstreet, Emily Dickinson, Adrienne Rich* (The University of North Carolina Press, 1984), Wendy Martin observes: "She [Anne Bradstreet] writes of her intense love for her husband and children, her grief at the loss of her parents and grandchildren, her joy in nature . . . the emphasis is on *this* life." After reading the brief biography of Anne Bradstreet, students might be asked to speculate as to why her poetry emphasizes daily life over spiritual transcendence.

Anne Bradstreet (1612–1672)

One of the most notable characteristics of American literature is the distinction of its women writers, particularly in poetry. The first accomplished poet on American soil, of *either* sex, was Anne Bradstreet. Who could have guessed that the poet who would begin the history of our literature would be an immigrant teen-aged bride? The question becomes less far-fetched when we know something of the life of the young woman who came to America when its claims to civilization were no more than a few muddy villages precariously perched between the ocean and the wilderness. Young as she was, Anne Bradstreet brought civilization with her.

Educated by tutors in her native England, she was immersed in the Bible. She also had access to the large library of the Earl of Lincoln, who employed her father, Thomas Dudley, as his estate manager. Shakespeare was still alive when Anne was born and, like many budding poets, she found in Shakespeare, and in other great poets of England, sources of inspiration and technique that would one day run like threads of gold through the fabric of her own work.

However, what most determined the course of her life was not a poetic influence but a religious one. Anne Bradstreet was born into a family of Puritans. Accepting their reformist views as naturally as most children accept the religious teachings of a parent, Anne married, at the age of sixteen, a well-educated and zealous young Puritan by the name of Simon Bradstreet. Two years later, in 1630, Simon brought his wife across the Atlantic to the part of New England around Salem that would become known as the Massachusetts Bay Colony. There, while her husband rose to prominence (he became a governor of the colony), Anne Bradstreet kept house in Cambridgeport and Ipswich. She raised four boys and four girls and, without seeking an audience or publication, found the time to write poems. These might never have come to light had it not been for John Woodbridge, her brother-in-law and a minister in Andover. He went to England in 1647 and there, in 1650, without consulting the author herself, published her poems under the title *The Tenth Muse Lately Sprung Up in America * * * By a Gentlewoman of Those Parts.*

In one stroke, an obscure housewife from the meadows of New England was placed among the nine Muses of art and learning sacred to the ancient Greeks. In itself, this was embarrassing enough. But in the middle of the seventeenth century, the real arrogance was that a woman would aspire to a place among the august company of established male poets. Conscious of the boldness she might be charged with, Bradstreet was resigned to criticism. "If what I do prove well," she wrote, "it won't advance; / They'll say it's stol'n, or else it was by chance." But *The Tenth Muse* fared better with critics and the public than she expected, and she felt encouraged to write for the rest of her life.

Today, Anne Bradstreet is remembered not for her elaborate earlier poems but for a few simple lyrics about the birth of children, the death of grandchildren, her love for her husband, her son's sailing to England, her own illnesses.

The following poem is about the burning of her home. Though she does not say so, 800 books were lost in this fire, a considerable library for a home in a raw New World. Destroyed also were all of Anne Bradstreet's papers and all her unpublished poems.

A cradle brought to Plymouth on the *Mayflower*.

Pilgrim Society, Plymouth, Massachusetts.

SUPPLEMENTARY SUPPORT MATERIALS
1. Vocabulary Activity Worksheet (*CCB*)
2. Review and Response Worksheet: Extended Metaphor (*CCB*)
3. Language Skills Worksheet: Sentence Inversion (*CCB*)
4. Selection Test (*CCB*)

DEVELOPING VOCABULARY
The following words from the poem are tested in the Selection Test. (See also Vocabulary Activity Worksheet.)

piteous	to recount
to repine	vanity
bereft	to chide

PREPARATION
1. ESTABLISHING A PURPOSE. You might ask students to read the poem to answer the following questions: What does the poet lose by the burning of her house? What does she gain?
2. PREREADING JOURNAL. Before students read, you might have them write a few lines in which they imagine their own feelings at seeing their home burn.

This poem is filled with *inversions*, a device especially common in English poetry written in earlier centuries. In an inversion, the words are wrenched out of the normal order of an English sentence. Poets used to use inversions frequently, to accommodate the demands of meter or rhyme. The second line here, for example, would normally be written:

I did not look for sorrow near

After you have read the poem, read it over a second time and look for the inverted word order. Once you rearrange the inverted sentences, you'll find the poem much easier to understand.

The poem portrays an internal debate, a type of dialogue between self and soul. As you read, note the points at which the speaker questions her own thoughts and emotions. What answers does she give to these questions? What conclusions does she reach? Note also your own responses: How would you "deal with" the destruction of a home?

Here Follow Some Verses upon the Burning of Our House, July 10, 1666

In silent night when rest I took
For sorrow near I did not look
I wakened was with thund'ring noise
And piteous shrieks of dreadful voice.
That fearful sound of "Fire!" and "Fire!"
Let no man know is my desire.
I, starting up, the light did spy,
And to my God my heart did cry
To strengthen me in my distress
And not to leave me succorless.°
Then, coming out, beheld a space
The flame consume my dwelling place.
And when I could no longer look,
I blest His name that gave and took,°
That laid my goods now in the dust.
Yea, so it was, and so 'twas just.
It was His own, it was not mine,
Far be it that I should repine;
He might of all justly bereft
But yet sufficient for us left.
When by the ruins oft I past
My sorrowing eyes aside did cast,
And here and there the places spy
Where oft I sat and long did lie:
Here stood that trunk, and there that chest,
There lay that store I counted best.
My pleasant things in ashes lie,
And them behold no more shall I.
Under thy roof no guest shall sit,
Nor at thy table eat a bit.
No pleasant tale shall e'er be told,
Nor things recounted done of old.
No candle e'er shall shine in thee,
Nor bridegroom's voice e'er heard shall be.
In silence ever shall thou lie,
A Adieu, adieu, all's vanity.
Then straight I 'gin my heart to chide,
And did thy wealth on earth abide?
Didst fix thy hope on mold'ring dust?
The arm of flesh didst make thy trust?
Raise up thy thoughts above the sky
That dunghill mists away may fly.
Thou hast a house on high erect,
Framed by that mighty Architect,
With glory richly furnished,
Stands permanent though this be fled.
It's purchased and paid for too
By Him who hath enough to do.
A price so vast as is unknown
Yet by His gift is made thine own;
There's wealth enough, I need no more,
Farewell, my pelf,° farewell my store.
The world no longer let me love,
My hope and treasure lies above.

10. **succorless:** without aid or assistance; helpless.
14. "The Lord gave, and the Lord hath taken away; blessed be the name of the Lord," (Job 1:21).
52. **pelf:** worldly goods.

A. Allusion
Some phrases are so common that it is hard to know whether they are allusions. For example, "silent night" in line 1 echoes a phrase in John Milton's *Paradise Lost,* but that may be a coincidence.
? The phrase "all's vanity" in line 36 almost certainly comes from a Biblical source. What is the allusion? ("Vanity of vanities; all is vanity." Ecclesiastes, 1:2; 12:8.)

CLOSURE
Have students summarize Bradstreet's thoughts and emotions as she watches her house burn.

ANALYZING THE POEM

Identifying Details

1. She mentions the loss of her dwelling place in line 12 and of her goods in line 15. In lines 23–26 she nostagically recalls the places where she used to sit and lie in the house, and she mentions a trunk and a chest. In lines 27–34 she laments the loss of future pleasant hours in the house.

2. The house is heaven, whose architect is God ("framed by that mighty Architect," line 44). It is more perfect than the poet's earthly home because it is richly furnished with glory. It has also been paid for with a price "so vast as is unknown" (line 49), probably a reference to the suffering, death, and resurrection of Christ.

Interpreting Meanings

3. Bradstreet uses this surprisingly negative word because she has come to regard her earthly treasures as insignificant—even bad—compared with the treasure of immortal life.

4. Answers will vary. Encourage students to express their opinions. Stress that there is no single right way to react *(Answers continue in left-hand column.)*

(Continued from top.) to or interpret a poem. It is a bit difficult, however, to argue for a meaning that the author seems not to have had in mind (note the word *unconsciously* in the queston). Within the context of the poem there is little reason to doubt Bradstreet's sincerity or religious beliefs. Her human impulse to lament misfortune seems, on her textual evidence, to have been conquered by her faith.

A Comment on the Poem

The poet first narrates an incident, then draws some conclusions from it. The incident is clear enough, but the conclusions are comprehensible only when we realize that they reflect an absolute faith in, and absolute submission to, the will of God. In fact, this poem reveals a typical pattern of Puritan thought. It is a series of steps that at first seem to be going anywhere the author chooses, but in the end, these steps always lead to the same affirmation—of the rightness of God's will and of the waywardness of human desires. In this poem, the speaker's anguish is unmistakable, and why not? Before her eyes, her house and all her beloved possessions are going up in flame. Like many people faced with calamity, she calls on God to give her the strength to endure and not to leave her without help. But she does not curse her bad luck. Instead almost at once she blesses God, who chose to inflict the anguish upon her. In doing this, she puts herself in the shoes of the Biblical figure of Job. In all his misery, Job was still able to say: "The Lord gave, and the Lord hath taken away; blessed be the name of the Lord."

This is the turning point of the poem, the point at which the speaker begins to scold herself for putting such value on the things of this world. It is the point at which she resigns herself to misfortune and embraces the test of faith that misfortune represents.

Responding to the Poem

Analyzing the Poem

Identifying Details

1. What are some of the specific losses that Bradstreet dwells on in the first half of the poem?
2. Bradstreet speaks of another "house" in an **extended metaphor** at the end of the poem. What is this house, who is its architect, and how is it more perfect than the house she has lost?

Interpreting Meanings

3. *Pelf*—a word designating riches or worldly goods—is usually used only when the riches or goods are considered to be slightly tainted, ill-gotten, or stolen. Why do you suppose Bradstreet uses such a bitter word in line 52 to describe her own cherished treasures?
4. At the very end of the poem, are you convinced that the speaker means what she says? Some readers have felt that, by so lovingly enumerating her losses, Bradstreet is "crying to heaven" in a way that, unconsciously, reveals more attachment to her earthly possessions than she would admit to. Do you think these readers have a point? Explain.

Writing About the Poem

A Critical Response

Analyzing the Writer's Attitude. Twice Bradstreet checks herself from mourning over the loss of her beloved possessions. The first instance is in lines 14–20; the second begins with line 37. Paraphrase lines 14–20; that is, restate each line in your own words. Then write a paragraph explaining what these lines reveal about Bradstreet's attitude toward earthly suffering and the Providence of God. Explain how such faith might have helped these first immigrants face a wilderness in a new world.

Analyzing Language and Style

The "Poetic" Style

During the time Anne Bradstreet wrote, and for many years after, people expected poetry to conform to a basic **meter,** or pattern of stressed and unstressed syllables. Most readers also looked for rhymes. Bradstreet's poem is rhymed in **couplets** and written in **iambic tetrameter.** This means that each line contains four iambs, an **iamb** being an unstressed syllable followed by a stressed syllable. Here is how the first line would be scanned:

In silent night when rest I took

You'll also see that to accommodate her meter, the poet often inverts words. In normal English word order, this sentence would read:

In [the] silent night when I took [my] rest

Continue scanning the poem to see how faithful, even slavish, Bradstreet has been to her basic beat. Then rewrite the lines to get rid of the inversions. What happens to the beat?

COMMENT FROM A CRITIC
In the first book-length study of this long-forgotten poet, *Edward Taylor* (Twayne Publishers, 1961), Norman S. Grabo writes that Taylor was ". . . a man of God in a land swarming with ministers . . . He knew there were devils and witches . . . He thought he was among God's chosen few and that by God's great design the great mass of men skidded to everlasting and inescapable damnation . . . [he] was a typical Puritan."

Edward Taylor (c. 1642–1729)

A The publication in 1939 of *The Poetical Works of Edward Taylor* was the third important instance in American literature of the discovery of buried poetic treasure. The first discovery occurred when Anne Bradstreet's brother-in-law carried her "private" poems to England and, without her consent, had them printed. The second occurred in 1890, when the heirs of Emily Dickinson decided to ignore her wishes and publish the poems she had carefully saved in little packets but that she expected would be destroyed after her death. (See Unit Five.)

Of these discoveries, the case of Edward Taylor is perhaps the most remarkable. For more than two hundred years, his brilliant poems simply moldered in the archives of the Yale College library. Then, once again, a body of work that the author had ordered his heirs never to publish came to light—in this case, with such compelling force as to cause the history of early poetry in America to be rewritten.

When scholars—particularly a man named Thomas H. Johnson—confronted this crucial addition to Colonial literature, they easily deduced Taylor's literary and religious background from the poems. But they had only a few meager clues to the personal life of the man himself, a life that spanned more than eighty years.

Edward Taylor was born in Leicestershire, England, near the town of Coventry. Like Anne Bradstreet, he was raised in a family that held dissenting views about many of the practices of the Church of England. Feeling more and more uncomfortable in the religious climate of his own country, where a royal Act of Uniformity had caused Puritans to be persecuted, he determined to seek the freedom that other Nonconformists before him had found in the New World. And so, in 1668, Edward Taylor sailed for Boston.

Gravestone rubbing of the Reverend Silas Biglow, Paxton, Massachusetts (1769).

Collection of Avon Neal and Ann Parker.

Friends had equipped Taylor with letters of introduction to some of the established Colonial leaders, among them the great Puritan minister Increase Mather (1639–1723). Impressed with the young man's credentials and charmed by his personality, Mather and other influential people eased the way toward Taylor's enrollment in Harvard College.

After training for the ministry, Taylor in 1671 accepted a call to become the pastor of a church in Westfield, Massachusetts. This town was one of the growing communities of settlers who had left the coastal towns of New England for richer farmlands in the Connecticut River valley. Taylor stayed in Westfield for the rest of his life. During those fifty-eight years in this frontier town, he faithfully tended to the spiritual needs of his flock. Taylor himself increased the flock by fourteen members—he had eight children by his first wife and six by his second. By the time he died in 1729, Taylor had outlived a number of his children. He could have had little notion that the poems he had scrupulously put away would outlive him with a radiance bright enough to penetrate the darkness of two centuries of obscurity.

A. Responding
The fact that Edward Taylor remained in obscurity for more than two hundred years might spark a discussion: How likely is it that other writers have remained undiscovered or unrecognized over a long period of time? Is it true, as Thomas Gray wrote in "Elegy Written in a Country Churchyard," that "in his narrow cell forever laid' . . ./Some mute, inglorious Milton here may rest . . ."?

Or was H. L. Mencken, the American journalist, correct in stating, "There are no mute, inglorious Miltons save in the hallucinations of poets. The one sound test of a Milton is that he functions as a Milton"? (Answers will vary but should include some discussion about the nature of literature—that is, what distinguishes "great" literature?)

PREPARATION

1. **BUILDING ON PRIOR KNOWLEDGE.** This poem begins with a parable, a brief, simple story used to make a point about morality or religion. Before they read, you might want students to discuss parables they already know, such as that of the grasshopper and the ant.

2. **ESTABLISHING A PURPOSE.** Have students read to identify the lesson that Taylor teaches through his parable.

SUPPLEMENTARY SUPPORT MATERIALS

1. Vocabulary Activity Worksheet (*CCB*)
2. Review and Response Worksheet: Rhyme and Alliteration (*CCB*)
3. Selection Test (*CCB*)

DEVELOPING VOCABULARY

The following words from the poem are tested in the Selection Test. (See also Vocabulary Activity Worksheet.)

nightingale
stratagem
entrails
gracious
venom

A. Parable/ Imagery

? At what point does the poem relate the spider and the fly to human beings and their fates? (Line 31)

B. Imagery/ Inversion

? Why is the nightingale an appropriate image for humanity that has been saved by God? (The nightingale is associated with higher, spiritual life.)

? Just as Anne Bradstreet uses inverted word order, so does Edward Taylor. Identify a simile in which the words are not in their usual sequence. (Line 46: "We'll nightingale sing like.")

Some of the meanings of the words in this poem are obsolete today; the footnotes should help you to understand them. Taylor also often used the parts of speech in unconventional ways. In conventional modern English, his first address to the spider would be expressed this way: "You sorrowful, venomous little creature." Reading the poem aloud will help clarify some of its harder passages.

Upon a Spider Catching a Fly

Thou sorrow, venom elf.
Is this thy play,
To spin a web out of thyself
To catch a fly?
For why?

I saw a pettish° wasp
Fall foul therein.
Whom yet thy whorl pins° did not clasp
Lest he should fling
His sting.

But as afraid, remote
Didst stand hereat
And with thy little fingers stroke
And gently tap
His back.

Thus gently him didst treat
Lest he should pet,
And in a froppish,° waspish heat
Should greatly fret
Thy net.

Whereas the silly fly,
Caught by its leg
Thou by the throat tookst hastily
And 'hind the head
Bite dead.

This goes to pot, that not
Nature doth call.
Strive not above what strength hath got
Lest in the brawl
Thou fall.

A This fray° seems thus to us.
Hell's spider gets
His entrails spun to whipcords° thus
And wove to nets
And sets

To tangle Adam's race
In's stratagems
To their destructions, spoiled, made base
By venom things
Damned sins.

But mighty, gracious Lord
Communicate
Thy grace to break the cord, afford
Us glory's gate
And state.

B We'll nightingale sing like
When perched on high
In glory's cage, thy glory, bright,
And thankfully,
For joy.

6. **pettish:** fretful.
8. **whorl pins:** projecting pins that hold thread on a spindle. The spider's whorl pins are his legs.
18. **froppish:** fretful (like pettish).
31. **fray:** battle.
33. **whipcords:** coarse strands of rope or animal entrails.

Closure
Have students orally give a prose paraphrase of the poem. (See A Creative Response, page 47.)

Analyzing The Poem
Identifying Details
1. The spider stays apart from the wasp and gently taps its back. When the fly is caught in the net, the spider catches it and kills it.
The spider is afraid of the wasp's sting, but the fly is defenseless and poses no threat.
2. Taylor urges us not to overestimate our own strength by struggling against nature and God, or by struggling against temptation without God's grace. We are likely to be destroyed, just as the fly is destroyed by the spider.
3. Hell's spider is the devil, or Satan, who seeks to trap humanity ("Adam's race") in a web of temptation and evil. God alone is powerful enough to break these cords.
4. The end rhyme scheme is generally *abacc,* although this is sometimes varied to *ababb* (in the sixth stanza, for example), and the rhymes are often slant rhymes (or half rhymes), as in *tap* and *back* in lines 14 and 15. Examples of internal rhyme occur in line 26, "this goes to pot, that not," and line 43, "Thy grace to break the cord, afford."

Interpreting Meanings
5. Taylor's parable teaches the lesson that to prevail against evil, we must have a strong defense (God's grace), similar to the wasp's defense (its sting) against the spider. If we try to prevail against evil on our own, without the help of God, we will be defenseless and doomed, like the fly.
The wasp represents the faithful person who strives against evil, using God's grace as a weapon to defeat Satan. The fly represents the foolish person who believes he or she can prevail without the help of God.
6. Answers will vary.

A Comment on the Poem

Perhaps the best way to approach this poem is to regard its intricate shape and technique as a kind of **metaphor** for the very thing it talks about: a cobweb, which stands for the devil's trap. Just as the spider spins a delicate web that is the scene of a natural conflict, so the author weaves an intricate little poem of short, interconnected lines that shows how the human race may escape the devil's trap.

In the sixth stanza, the expression "This goes to pot" sounds like modern slang curiously turning up in a poem written about three hundred years ago. But the expression meant then what it means now. When an animal was hunted down and killed, its flesh was dropped into a stewing pot. Like the dead animal, a person who "goes to pot" has lost vitality and is "washed up," finished. The expression takes on further meaning when we read it in the context of Taylor's poem: "This goes to pot, that not/Nature doth call." If we put this in normal word order, we have: "This goes to pot, that Nature doth not call." In Puritan theology, Nature, or "natural reason," was the term for an ability all humans were presumed to have been born with. "Natural reason" gave all people the means of perceiving God's truth by instinct, though not everyone heeded Nature's call. Just as the "silly fly" in this poem gets its head bitten off and "goes to pot," those people who do not heed the call of Nature, or "natural reason," will go to Hell. But those who listen to nature will be given the grace to break Satan's cords, to go through "glory's gate," and to rest "on high/In glory's cage" forever.

Responding to the Poem

Analyzing the Poem

Identifying Details

1. The poem begins with a **parable,** a brief story drawn from everyday life that is used to teach a lesson. This parable has three characters: the spider, the wasp, and the fly. How does the spider treat the wasp that has fallen into its net, and how does it treat the fly? Why does the spider treat its two victims differently?
2. Like the fly, who has no defenses against the spider, people have no strength of their own to fight sin. What warning does Taylor give in lines 28–30?
3. In line 31, the poet begins to talk about connections he notices between this natural scene and something in our own existence. What is "Hell's spider," and what does it do to "Adam's race"? Who alone can break the cords spun by Hell's spider?
4. Taylor uses **rhymes** to create an intricate network or "web" of repeated sounds. Describe the pattern of end rhymes in the poem. What examples can you find of internal rhymes, that is, rhyming words that occur within the lines?

Interpreting Meanings

5. Summarize the lesson Taylor is teaching in his parable of the spider, the wasp, and the fly. What kinds of people do you think the wasp and the fly represent?
6. Explain how you feel about poems like this one that teach lessons.

Writing About the Poem

A Creative Response

1. **Rewriting the Poem.** Recast this poem as a prose paragraph. Maintain the author's technique of addressing the spider directly, but phrase what he says in contemporary English. You will have to replace the **archaic** words (like *thou, thy,* and *didst*) and you will have to rewrite inversions so that they conform to normal English word order. You will also have to supply missing words, such as in line 5.

A Critical Response

2. **Comparing Spiders.** Can you see a resemblance between Edwards's spider (page 39) and Taylor's? Or are the insects used for very different purposes? Answer this question in a brief paragraph.

A. Expansion
One way to introduce conceits to your students is to write a few of them on the chalkboard before assigning page 48 or having it read in class. Here are two examples you may want to use:

Our hands were firmly cemented
By a fast balm, which thence did spring;
Our eye-beams twisted and did thread
Our eyes upon one double string.
—John Donne

When God at first made man,
Having a glass of blessings standing by—
"Let us," said he, "pour on him all we can;
—George Herbert

Elements of Literature

THE CONCEIT

In discussions of poetry. the term *conceit* does not mean an inflated opinion of oneself. In poetry, a **conceit** is a startling metaphor or other figure of speech—a surprising connection made between two different things. This connection may be especially witty, strange, exaggerated, or cleverly elaborated. The word *conceit* comes from the Italian *concetto,* meaning "bright idea," and this might be a good way to think about this special kind of figurative language.

A

In his poem about the spider and the fly, Edward Taylor ends with a little conceit, a clever and even shocking comparison between two things that seem to have nothing at all in common. First, he identifies the spider and its web with Satan and his web, which ensnares and entangles human beings. So far, the metaphor is not startling; it seems reasonable to associate a natural predator with Satan. But as Edwards continues, he creates an unusual metaphor. When the Lord breaks Satan's cords and Adam's race enters the gate to a state of glory, what is there but a *cage*! Most of us would never associate the idea of salvation with a cage, or with any kind of confinement.

Here we have a **conceit.** In this case, the conceit is based on a **paradox**—a statement that seems to contradict itself. If, in being saved, we are free from Satan, how is it that we are in a cage? But, like other paradoxes, this one reveals a complex truth, at least as the poet sees it. In order to be truly free, we must be protected, or "caged" by God and his glory. And if salvation is identified as a cage, it is a glorious cage—a cage that holds not dead flies, but joyfully singing nightingales.

Suppose a poet compares the evening sky to a transparent pink curtain: The poet has created a metaphor. The twentieth-century poet T. S. Eliot wrote that the evening was "spread out against the sky / Like a patient etherized upon a table." This is a simile so startling that we could call it a conceit. The nineteenth-century poet Emily Dickinson created another conceit when she compared the setting sun to a housewife sweeping up the sky with multicolored brooms and carelessly dropping shreds behind her.

Conceits, then, are startling figures of speech that are often extended as far as the poet can take them. They are exercises of the imagination, devices for making us see connections between vastly different things in the world. Conceits often give playful turns to common expressions so that they mean not only what they say on the surface, but something else as well, usually something much more profound.

Taylor's poems, full of conceits and elaborate imagery, are hardly the kinds of poems we might expect from a Puritan minister writing by candlelight in a pioneer village on the edge of a forest. But Edward Taylor, like all poets, was a product of his times. In poetry, he accepted the examples of the established English poets who immediately preceded him. The greatest among them—John Donne, George Herbert, and Richard Crashaw—were all masters of the poetical conceit. They saw no conflict in uniting religious devotion with a playful use of language that was sometimes so outrageous that it might seem to flirt with blasphemy.

Make up an original conceit. Begin by thinking of ordinary comparisons. Then try to match one half of a comparison with something no one is likely to have thought of before. Write your conceit in this format:

_____ is like _____.

SUPPLEMENTARY SUPPORT MATERIALS

1. Vocabulary Activity Worksheet (*CCB*)
2. Review and Response Worksheet: Paradox (*CCB*)
3. Selection Test (*CCB*)
4. Audiocassette recording

DEVELOPING VOCABULARY

The following words from the poem are tested in the Selection Test. (See also Vocabulary Activity Worksheet.)

bellows	to mete
canopy	aspen
lanthorn	

PREPARATION

1. ESTABLISHING A PURPOSE. As the headnote indicates, the first nineteen lines of the poem contain a series of questions. Have students read to identify the questions and then to find Taylor's answer.

2. PREREADING JOURNAL. (Challenging) A German philosopher suggested that while man is made in God's image, the image has nothing to do with man's physical appearance but is a divine "nucleus" of the soul, the purpose of which is to provide a point of contact between man and his Maker. Have students comment briefly on that suggestion.

(Less Challenging) Before they read, have students write at least two sentences about their understanding of infinity.

COMMENT FROM A CRITIC

A critic has noted that "the entire 'Preface' to *God's Determinations* turns primarily on the repetition of the words *all* and *nothing.*" You might ask students if they can find evidence to support the critic's statement. (Students should note how frequently the words appear in lines 1–2, 23–24, and 35–41 and should recognize that the subject of the poem is "Might Almighty." See also question 6 on page 51.)

These lines are from the "Preface" to a long series of poems that deal with the struggle between God and Satan for those human beings whom God has elected to save. The first nineteen lines contain a series of questions beginning with *Who.* All these questions have the same answer, given in line 20, and elaborated on in the lines that follow it. In line 1, Taylor uses the word *infinity* to refer to God. What work is God doing in the first four lines of the poem?

from God's Determinations Touching His Elect

Preface

Infinity, when all things it beheld
In nothing, and of nothing all did build,
Upon what base was fixed the lathe,° wherein
He turned this globe, and riggaled° it so trim?
Who blew the bellows of His furnace vast?
Or held the mold wherein the world was cast?
Who laid its cornerstone? Or whose command?
Where stand the pillars upon which it stands?
Who laced and filleted° the earth so fine,
With rivers like green ribbons smaragdine?°
Who made the seas its selfedge,° and its locks
Like a quilt ball within a silver box?
Who spread its canopy? Or curtains spun?
Who in this bowling alley bowled the sun?
Who made it always when it rises set
To go at once both down, and up to get?
Who the curtain rods made for this tapestry?
Who hung the twinkling lanthorns in the sky?
Who? Who did this? Or who is He? Why, know
It's only Might Almighty this did do.
His hand hath made this noble work which stands,
His glorious handiwork not made by hands.
Who spake all things from nothing; and with ease
Can speak all things to nothing, if He please.
Whose little finger at his pleasure can
Out mete ten thousand worlds with half a span:
Whose Might Almighty can by half a looks
Root up the rocks and rock the hills by the roots
Can take this mighty world up in his hand
And shake it like a squitchen° or a wand.
Whose single frown will make the Heavens shake
Like as an aspen leaf the wind makes quake.
Oh! what a might is this whose single frown
Doth shake the world as it would shake it down?
Which all from nothing fet,° from nothing, all:
Hath all on nothing set, lets nothing fall.
Gave all to nothing man indeed, whereby

3. **lathe:** a circular disk used by a potter.
4. **riggaled:** applied markings on the pot.
9. **filleted:** netted, meshed.
10. **smaragdine:** an emerald-green jewel.
11. **selfedge:** the finished edge of woven cloth.
30. **squitchen:** probably a switch.
35. **fet:** fetched.

A. Humanities Connection: Responding to the Illustration

? Why is this illustration especially appropriate to Taylor's poem? (Taylor describes the creation of the universe in terms of handicrafts. He mentions embroidery specifically in lines 9–12 and quilting in line 12. Have students note, too, that the New England quiltmaker created a little town (a miniature universe), complete with a church, houses, people, horses, and sheep.)

A

New England church (detail) (late 18th century). Applique quilt with embroidery.

From the collections of Henry Ford Museum & Greenfield Village.

Through nothing man all might him glorify.
In nothing then imbossed the brightest gem
More precious than all preciousness in them.
But nothing man did throw down all by sin:
And darkened that lightsome gem in him.
That now his brightest diamond is grown
Darker by far than any coalpit stone.

ANALYZING THE POEM

Identifying Details

1. It was built from nothing.

2. Taylor refers to pottery (lines 3–4), blowing the bellows of a furnace (line 5), casting an object in a mold (line 6), building (lines 7–8), embroidery (lines 9–12), and decorating the rooms of a house (lines 13–17).

3. In lines 25–26, Taylor says that God's "little finger at his pleasure can/Out mete ten thousand worlds with half a span." The whole passage from line 19 to line 30 stresses God's terrifying power.

4. The purpose of human existence is to glorify God.

Interpreting Meanings

5. The gem is the immortal soul of every human being.

The gem is line a diamond that has grown darker than a piece of coal.

The poet is probably referring to Adam's disobedience in the Garden of Eden.

6. He begins his answer at the end of line 19 ("Why, know . . ."). The answer stresses God's omnipotence and humanity's ingratitude and sinfulness.

The questions are intended to produce awe in man at God's great power in creating the universe. God is infinitely powerful, and man is puny and insignificant—even "nothing"—in comparison.

7. The paradox is that God has created "all" out of "nothing" (the void).

The poet puns on the noun *rocks,* meaning "stones," and the verb *rock,* meaning "to shake."

8. Answers will vary. You may suggest that students compare its likely effects on an audience with the effects mentioned for Jonathan Edwards's "Sinners in the Hands of an Angry God" (page 36).

Responding to the Poem

Analyzing the Poem

Identifying Details

1. According to the first two lines, what was the whole world built from?
2. The poet draws **images** from human life—specifically from life in a Puritan village—to talk about the act of creation, something that is impossible for human beings to imagine. Identify the various crafts and practical occupations that the poet refers to.
3. Find the lines in which the poet conveys to us the terrifying power of God, a power far greater than that of any human artisan.
4. According to lines 37–38, what is the purpose of human existence in God's world?

Interpreting Meanings

5. What is the "gem" that God sets in "nothing" (line 39)? In the last image of the poem, what has become of this gem? What Biblical event might the poet be referring to here?
6. The first part of the poem is a series of questions. How does Taylor answer his own questions? What feelings about God is this series of questions designed to create?
7. Taylor often uses **puns,** or plays on words, and **paradoxes,** or expressions that seem to be contradictory. What paradox do you find in line 36? What pun does the poet use in line 28?
8. It is possible that Taylor used this poem in one of his sermons. What effect do you think it would have had on a congregation?

Writing About the Poem

A Critical Response

Comparing the Poem with Job. The series of dramatic questions in Edward Taylor's "Preface" echoes a famous passage from the Book of Job, where God speaks to Job from a whirlwind. Job has asked why he has had to suffer so grievously at God's hands. God answers Job with questions of his own:

> Where wast thou when I laid the foundations of the earth? Declare, if thou hast understanding.
> Who hath laid the measures thereof, if thou knowest? Or who hath stretched the line upon it?
> Whereupon are the foundations thereof fastened? Or who laid the corner stone thereof;
> When the morning stars sang together, and all the sons of God shouted for joy?
> Or who shut up the sea with doors, when it brake forth, as if it had issued out of the womb? . . .
>
> —Job 38:4–8

Refer to the Book of Job, Chapters 38–41, for the rest of God's answer. Then write an essay in which you compare the text from Job with Taylor's poem. Before you write, consider these questions and organize your essay around the answers to them: What structure do the two passages have in common that makes them sound so much alike? What are the answers to the questions in each passage? How do both writers use familiar, homely images and metaphors to describe the unimaginable act of creation? What does each passage suggest about the significance of human beings in relation to the might of God?

Analyzing Language and Style

Imagery

Edwards's poetic nourishment came not from the spare plain style of Puritan writers like William Bradford, but from the great English poets of the seventeenth century. To get an idea of the richness of his imagery, make a list of all the **sights** you see in this poem. Are all the images connected with the sense of sight? Or do some reproduce **sounds,** or the feel of **textures**?

Of all the elaborate images in this poem, which one do you think is most fantastic and most successful in describing the world and its creation?

Edwards draws his imagery from the practical concerns of a simple Puritan village. Suppose he were writing this poem today. What crafts and occupations might he use to describe this indescribable act of creation?

A. Responding
? What do you think accounts for the fact that while excellent Puritan writings began to appear almost immediately, Southern Cavalier writings did not? Byrd's *The History of the Dividing Line* grew out of an event that occurred in 1728, nearly a hundred years after William Bradford began writing his history of the Plymouth Colony. (Possible reasons for the Puritan's early writing are the Puritan beliefs in self-examination and in writing as a means of glorifying God. Also, the harsh climate and the simple life the Puritans believed in may have meant fewer distractions from the self-discipline that writing requires.)

The Southern Planters

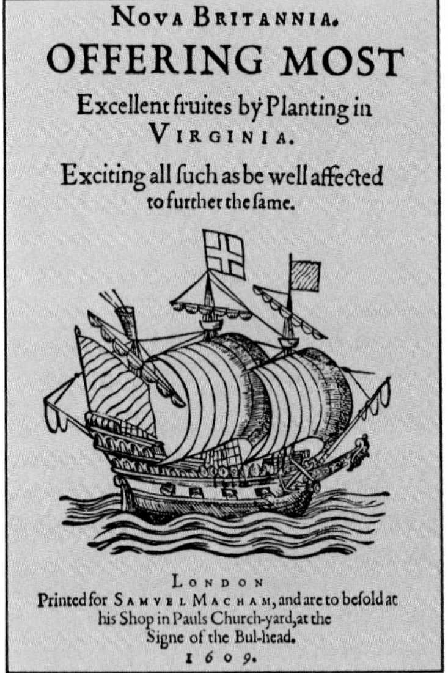
NOVA BRITANNIA.
OFFERING MOST
Excellent fruites by Planting in
VIRGINIA.
Exciting all such as be well affected
to further the same.

LONDON
Printed for SAMVEL MACHAM, and are to be sold at
his Shop in Pauls Church-yard, at the
Signe of the Bul-head.
1609.

Nova Britannia Offering Most Excellent Fruites by Planting in Virginia, London (1609). Woodcut.

Rare Books and Manuscripts Division, The New York Public Library. Astor, Lenox and Tilden Foundations.

A In addition to the Puritans of New England, there was another literary tradition in the New World. This literature came from the Southern planters, a group of people whose background and social views varied considerably from those of the Puritans.

Many reasons can be suggested for the differences. One factor may have been climate. The Southern climate was kinder; it was warm and soft and the land was enormously fertile. The Northern climate was harsh; springs and summers were brief and winters were long and cold. Even the land in New England was hard; its outcroppings of granite and bedrock broke plows and made farming difficult.

But economic and religious factors were even more important. The land holdings in New England were small for the most part; many colonists were small farmers or tradesmen who lived in villages and owned very little land. But the Southern planter was an aristocrat and the virtual ruler of a huge territory. He maintained this area by keeping a large number of slaves (though there were slaves in New England in those days too).

In religion, most Southerners belonged to the Church of England. In general, they were much more interested in the outside world—in literature, music, art, politics, and the world of nature—than they were in the scrupulous examination of their own souls. But the Puritans, who had rejected the established church, were constantly looking inward and questioning themselves. Where the Southerner saw the world as something to be conquered and enjoyed, the Puritan—who loved the world as much as anyone else did—feared that its beauties were lures and sources of temptation.

The Southern planters shared the world view of the English Renaissance, with its emphasis on classical literature and the growing spirit of scientific inquiry. Thus, when the Southerners wrote about the New World, they were apt to write about it in traditional ways. Characteristically, the first purely literary work of the South was a translation of a Latin classic, Ovid's collection of myths called the *Metamorphoses*. Even a work as original as *The Sotweed Factor* (1708), Ebenezer Cooke's humorous tale of a tobacco merchant, was written in bouncy couplets, the popular form for satirical verse in England.

In many ways, William Byrd is a representative figure for the Southern writers of the Colonial Period. Born in Virginia more than fifty years after the Pilgrims landed on Plymouth, Byrd was truly a Renaissance man in the New World. He translated Greek and Latin works, composed original poetry (mostly satiric verse), and wrote about mathematics and medicine. Writing a generation before Thomas Jefferson, Byrd displayed the same intellectual curiosity that his fellow Virginian would so strongly exemplify later.

Byrd described the pleasures of the life of the Southern planter: "I have a large family of my own, and my doors are open to everybody, yet I have no bills to pay. . . . I live in a kind of independence of everyone but Providence. . . . I must take care to keep all my people to their duty. . . . But then 'tis an amusement in this silent country."

William Byrd (1674–1744)

It is worth remembering that Jamestown, Virginia, was named for James I, the king who vowed to harry the Puritans out of England. Virginia itself was named for Elizabeth I, the "Virgin Queen." These place names—and many others in the South—remind us of an important difference between Virginia and the colonies of New England. New England was settled largely by those in conflict with British intellectual, theological, and social life; Virginia was settled by those in harmony with that life. By and large, the fervent, short-haired puritanical Roundheads went to New England; the aristocratic, long-haired, worldly Cavaliers went to Virginia.

William Byrd, a man of exceptional intellect and accomplishments, was a thorough Cavalier—worldly, sophisticated, and gentlemanly. Byrd was born in Virginia, the son of a wealthy landowner and merchant, but he was educated in England, where he spent half his life. In London, he acquired a passion for the theater, which the Puritans had once outlawed as immoral. Byrd had many scientific interests: He was even a member of the Royal Society, that pillar of the British scientific establishment.

Byrd alternated between living in England and Virginia. He preferred London, with its elegant homes, witty conversation, and gambling tables. During his visits to Westover, his 26,000-acre home in Virginia, he tried to keep alive both his social and intellectual life. Westover's gardens are still renowned, and its library of 3,600 volumes was rivaled in Byrd's time only by Cotton Mather's library in New England.

Byrd had little in common with the New Englanders. The contrasts between Byrd and the Puritans are instructive. For example, Byrd kept a diary, as many Puritans did. But the Puritans' diaries are primarily records of spiritual examination. Byrd's diary records the pleasures and practical concerns of a man of the world. Dinners, flirtations with women, literature, and natural science were of greater interest to him than matters of the spirit. In London in 1719, for example, he recorded a typical day:

William Byrd by Sir Godfrey Kneller.
Colonial Williamsburg Foundation.

May 28. I rose about 7 o'clock and read a chapter in Hebrew and some Greek. I neglected my prayers, but had milk for breakfast. The weather was still warm and clear and very dry, the wind north. About eleven came Annie Wilkinson but I would not speak with her. I was disappointed in the [absence] of Mrs. B—s who wrote me word she would come and breakfast with me, so I read some English and ate some bread and butter because I was to dine late and about 3 o'clock went to dine with Sir Wilfred Lawson and ate some mutton. After dinner we talked a little and about 6 o'clock went to Kensington in Sir Wilfred's coach where there was a ball in the gardens and several ladies and among the rest Miss Perry whom I stuck most to and she complained I squeezed her hand. Here I stayed till 1 o'clock and then came home and neglected my prayers.

In 1728, Byrd joined a survey expedition of the disputed boundary line between Virginia and North Carolina. *The History of The Dividing Line* is far more than a simple record of that expedition. Witty and elegantly written, it is filled with philosophical observations and barbed comments on American Colonial life.

FOR FURTHER READING
For Students
Your students might be interested in reading and reporting on the article about William Byrd that appears in the December 1959 issue of *American Heritage*—Marshall Fishwick's "The Pepys of the Old Dominion." The article focuses on Byrd's encoded diary, which, like *The History of the Dividing Line,* reveals a man of remarkable wit and candor. "Compared to his [Byrd's] prose," Fishwick writes, "the tedious sermonizing of the Puritan and Anglican ministers seems like copybook work in an understaffed grammar school."

PREPARATION

1. ESTABLISHING A PURPOSE. Because Byrd is the first non-New England writer in this unit, you might have students read for comparisons with the New England writers. Students can compare subject matter, tone, diction, and so on.

2. PREREADING JOURNAL. Students might write several sentences describing what they think would be an early Southern planter's attitude toward the Indians he encounters in his new life.

SUPPLEMENTARY SUPPORT MATERIALS

1. Vocabulary Activity Worksheet (*CCB*)
2. Review and Response Worksheet: Diction (*CCB*)
3. Selection Test (*CCB*)

DEVELOPING VOCABULARY

The following words from the history are tested in the Selection Test. (See also Vocabulary Activity Worksheet.)

frugality	enfeebled
reprobate	squeamish
faction	dissenter
to till	venerable
prudent	bliss

A. Tone

Have students answer the question about tone in the headnote. (Clearly, Byrd sounds more "modern.")

? What are some features of the writing that give the history its modern tone? (Colloquial word choice, lively rhythm, relatively simple style)

FROM THE HISTORY OF THE DIVIDING LINE

A **In the first extract from the *History,* Byrd ironically describes the "modish frenzy" of early travelers to America, a fashionable craze which he compares to a "distemper" or illness. Notice immediately how Byrd's *tone* differs from Bradford's, even though both men were writing about the same topic. Which writer do you think sounds more "modern"?**

Early Virginia Colonies

As it happened some ages before to be the fashion to saunter to the Holy Land and go upon other Quixote adventures,[1] so it was now grown the humor to take a trip to America. The Spaniards had lately discovered rich mines in their part of the West Indies, which made their maritime neighbors eager to do so too. This modish frenzy, being still more inflamed by the charming account given of Virginia by the first adventurers, made many fond of removing to such a Paradise.

Happy was he, and still happier she, that could get themselves transported, fondly expecting their coarsest utensils in that happy place would be of massy silver.

This made it easy for the Company to procure as many volunteers as they wanted for their new Colony, but, like most other undertakers who have no assistance from the public, they starved the design by too much frugality; for, unwilling to launch out at first into too much expense, they shipped off but few people at a time, and those but scantily provided. The adventurers were, besides, idle and extravagant and expected they might live without work in so plentiful a country.

These wretches were set ashore not far from Roanoke Inlet, but by some fatal disagreement or laziness were either starved or cut to pieces by the Indians.

Several repeated misadventures of this kind did for some time allay the itch of sailing to the new world, but the distemper broke out again about the year 1606. Then it happened that the Earl of Southampton and several other persons eminent for their quality and estates were invited into the Company who applied themselves once more to people the then almost abandoned Colony. For this purpose they embarked about a hundred men, most of them reprobates[2] of good families and related to some of the Company who were men of quality and fortune.

The ships that carried them made a shift to find a more direct way to Virginia and ventured through the capes into the Bay of Chesapeake. The same night they came to an anchor at the mouth of Powhatan, the same as James River, where they built a small fort at a place called Point Comfort.

This settlement stood its ground from that time forward, in spite of all the blunders and disagreement of the first adventurers and the many calamities that befell the Colony afterward. The six gentlemen who were first named of the Company by the Crown and who were empowered to choose an annual president from among themselves were always engaged in factions and quarrels, while the rest detested work more than famine. At this rate the Colony must have come to nothing had it not been for the vigilance and bravery of Captain Smith,[3] who struck a terror into all the Indians round about. This gentleman took some pains to persuade the men to plant Indian corn, but they

1. **Quixote adventures:** foolish adventures, after the madcap hero of Cervantes's novel, *Don Quixote* (1605–1615).

2. **reprobates** (rep′rə·bāts): people lost to all sense of duty or decency.

3. **Captain Smith:** John Smith (1579–1631), founder of Virginia.

A. Humanities Connection: Discussing the Map
Early maps of the New World are seldom accurate, but they do show the main topographic features. Have students look carefully at the de Bry map. Although called a "Map of Virginia," perceptive students may notice that the region shown is not in present-day Virginia—it is in North Carolina. The barrier islands are the Outer Banks. The large island is Roanoke. What appears to be a river to the interior is Albemarle Sound. This region was the home of the "lost colony," established twenty years before the first permanent white settlement at Jamestown. You might ask one or more volunteers to research the story of the lost colony, including Virginia Dare and "CROATOAN."

Theodore de Bry (1528–1598) was a Flemish engravèr and publisher. He never visited the New World, and his engravings are based on the drawings and paintings of explorers. The British geographer Richard Hakluyt assisted de Bry in obtaining these illustrations.

B. Tone
? What sort of tone does Byrd adopt when he makes the statement that the settlers, "like true Englishmen, . . . built a church that cost no more than fifty pounds and a tavern that cost five hundred." (The statement is satirical.)

A

Map of Virginia by Theodore de Bry (1590). Colored engraving. New York Public Library.

looked upon all labor as a curse. They chose rather to depend upon the musty provisions that were sent from England; and when they failed, they were forced to take more pains to seek for wild fruits in the woods than they would have taken in tilling the ground. Besides, this exposed them to be knocked in the head by the Indians and gave them fluxes [dysentery] into the bargain, which thinned the plantation very much. To supply this mortality, they were reinforced the year following with a greater number of people, along which were fewer gentlemen and more laborers, who, however, took care not to kill themselves with work. These found the first adventurers in a very starving condition but relieved their wants with the fresh supply they brought with them. From Kecoughtan[4] they extended themselves as far as Jamestown, where, like true Englishmen, B they built a church that cost no more than fifty pounds and a tavern that cost five hundred.

4. **Kecoughtan:** New Hampton, Virginia.

As the Colony grew, violence frequently erupted between the settlers and the Indians. Byrd offered his solution to the conflicts between the two cultures.

Intermarriage

They had now made peace with the Indians, but there was one thing wanting to make that peace lasting. The natives could by no means persuade themselves that the English were heartily their friends so long as they disdained to intermarry with them. And, in earnest, had the English consulted their own security and the good of the Colony, had they intended either to civilize or convert these gentiles, they would have brought their stomachs to embrace this prudent alliance.

The Indians are generally tall and well proportioned, which may make full amends for the darkness of their complexions. Add to this that they are healthy and strong, with constitutions un-

Closure
Have students write several sentences explaining why Byrd's history constituted a new form of literature for the New World.

A. Argument
? How might the Puritans have responded to Byrd's suggestion of intermarriage with the Indians? (Most of them would have been appalled. In the Puritans' eyes, the Native Americans were "savages" and very probably the instruments of Satan.)
? What evidence does Byrd use to support his argument for intermarriage? (The Indians are healthy and good-looking. They are no greater heathens than the explorers. Intermarriage promotes friendship between whites and Indians. The French have gained advantages through intermarriage.)

B. Humanities Connection: Discussing the Fine Art
This painting, executed by an unknown, self-taught artist, is marked by directness and naiveté. Such a work is considered *primitive* art.

tainted by lewdness and not enfeebled by luxury. Besides, morals and all considered, I cannot think the Indians were much greater heathens than the first adventurers, who, had they been good Christians, would have had the charity to take this only method of converting the natives to Christianity. For after all that can be said, a sprightly lover is the most prevailing missionary that can be sent among these or any other infidels.

A Besides, the poor Indians would have had less reason to complain that the English took away their land if they had received it by way of a portion with their daughters. Had such affinities been contracted in the beginning, how much bloodshed had been prevented and how populous would the country have been, and, consequently, how considerable! Nor would the shade of the skin have been any reproach at this day, for if a Moor may be washed white in three generations, surely an Indian might have been blanched.

The French, for their parts, have not been so squeamish in Canada, who upon trial find abundance of attraction in the Indians. Their late grand monarch thought it not below even the dignity of a Frenchman to become one flesh with this people and therefore ordered 100 livres for any of his subjects, man or woman, that would intermarry with a native.

By this piece of policy we find the French interest very much strengthened among the savages and their religion, such as it is, propagated just as far as their love. And I heartily wish this well-concerted scheme doesn't hereafter give the French an advantage over His Majesty's good subjects on the northern continent of America.

Byrd's History touches on other colonies besides Virginia. Here he presents a Cavalier's view of the Puritans of the northern colonies.

The New England Colonies

About the same time New England was pared off from Virginia by letters patent bearing [the] date April 10, 1608. Several gentlemen of the town and neighborhood of Plymouth obtained this grant, with the Lord Chief Justice Popham at their head.

Their bounds were specified to extend from 38 to 45 degrees of northern latitude, with a breadth of one hundred miles from the seashore. The first fourteen years this company encountered many difficulties and lost many men, though, far from being discouraged, they sent over numerous recruits of Presbyterians every year, who for all that

B

Hunting Party by an unknown artist (late 17th century). Oil on canvas, 25¾″ × 47⅛″.

The Metropolitan Museum of Art, Collection of Mr. and Mrs. Samuel Schwartz, 1979.

Reading Check Test

1. Byrd pictures the earliest Virginia settlers as (a) pious (b) lazy (c) timid (d) enterprising *(b)*

2. Intermarriage with the Indians, according to Byrd, would have served to (a) ensure peace (b) disgrace Captain Smith (c) promote trade (d) enrage the Puritans *(a)*

3. Byrd writes that, despite mistakes, the Plymouth Colony (a) was more prosperous than Virginia (b) encouraged intermarriage with the natives (c) revolted (d) succeeded *(d)*

4. Bearskin believes in (a) one supreme God (b) an angry god (c) many equal gods (d) predestination *(a)*

5. In hell, as Bearskin pictures it, the weather is always (a) warm (b) wintry (c) blazingly hot (d) rainy *(b)*

had much ado to stand their ground, with all their fighting and praying.

A But about the year 1620 a large swarm of dissenters fled thither from the severities of their stepmother, the church. These saints [the Puritan dissenters], conceiving the same aversion to the copper complexion of the natives as that of the first adventurers to Virginia, would on no terms contract alliances with them, afraid, perhaps, like the Jews of old, lest they might be drawn into idolatry by those strange women.

Whatever disgusted them I can't say, but this false delicacy, creating in the Indians a jealousy that the English were ill affected toward them, was the cause that many of them were cut off and the rest exposed to various distresses.

This reinforcement was landed not far from Cape Cod, where for their greater security they built a fort and near it a small town, which, in honor of the proprietors, was called New Plymouth. But they still had many discouragements to struggle with, though by being well supported from home they by degrees triumphed over them all.

Their brethren, after this, flocked over so fast that in a few years they extended the settlement one hundred miles along the coast, including Rhode Island and Martha's Vineyard.

Thus the Colony throve apace and was thronged with large detachments of Independents and Presbyterians who thought themselves persecuted at home.

Byrd's surveying party is guided by an Indian named Bearskin. Here, Byrd records Bearskin's religious beliefs.

The Native Religion

In the evening we examined our friend Bearskin concerning the religion of his country, and he explained it to us without any of that reserve to which his nation is subject. He told us he believed there was one supreme god, who had several subaltern[5] deities under him. And that this master god made the world a long time ago. That he told the sun, the moon, and stars their business in the beginning, which they, with good looking after, have faithfully performed ever since. That the same power that made all things at first has taken care to keep them in the same method and motion ever since. He believed that God had formed many worlds before he formed this, but that those worlds either grew old and ruinous or were destroyed for the dishonesty of the inhabitants. That God is very just and very good, ever well pleased with those men who possess those godlike qualities. That he takes good people into his safe protection, makes them very rich, fills their bellies plentifully, preserves them from sickness and from being surprised or overcome by their enemies. But all such as tell lies and cheat those they have dealings with he never fails to punish with sickness, poverty, and hunger and, after all that, suffers them to be knocked on the head and scalped by those that fight against them.

B He believed that after death both good and bad people are conducted by a strong guard into a great road, in which departed souls travel together for some time till at a certain distance this road forks into two paths, the one extremely level and the other stony and mountainous. Here the good are parted from the bad by a flash of lightning, the first being hurried away to the right, the other to the left. The right-hand road leads to a charming, warm country, where the spring is everlasting and every month is May; and as the year is always in its youth, so are the people, and particularly the women are bright as stars and never scold. That in this happy climate there are deer, turkeys, elks, and buffaloes innumerable, perpetually fat and gentle, while the trees are loaded with delicious fruit quite throughout the four seasons. That the soil brings forth corn spontaneously, without the curse of labor, and so very wholesome that none who have the happiness to eat of it are ever sick, grow old, or die. Near the entrance into this blessed land sits a venerable old man on a mat richly woven, who examines strictly all that are brought before him, and if they have behaved well, the guards are ordered to open the crystal gate and let them enter into the land of delight.

The left-hand path is very rugged and uneven, leading to a dark and barren country where it is always winter. The ground is the whole year round covered with snow, and nothing is to be seen upon the trees but icicles. All the people are hungry yet have not a morsel of anything to eat except a bitter kind of potato, that gives them the dry gripes [heaves] and fills their whole body with loathsome

5. **subaltern** (səb·ôl′tərn): subordinate; lower; of inferior rank or position.

A. Responding
? How accurate does Byrd's description of the early years of Puritan settlement seem to be? (Byrd glosses over the problems the "swarm of dissenters" faced, although he admits there were "discouragements.")

B. Responding
? How closely does Bearskin's picture of heaven correspond to your understanding of the Judeo-Christian idea of heaven? (Some similarities exist. Students' responses will depend in part on their personal beliefs.)

Analyzing The History
Identifying Facts
1. Byrd says that the entire idea of settling America was a "modish frenzy," that the company sponsoring the first expedition was too frugal, and that the first settlers were "starved or cut to pieces by the Indians."
2. Byrd thinks the expectations of the first colonists were unrealistic, that many settlers were encouraged to travel to Virginia by false accounts of explorers and adventurers.
3. Byrd thinks that intermarriage with the healthy and generally moral Native Americans would have brought lasting peace. The French benefited from intermarriage and the English would have, too.
Byrd's interests seem decidedly practical, although he "cannot think that the Indians were much greater heathens than the first adventurers, who, had they been good Christians, would have had the charity to take this only method of converting the natives to Christianity."

Interpreting Meanings
4. Byrd evidently admired a realistic outlook, practicality, industriousness, *(Answers continue in left-hand column.)*

(Continued from top.)
cooperation, bravery, and vigilance.
5. Byrd does not seem to be an admirer of the New England Puritans. He speaks of a "swarm of dissenters" fleeing there. A "false delicacy" made them "disgusted" with the Indians.
6. Byrd considers "three great articles of natural religion" important: belief in God, the moral distinction between good and evil, and the expectation of rewards and punishments in another world.
Whereas Mary Rowlandson shows the Puritan tendency to regard even the most mundane event as evidence of God's will, William Byrd is more worldly and practical. Students may agree, however, that Byrd's essential religious beliefs do not differ greatly from those of Rowlandson.
7. Answers will vary.

ulcers that stink and are insupportably painful. Here all the women are old and ugly, having claws like a panther with which they fly upon the men that slight their passion. For it seems these haggard old furies[6] are intolerably fond and expect a vast deal of cherishing. They talk much and exceedingly shrill, giving exquisite pain to the drum of the ear, which in that place of the torment is so tender that every sharp note wounds it to the quick. At the end of this path sits a dreadful old woman on a monstrous toadstool, whose head is covered with rattlesnakes instead of tresses, with glaring white eyes that strike a terror unspeakable into all that behold her. This hag pronounces sentence of woe upon all the miserable wretches that hold up their hands at her tribunal. After this they are delivered over to huge turkey buzzards, like harpies,[7] that fly away with them to the place above-mentioned. Here, after they have been tormented a certain number of years according to their several degrees of guilt, they are driven back into this world to try if they will mend their manners and merit a place the next time in the regions of bliss.

This was the substance of Bearskin's religion and was as much to the purpose as could be expected from a mere state of nature, without one glimpse of revelation or philosophy. It contained, however, the three great articles of natural religion: the belief of a god, the moral distinction between good and evil, and the expectation of rewards and punishments in another world. . . .

6. **furies:** in Greek and Roman mythology, fierce avenging goddesses.

7. **harpies:** in Greek and Roman mythology, filthy, evil creatures with women's heads and birds' bodies.

Responding to the History

Analyzing the History

Identifying Facts

1. What reasons does Byrd suggest for the failure of the first Virginia settlement?
2. According to Byrd, did the first colonists have realistic expectations of life in the New World? Explain his point of view.
3. For what reasons is Byrd in favor of intermarriage with Native Americans? Are his interests here primarily moral or primarily practical? Explain.

Interpreting Meanings

4. Like many English writers of his time, Byrd excels at **satire,** the use of ridicule to expose the faults or weaknesses of people or institutions. From his scathing portrait of the early settlers of Virginia in the first passage of this selection, what personal qualities do you think Byrd admired?
5. What is Byrd's attitude toward the Puritans of New England? Tell how his **diction,** or choice of words, reveals this attitude.
6. According to his description of the native religion, what "articles," or elements, of religion does Byrd consider most important? Consider Byrd's attitudes toward religion as revealed in his remarks on intermarriage, on the New England colonists, and on Native American theology. How closely do his views accord with those expressed by Mary Rowlandson (page 24)?
7. Did you find Byrd a more or less interesting writer than the other Colonials? Support your position with references to the selections you have read.

Writing About the History

A Critical Response

1. **Contrasting Two Histories.** In a brief essay, contrast the selection from Byrd's *History of the Dividing Line* with William Bradford's account of the Puritan landing at Plymouth (pages 15–20). In your essay, consider specifically how the two accounts differ in purpose, tone, and style.
2. **Analyzing the History.** Examine the references to women in this selection from Byrd's history. In a paragraph or two, mention the references and discuss what they reveal about the position of women in Byrd's world.

SUPPLEMENTARY SUPPORT MATERIALS

1. Review and Response Worksheet: Native American Myths and Ritual Songs (*CCB*)
2. Language Skills Worksheet: Plain Style (*CCB*)
3. Selection Test (*CCB*)

PREPARATION

1. BUILDING ON PRIOR KNOWLEDGE. Review with students that a myth is a traditional story that seeks to explain some aspect of the cosmos, nature, or human customs. Myths often center on the gods, creation, the meaning of life and death, natural phenomena, and heroic adventures.

2. ESTABLISHING A PURPOSE. Tell students they are about to read some Native American myths and songs. Ask them to look for the purposes of such literature as they read each piece.

A SAMPLE OF NATIVE AMERICAN MYTHS AND RITUAL SONGS

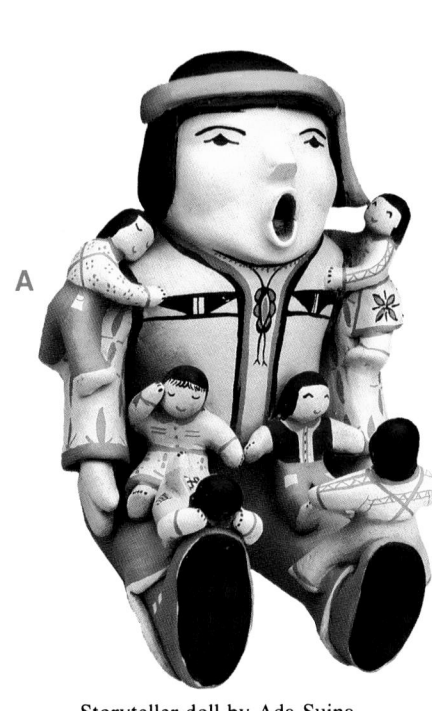

Storyteller doll by Ada Suina, Cochiti Pueblo, 1988.

Courtesy of the Amerind Foundation, Inc., Dragoon, Arizona. Photograph by Robin Stancliff.

Native American cultures were complex and diverse and encompassed a variety of arts. Their literary arts were oral. Generations of storytellers recited stories and poems over and over again, seldom in exactly the same way twice. For Native Americans, as for any culture, these stories served many purposes—to entertain, surely, but also to educate the young and to communicate the values of the culture.

The two most popular figures in Native American narratives are Grandmother Spider and Coyote, who are often portrayed as tricksters. Stories about these complex characters mix humor and seriousness, earthiness and abstract thought.

These figures, however, are not meant to be cartoon characters. They are believed in, since they represent a mythology and a set of religious beliefs carried forward from the past into the present.

Figures representing nature, such as the sun, moon, or earth, not only appear in Native American stories, but are directly invoked in a multitude of rituals.

Ramos Casas Grandes vessel (c. A.D. 1100).

Courtesy of the Amerind Foundation, Inc., Dragoon, Arizona. Photograph by Robin Stancliff.

A. Humanities Connection: About the Fine Art

Discuss with students how carving and pottery reflect a culture just as oral and written literature do. Southwest Indians began working in ceramics about 300 B.C., decorating practical objects, such as bowls, with animals, fantasy figures, and geometric designs. Native American artists also produced extraordinary paintings, weavings, baskets, jewelry, and feathered and beaded costumes.

B. Expansion

N. Scott Momaday (see page 1014) wrote, "The oral tradition of the Indian, even more than his plastic arts, is vast and various. His stories and songs, his legends and lore and prayers, are exceptionally rich and imaginative. They reflect an understanding of, and belief in, the power and beauty of language that is very nearly lost upon us who have, by and large, only the experience of a written tradition."

Expansion
Formal study of Native American folklore began with the work of Henry Rowe Schoolcraft (1793–1864), who collected stories from his Chippewa wife and through his work as an Indian agent. He was the first white man to translate Indian poetry. Schoolcraft's work had a significant influence on Henry Wadsworth Longfellow, whose narrative poem "The Song of Hiawatha" immortalized some of Schoolcraft's errors. (The story's origin is the Chippewa hero Manabozho, not the Iroquois Hiawatha.)

Research Project
Appoint a small group to research myths about the origin of sunlight told in other cultures.

A. Myth
? In explaining the origin of sunlight, what other natural phenomena does this myth also explain? (The bald tail of the possum and the bald head of the buzzard)

B. Responding
? What connection between the sun, fire, and pottery-making can you make? (Pottery is created by sun-drying or firing clay. Before the arrival of the sun and fire, people could not make pottery.)

C. Expansion
The Cherokee lived in the southeast part of North America, but they were forced to move to Indian Territory by 1839.

GRANDMOTHER SPIDER STEALS THE SUN

In the beginning there was only blackness, and nobody could see anything. People kept bumping into each other and groping blindly. They said: "What this world needs is light."

Fox said he knew some people on the other side of the world who had plenty of light, but they were too greedy to share it with others. Possum said he would be glad to steal a little of it. "I have a bushy tail," he said. "I can hide the light inside all that fur." Then he set out for the other side of the world. There he found the sun hanging in a tree and lighting everything up. He sneaked over to the sun, picked out a tiny piece of light, and stuffed it into his tail. But the light was hot and burned all the fur off. The people discovered his theft and took back the light, and ever since, Possum's tail has been bald.

A "Let me try," said Buzzard. "I know better than to hide a piece of stolen light in my tail. I'll put it on my head." He flew to the other side of the world and, diving straight into the sun, seized it in his claws. He put it on his head, but it burned his head feathers off. The people grabbed the sun away from him, and ever since that time Buzzard's head has remained bald.

Then Grandmother Spider said, "Let me try!" First she made a thick-walled pot out of clay. Next she spun a web reaching all the way to the other side of the world. She was so small that none of the people there noticed her coming. Quickly Grandmother Spider snatched up the sun, put it in the bowl of clay, and scrambled back home along one of the strands of her web. Now her side of the world had light, and everyone rejoiced.

Spider Woman brought not only the sun to the Cherokee, but
B fire with it. And besides that, she taught the Cherokee people the art of pottery making.

C —from a Cherokee tale reported by James Mooney in the 1890's

Writing Assignment

1. Have students write original myths involving Grandmother Spider or Coyote or explaining the origin of some natural phenomenon.

2. After students read the songs on page 62, have them write their own free-verse celebrations of Nature or of the human place in Nature.

Speaking Assignment

Have two students retell these myths orally, as they were originally transmitted. Students need not memorize word for word, but they should learn the stories well enough to retain their stylistic flavor and important details. Alternatively, have students find additional Native American myths and present them to the class orally.

COYOTE FINISHES HIS WORK

From the very beginning, Coyote was traveling around all over the earth. He did many wonderful things when he went along. He killed monsters and the evil spirits that preyed on the people. He made the Indians, and put them out in tribes all over the world because Old Man Above wanted the earth to be inhabited all over, not just in one or two places.

He gave all the people different names and taught them different languages. This is why Indians live all over the country now and speak in different ways.

He taught the people how to eat and how to hunt the buffalo and catch eagles. He taught them what roots to eat and how to make a good lodge and what to wear. He taught them how to dance. Sometimes he made mistakes, and even though he was wise and powerful, he did many foolish things. But that was his way.

Coyote liked to play tricks. He thought about himself all the time, and told everyone he was a great warrior, but he was not. Sometimes he would go too far with some trick and get someone killed. Other times, he would have a trick played on himself by someone else. He got killed this way so many times that Fox and the birds got tired of bringing him back to life. Another way he got in trouble was trying to do what someone else did.

Coyote (detail) by Susan Nagoda-Bergquist. **A**

Courtesy of the artist.

This is how he came to be called Imitator.

Coyote was ugly too. The girls did not like him. But he was smart. He could change himself around and trick the women. Coyote got the girls when he wanted.

One time, Coyote had done everything he could think of and was traveling from one place to another place, looking for other things that needed to be done. Old Man saw him going along and said to himself, "Coyote has now done almost everything he is capable of doing. His work is almost done. It is time to bring him back to the place where he started."

So Great Spirit came down and traveled in the shape of an old man. He met Coyote. Coyote said, "I am Coyote. Who are you?"

Old Man said, "I am Chief of the earth. It was I who sent you to set the world right."

"No," Coyote said, "you never sent me. I don't know you. If you are the Chief, take that lake over there and move it to the side of that mountain."

"No, If you are Coyote, let me see you do it."

Coyote did it.

"Now, move it back."

Coyote tried, but he could not do it. He thought this was strange. He tried again, but he could not do it.

Chief moved the lake back.

Coyote said, "Now I know you are the Chief."

Old Man said, "Your work is finished, Coyote. You have traveled far and done much good. Now you will go to where I have prepared a home for you."

Then Coyote disappeared. Now no one knows where he is anymore.

Old Man got ready to leave, too. He said to the Indians, "I will send messages to the earth by the spirits of the people

For Further Reading For Teachers and Students

The World of the American Indian, edited by Jules B. Billard (National Geographic Society, 1974); *Voices of the Wind: Native American Legends,* by Margot Edmonds and Ella C. Clark (Facts on File, 1990); and *Spider Woman's Granddaughters: Traditional Tales and Contemporary Writing by Native American Women,* edited by Paula Gunn Allen (Beacon Press, 1989).

A. Humanities Connection: About the Fine Art

Although she is of European descent, Susan Nagoda-Bergquist (b. 1943) heard Native American tales as a child, told to her by Papago, Hopi, and Apache women. The trickster tales of the hunter-gatherer tradition became her favorites and inspired an interest in anthropology and folklore. The character of Coyote figures in all of her work.

CLOSURE

Discuss with students what they can gain from understanding Native American traditions. They may touch on such issues as the history of their country, intercultural similarities and differences, respect for nature, and sheer enjoyment.

READING CHECK TEST

1. Grandmother Spider conceals the sun inside_______. *a clay pot*
2. Old Man proves to Coyote his claim to be Chief by _______. *moving a lake*
3. Old Man takes Coyote away to _______. *rest*
4. _______ possesses the "breath of life." *Mother Earth*
5. In "Song of the Sky Loom" the earth and the sky are spoken of as _______. *children*

A. Responding
What feature of Native American culture does this passage explain? (Mystical, out-of-body experiences)

B. Expansion
The Nez Percé Indians lived in the Northwest; the Tewa and Zuni were Pueblo Indians of the Southwest.

C. Cross-Curriculum Connections
According to N. Scott Momaday, the Native American "is deeply invested in the earth, committed to it both in his consciousness and in his instinct. In him the sense of place is paramount. Only in reference to the earth can he persist in his true identity."
What can be gained from an understanding of this view? (Students can agree with the Native American respect for the environment without having to agree with the religious values out of which this respect grew.)

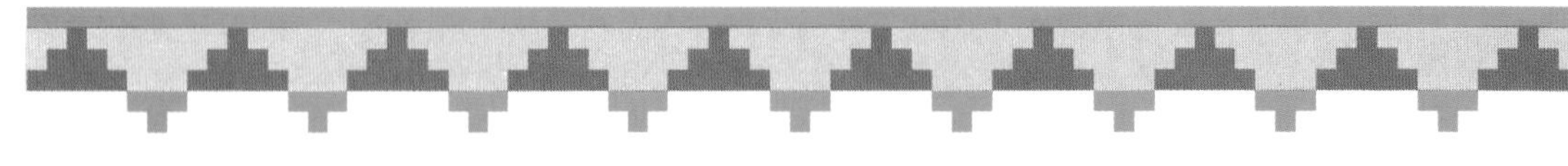

who reach me but whose time to die has not yet come. They will carry messages to you from time to time. When their spirits come back into their bodies, they will revive and tell you their experiences.

"Coyote and myself, we will not be seen again until Earth-woman is very old. Then we shall return to earth, for it will require a change by that time. Coyote will come along first, and when you see him you will know I am coming. When I come along, all the spirits of the dead will be with me. There will be no more Other Side Camp. All the people will live together. Earthmother will go back to her first shape and live as a mother among her children. Then things will be made right."

Now they are waiting for Coyote.

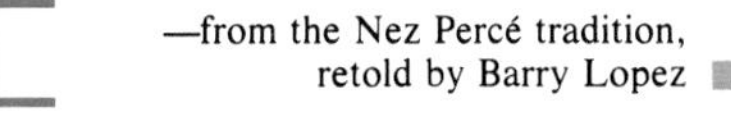

—from the Nez Percé tradition, retold by Barry Lopez

SONG of the SKY LOOM

Oh our Mother the Earth, oh our Father the Sky,
Your children are we, and with tired backs
We bring you the gifts that you love.
Then weave for us a garment of brightness;
May the warp be the white light of morning,
May the weft be the red light of evening,
May the fringes be the falling rain,
May the border be the standing rainbow.
Thus weave for us a garment of brightness
That we may walk fittingly where birds sing,
That we may walk fittingly where grass is green,
Oh our Mother the Earth, oh our Father the Sky!

—a traditional Tewa song translated by Herbert Joseph Spinden

BREATH of LIFE

We are grateful,
O Mother Earth
For the mountains
And the streams
Where the deer, by
command of thy
Breath of life, wander.

Wishing for you the
Fullness of life,
We shall go forth prayerfully
upon the trails of our
Earth Mother.

—a Zuni ritual song translated by Frank Hamilton Cushing

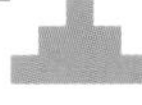

For Further Reading
For Teachers
The classic book on general semantics is S. I. Hayakawa's *Language in Thought and Action* (Harcourt Brace Jovanovich, 1964).

Exercises in Critical Thinking and Writing

DETERMINING THE PRECISE MEANINGS OF WORDS

Writing Assignment

Write a brief essay in which you discuss the precise meanings of two italicized words or phrases from one of the passages that follow on page 64.

Background

Understanding what you read and hear is the first necessity in developing critical thinking skills. We use language to communicate with one another, but language sometimes sets up obstacles to understanding. Remember that words are symbols. The word *ship* is not the reality ship. In fact, other languages use different groups of sounds to communicate the same reality (*vaisseau, bastimento*). Remembering that words are symbols, consider the following ways in which language is an imprecise tool for communication:

1. **Words are inexact.** Ask five people to describe very exactly the mental picture they get when they hear the word *ship*. Do any two people have the exact same mental image?
2. **Words have multiple meanings.** The word *ship* has at least twelve different meanings. It can refer to any number of seagoing vessels, an airplane, or a spacecraft. It can be a noun or a verb, and it is spelled the same as the suffix in such words as *friendship* and *leadership*.
3. A **Many words name intangible, abstract ideas.** When you say someone is "freckled," you are referring to a physical quality that can be proved by sensory evidence. When you say someone is "proud," however, you are referring to a quality that cannot be perceived by the senses. Words such as *pride* and *justice* involve value judgments, and people can disagree widely on them.
4. **Words and meanings change.** As long as English is used, it will continue to change. Reading something written hundreds of years ago often requires special effort because some of the words and meanings have become **archaic,** or obsolete.

Prewriting

When a regular dictionary does not cover the meaning of a word, particularly if it's from a passage written long ago, you should use an unabridged dictionary. The best sources are *Webster's Third New International Dictionary, Unabridged,* and the *Oxford English Dictionary (OED).* These dictionaries give complete lists of definitions and example sentences for each meaning; the *OED* also gives the dates the meanings were first recorded. Here is what *Webster's* says in part about *proud*:

> **proud** \'praud\ *adj* -ER/-EST [ME, fr. OE *prūd, prūt,* prob. fr. OF *prod, prud, prut, prou* good, capable, brave, fr. LL *prode* advantageous, advantage, fr. L *prodesse* to be useful, be beneficial, fr. *prod-* (var. of *pro-* before, forward) + *esse* to be—more at PRO-, IS] **1 :** feeling or showing pride: as **a :** having or displaying inordinate self-esteem <goaded the ~ baronage—J. R. Green> <his cold and ~ nature—A. Conan Doyle> **b :** highly satisfied or pleased **:** deeply gratified **:** ELATED, EXULTANT <~ to have such men—Sherwood Anderson> <a ~ boy . . . he has made something with his own hands—*Better Homes & Gardens*>—often used with *of* <~ of his success> <a record to be ~ of> **c** *chiefly Midland* **:** GLAD, DELIGHTED <we'd be ~ to have you stay for supper> **d :** marked by a proper or becoming self-respect <too ~ to fight—Woodrow Wilson> <brought a ~ . . . efficiency to everything she did—Fred Majdalany> **2 a :** marked by stateliness or magnificence **:** SPLENDID <~ princes and humble peasants—Vicki Baum> <~ old castles—E. O. Hauser> **b :** giving reason or occasion for pride **:** GLORIOUS <a ~ heritage> <our ~*est* feat—Joyce Cary> <his ~*est* moment—Paul Pickrel> **3 :** marked by great vitality or power **:** VIGOROUS, EXUBERANT: as **a** *of an animal* **:** full of spirit **:** METTLESOME <a ~ steed> **b** *of a body of water* **:** overflowing its banks **:** SWOLLEN <the ~ stream> **c** *of granulation tissue* **:** growing exuberantly <~ growth in an old wound>

Choose one of the following passages. Use an unabridged dictionary to investigate the meanings of each word in italics. Then, for each word, fill out a chart like the one on the next page.

A. Responding
? Define the word *patriotism* from each of the following points of view: (a) that of a candidate for President who favors increasing the military budget; (b) that of a candidate for President who favors decreasing the military budget; (c) a newly naturalized citizen; (d) a young adult who, as an act of conscience, refuses to register for the draft. (In forming these definitions, students should realize the value judgments involved in defining highly abstract words.)

Revising Essays
As students revise their essays, refer them to **Grammar, Usage, and Mechanics: A Reference Guide** at the back of their books.

A. Responding
? How is the sample paragraph organized? (The sample paragraph follows the organization of the prewriting chart on this page.)
? What are other possible methods of organization? (There are many other possible methods. A student paper might begin, for example, "In his *History,* Byrd uses a common word in an archaic way to criticize the Pilgrims' endeavors.")

Exercises in Critical Thinking and Writing /*cont.*

1.

He told me there was a bad river we were to ride through, which was so very fierce a horse could sometimes hardly *stem* it: but it was but narrow, and we should soon be over. I cannot express the concern of mind this *relation* set me in. . . .

—Sarah Kemble Knight

2.

I then *betook* me to my *apartment,* which was a little room parted from the kitchen by a single board partition; where, after I had noted the occurrences of the past day, I went to bed, which, though pretty hard, yet neat and *handsome.* But I could get no sleep, because of the clamor of some of the town *topers* in next room, who were entered into a strong debate concerning the signification of the name of their country (viz.), Narragansett.

—Sarah Kemble Knight

3.

As it happened some ages before to be the fashion to *saunter* to the Holy Land and go upon other Quixote adventures, so it was now *grown* the *humor* to take a trip to America. . . . This modish frenzy, being still more inflamed by the charming account given of Virginia by the first adventurers, made many fond of *removing to* such a Paradise. . . .

This made it easy for the Company to procure as many volunteers as they wanted for their new colony, but, like most other *undertakers* who have no assistance from the public, they starved the design by too much frugality. . . .

—William Byrd

Word ______	
Word's etymology	
Meaning in this context	
Is meaning still in use?	
Is word still in use?	
Other common meanings	
Does word imply a value judgment? If so, what evidence supports it?	
Dictionary (or dictionaries) used	

Writing

Choose two of the words from your Prewriting chart, and discuss each word in a separate paragraph. Include all the information you have learned in your research about the word.

Here is a sample paragraph from one writer's essay on the word *proud* as William Bradford uses it in the passage from his *History* (page 13). A

The word *proud* is from an Old English word *prūd,* from an Old French word meaning "good, capable, or brave," which ultimately comes from a Latin word *prodesse,* "to be useful or beneficial." In his comment about the lusty seaman who dies on the journey, Bradford uses the word *proud* in an unfavorable sense to mean "having inordinate self-esteem"; the seaman thinks of himself as superior to the *Mayflower's* passengers. We would still use the word *proud* to describe someone like the seaman, who has too high an opinion of himself. *Proud* can also mean "highly satisfied or pleased," as in "proud to have such men" (Sherwood Anderson). It can also mean "proper or becoming self-respect," as in "too proud to fight" (Woodrow Wilson). *Proud* is a word implying a value judgment on the part of the user. Bradford cites four or five examples of nasty behavior—specific incidents—to support his own judgment against the unfortunate sailor. He notes that the sailor scorned the passengers when they were sick; he cursed them daily; he told them he hoped to cast half of them overboard before the journey ended (as corpses, I presume) and to make merry with their money. I think Bradford means the word *proud* to contrast with the word *humble,* which would describe the kind of person a Puritan would hope to be: one who served others. To the Puritans, pride would be one of the seven deadly sins. It is interesting that none of the word's original meanings is negative. This information on *proud* comes from *Webster's Third International Dictionary, Unabridged.*

Revising and Proofreading

Use the guidelines in the section at the back of this book, called **Writing About Literature,** to revise and proofread your essay.

THE REVOLUTIONARY PERIOD
THE AGE OF REASON

The Spirit of the Colonists by Frank Schoonover. From *Washington* by Lucy Madison, Penn Publishing Company, 1925.

Collection of Harry Lynch, Wilmington, Delaware.

UNIT TWO

HUMANITIES CONNECTION: RESPONDING TO THE FINE ART

Frank E(arle) Schoonover (1877–1972), a student of the famous illustrator Howard Pyle, followed in his teacher's footsteps to become a successful illustrator for leading magazines.

The Spirit of the Colonists exhibits both technical skill and imaginative power. The highly particularized militiamen in the foreground are typical of the realistic style of illustration Pyle and Schoonover practiced; the ghostly figure of Washington on his horse in the background adds a symbolic aspect.

? Do you think this painting captures the spirit of the American Revolution? How so? (Student answers will vary. Students might note that the variously clothed figures suggest that the Revolution brought together for a common cause Americans of many kinds, both those in the militia and those who remained civilians. The determined look on the faces of these figures suggests the commitment of Americans to the cause. The ghostly figure of Washington, recognized as the father of the country, watches over the endeavor, lending his strength and courage.) Ask if the illustration suggests an age of "reason."

TEACHING THE REVOLUTIONARY PERIOD

From the plain prose of Benjamin Franklin to the impassioned oratory of Patrick Henry, this unit focuses on the founding of the American nation and the development of a distinct American character and philosophy. The theme of moral progress links each selection, and the selections, regardless of their stylistic differences, all emphasize self-examination and self-improvement.

Some of these early American writings have equivalents in such contemporary forms as the popular autobiography and the self-help book, making for interesting social and literary comparisons. Then, as now, America has been, in the words of art critic Harold Rosenberg, "the civilization of people engaged in attempting to transform themselves." You might ask students whether this perception of the American spirit matches their own perceptions and experiences. In addition to promoting discussion, the unit introduces literary devices and forms such as persuasion, propaganda, and the aphorism, or maxim, and the rhetorical devices characteristic of a literature derived from classical models.

The writings in this unit are by the men most closely associated with the American Enlightenment, men who used the written word to rail against Great Britain and to gain support for the Revolution. These men did not have the establishment of Great Britain or Europe to rest upon. They had to make a society and culture, build towns and banks and schools, wring a government from the conflicting needs of the variety of peoples who had emigrated to America, a government that would encompass the many religions and cultures that made up the colonies.

The Enlightenment spread throughout the western world, most noticeably in England, France, and Germany. It was an age that believed that there was virtually no limit to what well-intentioned people could accomplish when guided by reason. Reason could alter a corrupt government and even harmonize competing self-interests. Ignorance, prejudice, and unchecked power were considered primary factors in the corruption and sinfulness of human beings.

OBJECTIVES OF THE REVOLUTIONARY PERIOD UNIT

1. To improve reading proficiency and expand vocabulary
2. To gain exposure to notable Revolutionary writers
3. To define and identify significant literary techniques
4. To interpret and respond to forms of nonfiction, orally and in writing, through analysis of their elements
5. To recognize the growth of American English
6. To practice the following critical thinking and writing skills
   a. Comparing and contrasting writers
   b. Responding to critical comments
   c. Evaluating word connotations
   d. Comparing and contrasting speeches
   e. Evaluating a generalization
   f. Analyzing reasoning
   g. Responding to a point of view

SUPPLEMENTARY SUPPORT MATERIALS: UNIT TWO

1. Unit Introduction Test (*CCB*)
2. American Language Test (*CCB*)
3. Word Analogies Test (*CCB*)
4. Unit Review Test (*CCB*)
5. Critical Thinking and Writing Test (*CCB*)
6. Instructional Overhead Transparencies

A. Responding to the Quotation Michel Guillaume Jean de Crèvecoeur (krev KOOR) (1735–1813), from whose letter this quotation is taken, lived in America for many years, where he was better known as J. Hector St. John Crèvecoeur. A central idea in Crèvecoeur's writing is that life in the developing America created "new men"—different in manners, beliefs, and goals from those who remained in Europe. **?** What prediction does Crèvecoeur make about America's future? Has that prediction come true? (He predicts that Americans will cause "great changes" in the world. Encourage students to explain their opinions about the accuracy of this prediction.)

B. Expansion Mather's Puritan beliefs were not necessarily antithetical to his scientific interests. Daniel J. Boorstin comments that "the Puritan emphasis on sin thus seemed to reinforce the empirical emphasis of American science."

THE REVOLUTIONARY PERIOD
THE AGE OF REASON

by **Gary Q. Arpin**

A

What then is the American, this new man? . . .* He *is an American, who, leaving behind him all his ancient prejudices and manners, receives new ones from the new mode of life he has embraced, the new government he obeys, and the new rank he holds. He becomes an American by being received in the broad lap of our great* Alma Mater. *Here individuals of all nations are melted into a new race of men, whose labors and posterity will one day cause great changes in the world. Americans are the western pilgrims, who are carrying along with them that great mass of arts, sciences, vigor, and industry which began long since in the east; they will finish the great circle.

—from *Letters from an American Farmer,*
Michel Guillaume Jean de Crèvecoeur

Science in the New World

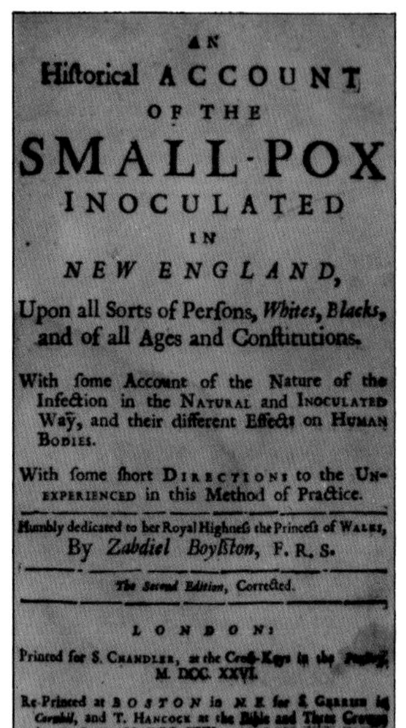
AN
Hiſtorical ACCOUNT
OF THE
SMALL-POX
INOCULATED
IN
NEW ENGLAND,
Upon all Sorts of Perſons, *Whites, Blacks,* and of all Ages and Conſtitutions.

With ſome Account of the Nature of the Infection in the NATURAL and INOCULATED Way, and their different Effects on HUMAN BODIES.

With ſome ſhort DIRECTIONS to the UNEXPERIENCED in this Method of Practice.

Humbly dedicated to her Royal Highneſs the Princeſs of WALES,
By *Zabdiel Boylston,* F. R. S.

The Second Edition, Corrected.

LONDON:
Printed for S. CHANDLER, at the Cross-Keys in the [illegible]. M. DCC. XXVI.

Re-Printed at *BOSTON* in *N. E.* for S. GERRISH in *Cornhill,* and T. HANCOCK at the Bible and Three Crowns in [illegible]. M. DCC. XXX.

In April of 1721, a ship from the West Indies docked in Boston Harbor. This was hardly an unusual occurrence, for trade with the West Indies was one of the foundations of New England economic life. This ship was different, though, and the consequences of its docking would illustrate some important currents in American social and intellectual life. For in addition to its customary cargo of sugar and molasses, this ship carried smallpox.

Smallpox was one of the scourges of civilized life in the seventeenth and eighteenth centuries. It spread rapidly, disfigured its victims, and was often fatal. The outbreak in Boston in 1721 was a major public-health problem. What was to be done?

The unlikely hero of this story is Cotton Mather (1663–1728), the great Puritan minister and historian, who was fifty-eight years old at the time and nearing the end of his life. Today Mather is commonly thought of as a conservative theologian, one of the last old-style Puritans. But Mather was also interested in natural science and medicine. He was a member of Britain's renowned Royal Society and the author of hundreds of essays on natural history. At the time of the smallpox epidemic, he was working on what would be the first scholarly essay on medicine written in America. B The opening sentence reveals his Puritan perspective: "Let us look upon sin as the cause of sickness."

His religious point of view did not, however, prevent Mather from seeking practical cures for specific diseases. He had heard of a method for dealing with smallpox that had been devised by a Turkish physician. The method seemed illogical, but it apparently worked. It was called inoculation. By this method, doctors infected people with fluid containing the virus, giving them a mild case of the disease. This made them immune to later attacks of the disease. In June of 1721, as the smallpox epidemic spread throughout Boston, Mather began a public campaign for inoculation.

The opposition was forceful. Boston's medical community, led by Dr. William Douglass, was violently opposed to such an experiment, especially one borrowed from the Moslems. Mather's medical opponents expressed themselves in language more religious than medical. Inoculation, the doctors argued, would violate "the all-wise Providence of God Almighty" by "trusting more the extra groundless machinations of men than to our Preserver in the ordinary course of nature." That is, human beings were daring to do the work of God.

The *New England Courant,* a newspaper founded by James Franklin (whose younger brother Benjamin had recently begun to assist him), added its voice to the chorus of opponents. Surprisingly, the clergy by and large supported Mather. The debate was vigorous, raging all that summer and into the fall. Dozens of pamphlets were written supporting each side of the question. Controversy developed into violence: In November, Mather's house was bombed.

Despite such fierce opposition, Mather succeeded in inoculating some three hundred people. By the time the epidemic was over, in March of the following year, only six of these had died. Of the five thousand other people who contracted the disease (nearly half of Boston's population), nine hundred had died. The evidence, according to Mather's figures, was clear: Whether or not inoculation made much sense to scientists, it worked.

An illustration from a book about the Salem witch trials called *The Wonders of the Invisible World* by Cotton Mather (1693).

Rare Books and Manuscripts Division, New York Public Library.

An American Pattern: Thought in Action

The episode of the smallpox controversy illustrates a number of interesting points about American life in the early eighteenth century. First, it is important to remember that seemingly opposite qualities of the American character often existed side by side. A Puritan theologian such as Mather was not necessarily guided only by religious principles. Mather may have been a devout Christian, but he was a practical scientist as well. And what was true of individuals was also true of historical periods. Puritan life was not characterized solely by Bible reading and witch hunting. Similarly, the period of rationalism that followed the Puritan era was not guided solely by the principles of reason.

A

Perhaps more important, Mather's experiment reveals that a practical approach to social change and scientific research was a necessity in America. From the earliest Colonial days, Americans had to be tinkerers. The frontier farmer with little access to tools shared a problem with the scientist who had few books and a new world of plants and animals to catalog. They both had to make do with what they had, and they had to get results.

"Puritan life was not characterized solely by Bible reading and witch hunting."

European thinkers had the leisure to specialize in nonproductive areas and to study the grand theoretical designs of scientists and philosophers. But Americans had to be generalists, and the evidence of experience had to come first. As Michel Guillaume Jean de Crèvecoeur wrote in his classic *Letters from an American Farmer* (1782), the American pioneer farmer "finds himself suddenly deprived of the assistance of friends, neighbors, tradesmen, and of all those inferior links which make a well-established society so

A. Responding

? What points about American life in the early eighteenth century are illustrated by the smallpox controversy episode? (It illustrates that seemingly opposite qualities of the American character often existed side by side and that a practical approach to social change and to scientific research was necessary.)

A. Expansion
This view of Newton's that God had created a well-ordered universe controlled by immutable laws, which thereafter operated without divine intervention, is the central belief of deism. This belief in the impossibility of divine intervention of course clashes directly with the traditional Christian belief in revelation, divine providence, and final judgment. In discussing the Bible, deists generally offered naturalistic explanations for miracles and allegorical interpretations for Old Testament prophecies. People such as Franklin and Jefferson saw deism as a way of reconciling religion and the new science, which seemed to undermine many traditional Christian beliefs. Deism also appealed to Americans because it embodied the American qualities of optimism and self-reliance.

beautiful and pleasing. He and his family are now alone. On their courage, perseverance, and skill their success depends."

American thought, then, had to be thought in action. And so at times even a Puritan theologian was willing, for practical reasons, to trust the "groundless machinations of men."

The Age of Reason in America

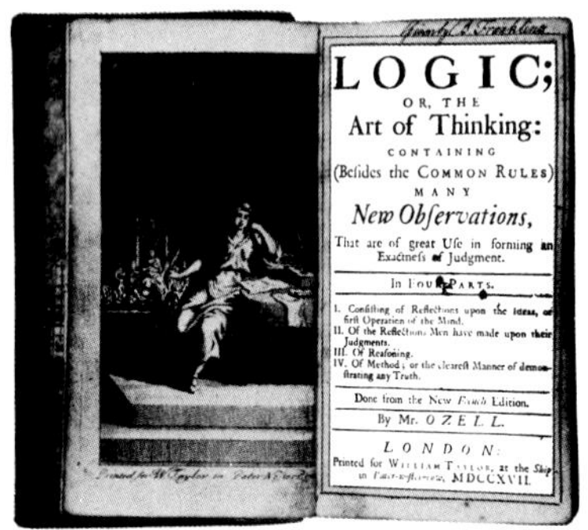
LOGIC;
OR, THE
Art of Thinking:
CONTAINING
(Besides the COMMON RULES)
MANY
New Observations,
That are of great Use in forming an Exactness of Judgment.
In FOUR PARTS.
I. Consisting of Reflections upon the Ideas, or first Operation of the Mind.
II. Of the Reflections Men have made upon their Judgments.
III. Of Reasoning.
IV. Of Method; or the clearest Manner of demonstrating any Truth.
Done from the New French Edition.
By Mr. OZELL.
LONDON:
Printed for WILLIAM TAYLOR, at the Ship in Pater-noster-Row, MDCCXVII.

Logic; or the Art of Thinking (1717). An English book owned by Benjamin Franklin.

The Library Company of Philadelphia.

The Age of Reason, or the Enlightenment, began in Europe with the rationalist philosophers and scientists of the seventeenth century. Rationalism is the belief that we can arrive at truth by using our reason rather than by relying on the authority of the past, on religious faith, or on intuition.

The emergence of modern science and the scientific method had much to do with this new emphasis on reason and free inquiry. Discoveries made by physical scientists and mathematicians were changing the ways people viewed the universe. Scientific investigation seemed to show that the universe was organized according to certain unchanging laws, and that people could discover those laws through the use of their reason.

The Puritans saw God as actively and mysteriously involved in the workings of the universe; the rationalists saw God differently. A Sir Isaac Newton (1642–1727), who discovered the laws of gravity, compared God to a clockmaker who, having created the perfect mechanism of this universe, then left His creation to run on its own. According to this view, God would not interfere with the operation of this perfect mechanism, and it made no sense to ask Him to do so.

God's special gift to humanity was reason—the ability to think in an ordered, logical manner. As the French philosopher and mathematician René Descartes affirmed in the opening sentence of his *Discourse on Method* (1637): "I think, therefore I am." This gift of reason enabled people to discover both scientific and spiritual truth. In the rationalist view, all human beings were born with an innate ethical sense, and all had the ability to regulate and improve their own lives.

The theoretical background for the Age of Reason, then, took shape in Europe in the work of such figures as Descartes, Newton, and John Locke. In America, however, as the story of Cotton Mather and the smallpox epidemic illustrates, a home-grown practicality already existed. This American pragmatism was characterized by an interest in the public welfare and a willingness to experiment, to try things out, no matter what the authorities might say.

"American pragmatism was characterized by an interest in the public welfare and a willingness to experiment, to try things out, no matter what the authorities might say."

The Age of Reason in America, then, combined common sense with ideas from European thinkers. From this mixture of ideas and outlooks came much of the triumph of eighteenth-century American life: the inventive and curious minds of Benjamin Franklin (see page 72) and Thomas Jefferson (see page 100); the drive to improve living conditions, forms of government, and individual minds; and the thinking behind the important statement "We hold these truths to be self-evident."

Deism and the Rationalist Mind

Like the Puritan, the rationalist also discovered God through the medium of the natural world, but in a different way. Newton's discovery of what seemed to be unchanging physical laws—gravity and the laws of motion—made many thinkers suspicious of claims that those laws were ever suspended by God.

Thus it seemed unlikely to rationalist thinkers that God would choose to reveal Himself only at particular times to particular people. It seemed much more reasonable to believe that God had made it possible for *all* people at *all* times to discover natural laws through their God-given faculty of reason. The title of a pamphlet attributed to Ethan Allen (1738–1789) gives a capsule summary of this point of view: *Reason the Only Oracle of Man.* (An *oracle* is someone through whom God speaks to the people.)

This outlook, called deism, was shared by many eighteenth-century thinkers, including Franklin, Jefferson, Thomas Paine (see page 93), and other founders of the American nation. American deists came from different religious backgrounds. Franklin, for example, had been raised a Presbyterian; Jefferson was an Anglican. But the deists avoided supporting specific religious sects. They sought, instead, the principles that united all religions.

"I never doubted," Franklin wrote in his *Autobiography,* "the existence of the deity, that He made the world, and governed it with His Providence; that the most acceptable service of God was the doing good to man; that our souls are immortal; and that all crime will be punished and virtue rewarded either here or hereafter; these I esteemed the essentials of every religion, and being to be found in all the religions we had in our country I respected them all."

Deists believed that the universe was orderly and good. In contrast to the Puritans, deists stressed humanity's inherent goodness. They believed in the perfectibility of every individual through the use of reason. God's objective, in the deist view, was the happiness of His creatures. Therefore, the best form of worship was to do good for others. There already existed in America an impulse to improve people's lives, as Cotton Mather's struggle to inoculate the citizens of Boston illustrates. But deism elevated this impulse to one of the nation's highest goals.

Deistic ideas were not shared by everyone in the Age of Reason. As rationalism spread in the 1730's and 1740's, a strongly emotional brand of religion, known as the Great Awakening, was flourishing (see page 36). Nevertheless, the rationalist point of view [A] was shared, in varying degrees, by the Founding Fathers. It provided the basis for the principles of the American Revolution and for our system of government. The struggle for independence was justified largely by appeals to rationalist principles.

Thomas Paine's *Common Sense* was such an appeal. Published in January of 1776, it was the most influential of many Revolutionary pamphlets and was read by virtually every American within months of its appearance. The very phrase *common sense* had come to mean the reasoning ability that all people share. Paine

> **"In contrast to the Puritans, deists stressed humanity's inherent goodness. They believed in the perfectibility of every individual through the use of reason."**

A clock made by Benjamin Franklin.

The Franklin Institute, Philadelphia, Pennsylvania.

A. Expansion
The Great Awakening is the name given to a series of religious revivals that swept America in the middle of the eighteenth century. Members of the Presbyterian and Baptist churches were among the first to feel the effects of this revival; the movement also contributed to the rapid spread of Methodism in the colonies. The general effect of the Great Awakening was to promote a more democratic spirit in religion and solidify opposition to the traditional Church of England in America.

A. Discussing the Time Line
The first line is significant less for its events than for being the period in which the principals of the American Revolution were born—Franklin, Washington, Jefferson, Patrick Henry, Thomas Paine—and of course George III.

The middle section is comprised of events leading up to the Revolutionary War and those of the war itself. You may wish to point out that in 1763, shortly after George III was crowned, the French and Indian War ended. This event was important in several ways. The British victory removed the threat of foreign invasion that had previously existed for the colonists, thus lessening their dependence on England. The fiscal problems resulting from the Seven Years' War (of which the French and Indian War was just one phase) were the reason for England's imposing the various tax laws, which so enraged the colonists.

The third line of the chart shows the revolutionary spirit sweeping across France and the establishment of the American nation. Call students' attention to the fact that the population of the U.S. almost doubled in the two decades from 1790 to 1810.

argued that we should seek independence in order to restore the natural rights that were evident to our reason but that had been taken away by the British. "'Tis repugnant to reason," he wrote, "to the universal order of things, to all examples from former ages, to suppose that this continent can long remain subject to any external power." Jefferson's Declaration of Independence based its arguments on the same rationalist assumptions about the relations between people, God, and the natural law.

American Literature in the Age of Reason

Most of the literature written in America during the Age of Reason was, understandably, rooted in reality rather than in the imagination. The best minds of this period were concentrating on social, political, and scientific improvements. This was an age of pamphlets, since most literature was intended to serve practical or political ends. Relations—and ultimately war—with England were major concerns for many years; following the Revolutionary War (1775–1783), the problems of organizing and governing the new nation were of the highest importance. *The Federalist Papers,* written by James Madison and Alexander Hamilton, may be thought of as the pamphlet form elevated to the highest level. These essays explain the ideas behind our Constitution.

An odometer (an instrument for measuring distance traveled) made by Benjamin Franklin.

The Franklin Institute, Philadelphia, Pennsylvania.

1706–1721	1722–1723	1725–1726	1728–1732
Benjamin Franklin born in Boston, 1706 Daniel Defoe's *Robinson Crusoe* published in London, 1719 Smallpox epidemic, 1721	Spain occupies Texas, 1722 **Benjamin Franklin arrives in Philadelphia 1723**	First American library established in Philadelphia, 1725 Jonathan Swift's *Gulliver's Travels* published in London, 1726	**William Byrd writes *History of the Dividing Line,* 1728** George Washington born in Virginia, 1732

A

1753–1755	1760–1762	1767–1768	1772–1773
Phyllis Wheatley born in Africa, c. 1753 Samuel Johnson completes his mammoth *Dictionary* in England, 1755	George III crowned King of England, 1760 Anne Franklin (Ben's sister-in-law) becomes first woman to edit a newspaper in America, 1762	Daniel Boone explores territory west of Appalachians, 1767 Boston citizens refuse to house British troops, 1768	Boston Assembly threatens to secede from Britain, 1772 Phyllis Wheatley's poems published, 1773 Boston Tea Party, 1773

1789–1790	1790–1791	1793	1793–1799
French Revolution begins, 1789 **Benjamin Franklin dies in Philadelphia, 1790**	First American census sets population at 3,929,214, 1790 **Thomas Paine writes *The Rights of Man,* 1791**	Invention of cotton gin leads to increase in slave labor, 1793 King Louis XVI and Marie Antoinette of France beheaded by revolutionaries, 1793	Samuel Taylor Coleridge publishes *Rime of the Ancient Mariner* in England, 1793 **Patrick Henry dies, 1799**

READING CHECK TEST

1. Cotton Mather proposed combatting the smallpox epidemic by (a) rounding up witches (b) inoculation (c) continuous prayer *(b)*
2. A scientist who greatly influenced the religious philosophy called deism was (a) Sir Isaac Newton (b) Louis Pasteur (c) Thomas Aquinas *(a)*
3. Deists believed that people were (a) inherently sinful (b) inherently good (c) not responsible for their actions *(b)*
4. The author of *Common Sense* was (a) Benjamin Franklin (b) Thomas Jefferson (c) Thomas Paine *(c)*
5. Most of the literature written in America during the Age of Reason consisted of (a) epic poetry (b) religious tracts (c) political tracts *(c)*

With a few exceptions, American poetry written during the eighteenth century was unoriginal. It was often written in direct imitation of British models. Thousands of broadsides, the poetic equivalent of pamphlets, were produced during this period. These poems and ballads printed on a single, large sheet of paper often ridiculed the British and urged Americans to take political action. They encouraged readers to drink no English tea, to wear domestically produced cloth, and, ultimately, to fight for liberty.

The unquestioned masterpiece of the American Age of Reason was Benjamin Franklin's *Autobiography* (see page 74). Franklin used the personal narrative, a form that was common in Colonial America. He separated it from much of its religious justification (the Puritan impulse toward self-examination). Then he molded it into what became a classic American pattern: the rags-to-riches story. Written in clear, witty prose, this charming account of the development of a self-made American provided the model for a story that would be told again and again. It appears in the moralistic stories about the office boy by Horatio Alger and in F. Scott Fitzgerald's novel *The Great Gatsby.* A

With the exception of Franklin's *Autobiography,* however, the many calls for an American literary independence to accompany its political independence were premature. The seeds had been sown, but the true flowering of American literature was still several generations in the future.

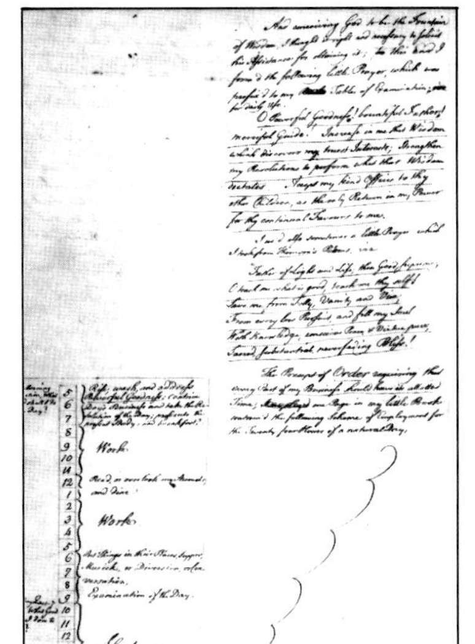

A page from Franklin's *Autobiography,* showing his daily schedule.

Henry Huntington Library, San Marino, California.

A. Connections Franklin's daily schedule, shown here on a page from his *Autobiography,* has been the model for similar schedules for countless people bent on self-improvement. One such person, Jay Gatsby, the protagonist of *The Great Gatsby* (page 1144), seems to have modeled his schedule closely after Franklin's. Some of Gatsby's entries: Rise from bed . . . 6.00 A.M. Dumbbell exercise and wallscaling . . . 6.15–6.30 Study electricity, etc. 7.15–8.15 A.M. Work . . . 8.30–4.30 P.M. . . . Study needed inventions 7.00–9.00 P.M.

1736–1737	1738–1741	1743–1744	1750
Patrick Henry born in Virginia, 1736 **Thomas Paine born in England, 1737**	The future King George III of England born, 1738 **Jonathan Edwards preaches "Sinners in the Hands of an Angry God," 1741**	**Thomas Jefferson born in Virginia, 1743** **William Byrd dies, 1744**	Franklin's experiments with a kite and key prove that lightening is a manifestation of electricity, 1750
1775	**1775–1783**	**1778–1783**	**1788–1789**
Patrick Henry persuades the Virginia Convention to put itself in a position of armed defense, 1775 Battle of Lexington and Concord, 1775	Revolutionary War, 1775–1783 American Declaration of Independence, July 4, 1776	Congress prohibits importation of slaves into the United States, 1778 American Revolution comes to an end, 1783	U.S. Constitution ratified, 1788 George Washington inaugurated as first President, 1789
1800	**1804–1806**	**1809–1810**	
Thomas Jefferson elected President, 1800 Washington, D.C., named capital of U.S., 1800	Lewis and Clark Expedition leaves to chart the Louisiana Purchase, 1804 **Noah Webster's dictionary published, 1806**	**Thomas Paine dies in New York state, 1809** U.S. population passes seven million, 1810	

A. Expansion
You may wish to explain briefly how the system of apprenticeship worked. A youth would sign a contract, called an *indenture*, obligating him to work for a craftsman or tradesman for board and room for a given number of years. In return, the apprentice gained skill in the craft or trade. During the final year of indenture, the apprentice was known as a *journeyman* and was paid wages.

B. Humanities Connection: Responding to the Fine Art
Subjects drawn from American history have a special attraction for Larry Rivers (b. 1923). He explained in connection with his painting *Washington Crossing the Delaware* that he "wanted to make a picture out of a national myth."
? Do you think that Rivers has succeeded in making a "real" picture out of the myth of Benjamin Franklin? How so? (Encourage students to explain their answers.)

Benjamin Franklin (1706–1790)

In many ways, Benjamin Franklin's life is the classic American success story—the tale of a self-made man who rose from poverty to eminence through his own industry and intelligence. One of seventeen children of a Boston candle and soap maker, Franklin had to leave school early in order to work. At twelve, he was apprenticed to his older brother James, a printer; at seventeen, chafing under the yoke of this apprenticeship, Ben journeyed to Philadelphia to seek his fortune. By the time he was twenty-four, he was a prosperous merchant, owner of a successful print shop, and publisher of the *Philadelphia Gazette*.

Few people have been so energetically devoted to improvement—both self-improvement and the improvement of society. Franklin's many accomplishments can only be summarized. He helped to found the American Philosophical Society, the University of Pennsylvania, and the first public library in America. He promoted numerous municipal projects in Philadelphia: paving streets, installing sewer lines, improving street lighting, and establishing a fire brigade. He was a scientist and an important inventor: his research, especially on electricity, resulted in his election to England's Royal Society. In addition, he invented an open heating stove (called a Franklin stove), bifocal eyeglasses, a musical instrument that used moistened glasses, and a rocking chair that could swat flies. Like Thomas Jefferson and many others of his age, Franklin was a tinkerer, constantly looking for ways to make things work a little better or more efficiently.

At forty-one, Franklin had made enough money to retire from business. He hoped to devote the rest of his life to study and scientific research, but this was not to be. Franklin possessed uncommon talents as a diplomat and negotiator, and for the rest of his life he used these skills in the service of his state and his country. As an agent of the Pennsylvania Assembly, Franklin lived in London in the 1750's, representing the interests of Pennsylvania. A decade later he was back in London lobbying for the Colonies in their dispute with Britain, hoping to bring about a reconciliation that would prevent

Sketch of Benjamin Franklin (detail) for *Philadelphia Now and Then* by Larry Rivers (1983). Right panel, ceramic-tile mural. J. C. Penney Collection.

A

war. Franklin's wit and charm made him enormously popular in London for many years; he once said that he was invited out to dinner there six nights a week. But by 1774, when he was sixty-eight, the stress between Britain and the Colonies had become too great for even this consummate diplomat to control. He was publicly attacked by the King's Privy Council for his policies; the British press called him an "old snake." Franklin finally relinquished his hopes for peace and sailed for America in 1775.

When Franklin arrived home, he was greeted with the news that the first battles in the Revolutionary War had been fought at Lexington and Concord, Massachusetts. The shot had been fired that "was heard around the world." After helping to draft the Declaration of Independence in 1776, Franklin left for Paris to negotiate the treaty that brought the French into the war on America's side. When Franklin landed in France, Lord Stormont, the British ambassador, caustically remarked: "I look upon him as a dangerous engine, and am very sorry that some British frigate did not meet with him by the way."

In Paris, Franklin was even more popular than he had once been in England. Playing the role of the sophisticated but homespun American, Franklin described himself as "an old man, with gray hair appearing under a marten fur cap, among the powdered heads of Paris." When the Revolution was over, he helped to negotiate the peace, and he was a member of the Constitutional Convention in 1787. His death three years later was the occasion for international mourning.

Franklin's practicality, like the success story of his life, is typically American, but it has not been universally admired throughout the nation's history. In a few words, American novelist Herman Melville (1819–1891) gave a remarkably complete picture of Franklin—as well as a fairly reasonable assessment of the man's limitations:

B

> Printer, postmaster, almanac maker, essayist, chemist, orator, tinker, statesman, humorist, philosopher, parlor man, political economist, professor of housewifery, ambassador, projector, maxim-monger, herb-doctor, wit: Jack of all trades, master of each and mastered by none—the type and genius of the land, Franklin was everything but a poet.
>
> —Herman Melville

Franklin did lack a poet's depth of imagination and emotion, but his literary talents and accomplishments were substantial. He was especially gifted as a wit. The lightly ironic tone of much of his *Autobiography* testifies to this talent, as do many of the aphorisms in his *Poor Richard's Almanack*. In fact, Franklin began his career as a comic writer, once slipping a satiric essay signed by "Silence Dogood" under the door of his brother's newspaper office. The following morning his brother read it to friends in Franklin's hearing. Franklin wrote in his *Autobiography:* "I had the exquisite pleasure of finding it met with their approbation. . . . I suppose now that I was rather lucky in my judges: And," he concluded with the light irony that characterizes his style, "that perhaps they were not really so very good ones as I then esteemed them."

His wit and self-mockery are also evident in a famous passage in which he rationalizes eating fish. He had thought of fishing as unprovoked murder, since fish had never done him any injury. But then he smelled fish frying one day off Block Island: C

> I balanced some time between principle and inclination; till I recollected that when the fish were opened, I saw smaller fish taken out of their stomachs. Then thought I, if you can eat one another, I don't see why we mayn't eat you. So I dined upon cod very heartily and continued to eat with other people, returning only now and then occasionally to a vegetable diet. So convenient a thing it is to be a *reasonable creature,* since it enables one to find or make a reason for everything one has a mind to do.

Franklin's talents were so great that he could have left his mark on any one of a half dozen areas of intellectual accomplishment. Biographer Carl Van Doren has written of him:

> Mind and will, talent and art, strength and ease, wit and grace met in him as if nature had been lavish and happy when he was shaped . . . . He moved through his world in a humorous mastery of it . . . . And sometimes, with his marvelous range, in spite of his personal tang, he seems to have been more than any single man: a harmonious human multitude.
>
> —Carl Van Doren

A. Expansion
Franklin only very reluctantly gave up his belief in the great future for an Anglo-American empire. His initial reaction to the Stamp Act was moderate, and he even sought the post of stamp tax collector for friends. He soon changed his mind, however, when he realized how deeply the tax law disturbed his fellow Americans.

B. Expansion
Franklin did try his hand at poetry as a youth, composing several ballads, which his brother printed and sent Benjamin out to hawk on the streets. At least one of these, "The Lighthouse Tragedy," sold well, but Franklin, in his *Autobiography*, dismisses these early attempts at poetry as "wretched stuff."

C. Expansion
Franklin had become a vegetarian while still an apprentice to his brother. Because his eating habits did not conform to those of his brother or his fellow workers, Benjamin often dined alone.

SUPPLEMENTARY SUPPORT MATERIALS
1. Vocabulary Activity Worksheet (*CCB*)
2. Review and Response Worksheet: Characterization (*CCB*)
3. Selection Test (*CCB*)

DEVELOPING VOCABULARY
These words from the autobiography are tested in the Selection Test. (See also Vocabulary Activity Worksheet.)

arbitrary	rectitude
indiscreet	avarice
impracticable	to annex
itinerant	unremitting
ingenious	subsequent

PREPARATION
ESTABLISHING A PURPOSE. Have students read question 5 on page 80 to help them establish a purpose for reading.

A. Expansion
Franklin often drew figures of speech from printing, reflecting his long experience with that trade. His use of *errata* ("printer's errors") to refer to mistakes in life is an example. Franklin uses a similar figure of speech in his epitaph, written in 1728: "The body of Benjamin Franklin, Printer (like the cover of an old book, its contents torn out and stripped of its lettering and gilding), lies here, food for worms; but the work shall not be lost, for it will . . . appear once more in a new and more elegant edition, revised and corrected by the Author."

FROM THE AUTOBIOGRAPHY

Franklin was apprenticed to his older brother James, who printed the *New England Courant*, a Boston newspaper. As an apprentice, Ben was treated more harshly than he thought was just. His brother's "tyrannical treatment," Franklin wrote, inspired "that aversion to arbitrary power that has stuck to me through my whole life." Following a dispute with the Massachusetts Assembly about something he had printed, James was imprisoned for a month and forbidden to publish his newspaper. In order to get around this order, James released Ben from his indenture, or contract of service, and made him the publisher, but he forced Ben to sign another, secret indenture. The newspaper was printed under Ben's name for a few months, until, in the fall of 1723, a new dispute arose between the brothers. Watch for the ways Franklin examines his actions and motives. Do you find such evaluations in autobiography today?

Leaving Boston

At length, a fresh difference arising between my brother and me, I took upon me to assert my freedom, presuming that he would not venture to produce the new indentures. It was not fair in me to take this advantage, and this I therefore reckon one of the first errata[1] of my life. But the unfairness of it weighed little with me, when under the *impressions of* resentment, for the blows his passion too often urged him to bestow upon me; though he was otherwise not an ill-natured man. Perhaps I was too saucy and provoking.

When he found I would leave him, he took care to prevent my getting employment in any other printing house of the town, by going round and speaking to every master, who accordingly refused to give me work. I then thought of going to New York as the nearest place where there was a printer; and I was the rather inclined to leave Boston when I reflected that I had already made myself a little obnoxious to the governing party; and from the arbitrary proceedings of the Assembly in my brother's case, it was likely I might if I stayed soon bring myself into scrapes; and farther that my indiscreet disputations about religion began to make me pointed at with horror by good people, as an infidel or atheist; I determined on the point; but my father now siding with my brother, I was sensible that if I attempted to go openly, means would be used to prevent me. My friend Collins therefore undertook to manage a little for me. He agreed with the captain of a New York sloop for my passage, under the notion of my being a young acquaintance of his that had got a naughty girl with child, whose friends would compel me to marry her, and therefore I could not appear or come away publicly. So I sold some of my books to raise a little money, was taken on board privately, and, as we had a fair wind, in three days I found myself in New York near 300 miles from home, a boy of but 17, without the least recommendation to or knowledge of any person in the place, and with very little money in my pocket.

My inclinations for the sea were by this time worn out, or I might now have gratified them. But having a trade, and supposing myself a pretty good workman, I offered my service to the printer of the place, old Mr. William Bradford.[2] He could give me no employment, having little to do and help enough already. But, says he, my son at Philadelphia has lately lost his principal hand, Aquila Rose, by death. If you go thither I believe he may employ you. Philadelphia was 100 miles farther. I set out, however, in a boat for Amboy,[3] leaving my chest and things to follow me round by sea.

1. **errata** (e·rät′ə): Latin for "errors," a printer's term.

2. **William Bradford:** one of the first American printers.
3. **Amboy:** Perth Amboy, New Jersey.

Second Street North from Market Street with Christ Church, Philadelphia by William Birch (1799). Colored line engraving.

Humanities Connection: Discussing the Fine Art
Explain to students that this Philadelphia scene was engraved about ten years after Franklin's death and therefore looks quite different from the way it did in 1729 when the young Franklin landed at the Market Street Wharf, a few blocks east of this long street (that is, to the right of this scene). George Washington, Franklin, Betsy Ross, and many other notables of the Revolutionary Era worshiped at Christ Church, only the steeple of which is visible in this picture. Christ Church Burial Ground, where Franklin and other Revolutionary leaders are buried, is a few blocks north and west of the church itself.

A. Expansion
Although the combining of dialogue with narrative was not common before John Bunyan's day (1628–1688), it was by no means unknown. Cervantes (1547–1616) and Rabelais (1490?–1553) mixed narration and dialogue to good effect. Another example, which Franklin obviously did not think of in this connection, is the Bible, in which dialogue and narration are often combined.

B. Expansion
Students may not understand why a run-away servant would be likely to be "taken up"—that is, arrested. Explain that many servants were bondsmen—indentured to their masters for passage to the colony or for debt. Servants who tried to escape from this condition of near slavery could be forcibly returned to their masters.

In crossing the bay we met with a squall that tore our rotten sails to pieces, prevented our getting into the kill,[4] and drove us upon Long Island. In our way a drunken Dutchman, who was a passenger too, fell overboard; when he was sinking I reached through the water to his shock pate[5] and drew him up so that we got him in again. His ducking sobered him a little, and he went to sleep, taking first out of his pocket a book which he desired I would dry for him. It proved to be my old favorite Author Bunyan's *Pilgrim's Progress*[6] in Dutch, finely printed on good paper with copper cuts [engravings], a dress better than I had ever seen it wear in its own language. I have since found that it has been translated into most of the languages of Europe, and suppose it has been more generally read than any other book except perhaps the Bible. Honest John was the first that I know of who mixed narration and dialogue, a method of writing very engaging to the reader, who in the most interesting parts finds himself, as it were, brought into the company and present at the discourse. . . .

A

When we drew near the island, we found it was at a place where there could be no landing, there being a great surf on the stony beach. So we dropped anchor and swung around toward the shore. Some people came down to the water edge and hallooed to us, as we did to them. But the wind was so high and the surf so loud that we could not hear so as to understand each other. There were canoes on the shore, and we made signs and hallooed that they should fetch us, but they either did not understand us or thought it impracticable. So they went away, and, night coming on, we had no remedy but to wait till the wind should abate, and in the meantime the boatman and I concluded to sleep if we could, and so crowded into the scuttle[7] with the Dutchman who was still wet, and the spray beating over the head of our boat, leaked through to us, so that we were soon almost as wet as he. In this manner we lay all night with very little rest. But the wind abating the next day, we made a shift to reach Amboy before night, having been 30 hours on the water without victuals [food], or any drink but a bottle of filthy rum, the water we sailed on being salt.

In the evening I found myself very feverish and went ill to bed. But having read somewhere that cold water drunk plentifully was good for a fever, I followed the prescription, sweat plentifully most of the night, my fever left me, and in the morning, crossing the ferry, proceeded on my journey on foot, having 50 miles to Burlington,[8] where I was told I should find boats that would carry me the rest of the way to Philadelphia.

It rained very hard all the day, I was thoroughly soaked, and by noon a good deal tired, so I stopped at a poor inn, where I stayed all night, beginning now to wish I had never left home. I cut so miserable a figure too, that I found by the questions asked me I was suspected to be some runaway servant, and in danger of being taken up on that suspicion. However, I proceeded the next day, and got in the evening to an inn within 8 to 10 miles of Burlington, kept by one Dr. Brown.

B

He entered into conversation with me while I took some refreshment, and, finding I had read a little, became very sociable and friendly. Our acquaintance continued as long as he lived. He had been, I imagine, an itinerant doctor, for there was no town in England, or country in Europe, of which he could not give a very particular account. He had some letters [education], and was ingenious, but much of an unbeliever, and wickedly undertook some years after to travesty the Bible in doggerel verse as Cotton had done Virgil.[9] By this means he set many of the facts in a very ridiculous light, and might have hurt weak minds if his work had been published; but it never was. At his house I lay that night, and the next morning reached Burlington—but had the mortification to find that the regular boats were gone a little before my coming, and no other expected to go till Tuesday, this being Saturday. Wherefore I returned to an old woman in the town of whom I had bought

4. **kill:** channel (from the Dutch *kil*). Here, the channel between Staten Island and the New Jersey coast.
5. **shock pate:** shaggy head.
6. John Bunyan's *Pilgrim's Progress* (1678) is a religious narrative, in which the hero, Christian, makes the journey to salvation. The work had great influence on Puritan lives and thought. Notice, however, that Franklin admires the book for literary and historical, rather than theological, reasons.
7. **scuttle:** area below the deck.
8. **Burlington:** Burlington, New Jersey, is about eighteen miles from Philadelphia.
9. **Cotton . . . Virgil:** Charles Cotton (1630–1687) wrote a parody of Virgil's Latin epic *The Aeneid*.

gingerbread to eat on the water, and asked her advice; she invited me to lodge at her house till a passage by water should offer; and, being tired with my foot traveling, I accepted the invitation. She, understanding I was a printer, would have had me stay at that town and follow my business, being ignorant of the stock necessary to begin with. She was very hospitable, gave me a dinner of ox cheek with great good will, accepting only of a pot of ale in return. And I thought myself fixed till Tuesday should come. However, walking in the evening by the side of the river, a boat came by, which I found was going toward Philadelphia, with several people in her. They took me in, and as there was no wind, we rowed all the way; and about midnight, not having yet seen the city, some of the company were confident we must have passed it, and would row no farther; the others knew not where we were, so we put toward the shore, got into a creek, landed near an old fence with the rails of which we made a fire, the night being cold, in October, and there we remained till daylight. Then one of the company knew the place to be Cooper's Creek, a little above Philadelphia, which we saw as soon as we got out of the creek, and arrived there about 8 or 9 on the Sunday morning, and landed at the Market Street wharf.

Arrival in Philadelphia

I have been the more particular in this description of my journey, and shall be so of my first entry into that city, that you may in your mind compare such unlikely beginnings with the figure I have since made there. I was in my working dress, my best clothes being to come round by sea. I was dirty from my journey; my pockets were stuffed out with shirts and stockings; I knew no soul, nor where to look for lodging. I was fatigued with traveling, rowing, and want of rest. I was very hungry, and my whole stock of cash consisted of a Dutch dollar and about a shilling in copper. The latter I gave the people of the boat for my passage, who at first refused it on account of my rowing; but I insisted on their taking it, a man being sometimes more generous when he has but a little money than when he has plenty, perhaps through fear of being thought to have but little. Then I walked up the street, gazing about, till near the Market House I met a boy with bread. I had made many a meal on bread, and inquiring where he got it, I went immediately to the baker's he directed me to in Second Street, and asked for biscuit, intending such as we had in Boston, but they, it seems, were not made in Philadelphia; then I asked for a three-penny loaf, and was told they had none such. So not considering or knowing the difference of money and the greater cheapness nor the names of his bread, I bade him give me three pennyworth of any sort. He gave me, accordingly, three great puffy rolls; I was surprised at the quantity, but took it, and having no room in my pockets, walked off, with a roll under each arm, and eating the other. Thus I went up Market Street as far as Fourth Street, passing by the door of Mr. Read, my future wife's father, when she, standing at the door, saw me, and thought I made, as I certainly did, a most awkward, ridiculous appearance. Then I turned and went down Chestnut Street and part of Walnut Street, eating my roll all the way, and, coming round, found myself again at Market Street wharf near the boat I came in, to which I went for a draught of the river water, and being filled with one of my rolls, gave the other two to a woman and her child that came down the river in the boat with us and were waiting to go farther. Thus refreshed, I walked again up the street, which by this time had many clean, dressed people in it who were all walking the same way; I joined them, and thereby was led into the great Meeting House of the Quakers near the market. I sat down among them, and after looking round a while and hearing nothing said, being very drowsy through labor and want of rest the preceding night, I fell fast asleep, and continued so till the meeting broke up, when one was kind enough to rouse me. This was therefore the first house I was in or slept in, in Philadelphia. . . .

Franklin did not find work with William Bradford's son, who needed no help. Instead, he began to work for a rival printer named Keimer. Eager to start his own print shop, though, Franklin left for England a year later to buy type and learn English printing methods. He spent eighteen months in England before returning to America and establishing his own business. Because of his skills in dealing with people and his abilities as a printer, his business prospered. In 1730, he married Deborah Read, the young woman who had watched him walking up Market Street with a roll under each arm on the day he arrived in Philadelphia.

A. Expansion
You may need to explain that by "the stock necessary to begin with," Franklin means the press, type, and other apparatus needed to equip a print shop.

B. Expansion
Point out to students that the bakery from which Franklin buys bread is situated on Second Street, near Market Street, the scene depicted on page 75.

C. Expansion
Explain that a Quaker meeting for worship has no set form or ritual. Any member may speak out in prayer or praise. Or, the entire congregation may sit silently in prayer or contemplation. It was during such a period of silent communion that the exhausted Benjamin Franklin fell asleep in the meeting house.

COMMENT FROM THE WRITER
Franklin believed that imitation of good models was an effective way of learning to write. In the following passage from his *Autobiography,* he describes how he learned from imitating the *Spectator* papers of the British writers Joseph Addison and Richard Steele: "I thought the writing excellent, and wished, if possible, to imitate it. With this view, I took some of the papers, and, making short hints of the sentiment in each sentence, laid them by a few days, and then without looking at the book, tried to complete the papers again. . . . Then I compared my *Spectator* with the original, discovered some of my faults, and corrected them."

Have students comment on the effectiveness of this method of learning to write as they see it.

CLOSURE
Have students suggest words or phrases that describe the character of the Benjamin Franklin they have met through the *Autobiography.* You might also want students to discuss how closely this image of Franklin corresponds to that of the "historical" Franklin.

A. Expansion
In introducing Franklin's scheme for attaining moral perfection, you may wish to inform students that during his two years in London, Franklin had led a rather free and easy life. It was to correct the "follies" of this period of his life that Franklin undertook this program of self-improvement.

B. Responding
Call students' attention to Virtue 4, *Resolution.*
? Think of a resolution of your own in the past (at New Year's, for example). What was it and how easily were you able to keep it? (Students probably will agree that resolutions are much more easily made than kept.)

ADDITIONAL WRITING ASSIGNMENT
Have students select two or three of Franklin's virtues to define in their own words. Suggest that they tell why each is an important virtue and give an everyday example of its application.

In the following section, Franklin explains his scheme for achieving moral perfection, which is perhaps the best-known passage of the Autobiography. *These ideas were originally intended to be included in a short book—one of the first of that now common American genre, the self-help book.*

Arriving at Moral Perfection

A It was about this time that I conceived the bold and arduous project of arriving at moral perfection. I wished to live without committing any fault at any time; I would conquer all that either natural inclination, custom, or company might lead me into. As I knew, or thought I knew, what was right and wrong, I did not see why I might not *always* do the one and avoid the other. But I soon found I had undertaken a task of more difficulty than I had imagined: while my care was employed in guarding against one fault, I was often surprised by another. Habit took the advantage of inattention. Inclination was sometimes too strong for reason. I concluded, at length, that the mere speculative conviction that it was our interest to be completely virtuous was not sufficient to prevent our slipping, and that the contrary habits must be broken, and good ones acquired and established, before we can have any dependence on a steady uniform rectitude of conduct. For this purpose I therefore contrived the following method.

In the various enumerations of the moral virtues I had met with in my reading, I found the catalog more or less numerous, as different writers included more or fewer ideas under the same name. Temperance, for example, was by some confined to eating and drinking, while by others it was extended to mean the moderating every other pleasure, appetite, inclination, or passion, bodily or mental, even to our avarice and ambition. I proposed to myself, for the sake of clearness, to use rather more names with fewer ideas annexed to each than a few names with more ideas; and I included after thirteen names of virtues all that at that time occurred to me as necessary or desirable, and annexed to each a short precept, which fully expressed the extent I gave to its meaning.

These names of virtues with their precepts were:

1. **Temperance.** Eat not to dullness. Drink not to elevation.
2. **Silence.** Speak not but what may benefit others or yourself. Avoid trifling conversation.
3. **Order.** Let all your things have their places. Let each part of your business have its time.
4. **Resolution.** Resolve to perform what you ought. Perform without fail what you resolve. B
5. **Frugality.** Make no expense but to do good to others or yourself; i.e., waste nothing.
6. **Industry.** Lose no time. Be always employed in something useful. Cut off all unnecessary actions.
7. **Sincerity.** Use no hurtful deceit. Think innocently and justly; and, if you speak; speak accordingly.
8. **Justice.** Wrong none, by doing injuries or omitting the benefits that are your duty.
9. **Moderation.** Avoid extremes. Forbear resenting injuries so much as you think they deserve.
10. **Cleanliness.** Tolerate no uncleanness in body, clothes, or habitation.
11. **Tranquillity.** Be not disturbed at trifles, or at accidents common or unavoidable.
12. **Chastity.** Rarely use venery [sex] but for health or offspring; never to dullness, weakness, or the injury of your own or another's peace or reputation.
13. **Humility.** Imitate Jesus and Socrates.[10]

My intention being to acquire the *habitude* of all these virtues, I judged it would be well not to distract my attention by attempting the whole at once, but to fix it on one of them at a time, and when I should be master of that, then to proceed to another, and so on till I should have gone through the thirteen. And as the previous acquisition of some might facilitate the acquisition of certain others, I arranged them with that view as they stand above. *Temperance* first, as it tends to procure that coolness and clearness of head, which is so necessary where constant vigilance was to be kept up, and guard maintained, against the unremitting attraction of ancient habits, and the force of perpetual temptations. This being acquired and established, *silence* would be more easy, and my desire being to gain knowledge at the same time that I improved in virtue, and considering that in conversation it was obtained rather

10. **Socrates:** Greek philosopher (469–399 B.C.), said to have lived a simple, virtuous life.

Reading Check Test

1. Franklin finds work as a printer in New York. *False*

2. While in Philadelphia, Franklin joins the Quaker church. *False*

3. In drawing up his list of virtues, Franklin decides to use "more names with fewer ideas." *True*

4. Each of the virtues received one month's attention from Franklin. *False*

5. Cleanliness and sincerity are among Franklin's virtues. *True*

Analyzing the Autobiography

Identifying Facts

1. He felt that his brother and father would prevent him from departing if he tried to leave openly. He sold some of his books.

2. He says that John Bunyan was the first to mix narration and dialogue.

3. Franklin provides vivid details of his shabby state: He is wearing dirty work clothes, their pockets bulging with shirts and stockings; he is tired and hungry and has only a few coins in his pocket.

(Answers continue top of next page.)

by the use of the ears than of the tongue, and therefore wishing to break a habit I was getting into of prattling, punning, and joking, which only made me acceptable to trifling company, I gave *silence* the second place. This, and the next, *order,* I expected would allow me more time for attending to my project and my studies; *resolution,* once become habitual, would keep me firm in my endeavors to obtain all the subsequent virtues; *frugality* and *industry,* by freeing me from my remaining debt, and producing affluence and independence, would make more easy the practice of *sincerity* and *justice,* etc., etc. Conceiving, then, that agreeable to the advice of Pythagoras[11] in his Golden Verses, daily examination would be necessary, I contrived the following method for conducting that examination.

I made a little book in which I allotted a page for each of the virtues. I ruled each page with red ink so as to have seven columns, one for each day of the week, marking each column with a letter for the day. I crossed these columns with thirteen red lines, marking the beginning of each line with the first letter of one of the virtues, on which line and in its proper column I might mark by a little black spot every fault I found, upon examination, to have been committed respecting that virtue upon that day.

I determined to give a week's strict attention to each of the virtues successively. Thus in the first week my great guard was to avoid every the least offence against temperance, leaving the other virtues to their ordinary chance, only marking every evening the faults of the day. Thus if in the first week I could keep my first line marked T clear of spots, I supposed the habit of that virtue so much strengthened and its opposite weakened, that I might venture extending my attention to include the next, and for the following week keep both lines clear of spots. Proceeding thus to the last, I could go through a course complete in thirteen weeks, and four courses in a year. And like him who, having a garden to weed, does not attempt to eradicate all the bad herbs at once, which would exceed his reach and his strength, but works on one of the beds at a time, and having accomplished the first proceeds to a second, so I should have (I hoped) the encouraging pleasure of seeing on my pages the progress I made in virtue, by clearing successively my lines of their spots, till in the end, by a number of courses, I should be happy in viewing a clean book after a thirteen weeks' daily examination.

Form of the Pages

Temperance							
Eat not to dullness. Drink not to elevation.							
	S	M	T	W	T	F	S
T							
S							
O							
R							
F							
I							
S							
J							
M							
CL							
T							
Ch							
H							

11. **Pythagoras:** Greek philosopher and mathematician of the sixth century B.C.

A. Expansion

Pythagoras attracted a number of disciples who followed rigorous ascetic practices intended to perfect the soul. Franklin's reference to Pythagoras's advice relates to the daily effort to perfect these virtues. Pythagoras's moral teaching contained many specific rules, some of which may have seemed arbitrary or ambiguous to the disciples. Questioning followers were answered with the famous reply *ipse dixit* (Greek, *autos epha*), meaning "He (himself) has said it." The words have come to refer to any arbitrary or dogmatic statement.

B. Responding

? On the basis of what you have read of Franklin so far, do you agree or disagree with scholar Moses Coit Tyler's evaluation of Franklin: ". . . Franklin's account of himself delineates a career of shrewd and somewhat selfish geniality, . . . of kindly systematic and most successful worldliness. . . ."? Why? (Student answers will vary.)

(*Answers begin top of page 79.*)
4. He places temperance at the head of his list, since it "tends to procure that coolness and clearness of head, which is so necessary where constant vigilance was to be kept up, and guard maintained, against the unremitting attraction of ancient habits, and the force of perpetual temptations."

Interpreting Meanings

5. Franklin's saving the Dutchman during the storm reveals that he is quick-thinking; his curing himself of a fever with a remembered "prescription" reveals that he is practical and self-reliant; his speed in locating lodgings when he misses the boat to Philadelphia reveals that he is resourceful and personable.

Student answers will vary. Many students may suggest that Franklin may be writing from both motives.

6. Franklin's scheme suggests that he believes that human beings *are* capable of improving themselves.

The scheme suggests that Franklin believes education should be methodically (*Answers continue in left-hand column.*)

(*Cont. from top.*) organized and planned.

Student answers will vary.

7. Student answers will vary. Most students will agree that Franklin is disarmingly direct, and that he does not hesitate to criticize his own feelings when he feels he deserves such criticism.

8. Student answers will vary.

9. Again, student answers will vary. Try to encourage students to name some specific "self-help" titles on subjects such as health, finance, diet, exercise, vocabulary development, etc. Most of the students will agree that these books have material accomplishments, rather than moral perfection, as their goal. Students may point out, however, that Franklin was certainly not immune to the appeal of material accomplishments and wordly success.

Responding to the Autobiography

Analyzing the Autobiography

Identifying Facts

1. Why did Franklin decide to leave Boston secretly? How did he raise some money for the journey from Boston to New York?
2. What method of writing in John Bunyan's *Pilgrim's Progress* does Franklin single out for praise?
3. Franklin's arrival in Philadelphia has become a favorite American anecdote. At the time he wrote this part of his life story, Franklin was living in England and was already one of the most famous Americans of his century. In contrast, what was Franklin's condition in life when he arrived in Philadelphia?
4. What virtue does Franklin place first on his list for achieving moral perfection? Why?

Interpreting Meanings

5. Though Franklin discusses his own character at length in his autobiography, many of his personality traits are revealed not through direct statements but through his actions. Explain what the events of the difficult journey from Boston to Philadelphia disclose about the **character** of the young Franklin. Do you feel Franklin is being honest, or is he trying to make himself look good?
6. What does Franklin's scheme for achieving moral perfection reveal about his views of human nature? What does it suggest about his attitudes toward education? What is your opinion of these views?
7. Franklin ends his list of virtues with humility. Did you find evidence of pride—the opposite of humility—in his history, and if so, where?
8. Which virtue on his list do you consider most important? Which is least important? Why?
9. How does Franklin's scheme for arriving at moral perfection compare with the self-help books available today?

Writing About the Autobiography

A Critical Response

1. **Comparing and Contrasting Two Writers.** Reread the selections from Jonathan Edwards (page 37), and write a brief essay in which you compare and contrast the Puritan preacher with Ben Franklin. Before you write, consider these points: each man's aims in life; his reasons for having them; and the means each man finds to achieve those aims. You quickly will be able to identify differences between the two men. But be sure to cite at least one way in which these two Americans, both heirs of the Puritan tradition, are alike.
2. **Responding to Critical Comments.** Reactions to Franklin's *Autobiography* have often been negative. Here is the response of a famous writer of a later period. Read this response and use a dictionary for any words you don't understand. Then write an essay about Twain's comments. In your first paragraph, restate in your own words how Twain feels about Franklin, and why. In your second paragraph, describe Twain's **tone.** In your third paragraph, give your own reaction to Twain's assessment of Franklin.

> [Franklin had] a malevolence which is without parallel in history; he would work all day and then sit up nights and let on to be studying algebra by the light of a smoldering fire, so that all other boys might have to do that also or else have Benjamin Franklin thrown up to them. Not satisfied with these proceedings, he had a fashion of living wholly on bread and water, and studying astronomy at meal time—a thing which has brought affliction to millions of boys since, whose fathers had read Franklin's pernicious biography.
>
> —Mark Twain

Analyzing Language and Style

American English

Franklin has some trouble communicating with the baker in Philadelphia. Finally, not knowing the names Philadelphians had for bread, he asks for three cents worth of any sort of bread at all. Franklin's troubles might be met by any traveler today.

1. People in different areas mean something different when they order a "roll," "coffee cake," "cinnamon bun," "crumb cake," "muffin," or "biscuit." What would you get in your area if you ordered these in a diner?
2. Use an unabridged dictionary to find out what you would get in England if you asked for a "biscuit."
3. Franklin uses the word *creek* to describe the waterway they pulled into one night. In England, the word meant "an arm of the sea." In America, people changed the word to mean "a shallow feeder of a river." Do you pronounce the word krēk or krik? Is the word used in your area, or do you say *brook, stream,* or *run*?

SUPPLEMENTARY SUPPORT MATERIALS
1. Vocabulary Activity Worksheet (*CCB*)
2. Review and Response Worksheet: Irony (*CCB*)
3. Selection Test (*CCB*)

DEVELOPING VOCABULARY
The following words from the maxims are tested in the Selection Test. (See also Vocabulary Activity Worksheet.)

almanac	to compose
investment	upright
interest	plowman
tart	to preach
to trample	bondage

PREPARATION
ESTABLISHING A PURPOSE. Ask students to read the sayings to determine, based on their own experience, whether or not they agree with each one.

A. Responding
? Do you think Poor Richard would agree or disagree with the following statements? (a) Even close friends need some privacy from each other. (Agree) (b) Live for tomorrow. (Disagree) (c) May all your wishes come true. (Disagree) (d) There is dignity in hard work. (Agree) (e) Beauty is in the eye of the beholder. (Agree) (f) A mind is a terrible thing to waste. (Agree)

SAYINGS OF POOR RICHARD

In 1732, Franklin wanted another income, and he turned to the business of publishing a yearly almanac. Almanacs were sure sellers: every house had one. An almanac was not only a calendar; it also calculated the tides and the phases of the moon, claimed to forecast the weather for the next year, and even provided astrological advice for those who believed in it. Many almanacs also supplied recipes, jokes, poems, and maxims.

***Poor Richard's Almanack* was Franklin's biggest publishing success, and it continued to appear for over twenty-five years. "Poor Richard" was an imaginary astrologer, who had a wife named Bridget. Over the years, a running dispute took place between Richard and the critical Bridget. One year, Bridget wrote the maxims, to answer those her husband had written the year before on female idleness. Once, Bridget went through the whole almanac and included better weather forecasts so that women would know the good days for drying their clothes.**

Franklin took Poor Richard's wit and widsom where he found it—from old sayings in other languages, from other writers, from popular adages. He never hesitated to rework the texts to suit his own purposes. For example, for the 1758 almanac, Franklin skimmed all his previous editions to compose a single speech on economy. Poor Richard claimed to have heard an old man, Father Abraham, deliver the speech at an auction. This speech, called "The Way to Wealth," has become one of the best known of Franklin's works. It has been mistakenly believed to be representative of Poor Richard's wisdom. Poor Richard often called for prudence and thrift, but he just as often favored extravagance.

1. Love your neighbor; yet don't pull down your hedge.

2. If a man empties his purse into his head, no man can take it away from him. An investment in knowledge always pays the best interest.

3. Three may keep a secret if two of them are dead.

4. Tart words make no friends; a spoonful of honey will catch more flies than a gallon of vinegar.

A **5.** Glass, china, and reputation are easily cracked and never well mended.

6. Fish and visitors smell in three days.

7. He that lieth down with dogs shall rise up with fleas.

8. One today is worth two tomorrows.

9. A truly great man will neither trample on a worm nor sneak to an emperor.

10. A little neglect may breed mischief; for want of a nail the shoe was lost; for want of a shoe the horse was lost; for want of a horse the rider was lost; for want of the rider the battle was lost.

11. If you would know the value of money, go and try to borrow some; he that goes a-borrowing goes a-sorrowing.

12. He that composes himself is wiser than he that composes books.

13. He that is of the opinion that money will do everything may well be suspected of doing everything for money.

14. If a man could have half his wishes, he would double his troubles.

15. 'Tis hard for an empty bag to stand upright.

16. A small leak will sink a great ship.

17. A plowman on his legs is higher than a gentleman on his knees.

18. None preaches better than the ant, and she says nothing.

19. There are no ugly loves nor handsome prisons.

20. Keep your eyes wide open before marriage, half shut afterward.

21. Nothing brings more pain than too much pleasure; nothing more bondage than too much liberty.

Reading Check Test

1. Poor Richard has a wife named Bridget. *True*
2. Poor Richard's sayings are original works of Franklin's. *False*
3. Poor Richard believes that people have difficulty keeping secrets. *True*
4. Poor Richard would enjoy having his family visit for a week. *False*
5. If Poor Richard were alive today, he might be president of a savings and loan institution. *False*

Analyzing The Maxims

Interpreting Meanings

1. The first, third, sixth, twelfth, thirteenth, seventeenth, eighteenth, and twentieth sayings may be said to reflect this attitude.
2. The eighth, tenth, eleventh, and fifteenth might be said to support that criticism.

The second saying points out that knowledge is more valuable and enduring than wealth, and the fourteenth cautions against placing too much importance on money.

3. Answers might suggest that Hawthorne may have felt that duties such as piety, charity, and kindness were omitted from Poor Richard's sayings.
4. Student answers will vary. Encourage the students to apply the maxims they select to as many diverse situations as they can.

Illustration from *Poor Richard's Almanack*. Engraving.

Yale University Library, New Haven, Connecticut.

Responding to the Maxims

Analyzing the Maxims

Interpreting Meanings

1. The sharpness of these sayings is partly due to Franklin's **ironic** view of human nature and human relationships. People, he implies, are not always what they would like to be (or what they think they are). Which of these sayings reflect this attitude?
2. Franklin is sometimes criticized for equating virtue with wealth and success. Which of these sayings support that criticism? Which do not?
3. A character in a story by Nathaniel Hawthorne says that he does not like Franklin's proverbs because "they are all about getting money or saving it." Hawthorne thought that the proverbs taught people only a very small proportion of their duties. What sorts of duties do you think Hawthorne felt were omitted from Poor Richard's sayings? Do you agree?
4. Take at least five of these maxims and apply each to a situation in contemporary life—to politics, society, family life, social and private morality, or business.

Writing About the Maxims

A Creative Response

Analyzing Contemporary Maxims. Contemporary Americans are still fond of maxims. Make a list of ten popular sayings or slogans; you'll find some on bumper stickers, some on tee shirts, and some in advertisements on TV and in magazines. Then make up at least three maxims of your own.

Primary Sources
A Letter to Samuel Mather

A Samuel Mather was Cotton Mather's son and the last of the Mather Dynasty, which comprised four generations of famous New England ministers and theologians. Samuel Mather was born the same year as Franklin, and both are believed to have studied penmanship under Mrs. Sarah Kemble Knight (see page 31). The occasion for this letter was Samuel Mather's gift to Franklin of his last book, *The Dying Legacy.* Franklin writes from his post in France.

". . . When I was a boy, I met with a book entitled *Essays to Do Good,* which I think was written by your father. It had been so little regarded by a former possessor that several leaves of it were torn out; but the remainder gave me such a turn of thinking, as to have an influence on my conduct through life; for I have always set a greater value on the character of a *doer of good* than on any other kind of reputation; and if I have been, as you seem to think, a useful citizen, the public owes the advantage of it to that book.

"You mention your being in your 78th year; I am in my 79th; we are grown old together. It is now more than 60 years since I left Boston, but I remember well both your father and grandfather, having heard them both in the pulpit, and seen them in their houses. The last time I saw your father was in the beginning of 1724, when I visited him after my first trip to Pennsylvania. He received me in his library, and on my taking leave showed me a shorter way out of the house through a narrow passage, which was crossed by a beam overhead. We were still talking as I withdrew, he accompanying me behind, and I turning partly toward him, when he said hastily, 'Stoop, stoop!' I did not understand him, till I felt my head hit against the beam. He was a man that never missed any occasion to giving instruction, and upon this he said to me, 'You are young, and have the world before you; stoop as you go through it, and you will miss many hard thumps.' This advice, thus beat into my head, has frequently been of use to me; and I often think of it, when I see pride mortified, and misfortunes brought upon people by their carrying their heads too high. B

"I long much to see again my native place, and to lay my bones there. I left it in 1723; I visited it in 1733, 1743, 1753, and 1763. In 1773 I was in England; in 1775 I had a sight of it, but could not enter, it being in possession of the enemy. I did hope to have been there in 1783, but could not obtain my dismissal from this employment here; and now I fear I shall never have that happiness. My best wishes however attend my dear country. *Esto perpetua* [May she endure forever]. It is now blest with an excellent constitution; may it last forever! . . ."

—B. Franklin

View of the Long Wharf and Part of Boston by Lt. Richard Byron (1764). Watercolor.

The Bostonian Society, Old State House, Boston.

A. Responding

? What influences on Benjamin Franklin by Cotton Mather are revealed in this letter? (Cotton Mather's writing and his advice influenced Franklin to attempt to do good and to be humble.)

B. Responding

? What do you think Cotton Mather meant when he said to Franklin about life, "Stoop as you go through it, and you will miss many hard thumps." (This advice has somewhat the same meaning as "Pride goeth before a fall." Encourage students to think of specific examples from their own experience that will help them to interpret Mather's statement.)

ADDITIONAL WRITING ASSIGNMENT

Have students write a brief account of their impressions of Franklin as man and writer now that they know more about him.

SUPPLEMENTARY SUPPORT MATERIALS
1. Vocabulary Activity Worksheet (*CCB*)
2. Review and Response Worksheet: Autobiography (*CCB*)
3. Language Skills Worksheet: Transitional Expressions (*CCB*)
4. Selection Test (*CCB*)

DEVELOPING VOCABULARY
These words from the autobiography are tested in the Selection Test. (See also Vocabulary Activity Worksheet.)

countenance	improvident
to indulge	avarice
salutation	to aggravate
copious	to procure
respiration	wretch

PREPARATION
ESTABLISHING A PURPOSE. Students undoubtedly have read about slavery in their social studies courses. Tell them they are about to read an account from someone who lived through it. Ask them to note their own feelings as they read.

FOR FURTHER READING FOR TEACHERS AND STUDENTS
Other first-person accounts of slavery include the following: *Bullwhip Days: The Slaves Remember,* edited by James Mellon (Avon); *Incidents in the Life of a Slave Girl: Written by Herself,* by Harriet A. Jacobs, edited by Maria . Child (Harvard, 1987); and *To Be a Slave*, by Julius Lester (Dial Books, 1968). Also see *The Narrative of the Life of Frederick Douglass, an American Slave,* by Frederick Douglass (Viking Penguin, 1982), an excerpt of which begins on page 386.

A. Irony
Encourage students to comment on the way in which Equiano views his captors, especially in comparison with the way the white slavers viewed their cargo. (Students may note that each viewed the other with suspicion on the basis of physical appearance.)

THE MIDDLE PASSAGE

Olaudah Equiano
(1745–1797)

Olaudah Equiano was still a child when he and his sister were kidnapped from their home in West Africa by slave traders. Over a period of six or seven months he was brought to a series of waystations, where he was a slave (although a well-treated one) in various African families, until he reached the coast. There he was put aboard one of the infamous slave ships bound for Barbados, an island in the West Indies. This part of the slave route, known as the middle passage, is described in Equiano's own words. (His autobiography was published in England in 1789 under the title* The Interesting Narrative of the Life of Olaudah Equiano, or Gustavus Vassa, the African.*)

It is estimated that about fifty million people were captured in Africa and shipped as slaves to South America, the United States, and the islands of the West Indies.

The first object that saluted[1] my eyes when I arrived on the coast was the sea, and a slave ship, which was then riding at anchor, and waiting for its cargo. These filled me with astonishment, which was soon converted into terror, which I am yet at a loss to describe, and the then feelings of my mind when I was carried on board. I was immediately handled and tossed up to see if I were sound, by some of the crew; and I was now persuaded that I had got into a world of bad spirits, and that they were going to kill me. Their complexions too, differing so much from ours, their long hair, and the language they spoke (which was very different from any I had ever heard), united to confirm me in this belief. [A] Indeed such were the horrors of my views and fears at the moment, that if ten thousand worlds had been my own, I would have freely parted with them all to have exchanged my condition with that of the meanest slave in my own country. When I looked round the ship too, and saw a large furnace or copper boiling, and a multitude of black people of every description chained together, every one of their countenances expressing dejection and sorrow, I no longer doubted of my fate; and, quite overpowered with horror and anguish, I fell motionless on the deck and fainted. When I recovered a little, I found some black people about me, who I believed were some of those who brought me on board, and had been receiving their pay; they talked to me in order to cheer me, but all in vain. I asked them if we were not to be eaten by those white men with horrible looks, red faces, and long hair. They told me I was not. . . .

Soon after this the blacks who brought me on board went off, and left me abandoned to despair. I now saw myself deprived of all chance of returning to my native country, or even the least glimpse of hope of gaining the shore, which I now considered as friendly; and I even wished for my former slavery in preference to my present situation, which was filled with horrors of every kind, still heightened by my ignorance of what I was to undergo. I was not long suffered to indulge my grief. I was soon put down under the decks, and there I received such a salutation to my nostrils as I had never experienced in my life; so that, with the loathsomeness of the stench, and crying together, I became so sick and low that I was not able to eat, nor had I the least desire to taste anything. I now wished for the last friend, death, to relieve me; but soon, to my grief, two of the white men offered me eatables; and, on my refusing to eat, one of them held me fast by the hands, and laid me across, I think, the windlass,[2] and tied my feet, while the other flogged me severely. I had never experienced anything of this kind before; and although, not being used to the water, I naturally feared that element the first time I saw it, yet nevertheless, could I have got over the nettings, I would have jumped over the side, but I could not; and besides the crew used to watch us very closely, who were not chained down to the decks, lest we should leap into the water; and I have seen some of these poor African prisoners most severely cut for

1. **saluted:** met.
2. **windlass** (wind′ləs): a crank with a handle, used to raise or lower the anchor.

Expansion

The enduring hymn "Amazing Grace" was written by John Newton (1725–1807) in response to his religious conversion, which he experienced while a captain of a slave ship headed for America. Newton returned his ship to Africa and freed his human cargo. Have students interpret the first two verses of the hymn in light of this background:

Amazing grace! How sweet the sound,
That saved a wretch like me!
I once was lost, but now am found,
Was blind, but now I see.

'Twas grace that taught my heart to fear,
And grace my fears relieved;
How precious did that grace appear
The hour I first believed!

attempting to do so, and hourly whipped for not eating. This indeed was often the case with myself. In a little time after, amongst the poor chained men, I found some of my own nation, which in a small degree gave ease to my mind. I inquired of these what was to be done with us; they gave me to understand we were to be carried to these white people's country to work for them. I was then a little revived, and thought if it were no worse than working, my situation was not so desperate: but still I feared I should be put to death, the white people looked and acted, as I thought, in so savage a manner; for I had never seen among any people such instances of brutal cruelty; and this not only shewn towards us blacks, but also to some of the whites themselves. A One white man in particular I saw, when we were permitted to be on deck, flogged so unmercifully with a large rope near the foremast, that he died in consequence of it; and they tossed him over the side as they would have done a brute. This made B me fear these people the more; and I expected nothing less than to be treated in the same manner. . . .

The slave quarters of a ship on its way to the West Indies, painted by one of the officers on board. Slave quarters were usually much more crowded than those shown here.

The Maritime Museum of Greenwich.

C

A. Responding
? How can some people be so cruel to others? Do we need the buffer of law to protect us from others' cruelty? (Answers will vary.)

B. Responding
? Why was the white man killed? (Presumably he was a sailor who had committed some infraction. Most captains ruled with absolute authority, and sailors had no recourse against their orders and judgments.)

C. Humanities Connection: Responding to the Fine Art
? Does the painting reflect the conditions described by Equiano? (Students will see the similarity but should note the caption comment regarding the actual conditions.)

Writing Assignment
Have students continue Equiano's account, describing the arrival of the ship in port and the sale of the slaves.

Closure
Have students summarize conditions on a slave ship as Equiano described them; have them explain their emotional reactions to this account.

Reading Check Test

1. The first things Equiano sees when he arrives at the coast are the sea and ________. *a slave ship*
2. Equiano is frightened as much by the crew's ________ as by their language and behavior. *appearance*
3. Refusing to eat, Equiano is ________. *flogged*
4. Below decks Equiano is greeted with a loathsome ________. *stench*
5. At the end two slaves jump overboard, preferring ________ to continued misery. *death*

A. Responding
Here, the slaves are not given food, yet Equiano earlier described slaves being beaten for not eating. How do you explain the difference in the way the slaves were treated in each instance? (Earlier, the slaves may have been forced to eat to keep them healthy and thus more valuable. Here, perhaps, the sailors were being cruel to the slaves by denying them food.)

B. Responding
Can you understand why some of the slaves would give up all hope? (Answers will vary.) Why would the rescued slaves be flogged? (As a lesson to other would-be jumpers)

While we stayed on the coast I was mostly on deck; and one day, to my great astonishment, I saw one of these vessels coming in with the sails up. As soon as the whites saw it, they gave a great shout, at which we were amazed; and the more so as the vessel appeared larger by approaching nearer. At last she came to an anchor in my sight, and when the anchor was let go, I and my countrymen who saw it were lost in astonishment to observe the vessel stop, and were now convinced it was done by magic. Soon after this the other ship got her boats out, and they came on board of us, and the people of both ships seemed very glad to see each other. Several of the strangers also shook hands with us black people, and made motions with their hands, signifying, I suppose, we were to go to their country; but we did not understand them. At last, when the ship we were in had got in all her cargo, they made ready with many fearful noises, and we were all put under deck, so that we could not see how they managed the vessel.

But this disappointment was the least of my sorrow. The stench of the hold,[3] while we were on the coast, was so intolerably loathsome that it was dangerous to remain there for any time, and some of us had been permitted to stay on the deck for the fresh air; but now that the whole ship's cargo were confined together, it became absolutely pestilential. The closeness of the place, and the heat of the climate, added to the number in the ship, which was so crowded that each had scarcely room to turn himself, almost suffocated us. This produced copious perspirations, so that the air soon became unfit for respiration, from a variety of loathsome smells, and brought on a sickness among the slaves, of which many died, thus falling victims to the improvident avarice, as I may call it, of their purchasers. This wretched situation was again aggravated by the galling of the chains, now become insupportable; and the filth of the necessary tubs, into which the children often fell, and were almost suffocated. The shrieks of the women, and the groans of the dying, rendered the whole a scene of horror almost inconceivable. Happily, perhaps, for myself, I was soon reduced so low here that it was thought necessary to keep me almost always on deck; and from my extreme youth, I was not put in fetters. In this situation I expected every hour to share the fate of my companions, some of whom were almost daily brought upon deck at the point of death, which I began to hope would soon put an end to my miseries. Often did I think many of the inhabitants of the deep much more happy than myself; I envied them the freedom they enjoyed, and as often wished I could change my condition for theirs. Every circumstance I met with served only to render my state more painful, and heighten my apprehensions and my opinion of the cruelty of the whites. One day they had taken a number of fishes; and when they had killed and satisfied themselves with as many as they thought fit, to our astonishment who were on the deck, rather than give any of them to us to eat, as we expected, they tossed the remaining fish into the sea again, although we begged and prayed for some as well as we could, but in vain; and some of my countrymen, being pressed by hunger, took an opportunity, when they thought no one saw them, of trying to get a little privately; but were discovered, and the attempt procured for them some very severe floggings. A

One day, when we had a smooth sea and moderate wind, two of my wearied countrymen, who were chained together (I was near them at the time), preferring death to such a life of misery, somehow made through the nettings and jumped into the sea; immediately another quite dejected fellow, who on account of his illness was suffered to be out of irons, also followed their example; and I believe many more would very soon have done the same, if they had not been prevented by the ship's crew, who were instantly alarmed. Those of us who were the most active were in a moment put down under the deck; and there was such a noise and confusion amongst the people of the ship as I never heard before, to stop her and get the boat out to go after the slaves. However, two of the wretches were drowned; but they got the other, and afterwards flogged him unmercifully, for thus attempting to prefer death to slavery. . . . B

3. **hold:** below-decks compartment for cargo.

Patrick Henry (1736–1799)

Patrick Henry's impressive oratorical powers made him famous in the public life of Virginia and the Colonies. Born in a frontier region of Virginia, Henry was raised in a cultured although modest environment. During his youth, the country was undergoing the religious revival known as the Great Awakening, and young Henry often accompanied his mother to hear the sermons of the great traveling preachers.

As a young man, Henry made several unsuccessful stabs at farming and merchant life before discovering his true calling: the law. In 1765, when he was twenty-nine, he was chosen to represent his region in the Virginia House of Burgesses. His first great speech was a declaration of resistance to the Stamp Act of that year, a form of taxation passed by the British Parliament that required stamps to be used on all newspapers and public documents. William Wirt, Henry's admirer and biographer, described the dramatic climax of this speech:

> A [Henry] exclaimed, in a voice of thunder, and with the look of a god, "Caesar had his Brutus—Charles I, his Cromwell—and George III—" ("Treason," cried the speaker—"treason, treason," echoed from every part of the house. It was one of those trying moments which is decisive of character. Henry faltered not for an instant; but rising to a loftier attitude, and fixing on the speaker an eye of the most determined fire, he finished his sentence with the firmest emphasis)—"may profit by their example. If this be treason, make the most of it."

This speech was so successful that Patrick Henry's political fortunes were secured. For the next ten years, he was one of the most powerful figures in Virginia politics.

Henry was tall and lank, "with a dark sour look," as the historian Gary Wills has written, "which his preacher's clothes made more intriguing. . . . He had the actor's trick, in his oratory, of lifting his whole body up toward climaxes, along with his voice, as if he could add cubits by wanting to. . . . No one who beheld him incandescent with a Cause ever forgot the experience . . ."

Patrick Henry by an unknown artist (early 19th century). Oil.

The Shelburne Museum, Shelburne, Vermont.

His famous "liberty or death" speech was made in 1775, when the Colonies were nearing the breaking point. Following the Boston Tea Party in December of 1773, the British had closed the port of Boston and inaugurated other harsh measures referred to by the colonists as the "Intolerable Acts." When the First Continental Congress protested these acts, the British Crown relieved the Colonies of taxation on a number of conditions. One condition was that the colonists fully support British rule and contribute toward the maintenance of British troops in America, whose numbers were increasing greatly. On March 20, 1775, the Virginia House of Burgesses held a convention in St. John's Episcopal Church in Richmond to decide how to respond to the growing British military threat. George Washington and Thomas Jefferson were both present.

On March 23, after several speeches in favor

A. Allusion
From their study of *Julius Caesar,* students are probably familiar with Brutus, Caesar's general and one of the conspirators who murdered him. Oliver Cromwell (1599–1658), Lord Protector of England, led an army against the king, Charles I, to become military dictator of England (1653). Under his direction, Charles I was beheaded. Henry alludes to these historical figures as a way of warning George III what might happen to him.

SUPPLEMENTARY SUPPORT MATERIALS
1. Vocabulary Activity Worksheet (*CCB*)
2. Review and Response Worksheet: Rhetorical Devices (*CCB*)
3. Selection Test (*CCB*)
4. Audiocassette recording

DEVELOPING VOCABULARY
The following words from the speech are tested in the Selection Test. (See also Vocabulary Activity Worksheet.)

arduous, remonstrance, temporal, inviolate, solace, supinely, insidious, invincible, comport, to extenuate

PREPARATION
ESTABLISHING A PURPOSE. The purpose of a persuasive speech is, of course, to move the audience to action. You might have students read to determine whether or not they would have been moved to action as an American colonist at this time.

A. Expansion
This speech was made in support of a resolution Henry had introduced calling for the formation of a local militia. Previous speakers had opposed the measure, arguing that it would provoke England to harsh actions. Although his listeners were moved by his speech, many minds remained unchanged: his resolution passed by a margin of only five votes.

B. Expansion
Students will be interested to know that no manuscript of Patrick Henry's famous speech exists. Henry apparently spoke extemporaneously, with some use of notes. The text generally accepted was compiled by William Wirt Henry, Patrick Henry's grandson and biographer from notes of people present at the delivery of the speech. Thomas Jefferson, who had heard the speech, read the text and suggested no changes. Although Jefferson differed with Henry politically, he considered Henry a great orator.

of compromise with the British, Patrick Henry rose to defend his resolution to take up arms against the British. A clergyman who was present later recalled that during Henry's speech he felt "sick with excitement." As the speech reached its climax, Patrick Henry is said to have grabbed an ivory letter opener and plunged it toward his breast with the word *Death.*

A Henry persuaded the delegation. The Virginia Convention voted to arm its people against England. A few weeks later, on April 19, the battle of Lexington, in Massachusetts, ignited the Revolutionary War. By June 15, the Revolution had been formalized by the raising of an army under General George Washington. On July 4 of the following year, the Declaration of Independence was adopted in Philadelphia.

Although this speech is one of the most famous in all American oratory, no manuscript of it exists. The traditionally accepted text was pieced together by Henry's biographer, William Wirt, forty years after the speech was given.

SPEECH TO THE VIRGINIA CONVENTION

B **As you read Henry's speech, try to envision the physical surroundings of its delivery: an eighteenth-century church in Richmond, Virginia. What elements in the speech remind you of the methods used by preachers such as Jonathan Edwards and his contemporaries, whom Henry himself may have heard as a boy? Are these features still current today in the speeches of preachers and politicians? What kind of effect are they intended to have on an audience?**

Mr. President: No man thinks more highly than I do of the patriotism, as well as abilities, of the very worthy gentlemen who have just addressed the House. But different men often see the same subject in different lights; and, therefore, I hope that it will not be thought disrespectful to those gentlemen, if, entertaining as I do, opinions of a character very opposite to theirs, I shall speak forth my sentiments freely and without reserve. This is no time for ceremony. The question before the House is one of awful moment to this country. For my own part I consider it as nothing less than a question of freedom or slavery; and in proportion to the magnitude of the subject ought to be the freedom of the debate. It is only in this way that we can hope to arrive at truth, and fulfill the great responsibility which we hold to God and our country. Should I keep back my opinions at such a time, through fear of giving offense, I should consider myself as guilty of treason toward my country, and of an act of disloyalty toward the majesty of heaven, which I revere above all earthly kings.

Mr. President, it is natural to man to indulge in the illusions of hope. We are apt to shut our eyes against a painful truth, and listen to the song of that siren, till she transforms us into beasts. Is this the part of wise men, engaged in a great and arduous struggle for liberty? Are we disposed to be of the number of those who, having eyes, see not, and having ears, hear not, the things which so nearly concern their temporal salvation? For my part, whatever anguish of spirit it may cost, I am willing to know the whole truth; to know the worst and to provide for it.

I have but one lamp by which my feet are guided; and that is the lamp of experience. I know of no way of judging of the future but by the past. And judging by the past, I wish to know what there has been in the conduct of the British ministry for the last ten years, to justify those hopes with which gentlemen have been pleased to solace

Literature and Language: Appealing to Emotions and Reason
In **persuasion,** a writer or speaker tries to convince an audience to think or act in a certain way. Effective persuasive writing appeals both to reason and to the emotions.

Ask students to find examples of the following emotional appeals in Patrick Henry's speech:

1. An appeal to patriotic feelings
2. A sense of urgency and danger
3. A sense of duty
4. An appeal to religious feelings, belief in God
5. A desire not to appear foolish

Students should also notice that Henry's argument uses a forceful example of *either-or* reasoning, which is considered a **fallacy,** an error in logical thinking (see page 113). Henry says that there are only two courses of action: *either* the colonists must fight, *or* they will be enslaved. Ask students to find passages in which he says slavery is the only alternative to war. (See the first and final paragraphs, in particular.)

Patrick Henry Speaking Against the Stamp Act in the Virginia House of Burgesses in 1765 by F. Rothermel (1851).

Humanities Connection: Responding to the Fine Art
Peter Frederick Rothermel (1817–1895) was an eminent painter of historical subjects. He is noted for his effective use of color and for his skillful management of large masses of figures. This painting exemplifies both features.

? How does Patrick Henry's appearance in this painting differ from that in the portrait on page 87? (Patrick Henry's dress and general appearance are much more dramatic in this painting.) What are some of the touches that the painter has used to dramatize the occasion? (The glove, seemingly flung onto the floor in the foreground is one such touch, as is the light streaming into the room in the background. The intense faces and postures of Henry and the other figures also contribute to the drama.)

READING CHECK TEST

1. Patrick Henry may have been influenced by the sermons of Jonathan Edwards. *True*
2. Henry says that it would be disastrous to know the whole truth. *False*
3. At the time of the speech, the First Continental Congress had already assembled. *True*
4. Henry says that the only recourse for the colonists is to arm themselves. *True*
5. Henry assumes there will be four million colonists fighting against the British. *False*

ANALYZING THE SPEECH

Identifying Facts

1. It is vital that the truth be known.
2. Henry compares the threat of subjugation to Britian to the threat of slavery and chains, saying that the British soldiers are "sent over to bind and rivet upon us those chains which the British ministry has been so long forging."

A. Sentence Structure (Challenging)

Call students' attention to the periodic sentence. Explain that a periodic sentence is one in which the main clause or some other essential grammatical element is postponed until the very end and that this device is often used in formal speeches. Have students recast this sentence, putting the main clause (*we must fight*) first and compare the effect.

ADDITIONAL WRITING ASSIGNMENT

As Henry uttered the words "Give me liberty . . .," he held up an ivory handled letter opener, which he let slowly sink toward his breast as he said " . . . or give me death." Ask students to react to this gesture, indicating whether or not they regard it as overly dramatic under the circumstances.

themselves and the House? Is it that insidious smile with which our petition[1] has been lately received? Trust it not, sir; it will prove a snare to your feet. Suffer not yourselves to be betrayed with a kiss. Ask yourselves how this gracious reception of our petition comports with these warlike preparations which cover our waters and darken our land. Are fleets and armies necessary to a work of love and reconciliation? Have we shown ourselves so unwilling to be reconciled, that force must be called in to win back our love? Let us not deceive ourselves, sir. These are the implements of war and subjugation; the last arguments to which kings resort.

I ask gentlemen, sir, what means this martial array, if its purpose be not to force us to submission? Can gentlemen assign any other possible motives for it? Has Great Britain any enemy, in this quarter of the world, to call for all this accumulation of navies and armies? No, sir, she has none. They are meant for us; they can be meant for no other. They are sent over to bind and rivet upon us those chains which the British ministry have been so long forging. And what have we to oppose to them? Shall we try argument? Sir, we have been trying that for the last ten years. Have we anything new to offer on the subject? Nothing. We have held the subject up in every light of which it is capable; but it has been all in vain. Shall we resort to entreaty and humble supplication? What terms shall we find which have not been already exhausted? Let us not, I beseech you, sir, deceive ourselves longer. Sir, we have done everything that could be done, to avert the storm which is now coming on. We have petitioned; we have remonstrated; we have supplicated; we have prostrated ourselves before the throne, and have implored its interposition to arrest the tyrannical hands of the ministry and Parliament. Our petitions have been slighted; our remonstrances have produced additional violence and insult; our supplications have been disregarded; and we have been spurned, with contempt, from the foot of the throne. In vain, after these things, may we indulge the fond hope of peace and reconciliation. There is no longer any room for hope. If we wish to be free—if we mean to preserve inviolate those inestimable privileges for which we have been so long contending—if we mean not basely to abandon the noble struggle in which we have been so long engaged, and which we have pledged ourselves never to abandon until the glorious object of our contest shall be obtained, we must fight! I repeat it, sir, we must fight! An appeal to arms and to the God of Hosts is all that is left us!

They tell us, sir, that we are weak; unable to cope with so formidable an adversary. But when shall we be stronger? Will it be the next week, or the next year? Will it be when we are totally disarmed, and when a British guard shall be stationed in every house? Shall we gather strength by irresolution and inaction? Shall we acquire the means of effectual resistance, by lying supinely on our backs, and hugging the delusive phantom of hope, until our enemies shall have bound us hand and foot? Sir, we are not weak, if we make proper use of the means which the God of nature hath placed in our power. Three millions of people, armed in the holy cause of liberty, and in such a country as that which we possess, are invincible by any force which our enemy can send against us. Besides, sir, we shall not fight our battles alone. There is a just God who presides over the destinies of nations; and who will raise up friends to fight our battles for us. The battle, sir, is not to the strong alone; it is to the vigilant, the active, the brave. Besides, sir, we have no election.[2] If we were base enough to desire it, it is now too late to retire from the contest. There is no retreat, but in submission and slavery! Our chains are forged! Their clanking may be heard on the plains of Boston! The war is inevitable—and let it come! I repeat it, sir, let it come!

It is in vain, sir, to extenuate the matter. Gentlemen may cry peace, peace—but there is no peace. The war is actually begun! The next gale that sweeps from the north will bring to our ears the clash of resounding arms! Our brethren are already in the field! Why stand we here idle? What is it that gentlemen wish? What would they have? Is life so dear, or peace so sweet, as to be purchased at the price of chains and slavery? Forbid it, Almighty God! I know not what course others may take; but as for me, give me liberty, or give me death!

1. **our petition:** Henry refers to the First Continental Congress's protest against new taxation laws, which led King George III to retract those laws conditionally.

2. **election:** choice.

3. They have no choice because their petitions have failed; if they wish to be free, they must fight.

Interpreting Meanings

4. The main idea is that, if the colonists don't act immediately to protect their freedoms, they will lose them completely.
5. Warlike preparations "cover our waters and darken our land," like clouds. The British army intends to "bind and rivet" the Americans on the chains which the British have been long forging. Finally, Henry compares the British threat to a storm.
6. The series of questions occurs near the beginning of the paragraph. The answer to each question implies that Henry believes that the Americans can no longer postpone their resistance to the British threat. "Irresolution and inaction" will be fatal to the American cause.

It is rhetorically more effective to let the audience draw its own conclusions, rather than for the speaker to assert his opinion directly. Provided that Henry is sure that the audience will answer the questions for themselves in a certain way, he will be able to count on their forceful support, since they will be convinced that their answers are their *own* opinion, rather than merely the speaker's view.
7. a. Henry's point is that illusory hopes are like the sirens and the beautiful maiden Circe in Homer's *Odyssey,* who were attractive on the surface but destructive in reality. Henry urges his listeners not to surrender their freedom in exchange for false hopes of peace. Students will probably agree that the statement might have equal relevance to some situations today. **b.** The allusion to the Old Testament is a graceful, but pointed, way for Henry to remind his listeners that they must not be like the heedless people whom the prophet upbraided in ancient Israel. **c.** The allusion is to the disloyal apostle Judas. Henry warns his listeners not to heed the apparently mild British reaction to their latest petition against the new taxation laws.
8. Student answers will vary. Suggest people in Eastern Europe, South Africa, Latin America.

Responding to the Speech

Analyzing the Speech

Identifying Facts

1. According to the first two paragraphs of this speech, why is Henry speaking out?
2. Countering the arguments of opponents is essential to any persuasive speech or essay. How does Henry deal with the fact that the British have yielded somewhat to the Continental Congress's petition?
3. According to Henry, why do the colonists have no choice but to go to war?

Interpreting Meanings

4. State in your own words the **main idea** of Henry's impassioned speech.
5. Throughout his speech, Henry uses **metaphors** to seize his listeners' feelings and at the same time to advance his arguments. In paragraph four, what metaphor does he use to describe the coming war?
6. Perhaps like the preachers whose sermons he heard as a child, Patrick Henry makes use of a time-honored device in this speech: the **rhetorical question.** This is a question for which no answer is provided because the answer is obvious. Find a series of rhetorical questions in the fifth paragraph of this speech. What is the answer to each question? Why do you think the speaker makes these points in the form of rhetorical questions rather than in the form of straightforward statements?
7. Because Henry's audience knew classical mythology and, especially, the Bible, the orator knew he could count on certain **allusions** to have emotional effects. Look up the classical and Biblical passages alluded to in each of the following statements. How would each one relate to the conflict in Virginia in 1775? Could any of them relate to life today?

   a. "We are apt to . . . listen to the song of that siren, till she transforms us into beasts." (*Odyssey,* Books 10 and 12)

   b. "Are we disposed to be of the number of those who, having eyes, see not, and having ears, hear not the things which so nearly concern their temporal salvation?" (Ezekiel 12:2)

   c. "Suffer not yourselves to be betrayed with a kiss." (Luke 22:47–48)
8. What contemporary people—individuals or groups—can you name who might use Henry's closing sentence as a slogan?

Writing About the Speech

A Creative Response

1. **Reporting on the Speech.** Pretend you are a reporter who listened to Henry's speech. Write a newspaper article about the event.

A Critical Response

2. **Comparing and Contrasting Speeches.** Compare and contrast Henry's speech with Jonathan Edwards's 1741 sermon "Sinners in the Hands of an Angry God" (see page 37). In your essay, consider the specific ways the speeches are similar and dissimilar. A chart like the following will help you organize your material.

	Edwards	Henry
Speaker's purpose		
Audience		
Metaphors and allusions		
Appeals to emotion		
Appeals to reason		
Use of rhetorical questions and repetition		
Main idea		

A. Expansion
As a class or group activity, you might want students to imagine themselves speaking before the U.S. Congress on a topic they find exciting. Students can outline the speech they might make, including a call to action and proof supporting their position and motives. Then, students might actually draft one or more paragraphs of the speech, using the kind of heightened style discussed here.

Elements of Literature

PERSUASION

Persuasion is a form of speaking or writing that aims to move a particular audience to take action. The goal of persuasion is not merely to win the audience's agreement but also to make the audience *act.* One of the most powerful examples of persuasion in American literature is Patrick Henry's "Give me liberty, or give me death!" speech. Jonathan Edwards's sermon on page 37 is another excellent example of persuasion. With that sermon, Edwards wanted to persuade his congregation to take the action necessary to save themselves from plummeting into the pit of hell. Patrick Henry wanted the Virginia legislators to put their state in a position of armed defense.

A persuasive speech or essay generally includes: (1) a call to action; (2) proof supporting the speaker's position and motives for taking the action; (3) a heightened style intended to move the audience emotionally. Here is what two critics have said about the style of persuasion. As you read their analysis, consider how well you think it applies to Patrick Henry's speech.

A Along with the emphasis on action and the fusion of proof and motive, the third characteristic stressed in persuasion is the emotional and imaginative appeal of the style. An old axiom states that you cannot move another person to laughter or to tears unless you first laugh or weep yourself. If you wish to excite an audience, you are probably going to be excited yourself, and accordingly you will adopt an exciting style. A plain unemotional style befits an exposition of facts, such as the working of a gasoline engine, and will be adopted just as naturally.

Persuasion, then, is notable for its emphasis on action, the coherence of proof and motive, and a heightened emotional and imaginative style. These are the three essential elements, and they point to other important characteristics. Because persuasion often aims at a specific audience, it is a more personal and direct form of discourse than exposition and argument. A persuasive writer speaks not only from mind to mind, but from heart to heart. In the final analysis an audience is won over not only by the speaker's arguments and explanations but by the speaker's personality. We do not judge persuasion by the morals of the writer, but we do judge the moral meaning of the speech. This means simply that we respond to ideas that appeal to our sense of honor, justice, and integrity, especially when those ideas are uttered in a manner that is appropriate to the importance of the subject, the dignity of the occasion, and the respect that a speaker owes to the opinions of mankind. At bottom we submit to a legitimate ethical appeal, the morality of mind, in the persuasive effort. No trick of style, no demagogic cleverness, no learning however wide can impart moral character to persuasion. This moral character stems from the writer's own reasoned conviction and passionate belief.

—Francis Connolly and Gerald Levin

Identify at least five examples of Patrick Henry's "heightened style." Look for expressions that don't sound as though they would have occurred to him in a casual conversation.

Eagle and snake sternboard attributed to Skillin Shop, Boston (1790). Gilded wood, metal, and glass.

Collection of Dr. William Greenspon. Photo: Whitney Museum of American Art.

A. Expansion
Paine's attempt to organize his fellow excise men to demand higher wages was regarded as revolutionary in the England of 1774. Although his part in this agitation cost him his job, it proved fortunate in the long run. It was while lobbying for his fellow excise men that Paine met and impressed Benjamin Franklin, who provided letters of reference which enabled Paine to make a start as a journalist in America.

B. Expansion
Even though British arms had shed American blood at Lexington and Bunker Hill, no one had publicly proposed that Americans should declare independence before *Common Sense* appeared.

Common Sense appeared originally without the author's name. (See the reproduction of the title page on page 95.) There was great speculation in America and abroad as to who the author might be. Authorship was generally ascribed either to John Adams, Samuel Adams, or Benjamin Franklin. As late as 1779, John Adams was welcomed in Paris as "le fameux Adams," author of *Common Sense.* In America, Franklin was the writer to whom most people ascribed the pamphlet. On one occasion, a woman with Tory sympathies chided Franklin for referring to their king as "the royal brute of Britain." Franklin denied having written *Common Sense* and then added, "Moreover, if I had written it, I would not have so dishonored—the brute creation."

Thomas Paine (1737–1809)

One of the most popular exponents of the Age of Reason—the most persuasive writer of the American Revolution—came from an unlikely background. The poorly educated son of a corset maker, Thomas Paine was born in England. He spent the first thirty-seven years of his life drifting through a number of occupations: corset maker, grocer, tobacconist, schoolteacher, and excise man (a government employee who examined goods and levied excise taxes on them). In 1774, Paine was dismissed from the excise for
A attempting to organize the employees in a demand for higher wages (an unusual activity in those days). Like many others at that time and since, he came to America to make a new start.

With a letter of introduction from Ben Franklin, whom he had met in London, Paine went to Philadelphia, where he worked as a journalist. In the disagreement between England and the Colonies, he instantly identified with the cause of the underdog. In January of 1776, he published the
B most important pamphlet in support of American independence: *Common Sense*.

In this forty-seven-page pamphlet, Paine denounced King George III as a "royal brute" and asserted that a continent should not remain tied to an island. The pamphlet sold half a million copies—in a country whose total population was roughly two and a quarter million.

That same year—1776—Paine joined the Continental Army as it retreated across New Jersey to Philadelphia. During the journey, he began writing what would be a series of sixteen pamphlets called *The American Crisis*. In these, he commented on the course of the war and urged his countrymen not to give up the fight. The first of these pamphlets was read to Washington's troops in December of 1776, a few days before they recrossed the Delaware River to attack Trenton.

After the Revolution, Paine lived peacefully in New York and New Jersey until 1787, when he returned to Europe. There he became involved once more in radical revolutionary politics.

Revolutionary times were over in America, but they were just beginning in France. On July

Thomas Paine by James Watson after Charles Willson Peale (late 18th century). Colored mezzotint.

14, 1789, the French Revolution began in Paris with the storming of the Bastille by an angry mob. Paine, who considered himself a citizen of the world, soon found a platform for his ideas. In France in 1791, he composed *The Rights of Man,* a reply to the English statesman Edmund Burke's condemnation of the French Revolution.

The Rights of Man was an impassioned defense of republican government and a call to the English people to overthrow their king. Although C
he was outside the country, Paine was tried for treason and outlawed from England. Safe in France from English law, he was briefly celebrated as a hero of the French Revolution but soon imprisoned for being a citizen of an enemy nation (England). James Monroe, the American minister to France at the time, secured Paine's release in 1794 by insisting that Paine was an American citizen.

The first part of Paine's last great work, *The Age of Reason,* appeared that year; the second part was published two years later. *The Age of Reason* was Paine's statement of belief and an explanation of the principles of deism (see page 69). The book was controversial in America, where it was not fully understood and was thought to be atheistic.

When the author of the book finally returned to America in 1802, he found himself an outcast.

C. Expansion
The Rights of Man had two main purposes: first, to justify the measures taken by the revolutionary government of France and second, to promote the overthrow of the monarchy in England. Paine hoped that *The Rights of Man* would have the same effect on the English as his *Common Sense* had had in America. The pamphlet became very popular with British radicals until it was officially suppressed by William Pitt's government in 1792.

SUPPLEMENTARY SUPPORT MATERIALS
1. Vocabulary Activity Worksheet (*CCB*)
2. Review and Response Worksheet: Argument (*CCB*)
3. Selection Test (*CCB*)

DEVELOPING VOCABULARY
The following words from the pamphlet are tested in the Selection Test. (See also Vocabulary Activity Worksheet.)

to esteem	apparition
celestial	apprehension
impious	martial
to relinquish	prudent
hypocrisy	to chastise

PREPARATION
ESTABLISHING A PURPOSE. Ask students to try as they read to determine to what audience Paine is addressing his arguments. When all have finished reading, discuss their ideas about the audience(s) that Paine had in mind. Follow up this discussion with question 3, page 99.

A. Expansion
You may want to explain that *dearness* here is the opposite of *cheap*; it means "difficulty of obtaining."

B. Irony
It is ironic that Paine quotes from a British act granting the colonies concessions as he indicts Britain for tyranny.

He had been stripped of his right to vote, he had no money, and he was continually harassed as a dangerous radical and atheist. When he died in New York, Paine was denied burial in consecrated ground. His body was buried in a corner of the farm he owned in New Rochelle.

Even in death, though, Thomas Paine was not allowed to rest. In 1819, an English sympathizer dug up Paine's body and removed it and the coffin to England, intending to erect a monument to the author of *The Rights of Man*. But no monument was ever built. The last record of Paine's remains shows that the coffin and the bones were acquired by a furniture dealer in England in 1844.

THE CRISIS, NO. 1

Patrick Henry's words were composed to be heard by an audience, but Thomas Paine wrote his pamphlets to be read. Nevertheless, parts of *The American Crisis* use vivid imagery and rhetorical techniques. You can better appreciate Paine's forceful style by trying an experiment. Read the first paragraph aloud, as if you were addressing a live audience.

These are the times that try men's souls. The summer soldier and the sunshine patriot will, in this crisis, shrink from the service of their country; but he that stands it now deserves the love and thanks of man and woman. Tyranny, like hell, is not easily conquered; yet we have this consolation with us, that the harder the conflict, the more glorious the triumph. What we obtain A too cheap, we esteem too lightly: it is dearness only that gives everything its value. Heaven knows how to put a proper price upon its goods; and it would be strange indeed if so celestial an article as freedom should not be highly rated. Britain, with an army to enforce her tyranny, has B declared that she has a right (not only to tax) but "to bind us in all cases whatsoever,"[1] and if being bound in that manner is not slavery, then is there not such a thing as slavery upon earth. Even the expression is impious; for so unlimited a power can belong only to God.

Whether the independence of the continent was declared too soon, or delayed too long, I will not now enter into as an argument; my own simple opinion is, that had it been eight months earlier, it would have been much better. We did not make a proper use of last winter, neither could we, while we were in a dependent state. However, the fault, if it were one, was all our own; we have none to blame but ourselves. But no great deal is lost yet. All that Howe[2] has been doing for this month past is rather a ravage than a conquest, which the spirit of the Jerseys,[3] a year ago, would have quickly repulsed, and which time and a little resolution will soon recover.

I have as little superstition in me as any man living, but my secret opinion has ever been, and still is, that God Almighty will not give up a people to military destruction, or leave them unsupportedly to perish, who have so earnestly and so repeatedly sought to avoid the calamities of war, by every decent method which wisdom could invent. Neither have I so much of the infidel in me as to suppose that He has relinquished the government of the world, and given us up to the care of devils; and as I do not, I cannot see on what grounds the King of Britain can look up to heaven for help against us: a common murderer, a highwayman, or a housebreaker has as good a pretense as he.

1. **"to bind . . . whatsoever":** Part of the British Parliament's response to Colonial protest over the "Intolerable Acts" was to rescind taxes while retaining the right to tax and "to bind [the Colonies] in all cases whatsoever."

2. **Howe:** Lord William Howe, commander of the British forces in America.
3. **Jerseys:** New Jersey was divided into East and West Jersey at the time.

Literature and Language: Writing Compound Sentences
Point out some of Paine's very short sentences that sound like **aphorisms,** or wise sayings. There's no fat in these sentences; not a word is wasted.

Sometimes Paine connects two such bare-boned sentences with a semicolon to create a **compound sentence.** Have students recall that a compound sentence contains two simple sentences connected with a semicolon or a coordinating conjunction. Students who wish to review this material should turn to **Grammar, Usage, and Mechanics: A Reference Guide.**

Ask students to find more examples of Paine's bare-boned sentences. Then have them write three compound sentences about the Revolution or about Tom Paine.

'Tis surprising to see how rapidly a panic will sometimes run through a country. All nations and ages have been subject to them: Britain has trembled like an ague[4] at the report of a French fleet of flat-bottomed boats; and in the fourteenth century the whole English army, after ravaging the kingdom of France, was driven back like men petrified with fear; and this brave exploit was performed by a few broken forces collected and headed by a woman, Joan of Arc. Would that heaven might inspire some Jersey maid to spirit up her countrymen, and save her fair fellow sufferers from ravage and ravishment! Yet panics, in some cases, have their uses; they produce as much good as hurt. Their duration is always short; the mind soon grows through them, and acquires
A a firmer habit than before. But their peculiar advantage is that they are the touchstones of sincerity and hypocrisy, and bring things and men to light, which might otherwise have lain forever undiscovered. In fact, they have the same effect on secret traitors, which an imaginary apparition would have upon a private murderer. They sift out the hidden thoughts of man, and hold them up in public to the world. Many a disguised Tory[5] has lately shown his head, that shall penitentially solemnize with curses the day on which Howe arrived upon the Delaware.

B As I was with the troops at Fort Lee, and marched with them to the edge of Pennsylvania, I am well acquainted with many circumstances, which those who live at a distance know but little or nothing of. Our situation there was exceedingly cramped, the place being a narrow neck of land between the North River[6] and the Hackensack. Our force was inconsiderable, being not one fourth so great as Howe could bring against us. We had no army at hand to have relieved the garrison, had we shut ourselves up and stood on our defense. Our ammunition, light artillery, and the best part of our stores had been removed on the apprehension that Howe would endeavor to penetrate the Jerseys, in which case Fort Lee could be of no use to us; for it must occur to every thinking man, whether in the army or not, that these kind of field forts are only for temporary purposes, and last in use no longer than the enemy directs his force against the particular object, which such forts are raised to defend. Such was our situation and condition at Fort Lee on the morning of the 20th of November, when an officer arrived with information that the enemy with 200 boats had landed about seven miles above. Major General Green, who commanded the garrison, immediately ordered them under arms, and sent express to General Washington at the town of Hackensack, distant, by the way of the ferry, six miles. Our first object was to secure the bridge over the Hackensack, which laid up the river between the enemy and us, about six miles from us, and three from them. General Washington arrived in about three quarters of an hour, and marched

COMMON SENSE;

ADDRESSED TO THE

INHABITANTS

OF

AMERICA,

On the following interefting

SUBJECTS.

I. Of the Origin and Defign of Government in general, with concife Remarks on the Englifh Conftitution.

II. Of Monarchy and Hereditary Succeffion.

III. Thoughts on the prefent State of American Affairs.

IV. Of the prefent Ability of America, with fome mifcellaneous Reflections.

Man knows no Mafter fave creating HEAVEN,
Or thofe whom choice and common good ordain.
THOMSON.

PHILADELPHIA;
Printed, and Sold, by R. BELL, in Third-Street.
MDCCLXXVI.

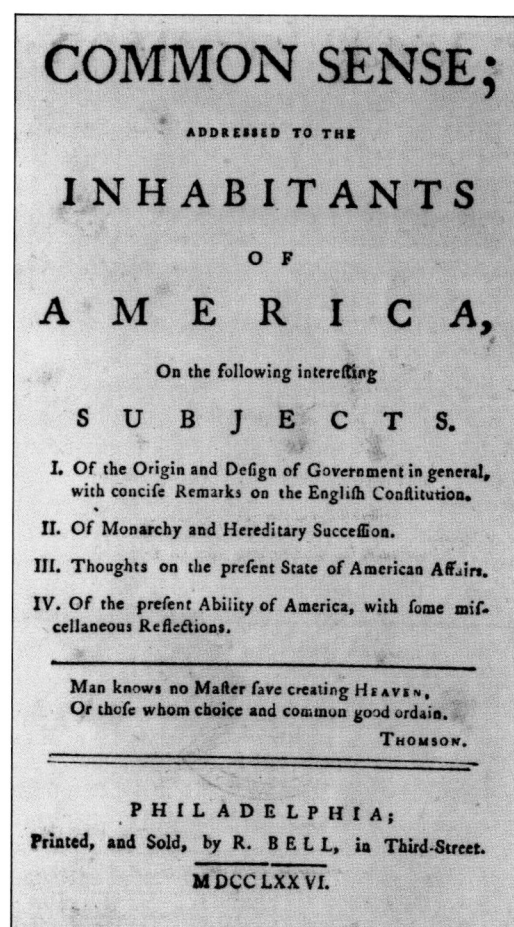

Title page of the first edition of *Common Sense* (1776).

The Library of Congress.

4. **ague:** fit of shivering.
5. **Tory:** supporter of British rule.
6. **North River:** the Hudson River.

A. Expansion
Explain to students that *touchstone* means "something that tests genuineness or value." You may wish to tell them that a touchstone was a kind of black stone used for testing the purity of gold or silver. The streak left by rubbing the precious metals against the touchstone indicated their purity.

B. Expansion (Challenging)
Ask students to research and report on Washington's early unsuccessful campaign around New York City in the late summer of 1776, the Battle of White Plains, and the retreat to Pennsylvania, which Paine briefly describes in *The Crisis, No. 1.*

A. Expansion
Paine thought it was a mistake for the British not to attack Brunswick (now New Brunswick, New Jersey) from Staten Island, where their troops were massed. Have students show on a map how such a move would have cut the American army off on their route to Pennsylvania as well as depriving them of the supplies stored at Brunswick.

B. Argument
Point out that Paine cleverly makes a harmless statement of the Tory tavern-keeper sound cowardly and selfish. It was, after all, quite reasonable of him to wish for peace in his day. Moreover, as a Tory, the tavern-keeper did not accept the inevitability of revolution and was therefore not asking that trouble be postponed for a later generation. This trick shows how ably Paine can fashion an argument out of the slightest materials.

at the head of the troops toward the bridge, which place I expected we should have a brush for; however, they did not choose to dispute it with us, and the greatest part of our troops went over the bridge, the rest over the ferry, except some which passed at a mill on a small creek, between the bridge and the ferry, and made their way through some marshy grounds up to the town of Hackensack, and there passed the river. We brought off as much baggage as the wagons could contain; the rest was lost. The simple object was to bring off the garrison. and march them on till they could be strengthened by the Jersey or Pennsylvania militia, so as to be enabled to make a stand. We stayed four days at Newark, collected our outposts with some of the Jersey militia, and marched out twice to meet the enemy, on being informed that they were advancing, though our numbers were greatly inferior to theirs. Howe, in my little opinion, committed a great error in generalship in not throwing a body of forces off from Staten Island through Amboy,[7] by which means he might have seized all our stores at Brunswick, and intercepted our march into Pennsylvania; but if we believe the power of hell to be limited, we must likewise believe that their agents are under some providential control.

A

I shall not now attempt to give all the particulars of our retreat to the Delaware; suffice it for the present to say, that both officers and men, though greatly harassed and fatigued, frequently without rest, covering, or provision, the inevitable consequences of a long retreat, bore it with a manly and martial spirit. All their wishes centered in one, which was that the country would turn out and help them to drive the enemy back. Voltaire[8] has remarked that King William[9] never appeared to full advantage but in difficulties and in action; the same remark may be made on General Washington, for the character fits him. There is a natural firmness in some minds which cannot be unlocked by trifles, but which, when unlocked, discovers a cabinet of fortitude; and I reckon it among those kind of public blessings, which we do not immediately see, that God hath blessed him with uninterrupted health, and given him a mind that can even flourish upon care.

7. **Amboy:** Perth Amboy, New Jersey.
8. **Voltaire:** French philosopher and writer (1694–1778), who had a great influence on Revolutionary thinkers.
9. **King William:** William III of England (reigned 1689–1702).

I shall conclude this paper with some miscellaneous remarks on the state of our affairs; and shall begin with asking the following question: Why is it that the enemy have left the New England provinces, and made these middle ones the seat of war? The answer is easy: New England is not infested with Tories, and we are. I have been tender in raising the cry against these men, and used numberless arguments to show them their danger, but it will not do to sacrifice a world either to their folly or their baseness. The period is now arrived, in which either they or we must change our sentiments, or one or both must fall. And what is a Tory? Good God! What is He? I should not be afraid to go with a hundred Whigs against a thousand Tories, were they to attempt to get into arms. Every Tory is a coward; for servile, slavish, self-interested fear is the foundation of Toryism; and a man under such influence, though he may be cruel, never can be brave.

But, before the line of irrecoverable separation be drawn between us, let us reason the matter together: Your conduct is an invitation to the enemy, yet not one in a thousand of you has heart enough to join him. Howe is as much deceived by you as the American cause is injured by you. He expects you will take up arms, and flock to his standard, with muskets on your shoulders. Your opinions are of no use to him, unless you support him personally, for 'tis soldiers, and not Tories, that he wants.

I once felt all that kind of anger, which a man ought to feel, against the mean principles that are held by the Tories: a noted one, who kept a tavern at Amboy, was standing at his door, with as pretty a child in his hand, about eight or nine years old, as I ever saw, and after speaking his mind as freely as he thought was prudent, finished with this unfatherly expression, "Well! Give me peace in my day." Not a man lives on the continent but fully believes that a separation must sometime or other finally take place, and a generous parent should have said, "If there must be trouble, let it be in my day, that my child may have peace;" and this single reflection, well applied, is sufficient to awaken every man to duty. Not a place upon earth might be so happy as America. Her situation is remote from all the wrangling world, and she has nothing to do but to trade with them. A man can distinguish himself between temper and principle, and I am as confident, as I am that God governs the world, that America will never be happy till

B

she gets clear of foreign dominion. Wars, without ceasing, will break out till that period arrives, and the continent must in the end be conqueror; for though the flame of liberty may sometimes cease to shine, the coal can never expire.

America did not, nor does not, want[10] force; but she wanted a proper application of that force. Wisdom is not the purchase of a day, and it is no wonder that we should err at the first setting off. From an excess of tenderness, we were unwilling to raise an army, and trusted our cause to the

A temporary defense of a well-meaning militia. A summer's experience has now taught us better; yet with those troops, while they were collected, we were able to set bounds to the progress of the enemy, and thank God! They are again assembling. I always considered militia as the best troops in the world for a sudden exertion, but they will not do for a long campaign. Howe, it is probable, will make an attempt on this city [Philadelphia], should he fail on this side the Delaware, he is ruined; if he succeeds, our cause is not ruined. He stakes all on his side against a part on ours; admitting he succeeds, the consequences will be that armies from both ends of the continent will march to assist their suffering friends in the middle states; for he cannot go everywhere: it is impossible. I consider Howe as the greatest enemy the Tories have; he is bringing a war into their country, which, had it not been for him and partly for themselves, they had been clear of. Should he now be expelled, I wish with all the devotion of a Christian that the names of Whig and Tory may never more be mentioned; but should the Tories give him encouragement to come, or assistance if he come, I as sincerely wish that our next year's arms may expel them from the continent, and the Congress appropriate their possessions to the relief of those who have suffered in well-doing. A single successful battle next year will settle the whole. America could carry on a two years' war by the confiscation of the property of disaffected persons, and be made happy by their expulsion. Say not that this is revenge; call it rather the soft resentment of a suffering people, who, having no object in view but the good of all, have staked their own all upon a seemingly doubtful event. Yet it is folly to argue against determined hardness; eloquence may strike the ear, and the language of sorrow draw forth the tear of compassion, but nothing can reach the heart that is steeled with prejudice.

Quitting this class of men, I turn with the warm ardor of a friend to those who have nobly stood, and are yet determined to stand the matter out. I call not upon a few, but upon all; not on this state or that state, but on every state: Up and help us; lay your shoulders to the wheel; better have too much force than too little, when so great an object is at stake. Let it be told to the future world that in the depth of winter, when nothing but hope and virtue could survive, that the city and the country, alarmed at one common danger, came forth to meet and to repulse it. Say not that thousands are gone, turn out your tens of thousands;[11] throw not the burden of the day upon Providence, but "show your faith by your works"[12] that God may bless you. It matters not where you live, or what rank B of life you hold, the evil or the blessing will reach you all. The far and the near, the home counties and the back,[13] the rich and poor will suffer or rejoice alike. The heart that feels not now is dead: the blood of his children will curse his cowardice who shrinks back at a time when a little might have saved the whole, and made them happy. I love the man that can smile in trouble, that can gather strength from distress, and grow brave by reflection. 'Tis the business of little minds to shrink; but he whose heart is firm, and whose conscience approves his conduct, will pursue his principles unto death. My own line of reasoning is to myself as straight and clear as a ray of light. Not all the treasures of the world, so far as I believe, could have induced me to support an offensive war, for I think it murder; but if a thief breaks into my house, burns and destroys my property, and kills or threatens to kill me, or those that are in it, and to "bind me in all cases whatsoever" to his absolute will, am I to suffer it? What signifies it to me, whether he who does it is a king or a common man; my countryman or not my countryman; whether it be done by an individual villain or an army of them? If we reason to the root of things we shall find no difference; neither can any just cause be assigned why we should punish in the one case and pardon in the other. Let them call me rebel, and welcome, I feel no

10. **want:** lack.

11. **thousands:** "Saul hath slain his thousands, and David his ten thousands" (1 Samuel 18:7).
12. **"show . . . works":** "Show me thy faith without thy works, and I will show thee my faith by my works" (James 2:18).
13. **back:** the back counties, or backwoods.

A. Expansion
Explain that by *militia* Paine means an army of citizens quickly raised to meet a temporary emergency. An army, by contrast, is better trained and equipped and more suitable for a long campaign.

B. Persuasion
Have a good reader read aloud the passage beginning "I call not upon a few . . ." and ending with ". . . and will pursue his principles unto death."

? Does this sound more like a persuasive speech or a political article? (Most will agree that it sounds like a speech.) Point out that it was such rousing rhetoric as this that raised the spirits of Washington's troops when *The Crisis, No. 1* was read aloud to them just before they crossed the Delaware to attack Trenton.

Reading Check Test

1. Paine believes that the colonies should have acted against Britain eight months before they did. *True*
2. Paine compares the king to a murderer and a thief. *True*
3. Paine describes the retreat to the Delaware as disorganized but courageous. *False*
4. Paine believed American isolation from Europe would create necessary hardship after gaining independence. *False*
5. Paine believed only those should fight who had nothing or no one to lose. *False*

Analyzing The Pamphlet
Identifying Facts

1. Paine says that the Americans have tried "every decent method" to avoid war; he also claims that the British king is evil and unjust.
2. Paine points out the military logic of the retreat, commends the fortitude of the retreating soldiers, and remarks that the hardship brings out people's best qualities.

Additional Writing Assignment
Explain that *mutual love* means the love that the colonies feel toward each other; similarly, *mutual fear* means the distrust each feels about the others. Then have students respond to the idea that "Mutual fear is the principal link in the chain of mutual love . . . ," indicating whether they agree or disagree. You may wish to point out that this epigrammatic statement closely resembles one made by John Donne, the English poet: "The best league between princes is a mutual fear of each other."

Closure
Have students list the arguments that Paine uses to convince his audience. Ask students, also, to summarize Paine's final, emotional appeal.

The Battle of Princeton, New Jersey by William Mercer (1777). Oil.
Historical Society of Pennsylvania.

concern from it; but I should suffer the misery of devils were I to make a whore of my soul by swearing allegiance to one whose character is that of a sottish, stupid, stubborn, worthless, brutish man. I conceive likewise a horrid idea in receiving mercy from a being, who at the last day shall be shrieking to the rocks and mountains to cover him, and fleeing with terror from the orphan, the widow, and the slain of America.

There are cases which cannot be overdone by language, and this is one. There are persons, too, who see not the full extent of the evil which threatens them; they solace themselves with hopes that the enemy, if he succeeds, will be merciful. It is the madness of folly to expect mercy from those who have refused to do justice; and even mercy, where conquest is the object, is only a trick of war; the cunning of the fox is as murderous as the violence of the wolf, and we ought to guard equally against both. Howe's first object is, partly by threats and partly by promises, to terrify or seduce the people to deliver up their arms and receive mercy. The ministry recommended the same plan to Gage,[14] and this is what the Tories call making their peace, "a peace which passeth all understanding"[15] indeed! A peace which would be the immediate forerunner of a worse ruin than any we have yet thought of. Ye men of Pennsylvania, do reason upon these things! Were the back counties to give up their arms, they would fall an easy prey to the Indians, who are all armed: this perhaps is what some Tories would not be sorry for. Were the home counties to deliver up their arms, they would be exposed to the resentment of the back counties, who would then have it in their power to chastise their defection at pleasure. And were any one state to give up its arms, that state must be garrisoned by all Howe's army of Britons and Hessians[16] to preserve it from the anger of the rest. Mutual fear is the principal link in the chain of mutual love, and woe be to that state that breaks the compact. Howe is mercifully inviting you to barbarous destruction, and men must be either rogues or fools that will not see it. I dwell not upon the vapors of imagination: I bring reason to your ears, and, in language as plain as A,B,C, hold up truth to your eyes.

I thank God that I fear not. I see no real cause for fear. I know our situation well, and can see the way out of it. While our army was collected, Howe dared not risk a battle; and it is no credit to him that he decamped from the White Plains,[17] and waited a mean opportunity to ravage the defenseless Jerseys; but it is great credit to us, that with a handful of men, we sustained an orderly retreat for near a hundred miles, brought off our ammunition, all our field pieces, the greatest part of our stores, and had four rivers to pass.

14. **Gage:** General Thomas Gage, Howe's predecessor.
15. **"a peace . . . understanding":** an ironic echo of St. Paul's Epistle to the Philippians 4:7.
16. **Hessians:** German mercenary troops from the region of Hesse and elsewhere who fought on the British side.
17. **White Plains:** Howe had defeated Washington at White Plains, New York, but had failed to press his advantage.

He suggests that only God could have prevented the British from attacking the troops at Perth Amboy and halting the march.

3. Paine is addressing "these middle provinces"—primarily those colonists who are Tory sympathizers.

Paine tries to persuade the Tories of their errors by asserting that self-interested fear is the foundation of Toryism and by warning them that their conduct is an invitation to the enemy.

4. The point of the anecdote is to emphasize that allegiance to the king, based on selfish fear, is merely deferring a conflict that is inevitable.

5. Paine states that the colonists' choice is between a "glorious issue"—that is, triumph and independence—and enslavement by the British.

To make it vivid, Paine draws a picture of enslavement that includes such details as ravaged country, depopulated cities, unsafe houses, and "our homes turned into barracks and bawdy houses for the Hessians."

Interpreting Meanings

6. Paine's main idea is that the Colonies must stand together against Britain. He supports this by saying that even the Tories will be crushed after their usefulness to the British is over. He also states that even if one colony is conquered by the British, all of the others will still be fighting.

7. Paine is suggesting that such people are willing to stand by their country only when it is as easy and pleasant as sunny summer weather to do so. The images are appropriate because they conjure up universal, easily understandable mental pictures.

8. In this metaphor, Paine suggests that self-interest—mutual protection—may be the most compelling reason for standing united.

9. Paine is arguing that it is as fair to rebel against England, which has trespassed on the colonists' rights, as it is to turn on a thief who trespasses on one's own property.

10. Student answers will vary. Direct them particularly to the first paragraph and to passage B on page 97.

None can say that our retreat was precipitate, for we were near three weeks in performing it, that the country[18] might have time to come in. Twice we marched back to meet the enemy, and remained out till dark. The sign of fear was not seen in our camp, and had not some of the cowardly and disaffected inhabitants spread false alarms through the country, the Jerseys had never been ravaged. Once more we are again collected and collecting; our new army at both ends of the continent is recruiting fast, and we shall be able to open the next campaign with sixty thousand men, well armed and clothed. This is our situation, and who will may know it. By perseverance and fortitude, we have the prospect of a glorious issue; by cowardice and submission, the sad choice of a variety of evils—a ravaged country—a depopulated city—habitations without safety, and slavery without hope—our homes turned into barracks and bawdy houses for Hessians, and a future race to provide for, whose fathers we shall doubt of. Look on this picture and weep over it! And if there yet remains one thoughtless wretch who believes it not, let him suffer it unlamented.

Common Sense
1776

18. **country:** local volunteers.

Responding to the Pamphlet

Analyzing the Pamphlet

Identifying Facts

1. What reasons does Paine give for his confidence that Divine help will be given to the Americans and not to the British?
2. Washington's march across New Jersey to the Delaware was actually a retreat from General Howe's British forces. Explain how Paine makes the event seem positive, even heroic. How does he link the results of the retreat to Divine Providence?
3. Find details in the middle of the essay that identify at least part of Paine's audience. What **arguments** does he use to persuade these readers of their errors?
4. Explain Paine's point in telling the anecdote about the Tory tavern keeper and his child.
5. What powerful emotional appeal does Paine make in the conclusion of his essay to sum up the choice facing the colonists? List the descriptive details that make this appeal especially vivid.

Interpreting Meanings

6. What is Paine's **main idea**? What are his chief supporting details?
7. The pamphlet opens with an emotional statement that is now famous, and it continues with two equally famous **images.** What kinds of people does Paine identify with summer and sunshine? Why are these images appropriate?
8. Explain the meaning of Paine's **metaphor,** "Mutual fear is the principal link in the chain of mutual love." Do you agree or disagree with this idea, and why?
9. An **analogy** is a comparison between two things that are alike in certain respects. Analogies are used often in argument and persuasion to demonstrate the logic of one idea by showing how it is similar to another, accepted idea. Analogies can be tricky, because few ideas or situations are completely alike in all aspects. What analogy does Paine draw when he talks about the thief (page 97)? What point is he making, and how might an opponent answer?
10. How do you think people today would respond to Paine's pamphlet? Are any of his arguments applicable to contemporary political situations? Explain.

Writing About the Pamphlet

A Creative Response

1. **Writing a Firsthand Account.** Imagine you are one of the volunteers who listened to this pamphlet being read a few days before Christmas 1776, just before you were to cross the frozen Delaware River and attack General Howe in Trenton. In a paragraph, explain how you felt while the pamphlet was being read, and describe the responses of the people around you.

A Critical Response

2. **Evaluating a Generalization.** "Not a place upon earth might be so happy as America. Her situation is remote from all the wrangling world, and she has nothing to do but to trade with them. . . . I am . . . confident . . . that America will never be happy till she gets clear of foreign dominion." In a brief essay, explain your evaluation of these words. How would you reply to Paine, in terms of the world as it exists today?

A. Expansion
It was a great tribute to Jefferson's reputation as a writer that he should have been chosen as the principal author of the Declaration of Independence when he had been a member of the Continental Congress for only a month.

B. Humanities Connection: Discussing the Fine Art
Like Thomas Jefferson, who is the subject of this portrait, Charles Willson Peale (1741–1827), its painter, was a man of universal interests and abilities. In his long life, Peale was an artist, inventor, naturalist, soldier, scientist, writer, and museum proprietor. This portrait, along with those of John Quincy Adams, George Washington, Benjamin Franklin, Henry Clay, John Paul Jones, and other distinguished Americans who sat for Peale formed the basis of the painter's Gallery of Distinguished Personages, a major attraction in his museum in Philadelphia.

Thomas Jefferson (1743–1826)

Architect, botanist, paleontologist, linguist, musician, and statesman, Thomas Jefferson displayed the wide range of interests that we associate with the eighteenth-century mind at its best. President John F. Kennedy reminded listeners of this once at an official dinner honoring winners of the Nobel Prize. Kennedy said that the White House had not seen such a great collection of talent since Thomas Jefferson dined there alone. Like Benjamin Franklin, Jefferson longed for time for his own research; also like Franklin, he was too valuable to his country to be spared such time for very long.

Jefferson was born in the red-clay country of what is now Albemarle County, Virginia, on 400 acres of land that his father had acquired for a bowl of punch. (Like many Virginians, Jefferson's father was land-hungry. When he died, he left his son more than 5,000 acres.) The elder Jefferson, a surveyor and magistrate, died when Thomas was fourteen. But he had provided his son with an excellent classical education and encouraged the many scientific interests that would occupy Jefferson for the rest of his life.

After attending the College of William and Mary, Jefferson became a lawyer. Soon he was a member of the Virginia House of Burgesses, where he established friendships with other young public servants, such as Patrick Henry. He was a spokesman for the rights of personal liberty and religious freedom, and a vocal opponent of institutions that infringed on those rights. In 1774, he wrote a pamphlet called *A Summary View of the Rights of British America,* in which he urged the rejection of all British Parliamentary authority over the Colonies. The House of Burgesses considered the pamphlet's proposals too radical, but *A Summary View* established Jefferson's reputation as a writer and a thinker. Two years later, when he was thirty-three, his fame as a writer brought him an extraordinary opportunity. The Continental Congress elected him one of the authors of the Declaration of Independence. [A]

Four other writers worked with him on the wording of the Declaration that was submitted to the Congress: John Adams of Massachusetts; Roger Sherman of Connecticut; Robert L. Livingston of New York; and Benjamin Franklin of Pennsylvania. Few changes were made by these other writers, but the Congress insisted on several major alterations. Jefferson was upset by what he called "mutilations" of his document.

[B]

Thomas Jefferson by Charles Willson Peale (late 18th century).

Independence National Historical Park Collection.

During the Revolution, Jefferson served for a time as governor of Virginia. When the British invaded Virginia, he retired to Monticello, the home he had designed himself. There he devoted himself to the pleasures of family life and to scientific research. He composed most of his *Notes on the State of Virginia* during this period.

Jefferson's beloved wife died in 1782. A year later he returned to public life, in part as an escape from private grief. He served as minister to France and, with Benjamin Franklin, helped to negotiate the treaty that formally ended the Revolutionary War in 1783. He later became George Washington's secretary of state. After losing the 1796 presidential election to John Adams, he served as Adams's vice-president (a post that, at

SUPPLEMENTARY SUPPORT MATERIALS
1. Vocabulary Activity Worksheet (*CCB*)
2. Review and Response Worksheet: Parallelism (*CCB*)
3. Selection Test (*CCB*)

DEVELOPING VOCABULARY
The following words from the autobiography are tested in the Selection Test. (See also Vocabulary Activity Worksheet.)

censure, to relinquish, complaisance, redress, to expunge

PREPARATION
ESTABLISHING A PURPOSE. You might ask students to read through the Declaration once, skipping the underlined parts as much as possible, and then reread the whole, paying special attention to the parts struck out. Ask them to try to decide whether the changes made by the Congress make the Declaration a stronger or a weaker statement.

A. Expansion
John Dickinson (1732–1808) had objected in his famous *Letters from a Farmer in Pennsylvania* to British laws he considered not only unfair to the colonists but also illegal under British law; however, Dickinson favored economic pressures and conciliation rather than revolt. For this reason, he refused to sign the Declaration. Dickinson was later the main author of the Articles of Confederation and a defender of the American Constitution.

that time, was awarded to the loser in the presidential contest).

In 1800, Jefferson was elected America's third president. A determined opponent of federal power, Jefferson was nevertheless responsible for one of the most sweeping federal actions of his age—the Louisiana Purchase. The acquisition from France of more than 820,000 square miles of western land would later be divided into thirteen states.

After his presidency ended in 1809, Jefferson retired once again to Monticello. Much of his energy during these years of retirement was devoted to establishing the University of Virginia. Jefferson helped to plan its courses of study and designed many of its buildings.

In 1826, both Jefferson (at eighty-three) and John Adams (at ninety) became gravely ill. Both hoped to live to see the fiftieth anniversary of the independence they had done so much to ensure. Jefferson died on the morning of July 4, several hours before Adams (whose last words were, "Thomas Jefferson still survives"). The epitaph Jefferson composed for himself clearly states which of his many accomplishments he considered most important:

> Here was buried Thomas Jefferson, Author of the Declaration of Independence, of the Statute of Virginia for religious freedom, and Father of the University of Virginia.

FROM THE AUTOBIOGRAPHY

In this extract from his *Autobiography*, Jefferson offers a fascinating glimpse of how the most celebrated document in American history was put together. The underlined passages in the Declaration show the parts omitted by Congress. The words added by Congress are in the margins. As you read, think about why Congress may have made the changes it did in the original draft.

The Declaration of Independence

Congress proceeded the same day to consider the Declaration of Independence, which had been reported and lain on the table the Friday preceding, and on Monday referred to a committee of the whole. The pusillanimous[1] idea that we had friends in England worth keeping terms with, still haunted the minds of many. For this reason, those passages which conveyed censures on the people of England were struck out, lest they should give them offense. The clause too, reprobating the enslaving the inhabitants of Africa, was struck out in complaisance to South Carolina and Georgia, who had never attempted to restrain the importation of slaves, and who, on the contrary, still wished to continue it. Our northern brethren also, I believe, felt a little tender under those censures; for though their people had very few slaves themselves, yet they had been pretty considerable carriers of them to others. The debates, having taken up the greater parts of the 2nd, 3rd, and 4th days of July, were, on the evening of the last, closed; the Declaration was reported by the committee, agreed to by the House, and signed by every member present, except Mr. Dickinson.[2] A As the sentiments of men are known not only by what they receive, but what they reject also, I will state the form of the Declaration as originally reported. The parts struck out by Congress shall be distinguished by a black line drawn under them, and those inserted by them shall be placed in the margin, or in a concurrent column.

1. **pusillanimous** (pyo͞o's'l·an'ə·məs): cowardly.

2. **Mr. Dickinson:** John Dickinson of Pennsylvania, who opposed the Declaration.

Literature and Language: Using Pronouns
Focus on a single passage in the Declaration of Independence; ask students to follow the written text as you read aloud a rewritten version with all pronouns omitted:

> The Founding Fathers hold these truths to be self-evident: that all men are created equal; that all men are endowed by all men's Creator with inherent and inalienable rights; that among these inherent and inalienable rights . . .

Continue with the rest of the passage, replacing all pronouns with the nouns they refer to. Students should see that pronouns make the sentences shorter and smoother by avoiding awkward repetition of nouns.

If necessary, have students use **Grammar, Usage, and Mechanics: A Reference Guide** to review pronoun forms. Then have students look at the first two paragraphs of the Declaration of Independence and identify each pronoun and antecedent they find.

A. Expansion (Challenging) Have students research and report on the Declaration of the Rights of Man and the Citizen, the "bill of rights" of the French Revolution. (An article including all or most of the text may be found in major encyclopedias.) Ask students to compare the principles set forth in the document with those contained in the Declaration of Independence. **(Less Challenging)** Have students summarize in their own words the political philosophy set forth in the second paragraph of the Declaration. Specifically, they should identify the following: the standard against which human laws can be measured ("laws of nature"); the natural rights of all people; the main function of a government; and the source of the powers of a government.

A Declaration by the Representatives of the United States of America, in General Congress Assembled

When, in the course of human events, it becomes necessary for one people to dissolve the political bands which have connected them with another, and to assume among the powers of the earth the separate and equal station to which the laws of nature and of nature's God entitle them, a decent respect to the opinions of mankind requires that they should declare the causes which impel them to the separation.

A We hold these truths to be self evident: that all men are created equal; that they are endowed by their Creator with inherent and inalienable rights (certain); that among these are life, liberty, and the pursuit of happiness; that to secure these rights, governments are instituted among men, deriving their just powers from the consent of the governed; that whenever any form of government becomes destructive of these ends, it is the right of the people to alter or to abolish it, and to institute new government, laying its foundation on such principles, and organizing its powers in such form, as to them shall seem most likely to effect their safety and happiness. Prudence, indeed, will dictate that governments long established should not be changed for light and transient causes; and accordingly all experience hath shown that mankind are more disposed to suffer while evils are sufferable, than to right themselves by abolishing the forms to which they are accustomed. But when a long train of abuses and usurpations, begun at a distinguished[3] period and pursuing invariably the same object, evinces a design to reduce them under absolute despotism, it is their right, it is their duty to throw off such government, and to provide new guards for their future security. Such has been the patient sufferance of these colonies; and such is now the necessity which constrains them to expunge (alter) their former systems of government. The history of the present king of Great Britain is a history of unremitting (repeated) injuries and usurpations, among which appears no solitary fact to contradict the uniform tenor of the rest, but all have (all having) in direct object the establishment of an absolute tyranny over these states. To prove this, let facts be submitted to a candid world for the truth of which we pledge a faith yet unsullied by falsehood.

He has refused his assent to laws the most wholesome and necessary for the public good.

He has forbidden his governors to pass laws of immediate and pressing importance, unless suspended in their operation till his assent should be obtained; and, when so suspended, he has utterly neglected to attend to them.

He has refused to pass other laws for the accommodation of large districts of people, unless those people would relinquish

3. **distinguished:** discernible.

The Declaration of Independence (detail) by John Trumbull (1786–1794). Oil.

Yale University Art Gallery, New Haven, Connecticut.

Humanities Connection: Discussing the Fine Art
John Trumbull (1756–1843), who as a young man served as an aide to George Washington during the Revolutionary War, dedicated his art to recording important events in his country's struggle for freedom. *The Declaration of Independence,* of which a detail is reproduced here, is a famous example of Trumbull's work. During the eight years he worked on this painting, Trumbull was meticulous in painting the likenesses of his subjects, visiting many of them long after the event to make sketches and working drawings. In the painting, Thomas Jefferson is shown handing the Declaration to the seated John Hancock, the president of the Continental Congress. Benjamin Franklin stands at Jefferson's left, and John Adams, dressed in brown, stands at the extreme left of the detail.

A. Expansion
The referent to the *he*'s on this page is "the present king of Great Britain" in the second paragraph of the Declaration.

B. Responding
? What effect does changing *suffered/totally to cease in some of these states* to *obstructed/by* have on the Declaration? (Answers will vary. Students should note that the change somewhat lessens the impact of the statement.)
? Why do you think the change was made? (Possibly as a political compromise with the delegates who did not want a complete break with the English people. See questions 6 and 7, page 107.)

the right of representation in the legislature, a right inestimable to them, and formidable to tyrants only.[4]

A He has called together legislative bodies at places unusual, uncomfortable, and distant from the depository of their public records, for the sole purpose of fatiguing them into compliance with his measures.

He has dissolved representative houses repeatedly and continually for opposing with manly firmness his invasions on the rights of the people.

He has refused for a long time after such dissolutions to cause others to be elected, whereby the legislative powers, incapable of annihilation, have returned to the people at large for their exercise, the state remaining, in the meantime, exposed to all the dangers of invasion from without and convulsions within.

He has endeavored to prevent the population of these states; for that purpose obstructing the laws for naturalization of foreigners, refusing to pass others to encourage their migrations hither, and raising the conditions of new appropriations of lands.

B He has suffered the administration of justice totally to cease in some of these states refusing his assent to laws for establishing judiciary powers. **obstructed / by**

He has made our judges dependent on his will alone for the tenure of their offices, and the amount and payment of their salaries.

He has erected a multitude of new offices, by a self-assumed power and sent hither swarms of new officers to harass our people and eat out their substance.

He has kept among us in time of peace standing armies and ships of war without the consent of our legislatures.

He has affected to render the military independent of, and superior to, the civil power.

He has combined with others[5] to subject us to a jurisdiction foreign to our constitutions and unacknowledged by our laws, giving his assent to their acts of pretended legislation for quartering large bodies of armed troops among us; for protecting them by a mock trial from punishment for any murders which they should commit on the inhabitants of these states; for cutting off our trade with all parts of the world; for imposing taxes on us without our consent; for depriving us [ ] of the benefits of trial by jury; for transporting us beyond seas to be tried for pretended offenses; for abolishing the free system of English laws in a neighboring province,[6] establishing therein an arbitrary government, and enlarging its boundaries, so as to render it at once an example and fit instrument for introducing the same absolute rule in to these states; for taking away our charters, abolishing our most valuable laws, and altering fundamentally the forms of our governments; for suspending our own legislatures, and declaring

in many cases

colonies

---

4. **formidable . . . only:** causing apprehension only to tyrants.
5. **others:** Parliament. Jefferson assumes throughout the Declaration that the British Parliament has no jurisdiction over America.
6. **province:** Quebec. French civil law was restored there in 1774.

CLOSURE
Have each student summarize, in two or three sentences, the purpose of the Declaration of Independence. Summaries should be shared orally in class.

READING CHECK TEST
1. The Declaration of Independence explains the necessity and right of the colonies to declare independence. *True*
2. Jefferson was unconcerned that Congress struck out passages of his draft. *False*
3. The Declaration blames the King of England, rather than the British people, for the state of war. *True*
4. Jefferson's draft of the Declaration states the king has waged war on human nature. *True*
5. The Declaration states that the colonies had declared allegience to the king, not to the jurisprudence of British Parliament. *True*

themselves invested with power to legislate for us in all cases whatsoever.

He has abdicated government here, withdrawing his governors, and declaring us out of his allegiance and protection.

by declaring us out of his protection, and waging war against us.

He has plundered our seas, ravaged our coasts, burnt our towns, and destroyed the lives of our people.

He is at this time transporting large armies of foreign mercenaries to complete the works of death, desolation, and tyranny already begun with circumstances of cruelty and perfidy[7] [ ] unworthy the head of a civilized nation.

scarcely paralleled in the most barbarous ages, and totally A

He has constrained our fellow citizens taken captive on the high seas, to bear arms against their country, to become the executioners of their friends and brethren, or to fall themselves by their hands.

He has [ ] endeavored to bring on the inhabitants of our frontiers, the merciless Indian savages, whose known rule of warfare is an undistinguished destruction of all ages, sexes and conditions of existence.

B **excited domestic insurrection among us, and has**

He has incited treasonable insurrections of our fellow citizens, with the allurements of forfeiture and confiscation of our property.

He has waged cruel war against human nature itself, violating its most sacred rights of life and liberty in the persons of a distant people who never offended him, captivating and carrying them into slavery in another hemisphere, or to incur miserable death in their transportation thither. This piratical warfare, the opprobrium of INFIDEL powers, is the warfare of the CHRISTIAN king of Great Britain. Determined to keep open a market where MEN should be bought and sold, he has prostituted his negative[8] for suppressing every legislative attempt to prohibit or to restrain this execrable commerce. And that this assemblage of horrors might want no fact of distinguished die,[9] he is now exciting those very people to rise in arms among us, and to purchase that liberty of which he has deprived them, by murdering the people on whom he also obtruded them: thus paying off former crimes committed against the LIBERTIES of one people, with crimes which he urges them to commit against the LIVES of another.

In every stage of these oppressions we have petitioned for redress in the most humble terms: our repeated petitions have been answered only by repeated injuries.

A prince whose character is thus marked by every act which may define a tyrant is unfit to be the ruler of a [ ] people who mean to be free. Future ages will scarcely believe that the hardiness of one man adventured, within the short compass of twelve years only, to lay a foundation so broad and so undisguised for tyranny over a people fostered and fixed in principles of freedom.

free

7. **perfidy:** betrayal of trust; treachery.
8. **negative:** veto.
9. **distinguished die:** clear stamp.

A. Responding
? What effect does adding the words *scarcely paralleled in the most barbarous ages, and totally* have on the Declaration? (Adding these words increases the severity of the charges made against George III.)

B. Parallelism
Notice that the final draft of the Declaration has eighteen paragraphs beginning with "He has" or "He is."
? What do these paragraphs have in common? (Each is an offense charged to the King of England.)

ANALYZING THE DECLARATION
Identifying Facts

1. The Congress felt that a "decent respect" for the opinions of others required them to explain the reasons for such a drastic and violent action.

2. Jefferson cites as truths that "all men are created equal," and have "certain inalienable rights" that include "life, liberty, and the pursuit of happiness."

3. Among these offenses are: the refusal to assent to necessary laws; the harassment of legislative bodies; the capricious dissolution of the "representative houses"; the attempt to prevent the states from being settled and populated; the coercion of judges; the maintenance of hostile standing armies and warships in the colonies without the colonists' consent; the plunder of the seas and coasts and the destruction of the towns; the coercion of citizens taken prisoner on the high seas; the inciting of the Indians to war and of the fellow citizens to insurrection.

A. Expansion
You may wish to explain that the parchment copy of the Declaration was badly damaged in an attempt in 1823 to make a copperplate facsimile and is now barely legible in parts. The Declaration is now on display in the National Archives Building in Washington, D.C.

Nor have we been wanting in attentions to our British brethren. We have warned them from time to time of attempts by their legislature to extend a jurisdiction over these our states. We have reminded them of the circumstances of our emigration and settlement here, no one of which could warrant so strange a pretension: that these were effected at the expense of our own blood and treasure, unassisted by the wealth or the strength of Great Britain: that in constituting indeed our several forms of government, we had adopted one common king, thereby laying a foundation for perpetual league and amity with them: but that submission to their parliament was no part of our constitution, nor ever in idea, if history may be credited: and, we [ ] appealed to their native justice and magnanimity as well as to the ties of our common kindred to disavow these usurpations which were likely to interrupt our connection and correspondence. They too have been deaf to the voice of justice and of consanguinity, and when occasions have been given them, by the regular course of their laws, of removing from their councils the disturbers of our harmony, they have, by the free election, reestablished them in power. At this very time too, they are permitting their chief magistrate to send over not only soldiers of our common blood, but Scotch and foreign mercenaries to invade and destroy us. These facts have given the last stab to agonizing affection, and manly spirit bids us to renounce forever these unfeeling brethren. We must endeavor to forget our former love for them, and hold them as we hold the rest of mankind, enemies in war, in peace friends. We might have been a free and a great people together; but a communication of grandeur and of freedom, it seems, is below their dignity. Be it so, since they will have it. The road to happiness and to glory is open to us, too. We will tread it apart from them, and acquiesce in the necessity which denounces[11] our eternal separation [ ]!

an unwarrantable / us

have

and we have conjured[10] them by

would inevitably

We must therefore

and hold them as we hold the rest of mankind, enemies in war, in peace friends.

We therefore the representatives of the United States of America in General Congress assembled, [ ] do in the name, and by the authority of the good people of these states reject and renounce all allegiance and subjection to the kings of Great Britain and all others who may hereafter claim by, through, or under them; we utterly dissolve all political connection which may heretofore have subsisted between us and the people or parliament of Great Britain: and finally we do assert and declare these colonies to be free and independent states, and that as free and independent states, they have full power to levy war, conclude peace, contract alliances, establish commerce, and to do all other acts and things which independent states may of right do.

appealing to the Supreme judge of the world for the rectitude of our intentions,

colonies, solemnly publish and declare, that these united colonies are, and of right ought to be, free and independent states; that they are absolved from all allegiance to the British crown, and that all political connection between them and the state of Great Britain is, and ought to be, totally dissolved;

And for the support of this declaration, [ ] we mutually pledge to each other our lives, our fortunes, and our sacred honor.

with a firm reliance on the protection of divine providence,

A [The Declaration thus signed on the 4th, on paper, was engrossed on parchment, and signed again on the 2d of August.

10. **conjured:** begged.
11. **denounces:** proclaims.

4. Jefferson refers to the deletion of the clause accusing the king of perpetuating the slave trade.

5. As one example students may point to the sentences listing grievances against the king. These sentences all begin with "He has. . . ." Parallelism also makes statements grand, formal, and memorable, as in the last line, where Jefferson speaks of "*our* lives, *our* fortunes, and *our* sacred honor."

Interpreting Meanings

6. Changes reflecting the colonists' desire to maintain ties to the English people include: the omission of the passage objecting to submission to the English Parliament; the change suggesting that the king's outrages "would inevitably" (rather than "were likely to") destroy the colonists' connection with the English people; the deletion of the passage swearing to "renounce forever these unfeeling brethren;" and the omission of mention of the *people* of Great Britain in the vow to "dissolve all political connection" with the English government.

Most of the citizens of the new country still felt close personal ties to England — many had relatives there.

7. Changes that seem to have been made for stylistic reasons include the change of "inherent and" to "certain"; the deletion of "begun at a distinguished period"; the change of "among which appears . . . have" to "all having"; the deletion of "and continually."

Changes that seem to have been made for political reasons include: the change from "expunge" to "alter"; the insertion of "in many cases"; the deletion of the reference to slavery; the change from "a people who mean to be free" to "a free people."

Responding to the Declaration

Analyzing the Declaration

Identifying Facts

1. The Declaration opens with a rational statement defending an act that was to have violent consequences. Explain why the Continental Congress wanted to publish its reasons for separating itself from Britain.
2. The word *self-evident* (added by Franklin) refers to the truths that are accessible to our common sense. List the truths that Jefferson cites in particular.
3. List the offenses charged to the King of England.
4. The omissions made by Congress are instructive. In the first paragraph of this passage from his *Autobiography,* Jefferson explains why one clause in particular was struck out. Which clause is it, and what precisely did it accuse the king of doing?
5. Jefferson frequently employs **parallelism,** which is the repeated use of sentences, clauses, or phrases with identical or similar structures. For example, when he cites the truths that are "self-evident," he begins each clause with *that.* The parallelism emphasizes Jefferson's view that all these truths are of equal importance. The parallel structure also creates a stately rhythm or cadence in the Declaration that you will hear if you listen to the words read aloud. Find at least two other sections of the Declaration in which parallel structures are repeated.

Interpreting Meanings

6. What changes indicate a desire on the part of the Congress not to make one last break—that is, with the English people themselves? Why do you think it would be important that the new country maintain its "consanguinity," or close kinship, with the English people?
7. The intent of the Congress is clarified when we examine the words that were changed in Jefferson's original draft. Which of the changes seem to have been adopted primarily for stylistic reasons (for clarity, or to avoid repetition, or to make greater impact)? Which seem to have been made for political reasons?

Writing About the Declaration

A Critical Response

1. **Analyzing Its Reasoning.** We think of the Declaration as a fundamentally political document, but it is also a carefully reasoned persuasive essay. In an essay of your own, explain how carefully reasoned the Declaration is and how persuasively it makes its points. Organize your own essay around answers to these questions: What are Jefferson's primary arguments? Where does he provide evidence to support his points? How does his conclusion effectively summarize and justify the arguments that have preceded it?
2. **Responding to a Point of View.** On March 31, 1776, Abigail Adams wrote this letter to her husband John Adams, who was on the committee preparing the Declaration of Independence. In a brief essay, explain your response to her letter. You might write in letter form to Abigail Adams herself.

> I long to hear that you have declared an independancy—and by the way, in the new Code of Laws which I suppose it will be necessary for you to make, I desire you would remember the ladies, and be more generous and favorable to them than your ancestors. Do not put such unlimited power into the hands of the husbands. Remember all men would be tyrants if they could. If particular care and attention is not paid to the ladies, we are determined to foment a rebellion, and will not hold ourselves bound by any laws in which we have no voice, or representation.
>
> —Abigail Adams

3. **Responding to Changes in the Document.** On July 14, 1776, Abigail Adams wrote to her husband again.

> I cannot but feel sorry that some of the most manly sentiments in the Declaration are expunged from the printed copy. Perhaps wise reasons induced it.
>
> —Abigail Adams

In a brief essay, give your opinion on at least two of the deleted passages. Is the document stronger or weaker because of these deletions? Why?

Analyzing Language and Style

Precise Meanings

Many words have been written in attempts to explain what Jefferson and the framers of the Declaration meant by the word *equal* and by the phrase *pursuit of happiness.*

1. Using a good dictionary, define what you think the word *equal* means in this document.
2. Write down at least three explanations of the phrase *pursuit of happiness.*
3. What does the word *equal* not mean?
4. What does *the pursuit of happiness* not mean?

A. Connections
As an alternative (or additional) approach to Jefferson's letter to Patsy, you might direct your students' attention to F. Scott Fitzgerald's letter to his daughter, Scotty, on page 552. Ask students to compare and contrast the two pieces of parental advice.

B. Expansion
By "more qualified than common," Jefferson means that he wishes his daughter to be more accomplished than young women of her class commonly were.

C. Expansion
By "loss after loss," Jefferson is referring to the death of his wife (Patsy's mother), discredit resulting from the British overrunning Virginia during his term as governor (1779–1781), and serious financial problems.

Primary Sources

A *A Letter from Jefferson to His Daughter*

In 1784, Jefferson was sent to Paris to work out the treaty ending the Revolutionary War. The next year he succeeded Benjamin Franklin as minister to France. He stayed in France for five years. His daughter Patsy was in a Catholic convent school in Paris when Jefferson wrote this letter from the south of France. (The wrist Jefferson complains of had been injured a few months earlier.)

Aix-en-Provence, March 28, 1787

"I was happy, my dear Patsy, to receive, on my arrival here, your letter, informing me of your good health and occupations. I have not written you sooner because I have been almost constantly on the road. My journey hitherto has been a very pleasing one. It was undertaken with the hope that the mineral waters of this place might restore strength to my wrist. Other considerations also concurred, instruction, amusement, and abstraction from business, of which I had too much at Paris. I am glad to learn that you are employed in things new and good, in your music and drawing. You know what have been my fears for some time past—that you do not employ yourself so closely as I could wish. You have promised me a more assiduous attention, and I have great confidence in what you promise. It is your future happiness which interests me, and nothing can contribute more to it (moral rectitude always excepted) than the contracting a habit of industry and activity. Of all the cankers of human happiness none corrodes with so silent, yet so baneful a tooth as indolence. . . . It is while we are young that the habit of industry is formed. If not then, it never is afterward. The fortune of our lives, therefore, depends on employing well the short period of youth. If at any moment, my dear, you catch yourself in idleness, start from it as you would from the precipice of a gulf. You are not, however, to consider yourself as unemployed while taking exercise. That is necessary for your health, and health is the first of all objects. For this reason, if you leave your dancing master for the summer, you must increase your other exercise.

"I do not like your saying that you are unable to read the ancient print of your Livy,[1] but [except] with the aid of your master. We are always equal to what we undertake with resolution. A little degree of this will enable you to decipher your Livy. If you always lean on your master, you will never be able to proceed without him. It is a part of the American character to consider nothing as desperate—to surmount every difficulty by resolution and contrivance. In Europe there are shops for every want: its inhabitants therefore have no idea that their wants can be furnished otherwise. Remote from all other aid, we are obliged to invent and to execute; to find means within ourselves, and not to lean on others. Consider, therefore, the conquering your Livy as an exercise in the habit of surmounting difficulties; a habit which will be necessary to you in the country where you are to live, and without which you will be thought a very helpless animal, and less esteemed. . . .

"You ask me to write you long letters. I will do it, my dear, on condition you will read them from time to time, and practice what they will inculcate. Their precepts will be dictated by experience, by a perfect knowledge of the situation in which you will be placed, and by the fondest love for you. This it is which makes me wish to see you more qualified than common. My expectations from you are high—yet not higher than you may attain. Industry and resolution are all that are wanting. Nobody in this world can make me so happy, or so miserable, as you. Retirement from public life will ere long become necessary for me. To your sister and yourself I look to render the evening of my life serene and contented. Its morning has been clouded by loss after loss, till I have nothing left but you. I do not doubt either your affection or dispositions. But great exertions are necessary, and you have little time to make them. Be industrious, then, my dear child. Think nothing unsurmountable by resolution and application and you will be all that I wish you to be.

". . . Continue to love me with all the warmth with which you are beloved . . . my dear Patsy."

1. **Livy:** Roman historian (59 B.C.–A.D. 17).

THE AMERICAN LANGUAGE

by Gary Q. Arpin

A In the years following the settlement of the New World, American English continued to develop, and differences between British and American usage became more and more apparent. British travelers to the New World noticed that Americans spoke with a nasality that was disagreeable to their British ears. The visitors also noticed what they thought of as "corruptions" of the language: words were being used in "barbarous" ways, and brand-new words were being coined.

Some of the differences between British and American English were caused by the simple fact of physical separation. Differences in pronunciation, for example, became marked as the accents of speakers on both sides of the ocean gradually changed. Differences are still apparent; for one example, British speakers omit the vowel before the second *r* in words like *secretary* and *laboratory,* but Americans deliberately pronounce all the syllables in such words.

Besides pronunciation, differences in usage also may result from physical separation. In the New World, for example, and especially in New England, it was (and is) common to hear someone speak of throwing a *rock.* In Britain, however, *rock* continued to refer only to a massive stone, such as Plymouth Rock. Throwing a rock would have seemed as odd to a British person as tossing a boulder.

Sometimes the meaning or usage of a word would change in England while Americans retained its older meaning. The American usage of *guess* to mean "suppose" is an example of this. In the eighteenth and nineteenth centuries, "I guess" sounded odd to British visitors, who would have said, "I suppose." But these visitors were unaware that "I guess" had been common in England until the eighteenth century. It even appears in the writings of Chaucer and Shakespeare. The British also criticized Americans for saying *fall* instead of *autumn,* apparently unaware that *fall* had been used in England until around 1750.

Americanisms and Their Critics

The word *Americanism* came into use to describe a word or expression that originated in the United States, or that was peculiar to the States. The word was first used in print in 1781 by the Reverend John Witherspoon, a Scottish clergyman who had come to this country in 1768 to become president of Princeton University. Witherspoon traveled a good deal and recorded words and phrases that were peculiar to the United States. Many of these words are so common today that it is hard to imagine a time when they might have been unusual. Among the Americanisms recorded by Witherspoon were *to notify,* meaning "to inform"; *mad,* in the

"Revolutionary" English

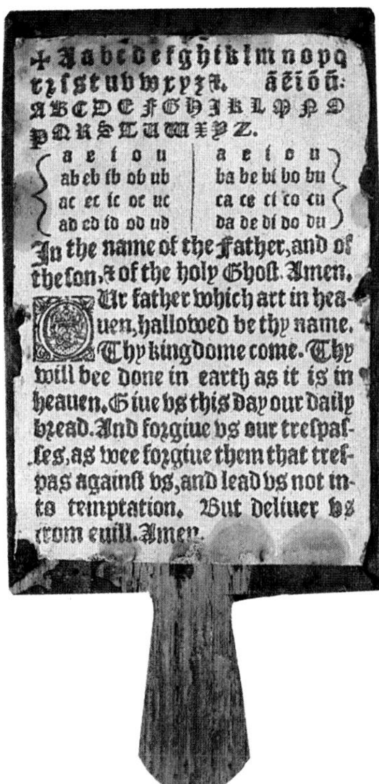

An English hornbook (17th century). A thin, transparent layer of horn protected the sheet of parchment. This was used as a child's textbook.

A. Expansion

? In what three fundamental ways do British and American English differ? (Pronounciation, usage, and vocabulary)

Comment From A Writer

While some language "purists" bemoaned the change from British to American English, Thomas Jefferson promoted it: "There are so many differences between us and England, of soil, climate, culture, productions, laws, religion and government, that we must be left far behind the march of circumstances, were we to hold ourselves rigorously to their standard. . . . Judicious neology can alone give strength and copiousness to language, and enable it to be the vehicle of new ideas."

A. Responding
Today, English language scholars know that English will never be a "complete" language. In the past few decades, for example, words have flooded into the English language with the advent of the space program and computers. Also, as new immigrant populations have entered the United States, their languages have had an effect on English.

? What events in this decade do you think will have a lasting effect on the English language? (Answers will vary. Students might note the popularity of home video movies and machines and the *glasnost* policy of the Soviet Union.)

B. Humanities Connection: Discussing the Illustration
The influence of the "blue-backed" speller, which sold more than eighty million copies in Webster's lifetime, was enormous. As a result of this speller, American spelling became simplified and uniform.

sense of "angry"; *chunks,* to describe big pieces of wood; *spell,* meaning "a period of time" (as in "a spell of bad weather"); *once in a while,* meaning "occasionally"; and *tote,* meaning "to carry."

A
Some critics considered English to be a complete language that had evolved through the centuries to a state of perfection in the eighteenth century. Any change was horrendous to them, especially any change brought about by a society of crude farmers in a barbarous land. As one writer put it in 1701, "A language, arrived at its zenith, requires no introduction of new words."

Twenty-seven years later, the same point was made by a British purist in response to a question put by Noah Webster. Webster had asked, "If a word becomes universally current in America . . . why should it not take its station in the language?" The British purist, a certain Captain Basil Hall, replied, "Because there are enough words already."

"If, as many people thought, literature was to be considered an authority for usage, then there was no authority in America."

But it is not hard to see the British point of view in this matter. An educated visitor to the former Colonies no doubt heard a great deal of crude and uneducated talk, as well as much that was simply strange or new. It would have been difficult to avoid negative judgments, much less to discover any richness in this language.

In addition, up until the mid-nineteenth century, there was no "American literature" to speak of. There was no demonstration, that is, of the *power* of the American idiom, no indication that American speech could lead to anything of lasting worth. If, as many people thought, literature was to be considered an authority for usage, then there was no authority in America.

Moreover, many people on both sides of the question expected, or feared, that the two forms of English would eventually grow separate until the two groups would no longer understand each other. They predicted that Americans, completely cut off from their past, would have to read the works of Shakespeare and Milton in translation!

B

94 AN EASY STANDARD

tually promiſed to aſſiſt each other, if they ſhould happen to be aſſaulted. They had not proceeded far, before they perceived a Bear making towards them with great rage. There were no hopes in flight; but one of them, being very active, ſprung up into a tree; upon which the other, throwing himſelf flat on the ground, held his breath, and pretended to be dead; remembering to have heard it aſſerted, that this creature will not prey upon a dead carcaſe. The bear came up, and after ſmelling to him ſome time, left him, and went on. When he was fairly out of ſight and hearing, the hero from the tree calls out—Well, my friend, what ſaid the bear? He ſeemed to whiſper you very cloſely. He did ſo, replied the other, and gave me this good piece of advice; never to aſſociate with a wretch, who in the hour of danger will deſert his friend.

TABLE XXXIII.

Words in which *ch* have the ſound of *k*.

CHRIST	cho-rus	chol-ic	char-ac-ter
chyle	te-trarch	chol-er	cat-e-chiſm
ſcheme	cha-os	ſchol-ar	pen-ta-teuch
ache	cho-ral	mon-arch	ſep-ul-cher
	e-poch	or-chal	tech-nic-al
chaſm	o-cher		al-chy-my
chriſm	tro-chee	ſchir-rous	an-cho-ret
tach			brach-i-al
	an-chor	ſtom-ach	lach-ry-mal
chord	chriſ-ten		mach-i-nate
loch	chym-iſt	pa-tri-arch	ſac-char-ine
	ech-o	eu-cha-riſt	ſyn-chro-niſm
ſchool	chal-ice		mich-ael-mas
or	ſched-ule	an-ar-chy	
choir	paſ-chal	chryſ-o-lite	chor-iſ-ter

OF PRONUNCIATION. 95

chron-i-cle	cha-lyb-e-rate	the-om-a-chy
or-cheſ-tra	a-nach-ro-niſm	
och-i-my	ſyn-ec-do-che	ar-chi-tec-ture
	pyr-rhich-i-us	an-ti-bac-chus
chi-me-ra	am-phib-ra-chus	
pa-ro-chi-al		cat-e-chet-ic-al
cha-mel-ion	mel-an-chol-y	
		bac-cha-nal-ian
tri-bach-us	chro-nol-o-gy	cat-e-chu-men
arch-an-gel	chi-rog-ra-phy	
me-chan-ic	cho-rog-ra-phy	ich-thy-ol-o-gy
ca-chex-y	chro-nom-e-ter	

FABLE VII.—*The* TWO DOGS.

HASTY and inconſiderate connections are generally attended with great diſadvantages; and much of every man's good or ill fortune depends upon the choice he makes of his friends.

A goodnatured Spaniel overtook a ſurly Maſtiff, as he was travelling upon the high road. Tray, although an entire ſtranger to Tyger, very civilly accoſted him; and if it would be no interruption, he ſaid, he ſhould be glad to bear him company on his way. Tyger

Spread from *The American Spelling Book* by Noah Webster, 1793 edition.

Rare Books and Manuscripts Division, New York Public Library.

COMMENT FROM A WRITER
A statement made by John Adams in 1780 about the growing influence of American English also explains why this form of English is spoken today in so many countries of the world: ". . . the increasing population in America, and their universal connection and correspondence with all nations will, aided by the influence of England in the world, whether great or small, force their language into general use. . . ."

"What language should Americans speak?"

The conflict between purists and advocates of change was especially heated in America in the eighteenth and nineteenth centuries, in part because of politics. On the American side, the rejection of English authority in language was for some an aspect of America's rejection of English political authority. In 1788, a march in New York supporting the ratification of the Constitution contained a language contingent. This group carried a scroll advocating the use of something called "Federal English."

The idea of a Federal English was supported by such notables as Noah Webster and John Adams. Advocates of Federal English were convinced that the importance of England in the world would decline and that of America would increase. A Federal English would establish the independence of American English and, at the same time, preserve the purity of the language in its new home.

The most radical political position on language argued for the establishment in America of a completely new language. At various times, French, Greek, and Hebrew were suggested as alternatives. Each had as its principal virtue, apparently, the fact that it was not English.

"Class distinctions were not marked by accent in America, as they were in Britain."

American English and American Democracy

Some proponents of American English were satisfied with things as they were. They pointed to the humble democratic character of the language as its greatest virtue: Class distinctions were not marked by accent in America, as they were in Britain, and geographical differences in speech were not nearly as important. ("America has no dialects," claimed one writer, somewhat overstating the case.) Because of this, an American would (in theory, at least) be immediately understood and accepted wherever he or she went in the country, which was not the case in England.

The American language had been democratized in other ways as well. For example, many English words denoting class had disappeared. In the best-known case, the words *master* and *servant* had been replaced by the less feudal-sounding *boss* and *help.* (British critics, though, pointed out that the differences here were simply a matter of custom. *Boss,* after all, comes from the Dutch *baas,* which also means "master.")

John Adams saw the connections between language and democracy when he recalled the historical links between oratory and opportunity in ancient Greece, the seat of democracy. Adams claimed that good language would be a means of establishing a natural aristocracy of merit. In 1780, he wrote:

> It is not to be disputed that the form of government has an influence upon language, and language in its turn influences not only the form of government, but the temper, the sentiments, and manners of the people.
>
> —John Adams

Rare books owned by Thomas Jefferson and given to start the Library of Congress.

Library of Congress.

READING CHECK TEST

1. A word or expression originating in the United States is called a(n) ________. *Americanism*
2. Noah Webster and John Adams advocated an American language, which they referred to as ________ English. *Federal*
3. The expression "to throw a rock" would sound strange to speakers in ________. *England*
4. The British criticized Americans for calling the season between summer and winter ________. *fall*
5. One American who opposed an academy to govern American English was ________. *Thomas Jefferson*

A. Responding
The fact that "language changes according to the way it is used" is a controversial idea among many language scholars. For example, while the word *author* is used by many Americans today as a verb as well as a noun, language purists continue to resist accepting the change.
? What are some other changes in language use that seem to be growing in acceptance? (Answers will vary. Students might mention the growing acceptance of *host* as a verb, the split infinitive, and *they* as a referent for *everyone.*)

He went on to predict that "eloquence will become the instrument for recommending men to their fellow citizens, and the principal means of advancement through the various ranks and offices."

Adams was arguing, when he wrote these words, for the establishment of an American Academy, which would try to govern the usage of English in America and protect it against whatever changes might originate in England in the future. Having established its independence from the British and its democratic purpose, American English would thereafter remain stable, or change only in approved ways. Adams, the political revolutionary, was a linguistic conservative.

"Language changes according to the way it is used, not the way authorities say it should be used."

But language tends to resist rules that people try to force on it. A [Language changes according to the way it is used, not the way authorities say it should be used.] Jefferson, perhaps the best linguist of the Revolutionary period, took the most reasonable view. Speaking of the foundations of an academy, he wrote:

> If, like the French Academicians, it were proposed to *fix* our language, it would be fortunate that the step was not taken in the days of our Saxon ancestors whose vocabulary would ill express the science of this day.
>
> —Thomas Jefferson

Thus Jefferson found himself at odds with both British and American purists. As is often the case in such circumstances, he was right. The move for an academy finally died, and the American language continued to develop in its own unpredictable and exuberant ways.

Analyzing Language

1. Each of the following American compounds contains a common English word whose meaning has been virtually lost in America, except in a very few specific usages. Use a dictionary to find the English meaning of the italicized words. Can you propose reasons why their meanings were lost in America?

   Chevy *Chase* | Boston *Common*
   cranberry *bog* | Berk*shire* Mountains

2. The following expressions are all Americanisms—they originated in America or have a usage peculiar to American speech. Refer to the *Dictionary of Americanisms* to find out what each word means and when it came into usage in American English. What do the words reveal about features and customs that were peculiar to American life?

   cold snap, dude, everglade, Indian summer, pot pie, ranch, salt lick, snowshoe

3. Eighteenth-century purists complained about the ways Americans adapted words to suit life in the New World. Their criticism was based on an assumption that words should develop historically from their roots, not in response to need and usage. Explain how the histories of the following words, all in common English usage, puncture the purists' argument. A good dictionary will give you the information you need.

   clue, companion, daughter, expedite, precocious, steward, town

4. Go to a library and look up the following words in the *Oxford Dictionary of the English Language,* or any other British dictionary. How is each word pronounced in England and in America?

   been, clerk, eat, laboratory, lieutenant, schedule

A. Expansion
As preparation for this assignment, you may want students to review Elements of Literature: Persuasion, page 92, and question 3, page 99. You may also find it helpful to ask students for examples from their own experience of the four fallacies listed on this page.

ANALYZING AND EVALUATING PERSUASION: LOGIC

Writing Assignment

A In a multi-paragraph essay, analyze and evaluate the logic used in Patrick Henry's "Speech to the Virginia Convention" (page 88).

Background

Persuasive writing or speaking attempts to influence people's beliefs and behavior. To be persuasive, speakers and writers use techniques that appeal both to reason and to the emotions. In this exercise, you will focus on **logic**, or the appeal to reason. (You will examine other persuasive techniques in the exercise that follows Unit Four, on page 321.)

Logic is correct reasoning; an error in logical thinking is called a **fallacy.** Watch for these common fallacies in persuasive speaking and writing.

1. **Either-or Fallacy.** This fallacy asserts that only two courses of action exist. "Either we invade Grenada, or Cuban Communism will take over the whole hemisphere." In almost every situation in life, there are more than two possible courses of action.
2. **False Analogy.** An **analogy** compares one situation with another. It suggests that, because there are certain similarities, the two situations are alike in all important respects. For example, Patrick Henry believed that the Colonists were being betrayed. He drew an analogy between their situation and Judas's betrayal of Jesus in the New Testament of the Bible: "Suffer not yourselves to be betrayed with a kiss." How alike are these two situations? Does the analogy strengthen or weaken his argument?
3. **Non Sequitur.** This Latin phrase means "It does not follow." The term refers to a conclusion that is forced onto an argument, even though it "does not necessarily follow" from what has been said. An example of a *non sequitur* would be saying that, because he deplores the way King George enslaves the Colonists, Patrick Henry also hates slavery of any kind (which was practiced in the Colonies).
4. **Appeal to Authority.** The opinion of an authority can lend weight to a persuasive argument, *when the authority is an expert in the matter being discussed.* But a movie star is not necessarily an expert in foreign affairs, so his or her endorsement of a political candidate shouldn't persuade you to vote for that candidate. Does Henry claim an authority for the Colonists' position? Could the British claim the same authority? What does that suggest about the logic of the appeal?

Prewriting

First, outline the main logical arguments in Patrick Henry's speech, beginning with paragraph 4, "I ask, gentlemen . . ." (page 90). **Paraphrase** (restate in your own words) Henry's reasons and his evidence. Here is one reader's work on the fourth paragraph. In the side notes, the reader comments on and responds to Henry's main idea.

I ask, gentlemen, sir, what means this martial array, if its purpose be not to force us to submission? Can gentlemen assign any other possible motive for it? Has Great Britain any enemy in this quarter of the world, to call for all this accumulation of navies and armies? No, sir, she has none. They are meant for us: They can be meant for no other. They are sent over to bind and rivet upon us those chains which the British ministry have been so long forging.

Henry's main idea is that there is only one reason for the presence of the British forces: to force the Colonists to submit to British demands.

Is this an either-or fallacy? Could there be another reason? It's possible, even if not probable, that the forces are there to protect the colonies. Maybe it's a show of force that would never be used. (There are contemporary parallels.)

Revising Essays As students revise their essays, refer them to **Grammar, Usage, and Mechanics: A Reference Guide** at the back of their books.

Exercises in Critical Thinking and Writing /*cont.*

Continue to outline Henry's arguments in paragraphs 5–8 in this same way. Write your own comments, questions, and responses beside the outline. Then evaluate the argument. Tell how effective you think the argument is, and why. Be sure to give reasons and examples to back up your evaluation.

Guidelines for Evaluating an Argument

1. What does the writer want me to do or think? (In other words, what is the writer's **purpose**?)
2. Does the writer **assume** (take for granted) anything that I don't think is true? If so, what are these assumptions?
3. What **reasons** does the writer give to try to convince me? (Outline the argument paragraph by paragraph.)
4. Are the reasons **opinions**, or are they provable **facts**? Are the reasons supported by specific **evidence** (incidents, examples, statistics)?
5. Are the writer's conclusions **logical**? That is, do they follow from the statements made?

Writing

Now write your essay analyzing and evaluating the logic of Patrick Henry's speech. You might follow this plan:

1. **Introduction:** Introduction identifying the title, the writer, and the writer's purpose. Give background information, if necessary. Include a **thesis statement** that gives your overall evaluation of the logic of the speech.
2. **Body:** Your **paraphrase** of Henry's main arguments along with your evaluation of the logic of each argument. (Are the reasons strong or weak? Is there sufficient evidence or not enough? Does the argument contain any fallacies?)
3. **Conclusion:** Concluding paragraph, summarizing your main points and stating your general response to the speech.

Here is one writer's introductory paragraph. Remember that your evaluation may be entirely different. Just be sure that you give specific evidence to support it.

When Patrick Henry stood up to make his speech to the Virginia Convention on March 23, 1775, his audience didn't know they were about to hear one of the all-time best examples of persuasive speaking. Henry's purpose was to persuade the delegates to the Convention that they must vote to arm the citizens and prepare for war with Britain. His speech was extremely effective because of its appeals to emotion, not because of its logic. In fact, some of Patrick Henry's logical arguments could be challenged.

Cites author, title, and date of speech.

Cites purpose of speech.

Ends with thesis statement.

Revising and Proofreading

Use the guidelines in the section at the back of this book, called **Writing About Literature,** to revise and proofread your essay.

AMERICAN ROMANTICISM

The Grand Canyon of Yellowstone (detail) by Thomas Moran (1872). Oil.

National Museum of American Art, Washington, D. C./Art Resource, N.Y. L.1968.84.1. Lent by the U.S. Dept. of the Interior.

UNIT THREE

Humanities Connection: Responding To The Fine Art

Thomas Moran (1837–1926) was one of the Hudson River school of painters, a group of American landscape painters whose favorite subjects were scenes of the Hudson River Valley. As with many other artists of that school, Moran's purpose was to bring moral and religious meaning to landscape.

? Compare this painting with the works of Thomas Cole (1801–1848) on pages 117 and 119. What is the subject matter of these three works? (Nature) How would you describe the way this subject is treated? (Student answers will vary. Students might suggest that nature is depicted as detailed, realistic, spacious, ominous, moody, or lonely.)

Teaching American Romanticism

The literature of Romanticism differs decisively from earlier American literature. Writers like Franklin and Jefferson were only secondarily men of letters, primarily builders of a nation. The entire nation's attention was on practical accomplishment—the opposite of Romanticism.

Romanticism, a movement that began in Europe, developed distinct American characteristics out of our colonial past and the development of the new nation. As students read the works in this and the following units, ask them to keep in mind the two principal ways in which the Romantic sensibility sought to rise above "dull realities": by exploring exotic settings, whether past or present; and by contemplating the natural world. Both activities were well suited to the luxuriant new land that faced Americans. It was inevitable that the first famous American novelist, James Fenimore Cooper, would be a Romantic celebrator of wilderness virtues.

Even while Cooper was taking Natty Bumppo into the frontier and celebrating American skill and initiative, the Fireside poets, as the text points out, "looked backward . . . at established European models." The first two poems in the unit, "To a Waterfowl" and "Thanatopsis," lend themsevles to a discussion of the question of whether poets such as Bryant were distinctively American. Students might agree that "Thanatopsis" could easily be mistaken for a British poem, whereas they may see the barrenness of the setting of "To a Waterfowl" as more suggestive of early New England.

The Romantic period fostered the beginning of what we consider today to be distinctively American literature. Pathfinders such as Irving, Cooper, and Bryant were to make way for such giants as Hawthorne, Melville, and Poe. But more significantly, as time went on, it was not only the writers but also their themes that attracted readers in Europe as well as in America.

Objectives Of The American Romanticism Unit

1. To improve reading proficiency and expand vocabulary
2. To gain exposure to notable authors and their works
3. To define and identify the elements of the story and poem
4. To define and identify significant literary techniques
5. To respond orally and in writing to stories and poetry
6. To analyze the language and style of notable authors
7. To write original works
8. To practice the following critical thinking and writing skills:
   - a. Analyzing conflict, style and imagery
   - b. Interpreting tone
   - c. Comparing and contrasting poems
   - d. Analyzing a poem
   - e. Analyzing the appeal of a literary work
   - f. Responding to a poem's message
   - g. Paraphrasing a poem

Supplementary Support Materials: Unit Three

1. Unit Introduction Test (*CCB*)
2. American Language Test (*CCB*)
3. Word Analogies Test (*CCB*)
4. Unit Review Test (*CCB*)
5. Critical Thinking and Writing Test (*CCB*)
6. Instructional Overhead Transparencies

A. Responding to the Quotation
Cooper is implicitly comparing Natty Bumppo with the pre-Fall Adam of the Bible, and the American Wilderness to Eden—a typically Romantic comparison in that it idealizes the subject.
? How does this view of the wilderness compare with your own? What movies, TV shows, or books can you think of in which the wilderness is idealized? (Encourage students to give specific titles. Students may feel that a contemporary view of an idealized wilderness focuses more on adventure or on ecological concerns than did the Romantic view.)

B. Humanities Connection: Discussing the Fine Art
Looking north, the lithograph shows the busy New York Bay of the sailing-ship era, and a pre-skyscraper Manhattan—the bustling center of a far smaller world.

AMERICAN ROMANTICISM

by **Gary Q. Arpin**

A

The imagination has no great task in portraying to itself a being removed from the everyday inducements to err, which abound in civilized life, while he retains the best and simplest of his early impressions; who sees God in the forest; hears Him in the winds; bows to Him in the firmament that o'er-canopies all; submits to His sway in a humble belief of His justice and mercy; in a word, a being who finds the impress of the Deity in all the works of nature, without any of the blots produced by the expedients, and passion, and mistakes of man.

—James Fenimore Cooper, in explaining why he created the character of Natty Bumppo

The Pattern of the "Journey"

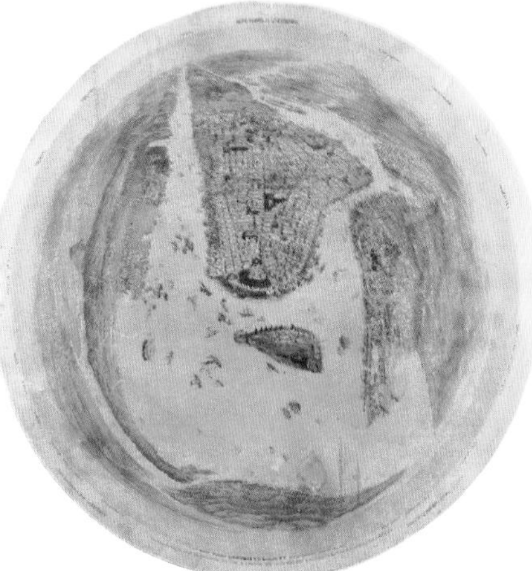

Bird's-Eye View of New York (1859). Colored lithograph.

Eno Collection, New York Public Library.

B

Very early in his *Autobiography,* Ben Franklin describes in great detail how he left his home in Boston and journeyed to Philadelphia. Journeys such as Franklin's reflect a classic narrative pattern—there is probably no pattern so common in all of narrative literature, from the days of the Greek epics and the Bible to the present. But an examination of the details of a particular journey can tell us a great deal about the sensibility of the traveler and the age in which he or she lives. The significance of Franklin's journey is clear—it is a journey away from the constraints of his family (a declaration of independence) and toward a city where he might prosper. Without stretching things too greatly, we may see in Franklin's journey not only his personal goals but the goals of eighteenth-century America as well: independence, prosperity, commerce, and urbane civilization.

The section of the *Autobiography* that recounts Franklin's journey was written in 1771. In 1799, Charles Brockden Brown described a quite different journey to Philadelphia in a novel called *Arthur Mervyn.* In this tale, the young farm-boy hero leaves his home for a plague-ridden Philadelphia, where he is plunged into a world of decay, corruption, and evil. *Arthur Mervyn* is seldom read now, but it illustrates the differences between the views of Franklin's era and that of the Romantic period. For Franklin, a journey to the city was an opportunity; for the Romantics, such a journey might be filled with unexpected dangers.

In Romantic literature, the city, far from being the seat of civilization, was often a place of moral ambiguity, and, worse, of corruption and death. The countryside became associated with independence, straightforward moral certainty, and health. This was especially true in America, where the idea of the frontier had taken on great importance. In the nineteenth century, this geography of the imagination—town, country, frontier—played a powerful role in American literature and life, and it continues to do so today.

The characteristic journey of the nineteenth century is the journey *away* from the town or city *to* the world of nature. Henry Thoreau (page 204) goes off to Walden Pond. Herman Melville's narrator in *Moby-Dick* (page 297), Ishmael, goes to sea. Walt Whitman (page 326) flees the "houses and rooms" that "are full of perfumes." Countless poets seek the beauties of nature. Each of these journeys is a flight both from something and to something. An understanding of this pattern of the "journey" in nineteenth-century American literature will take you a long way toward an understanding of American Romanticism. A

Autumn Landscape (Mount Chocorua) by Thomas Cole (1827). Oil.

Courtesy of Kennedy Galleries, Inc., New York.

B

"The characteristic journey of the nineteenth century is the journey *away* from the town or city *to* the world of nature."

The Romantic Escape

America's first truly popular professional writer was also one of the first New World Romantics. He was so successful in depicting an escape from the constraints of civilization that his story has made him immortal. The author was Washington Irving (page 123), and the escape was that of Rip Van Winkle. In order to understand some of the differences between Romanticism and rationalism, it is useful to contrast the fictional character of Rip with the historical figure of Ben Franklin.

Although both men have become almost mythical in the American mind, Rip is a kind of anti-Franklin figure, a do-nothing rather than a do-gooder. He has absolutely no ambition (other than to be free of his wife's nagging). He would rather "starve on a penny than work for a pound." His wife's attempts to force him into a Franklin-like sense of responsibility only drive him away from home and into the mountains. C

Whereas Franklin found freedom and prosperity through a journey to a great town, Rip's most urgent efforts are directed toward escaping from the town and the domestic concerns of his wife. His

A. Expansion
The journey *to* the town became a popular American theme later, during the realistic era of the 1890's and early twentieth century, perhaps partly in response to immigration and industrialization. Dreiser and Crane were the first great American storytellers of the city.

B. Humanities Connection: Responding to the Fine Art
? Look carefully at the man in the painting. Who might he be? What might he be doing? (Clearly he is not a backwoodsman, but a man of leisure whose communication with nature might be entirely too self-conscious.)

C. Expansion
In his lack of enthusiasm for the work ethic, Rip looks backward to the overworked peasantry, which was not such a remote memory in 1820; but he looks forward to Whitman's loafing and to Huck Finn's "lighting out for the territory."

A. Humanities Connection: Responding to the Fine Art Broadway at Spring Street is today a rather dirty but lively street at the edge of New York's "SoHo": a district of old cast-iron factories, some of which house artists' lofts, and some of which still produce clothing and other light manufactured goods.

? In what ways does Sebron's painting seem idealized? (The gracefulness of the human figures, the beautifully matched horses, the relatively clean slush, the overall air of stilled movement)

A

Broadway at Spring Street by Hyppolite Sebron (1855). Oil.

Private Collection.

journey from civilization begins in a familiar mountain landscape that soon becomes mysterious. Rip is given something to drink by a ghostly crew of Dutchmen, and he falls asleep. He wakes up twenty years later to discover that his wife is dead, that the American Revolution has taken place, and that he is, both literally and symbolically, a free man.

Irving's story is a whimsical fairy tale, much of it borrowed from a German source. But "Rip Van Winkle" contains a number of the attitudes and tendencies associated with American Romanticism: a distrust of "civilization," a nostalgia for the past, a concern with individual freedom, an interest in the supernatural, and a profound love for the beauties of the natural landscape.

The Romantic Sensibility

The Romantic sensibility is not easy to define, because Romanticism was a movement that went beyond national, chronological, and artistic boundaries. Its first stirrings were felt in Germany in the second half of the eighteenth century. Romanticism had a strong influence on literature, music, and painting in Europe and England well into the nineteenth century. Romanticism came relatively late to America, and, as you will see in this unit and in the units that follow, took different forms.

What is Romanticism? Because it is no single thing, it is not easy to define in capsule form. In general, though, *Romanticism* is the name given to those schools of thought that consider the rational inferior to the intuitive. For the Romantics, the imagination, spontaneity, individual feelings, and nature were of greater value than reason, logic, planning, and cultivation. Romanticism developed in part as a reaction against rationalism, as people realized the limits of reason. The Romantics believed that the imagination was able to discover truths that reason could not reach, truths usually accompanied by powerful emotion and associated with beauty. The Romantics did not flatly reject logical thought as invalid for all purposes. But for the purpose of art, they placed a new premium on nonrational experience.

Poetry was the highest work of the imagination for the Romantics. They often contrasted it with science, which was seen as destroying the very truth it claimed to seek. Edgar Allan Poe, for example, accused "science" of being a vulture:

> Who alterest all things with thy peering eyes!
> Why preyest thou thus upon the poet's heart,
> Vulture! Whose wings are dull realities!

The Romantic sensibility sought to rise above "dull realities" to a realm of higher truth. It would do this in two principal ways: first, by exploring exotic settings in the more "natural" past or in a world far removed from our sooty and noisy industrial age; second, by contemplating the natural world until dull reality falls away to reveal underlying beauty and truth. A

The Gothic novel, with its wild landscapes and mysterious castles, is one example of the first approach. Samuel Taylor Coleridge's poem "Kubla Khan" (1797) is a striking expression of this impulse to escape to a mysterious and magical landscape:

> In Xanadu did Kubla Khan
> A stately pleasure dome decree,
> Where Alph, the sacred river, ran
> Through caverns measureless to man
> Down to a sunless sea.

The second Romantic approach, the contemplation of the natural world, is evident in many lyric poems. In these, the poet views a commonplace object or event. A flower found by a stream or a waterfowl flying overhead brings the poet to some important, deeply felt insight, which is then recorded in the poem. In William Cullen Bryant's "To a Waterfowl" (see page 139), the lesson the poet takes from nature is clearly expressed in the final stanzas:

> He who, from zone to zone,
> Guides through the boundless sky thy certain flight,
> In the long way that I must tread alone
> Will lead my steps aright.

This contemplative process is similar to the Puritans' habit of drawing moral lessons from nature (see page 6). The difference is one of emphasis and goal. The Puritans' lessons were limited by their religion. They found in nature the God they knew from the Bible. The Romantics found in nature a far less clearly defined divinity; their experience is usually recorded as a more generalized emotional and intellectual awakening.

"Edgar Allan Poe accused 'science' of being a vulture."

B

White Pine Tree by Thomas Cole (c. 1840). Pen, brown ink, and wash, 15⅜" × 9⅝".

M. and M. Karolik Collection. Courtesy, Museum of Fine Arts, Boston.

A. Responding
Both of these Romantic strategies for seeking beauty are based on the premise that the actual present-day industrial world does not offer beauty to the beholder.
? Is this premise valid or not? (Student answers will vary.) Compare the attitude that seeks beauty in escape with the attitude that seeks beauty in reality. (Student answers will vary.)

B. Humanities Connection: Responding to the Fine Art
See Humanities Connection annotation, page 115.

A. Responding
This description of the typical hero of American Romanticism could well be applied to heroes from other eras and other forms of entertainment. Many such heroes are descended from the Romantic movement.
? Can you think of heroes from modern popular entertainment with similar Romantic traits? (Student answers will vary, but the typical hero of Westerns is a descendant of the Romantic hero, while the hard-boiled detective is a jaded, disillusioned version of him.)

B. Discussing the Time Line
This time line begins before the Romantic Era, in the Age of Enlightenment, and thus reminds us of the context in which Romanticism arose; and it looks forward to our own age with the births of Picasso and Einstein. You might point out that each brief entry stands for a number of other events or a historical or artistic movement. For instance, the potato famine of 1846 began a wave of Irish immigration to the United States, which was followed in turn by waves from other nations. Picasso's birth occurred at the time the Impressionist movement in French painting was thriving. *Great Expectations* was preceded by a host of Dickens novels beginning in 1836. If time permits, you might ask your students each to bring in an entry of his or her own for the time line, to deepen appreciation of the historical context of American Romanticism.

The American Hero in Romantic Fiction

A

The typical hero of American Romantic fiction is likely to have some or all of the following characteristics: youth (or childlike qualities); innocence; a love of nature and a distrust of town life; a corresponding uneasiness with women, who were usually taken (by male writers) to represent civilization and the impulse to "domesticate"; and the need to engage in a quest for some higher truth in the natural world. Although American Romantic poetry was heavily influenced by European writers, American novelists soon discovered that the subject matter available to them was very different from European materials. The novel in America moved toward a wilderness experience that Europe, so long settled, simply did not possess. The development of the American novel coincided with westward expansion, with the growth of a nationalist spirit, and with the rapid growth of cities. All these factors tended to reinforce the idealization of frontier life.

"Women were usually taken (by male writers) to represent civilization and the impulse to 'domesticate.'"

We can see how the novel developed by looking at the early career of James Fenimore Cooper. Cooper's first novel, *Precaution* (1820), describes life in an English country vicarage. His second novel, *The Spy* (1821), was influenced by the romances of the Scottish novelist Sir Walter Scott, though it is set during the American Revolution. It was in his third novel, *The Pioneers* (1823), that Cooper broke free of European constraints.

The Pioneers takes place in a frontier community in New York

B

1783–1789	1789–1803	1803–1811	1811–1812
Revolutionary War ends in America, 1783 Mob in Paris storms the Bastille, starting the French Revolution, 1789	George Washington becomes first U.S. President, 1789 Thomas Jefferson makes Lousiana Purchase, extending U.S. boundaries to the Rocky Mountains, 1803	Robert Fulton propels a boat by steam power, 1803 **William Cullen Bryant writes "Thanatopsis" at age 17, 1811**	**Jane Austen writes *Sense and Sensibility* in England, 1811** **The Brothers Grimm publish *Fairy Tales* in Germany, 1812**
1846–1848	**1847–1850**	**1851–1852**	**1854–1855**
Famine in Ireland caused by potato crop failure, 1846 War with Mexico, 1846–1848	Gold discovered in California, 1847 **Hawthorne publishes *The Scarlet Letter*, 1850**	**Melville publishes *Moby-Dick*, 1851** **Harriet Beecher Stowe publishes *Uncle Tom's Cabin*, 1852**	**Thoreau publishes *Walden*, 1854** **Frederick Douglass publishes his autobiography, 1855**
1862–1863	**1865**	**1866–1868**	**1870–1876**
Emily Dickinson first writes to Higginson, 1862 Abraham Lincoln delivers Gettysburg Address, 1863	Civil War ends, 1865 Lincoln assassinated while watching a play, April 14, 1865	**Whittier publishes *Snow-Bound*, 1866** **Louisa May Alcott publishes *Little Women*, 1868**	Robert E. Lee dies, 1870 Alexander Graham Bell patents the telephone, 1876

State. Among the characters are an old Indian, Chingachgook, the last of the tribe of the Mohicans, and an old frontiersman, a white man named Natty Bumppo. During the course of the novel, Natty is imprisoned for shooting a deer out of season; clearly, his frontier ethics are at odds with the artificial laws of the town. Eventually, he flees the town for the Western wilderness. Early in the book, Natty is almost a comic figure—a snaggletoothed and uncouth backwoodsman. But as the writing of the novel progressed, Cooper apparently forgot these aspects of his hero's character, and Natty became a heroic, virtuous, skillful frontiersman. It was this character who appeared in the rest of the Leatherstocking tales—a highly popular series of sequels that Cooper wrote over the next eighteen years.

Like Rip Van Winkle, Natty Bumppo is a triumph of American innocence. Most Europeans had an image of the American as an unsophisticated, uncivilized individual. This was a stereotype that Ben Franklin, when he lived in France, took great pains to demonstrate was unfair and untrue. But Cooper and the other Romantic novelists who followed him took no such pains. Instead, they turned the insult on its head. Virtue, they implied, was to be found in innocence, not in sophistication. Eternal truths were to be found not in dusty libraries or crowded cities or glittering court life, but in the wilderness that was unknown and unavailable to Europeans.

A

Natty Bumppo, from *The Last of the Mohicans* (1827). Engraving.

New York Public Library.

A. Humanities Connection: Responding to the Fine Art
Natty and Chingachgook are listening for sounds of movement on the trail.

? Why does Chingachgook have his ear to the ground, while Natty is standing? (The arrangement exemplifies the myth that Indians were innately more skillful trackers, yet shows the Indian in a subordinate posture.)

1812–1814	1820–1828	1836–1837	1839–1841
U.S. declares war on Britain, 1812 Francis Scott Key writes "The Star-Spangled Banner," 1814	**Washington Irving publishes *The Sketch Book*, 1820** **Noah Webster publishes his dictionary of the American language, 1828**	Davy Crockett dies in Texas at the Alamo, 1836 **Emerson delivers "The American Scholar" and asserts American independence, 1837**	**Poe publishes "The Fall of the House of Usher," 1839** **Emerson publishes "Self-Reliance," 1841**

1855	1858–1860	1861	1861–1862
Whitman publishes *Leaves of Grass*, 1855 **Longfellow publishes *The Song of Hiawatha*, 1855**	Lincoln-Douglas debates, 1858 South Carolina secedes from Union, 1860	U.S. population passes 32 million, 1861 **Charles Dickens publishes *Great Expectations* in England, 1861**	Civil War begins with firing on Ft. Sumter, 1861 Emancipation Proclamation frees all slaves, 1862

1877–1879	1879–1880	1881	1884–1886
Chief Joseph surrenders to U.S. troops with the Nez Percé, 1877 Josef Stalin born in Russia, 1879	Albert Einstein born in Germany, 1879 Thomas Alva Edison devises an electric lightbulb, 1880	Pablo Picasso born in Spain, 1881 **Henry James publishes *The Portrait of a Lady*, 1881**	**Twain publishes *Huckleberry Finn*, 1884** Dickinson dies and leaves nearly 1,800 unpublished poems, 1886

For Further Reading
The greatest English Gothic novel is Mary Shelley's *Frankenstein* (1818). Notable English Romantic poets include William Blake (1757–1827), William Wordsworth (1770–1850), Samuel Taylor Coleridge (1772–1834), Percy Bysshe Shelley (1792–1822), and John Keats (1795–1821).

Reading Check Test

1. Romantic literature is often about a journey from ______ to ______. *the city/nature*
2. America's first truly popular professional writer was ______. *Washington Irving*
3. Romanticism prefers feelings to ______. *reason*
4. The typical Romantic hero is ______. *young, innocent, nature-loving*
5. The Fireside poets were so called because ______. *their poems were read aloud at family firesides*

A. Humanities Connection: Responding to the Self-Portrait
? What kind of person does Longfellow want to make us think he is? (Student answers will vary.)

You might want to return to this portrait when discussing Longfellow's poems (page 146). Have students compare the image in the self-portrait with the kinds of poems Longfellow wrote.

Additional Writing Assignment
Have students write a paragraph stating their opinion of the relative values of feeling and reason.

American Romantic Poetry

A

Self-Portrait of Henry Wadsworth Longfellow in his study at Craigie House, Cambridge, Massachusetts (1847).

> "The Fireside Poets were unable to recognize the poetry of the future, which was being written right under their noses."

If the Romantic novelists looked for new subject matter and innovative themes, virtually the opposite tendency appears in the Romantic poets represented in this unit. Like Franklin, they wanted to prove that Americans were not unsophisticated hicks, but were as knowledgeable and polished as Europeans.

When an editor was shown the manuscript of Bryant's poem "Thanatopsis" (see page 142), he found it difficult to believe that such accomplished poetry could be the work of an American. Bryant had borrowed typically English themes, meter, and imagery to construct a poem with an American setting. In a sense, his poem was what a cultivated Englishman who had emigrated to America might be expected to write.

Each of the American poets in this unit, also, looked backward—over his shoulder, as it were—at established European literary models. Their poetry was limited by this tendency, and by their own facility with traditional meter and diction (leading to poems with "dum-de-dum" rhythms). But these poets used their talents fruitfully. Each wrote a few great poems, and each wrote many other poems that for generations were the staple of home and school reading.

In fact, the Fireside Poets, as the Boston group of Longfellow, Holmes, Lowell, and Whittier was called, were the last great popular poets in America. They were called "Fireside Poets" because their poems were so often read aloud at the family fireside as family entertainment. The works of the Fireside Poets appealed to the ordinary, literate man and woman, and their subjects—love, patriotism, nature, family, God, and religion—secured for these poets a well-loved place in almost every American home.

Nevertheless, their attempts to create a new American literature relied too reverently on the literature of the past. The Fireside Poets were unable to recognize the poetry of the future, which was being written right under their noses. Whittier's response in 1855 to reading the first volume of a certain new poet's work was to throw the book into the fire. Ralph Waldo Emerson's response was more farsighted. "I greet you," he wrote to this new poet, Walt Whitman, "at the beginning of a great career."

Washington Irving (1783–1859)

Washington Irving was born in New York City on April 8 in the year the Revolutionary War ended, and he was named for its hero, the victor of the critical Battle of Yorktown. When he was six years old, Irving and his nurse met the nation's new President in a New York City shop. When he was presented to his namesake, the child who was to become America's first professional writer was rewarded by the first President with a pat on the head.

Irving was the last of eleven children born to a successful and very religious hardware importer and his amiable wife. A small, sickly, but bright child, Irving was the darling of the family. He was indulgently allowed to slip away from the Irving home at 128 William Street to watch performances at the Little Theatre on John Street. And although his brothers attended college, he was kept at home and given a fragmentary education.

Still, the weight of his father's practical concerns forced Irving to study law. At sixteen, he was apprenticed to a law office, and at nineteen he began to work for a judge, Josiah Hoffman.

Irving's real interests, however, lay not in law offices but in the literary societies that were then popular among young men. He loved nothing more than friendly company in which he could try out his growing skill with humor. From an early age, Irving showed a genius for creating comic, fictional "narrators." Using the pseudonym Jonathan Oldstyle, Gent. (an abbreviation for *Gentleman*), he began to write letters for a newspaper published by his brothers. Oldstyle was a broad caricature of British tradition who could not accept the simple values of the new nation. The idea of a very young man hiding behind this pompous pen name was intended as irreverent fun. But Oldstyle's letters brought Irving favorable attention from his own family and from such prominent citizens as Aaron Burr.

The nineteenth century was the era of the Grand Tour, when fortunate young Americans were shipped off to visit European cathedrals and museums before settling down to a lifetime of moneymaking. At twenty-one, Irving visited

Portrait of Washington Irving by John Wesley Jarvis (1809). Oil.

Sleepy Hollow Restorations, Tarrytown, New York.

France, Italy, Holland, and England. He filled notebooks with accounts of his travels, including one story of his capture by pirates on his way to Sicily. The Grand Tour was the beginning of Irving's lifelong love affair with the rich culture and traditions of the Old World.

Back from Europe, Irving joined with other young men to publish *Salmagundi,* a humor magazine that made fun of the manners of the day and that greatly amused New Yorkers in 1807 and 1808. Still, Irving felt an obligation to do "real work," and thanks to Judge Hoffman he had passed the bar exams. When he found he was in love with the judge's daughter, Matilda, he began to make plans to marry. This forced Irving to take a serious view of his career and to admit that his preoccupation with writing was affecting it.

While he was dealing with this problem, Ma-

A. Humanities Connection: Responding to the Fine Art
This portrait is typically Romantic, a product of the era in which Byron and Bonaparte were the great heroes of the Western world. The windswept curls and sideburns are prototypically Byronic. The striking contrasts of light and shadow add glamor. ? How does this style of portrait resemble, and differ from, the rock-star posters of today? (Students may suggest that the portrait is more conservative than a rock-star poster; like many such posters, however, it depicts the subject looking directly at the viewer, in a somewhat intimate fashion.)

B. Expansion
Many other great writers have started out as lawyers or law students. Henry Fielding was a judge. Dickens was a court reporter. Flaubert studied law but broke off his studies because of a mysterious nervous illness. Kafka earned his living as an insurance lawyer.

A. Expansion
In addition, later in his career Irving published books of travel sketches of the West. While they don't match the greatness of his tales, they are still readable and provide a vivid glimpse of the exploration of the frontier as seen through the eyes of a citified Easterner. These works include *A Tour on the Prairie* (1835) and *The Adventures of Captain Bonneville* (1837) as well as portions of Irving's journals and notebooks.

tilda died of tuberculosis. Irving's grief turned him further from the law and thrust him into a new literary project, *A History of New York from the Beginning of the World to the End of the Dutch Dynasty.* This "history" was an elaborate hoax and was related by a highly unreliable narrator called Diedrich Knickerbocker. Published in 1809, this comic and irreverent "history" was a success and established Irving as the foremost young New York satirist.

In 1815, Irving was sent off to Liverpool, England, to look after the failing overseas branch of the family business. He found the business beyond repair, but he immersed himself in the British literary scene. He was particularly attracted to the Romantic novelist Sir Walter Scott, who gave the younger writer advice that was to make Irving's reputation. Scott's recommendation was that Irving read the German Romantics and make use of folklore and legends.

Now Irving made the decision he had previously lacked the courage to make. He decided against putting further energy into business and its "sordid, dusty, soul-killing way of life." He would give himself entirely to writing.

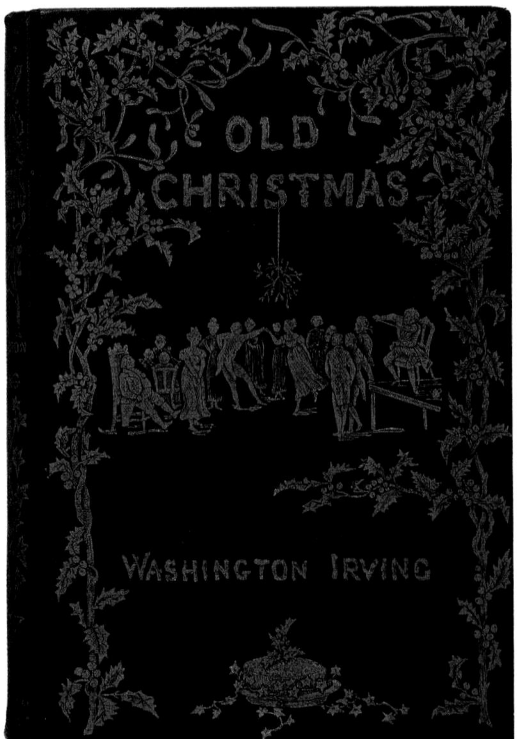

From the Max A. Polster Archive.

Returning to the United States in 1817, Irving brought with him the first drafts of stories based on German folk tales. "Rip Van Winkle" and "The Legend of Sleepy Hollow" became sketches in *The Sketch Book of Geoffrey Crayon, Gent.* (1819–1820). "Geoffrey Crayon" was a self-proclaimed American gentleman of "obscure origins"—another of Irving's comic voices. *The Sketch Book* carried Irving to the summit of international success. A

In Irving, the young nation had at last found a writer who provided positive answers to some urgent questions: Was America slavishly attached to British and European culture, or did it have a culture of its own? Would an authentic American literature be able to stand on its own legs?

Something about Irving's comic narrators touched a responsiveness in the American public. Even though Irving borrowed openly from a European past, he brought to his material a droll new voice, as inflated as a preacher's or a politician's at one moment, self-mocking the next. It was a voice a new nation recognized as its own.

Irving had also given his country its first international literary celebrity. In the British novelist William Thackeray's words, he was "the first ambassador from the New World of letters . . . to the old." This was a role that Irving enjoyed exploiting to the fullest, at home and abroad. He had always loved parties and people and praise. Now he had access to the literary circles of the world. It was a remarkable achievement for the unpromising child of a middle-class American family.

During the final years of his rich life, Irving lived as the "squire" of Sunnyside, his picturesque Dutch farmhouse in Tarrytown, New York. He behaved as a "man of letters," one whom Thackeray praised as "gentle, generous, good-humored . . . the complete gentleman." Though he wrote a popular biography of Columbus and a sort of Spanish "sketch book" called *The Alhambra,* Irving never again wrote anything that matched the success of the two great comic tales in *The Sketch Book.* We remember him today for the tale of Rip Van Winkle who slept for twenty years, and the tale of the Headless Horseman who met the Yankee schoolteacher in Sleepy Hollow, New York.

Supplementary Support Materials
1. Vocabulary Activity Worksheet (*CCB*)
2. Review and Response Worksheet: Tone (*CCB*)
3. Language Skills Worksheet: Revision Worksheet 1 (*CCB*)
4. Selection Test (*CCB*)

Developing Vocabulary
The following words from the story are tested in the Selection Test. (See also Vocabulary Activity Worksheet.)

malleable	dapper
impunity	to reciprocate
pestilent	to skulk
adherent	to desist
rubicund	to reiterate

Preparation
Establishing a Purpose. As the headnote suggests, have students read for the symbolic meanings in the story.

A. Expansion
The italicized opening of the story is known as a "frame device," written in a different voice from that of the main narrator. You might want to have students skim this opening and begin closer reading with "Whoever has made a voyage up the Hudson. . . ."

RIP VAN WINKLE
A POSTHUMOUS WRITING OF DIEDRICH KNICKERBOCKER

As you read the story, keep in mind its possible symbolic levels of meaning. Remember that Irving was born only two years after the Battle of Yorktown (1781), a battle which assured the success of the American Revolution. When the story was first published in 1819, John Adams and Thomas Jefferson were still alive. (*Posthumous* in the subtitle means "published after the writer's death.")

[The following tale was found among the papers of the late Diedrich Knickerbocker, an old gentleman of New York, who was very curious in the Dutch history of the province, and the manners of the descendants from its primitive settlers. His historical researches, however, did not lie so much among books as among men; for the former are lamentably scanty on his favorite topics; whereas he found the old burghers [citizens], *and still more their wives, rich in that legendary lore so invaluable to true history. Whenever, therefore, he happened upon a genuine Dutch family, snugly shut up in its low-roofed farmhouse, under a spreading sycamore, he looked upon it as a little clasped volume of blackletter, and studied it with the zeal of a bookworm.*

A *The result of all these researches was a history of the province during the reign of the Dutch governors, which he published some years since. There have been various opinions as to the literary character of his work, and, to tell the truth, it is not a whit better than it should be. Its chief merit is its scrupulous accuracy, which indeed was a little questioned on its first appearance, but has since been completely established; and it is now admitted into all historical collections as a book of unquestionable authority.*

The old gentleman died shortly after the publication of his work; and now that he is dead and gone, it cannot do much harm to his memory to say that his time might have been much better employed in weightier labors. He, however, was apt to ride his hobby his own way; and though it did now and then kick up the dust a little in the eyes of his neighbors, and grieve the spirit of some friends, for whom he felt the truest deference and affection, yet his errors and follies are remembered "more in sorrow than in anger," and it begins to be suspected that he never intended to injure or offend. But however his memory may be appreciated by critics, it is still held dear by many folk whose good opinion is well worth having; particularly by certain biscuit-bakers, who have gone so far as to imprint his likeness on their New Year cakes; and have thus given him a chance for immortality, almost equal to being stamped on a Waterloo Medal,[1] or a Queen Anne's farthing.]

Whoever has made a voyage up the Hudson must remember the Kaatskill[2] Mountains. They are a dismembered branch of the great Appalachian family, and are seen away to the west of the river, swelling up to a noble height, and lording it over the surrounding country. Every change of season, every change of weather, indeed, every hour of the day, produces some change in the magical hues and shapes of these mountains, and they are regarded by all the good wives, far and near, as perfect barometers. When the weather is fair and settled, they are clothed in blue and purple, and print their bold outlines on the clear evening sky; but sometimes, when the rest of the landscape is cloudless, they will gather a hood of gray vapors about their summits, which, in the last rays of the setting sun, will glow and light up like a crown of glory.

At the foot of these fairy mountains, the voyager may have descried the light smoke curling up from a village, whose shingle roofs gleam among

1. **Waterloo Medal:** a silver medal presented by the British government to the veterans of the Battle of Waterloo (1815).
2. **Kaatskill:** original Dutch spelling of Catskill.

Literature and Language: Using Precise Nouns

Suggest that students visualize the image created in these sentences. Which provides details that make it easier to imagine?

a. Rip saw a *person* dressed in strange *clothing* carrying *something.*

b. Rip saw a little *man* dressed in a *jerkin* and *breeches* carrying a *keg* on his *shoulder.*

Note that precise nouns *(fowling piece* instead of *gun; galligaskins* instead of *clothing; ninepins* instead of *sport* or *game)* help readers to picture what the writer is describing. When they write, students should choose precise nouns and verbs to create clear images.

Ask students to rewrite each of the following sentences, replacing general nouns with specific ones. They can also add modifiers to provide more details.

1. Rip heard *noises* in the *place.*

2. He saw *people* playing a *game.*

3. They were dressed in funny *clothing.*

4. When Rip awoke, he found his *gun* had changed.

5. The children laughed at Rip's *appearance.*

6. *Things* looked different in the village.

A. Setting

Each of the long descriptive paragraphs at the beginning of the story can be read aloud by a different student. If we imagine the story as a movie, each paragraph zooms in closer than the one before it: first an establishing shot of the Catskill Mountains, then the village, then the Van Winkle house, then Rip himself.

B. Tone

Irving's tone is often tongue-in-cheek: a cultured narrator smiling genially at his rustic characters.

? Can you find other examples of humorous or satirical tone? (This tone pervades the story; students should be able to find several examples—pertaining mostly to Rip and his wife—on this page.)

A the trees, just where the blue tints of the upland melt away into the fresh green of the nearer landscape. It is a little village, of great antiquity, having been founded by some of the Dutch colonists in the early times of the province, just about the beginning of the government of the good Peter Stuyvesant[3] (may he rest in peace!), and there were some of the houses of the original settlers standing within a few years, built of small yellow bricks brought from Holland, having latticed windows and gable fronts, surmounted with weathercocks.

In that same village, and in one of these very houses (which, to tell the precise truth, was sadly timeworn and weather-beaten), there lived, many years since, while the country was yet a province of Great Britain, a simple, good-natured fellow of B the name of Rip Van Winkle. He was a descendant of the Van Winkles who figured so gallantly in the chivalrous days of Peter Stuyvesant, and accompanied him to the siege of Fort Christina.[4] He inherited, however, but little of the martial character of his ancestors. I have observed that he was a simple, good-natured man; he was, moreover, a kind neighbor, and an obedient, henpecked husband. Indeed, to the latter circumstance might be owing that meekness of spirit which gained him such universal popularity; for those men are most apt to be obsequious and conciliating abroad, who are under the discipline of shrews at home. Their tempers, doubtless, are rendered pliant and malleable in the fiery furnace of domestic tribulation; and a curtain lecture[5] is worth all the sermons in the world for teaching the virtues of patience and long-suffering. A termagant[6] wife may, therefore, in some respects be considered a tolerable blessing; and if so, Rip Van Winkle was thrice blessed.

Certain it is that he was a great favorite among all the good wives of the village, who, as usual with the amiable sex, took his part in all family squabbles; and never failed, whenever they talked those matters over in their evening gossipings, to lay all the blame on Dame Van Winkle. The children of the village, too, would shout with joy whenever he approached. He assisted at their sports, made their playthings, taught them to fly kites and shoot marbles, and told them long stories of ghosts, witches, and Indians. Whenever he went dodging about the village, he was surrounded by a troop of them, hanging on his skirts, clambering on his back, and playing a thousand tricks on him with impunity; and not a dog would bark at him throughout the neighborhood.

The great error in Rip's composition was an insuperable aversion to all kinds of profitable labor. It could not be from the want of assiduity[7] or perseverance; for he would sit on a wet rock, with a rod as long and heavy as a Tartar's lance, and fish all day without a murmur, even though he should not be encouraged by a single nibble. He would carry a fowling-piece on his shoulder for hours together, trudging through woods and swamps, and up hill and down dale, to shoot a few squirrels or wild pigeons. He would never refuse to assist a neighbor even in the roughest toil, and was a foremost man at all country frolics for husking Indian corn, or building stone fences; the women of the village, too, used to employ him to run their errands, and to do such little odd jobs as their less obliging husbands would not do for them. In a word, Rip was ready to attend to anybody's business but his own; but as to doing family duty, and keeping his farm in order, he found it impossible.

In fact, he declared it was of no use to work on his farm; it was the most pestilent little piece of ground in the whole country; everything about it went wrong, and would go wrong, in spite of him. His fences were continually falling to pieces; his cow would either go astray or get among the cabbages; weeds were sure to grow quicker in his fields than anywhere else; the rain always made a point of setting in just as he had some outdoor work to do; so that though his patrimonial estate had dwindled away under his management, acre by acre, until there was little more left than a mere patch of Indian corn and potatoes, yet it was the worst conditioned farm in the neighborhood.

His children, too, were as ragged and wild as if they belonged to nobody. His son Rip, an urchin

---

3. **Peter Stuyvesant:** governor of New Amsterdam, 1646–1664.
4. **Fort Christina:** on the Delaware River, captured by Stuyvesant from the Swedes in 1655.
5. **curtain lecture:** reprimand given by a wife to her husband, originally delivered behind the curtains of one those old-fashioned beds.
6. **termagant** (tur'mə·gənt): violently abusive.
7. **assiduity** (əs·ə·dyōō'ə·tē): close and continuous application of effort.

Title page of "Rip Van Winkle" by Washington Irving. Illustration by N. C. Wyeth (1921). Lithograph.

David McKay Co. Inc.

Humanities Connection: Responding to the Fine Art

? Compare N. C. Wyeth's illustration of the story with that of John Quidor's (page 132). How do they differ in mood? (Wyeth emphasizes the whimsical fairy-tale aspect of the story, Quidor the demonic.) Do the two paintings make you think in different ways about the story? How can the same material lead to such diverse artistic interpretations? (Answers will vary, but the key difference lies in the artist's individual views of the story.)

A. Characterization

? What do you think of Rip as a person? (Answers will vary.) How is he unlike the typical American frontier hero? (He is not deliberately seeking to explore or do anything new, and is not animated by a spirit of either adventure or labor. If anything, he is helpless and passive.)

B. Stereotyping

? How would you describe Irving's view of marriage? (It is stereotyped. See question 11, page 137.)

begotten in his own likeness, promised to inherit the habits, with the old clothes, of his father. He was generally seen trooping like a colt at his mother's heels, equipped in a pair of his father's castoff galligaskins,[8] which he had much ado to hold up with one hand, as a fine lady does her train in bad weather.

A Rip Van Winkle, however, was one of those happy mortals, of foolish, well-oiled dispositions, who take the world easy, eat white bread or brown, whichever can be got with least thought or trouble, and would rather starve on a penny than work for a pound. If left to himself, he would have whistled life away in perfect contentment; but his wife kept continually dinning in his ears about his idleness, his carelessness, and the ruin he was bringing on his family. Morning, noon, and night, her tongue was incessantly going, and everything he said or did was sure to produce a torrent of household eloquence. Rip had but one way of replying to all lectures of the kind, and that, by frequent use, had grown into a habit. He shrugged his shoulders, shook his head, cast up his eyes, but said nothing. This, however, always provoked a fresh volley from his wife; so that he was fain to draw off his forces, and take to the outside of the house—the only side which, in truth, belongs to a henpecked husband.

Rip's sole domestic adherent was his dog Wolf, who was as much henpecked as his master; for Dame Van Winkle regarded them as companions in idleness, and even looked upon Wolf with an evil eye, as the cause of his master's going so often astray. True it is, in all points of spirit befitting an honorable dog, he was as courageous an animal as ever scoured the woods; but what courage can withstand the ever-during and all-besetting terrors of a woman's tongue? The moment Wolf entered the house his crest fell, his tail drooped to the ground or curled between his legs, he sneaked about with a gallows air, casting many a sidelong glance at Dame Van Winkle, and at the least flourish of a broomstick or ladle he would fly to the door with yelping precipitation.

B Times grew worse and worse with Rip Van Winkle as years of matrimony rolled on; a tart temper never mellows with age, and a sharp tongue is the only edged tool that grows keener with constant use. For a long while he used to console himself, when driven from home, by frequenting a kind of perpetual club of the sages, philosophers, and other idle personages of the village, which held its sessions on a bench before a small inn, designated by a rubicund portrait of His Majesty George the Third. Here they used to sit in the shade through a long, lazy summer's day, talking listlessly over village gossip, or telling endless sleepy stories about nothing. But it would have been worth any statesman's money to have heard the profound discussions that sometimes took place, when by chance an old newspaper fell into their hands from some passing traveler. How solemnly they would listen to the contents, as drawled out by Derrick Van Bummel, the schoolmaster, a dapper, learned little man, who was not to be daunted by the most gigantic word in the dictionary; and how sagely they would deliberate upon public events some months after they had taken place.

The opinions of this junto[9] were completely controlled by Nicholas Vedder, a patriarch of the village and landlord of the inn, at the door of which he took his seat from morning till night, just moving sufficiently to avoid the sun and keep in the shade of a large tree; so that the neighbors could tell the hour by his movements as accurately as by a sundial. It is true he was rarely heard to speak, but smoked his pipe incessantly. His adherents, however (for every great man has his adherents), perfectly understood him, and knew how to gather his opinions. When anything that was read or related displeased him, he was observed to smoke his pipe vehemently, and to send forth short, frequent, and angry puffs; but when pleased, he would inhale the smoke slowly and tranquilly, and emit it in light and placid clouds; and sometimes, taking the pipe from his mouth, and letting the fragrant vapor curl about his nose, would gravely nod his head in token of perfect approbation.

From even this stronghold the unlucky Rip was at length routed by his termagant wife, who would suddenly break in upon the tranquillity of the assemblage and call the members all to naught; nor was that august personage, Nicholas Vedder himself, sacred from the daring tongue of this terrible virago,[10] who charged him outright with encouraging her husband in habits of idleness.

8. **galligaskins** (gal·i·gas′kinz): loose, baggy trousers.

9. **junto** (hoon′tō): council.

10. **virago** (vi·rā′gō): a bad-tempered, quarrelsome woman.

128 **American Romanticism**

Poor Rip was at last reduced almost to despair; and his only alternative, to escape from the labor of the farm and clamor of his wife, was to take gun in hand and stroll away into the woods. Here he would sometimes seat himself at the foot of a tree, and share the contents of his wallet with Wolf, with whom he sympathized as a fellow-sufferer in persecution. "Poor Wolf," he would say, "thy mistress leads thee a dog's life of it; but never mind, my lad, while I live thou shalt never want a friend to stand by thee!" Wolf would wag his tail, look wistfully in his master's face; and if dogs can feel pity, I verily believe he reciprocated the sentiment with all his heart.

In a long ramble of the kind on a fine autumnal day, Rip had unconsciously scrambled to one of the highest parts of the Kaatskill Mountains. He was after his favorite sport of squirrel-shooting, and the still solitudes had echoed and reechoed with the reports of his gun. Panting and fatigued, he threw himself, late in the afternoon, on a green knoll, covered with mountain herbage, that crowned the brow of a precipice. From an opening between the trees he could overlook all the lower country for many a mile of rich woodland. He saw at a distance the lordly Hudson, far, far below him, moving on its silent but majestic course, with the reflection of a purple cloud, or the sail of a lagging bark, here and there sleeping on its glassy bosom, and at last losing itself in the blue highlands.

On the other side he looked down into a deep mountain glen, wild, lonely, and shagged, the bottom filled with fragments from the impending cliffs, and scarcely lighted by the reflected rays of the setting sun. For some time Rip lay musing on this scene; evening was gradually advancing; the mountains began to throw their long blue shadows over the valleys; he saw that it would be dark long before he could reach the village, and he heaved a heavy sigh when he thought of encountering the terrors of Dame Van Winkle.

As he was about to descend, he heard a voice from a distance, hallooing, "Rip Van Winkle, Rip Van Winkle!" He looked round, but could see nothing but a crow winging its solitary flight across the mountain. He thought his fancy must have deceived him, and turned again to descend, when he heard the same cry ring through the still evening air: "Rip Van Winkle! Rip Van Winkle!" At the same time Wolf bristled up his back, and giving a low growl, skulked to his master's side, looking fearfully down into the glen. Rip now felt a vague apprehension stealing over him; he looked anxiously in the same direction, and perceived a strange figure slowly toiling up the rocks, and bending under the weight of something he carried on his back. He was surprised to see any human being in this lonely and unfrequented place; but supposing it to be someone of the neighborhood in need of his assistance, he hastened down to yield it.

On nearer approach he was still more surprised at the singularity of the stranger's appearance. He was a short, square-built old fellow, with thick bushy hair and a grizzled beard. His dress was of the antique Dutch fashion—a cloth jerkin[11] strapped round the waist, several pair of breeches, the outer one of ample volume, decorated with rows of buttons down the sides, and bunches at the knees. He bore on his shoulder a stout keg, that seemed full of liquor, and made signs for Rip to approach and assist him with the load. Though rather shy and distrustful of this new acquaintance, Rip complied with his usual alacrity; and mutually relieving one another, they clambered up a narrow gully, apparently the dry bed of a mountain torrent. As they ascended, Rip every now and then heard long, rolling peals, like distant thunder, that seemed to issue out of a deep ravine, or rather cleft, between lofty rocks, toward which their rugged path conducted. He paused for an instant, but supposing it to be the muttering of one of those transient thundershowers which often take place in mountain heights, he proceeded. Passing through the ravine, they came to a hollow, like a small amphitheater, surrounded by perpendicular precipices, over the brinks of which impending trees shot their branches, so that you only caught glimpses of the azure sky and the bright evening cloud. During the whole time Rip and his companion had labored on in silence; for though the former marveled greatly what could be the object of carrying a keg of liquor up this wild mountain, yet there was something strange and incomprehensible about the unknown that inspired awe and checked familiarity. A

On entering the amphitheater, new objects of wonder presented themselves. On a level spot in the center was a company of odd-looking personages playing at ninepins.[12] They were dressed in B

11. **jerkin:** sleeveless jacket.
12. **ninepins:** a bowling game.

A. Characterization
? What do you expect to learn about this character as the story progresses? (He is magical.) What clues tell you that he is not an ordinary person? (He resembles the trolls, gnomes, elves, and leprechauns who populate European folk and fairy tales.)

B. Description
Part of the craft of fiction writing involves knowing when to linger over a description and when to make short order of it. Irving lovingly dwells on the description of the little men, the amphitheater, and the ninepins game.
? Why? (The extended description makes a fantasy environment real and draws the reader in.)

A. Plot/Suspense
This might be a good place to pause and briefly recapitulate what has gone on so far and ask the students for their reactions to the story.

? Has the story kept your interest despite your being familiar with the basic story line? What qualities of the story, and of Irving's handling of it, create suspense, or at least a feeling of pleasant anticipation, even when you know what's going to happen next? (Answers will vary, but students may suggest that Irving's vivid descriptions and frequent touches of humor hold the reader's interest.)

a quaint, outlandish fashion; some wore short doublets,[13] others jerkins, with long knives in their belts, and most of them had enormous breeches, of similar style with that of the guide's. Their visages, too, were peculiar; one had a large beard, broad face, and small piggish eyes; the face of another seemed to consist entirely of nose, and was surmounted by a white sugar-loaf hat, set off with a little red cock's tail. They all had beards, of various shapes and colors. There was one who seemed to be the commander. He was a stout old gentleman, with a weather-beaten countenance; he wore a laced doublet, broad belt and hanger,[14] high crowned hat and feather, red stockings, and high-heeled shoes, with roses[15] in them. The whole group reminded Rip of the figures in an old Flemish painting, in the parlor of Dominie Van Shaick, the village parson, and which had been brought over from Holland at the time of the settlement.

What seemed particularly odd to Rip was that, though these folks were evidently amusing themselves, yet they maintained the gravest faces, the most mysterious silence, and were, withal, the most melancholy party of pleasure he had ever witnessed. Nothing interrupted the stillness of the scene but the noise of the balls, which, whenever they were rolled, echoed along the mountains like rumbling peals of thunder.

As Rip and his companion approached them, they suddenly desisted from their play, and stared at him with such fixed, statue-like gaze, and such strange, uncouth, lackluster countenances, that his heart turned within him, and his knees smote together. His companion now emptied the contents of the keg into large flagons,[16] and made signs to him to wait upon the company. He obeyed with fear and trembling; they quaffed the liquor in profound silence, and then returned to their game.

By degrees Rip's awe and apprehension subsided. He even ventured, when no eye was fixed upon him, to taste the beverage, which he found had much of the flavor of excellent Hollands [Dutch gin]. He was naturally a thirsty soul, and was soon tempted to repeat the draft. One taste provoked another; and he reiterated his visits to the flagon so often that at length his senses were overpowered, his eyes swam in his head, his head gradually declined, and he fell into a deep sleep.

On waking, he found himself on the green knoll whence he had first seen the old man of the glen. He rubbed his eyes—it was a bright sunny morning. The birds were hopping and twittering among the bushes, and the eagle was wheeling aloft and breasting the pure mountain breeze. "Surely," thought Rip, "I have not slept here all night." He recalled the occurrences before he fell asleep. The strange man with a keg of liquor, the mountain ravine, the wild retreat among the rocks, the woebegone party at ninepins, the flagon—"Oh! that flagon! that wicked flagon!" thought Rip. "What excuse shall I make to Dame Van Winkle?"

He looked round for his gun, but in place of the clean, well-oiled fowling-piece, he found an old firelock lying by him, the barrel incrusted with rust, the lock falling off, and the stock worm-eaten. He now suspected that the grave roisters of the mountain had put a trick upon him, and, having dosed him with liquor, had robbed him of his gun. Wolf, too, had disappeared, but he might have strayed away after a squirrel or partridge. He whistled after him, and shouted his name, but all in vain; the echoes repeated his whistle and shout, but no dog was to be seen. A

He determined to revisit the scene of the last evening's gambol, and if he met with any of the party, to demand his dog and gun. As he rose to walk, he found himself stiff in the joints, and wanting in his usual activity. "These mountain beds do not agree with me," thought Rip, "and if this frolic should lay me up with a fit of the rheumatism, I shall have a blessed time with Dame Van Winkle." With some difficulty he got down into the glen: he found the gully up which he and his companion had ascended the preceding evening; but to his astonishment a mountain stream was now foaming down it, leaping from rock to rock, and filling the glen with babbling murmurs. He, however, made shift to scramble up its sides, working his toilsome way through thickets of birch, sassafras, and witchhazel, and sometimes tripped up or entangled by the wild grapevines that twisted their coils or tendrils from tree to tree, and spread a kind of network in his path.

At length he reached to where the ravine had opened through the cliffs to the amphitheater; but no traces of such opening remained. The rocks presented a high, impenetrable wall, over which

---

13. **doublets:** close-fitting jackets.
14. **hanger:** small, curved sword worn at the waist.
15. **roses:** rosettes.
16. **flagons:** large drinking vessels.

the torrent came tumbling in a sheet of feathery foam, and fell into a broad deep basin, black from the shadows of the surrounding forest. Here, then, poor Rip was brought to a stand. He again called and whistled after his dog; he was only answered by the cawing of a flock of idle crows, sporting high in the air about a dry tree that overhung a sunny precipice; and who, secure in their elevation, seemed to look down and scoff at the poor man's perplexities. What was to be done? The morning was passing away, and Rip felt famished for want of his breakfast. He grieved to give up his dog and gun; he dreaded to meet his wife; but it would not do to starve among the mountains. He shook his head, shouldered the rusty firelock, and, with a heart full of trouble and anxiety, turned his steps homeward. A

As he approached the village he met a number of people, but none whom he knew, which somewhat surprised him, for he had thought himself acquainted with everyone in the country round. Their dress, too, was of a different fashion from that to which he was accustomed. They all stared at him with equal marks of surprise, and whenever they cast their eyes upon him, invariably stroked their chins. The constant recurrence of this gesture induced Rip, involuntarily, to do the same, when, to his astonishment, he found his beard had grown a foot long!

He had now entered the skirts of the village. A troop of strange children ran at his heels, hooting after him, and pointing at his gray beard. The dogs, too, not one of which he recognized for an old acquaintance, barked at him as he passed. The very village was altered; it was larger and more populous. There were rows of houses which he had never seen before, and those which had been his familiar haunts had disappeared. Strange names were over the doors, strange faces at the windows—everything was strange. His mind now misgave him; he began to doubt whether both he and the world around him were not bewitched. Surely this was his native village, which he had left but the day before. There stood the Kaatskill Mountains, there ran the silver Hudson at a distance, there was every hill and dale precisely as it had always been. Rip was sorely perplexed. "That flagon last night," thought he, "has addled my poor head sadly!"

It was with some difficulty that he found the way to his own house, which he approached with silent awe, expecting every moment to hear the shrill voice of Dame Van Winkle. He found the house gone to decay—the roof fallen in, the windows shattered, and the doors off the hinges. A half-starved dog that looked like Wolf was skulking about it. Rip called him by name, but the cur snarled, showed his teeth, and passed on. This was an unkind cut indeed. "My very dog," sighed poor Rip, "has forgotten me!"

He entered the house, which, to tell the truth, Dame Van Winkle had always kept in neat order. It was empty, forlorn, and apparently abandoned. This desolateness overcame all his connubial fears; he called loudly for his wife and children—the lonely chambers rang for a moment with his voice, and then all again was silence. B

He now hurried forth, and hastened to his old resort, the village inn—but it too was gone. A large, rickety, wooden building stood in its place, with great gaping windows, some of them broken and mended with old hats and petticoats, and over the door was painted, "The Union Hotel, by Jonathan Doolittle." Instead of the great tree that used to shelter the quiet little Dutch inn of yore, there now was reared a tall naked pole, with something on the top that looked like a red nightcap,[17] and from it was fluttering a flag, on which was a singular assemblage of stars and stripes; all this was strange and incomprehensible. He recognized on the sign, however, the ruby face of King George, under which he had smoked so many a peaceful pipe; but even this was singularly metamorphosed.[18] The red coat was changed for one of blue and buff, a sword was held in the hand instead of a scepter, the head was decorated with a cocked hat, and underneath was painted in large characters, GENERAL WASHINGTON.

There was, as usual, a crowd of folk about the door, but none that Rip recollected. The very character of the people seemed changed. There was a busy, bustling, disputatious tone about it, instead of the accustomed phlegm and drowsy tranquillity. He looked in vain for the sage Nicholas Vedder, with his broad face, double chin, and fair long pipe, uttering clouds of tobacco smoke instead of idle speeches; or Van Bummel, the schoolmaster, doling forth the contents of an ancient newspaper. In place of these, a lean, bilious-looking fellow, with his pockets full of handbills,

17. **a red nightcap:** a "liberty cap," worn as a symbol of independence.

18. **metamorphosed** (met·ə·môr'fōzd): transformed.

A. Suspense

? What pieces of information does Irving give in these paragraphs that intrigue us as to Rip's fate? (The rust on the gun, the stiffness in Rip's joints, the changes in fashion, the unfamiliarity of faces, the length of Rip's beard—see question 4, page 136.)

B. Responding

? How would you feel in Rip's place, yourself in a world you no longer knew, which no longer knew you? What would you do in response? (Answers will vary.)

Humanities Connection: Discussing the Fine Art In this illustration by Quidor, Rip is seen as a glaring-eyed, ravaged, maddened old creature in the same mold as Ahab of *Moby-Dick,* or Shakespeare's Lear. The townspeople look like a singularly uncongenial lot, and the children at Rip's feet look as threatening as goblins. (See Humanities Connection annotation, page 127.)

The Return of Rip Van Winkle by John Quidor (1829). Oil on canvas.

National Gallery of Art, Washington, D.C. Andrew W. Mellon Collection.

was haranguing vehemently about rights of citizens, elections, members of Congress, liberty, Bunker's Hill, heroes of Seventy-six, and other words which were a perfect Babylonish[19] jargon to the bewildered Van Winkle. A

The appearance of Rip, with his long, grizzled beard, his rusty fowling-piece, his uncouth dress, and an army of women and children at his heels, soon attracted the attention of the tavern-politicians. They crowded round him, eyeing him from head to foot with great curiosity. The orator bustled up to him, and, drawing him partly aside, inquired "On which side he voted?" Rip stared in vacant stupidity. Another short but busy little fellow pulled him by the arm, and, rising on tiptoe, inquired in his ear, "Whether he was Federal or Democrat?" Rip was equally at a loss to comprehend the question; when a knowing, self-important old gentleman, in a sharp cocked hat, made his way through the crowd, putting them to the right and left with his elbows as he passed, and planting himself before Van Winkle, with one arm akimbo, the other resting on his cane, his keen eyes and sharp hat penetrating, as it were, into his very soul, demanded, in an austere tone, "What brought him to the election with a gun on his shoulder, and a mob at his heels; and whether he meant to breed a riot in the village?"—"Alas! gentlemen," cried Rip, somewhat dismayed, "I am a poor quiet man, a native of the place, and a loyal subject of the King, God bless him!"

Here a general shout burst from the bystanders—"A Tory! a Tory! a spy! a refugee! hustle him! away with him!" It was with great difficulty that the self-important man in the cocked hat restored order; and, having assumed a tenfold austerity of brow, demanded again of the unknown culprit, what he came there for, and whom he was seeking. The poor man humbly assured him that he meant no harm, but merely came there in search of some of his neighbors, who used to keep about the tavern. B

"Well, who are they? Name them."

Rip bethought himself a moment, and inquired, "Where's Nicholas Vedder?"

There was a silence for a little while, when an old man replied, in a thin piping voice, "Nicholas Vedder! Why, he is dead and gone these eighteen years! There was a wooden tombstone in the

A. Satire
Irving satirizes the politics of his day, and may be implying that the narrow partisanship of the people has led them to forget generosity. The line on page 131, "The very character of the people seemed changed," is also pertinent here. Irving may be nostalgic for the slower, friendlier pace of pre-Revolutionary America. (See page 136, questions 9 and 10.)

B. Dialogue
The passages in which Rip questions and is questioned by the townspeople, on this and the following page, are inherently dramatic and could be read aloud by students playing the different characters.

---

19. **Babylonish:** confusing (a confusion of languages occurred at the building of the Tower of Babel in the Book of Genesis).

A. Expansion
The deeper undercurrent beneath this seemingly comic tale is revealed by Rip's frightening confrontation with a son who has usurped him. "He doubted his own identity," Irving says. Beneath the charm of the telling, we are seeing a man at the end of his tether, alone, frightened, grief stricken. The multiplicity of layers in the story is surely one reason why it retains a grip on the imagination.

B. Tone
How does the tone change at this point? (It becomes less tense and dramatic, more genial and folklore-like, through the switch from dialogue to leisurely narration.)

churchyard that used to tell all about him, but that's rotten and gone, too."

"Where's Brom Dutcher?"

"Oh, he went off to the army in the beginning of the war; some say he was killed at the storming of Stony Point; others say he was drowned in a squall at the foot of Antony's Nose.[20] I don't know—he never came back again."

"Where's Van Bummel, the schoolmaster?"

"He went off to the wars, too, was a great militia general, and is now in Congress."

Rip's heart died away at hearing of these sad changes in his home and friends, and finding himself thus alone in the world. Every answer puzzled him, too, by treating of such enormous lapses of time, and of matters which he could not understand: war, Congress, Stony Point; he had no courage to ask after anymore friends, but cried out in despair, "Does nobody here know Rip Van Winkle?"

"Oh, Rip Van Winkle!" exclaimed two or three, "oh, to be sure! That's Rip Van Winkle yonder, leaning against the tree."

Rip looked, and beheld a precise counterpart of himself, as he went up the mountain; apparently as lazy, and certainly as ragged. The poor fellow A was now completely confounded. He doubted his own identity, and whether he was himself or another man. In the midst of his bewilderment, the man in the cocked hat demanded who he was, and what was his name.

"God knows," exclaimed he, at his wit's end, "I'm not myself—I'm somebody else—that's me yonder—no—that's somebody else got into my shoes. I was myself last night, but I fell asleep on the mountain, and they've changed my gun, and everything's changed, and I'm changed, and I can't tell what's my name, or who I am!"

The bystanders began now to look at each other, nod, wink significantly, and tap their fingers against their foreheads. There was a whisper, also, about securing the gun, and keeping the old fellow from doing mischief, at the very suggestion of which the self-important man in the cocked hat retired with some precipitation. At this critical moment a fresh, comely woman pressed through the throng to get a peep at the gray-bearded man. She had a chubby child in her arms, which, frightened at his looks, began to cry. "Hush, Rip," cried she, "hush, you little fool; the old man won't hurt you." The name of the child, the air of the mother, the tone of her voice, all awakened a train of recollections in his mind. "What is your name, my good woman?" asked he.

"Judith Gardenier."

"And your father's name?"

"Ah, poor man. Rip Van Winkle was his name, but it's twenty years since he went away from home with his gun, and never has been heard of since—his dog came home without him; but whether he shot himself, or was carried away by the Indians, nobody can tell. I was then but a little girl."

Rip had but one question more to ask; but he put it with a faltering voice:

"Where's your mother?"

"Oh, she too had died but a short time since; she broke a blood vessel in a fit of passion at a New England peddler."

There was a drop of comfort, at least, in this intelligence. The honest man could contain himself no longer. He caught his daughter and her child in his arms. "I am your father!" cried he. "Young Rip Van Winkle once, old Rip Van Winkle now! Does nobody know poor Rip Van Winkle?"

All stood amazed, until an old woman, tottering out from among the crowd, put her hand to her brow, and peering under it in his face for a moment, exclaimed, "Sure enough! It is Rip Van Winkle—it is himself! Welcome home again, old neighbor. Why, where have you been these twenty long years?"

Rip's story was soon told, for the whole twenty years had been to him but as one night. The neighbors stared when they heard it; some were seen to wink at each other, and put their tongues in their cheeks; and the self-important man in the cocked hat, who, when the alarm was over, had returned to the field, screwed down the corners of his mouth, and shook his head—upon which there was a general shaking of the head throughout the assemblage. B

It was determined, however, to take the opinion of old Peter Vanderdonk, who was seen slowly advancing up the road. He was a descendant of the historian of that name, who wrote one of the earliest accounts of the province. Peter was the most ancient inhabitant of the village, and well versed in all the wonderful events and traditions of the neighborhood. He recollected Rip at once, and corroborated his story in the most satisfactory manner. He assured the company that it was a

20. **Antony's Nose:** mountain near West Point.

Literature and Language: Using Participial Phrases
Review the definitions of **participle** and **participial phrase** (see page 1186); then ask students to identify them in this sentence:

He found the house *gone to decay*—the roof *fallen in,* the windows *shattered,* and the doors off the hinges.

Note that these are all past participles; present participles *(going, falling, shattering)* always end in *-ing.*

Demonstrate how participial phrases can be used to combine sentences. Ask students to change the first sentence in each pair into a participial phrase. Some words will be omitted.

1. Rip was puzzled at the changes in the village. Rip could not understand what had happened. (Hint: Begin with *Puzzled.*)
2. Rip was saddened to hear of his friends' deaths. Rip felt himself alone in the world.
3. Rip was beginning to understand what had happened. Rip asked Judith Gardenier where her mother was.
4. The villagers were amazed at his story. The villagers welcomed him home.
5. Rip was living with his daughter and her husband. Rip resumed his life of idleness.

fact, handed down from his ancestor the historian, that the Kaatskill Mountains had always been haunted by strange beings. That it was affirmed that the great Hendrick Hudson, the first discoverer of the river and country, kept a kind of vigil there every twenty years, with his crew of the Half Moon; being permitted in this way to revisit the scenes of his enterprise, and keep a guardian eye upon the river and the great city called by his name. That his father had once seen them in their old Dutch dresses playing at ninepins in a hollow of the mountain; and that he himself had heard, one summer afternoon, the sound of their balls, like distant peals of thunder.

A To make a long story short, the company broke up and returned to the more important concerns of the election. Rip's daughter took him home to live with her; she had a snug, well-furnished house, and a stout, cheery farmer for a husband, whom Rip recollected for one of the urchins that used to climb upon his back. As to Rip's son and heir, who was the ditto of himself, seen leaning against the tree, he was employed to work on the farm; but evinced an hereditary disposition to attend to anything else but his business.

Rip now resumed his old walks and habits; he soon found many of his former cronies, though all rather the worse for the wear and tear of time; and preferred making friends among the rising generation, with whom he soon grew into great favor.

Having nothing to do at home, and being arrived at that happy age when a man can be idle with impunity, he took his place once more on the bench at the inn door, and was reverenced as one of the patriarchs of the village, and a chronicle of the old times "before the war." It was some time before he could get into the regular track of gossip, or could be made to comprehend the strange events that had taken place during his torpor. How that there had been a revolutionary war, that the country had thrown off the yoke of old England, and that, instead of being a subject of his Majesty George the Third, he was now a free citizen of the United States. Rip, in fact, was no politician; the changes of states and empires made but little impression on him; but there was one species of despotism under which he had long groaned, and that was—petticoat government. Happily that was at an end; he had got his neck out of the yoke of matrimony, and could go in and out whenever he pleased, without dreading the tyranny of Dame Van Winkle. Whenever her name was mentioned, however, he shook his head, shrugged his shoulders, and cast up his eyes; which might pass either for an expression of resignation to his fate, or joy at his deliverance.

He used to tell his story to every stranger that arrived at Mr. Doolittle's hotel. He was observed, at first, to vary on some points every time he told it, which was, doubtless, owing to his having so recently awaked. It at last settled down precisely to the tale I have related, and not a man, woman, or child in the neighborhood but knew it by heart. Some always pretended to doubt the reality of it, and insisted that Rip had been out of his head, and that this was one point on which he always remained flighty. B The old Dutch inhabitants, however, almost universally gave it full credit. Even to this day they never hear a thunderstorm of a summer afternoon about the Kaatskill, but they say Hendrick Hudson and his crew are at their game of ninepins; and it is a common wish of all henpecked husbands in the neighborhood, when life hangs heavy on their hands, that they might have a quieting draft out of Rip Van Winkle's flagon.

Note. The foregoing tale, one would suspect, had been suggested to Mr. Knickerbocker by a little German superstition about the Emperor Frederick *der Rothbart,*[21] and the Kypphäuser C Mountain: the subjoined note, however, which he had appended to the tale, shows that it is an absolute fact, narrated with his usual fidelity.

"The story of Rip Van Winkle may seem incredible to many, but nevertheless I give it my full belief, for I know the vicinity of our old Dutch settlements to have been very subject to marvelous events and appearances. Indeed, I have heard many stranger stories than this, in the villages along the Hudson; all of which were too well authenticated to admit of a doubt. I have even talked with Rip Van Winkle myself, who, when last I saw him, was a very venerable old man, and so perfectly rational and consistent on every other point, that I think no conscientious person could refuse to take this into the bargain; nay, I have seen a certificate on the subject taken before a country justice and signed with a cross, in the justice's own handwriting. The story, therefore, is beyond the possibility of doubt.

"D. K."

21. ***der Rothbart:*** "the redbeard."

A. Tone
What words and phrases help restore the genial tone? (Words such as *snug* and *cheery* serve this purpose.)

B. Responding
At this point in the story, you might want to discuss with students how Rip's life has changed. (Responses will vary, but it may be that Rip's life returns to stasis: He once again spends his time at the inn, and a sense of complacency overcomes the former trauma. See question 6, page 136.)

C. Expansion
The "Note" returns us to the frame device.

CLOSURE
Have students discuss how reading the original story either changed or confirmed their pre-existing ideas of the tale of Rip Van Winkle.

READING CHECK TEST

1. Rip Van Winkle was a young man in the ______ century. *eighteenth*
2. His region of New York state had originally been settled by the ______. *Dutch*
3. The little men played a bowling game called ______. *ninepins*
4. When Rip returned from sleep, the colonies had ______. *become independent*
5. As an old man, Rip lived with his ______. *daughter*

A. Responding
The basic mythic pattern of departure, journey, and return, including such elements as the supernatural, disguises, and recognition scenes, was set forth by Joseph Campbell in his classic work of comparative mythology, *The Hero with a Thousand Faces.* Campbell specifies that the hero, on his return, brings a boon with him: something his society needs, like the fire brought back by Prometheus in the Greek myth, or a spiritual awakening such as that revealed by Buddha, or a victory in battle, or simply the inspiration of knowing that the hero has done great things.
? What boon does Rip bring with him? (Answers may vary, but some students may feel that he does not bring any boon, thus varying Campbell's pattern.)

A Comment on the Story

Like *Gulliver's Travels* and *Alice in Wonderland,* this story has perennially appealed to both children and adults. Part of its popularity may be traced to some age-old folk tale elements; in fact, Irving did borrow some of the plot from a German folk tale. Analyses of folk tales from all over the world have revealed an astonishing number of common narrative elements. Prominent among these elements are the following:

A
1. The perilous journey
2. The use of the supernatural
3. Disguise and recognition scenes

Just as in Homer's *Odyssey,* the hero of "Rip Van Winkle" embarks on a journey which keeps him away from home for twenty years. The journey involves some supernatural adventures. When the hero returns, few people recognize him. The comic conclusion portrays an elaborate recognition scene and the hero's reintegration into society.

"Rip Van Winkle," of course, varies these thematic strands in what is essentially a light-hearted, comic narrative. Rip's "journey" is hardly a heroic expedition, like that of Odysseus to the Trojan War. Instead of the faithful wife Penelope, we have the ill-tempered shrew, Mrs. Van Winkle, whose passing from the scene before Rip's return is a great relief to the hero. And the theme of the supernatural is limited to the mysterious appearance of Henry Hudson's Dutch crew, who themselves are presented as parodies of the silent, hard-working Dutch farmers who settled New Amsterdam. When Rip returns, it is not as the master of disguises and tricks, the "wily" Odysseus, but as a fumbling, disoriented old man who must plead his case before the suspicious townspeople. If Irving consciously evokes some aspects of the *Odyssey,* it is only to deflate them with a lightly satirical touch.

Nevertheless, a symbolic level to the story's meaning is unmistakable. Rip's enslavement to his wife parallels the country's colonial past; his awakening to a new life suggests the new condition of the United States after the Revolution. And the happy ending hints at Irving's optimism about the future. Irving's light touch does not insist on these parallels. But the roles of both history and setting in the story tend to reinforce them indirectly. The central incident of the plot is the supernatural vision of the early Dutch settlers. And the writer's pleasure and skill in his description of the natural landscape are evident in the story's leisurely exposition.

Responding to the Story

Analyzing the Story

Identifying Facts

1. Name Rip's positive **character** traits. What are his negative traits? Describe Rip's relationship with his wife.
2. What does the narrator himself say about the **character** of Dame Van Winkle?
3. Describe the appearance and behavior of the group that Rip meets on the mountain. What causes him to fall asleep?
4. When Rip awakens, what clues tell us that a great deal of time has passed?
5. Compare the appearance and activities of the inn before and after Rip's sleep. How does the inn reflect the political and social changes that have taken place in the country as a whole?
6. As Rip begins to understand what has happened to him, how does he react? Once he has adjusted to his situation, how does his new life compare to his old one?

Interpreting Meanings

7. In what ways is this a classic story of wish fulfillment? Do you think the **theme** of the story is still relevant to readers in the late twentieth century? Explain.
8. In his introductory note, the narrator (who is Geoffrey Crayon) explains that the manuscript of "Rip Van Winkle" was written by Diedrich Knickerbocker, the narrator of Irving's earlier *History of New York.* How does Irving use his two narrators—Geoffrey Crayon and Diedrich Knickerbocker—to defend the tale's credibility? What is Irving's **tone** in these introductory passages?
9. What details in "Rip Van Winkle" do you think reveal Irving's fascination with the past? Find some of Irving's descriptions of the **setting** which you think reflect a Romantic's view of nature.
10. Irving was a Romantic, but he was also a satirist. What elements of this story—including the narrator's commentaries—are **satirical?** Who or what are Irving's targets?

ANALYZING THE STORY

Identifying Facts

1. Rip is kind, helpful, and good-natured; however, he is also lazy and irresponsible.

His wife complains about his laziness.

2. She is a shrew and a termagant.

3. They are dressed in old-fashioned garb and are silently bowling at ninepins.

Drinking the group's liquor causes Rip to fall asleep.

4. Rip's gun has rusted; his dog Wolf has disappeared; his joints are stiff; and a new mountain stream has formed.

5. The crowd at the inn is livelier and more argumentative, and much political discussion is heard; an election is going on.

6. Rip is bewildered, but seems slightly relieved at the news of his wife's death!

His new life is more peaceful than his old, although just as "do-nothing." He is happy with a number of his former cronies, and delights in telling his story to anyone who will listen.

Interpreting Meanings

7. The idea of escape is at the heart of "Rip Van Winkle." Since Rip succeeds in that escape, the story is a classic example of wish fulfillment.

8. Knickerbocker's accuracy has been "completely established," according to Crayon.

The tone of the comments is lightly ironic, or mock-serious.

9. In his descriptions of the group on the mountain and in references to New York's Dutch past, Irving clothes history with an air of mystery and romance.

10. Irving satirizes the Van Winkles' way of life, and pokes fun at the townspeople.

11. Students should be able to suggest many examples of these popular character types. See "The Secret Life of Walter Mitty" (page 577 of this book). Talk about old TV shows like *I Love Lucy* and *All in the Family,* and about current "domestic" fare on TV. In classical literature there is *The Taming of the Shrew.*

11. Dame Van Winkle and Rip are **stereotyped characters** that have been found in literature throughout the ages—the nagging wife and the henpecked husband. Can you identify these character types in current literature and in popular movies and TV shows? What is your response to Irving's characterization of Dame Van Winkle? Was Irving (who remained a bachelor) biased in favor of the ne'er-do-well, Rip?

Writing About the Story

A Creative Response

1. **Writing an Epilogue.** Write an epilogue to this story called "Dame Van Winkle." Describe her response to Rip's disappearance. Was she also emancipated? Will you have Dame Van Winkle tell her own story, or let Diedrich Knickerbocker continue?

A Critical Response

2. **Modernizing the Story.** Suppose this story were reset in the late twentieth century. What elements of the story would have to change? In a paragraph, explain how the following story elements could be altered to set "Rip Van Winkle" in America today:

   a. Setting
   b. Characters
   c. Conflict

3. **Explaining a Parallel.** Rip's awakening has been seen by many critics as a parallel to the awakening of the new American nation. In a short essay, cite the specific elements in Rip's emancipation that reflect the country's emancipation from Great Britain. You may want to discuss the ideas of independence, peace, and maturity. Cite details from the story to prove that Irving is deliberately connecting Rip's emancipation with that of America.

4. **Analyzing a Conflict.** This story by America's first professional writer reflects a conflict that has been used by hundreds of other writers of comedy, before and after Irving. The conflict might be described as **the battle of the sexes.** In a brief essay, tell how Irving's story reflects this conflict; name other comedies that use the same conflict; and explain your own response to its continued use and popularity.

Analyzing Language and Style

Inflated Language

One of the elements of Irving's style is his use of comically inflated language to describe the commonplace. For example, rather than plainly saying Rip is "lazy," or that he "hates work," Irving states that Rip has "an insuperable aversion to all kinds of profitable labor."

1. Find at least two other comically inflated descriptions of Rip's family life.
2. How could each inflated description be phrased in plain English?
3. How did this element of Irving's style affect your reading of the story?

Primary Sources

A Traveler Comments on American Manners

Frances Trollope (1780–1863) visited America from her native England in 1832, and then went home and wrote a book about her adventures. Mrs. Trollope, like Dame Van Winkle, says what is on her mind.

"And now arrived the 4th of July, that greatest of all American festivals. On the 4th of July, 1776, the declaration of their independence was signed, at the State-house in Philadelphia.

"To me, the dreary coldness and want of enthusiasm in American manners is one of their greatest defects, and I therefore hailed the demonstrations of general feeling which this day elicits with real pleasure. On the 4th of July the hearts of the people seem to awaken from a three hundred and sixty-four days' sleep; they appear high-spirited, gay, animated, social, generous, or at least liberal in expense; and would they but refrain from spitting on that hallowed day, I should say, that on the 4th of July, at least, they appeared to be an amiable people. It is true that the women have but little to do with the pageantry, the splendor, or the gaiety of the day; but, setting this defect aside, it was indeed a glorious sight to behold a jubilee so heartfelt as this; and had they not the bad taste and bad feeling to utter an annual oration, with unvarying abuse of the mother country, to say nothing of the warlike manifesto called the Declaration of Independence, our gracious king himself might look upon the scene and say that it was good; nay, even rejoice, that twelve millions of bustling bodies, at four thousand miles distance from his throne and his altars, should make their own laws, and drink their own tea, after the fashion that pleased them best."

—from *Domestic Manners of the Americans,*
Frances Trollope

A. Expansion Bryant's life is interesting not because he was such a great poet that we ought to know about him in detail, but because his life typifies a pattern of the intellectual development of the professional classes in the United States at that time.

The combination of a strong foundation in Biblical religion with a growing curiosity about nature, the legal training, the eighteenth-century rationalistic deism merging into more intuitional, nineteenth-century views, and the later involvement in the question of slavery—all these things make Bryant prototypical, except, of course, for the fact that he was a gifted poet.

William Cullen Bryant (1794–1878)

Poetry is a lonely occupation, but not a solitary one. Poets of any consequence rarely write in isolation from the influence of their predecessors or from the influence of other poets of their own time. When William Cullen Bryant was still an adolescent, he read a book called *Lyrical Ballads*, published in 1798 by his great English contemporaries William Wordsworth and Samuel Taylor Coleridge. This volume of poetry and theory focused the expression and much of the philosophy of the Romantic era. The book was a powerful source of inspiration for poets who wanted to replace conventional poetic diction with the common speech of their own time. Bryant was one of these poets—the first mature American Romantic, the country boy who translated the messages of English Romanticism into his own native tongue.

Supporting the influence of the English Romantics were two factors of perhaps equal importance to Bryant's poetry. One factor was Bryant's growing attraction to deism, which held that divinity could be found in nature. The other factor was the geography of his surroundings, which placed Bryant in immediate contact with everything that supported this philosophy.

By the time of Bryant's birth, western Massachusetts was no longer a Colonial frontier, but a widely settled countryside. Over the next hundred years and more, its farms, steepled towns, and mountain forests would be the homes of many poets. These writers would find in their surroundings metaphors to express their sense of correspondence between human life and the life of nature. After Bryant, the same New England seasons would turn for Herman Melville, Emily Dickinson, and, later, for Robert Frost and Richard Wilbur. All these poets were intimate with the shadows and whispers of the Berkshires and the adjacent Green Mountains. All would make their own small plot of ground part of the permanent landscape of American poetry.

A Bryant was born in Cummington, Massachusetts, the son of a physician and a mother who came from a family of clergymen. As a child, he had access to his father's large library. By the age of nine, he was already writing poetry that earned him a reputation as a prodigy.

William Cullen Bryant, portrait by Samuel F. B. Morse (1825). Oil.

National Academy of Design, New York.

Along with conventional book learning, Bryant also had the advantage of his mother's faithful readings of Scripture and of his father's instruction in the close observation of the natural world. It was a kind of home-grown education, in which Christian piety was combined with scientific curiosity. After a year of formal study at Williams College, Bryant was tutored for a career as a lawyer. At the age of twenty-two, he entered the practice of law in the town of Great Barrington.

Just as it seemed that his new profession would replace his interest in literature, Bryant found a magazine that would publish "Thanatopsis," a poem he had worked on for six years. Almost at once, this poem established Bryant's reputation and soon made him famous. Widely reprinted, "Thanatopsis" was the keystone of a volume, entitled simply *Poems*, issued in Boston when Bryant was twenty-seven. Married by this time, he was soon persuaded to move to New York City. There, for many years, he played the triple role of editor, critic, and poet.

Supplementary Support Materials
1. Vocabulary Activity Worksheet (*CCB*)
2. Review and Response Worksheet: Theme (*CCB*)
3. Selection Test (*CCB*)

Developing Vocabulary
The following words from the poem are tested in the Selection Test. (See also Vocabulary Activity Worksheet.)
billow illimitable abyss

Preparation
Establishing a Purpose. To prepare students for this poem, you might ask them if they have ever watched birds flying across the sky. Have them describe the setting and how the experience made them feel. Then have them read to determine whether or not Bryant has captured that experience.

As the author of a poem that almost every schoolchild was able to recite by heart, Bryant became a famous literary figure. His influence extended even beyond literature, into religion and politics. As a convert to Unitarianism, Bryant believed in universal salvation, in the essential goodness of humankind, and in the ability to know God by intuition as well as by reason and conscience. As a liberal, Bryant supported the growing movement for the abolition of slavery; he was also one of the founders of the Republican Party, which, in his lifetime, would produce Abraham Lincoln. In 1870–1872, he published his translations of Homer's *Iliad* and *Odyssey.* When Bryant died at the age of eighty-four, he was a rich man, so widely honored at home and abroad that he had become a kind of national monument.

Today, Bryant's poems are not read as the spiritual counsels they were meant to be; instead, they are read as period pieces that authentically reflect their times. Bryant's moralizing is characteristic of the popular poetry of the nineteenth century; today, most readers prefer messages or themes that are implied, rather than explicitly stated. The appeal of Bryant's poems may have been due largely to the limited tastes of a particular time and place. Yet even when his poems seem more like moral fables than free expressions of the imagination, they ring with an air of piety and sincerity no one can doubt.

One of the aims of the Romantic poets was to discover and preach the moral lessons that could be found in nature. In a world swept by political revolution and already feeling the sooty touch of industrialism, the Romantics turned to nature for comfort and for proof of a Divine presence. The poem that follows is an example of this Romantic endeavor. It is addressed to a bird the speaker has seen flying overhead. A

Following the conventions of his time, the poet uses words like *whither, dost, thou,* and *thy.* Read *whither* in line 1 as meaning "To what place?"

To a Waterfowl

Whither, midst falling dew,
While glow the heavens with the last steps of day,
Far, through their rosy depths, dost thou pursue
Thy solitary way?

Vainly the fowler's° eye
Might mark thy distant flight to do thee wrong,
As, darkly seen against the crimson sky,
Thy figure floats along.

Seek'st thou the plashy° brink
Of weedy lake, or marge° of river wide,
Or where the rocking billows rise and sink
On the chafed oceanside?

There is a Power whose care
Teaches thy way along that pathless coast—
The desert and illimitable air—
B Lone wandering, but not lost.

5. **fowler:** hunter of wild birds.

9. **plashy:** watery.

10. **marge:** edge.

A. Apostrophe
A piece of writing addressed to a person, animal, or object is called an *apostrophe.*

B. Expansion
Line 16 is perhaps the most felicitous one in the poem, expressing a powerful philosophical and emotional attitude in five simple words. You might want students to paraphrase and discuss this line. Compare the paraphrases with the wording of the poem. The paraphrases are certain to be wordier and less powerful.

Closure

Have students summarize, in one or two sentences, Bryant's thoughts and feelings as he watches the waterfowl in flight.

Analyzing The Poem

Identifying Details

1. The hunter, or fowler (lines 5–8).

2. A "Power" (lines 13–14).

The bird will find a summer house in which to rest and be with its fellows.

3. "Plashy" (line 9); "billows" (line 11).

Humanities Connection: Writing About the Fine Art

You might use the photograph as the basis for a quick-write even before students read the poem itself. Ask students to look at the photograph for a minute and write down what they would like to ask, and tell, the birds. (This is much like what Bryant did after viewing real waterbirds. See Establishing a Purpose, page 139.)

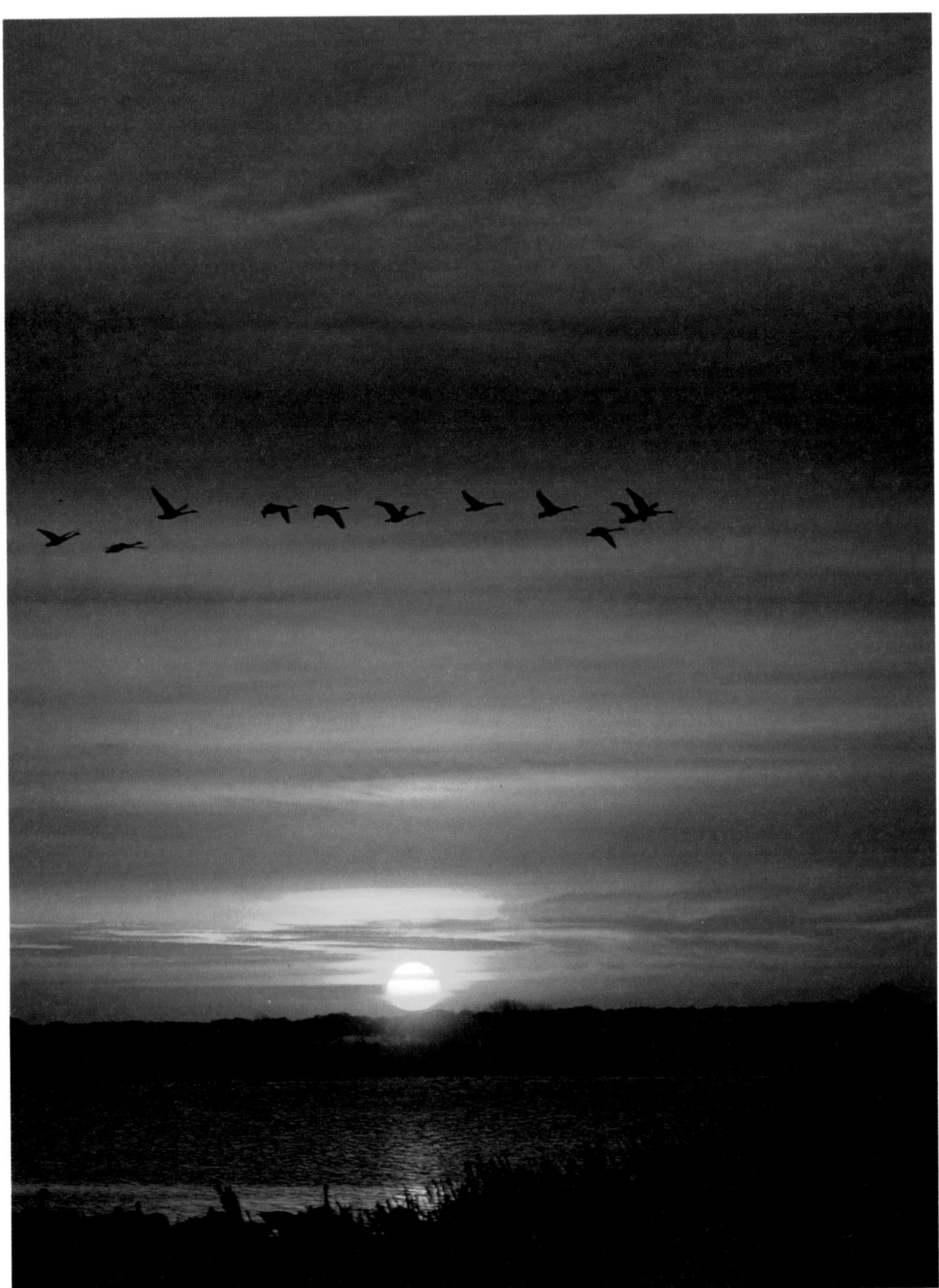

Interpreting Meanings

4. God will guide and protect us in our journey through life.

God, or to some supernatural power.

Parts of the sky or different climatic regions.

5. Misfortunes or evil forces in general, or the devil in particular.

6. "Pursue" (line 3), "distant flight" (line 6), "seek'st" (line 9), "summer home" (line 22), "certain flight" (line 30).

Lonely migration is a metaphor for one's pilgrimage through life.

7. This poem suggests that God actually intervenes in the universe to provide guidance for humanity.

8. Student answers will vary; most students may feel that the speaker gains at least some measure of peace and assurance from the experience.

9. Most students will agree that this is possible.

Students may suggest that the natural world is viewed more scientifically by many but that others speak of caring for nature with an almost religious zeal.

A All day thy wings have fanned,
At that far height, the cold, thin atmosphere,
Yet stoop not, weary, to the welcome land,
Though the dark night is near.

And soon that toil shall end;
Soon shalt thou find a summer home, and rest,
And scream among thy fellows; reeds shall bend,
Soon, o'er thy sheltered nest.

Thou'rt gone, the abyss of heaven
Hath swallowed up thy form; yet, on my heart
Deeply hath sunk the lesson thou hast given,
And shall not soon depart.

He who, from zone to zone,
Guides through the boundless sky thy certain flight,
B In the long way that I must tread alone
Will lead my steps aright.

A. Style
Note the very simple language: only *atmosphere* has more than one syllable.

B. Expansion
You might want students to compare the thoughts expressed in this stanza with those of Psalm 121 of the Bible. (You might want to remind students of Bryant's early grounding in the Bible.)

Responding to the Poem

Analyzing the Poem

Identifying Details

1. What danger to the bird is mentioned in the second stanza?
2. According to the speaker, what guides the waterfowl in its flight? Describe how the speaker envisions the end of the bird's "toil" in the sixth stanza.
3. The third stanza contains examples of **onomatopoeia,** or words that actually imitate the sounds of the things they refer to. Name these words.

Interpreting Meanings

4. In line 27, the point toward which the poem is building becomes explicit with the word *lesson.* In your own words, what is that lesson? Who is "He" in line 29? What are the "zones"?
5. The phrase "to do thee wrong" (line 6) is a curious way of describing what the fowler, or hunter, wants to do to the bird. What do you think Bryant intends the fowler to **symbolize,** other than just someone who is hunting birds?
6. Throughout the poem, certain words and phrases emphasize that the waterfowl is a migratory bird. What are some of these? What does the idea of a *lonely* migration contribute to the **theme** of the poem?
7. In the eighteenth century, rationalist thinkers had perceived the operations of nature as a "clockwork universe." They saw the universe as governed by "natural law," under which the stars and the seasons moved and rotated with mechanical precision. In their view, the creator of this mechanism did not control its workings but remained merely an indifferent spectator. In what way is this Romantic poem a rejection of that rationalist view?
8. Do you believe the lesson the speaker learns is a useful one? Explain.
9. Can Nature still present "lessons" to people today? How would you describe the way most people today view the natural world?

Writing About the Poem

A Critical Response

Analyzing the Poem. Do you think Bryant's main intention *was* to teach a lesson? If so, why does he spend so much time coming to the point? What does his extended description of the bird in flight do for you, as a reader, that a simple statement of his belief in Divine guidance would not have done? In a paragraph, explain your answers to these questions.

SUPPLEMENTARY SUPPORT MATERIALS
1. Vocabulary Activity Worksheet (*CCB*)
2. Review and Response Worksheet: Tone and Diction (*CCB*)
3. Selection Test (*CCB*)

DEVELOPING VOCABULARY
The following words from the poem are tested in the Selection Test. (See also Vocabulary Activity Worksheet.)

communion, blight, course, insensible, patriarch, pensive, unfaltering

PREPARATION
ESTABLISHING A PURPOSE. Before students read this poem, you might want to write on the board a list of words supplied by the students that convey their feelings about death. Then students can read to determine which words also describe Bryant's feelings.

A. Responding
? What if Bryant had titled his poem "Looking at Death"? What would have been gained? What lost? (Answers will vary, but students should understand that a show of classical learning was much more fashionable in Bryant's day than in ours. From the pen of a very young writer in a very young country, the title "Thanatopsis" was a self-conscious declaration of seriousness.)

B. Metaphor
Students should understand that "the last bitter hour" in line 9 is death, and that "the narrow house" in line 12 is the coffin.

C. Expansion
If you are having students read this poem orally, lines 17 and 31 are natural places to change readers.

D. Tone
Students should note that the tone becomes less chilling, more comforting at this point. (See question 4, page 145.)

Thanatopsis is a word Bryant coined by joining two Greek words, _thanatos_ ("death") and _opsis_ ("seeing"). The word is defined by the poem: a way of looking at death and a way of thinking about it. There are two speaking voices in the poem. The poet speaks the introduction. Then, beginning with "Yet a few days" (line 17), the "still voice" of nature speaks. In line 73, the poet's voice resumes with the words "So live. . . ."

In reading the poem, look for complete sentences. Remember that sometimes the subject is not at the beginning of a sentence. Do not stop at the end of a line if there is no punctuation mark. This poem uses many, many "run-on lines"; this means you have to "run-on" to the next line in order to complete the thought. (Notice that the first twelve lines are all run-on lines.) You'll find that many sentences will end in mid-line, indicating that you should pause there. If you read the poem aloud, you'll see how the run-on lines and the mid-line pauses (called _caesuras_) prevent the poem from having a sing-song rhythm.

A Thanatopsis

To him who in the love of Nature holds
Communion with her visible forms, she speaks
A various language: for his gayer hours
She has a voice of gladness, and a smile
And eloquence of beauty; and she glides
Into his darker musings with a mild
And healing sympathy that steals away
Their sharpness ere he is aware. When thoughts
Of the last bitter hour come like a blight
Over thy spirit, and sad images
B Of the stern agony and shroud and pall°
And breathless darkness and the narrow house
Make thee to shudder and grow sick at heart,
Go forth under the open sky and list°
To Nature's teachings, while from all around—
Earth and her waters and the depths of air—
Comes a still voice—Yet° a few days, and thee
The all-beholding sun shall see no more
In all his course; nor yet in the cold ground,
Where thy pale form was laid with many tears,
Nor in the embrace of ocean, shall exist
Thy image. Earth, that nourished thee, shall claim
Thy growth, to be resolved to earth again,
C And, lost each human trace, surrendering up
Thine individual being, shalt thou go
To mix forever with the elements,
To be a brother to the insensible rock
And to the sluggish clod, which the rude swain°
Turns with his share° and treads upon; the oak
Shall send his roots abroad and pierce thy mould.

Yet not to thine eternal resting place
Shalt thou retire alone, nor couldst thou wish
D Couch more magnificent. Thou shalt lie down
With patriarchs of the infant world, with kings,
The powerful of the earth, the wise, the good,

11. **pall:** coffin cover.
14. **list:** listen.
17. Here begins the voice of nature.
28. **rude swain:** country man, or farmer.
29. **share:** plow.

Fawn's Leap, Catskill, New York by John W. Hill (1868). Oil.

Munson-Williams-Proctor Institute, Museum of Art, Utica, New York.

Fair forms, and hoary seers° of ages past,
All in one mighty sepulcher.° The hills
Rock-ribbed and ancient as the sun; the vales
Stretching in pensive quietness between;
The venerable woods, rivers that move
In majesty, and the complaining brooks
That make the meadows green; and, poured round all,
Old Ocean's gray and melancholy waste—
Are but the solemn decorations all
Of the great tomb of man. The golden sun,
The planets, all the infinite host of heaven,
Are shining on the sad abodes of death,
Through the still lapse of ages. All that tread
The globe are but a handful to the tribes
That slumber in its bosom. Take the wings
Of morning,° pierce the Barcan wilderness,°
Or lose thyself in the continuous woods
Where rolls the Oregon,° and hears no sound
Save his own dashings; yet the dead are there,
And millions in those solitudes, since first

36. **hoary seers:** white-haired prophets.

37. **sepulcher:** tomb.

51. "Take the wings of morning" is an allusion to Psalm 139; **Barcan wilderness:** a vast desert in Libya.

53. **Oregon:** early name for the Columbia River.

A. Humanities Connection: Responding to the Fine Art

? Notice how tiny the human figures seem in comparison with their surroundings. Do they seem out of place? Why might they be thinking the thoughts that Bryant captures in this poem? (Answers will vary. Students should note lines 38–45, in particular, and Bryant's thoughts there about the majesty of the natural world.)

B. Responding

? How consoled are you by Bryant's words? If we are upset at the thought of death, is it consoling to think that everyone else has to die, too? (Answers will vary.)

Closure

Have students paraphrase lines 73–81 in their own language. Then ask students to replace this prose paraphrase with a statement of their own about death.

Reading Check Test

1. Nature can help you to confront death. *True*
2. Nature plays a part after death. *True*
3. Kings and peasants shall be as one after death. *True*
4. Life goes on after your death. *True*
5. Nothing can lessen the pain of death. *False*

Analyzing The Poem

Identifying Details

1. She speaks with gladness, a smile, and "eloquence of beauty."

She responds with a "mild and healing sympathy."

2. The "stern agony" of the ill, the "shroud" and "pall" in which a dead person and coffins are wrapped, the "breathless darkness," and a "narrow

A. Connections

Bryant is recommending an attitude of stoical, noble acceptance in the face of death. This, too, is a result of his knowledge of classical Greece and Rome, for it arises from the behavior of Socrates in the face of death in Plato's dialogue "Phaedo," and from the urgings of Marcus Aurelius's "Meditations." It is directly opposite to the refusal of resignation in Edna St. Vincent Millay's "Dirge Without Music," page 650.

B. Expansion

The fact that Bryant's view of the afterlife is subject to more than one interpretation may indicate that he himself was of two minds on the subject. You might use this as a jumping-off point for the idea that poets sometimes write poems not so much in order to report what they think, but to *find out* what they think.

The flight of years began, have laid them down
In their last sleep: the dead reign there alone.
So shalt thou rest; and what if thou withdraw
In silence from the living, and no friend
Take note of thy departure? All that breathe
Will share thy destiny. The gay will laugh
When thou art gone, the solemn brood of care
Plod on, and each one as before will chase
His favorite phantom; yet all these shall leave
Their mirth and their employments, and shall come
And make their bed with thee. As the long train
Of ages glide away, the sons of men—
The youth in life's green spring, and he who goes
In the full strength of years, matron and maid,
The speechless babe, and the gray-headed man—
Shall one by one be gathered to thy side
By those who in their turn shall follow them.

So° live that when thy summons comes to join
The innumerable caravan which moves
To that mysterious realm where each shall take
His chamber in the silent halls of death,
A Thou go not, like the quarry slave at night,
Scourged to his dungeon, but, sustained and soothed
By an unfaltering trust, approach thy grave
Like one who wraps the drapery of his couch
About him and lies down to pleasant dreams.

73. The poet resumes speaking here.

A Comment on the Poem

Considering the period in which "Thanatopsis" was written and the background of its author, the position this famous poem takes is remarkable. Instead of heaven and immortality, Bryant seems to envision an earthbound future. The poem seems to suggest ways by which humankind may become resigned to an afterlife without the heaven that is promised in the traditional notions of eternal life.

B Some readers, however, see indications of a more traditional faith in the poem. In line 79, they point to the "unfaltering trust" (in what or whom?). At the end of the poem, they think the "pleasant dreams" may suggest a hope of life or consciousness enduring after death.

The poet chose a meter to lend dignity to his subject. The poem is written in **blank verse,** or unrhymed iambic pentameter. ("Iambic pentameter" means that each line is composed of five iambs. An **iamb** is a pair of syllables in which an unstressed syllable is followed by a stressed syllable.) Blank verse closely echoes the rhythms of normal English speech, and for that reason, it has been widely used in poetic drama, from the plays of William Shakespeare to those of T. S. Eliot. Blank verse allows the poet to speak with the flow of prose, without losing the formality of poetry. Since blank verse also frees the poet from the obligation to find rhyming words, it makes it easier for the writer to use a number of lines to develop a complex thought.

It might be interesting to think about one detail in the poem which is no longer true. When Bryant points out that "All that tread / The globe are but a handful to the tribes / That slumber in its bosom," he is speaking as a man of the early nineteenth century. Were he alive today, he would know that there are now actually more people on earth than ever lived in all of recorded history.

house" all refer to death.

He advises us to go outdoors and listen to Nature's teachings.

3. Our individuality will be lost as we become mingled with the elements.

4. The poem shifts from a tone of stern finality to a tone of consolation.

We will not be alone in death; our resting place will be magnificent; we will lie down with the great of past generations; and everyone alive will share this fate.

5. "Couch . . . magnificent" (line 33), "mighty sepulcher" (line 37), "the great tomb of man" (line 45).

Other images include: "hills / Rock-ribbed and ancient as the sun" (lines 37–38); "rivers that move / In majesty" (lines 40–41); "Old Ocean's gray and melancholy waste" (line 43).

6. The dead are compared to the inhabitants of the wilderness. Death itself is a "last sleep" (line 57).

7. Enjambments occur often; for examples see lines 1, 2, 3, 4, 10, 14, 17, 22, 27, and 29.

Interpreting Meanings

8. This idea occurs at lines 17–30.

This view of creation is a comfort because it emphasizes the organic unity of all the living and the dead. The opposite view would suggest that death is final.

9. The poet advises readers to face the sleep of death with peaceful acceptance, rather than with fear and reluctance.

10. Most students will respond that the poem reads like the work of a more mature writer.

11. Student answers will vary. You might suggest the words *death* or *rest* or *nature,* or lines 14–15 or 54–58.

Responding to the Poem

Analyzing the Poem

Identifying Details

1. As the poem opens, Nature is **personified** as someone who speaks to us in various languages. What kind of language does Nature use to speak to us in our "gayer hours"? How does Nature respond to our "darker musings"?
2. In line 8, the **tone** of the poem grows more somber. The speaker refers to "sad **images**" that make us "shudder and grow sick at heart." What are these images? What does each image refer to? What does the speaker advise us to do when we have these thoughts?
3. A "still voice" is a phrase often used to refer to intuition, a perception of something not clearly defined—like the "still, small voice" of conscience. In this poem, the still voice is that of Nature. What does this still voice (lines 17–72) say will happen to our individuality at death?
4. In line 31, what shift in the **tone** of the poem occurs? What comfort is offered in this section of the poem?
5. Find at least two **metaphors** in lines 31–54 that are used to describe the earth as a whole. What are some other **images** in these lines that reinforce the impression of the earth's vastness and greatness?
6. Beginning with line 51, what is death compared with to make it seem less threatening?
7. Read the first thirty lines of the poem aloud, noting the **iambic pentameter** meter. Find at least three places in these lines where Bryant varies his meter to avoid a sing-song rhythm.

Interpreting Meanings

8. How does this poem reveal the Romantic conviction that the universe, far from being mechanical in nature, is really organic and undergoes constant cyclical changes? Why do you think this organic view of creation is a comfort to the speaker? What would the opposite view suggest about the speaker's ultimate fate?
9. At the conclusion of the speech of the "still voice" (line 73), the speaker's voice resumes for the concluding section, or summing up. What is the main thrust of his advice? What is your response to this advice? Do you find it wise and consoling? Do you find it disturbing? Or do you have some other reaction? Explain.
10. Bryant wrote "Thanatopsis" when he was sixteen years old. Does the poem seem to you to be the work of a teen-ager? Why or why not?
11. What do you think is the most important word or phrase in the poem?

Writing About the Poem

A Creative Response

1. **Writing a Letter.** How do you imagine a Puritan might respond to Bryant's meditation on death? Write a letter that a contemporary of Anne Bradstreet or Jonathan Edwards (see pages 42 and 36) might write to Bryant after reading "Thanatopsis" in the *North American Review.* Before you write, review the Puritans' view of the world.

A Critical Response

2. **Comparing and Contrasting Poems.** In an essay of several paragraphs, compare and contrast Bryant's view of nature in "Thanatopsis" and "To a Waterfowl." Cite the ways in which Nature speaks to the poet in both poems, and compare her lessons, or messages.
3. **Analyzing Imagery and Meaning.** In a brief essay, trace the images in "Thanatopsis" that identify death with sleep. Usually we wake from sleep. Do you think Bryant means to suggest a "waking" from the final sleep? Does the poem suggest an afterlife? Conclude your essay with your opinions on this question. (Be careful. Readers differ in their interpretation.)

Analyzing Language and Style

Inversions and Archaic Language

Like all poets, Bryant manipulates language to accommodate his rhymes and rhythms. Bryant's most obvious device in "Thanatopsis" is the use of **inversion**—the displacement of words, phrases, or clauses out of their normal English word order. Since Bryant wrote his poem in the early 1800's, some of his diction is now **archaic**—that is, the words are no longer in common use and are difficult for modern readers to understand.

1. Find at least five examples of inverted syntax in the poem. If the syntax were altered to conform to normal word order, what would happen to the poet's rhythm?
2. Find at least three examples of archaic language in the poem. How would you rephrase these lines in modern English?
3. List all the examples of archaic diction you can find in "To a Waterfowl." Replace these words with their modern equivalents and read the poem aloud. Is its effect different?

A. Responding
Discuss the changing role of poets in American life. There was a time when poetry was read by ordinary people as a form of entertainment, often read aloud by one family member to others or by one lover to another. Technological advance has replaced the fireside with the television set and the poem with the sitcom.

? Is a population nurtured on often-sentimental poetry better off than a population nurtured on television? Is poetry better off being written for an academic elite than for a wide audience? (Answers will vary, and some students may contend that there are many highly popular poets in America today, in the form of songwriters.)

B. Humanities Connection: Discussing the Fine Art
You might want students to compare this portrait of Longfellow with that on page 122.

Henry Wadsworth Longfellow (1807–1882)

A

Longfellow was and is the most popular poet America has ever produced. Perhaps with the exception of Robert Frost, not one of the great twentieth-century poets in America has ever remotely achieved the status of a "household name." Nor has one of them achieved the kind of recognition implicit in the word *popular.*

Longfellow's immense popularity—like that of the other Fireside Poets—was based largely on his appeal to an audience hungry for sermons and lessons. That audience wanted assurances that their cherished values would prevail over the new forces of history—such as industrialization—that were threatening to destroy them. In themselves, the values Longfellow endorsed were positive forces in the making of the American character. But his tendency to leave these values unexamined led to poetry that often offered easy comfort at the expense of illumination.

Longfellow's reputation today is based on a handful of poems so familiar that they are part of our national heritage. We could no more do without them than we could do without George Washington's cherry tree, Betsy Ross's flag, or Abraham Lincoln's log-cabin birthplace. There was a time when every schoolchild in America knew at least some of these opening lines:

> Listen, my children, and you shall hear
> Of the midnight ride of Paul Revere . . .
> —"Paul Revere's Ride"

> Under a spreading chestnut tree
> The village smithy stands . . .
> —"The Village Blacksmith"

> I shot an arrow into the air;
> It fell to earth, I knew not where . . .
> —"The Arrow and the Song"

The following selection of poems deliberately omits Longfellow's "old chestnuts," as these familiar old poems are called. Instead, it offers poems of Longfellow's that still speak to readers

B

An early photograph of Henry Wadsworth Longfellow.

of a later time and that show the poet in full command of his celebrated grace and skill.

Born in Portland, Maine, Longfellow was never far in his youth from the splashing waves and rocks of the Atlantic Coast or from the cultural and religious influences of the well-to-do families who lived "north of Boston." After attending Portland Academy, he continued his education at nearby Bowdoin College, where one of his classmates was Nathaniel Hawthorne (see page 263).

Longfellow's early interest in foreign languages and literature led naturally to an academic career. After three years of additional study in France, Spain, Italy, and Germany, he joined the Bowdoin faculty, married, and began to write a volume of prose sketches drawn from his experiences abroad.

During a second European trip in 1835, Longfellow's young wife died of a miscarriage. This death was, as time would tell, a foreshadowing of a second bitter loss. When he returned to America, the young widower moved to Harvard, where he had been appointed professor of French and Spanish. Seven years later, he married Frances Appleton, whom he had met in Eu-

Supplementary Support Materials
1. Vocabulary Activity Worksheet (*CCB*)
2. Review and Response Worksheet: Figurative Language (*CCB*)
3. Selection Test (*CCB*)
4. Audiocassette recording

Developing Vocabulary
The following word from the poem is tested in the Selection Test. (See also Vocabulary Activity Worksheet.)
watch

Preparation
Establishing a Purpose. Ask students to discuss whether or not they feel that nature reflects signs of our emotions. Then have students read to learn the speaker's ideas on this subject.

rope after his first wife's death. When his father-in-law made him a gift of the Cambridge mansion known as Craigie House, he settled into eighteen years of happily married life.

Longfellow produced some of his most celebrated poetry during this period, much of it based on American legends: *Evangeline* (1847), *The Song of Hiawatha* (1855), and *The Courtship of Miles Standish* (1858). On the first day of publication, this last poem sold 15,000 copies. By 1854, his poetry was bringing him enough income so that he could resign from Harvard to devote himself to writing full time. Seven years later, the second tragedy occurred: Longfellow's second wife died in a fiery accident at home, when a lighted match or hot sealing wax she was using on a letter ignited her summer dress.

Longfellow now devoted himself to his work with a religious and literary zeal. By the end of his long and productive life, he had become for Americans the symbolic figure of The Poet: mild, gray-bearded, haloed with goodness, and living in a world of still untold romance. This is the figure who was given honorary degrees by the universities of Cambridge and Oxford in England and who was received by Queen Victoria. Twelve years after his death, Longfellow's marble image was unveiled in the Poet's Corner in London's Westminster Abbey. He was the first American to be so honored.

Three years after writing this poem about his wife, Longfellow died without having shown it to anyone. Discovered among his papers, it was published four years later and immediately became one of his most famous poems. Since a large audience was waiting to read everything Longfellow wrote, it is puzzling that the poet simply put this lyric aside. Did he consider its expression of grief too personal to be made public? If so, why didn't he destroy it, instead of leaving it among papers he knew would be carefully sifted through and examined?

The Cross of Snow

In the long, sleepless watches of the night,
A gentle face—the face of one long dead—
Looks at me from the wall, where round its head
The night lamp casts a halo of pale light.
Here in this room she died; and soul more white
Never through martyrdom of fire was led
To its repose; nor can in books be read
The legend of a life more benedight.°
A There is a mountain in the distant West
That, sun-defying, in its deep ravines
Displays a cross of snow upon its side.
B Such is the cross I wear upon my breast
These eighteen years, through all the changing scenes
And seasons, changeless since the day she died.

8. **benedight:** an archaic word for "natural goodness," related to the word *beneficence*.

A. Imagery
The cross of snow is in the deepest ravines of the mountain. Similarly, the interior cross lies in the deepest part of Longfellow's heart, while his external face is deceptively sunny.

B. Symbolism
The cross of snow is a symbol worthy of Hawthorne. (See "The Minister's Black Veil," page 265.) In several of Hawthorne's works, a physical symbol of a moral or emotional state marks a character's appearance: the birthmark in the short story "The Birthmark," and the sewn letter *A* in *The Scarlet Letter.* Typically, Hawthorne's symbols are more troubling, more demonstrative of a sense of guilt. Longfellow's white cross connotes deep grief, but not personal guilt, and indeed can be seen as a bearer of hope. The minister's black veil causes his fiancée to recoil from the minister, but Longfellow's white cross invites only a tender sympathy.

Closure
Have students offer definitions for Longfellow's "cross of snow."

Analyzing The Poem
Identifying Details
1. He is speaking of his dead wife, who is pictured in a portrait on the wall.
2. A halo is usually associated with saints or angels.
The literal halo that the poet sees is the circular glow cast by the lamp on his wife's portrait. The lamplight makes it look as if she wears an angel's halo.
3. He tells us that his wife was gentle, pure, and kindly.

Interpreting Meanings
4. In the Christian tradition, martyrdom is usually associated with saints who have died for the faith.
The poet is emphasizing his wife's purity and spirituality.
(Answers continue in left-hand column.)

(Continued from top.)
5. These are the times when, unable to sleep, the poet broods on the past and mourns his wife.
6. The literal sense is untouched, or impenetrable, by sunlight. High altitudes and deep crags might result in a permanent cross of snow on a mountainside.
The poet's grief is too deep to be melted by any ray of happiness, just as the cross of snow in the deep crags cannot be melted by the rays of the sun.
7. The expression refers to Christ's carrying the cross on the way to the crucifixion.
Longfellow wears his "cross"—his grief—upon his breast because it is in his heart.
8. Student answers will vary.

Additional Writing Assignment
Have students write a group sonnet on the board, with the class deciding on a subject and as many students as possible contributing lines.

Responding to the Poem

Analyzing the Poem

Identifying Details

1. What precisely is Longfellow looking at when he refers to the "gentle face" in line 2?
2. What is a halo usually associated with? In line 4, what is the literal halo that the poet sees?
3. What does the poet tell us about his wife's character?

Interpreting Meanings

4. The words "martyrdom of fire" in line 6 might confuse readers who did not know that the poet's wife actually died in a fire. What is Longfellow suggesting about his wife's character when he uses such a powerful word to describe her death?
5. The phrase "watches of the night" usually refers to the rounds made by a watchman as he guards a house or a neighborhood. At certain hours, the watch would call, "All is well." What are Longfellow's **figurative** "watches of the night" (line 1)?
6. In line 10, explain how the phrase "sun-defying" suggests conditions of weather and geology that might actually produce a permanent cross of snow on the side of a mountain. How does the poet relate the idea of a "sun-defying" formation of snow to his own feelings?
7. What specific event does the expression "a cross to bear" refer to? In everyday speech, a cross, in the sense of a burden, is something to *bear* or *shoulder.* But Longfellow says that his is "the cross I wear upon my breast" (line 12). Why does he use that phrase instead of referring to it as a cross he bears?
8. Imagine that a contemporary celebrity had written a similar poem (or song) about a sad personal event. Would you think publication of the work appropriate? Why or why not?

Writing About the Poem

A Critical Response

Responding to the Poem. In a paragraph, describe your response to this poem. Before you write your paragraph, consider your responses to the following specific elements of the poem:

1. Message
2. Language
3. Rhyme and rhythm
4. Tone

At the end of your paragraph, tell whether or not you believe the poem has something to say to all people—not just to Longfellow's readers of a past era.

Elements of Literature

THE SONNET

"The Cross of Snow" is a **sonnet**—a fourteen-line poem usually written in iambic pentameter with an intricate pattern of rhyme. The sonnet is one of the oldest and most enduring poetic forms in world literature. Its most influential early master was the Italian poet Petrarch (1304–1374). During the Renaissance in England, Sir Thomas Wyatt (c. 1503–1542) introduced the form into English poetry, and the sonnet was taken up by such writers as Sir Philip Sidney, Edmund Spenser, and William Shakespeare. In later periods, distinguished sonnets were written by John Donne, John Milton, William Wordsworth, John Keats, Elizabeth Barrett Browning, Gerard Manley Hopkins, Edna St. Vincent Millay, and Robert Lowell, among others.

Two principal forms of the sonnet developed in English. In the first—called the **Petrarchan,** or **Italian,** sonnet—the fourteen lines are divided into two segments: the octave (first eight lines) and the sestet (last six lines). The rhyme scheme is most commonly abba, abba, cde, cde. In the **Elizabethan,** or **Shakespearean,** sonnet, there are three quatrains (groups of four lines), followed by a final rhyming couplet; the rhyme scheme of this type of sonnet is abab, cdcd, efef, gg.

For "The Cross of Snow," Longfellow (who knew Italian literature well) used the classic Italian form. What is the subject stated in the octave? What comment is made on the subject in the sestet? What is the rhyme scheme?

SUPPLEMENTARY SUPPORT MATERIALS
1. Vocabulary Activity Worksheet (*CCB*)
2. Review and Response Worksheet: Figurative Language (*CCB*)
3. Selection Test (*CCB*)

DEVELOPING VOCABULARY
The following words from the poem are tested in the Selection Test. (See also Vocabulary Activity Worksheet.)
dusky steed snare

PREPARATION
ESTABLISHING A PURPOSE. Have students discuss the following questions before reading the poem: Do poems have to be about intimate emotions or important events? Could a poet write about a factory? How?

A. Expansion
A ropewalk was a long path inside a rope factory, down which the strands were laid to be made into rope. The word can also refer to the building that contained the ropewalk. (See the painting on page 150).

B. Interpretation
? What is the Romantic element in these lines? (The assertion of the superiority of the poet's imagination to real life)

C. Responding
Discuss the contrast between the young maidens on the swing in stanza 4 and the faded trapeze artist in stanza 5.

The shape of this poem is simple. It opens with a description of an actual rope factory; then, hypnotized by the gleam of the long threads in the sun, the speaker imagines scene after scene in which rope-making plays a part. These imaginary pictures unreel like a movie until the final stanza, when the speaker returns us to the factory.

The dominant image of this poem is that of a spider: in this case, "human spiders" who spin rope on mechanical wheels.

At one time rope factories were common in New England. Often, like all industries of the time, they employed poor young children as laborers. Stark remnants of these factories can still be seen in states like Connecticut and Massachusetts today.

As you read the poem, keep two things in mind. First, the sight Longfellow is describing was a common one to someone who lived in the nineteenth century. Second, in Longfellow's time, thoughtful people were becoming increasingly aware of the dehumanizing effects of factory work.

A The Ropewalk

In that building, long and low,
With its windows all a-row,
  Like the portholes of a hulk,
Human spiders spin and spin,
Backward down their threads so thin
  Dropping, each a hempen° bulk.

At the end, an open door;
Squares of sunshine on the floor
  Light the long and dusky lane;
And the whirring of a wheel,
Dull and drowsy, makes me feel
  All its spokes are in my brain.

As the spinners to the end
Downward go and re-ascend,
  Gleam the long threads in the sun;
While within this brain of mine
B Cobwebs brighter and more fine
  By the busy wheel are spun.

Two fair maidens in a swing,
Like white doves upon the wing,
  First before my vision pass;
Laughing, as their gentle hands
Closely clasp the twisted strands,
  At their shadow on the grass.

Then a booth of mountebanks,°
With its smell of tan° and planks,
  And a girl poised high in air
C On a cord, in spangled dress,
With a faded loveliness,
  And a weary look of care.

6. **hempen:** made of hemp, a coarse-fibered shrub used for making rope.

25. **mountebanks:** "con men" who traveled with carnivals and circuses.
26. **tan:** a material used to give color and finish to raw leather.

Closure
Have students answer the following questions in class discussion: In what sense is this a poem of social comment? In what sense is it not a poem of social comment?

Reading Check Test
1. Workers in the factory are compared with spiders. *True*
2. The speaker feels that he weaves the same kinds of cobwebs in his brain as the workers. *False*
3. A *mountebank* is a trapeze artist. *False*
4. The man in the tower is almost hanged by the rope. *True*
5. The speaker does not support executions by hanging. *True*

A. Imagery
Have students note the imagery of the woman's face ascending in the bucket.

B. Expansion
Here, the poet calls for a "breath of Christian charity" to blow the gallows away.

C. Humanities Connection: Discussing the Fine Art
The painting shows a rope factory as a clean, airy place, and the workers as graceful and untroubled. You might ask your students to speculate on the degree of realism here.

Then a homestead among farms,
And a woman with bare arms
  Drawing water from a well;
A As the bucket mounts apace,°
With it mounts her own fair face,
  As at some magician's spell.

Then an old man in a tower,
Ringing loud the noontide hour,
  While the rope coils round and round
Like a serpent at his feet,
And again, in swift retreat,
  Nearly lifts him from the ground.

Then within a prison yard,
Faces fixed, and stern, and hard,
  Laughter and indecent mirth;
B Ah! it is the gallows tree!°
Breath of Christian charity,
  Blow, and sweep it from the earth!

34. **apace:** rapidly.

46. **gallows tree:** a simple structure of two posts and a crossbar on which criminals were once executed by hanging.

C

The Rope Walk by Charles Bird King (1830). Oil.

Bayly Art Museum at the University of Virginia, Charlottesville.

ANALYZING THE POEM
Identifying Details

1. The building is compared to a "hulk," or large ship, with windows in a row like portholes.

2. The spinners climb up and down as they operate the machines that spin out the lengths of rope.

The "cobwebs" are the images spun in the poet's own imagination.

3. The scenes are as follows: two young girls in a rope swing; a girl on a circus tightrope; a farm woman drawing water from a well; an old man ringing bells in a tower as the bell ropes almost drag him from the ground; prisoners in front of a gallows in a prison yard; a schoolboy flying a kite, with hunters and people fishing; ships sailing, wrecks aimlessly floating, anchors losing their grip in "faithless sand," and sailors "feeling for the land" by means of their slackening ropes.

Interpreting Meanings

4. The metaphor implies that the work has turned these people into mere, unthinking insects. It has dehumanized them.

5. The shifts in tone may be described as follows: playful and gay in stanza 4; hectic and tense in stanza 5; homely and peaceful in stanza 6; dramatic and tense in stanza 7; dark and bitter in stanza 8; a sudden shift to a lighthearted tone in stanza 9; rapid shifts in tone from light to dark to hopeful in stanza 10. Stanza 10 opens with a lighthearted scene of ships "rejoicing" in the breeze, then shifts to a grim picture of aimlessly floating wrecks, and of anchors losing their grip in the sand; the stanza closes with a hopeful tone, with sailors using rope leads to determine that they are approaching land. The shifts in tone in these stanzas suggest that the human condition is varied; great joy and great misery either exist at the same time or follow each other swiftly in succession.

The speaker seems to sympathize with their plight.

6. Student answers will vary. Think of mines, assembly lines, marathon word processing, garbage collection, highway construction, flying.

Then a schoolboy, with his kite
Gleaming in a sky of light,
  And an eager, upward look;
Steeds pursued through lane and field;
Fowlers with their snares concealed;
  And an angler by a brook.

Ships rejoicing in the breeze,
Wrecks that float o'er unknown seas,
  Anchors dragged through faithless sand;
Sea fog drifting overhead,
And, with lessening line and lead,°
  Sailors feeling for the land.

All these scenes do I behold,
These, and many left untold,
  In that building long and low;
While the wheel goes round and round,
With a drowsy, dreamy sound,
  And the spinners backward go.

59. **lead:** a nautical term for a weight used by sailors to take soundings to measure the water's depth.

Responding to the Poem

Analyzing the Poem

Identifying Details

1. In the first stanza, Longfellow uses a **simile.** What is the factory compared to?
2. By the end of stanza 3, the poet has presented a series of **images** of the factory and of the spinners at work. Describe what the workers are doing. What are the "cobwebs" mentioned at the end of this stanza?
3. Beginning with stanza 4, Longfellow takes an imaginary "ropewalk" and gives us a succession of pictures in which some kind of rope or cord plays a part. Briefly describe each of these scenes.

Interpreting Meanings

4. New England factories of the nineteenth century often were unpleasant places with working conditions that would be regarded as intolerable today. What is the implication of the **metaphor** comparing the factory workers to spiders?
5. Describe the changes of **tone** as the poet imagines scene after scene. What opposing aspects of human life is the poet holding "in balance"? How do you think he feels about the "human spiders"?
6. Can you think of any occupations today in which the workers could be compared to insects or animals?

Writing About the Poem

A Creative Response

Describing an Idyllic Scene. The famous printmakers Currier & Ives depicted rural nineteenth-century American scenes so charmingly and idealistically that we still find examples of their work on contemporary greeting cards as well as in art museums. Which idyllic scenes in "The Ropewalk" would you recommend to the attention of the printmakers? State your preference and describe the scene and its mood in a paragraph. Which scenes are definitely *not* Currier & Ives subjects?

Analyzing Language and Style

Trochaic Meter

The unusual sense of physical movement in this poem was not achieved by accident. Longfellow obviously wanted to give a bouncy spring to both his real ropewalk and his imaginary one, and so he decided on a rhythm based on the use of the *trochee.*

Trochaic meter is the exact opposite of iambic meter: Instead of the iambic da-DAH, the sound of trochaic meter is DAH-da. Once Longfellow has established his count of four of these trochees per line, does he faithfully repeat it from the first line to the last?

SUPPLEMENTARY SUPPORT MATERIALS

1. Vocabulary Activity Worksheet (*CCB*)
2. Review and Response Worksheet: Diction (*CCB*)
3. Selection Test (*CCB*)
4. Instructional Overhead Transparency

DEVELOPING VOCABULARY

The following word from the poem is tested in the Selection Test. (See also Vocabulary Activity Worksheet.)
to efface

PREPARATION

ESTABLISHING A PURPOSE. Before students read this poem, you might want them to brainstorm a list of qualities they associate with tides. Of these qualities, which do they often associate with poetry? (Rhythm, majesty, depth, and possibly simplicity) Which do they not associate with poetry? (Predictability)

A. Responding

? How does the title make you feel? What do you think the poem will be like, on the basis of the title alone? (Answers will vary.)

B. Atmosphere/ Theme

? What atmosphere is created by the images in this poem? (The darkness, the disappearing footprints, and the disappearance of the traveler suggest a mood of loneliness and isolation.)

? What quality of tides is important to understanding the theme of this poem? (Predictability—even though the day does return and the tides will continue to rise and fall, human life disappears.)

Read this poem aloud to hear how rhythm and sound effects contribute to a particular atmosphere. How do the first two lines even imitate the rhythmic rise and fall of the tide itself?

A

The Tide Rises, the Tide Falls

The tide rises, the tide falls,
The twilight darkens, the curlew° calls;
Along the sea sands damp and brown
The traveler hastens toward the town,
And the tide rises, the tide falls.

Darkness settles on roofs and walls,
But the sea, the sea in the darkness calls;
The little waves, with their soft, white
hands,
B
Efface the footprints in the sands,
And the tide rises, the tide falls.

The morning breaks; the steeds in their
stalls
Stamp and neigh, as the hostler° calls;
The day returns, but nevermore
Returns the traveler to the shore,
And the tide rises, the tide falls.

2. **curlew:** large, brown wading bird.
12. **hostler:** stable hand.

Sunlight on the Coast by Winslow Homer (1890). Oil.

Humanities Connection: Responding to the Fine Art

Winslow Homer (1836–1910) started as a free-lance illustrator but gave up illustrating for fine art in 1875. Largely self-taught, he had a naturalistic but strongly designed style. His innovative water-colors of outdoor life have grown in popularity since his death.

? How does this painting differ in mood from the poem? (Answers will vary, but the painting is less domestic than the poem—it shows neither town nor beach, only jagged rock. But its compositional simplicity and its evocation of the waves' ceaseless rhythm match the poem.)

Analyzing the Poem

Identifying Details

1. Stanza 1 presents twilight darkening into night; stanza 2 presents the passage of night; in stanza 3 morning is breaking.

Interpreting Meanings

2. It is implied that the traveler disappears or dies.

3. With this detail the poet suggests a feeling of renewed life.

With the information that the traveler never returns to the shore, the poet suggests a contrasting, somber hint of death.

4. The sound "alls" dominates the poem. It suggests a melancholy, mournful atmosphere.

The rising and falling of the tide is suggested by the rising and falling effect of the meter in the first and last halves of the refrain.

5. Answers will vary, but students should clearly express an opinion and give reasons.

6. Most students will agree that the poem could be both.

This detail implies a contrast between the permanence of nature and the transitoriness of human existence.

Closure

Have students state the theme of this poem in one or two sentences.

A. Expansion

Longfellow's poem is much calmer than Tennyson's; it notes the actions of nature and of people without comment. Tennyson delivers an impassioned address to nature. We can tell Tennyson is grieving for a lost loved one, though we are given no specific details; but we're given no idea at all of what experiences underlie Longfellow's muted melancholy.

Responding to the Poem

Analyzing the Poem

Identifying Details

1. How does the division into stanzas reflect the passage of time in the poem?

Interpreting Meanings

2. "Footsteps on the sands of time" is a common expression referring to mortality and the passing of time. What do you think is implied about the fate of the traveler when his footprints are washed away in the second stanza?
3. What feeling is suggested by the stamping and neighing of the horses the next morning? What contrasting feeling is suggested by what we are told about the traveler in this stanza?
4. **Onomatopoeia** is a poetic technique in which the sounds of words are used to echo their sense. If you have ever heard the call of a shore bird, you know that the words "curlew calls" in line 2 echo the sound the bird itself makes. (Its cry is particularly mournful when heard at dusk.) What sound do you think dominates this poem? What atmosphere or feeling does it suggest? How does the rhythm of the poem reflect the movement of the tides?
5. The waves are **personified** in stanza 2 as having "soft, white hands." This is an example of Longfellow's poetic style that some readers think is too cute, or too sentimental, to be effective. Do you think the personification is justified here? Why or why not?
6. Do you think this is a poem about one specific traveler? Or could it be seen as a "drama" about everyone's life? What do you think is suggested by the tide's continuing to rise and fall, despite the fact that the human traveler is gone?

The Cross of Snow.

In the long, sleepless watches of the night,
A gentle face,—the face of one long dead,—
Looks at me from the wall, where round its head
The night-lamp casts a halo of pale light.
Here in this room she died; and soul more white
Never through martyrdom of fire was led
To its repose; nor can in books be read
The legend of a life more benedight.
There is a mountain in the distant West,
That, sun-defying, in its deep ravines
Displays a cross of snow upon its side.
Such is the cross I wear upon my breast,
These eighteen years, through all the changing scenes
And seasons, changeless since the day she died.

July 10. 1879.

Writing About the Poem

A Critical Response

Comparing and Contrasting Poems. Alfred, Lord Tennyson, a British contemporary of Longfellow, wrote poetry that rivaled even Longfellow's in popularity. Read the following poem by Tennyson. Then, in a brief essay, compare and contrast this lyric with Longfellow's "The Tide Rises, the Tide Falls." Before you write, you might fill out a chart like the one following the poem.

Break, Break, Break

Break, break, break,
  On thy cold gray stones, O Sea!
And I would that my tongue could utter
  The thoughts that arise in me.

O, well for the fisherman's boy,
  That he shouts with his sister at play!
O, well for the sailor lad,
  That he sings in his boat on the bay!

And the stately ships go on
  To their haven under the hill;
But O for the touch of a vanish'd hand,
  And the sound of a voice that is still!

Break, break, break,
  At the foot of thy crags, O Sea!
But the tender grace of a day that is dead
  Will never come back to me.

—Alfred, Lord Tennyson

A

	Longfellow	Tennyson
What the sea represents		
Mood of the poem		
Message of the poem		
Sounds of the poem (rhymes and meter)		

Primary Sources
Visiting Mr. Longfellow

"These were distinguished visitors, but they did not outnumber the succession of simple, often touching, and sometimes afflicting callers, mostly Americans, who came to constitute a serious problem for Longfellow, but who were invariably received with courtesy and consideration—though some of them belonged in that category of 'books, bores, and beggars' which even he came to count as one of the principal vexations of daily life. Fortunately his humor was usually equal to the occasion, and he could describe some of his guests with characteristic good nature. There was the Englishman who remarked that, in other countries, you know, we go to see ruins and all that—'but you have no ruins in your country, and I thought I would call and see *you*.' There was the young Westerner who asked Longfellow how old he was, and when the poet answered, 'Seventy,' rejoined, 'I have seen a good many men of your age who looked much younger than you.' A German woman, with a strong accent, called to talk with him about 'The Building of the Ship,' which she was planning to read in public, and which she called 'The Lunch of the Sheep.' As he was standing at the front door one August morning, a woman in black came up to him and inquired whether this was the house in which Longfellow had been born; when he explained that it was not, she went on to ask, 'Did he die here?' "

—from *Longfellow: His Life and Work,*
Newton Arvin

Craigie House, Longfellow's home in Cambridge, Massachusetts. A

Additional Writing Assignment Have students imagine that they are paying a surprise visit to any author in this textbook and write down the conversation that might take place.

A. Expansion The photograph shows the house Longfellow's father-in-law gave him when Longfellow began teaching at Harvard at the age of thirty. Note that the house had been Washington's headquarters during 1775–1776.

A. Humanities Connection: Responding to the Fine Art Whittier's and Longfellow's portraits have been photographs; Irving's and Bryant's were paintings. ❓ How does seeing a photograph of a person make you feel, as opposed to seeing a painted portrait? What kind of person would you guess Whittier was, judging from his photograph alone? Is this borne out by his biography? How do you think an oil portrait of him would look, in comparison with his photograph? (Answers will vary, but the point is that art forms differ from each other. Each art form has its own strengths and weaknesses, embedded in the nature of the medium itself. Each form conveys a distinctive view of life and arouses a distinctive set of responses.)

John Greenleaf Whittier (1807–1892)

Whittier's poetic subjects and many of the qualities of his verse led him to be included in the group known as the Fireside Poets. But unlike Longfellow, Lowell, and Holmes, who were raised in privilege and enjoyed a distinguished education, Whittier was born into a poor Quaker family and had little formal schooling. He started to write poetry as an adolescent, heavily influenced by the popular Scottish poet Robert Burns (1759–1796). Burns had revived the Scottish literary heritage and written memorably of rural life. Significantly, the ballad and the song, two of Burns's favorite forms, were to remain favorites of Whittier as well.

With the assistance of the abolitionist William Lloyd Garrison (1805–1879), the young Whittier found work in Boston as a newspaper editor. In 1831, he published his first book, *Legends of New-England in Prose and Verse,* a collection of pieces on local Massachusetts history. But he soon immersed himself in current affairs, in total support of the antislavery cause.

In 1835, Whittier was elected to the state legislature. For the next quarter of a century, until the outbreak of the Civil War, Whittier never stopped working for the abolition of slavery. He contributed poems and articles to the *National Era,* which he also edited from 1847 to 1860. (It was this weekly newspaper that published Harriet Beecher Stowe's novel, *Uncle Tom's Cabin,* in installments during 1851–1852.)

Although much of Whittier's writing during this period was overtly political, he also produced a long work of fiction on the Salem witch trials and several books of nature poetry. "Barbara Frietchie," perhaps Whittier's best-known ballad, appeared in a collection called *In War Time and Other Poems,* published in 1864.

After the Civil War, Whittier turned again to nature for many of his subjects. In 1866, he completed *Snow-Bound,* a long poem (759 lines) which many critics consider his masterpiece and which made Whittier famous. Advancing age did not reduce his output; until he was well into his eighties, Whittier continued to publish poetry on homely incidents from rural life, episodes from

A

Colonial history, and the humanitarian ideals of justice, religious faith, and tolerance. As much as his poetry, his humane convictions and moral example left a mark for good on his time.

In *Snow-Bound,* Whittier looks back fondly on the life he spent as a boy in the farmhouse in Haverhill, Massachusetts, where his family had lived since 1688. Whittier remembers what we would call "an extended family," a gathering under one roof of eight to nine related people of varying ages, along with the male boarder who taught school nearby. Imprisoned by the storm, these people had to live for days without news of the outside world. Their rooms were dimly lighted by candles, or perhaps by lamps that burned the whale oil called macassar. Their food was stored in crocks and barrels and briny vats and kept in the cellar. Water came from a pump in the kitchen or a well in the yard. The bathroom as we know it today did not exist. For heat and cooking, they burned wood. Life, in a word, was hard. But like many people, Whittier found in his past a kind of benediction.

SUPPLEMENTARY SUPPORT MATERIALS

1. Vocabulary Activity Worksheet (*CCB*)
2. Review and Response Worksheet: Imagery (*CCB*)
3. Selection Test (*CCB*)
4. Audiocassette recording

DEVELOPING VOCABULARY

The following words from the poem are tested in the Selection Test. (See also Vocabulary Activity Worksheet.)

ominous	din
portent	sage
querulous	mute
firmament	mirth
supernal	knoll

PREPARATION

BUILDING ON PRIOR KNOWLEDGE. Ask your students what their own experiences with snow, if any, have been like and what comes to mind when they think of the word *snowbound.*

To be snowbound in the early 1800's, when this poem takes place, was quite different from being snowbound today. But for all of the hardships, being snowbound was something of an adventure, an interruption of the course of ordinary life. When snowbound, people became thoughtful, more deeply aware of one another and of the privileges of their security. Perhaps the main source of the poem's charm is the richness of its details—the lively reporting of Whittier's eye and the simple language by which he describes exactly what he sees. As you read, try to put yourself "there." (An *idyll* is a work describing a simple, pleasant rural scene, or a peaceful domestic setting.)

from Snow-Bound: A Winter Idyll

To the memory of the household it describes,
this poem is dedicated by the author

The sun that brief December day
Rose cheerless over hills of gray,
And, darkly circled, gave at noon
A sadder light than waning moon.
Slow tracing down the thickening sky
Its mute and ominous prophecy,
A portent seeming less than threat,
It sank from sight before it set.
A chill no coat, however stout,
Of homespun stuff could quite shut out,
A hard, dull bitterness of cold,
That checked, mid-vein, the circling race
Of lifeblood in the sharpened face,
The coming of the snowstorm told.
The wind blew east; we heard the roar
Of Ocean on his wintry shore,
And felt the strong pulse throbbing there
Beat with low rhythm our inland air.

Meanwhile we did our nightly chores—
Brought in the wood from out of doors,
Littered the stalls, and from the mows°
Raked down the herd's grass for the cows:
Heard the horse whinnying for his corn;
And, sharply clashing horn on horn,
Impatient down the stanchion° rows
The cattle shake their walnut bows;°
While, peering from his early perch
Upon the scaffold's pole of birch,
The cock his crested helmet bent
And down his querulous challenge sent.

Unwarmed by any sunset light
The gray day darkened into night,
A night made hoary° with the swarm
And whirl-dance of the blinding storm,
As zigzag, wavering to and fro,
Crossed and recrossed the wingëd snow:
And ere the early bedtime came
The white drift piled the window frame,
And through the glass the clothesline posts
Looked in like tall and sheeted ghosts.

So all night long the storm roared on:
The morning broke without a sun;
In tiny spherule° traced with lines
Of Nature's geometric signs,
In starry flake, and pellicle,°
All day the hoary meteor fell;
And, when the second morning shone,
We looked upon a world unknown,
On nothing we could call our own.
Around the glistening wonder bent
The blue walls of the firmament,
No cloud above, no earth below—
A universe of sky and snow!

The old familiar sights of ours
Took marvelous shapes; strange domes and towers
Rose up where sty or corncrib stood,
Or garden wall, or belt of wood;
A smooth white mound the brush pile showed,
A fenceless drift what once was road;
The bridle post an old man sat

21. **mows:** storage for feed.
25. **stanchion:** stall.
26. **walnut bows:** wooden yokes.
33. **hoary:** white, as with age or frost.
43. **spherule:** sphere.
45. **pellicle:** a coat or film.

A. Mood

? How would your expectations of the poem differ if the poem were titled "Blizzard" or "Shut In"?

B. Rhyme

The poem's rhyme-couplet form can make for a sing-song effect. If students read the poem aloud, have them emphasize a more natural, conversational style. (The audiocassette recording should help.) The stanza breaks are natural points for changing readers.

C. Imagery

Line 48 is a key line, marking a change from realistic description to magical imaginings.

Humanities Connection: Responding to the Fine Art
Charles Burchfield (1893–1967), an Ohio watercolorist, was known for the magical quality of his landscapes and his Sherwood Anderson-like debunking of small towns.

? Imagine that you are a textbook editor searching for a work of art to illustrate "Snow-Bound." What qualities in the Burchfield watercolor make you feel that this is the right piece of art? (Answers will vary. Students might mention the stillness and domesticity of the scene.)

Winter Landscape with Houses by Charles Burchfield (1916). Watercolor.

Courtesy of Kennedy Galleries, Inc., New York.

Closure

Have students discuss the question, Do you think you would have enjoyed being snowbound with the family in the poem? Why?

Reading Check Test

1. The family make their living by _______. *farming*
2. The father has his sons cut a _______ in the snow. *path*
3. The sharpest ear cannot hear the _______ outside. *brook*
4. The children have read of _______ cave. *Aladdin's*
5. At night the family _______. *sits by the fire*

With loose-flung coat and high cocked hat;
The well-curb° had a Chinese roof;
And even the long sweep,° high aloof,
In its slant splendor, seemed to tell
Of Pisa's leaning miracle.°

A prompt, decisive man, no breath
Our father wasted: "Boys, a path!"
Well pleased (for when did farmer boy
Count such a summons less than joy?),
Our buskins° on our feet we drew;
With mittened hands, and caps drawn low,
To guard our necks and ears from snow,
We cut the solid whiteness through.
And, where the drift was deepest, made
A tunnel walled and overlaid
With dazzling crystal: we had read
Of rare Aladdin's° wondrous cave,
And to our own his name we gave,
With many a wish the luck were ours
To test his lamp's supernal powers.
We reached the barn with merry din,
And roused the prisoned brutes within.
The old horse thrust his long head out,
And grave with wonder gazed about;
The cock his lusty greeting said,
And forth his speckled harem led;
The oxen lashed their tails, and hooked,
And mild reproach of hunger looked;
The hornëd patriarch of the sheep,
Like Egypt's Amun° roused from sleep,
Shook his sage head with gesture mute,
And emphasized with stamp of foot.

All day the gusty north wind bore
The loosening drift its breath before;
Low circling round its southern zone,
The sun through dazzling snow mist shone.
No church bell lent its Christian tone
To the savage air, no social smoke
Curled over woods of snow-hung oak.
A solitude made more intense
By dreary-voicëd elements,
The shrieking of the mindless wind,
The moaning tree boughs swaying blind,
And on the glass the unmeaning beat
Of ghostly fingertips of sleet.
Beyond the circle of our hearth
No welcome sound of toil or mirth
Unbound the spell, and testified
Of human life and thought outside.
We minded° that the sharpest ear
The buried brooklet could not hear,
The music of whose liquid lip
Had been to us companionship,
And, in our lonely life, had grown
To have an almost human tone.

As night drew on, and, from the crest
Of wooded knolls that ridged the west,
The sun, a snow-blown traveler, sank
From sight beneath the smothering bank,
We piled, with care, our nightly stack
Of wood against the chimney back—
The oaken log, green, huge, and thick,
And on its top the stout back stick;
The knotty forestick laid apart,
And filled between with curious art
The ragged brush; then hovering near,
We watched the first red blaze appear,
Heard the sharp crackle, caught the gleam
On whitewashed wall and sagging beam,
Until the old, rude-furnished room
Burst, flower-like, into rosy bloom;
While radiant with a mimic flame
Outside the sparkling drift became,
And through the bare-boughed lilac tree
Our own warm hearth seemed blazing free.
The crane and pendent trammels° showed,
The Turks' heads° on the andirons glowed;
While childish fancy, prompt to tell
The meaning of the miracle,
Whispered the old rhyme: *"Under the tree,*
When fire outdoors burns merrily,
There the witches are making tea."

---

62. **well-curb:** enclosing frame over a well.
63. **sweep:** a pole with a bucket attached to the end, used for dipping water from a well.
65. **Pisa's miracle:** a reference to the leaning tower of Pisa in Italy. Whittier refers to it as a miracle because it looks as if it should fall over.
70. **buskins:** high boots of leather.
77. **Aladdin:** a young man in the *Arabian Nights* who discovers treasure in a cave by means of a miraculous lamp.
90. **Amun:** an Egyptian god usually represented as a ram.
110. **minded:** understood.
136. **trammels:** the iron hooks that held cooking pots over a grate fire on a swinging arm (crane).
137. **Turks' heads:** the tops of the andirons resembled turbans.

A. Expansion/ Responding

Lines 66–73 return the description to the realistic level, but after the children make the tunnel, they're once again free to indulge their fantasies, up to line 92. Thus the poem establishes a rhythm of relatively burdensome farm work alternating with the relief of escape into the imagination. "Childish fancy" reappears on lines 137–142.

? This is being told by an old man remembering his boyhood. How do you think the boy's own narrative, at the time, would have resembled or differed from this? (It probably would not be a poem nor filled with as many extravagant adjectives.)

ANALYZING THE POEM

Identifying Details

1. Answers include the following: "The sun . . . Rose cheerless over hills of gray" (lines 1–2); "darkly circled, gave at noon/ A sadder light . . ." (lines 3–4); "the roar/Of Ocean on his wintry shore" (lines 15–16); "the strong pulse" of the "inland air" (lines 17–18).

2. Images include: "dreary-voiced elements," "shrieking of the mindless wind," "moaning tree boughs," "on the glass the unmeaning beat / Of ghostly fingertips of sleet."

The poet points out that the sound of the brook, now stilled, had provided companionship in their lonely life, and had come to have "an almost human tone."

3. The group sits contentedly before a cleanswept hearth; the logs give off a "tropic heat"; the wind roars in "baffled rage" outside, unable to get in; the dog and cat lie peacefully; mugs of cider are heating and apples roasting; a basket of nuts sits nearby.

Interpreting Meanings

4. Answers might include the *(Answers continue in left-hand column.)*

(Continued from top.) following: the reference to Chinese roof (line 62), and the allusion to the leaning tower of Pisa (lines 63–65).

5. They wish they could use Aladdin's lamp to grant wishes.

The other details include: the rhyme mentioning witches in lines 140–142; the cat's shadow appearing to be a tiger's in line 168; the chimney seeming to laugh in line 164.

6. Student answers will vary. Have them think of Jack London or John Steinbeck, two writers who might make us feel that human life is subject to the same indifferent laws that govern the natural world. Such writers might stress the hardships posed by the show, its blank, white indifference to human life. Instead of picturing cozy togetherness, another writer might describe the family as pawns of a hostile universe, where only the fittest survive.

160

The moon above the eastern wood
Shone at its full; the hill range stood
Transfigured in the silver flood,
Its blown snows flashing cold and keen,
Dead white, save where some sharp ravine
Took shadow, or the somber green
Of hemlocks turned to pitchy black
Against the whiteness at their back
For such a world and such a night
Most fitting that unwarming light,
Which only seemed where'er it fell
To make the coldness visible.

Shut in from all the world without,
We sat the clean-winged° hearth about,
Content to let the north wind roar
In baffled rage at pane and door,
While the red logs before us beat
The frost line back with tropic heat;
And ever, when a louder blast
Shook beam and rafter as it passed,
The merrier up its roaring draft
The great throat of the chimney laughed;
The house dog on his paws outspread
Laid to the fire his drowsy head,
The cat's dark silhouette on the wall
A couchant° tiger's seemed to fall;
And, for the winter fireside meet,
Between the andirons' straddling feet,
The mug of cider simmered slow,
The apples sputtered in a row,
And, close at hand, the basket stood
With nuts from brown October's wood.

156. **clean-winged:** turkey wings were used to brush ashes from the hearth.

168. **couchant:** reclining.

Responding to the Poem

Analyzing the Poem

Identifying Details

1. The first eighteen lines of the poem create a mood of foreboding and expectation. List the **images** that help build this suspenseful mood.
2. Cite the **images** of sound in lines 100–105 that help you imagine the storm outside the house. In lines 110–115, what details help you imagine the isolated quality of farm life in the nineteenth century?
3. In lines 155–174, what **images** show how the threatening situation outside is turned into a cozy and pleasant situation inside?

Interpreting Meanings

4. The poet emphasizes the fabulous nature of the snowbound world. What **images** help us see his farmyard as if it's an exotic sight from another world?
5. Another reference to folklore and to the fabulous occurs in the lines describing the crystal cave. In line 80, what do the boys wish they could do? What other details in the poem connect the fabulous or the imaginary with the snowbound farmhouse?
6. How might a realistic writer describe this storm?

Writing About the Poem

A Critical Response

Analyzing the Poem's Appeal. When *Snow-Bound* was published, it was an immediate best seller, and it continued to be reprinted well into the twentieth century. By then, the kind of life it pictures had all but vanished. In one paragraph or more, explain how you would account for this poem's continuing appeal. Consider whether such appeal to a "romantic past" is also made today in movies, books, and TV shows.

Analyzing Language and Style

Allusions

Snow-Bound was an enormously popular poem, and up until a few decades ago, parts of it could be recited by almost every schoolchild in America. However, *Snow-Bound* is not necessarily "easy"; what makes it difficult for some readers are its allusions. Go over the poem and find allusions to (1) architecture, (2) literature, and (3) history. What do these allusions tell you about the kind of education Whittier assumed his readers would have?

Oliver Wendell Holmes (1809–1894)

A One of the most dynamic men of his time, Oliver Wendell Holmes pursued two careers simultaneously—medicine and literature—and he made lasting contributions to each. A descendant of Anne Bradstreet, Holmes was born into an already distinguished family in Cambridge, Massachusetts—the town across the Charles River from Boston and the seat of Harvard College. Quite naturally, he assumed membership in that unofficial social order of "Boston Brahmins," a name taken from the high priests of the Hindu religion and humorously applied to Boston's upper classes. Their odd mixture of philosophical conservatism and intellectual boldness made these prominent Bostonians—Longfellow, Holmes, Lowell, Charles Eliot Norton, and others—part of an American legend extending into the twentieth century.

B Before turning to medicine, Holmes had graduated from Harvard and had studied law there, a subject he found "cold and cheerless." He was still a law student when the government's plan to destroy the American warship *Constitution* inspired him to write a poem that saved the ship and made him famous. This poem was the emotional "Old Ironsides," one of the most enduring pieces of verse in American literature.

In spite of this taste of literary glory, Holmes decided that he would become a physician—a profession he chose because it could teach him about humankind. He studied medicine at Harvard for three years. He followed that with three years of further work in Paris hospitals, where the world's best doctors were said to work. He was twenty-seven when, almost at the same time, he published his first book of poetry and was awarded a medical degree from Harvard. Combining poetry and medicine did not seem unusual to Dr. Holmes, who was said to hear poetic meter in the rhythm of the heart.

Practicing medicine proved less interesting to Holmes than teaching medical students. After two years as professor of anatomy at Dartmouth College, he returned to Harvard, and there began a career in medical education that would continue for over three decades.

Oliver Wendell Holmes by Mathew Brady.

One of the founders of the *Atlantic Monthly* magazine, Holmes gained his national reputation from a series of chatty, urbane, and sometimes irreverently witty essays. These were eventually collected under the title *The Autocrat of the Breakfast Table* (1858), in which the leading character (recognizable to most readers as the author himself) presided over the spirited table-talk at an imaginary Boston boarding house.

Holmes's poetry was, for the most part, light and even comic. It commented on the social and intellectual shortcomings of his contemporaries, particularly those who aspired to higher forms of verse than he himself dared to write. But, on the evidence of his serious poems such as "The Chambered Nautilus," Holmes had earned the right to judge, not from an envious spirit but in the confidence of an equal talent.

Today, Holmes is perhaps remembered more as a phenomenon—an aristocrat with the common touch, an artist with a passion for science—than as a poet. The sort of wit that made *The Autocrat of the Breakfast Table* and its sequels the equivalents of modern best sellers has long become outdated, but the benign figure of Oliver Wendell Holmes remains. It is impossible to forget the gentleness and humor of a man who, beginning his practice as a young physician, hung out a sign saying: "Grateful for Small Fevers."

A. Expansion The combination of literature and medicine is not as odd as it may sound. Medicine is good training for writers because it teaches them to strengthen their powers of observation and also provides some understanding of what makes human beings work. The great American poet William Carlos Williams was an obstetrician (see page 717). Arthur Conan Doyle, creator of Sherlock Holmes, was a doctor; John Keats was a surgeon's apprentice; and the great playwright and short-story writer Anton Chekhov was a physician who did some charitable medical work even after becoming a famous writer.

B. Expansion Holmes's son, Oliver Wendell Holmes, Jr., stuck to his legal studies. He became a justice of the United States Supreme Court and one of the greatest figures in American legal history.

PREPARATION

1. BUILDING ON PRIOR KNOWLEDGE. Interested students may wish to report on the early history of the American navy.

2. ESTABLISHING A PURPOSE. This is an "occasional" poem—one written to suit a specific occasion. Before students read, you might have them discuss what they think are the strengths and weaknesses of the genre. Students can then read to determine whether or not this poem shares those strengths and weaknesses.

SUPPLEMENTARY SUPPORT MATERIALS

1. Vocabulary Activity Worksheet (*CCB*)
2. Review and Response Worksheet: Word Connotations (*CCB*)
3. Selection Test (*CCB*)

DEVELOPING VOCABULARY

The following word from the poem is tested in the Selection Test. (See also Vocabulary Activity Worksheet.)
tattered

A. Metaphor

? How does the ship resemble a meteor? (It strikes quickly.) How realistic do you think this metaphor is? (Answers will vary. Remind students that a sailing ship was probably the fastest means of transportation in 1830.)

B. Metaphor

? What qualities of the eagle make it a fitting metaphor? (The eagle is the bird that rules the skies because of its swiftness, its strength, and its ability to strike its targets so well from a distance.)

C. Humanities Connection: Responding to the Photograph

The presence of Old Ironsides in a contemporary harbor suggests that Holmes's poem worked: it had its intended effect of saving the ship.

? What does the effect of the poem suggest about our ability to enact positive change through individual and group action? (Answers will vary. The fact that the ship *was* saved suggests that we can change things.)

In 1830, the 44-gun American warship *Constitution,* which had defeated the British warship *Guerrière* in the War of 1812, was scheduled to be scrapped. Holmes sent this poem to the Boston *Advertiser* in protest.

Suppose that a historic ship or building or site were about to be destroyed today. What sort of letters might come into the newspapers protesting the destruction?

Old Ironsides

Ay, tear her tattered ensign down!
Long has it waved on high,
And many an eye has danced to see
That banner in the sky;
Beneath it rung the battle shout,
And burst the cannon's roar—
A The meteor of the ocean air
Shall sweep the clouds no more.

Her deck, once red with heroes' blood,
Where knelt the vanquished foe,
Where winds were hurrying o'er the flood,
And waves were white below,
No more shall feel the victor's tread,
Or know the conquered knee—
The harpies° of the shore shall pluck
B The eagle of the sea!

Oh, better that her shattered hulk
Should sink beneath the wave;
Her thunders shook the mighty deep,
And there should be her grave;
Nail to the mast her holy flag,
Set every threadbare sail,
And give her to the god of storms,
The lightning and the gale!

15. **harpies:** an allusion to predatory flying creatures in Greek mythology, which have bodies of vultures and heads of women. The name meant "snatchers" or "robbers." Later, the harpies came to symbolize any creatures that prey on helpless victims.

"Old Ironsides" in Boston harbor today. C

CLOSURE
Have students write a one- or two-sentence description of Old Ironsides that has the same emotional power as the poem.

ANALYZING THE POEM
Identifying Details
1. In stanza 1, Holmes uses the metaphor of "the meteor of the ocean air" for the ship, and he calls it the "eagle of the sea."
2. Holmes proposes that it would be better to sink the ship and give her back to the sea and the "god of storms" than ignobly to rip her apart for scrap.

Interpreting Meanings
3. Old Ironsides has too noble a history, and too much patriotic meaning, to be scrapped.

Rather than begging that the ship not be destroyed, Holmes first urges the opposite of what he really means: "Ay, tear her tattered ensign down!" He then emphasizes the irony of his statement by evoking the ship's former glory.
4. Holmes is suggesting that those who are responsible for arranging that the ship be scrapped, and who will profit from it, are the vulture-like harpies.
5. Students may suggest that the ship symbolizes the nation's heroic past, threatened by "progress" and "modern ways."
6. Holmes uses irony and fiery rhetoric to make an angry statement appealing to readers' emotions, rather than offering a humbler prayer or a reasoned petition.
7. Student answers will vary. Have students discuss our sensitivity to the destruction of other historical landmarks or of the environment.
8. Encourage a lively discussion among the students, and urge them to support their opinions with convincing arguments.

ADDITIONAL WRITING ASSIGNMENT
Have students write an occasional poem about a contemporary event.

Responding to the Poem

Analyzing the Poem

Identifying Details

1. What **metaphors** does Holmes use to describe the ship in stanzas 1 and 2?
2. What proposal concludes the poem?

Interpreting Meanings

3. In simple terms, what message does the first stanza present? What is **ironic** about the way Holmes states his message?
4. When a ship is broken up in the dockyards, she is said to be scrapped—that is, stripped of everything valuable or reusable. Is Holmes comparing the directors of the scrapping business to harpies in stanza 2, or is his scorn directed at someone else? Explain.
5. What do you think the poet wants the ship to **symbolize**?
6. In many circumstances where poets have seen things they love threatened by "progress," they have composed prayers or made petitions. How does Holmes's response differ from a prayer or a petition?
7. If, next year, Old Ironsides should be found to be in danger of sinking at her dock, do you think most Americans would let her go?
8. Do you think other historical relics like this old ship should be preserved? Or do you think they should be destroyed? Why?

Writing About the Poem

A Creative Response

1. **Applying the Poem to Other Situations.** In a paragraph, tell how this poem might be read to apply to a situation involving a human being. In your paragraph, explain what the ship's parts might symbolize in human terms: her flag, her deck red with blood, her shattered hulk, her thunders, her threadbare sails.

A Critical Response

2. **Finding Contemporary Parallels.** Specifically, this poem is an expression of outrage at the thought of a ship that has become a national treasure and a reminder of past glory being regarded as nothing more than an object to be dismantled and sold at a profit. More broadly, however, the poem can be read as a call to honor the past. In a brief essay, explain how that same appeal is sometimes made today. What are some specific issues that have inspired such appeals? Are these appeals still made in the form of poetry? What other forms of expression have contemporary patriots and lovers of the past found effective?

Analyzing Language and Style

Connotations

With his poem, Holmes wanted to persuade people to do something, so he deliberately chose words for their emotional overtones and associations. These emotional shadings that are attached to some words are called **connotations.** For example, in line 1, Holmes describes the ship's flag as a "tattered ensign." *Tattered* suggests many months facing the lashing gale of winds, perhaps in the line of duty. The image of a "tattered flag" (ensign) is likely to stir our hearts. But suppose instead he had called it a "rotting flag" or a "ragged flag" or just a "worn-out flag"? How would the emotional content of the line change?

Suggest substitute wording for each of these lines from the poem, to call forth completely different emotional responses from a reader:

1. meteor of the ocean air
2. red with heroes' blood
3. harpies of the shore
4. eagle of the sea
5. shattered hulk
6. holy flag
7. threadbare sail

Supplementary Support Materials
1. Vocabulary Activity Worksheet (*CCB*)
2. Review and Response Worksheet: Metaphor (*CCB*)
3. Selection Test (*CCB*)

Developing Vocabulary
The following word from the poem is tested in the Selection Test. (See also Vocabulary Activity Worksheet.)
vaulted

Preparation
Establishing a Purpose. Before students read, have them discuss the question, How is human life like the growth of a seashell? Then have them read to find the analogy that Holmes draws in this poem.

A. Connections
Holmes's choice of a seashell as subject goes along with his interest in science. A contemporary writer who continues this tradition of musing upon natural history is the essayist Lewis Thomas (page 994).

B. Expansion
Because this poem contains much archaic language and diction, you might want to turn to the Analyzing Language and Style exercise, page 166, at the very beginning, using it to "modernize" the poem stanza by stanza or line by line.

C. Responding
? In the phrase "dim dreaming life," is Holmes also commenting on human life? What evidence is there in the poem to support your answer? (The metaphor of the nautilus as a "tenant" in line 12 suggests that Holmes is drawing parallels between the nautilus and humanity.)

A nautilus is a creature that lives in a seashell, one of those mollusks that grow year by year, from the size of a tiny bead to the size of a pumpkin. In Holmes's own description, the nautilus shell is composed of a "series of enlarging compartments successively dwelt in by the animal that inhabits the shell, which is built in a widening spiral." The word *nautilus* comes from the Greek word for "sailor," reminding us that the Greeks thought this shell could actually move on the surface of the water, using a membrane as its sail. Ancient drawings often represent the nautilus as a little boat with its sail billowing in the wind, blown by one of those fat-cheeked figures on the "four corners" of the earth. The nautilus is one of the most beautiful objects in nature and one of the most fragile of life-containing vessels.

The first three stanzas of the poem are a meditation upon the life and death of the shell. In the next-to-last stanza, the poet begins an apostrophe (a direct address to an object or to someone who is not present). The visual description here is like the scene in Shakespeare's *Hamlet* (Act V) in which a gravedigger unearths the skull of a man Hamlet knew. Hamlet holds the skull up to the light and speaks words about life and destiny that the skull evokes for him. In "The Chambered Nautilus," the poet might be pictured holding the shell before him and speaking.

Like most poems written in the 1800's, "The Chambered Nautilus" contains some words that are now archaic, or not in common use. When you come to a word you don't know, stop and think about it; try to use the context to figure out its meaning if a dictionary isn't handy. Remember to pause in reading the poem only when you come to a comma, period, or other mark of punctuation.

The Chambered Nautilus

This is the ship of pearl, which poets feign,°
  Sails the unshadowed main—
  The venturous bark that flings
On the sweet summer wind its purpled wings
In gulfs enchanted, where the siren° sings,
  And coral reefs lie bare,
Where the cold sea maids rise to sun their streaming hair.

Its webs of living gauze no more unfurl;
  Wrecked is the ship of pearl!
  And every chambered cell,
Where its dim dreaming life was wont to dwell,
As the frail tenant shaped his growing shell,
  Before thee lies revealed—
Its irised° ceiling rent,° its sunless crypt unsealed!

Year after year beheld the silent toil
  That spread his lustrous coil;
  Still, as the spiral grew,
He left the past year's dwelling for the new,
Stole with soft step its shining archway through,
  Built up its idle door,
Stretched in his last-found home, and knew the old no more.

1. **feign:** imagine.

5. **siren:** an allusion to a mythical sea maiden. The sirens' songs were so seductive that sailors would wreck their ships on the rocks in order to hear them.

14. **irised:** iridescent; from Iris, goddess of the rainbow; **rent:** torn.

Closure

Ask students to answer the question, Are you convinced that your personal development resembles that of a nautilus shell? Why or why not?

A

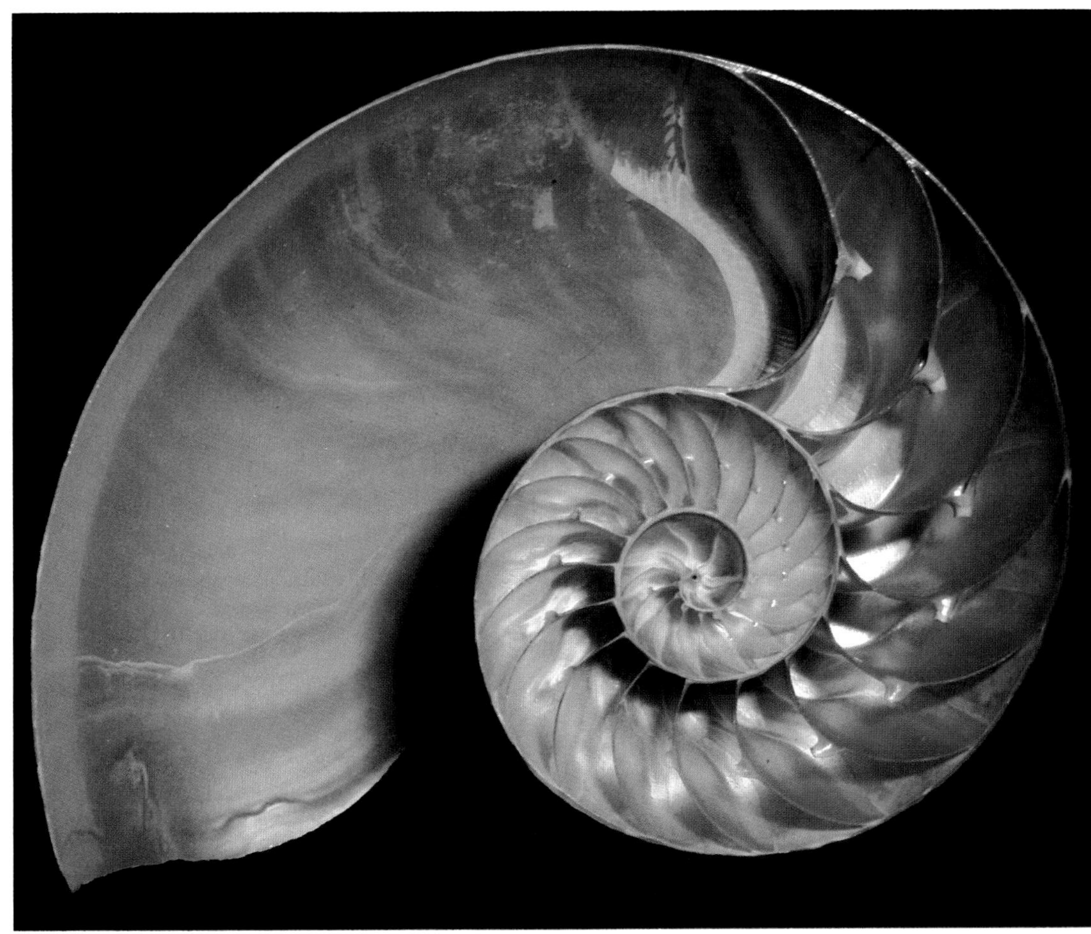

Thanks for the heavenly message brought by thee,
   Child of the wandering sea,
   Cast from her lap, forlorn!
From thy dead lips a clearer note is born
B Than ever Triton blew from wreathéd horn!°
   While on mine ear it rings,
Through the deep caves of thought I hear a voice that
      sings—

C Build thee more stately mansions, O my soul,
   As the swift seasons roll!
   Leave thy low-vaulted past!
Let each new temple, nobler than the last,
Shut thee from heaven with a dome more vast,
   Till thou at length art free,
Leaving thine outgrown shell by life's unresting sea!

26. This line echoes a famous line from "The World Is Too Much with Us," a sonnet by William Wordsworth: "Or hear old Triton blow his wreathéd horn." Triton was a mythical sea god, often represented as blowing a conch-shell horn.

A. Humanities Connection: Discussing the Photograph
Students may wish to bring in photographs or drawings of natural objects with which they feel emotional connections.

B. Apostrophe
? What is Holmes apostrophizing in stanza 4? (The shell) In stanza 5? (His own soul)

C. Expansion
The Biblical phrase "more stately mansions" was later used by Eugene O'Neill as the title of a play.

ANALYZING THE POEM
Identifying Details
1. The nautilus is compared to a "ship of pearl," sailing on the ocean.
2. "Gulfs enchanted" (line 5) and "coral reefs" (line 6).
3. These are the membranes of the animal inside the nautilus shell.
The nautilus has been "wrecked" (line 9)—taken from the sea and split open.
4. The "frail tenant" is the mollusk who lived inside the nautilus.
5. "Silent toil / That spread his lustrous coil" (lines 15–16); "the spiral grew" (line 17); "left the past year's dwelling for the new" (line 18); moved through its "shining archway" (line 19); "built up its idle door" (line 20).
6. The poet is grateful to the nautilus for its lesson.

Interpreting Meanings
7. This is revealed in the last stanza.
The soul is told to reach higher and higher as time passes until it finally leaves its body behind and becomes free.
8. The creature building its nautilus shell is a metaphor for the human soul striving toward heaven. The "stately mansions,"
(Answers continue in left-hand column.)

(Continued from top.)
or nautilus chambers, represent the spiritual achievements of the soul; the "low-vaulted past," or previous chamber, represents the earlier, less spiritual state of the soul; "each new temple," or chamber, represents each step of the soul toward heaven; the "outgrown shell" is a suggestion of the body discarded by the soul in death; the "unresting sea" represents life.
9. Answers will vary. Encourage students to compare the tone and specific motifs of the two poems in some detail.
10. Answers will vary. Have students support their candidates by comparing them in detail with some of the other poems in the unit.

Responding to the Poem

Analyzing the Poem

Identifying Details

1. What **metaphor** describes the nautilus in line 1?
2. The poet says that the "main," or open sea, over which the nautilus sailed is "unshadowed" (line 2). What other **images** in the first stanza help you picture where the nautilus once sailed?
3. What are the "webs of living gauze" referred to in line 8? According to the second stanza, what has happened to the nautilus?
4. Who is the "frail tenant" of the shell?
5. Stanza 3 describes the way the nautilus grows. The poet speaks of the nautilus **metaphorically,** as a person who changes homes. What details describe how this happens year after year?
6. Why does the speaker thank the nautilus in the fourth stanza?

Interpreting Meanings

7. In what part of the poem is the "heavenly message" of the shell revealed? **Paraphrase** this message—that is, state in your own words what the "voice that sings" says to the poet.
8. The central extended **metaphor** of the poem is revealed in the last stanza. What is that metaphor? Step by step, how is it extended—that is, what are the "stately mansions," the "low-vaulted past," "each new temple," the "outgrown shell," and the "unresting sea"?
9. Did you find this poem more optimistic than "Thanatopsis"?
10. Of all the nature poems you've read in this unit, which did you like best? Least?

Writing About the Poem

A Creative Response

1. **Taking Another Point of View.** Holmes himself was a scientist, but he addresses the shell here as a poet. Imagine that he takes a second look at it as a scientist. What would he then think of the shell? What questions might he ask it? Would it have a message for Holmes the scientist? Write a paragraph answering these questions.

A Critical Response

2. **Responding to a "Message."** In weak poems containing a well-meant message or moral, the reader often feels that the message or moral has been "tacked on" at the last minute. In good poems of the same kind, the message or moral is a natural outgrowth of the premises of the poem and is inseparable from these premises. In reading "The Chambered Nautilus," do you feel that the message in the last stanza is merely tacked on to give the poem a moral? Or do you feel that the poem is "all of a piece," that this message is an inevitable conclusion that has been led up to throughout the poem? State and support your opinion in a brief essay.
3. **Analyzing the Poem's Appeal.** "The Chambered Nautilus" is one of the most enduring poems in American literature and, as such, is a part of the national heritage. (Abraham Lincoln is said to have known it by heart.) Why do you think this poem has endured while so many other poems by Holmes and his contemporaries have disappeared? Write at least one paragraph suggesting reasons for the poem's appeal. Consider its (a) message and (b) sounds.

Analyzing Language and Style

Poetic and Archaic Language

In Holmes's time, certain words, as well as certain subjects, were considered correct for poetry. (Certain other words and subjects were taboo in poetry.) Holmes makes use of some of these "poetic" words, as well as of some **archaic** words—that is, words no longer in common use. What plain, everyday English words could be substituted for the following "poetic" or archaic words from "The Chambered Nautilus"? Put your substitutes in the poem: Does it sound more "modern"?

feign	wont	thou
main	thee	beheld
bark	thine	art

Now find lines that use **inverted syntax** in the poem, and put these passages in normal English sentence order. Does the poem now seem less inflated, less archaic?

Which of the archaic words in the list above are used today in other senses?

James Russell Lowell (1819–1891)

Ancestor of two twentieth-century American poets, Amy Lowell and Robert Lowell, James Russell Lowell belonged to an aristocratic class and a conservative poetic tradition. His two famous descendants vehemently detached themselves from this tradition, but James Russell Lowell reveled in his heritage.

Born to a Unitarian clergyman in Concord, Massachusetts, James Russell Lowell was identified throughout his life with the literary and academic eminence of his native town. He graduated from Harvard College as the class poet in 1838 and continued his studies at Harvard Law School. His literary activity was partly prompted by his wife, Maria White Lowell, who successfully enlisted his support as a writer for the Abolitionists.

Like John Greenleaf Whittier and many other New England writers of his time, Lowell was a man of strong political and social convictions. Abandoning the law (without regrets), Lowell turned to writing. He expressed himself forcefully in articles, essays, and poems. His editorial career included a term with an antislavery publication, *The Pennsylvania Freeman,* and a longer term as the first editor of the *Atlantic Monthly.* Lowell shared the progressive spirit of his time, which found its clearest identity in the Abolitionist movement and in fighting the problems of post-Civil War industrialism.

By 1848, when Lowell was only twenty-nine, he had published the four books of poetry that would establish his literary reputation. One of these was *A Fable for Critics,* a collection of witty, satirical verses about contemporary writers (including one named James Russell Lowell). The *Fable* takes American writers to task for not being more American:

> You steal Englishmen's books and think Englishmen's thought,
> With their salt on her tail your wild eagle is caught;
> Your literature suits its each whisper and motion
> To what will be thought of it over the ocean.

James Russell Lowell by Mathew Brady.

In 1853, Maria died, and Lowell was devastated. Retreating for over ten years, he published nothing until 1864. In effect, he stopped writing poetry almost completely. Instead, he began a new career—teaching. He succeeded Longfellow as Smith Professor of French and Spanish at Harvard, where he taught for more than twenty years. One of Lowell's greatest poems, "Ode Recited at the Harvard Commemoration," was composed in 1865 to honor the graduates of Harvard who had died in the Civil War. But as he grew older, Lowell's time was increasingly occupied with scholarly interests, literary criticism, and diplomatic service, and he never again wrote a poem that had wide appeal.

Lowell's public spirit was recognized by his appointments as minister (we would now say ambassador) to Spain in 1877 and to Britain in 1880. In Britain, he won many friends, including the distinguished critic and scholar Leslie Stephen. When Stephen needed a suitable godfather for his first daughter by his second wife, he asked Lowell to accept that honor. And so the pillar of conservative American literature became the godfather of a woman whose innovations would decisively change the nature of the English nov '—Virginia Woolf.

A

B

A. Humanities Connection: Responding to the Photograph

? How is Lowell's appearance typical of the Romantic era? (Answers will vary, but Lowell's hair and beard would not look unusual on a contemporary college campus (we ourselves may be living in a Romantic era) and his several layers of loosely fitting outerwear were probably intended to look dashing.)

B. Expansion

Lowell's biography shows him to be an imposing person, and his photograph shows him as a piercing-eyed Romantic. The poem shows another side of him. You might discuss with students the idea that despite their now archaic language and dress, the early American writers were human beings like ourselves, with all the feelings we have—in this case, the grief of a father for his daughter.

Supplementary Support Materials
1. Vocabulary Activity Worksheet (*CCB*)
2. Review and Response Worksheet: Imagery (*CCB*)
3. Selection Test (*CCB*)

Developing Vocabulary
The following word from the poem is tested in the Selection Test. (See also Vocabulary Activity Worksheet.)
thrilled

Preparation
Establishing a Purpose. In good poetry, style befits subject, enhancing tone. Ask students to read to determine how the style and subject of this poem complement each other.

A. Simile
? In what way are the trembling twig and the unbent leaves important to the simile? (The trembling represents the effect that the young child had on her father. She was so young, however, that she left life "unbent" by her presence on earth.)

B. Metaphor
? In what sense does the child have a "May"? (In northern climates May is the time of year when trees and flowers are becoming green and have not yet begun to burn from the sun. Thus the child represents the fullness and the promise of new life.)

C. Refrain
? What effect does the change of refrain in the last stanza have on the poem? (It makes the poem seem less personal, more applicable to human experience.)

When James Russell Lowell's first child, Blanche, was only four months old, the poet was so pleased with the lively infant that he could not resist boasting about her. As he wrote to a friend, "Miss Blanche Lowell, in the freshness of her morning spirits, is, in my opinion, a sight well worth a journey from Philadelphia to look upon. Why, she laughs all over. You can see it through her clothes. The very tips of her toes twinkle for joy. . . . She has another grace which I might in modesty omit, but I love truth! She is exceedingly fond of her father!"

Less than a year later, the infant who had been the joy of his life was dead. It took Lowell many months to find words for his grief. When they came, he produced a short elegiac lyric that, in its purity and simplicity, stands apart from the bulk of his collected works.

She Came and Went

A [As a twig trembles, which a bird
 Lights on to sing, then leaves unbent,
So is my memory thrilled and stirred—
 I only know she came and went.

As clasps some lake, by gusts unriven,
 The blue dome's measureless content,
So my soul held that moment's heaven—
 I only know she came and went.

As, at one bound, our swift spring heaps
 The orchards full of bloom and scent,
B [So clove her May my wintry sleeps—
 I only know she came and went.

An angel stood and met my gaze,
 Through the low doorway of my tent;
The tent is struck, the vision stays—
 I only know she came and went.

Oh, when the room grows slowly dim,
 And life's last oil is nearly spent,
One gush of light these eyes will brim,
 Only to think she came and went.] C

Responding to the Poem

Analyzing the Poem

Identifying Details

1. Each of the first three stanzas makes a comparison that describes the effect Lowell's daughter has had on his life. Restate these three **similes** in your own words.
2. What time of life does the last stanza refer to? What does the poet say will happen when this time of his life arrives?

Interpreting Meanings

3. What words and **images** in the poem emphasize the brevity of the daughter's life? What words and images express the joy she gave her father?
4. How would you **paraphrase** the **refrain**?
5. This is a very personal poem. Do you think the ideas Lowell expresses apply only to his own personal tragedy? Or does the poem's meaning transcend the limits of this one personal experience—and, if so, what other experiences might the poem speak for?

Writing About the Poem

A Critical Response

Comparing Two Poems on the Same Theme. In a brief essay, compare and contrast Lowell's "She Came and Went" with Longfellow's "The Cross of Snow" (page 147). What image does each poet use to evoke the emotion of grief? How do the poems differ in structure? Which lyric do you think evokes a more vivid picture of the loved one who was lost?

CLOSURE

Have students suggest other experiences that this poem might speak for. (See question 5, page 168.)

ANALYZING THE POEM

Identifying Details

1. The poet's memory is "thrilled and stirred" by thoughts of his daughter as a twig is made to tremble by a bird alighting on it. The poet's soul clasped his daughter's presence as a still lake clasps the sky. The daughter's presence revived the poet's life as spring awakens the world after winter.

2. It refers to the end of life.

The memory of his daughter will be a final "gush of light" that will cause the poet's eyes to brim with tears.

Interpreting Meanings

3. The repeated line "she came and went"; the image of a twig unbent by the brief perch of a bird; the word "moment's" in line 7.

Words and images expressing joy include: the image of a bird singing; the words "thrilled and stirred" (line 3); "measureless content" (line 6); "bloom and scent" (line 10); the images of spring and May; the image of the angel; the image of a gush of light (line 19).

4. One possibility: "My grief is so great that I only remember two moments in my daughter's life: her birth and her death."

5. Answers will vary. The feeling of loss is one shared by all people. The fact that the references are so general (he never states that "she" was a child) make it possible to think "she" was a lost love.

Humanities Connection: Writing About the Fine Art

? Looking at the painting, quickly write down a few adjectives that describe how it makes you feel. How do these feelings resemble, and differ from, the feelings aroused in you by the poem? (Answers will vary. The picture concretely identifies its subjects and their relationship. In both art forms, feelings are only implied.)

Mother and Child by Mary Cassatt (1890's). Oil.

Private Collection.

SUPPLEMENTARY SUPPORT MATERIALS
1. Vocabulary Activity Worksheet (*CCB*)
2. Review and Response Worksheet: Characterization (*CCB*)
3. Selection Test (*CCB*)

DEVELOPING VOCABULARY
The following words from the poem are tested in the Selection Test. (See also Vocabulary Activity Worksheet.)
robust gnarled

PREPARATION
ESTABLISHING A PURPOSE. Have students read to learn Lowell's assessment of Longfellow, Hawthorne, and Poe. As students read selections from Hawthorne and Poe in Unit Four, they can decide if they agree with Lowell's criticisms.

A. Responding
Based on this description of Poe, why is the cartoon on page 171 particularly appropriate? (It is "fudge" that Poe would have had a raven with him in a boarding house.)

B. Responding
Based on these descriptions, which poet would you prefer, Hawthorne or Poe? Why? (Answers will vary. Some students will be swayed by the clear shots at Poe; others may find the description of Hawthorne too confusing to appeal.)

C. Noting Details
What are some details in the poem that indicate that Lowell knew the poets he describes? (Lowell is obviously familiar with such details as Hawthorne's appearance and Poe's manner of speaking.)

The lively bounce of his lines sometimes disguises the sharp criticism Lowell directed at his contemporaries. In the following excerpts from *A Fable for Critics,* his targets are a novelist—Nathaniel Hawthorne (see page 263)—and a poet who also wrote stories and literary criticism, Edgar Allan Poe (see page 226). To appreciate fully the bite of Lowell's wit as he sums up the virtues and shortcomings of his fellow writers, a reader must know at least some of the works of these men. However, even without firsthand knowledge, most readers will recognize the fun Lowell is having and respond to the generosity of spirit that informs even his moments of ridicule.

Since Lowell was a highly learned man, it is not surprising that his verse is full of allusions. What *is* surprising to twentieth-century readers is the assumption that his audience would immediately grasp the meanings of these allusions. Some are from classical literature; others are from works generally available to Americans in the mid-nineteenth century.

Today, satirical poems written in the manner of *A Fable for Critics* have all but disappeared. We find their counterparts occasionally in magazines or in newspaper columns that feature comic verse contributed by subscribers.

from A Fable for Critics

There is Hawthorne, with genius so shrinking and rare
That you hardly at first see the strength that is there;
A frame so robust, with a nature so sweet,
So earnest, so graceful, so lithe and so fleet,
Is worth a descent from Olympus to meet;
'Tis as if a rough oak that for ages had stood,
With his gnarled bony branches like ribs of the wood,
Should bloom, after cycles of struggle and scathe,°
With a single anemone trembly and rathe;°
His strength is so tender, his wildness so meek,
That a suitable parallel sets one to seek—
He's a John Bunyan Fouqué, a Puritan Tieck;°
When Nature was shaping him, clay was not granted
For making so full-sized a man as she wanted,
So, to fill out her model, a little she spared
From some finer-grained stuff for a woman prepared,
And she could not have hit a more excellent plan
For making him fully and perfectly man.

. . .

There comes Poe, with his raven, like Barnaby Rudge,°
Three-fifths of him genius and two-fifths sheer fudge,
Who talks like a book of iambs and pentameters,
In a way to make people of common sense damn meters,
Who has written some things quite the best of their kind,
But the heart somehow seems all squeezed out by the
   mind,
Who—But hey-day! What's this? Messieurs Mathews°
   and Poe,
You mustn't fling mud balls at Longfellow so,
Does it make a man worse that his character's such

8. **scathe:** injury.

9. **rathe:** an obsolete word meaning "short-lived" or "appearing early in a day or a season."

12. **John Bunyan Fouqué** combines the name of John Bunyan, the Puritan author of *The Pilgrim's Progress,* with that of Friedrich Fouqué, author of a Romantic novel called *Undine.* **Ludwig Tieck** is another Romantic author.

35. **Barnaby Rudge:** hero of Charles Dickens's novel of the same name; Rudge kept a pet raven.

41. **Mathews:** Cornelius Mathews, a writer and editor whose criticism of Longfellow was notably harsh.

CLOSURE

Have students suggest one-sentence summaries of Lowell's comments on each poet.

ANALYZING THE POEM

Identifying Details

1. Lowell compares Hawthorne to something rough and powerful and to something delicate and fragile.

Hawthorne is described as having "tender strength" and "meek wildness."

2. Lowell calls Hawthorne a "John Bunyan Fouqué," combining the names of Puritan and Romantic authors, and a "Puritan Tieck," which presents the same contradiction. He says that Hawthorne was made "fully and perfectly man" by the addition of a little "finer-grained stuff for a woman prepared."

3. In Poe the "heart" is overcome by the "mind."

4. He says that Longfellow is generous to his fellow bards and even to his critics.

Lowell reminds Longfellow's critics that "elegance also is force."

Interpreting Meanings

5. Lowell suggests that Poe's work contains much that is mere embellishment. (The original sense of *fudge* is "nonsense" or "empty talk.")

6. Answers will vary.

7. Answers will vary. Most will choose Longfellow or Hawthorne.

A. Responding

? Based on your reading of Longfellow, do you agree or disagree with this assessment of his work?

ADDITIONAL WRITING ASSIGNMENT

Write a satirical stanza about any writer you have encountered in this textbook.

As to make his friends love him (as you think) too
  much?
Why, there is not a bard at this moment alive
More willing than he that his fellows should thrive;
A While you are abusing him thus, even now
He would help either one of you out of a slough;
You may say that he's smooth and all that till you're
  hoarse,
But remember that elegance also is force. . . .

Responding to the Poem

Analyzing the Poem

Identifying Details

1. Hawthorne is described as having qualities that seem **incongruous,** or not matched. What is contradictory about the image of the oak and the anemone (lines 6–9)? What details in line 10 emphasize that **paradox,** or apparent contradiction, in Hawthorne's character?
2. What other details in Lowell's discussion of Hawthorne present **paradoxes?**
3. What is Lowell's chief criticism of Poe's work, given in line 40?
4. How does Lowell defend Longfellow's character? How does he defend Longfellow's work?

Interpreting Meanings

5. How would you explain what Lowell means by saying that Poe is "two-fifths sheer fudge"?
6. Longfellow has endured a great deal of criticism, then and now. What passages from Longfellow (pages 147–152) support Lowell's point that "elegance also is force"?
7. Of these writers, which do you think Lowell most admires, for both his character and his work?

Writing About the Poem

A Critical Response

Summarizing a Verse. Lowell did not spare himself in his *Fable for Critics.* Read this self-assessment, and then briefly summarize Lowell's criticism of his own poetry. Use an encyclopedia to learn the meaning of the allusion to Parnassus. Can you cite any other writers who, in your own opinion, have not learned the distinction between singing and preaching?

There is Lowell, who's striving Parnassus to climb
With a whole bale of *isms* tied together with rhyme,
He might get on alone, spite of brambles and boulders,
But he can't with that bundle he has on his shoulders,
The top of the hill he will never come nigh reaching
Till he learns the distinction 'twixt singing and
  preaching. . . .

—from "A Fable for Critics,"
James Russell Lowell

"I'm sorry, Mr. Poe, but you know very well you can't keep a pet in your room."

From a series, *Through History with J. Wesley Smith. Saturday Review of Literature,* 1957.

A. Expansion
The battle between linguistic purists and linguistic liberals is almost as old as the language itself, since language is always in a state of change, and any change will be welcomed by some people more than others. Today the battle has been taken up by certain critics who make a practice of collecting examples of, in their view, linguistic barbarisms, and publicly decrying them. You might want to bring in some of the works of Edwin Newman, William Safire, and others on this subject, and discuss examples of questionable usage that these writers have found.

THE AMERICAN LANGUAGE

by Gary Q. Arpin

"Noah's Ark": Webster's Dictionary

"The ultimate authority was royal —the King's English (though one king of England, the German George I, could not speak English at all)."

John Adams's proposal to establish an American Academy to guard the language from corruption (see page 111) was a response to a problem of increasing importance—the need many Americans felt to have some kind of authority governing matters of usage.

A In England, linguistic authority had traditionally rested in literature and in the aristocracy. The English felt that words should be used the way great writers and the nobility used them. The ultimate authority was royal—the King's English (though one king of England, the German George I, could not speak English at all). This was beginning to change in England in the eighteenth century, however; and of course in America matters were very different. In America, up until the mid-ninteenth century, there was very little literature and, needless to say, a good deal of disagreement about the scope of royal authority.

Why was an authority necessary at all? People had not always felt the need for one. The Roman poet Horace wrote that "usage is the law and rule of speech." Horace meant that the *speakers* of a language determine matters of usage by common agreement. In a relatively stable social structure, this is what happens: People of a particular class will speak exactly the way their friends and associates speak, and matters of right and wrong won't even be raised. But in societies where social structure is fluid, the matter becomes more complex.

Imagine that you are a baker in London in the eighteenth century. Your cakes and pastries suddenly become very popular, and in a few years you have become a moderately wealthy member of a growing middle class. But your own speech patterns reveal your humbler origins, just as clearly as a caste mark would. Now, how about your children? Well, what you want for your children is a different matter.

"Written grammars dictating English usage became popular in England, and schoolmasters began to take over authority in matters of English language usage."

In fact, hundreds of eighteenth-century English found themselves in this situation, and they did what you might expect them to do. They sent their children to newly founded schools that, among other things, taught the children for the first time the language habits of the class they wanted to imitate. English grammar now became a subject to be taught to youngsters. Before this, children would be taught Latin and Greek; it was assumed they could speak their own language and needed no instruction in it. The teachers in these new schools were probably not from the nobility and thus did not come by upper-class language usage naturally; but they had *books*. In this way, written grammars dictating English usage became popular in England, and schoolmasters began to take over authority in matters of English language usage. What one writer has called "the schoolmastering of English" had begun.

The teaching of English arose for similar reasons in America. Before the Revolution, it would have been difficult to find an "English School" in the Colonies—that is, a school that taught English grammar rather than Latin grammar. Benjamin Franklin tried to establish a school to teach English in Philadelphia in the 1750's, but his Latin School overwhelmed it, and the English school went out of business. After the Revolution, though, regular instruction in English grammar became common in the public schools. However, the only available textbooks came from England. This was clearly an awkward situation for a new nation that wanted to establish linguistic independence and justify its use of language to carping British critics.

> **"The spelling book turned out to be a major force in the drive for American linguistic independence."**

An American Spelling Book

Enter Noah Webster, a young schoolmaster from Connecticut. Webster was looking for a way to finance his legal education, and he was also passionately dedicated to the cause of American English. To help advance these two causes, Webster wrote a spelling book, which he first published in 1783, when he was twenty-five. The spelling book turned out to be a major force in the drive for American linguistic independence. Over the generations, *The American Spelling Book* was used in numerous editions, and over a hundred million copies of it were sold. A

Webster believed that "a national language is a band of national union," and he prepared his speller and his later textbooks for a purpose:

> . . . to reform the abuses and corruption which . . . tincture the conversation of the polite part of Americans . . . and especially to render the pronunciation . . . accurate and uniform by demolishing those obvious distinctions of provincial dialects.

Webster reasoned that accurate and uniform American spelling would lead to uniform American speech, and that uniformity in speech would "reconcile the people of America to each other."

The whole idea of consistency in spelling was fairly new in Webster's time and was directly related to the increasing use of the printing press. Until the 1700's, people followed rather flexible rules of spelling, and in fact some letters of the alphabet were not completely fixed: *i, j,* and *y,* and *u, v,* and *w* were not yet distinct letters. Sometimes a word would be written with an *e* at the end and sometimes not. Thus, *join* might be written *ioyn* or *joyne* or *ioyne.* The word *the* was frequently written *ye,* the *y* in this case being a form of a Middle English letter that stood for the sound *th* and that had disappeared. (These spellings are now used by some store owners who want to give an old-fashioned appearance to their store's name; for example, Ye Olde Noveltie Shoppe.)

In 1755, in England, Samuel Johnson's great *Dictionary of the English Language* was published. Dr. Johnson also wished to reg-

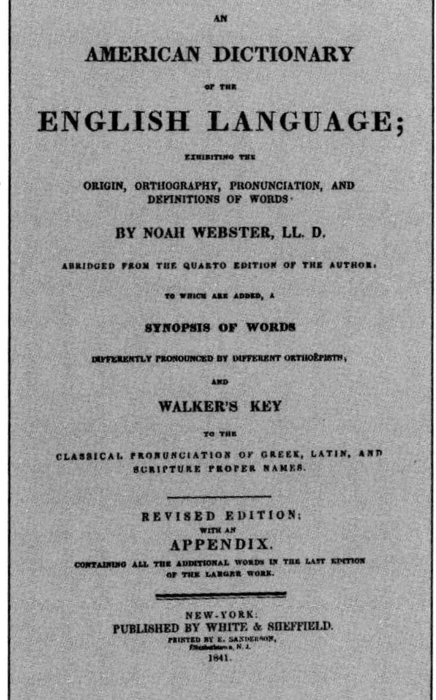
AN
AMERICAN DICTIONARY
OF THE
ENGLISH LANGUAGE;
EXHIBITING THE
ORIGIN, ORTHOGRAPHY, PRONUNCIATION, AND DEFINITIONS OF WORDS
BY NOAH WEBSTER, LL. D.
ABRIDGED FROM THE QUARTO EDITION OF THE AUTHOR:
TO WHICH ARE ADDED, A
SYNOPSIS OF WORDS
DIFFERENTLY PRONOUNCED BY DIFFERENT ORTHOËPISTS;
AND
WALKER'S KEY
TO THE
CLASSICAL PRONUNCIATION OF GREEK, LATIN, AND SCRIPTURE PROPER NAMES.

REVISED EDITION;
WITH AN
APPENDIX,
CONTAINING ALL THE ADDITIONAL WORDS IN THE LAST EDITION OF THE LARGER WORK.

NEW-YORK:
PUBLISHED BY WHITE & SHEFFIELD.
PRINTED BY E. SANDERSON,
1841.

Title page, *An American Dictionary of the English Language* by Noah Webster (1841).

A. Expansion
Noah Webster (1758–1843) had an extremely varied and busy career. He fought beside his father in the Revolution, owned and edited a daily newspaper in New York City, wrote influential pamphlets in favor of ratification of the Constitution (and on subjects from banking to epidemiology), worked for the enactment of copyright laws, wrote and published a revised version of the Bible, served in the General Assembly of Connecticut and the General Court of Massachusetts, and campaigned for the introduction of an adequate water supply in New Haven—among other activities.

A. Responding
While many of Webster's spelling innovations seem funny today, some of them, such as *music,* were so successful that they crossed the Atlantic and changed British as well as American spelling.

A more recent, and even more quixotic, attempt to reform spelling was made by the playwright George Bernard Shaw around the turn of the century. Shaw wanted English to be spelled phonetically. He was fond of pointing out that English spelling is so nonsensical that the word *fish* could conceivably be spelled *ghoti—gh* as in *rough, o* as in *women,* and *ti* as in all words ending in *tion.*

? How would you change the rules of spelling if you could? (Answers will vary, but will probably tend toward a phonetic approach.)

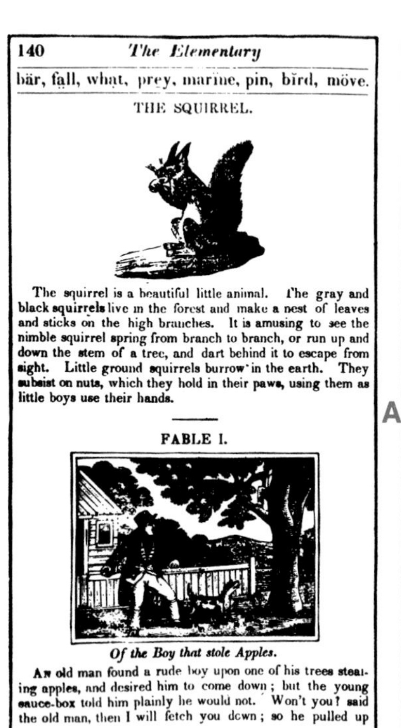

140 *The Elementary*

bär, fall, whạt, prey, marïne, pin, bĭrd, möve.

THE SQUIRREL.

The squirrel is a beautiful little animal. The gray and black squirrels live in the forest and make a nest of leaves and sticks on the high branches. It is amusing to see the nimble squirrel spring from branch to branch, or run up and down the stem of a tree, and dart behind it to escape from sight. Little ground squirrels burrow in the earth. They subsist on nuts, which they hold in their paws, using them as little boys use their hands.

FABLE I.

Of the Boy that stole Apples.

An old man found a rude boy upon one of his trees stealing apples, and desired him to come down; but the young sauce-box told him plainly he would not. Won't you? said the old man, then I will fetch you down; so he pulled up

The American Spelling Book
by Noah Webster (1783). Engraving (from 1793 edition).

Rare Books and Manuscripts Division, New York Public Library.

ularize spelling, and Webster's attempts to regularize American spelling were partly an attempt to refine Johnson's methods. Early editions of Webster's American speller were quite conservative—that is, most of the spellings were consistent with Johnson's English spellings. The main exception was Webster's omission of the *k* in words ending in *-ck.* Where Johnson's dictionary had *publick* and *musick,* Webster's speller had *public* and *music.* By 1789, though, Webster's more radical ideas regarding spelling had aroused a great deal of mocking resistance, even in his own country. His proposals resulted in spellings that were too different from common usage to be acceptable to many people.

Webster's first principle was the "omission of all superfluous or silent letters"—such as the *k* in *musick* and all silent vowels and consonants. *Bread, give, friend, programme, travelled,* and *built* thus became *bred, giv, frend, program, traveled,* and *bilt.*

Webster's second principle was to regularize spelling and sound. For example, *grieve* and *mean* contain the same vowel sounds spelled differently. Webster used *ee* for both as well as anywhere that sound occurred—*greev* and *meen,* and also *pleez* and *bleet.* Similarly, *laugh* and *draught* became *laf* and *draft, plough* became *plow,* and *women* became *wimmin.*

Webster's batting average was not very high, as these examples show, and he gradually yielded to public pressure and modified his more radical spellings. Still, he had some successes, and virtually all of the present differences between British and American spelling were advocated by Webster.

"Webster disliked fashionable and urban people and manners almost as much as he disliked British ways."

Webster's Dictionary

Webster's first dictionary, published in 1806, contained all of these spellings and others. Readers no doubt experienced a good deal of surprise when they came across words like *tung, fether, soop,* and *definit.*

Many of Webster's recommended pronunciations must have been surprising as well. Webster disliked fashionable and urban people and manners almost as much as he disliked British ways. At times, in fact, his praise of the common people and their simple ways sounded Whitmanesque, years before Whitman was born. He praised "the great body of farmers and mechanics" in the United States, writing in 1789:

> A man of great soul would sooner imitate the virtues of a cottage than the vices of a court; would deem it more honorable to gain one useful idea from the humble laborer, than to copy the vicious pronunciation of a splendid court.

These words didn't simply express an opinion; they launched a crusade. Any pronunciation that smacked of being affected or too fashionable was hateful to Webster. He rejected the *yu* sound in words such as *lecture, nature, figure,* and *tenure* as affectations. He recommended that they be pronounced *lecter, nater, figger,* and *tenor.*

Webster was an odd mixture of conservative and radical. In matters of spelling and pronunciation, he laid down stern rules; and yet in matters of grammar and usage, he was often willing to bow to the usage of the common people. The single thread running through these two contradictory attitudes was Webster's democratic desire for a common, regular American language.

Many of Webster's spelling reforms and odd pronouncements make him appear to be a crackpot, and there is no question that there was something of the crackpot about him. He had a degree from Yale, but as a linguist he was self-taught. Like many self-taught people, he had odd gaps in his learning. As a result, his etymologies, or word derivations, were frequently incorrect.

Despite the fact that his enthusiasms and spotty knowledge led him astray, Webster was no fool, and he was enormously energetic. *The American Dictionary of the English Language* was an incredible accomplishment for one person. His 1806 dictionary had defined 28,000 words and indicated their pronunciation. The 1828 dictionary defined 70,000 words and provided etymologies as well as pronunciations. This was the first dictionary to include Americanisms such as *lot, to spell* ("to relieve someone at work"), and *clever* ("good-natured"). "Such local terms exist," he had written some years before, "in spite of lexicographers and critics. Is this *my* fault? And if local terms exist, why not explain them? . . . How are such words to be understood without the aid of a dictionary?"

The *American Dictionary* also included the new American meanings of older English words such as *congress, court,* and *plantation,* and settled for all time the changes in word endings that distinguish American from British usage: *-er* for *-re* (*center* rather than *centre*); *-or* for *-our* (*favor* rather than *favour*); *-c* for *-ck* (*music* rather than *musick*); *-ck* for *-que* (*check* rather than *cheque*); *-ize* for *-ise* (*legalize* rather than *legalise*); and *-ler* for *-ller* (*traveler* rather than *traveller*). The 1828 dictionary decided firmly that Americans would spell and pronounce the name of the newly produced metal *aluminum* (the British favored *aluminium,* like *sodium* and *potassium*). We say *skedule* rather than *shedule* because Webster thought the pronunciation of *schedule* should follow the example of *school.*

"Many of Webster's spelling reforms and odd pronouncements make him appear to be a crackpot, and there is no question that there was something of the crackpot about him."

"Noah's Ark"

For all of its eccentricities, then, the *American Dictionary* was a landmark in the development of American English. When Webster had announced, early in the 1800's, that he was preparing a dictionary that would include American words and usages, he was attacked by purists. One wrote in the *New England Palladium:* A

> If the Connecticut Lexicographer considers retaining the English language as a badge of slavery, let him not give us a Babylonish dialect in its stead, but adopt at once the language of the aborigines . . . . Let, then, the projected volume of *foul* and *unclean* things bear his own Christian name, and be called—Noah's Ark.

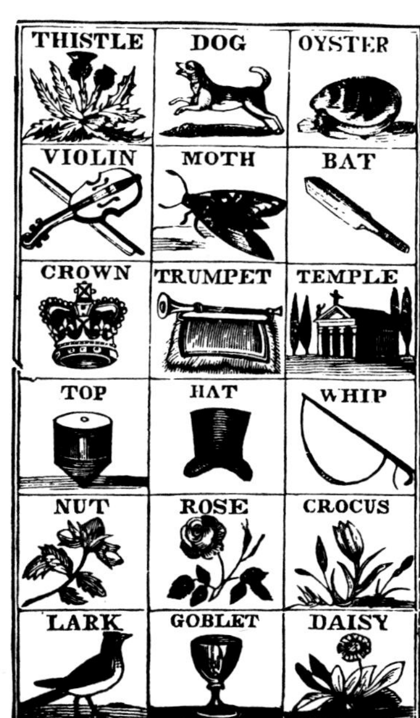

Picture Lessons, a nineteenth-century teaching aid. Engraving.

A. Responding *Webster's Third New International Dictionary* was published in 1971 and aroused debate in linguistic and literary circles for the same reason Webster's original dictionary had: the battle between purists and liberals. *Webster's Third* allowed many usages and pronunciations that purists considered substandard, as well as including slang terms that had previously been excluded from dictionaries. Many purists still cling to the *Second New International Dictionary* as the upholder of strict standards.

? Do you think a dictionary should record a language as it is spoken, or as it *should* be spoken? (Answers will vary: encourage students to defend their views.)

Reading Check Test

1. The English felt that words should be used the way ________ and ________ used them. *great writers/nobility*

2. The Roman poet Horace believed that "________ is the law and rule of speech." *usage*

3. The new idea of consistency in spelling was directly related to the increasing use of the ________. *printing press*

4. The two books of Webster's that had the biggest influence on American language were a ________ and a ________. *spelling book/dictionary*

5. Webster had rules about spelling and pronunciation, but he would bow to the usage of ________. *common people*

> **"Generations of Americans decided on the correctness of a word or a usage or a spelling by 'looking it up in Webster's,' and every household had to have a copy of Webster's dictionary next to the Bible."**

Despite such criticism, the foul Americanisms found their way aboard Noah's Ark and gained thereby a legitimacy they would otherwise not have had. And Webster's pronouncements, even when they had little sound linguistic reasoning behind them, settled the uncertainties about authority in American English. Generations of Americans decided on the correctness of a word or a usage or a spelling by "looking it up in Webster's," and every household had to have a copy of Webster's dictionary next to the Bible.

Early in his career, Webster had been one of those who thought that American English would become as distinct from British English as Dutch is from German. By 1828, although his patriotism had not diminished, his views of the development of American English had moderated. "The body of the language is the same as in England," he wrote in the Preface to the *American Dictionary,* "and it is desirable to perpetuate that sameness." In the same Preface, though, he pointed proudly at the burgeoning American literature as a source of richness and at the growth of the language as a source of pride. He would have been pleased to have seen the fruits of his labors.

Analyzing Language

1. One of the reasons Webster advocated spelling reform was to provide consistency. He thought that words that sounded the same should be spelled the same. This was not as easy as it seemed, though. Here is a selection written by Webster in his reformed spelling. Read it carefully; then find the places where he was inconsistent. Consider these inconsistencies: the use of *r* instead of *wr* to indicate an *r* sound; the use of *s* instead of *c* to indicate an *s* sound; elimination of unsounded double consonants; elimination of silent letters.

> In the essays, ritten within the last year, a considerable change of spelling iz introduced by way of experiment. The liberty waz taken by the writers before the age of Queen Elizabeth, and to this we are indeted for the preference of modern spelling over that of Gower and Chaucer. The man who admits that the change of *housbonde, mynde, ygone, moneth* into *husband, mind, gone, month,* iz an improovment, must acknowledge also the riting of *helth, breth, rong, tung, munth,* to be an improovment. There iz no alternativ. Every possible reezon that could ever be offered for altering the spelling of wurds, stil exists in full force; and if a gradual reform should not be made in our language, it wil proov that we are less under the influence of reezon than our ancestors.

2. Make a list of words in which the sounds represented by the letters *a, e,* and *i* are very different. (For example, the letter *a* represents three different sounds in the words *mate, mat,* and *all.*)
3. Most efforts at spelling reform have been failures, and we find inconsistencies in English spelling still with us. List pairs of words that are still spelled in similar ways but that are pronounced differently (such as *tough* and *bough*). Then list pairs of words that are still spelled differently but that are pronounced the same (such as *dead* and *bed*).
4. Webster's simplified spelling never completely succeeded, but nonstandard forms of simplified spelling have flourished in product names, in advertising signs ("All-Nite Diner"), and in road signs ("Thruway North"). Make a list of five such simplified spellings from examples you have seen. Explain whether or not you think they are useful.
5. Make a list of school subjects or jobs that you think could be spelled more simply. Next to each word, write its simpler spelling. Then use the words in a paragraph, in their simpler forms, and exchange your paragraphs in class. Does everyone understand the new simplified spellings?

Exercises in Critical Thinking and Writing

RESPONDING TO LITERATURE

Writing Assignment

Write an essay of at least four paragraphs, in which you discuss your response to the lines from Phillis Wheatley's poem "To the Right Honorable William, Earl of Dartmouth . . ." which follow. Consider in your resonse the facts of Wheatley's life, which follow the poem.

A

From **To the Right Honorable William, Earl of Dartmouth, His Majesty's Principal Secretary of State for North America, etc.**

Should you, my lord, while you peruse my song
Wonder from whence my love of *Freedom* sprung,
Whence flow these wishes for the common good,
By feeling hearts alone best understood,
I, young in life, by seeming cruel fate
Was snatched from *Afric's* fancied happy seat:
What pangs excruciating must molest,
What sorrows labor in my parent's breast?
Steeled was the soul and by no misery moved
That from a father seized his babe beloved
Such, such my case. And can I then but pray
Others may never feel tyrannic sway?

For favors past, great Sir, our thanks are due,
And thee we ask thy favors to renew,
Since in thy power, as in thy will before,
To soothe the griefs, which thou didst once deplore.
May heav'nly grace the sacred sanction give
To all thy works, and thou forever live
Not only on the wings of fleeting *Fame,*
Though praise immortal crowns the patriot's name,
But to conduct to heav'ns refulgent fane,
May fiery coursers sweep th' ethereal plain,
And bear thee upwards to that blest abode,
Where, like the prophet, thou shalt find thy God.

Phillis Wheatley

Phillis Wheatley was born in Africa, probably in what is now Senegal or Ghana. She arrived on a slave ship in Boston in 1761 and was purchased by John Wheatley. She was probably only about seven years old at the time (there is a reference to the loss of her baby teeth). She became Mrs. Wheatley's servant. Named Phillis, and assuming her owners' surname, the young girl showed tremendous precocity. She learned not only English but also Latin, and she often read the Bible and the English poets popular in her time. In 1773 her only book of poetry was published with much fanfare in England. After the Wheatleys died, Phillis was freed, and she married John Peters, a free man. But all the attention lavished on her in her early life dried up the moment she was on her own. She died destitute when she was only about thirty-five years old. B

Wheatley's style is like the style popular in poetry of her time: She uses a Latinate vocabulary, inversions, and elevated diction. Here she addresses a man who had just been appointed secretary in charge of the American Colonies (1772). Dartmouth, she hoped, would be more open to the Colonists' grievances.

Background

Whenever you read something, you respond in some personal way. Your response might be "Terrific!" or "This is boring," or "This character reminds me of my Uncle Paul."

Personal responses are not necessarily based on objective criteria, or standards. For that reason, there are no "right" or "wrong" responses to a piece of writing. Your reactions are as valid as anyone else's.

In planning an essay of response, you might want to consider the following questions.

1. **Enjoyment.** Did you like reading the selection, or not? Can you determine why?
2. **Emotions.** How did the selection make you feel? What did the writer do to evoke these feelings?
3. **Similarity to Your Experience.** Did the characters, scenes, or situations remind you of anything you have experienced or heard about? Did they seem credible? Why or why not?
4. **Style.** How would you describe the writer's style—that is, his or her diction, or word choice; sentence structure; and clarity of expression? How did the style affect your response?
5. **Meanings.** Beyond the surface details of the selection, what is the writer's meaning or **purpose**? (If you aren't sure, say so in your essay.) How effectively is this meaning conveyed? Do you agree with the writer's message? Did the selection make you think about something that had not occurred to you before?

A. Expansion
In the first stanza, Wheatley explains her love of freedom, which arises from the fact that she was captured and enslaved as a child. Because of her experiences, she prays that other people will not be subjected to tyranny.

In the second stanza, Wheatley thanks the Earl of Dartmouth for his past kindness to the American colonists, and asks him to renew his favorable policies. She assures him that immortal fame and a place in heaven will be his reward.

B. Connections
You might want to compare Wheatley's career with that of Bryant, another teenage prodigy of verse (page 138).

Revising Essays
As students revise their essays, refer them to **Grammar, Usage, and Mechanics: A Reference Guide** at the back of their books.

A. Connections
The question, "What would Phillis Wheatley have written if she'd felt free to be personal?" is tragically appropriate not only to black writers and writers from other disadvantaged groups, but also to writers from backgrounds that society considers elite. It is arguable that for all their intelligence and ability, poets like Lowell and Bryant were emotionally constricted by their environments. The freedom to express unconventional feelings in print is a fairly recent development. English Romantic poets like Wordsworth and Blake first championed it, but not until Whitman (page 326) did it reach full expression. In our own time, the freedom to express one's deepest feelings has become poetry's first article of faith, exemplified by, among others, Robert Lowell (page 1102), Sylvia Plath (page 1119), Allen Ginsberg (page 1134), and Anne Sexton (page 1122).

Exercises in Critical Thinking and Writing/*cont.*

Prewriting

The first step in writing an essay of response is to read the selection carefully. While you read, you should make comments and ask questions. Because you will eventually write about your response, you should write out these comments and questions, so you can make use of them later.

Here is an example of one reader's responses to the first few lines of the poem. They may or may not be similar to your own responses.

Lines 1–2: The first thing I have to do is figure out these archaic words: "Should you . . . wonder from whence my love of *Freedom* sprung." Right away I can say that the style is very old-fashioned.

Frontispiece for *Poems on Various Subjects, Religious and Moral* by Phillis Wheatley (c. 1772). Engraving.

American Antiquarian Society, Worcester, Massachusetts.

After you have written your comments and questions about the rest of the poem, look again at the five sets of questions under **Background.** Apply those questions to Wheatley's poem.

Sort through your questions and comments. Think about how you reacted to the poem. Then write a **topic statement** that expresses your overall response. (The topic statement can consist of more than one sentence.)

Writing

Here is the first paragraph of one reader's response to Wheatley's poem. You might use it as a model for your own opening paragraph. Then complete your essay with further information on how you responded to the poem. Notice that the first paragraph summarizes very generally the writer's response. Subsequent paragraphs should develop specific aspects of the response.

When I first read it, I thought Phillis Wheatley's poem "To the Right Honorable William, Earl of Dartmouth . . ." took a long time to say very little. I thought her style was really tough and old-fashioned and hard to understand. After each additional reading, however, I came to find the poem easier, and I liked it more. The message is made clear and so are the poet's feelings. I was moved by her feelings about tyranny. People may ask: How would you feel about the poem if you knew nothing about the writer? I'm not interested in that question. I'm interested in this one: What would Phillis Wheatley have written if she'd felt free to be personal? A

Revising and Proofreading

Use the guidelines in the section at the back of this book, called **Writing About Literature,** to revise and proofread your essay.

THE AMERICAN RENAISSANCE
FIVE MAJOR WRITERS

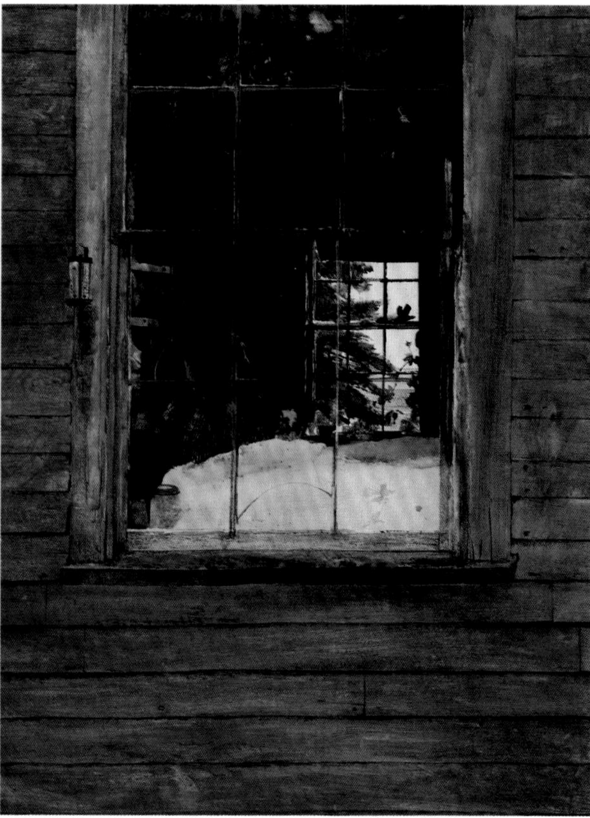

Geraniums by Andrew Wyeth (1960). Drybrush watercolor. Private collection.

UNIT FOUR

HUMANITIES CONNECTION: RESPONDING TO THE FINE ART

Andrew Wyeth (b. 1917), the American painter whose work is represented here, is best known for his meticulously drawn figures and rural landscapes. Wyeth was trained by his father, N. C. Wyeth (see pages 127 and 205). Andrew Wyeth has a son, Jamie, who is also an artist (see page 989).

? The rough-hewn texture of this shelter suggests a cabin set apart from civilization. Through the windows you can see trees and perhaps a glimpse of water. What do you see in the cabin? (There are jars on the windowsill, and red flowers. The white shape is probably a bed.) Do the jars in the forefront suggest that someone has been preserving fruit? (Yes.) Have the geraniums been cultivated, or do they grow wild? Has the cabin been deserted? (Not if the flowers are still blooming) Why do you suppose this painting was chosen to represent a unit of American writers who are among the first to step from behind the shadow of European dominance into their own light as world leaders in literature? (It has a look that is rough-hewn yet civilized, and it is a distinctively "American" look.)

TEACHING THE AMERICAN RENAISSANCE UNIT

Each of the five writers in this unit is essentially Romantic. None deals very much with ordinary life. Hawthorne, of the five, dwells most upon male/female relationships, but almost always in a historical or supernatural setting, highly charged with symbolism. Poe employs the emotion of love—usually lost love—primarily as a catalyst to terror. Women scarcely figure in Melville's work at all. And while Thoreau writes about the most humdrum daily occupations, he is elevating the humdrum to the level of meditative bliss.

The similarities and differences among these writers can be seen in their different relationships to Transcendentalism. Transcendentalists sought to create religious consciousness that would exhibit the freedom and democracy of the new nation. They felt that the way to God led through the self: contemplation of one's own thoughts would lead one to a perception of the infinite.

Emerson is the central Transcendentalist. Thoreau, his protégé, takes to its furthest point the search for ecstatic experience in nature, while Emerson mostly contemplates his own mind. Of the three fiction writers in the unit, none embraced Transcendentalism, yet all show its influence. Hawthorne lived for a while at the Utopian community Brook Farm, but he satirized it in *The Blithedale Romance.* Melville outwardly mocked the movement, yet nothing is more Transcendentalist than Ahab's great line, "Strike through the mask!" Poe expressed scorn for the movement, but a philosophical essay of his comes to the conclusion that everything is part of God and that God is reflected in the human mind.

Both Poe and Hawthorne wrote symbolic, often supernatural tales filled with atmosphere. Hawthorne, however, was burdened by a sense of sin from a specific time and place in history, while Poe was burdened by the sheer terror of the human soul facing the fact of death. Poe's settings are often mere window-dressing, while the background of Puritan New England is central to Hawthorne. Alfred Kazin identifies Hawthorne with the sense of guilt and Poe with the sense of anxiety. In *The Scarlet Letter,* Kazin says, Hawthorne achieved the "unity of effect" that Poe preached.

OBJECTIVES OF THE AMERICAN RENAISSANCE UNIT

1. To improve reading proficiency and expand vocabulary
2. To gain exposure to notable authors and their works
3. To define and identify significant literary techniques
4. To define and identify elements of nonfiction, fiction, and poetry
5. To interpret and respond to nonfiction, fiction, and poetry, orally and in writing
6. To practice the following critical thinking and writing skills:
   a. Comparing and contrasting literary forms
   b. Responding to a writer's views
   c. Paraphrasing a poem
   d. Analyzing and interpreting poetic elements
   e. Analyzing a poem
   f. Analyzing and evaluating persuasive writing

Supplementary Support Materials: Unit Four

1. Unit Introduction Test (*CCB*)
2. Word Analogies Test (*CCB*)
3. Unit Review Test (*CCB*)
4. Critical Thinking and Writing Test (*CCB*)
5. Study Guide to *The Scarlet Letter*
6. Instructional Overhead Transparencies

A. Responding to the Quotation
In this quotation, Emerson asserts his belief that individual creativity is, on a smaller scale, akin to the divine creativity that made the universe. This belief is derived from the Hindu idea of *atman,* which means that each individual soul is made of the same stuff as the universal World-Soul.

You might have students discuss their own creativity. What feelings does such an act of creativity, even a minor one, arouse in them?

B. Expansion
Later, Melville was to say in print that Hawthorne was close to being an American Shakespeare (see page 181). The claim would have seemed exaggerated to most people even then, given Hawthorne's much more limited range.

C. Humanities Connection: Discussing the Fine Art
Typee was autobiographical, so it's valid to see the oarsman in the picture as the artist's rendering of the young Melville.

THE AMERICAN RENAISSANCE FIVE MAJOR WRITERS

by **Gary Q. Arpin**

Five Famous Writers

A *To create—to create—is the proof of a divine presence.*

—from "The American Scholar," Ralph Waldo Emerson

On August 5, 1850, a remarkable party took place in Stockbridge, Massachusetts, at the home of an attorney named David Dudley Field. Among those attending were the Boston publisher James Fields; two of his authors, Oliver Wendell Holmes and Nathaniel Hawthorne; the New York editor and publisher Evert Duyckinck; and two of *his* authors, Cornelius Mathews and Herman Melville. The party began in the morning with a climb up Monument Mountain, a peak in the Berkshires made famous by William Cullen Bryant's poem "The Story of an Indian Girl." Although several members of the party had never met before, the group was in good humor—perhaps, in part, because of a champagne picnic lunch. During the climb, Melville, the bravest of the group, leaned out over precipices to demonstrate how sailors took in sail; Hawthorne, usually the most restrained of men, loosened up enough to look wildly about for the great carbuncle (a deep-red gem), the subject of a tale, based on a local legend, which he had written many years before.

The afternoon continued with a long, wine-filled dinner at Field's house. The conversation turned, not surprisingly, to American literature. B In response to a mischievous statement by Holmes in praise of English writers, Melville vigorously defended American writers. The question of whether there would ever be an American writer as great as Shakespeare provoked a heated discussion, with Melville again firmly supporting the American side. Hawthorne found himself agreeing with Melville, whom he had never met before, and who, he discovered, was currently living in Pittsfield, not far from Hawthorne's own home in Lenox.

C 

Illustration (detail) by Mead Shaeffer for *Typee* (1920) by Herman Melville.

Columbia University Library, New York.

Melville and Hawthorne: An Unlikely Friendship

The possibility of a friendship between these two celebrated writers would have seemed highly unlikely. Herman Melville (see page 294) was a sociable ex-sailor, best known at this time for having lived among cannibals in the South Seas and for having written a remarkable first novel, *Typee* (1846), about the experience. Since the publication of that novel, he had written three moderately successful short novels about the sea. He had also written one immensely long, "experimental" novel, *Mardi,* about . . . well, no one had been quite sure what it was about. At the time of Field's party, Melville was at work on his fifth novel, which, it appeared, was also going to be fairly long.

Nathaniel Hawthorne (see page 263) was fifteen years older than Melville. He had had a slightly more conventional career as a writer of fiction, especially of short tales that had been published in a variety of magazines. Magazines, and the short stories required to fill them, had become very popular with a growing audience of prosperous and educated readers. Hawthorne had already collected two volumes of his stories in book form. His recently published novel, *The Scarlet Letter,* displayed his fascination with the dark side of New England's Puritan past. And he was at work on another novel, *The House of the Seven Gables.*

Hawthorne was reserved and little given to social activity of any kind. But despite the differences in the two writers' temperaments and interests, a friendship sprang up between them. "I met Melville the other day," Hawthorne wrote to a friend, "and liked him so much that I have asked him to spend a few days with me before leaving these parts." This was the beginning of a remarkable association that came at a critical point in Melville's life, when he was hard at work on *Moby-Dick.* Melville was exposed to what he called the power of darkness in Hawthorne's work, which he began to read avidly following their meeting. This exposure had a powerful effect on what would become the greatest novel written by an American in the nineteenth century.

Puritan children averting their eyes from Hester Prynne. From *The Scarlet Letter* by Nathaniel Hawthorne. Engraving after a painting by George Boughton (mid-19th century).

A Declaration of Literary Independence

The immediate result of this meeting was a magazine essay Melville wrote two weeks later. In addition to extravagant praise of its subject, the essay contained a stirring defense of American literature over English literature. Stating that "England, after all, is, in many things, an alien to us," Melville urged American readers to "prize and cherish her [America's] writers." He claimed that in Hawthorne, America was very close to producing her own Shakespeare, and he went on to add in a burst of literary patriotism that "even if there were no Hawthorne, no Emerson, no Whittier, no Irving, no Bryant, no Dana, no Cooper . . . nevertheless, let America first praise mediocrity, even, in her own children, before she praises . . . the best excellence in the children of any other land." A

This was only the latest expression of a common theme that went back to the earliest days of the Republic. As Noah Webster had put it in 1783, "America must be as independent in *literature* as she is in *politics,* as famous for *arts* as for *arms.*" The difference now was that the high expectations for an American literature of the first rank were finally justified. The members of that party in the Berkshires were themselves proof that America did, in fact, finally possess a powerful class of imaginative writers.

"Melville claimed that in Hawthorne, America was very close to producing her own Shakespeare."

Melville's hornblowing for American literature coincided with the beginning of an extraordinary explosion of American literary genius. It was a time when the American landscape and American culture would finally find their place in a native and original literature. Writers of the time were aware of this, and they sometimes used the word *renaissance* to describe the phenomenon.

The American Renaissance was not literally a "rebirth"; rather, it was an equivalent to the earlier European Renaissance, in the sense that it marked the arrival of cultural maturity. "There is a B

A. Expansion
Melville was noted for wild mood swings alternating between grandiose exuberance and melancholic dejection. His essay on Hawthorne was the fruit of the former—as were many of his finest creative passages.

B. Responding
? What was the European Renaissance? (The European Renaissance, a great revival of classical learning, began in Italy in the 1400's, spread north to Germany and Holland, and reached England by Shakespeare's time.)

A. Humanities Connection: Responding to the Fine Art

? Look carefully at the people in the illustration. What attitude do you think the artist was taking toward his subject? (The satire is unmistakable. A man in the front row of the audience is asleep. Several other audience members are obviously interested in concerns of their own, and the myopic speaker seems oblivious.)

? How would an artist of similar spirit depict a present-day American high school classroom?

B. Expansion

We should not assume that the intellectual level of the average person in 1826 was notably higher than our own. The Lyceum movement began because its founders saw a need. Critic Alfred Kazin quotes an earlier reminiscence as saying that the townspeople of Concord were ignorant, materialistic, and excessively given to drink.

moment in the history of every nation," Emerson wrote, "when, proceeding out of . . . brute youth, the perceptive powers reach their ripeness . . . so that man, at that instant, extends across the entire scale and, with his feet still planted on the immense forces of night, converses by his eyes and brain with solar and stellar creation. That is the moment of adult health, the culmination of power."

This was the moment America had reached, at least in its literature. The confidence these writers felt in the vitality of their time is evidenced in the remarkable body of work they produced. In the period from 1849 to 1855, the following works were published: Emerson's *Representative Men,* Hawthorne's *The Scarlet Letter* and *The House of the Seven Gables,* Melville's *Moby-Dick* and *Pierre,* Thoreau's *Walden,* and Whitman's *Leaves of Grass* (see page 331)—enough masterpieces for any national literature. How had this come about?

The Intellectual and Social Life of New England

One of the most important reasons for the rise of American literature in the mid-nineteenth century was the intellectual and social ferment in New England. This region had been traditionally noted for its interests in self-improvement and in intellectual pursuits; the prosperity of the century's early decades created an especially fertile soil for their growth.

A

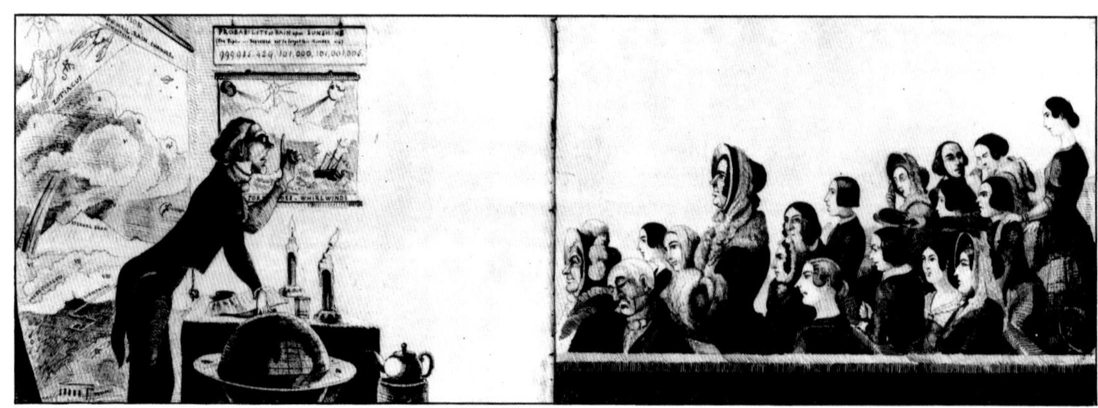

Lyceum Lecture by James Pollard Espy at Clinton Hall by an unknown artist (1841). Pen and ink.

Museum of the City of New York.

B

These interests found expression in the Lyceum movement, which was founded in 1826 to improve American education. The Lyceum organizations were named for the school of the Greek philosopher Aristotle. They had a number of goals, ranging from training teachers to establishing museums. One part of the Lyceum program was a course of winter lectures, which became immensely popular in New England and throughout the Midwest. The topics ranged from the practical ("The Honey Bee") to the educational ("The Life and Times of Oliver Cromwell") to the inspirational

("The Capacity of the Human Mind for Culture and Improvement"). One of the most popular speakers in this series, from the 1830's to the 1870's, was Ralph Waldo Emerson (see page 187). A

"There is something about this familial innocent chapter in American life," the twentieth-century critic Alfred Kazin has written of these times, "that suddenly takes one back to the classic, the prophetic beginning of nations. Emerson was on a mission to his own people; he was preaching now to the whole American congregation. To recall these village lyceums, these rude country halls, evening meetings in odd churches, barns, schools, and banquet rooms, tents spread in preparation for the idyllic summer's opening of the college year . . . is to imagine a time when people still looked to literary men for guidance. . . . Emerson made a thousand appearances, crossed the Mississippi on ice in dead winter to deliver a lecture in Iowa, was bumped, jostled, frozen in wagons, carriages, flatboats, steamboats, trains (where he felt so solitary that he vowed he would go over to any man reading a book and hug him)."

This was a time of social improvement in other ways as well. New England was a center of numerous reform movements. Horace Mann and others were dedicated to improving public education; Dorothea Dix devoted herself to alleviating the horrible conditions in insane asylums; others addressed themselves to the problems of the blind and the deaf. Abolitionist groups led by the radical William Lloyd Garrison sought the immediate abolition of slavery. Feminists such as Elizabeth Peabody, Margaret Fuller, and Emma Willard campaigned for women's rights. (Women were still not allowed to vote, and their other legal rights were greatly limited.) B

Southerners called New England the home of "isms," and they were right—social causes, both reasonable and crackpot, abounded. Numerous utopian projects aimed at reforming society completely. In 1840, Emerson wrote to the British writer Thomas Carlyle that "not a reading man but has a draft [plan] of a new community in his waistcoat pocket." Emerson was speaking from personal experience, for the most influential of these utopian groups had been meeting in his own home since 1836. C

Emerson's School of Philosophy, called "Sylvan," in Concord, Massachusetts.

The Transcendentalists

Emerson's friend, Dr. Frederic Hedge, had first proposed the group, which called itself "Hedge's Club" or "The Symposium." But to outsiders it quickly became known as "The Transcendental Club." The term **transcendental** came from the German Romantic philosopher Immanuel Kant. The word referred to the idea that matters of ultimate reality—God, the cosmos, the self—transcend, or go beyond, human experience.

For Emerson, Transcendentalism was not a new idea but, as he wrote in 1842, "the very oldest of thoughts cast into the mold of these new times." That "oldest of thoughts" was Idealism, which originated with Plato in ancient Greece. Idealism asserted that the true reality was spiritual or "ideal," rather than physical. The

> **"*Transcendental* referred to the idea that matters of ultimate reality transcend, or go beyond, human experience."**

A. Expansion Emerson's success as a lecturer was partly due to the experience in public sermonizing he had gained as a minister.

B. Responding ? How do these reformist issues compare with those of our own day? (Reforms in many of these areas have been achieved, although the drive to reform education continues. New reform movements, such as those for equal rights and consumer protection, have developed.)

C. Expansion The great essayist and social critic Carlyle was a kindred spirit to Emerson, except for differences on political issues. Both Emerson and Carlyle were aphoristic stylists and unabashed proponents of the importance of individual genius.

A. Expansion (More Challenging) Your more advanced students might want to start a discussion group of their own, examining such wide-ranging questions as how education ought to be conducted and what constitutes the good life. They might use readings in Emerson and Thoreau as their starting point.

B. Humanities Connection: Discussing the Fine Art The element of elitism in Transcendentalism can be clearly seen in this photograph.

> "Transcendentalists optimistically believed in human perfectibility."

Transcendentalists were Idealists in this philosophical sense. They sought the permanent spiritual reality that lay behind transitory physical appearances. They were also idealists in a broader sense. They optimistically believed in human perfectibility, and they were often engaged in projects intended to make this ideal a reality.

A The club that met in Emerson's house comprised a wide range of members and beliefs. There were a number of ministers, including George Ripley, founder of *The Dial,* the Transcendentalists' periodical, and of Brook Farm, a self-governing, experimental community. (Brook Farm survived for six years and became the setting for Hawthorne's *Blithedale Romance.* Hawthorne lived at the Farm for a few months but could not stand all the elevated conversation.) There were radical educators like Bronson Alcott (the father of Louisa May Alcott), who ran the Temple School in Boston. Alcott also founded an experimental community, Fruitlands, a vegetarian group that lasted only seven months. Another member was Margaret Fuller, a feminist and an influential critic, who edited *The Dial* for several years.

These were powerful and independent thinkers, not so much under Emerson's influence as in his circle. When we think of Transcendentalism today, we think almost automatically of Emerson. But in fact, Transcendentalist ideas were as wide-ranging as these minds; they were educational, practical, mystical, poetical, and political. The Transcendentalists shared an idealism and a commitment to the spiritual and the hopeful, but that commitment took many forms.

B

Ralph Waldo Emerson's home, Concord, Massachusetts.

Emerson and Transcendentalism: The American Roots

Emerson himself remained skeptical of many of the Transcendentalists' ideas and projects. Although he edited *The Dial* for two years, both Brook Farm and Fruitlands were founded (and collapsed) without his participation. Nevertheless, he was the most influential and well known of the Transcendentalists, largely because of his lectures and books.

Transcendental thought was most clearly and forcefully expressed in Emerson's writings and in those of his disciple, Henry David Thoreau (see page 204). As developed by Emerson, Transcendentalism grafted ideas from Europe and the Far East onto a native American philosophical stem. Perhaps the best way of viewing this school of thought is by examining its American roots, especially the ideas about the relations between God, humanity, and nature held by Emerson's New England ancestors.

For the Puritans, there were basically two ways in which God was revealed to people. The first was through the Bible, the word of God. The second was through the physical world; to William Bradford, for example, the death of a scoffing sailor on the *Mayflower* was the direct action of God in the human world. God existed in a less clearly defined way for some other Puritans. Jonathan Edwards found God's "excellency, His wisdom, His purity and love

. . . in the sun, moon, and stars . . . in the grass, flowers, trees; in the water, and all nature." This native mysticism—which was typical as well of Romanticism—would reappear in Emerson's thought.

A rational thinker like Benjamin Franklin, on the other hand, saw nature differently. Far from recognizing in nature any direct manifestation of God, he viewed it as something to be examined scientifically and to be used for the betterment of humanity.

For Emerson, both of these ways of viewing the world around us were important; but the mystical outlook was "higher" than the practical one. The mystical view did not spring from logic; it came, rather, from intuition. It was spontaneous and emotional, not deliberate and rational.

Emerson followed in the Romantic tradition of William Cullen Bryant (see page 138) by holding that the physical facts of the natural world were the doorway to the spiritual or ideal world. Like Jonathan Edwards, he found God's presence in the world around him. Alone in nature, the logical part of his mind gave way, to allow direct, visionary contact with the world of the spirit. Emerson gave memorable expression to this moment: "Standing on the bare ground, all mean egotism vanishes. I become a transparent eyeball. I am nothing. I see all. The currents of the Universal Being circulate through me; I am part or parcel of God."

One product of Emerson's conviction that we can find God directly in nature was a profound optimism. God is good, and God works through nature. Therefore, even the natural events that seem most tragic—pestilence, death, disaster—can be explained on a spiritual level. Death is simply a part of the cycle of life. To the extent that we are separated from a direct, intuitive knowledge of God, we are capable of evil. But if we simply trust ourselves—that is, trust in the power each of us has to know God directly—then we will realize that each of us is also part of the Divine Soul, the source of all good. "That is always best which gives me to myself," Emerson wrote in an address to the Harvard Divinity School. "That which shows God in me, fortifies me. That which shows God out of me, makes me a wart and a wen [cyst]."

Emerson's optimism struck a sympathetic chord with audiences that might have had difficulty with the more complex aspects of his thought. Your condition today, he seemed to tell his readers and listeners, may be mean, dull, and routine, but it need not be. All we need do is discover the God within each of us, he suggested, and our lives will partake of the grandeur of the universe.

Melville, Hawthorne, and Poe: The Power of Darkness

Emerson's idealism was exciting stuff for his audiences, but not all the writers and thinkers of the time were in agreement with Transcendentalist thought. "To one who has weathered Cape Horn as a common sailor," Herman Melville wrote of Emerson's ideas, "what stuff all this is."

> "The mystical view did not spring from logic; it came, rather, from intuition."

An illustration from a French translation of Poe's "The Masque of the Red Death."

A. Connections
You might remind your students of Edwards's sermon, "Sinners in the Hands of An Angry God" (page 37). This quotation may reassure them that life was not always bleak even for the Puritans.

B. Expansion
Franklin's view exemplifies deism, the idea that the universe was rationally designed by a divinity who endowed us with reason but who does not interfere with the minute workings of the universe.

C. Expansion
This view can also be found in such British Romantic poets as Wordsworth.

D. Expansion
Here we can see one of the origins of the "positive thinking" and "self-realization" trends of our own century. Emerson's influence runs deep: "Trust Yourself" is the title of a 1985 song by Bob Dylan.

Reading Check Test

1. Hawthorne and Melville became friends when Melville was at work on *Moby-Dick. True*
2. Melville believed that American writers should look to the best literary models from every land rather than focusing narrowly on American literature. *False*
3. Transcendentalism began as a club. *True*
4. Emerson's belief that we can find God in nature made him an optimist. *True*
5. Melville, Hawthorne, and Poe are sometimes called "anti-Transcendentalists." *True*

A. Humanities Connection: Discussing the Fine Art You might use this illustration as an opportunity to give your class "coming attractions" of *Moby-Dick.* Kent portrays the whale as a monumental force of nature, looming and mountainous, whose teeth, eyes, and pulverized food are matched with the stars.

B. Connections Students have many opportunities to discuss symbolism in this unit. The symbolism of specific works is discussed in end-of-selection questions on pages 260 (Poe, "The Raven"), 274 (Hawthorne, "The Minister's Black Veil"), 292 (Hawthorne, "Rappaccini's Daughter"), and in two questions on page 316 (Melville, *Moby-Dick*).

C. Expansion (Less Challenging) Your less advanced students may be assisted in understanding Transcendentalism if you do a semantic map of the term.

A

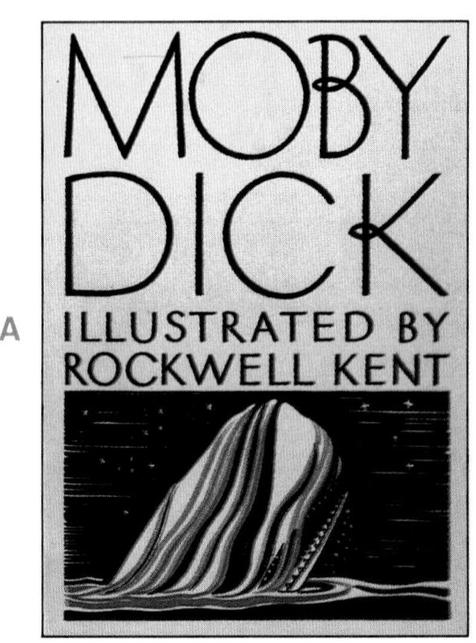

And yet there is no novel so Transcendental in its theme and content as Melville's own *Moby-Dick.* For the central premise of that novel is also one of the most important ideas in Emerson's "Nature." In that essay, Emerson wrote, "Every natural fact is a symbol of some spiritual fact." There is little doubt that Melville would agree with his character Ahab when Ahab says: "All visible objects . . . are but as pasteboard masks. But in each event—in the living act, the undoubted deed—there, some unknown but still reasoning thing puts forth the moldings of its features from behind the unreasoning mask."

Where Melville disagreed with Emerson was not in the notion that spiritual facts lie behind the appearances of nature; he disagreed with the premise that those facts are necessarily benign, or good. Indeed, what attracted Melville to Hawthorne at that party in the Berkshires was the sense that they shared a dark view of the nature of things. In his essay "Hawthorne and His Mosses," Melville says that this great power of darkness in Hawthorne "derives its force from its appeals to that Calvinistic sense of innate depravity and Original Sin, from whose visitations, in some shape or other, no deeply thinking mind is always and wholly free. For, in certain moods, no man can weigh this world, without throwing in something, somehow like Original Sin, to strike the uneven balance."

Hawthorne and Edgar Allan Poe (see page 226), in their own ways, would have agreed with Melville. These three writers are sometimes considered "anti-Transcendentalists." However, this does not mean there was no element of Transcendentalism in their work. Moreover, their work had common roots in America's past.

Emerson had taken the ecstatic, mystical elements of Puritan thought and ignored its dark side. The ideas of Melville, Hawthorne, and Poe developed from both the mystical and the melancholy aspects of Puritan thought. Melville emphasized the conflict between good and evil in his work; Hawthorne was concerned with the psychological effects of sin; Poe sought the mystical realm in the derangement of the senses. Although their subjects differed greatly, **symbolism** was important to each of them. B

Symbolism was also a technical strategy in their writing. This is especially evident in the work of Melville and Hawthorne, whose characters live simultaneously on two levels, as real people and as representatives of something larger. The Puritans would have understood this. The fire that destroyed Anne Bradstreet's house (see page 43) was both a natural fact and a spiritual fact. It was different in content, but not in form, from the whale that severed Ahab's leg in Melville's *Moby-Dick.*

Despite their differences, Hawthorne, Melville, and Poe share with Emerson and Thoreau a vision of the world that ultimately came from their Puritan ancestors and that was shaped by the American experience. C Theirs was an imaginative vision that was essentially Romantic, in that it stressed intuition, the powers of nature, and individual emotion (see Unit Three, pages 116–122). And despite this vision's borrowings from other cultures, it was uniquely American.

"Theirs was an imaginative vision that was essentially Romantic, in that it stressed intuition, the powers of nature, and individual emotion."

A **TWO IDEALISTS**

TWO IDEALISTS

Ralph Waldo Emerson (1803–1882)

Shortly before the poet Walt Whitman died (see page 326), he honored a man whose ideas had influenced him profoundly throughout his own long and controversial career. "America in the future," he wrote, "in her long train of poets and writers, while knowing more vehement and luxurious ones, will, I think, acknowledge nothing nearer [than] this man, the actual beginner of the whole procession."

"This man" was Ralph Waldo Emerson. Better than anyone before him, Emerson expressed the advantages of a young land—its freedom from the old, corrupt, and moribund thought and customs of Europe; its access to higher laws directly through nature rather than indirectly through books and the teachings of the past; its energy; and its opportunity to reform the world. In "Self-Reliance," Emerson called for a philosopher "who shall reveal the resources of man, and tell men . . . that with the exercise of self-trust, new powers shall appear; that man is the word made flesh . . . and that the moment he acts from himself, tossing the laws, the books, idolatries, and customs out the window—we pity him no more, but thank and revere him." Emerson himself fit that description of the new philosopher very well.

Emerson was one of those rare writers who appealed both to intellectuals and to the general public. He helped open the door between the commonplace and "uncivilized" world of nineteenth-century America and the realm of philosophical and religious truth. In this way, he influenced contemporaries such as Thoreau, Melville, Whitman, and Dickinson, each of whom claimed a slightly different aspect of the crude and rich American experience for subject matter. His influence has continued into the twentieth century and can be seen, among other places, in Robert Frost's simple nature lyrics (see page 670) and in Wallace Stevens's philosophical poems (see page 768). Both these poets, in their ways, emphasize the connections between humans, nature, and a higher order.

Emerson's influence on the popular mind—spread through the thousands of lectures he gave throughout the United States during a long career—was equally strong. He had something of a reputation for being difficult to understand and, partly as a result of this, was considered "good for you" in a cultural sense. In fact, though, Emerson's lectures were usually quite understandable.

"I had heard of him as full of transcendentalisms, myths, & oracular gibberish," Melville wrote a friend after hearing Emerson lecture for the first time. "To my surprise, I found him quite intelligible." Then Melville added wryly, "To say truth, they told me that that night he was unusually plain."

Emerson's work is often "plain" in the sense that he offers a perfectly understandable surface, though there is much substance beneath it. His essays sometimes appear to be collections of memorable sentences rather than organized expositions of thought. Such a style betrays Emerson's habit of piecing together his lectures and essays from his journals. B

But in some ways, this style was appropriate to a lecture. If one sentence was unclear, the listener need only wait for the next one, which might contain thought enough to consider for the entire evening.

Moreover, one of Emerson's stirring sentences might satisfy the intellectual and emotional needs of many different people. "Trust thyself; every heart vibrates to that iron string." No one had to delve deeply into Emerson's philosophy to respond to such confident optimism. Whether or not Emerson intended it, that sentence served equally well as a motto for businessmen and as an encouragement to a young man to go off and live alone in the woods.

Oddly, despite his great influence, it is difficult even to classify what kind of writer Emerson was. *Essayist* is too limited; *philosopher* is

A. Expansion
The word *idealist* is used here in two senses: in our everyday sense, meaning someone who holds high and sometimes unrealistic ideals; and in the technical philosophical sense, meaning someone who believes that the essence of objects is spiritual rather than physical.

B. Expansion
Emerson was a thinker who naturally thought in fragments, observations, and aphorisms, rather than in sustained passages. Most of his works originated as journal jottings. When lecturing, he sometimes exasperated his family and friends by shuffling his pages in full view of the audience. On his deathbed he was heard reciting fragments of sentences, as if lecturing.

A. Responding
What is a poet? What is a philosopher? Can someone be a strong poet yet a weak versifier? (The latter question is applicable not only to Emerson but also to Melville, Edgar Lee Masters, and sometimes even Whitman.)

B. Expansion
What do you think Emerson would have been like to know? (Students may conclude that those who knew Emerson would have to be prepared for his unconventional attitudes.)

C. Responding
Can you see echoes of Emerson's words in the attitudes of Americans today? (Answers will vary, but Americans, having firmly established their independence, seem somewhat more accepting of their "historical associations.")

A

too broad. The best term, perhaps, is *poet,* not in the sense of *versifier,* but in the sense Melville intended when he wrote that Benjamin Franklin was "everything but a poet." (See page 73.)

"I am a poet," Emerson wrote to his fiancée, Lydia Jackson, in 1835, "of a low class without doubt but yet a poet. That is my nature & vocation. My singing be sure is very 'husky,' & is for the most part in prose. Still am I a poet in the sense of a perceiver & dear lover of the harmonies that are in the soul & in matter. . . ."

This poet was born in Boston in 1803 to a family that was cultured, but poor. When he was only eight years old, his father, a Unitarian minister, died of tuberculosis. His mother was left with four growing boys to care for. A fifth son was mentally retarded and raised by relatives. Mrs. Emerson opened a boardinghouse and depended on the generosity of the Church.

The father's place in the lives of the Emerson children was taken by their aunt. Mary Moody Emerson was a strict Calvinist whose rigid piety emphasized self-sacrifice and whose enormous energy drove the Emerson boys to achievement. "She had the misfortune," Emerson later wrote, "of spinning with a greater velocity than any of the other tops."

Despite Aunt Mary's example of self-reliance in the family, every step of Emerson's own life had been laid out for him from an early age. He was to go to Harvard and become a minister like his father and the seven generations of Emersons before him. Emerson uncomfortably obeyed. His life consisted of a series of attempts to establish his own identity against this background of expectation.

When he was fourteen, Emerson entered Harvard. He was an indifferent student, especially weak at science and mathematics, but he read widely in philosophy and theology. The most significant events of his college career occurred during his junior year. He dropped the name Ralph, a gesture toward establishing his identity, and he began keeping a journal. Eventually reaching monumental proportions (the published version consists of fourteen volumes), that journal would be the source of Emerson's lectures and essays for the rest of his life.

Emerson's academic record at Harvard was so weak that upon graduation he failed to get a teaching post in the prestigious Boston Public Latin School. Instead, he took a teaching job at a school run by his uncle, and he prepared himself, with many doubts, for the Unitarian ministry. In 1826, he was licensed to preach. Three years later, at the age of twenty-six, he accepted a post at Boston's Second Church, which had been Cotton Mather's church a century before. That year, he married Ellen Tucker, a beautiful but fragile seventeen-year-old already in the early stages of tuberculosis, that curse of nineteenth-century life. Sixteen months later Ellen died.

B

Emerson's grief coincided with a growing disbelief in some of the central doctrines of his religion. As a result, he distrusted his own vocation as a minister. In June of 1832, he shocked his congregation by resigning the ministry and setting off for an extended tour of Europe.

Long influenced by European thinkers, Emerson had read the work of German philosopher Immanuel Kant and admired the writings of British historian Thomas Carlyle, who was in Scotland thundering out calls for individual greatness and denouncing the evils of modern society. Emerson had also read the Romantic poets William Wordsworth and Samuel Taylor Coleridge. From Kant he would adopt the term *transcendentalism;* from Coleridge he would take up the crucial distinction between logical thought and intuition, a poetic form of thought that enables us to see the correspondences between the physical world and spiritual reality. In Europe Emerson met and conversed with Coleridge and Wordsworth, and he visited Carlyle at his remote farmhouse.

When he returned to America in 1834, Emerson settled in Concord, Massachusetts, and soon married Lydia Jackson. He began to supplement his meager income by giving lectures. In fact, he found in the lectern "a second pulpit," as he wrote Carlyle. After a short time, the major works by which we have come to know Emerson's thought began to appear.

C

The announced subject of Emerson's first series of lectures was the philosophy of history. Emerson's view was distinctively American, in that he denied the importance of the past. "The ancients are dead," he said in one of these early lectures, "but for us the earth is new today and heaven is raining influences. Let us unfetter ourselves of our historical associations and find a pure standard in the idea of man."

The last phrase points to Emerson's focus on

Ralph Waldo Emerson and his family.

the nature of our humanity—a subject that really interested him more in these lectures than any philosophy of history. Individual men and women were part of this "idea of man" in the same way that individual souls were part of a larger entity, which Emerson would later call the "Over-Soul."

The idea of nature corresponded to the idea of man—both were part of a universal whole. "There is in nature," he wrote in the "Humanity of Science," "a parallel unity, which corresponds to this unity in the mind, and makes it available. . . . Not only man puts things in a row, but things belong in a row."

In 1836, there occurred three major events in Emerson's life: the publication of *Nature,* the most complete exposition of his philosophy; the birth of his son Waldo, who would become the center of Emerson's life; and the first meeting of a conversation group of like-minded thinkers in Emerson's drawing room, which would come to be called "The Transcendental Club."

Over the following years, Emerson's influence as a lecturer and an intellectual leader continued to grow. In 1837, he excited his student audience at Harvard with the lecture now known as "The American Scholar." Oliver Wendell Holmes (see page 161) called this speech "our intellectual Declaration of Independence." In the speech, Emerson demanded that American scholars free themselves from the shackles of the past. "Our day of dependence," Emerson declared, "our long apprenticeship to the learning of other lands, draws to a close." He reminded scholars of the importance of the present and of things that were apparently insignificant. Since all things are part of a larger whole, even the commonest matters could open a door to the eternal.

A year later, in 1838, he was invited back to Harvard by a small group of divinity students to speak to them on the eve of their graduation. His speech—"The Divinity School Address"—called for a rejection of institutional religion in favor of a personal relation with God. Religious

A

A. Expansion
What excited Emerson's fellow American intellectuals then—and now—was not so much his originality, for, in fact, his philosophical ideas can all be traced to others, but the infectiousness of his style and the sheer confidence with which he took up the self-appointed task of founding a new culture for the new nation.

A. Expansion As the drawing shows, Emerson was sometimes the object of satire, even in his own day, for the extravagance of his claims and his language. You might want to return to this caricature when discussing "Nature," particularly with regard to the "transparent eyeball" metaphor on page 192.

B. Expansion *Representative Men* is a series of character studies of great men such as Napoleon Bonaparte and the great German poet Goethe (pronounced, in English, gʉr'tə). The only American Emerson included among his representative great men was—himself.

Additional Writing Assignment Your students have now read about Transcendentalism and Emerson without yet reading his actual words. Ask them to write a brief statement of their reaction to this philosophy, and to anticipate what Emerson might say about nature.

A

"Standing on the bare ground, — my head
bathed by the blithe air, & uplifted into
infinite space, — all mean egotism
vanishes. I become a transparent
Eyeball."
Nature, p. 13.

A caricature by Christopher Pearce Cranch from *Illustrations of the New Philosophy.*

By permission of the Houghton Library, Harvard University, Cambridge.

truth, Emerson said, was "an intuition. It cannot be received at second hand." Like the scholar's books, the pulpit was for inspiration, not indoctrination. Emerson called upon the young divinity students before him to "cast behind . . . all conformity, and acquaint men at first hand with the Deity." This lecture so outraged Harvard authorities (who seized on what they thought was its denial of the divinity of Christ) that three decades passed before Emerson was allowed to speak there again.

By this time, Emerson's life had settled into a consistent pattern: an ever-widening series of lecture tours, punctuated by the publication of B his lectures in essay form. *Essays* appeared in 1841; *Essays: Second Series* in 1844; *Representative Men* in 1850. There was something for everyone in his lectures and essays, but especially for the legions of people who were disappointed with the narrowing material or spiritual condition of their lives.

It was to these people, perhaps, that Emerson spoke most intensely. Concord became a kind of Mecca to a rising class of disaffected and truth-seeking young. They sought out Emerson as a kind of guru. But Emerson's genius was such that he appealed to a broad spectrum of American society. Intellectuals responded to his philosophy, his ideas about the relations between humanity, nature, and God; the young responded to his hope, his declarations that they were on the verge of a great new age; while society at large responded to his optimism, his claims that all was really for the best.

That optimism was dealt a severe blow in 1842 when Emerson's son Waldo died at the age of six from scarlet fever. Emerson was profoundly moved. By nature a rather cold, restrained man, he had found in Waldo someone to whom he could demonstrate his love directly and unaffectedly. At the child's death, Emerson shrank back into an emotional shell from which he never reemerged. "How can I hope for a friend," he wrote in his journal during his middle years, "who have never been one?"

In his later years, Emerson suffered from a severe loss of memory and had difficulty recalling the most ordinary words. This affliction resulted in his increasing public silence, and when he did appear in public, he read from notes. Near the end of his life, agreeing to such a performance, he remarked, "A queer occasion it will be—a lecturer who has no idea of what he is lecturing about, and an audience who don't know what he *can* mean."

In the autumn of 1881, Walt Whitman paid Emerson a visit of respect and was asked to dinner. In Whitman's report of this "blessed evening with Emerson," he wrote that Emerson "seated himself in his chair, a trifle pushed back, and, though a listener and apparently an alert one, remained silent through the whole talk and discussion. A lady friend [Louisa May Alcott] quietly took a seat next to him, to give special attention. A good color in his face, eyes clear, with the well-known expression of sweetness, and the old clear-peering aspect quite the same." Six months later, Emerson was dead.

Supplementary Support Materials
1. Vocabulary Activity Worksheet (*CCB*)
2. Review and Response Worksheet: Imagery (*CCB*)
3. Selection Test (*CCB*)

Developing Vocabulary
The following words from the essay are tested in the Selection Test. (See also Vocabulary Activity Worksheet.)

sublime	to integrate
admonishing	superficial
kindred	decorum
manifold	

Preparation
Establishing a Purpose. A quotation from Emerson in the explanatory note on this page includes the phrase "an original relation to the universe." From their study of Unit Three, students are familiar with the American Romantic writers, who found renewal through contemplation of nature. Ask students to read this selection to determine what will be Emerson's "original relation to nature."

A. Expansion
You might pause here to ask students to paraphrase the first paragraph. Essentially, Emerson is merely saying that the stars are sublime.

The sentence "If the stars should appear one night in a thousand years . . ." was used by Isaac Asimov as the premise for the classic science-fiction story "Nightfall."

B. Responding
? Do you agree or disagree with Emerson's claim that children have a deeper wisdom than adults? (Emerson seems to mean that children's ability to perceive has not yet been clouded by what they will learn as they grow older.) Do you agree with his portrayal of nature as always benign? Explain. (Emerson's ability to overlook hurricanes and snowstorms may reflect his comfortable lifestyle. On the other hand, it may reflect his view that nature can, in effect, do no wrong.)

FROM NATURE

In his introduction to the book *Nature,* from which the following chapter is taken, Emerson offers a clue to the underlying purpose of his work when he encourages us, his contemporaries, to look directly at Nature:

"Our age is retrospective. It builds the sepulchres of the fathers. It writes biographies, histories, and criticism. The foregoing generations beheld God and nature face to face; we, through their eyes. Why should we not also enjoy an original relation to the universe? Why should we not have a poetry and philosophy of insight and not of tradition, and a religion by revelation to us, and not the history of theirs?"

As you read this first chapter from *Nature,* think about whether people can still achieve this mystical relationship with the natural universe. Since 1836, when the essay was first published, how has the natural world changed? What has happened to "the plantations of God"?

A To go into solitude, a man needs to retire as much from his chamber [room] as from society. I am not solitary while I read and write, though nobody is with me. But if a man would be alone, let him look at the stars. The rays that come from those heavenly worlds will separate between him and what he touches. One might think the atmosphere was made transparent with this design, to give man, in the heavenly bodies, the perpetual presence of the sublime. Seen in the streets of cities, how great they are! If the stars should appear one night in a thousand years, how would men believe and adore; and preserve for many generations the remembrance of the city of God which had been shown! But every night come out these envoys of beauty, and light the universe with their admonishing smile.

The stars awaken a certain reverence, because though always present, they are inaccessible; but all natural objects make a kindred impression, when the mind is open to their influence. Nature never wears a mean appearance. Neither does the wisest man extort her secret, and lose his curiosity by finding out all her perfection. Nature never became a toy to a wise spirit. The flowers, the animals, the mountains, reflected the wisdom of his best hour, as much as they had delighted the simplicity of his childhood.

When we speak of nature in this manner, we have a distinct but most poetical sense in the mind. We mean the integrity of impression made by manifold natural objects. It is this which distinguishes the stick of timber of the woodcutter from the tree of the poet. The charming landscape which I saw this morning is indubitably made up of some twenty or thirty farms. Miller owns this field, Locke that, and Manning the woodland beyond. But none of them owns the landscape. There is a property in the horizon which no man has but he whose eye can integrate all the parts, that is, the poet. This is the best part of these men's farms, yet to this their warranty deeds give no title.

To speak truly, few adult persons can see nature. Most persons do not see the sun. At least B they have a very superficial seeing. The sun illuminates only the eye of the man, but shines into the eye and the heart of the child. The lover of nature is he whose inward and outward senses are still truly adjusted to each other; who has retained the spirit of infancy even into the era of manhood. His intercourse with heaven and earth becomes part of his daily food. In the presence of nature, a wild delight runs through the man, in spite of real sorrows. Nature says—he is my creature, and maugre [despite] all his impertinent griefs, he shall be glad with me. Not the sun or the summer alone, but every hour and season yields its tribute of delight; for every hour and change corresponds to and authorizes a different state of the mind, from breathless noon to grimmest midnight.

Nature is a setting that fits equally well a comic or a mourning piece. In good health, the air is a cordial of incredible virtue. Crossing a bare common, in snow puddles, at twilight, under a clouded sky, without having in my thoughts any occurrence of special good fortune, I have enjoyed a perfect exhilaration. I am glad to the brink of fear.

CLOSURE

In class discussion, have students pose a series of questions whose answers will reveal Emerson's basic views about our relationships to nature and to God. You may want to have other students answer the questions.

READING CHECK TEST

1. People would look at the stars each night with the same wonder they would if the stars appeared only once in a thousand years. *False*

2. Adults do not delight in nature as much as children do. *True*

3. People see nature only superficially. *True*

4. In nature, there is perpetual age and wisdom. *False*

5. If we use our intuition, we will see that there is a very real relationship between ourselves and the plant world. *True*

A. Responding

? Do you find it contradictory that, in the same breath, Emerson says, "All mean egotism vanishes," and, "I see all; the currents of the Universal Being circulate through me"? (There is no contradiction. He means that he has become part of something far greater.)

B. Humanities Connection: Discussing the Fine Art

Thomas Cole (1801–1848) was a founder of the Hudson River school. Like others of that school, he sought moral and religious meaning in the landscape. This painting shows New Hampshire in autumn. The beautiful view is a backdrop for the work of a settler whose land is studded with the stumps of trees he has felled. You might ask if students can discern a moral or religious meaning in this painting. What, for example, do they make of the dead trees at the edge of the clearing? (We have seen Cole's work in Unit Three, pages 117 and 119.)

In the woods, too, a man casts off his years, as the snake his slough, and at what period soever of life, is always a child. In the woods is perpetual youth. Within these plantations of God, a decorum and sanctity reign, a perennial festival is dressed, and the guest sees not how he should tire of them in a thousand years. In the woods, we return to reason and faith. There I feel that nothing can befall me in life—no disgrace, no calamity (leaving me my eyes), which nature cannot repair. Standing on the bare ground—my head bathed by the blithe air, and uplifted into infinite space—all mean egotism vanishes. I become a transparent eyeball; I am nothing; I see all; the currents of the Universal Being circulate through me; I am part or parcel of God. A The name of the nearest friend sounds then foreign and accidental: to be brothers, to be acquaintances, master, or servant, is then a trifle and a disturbance. I am the lover of uncontained and immortal beauty. In the wilderness, I find something more dear and connate [inborn] than in streets or villages. In the tranquil landscape, and especially in the distant line of the horizon, man beholds somewhat [something] as beautiful as his own nature.

The greatest delight which the fields and woods

B

The Notch of the White Mountains (Crawford Notch) (detail) by Thomas Cole (1839). Oil on canvas.

National Gallery of Art, Washington, D.C. Andrew W. Mellon Fund.

Analyzing The Essay
Identifying Facts
1. Emerson says that people would surely believe in and adore God, and they would preserve for many generations the memory of the stars as showing the "city of God."
2. Emerson says that all nature deserves our attention and reverence. The stars are an especially dramatic example because they are inaccessible.
3. According to Emerson, children have the "inward and outward senses still truly adjusted to each other." He urges adults to become like children in their pure and unfettered joy in nature.

Interpreting Meanings
4. He says that he means the "integrity of impression made by manifold natural objects." He probably refers to an imaginative sense of looking at nature directly, in all its beauty and wholeness.
Emerson says that, while a wood-cutter will see a stack of timber, a poet will see a tree; while an ordinary person will see a collection of farms, the poet will see them as an entire landscape, bounded by the horizon.
5. Emerson says he becomes "part or parcel of God" when his own ego vanishes. Then he becomes the transparent eyeball, seeing all. The Universal Being circulates through him. Note the importance Emerson placed on the eyes (page 192, column 1).
God is found in the perfect harmony between people and nature. (Notice the paradox: "I am nothing; I see all.")
6. Student answers will vary. Encourage the students to reread the essay carefully before they begin to answer each part of the question.

minister is the suggestion of an occult relation between man and the vegetable. I am not alone and unacknowledged. They nod to me, and I to them. The waving of the boughs in the storm is new to me and old. It takes me by surprise, and yet is not unknown. Its effect is like that of a higher thought or a better emotion coming over me, when I deemed I was thinking justly or doing right.

Yet it is certain that the power to produce this delight does not reside in nature, but in man, or in a harmony of both. It is necessary to use these pleasures with great temperance. For nature is not always tricked [dressed] in holiday attire, but the same scene which yesterday breathed perfume and glittered as for the frolic of the nymphs, is overspread with melancholy today. Nature always wears the colors of the spirit. To a man laboring under calamity, the heat of his own fire hath sadness in it. Then there is a kind of contempt of the landscape felt by him who has just lost by death a dear friend. The sky is less grand as it shuts down over less worth in the population.

Responding to the Essay

Analyzing the Essay

Identifying Facts

1. Emerson wants his audience to look at some of the commonest elements of their lives—the natural environment that they see every day—in a new way. How would our attitude toward the stars change if they appeared only once every thousand years?
2. The second paragraph makes clear that Emerson is using the stars as an attention-getting example for a point about nature. What point is he making?
3. "To speak truly," Emerson says, "few adult persons can see nature." He says that children somehow have the advantage over adults in this matter. Read carefully the paragraph that begins with that sentence. What do adults seem to lose as they grow older?

Interpreting Meanings

4. What do you think Emerson means by a "poetical sense" of looking at nature? What **images** illustrate the distinction between nature used for practical benefits and nature viewed in this poetic way?
5. The most famous passage in *Nature,* and perhaps in all of Emerson's work, begins, "Standing on the bare ground . . . " and ends, "I am part or parcel of God." In what way is the **image** of a "transparent eyeball" a description of a visionary experience of God? Describe the relation presented here between people, nature, and God. According to Emerson, is God to be found only in nature, only in people, or in some common element that they both share?
6. Describe your response to Emerson's essay. Cite the passages you found yourself agreeing with and those you are doubtful about.

Writing About the Essay

A Critical Response

Comparing Two Descriptions. One of the roots of Emerson's Transcendentalist thought is to be found in the Puritan view of the relations between God, people, and nature. Reread Jonathan Edwards's description of his experience of a thunderstorm (page 41), and in a brief essay compare it to Emerson's description of nature. What similarities do you find? What differences?

Analyzing Language and Style

Paradoxes

Emerson's epigrammatic sentences are justly famous. One aspect of his style that is often overlooked, though, is his use of **paradox**, the linking of seemingly contradictory elements (as in the expression from *Romeo and Juliet*: "Parting is such sweet sorrow"). Read the following sentences from *Nature* and discuss their use of paradox. How would you express each statement in your own words?

1. "I am not solitary while I read and write, though nobody is with me."
2. "But every night come out these envoys of beauty, and light the universe with their admonishing smile."
3. "Most persons do not see the sun."
4. "I am glad to the brink of fear."

Supplementary Support Materials
1. Vocabulary Activity Worksheet (*CCB*)
2. Review and Response Worksheet: Figurative Language (*CCB*)
3. Selection Test (*CCB*)
4. Audiocassette recording

Developing Vocabulary
The following words from the essay are tested in the Selection Test. (See also Vocabulary Activity Worksheet.)
manifest aspirant aversion

Preparation
1. **Building On Prior Knowledge.** Before students read, you may want them to write out their definitions of *self-reliance*.

2. **Establishing A Purpose.** Have students read to discover how Emerson's views on self-reliance differ from or extend their own.

A. Responding
? What does Emerson mean by "this sculpture in the memory?" (He seems to be saying that some people strike a responsive chord in us at first meeting, a "preestablished harmony," almost as if we knew them already. This is in agreement with his Platonic Idealism.)

B. Responding
? Do you agree that people only half express themselves? What examples can you cite supporting or refuting this from your own experience or knowledge?

C. Responding
Emerson is saying that greatness comes not so much through striving as through acceptance of one's fate.
? Do you agree? (Answers will vary. Many students may identify greatness with fame and economic success rather than simply doing one's best.)

FROM SELF-RELIANCE

In an essay published in 1841, Emerson addressed one of the central characteristics of the American sensibility: individualism. Before you read, think about your own definition of "self-reliance."

There is a time in every man's education when he arrives at the conviction that envy is ignorance; that imitation is suicide; that he must take himself for better, for worse, as his portion; that though the wide universe is full of good, no kernel of nourishing corn can come to him but through his toil bestowed on that plot of ground which is given to him to till. The power which resides in him is new in nature, and none but he knows what that is which he can do, nor does he know until he has tried. Not for nothing one face, one character, one fact makes much impression on him, and another none. It is not without preestablished harmony, this sculpture in the memory. The eye was placed where one ray should fall, that it might testify of that particular ray. Bravely let him speak the utmost syllable of his confession. We but half express ourselves, and are ashamed of that divine idea which each of us represents. It may be safely trusted as proportionate and of good issues, so it be faithfully imparted, but God will not have his work made manifest by cowards. It needs a divine man to exhibit any thing divine. A man is relieved and gay when he has put his heart into his work and done his best; but what he has said or done otherwise, shall give him no peace. It is a deliverance which does not deliver. In the attempt his genius deserts him; no muse befriends; no invention, no hope.

Trust thyself: every heart vibrates to that iron string. Accept the place the divine Providence has found for you; the society of your contemporaries, the connection of events. Great men have always done so and confided themselves childlike to the genius of their age, betraying their perception that the Eternal was stirring at their heart, working through their hands, predominating in all their being. And we are now men, and must accept in the highest mind the same transcendent destiny; and not pinched in a corner, not cowards fleeing before a revolution, but redeemers and benefactors, pious aspirants to be noble clay plastic under the Almighty effort, let us advance and advance on Chaos and the Dark. . . .

These are the voices which we hear in solitude, but they grow faint and inaudible as we enter into the world. Society everywhere is in conspiracy against the manhood of every one of its members. Society is a joint-stock company in which the members agree for the better securing of his bread to each shareholder, to surrender the liberty and culture of the eater. The virtue in most request is conformity. Self-reliance is its aversion. It loves not realities and creators, but names and customs.

Whoso would be a man must be a nonconformist. He who would gather immortal palms must not be hindered by the name of goodness, but must explore if it be goodness. Nothing is at last sacred but the integrity of our own mind. Absolve you to yourself, and you shall have the suffrage of the world. . . .

A foolish consistency is the hobgoblin of little minds, adored by little statesmen and philosophers and divines. With consistency a great soul has simply nothing to do. He may as well concern himself with his shadow on the wall. Out upon your guarded lips! Sew them up with packthread, do. Else, if you would be a man, speak what you think today in words as hard as cannon balls, and tomorrow speak what tomorrow thinks in hard words again, though it contradict every thing you said today. Ah, then, exclaim the aged ladies, you shall be sure to be misunderstood. Misunderstood! It is a right fool's word. Is it so bad then to be misunderstood? Pythagoras was misunderstood, and Socrates, and Jesus, and Luther, and Copernicus, and Galileo, and Newton, and every pure and wise spirit that ever took flesh. To be great is to be misunderstood.

Closure
Have students write several sentences explaining how the phrase "imitation is suicide" is central to Emerson's views on self-reliance.

Reading Check Test
1. Imitation of others is "ignorance." *True*
2. We must trust ourselves, for within each of us is a divine being. *True*
3. To be great is to be understood by those around you. *False*
4. We should speak in "strong words" even if we contradict ourselves. *True*
5. We should listen to our intuition before the wisdom of sages from our past. *True*

Responding to the Essay

Analyzing the Essay

Identifying Facts

1. According to the first sentence, what does every person realize at some moment in his or her education?
2. According to the second paragraph, what is the destiny of every human being?
3. Explain what Emerson thinks of society as a whole, according to the third paragraph.
4. What is the opposite of "self-reliance," according to the third paragraph?
5. In the fourth paragraph, what does Emerson see as the most sacred aspect of a person?
6. What does Emerson think of people who call for consistency in thought and action and who fear being misunderstood?

Interpreting Meanings

7. What do you think Emerson means by "the divine idea which each of us represents" (paragraph 1)?
8. How do you think self-reliance differs from selfishness or self-centeredness?
9. Suppose this essay were to be delivered as a major political address during a Presidential campaign today. How do you think people would respond?

Writing About the Essay

A Creative Response

1. **Writing an Essay.** Take one of these statements and write your own essay. Remember that an essayist expresses personal views on some limited topic.
   a. "Envy is ignorance."
   b. "God will not have His work made manifest by cowards."
   c. "Trust thyself: every heart vibrates to that iron string."
   d. "A foolish consistency is the hobgoblin of little minds."
   e. "To be great is to be misunderstood."

A Critical Response

2. **Writing a Response.** In at least three paragraphs, write an essay called "On Emerson's Self-Reliance." Explain your own responses to Emerson's views on self-reliance. Which of his ideas are most significant today? Are any of his ideas dated? Some readers find nineteenth-century writers are frequently condescending to women; what do you think?

Analyzing Language and Style

Figurative Language

Emerson makes many of his points through a series of **figures of speech**—comparisons between two things that are basically unlike.

1. In "Self-Reliance," what does he compare with these ordinary things and events:
   a. planting corn
   b. an iron string
   c. clay
   d. a stock-company
   e. cannon balls
2. What do you think is the significance of the word *iron* to describe the string? How would the effect and meaning differ if the string were described as silken, golden, or silver?
3. The most famous **metaphor** in "Self-Reliance" is the one that opens the final paragraph. How would you explain what Emerson means by this metaphor? What exactly is a hobgoblin? What is a "little mind"? What would be a "wise" consistency? What would be a "foolish" consistency?

Pat Lyon at the Forge by John Neagle (1829). Oil.

Courtesy of the Pennsylvania Academy of the Fine Arts, Philadelphia. Gift of the Lyon family.

Analyzing The Essay

Identifying Facts

1. Every person must come to terms with his or her identity.
2. Every human being must accept the place that Providence has accorded.
3. He believes society conspires to suppress the individuality of its members, pressuring us to conform rather than to fulfill ourselves as individuals.
4. The opposite of self-reliance is conformity—bowing to the pressures of society.
5. The integrity of one's own mind.
6. He calls them "aged ladies," and urges us to ignore them, saying, "to be great is to be misunderstood."

Interpreting Meanings

7. The "divine idea" is the potential in each of us for expression and fulfillment.
8. Answers will vary. Doing one's best is not necessarily selfish.
9. Answers will vary.

SUPPLEMENTARY SUPPORT MATERIALS
1. Vocabulary Activity Worksheet (*CCB*)
2. Review and Response Worksheet: Apostrophe (*CCB*)
3. Selection Test (*CCB*)

DEVELOPING VOCABULARY
The following word from the poem is tested in the Selection Test. (See also Vocabulary Activity Worksheet.)
unfurled

PREPARATION
BUILDING ON PRIOR KNOWLEDGE. Before students read the poem, you might elicit from them what they already know about the first battle of the Revolutionary War. Then have students suggest words or phrases that reflect the meaning of this historic occasion for Americans.

A. Expansion
Note that the poem was originally written to be sung.

B. Alliteration
? What sounds are alliterated in lines 5 and 6? (s's) What effect does this repetition have at this point in the poem? (It emphasizes the silence that hovers around the place.)

C. Responding
? What is the spirit that the poet addresses here? (The Transcendentalist Spirit—the ultimate reality)

The "Concord Hymn" is an example of *occasional poetry,* poetry written to commemorate an "occasion" of historical or local importance. This poem was written for the dedication of a monument to the Minutemen, the colonial farmers who, on April 19, 1775, routed the red-coated ranks of the British Militia and signaled the start of the Revolutionary War. Over the generations, millions of Americans have made their pilgrimage to the monument at Concord. This poem was sung at the ceremonies to the tune of "Old Hundredth" ("Praise God, from whom all blessings flow . . .") A

Concord Hymn

Sung at the Completion of the Battle Monument, July 4, 1837

By the rude° bridge that arched the flood,
Their flag to April's breeze unfurled,
Here once the embattled farmers stood
And fired the shot heard round the world.

B The foe long since in silence slept;
Alike the conqueror silent sleeps;
And Time the ruined bridge has swept
Down the dark stream which seaward creeps.

On this green bank, by this soft stream,
We set today a votive stone;°
That memory may their deed redeem,
When, like our sires, our sons are gone.

C Spirit, that made those heroes dare
To die, and leave their children free,
Bid Time and Nature gently spare
The shaft° we raise to them and thee.

1. **rude:** crude, or roughly built.

10. **votive stone:** a marker made of stone, which fulfills a promise or a pledge.

16. **shaft:** column; here, the monument.

Responding to the Poem

Analyzing the Poem

Identifying Details

1. Identify the "foe" and the "conqueror" mentioned in the second stanza. What has happened to them and to the bridge?
2. According to Stanza 3, why are they putting up a monument here?
3. According to Stanza 4, why did the heroes die?
4. What does the speaker ask of the Spirit in Stanza 4?

Interpreting Meanings

5. The poem ends in an **apostrophe**—words spoken to a person or object who cannot or does not answer. How would you define the Spirit addressed in line 13?
6. To say that the shot of the Minutemen was "heard round the world" is, on a literal level, to indulge in **hyperbole**, or exaggeration for effect. On a **figurative** level, how is this statement true? What other "shots" can you think of that might be said to have been heard around the world?

Closure

Have students paraphrase the poem. (See A Critical Response, below.)

Analyzing The Poem

Identifying Details

1. The foe is the British; the conqueror is the American force of Minutemen that repelled the British at Concord.

Both foe and conqueror lie silent in their graves, and the bridge has collapsed with time.

2. The purpose of the monument is to ensure that people throughout the ages will remember the heroism of the first small band of Revolutionaries, the Minutemen.

3. They died to "leave their children free."

4. He asks the Spirit to plead with "Time and Nature" to "gently spare the shaft" the people raise: In other words, he asks that the monument be allowed to endure through the ages.

Interpreting Meanings

5. Emerson might mean God, or he may be addressing the spirit of courage.

6. On a figurative level the statement is true because the American struggle for independence has served, over the course of two hundred years, as an example for many other nations fighting oppression and injustice.

Student answers will vary.

7. Students will mention local war memorial monuments, and national monuments they have visited.

Student answers will vary.

8. Student answers will vary. The last two stanzas are general enough for anything. The second might be applied to some World War II battles.

A. Humanities Connection: Responding to the Photograph

This photograph shows a "rude bridge" similar to the one where the Battle of Concord was fought.

? Do you feel that this bridge is imposing, monumental, or, on the other hand, modest and of small scale? (Most students will probably say the latter. Emphasize that Emerson himself was making the same point, comparing the unassuming scale and perishable nature of the bridge to its lasting impact on history.)

A

7. What other monuments have been erected to the dead so that "memory may their deed redeem"? Do you believe that memory actually *can* "redeem" or recover the dead? Explain.
8. Could any stanzas of this hymn be sung at other war memorials erected in the years since 1837?

Writing About the Poem

A Creative Response

1. **Writing a Letter.** Imagine that you are an aged veteran of the battle described in the poem. Write a letter to a friend, describing your reaction to hearing the poem sung at the dedication.

A Critical Response

2. **Paraphrasing the Poem.** Paraphrase—state in your own words—the text of this poem, taking it line by line.
   a. Substitute simpler, modern words for the archaic or old-fashioned ones.
   b. Provide any missing words.
   c. Put the inverted (or reversed) words in standard English word order.
   d. Rephrase the figures of speech, using plain, literal language.

   Paraphrase the poem as if you are doing it for someone who does not understand it at all—perhaps for someone who is much younger than you are.

Supplementary Support Materials

1. Vocabulary Activity Worksheet (*CCB*)
2. Review and Response Worksheet: Apostrophe (*CCB*)
3. Selection Test (*CCB*)

Developing Vocabulary

The following word from the poem is tested in the Selection Test. (See also Vocabulary Activity Worksheet.)

nook

Preparation

Establishing a Purpose. Have students read to determine how Emerson answers these questions: Where did the rhodora come from? Why is it here?

A. Expansion

"Pierced our solitudes" is a striking image for what the wind does. Solitude must be very deep if a mere wind seems like a visitor.

B. Personification

? What is the personification in line 4? ("To please the desert and the sluggish brook") What is the effect of this personification? (Answers will vary. Personifying the rhodora raises it to a level with humans.)

C. Expansion

The poem's message echoes the biblical parallel of the lilies of the field, and thus suggests that beauty has a divine origin.

Like the Romantics, the Transcendentalists saw in nature signs of divinity and answers to questions about the meaning of life.

"Whence is the flower?" means "Where did the flower come from?" How would most people answer this question?

The Rhodora:

On Being Asked, Whence Is the Flower?

A In May, when sea winds pierced our solitudes,
I found the fresh Rhodora in the woods,
Spreading its leafless blooms in a damp nook,
B To please the desert and the sluggish brook.
The purple petals, fallen in the pool,
Made the black water with their beauty gay;
Here might the redbird come his plumes to cool,
And court the flower that cheapens his array.
Rhodora! if the sages ask thee why
This charm is wasted on the earth and sky,
Tell them, dear, that if eyes were made for seeing,
Then Beauty is its own excuse for being:
Why thou wert there, O rival of the rose!
I never thought to ask, I never knew;
But, in my simple ignorance, suppose
The selfsame Power that brought me there brought you.

CLOSURE

Have students, in class discussion, outline a brief speech that Emerson might give to explain his musings about the rhodora to high-school-age members of a transcendentalist club.

ANALYZING THE POEM

Identifying Details

1. He finds the rhodora in a damp nook in the woods, by the side of a brook.

The flower was pleasing the "desert and the sluggish brook."

2. The sages are probably philosophers.

The sages question why the charming flower has been "wasted"—that is, placed where no one, or few people, will appreciate it. The poet answers this question by claiming that beauty is its own justification, or its own "excuse for being."

3. In line 4 the rhodora is personified when the poet says that it spreads its blossoms "to please" the desert and the brook. In line 8, the redbird is said to pay "court" to the flower whose blooms are more beautiful than its plumage.

4. The apostrophe occurs in lines 9–16, where the poet directly addresses the flower.

Responding to the Poem

Analyzing the Poem

Identifying Details

1. Describe where the poet comes upon the rhodora. Until then, whom or what had the flower been pleasing with its beauty?
2. In line 9, who might the "sages" be? What is their question, and how does the poet answer it?
3. There are several instances of **personification** in the poem. Identify and explain at least three of these.
4. Part of this poem is an **apostrophe**—a direct address to something that cannot answer. Where is the apostrophe?

Interpreting Meanings

5. How does Emerson say he is like the rhodora?
6. Line 12 is the key to the poem's meaning and one of Emerson's most famous sayings. How would you rephrase the line in your own words? Do you agree with its statement?
7. Do you think everything in the world, including beauty, has to have a utilitarian purpose? Do many people behave as if they believe that usefulness is more important than beauty? Explain.
8. The poet indicates in his subtitle that someone has asked him where the rhodora came from. What is the poet's answer? If you were the questioner, would this answer satisfy you? How would you have answered the question?
9. What do you think the poet means by "Power" in the last line?
10. How might a rationalist writer like Benjamin Franklin have answered the question "Whence is the flower?"

Writing About the Poem

A Critical Response

1. **Analyzing the Poem.** A poem written in **iambic pentameter** has five iambs in a line: that is, the poem has five groups of syllabic pairs in which an unstressed syllable alternates with a stressed syllable (daDUM, daDUM, daDUM, daDUM, daDUM). If you were scanning this poem, you might mark the first line like this:

   In May, when sea winds pierced our solitudes

   In a brief essay, analyze the poem's metrical structure and rhyme scheme. Is it written entirely in iambic pentameter? Does every line rhyme with another line? At the end of your essay, describe your response to Emerson's rhymes and metrics.

2. **Comparing Philosophies.** In Act III, Scene 1, of Shakespeare's *As You Like It,* a character speaks of the compensations he finds in his forest life:

   > . . . this our life, exempt from public haunt,
   > Finds tongues in trees, books in the running brooks,
   > Sermons in stones, and good in every thing.
   >
   > —from *As You Like It,*
   > William Shakespeare

   In an essay, tell whether this philosophy of nature is like Emerson's. Emerson's simplicity in "The Rhodora" opens him to intuition and to a sense of the presence of God. Is there any hint that nature contains signs of divinity in the Shakespeare quotation?

Analyzing Language and Style

Inversions

Inversions are "reversals." Emerson frequently inverts or reverses the normal English word order of a sentence in order to accommodate his meters and rhymes. Lines 5–8 are one complete sentence. What words are wrenched out of their normal order to make the rhymes and meter "come out right"?

Rewrite this sentence in normal English word order. To do this, you have to be sure you know exactly what word or phrase each modifier refers to.

Interpreting Meanings

5. Emerson is like the rhodora in that he, too, was created by God—the "selfsame Power" of line 16.

6. Beauty needs no practical justification for its existence; it is an end in itself.

Student answers will vary.

7. Again, students may be divided in their opinions.

8. The poet implies in the last line that the rhodora comes from a creative "Power"—that is, the rhodora is one of God's creations.

Student answers will vary.

9. Students will probably agree that the poet refers either to God or—possibly—to a less specific, divine, creative force.

10. A rationalist writer might have discussed the flower's origins in a seed or its botanical relationship to other plants. Or such a writer might have simply presented the flower as part of the variety of the universe.

SUPPLEMENTARY SUPPORT MATERIALS
1. Vocabulary Activity Worksheet (*CCB*)
2. Review and Response Worksheet: Personification (*CCB*)
3. Selection Test (*CCB*)

DEVELOPING VOCABULARY
The following words from the poem are tested in the Selection Test. (See also Vocabulary Activity Worksheet.)
radiant tumultuous bastion

PREPARATION
ESTABLISHING A PURPOSE. Have students brainstorm a list of words and phrases that suggest what a snowstorm means to them. Then have them read to determine what a snowstorm means to Emerson.

A. Expansion
If you live in a snowy area, you might ask your students what their first reaction is when they hear a prediction for a snowstorm. (Children and teenagers tend to be pleased at the prospect, adults to be displeased. It's a sign of typically Emersonian optimism that he seizes upon a snowstorm as an occasion for delight and an opportunity for large reflections on the idea of art.)

B. Tone
? What effect do the words "come see" have on the tone of the poem? (The friendly invitation draws the reader into the poem and makes for a somewhat endearing tone.)

C. Interpretation
? In what sense is the snow a "fierce artificer"? (See question 8, page 201.)

D. Mood
Note Emerson's use of adjectives and adverbs to create a mood: *fanciful, mockingly, swanlike, mad, frolic.*

If you have ever witnessed a heavy snow, you will understand at once the message of this poem—which is about the ways that art imitates nature. Emerson probably wrote the poem in 1834, the year after a particularly heavy snow hit Concord. Note again how Emerson sees a correspondence between nature and human life.

The Snow-Storm

A
Announced by all the trumpets of the sky,
Arrives the snow, and, driving o'er the fields,
Seems nowhere to alight: the whited air
Hides hills and woods, the river, and the heaven,
And veils the farmhouse at the garden's end.
The sled and traveler stopped, the courier's feet
Delayed, all friends shut out, the housemates sit
Around the radiant fireplace, enclosed
In a tumultuous privacy of storm.

B
Come see the north wind's masonry.
Out of an unseen quarry evermore
C
Furnished with tile, the fierce artificer
Curves his white bastions with projected roof
Round every windward stake, or tree, or door.
Speeding, the myriad-handed, his wild work
So fanciful, so savage, naught cares he
For number or proportion. Mockingly,
On coop or kennel he hangs Parian° wreaths;
A swanlike form invests the hidden thorn;
Fills up the farmer's lane from wall to wall,
Maugre° the farmer's sighs; and at the gate
D
A tapering turret overtops the work.
And when his hours are numbered, and the world
Is all his own, retiring, as he were not,
Leaves, when the sun appears, astonished Art
To mimic in slow structures, stone by stone,
Built in an age, the mad wind's night work,
The frolic architecture of the snow.

18. **Parian:** fine marble from the island of Paros in Greece.

21. **Maugre:** despite.

Closure
Have students generate a list of brief (fewer than ten words), simple sentences about Emerson's views, as they are revealed in "The Snow-Storm," on nature and art. Taken together, the sentences should summarize the poet's views.

Analyzing The Poem
Identifying Details

1. The "trumpets of the sky" announce the storm.
2. The fields, the hills and the woods, the river, the farmhouse, the sled and the traveler, and the courier.
They sit by the fireplace.
3. The north wind is compared with an architect.
Details include "masonry" (line 10), "quarry" (line 11), "artificer" (line 12), the mention of "bastions" and a "projected roof" (line 13). "Parian wreaths" (line 18), "tapering turret" (line 22), and "frolic architecture" (line 28).
4. The madness is demonstrated in the overwhelming speed and wildness with which the wind has piled up the snow in "architectural" forms.
Details include "fanciful" (line 16), the mention of a "swan-like form" (line 19), and the adjective "frolic" in the last line.

Interpreting Meanings
5. The adjective "tumultuous" suggests violence, noise, and anxiety; the noun "privacy" suggests quiet and peace. The phrase is virtually an oxymoron, or yoking together of opposites.
6. They are described as slow because it takes many years, or centuries to build in stone on a comparable scale to what nature builds in snow in a few hours.
7. Art is astonished at the beauty of the snow's "frolic architecture."
The poem suggests the awesome power, and equally awesome beauty, of the forces of nature. People can only sit quietly by in wonder.
8. Most students will agree that the phrase might be an apt description for some artists.
9. Think of how castles and cathedrals imitate soaring mountains; how paintings imitate nature; how some sculpture looks like stones or boulders or trees.

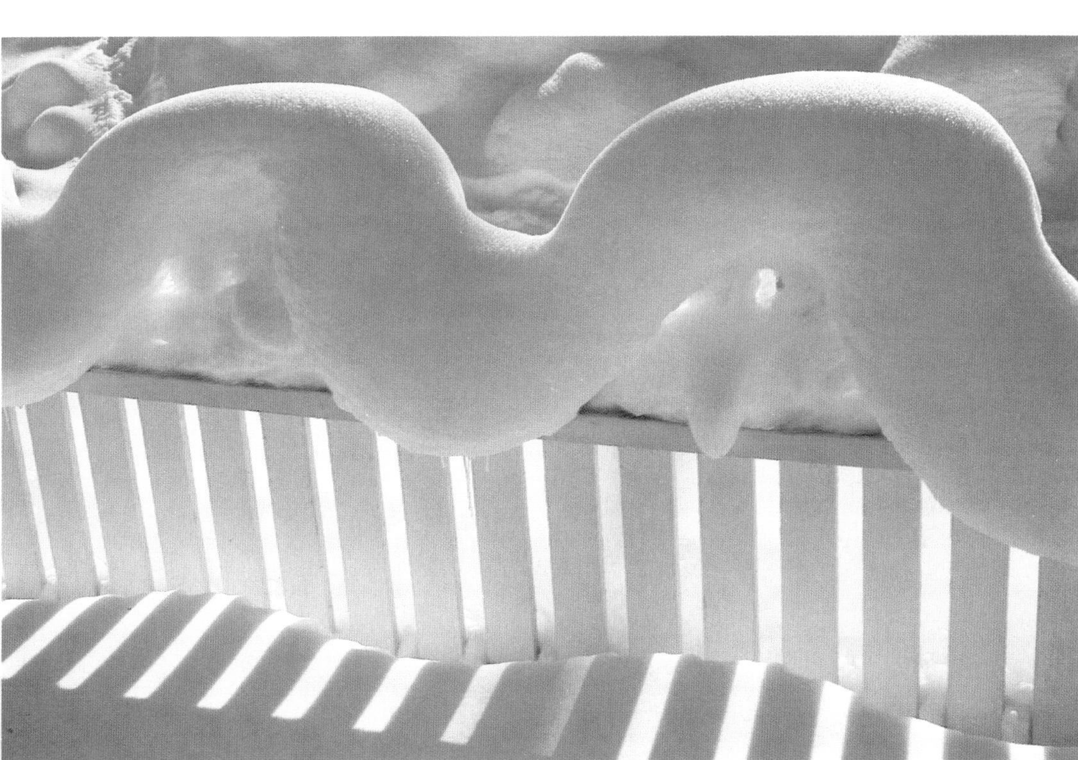

Responding to the Poem

Analyzing the Poem

Identifying Details

1. What precedes the snow, according to line 1?
2. Name some of the things and people that the snow affects in lines 1–9. Where do the people inside the house sit?
3. The second part of the poem (lines 10–28) is a lengthy **personification.** What type of person is the north wind personified as? Point out at least three details that extend the personification.
4. The final adjective applied to the north wind is "mad" in line 27. How has that "madness" been demonstrated? What details in the poem suggest that this madness is also imaginative and joyful?

Interpreting Meanings

5. Explain how the meanings of the words "tumultuous privacy" (line 9) make this a startling and vivid phrase.
6. According to the last four lines, human art only mimics the work of nature. Why do you think Art's structures are described as "slow" (line 26)?
7. Art is **personified** in this poem as "astonished." What is Art, or human work and creation, astonished at? What overall idea about nature and human work is suggested by the poem?
8. Could artists, writers, and composers also be called "fierce artificers"? Explain.
9. Can you think of other instances where art "mimics" nature?

Writing About the Poem

A Critical Response

Comparing Poems. Compare the transformations of outdoor and indoor worlds in Emerson's "The Snow-Storm" and Whittier's "Snow-Bound" (page 157). In particular, explain how **figurative** and **sensory language** contribute to the mood of each poem.

SUPPLEMENTARY SUPPORT MATERIALS
1. Review and Response Worksheet: Aphorisms (*CCB*)
2. Selection Test (*CCB*)

PREPARATION
ESTABLISHING A PURPOSE. Have students read the aphorisms to determine which ones ring true according to their own experience.

CLOSURE
Have students write one- or two-sentence restatements of the four longest aphorisms. You might also want students to suggest aphorisms of their own.

A. Responding
? This aphorism is from Emerson's 1824 *Journals.* Why might the country have been "roaring Patriotism at the top of its voice" at that time? (Following the War of 1812, the country began to expand, adding many new states. A whole generation had now been born in the "United States.")

B. Responding
? If Emerson were alive today, do you think he would still believe this aphorism? Why? (Answers may vary, now that the world seems to be more interested in peace.)

C. Responding
? Based on the Emerson poems you have read, would you say that the poet practices this philosophy? What about his poetry is new? What is old? (Answers will vary. Emerson's poetry is "new" in the sense that it offers his own unique perspective on his subject. His poetry is "old" in its use of traditional subject matter, verse forms, and poetic devices.)

EMERSON'S APHORISMS

An *aphorism* is a short statement that expresses a wise or clever observation about life. (Aphorisms might also be called "maxims," "adages," or just "sayings.") Try paraphrasing these aphorisms in your own words: you'll see how much meaning the writer has packed into a few words. That, of course, is what makes an aphorism memorable.

A [I confess I am a little cynical on some topics, and when a whole nation is roaring Patriotism at the top of its voice, I am fain [inclined] to explore the] cleanness of its hands and purity of its heart. I have generally found the gravest and most useful citizens are not the easiest provoked to swell the noise, though they may be punctual at the polls.

—*Journals,* 1824

B [Don't trust children with edge tools. Don't trust man, great God, with more power than he has, until he has learned to use that little better.] What a hell should we make of the world if we could do what we would! Put a button on the foil [sword] till the young fencers have learned not to put each other's eyes out.

—*Journals,* 1832

The maker of a sentence, like the other artist, launches out into the infinite and builds a road into Chaos and old Night, and is followed by those who hear him with something of wild, creative delight.

—*Journals,* 1834

C [Poetry must be as new as foam, and as old as the rock.]

—*Journals,* 1844

The invariable mark of wisdom is to see the miraculous in the common.

—*Nature*

A man is a god in ruins.

—*Nature*

Nothing can bring you peace but yourself. Nothing can bring you peace but the triumph of principles.

—"Self-Reliance"

. . . prayer as a means to effect a private end is meanness and theft. It supposes dualism and not a unity in nature and consciousness. As soon as the man is at one with God, he will not beg. He will then see prayer in all action.

—"Self-Reliance"

This time, like all times, is a very good one, if we but know what to do with it.

—"The American Scholar"

Books are the best of things, well used; abused, among the worst.

—"The American Scholar"

Public and private avarice make the air we breathe thick and fat.

—"The American Scholar"

Primary Sources
Hawthorne Talks About Emerson

Emerson, who thought of sin as merely a child's case of measles on the world, and Hawthorne, who plumbed the nature of evil, could never talk together. Hawthorne did live at Brook Farm for a few months, but he left, finding the high-minded discussions stifling. He then lived for a time in a house called the Old Manse in Concord, the same house where Emerson had written his first book, *Nature.* Here, in a passage from his essay called "The Old Manse," Hawthorne talks about Emerson and the "hobgoblins" who came to Concord seeking answers to the riddle of the world.

"These hobgoblins of flesh and blood were attracted thither by the widespreading influence of a great original thinker, who had his earthly abode at the opposite extremity of our village. His mind acted upon other minds of a certain constitution with wonderful magnetism, and drew many men upon long pilgrimages to speak with him face to face. Young visionaries—to whom just so much of insight had been imparted as to make life all a labyrinth [maze] around them—came to seek the clue that should guide them out of their self-involved bewilderment. Gray-headed theorists—whose systems, at first air, had finally imprisoned them in an iron framework—traveled painfully to his door, not to ask deliverance, but to invite the free spirit into their own thraldom [servitude]. People that had lighted on a new thought, or a thought that they fancied new, came to Emerson, as the finder of a glittering gem hastens to a lapidary [gem dealer], to ascertain its quality and value. Uncertain, troubled, earnest wanderers through the midnight of the moral world beheld his intellectual fire as a beacon burning on a hilltop, and, climbing the difficult ascent, looked forth into the surrounding obscurity more hopefully than hitherto. The light revealed objects unseen before—mountains, gleaming lakes, glimpses of a creation among the chaos; but also, as was unavoidable, it attracted bats and owls and the whole host of night birds, which flapped their dusky wings against the gazer's eyes, and sometimes were mistaken for fowls of angelic feather. Such delusions always hover nigh whenever a beacon fire of truth is kindled.

A "For myself, there had been epochs of my life when I, too, might have asked of this prophet the master word that should solve me the riddle of the universe; but now, being happy, I felt as if there were no question to be put, and therefore admired Emerson as a poet of deep beauty and austere tenderness, but sought nothing from him as a philosopher. It was good, nevertheless, to meet him in the wood paths, or sometimes in our avenue, with that pure intellectual gleam diffused about his presence like the garment of a shining one; and he so quiet, so simple, so without pretension, encountering each man alive as if expecting to receive more than he could impart. And, in truth, the heart of many an ordinary man had, perchance, inscriptions which he could not read. But it was impossible to dwell in his vicinity without inhaling more or less the mountain atmosphere of his lofty thought, which, in the brains of some people, wrought a singular giddiness—new truth being as heady as new wine. Never was a poor little country village infested with such a variety of queer, strangely dressed, oddly behaved mortals, most of whom took upon themselves to be important agents of the world's destiny, yet were simply bores of a very intense water. . . ."

—from "The Old Manse,"
Nathaniel Hawthorne

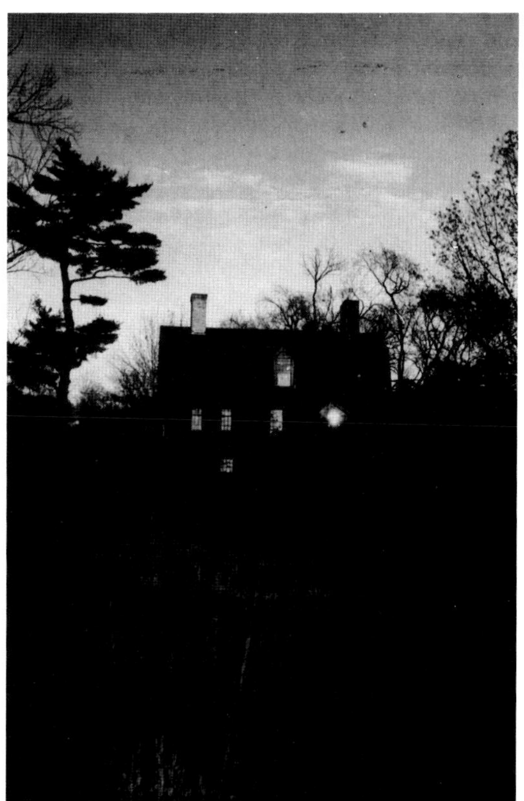

"The Old Manse," the home of Nathaniel Hawthorne in Concord, Massachusetts.

A. Expansion Hawthorne was happy because he had recently married Sophia Peabody, ending his long solitude at the age of thirty-eight. Sophia and Nathaniel were both extremely retiring by nature, so the courtship was a rather awkward one, but they were both ecstatic with the results. Hawthorne described his life with Sophia as "paradise," and wrote many of his best short stories in the Old Manse. Referring to the accidental nature of their courtship, Sophia etched this message on a windowpane with her ring: "Man's accidents are God's purposes"—in itself an aphorism worthy of Emerson.

COMMENT FROM A CRITIC
Alfred Kazin says that Thoreau, like many American writers, sought to create his own life in the act of writing about it. His life was short on external experience, and he was not well-traveled, but he focused obsessively on those experiences he did have and on the few, rather repetitious landscapes he did encounter. His major activity was to turn all this into prose, and he did so in the form of journals which, in print, exceed seven thousand pages. (He died at forty-five.) Like Emerson, he was a ceaseless honer of sentences, who prospected in his own journals for the choicest nuggets amid the sand.

A. Expansion
As a young man, Thoreau worked briefly in his father's pencil factory, and while there he made innovations in pencilmaking which improved the quality of the company's pencils enormously.

Henry David Thoreau (1817–1862)

On July 4, 1845 (the date was deliberately chosen), a young man ended a three-year stay at the house of a friend and moved to a cabin on the shores of Walden Pond in Massachusetts. He was twenty-eight years old and, to all appearances, a failure. He had lasted only two weeks as a schoolteacher (he refused to whip a child, then a mandatory form of punishment); his public lectures had been uninspiring; the woman to whom he had proposed marriage had turned him A down; he had little interest in the family business. Despite his impressive Harvard education, he had not realized his literary ambitions.

The pattern of his life had been, and would continue to be, precisely the opposite of the great American success story of the self-made man. If ever a person looked like a self-*un*made man, a man who had squandered the advantages of intelligence, education, and the friendship of brilliant and successful people, it was Henry David Thoreau. On top of all his other problems, Thoreau was difficult to get along with. He was admired, but from a distance—for he kept people at a distance. Three days before Thoreau went to Walden, Hawthorne wrote to a New York publisher that Thoreau was "tedious, tiresome, and intolerable." And yet, Hawthorne added, "he has great qualities of intellect and character."

Even his closest friends had doubts about Thoreau. "He seemed born for great enterprise and for command," Emerson said years later at Thoreau's funeral, "and I so much regret the loss of his rare powers of action, that I cannot help counting it a fault in him that he had no ambition. Wanting [lacking] this, instead of engineering for all America, he was the captain of a huckleberry party."

What Emerson failed to see, and what Thoreau knew (or at least hoped) all along, was that by leading a berry-picking party on a jaunt in the woods he could "engineer for all America" in the most profound way. This paradox is at the center of Thoreau's life and work.

He was born David Henry Thoreau in Concord, Massachusetts, in 1817. (He changed the order of his names after graduating from college.) His father was a moderately successful manufacturer of pencils. His mother took in boarders, among them the sister of Emerson's wife, thus establishing the relationship between the two families. As a boy, Thoreau tramped the woods and fields around Concord, often with a fishing rod, seldom with a gun. No one knew Concord as well as he did, and his attachment to this region was established early in his life.

Thoreau entered Harvard in 1833 and graduated four years later (without any literary distinction). Independent and eccentric even then, he attended chapel in a green coat, "because," he wrote, "the rules required black." He never ranked higher than the middle of his class, but he was extremely well read. At Harvard, mostly on his own, he became thoroughly familiar with English literature and with the German philosophers who provided much of the underpinnings of Transcendentalism.

After graduation, Thoreau went to New York, but he pined after his hometown. ("Am I not made of Concord dust?" he wrote to Emerson's wife.) After a year of struggling, he gave up and came home. Thoreau appeared to be floundering. But, in fact, he knew what he was doing; at least he knew that internally he was heading in the right direction, even if his external navigation looked aimless. A friend proposed that Henry and he sail to Europe and work their way across the continent, but Henry turned him down emphatically:

> I have been surprised when one has with confidence proposed to me, a grown man, to embark in some enterprise of his, as if I had absolutely nothing to do, my life having been a complete failure hitherto. What a doubtful compliment this to pay me! As if he had met me halfway across the ocean beating up against the wind, but bound nowhere, and proposed to me to go along with him! . . . No, no! I am not without employment at this stage of the voyage. To tell the truth, I saw an advertisement for able-bodied seamen, when I was a boy, sauntering in my native port, and as soon as I came of age I embarked.

That last sentence, in what would become Thoreau's typically metaphoric style, expressed the real truth: Thoreau knew where he was going. His voyage would be inward, and it would depart from Walden Pond, where Emerson had offered him the use of some land.

The experiment at Walden Pond was an attempt to rediscover the grandeur and heroism inherent in a simple life led close to Nature. The fact that Thoreau's cabin was only two miles from town—that he had really only set himself up in the suburbs of Concord, to which he commuted almost daily—was not really the point. Walden offered a focus for his contemplative urge. "I wish to meet the facts of life," he wrote in his journal, "the vital facts, which are the phenomena or actuality the gods meant to show us . . . and so I came down here."

This private confrontation was to Thoreau's mind the truly heroic enterprise of his time. "I am glad to remember as I sit by my door tonight," he wrote on the evening of July 7, "that I too am at least a remote descendant of that heroic race of men of whom there is a tradition. I too sit here on the shore of my Ithaca, a fellow wanderer and survivor of Ulysses." Again and again in *Walden,* Thoreau would return to these same images drawn from the Greek and Latin epics, asserting the essential brotherhood between the adventurers of the mythic past and the truth-seeking voyager of the present. A

"The mass of men," as one of the most famous sentences in *Walden* puts it, "lead lives of quiet desperation." When he looked toward

B

Thoreau at Walden by N. C. Wyeth (1936). Tempera on panel, 42″ × 48″.

Private Collection, photograph courtesy of the Brandywine River Museum, Chadds Ford, Pennsylvania.

A. Connections
Another great writer who compared the life of the obscure modern individual with the heroic journeys of a Greek hero was James Joyce, in *Ulysses* (1922).

B. Humanities Connection: Responding to the Fine Art
? Look closely at Wyeth's rendering of Thoreau and his surroundings. What kind of person does Thoreau seem to be? What adjectives would you apply to him: Interesting? Thoughtful? Likable? Sociable? Lonely? Notice how Wyeth's use of light and shade helps to create a link between Thoreau and the landscape, and an aura around both.

A. Expansion
Despite his solitariness, Thoreau had many contacts with people, and most of the time he lived close to his extended family, which was large and full of interesting, eccentric characters. (Some of them were the kinds of followers of Emerson that Hawthorne complains about on page 203.) Thoreau, however, never wrote about his family—a fact that says a great deal about him.

B. Expansion
Thoreau's books did not do well in his lifetime. Of *A Week on the Concord and Merrimack Rivers,* only 294 copies were sold out of an edition of 1000. Thoreau had his publisher send him the remaining copies. He wrote in his journal: "I have now a library of nearly nine hundred volumes, over seven hundred of which I wrote myself."

town, Thoreau saw his prosperous fellow citizens so caught up in the material pursuits of making a living that they had become one-dimensional. When he looked along the site of the Fitchburg railway under construction within view of his cabin, he saw Irish railway workers in shanties living desperately poor lives, materially and spiritually. He hoped to wake them all up and show them that the heroic enterprise of confronting the "vital facts of life" lay literally in their own back yards.

Walden—one of the greatest works ever produced in America—owes much of its artistic success to Thoreau's successful blending of style and content. He looked to Nature, rather than to the stylists of the past, for a model. His style would be simple—at least on the surface. "Nature never indulges in exclamations," he wrote, "never says ah! or alas! She is not French. She is a plain writer, uses few gestures, does not add to her verbs, uses few adverbs, no expletives."

For Thoreau, as for Emerson and the Romantics who had preceded them, Nature itself was a form of language; behind its outward appearance, Nature contained spiritual reality. Nature spoke to us, if we could but understand the messages about those "vital facts" which "the gods meant to show us." A style that imitated Nature would also speak fundamental truths. Thoreau wished to write sentences "which lie like boulders on the page, up and down or across; which contain the seed of other sentences, not mere repetition, but creation; which a man might sell his grounds and castles to build."

Such a style rewards careful reading. Its paradoxes are not mere playfulness, but point to what Thoreau sees as a higher truth. A phrase like "I have traveled a good deal in Concord" contains in its apparent paradox the seeds of much of the book.

It was while he was at Walden that Thoreau's other famous act took place. As a protest against the Mexican War, which he and many others saw as an attempt to extend American slave-owning territory, Thoreau refused to pay his poll tax. He then spent a night in jail before someone paid the tax for him. Thoreau was vocally and radically opposed to slavery. While at Walden, and again in 1851 (after the Fugitive Slave Act had been passed), he helped fugitive slaves make their way to Canada. Near the end of his life, in 1859, he was one of the first defenders of John Brown, the radical abolitionist who staged a famous raid on the Federal arsenal at Harpers Ferry in Virginia.

Thoreau remained at Walden for a little more than two years. In 1847, he left the cabin and moved back into the Emersons' house, where he had received room and board before, in exchange for a few hours a day of odd jobs and gardening. During the next few years, he worked on *Walden* and "Resistance to Civil Government," which was delivered as a lecture in 1848 and published in 1849. Later called "Civil Disobedience," this essay asserted the primacy of the individual conscience and the need for action in keeping with that conscience. It had little immediate influence, but few essays have had such an overwhelming, long-range effect on human history. It was especially important in helping to inspire the form of passive resistance used by Mahatma Gandhi in India and, later, by Martin Luther King, Jr., in the United States.

Thoreau moved back into his father's house in 1849 and lived there the rest of his life. He supported himself by making pencils, taking odd jobs—he was an excellent carpenter, mason, and gardener—and doing survey work on the land around Concord that he knew so well. He became a kind of Concord recordkeeper, a fount of local knowledge about the amount of rainfall and snowfall and the first days of frost. He could predict to the day when each wildflower in the area would bloom. A

Walden was published in 1854 and was well enough received to expand Thoreau's reputation. His most widely read works, though, were his antislavery tract, "Slavery in Massachusetts," and "A Plea for Captain John Brown" (1860). B

In 1861, Thoreau caught a cold, and it soon became clear that beneath the cold lay incurable tuberculosis. He traveled that year to the Midwest in hopes that the change of air would help, but it did not. When he returned to Concord, he began working feverishly to put his work in final shape. He faced his coming death with great calm. The town constable, Sam Staples (who had jailed him for refusing to pay his poll tax), told Emerson that he "never saw a man dying with so much pleasure and peace."

"Henry, have you made your peace with God?" his aunt is said to have asked him toward his end. "Why, Aunt," he replied, "I didn't know we had ever quarreled."

SUPPLEMENTARY SUPPORT MATERIALS
1. Vocabulary Activity Worksheet (*CCB*)
2. Review and Response Worksheet: Theme (*CCB*)
3. Selection Test (*CCB*)

DEVELOPING VOCABULARY
The following words from the essays are tested in the Selection Test. (See also Vocabulary Activity Worksheet.)

impertinent	transient
dearth	superfluous
impervious	invidious
faculty	internecine
squatter	assiduously

PREPARATION
1. BUILDING ON PRIOR KNOWLEDGE. Elicit from students what they already know about *Walden.* Even if students have not read the selection, they may be familiar with the name of the pond from such sources as Trudeau's comic strip *Doonesbury.* Have students discuss their predictions about the content of the selection.

2. ESTABLISHING A PURPOSE. Have students read to determine the accuracy of their predictions.

Humanities Connection: Discussing the Photograph
Edward Steichen (1879–1973) was one of the great pioneers of photography who helped gain acceptance for it as an art form. In this photograph, Steichen is showing the pattern of light and shade and of the shapes of round stones at the bottom of the pond. If, however, the viewer forgets that these are specific objects in a specific place, and views them as a pattern, the photograph then becomes a work of abstract art, with design, movement, and harmony. It is no longer a representation of nature, but an object with an existence of its own.

WALDEN, OR LIFE IN THE WOODS

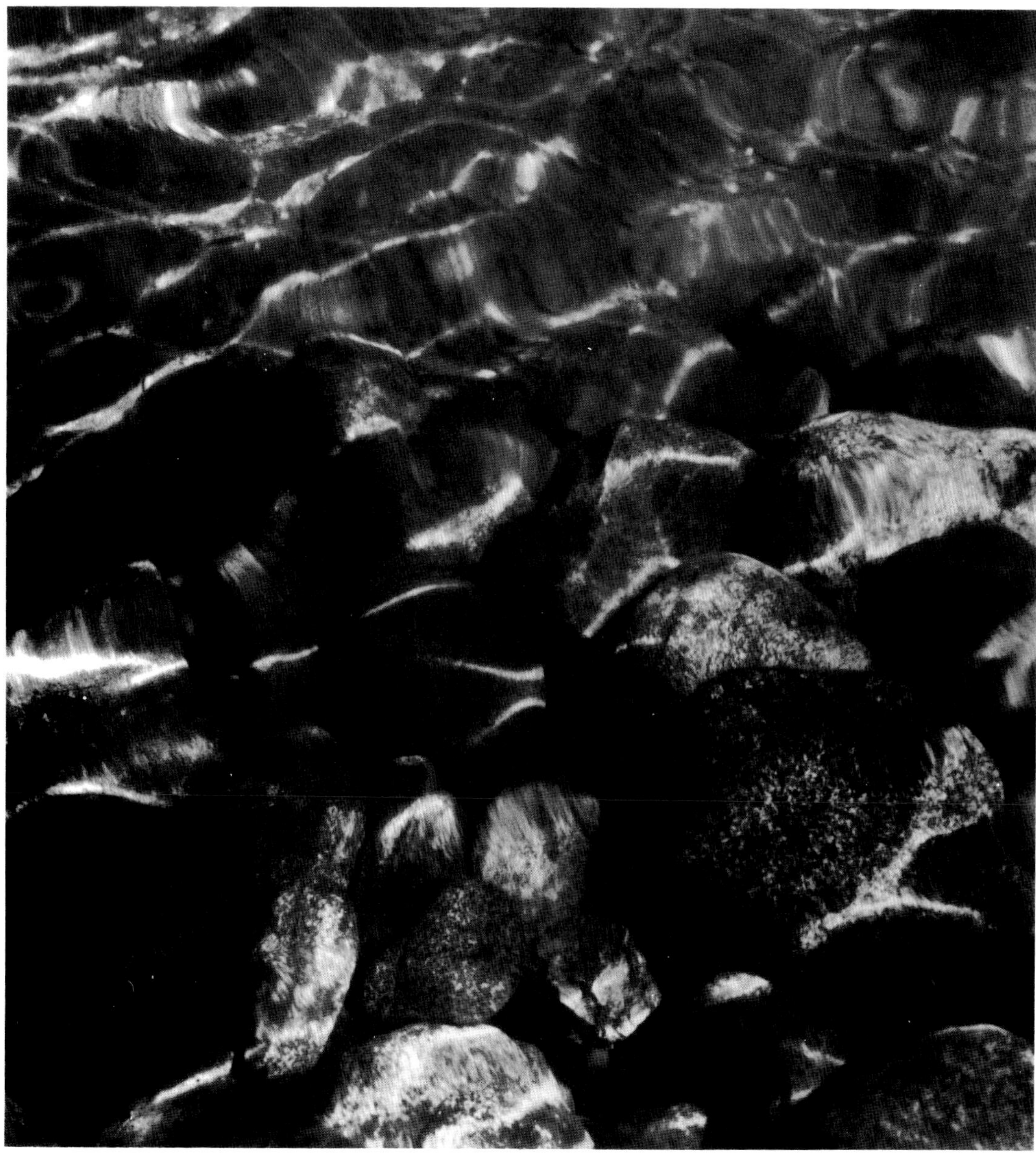

A photograph from the Walden Pond series by Edward Steichen (early 20th century).

International Museum of Photography at George Eastman House, Rochester, New York. Reprinted with the permission of Joanna T. Steichen.

Summary of excerpt from "Economy":
Thoreau describes the construction of his house at Walden Pond and his garden work there, in order to show the importance and feasibility of living a "stripped-down" lifestyle.

A. Responding
Do great works of literature have to be based upon great events? Can you think of others that are not? (In many cases, heroic subject matter does enhance the greatness of a work—*Moby-Dick*, page 297, is one of the outstanding examples in all literature. But many writers, such as E. B. White in "Death of a Pig," page 988, have found heroic meanings in the commonplace.)

B. Expansion
Chanticleer is the vain rooster in Chaucer's "The Nun's Priest's Tale."

C. Responding
Do you agree that the foremost requirement of a writer is "a simple and sincere account of his own life"? (It does seem to limit one's reading. And even if all autobiographies were sincere, it would still be useful to have biographies.)

A

A temporary move to a site on a large pond in Concord, Massachusetts, resulted in a work of literature that was to become an American classic. Thoreau moved to Walden because he wanted to find out what life is. That is a question people still ask; it is something people the world over have always asked, when they have had the leisure to think about it. As you read, imagine yourself in the woods near this pond. How would you have responded to a life that offered little more in excitement than a battle between ants, little more in company than the visit of a bird?

B

I do not propose to write an ode to dejection, but to brag as lustily as chanticleer in the morning, standing on his roost, if only to wake my neighbors up.

From
Economy

When I wrote the following pages, or rather the bulk of them, I lived alone, in the woods, a mile from any neighbor, in a house which I had built myself, on the shore of Walden Pond, in Concord, Massachusetts, and earned my living by the labor of my hands only. I lived there two years and two months. At present I am a sojourner in civilized life again.

I should not obtrude my affairs so much on the notice of my readers if very particular inquiries had not been made by my townsmen concerning my mode of life, which some would call impertinent, though they do not appear to me at all impertinent, but, considering the circumstances, very natural and pertinent. Some have asked what I got to eat; if I did not feel lonesome; if I was not afraid; and the like. Others have been curious to learn what portion of my income I devoted to charitable purposes; and some, who have large families, how many poor children I maintained. I will therefore ask those of my readers who feel no particular interest in me to pardon me if I undertake to answer some of these questions in this book. In most books, the *I*, or first person, is omitted; in this it will be retained; that, in respect to egotism, is the main difference. We commonly do not remember that it is, after all, always the first person that is speaking. I should not talk so much about myself if there were anybody else whom I knew as well. Unfortunately, I am confined to this theme by the narrowness of my experience. Moreover, I, on my side, require of every writer, first or last, a simple and sincere account of his own life, and not merely what he has heard of other men's lives; some such account as he would send to his kindred from a distant land; for if he has lived sincerely, it must have been in a distant land to me. Perhaps these pages are more particularly addressed to poor students. As for the rest of my readers, they will accept such portions as apply to them. I trust that none will stretch the seams in putting on the coat, for it may do good service to him whom it fits. . . . C

By the middle of April, for I made no haste in my work, but rather made the most of it, my house was framed and ready for the raising. I had already bought the shanty of James Collins, an Irishman who worked on the Fitchburg Railroad, for boards. James Collins' shanty was considered an uncommonly fine one. When I called to see it, he was not at home. I walked about the outside, at first unobserved from within, the window was so deep and high. It was of small dimensions, with a peaked cottage roof, and not much else to be seen, the dirt being raised five feet all around as if it were a compost heap. The roof was the soundest part, though a good deal warped and made brittle by the sun. Doorsill there was none, but a perennial passage for the hens under the door board. Mrs. C. came to the door and asked me to view it from the inside. The hens were driven in by my approach. It was dark, and had a dirt floor for the most part, dank, clammy, and aguish,[1] only here a board and there a board which would not bear removal. She lighted a lamp to show me the inside of the roof and the walls, and also that the board floor extended under the bed, warning me not to step into the cellar, a sort of dust hole two feet deep. In her own words, they were "good boards overhead, good boards all around, and a good window"—of two whole squares originally, only the cat had passed out that way lately. There was a stove, a bed, and a place to sit an infant in the house where it was born, a silk parasol, gilt-framed looking glass, and a patent new coffee mill nailed to an oak sapling, all told. The bargain was

1. **aguish:** likely to cause ague, or fever and chills.

Literature and Language: Supporting Main Ideas
Thoreau's aim in *Walden* is clearly expository: He wants to inform the reader about his experiences in the woods beside Walden Pond. Explain to students that the general formula for exposition is a series of main ideas supported by details, such as facts, examples, and statistics. (See also "Using the Expository and Persuasive Aims," page 1163.)

In the excerpt from "Economy," ask students to discover some support for each of these main ideas:

1. Thoreau's house did not cost much money. (page 211)

2. People can grow enough food for themselves on a small piece of land. (page 211)

After they read the excerpt from "Where I Lived and What I Lived For" (page 211), ask students to write a single sentence summarizing in their own words one of Thoreau's main ideas. Beneath this statement of main idea, have them list some supporting details. Students may work in pairs or small groups and compare their answers.

soon concluded, for James had in the meanwhile returned. I to pay four dollars and twenty-five cents tonight, he to vacate at five tomorrow morning, selling to nobody else meanwhile: I to take possession at six. It were well, he said, to be there early; and anticipate certain indistinct but wholly unjust claims on the score of ground rent and fuel. This he assured me was the only encumbrance. At six I passed him and his family on the road. One large bundle held their all—bed, coffee mill, looking glass, hens—all but the cat; she took to the woods and became a wild cat, and, as I learned afterward, trod in a trap set for woodchucks, and so became a dead cat at last. A

I took down this dwelling the same morning, drawing the nails, and removed it to the pond-side by small cartloads, spreading the boards on the grass there to bleach and warp back again in the sun. One early thrush gave me a note or two as I drove along the woodland path. I was informed treacherously by a young Patrick that neighbor Seeley, an Irishman, in the intervals of the carting, transferred the still tolerable, straight, and drivable nails, staples, and spikes to his pocket, and then stood when I came back to pass the time of day, and look freshly up, unconcerned, with spring thoughts, at the devastation; there being a dearth of work, as he said. He was there to represent spectatordom, and help make this seemingly insignificant event one with the removal of the gods of Troy.[2]

I dug my cellar in the side of a hill sloping to the south, where a woodchuck had formerly dug his burrow, down through sumach and blackberry roots, and the lowest stain of vegetation, six feet square by seven deep, to a fine sand where potatoes would not freeze in any winter. The sides were left shelving, and not stoned; but the sun having never shone on them, the sand still keeps its place. It was but two hours' work. I took particular pleasure in this breaking of ground, for in almost all latitudes men dig into the earth for an equable temperature. Under the most splendid house in the city is still to be found the cellar where they store their roots as of old, and long after the superstructure has disappeared posterity remark its dent in the earth. The house is still but a sort of porch at the entrance of a burrow.

At length, in the beginning of May, with the help of some of my acquaintances, rather to improve so good an occasion for neighborliness than from any necessity, I set up the frame of my house. No man was ever more honored in the character of his raisers[3] than I. They are destined, I trust, to assist at the raising of loftier structures one day. I began to occupy my house on the 4th of July, as soon as it was boarded and roofed, for the boards were carefully feather-edged and lapped,[4] so that it was perfectly impervious to rain; but before boarding I laid the foundation of a chimney at one end, bringing two cartloads of stones up the hill from the pond in my arms. I built the chimney after my hoeing in the fall, before a fire became necessary for warmth, doing my cooking in the meanwhile out of doors on the ground, early in the morning: which mode I still think is in some respects more convenient and agreeable than the usual one. When it stormed before my bread was baked, I fixed a few boards over the fire, and sat under them to watch my loaf, and passed some pleasant hours in that way. In those days, when my hands were much employed, I read but little, but the least scraps of paper which lay on the ground, my holder, or tablecloth, afforded me as much entertainment, in fact answered the same purpose as the *Iliad*.[5]

It would be worth the while to build still more deliberately than I did, considering, for instance, what foundation a door, a window, a cellar, a garret, have in the nature of man, and perchance never raising any superstructure until we found a better reason for it than our temporal necessities even. There is some of the same fitness in a man's building his own house that there is in a bird's building its own nest. Who knows but if men constructed their dwellings with their own hands, and provided food for themselves and families simply and honestly enough, the poetic faculty would be universally developed, as birds universally sing when they are so engaged? But alas! we do like cowbirds and cuckoos, which lay their eggs in B

2. **the gods of Troy:** the household gods of Aeneas, which he took with him after the fall of Troy (Virgil's *Aeneid*, Book II).

3. **raisers:** Thoreau's helpers included Emerson and the Transcendentalist writers Bronson Alcott and William Ellery Channing. Hence the pun in the next sentence.

4. **feather-edged and lapped:** the edges were cut at a 45-degree angle and overlapped.

5. **the *Iliad*:** Homer's epic about the Greek siege of Troy.

A. Responding
". . . and so became a dead cat at last." Thoreau's pungent style lent itself to humor.

? What does Thoreau's brand of humor say to you about Thoreau? (Students may suggest that it reinforces his practical nature; even his joke has a basis in factual reporting.)

B. Expansion
This passage indicates Thoreau's extreme scrupulousness. He wishes he had built his house—and, by implication, lived his life—even more deliberately than he did. "Temporal necessities"—what most people call "the realities of life"—seemed almost beneath his consideration, even in so practical a task as putting a roof over his head.

A. Humanities Connection: Responding to the Fine Art

? Why is the photograph metaphorically appropriate? (It depicts a nest, and Thoreau compares his house-raising to nest-building.)

A

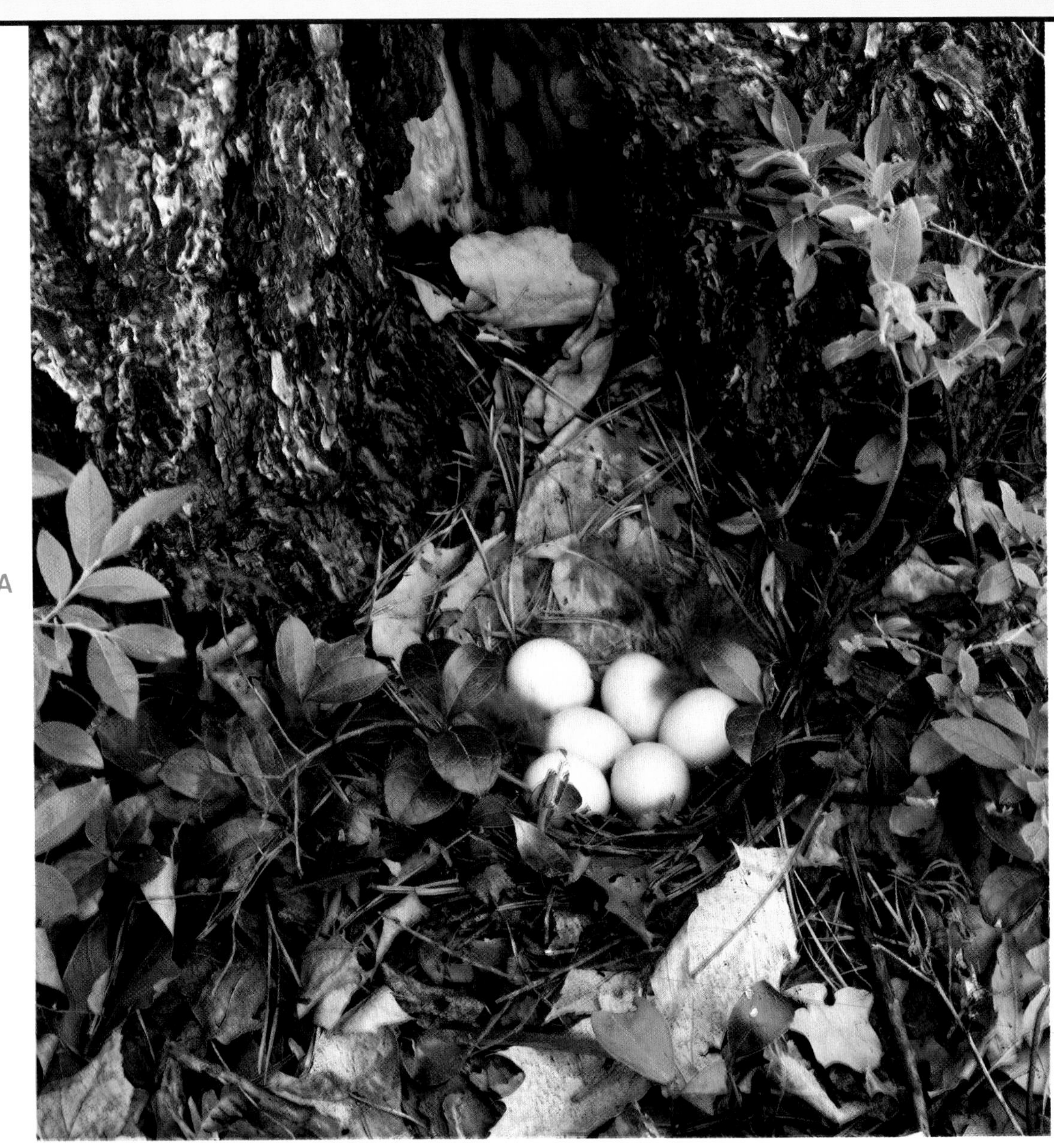

Photograph taken by Eliot Porter to illustrate the writings of Thoreau, 1962.

Eliot Porter Archives, Amon Carter Museum, Forth Worth, Texas.

nests which other birds have built, and cheer no traveler with their chattering and unmusical notes. Shall we forever resign the pleasure of construction to the carpenter? What does architecture amount to in the experience of the mass of men? I never in all my walks came across a man engaged in so simple and natural an occupation as building his house. . . .

Before winter I built a chimney and shingled the sides of my house, which were already impervious to rain, with imperfect and sappy shingles made of the first slice of the log, whose edges I was obliged to straighten with a plane.

I have thus a tight-shingled and plastered house, ten feet wide by fifteen long, and eight-feet posts, with a garret and a closet, a large window on each side, two trapdoors, one door at the end, and a brick fireplace opposite. The exact cost of my house, paying the usual price for such materials as I used, but not counting the work, all of which was done by myself, was as follows; and I

Summary of excerpt from "Where I Lived and What I Lived For": Thoreau wants to live "deliberately" and "front only the essential facts of life."

give the details because very few are able to tell exactly what their houses cost, and fewer still, if any, the separate cost of the various materials which compose them:

A

Boards,	$8 03½	Mostly shanty boards
Refuse shingles for roof and sides,	4 00	
Laths,	1 25	
Two secondhand windows with glass,	2 43	
One thousand old brick,	4 00	
Two casks of lime,	2 40	That was high
Hair,	0 31	More than I needed
Mantle-tree iron,	0 15	
Nails,	3 90	
Hinges and screws,	0 14	
Latch,	0 10	
Chalk,	0 01	
Transportation,	1 40	I carried a good
In all,	$28 12½	part on my back

. . . Before I finished my house, wishing to earn ten or twelve dollars by some honest and agreeable method, in order to meet my unusual expenses, I planted about two acres and a half of light and sandy soil near it chiefly with beans, but also a small part with potatoes, corn, peas, and turnips. The whole lot contains eleven acres, mostly growing up to pines and hickories, and was sold the preceding season for eight dollars and eight cents an acre. One farmer said that it was "good for nothing but to raise cheeping squirrels on." I put no manure on this land, not being the owner, but merely a squatter, and not expecting to cultivate so much again, and I did not quite hoe it all once. I got out several cords of stumps in plowing, which supplied me with fuel for a long time, and left small circles of virgin mold, easily distinguishable through the summer by the greater luxuriance of the beans there. The dead and for the most part unmerchantable wood behind my house, and the driftwood from the pond, have supplied the remainder of my fuel. I was obliged to hire a team and a man for the plowing, though I held the plow myself. My farm outgoes for the first season were, for implements, seed, work, &c., $14.72½. The seed corn was given me. This never costs anything to speak of, unless you plant more than enough. I got twelve bushels of beans, and eighteen bushels of potatoes, beside some peas and sweet corn. The yellow corn and turnips were too late to come to anything. My whole income from the farm was

	$23 44,
Deducting the outgoes,	14 72½
there are left,	$ 8 71½

beside produce consumed and on hand at the time this estimate was made of the value of $4.50—the amount on hand much more than balancing a little grass which I did not raise. All things considered, that is, considering the importance of a man's soul and of today, notwithstanding the short time occupied by my experiment, nay, partly even because of its transient character, I believe that that was doing better than any farmer in Concord did that year. . . . B

From

Where I Lived and What I Lived For

C

I went to the woods because I wished to live deliberately, to front only the essential facts of life, and see if I could not learn what it had to teach, and not, when I came to die, discover that I had not lived. I did not wish to live what was not life, living is so dear; nor did I wish to practice resignation, unless it was quite necessary. I wanted to live deep and suck out all the marrow of life, to live so sturdily and Spartan-like as to put to rout all that was not life, to cut a broad swath and shave close, to drive life into a corner, and reduce it to its lowest terms, and, if it proved to be mean, why then to get the whole and genuine meanness of it, and publish its meanness to the world; or if it were sublime, to know it by experience, and be able to give a true account of it in my next excursion. For most men, it appears to me, are in a strange uncertainty about it, whether it is of the devil or of God, and have *somewhat hastily* concluded that it is the chief end of man here to "glorify God and enjoy Him forever."[6]

---

6. **"glorify . . . forever":** the answer to the question, Why did God make us?, from the *New England Primer.*

A. Responding
? We are reading the minute details of expenditures a man made on his house over a hundred years ago, yet it says something to us today. What does it say? Imagine that the average contemporary American homeowner presents, alongside Thoreau's, a list of his or her expenses for home improvement during a year. Which list would "grab" us more? Why should there be so much emotional difference between two simple lists? (Thoreau actually *built* his house.)

B. Responding
? Why does Thoreau believe that he did better with his small profit than any other farmer in Concord? (Because the experiment was good for his soul)

C. Expansion
The first paragraph of "Where I Lived and What I Lived For," in which Thoreau explains why he goes to the woods, is excellent for reading aloud.

Summary of excerpt from "Solitude": Thoreau describes his pleasure at being alone in nature and says that it is minds rather than space that separates people.

A. Responding
"Simplify, simplify" is one of Thoreau's most famous aphorisms. Another on this page is, "We do not ride on the railroad; it rides upon us."
? Based on your own experience, what application do these aphorisms have for modern life? (Answers will vary. Class discussion should include students' thoughts on materialism in contemporary American society)

B. Responding
? Do Americans need more solitude? As a nation, do you feel that we are too obsessed with not spending our hours in solitude, with spending them instead with the electronic company of television or video movies or with disembodied company via telephone? (Answers will vary; encourage class discussion.)

Still we live meanly, like ants; though the fable tells us that we were long ago changed into men;[7] like pygmies we fight with cranes; it is error upon error, and clout upon clout, and our best virtue has for its occasion a superfluous and evitable wretchedness. Our life is frittered away by detail. An honest man has hardly need to count more than his ten fingers, or in extreme cases he may add his ten toes, and lump the rest. Simplicity, simplicity, simplicity! I say, let your affairs be as two or three, and not a hundred or a thousand; instead of a million count half a dozen, and keep your accounts on your thumbnail. In the midst of this chopping sea of civilized life, such are the clouds and storms and quicksands and thousand-and-one items to be allowed for, that a man has to live, if he would not founder and go to the bottom and not make his port at all, by dead reckoning, and he must be a great calculator indeed

A who succeeds. Simplify, simplify. Instead of three meals a day, if it be necessary eat but one; instead of a hundred dishes, five; and reduce other things in proportion. Our life is like a German Confederacy[8] made up of petty states, with its boundary forever fluctuating, so that even a German cannot tell you how it is bounded at any moment. The nation itself, with all its so-called internal improvements, which, by the way, are all external and superficial, is just such an unwieldy and overgrown establishment, cluttered with furniture and tripped up by its own traps, ruined by luxury and heedless expense, by want of calculation and a worthy aim, as the million households in the land; and the only cure for it as for them is in a rigid economy, a stern and more than Spartan simplicity of life and elevation of purpose. It lives too fast. Men think that it is essential that the *Nation* have commerce, and export ice, and talk through a telegraph, and ride thirty miles an hour, without a doubt, whether *they* do or not; but whether we should live like baboons or like men, is a little uncertain. If we do not get out sleepers,[9] and forge rails, and devote days and nights to the work, but go to tinkering upon our *lives* to improve *them,* who will build railroads? And if railroads are not built, how shall we get to heaven in season? But if we stay at home and mind our business, who will want railroads? We do not ride on the railroad; it rides upon us. Did you ever think what those sleepers are that underlie the railroad? Each one is a man, an Irishman, or a Yankee man. The rails are laid on them, and they are covered with sand, and the cars run smoothly over them. They are sound sleepers, I assure you. And every few years a new lot is laid down and run over; so that, if some have the pleasure of riding on a rail, others have the misfortune to be ridden upon. And when they run over a man that is walking in his sleep, a supernumerary sleeper in the wrong position, and wake him up, they suddenly stop the cars, and make a hue and cry about it, as if this were an exception. I am glad to know that it takes a gang of men for every five miles to keep the sleepers down and level in their beds as it is, for this is a sign that they may sometime get up again.

7. **the fable . . . men:** in a Greek fable, Zeus changed ants into men. In the *Iliad,* Homer compares the Trojans to cranes fighting with pygmies.
8. **German Confederacy:** at the time Thoreau was writing, Germany was not yet a unified nation.
9. **sleepers:** railroad ties, so called because they lie flat.

From
Solitude

Some of my pleasantest hours were during the long rainstorms in the spring or fall, which confined me to the house for the afternoon as well as the forenoon, soothed by their ceaseless roar and pelting; when an early twilight ushered in a long evening in which many thoughts had time to take root and unfold themselves. In those driving northeast rains which tried the village houses so, when the maids stood ready with mop and pail in front entries to keep the deluge out; I sat behind my door in my little house, which was all entry, and thoroughly enjoyed its protection. In one heavy thundershower the lightning struck a large pitch pine across the pond, making a very conspicuous and perfectly regular spiral groove from top to bottom, an inch or more deep, and four or five inches wide, as you would groove a walking stick. I passed it again the other day, and was struck with awe on looking up and beholding that mark, now more distinct than ever, where a terrific and resistless bolt came down out of the harmless sky eight years ago. Men frequently say to me, "I should think you would feel B lonesome down there, and want to be nearer folks, rainy and snowy days and nights especially." I am tempted to reply to such—This whole earth which we inhabit is but a point in space. How far apart, think you, dwell the two most distant inhabitants of yonder star, the breadth of whose disk cannot be appreciated by our instruments? Why should I feel lonely? is not our planet in the Milky Way? This which you put seems to me not to be the most important question. What sort of space is that which separates a man from his fellows and makes him solitary? I have found that no exertion of the legs can bring two minds much nearer to one another. What do we want most to dwell near to? Not to many men surely, the depot, the post office, the barroom, the meetinghouse, the schoolhouse, the grocery, Beacon Hill, or the Five Points,[10] where men most congregate, but to the perennial source of our life, whence in all our experience we have found that to issue; as the willow stands near the water and sends out its roots in that direction. This will vary with different natures, but this is the place where a wise man will dig his cellar. . . .

A

From

The Bean-Field

Meanwhile my beans, the length of whose rows, added together, was seven miles already planted, were impatient to be hoed, for the earliest had grown considerably before the latest were in the ground; indeed they were not easily to be put off. What was the meaning of this so steady and self-respecting, this small Herculean labor, I knew not. I came to love my rows, my beans, though so many more than I wanted. They attached me to the earth, and so I got strength like Antæus.[11] But why should I raise them? Only Heaven knows. This was my curious labor all summer—to make this portion of the earth's surface, which had yielded only cinquefoil, blackberries, johnswort, and the like, before, sweet wild fruits and pleasant flowers, produce instead this pulse.[12] What shall I learn of beans or beans of me? I cherish them, I hoe them, early and late I have an eye to them; and this is my day's work. It is a fine broad leaf to look on. My auxiliaries are the dews and rains which water this dry soil, and what fertility is in the soil itself, which for the most part is lean and effete. My enemies are worms, cool days, and most of all woodchucks. The last have nibbled for me a quarter of an acre clean. But what right had I to oust johnswort and the rest, and break up their ancient herb garden? Soon, however, the remaining beans will be too tough for them, and go forward to meet new foes. . . .

It was a singular experience that long acquaintance which I cultivated with beans, what with planting, and hoeing, and harvesting, and threshing, and picking over, and selling them—the last was the hardest of all—I might add eating, for I did taste. I was determined to know beans. When they were growing, I used to hoe from five o'clock in the morning till noon, and commonly spent the rest of the day about other affairs. Consider the intimate and curious acquaintance one makes with various kinds of weeds—it will bear some iteration in the account, for there was no little iteration in the labor—disturbing their delicate organizations so ruthlessly, and making such invidious distinctions with his hoe, leveling whole ranks of one species, and sedulously cultivating another. That's Roman wormwood, that's pigweed, that's sorrel, that's pipergrass—have at him, chop him up, turn his roots upward to the sun, don't let him have a fiber in the shade; if you do he'll turn himself t'other side up and be as green as a leek in two days. A long war, not with cranes, but with weeds, those Trojans who had sun and rain and dews on their side. Daily the beans saw me come to their rescue armed with a hoe, and thin the ranks of their enemies, filling up the trenches with weedy dead. Many a lusty, crest-waving Hector,[13] that towered a whole foot above his crowding comrades, fell before my weapon and rolled in the dust. . . .

B

C

10. **Beacon Hill . . . Five Points:** well-known busy areas of nineteenth-century Boston and New York.

11. **Antaeus** (an·tē′əs): in Greek mythology, the giant who drew strength from the earth, his mother.

12. **pulse:** beans, peas, and other legumes.

13. **Hector:** in the *Iliad,* Hector was the Trojan prince killed by the Greek hero Achilles.

Summary of excerpt from "The Bean-Field": Thoreau describes his planting and hoeing of beans and his battles against weeds, using metaphors from Greek mythology.

A. Responding
? Do you agree that "no exertion of the legs can bring two minds much nearer to one another"? (Student answers may include a discussion of what constitutes a basis for mutual understanding.)

B. Expansion
"I was determined to know beans" is a witticism aimed at the common saying, "He doesn't know beans." Thoreau may have been responding to his Concord neighbors who thought of him as a crank.

C. Expansion
In this chapter Thoreau again draws the comparison between the ordinary labors of ordinary people and the heroic acts of Greek myth, making ordinary labor also seem heroic.

Summary of excerpt from "Brute Neighbors": Thoreau describes a battle between black ants and red ants, drawing parallels with human warfare. He also describes loons and hunters trying to outwit each other on Walden Pond.

A. Responding
? How do you feel about Thoreau's depiction of the ant war? Do you think that he is making too much out of a small thing? Or that he is revealing an important truth? What impression do you have of Thoreau's personality, based on this section? In particular, based on his comparisons between ants and people? (Thoreau's account makes us realize that, although they are tiny insects, they are giving up their lives for some reason. Thoreau appears to take *all* life seriously, yet he ridicules the great battles of our own past.)

From
Brute Neighbors

A One day when I went out to my woodpile, or rather my pile of stumps, I observed two large ants, the one red, the other much larger, nearly half an inch long, and black, fiercely contending with one another. Having once got hold they never let go, but struggled and wrestled and rolled on the chips incessantly. Looking farther, I was surprised to find that the chips were covered with such combatants, that it was not a *duellum,* but a *bellum,*[14] a war between two races of ants, the red always pitted against the black, and frequently two red ones to one black. The legions of these Myrmidons[15] covered all the hills and vales in my wood-yard, and the ground was already strewn with the dead and dying, both red and black. It was the only battle which I have ever witnessed, the only battlefield I ever trod while the battle was raging; internecine war; the red republicans on the one hand, and the black imperialists on the other. On every side they were engaged in deadly combat, yet without any noise that I could hear, and human soldiers never fought so resolutely. I watched a couple that were fast locked in each other's embraces, in a little sunny valley amid the chips, now at noonday prepared to fight till the sun went down, or life went out. The smaller red champion had fastened himself like a vice to his adversary's front, and through all the tumblings on that field never for an instant ceased to gnaw at one of his feelers near the root, having already caused the other to go by the board; while the stronger black one dashed him from side to side, and, as I saw on looking nearer, had already divested him of several of his members. They fought with more pertinacity than bulldogs. Neither manifested the least disposition to retreat. It was evident that their battle cry was Conquer or die. In the meanwhile there came along a single red ant on the hillside of this valley, evidently full of excitement, who either had despatched his foe, or had not yet taken part in the battle; probably the latter, for he had lost none of his limbs: whose mother had charged him to return with his shield or upon it.[16] Or perchance he was some Achilles, who had nourished his wrath apart, and had now come to avenge or rescue his Patroclus.[17] He saw this unequal combat from afar—for the blacks were nearly twice the size of the red—he drew near with rapid pace till he stood on his guard within half an inch of the combatants; then, watching his opportunity, he sprang upon the black warrior, and commenced his operations near the root of his right foreleg, leaving the foe to select among his own members; and so there were three united for life, as if a new kind of attraction had been invented which put all other locks and cements to shame. I should not have wondered by this time to find that they had their respective musical bands stationed on some eminent chip, and playing their national airs the while, to excite the show and cheer the dying combatants. I was myself excited somewhat even as if they had been men. The more you think of it, the less the difference. And certainly there is not the fight recorded in Concord history, at least, if in the history of America, that will bear a moment's comparison with this, whether for the numbers engaged in it, or for the patriotism and heroism displayed. For numbers and for carnage it was an Austerlitz or Dresden.[18] Concord Fight! Two killed on the patriots' side, and Luther Blanchard wounded! Why here every ant was a Buttrick—"Fire! for God's sake fire!"—and thousands shared the fate of Davis and Hosmer.[19] There was not one hireling there. I have no doubt that it was a principle they fought for, as much as our ancestors, and not to avoid a three-penny tax on their tea; and the results of this battle will be as important and memorable to those whom it concerns as those of the battle of Bunker Hill, at least.

I took up the chip on which the three I have particularly described were struggling, carried it into my house, and placed it under a tumbler on my windowsill, in order to see the issue. Holding a microscope to the first-mentioned red ant, I saw

14. **not a *duellum,* but a *bellum:*** not a duel, but a war.
15. **Myrmidons:** Achilles' soldiers in the *Iliad. Myrmex* is Greek for "ant."
16. **return . . . upon it:** the traditional charge of Spartan mothers to their warrior sons.
17. **Achilles . . . Patroclus:** Achilles withdrew from the battle at Troy but returned after his friend Patroclus was killed.
18. **Austerlitz or Dresden:** major battles of the Napoleonic Wars.
19. **Concord . . . Hosmer:** at the battle of Concord, Major John Buttrick led the Minutemen, who defeated the British. Davis and Hosmer were the two Americans killed.

that, though he was assiduously gnawing at the near foreleg of his enemy, having severed his remaining feeler, his own breast was all torn away, exposing what vitals he had there to the jaws of the black warrior, whose breastplate was apparently too thick for him to pierce; and the dark carbuncles of the sufferer's eyes shone with ferocity such as war only could excite. They struggled half an hour longer under the tumbler, and when I looked again the black soldier had severed the heads of his foes from their bodies, and the still-living heads were hanging on either side of him like ghastly trophies at his saddlebow, still apparently as firmly fastened as ever, and he was endeavoring with feeble struggles, being without feelers and with only the remnant of a leg, and I know not how many other wounds, to divest himself of them; which at length, after half an hour more, he accomplished. I raised the glass, and he went off over the windowsill in that crippled state. Whether he finally survived that combat, and spent the remainder of his days in some Hotel des Invalides,[20] I do not know; but I thought that his industry would not be worth much thereafter. I never learned which party was victorious, nor the cause of the war; but I felt for the rest of that day as if I had had my feelings excited and harrowed by witnessing the struggle, the ferocity and carnage, of a human battle before my door.

A

In the fall the loon *(Colymbus glacialis)* came, as usual, to molt and bathe in the pond, making the woods ring with his wild laughter before I had risen. At rumor of his arrival all the Mill-dam sportsmen are on the alert, in gigs and on foot, two by two and three by three, with patent rifles and conical balls and spyglasses. They come rustling through the woods like autumn leaves, at least ten men to one loon. Some station themselves on this side of the pond, some on that, for the poor bird cannot be omnipresent; if he dive here he must come up there. But now the kind October wind rises, rustling the leaves and rippling the surface of the water, so that no loon can be heard or seen, though his foes sweep the pond with spyglasses, and make the woods resound with their discharges. The waves generously rise and dash angrily, taking sides with all waterfowl, and our sportsmen must beat a retreat to town and shop and unfinished jobs. But they were too often successful. When I went to get a pail of water early in the morning, I frequently saw this stately bird sailing out of my cove within a few rods. If I endeavored to overtake him in a boat, in order to see how he would maneuver, he would dive and be completely lost, so that I did not discover him again, sometimes, till the latter part of the day. But I was more than a match for him on the surface. He commonly went off in a rage.

B

As I was paddling along the north shore one very calm October afternoon—for such days especially they settle on to the lakes, like the milkweed down—having looked in vain over the pond for a loon, suddenly one, sailing out from the shore toward the middle a few rods in front of me, set up his wild laugh and betrayed himself. I pursued with a paddle and he dived, but when he came up I was nearer than before. He dived again, but I miscalculated the direction he would take, and we were fifty rods apart when he came to the surface this time, for I had helped to widen the interval; and again he laughed long and loud, and with more reason than before. He maneuvered so cunningly that I could not get within half a dozen rods of him. Each time, when he came to the surface, turning his head this way and that, he coolly surveyed the water and the land, and apparently chose his course so that he might come up where there was the widest expanse of water and at the greatest distance from the boat. It was surprising how quickly he made up his mind and put his resolve into execution. He led me at once to the widest part of the pond, and could not be driven from it. While he was thinking one thing in his brain, I was endeavoring to divine his thought in mine. It was a pretty game, played on the smooth surface of the pond, a man against a loon. Suddenly your adversary's checker disappears beneath the board, and the problem is to place yours nearest to where his will appear again. Sometimes he would come up unexpectedly on the opposite side of me, having apparently passed directly under the boat. So long-winded was he and so unweariable, that when he had swum farthest he would immediately plunge again, nevertheless; and then no wit could divine where in the deep pond, beneath the smooth surface, he might be speeding his way like a fish, for he had time and ability to visit the bottom of the pond in its deepest part. It is said that loons have been caught in the New York lakes eighty feet beneath the surface, with hooks set for trout—though Walden is deeper

20. **Hotel des Invalides:** the old soldiers' home in Paris.

A. Attitude
? Are Thoreau's sympathies with the loon or the hunters? How can you tell? (The writer's sympathies are obviously with the loon. The loons are depicted as the natural inhabitants, the hunters as the intruders who outnumber the birds ten to one. Also, the woods ring with the laughter of the loons and resound with the discharges of the hunters' guns. Even the waves take sides with the "poor" birds.)

B. Expansion
Thoreau's description of the loon is a relatively discursive piece of nature writing, in contrast with his more compact, aphoristic philosophical passages. But the loon passage in its entirety can be read as a philosophical metaphor on the relationship between people and nature, or between people and the underlying realities of existence.

Summary of excerpt from "Conclusion":
Thoreau summarizes and universalizes the experiences of his two years at Walden Pond.

CLOSURE
In class discussion, elicit from students how the ideas expressed in each of the following sentences from *Walden* is central to the ideas expressed in the essay.

- "How worn and dusty, then, must be the highways of the world, how deep the ruts of tradition and conformity."
- "In proportion as he simplifies his life, the laws of the universe will appear less complex, and solitude will not be solitude."

than that. How surprised must the fishes be to see this ungainly visitor from another sphere speeding his way amid their schools! Yet he appeared to know his course as surely under water as on the surface, and swam much faster there. Once or twice I saw a ripple where he approached the surface, just put his head out to reconnoiter, and instantly dived again. I found that it was as well for me to rest on my oars and wait his reappearing as to endeavor to calculate where he would rise; for again and again, when I was straining my eyes over the surface one way, I would suddenly be startled by his unearthly laugh behind me. But why, after displaying so much cunning, did he invariably betray himself the moment he came up by that loud laugh? Did not his white breast enough betray him? He was indeed a silly loon, I thought. I could commonly hear the plash of the water when he came up, and so also detected him. But after an hour he seemed as fresh as ever, dived as willingly and swam yet farther than at first. It was surprising to see how serenely he sailed off with unruffled breast when he came to the surface, doing all the work with his webbed feet beneath. His usual note was this demoniac laughter, yet somewhat like that of a waterfowl; but occasion-

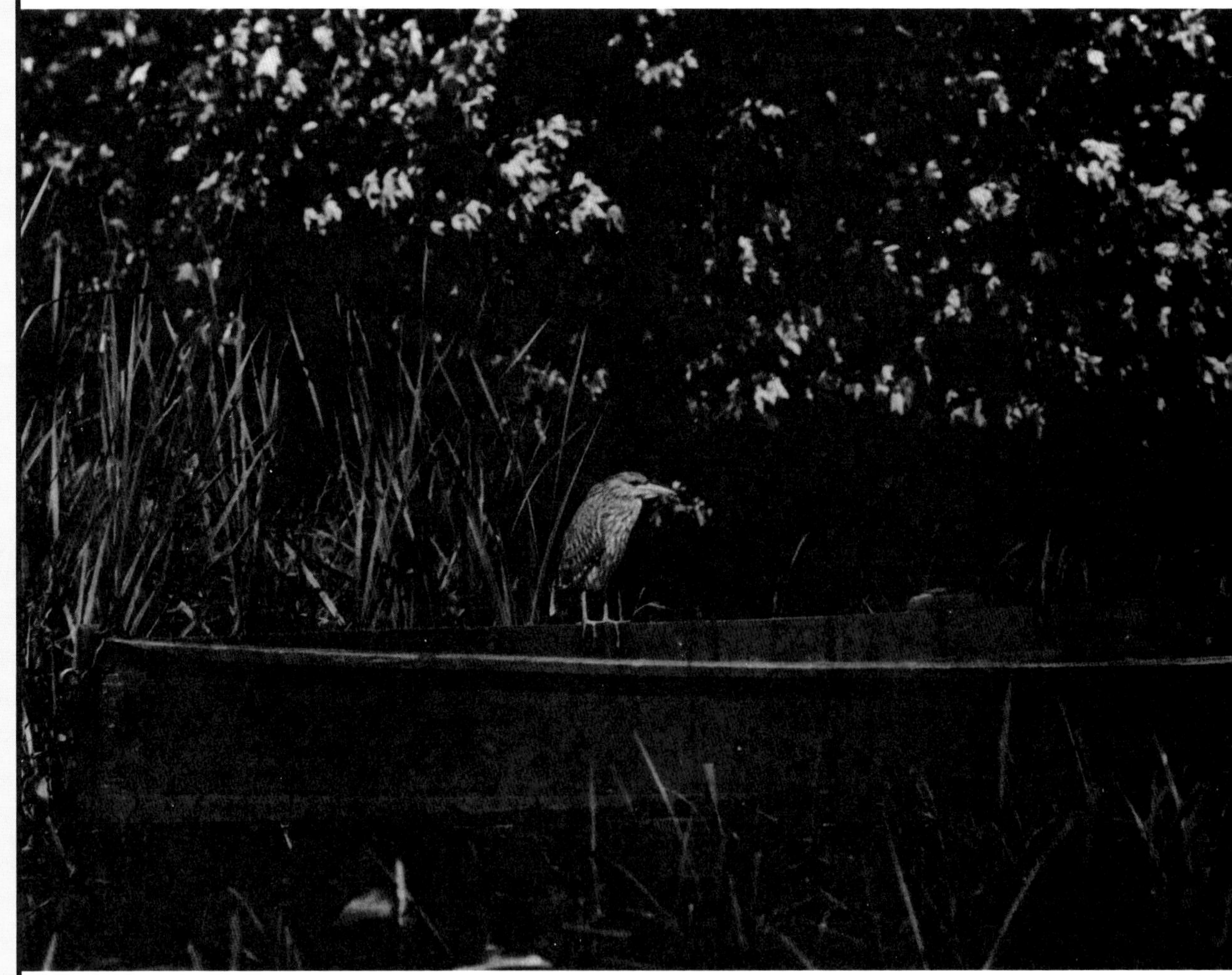

On the Concord Banks, a River Boat, and American Bittern, a photograph by Herbert W. Gleason (early 20th century).

Concord Free Public Library, Concord, Massachusetts.

Reading Check Test

1. Thoreau gathers the material and builds the house without help from neighbors. *False*
2. Thoreau hoped to earn some money from his crops; however, he just breaks even after deducting planting and seed costs. *False*
3. A laughing loon easily outwits the naturalist as he chases the bird around Walden Pond in a small boat. *True*
4. Thoreau says he left Walden Pond because he had other lives to lead and did not want to fall into a worn routine. *True*
5. Thoreau tells his readers they should all live as he did, for only by living away from society and with nature is man able to know his possibilities. *False*

ally, when he had balked me most successfully and come up a long way off, he uttered a long-drawn unearthly howl, probably more like that of a wolf than any bird; as when a beast puts his muzzle to the ground and deliberately howls. This was his looning—perhaps the wildest sound that is ever heard here, making the woods ring far and wide. I concluded that he laughed in derision of my efforts, confident of his own resources. Though the sky was by this time overcast, the pond was so smooth that I could see where he broke the surface when I did not hear him. His white breast, the stillness of the air, and the smoothness of the water were all against him. At length, having come up fifty rods off, he uttered one of those prolonged howls, as if calling on the god of loons to aid him, and immediately there came a wind from the east and rippled the surface, and filled the whole air with misty rain, and I was impressed as if it were the prayer of the loon answered, and his god was angry with me; and so I left him disappearing far away on the tumultuous surface.

From
Conclusion

I left the woods for as good a reason as I went there. Perhaps it seemed to me that I had several more lives to live, and could not spare any more time for that one. It is remarkable how easily and insensibly we fall into a particular route, and make a beaten track for ourselves. I had not lived there a week before my feet wore a path from my door to the pond-side; and though it is five or six years since I trod it, it is still quite distinct. It is true, I fear that others may have fallen into it, and so helped to keep it open. The surface of the earth is soft and impressible by the feet of men; and so with the paths which the mind travels. How worn and dusty, then, must be the highways of the world, how deep the ruts of tradition and conformity! I did not wish to take a cabin passage, but rather to go before the mast and on the deck of the world, for there I could best see the moonlight amid the mountains. I do not wish to go below now.

I learned this, at least, by my experiment; that if one advances confidently in the direction of his dreams, and endeavors to live the life which he has imagined, he will meet with a success unexpected in common hours. He will put some things behind, will pass an invisible boundary; new, universal, and more liberal laws will begin to establish themselves around and within him; or the old laws be expanded, and interpreted in his favor in a more liberal sense, and he will live with the license of a higher order of beings. In proportion as he simplifies his life, the laws of the universe will appear less complex, and solitude will not be solitude, nor poverty poverty, nor weakness weakness. If you have built castles in the air, your work need not be lost; that is where they should be. Now put the foundations under them. . . .

Some are dinning in our ears that we Americans, and moderns generally, are intellectual dwarfs compared with the ancients, or even the Elizabethan men. But what is that to the purpose? A living dog is better than a dead lion.[21] Shall a man go and hang himself because he belongs to the race of pygmies, and not be the biggest pygmy that he can? Let everyone mind his own business, and endeavor to be what he was made.

Why should we be in such desperate haste to succeed, and in such desperate enterprises? If a man does not keep pace with his companions, perhaps it is because he hears a different drummer. Let him step to the music which he hears, however measured or far away. It is not important that he should mature as soon as an apple tree or an oak. Shall he turn his spring into summer? If the condition of things which we were made for is not yet, what were any reality which we can substitute? We will not be shipwrecked on a vain reality. Shall we with pains erect a heaven of blue glass over ourselves, though when it is done we shall be sure to gaze still at the true ethereal heaven far above, as if the former were not? . . .

The life in us is like the water in the river. It may rise this year higher than man has ever known it, and flood the parched uplands; even this may be the eventful year, which will drown out all our muskrats. It was not always dry land where we dwell. I see far inland the banks which the stream anciently washed, before science began to record its freshets. Everyone has heard the story which has gone the rounds of New England, of a strong and beautiful bug which came out of the dry leaf of an old table of apple-tree wood, which had

21. **living dog . . . dead lion:** from Ecclesiastes 9:4.

ANALYZING THE ESSAYS
Identifying Facts

1. Because so many of his neighbors have asked him questions about his experiment in living at Walden.

That he does not know anybody else as well as he knows himself, and that—when *he* reads a book—he requires of every writer "a simple and sincere account of his own life."

2. People building their own houses might resemble birds, who build their own nests; perhaps "the poetic faculty" would be "universally developed."

3. He says he went to the woods to live because he wanted to live simply enough to confront the essential facts of life.

4. Since the earth is but a point in space, it is nonsense to assume that he would be lonely while at Walden.

That which really isolates them, Thoreau argues, is their removal from nature, the "perennial source of our life."

5. Thoreau rejoices in looking at the fine plants; he takes pleasure in battling worms, cool days, and woodchucks.

He compares his weeding to an epic battle against the Trojans.

6. That if we advance confidently in the direction of our dreams, we will meet with

A. Expansion
The last four sentences are ringing and apocalyptic. You might ask students to paraphrase them in order to discuss their meaning.

stood in a farmer's kitchen for sixty years, first in Connecticut, and afterward in Massachusetts—from an egg deposited in the living tree many years earlier still, as appeared by counting the annual layers beyond it; which was heard gnawing out for several weeks, hatched perchance by the heat of an urn. Who does not feel his faith in a resurrection and immortality strengthened by hearing of this? Who knows what beautiful and winged life, whose egg has been buried for ages under many concentric layers of woodenness in the dead, dry life of society, deposited at first in the alburnum[22] of the green and living tree, which has been gradually converted into the semblance of its well-seasoned tomb—heard perchance gnawing out now for years by the astonished family of man, as they sat round the festive board—may unexpectedly come forth from amid society's most trivial and handselled[23] furniture, to enjoy its perfect summer life at last!

I do not say that John or Jonathan[24] will realize all this; but such is the character of that morrow which mere lapse of time can never make to dawn. The light which puts out our eyes is darkness to us. Only that day dawns to which we are awake. There is more day to dawn. The sun is but a morning star. A

THE END

22. **alburnum:** sapwood.

23. **handselled:** given as a mere token of good wishes; hence, of no great value in itself.

24. **John or Jonathan:** John Bull and Brother Jonathan were traditional personifications of Britain and the United States.

Responding to the Essays

Analyzing the Essays

Identifying Facts

1. According to the second paragraph in "Economy," why has Thoreau decided to write about his life? How does he justify talking primarily about himself?
2. What does Thoreau think would happen if we made our houses with our own hands?
3. How does Thoreau answer the questions implied in the title "Where I Lived and What I Lived For"?
4. What arguments does Thoreau present in "Solitude" to demonstrate that he is not lonely in his isolated situation? What kind of space does he suggest *really* isolates human beings?
5. What satisfactions does Thoreau find in the labor of raising beans (in "The Bean-Field")? How does he find humor and whimsy even in the task of weeding?
6. In his "Conclusion," what does Thoreau say he learned from his experiment?

Interpreting Meanings

7. Why do you think Thoreau goes to the trouble of itemizing the exact cost of his house? What might he have wanted to prove to his Concord neighbors?
8. What does Thoreau mean when he says "Simplify, simplify" (page 212)? Do you think he has a valid point here? Explain.
9. How would you summarize Thoreau's ideas on progress, as exemplified by what he says about the railroad and other forms of new technology? Do you agree with him? Why or why not?
10. Thoreau was a great observer of nature, though he was not a scientist. Compare Thoreau's description of the war between the ants and his game with the loon in "Brute Neighbors." In each case, what does he find in the natural occurrence that is remarkable or valuable?
11. What do you think is the lesson of the fable of the apple-wood table at the conclusion of *Walden*?
12. Do you see evidences of the Romantic point of view in *Walden*—the emphasis on intuition, on the power in nature, and on human emotions? Explain.
13. What do you think Thoreau means in his final paragraph by the words, "Only that day dawns to which we are awake"?
14. Find at least two passages from these essays that you think pertain to life today. Describe the situations or the people each quotation might apply to or appeal to.
15. Suppose a Puritan, like William Bradford (page 11), Mary Rowlandson (page 23), Jonathan Edwards (page 36), or Anne Bradstreet (page 42), had spent time in Walden and were recording these same experiences. How might their journal entries differ from Thoreau's?

a success we never imagined. If we simplify our life, we will be able to live in harmony with higher laws and at peace with ourselves.

Interpreting Meanings

7. Students may have differing opinions. Possibly, that very few things are really essential for life, and that it is possible for human beings to shelter themselves for a very small outlay.

8. We should always strive to cut through the nonessential aspects of our lives so that we can concentrate on the most important things.
Student answers will vary.

9. Thoreau is skeptical about progress.
Student answers will vary.

10. In the war between the ants, Thoreau marvels at the tenacity of the two warring parties. The battle suggests to Thoreau the carnage and waste of human battles and wars. Perhaps he implies that all wars are futile.

In his game with the loon, Thoreau is struck by the wild laughter and the cunning maneuvers of the bird. Thoreau wonders why the bird announces its whereabouts; but he then concludes that the loon's laughter mocks his efforts to come closer to it.

11. Thoreau's lesson concerns resurrection and immortality: he says that beauty may come forth from even the most trivial things in life, "to enjoy its perfect summer life at last."

12. Students should be able to identify numerous instances of a Romantic point of view in *Walden.*

13. In order to enjoy the role of nature in our lives, we must take the trouble to observe nature carefully—or, in his metaphor, to actually "awake" to the "dawn" of each day.

14. Student answers will vary. Try "Why should we be in such desperate haste to succeed . . .?" (page 217)

15. A Puritan would have (a) seen examples of God's providence, (b) read moral lessons in nature, and (c) read allegorical meaning in his or her experiences.

Writing About the Essays

A Creative Response

1. **Writing a Journal Entry.** *Walden* does not record monumental events; it records the day-to-day ordinary events that most people would let pass by unnoticed. But in these events, Thoreau can find something interesting. Try to think like Thoreau for a day: At the end of the day, record in a journal what you saw, what you heard, and what you thought. Did anything remind you of books you have read? Did anything convey a lesson? Did you find a message in any event?
2. **Writing from Another Point of View.** Suppose Benjamin Franklin (see page 72) had lived at Walden Pond for a time. Write an entry that Franklin might have recorded in his journal. What lessons or morals might the rationalist Franklin have found in his experience?

A Critical Response

3. **Developing a Topic.** "The invariable mark of wisdom," Emerson wrote, "is to find the miraculous in the common." Using Emerson's statement as your topic sentence, choose a scene from *Walden* and discuss how Thoreau finds "the miraculous in the common."
4. **Comparing a Poem with Walden.** The Irish poet William Butler Yeats (1865–1939) was supposed to have based one of his famous poems on Thoreau's *Walden,* specifically on the entry about the bean-fields. (When he was a little boy, Yeats listened to his father read Thoreau aloud.) Here is Yeats's poem. In an essay, tell how it compares with Thoreau's writings in terms of **imagery, tone,** and **subject matter.**

The Lake Isle of Innisfree

I will arise and go now, and go to Innisfree,
And a small cabin build there, of clay and wattles made:
Nine bean-rows will I have there, a hive for the honeybee,
And live alone in the bee-loud glade.

And I shall have some peace there, for peace comes dropping slow,
Dropping from the veils of the morning to where the cricket sings;
There midnight's all a glimmer, and noon a purple glow,
And evening full of the linnet's wings.

I will arise and go now, for always night and day
I hear lake water lapping with low sounds by the shore;
While I stand on the roadway, or on the pavements gray,
I hear it in the deep heart's core.

—William Butler Yeats

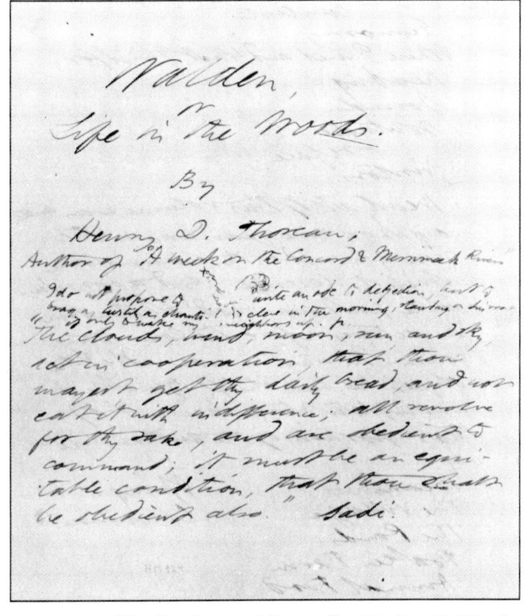
Walden,
or
Life in the Woods.
By
Henry D. Thoreau,
Author of "A Week on the Concord & Merrimack Rivers"

"The clouds, wind, moon, sun and sky act in cooperation, that thou mayest get thy daily bread, and not eat it with indifference; all revolve for thy sake, and are obedient to command; it must be an equitable condition, that thou shouldst be obedient also." Sadi.

The Huntington Library, San Marino, California.

Analyzing Language and Style

A Metaphorical Style

Walden is not a simple book; Thoreau's typical style is metaphorical. For each passage that follows, identify the **metaphor** or **simile** and explain what is being compared with what. (Notice how visual each figure of speech is.) How would you express each idea in your own words?

1. "As for the rest of my readers, they will accept such portions as apply to them. I trust that none will stretch the seams in putting on the coat, for it may do good service to him whom it fits." (Page 208)
2. "I wanted to live deep and suck out all the marrow of life. . . ." (Page 211)
3. "Our life is like a German Confederacy, made up of petty states, with its boundary forever fluctuating. . . ." (Page 212)
4. "I did not wish to take a cabin passage, but rather to go before the mast and on the deck of the world, for there I could best see the moonlight amid the mountains. I do not wish to go below now." (Page 217)
5. "If a man does not keep pace with his companions, perhaps it is because he hears a different drummer. Let him step to the music which he hears, however measured or far away." (Page 217)
6. "The life in us is like the water in the river. It may rise this year higher than man has ever known it, and flood the parched uplands; even this may be the eventful year, which will drown out all our muskrats." (Page 217)

SUPPLEMENTARY SUPPORT MATERIALS
1. Vocabulary Activity Worksheet (*CCB*)
2. Review and Response Worksheet: Style (*CCB*)

DEVELOPING VOCABULARY
The following words from the essay are tested in the Selection Test. (See also Vocabulary Activity Worksheet.)

expedient	insurrection
vitality	impetuous
alacrity	domesticated
to cultivate	sanction
eradication	aloof

PREPARATION
BUILDING ON PRIOR KNOWLEDGE. Discuss with students what they already know about the idea of civil disobedience from their study of history and from the news. What feelings are immediately summoned up when they hear the phrase *civil disobedience*? (Students may suggest leaders such as Gandhi and King.)

A. Humanities Connection: Discussing the Fine Art
Horace Pippin (1888–1946) was a self-taught African American artist from Westchester, Pennsylvania, who began painting at the age of forty-two. He is known for the emotional depth of his work, which he achieved through a sophisticated use of form, color, and detail. John Brown was an important figure in the abolitionist movement.

FROM RESISTANCE TO CIVIL GOVERNMENT

In July of 1846, Thoreau's stay at Walden Pond was interrupted by a night in jail. Thoreau was arrested because he refused, on principle, to pay a tax to the state. He refused primarily because he was opposed to the government's support of slavery. The police in Concord offered to pay the tax for Thoreau, but he refused that also. He was forced, therefore, to spend the night in jail, and he might have spent more time there, except that someone, probably his aunt, paid the tax for him. This night in jail was the inspiration for the essay known as "Resistance to Civil Government" or "Civil Disobedience." Some people have suggested that the essay shows that Thoreau merely wanted to withdraw from life and all its hard questions. Others see Thoreau's position as the only one he could logically take to justify his stand. You will have to decide for yourself how the essay affects you.

A

John Brown Going to His Hanging by Horace Pippin (1942). Oil on canvas.

Accession #1943.11. Courtesy of the Pennsylvania Academy of the Fine Arts, Philadelphia. John Lambert Fund.

A I heartily accept the motto—"That government is best which governs least;"[1] and I should like to see it acted up to more rapidly and systematically. Carried out, it finally amounts to this, which also I believe—"That government is best which governs not at all;" and when men are prepared for it, that will be the kind of government which they will have. Government is at best but an expedient; but most governments are usually, and all governments are sometimes, inexpedient. The objections which have been brought against a standing army, and they are many and weighty, and deserve to prevail, may also at last be brought against a standing government. The standing army is only an arm of the standing government. The government itself, which is only the mode which the people have chosen to execute their will, is equally liable to be abused and perverted before the people can act through it. Witness the present Mexican war, the work of comparatively a few individuals using the standing government as their tool; for, in the outset, the people would not have consented to this measure.[2]

This American government—what is it but a tradition, though a recent one, endeavoring to transmit itself unimpaired to posterity, but each instant losing some of its integrity? It has not the vitality and force of a single living man; for a single man can bend it to his will. It is a sort of wooden gun to the people themselves; and, if ever they should use it in earnest as a real one against each other, it will surely split. But it is not the less necessary for this; for the people must have some complicated machinery or other, and hear its din, to satisfy that idea of government which they have. Governments show thus how successfully men can be imposed on, even impose on themselves, for their own advantage. It is excellent, we must all allow; yet this government never of itself furthered any enterprise, but by the alacrity with which it got out of its way. *It* does not keep the country free. *It* does not settle the West. *It* does not educate. The character inherent in the American people has done all that has been accomplished; and it would have done somewhat more, if the government had not sometimes got in its way. For government is an expedient by which men would fain[3] succeed in letting one another alone; and, as has been said, when it is most expedient, the governed are most let alone by it. Trade and commerce, if they were not made of India rubber, would never manage to bounce over the obstacles which legislators are continually putting in their way; and, if one were to judge these men wholly by the effects of their actions, and not partly by their intentions, they would deserve to be classed and punished with those mischievous persons who put obstructions on the railroads.

But, to speak practically and as a citizen, unlike those who call themselves no-government men, I ask for, not at once no government, but *at once* a better government. Let every man make known what kind of government would command his respect, and that will be one step toward obtaining it.

After all, the practical reason why, when the power is once in the hands of the people, a majority are permitted, and for a long period continue, to rule, is not because they are most likely to be in the right, nor because this seems fairest to the minority, but because they are physically the strongest. But a government in which the majority rule in all cases cannot be based on justice, even as far as men understand it. Can there not be a government in which majorities do not virtually decide right and wrong, but conscience?—in which majorities decide only those questions to which the rule of expediency is applicable? Must the citizen ever for a moment, or in the least degree, resign his conscience to the legislator? Why has every man a conscience, then? I think that we should be men first, and subjects afterward. It is not desirable to cultivate a respect for the law, so much as for the right. The only obligation which I have a right to assume, is to do at any time what I think right. . . . B

It is not a man's duty, as a matter of course, to devote himself to the eradication of any, even the most enormous wrong; he may still properly have other concerns to engage him; but it is his duty, at least, to wash his hands of it, and, if he gives it no thought longer, not to give it practically his support. If I devote myself to other pursuits and C

1. **"That . . . least":** this Jeffersonian statement was the motto of the New York *Democratic Review,* which had published two of Thoreau's essays.
2. **this measure:** President Polk initiated hostilities against Mexico without a Congressional declaration of war.

3. **fain:** willingly.

A. Responding
? Would Thoreau's dictum "That government is best which governs not at all" be workable in a complex society? (Although many people today claim to approve of the dictum, few would be willing to give up those parts of the government that are useful to them.)

B. Responding
? How can a balance be created between the will of the majority and the rights of the minority? What would happen if we all did what we thought was right? (Answers will vary. Ask for specific examples.)

C. Responding
? Thoreau makes a characteristically scrupulous distinction: We don't have to oppose wrongdoing actively, but we have to refuse to engage in it. How does this fit in with other aspects of his personality you know about? (He felt that we should work out our own beliefs without interference.)

A. Responding
What one person symbolizes the government for Thoreau? (His neighbor the tax collector) Note that Thoreau lived in a much simpler, smaller-scale society than ours.

B. Expansion
The idea that a single righteous person, or a small group of such persons, can redeem a whole society has strong biblical echoes—see Genesis 18.

C. Imagery
What is the point of Thoreau's image of a lone woman with silver spoons? (Such a person would be so frightened of losing her possessions she would not be able to tell who she could trust. Thoreau uses this image to make a similar point about the government.)

contemplations, I must first see, at least, that I do not pursue them sitting upon another man's shoulders. I must get off him first, that he may pursue his contemplations too. See what gross inconsistency is tolerated. I have heard some of my townspeople say, "I should like to have them order me out to help put down an insurrection of the slaves, or to march to Mexico—see if I would go;" and yet these very men have each, directly by their allegiance, and so indirectly, at least, by their money, furnished a substitute. The soldier is applauded who refuses to serve in an unjust war by those who do not refuse to sustain the unjust government which makes the war; is applauded by those whose own act and authority he disregards and sets at nought; as if the State were penitent to that degree that it hired one to scourge it while it sinned, but not to that degree that it left off sinning for a moment. Thus, under the name of order and civil government, we are all made at last to pay homage to and support our own meanness. After the first blush of sin, comes its indifference; and from immoral it becomes, as it were, *un*moral, and not quite unnecessary to that life which we have made. . . .

I meet this American government, or its representative the State government, directly, and face to face, once a year, no more, in the person of its tax-gatherer; this is the only mode in which a man situated as I am necessarily meets it; and it then says distinctly, Recognize me; and the simplest, the most effectual, and, in the present posture of affairs, the indispensablest mode of treating with it on this head, of expressing your little satisfaction with and love for it, is to deny it then. My civil neighbor, the tax-gatherer,[4] is the very man I have to deal with—for it is, after all, with men and not with parchment that I quarrel—and he has voluntarily chosen to be an agent of the government. How shall he ever know well what he is and does as an officer of the government, or as a man, until he is obliged to consider whether he shall treat me, his neighbor, for whom he has respect, as a neighbor and well-disposed man, or as a maniac and disturber of the peace, and see if he can get over this obstruction to his neighborliness without a ruder and more impetuous thought or speech corresponding with his action? A

I know this well, that if one thousand, if one hundred, if ten men whom I could name—if ten *honest* men only—aye, if *one* HONEST man, in this State of Massachusetts, *ceasing to hold slaves,* were actually to withdraw from this copartnership, and be locked up in the county jail therefore, it would be the abolition of slavery in America. For it matters not how small the beginning may seem to be: what is once well done is done forever. . . . B

I have paid no poll tax[5] for six years. I was put into a jail once on this account, for one night; and, as I stood considering the walls of solid stone, two or three feet thick, the door of wood and iron, a foot thick, and the iron grating which strained the light, I could not help being struck with the foolishness of that institution which treated me as if I were mere flesh and blood and bones, to be locked up. I wondered that it should have concluded at length that this was the best use it could put me to, and had never thought to avail itself of my services in some way. I saw that, if there was a wall of stone between me and my townsmen, there was a still more difficult one to climb or break through, before they could get to be as free as I was. I did not for a moment feel confined, and the walls seemed a great waste of stone and mortar. I felt as if I alone of all my townsmen had paid my tax. They plainly did not know how to treat me, but behaved like persons who are underbred. In every threat and in every compliment there was a blunder; for they thought that my chief desire was to stand the other side of that stone wall. I could not but smile to see how industriously they locked the door on my meditations, which followed them out again without let or hinderance, and *they* were really all that was dangerous. As they could not reach me, they had resolved to punish my body; just as boys, if they cannot come at some person against whom they have a spite, will abuse his dog. I saw that the State was half-witted, that it was timid as a lone woman with her silver spoons, C
and that it did not know its friends from its foes, and I lost all my remaining respect for it, and pitied it. . . .

The night in prison was novel and interesting enough. The prisoners in their shirt sleeves were enjoying a chat and the evening air in the doorway,

4. Sam Staples, who sometimes assisted Thoreau in his surveying.

5. **poll tax:** some states and localities required each citizen to pay a "poll tax" (or head tax) to qualify for voting.

Closure

Have students describe the extent to which they think Thoreau, based on the essay, would approve of the federal government as it exists today.

Reading Check Test

1. We would lead better lives if there were stronger state governments. *False*
2. We need government for directing the tasks of educating, settling territories, and keeping the country free. *False*
3. Thoreau feels that jail is a ridiculous institution that locks up his body, but not his mind. *True*
4. Thoreau feels that he gets a closer view of his town and understands its people better because of his night in jail. *True*
5. The ideal state is one in which individuals are free to be themselves even if they wish to live away from the society of others. *True*

when I entered. But the jailer said, "Come, boys, it is time to lock up;" and so they dispersed, and I heard the sound of their steps returning into the hollow apartments. My roommate was introduced to me by the jailer, as "a first-rate fellow and a clever man." When the door was locked, he showed me where to hang my hat, and how he managed matters there. The rooms were whitewashed once a month; and this one, at least, was the whitest, most simply furnished, and probably the neatest apartment in the town. He naturally wanted to know where I came from, and what brought me there; and, when I told him, I asked him in my turn how he came there, presuming him to be an honest man, of course; and, as the world goes, I believe he was. "Why," said he, "they accuse me of burning a barn; but I never did it." As near as I could discover, he had probably gone to bed in a barn when drunk, and smoked his pipe there; and so a barn was burnt. He had the reputation of being a clever man, had been there some three months waiting for his trial to come on, and would have to wait as much longer; but he was quite domesticated and contented, since he got his board for nothing, and thought that he was well treated.

He occupied one window, and I the other; and I saw, that, if one stayed there long, his principal business would be to look out the window. I had soon read all the tracts that were left there, and examined where former prisoners had broken out, and where a grate had been sawed off, and heard the history of the various occupants of that room; for I found that even here there was a history and a gossip which never circulated beyond the walls of the jail. Probably this is the only house in the town where verses are composed, which are afterward printed in a circular form, but not published. I was shown quite a long list of verses which were composed by some young men who had been detected in an attempt to escape, who avenged themselves by singing them.

I pumped my fellow prisoner as dry as I could, for fear I should never see him again; but at length he showed me which was my bed, and left me to blow out the lamp.

A It was like traveling into a far country, such as I had never expected to behold, to lie there for one night. It seemed to me that I never had heard the town clock strike before, nor the evening sounds of the village; for we slept with the windows open, which were inside the grating. It was to see my native village in the light of the Middle Ages, and our Concord was turned into a Rhine stream, and visions of knights and castles passed before me. They were the voices of old burghers that I heard in the streets. I was an involuntary spectator and auditor of whatever was done and said in the kitchen of the adjacent village inn—a wholly new and rare experience to me. It was a closer view of my native town. I was fairly inside of it. I never had seen its institutions before. This is one of its peculiar institutions; for it is a shire town.[6] I began to comprehend what its inhabitants were about.

In the morning, our breakfasts were put through the hole in the door, in small oblong-square tin pans, made to fit, and holding a pint of chocolate, with brown bread, and an iron spoon. When they called for the vessels again, I was green enough to return what bread I had left; but my comrade seized it, and said that I should lay that up for lunch or dinner. Soon after, he was let out to work at haying in a neighboring field, whither he went every day, and would not be back till noon; so he bade me good day, saying that he doubted if he should see me again.

When I came out of prison—for someone interfered, and paid the tax—I did not perceive that great changes had taken place on the common, such as he observed who went in a youth, and emerged a tottering and gray-headed man; and yet a change had to my eyes come over the scene—the town, and State, and country—greater than any that mere time could effect. I saw yet more distinctly the State in which I lived. I saw to what extent the people among whom I lived could be trusted as good neighbors and friends; that their friendship was for summer weather only; that they did not greatly purpose to do right; that they were a distinct race from me by their prejudices and superstitions, as the Chinamen and Malays are; that, in their sacrifices to humanity, they ran no risks, not even to their property; that, after all, they were not so noble but they treated the thief as he had treated them, and hoped, by a certain outward observance and a few prayers, and by walking in a particular straight though useless path from time to time, to save their souls. This may be to judge my neighbors harshly; for I believe that most of them are not aware that they have such an institution as the jail in their village. B

6. **shire town:** a town where a court sits, like a county seat.

A. Connections
This paragraph has a lyrical quality that lends itself to being read aloud. Thoreau is saying that his one night in jail, while not changing either him or the town physically, has changed his way of seeing. Compare this to the experience of Rip Van Winkle (page 125), who did go through profound physical changes during his much longer separation from his townspeople but who at the end fit in comfortably with them as before.

B. Irony/ Characterization
The last sentence of this paragraph is ironic. What does the unawareness regarding a jail say about Thoreau's townspeople? (It suggests both insensitivity and intolerance.)

Analyzing The Essay
Identifying Facts
1. He says that a government based on majority rule in all cases cannot be based on justice, since the majority will, sooner or later, inevitably harm the minority.

Thoreau says that his only obligation is to do what he thinks right.

2. He predicts that if even only one honest man were to fight against slavery by going to jail in protest, it would lead to the abolition of slavery in America.

3. He refused to pay his poll-tax.

4. He says that the night was "novel and interesting." He describes his fellow prisoners and his conversation with his roommate. When his roommate retired to bed, Thoreau listened to the town clock and the evening sounds of the village, which became transformed in his mind to a medieval town.

5. Thoreau says that an ideal state will recognize the individual as a "higher and independent power," from which all the state's authority is derived. The perfect state will be just to all men, and will even allow some individuals to withdraw and live aloof from it.

A. Connections
See Emerson's comment about Thoreau's huckleberry party, in the biography on page 204. How do you think Thoreau felt about the relative importance of private and public life? (He had a marked preference for privacy in his own life.)

B. Expansion
The last paragraph is the central exposition of Thoreau's political ideas in this essay. It might be read aloud. Two sentences worth special attention and discussion are the ones beginning "The progress from an absolute to a limited monarchy . . ." and "There will never be a really free and enlightened State. . . ."

It was formerly the custom in our village, when a poor debtor came out of jail, for his acquaintances to salute him, looking through their fingers, which were crossed to represent the grating of a jail window, "How do ye do?" My neighbors did not thus salute me, but first looked at me, and then at one another, as if I had returned from a long journey. I was put into jail as I was going to the shoemakers to get a shoe which was mended. When I was let out the next morning, I proceeded to finish my errand, and, having put on my A mended shoe, joined a huckleberry party, who were impatient to put themselves under my conduct; and in half an hour—for the horse was soon tackled[7]—was in the midst of a huckleberry field, on one of our highest hills, two miles off; and then the State was nowhere to be seen.

This is the whole history of "My Prisons."

B The authority of government, even such as I am willing to submit to—for I will cheerfully obey those who know and can do better than I, and in many things even those who neither know nor can do so well—is still an impure one: to be strictly just, it must have the sanction and consent of the governed. It can have no pure right over my person and property but what I concede to it. The progress from an absolute to a limited monarchy, from a limited monarchy to a democracy, is a progress toward a true respect for the individual. Is a democracy, such as we know it, the last improvement possible in government? Is it not possible to take a step further toward recognizing and organizing the rights of man? There will never be a really free and enlightened State, until the State comes to recognize the individual as a higher and independent power, from which all its own power and authority are derived, and treats him accordingly. I please myself with imagining a State at last which can afford to be just to all men, and to treat the individual with respect as a neighbor; which even would not think it inconsistent with its own repose, if a few were to live aloof from it, not meddling with it, nor embraced by it, who fulfilled all the duties of neighbors and fellow men. A State which bore this kind of fruit, and suffered it to drop off as fast as it ripened, would prepare the way for a still more perfect and glorious State, which also I have imagined, but not yet anywhere seen.

7. **tackled:** harnessed.

Responding to the Essay

Analyzing the Essay

Identifying Facts

1. Explain what Thoreau thinks is wrong with majority rule. What does he say is the only obligation he has a right to assume?
2. What does Thoreau predict about slavery in America?
3. Explain why Thoreau was put in jail. What were his feelings about the government when he was in jail?
4. How does Thoreau describe his sensations and thoughts as he lies in jail during the night?
5. At the end of the essay, what qualities does Thoreau envision in an ideal "perfect and glorious State"?

Interpreting Meanings

6. **Paradox** is a statement or expression that presents an apparent contradiction which actually contains a truth. What is the truth behind these two paradoxes?
   a. "I saw that, if there was a wall of stone between me and my townsmen, there was a still more difficult one to climb or break through, before they could get to be as free as I was." (Page 222)
   b. "I felt as if I alone of all my townsmen had paid my tax." (Page 222)
7. How are Thoreau's perceptions of his fellow citizens changed by his night in jail? What idea do you think he is stressing in telling us about getting his shoe fixed and leading the huckleberry party on the day he was released?
8. From what you know about American Romanticism, would you say that Thoreau's assumptions and points in this essay are fundamentally Romantic? Explain.
9. What influences of Emerson can you find in Thoreau's "Resistance to Civil Government"?
10. Which of Thoreau's arguments did you find convincing, and which did you disagree with? Are you convinced that there could be civil order if each person followed his or her own conscience? Explain.
11. Comment on how Thoreau's main points in this essay relate to contemporary life. What would happen to a Thoreau-type protest today?

Interpreting Meanings

6. a. Thoreau means that the townsmen are imprisoned by conformity.

b. Thoreau means that, by following his own conscience, he has figuratively paid his tax—that is, he has rendered a service to the state and to his fellow townsmen.

7. Thoreau comes to feel that the friendship of his fellow townsmen is "for summer weather only"—perhaps he is consciously echoing Thomas Paine's phrase about "the summer soldier and the sunshine patriot" from *The American Crisis.* He says that he now feels that his neighbors are narrowminded and hypocritical.

Thoreau stresses that he is not allowing the experience of being jailed to disrupt his normal life or his enjoyment of nature.

8. Student answers will vary, but most students will see Thoreau's assumptions and points as Romantic. Note particularly the stress on the integrity of the individual, the emphasis on conscience as a higher imperative than the rules of the state, his vision of Concord at night as a medieval town on the Rhine, and the visionary conclusion describing an ideal government.

Writing About the Essay

A Creative Response

1. **Taking Another Point of View.** Imagine that you are the police officer who arrested Thoreau. Write a short speech explaining why it was necessary to do so. Include your response to Thoreau's purpose in defying the law.

A Critical Response

2. **Supporting a Statement.** Write an essay either in support of or in opposition to this statement from "Resistance to Civil Government": "That government is best which governs not at all."
3. **Comparing or Contrasting Two Political Statements.** In an essay, compare or contrast Thoreau's ideas in this essay with the ideas in the Declaration of Independence (page 101). Cite specific passages from both documents to support what you say about them. You might find similarities in the two works, or you might find that they are completely divergent.

Analyzing Language and Style

Precise Meanings

"After the first blush of sin," writes Thoreau on page 222, "comes its indifference; and from immoral it becomes, as it were, *un*moral . . ."

1. The word *indifference* can mean "neutrality" or "apathy." What is the difference between the two meanings? Which meaning does the word have here?
2. How is *unmoral* different from *immoral*?
3. Reread the passage in its context. How would you paraphrase it?

Thoreau was arrested because he did not pay "poll tax."

4. The word *poll* comes from a Middle English word for "top of the head." Usage has added other meanings, including the sense of "individual" ("one head"). What do you think a "poll tax" is?
5. What do the words *poll, pollster,* and *poll booth* mean today? How are they related to the sense of "head"?

9. In general, Emerson's faith in the power of the individual to shape his or her own destiny seems to be reflected in Thoreau's essay. Students will probably also point to echoes of Emerson's emphasis on the values of integrity and self-reliance.

10. Again, student answers will vary. Urge the students to discuss a variety of concrete situations in historical and contemporary contexts. You may want to point out that many celebrated works of literature have dealt with the conflict of individual conscience with the demands of the state or of civil order: for example, Sophocles's tragedy *Antigone,* T. S. Eliot's *Murder in the Cathedral,* and Henrik Ibsen's *An Enemy of the People.*

11. Student answers will vary. While jails are no longer as pleasant as the one in Concord, Thoreau's example did inspire Gandhi, Martin Luther King, Jr., and others to use the same kind of protest—successfully.

Primary Sources

Two Journals

On August 30, 1842, the young Thoreau had dinner with Nathaniel Hawthorne. In his notebooks, Hawthorne gave this description of his guest. Neither man at this point had written the books that were to make him famous.

"Mr. Thorow dined with us yesterday. He is a singular character—a young man with much of wild original stuff still remaining in him; and so far as he is sophisticated, it is in a way and method of his own. He is as ugly as sin, long-nosed, queer-mouthed, and with uncouth and somewhat rustic, although courteous manners, corresponding very well with such an exterior. But his ugliness is of an honest and agreeable fashion, and becomes him much better than beauty. He was educated, I believe at Cambridge, and formerly kept school in this town; but for two or three years back, he has repudiated all regular modes of getting a living, and seems inclined to lead a sort of Indian life . . . He has been for sometime an inmate of Mr. Emerson's family; and, in requital, he labors in the garden, and performs such other offices as may suit him—being entertained by Mr. Emerson for the sake of what true manhood there is in him. Mr. Thorow is a keen and delicate observer of nature—a genuine observer, which, I suspect, is almost as rare a character as even an original poet; and Nature, in return for his love, seems to adopt him as her special child, and shows him secrets which few others are allowed to witness. He is familiar with beast, fish, fowl, and reptile, and has strange stories to tell of his adventures, and friendly passages with these lower brethren of mortality. . . . With all this he has more than a tincture of literature—a deep and true taste for poetry, especially the elder poets. . . . On the whole I find him a healthy and wholesome man to know."

—Nathaniel Hawthorne

Hawthorne's daughter described a skating trio on the Concord River: Emerson, Thoreau, and Hawthorne are on the ice. (In ancient Greece, a *dithyramb* was a wild, emotional hymn. Bacchus was the god of wine and merrymaking.)

"One afternoon Mr. Emerson and Mr. Thoreau went with him [Hawthorne] down the river. Henry Thoreau is an experienced skater, and was figuring dithyrambic dances and Bacchic leaps on the ice—very remarkable, but very ugly, methought. Next him followed Mr. Hawthorne, wrapped in his cloak, moved like a self-impelled Greek statue, stately and grave. Mr. Emerson closed the line, evidently too weary to hold himself erect, pitching headforemost, half lying on the air."

—Rose Hawthorne Lathrop

A. Humanities Connection: Responding to the Photograph

? What kind of person does Poe appear to be in this photograph? (Students may see both gentility and an air of seeming haunted.)

THE DARK SIDE OF ROMANTICISM

Edgar Allan Poe (1809–1849)

"The want of parental affection," wrote Poe, "has been the heaviest of my trials." Edgar Poe was born in Boston, and he was, indeed, most unfortunate in his parents. His father, David Poe, was a mediocre traveling actor who drank heavily. His mother, Elizabeth Arnold, was a talented actress who was deserted by her husband when Edgar was an infant. She died soon after the desertion in a rooming house in Richmond, Virginia, leaving Edgar an orphan before his third birthday.

The boy was taken in by John and Frances Allan, a charitable and childless couple in Richmond. John Allan, an ambitious and self-righteous tobacco merchant, became Edgar's guardian (and the source of the writer's middle name). He provided generously for Edgar's education, but he did not formally adopt him.

Although Frances Allan was sympathetic to Edgar, the boy grew up feeling both the lack of a natural father and the disapproval of his foster father. And John Allan made no secret of his disappointment in Edgar—in his idleness, in his indifference to business life, and in his literary ambitions. Surely Allan's unfavorable opinion contributed to Edgar's growing moodiness.

At seventeen, when he entered the University of Virginia, Edgar fell in love with and became secretly engaged to a girl named Elmira Royster. On discovering the romance, however, her family put an end to it—probably because they had heard that Edgar would never be the heir to John Allan's fortune.

Throughout his schooling, Poe had shown signs of brilliance, and at the university he did well in his studies. But he was resentful of the meager allowance Allan provided him. When he tried to increase his income by gambling, he went deep into debt. On discovering this, Allan refused to help his foster son and instead withdrew him from college.

After a particularly bitter quarrel with Allan, Poe ran off to Boston to make his own way in the world. There, in 1827, he published a small volume of poems, *Tamerlane,* inspired by his ruined romance with Elmira Royster. The book did not attract much attention, and Poe could find no work. In despair, he joined the army. He earned promotion to the rank of Sergeant Major, but he developed a distaste for the enlisted man's life and appealed to Allan for help. At the request of his wife, who was dying, Allan interceded for Edgar (for the last time) and agreed to help him enter West Point.

Awaiting his appointment to the Academy, Poe published a second volume of poems, *El Aaraaf,* in 1829 and received his first real recognition as a writer. The following year, while he was at West Point, he learned that Allan, now a widower, had married a wife young enough to provide him with children. Since this appeared to end all of Poe's hopes of becoming Allan's heir, he had himself dismissed from West Point.

He moved in with an aunt, Maria Poe Clemm, in Baltimore. In 1835, he married her thirteen-year-old daughter, Virginia. The disparity in their ages and Virginia's chronic poor health resulted in a very odd marriage, but need and a strong sense of family drew the three housemates together.

Poe found work as editor of the *Southern Literary Messenger* and proved expert at it. He increased the circulation so dramatically that he was sought after by other magazines. He wrote when he could find the time, completing his only full-length novel, *The Narrative of Arthur Gordon Pym,* several years after his marriage. He decided that, however difficult it might be, he would support himself and his family by writing.

Many readers think of Poe as bringing to a peak the Gothic tradition. This was a central aspect of the European Romantic movement. The word *Gothic* comes from the name of an architectural style of the late Middle Ages. The term has come to be applied to writings that try to reproduce the mysterious atmosphere suggested by the medieval castles, with their dungeons and secret passages. Gothic novels featured mysterious settings and had strong elements of the bizarre and the supernatural. Poe compressed these elements into the narrower confines of the short story.

Poe's reputation as a Gothic writer is justly earned in his tales of the ghastly and the grotesque: in "The Masque of the Red Death," "The Pit and the Pendulum," "The Fall of the House of Usher," and his own favorite, "Ligeia." Death stalks in each story, pointing a bony finger and sending chills through one generation of readers after another.

In "The Gold Bug" and in the tales built around that intuitive sleuth Auguste Dupin, "The Purloined Letter" and "The Murders in the Rue Morgue," Poe laid the foundations for the modern detective story. He inspired Sir Arthur Conan Doyle to create Sherlock Holmes, and he inspired Russian novelist Feodor Dostoevski (1821–1881) to explore the criminal mind.

In fact, Poe was more admired abroad than at home. While his American contemporaries dismissed him as a lightweight, the French poet Charles Baudelaire (1821–1867) praised Poe's probings of the human heart and imagination. (See also page 724.)

These excursions into the workings of the human mind make up Poe's primary contributions to literature. But despite his unquestioned mastery of terror and suspense, Poe was not merely a writer of horror stories. What he desired most in his writing was to cut free from reality or actuality in order to enter the world of the imagination. In this quest he was essentially Romantic, although the world the imagination opened for him was chaotic and potentially evil, rather than a creative source of dreams and visions.

Poe created his imaginative worlds through a masterful use of ambiguity and atmosphere. His distraught narrators, deranged heroes, and death-obsessed heroines bear little resemblance to the humans we know. Poe's purpose in creating them was neither to frighten his readers nor to present them with a convincing likeness of human behavior. Instead, he wanted to get behind the face of the everyday—to leave the tangible, sunlit aspect of the rational world and show us the truth that lies in the dark and irrational depths of the human mind.

Poe produced a considerable outpouring of poems and tales even as he worked at a demanding career as a magazine editor, and in spite of humiliating poverty and the serious consequences of his drinking. The slightest amount of alcohol deranged him; yet he drank to escape a reality he found agonizing. Publication of "The Raven" in 1845 brought him some fame at last, but financial security still eluded him.

When Virginia died of tuberculosis in 1847, Poe grew more unstable and contracted illnesses of his own. He developed a brain lesion that would leave him little time to live. Nevertheless, he pursued romance relentlessly, always looking for someone to "adopt" him. In 1849, during a visit to Baltimore, he began to drink and disappeared for five days. He was found on a rainy sidewalk on October 3, delirious, his clothing torn. Hospitalized, he regained enough consciousness to say the words "Lord help my poor soul" before he died.

A. Connections
Gothic novels are plentiful in bookstores today, usually in the form of paperback gothic romances. Prominent practitioners of the art include Georgette Heyer, Victoria Holt, and Phyllis Whitney. The horror fiction of Stephen King and Ira Levin is also descended from Poe. Many students will have read one or more of these novels, or, if not, may well have seen movies based on them. Ask students to list gothic elements from contemporary fiction and film and look for these as they read the selections by Poe.

B. Expansion
Interested students might want to compare Dostoevsky's novella *The Double* with another of Poe's short stories, "William Wilson." Both explore the theme of the *doppelganger,* or mysterious double who follows and frightens the protagonist.

SUPPLEMENTARY SUPPORT MATERIALS
1. Vocabulary Activity Worksheet (*CCB*)
2. Review and Response Worksheet: Imagery and Theme (*CCB*)
3. Selection Test (*CCB*)
4. Audiocassette recording

DEVELOPING VOCABULARY
The following words from the story are tested in the Selection Test. (See also Vocabulary Activity Worksheet.)

profuse	wanton
dauntless	revel
reverie	disapprobation
tremulousness	spectral
phantasm	prostrate

PREPARATION
ESTABLISHING A PURPOSE. Scholars have said that this story reveals the "darker side of romanticism." Have students read to find these "darker" elements of romanticism.

A. Connections
Poe's view of the effects of the plague—a time when the great and wealthy shut themselves off from the poor and diseased and lived lives of luxury and self-indulgence—parallels in many respects Boccaccio's point of view in *Decameron* (1351–1353).

B. Responding
The change in tone from the first paragraph to the second paragraph sets up a tension that will build throughout the story.
? What evidence can you find as you read the story of the growing menace? (The striking of the clock seems to affect everyone; people avoid the seventh chamber; the crowd becomes aware of a masked figure who resembles a corpse.)

THE MASQUE OF THE RED DEATH

The word *masque* in the title refers to a masked ball, an entertainment that was popular in Europe during the fourteenth and fifteenth centuries. It also refers to a mask that disguises the face. To understand what is happening on a literal level in this story, think about the Black Death, or bubonic plague, an epidemic that killed seventy-five percent of Europe's population during the fourteenth century. The plague lasted twenty years and was spread by fleas that lived on humans and rats. Some critics think the specific source of this story was a news article about a masked ball that was held in Paris in 1832 while a cholera epidemic raged in the city.

The "Red Death" had long devastated the country. No pestilence had ever been so fatal, or so hideous. Blood was its avatar[1] and its seal—the redness and the horror of blood. There were sharp pains, and sudden dizziness, and then profuse bleeding at the pores, with dissolution. The scarlet stains upon the body and especially upon the face of the victim, were the pest ban which shut him out from the aid and from the sympathy of his fellow men. And the whole seizure, progress, and termination of the disease, were the incidents of half an hour.

But the Prince Prospero was happy and dauntless and sagacious. When his dominions were half depopulated, he summoned to his presence a thousand hale and lighthearted friends from among the knights and dames of his court, and with these retired to the deep seclusion of one of his castellated[2] abbeys. This was an extensive and magnificent structure, the creation of the prince's own eccentric yet august taste. A strong and lofty wall girdled it in. This wall had gates of iron. The courtiers, having entered, brought furnaces and massy hammers and welded the bolts. They resolved to leave means neither of ingress or egress to the sudden impulses of despair or of frenzy from within. The abbey was amply provisioned. With such precautions the courtiers might bid defiance to contagion. The external world could take care of itself. In the meantime it was folly to grieve, or to think. The prince had provided all the appliances of pleasure. There were buffoons, there were improvisatori,[3] there were ballet dancers, there were musicians, there was Beauty, there was wine. All these and security were within. Without was the "Red Death."

It was toward the close of the fifth or sixth month of his seclusion, and while the pestilence raged most furiously abroad, that the Prince Prospero entertained his thousand friends at a masked ball of the most unusual magnificence.

It was a voluptuous scene, that masquerade. But first let me tell of the rooms in which it was held. There were seven—an imperial suite. In many palaces, however, such suites form a long and straight vista, while the folding doors slide back nearly to the walls on either hand, so that the view of the whole extent is scarcely impeded. Here the case was very different; as might have been expected from the duke's love of the bizarre. The apartments were so irregularly disposed that the vision embraced but little more than one at a time. There was a sharp turn at every twenty or thirty yards, and at each turn a novel effect. To the right and left, in the middle of each wall, a tall and narrow Gothic window looked out upon a closed corridor which pursued the windings of the suite. These windows were of stained glass whose color varied in accordance with the prevailing hue of the decorations of the chamber into which it opened. That at the eastern extremity was hung, for example, in blue—and vividly blue were its

1. **avatar:** embodiment, or concrete form.
2. **castellated:** built with turrets and battlements, like a castle.
3. **improvisatori:** performers who improvise their acts.

Lord, haue mercy
on London.
I follow.
We fly.
Wee dye.
Keepe out.

The Great Plague of London (1665). Colored woodcut.

A. **Humanities Connection: Discussing the Fine Art** Despite the quaint spellings, this is a picture of true horror. In order to bring this fact home, ask students to imagine this scene of the plague transferred to modern times. Interested students may want to draw their own sketches.

B. **Symbolism** What significance does the color of the windows in the last chamber have? (They are the color of the Red Death, and it is in this chamber that he will triumph.)

windows. The second chamber was purple in its ornaments and tapestries, and here the panes were purple. The third was green throughout, and so were the casements. The fourth was furnished and lighted with orange—the fifth with white—the sixth with violet. The seventh apartment was closely shrouded in black velvet tapestries that hung all over the ceiling and down the walls, falling in heavy folds upon a carpet of the same material and hue. But in this chamber only, the color of the windows failed to correspond with the decorations. The panes here were scarlet—a deep blood color. Now in no one of the seven apartments was there any lamp or candelabrum, amid the profusion of golden ornaments that lay scattered to and fro or depended from the roof. There was no light of any kind emanating from lamp or candle within the suite of chambers. But in the corridors that followed the suite, there stood, opposite to each window, a heavy tripod, bearing a brazier of fire that projected its rays through the tinted glass and so glaringly illumined the room. And thus were produced a multitude of gaudy and fantastic appearances. But in the western or black chamber the effect of the firelight that streamed upon the dark hangings through the blood-tinted panes, was ghastly in the extreme, and produced so wild a look upon the countenances of those who entered, that there were few of the company bold enough to set foot within its precincts at all.

It was in this apartment, also, that there stood against the western wall, a gigantic clock of ebony. Its pendulum swung to and fro with a dull, heavy, monotonous clang; and when the minute hand made the circuit of the face, and the hour was to be stricken, there came from the brazen lungs of the clock a sound which was clear and loud and deep and exceedingly musical, but of so peculiar a note and emphasis that, at each lapse of an hour, the musicians of the orchestra were constrained

A. Characterization
? How is our feeling about Prince Prospero changed by this sentence? (Initially, he was described as "happy and dauntless and sagacious," but now Poe tells us there is a possibility of madness in his character.)

B. Responding
A good passage to read aloud.
? How does Poe's use of "and" and "but" at the beginnings of sentences affect the mood and pace? What else does Poe do to create this mood? (The pace quickens as the clock strikes twelve. Using "and" and "but" to begin the sentences gives a sense of time rushing on without pause. This mood is also accentuated by the piling up of adverbs such as "feverishly," "whirlingly," and "whisperingly.")

to pause, momentarily, in their performance, to hearken to the sound; and thus the waltzers perforce ceased their evolutions; and there was a brief disconcert[4] of the whole gay company; and, while the chimes of the clock yet rang, it was observed that the giddiest grew pale, and the more aged and sedate passed their hands over their brows as if in confused reverie or meditation. But when the echoes had fully ceased, a light laughter at once pervaded the assembly; the musicians looked at each other and smiled as if at their own nervousness and folly, and made whispering vows, each to the other, that the next chiming of the clock should produce in them no similar emotion; and then, after the lapse of sixty minutes (which embrace three thousand and six hundred seconds of the Time that flies), there came yet another chiming of the clock, and then were the same disconcert and tremulousness and meditation as before.

But, in spite of these things, it was a gay and magnificent revel. The tastes of the duke were peculiar. He had a fine eye for colors and effects. He disregarded the *decora*[5] of mere fashion. His plans were bold and fiery, and his conceptions glowed with barbaric luster. There are some who would have thought him mad. His followers felt that he was not. It was necessary to hear and see and touch him to be *sure* that he was not.

A

He had directed, in great part, the moveable embellishments of the seven chambers, upon occasion of this great *fête;*[6] and it was his own guiding taste which had given character to the masqueraders. Be sure they were grotesque. There were much glare and glitter and piquancy and phantasm—much of what has been since seen in *Hernani.*[7] There were arabesque figures with unsuited limbs and appointments. There were delirious fancies such as the madman fashions. There was much of the beautiful, much of the wanton, much of the bizarre, something of the terrible, and not a little of that which might have excited disgust. To and fro in the seven chambers there stalked, in fact, a multitude of dreams. And these—the dreams—writhed in and about, taking hue from the rooms, and causing the wild music of the orchestra to seem as the echo of their steps.

And, anon,[8] there strikes the ebony clock which stands in the hall of the velvet. And then, for a moment, all is still, and all is silent save the voice of the clock. The dreams are stiff-frozen as they stand. But the echoes of the chime die away—they have endured but an instant—and a light, half-subdued laughter floats after them as they depart. And now again the music swells, and the dreams live, and writhe to and fro more merrily than ever, taking hue from the many-tinted windows through which stream the rays from the tripods. But to the chamber which lies most westwardly of the seven, there are now none of the maskers who venture; for the night is waning away; and there flows a ruddier light through the blood-colored panes; and the blackness of the sable drapery appalls; and to him whose foot falls upon the sable carpet, there comes from the near clock of ebony a muffled peal more solemnly emphatic than any which reaches *their* ears who indulge in the more remote gaieties of the other apartments.

But these other apartments were densely crowded, and in them beat feverishly the heart of life. And the revel went whirlingly on, until at length there commenced the sounding of midnight upon the clock. And then the music ceased, as I have told; and the evolutions of the waltzers were quieted; and there was an uneasy cessation of all things as before. But now there were twelve strokes to be sounded by the bell of the clock; and thus it happened, perhaps, that more of thought crept, with more of time, into the meditations of the thoughtful among those who reveled. And thus, too, it happened, perhaps, that before the last echoes of the last chime had utterly sunk into silence, there were many individuals in the crowd who had found leisure to become aware of the presence of a masked figure which had arrested the attention of no single individual before. And the rumor of this new presence having spread itself whisperingly around, there arose at length from the whole company a buzz, or murmur, expressive of disapprobation and surprise—then, finally, of terror, of horror, and of disgust.

B

In an assembly of phantasms such as I have painted, it may well be supposed that no ordinary

4. **disconcert:** embarrassment, confusion.
5. ***decora:*** here, proper good taste.
6. ***fête*** (fāt): French for party.
7. ***"Hernani":*** a romantic play by the French writer Victor Hugo (1802–1885), first presented in 1830.
8. **anon:** soon.

CLOSURE

On one side of a sheet of paper, have students list the events that make up the plot of this story. On the other side, have them write a list of words and phrases that convey the atmosphere of the story. In class discussion, elicit from students how Poe used these basic events to communicate such horror and repulsion.

READING CHECK TEST

1. Prince _______ and his friends lock themselves in the abbey to escape the Red Death. *Prospero*

2. In all but one of the seven rooms of the imperial suite, there is a _______ of the same color as the furnishings. *stained-glass window*

3. During the masked ball, the revelers enjoy themselves except when the _______ sounds. *ebony clock*

4. At midnight, the Prince becomes infuriated when he notices a reveler in the costume of _______. *the Red Death*

appearance could have excited such sensation. In truth the masquerade license of the night was nearly unlimited; but, the figure in question had out-Heroded Herod,[9] and gone beyond the bounds of even the prince's indefinite decorum. There are chords in the hearts of the most reckless which cannot be touched without emotion. Even with the utterly lost, to whom life and death are equally jests, there are matters of which no jest can be made. The whole company, indeed, seemed now deeply to feel that in the costume and bearing of the stranger neither wit nor propriety existed. The figure was tall and gaunt, and shrouded from head to foot in the habiliments[10] of the grave. The mask which concealed the visage was made so nearly to resemble the countenance of a stiffened corpse that the closest scrutiny must have had difficulty in detecting the cheat. And yet all this might have been endured, if not approved, by the mad revelers around. But the mummer[11] had gone so far as to assume the type of the Red Death. His vesture was dabbled in *blood*—and his broad brow, with all the features of the face, was besprinkled with the scarlet horror. A

When the eyes of Prince Prospero fell upon this spectral image (which with a slow and solemn movement, as if more fully to sustain its role, stalked to and fro among the waltzers), he was seen to be convulsed, in the first moment with a strong shudder either of terror or distaste; but, in the next, his brow reddened with rage.

"Who dares?" he demanded hoarsely of the courtiers who stood near him—"who dares insult us with this blasphemous mockery? Seize him and unmask him—that we may know whom we have to hang at sunrise, from the battlements!"

It was in the eastern or blue chamber in which stood the Prince Prospero as he uttered these words. They rang throughout the seven rooms loudly and clearly—for the prince was a bold and robust man, and the music had become hushed at the waving of his hand.

It was in the blue room where stood the prince, with a group of pale courtiers by his side. At first, as he spoke, there was a slight rushing movement of this group in the direction of the intruder, who at the moment was also near at hand, and now, with deliberate and stately step, made closer approach to the speaker. But from a certain nameless awe with which the mad assumptions of the mummer had inspired the whole party, there were found none who put forth hand to seize him; so that, unimpeded, he passed within a yard of the prince's person; and, while the vast assembly, as if with one impulse, shrank from the centers of the rooms to the walls, he made his way uninterruptedly, but with the same solemn and measured step which had distinguished him from the first, through the blue chamber to the purple—through the purple to the green—through the green to the orange—through this again to the white—and even thence to the violet, ere a decided movement had been made to arrest him. It was then, however, that the Prince Prospero, maddening with rage and the shame of his own momentary cowardice, rushed hurriedly through the six chambers, while none followed him on account of a deadly terror that had seized upon all. He bore aloft a drawn dagger, and had approached, in rapid impetuosity, to within three or four feet of the retreating figure, when the latter, having attained the extremity of the velvet apartment, turned suddenly and confronted his pursuer. There was a sharp cry—and the dagger dropped gleaming upon the sable carpet, upon which, instantly afterward, fell prostrate in death the Prince Prospero. Then, summoning the wild courage of despair, a throng of the revelers at once threw themselves into the black apartment, and seizing the mummer, whose tall figure stood erect and motionless within the shadow of the ebony clock, gasped in unutterable horror at finding the grave-cerements[12] and corpselike mask which they handled with so violent a rudeness, untenanted by any tangible form.

And now was acknowledged the presence of the Red Death. He had come like a thief in the night. And one by one dropped the revelers in the C blood-bedewed halls of their revel, and died each in the despairing posture of his fall. And the life of the ebony clock went out with that of the last of the gay. And the flames of the tripods expired. And Darkness and Decay and the Red Death held illimitable dominion over all.

B 9. **Herod:** the Biblical king who massacred babies in his attempt to kill the infant Jesus. To "out-Herod Herod" (from Hamlet's advice to the players) is to go to excess.

10. **habiliments:** clothing.

11. **mummer:** masked person.

12. **grave-cerements:** shrouds, cloths that cover a body.

A. Responding

? What is the emotional impact of the descriptions? Do you feel the story has "paid off" on its promise of horror? If so, how? If not, why not? Given Poe's predilection for ornate, lurid descriptions, is there a danger of his tone becoming unintentionally comic through overstatement? Do you think he himself might have been aware of that? (See the line, "Even with the utterly lost, to whom life and death are equally jests, there are matters of which no jest can be made.")

B. Expansion

In the morality plays of the Middle Ages, the character of Herod was presented as a raving, bellowing madman.

C. Responding

? What does this thief (the Red Death) steal? (Life)

ANALYZING THE STORY
Identifying Facts
1. Sharp pains, sudden dizziness, profuse bleeding at the pores, and then death. The disease appalls people and prevents them from offering aid.
2. He summons a thousand of his subjects to an old abbey, where they hope to defy the plague by sealing themselves off.
3. The suite of seven rooms in which the ball is held is decorated in various colors, and Poe details the nature of the tapestries, stained-glass windows, ornaments, and carpets. The seventh chamber, decorated in black, is particularly striking; the window panes here are of scarlet.
4. The Red Death confronts Prince Prospero and the revelers. The Prince pursues the specter with a dagger. Finally, the Red Death turns on the nobleman in the velvet apartment, and the Prince falls dead.
5. The Red Death is compared to a thief in the night; the halls are described as "blood-bedewed"; the revelers drop in "despairing postures"; the clock ceases to run; and the flames of the tripods are extinguished.

Responding to the Story

Analyzing the Story

Identifying Facts

1. According to the first paragraph, what characteristics of the "Red Death" make it a horrifying disease?
2. Describe Prospero's plan for surviving the epidemic.
3. Poe gives a great deal of space in the story to the palace plans and decorations, providing us with textures and colors in profusion. What are some of the sensory **images** that create a vivid, concrete impression of Prince Prospero's hall?
4. What happens at the **climax** of the story?
5. The story concludes, "And Darkness and Decay and the Red Death held illimitable dominion over all." List the specific **images** of darkness, decay, and death in the final paragraph.

Interpreting Meanings

6. What do the ebony clock and its arresting chimes add to the plot? Can you think of any **symbolic** value the clock might have?
7. What **symbolic** significance can you find in Poe's use of numbers? In his use of colors, especially the black and the scarlet in the seventh room? In the movement from east to west in the sequence of rooms?
8. Poe's story is clearly not meant to be realistic; instead, it is a masterpiece of imaginative atmosphere that may be read as an **allegory**—a story in which characters, objects, and events symbolize various ideas and qualities. The mysterious guest, for example, turns out not to be a real person, but the embodiment of the Red Death. What, in a still larger sense, might this figure symbolize? What attitudes toward life and death do you think the Prince and his party-goers might symbolize?
9. In the last paragraph, Poe **alludes** to a prophecy from the Bible: "For yourselves know perfectly that the Day of the Lord so cometh as a thief in the night." (1 Thessalonians 5:2) "The Day of the Lord" is a way of referring to the last day of the world, or Judgment Day. Explain how the allusion adds a layer of meaning to Poe's story.
10. How would you state the **theme** of this story—the main idea about human behavior that is revealed by the fictional events? How do you feel about this theme—is it a valid one, in your experience?
11. Poe felt strongly that the main concern of any story was its **psychological effect.** He believed that neither narrative nor characterization was as important as the reader's emotional response. What emotional effect did the first paragraph of this story have on you? How does Poe produce this effect?

Writing About the Story

A Creative Response

1. **Staging the Story.** Suppose you were planning a movie or stage adaptation of "The Masque of the Red Death." Write a brief description of the first thing the audience would see. What would they hear?
2. **Writing an Opening Sentence.** In a review of Nathaniel Hawthorne's *Twice-Told Tales,* Poe said that the very first sentence in a story should create a particular effect. Reread the first sentence of this story. Then write three original sentences that you think would be good story openers. What effect do you want to create by each sentence?

A Critical Response

3. **Commenting on a Criticism.** Richard Wilbur, an American poet and an authority on Poe, has said this about "The Masque of the Red Death":

> Prince Prospero's flight from the Red Death is the poetic imagination's flight from temporal and worldly consciousness into dream. The thousand dancers of Prince Prospero's costume ball are just what Poe says they are—"dreams" or "phantasms," veiled and vivid creatures of Prince Prospero's rapt imagination. Whenever there is a feast, or carnival, or costume ball in Poe, we may be sure that a dream is in progress.
>
> —Richard Wilbur

Write an essay commenting on this remark. If you agree with it, explain what the events of the story suggest about the conflict between the dream world and the temporal world, or between illusion and reality. If you disagree, explain why.

Analyzing Language and Style

Emotional Effects

Poe was a master at finding words that created specific emotional effects. In this story, perhaps the most prominent word is *blood.* In his third sentence, Poe names the emotion he associates with blood: horror.

1. Find at least three passages in which blood is used to describe the color red. Think of at least one other descriptive word that might have been used in each case to create a different emotional effect. (For example, would "tomato red" make you feel horror?)

Interpreting Meanings

6. The clock and its chimes contribute elements of mystery and suspense. We wonder what the significance of the revelers' sudden confusion may be when they hear the chimes.

The clock may represent the inevitable passage of time for the revelers.

7. Note that Prospero's mansion has seven apartments; the number seven has often been regarded as symbolic or magical (as in the seven ages of man or the seven deadly sins). The Red Death makes his first appearance when the clock chimes midnight—again, perhaps, a symbol of the "witching hour."

The scarlet and black of the seventh chamber might be held to symbolize blood and death.

Perhaps this movement should be associated with the regions of the rising and setting sun, and hence, by extension, with birth and death.

8. The fact of mortality itself—that is, the death which awaits every human being.

The Prince and the revelers perhaps symbolize the universal temptation to deny the fact of death and to devote our lives to carefree pleasures.

9. Just as the prophecy implies that the end of the world may come when we least expect it, so the Prince and his revelers are surprised by the Red Death, although they believed themselves immune to it.

10. Students will suggest various answers. In general, the theme seems to be that those who try to insulate themselves against such universal ills as disease and death are only cherishing an illusion.

Student answers will vary.

11. The intended effect was one of terror or horror.

He produces this effect through carefully chosen words: *devastated, fatal, hideous,* and *dissolution* are some examples.

2. Given the nature of the enemy in the story, why do you think Poe keeps using the word *blood* as he does?
3. Poe uses the French word *bizarre* twice. *Bizarre* means "strange, odd, eccentric, outrageous, grotesque." Here are the two passages in which *bizarre* is used. Read each passage in context and suggest another word that could have been used to suggest a completely different emotional effect:

   a. ". . . the duke's love of the bizarre." (Page 228)
   b. "There was much of the . . . bizarre. . . ." (Page 230)
4. "There were delirious fancies such as the madman fashions. There was much of the beautiful, much of the wanton, much of the bizarre, something of the terrible, and not a little of that which might have excited disgust." Define the words in this passage, besides *bizarre,* that create a particular emotional tone. How would you describe that tone? What effect is Poe looking for?
5. Reread the very last sentence of the story. What is its emotional effect? What things do you associate with the word *decay*? What word means the opposite of decay?

Primary Sources
A Visit to the Poes

Mrs. Gove Nichols visited Poe's cottage in New York and recorded her impressions.

"The cottage had an air of gentility that must have been lent to it by the presence of its inmates. So neat, so poor, so unfurnished, and yet so charming a dwelling I never saw. The floor of the kitchen was white as wheaten flour. A table, a chair, and a little stove it contained seemed to furnish it completely. The sitting room was laid with check matting; four chairs, a light stand, and a hanging bookshelf completed its furniture. There were pretty presentation copies of books on the little shelves, and the Brownings had posts of honor on the stand. With quiet exultation Poe drew from his inside pocket a letter he had recently received from Elizabeth Barrett Browning. He read it to us. It was very flattering. . . . On the bookshelf there lay a volume of Poe's poems. He took it down, wrote my name in it and gave it to me. . . . He was at this time greatly depressed. Their extreme poverty, the sickness of his wife, and his own inability to write sufficiently accounted for this. We spent half an hour in the house, when some more company came, which included ladies, and then we all went to walk.

"We strolled away into the woods, and had a very cheerful time, till someone proposed a game at leaping. I think it must have been Poe, as he was expert in the exercise. Two or three gentlemen agreed to leap with him, and though one of them was tall and had been a hunter in times past, Poe still distanced them all. But alas! his gaiters [cloth or leather coverings that went over the shoes and covered the ankle], long worn and carefully kept, were both burst in the grand leap that made him victor. . . . I was certain he had no other shoes, boots, or gaiters. Who among us could offer him money to buy a new pair? . . . When we reached the cottage, I think all felt that we must not go in, to see the shoeless unfortunate sitting or standing in our midst. I had an errand, however—and I entered the house to get it. The poor old mother looked at his feet with a dismay that I shall never forget. 'Oh, Eddie!' said she, 'how did you burst your gaiters?' Poe seemed to have come into a semi-torpid state as soon as he saw his mother. 'Do answer Muddie,' now said she coaxingly—I related the cause of the mishap, and she drew me into the kitchen.

" 'Will you speak to Mr. ______ [an editor],' she said, 'about Eddie's last poem? . . . If he will only take the poem, Eddie can have a pair of shoes. He has it—I carried it last week, and Eddie says it is his best. You will speak to him about it, won't you?'

"We had already read the poem in conclave, and Heaven forgive us, we could not make head or tail of it. It might as well have been in any of the lost languages, for any meaning we could extract from its melodious numbers. I remember saying that I believed it was only a hoax that Poe was passing off for poetry, to see how far his name would go in imposing upon people. But here was a situation. The reviewer had been actively instrumental in the demolition of the gaiters.

" 'Of course, they will publish the poem,' said I, 'and I will ask C______ to be quick about it.'

"The poem was paid for at once and published soon after. I presume it is regarded as genuine poetry in the collected poems of its author, but then it bought the poet a pair of gaiters, and twelve shillings over."

—from *Israfel: The Life and Times of Edgar Allan Poe,* Hervey Allen

SUPPLEMENTARY SUPPORT MATERIALS
1. Vocabulary Activity Worksheet (*CCB*)
2. Review and Response Worksheet: Setting (*CCB*)
3. Selection Test (*CCB*)

DEVELOPING VOCABULARY
The following words from the story are tested in the Selection Test. (See also Vocabulary Activity Worksheet.)

munificent | hypochondriac
wan | to allude
incoherence

PREPARATION
ESTABLISHING A PURPOSE. As indicated in the explanatory note on this page, this story has been seen as a journey into "the unexplored world of the human mind." You might suggest that students read this story to decide if they agree with this statement. Is Poe exploring a part of the human mind that we all share?

A. Titles and Names
Choice of title and characters' names is an important, if minor, part of the writer's craft.
? How does the title strengthen this story? What other words might have been used instead of "fall"? Why is "fall" best? Why is the word "house" included in the title? On the other hand, could the story simply have been called "The House of Usher"? (Explain to students that noble and royal families are often designated as "the house of ________." For instance, the British royal family belongs to the House of Windsor.)

B. Expansion
The first sentence of this story is a classic example of atmospheric language. (See Analyzing Language and Style, page 247.)

C. Expansion
Words like *mere* and *sedges* all come from Middle English and were considered antiquated and "poetic" even when Poe wrote this.

A

THE FALL OF THE HOUSE OF USHER

"The Fall of the House of Usher" is probably Poe's best and most famous story. The story exhibits so many trappings of the Gothic tale that a list of them would stretch to the bottom of the page. We have a mysterious setting, mysterious illnesses, mysterious sounds in the night, the possibility of live burial, and the suggestion of the supernatural at work. But despite all its Gothic touches, the story aims for much more than mere thrills. The narrator's journey to the House of Usher has been seen as a symbolic psychological journey out of the world of reason and sanity into the unexplored world of the human mind.

Notice how Poe begins by establishing the mood of his story. Which words and phrases in the opening paragraph make you aware that the narrator is leaving one region and entering another, uncertain one?

Son cœur est un luth suspendu;
Sitôt qu'on le touche il résonne.[1]
—De Béranger.

B During the whole of a dull, dark, and soundless day in the autumn of the year, when the clouds hung oppressively low in the heavens, I had been passing alone, on horseback, through a singularly dreary tract of country; and at length found myself, as the shades of the evening drew on, within view of the melancholy House of Usher. I know not how it was—but, with the first glimpse of the building, a sense of insufferable gloom pervaded my spirit. I say insufferable; for the feeling was unrelieved by any of that half-pleasurable, because poetic, sentiment, with which the mind usually receives even the sternest natural images of the desolate or terrible. I looked C upon the scene before me—upon the mere[2] house, and the simple landscape features of the domain—upon the bleak walls—upon the vacant eyelike windows—upon a few rank sedges[3]—and upon a few white trunks of decayed trees—with an utter depression of soul which I can compare to no earthly sensation more properly than to the afterdream of the reveler upon opium—the bitter lapse into everyday life—the hideous dropping off of the veil. There was an iciness, a sinking, a sickening of the heart—an unredeemed dreariness of thought which no goading of the imagination could torture into aught[4] of the sublime. What was it—I paused to think—what was it that so unnerved me in the contemplation of the House of Usher? It was a mystery all insoluble; nor could I grapple with the shadowy fancies that crowded upon me as I pondered. I was forced to fall back upon the unsatisfactory conclusion, that while, beyond doubt, there *are* combinations of very simple natural objects which have the power of thus affecting us, still the analysis of this power lies among considerations beyond our depth. It was possible, I reflected, that a mere different arrangement of the particulars of the scene, of the details of the picture, would be sufficient to modify, or perhaps to annihilate its capacity for sorrowful impression; and, acting upon this idea, I reined my horse to the precipitous brink of a black and lurid tarn[5] that lay in unruffled luster by the dwelling, and gazed down—but with a shudder even more thrilling than before—upon the remodeled and inverted images of the gray sedge, and the ghastly tree stems, and the vacant and eyelike windows.

Nevertheless, in this mansion of gloom I now

1. ***Son coeur . . . il résonne:*** "His heart is a suspended lute; / Whenever one touches it, it resounds." From "Le Refus" ("The Refusal") by Pierre Jean de Béranger (1780–1857).
2. **mere:** lake.
3. **sedges:** grasslike plants that grow in watery ground.
4. **aught:** anything.
5. **tarn:** small mountain lake or pond with dark waters.

Illustration of a scene from "The Fall of the House of Usher" by Arthur Rackham (1935).

Humanities Connection: Responding to the Fine Art
Arthur Rackham was one of the greatest illustrators of the Victorian age. He specialized in illustrating fairy tales.

? Turn back to this picture when reading the description of Usher's house on page 236, paragraph three. Has Rackham done Poe's words justice? Has he transcribed the description exactly? (Students should note the gloomy mood of Rackham's art but may find that his "house of Usher" differs from their own vision of it.)

A. Responding
? What does the phrase "the entire family lay in the direct line of descent" mean? (That each generation of Ushers had only one son to carry on the family name)

B. Responding
? What does Poe accomplish by blurring the boundaries between the family and its house? (It will have symbolic value at the end of the story when the house, like the family, collapses.) Is this "blurring" realistic? Is it effective? (Some will find it rather confusing.)

C. Expansion
See illustration and Humanities Connection annotation, page 235.

proposed to myself a sojourn of some weeks. Its proprietor, Roderick Usher, had been one of my boon companions in boyhood; but many years had elapsed since our last meeting. A letter, however, had lately reached me in a distant part of the country—a letter from him—which, in its wildly importunate nature, had admitted of no other than a personal reply. The MS.[6] gave evidence of nervous agitation. The writer spoke of acute bodily illness—of a mental disorder which oppressed him—and of an earnest desire to see me, as his best, and indeed his only personal friend, with a view of attempting, by the cheerfulness of my society, some alleviation of his malady. It was the manner in which all this, and much more, was said—it was the apparent *heart* that went with his request—which allowed me no room for hesitation; and I accordingly obeyed forthwith what I still considered a very singular summons.

Although, as boys, we had been even intimate associates, yet I really knew little of my friend. His reserve had been always excessive and habitual. I was aware, however, that his very ancient family had been noted, time out of mind, for a peculiar sensibility of temperament, displaying itself, through long ages, in many works of exalted art, and manifested, of late, in repeated deeds of munificent yet unobtrusive charity, as well as in a passionate devotion to the intricacies, perhaps even more than to the orthodox and easily recognizable beauties, of musical science. I had learned, too, the very remarkable fact, that the stem of the Usher race, all time-honored as it was, had put forth, at no period, any enduring branch; A in other words, that the entire family lay in the direct line of descent, and had always, with very trifling and very temporary variation, so lain. It was this deficiency, I considered, while running over in thought the perfect keeping of the character of the premises with the accredited character of the people, and while speculating upon the possible influence which the one, in the long lapse of centuries, might have exercised upon the other—it was this deficiency, perhaps, of collateral issue,[7] and the consequent undeviating transmission, from sire to son, of the patrimony with the name, B which had at length, so identified the two as to merge the original title of the estate in the quaint and equivocal appellation of the "House of Usher"—an appellation which seemed to include, in the minds of the peasantry who used it, both the family and the family mansion.

I have said that the sole effect of my somewhat childish experiment—that of looking down within the tarn—had been to deepen the first singular impression. There can be no doubt that the consciousness of the rapid increase of my superstition—for why should I not so term it?—served mainly to accelerate the increase itself. Such, I have long known, is the paradoxical law of all sentiments having terror as a basis. And it might have been for this reason only, that, when I again uplifted my eyes to the house itself, from its image in the pool, there grew in my mind a strange fancy—a fancy so ridiculous, indeed, that I but mention it to show the vivid force of the sensations which oppressed me. I had so worked upon my imagination as really to believe that about the whole mansion and domain there hung an atmosphere peculiar to themselves and their immediate vicinity—an atmosphere which had no affinity with the air of heaven, but which had reeked up from the decayed trees, and the gray wall, and the silent tarn—a pestilent and mystic vapor, dull, sluggish, faintly discernible, and leaden-hued.

Shaking off from my spirit what *must* have been a dream, I scanned more narrowly the real aspect of the building. Its principal feature seemed to be that of an excessive antiquity. The discoloration of ages had been great. Minute fungi overspread the whole exterior, hanging in a fine tangled web-work from the eaves. Yet all this was apart from any extraordinary dilapidation. No portion of the masonry had fallen; and there appeared to be a wild inconsistency between its still perfect adaptation of parts, and the crumbling condition of the individual stones. In this there was much that reminded me of the specious totality of old wood-work which has rotted for long years in some neglected vault, with no disturbance from the breath of the external air. Beyond this indication of extensive decay, however, the fabric gave little token of instability. Perhaps the eye of a scrutinizing observer might have discovered a barely perceptible fissure, which, extending from the roof of the building in front, made its way down the wall in a zigzag direction, until it became lost in the sullen waters of the tarn. C

Noticing these things, I rode over a short causeway to the house. A servant-in-waiting took my horse, and I entered the Gothic archway of the

6. **MS.:** an abbreviation of the word *manuscript*.
7. **collateral issue:** descendants.

Literature and Language: Using Dashes
A glance at the text—without even pausing to read—will show students that Poe peppers his story with dashes. We use dashes today for the same purpose that Poe used them: to indicate an abrupt break in thought or speech. Dashes also show an unfinished statement or question, though Poe doesn't use them for that purpose in this story.

Read aloud some of the dash-filled sentences (see bottom left column, page 234, for example) while students listen carefully. Ask them to determine what mood or feeling the sentences suggest. Students should observe that the dashes make the narrator sound nervous, agitated, high-strung. Even more so is Usher at the story's end; see the top left column, page 245.

Ask students to calm down the narrator, rewriting three of Poe's dash-filled sentences. When they remove the dashes, students may omit some words or break long sentences into shorter ones.

hall.[8] A valet, of stealthy step, thence conducted me, in silence, through many dark and intricate passages in my progress to the *studio* of his master. Much that I encountered on the way contributed, I know not how, to heighten the vague sentiments of which I have already spoken. While the objects around me—while the carvings of the ceilings, the somber tapestries of the walls, the ebon blackness of the floors, and the phantasmagoric[9] armorial trophies which rattled as I strode, were but matters to which, or to such as which, I had been accustomed from my infancy—while I hesitated not to acknowledge how familiar was all this—I still wondered to find how unfamiliar were the fancies which ordinary images were stirring up. On one of the staircases, I met the physician of the family. His countenance, I thought, wore a mingled expression of low cunning and perplexity. He accosted me with trepidation and passed on. The valet now threw open a door and ushered me into the presence of his master.

The room in which I found myself was very large and lofty. The windows were long, narrow, and pointed, and at so vast a distance from the black oaken floor as to be altogether inaccessible from within. Feeble gleams of encrimsoned light made their way through the trellised panes, and served to render sufficiently distinct the more prominent objects around; the eye, however, struggled in vain to reach the remoter angles of the chamber, or the recesses of the vaulted and fretted[10] ceiling. Dark draperies hung upon the walls. The general furniture was profuse, comfortless, antique, and tattered. Many books and musical instruments lay scattered about, but failed to give any vitality to the scene. I felt that I breathed an atmosphere of sorrow. An air of stern, deep, and irredeemable gloom hung over and pervaded all.

A Upon my entrance, Usher arose from a sofa on which he had been lying at full length, and greeted me with a vivacious warmth which had much in it, I at first thought, of an overdone cordiality—of the constrained effort of the *ennuyé*[11] man of the world. A glance, however, at his countenance, convinced me of his perfect sincerity. We sat down; and for some moments, while he spoke not, I gazed upon him with a feeling half of pity, half of awe. Surely, man had never before so terribly altered, in so brief a period, as had Roderick Usher! It was with difficulty that I could bring myself to admit the identity of the wan being before me with the companion of my early boyhood. Yet the character of his face had been at all times remarkable. A cadaverousness[12] of complexion, an eye large, liquid, and luminous beyond comparison; lips somewhat thin and very pallid, but of a surpassing beautiful curve; a nose of a delicate Hebrew model, but with a breadth of nostril unusual in similar formations; a finely molded chin, speaking, in its want of prominence, of a want of moral energy; hair of a more than weblike softness and tenuity;[13] these features, with an inordinate expansion above the regions of the temple, made up altogether a countenance not easily to be forgotten. And now in the mere exaggeration of the prevailing character of these features, and of the expression they were wont to convey, lay so much of change that I doubted to whom I spoke. The now ghastly pallor of the skin, and the now miraculous luster of the eye, above all things startled and even awed me. The silken hair, too, had been suffered to grow all unheeded, and as, in its wild gossamer texture, it floated rather than fell about the face, I could not, even with effort, connect its Arabesque[14] expression with any idea of simple humanity.

In the manner of my friend I was at once struck with an incoherence—an inconsistency; and I soon found this to arise from a series of feeble and futile struggles to overcome a habitual trepidancy—an excessive nervous agitation. For something of this nature I had indeed been prepared, no less by his letter, than by reminiscences of certain boyish traits, and by conclusions deduced from his peculiar physical conformation and temperament. His action was alternately vivacious and sullen. His voice varied rapidly from a tremulous indecision (when the animal spirits seemed B utterly in abeyance) to that species of energetic concision—that abrupt, weighty, unhurried, and

8. The archway looked like a doorway in a Gothic cathedral—high, pointed, and elaborately carved.
9. **phantasmagoric** (fan·taz·mə·gor′ik): dreamlike, bizarre.
10. **fretted:** carved in an intricate pattern.
11. ***ennuyé*** (än·nwē′ā): a French word meaning "bored" or "jaded."
12. **cadaverousness** (kə·dav′ər·əs·nes): corpselike quality.
13. **tenuity** (tə·no͞o′ə·tē): thinness, fineness.
14. **Arabesque:** elaborately intricate, as in Moorish or Arabic ornamentation.

A. Characterization
On this page and the next, Poe relies on description rather than dramatization—on telling us rather than showing us what Roderick Usher is like.
? How effective is this telling? How could Usher's characterization have been made more vivid? (The extended description seems effective; it might be more vivid if the speaker had quoted some of Usher's words.)

B. Expansion (Challenging)
Students who are interested in human behavior might want to look up Usher's symptoms in the psychiatric section of a medical handbook and report their diagnoses to the class. Manic depression might be a likely choice.

A. Expansion Students might be interested to know that recent research indicates that a predisposition to certain mental illnesses such as clinical depression and schizophrenia is almost certainly inherited.

B. Expansion Here Poe seems to be describing a form of schizophrenia, sometimes called catatonia, in which the patient may alternate between states of agitation and stupor.

hollow-sounding enunciation—that leaden, self-balanced, and perfectly modulated guttural utterance, which may be observed in the lost drunkard, or the irreclaimable eater of opium, during the periods of his most intense excitement.

It was thus that he spoke of the object of my visit, of his earnest desire to see me, and of the solace he expected me to afford him. He entered, at some length, into what he conceived to be the nature of his malady. It was, he said, a constitutional and a family evil, and one for which he despaired to find a remedy—a mere nervous affection,[15] he immediately added, which would undoubtedly soon pass off. It displayed itself in a host of unnatural sensations. Some of these, as he detailed them, interested and bewildered me; although, perhaps, the terms, and the general manner of the narration had their weight. He suffered much from a morbid acuteness of the senses; the most insipid food was alone endurable; he could wear only garments of certain texture; the odors of all flowers were oppressive; his eyes were tortured by even a faint light; and there were but peculiar sounds, and these from stringed instruments, which did not inspire him with horror.

To an anomalous[16] species of terror I found him a bounden slave. "I shall perish," said he, "I *must* perish in this deplorable folly. Thus, thus, and not otherwise, shall I be lost. I dread the events of the future, not in themselves, but in their results. I shudder at the thought of any, even the most trivial, incident, which may operate upon this intolerable agitation of soul. I have, indeed, no abhorrence of danger, except in its absolute effect—in terror. In this unnerved—in this pitiable condition—I feel that the period will sooner or later arrive when I must abandon life and reason together, in some struggle with the grim phantasm, FEAR."

I learned, moreover, at intervals, and through broken and equivocal hints, another singular feature of his mental condition. He was enchained by certain superstitious impressions in regard to the dwelling which he tenanted, and whence, for many years, he had never ventured forth—in regard to an influence whose supposititious[17] force was conveyed in terms too shadowy here to be restated—an influence which some peculiarities in the mere form and substance of his family mansion, had, by dint of long sufferance, he said, obtained over his spirit—an effect which the *physique* of the gray walls and turrets, and of the dim tarn into which they all looked down, had, at length, brought about upon the *morale* of his existence.

He admitted, however, although with hesitation, that much of the peculiar gloom which thus afflicted him could be traced to a more natural and far more palpable origin—to the severe and long-continued illness—indeed to the evidently approaching dissolution—of a tenderly beloved sister—his sole companion for long years—his last and only relative on earth. "Her decease," he said, with a bitterness which I can never forget, "would leave him (him the hopeless and the frail) the last of the ancient race of the Ushers." While he spoke, the lady Madeline (for so was she called) passed slowly through a remote portion of the apartment, and, without having noticed my presence, disappeared. I regarded her with an utter astonishment not unmingled with dread—and yet I found it impossible to account for such feelings. A sensation of stupor oppressed me, as my eyes followed her retreating steps. When a door, at length, closed upon her, my glance sought instinctively and eagerly the countenance of the brother—but he had buried his face in his hands, and I could only perceive that a far more than ordinary wanness had overspread the emaciated fingers through which trickled many passionate tears.

The disease of the lady Madeline had long baffled the skill of her physicians. A settled apathy, a gradual wasting away of the person, and frequent although transient affections of a partially cataleptical[18] character, were the unusual diagnosis. Hitherto she had steadily borne up against the pressure of her malady, and had not betaken herself finally to bed; but, on the closing in of the evening of my arrival at the house, she succumbed (as her brother told me at night with inexpressible agitation) to the prostrating power of the destroyer; and I learned that the glimpse I had obtained of her person would thus probably be the last I should obtain—that the lady, at least while living, would be seen by me no more.

15. **affection:** here, affliction.
16. **anomalous:** abnormal.
17. **supposititious:** supposed.
18. **cataleptical:** in catalepsy, the victim loses sensation and the ability to move the limbs, or even the entire body. In a cataleptic attack, Madeline could be as stiff as a corpse.

A

The Dead Wife by George Cochran Lambdin (late 19th century). Oil. North Carolina Museum of Art, Raleigh. Gift of Peter A. Vogt.

For several days ensuing, her name was unmentioned by either Usher or myself: and during this period I was busied in earnest endeavors to alleviate the melancholy of my friend. We painted and read together; or I listened, as if in a dream, to the wild improvisations of his speaking guitar. And thus, as a closer and still closer intimacy admitted me more unreservedly into the recesses of his spirit, the more bitterly did I perceive the futility of all attempt at cheering a mind from which darkness, as if an inherent positive quality, poured forth upon all objects of the moral and physical universe, in one unceasing radiation of gloom.

I shall ever bear about me a memory of the many solemn hours I thus spent alone with the master of the House of Usher. Yet I should fail in any attempt to convey an idea of the exact character of the studies, or of the occupations, in which he involved me, or led me the way. An excited and highly distempered ideality[19] threw a sulfureous[20] luster over all. His long, improvised dirges will ring forever in my ears. Among other things, I hold painfully in mind a certain singular perversion and amplification of the wild air of the

19. **distempered ideality:** disturbed or disordered idea.
20. **sulfureous:** yellowish, like sulfur.

A. Humanities Connection: Responding to the Fine Art
The painting seems to follow Poe's precept that the most powerful subject for a work of art is the death of a beautiful young woman; it shows that in the nineteenth century, Poe was not alone in this idea.
? How would you describe the mood of this painting? (Dark and heavy) Other than the fact that the subject of the painting is a dead woman, why do you suppose this painting was chosen to illustrate the story? (The rooms, the darkness, and the heavy drapery seem consistent with the description of the House of Usher.)

A. Expansion
Note Poe's anticipation of abstract painting, more than half a century before it appeared on any real canvas.

B. Allegory
Remind students of the way in which Poe identifies the family and the house of Usher. (See annotation B, page 236.) The personification of the house in this poem ("reared its head") strengthens the parallel between it and Usher himself. The poem may be read as an allegory of Usher's loss of reason and the fall of his house and family into utter disarray.

last waltz of Von Weber.[21] From the paintings over which his elaborate fancy brooded, and which grew, touch by touch, into vaguenesses at which I shuddered the more thrillingly, because I shuddered knowing not why—from these paintings (vivid as their images now are before me) I would in vain endeavor to educe more than a small portion which should lie within the compass of merely written words. By the utter simplicity, by the nakedness of his designs, he arrested and overawed attention. If ever mortal painted an idea, that mortal was Roderick Usher. For me at least—in the circumstances then surrounding me—there arose out of the pure abstractions which the hypochondriac contrived to throw upon his canvas, an intensity of intolerable awe, no shadow of which felt I ever yet in the contemplation of the certainly glowing yet too concrete reveries of Fuseli.[22]

One of the phantasmagoric conceptions of my friend, partaking not so rigidly of the spirit of abstraction, may be shadowed forth, although feebly, in words. A small picture presented the interior of an immensely long and rectangular vault or tunnel, with low walls, smooth, white, and without interruption or device. Certain accessory points of the design served well to convey the idea that this excavation lay at an exceeding depth below the surface of the earth. No outlet was observed in any portion of its vast extent, and no torch, or other artificial source of light was discernible; yet a flood of intense rays rolled throughout, and bathed the whole in a ghastly and inappropriate splendor.

I have just spoken of that morbid condition of the auditory nerve which rendered all music intolerable to the sufferer, with the exception of certain effects of stringed instruments. It was, perhaps, the narrow limits to which he thus confined himself upon the guitar, which gave birth, in great measure, to the fantastic character of his performances. But the fervid *facility* of his *impromptus*[23] could not be so accounted for. They must have been, and were, in the notes, as well as in the words of his wild fantasias (for he not unfrequently accompanied himself with rhymed verbal improvisations), the result of that intense mental collectedness and concentration to which I have previously alluded as observable only in particular moments of the highest artificial excitement. The words of one of these rhapsodies I have easily remembered. I was, perhaps, the more forcibly impressed with it, as he gave it, because, in the under or mystic current of its meaning, I fancied that I perceived, and for the first time, a full consciousness on the part of Usher, of the tottering of his lofty reason upon her throne. The verses, which were entitled "The Haunted Palace," ran very nearly, if not accurately, thus:

I

In the greenest of our valleys,
By good angels tenanted,
Once a fair and stately palace—
Radiant palace—reared its head.
In the monarch Thought's dominion—
It stood there!
Never seraph spread a pinion[24]
Over fabric half so fair.

II

Banners yellow, glorious, golden,
On its roof did float and flow;
(This—all this—was in the olden
Time long ago)
And every gentle air that dallied,
In that sweet day,
Along the ramparts plumed and pallid,
A winged odor went away.

III

Wanderers in that happy valley
Through two luminous windows saw
Spirits moving musically
To a lute's well-tuned law,
Round about a throne, where sitting
(Porphyrogene!)[25]
In state his glory well befitting,
The ruler of the realm was seen.

21. **Von Weber:** Carl Maria von Weber (1786–1826), a German composer of Romantic music.
22. **Fuseli:** Johann Heinrich Fuseli, a Swiss painter (1741–1825) who lived in England and illustrated the epics of Milton and the tragedies of Shakespeare. He often painted scenes of horror and the supernatural.
23. ***impromptus:*** improvised performances.
24. **pinion** (pin′yən): wing (a seraph is an angel).
25. **Porphyrogene:** someone "born to the purple," or of royal blood. Porphyry was a purple dye reserved for royalty. (Poe coined the word *Porphyrogene.*)

IV

And all with pearl and ruby glowing
  Was the fair palace door,
Through which came flowing, flowing, flowing
  And sparkling evermore,
A troop of Echoes whose sweet duty
  Was but to sing,
In voices surpassing beauty,
  The wit and wisdom of their king.

V

But evil things, in robes of sorrow,
  Assailed the monarch's high estate;
(Ah, let us mourn, for never morrow
  Shall dawn upon him, desolate!)
And, round about his home, the glory
  That blushed and bloomed
Is but a dim-remembered story
  Of the oldtime entombed.

VI

And travelers now within that valley,
  Through the red-litten[26] windows, see
Vast forms that move fantastically
  To a discordant melody;
While, like a rapid ghastly river,
  Through the pale door,
A hideous throng rush out forever,
  And laugh—but smile no more.

I well remember that suggestions arising from this ballad led us into a train of thought wherein there became manifest an opinion of Usher's which I mention not so much on account of its novelty (for other men have thought thus); as on account of the pertinacity with which he maintained it. This opinion, in its general form, was that of the sentience[27] of all vegetable things. But, in his disordered fancy, the idea had assumed a more daring character, and trespassed, under certain conditions, upon the kingdom of inorganization.[28] I lack words to express the full extent, of the earnest *abandon* of his persuasion. The belief, however, was connected (as I have previously hinted) with the gray stones of the home of his forefathers. The conditions of the sentience had been here, he imagined, fulfilled in the method of collocation of these stones—in the order of their arrangement, as well as in that of the many *fungi* which overspread them, and of the decayed trees which stood around—above all, in the long undisturbed endurance of this arrangement, and in its reduplication in the still waters of the tarn. Its evidence—the evidence of the sentience—was to be seen, he said (and I here started as he spoke), in the gradual yet certain condensation of an atmosphere of their own about the waters and the walls. The result was discoverable, he added, in that silent, yet importunate and terrible influence which for centuries had molded the destinies of his family, and which made *him* what I now saw him—what he was. Such opinions need no comment, and I will make none.

A

Our books—the books which, for years, had formed no small portion of the mental existence of the invalid—were, as might be supposed, in strict keeping with this character of phantasm. We pored together over such works as the Ververt et Chartreuse[29] of Gresset; the Belphegor of Machiavelli; the Heaven and Hell of Swedenborg; the Subterranean Voyage of Nicholas Klimm by Holberg; the Chiromancy of Robert Flud, of Jean D'Indaginé, and of De la Chambre; the Journey into the Blue Distance of Tieck; and the City of the Sun of Campanella. One favorite volume was a small octavo edition of the *Directorium Inquisitorum,* by the Dominican Eymeric de Gironne; and there were passages in Pomponius Mela, about the old African Satyrs and Ægipans, over which Usher would sit dreaming for hours. His chief delight, however, was found in the perusal of an exceedingly rare and curious book in quarto Gothic—the manual of a forgotten church—the *Vigiliæ Mortuorum secundum Chorum Ecclesiæ Maguntinæ.*[30]

I could not help thinking of the wild ritual of this work, and of its probable influence upon the hypochondriac, when, one evening, having informed me abruptly that the lady Madeline was no more, he stated his intention of preserving her corpse for a fortnight (previously to its final interment), in one of the numerous vaults within the

B

26. **red-litten:** red-lighted.
27. **sentience** (sen′shəns): consciousness.
28. **kingdom of inorganization:** the world of inorganic objects.

29. **Ververt et Chartreuse,** etc.: the books listed include works of mysticism, of magic, or of horror. Most of them foreshadow what is to happen to Madeline Usher.
30. ***Vigiliae Mortuorum*** means "vigil of the dead."

A. Personification
Make sure students penetrate Poe's language here and understand that Roderick Usher believes his house is alive and that it is destroying him and his family.
? What clues have you had that the Usher family and its house are completely identified with each other? (See, for example, annotation A, page 234, annotation B, page 236, and annotation B, page 240.)

B. Plot
Point out to students that, after a long digression, the plot per se resumes with the words, ". . . one evening."

A. Connections Here Poe seems to be describing the brother and sisters as *doppelgangers,* a theme he also uses in "William Wilson." (See annotation B, page 227.)

B. Responding Up until now the narrator has represented reason and sanity.

? What is happening to the narrator here? (He's falling prey to Roderick's delusions and madness.) How do you think you would have felt by this time if you were in the narrator's place?

main walls of the building. The worldly reason, however, assigned for this singular proceeding, was one which I did not feel at liberty to dispute. The brother had been led to his resolution (so he told me) by consideration of the unusual character of the malady of the deceased, of certain obtrusive and eager inquiries on the part of her medical men, and of the remote and exposed situation of the burial ground of the family. I will not deny that when I called to mind the sinister countenance of the person whom I met upon the staircase,[31] on the day of my arrival at the house, I had no desire to oppose what I regarded as at best but a harmless, and by no means an unnatural, precaution.[32]

At the request of Usher, I personally aided him in the arrangements for the temporary entombment. The body having been encoffined, we two alone bore it to its rest. The vault in which we placed it (and which had been so long unopened that our torches, half smothered in its oppressive atmosphere, gave us little opportunity for investigation) was small, damp, and entirely without means of admission for light; lying, at great depth, immediately beneath that portion of the building in which was my own sleeping apartment. It had been used, apparently, in remote feudal times, for the worst purposes of a dungeon-keep,[33] and, in later days, as a place of deposit for powder, or some other highly combustible substance, as a portion of its floor, and the whole interior of a long archway through which we reached it, were carefully sheathed with copper. The door, of massive iron, had been, also, similarly protected. Its immense weight caused an unusually sharp grating sound, as it moved upon its hinges.

Having deposited our mournful burden upon tressels within this region of horror, we partially turned aside the yet unscrewed lid of the coffin, and looked upon the face of the tenant. A striking similitude between the brother and sister now first arrested my attention; and Usher, divining, perhaps, my thoughts, murmured out some few words from which I learned that the deceased and himself had been twins, and that sympathies of a scarcely intelligible nature had always existed between them. Our glances, however, rested not long upon the dead—for we could not regard her unawed. The disease which had thus entombed the lady in the maturity of youth, had left, as usual in all maladies of a strictly cataleptical character, the mockery of a faint blush upon the bosom and the face, and that suspiciously lingering smile upon the lip which is so terrible in death. We replaced and screwed down the lid, and, having secured the door of iron, made our way, with toil, into the scarcely less gloomy apartments of the upper portion of the house.

And now, some days of bitter grief having elapsed, an observable change came over the features of the mental disorder of my friend. His ordinary manner had vanished. His ordinary occupations were neglected or forgotten. He roamed from chamber to chamber with hurried, unequal, and objectless step. The pallor of his countenance had assumed, if possible, a more ghastly hue—but the luminousness of his eye had utterly gone out. The once occasional huskiness of this tone was heard no more; and a tremulous quaver, as if of extreme terror, habitually characterized his utterance. There were times, indeed, when I thought his unceasingly agitated mind was laboring with some oppressive secret, to divulge which he struggled for the necessary courage. At times, again, I was obliged to resolve all into the mere inexplicable vagaries[34] of madness, for I beheld him gazing upon vacancy for long hours, in an attitude of the profoundest attention, as if listening to some imaginary sound. It was no wonder that his condition terrified—that it infected me. I felt creeping upon me, by slow yet certain degrees, the wild influences of his own fantastic yet impressive superstitions.

It was, especially, upon retiring to bed late in the night of the seventh or eighth day after the placing of the lady Madeline within the dungeon, that I experienced the full power of such feelings. Sleep came not near my couch—while the hours waned and waned away. I struggled to reason off the nervousness which had dominion over me. I endeavored to believe that much, if not all of what I felt, was due to the bewildering influence of the gloomy furniture of the room—of the dark and tattered draperies, which, tortured into motion by the breath of a rising tempest, swayed fitfully to

31. This person is the doctor.
32. Usher wishes to be sure his sister's body will not be dissected by doctors. At the time, bodies were often stolen and sold to medical students.
33. **dungeon-keep:** dungeon.

34. **vagaries:** whims.

A. Pathetic Fallacy
The luminous gas is an important atmospheric effect. It, and the whirlwind, exemplify the "pathetic fallacy"—the idea that the external environment mirrors human emotions.

B. Story Structure
The thematically appropriate story-within-a-story is a typically Gothic touch, and not much to modern taste. Poe's quotation from *Mad Trist* has more than a touch of parody to it.

? Why might Poe include a long passage from a made-up book at this point? (One of the devices Poe uses to build suspence is stopping and starting the action of the story. Inserting this scene has this effect, with the added benefit that the words he is quietly reading to Roderick are suddenly echoes of reality.)

C. Responding
The narrator dislikes the "unimaginative prolixity" of *Mad Trist.* Could the same phrase be used to describe Poe's writing? (Though Poe could certainly be accused of prolixity, he was hardly unimaginative.)

and fro upon the walls, and rustled uneasily about the decorations of the bed. But my efforts were fruitless. An irrepressible tremor gradually pervaded my frame; and, at length, there sat upon my very heart an incubus[35] of utterly causeless alarm. Shaking this off with a gasp and a struggle, I uplifted myself upon the pillows, and, peering earnestly within the intense darkness of the chamber, hearkened—I know not why, except that an instinctive spirit prompted me—to certain low and indefinite sounds which came, through the pauses of the storm, at long intervals, I knew not whence. Overpowered by an intense sentiment of horror, unaccountable yet unendurable, I threw on my clothes with haste (for I felt that I should sleep no more during the night), and endeavored to arouse myself from the pitiable condition into which I had fallen, by pacing rapidly to and fro through the apartment.

I had taken but few turns in this manner, when a light step on an adjoining staircase arrested my attention. I presently recognized it as that of Usher. In an instant afterward he rapped, with a gentle touch, at my door, and entered, bearing a lamp. His countenance was, as usual, cadaverously wan—but, moreover, there was a species of mad hilarity in his eyes—an evidently restrained *hysteria* in his whole demeanor. His air appalled me—but anything was preferable to the solitude which I had so long endured, and even welcomed his presence as a relief.

"And you have not seen it?" he said abruptly, after having stared about him for some moments in silence—"you have not then seen it?—but, stay! you shall." Thus speaking, and having carefully shaded his lamp, he hurried to one of the casements, and threw it freely open to the storm.

The impetuous fury of the entering gust nearly lifted us from our feet. It was, indeed, a tempestuous yet sternly beautiful night, and one wildly singular in its terror and its beauty. A whirlwind had apparently collected its force in our vicinity; for there were frequent and violent alterations in the direction of the wind; and the exceeding density of the clouds (which hung so low as to press upon the turrets of the house) did not prevent our perceiving the lifelike velocity with which they flew careering from all points against each other, without passing away into the distance. I say that even their exceeding density did not prevent our perceiving this—yet we had no glimpse of the moon or stars—nor was there any flashing forth of the lightning. But the under surfaces of the huge masses of agitated vapor, as well as all terrestrial objects immediately around us, were glowing in the unnatural light of a faintly luminous and distinctly visible gaseous exhalation which hung about and enshrouded the mansion. A

"You must not—you shall not behold this!" said I, shudderingly, to Usher, as I led him, with a gentle violence, from the window to a seat. "These appearances, which bewilder you, are merely electrical phenomena not uncommon—or it may be that they have their ghastly origin in the rank miasma[36] of the tarn. Let us close this casement—the air is chilling and dangerous to your frame. Here is one of your favorite romances. I will read, and you shall listen—and so we will pass away this terrible night together."

The antique volume which I had taken up was the *Mad Trist* of Sir Launcelot Canning;[37] but I B called it a favorite of Usher's more in sad jest than in earnest; for, in truth, there is little in its uncouth and unimaginative prolixity[38] which could have C had interest for the lofty and spiritual ideality of my friend. It was, however, the only book immediately at hand; and I indulged a vague hope that the excitement which now agitated the hypochondriac, might find relief (for the history of mental disorder is full of similar anomalies) even in the extremeness of the folly which I should read. Could I have judged, indeed, by the wild, overstrained air of vivacity with which he hearkened, or apparently hearkened, to the words of the tale, I might well have congratulated myself upon the success of my design.

I had arrived at that well-known portion of the story where Ethelred, the hero of the Trist, having sought in vain for peaceable admission into the dwelling of the hermit, proceeds to make good an entrance by force. Here, it will be remembered, the words of the narrative run thus:

"And Ethelred, who was by nature of a doughty[39] heart, and who was now mighty withal,

35. **incubus** (in′kyə·bəs): nightmare. At one time, people believed nightmares were caused by demons who lay on top of sleeping persons.

36. **rank miasma:** marsh gas, arising from rotting vegetable or animal matter.
37. ***Mad Trist* of Sir Launcelot Canning:** an invented book.
38. **prolixity:** wordiness.
39. **doughty** (dout′ē): courageous.

A. Expansion
Point out to students how Poe continues to weave his own story around the story of Ethelred, so that increasingly dreadful sounds heard by the narrator are anticipated by sounds described in his reading. (See annotation B, page 243.)

on account of the powerfulness of the wine which he had drunken, waited no longer to hold parley with the hermit, who, in sooth, was of an obstinate and maliceful turn, but, feeling the rain upon his shoulders, and fearing the rising of the tempest, uplifted his mace outright, and, with blows, made quickly room in the plankings of the door for his gauntleted hand; and now pulling therewith sturdily, he so cracked, and ripped, and tore all asunder, that the noise of the dry and hollow-sounding wood alarmed and reverberated throughout the forest."

At the termination of this sentence I started, and for a moment, paused; for it appeared to me (although I at once concluded that my excited fancy had deceived me)—it appeared to me that, from some very remote portion of the mansion, there came, indistinctly, to my ears, what might have been, in its exact similarity of character, the echo (but a stifled and dull one certainly) of the very cracking and ripping sound which Sir Launcelot had so particularly described. It was, beyond doubt, the coincidence alone which had arrested my attention; for, amid the rattling of the sashes of the casements, and the ordinary commingled noises of the still increasing storm, the sound, in itself, had nothing, surely which should have interested or disturbed me. I continued the story:

"But the good champion Ethelred, now entering within the door, was sore enraged and amazed to perceive no signal of the maliceful hermit; but, in the stead thereof, a dragon of a scaly and prodigious demeanor, and of a fiery tongue, which sat in guard before a palace of gold, with a floor of silver; and upon the wall there hung a shield of shining brass with this legend enwritten—

Who entereth herein, a conqueror hath bin;
Who slayeth the dragon, the shield he shall win;

And Ethelred uplifted his mace, and struck upon the head of the dragon, which fell before him, and gave up his pesty breath, with a shriek so horrid and harsh, and withal so piercing, that Ethelred had fain to close his ears with his hands against the dreadful noise of it, the like whereof was never before heard."

Here again I paused abruptly, and now with a feeling of wild amazement—for there could be no doubt whatever that, in this instance, I did actually hear (although from what direction it proceeded I found it impossible to say) a low and apparently distant, but harsh, protracted, and most unusual screaming or grating sound—the exact counterpart of what my fancy had already conjured up for the dragon's unnatural shriek as described by the romancer.

Oppressed, as I certainly was, upon the occurrence of the second and most extraordinary coincidence, by a thousand conflicting sensations, in which wonder and extreme terror were predominant, I still retained sufficient presence of mind to avoid exciting, by any observation, the sensitive nervousness of my companion. I was by no means certain that he had noticed the sounds in question; although, assuredly, a strange alteration had, during the last few minutes, taken place in his demeanor. From a position fronting my own, he had gradually brought round his chair, so as to sit with his face to the door of the chamber; and thus I could but partially perceive his features, although I saw that his lips trembled as if he were murmuring inaudibly. His head had dropped upon his breast—yet I knew that he was not asleep, from the wide and rigid opening of the eye as I caught a glimpse of it in profile. The motion of his body, too, was at variance with this idea—for he rocked from side to side with a gentle yet constant and uniform sway. Having rapidly taken notice of all this, I resumed the narrative of Sir Launcelot, which thus proceeded:

"And now, the champion, having escaped from the terrible fury of the dragon, bethinking himself of the brazen shield, and of the breaking up of the enchantment which was upon it, removed the carcass from out of the way before him, and approached valorously over the silver pavement of the castle to where the shield was upon the wall; which in sooth tarried not for his full coming, but fell down at his feet upon the silver floor, with a mighty great and ringing sound."

No sooner had these syllables passed my lips, than—as if a shield of brass had indeed, at the moment, fallen heavily upon a floor of silver—I became aware of a distinct, hollow, metallic, and clangorous, yet apparently muffled reverberation. Completely unnerved, I leaped to my feet; but the measured rocking movement of Usher was undisturbed. I rushed to the chair in which he sat. His eyes were bent fixedly before him, and throughout his whole countenance there reigned a stony rigidity. But, as I placed my hand upon his shoulder, there came a strong shudder over his whole person; a sickly smile quivered about his lips; and I saw that he spoke in a low, hurried, and gibbering

A

CLOSURE

Have students write out, without pausing to think much beforehand, their emotional reactions to the story.

READING CHECK TEST

1. Because of Roderick's nervous affliction, he can eat only the most bland foods. *True*

2. After Roderick introduces Madeline to the narrator, the narrator comments on her charming beauty and her frail physical appearance. *False*

3. While burying Madeline, the narrator realizes that Roderick and his sister are twins. *True*

4. Roderick seems less depressed after his sister's death. *False*

5. After Roderick's death, the narrator flees the Usher house. *True*

murmur, as if unconscious of my presence. Bending closely over him, I at length drank in the hideous import of his words.

"Not hear it?—yes, I hear it, and *have* heard it. Long—long—long—many minutes, many hours, many days, have I heard it—yet I dared not—oh, pity me, miserable wretch that I am!—I
A dared not—I *dared* not speak! *We have put her living in the tomb!* Said I not that my senses were acute? I *now* tell you that I heard her first feeble movements in the hollow coffin. I heard them—many, many days ago—yet I dared not—*I dared not speak!* And now—tonight—Ethelred—ha! ha!—the breaking of the hermit's door, and the death-cry of the dragon, and the clangor of the shield!—say, rather, the rending of her coffin, and the grating of the iron hinges of her prison, and her struggles within the coppered archway of the vault! Oh whither shall I fly? Will she not be here anon? Is she not hurrying to upbraid me for my haste? Have I not heard her footstep on the stair? Do I not distinguish that heavy and horrible beating of her heart? MADMAN!" here he sprang furiously to his feet, and shrieked out his syllables, as if in the effort he were giving up his soul—"MADMAN! I TELL YOU THAT SHE NOW STANDS WITHOUT THE DOOR!"

As if in the superhuman energy of his utterance there had been found the potency of a spell—the huge antique panels to which the speaker pointed, threw slowly back, upon the instant, their ponderous and ebony jaws. It was the work of the rushing gust—but then without those doors there DID stand the lofty and enshrouded figure of the lady Madeline of Usher. There was blood upon her white robes, and the evidence of some bitter struggle upon every portion of her emaciated frame. For a moment she remained trembling and reeling to and fro upon the threshold, then, with a low, moaning cry, fell heavily inward upon the person of her brother, and in her violent and now final death-agonies, bore him to the floor a corpse, and a victim to the terrors he had anticipated.

From that chamber, and from that mansion, I fled aghast. The storm was still abroad in all its wrath as I found myself crossing the old causeway. Suddenly there shot along the path a wild light, and I turned to see whence a gleam so unusual could have issued; for the vast house and its shadows were alone behind me. The radiance was that of the full, setting, and blood-red moon which now shone vividly through the once barely discernible fissure of which I have before spoken as extending from the roof of the building, in a zigzag direction, to the base. While I gazed, this fissure rapidly widened—there came a fierce breath of the whirlwind—the entire orb of the satellite burst at once upon my sight—my brain reeled as I saw the mighty walls rushing asunder—there was a long tumultuous shouting sound like the voice of a thousand waters—and the deep and dank tarn at my feet closed sullenly and silently over the fragments of the "HOUSE OF USHER."

B

A Comment on the Story

Nature seems to have provided us with an emotional circuit for the registering of fright. Presumably, it is an alarm system that will send us flying toward a less threat-
C ening environment. It might be the need to flush out that fright system under controlled circumstances that sends us to scary movies and terrifying stories. Imagine yourself seated in a dark theater watching a scene take place on stage. An innocent young woman is brushing her hair at a mirror as she prepares for bed. Suddenly we see, although she does not, a sinister face appear at her window. What would be the impact on you at the time? What would it be after you had left the theater and begun your long walk home in the dark?

It must have been some knowledge of this human susceptibility that led Edgar Allan Poe to explore the uses of the horror tale, a story that exploits our subconscious fears. Although we each have different furnishings for our nightmares, we all respond the same way to such universal images as remote, crumbling houses set in the midst of swamps or lonely moors; stormy skies; thick mists; eerie sounds; characters who are sick in mind and body, who speak little and never hum or whistle.

It is the relationship of Roderick and Madeline that first claims our attention in this story. Twins united by sensibility and temperament, they suffer from similar illnesses (hers physical, his mental); at the end of the story, they embrace a common fate. But it may gradually dawn on us that the relationship of Roderick and the narrator may be even more fascinating, and ominous. The unnamed storyteller seems to be a relatively de-

A. Connections
Premature burial was a favorite theme of Poe's, appearing also in "The Cask of Amontillado" and "The Premature Burial." Usher's climactic mad speech echoes the narrator's in "The Tell-Tale Heart."

B. Responding
? How do you feel at the end of the story? Did you experience a "satisfying" horror? If not, why not, and what does this say about the changing "threshold of horror" in audiences at different times in history? What kinds of things are most likely to frighten modern audiences? (Answers will vary. Many students will feel that the more spectacular scares seen in movies today make it difficult to be moved by Poe's more refined horrors.)

C. Responding
? The comment provides one plausible reason why people may seek frightening entertainment. What other reasons might there be? (Answers will vary.)

ANALYZING THE STORY
Identifying Facts
1. He feels "a sense of insufferable gloom."

Evocative adjectives in the first paragraph include: dull, dark, alone, dreary, melancholy, insufferable, bleak, rank, decayed, bitter, hideous, unredeemed, shadowy, sorrowful, precipitous, black, lurid, gray, ghastly.

2. He has come because his old childhood friend, Roderick Usher, has written him an urgent letter, saying that he is ill and begging the narrator to visit him.

3. The symptoms include paleness, nervous agitation, sudden shifts of mood, and a morbid acuteness of the senses.

Madeline is apathetic; her body is gradually wasting away; and she has occasional cataleptic seizures.

4. At first, the narrator tries to comfort Roderick, his friend, by joining him in his pursuits and trying to understand his malady. Little by little, however, the narrator succumbs to melancholy and a vague feeling of apprehension. The news that Madeline has died from her illness depresses both characters still more. The narrator helps Roderick with his arrangements to preserve the corpse of Made-

tached observer at the beginning. He goes out of his way to tell us that he "really knew little" of his friend. Gradually, however, we discover that the narrator is not only fascinated by Usher's mental degeneration; he also finds himself participating in it. The first-person point of view in the story becomes not only a technical device, but also part of its very theme.

In describing the narrator's deteriorating mental state, Poe seems to recognize the fact that we are fascinated by tales of horror because, below the surface, the forces of chaos bubble in all of us. Like the narrator, we enjoy approaching the brink—and then drawing back. The problem, of course, is that we may withdraw too late from a glimpse of the dark elements of human nature—elements which we may imagine exist in ourselves as well. Usher, who enjoyed confronting his own extremes, was condemned to madness and death. The narrator, whom Poe may have intended to represent "normal" people, watched in fascination and then "fled aghast," just in time, with the "deep and dank tarn" at his feet.

In some sense, then, the narrator of Poe's tale has followed our emotional course as we read a horror story. At first disclaiming any identification or sympathy, Poe's storyteller is inexorably drawn into the situation. He is both observer and participant. As if to underline his ambiguous status, this narrator indulges repeatedly in paradoxical expressions, such as "sad jest," "gentle violence," and "[a night] wildly singular for its terror and its beauty." Terror is repellent; it is also, in some guises, fascinating and pleasurable. Just in the nick of time, the narrator escapes. In the same way, we the readers, after taking pleasure in a tale that is discomforting and even terrifying, can close our books with the thought that "it's all only a story after all."

Responding to the Story

Analyzing the Story

Identifying Facts

1. As the story opens, how does the narrator respond to his first sight of the House of Usher? What **images** help you to see and hear this **setting**?
2. Explain why the narrator has come to this house.
3. Describe the symptoms of Roderick Usher's illness. What are his sister Madeline's symptoms?
4. Summarize what happens during the narrator's visit to the House of Usher.

Interpreting Meanings

5. What do you think Roderick's artistic efforts—his guitar solo, his painting, and his poem "The Haunted Palace"—reveal about his state of mind?
6. Why do you think Poe had Roderick and Madeline be *twins* instead of merely brother and sister?
7. The story is presented from the **point of view** of a typical Poe narrator—a character who claims to provide an objective, rational view of events, but whose rationality becomes suspect during the course of the tale. What evidence can you find suggesting that the narrator's state of mind may be approaching that of his friend Roderick? How does this uncertainty about the narrator's objectivity affect your response to the events of the plot?
8. What do you think is happening at the end of the story, when Madeline Usher appears? Is she a hallucination of the narrator? Is she a ghost? Or is she a real, living person who has been buried alive? How do you interpret Madeline's appearance?
9. Poe wrote of the poem within the story, ". . . by the Haunted Palace I mean to imply a mind haunted by phantoms—a disordered brain." How might the whole story be seen as an **allegory** of a journey into the human mind in its conscious and unconscious states? In this light, what, for example, would the final *fall* of the house represent?
10. Do you think a filmed version of Poe's story would be popular today? Why?

Writing About the Story

A Creative Response

1. **Using Another Point of View.** Select one incident from the story. Retell the incident from Madeline's point of view.

A Critical Response

2. **Analyzing the Story's Effect.** Poe wrote that a skillful literary artist fashions a tale to achieve

> a certain unique or single *effect*. . . . In the whole composition there should be no word written, of which the tendency, direct or indirect, is not to the one pre-established design.
>
> —Edgar Allan Poe

line for a period of two weeks in one of the vaults of the castle. Finally, during a stormy night, the narrator is seized by a feeling of horror. Roderick joins him and they seek distraction in the reading of a medieval romance. But at the height of the storm, an apparition of Madeline confronts them. Roderick collapses dead in the arms of his sister. The narrator flees the house as it collapses into the tarn.

Interpreting Meanings

5. All of Roderick Usher's artistic efforts display a tortured sensibility and a disordered mind.

6. Some critics have proposed that Poe intended the reader to conclude that Roderick and Madeline were two closely related sides of the same personality.

7. The narrator seems more and more drawn to Usher, as he tries to understand and sympathize with his old friend's malady. He emphasizes that he takes part with Roderick in his artistic pursuits. The experience of conveying the body of Madeline to the vault seems to unnerve him profoundly. Finally, the narrator admits, "I felt creeping upon me, by slow yet certain degrees, the wild influences of his own fantastic yet impressive superstitions." Despite his efforts to cling to sanity, he is addressed twice by Usher in the concluding scene as "Madman!"

Student responses will vary.

8. Student answers will vary.

Some students will agree that the very ambiguity of the situation serves to increase our response of awe and horror.

9. Note that we follow the narrator into Usher's disordered imagination which eventually shuts out all light from the outer or upper world. Usher's world collapses because it loses connection with the other aspects of reality. Allegorically, we see how fantasy replaces reality and results in destruction and madness.

The fall of the house might be held to symbolize the final collapse of Usher (and by extension, of his family) into a maelstrom of chaos and death. In a more general sense, Poe's symbolism may suggest that if undisciplined, overrefined aesthetic impulses are given free reign in the human mind, the

(Continued on page 248)

Analyze "The Fall of the House of Usher" to show whether or not every detail builds and heightens the story's mood of terror.

3. **Comparing Two Stories.** In an essay, compare the **themes** of "The Masque of the Red Death" and "The Fall of the House of Usher." In particular, consider how each story might be about the impossibility of achieving the Romantic ideal—that is, the transcendence of imagination over reality.
4. **Analyzing the Story's Meaning.** In a brief essay, develop one of the following statements about the meaning of "The Fall of the House of Usher." Quote from the story to support your position.
   a. The narrator becomes insane under the influence of Roderick, and at the end of the story he is hallucinating.
   b. The story is symbolic. Roderick is identified with the house, and both are ruined when the story ends as Madeline gets her revenge.
   c. The story is about an artist who leaves the real world and journeys through the underside of the human mind.

Analyzing Language and Style

Suggestive Words

1. Reread the famous first paragraph of this story and list all the words that suggest decay, sterility, finality, and emptiness.
2. What sound do you hear repeated in this paragraph? What might this repeated sound remind you of?
3. Which words in this description do you think characterize the mind of the narrator? Which adverbs and adjectives reveal his feelings?
4. What details in this first paragraph suggest that the house and its occupants are tied together? (Look for details that **personify** the house.)
5. How would your feelings about the house have been different if the narrator had come upon it on a sunny morning in springtime?
6. Rewrite the first sentence, and change the time of day, the time of year, the weather, and the adjectives and adverbs that suggest the narrator's feelings rather than actuality. Can you change the sentence's emotional effect?

Elements of Literature

SYMBOLS

A **symbol** in literature is a concrete object, person, place, or action that operates on at least two levels of meaning: It functions as itself, and it stands for a larger meaning or quality.

Certain symbols are so well known and their meanings so broadly agreed upon that they may be called conventional. For example, most people accept the flag of their nation as a symbol of unity and patriotism. In Western cultures, the rose is a conventional symbol of beauty or love, the color white of purity or innocence, and the color green of hope.

The underlying meanings of other symbols arise from the context that writers create. In Poe's "The Fall of the House of Usher," for example, the opening description of Roderick's decaying mansion inspires certain responses in both the narrator and the reader. However, it is not until later in the story, when Roderick mentions his strange theory of the "sentience" of the building's stones (page 241), that we realize that the decaying house also symbolizes the degeneration of Usher's own mind. At the end of the story, Poe further emphasizes this symbolic meaning with a stroke of fantasy: immediately after Roderick and Madeline collapse in death, the horrified narrator watches the house itself collapse into the tarn.

Symbolism in literature is often more complex than this example would suggest. In fact, the most interesting symbols may be those that provoke different, sometimes conflicting, interpretations. For instance, does Poe hint in this story that Roderick and Madeline, as twins who suffer from similar maladies, are symbolic of two halves of the same mind? Or does he suggest, through the narrator's growing apprehension, that the narrator sees the dark side of his own mind symbolized in Usher? Is the narrator's situation in the story unique and grotesque? Or is it indirectly symbolic of a universal fascination with evil? And exactly what is suggested in the story by Roderick's use of the arts of painting and music? If there were one, definitive, undeniable answer to each of these questions, much of the mysterious power of the story's symbolism might disappear.

Symbols are as old as literature itself. Folk tales, parables, and allegories have always depended on the use of symbols. But there is no point in trying to squeeze symbolic meaning out of everything we read. To convey several levels of abstract meaning successfully, symbols must be supported by a context that sparks our imagination. In their ability to evoke responses from our unconscious emotions, symbols can be a writer's most effective tools.

Did you find other symbols in the story of the House of Usher that have not been mentioned? Can you justify your responses?

Supplementary Support Materials

1. Vocabulary Activity Worksheet (*CCB*)
2. Review and Response Worksheet: Tone (*CCB*)
3. Selection Test (*CCB*)
4. Audiocassette recording
5. Instructional Overhead Transparency

Developing Vocabulary

The following word from the poem is tested in the Selection Test. (See also Vocabulary Activity Worksheet.)
pilgrim

Preparation

Building On Prior Knowledge. Some students will have heard the word "Eldorado" before. What does it mean to them? What expectations does it set up as the title of a poem?

(Continued from page 247.)

result may be that the mind will crack and disintegrate in insanity or death.

10. Student answers will vary. Several of Poe's stories have been filmed with some success.

A. Word Connotations
? What is the meaning of the word *shadow* in this stanza? (Absence of light)

B. Word Connotations
? What is the connotation of "shadow" in this stanza? (Disappointment; a darkness of the heart)

C. Responding
? Why is the shadow called a "pilgrim" shadow? (It is a spirit who is eternally searching, perhaps as we all are.)

D. Responding
? Where will the knight find Eldorado? (In death)

El Dorado is Spanish for "the gilded one" or "the man of gold," from the Spanish word for gold, _oro_. The term is associated with the conquistadors, who had heard repeatedly about a ruler who lived in what is now Colombia. Every year, the ruler would be covered in gold which would then be rinsed from his body in Lake Guatavitá. During the ceremony, emeralds and other precious stones would be sacrificially washed into the depths of the lake. The conquistadors became convinced that, if only they could find it, a country of vast riches would be theirs. "Eldorado" was never found. But in 1849, the year in which this poem was written, Eldorado took on a new meaning.

The discovery of gold in California convinced thousands of Americans that a land of golden opportunity was at hand. Thus began the great rush that would take the gold seekers to the vicinity of Sutter's Mill and the muddy streets of San Francisco.

Behind this poem, then, lie both the legend passed on by the frustrated conquistadors and the reality reported in the daily papers. Yet for Poe, Eldorado was predominantly an idea, as it remains for us today. "El Dorado" speaks to our hopes that somewhere lies a great good place, the land of our heart's desire.

Eldorado

Gaily bedight,°
A gallant knight,
A In sunshine and in shadow,
Had journeyed long,
Singing a song,
In search of Eldorado.

But he grew old—
This knight so bold—
B And o'er his heart a shadow
Fell as he found
No spot of ground
That looked like Eldorado.

And, as his strength
Failed him at length,
C He met a pilgrim shadow—
"Shadow," said he,
"Where can it be—
This land of Eldorado?"

"Over the Mountains
Of the Moon,°
D Down the Valley of the Shadow,°
Ride, boldly ride,"
The shade replied,
"If you seek for Eldorado!"

1. **bedight:** bedecked (dressed).

20. **Mountains of the Moon:** the legendary source of the Nile River.
21. **Valley of the Shadow:** the "valley of the shadow of death" is mentioned in Psalm 23.

CLOSURE

Have students write a one-line paraphrase for each of the four stanzas.

ANALYZING THE POEM

Identifying Details

1. The knight grows old in his search for Eldorado.

2. The shadow tells him to ride boldly "over the Mountains of the Moon" and "down the Valley of the Shadow."

Interpreting Meanings

3. He uses the adjective "pilgrim."
The word suggests that the shadow, too, is on a journey or quest, but that this quest is perhaps of a spiritual, rather than a material, nature.

4. The meter of the poem is predominantly duple, except for the first stanza. Lines 1, 5, 6, 10, 14, 16, 18, and 22 are each a trochee plus an iamb. This bumpety-bump rhythm may suggest the movement of the knight on his quest.

5. In the first stanza, *shadow* is used literally, as in "shade." In the second, it has a figurative meaning: a shadow over the heart (line 9). In the third stanza, it refers to the mysterious pilgrim figure who speaks to the knight. In the last stanza Poe echoes a phrase in Psalm 23, the "valley of the shadow of death."
Just as the uses of the word *shadow* gradually suggest ominous and mysterious connotations, so the poem's tone gradually shifts from bright gaiety to one of somber melancholy.

6. Answers may vary. The knight seems to represent active optimism; the shadow may represent death, wisdom, or something else, depending on how one interprets the shadow's advice.

7. Answers will vary. Some may feel the shadow's response indicates that the knight's perseverance will be rewarded; others may say the shadow is cryptically telling the knight that Eldorado exists only in people's dreams. Urge students to express their own opinions.

8. Answers will vary. Think of success in business, cures for disease, peace on earth, the perfect society.

Responding to the Poem

Analyzing the Poem

Identifying Details

1. Describe what happens to the knight in the course of the first two stanzas.
2. What directions does the shadow give him?

Interpreting Meanings

3. What adjective does Poe use to describe the shadow the knight meets? What do you think this word suggests about the nature of the shadow?
4. Describe the **meter** of the poem. Do you think the poem's beat is appropriate to its subject? Explain.
5. The words *Eldorado* and *shadow* are rhymed in each stanza, creating a pleasant echo throughout the poem. How do the meaning and the **connotations** of the word *shadow* change from stanza to stanza? How do these changes reflect a gradual change in the poem's **tone**?
6. The characters of the knight and the shadow have a **symbolic** meaning. What types of people, attitudes, or concepts might these two characters represent?
7. The response the shadow makes to the knight's question is open to interpretation. Explain what *you* think the shadow's answer means.
8. Name some "Eldorados" that contemporary people might search for. Would the shadow's advice pertain to these quests?

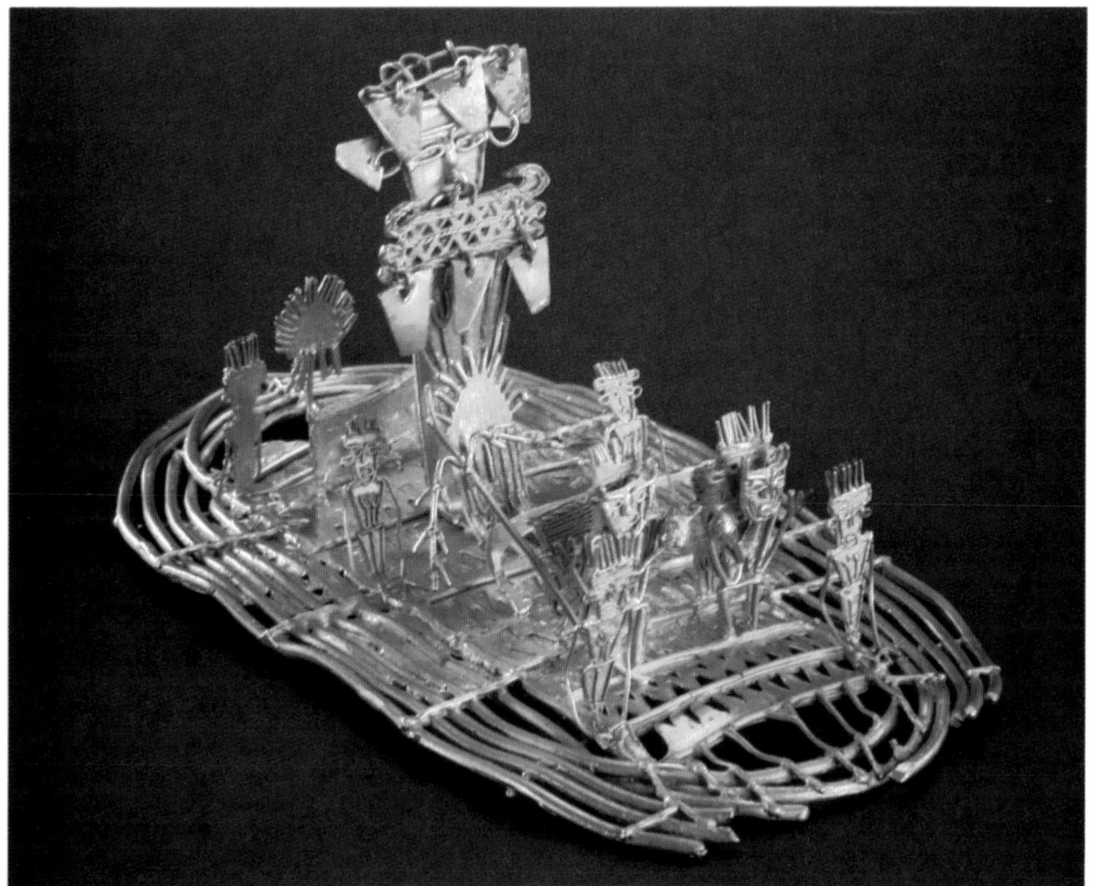

The raft of El Dorado. Pre-Colombian gold (late 16th century).

Museo del Oro, Bogota, Colombia.

Supplementary Support Materials
1. Vocabulary Activity Worksheet (*CCB*)
2. Review and Response Worksheet: Repetition and Rhyme (*CCB*)
3. Selection Test (*CCB*)

Developing Vocabulary
The following words from the poem are tested in the Selection Test. (See also Vocabulary Activity Worksheet.)
seraph sepulcher
to covet to dissever
kinsmen

Preparation
Establishing a Purpose. This poem is about a kind of love that many people do not think is a healthy, positive love. Have students read the poem to decide whether they agree with these people.

A. Responding
Most contemporary poetry does not use rhyme and rhythm as Poe does.
? What might be the purpose of rhyme and rhythm in "Annabel Lee"? (One purpose might be that they echo the cadences of nursery rhymes, thus emphasizing the youth and innocence of both the heroine and the narrator. Students might also note the line "*I* was a child and *she* was a child" as further evidence of the poem's tone.)

B. Setting
? What effect does the remote setting in time and place have on the poem? (It makes it seem like a fairy tale and, again, emphasizes the youth and innocence of the heroine and the narrator.)

Not long before his own death, Poe wrote this poem about the death of his wife Virginia. Like other fairy tales, the poem is set far away and long ago. Its details nevertheless reflect some of the actual circumstances of Virginia's life and death. When barely an adult, she contracted tuberculosis, a disease for which there was then no known cure. Slowly wasting away, she managed to live a fairly normal life until the fatal stage of her illness became apparent. In the midst of singing a song for a family gathering, she lost her voice as blood came gushing from her mouth. Lingering for months as an invalid, she died near the end of 1847. Her body was placed in a burial vault—if not exactly "by the sea," at least close to the Hudson River at a point where it approaches the Atlantic Ocean. Read the poem aloud to hear its rhymes and feel its rhythm. A

Annabel Lee

B It was many and many a year ago,
In a kingdom by the sea,
That a maiden there lived whom you may know
By the name of Annabel Lee;
And this maiden she lived with no other thought
Than to love and be loved by me.

I was a child and *she* was a child,
In this kingdom by the sea,
But we loved with a love that was more than love—
I and my Annabel Lee—
With a love that the wingèd seraphs of Heaven
Coveted her and me.

And this was the reason that, long ago,
In this kingdom by the sea,
A wind blew out of a cloud, chilling
My beautiful Annabel Lee;
So that her highborn kinsmen° came
And bore her away from me,
To shut her up in a sepulcher
In this kingdom by the sea.

The angels, not half so happy in Heaven,
Went envying her and me:—
Yes!—all that was the reason (as all men know,
In this kingdom by the sea)
That the wind came out of the cloud by night,
Chilling and killing my Annabel Lee.

But our love it was stronger by far than the love
Of those who were older than we—
Of many far wiser than we—
And neither the angels in Heaven above,
Nor the demons down under the sea,
Can ever dissever my soul from the soul
Of the beautiful Annabel Lee:—

17. **highborn kinsmen:** angels.

A

Sissy, a drawing attributed to Edgar Allan Poe. Sissy was a nickname for Poe's wife, Virginia.

Valentine Museum, Richmond.

For the moon never beams, without bringing me dreams
  Of the beautiful Annabel Lee;
And the stars never rise, but I feel the bright eyes
  Of the beautiful Annabel Lee:
And so, all the nighttide, I lie down by the side
Of my darling—my darling—my life and my bride,
  In the sepulcher there by the sea—
  In her tomb by the sounding sea.

B

A. Humanities Connection: Responding to the Fine Art

If this portrait was drawn by Poe himself, it probably contains elements of the same sensibility he brought to his writing.

? What aspects of the drawing seem particularly Poe-like? (Students may cite among other answers, the idealized beauty of the young woman and the deathlike, depersonalized closing of her eyes.)

B. Responding

? What do you think of the kind of love expressed in this poem? Is it a kind of love you would like to give and receive? Does it sound genuine, false, or some combination of the two? (Answers will vary. Many will find it obsessive to the point of morbidity; some may like the idea of eternal love.)

CLOSURE

Have students write out several sentences that encapsulate the speaker's feelings for Annabel Lee.

ANALYZING THE POEM

Identifying Details

1. The narrator says that a wind came from a cloud and gave the girl a fatal chill.

2. The speaker says that their love was stronger by far than the love of those who were older and wiser, and that neither angels nor demons can separate his soul from that of his beloved.

He says that the moon and the stars remind him of the eyes of his beloved every night, and that he lies nightly by her grave.

3. The pattern of end rhymes varies from stanza to stanza. In the first stanza it is *ababcb.* The long "e" sound of rhyme *b* is repeated at regular intervals in each succeeding stanza. Some internal rhymes are: "chilling" and "killing" (line 26), "beams" and "dreams" (line 34), "rise" and "eyes" (line 36), "nighttide" and "side" (line 38).

(Answers continue in left-hand column.)

(Continued from top.)

Interpreting Meanings

4. Student answers will vary. Some students may suggest that the two elements—musical language and a haunting story—are effectively combined.

5. Student answers will vary.

A Comment on the Poem

The relationship between fact and imagination is a minor part of this poem. Its larger concern is with the spiritual qualities of love that endure even beyond death. In Poe's conception, the love he shared was "more than love." It was not only love between a man and a woman, but a kind of love that transcends mortal considerations because it is part of the God-given innocence of childhood. This is the love possible in that state of being which William Wordsworth wrote about:

> Not in entire forgetfulness,
> And not in utter nakedness,
> But trailing clouds of glory do we come
> From God, who is our home;
> Heaven lies about us in our infancy!
> —from "Intimations of Immortality,"
> William Wordsworth

By transforming his child bride, Virginia Clemm, into the fantasy of Annabel Lee, Poe created a fable in which an actual person becomes a character unrelated to a particular place or time. Annabel Lee is one of many figures in the imaginative history of love and loss.

A Vision of Dead Desire by Clarence John Laughlin (1954). Photograph.

The Historic New Orleans Collection and the Estate of Clarence John Laughlin. Robert Miller Gallery, New York.

Responding to the Poem

Analyzing the Poem

Identifying Details

1. What explanation does the narrator give for Annabel Lee's death?
2. In Stanza 5, how does the speaker defy both the angels and the demons who succeed in separating him from his beloved? In Stanza 6, how does he attempt to show that loving memory can defeat death and absence?
3. Describe the pattern of **end rhymes** in the poem. How many **internal rhymes**—rhymes within lines—can you find?

Interpreting Meanings

4. The poem's singsong **meter,** together with its **rhymes** and **repetition,** gives it the effect of an old ballad. Some critics have felt that Poe was more concerned with the music of his composition than with the story it tells or the emotion it expresses. Do you feel that the poem is primarily memorable as "word music," or that it is primarily a haunting story of lost love? Give reasons for your opinion.
5. Grief is one kind of emotion; sadness is another. Which emotion do you think this poem more effectively expresses?

Writing About the Poem

A Creative Response

1. **Imitating the Poem.** Write at least one stanza—about any topic—imitating the meter and rhyme scheme of "Annabel Lee." Begin with Poe's first line.

A Critical Response

2. **Comparing Poems.** In one paragraph, cite a way in which Poe's "Annabel Lee" is like the lines from Wordsworth's "Intimations of Immortality." In a second paragraph, tell how "Annabel Lee" is different: In other words, what does Poe go on to imagine that is not mentioned by Wordsworth?

SUPPLEMENTARY SUPPORT MATERIALS
1. Vocabulary Activity Worksheet (*CCB*)
2. Review and Response Worksheet: Allusion (*CCB*)
3. Selection Test (*CCB*)
4. Audiocassette recording

DEVELOPING VOCABULARY
The following words from the poem are tested in the Selection Test. (See also Vocabulary Activity Worksheet.)

wont	niche
yon	agate

PREPARATION
ESTABLISHING A PURPOSE. Have students read the poem to learn why Poe thinks of Helen as the ideal woman.

This poem is addressed to a woman, but whether it is a real woman or an idealized woman no one knows. The poem is filled with allusions; read it once, aloud, and then, after you have read the comment following it, read it again. Is "Helen" real, or is she an ideal? Or is she a beautiful statue the poet is looking at?

To Helen

Helen, thy beauty is to me
  Like those Nicéan barks of yore,
That gently, o'er a perfumed sea,
A The weary, way-worn wanderer bore
  To his own native shore.

On desperate seas long wont to roam,
  Thy hyacinth hair, thy classic face,
Thy Naiad airs have brought me home
  To the glory that was Greece,
  And the grandeur that was Rome.

Lo! in yon brilliant window-niche
  How statue-like I see thee stand,
The agate lamp within thy hand!
  Ah, Psyche, from the regions which
  Are Holy Land!

B

Funeral Stele of a Young Girl (5th century B.C.) Greek sculpture.

Museo Nazionale, Athens.

A. Alliteration
? What is the effect of the alliteration in these lines? (It draws out, or extends, the word *weary,* thus creating a feeling of weariness and making Helen even more meaningful.)

B. Humanities Connection: Responding to the Fine Art
Have your students look at the Greek sculpture before reading the poem.
? How do you think this bas-relief exemplifies themes of Poe's you have already encountered? (The juxtaposition of young female beauty with ruin is prominent in both "Annabel Lee" and "The Fall of the House of Usher.")

CLOSURE

Have students, without using the word *classic,* describe Poe's ideal of beauty.

ANALYZING THE POEM

Identifying Details

1. The speaker compares Helen's beauty to the "Nicéan barks of yore" (ancient Greek ships), which carried wanderers home over the "perfumed sea."

2. He says they have brought him "home" to the glory and grandeur of Greek and Roman culture.

3. The speaker had roamed on these seas.

4. He pictures her as a statue, holding a lamp in a window-niche.

5. Alliteration occurs in line 4 ("weary, way-worn wanderer"), line 7 ("hyacinth hair"), lines 9–10 ("glory that was Greece, / And the grandeur . . ."), line 12 ("statue-like I see thee stand").

The end-rhyme scheme is different in all three stanzas. Stanza 1: *ababb.* Stanza 2: *ababa.* Stanza 3: *abbaa.* Among the internal rhyming sounds are "beauty" and "me" in line 1, "gently" and "sea" in line 3, "way-worn" and "bore" in line 4, "brilliant" and "window-niche" in *(Answers continue in left-hand column.)*

(Continued from top.) line 11, "lamp" and "hand" in line 13. (Some of these are slant rhymes.)

Interpreting Meanings

6. Her beauty reminds him of the beauty of classical art. He may mean "brought home" in the sense of "back to one's roots," since classical culture influenced the development of Western civilization.

The poem expresses the general idea that classical culture is to be revered for its harmonious expression of beauty.

Answers will vary. You might begin by showing some examples of classical art.

7. The speaker addresses Helen by the name Psyche. The allusion emphasizes the woman's beauty, both in herself and in her role as the chosen lover of Cupid, god of love.

8. Student answers will vary. Ask students to cite women in other works by Poe as examples.

A Comment on the Poem

In "To Helen," Poe takes advantage of the suggestive power of *allusions*. Six allusions occur in a poem of only fifteen lines. To understand the poem, you must recognize each of these allusions.

The first allusion, the name *Helen* itself, has two possible interpretations. Poe said that Helen is really Jane Stith Stanard, the mother of a teen-aged friend. But according to an old tradition, Helen, the wife of King Menelaus of Sparta, was the most beautiful woman in the world. She ran off with Paris, a Prince of Troy, and her husband's efforts to get her back resulted in the ten-year-long Trojan War.

The word *Nicean* (line 2) has puzzled Poe scholars because it does not easily fit into the poem's context. Nicaea was a colony of ancient Greece. Nicaea would have used "barks," or ships, to maintain its economic and political life; however, it is not, as Poe suggests, identified with Odysseus, the most famous "way-worn wanderer" of ancient literature. The bark that *did* bear the wanderer to his native shore was supplied by the people of Phaeacia.

Hyacinth, or *hyacinthine,* hair (line 7) is a term that occurs frequently in descriptions of classical beauty. If you've ever seen Greek statues, you might have noticed how the curls of the hair look like the thick layers of petals on the hyacinth flower. A Naiad (nā'ad) (line 8) is a nymph identified with fertility and fresh water in Greek mythology.

In Greek legend, Psyche (line 14), whose name means "soul," was a woman of uncommon beauty. She was the chosen lover of Cupid, the god of love himself. To keep his identity secret, Cupid asked Psyche never to look at him, and he came to her only at night in order to keep his face hidden. But Psyche was curious. Once, when Cupid was asleep, she brought an oil-burning lamp made of agate (a semiprecious stone) close to his face and spilled a drop of hot oil on his shoulder. While this incident caused discord between them, eventually Cupid and Psyche were united as ideal lovers and were taken to live with the gods. They are often represented in paintings and sculpture, in which "statue-like" Psyche bends over Cupid with a lamp in her hand.

Finally, the term *Holy Land* here (line 15) does not refer to the land of the Bible, but to the imaginative regions of classical literature which, like most poets, Poe considered sacred.

Responding to the Poem

Analyzing the Poem

Identifying Details

1. In Stanza 1, find the extended **simile** the speaker uses to describe Helen's beauty.
2. In Stanza 2, where does the speaker say Helen's "Naiad," or nymphlike, airs have brought him?
3. In Stanza 2, who was "wont to roam on desperate seas"?
4. Where does the speaker picture Helen in Stanza 3?
5. Subtle musical effects are created in the poem by **alliteration** and **rhyme.** List all the uses of alliteration you can find. What is the end-rhyme scheme, and where do you hear internal rhyming sounds?

Interpreting Meanings

6. How would you explain what the speaker means when he says that Helen's beauty has brought him "home" to Greece and Rome? What general ideas about beauty and classical civilization do you think the poem expresses? How do you feel about these ideas?
7. In Stanza 3, by what name does the speaker address Helen? Reread the Comment on the Poem, and explain why you think the speaker chose this **allusion.**
8. Critics often claim that Poe turns his women characters into statues. They say he is more concerned with idealized and unresponsive beauty than with beauty as it appears in the faces of real human beings. Do you feel that this poem is really a love poem addressed to an individual woman? Or does it seem to be the expression of an ideal? Explain.

Writing About the Poem

A Critical Response

Analyzing the Poem. In at least three paragraphs, analyze these aspects of the poem: the **extended simile** in Stanza 1 (is it strained, or does it work?); the word *desperate* in Stanza 2 (why "desperate" seas?); the vision in Stanza 3 (why does the speaker imagine Helen as a statue?).

SUPPLEMENTARY SUPPORT MATERIALS
1. Vocabulary Activity Worksheet (*CCB*)
2. Review and Response Worksheet: Tone and Imagery (*CCB*)
3. Selection Test (*CCB*)

DEVELOPING VOCABULARY
The following words from the poem are tested in the Selection Test. (See also Vocabulary Activity Worksheet.)

surcease	craven
to implore	gaunt
obeisance	censer
mien	to quaff
beguiling	undaunted

PREPARATION
ESTABLISHING A PURPOSE. The strong rhythm and rhyme of this poem sometimes make it easy for the narrative to become lost. You might suggest that students read this poem twice. The first time have them read it for the story. The second time have them concentrate on the poetic effects.

"The Raven"—probably the most famous poem in American literature—has captivated artists and illustrators. You might have seen some of the many drawings and cartoons that present a poetic figure of a man in conversation with a black bird perched on the head of a white marble statue.

"The Raven" has the sound of a lyric, but actually, it is a narrative poem with a plot that leads the reader from curiosity to horror. As you read the story, notice how the speaker's amusement with his visitor does not last for long. Annoyed, then infuriated by the stolid and all but silent presence of the bird, he gives in to what Poe himself has called "that species of despair which delights in self-torture." As we say in the current jargon of psychology, he "projects" onto the bird whatever his own wild imagination dredges up.

The Raven

1.

Once upon a midnight dreary, while I pondered, weak and weary,
Over many a quaint and curious volume of forgotten lore—
A While I nodded, nearly napping, suddenly there came a tapping,
As of someone gently rapping, rapping at my chamber door.
" 'Tis some visitor," I muttered, "tapping at my chamber door—
Only this and nothing more."

2.

Ah, distinctly I remember it was in the bleak December;
And each separate dying ember wrought its ghost upon the floor.
Eagerly I wished the morrow—vainly I had sought to borrow
From my books surcease of sorrow—sorrow for the lost Lenore—
For the rare and radiant maiden whom the angels name Lenore—
Nameless *here* for evermore.

3.

And the silken, sad, uncertain rustling of each purple curtain
Thrilled me—filled me with fantastic terrors never felt before;
So that now, to still the beating of my heart, I stood repeating,
B " 'Tis some visitor entreating entrance at my chamber door—
Some late visitor entreating entrance at my chamber door
This it is and nothing more."

4.

Presently my soul grew stronger; hesitating then no longer,
"Sir," said I, "or Madam, truly your forgiveness I implore;
But the fact is I was napping, and so gently you came rapping,
And so faintly you came tapping, tapping at my chamber door,
That I scarce was sure I heard you"—here I opened wide the door—
Darkness there and nothing more.

A. Setting/Rhyme
? What details of setting on this page create an atmosphere of mystery or foreboding? (The poem opens on a "dreary" midnight. The speaker is reading a "strange" book and is suddenly interrupted by a mysterious tapping.)

Have students note the internal rhymes in this stanza: dreary / weary; napping / tapping / rapping; remember / December; morrow / borrow / sorrow. You might have students experiment with ways of reading this stanza so that the "singsong" effect of these rhymes does not destroy the atmosphere.

B. Alliteration / Suspense
Note alliteration of *s* sounds in "silken, sad, uncertain rustling."
? Does the alliteration itself help to create a feeling of suspense? What details add to the suspense? (The speaker is filled with "fantastic terrors" by the curtain rustlings.)

Humanities Connection: Responding to the Fine Art

The woodcut illustrates stanza 5. Turn to it after reading the entire poem, and discuss how successfully the artist summons up the emotional effect of the relentlessly, morbidly mocking raven.

? Why has the artist chosen to make the raven purple instead of black? (Perhaps because the incongruity makes the bird seem even more strikingly menacing)

The Raven III by Antonio Frasconi (1959). Colored woodcut.

5.

Deep into that darkness peering, long I stood there wondering, fearing,
A Doubting, dreaming dreams no mortal ever dared to dream before;
But the silence was unbroken, and the stillness gave no token,
And the only word there spoken was the whispered word, "Lenore?"
This I whispered, and an echo murmured back the word "Lenore!"
Merely this and nothing more.

6.

Back into the chamber turning, all my soul within me burning,
Soon again I heard a tapping somewhat louder than before.
"Surely," said I, "surely that is something at my window lattice;
Let me see, then, what thereat is, and this mystery explore—
Let my heart be still a moment and this mystery explore—
'Tis the wind and nothing more!"

7.

B Open here I flung the shutter, when, with many a flirt and flutter,
In there stepped a stately Raven of the saintly days of yore;°
Not the least obeisance made he; not a minute stopped or stayed he;
But, with mien of lord or lady, perched above my chamber door—
Perched upon a bust of Pallas° just above my chamber door—
Perched, and sat, and nothing more.

8.

Then this ebony bird beguiling my sad fancy into smiling,
By the grave and stern decorum of the countenance it wore,
C "Though thy crest be shorn and shaven, thou," I said, "art sure no craven,
Ghastly grim and ancient Raven wandering from the Nightly shore—
Tell me what thy lordly name is on the Night's Plutonian shore!"°
Quoth the Raven, "Nevermore."

9.

Much I marveled this ungainly fowl to hear discourse so plainly,
Though its answer little meaning—little relevancy bore;
For we cannot help agreeing that no living human being
Ever yet was blessed with seeing bird above his chamber door—
Bird or beast upon the sculptured bust above his chamber door,
With such name as "Nevermore."

---

38. In early Christian legends, holy men who withdrew from the world and lived in isolation in the desert were visited by ravens who brought them bread in their beaks. (*Of yore* means "of time long past.")
41. **Pallas:** Pallas Athena, the Greek goddess of wisdom.
47. **Plutonian shore:** Pluto was the Greek god of the underworld—the land of darkness. The underworld, also called Hades, was surrounded by the River Styx: hence the mention of a shore.

A. Responding
? Is "dreaming dreams no mortal ever dared to dream before" a good description of how Poe saw himself? (Many students will agree; encourage them to defend their response.)

B. Responding
? What impact does the phrase "flirt and flutter" have? Is it possible that by binding himself to a very strict pattern of rhyme and alliteration, Poe has forced himself to settle for word choices that don't convey the appropriate tone? (Both are "bird words." In Poe's time, "flirt" also meant the opening and shutting of a bird's tail. "Flutter" refers to moving the feathers without actually flying.)

C. Expansion
The internal rhyme of "shaven" and "craven" in line 45 risks unintentional humor. This doesn't mean Poe was wrong to choose his strict metrical and rhyme scheme; it means that even good artistic choices have their downsides.

A. Connections
Lines 58–59: Poe makes the point that the good things in life cannot last. Compare to Robert Frost's "Nothing Gold Can Stay," page 670.

B. Expansion
Lines 62–66: the narrator tries to rationalize his fear away, telling himself that "nevermore" is the only word the raven learned from a previous, unhappy master.

C. Alliteration
In line 71 Poe's alliteration works. The repeated *g* sounds, in a string of terse adjectives, build tension.

D. Expansion
Lines 76–77: the repetition of "velvet lining that the lamplight gloated o'er" shows the narrator's increasingly maddened state.

10.

But the Raven, sitting lonely on the placid bust, spoke only
That one word, as if his soul in that one word he did outpour.
Nothing farther then he uttered—not a feather then he fluttered—
A Till I scarcely more than muttered, "Other friends have flown before—
On the morrow *he* will leave me, as my Hopes have flown before."
Then the bird said, "Nevermore."

11.

Startled at the stillness broken by reply so aptly spoken,
"Doubtless," said I, "what it utters is its only stock and store
Caught from some unhappy master whom unmerciful Disaster
B Followed fast and followed faster till his songs one burden bore—
Till the dirges of his Hope that melancholy burden bore
Of 'Never—nevermore.' "

12.

But the Raven still beguiling all my fancy into smiling,
Straight I wheeled a cushioned seat in front of bird, and bust and door;
Then, upon the velvet sinking, I betook myself to linking
Fancy unto fancy, thinking what this ominous bird of yore—
C What this grim, ungainly, ghastly, gaunt, and ominous bird of yore
Meant in croaking "Nevermore."

13.

This I sat engaged in guessing, but no syllable expressing
To the fowl whose fiery eyes now burned into my bosom's core;
This and more I sat divining, with my head at ease reclining
D On the cushion's velvet lining that the lamplight gloated o'er,
But whose velvet-violet lining with the lamplight gloating o'er,
She shall press, ah, nevermore!

14.

Then, methought, the air grew denser, perfumed from an unseen censer
Swung by Seraphim° whose footfalls tinkled on the tufted floor.
"Wretch," I cried, "thy God hath lent thee—by these angels he hath sent thee
Respite—respite and nepenthe° from thy memories of Lenore;
Quaff, oh, quaff this kind nepenthe and forget this lost Lenore!"
Quoth the Raven, "Nevermore."

---

80. **Seraphim:** the highest of the nine ranks of angels, often pictured as having three sets of wings.
82. **nepenthe** (ni·pen′thē): a sleeping potion which people long ago believed would relieve pain and sorrow; eventually, it came to stand for anything causing oblivion.

CLOSURE
Have students list, in class discussion, the images that create the atmosphere of mystery or fear in the poem.

15.

A "Prophet!" said I, "thing of evil!—prophet still, if bird or devil!—
Whether Tempter sent, or whether tempest tossed thee here ashore,
Desolate yet all undaunted, on this desert land enchanted—
On this home by Horror haunted—tell me truly, I implore—
Is there—*is* there balm in Gilead?°—tell me—tell me, I implore!"
Quoth the Raven, "Nevermore."

16.

"Prophet!" said I, "thing of evil!—prophet still, if bird or devil!
By that Heaven that bends above us—by that God we both adore—
Tell this soul with sorrow laden if, within the distant Aidenn,°
It shall clasp a sainted maiden whom the angels name Lenore—
Clasp a rare and radiant maiden whom the angels name Lenore."
B Quoth the Raven, "Nevermore."

17.

"Be that word our sign of parting, bird or fiend!" I shrieked, upstarting—
"Get thee back into the tempest and the Night's Plutonian shore!
Leave no black plume as a token of that lie thy soul hath spoken!
Leave my loneliness unbroken!—quit the bust above my door!
C Take thy beak from out my heart, and take thy form from off my door!"
Quoth the Raven, "Nevermore."

18.

D And the Raven, never flitting, still is sitting, *still* is sitting
On the pallid bust of Pallas just above my chamber door;
And his eyes have all the seeming of a demon's that is dreaming,
And the lamplight o'er him streaming throws his shadow on the floor;
And my soul from out that shadow that lies floating on the floor
Shall be lifted—nevermore!

E

---

89. **Is there balm in Gilead?:** a line from the Bible (Jeremiah 8:22). A *balm* is any healing ointment. Gilead was a region in ancient Palestine. Literally, the question means, "Is there relief from my sorrow?"
93. **Aidenn:** an Arabic word meaning "Eden" or "Heaven."

A. Expansion
The short, broken phrases separated by dashes indicate the narrator's increasing frenzy.

B. Expansion
Line 96: This "nevermore" cruelly dashes the narrator's fondest hope: that he will meet Lenore again in the afterlife.

C. Imagery
Line 101: Note the emotional power of "take thy beak from out my heart."

D. Expansion
Line 103: the repetition of "still is sitting" adds emotional force by making us feel the unending presence of the raven.

E. Responding
Your students have now read one of the classic poems of psychological horror.
? How did this poem make you feel? Were you able to take it seriously? (Answers will vary. Some may feel the concentration required by the rhyme makes it difficult to feel anything.)

Analyzing The Poem

Identifying Details

1. He seeks a remedy for, or a distraction from, his sorrow at the death of his beloved, the radiant maiden Lenore.

2. He says that he peers into the darkness outside the door. His imagination is prey to wild fancies, and he whispers the name "Lenore." But nothing except an echo of this name resounds.

In his wild, distracted state, the narrator may have expected that the spirit or soul of his beloved had come to visit him.

3. The Raven is immobile, sitting on the bust of Pallas. When the narrator mutters that the bird will doubtless leave on the morrow, the bird responds, "Nevermore."

Interpreting Meanings

4. The narrator describes the time of the events as "bleak December." The dying embers in the fireplace produce "ghosts" on the floor. The curtains rustle sadly, and the narrator is "thrilled . . . with fantastic terrors." He repeats to himself the statement that the noise at the door is merely being caused by a visitor—as if to reassure himself that the sound is not supernatural. Thus, many of the images in these stanzas contribute to a mysteri-

A. Expansion

When your students have read Poe's explanation of his own writing process, you might ask, "Do you believe it? Or is this simply another tale Poe has invented?" Assuming that it is true, and that Poe was such a strange writer that he predetermined an intellectual structure for his poem before arriving at his inspiration, is this the way most poets work, or should work? Further, is it possible that a great writer can fool himself about his own work habits?

Responding to the Poem

Analyzing the Poem

Identifying Details

1. What experience has made the speaker seek "surcease of sorrow" in his old books?
2. What does the speaker say in Stanza 5? What do you think he may have expected to find at his door?
3. What is the first hint, in Stanza 10, that the Raven is here to stay?

Interpreting Meanings

4. Which **images** describing the setting in Stanzas 2 and 3 create an atmosphere of mystery or fear?
5. In Stanza 14, the speaker talks to himself. What does he suggest is happening, and what is the nature of the "nepenthe" he is tempted to indulge in? What does the Raven's inevitable answer tell him about the possibility of this kind of oblivion?
6. In Stanza 17, what could the speaker mean by begging the bird, "Take thy beak from out my heart"?
7. The speaker's **tone** changes as the Raven gradually turns from a comic figure into a demonic figure. Trace these changes in tone. Is there evidence in Stanza 18 that the speaker goes mad? Explain.
8. The Raven in this poem is a **symbol**—it functions as a real raven in the story, but it also has a broader, figurative meaning. What, in your opinion, does the Raven symbolize? Why do you suppose Poe chose a raven to carry this meaning, rather than—for example—a dove, a nightingale, or a chicken?

Writing About the Poem

A Creative Response

1. **Describing an Alternate Setting.** In his comment on the composition of "The Raven" (which follows), Poe gives the reasons why he chose to introduce the speaker and the Raven in a *room.* Write your own descriptive paragraph of another setting in which the speaker and the Raven might have met. Describe this setting so that it will allow the events in the poem to remain as disturbing as they are.
2. **Imitating Poe's Techniques.** Poe's poem has been subject to many parodies. Write at least two verses imitating his **rhyme scheme** and **meter.** Open with his first line. Replace the name *Lenore* (the rhyming sounds for Lenore might all be used up in the original).

A Critical Response

3. **Comparing Poems.** Both "The Raven" and "Annabel Lee" are about love and loss. In a brief essay, compare the overall effects of the two poems. First compare and contrast the poems in terms of their **meaning** and **message;** then compare Poe's use of **speaker, tone,** and **sound effects** to convey meaning in each poem.
4. **Analyzing the Poem.** In the material under Primary Sources (which follows), Poe is quoted as saying that this speaker is impelled "by the human thirst for self-torture." In a paragraph, explain what you think this statement means, and tell whether or not you think the speaker in the poem exhibits this compulsion.

Primary Sources

Poe's Essay on the Writing Process: "I Asked Myself—What Is the Most Melancholy Topic?"

"The Raven" was an instant popular success. Several years after its publication, Poe wrote an essay describing how the poem was composed. He claims that he approached the poem as if he were solving a mathematical problem. Few critics seriously believe that "The Raven" began exactly the way Poe says it did—he describes the writing process in reverse. But what he tells us about how he chose details in the poem is fascinating. A

First, Poe decided he wanted to write a poem with a melancholy effect. Then he decided that the melancholy would be reinforced by the refrain "Nevermore" (he liked its sound) and that a raven would utter the refrain. Finally, he decided his subject would be the most melancholy subject in the world: a lover's mourning for a beautiful woman.

Now Poe was ready to write. The first stanza he wrote, he claimed, was the climactic one (Stanza 15).

"The next point to be considered was the mode of bringing together the lover and the Raven—and the first ous, ominous atmosphere.

5. The narrator suggests that this supernatural visitation is meant to comfort and console him for the loss of Lenore. Just as nepenthe provides oblivion from sorrows, he will forget the maiden.

The Raven's repetition of "Nevermore" tells the narrator that his hope for oblivion is illusory.

6. The bird has become a demonic force for the narrator; its prophecy that he may never forget his sorrow makes it seem to the narrator as if the raven wounds his heart with its beak.

7. Although the poem starts somberly, the first appearance of the Raven evokes a kind of bemusement in the narrator (Stanzas 7–9); he even jokes that the Raven seems like a prodigy. The narrator's mood becomes more reflective in stanzas 10–13; he wonders what misfortune can have befallen the Raven's master. It is only in Stanza 14 that the narrator realizes that the visit of the Raven may be specifically intended for him. In stanzas 15 and 16, he tries desperately to wring some shred of hope or consolation from the bird, but in vain. In the final two stanzas, he gives full vent to his fury and despair.

The narrator tells us that the Raven has remained on the bust of Pallas to this day, his eyes resembling those of a demon. He also tells us that his own soul is in the shadow of the Raven and will never be lifted up again. The exaggerated nature of both claims perhaps suggests that the speaker has gone mad.

8. Perhaps death, the pain of loss, despair itself. In his own comment, Poe says the Raven is "emblematical of Mournful and Never-Ending Remembrance" (page 261).

Poe himself, in another part of "The Philosophy of Composition," says he thought of using a parrot because it was capable of speech but that a Raven, also capable of speech, was more in keeping with the tone he wanted. It is said that Poe also thought of an owl because it is associated with Athena, the classical goddess of wisdom.

branch of this consideration was the *locale.* For this the most natural suggestion might seem to be a forest, or the fields—but it has always appeared to me that a close *circumscription of space* is absolutely necessary to the effect of insulated incident—it has the force of a frame to a picture. It has an indisputable moral power in keeping concentrated the attention. . . .

"I determined, then, to place the lover in his chamber—in chamber rendered sacred to him by memories of her who had frequented it. The room is represented as richly furnished—this in mere pursuance of the ideas I have already explained on the subject of Beauty, as the sole true poetical thesis.

"The *locale* being thus determined, I had now to introduce the bird—and the thought of introducing him through the window, was inevitable. The idea of making the lover suppose, in the first instance, that the flapping of the wings of the bird against the shutter, is a 'tapping' at the door, originated in a wish to increase, by prolonging, the reader's curiosity, and in a desire to admit the incidental effect arising from the lover's throwing open the door, finding all dark, and thence adopting the half-fancy that it was the spirit of his mistress that knocked.

"I made the night tempestuous, first, to account for the Raven's seeking admission, and secondly, for the effect of contrast with the (physical) serenity within the chamber.

"I made the bird alight on the bust of Pallas, also for the effect of contrast between the marble and the plumage—it being understood that the bust was absolutely *suggested* by the bird—the bust of Pallas being chosen, first, as most in keeping with the scholarship of the lover, and secondly, for the sonorousness of the word, *Pallas,* itself.

". . . So far, everything is within the limits of the accountable—of the real. A raven, having learned by rote the single word *Nevermore,* and having escaped from the custody of its owner, is driven at midnight, through the violence of a storm, to seek admission at a window from which a light still gleams—the chamber window of a student, occupied half in poring over a volume, half in dreaming of a beloved mistress deceased. The casement being thrown open at the fluttering of the bird's wings, the bird itself perches on the most convenient seat out of the immediate reach of the student, who, amused by the incident and the oddity of the visitor's demeanor, demands of it, in jest and without looking for a reply, its name. The raven addressed, answers with its customary word, 'Nevermore'—a word which finds immediate echo in the melancholy heart of the student, who, giving utterance aloud to certain thoughts suggested by the occasion, is again startled by the fowl's repetition of 'Nevermore.' The student now guesses the state of the case, but is impelled, as I have before explained, by the human thirst for self-torture, and in part by superstition, to propound such queries to the bird as will bring him,

"One more time."

Drawing by Chas. Addams. © 1984 The New Yorker Magazine, Inc.

the lover, the most of the luxury of sorrow, through the anticipated answer 'Nevermore.' With the indulgence, to the extreme, of this self-torture, the narration, in what I have termed its first or obvious phase, has a natural termination, and so far there has been no overstepping of the limits of the real.

"But in subjects so handled, however skillfully, or with however vivid an array of incident, there is always a certain hardness or nakedness, which repels the artistic eye. Two things are invariably required—first, some amount of complexity . . . ; and, secondly, some amount of suggestiveness—some undercurrent, however indefinite, of meaning. . . .

"Holding these opinions, I added the two concluding stanzas of the poem—their suggestiveness being thus made to pervade all the narrative which has preceded them. . . .

"It will be observed that the words 'from out my heart,' involve the first metaphorical expression in the poem. They, with the answer, 'Nevermore,' dispose the mind to seek a moral in all that has been previously narrated. The reader begins now to regard the Raven as emblematical [symbolic]—but it is not until the very last line of the very last stanza, that the intention of making him emblematical of *Mournful and Never-Ending Remembrance* is permitted distinctly to be seen. . . ."

—Edgar Allan Poe

A. Expansion
The answers to these questions need not be mutually exclusive: Poe's use of sound has its positive and negative aspects. See annotations throughout the poem.

Elements of Literature

SOUND EFFECTS

In writing "The Raven," Poe deliberately set out to produce an original verse form and to create novel effects using rhyme and alliteration.

For his basic meter, he chose the **trochee**—that is, a stressed syllable followed by an unstressed syllable, as in the word *dreary.* Poe says his stanzas are organized into this pattern of trochees:

Line 1: eight trochees
Line 2: seven and a half
Line 3: eight
Line 4: seven and a half
Line 5: seven and a half
Line 6: three and a half

Read two or three stanzas aloud and listen to the pattern of stressed and unstressed syllables. Does each line fit the description above?

The poem is a virtuoso performance in the use of **internal rhyme**—rhyme that occurs within the lines, or repetition within a line of an end rhyme. "Dreary" and "weary" in line 1 prepare us for a pattern of internal rhyming sounds. "Napping," "tapping," and "rapping" in lines 3 and 4 make us expect more. What other uses of internal rhyme can you find?

Some of the rhymes are ingenious. Not many writers, for example, would think of rhyming "window lattice" with "what thereat is" (lines 33–34). Can you locate two other clever internal rhymes in stanzas 14 and 16?

The refrain "Nevermore" is an important element in the rhyme scheme of the poem. How does Poe keep the sound of the word echoing in our ears? What other word are we reminded of when we hear the repeated "Nevermore"? What effect does this echo have?

The technique of **alliteration** (the repetition of a consonant sound) is sometimes used to create **onomatopoeia**—the use of words with sounds that actually echo their sense. But often alliteration is used merely to create a striking sound effect. At times it becomes so exaggerated that we might even wonder if Poe is mocking himself. A good example of the excessive use of alliteration is in line 71, where the hard *g* is repeated four times, almost resulting in a tongue twister: "this grim, ungainly, ghastly, gaunt, and ominous bird of yore." Find at least six other uses of alliteration that you think are unusual. Where in Stanzas 1 and 3 is alliteration used to create onomatopoeia?

Poe wanted all these sound effects to influence the reader's mood and to create music that would contribute to the beauty of the poem. In your opinion, what is the effect of this play with sounds? Do you feel that the use of rhyme and alliteration seems forced and overdone? Or do the poem's sound effects please you and stay with you—just as a witty, inventive musical score might echo in your ears long after the sounds have stopped? A

Nathaniel Hawthorne (1804–1864)

Nathaniel Hawthorne was an unusually handsome man, with a loving and beloved wife. By mid-life he had earned recognition as a writer and won the admiration of his contemporaries. Nevertheless, he became increasingly dissatisfied, remote, and disappointing to his friends. It was as if his dark insights into the human heart cast gloom into his own. His fiction, which has survived the changing tastes of many generations and is more admired today than when it was written, is fueled by a moral intuition, an awareness of the guilt that goes along with a Puritan conscience. The shadow of guilt appears to have darkened Hawthorne's life.

The source of this darkness is thought to lie in Hawthorne's illustrious ancestors. The American branch of the family began with William Hathorne, a serious soldier and judge who came to the Massachusetts colony in 1630. Hawthorne describes him in the preamble to *The Scarlet Letter* as "the bearded, sable-cloaked, and steeple-crowned progenitor." William Hathorne's son, John, was also a judge. During the Salem witch trials of 1692, he sentenced nineteen of the accused to death.

By 1804, however, the year of Hawthorne's birth, the family had lost its wealth and renown. His own father, a sea captain, died during a voyage and left his grief-stricken wife with three infants to raise and few resources beyond the charity of relatives. As he grew up, Hawthorne experienced a sense of deprivation, bearing a name whose greatness and influence had long since passed. It was he who added the *w* to its spelling to insure a broad *a* in its pronunciation.

Hawthorne attended Salem schools and college at Bowdoin in Maine. Here, by his own judgment, he was an idle student, "rather choosing to nurse my own fancies than to dig into Greek roots." He chewed tobacco, played cards, drank wine at the taverns, and avoided intellectual company in favor of pleasure.

Henry Wadsworth Longfellow (see page 146), already a literary figure, was also a Bowdoin student. Yet Hawthorne preferred the company

of men like Franklin Pierce, whose interests lay more in living life than in writing about it.

In the spring of 1825, he graduated in the middle of his class, determinedly unhonored. He wrote to his sister Louise, "I shall never make a distinguished figure in the world and all I hope or wish is to plod along with the multitude." There is good reason to believe that this was an ironic statement, concealing an ambition that burned intensely.

Returning to Salem, Hawthorne set himself up in what he called the "dismal chamber," a room on the third floor of the family house. He kept himself prisoner there until he had learned the craft of fiction and had begun to understand what he, as an American, might have to say through it. This lonely apprenticeship took him twelve years.

A. Developing Vocabulary
"Sable-cloaked" means "black-cloaked," not "cloaked in sable furs." "Steeple-crowned" refers to his wearing a tall hat.

B. Expansion
With regard to Hawthorne's relative lack of classical learning, note how few Latin and Greek allusions there are in his works as compared to Poe's.

C. Connections
Compare Hawthorne's reclusiveness to Emily Dickinson's. (See Dickinson biography, page 352.) Contrast it also to Thoreau's isolation, which took him out of town but did not impair his social life, and to Melville's isolation at the end of his career, which impaired his work rather than strengthened it as had Hawthorne's time of withdrawal.

A. Expansion
Hawthorne worked on several unfinished novels during those years, *Dr. Grimshae's Secret; Septimius Felton, or The Elixir of Life;* and *The Ancestral Footstep* among them. Alfred Kazin quips that Hawthorne lived out his last years as a Hawthorne character. He was certainly in failing spirits and emotionally isolated from the society around him. Kazin also suggests that Hawthorne, in the intellectually solemn atmosphere of Transcendentalism, felt low self-esteem for being a "mere" storyteller. Emerson, for one, had little use for fiction and thought Hawthorne's success arose from his personal qualities rather than his writing.

He emerged from this seclusion in 1837 to publish a collection of stories with the unassuming title, *Twice-Told Tales.* If they were conventionally presented, they nonetheless offered a unique foretaste of Hawthorne's singular vision, that of the human heart as a lurking place for the secrets of past violence. The book was favorably reviewed by his friend Longfellow and, in a later edition, by Poe. Hawthorne had achieved just enough success to encourage further work.

In 1839, he became engaged to Sophia Peabody, but the couple heeded traditional warnings against hasty marriage. Meanwhile, Hawthorne went off to West Roxbury to join the utopian experiment in communal living at Brook Farm. It did not suit him. Neither the shoveling of manure nor the endless, lofty discussions of the Transcendentalists appealed to him (see page 183). Although he left after a few months, he made good use of the experience later, in his novel *The Blithedale Romance* (1852).

When they were married in 1842, Hawthorne and his wife moved into the Old Manse in Concord, where Emerson had lived before them. Concord was the home of many prominent writers, and we might imagine that Hawthorne would have found it more congenial than Brook Farm. However, although he often walked with Thoreau and Emerson, neither creativity nor warm friendship came from these relationships.

Since he was making only the barest living from his stories, Hawthorne had to accept a political appointment as surveyor to the Salem customhouse in 1846. This appointment freed him from financial worry for three years, but in 1849 he lost the job. Despite this loss and the simultaneous death of his mother, he somehow found the energies for his masterwork, *The Scarlet Letter.* It was, he said, "a particularly hell-fired story into which I found it almost impossible to throw a cheering light."

The Scarlet Letter is set in Puritan Boston during the mid-seventeenth century. The title refers to a cloth letter, *A,* which the narrator finds in a customhouse, along with documents outlining the tragic story of Hester Prynne, who bore an illegitimate child. Refusing to name its father, she was sentenced to wear the scarlet *A* (for adultery) on her breast. The story is about sin and redemption, and the tragic consequences of hypocrisy and concealed guilt.

When *The Scarlet Letter* was published in 1850, it brought Hawthorne wide acclaim, some money, and the admiration and friendship of Herman Melville. This success continued. Another novel, *The House of the Seven Gables,* appeared the following year, as well as another collection of stories, *The Snow-Image.*

In 1853, Hawthorne's friend Franklin Pierce became President and offered Hawthorne the post of United States consul at Liverpool. Hawthorne accepted willingly. He and his family lived in Europe for seven years. Hawthorne wrote, traveled, filled his notebooks, and worked on an ambitious novel, *The Marble Faun,* a romance set in Italy and published in 1860, when he returned to America.

As an exile, however, Hawthorne found his creativity dwindling, and he had become inexplicably dejected. Arriving back in America, he was further discouraged by his own judgment of *The Marble Faun,* which he decided was a failure. Even his return home was oddly cheerless. After his years abroad, he was disenchanted with both the Europe where he had been and the America from which he now felt estranged. His old friend Pierce, for whom he had written a campaign biography in 1852, had been defeated for reelection. Abraham Lincoln was in the White House, and with the onset of the Civil War, Hawthorne felt entirely out of harmony with his times.

Back in Concord, he did manage to convert his English journals into the book *Our Old Home* (1863); but he found himself unable to complete the several fiction projects he had promised his publisher. His health declined. A Glimpsing Hawthorne at a social gathering (which he hated), the elder Henry James noted that he had the look "of a rogue who suddenly finds himself in the company of detectives." On the night of May 18, 1864, while on a trip with Franklin Pierce, Hawthorne died in a New Hampshire hotel room.

Emerson felt that Hawthorne, no longer able to endure his painful solitude, "died of it." Emerson also noted in his journal, after attending Hawthorne's funeral, that he was sorry he hadn't known Hawthorne better. And he recorded this sadly ironic anecdote: "One day, when I found him on the top of his hill, in the woods, he paced back the path to his house, and said, *'This path is the only remembrance of me that will remain.'* "

SUPPLEMENTARY SUPPORT MATERIALS

1. Vocabulary Activity Worksheet (*CCB*)
2. Review and Response Worksheet: Characterization (*CCB*)
3. Selection Test (*CCB*)

DEVELOPING VOCABULARY

The following words from the story are tested in the Selection Test. (See also Vocabulary Activity Worksheet.)

perturbation	vagary
iniquity	to portend
indecorous	remonstrance
ostentatious	to intimate
sagacious	antipathy

PREPARATION

ESTABLISHING A PURPOSE. Have students read the story to determine why Hawthorne called it a "parable." What is the parable of the story?

THE MINISTER'S BLACK VEIL

Winter Sunday in Norway, Maine, by an unknown artist (c. 1860). Oil.

New York State Historical Association, Cooperstown.

Humanities Connection: Responding to the Fine Art

This painting is an example of "primitive" or "naive" painting. It is by a self-taught artist unversed in techniques such as perspective. Early America had many naive painters whose work has great charm and vigor. The Horace Pippin painting on page 220 is modern but has naive elements.

? Compare these two paintings with the Andrew Wyeth on page 179, the Thomas Cole on page 192, and the Martin Johnson Heade on page 284. What are the relative strengths and weaknesses of naive and sophisticated painting? (Naive art may have a freshness of vision and may reflect the feeling of a time and place better than a sophisticated work. However, naive works without vision tend to merely look childish. Sophisticated works like Wyeth's can dazzle us with their technique but lack the boldness of the naive.)

A. Responding
? What is a parable? Why do you think Hawthorne might have called his story a parable? (Because it is a short story with a moral) What expectations does this heading arouse in you as a reader? (The word is associated with the Bible, so one might expect a religious message.) What do you think it might have to do with the environment in which Hawthorne lived? (Massachusetts still had a strong Puritan tradition.) Why don't modern writers usually put headings like "A Parable" on their stories? (It probably would sound too pretentious.)

B. Expansion
Stop and discuss why Mr. Hooper might have put on the veil. Ask your students whether they feel pulled in by the suspense. (At this point, allow the discussion to be open-ended, although you might want to reevaluate students' responses as the story progresses.)

Hawthorne added the following note to this story: "Another clergyman in New England, Mr. Joseph Moody, of York, Maine, who died about eighty years since, made himself remarkable by the same eccentricity that is here related of the Reverend Mr. Hooper. In his case, however, the symbol had a different import. In early life he had accidentally killed a beloved friend; and from that day till the hour of his own death, he hid his face from men." When you get to Goodman Gray's line: "Our parson has gone mad," stop and try to imagine why the minister has draped his face with the black material ordinarily used by mourners. Think of at least three possible reasons for the veil. Remember that one of Hawthorne's concerns was the existence of sin.

A

A Parable

The sexton stood in the porch of Milford meetinghouse, pulling busily at the bell rope. The old people of the village came stooping along the street. Children, with bright faces, tripped merrily beside their parents, or mimicked a graver gait, in the conscious dignity of their Sunday clothes. Spruce bachelors looked sidelong at the pretty maidens, and fancied that the Sabbath sunshine made them prettier than on weekdays. When the throng had mostly streamed into the porch, the sexton began to toll the bell, keeping his eye on the Reverend Mr. Hooper's door. The first glimpse of the clergyman's figure was the signal for the bell to cease its summons.

B "But what has good Parson Hooper got upon his face?" cried the sexton in astonishment.

All within hearing immediately turned about, and beheld the semblance of Mr. Hooper, pacing slowly his meditative way toward the meetinghouse. With one accord they started, expressing more wonder than if some strange minister were coming to dust the cushions of Mr. Hooper's pulpit.

"Are you sure it is our parson?" inquired Goodman[1] Gray of the sexton.

"Of a certainty it is good Mr. Hooper," replied the sexton. "He was to have exchanged pulpits with Parson Shute, of Westbury; but Parson Shute sent to excuse himself yesterday, being to preach a funeral sermon."

The cause of so much amazement may appear sufficiently slight. Mr. Hooper, a gentlemanly person, of about thirty, though still a bachelor, was dressed with due clerical neatness, as if a careful wife had starched his band, and brushed the weekly dust from his Sunday's garb. There was but one thing remarkable in his appearance. Swathed about his forehead, and hanging down over his face, so low as to be shaken by his breath, Mr. Hooper had on a black veil. On a nearer view it seemed to consist of two folds of crape,[2] which entirely concealed his features, except the mouth and chin, but probably did not intercept his sight, further than to give a darkened aspect to all living and inanimate things. With this gloomy shade before him, good Mr. Hooper walked onward, at a slow and quiet pace, stooping somewhat, and looking on the ground, as is customary with abstracted men, yet nodding kindly to those of his parishioners who still waited on the meetinghouse steps. But so wonder-struck were they that his greeting hardly met with a return.

"I can't really feel as if good Mr. Hooper's face was behind that piece of crape," said the sexton.

"I don't like it," muttered an old woman, as she hobbled into the meetinghouse. "He has changed himself into something awful, only by hiding his face."

"Our parson has gone mad!" cried Goodman Gray, following him across the threshold.

A rumor of some unaccountable phenomenon had preceded Mr. Hooper into the meetinghouse, and set all the congregation astir. Few could refrain from twisting their heads toward the door; many stood upright, and turned directly about; while several little boys clambered upon the seats, and came down again with a terrible racket. There was a general bustle, a rustling of the women's gowns and shuffling of the men's feet, greatly at variance with that hushed repose which should attend the entrance of the minister. But Mr. Hooper appeared not to notice the perturbation of his people. He entered with an almost noiseless step, bent his head mildly to the pews on each

1. **Goodman:** a form of polite address, like "good sir."

2. **crape** (krāp): black cloth worn as a sign of mourning (usually pinned on the sleeve). In French, it's spelled *crêpe*.

side, and bowed as he passed his oldest parishioner, a white-haired great-grandsire, who occupied an armchair in the center of the aisle. It was strange to observe how slowly this venerable man became conscious of something singular in the appearance of his pastor. He seemed not fully to partake of the prevailing wonder, till Mr. Hooper had ascended the stairs, and showed himself in the pulpit, face to face with his congregation, except for the black veil. That mysterious emblem was never once withdrawn. It shook with his measured breath, as he gave out the psalm; it threw its obscurity between him and the holy page, as he read the Scriptures; and while he prayed, the veil lay heavily on his uplifted countenance. Did he seek to hide it from the dread Being whom he was addressing?

Such was the effect of this simple piece of crape, that more than one woman of delicate nerves was forced to leave the meetinghouse. Yet perhaps the pale-faced congregation was almost as fearful a sight to the minister as his black veil to them.

A Mr. Hooper had the reputation of a good preacher, but not an energetic one: he strove to win his people heavenward by mild, persuasive influences, rather than to drive them thither by the thunders of the Word. The sermon which he now delivered was marked by the same characteristics of style and manner as the general series of his pulpit oratory. But there was something, either in the sentiment of the discourse itself, or in the imagination of the auditors, which made it greatly the most powerful effort that they had ever heard from their pastor's lips. It was tinged, rather more darkly than usual, with the gentle gloom of Mr. Hooper's temperament. The subject had reference to secret sin, and those sad mysteries which we hide from our nearest and dearest, and would fain conceal from our own consciousness, even forgetting that the Omniscient[3] can detect them. A subtle power was breathed into his words. Each member of the congregation, the most innocent girl, and the man of hardened breast, felt as if the preacher had crept upon them, behind his awful veil, and discovered their hoarded iniquity of deed or thought. Many spread their clasped hands on their bosoms. There was nothing terrible in what Mr. Hooper said, at least, no violence; and yet, with every tremor of his melancholy voice, the hearers quaked. An unsought pathos came hand in hand with awe. So sensible were the audience of some unwonted attribute in their minister, that they longed for a breath of wind to blow aside the veil, almost believing that a stranger's visage would be discovered, though the form, gesture, and voice were those of Mr. Hooper.

At the close of the services, the people hurried out with indecorous confusion, eager to communicate their pent-up amazement, and conscious of lighter spirits the moment they lost sight of the black veil. Some gathered in little circles, huddled closely together, with their mouths all whispering in the center; some went homeward alone, wrapt in silent meditation; some talked loudly, and profaned the Sabbath day with ostentatious laughter. A few shook their sagacious heads, intimating that they could penetrate the mystery; while one or two affirmed that there was no mystery at all, but only that Mr. Hooper's eyes were so weakened by the midnight lamp, as to require a shade. After a brief interval, forth came good Mr. Hooper also, in the rear of his flock. Turning his veiled face from one group to another, he paid due reverence to the hoary heads, saluted the middle-aged with kind dignity as their friend and spiritual guide, greeted the young with mingled authority and love, and laid his hands on the little children's heads to bless them. Such was always his custom on the Sabbath day. Strange and bewildered looks B repaid him for his courtesy. None, as on former occasions, aspired to the honor of walking by their pastor's side. Old Squire Saunders, doubtless by an accidental lapse of memory, neglected to invite Mr. Hooper to his table, where the good clergyman had been wont to bless the food, almost every Sunday since his settlement. He returned, therefore, to the parsonage, and, at the moment of closing the door, was observed to look back upon the people, all of whom had their eyes fixed upon the minister. A sad smile gleamed faintly from beneath the black veil, and flickered about his mouth, glimmering as he disappeared.

"How strange," said a lady, "that a simple black veil, such as any woman might wear on her bonnet, should become such a terrible thing on Mr. Hooper's face!"

"Something must surely be amiss with Mr. Hooper's intellects," observed her husband, the physician of the village. "But the strangest part of the affair is the effect of this vagary, even on a

3. **the Omniscient:** the all-knowing God.

A. Theme
This paragraph is a good one to read aloud. The sentence, "The subject had reference to secret sin," is thematically crucial. You might stop and ask your students what they think Hawthorne might mean by secret sin.

B. Expansion
Note that Mr. Hooper is not changing his life or manners in any way except to wear the veil. This makes it a kind of controlled scientific experiment in which only one variable is altered. Hawthorne had a fascination for the experimental process, as "Rappaccini's Daughter" (page 275) will show.

A. Connections
In this paragraph Hawthorne inserts macabre effects: the death of a young woman, and a suggestion of the supernatural when the corpse appears to shudder.
? At this point, how would you compare Hawthorne's writing with Poe's? (Answers will vary. You might have students re-read the description of the masked figure in *Red Death* [p. 231] and compare it to this. Poe's style seems more intense, his choice of words more affected, his sentences longer, and his events more dramatic than Hawthorne's.)

B. Dialogue
? What effect does the dialogue have on the pace of the story? (It quickens it. Hawthorne keeps the narrative moving with a series of contrasts, alternating dramatic, dialogue-based scenes with longer narrative passages.)

sober-minded man like myself. The black veil, though it covers only our pastor's face, throws its influence over his whole person, and makes him ghostlike from head to foot. Do you not feel it so?"

"Truly do I," replied the lady, "and I would not be alone with him for the world. I wonder he is not afraid to be alone with himself!"

"Men sometimes are so," said her husband.

A

The afternoon service was attended with similar circumstances. At its conclusion, the bell tolled for the funeral of a young lady. The relatives and friends were assembled in the house, and the more distant acquaintances stood about the door, speaking of the good qualities of the deceased, when their talk was interrupted by the appearance of Mr. Hooper, still covered with his black veil. It was now an appropriate emblem. The clergyman stepped into the room where the corpse was laid, and bent over the coffin, to take a last farewell of his deceased parishioner. As he stooped, the veil hung straight down from his forehead, so that, if her eyelids had not been closed forever, the dead maiden might have seen his face. Could Mr. Hooper be fearful of her glance, that he so hastily caught back the black veil? A person who watched the interview between the dead and living scrupled[4] not to affirm that, at the instant when the clergyman's features were disclosed, the corpse had slightly shuddered, rustling the shroud and muslin cap, though the countenance retained the composure of death. A superstitious old woman was the only witness of this prodigy. From the coffin Mr. Hooper passed into the chamber of the mourners, and thence to the head of the staircase, to make the funeral prayer. It was a tender and heart-dissolving prayer, full of sorrow, yet so imbued with celestial hopes that the music of a heavenly harp, swept by the fingers of the dead, seemed faintly to be heard among the saddest accents of the minister. The people trembled, though they but darkly understood him when he prayed that they, and himself, and all of mortal race, might be ready, as he trusted this young maiden had been, for the dreadful hour that should snatch the veil from their faces. The bearers went heavily forth, and the mourners followed, saddening all the street, with the dead before them, and Mr. Hooper in his black veil behind.

B

"Why do you look back?" said one in the procession to his partner.

"I had a fancy," replied she, "that the minister and the maiden's spirit were walking hand in hand."

"And so had I, at the same moment," said the other.

That night, the handsomest couple in Milford village were to be joined in wedlock. Though reckoned a melancholy man, Mr. Hooper had a placid cheerfulness for such occasions, which often excited a sympathetic smile where livelier merriment would have been thrown away. There was no quality of his disposition which made him more beloved than this. The company at the wedding awaited his arrival with impatience, trusting that the strange awe which had gathered over him throughout the day would now be dispelled. But such was not the result. When Mr. Hooper came, the first thing that their eyes rested on was the same horrible black veil, which had added deeper gloom to the funeral, and could portend nothing but evil to the wedding. Such was its immediate effect on the guests that a cloud seemed to have rolled duskily from beneath the black crape, and dimmed the light of the candles. The bridal pair stood up before the minister. But the bride's cold fingers quivered in the tremulous hand of the bridegroom, and her deathlike paleness caused a whisper that the maiden who had been buried a few hours before was come from her grave to be married. If ever another wedding were so dismal, it was that famous one where they tolled the wedding knell.[5] After performing the ceremony, Mr. Hooper raised a glass of wine to his lips, wishing happiness to the new-married couple in a strain of mild pleasantry that ought to have brightened the features of the guests, like a cheerful gleam from the hearth. At that instant, catching a glimpse of his figure in the looking glass, the black veil involved his own spirit in the horror with which it overwhelmed all others. His frame shuddered, his lips grew white, he spilled the untasted wine upon the carpet, and rushed forth into the darkness. For the earth, too, had on her Black Veil.

The next day, the whole village of Milford talked of little else than Parson Hooper's black veil. That, and the mystery concealed behind it, supplied a topic for discussion between acquaint-

4. **scrupled:** here, refrained.

5. **If . . . knell:** a reference to Hawthorne's story, "The Wedding Knell." A *knell* is the ringing of a bell.

ances meeting in the street, and good women gossiping at their open windows. It was the first item of news that the tavern keeper told to his guests. The children babbled of it on their way to school. One imitative little imp covered his face with an old black handkerchief, thereby so frightening his playmates that the panic seized himself, and he well-nigh lost his wits by his own waggery.

A It was remarkable that of all the busybodies and impertinent people in the parish, not one ventured to put the plain question to Mr. Hooper, wherefore he did this thing. Hitherto, whenever there appeared the slightest call for such interference, he had never lacked advisers, nor shown himself averse to be guided by their judgment. If he erred at all, it was by so painful a degree of self-distrust that even the mildest censure would lead him to consider an indifferent action as a crime. Yet, though so well acquainted with this amiable weakness, no individual among his parishioners chose to make the black veil a subject of friendly remonstrance. There was a feeling of dread, neither plainly confessed nor carefully concealed, which caused each to shift the responsibility upon another, till at length it was found expedient to send a deputation of the church, in order to deal with Mr. Hooper about the mystery, before it should grow into a scandal. Never did an embassy so ill discharge its duties. The minister received them with friendly courtesy, but became silent, after they were seated, leaving to his visitors the whole burden of introducing their important business. The topic, it might be supposed, was obvious enough. There was the black veil swathed round Mr. Hooper's forehead, and concealing every feature above his placid mouth, on which, at times, they could perceive the glimmering of a melancholy smile. But that piece of crape, to their imagination, seemed to hang down before his heart, the symbol of a fearful secret between him and them. Were the veil but cast aside, they might speak freely of it, but not till then. Thus they sat a considerable time, speechless, confused, and shrinking uneasily from Mr. Hooper's eye, which they felt to be fixed upon them with an invisible glance. Finally, the deputies returned abashed to their constituents, pronouncing the matter too weighty to be handled, except by a council of the churches, if, indeed, it might not require a general synod.[6]

6. **synod** (sin'əd): a council of churches.

But there was one person in the village unappalled by the awe with which the black veil had impressed all beside herself. When the deputies B returned without an explanation, or even venturing to demand one, she, with the calm energy of her character, determined to chase away the strange cloud that appeared to be settling round Mr. Hooper, every moment more darkly than before. As his plighted wife,[7] it should be her privilege to know what the black veil concealed. At the minister's first visit, therefore, she entered upon the subject with a direct simplicity, which made the task easier both for him and her. After he had seated himself, she fixed her eyes steadfastly upon the veil, but could discern nothing of the dreadful gloom that had so overawed the multitude: it was but a double fold of crape, hanging down from his forehead to his mouth, and slightly stirring with his breath.

"No," said she aloud, and smiling, "there is nothing terrible in this piece of crape, except that it hides a face which I am always glad to look upon. Come, good sir, let the sun shine from behind the cloud. First lay aside your black veil; then tell me why you put it on."

Mr. Hooper's smile glimmered faintly.

"There is an hour to come," said he, "when all of us shall cast aside our veils. Take it not amiss, beloved friend, if I wear this piece of crape till then."

"Your words are a mystery, too," returned the young lady. "Take away the veil from them, at least."

"Elizabeth, I will," said he, "so far as my vow may suffer me. Know, then, this veil is a type and a symbol, and I am bound to wear it ever, both in light and darkness, in solitude and before the gaze of multitudes, and as with strangers, so with my familiar friends. No mortal eye will see it withdrawn. This dismal shade must separate me from the world: even you, Elizabeth, can never come behind it!"

"What grievous affliction hath befallen you," she earnestly inquired, "that you should thus darken your eyes forever?"

"If it be a sign of mourning," replied Mr. Hooper, "I, perhaps, like most other mortals, have sorrows dark enough to be typified by a black veil."

"But what if the world will not believe that it

7. **plighted wife:** intended wife.

A. Responding
Hawthorne explains why no one simply asked Mr. Hooper his reasons for putting on the veil.
? Is Hawthorne's explanation convincing in real-life terms? Is it convincing in terms of the story? (The answers are probably no and yes, respectively. This demonstrates how an author achieves suspension of disbelief by means of well-narrated detail.)

B. Responding
? How would you feel if you were Elizabeth? (Answers will vary. She is clearly stunned by his strange behavior and his refusal to change.) How would you feel if you were Mr. Hooper, loving her yet feeling compelled to repel her? (Answers will vary even more. People obsessed with sin—or duty—are sometimes difficult to figure out.)

A. Humanities Connection: Responding to the Fine Art

? In this illustration, Mr. Hooper seems to be walking with his head bowed. Why? Is he ashamed of his action? (No. He is probably weighed down with the sin his veil symbolizes.) How are the other figures in the illustration behaving? Is their behavior consistent with details in the selection? (The other figures, especially the child, seem frightened or apprehensive of Mr. Hooper, behavior that is certainly consistent with the story.)

A

Illustration for "The Minister's Black Veil" from *Hawthorne's Short Stories* published by Dodd, Mead & Co., 1964.

is the type of an innocent sorrow?" urged Elizabeth. "Beloved and respected as you are, there may be whispers that you hide your face under the consciousness of secret sin. For the sake of your holy office, do away with this scandal!"

The color rose into her cheeks as she intimated the nature of the rumors that were already abroad in the village. But Mr. Hooper's mildness did not foresake him. He even smiled again—that same sad smile, which always appeared like a faint glimmering of light, proceeding from the obscurity beneath the veil.

"If I hide my face for sorrow, there is cause enough," he merely replied; "and if I cover it for secret sin, what mortal might not do the same?"

And with this gentle but unconquerable obstinacy did he resist all her entreaties. At length Elizabeth sat silent. For a few moments she appeared lost in thought, considering, probably, what new methods might be tried to withdraw her lover from so dark a fantasy, which, if it had no other meaning, was perhaps a symptom of mental disease. Though of a firmer character than his own, the tears rolled down her cheeks. But, in an instant, as it were, a new feeling took the place of sorrow: her eyes were fixed insensibly on the black veil, when, like a sudden twilight in the air, its terrors fell around her. She arose, and stood trembling before him.

"And do you feel it then, at last?" said he mournfully.

She made no reply, but covered her eyes with her hand, and turned to leave the room. He rushed forward and caught her arm.

A "Have patience with me, Elizabeth!" cried he, passionately. "Do not desert me, though this veil must be between us here on earth. Be mine, and hereafter there shall be no veil over my face, no darkness between our souls! It is but a mortal veil—it is not for eternity! Oh! you know not how lonely I am, and how frightened, to be alone behind my black veil. Do not leave me in this miserable obscurity forever!"

"Lift the veil but once, and look me in the face," said she.

"Never! It cannot be!" replied Mr. Hooper.

"Then farewell!" said Elizabeth.

She withdrew her arm from his grasp, and slowly departed, pausing at the door, to give one long, shuddering gaze, that seemed almost to penetrate the mystery of the black veil. But, even amid his grief, Mr. Hooper smiled to think that only a material emblem had separated him from happiness, though the horrors which it shadowed forth must be drawn darkly between the fondest of lovers.

From that time no attempts were made to remove Mr. Hooper's black veil, or, by a direct appeal, to discover the secret which it was supposed to hide. By persons who claimed a superiority to popular prejudice, it was reckoned merely an eccentric whim, such as often mingles with the sober actions of men otherwise rational, and tinges them all with its own semblance of insanity. But with the multitude, good Mr. Hooper was irreparably a bugbear.[8] He could not walk the street with any peace of mind, so conscious was he that the gentle and timid would turn aside to avoid him, and that others would make it a point B of hardihood to throw themselves in his way. The impertinence of the latter class compelled him to give up his customary walk at sunset to the burial ground; for when he leaned pensively over the gate, there would always be faces behind the gravestones, peeping at his black veil. A fable went the rounds that the stare of the dead people drove him thence. It grieved him, to the very depth of his kind heart, to observe how the children fled from his approach, breaking up their merriest sports, while his melancholy figure was yet afar off. Their instinctive dread caused him to feel more strongly than aught else that a preternatural horror was interwoven with the threads of the black crape. In truth, his own antipathy to the veil was known to be so great that he never willingly passed before a mirror, nor stooped to drink at a still fountain, lest, in its peaceful bosom, he C should be affrighted by himself. This was what gave plausibility to the whispers that Mr. Hooper's conscience tortured him for some great crime too horrible to be entirely concealed, or otherwise than so obscurely intimated. Thus, from beneath the black veil, there rolled a cloud into the sunshine, an ambiguity of sin or sorrow, which enveloped the poor minister, so that love or sympathy could never reach him. It was said that ghost and fiend consorted with him there. With self-shudderings and outward terrors, he walked continually in its shadow, groping darkly within his own soul, or gazing through a medium that saddened the whole world. Even the lawless wind, it was believed, respected his dreadful secret, and never blew aside the veil. But still good Mr. Hooper sadly smiled at the pale visages of the wordly throng as he passed by.

D Among all its bad influences, the black veil had the one desirable effect of making its wearer a very efficient clergyman. By the aid of his mysterious emblem—for there was no other apparent cause—he became a man of awful power over souls that were in agony for sin. His converts always regarded him with a dread peculiar to themselves, affirming, though but figuratively, that before he brought them to celestial light, they had been with him behind the black veil. Its gloom, indeed, enabled him to sympathize with all dark affections. Dying sinners cried aloud for Mr. Hooper, and would not yield their breath till he appeared; though ever, as he stooped to whisper consolation, they shuddered at the veiled face so near their own. Such were the terrors of the black veil, even when Death had bared his visage! Strangers came long distances to attend service at his church, with the mere idle purpose of gazing at his figure, because it was forbidden them to behold his face. But many were made to quake

8. **bugbear:** source of fears, often groundless ones.

A. Expansion
This paragraph shows Hooper's anguish at its deepest. He genuinely loves Elizabeth, and wishes he did not feel compelled to act as he does.

B. Expansion
Note that even before putting on the veil, Mr. Hooper had been melancholy—his favorite recreation had been walking to the cemetery.

C. Responding
? Do you think Hooper's conscience was torturing him for a specific sin, or for a vague sense of personal and universal sin, or both? (Note that Hawthorne is deliberately ambiguous on this point.)

D. Irony
A very effective irony, making the point that consciousness of sin brings one closer to God.

CLOSURE

Have students write a two- or three-sentence statement of the theme of the story. Statements should be shared orally in class.

READING CHECK TEST

1. The veil makes Hooper a more effective minister. *True*

2. Hooper refuses to drink from a fountain where he might see his own reflection. *True*

3. Governor Belcher, who has asked that Hooper give the election-day sermon, withdraws the offer when Hooper refuses to remove the veil. *False*

4. Elizabeth, who after all these years still loves Hooper, is the only person with him at his death. *False*

5. Hooper momentarily withdraws the veil just before his death. *False*

A. Expansion

The minister of Westbury is metaphorically referring to the spiritual veil between life and death, not the physical veil Hooper is wearing.

ere they departed! Once, during Governor Belcher's[9] administration, Mr. Hooper was appointed to preach the election sermon. Covered with his black veil, he stood before the chief magistrate, the council, and the representatives, and wrought so deep an impression that the legislative measures of that year were characterized by all the gloom and piety of our earliest ancestral sway.

In this manner Mr. Hooper spent a long life, irreproachable in outward act, yet shrouded in dismal suspicions; kind and loving, though unloved, and dimly feared; a man apart from men, shunned in their health and joy, but ever summoned to their aid in mortal anguish. As years wore on, shedding their snows above his sable veil, he acquired a name throughout the New England churches, and they called him Father Hooper. Nearly all his parishioners who were of mature age when he was settled had been borne away by many a funeral: he had one congregation in the church, and a more crowded one in the churchyard; and having wrought so late into the evening, and done his work so well, it was now good Father Hooper's turn to rest.

Several persons were visible by the shaded candlelight, in the death chamber of the old clergyman. Natural connections he had none. But there was the decorously grave, though unmoved physician, seeking only to mitigate the last pangs of the patient whom he could not save. There were the deacons, and other eminently pious members of his church. There, also, was the Reverend Mr. Clark, of Westbury, a young and zealous divine, who had ridden in haste to pray by the bedside of the expiring minister. There was the nurse, no hired handmaiden of death, but one whose calm affection had endured thus long in secrecy, in solitude, amid the chill of age, and would not perish, even at the dying hour. Who, but Elizabeth! And there lay the hoary head of good Father Hooper upon the death pillow, with the black veil still swathed about his brow, and reaching down over his face, so that each more difficult gasp of his faint breath caused it to stir. All through life that piece of crape had hung between him and the world: it had separated him from cheerful brotherhood and woman's love, and kept him in that saddest of all prisons, his own heart; and still it lay upon his face, as if to deepen the gloom of his darksome chamber, and shade him from the sunshine of eternity.

For some time previous, his mind had been confused, wavering doubtfully between the past and the present, and hovering forward, as it were, at intervals, into the indistinctness of the world to come. There had been feverish turns, which tossed him from side to side, and wore away what little strength he had. But in his most convulsive struggles, and in the wildest vagaries of his intellect, when no other thought retained its sober influence, he still showed an awful solicitude lest the black veil should slip aside. Even if his bewildered soul could have forgotten, there was a faithful woman at his pillow, who, with averted eyes, would have covered that aged face, which she had last beheld in the comeliness of manhood. At length the death-stricken old man lay quietly in the torpor of mental and bodily exhaustion, with an imperceptible pulse, and breath that grew fainter and fainter, except when a long, deep, and irregular inspiration seemed to prelude the flight of his spirit.

The minister of Westbury approached the bedside.

"Venerable Father Hooper," said he, "the moment of your release is at hand. Are you ready for the lifting of the veil that shuts in time from eternity?" A

Father Hooper at first replied merely by a feeble motion of his head; then, apprehensive, perhaps, that his meaning might be doubtful, he exerted himself to speak.

"Yea," said he, in faint accents, "my soul hath a patient weariness until that veil be lifted."

"And is it fitting," resumed the Reverend Mr. Clark, "that a man so given to prayer, of such a blameless example, holy in deed and thought, so far as mortal judgment may pronounce; is it fitting that a father in the church should leave a shadow on his memory that may seem to blacken a life so pure? I pray you, my venerable brother, let not this thing be! Suffer us to be gladdened by your triumphant aspect as you go to your reward. Before the veil of eternity be lifted, let me cast aside this black veil from your face!"

And thus speaking, the Reverend Mr. Clark bent forward to reveal the mystery of so many years. But, exerting a sudden energy, that made all the beholders stand aghast, Father Hooper snatched both his hands from beneath the bedclothes, and pressed them strongly on the black

9. **Governor Belcher:** Jonathan Belcher was governor of the Massachusetts Bay Colony from 1730 to 1741.

ANALYZING THE STORY
Identifying Facts

1. They are shocked.
2. Hooper is neat, gentle, and kind. They seem to have been well disposed toward him.
3. At the funeral, Hooper bends over the body of the dead girl to take his last farewell. The veil shifts momentarily to reveal his face; an old woman later affirms that the corpse gave a shudder at that moment. But Mr. Hooper's funeral prayer deeply moves those of his congregation who are present. At the wedding, the guests regard the veil as an ominous portent that spreads a shadow over such a happy occasion. The mood is heightened when Mr. Hooper, just as he raises a glass to toast the couple, catches sight of his veiled face in a looking glass. Terrified, he spills the wine on the carpet and rushes out into the night.
4. The passage is on page 269.

Elizabeth says that the world may not believe that the veil is the sign of an innocent sorrow. She warns Hooper that people will gossip about him, whispering that he has been involved in some scandal. She then appeals to their love, and *(Answers continue on top of next page.)*

veil, resolute to struggle, if the minister of Westbury would contend with a dying man.

"Never!" cried the veiled clergyman. "On earth, never!"

"Dark old man!" exclaimed the frightened minister, "with what horrible crime upon your soul are you now passing to the judgment?"

Father Hooper's breath heaved; it rattled in his throat; but, with a mighty effort, grasping forward with his hands, he caught hold of life, and held it back till he should speak. He even raised himself in bed; and there he sat, shivering with the arms of death around him, while the black veil hung down, awful at that last moment, in the gathered terrors of a lifetime. And yet the faint, sad smile, so often there, now seemed to glimmer from its obscurity, and linger on Father Hooper's lips.

"Why do you tremble at me alone?" cried he, turning his veiled face round the circle of pale spectators. "Tremble also at each other! Have men avoided me, and women shown no pity, and children screamed and fled, only for my black veil? What, but the mystery which it obscurely typifies, has made this piece of crape so awful? When the friend shows his inmost heart to his friend; the lover to his best beloved; when man does not vainly shrink from the eye of his Creator, loathsomely treasuring up the secret of his sin; then deem me a monster, for the symbol beneath which I have lived, and die! I look around me, and, lo! on every visage a Black Veil!"

While his auditors shrank from one another, in mutual fright, Father Hooper fell back upon his pillow, a veiled corpse, with a faint smile lingering on the lips. Still veiled, they laid him in his coffin, and a veiled corpse they bore him to the grave. The grass of many years has sprung up and withered on that grave, the burial stone is moss-grown, and good Mr. Hooper's face is dust; but awful is still the thought that it moldered beneath the Black Veil! A

B

ADDITIONAL WRITING ASSIGNMENT
Have students write a new ending for the story in which Mr. Hooper, on his deathbed, agrees to have his veil removed.

A. Expansion
Hawthorne imagines the veil remaining unchanged above a decaying corpse. Elicit from students the idea that Hawthorne views sin as more enduring than life.

B. Responding
? If everyone were as sin-conscious as Mr. Hooper, would this be a better world? (Answers will vary. Like any other single-issue agenda, sin-consciousness may offer little help in dealing with most of life's everyday problems.)

A Comment on the Story

About a century before Hawthorne wrote this story, the fiery Jonathan Edwards reminded his congregation of their "sinful, wicked manner of attending [God's] solemn worship." Those who listened to Edwards's famous sermon, "Sinners in the Hands of an Angry God" (see page 37), heard their preacher's powerful images of God's anger: it was "great waters that are dammed for the present"; it was a bow that was already bent to pierce them with the arrow of justice; it was the fire into which a spider or loathsome insect would be cast. It did not take the citizens of Northampton, Massachusetts, long to decide that Edwards's theology was overly harsh, and he was soon dismissed from his post.

In "The Minister's Black Veil," the kindly and gentle Hooper might at first seem the very opposite of Edwards. But it is soon clear that Hooper's actions, perhaps even more effectively than Edwards's words, inspired his congregation with dread. It is Hooper's sermon, outwardly mild but profoundly disturbing, that provides the best clue to the black veil's symbolic meaning. By wearing the veil, Hooper physically declares his kinship with all human beings as secret sinners. Instead of denouncing, as Edwards did, our illusion that we can somehow hide our wickedness from God, Hawthorne's hero humbly wears a visual reminder to all of his own guilt.

Paradoxically, the minister's symbolic confession that he too is a secret sinner has the opposite effect from what he intended; his parishioners, unwilling to face an uncomfortable truth about themselves, are alienated from him. It does not occur to them that the black veil could represent a general truth about human nature; they prefer to speculate instead on Hooper's sanity and on his guilt for some mysterious past crime. Only sinners who must confront death seem to find comfort in his ministry. Instead of dismissal, Hooper lives out his life suffering a harsher fate: though grudgingly respected, he must bear isolation, mockery, and "dismal suspicions."

In the note on page 266, Hawthorne reveals that he knew of a clergyman in Maine who had worn a black veil as a symbol of his sorrow and penance for having accidentally killed a friend. At the same time, by pointedly describing his own tale as a "parable," Hawthorne emphasizes his own distance from realism and his story's significance as a moral tale. We know that very few clergymen in real life would go to the extreme of Parson Hooper. Nevertheless, Hawthorne's story, precisely attuned to the American Puritan past, remains a haunting exploration of the nature of evil and of the Puritan's need to satisfy the demands of a hidden, ungraspable God.

(*Continued from previous page.*)
asks him to cast aside the veil once for her sake.
5. Although the veil continually inspired fear, Hawthorne emphasizes that its one desirable effect was to make Hooper an even better clergyman than before.

Interpreting Meanings
6. Probably because they are still so frightened.
7. Poe implies that Hooper and Elizabeth had been guilty of some indiscretion or sin together while they were still unmarried.
Student answers will vary.
8. Elizabeth is the one person in the village who is not appalled by Hooper's veil. She dares what all the villagers had been afraid to do: she asks Hooper with a direct simplicity why he wears the veil. Up to this point, Elizabeth seems loving, caring, and full of common sense. But in the course of her interview with Hooper, Elizabeth's attitude changes. When Hooper obstinately resists her entreaties, Elizabeth becomes sorrowful, and then terrified. Hawthorne never directly explains her change of attitude, and stu-
(*Answers continue in left-hand column.*)

(*Continued from top.*)
dents may have various opinions for its cause.
9. Hooper seems to assert that all those around him are secret sinners, who deny to themselves and to God the fact of their evil. Students will have different opinions on the symbolism of the veil. Students may also suggest that the veil acquires various subsidiary symbolic meanings throughout the story.
10. Students will have various opinions, but in general it can be said that Hawthorne injects emotional language into the story to darken the atmosphere and the tone.
11. Probably that the torment of a guilty conscience, or simply the acute awareness of one's own sinfulness, is like a "prison," confining a person in his or her own melancholy.
Student answers will vary.
12. Perhaps that we are all secret sinners who fail to acknowledge our guilt.

Responding to the Story

Analyzing the Story

Identifying Facts

1. Describe the congregation's response to their first sight of Mr. Hooper's black veil.
2. Briefly describe Hooper's **character,** based on the picture of him offered in the story's opening paragraphs. What does the congregation's attitude toward him seem to have been up to this point?
3. In a single afternoon, Hooper presides at both a funeral and a wedding. Explain how the veil is responsible for a shudder and a general heightening of mood at each event.
4. Elizabeth, Hooper's fiancée, demands to know why he must wear the veil. Locate the passage that gives Hooper's explanation. What arguments against the veil does Elizabeth make?
5. Does the black veil have any positive effects throughout Hooper's long ministry? Explain.

Interpreting Meanings

6. Why do you think the villagers bury Hooper without removing the veil?
7. Poe said that Hooper wore the veil because:

> . . . a crime of dark dye (having reference to the "young lady") has been committed . . .
>
> —Edgar Allan Poe

   What do you think Poe refers to? What is your response to this explanation for the veil?
8. Describe Elizabeth's first response to the sight of her fiancé's veil, and tell how her reaction changes. How would you explain her sudden change of attitude?
9. From his deathbed, Hooper makes it clear that he is not the only wearer of the veil, but that he sees similar veils all around him. Explain what you think the minister means by this deathbed statement. What does the veil **symbolize,** in your opinion?
10. Would you describe the narrator's **tone** as neutral or emotional? Explain how the words the narrator chooses in referring to the veil affect the story's tone.
11. On page 272, the narrator remarks that the "saddest of all prisons" is a person's "own heart." What does this mean? Do you agree? Explain your response.
12. What do you think is this story's **theme,** or main idea? In your answer, consider that Hawthorne subtitled the story "A Parable" and that a **parable** is a short, usually simple story from which a moral or religious lesson can be drawn.

Writing About the Story

A Creative Response

1. **Using Another Point of View.** This story would be very different if we were to hear it told from Reverend Hooper's point of view. Write a paragraph of the story as it might be told by Reverend Hooper himself. Let Hooper explain the significance of the veil, and how he first thought of wearing it. Let him describe how he feels wearing it all the time.

A Critical Response

2. **Comparing the Story to a Sermon.** In an essay, compare Hawthorne's story to Jonathan Edwards's sermon "Sinners in the Hands of an Angry God" (page 37). Consider the attitude toward sin revealed in each selection, the attitude toward hypocrisy, and the conditions needed for salvation. If you think the two selections are radically different, then construct your essay as a series of contrasts.
3. **Comparing the Story to an Essay.** On page 192, in *Nature,* Emerson says that we are "part or parcel of God," and that in the beauties of nature we can behold something "as beautiful as our own nature." In an essay, explain how Emerson's views of human nature compare or contrast with Hawthorne's. Cite specific passages from both writers to support what you say. Do you agree with either writer?

Analyzing Language and Style

Archaic and Old-Fashioned Words

Hawthorne's story, though symbolic and ambiguous in meaning, is told in a plain, accessible style. If modern readers have trouble with Hawthorne, it is with his archaic or old-fashioned language. Context clues should help you figure out any language that is strange. Which word or words in each of the following passages from the story are rarely used today? How would you rephrase each passage in a modern idiom? Are any of these words used today in different senses?

1. "On a nearer view it seemed to consist of two folds of crape. . . ." (Page 266)
2. "A superstitious old woman was the only witness of this prodigy." (Page 268)
3. ". . . he well-nigh lost his wits from his own waggery." (Page 269)
4. ". . . having wrought so late into the evening. . . ." (Page 272)

SUPPLEMENTARY SUPPORT MATERIALS
1. Vocabulary Activity Worksheet (*CCB*)
2. Review and Response Worksheet: Ambiguity (*CCB*)
3. Selection Test (*CCB*)
4. Audiocassette recording

DEVELOPING VOCABULARY
The following words from the story are tested in the Selection Test. (See also Vocabulary Activity Worksheet.)

vicissitudes	to assuage
resplendent	equanimity
assiduous	to imbue
baneful	to quell
lurid	vivacity

PREPARATION
ESTABLISHING A PURPOSE. Have students read this story to learn if it, too, like "The Minister's Black Veil," might be called "a parable." If so, what is the parable?

A. Expansion
You might stop after the first sentence and ask students to compare it with the first sentence of "The Minister's Black Veil." The latter is much more concise, direct, and realistic; the former, more self-consciously exotic and Romantic. (The Renaissance Italian setting is doubtless influenced by Shakespeare.)

RAPPACCINI'S DAUGHTER

This story reflects Hawthorne's ideas about scientific experimentation. Science had taken a strong hold on people's imaginations in his time: Here he describes a perversion of the art. Watch for hints in the story that Hawthorne imagines Rappaccini's garden as another Eden, with an Adam, an Eve, and a serpent. Given Hawthorne's concerns, what would you predict his attitude would be toward a scientist who misuses his powers?

A A young man, named Giovanni Guasconti,[1] came, very long ago, from the more southern region of Italy, to pursue his studies at the University of Padua. Giovanni, who had but a scanty supply of gold ducats in his pocket, took lodgings in a high and gloomy chamber of an old edifice which looked not unworthy to have been the palace of a Paduan noble, and which, in fact, exhibited over its entrance the armorial bearings of a family long since extinct. The young stranger, who was not unstudied in the great poem of his country, recollected that one of the ancestors of this family, and perhaps an occupant of this very mansion, had been pictured by Dante as a partaker of the immortal agonies of his Inferno.[2] These reminiscences and associations, together with the tendency to heartbreak natural to a young man for the first time out of his native sphere, caused Giovanni to sigh heavily as he looked around the desolate and ill-furnished apartment.

"Holy Virgin, signor!" cried old Dame Lisabetta, who, won by the youth's remarkable beauty of person, was kindly endeavoring to give the chamber a habitable air, "what a sigh was that to come out of a young man's heart! Do you find this old mansion gloomy? For the love of Heaven, then, put your head out of the window, and you will see as bright sunshine as you have left in Naples."

Guasconti mechanically did as the old woman advised, but could not quite agree with her that the Paduan sunshine was as cheerful as that of southern Italy. Such as it was, however, it fell upon a garden beneath the window and expended its fostering influences on a variety of plants, which seemed to have been cultivated with exceeding care.

"Does this garden belong to the house?" asked Giovanni.

"Heaven forbid, signor, unless it were fruitful of better pot herbs than any that grow there now," answered old Lisabetta. "No, that garden is cultivated by the own hands of Signor Giacomo Rappaccini,[3] the famous doctor, who, I warrant him, has been heard of as far as Naples. It is said that he distills these plants into medicines that are as potent as a charm. Oftentimes you may see the signor doctor at work, and perchance the signora,[4] his daughter, too, gathering the strange flowers that grow in the garden."

The old woman had now done what she could for the aspect of the chamber; and, commending the young man to the protection of the saints, took her departure.

Giovanni still found no better occupation than to look down into the garden beneath his window. From its appearance, he judged it to be one of those botanic gardens which were of earlier date in Padua than elsewhere in Italy or in the world. Or, not improbably, it might once have been the pleasure place of an opulent family; for there was the ruin of a marble fountain in the center, sculptured with rare art, but so woefully shattered that it was impossible to trace the original design from the chaos of remaining fragments. The water, however, continued to gush and sparkle into the

1. **Giovanni Guasconti** (jô·vän'nē gwä·skôn'tē).
2. **Dante . . . Inferno:** the *Inferno* is the first of the three major sections of *The Divine Comedy,* the great Italian epic poem written by Dante Alighieri (1265–1321). The *Inferno* describes the souls in Hell, many of whom are real people of Dante's day.
3. **Signor Giacomo Rappaccini** (sē·nyôr' jä'kô·mô rap·a·chē'nē).
4. **signora** (sē·nyô'rä): a title of respect for a lady.

A. Responding
You might stop here to paraphrase what's been read and to answer student questions.
? What is your opinion of Giovanni so far? (There isn't much to go on yet, but he seems almost as melancholy as other "typical" Hawthorne characters.)

B. Description
Note that physical description of Rappaccini's movements leads into the crucial description of his garden.

C. Responding
? What effect does Hawthorne achieve by having Beatrice's first lines spoken "offstage"? (The result is a dramatic touch aimed at creating an air of romantic mystery.)

sunbeams as cheerfully as ever. A little gurgling sound ascended to the young man's window, and made him feel as if the fountain were an immortal spirit that sung its song unceasingly and without heeding the vicissitudes around it, while one century embodied it in marble and another scattered the perishable garniture on the soil. All about the pool into which the water subsided grew various plants, that seemed to require a plentiful supply of moisture for the nourishment of gigantic leaves, and, in some instances, flowers gorgeously magnificent. There was one shrub in particular, set in a marble vase in the midst of the pool, that bore a profusion of purple blossoms, each of which had the luster and richness of a gem; and the whole together made a show so resplendent that it seemed enough to illuminate the garden, even had there been no sunshine. Every portion of the soil was peopled with plants and herbs, which, if less beautiful, still bore tokens of assiduous care, as if all had their individual virtues, known to the scientific mind that fostered them. Some were placed in urns, rich with old carving, and others in common garden pots; some crept serpentlike along the ground or climbed on high, using whatever means of ascent was offered them. One plant had wreathed itself round a statue of Vertumnus,[5] which was thus quite veiled and shrouded in a drapery of hanging foliage, so happily arranged that it might have served a sculptor for a study.

While Giovanni stood at the window, he heard a rustling behind a screen of leaves, and became aware that a person was at work in the garden. His figure soon emerged into view, and showed itself to be that of no common laborer, but a tall, emaciated, sallow, and sickly looking man, dressed in a scholar's garb of black. He was beyond the middle term of life, with gray hair, a thin, gray beard, and a face singularly marked with intellect and cultivation, but which could never, even in his more youthful days, have expressed much warmth of heart.

Nothing could exceed the intentness with which this scientific gardener examined every shrub which grew in his path: it seemed as if he was looking into their inmost nature, making observations in regard to their creative essence, and discovering why one leaf grew in this shape and another in that, and wherefore such and such flowers differed among themselves in hue and perfume. Nevertheless, in spite of this deep intelligence on his part, there was no approach to intimacy between himself and these vegetable existences. On the contrary, he avoided their actual touch or the direct inhaling of their odors with a caution that impressed Giovanni most disagreeably; for the man's demeanor was that of one walking among malignant influences, such as savage beasts, or deadly snakes, or evil spirits, which, should he allow them one moment of license, would wreak upon him some terrible fatality. It was strangely frightful to the young man's imagination to see this air of insecurity in a person cultivating a garden, that most simple and innocent of human toils, and which had been alike the joy and labor of the unfallen parents of the race. Was this garden, then, the Eden of the present world? And this man, with such a perception of harm in what his own hands caused to grow—was he the Adam?

The distrustful gardener, while plucking away the dead leaves or pruning the too luxuriant growth of the shrubs, defended his hands with a pair of thick gloves. Nor were these his only armor. When, in his walk through the garden, he came to the magnificent plant that hung its purple gems beside the marble fountain, he placed a kind of mask over his mouth and nostrils, as if all this beauty did but conceal a deadlier malice; but, finding his task still too dangerous, he drew back, removed the mask, and called loudly, but in the infirm voice of a person affected with inward disease:

"Beatrice! Beatrice!"

"Here am I, my father. What would you?" cried a rich and youthful voice from the window of the opposite house—a voice as rich as a tropical sunset, and which made Giovanni, though he knew not why, think of deep hues of purple or crimson and of perfumes heavily delectable. "Are you in the garden?"

"Yes, Beatrice," answered the gardener, "and I need your help."

Soon there emerged from under a sculptured portal the figure of a young girl, arrayed with as much richness of taste as the most splendid of the flowers, beautiful as the day, and with a bloom so deep and vivid that one shade more would have been too much. She looked redundant with life, health, and energy; all of which attributes were bound down and compressed, as it were, and girdled tensely, in their luxuriance, by her virgin

5. **Vertumnus:** Roman god of gardens and orchards.

Isabella and the Pot of Basil
by John White Alexander (1897). Oil.

Museum of Fine Arts, Boston.
Gift of Ernest Wadsworth Longfellow.

Humanities Connection: Responding to the Fine Art
John White Alexander (1856–1915) was a leader of the Art Nouveau movement, a late nineteenth- and early twentieth-century style notable for its use of sinuous, organic curves and its sensuous elegance. *Isabella and the Pot of Basil* is based on a poem by John Keats.

? Compare this work with *Sissy,* page 251. (*Isabella* and *Sissy* share a sensual treatment of line, strong modeling, and a somewhat classical look, and both have their eyes closed.) Or compare it with Horace Pippin's "naive" painting on page 220. (Pippin's painting is harder, flatter, and brighter.) In what ways do these paintings strive for the common goal of beauty and emotional power? (Pippin is concerned with the emotional power of the event he is recording, the others with the emotional power of form and technique.)

A. Responding
? What is Hawthorne showing here? (Beatrice's affinity for the poisonous plants) What does this foreshadow? (Beatrice's poisoned nature)

B. Plot
? What is Giovanni's reaction to his glimpse of Beatrice? (He is enchanted.)

C. Expansion
The crucial secondary character, Baglioni, is introduced. Have students paraphrase the long conversation between Giovanni and Baglioni.

zone. Yet Giovanni's fancy must have grown morbid while he looked down into the garden; for the impression which the fair stranger made upon him was as if here were another flower, the human sister of those vegetable ones, as beautiful as they, more beautiful than the richest of them, but still to be touched only with a glove, nor to be approached without a mask. As Beatrice came down the garden path, it was observable that she handled and inhaled the odor of several of the plants which her father had most sedulously avoided.

"Here, Beatrice," said the latter, "see how many needful offices require to be done to our chief treasure. Yet, shattered as I am, my life might pay the penalty of approaching it so closely as circumstances demand. Henceforth, I fear, this plant must be consigned to your sole charge."

A "And gladly will I undertake it," cried again the rich tones of the young lady, as she bent toward the magnificent plant and opened her arms as if to embrace it. "Yes, my sister, my splendor, it shall be Beatrice's task to nurse and serve thee; and thou shalt reward her with thy kisses and perfumed breath, which to her is as the breath of life."

Then, with all the tenderness in her manner that was so strikingly expressed in her words, she busied herself with such attentions as the plant seemed to require; and Giovanni, at his lofty window, rubbed his eyes and almost doubted whether it were a girl tending her favorite flower, or one sister performing the duties of affection to another. The scene soon terminated. Whether Dr. Rappaccini had finished his labors in the garden, or that his watchful eye had caught the stranger's face, he now took his daughter's arm and retired. B Night was already closing in; oppressive exhalations seemed to proceed from the plants and steal upward past the open window; and Giovanni, closing the lattice, went to his couch and dreamed of a rich flower and beautiful girl. Flower and maiden were different, and yet the same, and fraught with some strange peril in either shape.

But there is an influence in the light of morning that tends to rectify whatever errors of fancy, or even of judgment, we may have incurred during the sun's decline, or among the shadows of the night, or in the less wholesome glow of moonshine. Giovanni's first movement, on starting from sleep, was to throw open the window and gaze down into the garden which his dreams had made so fertile of mysteries. He was surprised and a little ashamed to find how real and matter-of-fact an affair it proved to be, in the first rays of the sun which gilded the dewdrops that hung upon leaf and blossom, and, while giving a brighter beauty to each rare flower, brought everything within the limits of ordinary experience. The young man rejoiced that, in the heart of the barren city, he had the privilege of overlooking this spot of lovely and luxuriant vegetation. It would serve, he said to himself, as a symbolic language to keep him in communion with Nature. Neither the sickly and thought-worn Dr. Giacomo Rappaccini, it is true, nor his brilliant daughter was now visible; so that Giovanni could not determine how much of the singularity which he attributed to both was due to their own qualities and how much to his wonder-working fancy; but he was inclined to take a most rational view of the whole matter.

In the course of the day, he paid his respects to Signor Pietro Baglioni, professor of medicine in the university, a physician of eminent repute, to whom Giovanni had brought a letter of introduction. The professor was an elderly personage, apparently of genial nature, and habits that might almost be called jovial. He kept the young man to dinner, and made himself very agreeable by the freedom and liveliness of his conversation, especially when warmed by a flask or two of Tuscan wine. Giovanni, conceiving that men of science, inhabitants of the same city, must needs be on familiar terms with one another, took an opportunity to mention the name of Dr. Rappaccini. But the professor did not respond with so much cordiality as he had anticipated.

"Ill would it become a teacher of the divine art of medicine," said Professor Pietro Baglioni, in answer to a question of Giovanni, "to withhold due and well-considered praise of a physician so eminently skilled as Rappaccini; but, on the other hand, I should answer it but scantily to my conscience were I to permit a worthy youth like yourself, Signor Giovanni, the son of an ancient friend, to imbibe erroneous ideas respecting a man who might hereafter chance to hold your life and death in his hands. The truth is, our worshipful Dr. Rappaccini has as much science as any member of the faculty—with perhaps one single exception—in Padua, or all Italy; but there are certain grave objections to his professional character." C

"And what are they?" asked the young man.

"Has my friend Giovanni any disease of body or heart, that he is so inquisitive about physicians?" said the professor, with a smile. "But as for Rappaccini, it is said of him—and I, who know the man well, can answer for its truth—that he cares infinitely more for science than for mankind. His patients are interesting to him only as subjects for some new experiment. He would sacrifice human life, his own among the rest, or whatever else was dearest to him, for the sake of adding so much as a grain of mustard seed to the great heap of his accumulated knowledge."

"Methinks he is an awful man indeed," remarked Guasconti, mentally recalling the cold and purely intellectual aspect of Rappaccini. "And yet, worshipful professor, is it not a noble spirit? Are there many men capable of so spiritual a love of science?"

"God forbid," answered the professor, somewhat testily, "at least, unless they take sounder views of the healing art than those adopted by Rappaccini. It is his theory that all medicinal virtues are comprised within those substances which we term vegetable poisons. These he cultivates with his own hands, and is said even to have produced new varieties of poison, more horribly deleterious than Nature, without the assistance of this learned person, would ever have plagued the world withal. That the signor doctor does less mischief than might be expected with such dangerous substances is undeniable. Now and then, it must be owned, he has effected, or seemed to effect, a marvelous cure; but, to tell you my private mind, Signor Giovanni, he should receive little credit for such instances of success—they being probably the work of chance—but should be held strictly accountable for his failures, which may justly be considered his own work."

The youth might have taken Baglioni's opinions with many grains of allowance had he known that there was a professional warfare of long continuance between him and Dr. Rappaccini, in which the latter was generally thought to have gained the advantage. If the reader be inclined to judge for himself, we refer him to certain black-letter tracts on both sides, preserved in the medical department of the University of Padua.

"I know not, most learned professor," returned Giovanni, after musing on what had been said of Rappaccini's exclusive zeal for science, "I know not how dearly this physician may love his art, but surely there is one object more dear to him. He has a daughter."

"Aha!" cried the professor, with a laugh. "So now our friend Giovanni's secret is out. You have heard of this daughter, whom all the young men in Padua are wild about, though not half a dozen have ever had the good hap to see her face. I know little of Signora Beatrice save that Rappaccini is said to have instructed her deeply in his science, and that, young and beautiful as fame reports her, she is already qualified to fill a professor's chair. Perchance her father destines her for mine! Other absurd rumors there be, not worth talking about or listening to. So now, Signor Giovanni, drink off your glass of Lachryma."

Guasconti returned to his lodgings somewhat heated with the wine he had quaffed, and which caused his brain to swim with strange fantasies in reference to Dr. Rappaccini and the beautiful Beatrice. On his way, happening to pass by a florist's, he bought a fresh bouquet of flowers. A

Ascending to his chamber, he seated himself near the window, but within the shadow thrown by the depth of the wall, so that he could look down into the garden with little risk of being discovered. All beneath his eye was a solitude. The strange plants were basking in the sunshine, and now and then nodding gently to one another, as if in acknowledgment of sympathy and kindred. In the midst, by the shattered fountain, grew the magnificent shrub, with its purple gems clustering all over it; they glowed in the air, and gleamed back again out of the depths of the pool, which thus seemed to overflow with colored radiance from the rich reflection that was steeped in it. At first, as we have said, the garden was a solitude. Soon, however—as Giovanni had half hoped, half feared would be the case—a figure appeared beneath the antique sculptured portal, and came down between the rows of plants, inhaling their various perfumes as if she were one of those beings of old classic fable that lived upon sweet odors. On again beholding Beatrice, the young man was even startled to perceive how much her beauty exceeded his recollection of it; so brilliant, so vivid, was its character, that she glowed amid the sunlight, and, as Giovanni whispered to himself, positively illuminated the more shadowy intervals of the garden path. Her face being now more revealed than on the former occasion, he was struck by its expression of simplicity and sweetness—qualities that had not entered into his idea of her character, and which made him ask anew what manner of mortal she might be. Nor did he fail again to observe, or imagine, an analogy B

A. Plot
The bouquet is an important plot device, subtly introduced.

B. Characterization
This scene repeats that on the top of page 278, but at a higher emotional pitch.

? How do you respond to Giovanni's feelings about Beatrice? (Answers will vary. Some students may admit to having experienced similar feelings; others may think Giovanni is hallucinating.)

A. Responding

? What does the lizard's death reveal about the plants? (That they are unnatural)

B. Expansion

You might want to return to this question at the end of the story, and have students answer it.

C. Plot

? What effect does the withering of the bouquet have on Giovanni? On the story? (It alarms Giovanni, though he tries to view it casually. It deepens the story's mood of supernatural suspense.)

between the beautiful girl and the gorgeous shrub that hung its gemlike flowers over the fountain—a resemblance which Beatrice seemed to have indulged a fantastic humor in heightening, both by the arrangement of her dress and the selection of its hues.

Approaching the shrub, she threw open her arms, as with a passionate ardor, and drew its branches into an intimate embrace—so intimate that her features were hidden in its leafy bosom and her glistening ringlets all intermingled with the flowers.

"Give me thy breath, my sister," exclaimed Beatrice, "for I am faint with common air. And give me this flower of thine, which I separate with gentlest fingers from the stem and place it close beside my heart."

With these words, the beautiful daughter of Rappaccini plucked one of the richest blossoms of the shrub, and was about to fasten it in her bosom. But now, unless Giovanni's draughts of wine had bewildered his senses, a singular incident occurred. A small orange-colored reptile, of the lizard or chameleon species, chanced to be creeping along the path, just at the feet of Beatrice. It appeared to Giovanni—but, at the distance from which he gazed, he could scarcely have seen anything so minute—it appeared to him, however, that a drop or two of moisture from the broken stem of the flower descended upon the lizard's head. For an instant the reptile contorted itself violently, and then lay motionless in the sunshine. Beatrice observed this remarkable phenomenon, and crossed herself, sadly, but without surprise; nor did she therefore hesitate to arrange the fatal flower in her bosom. There it blushed, and almost glimmered with the dazzling effect of a precious stone, adding to her dress and aspect the one appropriate charm which nothing else in the world could have supplied. But Giovanni, out of the shadow of his window, bent forward and shrank back, and murmured and trembled.

A

"Am I awake? Have I my senses?" said he to himself. "What is this being? Beautiful shall I call her, or inexpressibly terrible?"

B

Beatrice now strayed carelessly through the garden, approaching closer beneath Giovanni's window, so that he was compelled to thrust his head quite out of its concealment in order to gratify the intense and painful curiosity which she excited. At this moment, there came a beautiful insect over the garden wall; it had, perhaps, wandered through the city, and found no flowers or verdure among those antique haunts of men until the heavy perfumes of Dr. Rappaccini's shrubs had lured it from afar. Without alighting on the flowers, this winged brightness seemed to be attracted by Beatrice, and lingered in the air and fluttered about her head. Now, here it could not be but that Giovanni Guasconti's eyes deceived him. Be that as it might, he fancied that, while Beatrice was gazing at the insect with childish delight, it grew faint and fell at her feet; its bright wings shivered; it was dead—from no cause that he could discern, unless it were the atmosphere of her breath. Again Beatrice crossed herself and sighed heavily as she bent over the dead insect.

An impulsive movement of Giovanni drew her eyes to the window. There she beheld the beautiful head of the young man—rather a Grecian than an Italian head, with fair, regular features, and a glistening of gold among his ringlets—gazing down upon her like a being that hovered in midair. Scarcely knowing what he did, Giovanni threw down the bouquet which he had hitherto held in his hand.

"Signora," said he, "these are pure and healthful flowers. Wear them for the sake of Giovanni Guasconti."

"Thanks, signor," replied Beatrice, with her rich voice, that came forth as it were like a gush of music, and with a mirthful expression half childish and half womanlike. "I accept your gift, and would fain recompense it with this precious purple flower; but if I toss it into the air, it will not reach you. So Signor Guasconti must even content himself with my thanks."

She lifted the bouquet from the ground, and then, as if inwardly ashamed at having stepped aside from her maidenly reserve to respond to a stranger's greeting, passed swiftly homeward through the garden. But few as the moments were, it seemed to Giovanni, when she was on the point of vanishing beneath the sculptured portal, that his beautiful bouquet was already beginning to wither in her grasp. It was an idle thought; there could be no possibility of distinguishing a faded flower from a fresh one at so great a distance. C

For many days after this incident, the young man avoided the window that looked into Dr. Rappaccini's garden, as if something ugly and monstrous would have blasted his eyesight had he

A been betrayed into a glance. He felt conscious of having put himself, to a certain extent, within the influence of an unintelligible power by the communication which he had opened with Beatrice. The wisest course would have been, if his heart were in any real danger, to quit his lodgings and Padua itself at once; the next wiser, to have accustomed himself, as far as possible, to the familiar and daylight view of Beatrice—thus bringing her rigidly and systematically within the limits of ordinary experience. Least of all, while avoiding her sight, ought Giovanni to have remained so near this extraordinary being that the proximity and possibility even of intercourse should give a kind of substance and reality to the wild vagaries which his imagination ran riot continually in producing. Guasconti had not a deep heart—or, at all events, its depths were not sounded now; but he had a quick fancy, and an ardent southern temperament, which rose every instant to a higher fever pitch. Whether or no Beatrice possessed those terrible attributes, that fatal breath, the affinity with those so beautiful and deadly flowers which were indicated by what Giovanni had witnessed, she had at least instilled a fierce and subtle poison into his system. It was not love, although her rich beauty was a madness to him; nor horror, even while he fancied her spirit to be imbued with the same baneful essence that seemed to pervade her physical frame; but a wild offspring of both love and horror that had each parent in it, and burned like one and shivered like the other. Giovanni knew not what to dread; still less did he know what to hope; yet hope and dread kept a continual warfare in his breast, alternately vanquishing one another and starting up afresh to renew the contest. Blessed are all simple emotions, be they dark or bright! It is the lurid intermixture of the two that produces the illuminating blaze of the infernal regions.

Sometimes he endeavored to assuage the fever of his spirit by a rapid walk through the streets of Padua or beyond its gates: his footsteps kept time with the throbbings of his brain, so that the walk was apt to accelerate itself to a race. One day he found himself arrested; his arm was seized by a portly personage, who had turned back on recognizing the young man and expended much breath in overtaking him.

"Signor Giovanni! Stay, my young friend!" cried he. "Have you forgotten me? That might well be the case if I were as much altered as yourself."

It was Baglioni, whom Giovanni had avoided ever since their first meeting, from a doubt that the professor's sagacity would look too deeply into his secrets. Endeavoring to recover himself, he stared forth wildly from his inner world into the outer one and spoke like a man in a dream.

"Yes, I am Giovanni Guasconti. You are Professor Pietro Baglioni. Now let me pass!"

"Not yet, not yet, Signor Giovanni Guasconti," said the professor, smiling, but at the same time scrutinizing the youth with an earnest glance. "What! did I grow up side by side with your father, and shall his son pass me like a stranger in these old streets of Padua? Stand still, Signor Giovanni; for we must have a word or two before we part."

"Speedily, then, most worshipful professor, speedily," said Giovanni, with feverish impatience. "Does not your worship see that I am in haste?"

Now, while he was speaking, there came a man in black along the street, stooping and moving feebly like a person in inferior health. His face was all overspread with a most sickly and sallow hue, but yet so pervaded with an expression of piercing and active intellect that an observer might easily have overlooked the merely physical attributes and have seen only this wonderful energy. As he passed, this person exchanged a cold and distant salutation with Baglioni, but fixed his eyes upon Giovanni with an intentness that seemed to bring out whatever was within him worthy of notice. Nevertheless, there was a peculiar quietness in the look, as if taking merely a speculative, not a human, interest in the young man.

"It is Dr. Rappaccini!" whispered the professor when the stranger had passed. "Has he ever seen your face before?"

"Not that I know," answered Giovanni, starting at the name.

"He *has* seen you! he must have seen you!" said Baglioni, hastily. "For some purpose or other, this man of science is making a study of you. I know that look of his! It is the same that coldly illuminates his face as he bends over a bird, a mouse, or a butterfly, which, in pursuance of some experiment, he has killed by the perfume of a flower; a look as deep as Nature itself, but without Nature's warmth of love. Signor Giovanni, I B

A. Connections

? Are there similarities between Hawthorne's treatment of Giovanni's feelings and Poe's treatment of similar subjects? (Yes, in the mixture of love and horror) Are there differences? (Hawthorne's is probably more psychological.)

Giovanni grows increasingly frenzied—elicit the perception that this, too, is reminiscent of Poe.

B. Plot

? What does Baglioni reveal about Giovanni's function in the plot? (He reveals that Giovanni may not be an innocent bystander, but the subject of an experiment.)

A. Expansion A helpful servant provides useful information—a stock device of classic drama and storytelling.

B. Expansion (Less Challenging) At this point, for recap, you might ask your less advanced students: "What danger is Giovanni in? How much does he realize of it? What would you do now if you were Giovanni?"

will stake my life upon it, you are the subject of one of Rappaccini's experiments!"

"Will you make a fool of me?" cried Giovanni, passionately. "*That,* signor professor, was an untoward experiment."

"Patience! patience!" replied the imperturbable professor. "I tell thee, my poor Giovanni, that Rappaccini has a scientific interest in thee. Thou hast fallen into fearful hands! And the Signora Beatrice—what part does she act in this mystery?"

But Guasconti, finding Baglioni's pertinacity intolerable, here broke away, and was gone before the professor could again seize his arm. He looked after the young man intently and shook his head.

"This must not be," said Baglioni to himself. "The youth is the son of my old friend, and shall not come to any harm from which the arcana[6] of medical science can preserve him. Besides, it is too insufferable an impertinence in Rappaccini, thus to snatch the lad out of my own hands, as I may say, and make use of him for his infernal experiments. This daughter of his! It shall be looked to. Perchance, most learned Rappaccini, I may foil you where you little dream of it!"

Meanwhile Giovanni had pursued a circuitous route, and at length found himself at the door of his lodgings. As he crossed the threshold, he was met by old Lisabetta, who smirked and smiled, and was evidently desirous to attract his attention; vainly, however, as the ebullition of his feelings had momentarily subsided into a cold and dull vacuity. He turned his eyes full upon the withered face that was puckering itself into a smile, but seemed to behold it not. The old dame, therefore, laid her grasp upon his cloak.

A "Signor! signor!" whispered she, still with a smile over the whole breadth of her visage, so that it looked not unlike a grotesque carving in wood, darkened by centuries. "Listen, signor! There is a private entrance into the garden!"

"What do you say?" exclaimed Giovanni, turning quickly about, as if an inanimate thing should start into feverish life. "A private entrance into Dr. Rappaccini's garden?"

"Hush! hush! not so loud!" whispered Lisabetta, putting her hand over his mouth. "Yes, into the worshipful doctor's garden, where you may see all his fine shrubbery. Many a young man in Padua would give gold to be admitted among those flowers."

Giovanni put a piece of gold into her hand.

"Show me the way," said he.

A surmise, probably excited by his conversation with Baglioni, crossed his mind that this interposition of old Lisabetta might perchance be connected with the intrigue, whatever was its nature, in which the professor seemed to suppose that Dr. Rappaccini was involving him. But such a suspicion, though it disturbed Giovanni, was inadequate to restrain him. The instant that he was aware of the possibility of approaching Beatrice, it seemed an absolute necessity of his existence to do so. It mattered not whether she was angel or demon; he was irrevocably within her sphere, and must obey the law that whirled him onward, in ever lessening circles, toward a result which he did not attempt to foreshadow; and yet, strange to say, there came across him a sudden doubt whether this intense interest on his part was not delusory; whether it was really of so deep and positive a nature as to justify him in now thrusting himself into an incalculable position; whether it was not merely the fantasy of a young man's brain, only slightly or not at all connected with his heart.

He paused, hesitated, turned half about, but again went on. His withered guide led him along several obscure passages, and finally undid a door, through which, as it was opened, there came the sight and sound of rustling leaves, with the broken sunshine glimmering among them. Giovanni stepped forth, and, forcing himself through the entanglement of a shrub that wreathed its tendrils over the hidden entrance, stood beneath his own window in the open area of Dr. Rappaccini's garden. B

How often is it the case that, when impossibilities have come to pass and dreams have condensed their misty substance into tangible realities, we find ourselves calm, and even coldly self-possessed, amid circumstances which it would have been a delirium of joy or agony to anticipate! Fate delights to thwart us thus. Passion will choose his own time to rush upon the scene, and lingers sluggishly behind when an appropriate adjustment of events would seem to summon his appearance. So was it now with Giovanni. Day after day, his pulses had throbbed with feverish blood at the improbable idea of an interview with

6. **arcana** (är·kā′nə): secret or hidden knowledge.

Beatrice, and of standing with her, face to face, in this very garden, basking in the Oriental sunshine of her beauty, and snatching from her full gaze the mystery which he deemed the riddle of his own existence. But now there was a singular and untimely equanimity within his breast. He threw a glance around the garden to discover if Beatrice or her father was present, and, perceiving that he was alone, began a critical observation of the plants.

The aspect of one and all of them dissatisfied him; their gorgeousness seemed fierce, passionate, and even unnatural. There was hardly an individual shrub which a wanderer, straying by himself through a forest, would not have been startled to find growing wild, as if an unearthly face had glared at him out of the thicket. Several also would have shocked a delicate instinct by an appearance of artificialness indicating that there had been such commixture and, as it were, adultery of various vegetable species that the production was no longer of God's making, but the monstrous offspring of man's depraved fancy, glowing with only an evil mockery of beauty. They were probably the result of experiment, which in one or two cases had succeeded in mingling plants individually lovely into a compound possessing the questionable and ominous character that distinguished the whole growth of the garden. In fine, Giovanni recognized but two or three plants in the collection, and those of a kind that he well knew to be poisonous. While busy with these contemplations, he heard the rustling of a silken garment, and, turning, beheld Beatrice emerging from beneath the sculptured portal.

Giovanni had not considered with himself what should be his deportment; whether he should apologize for his intrusion into the garden, or assume that he was there with the privity,[7] at least, if not by the desire, of Dr. Rappaccini or his daughter; but Beatrice's manner placed him at his ease, though leaving him still in doubt by what agency
A he had gained admittance. She came lightly along the path and met him near the broken fountain. There was surprise in her face, but brightened by a simple and kind expression of pleasure.

"You are a connoisseur in flowers, signor," said Beatrice, with a smile, alluding to the bouquet which he had flung her from the window. "It is no marvel, therefore, if the sight of my father's rare collection has tempted you to take a nearer view. If he were here, he could tell you many strange and interesting facts as to the nature and habits of these shrubs; for he has spent a lifetime in such studies, and this garden is his world."

"And yourself, lady," observed Giovanni, "if fame says true, you likewise are deeply skilled in the virtues indicated by these rich blossoms and these spicy perfumes. Would you deign to be my instructress, I should prove an apter scholar than if taught by Signor Rappaccini himself."

"Are there such idle rumors?" asked Beatrice, with the music of a pleasant laugh. "Do people say that I am skilled in my father's science of plants? What a jest is there! No, though I have grown up among these flowers, I know no more of them than their hues and perfume; and sometimes methinks I would fain rid myself of even that small knowledge. There are many flowers here, and those not the least brilliant, that shock and offend me when they meet my eye. But pray, signor, do not believe these stories about my science. Believe nothing of me save what you see with your own eyes."

"And must I believe all that I have seen with my own eyes?" asked Giovanni, pointedly, while the recollection of former scenes made him shrink. "No, signora; you demand too little of me. Bid me believe nothing save what comes from your own lips."

It would appear that Beatrice understood him. There came a deep flush to her cheek; but she looked full into Giovanni's eyes, and responded to his gaze of uneasy suspicion with a queenlike haughtiness.

"I do so bid you, signor," she replied. "Forget whatever you may have fancied in regard to me. If true to the outward senses, still it may be false in its essence; but the words of Beatrice Rappaccini's lips are true from the depths of the heart outward. Those you may believe."

A fervor glowed in her whole aspect and beamed upon Giovanni's consciousness like the light of truth itself; but while she spoke, there was a fragrance in the atmosphere around her, rich and delightful, though evanescent, yet which the young man, from an indefinable reluctance, scarcely dared to draw into his lungs. It might be the odor of the flowers. Could it be Beatrice's breath which thus embalmed her words with a

B

7. **privity:** private knowledge.

A. Responding
The first face-to-face meeting between Giovanni and Beatrice in the garden is a crucial dramatic scene. Hawthorne builds up to it with some rather thick expository and descriptive paragraphs.
? Why does Hawthorne build up to the Giovanni/Beatrice meeting with so much exposition and description? (For pacing and suspense) What do you think will result from the conversation? (From her happy expression when finding a stranger in her garden, we may expect that they will fall in love.)

B. Expansion
See A Critical Response, page 292, question 5, for an exploration of the Biblical parallels that are especially prominent in this scene. There are also parallels here with *Romeo and Juliet.* (Hawthorne may be deliberately debunking classic love stories.)

Humanities Connection: Responding to the Fine Art
Martin Johnson Heade (1819–1904) was born in Lumberville, Pennsylvania, but spent much of his life traveling, especially to South America. He was known for his lush portrayals of landscapes, flowers, and birds.

? The orchid in this painting is not intended to be poisonous. Why do you suppose, then, that this painting was chosen to illustrate the story? Is there something inherently dangerous-looking about overlush beauty? (In addition to its exotic appearance, the orchid is in a wild, jungle setting.)

Orchids, Passion Flowers, and Hummingbird by Martin Johnson Heade (1865). Oil.

strange richness, as if by steeping them in her heart? A faintness passed like a shadow over Giovanni and flitted away; he seemed to gaze through the beautiful girl's eyes into her transparent soul, and felt no more doubt or fear.

A The tinge of passion that had colored Beatrice's manner vanished; she became gay, and appeared to derive a pure delight from her communion with the youth not unlike what the maiden of a lonely island might have felt conversing with a voyager from the civilized world. Evidently her experience of life had been confined within the limits of that garden. She talked now about matters as simple as the daylight or summer clouds, and now asked questions in reference to the city, or Giovanni's distant home, his friends, his mother, and his sisters—questions indicating such seclusion, and such lack of familiarity with modes and forms, that Giovanni responded as if to an infant. Her spirit gushed out before him like a fresh rill that was just catching its first glimpse of the sunlight and wondering at the reflections of earth and sky which were flung into its bosom. There came thoughts, too, from a deep source, and fantasies of a gemlike brilliancy, as if diamonds and rubies sparkled upward among the bubbles of the fountain. Ever and anon there gleamed across the young man's mind a sense of wonder that he should be walking side by side with the being who had so wrought upon his imagination, whom he had idealized in such hues of terror, in whom he had positively witnessed such manifestations of dreadful attributes—that he should be conversing with Beatrice like a brother, and should find her so human and so maidenlike. But such reflections were only momentary; the effect of her character was too real not to make itself familiar at once.

In this free intercourse, they had strayed through the garden, and now, after many turns among its avenues, were come to the shattered fountain, beside which grew the magnificent shrub, with its treasury of glowing blossoms. A fragrance was diffused from it which Giovanni recognized as identical with that which he had attributed to Beatrice's breath, but incomparably more powerful. As her eyes fell upon it, Giovanni beheld her press her hand to her bosom as if her heart were throbbing suddenly and painfully.

B "For the first time in my life," murmured she, addressing the shrub, "I had forgotten thee."

"I remember, signora," said Giovanni, "that you once promised to reward me with one of these living gems for the bouquet which I had the happy boldness to fling to your feet. Permit me now to pluck it as a memorial of this interview."

He made a step toward the shrub with extended hand; but Beatrice darted forward, uttering a shriek that went through his heart like a dagger. She caught his hand and drew it back with the whole force of her slender figure. Giovanni felt her touch thrilling through his fibers.

"Touch it not!" exclaimed she, in a voice of agony. "Not for thy life! It is fatal!"

Then, hiding her face, she fled from him and vanished beneath the sculptured portal. As Giovanni followed her with his eyes, he beheld the emaciated figure and pale intelligence of Dr. Rappaccini, who had been watching the scene, he knew not how long, within the shadow of the entrance. C

No sooner was Guasconti alone in his chamber than the image of Beatrice came back to his passionate musings, invested with all the witchery that had been gathering around it ever since his first glimpse of her, and now likewise imbued with a tender warmth of girlish womanhood. She was human; her nature was endowed with all gentle and feminine qualities; she was worthiest to be worshiped; she was capable, surely, on her part, of the height and heroism of love. Those tokens which he had hitherto considered as proofs of a frightful peculiarity in her physical and moral system were now either forgotten, or, by the subtle sophistry[8] of passion, transmitted into a golden crown of enchantment, rendering Beatrice the more admirable by so much as she was the more unique. Whatever had looked ugly was now beautiful; or, if incapable of such a change, it stole away and hid itself among those shapeless half ideas which throng the dim region beyond the daylight of our perfect consciousness. Thus did he spend the night, nor fell asleep until the dawn had begun to awake the slumbering flowers in Dr. Rappaccini's garden, whither Giovanni's dreams doubtless led him. Up rose the sun in his due season, and, flinging his beams upon the young man's eyelids, awoke him to a sense of pain. When thoroughly aroused, he became sensible of a burning and tingling agony in his hand—in his right hand—the very hand which Beatrice had grasped in her own when he was on the point of plucking one of the gemlike flowers. On the back D

8. **sophistry** (säf'is·trē): clever but unsound arguments.

A. Characterization
Hawthorne is bringing out Beatrice's innocent side. How convincing is this passage as a description of a real young woman? Note that her actual words are not recorded. (The mixture of simple and deep thoughts seems contradictory, as does her expressiveness after years of confinement. It is more convincing as Giovanni's reaction to her.)

B. Responding
How does this sentence, addressed to a plant, make you feel? (Answers will vary. Some students will feel Beatrice has been too isolated.)

C. Plot
Why does Hawthorne show us that Rappaccini is watching? (Perhaps to confirm that Giovanni is the subject of an experiment)

D. Plot
What does the burning in Giovanni's hand mean? (Beatrice's touch may be poisonous.)

A. Responding
? Do you agree with Hawthorne's remark on love? (Most will probably agree that once we decide we are in love it is difficult to discourage us.)

B. Expansion
With the phrase "that Eden of poisonous flowers," Hawthorne makes the Biblical parallel explicit.

C. Connections
? Where else have we seen a story-within-a-story? (*Mad Trist,* in "The Fall of the House of Usher," page 234) It's entirely possible that Hawthorne learned some techniques of supernatural horror from Poe.

of that hand there was now a purple print like that of four small fingers, and the likeness of a slender thumb upon his wrist.

A Oh, how stubbornly does love—or even that cunning semblance of love which flourishes in the imagination, but strikes no depth of root into the heart—how stubbornly does it hold its faith until the moment comes when it is doomed to vanish into thin mist! Giovanni wrapped a handkerchief about his hand and wondered what evil thing had stung him, and soon forgot his pain in a reverie of Beatrice.

After the first interview, a second was in the inevitable course of what we call fate. A third; a fourth; and a meeting with Beatrice in the garden was no longer an incident in Giovanni's daily life, but the whole space in which he might be said to live; for the anticipation and memory of that ecstatic hour made up the remainder. Nor was it otherwise with the daughter of Rappaccini. She watched for the youth's appearance, and flew to his side with confidence as unreserved as if they had been playmates from early infancy—as if they were such playmates still. If, by any unwonted chance, he failed to come at the appointed moment, she stood beneath the window and sent up the rich sweetness of her tones to float around him in his chamber and echo and reverberate throughout his heart: "Giovanni! Giovanni! Why tarriest B thou? Come down!" And down he hastened into that Eden of poisonous flowers.

But, with all this intimate familiarity, there was still a reserve in Beatrice's demeanor, so rigidly and invariably sustained that the idea of infringing it scarcely occurred to his imagination. By all appreciable signs, they loved; they had looked love with eyes that conveyed the holy secret from the depths of one soul into the depths of the other, as if it were too sacred to be whispered by the way; they had even spoken love in those gushes of passion when their spirits darted forth in articulated breath like tongues of long-hidden flame; and yet there had been no seal of lips, no clasp of hands, nor any slightest caress such as love claims and hallows. He had never touched one of the gleaming ringlets of her hair; her garment—so marked was the physical barrier between them—had never been waved against him by a breeze. On the few occasions when Giovanni had seemed tempted to overstep the limit, Beatrice grew so sad, so stern, and withal wore such a look of desolate separation, shuddering at itself, that not a spoken word was requisite to repel him. At such times, he was startled at the horrible suspicions that rose, monsterlike, out of the caverns of his heart and stared him in the face; his love grew thin and faint as the morning mist; his doubts alone had substance. But, when Beatrice's face brightened again after the momentary shadow, she was transformed at once from the mysterious, questionable being whom he had watched with so much awe and horror; she was now the beautiful and unsophisticated girl whom he felt that his spirit knew with a certainty beyond all other knowledge.

A considerable time had now passed since Giovanni's last meeting with Baglioni. One morning, however, he was disagreeably surprised by a visit from the professor, whom he had scarcely thought of for whole weeks, and would willingly have forgotten still longer. Given up as he had long been to a pervading excitement, he could tolerate no companions except upon condition of their perfect sympathy with his present state of feeling. Such sympathy was not to be expected from Professor Baglioni,

The visitor chatted carelessly for a few moments about the gossip of the city and the university, and then took up another topic.

"I have been reading an old classic author lately," said he, "and met with a story that strangely interested me. Possibly you may remember it. It is of an Indian prince, who sent a beautiful woman as a present to Alexander the Great. She was as lovely as the dawn and gorgeous as the sunset, but what especially distinguished her was a certain rich perfume in her breath—richer than a garden of Persian roses. Alexander, as was natural to a youthful conqueror, fell in love at first sight with this magnificent stranger; but a certain sage physician, happening to be present, discovered a terrible secret in regard to her." C

"And what was that?" asked Giovanni, turning his eyes downward to avoid those of the professor.

"That this lovely woman," continued Baglioni, with emphasis, "had been nourished with poisons from her birth upward, until her whole nature was so imbued with them that she herself had become the deadliest poison in existence. Poison was her element of life. With that rich perfume of her breath she blasted the very air. Her love would have been poison—her embrace death. Is not this a marvelous tale?"

"A childish fable," answered Giovanni, nervously starting from his chair. "I marvel how your worship finds time to read such nonsense among your graver studies."

"By the by," said the professor, looking uneasily about him, "what singular fragrance is this in your apartment? Is it the perfume of your gloves? It is faint, but delicious; and yet, after all, by no means agreeable. Were I to breathe it long, methinks it would make me ill. It is like the breath of a flower, but I see no flowers in the chamber."

"Nor are there any," replied Giovanni, who had turned pale as the professor spoke, "nor, I think, is there any fragrance except in your worship's imagination. Odors, being a sort of element combined of the sensual and the spiritual, are apt to deceive us in this manner. The recollection of a perfume, the bare idea of it, may easily be mistaken for a present reality."

"Ay, but my sober imagination does not often play such tricks," said Baglioni, "and, were I to fancy any kind of odor, it would be that of some vile apothecary drug wherewith my fingers are likely enough to be imbued. Our worshipful friend Rappaccini, as I have heard, tinctures his medicaments with odors richer than those of Araby. Doubtless, likewise, the fair and learned Signora Beatrice would minister to her patients with draughts as sweet as a maiden's breath; but woe to him that sips them."

Giovanni's face evinced many contending emotions. The tone in which the professor alluded to the pure and lovely daughter of Rappaccini was a torture to his soul; and yet the intimation of a view of her character opposite to his own gave instantaneous distinctness to a thousand dim suspicions, which now grinned at him like so many demons. But he strove hard to quell them and to respond to Baglioni with a true lover's perfect faith.

"Signor professor," said he, "you were my father's friend; perchance, too, it is your purpose to act a friendly part toward his son. I would fain feel nothing toward you save respect and deference; but I pray you to observe, signor, that there is one subject on which we must not speak. You know not the Signora Beatrice. You cannot, therefore, estimate the wrong—the blasphemy, I may even say—that is offered to her character by a light or injurious word."

"Giovanni! my poor Giovanni!" answered the professor, with a calm expression of pity, "I know this wretched girl far better than yourself. You shall hear the truth in respect to the poisoner Rappaccini and his poisonous daughter; yes, poisonous as she is beautiful. Listen; for, even should you do violence to my gray hairs, it shall not silence me. That old fable of the Indian woman has become a truth by the deep and deadly science of Rappaccini and in the person of the lovely Beatrice."

Giovanni groaned and hid his face.

"Her father," continued Baglioni, "was not restrained by natural affection from offering up his child in this horrible manner as the victim of his insane zeal for science; for, let us do him justice, he is as true a man of science as ever distilled his own heart in an alembic.[9] What, then, will be your fate? Beyond a doubt you are selected as the material of some new experiment. Perhaps the result is to be death; perhaps a fate more awful still. Rappaccini, with what he calls the interest of science before his eyes, will hesitate at nothing."

"It is a dream," muttered Giovanni to himself. "Surely it is a dream."

"But," resumed the professor, "be of good cheer, son of my friend. It is not yet too late for the rescue. Possibly we may even succeed in bringing back this miserable child within the limits of ordinary nature, from which her father's madness has estranged her. Behold this little silver vase! It was wrought by the hands of the renowned Benvenuto Cellini,[10] and is well worthy to be a love gift to the fairest dame in Italy. But its contents are invaluable. One little sip of this antidote would have rendered the most virulent poisons of the Borgias[11] innocuous. Doubt not that it will be as efficacious against those of Rappaccini. Bestow the vase, and the precious liquid within it, on your Beatrice, and hopefully await the result."

Baglioni laid a small, exquisitely wrought silver vial on the table and withdrew, leaving what he had said to produce its effect upon the young man's mind.

"We will thwart Rappaccini yet," thought he, chuckling to himself, as he descended the stairs. "But, let us confess the truth of him, he is a wonderful man—a wonderful man indeed; a vile empiric,[12] however, in his practice, and therefore

9. **alembic:** an apparatus made of glass or metal.
10. **Benvenuto Cellini:** sculptor and goldsmith (1500–1571).
11. **Borgias:** an aristocratic Italian family of the Renaissance; many Borgias were accused of poisoning their enemies.
12. **empiric:** charlatan or quack.

A. Expansion (Less Challenging) Less advanced students may have trouble wading through this scene. Paraphrase it by saying that the older man, Baglioni, is cautioning the younger one, Giovanni, against the dangers of associating with his beloved, and that Giovanni takes offense.

A. Characterization
What new feelings toward Beatrice does Giovanni reveal here? (That he mistrusts her and must test her)
? How do you respond to his feelings?

B. Plot
? What new crucial plot development happens here? (Giovanni's system, too, has apparently become poisonous to other living things.)

not to be tolerated by those who respect the good old rules of the medical profession."

A Throughout Giovanni's whole acquaintance with Beatrice, he had occasionally, as we have said, been haunted by dark surmises as to her character; yet so thoroughly had she made herself felt by him as a simple, natural, most affectionate, and guileless creature, that the image now held up by Professor Baglioni looked as strange and incredible as if it were not in accordance with his own original conception. True, there were ugly recollections connected with his first glimpses of the beautiful girl; he could not quite forget the bouquet that withered in her grasp, and the insect that perished amid the sunny air, by no ostensible agency save the fragrance of her breath. These incidents, however, dissolving in the pure light of her character, had no longer the efficacy of facts, but were acknowledged as mistaken fantasies, by whatever testimony of the senses they might appear to be substantiated. There is something truer and more real than what we can see with the eyes and touch with the finger. On such better evidence had Giovanni founded his confidence in Beatrice, though rather by the necessary force of her high attributes than by any deep and generous faith on his part. But now his spirit was incapable of sustaining itself at the height to which the early enthusiasm of passion had exalted it; he fell down, groveling among earthly doubts, and defiled therewith the pure whiteness of Beatrice's image. Not that he gave her up; he did but distrust. He resolved to institute some decisive test that should satisfy him, once for all, whether there were those dreadful peculiarities in her physical nature which could not be supposed to exist without some corresponding monstrosity of soul. His eyes, gazing down afar, might have deceived him as to the lizard, the insect, and the flowers; but if he could witness, at the distance of a few paces, the sudden blight of one fresh and healthful flower in Beatrice's hand, there would be room for no further question. With this idea, he hastened to the florist's and purchased a bouquet that was still gemmed with the morning dewdrops.

It was now the customary hour of his daily interview with Beatrice. Before descending into the garden, Giovanni failed not to look at his figure in the mirror—a vanity to be expected in a beautiful young man, yet, as displaying itself at that troubled and feverish moment, the token of a certain shallowness of feeling and insincerity of character. He did gaze, however, and said to himself that his features had never before possessed so rich a grace, nor his eyes such vivacity, nor his cheeks so warm a hue of superabundant life.

"At least," thought he, "her poison has not yet insinuated itself into my system. I am no flower to perish in her grasp."

With that thought, he turned his eyes on the bouquet, which he had never once laid aside from his hand. A thrill of indefinable horror shot through his frame on perceiving that those dewy flowers were already beginning to droop; they wore the aspect of things that had been fresh and lovely yesterday. B Giovanni grew white as marble, and stood motionless before the mirror, staring at his own reflection there as at the likeness of something frightful. He remembered Baglioni's remark about the fragrance that seemed to pervade the chamber. It must have been the poison in his breath! Then he shuddered—shuddered at himself. Recovering from his stupor, he began to watch with curious eye a spider that was busily at work hanging its web from the antique cornice of the apartment, crossing and recrossing the artful system of interwoven lines—as vigorous and active a spider as ever dangled from an old ceiling. Giovanni bent toward the insect, and emitted a deep, long breath. The spider suddenly ceased its toil; the web vibrated with a tremor originating in the body of the small artisan. Again Giovanni sent forth a breath, deeper, longer, and imbued with a venomous feeling out of his heart; he knew not whether he were wicked, or only desperate. The spider made a convulsive grip with his limbs and hung dead across the window.

"Accursed! accursed!" muttered Giovanni, addressing himself. "Hast thou grown so poisonous that this deadly insect perishes by thy breath?"

At that moment, a rich, sweet voice came floating up from the garden.

"Giovanni! Giovanni! It is past the hour! Why tarriest thou? Come down!"

"Yes," muttered Giovanni again. "She is the only being whom my breath may not slay! Would that it might!"

He rushed down, and in an instant was standing before the bright and loving eyes of Beatrice. A moment ago, his wrath and despair had been so fierce that he could have desired nothing so much as to wither her by a glance; but with her actual presence there came influences which had too real an existence to be at once shaken off: recollections of the delicate and benign power of her feminine nature, which had so often enveloped him in a religious calm; recollections of many a holy and passionate outgush of her heart, when the pure fountain had been unsealed from its depths and made visible in its transparency to his mental eye; recollections which, had Giovanni known how to estimate them, would have assured him that all this ugly mystery was but an earthly illusion, and that, whatever mist of evil might seem to have gathered over her, the real Beatrice was a heavenly angel. Incapable as he was of such high faith, still her presence had not utterly lost its magic. Giovanni's rage was quelled into an aspect of sullen insensibility. Beatrice, with a quick spiritual sense, immediately felt that there was a gulf of blackness between them which neither he nor she could pass. They walked on together, sad and silent, and came thus to the marble fountain and to its pool of water on the ground, in the midst of which grew the shrub that bore gemlike blossoms. Giovanni was affrighted at the eager enjoyment—the appetite, as it were—with which he found himself inhaling the fragrance of the flowers.

"Beatrice," asked he, abruptly, "whence came this shrub?"

A "My father created it," answered she, with simplicity.

"Created it! created it!" repeated Giovanni. "What mean you, Beatrice?"

"He is a man fearfully acquainted with the secrets of Nature," replied Beatrice, "and, at the hour when I first drew breath, this plant sprang from the soil, the offspring of his science, of his intellect, while I was but his earthly child. Approach it not!" continued she, observing with terror that Giovanni was drawing nearer to the shrub. "It has qualities that you little dream of. But I, dearest Giovanni, I grew up and blossomed with the plant and was nourished with its breath. It was my sister, and I loved it with a human affection; for, alas!—hast thou not suspected it?—there was an awful doom."

Here Giovanni frowned so darkly upon her that Beatrice paused and trembled. But her faith in his tenderness reassured her, and made her blush that she had doubted for an instant.

"There was an awful doom," she continued, "the effect of my father's fatal love of science, which estranged me from all society of my kind. Until Heaven sent thee, dearest Giovanni, oh, how lonely was thy poor Beatrice!"

"Was it a hard doom?" asked Giovanni, fixing his eyes upon her.

"Only of late have I known how hard it was," answered she, tenderly. "Oh, yes, but my heart was torpid, and therefore quiet."

Giovanni's rage broke forth from his sullen gloom like a lightning flash out of a dark cloud.

"Accursed one!" cried he, with venomous scorn and anger. "And, finding thy solitude wearisome, thou hast severed me likewise from all the warmth of life and enticed me into thy region of unspeakable horror!"

"Giovanni!" exclaimed Beatrice, turning her large, bright eyes upon his face. The force of his words had not found its way into her mind; she was merely thunderstruck.

"Yes, poisonous thing!" repeated Giovanni, beside himself with passion. "Thou hast done it! Thou hast blasted me! Thou hast filled my veins with poison! Thou hast made me as hateful, as ugly, as loathsome and deadly a creature as thyself—a world's wonder of hideous monstrosity! Now, if our breath be happily as fatal to ourselves as to all others, let us join our lips in one kiss of unutterable hatred, and so die!" B

"What has befallen me?" murmured Beatrice, with a low moan out of her heart. "Holy Virgin, pity me, a poor heartbroken child!"

"Thou—dost thou pray?" cried Giovanni, still with the same fiendish scorn. "Thy very prayers, as they come from thy lips, taint the atmosphere with death. Yes, yes, let us pray! Let us to church and dip our fingers in the holy water at the portal! They that come after us will perish as by a pestilence! Let us sign crosses in the air! It will be scattering curses abroad in the likeness of holy symbols!"

"Giovanni," said Beatrice, calmly, for her grief was beyond passion, "why dost thou join thyself with me thus in those terrible words? I, it is true, am the horrible thing thou namest me. But thou—what hast thou to do, save with one other shudder at my hideous misery to go forth out of the garden and mingle with thy race, and forget that there ever crawled on earth such a monster as poor Beatrice?"

"Dost thou pretend ignorance?" asked Giovanni, scowling upon her. "Behold! this power have I gained from the pure daughter of Rappaccini." C

There was a swarm of summer insects flitting through the air in search of the food promised by

A. Expansion
Note the chillingly dramatic effect of the phrase "My father created it," as opposed to the ordinary alternative, "My father grew it."

B. Responding
Giovanni becomes enraged at his loved one. How does this quarrel compare with lovers' quarrels in realistic environments? (Students probably will note the poetic language and the appeals to abstract concepts rather than matter-of-fact concerns.)

C. Sarcasm
What is sarcastic about Giovanni's "this power have I gained" statement? (In search of the power of love, he gained instead the power of death.) What is his new attitude toward Beatrice? (That she is not pure at all, but evil)

Closure
Have students jot down the romantic elements in this story. In class discussion, ask them to give specific examples of these elements.

Reading Check Test
1. A large, magnificent plant with purple, gem-like flowers is a "breath of life" to Beatrice, who refers to the plant as her sister. *True*
2. Professor Pietro Baglioni, a friend of Giovanni's father, is pleased to notice Giovanni's interest in Beatrice. *False*
3. Professor Baglioni believes that Giovanni is certainly part of one of Rappaccini's experiments. *True*
4. Although they never kiss or hold hands, the love grows between Giovanni and Beatrice. *True*
5. In her dying words, Beatrice claims that there is more poison in Giovanni's nature than in hers. *False*

A. Responding
? What is your response to the line "Oh, what is death after such words as thine?"
If Poe had written this story, how might he have treated the relationship between Beatrice and Giovanni at this point? Note the subtlety of Hawthorne's psychological insights. (Answers will vary. Poe might, as Giovanni suggested on the previous page, have had the deadly female kiss the poor male passionately, thus causing them to die in a violent embrace.)

B. Connections
? This scene echoes the lovers' deaths in *Romeo and Juliet.* What do you think will happen now?

C. Paraphrase
Paraphrase: "I would rather have been loved than feared."
? How is this statement applicable to circumstances outside the particular ones of this story? (Answers may include contemporary applications as well as those pertaining to Hawthorne personally.)

the flower odors of the fatal garden. They circled round Giovanni's head, and were evidently attracted toward him by the same influence which had drawn them for an instant within the sphere of several of the shrubs. He sent forth a breath among them, and smiled bitterly at Beatrice as at least a score of the insects fell dead upon the ground.

"I see it! I see it!" shrieked Beatrice. "It is my father's fatal science! No, no, Giovanni; it was not I! Never! never! I dreamed only to love thee and be with thee a little time, and so to let thee pass away, leaving but thine image in mine heart; for, Giovanni, believe it, though my body be nourished with poison, my spirit is God's creature, and craves love as its daily food. But my father—he has united us in this fearful sympathy. Yes, spurn me, tread upon me, kill me! Oh, what is death after such words as thine? But it was not I. Not for a world of bliss would I have done it." A

Giovanni's passion had exhausted itself in its outburst from his lips. There now came across him a sense, mournful, and not without tenderness, of the intimate and peculiar relationship between Beatrice and himself. They stood, as it were, in an utter solitude, which would be made none the less solitary by the densest throng of human life. Ought not, then, the desert of humanity around them to press this insulated pair closer together? If they should be cruel to one another, who was there to be kind to them? Besides, thought Giovanni, might there not still be a hope of his returning within the limits of ordinary nature, and leading Beatrice, the redeemed Beatrice, by the hand? Oh, weak, and selfish, and unworthy spirit, that could dream of an earthly union and earthly happiness as possible, after such deep love had been so bitterly wronged as was Beatrice's love by Giovanni's blighting words! No, no, there could be no such hope. She must pass heavily, with that broken heart, across the borders of Time—she must bathe her hurts in some fount of paradise, and forget her grief in the light of immortality, and *there* be well.

But Giovanni did not know it.

"Dear Beatrice," said he, approaching her, while she shrank away as always at his approach, but now with a different impulse, "dearest Beatrice, our fate is not yet so desperate. Behold! there is a medicine, potent, as a wise physician has assured me, and almost divine in its efficacy. It is composed of ingredients the most opposite to those by which thy awful father has brought this calamity upon thee and me. It is distilled of blessed herbs. Shall we not quaff it together, and thus be purified from evil?"

"Give it me!" said Beatrice, extending her hand to receive the little silver vial which Giovanni took from his bosom. She added, with a peculiar emphasis, "I will drink, but do thou await the result." B

She put Baglioni's antidote to her lips; and, at the same moment, the figure of Rappaccini emerged from the portal and came slowly toward the marble fountain. As he drew near, the pale man of science seemed to gaze with a triumphant expression at the beautiful youth and maiden, as might an artist who should spend his life in achieving a picture or a group of statuary and finally be satisifed with his success. He paused; his bent form grew erect with conscious power; he spread out his hands over them in the attitude of a father imploring a blessing upon his children; but those were the same hands that had thrown poison into the stream of their lives. Giovanni trembled. Beatrice shuddered nervously, and pressed her hand upon her heart.

"My daughter," said Rappaccini, "thou art no longer lonely in the world. Pluck one of those precious gems from thy sister shrub and bid thy bridegroom wear it in his bosom. It will not harm him now. My science and the sympathy between thee and him have so wrought within his system that he now stands apart from common men, as thou dost, daughter of my pride and triumph, from ordinary women. Pass on, then, through the world, most dear to one another and dreadful to all besides!"

"My father," said Beatrice, feebly, and still as she spoke she kept her hand upon her heart, "wherefore didst thou inflict this miserable doom upon thy child?"

"Miserable!" exclaimed Rappaccini. "What mean you, foolish girl? Dost thou deem it misery to be endowed with marvelous gifts against which no power nor strength could avail an enemy—misery, to be able to quell the mightiest with a breath—misery, to be as terrible as thou art beautiful? Wouldst thou, then, have preferred the condition of a weak woman, exposed to all evil and capable of none?"

"I would fain have been loved, not feared," C murmured Beatrice, sinking down upon the ground. "But now it matters not. I am going,

Analyzing the Story

Identifying Facts

1. Dr. Rappaccini intently examines the plants and shrubs, but with cold, scientific detachment: Giovanni notes that he avoids any contact with the flowers, and is even cautious not to breathe their odors. By contrast, Beatrice (who herself resembles a flower in Giovanni's eyes) handles and inhales the odor of several plants which her father avoids.

When he comes to the magnificent plant, Dr. Rappaccini supplements the thick gloves he wears on his hands with a mask, which he ties about his mouth and nostrils. But when he summons his daughter, Beatrice tenderly attends to the plant, calling it her "sister" and her "splendor."

2. A small lizard dies in the garden when struck by a tiny drop of liquid that falls from one of the purple flowers of the plant by the fountain. Likewise, a butterfly falls dead when it comes in contact with Beatrice's breath. And the fresh flowers which Giovanni throws to Beatrice at their first meeting begin to wither a few moments later, as Beatrice withdraws from the garden into the house.

(Answers continue top of page 292.)

Father, where the evil which thou hast striven to mingle with my being will pass away like a dream—like the fragrance of these poisonous flowers, which will no longer taint my breath among the flowers of Eden. Farewell, Giovanni! Thy words of hatred are like lead within my heart; but they, too, will fall away as I ascend. Oh, was there not, from the first, more poison in thy nature than in mine?"

To Beatrice—so radically had her earthly part been wrought upon by Rappaccini's skill—as poison had been life, so the powerful antidote was death; and thus the poor victim of man's ingenuity and of thwarted nature, and of the fatality that attends all such efforts of perverted wisdom, perished there, at the feet of her father and Giovanni. Just at that moment, Professor Pietro Baglioni looked forth from the window, and called loudly, in a tone of triumph mixed with horror, to the thunderstricken man of science: A

"Rappaccini! Rappaccini! and is *this* the upshot of your experiment!"

B

A. Tone

? Note that Baglioni's tone mixes triumph with horror. What is Hawthorne implying with this mixture? (Baglioni, and therefore by extension "normal" humanity, may be as meddlesome and wicked as the mad scientist.)

B. Responding

? Do you like the ending of the story? What alternative ending can you imagine that would be more satisfying for you? (See Writing About the Story, question 1, page 292.)

C. Humanities Connection: Discussing the Fine Art

René Lalique (1860–1945) was a pioneer modern goldsmith, jewelry designer, and glassblower. He designed glass perfume bottles, revolutionizing that industry, and was a leader in the use of glass as decor in modern architecture. This piece shows a woman and a poisonous (opiate-containing) flower.

A Comment on the Story

Hawthorne's style in this story anticipates the twentieth-century blend of fantasy and realism of such modern Latin American novelists as Gabriel García Márquez and Jorgé Luis Borges. Dr. Rappaccini's obsession with science has led him to the brink of magic, and certain details of the story's plot are so mysterious that they must be regarded as supernatural. On the other hand, Hawthorne's descriptions of the setting are lovingly detailed and realistic.

Part of the appeal of the story might lie in its **ambiguity**—its refusal to be pinned down to one interpretation. On one level, the story's theme reveals how a perverted use of science can lead us beyond morality into confrontation with evil. On another level, the story is about the tragic destruction of innocence, and on yet another, about the dangers of intellectual arrogance. Too late, Giovanni Guasconti realizes that he has been the subject of a bizarre scientific experiment and that he has been lured into his situation by an innocent creature who has been ruined for ordinary human life by her father's sinister science.

Through various references in the story, Hawthorne implies that our awareness of two other classic tales may contribute to an understanding of "Rappaccini's Daughter."

First, in the story's opening paragraph Hawthorne refers to Dante's epic poem, *The Divine Comedy.* The name *Beatrice* ("the blessed one") has an important set of connotations. It was Beatrice who guided Dante in the last of his three great journeys to Hell, Purgatory, and Paradise. The associations of Beatrice in Dante's poem—with innocence, radiant beauty, and eternal life—seem to be ironically twisted in Hawthorne's tale. But then we learn, in a further ironic twist, that his Beatrice may be a far more accurate emblem of these qualities than she appeared at first to be.

Female Head with Poppy Blossoms by René Lalique (1898–1900).

Calouste Gulbenkian Museum, Lisbon, Portugal.

C

Second, the description of Rappaccini's marvelous garden and Beatrice's confinement to it suggest the account of Eden in the Bible. Hawthorne's tale is an allegorical reenactment of the world's fall from original innocence and purity. In the Bible, the Original Sin of Adam and Eve was disobedience that resulted from pride. Readers of Hawthorne's story must decide what Hawthorne considers our greatest fault, and how Rappaccini, Baglioni, and perhaps Giovanni himself exemplify it.

Readers might also think about the one part of Beatrice's character that was not poisoned by the science of her father. Though her father had poisoned her body, he could not pervert her soul, nor could he destroy her need for love and her capacity for giving it.

(Answers begin top of page 291.)

3. Baglioni says that Dr. Rappaccini is a brilliant physician but is gravely flawed. He tells Giovanni that Rappaccini considers his patients merely as subjects for experimental science. Rappaccini is not to be trusted.

4. Among other passages, students may cite the opening scene, where Rappaccini commits the flower to his daughter's care; the scene in the garden between Giovanni and Beatrice, where Beatrice tenderly addresses the flower and then warns Giovanni not to touch it; and the final scene in the garden.

5. He begins to experience emotions of both love and horror.

6. Baglioni tells Giovanni to persuade Beatrice to drink some of the liquid he keeps in a silver vial. He claims that the liquid is an antidote to Rappaccini's poisons.

7. Giovanni believes that he has contracted Beatrice's deadly powers. He breathes on some flowers and on a spider, and both die.

Giovanni becomes deeply distrustful and angry. He believes that Beatrice has cursed him.

(Answers continue in left-hand column.)

(Cont. from top.)

8. Rappaccini wanted to endow both of them with "marvelous gifts" that would set them apart from ordinary people. These gifts appear to be the power to destroy their enemies.

9. She implies that the real poison is mental and emotional, rather than physical.

Interpreting Meanings

10. These details of setting suggest a mood of decay, torture, corruption, and death.

The first paragraph, by emphasizing the gloominess of Giovanni's lodgings, the link with Dante's Inferno, and the extinction of the notable Paduan family, evokes a mood of decay and corruption.

11. Most students will agree that Beatrice dies from a lack of love. She is smothered by her father's obsessions and by Giovanni's suspicious distrust.

12. The circumstances of Beatrice's

(Answers continue top of page 293.)

Responding to the Story

Analyzing the Story

Identifying Facts

1. Describe Dr. Rappaccini's behavior toward the plants in his garden. How does his daughter's behavior toward the plants differ from his own? In particular, how does each treat the large plant by the fountain?
2. Name three of the early hints in the story that Beatrice may have deadly powers.
3. Explain what we learn from Baglioni about the **character** of Dr. Rappaccini.
4. Cite the passages in the story that reveal Beatrice's relationship with the large flower.
5. As a result of his first talk with Beatrice in the garden, how does Giovanni begin to feel about her?
6. Describe Baglioni's plan to save both Beatrice and Giovanni.
7. After Baglioni's visit, what physical change does Giovanni recognize in himself? What change in attitude toward Beatrice begins to grow in his mind? What does he accuse her of?
8. Explain what Dr. Rappaccini wanted to do for Giovanni and Beatrice with his science.
9. In Beatrice's last words, at the story's **climax,** what does she imply is the real poison that has spread through Giovanni's nature?

Interpreting Meanings

10. Giovanni's lodgings are in the house of an old Paduan family, "long extinct," one of whose members had been assigned by Dante to a place in Hell. What mood is established by the **setting**? How does the first paragraph set the mood for the whole story?
11. What do you think actually killed Beatrice?
12. How are the circumstances of Beatrice's death **ironic**? In your opinion, which character or characters bear most responsibility for her fate, and why?
13. During Giovanni's first meeting with Beatrice, what warning does she issue about truth and appearance? Consider Beatrice's appearance, her physical nature, and her soul, and explain the **moral** about beauty and appearances the story might be teaching.
14. How are Rappaccini and Baglioni **foils**—or contrasting characters—both in personality and in the uses they make of science? On a **symbolic** level, what contrasting uses of science might these two characters represent?
15. What warning about our relation to science and nature might Hawthorne be implying in this story? Is the warning any more or less relevant today than it was in the mid-nineteenth century? Explain.

Writing About the Story

A Creative Response

1. **Ending the Story.** What happens to Giovanni? In at least a paragraph, provide an ending to Hawthorne's story that accounts for Giovanni. You might also want to suggest what will happen to Dr. Rappaccini and his garden.

A Critical Response

2. **Analyzing the Story's Romantic Elements.** Hawthorne's fiction, while deeply individualistic, represents one of the most brilliant flowerings of American Romanticism. The Romantic outlook is often marked by (a) a belief that the beauties and mysteries of nature are a source of moral lessons; (b) a fascination with the exotic and with the past; (c) an interest in the supernatural; and (d) an interest in human emotions and the psychological depths of human nature. Write a brief essay explaining how "Rappaccini's Daughter" displays each of these characteristics of Romantic literature.
3. **Comparing Stories.** Hawthorne, who spent years of his life in seclusion, wrote in "The Minister's Black Veil" that every human being is alone "in that saddest of all prisons, the human heart." Many of his writings reveal a deep conviction of the essential isolation of each individual. In an essay, compare the images of human isolation presented in "The Minister's Black Veil" and in "Rappaccini's Daughter." Which character is isolated in each story, and for what purpose?
4. **Comparing Stories.** In an essay, show how both "The Minister's Black Veil" and "Rappaccini's Daughter" deal with the idea that evil can exist behind a facade of normalcy or beauty. At the end of your essay, explain your own response to this idea.
5. **Describing Biblical Parallels.** In an essay, trace the parallels between "Rappaccini's Daughter" and the account of Adam and Eve in Genesis 1–3. Answer these questions in your essay:

   a. How are the gardens similar?
   b. How are they different?
   c. What is Hawthorne's equivalent of the forbidden tree in Genesis?
   d. Who is Adam in Hawthorne's story?
   e. Who is Eve?
   f. Who is the serpent?

   Find passages of Hawthorne's story in which these elements of the Biblical account are alluded to.

death are ironic in at least two ways. First, Baglioni had promised an antidote when he gave the drink to Giovanni. When Beatrice falls dead, we realize that the liquid was an antidote only in an ironic, figurative sense: The death that it causes is a release from the evil that Dr. Rappaccini had inflicted upon her. Second, Beatrice's death is ironic because, as she says just before she dies, she would rather have been loved than feared. Rappaccini is perverted; Giovanni is weak and distrustful; and Baglioni, while professing to honor humane science, is consumed with jealousy. It seems especially ironic, given the other characters' faults, that it is Beatrice who should die.

Student answers will vary. All three men bear some responsibility.

13. She tells him to believe only the words from her lips, not what he has heard or what he may have fancied about her.

Student answers will vary. Encourage them to present and support their own opinions. Some may argue that the moral is that appearances are deceptive or even that beauty is dangerous. Others may argue that Beatrice was as pure as she was beautiful and that Giovanni therefore should have trusted her.

14. Rappaccini might represent the detached use of science for the sole purpose of increasing knowledge, regardless of human consequences. Baglioni, however, represents a more humane use of science. The picture of Baglioni gloating over Beatrice's death at the end of the story is disconcerting: We realize that he caused her death, and we suspect that he is more moved by his professional rivalry with Rappaccini at this moment than by the death of the girl.

15. Hawthorne seems to say that humanity trifles with nature at its peril. Rappaccini perverted beauty into poisons and changed regenerative symbols of life (plants) into agents of death.

Most will agree that the implied warning is more relevant today than when the story was written. Consider nuclear weapons and wastes as well as genetic engineering and the like.

Analyzing Language and Style

Connotations

Connotations are the associations and feelings attached to certain words—associations and feelings that go well beyond the word's strict dictionary definition. Connotations become attached to certain words because of shared usage.

Hawthorne does not state outright how he wants his reader to feel about Rappaccini. However, the connotations of the words he uses to describe Dr. Rappaccini when he first appears in the story alert us at once to the nature of the doctor's character. Read again the passage beginning "While Giovanni stood at the window" on page 276.

1. What associations and feelings do you have when you hear these words?
   a. emaciated
   b. sallow
   c. sickly looking
   d. scholar's garb of black
2. In the next paragraph, beginning "Nothing could exceed," find the extended **figure of speech** that describes Rappaccini's demeanor. What associations or feelings does this figure of speech create? How does it make you feel about the doctor?
3. What words in the paragraph beginning "The distrustful gardener" on page 276 suggest something unhealthy in the doctor's spirit?
4. In contrast to her father, what words and **figures of speech** describe Beatrice when she enters, in the paragraph beginning "'Here am I, my father!'"
5. In the next paragraph, beginning "Soon there emerged," what words and **figures of speech** describe Beatrice?
6. Is there any suggestion in the description of Beatrice that she too is evil? How would you describe the emotional effect of the description of Beatrice?
7. Can you find additional words and **figures of speech** describing the doctor and his daughter that reinforce your first impression of them? Do any descriptions make you question your evaluation of their characters?

Primary Sources

Hawthorne and the Monument at Concord

In 1846, in an essay called "The Old Manse," Hawthorne writes of the years he lived in an old home that lay near the Concord River and the famous battle monument. He has just described the graves of two nameless British soldiers buried near the monument.

"Lowell, the poet, as we were once standing over this grave, told me a tradition in reference to one of the inhabitants below. The story has something deeply impressive, though its circumstances cannot altogether be reconciled with probability. A youth in the service of the clergymen happened to be chopping wood, that April morning [the day the first battle of the Revolution was fought], at the back door of the Manse, and when the noise of battle rang from side to side of the bridge he hastened across the intervening field to see what might be going forward. It is rather strange, by the way, that this lad should have been so diligently at work when the whole population of town and country were startled out of their customary business by the advance of the British troops. Be that as it might, the tradition says that the lad now left his task and hurried to the battlefield with the axe still in his hand. The British had by this time retreated, the Americans were in pursuit; and the late scene of strife was thus deserted by both parties. Two soldiers lay on the ground—one was a corpse; but, as the young New Englander drew nigh, the other Briton raised himself painfully upon his hands and knees and gave a ghastly stare into his face. The boy—it must have been a nervous impulse, without purpose, without thought, and betokening a sensitive and impressible nature rather than a hardened one—the boy uplifted his axe and dealt the wounded soldier a fierce and fatal blow upon the head.

"I could wish that the grave might be opened; for I would fain know whether either of the skeleton soldiers has the mark of an axe in his skull. The story comes home to me like truth. Oftentimes, as an intellectual and moral exercise, I have sought to follow that poor youth through his subsequent career, and observe how his soul was tortured by the blood stain, contracted as it had been before the long custom of war had robbed human life of its sanctity, and while it still seemed murderous to slay a brother man. This one circumstance has borne more fruit for me than all that history tells us of the fight. . . ."

—from "The Old Manse,"
Nathaniel Hawthorne

A. Expansion
The experience of losing his father at the age of twelve, under circumstances connected with bankruptcy, scarred Melville deeply. Throughout his books characters appear who are, either literally or figuratively, orphans looking for their fathers. In *Moby-Dick,* Ahab is a mad father-figure to the orphan Ishmael. In real life, Hawthorne was a disappointingly remote father figure to the eager Melville.

B. Responding
You might briefly discuss the subject of literary apprenticeships. Hawthorne's apprenticeship was twelve years in seclusion; Melville's was five years traveling the world on sailing ships.
? What different kinds of results might these different apprenticeships be expected to produce? Is one necessarily "better" than another? (Teaching and writing would develop his contemplative side and writing skills. Sailing would develop his physical skills and give him material to write about.)

Herman Melville (1819–1891)

It is the central irony of Herman Melville's career that his triumphant achievement, now widely recognized as one of the greatest American novels, was almost wholly ignored while its author was alive. Melville's countrymen—so absorbed with success; so eager to discover it, bestow it, reward it, celebrate it—passed by *Moby-Dick* without the barest recognition.

As a result, Melville spent the last third of his life in poverty and despair, thinking himself a failure. His disappointment was even more painful because he had known easy, early success with his adventure stories; with ambitious, serious work, he met only failure and humiliation.

It is a further irony that Melville became resigned to the contempt of the world; that in spite of its painfulness, he deliberately decided in the world's favor. In a statement that was to be echoed by the twentieth-century novelist William Faulkner, Melville once remarked that failure "is the true test of greatness."

Herman Melville was born in New York City on August 1, into a distinguished family. His father, Allan Melville, came from a line of wealthy Boston merchants, and his mother, Maria Gansevoort, had even more prosperous and aristocratic ancestors among the Hudson River landlords. There were Revolutionary heroes in both families. General Peter Gansevoort had fought off the British and the Indians at Fort Stanwix; Major Melville, Herman's grandfather, had taken part in the Boston Tea Party.

In 1830, when Melville was ten, his father went bankrupt and the family fled New York City for a less secure life in Albany. Herman and his brothers attended Albany Academy until 1832, when their father collapsed under his anxieties, grew ill, then insane, and quite suddenly, died. [A] Maria Melville was an austere, God-fearing woman, and under these circumstances she became even more remote from her children. Melville went off to visit an uncle in the Berkshires near Pittsfield, Massachusetts. He enjoyed himself so much that he remained to teach and to try his hand at writing articles and stories.

When he returned to his family, he had some of his pieces published in the local paper. However, the poverty-stricken life he faced with his family turned his thoughts toward the age-old dream of going to sea.

Herman Melville by Wyatt Eaton. Oil.

He made his first voyage in 1839, serving as cabin boy aboard the merchantman *St. Lawrence*. He remained at sea for five years. In January of 1841, he signed on the whaler *Acushnet,* [B] bound for the South Pacific. A year and a half later, he jumped ship in the Marquesas Islands and found himself in the Typee Valley of Nuku Hiva, captive of a cannibal tribe.

He escaped on the whaler *Lucy Ann* for a voyage to Tahiti and later did a hitch as a sailor aboard the man-of-war *United States*. When this Navy ship returned him to Boston in October of 1844, the principal sea-going era of his life ended. Ishmael, the young narrator of *Moby-Dick,* surely voices Melville's own sentiments when he says, "A whale ship was my Yale College and my Harvard."

Despite Melville's lack of formal education, he had gathered a thorough knowledge of the Bible and become a voracious reader, drawn to the best of English and American literature and philosophy. He had been storing his seafaring experiences with the idea of writing about them. Now, returned to the family house, he began to do just that.

In less than two years, he produced his first novel, *Typee*. It was autobiographical and described his experiences at sea and on Nuku Hiva with the cannibals. When it was published in 1846, it met with immediate success. Melville dedicated the book to an old friend of his father, Lemuel Shaw, chief justice of Massachusetts; in 1847, Melville married Judge Shaw's daughter, Elizabeth. The couple moved to New York City, where they settled in a house on lower Fourth Avenue.

Lizzie Shaw was no intellectual match for her husband, but she was an amiable housewife, proud of Melville's accomplishments even when his literary themes seemed to scorn the homely comforts and securities she provided. In the course of their long and often troubled marriage, she bore four children and was never more loyal and devoted than at times of crisis.

The years after the success of *Typee* were enormously productive. In 1847, Melville published a sequel, entitled *Omoo*. Two years later he produced *Mardi,* the work in which he began to experiment with allegory and symbolism. The year 1849 also saw the publication of *Redburn,* which drew upon his experiences aboard the *St. Lawrence,* but in less realistic, more imaginative terms than those of the early romances. In 1850, he used his service on the *United States* as the basis for another, semi-autobiographical novel, entitled *White-Jacket*.

In the summer of 1850, Melville bought a farm near Pittsfield, Massachusetts, and settled his growing family there. He had already met Nathaniel Hawthorne, who lived in nearby Lenox, and Melville sensed a strong kinship with the older writer. While Hawthorne responded to Melville's admiration and they saw much of each other, Melville found Hawthorne's reserve disappointing.

Melville was in particular need of encouragement, for he was working on a book that would

Painted sternboard from the ship *Mary and Susan*. Old Lighthouse Museum, Stonington, Connecticut.

A. Expansion
In later life, Melville was scornful of his early success and cynical about the prospect of pursuing a remunerative literary career. Readers could not follow his ambiguities and symbols, and he felt that attracting an audience would mean betraying his artistic ideals.

B. Humanities Connection: Responding to the Fine Art
Folk art can be found in unsuspected places—not only on canvas, but, as in this case, on the side of a ship.

? Do people today engage in similar folk-art practices? What about the painting of vans and customized cars? Can you think of other examples of folk art? (Designs on jeans, jackets, and T-shirts, for example)

A. Expansion
Melville's increasing depression in later life was a considerable strain on his family. His granddaughter, Eleanor Metcalf, remembered him as an oppressive presence. Relatives urged his wife to separate from him, though she resisted on grounds of propriety. Even while still in Massachusetts, Melville had been examined by Dr. Oliver Wendell Holmes, who had an early interest in psychiatry.

B. Expansion
The street on which the customs house stood was Gansevoort (pronounced Gainsvoort) Street—named after Melville's grandfather, a hero of the American Revolution. Melville was bitterly conscious of the ironic contrast between his family's past glory and his own obscurity.

both exploit his whaling experience and, on a far more ambitious plane, seek the ultimate truth of human existence. That truth, and the mystery of whether it is benign or evil in nature, is embodied in Moby-Dick, the great white whale that gives the book its title and central symbol.

Melville found the perfect narrator for his whale story in a young man named Ishmael, who has a keen eye and a questioning voice. Moreover, he saw his main character clearly: Captain Ahab, standing on the *Pequod*'s quarter-deck with his peg leg jammed into that accommodating hole and his heart full of brooding vengeance. In Ahab, Melville created a giant of a character, one with very few equals in American literature.

When he finished *Moby-Dick* in July of 1851, Melville sensed that he had taken a great risk and won, that he had written a sublime novel. He dedicated it to Hawthorne and wrote him, "I have written a wicked book but I feel spotless as a lamb."

Yet for all his bright expectations, *Moby-Dick* was a failure. Critics and readers alike were either puzzled or indifferent, and Melville finally had to admit that his literary career had foundered. He wrote to Hawthorne:

> The calm, the coolness, the silent, grass-growing mood in which a man *ought* always to compose—that, I fear can seldom be mine. Dollars damn me; and the malicious Devil is forever grinning in upon me, holding the door ajar. My dear Sir, a presentiment [feeling of fear about the future] is on me—I shall at last be worn out and perish . . . What I feel most moved to write, that is banned—it will not pay. Yet, altogether, write the other way I cannot. So the product is a final hash, and all my books are botches.

A [He was in debt, unable to meet the needs of his family, and in ill health, quite possibly falling toward the mental derangement that had ended his father's life.] However, he continued to hope for a change in his fortunes. He published the poorly received novels *Pierre* in 1852, *Israel Potter* in 1855, and *The Confidence Man* in 1857.

In 1856, he scraped together enough money for a trip to Europe, visiting Hawthorne in England and going on to Italy and Palestine. He returned home feeling somewhat restored by his travels, but he still could find no way out of the hopeless, impoverished life that had been thrust upon him. This same year he published a collection of stories, entitled *The Piazza Tales,* which included one of his finest short pieces of fiction, "Bartleby the Scrivener." It is tempting to see in the stubborn pathos of the title character something of Melville's own bitterly stung emotions.

In 1866, he found a job, much as Hawthorne had, with the customhouse. [As an inspector, he] B visited the North River steamship piers each day to examine the incoming freight and passenger luggage. But if the customhouse gave him the financial security he yearned for, the "grass-growing" peace of mind was still denied him. A different kind of tragedy hit the following year, when his son Malcolm took to his room and killed himself with a pistol.

Nevertheless, during this dark period—during the twenty years in which he worked at the most routine of jobs—Melville never stopped writing, producing in particular a number of notable poems. Almost none of his work found a publisher, and he was obliged to bring it out in private editions of only a few copies. To end this period in Melville's life, there was further tragedy. In 1886, his son Stanwix, always an unstable wanderer, died in San Francisco.

At about the same time, Lizzie Melville came into a small inheritance which allowed her husband, at the age of sixty-seven, to retire from the customhouse and begin work on a book that would become another masterpiece. This was *Billy Budd.* When Melville died on September 28, 1891, the novella lay unwanted in his desk drawer. In 1924, thirty-three years later, it was published and acclaimed. Near the desk where Melville had composed it, a note was found. It read, "Be true to the dreams of thy youth."

FROM MOBY-DICK

"Now the Lord had prepared a great fish to swallow up Jonah."

—The Book of Jonah

*"Whales in the sea
God's voice obey."*

—The New England Primer

Whaleboat Comes to Grief (detail) after a painting by Ambrose Garneray (mid-19th century). Lithograph.

Shelburne Museum, Shelburne, Vermont.

Humanities Connection: Responding to the Fine Art
Ambrose Garneray (1783–1857) was a popular British watercolorist. This work is part of a lithograph that was copied from one of his paintings. Before the age of photographic reproduction, copying by hand was a common means of reproducing paintings.

? Based on this illustration and on the quotations superimposed on it, what predictions can you make about the plot of *Moby-Dick?* (It will involve whales and the dangers faced by whalers.) About the theme? (You may want to return to the illustration from time to time as you discuss the selections from the novel that appear here.)

SUPPLEMENTARY SUPPORT MATERIALS
1. Vocabulary Activity Worksheet (*CCB*)
2. Review and Response Worksheet: Point of View (*CCB*)
3. Selection Test (*CCB*)
4. Audiocassette recording

DEVELOPING VOCABULARY
The following words from the novel are tested in the Selection Test. (See also Vocabulary Activity Worksheet.)

sentinel	abominate
nigh	perdition
infallibly	surveillance
cataract	to induce
phantom	cajoling

PREPARATION
ESTABLISHING A PURPOSE. As indicated in the explanatory note on this page, "Loomings" is Ishmael's narrative. Have students read this chapter to learn about the narrator's character.

Plot of "Loomings": *Moby-Dick* begins with the three words, "Call me Ishmael." Ishmael says that some years ago, he sought escape from his life at sea as an

A. Responding
The name Ishmael, derived from the Bible, has great symbolic meaning. The son of Abraham and Hagar, a serving maid of Abraham's wife Sarah, Ishmael is an outcast whose name has come to be symbolic of a displaced person or wanderer. In *Moby-Dick,* Ishmael is not only a wanderer in the physical world of the sea, but also a spiritual wanderer, in search of the meaning of life.
? Why does Ishmael begin with "Call me Ishmael" rather than "My name is Ishmael"? (The opening makes Ishmael every man and vice versa.)

Four chapters from Melville's great novel will give you only a taste of its characters, setting, and conflict between a sea captain and a mysterious white whale. The first chapter is called "Loomings," a word that suggests something indistinct, perhaps threatening or ominous, like a ship that suddenly looms out of the mist. Listen now to Ishmael's narrative and try to form a picture of this narrator who is driven to seek passage as a sailor on a whaling ship. Remember that Melville himself did the same thing when he was twenty-two years old.

Loomings

A Call me Ishmael. Some years ago—never mind how long precisely—having little or no money in my purse, and nothing particular to interest me on shore, I thought I would sail about a little and see the watery part of the world. It is a way I have of driving off the spleen, and regulating the circulation. Whenever I find myself growing grim about the mouth; whenever it is a damp, drizzly November in my soul; whenever I find myself involuntarily pausing before coffin warehouses, and bringing up the rear of every funeral I meet; and especially whenever my hypos[1] get such an upper hand of me, that it requires a strong moral principle to prevent me from deliberately stepping into the street, and methodically knocking people's hats off—then, I account it high time to get to sea as soon as I can. This is my substitute for pistol and ball. With a philosophical flourish Cato[2] throws himself upon his sword; I quietly take to the ship. There is nothing surprising in this. If they but knew it, almost all men in their degree, some time or other, cherish very nearly the same feelings toward the ocean with me.

There now is your insular city of the Manhattoes,[3] belted round by wharves as Indian isles by coral reefs—commerce surrounds it with her surf. Right and left, the streets take you waterward. Its extreme downtown is the Battery, where that noble mole is washed by waves, and cooled by breezes, which a few hours previous were out of sight of land. Look at the crowds of water-gazers there.

Circumambulate[4] the city of a dreamy Sabbath afternoon. Go from Corlears Hook to Coenties Slip, and from thence, by Whitehall, northward. What do you see?—Posted like silent sentinels all around the town, stand thousands upon thousands of mortal men fixed in ocean reveries. Some leaning against the spiles; some seated upon the pierheads; some looking over the bulwarks of ships from China; some high aloft in the rigging, as if striving to get a still better seaward peep. But these are all landsmen; of week days pent up in lath and plaster—tied to counters, nailed to benches, clinched to desks. How then is this? Are the green fields gone? What do they here?

But look! here come more crowds, pacing straight for the water, and seemingly bound for a dive. Strange! Nothing will content them but the extremest limit of the land; loitering under the shady lee of yonder warehouses will not suffice. No. They must get just as nigh the water as they possibly can without falling in. And there they stand—miles of them—leagues. Inlanders all, they come from lanes and alleys, streets and avenues—north, east, south, and west. Yet here they all unite. Tell me, does the magnetic virtue in the needles of the compasses of all those ships attract them thither?

Once more. Say, you are in the country; in some high land of lakes. Take almost any path you please, and ten to one it carries you down in a dale, and leaves you there by a pool in the stream. There is magic in it. Let the most absent-minded of men be plunged in his deepest reveries—stand that man on his legs, set his feet a-going, and he will infallibly lead you to water, if water there be in all that region. Should you ever be athirst in the great American desert, try this experiment, if

1. **hypos:** short for hypochondria, or depression and imagined sickness.
2. **Cato:** Marcus Porcius Cato, or Cato the Younger (95–46 B.C.), Roman statesman famous for his integrity. In the conflict between the Roman generals Caesar and Pompey, Cato supported Pompey and took his own life when Caesar triumphed.
3. **Manhattoes:** Washington Irving's term, in his *Knickerbocker's History of New York,* for the residents of Manhattan.
4. **circumambulate:** walk around.

ordinary seaman. He cannot explain, though, why he chose a whaling ship. Directed by "the Fates," he assumes that he has been selected for some role in a grand performance they are staging.

your caravan happen to be supplied with a metaphysical professor. Yes, as everyone knows, meditation and water are wedded forever.

A But here is an artist. He desires to paint you the dreamiest, shadiest, quietest, most enchanting bit of romantic landscape in all the valley of the Saco.[5] What is the chief element he employs? There stand his trees, each with a hollow trunk, as if a hermit and a crucifix were within; and here sleeps his meadow, and there sleep his cattle; and up from yonder cottage goes a sleepy smoke. Deep into distant woodlands winds a mazy way, reaching to overlapping spurs of mountains bathed in their hillside blue. But though the picture lies thus tranced, and though this pine tree shakes down its sighs like leaves upon this shepherd's head, yet all were vain, unless the shepherd's eye were fixed upon the magic stream before him. Go visit the Prairies in June, when for scores on scores of miles you wade knee-deep among Tiger lilies—what is the one charm wanting?—Water—there is not a drop of water there! Were Niagara but a cataract of sand, would you travel your thousand miles to see it? Why did the poor poet of Tennessee, upon suddenly receiving two handfuls of silver, deliberate whether to buy him a coat, which he sadly needed, or invest his money in a pedestrian trip to Rockaway Beach? Why is almost every robust, healthy boy with a robust, healthy soul in him, at some time or other crazy to go to sea? Why upon your first voyage as a passenger, did you yourself feel such a mystical vibration, when first told that you and your ship were now out of sight of land? Why did the old Persians hold the sea holy? Why did the Greeks give it a separate deity, and make him the own brother of Jove?[6] Surely all this is not without meaning. And still deeper the meaning of that story of Narcissus,[7] who because he could not grasp the tormenting, mild image he saw in the fountain, plunged into it and was drowned. But that same image, we ourselves see in all rivers and oceans. It is the image of the ungraspable phantom of life; and this is the key to it all.

Now, when I say that I am in the habit of going to sea whenever I begin to grow hazy about the eyes, and begin to be over conscious of my lungs, I do not mean to have it inferred that I ever go to sea as a passenger. For to go as a passenger you must needs have a purse, and a purse is but a rag unless you have something in it. Besides, passengers get seasick—grow quarrelsome—don't sleep of nights—do not enjoy themselves much, as a general thing—no, I never go as a passenger; nor, though I am something of a salt, do I ever go to sea as a Commodore, or a Captain, or a Cook. I abandon the glory and distinction of such offices to those who like them. For my part, I abominate all honorable, respectable toils, trials, and tribulations of every kind whatsoever. It is quite as much as I can do to take care of myself, without taking care of ships, barques, brigs, schooners, and what not. And as for going as cook—though I confess there is considerable glory in that, a cook being a sort of officer on shipboard—yet, somehow, I never fancied broiling fowls—though once broiled, judiciously buttered, and judgmatically salted and peppered, there is no one who will speak more respectfully, not to say reverentially, of a broiled fowl than I will. It is out of the idolatrous dotings of the old Egyptians upon broiled ibis and roasted river horse, that you see the mummies of those creatures in their huge bake-houses the pyramids. B

No, when I go to sea, I go as a simple sailor, right before the mast, plumb down into the forecastle, aloft there to the royal masthead. True, they rather order me about some, and make me jump from spar to spar, like a grasshopper in a May meadow. And at first, this sort of thing is unpleasant enough. It touches one's sense of honor, particularly if you come of an old established family in the land, the Van Rensselaers, or Randolphs, or Hardicanutes. And more than all, if just previous to putting your hand into the tarpot, you have been lording it as a country schoolmaster, making the tallest boys stand in awe of you. The transition is a keen one, I assure you, from a schoolmaster to a sailor, and requires a strong decoction of Seneca and the Stoics[8] to en-

5. **Saco:** river in Maine.
6. **a separate deity . . . Jove:** Neptune, Roman god of the sea (the Greek Poseidon), was brother of Jove, or Jupiter (the Greek Zeus), ruler of the gods.
7. **Narcissus:** youth of Greek legend who fell in love with his own reflection in a pool and pined away with longing for it. On his death, he was changed into a narcissus flower.

8. **Seneca and the Stoics:** Lucius Annaeus Seneca (4 B.C.–A.D. 65) was a Roman philosopher of the Stoic school, which advocated bravery and austerity as a way of achieving inner harmony. When suspected of treason and ordered by the Emperor Nero to kill himself, Seneca took his own life with great calm.

A. Responding

? What argument about the artist does Ishmael use to support his belief in humanity's longing for the sea? (That the chief element a landscape artist will use to show the romance of the scene is water)

B. Responding

? Why does Ishmael prefer going to sea as a sailor than as a passenger? (Passengers must have money, and, besides, they do not enjoy themselves as sailors do.) Would you prefer going to sea as a sailor or as a passenger? Why? (Be sure students give reasons for their answers.)

CLOSURE
In class discussion, have students suggest phrases and sentences that characterize Ishmael.

READING CHECK TEST
1. Ishmael believes that people would not travel so far to see Niagara if it were a desert. *True*
2. Ishmael sometimes goes to sea as a passenger. *False*
3. According to Ishmael, we are all, in some sense, slaves. *True*
4. The *Pequod* is the first ship Ishmael has sailed on. *False*
5. Curiosity about the whale is one motive for Ishmael's going on a whaling ship. *True*

A. Responding
? When Ishmael says "Who ain't a slave?" is he stating a universal truth, or merely excusing his own lack of ambition, or both? (He is stating a universal truth. Most people have a boss and/or someone else to whom they are responsible. In that sense, they take orders.)

B. Irony
? Which kind of person is usually better off financially: a passenger on an ocean liner, or a common sailor? (Elicit the perception that Ishmael is being ironic in saying he would rather be the one who is paid.)

Sailor (detail) by John Cranch (mid-19th century). Oil on wood panel. Peabody Museum of Salem, Salem, Massachusetts.

able you to grin and bear it. But even this wears off in time.

What of it, if some old hunks of a sea captain orders me to get a broom and sweep down the decks? What does that indignity amount to, weighed, I mean, in the scales of the New Testament? Do you think the archangel Gabriel thinks anything the less of me, because I promptly and respectfully obey that old hunks in that particular
A instance? Who ain't a slave? Tell me that. Well, then, however the old sea captains may order me about—however they may thump and punch me about, I have the satisfaction of knowing that it is all right; that everybody else is one way or other served in much the same way—either in a physical or metaphysical point of view, that is; and so the universal thump is passed round, and all hands should rub each other's shoulderblades, and be content.

B Again, I always go to sea as a sailor, because they make a point of paying me for my trouble, whereas they never pay passengers a single penny that I ever heard of. On the contrary, passengers themselves must pay. And there is all the difference in the world between paying and being paid. The act of paying is perhaps the most uncomfortable infliction that the two orchard thieves[9] entailed upon us. But *being paid*—what will compare with it? The urbane activity with which a man receives money is really marvelous, considering that we so earnestly believe money to be the root of all earthly ills, and that on no account can a monied man enter heaven. Ah! how cheerfully we consign ourselves to perdition!

Finally, I always go to sea as a sailor, because of the wholesome exercise and pure air of the forecastle deck. For as in this world, head winds are far more prevalent than winds from astern (that is, if you never violate the Pythagorean maxim), so for the most part the Commodore on the quarter-deck[10] gets his atmosphere at second hand from the sailors on the forecastle. He thinks he breathes it first; but not so. In much the same way do the commonalty lead their leaders in many other things, at the same time that the leaders little suspect it. But wherefore it was that after having

9. **the two orchard thieves:** Adam and Eve.
10. **quarter-deck:** a part of the upper deck normally reserved for officers.

ANALYZING THE NOVEL
Identifying Facts
1. The first paragraph makes it clear that the novel will be told from the first-person point of view.

Ishmael is morbidly depressed. Furthermore, he has no money, and nothing to interest him on shore.

2. He mentions the crowd of watergazers at the Battery in Manhattan, the paths in the countryside that lead to pools and streams, the streams in painted landscapes, the allure of Niagara Falls, and the reverence of the ancients for water.

3. The writer mentions "one grand hooded phantom," which he compares to a snow hill in the air. These details foreshadow the appearance of Moby-Dick, the great white whale.

Interpreting Meanings
4. He says that he has enough trouble taking care of himself, without having to worry about the welfare of a ship. He says that he does not mind being ordered around by the officers, since every human being is—in a metaphysical sense—a slave to destiny.

The choice suggests that Ishmael is modest about his own abilities; perhaps it also suggests that he has a metaphysical, or philosophical, strain of resignation.

5. Ishmael says that the idea of the whale aroused all of his curiosity.

Ishmael is insatiably curious, especially about remote settings. He also has an itch to see the horrible and the forbidden.

6. Ishmael's speculations introduce the theme of fate and free will, which will be prominent throughout the novel. His remarks show us that the voyage he is about to undertake turned out to be highly unusual; the passage prepares us to pay close attention to the narrative.

7. He means that the great size of the whale in the ocean makes it look like an island.

8. Student answers will vary. (The sea in the Bible has traditionally been seen as demonic.)

repeatedly smelled the sea as a merchant sailor, I should now take it into my head to go on a whaling voyage; this the invisible police officer of the Fates, who has the constant surveillance of me, and secretly dogs me, and influences me in some unaccountable way—he can better answer than anyone else. And, doubtless, my going on this whaling voyage, formed part of the grand program of Providence that was drawn up a long time ago. It came in as a sort of brief interlude and solo between more extensive performances. I take it that this part of the bill must have run something like this:

Grand Contested Election for the Presidency of the United States.
WHALING VOYAGE BY ONE ISHMAEL.
BLOODY BATTLE IN AFFGHANISTAN.

Though I cannot tell why it was exactly that those stage managers, the Fates, put me down for this shabby part of a whaling voyage, when others were set down for magnificent parts in high tragedies, and short and easy parts in genteel comedies, and jolly parts in farces—though I cannot tell why this was exactly; yet, now that I recall all the circumstances, I think I can see a little into the springs and motives which being cunningly presented to me under various disguises, induced me to set about performing the part I did, besides cajoling me into the delusion that it was a choice resulting from my own unbiased free will and discriminating judgment.

Chief among these motives was the overwhelming idea of the great whale himself. Such a portentous and mysterious monster roused all my curiosity. Then the wild and distant seas where he rolled his island bulk; the undeliverable, nameless perils of the whale; these, with all the attending marvels of a thousand Patagonian[11] sights and sounds, helped to sway me to my wish. With other men, perhaps, such things would not have been inducements; but as for me, I am tormented with an everlasting itch for things remote. I love to sail forbidden seas, and land on barbarous coasts. Not ignoring what is good, I am quick to perceive a horror, and could still be social with it—would they let me—since it is but well to be on friendly terms with all the inmates of the place one lodges in.

By reason of these things, then, the whaling voyage was welcome; the great floodgates of the wonder-world swung open, and in the wild conceits that swayed me to my purpose, two and two there floated into my inmost soul, endless processions of the whale, and, midmost of them all, one grand hooded phantom, like a snow hill in the air.

11. **Patagonian:** Patagonia is a region east of the Andes mountains, covering the southern parts of Argentina and Chile. *Patagonian* suggested a place very exotic and far away.

Responding to the Novel

Analyzing the Novel

Identifying Facts

1. What **point of view** will the novel be told from? What does the narrator tell us about himself and the mood that moves him to go to sea?
2. What details does the narrator offer to prove that waters and oceans hold a mysterious allure for humanity?
3. What details in the final paragraph **foreshadow** the fact that Ishmael's quest will be for the white whale?

Interpreting Meanings

4. Ishmael prefers the lowliest of shipboard roles. What reasons does he give for this choice? What does this choice suggest about his **character**?
5. What role does the idea of the whale play in Ishmael's decision? What does this information contribute to our knowledge of Ishmael's **character**?
6. Ishmael wonders whether leaving the comparative safety of the merchant fleet for a whaling voyage was decided by fate or by his own free will. Why would this be a matter of importance to him? Or to us as readers?
7. What does Ishmael mean by the whale's "island bulk" (page 301)?
8. Ishmael calls us all "water-gazers"; he says we are fixed in "ocean reveries." Do you agree? What reasons can you suggest for our fascination with the ocean? Why do you think the sea and the large creatures that inhabit it are so often used to symbolize evil or destructiveness?

SUPPLEMENTARY SUPPORT MATERIALS
1. Vocabulary Activity Worksheet (*CCB*)
2. Review and Response Worksheet: Figurative Language (*CCB*)
3. Selection Test (*CCB*)

DEVELOPING VOCABULARY
The following words from the novel are tested in the Selection Test. (See also Vocabulary Activity Worksheet.)

peremptory	vindictive
diabolical	tacit
outlandish	to insinuate
motley	discernment
to ascribe	misanthropic

PREPARATION
ESTABLISHING A PURPOSE In this chapter, Ahab, with his "barbaric white leg," is introduced. Remind students that they will be learning about Ahab from Ishmael's point of view. Then have them read to learn about the several sides of Ahab's character.

Plot of "Ahab": Several days after leav-

A. Plot
? What effect does Ahab's delayed appearance have? (It builds suspense, especially when Ishmael's "vague disquietude" becomes "almost a perturbation.")

B. Responding
? What does Ahab do when he does appear? (Nothing—he merely appears.) Yet the characterization is powerful. It is achieved entirely through portents and physical details.

C. Simile
? What simile does Ishmael use to describe Ahab's first appearance? (He says that Ahab is "like a man cut away from the stake.") What effect does this simile have on the reader's perception of Ahab? (It associates Ahab with great torment.)

Ishmael leaves New York for the Massachusetts seaport of New Bedford. At an inn there, he makes the acquaintance of a South Sea islander named Queequeg, and the two become friends. The would-be sailors journey next to Nantucket, Massachusetts, where they sign on for a three-year voyage on the whaling ship, the Pequod, *under the command of a mysterious Captain Ahab. The ship sets sail on an icy Christmas Day; she is weirdly decorated with whale bones, and her crew is an assortment of officers and men from all over the world. It is not until the voyage is under way for several days, however, that we first glimpse the mysterious, forbidding figure of the captain.*

Ahab

A For several days after leaving Nantucket, nothing above hatches was seen of Captain Ahab. The mates regularly relieved each other at the watches, and for aught that could be seen to the contrary, they seemed to be the only commanders of the ship; only they sometimes issued from the cabin with orders so sudden and peremptory, that after all it was plain they but commanded vicariously.[1] Yes, their supreme lord and dictator was there, though hitherto unseen by any eyes not permitted to penetrate into the now sacred retreat of the cabin.

Every time I ascended to the deck from my watches below, I instantly gazed aft to mark if any strange face was visible; for my first vague disquietude touching the unknown captain, now in the seclusion of the sea, became almost a perturbation. This was strangely heightened at times by the ragged Elijah's diabolical incoherences uninvitedly recurring to me,[2] with a subtle energy I could not have before conceived of. But poorly could I withstand them, much as in other moods I was almost ready to smile at the solemn whimsicalities of that outlandish prophet of the wharves. But whatever it was of apprehensiveness or uneasiness—to call it so—which I felt, yet whenever I came to look about me in the ship, it seemed against all warranty to cherish such emotions. For though the harpooneers, with the great body of the crew, were a far more barbaric, heathenish, and motley set than any of the tame merchant-ship companies which my previous experiences had made me acquainted with, still I ascribed this—and rightly ascribed it—to the fierce uniqueness of the very nature of that wild Scandinavian vocation in which I had so abandonedly embarked. But it was especially the aspect of the three chief officers of the ship, the mates, which was most forcibly calculated to allay these colorless misgivings, and induce confidence and cheerfulness in every presentment[3] of the voyage. Three better, more likely sea officers and men, each in his own different way, could not readily be found, and they were every one of them Americans: a Nantucketer, a Vineyarder, a Cape man. Now, it being Christmas when the ship shot from out her harbor, for a space we had biting Polar weather, though all the time running away from it to the southward; and by every degree and minute of latitude which we sailed, gradually leaving that merciless winter, and all its intolerable weather behind us. It was one of those less lowering, but still gray and gloomy enough mornings of the transition, when with a fair wind the ship was rushing through the water with a vindictive sort of leaping and melancholy rapidity, that as I mounted to the deck at the call of the forenoon watch, so soon as I leveled my glance toward the taffrail,[4] foreboding shivers ran over me. Reality outran apprehension: Captain Ahab stood upon his quarter-deck. B

There seemed no sign of common bodily illness about him, nor of the recovery from any. He looked like a man cut away from the stake, when the fire has overrunningly wasted all the limbs without consuming them, or taking away one particle from their compacted, aged robustness. His whole high, broad form, seemed made of solid bronze, and shaped in an unalterable mold, like Cellini's cast Perseus.[5] Threading its way out from among his gray hairs, and continuing right down one side of his tawny scorched face and neck, till it disappeared in his clothing, you saw a slender C

1. **vicariously:** as substitutes for another (in this case, for Captain Ahab).
2. Before the *Pequod* sailed, an old man named Elijah had asked Ishmael how much he knew about Ahab. "Look ye," Elijah had said ominously, "when Captain Ahab is all right, then this left arm of mine will be all right."
3. **presentment:** here, prediction.
4. **taffrail:** the rail around a ship's stern.
5. **Cellini's cast Perseus:** Benvenuto Cellini (1500–1571), famous Italian sculptor, created an imposing bronze statue of Perseus, a hero of Greek mythology.

ing Nantucket, Ishmael sees Ahab for the first time. Shivering, Ishmael is shocked by Ahab's appearance, but realizes the barbaric leg must account for some of his grim appearance. Before long, Ahab retreats to his cabin, but is seen every day thereafter.

READING CHECK TEST

1. Once the ship leaves Nantucket, Ahab is seen daily. *False*
2. The "elite" of the ship are the harpooners. *False*
3. Ahab's scar runs down one side of his face and neck. *True*
4. Ahab's leg was made from the bone of a sperm whale's jaw. *True*
5. Ahab never loses his appearance of grim determination. *False*

Leonard's Oil Works by William Wall (1855). Oil. Private Collection.

A

A. Humanities Connection: Discussing the Fine Art
William Allen Wall (1801–1885) was an American watercolorist specializing in scenes of New Bedford. (Not to be confused with William Guy Wall [b. 1792], an Irish-American painter of the Hudson River school.) This painting shows the industrial ramifications of the whaling industry in nineteenth-century America: Candles are being made from tallow derived from sperm whale oil.

CLOSURE
Have students brainstorm examples of figurative language used to describe Ahab. Then have them draw one-sentence generalizations about Ahab based on the figurative language.

rodlike mark, lividly whitish. It resembled that perpendicular seam sometimes made in the straight, lofty trunk of a great tree, when the upper lightning tearingly darts down it, and without wrenching a single twig, peels and grooves out the bark from top to bottom, ere running off into the soil, leaving the tree still greenly alive, but branded. Whether that mark was born with him, or whether it was the scar left by some desperate wound, no one could certainly say. By some tacit consent, throughout the voyage little or no allusion was made to it, especially by the mates. But once Tashtego's senior, an old Gay-Head Indian[6] among the crew, superstitiously asserted that not till he was full forty years old did Ahab become that way branded, and then it came upon him, not in the fury of any mortal fray, but in an elemental strife at sea. Yet, this wild hint seemed inferentially negatived, by what a gray Manxman[7] insinuated, an old sepulchral man, who, having never before sailed out of Nantucket, had never ere this laid eye upon wild Ahab. Nevertheless, the old sea traditions, the immemorial credulities, popularly invested this old Manxman with preternatural powers of discernment. So that no white sailor seriously contradicted him when he said that if ever Captain Ahab should be tranquilly laid out—which might hardly come to pass, so he muttered—then, whoever should do that last office for the dead, would find a birthmark on him from crown to sole.

So powerfully did the whole grim aspect of Ahab affect me, and the livid branch which streaked it, that for the first few moments I hardly noted that not a little of this overbearing grimness was owing to the barbaric white leg upon which he partly stood. It had previously come to me that this ivory leg had at sea been fashioned from the polished bone of the sperm whale's jaw. "Aye, he was dismasted off Japan," said the old Gay-Head Indian once; "but like his dismasted craft, he shipped [8] another mast without coming home for it. He has a quiver of 'em."

I was struck with the singular posture he main-

6. **Gay-Head Indian:** an Indian from the town of Gay-Head, Massachusetts.
7. **Manxman:** a man from the Isle of Man, one of the islands located between Northern Ireland and England.
8. **shipped:** took aboard.

Analyzing The Novel

Identifying Facts

1. Ishmael observes the mates suddenly emerging from the captain's cabin with peremptory orders.

2. Ishmael says that the harpooners, although savage-looking, are appropriate crewmen for such a wild voyage. As for the mates, he says that one could hardly wish for better officers.

3. The old Gay-Head Indian asserts that Ahab acquired the brand, or scar, when the captain was forty years old, "in an elemental strife at sea." The Manxman contends that the scar is a birthmark running the length of Ahab's body.

4. Ahab steadies his boneleg in one of two holes on either side of the quarter-deck.

5. Ishmael says that as the weather grew warmer, Ahab's personality seemed to unbend slightly.

Melville uses an extended metaphor for the coming of spring.

Interpreting Meanings

6. Ishmael compares Ahab to a man who is released from the stake. Secondly, he compares the captain to a form of *(Answers continue in left-hand column.)*

(Continued from top.) solid bronze. Finally, he likens the scar on Ahab's body to the mark made by lightning on the trunk of a great tree.

The comparisons suggest the qualities of grimness, impermeable strength, and heroism. The lightning and tree might suggest pride and retribution.

7. Feelings of awe and the idea that Ahab has been involved in an elemental strife at sea. Ishmael also mentions Ahab's immobility and silence. The use of the word "crucifixion" suggests Christ's suffering and martyrdom.

8. The Indian uses an implied metaphor to suggest that Ahab's leg is like the mast of a ship.

The Indian uses a simile to compare Ahab to a craft, or a ship. He then uses a figure of speech to compare Ahab's ivory leg to an arrow in a "quiver."

Student answers will vary.

tained. Upon each side of the Pequod's quarter-deck, and pretty close to the mizen shrouds,[9] there was an auger-hole, bored about half an inch or so, into the plank. His bone leg steadied in that hole; one arm elevated, and holding by a shroud; Captain Ahab stood erect, looking straight out beyond the ship's ever-pitching prow. There was an infinity of firmest fortitude, a determinate, unsurrenderable willfulness, in the fixed and fearless, forward dedication of that glance. Not a word he spoke; nor did his officers say aught to him; though by all their minutest gestures and expressions, they plainly showed the uneasy, if not painful, consciousness of being under a troubled master-eye. And not only that, but moody, stricken Ahab stood before them with a crucifixion in his face; in all the nameless, regal, overbearing dignity of some mighty woe.

Ere long, from his first visit in the air, he withdrew into his cabin. But after that morning, he was every day visible to the crew; either standing in his pivot-hole, or seated upon an ivory stool he had; or heavily walking the deck. As the sky grew less gloomy, indeed, began to grow a little genial, he became still less and less a recluse; as if, when the ship had sailed from home, nothing but the dead, wintry bleakness of the sea had then kept him so secluded. And, by and by, it came to pass, that he was almost continually in the air; but, as yet, for all that he said, or perceptibly did, on the at last sunny deck, he seemed as unnecessary there as another mast. But the Pequod was only making a passage now; not regularly cruising; nearly all whaling preparatives needing supervision the mates were fully competent to, so that there was little or nothing, out of himself to employ or excite Ahab, now; and thus chase away, for that one interval, the clouds that layer upon layer were piled upon his brow, as ever all clouds choose the loftiest peaks to pile themselves upon.

Nevertheless, ere long, the warm, warbling persuasiveness of the pleasant holiday weather we came to seemed gradually to charm him from his mood. For, as when the red-cheeked, dancing girls, April and May, trip home to the wintry, misanthropic woods, even the barest, ruggedest, most thunder-cloven old oak will at least send forth some few green sprouts, to welcome such glad-hearted visitants; so Ahab did, in the end, a little respond to the playful allurings of that girlish air. More than once did he put forth the faint blossom of a look, which, in any other man, would have soon flowered out in a smile.

9. **mizen shrouds:** the sails on the mast closest to the stern.

Responding to the Novel

Analyzing the Novel

Identifying Facts

1. Even before Ahab makes his first appearance on deck, what evidence of his presence does Ishmael observe?
2. Apprehensions regarding the mysterious captain make Ishmael uneasy. By contrast, why does he find the presence of the rest of the ship's company reassuring?
3. Describe Ahab's "brand," or scar. What superstitions surround the scar?
4. Describe the "posture" Ahab maintains on the quarter-deck.
5. In the final paragraph, what hint is offered that Ahab's personality may have a gentler side? Find the examples of **figurative language** in this paragraph that help make this point about Ahab's character.

Interpreting Meanings

6. Find the three **similes** that describe Ahab's appearance as he stands on the quarter-deck. What do you think each simile implies about Ahab's **character**?
7. Ishmael's first impression of Ahab is of terrifying grimness, in part because of Ahab's "barbaric white leg," crafted from the jawbone of a sperm whale. What additional feelings about Ahab are suggested by Ishmael's description of the captain at his post?
8. The old Gay-Head Indian says that Ahab "was dismasted off Japan" (see page 303). What **figure of speech** is implied in the word *dismasted*? (What is the Indian comparing to a mast?) What other figures of speech does the Indian use in this speech to describe Ahab's affliction? Why are his figures of speech particularly suitable?

SUPPLEMENTARY SUPPORT MATERIALS
1. Vocabulary Activity Worksheet (*CCB*)
2. Review and Response Worksheet: Point of View (*CCB*)
3. Selection Test (*CCB*)

DEVELOPING VOCABULARY
The following words from the novel are tested in the Selection Test. (See also Vocabulary Activity Worksheet.)

pedestrian	imprecation
rejoinder	to dilate
tarpaulin	volition
harpoon	to quail
squall	condescension

PREPARATION
ESTABLISHING A PURPOSE. In this chapter, Ahab reveals that his quest for Moby-Dick is the true purpose of the voyage. Have students read to learn what Moby-Dick symbolizes for Ahab.

Plot of "The-Quarter-Deck": Ahab uses oratory to excite the crew's passion for whale-killing and offers a doubloon to the first man who spots Moby-Dick. Except for Starbuck, the men are enthusiastic. At the end of the chapter, Ahab drinks wine from the harpooners' shafts in a blasphemous mock-communion.

Stubb and Ahab quarrel violently, and an ominous dream suggests to the mate that he had better beware of the captain's anger. Hinting at the true nature of his quest over the oceans of the world, Ahab orders the crew to be on the lookout for a great white whale. Notice that, as the narrative gathers dramatic momentum, Melville introduces several chapters, like this one, with stage directions.

The Quarter-Deck

A *(Enter Ahab: Then, all.)*

It was not a great while after the affair of the pipe,[1] that one morning shortly after breakfast, Ahab, as was his wont, ascended the cabin-gangway to the deck. There most sea captains usually walk at that hour, as country gentlemen, after the same meal, take a few turns in the garden.

Soon his steady, ivory stride was heard, as to and fro he paced his old rounds, upon planks so familiar to his tread, that they were all over B dented, like geological stones, with the peculiar mark of his walk. Did you fixedly gaze, too, upon that ribbed and dented brow, there also, you would see still stranger footprints—the footprints of his one unsleeping, ever-pacing thought.

But on the occasion in question, those dents looked deeper, even as his nervous step that morning left a deeper mark. And, so full of his thought was Ahab, that at every uniform turn that he made, now at the main-mast and now at the binnacle,[2] you could almost see that thought turn in him as he turned, and pace in him as he paced; so completely possessing him, indeed, that it all but seemed the inward mold of every outer movement.

"D'ye mark him, Flask?" whispered Stubb, "the chick that's in him pecks the shell. 'Twill soon be out."

The hours wore on—Ahab now shut up within his cabin; anon, pacing the deck, with the same intense bigotry of purpose[3] in his aspect.

It drew near the close of day. Suddenly he came to a halt by the bulwarks, and inserting his bone leg into the auger-hole there, and with one hand grasping a shroud, he ordered Starbuck to send everybody aft.

"Sir!" said the mate, astonished at an order seldom or never given on shipboard except in some extraordinary case.

"Send everybody aft," repeated Ahab. "Mast-heads, there! come down!"

When the entire ship's company were assembled, and with curious and not wholly unapprehensive faces, were eyeing him, for he looked not unlike the weather horizon when a storm is coming up, Ahab, after rapidly glancing over the bulwarks, and then darting his eyes among the crew, started from his stand-point; and as though not a soul were nigh him resumed his heavy turns upon the deck. With bent head and half-slouched hat he continued to pace, unmindful of the wondering whispering among the men; till Stubb cautiously whispered to Flask that Ahab must have summoned them there for the purpose of witnessing a pedestrian feat. But this did not last long. Vehemently pausing, he cried—

"What do ye do when ye see a whale, men?"

"Sing out for him!" was the impulsive rejoinder from a score of clubbed voices.

"Good!" cried Ahab, with a wild approval in his tones; observing the hearty animation into which his unexpected question had so magnetically thrown them.

"And what do ye next, men?"

"Lower away, and after him!"

"And what tune is it ye pull to, men?"

"A dead whale or a stove[4] boat!"

More and more strangely and fiercely glad and approving, grew the countenance of the old man at every shout; while the mariners began to gaze curiously at each other, as if marveling how it was that they themselves became so excited at such seemingly purposeless questions.

But, they were all eagerness again, as Ahab, now half-revolving in his pivot-hole, with one hand reaching high up a shroud, and tightly, almost convulsively grasping it, addressed them thus—

1. Ahab had thrown his pipe overboard one evening, when he realized that he had no business "with the thing that is meant for sereneness."
2. **binnacle:** case containing the compass.
3. **bigotry of purpose:** intense single-mindedness (bigotry suggests narrowness or exclusion of other ideas).
4. **stove:** with a hole smashed in it.

A. Expansion
As the stage direction, "Enter Ahab: Then, all," shows, this scene is dramatized almost as if it were a play. (It also shows Melville's debt to Shakespeare.) Have student volunteers play the roles of the characters, reading their lines at the front of the room. The rest of the class, at their seats, can play the crew, reading such lines as, "Sing out for him!" in unison.

B. Simile
? What effect does comparing the dents Ahab's ivory leg makes in the planks to "geological stones" have? (It magnifies Ahab's effect on his environment and continues to emphasize the symbolic nature of events.)

A. Noting Details
? How do Tashtego, Daggoo, and Queequeg react to Ahab's description of the white whale? (They realize the whale must be Moby-Dick.)

B. Characterization
? What is Ahab's response to Starbuck's query that it was Moby-Dick who took Ahab's leg? (He acknowledges in a frenzied manner that it was Moby-Dick.) What does the manner of his response suggest about Ahab? (That he is fixated on taking revenge for his leg)

"All ye mastheaders have before now heard me give orders about a white whale. Look ye! d'ye see this Spanish ounce of gold?"—holding up a broad, bright coin to the sun—"it is a sixteen dollar piece, men, a doubloon. D'ye see it? Mr. Starbuck, hand me yon top-maul."

While the mate was getting the hammer, Ahab, without speaking, was slowly rubbing the gold piece against the skirts of his jacket, as if to heighten its luster, and without using any words was meanwhile lowly humming to himself, producing a sound so strangely muffled and inarticulate that it seemed the mechanical humming of the wheels of his vitality in him.

Receiving the top-maul from Starbuck, he advanced toward the main-mast with the hammer uplifted in one hand, exhibiting the gold with the other, and with a high, raised voice exclaiming: "Whosoever of ye raises me a white-headed whale with a wrinkled brow and a crooked jaw; whosoever of ye raises me that white-headed whale, with three holes punctured in his starboard fluke—look ye, whosoever of ye raises me that same white whale, he shall have this gold ounce, my boys!"

"Huzza! huzza!" cried the seamen, as with swinging tarpaulins they hailed the act of nailing the gold to the mast.

"It's a white whale, I say," resumed Ahab, as he threw down the top-maul: "a white whale. Skin your eyes for him, men; look sharp for white water; if ye see but a bubble, sing out."

A All this while Tashtego, Daggoo, and Queequeg had looked on with even more intense interest and surprise than the rest, and at the mention of the wrinkled brow and crooked jaw they had started as if each was separately touched by some specific recollection.

"Captain Ahab," said Tashtego, "that white whale must be the same that some call Moby-Dick."

"Moby-Dick?" shouted Ahab. "Do ye know the white whale then, Tash?"

"Does he fan-tail[5] a little curious, sir, before he goes down?" said the Gay-Header deliberately.

"And has he a curious spout, too," said Daggoo, "very bushy, even for a parmacetty,[6] and mighty quick, Captain Ahab?"

"And he have one, two, tree—oh! good many iron in him hide, too, Captain," cried Queequeg disjointedly, "all twiske-tee betwisk, like him—him—" faltering hard for a word, and screwing his hand round and round as though uncorking a bottle—"like him—him—"

"Corkscrew!" cried Ahab, "aye, Queequeg, the harpoons lie all twisted and wrenched in him; aye, Daggoo, his spout is a big one, like a whole shock of wheat, and white as a pile of our Nantucket wool after the great annual sheepshearing; aye, Tashtego, and he fan-tails like a split jib in a squall. Death and devils! men, it is Moby-Dick ye have seen—Moby-Dick—Moby-Dick!"

"Captain Ahab," said Starbuck, who, with Stubb and Flask, had thus far been eyeing his superior with increasing surprise, but at last seemed struck with a thought which somewhat explained all the wonder. "Captain Ahab, I have heard of Moby-Dick—but it was not Moby-Dick that took off thy leg?"

"Who told thee that?" cried Ahab; then pausing, "Aye, Starbuck; aye, my hearties all round; it was Moby-Dick that dismasted me; Moby-Dick that brought me to this dead stump I stand on now. Aye, aye," he shouted with a terrific, loud, animal sob, like that of a heart-stricken moose; "Aye, aye! it was that accursed white whale that razeed me; made a poor, pegging lubber of me forever and a day!" Then tossing both arms, with measureless imprecations he shouted out: "Aye, aye! and I'll chase him round Good Hope, and round the Horn, and round the Norway Maelstrom, and round perdition's flames before I give him up. And this is what ye have shipped for, men! to chase that white whale on both sides of land, and over all sides of earth, till he spouts black blood and rolls fin out. What say ye, men, will ye splice[7] hands on it, now? I think ye do look brave." B

"Aye, aye!" shouted the harpooneers and seamen, running closer to the excited old man: "A sharp eye for the White Whale; a sharp lance for Moby-Dick!"

"God bless ye," he seemed to half sob and half shout. "God bless ye, men. Steward! go draw the great measure of grog.[8] But what's this long face about, Mr. Starbuck; wilt thou not chase the white whale? art not game for Moby-Dick?"

"I am game for his crooked jaw, and for the

5. **fan-tail:** spread the tail like a fan.
6. **parmacetty:** a sperm whale; dialect for *spermaceti.*
7. **splice:** join; a nautical term for the weaving of rope ends.
8. **grog:** watered-down liquor drunk by sailors.

CLOSURE

In class discussion, have students suggest words and phrases that characterize Ahab and his relationship to Moby-Dick.

READING CHECK TEST

1. Ahab offers an ounce of ______ to the one who first sights Moby-Dick. *gold*
2. Queequeg says that Moby-Dick has many ______ in him. *irons* or *harpoons*
3. All the crew except ______ join in the excitement of the search for Moby-Dick. *Starbuck*
4. Ahab says that all visible objects are but as ______ masks. *pasteboard*
5. Ahab uses the inverted heads of ______ as a chalice from which to drink wine. *harpoon shafts*

jaws of Death too, Captain Ahab, if it fairly comes in the way of the business we follow: but I came here to hunt whales, not my commander's vengeance. How many barrels will thy vengeance yield thee even if thou gettest it, Captain Ahab? It will not fetch thee much in our Nantucket market."

"Nantucket market! Hoot! But come closer, Starbuck; thou requirest a little lower layer. If money's to be the measurer, man, and the accountants have computed their great counting-house the globe by girdling it with guineas, one to every three parts of an inch; then, let me tell thee, that my vengeance will fetch a great premium *here*!"

"He smites his chest," whispered Stubb, "what's that for? Methinks it rings most vast, but hollow."

"Vengeance on a dumb brute!" cried Starbuck, "that simply smote thee from blindest instinct! Madness! To be enraged with a dumb thing, Captain Ahab, seems blasphemous."

A "Hark ye yet again—the little lower layer. All visible objects, man, are but as pasteboard masks. But in each event—in the living act, the undoubted deed—there, some unknown but still reasoning thing puts forth the moldings of its features from behind the unreasoning mask. If man will strike, strike through the mask! How can the prisoner reach outside except by thrusting through the wall? To me, the white whale is that wall, shoved near to me. Sometimes I think there's naught beyond. But 'tis enough. He tasks me; he heaps me; I see in him outrageous strength, with an inscrutable malice sinewing it. That inscrutable thing is chiefly what I hate; and be the white whale agent, or be the white whale principal, I will wreak that hate upon him. Talk not to me of blasphemy, man; I'd strike the sun if it insulted me. For could the sun do that, then could I do the other; since there is ever a sort of fair play herein, jealousy presiding over all creations. But not my master, man, is even that fair play. Who's over me? Truth hath no confines. Take off thine eye! More intolerable than fiends' glarings is a doltish stare! So, so; thou reddenest and palest; my heat has melted thee to anger-glow. But look ye, Starbuck, what is said in heat, that thing unsays itself. There are men from whom warm words are small indignity. I meant not to incense thee. Let it go. Look! see yonder Turkish cheeks of spotted tawn—living, breathing pictures painted by the sun. The pagan leopards—the unrecking and unworshiping things, that live, and seek, and give no reasons for the torrid life they feel! The crew, man, the crew! Are they not one and all with Ahab, in this matter of the whale? See Stubb! he laughs! See yonder Chilean! he snorts to think of it. Stand up amid the general hurricane, thy one tossed sapling cannot, Starbuck! And what is it? Reckon it. 'Tis but to help strike a fin; no wondrous feat for Starbuck. What is it more? From this one poor hunt, then, the best lance out of all Nantucket, surely he will not hang back, when every foremast-hand has clutched a whetstone? Ah! constrainings seize thee; I see! the billow lifts thee! Speak, but speak!—Aye, aye! thy silence, then, *that* voices thee. (*Aside*) Something shot from my dilated nostrils, he has inhaled it in his lungs. Starbuck now is mine; cannot oppose me now, without rebellion."

"God keep me!—keep us all!" murmured Starbuck, lowly.

But in his joy at the enchanted, tacit acquiescence of the mate, Ahab did not hear his foreboding invocation; nor yet the low laugh from the hold; nor yet the presaging vibrations of the winds in the cordage; nor yet the hollow flap of the sails against the masts, as for a moment their hearts sank in. For again Starbuck's downcast eyes lighted up with the stubborness of life; the subterranean laugh died away; the winds blew on; the sails filled out; the ship heaved and rolled as before. Ah, ye admonitions and warnings! why stay ye not when ye come? But rather are ye predictions than warnings, ye shadows! Yet not so much predictions from without, as verifications of the foregoing things within. For with little external to constrain us, the innermost necessities in our being, these still drive us on.

"The measure! the measure!" cried Ahab.

B Receiving the brimming pewter, and turning to the harpooneers, he ordered them to produce their weapons. Then ranging them before him near the capstan,[9] with their harpoons in their hands, while his three mates stood at his side with their lances, and the rest of the ship's company formed a circle round the group; he stood for an instant searchingly eyeing every man of his crew. But those wild eyes met his, as the bloodshot eyes of the prairie wolves meet the eye of their leader, ere he rushes on at their head in the trail of the bison; but, alas! only to fall into the hidden snare of the Indian.

9. **capstan:** a large cylinder around which cables are wound.

A. Metaphor
The passage beginning, "Hark ye yet again" is one of Ahab's great soliloquies. Its vision of the world as pasteboard masks, and its exhortation, "Strike through the mask!" are the pinnacles of Melville's negative transcendentalism (see page 186). Discuss the metaphor of the masks—do your students feel it is applicable to life as they know it? How can we live according to the directive, "Strike through the mask"?

B. Expansion
Here begins the "communion" scene with its powerful allusion to a religious sacrament. (Some students may need the ceremony of communion explained to them.)

ANALYZING THE NOVEL

Identifying Facts

1. To assemble so that he can address them.

2. According to Ahab, Moby-Dick has a white head, a wrinkled brow, and a crooked jaw. He also has three holes punctured in his starboard (right) fluke. He fantails curiously, and many harpoons are twisted in him.

3. To sharpen the crew's eagerness to chase and kill the great white whale.

4. He orders them to tilt their harpoons upwards, so that liquor can be poured into the sockets. He then orders them to drink and swear to the death of Moby-Dick.

5. The premonitions of the low laugh in the hold and the vibrations of the winds in the cordage, and the comparison of the Leyden jar.

Interpreting Meanings

6. Starbuck says that Ahab's thirst for vengeance on a dumb brute seems blasphemous.

Starbuck's misgivings suggest that he also has a balanced sense of the order of the universe, and that he foresees that Ahab's unnatural quest for vengeance

A. Humanities Connection: Discussing the Illustration

Contrast this ship's log with the way a ship's log would look today. The antique log looks charming, but critic Alfred Kazin points out that "New Bedford whaling captains were the worst slave drivers on the seven seas."

A

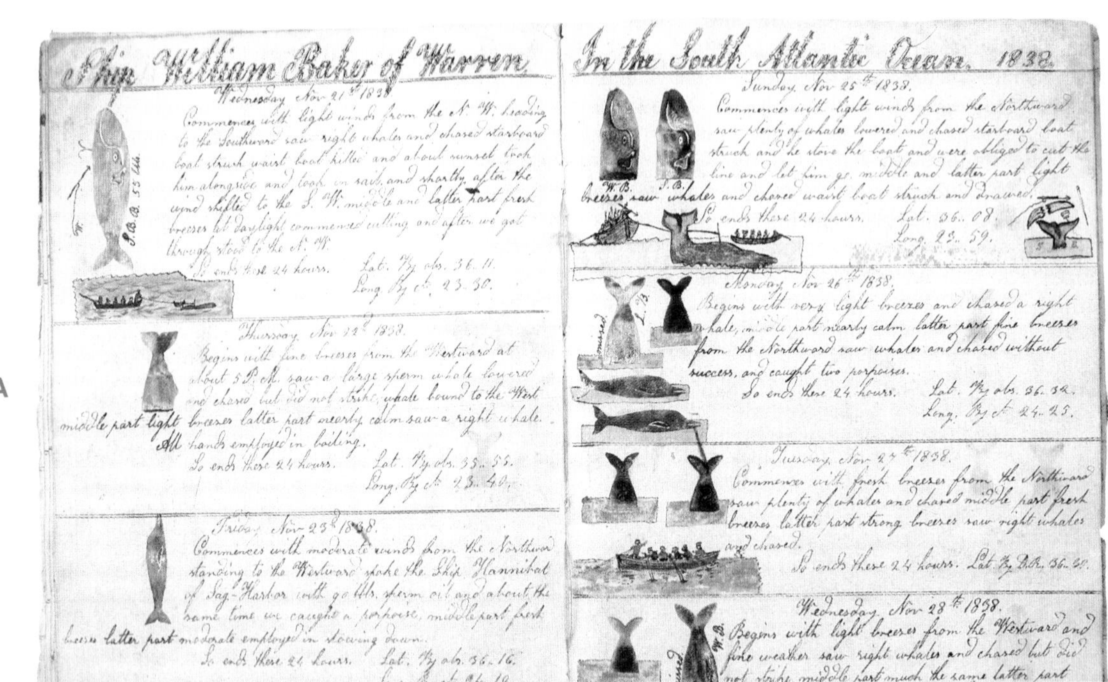

Ship William Baker of Warren

Wednesday Nov 21st 1838

Commences with light winds from the N. W. heading to the Southward saw right whales and chased starboard boat struck waist boat killed and about sunset took him alongside and took in sail, and shortly after the wind shifted to the S. W. middle and latter part fresh breezes at daylight commenced cutting and after we got through stood to the N. W.

So ends these 24 hours. Lat. By obs. 36. 11. Long. By ch. 23. 30.

Thursday Nov 22d 1838.

Begins with fine breezes from the Westward at about 5 P. M. saw a large sperm whale lowered and chased but did not strike, whale bound to the West middle part light breezes latter part nearly calm saw a right whale. All hands employed in boiling.

So ends these 24 hours. Lat. By obs. 35. 55. Long. By ch. 23. 40.

Friday Nov 23d 1838.

Commences with moderate winds from the Northward standing to the Westward spoke the Ship Hannibal of Sag-Harbor with 90 bbls. sperm oil and about the same time we caught a porpoise, middle part fresh breezes latter part moderate employed in stowing down.

So ends these 24 hours. Lat. By obs. 36. 16. Long. By ch. 24. 10

In the South Atlantic Ocean. 1838.

Sunday Nov 25th 1838.

Commences with light winds from the Northward saw plenty of whales lowered and chased starboard boat struck and he stove the boat and were obliged to cut the line and let him go. middle and latter part light breezes saw whales and chased waist boat struck and drawed.

So ends these 24 hours. Lat. 36. 08. Long. 23. 59.

Monday Nov 26th 1838.

Begins with very light breezes and chased a right whale, middle part nearly calm latter part fine breezes from the Northward saw whales and chased without success, and caught two porpoises.

So ends these 24 hours. Lat. By obs. 36. 32. Long. By ch. 24. 25.

Tuesday Nov 27th 1838.

Commences with fresh breezes from the Northward saw plenty of whales and chased middle part fresh breezes latter part strong breezes saw right whales and chased.

So ends these 24 hours. Lat. By D. R. 36. 40.

Wednesday Nov 28th 1838.

Begins with light breezes from the Westward and fine weather saw right whales and chased but did not strike, middle part much the same latter part

Two pages from the daily logbook of the ship *William Baker* for November 1838. These pages chronicle nine days and the images symbolize successes and failures in the hunting of whales.

New Bedford Whaling Museum, New Bedford, Massachusetts.

"Drink and pass!" he cried, handing the heavy, charged flagon to the nearest seaman. "The crew alone now drink. Round with it, round! Short drafts—long swallows, men; 'tis hot as Satan's hoof. So, so; it goes round excellently. It spiralizes in ye; forks out at the serpent-snapping eye. Well done; almost drained. That way it went, this way it comes. Hand it me—here's a hollow! Men, ye seem the years; so brimming life is gulped and gone. Steward, refill!

"Attend now, my braves. I have mustered ye all round this capstan; and ye mates, flank me with your lances; and ye harpooneers, stand there with your irons; and ye, stout mariners, ring me in, that I may in some sort revive a noble custom of my fisherman fathers before me. O men, you will yet see that——Ha! boy, come back? bad pennies come not sooner. Hand it me. Why, now, this pewter had run brimming again, wert not thou St. Vitus' imp[10]—away, thou ague!

"Advance, ye mates! Cross your lances full before me. Well done! Let me touch the axis." So saying, with extended arm, he grasped the three level, radiating lances at their crossed center; while so doing, suddenly and nervously twitched them, meanwhile glancing intently from Starbuck to Stubb, from Stubb to Flask. It seemed as though, by some nameless, interior volition, he would fain have shocked into them the same fiery emotion accumulated within the Leyden jar[11] of his own magnetic life. The three mates quailed before his strong, sustained, and mystic aspect. Stubb and Flask looked sideways from him; the honest eye of Starbuck fell downright.

"In vain!" cried Ahab; "but, maybe, 'tis well. For did ye three but once take the full-forced shock, then mine own electric thing, *that* had perhaps expired from out me. Perchance, too, it would have dropped ye dead. Perchance ye need it not. Down lances! And now, ye mates, I do

10. **St. Vitus' imp:** Saint Vitus is the patron saint of people ill with chorea, a nervous disorder characterized by irregular, jerking movements.

11. **Leyden jar:** a device for storing electrical charges, consisting of a glass jar coated with tinfoil on the outside, and a metal rod connected to the lining and passing through the lid.

will lead to disaster.

7. Starbuck is probably afraid of the captain.

8. One paraphrase might be: People, objects, and events are lifeless, irrational, and static until the energy of an action or deed gives them meaning.

Ahab says that men are imprisoned by a wall until they "strike through the mask"; presumably, he means that men achieve freedom only through actions or deeds.

9. He says he sees in the whale "outrageous strength" and "inscrutable malice." He hates above all the inscrutable quality of the whale, and he vows that he will bring the beast and its hatred under control.

Perhaps that nothingness is behind the face of evil.

10. Note especially Ahab's comparison of himself to the Pope and of the mates to his "cardinals." Melville's allusion to washing "the feet of beggars" refers to a traditional ceremony on Maundy Thursday when the Pope, as a sign of humility, washes the feet of twelve poor men.

Many students may suggest that the details of the scene signify that Ahab's quest is somehow blasphemous.

11. Students' answers will differ, although for most of them the drinking scene will probably create an impression of Ahab as a madman.

12. The statement suggests Ahab's qualities of pride, determination, and ferocity. In his prior statement, he said that he would "wreak . . . hate" upon the "inscrutable thing"—perhaps this statement suggests that he regards the power of the whale (and maybe the inscrutable power of God?) as hateful and worthy of attack.

13. Students may again point to the premonitions on page 307 (the "low laugh from the hold" and the "presaging vibrations of the winds in the cordage"), as well as to Melville's apostrophe beginning "Ah, ye admonitions and warnings!"

appoint ye three cupbearers to my three pagan kinsmen there—you three most honorable gentlemen and noblemen, my valiant harpooneers. Disdain the task? What, when the great Pope washes the feet of beggars, using his tiara for ewer?[12] Oh, my sweet cardinals! your own condescension, *that* shall bend ye to it. I do not order ye; ye will it. Cut your seizings and draw the poles, ye harpooneers!"

Silently obeying the order, the three harpooneers now stood with the detached iron part of their harpoons, some three feet long, held, barbs up, before him.

"Stab me not with that keen steel! Cant[13] them; cant them over! know ye not the goblet end? Turn up the socket? So, so; now, ye cupbearers, advance. The irons! take them; hold them while I fill!" Forthwith, slowly going from one officer to the other, he brimmed the harpoon sockets with the fiery waters from the pewter.

"Now, three to three, ye stand. Commend the murderous chalices! Bestow them, ye who are now made parties to this indissoluble league. Ha! Starbuck! but the deed is done! Yon ratifying sun now waits to sit upon it. Drink, ye harpooneers! drink and swear, ye men that man the deathful whaleboat's bow—Death to Moby-Dick! God hunt us all, if we do not hunt Moby-Dick to his death!" The long, barbed steel goblets were lifted; and to cries and maledictions against the white whale, the spirits were simultaneously quaffed down with a hiss. Starbuck paled, and turned, and shivered. Once more, and finally, the replenished pewter went the rounds among the frantic crew, when, waving his free hand to them, they all dispersed; and Ahab retired within his cabin.

12. **tiara for ewer:** crown for a pitcher; a reference to the practice of washing the feet of the poor on Holy Thursday, in imitation of Jesus's washing the feet of his disciples.
13. **cant:** overturn or tilt.

Responding to the Novel

Analyzing the Novel

Identifying Facts

1. After his endless, obsessive pacing of the deck, what unprecedented command does Ahab issue to the crew?
2. What do you learn from Ahab's dialogue with his crew about Moby-Dick's appearance?
3. Explain Ahab's purpose in meeting with the crew.
4. Toward the end of the chapter, what does Ahab order the mates to do with their lances?
5. After the story is underway, Melville shifts his **point of view.** Though Ishmael is still the narrator, some passages seem to be told from an **omniscient point of view.** What details in this chapter seem to be those that only an omniscient narrator would know?

Interpreting Meanings

6. Only Starbuck has misgivings about Ahab's pursuit of the great white whale. What are these misgivings? What do they tell us about Starbuck's **character**?
7. Why do you think Starbuck gives in to Ahab?
8. In your own words, explain the idea Ahab expresses in his famous **metaphor** comparing visible objects to "pasteboard masks" (page 307). In what way does Ahab see human beings as prisoners, and how does he hope to break out of his own "prison"?
9. Describe the qualities and mysteries that the white whale represents for Ahab. What do you think Ahab means when he says the white whale "is that wall . . . Sometimes I think there's naught beyond"? (See page 307.)
10. What details in the drinking scene suggest a **parody** or mockery of a religious ritual? What do you think the scene signifies about Ahab's quest?
11. What has the drinking scene revealed about Ahab's **character**? Do you have the impression that he is a clear-headed, if impassioned, crusader? Or that he is an unstable madman? Do you pity him or fear him? Cite specific details that contribute to your impression of Ahab.
12. What is suggested about Ahab's **character** when he says "Talk not to me of blasphemy, man; I'd strike the sun if it insulted me"? (See page 307.) What did he say prior to this that sounded like blasphemy—that is, mockery of God?
13. What details in this chapter do you think **foreshadow** disaster and destruction for the *Pequod* and her crew?

Supplementary Support Materials
1. Vocabulary Activity Worksheet (*CCB*)
2. Review and Response Worksheet: Theme (*CCB*)
3. Selection Test (*CCB*)

Developing Vocabulary
The following words from the novel are tested in the Selection Test. (See also Vocabulary Activity Worksheet.)

malignity	laceration
ignoble	to dissemble
ubiquitous	ire

Preparation
Establishing a Purpose. Question 11, page 316, suggests that the *Pequod* and her company can be seen as a microcosm—a world in miniature. Have students read this chapter to decide whether they agree with this statement.

A. Foreshadowing
? What indications are there, in Ishmael's opening statement, that disaster looms? (Ishmael mentions the "dread in my soul" and the "wild, mystical" feeling. Also, by this time, the reader realizes just what men who undertake revenge against the "murderous monster" are in for.)

B. Responding
? Given the horrible stories that are known about Moby-Dick, why do you suppose the men are willing to continue the search? (They have been worked to a fevered pitch by Ahab; they have their reputations as whalers to consider; they are afraid, to some extent, of Ahab.)

Following the ritual on the quarter-deck, when Ahab baptized the harpoons in liquor and revealed the object of his chase, we hear three characters privately reflect on their journey's goal. Ahab recognizes himself as a driven man; Starbuck reflects on what he sees as the captain's insanity; and Stubb fatalistically resigns himself to whatever destiny may bring. That night a squall threatens to strike the ship, and the crew become tense. Now at last, however, we are about to meet the object of Ahab's obsession—the white whale, Moby-Dick.

Moby-Dick

A I, Ishmael, was one of that crew; my shouts had gone up with the rest; my oath had been welded with theirs; and stronger I shouted, and more did I hammer and clinch my oath, because of the dread in my soul. A wild, mystical, sympathetical feeling was in me; Ahab's quenchless feud seemed mine. With greedy ears I learned the history of that murderous monster against whom I and all the others had taken our oaths of violence and revenge.

For some time past, though at intervals only, the unaccompanied, secluded White Whale had haunted those uncivilized seas mostly frequented by the Sperm Whale fishermen. But not all of them knew of his existence; only a few of them, comparatively, had knowingly seen him; while the number who as yet had actually and knowingly given battle to him, was small indeed. For, owing to the large number of whale-cruisers; the disorderly way they were sprinkled over the entire watery circumference, many of them adventurously pushing their quest along solitary latitudes, so as seldom or never for a whole twelvemonth or more on a stretch, to encounter a single news-telling sail of any sort; the inordinate length of each separate voyage; the irregularity of the times of sailing from home; all these, with other circumstances, direct and indirect, long obstructed the spread through the whole worldwide whaling-fleet of the special individualizing tidings concerning Moby-Dick. It was hardly to be doubted that several vessels reported to have encountered, at such or such a time, or on such or such a meridian, a Sperm Whale of uncommon magnitude and malignity,[1] which whale, after doing great mischief to his assailants, had completely escaped them; to some minds it was not an unfair presumption, I say, that the whale in question must have been no other than Moby-Dick. Yet as of late the Sperm Whale fishery had been marked by various and not unfrequent instances of great ferocity, cunning, and malice in the monster attacked; therefore it was, that those who by accident ignorantly gave battle to Moby-Dick; such hunters, perhaps, for the most part, were content to ascribe the peculiar terror he bred, more, as it were, to the perils of the Sperm Whale fishery at large, than to the individual cause. In that way, mostly, the disastrous encounter between Ahab and the whale had hitherto been popularly regarded.

And as for those who, previously hearing of the White Whale, by chance caught sight of him, in the beginning of the thing they had every one of them, almost, as boldly and fearlessly lowered for him, as for any other whale of that species. But at length, such calamities did ensue in these assaults—not restricted to sprained wrists and ankles, broken limbs, or devouring amputations—but fatal to the last degree of fatality; those repeated disastrous repulses, all accumulating and piling their terrors upon Moby-Dick; those things had gone far to shake the fortitude of many brave hunters, to whom the story of the White Whale had eventually come.

Nor did wild rumors of all sorts fail to exaggerate and still the more horrify the true histories B of these deadly encounters. For not only do fabulous rumors naturally grow out of the very body of all surprising terrible events—as the smitten tree gives birth to its fungi—but, in maritime life, far more than in that of terra firma, wild rumors abound, wherever there is any adequate reality for them to cling to. And as the sea surpasses the land in this matter, so the whale fishery surpasses every other sort of maritime life, in the wonderfulness and fearfulness of the rumors which sometimes circulate there. For not only are whalemen as a body unexempt from that ignorance and superstitiousness hereditary to all sailors; but of all sailors, they are by all odds the most directly brought into contact with whatever is appallingly astonishing in the sea; face to face they not only eye its greatest marvels, but, hand to jaw, give battle to them. Alone, in such remotest waters, that though you sailed a thousand miles, and passed a thousand shores, you would not come to

1. **malignity:** intense ill will.

Plot of "Moby-Dick": Ishmael learns more about Moby-Dick, partly from stories about him that pass from ship to ship, and about Ahab's loss of his leg and his subsequent fixation on the great white whale.

any chiseled hearthstone, or aught hospitable beneath that part of the sun; in such latitudes and longitudes, pursuing too such a calling as he does, the whaleman is wrapped by influences all tending to make his fancy pregnant with many a mighty birth.

A No wonder, then, that ever gathering volume from the mere transit over the widest watery spaces, the outblown rumors of the White Whale did in the end incorporate with themselves all manner of morbid hints and half-formed fetal suggestions of supernatural agencies, which eventually invested Moby-Dick with new terrors unborrowed from anything that visibly appears. So that in many cases such a panic did he finally strike, that few who by those rumors, at least, had heard of the White Whale, few of those hunters were willing to encounter the perils of his jaw.

But there were still other and more vital practical influences at work. Not even at the present day has the original prestige of the Sperm Whale, as fearfully distinguished from all other species of the leviathan,[2] died out of the minds of the whalemen as a body. There are those this day among them, who, though intelligent and courageous enough in offering battle to the Greenland or Right whale, would perhaps—either from professional inexperience, or incompetency, or timidity, decline a contest with the Sperm Whale; at any rate, there are plenty of whalemen, especially among those whaling nations not sailing under the American flag, who have never hostilely encountered the Sperm Whale, but whose sole knowledge of the leviathan is restricted to the ignoble monster primitively pursued in the North; seated on their hatches, these men will hearken with a childish fireside interest and awe, to the wild, strange tales of Southern whaling. Nor is the preeminent tremendousness of the great Sperm Whale anywhere more feelingly comprehended than on board of those prows which stem him. . . .

So that overawed by the rumors and portents concerning him, not a few of the fishermen recalled, in reference to Moby-Dick, the earlier days of the Sperm Whale fishery, when it was oftentimes hard to induce long-practiced Right whalemen to embark in the perils of this new and daring warfare; such men protesting that although other leviathans might be hopefully pursued, yet to chase and point lance at such an apparition as the Sperm Whale was not for mortal man. That to attempt it, would be inevitably to be torn into a quick eternity. On this head, there are some remarkable documents that may be consulted.

Nevertheless, some there were, who even in the face of these things, were ready to give chase to Moby-Dick; and a still greater number who, chancing only to hear of him distantly and vaguely, without the specific details of any certain calamity, and without superstitious accompaniments, were sufficiently hardy not to flee from the battle if offered.

One of the wild suggestions referred to, as at last coming to be linked with the White Whale in the minds of the superstitiously inclined, was the unearthly conceit that Moby-Dick was ubiquitous; that he had actually been encountered in opposite latitudes at one and the same instant of time.

Nor, credulous as such minds must have been, was this conceit altogether without some faint show of superstitious probability. For as the secrets of the currents in the seas have never yet been divulged, even to the most erudite research, so the hidden ways of the Sperm Whale when beneath the surface remain, in great part, unaccountable to his pursuers; and from time to time have originated the most curious and contradictory speculations regarding them, especially concerning the mystic modes whereby, after sounding to a great depth, he transports himself with such vast swiftness to the most widely distant points.

It is a thing well known to both American and English whaleships, and also a thing placed upon authoritative record years ago by Scoresby, that some whales have been captured far north in the Pacific, in whose bodies have been found the barbs of harpoons darted in the Greenland seas. Nor is it to be gainsaid, that in some of these instances it has been declared that the interval of time between the two assaults could not have exceeded very many days. Hence, by inference, it has been believed by some whalemen, that the Nor' West Passage,[3] so long a problem to man, was never a problem to the whale. . . .

Forced into familiarity, then, with such prodigies as these, and knowing that after repeated, intrepid

2. **leviathan** (lə·vī′ə·thən): huge sea monster.

3. **Nor' West Passage:** sailors long hoped to discover a river joining the Atlantic and Pacific oceans through Canada.

A. Supernatural Elements
Note how elements of the supernatural are brought into the work.

? Compare Melville's use of the supernatural with that of Hawthorne and Poe. Does Melville intend for the reader to believe it? Do Hawthorne and Poe? (Melville uses the supernatural in a symbolic way to emphasize the conflict between good and evil. Hawthorne is more concerned with the psychological effects of sin. Poe's Gothic tales are not to be taken literally.)

A. Expansion
In fact, whales in flight do not turn around and attack pursuing boats.

assaults, the White Whale had escaped alive, it cannot be much matter of surprise that some whalemen should go still further in their superstitions, declaring Moby-Dick not only ubiquitous, but immortal (for immortality is but ubiquity in time); that though groves of spears should be planted in his flanks, he would still swim away unharmed; or if indeed he should ever be made to spout thick blood, such a sight would be but a ghastly deception; for again in unensanguined[4] billows hundreds of leagues away, his unsullied jet would once more be seen.

But even stripped of these supernatural surmisings, there was enough in the earthly make and incontestable character of the monster to strike the imagination with unwonted power. For, it was not so much his uncommon bulk that so much distinguished him from other sperm whales, but, as was elsewhere thrown out—a peculiar snow-white, wrinkled forehead, and a high, pyramidical white hump. These were his prominent features; the tokens whereby, even in the limitless, uncharted seas, he revealed his identity, at a long distance, to those who knew him.

The rest of his body was so streaked, and spotted, and marbled with the same shrouded hue, that, in the end, he had gained his distinctive appellation of the White Whale; a name, indeed, literally justified by his vivid aspect, when seen gliding at high noon through a dark blue sea, leaving a milky-way wake of creamy foam, all spangled with golden gleamings.

Nor was it his unwonted magnitude, nor his remarkable hue, nor yet his deformed lower jaw, that so much invested the whale with natural terror, as that unexampled, intelligent malignity which, according to specific accounts, he had over and over again evinced in his assaults. More than all, his treacherous retreats struck more of dismay than perhaps aught else. For, when swimming before his exulting pursuers, with every apparent
A symptom of alarm, he had several times been known to turn round suddenly, and, bearing down upon them, either stave[5] their boats to splinters, or drive them back in consternation to their ship.

Already several fatalities had attended his chase. But though similar disasters, however little bruited[6] ashore, were by no means unusual in the

4. **unensanguined:** unbloodied.
5. **stave:** smash.
6. **bruited:** reported.

Capturing the Sperm Whale after Ambrose Garneray (c. 1850). Colored lithograph.

Peabody Museum of Salem, Salem, Massachusetts.

Humanities Connection: Discussing the Fine Art

Another Garneray copy (see page 297). The size of the whale compared with that of the men is, if anything, underestimated. Note the man on top of the whale. The ship at right has a dead whale floating beside it in preparation for processing, while birds hover above and another boat sets out. This illustration shows why whaling was such a hazardous undertaking.

A. Expansion
Note the prejudices of the day: Whales were considered unintelligent and malign, whereas we today believe them to be the opposite.

B. Responding
? What is the definition of *monomania*? (A concentration on a single idea or object that becomes excessive to the point of derangement.) Can you imagine a story of monomania and of a quest for an elusive, unfathomable, fateful truth being set in some other place or time? (Perhaps someone's search today for the wisest guru; the artist's struggle to produce the perfect work of art)

A fishery; yet, in most instances, such seemed the White Whale's infernal aforethought of ferocity, that every dismembering or death that he caused was not wholly regarded as having been inflicted by an unintelligent agent.

Judge, then, to what pitches of inflamed, distracted fury the minds of his more desperate hunters were impelled, when amid the chips of chewed boats, and the sinking limbs of torn comrades, they swam out of the white curds of the whale's direful wrath into the serene, exasperating sunlight, that smiled on, as if at a birth or a bridal.

His three boats stove around him, and oars and men both whirling in the eddies, one captain, seizing the line-knife from his broken prow, had dashed at the whale, as an Arkansas duelist at his foe, blindly seeking with a six-inch blade to reach the fathom-deep life of the whale. That captain was Ahab. And then it was, that suddenly sweeping his sickle-shaped lower jaw beneath him, Moby-Dick had reaped away Ahab's leg, as a mower a blade of grass in the field. No turbaned Turk, no hired Venetian or Malay, could have smote him with more seeming malice. Small reason was there to doubt, then, that ever since that almost fatal encounter, Ahab had cherished a wild vindictiveness against the whale, all the more fell for that in his frantic morbidness he at last came to identify with him, not only all his bodily woes, but all his intellectual and spiritual exasperations. The White Whale swam before him as the monomaniac incarnation of all those malicious agencies which some deep men feel eating in them, till they are left living on with half a heart and half a lung. That intangible malignity which has been from the beginning; to whose dominion even the modern Christians ascribe one-half of the worlds; which the ancient Ophites of the east reverenced in their statue devil—Ahab did not fall down and worship it like them; but deliriously transferring its idea to the abhorred white whale, he pitted himself, all mutilated, against it. All that most maddens and torments; all that stirs up the lees of things; all truth with malice in it; all that cracks the sinews and cakes the brain; all the subtle demonisms of life and thought; all evil, to crazy Ahab, were visibly personified and made practically assailable in Moby-Dick. He piled upon the whale's white hump the sum of all the general rage and hate felt by his whole race from Adam down; and then, as if his chest had been a mortar, he burst his hot heart's shell upon it.

It is not probable that this monomania in him took its instant rise at the precise time of his bodily dismemberment. Then, in darting at the monster, knife in hand, he had but given loose to a sudden, passionate, corporal animosity; and when he received the stroke that tore him, he probably but felt the agonizing bodily laceration, but nothing more. Yet, when by this collision forced to turn toward home, and for long months of days and weeks, Ahab and anguish lay stretched together in one hammock, rounding in mid-winter that dreary, howling Patagonian Cape; then it was, that his torn body and gashed soul bled into one another; and so interfusing, made him mad. That it was only then, on the homeward voyage after the encounter, that the final monomania seized him, seems all but certain from the fact that, at intervals during the passage, he was a raving lunatic; and, though unlimbed of a leg, yet such vital strength yet lurked in his Egyptian chest, and was moreover intensified by his delirium, that his mates were forced to lace him fast, even there, as he sailed, raving in his hammock. In a straitjacket, he swung to the mad rockings of the gales. And, when running into more sufferable latitudes, the ship, with mild stun'sails spread, floated across the tranquil tropics, and, to all appearances, the old man's delirium seemed left behind him with the Cape Horn swells, and he came forth from his dark den into the blessed light and air; even then, when he bore that firm, collected front, however pale, and issued his calm orders once again; and his mates thanked God the direful madness was now gone; even then, Ahab, in his hidden self, raved on. Human madness is oftentimes a cunning and most feline thing. When you think it fled, it may have but become transfigured into some still subtler form. Ahab's full lunacy subsided not, but deepeningly contracted; like the unabated Hudson, when that noble Northman flows narrowly, but unfathomably through the Highland gorge. But, as in his narrow-flowing monomania, not one jot of Ahab's broad madness had been left behind; so in that broad madness, not one jot of his great natural intellect had perished. That before living agent, now became the living instrument. If such a furious trope[7] may stand, his special lunacy stormed his general sanity, and carried it, and turned all its concentrated cannon upon its own mad mark; so that far from having lost his

7. **trope:** a figure of speech.

CLOSURE

In class discussion, have students suggest phrases and sentences that describe Moby-Dick as Ishmael has heard about him.

READING CHECK TEST

1. Ishmael shares the crew's excitement about hunting for Moby-Dick. *False*

2. The white color is not the only distinctive feature of Moby-Dick. *True*

3. When the whale takes his leg, Ahab loses all will to live. *False*

4. The people of Nantucket know Ahab as a demented man. *False*

5. Ishmael believes that nothing good can come of the search for Moby-Dick. *True*

strength, Ahab, to that one end, did now possess a thousandfold more potency than ever he had sanely brought to bear upon any one reasonable object. . . .

A Now, in his heart, Ahab had some glimpse of this, namely: all my means are sane, my motive and my object mad. Yet without power to kill, or change, or shun the fact, he likewise knew that to mankind he did long dissemble; in some sort, did still. But that thing of his dissembling was only subject to his perceptibility, not to his will determinate. Nevertheless, so well did he succeed in that dissembling, that when with ivory leg he stepped ashore at last, no Nantucketer thought him otherwise than but naturally grieved, and that to the quick, with the terrible casualty which had overtaken him.

The report of his undeniable delirium at sea was likewise popularly ascribed to a kindred cause. And so too, all the added moodiness which always afterward, to the very day of sailing in the Pequod on the present voyage, sat brooding on his brow. Nor is it so very unlikely that, far from distrusting his fitness for another whaling voyage, on account of such dark symptoms, the calculating people of that prudent isle were inclined to harbor the conceit that for those very reasons he was all the better qualified and set on edge for a pursuit so full of rage and wildness as the bloody hunt of whales. Gnawed within and scorched without, with the infixed, unrelenting fangs of some incurable idea, such a one, could he be found, would seem the very man to dart his iron and lift his lance against the most appalling of all brutes. Or, if for any reason thought to be corporeally incapacitated for that, yet such a one would seem superlatively competent to cheer and howl on his underlings to the attack. But be all this as it may, certain it is that with the mad secret of his unabated rage bolted up and keyed in him, Ahab had purposely sailed upon the present voyage with the one only and all-engrossing object of hunting the White Whale. Had any of his old acquaintances on shore but half dreamed of what was lurking in him then, how soon would their aghast and righteous souls have wrenched the ship from such a fiendish man! They were bent on profitable cruises, the profit to be counted down in dollars from the mint. He was intent on an audacious, immitigable, and supernatural revenge.

Here, then, was this gray-headed, ungodly old man, chasing with curses a Job's whale[8] round the world, at the head of a crew, too, chiefly made up of mongrel renegades and castaways and cannibals—morally enfeebled also by the incompetence of mere unaided virtue or right-mindedness in Starbuck, the invulnerable jollity of indifference and recklessness in Stubb, and the prevading mediocrity in Flask. Such a crew, so officered, seemed specially picked and packed by some infernal fatality to help him to his monomaniac revenge. How it was that they so aboundingly responded to the old man's ire—by what evil magic their souls were possessed, that at times his hate seemed almost theirs; the White Whale as much their insufferable foe as his; how all this came to be—what the White Whale was to them, or how to their unconscious understandings, also, in some dim, unsuspected way, he might have seemed the gliding great demon of the seas of life—all this to explain, would be to dive deeper than Ishmael can go. The subterranean miner that works in us all, how can one tell whither leads his shaft by the ever-shifting, muffled sound of his pick? Who does not feel the irresistible arm drag? B What skiff in tow of a seventy-four[9] can stand still? For one, I gave myself up to the abandonment of the time and the place; but while yet all arush to encounter the whale, could see naught in that brute but the deadliest ill.

8. **a Job's whale:** a curse or affliction. Job, in the Bible, was visited with grievous afflictions as a test of his faith in God.

9. **skiff . . . seventy-four:** a small boat being pulled by a large one.

A. Narration

Note that the first-person narrator, Ishmael, shows us the inner thoughts of another character, Ahab. This is technically a violation of sound creative writing principles. There is no confrontation scene between Ishmael and Ahab in *Moby-Dick,* yet it was important to show us something of Ahab's inner life, so Melville resorted to this method.

? Does this method work? Would you recommend it to other writers? (*Moby-Dick* burst the bounds of conventional narrative, and got away with it through its intellectual and emotional power.)

B. Interpretation

? What does Ishmael mean by "the subterranean miner that works in us all?" (Answers may vary. It may mean our ceaseless desire for knowledge and self-knowledge, or our unconscious, or fate.)

ANALYZING THE NOVEL
Identifying Facts
1. Ishmael has been caught up in the crew's excitement, even though he feels a "dread" in his soul.
2. Because of the great length of individual whaling voyages and the wide diffusion of whaling vessels.
3. Because of whalers' direct contact with the most terrifying creatures of the sea, and because of their long periods of isolation.
4. He is uncommonly large, with an odd, snow-white wrinkled forehead and a high white hump. The rest of his body is streaked and marbled, and his lower jaw is deformed.
5. He transferred to the whale all his bodily woes, as well as his "intellectual and spiritual exasperations."
The whale personified all evil for Ahab.
6. Monomania is a mental disorder characterized by a consuming obsession with one idea or action.
According to Ishmael, Ahab became monomaniacal sometime after his encounter with Moby-Dick, during the long months of his recuperation.
7. Ahab only pretends to have recovered from his madness.

Responding to the Novel

Analyzing the Novel

Identifying Facts

1. Describe how Ahab's talk on the quarter-deck has affected Ishmael.
2. Why has the spread of news about Moby-Dick through the world's whaling fleet been slow?
3. According to Ishmael, why is superstition more powerful among whalers than among ordinary people?
4. Describe the actual, observable characteristics of the white whale.
5. According to the passage beginning "His three boats" on page 314, what did Ahab "transfer" to the white whale? What did the whale **personify** to Ahab?
6. What is monomania? According to Ishmael, how did Ahab become monomaniacal?
7. After Ahab recovers from the delirium brought on by Moby-Dick's attack, he seems to regain his sanity. In what way is his rational demeanor deceptive? How does it help him toward his goal?

Interpreting Meanings

8. What supernatural qualities are attributed to Moby-Dick by the sailors? What is the effect of turning Moby-Dick into a mythical monster?
9. What **images** used to describe Moby-Dick in this chapter suggest beauty as well as horror? Can you think of any other instances (from life or literature) where these two qualities are combined in one person or event or thing?
10. The final paragraph draws a picture of the *Pequod*'s crew as they travel the world's oceans on Ahab's quest. What is the narrator's **attitude** here toward the ship's captain, her crew, and her quest?
11. Explain how the ship and her company can be seen as a *microcosm*—a world in miniature—and as a **symbol** for the "ship" of humanity.

Writing About the Novel

A Creative Response

1. **Describing an Event from Another Point of View.** We hear the story of *Moby-Dick* from Ishmael's point of view. Now let Captain Ahab speak. In two or three paragraphs, record what the captain might write in his log one night. You might try the night the *Pequod* set sail from Nantucket or the night after the ritual on the quarter-deck. What does Ahab fear? What does he want? How does he feel about the crew?

A Critical Response

2. **Comparing Ahab's Speech with Transcendental Ideas.** Write an essay comparing Ahab's monologue in "The Quarter-Deck" (beginning on page 307 with "Hark ye yet again . . .") to Transcendentalist ideas. In what ways does the speech agree with Transcendentalist thought? In what ways does it reject it?
3. **Analyzing a Character.** In at least one paragraph, analyze the character of Captain Ahab, given what you know of him from these chapters. Before you write, gather your data in a chart like the following:

What we know about Ahab:	
From his speech	
From his actions	
From his appearance	
From his thoughts	

4. **Explaining a Symbol.** British novelist and poet D.H. Lawrence wrote this about *Moby-Dick:*

> A hunt. The last great hunt.
> For what?
> For Moby-Dick, the huge white sperm whale: who is old, hoary, monstrous and swims alone; who is unspeakably terrible in his wrath, having so often been attacked; and snow-white.
> Of course he is a symbol.
> Of what?
> I doubt that even Melville knew exactly. That's the best of it.
> —D.H. Lawrence

In a brief essay, explain what you think Moby-Dick symbolizes—insofar as you can tell from what you've read. Cite passages to support your interpretation.

Analyzing Language and Style

Names and Their Significance

The name *Ahab* has come to signify a wicked king, and the name *Ishmael* has come to signify a wanderer or outcast. The names are from the Bible. Who are Ahab and Ishmael in the Bible? Why do you think Melville chose their names for his captain and narrator? Ahab's story is found in 1 Kings 16:29–22:40, and Ishmael's story is in Genesis 21:9–21.

Ahab's rational demeanor persuades the people of Nantucket that he is fit to be captain of another whaling voyage.

Interpreting Meanings

8. They suggest that he is ubiquitous, or present everywhere, and that he is immortal.

The effect is to build up suspense and horror.

9. One such image occurs in the physical description of Moby-Dick, where Melville pictures the whale "seen gliding at high noon through a dark blue sea, leaving a milky-way wake of creamy foam, all spangled with golden gleamings."

Some see these contradictory qualities in volcanoes, storms, fires, and predators.

10. The narrator's attitude seems ambiguous. On the one hand, he says he is "all a-rush to encounter the whale." On the other hand, he calls Ahab an "ungodly old man," and refers to the crew as a collection of "mongrel renegades, and castaways, and cannibals." He feels that the whale itself represents the "deadliest ill." Ishmael repeatedly underlines the idea of fate in this paragraph, referring to the "infernal fatality" of this particular crew turning up to help the captain in his "monomaniac revenge."

11. Melville refers several times to the diversity of races, outlooks, and backgrounds among the members of the ship's crew, and several references in the last paragraph of this chapter convey a generalized picture of the *Pequod*'s voyage, so that it may be regarded as symbolic of the voyage of humanity as a whole. Ishmael refers to Ahab chasing a Job's whale "round the world." And in wondering about his mixed feelings, he uses the arresting image of "the subterranean miner that works in us all"—doubt and fear are compared to the sounds of a miner's pick deep below the surface of our conscious minds.

Primary Sources

A Letter and a Journal Entry

While he was writing *Moby-Dick,* Melville wrote this letter to Hawthorne. As you can see, Melville missed the company of other writers.

Pittsfield, June 29, 1851.

"My Dear Hawthorne—

The clear air and open window invite me to write to you. For some time past I have been so busy with a thousand things that I have almost forgotten when I wrote you last, and whether I received an answer. This most persuasive season has now for weeks recalled me from certain crotchety and over-doleful chimeras,[1] the like of which men like you and me, and some others, forming a chain of God's posts round the world, must be content to encounter now and then, and fight them the best way we can. . . .

"Not entirely yet, though, am I without something to be urgent with. The 'Whale' is only half through the press; for, wearied with the long delays of the printers, and disgusted with the heat and dust of the Babylonish[2] brick-kiln of New York, I came back to the country to feel the grass—and end the book reclining on it, if I may. I am sure you will pardon this speaking all about myself; for if I *say* so much on that head, be sure all the rest of the world are thinking about themselves ten times as much. Let us speak, though we show all our faults and weaknesses—for it is a sign of strength to be weak, to know it, and out with it—not in set way and ostentatiously, though, but incidentally and without premeditation. But I am falling into my old foible—preaching. I am busy, but shall not be very long. Come and spend a day here, if you can and want to; if not, stay in Lenox, and God give you long life. When I am quite free of my present engagements, I am going to treat myself to a ride and a visit to you. . . .

"Shall I send you a fin of the 'Whale' by way of a specimen mouthful? The tail is not yet cooked—though the hellfire in which the whole book is broiled might not unreasonably have cooked it all ere this. This is the book's motto (the secret one): Ego non baptiso te in nomine[3]—but make out the rest yourself. . . ."

H.M.

1. **chimeras:** monsters (Melville means troublesome thoughts).
2. **Babylonish:** Babylon was an ancient city infamous in the Bible for evil and corruption.
3. **Ego non baptiso te in nomine:** "I do *not* baptize you in the name of . . ."; Melville is suggesting that the book is about the workings of evil.

When *Moby-Dick* was published, Melville sent Hawthorne a copy. Hawthorne's response must have been positive, for Melville calls Hawthorne's letter "joy-giving and exultation-breeding." None of Hawthorne's letters to Melville have survived, but in 1856, Hawthorne did write about Melville in his notebook while he was in England.

November 20th [1856]

"A week ago last Monday, Herman Melville came to see me at the Consulate, looking much as he used to do (a little paler, and perhaps a little sadder), in a rough outside coat, and with his characteristic gravity and reserve of manner. . . . I felt rather awkward at first; because this is the first time I have met him since my ineffectual attempt to get him a consular appointment from General Pierce. . . . Melville has not been well, of late; he has been affected with neuralgic complaints in his head and limbs, and no doubt has suffered from too constant literary occupation, pursued without much success, latterly; and his writings, for a long while past, have indicated a morbid state of mind. . . . I invited him to come and stay with us at Southport, as long as he might remain in this vicinity; and accordingly, he did come, the next day, taking with him, by way of baggage, the least little bit of a bundle, which, he told me, contained a nightshirt and a toothbrush. He is a person of very gentlemanly instincts in every respect, save that he is a little heterodox in the matter of clean linen.

"He stayed with us from Tuesday till Thursday; and, on the intervening day, we took a pretty long walk together, and sat down in a hollow among the sand hills (sheltering ourselves from the high, cool wind) and smoked a cigar. Melville, as he always does, began to reason of Providence and futurity, and of everything that lies beyond human ken, and informed me that he had 'pretty much made up his mind to be annihilated'; but still he does not seem to rest in that anticipation; and, I think, will never rest until he gets hold of a definite belief. It is strange how he persists—and has persisted ever since I knew him, and probably long before—in wandering to and fro over these deserts, as dismal and monotonous as the sand hills amid which we were sitting. He can neither believe, nor be comfortable in his unbelief; and he is too honest and courageous not to try to do one or the other. If he were a religious man, he would be one of the most truly religious and reverential; he has a very high and noble nature, and better worth immortality than most of us."

N.H.

Supplementary Support Materials
1. Review and Response Worksheet: Diction (*CCB*)
2. Selection Test (*CCB*)

Preparation
Establishing a Purpose. Have students read to learn how Melville commemorates the dead at Shiloh.

Closure
Have students paraphrase the poem, orally or in writing.

Analyzing the Poem
Identifying Details
1. "April rain" solaced the wounded (lines 5–6).
2. The swallows.

Interpreting Meanings
3. The soldiers on both sides meet death, a common fate, in the course of the day; the poet thus calls them "friends at eve."
4. One paraphrase might be: There is nothing so concrete as a bullet to show us the brutal reality of war.
5. The religious teachings of the church stress peace, not war. According to the Bible, Sunday is the "Lord's day," and should be observed as a day of rest and worship, not of battle.
6. The repetitions of *l* and *w* sounds suggest the movement of birds.
The repetition of the long *o* sounds.
7. The circular effect stresses that the natural world goes on, despite the tragic deaths of so many men.

Like all requiems, this poem commemorates the dead in a spirit of peace and acceptance. The occasion for it was the Civil War battle at Tennessee's Shiloh Church in April, 1862. During the two-day battle, more than twenty thousand lives were lost. Melville's subject is not the battle itself, or the righteousness of one cause over the other. His subject is the power of the great leveler, death, to join friend and foe in eternal silence.

Suppressing his own deep feelings of partisanship, Melville deliberately ignores the issues that had brought Americans of the North and South into bloody conflict. Instead, he composes a kind of song or chant to remind his readers that the waste of life in battle can never be undone. To give his song its own internal music, he chooses the device of onomatopoeia, so that the sounds of the requiem literally moan and whisper its somber message. Read the poem aloud and you will hear how it is based on the onomatopoetic use of the vowel *o* and the consonant *s*. Melville could have written about any number of other Civil War battles; he may have chosen this one because his poet's ear found the lovely word *Shiloh* especially evocative. The Battle of Shiloh is also known as the Battle of Pittsburg Landing. To appreciate how much Melville's poetic effects are enhanced by the name *Shiloh,* simply substitute *Pittsburg Landing* in the places in the poem where the name is used.

Shiloh

A Requiem (April, 1862)

Skimming lightly, wheeling still,
  The swallows fly low
Over the field in clouded days,
  The forest-field of Shiloh—
Over the field where April rain
Solaced the parched ones stretched in pain
Through the pause of night
That followed the Sunday fight
  Around the church of Shiloh—
The church so lone, the log-built one,
That echoed to many a parting groan
    And natural prayer
  Of dying foemen mingled there—
Foemen at morn, but friends at eve—
  Fame or country least their care:
(What like a bullet can undeceive!)
  But now they lie low,
While over them the swallows skim,
  And all is hushed at Shiloh.

Responding to the Poem

Analyzing the Poem

Identifying Details

1. According to the poem, what natural element comforted the dying soldiers?
2. What are the only moving things in the poem?

Interpreting Meanings

3. Explain how "foemen at morn" (line 14) could become "friends at eve."
4. The most forthright statement in the poem occurs in line 16. How would you **paraphrase** this statement?
5. Shiloh Church is named after the place where the Israelites worshiped after they reached the Promised Land. What is **ironic** about a battle occurring at a church and on a Sunday?
6. Find the sounds in the poem's first two lines that suggest the movement of birds. What sounds in the poem suggest moaning and hushed silence?
7. What is the effect of ending the poem as it begins, with the flight of swallows?

Supplementary Support Materials
1. Review and Response Worksheet: Diction (*CCB*)
2. Selection Test (*CCB*)

Preparation

Establishing a Purpose. Have students read to learn how the poet believes that art is created.

An allusion provides the metaphor for the basis of this poem. The allusion is Biblical. Jacob wrestled with a stranger on the bank of the River Jabbok and would not release him until the stranger blessed him. The stranger turned out to be an angel and, in blessing Jacob, gave him the name of Israel (Genesis 32). The incident is frequently used as a metaphor for the struggle to create art.

Art

In placid hours well pleased we dream
Of many a brave unbodied scheme.
But form to lend, pulsed life create,
What unlike things must meet and mate:
A flame to melt—a wind to freeze;
Sad patience—joyous energies;
Humility—yet pride and scorn;
Instinct and study; love and hate;
Audacity—reverence. These must mate,
And fuse with Jacob's mystic heart,
To wrestle with the angel—Art.

Jacob Wrestling with the Angel by Jack Levine (1975). Oil.

Private collection.

A. Expansion
An "unbodied scheme" is a scheme that is not brought to fruition.

B. Responding
? What statement is the poet making about art? (That in order to bring artistic forms to life, the artist must combine contradictory elements, such as those listed in lines 5–9.)

C. Humanities Connection: Discussing the Fine Art
Jack Levine (b. 1915) is an artist who began as a child prodigy—his painting *String Quartette,* done when he was sixteen, is in the collection of the Metropolitan Museum of Art. He is known for building groups of human forms into complex designs. His early work often featured social comment; later he turned to Biblical themes, as in this picture.

CLOSURE
Have students list the sets of opposites in this poem. Then have them write a brief statement to be shared in class explaining how these opposites are significant to the theme of the poem.

ANALYZING THE POEM
Identifying Details
1. The meaning is "formless" or "abstract."
2. Six sets of opposites are: melting and freezing, sadness and joy, humility and pride, instinct (or intuition) and study, love and hate, audacity and reverence.

Interpreting Meanings
3. Students' answers will vary. Urge them to express their own opinions, and to support their views with appropriate examples from literature and the other arts. Can students think of a painting or book or character they would call both flame and wind, or patience and energy, humility and pride, instinct and education, love and hate, daring and reverence?
4. Some possibilities might include: a groan and a prayer (lines 11–12) and foemen and friends (line 14).

A Comment on the Poem

The idea that the creation of a work of art requires wrestling with unknown forces is an old one. Many great artists have described their struggles to give form to ideas and shape to raw materials. These struggles are often compared to hand-to-hand conflicts with the same mysterious powers that religious mystics encounter in their efforts to know God.

Melville gives specific detail and a new twist to this idea of a struggle. In the first two lines, he quietly evokes a feeling that almost everyone has experienced—the self-congratulatory notion that we too could create art, even though, for the moment, our artistic schemes remain only daydreams.

But then he shatters such a notion by suggesting what it takes to transform an "unbodied scheme" into something that is real art. In a work of art, Melville asserts, opposites must somehow be reconciled; mutually antagonistic qualities must somehow "mate." Then, and only then, can the would-be artist wrestle with the angel of Art and, like Jacob, prove himself or herself worthy of receiving the angel's blessing.

Responding to the Poem

Analyzing the Poem

Identifying Details

1. Define the word *unbodied* as it is used in line 2 to describe a daydream.
2. The core of the poem is Melville's listing of opposites—most of them feelings that, at first glance, would seem to be contrary to one another. Find six of these sets of opposites in the poem.

Interpreting Meanings

3. For the purposes of artistic creation, how might these opposites work together—that is, how might they become equal contributions to one work of art?
4. Reread Melville's poem "Shiloh." Can you name some opposite feelings, conditions, or qualities that are brought together in this requiem?

Writing About the Poem

A Critical Response

Comparing Poems. Ralph Waldo Emerson also wrote a poem called "Art." Here are its opening lines:

Give to barrows, trays, and pans
Grace and glimmer of romance;
Bring the moonlight into noon
Hid in gleaming piles of stone;
On the city's paved street
Plant gardens lined with lilacs sweet;
Let spouting fountains cool the air,
Singing in the sun-baked square;
Let statue, picture, park and hall,
Ballad, flag and festival,
The past restore, the day adorn,
And make tomorrow a new morn. . . .

—from "Art,"
Ralph Waldo Emerson

In an essay, compare and contrast Emerson's ideas about art with Melville's. Before you write, think about the ways that the two poets' ideas about art and the role of the artist are similar, and in what ways they are different. Which poet calls for a return to an ideal past, and which calls for new, imaginative transformations? Both poets offer advice as to what an artist should do. What sort of artist do you think would be more likely to take Emerson's advice? What sort of artist would take Melville's?

Exercises in Critical Thinking and Writing

ANALYZING AND EVALUATING PERSUASIVE WRITING: RHETORIC

Writing Assignment

In a brief essay, analyze and evaluate the rhetoric used in the following excerpt from "Self-Reliance" by Ralph Waldo Emerson.

Background

In the exercise following Unit Two, you looked at logic as a means of persuasion. In this exercise, you'll focus on how rhetoric is used in persuasive writing. **Rhetoric** is the art of using language effectively. Where logic appeals to our reason, rhetoric often appeals to our emotions. Some common rhetorical devices follow, each one illustrated with an example from Thoreau's essay "Resistance to Civil Government."

1. A **rhetorical question** is one for which no answer is expected. Rhetorical questions presume that the reader agrees with the writer.

   "This American government—what is it but a tradition, though a recent one, endeavoring to transmit itself unimpaired to posterity, but each instant losing some of its integrity?"

   Thoreau suggests that no one could possibly disagree with his belief that the government is losing its integrity.
2. **Hyperbole** is the use of exaggeration for effect; it is not meant to be taken literally. Hyperbole overstates the case to make a point.

   "It [the government] has not the vitality and force of a single living man; for a single man can bend it to his will."
3. **Ridicule** makes us laugh at something by presenting it as absurd. Thoreau belittles the government when he compares it to a child's toy. He also belittles governments (and the people governed) when he suggests that governments are necessary only because "people must have some complicated machinery or other, and hear its din. . . ."
4. The **connotations** of a word are the associations and emotional overtones we attach to it. Words with strong connotations are sometimes called "loaded words." *Din,* for example, is a loaded word, with strong negative connotations. It suggests a long, loud sound that is confusing or uproarious and likely to make us want to cover our ears. Try replacing *din* with the phrase *busy hum* or *whirring wheels.* How would the connotations of these phrases change the impact of Thoreau's description of government?
5. **Rhythm, repetition,** and **parallel structure** have a twofold effect on an audience. First, these techniques lend a pleasurable quality to prose, just as they do to poetry. Second, they make people remember certain ideas. These devices can make prose seem like an "incantation"—a chant or prayer. They make certain ideas resound in our heads.

   "*It does not* keep the country free. *It does not* settle the West. *It does not* educate."

Prewriting

Read the following excerpt from Emerson's "Self-Reliance." (It is not part of the excerpt you have already read.) Note your responses as you read.

> I read the other day some verses written by an eminent painter which were original and not conventional. The soul always hears an admonition in such lines, let the subject be what it may. The sentiment they instill is of more value than any thought they may contain. To believe your own thought, to believe that what is true for you in your private heart is true for all men—that is genius. Speak your latent conviction, and it shall be the universal sense; for the inmost in due time becomes the outmost—and our first thought is rendered back to us by the trumpets of the Last Judgment. Familiar as the voice of the mind is to each, the highest merit we ascribe to Moses, Plato, and Milton is that they set at naught books and traditions, and spoke not what men, but what *they* thought. A man should learn to detect and watch that gleam of light which flashes across his mind from within, more than the luster of the firmament of bards and sages. Yet he dismisses

A

A. Expansion
This passage itself is an example of a work whose greatness is largely in its power of expression, whether or not its message is true. Therefore, the existence of the essay in itself supports Emerson's assertion that greatness comes from daring to speak one's own thoughts, rather than from being right. This is something of a logical conundrum. (The fourth sentence, "To believe your own thought . . ." is crucial.)

Revising Essays
As students revise their essays, refer them to **Grammar, Usage, and Mechanics:** A Reference Guide at the back of their books.

Exercises in Critical Thinking and Writing/*cont.*

without notice his thought, because it is his. In every work of genius we recognize our own rejected thoughts; they come back to us with a certain alienated majesty. Great works of art have no more affecting lesson for us than this. They teach us to abide by our spontaneous impression with good-humored inflexibility then most when the whole cry of voices is on the other side. Else, tomorrow a stranger will say with masterly good sense precisely what we have thought and felt all the time, and we shall be forced to take with shame our own opinion from another.

There is a time in every man's education when he arrives at the conviction that envy is ignorance; that imitation is suicide; that he must take himself for better, for worse, as his portion; that though the wide universe is full of good, no kernel of nourishing corn can come to him but through his toil bestowed on that plot of ground which is given to him to till. The power which resides in him is new in nature, and none but he knows what that is which he can do, nor does he know until he has tried. Not for nothing one face, one character, one fact, makes much impression on him, and another none. This sculpture in the memory is not without pre-established harmony. The eye was placed where one ray should fall, that it might testify of that particular ray. We but half express ourselves, and are ashamed of that divine idea which each of us represents. It may be safely trusted as proportionate and of good issues, so it be faithfully imparted, but God will not have his work made manifest by cowards.

—from "Self-Reliance,"
Ralph Waldo Emerson

1. What is Emerson's **purpose** in this excerpt? What is he trying to convince his audience to believe or to do?
2. **Paraphrase** his main argument in your own words.
3. How does he **develop** his argument? What does he say to support his main points?
4. Now, focus on the **rhetorical devices** you have just read about. List as many examples as you can.
5. **Evaluate** the excerpt as a whole. Were you persuaded? Why—or why not? How effective is Emerson's language? How strong or weak is his argument?
6. Write a **thesis statement** in which you summarize your evaluation. In the rest of your essay, give specific examples and quotations to support your opinion.

Writing

Here is the beginning of an essay on the rhetorical devices used in Thoreau's "Resistance to Civil Government." Notice that in the first paragraph, the writer identifies Thoreau's purpose and gives a brief summary of his argument. The second paragraph (only part of which is given here) goes on to identify some rhetorical devices.

In "Resistance to Civil Government," Henry David Thoreau wants to persuade us that it is a citizen's duty to protest an unjust government, and that he is therefore justified in not paying his taxes. He begins by stating his view of government: "That government is best which governs least"—or "not at all." Thoreau believes that if government can't be abolished altogether, individuals must work to make it better. And since people should be governed by their own consciences (not by majority rule), we should not support a government action we think is wrong. The Mexican War, he says, is "the work of comparatively a few individuals using the standing government as their tool." Given a chance, he says, the people in general would never agree to it.

Thoreau uses words well, and he persuades as much by rhetoric as by logical reasoning. For example, he makes two comparisons that ridicule the government. He says it is a wooden gun, a harmless child's toy. And he says it is some kind of "complicated machinery" created by people only to produce loud, confusing noises. This "din" satisfies the people's notion of what a government should be doing....

Revising and Proofreading

Use the guidelines in the section at the back of this book, called **Writing About Literature,** to revise and proofread your essay.

A NEW AMERICAN POETRY

WHITMAN AND DICKINSON

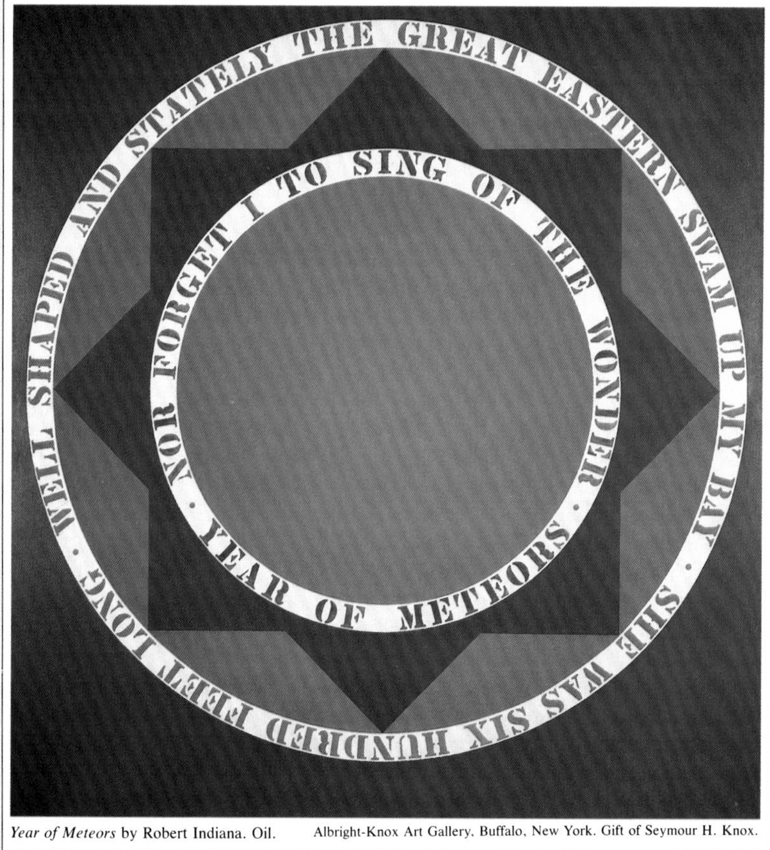

Year of Meteors by Robert Indiana. Oil. Albright-Knox Art Gallery, Buffalo, New York. Gift of Seymour H. Knox.

UNIT FIVE

HUMANITIES CONNECTION: RESPONDING TO THE FINE ART

The works of Robert Indiana (b. 1928), an influential American "pop artist," are distinguished by bold, contrasting images and colors. Heavily influenced by road signs and billboards, Indiana's paintings and prints, such as *Demuth American Dream No. 5* and *Years of Meteors,* shown here, frequently consist of figures within figures that tend to draw the viewer into the work.

? After studying the painting carefully, what do you see? (Perhaps a ship's logo or star shape for meteors) Is the painting art, poetry, or both? (Both. Consider the evocative personification, "Swam up my bay.")

Have students explain why they do or do not see the art as a poem, but leave the discussion open-ended—it's not necessary to define "poetry" firmly at this point. You may also want students to make predictions about the kind of poetry they will study in this unit, based on this art. When students have completed their study of Whitman and Dickinson, they can return to the art to discuss why it is an appropriate choice to represent the poetry of the unit.

TEACHING THE NEW AMERICAN POETRY UNIT

The unit introduction (pages 324–325) can help students focus both on the poets' uniqueness and on their places in American literature. The first part of the introduction presents Whitman and Dickinson as representing "two distinct seams in the fabric of American poetry." Help students note the contrasts between the two poets by having them prepare a chart summary such as the following one:

	WHITMAN	DICKINSON
Personality	social, gregarious	private, shy
Expectations	message to be carried to the world	message to die in oblivion
When Famous	during his lifetime	after her death
Poetic Style	sweeping catalogs and the cadences of free verse	meticulous word choice, rhyme, hymnbook meters

The seventh paragraph of the unit introduction ("As the history of our poetry shows . . .") makes generalizations on American poetry subsequent to Whitman and Dickinson. Alert students to the fact that understanding Whitman and Dickinson will prepare them for units Eight, Nine, and Thirteen, where they will encounter poets who owe to Whitman and Dickinson their freedom and range of subjects and styles.

Finally, the concluding paragraph of the unit introduction and the poem by Ezra Pound stress the "co-equal importance" of free verse and traditional forms. You may need to stress "co-equal"—some students may be biased for or against one of the verse forms. (Students might benefit from Miller William's definition of free verse: "Poetry in which line length and rhyme [if any] to come [are] not predictable from what has gone before nor prescribed by tradition.") You might end by reading aloud Pound's poem and asking students to jot down in their journals their immediate interpretation of Pound's meaning—a "best guess." Ask two or three students to share what they have written. Make no judgments at this time, but ask students to leave space to write a second response after they have completed the unit.

OBJECTIVES OF THE NEW AMERICAN POETRY UNIT

1. To improve reading proficiency and expand vocabulary
2. To gain exposure to notable poets and their works
3. To define and identify elements of poetry
4. To express and explain responses to poetry, orally and in writing
5. To practice the following critical thinking and writing skills
   - a. Comparing and contrasting poetry and other forms
   - b. Rewriting a paragraph as a poem
   - c. Comparing and contrasting poems
   - d. Analyzing responses to poetry
   - e. Evaluating a title
   - f. Commenting on criticism
   - g. Interpreting metaphors
   - h. Interpreting poems

SUPPLEMENTARY SUPPORT MATERIALS: UNIT FIVE

1. Unit Introduction Test (*CCB*)
2. Word Analogies Test (*CCB*)
3. Unit Review Test (*CCB*)
4. Critical Thinking and Writing Test (*CCB*)
5. Instructional Overhead Transparencies

A. Responding to the Quotation

? The Whitman quote, from #52, *Song of Myself,* page 341, strikes the great Whitman theme of the poet's oneness with the universe—and with the reader. The Dickinson quote, the opening lines of an eight-line poem not in the textbook, has the poignancy of a note in a bottle cast into the ocean by an island exile. Since at this point students have no context in which to evaluate the poets' meanings, you may wish simply to have them jot down in their journals a list of questions (however facetious) raised by the lines. (Is Whitman saying he is part of the earth? A road? Is Dickinson lonely? Bitter? Hurt?) Return to these questions after discussing the two-page unit introduction and ask students how these lines now seem to fit each poet. (Whitman's confidence that his message will endure—be "underfoot"; Dickinson's poems written with no immediate response)

A NEW AMERICAN POETRY
WHITMAN AND DICKINSON

by **John Malcolm Brinnin**

AMERICA'S FIRST DISTINCTIVE POEM.

WALT WHITMAN'S

LEAVES OF GRASS

(NOW COMPLETE.)

INCLUDING, AS PART OF CONTENTS,

Proto-Leaf,
Chants Democratic,
Enfans d'Adam,
Poem of Joys,
Messenger Leaves,
Calamus,
So Long,
&c., &c.

Portrait of the Poet,
ENGRAVED BY SCHOFF.

TO BE READY ABOUT 1st OF MAY.

In one volume, 456 pages, 12mo, best paper, print, and electrotyping Boston can turn out.

Price, $1 25.

THAYER & ELDRIDGE,
PUBLISHERS,
116 WASHINGTON STREET,
BOSTON, MASS.

Agents Wanted
To obtain Subscribers for
LOSSING'S

"Whitman and Dickinson represent two distinct seams in the fabric of American poetry, one slightly uneven and the other carefully measured and stitched tight."

A

If you want me again look for me under your boot-soles.

—Walt Whitman

This is my letter to the World
That never wrote to Me—

—Emily Dickinson

The two greatest American poets of the nineteenth century were so different from one another, both as artists and as personalities, that only a nation as varied in character as the United States could possibly contain them.

Walt Whitman worked with bold strokes on a broad canvas; Emily Dickinson worked with the delicacy of a miniaturist. Whitman was sociable and gregarious, a traveler; Dickinson was private and shy, content to remain in one secluded spot through all of her lifetime.

While both poets were close observers of people and of life's daily activities, the emphasis they gave to what impressed them was so distinct as to make them opposites. Whitman was the public spokesman of the masses and the prophet of progress. "I hear America singing," he said, and he joined his eloquent voice to that chorus. Dickinson was the obscure homebody, peering through the curtains of her house in a country village, who found in nature metaphors for the spirit and recorded them with no thought of an audience. Whitman expected that his celebration of universal brotherhood and the bright destiny of democracy would be carried like a message into the future. Dickinson expected nothing but oblivion for the poetry that was her "letter to the world."

Whitman's career might be regarded as another American success story—the story of an amiable young man who drifted into middle age, working at one job after another, never "finding himself" until, at his own expense, he boldly published *Leaves of Grass* (1855). The book made him famous around the world. Dickinson's career as a poet began after her death. It is one of those ironies of history in which a writer dies unknown, only to have fame thrust upon her by succeeding generations.

Whitman and Dickinson represent two distinct seams in the fabric of American poetry, one slightly uneven and the other carefully measured and stitched tight. Whitman was as extravagant with words as he was careless with repetition and self-contradiction. Aiming for the large, overall impression, he filled his pages with long lists as he strained to catalogue everything in sight. His technique is based on the **cadence**—the long, easy sweep of sound that echoes the Bible and the speeches of orators and preachers. This cadence is the basis for his **free verse:** poetry without rhyme or meter.

Dickinson, on the other hand, wrote with the precision of a diamond cutter. Meticulous in her choice of words, she aimed to evoke the feelings of things rather than simply to name them. She

Reading Check Test

1. Who is described as "spokesman of the masses and the prophet of progress"? (Whitman)
2. Who apparently attempted to catalogue the entire range of American life? (Whitman)
3. Who is remembered as living a hidden, obscure life? (Dickinson)
4. Who wrote in the broad cadences of free verse? (Whitman)
5. Who is praised for meticulously crafted verses of "gem-like artistry"? (Dickinson)

was always searching for the one right phrase that would fix a thought in the mind. Her technique is economical, and her neat stanzas are controlled by the demands of rhyme and the meters she found in her hymn book.

As the history of our poetry shows, both modes of expression have continued to be used by American writers. Both poets have served as models for twentieth-century poets who have been drawn to the visions they fulfilled and the techniques they mastered. [A] Poetry as public speech written in the cadences of free verse remains a part of our literature; poetry as private observation, carefully crafted in rhyme and meter, still attracts young writers who tend to regard poems as experiences rather than as statements.

A. Responding

? Which poet, so far, better fits your "image" of a poet? Why? Or does each capsule biography suggest different stereotypes of a poet? (For example, Whitman as the long-haired, out-of-work type; Dickinson as the shy, dreamy type)

The co-equal importance of the two poetic methods has never been more clearly affirmed than in the following words by Ezra Pound (see Unit Nine). Pound speaks for himself here as a poet more attuned to the abbreviations of Dickinson than to the expansiveness of Whitman. Nevertheless, he offers in this poem a benediction that represents the feeling of every poet who has envied the gem-like artistry of Dickinson and the all-embracing power of Whitman:

A Pact

I make a pact with you, Walt Whitman—
I have detested you long enough.
I come to you as a grown child
Who has had a pig-headed father;
I am old enough now to make friends.
It was you that broke the new wood,
Now is a time for carving.
We have one sap and one root—
Let there be commerce between us.

—Ezra Pound

"Pound offers a benediction that represents the feeling of every poet who has envied the gem-like artistry of Dickinson and the all-embracing power of Whitman."

Before I leave
america I must see
You again - there is no
one in this wide great
world of america
whom I love and
honour so much.
With warm
affection, and honourable
admiration,
Oscar Wilde

A letter from British writer Oscar Wilde to Walt Whitman.

A. Humanities Connection: Responding to the Illustration

? What details "date" this picture? (Its oval shape suggests it is a daguerrotype. The man wears an old-fashioned hat, shirt, and tie.)

B. Connections

Whitman's travels on foot, train, coach, and riverboat are captured in his "Song of the Open Road," source of the lines "Afoot and light-hearted I take to the open road,/Healthy, free, the world before me,/The long brown path before me leading wherever I choose"—an often quoted expression of the perennial American yearning to expand frontiers, to "go West," to "see the elephant." It is a theme later captured in fiction by Twain's Huck Finn, who plans to "light out for the territory," and in everyday American life by the cars of the fifties designed, with their stabbing fins, like yachts for cruising; by the TV reports of Charles Kuralt "on the road"; by Ginsberg (page 1134) and the other Beat poets who took off for distant parts whenever the scene grew dull; in our own time by writer-travelers like William Least Heat Moon (page 1070), whose record of his wanderings appeared in 1982.

Walt Whitman (1819–1892)

A

Less than a hundred years after the vast and largely uninhabited territory of America had become the United States, the new nation found its voice in a poet who spoke to all the world. His name was Walt Whitman, and he struck a note in literature that was as forthright, as original, and as deeply charged with democracy's energies as the land that produced him.

But the appearance of something radically different in poetry is always greeted with a mixed response; Whitman's work was no exception. What he said and how he said it troubled guardians of tradition as much as it excited readers for whom he was the master of a new language and the author of a national identity.

Whitman was a curious mixture of the homespun and the theatrical; he had the earthy spirit of the born democrat and the self-dramatizing disposition of the aristocratic dandy. At times he was the man on the street wearing rolled-up sleeves and unpressed corduroys. At other times he was the artist in a slouch felt hat and the sort of flowing silk tie associated with the affectations of Romanticism.

Whitman's two-sided image of himself is a clue to his poetry. Much of it has the simplicity of folk literature. He takes delight in *catalogues*—in the long listings of things, names, and activities found in ancient epics and sagas. Yet the greater part of Whitman's poetry escapes all categories; it demands to be read with the same attention that we give to the most sophisticated poetry in our language.

Whitman was born on May 31, 1819, to parents of Dutch and English descent. They kept a farm in West Hills, Long Island, in what is today the township of Huntington. His father's ancestors had come from England only twenty years after the landing of the *Mayflower* and had settled in Connecticut. On his mother's side, his ancestors were among the early immigrants from Holland who settled on Manhattan Island and along the Hudson River. Whitman and his eight brothers and sisters were able to assume their essential American-ness with an uncommon confidence. They knew their American grandparents, and they grew up in circumstances that allowed them both the communal experience of country life and the experience of a new city on its way to becoming a metropolis.

This city was Brooklyn, which, by 1855, would become the third largest city in America. It was there that Walter Whitman, Sr., hoped to prosper as a carpenter and builder of houses. He moved there with his wife Louisa and their family in 1823. Young Walter went to school until he was eleven. He then worked as an office boy and printer's assistant, and for a time he taught school.

On weekends spent along the beaches and in the woods of Long Island, Whitman read Sir Walter Scott, the Bible, Shakespeare, Homer, Dante, and "the ancient Hindoo poems." He never became a scholar; he never went to college.

Before he was twenty, his feeling for the written word and his fascination with the boom-town atmosphere of Brooklyn led him into journalism. After ten years of this, he took a kind of working vacation—a difficult overland trip by train, horse-drawn coach, and riverboat to New Orleans. There he put his newspaperman's talent to work for the *Crescent* and his own talent for ob- B

A. Responding

? Why would a letter from Emerson be more important than one from any other American of this period? (Emerson's reputation as a preeminent thinker and writer was firmly established. A biography of Emerson begins on page 187.)

B. Humanities Connection: Responding to the illustration

? Imagine that you are the typesetter. What would you do with the changes written in by Whitman? (A slash indicates the end of a line; the *d* after line 2 means "delete.") Do you think Whitman's changes improve the poem? Why? (Why not?)

servation to work for himself. After a few months, he returned to New York by way of the Great Lakes and a side trip to Niagara Falls. By this time, Whitman had added to his limited sense of America the experience of a wilderness surrendering its vastness to civilization. He also had become acquainted with the entirely alien culture that French Catholic New Orleans represented.

Back in Brooklyn, Whitman accepted an offer to become editor of *The Freeman*. For the next six or seven years, he supplemented his income as a part-time carpenter and building contractor. All this while, he was keeping notebooks and quietly putting together the sprawling collection of poems that would transform his life and change the course of American literature.

In 1855, he published this collection at his own expense, under the title *Leaves of Grass*. Since the book was too boldly new and strange to win the attention of reviewers or readers with fixed ideas about poetry, its publication went all but unnoticed. Disappointed but not defeated, Whitman bided his time and was rewarded for his patience and his own efforts at self-promotion. He was not only his own publisher, but also his own salesman. To stir up interest in the product he sent samples to people whose endorsement he thought might be useful. One of these samples reached Ralph Waldo Emerson (see page 187), who at once wrote to Whitman the most important letter he would ever receive:

Concord, Massachusetts, 21 July, 1855

Dear Sir—I am not blind to the worth of the wonderful gift of *Leaves of Grass*. I find it the most extraordinary piece of wit and wisdom that America has yet contributed. I am very happy in reading it, as great power makes us happy. It meets the demand I am always making of what seemed the sterile and stingy Nature, as if too much handiwork, or too much lymph in the temperament, were making our Western wits fat and mean.

I give you joy of your free and brave thought. I have great joy in it. I find incomparable things said incomparably well, as they must be. I find the courage of treatment which so delights us, and which large perception only can inspire.

I greet you at the beginning of a great career, which yet must have had a long foreground somewhere, for such a start. I rubbed my eyes a little, to see if this sunbeam were no illusion; but the solid sense of the book is a sober certainty. It has the best merits, namely, of fortifying and encouraging.

I did not know until I last night saw the book advertised in a newspaper that I could trust the name as real and available for a post-office. I wish to see my benefactor, and have felt much like striking my tasks and visiting New York to pay you my respects.

R. W. Emerson

The "long foreground" of which Emerson spoke had not been the careful, confident period of preparation to which many poets devote themselves before they are ready to publish. Instead, it had been a precarious existence. Journalism had kept Whitman going financially, but not even the editorials he

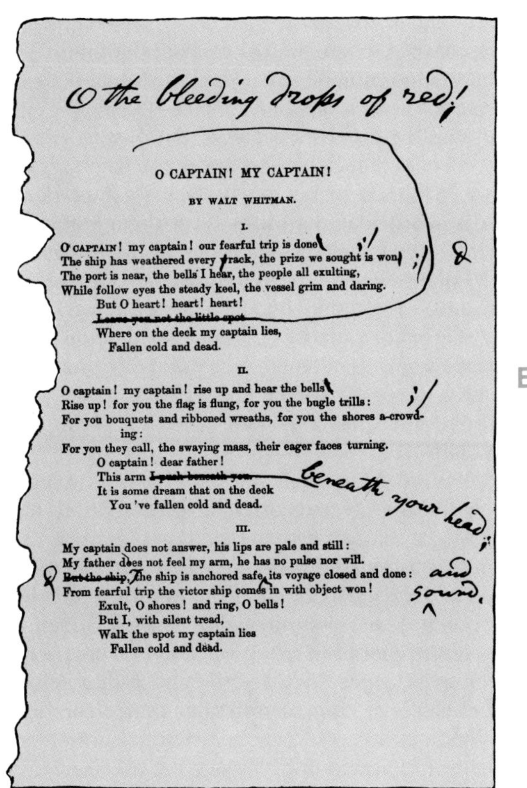

O the bleeding drops of red!

O CAPTAIN! MY CAPTAIN!

BY WALT WHITMAN.

I.

O CAPTAIN! my captain! our fearful trip is done;
The ship has weathered every rack, the prize we sought is won;
The port is near, the bells I hear, the people all exulting,
While follow eyes the steady keel, the vessel grim and daring.
But O heart! heart! heart!
~~Leave you not the little spot~~
Where on the deck my captain lies,
Fallen cold and dead.

II.

O captain! my captain! rise up and hear the bells;
Rise up! for you the flag is flung, for you the bugle trills:
For you bouquets and ribboned wreaths, for you the shores a-crowding:
For you they call, the swaying mass, their eager faces turning.
O captain! dear father!
This arm ~~I push beneath you~~ beneath your head;
It is some dream that on the deck
You 've fallen cold and dead.

III.

My captain does not answer, his lips are pale and still:
My father does not feel my arm, he has no pulse nor will.
~~But the ship~~, The ship is anchored safe and sound, its voyage closed and done:
From fearful trip the victor ship comes in with object won!
Exult, O shores! and ring, O bells!
But I, with silent tread,
Walk the spot my captain lies
Fallen cold and dead.

Manuscript of "O Captain! My Captain!" by Walt Whitman.

The Library of Congress, Washington, D.C.

ADDITIONAL WRITING ASSIGNMENT

(Less Challenging)

"O Captain! My Captain!" (1865) commemorated the death of Lincoln. Once standard schoolbook fare for student memorization, it is now considered inferior to Whitman's later free-verse elegy commemorating Lincoln, "When Lilacs Last in the Dooryard Bloom'd" (1867). Nevertheless it expresses a frequently cited metaphor, the president as captain of the ship of state. Have students write out their personal responses to the poem.

(Challenging)

Have more advanced students locate and respond to "When Lilacs Last in the Dooryard Bloom'd" as well, and then compare their responses to the two poems, and write an analysis of why they think the latter elegy is considered by critics today to be the better poem.

A. Expansion
The Good Gray Poet, an image supported by this quotation, was a book by William O'Connor that depicted Whitman as a saint for his Civil War work. Coming out simultaneously with Whitman's *Drum-Taps* (1865), poems *not* glorifying war, as was then the custom, the book helped polarize opinion for or against Whitman. In the long run, however, it drew disciples who looked after Whitman's physical needs and worked to promote his reputation.

B. Expansion
He began nursing Civil War wounded after visiting his mildly wounded brother George in Washington, D.C. He later rented a room and got a job in Washington so he could visit hospitalized Brooklyn soldiers. Only in his early 40's, he looked older, and served as sympathetic father figure to the young men. He was so loved that recovered soldiers often stopped him in the street to hug and kiss him.

wrote for the *Brooklyn Eagle* had brought him distinction. On the surface, at least, his "long foreground" of preparation had been a mixture of hack work and jack-of-all-trades ingenuity.

But surfaces can be deceptive. Behind the scenes, Whitman's wide reading and lively contemplation had shaped a character that would not be denied expression. What he saw and heard on the crowded streets of New York somehow fused with his knowledge of European philosophy and Oriental mysticism. The result was a vision—realistic in its immediate concerns and cosmic in implication.

By the time he was ready to declare himself a poet and to publish the first version of his book, Walt Whitman was unique. *Leaves of Grass* is a masterpiece that Whitman was to expand and revise through many editions. Its process of growth did not end until the ninth, "deathbed" edition was published in 1891, thirty-six years after its first appearance.

The figure we know today as Walt Whitman was conceived and created by the poet himself. Whitman promoted his "image" and sold it to the public with a pitchman's skill worthy of P. T. Barnum, the great showman of the century. At first glance, that figure is a bundle of contradictions. Whitman seems to have had the theatrical flair of a con man and the selfless dignity of a saint; the sensibility of an artist and the carefree spirit of a hobo; the blustery egotism of a braggart and the demure shyness of a shrinking violet. On second glance, these contradictions disappear: Walt Whitman was everything he seemed to be. The figure he so carefully crafted and put on display was not a surrogate, but the man himself.

A "One would see him afar off," wrote the great naturalist John Burroughs, "in the crowd but not of it—a large, slow-moving figure, clad in gray, with broad-brimmed hat and gray beard—or, quite as frequently, on the front platform of the street horse-cars with the driver. . . . Whitman was of large mold in every way, and of bold, far-reaching schemes, and is very sure to fare better at the hands of large men than of small. The first and last impression which his personal presence always made upon one was of a nature wonderfully gentle, tender, and benignant. . . . I was impressed by the fine grain and clean, fresh quality of the man. . . . He always had the look of a man who had just taken a bath."

The extraordinary thing about that man "in the crowd but not of it" was that, in defining himself, he created a hero of epic stature and singlehandedly added the myth of America to the world's mythology. If there is a side of Whitman that today we would associate with "image building," or self-promotion, there is nothing in his poetry to suggest that it was anything but the product of the kind of genius that permanently changes the history of art.

Other American poets—notably Ralph Waldo Emerson—had already begun to give expression to American democratic ideals and aspirations. But these poets still wrote in the formal measures of traditional English poetry and in the diction of the "King's English," which educated Americans had quite naturally adopted. Whitman modified that diction and abandoned traditional rhyme schemes and formal meters in favor of the natural rhythms and speech patterns of free verse.

The result was poetry that could sing and speak of anything under the sun. Its sweep was easy and its range was broad. Suddenly, poetry was no longer a matter of organized word-structures that neatly clicked shut at the last line; instead, it was a series of open-ended units of rhythm that flowed one into the other and demanded to be read in their totality.

"Whitman throws his chunky language at the reader," says critic Paul Zweig. "He cajoles and thunders; he chants, celebrates, chuckles, and caresses. He spills from his capacious American soul every dreg of un-Englishness, every street sound thumbing its nose at traditional subject matter and tone. Here is Samson pulling the house of literature down around his ears, yet singing in the ruins."

Walt Whitman had invented a way of writing poetry that perfectly accommodated his way of seeing. His form is loose enough to allow for long lists and catalogues abundant in detail; it is also flexible enough to include delicate moments of lyricism as well as stretches of blustering oratory. This form served Whitman as observer and prophet—as a private man tending the wounded in the hospital wards of the Civil War, and as the public man who gave voice to the grief of a nation in his great elegy for the slain Lincoln, "When Lilacs Last in the Dooryard Bloom'd." Most important, Whitman's technique was the instrument by which the message of one man in B

Leaves

of

Grass.

Brooklyn, New York:
1855.

TITLE PAGE OF THE FIRST EDITION

Whitman himself set some of the type for the original issue of Leaves of Grass

his time became, for all time, news of America the world wanted to hear.

A When Whitman died in 1892, he had fulfilled a great personal intention. He had enlarged the possibilities of American poetry to include the

B lyricism of simple speech and the grand design of the epic. The epic is that rare kind of poetry in which the ideals and values of a society are embodied in the experiences of a hero or a heroine. Usually, these epic heroes set out on a quest for knowledge that involves them deeply, sometimes secretly, in the ordinary life of their times. But their adventures, however day-to-day and down to earth, eventually become metaphors for tests of character and moments of spiritual enlightenment.

How is *Leaves of Grass* like an epic? Who is its hero? What is its action? The hero is the poet, and he is a hero not of the ancient past but of the future. As in all epics, the action takes the form of a journey. In *Leaves of Grass,* the journey is the one the speaker takes as he becomes a poet:

> I am the poet of the Body, and I am the poet
> of the Soul . . .
> I am the poet of the woman the same as the
> man . . .
> I am not the poet of goodness only, I do not
> decline to be the poet of wickedness
> also . . .

By the end of his epic journey, which even takes him down into the depths of a kind of Hell, the poet has also been transformed. The "I" has become identified with every element in the universe and has been reborn as something divine. He has become the saving force which Whitman believed it was the true role of the American poet to be.

Nothing quite like it had ever been done before.

Those who came after Whitman would also bring the vernacular of farmers, steel workers, and small-town housewives into literature. Other poets—notably Hart Crane and William Carlos Williams—would base their own epics on that American experience whose dimensions Whitman was the first to explore.

Yet Whitman's greatest contribution to literature may be the gift that only he could have given. He brought a humanizing touch that unites poetry as an art with poetry as an aspiration that runs through the life of every person. His poetry is an attempt to break the bounds of poetry, to desanctify the art of words by lending it the artlessness of feelings prodded into statement. The volume containing his life's work is not a collection of polished aphorisms or rhymed nuggets of wisdom that may be quoted in support of this idea or that. Instead, it is a spiritual autobiography that tells the story of an enchanted observer who says who he is at every opportunity and claims what he loves by naming it. Walt Whitman found his place in our literature and yet, pre-eminent as it was, refused to be confined there. "Camerado," he said, "this is no book / Who touches this touches a man."

A. Expansion
Whitman's Civil War nursing undercut his own health, and his Washington years (a time when his reputation as a poet underwent slow, faltering growth) ended in 1873 with a paralytic stroke. Whitman moved to the home of his brother George in Camden, N.J., living there until his death March 26, 1892.

B. Responding
? Name some literary epics and identify the heroes and journeys involved in each. What movies or television specials have you also heard touted as "epic" in scope? Which of these, if any, did involve a genuine hero, heroic journey, and some kind of transformation of the hero? (*Iliad, Odyssey, Beowulf, Inferno.* The heroes endure hardships to reach a destination, vanquish an enemy, and find philosophic answers.)

Humanities Connection: Responding to the Fine Art

Forge welding, or forging, is a process of heating and shaping separate pieces of metal in order to join them in a continuous metallic bond. Students will be familiar with the process on the smaller scale of the blacksmith (if only from seeing it depicted in westerns) and should be able to imagine the heat and laborious effort involved in the scene shown in *Forging the Shaft: A Welding Heat.*

? Imagine that you are a part of the scene in this painting. What do you see? Smell? Hear? Feel on your skin? How do the colors used by the painter communicate these impressions and feelings? What do the words of the title add to these impressions? (Answers will vary; encourage imaginative responses.)

Forging the Shaft: A Welding Heat by John Ferguson Weir (1877). Oil.

The Metropolitan Museum of Art, New York, Purchase. Gift of Lyman G. Bloomingdale.

Supplementary Support Materials
1. Review and Response Worksheet: Free Verse (*CCB*)
2. Selection Test (*CCB*)

Preparation
Establishing a Purpose. Ask students to recall the kinds of work done by Whitman himself, and to think about other occupations of his era, in order to predict types of work Whitman might celebrate.

Closure
Have students write one- or two-sentence statements that tell, without paraphrasing, what this poem is about.

This famous lyric appears in the front of *Leaves of Grass* and serves to introduce one of the poet's major themes. The poem celebrates work. In a truly American epic, what sort of work would you expect to be celebrated?

I Hear America Singing

I hear America singing, the varied carols I hear,
Those of mechanics, each one singing his as it should be blithe and strong,
The carpenter singing his as he measures his plank or beam,
The mason singing his as he makes ready for work, or leaves off work,
The boatman singing what belongs to him in his boat, the deck-hand singing on the steamboat deck,
The shoemaker singing as he sits on his bench, the hatter singing as he stands,
The wood-cutter's song, the ploughboy's on his way in the morning, or at noon intermission or at sundown,
The delicious singing of the mother, or of the young wife at work, or of the girl sewing or washing,
Each singing what belongs to him or her and to none else,
The day what belongs to the day—at night the party of young fellows, robust, friendly,
Singing with open mouths their strong melodious songs.

Responding to the Poem

Analyzing the Poem

Identifying Details

1. Name the people whom the poet hears in lines 2–8. What does each person sing, according to line 9?
2. Most of the poem describes the songs of the day. What is the setting for the songs of the night in the concluding lines?

Interpreting Meanings

3. What Whitman has in mind here are not the actual work songs once associated with various trades and kinds of physical labor, but something more subtle. What would you say this poem is really about?
4. A feeling of acceptance, even of contentment, runs through the sounds of these many voices. Remembering the long hours and small pay of tradespeople and manual laborers in the nineteenth century, would you say that the poet is romanticizing or idealizing their lot? Or would you say that the songs he hears are expressions of independence and joy in life? Explain your response, and support it with specific references to the poem.
5. If the poet of *Leaves of Grass* were alive today, what kinds of singing do you think he would hear? In what ways would these "songs" be different from those he heard in his own time? In what ways would they be the same as what Whitman heard? Explain your answers with references to Whitman's poems.

Analyzing the Poem
Identifying Details
1. The people whom Whitman hears include mechanics, the carpenter, the mason, the boatman, the deck-hand, the shoemaker, the hatter, the wood-cutter, the ploughboy, the mother, the young wife, and the girl sewing or washing.
Each person sings "what belongs to him or her and to none else." That is, the song of each person is unique.
2. The setting is a party of young fellows, singing "strong melodious songs."

Interpreting Meanings
3. Student answers will vary. Most students will suggest that the poem is really about the vast diversity of the American people.
4. It is a romantic vision, for these people do not have the control over their lives that is implied.
5. The romantic poet would idealize the office worker and the person on the assembly line. The poet's attitude, not the work, is important.

SUPPLEMENTARY SUPPORT MATERIALS
1. Review and Response Worksheet: Parallelism (*CCB*)
2. Selection Test (*CCB*)
3. Audiocassette recording

PREPARATION
ESTABLISHING A PURPOSE. Have students read to learn what the poem reveals about the speaker: Is he an optimist or a pessimist? What spiritual or religious beliefs would such a man find congenial? How do the answers to these questions fit with what students already know about Whitman himself?

CLOSURE
In class discussion have individual students answer these questions: Who is the speaker? What are his thoughts and feelings?

ANALYZING THE POEM
Identifying Details
1. All the readers of Whitman's poems, both singly and collectively.
2. That he is the great-grandchild of American-born ancestors, that he is thirty-seven years old, and that he is in good health.

Interpreting Meanings
3. The image suggests delicacy and individuality.
By "loafing," Whitman seems to be inviting his soul to communicate freely and intuitively with himself.
4. Philosophies and universities, or schools of thought about poetry.
In order to be able to absorb all sorts of diverse experiences and opinions.
5. To inspire original poetry and "energy."
Student answers will vary. Whitman's style is as open and comprehensive and "wild" as nature itself.
6. Students may cite lines 3, 6, and 12–13.

The varied subjects of these selections from Whitman's boldly entitled poem reveal the mind and character of the poet whose sensibilities hold the "song" together. "Song of Myself" employs a form so rarely practiced in Whitman's time that it did not even have a name. Today we know it as *free verse*—a kind of expression that ignores the many available forms of meter and the music of rhyme in favor of cadences meant to imitate the natural flow of thought and feeling.

The first poem—number 1 of the 52 that make up "Song of Myself"—is a kind of opening prayer. It answers three questions: Who is the speaker? What are his intentions? How will he compose his "song"?

Song of Myself

1.

I celebrate myself, and sing myself,
And what I assume you shall assume,
For every atom belonging to me as good belongs to you.

I loaf and invite my soul,
I lean and loaf at my ease observing a spear of summer grass.

My tongue, every atom of my blood, formed from this soil, this air,
Born here of parents born here from parents the same, and their parents the same,
I, now thirty-seven years old in perfect health begin,
Hoping to cease not till death.

Creeds and schools in abeyance,
Retiring back a while sufficed at what they are, but never forgotten,
I harbor for good or bad, I permit to speak at every hazard,
Nature without check with original energy.

Responding to the Poem

Analyzing the Poem

Identifying Details

1. Who is "you" in lines 2 and 3?
2. What autobiographical facts does the speaker reveal in lines 7–9?

Interpreting Meanings

3. What is the connection between the "soul" and "a spear of summer grass" (lines 4–5)? How is this speaker's "loafing" more than mere idleness?
4. What other terms could you substitute for "creeds" and "schools" in line 10? For what purpose does the speaker hold these "in abeyance"?
5. In Whitman's time, as never before, nature was being explored, analyzed, harnessed, exploited, and otherwise "used" to serve humankind. How is this poet going to "use" nature? How could this statement be seen as a description of the poet's style?
6. What lines of this poem show that the speaker wants to share his being or individuality with all of the natural world? What do you think of the idea expressed in line 3?

The Elements of Literature

FREE VERSE

Today we are so used to poetry written in free verse that we take it for granted. But in Whitman's time, Americans preferred poetry that was just like the poetry being written in England; they expected a poem to show the very strictest concern for meter and rhyme. Thus, Whitman's sprawling lines were revolutionary, as was his daring use of American slang, of foreign words, or of words he simply made up to suit his purpose. Whitman's "free verse" is said to have been inspired by the roll and sweep of passages from the Bible and even by the measured cadences of Emerson's essays (see page 191).

Free verse is poetry that is written without concern for regular rhyme schemes and meter. But free verse is not really free at all. Whitman abandoned meter and regular rhyme schemes, but he made full use of these other poetic elements:

1. **Assonance:** the repetition of similar vowel sounds.
2. **Alliteration:** the repetition of similar sounds, usually consonants.
3. **Onomatopoeia:** the use of words whose sounds echo their sense (such as *buzz*).
4. **Parallel structure:** the repetition of similarly constructed phrases or clauses or sentences, one after the other.
5. **Imagery:** the use of language to evoke visual images, as well as sensations of smell, hearing, taste, and touch.

What you hear when you read Whitman's lines aloud is **cadence**—the run of words that rise and fall in emphasis when he has a particular point to make and measures his lines to make it. As you can see from Whitman's poems, cadence does not depend on any strict count of stressed syllables. In traditional poetry, line length is determined by the demands of the meter.

For example, look at *The Song of Hiawatha,* an epic poem by Henry Wadsworth Longfellow (see page 146), which was published in the same year as Whitman's epic, *Leaves of Grass* (1855). Longfellow's poem, which was far more popular than Whitman's, is written in strict **trochaic tetrameter;** that is, each line has four trochees. A **trochee** is an accented syllable followed by an unaccented syllable (DAH da). Read aloud these lines from *The Song of Hiawatha,* to hear how different they sound from the opening lines of "Song of Myself":

> By the shores of Gitche Gumee,
> By the shining Big-Sea-Water,
> Stood the wigwam of Nokomis,
> Daughter of the moon, Nokomis.

In Whitman's poetry, lines can be any length at all—three syllables or thirty syllables, depending on the emphasis he wants. In the same poem, Whitman can write in one line

> Now I will do nothing but listen

and in a subsequent line

> I hear the bravuras of birds, bustle of growing wheat, gossip of flames, clack of sticks cooking my meals

Poets, who, like Whitman, choose to write in cadence have nothing but their own sense of balance and proportion to tell them when a line should end and when it should go on. With no meter to work against, and no other count to give their poems a semblance of order, they are, so to speak, on their own. They must rely completely on their own sense of spacing and timing, on their own feelings as to the "rightness" of sound and movement in every poem.

Traditional poets have found this freedom to be a handicap. Robert Frost has said that writing in this manner is "like playing tennis with the net down." Frost meant that the net on the tennis court is like the meter in poetry—the essential thing that the player and the poet must both respect and overcome. But in the twentieth century, poets have more and more accepted the challenge of writing in cadence. Instead of conforming to a chosen meter or a count of stressed syllables, they write in cadences which follow "curves of thought" or "shapes of speech." They are trusting that their own sense of balance and measure will lead to poems as well-composed as any written in meter. A poem written in regular meter might be compared to a metronome, which keeps a predictable, mechanical beat. Free verse, on the other hand, might be compared to the style of a jazz drummer, who varies the beat throughout a performance.

To hear Whitman's cadences, you must read his poems aloud. In the short opening passage (number 1), you should hear no fewer than thirty-three occurrences of the same consonant sound. What sound is it? What other examples of repetition (including parallel sentence constructions) help create the rhythms and music in this supposedly "free" verse?

A

A. Expansion
After discussing the content of the page, help students internalize the concepts by breaking a passage of poetic prose from Thoreau into lines of free verse as Whitman might have done, were he the author. A suitable passage is the opening paragraph of the selection from "Where I Lived and What I Lived For," text page 211. Have students work in small groups to break the paragraph into free verse lines, with each group responsible for explaining elements of cadence, alliteration, parallel structure, and imagery that guided group choices.

Supplementary Support Materials

1. Review and Response Worksheet: Imagery and Tone (*CCB*)
2. Selection Test (*CCB*)
3. Audiocassette recording

Preparation

Establishing a Purpose. As the headnote indicates, ask students as they read to form mental images of the scenes in the poem.

A. Imagery

? Describe the images evoked by the two brief scenes glimpsed in lines 6–10. (The poet sees himself at the bow of the ship looking toward land. He goes clamming. This evokes the image of men digging into the wet sand with toes and fingers.)

B. Noting Details

? Explain what the men in lines 15–24 are like. What is the slave's physical condition? (Weak, ragged, limping) What shows that both men are courageous? (The slave has dared to run away; the speaker dares to shelter him.) Note: Some students may wish to look ahead to the firsthand account of a runaway slave in Unit Six, Frederick Douglass's "The Battle with Mr. Covey," page 386. You may wish also to refer to the Moran oil reproduced in this unit on page 339, *Slaves Escaping Through the Swamps,* and ask students what it adds to their interpretation of this scene.

Here we have the poet as both observer and participant. In these movie-like glimpses into the broad American scene, he sees what he knows. The poet speaks as though he were not only the cameraman who shoots the pictures but also the director behind each scene who "arranges" just what it will look like. As you read, try to form mental pictures of each of these scenes.

10.

Alone far in the wilds and mountains I hunt,
Wandering amazed at my own lightness and glee,
In the late afternoon choosing a safe spot to pass the night,
Kindling a fire and broiling the fresh-killed game,
Falling asleep on the gathered leaves with my dog and gun by
my side.

A

The Yankee clipper is under her sky-sails, she cuts the sparkle
and scud,
My eyes settle the land, I bend at her prow or shout joyously
from the deck.

The boatmen and clam-diggers arose early and stopped for me,
I tucked my trowser-ends in my boots and went and had a good
time;
You should have been with us that day round the chowder-kettle.

I saw the marriage of the trapper in the open air in the far west,
the bride was a red girl,
Her father and his friends sat near cross-legged and dumbly
smoking, they had moccasins to their feet and large thick
blankets hanging from their shoulders,
On a bank lounged the trapper, he was dressed mostly in skins,
his luxuriant beard and curls protected his neck, he held
his bride by the hand.
She had long eyelashes, her head was bare, her coarse straight
locks descended upon her voluptuous limbs and reached
to her feet.

B

The runaway slave came to my house and stopped outside,
I heard his motions crackling the twigs of the woodpile,
Through the swung half-door of the kitchen I saw him limpsy
and weak,
And went where he sat on a log and led him in and assured him,
And brought water and filled a tub for his sweated body and
bruised feet,
And gave him a room that entered from my own, and gave him
some coarse clean clothes,
And remember perfectly well his revolving eyes and his awk-
wardness,
And remember putting plasters on the galls° of his neck and
ankles;
He staid with me a week before he was recuperated and passed
north,
I had him sit next me at table, my fire-lock leaned in the corner.

22. **galls:** sores.

ANALYZING THE POEM
Identifying Details
1. The scene in the first stanza is the wilds and the mountains, where the speaker, accompanied by his dog, is hunting. In the second stanza, the setting is aboard a Yankee clipper ship. In the third stanza, the poet is with boatmen and clamdiggers, with whom he has a "good time" around the chowder-kettle. In the fourth, the speaker witnesses the marriage of an Indian girl and a trapper outdoors in the Far West. Finally, in the fifth stanza, the speaker is at his own house, where he aids a runaway slave.
2. Among the images students may cite are kindling the fire and cooking (line 4), the picture of the ship under sail (line 6), the description of the Indian girl's father and his friends (line 12), and the portrait of the girl (line 14).
3. See the sequence of participles in lines 4–5 and the verbs connected by "and" in lines 16–22.
4. A "Yankee Clipper" is a nineteenth-century sailing ship with tall masts. "Scud" here may mean the wind-driven spray.

"Dumbly" means "mutely." "Limpsy" is a variation of "limp," in the sense of "weak" or "swaying." "Revolving eyes" refers to the man's eyes rolling in fear or pain; "galls" is equivalent to "chronic sores."

Interpreting Meanings
5. In the fourth scene, the speaker might imply a threat to the marriage with the phrase "dumbly smoking" in line 12. Perhaps it is an arranged match. In the last scene, the pathetic plight of the runaway slave moves the speaker deeply; there is no room for joy.
6. The stanza shows that the speaker is profoundly sensitive, caring, and compassionate.
7. He admires the girl's beauty. He pities the slave.

Hunter in the Adirondacks by Winslow Homer (1892). Watercolor.

Courtesy of the Harvard University Art Museums (Fogg Art Museum), Cambridge, Massachusetts. Anonymous Gift.

Responding to the Poem

Analyzing the Poem

Identifying Details

1. In the five stanzas of this poem, the speaker observes and participates in five far-ranging American scenes. Identify the "scene" in each stanza.
2. What **images** of sight, touch, and sound bring the reader into each of these scenes?
3. What repetitions of sentence patterns help create a sense of **cadence** in this poem—a rhythmic rise and fall of your voice as the lines are spoken aloud?
4. To read poetry, you need to keep a dictionary handy. What is the meaning of a "Yankee Clipper" and of "scud" (line 6)? Does "dumbly" in line 12 mean "stupidly" or "mutely"? What do you guess "limpsy" is in line 17? What are "revolving eyes" (line 21) and "galls" (line 22)?

Interpreting Meanings

5. In the first scene, the speaker says that he was "amazed" at his own "lightness and glee." In the second scene, he shouts "joyously from the deck." In the third, he "went and had a good time." In the fourth and fifth scenes, such expressions of personal delight are absent. What is the **tone** of these scenes? How do you account for this?
6. In the last scene, the "runaway slave" is one of thousands who entrusted their lives to the compassion of men and women who might feed and clothe them and otherwise assist their attempts to escape bondage. With this fact in mind, what do you think the stanza—especially the last line—shows about the speaker's character?
7. How would you describe the speaker's **attitude** toward the red girl and the runaway slave?

SUPPLEMENTARY SUPPORT MATERIALS
1. Review and Response Worksheet: Cataloguing (*CCB*)
2. Selection Test (*CCB*)

PREPARATION

ESTABLISHING A PURPOSE. Call students' attention to the definition of *fakes* in the headnote, but alert them mainly to listen for the *sounds* of this poem. You may wish to enhance this focus by having students close their books and their eyes as you or assigned students read the poem aloud.

CLOSURE

In class discussion have students brainstorm the sounds in the poem. Then have individual students describe an image used by Whitman to evoke each sound.

A. Humanities Connection: Discussing the Photogravure
Alfred Stieglitz (stēg′lits), 1864–1946, was an American photographer, editor, and art exhibitor credited with a leading role in recognition of photography as a fine art.

Depicted here is a scene in which one can easily place Whitman, who frequented the horse-drawn public transportation of the late 1800's. After students have read the poem, you might ask them how the photogravure affects or modifies their initial mental image of the engines, hose-carts, and train cars mentioned in lines 11 and 12 on text page 337.

The speaker introduces this selection by telling us what *he* is going to do—*we* must stay with him and, like Whitman, "do nothing but listen." Whitman's allusion to Uranus in line 23 serves him well, since it refers to a remote planet with a broad orbit. The word *fakes* in line 27 shows his knowledge of nautical terms: A *fake* is a loop of coiled rope, especially the kind of "running" rope used on cargo ships. In reading this "song," you will have to hear the sounds that are evoked by the images.

26.

Now I will do nothing but listen,
To accrue what I hear into this song, to let sounds contribute
toward it.

I hear bravuras of birds, bustle of growing wheat, gossip of
flames, clack of sticks cooking my meals.
I hear the sound I love, the sound of the human voice,
I hear all sounds running together, combined, fused or following,
Sounds of the city and sounds out of the city, sounds of the day
and night,
Talkative young ones to those that like them, the loud laugh of
work-people at their meals,
The angry base of disjointed friendship, the faint tones of the
sick,
The judge with hands tight to the desk, his pallid lips pronoun-
cing a death-sentence,
The heave'e'yo of stevedores unlading ships by the wharves,
the refrain of the anchor-lifters,

The Terminal by Alfred Stieglitz (1892), from *Camera Work* No. 36, October, 1911. Photogravure, 10″ × 13″.

Collection, The Museum of Modern Art, New York. Gift of Georgia O'Keeffe.

A

Analyzing The Poem

Identifying Details

1. Through alliteration of sounds.

2. That of the human voice (line 4).

3. Morphine, a drug that takes away pain, may be called "honeyed" or sweet because of its analgesic effects.

4. Sounds of joy: bravuras of birds (line 3), the sound of the human voice (line 4), the loud laugh of the working people (line 7), the sound of the orchestra (line 23). Sounds of sorrow: the faint tones of the sick (line 8), the ring of alarm-bells (line 11), the slow death march (lines 13–14). Sounds of work: the bustle of growing wheat (line 3), the clack of sticks cooking (line 3), the stevedores and the refrain of the anchor-lifters (line 10), the whirr of the engines and carts (line 11). Sounds of art: the musical instruments (lines 15–17), the chorus of the opera (lines 18–19), the voices of the tenor and the soprano (lines 20–22), the sound of the orchestra (line 23). Sounds of nature: the birds (line 3), the wheat (line 3).

5. Students may mention the following examples: the infinitives "to accrue" and "to let" (line 2), the repetition of "I hear" (lines 3–5, 15, 16, 18, 22), the "sounds" (line 6), and the series of clauses beginning with "it" (lines 24–25).

6. Students should point to the phrase "crackle of sticks cooking my meals."

Have students sound these words especially: *chorus, grand opera; music, suits; tenor, large, creation, me, orbic, mouth, pouring, full; soprano, orchestra, whirls, wider, Uranus, wrenches, ardor, know, sails, indolent, waves, angry, hail, lose, steeped, honeyed, morphine, throttled, feel, being.*

Interpreting Meanings

7. Lines 3 and 11.

The last line concisely sums up in one phrase the immense diversity conveyed in the preceding lines of the poem.

8. Because Whitman has just catalogued an astounding variety of different sounds in lines 5–17.

9. Whitman regards life itself as a mystery.

10. A "wrenching" sensation and a feeling of breathlessness.

Probably ecstasy.

The ring of alarm-bells, the cry of fire, the whirr of swift-streaking engines and hose-carts with premonitory tinkles and colored lights,
The steam-whistle, the solid roll of the train of approaching cars,
The slow march played at the head of the association marching two and two,
(They go to guard some corpse, the flag-tops are draped with black muslin.)
I hear the violincello ('tis the young man's heart's complaint),
I hear the keyed cornet, it glides quickly in through my ears,
It shakes mad-sweet pangs through my belly and breast.

I hear the chorus, it is a grand opera,
Ah this indeed is music—this suits me.

A tenor large and fresh as the creation fills me,
The orbic flex of his mouth is pouring and filling me full.

I hear the trained soprano (what work with hers is this?)
The orchestra whirls me wider than Uranus flies,
It wrenches such ardors from me I did not know I possessed them,
It sails me, I dab with bare feet, they are licked by the indolent waves,
I am cut by bitter and angry hail, I lose my breath,
Steeped amid honeyed morphine, my windpipe throttled in fakes of death,
At length let up again to feel the puzzle of puzzles,
And that we call Being.

Responding to the Poem

Analyzing the Poem

Identifying Details

1. The speaker says in line 2 that he will let sounds "contribute" to his own song. How does he *describe* the sounds he hears in line 3?
2. What is the sound that the speaker says he loves?
3. What is "honeyed morphine" (line 27)?
4. The sounds in this poem tend to fall into categories. Break Whitman's long **catalogue**—or list—of sounds into these categories: sounds of joy, sorrow, work, art, and nature.
5. How many examples of **parallel sentence construction** can you find in this poem of 29 lines?
6. What sound in line 3 is an example of **onomatopoeia**—the use of a word with a sound that echoes its sense? What open vowel sounds contribute to the majestic sounds of the last three stanzas?

Interpreting Meanings

7. Whitman's lines are not long or short by accident. He had a reason for stopping each line as he did, or for extending it as long as he did. What long lines suggest a medley of many different sounds? What does the poet gain by making the last line so short?
8. Whitman had a great love for grand opera, especially Italian opera. In opera, many different characters may sing simultaneously of their own emotions. What makes the mention of an operatic chorus particularly appropriate at lines 18–19?
9. Why do you think the speaker calls "Being" the "puzzle of puzzles" in the last two lines?
10. In the final section of this selection, the speaker describes the physical effect that operatic singing has upon him, and he attempts to suggest its spiritual effect. What is the physical effect? What would you say the spiritual effect is?

Supplementary Support Materials
1. Review and Response Worksheet: Tone and Imagery (*CCB*)
2. Selection Test (*CCB*)
3. Audiocassette recording

Preparation

Establishing a Purpose. After students have read the headnote, ask them to recall a time when they were able deeply to feel the pain of another person. Ask students who are willing to do so to describe that time in general terms.

Closure

Have students write a brief journal entry describing, from the point of view of the speaker, the speaker's feelings about one of the people he describes.

A. Noting Details
? Why was the skipper a hero to Whitman? (After three days and nights, he saved a steamship set adrift in a storm.)

B. Noting Details
? Who are the two martyrs that the poet mentions? (A condemned witch and an escaped slave)

C. Interpretation
Blood dribbles down, diluted with sweat.

D. Responding
? What evidence is there in these lines of the poet's empathy? (The poet says that he "wears" the agonies of others. He becomes the wounded person and thus feels the agony firsthand.)

In this excerpt from the thirty-third section of "Song of Myself," we come upon one of the poet's most famous lines: "I am the man, I suffered, I was there." The line not only shows the poet as a man of sympathetic disposition, but as one capable of *empathy*—the ability to project one's own feelings into the consciousness of others. A great part of Whitman's work is distinguished by his attempts to erase the line between observer and object. Whitman does this in order that, imaginatively speaking, he might *become* the thing or person he is talking about. This is why his poems strike even his most resistant readers with an urgency they cannot ignore.

From 33.

A
I understand the large hearts of heroes,
The courage of present times and all times,
How the skipper saw the crowded and rudderless wreck of the
  steam-ship, and Death chasing it up and down the storm,
How he knuckled tight and gave not back an inch, and was
  faithful of days and faithful of nights,
And chalked in large letters on a board, *Be of good cheer, we
  will not desert you;*
How he followed with them and tacked with them three days
  and would not give it up.
How he saved the drifting company at last.
How the lank loose-gowned women looked when boated from
  the side of their prepared graves,
How the silent old-faced infants and the lifted sick, and the
  sharp-lipped unshaved men;
All this I swallow, it tastes good, I like it well, it becomes mine,
I am the man, I suffered, I was there.

B
The disdain and calmness of martyrs,
The mother of old, condemned for a witch, burnt with dry
  wood, her children gazing on,
The hounded slave that flags in the race, leans by the fence,
  blowing, covered with sweat,
The twinges that sting like needles his legs and neck, the
  murderous buckshot and the bullets,
All these I feel or am.

I am the hounded slave, I wince at the bite of the dogs,
C
Hell and despair are upon me, crack and again crack the
  marksmen,
I clutch the rails of the fence, my gore dribs, thinned with the
  ooze of my skin,
I fall on the weeds and stones,
The riders spur their unwilling horses, haul close,
Taunt my dizzy ears and beat me violently over the head with
  whip-stocks.

D
Agonies are one of my changes of garments.
I do not ask the wounded person how he feels, I myself become
  the wounded person,
My hurts turn livid upon me as I lean on a cane and observe.
I am the mashed fireman with breast-bone broken,

Literature and Language: Structuring Series

Many of Whitman's poems contain catalogues—long lists of names, things, or activities at the end of a sentence. These items make up a series and are separated by commas. When the items in a series contain commas themselves, they are separated by semicolons, as in the first stanza of "from 33" on page 338.

Ask students to notice the series in "I Hear America Singing." (The whole poem, from line 2 to the end, is a series of the workers' songs, the "varied carols" the speaker hears.) Then ask them to notice the catalogue/series structure in other Whitman poems in this unit (see especially "26," "from 33," and "On the Beach at Night Alone.")

After writing these sentence starters on the board, ask students to complete them with a series of items punctuated correctly.

1. As I flip through the TV channels, I see and hear. . . .

2. My favorite times are. . . .

3. On a hot, summer day, ...

Slaves Escaping Through the Swamps by Thomas Moran (c. 1870). Oil.

Philbrook Art Center, Tulsa, Oklahoma.

Humanities Connection: Responding to the Fine Art

Thomas Moran (1837–1926) was one of three brothers noted for historical, maritime, landscape, and animal paintings. His specialty was the mood-evoking landscape done in the style of the Romantic English landscape artist Joseph Turner (1775–1851). Like Turner, he attempted to convey not just the details of a scene, but atmospheric effects that revealed the elemental power of nature.

? Imagine that you are in this scene: What time is it? What noises spook you? What dangers terrify you? What is your physical condition? What are you carrying? How far have you come and how far must you go? (Students may wish to follow this exercise by writing an interior monologue as a runaway slave.)

ANALYZING THE POEM
Identifying Details
1. The selfless courage of the ship's captain who saves a ship in a ferocious storm; martyrs who are condemned witches and runaway slaves; a fireman who has risked death to battle a blaze; a dying general in war, who urges his troops to "mind the entrenchments" rather than come to his aid.
2. The speaker restates this point at several places in the poem: see particularly "I am the hounded slave" (line 17); "I am the mashed fireman" (line 26); "I am the clock myself" (line 36); "I am an old artillerist" (line 37); "I take part, I see and hear the whole" (line 42).
3. The hounded slave is similar to the "runaway slave" of "10" (see page 334): He is probably one of the numerous slaves who attempted to escape from the South to the North on the "underground railroad" of the 1840's and 1850's.
The poet is probably imagining the bombardment of Fort Sumter in April, 1861—the conflict which started the Civil War.
4. The word means "pay attention to."
(Answers continue in left-hand column.)

(Continued from top.)
5. Among the repeated sentence structures that students may mention are the following: the clauses beginning with "how" (lines 3–9), the parallel clauses of line 11, the sequence of nouns at the beginning of lines 12–15, the parallel clauses beginning with "I" in lines 37–38, and the series of nouns and phrases in lines 43–47.
6. Students can easily find at least ten of each in the poem.

Interpreting Meanings
7. Imaginative empathy; admiration for the heroes' courage; compassion for their suffering.
8. Short lines are usually the most emphatic and thus most important. See lines 11, 16, 38. Often they are meant to be said more slowly.

Tumbling walls buried me in their debris,
Heat and smoke I inspired, I heard the yelling shouts of my comrades,
I heard the distant click of their picks and shovels,
They have cleared the beams away, they tenderly lift me forth.

I lie in the night air in my red shirt, the pervading hush is for my sake,
Painless after all I lie exhausted but not so unhappy.
White and beautiful are the faces around me, the heads are bared of their fire-caps,
The kneeling crowd fades with the light of the torches.

Distant and dead resuscitate,
They show as the dial or move as the hands of me, I am the clock myself.

I am an old artillerist, I tell of my fort's bombardment,
I am there again.

Again the long roll of the drummers,
Again the attacking cannon, mortars,
Again to my listening ears the cannon responsive.

I take part, I see and hear the whole,
The cries, curses, roar, the plaudits for well-aimed shots,
The ambulanza slowly passing trailing its red drip.
Workmen searching after damages, making indispensable repairs,
The fall of grenades through the rent roof, the fan-shaped explosion,
The whizz of limbs, heads, stone, wood, iron, high in the air.

Again gurgles the mouth of my dying general, he furiously waves with his hand,
He gasps through the clot *Mind not me—mind—the entrenchments.*

Responding to the Poem

Analyzing the Poem

Identifying Details

1. "The large hearts of heroes" is the keynote for this passage. What kinds of heroism does the speaker describe here? List the people he identifies with.
2. At what moments does the speaker restate the point of "I am the man, I suffered, I was there"?
3. Remembering the historical background against which this poem was written, how would you explain the incident described in lines 17–22? What conflict is the poet describing in the account of the old artillerist in lines 37–49?
4. What does "mind" mean in the last line?
5. Find at least five **sentence structures** that Whitman repeats in this poem to create his **rhythm.**
6. The poet wants us to share his empathy. What **images** of sight and sound help us feel we also "are there"?

Interpreting Meanings

7. How would you describe the speaker's **tone** in this passage—what are his feelings for these "heroes"?
8. Notice the alternation of very long lines and very short lines. Can you see the reason for each short line? How would you use your voice in reading each short line aloud?

Supplementary Support Materials

1. Review and Response Worksheet: The Speaker (*CCB*)
2. Selection Test (*CCB*)
3. Audiocassette recording

Preparation

Establishing a Purpose. Have students read the headnote before listening to the audiocassette or a live reading of the poem. Note the final question: What *is* happening to the speaker?

The final poem of "Song of Myself" is a *coda*—a brief restatement and summing up of the themes of the entire song. Since none of these themes is more insistently present throughout the poem than the mind and spirit of the speaker himself, the passage is highly personal. True to his nature, the poet mocks his own egotism; but, just as true to his confidence in himself, he proclaims his importance—and his inescapability. What is happening to the speaker in this famous passage?

52.

The spotted hawk swoops by and accuses me, he complains
 of my gab and my loitering.

I too am not a bit tamed, I too am untranslatable,
I sound my barbaric yawp over the roofs of the world.

A The last scud of day holds back for me,
It flings my likeness after the rest and true as any on the
 shadowed wilds,
It coaxes me to the vapor and the dusk.

I depart as air, I shake my white locks at the runaway sun,
I effuse my flesh in eddies, and drift it in lacy jags.

I bequeath myself to the dirt to grow from the grass I love,
If you want me again look for me under your boot-soles.

You will hardly know who I am or what I mean,
B But I shall be good health to you nevertheless,
And filter and fiber your blood.

Failing to fetch me at first keep encouraged,
Missing me one place search another,
I stop somewhere waiting for you.

A. Metaphor
You may wish to pause after reading lines 1–8, or after discussion of response questions 1, 3, and 4 on page 342, to examine the photograph and further discuss the hawk metaphor and its applicability to the speaker—clearly Whitman himself. **?** How do the lines evoke the soaring freedom sought by both hawk and poet? (Choices such as "depart as air," "eddies," "drift in lacy jags")

B. Responding
? What evidence is there in these lines that Whitman considers himself a poet "for the masses"? (He uses images such as dirt, boot-soles, and blood to describe his nearness to the people. "I stop somewhere waiting for you" indicates his accessibility.)

Closure
Have students paraphrase the poem orally, and then, in brief statements, tell the author's purpose in writing the poem.

Analyzing The Poem
Identifying Details
1. He says in lines 2–3 that he is not tamed, that he is untranslatable, and that he sounds a "barbaric yawp."

2. Whitman imagines himself as melting into the dirt "to grow from the grass I love." He tells his readers that they may not know or understand him well, but that he will remain—through his poetry—as a salutary influence on them. If readers fail to "reach" him at first, they should be encouraged and search for him in another place; they will eventually find him.

Interpreting Meanings
3. The poet writes in a wild, free style people do not understand. His language, his art, is still powerful.
4. Again, students will have different opinions. Encourage the students to support their answers with specific facts and/or arguments.
5. He probably means that he intends
(Answers continue in left-hand column.)

(Continued from top.)
his poetry to be as accessible and nearby as the earth or the dust under the boot-soles of the average working person of the day.
6. The connection of the words "I" (the first word in the second line) and "you" (the final word in the last line) serves as an emblem for Whitman's profound empathy; the ability to inject his own personality into those of other people in order to experience their emotions more deeply. He intends all his readers, as far as possible, to accept his "search" for them and to empathize with him in return.
7. He consistently uses the present tense.
The effect would have lost much of its immediacy and intensity.

Responding to the Poem

Analyzing the Poem

Identifying Details

1. What qualities does the speaker say he shares with the spotted hawk?
2. Beginning with line 9, the speaker makes one of his most direct addresses to his readers. What, in your own words, is his parting message?

Interpreting Meanings

3. Considering what you know of the work of poets who preceded him, what does the poet mean when he describes his own poetry as "barbaric yawp"? Do you agree? Describe your response to Whitman's language. Do you think its effect on people has changed with the passage of time?
4. Could Whitman also be using the phrase "barbaric yawp" to refer to the way the Old World might have regarded the experiment of democracy itself? Explain your answer.
5. What do you think the poet means when he says, in line 10, "If you want me again look for me under your boot-soles"?
6. The first line of "Song of Myself" is "I celebrate myself, and sing myself"; the last line is "I stop somewhere waiting for you." Taking into account all that you have learned of the poet's character and the range of his poem, tell what you think the last words in the poem reveal about Whitman's overall **purpose** in writing the poem.
7. What tense does the poet use in these selections from "Song of Myself"? How would the effect have differed if he had spoken in the past tense?

Writing About "Song of Myself"

A Creative Response

1. **Writing an Essay as a Poem.** Whitman is said to have been influenced by the rolling cadences of Emerson's essays. Take a paragraph from one of Emerson's essays, and write it in the shape of a poem. Pay special attention to where you will break the lines: Which lines will you run long and which will you run short?

A Critical Response

2. **Comparing Whitman to Emerson.** In a brief essay, compare these selections from "Song of Myself" with Emerson's essay "Nature" (page 191). First, compare Whitman's message about people and their relationship to nature with Emerson's views on the same subject. Second, compare the style and diction of the writings. Quote from the poems and the essay to support what you say.
3. **Comparing a Poem to a Psalm.** Whitman knew his Bible very well. In a brief essay, tell whether or not you detect similarities between Song 33 and Psalm 22. Quote from the psalm and the poem to support your opinions. Fill out a chart like the following one before you write.

	Psalm 22	Song 33
Parallel structures		
Cadences		
Message		
Tone		

Supplementary Support Materials
1. Review and Response Worksheet: Symbols (*CCB*)
2. Selection Test (*CCB*)

Preparation

Establishing a Purpose. The headnote, especially its final question, can be used to focus students' attention as they read the poem quietly or listen as it is read.

Closure

Have students jot down on a sheet of paper adjectives and adverbs that describe the sky images in the poem. Then have students write two one-sentence statements that contrast each of the two figures with the sky images. Images and statements should be shared orally.

A. Humanities Connection: Discussing the Fine Art

Marsden Hartley (1877–1943) was an American painter of landscapes and still lifes, best known for his paintings of the people and scenery of his native Maine.

You might ask students, before they read the poem, briefly to describe the mood conveyed by the painting. After reading, ask which lines the painting seems intended to illustrate. (Suitable responses: lines 4–6, 7–10, 17–21)

Many of Whitman's poems are set on the same Long Island beach, and several of them focus on a child. In this poem, we are aware that the child is crying over something. What is it?

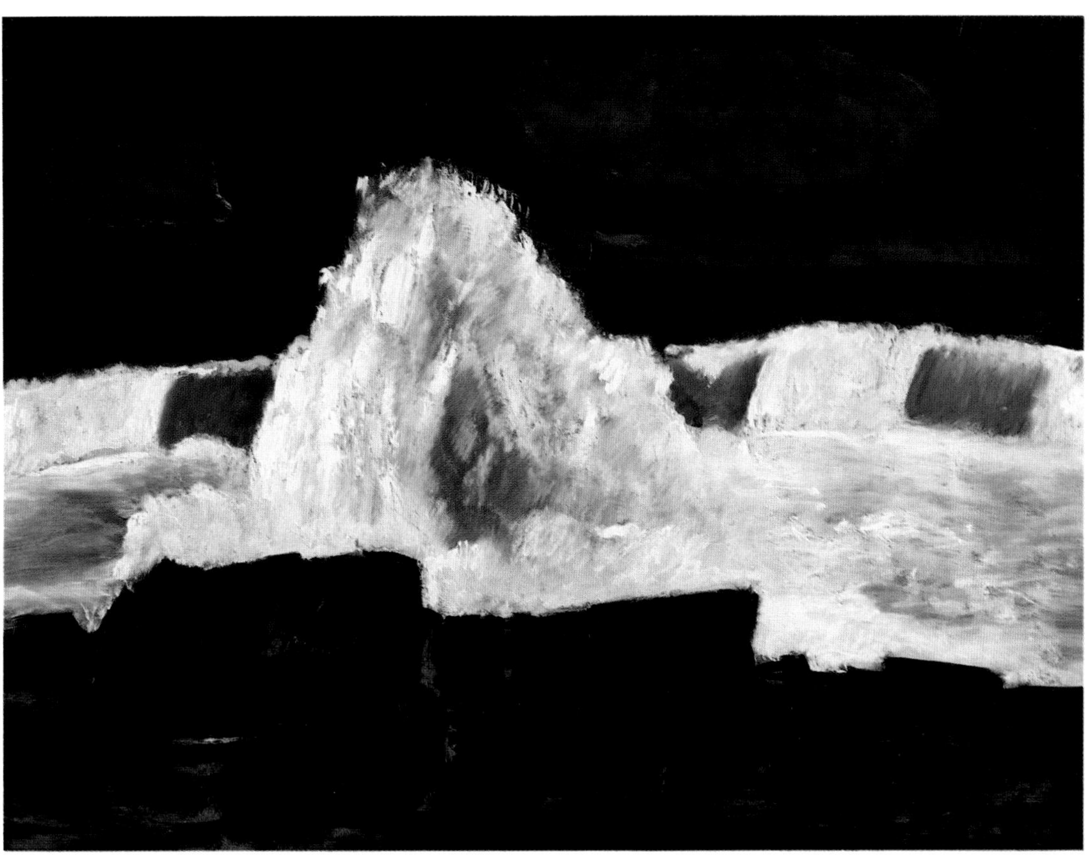

Evening Storm, Schoodic, Maine by Marsden Hartley (1942). Oil on composition board, 30″ × 40″.

Collection, The Museum of Modern Art, New York. Acquired through the Lillie P. Bliss Bequest.

On the Beach at Night

On the beach at night,
Stands a child with her father,
Watching the east, the autumn sky.

Up through the darkness,
While ravening clouds, the burial clouds, in black masses
   spreading,
Lower sullen and fast athwart and down the sky,
Amid a transparent clear belt of ether° yet left in the east,
Ascends large and calm the lord-star Jupiter,
And nigh at hand, only a very little above,
Swim the delicate sisters the Pleiades.°

7. **ether:** sky.

10. **Pleiades** (plē′ə·dēz): a cluster of seven stars in the constellation Taurus, imagined to be seven sisters.

Analyzing The Poem
Identifying Details
1. Voracious hunger.
2. She is afraid that the clouds will "devour" Jupiter and the stars.
3. The poet tells the child that the clouds will not obscure the bright stars and the planet for long.

Interpreting Meanings
4. The forces of evil and destruction in the world, which threaten to overwhelm good.

In general, Jupiter and the immortal stars in this poem are images of light, perhaps symbolizing radiance, justice, and the triumph of good over evil.
5. From the statement in the last stanza that "something will endure longer even than lustrous Jupiter" (line 30), we may infer that Whitman is talking about the soul—or perhaps about a higher, divine power. The lesson the speaker is teaching the child concerns the profound issues of good and evil, life and death.
6. The "black masses" (line 5), the transparent "belt of ether" in the east (line 7), the description of the planet *(Answers continue in left-hand column.)*

(Continued from top.) Jupiter rising (line 8), and the "delicate sisters" of the Pleiades (line 10).

They seem small and insignificant.

The theme of the poem emphasizes that "something" more immortal than the stars persists in nature and watches over us.
7. Student answers will vary.

He might mean God, or love, or the creative imagination, or life itself. He might even mean poetry and vision. He might also mean the soul of each individual. You might compare this sentiment to that in Cummings's poem on page 738, or in Moore's poem on 725.

A. Imagery
? What scene is depicted through the images in these lines? (The scene is the planet Jupiter appearing just below the Pleiades in a sky filled with dark clouds.)

From the beach the child holding the hand of her father,
Those buried clouds that lower victorious soon to
  devour all,
Watching, silently weeps.

Weep not, child,
Weep not, my darling,
With these kisses let me remove your tears,
The ravening clouds shall not long be victorious,
They shall not long possess the sky, they devour the
  stars only in apparition,
Jupiter shall emerge, be patient, watch again another
  night, the Pleiades shall emerge,
They are immortal, all those stars both silvery and
  golden shall shine out again,
The great stars and the little ones shall shine out again,
  they endure,
The vast immortal suns and the long-enduring pensive
  moons shall again shine.

Then dearest child mournest thou only for Jupiter?
Considerest thou alone the burial of the stars?
Something there is,
(With my lips soothing thee, adding I whisper,
I give thee the first suggestion, the problem and indirec-
  tion),
Something there is more immortal even than the stars,
(Many the burials, many the days and nights, passing
  away),
Something that shall endure longer even than lustrous
  Jupiter,
Longer than sun or any revolving satellite,
Or the radiant sisters the Pleiades.

A

Responding to the Poem

Analyzing the Poem

Identifying Details

1. What does *ravening* mean in lines 5 and 17?
2. Why does the child weep silently in lines 11–13?
3. How does the poet reassure the child in the fourth stanza?

Interpreting Meanings

4. The last stanza implies that the poem is intended to be read on a **symbolic,** as well as on a literal, level. What do you think the "ravening clouds" might symbolize? What might Jupiter and the "immortal stars" symbolize?
5. When the poet says in line 27 that he is giving "the first suggestion, the problem and indirection," it is as if he were teaching the child her first lesson on an important, and possibly difficult subject. What do you think the subject is, and what is the lesson the poet wants to teach the child?
6. What specific **images** help you to visualize what is happening in the sky? How do the two figures on the beach contrast with these distant sky images? How is this contrast important to the poem?
7. What do you think he means by the "something" in the last stanza—the "something" that is immortal and will endure? Do you think the lesson he intends for the child is clear? How would you respond to Whitman's main point in this poem?

Supplementary Support Materials

1. Review and Response Worksheet: Symbols (*CCB*)
2. Selection Test (*CCB*)
3. Instructional Overhead Transparency

Preparation

Establishing A Purpose. Before students read the poem, you might want them to share their thoughts and impressions from visits to the sea.

Closure

Have students explain why the term "vast similitude" is central to the theme of this poem.

Analyzing The Poem

Identifying Details

1. The "old mother" is the sea. The "to and fro" is the ebb and flow of the ocean waves or the tides.
2. The song is probably the noise of the waves.
3. Student answers will vary. One possible definition is "sameness" or "oneness."

Interpreting Meanings

4. One might compare it to the cycle of birth, life, and death.
5. He means that everything in nature is bound together.

Some of the categories include: celestial bodies, human beings, aspects of culture, and inanimate objects.

6. Student answers will vary. Many students may point out that "spans"—in the sense of "bridges"—has a slightly different (and weaker) meaning than "interlocks"—in the sense of "unifies closely."
7. Student answers will vary.

Such thoughts seem to be prompted by the image of the "edge of the world," suggested by the meeting of sea and sky at a beach. Also, the sea traditionally suggests both life and death, time and eternity.

"Even as a boy," wrote Whitman in his *Specimen Days* (see page 350), "I had the fancy, the wish, to write a piece, perhaps a poem, about the seashore—that suggesting, dividing line, contact, junction, the solid marrying the liquid . . . blending the real and ideal, and each made portion of the other. Hours, days, in my Long Island youth and early manhood, I haunted the shores of Rockaway or Coney Island, or away east to the Hamptons or Montauk. Once, at the latter place (by the old lighthouse, nothing but sea-tossings in sight in every direction as far as the eye could reach), I remember well, I felt that I must one day write a book expressing this liquid, mystic theme."

On the Beach at Night Alone

On the beach at night alone,
As the old mother sways her to and fro singing her husky song,
As I watch the bright stars shining, I think a thought of the clef
  of the universes and of the future.
A vast similitude interlocks all,
All spheres, grown, ungrown, small, large, suns, moons, planets,
All distances of place however wide,
All distances of time, all inanimate forms,
All souls, all living bodies though they be ever so different, or in
  different worlds,
All gaseous, watery, vegetable, mineral processes, the fishes, the
  brutes,
All nations, colors, barbarisms, civilizations, languages,
All indentities that have existed or may exist on this globe, or
  any globe
All lives and deaths, all of the past, present, future,
This vast similitude spans them, and always has spanned,
And shall forever span them and compactly hold and enclose
  them.

Responding to the Poem

Analyzing the Poem

Identifying Details

1. Who is the "old mother"? (The title gives you the clue.) What is her "to and fro"?
2. What is the old mother's "husky song"?
3. How would you define "similitude"?

Interpreting Meanings

4. What in human life might the old mother's "to and fro" be compared with?
5. What does the poet mean by a "vast similitude" that "interlocks" all? The **catalogue** that Whitman cites includes many categories. Name some of them.
6. What distinction can you make between a "vast similitude" that "*interlocks* all" and a "vast similitude" that "*spans* them"? Do the verbs merely suggest two aspects of the same phenomenon? Explain.
7. Why do you think thoughts like these came to the poet while he was on the beach?

Writing About the Poem

A Critical Response

Comparing the Poem to "Thanatopsis." In a brief essay, explain whether or not you think Whitman's "vast similitude" has anything in common with the view of the universe expressed in "Thanatopsis" (see page 142).

Humanities Connection: Responding to the Fine Art
(You might want to defer discussion of the art until students have read and responded to the poem on the facing page, 347.)
? How does the painting manage to convey the attitudes and methods of Whitman's "learned astronomer," even though it depicts a laboratory rather than an observatory? (Orderly instruments, devices, and containers; focus on what is measurable or observable; the man's seriousness) Is there another type of illustration you might have chosen to accompany this poem? What is it, and why would it be a good choice?

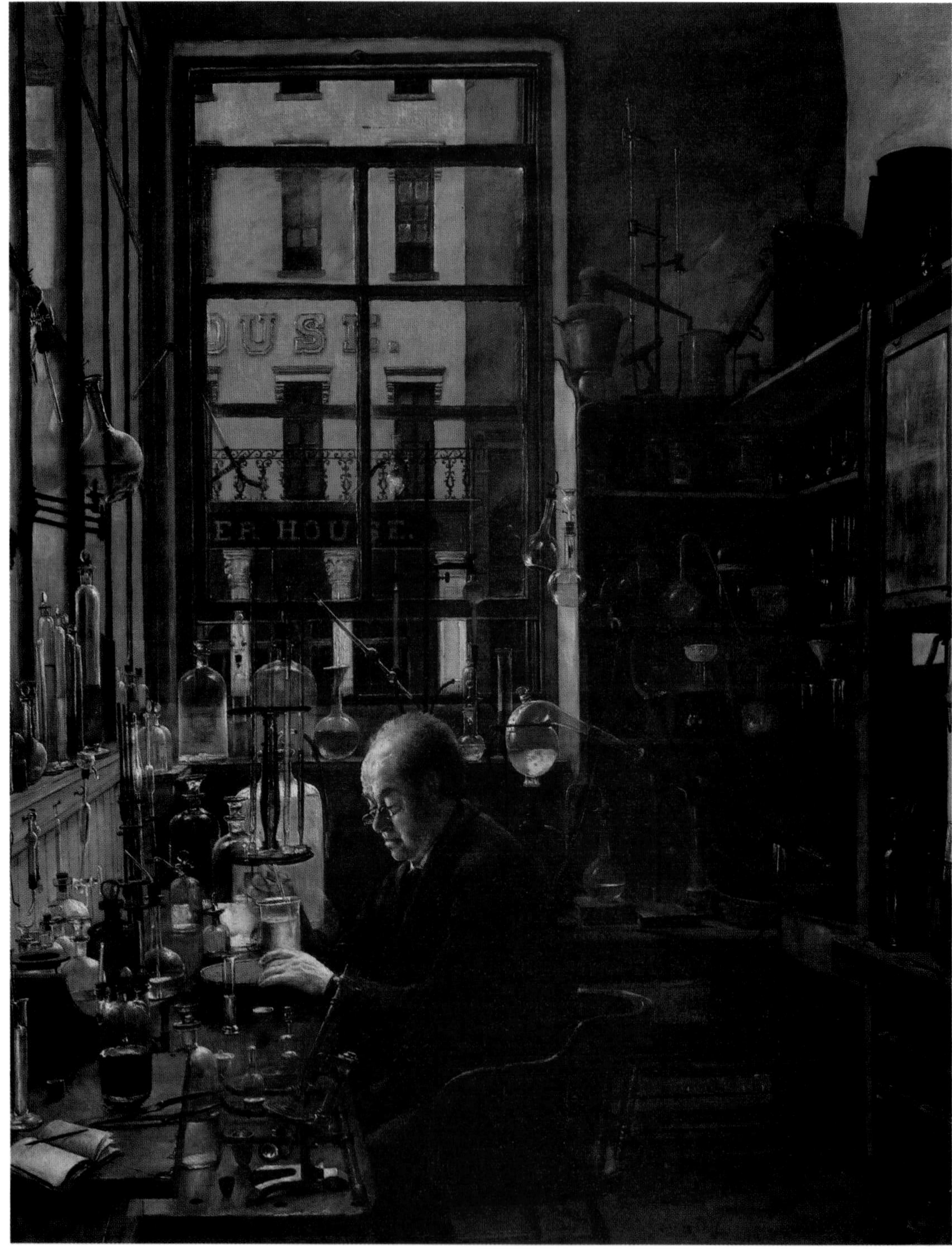

In the Laboratory of Thomas Price by Henry Alexander (c. 1887). Oil.

The Metropolitan Museum of Art, New York City. Alfred N. Punnett Fund, 1939.

Supplementary Support Materials
1. Review and Response Worksheet: Diction (*CCB*)
2. Selection Test (*CCB*)

Preparation
Establishing a Purpose. Read the headnote with the class, noting the extreme interest in astronomical lectures at Whitman's time. From what students already know about Whitman, do they think he will have a greater interest in the facts and numbers of astronomy, or in something else about the stars?

Closure
In class discussion have individual students answer this question: Why did the speaker leave the lecture room?

This poem, made up of a single sentence, moves with sure steps from its quiet opening line to its abrupt, yet carefully calculated, conclusion.

To place the poem in its time—and to anticipate Whitman's attitude toward its subject—remember that astronomy was of great interest to many nineteenth-century Americans, who followed scientific lectures and debates as eagerly as their great-grandchildren would follow television serials.

When I Heard the Learned Astronomer

When I heard the learned astronomer,
When the proofs, the figures, were ranged in columns before me,
When I was shown the charts and diagrams, to add, divide, and measure them,
When I sitting heard the astronomer where he lectured with much applause in the lecture-room,
How soon unaccountable I became tired and sick,
Till rising and gliding out I wandered off by myself,
In the mystical moist night air, and from time to time,
Looked up in perfect silence at the stars.

Responding to the Poem

Analyzing the Poem

Identifying Details

1. How does the audience's reaction to the astronomer's lecture differ from the speaker's reaction?

Interpreting Meanings

2. Listening to a lecture that he had obviously wanted to attend, the speaker finds it puzzling—"unaccountable"—that he "became tired and sick." What do you think might have been the reason for such an unexpected reaction? How is this reaction typical of the Romantic attitude toward a scientific dissection of nature?
3. In terms of the conflict of reality versus imagination, of science versus art, what is the significance of the poem's final line? What do you think the poet gained from watching the stars in "perfect silence" that he couldn't get from the astronomer?

Writing About the Poem

A Critical Response

Comparing Poems. In "On the Beach at Night" (page 343), the poet also uses the stars. In a brief essay, explain how that speaker's way of looking at the stars in that poem is different from the method used by the learned astronomer.

Analyzing the Poem
Identifying Details
1. The audience applauds enthusiastically, whereas the speaker feels "tired and sick."

Interpreting Meanings
2. Whitman's unease can probably be explained by his feeling that the astronomer has reduced the mystery of the universe to proofs, figures, columns, charts, and diagrams.

Whitman's reaction is typically Romantic in that the Romantics prized mystery, subjectivity, and intuition as ways to higher truth.
3. In general, the final line contrasts silence and mystery with rational discourse and objectivity; Whitman evidently believes that the universe is a far vaster, more mysterious place than the astronomer would say it is.

He gained peace and a sense of the beautiful majesty of nature. He might have become Emerson's "transparent eyeball" (page 192).

SUPPLEMENTARY SUPPORT MATERIALS
1. Review and Response Worksheet: Free Verse (*CCB*)
2. Selection Test (*CCB*)

PREPARATION
ESTABLISHING A PURPOSE. Read the headnote with the class and suggest that they listen for gentleness and empathy as the poem is read aloud (it is not on the audiocassette).

A. Setting
? Does the "gray and dim" refer to the daybreak or to the sight in camp? (Answers will vary. "Gray and dim" is probably deliberately ambiguous. Referring to the daybreak, the phrase is a form of pathetic fallacy, reflecting the dismal sight of the wounded men. As a reference to the wounded men themselves, the phrase parallels the way the speaker first sees the men, covered with "gray and heavy blanket.")

B. Noting Details
? What is significant about the ages of the first two wounded men? (One is very old, and the other very young.) What effect does the poet achieve by spanning the upper and lower age limits of soldiers? (He makes the men seem symbolically to represent all soldiers.)

During the Civil War, Whitman spent several years as a volunteer assistant to the staffs of hospitals and medical field units of the Union army. Without an official position or title, he came to know the wounded as persons, rather than as casualties or "cases"—an experience that profoundly affected his life and work. His association with dying men, whom he tried to comfort with words, little gifts, and offers to write letters, brought a wider dimension of tragedy into his thinking. In his poetry, a gentle poignancy began to balance his bluster.

A Sight in Camp in the Daybreak Gray and Dim

A [A sight in camp in the daybreak gray and dim,
As from my tent I emerge so early sleepless,
As slow I walk in the cool fresh air the path near by the hospital tent,
Three forms I see on stretchers lying, brought out there untended lying,
Over each the blanket spread, ample brownish woolen blanket,
Gray and heavy blanket, folding, covering all.

Curious I halt and silent stand,
Then with light fingers I from the face of the nearest the first just lift the blanket;
B Who are you elderly man so gaunt and grim, with well-grayed hair, and flesh all sunken about the eyes?
Who are you my dear comrade?

Then to the second I step—and who are you my child and darling?
Who are you sweet boy with cheeks yet blooming?

Then to the third—a face nor child nor old, very calm, as of beautiful yellow-white ivory;
Young man I think I know you—I think this face is the face of the Christ himself,
Dead and divine and brother of all, and here again he lies.

CLOSURE

In class discussion have students suggest adjectives that reveal the speaker's attitude toward each of the three figures in the poem.

ANALYZING THE POEM

Identifying Details

1. The hospital tent and the stretchers identify the setting as a battlefield.

2. He sees three people lying untended on the stretchers.

The first is the gaunt and grim face of an elderly man. The second is the innocent face of an adolescent boy. The third face is beautifully calm.

Interpreting Meanings

3. Student answers will vary. Some students will suggest that the Civil War setting, in which brothers were pitted against brothers, makes the apparition of the face of Christ—who bade men love one another—especially ironic and effective. Others may simply think of bearded faces.

4. Students may want to emphasize the fundamental theme of camaraderie and brotherhood in the poem. Whitman's *(Answers continue on next page.)*

Burial place for the Civil War dead, Fredericksburg, Virginia, May 12, 1861.

Photograph by Timothy O'Sullivan.

Responding to the Poem

Analyzing the Poem

Identifying Details

1. Find the details that identify the **setting** of the poem.
2. What is the sight that the speaker sees in the daybreak? Describe the three faces he sees.

Interpreting Meanings

3. The poem moves from anonymity to identity, from mere "forms," each hidden by an "ample brownish woolen blanket," to individuals with particular physical features. One of these strikes the speaker as having the features of "the Christ himself." Why, given the circumstances of this particular war, might the poet have seen this face on one of the dead soldiers?
4. The point of the poem is never openly stated; that is, it remains implicit. How would you make the poet's **message** explicit? Is there any significance to the fact that the "forms" who become persons in the eyes of the speaker are a trio? Explain.
5. Whitman's poetry, technically speaking, is all of a piece—a body of work easily identified by rolling **cadences,** by **catalogues** of things and activities, and by self-assertive expostulations. What most distinguishes one of his poems from another lies in the **tone:** in modulations of voice that indicate his attitude toward different subjects, and in a kind of timing that suggests that the reader is overhearing a man's conversation with himself. How would you describe the tone of this poem? What are the main elements that support your description?

The Poems as a Whole

1. Describe your own response to Whitman's poetry. How do you respond to his **rhythms, diction, catalogues, subject matter,** and **tone?**
2. Whitman's biographer Paul Zweig says that Whitman had a genius for the single line, "the verbal snapshot." Find at least five **images** from the poems that you think make particularly unusual and evocative "verbal snapshots."
3. Suppose you had to select a line or word from Whitman's own works to characterize him. Which line or lines from these poems would you select, and why?

Humanities Connection: Responding to the Photograph

Timothy H. O'Sullivan (c. 1840–1882) was a New York-born pioneer photographer who worked with the Civil War photographer Mathew Brady as well as on his own on the battlefronts of the Civil War.

? What relationship do you see between this photograph and the poem on text page 348? Is the effect of the poem enhanced by the starkness of the black and white photography (all that was available then), or would a color photograph have greater impact? Explain your reasoning. (The effect is enhanced by the black and white. Color adds brightness and liveliness—qualities that should not be part of this scene.)

(Answers begin on page 349.)
point is that the Civil War has ruthlessly violated the brotherhood of mankind.

Whitman may be using the trio symbolically to evoke the Christian notion of the Trinity: Three persons—Father, Son, and Holy Spirit—in one God.

5. The tone is somber, both at the beginning and the end. In the opening lines, Whitman is "sleepless" and walks "slowly" as he spies the forms lying on stretchers. His sympathy for the wounded is clear in the body of the poem. At the end, he evokes the memory of the Crucifixion, as he comments that Christ, "brother of all," has been newly killed in the Civil War, which pitted brother against brother.

THE POEMS AS A WHOLE

1. Answers will be highly individual. You might have students use this question in small-group discussion.

2. You might divide the class into pairs or triads, and have each group offer one image they find particularly evocative.

3. This question makes a good individual assignment, as part of a general review of Whitman.

Writing About the Poems

A Creative Response

1. **Writing a Free-Verse Poem.** Write a free-verse poem, beginning with one of Whitman's openers.

   I was there . . .
   You will hardly know who I am . . .
   I hear America singing . . .
   On the beach . . .

   In free verse, you are not restricted to the use of rhymes and regular meters, but you will want to use imagery and sound effects, including alliteration, parallel structures, and other forms of repetition.

A Critical Response

2. **Analyzing the Ideas in the Poems.** In a brief essay, show how Whitman expresses the following ideas in the poems you have read.
   a. The notion of "similitudes."
   b. The notion that the poet is "with us" or "is there."
   c. The notion that imagination can discover truths not necessarily accessible to reason.
3. **Explaining the Poet's Statement.** In an essay, explain how the poems you have read here can be used to illustrate and justify the following statement by Whitman.

> I know very well that my "Leaves" could not possibly have emerged . . . from . . . any other land than democratic America.
>
> —Walt Whitman

4. **Contrasting Whitman with a Fireside Poet.** In an essay, contrast Whitman's subject matter and style with those of one of the Fireside Poets (see pages 146–171). Use the following statement by Whitman as your thesis statement.

> For grounds for "Leaves of Grass," as a poem, I abandoned conventional themes, which do not appear in it; none of the stock ornamentation or choice plots of love or war, or high, exceptional personages of Old World song . . . no legend, or myth, or romance, nor euphemism, nor rhyme.
>
> —Walt Whitman

5. **Comparing Whitman to Taylor and Emerson.** You have seen that it was a habit of the Puritans to "read" nature for signs of divinity. You have also seen how the Transcendentalists "read" nature. In an essay, compare and contrast Whitman's "reading" of nature with that of Edward Taylor (see page 45) and Ralph Waldo Emerson (see page 187).
6. **Analyzing the Prose.** Some samples of Whitman's prose writings follow (see "Primary Sources"). In a brief essay, compare the prose with the poems you have read. Before you write, collect your data on a chart such as the following:

	Prose	Poetry
Tone		
Democratic feelings		
Use of list and catalogues		
Use of vigorous language		

Primary Sources
From Specimen Days

The following extracts are from Whitman's "memoranda book," which he called *Specimen Days.*

The Inauguration

"March 4, 1865—The President[1] very quietly rode down to the capitol in his own carriage, by himself, on a sharp trot, about noon, either because he wished to be on hand to sign bills, or to get rid of marching in line with the absurd procession, the muslin temple of liberty, and pasteboard monitor. I saw him on his return, at three o'clock, after the performance was over. He was in his plain two-horse barouche,[2] and looked very much worn and tired; the lines, indeed, of vast responsibilities, intricate questions, and demands of life and death, cut deeper than ever upon his dark brown face; yet all the old goodness, tenderness, sadness, and canny shrewd-

1. **The President:** Abraham Lincoln. He would be assassinated in April, just a month after Whitman wrote this.

2. **barouche** (bə·ro͞osh′): four-wheeled, horse-drawn carriage.

ness, underneath the furrows. (I never see that man without feeling that he is one to become personally attached to, for his combination of purest, heartiest tenderness, and native western form of manliness.) By his side sat his little boy, of ten years. There were no soldiers, only a lot of civilians on horseback, with huge yellow scarfs over their shoulders, riding around the carriage. (At the inauguration four years ago, he rode down and back again surrounded by a dense mass of armed cavalrymen eight deep, with drawn sabres; and there were sharpshooters stationed at every corner on the route.) I ought to make mention of the closing levee[3] of Saturday night last. Never before was such a compact jam in front of the White House—all the grounds filled, and away out to the spacious sidewalks. I was there, as I took a notion to go—was in the rush inside with the crowd—surged along the passage-ways, the blue and other rooms, and through the great east room. Crowds of country people, some very funny. Fine music from the Marine band, off in a side place. I saw Mr. Lincoln, dressed all in black, with white kid gloves and a claw-hammer coat, receiving, as in duty bound, shaking hands, looking very disconsolate, and as if he would give anything to be somewhere else."

The Real War Will Never Get in the Books

"And so goodbye to the war. I know not how it may have been, or may be, to others—to me the main interest I found (and still, on recollection, find), in the rank and file of the armies, both sides, and in those specimens amid the hospitals, and even the dead on the field. To me the points illustrating the latent personal character and eligibilities of these States, in the two or three millions of American young and middle-aged men, North and South, embodied in those armies—and especially the one-third or one-fourth of their number, stricken by wounds or disease at some time in the course of the contest—were of more significance even than the political interests involved. (As so much of a race depends on how it faces death, and how it stands personal anguish and sickness. As, in the glints of emotions under emergencies, and the indirect traits and asides in Plutarch, we get far profounder clues to the antique world than all its more formal history.)

"Future years will never know the seething hell and the black infernal background of countless minor scenes and interiors (not the official surface-courteousness of the Generals, not the few great battles) of the Secession war; and it is best they should not—the real war will never get in the books. In the mushy influences of current times, too, the fervid atmosphere and typical events of those years are in danger of being totally forgotten. I have at night watched by the side of a sick man in the hospital, one who could not live many hours. I have seen his eyes flash and burn as he raised himself and recurred to the cruelties on his surrendered brother, and mutilations of the corpse afterward. (See, in the preceding pages, the incident at Upperville—the seventeen killed as in the description, were left there on the ground. After they dropped dead, no one touched them—all were made sure of, however. The carcasses were left for the citizens to bury or not, as they chose.)

"Such was the war. It was not a quadrille[4] in a ballroom. Its interior history will not only never be written—its practicality, minutiae of deeds and passions, will never be even suggested. The actual soldier of 1862–'65, North and South, with all his ways, his incredible dauntlessness, habits, practices, tastes, language, his fierce friendship, his appetite, rankness, his superb strength and animality, lawless gait, and a hundred unnamed lights and shades of camp, I say, will never be written—perhaps must not and should not be. A

"The preceding notes may furnish a few stray glimpses into that life, and into those lurid interiors, never to be fully conveyed to the future. The hospital part of the drama from '61 to '65, deserves indeed to be recorded. Of that many-threaded drama, with its sudden and strange surprises, its confounding of prophecies, its moments of despair, the dread of foreign interference, the interminable campaigns, the bloody battles, the mighty cumbrous and green armies, the drafts and bounties—the immense money expenditure, like a heavy-pouring constant rain—with, over the whole land, the last three years of the struggle, an unending, universal mourning-wail of women, parents, orphans—the marrow of the tragedy concentrated in those Army Hospitals—(it seemed sometimes as if the whole interest of the land, North and South, was one vast central hospital, and all the rest of the affair but flanges)—those forming the untold and unwritten history of the war—infinitely greater (like life's) than the few scraps and distortions that are ever told or written. Think how much, and of importance, will be—how much, civic and military, has already been—buried in the grave, in eternal darkness." B

—Walt Whitman

3. **levee:** reception.

4. **quadrille** (kwə·dril′): a French dance for four couples.

A. Expansion Whitman was perhaps premature in his judgment. Veterans of the Civil War were astounded at the accuracy of Stephen Crane's 1893 novel, *The Red Badge of Courage.*

B. Connections Students may wish to compare this descriptive paragraph with Lincoln's "Gettysburg Address" (page 444).

A. Humanities Connection: Responding to the Photograph

? Look carefully at the person in the photograph. What do you think she is like? What interests her? Where would you be likelier to find her—at a party or in a library? What details influenced your responses? (After students have completed this exercise, you may want them to turn to page 372, to Dickinson's short note of July 1862 to Higginson, to see how Dickinson describes herself.)

B. Expansion

You may wish at this point to pause for the poem "Heart! We will forget him!" on page 355 and the painting on the facing page, 354. Ask students how the poem and the painting convey the poignant sadness of a young woman's attempt to forget a love she must set aside.

Emily Dickinson (1830–1886)

A brief outline of Emily Dickinson's life reads like the plot of a story destined to become a legend. Once upon a time there was born to a religious and well-to-do New England family a daughter they named Emily. As a child she was lively, well-behaved, and obedient; she took pleasure in the busy household of which she was a part and in the seasonal games, parties, and outings of a village snowy cold in winter and brilliantly green and flowering in the summer.

At home she learned to cook and sew. When she was old enough, she was sent to a school where strict rules did not keep Emily and the other girls from displaying their high spirits as they enjoyed the entertainments of boarding-school life. Emily took part in these, but not always with as much enthusiasm as she might have. As she said many years later, something sad and reserved in her nature made her "a mourner among the children."

To her family and friends, everything about the young Dickinson seemed normal. No one doubted that she would grow gracefully into womanhood, make a good marriage, and settle into a village life of churchgoing, holiday gatherings, and neighborly harmony. But something happened in her life that has been the subject of speculation for decades.

When Dickinson was twenty-three years old, her father, who had become a United States Congressman, took her with him to Washington, D.C., and then on to Philadelphia. The journey seems to have marked the start of the turning point of her existence. Her father may have taken her with him because she had fallen in love with someone she could never marry. This was a married lawyer, older than Emily, a man who would die that year of tuberculosis.

Whatever happened, it seems likely that in the course of the journey, Emily fell in love with someone else. This was Charles Wadsworth, who was also married and who was pastor of the Arch Street Presbyterian Church in Philadelphia. Letters to the Reverend Wadsworth show that Dickinson saw him as a "muse," someone who could help her with her feelings and her writings,

A

The only authentic photograph of Emily Dickinson. She is about seventeen years old here.

someone she could love passionately in her imagination.

But in 1861 Wadsworth took up a new assignment in San Francisco. His leaving seems to have caused the great crisis in Dickinson's life: B "I sing," she wrote around this time, "as the boy does by the burying ground, because I am afraid."

The young woman quietly and abruptly withdrew from all social life except that involving her immediate family. Within a few years, dressed always in white—like the bride she would never become—she had gone into a state of seclusion. Her only activities were household tasks and the writing of poems that she either kept to herself or sent out as valentines, birthday greetings, or notes to go with the gift of a cherry pie or a batch of cookies.

Around the time that Wadsworth was preparing to move to California, Dickinson sent a few of her poems to Thomas Wentworth Higginson. (Her letter is on page 372.) As editor of the *Atlantic Monthly,* Higginson had been encouraging the work of younger poets. Higginson never became a substitute for Wadsworth, but he was kindly, and he did serve as a distant "teacher" and "mentor." Eventually, Dickinson gave up hope of ever finding a wider audience than her few friends and relatives. About 1861, she wrote "I'm Nobody! Who are you?/Are you—Nobody—too?"

During her lifetime, Emily Dickinson published no more than a handful of her typically brief poems. She seemed to lack all concern for an audience, and she went so far as to instruct her family to destroy any poems she might leave behind. Still, she saw to it that bundles of handwritten poems were carefully wrapped and put away in places where friendly, appreciative, and, finally, astonished eyes would find them. The poems were assembled and edited by different members of her family and friends; they were then published in installments so frequent that readers began to wonder when they would ever end.

Then, in 1955, a collection called *The Poems of Emily Dickinson* was finally made available. This was the devoted work of Thomas H. Johnson, a scholar who, unlike Dickinson's earlier editors, refrained from making "presentable" entities of poems whose punctuation, rhyme schemes, syntax, and word choice were frequently baffling.

As a result of Johnson's research, whole generations of readers who had grown up on Dickinson poems were faced with new versions of poems that sometimes "rescued" meanings from the tamperings of her first editors. And sometimes, these originals made emphases which, in the interests of "smoothness," those editors had overlooked. Yet, at other times, comparisons also revealed that Dickinson's first editors had often served her well—in spirit, if not always in the way demanded by scholarship.

Here is an example of how one stanza was changed by the original editors. Johnson's version is first:

We passed the School, where Children strove
At Recess—in the Ring—
We passed the Fields of Gazing Grain—
We passed the Setting Sun—

And this is how the early editor changed it:

We passed the school where children played
Their lessons scarcely done;
We passed the fields of gazing grain,
We passed the setting sun.

When Dickinson died at the age of fifty-six, hardly anyone knew that the strange, shy woman in their midst, the perpetual bride who never crossed her own doorstep, was a poet whose sharp and delicate voice would echo for generations to come. Some eighty years after her death, when the quarrels among her relatives who had inherited her manuscripts had died down and all of her work was finally published, she was recognized as one of the greatest poets America, and perhaps the world, had produced. A

The self-imposed restrictions of Dickinson's actual life were more than matched by her ability to see the universal in the particular, and vice versa. She perceived the relationship between a drop of dew and a flood, between a desert and a grain of sand. These perceptions helped her to make metaphors that embraced experiences far beyond the limited compass of Amherst village life.

Yet, no matter how far her imagination ranged, Dickinson never denied those experiences their truth as aspects of a cycle of existence important in itself. When an Amherst neighbor's barn caught fire and lit up the sky, it was a real barn at the edge of a real pasture, and its loss became a matter of local anguish. But these local actualities did not prevent Dickinson from regarding the incident as a reminder of ultimate doom, of the Biblical prophecies of destruction of the earth by fire.

Behind the now famous legend of Emily Dickinson, and the plays and novels that have romanticized and sentimentalized her life, is a woman whose genius made its own rules, followed its own commands, and found its own fulfillment. B Tears for the once cheerful young woman whose supposed broken heart drove her into self-imposed exile do not apply. Emily Dickinson's life as a recluse was richer, more varied and—in the satisfactions that come with the exercise of God-given talent—even happier than the lives of those around her. In the prospect of history, we can see that the untold secret of Emily Dickinson's emotional life is secondary to the great secret of her genius, the secret destiny would not let her keep.

A. Expansion
After discussing this paragraph, have students reconsider the Dickinson quotation at the beginning of the unit, page 324. What do they now see as the meaning of her "letter" to a world that never wrote back? (She resigned herself to not being recognized in her lifetime. She carefully saved her poems, however, so it is possible that she hoped for posthumous fame.)

B. Connections
One of Dickinson's literary influences was Ralph Waldo Emerson. You might ask students to explain how the information in these lines relates to his advice in "Self-Reliance" (text page 194).

Humanities Connection: Responding to the Fine Art
Eastman Johnson (1824–1906) was a genre painter known for such paintings as *Old Kentucky Home* and *Corn Husking at Nantucket,* but he is primarily remembered for the portrait work to which he devoted himself exclusively after 1885. His famous sitters include Presidents Hayes, Cleveland, and Harrison, as well as the railroad magnate Cornelius Vanderbilt and the writers Emerson and Longfellow.

? Think about the setting—what lies under the wisps of fog or cloud?—and the situation of the girl standing there in what appears to be a stiff breeze. Then look at the title: How does it affect your view of the painting? Is it the painter who has the romantic imagination, while the girl herself may scarcely be thinking of him? Consider, too, how a painting differs from a photograph. What effects can a painter achieve (for example, the misty background) that would be difficult with an unretouched photograph? (The title obliges the viewer to see the picture in a certain way. Had the title been *Looking to the Future,* the viewer's interpretation would be totally different. This shows how influential titles can be.)

The Girl I Left Behind Me
by Eastman Johnson (1907). Oil.

SUPPLEMENTARY SUPPORT MATERIALS
1. Review and Response Worksheet: Tone (*CCB*)
2. Selection Test (*CCB*)

PREPARATION

ESTABLISHING A PURPOSE. Suggest that students read to understand what the two things about "him" are that the speaker wants to forget and whether or not she is successful in doing so.

CLOSURE

Have students write brief statements explaining the conflict in this poem. Responses should be shared orally.

The poems are reprinted here exactly as the poet wrote them. After Dickinson died, her sister Lavinia and a family friend took forty-nine packets of poems, all carefully tied with thread so that they looked like little "books," and worked for several years to prepare them for publication. In the process, the editors changed some of Dickinson's words and her unusual punctuation and capitalization. Only recently have we been able to read Dickinson's poems just as they appear in her manuscript. As you read, be alert to her use of dashes—they indicate a pause in thought or rhythm.

Here we have Emily Dickinson's version of the old story of unrequited love—or of love that is impossible because of the circumstances of the potential lovers. The substance of the poem is conflict: between will and emotion, between the thinking mind and the feeling heart. Which of these do you think is more powerful—the mind or the heart?

Heart! We will forget him!

Heart! We will forget him!
You and I—tonight!
You may forget the warmth he gave—
I will forget the light!

When you have done, pray tell me
That I may straight begin!
Haste! lest while you're lagging
I remember him!

Responding to the Poem

Analyzing the Poem

Identifying Details

1. Assume that the speaker is the mind. What does it order the heart to do?
2. Which word describes what "he" gave the heart? Which word describes what "he" gave the mind?
3. Exclamation points punctuate this little poem, as if the poem were saying, "Hurry up! We must get this over with!" Why is she in such a hurry?

Interpreting Meanings

4. Why do you think the heart is asked to take the lead in this situation?
5. How would you **paraphrase** what the speaker means by warmth and light?
6. If you wanted to forget someone, would you first try to forget his or her "warmth" or "light"? Why?
7. What feeling or **tone** would you say this lyric expresses?

ANALYZING THE POEM

Identifying Details

1. The mind orders the heart to forget the warmth that the beloved gave.
2. "Warmth" (line 3).
"Light" (line 4).
3. The matter cannot wait because the speaker is half afraid that she will weaken in her resolution to forget the lover.

Interpreting Meanings

4. Students may suggest that the speaker feels it will be harder for the heart than for the mind to forget; therefore, the heart is asked to take the lead.
5. Answers may vary. One paraphrase for "warmth" might be "passion"; one paraphrase for "light" might be "intelligence."
6. Students may make their decision based on an interpretation of "light" as "guidance" or "mentor," harder perhaps to give up and forget than abstract intelligence.
7. Among the suggestions students may offer are regret, determination, and impatience.

SUPPLEMENTARY SUPPORT MATERIALS

1. Review and Response Worksheet: Imagery (*CCB*)
2. Language Skills Worksheet: Revision Worksheet 2 (*CCB*)
3. Selection Test (*CCB*)
4. Audiocassette recording

PREPARATION

ESTABLISHING A PURPOSE. Read the headnote in class and briefly discuss the mixed feelings Dickinson may have had about remaining true to her own poetic vision when it seemed to require that no one publish her poems.

CLOSURE

Have individual students paraphrase this poem orally.

ANALYZING THE POEM

Identifying Details

1. The defeated, or those who never succeed, count success sweetest.
2. Purple was the imperial color of ancient Rome. Dickinson associates the conquering army with the Roman host that conquered the known world in ancient times.
3. A defeated army.
4. A defeated, dying warrior.

Interpreting Meanings

5. The first kind is abstract—the desire for success. The second kind of desire is concrete—the extreme need or thirst for a "nectar." In both cases the idea of "need" is present.
6. He won't ever hear the sounds of triumph directed to him.
7. Certainly it seems to be universal and true. (You might compare this poem to Dickinson's "Fame is a bee.")
8. Answers will vary. Try finding imagery from a sports event or a test for college admission or a job.

Dickinson sent this poem along with three others to Higginson in 1862 to ask his advice about publication. It is one of several poems that show Dickinson's concern with fame. Could the feeling expressed here reflect the poet's sense of failure to win an audience for her poems? What kind of endeavor does she use as a concrete illustration of success? What might this illustration suggest about the way she thought of her own struggles with the world?

Success is counted sweetest

Success is counted sweetest
By those who ne'er succeed.
To comprehend a nectar°
Requires sorest° need.

Not one of all the purple Host°
Who took the Flag today
Can tell the definition
So clear of Victory

As he defeated—dying—
On whose forbidden ear
The distant strains of triumph
Burst agonized and clear!

3. **nectar:** once a name for the drink of the gods of classical literature, now a term applied to any delicious beverage.
4. **sorest:** as used here, "deepest" or "most extreme."
5. **Host:** an archaic word for an army.

Responding to the Poem

Analyzing the Poem

Identifying Details

1. According to the poet, who is likely to count success sweetest?
2. Purple is a color associated with blood shed in battle. What is the "purple Host" in line 5?
3. What example does the poet supply to illustrate her statement about those who know success best?
4. What **image** does the poet present in the last stanza?

Interpreting Meanings

5. Two kinds of desire are balanced in the first stanza. How would you define them? What is their relationship to each other?
6. Why is the ear "forbidden" in line 10?
7. Do you think the feeling expressed in this poem is valid? Is it common? Explain.
8. "Victory" is considered in military terms here. Can you think of other circumstances—perhaps a circumstance in your own life—in which the situation in this poem, and its conclusion, might be repeated?

Robert Gould Shaw Memorial (detail) by Augustus Saint-Gaudens (1894–1897). Bronze.

Boston Common, Boston, Massachusetts.

SUPPLEMENTARY SUPPORT MATERIALS
1. Review and Response Worksheet: Imagery (*CCB*)
2. Selection Test (*CCB*)
3. Audiocassette recording

PREPARATION

ESTABLISHING A PURPOSE. After reading the headnote, explore with the class the idea that each of us has unwritten, internal "rules" by which we choose our friends or our vocations.

CLOSURE

Have individual students paraphrase the first line of this poem.

ANALYZING THE POEM

Identifying Details

1. Decides its preferences and then firmly "shuts the door."
2. The subject and the verb.
3. That of an emperor or ruler, pausing in a chariot to beg the soul to admit him.
4. In line 7, the phrase "an Emperor be kneeling."
5. She chooses one person and then she closes off everybody else.

Interpreting Meanings

6. Dickinson's biographer Richard Sewell calls this one of her "poet poems." "Divine majority" then would mean "having come into one's own." The poet could be declaring herself a poet here. She has found her vocation; she has "selected her own Society," her own vision.

"Divine" suggests an immortal. (She joins the ranks of the immortals.)

7. Answers will vary. (We favor the image of the tightly sealed clam.)
8. The word "lids" metaphorically suggests that the soul has eyes. Note that eyes can be forced open much more easily than a closed bivalve can be.
9. Lines 10 and 12 are reduced from four to two syllables, with approximately equal stress.

It slows down the rhythm.

10. It chooses and accepts only what it wants.

It could easily isolate itself.

This poem is about choices and the mysterious instinct that leads each one of us to prefer certain things and cherish certain people above all others. In Emily Dickinson's view, this instinct has less to do with the discriminations of the mind than with the inclinations of that spiritual part of us that we call the soul. When you select friends, do you do it because of what your intellect tells you or because of what your soul prompts you to do?

The Soul selects her own Society

The Soul selects her own Society—
Then—shuts the Door—
To her divine Majority—
Present no more—

Unmoved—she notes the Chariots—pausing—
At her low Gate—
Unmoved—an Emperor be kneeling
Upon her Mat—

I've known her—from an ample nation—
Choose One—
Then—close the Valves of her attention—
Like Stone—

Responding to the Poem

Analyzing the Poem

Identifying Details

1. In the first stanza, what does the soul do?
2. What words have to be added to lines 3-4 to make a complete sentence?
3. What is the principal **image** of the second stanza?
4. In stanza 2, where does the poet sacrifice correct syntax in order to make her point? How would you put this stanza into conventional English?
5. In the last stanza, what does the soul do?

Interpreting Meanings

6. "Majority" as used here has at least two meanings. It could mean having reached the full legal age, or having "come into one's own"; or it could mean superiority (an obsolete usage); or it could mean "the greater part of something." What do you think it means? What kind of person does the adjective "divine" suggest?
7. Look up the word *valve* in a dictionary. Do you think the phrase "Valves of her attention" is drawn from the world of organic things (the valves of a clamshell)? Or from the world of mechanical things (the valve of a faucet)? What do you picture happening here?
8. The editors changed the word *valves* to the word *lids*. How does this change the **metaphor?** How does it change your **image** of what is happening?
9. Look carefully at the **meter** of lines 10 and 12. How does the rhythmical pattern of these lines differ from the corresponding lines in the first and second stanzas? What is the effect of this difference?
10. What advantage may lie in a "selection" as strict as this "soul"makes? What are its disadvantages?

Writing About the Poem

A Critical Response

Evaluating a Title. Dickinson did not give her poems titles. The editors titled this poem "Exclusion." In a brief essay, give your evaluation of this as the title of the poem. In what ways does it apply? Are there any ways in which it is too limiting? What titles would you suggest?

SUPPLEMENTARY SUPPORT MATERIALS
1. Review and Response Worksheet: Imagery (*CCB*)
2. Selection Test (*CCB*)
3. Audiocassette recording

PREPARATION
ESTABLISHING A PURPOSE. Challenge students to seek an answer to the final question of the headnote as they read: What phrase strikes them as most significant?

CLOSURE
In class discussion have students choose the most significant phrase in the poem and explain its significance.

A. Expansion
Help students grasp the point of the final paragraph by rereading the last stanza of "The Soul selects her own Society" twice: first substituting "and be done" for the final line, and second, as given in the text.

B. Responding
? What *kind* of bird do you visualize as you hear the poem? Does the Fuertes watercolor and ink match or contrast with your own mental image? Why or why not? (Ask students to cite details from the poem in their responses.)

C. Interpretation
? What is the relationship between the speaker and the bird? (The speaker is an unknown onlooker until she offers the bird a crumb, and the bird, frightened, flies off. The speaker and the bird never achieve a relationship.) What might the poet be saying about our relationship with nature? (We can observe it, but our actions cannot or do not have an effect on it. See question 9, page 359.)

The Elements of Literature

SLANT RHYME

Not long ago, rhyme was part of every poet's craft. Today it is still the most familiar aspect of sound in poetry; but rhyme has, over the years, fallen out of favor with many poets. This is because these poets feel that almost all the rhymes in English have been used over and over again. Some poets, as a solution, have abandoned rhyme altogether. Other poets, like Dickinson, use slant rhyme.

Exact rhyme is the use of two or more words with identical sounds to their accented syllables and all succeeding syllables. Exact rhymes are found in words like *cat/mat, tarnished/varnished,* and *dreary/weary.*

When the rhyming sound is *not* exact—as in *follow/fellow, morn/spurn,* or *mystery/mastery*—it is called **slant rhyme, off-rhyme,** or **half rhyme.** Slant rhyme makes many readers uncomfortable—in the way that a sharp or flat note on a piano would disturb a listener who wasn't expecting it.

Part of the shock value of Dickinson's poems comes from her use of slant rhyme. In "The Soul selects her own Society," only one perfect rhyme is used: *door/more.* How many slant rhymes can you find? What rhyming sounds were you expecting to hear?

A Slant rhyme is a subtle use of sound. It is often used to force our attention onto particular words. For example, the last word in this poem, *stone,* stands out because it doesn't match exactly in sound the word *one.* Why is it important that the word *stone* be emphasized? To hear and understand the difference, imagine that Dickinson had ended her poem with the words "And be done."

Here is a poem that seems to have no message, nothing but an invitation to share an experience in which, step by step, we are guided by the poet's acute observations. Dickinson wrote many poems about nature, but they are always more than simple appreciations of natural beauty. If you had to select the most significant phrase in this poem, which would it be?

A Bird came down the Walk

B A Bird came down the Walk—
He did not know I saw—
He bit an Angleworm in halves
And ate the fellow, raw,

And then he drank a Dew
From a convenient Grass—
And then hopped sidewise to the Wall
To let a Beetle pass—

He glanced with rapid eyes
That hurried all around—
They looked like frightened Beads, I thought—
He stirred his Velvet Head

Like one in danger, Cautious,
I offered him a Crumb
And he unrolled his feathers
And rowed him softer home—

Than Oars divide the Ocean,
Too silver for a seam—
Or Butterflies, off Banks of Noon
Leap, plashless° as they swim.

20. **plashless:** without splashing.

C

ANALYZING THE POEM

Identifying Details

1. The bird bites and eats a raw angleworm, and drinks a drop of dew from a blade of grass. Then he hops sideways on the walk to allow a beetle to pass. He glances around rapidly and hurries. He stirs his head cautiously.

2. When the speaker offers it a crumb, the bird "unrolls" its feathers and flies away.

3. The simile compares the bird's eyes to "frightened Beads."

4. The poet compares the bird to a boat and to butterflies.

5. The bird seems nervous and hurried on the ground. In contrast, when it is in the air, it is graceful and streamlined.

Interpreting Meanings

6. Dickinson's complex imagery first relates the bird's feathered wings to the oars of a boat, spreading apart to divide the water. The wings "unroll" as if they are to "row" the bird's body, as oars would row a boat. The phrase "Banks of Noon" implies a related image; noon, a time of day, is pictured as a river or stream, upon whose banks butterflies "leap." The butterflies themselves, in their playful movement, are in turn imagined as water creatures that "swim," rather than fly.

7. The phrase implies a beautifully calm, tranquil ocean.

8. The long "o" sounds occur in "unrolled," "rowed," "home," "ocean." Students may also note the "o" sounds in "softer," "oars," and "noon."

Answers will vary. Among the words that students may note are: "feathers," "silver," "seam," "leap," "plashless," and "swim."

9. Student answers will vary.

10. Students may be divided on this question. The title "In the Garden" supplies an explicit setting for the poem, and some students may feel that such a title helps to make the poem more concrete. Other students may disagree, arguing that a specific setting detracts from the suggestive power of the poem.

Responding to the Poem

Analyzing the Poem

Identifying Details

1. What various things does the bird do while the speaker watches?
2. What happens when the speaker tries to be friendly with the bird?
3. The poem is purely descriptive until the third stanza, when one daring **simile** lifts it into the realm of the imagination. What is that simile and what two distinct things is it comparing?
4. The two **figures of speech** in lines 15–20 are also strikingly unusual. What is the bird compared to here?
5. Describe how the actions of the bird in the air contrast with its actions on the ground.

Interpreting Meanings

6. Explain what you think the poet means by "unrolled," "rowed him," "Banks of Noon," and butterflies that "swim." What **images** do these words put in your mind?
7. What kind of ocean do you think would be "Too silver for a seam"?
8. Beginning with line 15, how many "o" sounds can you hear? What other sounds in lines 15–20 do you think help create a soft, "liquid" music?
9. Some readers feel that this poem dramatizes the unbridgeable distance between the human world and the natural world. Do you agree? Explain.
10. When this poem was first published, it was entitled "In the Garden." Do you think this title adds or subtracts from the impact of the poem? Explain.

Head of a Squawking Bird by Louis Agassiz Fuertes (early 20th century). Watercolor and ink on paper.

Supplementary Support Materials
1. Review and Response Worksheet: Theme (*CCB*)
2. Selection Test (*CCB*)
3. Audiocassette recording
4. Instructional Overhead Tranparency

Preparation

Establishing a Purpose. Suggest that students read the poem to determine the poet's message about beauty and truth.

Closure

Have individual students explain, in their own words, what they believe is the message of this poem.

A. Expansion
Keat's famous ode (1819) describes the perfection and timelessness of art as contrasted with the living, changing world. The contrast is suggested by the eternally still figures on an imaginary Greek urn with a pastoral theme. One figure is a youth who, while he can never possess his beloved, will always be near his goal. Her beauty, in turn, will never fade. The 50-line poem ends with the two lines quoted in the headnote, the urn's response to the speaker of the poem.

B. Interpretation
? Is the man directing this question toward himself or toward the speaker? (Either reading results in the equating of truth and beauty.)

C. Connections
Some students may wish to look up Carl Sandburg's poem "Grass," in which the image of green life covering all is used to a different purpose.

A **"Beauty is truth, truth beauty"—that is all**
Ye know on earth, and all ye need to know.

These concluding lines of John Keats's "Ode on a Grecian Urn" are among the most famous in English poetry. Emily Dickinson knew them, of course, and here she presents her own version of the theme suggested by Keats. Before you read the poem, decide how you would define these two concepts: beauty and truth.

I died for Beauty—but was scarce

I died for Beauty—but was scarce
Adjusted in the Tomb
When One who died for Truth, was lain
In an adjoining Room—

He questioned softly "Why I failed?"
B "For Beauty," I replied—
"And I—for Truth—Themself are One—
We Bretheren, are," He said—

And so, as Kinsmen, met at Night—
We talked between the Rooms—
C Until the Moss had reached our lips—
And covered up—our names—

Responding to the Poem

Analyzing the Poem

Identifying Details

1. What situation does the speaker imagine happening in the first stanza? Where is this situation taking place?
2. What do the two speakers have in common that allows one of them to claim that they are "Bretheren," that is, brothers?
3. What event is described in the last two lines of the poem?
4. The **meter** in this poem is so regular and the rhyme arranged so like clockwork that only the use of two **slant rhymes** saves it from a sing-song quality. Where are the slant rhymes? What sound do you *expect* to hear?

Interpreting Meanings

5. How does the **slant rhyme** make the last word stand out? Do you think this is an important word? Why?
6. What are the "rooms" in lines 4 and 10?
7. In the third stanza, "the moss" is real, in the sense that it is a kind of green growth likely to be found in a cemetery, or in any other place of stones and shade. But "the moss" is also a **metaphor.** For what? What is significant in the fact that it covered up the speaker's names?
8. The incident recounted here is imaginary. Nevertheless, Dickinson seems to have a **message** in mind. What would you say that message is? Would you say that it is optimistic or pessimistic?
9. Poetry gives form to feelings. What feelings would you say are expressed in this poem?

Analyzing The Poem

Identifying Details

1. The speaker imagines that she is dead, having died "for Beauty," and that she is newly laid to rest in the tomb. Next to her, one who has died "for Truth" is buried.

The setting is a tomb or mausoleum.

2. Both speakers died for abstract concepts—truth and beauty—that are really two aspects of the same whole.

3. In the third stanza, the speaker pictures a regular series of conversations between the two dead persons. She compares these to the talks kinsmen might have when they meet at night. In the last two lines, the moss of the cemetery reaches the speakers' lips and covers up their names on their tombstones.

4. The slant rhymes occur in lines 6 and 8 ("replied" and "said") and in lines 10 and 12 ("Rooms" and "names"). In each case, we expect the second word of the pair to echo the end sound of the first word.

Interpreting Meanings

5. The sound of the last word, "names," clashes a bit with the sound of the word "rooms." This clash helps to draw attention to the word "names." Most students will agree that it is an important word, because a person's name is a clue to his or her identity.

6. The rooms are probably tombs or graves.

7. The moss metaphorically suggests a passage of time that results in oblivion. The speaker seems to suggest that death is a kind of oblivion for those who die, who are destined to be forgotten by the living as well.

8. Student opinions will differ. Supporting an optimistic interpretation might be that those people who have supported goodness—truth and beauty—during their lives will meet together after death for mutual comfort. Pessimistic interpretations might point to the fact that the poem ends with the apparent oblivion of the speakers.

9. Answers will vary. (Love, kinship, dedication, regret)

SUPPLEMENTARY SUPPORT MATERIALS
1. Review and Response Worksheet: Situational Irony (*CCB*)
2. Selection Test (*CCB*)
3. Audiocassette recording

PREPARATION
ESTABLISHING A PURPOSE. Note the title and ask students to predict the kind of poem this will be. Then have students read to verify their predictions.

ANALYZING THE POEM
Identifying Details
1. At the moment of my death, I heard a fly in the room. (Answers will vary.)
2. She had made her will. The people around her had stopped crying and had steeled themselves for death.
3. They are expecting death. Instead, the fly "interposes."
The fly reverses momentarily the expectation of a solemn event, death.
4. Probably God or Christ.
5. The speaker's eyes cloud over.
(Answers continue in left-hand column.)

(Continued from top.)
6. The people had finished weeping.

Interpreting Meanings
7. "Gusts" or "bursts." "Heaves" suggests bodily agony.
8. The pause in line 13 divides the description of the fly. "Interposed" is unexpected and formal. In line 13, "uncertain stumbling Buzz" displays alliteration, assonance, and onomatopoeia.
9. She cannot assign her soul.
10. Some might find the tone bizarrely comic or even cold. Certainly the fly adds a note of reality. (Compare Dickinson's control of her feelings with the openly sentimental "O Captain! My Captain!" on page 327. Compare the points of view of the two poems as well.)
11. Student answers will vary.

CLOSURE
Ask two students to discuss how this poem is different from popular romantic poems and songs about death and dying.

One of Dickinson's most brilliantly original works, this poem begins with such boldness and continues with such quick shifts of attention that we find ourselves reading it without stopping to think that we are hearing a voice from the dead.

Once we have accepted Dickinson's poetic license, we take the poem for what it is—an imaginative report of what it might feel like to die. What would you expect someone to sense in that ultimate moment when we cannot "see to see"?

I heard a Fly buzz—when I died—

I heard a Fly buzz—when I died—
The Stillness in the Room
Was like the Stillness in the Air—
Between the Heaves of Storm—

The Eyes around—had wrung them dry—
And Breaths were gathering firm
For that last Onset—when the King
Be witnessed—in the Room—

I willed my Keepsakes—Signed away
What portion of me be
Assignable—and then it was
There interposed a Fly—

With Blue—uncertain stumbling Buzz—
Between the light—and me—
And then the Windows failed—and then
I could not see to see—

Responding to the Poem

Analyzing the Poem

Identifying Details

1. Paraphrase the statement made in stanza 1.
2. According to the second and third stanzas, how had the speaker and those around her prepared for death?
3. According to stanza 2, what are the dying person and those around her *expecting* to find in the room? What appears instead? In what way is this appearance **ironic**?
4. Who do you think the "King" of line 7 is?
5. What does the poet mean by the phrase "the Windows failed" in line 15?
6. In order to clarify the syntax, how would you **paraphrase** line 5?

Interpreting Meanings

7. In reference to the behavior of storms, what word other than "Heaves" might have been useful in line 4? Why is "Heaves" an appropriate word, in regard to what is happening in the poem?
8. How does the poet use pauses and specific words in lines 12 and 13 to make the appearance of the fly dramatic and lively?
9. In the third stanza, the poet speaks of signing away the portion that is "assignable." What portion of the speaker, by implication, is *not* assignable?
10. What is the **tone** of the poem—what feeling do you think the poet expresses by inserting the fly into a deathbed scene?
11. Do you find this poem grotesque or moving? Or do you have some other reaction?

SUPPLEMENTARY SUPPORT MATERIALS
1. Review and Response Worksheet: Tone (*CCB*)
2. Selection Test (*CCB*)
3. Audiocassette recording

PREPARATION
ESTABLISHING A PURPOSE. Check for understanding of the concept of metaphysical poetry, and ask students to listen, in this poem, for extensions of time periods as the key metaphor.

CLOSURE
Have individual students state the theme of the poem.

Poetry becomes metaphysical when its imagery and figures of speech become very intellectual and sometimes very far-fetched and fantastic. In metaphysical poetry, ordinary things are often seen in relation to the universal, and private emotions are often regarded as world-shaking events. See if you think this poem meets these requirements. The theme is the hope of romantic fulfillment—a hope so profound that it can be maintained almost forever.

If you were coming in the Fall

If you were coming in the Fall,
I'd brush the Summer by
With half a smile, and half a spurn,
As Housewives do, a Fly.

If I could see you in a year,
I'd wind the months in balls—
And put them each in separate Drawers,
For fear the numbers fuse—

If only Centuries, delayed,
I'd count them on my Hand,
Subtracting, till my fingers dropped
Into Van Dieman's Land.

If certain, when this life was out—
That your's and mine, should be
I'd toss it yonder, like a Rind,
And take Eternity—

But, now, uncertain of the length
Of this, that is between,
It goads me, like the Goblin Bee—
That will not state—its sting.

Responding to the Poem

Analyzing the Poem

Identifying Details

1. What is the **simile** in the first stanza? What two things are being compared?
2. In the second stanza, what domestic articles are the months compared to? Why does the speaker put them in separate drawers?
3. "Van Dieman's Land" in stanza 3 is the old name for Tasmania, the large island south of Australia. It is used to mean those places on the globe furthest away from us. Given this fact, can you **paraphrase** the third stanza?
4. The fourth stanza contains a daring but simple **simile.** What would the speaker toss away as if it were the rind of an orange?
5. The speaker's **tone** changes in stanza 5 and her exaggerations disappear. Conscious of how long her hope must be maintained, the speaker is goaded, or pushed and prodded against her will. What is she goaded by?

Interpreting Meanings

6. How would the bee in the last stanza be different from the fly in the first stanza?
7. A goblin is a grotesque creature in folklore. What does it mean that the bee is a "Goblin" and will not "state" its sting?
8. Who might "you" be? How would you describe the speaker's situation, and how does she feel about it?
9. If you were the editor of this poem, would you suggest any corrections in spelling and punctuation?

ANALYZING THE POEM
Identifying Details
1. The summer is compared with a fly.
2. Months are compared to clothes that are put in storage and to balls of yarn that are separated so they won't become tangled.
3. I would count off the centuries on my fingers until they dropped to the place on earth which is furthest away.
4. Her life.
5. By her own uncertainty about how long her wait must be.

Interpreting Meanings
6. The fly is easily brushed aside. But the *threat* of a bee sting is compared to the gnawing uncertainty in the speaker's mind.
7. It suggests that fanciful fears nag her. The unstated sting is the length of inquietude left to endure.
8. A friend or lover. The speaker's situation seems uncertain.
9. Omit commas in lines 4, 9, 14, and 18. Change "your's" to "yours" (line 14).

Supplementary Support Materials

1. Review and Response Worksheet: Personification and Theme (*CCB*)
2. Selection Test (*CCB*)
3. Audiocassette recording

Preparation

Establishing a Purpose. Call students' attention to the poem's basic metaphor, Death as a ride in a horse-drawn carriage. Ask them to listen for details that extend the metaphor.

Closure

Have individual students explain the irony that is so central to the meaning of the poem.

A. Interpretation

? Why could the speaker not "stop for Death"? (Answers will vary, but the implication is that she, like all of us, was too busy, perhaps too attached to earthly life.)

B. Interpretation

? What evidence is there in these lines that Death is personified as a suitor? (He picks up the speaker in a carriage, and he behaves with great civility. They drive slowly. The speaker makes accommodation in her life for him.) If death is seen as a suitor, what does this say about our acceptance of death? (Perhaps that it is a natural way of moving from one state of life to another, just as one would move from being single to being married.)

C. Expansion

Some critics have noted that these lines are metaphors for the three periods of life: youth, adulthood, and old age.

Like many other metaphors in Dickinson's poetry, this one "tames" or "domesticates" the most awesome and inevitable of human experiences, and does so with playfulness and wit.

The literal elements of the metaphor are simple: Dying is compared to an unexpected ride in a horse-drawn carriage. But these are just about the only simple elements in a poem that depends for its effect on irony, on gradual comprehension, and on a blithe tone that is much at odds with the story being told.

Because I could not stop for Death—

A Because I could not stop for Death—
He kindly stopped for me—
The Carriage held but just Ourselves—
And Immortality.

B We slowly drove—He knew no haste
And I had put away
My labor and my leisure too,
For His Civility—

We passed the School, where Children strove
At Recess—in the Ring—
C We passed the Fields of Gazing Grain—
We passed the Setting Sun—

Or rather—He passed Us—
The Dews drew quivering and chill—
For only Gossamer,° my Gown—
My Tippet—only Tulle°—

We paused before a House that seemed
A Swelling of the Ground—
The Roof was scarcely visible—
The Cornice—in the Ground—

Since then—'tis Centuries—and yet
Feels shorter than the Day
I first surmised the Horses Heads
Were toward Eternity—

15. **Gossamer:** a very thin, soft material.
16. **Tippet . . . Tulle:** her shawl was made only of fine netting.

ANALYZING THE POEM

Identifying Details

1. There are three passengers: the speaker, Death, and immortality.

2. Death is personified as a courteous suitor who kindly stops to take the speaker for a ride in his carriage.

3. They pass a school where children play, fields of grain, and the setting sun.

4. The "setting of the sun" suggests both the coming of night and the darkness of death. The temperature now becomes chilly.

5. The speaker realizes that this is the day of her death and that the carriage ride is her journey to eternity.

Interpreting Meanings

6. One possibility might be: Because I was too busy to think about death, he kindly came of his own accord.

The ironic word is "kindly."

7. The notion of "civility"—unexpectedly connected with death—extends the irony of the word "kindly" in the first stanza.

8. Student answers will vary. The children and the grain may be held to suggest growth and life.

The stalks of grain, bowed in one direction or another by the wind, may be imagined as heads and eyes that "gaze."

9. The "House" that is a "Swelling of the Ground" is the tomb, or mausoleum, of the speaker.

10. You might introduce a new interpretation here. (See Kazin's comment.) Some critics see this poem as a committment to a life of poetry, in which Dickinson shuts the door to marriage. Sewell, Dickinson's biographer, thinks that the poem may have as much to do with life as with death, that it commemorates the moment when the idea of "eternity" struck with full force and Dickinson saw her poetic mission before her. In this reading, Sewell says, the fourth stanza suggests the poet's sense of unpreparedness for her great mission. (The original editors had omitted the fourth stanza and had called the poem "The Chariot," which reduced it to a conventional poem on death.) Sewell calls the meaning of eternity Dickinson's "flood subject," her all-encompassing theme.

Portland Place, London by Alvin Langdon Coburn.

Responding to the Poem

Analyzing the Poem

Identifying Details

1. How many passengers are in Death's carriage? Who are they?
2. As what kind of person is Death **personified**—what are his characteristics?
3. What three things do the riders pass in stanza 3?
4. What is significant about the fact that the carriage passes the sun in stanza 4? How does the temperature now change?
5. What has the speaker surmised, or guessed, in the last stanza?

Interpreting Meanings

6. Can you paraphrase the first two lines in a way that emphasizes their **irony?** What word in line 2 tells you unmistakably that the **tone** is ironic?
7. In stanza 2, "civility" means politeness, or formal good manners. How does this kind of behavior on the part of both Death and the speaker extend the **irony** of stanza 1?
8. Of all the things the poet might have had the carriage pass, why do you think she chooses the children and the grain in stanza 3? How can grain be imagined as "gazing"?
9. Stanza 5 is a riddle in itself. Can you solve it by identifying what the nearly buried house is?
10. Some readers think the concluding stanza subtly introduces a **tone** of terror, because the speaker has suddenly realized she will ride on forever, conscious of being dead. Some think that the whole poem is an expression of trust and even triumph. Which group do you agree with, and why?

Writing About the Poem

A Critical Response

Commenting on a Critic. Alfred Kazin said of the last stanza in this poem:

> What that famous Eternity is, we cannot say.

In a paragraph, explain what *you* think Dickinson meant by the Eternity the horses were going toward.

SUPPLEMENTARY SUPPORT MATERIALS

1. Review and Response Worksheet: Meter (*CCB*)
2. Selection Test (*CCB*)
3. Audiocassette recording

PREPARATION

ESTABLISHING A PURPOSE. You may wish first to clarify vocabulary ("Moor" means rolling land, not a person; "Checks" are railway tickets), and then use the headnote to direct students to consider whether the tone is playful or serious, as they listen to the audiocassette.

CLOSURE

Have individual students explain how this poem could be interpreted as a confirmation of faith, or as a tribute to the powers of imagination.

ANALYZING THE POEM

Identifying Details

1. She has never seen either a moor or the sea. By extension, she has never seen heather or waves.

In spite of this, she can imagine how the heather must look on a moor and how the billows, or waves, look on the ocean.

2. She says she has never spoken with God or visited heaven.

She is certain that heaven exists, and she says she knows the spot "As if the Checks were given."

Interpreting Meanings

3. Students will have various responses. This may be a good time to discuss with students the notion of ambiguity in poetry. A poem's richness is often increased when we consider multiple interpretations. Perhaps Dickinson left the matter open intentionally.

4. Probably by riding on a train with your tickets in hand.

Brought up in a household which reflected the Puritan piety of earlier centuries, Emily Dickinson was both "one of the faithful" and a free spirit. As an obedient and conservative young woman, she accepted what she was taught and valued what she learned. But her imagination led her to examine all conventions, and an element of playfulness in her temperament often made her treat sober matters with a touch of frivolity.

There is nothing frivolous in the following poem, and yet we are left to wonder if its intent is wholly religious. Is it a confirmation of faith, or is Dickinson once more paying tribute to the powers of imagination?

I never saw a Moor—

I never saw a Moor—
I never saw the Sea—
Yet know I how the Heather looks
And what a Billow be.

I never spoke with God
Nor visited in Heaven—
Yet certain am I of the spot
As if the Checks were given—

Responding to the Poem

Analyzing the Poem

Identifying Details

1. What does the speaker say she has never seen in the first stanza? What does she know in spite of this?
2. What does the speaker say she has never done in the second stanza? What is she certain of in spite of this?

Interpreting Meanings

3. Do you think Dickinson is professing a belief in heaven based on religious conviction? Or is she celebrating the power of the imagination to confirm what she could not have experienced during her life? Explain.
4. "Checks" were colored railway tickets given to passengers to assure the conductor that they were heading in the right direction. Dickinson's editors wanted to change the word to "charts," which was more conventionally poetic. A *chart* is a map. Which way would you be more likely to get to a destination: by riding on a train with your tickets in hand, or by following a map?

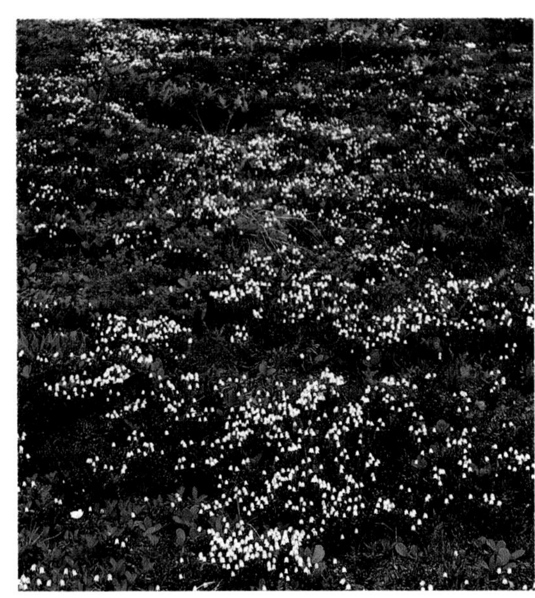

Supplementary Support Materials

1. Review and Response Worksheet: Implied Metaphor (*CCB*)
2. Selection Test (*CCB*)
3. Audiocassette recording

Analyzing the Poem

Identifying Details

1. Suggestions might include "indirect," "changed," "toned down."
2. "Circuit" suggests a way that is circuitous or roundabout. Line 2 might be paraphrased: "If you want to be successful, tell the truth in a roundabout way, rather than directly."
3. The surprise of truth is too bright.
4. The lines might be paraphrased as follows: "Truth is so bright and dangerous that it may be compared to lightning: just as lightning is less scary when it is explained carefully and kindly to children, so truth is more approachable from a roundabout way."

Interpreting Meanings

5. The reason is that truth is so bright that a direct revelation of it would blind all of us. "Dazzle" could mean "enlighten" or "overpower." "Blind" could mean "ignorant."
6. Truth is being compared to an intensely bright light.
7. To spare someone's feelings, to support someone's efforts; perhaps it differs because of its motivation.
8. Some students may feel that a "slant" truth is always a lie; others may point out that the "whole" truth may be incomprehensible to those who are too inexperienced to understand it.

A. Expansion
The metaphor of truth as a dazzling light is discussed in question 6. Invert lines 5–8 and paraphrase them to make the analogy clear also: Truth must show its light gradually lest it blind people, *just as* kind explanations are used to lessen children's terror of lightning.

Some people think these two quatrains express the essence of Dickinson's own poetry. How can this lyric be seen as a reference to the way all poetry "works"?

Tell all the Truth

Tell all the Truth but tell it slant—
Success in Circuit lies
Too bright for our infirm Delight
The Truth's superb surprise

A As Lightning to the Children eased
With explanation kind
The Truth must dazzle gradually
Or every man be blind—

Responding to the Poem

Analyzing the Poem

Identifying Details

1. How would you define the word *slant* as it is used in line 1?
2. What is "Circuit"? How would you **paraphrase** line 2?
3. In line 3, what is "too bright for our infirm Delight"?
4. Lines 5 and 6 provide an example to illustrate the poet's point about truth. As is typical of Dickinson's technique, she omits several words in these lines. How would you rephrase the lines to make a full sentence?

Interpreting Meanings

5. The last two lines explain why the truth must be told "slant." What is the reason? How would you define the words *dazzle* and *blind* here?
6. The poet says that Truth is "bright" and that it can "dazzle." What **metaphor** is implied here—what is Truth being compared with?
7. Can you think of some cases where the truth might be told "slant"? How is this different from a lie?
8. Do you agree with the poet's message? Explain your response to Dickinson's poem.

Supplementary Support Materials
1. Review and Response Worksheet: Personification and Theme (*CCB*)
2. Selection Test (*CCB*)
3. Audiocassette recording

Preparation

Establishing a Purpose. The audiocassette will help students listen for the tone as the poem moves from "happy Flower" to the chilling "blonde Assassin" and the cold, ironic, "Approving God."

Closure

Have individual students state the theme of the poem.

Analyzing the Poem

Identifying Details

1. The power of the frost "beheads" a happy flower and kills it. Meanwhile, the sun—and by implication, God Himself—take no notice of the event.
2. The sun is said to proceed "unmoved."

God is apparently "approving."

(Answers continue in left-hand column.)

(Continued from top.)

Interpreting Meanings

3. The frost, called "blonde" because of its whiteness.
4. The flower is personified as a laughing, happy child, unaware of the danger that threatens it. The frost is called an "assassin," a grim, powerful figure who beheads the flower. The sun is personified as an impersonal, uncaring figure who "proceeds unmoved" in measuring off "another Day."
5. The theme relates to the sadness of death in the natural world. Students may find it shocking in that it can be read as a criticism of God.
6. The word *unmoved* could mean "motionless" (in the physical sense) or "without feeling" (in an emotional sense).
7. Probably she's sympathetic.
8. Emerson focuses on the positive aspects of nature. In this poem, the speaker focuses on the negative.

Listen for the poet's tone as she describes how frost kills a flower. Is it somber, or is it playful?

Apparently with no surprise

Apparently with no surprise
To any happy Flower
The Frost beheads it at its play—
In accidental power—
The blonde Assassin passes on—
The Sun proceeds unmoved
To measure off another Day
For an Approving God.

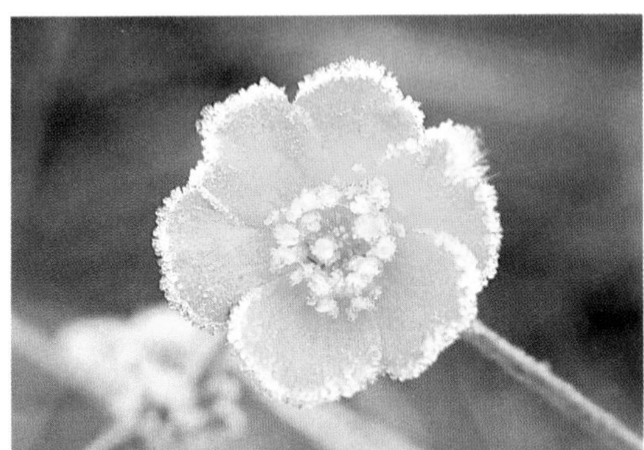

Responding to the Poem

Analyzing the Poem

Identifying Details

1. What happens in the poem?
2. What word tells how the sun feels about the incident? How does God feel?

Interpreting Meanings

3. Who *is* the "blonde Assassin"?
4. Aside from the use of capital letters, how are the flower, the frost, and the sun **personified** in this poem? What kind of person does each seem to be?
5. What do you think is the **theme** of this poem? Is the theme shocking or reassuring? Explain.
6. A **pun** is a play on words with similar meanings. What pun is in line 6? How would you explain it?
7. The speaker describes how she thinks God feels about the flower's beheading. How do you think the speaker feels?
8. How does the speaker's attitude toward nature in this poem differ from Emerson's attitude in the selection from "Nature" (page 191)? Which point of view do you favor, and why?

SUPPLEMENTARY SUPPORT MATERIALS
1. Review and Response Worksheet: The New Poetry (*CCB*)
2. Selection Test (*CCB*)
3. Audiocassette recording

PREPARATION
ESTABLISHING A PURPOSE. Ask students to read the poem to decide what the poet is saying about imagination.

Look up the word *revery* (reverie) in a dictionary. How could revery be equated with imagination?

To make a prairie it takes a clover and one bee

To make a prairie it takes a clover and one bee,
One clover, and a bee,
And revery.
The revery alone will do,
If bees are few.

A

A. Expansion
The poem can be read almost at a glance, but depending on the philosophical bent of your class, discussion of the nature of creativity and the power of the imagination may go on for some time. Before waxing too philosophical, ask students what scientific knowledge is assumed by line 1 and the photograph that illustrates it; without specific awareness of that knowledge, the poem loses its impact. (Knowledge that bees carry from plant to plant the pollen that is necessary for fertilization)

CLOSURE
Have individual students make brief statements explaining the message of the poem.

Analyzing The Poem

Identifying Details

1. The notion is that both bees and clover would eventually multiply.

2. Dickinson seems to be implying a union between the concrete and the abstract. She celebrates the power of the imagination to create one's own universe, and even implies—in the last two lines—that the imagination is so powerful that "revery alone will do."

Interpreting Meanings

3. Student answers will vary. Most students will agree that Dickinson is emphasizing the almost infinite power of the imagination.

The Poems as a Whole

1. Student answers will vary. Create a chalkboard chart using "success," "failure," "religion," "love," "death," and "imagination" as the headings. Brainstorm for one (or two) of the categories a short list of what students believe Dickinson says about the topic. Then ask students to cite poems supporting their ideas. Continue with general discussion of the remaining topics, noting that while all readers do not agree on Dickinson's

Responding to the Poem

Analyzing the Poem

Identifying Details

1. Scientifically speaking, how could one bee and one clover "make a prairie"?
2. How, if "bees are few," could "revery" accomplish the same thing?

Interpreting Meanings

3. What idea or message about the imagination do you think Dickinson wanted to convey in this poem?

The Poems as a Whole

1. About Dickinson's cycle of poems, a critic says this:

> . . . we cannot help reading [this] tumultuous cycle as one of the fullest records ever left of a *life,* whose outlet more and more became poetry.
>
> —Alfred Kazin

From the poems you have read, what have *you* learned about the poet and her responses to success and failure? Religion? Love? Death? Imagination? Do all readers agree on what the poems mean?

2. Did you find Dickinson's poems understandable or difficult? Try to explain your response to them.
3. Dickinson's poems are known for their unusual **metaphors.** Find at least five metaphors from this collection of her poems that strike you as particularly effective. For each example of a metaphor, identify the two distinct things the poet is comparing. In what ways are the two things alike?
4. Dickinson is also known for her precise **imagery.** Find at least five examples of images from these poems that you found particularly effective. Explain why each image is effective.
5. Here is what another critic says about Dickinson's poetry:

> The most cursory glance at Emily Dickinson will reveal that she is a deeply religious poet, preoccupied, to the verge of obsession, with the themes of death and immortality.
>
> —Northrop Frye

Based on the poems you've read, discuss this statement. How did *you* feel about Dickinson's **themes** and the **tone** she used to talk about them?

Writing About the Poems

A Creative Response

1. **Writing Quatrains.** A quatrain is four lines of verse, usually unified by a rhyme scheme. Write a poem of your own on one of the subjects Dickinson used in the poems you've read. You might use one of these lines as your opening:

Apparently with no surprise . . .
I never saw a . . .
Heart! We will forget . . .

Use meter and rhyme in the quatrain that you write. But introduce variations in the meter and use some slant rhymes to prevent your quatrain from sounding sing-song and mechanical.

A Critical Response

2. **Analyzing a Poem.** Dickinson let the strict meters she found in her hymn book provide the basic beat for her poems, but the variations she introduced gave her poems subtlety and prevented monotony. In a brief essay, analyze at least two of her poems to show how she uses this traditional hymn stanza:

8 syllables in line 1 8 syllables in line 3
6 syllables in line 2 6 syllables in line 4

Then show how she also uses the short hymn meter of 6, 6, 8, and 6 syllables. To see how closely some of the poems conform to a hymn meter, you might try singing "If you were coming in the Fall" to the tune of "O God Our Help in Ages Past." The music for this hymn follows.

3. **Analyzing an Edited Version.** As you know, the editors of Dickinson's poems frequently altered them, often to make them more conventionally "poetic"—that is, to provide conventional rhymes and rhythms and to get rid of what they thought were awkward phrasings. Here is a copy of a poem as Dickinson wrote it. The editors felt it needed many improvements; their alterations are shown. In an essay, describe the kinds of changes the editors made and evaluate them. Why do you think they made them, and what effect do they have on the original poem?

meaning, a valid interpretation must be backed by the poet's words.

2. Student answers will vary.

3. Student answers will vary. Brainstorm one or two metaphors and identify the things being compared; then have students continue on their own.

4. Follow the same procedure as for question 3.

5. Students will have to acknowledge that Dickinson does focus on death and immortality, but beyond that, answers will be personal.

If you were coming in the Fall,
I'd brush the Summer by
With half a smile, and half a spurn,
As Housewives do, a Fly.

If I could see you in a year,
I'd wind the months in balls—
And put them each in separate Drawers,
For fear the numbers fuse—

If only Centuries, delayed,
I'd count them on my Hand,
Subtracting, till my fingers dropped
Into Van Dieman's Land.

If certain, when this life was out—
That your's and mine, should be
I'd toss it yonder, like a Rind,
And take Eternity—

But, now, uncertain of the length
Of this, that is between,
It goads me, like the Goblin Bee—
That will not state—it's sting.

Comparing Poems. In a brief essay, compare and contrast one of Emily Dickinson's poems with the poems by Edward Taylor (pages 45–51) or with "Thanatopsis" by William Cullen Bryant (page 142). In your essay, consider such elements as **subject matter, message, tone, metaphors, rhythms,** and **rhymes.**

Analyzing Language and Style

Diction and Syntax

Dickinson's poems were looked upon as eccentric because they did not conform to standards of correct usage. Examine the poems here to see if they exhibit any of these characteristics. In each case, try to explain the effects of Dickinson's "rule-breaking." Does her eccentric punctuation ever affect the poem's meaning?

1. The *-s* is often not added to the third person singular of verbs.
2. There may be no agreement between subject and verb.
3. A word might be made up.
4. Punctuation is not standard.
5. Articles *(a, an, the)* are sometimes omitted.
6. Some words are misspelled.

Primary Sources
Higginson's Account of Dickinson

In 1862, Emily Dickinson sent critic Thomas Wentworth Higginson a letter and four poems, asking for critical help. Dickinson saw him as a mentor, and they corresponded for several years. Four years after Dickinson's death, Higginson assisted Mable Loomis Todd (a friend of Austin Dickinson's) in editing the poems. The next year, Higginson wrote an article in the *Atlantic Monthly* about his experiences with Emily Dickinson. This is the only contemporary account we have of the poet.

". . . On April 16, 1862, I took from the post office the following letter:

> Mr. Higginson,—Are you too deeply occupied to say if my verse is alive?
>
> The mind is so near itself it cannot see distinctly, and I have none to ask.
>
> Should you think it breathed, and had you the leisure to tell me, I should feel quick gratitude.
>
> If I make the mistake, that you dared to tell me would give me sincerer honor toward you.
>
> I inclose my name, asking you, if you please, sir, to tell me what is true?
>
> That you will not betray me it is needless to ask, since honor is its own pawn.

"The letter was postmarked 'Amherst,' and it was in a handwriting so peculiar that it seemed as if the writer might have taken her first lessons by studying the famous fossil bird tracks in the museum of that college town. Yet it was not in the slightest degree illiterate, but cultivated, quaint, and wholly unique. Of punctuation there was little; she used chiefly dashes, and it has been thought better, in printing these letters, as with her poems, to give them the benefit in this respect of the ordinary usages; and so with her habit as to capitalization. . . . But the most curious thing about the letter was the total absence of a signature. It proved, however, that she had

A. Responding
? How does Dickinson's use of the word *surgery* suggest her feelings? Have you ever felt that way when your writing was critiqued? (The English language reflects this image. Criticism "cuts" and "wounds.")

B. Responding
Except for *Revelation,* the final, apocalyptic book of the Bible, all of the references are to English writers: the poets John Keats (1795–1821), Robert Browning (1812–1889), and Elizabeth Barrett Browning (1806–1861); the essayist and critic John Ruskin (1819–1900); and the physician-author of *Religio Medici* and *Christian Morals,* Sir Thomas Browne (1605–1682).
? What does this reading list suggest about Americans' views of "culture" as late as the end of the nineteenth century? (They still revered things English and/or Old World.)

C. Responding
? Would Dickinson have found the textbook's selections from *Leaves of Grass* offensive? Why or why not? (She may have found the subject matter surprising but may have accepted his emotion.)

written her name on a card, and put it under the shelter of a smaller envelope inclosed in the larger; and even this name was written—as if the shy writer wished to recede as far as possible from view—in pencil, not in ink. The name was Emily Dickinson. Enclosed with the letter were four poems. . . . I remember to have ventured
A on some criticism which she afterwards called 'surgery,' and on some questions, part of which she evaded, as will be seen, with a naïve skill such as the most experienced and worldly coquette might envy. Her second letter (received April 26, 1862) was as follows:—

Mr. Higginson,—Your kindness claimed earlier gratitude, but I was ill, and write to-day from my pillow.

Thank you for the surgery; it was not so painful as I supposed. I bring you others, as you ask. . . .

You asked how old I was? I made no verse, but one or two, until this winter, sir.

I had a terror since September, I could tell to none; and so I sing, as the boy does by the burying ground, because I am afraid.

B You inquire my books. For poets, I have Keats, and Mr. and Mrs. Browning. For prose, Mr. Ruskin, Sir Thomas Browne, and the Revelations. I went to school, but in your manner of the phrase had no education. When a little girl, I had a friend who taught me Immortality; but venturing too near, himself, he never returned. Soon after my tutor died, and for several years my lexicon was my only companion. Then I found one more,[1] but he was not contented I be his scholar, so he left the land.

You ask of my companions. Hills, sir, and the sundown, and a dog large as myself, that my father bought me. They are better than beings because they know, but do not tell; and the noise in the pool at noon excels my piano.

I have a brother and sister; my mother does not care for thought, and father, too busy with his briefs to notice what we do. He buys me many books, but begs me not to read them, because he fears they joggle the mind. They are religious, except me. . . .

But I fear my story fatigues you. I would like to learn. Could you tell me how to grow, or is it unconveyed, like melody or witchcraft?

C You speak of Mr. Whitman. I never read his book, but was told that it was disgraceful.

". . . I must soon have written to ask her for her picture, that I might form some impression of my enigmatical correspondent. To this came the following reply, in July, 1862:

Could you believe me without? I had no portrait, now, but am small, like the wren; and my hair is bold like the chestnut bur; and my eyes, like the sherry in the glass, that the guest leaves. Would this do just as well?

It often alarms father. He says death might occur and he has molds [photographs] of all the rest, but has no mold of me. . . .' "

—from "Emily Dickinson,"
Thomas Wentworth Higginson

1. Probably Charles Wadsworth.

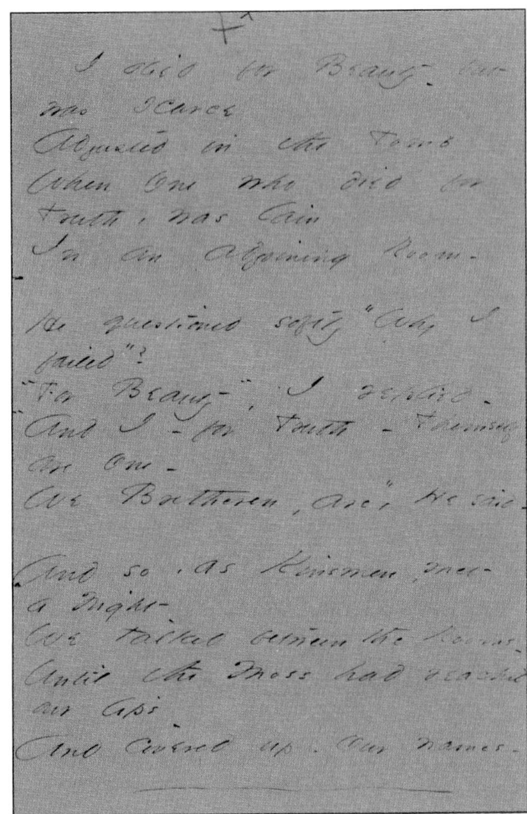
I died for Beauty – but was scarce
Adjusted in the Tomb
When One who died for Truth, was lain
In an adjoining Room –
He questioned softly "Why I failed"?
"For Beauty", I replied –
And I – for Truth – Themself are One –
We Brethren, are", He said –
And so, as Kinsmen, met a Night –
We talked between the Rooms –
Until the Moss had reached our lips –
And covered up – our names –

Manuscript for "I died for Beauty."

By permission of the Houghton Library, Harvard University, Cambridge.

Exercises in Critical Thinking and Writing

COMPARING AND CONTRASTING POEMS

Writing Assignment

Write a brief essay in which you compare and contrast Walt Whitman's "Song Number 6" and Emily Dickinson's "This quiet Dust Was Gentlemen and Ladies."

Background

When you **compare** two poems, you point out the ways in which they are alike; when you **contrast** them, you tell how they're different. But first you must be able to *see* the similarities and differences. The easiest way to approach this assignment is to focus on the **elements** of poetry: **subject, figurative language, imagery, sound effects, form,** and **theme.**

When you write a comparison and/or contrast essay, it's important to decide how you're going to present your ideas. Here are three possible ways to organize your essay:

1. **Similarities and differences.** You can discuss all of the ways the poems are similar, then go on to discuss all of the ways they're different.
2. **Block method.** You can discuss all of the elements of one poem first and then discuss all of the elements of the second poem.
3. **Point-by-point method.** You can discuss each element in both poems, one element at a time. For example, you can first deal with the subject in both poems, then figurative language in both poems, etc. Each element might take a single paragraph.

Prewriting

1. Read both poems carefully several times. At least one reading should be aloud so that you can listen to the poems' sound effects.

6

A child said *What is the grass?* fetching it to me with full hands;
How could I answer the child? I do not know what it is anymore than he.

I guess it must be the flag of my disposition, out of hopeful green stuff woven.
Or I guess it is the handkerchief of the Lord,
A scented gift and remembrancer designedly dropt,
Bearing the owner's name someway in the corners, that we may see and remark, and say *Whose?*

Or I guess the grass is itself a child, the produced babe of the vegetation. . . .

And now it seems to me the beautiful uncut hair of graves.

Tenderly will I use you curling grass,
It may be you transpire from the breasts of young men,
It may be if I had known them I would have loved them,
It may be you are from old people, or from offspring taken soon out of their mothers' laps,
And here you are the mothers' laps. . . . A

What do you think has become of the young and old men?
And what do you think has become of the women and children? B

They are alive and well somewhere,
The smallest sprout shows there is really no death,
And if ever there was it led forward life, and does not wait at the end to arrest it,
And ceased the moment life appeared.

All goes onward and outward, nothing collapses,
And to die is different from what anyone supposed, and luckier.

—from *Song of Myself,*
Walt Whitman

This quiet Dust was Gentlemen and Ladies
And Lads and Girls
Was Laughter and Ability and Sighing
And Frocks and Curls—
This passive place a Summer's nimble Mansion C
Where Bloom and Bees
Fulfilled their Oriental Circuit
Then ceased, like these.

—Emily Dickinson

2. Now, for each poem, jot down answers to the following questions. Note line numbers that will serve as examples.

A. Expansion Students might note that in these lines Whitman's poem comes closest in meaning to Dickinson's poem. It is here that the poet associates nature and death.

B. Expansion The fact that Whitman poses a question here, rather than making a statement as Dickinson does, may be a significant difference in the two poems.

C. Expansion The "quiet dust" and the "passive place" probably refer to human remains and to the grave site where grass and bees once flourished. The last line of the poem is usually interpreted as a considerably more pessimistic statement about the nature of death than is Whitman's poem.

Revising Essays
As students revise their essays, refer them to **Grammar, Usage, and Mechanics: A Reference Guide** at the back of their books.

Exercises in Critical Thinking and Writing/*cont.*

a. What is the poem's **subject?**
b. Does the poem use **figures of speech?** What is the effect of the figures?
c. Does the poem use **imagery?** What is the emotional effect of the imagery?
d. Does the poem use **meter** and **rhyme,** or is it written in **free verse?** What is the effect of the poem's sounds?
e. What is the poet's **tone**—or attitude toward the subject?
f. What is the poet's message, or **theme?**

3. Once you've answered these questions, organize your information into two lists: Similarities and Differences. For example:

Similarities	Differences
a. Both poems are about time and loss.	a. Whitman's poem is in free verse; Dickinson's conforms to meter and uses rhyme.
Etc.	Etc.

4. When you have finished your lists, think of a **thesis statement** which will summarize your main idea. Say whether you think the poems are more alike or more different. Here are two examples:

> a. Whitman's poem and Dickinson's poem are totally different in form, but they are similar in subject and tone.
> b. Whitman's poem about grass and Dickinson's poem about "quiet dust" may share the same subject matter, but they are as different as two poems can possibly be.

Writing

With your thesis statement and lists in front of you, you're ready to decide on your method of organization. Here is one possible plan:

Paragraph 1: Cite the titles and authors of the two poems. Include your thesis statement.
Paragraph 2: Discuss the poems' similarities. (If you have a lot to say, this may take more than one paragraph.)
Paragraph 3: Discuss the poems' differences. (Again, this may take more than one paragraph.)
Concluding paragraph: State your response to the two poems. Tell which one you liked better, and why.

Remember to cite specific examples (lines, words, or phrases) from the poems to support your points. Whenever you quote directly, use quotation marks, and check the text to make sure you've quoted accurately.

Revision and Proofreading

Don't hand in your first draft. Take the time to revise and proofread your essay, using the guidelines in the section at the back of this book called **Writing About Literature.**

THE RISE OF REALISM
THE CIVIL WAR AND POST-WAR PERIOD

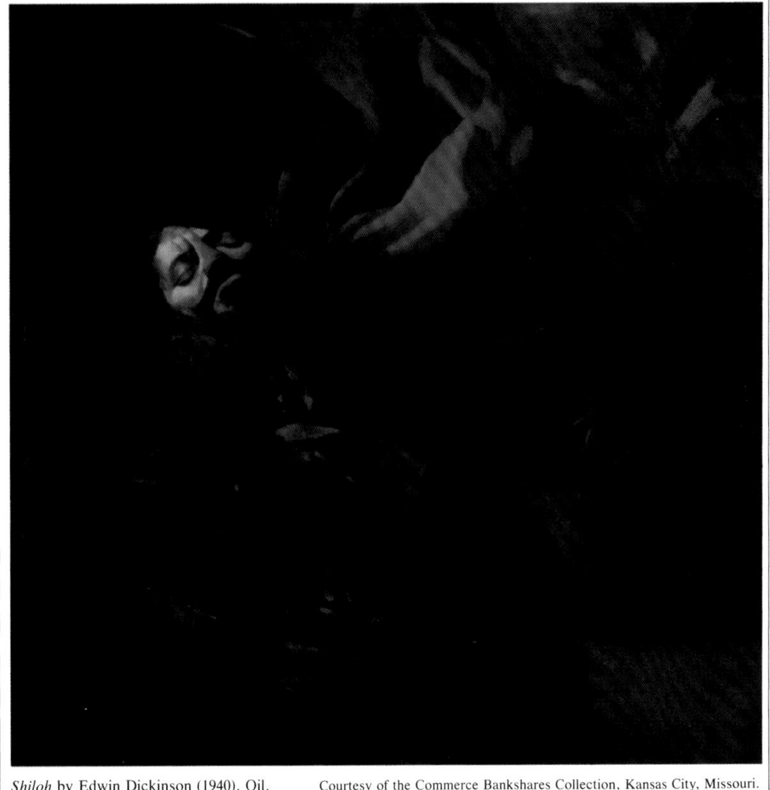

Shiloh by Edwin Dickinson (1940). Oil. Courtesy of the Commerce Bankshares Collection, Kansas City, Missouri.

UNIT SIX

HUMANITIES CONNECTION: RESPONDING TO THE FINE ART

The dark, swirling forms and skull-like face in this oil painting by the twentieth-century Romantic painter Edwin Dickinson (1891–1978) evoke a somber mood appropriate to the painting's title. Each side lost over 10,000 men at the battle of Shiloh (April 6–7, 1862) in Tennessee, one of the bloodiest battles of the Civil War and second only to Gettysburg as a subject of controversy.

? What first strikes you about the painting? (The face draws most viewers like a bull's-eye.) What clues to the Civil War setting do you see? (Uniform coat, huge boot at the right) Do you think the other shapes are realistic objects such as sheets or blankets, or are they shapes chosen for their sobering effect? Do you find the painting more *realistic* (representing an actual death scene at Shiloh) or more *symbolic* (representing the war in general)? Explain your response. (For example, the swirling shapes could symbolically represent winding sheets or shrouds for the dead.)

TEACHING THE RISE OF REALISM UNIT

The change from romanticism to realism in American fiction was in large part due to historical and social changes. The Civil War, the growth of the railroads, the telegraph, mass immigration, and rapid industrialization all combined, in the latter half of the nineteenth century, to transform the United States from a mostly agrarian, decentralized nation to an urbanized, more centralized one. Transportation and communication brought people into closer contact with the various regions of the country at precisely the same time that regional differences began to fade away. The result was nostalgia, a feeling that expressed itself in fiction as regionalism, or local color.

The hardships of the Civil War and its aftermath, and the grim conditions that prevailed in the burgeoning urban slums, factories, railroad camps, and mines, impressed themselves upon writers who felt that the depiction of this form of human suffering was an important artistic end in itself. The influence of foreign literature was also important in the development of realism in American writing. American Romanticism had followed in the footsteps of its European models, and when European writers turned to realism, Americans, who at that time still represented the "junior" nation, followed suit. Frank Norris studied Emile Zola. Henry James was influenced by Flaubert and Turgenev in his striving toward ever more subtle psychological realism. Stephen Crane and Joseph Conrad, who knew each other in England, strengthened each other in their development of an impressionistic descriptive style. Kipling was another strong influence on Crane, who took his famous "wafer" simile from a line in *The Light That Failed:* ". . . the sun shone, a blood-red wafer. . . ." And the journalistic, sentimental, comic melodrama of Dickens influenced a whole generation of writers, from Dostoevsky in Russia to Mark Twain and Bret Harte in the United States.

OBJECTIVES OF THE RISE OF REALISM UNIT

1. To increase proficiency and expand vocabulary
2. To gain exposure to notable authors and their works
3. To define and identify elements of nonfiction, fiction, and spirituals
4. To define and identify significant literary techniques
5. To interpret and respond to autobiography, spirituals, stories, and novels, through analysis of their elements
6. To practice the following critical thinking and writing skills:
   a. Responding to an idea
   b. Comparing and contrasting forms of literature
   c. Comparing and contrasting writers
   d. Analyzing euphemism and irony
   e. Comparing and contrasting tone and theme
   f. Analyzing features of impressionistic style
   g. Analyzing inferences and point of view

A. Discussing the Quotation
The quotation is from Crane's *War is Kind* (1899), a collection of epigrammatic free verse anticipating some strands of twentieth-century poetry. Tell students that they will later experience, with the narrator of Crane's "The Open Boat," a universe that does seem either hostile or indifferent to human concerns.

Supplementary Support Materials: Unit Six

1. Unit Introduction Test (*CCB*)
2. American Language Test (*CCB*)
3. Word Analogies Test (*CCB*)
4. Unit Review Test (*CCB*)
5. Critical Thinking and Writing Test (*CCB*)
6. Instructional Overhead Transparencies

B. Humanities Connection: Responding to the Illustration
The ordinance proclaims the secession of South Carolina. Have students study the Charleston scene of four months later, page 378, and imagine the feelings of South Carolinians, as contrasted with the reactions of Whitman (text page 377). Americans today are unlikely to consider seriously any state's withdrawal from the Union.
? Was the issue clear-cut for people living *before* the Civil War? Consider a secessionist's reaction to passages such as this one in our Declaration of Independence: "united colonies [which] are, and of right ought to be, free and independent states" (text page 106).

C. Responding
? Note Emerson's earlier warning, restated in paragraph 3, that war was inevitable if slavery were not abolished. From your studies, do you also consider slavery the key issue?

THE RISE OF REALISM
THE CIVIL WAR AND POST-WAR PERIOD

by **Gary Q. Arpin**

A

> *A man said to the universe:*
> *"Sir, I exist!"*
> *"However," replied the universe,*
> *"The fact has not created in me*
> *"A sense of obligation."*
>
> —Stephen Crane

The Civil War

On the evening of April 13, 1861, Walt Whitman went to the opera at the Academy of Music in Manhattan. After the opera, he was walking down Broadway toward Brooklyn when, as he later wrote, "I heard in the distance the loud cries of the newsboys, who came presently tearing and yelling up the street, rushing from side to side even more furiously than usual. I bought an extra and crossed to the Metropolitan Hotel . . . where the great lamps were still brightly blazing, and, with a crowd of others, who gathered impromptu, read the news, which was evidently authentic."

The news that Whitman and the others read so avidly was of the Confederate attack on Fort Sumter, the opening shots of the Civil War. Thus solemnly began, for one of the few American writers who would witness it firsthand, the greatest cataclysm in United States history.

B

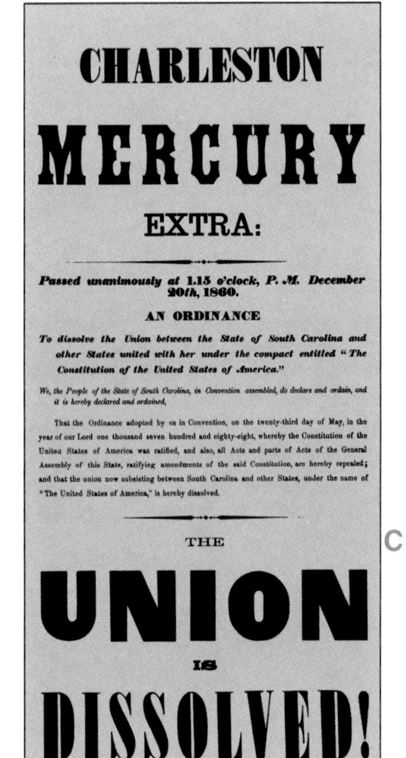

CHARLESTON

MERCURY

EXTRA:

Passed unanimously at 1.15 o'clock, P. M. December 20th, 1860.

AN ORDINANCE

To dissolve the Union between the State of South Carolina and other States united with her under the compact entitled "The Constitution of the United States of America."

We, the People of the State of South Carolina, in Convention assembled, do declare and ordain, and it is hereby declared and ordained,

That the Ordinance adopted by us in Convention, on the twenty-third day of May, in the year of our Lord one thousand seven hundred and eighty-eight, whereby the Constitution of the United States of America was ratified, and also, all Acts and parts of Acts of the General Assembly of this State, ratifying amendments of the said Constitution, are hereby repealed; and that the union now subsisting between South Carolina and other States, under the name of "The United States of America," is hereby dissolved.

THE

UNION

IS

DISSOLVED!

Rare Books and Manuscripts Division, New York Public Library.

Responses to the War: Idealism . . .

C

In Concord, Massachusetts, home of Emerson, Thoreau, Hawthorne, Bronson Alcott, and many other intellectual leaders of the nation, army volunteers met at the bridge that Emerson had immortalized in "The Concord Hymn" (page 196), his famous poem about the beginning of the American Revolution. Emerson had for decades warned that this day would come if slavery were not abolished. Now that the day had arrived, he was filled with patriotic fervor. "Now we have a country again," he had said when he heard of the outbreak of hostilities. He watched the Concord volunteers march to Boston, and he visited a navy yard, declaring that "sometimes gunpowder smells good."

Emerson had great respect for the Southern will to fight, and he suspected, quite rightly, that the war would not be over in a few months as some people had predicted. He expected setbacks during the war, but he would not let them dampen his faith in the Union cause. When the Concord volunteers returned a few months later from the Battle of Bull Run, defeated and disillusioned, many of them unwilling to re-enlist, Emerson maintained his conviction that the war must be pursued. "The war with its defeats and uncertainties," he wrote, "is immensely better than what we lately called the integrity of the Republic, as amputation is better than cancer."

A. Humanities Connection: Responding to the Fine Art
Though Thomas Nast (1840–1902) was a thoroughly competent painter, he is best known for his political cartoons. His cartoons of the Civil War in *Harper's Weekly* attracted wide attention, and it was he who created the tiger, the elephant, and the donkey as symbols of Tammany Hall and the Republican and Democratic parties. The painting reproduced here demonstrates Nast's mastery of realistic draftsmanship.
? Contrast the excited, jubilant air of this painting with the soberness of the indented quote from Walt Whitman on this page, or with the somber quality of Dickinson's *Shiloh* (page 375). If you have read or viewed Margaret Mitchell's Civil War story, *Gone with the Wind* (1936, motion picture 1939), which of these visual or mental scenes remind you of the innocent excitement of Mitchell's opening scenes? What reminds you of the desolation in Atlanta and at Tara later on? (Answers will vary.)

A

New York's Seventh Regiment marching down Broadway on April 19, 1861, by Thomas Nast (1869). Oil.

Seventh Regiment Armory, New York City.

Still, Northern disillusionment after a defeat so early in the war was strong. With a keen eye for the sad details, Whitman recorded the sense of gloomy defeat in Washington at the end of June when Northern troops returned from the disaster of Bull Run:

> The defeated troops commenced pouring into Washington over the Long Bridge at daylight on Monday, 22nd—day drizzling all through with rain. The Saturday and Sunday of the battle (20th, 21st) had been parched and hot to an extreme—the dust, the grime and smoke, in layers, sweated in followed by other layers again sweated in, absorbed by those excited souls—their clothes all saturated with the clay-powder filling the air—stirred up everywhere on the dry roads and trodden fields by the regiments, swarming wagons, artillery, etc.—all the men with this coating of murk and sweat and rain, now recoiling back, pouring over the Long Bridge—a horrible march of twenty miles, returning to Washington baffled, humiliated, panic-struck. Where are the vaunts, and the proud boasts with which you went forth? Where are your banners, and your bands of music, and your ropes to bring back your prisoners? Well, there isn't a band playing—and there isn't a flag but clings ashamed and lank to its staff.
>
> —Walt Whitman

Late in 1862, Whitman traveled to Virginia to find his brother George, who had been wounded in battle. After George was nursed back to health, Whitman remained in Washington off and on, working part-time and serving as a volunteer hospital visitor, com-

A. Humanities Connection: Discussing the Photograph
(See also Humanities Connection annotation B, page 376.) Notice the date, a day after the reaction of Whitman cited on page 376. On April 14, Confederate forces took Fort Sumter in the Charleston harbor after a 34-hour bombardment. The U.S. flag did not again fly over the fort for 4 years—April 14, 1865.

B. Responding
Melville's *Battle-Pieces and Aspects of the War* (1866) contains 72 elegaic Civil War poems. Compare the poems with those of Whitman in *Drum-taps* (1865, found in inclusive editions of *Leaves of Grass*). ? Comment on the different attitudes of Whitman and Melville toward young soldiers, as suggested by the quote from Whitman in the paragraph beginning "Future years," and by the final couplet of the Melville verse.

"Whitman wrote, '. . . the real war will never get in the books.' "

A

Confederate flag at Fort Sumter, Charleston, South Carolina, April 14, 1861.

forting the wounded and writing to their loved ones. The condition of the wounded was appalling. The medical teams of both sides were overwhelmed by the dead and dying. Many of the injured had to remain on the battlefield for two or three days, until the camp hospitals had room for them. Antiseptics were primitive, as were operating-room techniques. Anesthesia was virtually unknown. A major wound meant amputation or even death.

Whitman estimated that in three years as a camp hospital volunteer, he visited tens of thousands of wounded men. "I am the man," he had written in *Song of Myself* (page 338), "I suffered . . . I was there," and now he *was* there, in the real heart of America. In his poems, he had presented a panoramic vision of America; now America passed through the hospital tents in the form of wounded men from every state in the Union and the Confederacy. The horrifying experience was one of the most moving and painful of Whitman's life, but it confirmed his belief in the "true *ensemble* and extent of the States," as the poems in *Drum-Taps* demonstrate.

"Future years," he wrote, "will never know the seething hell and the black infernal background of the countless minor scenes and interiors (not the official surface-courteousness of the Generals, not the few great battles of the Secession war); and it is best they should not—the real war will never get in the books." Nevertheless, out of the horror that he viewed, Whitman was able to derive an optimistic vision of the American character, of "the actual soldier of 1862–65 . . . with all his ways, his incredible dauntlessness, habits, practices, tastes, language, his fierce friendship, his appetite, rankness, his superb strength—and a hundred unnamed lights and shades."

. . . and Disillusionment

B

The war that strengthened Whitman's optimism served at the same time to justify Herman Melville's pessimism. Melville's poems about the war, collected in *Battle-Pieces,* were often dark and foreboding. Of the elation following the firing on Fort Sumter, Melville wrote:

> O, the rising of the People
> Came with the springing of the grass,
> They rebounded from dejection
> After Easter came to pass.
> And the young were all elation
> Hearing Sumter's cannon roar. . . .
> But the elders with foreboding
> Mourned the days forever o'er,
> And recalled the forest proverb,
> The Iroquois' old saw:
> *Grief to every graybeard*
> *When young Indians lead the war.*
>
> —Herman Melville

A. Expansion
In some families, diaries kept by Civil War soldiers have been handed on as family heirlooms. If such a record or a published Civil War journal is available from a local library, have students read it and write in their journals about the feelings and reactions the account arouses.

B. Responding
? How does this tradition help account for Whitman's remark, "the real war will never get in the books" (page 378)? (The realistic novel did not yet exist.)

C. Responding
? How is this view also expressed in the Crane quotation that opens the unit (page 376)? (Both suggest that the universe has no interest in any individual.)

Melville was fascinated by the war, but he never wrote a novel about it. The poems in *Battle-Pieces,* based on newspaper accounts of the battles as well as visits to battlefields, record the heroism and futility of the fighting on both sides, and demonstrate respect for the Southern soldiers as well as the Northern ones. But in some of the best poems there is a sense of human nature being stripped bare, revealing not the heroism and strength that Whitman found, but, rather, humanity's basic evil.

"Melville was fascinated by the war, but he never wrote a novel about it."

The War and Literature

There was enough atrocity and heroism in the war to feed the views of both Melville and Whitman. What is odd, though, is that Melville's *Battle-Pieces* (which was ignored until the twentieth century) and Whitman's *Drum-Taps* and *Specimen Days* comprise the bulk of the war's literary legacy. There were many accounts of soldiers' experiences, but virtually all of them were the work of amateur writers; they had historical value, but no literary significance. Why did an event of such magnitude result in so little valuable literature at the time? A

One reason is that few major American writers saw the Civil War firsthand. Emerson was in Concord during most of the war, "knitting socks and mittens for soldiers," as he wrote to his son, and "writing patriotic lectures." Thoreau, who had been a fervent abolitionist, died in 1862, and Hawthorne died two years later. Emily Dickinson seems almost to have missed the war altogether; from her peaceful room in Amherst, Massachusetts, the carnage must have seemed very far away. Of the younger generation, William Dean Howells, Henry James, and Henry Adams were abroad.

But more importantly, the literary form most appropriate for handling such strong material—the realistic novel—had not yet been fully developed in the United States. War, with its life-and-death struggles, its defeats and victories, its indifference to the fate of individuals, would for later fiction writers be a subject of central importance. But for writers of the 1860's, war was more appropriate for poetry or pamphlets.

Modern readers think that one by-product of a war is a literary account of it, largely in the form of novels by young men who had survived the war. Modern writers like Ernest Hemingway went to war intending to return with the material for novels. This was not the case with the Civil War because traditional literary forms and sensibility could not easily deal with such material. There was no place for "the real war" in the fiction of the time. The traditional romantic novel of chivalry and high adventure simply could not accept the horrifying details of the Civil War. B

To those who lived through it, the war was a great tragedy. But for later writers, war confirmed a view of the world that saw all existence as a battle with an indifferent and often hostile environment. Thus, the great novel of the Civil War, *The Red Badge of Courage,* had to wait to be written by a man who was not born until six years after the war had ended: Stephen Crane. C

Dead Confederate gunners at Dunker Church after the Battle of Antietam, September 17, 1862. Photograph by Mathew Brady. D

D. Humanities Connection: Responding to the Photograph
When the Civil War began, Mathew B. Brady (c. 1828–1896) was already famous for photographs of the illustrious. He had begun photographing President Lincoln in 1860, and when war broke out, was authorized to accompany and photograph the army. The result was a vast visual record of the war. The Antietam campaign, source of this photograph, was so fierce that September 17, 1862, is said to have been the bloodiest single day of the war (a total of some 23,000 dead or wounded).
? Imagine that you are Brady. What happened before you took this photograph? What will happen next? What lies off-camera? Does the camera catch the horror you and others feel? What personal qualities have you had to develop in order to take pictures at the front?

A. Humanities Connection: Responding to the Photograph
The photograph dramatizes the societal focus of realism. Documentary photographer Lewis Hine (1874–1940) dedicated himself to exposing the evils of the industrial revolution in America—especially the poverty of new immigrants and the work lives of children. In earlier ages children were apprenticed in a trade or worked within the family, but the rapid growth of cities and expansion of industry after the Civil War led to their virtual enslavement in mines and factories. Despite early attempts to legislate child labor, not until the First Labor Standards Act of 1938 were minimum age limits even set.

? Imagine the lives of children in this scene. What time of day is it? What were they doing before they were asked to pose? What will they do next? What are their hopes and ambitions while they are working underground, or have all their dreams been crushed?

Additional Writing Assignment
Have students review the descriptions of romantic fiction on pages 120–121 (Unit Three) and pages 185–186 (Unit Four). In one or two paragraphs, have students discuss why the Civil War would have made the romantic approach, with its innocence and quest for spiritual meaning, seem dated and inappropriate.

The Rise of Realism

One of the most enduring subjects for prose fiction has always been the exploits of larger-than-life heroes. Born of the chivalric romance, the **romantic novel** presents the ordinary readers with lives lived at an idealistic level. The heroes and heroines of the novels of James Fenimore Cooper (1789–1851), for example, engage in romantic adventures filled with courageous acts, daring chases, and exciting escapes. Cooper's Leatherstocking, like his modern-day heir James Bond, has uncommon abilities that enable him to survive and prevail. His adventures are a far cry from the ordinary lives led by his readers. Such exciting exploits have always been a staple of prose fiction (and before that, of epic poetry).

In America, the great fiction writers of the mid-nineteenth century, Poe (page 226), Hawthorne (page 263), and Melville (page 294), shared an aversion to realism. These writers used romance not simply to entertain readers, but to reveal truths that would be hidden in a realistic story that limited itself to what actually could happen.

However, after the Civil War, a new generation of writers came of age. They were known as **realists,** writers who looked at "local manners" very closely and who aimed at a "very minute fidelity" to the common course of ordinary life. Their subjects were drawn from the slums of the rapidly growing cities, from the factories that were replacing farmlands. Their characters might include shop girls, poor factory workers, corrupt politicians, even prostitutes. But realism was not solely an American movement. In fact, it was well-entrenched in Europe by the time it began to develop widely in the United States.

Boys working in a mine in South Pittston, Pennsylvania, January 10, 1911. Photograph by Lewis Hine.

For Further Reading
For The Student
Students can sample European realism in Defoe's *Moll Flanders* (1722), Eliot's *Silas Marner* (1861), Trollope's *Barchester Towers* (1857), Balzac's *Le Pere Goriot* (1834), Tolstoy's *Anna Karenina* (1873–76), or their own selections from the works of Stendhal (1783–1842) or Flaubert (1821–1880). They should watch for the author's realistic treatment of daily life and probing of motivation.

A. Responding
Pause to clarify major points.
? How were regional writers realistic? (In speech and manners) How were they romantic? (In characterization and in social environment) How does literary realism go beyond regionalism? (It attempts more accurately to reveal social conditions and motivation.)

The European Roots of Realism

In Europe, realism developed in the work of such writers as Daniel Defoe, George Eliot, Anthony Trollope, Honoré de Balzac, Stendhal, Gustave Flaubert, and Leo Tolstoy. All of these writers faithfully reproduced the environment and the manners of everyday life: the way ordinary people lived and dressed, and what they thought and felt and talked about.

But realism was not simply concerned with recording wallpaper patterns, hairstyles, or the subjects of conversations. It sought also to explain *why* ordinary people behave the way they do. What, for example, fuels the ambitions of a young man who has come from the country to the city to make his fortune? Why does an apparently happily married woman decide to have a love affair? What leads a woman to accept or reject a particular man? In trying to answer these questions, realistic novelists often relied on the emerging sciences of human and animal behavior—biology, psychology, and sociology—as well as on their own insights and observations.

"Realism was not simply concerned with recording wallpaper patterns, hairstyles, or the subjects of conversations."

American Regional Writing

In America, realism had its roots in—though it was not synonymous with—**regionalism,** literature that emphasizes a specific geographic setting and that reproduces the speech and manners of people who live in that region. Harriet Beecher Stowe (1811–1896) is an example of a regional writer (though her greatest novel, *Uncle Tom's Cabin,* was one of the few that did not take place in her native New England). Joel Chandler Harris, Bret Harte (page 393), Sarah Orne Jewett, and Mark Twain (page 402) also recorded the peculiarities of speech and temperament in their parts of a rapidly expanding nation.

A However, while regional writers might be realistic in their depiction of speech patterns and manners, they were often unrealistic in their depiction of character and social environment. For example, a Southern writer like Thomas Nelson Page, who wrote very popular post-Civil War novels about the South, stressed the romantic "moonlight and magnolia" environment at the expense of the realities of a social world that relied on slavery. Realism as a literary movement in the United States went far beyond regionalism in its concern for accuracy in social conditions and human motivation.

Mark Twain is the best-known example of a regional writer whose realism far surpassed local bounds. Although he first established his reputation as a regional humorist, Twain evolved into a writer whose comic view of society became increasingly satiric. His best novel, *The Adventures of Huckleberry Finn,* describes the moral growth of a comic character in an environment that is at the same time physically beautiful and morally repugnant. *Huckleberry Finn* combines a biting picture of some of the injustices inherent in pre-Civil War American life with a lyrical portrait of the American landscape.

B

Addie Laud, a twelve-year-old spinner in a cotton mill in North Pownal, Vermont, February 9, 1910. Photograph by Lewis Hine.

B. Humanities Connection: Discussing the Photograph
Another photograph by Lewis Hine, this one shows a girl typical of an estimated 40,000 children under age 16 who worked in cotton mills in 1908. Many families, especially newly arrived immigrants, depended on the children's wages for survival. Some children working in textile mills were so small that they had to stand on their machines to work. Conditions were little better for their mothers who ran sewing machines in hot garment district workshops to earn a profit for their employer (their "sweater") and his "sweat-shop."

A. Discussing the Time Line
To enhance students' grasp of the time spans, draw a line entirely across a chalkboard, labeling one end 1800, the middle 1850, and the other end 1900. Divide the halves into five decades each. Then elicit from students, and write in the appropriate space, the major historical events from the time line (e.g., "N.T." just past your 1830 divider for Nat Turner's uprising in 1831; "URR" and a bracket for the entire 1850's for Harriet Tubman's underground railroad activity). Next add major social or business events (e.g., "S.O." for Rockefeller's founding of Standard Oil). Finally, relate writers' careers to the sociohistorical background by asking questions like these: What was happening in the U.S. when Londoners were reading *Great Expectations* for the first time? What was happening here when Tolstoy's *War and Peace* was published?

Representative American Realists

William Dean Howells

The most active proponent of realism in American fiction was William Dean Howells (1837–1920). Howells, who lived most of his life in Boston, was the editor of the influential magazine *The Atlantic Monthly,* which was published in Boston. He was also the author of several novels, including *The Rise of Silas Lapham* (1885). In both his fiction and his critical writings, Howells insisted that realism should deal with the lives of ordinary people, be faithful to the development of character even at the expense of action, and reveal the strength of good over evil. Howells's "smiling realism" portrayed an America where people may act foolishly but where their good qualities eventually win out. In *The Rise of Silas Lapham,* for example, the *nouveau riche* character Silas Lapham, whose fortune is based on manufacturing paint, must choose between bankruptcy and shady business dealings. Although Silas is tempted, his integrity wins out, and he returns to his former life as a farmer, a poorer but morally better man.

"Ah! poor Real Life, which I love," Howells wrote in one of his many essays, "can I make others share the delight I find in thy foolish and insipid face?" For Howells, life *was,* even at its worst, merely "foolish and insipid," and this proved to be his greatest limitation as a novelist.

1830–1835	1836–1839	1840–1848	1850
Nat Turner leads unsuccessful slave uprising in Virginia, 1831 **Mark Twain born, 1835**	Frederick Douglass runs away from his master in Baltimore, 1836 **Poe publishes "The Fall of the House of Usher," 1839**	Dorothea Dix campaigns for better treatment for mentally ill, 1840's Women's Rights Convention held in Seneca Falls, N.Y., 1848	Half of 30 states in Union permit slavery, 1850 Harriet Tubman leads hundreds of slaves to freedom on Underground Railroad, 1850's

A

1861	1861	1861–1862	1863
Abraham Lincoln inaugurated President of U.S., 1861 Confederates attack Fort Sumter in Charleston Harbor, April 12, 1861	Civil War in U.S., 1861–1865 Battle of Bull Run: Confederates under "Stonewall" Jackson beat Union army, July 21, 1861	Robert E. Lee named leader of army of Northern Virginia, 1861 Grant defeated at Battle of Shiloh, April 6, 1862	Emancipation Proclamation frees all slaves, 1863 Lee victorious at Battle of Chancellorsville, May 1-5, 1863

1865–1870	1871–1875	1876	1877–1883
Tolstoy writes *War and Peace* in Russia, 1865–1869 Rockefeller founds Standard Oil Company, 1870	**Stephen Crane born, 1871** **Mark Twain publishes *The Adventures of Tom Sawyer,* 1875**	Sitting Bull and 2500-4000 Sioux warriors defeat Custer and 264 cavalry at the Battle of Little Big Horn, June 25, 1876	Chief Joseph and the Nez Percé surrender and are settled on reservations, 1877 **Twain publishes *Life on the Mississippi,* 1883**

Frank Norris and Naturalism

Other novelists viewed life as more complex. Californian Frank Norris (1870–1902), for example, who agreed with Howells that the proper subject for fiction was the ordinary person, found Howells's fiction too strait-laced and narrow. It was, Norris said, "as respectable as a church and proper as a deacon." Norris was interested in the earthier aspects of life, with the impact of large social forces on individuals. His best-known novel, *The Octopus,* is about the struggles between wheat farmers and the railroad monopoly in California. Norris was not the first to use the novel to examine social institutions (usually with the aim of reforming them). Harriet Beecher Stowe's *Uncle Tom's Cabin* had been published before the Civil War (and was credited by Lincoln with helping to cause it). But *Uncle Tom's Cabin* was as much melodrama as it was realistic fiction, and by Norris's time the techniques of realistic fiction had developed a good deal.

Norris, whose principal model was the French novelist Emile Zola, is generally considered to be a **naturalist.** Following Zola's lead, naturalists relied heavily on the growing scientific disciplines of psychology and sociology. In their fiction, they attempted to dissect human behavior with as much objectivity as a scientist would dissect a frog or a cadaver. For naturalists, human behavior was determined by forces beyond the individual's power, especially

> **"Naturalists attempted to dissect human behavior with as much objectivity as a scientist would dissect a frog."**

1850–1852	1855	1860	1861
Susan B. Anthony campaigns for equal rights for women, 1850's **Harriet Beecher Stowe publishes *Uncle Tom's Cabin,* 1852**	**Walt Whitman publishes *Leaves of Grass,* 1855** **Frederick Douglass publishes *My Bondage and My Freedom,* 1855**	Slave population in U.S. reaches nearly 4 million, 1860 80 percent of 31 million people in U.S. live on farms, 1860	**Charles Dickens publishes *Great Expectations* in England, 1861** Confederate States of America formed, 1861
1863	**1863–1864**	**1865**	**1866–1869**
Lee defeated at Battle of Gettysburg, July 3, 1863 Lincoln delivers Gettysburg Address, November 19, 1863	**Novelist Henry James born in New York, 1863** Sherman's Union army marches into Atlanta and burns city to ground, September 2, 1864	Lee surrenders to Grant at Appomattox Court House in Virginia, April 9, 1865 Lincoln assassinated in Ford's Theater in Washington, April 14, 1865	Fourteenth Amendment forbids voting discrimination, 1866 **Harte publishes "The Outcasts of Poker Flat," 1869**
1884–1892	**1895**	**1890–1900**	**1897–1900**
Twain publishes *The Adventures of Huckleberry Finn,* 1884 Tchaikovsky writes *The Nutcracker* in Russia, 1892	**Crane publishes *The Red Badge of Courage,* 1895** Frontier is gone by 1890's	5 million Americans work in factories, 1890's 50 buffalo are left in U.S., 1900	40 percent of 76 million people in U.S. live in towns and cities, 1900 **Ernest Hemingway born, 1897**

Reading Check Test

1. What kind of novel presents lives lived on an idealistic plane? *romantic*
2. What kind of novel reproduces daily life, probes motivation, and examines social issues? *realistic*
3. Who liked to put a straightforward American into the complex society of a European drawing room? *Henry James*
4. Whose novels, such as *Octopus,* dealt with the impact of social forces on individuals? *Frank Norris*
5. What school of thought views human behavior as determined by biological and environmental forces? *naturalism*

A. Responding

State the major focus of "Jamesian realism." (Psychological motivation)

B. Responding

Distinguish Crane's use of psychology from that of James. (Crane focuses on people severely stressed, James on the drawing room.) Identify the irony in the example from "The Blue Hotel."

C. Humanities Connection: Responding to the Fine Art

This oil blends pictorial realism (flapping laundry, sagging trousers, waiting for a kettle to boil) with an ironic title. The sentimental ballad "Home, Sweet Home" had been popular in England and America since it was composed for an 1823 opera by John Howard Payne and Henry Bishop.

Imagine the camp life of a Civil War soldier. How many such tents does the encampment contain? What is the weather like? How does a soldier fill time while waiting?

by biology and environment. The naturalists tended to look at human life bluntly and crudely. Their characters often had only limited choices and motivations. In the eyes of some naturalist writers, human beings were totally subject to the natural laws of the universe; like animals, they lived crudely, by instinct, unable to control their own destinies.

Henry James and Psychological Realism

A New York-born Henry James (1843–1916), America's greatest psychological novelist, concentrated principally on fine distinctions in character motivation. James was a realist, but no realist could be further from the blunt naturalistic view that people were driven by animal-like instincts. In his finely tuned studies of human motivation, James opened the inner mind to the techniques of fiction. He was principally interested in complex social and psychological situations. His novels (such as *Daisy Miller* and *The Portrait of a Lady*) most often took place in Europe, because he considered European society, with its long-evolved systems of class and nobility, to be both more complex and more sinister than American society. In a typically "Jamesian" fiction, a straightforward American confronts the complexities of European society and either defeats or is defeated by them.

"When we confront recent writers like Kurt Vonnegut and Thomas Pynchon, we are reminded of the strong tradition of American Romance."

Stephen Crane and the Uses of Irony

B Stephen Crane (1871–1900) was as profound a psychologist as James, but his principal interest was in character at moments of stress. For James the proper setting for an examination of human behavior under pressure was the drawing room; for Crane it was the battlefield, or the streets of a slum, or a western outpost, or a lifeboat lost somewhere at sea. Crane's view of life was as bleak as Howells's vision was bright. Although Crane is sometimes referred to as a naturalist, he is probably best thought of as an **ironist**; he was the first of many modern American writers—from Ernest Hemingway to Kurt Vonnegut—to juxtapose human pretensions with the indifference of the universe. Of all the nineteenth-century realists, only Crane could describe a stabbing death (in his story "The Blue Hotel") in this coolly cynical manner: "[The blade] shot forward, and a human body, this citadel of virtue, wisdom, power, was pierced as easily as if it had been a melon." It would take this sensibility to get the "real war" in the books.

Crane's ironic view of life was a far cry from the "smiling realism" of Howells, but they were two branches of the same trunk. Realism—whether it was psychological realism, naturalism, social realism, or smiling realism—was a powerful way of looking at human life. In fact, realism would virtually control fiction from the 1890's to the middle of the twentieth century. Only when we confront recent writers like Kurt Vonnegut and Thomas Pynchon are we reminded of the strong tradition of American Romance.

Home Sweet Home by Winslow Homer (1863). Oil. C

Private collection.

Frederick Douglass (1818–1895)

Frederick Douglass was born into slavery in Talbot County on the Eastern Shore of Maryland, and was separated from his mother soon after his birth. "The practice of separating children from their mothers," wrote Douglass years later, "and hiring the latter out at distances too great to admit of their meeting, except at long intervals, is a marked feature of the cruelty and barbarity of the slave system. But it is in harmony with the grand aim of slavery, which, always and everywhere, is to reduce man to a level with the brute. It is a successful method of obliterating from the mind and heart of the slave all just ideas of the sacredness of *the family. . . .*"

Since records were not kept of the birth of slaves, Douglass was never sure of his exact age: "Genealogical trees do not flourish among slaves," he was to remark ironically later. Although Douglass received no formal education as a child, he did teach himself to read with the help, at first, of members of the household he served. Later, these same people became furious when they saw Douglass reading a book or a newspaper; "education and slavery," they decided, "are incompatible with each other."

When Douglass was about twenty-one, he satisfied his hunger for freedom by escaping to Massachusetts, where he married and soon started to make public speeches in support of the abolitionist cause. He took the name "Douglass" from the hero of Sir Walter Scott's romantic novel *The Lady of the Lake*.

Largely because of the danger he faced as a fugitive slave, Douglass spent several years in England in the 1840's. There he mobilized antislavery sentiment and became independent when British friends purchased his freedom.

Back in the United States, Douglass founded a newspaper, the *North Star.* (The name was chosen because escaping slaves used this star as a guide north.) In his newspaper, Douglass championed the abolition of slavery. In 1855, he published a revised version of his life's story, entitled *My Bondage and My Freedom*. These "escape" narratives, like the earlier "captivity" stories (page 23), were enormously popular, and

Douglass's were widely read and most influential in the abolitionist cause.

When the war came, Douglass worked ardently for the Underground Railroad, the secret network of abolitionists and their sympathizers that helped many slaves escape to the North. He also energetically helped to recruit black soldiers for the Union armies.

Continuing to write and lecture after the war, Douglass argued that the surest way to rehabilitate his tragically scarred people was through education. He served in several government posts, most notably the diplomatic corps in Haiti. In 1882, he published yet another version of his autobiography, entitled *Life and Times of Frederick Douglass.*

Douglass has been compared with Benjamin Franklin, another self-made man who struggled against tremendous odds to achieve distinction at a critical time in his nation's history. But Douglass's story, of course, is different from Franklin's. Franklin was never a slave. He was never "owned" by another human being, considered to be of no more moral significance than a beast or a piece of land. Today Douglass is revered for the courage with which he insistently proclaimed his profoundly humane values, and admired for the quiet eloquence of his writing style.

A. Expansion
The success of Alex Haley in the 1970's testifies to the accuracy of Douglass's remarks on lack of concern previously felt for the origins of black American families. His 1976 novel, *Roots,* based on his own family tree, won a special Pulitzer Prize in 1977 and was also enacted as a television miniseries.

B. Allusion
The Lady of the Lake (1810) by Sir Walter Scott (1771–1832), a Scottish novelist whose great achievement was the exploitation of history as material for novels, is set in Scotland during a troubled period of border warfare.

Supplementary Support Materials
1. Vocabulary Activity Worksheet (*CCB*)
2. Review and Response Worksheet: Narrative (*CCB*)
3. Selection Test (*CCB*)

Developing Vocabulary
The following words from the autobiography are tested in the Selection Test. (See also Vocabulary Activity Worksheet.)

epoch	sundry
exceedingly	entreating
to subject	compensation

Preparation
Establishing a Purpose. Use the headnote to establish a context for the selection and to prepare students to learn "how a slave was made a man."

A. Motivation
? Why did Douglass decide to walk seven miles in his condition? (He had been mistreated once too often.) Was he right to choose to complain? Why or why not?

Comment From The Writer
Douglass was proud of his ancestry, even when denying it would have been useful to him. A story is told of a night when he was traveling by boat from New York to Boston. American Indians were allowed to occupy cabins or public rooms, but Negroes were not. A kind-hearted officer, finding Douglass curled up in a corner of the deck in a storm, said to him, "You're an Indian, aren't you?" Immediately grasping the officer's point, Douglass said, "No, sir, I'm a nigger"—and remained on deck.

THE BATTLE WITH MR. COVEY

In the following selection from *The Narrative of the Life of Frederick Douglass* (1845), Douglass provides a graphic account of a critical incident in his youth. He has previously explained to his readers "how a man was made a slave"; now he sets out to tell us "how a slave was made a man." At this time, when he was about sixteen, Douglass was owned by a man named Thomas and had been rented out to work for a year for a man named Covey.

I have already intimated that my condition was much worse, during the first six months of my stay at Mr. Covey's, than in the last six. The circumstances leading to the change in Mr. Covey's course toward me form an epoch in my humble history. You have seen how a man was made a slave; you shall see how a slave was made a man. On one of the hottest days of the month of August, 1833, Bill Smith, William Hughes, a slave named Eli, and myself were engaged in fanning wheat. Hughes was clearing the fanned wheat from before the fan, Eli was turning, Smith was feeding, and I was carrying wheat to the fan. The work was simple, requiring strength rather than intellect; yet, to one entirely unused to such work, it came very hard.

About three o'clock of that day, I broke down; my strength failed me; I was seized with a violent aching of my head, attended with extreme dizziness; I trembled in every limb. Finding what was coming, I nerved myself up, feeling it would never do to stop work. I stood as long as I could stagger to the hopper with grain. When I could stand no longer, I fell, and felt as if held down by an immense weight. The fan of course stopped; every one had his own work to do; and no one could do the work of the other, and have his own go on at the same time.

Mr. Covey was at the house, about one hundred yards from the treading-yard where we were fanning. On hearing the fan stop, he left immediately, and came to the spot where we were. He hastily inquired what the matter was. Bill answered that I was sick, and there was no one to bring wheat to the fan. I had by this time crawled away under the side of the post-and-rail fence by which the yard was enclosed, hoping to find relief by getting out of the sun. He then asked where I was. He was told by one of the hands.

He came to the spot, and, after looking at me awhile, asked me what was the matter. I told him as well as I could, for I scarce had strength to speak. He then gave me a savage kick in the side, and told me to get up. I tried to do so, but fell back in the attempt. He gave me another kick, and again told me to rise. I again tried, and succeeded in gaining my feet; but stooping to get the tub with which I was feeding the fan, I again staggered and fell. While down in this situation, Mr. Covey took up the hickory slat with which Hughes had been stroking off the half-bushel measure, and with it gave me a heavy blow upon the head, making a large wound, and the blood ran freely; and with this again told me to get up. I made no effort to comply, having now made up my mind to let him do his worst. In a short time after receiving this blow, my head grew better. Mr. Covey had now left me to my fate.

At this moment I resolved, for the first time, to go to my master, enter a complaint, and ask his protection. In order to do this, I must that afternoon walk seven miles; and this, under the circumstances, was truly a severe undertaking. I was exceedingly feeble; made so as much by the kicks and blows which I received, as by the severe fit of sickness to which I had been subjected. I, however, watched my chance, while Covey was looking in an opposite direction, and started for St. Michael's. I succeeded in getting a considerable distance on my way to the woods, when Covey A

Frederick Douglass Planning His Escape (in 1836) by Jacob Lawrence (c. 1938). Casein on gessoed hardboard.

Hampton University Museum, Hampton, Virginia.

Humanities Connection: Responding to the Fine Art

This oil is done in what is called a *primitive* style—a fresh, fanciful, strong, often colorful style suggesting that the work is by an untrained painter, even if the painter is trained. Have students compare this work with the Moran oil on page 339, *Slaves Escaping Through the Swamps.*

? What different aspects of escape are emphasized? (This oil shows the stealthy, determined planning; Moran's oil suggests the terrors of the escape itself. Both suggest the use of night hours.)

Direct students also to a second oil by Lawrence on page 390.

? Do the subjects of Lawrence's oils—survival and freedom—seem especially suited to a primitive style? Why? (Students may suggest that because survival and freedom are basic needs, a primitive style is suitable.)

A. Characterization
What traits of character are shown by Douglass in his journey to his master? (Courage, perseverance) In the conversation with Master Thomas that Douglass relates on this page, what traits of character are shown by Thomas? (He will listen, but needs to rationalize the system, assert his authority.) Is Thomas an evil man? Why or why not? (He is a man of his time, doing business as a slaver. He is governed by economic considerations rather than by sympathy.)

B. Expansion
Note that response question 4, page 390, focuses on the talisman and on Douglass's character.

discovered me, and called after me to come back, threatening what he would to if I did not come. I disregarded both his calls and his threats, and made my way to the woods as fast as my feeble state would allow; and thinking I might be overhauled by him if I kept the road, I walked through the woods, keeping far enough from the road to avoid detection, and near enough to prevent losing my way.

I had not gone far before my little strength again failed me. I could go no farther. I fell down, and lay for a considerable time. The blood was yet oozing from the wound on my head. For a time I thought I should bleed to death; and think now that I should have done so, but that the blood so matted my hair as to stop the wound. After lying there about three quarters of an hour, I nerved myself up again, and started on my way, through bogs and briers, barefooted and bareheaded, tearing my feet sometimes at nearly every step; and after a journey of about seven miles, occupying some five hours to perform it, I arrived at master's store. I then presented an appearance enough to affect any but a heart of iron. From the crown of my head to my feet, I was covered with blood. My hair was all clotted with dust and blood; my shirt was stiff with blood. My legs and feet were torn in sundry places with briers and thorns, and were also covered with blood. I suppose I looked like a man who had escaped a den of wild beasts, and barely escaped them.

In this state I appeared before my master, humbly entreating him to interpose his authority for my protection. I told him all the circumstances as well as I could, and it seemed, as I spoke, at times to affect him. He would then walk the floor, and seek to justify Covey by saying he expected I deserved it. He asked me what I wanted. I told him, to let me get a new home; that as sure as I lived with Mr. Covey again, I should live but to die with him; that Covey would surely kill me; he was in a fair way for it. Master Thomas ridiculed the idea that there was any danger of Mr. Covey's killing me, and said that he knew Mr. Covey; that he was a good man, and that he could not think of taking me from him; that, should he do so, he would lose the whole year's wages; that I belonged to Mr. Covey for one year, and that I must go back to him, come what might; and that I must not trouble him with any more stories, or that he would himself *get hold of me*. After threatening me thus, he gave me a very large dose of salts, telling me that I might remain in St. Michael's that night (it being quite late), but that I must be off back to Mr. Covey's early in the morning; and that if I did not, he would *get hold of me,* which meant that he would whip me.

I remained all night, and, according to his orders, I started off to Covey's in the morning (Saturday morning), wearied in body and broken in spirit. I got no supper that night, or breakfast that morning. I reached Covey's about nine o'clock; and just as I was getting over the fence that divided Mrs. Kemp's fields from ours, out ran Covey with his cowskin, to give me another whipping. Before he could reach me, I succeeded in getting to the cornfield; and as the corn was very high, it afforded me the means of hiding. He seemed very angry, and searched for me a long time. My behavior was altogether unaccountable. He finally gave up the chase, thinking, I suppose, that I must come home for something to eat; he would give himself no further trouble in looking for me. I spent that day mostly in the woods, having the alternative before me—to go home and be whipped to death, or stay in the woods and be starved to death.

That night, I fell in with Sandy Jenkins, a slave with whom I was somewhat acquainted. Sandy had a free wife who lived about four miles from Mr. Covey's; and it being Saturday, he was on his way to see her. I told him my circumstances, and he very kindly invited me to go home with him. I went home with him, and talked this whole matter over, and got his advice as to what course it was best for me to pursue. I found Sandy an old adviser.[1] He told me, with great solemnity, I must go back to Covey; but that before I went, I must go with him into another part of the woods, where there was a certain *root,* which, if I would take some of it with me, carrying it *always on my right side,* would render it impossible for Mr. Covey, or any other white man, to whip me. He said he had carried it for years; and since he had done so, he had never received a blow, and never expected to while he carried it. I at first rejected the idea, that the simple carrying of a root in my pocket would have any such effect as he had said, and was not disposed to take it; but Sandy impressed the necessity with much earnestness, telling me it could do no harm, if it did no good. To please him, I at

1. **an old adviser:** here, an old friend, someone who could be trusted.

READING CHECK TEST

1. Frederick Douglass did not know how old he was when the battle with Mr. Covey occurs. *True*

2. His fellow slave, Bill, joins in the beating to which Douglass is subjected. *False*

3. The slave Sandy Jenkins has a free wife. *True*

4. After beating Mr. Covey, Douglass is forced to flee for his life, and goes immediately north to freedom. *False*

5. When Douglass flees to Thomas's farm, Thomas gives him yet another beating. *False.*

CLOSURE

Have individual students explain the elements of Douglass's character that most impressed them. What did this selection add to their understanding of a theme present not only in this selection, but also earlier, in poems by Whitman—the degrading influence of slavery on both owner and slave?

length took the root, and, according to his direction, carried it upon my right side. This was Sunday morning.

A I immediately started for home; and upon entering the yard gate, out came Mr. Covey on his way to meeting. He spoke to me very kindly, bade me drive the pigs from a lot near by, and passed on towards the church. Now, this singular conduct of Mr. Covey really made me begin to think that there was something in the root which Sandy had given me; and had it been on any other day than Sunday, I could have attributed the conduct to no other cause than the influence of that root; and as it was, I was half inclined to think the root to be something more than I at first had taken it to be. All went well till Monday morning. On this morning, the virtue of the root was fully tested.

Long before daylight, I was called to go and rub, curry, and feed the horses. I obeyed, and was glad to obey. But whilst thus engaged, whilst in the act of throwing down some blades from the loft, Mr. Covey entered the stable with a long rope; and just as I was half out of the loft, he caught hold of my legs, and was about tying me. As soon as I found what he was up to, I gave a sudden spring, and as I did so, he holding to my legs, I was brought sprawling on the stable floor. Mr. Covey seemed now to think he had me, and could do what he pleased; but at this moment—from whence came the spirit I don't know—I resolved to fight; and, suiting my action to the resolution, I seized Covey hard by the throat; and as I did so, I rose. He held on to me, and I to him. My resistance was so entirely unexpected, that Covey seemed taken all aback. He trembled like a leaf. This gave me assurance, and I held him uneasy, causing the blood to run where I touched him with the ends of my fingers. Mr. Covey soon called out to Hughes for help. Hughes came, and, while Covey held me, attempted to tie my right hand. While he was in the act of doing so, I watched my chance, and gave him a heavy kick close under the ribs.

This kick fairly sickened Hughes, so that he left me in the hands of Mr. Covey. This kick had the effect of not only weakening Hughes, but Covey also. When he saw Hughes bending over with pain, his courage quailed. He asked me if I meant to persist in my resistance. I told him I did, come what might; that he had used me like a brute for six months, and that I was determined to be used so no longer. With that, he strove to drag me to a stock that was lying just out of the stable door. He meant to knock me down. But just as he was leaning over to get the stick, I seized him with both hands by his collar, and brought him by a sudden snatch to the ground. By this time, Bill came. Covey called upon him for assistance. Bill wanted to know what he could do. Covey said, "Take hold of him, take hold of him!" Bill said his master hired him out to work, and not to help to whip me; so he left Covey and myself to fight our own battle out. We were at it for nearly two hours. Covey at length let me go, puffing and blowing at a great rate, saying that if I had not resisted, he would not have whipped me half so much. The truth was, that he had not whipped me at all. I considered him as getting entirely the worst end of the bargain; for he had drawn no blood from me, but I had from him. The whole six months afterwards, that I spent with Mr. Covey, he never laid the weight of his finger upon me in anger. He would occasionally say he didn't want to get hold of me again. "No," thought I, "you need not; for you will come off worse than you did before." B

This battle with Mr. Covey was the turning-point in my career as a slave. It rekindled the few expiring embers of freedom, and revived within me a sense of my own manhood. It recalled the departed self-confidence, and inspired me again with a determination to be free. The gratification afforded by the triumph was a full compensation for whatever else might follow, even death itself. He only can understand the deep satisfaction which I experienced, who has himself repelled by force the bloody arm of slavery. I felt as I never felt before. It was a glorious resurrection, from the tomb of slavery, to the heaven of freedom. C My long-crushed spirit rose, cowardice departed, bold defiance took its place; and I now resolved that, however long I might remain a slave in form, the day had passed forever when I could be a slave in fact.

A. Characterization

? Notice what Douglass interprets as the cause of Covey's change in behavior. Do you find his idea humorous? How do you account for the change? (Perhaps Mr. Thomas said something about his treatment of Douglass.)

B. Analyzing an Outcome

? The two-hour battle worked out well for Douglass. How else could it have gone for him? What other kinds of action might Mr. Covey have been within his rights to take? (Covey might have beaten him. Since Douglass was Covey's property, Covey was free to do whatever he wished.)

C. Expansion

This metaphor is discussed in Analyzing Language and Style, question 3, page 390.

ANALYZING THE AUTOBIOGRAPHY
Identifying Facts
1. Douglass decided to enter a complaint with his master. Weak and seriously wounded, he walked seven miles to St. Michael's.

Thomas said that he expected that Douglass deserved the beating. He told Douglass to return to Covey, whom he called a "good man," and to cause no more trouble.

2. Sandy told Douglass to return to Covey, carrying a certain root from the woods on his right side. The root would protect Douglass against Covey's violence.

3. Douglass's stout resistance when Covey and Hughes attempted to tie him up evidently inspired Covey's grudging respect. Douglass says that this episode revived in him a sense of his own manhood.

Interpreting Meanings
4. According to Douglass, his own fighting spirit was more powerful than the root.

Students will have various answers. Many students will point to Douglass's *(Answers continue in left-hand column.)*

(Continued from top.)
fierce determination and pride.

5. Douglass recounts with wry humor how Mr. Covey's apparently gentle behavior on Sunday almost convinced him that the root had supernatural powers.

6. Most students will agree that the passage reveals that Covey was a violent bully. Like many bullies, he became cowed when faced with firm resistance.

7. By a slave "in form," Douglass means his outer, legal designation as a slave. By saying that he was no longer a slave "in fact," he refers to the pride and independence of his inner spirit.

8. Students may suggest that when people in charge refuse to acknowledge injustice, victims must think of ways to help themselves.

Responding to the Autobiography

Analyzing the Autobiography

Identifying Facts

1. What action did Douglass take after being struck by Covey? What did Thomas advise Douglass to do?
2. Explain how Sandy Jenkins helped Douglass.
3. Describe what Douglass calls the turning point in his life as a slave.

Interpreting Meanings

4. Sandy Jenkins's "root" was a talisman, an object invested with supernatural powers. Explain what Douglass discovered that was even more powerful than the root. What personal **characteristics** would you say impelled Douglass to revolt against Covey?

Frederick Douglass Edits the North Star by Jacob Lawrence (c. 1938). Casein on hardboard.

Hampton University Museum, Hampton, Virginia.

5. What elements of humor are found in Douglass's account of Sandy Jenkins's advice? Explain.
6. What does this passage reveal about Covey's **character?**
7. Explain the distinction between being a slave "in form" and a slave "in fact."
8. Do you think any aspects of Douglass's narrative are relevant to the problem of racism in modern society? Explain.

Writing About the Autobiography

A Creative Response

1. **Applying Meanings.** Reread Emerson's essay "Self-Reliance" (page 194), and write a brief essay in which you tell whether or not any of Emerson's passages relate to Douglass's experience. Does anything in Douglass's narrative negate Emerson's ideas?

A Critical Response

2. **Responding to an Idea.** *"He only can understand the deep satisfaction which I experienced, who has himself repelled by force the bloody arm of slavery."* In a paragraph, describe your response to this idea. What are its implications? In what ways is it true? In what ways might it not be true?

Analyzing Language and Style

Metaphors

At the end of this passage, Douglass uses images and metaphors that suggest resurrection and rebirth.

1. Define the terms of the comparison implied in this line: "It [the battle] rekindled the few expiring embers of freedom." How are these images related to the idea of rebirth?
2. What is Douglass implicitly comparing slavery with when he refers to "the bloody arm of slavery"?
3. Find the passage that specifically compares Douglass's experience to a rebirth. What are the terms of the comparisons here?

SUPPLEMENTARY SUPPORT MATERIALS

1. Review and Response Worksheet: Spirituals (*CCB*)
2. Selection Test (*CCB*)
3. Audiocassette recording

PREPARATION

1. **BUILDING ON PRIOR KNOWLEDGE.** For some students, spirituals are a part of their religious or cultural heritages. Have these students share what they already know about the forms and themes of spirituals.

2. **ESTABLISHING A PURPOSE.** Have students read to determine why these spirituals had the effect on Douglass that he describes in the headnote.

SPIRITUALS AND "CODE" SONGS

Frederick Douglass wrote eloquently about the songs of slavery in this passage from *My Bondage and My Freedom* (1855).

"Slaves are generally expected to sing as well as to work. A silent slave is not liked by masters or overseers. *'Make a noise, make a noise,'* and *'bear a hand,'* are the words usually addressed to the slaves when there is silence amongst them. This may account for the almost constant singing heard in the southern states. . . . On allowance day, those who visited the great house farm were peculiarly excited and noisy. While on their way, they would make the dense old woods, for miles around, reverberate with their wild notes. These were not always merry because they were wild. On the contrary, they were mostly of a plaintive cast, and told a tale of grief and sorrow. In the most boisterous outbursts of rapturous sentiment, there was ever a tinge of deep melancholy. I have never heard any songs like those anywhere since I left slavery, except when in Ireland. There I heard the same *wailing notes,* and was much affected by them. It was during the famine of 1845–1846. In all the songs of the slaves, there was ever some expression in praise of the great house farm; something which would flatter the pride of the owner, and, possibly, draw a favorable glance from him. . . .

"The hearing of those wild notes always depressed my spirits, and filled my heart with ineffable sadness. The mere recurrence, even now, afflicts my spirit, and while I am writing these lines, my tears are falling. To those songs I trace my first glimmering conceptions of the dehumanizing character of slavery. I can never get rid of that conception. Those songs still follow me, to deepen my hatred of slavery, and quicken my sympathies for my brethren in bonds. If any one wishes to be impressed with a sense of the soul-killing power of slavery, let him go to Col. Lloyd's plantation, and, on allowance day, place himself in the deep pine woods, and there let him, in silence, thoughtfully analyze the sounds that shall pass through the chambers of his soul, and if he is not thus impressed, it will only be because 'there is no flesh in his obdurate heart.' "

—Frederick Douglass

Go Down, Moses

Go down, Moses,
Way down in Egypt land
Tell old Pharaoh
To let my people go.

When Israel was in Egypt land
Let my people go
Oppressed so hard they could not stand
Let my people go.

Go down, Moses,
Way down in Egypt land
Tell old Pharaoh
"Let my people go."

"Thus saith the Lord," bold Moses said,
"Let my people go;
If not I'll smite your first-born dead
Let my people go."

Go down, Moses,
Way down in Egypt land,
Tell old Pharaoh,
"Let my people go!"

A

A. Expansion
Most students are probably familiar with the Biblical story in which Moses announces to the Pharaoh Rameses that God has commanded that the Hebrews be allowed to leave Egypt. At Rameses' first refusal, Moses' staff is turned into a serpent, and the waters of the Nile are turned blood red. When Rameses remains adamant, Egypt is cursed with plagues of frogs, gnats, and flies. Next, the Egyptian animals suffer from an epidemic, and a plague of boils descends on both people and animals, followed by fierce lightning and hail storms, an invasion of locusts, and daylight darkness. Rameses agrees to free the Hebrews, however, only when the first-born sons of the Egyptians, including that of Rameses, are smitten.

CLOSURE
Have individual students suggest words and phrases that capture the spirit of these songs.

A. Expansion
As explained in Writing About the Songs, number 5, below, the "drinking gourd" is the Big Dipper constellation. This stanza also gives information about the time for the escape.

B. Expansion
If students imagine someone dragging a "peg" foot behind while walking, they can visualize the kind of trail that would be left for slaves to follow.

C. Responding
? Think of a situation where this song might have been sung by one or more slaves to convey information about an escape route. Describe the setting. Describe the slaves who are singing and those who are listening. Why do you suppose the slave owners did not understand the codes in these songs? (Perhaps they did not credit slaves with the intelligence or imagination to create coded messages.)

Follow the Drinking Gourd

A
When the sun comes back and the first quail calls,
Follow the drinking gourd,
For the old man is a-waiting for to carry you to freedom
If you follow the drinking gourd.

[Refrain] Follow the drinking gourd,
Follow the drinking gourd,
For the old man is a-waiting for to carry you to freedom
If you follow the drinking gourd.

The river bank will make a very good road,
The dead trees show you the way,
B
Left foot, peg foot traveling on
Follow the drinking gourd. [Refrain]

The river ends between two hills
Follow the drinking gourd.
There's another river on the other side,
Following the drinking gourd. [Refrain]

Where the little river meets the great big river,
Follow the drinking gourd.
The old man is a-waiting for to carry you to freedom,
If you follow the drinking gourd. [Refrain]
C

Responding to the Songs

Writing About the Songs

A Creative Response

1. **Writing a Stanza.** Write an original stanza for "Follow the Drinking Gourd." Use as a basis for your stanza the analysis you make in item 5 below. Include a coded piece of information.

A Critical Response

2. **Analyzing Allusions.** Many people during the time of slavery were called "Moses" by slaves who were looking for someone to deliver them from their chains. Harriet Tubman, for example, used "Moses" as her code name in her work with the Underground Railroad. A Methodist minister named Francis Asbury was also known as "Moses," and according to some scholars, "Go Down, Moses" really refers to the slaves' (vain) hope that he would win liberty for them. Ultimately, of course, the name Moses refers back to the deliverer of Israel, who dominates the Book of Exodus in the Bible. And it is the Book of Exodus that provided the spiritual singers with their most compelling images of freedom. In an essay, explain why Moses would be seen as the prototype of the rescuer (see Exodus 7–12). What, in the slaves' terms, would "Egypt" and "Pharaoh" stand for? Explain the other allusions to the Exodus story found in this spiritual.
3. **Reporting on Other Spirituals.** Find the texts of the following spirituals and in a brief essay explain the Biblical allusions in them. What would each Biblical image or event stand for in the singers' experience?
   a. "Pharaoh's Army Got Drownded"
   b. "Swing Low, Sweet Chariot"
   c. "We Are Crossing Jordan River"
4. **Comparing the Spirituals to the Puritans' Writings.** Like the singers of spirituals, the Puritans also read the Bible with a "double vision"; that is, they saw in the Biblical narratives and images "types" of their own experiences. In a brief essay, compare and contrast one of the Puritan writer's methods with the method used in at least two spirituals.
5. **Analyzing a Code Song.** Some of the slaves' songs were "code songs"—they provided runaway slaves with directions, times, and meeting places for their escape. For example, the drinking gourd in this song is the Big Dipper constellation; it points to the North Star, which gave runaways their direction to the North. What other "codes" can you find in this song? Describe them in a paragraph.

Bret Harte (1836–1902)

Mark Twain (see page 402) once wrote, "Bret Harte was one of the pleasantest men I have ever known. He was also one of the unpleasantest men I have ever known." Twain's evaluation not only reflects his relationship with Harte, which began in warm friendship and deteriorated into near-hatred; it also hints at the eventual decline of Harte's reputation.

Francis Brett Hart (he later dropped the *t* in Brett and added the *e* to Hart) arrived in California from Albany, New York, when he was about eighteen years old. Seemingly without a sense of direction, he worked as a miner, a teacher, and a druggist's assistant. In 1859, when he took a newspaper job with the *Northern Californian,* he began to think of himself as a writer. By the time Twain met him, in 1863, Harte was a respected newspaper editor and a popular writer. Although Twain was a year older, he admired the more experienced Harte and looked to him for criticism and advice.

From 1868 to 1871, Harte edited the *Overland Monthly,* a magazine published in San Francisco. Some of his best-known stories appeared during these years. "The Luck of Roaring Camp" (1868) and "The Outcasts of Poker Flat" (1869) brought him acclaim on both coasts.

Curiosity about the Western frontier had existed for a long time among Americans, and it had increased enormously with the Gold Rush that began in 1849. When Harte began writing, nearly twenty years after the Rush, the American reading public was still hungry for tales about the colorful characters inhabiting the Wild West. Harte's ability to satisfy that hunger earned him nationwide fame as a realistic regionalist, a writer of "local color." It also earned him a good deal of money.

To readers of the time, Harte's stories seemed daringly realistic; unlike most contemporary writers, he described scenes of violence in graphic detail, and he appeared to write frankly about love and sex. Readers also loved his stories because, with all their surface "realism," they always carried a neat, moralistic message. In a typical Harte story, good triumphs and evil is driven out. As time would tell, Harte actually had more in common as a storyteller with Washington Irving than he had with Twain or the great realists who would dominate the next century.

A

The most important basis for Harte's enormous popularity was one of the very things Mark Twain later became irate about. Harte's Western characters were almost invariably noble, upstanding, and admirable. Beneath their rough exteriors, they were gentlemen and ladies who never abandoned their dignity, even though they found themselves in primitive surroundings. The gambler with a heart of gold, the gentle farmer driven to using a gun to fight evil, the tough dance-hall woman secretly motivated by compassion—these and other characters still inhabit Westerns written for movies and television. Most of them were invented by Bret Harte. B

The reading public liked to imagine that the actual West was populated by this kind of character, but Twain knew better. He grouped Harte's stories with James Fenimore Cooper's novels, which Twain detested. From Twain's point of view, Cooper's Indians talked like British professors—"scholarly savages" he called them. Twain's Western characters, on the other hand, were "treacherous, filthy, and repulsive." No wonder that he sometimes fumed over the romanticized, squeaky-clean vision of the West that Harte popularized.

A. Humanities Connection: Responding to the Photograph
? Having read the biography, do you think this picture exhibits the personality of Bret Harte? Why or why not? (Answers will vary.)

B. Responding
? What western movies or television re-runs can you cite that feature these stereotypical characters? (Answers will vary; e.g., "Gunsmoke.")

SUPPLEMENTARY SUPPORT MATERIALS
1. Vocabulary Activity Worksheet (*CCB*)
2. Review and Response Worksheet: Foreshadowing (*CCB*)
3. Language Skills Worksheet: Fragments and Run-On Sentences (*CCB*)
4. Selection Test (*CCB*)

DEVELOPING VOCABULARY
The following words from the story are tested in the Selection Test. (See also Vocabulary Activity Worksheet.)

predisposing	sylvan
impropriety	tethered
expatriated	to extemporize
coquetry	ostentatiously
anathema	wan

PREPARATION
ESTABLISHING A PURPOSE. Have students read to answer the questions posed in the headnote.

A. Interpretation
? What established categories of professions would a western town be likely to reject as "objectionable"? (Possible answers: cardplayers, drunkards, gamblers, saloon entertainers of various types, prostitutes)

In 1871, with a $10,000 contract to write for the Boston-based *Atlantic Monthly* magazine, Harte left San Francisco. He was at the height of his literary career. His cross-country trip with his family was covered by daily newspapers from California to Boston, where he was the guest of honor at a literary dinner.

The attention Harte received at this dinner—as well as his $10,000 contract—so irritated Mark Twain that it probably triggered the decline of the friendship between the two men. Twain became increasingly outspoken about Harte's failure to pay his debts, his rude behavior, and his heavy drinking.

Harte disappointed the editors of *The Atlantic Monthly,* for his creative ability was a thing of the past. With his marriage foundering, he left his family and accepted an appointment as a diplomat in Germany. By the time he died of cancer in 1902, in London, the public was reading novels by writers who made Harte seem tame and old-fashioned. Few people even remembered him as one of the shapers of the myth of the American West.

THE OUTCASTS OF POKER FLAT

As you read this story, look for the familiar Western "types." Which characters are still around, in almost every Western movie and TV show? Look also for Harte's method of characterization. The first two paragraphs, for example, don't contain a single direct reference to what kind of man John Oakhurst is. In spite of that, the reader gets a pretty clear picture of him. How does Harte manage this?

As Mr. John Oakhurst, gambler, stepped into the main street of Poker Flat on the morning of the twenty-third of November, 1850, he was conscious of a change in its moral atmosphere since the preceding night. Two or three men, conversing earnestly together, ceased as he approached and exchanged significant glances. There was a Sabbath lull in the air, which, in a settlement unused to Sabbath influences, looked ominous.

Mr. Oakhurst's calm, handsome face betrayed small concern in these indications. Whether he was conscious of any predisposing cause was another question. "I reckon they're after somebody," he reflected; "likely it's me." He returned to his pocket the handkerchief with which he had been whipping away the red dust of Poker Flat from his neat boots, and quietly discharged his mind of any further conjecture.

In point of fact, Poker Flat was "after somebody." It had lately suffered the loss of several thousand dollars, two valuable horses, and a prominent citizen. It was experiencing a spasm of virtuous reactions, quite as lawless and ungovernable as any of the acts that had provoked it. A secret committee had determined to rid the town of all improper persons. This was done permanently in regard to two men who were then hanging from the boughs of a sycamore in the gulch, and temporarily in the banishment of certain other objectionable characters. I regret to say that some of these were ladies. It is but due to the sex, however, to state that their impropriety was professional, and it was only in such easily established standards of evil that Poker Flat ventured to sit in judgment. A

Mr. Oakhurst was right in supposing that he was included in this category. A few of the com-

A

When Guns Speak, Death Settles Dispute . . . by Charles Russell (1911). Oil.

The Thomas Gilcrease Institute of American History and Art, Tulsa, Oklahoma.

mittee had urged hanging him as a possible example and a sure method of reimbursing themselves from his pockets of the sums he had won from them. "It's agin justice," said Jim Wheeler, "to let this yer young man from Roaring Camp—an entire stranger—carry away our money." But a crude sentiment of equity residing in the breasts of those who had been fortunate enough to win from Mr. Oakhurst overruled this narrower local prejudice.

Mr. Oakhurst received his sentence with philosophic calmness, none the less coolly that he was aware of the hesitation of his judges. He was too much of a gambler not to accept fate. With him life was at best an uncertain game, and he recognized the usual percentage in favor of the dealer.

A body of armed men accompanied the deported wickedness of Poker Flat to the outskirts of the settlement. Besides Mr. Oakhurst, who was known to be a coolly desperate man, and for whose intimidation the armed escort was intended, the expatriated party consisted of a young woman familiarly known as "The Duchess"; another who had won the title of "Mother Shipton";[1] and "Uncle Billy," a suspected sluice robber[2] and confirmed drunkard. The cavalcade provoked no comments from the spectators, nor

1. **"Mother Shipton":** an English woman who was accused of witchcraft.
2. **sluice robber:** Sluices were channels in which gold ore was washed. Robbing a sluice was a low form of stealing.

A. Humanities Connection: Responding to the Fine Art
Together with Frederic Remington, Charles Russell (1864–1926) was one of the greatest and most popular painters of the American West. He himself had worked as a trapper and cowboy and lived for a time with Indians before translating his passion for things western to canvas.

? What story is suggested by the scattered cards, bottle, and violent action? Where were these men till a few minutes ago? What is their profession? Who is shooting at them? Why? (One good guess is that local citizens have accused some cowboys of cheating at cards at The Long Horn.) What connection do you see between this painting and Harte's story? (Stereotypes of the West, gambling)

A. Tone/Diction

What sarcasm or irony do you detect in the narrator's use of the word "regenerating" to characterize the attitudes of the people of Poker Flat? (They saw themselves as moral, respectable people while the narrator does not. See Analyzing Language and Style, question 2, page 401.)

The narrator's use of polysyllabic words such as "regenerating," "precipitous," and "equanimity" indicates "educated" diction. What does such word choice tell you about the narrator and his intended audience? (He is writing for educated readers and displaying his own erudition.) Judging by the few examples of Mr. Oakhurst's speech (see second paragraph of story and the next to last paragraph on page 398), how would the tone of the story differ if he were telling it? Substitute words he might use for the "educated" ones and describe the effect. (The tone would be more realistic; the story would have more natural energy.)

was any word uttered by the escort. Only when the gulch which marked the uttermost limit of Poker Flat was reached, the leader spoke briefly and to the point. The exiles were forbidden to return at the peril of their lives.

As the escort disappeared, their pent-up feelings found vent in a few hysterical tears from the Duchess, some bad language from Mother Shipton, and a Parthian[3] volley of expletives from Uncle Billy. The philosophic Oakhurst alone remained silent. He listened calmly to Mother Shipton's desire to cut somebody's heart out, to the repeated statements of the Duchess that she would die in the road, and to the alarming oaths that seemed to be bumped out of Uncle Billy as he rode forward. With the easy good humor characteristic of his class, he insisted upon exchanging his own riding horse, "Five-Spot," for the sorry mule which the Duchess rode. But even this act did not draw the party into any closer sympathy. The young woman adjusted her somewhat draggled plumes with a feeble, faded coquetry; Mother Shipton eyed the possessor of Five-Spot with malevolence, and Uncle Billy included the whole party in one sweeping anathema.

A The road to Sandy Bar—a camp that, not having as yet experienced the regenerating influences of Poker Flat, consequently seemed to offer some invitation to the emigrants—lay over a steep mountain range. It was distant a day's severe travel. In that advanced season the party soon passed out of the moist, temperate regions of the foothills into the dry, cold, bracing air of the Sierras. The trail was narrow and difficult. At noon the Duchess, rolling out of her saddle upon the ground, declared her intention of going no farther, and the party halted.

The spot was singularly wild and impressive. A wooded amphitheater, surrounded on three sides by precipitous cliffs of naked granite, sloped gently toward the crest of another precipice that overlooked the valley. It was, undoubtedly, the most suitable spot for a camp, had camping been advisable. But Mr. Oakhurst knew that scarcely half the journey to Sandy Bar was accomplished, and the party were not equipped or provisioned for delay. This fact he pointed out to his companions curtly, with a philosophic commentary on the folly of "throwing up their hand before the game was played out." But they were furnished with liquor, which in this emergency stood them in place of food, fuel, rest, and prescience. In spite of his remonstrances, it was not long before they were more or less under its influence. Uncle Billy passed rapidly from a bellicose state into one of stupor, the Duchess became maudlin, and Mother Shipton snored. Mr. Oakhurst alone remained erect, leaning against a rock, calmly surveying them.

Mr. Oakhurst did not drink. It interfered with a profession which required coolness, impassiveness, and presence of mind, and, in his own language, he "couldn't afford it." As he gazed at his recumbent fellow exiles, the loneliness begotten of his pariah[4] trade, his habits of life, his very vices, for the first time, seriously oppressed him. He bestirred himself in dusting his black clothes, washing his hands and face, and other acts characteristic of his studiously neat habits, and for a moment forgot his annoyance. The thought of deserting his weaker and more pitiable companions never perhaps occurred to him. Yet he could not help feeling the want of that excitement which, singularly enough, was most conducive to that calm equanimity for which he was notorious. He looked at the gloomy walls that rose a thousand feet sheer above the circling pines around him, at the sky ominously clouded, at the valley below, already deepening into shadow; and, doing so, suddenly he heard his own name called.

A horseman slowly ascended the trail. In the fresh, open face of the newcomer Mr. Oakhurst recognized Tom Simson, otherwise known as "The Innocent," of Sandy Bar. He had met him some months before over a "little game" and had, with perfect equanimity, won the entire fortune—amounting to some forty dollars—of that guileless youth. After the game was finished, Mr. Oakhurst drew the youthful speculator behind the door and thus addressed him: "Tommy, you're a good little man, but you can't gamble worth a cent. Don't try it over again." He then handed him his money back, pushed him gently from the room, and so made a devoted slave of Tom Simson.

There was a remembrance of this in his boyish and enthusiastic greeting of Mr. Oakhurst. He had

3. **Parthian:** In ancient times, the Parthians were said to have turned about during their retreats and fired arrows at their enemy.

4. **pariah** (pə·rī′ə): outcast, despised.

Literature and Language: Choosing the Right Word
Point out Harte's diction—his choice of words—as students read. Note that besides developing a plot, characters, and setting, short-story writers have to make every word count in telling their tales.

Have students, working in pairs, select five sentences from "The Outcasts of Poker Flat" and discuss Harte's diction. Has Harte made the best possible word choices? Can students think of better choices? Encourage students to rewrite the sentences and compare the results.

started, he said, to go to Poker Flat to seek his fortune. "Alone?" No, not exactly alone; in fact A (a giggle), he had run away with Piney Woods. Didn't Mr. Oakhurst remember Piney? She that used to wait on the table at the Temperance House? They had been engaged a long time, but old Jake Woods had objected, and so they had run away, and were going to Poker Flat to be married, and here they were. And they were tired out, and how lucky it was they had found a place to camp, and company. All this the Innocent delivered rapidly, while Piney, a stout, comely damsel of fifteen, emerged from behind the pine tree, where she had been blushing unseen, and rode to the side of her lover.

Mr. Oakhurst seldom troubled himself with sentiment, still less with propriety; but he had a vague idea that the situation was not fortunate. He retained, however, his presence of mind sufficiently to kick Uncle Billy, who was about to say something, and Uncle Billy was sober enough to recognize in Mr. Oakhurst's kick a superior power that would not bear trifling. He then endeavored to dissuade Tom Simson from delaying further, but in vain. He even pointed out the fact that there was no provision, nor means of making a camp. But, unluckily, the Innocent met this objection by assuring the party that he was provided with an extra mule loaded with provisions, and by the discovery of a rude attempt at a log house near the trail. "Piney can stay with Mrs. Oakhurst," said the Innocent, pointing to the Duchess, "and I can shift for myself."

Nothing but Mr. Oakhurst's admonishing foot saved Uncle Billy from bursting into a roar of laughter. As it was, he felt compelled to retire up the canyon until he could recover his gravity. There he confided the joke to the tall pine trees, with many slaps of his leg, contortions of his face, and the usual profanity. But when he returned to the party, he found them seated by a fire—for the air had grown strangely chill and the sky overcast—in apparently amicable conversation. Piney was actually talking in an impulsive girlish fashion to the Duchess, who was listening with an interest and animation she had not shown for many days. The Innocent was holding forth, apparently with equal effect, to Mr. Oakhurst and Mother Shipton, who was actually relaxing into amiability. "Is this yer a d—d[5] picnic?" said Uncle Billy, with inward scorn, as he surveyed the sylvan group, the glancing firelight, and the tethered animals in the foreground. Suddenly an idea mingled with the alcoholic fumes that disturbed his brain. It was apparently of a jocular nature, for he felt impelled to slap his leg again and cram his fist into his mouth.

As the shadows crept slowly up the mountain, a slight breeze rocked the tops of the pine trees and moaned through their long and gloomy aisles. B The ruined cabin, patched and covered with pine boughs, was set apart for the ladies. As the lovers parted, they unaffectedly exchanged a kiss, so honest and sincere that it might have been heard above the swaying pines. The frail Duchess and the malevolent Mother Shipton were probably too stunned to remark upon this last evidence of simplicity, and so turned without a word to the hut. The fire was replenished, the men lay down before the door, and in a few minutes were asleep.

Mr. Oakhurst was a light sleeper. Toward morning he awoke benumbed and cold. As he stirred the dying fire, the wind, which was now blowing strongly, brought to his cheek that which caused the blood to leave it—snow!

He started to his feet with the intention of awakening the sleepers, for there was no time to lose. But, turning to where Uncle Billy had been lying, he found him gone. A suspicion leaped to his brain, and a curse to his lips. He ran to the spot where the mules had been tethered—they were no longer there. The tracks were already rapidly disappearing in the snow.

The momentary excitement brought Mr. Oakhurst back to the fire with his usual calm. He did not waken the sleepers. The Innocent slumbered peacefully, with a smile on his good-humored, freckled face; the virgin Piney slept beside her frailer sisters as sweetly as though attended by celestial guardians; and Mr. Oakhurst, drawing his blanket over his shoulders, stroked his mustaches and waited for the dawn. It came slowly in a whirly mist of snowflakes that dazzled and confused the eye. What could be seen of the landscape appeared magically changed. He looked over the valley and summed up the present and future in two words, "Snowed in!"

A careful inventory of the provisions, which, fortunately for the party, had been stored within the hut, and so escaped the felonious fingers of Uncle Billy, disclosed the fact that with care and prudence, they might last ten days longer. "That

5. Harte himself omitted the expletive.

A. Expansion
It is a curious fact that in real life as in fiction, parents often bestow upon their children first names or initials that humorously complement the family surname, as in, for example, the real name "I. Doctor." You might have students invent similar names for the other characters of Harte's story, and comment on how use of these names would have affected the tone of the story. (The change would be in the direction of total farce.)

B. Personification
Which words in this sentence attribute human qualities to Nature? (Crept, rocked, moaned) Watch for additional examples of personification as you read. (Page 398, "the sun, looking"; page 400, "The moon . . . looked down")

CLOSURE
Conduct a brief oral review before going on to the responding and writing questions. The outcasts form a memorable group. Have students quickly list them. Which ones exemplify an Old West stereotype they expected? How?

READING CHECK TEST

1. Oakhurst, the gambler, is the only member of the group who survives the snowstorm. *False*

2. Tom Simson runs away with the mules, leaving his sweetheart behind. *False*

3. The narrator calls Mother Shipton "the strongest and yet the weakest of the outcasts of Poker Flat." *False*

4. Oakhurst once returned to Tom some money he had won from him in a card game. *True*

5. Uncle Billy was run out of Poker Flat on suspicion of stealing gold ore. *True*

A. Characterization
Why do you suppose that Oakhurst discloses "Uncle Billy's rascality" only to the Duchess and Mother Shipton? (Probably to keep from alarming the others) What does this action reveal about Oakhurst's character? (That he is a person of compassion)

B. Expansion
For a sober depiction of an Old West poker game, see the photograph on page 401.

is," said Mr. Oakhurst *sotto voce*[6] to the Innocent, "if you're willing to board us. If you ain't—and perhaps you'd better not—you can wait till Uncle Billy gets back with provisions." For some occult reason, Mr. Oakhurst could not bring himself to disclose Uncle Billy's rascality, and so offered the hypothesis that he had wandered from the camp and had accidentally stampeded the animals. He dropped a warning to the Duchess and Mother Shipton, who of course knew the facts of their associate's defection. "They'll find out the truth about us *all* when they find out anything," he added significantly, "and there's no good frightening them now."

A

Tom Simson not only put all his worldly store at the disposal of Mr. Oakhurst, but seemed to enjoy the prospect of their enforced seclusion. "We'll have a good camp for a week, and then the snow'll melt, and we'll all go back together." The cheerful gaiety of the young man and Mr. Oakhurst's calm infected the others. The Innocent, with the aid of pine boughs, extemporized a thatch for the roofless cabin, and the Duchess directed Piney in the rearrangement of the interior with a taste and tact that opened the blue eyes of that provincial maiden to their fullest extent. "I reckon now you're used to fine things at Poker Flat," said Piney. The Duchess turned away sharply to conceal something that reddened her cheeks through their professional tint, and Mother Shipton requested Piney not to "chatter." But when Mr. Oakhurst returned from a weary search for the trail, he heard the sound of happy laughter echoed from the rocks. He stopped in some alarm, and his thoughts first naturally reverted to the whiskey, which he had prudently cached.[7] "And yet it don't somehow sound like whiskey," said the gambler. It was not until he caught sight of the blazing fire through the still blind storm, and the group around it, that he settled to the conviction that it was "square fun."

Whether Mr. Oakhurst had cached his cards with the whiskey as something debarred the free access of the community, I cannot say. It was certain that, in Mother Shipton's words, he "didn't say 'cards' once" during that evening. Haply the time was beguiled by an accordion, produced somewhat ostentatiously by Tom Simson from his pack. Notwithstanding some difficulties attending the manipulation of this instrument, Piney Woods managed to pluck several reluctant melodies from its keys, to an accompaniment by the Innocent on a pair of bone castanets. But the crowning festivity of the evening was reached in a rude camp-meeting hymn, which the lovers, joining hands, sang with great earnestness and vociferation. I fear that a certain defiant tone and Covenanters'[8] swing to its chorus, rather than any devotional quality, caused it speedily to infect the others, who at last joined in the refrain:

I'm proud to live in the service of the Lord,
And I'm bound to die in His army.

The pines rocked, the storm eddied and whirled above the miserable group, and the flames of their altar leaped heavenward, as if in token of the vow.

At midnight the storm abated, the rolling clouds parted, and the stars glittered keenly above the sleeping camp. Mr. Oakhurst, whose professional habits had enabled him to live on the smallest possible amount of sleep, in dividing the watch with Tom Simson, somehow managed to take upon himself the greater part of that duty. He excused himself to the Innocent by saying that he had "often been a week without sleep." "Doing what?" asked Tom. "Poker!" replied Oakhurst sententiously. "When a man gets a streak of luck, he don't get tired. The luck gives in first. Luck," continued the gambler reflectively, "is a mighty queer thing. All you know about it for certain is that it's bound to change. And it's finding out when it's going to change that makes you. We've had a streak of bad luck since we left Poker Flat—you come along, and slap, you get into it, too. If you can hold your cards right along, you're all right. For," added the gambler, with cheerful irrelevance,

B

"I'm proud to live in the service of the Lord,
And I'm bound to die in His army."

The third day came, and the sun, looking through the white-curtained valley, saw the outcasts dividing their slowly decreasing store of provisions for the morning meal. It was one of the peculiarities of that mountain climate that its rays

6. ***sotto voce*** (sät'ō vō'chē): a low voice.
7. **cached** (kasht): hidden (from the French word *cacher*, meaning "to hide or conceal.")
8. **Covenanters:** Scottish Presbyterians who had made a covenant, or promise, to resist the rule of the Anglican Church.

FOR FURTHER READING
FOR THE STUDENT

Harte's sentimental melodrama, eccentric characters, and multisyllable words are reminiscent of Charles Dickens (1812–1870), and his regional color looks forward to Twain and Crane. Students may wish to compare and contrast Harte's story with Dickens's *Oliver Twist,* Twain's "The Celebrated Jumping Frog of Calaveras County," or Crane's "The Bride Comes to Yellow Sky."

diffused a kindly warmth over the wintry landscape, as if in regretful commiseration of the past. But it revealed drift on drift of snow piled high around the hut—a hopeless, uncharted, trackless sea of white lying below the rocky shores to which the castaways still clung. Through the marvelously clear air the smoke of the pastoral village of Poker Flat rose miles away. Mother Shipton saw it and, from a remote pinnacle of her rocky fastness, hurled in that direction a final malediction. It was her last vituperative attempt and, perhaps for that reason, was invested with a certain degree of sublimity. It did her good, she privately informed the Duchess. "Just you go out there and cuss, and see." She then set herself to the task of amusing "the child," as she and the Duchess were pleased to call Piney. Piney was no chicken, but it was a soothing and original theory of the pair thus to account for the fact that she didn't swear and wasn't improper.

When night crept up again through the gorges, the reedy notes of the accordion rose and fell in fitful spasms and long-drawn gasps by the flickering campfire. But music failed to fill entirely the aching void left by insufficient food, and a new diversion was proposed by Piney—storytelling. Neither Mr. Oakhurst nor his female companions caring to relate their personal experiences, this plan would have failed too, but for the Innocent. Some months before he had chanced upon a stray copy of Mr. Pope's[9] ingenious translation of the *Iliad*. He now proposed to narrate the principal incidents of that poem—having thoroughly mastered the argument and fairly forgotten the words—in the current vernacular of Sandy Bar. And so, for the rest of that night, the Homeric demigods again walked the earth. Trojan bully and wily Greek wrestled in the winds, and the great pines in the canyon seemed to bow to the wrath of the son of Peleus.[10] Mr. Oakhurst listened with great satisfaction. Most especially was he interested in the fate of "Ashheels," as the Innocent persisted in denominating the "swift-footed Achilles." A

So, with small food and much of Homer and the accordion, a week passed over the heads of the outcasts. The sun again forsook them, and again from leaden skies the snowflakes were sifted over the land. Day by day closer around them drew the snowy circle, until at last they looked from their prison over drifted walls of dazzling white that towered twenty feet above their heads. It became more and more difficult to replenish their fires, even from the fallen trees beside them, now half hidden in the drifts. And yet no one complained. The lovers turned from the dreary prospect and looked into each other's eyes, and were happy. Mr. Oakhurst settled himself coolly to the losing game before him. The Duchess, more cheerful than she had been, assumed the care of Piney. Only Mother Shipton—once the strongest of the party—seemed to sicken and fade. At midnight on the tenth day, she called Oakhurst to her side. "I'm going," she said, in a voice of querulous weakness, "but don't say anything about it. Don't waken the kids. Take the bundle from under my head, and open it." Mr. Oakhurst did so. It contained Mother Shipton's rations for the last week, untouched. "Give 'em to the child," she said, pointing to the sleeping Piney. "You've starved yourself," said the gambler. "That's what they call it," said the woman querulously, as she lay down again and, turning her face to the wall, passed quietly away. B

The accordion and the bones were put aside that day, and Homer was forgotten. When the body of Mother Shipton had been committed to the snow, Mr. Oakhurst took the Innocent aside and showed him a pair of snowshoes, which he had fashioned from the old packsaddle. "There's one chance in a hundred to save her yet," he said, pointing to Piney; "but it's there," he added, pointing toward Poker Flat. "If you can reach there in two days, she's safe." "And you?" asked Tom Simson. "I'll stay here," was the curt reply.

The lovers parted with a long embrace. "You are not going, too?" said the Duchess, as she saw Mr. Oakhurst apparently waiting to accompany him. "As far as the canyon," he replied. He turned suddenly and kissed the Duchess, leaving her pallid face aflame and her trembling limbs rigid with amazement.

Night came, but not Mr. Oakhurst. It brought the storm again and the whirling snow. Then the Duchess, feeding the fire, found someone had quietly piled beside the hut enough fuel to last a few days longer. The tears rose to her eyes, but she hid them from Piney.

The women slept but little. In the morning, looking into each other's faces, they read their

9. **Mr. Pope:** Alexander Pope (1688–1744), an English poet.
10. **son of Peleus:** Achilles, whose wrath causes the conflict in Homer's *Iliad*.

A. Humor
? What might Tom have made of the names of other characters from *The Iliad,* such as Patroclus, Odysseus, Menelaos, or the gods and goddesses Poseidon, Hermes, Aphrodite, and Artemis? (Perhaps Rockless, O'Dishes, Manny Louse, Posey Dan, Herman, Afterdate, and Arty Miss.)

B. Theme
? What moral code underlies Mother Shipton's actions? Judging from the behavior of other characters as well, what does this story outline as the moral code of the West? Include comments on the distinctions to be made in dealing with people of different types, and "sins" that are allowable in some circumstances but not others.

Analyzing the Story
Identifying Facts

1. The outcasts are Oakhurst (a gambler), the "Duchess," Mother Shipton, and Uncle Billy (a suspected robber and a drunkard).

2. They are all targets of the town's determination to exile all "improper persons."

3. Tom Simson and Piney Woods are a young couple who have eloped together from Sandy Bar. They are on their way to Poker Flat.

Tom thinks of Oakhurst as a friend because Oakhurst had returned the money that Tom had lost to him in a card game. He thinks the meeting is lucky because he and Piney, tired out from their journey, can make camp and rest with good company.

4. Uncle Billy steals the mules, leaving the characters stranded. A heavy snowstorm traps the travelers in the valley. Food and fuel become increasingly more scarce.

5. Mother Shipton grows ill and dies. The Duchess and Piney Woods perish in the cold. Oakhurst commits suicide with his pistol. Uncle Billy and Tom may still be alive.

fate. Neither spoke, but Piney, accepting the position of the stronger, drew near and placed her arm around the Duchess's waist. They kept this attitude for the rest of the day. That night the storm reached its greatest fury and, rending asunder the protecting vines, invaded the very hut.

Toward morning they found themselves unable to feed the fire, which gradually died away. As the embers slowly blackened, the Duchess crept closer to Piney and broke the silence of many hours: "Piney, can you pray?" "No, dear," said Piney simply. The Duchess, without knowing exactly why, felt relieved and putting her head upon Piney's shoulder, spoke no more. And so reclining, the younger and purer pillowing the head of her soiled sister upon her virgin breast, they fell asleep.

The wind lulled as if it feared to waken them. Feathery drifts of snow, shaken from the long pine boughs, flew like white-winged birds and settled about them as they slept. The moon through the rifted clouds looked down upon what had been the camp. But all human stain, all trace of earthly travail, was hidden beneath the spotless mantle mercifully flung from above.

They slept all that day and the next, nor did they waken when voices and footsteps broke the silence of the camp. And when pitying fingers brushed the snow from their wan faces, you could scarcely have told from the equal peace that dwelt upon them which was she that had sinned. Even the law of Poker Flat recognized this and turned away, leaving them still locked in each other's arms.

But at the head of the gulch, on one of the largest pine trees, they found the deuce of clubs[11] pinned to the bark with a bowie knife. It bore the following, written in pencil in a firm hand:

BENEATH THIS TREE
LIES THE BODY
OF
JOHN OAKHURST,
WHO STRUCK A STREAK OF BAD LUCK
ON THE 23RD OF NOVEMBER, 1850,
AND
HANDED IN HIS CHECKS
ON THE 7TH DECEMBER, 1850.

And pulseless and cold, with a Derringer by his side and a bullet in his heart, though still calm as in life, beneath the snow lay he who was at once the strongest and yet the weakest of the outcasts of Poker Flat.

---

11. **deuce of clubs:** the two of clubs, the card with the lowest value in the deck.

Responding to the Story

Analyzing the Story

Identifying Facts

1. Who are the outcasts of Poker Flat?
2. Why are Oakhurst and the others forced to leave town?
3. Who are Tom Simson and Piney Woods, and where are they going? Why is Tom so glad to run into Oakhurst?
4. What **complications** result to make the characters' problem difficult to resolve?
5. What has happened to each character by the story's end? Which two might still be alive?

Interpreting Meanings

6. When Piney first reveals herself to the group, Oakhurst has a vague idea that the situation is not "fortunate." What might be unfortunate about having Piney and Tom join them? What is Uncle Billy's reaction?
7. Why doesn't Oakhurst want Piney and Tom to know what Uncle Billy has done?
8. How does each of the outcasts—except for Uncle Billy—change in the course of the story? What causes the changes? What early clues **foreshadow** the fact that Billy might be the one character not to undergo a change?

Interpreting Meanings

6. Oakhurst has a premonition that the company may be in for hard times. Apparently, he fears that the two innocent young people may have to share the hardships of the others.

Uncle Billy cynically guffaws when Tom makes the innocent mistake of referring to the Duchess as Mrs. Oakhurst.

7. He may be afraid that they will panic.

8. The pressure of hardship brings out generosity and self-sacrifice in each of the characters, who were previously cynical and hard-boiled.

Uncle Billy's alcoholism and cynical attitude toward the innocent young lovers are clues.

9. Because Oakhurst sees the situation as hopeless, he is going to the head of the gulch to commit suicide, apart from the others.

Oakhurst organizes the camp and exercises leadership among the outcasts.

On the other hand, Oakhurst yields to despair at the end of the story and commits suicide.

10. The story shows that the innocence of Tom and Piney Woods had the effect of keeping up the other characters' spirits and of inspiring them to become generous and self-sacrificing. Students will differ on whether or not they think this result is believable.

11. One statement of the theme might be: Under the pressure of hardship, even people whom the world at large condemns as "evil" or "improper" can show themselves as generous and humane. The story is certainly somewhat moralistic.

12. A contemporary realist might change some or all of the following: the innocence and purity of the young lovers' relationship; the dramatic changes of heart in the Duchess and Mother Shipton; the descriptions of nature and of the snowstorms; and the melodramatic epitaph of Oakhurst. Encourage students to discuss what form these changes might take.

13. He seems fair. Certainly they behaved nobly.

9. Why does Oakhurst leave the camp with Tom? In what ways is he the strongest of the outcasts? In what way might he be considered the weakest?
10. What does this story reveal about the power of innocence? Do you find what it says believable?
11. How would you state the **theme** of this story? Do you think the story is strongly moralistic? Explain.
12. If this story were being told by a contemporary realist, how do you think it might change?
13. How do you feel about Harte's depiction of the women characters in this story? Can you find any attitudes toward the women that might be labeled sexist today?

Poker game (c. 1890).

Writing About the Story

A Creative Response

1. **Casting a Film.** Imagine that you are the producer of a movie version of "The Outcasts of Poker Flat," being made either for TV or for theatrical release. Imagine further that you have no financial restrictions and can hire any actors you want. Write a list naming the actors you would hire for parts in the story. Then, for each of your choices, write a brief paragraph explaining why that actor would be right for the role.

A Critical Response

2. **Comparing Depictions of the Frontier.** In a library, find another book of fiction about the Old West by one of the following twentieth-century writers. Then write a report in which you compare that writer's characters and themes with Harte's. Does the contemporary writer also perpetuate myths about the Old West? Or is the other story more realistic?
   a. Louis L'Amour
   b. Jack Schaefer
   c. Walter van Tilburg Clark
   d. Dorothy Johnson

Analyzing Language and Style

Euphemisms and Comic Irony

Harte's style is marked by two characteristics: (1) **euphemism**—the use of language to conceal an unpleasant reality, and (2) **irony,** the use of language to contrast appearances with reality. Both stylistic devices account for the humor in the story.

1. "It is but due to the sex, however, to state that their impropriety was professional. . . ." (Page 394)
   a. What does Harte mean by *professional*?
   b. What *is* their "impropriety"?
2. ". . . Sandy Bar—a camp that, not having as yet experienced the regenerating influences of Poker Flat. . . ." (Page 396)
   a. What does *regenerating* mean, and how is the word usually used?
   b. What does Harte really mean here?
3. "Mr. Oakhurst did not drink. It interfered with a profession which required coolness. . . ." (Page 396)
   a. What do we usually mean when we refer to a *profession*?
   b. What is Mr. Oakhurst's real profession?
4. ". . . the virgin Piney slept beside her frailer sisters as sweetly as though attended by celestial guardians. . . ." (Page 397)
   a. In what ways are Mother Shipton and the duchess "frailer" than Piney?
   b. What is ironic about the use of the phrase "celestial guardians" here?
5. ". . . the Duchess directed Piney in the rearrangement of the interior with a taste and tact that opened the blue eyes of that provincial maiden. . . ." (Page 398)
   a. What is actually taking place here?
   b. Why is this description of the Duchess's interior decorating humorously ironic?
6. ". . . something that reddened her [the Duchess's] cheeks through their professional tint. . . ." (Page 398)
   a. What does Harte mean by "professional tint"?
   b. Why is it "professional"?

A. Humanities Connection: Discussing the Illustration
The caricature catches Twain's "faintly pompous platform manner" and the gaslighting of nineteenth-century stages, and shows flitting off at the left several of Twain's books—*Huckleberry Finn, Innocents Abroad, A Tramp Abroad.* Born in Vienna, Joseph Keppler (1838–1894) emigrated to the United States in 1867 and co-founded in St. Louis a humorous periodical, *Puck* (1871). When it failed, Keppler joined the staff of the famous *Frank Leslie's Illustrated Newspaper* in New York City. In 1876 he started a second *Puck,* following with an English edition in 1877, both of which became famous for political cartoons. Keppler's cartoons were skillfully drawn and bitingly satiric. He was also the first in America to apply color to lithography. Lithography requires drawing in reverse on stone with a crayon or ink that contains grease or oil. These areas bond chemically with the stone and accept ink in the printing process. A separate stone is required for each color.

B. Expansion
Artemus Ward was the pseudonym of Charles Farrar Browne (1834–1867), a humorist known on both sides of the Atlantic for his series in the Cleveland *Plain Dealer,* "Artemus Ward's Letters." Supposedly written by a carnival manager, the letters commented on current events in a New England dialect augmented by bad grammar and misspellings. Browne joined the humorous New York weekly *Vanity Fair* in 1859, and later proved successful on the lecture circuit.

Mark Twain (1835–1910)

Mark Twain is the most celebrated humorist in American history. His ability to make us laugh has contributed to the singular popularity of his books, not just in Twain's own time but in following generations. Since humor is by nature very difficult to translate from language to language, it is even more surprising to find that Twain's appeal has traveled throughout the world.

The great humorist is also, ironically, our great realist. Behind the backwoods humor—especially in his novel *The Adventures of Huckleberry Finn*—is a revelation of the illusions that exist in American life. Huck's journey on a raft with the escaped slave Jim is not a "hymn to boyhood." It is a dramatization of the grim realities of a slave-holding society.

Although Twain became remarkably successful, his later life was shadowed by disappointment and tragedy, and as he grew older he turned into a bitter man. He once told his friend William Dean Howells, the influential novelist and editor of *The Atlantic Monthly,* "Everyone is a moon and has a dark side which he never shows to anybody."

He was born Samuel Langhorne Clemens on November 30, 1835, in the backwoods settlement of Florida, Missouri. His father, John Clemens, was a bright, ambitious, but impractical Virginian who had married Jane Lampton, a witty, dynamic woman who was also a great beauty. With the failure of his store in 1839, John Clemens moved his hopes and his family thirty miles to Hannibal, Missouri. This was the Mississippi River town where young Sam would live from the age of five until he was eighteen; later, he would fashion the town into the scene of the most renowned boyhood in American literature.

Sam's own carefree boyhood, and his formal education, came to an end with his father's death in 1847. Hoping to support their mother and sister, his older brother Orion started a newspaper, and Sam, eleven years old, went to work setting type and editing copy. When he turned eighteen, he set forth to find his place in

Mark Twain speaking in front of an audience, by J. Keppler. Late 19th century. Lithograph. A

the world, and over the next fifteen years he worked as a printer in St. Louis, New York, Philadelphia, Washington, and the Iowa towns of Muscatine and Keokuk. Smitten by a love for the magical steamboats that plied the Mississippi, he even for a time apprenticed himself to the greatest of the steamboat pilots, Horace Bixby. From Bixby, Sam Clemens learned the bends and shallows of the great river from Minnesota to the Louisiana delta. It was the leadsman's cry of "Mark twain!" announcing a water depth of two fathoms (twelve feet) that provided him with his celebrated pen name.

During the Civil War, Twain was for a short time a soldier with a company of Confederate irregulars. (He said he learned more about retreating than fighting.) But he soon abandoned the military life for that of a gold prospector in Nevada. While he found little gold there, he did discover the rich mine of storytelling that lay within him. With his Missouri drawl and relaxed manner he was a natural actor. He took to the easy style and regional humor of Artemus Ward B and Bret Harte (page 393), fellow lecturers and storytellers who encouraged his work. Twain found that he could make delighted captives of an audience. The secret lay in his deft use of a faintly pompous platform manner: In pretending not to recognize the coarseness or absurdity of his material, Twain's deadpan attitude added to his material's hilarity.

Twain soon discovered that this voice could also be turned to prose. In 1862, he took a job as reporter for the *Territorial Enterprise,* in Virginia City, Nevada, and for the next nine years he wrote for a variety of newspapers. In 1865, he achieved wide recognition as a humorist with the publication of his hilarious version of an old tall tale, "The Celebrated Jumping Frog of Calaveras County." Four years later, Twain's dispatches from a Mediterranean tour were published as a book entitled *The Innocents Abroad.* This satirical travelogue poked fun at the traditional American pilgrimage to the monuments of European civilization. The book was funny, but it also told the nation exactly what it wished to believe about its own youthful reflection in a mirror of Old World decadence. Twelve thousand copies were sold in the first month, and sixty-seven thousand within the year. Twain was launched on a literary career and a prosperity that was the prize of his expansive times.

At thirty-five, with a raffish, barroom air about him, Twain was a dubious candidate for marriage, but he courted Olivia Langdon, the daughter of an affluent family from Elmira, New York. She was a delicate, proper woman, but Twain overcame all resistance, and in 1870 Livvy's father gave them his consent and a lavish wedding. Twain was embarked on a marriage of unceasing devotion.

In 1871, he moved to Hartford, Connecticut, where he built an enormous home that is still visited today by thousands of tourists. The next year, he published *Roughing It,* a sequel to *The Innocents Abroad,* which drew on his experiences as a tenderfoot in the West. He soon had an invitation from William Dean Howells to do a series for *The Atlantic Monthly* on his days as a Mississippi pilot. This series eventually was expanded into the book *Life on the Mississippi* (1883); his work on it turned Twain's thoughts further toward his own past and to recollections of prewar innocence.

By the mid-1870's he was also at work on *The Adventures of Tom Sawyer.* This hymn to boyhood absorbed him but presented difficulties of voice and point of view. Twain could not be sure if he was writing a book for children or for adults. Nevertheless, in writing the book, he made an imaginative return to the Hannibal of his boyhood and succeeded in transforming it into a compelling myth. The book was well received when it was published in 1876.

In *Huckleberry Finn,* which was completed and published in 1884, Twain had triumphed in finding exactly the voice he had sought in *Tom Sawyer.* The first-person narration of the hero, natural and slangy, established an altogether new relation between expression and content; it also caused a revolution in American literature. As Ernest Hemingway (speaking through a fictional character) later put it, "All modern American literature comes from one book by Mark Twain called *Huckleberry Finn.*" T. S. Eliot, a fellow Missourian, added that Twain's was "a new way of writing . . . a literary language based on American colloquial speech."

At the age of fifty, Mark Twain had brought forth a masterwork from the most modest materials. But in the years that followed, he was never to equal it, despite his continued popularity with such books as *A Connecticut Yankee in King Arthur's Court* (1889) and *Pudd'nhead Wilson* (1894). Twain's later years were marked by financial and professional disappointment and personal tragedy. His fascination with business and getting ahead financially, so typical of the young nation and its new middle class, led him to invest heavily and disastrously in the Paige typesetting machine. The panic of 1893 bankrupted him.

Then illness overtook the close-knit Clemens family. Suzy, his eldest daughter, died of meningitis in 1896. His wife, a permanent invalid during her last years, died in 1904. In a final blow, Jean, his youngest daughter, died in an epileptic seizure in 1909. "Possibly," said Twain after Jean's death, "I know now what the soldier feels when a bullet crashes through his heart." Four months later, he too was dead.

As loss followed loss, and as the whole country seemed to lose its vitality and become more complex, Twain turned into an obsessive, embittered old man. In his final years, the subject matter of his work was his own disillusionment on a grand scale; the great comic writer appeared to be at war not only with the human race, but with the God who had created it.

For Further Reading For The Teacher

An example of Twain's darker work is "The Mysterious Stranger," found in *Great Short Works of Mark Twain,* edited by Justin Kaplan (Harper & Row, 1967). A recent, new Twain collection edited by Charles Neider is *The Outrageous Mark Twain* (Doubleday, 1987). Its pieces take on such issues as racism, fundamentalism, and Christian Science. (One piece—"Is Shakespeare Dead?"—attempts to bury the bard.)

SUPPLEMENTARY SUPPORT MATERIALS
1. Vocabulary Activity Worksheet (*CCB*)
2. Review and Response Worksheet: Dialect (*CCB*)
3. Selection Test (*CCB*)

DEVELOPING VOCABULARY
The following words from the novel are tested in the Selection Test. (See also Vocabulary Activity Worksheet.)

tediously
prodigious
stoicism
picturesquely
elephantinely

PREPARATION

1. BUILDING ON PRIOR KNOWLEDGE. Some students may have visited a steamboat at a theme park or restored riverfront; others will know of steamboats only from reading and video. Briefly discuss their impressions of steamboat life and the importance of the Mississippi River as a trade and communications channel.

2. ESTABLISHING A PURPOSE. Use the headnote to alert students to the appearance of the fictional Huck Finn in a humorous but basically autobiographical account of Twain's own boyhood.

3. PREREADING JOURNAL. What is the reason for the continued attraction of floating down a river? Why do so many people sail or cruise on holidays, or dream of living on a houseboat? Have students write about what they think makes river life so attractive.

FROM LIFE ON THE MISSISSIPPI

In *Life on the Mississippi,* Twain offers a sometimes humorous account of his boyhood days in Hannibal, Missouri, and of his adventures as an apprentice pilot on a steamboat on the great river. As a youth, Twain was so fascinated by the riverboats that he persuaded Horace Bixby, the locally famous pilot of the *Paul Jones,* to teach him how to navigate the river between New Orleans and St. Louis (a distance of about seven hundred miles) for five hundred dollars. In the following excerpt, taken from an early chapter called "Frescos from the Past," Twain provides a colorful portrait of life on the river by incorporating a passage intended as part of *The Adventures of Huckleberry Finn,* a novel which he had in progress at the time. The story is told in dialect. For greatest pleasure, you should read it aloud, or listen to an oral reading.

Frescos from the Past: The Raftsmen

Seventy years elapsed after the exploration before the river's borders had a white population worth considering; and nearly fifty more before the river had a commerce. Between La Salle's opening of the river and the time when it may be said to have become the vehicle of anything like a regular and active commerce, seven sovereigns had occupied the throne of England, America had become an independent nation, Louis XIV and Louis XV had rotted and died,[1] the French monarchy had gone down in the red tempest of the Revolution, and Napoleon[2] was a name that was beginning to be talked about. Truly, there were snails in those days.

The river's earliest commerce was in great barges—keelboats, broadhorns.[3] They floated and sailed from the upper rivers to New Orleans, changed cargoes there, and were tediously warped and poled back by hand. A voyage down and back sometimes occupied nine months. In time this commerce increased until it gave employment to hordes of rough and hardy men; rude, uneducated, brave, suffering terrific hardships with sailor-like stoicism; heavy drinkers, coarse frolickers in moral sties like the Natchez-under-the-hill of that day, heavy fighters, reckless fellows, every one, elephantinely jolly, foul-witted, profane, prodigal of their money, bankrupt at the end of the trip, fond of barbaric finery, prodigious braggarts; yet, in the main, honest, trustworthy, faithful to promises and duty, and often picturesquely magnanimous.

By and by the steamboat intruded. Then, for fifteen or twenty years, these men continued to run their keelboats downstream, and the steamers did all of the upstream business, the keelboatmen selling their boats in New Orleans, and returning home as deck-passengers in the steamers.

But after a while the steamboats so increased in number and in speed that they were able to absorb the entire commerce; and then keelboating died a permanent death. The keelboatman became a deckhand, or a mate, or a pilot on the steamer; and when steamer-berths were not open to him, he took a berth on a Pittsburgh coal-flat, or on a pine raft constructed in the forests up toward the sources of the Mississippi.

In the heyday of the steamboating prosperity, the river from end to end was flaked with coal-fleets and timber-rafts, all managed by hand, and employing hosts of the rough characters whom I have been trying to describe. I remember the annual processions of mighty rafts that used to glide by Hannibal when I was a boy—an acre or so of

1. **Louis XIV . . . died:** Louis XIV and Louis XV ruled France from 1643 to 1774.
2. **Napoleon:** Napoleon Bonaparte (1769–1821), conquering general and Emperor of France from 1804 to 1814.
3. **broadhorns:** river barges without keels.

A. Characterization

? How does the slave, Jim, demonstrate what today would be called "street smarts"—a very practical kind of intelligence? (He devises a simple plan to get the information he and Huck need with no real danger to either of them.)

white, sweet-smelling boards in each raft, a crew of two dozen men or more, three or four wigwams scattered about the raft's vast level space for storm-quarters—and I remember the rude ways and the tremendous talk of their big crews, the ex-keelboatmen and their admiringly patterning successors; for we used to swim out a quarter or a third of a mile and get on these rafts and have a ride.

By way of illustrating keelboat talk and manners, and that now departed and hardly remembered raft life, I will throw in, in this place, a chapter from a book which I have been working at, by fits and starts, during the past five or six years, and may possibly finish in the course of five or six more. The book is a story which details some passages in the life of an ignorant village boy, Huck Finn, son of the town drunkard of my time out West, there. He has run away from his persecuting father, and from a persecuting good widow who wishes to make a nice, truth-telling, respectable boy of him; and with him a slave of the widow's has also escaped. They have found a fragment of a lumber-raft (it is high water and dead summer-time), and are floating down the river by night, and hiding in the willows by day—bound for Cairo,[4] whence the Negro will seek freedom in the heart of the free states. But, in a fog, they pass Cairo without knowing it. By and by they begin to suspect the truth, and Huck Finn is persuaded to end the dismal suspense by swimming down to a huge raft which they have seen in the distance ahead of them, creeping aboard under cover of the darkness, and gathering the needed information by eavesdropping:

A But you know a young person can't wait very well when he is impatient to find a thing out. We talked it over, and by and by Jim said it was such a black night, now, that it wouldn't be no risk to swim down to the big raft and crawl aboard and listen—they would talk about Cairo, because they would be calculating to go ashore there for a spree, maybe; or anyway they would send boats ashore to buy whiskey or fresh meat or something. Jim has a wonderful level head . . . he could most always start a good plan when you wanted one.

I stood up and shook my rags off and jumped into the river, and struck out for the raft's light. By and by, when I got down nearly to her, I eased up and went slow and cautious. But everything was all right—nobody at the sweeps. So I swum down along the raft till I was most abreast the campfire in the middle, then I crawled aboard and inched along and got in among some bundles of shingles on the weather side of the fire. There was thirteen men there—they was the watch on deck of course. And a mighty rough-looking lot, too. They had a jug, and tin cups, and they kept the jug moving. One man was singing—roaring, you may say; and it wasn't a nice song—for a parlor, anyway. He roared through his nose, and strung out the last word of every line very long. When he was done they all fetched a kind of Injun war-whoop, and then another was sung. It begun:

"There was a woman in our towdn,
In our towdn did dwed'l [dwell],
She loved her husband dear-i-lee,
But another man twyste as wed'l.

"Singing too, riloo, riloo, riloo,
Ri-too, riloo, rilay - - - e,
She loved her husband dear-i-lee,
But another man twyste as wed'l."

And so on—fourteen verses. It was kind of poor, and when he was going to start on the next verse one of them said it was the tune the old cow died on; and another one said: "Oh, give us a rest!" And another one told him to take a walk. They made fun of him till he got mad and jumped up and began to cuss the crowd, and said he could lam[5] any thief in the lot.

They was all about to make a break for him, but the biggest man there jumped up and says:

"Set whar you are, gentlemen. Leave him to me; he's my meat."

Then he jumped up in the air three times, and cracked his heels together every time. He flung off a buckskin coat that was all hung with fringes, and says, "You lay thar tell the chawin-up's done"; and flung his hat down, which was all over ribbons, and says, "You lay thar tell his sufferin's is over."

Then he jumped up in the air and cracked his heels together again, and shouted out:

"Whoo-oop! I'm the old original iron-jawed, brass-mounted, copper-bellied corpse-maker from

4. **Cairo:** town in Southern Illinois, the destination in free territory of many runaway slaves.

5. **lam:** beat, thrash.

Humanities Connection: Responding to the Fine Art George Caleb Bingham (1811–1879) was an American politician and genre painter, focusing not on "great" events but on scenes of everyday life. Born in Virginia, he grew up (like Twain) in Missouri and traveled widely on the Mississippi and throughout the South. His paintings, faithfully reflecting their time and locale, were so popular that engravings from them sold widely.

? Mention details from the painting in each of your answers. How does the raft in this scene compare with the rafts and keelboats Twain describes (page 404)? What might account for the jolliness of the scene? Why are no women present? Do all these men work on the boat, or are some just visiting? What is there about the scene to make a small boy in Twain's day yearn for a life on the river?

The Jolly Flatboatmen in Port by George Caleb Bingham (1857). Oil.

The Saint Louis Art Museum, St. Louis, MO, Museum Purchase.

the wilds of Arkansaw! Look at me! I'm the man they call Sudden Death and General Desolation! Sired by a hurricane, dam'd[6] by an earthquake, half-brother to the cholera, nearly related to the smallpox on the mother's side! Look at me! I take nineteen alligators and a bar'l of whiskey for breakfast when I'm in robust health, and a bushel of rattlesnakes and a dead body when I'm ailing. I split the everlasting rocks with my glance, and I squench the thunder when I speak! Whoo-oop! Stand back and give me room according to my strength! Blood's my natural drink, and the wails of the dying is music to my ear. Cast your eye on me, gentlemen! and lay low and hold your breath, for I'm 'bout to turn myself loose! A

All the time he was getting this off, he was shaking his head and looking fierce, and kind of swelling around in a little circle, tucking up his wristbands, and now and then straightening up and beating his breast with his fist, saying, "Look at me, gentlemen!" When he got through, he jumped up and cracked his heels together three times, and let off a roaring "Whoo-oop! I'm the bloodiest son of a wildcat that lives!" B

Then the man that had started the row tilted his old slouch hat down over his right eye; then he bent stooping forward, with his back sagged and his south end sticking out far, and his fists a-shoving out and drawing in in front of him, and so went around in a little circle about three times, swelling himself up and breathing hard. Then he straightened, and jumped up and cracked his heels together three times before he lit[7] again (that made them cheer), and he began to shout like this:

"Whoo-oop! bow your neck and spread, for the kingdom of sorrow's a-coming! Hold me down to the earth, for I feel my powers a-working! Whoo-oop! I'm a child of sin, *don't* let me get a start! Smoked glass, here, for all! Don't attempt to look at me with the naked eye, gentlemen! When I'm playing I use the meridians of longitude and parallels of latitude for a seine,[8] and drag the Atlantic Ocean for whales! I scratch my head with the lightning and purr myself to sleep with the thunder! When I'm cold, I bile the Gulf of Mexico and bathe in it; when I'm hot I fan myself with an equinoctial storm; when I'm thirsty I reach up and suck a cloud dry like a sponge; when I range the C

6. **dam'd:** mothered.
7. **lit:** landed.
8. **seine** (sān): a large fishing net.

A. Oral Interpretation
The riverman's boast (which begins at the bottom of page 405 and continues through the first paragraph on this page) begs to be read aloud—by you, or by a student. Another boast begins at the bottom of page 407 and continues to the top of 408. The first boaster's name is Bob; the second is called the Child of Calamity.

B. Imagery
? In the boasts themselves and in this descriptive paragraph, there is a great deal of animal imagery. Is there any particular animal this paragraph calls to your mind? (Perhaps a fighting cock or moviedom's King Kong)

C. Exaggeration
? In both the first boast and in this one, the speaker lays claim to powers that belong only to nature or a god. How many such claims can you identify?

A. Responding

? How do the arrival and opening words of the little man differ markedly from the approach of Bob and the Child of Calamity? (No boasts or exaggerating; just a straight statement of intent) Read what the small man does in the next paragraph. Whom do you like better—little Davy, Bob, or the Child of Calamity? Why?

B. Connections

? What similarities are there between this passage and the oil painting on pages 406–407? (The fiddling, dancing, and singing) Do the characters and situation also differ in any way? (Twain's men seem rougher; his raft is not yet in port.)

earth hungry, famine follows in my tracks! Whoo-oop! Bow your neck and spread! I put my hand on the sun's face and make it night in the earth; I bite a piece out of the moon and hurry the seasons; I shake myself and crumble the mountains! Contemplate me through leather—*don't* use the naked eye! I'm the man with a petrified heart and biler-iron bowels! The massacre of isolated communities is the pastime of my idle moments, the destruction of nationalities the serious business of my life! The boundless vastness of the great American desert is my inclosed property, and I bury my dead on my own premises!'' He jumped up and cracked his heels together three times before he lit (they cheered him again), and as he come down he shouted out: ''Whoo-oop! Bow your neck and spread, for the Pet Child of Calamity's a-coming!''

Then the other one went to swelling around and blowing again—the first one—the one they called Bob; next, the Child of Calamity chipped in again, bigger than ever; then they both got at it at the same time, swelling round and round each other and punching their fists into each other's faces, and whooping and jawing . . . , then Bob called the Child names, and the Child called him names back again; next, Bob called him a heap rougher names, and the Child came back at him with the very worst kind of language; next, Bob kicked the Child's hat off, and the Child picked it up and kicked Bob's ribbony hat about six foot; Bob went and got it and said never mind, this warn't going to be the last of this thing, because he was a man that never forgot and never forgive, and so the Child better look out, for there was a time a-coming, just as sure as he was a living man, that he would have to answer to him with the best blood in his body. The Child said no man was willinger than he for that time to come, and he would cross his path again, for he could never rest till he had waded in his blood, for such was his nature, though he was sparing him now on account of his family, if he had one.

Both of them was edging away in different directions, growling and shaking their heads and going on about what they was going to do; but a little black-whiskered chap skipped up and says:

A

''Come back here, you couple of chicken-livered cowards, and I'll thrash the two of ye!''

And he done it, too. He snatched them, he jerked them this way and that, he booted them around, he knocked them sprawling faster than they could get up. Why, it warn't two minutes till they begged like dogs—and how the other lot did yell and laugh and clap their hands all the way through, and shout, ''Sail in, Corpse-Maker!'' ''Hi! At him again, Child of Calamity!'' ''Bully for you, little Davy!'' Well, it was a perfect powwow for a while. Bob and the Child had red noses and black eyes when they got through. Little Davy made them own up that they was sneaks and cowards and not fit to eat with a dog . . . ; then Bob and the Child shook hands with each other, very solemn, and said they had always respected each other and was willing to let bygones be bygones. So then they washed their faces in the river; and just then there was a loud order to stand by for a crossing, and some of them went forward to man the sweeps there, and the rest went aft to handle the after sweeps.

I lay still for fifteen minutes, and had a smoke out of a pipe that one of them left in reach; then the crossing was finished, and they stumped back and had a drink around and went to talking and singing again. Next they got out an old fiddle, and one played, and another patted juba,[9] and the rest turned themselves loose on a regular old-fashioned keelboat breakdown. They couldn't keep that up very long without getting winded, so by and by they settled around the jug again.

B

They sung ''Jolly, Jolly Raftsman's the Life for Me,'' with a rousing chorus, and then they got to talking about differences betwixt hogs, and their different kind of habits; and next about women and their different ways; and next about the ways to put out houses that was afire; and next about what ought to be done with the Indians; and next about what a king had to do, and how much he got; and next about how to make cats fight; and next about what to do when a man has fits; and next about differences betwixt clear-water rivers and muddy-water ones. The man they called Ed said the muddy Mississippi water was wholesomer to drink than the clear water of the Ohio; he said if you let a pint of this yaller Mississippi water settle, you would have about a half to three-quarters of an inch of mud in the bottom, according to the stage of the river, and then it warn't no better than Ohio water—what you wanted to do was to keep it stirred up—and when the river was low, keep mud on hand to put in and thicken the water up the way it ought to be.

9. **juba:** a lively Southern black dance, accompanied by hand clapping.

The Child of Calamity said that was so; he said there was nutritiousness in the mud, and a man that drunk Mississippi water could grow corn in his stomach if he wanted to. He says:

"You look at the graveyards; that tells the tale. Trees won't grow worth shucks in a Cincinnati graveyard, but in a Sent Louis graveyard they grow upwards of eight hundred foot high. It's all on account of the water the people drunk before they laid up. A Cincinnati corpse don't richen a soil any."

A

And they talked about how Ohio water didn't like to mix with Mississippi water. Ed said if you take the Mississippi on a rise when the Ohio is low, you'll find a wide band of clear water all the way down the east side of the Mississippi for a hundred mile or more, and the minute you get out a quarter of a mile from shore and pass the line, it is all thick and yaller the rest of the way across. Then they talked about how to keep tobacco from getting moldy, and from that they went into ghosts and told about a lot that other folks had seen; but Ed says:

"Why don't you tell something that you've seen yourselves? Now let me have a say. Five years ago I was on a raft as big as this, and right along here it was a bright moonshiny night, and I was on watch and boss of the stabboard oar forrard, and one of my pards was a man named Dick Allbright, and he come along to where I was sitting, forrard[10]—gaping and stretching, he was—and stopped down on the edge of the raft and washed his face in the river, and come and set down by me and got out his pipe, and had just got it filled, when he looks up and says:

"'Why looky-here,' he says, 'ain't that Buck Miller's place, over yander in the bend?'

"'Yes,' says I, 'it is—why?' He laid his pipe down and leaned his head on his hand, and says:

"'I thought we'd be furder down.' I says:

"'I thought it, too, when I went off watch'—we was standing six hours on and six off—'but the boys told me,' I says, 'that the raft didn't seem to hardly move, for the last hour,' says I, 'though she's a-slipping along all right now,' says I. He give a kind of a groan, and says:

"'I've seed a raft act so before, along here,' he says, "pears to me the current has most quit above the head of this bend durin' the last two years,' he says.

"Well, he raised up two or three times, and looked away off and around on the water. That started me at it, too. A body is always doing what he sees somebody else doing, though there mayn't be no sense in it. Pretty soon I see a black something floating on the water away off to stabboard and quartering behind us. I see he was looking at it, too. I says:

"'What's that?' He says, sort of pettish:

"'Tain't nothing but an old empty bar'l.'

"'An empty bar'l!' says I, 'why,' says I, 'a spy-glass is a fool to *your* eyes. How can you tell it's an empty bar'l?' He says:

"'I don't know; I reckon it ain't a bar'l, but I thought it might be,' says he.

"'Yes,' I says, 'so it might be, and it might be anything else, too; a body can't tell nothing about it, such a distance as that,' I says.

"We hadn't nothing else to do, so we kept on watching it. By and by I says:

"'Why, looky-here, Dick Allbright, that thing's a-gaining on us, I believe.'

"He never said nothing. The thing gained and gained, and I judged it must be a dog that was about tired out. Well, we swung down into the crossing, and the thing floated across the bright streak of the moonshine, and by George, it *was* a bar'l. Says I:

"'Dick Allbright, what made you think that thing was a bar'l, when it was half a mile off?' says I. Says he:

"'I don't know,' Says I:

"'You tell me, Dick Allbright,' Says he:

"'Well, I knowed it was a bar'l; I've seen it before; lots has seen it, they say it's a ha'nted bar'l.'

"I called the rest of the watch, and they come and stood there, and I told them what Dick said. It floated right along abreast, now, and didn't gain any more. It was about twenty foot off. Some was for having it aboard, but the rest didn't want to. Dick Allbright said rafts that had fooled with it had got bad luck by it. The captain of the watch said he didn't believe in it. He said he reckoned the bar'l gained on us because it was in a little better current than what we was. He said it would leave by and by. B

"So then we went to talking about other things, and we had a song, and then a breakdown; and after that the captain of the watch called for another song; but it was clouding up now, and the bar'l stuck right thar in the same place, and the

10. **stabboard . . . forrard:** *starboard* (right side) and *forward*.

A. Responding

? Trace the train of thought in the conversation reported from the middle of the second column on page 408 to the middle of the first column on this page. Although topics may differ, how is the process exactly like an extended conversation at, say, a picnic or a party? (The movement from topic to topic by very loose association; variety and range of topics covered)

B. Interpretation

? What two theories have been offered to account for the barrel's behavior? (That it is haunted and that it is in a stronger current) Which theory is more rational? (The second) Why might the other theory come to appeal even to a rational person in the middle of the night? (People seem to be more susceptible to ghost stories and superstitions in the dark.)

For Further Reading
For The Student

Students may enjoy reading anecdotes about Twain from *The Little, Brown Book of Anecdotes* (Clifton Fadiman, general editor, 1985). One example: Told as a cub reporter never to state as true anything he could not personally verify, Twain wrote this account of a gala social event: "A woman giving the name of Mrs. James Jones, who is reported to be one of the society leaders of the city, is said to have given what purported to be a party yesterday to a number of alleged ladies. The hostess claims to be the wife of a reputed attorney."

Famous Twain remarks can also be found in *Bartlett's* and other books of quotations.

A. Interpretation
? Why does Ed make such a point of the men's drinking behavior? (Drinking together suggests fun and sociability; drinking in private suggests their growing anxiety.)

B. Expansion
There is a flavor of the story of Jonah in Ed's story—a ship bedeviled by storm until the man responsible goes overboard.

song didn't seem to have much warm-up to it, somehow, and so they didn't finish it, and there warn't any cheers, but it sort of dropped flat, and nobody said anything for a minute. Then everybody tried to talk at once, and one chap got off a joke, but it warn't no use, they didn't laugh, and even the chap that made the joke didn't laugh at it, which ain't usual. We all just settled down glum, and watched the bar'l, and was oneasy and oncomfortable. Well, sir, it shut down black and still, and then the wind began to moan around, and next the lightning began to play and the thunder to grumble. And pretty soon there was a regular storm, and in the middle of it a man that was running aft stumbled and fell and sprained his ankle so that he had to lay up. This made the boys shake their heads. And every time the lightning come, there was that bar'l, with the blue lights winking around it. We was always on the lookout for it. But by and by, toward dawn, she was gone. When the day come we couldn't see her anywhere, and we warn't sorry, either.

"But next night about half past nine, when there was songs and high jinks going on, here she comes again, and took her old roost on the stabboard side. There warn't no more high jinks. Everybody got solemn; nobody talked; you couldn't get anybody to do anything but set around moody and look at the bar'l. It begun to cloud up again. When the watch changed, the off watch stayed up, 'stead of turning in. The storm ripped and roared around all night, and in the middle of it another man tripped and sprained his ankle, and had to knock off. The bar'l left toward day, and nobody see it go.

A "Everybody was sober and down in the mouth all day. I don't mean the kind of sober that comes of leaving liquor alone—not that. They was quiet, but they all drunk more than usual—not together, but each man sidled off and took it private, by himself.

"After dark the off watch didn't turn in; nobody sung, nobody talked; the boys didn't scatter around, neither; they sort of huddled together, forrard; and for two hours they set there, perfectly still, looking steady in the one direction, and heaving a sigh once in a while. And then, here comes the bar'l again. She took up her old place. She B stayed there all night; nobody turned in. The storm come on again, after midnight. It got awful dark; the rain poured down; hail, too; the thunder boomed and roared and bellowed; the wind blowed a hurricane; and the lightning spread over everything in big sheets of glare, and showed the whole raft as plain as day; and the river lashed up white as milk as far as you could see for miles, and there was that bar'l jiggling along, same as ever. The captain ordered the watch to man the after sweeps for a crossing, and nobody would go—no more sprained ankles for them, they said. They wouldn't even *walk* aft. Well, then, just then the sky split wide open, with a crash, and the lightning killed two men of the after watch, and crippled two more. Crippled them how, say you? Why, *sprained their ankles!*

"The bar'l left in the dark betwixt lightnings, toward dawn. Well, not a body eat a bite at breakfast that morning. After that the men loafed around, in twos and threes, and talked low together. But none of them herded with Dick Allbright. They all give him the cold shake. If he come around where any of the men was, they split up and sidled away. They wouldn't man the sweeps with him. The captain had all the skiffs hauled up on the raft, alongside of his wigwam, and wouldn't let the dead men be took ashore to be planted; he didn't believe a man that got ashore would come back, and he was right.

"After night come, you could see pretty plain that there was going to be trouble if that bar'l come again; there was such a muttering going on. A good many wanted to kill Dick Allbright, because he'd seen the bar'l on other trips, and that had an ugly look. Some wanted to put him ashore. Some said: 'Let's all go ashore in a pile, if the bar'l comes again.'

"This kind of whispers was still going on, the men being bunched together forrard watching for the bar'l, when lo and behold you! here she comes again. Down she comes, slow and steady, and settles into her old tracks. You could'a heard a pin drop. Then up comes the captain, and says:

" 'Boy's don't be a pack of children and fools; I don't want this bar'l to be dogging us all the way to Orleans, and *you* don't: Well, then, how's the best way to stop it? Burn it up—that's the way. I'm to fetch it aboard,' he says. And before anybody could say a word, in he went.

"He swum to it, and as he come pushing it to the raft, the men spread to one side. But the old man got it aboard and busted in the head, and there was a baby in it! Yes, sir; a stark-naked baby. It was Dick Allbright's baby; he owned up and said so.

CLOSURE
Have individual students suggest words and phrases that describe the characters of the keelboatmen.

READING CHECK TEST

1. The rafts Twain is describing were a kind of steamboat. *False*
2. Huck and Jim swim together from their own raft to the boatmen's raft. *False*
3. Dick Allbright felt that he was pursued by a haunted barrel. *True*
4. The winner of the fight was the man called Little Davy. *True*
5. The raftsmen made Huck clean their deck before they let him go. *False*

"'Yes,' he says, a-leaning over it, 'yes, it is my own lamented darling, my poor lost Charles William Allbright deceased,' says he—for he could curl his tongue around the bulliest words in the language when he was a mind to, and lay them before you without a jint started anywheres. Yes, he said, he used to live up at the head of this bend, and one night he choked his child, which was crying, not intending to kill it—which was prob'ly a lie—and then he was scared, and buried it in a bar'l, before his wife got home, and off he went, and struck the northern trail and went to rafting; and this was the third year that the bar'l had chased him. He said the bad luck always begun light, and lasted till four men was killed, and then the bar'l didn't come any more after that. He said if the men would stand it one more night—and was a-going on like that—but the men had got enough. They started to get out a boat to take him ashore and lynch him, but he grabbed the little child all of a sudden and jumped overboard with it, hugged up to his breast and shedding tears, and A we never see him again in this life, poor old suffering soul, nor Charles William neither."

"*Who* was shedding tears?" says Bob; "was it Allbright or the baby?"

"Why, Allbright, of course; didn't I tell you the baby was dead? Been dead three years—how could it cry?"

"Well, never mind how it could cry—how could it *keep* all that time?" says Davy. "You answer me that."

"I don't know how it done it," says Ed. "It done it, though—that's all I know about it."

"Say—what did they do with the bar'l?" says the Child of Calamity.

"Why, they hove it overboard, and it sunk like a chunk of lead."

"Edward, did the child look like it was choked?" says one.

"Did it have its hair parted?" says another.

"What was the brand on that bar'l, Eddy?" says a fellow they called Bill.

"Have you got the papers for them statistics, Edmund?" says Jimmy.

"Say, Edwin, was you one of the men that was killed by the lightning?" says Davy.

"Him? Oh, no! he was both of 'em," says Bob. Then they all haw-hawed.

"Say, Edward, don't you reckon you'd better take a pill? You look bad—don't you feel pale?" says the Child of Calamity.

Let a Leadsman Cry by Thomas Hart Benton (1944). Lithograph from *Life on the Mississippi* by Mark Twain.

Limited Editions Club, New York City. The New York Public Library.

B

"Oh, come, now, Eddy," says Jimmy, "show up; you must'a kept part of that bar'l to prove the thing by. Show us the bunghole—*do*—and we'll all believe you."

"Say, boys," says Bill, "less divide it up. Thar's thirteen of us. I can swaller a thirteenth of the yarn, if you can worry down the rest."

Ed got up mad and said they could all go to some place which he ripped out pretty savage, and then walked off aft, cussing to himself, and they yelling and jeering at him, and roaring and laughing so you could hear them a mile.

"Boys, we'll split a watermelon on that," says the Child of Calamity; and he came rummaging around in the dark amongst the shingle bundles

A. Predicting an Outcome
? What elements of Ed's story did you find particularly amusing or far fetched? Will the other boatmen accept Ed's story at face value or pick it apart?

B. Humanities Connection: Discussing the Illustration
A leadsman is the man who lowers a weight on a rope to determine the depth of the water. Thomas Hart Benton, the 20th-century American painter (1889–1975), was a grandnephew of a famous nineteenth-century senator of the same name, and the son of a congressman. He studied art in Chicago and Paris, but returned to the United States to work. He is especially known for his murals in public buildings, his dramatization of American themes, and a strongly rhythmic, graphic style.

ANALYZING THE STORY
Identifying Facts

1. He wants to illustrate "keelboat talk and manners" for his readers.
2. Huck and Jim are bound for Cairo, but a fog causes them to pass the city on the river. Huck hopes to eavesdrop on the men's conversation in order to find out their true location. When he climbs aboard, Huck sees from his hiding place a collection of rough men, singing and drinking. The men are fierce-looking and vie with each other in profanity and boasting.
3. They sing, drink, curse, and tell stories.

Interpreting Meanings

4. Among the adjectives Twain uses to describe the keelboatmen are the following: rude, uneducated, brave, stoic, coarse, reckless, foul-witted, profane, prodigal, bankrupt, honest, trustworthy, faithful, and magnanimous. The men were heavy drinkers, fighters, and braggarts. This passage resembles Walt Whitman's catalogue style in that it contains a list of vivid, contrasting qualities.
5. Bob claims that he was "sired by a hurricane" and "dam'd (mothered) by an

A. Interpretation
? Why are Davy's words likely to gain Huck a reprieve? (Davy can whip anyone.) In the scene that follows, why does Huck lie to the men? (He doesn't want to lead them to his slave friend, Jim.)

where I was, and put his hand on me. I was warm and soft and naked; so he says "Ouch!" and jumped back.

"Fetch a lantern or a chunk of fire here, boys—there's a snake here as big as a cow!"

So they run there with a lantern, and crowded up and looked in on me.

"Come out of that, you beggar!" says one.

"Who are you?" says another.

"What are you after here? Speak up prompt, or overboard you go."

"Snake him out, boys. Snatch him out by the heels."

I began to beg, and crept out amongst them trembling. They looked me over, wondering, and the Child of Calamity says:

"A cussed thief! Lend a hand and less heave him overboard!"

"No," says Big Bob, "less get out the paint-pot and paint him a sky-blue all over from head to heel, and *then* heave him over."

"Good! that's it. Go for the paint, Jimmy."

When the paint come, and Bob took the brush and was just going to bend, the others laughing and rubbing their hands, I begun to cry, and that sort of worked on Davy, and he says:

A "'Vast[11] there. He's nothing but a cub. I'll paint the man that teches him!"

So I looked around on them, and some of them grumbled and growled, and Bob put down the paint, and the others didn't take it up.

"Come here to the fire, and less see what you're up to here," says Davy. "Now set down there and give an account of yourself. How long have you been aboard here?"

"Not over a quarter of a minute, sir," says I.

"How did you get dry so quick?"

"I don't know, sir. I'm always that way, mostly."

"Oh, you are, are you? What's your name?"

I warn't going to tell my name. I didn't know what to say, so I just says:

"Charles William Allbright, sir."

Then they roared—the whole crowd; and I was mighty glad I said that, because, maybe, laughing would get them in a better humor.

When they got done laughing, Davy says:

"It won't hardly do, Charles William. You couldn't have growed this much in five years, and you was a baby when you come out of the bar'l, you know, and dead at that. Come, now, tell a straight story, and nobody'll hurt you, if you ain't up to anything wrong. What *is* your name?"

"Aleck Hopkins, sir. Aleck James Hopkins."

"Well, Aleck, where did you come from, here?"

"From a trading-scow.[12] She lays up the bend yonder. I was born on her. Pap has traded up and down here all his life; and he told me to swim off here, because when you went by he said he would like to get some of you to speak to a Mr. Jonas Turner, in Cairo, and tell him—"

"Oh, come!"

"Yes, sir, it's as true as the world. Pap he says—"

"Oh, your grandmother!"

They all laughed, and I tried again to talk, but they broke in on me and stopped me.

"Now, looky-here," says Davy; "you're scared, and so you talk wild. Honest, now, do you live in a scow, or is it a lie?"

"Yes, sir, in a trading-scow. She lays up at the head of the bend. But I warn't born in her. It's our first trip."

"Now you're talking! What did you come aboard here for? To steal?"

"No, sir, I didn't. It was only to get a ride on the raft. All boys does that."

"Well, I know that. But what did you hide for?"

"Sometimes they drive the boys off."

"So they do. They might steal. Looky-here; if we let you off this time, will you keep out of these kind of scrapes hereafter?"

"'Deed I will, boss. You try me."

"All right, then. You ain't but little ways from shore. Overboard with you, and don't you make a fool of yourself another time this way. Blast it, boy, some raftsmen would rawhide you till you were black and blue!"

I didn't wait to kiss goodbye, but went overboard and broke for shore. When Jim come along by and by, the big raft was away out of sight around the point. I swum out and got aboard, and was mighty glad to see home again.

The boy did not get the information he was after, but his adventure has furnished the glimpse of the departed raftsman and keelboatman which I desire to offer in this place.

11. **vast:** a contraction of *avast,* a cry meaning "Stop!"

12. **trading-scow:** a large, flat-bottomed boat.

earthquake." He says his relations are diseases (cholera and smallpox), and that he eats alligators and drinks a barrel of whiskey for breakfast. His voice and his glance split the rocks and drown out the thunder, and he drinks blood. The Child of Calamity tries to outdo Bob by bragging that he is superior to the cosmic forces of lightning, thunder, cloud, storm, and ocean. The outlandish hyperbole of the boasts of simple keelboatmen, when compared with the vaunting of mythological heroes, is a source of comic irony.

6. The lightning plays around the barrel as it floats nearby. The appearances of the barrel seem to cause the crewmen to sprain their ankles. Dick Allbright claims that the barrel has been chasing him since he accidentally choked his child, and that every time it appears four men die. At the end of the tale, Allbright jumps overboard with the dead baby in the barrel and is never seen again.

The motifs of Allbright's love for the baby and of its accidental death are pathetic. But the story is dominated by gallows humor, in which the corpse of the dead baby becomes a curse that demands expiation through the deaths of others.

7. Huck wins Davy's sympathy by bursting into tears when he is discovered. Then he pretends he has only been on board for a quarter of a minute. The men roar with laughter when Huck tells them that his real name is Charles William Allbright. He then pretends that his name is Aleck Hopkins and that he is bearing a message from his father on a trading-scow. Although the men do not believe him, they good-naturedly let him go, making him promise that he will keep out of scrapes in the future.

8. Student answers will vary. Ask them to explain their answers with specific examples. (Review current movies and TV shows.)

Responding to the Story

Analyzing the Story

Identifying Facts

1. What is Twain's purpose in presenting a chapter from his work in progress?
2. Explain why Huck Finn swims to the huge raft. Describe what he observes when he climbs aboard.
3. Describe how the keelboatmen seem to pass their time.

Interpreting Meanings

4. List the words Twain uses to describe the keelboatmen in the opening passage of this selection. How is this litany like Whitman's **catalogue** style? (See page 326.)
5. In ancient epics and romances, the heroes had supernatural powers and were often identified with the forces of nature. Find the **images** and details in the boasts of Bob and the Child of Calamity that show they are the backwoods equivalents of these heroes.
6. What supernatural elements are in the story of Dick Allbright and the baby? How does this combine "gallows humor" (morbid humor) and pathos?
7. In the *Odyssey,* Homer's epic, Odysseus is a prototype of the cunning hero, one who often escapes from tight or dangerous situations by using his wits rather than brute force. Odysseus has been called the master "artificer," meaning that he is a skilled liar. Explain how this boy narrator is also a master "artificer."
8. How would you describe the **characters** of the keelboatmen? Are such character types evident in any occupation in American life today? Explain.

Writing About the Story

A Creative Response

1. **Writing an Exaggerated Boast.** In the shouting contest between Bob and the Child of Calamity, each man tries to top the other with boasts and insults. There is a long oral tradition behind such contests, dating back ultimately to the boasts of the heroes in ancient epic poems. For example, Odysseus opens his remarks to the king of the Phaiakians with a kind of boast:

> I am Laertes' son, Odysseus.
> Men hold me
> formidable for guile in peace and war:
> this fame has gone abroad to the sky's rim.
> —from the *Odyssey,* Book 9,
> by Homer

In the American South and Southwest, the tradition of boasting continued in its own special way. Speakers would try to top each other with tall tales, jokes, anecdotes, and boastings about their achievements. (See Davy Crockett's speech on page 510.) Write a boast for a speaker who is "vying for supremacy." Give your speaker a name and try to include as much humor in the boast as possible. Open with the words "I am." What **metaphors** will your boaster use to exaggerate his or her achievements and prowess?

2. **Rewriting Dialect.** The dialect in this selection comprises a mixture of regional vernaculars: the backwoodsmen's speech, the dialect of the American Southwest, and the raftsmen's jargon. Choose a speech or an exchange in dialogue from the selection that you find especially colorful, and rewrite it in standard English. Then compare the two versions. What has been lost when standard English is used in this specific context?

Analyzing Language Style

Dialect and Frontier Humor

Twain, who is celebrated for his reproductions of dialect, claims in the introduction to *The Adventures of Huckleberry Finn* that he has used seven dialects in that book (a boast that might have to be taken as a slight exaggeration). Dialect may differ from standard English in vocabulary, in pronunciation, and in grammar. "Frontier humor" uses dialect plus a few humorous devices:

a. **Hyperbole,** or exaggeration for effect
b. Colorful and often comic **metaphors,** which usually create hilarious images through the terms of comparisons
c. **Incongruity,** whereby two opposites—two images or events or elements that seem inappropriately matched—are unexpectedly joined
d. **Boasts**
e. **Digressions** from the point of the story

1. Locate at least five examples of each characteristic of dialect in the selection from *Life on the Mississippi.*
2. Locate at least one example of Twain's use of each of the techniques of frontier humor.
3. Which humorous techniques are most prevalent in this episode from *Life on the Mississippi?*
4. Which of these humorous techniques are used by humorists and comics today? What variations do contemporary comics use to appeal to their particular audiences?

SUPPLEMENTARY SUPPORT MATERIALS
1. Vocabulary Activity Worksheet (*CCB*)
2. Review and Response Worksheet: Tone (*CCB*)
3. Selection Test (*CCB*)
4. Audiocassette recording

DEVELOPING VOCABULARY
The following words from the novel are tested in the Selection Test. (See also Vocabulary Activity Worksheet.)

temperance	shanty
stanchion	slough
skiff	monstrous
ramrod	stern
gully	quicksilver

PREPARATION
BUILDING ON PRIOR KNOWLEDGE. Discuss with students the elements that, based on the biography of Twain, the selection from *Life on the Mississippi,* and the Analyzing Language Style exercise on page 413, they expect to find in *Huckleberry Finn.* (Possible answers: the characters of Jim and Huck and the use of dialect)

A. Humanities Connection: Discussing the Illustrations
Edward Winslow Kemble (1861–1933) was an illustrator and cartoonist best known for his light but sympathetic interpretations of mischievous boys, as in his drawings for the first (1884) edition of *Huckleberry Finn.* Drawings for the chapters reprinted here appear on almost every page. Have students identify the passages illustrated by each drawing and comment on the accuracy of Kemble's interpretation. Do the drawings contribute to their impressions of Pap as despicable and Huck as likable? (Students probably will agree but may note that the same traits might be illustrated differently today.)

FROM THE ADVENTURES OF HUCKLEBERRY FINN

The following selections come from the early part of Twain's novel. Huck Finn describes his brutal treatment at the hands of his father, his ingenious escape, the first few exhilarating days of life on the river alone, and the meeting with the runaway slave Jim. As you read, note that Twain tells the story from Huck's point of view, using the boy's own "voice." You will encounter numerous examples of dialect in the selection: reading the first two or three paragraphs aloud will help prepare you for the colorful vernacular of Huck's language.

Up to this point in the novel (Chapter 5), Huck has been taken away from his shiftless, drunken father and placed with a pious widow who is attempting to "civilize" him. Huck's father has heard that he has gotten some money, and the old man comes creeping into Huck's room one night in search of it. When Huck goes to his room and lights his candle, "there sat Pap—his own self!"

Pap Starts in on a New Life

I had shut the door to. Then I turned around, and there he was. I used to be scared of him all the time, he tanned[1] me so much. I reckoned I was scared now, too; but in a minute I see I was mistaken—that is, after the first jolt, as you may say, when my breath sort of hitched, he being so unexpected; but right away after I see I warn't scared of him worth bothring about.

He was most fifty, and he looked it. His hair was long and tangled and greasy, and hung down, and you could see his eyes shining through like he was behind vines. It was all black, no gray; so was his long, mixed-up whiskers. There warn't no color in his face, where his face showed; it was white; not like another man's white, but a white to make a body sick, a white to make a body's flesh crawl—a tree-toad white, a fish-belly white. As for his clothes—just rags, that was all. He had one ankle resting on t'other knee; the boot on that foot was busted, and two of his toes stuck through, and he worked them now and then. His hat was laying on the floor—an old black slouch with the top caved in, like a lid.

I stood a-looking at him; he set there a-looking at me, with his chair tilted back a little. I set the candle down. I noticed the window was up; so he

A

The illustrations in this extract are by E. W. Kemble for the 1884 edition of *The Adventures of Huckleberry Finn.*

1. **tanned:** whipped.

had clumb in by the shed. He kept a-looking me all over. By and by he says:

"Starchy clothes—very. You think you're a good deal of a big-bug, *don't* you?"

"Maybe I am, maybe I ain't," I says.

"Don't you give me none o' your lip," says he. "You've put on considerable many frills since I been away. I'll take you down a peg before I get done with you. You're educated, too, they say—can read and write. You think you're better'n your father, now, don't you, because he can't? *I'll* take it out of you. Who told you you might meddle with such hi-falut'n foolishness, hey?—who told you you could?"

"The widow. She told me."

"The widow, hey?—and who told the widow she could put in her shovel about a thing that ain't none of her business?"

"Nobody never told her."

"Well, I'll learn her how to meddle. And looky here—you drop that school, you hear? I'll learn people to bring up a boy to put on airs over his own father and let on to be better'n what *he* is. You lemme catch you fooling around that school again, you hear? Your mother couldn't read, and she couldn't write, nuther, bother she died. None of the family couldn't before *they* died. *I* can't, and here you're a-swelling yourself up like this. I ain't the man to stand it—you hear? Say, lemme hear you read."

I took up a book and begun something about General Washington and the wars. When I'd read about a half a minute, he fetched the book a whack with his hand and knocked it across the house. He says:

"It's so. You can do it. I had my doubts when you told me. Now looky here; you stop that putting on frills. I won't have it. I'll lay for you, my smarty; and if I catch you about that school I'll tan you good. First you know you'll get religion, too. I never see such a son."

He took up a little blue and yaller picture of some cows and a boy, and says:

"What's this?"

"It's something they give me for learning my lessons good."

He tore it up, and says:

"I'll give you something better—I'll give you a cowhide."

He set there a-mumbling and a-growling a minute, and then he says:

"*Ain't* you a sweet-scented dandy, though? A bed; and bed-clothes; and a look'n'-glass; and a piece of carpet on the floor—and your own father got to sleep with the hogs in the tanyard. I never see such a son. I bet I'll take some o' these frills out o' you before I'm done with you. Why, there ain't no end to your airs—they say you're rich. Hey?—how's that?"

"They lie—that's how."

"Looky here—mind how you talk to me; I'm a-standing about all I can stand now—so don't gimme no sass. I've been in town two days, and I hain't heard nothing but about you bein' rich. I heard about it away down the river, too. That's why I come. You git me that money tomorrow—I want it."

"I hain't got no money."

"It's a lie. Judge Thatcher's got it. You git it. I want it."

"I hain't got no money, I tell you. You ask Judge Thatcher; he'll tell you the same."

"All right. I'll ask him; and I'll make him pungle,[2] too, or I'll know the reason why. Say, how much you got in your pocket? I want it."

"I hain't got only a dollar, and I want that to—"

"It don't make no difference what you want it for—you just shell it out."

He took it and bit it to see if it was good, and then he said he was going downtown to get some whiskey, said he hadn't had a drink all day. When he had got out on the shed he put his head in again, and cussed me for putting on frills and trying to do better than him; and when I reckoned he was gone he came back and put his head in again, and told me to mind about that school, because he was going to lay for me and lick me if I didn't drop that.

Next day he was drunk, and he went to Judge Thatcher's and bullyragged him, and tried to make him give up the money; but he couldn't, and then he swore he'd make the law force him.

The judge and the widow went to law to get the court to take me away from him and let one of them be my guardian; but it was a new judge that had just come, and he didn't know the old man; so he said courts mustn't interfere and separate families if they could help it; said he'd druther not take a child away from its father. So Judge Thatcher and the widow had to quit on the business. A

2. **pungle:** pay the money.

A. Responding

What happens when Judge Thatcher and the widow ask the court for guardianship of Huck? (The judge, not knowing about Huck's father, says that he doesn't like to break up families, and refuses the request.)

A. Irony/Characterization
Pause to discuss the insights into Pap conveyed by the chapter, and the irony of the chapter title, "Pap Starts in on a New Life" (see question 6, page 428).
? What has the new judge learned about Pap that Huck, Judge Thatcher, and the widow already knew? (Pap will never change.) Do you agree with Alexander Butrym, who says of this chapter, "We are struck by the old man's meanness. We also note the peculiar pride he has in his ignorance and slovenliness"? (Students may disagree, pointing out that Pap is uneducated and unskilled and that he has no real options.)

B. Responding
? What psychological truth about people's reasons for doing things does Twain hit upon here? (Out of rebelliousness and individuality, people often do exactly the opposite of what someone in authority suggests or demands.)

C. Allusion
In the Bible (Genesis 4), Cain, the first son of Adam and Eve, commits the first murder when he kills his brother Abel. "To raise Cain" can be taken as direct allusion to Cain's violence.

That pleased the old man till he couldn't rest. He said he'd cowhide me till I was black and blue if I didn't raise some money for him. I borrowed three dollars from Judge Thatcher, and Pap took it and got drunk, and went a-blowing around and cussing and whooping and carrying on; and he kept it up all over town, with a tin pan, till most midnight; then they jailed him, and the next day they had him before court, and jailed him again for a week. But he said *he* was satisfied; said he was boss of his son, and he'd make it warm for *him*.

When he got out the new judge said he was a-going to make a man of him. So he took him to his own house, and dressed him up clean and nice, and had him to breakfast and dinner and supper with the family, and was just old pie to him, so to speak. And after supper he talked to him about temperance and such things till the old man cried, and said he'd been a fool, and fooled away his life; but now he was a-going to turn over a new leaf and be a man nobody wouldn't be ashamed of, and he hoped the judge would help him and not look down on him. The judge said he could hug him for them words; so *he* cried, and his wife she cried again; Pap said he'd been a man that had always been misunderstood before, and the judge said he believed it. The old man said that what a man wanted that was down was sympathy, and the judge said it was so; so they cried again. And when it was bedtime the old man rose up and held out his hand, and says:

"Look at it, gentlemen and ladies all; take a-hold of it; shake it. There's a hand that was the hand of a hog; but it ain't so no more; it's the hand of a man that's started in on a new life, and'll die before he'll go back. You mark them words—don't forget I said them. It's a clean hand now; shake it—don't be afeared."

So they shook it, one after the other, all around, and cried. The judge's wife she kissed it. Then the old man he signed a pledge—made his mark. The judge said it was the holiest time on record, or something like that. Then they tucked the old man into a beautiful room, which was the spare room, and in the night some time he got powerful thirsty and clumb out on to the porch roof and slid down a stanchion and traded his new coat for a jug of forty-rod, and clumb back again and had a good old time; and toward daylight he crawled out again, drunk as a fiddler, and rolled off the porch and broke his left arm in two places, and was most

froze to death when somebody found him after sun-up. And when they come to look at that spare room they had to take soundings before they could navigate it.

The judge he felt kind of sore. He said he reckoned a body could reform the old man with a shotgun, maybe, but he didn't know no other way. A

Pap Struggles with the Death Angel

Well, pretty soon the old man was up and around again, and then he went for Judge Thatcher in the courts to make him give up that money, and he went for me, too, for not stopping school. He catched me a couple of times and thrashed me, but I went to school just the same, and dodged him or outrun him most of the time. I didn't want to go to school much before, but I reckoned I'd go now to spite Pap. B That law trial was a slow business—appeared like they warn't ever going to get started on it; so every now and then I'd borrow two or three dollars off of the judge for him, to keep from getting a cowhiding. Every time he got money he got drunk: and every time he got drunk he raised Cain around town; and every time he raised Cain he C got jailed. He was just suited—this kind of thing was right in his line.

He got to hanging around the widow's too much, and so she told him at last that if he didn't quit using around there she would make trouble for him. Well, *wasn't* he mad? He said he would show who was Huck Finn's boss. So he watched out for me one day in the spring, and catched me, and took me up the river about three mile in a skiff, and crossed over to the Illinois shore where it was woody and there warn't no houses but an old log hut in a place where the timber was so thick you couldn't find it if you didn't know where it was.

A He kept me with him all the time, and I never got a chance to run off. We lived in that old cabin, and he always locked the door and put the key under his head nights. He had a gun which he had stole, I reckon, and we fished and hunted, and that was what we lived on. Every little while he locked me in and went down to the store, three miles, to the ferry, and traded fish and game for whiskey, and fetched it home and got drunk and had a good time, and licked me. The widow she found out where I was by and by, and she sent a man over to try to get hold of me; but Pap drove him off with the gun, and it warn't long after that till I was used to being where I was, and liked it—all but the cowhide part.

It was kind of lazy and jolly, laying off comfortable all day, smoking and fishing, and no books nor study. Two months or more run along, and my clothes got to be all rags and dirt, and I didn't see how I'd ever got to like it so well at the widow's, where you had to wash, and eat on a plate, and comb up, and go to bed and get up regular, and be forever bothering over a book, and have old Miss Watson pecking at you all the time. I didn't want to go back no more. I had stopped cussing, because the widow didn't like it; but now I took to it again because Pap hadn't no objections. It was pretty good times up in the woods there, take it all around.

But by and by Pap got too handy with his hick'ry, and I couldn't stand it. I was all over welts. He got to going away so much, too, and locking me in. Once he locked me in and was gone three days. It was dreadful lonesome. I judged he had got drownded, and I wasn't ever going to get out anymore. I was scared. I made up my mind I would fix up some way to leave there. I had tried B to get out of that cabin many a time, but I couldn't find no way. There warn't a window to it big enough for a dog to get through. I couldn't get up the chimbly; it was too narrow. The door was thick, solid oak slabs. Pap was pretty careful not to leave a knife or anything in the cabin when he was away; I reckon I had hunted the place over as much as a hundred times; well, I was most all the time at it, because it was about the only way to put in the time. But this time I found something at last; I found an old rusty wood saw without any handle; it was laid in between a rafter and the clapboards of the roof. I greased it up and went to work. There was an old horse blanket nailed against the logs at the far end of the cabin behind the table, to keep the wind from blowing through the chinks and putting the candle out. I got under the table and raised the blanket, and went to work to saw a section of the big bottom log out—big enough to let me through. Well, it was a good long job, but I was getting toward the end of it when I heard Pap's gun in the woods. I got rid of the signs of my work, and dropped the blanket and hid my saw, and pretty soon Pap come in.

Pap warn't in a good humor—so he was his natural self. He said he was downtown, and everything was going wrong. His lawyer said he reckoned he would win his lawsuit and get the money if they ever got started on the trial; but then there was ways to put it off a long time, and Judge Thatcher knowed how to do it. And he said people allowed there'd be another trial to get me away from him and give me to the widow for my guardian, and they guessed it would win this time. This shook me up considerable, because I didn't want to go back to the widow's any more and be so cramped up and civilized, as they called it. Then the old man got to cussing, and cussed everything and everybody he could think of, and then cussed them all over again to make sure he hadn't skipped any, and after that he polished off with a kind of a general cuss all round, including a considerable

A. Expansion
Huck's mixed feelings about his life with Pap are discussed in response question 2, page 428. You may also wish to call to students' attention the repeated violence Huck is experiencing, however humorously presented it may be, and look ahead to Philip Young's comment (page 427) and the related writing assignment (number 3, page 428). Response question 10 also addresses the idea that many incidents of the novel could equally well have served as the basis of tragedy rather than comedy.

B. Plot
The strategy Huck ultimately uses to escape, begun here and continuing into Chapter 7 ("I Fool Pap and Get Away"), is addressed in response question 3, page 428.

A. Allusion
Even the irreligious Huck would have been familiar with the great stories from the King James (1611) translation of the Bible, as this allusion to Genesis 2:7 indicates: "And the Lord God formed man of the dust of the ground, and breathed into his nostrils the breath of life; and man became a living soul." The more recent New American Bible interprets "dust" as "clay," more clearly portraying God as a creative potter. See also the note on the allusion on text page 419.

ADDITIONAL WRITING ASSIGNMENT
Pap's propensity to rail against the government is a consummately American trait, a cherished form of freedom of speech. You may wish to have students use the passage as the basis of one of these brief writing assignments: (a) an exercise in translating dialectal speech to standard English; (b) as the basis of an updated diatribe from someone like television's Archie Bunker.

parcel of people which he didn't know the names of, and so called them what's-his-name when he got to them, and went right along with his cussing.

He said he would like to see the widow get me. He said he would watch out, and if they tried to come any such game on him he knowed of a place six or seven mile off to stow me in, where they might hunt till they dropped and they couldn't find me. That made me pretty uneasy again, but only for a minute; I reckoned I wouldn't stay on hand till he got that chance.

The old man made me go to the skiff and fetch the things he had got. There was a fifty-pound sack of corn meal, and a side of bacon, ammunition, and a four-gallon jug of whiskey, and an old book and two newspapers for wadding, besides some tow. I toted up a load, and went back and set down on the bow of the skiff to rest. I thought it all over, and I reckoned I would walk off with the gun and some lines, and take to the woods when I run away. I guessed I wouldn't stay in one place, but just tramp right across the country, mostly nighttimes, and hunt and fish to keep alive, and so get so far away that the old man nor the widow couldn't ever find me any more. I judged I would saw out and leave that night if pap got drunk enough, and I reckoned he would. I got so full of it I didn't notice how long I was staying till the old man hollered and asked me whether I was asleep or drownded.

I got the things all up to the cabin, and then it was about dark. While I was cooking supper the old man took a swig or two and got sort of warmed up, and went to ripping again. He had been drunk over in town, and laid in the gutter all night, and he was a sight to look at. A body would 'a' thought he was Adam—he was just all mud. Whenever his liquor begun to work he most always went for the govment. This time he says: A

"Call this a govment! why, just look at it and see what it's like. Here's the law a-standing ready to take a man's son away from him—a man's own son, which he has had all the trouble and all the anxiety and all the expense of raising. Yes, just as that man has got that son raised at last, and ready to go to work and begin to do suthin' for *him* and give him a rest, the law up and goes for him. And they call *that* govment! That ain't all, nuther. The law backs that old Judge Thatcher up and helps him to keep me out o' my property. Here's what the law does: The law takes a man worth six thousand dollars and up'ards, and jams him into an old trap of a cabin like this, and lets him go round in clothes that ain't fitten for a hog. They call that govment! A man can't get his rights in a govment like this. Sometimes I've a mighty notion to just leave the country for good and all. Yes, and I *told* 'em so; I told old Thatcher so to his face. Lots of 'em heard me, and can tell what I said. Says I, for two cents I'd leave the blamed country and never come a-near it ag'in. Them's the very words. I says, look at my hat—if you call it a hat—but the lid raises up and the rest of it goes down till it's below my chin, and then it ain't rightly a hat at all, but more like my head was shoved up through a jint o' stove-pipe. Look at it, says I—such a hat for me to wear—one of the wealthiest men in this town if I could git my rights. . . .

Pap was a-going on so he never noticed where his old limber legs was taking him to, so he went head over heels over the tub of salt pork and barked[3] both shins, and the rest of his speech was all the hottest kind of language. . . . He hopped around the cabin considerable, first on one leg and then on the other, holding first one shin and then the other one, and at last he let out with his left foot all of a sudden and fetched the tub a rattling

3. **barked:** bumped.

A. Responding

? In this and following paragraphs, Pap experiences the D.T.'s or delirium tremens of advanced alcoholism. Do you find the scene more sad than funny? Do you feel any sympathy for Pap, despite the real danger he is to Huck? What do your reactions suggest about changes in society's attitudes toward alcoholism since the 1880's? (Today alcoholics are treated as people with a disease. They may receive more understanding than Pap did.)

B. Allusion

The Talmudists (specialists in Hebrew tradition) report the belief that Adam lived in Paradise only 12 hours before he sinned and was thrust out. Mohammedan legend expands upon the story, adding that, for the creation of Adam, God sent the archangels Gabriel, Michael, and Israfel to fetch seven differently colored handfuls of earth from different depths, but they returned empty-handed. God then sent the archangel Azrael, who succeeded. As a reward, Azrael was made the Angel of Death, whose job it would be once again to separate men's souls from the clay of their bodies.

kick. But it warn't good judgment, because that was the boot that had a couple of toes leaking out of the front end of it; so now he raised a howl that fairly made a body's hair raise, and down he went in the dirt, and rolled there, and held his toes; and the cussing he done then laid over anything he had ever done previous. He said so his own self afterwards. He had heard old Sowberry Hagan in his best days, and he said it laid over him, too; but I reckon that was sort of piling it on, maybe.

After supper Pap took the jug, and said he had enough whiskey there for two drunks and one delirium tremens.[4] That was always his word. I judged he would be blind drunk in about an hour, and then I would steal the key, or saw myself out, one or t'other. He drank and drank, and tumbled down on his blankets by and by; but luck didn't run my way. He didn't go sound asleep, but was uneasy. He groaned and moaned and thrashed around this way and that for a long time. At last I got so sleepy I couldn't keep my eyes open all I could do, and so before I knowed what I was about I was sound asleep, and the candle burning.

A I don't know how long I was asleep, but all of a sudden there was an awful scream and I was up. There was Pap looking wild, and skipping around every which way and yelling about snakes. He said they was crawling up his legs; and then he would give a jump and scream, and say one had bit him on the cheek—but I couldn't see no snakes. He started and run round and round the cabin, hollering, "Take him off! take him off! he's biting me on the neck!" I never see a man look so wild in the eyes. Pretty soon he was all fagged out, and fell down panting; then he rolled over and over wonderful fast, kicking things every which way, and striking and grabbing at the air with his hands, and screaming and saying there was devils a-hold of him. He wore out by and by, and laid still awhile, moaning. Then he laid stiller, and didn't make a sound. I could hear the owls and the wolves away off in the woods, and it seemed terrible still. He was laying over by the corner. By and by he raised up part way and listened, with his head to one side. He says, very low:

"Tramp—tramp—tramp; that's the dead; tramp—tramp—tramp; they're coming after me, but I won't go. Oh, they're here! don't touch me—don't! hands off—they're cold; let go. Oh, let a poor devil alone!"

Then he went down on all fours and crawled off, begging them to let him alone, and he rolled himself up in his blanket and wallowed in under the old pine table, still a-begging; and then he went crying. I could hear him through the blanket.

By and by he rolled out and jumped up to his feet looking wild, and he sees me and went for me. He chased me round and round the place with a clasp knife, calling me the Angel of Death, and B saying he would kill me, and then I couldn't come for him no more. I begged, and told him I was only Huck; but he laughed *such* a screechy laugh, and roared and cussed, and kept on chasing me up. Once when I turned short and dodged under his arm he made a grab and got me by the jacket between my shoulders, and I thought I was gone; but I slid out of the jacket quick as lightning, and saved myself. Pretty soon he was all tired out, and dropped down with his back against the door, and said he would rest a minute and then kill me. He put his knife under him, and said he would sleep and get strong, and then he would see who was who.

So he dozed off pretty soon. By and by I got the old split-bottom chair and clumb up as easy as I could, not to make any noise, and got down the gun. I slipped the ramrod down it to make sure

4. **delirium tremens:** an illness caused by alcohol, characterized by sweating, trembling, anxiety, and hallucinations.

Literature and Language: Writing Dialect
Have students read the discussion of *dialect* in the Handbook of Literary Terms (page 1172) and review the term *regionalism* (page 381). Some words and expressions in *Huck Finn* may be so unfamiliar that students will benefit from "translating" Twain's sentences into modern English. Read aloud three or four such sentences and ask students to notice how pronunciation, vocabulary, and/or grammar differ from the dialect they speak. Then have students find and "translate" ten more sentences in which the dialect clearly differs from modern standard English.

A. Interpretation
Pap is exhibiting an effect of alcoholism called a blackout, a complete memory loss with regard to events during a period of drunkenness. He genuinely does not know that he attacked Huck.

B. Characterization/Plot
? This is not the first lie Huck has told. What is another? (His lie to Pap at the beginning of this chapter) How do the circumstances of Huck's life account for his development of such adroitness at lying? (It is a survival skill.) What does Huck's ability to lie quickly and plausibly suggest about him? (He is quite intelligent.) Notice, in the section that follows, how one of Huck's lies—the one about a prowler—becomes a plot element.

it was loaded, and then I laid it across the turnip barrel, pointing towards pap, and set down behind it to wait for him to stir. And how slow and still the time did drag along.

I Fool Pap and Get Away

"Git up! What you 'bout?"

I opened my eyes and looked around trying to make out where I was. It was after sun-up, and I had been sound asleep. Pap was standing over me looking sour—and sick, too. He says:

"What you doin' with this gun?"

A I judged he didn't know nothing about what he had been doing, so I says:

"Somebody tried to get in, so I was laying for him."

"Why didn't you roust me out?"

"Well, I tried to, but I couldn't; I couldn't budge you."

"Well, all right. Don't stand there palavering[5] all day, but out with you and see if there's a fish on the lines for breakfast. I'll be along in a minute."

He unlocked the door, and I cleared out up the riverbank. I noticed some pieces of limbs and such things floating down, and a sprinkling of bark; so I knowed the river had begun to rise. I reckoned I would have great times now if I was over at the town. The June rise used to be always luck for me; because as soon as that rise begins here comes cordwood floating down, and pieces of log rafts—

5. **palavering** (pə·lav′ər·ing): chatting idly.

sometimes a dozen logs together; so all you have to do is to catch them and sell them to the woodyards and the sawmill.

I went along up the bank with one eye out for pap and t'other one out for what the rise might fetch along. Well, all at once here comes a canoe; just a beauty, too, about thirteen or fourteen foot long, riding high like a duck. I shot headfirst off of the bank like a frog, clothes and all on, and struck out for the canoe. I just expected there'd be somebody laying down in it, because people often done that to fool folks, and when a chap had pulled a skiff out most to it they'd raise up and laugh at him. But it warn't so this time. It was a drift-canoe sure enough, and I clumb in and paddled her ashore. Thinks I, the old man will be glad when he sees this—she's worth ten dollars. But when I got to shore Pap wasn't in sight yet, and as I was running her into a little creek like a gully, all hung over with vines and willows, I struck another idea: I judged I'd hide her good, and then, 'stead of taking to the woods when I run off, I'd go down the river about fifty mile and camp in one place for good, and not have such a rough time tramping on foot.

It was pretty close to the shanty, and I thought I heard the old man coming all the time; but I got her hid; and then I out and looked around a bunch of willows, and there was the old man down the path a piece just drawing a bead on a bird with his gun. So he hadn't seen anything.

When he got along I was hard at it taking up a "trot" line. He abused me a little for being so slow; but I told him I fell in the river, and that was what made me so long. I knowed he would see I was wet, and then he would be asking questions. We got five catfish off the lines and went home. B

While we laid off after breakfast to sleep up, both of us being about wore out, I got to thinking that if I could fix up some way to keep Pap and the widow from trying to follow me, it would be a certainer thing than trusting to luck to get far enough off before they missed me; you see, all kinds of things might happen. Well, I didn't see no way for a while, but by and by Pap raised up a minute to drink another barrel of water, and he says:

"Another time a man comes a-prowling round here you roust me out, you hear? That man warn't here for no good. I'd a shot him. Next time you roust me out, you hear?"

Then he dropped down and went to sleep again; what he had been saying give me the very idea I wanted. I says to myself, I can fix it now so nobody won't think of following me.

About twelve o'clock we turned out and went along up the bank. The river was coming up pretty fast, and lots of driftwood going by on the rise. By and by along comes part of a log raft—nine logs fast together. We went out with the skiff and towed it ashore. Then we had dinner. Anybody but Pap would 'a' waited and seen the day through, so as to catch more stuff; but that warn't Pap's style. Nine logs was enough for one time; he must shove right over to town and sell. So he locked me in and took the skiff, and started off towing the raft about half past three. I judged he wouldn't come back that night. I waited till I reckoned he had got a good start; then I out with my saw, and went to work on that log again. Before he was t'other side of the river I was out of the hole; him and his raft was just a speck on the water away off yonder.

A I took the sack of corn meal and took it to where the canoe was hid, and shoved the vines and branches apart and put it in; then I done the same with the side of bacon; then the whiskey jug. I took all the coffee and sugar there was, and all the ammunition; I took the wadding; I took the bucket and gourd; took a dipper and a tin cup, and my old saw and two blankets, and the skillet and the coffee pot. I took fish lines and matches and other things—everything that was worth a cent. I cleaned out the place. I wanted an ax, but there wasn't any, only the one out at the woodpile, and I knowed why I was going to leave that. I fetched out the gun, and now I was done.

I had wore the ground a good deal crawling out of the hole and dragging out so many things. So I fixed that as good as I could from the outside by scattering dust on the place, which covered up the smoothness and the sawdust. Then I fixed the piece of log back into its place, and put two rocks under it and one against it to hold it there, for it was bent up at that place and didn't quite touch ground. If you stood four of five foot away and didn't know it was sawed, you wouldn't never notice it; and besides, this was the back of the cabin, and it warn't likely anybody would go fooling around there.

It was all grass clear to the canoe, so I hadn't left a track. I followed around to see. I stood on the bank and looked out over the river. All safe.

So I took the gun and went up a piece into the woods, and was hunting around for some birds when I see a wild pig; hogs soon went wild in them bottoms after they got away from the prairie-farms. I shot this fellow and took him into camp.

I took the ax and smashed in the door. I beat it and hacked it considerable a-doing it. I fetched the pig in, and took him back nearly to the table and hacked into his throat with the ax, and laid him down on the ground to bleed; I say ground because it *was* ground—hard packed, and no boards. Well, next I took an old sack and put a lot of big rocks in it—all I could drag—and I started it from the pig, and dragged it to the door and through the woods down to the river and dumped it in, and down it sunk, out of sight. You could easy see that something had been dragged over the ground. I did wish Tom Sawyer was B
there; I knowed he would take an interest in this kind of business, and throw in the fancy touches. Nobody could spread himself like Tom Sawyer in such a thing as that.

Well, last I pulled out some of my hair, and blooded the ax good, and stuck it on the back side, and slung the ax in the corner. Then I took up the pig and held him to my breast with my jacket (so he couldn't drip) till I got a good piece below the house and then dumped him into the river. Now I thought of something else. So I went and got the bag of meal and my old saw out of the canoe, and fetched them to the house. I took the bag to where it used to stand, and ripped a hole in the bottom of it with the saw, for there warn't no knives and forks on the place—Pap done every-

A. Responding
James M. Cox remarks of the plot as a whole (Huck's revolt and the freeing of a slave in the process), "He is involved in a subversive project which has the reader's complete approval."
? How could this comment also be applied here, to Huck's theft of goods from the cabin? (Most students will see Huck as fully justified in escaping Pap and taking supplies he will need, especially given the inability of the courts to help him.)

B. Allusion
Students who have read *The Adventures of Tom Sawyer* (1876) will recognize Huck as the more truly intelligent of the two. Tom's showy escapades involve pointless details drawn from romantic tales of knights and robbers and kings, while everything Huck does has a purpose.

A. Responding
In the first column on this page, Huck completes his escape strategy and reviews its probable effect on those who might look for him.
? Examine carefully everything Huck has done. Can you find any flaws? Are there any false leads or clues he has planted which would *not* fool one of television's sleuths? (Encourage students to share and expand on their various responses.)

B. Plot
? Why does Pap fail to see Huck? (He pulled his canoe into some overhanging willow branches along the bank.)

C. Responding
? Does Kemble's drawing on this page capture Huck's peace at this point? Have you had feelings similar to Huck's while looking up at the sky? (Answers will vary.)

thing with his clasp knife about the cooking. Then I carried the sack about a hundred yards across the grass and through the willows east of the house, to a shallow lake that was five mile wide and full of rushes—and ducks too, you might say, in the season. There was a slough or a creek leading out of it on the other side that went miles away, I don't know where, but it didn't go to the river. The meal sifted out and made a little track all the way to the lake. I dropped pap's whetstone there too, so as to look like it had been done by accident. Then I tied up the rip in the meal sack with a string, so it wouldn't leak no more, and took it and my saw to the canoe again.

It was about dark now; so I dropped the canoe down the river under some willows that hung over the bank, and waited for the moon to rise. I made fast to a willow; then I took a bit to eat, and by and by laid down in the canoe to smoke a pipe and lay out a plan. I says to myself, they'll follow

the track of that sackful of rocks to the shore and then drag the river for me. And they'll follow that meal track to the lake and go browsing down the creek that leads out of it to find the robbers that killed me and took the things. They won't ever hunt the river for anything but my dead carcass. They'll soon get tired of that, and won't bother no more about me. All right; I can stop anywhere I want to. Jackson's Island is good enough for me; I know that island pretty well, and nobody ever comes there. And then I can paddle over to town nights, and slink around and pick up things I want. Jackson's Island's the place.

A I was pretty tired, and the first thing I knowed I was asleep. When I woke up I didn't know where I was for a minute. I set up and looked around, a little scared. Then I remembered. The river looked miles and miles across. The moon was so bright I could 'a' counted the drift logs that went a-slipping along, black and still, hundreds of yards out from shore. Everything was dead quiet, and it looked late, and *smelt* late. You know what I mean—I don't know the words to put it in.

I took a good gap and a stretch, and was just going to unhitch and start when I heard a sound away over the water. I listened. Pretty soon I made it out. It was that dull kind of a regular sound that comes from oars working in rowlocks when it's a still night. I peeped out through the willow branches, and there it was—a skiff, away across the water. I couldn't tell how many was in it. It kept a-coming, and when it was abreast of me I see there warn't but one man in it. Thinks I, maybe it's Pap, though I warn't expecting him. He dropped below me with the current, and by and by he came a-swinging up shore in the easy water, and he went by so close I could 'a' reached out the gun and touched him. Well it *was* Pap, sure enough—and sober, too, by the way he laid his oars. B

I didn't lose no time. The next minute I was a-spinning downstream soft, but quick, in the shade of the bank. I made two mile and a half, and then struck out a quarter of a mile or more toward the middle of the river, because pretty soon I would be passing the ferry landing, and people might see me and hail me. I got out amongst the driftwood, and then laid down in the bottom of the canoe and let her float. I laid there, and had a good rest and a smoke out of my pipe, looking away into the sky; not a cloud in it. The sky looks ever so deep when you lay down on your back in the moonshine; I never knowed it before. C And how far a body can hear on the water such nights! I heard people talking at the ferry landing. I heard what they said, too—every word of it. One man said it was getting towards the long days and the short nights now. T'other one said *this* warn't one of the short ones, he reckoned—and then they laughed, and he said it over again, and they laughed again; then they waked up another fellow and told him, and laughed, but he didn't laugh; he ripped out something brisk, and said let him alone. The first fellow said he 'lowed to tell it to his old woman—she would think it was pretty good; but he said that warn't nothing to some things he had said in his time. I heard one man say it was nearly

A. Simile

? With what does Huck compare Jackson's Island? (A big, dark steamboat) What mental image of the island does this create in your mind? (Perhaps an island with a blocky shape, some cliffs rising straight up from the river, some trees sticking up higher than others)

B. Word Choice

? Earlier (page 422) Huck spoke disparagingly of his ability to find the right words. How does this sentence demonstrate his ability to choose exactly the right words? ("Freckled" conveys the size and shape of scattered spots of light, and "swapped about" suggests the movement of the dappled spots of sunlight as the breeze shifts the branches.)

C. Responding

? As Twain once cabled in response to a premature query about his death, "Report of my death greatly exaggerated." In the second column on this page, what amusement—and practical benefit—does Huck derive from his presumed death? (He eats a loaf of bread plugged with quicksilver that floated down the river and was meant to stop over his drowned body.)

three o'clock, and he hoped daylight wouldn't wait more than about a week longer. After that the talk got further and further away, and I couldn't make out the words anymore; but I could hear the mumble, and now and then a laugh, too, but it seemed a long ways off.

A I was away below the ferry now. I rose up, and there was Jackson's Island, about two mile and a half downstream, heavy-timbered and standing up out of the middle of the river, big and dark and solid, like a steamboat without any lights. There warn't any signs of the bar at the head—it was all underwater now.

It didn't take me long to get there. I shot past the head at a ripping rate, the current was so swift, and then I got into the deadwater and landed on the side towards the Illinois shore. I run the canoe into a deep dent in the bank that I knowed about; I had to part the willow branches to get in; and when I made fast nobody could 'a' seen the canoe from the outside.

I went up and set down on a log at the head of the island, and looked out on the big river and the black driftwood and away over to the town, three mile away, where there was three or four lights twinkling. A monstrous big lumber raft was about a mile upstream, coming along down, with a lantern in the middle of it. I watched it come creeping down, and when it was most abreast of where I stood I heard a man say, "Stern oars, there! heave her head to stabboard!" I heard that just as plain as if the man was by my side.

There was a little gray in the sky now; so I stepped into the woods, and laid down for a nap before breakfast.

I Spare Miss Watson's Jim

The sun was up so high when I waked that I judged it was after eight o'clock. I laid there in the grass and the cool shade thinking about things, and feeling rested and ruther comfortable and satisfied. I could see the sun out at one or two holes, but mostly it was big trees all about, and gloomy in there amongst them. B There was freckled places on the ground where the light sifted down through the leaves, and the freckled places swapped about a little, showing there was a little breeze up there. A couple of squirrels set on a limb and jabbered at me very friendly.

I was powerful lazy and comfortable—didn't want to get up and cook breakfast. Well, I was dozing off again when I thinks I hears a deep sound of "boom!" away up the river. I rouses up, and rests on my elbow and listens; pretty soon I hears it again. I hopped up, and went and looked out at a hole in the leaves, and I see a bunch of smoke lay on the water a long ways up—about abreast the ferry. And there was the ferryboat full of people floating along down. I knowed what was the matter now. "Boom!" I see the white smoke squirt out of the ferryboat's side. You see, they was firing cannon over the water, trying to make my carcass come to the top.

I was pretty hungry, but it warn't going to do for me to start a fire, because they might see the smoke. So I set there and watched the cannon smoke and listened to the boom. The river was a mile wide there, and it always looks pretty on a summer morning—so I was having a good enough time seeing them hunt for my remainders if I only had a bit to eat. When, then I happened to think how they always put quicksilver in loaves of bread and float them off, because they always go right to the drowned carcass and stop there. So, says I, I'll keep a lookout, and if any of them's floating around after me I'll give them a show. I changed to the Illinois edge of the island to see what luck I could have, and I warn't disappointed. A big double loaf come along, and I most got it with a long stick, but my foot slipped and she floated out further. Of course I was where the current set in the closest to the shore—I knowed enough for that. But by and by along comes another one, and this time I won. I took out the plug and shook out the little dab of quicksilver, and set my teeth in. It was "baker's bread"—what the quality eat; none of your low-down cornpone.

I got a good place amongst the leaves, and set there on a log, munching the bread and watching the ferryboat, and very well satisfied. And then something struck me. I says, now I reckon the widow or the parson or somebody prayed that this bread would find me, and here it has gone and done it. So there ain't no doubt but there is something in that thing—that is, there's something in it when a body like the widow or the parson prays, but it don't work for me, and I reckon it don't work for only just the right kind.

I lit a pipe and had a good long smoke, and went on watching. The ferryboat was floating with the current, and I allowed I'd have a chance to

C

COMMENT FROM A CRITIC

The authors of *The Story of English* (1986) remark on the gifts of two writers in forming American English: "Twain was the writer who brought the newly forged American language back from the frontier to the teeming cities of the East Coast. By a quirk of history, the only writer to touch Twain when it came to the naturalness and vitality of American speech was already making a name for himself among the more discriminating members of the East Coast poetry-reading public. This was Walt Whitman. . . ."

? How could Mark Twain be compared with Walt Whitman for introducing natural, lively language into American writing? (Twain's direct prose, as on page 404; his use of dialect; Whitman's use of the cadences of free verse)

see who was aboard when she come along, because she would come in close, where the bread did. When she'd got pretty well along down towards me, I put out my pipe and went to where I fished out the bread, and laid down behind a log on the bank in a little open place. Where the log forked I could peep through.

By and by she come along, and she drifted in so close that they could 'a' run out a plank and walked ashore. Most everybody was on the boat. Pap, and Judge Thatcher, and Bessie Thatcher, and Joe Harper, and Tom Sawyer, and his old Aunt Polly, and Sid and Mary, and plenty more. Everybody was talking about the murder, but the captain broke in and says:

"Look sharp, now; the current sets in the closest here, and maybe he's washed ashore and got tangled amongst the brush at the water's edge. I hope so, anyway."

I didn't hope so. They all crowded up and leaned over the rails, nearly in my face, and kept still, watching with all their might. I could see them first-rate, but they couldn't see me. Then the captain sung out: "Stand away!" and the cannon let off such a blast right before me that it made me deef with the noise and pretty near blind with

the smoke, and I judged I was gone. If they'd 'a' had some bullets in, I reckon they'd 'a' got the corpse they was after. Well, I see I warn't hurt, thanks to goodness. The boat floated on and went out of sight around the shoulder of the island. I could hear the booming now and then, further and further off, and by and by, after an hour, I didn't hear it no more. The island was three mile long. I judged they had got to the foot, and was giving it up. But they didn't yet awhile. They turned around the foot of the island and started up the channel on the Missouri side, under steam, and booming once in a while as they went. I crossed over to that side and watched them. When they got abreast the head of the island they quit shooting and dropped over to the Missouri shore and went home to the town.

I knowed I was all right now. Nobody else would come a-hunting after me. I got my traps out of the canoe and made me a nice camp in the thick woods. I made a kind of a tent out of my blankets to put my things under so the rain couldn't get at them. I catched a catfish and haggled him open with my saw, and towards sundown I started my campfire and had supper. Then I set out a line to catch some fish for breakfast.

When it was dark I set by my campfire smoking, and feeling pretty well satisfied; but by and by it got sort of lonesome, and so I went and set on the bank and listened to the current swashing along, and counted the stars and drift logs and rafts that come down, and then went to bed; there ain't no better way to put in time when you are lonesome; you can't stay so, you soon get over it.

And so for three days and nights. No difference—just the same thing. But the next day I went exploring around down through the island. I was boss of it; it all belonged to me, so to say, and I wanted to know all about it; but mainly I wanted to put in the time. I found plenty strawberries, ripe and prime; and green summer grapes, and green razberries; and the green blackberries was just beginning to show. They would all come handy by and by, I judged.

Well, I went fooling along in the deep woods till I judged I warn't far from the foot of the island. I had my gun along, but I hadn't shot nothing; it was for protection; thought I would kill some game nigh home. About this time I mighty near stepped on a good-sized snake, and it went sliding off through the grass and flowers, and I after it, trying to get a shot at it. I clipped along, and all

For Further Reading
For The Teacher

A number of collections of critical essays on *Huckleberry Finn* are available. Still of great value is the 1968 Prentice-Hall collection edited by Claude M. Simpson, *Twentieth Century Interpretations of Adventures of Huckleberry Finn.* Authors include Bernard DeVoto and Leo Marx; a second section contains viewpoints of William Dean Howells, Van Wyck Brooks, F. Scott Fitzgerald, T.S. Eliot, F.R. Leavis, Richard Chase, and Ralph Ellison, as well as a good portion of Philip Young's comment on page 427.

of a sudden I bounded right on to the ashes of a campfire that was still smoking.

A

My heart jumped up amongst my lungs. I never waited for to look further, but uncocked my gun and went sneaking back on my tiptoes as fast as ever I could. Every now and then I stopped a second amongst the thick leaves and listened, but my breath come so hard I couldn't hear nothing else. I slunk along another piece further, then listened again; and so on, and so on. If I see a stump, I took it for a man; if I trod on a stick and broke it, it made me feel like a person had cut one of my breaths in two and I only got half, and the short half, too.

When I got to camp I warn't feeling very brash, there warn't much sand in my craw; but I says, this ain't no time to be fooling around. So I got B all my traps into my canoe again so as to have them out of sight, and I put out the fire and scattered the ashes around to look like an old last-year's camp, and then clumb a tree.

I reckon I was up in the tree two hours; but I didn't see nothing. I didn't hear nothing—I only *thought* I heard and seen as much as a thousand things. Well, I couldn't stay up there forever; so at last I got down, but I kept in the thick woods and on the lookout all the time. All I could get to eat was berries and what was left over from breakfast.

By the time it was night I was pretty hungry. So when it was good and dark I slid out from shore before moonrise and paddled over to the Illinois bank—about a quarter of a mile. I went out in the woods and cooked a supper, and I had about made up my mind I would stay there all night when I hear a *plunkety-plunk, plunkety-plunk,* and says to myself, horses coming; and next I hear people's voices. I got everything into the canoe as quick as I could, and then went creeping through the woods to see what I could find out. I hadn't got far when I hear a man say:

"We better camp here if we can find a good place; the horses is about beat out. Let's look around."

I didn't wait, but shoved out and paddled away easy. I tied up in the old place, and reckoned I would sleep in the canoe.

I didn't sleep much. I couldn't, somehow, for thinking. And every time I waked up I thought somebody had me by the neck. So the sleep didn't do me no good. By and by I says to myself, I can't live this way; I'm a-going to find out who it is that's here on the island with me; I'll find it out or bust. Well, I felt better right off.

So I took my paddle and slid out from shore just a step or two, and then let the canoe drop along down amongst the shadows. The moon was shining, and outside of the shadows it made it most as light as day. I poked along well on to an hour, everything still as rocks and sound asleep. Well, by this time I was most down to the foot of the island. A little ripply, cool breeze begun to blow, and that was as good as saying the night was about done. I give her a turn with the paddle and brung her nose to shore; then I got my gun and slipped out and into the edge of the woods. I sat down there on a log, and looked out through the leaves. I see the moon go off watch, and the darkness begin to blanket the river. But in a little while I see a pale streak over the treetops, and knowed the day was coming. So I took my gun and slipped off towards where I had run across that campfire, stopping every minute or two to listen. But I hadn't no luck somehow; I couldn't seem to find the place. But by and by, sure enough, I catched a glimpse of fire away through the trees. I went for it, cautious and slow. By and by I was close enough to have a look, and there

A. Responding

? Imagine Huck's fright. Can you recall a time when you thought you heard footsteps behind you on a dark night, or a time as a small child when you woke from a nightmare and every shape in your room looked menacing? How were your feelings like Huck's as he discovers evidence of another person on "his" island?

B. Word Choice

? Huck has used the expression "my traps" before (page 424, second column, second paragraph). Does it mean animal snares, or something else? (It means "things" as in "all my gear" or "all my belongings.") How do you know? (Context. It clearly means everything he has with him, none of which includes a snare or animal trap.)

CLOSURE

Call students' attention to the lithograph on page 429, which continues the story. Then have students form pairs and briefly explain to each other why it would be right to say that (a) Huck's meeting up with Jim is the most important of the many events of these chapters, and (b) the ending clearly sets the stage for adventures to come.

READING CHECK TEST

1. Huck's father returned in order to give Huck money. *False*
2. Judge Thatcher took Huck away from Pap and gave him to a guardian. *True*
3. When Pap got drunk, he usually started to complain about the government. *True*
4. As part of his deception, Huck bashed the door of his cabin with an axe. *True*
5. Huck acquired his name because he survived mainly on huckleberries while on Jackson's Island. *False*

A. Dialect

In an explanatory note at the beginning of *Huckleberry Finn,* Twain lists seven dialects he specifically reproduces in the book, lest readers "suppose that all these characters were trying to talk alike and not succeeding." The Missouri Negro dialect of the time was thicker than that spoken by Huck. You might have students orally translate Jim's words to standard English to be sure they understand the reason for the strange scene illustrated by Kemble—a grown man on his knees before a mere boy. In fairness to Twain, you might also explain that despite this stereotypical portrayal of a slave as overly superstitious, Twain for the most part depicts Jim as a dignified, level-headed man.

laid a man on the ground. It most give me the fantods.[6] He had a blanket around his head, and his head was nearly in the fire. I set there behind a clump of bushes in about six foot of him, and kept my eyes on him steady. It was getting gray daylight now. Pretty soon he gapped and stretched himself and hove off the blanket, and it was Miss Watson's Jim! I bet I was glad to see him. I says:

"Hello, Jim!" and skipped out.

He bounced up and stared at me wild. Then he drops down on his knees, and puts his hands together and says:

A "Doan' hurt me—don't! I hain't ever done no harm to a ghos'. I alwuz liked dead people, en done all I could for 'em. You go en git in de river ag'in, whah you b'longs, en doan' do nuffn to Ole Jim, 'at 'uz alwuz yo' fren'."

Well, I warn't long making him understand I warn't dead. I was ever so glad to see Jim. I warn't lonesome now. I told him I warn't afraid of *him* telling the people where I was. I talked along, but he only set there and looked at me; never said nothing. Then I says:

"It's good daylight. Le's get breakfast. Make up your campfire good."

"What's de use er makin' up de campfire to cook strawbries en sich truck? But you got a gun, hain't you? Den we kin git sumfn better den strawbries."

"Strawberries and such truck," I says. "Is that what you live on?"

"I couldn't git nuffn else," he says.

"Why, how long you been on the island, Jim?"

"I come heah de night arter you's killed."

"What, all that time?"

"Yes-indeedy."

"And ain't you had nothing but that kind of rubbage to eat?"

"No, sah—nuffn else."

"Well, you must be most starved, ain't you?"

"I reck'n I could eat a hoss. I think I could. How long you ben on de islan'?"

"Since the night I got killed."

"No! W'y, what has you lived on? But you got a gun. Oh, yes, you got a gun. Dat's good. Now you kill sumfn en I'll make up de fire."

So we went over to where the canoe was, and while he built a fire in a grassy open place amongst the trees, I fetched meal and bacon and coffee, and coffee pot and frying pan, and sugar and tin cups. . . . I catched a good big catfish, too, and Jim cleaned him with his knife, and fried him.

When breakfast was ready we lolled on the grass and eat it smoking hot. Jim laid it in with all his might, for he was most about starved. Then when we had got pretty well stuffed, we laid off and lazied.

By and by Jim says:

"But looky here, Huck, who wuz it dat 'uz killed in dat shanty ef it warn't you?"

Then I told him the whole thing, and he said it was smart. He said Tom Sawyer couldn't get up no better plan than what I had. Then I says:

"How do you come to be here, Jim, and how'd you get here?"

He looked pretty uneasy, and didn't say nothing for a minute. Then he says:

"Maybe I better not tell."

"Why, Jim?"

"Well, dey's reasons. But you wouldn't tell on me ef I 'uz to tell you, would you, Huck?"

"Blamed if I would, Jim."

"Well, I b'lieve you, Huck I—I *run off.*"

"Jim!"

"But mind, you said you wouldn' tell—you know you said you wouldn' tell, Huck."

"Well, I did. I said I wouldn't, and I'll stick to it. Honest *injun,* I will. People would call me a low-down Abolitionist and despise me for keeping mum—but that don't make no difference. I ain't a-going to tell, and I ain't a-going back there, anyways. So, now, le's know all about it." . . .

6. **fantods:** anxiety attacks.

ANALYZING THE STORY

Identifying Facts

1. Huck's father wants him to stop attending school. He abducts Huck in order to ensure that he can control him.

2. Pap locks up the boy and leaves him alone for long periods.

On the one hand, Huck is relieved not to have to go to school and to be subject to the widow's discipline. On the other hand, he is often lonely and terrified of his father, who often beats him in his drunken rages.

3. Huck fools Pap by sawing though a log in the cabin and crawling through the hole to liberty. He collects all the goods that are worth taking from the cabin and carries them to a canoe that he has found and hidden on the river. He shoots a wild pig and uses its blood to stage a "murder scene," so that Pap and others will believe that Huck has been killed; he also creates a false trail with a sack of meal, so that those who hunt for the robbers will be misled.

He hides on Jackson's Island.

4. Jim is hiding there as a runaway slave.

Huck promises Jim that he will not betray his whereabouts.

A Comment on the Novel

"*The Adventures of Huckleberry Finn* has so much about it that is hilarious or idyllic that our attention is easily diverted from the spill of blood that seeps through its pages, giving them a large part of their meaning. Life on the Mississippi around 1845 could be gory: Twain based the novel largely on experiences he himself had undergone as a boy or had known intimately of, and had never quite got over. We are often disinclined to consider how peaceful and restricted, aside from television, is the average recent American childhood compared to childhoods of other times and of other places today. Many people have become adults without ever having seen 'live' a human being killed. Plenty of boys have never looked at a corpse, and very few of them have witnessed a murder.

"Things were different with young Clemens and thus with Huck. The difference is profoundly important to the novel. Sam often looked hard at slaves chained together flat on the dirt in the baking summer sun, awaiting shipment to the market. He was a boy in Hannibal during a time when that town was terrorized by a lynching, murderous gang ludicrously called 'The Black Avengers of the Spanish Main.' A cave near Hannibal contained as a public amusement the body of a young girl preserved in alcohol; it was arranged so that one could seize the corpse by the hair, and drag it to the surface in order to study the face. When he was ten years old the boy saw a man take a lump of iron and crush a Negro's skull with it. . . . On another occasion he was playing near the spot where a runaway slave had drowned days before, and by accident he jarred loose the body, which had not been located, but which now popped up at him headfirst half out of the water, and seemed certainly to be chasing him as he fled. He watched knife fights in Hannibal, and at the end of one of them the loser fell dead at the feet of the boy who had wormed his way in for a good look. He was also witness, at noon on Main Street, to the murder of a man named Smarr. Kind persons placed a large Bible on the chest of the dying man. As he wrote years later, Sam 'gasped and struggled for breath under the crush of that vast book for many a night.'

" . . . Of the shocks young Clemens was exposed to as a boy, many others found their way, years later, into the novel. These facts help explain what might otherwise seem a very curious thing: That with no exceptions but the rather irrelevant Tom Sawyer scenes which open and close *Huckleberry Finn,* every major episode in the novel ends in violence, in physical brutality, and usually in death. All along the way there is bloodshed and pain. There are thirteen separate corpses. All this despite the fact that Twain, in planning his book, made many notes for similar episodes which he did not use. . . .

"The aspect of these brutal episodes that is most relevant to the main plot of a boy going down a river on a raft is quite simply this: They serve to *wound* him. His experience of violence has made him sick. Innumerable readers have tried it, but the plain truth is that Huckleberry Finn, boy or book, cannot really be understood without this clear perception. *Now* we may look at what has happened to this uncomplicated 'child of nature.' He may be still 'unspoiled,' but from having been knocked about so much he is very bruised. Better he had never come ashore that night to see such things, but he came. Now exposed to more bloodshed, drowning, and sudden death than he can handle, he is himself their casualty. And Twain—working from his own bitter experience—could predict with unhappy confidence: He isn't ever going to get shut of them. Lots of times he dreams about them.

"There are other things besides bad dreams which interfere with Huck's peace. Among them are a very active mind which he cannot put to rest, and a growing bitterness about human nature. He cannot sleep, he tells us: 'I couldn't, somehow, for thinking.' His encounter with the frauds called the Duke and the Dauphin is supposed to be funny. But Huck is not amused; they disgust him with mankind in general. He is wounded, and bitter, and suffering from both insomnia and nightmare, and he rebels. His rebellion brings about the crisis of the novel when he, utterly perplexed and sickened by his experiences, tries to decide whether he will steal a poor old woman's slave or protect him. He is all conflict, and tries to pray, but the words won't come. Finally, tortured, he decides. He will protect the slave, although to him this means taking up wickedness again, and eternal punishment in the hereafter. He has deserted the values of the society of his time.

"This is of course his second desertion, really. Completely dissatisfied with his pious foster mother and the effeminate respectability which surrounded her, he had already run away from St. Petersburg. Now, off on his own, and exposed to the violence and evil of society as a whole, he renounces it. He goes on now outside its ways. If it is good, he is wicked. And if it aims for heaven, he will go elsewhere."

—from *"Huckleberry Finn:* The Little Lower Layer,"
Philip Young

Interpreting Meanings

5. The language reveals that Huck feels disgust for his father's appearance.

Students will generally agree that Pap looks and behaves like a cruel, dissolute character.

6. The new judge believes that he can make a man of Pap and reform him. He gives Pap new clothes, feeds him, lodges him in his own house, and lectures him on temperance. In an emotional scene, Pap promises that he will turn over a new leaf. That night, however, Pap escapes from his room, trades his new coat for some liquor, and gets "drunk as a fiddler." The new judge says that he reckons that the only way Pap can be reformed is with a shotgun.

Pap's "change of heart" lasts for barely a day, rather than a lifetime.

7. Student answers will vary. On the one hand, Huck is practical and observant,

(Answers continue top of page 428.)

(Answers begin top of page 427.) cleverly evading his pursuers. On the other hand, he uses a variety of poetic phrases to describe his surroundings. Some of the phrases that students may single out include "Everything was dead quiet and it looked late, and it *smelt* late"; "The sky looks ever so deep when you lay down on your back in the moonshine; I never knowed it before"; "There was freckled places on the ground where the light sifted down through the leaves. . . ."

8. Although Huck is forced to rely entirely on himself, he is now free and uninhibited, either by the widow's efforts to educate him or by Pap's cruelty. His clever strategies to conceal himself and avoid discovery mingle with his wonder at nature to establish an exciting, optimistic tone.

9. Huck's simulation of his own death is readily apparent in the trick which he uses to fool Pap and get away. He is symbolically reborn on the river, where he throws off the "bonds" of discipline and control—both good (the widow) and bad (Pap).

10. Student answers will vary. Pap's drunkenness and cruelty to Huck are

Responding to the Story

Analyzing the Story

Identifying Facts

1. In the opening scene, explain what Huck's father wants. Why does he abduct Huck?
2. Describe how Pap treats Huck at the old cabin. What are Huck's mixed feelings about life with Pap and the widow at this point in the story?
3. Describe the strategy Huck devises to escape from Pap. Where does Huck hide from his pursuers?
4. What had brought Jim to the island? Explain what it is that Huck promises Jim.

Interpreting Meanings

5. What do the **images** and **figures of speech** used to describe Pap in the passage beginning "He was most fifty" on page 414 reveal about Huck's feelings for his father? How would you **characterize** Pap?
6. What is **ironic** about the episode involving Pap and the new judge? What is ironic about the title "Pap Starts in on a New Life"?
7. As Huck tells us about his first few days on the island, his language blends the colloquial with the poetic. From the way he describes river, woods, and sky, in this and other passages, how do you think Huck feels toward his natural surroundings? What details support your interpretation?
8. From what you have seen so far, how do Huck's first days on the river contrast with the life he knew with the widow and with Pap?
9. Explain how this part of the novel **symbolically** describes Huck's "death" and subsequent "rebirth." In being "reborn," what "bonds" or "chains" has he thrown off?
10. Identify several scenes in this excerpt that might easily have been used as the basis for tragedy. What devices does Mark Twain use to establish and consistently maintain a **comic tone** in this excerpt?
11. Explain how the characters and events in this part of Huck's story are relevant to contemporary life. If any events in the chapters you've just read could not happen today, explain the broad ways in which they may still be relevant.

Writing About the Story

A Creative Response

1. **Imitating a Writer's Technique.** In a paragraph, describe a character in such a way as to reveal the way you feel about him or her. Imitate the description of Pap on page 414, and describe hair, eyes, color, face, and clothes.
2. **Writing a Journal Entry.** Suppose Huck Finn lives to be a very old man and writes his reflections on his escape from the clutches of his pathetically ill father. (See Twain's comment in "Primary Sources," page 429.) Write the journal entry as Huck might write it, using Huck's voice, just as Twain did, and identifying the time and place when the entry is recorded. Try to characterize Huck in his old age.

A Critical Response

3. **Responding to a Critic.** Reread the "Comment on the Novel" by Philip Young on page 427. Then, in a short essay, respond to Young's comment by referring to the excerpt from *The Adventures of Huckleberry Finn.* In your opinion, is Young correct when he claims that repeated exposures to violence, injustice, and brutality "wound" young Huck? What passages in this extract from the novel might be used either to support or to refute this claim?
4. **Analyzing the Selection.** In a brief essay, explain why this novel can be called realistic. Include in your essay an explanation of how the story would have to change, or end, if it were told by an earlier Romantic writer. What do you think a Romantic like Washington Irving (page 123) would have done with Huck's problems with Pap and his escape to the river?
5. **Evaluating "Voice."** If Huck had been ten years older when he experienced these adventures, what elements in the narrator's "voice" do you think Twain might have altered? Evaluate the "voice" used in the novel in a brief essay.

Analyzing Language and Style

Descriptive Language

In a marvelously ironic passage, Huck laments his limited use of language:

> Everything was dead quiet, and it looked late, and *smelt* late. You know what I mean—I don't know the words to put it in.

Which detail in this very passage indicates that Huck did, in fact, know exactly the words "to put it in"?

Find at least five other passages from these chapters that show how Huck was capable of poetic language—of descriptive details, in particular. Look particularly for **imagery** that attaches to some sensory experience: to sight, hearing, smell, taste, or feeling.

minimized by Twain. But he blends realism with comic detachment by exaggerating Pap's rantings, by inserting the ironic episode of the new judge and showing the judge's naivete, and by making Huck more than a match for Pap. Similarly, Huck's loneliness and desperation are realistically portrayed, but are offset by his spirit of adventure, his practicality, and Twain's descriptions of the river's beauty. The plan with which Huck outwits Pap and the pursuers is somewhat grotesque, in that the boy stages his own "death"; the reader, on the other hand, is brought to sympathize with the boy and to applaud his ingenuity. Toward the end, the ironically comic scene in which Huck and Jim, both scared to death, are reunited helps to distract the reader's attention from Jim's life-and-death situation as a runaway slave. Encourage students to offer other suggestions on Twain's tone in this selection.

11. Students will have various answers. It would be hard to imagine certain aspects of the tale today: for example, those parts of the story dealing with the river, with the custody of a minor child, or with slavery. On the other hand, some key aspects of Twain's story remain broadly relevant, such as the motifs of child abuse and alcoholism. On the thematic level, Huck's struggle to break away from restraints and to achieve freedom is probably part of every child's psychological make-up at a certain stage.

Primary Sources
The "Original" Huckleberry Finn

In his autobiography, Twain remarks that he received a letter from a man from Hannibal who wanted to know if his brother was really the original of Huckleberry Finn. Here is Twain's reply.

"I have replied that Huckleberry Finn was Tom Blankenship. As this writer evidently knew the Hannibal of the 'forties, he will easily recall Tom Blankenship. Tom's father was at one time Town Drunkard, an exceedingly well-defined and unofficial office of those days. He succeeded General——(I forget the General's name) and for a time he was sole and only incumbent of the office; but afterward Jimmy Finn proved competency and disputed the place with him, so we had two town drunkards at one time—and it made as much trouble in that village as Christendom experienced in the fourteenth century, when there were two Popes at the same time.

"In *Huckleberry Finn* I have drawn Tom Blankenship exactly as he was. He was ignorant, unwashed, insufficiently fed; but he had as good a heart as ever any boy had. His liberties were totally unrestricted. He was the only really independent person—boy or man—in the community, and by consequence he was tranquilly and continuously happy and was envied by all the rest of us. We liked him; we enjoyed his society. And as his society was forbidden us by our parents, the prohibition trebled and quadrupled its value, and therefore we sought and got more of his society than of any other boy's. I heard, four years ago, that he was justice of the peace in a remote village in Montana and was a good citizen and greatly respected."

—from *The Autobiography of Mark Twain*, Samuel Clemens

Huckleberry Finn and Jim by Thomas Hart Benton. Lithograph.

The Nelson-Atkins Museum, Kansas City, Missouri. Gift of Mrs. Peter T. Bohan.

A. Expansion
For information about the battle of Shiloh, see the Humanities Connection annotation, page 375.

B. Humanities Connection: Responding to the Photograph
? Having read the biography of Bierce, tell what aspects of his life you think this pose illustrates. Is there anything about Bierce that doesn't appear to fit the man in the picture? (Answers will vary.)

Ambrose Bierce (1842–1914?)

The belief that life will prove gratifying and will reward our virtues is so strong that it has become a main current in storytelling. But this romantic notion has its inevitable counterpart in realism and naturalism—fiction which conforms to the truth as seen, rather than as we would like it to be.

"Telling it like it is," as latter-day reporters put it, is a powerful force in American literature, and nowhere is it more evident than in our fiction about wartime.

Ambrose Bierce infused his writing with an attitude of scorn for all our sentimental illusions. His dark vision of life centers on warfare and the cruel joke it plays on humanity. This vision assures Bierce's place in our literary history.

Bierce was born in 1842, youngest of ten children in the family of an eccentric and unsuccessful farmer named Marcus Aurelius Bierce. The Bierces lived in a log cabin in Meigs County, Ohio, where Marcus's small library provided Ambrose with his principal means of education. Aside from a year at a Kentucky military academy, he never went to school, and his reticence about his humble origins leaves us scant knowledge of his life prior to the Civil War.

At nineteen, Bierce volunteered for the Ninth Indiana Infantry and saw action at the bloody
A battles of Shiloh and Chickamauga. He was severely wounded at Kenesaw Mountain and cited for bravery no fewer than fifteen times on General Sherman's march to the sea in 1864. Bierce found comfort in the army's well-defined purpose and code of behavior, and at the war's end he reenlisted.

Several years in the peacetime army left Bierce discouraged about his prospects. He left the army and joined his brother Albert to work at the United States Mint in San Francisco. He began to contribute short pieces to the city's weeklies, the *Argonaut* and the *Newsletter.* These efforts revealed a caustic wit and a delight in satirizing human follies. Bierce found plenty of targets in a postwar America that, in a rush for profit, had forgotten the ideals for which the war had been fought.

B

A growing reputation as a muckraking reporter brought him the editorship of the *Newsletter* and the acquaintance of the literary community, including Bret Harte and Mark Twain. When the financier Collis P. Huntington, head of the Southern Pacific Railroad, asked Bierce's price for silence on the railroad's tax fraud case, Bierce is said to have replied: "My price is about seventy-five million dollars, to be handed to the Treasurer of the United States." Bierce's disillusionment with the deceit and greed of his times continued to spur his pen and earned him the nickname "Bitter Bierce."

On Christmas, 1871, he married Mary Day of San Francisco; within a few months they moved to England, where Bierce spent the next four years editing and contributing to humor magazines and starting to write fiction. On his return to San Francisco in 1876 he wrote a regular column, "Prattler," which offered an assortment of reviews, commentary of every sort, and his first short stories.

This was the most active and fruitful time of Bierce's life. He became the witty scholar and literary dictator of the West Coast, but he never achieved wide recognition for his stories.

Supplementary Support Materials
1. Vocabulary Activity Worksheet (*CCB*)
2. Review and Response Worksheet: Point of View (*CCB*)
3. Language Skills Worksheet: Misplaced and Dangling Modifiers (*CCB*)
4. Selection Test (*CCB*)

Developing Vocabulary
The following words from the story are tested in the Selection Test. (See also Vocabulary Activity Worksheet.)

traversed	effaced
imperious	oscillation
summarily	preternaturally

Preparation
1. **Establishing a Purpose.** Tell students to imagine the story as a movie. Have them jot down notes on scenes where they would recommend panoramic shots, close-ups, slow motion, or other movie techniques.

2. **Prereading Journal.** In the biography of Bierce on page 430, the authors state that Bierce's "dark vision of life centers on warfare and the cruel joke it plays on humanity." In a journal entry, have students write about the "cruel jokes" of warfare.

A. Title
? The original title of this book was *The Cynic's Word Book.* Judging by the sample entries, which title do you prefer? Or do both titles have merit? Explain your thinking. (Encourage students to defend their responses—or to suggest other titles.)

B. Plot/Setting
? What do you learn about the situation from the first paragraph of the story? (A man is about to be hanged from a railroad bridge by soldiers in the Federal [Union] army. The setting is northern Alabama, sometime during the Civil War.)

A *The Devil's Dictionary,* published in 1906, was more successful. Bierce offered in his "dictionary" a collection of definitions filled with irony and sardonic humor. The book was addressed to "enlightened souls who prefer dry wine to sweet, sense to sentiment, wit to humor, and clean English to slang." He defined war as a "by-product of the arts of peace," and peace as "a period of cheating between two periods of fighting." A cynic was a person who "sees things as they are, not as they ought to be. Hence the custom among the Scythians of putting out a cynic's eyes to improve his vision." Duty was "that which sternly impels us in the direction of profit along the line of desire"; to pray was "to ask that the laws of the universe be annulled in behalf of a single petitioner confessedly unworthy."

In 1913, when Bierce was a lonely and weary old man, he asked his few friends to "forgive him in not perishing where he was." He set off for Mexico to report on, or join in, its revolution. "Goodbye," he wrote. "If you ever hear of my being stood up against a Mexican stone wall and shot to rags please know that I think it a pretty good way to depart this life. It beats old age, disease, or falling down the cellar stairs." No further word was ever heard from him.

AN OCCURRENCE AT OWL CREEK BRIDGE

Bierce's story is set in the deep South during the Civil War. He invites us to sympathize with the hero, a Southerner who has tried to help the Confederate cause, and he portrays the Union side as brutal and treacherous. But the shifting points of view and the elements of fantasy in the story transcend any taking of sides. As you read "An Occurrence at Owl Creek Bridge," you may conclude that the story's interest is really psychological. The horrors of war may serve only as an external setting for the landscape that really interests the writer. That landscape is the inside of the mind of a man condemned to death.

I

A man stood upon a railroad bridge in northern Alabama, looking down into the swift water twenty feet below. The man's hands were behind his back, the wrists bound with a cord. A rope closely encircled his neck. It was attached to a stout cross-timber above his head and the slack fell to the level of his knees. Some loose boards laid upon the sleepers[1] supporting the metals of the railway supplied a footing for him and his executioners—two private soldiers of the Federal army, directed by a sergeant who in civil life may have been a deputy sheriff. At a short remove upon the same temporary platform was an officer in the uniform of his rank, armed. He was a captain. A sentinel at each end of the bridge stood with his rifle in the position known as "support," that is to say, vertical in front of the left shoulder, the hammer resting on the forearm thrown straight across the chest—a formal and unnatural position, enforcing an erect carriage of the body. It did not appear to be the duty of these two men to know what was occurring at the center of the bridge; they merely blockaded the two ends of the foot planking that traversed it.

B Beyond one of the sentinels nobody was in sight; the railroad ran straight away into a forest

1. **sleepers:** pieces of timber which secured railroad tracks.

A. Word Choice

? What effect does the phrase "engaged in being hanged" have on you? Does it trivialize the hanging, making it seem like a business appointment, or does the understatement make the situation seem even crueler? (It is a matter of business to those who are doing the hanging, which makes the act even crueler.)

B. Expansion

The following sentences explain how efficiently this arrangement works. The plank is like a seesaw, evenly balanced by the sergeant and the civilian, until the sergeant steps off and the civilian's end of the plank drops.

C. Description

? Reread the first three paragraphs of the story (through "gentlemen are not excluded" on this page). Can you see how Bierce begins with a tight focus on the man to be hanged, then uses spatial cues ("at a short remove," "at each end of the bridge") to lead your mental eye to a panoramic view of the scene, and finally returns the focus to the man? What details give you an almost photographic idea of the man, the bridge, and the broader scene? (Descriptions of the man, the disposition of the rope, the riverbank, the exact position of the participants and viewers) How could you use a similar approach to describe someone and some place you know about? (Answers will vary. Ask volunteers for examples.)

for a hundred yards, then, curving, was lost to view. Doubtless there was an outpost farther along. The other bank of the stream was open ground—a gentle acclivity topped with a stockade of vertical tree trunks, loopholed for rifles, with a single embrasure through which protruded the muzzle of a brass cannon commanding the bridge. Midway of the slope between bridge and fort were the spectators—a single company of infantry in line, at "parade rest," the butts of the rifles on the ground, the barrels inclining slightly backward against the right shoulder, the hands crossed upon the stock. A lieutenant stood at the right of the line, the point of his sword upon the ground, his left hand resting upon his right. Excepting the group of four at the center of the bridge, not a man moved. The company faced the bridge, staring stonily, motionless. The sentinels, facing the banks of the stream, might have been statues to adorn the bridge. The captain stood with folded arms, silent, observing the work of his subordinates, but making no sign. Death is a dignitary who when he comes announced is to be received with formal manifestations of respect, even by those most familiar with him. In the code of military etiquette silence and fixity are forms of deference.

A The man who was engaged in being hanged was apparently about thirty-five years of age. He was a civilian, if one might judge from his habit, which was that of a planter. His features were good—a straight nose, firm mouth, broad forehead, from which his long, dark hair was combed straight back, falling behind his ears to the collar of his well-fitting frock coat. He wore a mustache and pointed beard, but no whiskers; his eyes were large and dark gray, and had a kindly expression which one would hardly have expected in one whose neck was in the hemp. Evidently this was no vulgar assassin. The liberal military code makes provision for hanging many kinds of persons, and gentlemen are not excluded.

The preparations being complete, the two private soldiers stepped aside and each drew away the plank upon which he had been standing. The sergeant turned to the captain, saluted and placed himself immediately behind that officer, who in B turn moved apart one pace. These movements left the condemned man and the sergeant standing on the two ends of the same plank, which spanned three of the cross-ties of the bridge. The end upon

C

The Red Bridge by Julian Alden Weir (1896). Oil.

The Metropolitan Museum of Art, New York. Gift of Mr. and Mrs. John A. Rutherford, 1914.

Humanities Connection: Responding to the Fine Art
Julian Alden Weir (1852–1919) was born at West Point, where his painter father, Robert Walter Weir, was teaching drawing at the U.S. Military Academy. Julian studied with his father and with a teacher in Paris, becoming one of the earliest American impressionist painters. As a rule, impressionists observed nature closely and painted everyday subjects, but avoided ugly scenes. Together with *Idle Hours* and *The Green Bodice, The Red Bridge* is one of Weir's best-known paintings.

? Imagine that this is the bridge at Owl Creek and that you are one of the soldiers. What kinds of activities might a place like this usually invite? (Fishing, swimming—certainly not an execution)

A. Point of View
The reportorial tone shifts here to the bemused psychological state of the prisoner as he calmly observes the proceedings.
? How slowly or rapidly does time move for the man? Do his senses seem dulled or sharpened? How do you account for this change? (Time is slower and his senses are acute—a state often reported by people at points of crisis.) What details of the paragraph on the metallic sound especially struck you? Did you identify the source of the sound before the man did? Did the ticking really slow down, or were the "delays" a trick of the man's mental state? (The latter; he seems to be feeling so much each millisecond that time is slowed for him.)

B. Flashback
The story breaks abruptly at the end of Part I. Part II is a flashback that explains who the civilian is and how he arrived at his present dire circumstances.

which the civilian stood almost, but not quite, reached a fourth. This plank had been held in place by the weight of the captain; it was now held by that of the sergeant. At a signal from the former the latter would step aside, the plank would tilt and the condemned man go down between two ties. The arrangement commended itself to his judgment as simple and effective. His face had not been covered nor his eyes bandaged. He looked a moment at his "unsteadfast footing," then let his gaze wander to the swirling water of the stream racing madly beneath his feet. A piece of dancing driftwood caught his attention and his eyes followed it down the current. How slowly it appeared to move! What a sluggish stream!

A

He closed his eyes in order to fix his last thoughts upon his wife and children. The water, touched to gold by the early sun, the brooding mists under the banks at some distance down the stream, the fort, the soldiers, the piece of drift—all had distracted him. And now he became conscious of a new disturbance. Striking through the thought of his dear ones was a sound which he could neither ignore nor understand, a sharp, distinct, metallic percussion like the stroke of a blacksmith's hammer upon the anvil; it had the same ringing quality. He wondered what it was, and whether immeasurably distant or near by—it seemed both. Its recurrence was regular, but as slow as the tolling of a death knell. He awaited each stroke with impatience and—he knew not why—apprehension. The intervals of silence grew progressively longer; the delays became maddening. With their greater infrequency the sounds increased in strength and sharpness. They hurt his ear like the thrust of a knife; he feared he would shriek. What he heard was the ticking of his watch.

He unclosed his eyes and saw again the water below him. "If I could free my hands," he thought, "I might throw off the noose and spring into the stream. By diving I could evade the bullets and, swimming vigorously, reach the bank, take to the woods and get away home. My home, thank God, is as yet outside their lines; my wife and little ones are still beyond the invader's farthest advance."

B

As these thoughts, which have here to be set down in words, were flashed into the doomed man's brain rather than evolved from it the captain nodded to the sargeant. The sergeant stepped aside.

II

Peyton Farquhar was a well-to-do planter, of an old and highly respected Alabama family. Being a slave owner and like other slave owners a politician he was naturally an original secessionist and ardently devoted to the Southern cause. Circumstances of an imperious nature, which it is unnecessary to relate here, had prevented him from taking service with the gallant army that had fought the disastrous campaigns ending with the fall of Corinth,[2] and he chafed under the inglorious restraint, longing for the release of his energies, the larger life of the soldier, the opportunity for distinction. That opportunity, he felt, would come, as it comes to all in wartime. Meanwhile he did what he could. No service was too humble for him to perform in aid of the South, no adventure too perilous for him to undertake if consistent with the character of a civilian who was at heart a soldier, and who in good faith and without too much qualification assented to at least a part of the frankly villainous dictum that all is fair in love and war.

One evening while Farquhar and his wife were sitting on a rustic bench near the entrance to his grounds, a gray-clad soldier rode up to the gate and asked for a drink of water. Mrs. Farquhar was only too happy to serve him with her own white hands. While she was fetching the water her husband approached the dusty horseman and inquired eagerly for news from the front.

"The Yanks are repairing the railroads," said the man, "and are getting ready for another advance. They have reached the Owl Creek bridge, put it in order and built a stockade on the north bank. The commandant has issued an order, which is posted everywhere, declaring that any civilian caught interfering with the railroad, its bridges, tunnels, or trains will be summarily hanged. I saw the order."

"How far is it to the Owl Creek bridge?" Farquhar asked.

"About thirty miles."

"Is there no force on this side the creek?"

"Only a picket post half a mile out, on the railroad, and a single sentinel at this end of the bridge."

"Suppose a man—a civilian and student of

2. **Corinth:** General Grant took Corinth, Mississippi, on April 7, 1862, after the Battle of Shiloh.

hanging—should elude the picket post and perhaps get the better of the sentinel,'' said Farquhar, smiling, ''what could he accomplish?''

A The soldier reflected. ''I was there a month ago,'' he replied. ''I observed that the flood of last winter had lodged a great quantity of driftwood against the wooden pier at this end of the bridge. It is now dry and would burn like tow.''

The lady had now brought the water, which the soldier drank. He thanked her ceremoniously, bowed to her husband and rode away. An hour later, after nightfall, he repassed the plantation, going northward in the direction from which he had come. He was a Federal scout.

III

As Peyton Farquhar fell straight downward through the bridge he lost consciousness and was as one already dead. From this state he was awakened—ages later, it seemed to him—by the pain of a sharp pressure upon his throat, followed by a sense of suffocation. Keen, poignant agonies seemed to shoot from his neck downward through every fiber of his body and limbs. These pains appeared to flash along well-defined lines of ramification and to beat with an inconceivably rapid periodicity. They seemed like streams of pulsating fire heating him to an intolerable temperature. As to his head, he was conscious of nothing but a feeling of fullness—of congestion. These sensations were unaccompanied by thought. The intellectual part of his nature was already effaced; he had power only to feel, and feeling was torment. He was conscious of motion. Encompassed in a luminous cloud, of which he was now merely the fiery heart, without material substance, he swung through unthinkable arcs of oscillation, like a vast pendulum. Then all at once, with terrible suddenness, the light about him shot upward with the noise of a loud plash; a frightful roaring was in his ears, and all was cold and dark. The power of thought was restored; he knew that the rope had broken and he had fallen into the stream. There was no additional strangulation; the noose about his neck was already suffocating him and kept the water from his lungs. To die of hanging at the bottom of a river!—the idea seemed to him ludicrous. He opened his eyes in the darkness and saw above him a gleam of light, but how distant, how inaccessible! He was still sinking, for the light became fainter until it was a mere glimmer. Then it began to grow and brighten, and he knew that he was rising toward the surface—knew it with reluctance, for he was now very comfortable. ''To be hanged and drowned,'' he thought, ''that is not so bad; but I do not wish to be shot. No; I will not be shot; that is not fair.''

He was not conscious of an effort, but a sharp pain in his wrist apprised him that he was trying to free his hands. He gave the struggle his attention, as an idler might observe the feat of a juggler, without interest in the outcome. What splendid effort!—what magnificent, what superhuman strength! Ah, that was a fine endeavor! Bravo! The cord fell away; his arms parted and floated upward, the hands dimly seen on each side in the growing light. He watched them with a new interest as first one and then the other pounced upon the noose at his neck. They tore it away and thrust it fiercely aside, its undulations resembling those of a water snake. ''Put it back, put it back!'' He thought he shouted these words to his hands, for the undoing of the noose had been succeeded by the direst pang that he had yet experienced. His neck ached horribly; his brain was on fire; his heart, which had been fluttering faintly, gave a great leap, trying to force itself out at his mouth. His whole body was racked and wrenched with an insupportable anguish! But his disobedient hands gave no heed to the command. They beat the water vigorously with quick, downward strokes, forcing him to the surface. He felt his head emerge; his eyes were blinded by the sunlight; his chest expanded convulsively, and with a supreme and crowning agony his lungs engulfed a great draught of air, which instantly he expelled in a shriek!

He was now in full possession of his physical senses. They were, indeed, preternaturally keen and alert. Something in the awful disturbance of his organic system had so exalted and refined them that they made record of things never before perceived. He felt the ripples upon his face and heard their separate sounds as they struck. He looked at the forest on the bank of the stream, saw the individual trees, the leaves and the veining of each leaf—saw the very insects upon them: the locusts, the brilliant-bodied flies, the gray spiders stretching their webs from twig to twig. He noted the prismatic colors in all the dewdrops upon a million blades of grass. The humming of the gnats that danced above the eddies of the stream, the beating B

A. Plot

? How do these two paragraphs, together with earlier parts of Farquhar's conversation with the soldier in Confederate garb, explain how Farquhar came to be standing on Owl Creek bridge with a rope around his neck? (A Union scout trapped him into attempting to sabotage the position, held by the Union.) What information is left out? (Motivation: Why Farquhar? Was he a leader among the planters? Or did the Union simply want to make an example of someone?)

B. Identifying Details

? What images especially strike you as a good basis for camera close-ups? Could a man, even in such extreme danger, really see all that detail? (Answers will vary.)

CLOSURE

Have students discuss what, if anything, the story has to say about human beings. Does this story belong in the canon of "good literature," or is it a trick story with little or no message?

READING CHECK TEST

1. Farquhar is a Confederate captain who has been captured in a sabotage attempt. *False*
2. Farquhar has been condemned to death by firing squad. *False*
3. Farquhar was entrapped by a Union scout into sabotaging a bridge. *True*
4. In the middle part of the story, Bierce uses flashback to explain why Farquhar is being executed. *True*
5. While waiting to be executed, Farquhar is very much disturbed by a sound that turns out to be the ticking of his watch. *True*

A. Identifying Details

Students new to this story are likely first to read Part III as intensely suspenseful action, even if they see Farquhar as incredibly lucky. ? Locate the single earlier paragraph which summarizes all of Part III except the final sentence. (The final paragraph of Part I, the end of column 1 on page 434.) Can you identify a whole series of odd details you at first took as simply indicative of Farquhar's mental state, but which you now see as clues to the fantasy nature of the episode? (A partial list: the rope's breaking in the first place, Farquhar's preternaturally sharp senses, the soldiers' poor marksmanship, a civilian's ability accurately to predict every military move, a cannon's not injuring Farquhar, the "giant garden plants" he sees when he comes ashore, the unfamiliarity of the landscape, road, and stars)

of the dragonflies' wings, the strokes of the water spiders' legs, like oars which had lifted their boat—all these made audible music. A fish slid along beneath his eyes and he heard the rush of its body parting the water.

He had come to the surface facing down the stream; in a moment the visible world seemed to wheel slowly round, himself the pivotal point, and he saw the bridge, the fort, the soldiers upon the bridge, the captain, the sergeant, the two privates, his executioners. They were in silhouette against the blue sky. They shouted and gesticulated, pointing at him. The captain had drawn his pistol, but did not fire; the others were unarmed. Their movements were grotesque and horrible, their forms gigantic.

Suddenly he heard a sharp report and something struck the water smartly within a few inches of his head, spattering his face with spray. He heard a second report, and saw one of the sentinels with his rifle at his shoulder, a light cloud of blue smoke rising from the muzzle. The man in the water saw the eye of the man on the bridge gazing into his own through the sights of the rifle. He observed that it was a gray eye and remembered having read that gray eyes were keenest, and that all famous marksmen had them. Nevertheless, this one had missed.

A counter-swirl had caught Farquhar and turned him half round; he was again looking into the forest on the bank opposite the fort. The sound of a clear, high voice in a monotonous singsong now rang out behind him and came across the water with a distinctness that pierced and subdued all other sounds, even the beating of the ripples in his ears. Although no soldier, he had frequented camps enough to know the dread significance of that deliberate, drawling, aspirated chant; the lieutenant on shore was taking a part in the morning's work. How coldly and pitilessly—with what an even, calm intonation, presaging, and enforcing tranquility in the men—with what accurately measured intervals fell those cruel words:

"Attention, company! . . . Shoulder arms! . . . Ready! . . . Aim! . . . Fire!"

Farquhar dived—dived as deeply as he could. The water roared in his ears like the voice of Niagara, yet he heard the dulled thunder of the volley and, rising again toward the surface, met shining bits of metal, singularly flattened, oscillating slowly downward. Some of them touched him on the face and hands, then fell away, continuing their descent. One lodged between his collar and neck; it was uncomfortably warm and he snatched it out.

As he rose to the surface, gasping for breath, he saw that he had been a long time under water; he was perceptibly farther down stream—nearer to safety. The soldiers had almost finished reloading; the metal ramrods flashed all at once in the sunshine as they were drawn from the barrels, turned in the air, and thrust into their sockets. The two sentinels fired again, independently and ineffectually.

The hunted man saw all this over his shoulder; he was now swimming vigorously with the current. His brain was as energetic as his arms and legs; he thought with the rapidity of lightning.

"The officer," he reasoned, "will not make this martinet's[3] error a second time. It is as easy to dodge a volley as a single shot. He has probably already given the command to fire at will. God help me, I cannot dodge them all!"

An appalling plash within two yards of him was followed by a loud, rushing sound, *diminuendo,*[4] which seemed to travel back through the air to the fort and died in an explosion which stirred the very river to its deeps! A rising sheet of water curved over him, fell down upon him, blinded him, strangled him! The cannon had taken a hand in the game. As he shook his head free from the commotion of the smitten water he heard the deflected shot humming through the air ahead, and in an instant it was cracking and smashing the branches in the forest beyond.

"They will not do that again," he thought; "the next time they will use a charge of grape.[5] I must keep an eye upon the gun; the smoke will apprise me—the report arrives too late; it lags behind the missile. That is a good gun."

Suddenly he felt himself whirled round and round—spinning like a top. The water, the banks, the forests, the now distant bridge, fort and men—all were commingled and blurred. Objects were represented by their colors only; circular horizontal streaks of color—that was all he saw. He had been caught in a vortex and was being whirled on with a velocity of advance and gyration that made him giddy and sick. In a few moments he was flung upon the gravel at the foot of the left bank

3. **martinet** (mär·t'n·et'): a strict military disciplinarian.
4. ***diminuendo*** (də·min·yo͞o·wen'dō): decreasing in loudness.
5. **a charge of grape:** a cannon charge of small iron balls, called grapeshot.

A

ANALYZING THE STORY
Identifying Facts
1. Probably only several seconds elapse between the time that Farquhar falls through the bridge and his actual death.
2. The story is set during the Civil War. Soldiers surround a prisoner on a railroad bridge in northern Alabama. Spectators line one bank of the river which is spanned by the bridge. Peyton Farquhar, the prisoner, is about to be hanged.
3. He thinks of his wife and children.

Farquhar hears a sharp, regular percussion like the sound of a blacksmith's anvil. The sound turns out to be the ticking of his watch in the silence just before the signal is given for the hanging.
4. A gray-clad soldier visits Farquhar at his plantation. The soldier tells him that the Union forces have repaired Owl Creek Bridge, and have issued an order that provides that anyone caught interfering with the bridge will be summarily hanged.

Eager to serve the Confederate cause, Farquhar decides to try to elude the guards and burn the bridge.
5. Farquhar imagines that he falls into the river with the noose around his neck, frees his hands, and swims underwater to evade the soldier's bullets. Some distance downstream, he reaches the river bank. He travels through a forest all day and all night to reach the front gate of his own house the next morning. He stretches out his arms to embrace his wife, who is awaiting him.

Farquhar is hanged.

Interpreting Meanings
6. Student answers will vary. The story shows that, despite Farquhar's apparent calm, the unconscious terror of death has the effect of heightening his sense perceptions and of distorting time and distance. The story also shows that at the moment of death we may be prompted to fix our thoughts on those who are dearest to us. Ask students to defend their evaluations of these psychological points.
7. Bierce uses third-person limited point of view, recounting the events as they are *(Answers continue top of page 438.)*

of the stream—the southern bank—and behind a projecting point which concealed him from his enemies. The sudden arrest of his motion, the abrasion of one of his hands on the gravel, restored him, and he wept with delight. He dug his fingers into the sand, threw it over himself in handfuls and audibly blessed it. It looked like diamonds, rubies, emeralds; he could think of nothing beautiful which it did not resemble. The trees upon the bank were giant garden plants; he noted a definite order in their arrangement, inhaled the fragrance of their blooms. A strange, roseate light shone through the spaces among their trunks and the wind made in their branches the music of aeolian harps.[6] He had no wish to perfect his escape—was content to remain in that enchanting spot until retaken.

A whiz and rattle of grapeshot among the branches high above his head roused him from his dream. The baffled cannoneer had fired him a random farewell. He sprang to his feet, rushed up the sloping bank, and plunged into the forest.

All that day he traveled, laying his course by the rounding sun. The forest seemed interminable; nowhere did he discover a break in it, not even a woodsman's road. He had not known that he lived in so wild a region. There was something uncanny in the revelation.

By nightfall he was fatigued, footsore, famishing. The thought of his wife and children urged him on. At last he found a road which led him in what he knew to be the right direction. It was as wide and straight as a city street, yet it seemed untraveled. No fields bordered it, no dwelling anywhere. Not so much as the barking of a dog suggested human habitation. The black bodies of the trees formed a straight wall on both sides, terminating on the horizon in a point, like a diagram in a lesson in perspective. Overhead, as he looked up through this rift in the wood, shone great golden stars looking unfamiliar and grouped in strange constellations. He was sure they were arranged in some order which had a secret and malign significance. The wood on either side was full of singular noises, among which—once, twice, and again—he distinctly heard whispers in an unknown tongue.

His neck was in pain and lifting his hand to it he found it horribly swollen. He knew that it had a circle of black where the rope had bruised it. His eyes felt congested; he could no longer close them. His tongue was swollen with thirst; he relieved its fever by thrusting it forward from between his teeth into the cold air. How softly the turf had carpeted the untraveled avenue—he could no longer feel the roadway beneath his feet!

Doubtless, despite his suffering, he had fallen asleep while walking, for now he sees another scene—perhaps he has merely recovered from a delirium. He stands at the gate of his own home. All is as he left it, and all bright and beautiful in the morning sunshine. He must have traveled the entire night. As he pushes open the gate and passes up the wide white walk, he sees a flutter of female garments; his wife, looking fresh and cool and sweet, steps down from the veranda to meet him. At the bottom of the steps she stands waiting, with a smile of ineffable joy, an attitude of matchless grace and dignity. Ah, how beautiful she is! He springs forward with extended arms. As he is about to clasp her he feels a stunning blow upon the back of the neck; a blinding white light blazes all about him with a sound like the shock of a cannon—then all is darkness and silence!

Peyton Farquhar was dead; his body, with a broken neck, swung gently from side to side beneath the timbers of the Owl Creek bridge.

6. **aeolian harps:** stringed instruments that are played by the wind. Aeolus was the king of the winds in Greek mythology.

(Answers begin top of page 437.)
seen by Farquhar in his imagination.

Bierce refers several times to the pain in Farquhar's neck and his sense of suffocation. The heightening of sensory details, like the unfamiliar stars and singular noises in the forest, also suggests an unreal, dream-like atmosphere.

8. Student answers will vary. Most students will probably call the end shocking, even though they may have suspected that Farquhar was only imagining his escape.

Student answers will vary.

9. Again, students will have different opinions. The description of Farquhar's gentlemanly bearing and the account of the Union soldier's trick both prejudice the reader somewhat toward the Confederate side. On the other hand, Bierce's ironic comment about the "liberal military code" suggests that he thinks war is brutal.

10. The story opens with a "close-up" shot of Peyton Farquhar. Bierce then uses a "group shot" to show the two ends of the railroad bridge. A "panoramic shot" describes the spectators of the execution in the second paragraph. Another *(Answers continue in left-hand column.)*

(Cont. from top.) "close-up" in the third paragraph gives a physical description of Farquhar. "Slowed motion" appears in Farquhar's hearing the ticking sound of his own watch in Part I and in the fantasy of Part II, while "fast motion" frames Part III in the description of the falling body and Farquhar's death of a broken neck. Much of Part III consists of "dream sequences," while "sound effects" are used in the ticking of the watch and in the reports of the rifles of the soldiers. Encourage students to discuss their movie adaptations in detail.

Responding to the Story

Analyzing the Story

Identifying Facts

1. How much time actually elapses between the opening and closing lines of Part III?
2. Describe the **setting** at the opening of the story. What is Peyton Farquhar's situation?
3. Describe Farquhar's last thoughts. Identify and describe the sound that disturbs the thoughts going through his mind.
4. In the **flashback** of the story's second section, who visits Peyton Farquhar? What plan does Farquhar conceive as a result of this visit?
5. What does Farquhar imagine in the story's last section? Ironically, what is his real fate?

Interpreting Meanings

6. Summarize what you think this story reveals about the psychology of a person facing death. Do you find the psychology believable? Explain.
7. The third part of the story, which occurs within the few seconds before Farquhar dies, is presumably a fantasy. What **point of view** does the writer use here? How does Bierce prepare us for the final outcome of the story?
8. When you discovered Farquhar had not actually escaped but had only imagined it, what were your own emotions? Did you feel that this outcome was more credible and more powerful than the one you had been led to anticipate? Or did you feel cheated by the surprise ending? Explain your response.
9. Do you think the writer tries to enlist your sympathies toward either the Union or the Confederate side? Or does the story seem to be focused on a more general **theme** about the nature of the war? Cite details from the story to support your response.
10. Review the story closely and comment on how Bierce has used a cinematic style, including the following techniques:

    a. close-up shots
    b. group shots
    c. panoramic shots
    d. fast motion
    e. slowed motion
    f. dream sequences
    g. sound effects
    h. quick cuts
    i. moving camera shots

    Discuss how you think the story might be adapted into a movie.

Writing About the Story

A Creative Response

1. **Imitating a Technique.** An outstanding aspect of Bierce's narrative technique in this story is his ability to "slow time down" as he dramatizes, almost second by second, the thoughts that flash through Farquhar's mind immediately before and after he is hanged. Bierce's technique anticipates, at least to some degree, the more modern mode of narration known as "stream-of-consciousness." Imagine that you, or a character you create, are subjected to an extraordinary crisis or moment of pressure. Define the nature of this pressure in a sentence or two. Then write an account, either in the first or third person, of the thoughts inside your character's mind over a very short period of time. Try to imitate Bierce by making this account as varied and as suspenseful as possible.

A Critical Response

2. **Analyzing Suspense.** Bierce is noted for the surprise endings of many of his stories and for his ability to keep the reader uncertain and tense about the outcome. In a brief essay, explain how Bierce increases the reader's suspense in two different ways in the second and the third parts of this story.
3. **Responding to a Critical Comment.** The following comment on Bierce's story was made by two prominent critics:

> The plot that depends on some peculiarity of human psychology—as does "An Occurrence at Owl Creek Bridge"—may give us a shock of surprise, but it does not carry a fictional meaning. The peculiar quirk of psychology—the "case study"—must also involve some significant human evaluation, some broadening or deepening of our human attitudes, if it is to be acceptable as fiction. Fiction involves all kinds of human characters and human experiences, common and uncommon, but it is concerned to do more than make a clinical report, medical or psychological.
>
> —Cleanth Brooks and Robert Penn Warren

In a brief essay, respond to these critical remarks. If you agree that the story is merely a "case study" in psychology and therefore not true fiction, cite details from the story to support your response. If you feel, on the other hand, that the story uses psychology to reveal something important about character or human nature in general, explain your reasons for holding that opinion.

PREPARATION

1. PREREADING JOURNAL. Have students note in their journals their reactions to the words *Civil War.*

2. ESTABLISHING A PURPOSE. Have students read the headnote. Then, as they read, encourage them to place the accounts in context with what they already know about the Civil War.

SUPPLEMENTARY SUPPORT MATERIALS

1. Vocabulary Activity Worksheet (*CCB*)
2. Review and Response Worksheet: Tone and Style (*CCB*)
3. Language Skills Worksheet: The Narrative Paragraph (*CCB*)
4. Selection Test (*CCB*)

DEVELOPING VOCABULARY

The following words from the excerpts are tested in the Selection Test. (See also Vocabulary Activity Worksheet.)

foreboding	query
impalpable	eloquent
to consecrate	arduous
tumult	fortitude
to implore	to alleviate

VOICES FROM THE CIVIL WAR

There are few literary records of the Civil War, but there are many personal testimonies in the forms of letters, diaries, and memoirs. Some of these were written by well-known figures, but most were the work of ordinary people caught up in the most extraordinary

and painful events in America's history. The following excerpts provide a brief history of the War in the voices of those who experienced it, including an Indiana farm boy, a Southern gentlewoman, Frederick Douglass, President Lincoln, and General Robert E. Lee.

A

FOR FURTHER READING FOR TEACHERS AND STUDENTS

The American Heritage Picture History of the Civil War, edited by Richard M. Ketchum (American Heritage Publishing Co., Inc., 1960); *They Were There: The Civil War in Action as Seen by its Combat Artists,* by Phillip Van Doren Stern (Crown Publishers, Inc., 1959).

A. Humanities Connection: Responding to the Photographs

Photography allowed people who were far from the battlefields to see the stark reality of warfare—captured at the moment by the camera rather than painted (and often glamorized) sometime later.

? How might these photographs dispel glamorous notions about warfare? (They show that soldiers are everyday people rather than idealized heroes; they also suggest the seriousness of war.)

Cross-Curriculum Connection
The first shots of the Civil War were fired at Fort Sumter, a Federal fort, in April 1861. After the fort surrendered, the Confederate flag was raised; it flew over Charleston harbor for most of the war.

A. Responding
? For what do you think Mary Chesnut prayed? (Students may suggest that she prayed for peace, for victory, for the safety of her family and friends.)

B. Humanities Connection: Responding to the Fine Art
Conrad Wise Chapman (1842–1910) is considered one of the principal painters of the Civil War Confederacy. Wounded at Shiloh, he was transferred to Charleston; there he was ordered to illustrate the city's forts and batteries. The resulting paintings, noted for their clear color, contrast, and deep perspective, became important historical documents.
? Is the painting simply a record of the scene, or does it convey a mood? (It suggests loneliness and perhaps uncertainty about the future.)

VOICES FROM THE CIVIL WAR

THE FIRST SHOTS: FORT SUMTER

Mary Chesnut

Mary Boykin Chesnut was the wife of James Chesnut, ex-Senator from South Carolina and aide to Jefferson Davis, President of the Confederacy. During the course of the War, Mary Chesnut traveled from city to city in the South as the capital of the Confederacy was changed. She kept up with the latest war news through her husband and their wide circle of knowledgeable and influential friends. Mary Chesnut was sophisticated, witty, and sensitive. Her diaries present an invaluable firsthand view of the War.

In April of 1861, several months after seven Southern states had formally seceded from the Union, Confederate forces demanded the surrender of the Union garrison on Fort Sumter, located on an island in the harbor of Charleston, South Carolina. Mary Chesnut was in Charleston when, at dawn on the twelfth of April, fighting began.

“APRIL 12, 1861 . . . Yesterday's was the merriest, maddest dinner we have had yet. Men were audaciously wise and witty. We had an unspoken foreboding that it was to be our last pleasant evening. . . .

I do not pretend to go to sleep. How can I? If Anderson [the Federal commander at Fort Sumter] does not accept terms at four, the orders are he shall be fired upon. I count four, St. Michael's bells chime out, and I begin to hope. At half past four the heavy booming of a cannon. A I sprang out of bed, and on my knees prostrate I prayed as I never prayed before.”

—from *A Diary from Dixie* by Mary Chesnut

Mary Boykin Chesnut by Samuel Osgood (1856). Oil.

National Portrait Gallery, Smithsonian Institution, Washington, D.C. On loan from Serena Williams Miles Van Rensselaer.

B

The Flag of Sumter, Oct. 20, 1863 by Conrad Wise Chapman (1864). Oil on board.

The Museum of the Confederacy, Richmond. Photograph, Katherine Wetzel.

VOICES FROM THE CIVIL WAR

Theodore Upson

It is often said that any civil war is a war of brother against brother, but one must think a moment to realize exactly what this meant in nineteenth-century America. America at the time was a mobile society, and many families, especially in the border states, had friends and relatives in both the North and the South. For such families especially the Civil War was a profoundly personal conflict. Here is the response of Theodore Upson, a teen-age farm boy in Indiana, to the news of the attack on Fort Sumter.

"April, 1861

Father and I were husking out some corn. We could not finish before it wintered up. When William Cory came across the field (he had been down after the Mail) he was excited and said, "Jonathan, the Rebs have fired upon and taken Fort Sumter." Father got white and couldn't say a word.

William said, "The President will soon fix them. He has called for 75,000 men and is going to blockade their ports, and just as soon as those fellows find out that the North means business they will get down off their high horse." A

Father said little. We did not finish the corn and drove to the barn. Father left me to unload and put out the team and went to the house. After I had finished I went in to dinner. Mother said, "What is the matter with Father?" He had gone right upstairs. I told her what we had heard. She went to him. After a while they came down. Father looked ten years older. We sat down to the table. Grandma wanted to know what was the trouble. Father told her and she began to cry. "Oh my poor children in the South! Now they will suffer! God knows how they will suffer! I knew it would come! Jonathan, I told you it would come!"

"They can come here and stay," said Father.

"No, they will not do that. There is their home. There they will stay. Oh to think that I should have lived to see the day when Brother should rise against Brother." . . .

Mother had a letter from the Hales. Charlie and his father are in their [i.e., the Confederate] army and Dayton wanted to go but was too young. I wonder if I were in our army and they should meet me would they shoot me. I suppose they would." B

—from *The Blue and the Gray: The Story of the Civil War as Told by Participants* edited by Henry Steele Commager

A. Expansion
Many people believed that this would be a quick conflict. In fact, the Civil War lasted four years and claimed some 618,000 lives, an average of 423 per day—more than were killed in all of America's other wars combined.

B. Writing Assignment
Imagine that you are young Dayton Hale. Write a journal entry for the day you were turned down for the Confederate army. In your entry, refer to your Indiana friend Theodore Upson.

Connections
"A Mystery of Heroism," by Stephen Crane (page 457), also describes the carnage of battle. Both the 1951 film version of Crane's *The Red Badge of Courage,* starring Audie Murphy, and the 1974 television remake, starring Richard Thomas, are well regarded by critics.

A. Expansion
During the war, Whitman estimated, he made more than 600 visits to hospitals and camps and ministered to 100,000 sick and wounded soldiers, Union and Confederate. He nursed the injured, read to them, and distributed small gifts of food, clothing, stamps, and so on. Whitman's prose account of his experiences, *Memoranda During the War,* was privately published many years later and in 1882 was combined with other prose writings in a book called *Specimen Days.* (Another excerpt from *Specimen Days,* which recalls Lincoln's second inauguration and Whitman's thoughts on the "real war," begins on page 350.)

Whitman's experiences convinced him of the horrors of war. In 1863 he wrote, "My opinion is *to stop the war now.*"

VOICES FROM THE CIVIL WAR

VIEWS FROM THE BATTLEFIELD AND THE HOME FRONT

Walt Whitman

The poet Walt Whitman (1819–1892) was too old to fight in the Civil War, but he did volunteer his services as a nurse in army hospitals. (See text page 348 for additional information on Whitman.) Here is Whitman's description of the battle of Chancellorsville. This was one of the bloodiest battles of the War, the one that Stephen Crane depicted in his novel **The Red Badge of Courage.**

A NIGHT BATTLE, OVER A WEEK SINCE

"MAY 12, 1863—There was part of the late battle at Chancellorsville (second Fredericksburgh) a little over a week ago, Saturday, Saturday night and Sunday, under Gen. Joe Hooker, I would like to give just a glimpse of—(a moment's look in a terrible storm at sea—of which a few suggestions are enough, and full details impossible). The fighting had been very hot during the day, and after an intermission the latter part was resumed at night and kept up with furious energy till 3 o'clock in the morning. That afternoon (Saturday) an attack sudden and strong by Stonewall Jackson had gain'd a great advantage to the southern army, and broken our lines, entering us like a wedge and leaving things in that position at dark. But Hooker at 11 at night made a desperate push, drove the secesh[1] forces back, restored his original lines, and resumed his plans. This night scrimmage was very exciting and afforded countless strange and fearful pictures. The fighting had been general both at Chancellorsville and northeast at Fredericksburgh. (We hear of some poor fighting, episodes, skedaddling on our part. I think not of it. I think of the fierce bravery, the general rule.) One corps, the 6th, Sedgwick's, fights four dashing and bloody battles in thirty-six hours, retreating in great jeopardy, losing largely but maintaining itself, fighting with the sternest desperation under all circumstances, getting over the Rappahannock only by the skin of its teeth, yet getting over. It lost many, many brave men, yet it took vengeance, ample vengeance.

But it was the tug of Saturday evening, and through the night and Sunday morning, I wanted to make a special note of. It was largely in the woods, and quite a general engagement. The night was very pleasant, at times the moon shining out full and clear, all Nature so calm in itself, the early summer grass so rich, and foliage of the trees—yet there the battle raging, and many good fellows lying helpless, with new accessions to them, and every minute amid the rattle of muskets and crash of cannon (for there was an artillery contest too) the red life blood oozing out from heads or trunks or limbs upon that green and dew-cool grass. Patches of the woods take fire, and several of the wounded, unable to move, are consumed—quite large spaces are swept over, burning the dead also—some of the men have their hair and beards singed—some, burns on their faces and hands—others, holes burnt in their clothing. The flashes of fire from the cannon, the quick flaring flames and smoke, and the immense roar—the musketry so general, the light nearly bright enough for each side to see the other—the crashing, tramping of men—the yelling—close quarters—we hear the secesh yells—our men cheer loudly back, especially if Hooker is in sight—hand to hand conflicts, each side stands up to it, brave, determin'd as demons, they often charge upon us—a thousand deeds are done worth to write newer greater poems on—and still the woods on fire—still many are not only scorch'd—too many, unable to move, are burn'd to death. A

1. **secesh** (sē·sĕsh′): short for secessionist; that is, the Southern states that seceded from the Union.

442

Speech Assignment
One of Whitman's war poems appears on page 348. Have students find additional examples of Whitman's war verse (like "The Wound Dresser," "By the Bivouac's Fitful Flame,"or "Beat! Beat! Drums!") and read them to the class. These poems, originally collected in *Drum-Taps* (1865), were later incorporated into *Leaves of Grass.*

A. Responding
What is your reaction to the scene Whitman describes here? Would a picture provide more vivid testimony, or are Whitman's words vivid enough? (Many students may find Whitman's description quite graphic enough.)

B. Irony
What irony does Nature herself provide on this night? (The "softly, quietly shining" moon, the buoyant sky, and the placid stars provide an ironic contrast to the wild carnage of the scene below.)

C. Expansion/ Writing Assignment
The reading of this letter was one of the most poignant moments in Ken Burns's 1990 PBS documentary *The Civil War*. As a writing assignment, have students write Sarah's response to her husband's letter, either before or after she has learned of his death.

VOICES FROM THE CIVIL WAR

Then the camps of the wounded—O heavens, what scene is this?—is this indeed *humanity*—these butchers' shambles? There are several of them. There they lie, in the largest, in an open space in the woods, from 200 to 300 poor fellows—the groans and screams—the odor of blood, mixed with the fresh scent of the night, the grass, the trees—that slaughterhouse! O well is it their mothers, their sisters cannot see them—cannot conceive, and never conceiv'd, these things. One man is shot by a shell, both in the arm and leg—both are amputated—there lie the rejected members. Some have their legs blown off—some bullets through the breast—some indescribably horrid wounds in the face or head, all mutilated, sickening, torn, gouged out—some in the abdomen—some mere boys—many rebels, badly hurt—they take their regular turns with the rest, just the same as any—the surgeons use them just the same. Such is the camp of the wounded—such a fragment, a reflection afar off of the bloody scene—while over all the clear, large moon comes out at times softly, quietly shining. Amid the woods, that scene of flitting souls—amid the crack and crash and yelling sounds—the impalpable perfume of the woods—and yet the pungent, stifling smoke—the radiance of the moon, looking from heaven at intervals so placid—the sky so heavenly—the clear-obscure up there, those buoyant upper oceans—a few large placid stars beyond, coming silently and languidly out, and then disappearing—the melancholy, draperied night above, around. And there, upon the roads, the fields, and in those woods, that contest, never one more desperate in any age or land—both parties now in force—masses—no fancy battle, no semiplay, but fierce and savage demons fighting there—courage and scorn of death the rule, exceptions almost none. ”

—from *Specimen Days* by Walt Whitman

Major Sullivan Ballou

In July of 1861 Major Ballou wrote to his wife, Sarah, in Rhode Island. One week after he wrote this letter, Major Ballou was killed in the first Battle of Bull Run, Virginia.

“ . . . I have, I know, but few and small claims upon Divine Providence, but something whispers to me—perhaps it is the wafted prayer, of my little Edgar, that I shall return to my loved ones unharmed. If I do not, my dear Sarah, never forget how much I love you, and when my last breath escapes me on the battlefield, it will whisper your name. Forgive my many faults, and the many pains I have caused you. How thoughtless and foolish I have oftentimes been! How gladly would I wash out with my tears every little spot upon your happiness. . . .

But, O Sarah! If the dead can come back to this earth and flit unseen around those they loved, I shall always be near you; in the gladdest days and in the darkest nights . . . *always, always,* and if there be a soft breeze upon your cheek, it shall be my breath, as the cool air fans your throbbing temple, it shall be my spirit passing by. Sarah, do not mourn me dead: think I am gone and wait for thee, for we shall meet again. . . . ”

—from *The Civil War: An Illustrated History* by Geoffrey C. Ward, with Ric Burns and Ken Burns

A. Humanities Connection: Responding to the Fine Art
Peter Frederick Rothermel (1817–1895) was in his day a highly regarded historical painter (see page 89), but his reputation later waned. After the Civil War he was commissioned by the Pennsylvania legislature to do a colossal work on the Battle of Gettysburg. "Pickett's Charge" is a section of that work.

The Battle of Gettysburg, July 1–3, 1863, was the greatest single battle and turning point of the war. The Confederate army was taking a heavy toll, but could not quite smash the Army of the Potomac. Then Major General George Pickett led a force of 15,000 against the main body of Union Troops. The assault did not succeed, and the Confederate army—now one third smaller—retreated. In all, the toll at Gettysburg was 5,660 dead, 27,000 wounded, and 10,500 missing.

? What is your reaction to the scene depicted in the painting? How does it compare with Whitman's battlefield account (page 442)? (Answers will vary; students should find many similarities.)

B. Expansion/ Theme
Most students will know the legend—not the fact—that Lincoln scribbled this speech on the back of an envelope on his way to Gettysburg. When he presented it, the speech disappointed many listeners, who were used to long, flowery orations. Later, however, the speech came to be regarded as a masterpiece.

? What are the main themes of Lincoln's speech? (Respect for the dead; the value of democracy; the need for peace)

C. Style
? What techniques contribute to the overall effect of Lincoln's speech? (Students may cite its rhythmic cadences; its use of parallel structures; its linking of past and present, war and peace; its restrained, dignified language; and its economy of expression.)

Pickett's Charge at the Battle of Gettysburg by Peter F. Rothermel. Oil on canvas. A The State Museum of Pennsylvania, Harrisburg.

B THE GETTYSBURG ADDRESS

Abraham Lincoln

On July 7, 1863, a few days after the Battle of Gettysburg, Lincoln noted in an informal address how important this battle had been, but concluded that he was "not prepared to make [a speech] worthy of the occasion."

Several months later, in November of that year, Lincoln in fact delivered a speech on this theme, perhaps the most memorable of his career, at the dedication of the cemetery at Gettysburg.

"Four score and seven years ago our fathers brought forth on this continent a new nation, conceived in Liberty, and dedicated to the proposition that all men are created equal.

Now we are engaged in a great civil war, testing whether that nation, or any nation so conceived and so dedicated, can long endure. We are met on a great battlefield of that war. We have come to dedicate a portion of that field as a final resting place for those who here gave their lives that that nation might live. It is altogether fitting and proper that we should do this.

But, in a larger sense, we can not dedicate—we can not consecrate—we can not hallow—this ground. The brave men, living and dead, who struggled here, have consecrated it far above our poor power to add or detract. The world will little note nor long remember what we say here, but it can never forget what they did here. It is for us the living, rather, to be dedicated here to the unfinished work which they who fought here have thus far so nobly advanced. It is rather for us to be here dedicated to the great task remaining before us—that from these honored dead we take increased devotion to that cause for which they gave the last full measure of devotion—that we here highly resolve that these dead shall not have died in vain—that this nation, under God, shall have a new birth of freedom—and that government of the people, by the people, for the people, shall not perish from the earth." C

Cross-Curriculum Connection
Stirring patriotic songs like "The Battle Hymn of the Republic" and "The Battle Cry of Freedom" ("We'll rally round the flag; boys, we'll rally once again") were more often sung by people at home. Soldiers at the front preferred sentimental songs like "Just Before the Battle, Mother" or "Somebody's Darling." Many of their songs spoke of yearning for their sweethearts ("The Yellow Rose of Texas"), of loneliness ("All Quiet on the Potomac"), or of homesickness ("Tenting Tonight on the Old Camp Ground").

Recorded collections of Civil War songs are widely available. A PBS documentary, *Songs of the Civil War,* is available as a video, audiocassette, or compact disc.

VOICES FROM THE CIVIL WAR

THE BATTLE HYMN OF THE REPUBLIC

Julia Ward Howe

A *One of the greatest songs to come out of the Civil War was "The Battle Hymn of the Republic," written by Julia Ward Howe, wife of reformer Samuel Gridley Howe and an energetic supporter of abolition and women's rights. The lyrics follow.*

Mine eyes have seen the glory of the coming of the Lord:
He is trampling out the vintage where the grapes of wrath are stored;
He hath loosed the fateful lightning of his terrible swift sword:
His truth is marching on.

I have seen Him in the watch fires of a hundred circling camps;
They have builded Him an altar in the evening dews and damps;
I can read His righteous sentence by the dim and flaring lamps.
His day is marching on.

I have read a fiery gospel writ in burnished rows of steel;
"As ye deal with my contemners, so with you my grace shall deal;
Let the Hero, born of woman, crush the serpent with his heel,
Since God is marching on."

He has sounded forth the trumpet that shall never call retreat;
He is sifting out the hearts of men before his judgment seat:
Oh! be swift, my soul, to answer Him! be jubilant, my feet!
Our God is marching on.

In the beauty of the lilies Christ was born across the sea,
With a glory in His bosom that transfigures you and me:
As He died to make men holy, let us die to make men free,
While God is marching on.

—Julia Ward Howe

B

"THE BATTLE HYMN" IN LIBBY PRISON

Among the singers of the "Battle Hymn" was Chaplain McCabe of the Union Army, who took it to the front and in due time to Libby Prison, whither he was sent after being captured. One night came a rumor of disaster to the Union arms. A great battle, their jailers told them; a great Confederate victory. Sadly the Northern men gathered, talking in low tones. Suddenly, one of the Negroes who brought food for the prisoners whispered that the news was false: there had, indeed, been a great battle, but the Union Army had won.

Like a flame the word flashed through the prison. Men leaped to their feet, shouted, embraced one another in a frenzy of joy and triumph; and Chaplain McCabe, standing in the middle of the room, lifted up his great voice and sang:

"Mine eyes have seen the glory
of the coming of the Lord!"

Every voice took up the chorus, and Libby Prison rang with the shout of "Glory, glory, hallelujah!"

The victory was that of Gettysburg. Some time after, McCabe told in Washington the story of his wartime experiences; and when he came to that night in Libby Prison, he sang the "Battle Hymn" once more. The effect was magical; people shouted, wept, and sang, all together; and when the song was ended, above the tumult of applause was heard the voice of Abraham Lincoln, exclaiming, while the tears rolled down his cheeks—

"Sing it again!"

—from *Julia Ward Howe*
by Laura E. Richards and Maude H. Elliott

A. Expansion
"The Battle Hymn of the Republic" was set to the tune of "John Brown's Body," another Civil War song. The melody, ironically, was that of a Southern camp-meeting hymn.

Howe wrote her lyrics after a visit to a Union camp. She was paid only four dollars for the lyrics by the *Atlantic Monthly.* Much later Howe wrote, "The wild echoes of that fearful struggle have long since died away, and with them all memories of unkindness between ourselves and our Southern brethren. But those who once loved my hymn still sing it. I hope and I believe that it stands for what our whole country now believes in—in the sacredness of human liberty."

B. Interpretation
Have students interpret each stanza in light of what they have learned about the Civil War. (Be prepared to assist students with unfamiliar allusions to the Bible.)

A. Expansion
The regiment was organized in Boston, then a center of abolitionist activity. Their story is also told in the PBS documentary *The Massachusetts 54th Colored Infantry* (part of *The American Experience* series). The unit is further honored by the Shaw Memorial (named for commander, Colonel Robert Gould Shaw), a bronze bas-relief in Boston Common by Augustus Saint-Gaudens (1848–1907).

B. Expansion
Because of Northern racism, Lincoln was not persuaded to send such a regiment into combat until after he issued the Emancipation Proclamation in 1863. Most African American soldiers performed noncombat roles. African Americans did noncombat duty even in the South, and in March 1865 were authorized to serve in the Confederate army—but shortly thereafter the war ended.

VOICES FROM THE CIVIL WAR

Frederick Douglass

The most famous African American spokesman during the Civil War was Frederick Douglass (see page 385). Douglass used all of his eloquence and passionate oratory to persuade African Americans in the North to enlist in the Union Army. Eventually a number of all-black regiments of volunteers were formed and trained. (The 1989 film Glory *re-enacts the tragic exploits of one such regiment.) About 180,000 African Americans enlisted, including two of Douglass's sons.*

The following call to action first appeared in Douglass's own newspaper in March, 1863.

Frederick Douglass by unidentified photographer. Daguerreotype, $3\frac{1}{8}'' \times 2\frac{3}{4}''$, c. 1850. National Portrait Gallery, Smithsonian Institution, Washington, D.C. (NPG.80.21)

"When first the rebel cannon shattered the walls of Sumter and drove away its starving garrison, I predicted that the war then and there inaugurated would not be fought out entirely by white men. Every month's experience during these dreary years has confirmed that opinion. A war undertaken and brazenly carried on for the perpetual enslavement of colored men, calls logically and loudly for colored men to help suppress it. Only a moderate share of sagacity was needed to see that the arm of the slave was the best defense against the arm of the slaveholder. Hence with every reverse to the national arms, with every exulting shout of victory raised by the slaveholding rebels, I have implored the imperiled nation to unchain against her foes her powerful black hand. Slowly and reluctantly that appeal is beginning to be heeded. Stop not now to complain that it was not heeded sooner. It may or it may not have been best that it should not. This is not

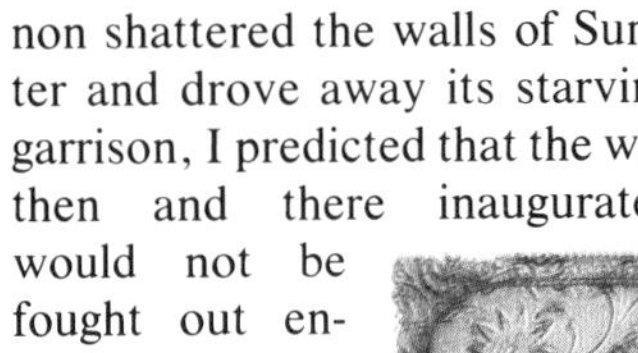

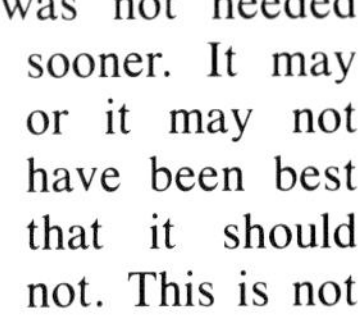

The Provost Guard of the 107th Colored Infantry, one of the regiments assigned to defend Washington, D.C.

Research Projects
Delegate one third of the class to report on the condition and treatment of former slaves in the period immediately following the Civil War. Have another third of the class report on the legal status of African Americans from the end of the Civil War to the civil rights movement of the 1960's. (See "Choice: A Tribute to Dr. Martin Luther King, Jr.," page 1041.) Have the final third group compare the words of Frederick Douglass to some of the speeches of Dr. King.

VOICES FROM THE CIVIL WAR

the time to discuss that question. Leave it to the future. When the war is over, the country is saved, peace is established, and the black man's rights are secured, as they will be, history with an impartial hand will dispose of that and sundry other questions. Action! Action! not criticism, is the plain duty of this hour. Words are now useful only as they stimulate to blows. The office of speech now is only to point out when, where, and how to strike to the best advantage. There is no time to delay. The tide is at its flood that leads on to fortune. From East to West, from North to South, the sky is written all over, "Now or never." Liberty won by white men would lose half its luster. "Who would be free themselves must strike the blow." "Better even die free, than to live slaves." This is the sentiment of every brave colored man amongst us. ❞

—from *Life and Times of Frederick Douglass, Written by Himself*

The following are just a small sample of memorable quotations from Frederick Douglass's speeches and writings.

❝ We are *Americans,* speaking the same language, adopting the same customs, holding the same general opinions . . . and shall rise and fall with Americans.

* * * * *

Once let the black man get upon his person the brass letters "U.S.," let him get an eagle on his buttons and a musket on his shoulder and bullets in his pocket, and there is no power on earth which can deny that he has earned the right to citizenship in the United States. A

* * * * *

The day dawns; the morning star is bright upon the horizon! The iron gate of our prison stands half open. One gallant rush from the North will fling it wide open, while four millions of our brothers and sisters shall march out into liberty. The chance is now given you to end in a day the bondage of centuries, and to rise in one bound from social degradation to the plane of common equality with all other varieties of men. ❞

—from *Life and Times of Frederick Douglass, Written by Himself*

B

Young "Contraband" Jackson (left) joined an African American regiment of the Union Army as a drummer (right).

A. Interpreting
Based on this argument, how do you think Douglass would define the word *citizen*? (As someone who loves his or her country enough to fight for it)

B. Humanities Connection: Responding to the Photographs
Notice the difference in Jackson's attire. Why do you think someone would purposely want to take and display both photographs? (Students should note their propaganda value and how such photographs would have helped the abolitionist cause.)

Expansion
Women on both sides made heroic contributions during the Civil War. Clara Barton (1821–1912), the "Angel of the Battlefield," ministered to the wounded even without official authorization. She eventually was appointed superintendent of nurses with the Army of the James. After the war Barton gathered records on missing Union soldiers and was able to identify many thousands of them, particularly victims of the notorious Andersonville Prison in Georgia. In 1881 Barton founded the American branch of the International Association of the Red Cross.

A. Cross-Curriculum Connection
? Do you think that this is one of the first civil rights demonstrations? Were the soldiers right to insist on full pay? What groups today are still fighting for equal pay? (Answers will vary, though most students probably will agree that the soldiers deserved full pay.)

B. Humanities Connection: About the Fine Art
An annotation on Jacob Lawrence appears on page 691; other paintings appear on pages 387 and 390.

Harriet Tubman (?1821–1913) worked as a field hand until she escaped from slavery about 1849. Soon after, she became a leading figure in the Underground Railroad, which helped slaves escape beyond the reach of the Fugitive Slave Law. During the war she served with the Union forces in South Carolina as a laundress, cook, guide, and spy behind enemy lines.

VOICES FROM THE CIVIL WAR

Susie King Taylor

Susie King Taylor was born in slavery near Savannah, Georgia, in 1848. In April of 1862, when she was fourteen, her uncle took her and his own seven children behind the Union lines to work as a laundress for an African American troop. Young Susie soon found herself doing emergency work tending the wounded. It was the hope of many African Americans to secure their freedom by working for the Union Army.

After the war was over, Taylor returned to Savannah and opened a school for children of former slaves. In 1902, after she had moved to Boston, she wrote down her memory of her experiences with an African American regiment at Camp Saxton in Georgia.

"The first colored troops did not receive any pay for eighteen months, and the men had to depend wholly on what they received from the commissary, established by General Saxton. A great many of these men had large families, and as they had no money to give them, their wives were obliged to support themselves and children by washing for the officers of the gunboats and the soldiers, and making cakes and pies which they sold to the boys in camp. A Finally, in 1863, the government decided to give them half pay, but the men would not accept this. They wanted "full pay" or nothing. They preferred rather to give their services to the state, which they did until 1864, when the government granted them full pay, with all the back pay due. . . .

While at Camp Shaw, Chaplain Fowler, Robert Defoe, and several of our boys were captured while tapping some telegraph wires. Robert Defoe was confined in the jail at Walterborough, S.C., for about twenty months. When Sherman's army reached Pocotaligo he made his escape and joined his company (Company G). He had not been paid, as he had refused the reduced pay offered by the government. Before we got to camp, where the payrolls could be made out, he sickened and died of smallpox and was buried at Savannah, never having been paid one cent for nearly three years of service. He left no heirs and his account was never settled. . . .

About four o'clock, July 2, the charge into battle was made. The first of the wounded to be brought in was Samuel Anderson of our company; then others of our boys, some with their legs off, arm gone, foot off, and wounds of all kinds imaginable. They had to wade through creeks and marshes, as they were discovered by the enemy and shelled very badly. A number of the men were lost. . . .

My work now began. I gave my assistance to try to <u>alleviate</u> their sufferings. I asked the doctor at the hospital what I could get for them to eat. They wanted soup, but that I could not get; but I had a few cans of condensed milk and some turtle eggs, so I thought I would try to make some custard. I had doubts as to my success, for cooking with turtle eggs was something new to me, but the adage has it, "Nothing ventured, nothing done," so I made a venture and the result was a very delicious custard. This I carried to the men, who enjoyed it very much. My services were given at all times for the comfort of these men. I was on hand to assist whenever needed. I was enrolled as company laundress, but I did very little of it, because I was always busy doing other things through camp, and was employed all the time doing something for the officers and comrades."

—from *Reminiscences of My Life in Camp* by Susie King Taylor

B *Harriet Tubman Series, No. 29* by Jacob Lawrence (1939–40). Tempera on hardboard.

Hampton University Museum, Hampton, Virginia. Photograph by Reuben Burrell.

Expansion
Many soldiers on both sides have written about the interminable boredom of camp life between battles and during winter quarters. "The first thing in the morning is drill, then drill, then drill again," wrote a Pennsylvanian. "Between drills, we drill and sometimes we stop to eat a little and have a roll call." And a Mississippi soldier wrote, "Oh how tiresome this camp life is to me, one everlasting monotone, yesterday, today, and tomorrow."

VOICES FROM THE CIVIL WAR

LIFE IN THE ARMY

John Billings

John Billings was a member of the 10th Massachusetts battery of light artillery. In his book, Hardtack and Coffee, *he described the ordinary life of a Union soldier.*

A

HARDTACK AND COFFEE

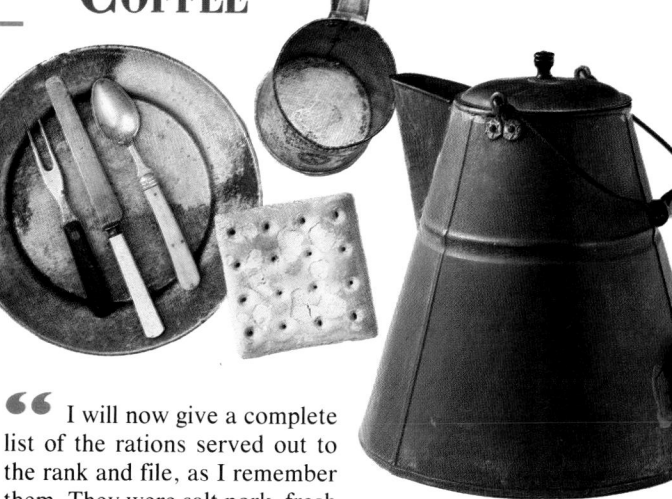

"I will now give a complete list of the rations served out to the rank and file, as I remember them. They were salt pork, fresh beef, salt beef, rarely ham or bacon, hard bread, soft bread, potatoes, an occasional onion, flour, beans, split pease, rice, dried apples, dried peaches, desiccated vegetables, coffee, tea, sugar, molasses, vinegar, candles, soap, pepper and salt.

It is scarcely necessary to state that these were not all served out at one time. There was but one kind of meat served at once, and this . . . was usually pork. When it was hard bread, it wasn't *soft* bread or flour, and when it was pease or beans it wasn't rice. . . .

I will speak of the rations more in detail, beginning with the hard bread, or, to use the name by which it was known in the Army of the Potomac, *Hardtack*. What was hardtack? It was a plain flour-and-water biscuit. Two which I have in my possession as mementos measure three and one-eighth by two and seven-eighths inches, and are nearly half an inch thick. Although these biscuits were furnished to organizations by weight, they were dealt out to the men by number, nine constituting a ration in some regiments, and ten in others; but there were usually enough for those who wanted more, as some men would not draw them. While hardtack was nutritious, yet a hungry man could eat his ten in a short time and still be hungry. . . .

The coffee ration was most heartily appreciated by the soldier. When tired and foot-sore, he would drop out of the marching column, build his little camp-fire, cook his mess of coffee, take a nap behind the nearest shelter, and when he woke, hurry on to overtake his company. Such men were sometimes called stragglers; but it could, obviously, have no offensive meaning when applied to them. . . .

One of the most interesting scenes presented in army life took place at night when the army was on the point of bivouacking. As soon as this fact became known along the column, each man would seize a rail from the nearest fence, and with this additional arm on the shoulder would enter the proposed camping-ground. In no more time than it takes to tell the story, the little camp-fires, rapidly increasing to hundreds in number, would shoot up along the hills and plains, and as if by magic acres of territory would be luminous with them. Soon B they would be surrounded by the soldiers, who made it an almost invariable rule to cook their coffee first, after which a large number, tired out with the toils of the day, would make their supper of hardtack and coffee, and roll up in their blankets for the night."

—from *Hardtack and Coffee* by John Billings

A. Expansion
Soldiers supplemented a monotonous diet of hardtack, salt pork, and coffee by foraging in the countryside as they passed through. Often however, their foraging took the form of looting and pillaging. "If God Almighty had yet in store another plague worse than all the others," wrote the governor of North Carolina, "I am sure it must have been a regiment or so of half-armed, half-disciplined Confederate Cavalry."

B. Writing Assignment
Have students recreate the dialogue of soldiers sitting around the campfire during a noncombat period. What did the men talk about—conditions in camp? Letters from home? Past battles and present worries?

A. Responding
? What practical purposes did such dialogues as these between Rebels and Yanks serve? (Exchanges of information; trading of supplies) How do you think Hunter will feel the next day or the day after, when he goes into battle against these same Yankees? (He probably will have conflicting feelings.)

B. Writing Assignment
Have students imagine they are Alexander Hunter or his Yankee counterpart and write a letter home. Students should describe these events in a more condensed form and include the soldier's reflections upon the unusual encounter.

VOICES FROM THE CIVIL WAR

Alexander Hunter

Alexander Hunter was a college boy who joined the 17th Virginia Regiment at the outbreak of the War. His later book, **Johnny Reb and Billy Yank,** *provides a lively look at life in the Confederate Army. Here he describes a meeting between Union and Confederate soldiers.*

Johnny Reb AND Billy Yank

“It was the latter part of August [1863]; orders were given to be prepared to go on [guard duty] early in the morning; and until a late hour the men were busy cooking rations and cleaning equipment.

Before the mists had been chased by the rising sun, the company in close column of fours marched down the road. Man and animals were in perfect condition, brimful of mettle and in buoyant spirits.

The route lay along the banks of the river; upon the winding course of which, after several hours riding, the regiment reached its destination and relieved the various [guards]. A sergeant and squad of men were left at each post . . . to watch the enemy on the other side of the Rappahannock.

The Rappahannock, which was at this place about two hundred yards wide, flowing oceanward, its bosom reflecting the roseate-hued morn, was as lovely a body of water as the sun ever shone upon. The sound of the gentle ripple of its waves upon the sand was broken by a faint ''halloo'' which came from the other side.

''Johnny Reb; I say, J-o-h-n-n-y R-e-b, don't shoot!''

Joe Reid shouted back, ''All right!''

''What command are you?''

The spoken words floated clear and distant across the water, ''The Black Horse cavalry. Who are you?''

''The Second Michigan Cavalry.''

''Come to the bank,'' said our spokesman, ''and show yourself; we won't fire.''

''On your honor, Johnny Reb?''

''On our honor, Billy Yank.''

In a second a large squad of blue-coats across the way advanced to the water's brink. The Southerners did the same; then the former put the query.

''Have you any tobacco?''

''Plenty of it,'' went our reply.

''Any sugar or coffee?'' they questioned.

''Not a taste nor a smell.''

''Let's trade,'' was shouted with eagerness.

''Very well,'' was the reply, ''. . . meet us here this evening.''

''All right,'' they answered; then added, ''Say, Johnny, want some newspapers?''

''Y-e-s!''

''Then look out, we are going to send you some.''

''How are you going to do it?''

''Wait and see.'' . . .

Eagerly he watched. . . . Presently he shouted:

''Here they come!'' and then in a tone of intense admiration, ''I'll be doggoned if these Yanks are not the smartest people in the world.''

On the other side were several miniature boats and ships—such as school-boys delight in—with sails set; the gentle breeze impelled the little crafts across the river, each freighted with a couple of newspapers. . . .

Drawing lots, Joe Boteler, who found luck against him, started to town, with a muttered curse, to buy tobacco. . . .

Joe returned in the evening with a box of plug tobacco about a foot square; but how to get it across was the question. The miniature boats could not carry it, and we shouted across to the Yanks that we had about twenty pounds of cut plug, and asked them what we must do? They hallooed back to let one of us swim across, and declared it was perfectly safe. . . . I volunteered. Having lived on the banks of the Potomac all my life, I was necessarily a swimmer. . . .

As I approached the shore the news of my coming reached camp, and nearly all the Second Michigan were lined up along the bank.

I felt a little queer, but had perfect faith in their promise and kept on without missing a stroke. . . . The blue-coats crowded around me and gave me a hearty welcome, . . . and heaped offerings of sugar, coffee, lemons, and even candy.

Bidding my friends the enemy good-by, I swam back with the precious cargo, and we had a feast that night.” A B

Expansion
Thomas Jonathan Jackson (1824–1863), a prominent Confederate officer, was promoted to brigadier general after his success at the Battle of Bull Run. Also during that battle he won the nickname "Stonewall" because of the determination with which he fought and that he inspired in his troops.

Jackson served at Harper's Ferry, Antietam, Fredericksburg, and Chancellorsville. In Chancellorsville, however, he was inadvertently wounded by his own men; he died when pneumonia set in. The South never found another officer of Jackson's valor and skill to replace him.

A. Responding

? What qualities of leadership are credited to Jackson in this tribute? (His discipline; his focus; his ability to inspire obedience)

Are these important to any leader, or are they strictly military? (Within the context, at least, the qualities seem best suited to a military leader.)

VOICES FROM THE CIVIL WAR

Mary Chesnut

Mrs. Chesnut describes Stonewall Jackson, commander of the Confederate Army.

"DECEMBER 8, 1863
General Lawton was here last night. He superseded Colonel Myers last winter, in spite of Miles with the Congress at his heels. He was one of Stonewall's generals, so I listened with all my ears. "Stonewall could not sleep, so every two or three nights you were waked up by orders to have your brigade in marching order before daylight, and to report in person to the Commander. Then you were marched a few miles out and then a few miles in again."

"A little different from the western stories, and some generals nearer Richmond asleep several hours after they have been expected to attack."

General Lawton said: "The restless, discontented spirits move the world. All this of Stonewall's was to make us always ready, ever on the alert; and the end of it was this: Jackson's men had gone half a day's march before Pete Longstreet waked and breakfasted." He added: "I think there is a popular delusion about the amount of praying Jackson did. He certainly preferred a fight on Sunday to a sermon. Failing to manage a fight, he loved next best a long Presbyterian sermon, Calvinistic to the core.

"He had no sympathy with human infirmity. He was a one-idea man. He looked upon broken-down men and stragglers as the same thing. He classed all who were weak and weary, who fainted by the wayside, as men wanting in patriotism. If a man's face was white as cotton and his pulse so low that you could not feel it, he merely looked upon him impatiently as an inefficient soldier, and rode off out of patience. He was the true type of all great soldiers. He did not value human life where he had an object to accomplish. He could order men to their death as a matter of course. Napoleon's French conscription could not have kept him supplied with men, he used up his command so rapidly. Hence, while he was alive there was more pride than truth in the talk of his soldier's love for him. They feared him, and obeyed him to the death; faith they had in him, a faith stronger than death. But I doubt if he had their love, though their respect he did command. And now that they begin to see that a few years more of Stonewall Jackson would have freed them from the yoke of the hateful Yankee, they deify him. They are proud to have been one of the famous Stonewall Brigade, to have been a brick in that wall. A

"But be ye sure, it was bitter hard work to keep up with Stonewall Jackson, as all know who ever served with him. He gave his orders rapidly and distinctly, and rode away without allowing answer or remonstrance. When you failed, you were apt to be put under arrest. When you succeeded, he only said *good.*"

—from *A Diary from Dixie*
by Mary Chesnut

A. Allusion
Chesnut alludes to II Samuel 12, where King David is punished for arranging for the murder of Uriah the Hittite and marrying Uriah's wife Bathsheba. When David's child by Bathsheba falls ill, David weeps and prays, but after the child dies, "then David arose from the earth, and washed, and anointed himself, and changed his apparel, and came into the house of the LORD, and worshipped. Then he came to his own house; and when he required, they set bread before him, and he did eat" (v. 20). Asked why he cried before the child died and not after, David replies (v. 22–23), "While the child was yet alive, I fasted and wept; for I said, Who can tell whether God will be gracious to me, that the child may live? But now he is dead, wherefore should I fast? Can I bring him back again? I shall go to him, but he shall not return to me."

Have students apply this story to Mary Chesnut's situation. (Like David, she feels that the waiting is over and that it is time for life to go on.)

B. Cross-Curriculum Connection
Jefferson Davis (1808–1889) served as a U.S. Senator and as secretary of war under President Franklin Pierce. Elected President of the Confederacy in 1861, he exhibited able executive leadership and was at least partly responsible for the South's powerful showing against the much larger Northern forces. He often clashed with Southern governors, however, as they defended their own states' rights. Davis was captured in Georgia in April 1865, imprisoned for two years, and indicted for treason, but he was never tried.

C. Cross-Curriculum Connection
William Tecumseh Sherman's march through Georgia began with the fall of Atlanta in September 1864. Atlanta's mills, munitions factories, and railroad connections made it vital to the South; so Sherman ordered Atlanta evacuated and burned.

VOICES FROM THE CIVIL WAR

THE END OF THE WAR

Mary Chesnut

As she had been present at the beginning of the war, Mary Chesnut was also present at its end. In Columbia, South Carolina, she received the news, increasingly depressing, from the field.

"SEPTEMBER 1, 1864
The battle is raging at Atlanta, our fate hanging in the balance.

SEPTEMBER 2, 1864
Atlanta is gone. Well that agony [A] is over. Like David, when the child was dead, I will get up from my knees, will wash my face and comb my hair. There is no hope, but we will try to have no fear. . . .

SEPTEMBER 21, 1864
[B] The President [of the Confederacy] has gone West. He sent for Mr. Chesnut.

I went with Mrs. Rhett to hear Dr. Palmer [a minister]. I did not know before how utterly hopeless was our situation. This man is so eloquent; it was hard to listen and not give way. Despair was his word, and martyrdom. He offered us nothing more in this world than the martyr's crown. He is not for slavery, he says; he is for freedom, the freedom to govern our own country as we see fit. He is against foreign interference in our state matters. That is what Mr. Palmer went to war for, it appears. Every day shows that slavery is doomed the world over. For that he thanked God. He spoke of this time of our agony; and then came the cry: "Help us, Oh God! Vain is the help of man." So we came away shaken to the depths. . . .

The end has come, no doubt of the fact. . . . We are going to be wiped off the face of the earth. Now what is there to prevent Sherman taking General Lee in the rear? We have but two armies, and Sherman is between them now.

SEPTEMBER 29, 1864
These stories of our defeats in the Valley fall like blows upon a dead body. Since Atlanta, I have felt as if all were dead within me, forever. Captain Ogden of General Chesnut's staff dined here today. Had ever a Brigadier with little or no brigade so magnificent a staff? The reserves, as somebody said, are gathered by robbing the cradle and the graves of men too old and boys too young.

Every man is being hurried to the front. Today Mr. Chesnut met a poor creature coming from the surgeon's with a radiant face and a certificate. "General, see! I am exempt from service; one leg utterly useless the other not warranted to last three months."

—from *A Diary from Dixie* by Mary Chesnut

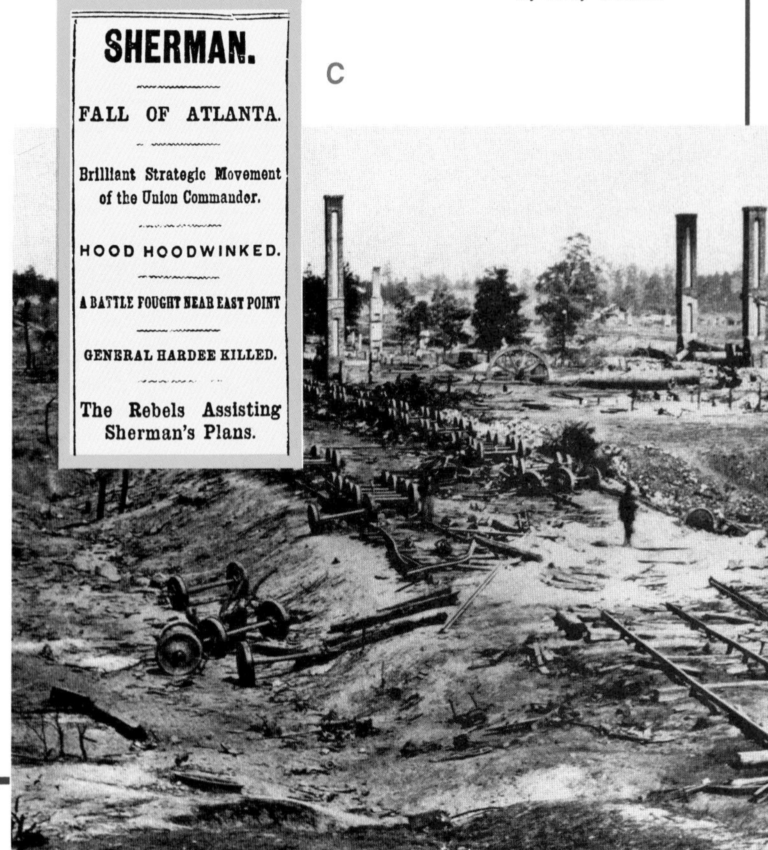
[C]

SHERMAN.

FALL OF ATLANTA.

Brilliant Strategic Movement of the Union Commander.

HOOD HOODWINKED.

A BATTLE FOUGHT NEAR EAST POINT

GENERAL HARDEE KILLED.

The Rebels Assisting Sherman's Plans.

Cross-Curriculum Connection
Both Ulysses S. Grant (1822–1885) and Robert E. Lee (1807–1870) were graduates of West Point, and both had served in the Mexican War. Not until March 1864 was Grant made commander of the Union forces. He at once planned to confront the enemy aggressively at every point so that the Confederate armies could not support each other. He himself led the main charge against Lee, and their two armies engaged in a number of terrible battles before the surrender at Appomattox. In 1868 Grant was elected 18th President of the United States; he was reelected in 1872. He is buried in New York City, in a magnificent tomb overlooking the Hudson River.

Abraham Lincoln

The fall of Richmond, Virginia, signaled the end of the war. On April 3, 1865, just six days before Lee surrendered, President Lincoln visited Richmond, now in Union hands.

On April 3 [1865], Abraham Lincoln and his son Tad arrived at Rockett's Wharf [in Richmond, Virginia] aboard a small barge. "Thank God I have lived to see this," he said. "It seems to me that I have been dreaming a horrid nightmare for four years, and now the nightmare is over."

Blacks mobbed the President, laughing, singing, weeping for joy, kneeling before him, straining to touch his hand. "I know I am free," said one man, "for I have seen Father Abraham and felt him."

Lincoln was taken aback. "Don't kneel to me," he said. "You must kneel to God only, and thank Him for your freedom." A

—from *The Civil War: An Illustrated History*
by Geoffrey C. Ward, with Ric Burns and Ken Burns

A. Responding
? What does this anecdote say about Lincoln's reputation among African Americans? About Lincoln himself? (Lincoln was revered by grateful ex-slaves, but he did not want to be deified.)

Seth Flint

On April 9, 1865, Lee surrendered to Grant at Appomattox Court House. Seth Flint, a Union soldier who witnessed the event, described the scene.

I Saw Lee Surrender

"Grant looked like an old and battered campaigner as he rode into the yard. His blue blouse was unbuttoned and underneath could be seen his undershirt. He was unlike Lee.

What a brave pair of thoroughbreds Lee and Traveler were. That horse would have attracted attention anywhere. General Lee's uniform was immaculate and he presented a superb martial figure. But it was the face beneath the gray felt hat that made the deepest impression on me. I have been trying to find a single word that describes it and I have concluded that "benign" is the adjective I'm after, because it means kindly and gracious. There was something else about him that aroused my deep pity that so great a warrior should be acknowledging defeat. . . .

Four o'clock—the door opened. Out came General Lee, his soldierly figure erect, even in defeat. We stiffened and gave him a salute, and the man in gray courteously returned it. At the moment his soul must have been heavy with sorrow—the years of desperate struggle fruitless—and yet he could return the salute of some Yankee troopers. B

After the departure of General Lee, we quickly learned the happy news of the surrender and it spread like wildfire through the army. That night was one of the happiest I have ever known.

When I sounded taps, the sweetest of all bugle calls, the

B. Cross-Curriculum Connection
Lee was offered command of the Union army, but he chose to stay with the Confederacy when his home state of Virginia seceded in 1861. He became commander of the Confederate army in May 1862 and made a number of daring and successful raids northward. After Gettysburg, however, he gradually fell back until he was forced to surrender at Appomattox. Like Jefferson Davis, he was indicted for treason but never tried.

In one of the ironies of the war, Lee's home in Virginia became the site of the Arlington National Cemetery.

CLOSURE

Have students discuss how their understanding of the Civil War era has changed. Consider these questions:

- What can you learn about an event from someone who actually lived through it? How does that differ from a historian's account of the same event?
- Which selection did you find most informative? Most moving?

READING CHECK TEST

1. Upson's story mainly shows how the war **(a)** delayed harvest, **(b)** divided families, or **(c)** disrupted the mail. **b**
2. Whitman emphasizes the suffering of the **(a)** wounded, **(b)** entire families, or **(c)** animals. **a**
3. According to Lincoln, the cemetery at Gettysburg will be consecrated by **(a)** himself, **(b)** Congress, or **(c)** those who fought there. **c**
4. Douglass wanted African Americans to **(a)** join the Union army, **(b)** unmask slavery, or **(c)** execute their masters. **a**
5. Chesnut's last diary entry describes **(a)** a soldier's diet, **(b)** the fall of Atlanta, or **(c)** John Billings. **b**

A. Humanities Connection: Responding to the Fine Art

? There is a quiet kind of dignity in these two scenes. How would you describe their difference in mood? (Answers will vary, but students should note the sense of sorrow in *Furling the Flag* and the quiet pride and restraint of *The Surrender of General Lee to General Grant, April 9, 1865.*)

B. Responding/Writing Assignment

? Do you agree with Seth Flint's perception? (Answers will vary.)

Have students imagine that they are Union or Confederate soldiers now free to go. In character, they should write a letter home, telling their families of this day and of their return.

C. Expansion

A few months later Lee would write, "The war being at an end . . . I believe it to be the duty of every one to unite in the restoration of the country, and the establishment of peace and harmony."

Furling the Flag by Richard N. Brooke (1872). Oil.
Courtesy of the West Point Museum, United States Military Academy, West Point, New York.

notes had scarcely died away when from the distance—it must have come from General Lee's headquarters—came, silvery clear, the same call. The boys on the other side welcomed peace.

Soldiers don't carry hatred. ❞

—from "I Saw Lee Surrender" by Seth M. Flint

The Surrender of General Lee to General Grant, April 9, 1865 by Louis Mathieu Didier Guillaume (c. 1867–68). Oil on canvas.

Robert E. Lee

On April 10, 1865, one day after General Lee surrendered to General Grant at the Appomattox Court House in Virginia, Lee said goodbye to his troops. It was an emotional occasion—the troops were overjoyed at seeing their leader but were saddened by the memory of defeat. General Lee, with head bare and tears in his eyes, proceeded to address his troops:

General Lee Bids Farewell to His Troops

❝ After four years' of arduous service, marked by unsurpassed courage and fortitude, the Army of Northern Virginia has been compelled to yield to overwhelming numbers and resources. I need not tell the survivors of so many hard-fought battles, who have remained steadfast to the last, that I have consented to this result from no distrust of them; but, feeling that valour and devotion could accomplish nothing that could compensate for the loss that would have attended the continuation of the contest, I have determined to avoid the useless sacrifice of those whose past services have endeared them to their countrymen. By the terms of the agreement, officers and men can return to their homes and remain there until exchanged. You will take with you the satisfaction that proceeds from the consciousness of duty faithfully performed; and I earnestly pray that a merciful God will extend to you His blessing and protection. With an increasing admiration of your constancy and devotion to your country, and a grateful remembrance of your kind and generous consideration of myself, I bid you an affectionate farewell. ❞

—from *Recollections and Letters of General Robert E. Lee,* by his son, Captain Robert E. Lee

Stephen Crane (1871–1900)

Stephen Crane was the youngest of the fourteen children of Jonathan Townley Crane, a Methodist minister, and his devout wife Mary. Stephen's frail health as a child was one reason for the family's move from the parsonage in Newark, New Jersey, to Port Jervis in upstate New York. Here the child grew up with a yearning to become a baseball star. He put in a term first at Lafayette College and then at Syracuse University (where he was made captain of the baseball team) before he decided to try earning a living as a writer.

In the spring of 1891 he went to work for his brother Townley's news agency in Asbury Park, New Jersey; he soon caused a scandal in that pious and conservative seaside resort with an ironic story about a workingmen's parade. Later, struggling to make a living as a reporter in New York City, he was drawn to the city's underside. What he called his "artistic education on the Bowery" (the city's skid row) kept him hungry and often ill.

He lived at the Art Students' League on Twenty-third Street, reporting intermittently for the *Herald* and the *Tribune,* exploring the city's slums and saloons, and writing his first significant fiction about his experiences. This was *Maggie: A Girl of the Streets,* a somber, somewhat shocking novel, whose plot involved brutality, alcoholism, prostitution, and suicide.

A Crane's subject matter and style in *Maggie* revealed him as a pioneer of naturalism, the literary movement which went beyond realism in its dissection of human instincts and behavior, and of the social environment that was believed to "condition" people to be what they are. Furthermore, *Maggie* broke other new ground; it was one of the first novels to use the city and its all-too-real slums as a setting. *Maggie* was impossibly grim for the popular magazines, and Crane borrowed $700 to have it printed in 1893. The copies of the little yellow paperback lay piled in his rented room for want of readers.

But a literary triumph followed soon after Crane's apparent failure with *Maggie.* In the summer of 1893, he finished a short novel entitled *The Red Badge of Courage.* This story focused on the impressions of Henry Fleming, a young soldier at the Civil War battle of Chancellorsville. B As William Dean Howells (see page 382) observed, Crane's genius seemed to "spring to life fully armed" with this book. He had been born well after the end of the Civil War and had had no direct experience with battle. But he had read the popular anthology *Battles and Leaders of the Civil War,* and he had seen Mathew Brady's famous battle photographs. "I have never been in a battle, of course," wrote Crane later, "and I believe that I got my sense of the rage of conflict on the football field. The psychology is the same. The opposing team is an enemy tribe."

Whatever his sources, Crane managed to produce an extraordinary work that not only persuaded the war's veterans of its essential truth but also provided an arresting psychological study of the ordinary man thrust into war. The impressionistic technique used by Crane in the novel would have an important influence on the fiction of the next several decades.

In fiction, **impressionism** is a technique whereby the writer gives us not objective reality, but one character's impression of that reality. In other words, in *The Red Badge of Courage,* we get Henry Fleming's impressions of what he sees

A. Expansion
You may wish to review the basic elements of naturalism, outlined on pages 383–384, in the second paragraph of the section titled "Frank Norris and Naturalism."

B. Expansion
The Battle of Chancellorsville, May 2–4, 1863, was the last great victory of Confederate General Robert E. Lee, but the victory was marred by the mortal wounding of Confederate General T. J. (Stonewall) Jackson by his own men. The victory led Lee to invade the North for the Gettysburg campaign. The larger Union army at Chancellorsville was commanded by Joseph Hooker. On hearing that Hooker had lost his nerve, some 17,000 men, and the battle, President Lincoln cried out, "My God, my God! What will the country say!"

A. Humanities Connection: About the Illustration
It is said that Crane thought out his work so thoroughly before committing words to paper that he was able to write steadily, as if simply copying an already existing manuscript, in handwriting neat enough for a bank bill.

B. Expansion
There are two movie versions, both titled *The Red Badge of Courage.* The 1951 black-and-white film, directed by John Huston, is a realistic drama starring Audie Murphy, Bill Mauldin, John Dierkes, Royal Dano, Arthur Hunnicutt, and Andy Devine. Production of the film was so troubled that Lillian Ross wrote a book about it entitled *Picture.* The 1974 re-make for television is an adaptation by John Gay directed by Lee Phillips. This re-make stars Richard Thomas, Michael Brandon, Wendell Burton, Charles Aidman, and Warren Berlinger.

The Red Badge of Courage.
An Episode of the American Civil War.
By Stephen Crane.

The cold passed reluctantly from the earth and the retiring fogs revealed an army stretched out on the hills, resting. As the landscape changed from brown to green the army awakened and began to tremble with eagerness at the noise of rumors. It cast its eyes upon the roads which were growing from long troughs of liquid mud to proper thoroughfares. A river, amber-tinted in the shadow of its banks, purled at the army's feet and at night when the stream had become of a sorrowful blackness one could see across, the red eye-like gleam of hostile camp-fires set in the low brows of distant hills.

Once, a certain soldier developed virtues and went resolutely to wash a shirt. He came flying back from a brook waving his garment, banner-like. He was swelled with a tale he had heard from a reliable friend who had heard it from a truthful cavalryman who had heard it from his trust-worthy brother, one of the orderlies at division head-quarters. He adopted the important air of a herald in red and gold.

"We're goin' t' move t'morrah - sure," he said

and feels and hears of the war, not a description of what is actually happening.

The Red Badge of Courage, published in 1895, sold so widely that in the following year Crane's publishers reissued *Maggie*. The renown of *The Red Badge of Courage* made Crane into a national expert on war, and he was to spend the rest of his short life writing about it for the newspapers. His celebrity was such that he also became the prototype of the adventurous correspondent who not only writes about sensational events but also lives a sensational life, delighting in shocking conservative readers.

One of the fascinating elements of Crane's life was the degree to which he interwove his fiction and his real-life experiences. It was as if he had invented a war in his novel, and then had to pursue the brushfire wars of his own times in order to confirm what he had written. Nor was experience wasted on him. When he sailed from Florida to cover a gun-running operation to Cuba, he was shipwrecked off the Florida coast and endured a fifty-four-hour struggle against the sea. The result was his superb story "The Open Boat" (1898).

Before this ill-fated journey, he had stopped off at the Hotel de Dream in Jacksonville, Florida, and taken up with the hostess, Cora Taylor. She soon decided that she would stay with him and become the first female war correspondent. This oddly matched couple later went off to Greece to cover a war. They settled eventually in England, renting a huge, dilapidated, medieval house in Sussex.

All of these adventures were taking their toll on Crane's always delicate health. When he returned to England from another trip to Cuba, this time to cover the Spanish-American War, he was in the last year of his life. Still he continued to write, desperate now to pay for Cora's extravagant domestic life. In his last year he produced his second volume of poems (he called them "lines"), *War Is Kind* (page 463). But tuberculosis was sapping his strength. He suffered a serious hemorrhage in March 1900. After a hurried journey to a sanitarium in the Black Forest of Germany, Stephen Crane died there in May, not quite thirty years old.

SUPPLEMENTARY SUPPORT MATERIALS
1. Vocabulary Activity Worksheet (*CCB*)
2. Review and Response Worksheet: Irony (*CCB*)
3. Language Skills Worksheet: Adverb Phrases (*CCB*)
4. Selection Test (*CCB*)

DEVELOPING VOCABULARY
The following words from the story are tested in the Selection Test. (See also Vocabulary Activity Worksheet.)

incessant	calamity
conflagration	gesticulating
demeanor	furtive
to obliterate	blanched

PREPARATION
1. ESTABLISHING A PURPOSE. Have students respond to the headnote and then read the story to see if Fred Collins demonstrates the qualities of a hero.

2. BUILDING ON PRIOR KNOWLEDGE. Review *irony* with students (see page 612 and the entry in the Handbook of Literary Terms, page 1175) and ask students to look out for irony in this story.

A MYSTERY OF HEROISM

What *is* heroism? Is it exceptional courage? How about an act in which a person ignores normal human fear and risks his or her life for something trivial, which, for the moment, seems more important than survival?

A **That kind of risk is what we have in this Stephen Crane story. In the midst of all the frightful noise and bloody destruction of a Civil War battlefield, with death all around, a soldier suddenly has a mind to run straight into the battle on an impulse which, to his comrades, seems simply crazy. Right into the line of enemy fire—for *that?***

In the story's ending, you will recognize a classic irony: That which is sought by one man as more precious than his life, to another is just a joke.

Before you read, write down three characteristics that you think would qualify someone to be called a hero.

The dark uniforms of the men were so coated with dust from the incessant wrestling of the two armies that the regiment almost seemed a part of the clay bank which shielded them from the shells. On the top of the hill a battery[1] was arguing in tremendous roars with some other guns, and to the eye of the infantry the artillerymen, the guns, the caissons,[2] the horses, were distinctly outlined upon the blue sky. When a piece was fired, a red streak as round as a log flashed low in the heavens, like a monstrous bolt of lightning. The men of the battery wore white duck trousers, which somehow emphasized their legs; and when they ran and crowded in little groups at the bidding of the shouting officers, it was more impressive than usual to the infantry.

Fred Collins, of A Company, was saying: "Thunder! I wisht I had a drink. Ain't there any water round here?" Then somebody yelled: "There goes th' bugler!"

As the eyes of half the regiment swept in one machine-like movement, there was an instant's picture of a horse in a great convulsive leap of a death-wound and a rider leaning back with a crooked arm and spread fingers before his face. On the ground was the crimson terror of an exploding shell, with fibers of flame that seemed like lances. A glittering bugle swung clear of the rider's back as fell headlong the horse and the man. In the air was an odor as from a conflagration.

Sometimes they of the infantry looked down at a fair little meadow which spread at their feet. Its long green grass was rippling gently in a breeze. Beyond it was the gray form of a house half torn to pieces by shells and by the busy axes of soldiers who had pursued firewood. The line of an old fence was now dimly marked by long weeds and by an occasional post. A shell had blown the well-house to fragments. Little lines of gray smoke ribboning upward from some embers indicated the place where had stood the barn. B

From beyond a curtain of green woods there came the sound of some stupendous scuffle, as if two animals of the size of islands were fighting. At a distance there were occasional appearances of swift-moving men, horses, batteries, flags, and with the crashing of infantry volleys were heard, often, wild and frenzied cheers. In the midst of it all Smith and Ferguson, two privates of A Company, were engaged in a heated discussion which involved the greatest questions of the national existence.

The battery on the hill presently engaged in a frightful duel. The white legs of the gunners scampered this way and that way, and the officers redoubled their shouts. The guns, with their demeanors of stolidity and courage, were typical of something infinitely self-possessed in this clamor or of death that swirled around the hill.

One of a "swing" team was suddenly smitten quivering to the ground, and his maddened brethren dragged his torn body in their struggle to escape from this turmoil and danger. A young soldier astride one of the leaders swore and fumed in his saddle and furiously jerked at the bridle. An C

1. **battery:** group of heavy guns.
2. **caissons** (kā′sənz): two-wheeled wagons for ammunition.

A. Expansion
This story, like *The Red Badge of Courage,* was written before Crane had experienced war. He had interviewed Civil War veterans, but they told him only dry facts and statistics. They seemed unable to recall—or at least to articulate—their thoughts and feelings about war. Crane drew upon his own imagination to fill in those thoughts and feelings. He succeeded so well that many veterans wrote to ask Crane what regiment he had served in, and others were convinced that they had served with him.

B. Description
Here and on page 458, have students notice the utter devastation visited on the "fair little meadow."

C. Vocabulary
The "swing" team are horses harnessed to swing guns in another direction.

A. Humanities Connection: Responding to the Fine Art
This illustration depicts the Battle of Antietam (September 1862), one of the bloodiest of the Civil War. About 12,500 Northerners and almost 11,000 Southerners were killed or wounded before the Confederates withdrew. Confederate retreat gave the North the victory that Lincoln had been waiting for. On September 22, he announced the preliminary Emancipation Proclamation.

? How does the painting compare to the description of battle in the story? (In the painting, the battle seems fairly organized and somewhat distant; Crane, on the other hand, brings all of the unpleasant details to life in the story.)

B. Expansion
Two lieutenants in *The Red Badge of Courage* are similarly wounded, one in the hand and the other in the arm. In another story by Crane, "An Episode of War," a lieutenant some distance from direct battle is shot in the hand. He goes to the field hospital protesting that he wants his hand saved but arrives home minus his entire arm.

C. Contrast
Have students note the strange contrast as Crane interrupts the powerful descriptions of war with joking dialogue about thirst.

D. Simile
Ask students to notice Crane's startlingly original metaphors and similes throughout this story.

A

Battle of Antietam.

officer screamed out an order so violently that his voice broke and ended the sentence in a falsetto shriek.

The leading company of the infantry regiment was somewhat exposed, and the colonel ordered it moved more fully under the shelter of the hill. There was the clank of steel against steel.

B A lieutenant of the battery rode down and passed them, holding his right arm carefully in his left hand. And it was as if this arm was not at all a part of him, but belonged to another man. His sober and reflective charger went slowly. The officer's face was grimy and perspiring, and his uniform was tousled as if he had been in direct grapple with an enemy. He smiled grimly when the men stared at him. He turned his horse toward the meadow.

Collins, of A Company, said: "I wisht I had a drink. I bet there's water in that there ol' well yonder!" C

"Yes; but how you goin' to git it?"

For the little meadow which intervened was now suffering a terrible onslaught of shells. Its green and beautiful calm had vanished utterly. Brown earth was being flung in monstrous handfuls. And there was a massacre of the young blades of grass. They were being torn, burned, obliterated. Some curious fortune of the battle had made this gentle little meadow the object of the red hate of the shells, and each one as it exploded seemed like an imprecation[3] in the face of a maiden. D

3. **imprecation:** curse.

The wounded officer who was riding across this expanse said to himself: "Why, they couldn't shoot any harder if the whole army was massed here!"

A A shell struck the gray ruins of the house, and as, after the roar, the shattered wall fell in fragments, there was a noise which resembled the flapping of shutters during a wild gale of winter. Indeed, the infantry paused in the shelter of the bank appeared as men standing upon a shore contemplating a madness of the sea. The angel of calamity had under its glance the battery upon the hill. Fewer white-legged men labored about the guns. A shell had smitten one of the pieces, and after the flare, the smoke, the dust, and wrath of this blow were gone, it was possible to see white legs stretched horizontally upon the ground. And at the interval to the rear where it is the business of battery horses to stand with their noses to the fight, awaiting the command to drag their guns out of the destruction, or into it, or wheresoever these incomprehensible humans demanded with whip and spur—in this line of passive and dumb spectators, whose fluttering hearts yet would not let them forget the iron laws of man's control of them—in this rank of brute-soldiers there had been relentless and hideous carnage. From the ruck of bleeding and prostrate horses, the men of the infantry could see one animal raising its stricken body with its forelegs and turning its nose with mystic and profound eloquence toward the sky.

Some comrades joked Collins about his thirst. "Well, if yeh want a drink so bad, why don't yeh go git it?" B

"Well, I will in a minnet, if yeh don't shut up!"

A lieutenant of artillery floundered his horse straight down the hill with as little concern as if it were level ground. As he galloped past the colonel of the infantry, he threw up his hand in swift salute. "We've got to get out of that," he roared angrily. He was a black-bearded officer, and his eyes, which resembled beads, sparkled like those of an insane man. His jumping horse sped along the column of infantry.

The fat major, standing carelessly with his sword held horizontally behind him and with his legs far apart, looked after the receding horseman and laughed. "He wants to get back with orders pretty quick, or there'll be no batt'ry left," he observed.

The wise young captain of the second company hazarded to the lieutenant-colonel that the enemy's infantry would probably soon attack the hill, and the lieutenant-colonel snubbed him.

A private in one of the rear companies looked out over the meadow, and then turned to a companion and said, "Look there, Jim!" It was the wounded officer from the battery, who some time before had started to ride across the meadow, supporting his right arm carefully with his left hand. This man had encountered a shell, apparently, at a time when no one perceived him, and he could now be seen lying face downward with a stirruped foot stretched across the body of his dead horse. A leg of the charger extended slantingly upward, precisely as stiff as a stake. Around this motionless pair the shells still howled.

A. Setting

? What do you suppose is the point of describing the devastation of the house? (It is a poignant reminder of how war destroys the ordinary, natural way of human life. Later we find that the well at the house is important to the plot.)

B. Conflict

? Why are Collins's comrades joking him about getting a drink? (They are probably tired of hearing him complain and are daring him to do something about it.) What is the nature of the conflict here? (It is external—Collins against his fellow soldiers. Their teasing forces him to make a decision that he may not have intended to make.)

A. Dialect
Note that "medder" is "meadow."
? Why does Crane use dialect with Collins and the other soldiers but not with the officers? (It shows the soldiers as ordinary, uneducated men and emphasizes the social distance between the officers and the ordinary soldiers.)

B. Characterization
? Why is Collins's resentment beginning to fade? (He is coming closer to having to act upon his complaint—something that perhaps he doesn't really want to do.)

C. Metaphor
? Why is Collins's pride described as "a chasm"? (It separates him from the other soldiers; it is very deep, perhaps central to his being.)

D. Theme
? What are the "quaint emotions" that rule him? (Students may suggest daring or boastful pride.)
? Crane describes Collins as "being led." Does this mean he has not exercised free will in his decision? (Answers will vary, but Crane did believe that one's makeup and environment determine one's choices—a major tenet of the Naturalists.)

There was a quarrel in A Company. Collins was shaking his fist in the faces of some laughing comrades. "Dern yeh! I ain't afraid t' go. If yeh say much, I will go!"

"Of course, yeh will! You'll run through that there medder, won't yeh?"

Collins said, in a terrible voice: "You see now!"

At this ominous threat his comrades broke into renewed jeers.

Collins gave them a dark scowl, and went to find his captain. The latter was conversing with the colonel of the regiment.

"Captain," said Collins, saluting and standing at attention—in those days all trousers bagged at the knees—"Captain, I want t' get permission to go git some water from that there well over yonder!"

The colonel and the captain swung about simultaneously and stared across the meadow. The captain laughed. "You must be pretty thirsty, Collins?"

"Yes, sir, I am."

"Well—ah," said the captain. After a moment, he asked, "Can't you wait?"

"No, sir."

The colonel was watching Collins's face. "Look here, my lad," he said, in a pious sort of voice—"Look here, my lad"—Collins was not a lad—"don't you think that's taking pretty big risks for a little drink of water?"

"I dunno," said Collins uncomfortably. Some of the resentment toward his companions, which perhaps had forced him into this affair, was beginning to fade. "I dunno w'ether 'tis."

The colonel and the captain contemplated him for a time.

"Well," said the captain finally.

"Well," said the colonel, "if you want to go, why, go."

Collins saluted. "Much obliged t' yeh."

As he moved away the colonel called after him. "Take some of the other boys' canteens with you, an' hurry back, now."

"Yes, sir, I will."

The colonel and the captain looked at each other then, for it had suddenly occurred that they could not for the life of them tell whether Collins wanted to go or whether he did not.

They turned to regard Collins, and as they perceived him surrounded by gesticulating comrades, the colonel said: "Well, by thunder! I guess he's going."

Collins appeared as a man dreaming. In the midst of the questions, the advice, the warnings, all the excited talk of his company mates, he maintained a curious silence.

They were very busy in preparing him for his ordeal. When they inspected him carefully, it was somewhat like the examination that grooms give a horse before a race; and they were amazed, staggered, by the whole affair. Their astonishment found vent in strange repetitions.

"Are yeh sure a-goin'?" they demanded again and again.

"Certainly I am," cried Collins at last, furiously.

He strode sullenly away from them. He was swinging five or six canteens by their cords. It seemed that his cap would not remain firmly on his head, and often he reached and pulled it down over his brow.

There was a general movement in the compact column. The long animal-like thing moved slightly. Its four hundred eyes were turned upon the figure of Collins.

"Well, sir, if that ain't th' derndest thing! I never thought Fred Collins had the blood in him for that kind of business."

"What's he goin' to do, anyhow?"

"He's goin' to that well there after water."

"We ain't dyin' of thirst, are we? That's foolishness."

"Well, somebody put him up to it, an' he's doin' it."

"Say, he must be a desperate cuss."

When Collins faced the meadow and walked away from the regiment, he was vaguely conscious that a chasm, the deep valley of all prides, was suddenly between him and his comrades. It was provisional, but the provision was that he return as a victor. He had blindly been led by quaint emotions, and laid himself under an obligation to walk squarely up to the face of death.

But he was not sure that he wished to make a retraction, even if he could do so without shame. As a matter of truth, he was sure of very little. He was mainly surprised.

It seemed to him supernaturally strange that he had allowed his mind to maneuver his body into such a situation. He understood that it might be called dramatically great.

Closure
Have students discuss questions 6 and 7, page 463, and then briefly answer these questions in writing: Is Collins a hero? Why or why not?

Reading Check Test
1. The occasion of the story is **(a)** a dress parade, **(b)** a furious battle, or **(c)** a military retreat. *(b)*
2. As they wait, the infantry are witnessing **(a)** an artillery exchange, **(b)** a tank attack, or **(c)** an aircraft attack. *(a)*
3. Collins ventures into the bombardment in order to **(a)** save a wounded comrade, **(b)** spy on the enemy, or **(c)** get some water. *(c)*
4. The wounded officer asks Collins to **(a)** drag him to shelter, **(b)** give him some of the water, or **(c)** call for help. *(b)*
5. At the end the two young lieutenants **(a)** reprimand Collins, **(b)** praise Collins's heroism, or **(c)** spill the water. *(c)*

A However, he had no full appreciation of anything, excepting that he was actually conscious of being dazed. He could feel his dulled mind groping after the form and color of this incident. He wondered why he did not feel some keen agony of fear cutting his sense like a knife. He wondered at this, because human expression had said loudly for centuries that men should feel afraid of certain things, and that all men who did not feel this fear were phenomena—heroes.

He was, then, a hero. He suffered that disappointment which we would all have if we discovered that we were ourselves capable of those deeds which we most admire in history and legend. This, then, was a hero. After all, heroes were not much.

B No, it could not be true. He was not a hero. Heroes had no shames in their lives, and, as for him, he remembered borrowing fifteen dollars from a friend and promising to pay it back the next day, and then avoiding that friend for ten months. When, at home, his mother had aroused him for the early labor of his life on the farm, it had often been his fashion to be irritable, childish, diabolical; and his mother had died since he had come to the war.

C He saw that, in this matter of the well, the canteens, the shells, he was an intruder in the land of fine deeds.

He was now about thirty paces from his comrades. The regiment had just turned its many faces toward him.

From the forest of terrific noises there suddenly emerged a little uneven line of men. They fired fiercely and rapidly at distant foliage on which appeared little puffs of white smoke. The spatter of skirmish firing was added to the thunder of the guns on the hill. The little line of men ran forward. A color-sergeant fell flat with his flag as if he had slipped on ice. There was hoarse cheering from this distant field.

Collins suddenly felt that two demon fingers were pressed into his ears. He could see nothing but flying arrows, flaming red. He lurched from the shock of this explosion, but he made a mad rush for the house, which he viewed as a man submerged to the neck in a boiling surf might view the shore. In the air little pieces of shell howled, and the earthquake explosions drove him insane with the menace of their roar. As he ran the canteens knocked together with a rhythmical tinkling.

As he neared the house, each detail of the scene became vivid to him. He was aware of some bricks of the vanished chimney lying on the sod. There was a door which hung by one hinge.

Rifle bullets called forth by the insistent skirmishers came from the far-off bank of foliage. They mingled with the shells and the pieces of shells until the air was torn in all directions by hootings, yells, howls. The sky was full of fiends who directed all their wild rage at his head.

When he came to the well, he flung himself face downward and peered into its darkness. There were furtive silver glintings some feet from the surface. He grabbed one of the canteens and, unfastening its cap, swung it down by the cord. The water flowed slowly in with an indolent[4] gurgle.

And now, as he lay with his face turned away, he was suddenly smitten with the terror. It came upon his heart like the grasp of claws. All the power faded from his muscles. For an instant he was no more than a dead man. D

The canteen filled with a maddening slowness, in the manner of all bottles. Presently he recovered his strength and addressed a screaming oath to it. He leaned over until it seemed as if he intended to try to push water into it with his hands. His eyes as he gazed down into the well shone like two pieces of metal, and in their expression was a great appeal and a great curse. The stupid water derided him.

There was the blaring thunder of a shell. Crimson light shone through the swift-boiling smoke and made a pink reflection on part of the wall of the well. Collins jerked out his arm and canteen with the same motion that a man would use in withdrawing his head from a furnace.

He scrambled erect and glared and hesitated. On the ground near him lay the old well bucket, with a length of rusty chain. He lowered it swiftly into the well. The bucket struck the water and then, turning lazily over, sank. When, with hand reaching tremblingly over hand, he hauled it out, it knocked often against the walls of the well and spilled some of its contents.

In running with a filled bucket, a man can adopt but one kind of gait. So, through this terrible field over which screamed practical angels of death, Collins ran in the manner of a farmer chased out of a dairy by a bull.

---

4. **indolent** (in′də·lənt): lazy.

A. Irony
What is ironic about Collins's quest? (He risks his life for something trivial; furthermore, his decision to do so is not even a conscious one.)

B. Connections
Can you think of historical or literary heroes who had imperfections or who faced shame? (Examples include Hercules, who had a violent temper; Moses, who was impatient; Arthur, who was blind to the deception of his court.)

C. Interpreting
What does this sentence mean? (Collins realizes that his quest is trivial.)

D. Conflict
Many of Crane's stories explore a character's inner conflict, a confrontation of his own fear.
Why is Collins suddenly afraid now that his mission is half over? (Until this point, Collins has felt dazed and dull-minded, removed from any sense of the reality of his peril.)

Analyzing the Story

Identifying Facts

1. The lieutenant, shot, lies in the no-man's land, crying for water as Collins passes. We assume that he later dies.

2. Collins is disappointed because he does not feel heroic, only dazed. He knows himself to be ordinary; and if he is heroic, then heroes are "not much."

3. Collins first screams that he can't help the wounded man. He runs on but turns back and tries to help the man drink from the shaking bucket.

The other men roar in welcome as Collins returns; they laugh and play with the bucket. They do not recognize his heroism. They are hardened to the agony of the dying officer.

Interpreting Meanings

4. Collins's low rank makes him representative of ordinary people caught up in the insanity of war. It also makes his rejection of his own heroism more poignant.

5. White is associated with innocence and purity and is therefore ironic on a battlefield.

The color contrasts dramatically with

A. Theme

? Why does Collins return? (Perhaps the dying man's plea has touched a chord of humanity in Collins. Brotherhood, particularly in the face of danger, is a theme of many of Crane's stories, including "The Open Boat.")

B. Irony

See question 8, page 463.

His face went staring white with anticipation—anticipation of a blow that would whirl him around and down. He would fall as he had seen other men fall, the life knocked out of them so suddenly that their knees were no more quick to touch the ground than their heads. He saw the long blue line of the regiment, but his comrades were standing looking at him from the edge of an impossible star. He was aware of some deep wheel-ruts and hoof-prints in the sod beneath his feet.

The artillery officer who had fallen in this meadow had been making groans in the teeth of the tempest of sound. These futile cries, wrenched from him by his agony, were heard only by shells, bullets. When wild-eyed Collins came running, this officer raised himself. His face contorted and blanched from pain, he was about to utter some great beseeching cry. But suddenly his face straightened, and he called: "Say, young man, give me a drink of water, will you?"

Collins had no room amid his emotions for surprise. He was mad from the threats of destruction.

"I can't!" he screamed, and in his reply was a full description of his quaking apprehension. His cap was gone and his hair was riotous. His clothes made it appear that he had been dragged over the ground by the heels. He ran on.

The officer's head sank down, and one elbow crooked. His foot in its brass-bound stirrup still stretched over the body of his horse, and the other leg was under the steed.

A [But Collins turned. He came dashing back. His face had now turned gray, and in his eyes was all terror. "Here it is! Here it is!"]

The officer was as a man gone in drink. His arm bent like a twig. His head drooped as if his neck were of willow. He was sinking to the ground, to lie face downward.

Collins grabbed him by the shoulder. "Here it is. Here's your drink. Turn over. Turn over, man, for God's sake!"

With Collins hauling at his shoulder, the officer twisted his body and fell with his face turned toward that region where lived the unspeakable noises of the swirling missiles. There was the faintest shadow of a smile on his lips as he looked at Collins. He gave a sigh, a little primitive breath like that from a child.

Collins tried to hold the bucket steadily, but his shaking hands caused the water to splash all over the face of the dying man. Then he jerked it away and ran on.

The regiment gave him a welcoming roar. The grimed faces were wrinkled in laughter.

His captain waved the bucket away. "Give it to the men!"

The two genial, skylarking young lieutenants were the first to gain possession of it. They played over it in their fashion.

When one tried to drink, the other teasingly knocked his elbow. "Don't Billie! You'll make me spill it," said the one. The other laughed.

[Suddenly there was an oath, the thud of wood on the ground, and a swift murmur of astonishment among the ranks. The two lieutenants glared at each other. The bucket lay on the ground, empty.] B

Responding to the Story

Analyzing the Story

Identifying Facts

1. What happens to that lieutenant who holds his right arm carefully in his left hand as he passes the battery?
2. When the thought occurs to Collins that he is a hero, he is disappointed. Why?
3. Describe what Collins, "mad from the threats of destruction," does as the lieutenant cries for water. How do the other men respond to his act of mercy?

Interpreting Meanings

4. There is a lot of "rank" in this story—several lieutenants, a captain, a major, a lieutenant-colonel, and a colonel. But the hero is a private. Discuss whether or not you think his lowly rank is significant in any way.
5. In the author's "painting" of the battlefield, our attention is drawn several times to the white legs of the soldiers—to their duck (white linen) trousers. What point, if any, can you see to that **image?** (What does the white contrast with?)

the red of exploding shells and with the blood and gore of the wounded and dying.

6. Answers will vary. The question of his motive is probably the "mystery" of the title. Thirst alone is not motive enough; the other soldiers do not seem particularly thirsty. The jeers of his comrades force him to declare his fearlessness—though, to himself, he questions his courage.

7. Most students will agree that his quest for water is not heroic. His heroism lies in returning under fire to give the dying man water. As frenzied as he is with fear, he feels an impulse to do "what must be done."

8. Answers will vary. If the officers spill the water, they have "undone" Collins's deed. If the bucket is already empty, Collins's ordeal was pointless. In either case, it is ironic that after Collins's fearsome journey, no one living gets water.

9. Students may suggest that Collins probably wouldn't have dared express anger at the lieutenants. Perhaps he shrugged and made a joke.

10. The artillery argues with other guns; the guns are called "stolid" and "courageous." The soldiers' eyes sweep in a "machine-like movement." Students should find other examples.

Students will agree that war dehumanizes. You might refer them ahead to Tim O'Brien's story "Speaking of Courage" (page 935).

6. Collins, the soldier who takes center stage in the story, must have had a powerful **motive** for his daring act. Is this the mystery in the title? Do you think his motive is thirst? Or the jeers of his comrades? Or some other force in his nature? Discuss your answers.
7. What do you think is heroic in Collins's behavior? Is it the fetching of the water? Or his return to the wounded officer? Or perhaps neither?
8. The ending of the story is **ambiguous**—that is, it suggests several interpretations. Do you think the lieutenants spilled the water? Or was the bucket empty by the time Collins got back? What significance do you read into that empty bucket—into the spilled water that Collins had risked his life for?
9. We are not told how Collins reacts to the "skylarking lieutenants' " carelessness, but what do you imagine he said or did when he saw what had happened?
10. In modern war, it has been said, machines resemble humans and humans resemble machines. Find two or three examples from this story showing that Crane also feels that war **personifies** machines and dehumanizes people. What do you think of this idea about the dehumanizing effects of war and the glorification of its machines?

Writing About the Story

A Critical Response

1. **Comparing a Poem and a Story.** Write a brief essay in which you summarize Stephen Crane's attitude toward war, based on your reading of "A Mystery of Heroism" and the following poem. In your essay, be sure to cover these questions:

	Poem	Story
1. Is anyone a hero in the sense of being noble, or willing to risk his life for a high moral principle?		
2. Does any scene in the poem remind you of a scene in the story?		
3. Does Crane really show you that war is kind?		

War Is Kind

Do not weep, maiden, for war is kind.
Because your lover threw wild hands toward the sky
And the affrighted steed ran on alone,
Do not weep.
War is kind.

Hoarse, booming drums of the regiment,
Little souls who thirst for fight,
These men were born to drill and die.
The unexplained glory flies above them,
Great is the battle-god, great, and his kingdom—
A field where a thousand corpses lie.

Do not weep, babe, for war is kind.
Because your father tumbled in the yellow trenches,
Raged at his breast, gulped and died,
Do not weep.
War is kind.

Swift blazing flag of the regiment,
Eagle with crest of red and gold,
These men were born to drill and die.
Point for them the virtue of slaughter,
Make plain to them the excellence of killing
And a field where a thousand corpses lie.

Mother whose heart hung humble as a button
On the bright splendid shroud of your son,
Do not weep.
War is kind.

—Stephen Crane, 1896

2. **Responding to a Critic.** Critic J. C. Levenson says this about Crane's stories:

> The casting out of fear and the finding of brotherly love are the touchstones of his naturalistic parables.

Do you think this statement applies to "A Mystery of Heroism"? If so, can you detect **irony** in the fact that a person discovers brotherhood in the midst of a *civil* war? In a brief essay, discuss your response to these questions.

Supplementary Support Materials
1. Vocabulary Activity Worksheet (*CCB*)
2. Review and Response Worksheet: Conflict and Theme (*CCB*)
3. Language Skills Worksheet: The Descriptive Paragraph (*CCB*)
4. Selection Test (*CCB*)

Developing Vocabulary
The following words from the story are tested in the Selection Test. (See also Vocabulary Activity Worksheet.)

scrutiny	contritely
cynical	abominable
impetuous	tangible
ingenuously	plausible
composite	simultaneously

Preparation
Establishing a Purpose. After students read the headnote, ask them how they think they would feel in such a life-and-death situation, how they would respond to their fellow castaways and to the danger. Ask them to compare their responses to those of the characters in the story.

A. Expansion
Crane's news report of this event appears in the Great Illustrated Classics edition of *The Red Badge of Courage and Other Stories* by Stephen Crane (Dodd, Mead & Company, 1957). In his news report Crane said, "The history of life in an open boat for thirty hours would no doubt be instructive for the young, but none is to be told here and now." Perhaps he was already planning this short story.

B. Comparison
Note how Crane describes the captain's feelings by comparing his loss to other kinds of defeats.

C. Plot
This indirect reference is the only mention of the ship's sinking—a dramatic event, but not the focus of this story.

THE OPEN BOAT

Writers are often advised to focus on what they know best. Stephen Crane surely did that in the following story. On New Year's Day, 1897, Crane was a news correspondent aboard the *Commodore*, a ship carrying arms and ammunition from Jacksonville, Florida, to rebels in Cuba. Off the Florida coast the ship went off course, rammed a sandbar, developed a leak, and sank. Crane and three (or possibly four) members of the crew spent a worrisome day and night in a ten-foot dinghy. They came ashore finally at Daytona Beach; one man was drowned. Crane's first account of the incident was a news dispatch. His second was this short story, perhaps his finest. A

This story of four castaways is a perfect example of humans in conflict with nature. As you read, see how Crane wrings every wet inch of suspense out of the situation. Will these poor fellows survive the shipwreck, or won't they? Theirs is such a little chip of a boat. Imagine, ten feet. Two of those survivors, laid head to toe, would be longer than that boat. And what a frightening description of the sea's power to swallow them! What a lot of angry water! And how miserably hungry, soaked, tired, and cold they are. It's not surprising that, before long, we begin to share in the survivors' terror.

When it seems as if we cannot bear another whitecap, there is sudden hope on the horizon. So we row on, shipping more water, all but goners. Rescue seems at hand, but no, there's more, much more, to be endured. See if you agree that, once you read "The Open Boat," you will never again take dry land for granted.

A Tale Intended to be after the Fact: Being the Experience of Four Men from the Sunk Steamer Commodore

I

None of them knew the color of the sky. Their eyes glanced level, and were fastened upon the waves that swept toward them. These waves were of the hue of slate, save for the tops, which were of foaming white, and all of the men knew the colors of the sea. The horizon narrowed and widened, and dipped and rose, and at all times its edge was jagged with waves that seemed thrust up in points like rocks.

Many a man ought to have a bathtub larger than the boat which here rode upon the sea. These waves were most wrongfully and barbarously abrupt and tall, and each froth-top was a problem in small-boat navigation.

The cook squatted in the bottom, and looked with both eyes at the six inches of gunwale[1] which separated him from the ocean. His sleeves were rolled over his fat forearms, and the two flaps of his unbuttoned vest dangled as he bent to bail out the boat. Often he said, "Gawd! that was a narrow clip." As he remarked it he invariably gazed eastward over the broken sea.

The oiler, steering with one of the two oars in the boat, sometimes raised himself suddenly to keep clear of water that swirled in over the stern. It was a thin little oar, and it seemed often ready to snap.

The correspondent, pulling at the other oar, watched the waves and wondered why he was there.

The injured captain, lying in the bow, was at this time buried in that profound dejection and indifference which comes, temporarily at least, to even the bravest and most enduring when, willy-nilly, the firm fails, the army loses, the ship goes down. The mind of the master of a vessel is rooted deep in the timbers of her, though he command for a day or a decade; and this captain had on him the stern impression of a scene in the grays of dawn of seven turned faces, and later a stump of a topmast with a white ball on it, that slashed to and fro at the waves, went low and lower, and down. Thereafter there was something strange in his voice. Although steady, it was deep with

1. **gunwale** (gun'l): the side of the boat.

mourning, and of a quality beyond oration or tears.

"Keep 'er a little more south, Billie," said he.

"A little more south, sir," said the oiler in the stern.

A seat in his boat was not unlike a seat upon a bucking bronco, and by the same token a bronco is not much smaller. The craft pranced and reared and plunged like an animal. As each wave came, and she rose for it, she seemed like a horse making at a fence outrageously high. The manner of her scramble over these walls of water is a mystic thing, and, moreover, at the top of them were ordinarily these problems in white water, the foam racing down from the summit of each wave requiring a new leap, and a leap from the air. Then, after scornfully bumping a crest, she would slide and race and splash down a long incline, and arrive bobbing and nodding in front of the next menace.

A singular disadvantage of the sea lies in the fact that after successfully surmounting one wave you discover that there is another behind it just as important and just as nervously anxious to do something effective in the way of swamping boats. In a ten-foot dinghy one can get an idea of the resources of the sea in the line of waves that is not probable to the average experience which is never at sea in a dinghy. As each slaty wall of water approached, it shut all else from the view of the men in the boat, and it was not difficult to imagine that this particular wave was the final outburst of the ocean, the last effort of the grim water. There was a terrible grace in the move of the waves, and they came in silence, save for the snarling of the crests.

In the wan light the faces of the men must have been gray. Their eyes must have glinted in strange ways as they gazed steadily astern. Viewed from a balcony, the whole thing would doubtless have been weirdly picturesque. But the men in the boat had no time to see it, and if they had had leisure, there were other things to occupy their minds. The sun swung steadily up the sky, and they knew it was broad day because the color of the sea changed from slate to emerald green streaked with amber lights, and the foam was like tumbling snow. The process of the breaking day was unknown to them. They were aware only of this effect upon the color of the waves that rolled toward them.

In disjointed sentences the cook and the correspondent argued as to the difference between a life-saving station and a house of refuge. The cook had said: "There's a house of refuge just north of the Mosquito Inlet Light, and as soon as they see us they'll come off in their boat and pick us up."

"As soon as who see us?" said the correspondent.

"The crew," said the cook.

"Houses of refuge don't have crews," said the correspondent. "As I understand them, they are only places where clothes and grub are stored for the benefit of shipwrecked people. They don't carry crews."

"Oh, yes, they do," said the cook.

"No, they don't," said the correspondent.

"Well, we're not there yet, anyhow," said the oiler, in the stern.

"Well," said the cook, "perhaps it's not a house of refuge that I'm thinking of as being near Mosquito Inlet Light; perhaps it's a life-saving station."

"We're not there yet," said the oiler in the stern.

II

As the boat bounced from the top of each wave the wind tore through the hair of the hatless men, and as the craft plopped her stern down again the spray slashed past them. The crest of each of these waves was a hill, from the top of which the men surveyed for a moment a broad tumultuous expanse, shining and wind-riven. It was probably splendid, it was probably glorious, this play of the free sea, wild with lights of emerald and white and amber.

"Bully good thing it's an on-shore wind," said the cook. "If not, where would we be? Wouldn't have a show."

"That's right," said the correspondent.

The busy oiler nodded his assent.

Then the captain, in the bow, chuckled in a way that expressed humor, contempt, tragedy, all in one. "Do you think we've got much of a show now, boys?" said he.

Whereupon the three were silent, save for a trifle of hemming and hawing. To express any particular optimism at this time they felt to be childish and stupid, but they all doubtless possessed this sense of the situation in their minds.

A. Figurative Language Have students note the extended simile here (the craft is like a bronco) and the personification of the waves in the next paragraph.

B. Impressionism Crane is considered an impressionist writer because of his faithful account of characters' impressions of a scene. Have students apply the definition (page 455) to "The Open Boat." Have students also note, however, that Crane is often "painterly" in his physical descriptions, like this one.

C. Expansion Before 1871 only volunteers conducted rescue efforts and built shelter huts ("houses of refuge") along isolated stretches of coast. The Coast Guard (then known as the Revenue Marine) engaged only in antismuggling efforts; but in 1871 the service began to organize lifesaving stations and rescue crews. In 1878 it became the U.S. Lifesaving Service and in 1915, the U. S. Coast Guard.

Humanities Connection: Responding to the Fine Art
See page 153 for another Winslow Homer seascape and more information about him.

Homer's early work, apart from his genre paintings of the Civil War, were etchings for *Harper's Weekly* Magazine, portraying the aristocratic social scene. Two years spent in a fishing village in England in the 1880's, however, turned him to graver subjects. A year after his return to America, Homer moved to Prout's Neck, Maine, where he lived for the rest of his life. Again within sight and sound of the sea, Homer produced what many critics believe are his greatest works.

? Compare Homer's seascape with Crane's verbal description. What conflicts does this painting suggest, and how does it make you feel? (Answers will vary, but students will agree that the rugged seascape suggests conflicts within nature and creates an intensity of feeling.)

Maine Coast by Winslow Homer (1896). Oil on canvas.

The Metropolitan Museum of Art, New York. Gift of George A. Hearn, in memory of Arthur Hoppock Hearn, 1911. (11.116.1).

A young man thinks doggedly at such times. On the other hand, the ethics of their condition was decidedly against any open suggestion of hopelessness. So they were silent. A

"Oh, well," said the captain, soothing his children, "we'll get ashore all right."

But there was that in his tone which made them think; so the oiler quoth, "Yes! if this wind holds."

The cook was bailing. "Yes! if we don't catch hell in the surf."

Canton-flannel gulls flew near and far. Sometimes they sat down on the sea, near patches of brown seaweed that rolled over the waves with a movement like carpets on a line in a gale. The birds sat comfortably in groups, and they were envied by some in the dinghy, for the wrath of the sea was no more to them than it was to a covey of prairie chickens a thousand miles inland. Often they came very close and stared at the men with black bead-like eyes. At these times they were uncanny and sinister in their unblinking scrutiny, B and the men hooted angrily at them, telling them to be gone. One came, and evidently decided to alight on the top of the captain's head. The bird flew parallel to the boat and did not circle, but made short sidelong jumps in the air in chicken-fashion. His black eyes were wistfully fixed upon the captain's head. "Ugly brute," said the oiler to the bird. "You look as if you were made with a jackknife." The cook and the correspondent swore darkly at the creature. The captain naturally wished to knock it away with the end of the heavy painter, but he did not dare do it, because anything C resembling an emphatic gesture would have capsized this freighted boat; and so, with his open hand, the captain gently and carefully waved the gull away. After it had been discouraged from the pursuit the captain breathed easier on account of his hair, and others breathed easier because the bird struck their minds at this time as being somehow gruesome and ominous.

In the meantime the oiler and the correspondent rowed. And also they rowed. They sat together in the same seat, and each rowed an oar. Then the oiler took both oars; then the correspondent took both oars; then the oiler; then the correspondent. They rowed and they rowed. The very ticklish part of the business was when the time came for the reclining one in the stern to take his turn at the oars. By the very last star of truth, it is easier

A. Theme

? What are the men thinking of? Why don't they discuss their thoughts? (They are at this point optimistic, but optimism seems foolish under the circumstances. On the other hand, they cannot say anything pessimistic; their growing sense of comradeship prevents them from saying anything that might discourage the others.)

B. Word Choice

Have students notice the frequent use of the word *sinister* in the story.

? Why are the gulls described as sinister? (Gulls are carrion eaters, and they seem to be eyeing the men as possible meals, anticipating their deaths. Note that later in this paragraph, one gull is "wistfully" eyeing the captain's head.)

C. Expansion

The "painter," a heavy rope attached to the bow, is used to tie a boat to its mooring.

A. Symbol
What does the seaweed symbolize? (It looks like the land and therefore symbolizes safety.) What practical help does it provide? (The men can measure their forward movement as they pass the apparently stationary mats.)

B. Symbol
Have students look for another image of something that is small and pointed. (The pencil point on page 474) What do you think is the significance of these images? (They represent the fragility of human effort and human life, stacked against the chaos of nature and fate.)

C. Theme
How does Crane describe the "subtle brotherhood of men"? (Answers will vary, focusing on one or more details in this paragraph and elsewhere. Note, however, that although the men are wet and cold, this sense of brotherhood warms them.)

to steal eggs from under a hen than it was to change seats in the dinghy. First the man in the stern slid his hand along the thwart[2] and moved with care, as if he were of Sèvres.[3] Then the man in the rowing-seat slid his hand along the other thwart. It was all done with the most extraordinary care. As the two sidled past each other, the whole party kept watchful eyes on the coming wave, and the captain cried: "Look out, now! Steady, there!"

A The brown mats of seaweed that appeared from time to time were like islands, bits of earth. They were traveling, apparently, neither one way nor the other. They were, to all intents, stationary. They informed the men in the boat that it was making progress slowly toward the land.

The captain, rearing cautiously in the bow after the dinghy soared on a great swell, said that he had seen the lighthouse at Mosquito Inlet. Presently the cook remarked that he had seen it. The correspondent was at the oars then, and for some reason he too wished to look at the lighthouse; but his back was toward the far shore, and the waves were important, and for some time he could not seize an opportunity to turn his head. But at last there came a wave more gentle than the others, and when at the crest of it he swiftly scoured the western horizon.

"See it?" said the captain.

"No," said the correspondent, slowly; "I didn't see anything."

"Look again," said the captain. He pointed. "It's exactly in that direction."

At the top of another wave the correspondent did as he was bid, and this time his eyes chanced
B on a small, still thing on the edge of the swaying horizon. It was precisely like the point of a pin. It took an anxious eye to find a lighthouse so tiny.

"Think we'll make it, Captain?"

"If this wind holds and the boat don't swamp, we can't do much else," said the captain.

The little boat, lifted by each towering sea and splashed viciously by the crests, made progress that in the absence of seaweed was not apparent to those in her. She seemed just a wee thing wallowing, miraculously top up, at the mercy of five oceans. Occasionally a great spread of water, like white flames, swarmed into her.

"Bail her, cook," said the captain, serenely.

"All right, Captain," said the cheerful cook.

III

It would be difficult to describe the subtle brotherhood of men that was here established on the seas. No one said that it was so. No one mentioned it. But it dwelt in the boat, and each man felt it warm him. They were a captain, an oiler, a cook, and a correspondent, and they were friends—friends in a more curiously iron-bound degree than may be common. The hurt captain, lying against the water-jar in the bow, spoke always in a low voice and calmly; but he could never command a more ready and swiftly obedient crew than the motley three of the dinghy. It was more than a mere recognition of what was best for the common safety. There was surely in it a quality that was personal and heart-felt. And after this devotion to the commander of the boat, there was this comradeship, that the correspondent, for instance, who had been taught to be cynical of men, knew even at the time was the best experience of his life. But no one said that it was so. No one mentioned it. C

"I wish we had a sail," remarked the captain. "We might try my overcoat on the end of an oar, and give you two boys a chance to rest." So the cook and the correspondent held the mast and spread wide the overcoat; the oiler steered; and the little boat made good way with her new rig. Sometimes the oiler had to scull sharply to keep a sea from breaking into the boat, but otherwise sailing was a success.

Meanwhile the lighthouse had been growing slowly larger. It had now almost assumed color, and appeared like a little gray shadow on the sky. The man at the oars could not be prevented from turning his head rather often to try for a glimpse of this little gray shadow.

At last, from the top of each wave, the men in the tossing boat could see land. Even as the lighthouse was an upright shadow on the sky, this land seemed but a long black shadow on the sea. It certainly was thinner than paper. "We must be about opposite New Smyrna," said the cook, who had coasted this shore often in schooners. "Captain, by the way, I believe they abandoned that life-saving station there about a year ago."

"Did they?" said the captain.

2. **thwart:** a seat, going crosswise, for a rower.
3. **Sèvres** (sev′rə): a fine porcelain china made in Sèvres, France.

The wind slowly died away. The cook and the correspondent were not now obliged to slave in order to hold high the oar. But the waves continued their old impetuous swooping at the dinghy, and the little craft, no longer under way, struggled woundily over them. The oiler or the correspondent took the oars again.

A Shipwrecks are apropos of nothing. If men could only train for them and have them occur when the men had reached pink condition, there would be less drowning at sea. Of the four in the dinghy none had slept any time worth mentioning for two days and two nights previous to embarking in the dinghy, and in the excitement of clambering about the deck of a foundering ship they had also forgotten to eat heartily.

B For these reasons, and for others, neither the oiler nor the correspondent was fond of rowing at this time. The correspondent wondered ingenuously how in the name of all that was sane could there be people who thought it amusing to row a boat. It was not an amusement; it was a diabolical punishment, and even a genius of mental aberrations could never conclude that it was anything but a horror to the muscles and a crime against the back. He mentioned to the boat in general how the amusement of rowing struck him, and the weary-faced oiler smiled in full sympathy. Previously to the foundering, by the way, the oiler had worked a double watch in the engine-room of the ship.

"Take her easy now, boys," said the captain. C "Don't spend yourselves. If we have to run a surf you'll need all your strength, because we'll sure have to swim for it. Take your time."

Slowly the land arose from the sea. From a black line it became a line of black and a line of white—trees and sand. Finally the captain said that he could make out a house on the shore. "That's the house of refuge, sure," said the cook. "They'll see us before long, and come out after us."

The distant lighthouse reared high. "The keeper ought to be able to make us out now, if he's looking through a glass," said the captain. "He'll notify the life-saving people."

"None of those other boats could have got ashore to give word of this wreck," said the oiler, in a low voice, "else the lifeboat would be out hunting us."

Slowly and beautifully the land loomed out of the sea. The wind came again. It had veered from the northeast to the southeast. Finally a new sound struck the ears of the men in the boat. It was the low thunder of the surf on the shore. "We'll never be able to make the lighthouse now," said the captain. "Swing her head a little more north, Billie."

"A little more north, sir," said the oiler.

Whereupon the little boat turned her nose once more down the wind, and all but the oarsman watched the shore grow. Under the influence of this expansion doubt and direful apprehension were leaving the minds of the men. The management of the boat was still most absorbing, but it could not prevent a quiet cheerfulness. In an hour, perhaps, they would be ashore. D

Their backbones had become thoroughly used to balancing in the boat, and they now rode this wild colt of a dinghy like circus men. The correspondent thought that he had been drenched to the skin, but happening to feel in the top pocket of his coat, he found therein eight cigars. Four of them were soaked with sea-water; four were perfectly scatheless. After a search, somebody produced three dry matches; and thereupon the four waifs rode impudently in their little boat and, with an assurance of an impending rescue shining in their eyes, puffed at the big cigars, and judged well and ill of all men. Everybody took a drink of water. E

IV

"Cook," remarked the captain, "there don't seem to be any signs of life about your house of refuge."

"No," replied the cook. "Funny they don't see us!"

A broad stretch of lowly coast lay before the eyes of the men. It was of low dunes topped with dark vegetation. The roar of the surf was plain, and sometimes they could see the white lip of a wave as it spun up the beach. A tiny house was blocked out black upon the sky. Southward, the slim lighthouse lifted its little gray length.

Tide, wind, and waves were swinging the dinghy northward. "Funny they don't see us," said the men.

The surf's roar was here dulled, but its tone was nevertheless thunderous and mighty. As the boat swam over the great rollers the men sat listening to this roar. "We'll swamp sure," said everybody.

It is fair to say here that there was not a life-

A. Theme
? What do you think this startling sentence means? (Answers will vary. *Apropos of* means "connected to" or "with reference to." Shipwrecks are random events, part of the overall indifference—or even malevolence—of nature.)

B. Tone
Note the satiric tone, humorous because of its understatement.

C. Foreshadowing
? What problem does the captain foresee? (The greatest danger will be closest to shore—the surf.)

D. Plot
? At this point, how do the men expect their story to turn out? (Happily, with all safely on shore)
? What do you expect will happen? (Ask students to keep alert to clues to the story's ending. You might review the terms *situational irony* (page 1175) and *foreshadowing* (page 1173).

E. Impressionism
Here is a vivid image, worthy of Winslow Homer's brush.

A. Expansion
As the *Commodore* sank, one of the men left on board without a lifeboat jumped to his death in the open seas. In his newspaper account of the *Commodore*'s sinking, Crane wrote, "I somehow felt that I could see in the expression of his hands, and in the very toss of his head, as he leaped thus to death, that it was rage, rage, rage unspeakable that was in his heart at the time."

B. Leitmotif
A *leitmotif* is a recurring phrase or passage, especially in music, that is important to the meaning or structure of a work. Ask students to look for this passage repeated in the story and to consider what it has to do with the story's theme. (Dying seems absurd with the shore in sight. The contrast emphasizes that life is neither fair nor reasonable.)

C. Metaphor
Note the metaphors for Fate or Destiny. ("an old ninny-woman"; "an old hen")

D. Irony
Even an image—here, a tiny man threatening the vast, uncaring sky—can be ironic.

E. Dialogue
? Why do you suppose Crane doesn't use dialogue tags for most of the conversation that follows? (Neither the speaker nor the tone of voice matters. The dialogue moves more rapidly without tags.)

saving station within twenty miles in either direction; but the men did not know this fact, and in consequence they made dark and opprobrious remarks concerning the eyesight of the nation's lifesavers. Four scowling men sat in the dinghy and surpassed records in the invention of epithets.

"Funny they don't see us."

The lightheartedness of a former time had completely faded. To their sharpened minds it was easy to conjure pictures of all kinds of incompetency and blindness and, indeed, cowardice. There was the shore of the populous land, and it was bitter and bitter to them that from it came no sign.

"Well," said the captain, ultimately, "I suppose we'll have to make a try for ourselves. If we stay out here too long, we'll none of us have strength left to swim after the boat swamps."

And so the oiler, who was at the oars, turned the boat straight for the shore. There was a sudden tightening of muscles. There was some thinking.

"If we don't all get ashore," said the captain—"if we don't all get ashore, I suppose you fellows know where to send news of my finish?"

A They then briefly exchanged some addresses and admonitions. As for the reflections of the men, there was a great deal of rage in them. Perchance B they might be formulated thus: "If I am going to be drowned—if I am going to be drowned—if I am going to be drowned, why, in the name of the seven mad gods who rule the sea, was I allowed to come thus far and contemplate sand and trees? Was I brought here merely to have my nose dragged away as I was about to nibble the sacred C cheese of life? It is preposterous. If this old ninny-woman, Fate, cannot do better than this, she should be deprived of the management of men's fortunes. She is an old hen who knows not her intention. If she has decided to drown me, why did she not do it in the beginning and save me all this trouble? The whole affair is absurd.—But no; she cannot mean to drown me. She dare not drown me. She cannot drown me. Not after all this D work." Afterward the man might have had an impulse to shake his fist at the clouds. "Just you drown me, now, and then hear what I call you!"

The billows that came at this time were more formidable. They seemed always just about to break and roll over the little boat in a turmoil of foam. There was a preparatory and long growl in the speech of them. No mind unused to the sea would have concluded that the dinghy could ascend these sheer heights in time. The shore was still afar. The oiler was a wily surfman. "Boys," he said swiftly, "she won't live three minutes more, and we're too far out to swim. Shall I take her to sea again, Captain?"

"Yes; go ahead!" said the captain.

This oiler, by a series of quick miracles and fast and steady oarsmanship, turned the boat in the middle of the surf and took her safely to sea again.

There was a considerable silence as the boat bumped over the furrowed sea to deeper water. Then somebody in gloom spoke: "Well, anyhow, they must have seen us from the shore by now."

The gulls went in slanting flight up the wind toward the gray, desolate east. A squall, marked by dingy clouds and clouds brick-red like smoke from a burning building, appeared from the southeast.

"What do you think of those life-saving people? Ain't they peaches?" E

"Funny they haven't seen us."

"Maybe they think we're out here for sport! Maybe they think we're fishin'. Maybe they think we're damned fools."

It was a long afternoon. A changed tide tried to force them southward, but wind and wave said northward. Far ahead, where coastline, sea, and sky formed their mighty angle, there were little dots which seemed to indicate a city on the shore.

"St. Augustine?"

The captain shook his head. "Too near Mosquito Inlet."

And the oiler rowed, and then the correspondent rowed; then the oiler rowed. It was a weary business. The human back can become the seat of more aches and pains than are registered in books for the composite anatomy of a regiment. It is a limited area, but it can become the theater of innumerable muscular conflicts, tangles, wrenches, knots, and other comforts.

"Did you ever like to row, Billie?" asked the correspondent.

"No," said the oiler; "hang it!"

When one exchanged the rowing-seat for a place in the bottom of the boat, he suffered a bodily depression that caused him to be careless of everything save an obligation to wiggle one finger. There was cold sea-water swashing to and fro in the boat, and he lay in it. His head, pillowed on a thwart, was within an inch of the swirl of a wave-crest, and sometimes a particularly obstreperous[4] sea came inboard and drenched him once more. But these matters did not annoy him. It is almost certain that if the boat had capsized he would have tumbled comfortably out upon the ocean as if he felt sure that it was a great soft mattress.

"Look! There's a man on the shore!"

"Where?"

"There! See 'im? See 'im?"

"Yes, sure! He's walking along."

"Now he's stopped. Look! He's facing us!"

"He's waving at us!"

"So he is! By thunder!"

"Ah, now we're all right! Now we're all right! There'll be a boat out here for us in half an hour."

A "He's going on. He's running. He's going up to that house there."

The remote beach seemed lower than the sea, and it required a searching glance to discern the little black figure. The captain saw a floating stick, and they rowed to it. A bath towel was by some weird chance in the boat, and, tying this on the stick, the captain waved it. The oarsman did not dare turn his head, so he was obliged to ask questions.

"What's he doing now?"

B "He's standing still again. He's looking, I think.—There he goes again—toward the house.—Now he's stopped again."

"Is he waving at us?"

"No, not now; he was, though."

"Look! There comes another man!"

"He's running."

"Look at him go, would you!"

"Why, he's on a bicycle. Now he's met the other man. They're both waving at us. Look!"

"There comes something up the beach."

"What the devil is that thing?"

"Why, it looks like a boat."

"Why, certainly, it's a boat."

"No; it's on wheels."

"Yes, so it is. Well, that must be the lifeboat. They drag them along shore on a wagon."

"That's the lifeboat, sure."

"No, by God, it's—it's an omnibus."[5]

4. **obstreperous** (əb·strep′ər·əs): unruly.

5. **omnibus:** a vehicle for carrying many passengers. At the time the story was written, it would have been drawn by horses.

"I tell you it's a lifeboat."

"It is not! It's an omnibus. I can see it plain. See? One of these big hotel omnibuses."

"By thunder, you're right. It's an omnibus, sure as fate. What do you suppose they are doing with an omnibus? Maybe they are going around collecting the life-crew, hey?"

"That's it, likely. Look! There's a fellow waving a little black flag. He's standing on the steps of the omnibus. There come those other two fellows. Now they're all talking together. Look at the fellow with the flag. Maybe he ain't waving it!"

"That ain't a flag, is it? That's his coat. Why, certainly, that's his coat."

"So it is; it's his coat. He's taken it off and is waving it around his head. But would you look at him swing it!"

"Oh, say, there isn't any life-saving station there. That's just a winter-resort hotel omnibus that has brought over some of the boarders to see us drown."

"What's that idiot with the coat mean? What's he signaling, anyhow?"

"It looks as if he were trying to tell us to go north. There must be a life-saving station up there."

"No; he thinks we're fishing. Just giving us a merry hand. See? Ah, there, Willie!"

"Well, I wish I could make something out of those signals. What do you suppose he means?"

"He don't mean anything; he's just playing."

"Well, if he'd just signal us to try the surf again, or to go to sea and wait, or go north, or go south, or go to hell, there would be some reason in it. But look at him! He just stands there and keeps his coat revolving like a wheel. The ass!"

"There come more people."

"Now there's quite a mob. Look! Isn't that a boat?"

"Where? Oh, I see where you mean. No, that's no boat."

"That fellow is still waving his coat."

"He must think we like to see him do that. Why don't he quit it? It don't mean anything."

"I don't know. I think he is trying to make us go north. It must be that there's a life-saving station there somewhere."

"Say, he ain't tired yet. Look at 'im wave!"

"Wonder how long he can keep that up. He's been revolving his coat ever since he caught sight

A. Dialogue

? What excuse does Crane offer for this long, repetitive conversation, with the men discussing each detail of the situation on shore? (The speakers are explaining what's happening to the rower, who is seated with his back to shore. Crane also is giving us some variety by reporting the action by means of dialogue rather than the narrator's voice.)

B. Irony

Throughout the scene that follows, from here to the end of Part IV, have students note how the men's expectations are repeatedly thwarted: The man is not telling them anything with his gestures; the lifesaving boat turns out to be a hotel omnibus; there is no rescue.)

A. Syntax/ Repetition

? Why do you think Crane uses this same description, almost word for word, on pages 467 and 470? (For the oiler and the correspondent, rowing is the sum of their existence. Note also that the rhythm of the words matches the rhythm of the rowing.)

B. Figurative Language/Theme

? To what is the speaker comparing himself? (To a mouse that is being tormented) How does this comparison fit the theme of the story? (A mouse is usually regarded as a helpless creature, highly subject to the vagaries of fate.)

C. Imagery

? What mood do these images create? (Vast emptiness, desolation, a feeling of one's unimportance in the universe) Encourage student artists to try to depict a scene such as this from the story.

of us. He's an idiot. Why aren't they getting men to bring a boat out? A fishing-boat—one of those big yawls—could come out here all right. Why don't he do something?"

"Oh, it's all right now."

"They'll have a boat out here for us in less than no time, now that they've seen us."

A faint yellow tone came into the sky over the low land. The shadows on the sea slowly deepened. The wind bore coldness with it, and the men began to shiver.

"Holy smoke!" said one, allowing his voice to express his impious mood, "if we keep on monkeying out here! If we've got to flounder out here all night!"

"Oh, we'll never have to stay here all night! Don't you worry. They've seen us now, and it won't be long before they'll come chasing out after us."

The shore grew dusky. The man waving a coat blended gradually into this gloom, and it swallowed in the same manner the omnibus and the group of people. The spray, when it dashed uproariously over the side, made the voyagers shrink and swear like men who were being branded.

"I'd like to catch the chump who waved the coat. I feel like socking him one, just for luck."

"Why? What did he do?"

"Oh, nothing, but then he seemed so damned cheerful."

A In the meantime the oiler rowed, and then the correspondent rowed, and then the oiler rowed. Gray-faced and bowed forward, they mechanically, turn by turn, plied the leaden oars. The form of the lighthouse had vanished from the southern horizon, but finally a pale star appeared, just lifting from the sea. The streaked saffron in the west passed before the all-merging darkness, and the sea to the east was black. The land had vanished, and was expressed only by the low and drear thunder of the surf.

"If I am going to be drowned—if I am going to be drowned—if I am going to be drowned, why, in the name of the seven mad gods who rule the sea, was I allowed to come thus far and contemplate sand and trees? Was I brought here merely B to have my nose dragged away as I was about to nibble the sacred cheese of life?"

The patient captain, drooped over the water-jar, was sometimes obliged to speak to the oarsman.

"Keep her head up! Keep her head up!"

"Keep her head up, sir." The voices were weary and low.

This was surely a quiet evening. All save the oarsman lay heavily and listlessly in the boat's bottom. As for him, his eyes were just capable of noting the tall black waves that swept forward in a most sinister silence, save for an occasional subdued growl of a crest.

The cook's head was on a thwart, and he looked without interest at the water under his nose. He was deep in other scenes. Finally he spoke. "Billie," he murmured, dreamfully, "what kind of pie do you like best?"

V

"Pie!" said the oiler and the correspondent, agitatedly. "Don't talk about those things, blast you!"

"Well," said the cook, "I was just thinking about ham sandwiches and—"

A night on the sea in an open boat is a long night. As darkness settled finally, the shine of the light, lifting from the sea in the south, changed to full gold. On the northern horizon a new light appeared, a small bluish gleam on the edge of the waters. These two lights were the furniture of the world. Otherwise there was nothing but waves. C

Two men huddled in the stern, and distances were so magnificent in the dinghy that the rower was enabled to keep his feet partly warm by thrusting them under his companions. Their legs indeed extended far under the rowing-seat until they touched the feet of the captain forward. Sometimes, despite the efforts of the tired oarsman, a wave came piling into the boat, an icy wave of the night, and the chilling water soaked them anew. They would twist their bodies for a moment and groan, and sleep the dead sleep once more, while the water in the boat gurgled about them as the craft rocked.

The plan of the oiler and the correspondent was for one to row until he lost the ability, and then arouse the other from his sea-water couch in the bottom of the boat.

The oiler plied the oars until his head drooped forward and the overpowering sleep blinded him; and he rowed yet afterward. Then he touched a man in the bottom of the boat, and called his name. "Will you spell me for a little while?" he said, meekly.

"Sure, Billie," said the correspondent, awaking and dragging himself to a sitting position. They

A. Theme

What is the significance of this short description? (It reflects the sense of brotherhood that the men feel.)

B. Theme

What is the significance of this short dialogue? (It again reflects brotherhood. Even in their misery, the men remain polite and sensitive to each other.)

exchanged places carefully, and the oiler, cuddling down in the seawater at the cook's side, seemed to go to sleep instantly.

The particular violence of the sea had ceased. The waves came without snarling. The obligation of the man at the oars was to keep the boat headed so that the tilt of the rollers would not capsize her, and to preserve her from filling when the crests rushed past. The black waves were silent and hard to be seen in the darkness. Often one was almost upon the boat before the oarsman was aware.

In a low voice the correspondent addressed the captain. He was not sure that the captain was awake, although this iron man seemed to be always awake. "Captain, shall I keep her making for that light north, sir?"

The same steady voice answered him. "Yes. Keep it about two points off the port bow."

The cook had tied a life belt around himself in order to get even the warmth which this clumsy cork contrivance could donate, and he seemed almost stove-like when a rower, whose teeth invariably chattered wildly as soon as he ceased his labor, dropped down to sleep.

A The correspondent, as he rowed, looked down at the two men sleeping underfoot. The cook's arm was around the oiler's shoulders, and, with their fragmentary clothing and haggard faces, they were the babes of the sea—a grotesque rendering of the old babes in the wood.[6]

Later he must have grown stupid at his work, for suddenly there was a growling of water, and a crest came with a roar and a swash into the boat, and it was a wonder that it did not set the cook afloat in his life belt. The cook continued to sleep, but the oiler sat up, blinking his eyes and shaking with the new cold.

B "Oh, I'm awful sorry, Billie," said the correspondent, contritely.

"That's all right, old boy," said the oiler, and lay down again and was asleep.

Presently it seemed that even the captain dozed, and the correspondent thought that he was the one man afloat on all the oceans. The wind had a voice as it came over the waves, and it was sadder than the end.

There was a long, loud swishing astern of the boat, and a gleaming trail of phosphorescence, like blue flame, was furrowed on the black waters. It might have been made by a monstrous knife.

Then there came a stillness, while the correspondent breathed with open mouth and looked at the sea.

Suddenly there was another swish and another long flash of bluish light, and this time it was alongside the boat, and might almost been reached with an oar. The correspondent saw an enormous fin speed like a shadow through the water, hurling the crystalline spray and leaving the long glowing trail.

The correspondent looked over his shoulder at the captain. His face was hidden, and he seemed to be asleep. He looked at the babes of the sea. They certainly were asleep. So, being bereft of sympathy, he leaned a little way to one side and swore softly into the sea.

But the thing did not then leave the vicinity of the boat. Ahead or astern, on one side or the other, at intervals long or short, fled the long sparkling streak, and there was to be heard the *whirroo* of the dark fin. The speed and power of the thing was greatly to be admired. It cut the water like a gigantic and keen projectile.

The presence of this biding thing did not affect the man with the same horror that it would if he had been a picnicker. He simply looked at the sea dully and swore in an undertone. C

Nevertheless, it is true that he did not wish to be alone with the thing. He wished one of his companions to awake by chance and keep him company with it. But the captain hung motionless over the water-jar, and the oiler and the cook in the bottom of the boat were plunged in slumber.

VI

"If I am going to be drowned—if I am going to be drowned—if I am going to be drowned, why, in the name of the seven mad gods who rule the sea, was I allowed to come thus far and contemplate sand and trees?" D

During this dismal night, it may be remarked that a man would conclude that it was really the intention of the seven mad gods to drown him, despite the abominable injustice of it. For it was certainly an abominable injustice to drown a man who had worked so hard, so hard. The man felt it would be a crime most unnatural. Other people had drowned at sea since galleys swarmed with painted sails, but still—

6. **babes in the wood:** a reference to an old story about two children left to die in the woods, who were ministered to by friendly birds. The two abandoned children were often depicted by artists as lying in the forest, covered with leaves and entwined in each other's arms.

C. Theme

Why does the correspondent repond to the shark with less horror than he felt toward the gulls? (He has endured too much to be surprised at this new threat.)

Why does he wish one of the others would waken "by chance"? (Sharing their experience has been good. Now he would prefer to share this, too. Out of consideration for his companions, however, he won't wake them.)

D. Repetition

Again Crane repeats the leitmotif introduced on page 470 and repeated on page 472. Why? (He is suggesting that the men are obsessing about this question; it is all they can think about. And it stresses one of the themes of the story—that nature has no concern for humanity.)

A. Theme

? Why does Crane switch to present tense? (He is expressing directly to the reader what he believes are general truths, applicable to all people, not just the men in the boat.)

B. Personification

? How does Crane personify nature here? (Nature speaks to a person; a star is what she speaks.)

? Why is a star appropriate as nature's word? (It is high, cold, and indifferent.)

? How do you react when you look at a starry sky? (Answers will vary, but some students will probably note that many people feel the insignificance of human life when they contemplate the stars.)

C. Expansion

This is the first stanza of "Bingen on the Rhine" by the English poet Caroline Elizabeth Sheridan North (1808–1877). Algiers is the capital of Algeria, a North African country colonized by the French in the 19th century. Algeria gained its independence in 1962.

A When it occurs to a man that nature does not regard him as important, and that she feels she would not maim the universe by disposing of him, he at first wishes to throw bricks at the temple, and he hates deeply the fact that there are no bricks and no temples. Any visible expression of nature would surely be pelleted with his jeers.

Then, if there be no tangible thing to hoot, he feels, perhaps, the desire to confront a personification and indulge in pleas, bowed to one knee, and with hands supplicant, saying, "Yes, but I love myself."

B A high cold star on a winter's night is the word he feels that she says to him. Thereafter he knows the pathos of his situation.

The men in the dinghy had not discussed these matters, but each had, no doubt, reflected upon them in silence and according to his mind. There was seldom any expression upon their faces save the general one of complete weariness. Speech was devoted to the business of the boat.

To chime the notes of his emotion, a verse mysteriously entered the correspondent's head. He had even forgotten that he had forgotten this verse, but it suddenly was in his mind.

C
A soldier of the Legion[7] lay dying in Algiers;
There was lack of woman's nursing, there was dearth of woman's tears;
But a comrade stood beside him, and he took that comrade's hand,
And he said, "I never more shall see my own, my native land."

In his childhood the correspondent had been made acquainted with the fact that a soldier of the Legion lay dying in Algiers, but he had never regarded the fact as important. Myriads of his schoolfellows had informed him of the soldier's plight, but the dinning had naturally ended by making him perfectly indifferent. He had never considered it his affair that a soldier of the Legion lay dying in Algiers, nor had it appeared to him as a matter for sorrow. It was less to him than the breaking of a pencil's point.

Now, however, it quaintly came to him as a human, living thing. It was no longer merely a picture of a few throes in the breast of a poet, meanwhile drinking tea and warming his feet at the grate; it was an actuality—stern, mournful, and fine.

The correspondent plainly saw the soldier. He lay on the sand with his feet out straight and still. While his pale left hand was upon his chest in an attempt to thwart the going of his life, the blood came between his fingers. In the far Algerian distance, a city of low square forms was set against a sky that was faint with the last sunset hues. The correspondent, plying the oars and dreaming of the slow and slower movements of the lips of the soldier, was moved by a profound and perfectly impersonal comprehension. He was sorry for the soldier of the Legion who lay dying in Algiers.

The thing which had followed the boat and waited had evidently grown bored at the delay. There was no longer to be heard the slash of the cutwater, and there was no longer the flame of the long trail. The light in the north still glimmered, but it was apparently no nearer to the boat. Sometimes the boom of the surf rang in the correspondent's ears, and he turned the craft seaward then and rowed harder. Southward, someone had evidently built a watch-fire on the beach. It was too low and too far to be seen, but it made a shimmering, roseate reflection upon the bluff in back of it, and this could be discerned from the boat. The wind came stronger, and sometimes a wave suddenly raged out like a mountain cat, and there was to be seen the sheen and sparkle of a broken crest.

The captain, in the bow, moved on his water-jar and sat erect. "Pretty long night," he observed to the correspondent. He looked at the shore. "Those life-saving people take their time."

"Did you see that shark playing around?"

"Yes, I saw him. He was a big fellow, all right."

"Wish I had known you were awake."

Later the correspondent spoke into the bottom of the boat. "Billie!" There was a slow and gradual disentanglement. "Billie, will you spell me?"

"Sure," said the oiler.

As soon as the correspondent touched the cold, comfortable sea-water in the bottom of the boat and had huddled close to the cook's life belt he was deep in sleep, despite the fact that his teeth played all the popular airs. This sleep was so good to him that it was but a moment before he heard a voice call his name in a tone that demonstrated the last stages of exhaustion. "Will you spell me?"

"Sure, Billie."

7. **Legion:** the French Foreign Legion, an army composed of volunteers from many countries, originally based in North Africa.

The light in the north had mysteriously vanished, but the correspondent took his course from the wide-awake captain.

Later in the night they took the boat farther out to sea, and the captain directed the cook to take one oar at the stern and keep the boat facing the seas. He was to call out if he should hear the thunder of the surf. This plan enabled the oiler and the correspondent to get respite together. "We'll give those boys a chance to get into shape again," said the captain. They curled down and, after a few preliminary chatterings and trembles, slept once more the dead sleep. Neither knew they had bequeathed to the cook the company of another shark, or perhaps the same shark.

As the boat caroused on the waves, spray occasionally bumped over the side and gave them a fresh soaking, but this had no power to break their repose. The ominous slash of the wind and the water affected them as it would have affected mummies.

"Boys," said the cook, with the notes of every reluctance in his voice, "she's drifted in pretty close. I guess one of you had better take her to sea again." The correspondent, aroused, heard the crash of the toppled crests.

As he was rowing, the captain gave him some whiskey-and-water, and this steadied the chills out of him. "If I ever get ashore and anybody shows me even a photograph of an oar—"

At last there was a short conversation.

"Billie!—Billie, will you spell me?"

"Sure," said the oiler.

VII

When the correspondent again opened his eyes, the sea and the sky were each of the gray hue of the dawning. Later, carmine and gold was painted upon the waters. The morning appeared finally, in its splendor, with a sky of pure blue, and the sunlight flamed on the tips of the waves.

On the distant dunes were set many little black cottages, and a tall white windmill reared above them. No man, nor dog, nor bicycle appeared on the beach. The cottages might have formed a deserted village.

The voyagers scanned the shore. A conference was held in the boat. "Well," said the captain, "if

A

Kissing the Moon by Winslow Homer (1904). Oil on canvas (30¼″ × 40⅜″).

A. Humanities Connection: Responding to the Fine Art
Kissing the Moon is one of Winslow Homer's late works. It represents what art historian Vincent Price referred to in *The Vincent Price Treasury of American Art* as "a facing up to nature, not as it might seem through sentiment, but rather as it is, the force of life that is always there for man to wage war against." **?** Apply these comments to both the painting and the story. How do the details of the picture compare to details in the story? (Students may comment on how low the boat is riding, how the waves create walls, and how still and stoical the men seem.) Is the moon rising or setting? (The pattern of light and clouds in the sky and the ruddy glow on the men's faces suggest sunset; therefore, the moon is rising.) Why do you think the painting is called *Kissing the Moon*? (The sea appears to be kissing the moon.)

CLOSURE
Ask students to decide which of the two Crane stories they like better—"The Open Boat" or "A Mystery of Heroism" (page 457)—and why.

READING CHECK TEST

1. The story narrates the experience of four men in a ten-foot boat. *True*

2. The men were surprised by a storm while fishing on a lake. *False*

3. Among their unwelcome visitors are a seabird and a large shark. *True*

4. At one point people wave to the men, from the shore, but do not help them. *True*

5. Two of the men—the oiler and the captain—drown in high waves. *False*

A. Symbol/Theme
What does the wind-tower symbolize? (To the correspondent, it symbolizes the indifference of nature. The winds go on, unconcerned about attempts to harness them.)

B. Theme
Why is the shore described as indifferent? (Though the men long for the shore, it does not seem to care whether they live or die.) Have students compare this passage with the passage on page 478, where the land welcomes the survivors but is indifferent to the dead Billy.

C. Theme
In personifying the wave, has Crane made it evil? Has nature moved from being indifferent to being an actual enemy? ("Furious, implacable" does suggest enmity.)

D. Responding
Why do you think the coldness of the water makes the correspondent sad? (It contrasts so brutally with the warmth of comradeship among the men on the boat. It is like a "last straw.")

no help is coming, we might better try a run through the surf right away. If we stay out here much longer we will be too weak to do anything for ourselves at all." The others silently acquiesced in this reasoning. The boat was headed for the beach. The correspondent wondered if none ever ascended the tall wind-tower, and if then they never looked seaward. This tower was a giant, standing with its back to the plight of the ants. It represented in a degree, to the correspondent, the serenity of nature amid the struggles of the individual—nature in the wind, and nature in the vision of men. She did not seem cruel to him then, nor beneficent, nor treacherous, nor wise. But she was indifferent, flatly indifferent. It is, perhaps, plausible that a man in this situation, impressed with the unconcern of the universe, should see the innumerable flaws of his life, and have them taste wickedly in his mind, and wish for another chance. A distinction between right and wrong seems absurdly clear to him, then, in this new ignorance of the grave-edge, and he understands that if he were given another opportunity he would mend his conduct and his words, and be better and brighter during an introduction or at a tea.

"Now, boys," said the captain, "she is going to swamp sure. All we can do is to work her in as far as possible, and then when she swamps, pile out and scramble for the beach. Keep cool now, and don't jump until she swamps sure."

The oiler took the oars. Over his shoulders he scanned the surf. "Captain," he said, "I think I'd better bring her about and keep her head-on to the seas and back her in."

"All right, Billie," said the captain. "Back her in." The oiler swung the boat then, and, seated in the stern, the cook and the correspondent were obliged to look over their shoulders to contemplate the lonely and indifferent shore.

The monstrous inshore rollers heaved the boat high until the men were again enabled to see the white sheets of water scudding up the slanted beach. "We won't get in very close," said the captain. Each time a man could wrest his attention from the rollers, he turned his glance toward the shore, and in the expression of the eyes during this contemplation there was a singular quality. The correspondent, observing the others, knew that they were not afraid, but the full meaning of their glances was shrouded.

As for himself, he was too tired to grapple fundamentally with the fact. He tried to coerce his mind into thinking of it, but the mind was dominated at this time by the muscles, and the muscles said they did not care. It merely occurred to him that if he should drown it would be a shame.

There were no hurried words, no pallor, no plain agitation. The men simply looked at the shore. "Now, remember to get well clear of the boat when you jump," said the captain.

Seaward the crest of a roller suddenly fell with a thunderous crash, and the long white comber came roaring down upon the boat.

"Steady now," said the captain. The men were silent. They turned their eyes from the shore to the comber and waited. The boat slid up the incline, leaped at the furious top, bounced over it, and swung down the long back of the wave. Some water had been shipped, and the cook bailed it out.

But the next crest crashed also. The tumbling, boiling flood of white water caught the boat and whirled it almost perpendicular. Water swarmed in from all sides. The correspondent had his hands on the gunwale at this time, and when the water entered at that place he swiftly withdrew his fingers, as if he objected to wetting them.

The little boat, drunken with this weight of water, reeled and snuggled deeper into the sea.

"Bail her out, cook! Bail her out!" said the captain.

"All right, Captain," said the cook.

"Now, boys, the next one will do for us sure," said the oiler. "Mind to jump clear of the boat."

The third wave moved forward, huge, furious, implacable. It fairly swallowed the dinghy, and almost simultaneously the men tumbled into the sea. A piece of life belt had lain in the bottom of the boat, and as the correspondent went overboard he held this to his chest with his left hand.

The January water was icy, and he reflected immediately that it was colder than he had expected to find it off the coast of Florida. This appeared to his dazed mind as a fact important enough to be noted at the time. The coldness of the water was sad; it was tragic. This fact was somehow mixed and confused with his opinion of his own situation, so that it seemed almost a proper reason for tears. The water was cold.

When he came to the surface he was conscious of little but the noisy water. Afterward he saw his companions in the sea. The oiler was ahead in the race. He was swimming strongly and rapidly. Off to the correspondent's left, the cook's great white

Analyzing the Story

Identifying Facts

1. The men see only the enormous waves as they struggle to keep their little craft afloat. They have neither the time nor the desire to look up at the sky.

2. The external conflict is between man and nature; specifically, four men in a ten-foot dinghy against high, rolling waves and a dangerous surf.

The internal conflicts involve the men's fear, their outcries against fate, their resistance to accept death.

3. The patches of seaweed show that land is not far away.

The men envy the gulls because they are at home on the sea and in no danger. The men also dislike the gulls because they are a nuisance and seem "gruesome and ominous," perhaps like birds of prey.

4. The surf is dangerous to the little boat. When the dinghy is close to shore, it can be swamped.

Various solutions don't work out. There is no one at the refuge station; the man waving his coat gives them no help, nor do the people on the omnibus. The shark adds to their problems.

(Answers continue on next page.)

and corked back bulged out of the water; and in the rear the captain was hanging with his one good hand to the keel of the overturned dinghy.

There is a certain immovable quality to a shore, and the correspondent wondered at it amid the confusion of the sea.

It seemed also very attractive; but the correspondent knew that it was a long journey, and he paddled leisurely. The piece of life preserver lay under him, and sometimes he whirled down the incline of a wave as if he were on a hand-sled.

But finally he arrived at a place in the sea where travel was beset with difficulty. He did not pause swimming to inquire what manner of current had caught him, but there his progress ceased. The shore was set before him like a bit of scenery on a stage, and he looked at it and understood with his eyes each detail of it.

As the cook passed, much farther to the left, the captain was calling to him, "Turn over on your back, cook! Turn over on your back and use the oar."

"All right, sir." The cook turned on his back, and, paddling with an oar, went ahead as if he were a canoe.

Presently the boat also passed to the left of the correspondent, with the captain clinging with one hand to the keel. He would have appeared like a man raising himself to look over a board fence if it were not for the extraordinary gymnastics of the boat. The correspondent marveled that the captain could still hold to it.

They passed on nearer to shore—the oiler, the cook, the captain—and following them went the water-jar, bouncing gaily over the seas.

The correspondent remained in the grip of this strange new enemy—a current. The shore, with its white slope of sand and its green bluff topped with little silent cottages, was spread like a picture before him. It was very near to him then, but he was impressed as one who, in a gallery, looks at a scene from Brittany or Algiers.

A He thought: "I am going to drown? Can it be possible? Can it be possible? Can it be possible?" Perhaps an individual must consider his own death to be the final phenomenon of nature.

But later a wave perhaps whirled him out of this small deadly current, for he found suddenly that he could again make progress toward the shore. Later still he was aware that the captain, clinging with one hand to the keel of the dinghy, had his face turned away from the shore and toward him, and was calling his name. "Come to the boat! Come to the boat!"

In his struggle to reach the captain and the boat, he reflected that when one gets properly wearied, drowning must really be a comfortable arrangement—a cessation of hostilities accompanied by a large degree of relief; and he was glad of it, for the main thing in his mind for some moments had been horror of the temporary agony. He did not wish to be hurt.

Presently he saw a man running along the shore. He was undressing with most remarkable speed. Coat, trousers, shirt, everything flew magically off him.

"Come to the boat!" called the captain.

"All right, Captain." As the correspondent paddled, he saw the captain let himself down to bottom and leave the boat. Then the correspondent performed his one little marvel of the voyage. A large wave caught him and flung him with ease and supreme speed completely over the boat and far beyond it. It struck him even then as an event in gymnastics and a true miracle of the sea. An overturned boat in the surf is not a plaything to a swimming man. B

The correspondent arrived in water that reached only to his waist, but his condition did not enable him to stand for more than a moment. Each wave knocked him into a heap, and the undertow pulled at him.

Then he saw the man who had been running and undressing, and undressing and running, come bounding into the water. He dragged ashore the cook, and then waded toward the captain; but the captain waved him away and sent him to the correspondent. He was naked—naked as a tree in winter; but a halo was about his head, and he shone like a saint. He gave a strong pull, and a long drag, and a bully heave at the correspondent's hand. The correspondent, schooled in the minor formulae, said, "Thanks, old man." But suddenly the man cried, "What's that?" He pointed a swift finger. The correspondent said, "Go."

In the shallows, face downward, lay the oiler. His forehead touched sand that was periodically, between each wave, clear of the sea. C

The correspondent did not know all that transpired afterward. When he achieved safe ground he fell, striking the sand with each particular part of his body. It was as if he had dropped from a roof, but the thud was grateful to him.

A. Characterization

? What does the correspondent face at this moment? (He faces his own death, but the question marks indicate that he still cannot believe that he will die.)

B. Theme

? How is the correspondent saved? (A wave carries him over the boat instead of hurling him against it.)

? Does this represent a kindly side of nature? (No; it is just chance.)

C. Responding

? Why do you think the oiler is the only character who is named in the story? (The other three represent all human beings who face the indifference of nature and endure. Billy is an individual, the victim of the vagaries of chance, just as the dying soldier in Algiers was.)

(*Continued from previous page.*)

Interpreting Meanings

5. The two major reflections are the long paragraph on page 470 (bracketed by B) and the first two paragraphs on page 474. Students may cite other passages, including the passage about the tower (bracketed by A, page 476).

The oiler contributed the most of anyone to keeping the dinghy afloat. His death shows that any—or all—of them could have died; nature made no thoughtful choice.

6. The sea represents external nature, implacable, indifferent, powerful. The gulls, "comfortably" at home, could symbolize nature's indifference to the plight of humans. The tower could show the unconcern of the universe, representing nature's indifference to human struggles.

7. Crane conveys the deepening brotherhood by stating it directly at the beginning of Section III. It is also conveyed by many incidents, such as their sharing the cigars and spelling one another.

Note the details describing the rescuer as a saint with a halo.

8. Other examples are the observation about a balcony view (page 465) and the generalizations on the top of page 474.

It seemed that instantly the beach was populated with men with blankets, clothes, and flasks, and women with coffeepots and all the remedies sacred to their minds. The welcome of the land to the men from the sea was warm and generous; but a still and dripping shape was carried slowly up the beach, and the land's welcome for it could only be the different and sinister hospitality of the grave.

When it came night, the white waves paced to and fro in the moonlight, and the wind brought the sound of the great sea's voice to the men on the shore, and they felt that they could then be interpreters.

Responding to the Story

Analyzing the Story

Identifying Facts

1. The story opens with one of Crane's memorable sentences: "None of them knew the color of the sky." What keeps the men from knowing the sky's color?
2. **External conflict** is immediately apparent in the description of the waves as "wrongfully and barbarously abrupt and tall." How would you describe the story's external conflict? What **internal conflicts** do the men also struggle against?
3. Why do the men in the dinghy regard the patches of seaweed as an encouraging sign? Do they view the seagulls with equal favor? Expain why or why not.
4. Every story has **complications,** which hook us by building up our **suspense.** Just when success seems near at hand, something goes wrong. In this story, rowing straight to shore would seem to be a simple matter. It proves not to be. Why? Name the various possibilities of rescue that turn out, one after the other, to be fruitless.

Interpreting Meanings

5. Crane is a master of **naturalism.** Naturalists believe that human beings are no freer than animals, that we are in the grip of indifferent natural forces beyond our comprehension or control. Find at least two passages in this story which reveal the men's feelings about nature or fate. How does the death of the oiler (the only character given a name) demonstrate a naturalist's ironic outlook on life?
6. Crane's story is rich in **symbols**, which, like stones thrown into a pond, create circles of ever-widening meaning. The symbols here are the sea, the gulls, and the tower. What do you think each one means?
7. Despite his naturalism, Crane often uses religious details. How does Crane convey the deepening sense of brotherhood among the four men in the dinghy? What religious details describe the rescuer?
8. Think about the **point of view** in the story, which occasionally shifts. Most of the time the narrator, though **omniscient**, seems to be right there with the men in the boat. But then he draws back and mentions the remoteness of a life-saving station, adding, "but the men did not know this fact." Point out another example of such a change in perspective. Why do you think Crane decided not to have the correspondent tell the story?
9. Near the end of the story, the correspondent recalls a poem, read in childhood, about a soldier dying in Algiers. Why does the poem have new meaning for him now?
10. What do you make of the statement on page 468, that the correspondent knew this was the "*best* experience of his life"?
11. At the story's end, why do you think the correspondent believes that the men can now be "interpreters"? What will they interpret?
12. Suppose you had been one of the four people adrift in the ten-foot boat. Would you have done things differently? What do you think would have been the worst aspect of the experience? The best?

Writing About the Story

A Creative Response

1. **Reporting the Facts.** Five days after the sinking of the *Commodore*, Crane filed his news story about the disaster. Pretend you are a news reporter sent to cover the rescue of the men in the open boat. Write a news story describing the ordeal of the four men in the dinghy, as if it just occurred. Include details of the rescue. You will have to invent a few facts, such as the full names of the people and some exact times. Otherwise, stick closely to the events that Crane narrates (minus his interpretations, of course). Use a front-page story from a real newspaper as your model for length and style. Remember to cover the "four W's and an H" of news reporting: **What** happened? **When** did it happen? **Where** did it happen? **Whom** did it happen to? **How** did it happen? Submit your story under an appropriate, catchy headline.

(Note the shift to present tense.)

This omniscient point of view allows Crane to make observations that the correspondent, confined to the dinghy, could not make. It also helps us to view the men as if from a godlike perspective.

9. As a child, death had been remote from his experience. Now, however, the correspondent himself faces death. Perhaps it is this change that makes the experience in the boat so important.

10. He realizes that his suffering has given him a deep sense of brotherhood and an appreciation of life. Students may suggest other answers.

11. He feels that their ordeal has given them the insight to comment on what happened.

Presumably they can interpret to others the great lessons they learned—the indifference of nature, the frailty of human beings, and the brotherhood of humanity.

12. Answers will vary. Most will agree that the captain directed the journey well, that the physical hardships and the oiler's death were the worst part; that the men's brotherhood was the best.

A Critical Response

2. **Explaining the Theme.** Robert Wooster Stallman, a noted critic and biographer of Stephen Crane, wrote the following commentary on "The Open Boat."

> This theme of insight through suffering is prepared for by the very first image of the story: "None of them knew the color of the sky." It is foreshadowed and epitomized in the song that the correspondent recites to himself: "A soldier of the Legion lay dying in Algiers." The correspondent had known this verse when a child, but *then* had not regarded the death of that soldier as important or meaningful. He had never felt any sympathy for the soldier's plight because he himself had not yet experienced it. "It was less to him than the breaking of a pencil's point." The soldier's plight parallels and foremirrors the oiler's plight. The image of the delicate pencil point correlates with the image of the thin oar of the oiler that "seemed often ready to snap." The whole meaning of "The Open Boat" is focused in the death of the oiler.
>
> —Robert Wooster Stallman

Do you agree with Stallman? Is the theme of the story "insight through suffering"? Is the "whole meaning" of the story "focused in the death of the oiler"? Write a brief essay in which you respond to each of Stallman's observations. Cite passages from the story to support your opinions.

3. **Comparing the Story with a Poem.** Nine months before the *Commodore* sank, Stephen Crane wrote this poem:

> To the maiden
> The sea was blue meadow,
> Alive with little froth-people
> Singing.
>
> To the sailor, wrecked,
> The sea was dead gray walls
> Superlative in vacancy,
> Upon which nevertheless at fateful time
> Was written
> The grim hatred of nature.
>
> —Stephen Crane

In a brief essay, explain how this poem connects with "The Open Boat" in terms of the way it views *nature*. You might want to conclude your essay with a statement of your own feelings about nature—whether you agree with the maiden or the sailor.

4. **Contrasting Two Views of Nature.** In its view of nature, Stephen Crane's naturalism has very little in common with the Romantic Transcendentalism of Ralph Waldo Emerson. Review Emerson's thoughts about nature as expressed in his essay on page 191. Then write a brief essay in which you contrast the way Emerson and Crane feel about the natural world. Be sure to quote directly from Emerson and Crane as you make your points.

Primary Sources
"Plenty of grit"

Two days before Stephen Crane's news report of the sinking of the *Commodore* had appeared in the *New York Press*, an unsigned article in the same paper carried an interview with the captain of the lost steamer.

". . . Captain Murphy had his arm in a sling, but otherwise seemed all right. All of them looked tired and worn out.

"The captain paid a marked compliment to his men for their orderly conduct. He said that Higgins [the oiler] was a game man, and fought hard for his life and to aid his shipmates. Higgins was buried at Daytona yesterday.

. . .

" 'That man Crane is the spunkiest fellow out,' said Captain Murphy tonight to The Press correspondent, in speaking of the wreck and incidents pertaining to it. 'The sea was so rough that even old sailors got seasick when we struck the open sea after leaving the bar, but Crane behaved like a born sailor. He and I were about the only ones not affected by the big seas which tossed us about.'

. . .

" 'When we went over I called to him to see that his life preserver was on all right and he replied in his usual tones, saying that he would obey orders. He was under the boat once, but got out in some way. He held up Higgins when the latter got so terribly tired and endeavored to bring him in, but the sailor was so far gone that he could hardly help himself. When we were thrown up by the waves, Crane was the first man to stagger up the beach looking for houses. He's a thoroughbred,' concluded the captain, 'and a brave man, too, with plenty of grit.' "

—The *New York Press*,
Tuesday, January 5, 1897

Supplementary Support Materials
1. Vocabulary Activity Worksheet (*CCB*)
2. Review and Response Worksheet: Motivation (*CCB*)
3. Language Skills Worksheet: Prepositions and Prepositional Phrases (*CCB*)
4. Selection Test (*CCB*)

Developing Vocabulary
The following words from the story are tested in the Selection Test. (See also Vocabulary Activity Worksheet.)

speculation	fastidious
judicious	preposterous
veritable	deft
gaunt	profusion
to revel	to decipher

A. Expansion
Kate Chopin's own "awakening" came after the death of her husband and, two years later, that of her mother. She was financially comfortable and, for the first time in her life, independent. She had long been an admirer of French writer Guy de Maupassant and of American women regional writers Sarah Orne Jewett and Willa Cather.

By the late 19th century, many women had established themselves as professional writers, particularly in women's magazines, such as *Vogue* (see page 485).

B. Expansion
Many of Chopin's stories deal with both the pleasures and pains of marriage and family life. Chopin said that the artist's focus should be the subtle and complex "true meaning" of human life, stripped of society's moral conventions.

Kate Chopin (1851–1904)

Kate Chopin's life is a study in the kind of literary pioneering which goes unrecognized, and is even scorned, in a writer's own time, but which is understood and acclaimed long after the writer has died and is denied a vindication.

Chopin was born Katherine O'Flaherty in St. Louis, Missouri, to an Irish immigrant father and a mother of French descent. Her prosperous parents encouraged her early interest in music and reading, and she was educated in French for a time by her worldly great-grandmother. Kate became a beautiful, witty, and popular young woman with a notably independent turn of mind.

At nineteen, Kate married Oscar Chopin, a French Creole from New Orleans, and they enjoyed a long European honeymoon, visiting art galleries and attending operas. The Chopins settled in Louisiana and reared a family of six children, but it was not until Oscar's early death and her return to St. Louis that Kate Chopin began to write. She published a poem when she was thirty-eight and followed it with some short stories. In 1890 she published her first novel.

Chopin's stories concern the life of French Creoles in Louisiana. Published in national magazines and collected in two volumes called *Bayou Folk* (1894) and *A Night in Acadie* (1897), the stories were praised for their accurate portrayal of this French strain in the national culture. Chopin's theme, however, was a much more controversial matter: it was the repression of women in Victorian America.

A This theme was most dramatically presented in her novel *The Awakening,* which appeared in 1899. The novel portrays a dissatisfied New Orleans wife who breaks from the confines of her marriage and, in her quest for freedom, flagrantly defies the Victorian ideals of motherhood and domesticity. Although the concern of Chopin's novel was somewhat similar to Gustave Flaubert's widely praised novel *Madame Bovary,* published in France in 1856, American critics responded to the story with hostility. *The Awakening* was condemned as sordid and vulgar. Victorians, who looked to literature for moral lessons, saw only an immoral lesson in *The Awakening*.

Kate Chopin was disheartened enough by this rejection to allow her writing to languish, and she produced little more before her death in 1904.

The Awakening and many of Chopin's other works were rediscovered a generation after her death. With the help of discerning critics and the women's movement of the 1960's, Kate Chopin is now recognized as a novelist of skill and perception, whose work first appeared half a century before its time. B

PREPARATION

1. **ESTABLISHING A PURPOSE.** After students have responded to the headnote and written down what they would do with such a windfall, have them read the story to compare their motivations and choices with those of Mrs. Sommers.

2. **BUILDING ON PRIOR KNOWLEDGE.** Ask students about the kinds of aid available in your community to help women who are single parents trying to support minor children. Did such programs exist in the 1890's, when this story takes place? Ask for a volunteer to find out when these programs began.

A PAIR OF SILK STOCKINGS

Here is a story of escape—escape from the humdrum, from the obligations and boredom of day-to-day existence. Virtually all of us, probably even lion tamers, have wanted to escape like this in one way or another.

For Mrs. Sommers, the humdrum comes from trying to satisfy the needs of her poor family. Here we see a woman who has been doing her best to clothe and feed four children for a long time.

Her escape is sudden, and it is as surprising to her as it is to us. As you read, see if you are ever told that Mrs. Sommers makes a rational decision to embark on a pleasure binge. Does she think she deserves a break from routine? Or does she just go ahead and *do* it?

What is interesting in this story (since we've all known feelings like hers) is Mrs. Sommers's reaction to her escape. When her afternoon is ended and she must return to the reality of her family—with just those silk stockings, what does she feel? Guilt? Happiness? A need for penance, or for *more* silk stockings in those gorgeous colors she failed to buy?

All of these feelings are possible to her, and Mrs. Sommers is surely experiencing one or another of them, but they are subtly shown here. Like many a good story, this one leaves us to do some guessing on our own about what Mrs. Sommers is feeling as we leave her on the streetcar.

You should know that in the 1890's silk stockings were a great luxury. (Nylon wasn't invented yet, and most women wore thick cotton stockings.) Also, fifteen dollars was a princely week's salary. As you'll see, it could buy far more than two tickets to the movies.

Read the story's first sentence, and then stop. Write down what *you* would do with an unexpected gift of money that amounted to a week's salary today.

Little Mrs. Sommers one day found herself the unexpected possessor of fifteen dollars. It seemed to her a very large amount of money, and the way in which it stuffed and bulged her worn old *porte-monnaie*[1] gave her a feeling of importance such as she had not enjoyed for years.

The question of investment was one that occupied her greatly. For a day or two she walked about apparently in a dreamy state, but really absorbed in speculation and calculation. She did not wish to act hastily, to do anything she might afterward regret. But it was during the still hours of the night when she lay awake revolving plans in her mind that she seemed to see her way clearly toward a proper and judicious use of the money.

A A dollar or two should be added to the price usually paid for Janie's shoes, which would insure their lasting an appreciable time longer than they usually did. She would buy so and so many yards of percale[2] for new shirtwaists for the boys and Janie and Mag. She had intended to make the old ones do by skillful patching. Mag should have another gown. She had seen some beautiful patterns, veritable bargains in the shop windows. And still there would be left enough for new stockings—two pairs apiece—and what darning that would save for a while! She would get caps for the boys and sailor hats for the girls. The vision of her little brood looking fresh and dainty and new for once in their lives excited her and made her restless and wakeful with anticipation. B

The neighbors sometimes talked of certain "better days" that little Mrs. Sommers had known before she had ever thought of being Mrs. Sommers. She herself indulged in no such morbid retrospection.[3] She had no time—no second of time to devote to the past. The needs of the present absorbed her every faculty. A vision of the future like some dim, gaunt monster sometimes appalled her, but luckily tomorrow never comes. C

1. ***porte-monnaie*** (pôrt' môn·nĕ'): a purse.
2. **percale** (pər·kāl'): cloth made of cotton.
3. **morbid retrospection:** brooding on unpleasant things in the past.

A. Characterization

? What do these thoughts reveal about Mrs. Sommers's life? (Money is a constant worry. Mrs. Sommers must often compromise on clothes for the children; she spends a great deal of time mending and patching what she does buy.)

B. Responding

? What stereotype does this vision represent? (That of a selfless mother devoted to her children with no concern for her own needs and wants)

C. Responding

? What do you make of this sentence? How does Mrs. Sommers's image of her future compare with your own? (Answers will vary, but most students will be more hopeful and optimistic. Ask them to try to think of an image, as Chopin has, to express their view.)

? Why does tomorrow never come? (Probably because Mrs. Sommers just deals with one day at a time.)

A. Humanities Connection: Responding to the Fine Art
Maurice Prendergast (1859–1924) was a member of The Eight, a group of eight American artists who stressed American themes in their work and sought to break with European traditions.

Prendergast is known for his post-impressionist watercolors, monotypes, and oil paintings. His watercolors of urban life often feature animated figures, bold areas of color, and a rather flat perspective.

? In what way does this seem a particularly American picture? (The poster, with happy, young women pursuing active pastimes, is advertising an American brand of bicycle.) What is the effect of the colors? (The bold colors suggest vitality and perhaps freedom.) Why do you think the woman is examining the poster? (Answers will vary. Perhaps she is considering the possibility of taking up cycling or even buying a bicycle for herself.) Are there any similarities between the woman in the painting and Mrs. Sommers? (Answers will vary. Many students will note some similarities between the two; possible answers include: a shared interest in fashion; self-indulgence; sense of guilt.)

A

Woman in veiled hat looking at a poster for Columbia bicycles. Page 5 from *Large Boston Public Garden Sketchbook* by Maurice Prendergast (c. 1895). Watercolor on paper.

The Metropolitan Museum of Art, New York. Robert Lehman Collection, 1975. (1975.1.928).

Mrs. Sommers was one who knew the value of bargains, who could stand for hours making her way inch by inch toward the desired object that was selling below cost. She could elbow her way if need be; she had learned to clutch a piece of goods and hold it and stick to it with persistence and determination till her turn came to be served, no matter when it came.

But that day she was a little faint and tired. She had swallowed a light luncheon—no! when she came to think of it, between getting the children fed and the place righted, and preparing herself for the shopping bout, she had actually forgotten to eat any luncheon at all!

She sat herself upon a revolving stool before a counter that was comparatively deserted, trying to gather strength and courage to charge through an eager multitude that was besieging breastworks[4] of shirting and figured lawn. An all-gone limp feeling had come over her and she rested her hand aimlessly upon the counter. She wore no gloves. By degrees she grew aware that her hand had encountered something very soothing, very pleasant to touch. She looked down to see that her hand lay upon a pile of silk stockings. A placard nearby announced that they had been reduced in price from two dollars and fifty cents to one dollar and ninety-eight cents; and a young girl who stood behind the counter asked her if she wished to examine their line of silk hosiery. She smiled, just as if she had been asked to inspect a tiara of diamonds with the ultimate view of purchasing it. But she went on feeling the soft, sheeny luxurious things—with both hands now, holding them up to see them glisten, and to feel them glide serpentlike through her fingers.

Two hectic blotches came suddenly into her pale cheeks. She looked up at the girl.

"Do you think there are any eights-and-a-half among these?"

There were any number of eights-and-a-half. In fact, there were more of that size than any other. Here was a light-blue pair; there were some lavender, some all black and various shades of tan and gray. Mrs. Sommers selected a black pair and looked at them very long and closely. She pretended to be examining their texture, which the clerk assured her was excellent.

"A dollar and ninety-eight cents," she mused aloud. "Well, I'll take this pair." She handed the girl a five-dollar bill and waited for her change and for her parcel. What a very small parcel it was! It seemed lost in the depths of her shabby old shopping bag.

Mrs. Sommers after that did not move in the direction of the bargain counter. She took the el-

4. **breastworks:** low walls put up as barricades. The bolts of shirting material and fine, patterned cotton ("figured lawn") are compared to barricades being stormed by shoppers.

CLOSURE

Have students compare Mrs. Sommers's choices with those they made in response to the headnote. Does the writer pass judgment on Mrs. Sommers's behavior or simply tell us her story? (The writer does not judge Mrs. Sommers.)

READING CHECK TEST

1. Mrs. Sommers finds herself in possession of fifteen hundred dollars. *False*
2. Mrs. Sommers spends the entire amount on clothes for her children. *False*
3. She starts her spending spree at a counter display of stockings. *True*
4. She buys two expensive magazines to read in a restaurant. *True*
5. Leaving a theater, she boards a cable car and runs away from home. *False*

evator, which carried her to an upper floor into the region of the ladies' waiting rooms. Here, in a retired corner, she exchanged her cotton stockings for the new silk ones which she had just bought. She was not going through any acute mental process or reasoning with herself, nor was she striving to explain to her satisfaction the motive of her action. She was not thinking at all. She seemed for the time to be taking a rest from that laborious and fatiguing function and to have abandoned herself to some mechanical impulse that directed her actions and freed her of responsibility.

How good was the touch of the raw silk to her flesh! She felt like lying back in the cushioned chair and reveling for a while in the luxury of it. She did for a little while. Then she replaced her shoes, rolled the cotton stockings together and thrust them into her bag. After doing this she crossed straight over to the shoe department and took her seat to be fitted.

She was fastidious. The clerk could not make her out; he could not reconcile her shoes with her stockings, and she was not too easily pleased. She held back her skirts and turned her feet one way and her head another as she glanced down at the polished, pointed-tipped boots. Her foot and ankle looked very pretty. She could not realize that they belonged to her and were a part of herself. She wanted an excellent and stylish fit, she told the young fellow who served her, and she did not mind the difference of a dollar or two more in the price so long as she got what she desired.

It was a long time since Mrs. Sommers had been fitted with gloves. On rare occasions when she had bought a pair they were always "bargains," so cheap that it would have been preposterous and unreasonable to have expected them to be fitted to the hand.

Now she rested her elbow on the cushion of the glove counter, and a pretty, pleasant young creature, delicate and deft of touch, drew a long-wristed "kid" over Mrs. Sommers' hand. She smoothed it down over the wrist and buttoned it neatly, and both lost themselves for a second or two in admiring contemplation of the little symmetrical gloved hand. But there were other places where money might be spent.

There were books and magazines piled up in the window of a stall a few paces down the street. Mrs. Sommers bought two high-priced magazines such as she had been accustomed to read in the days when she had been accustomed to other pleasant things. She carried them without wrapping. As well as she could she lifted her skirts at the crossings. Her stockings and boots and well-fitting gloves had worked marvels in her bearing—had given her a feeling of assurance, a sense of belonging to the well-dressed multitude.

She was very hungry. Another time she would have stilled the cravings for food until reaching her own home, where she would have brewed herself a cup of tea and taken a snack of anything that was available. But the impulse that was guiding her would not suffer her to entertain any such thought.

There was a restaurant at the corner. She had never entered its doors; from the outside she had sometimes caught glimpses of spotless damask and shining crystal, and soft-stepping waiters serving people of fashion.

When she entered her appearance created no surprise, no consternation, as she had half feared it might. She seated herself at a small table alone, and an attentive waiter at once approached to take her order. She did not want a profusion; she craved a nice and tasty bite—a half dozen bluepoints,[5] a plump chop with cress, a something sweet—a crème-frappée,[6] for instance; a glass of Rhine wine, and after all a small cup of black coffee.

While waiting to be served she removed her gloves very leisurely and laid them beside her. Then she picked up a magazine and glanced through it, cutting the pages with a blunt edge of her knife.[7] It was all very agreeable. The damask was even more spotless than it had seemed through the window, and the crystal more sparkling. There were quiet ladies and gentlemen, who did not notice her, lunching at the small tables like her own. A soft, pleasing strain of music could be heard, and a gentle breeze was blowing through the window. She tasted a bite, and she read a word or two, and she sipped the amber wine and wiggled her toes in the silk stockings. The price of it made no difference. She counted the money out to the waiter and left an extra coin on his tray,

5. **bluepoints:** small oysters.
6. **crème-frappée** (krĕm fră·pā′): a dessert similar to ice cream.
7. Magazines and books were often printed with pages joined at their outer edges and had to be cut apart to be read.

A. Motivation

What do you think is making Mrs. Sommers behave so unusually? (Students should note that she is exhausted from years of penny-pinching worry and is taking a holiday from her real life.)

B. Vocabulary

A kid glove is made of kidskin, leather from the skin of a young goat. The expression "to handle with kid gloves" means to treat someone or something tactfully and considerately.

C. Theme

What do Mrs. Sommers's purchases mean to her? (They give her pleasure in themselves and perhaps symbolize her earlier, "better" life. They represent self-esteem and freedom.)

Analyzing The Story

Identifying Facts

1. At first Mrs. Sommers intends to buy clothes and shoes for the children.

Instead, she treats herself for a day. She buys silk stockings, shoes, gloves, and magazines; eats in a fine restaurant; and attends a play.

Interpreting Meanings

2. She wants to run away, abandon her worries and deprivations, and lead a pleasurable life without worrying about money.

Most students will agree that she will, however reluctantly, return home to resume her difficult life.

3. Answers will vary. Most students will feel pity and sympathy for Mrs. Sommers, but some may judge her, saying she has selfishly indulged herself at the expense of her children. Others may say that she well deserves a day off and a bit of self-indulgence.

4. Mrs. Sommers apparently was better off before her marriage: She didn't have to scrimp and compromise to make purchases. Her behavior in the shoe store suggests she used to be very particular

A. Point of View

? Why does Chopin introduce this man and his thoughts? (The man offers a different viewpoint, enabling us to see Mrs. Sommers as strangers see her. His unknowing view of Mrs. Sommers also suggests that every person we see has a "story" we don't know anything about.)

B. Plot

? Why do you think Mrs. Sommers's husband is never mentioned, either in the narration or in her thoughts? (Mr. Sommers is probably so long gone from her life that she never thinks of him. Unlike Amanda Wingfield in "The Glass Menagerie" (page 769), Mrs. Sommers focuses intently on the "here and now," getting through each day, rather than dwelling on the past. Students may speculate whether Mr. Sommers died or abandoned his family but should remember that the story is not about Mrs. Sommers's whole life—only about her day of pleasure.)

whereupon he bowed before her as before a princess of royal blood.

There was still money in her purse, and her next temptation presented itself in the shape of a matinée poster.

It was a little later when she entered the theater, the play had begun and the house seemed to her to be packed. But there were vacant seats here and there, and into one of them she was ushered, between brilliantly dressed women who had gone there to kill time and eat candy and display their gaudy attire. There were many others who were there solely for the play and acting. It is safe to say there was no one present who bore quite the attitude which Mrs. Sommers did to her surroundings. She gathered in the whole—stage and players and people in one wide impression, and absorbed it and enjoyed it. She laughed at the comedy and wept—she and the gaudy woman next to her wept over the tragedy. And they talked a little together over it. And the gaudy woman wiped her eyes and sniffled on a tiny square of filmy, perfumed lace and passed little Mrs. Sommers her box of candy.

The play was over, the music ceased, the crowd filed out. It was like a dream ended. People scattered in all directions. Mrs. Sommers went to the corner and waited for the cable car.

A man with keen eyes, who sat opposite to her, A seemed to like the study of her small, pale face. It puzzled him to decipher what he saw there. In truth, he saw nothing—unless he were wizard enough to detect a poignant wish, a powerful longing that the cable car would never stop anywhere, but go on and on with her forever.

B

Responding to the Story

Analyzing the Story

Identifying Facts

1. What at first does Mrs. Sommers intend to do with the money? What does she end up doing with it instead?

Interpreting Meanings

2. How do you interpret that final wish of Mrs. Sommers—that the cable car will go on and on without ever stopping? What do you predict will happen next?
3. The author describes her as "Little Mrs. Sommers." We are given a few further details about her—four children, no mention of a husband or job, a future she regards as a "dim, gaunt monster." She lacks the time to recall her "better days." What do you think of the **character** of Mrs. Sommers? How do you feel about what she does with the fifteen dollars?
4. What details about Mrs. Sommers's earlier life might help explain the **motivation** for her shopping spree?
5. What do you think the rest of Mrs. Sommers's life will be like? (Do you think she'll ever wear those black stockings again?) Discuss your answers.
6. When Mrs. Sommers feels the black stockings, they "glide serpentlike" through her fingers. What does a serpent often **symbolize** in Western culture? Explain whether or not you think the use of the word here is significant.
7. A **feminist critic** might say that this story is about a woman who strikes out for personal freedom and identity. A **Marxist critic** might say it is about the class struggle. Critic Barbara C. Ewell says:

> The power of money to enhance self-esteem and confidence is the core of this poignant tale.

Which critic do you agree with? What do *you* think is the core of the story?

8. This story is over a hundred years old. Do you think it is an old-fashioned story, which could not happen today? Or is the story still modern? (Could you see little Mrs. Sommers in a TV sitcom?) Could Mrs. Sommers's **conflict** also be experienced by a man? (What of her unnamed husband?) Discuss your responses.

about style and fit, with price no object. There were "pleasant things" in those days, including high-priced magazines.

5. Answers will vary. Have students consider their responses to question 2. Some students may suggest that she may feel ashamed of her spending spree and not wear the stockings again, but occasionally take them out to look at wistfully.

6. A serpent often symbolizes sin, temptation, or evil. The word *serpentlike* is appropriate because the luxurious stockings tempt Mrs. Sommers away from her selfless intention to buy clothing for her children into a day's self-indulgent spending.

7. Student opinions will vary, but clearly money (or the lack of it) is central to the story. Ask students to defend their views with details from the story. Those who defend the feminist view might note that she struggles for freedom from overwhelming, never-ending burdens.

8. Students should realize that her plight continues today, for men as well as women. It may be that Mr. Sommers once acted on the same impulse that his wife feels at the story's end—to run from responsibilities.

Writing About the Story

A Creative Response

1. **Writing the Next Scene.** Write one paragraph or more telling what Mrs. Sommers does and what she thinks as she continues on the cable car. Does she stay on? Does she get off and go home? Does she go someplace else? Whatever you decide to have Mrs. Sommers do, try to make her decision consistent with the character created in the story.

A Critical Response

2. **Comparing Stories.** Is Mrs. Sommers's experience like the experience of Aunt Georgiana in Willa Cather's story "A Wagner Matinée" (page 518)? Write a brief essay comparing the two women and their afternoons of escape into new, more beautiful worlds. Before you write, review each story carefully. Gather your details of comparison in some sort of chart, perhaps like the following:

	Aunt Georgiana	Mrs. Sommers
1. Her real life when story opens.		
2. Her past life.		
3. Her wants and needs.		
4. Her new experiences. (How does she "escape"?)		
5. Effects of new experiences. (How did they change her?)		

Primary Sources

Vogue *Stories*

A [Chopin had trouble selling her stories. *Vogue* magazine, whose readership consisted mainly of young women from wealthy families, published much of her work.

"The title of Chopin's last *Vogue* story of the 1890's, 'A Pair of Silk Stockings,' suggests a tale for the rich—but it is really a message to *Vogue* readers about how the other half lives. Its central character, a struggling mother who once had 'certain better days,' must now scrimp to buy necessities for her children. But when Mrs. Sommers suddenly finds herself with fifteen dollars, she yields to temptation and spends all the money on herself: silk stockings, new boots, kid gloves, a tasty lunch, and a matinee. On the streetcar home, she feels 'a poignant wish, a powerful longing that the cable car would never stop anywhere, but go on and on with her forever.'

"Mrs. Sommers was the kind of woman that *Vogue* readers might pass by on the street without noticing—but by the late 1890's, living frugally in St. Louis, Kate Chopin had seen the effects of poverty and urban strife on women. *Vogue*, unlike other magazines, did not expect her to write for "the young person" about domesticity and womanly self-sacrifice. *Vogue* allowed her to describe what she had seen, honestly and fearlessly.

"*Vogue* moved with her; other magazines refused."

—from *Kate Chopin,*
Emily Toth

A. Expansion
Have several students do some research to find out which magazines still encourage new writers to send manuscripts and which rely primarily on material sent by literary agents. Students can consult professional guides such as *Writer's Market, The Writer's Handbook,* and *Literary Market Place.* Encourage students to share their findings with the class, perhaps in an information sheet.

A. Expansion
Westerners favored other colorful polysyllabic words as well: *discombobulate* (confuse), *hornswoggle* (swindle), *squabblification* (quarreling), *lallapalooza* (extraordinary person or thing), *absquatulate* (go away, skedaddle).

B. Expansion
The theme continues. In the opening credits of *McCloud,* a television series still rerun on late night channels, Dennis Weaver as a westerner new to the big city draws stares. The success of the original *Crocodile Dundee* movie in the 1980's owed much of its success to the coming of a man from the Australian outback to New York City.

C. Expansion
A number of frontier expressions still in existence derive from the game of poker, the French origins of which were quickly forgotten as its popularity spread like a new religion: *you bet, call one's bluff, square deal* (and other kinds of deals), *poker face, up the ante, throw in one's hand, ace up one's sleeve, stacked deck.* Trade in beaver pelts contributed *eager beaver* and *work like a beaver.* The gold rush contributed *bonanza, diggings, el dorado, pan out, stake a claim, strike it rich.*

THE AMERICAN LANGUAGE

by Gary Q. Arpin

A Period of Vocabulary Growth

The word *backwoods* was first recorded in America in 1709. Seventy-five years later the word *backwoodsman* appeared. John Pickering, a linguist in the nineteenth century, wrote that the word was applied "by people of the commercial towns to those who inhabit the territory westward of the Allegheny mountains." A Backwoodsmen themselves used more colorful terms. They called themselves *ring-tailed roarers* or *mollagausaugers* ("courageous men"); they were known for their ability to track game, shoot, and fight. The backwoodsmen were a new breed of American—almost as different from Easterners as Easterners were from the English—and they captured the American imagination.

"The backwoodsmen called themselves *ring-tailed roarers.*"

CROCKETT DELIVERING HIS CELEBRATED WAR SPEECH.

Congressman Davy Crockett giving a speech. Woodcut from *Davy Crockett Almanac* (1835).

American Antiquarian Society, Worcester, Massachusetts.

Backwoods English Comes East

B The exploits of the backwoodsmen during the War of 1812 made them famous, and when Davy Crockett came to Washington in 1827 as a Congressman from Tennessee, he was stared at in the street. The following year, another backwoodsman, Andrew Jackson, was elected President. Jackson's partisans brought muddy boots to Washington, as the stained upholstery in the White House testified. They also brought a new form of English that sedate Easterners sometimes found hard to understand—for these pioneers were well-known for their feats with language.

Backwoods English was filled with exaggerated slang and exuberant bragging—language equal to the awesome task of conquering the raw West. "Crockett Almanacs," published between the 1830's and 1850's, were popular collections of speeches supposedly given by Davy Crockett that brought this backwoods language into Eastern homes. Compare Patrick Henry's "Give me liberty or give me death" (page 88) to this oration.

> Hosses, I am with you! and while the stars of Uncle Sam, and the stripes of his country wave triumphantly in the breeze, whar, whar, whar, is the craven, low-lived, chicken-bred, toad-hoppin', red-mounted, bristle-headed mother's son of ye who will not raise the beacon light of triumph, smouse the citadel of the aggressor, and squeeze ahead for Liberty and Glory! Whoop! h-u-rah, hosses, come along—Crockett's with you—show us the enemy!
>
> —Davy Crockett

C Most backwoods slang had a short life, although some words and phrases have survived. Phrases like *fly off the handle, pull up stakes, a knock-down-drag-out fight, up a tree,* and *doing a land-office business* all date from this period.

The American Vernacular in Literature

American English was being recorded in a slightly different fashion in the nineteenth century than it had been earlier. Students of the language were still compiling lists of Americanisms, but writers were also beginning to use American English in literature. The first half of the century resounded with calls to establish an independent literature describing the American landscape and dealing with American manners and interests, and by the mid-nineteenth century American literature had begun to flower. To describe American phenomena, writers began to turn to the American **vernacular**—the common spoken language of a region. The "Crockett Almanacs" were a kind of sub-literature, but only a little later Mark Twain was recording the language of the American West in books like *Roughing It* and *Life on the Mississippi.* The backwoodsmen on the raft in *Life on the Mississippi* (page 404) were obviously capable of facing off with Davy Crockett himself.

In *The Adventures of Huckleberry Finn* (page 414), Twain showed that the vernacular could be used for more than just bluster, as this brief poetic description of a night on the river shows:

> Once or twice of a night we would see a steamboat slipping along in the dark, and now and then she would belch a whole world of sparks up out of her chimbleys, and they would rain down in the river and look awful pretty; then she would turn a corner and her lights would wink out and her pow-wow shut off and leave the river still again; and by-and-by her waves would get to us, a long time after she was gone, and joggle the raft a bit, and after that you wouldn't hear nothing for you couldn't tell how long, except maybe frogs or something.
>
> —from *The Adventures of Huckleberry Finn,* Mark Twain

Another writer who used American vernacular to create literature of a high order was Walt Whitman (page 326). Here he proclaims the virtues of American English:

> The English language befriends the grand American expression . . . it is the powerful language of resistance . . . it is the dialect of common sense. It is the speech of the proud and melancholy races and of all who aspire. It is the chosen tongue to express growth faith self-esteem freedom justice equality friendliness amplitude prudence decision and courage. It is the medium that shall well nigh express the inexpressible.
>
> —from *Leaves of Grass,* Walt Whitman

The American vernacular was also the medium that Whitman used in his verse. Whitman quite pointedly used an Americanism *(to loaf)* in the first lines of "Song of Myself" (see page 332):

> I loaf and invite my soul,
> I lean and loaf . . . observing a spear of summer grass.

A

Huck Finn. Drawing by E. W. Kemble, 1884.

"The American vernacular was the medium that Whitman used in his verse."

A. Humanities Connection: Responding to the Illustrations (See Humanities Connection annotation A, page 414.) You might ask students to imagine the boy in the Kemble drawing reciting the passage from *The Adventures of Huckleberry Finn.* See also the woodcut on page 486, *Congressman Davy Crockett Giving a Speech.*

? What similarities do you find between this picture and the boasts of Bob and the Child of Calamity (pages 405 and 407–408) in the episode from Twain's *Life on the Mississippi?* (Answers will vary but should include mastery of thunder and lightning, "iron-jawed, brass-mounted copper-bellied corpse maker," and also general descriptions of personal impregnability.)

A. Humanities Connection: Responding to the Illustration
A Humanities Connection annotation on Bingham, himself a successful politician, appears on page 406.
? Can you imagine this speaker as the Oregon candidate quoted at the right? What details make the drawing and the speech a good match? (The intensity suggested by the leaning forward and the hand gesture) Would you trust this speaker? Why or why not? (Answers will vary. Some students may see an almost devilish air to the man's ears, eyebrows, and general features.)

In *Two Years Before the Mast* (1840), Richard Henry Dana called *loafer* "the newly invented Yankee word." Four years later, in *Martin Chuzzlewit,* some of which takes place in America, Charles Dickens put *loaf* in quotation marks to show that it was a peculiarly American term. Whitman's use of *loaf* eleven years later proclaimed his Americanness just as surely as if he had called himself a ring-tailed roarer.

The Language of the Stump: Political Coinages

"'Boys, I go in for the American Eagle, claws, stars, stripes, and all.'"

A

A stump-speaking politician. Drawing by George Caleb Bingham (1853). Brush, black ink, and wash over pencil, 11½ × 9½″.

The Saint Louis Art Museum, St. Louis, Missouri. Courtesy of the People of Missouri.

The American vernacular was not only used in literature. It was also being used on the political platform, or "stump." (Candidates for offices would stand on tree stumps to deliver their speeches.) Candidates in the West used Crockett-style language to capture the attention of their rough-hewn audiences. Here is a part of a speech made by an Oregon candidate for office in 1858:

> Fellow-citizens, you might as well try to dry up the Atlantic Ocean with a broomstraw, or draw this 'ere stump from under my feet with a harnessed gadfly, as to convince me that I ain't gwine to be elected this heat [race]. My opponent don't stand a chance; not a sniff. Why, he ain't as intellectual as a common sized shad. . . . If thar's anybody this side of whar the sun begins to blister the yea'th [heath] that can wallop me, let him show himself—I'm ready. Boys, I go in for the American Eagle, claws, stars, stripes, and all; and may I bust my everlastin' button-holes ef I don't knock down, drag out, and gouge everybody as denies me!

This so-called "stump style" is long gone, but many phrases coined by politicians of the period have lasted.

The word *gerrymander* was coined in 1812 after Massachusetts Governor Gerry reorganized the election districts in his state in order to maintain control of the state senate. One of the districts was absurdly long and serpentine, and Gilbert Stuart, noting its resemblance to a salamander, drew a map for a newspaper giving this district a head, wings, and claws. "A Gerrymander," proclaimed the newspaper's editor, and thus the word was born.

Filibuster comes from the Dutch *vribuiter* ("freebooter" or "pirate"). The word was first used in the nineteenth century to refer to attempts by Americans to encourage revolutions in Latin America by running in guns.

The Language of the Press

Newspapers began to flourish in America in the late 1830's, thanks to improved printing methods which made a penny newspaper profitable. Dickens's satirical scene in *Martin Chuzzlewit* gives some indication of the flavor of many newspapers of the day. When Martin Chuzzlewit lands in New York, he is confronted by a mass of newsboys:

A. Humanities Connection: Responding to the Fine Art

? How does the painting relate to or expand upon the section titled "Language of the Press"? (It shows the eager newsboys getting the papers they will sell.) What time and kind of day is it? (Some may suggest early morning or a cloudy day because of the grayish sky and the predominance of dark reds and browns in the painting.) Why do you think the boys are reaching so eagerly for the papers? (Most likely to earn money selling them, although the older boy at the right seems quite interested in the news itself or perhaps a serial story of some kind)

B. Expansion

Once the Chisholm trail had been established by livestock trader Joseph McCoy (the original "real McCoy") in 1867, *cow-* and ranch-related terms also flooded the language: *cowboy, cow camp, cow hand, cowpuncher, cowpoke, bronco-buster, wrangler, range rider, cattle baron.* Frontiersmen dealing with Indians and Spanish-speaking Mexicans contributed enduring pidgin phrases such as *no can do* and *long time no see.*

> "Here's this morning's *New York Sewer!*" cried one. "Here's this morning's *New York Stabber!* Here's the *New York Family Spy!* Here's the *New York Private Listener!* Here's the *New York Peeper!* . . . Here's full particulars of the patriotic loco-foco movement yesterday in which the whigs was so chawed up, and the last Alabama gouging case, and the interesting Arkansas dooel with bowie-knives, and all the political, commercial, and fashionable news!"
>
> —from *Martin Chuzzlewit,* Charles Dickens

The Last Edition by George Loring Brown (undated). Oil.

Carnegie Museum of Art, Pittsburgh, Pennsylvania. Gift of Mr. and Mrs. Henry J. Heinz II. 57.6.2.

A

Newspapers tried to attract readers with colorful language. One of the ways they did this was to invent whimsical abbreviations. The earliest recorded use of the most famous Americanism of them all—*OK*—shows that it had its origin in the fad for witty abbreviations. *OK* was first used in a Boston newspaper in 1839, to mean "all correct" ("oll korrect"). But *OK* might never have survived if the New York Democratic Club, during the 1840 presidential election, had not dubbed themselves *The OK Club.* The Democrats intended *OK* to stand for "Old Kinderhook," a nickname for their candidate, President Martin Van Buren, who had been born in Kinderhook, New York. But their opponents claimed that *OK* stood for "oll korrect" and that the letters had been coined by former President Andrew Jackson, who had misspelled "all correct." (This was to remind voters that Van Buren had been Jackson's handpicked successor and to make fun of Jackson's lack of education.) "OK!" became a Democratic rallying cry during that boisterous election year and from then on came into widespread popular use. But its true derivation—in that Boston newspaper—eluded researchers for over a hundred years.

The Influence of the Immigrants

The late 1840's saw a tremendous increase in the number of immigrants to the United States. In 1845, about 100,000 immigrants arrived; in 1854, this number had grown to 500,000. A majority of immigrants during the mid-nineteenth century were either Germans, seeking haven from political disorder, or Irish, fleeing the devastating famine. The influence of Irish words on American English was small—Irish immigrants also spoke English, since their own language had been suppressed by the British. The German influence was stronger, especially in words for foods (*sauerkraut, frankfurter, hamburger, noodle.*) German has also given us *kindergarten* ("garden of children"); *bum* (from *bummeln,* "to waste time"); *dumb,* in the sense of "stupid" (from *dumm*); and *fresh,* meaning "impertinent" (from *frech,* "impudent").

However, the greatest source of loan words in the nineteenth century was Spanish. As Americans moved westward into territory originally settled by the Spanish, they came upon a host of novelties with Spanish names. *Mustang, lasso, ranch, fiesta, plaza, bronco, canyon,* and *patio* are just a few words of Spanish origin.

B

489

A. Expansion
Most railroad terminology was borrowed from nautical jargon (e.g., *berth, purser, steward, fare, cabin, freight*), a practice that has continued with today's airlines in such terms as *boarding* and *landing.* Some new phrases did, however, derive from railroading: *railroad* as a verb (meaning "coerce"), *sidetrack, streamline, make the grade, highball, right of way, backtrack, end of the line,* and of course, *go off the rails.*

"The rapid growth of the railroad created a unique problem—an urgent need for new place names. Every station had to have a name."

A

The Language of the Rails

The rapid growth of the railroad created a unique problem—an urgent need for new place names. Every station had to have a name, and many sparsely settled areas where the railroad stopped were nameless. The responsibility for providing these new names often fell to railroad executives. As historian Daniel Boorstin writes, one executive who was assigned to name thirty-two stations in the state of Washington performed his task in this way:

> By a strenuous exercise of free-association, [the executive] christened the required number of stations with a variety of names ranging from Warden (''after a heavy stockholder''), to Othello (''after the play''), Ralston (''after a health food''), Horlick (''after the malted milk''), Whittier (''after the poet''), and Laconia (''on account of its location at the summit—after what I thought was Laconia in Switzerland located high up among the Alps, but in looking over the Swiss map this morning I am unable to find a place of that name there'').
>
> —from *The Americans,*
> Daniel Boorstin

The executive may have been weak in European geography, but the name he gave the mountain station had its own nobility. If we assume that it required hardy people to live in the Washington mountains, it was appropriate as well, for in ancient Greece, the dominant people of Laconia were the Spartans.

Analyzing Language

1. One characteristic of English that is common in American speech is the fluidity of parts of speech. Americans change nouns into verbs or adjectives, and verbs into nouns or adjectives. These changes are often brought about by the addition of a suffix. The first suffix popularly used in the United States to make new nouns was *-ery. Printery* was coined in 1638, *grocery* in 1791. Other suffixes used to change a word's function are *-logy, -ism, -ize,* and *-ish.* Make a list of five words that have been formed by the addition of each of these suffixes. What information is given in the dictionary about each word's origin?
2. Nearly every occupation coins its own special vocabulary, which may then find its way into general usage. Short-order cooks, for example, have developed an imaginative vocabulary for the food they serve. You probably use many of the terms yourself: *BLT* (''bacon, lettuce, and tomato sandwich''), *two eggs sunny side up* (''two eggs fried on one side only''), *one medium burger without* (''one hamburger medium-cooked without onions''). Compile a brief dictionary of the special vocabulary of people in a business or industry you are familiar with (stockbrokers, doctors, lawyers, news reporters, weather forecasters, computer programmers, athletes, singers, and so on). Explain the meaning of each word or phrase and, if you can, cite its derivation. Have any of these words or phrases been picked up and used by people outside the occupation?
3. In his book on language, *Word Play: What Happens When People Talk* (Knopf, 1974), Peter Farb says that ''even the menu for an American breakfast emphasizes that English is a patchwork of words borrowed from other languages.'' Here is a menu for what might be called a typical American breakfast. Use a dictionary to find the language that the name of each breakfast food is borrowed from, and write a paragraph explaining your findings.

   Orange juice or tomato juice
   Cereal
   Waffles with syrup
   Bacon
   Coffee or tea

MAKING INFERENCES AND ANALYZING POINT OF VIEW

Writing Assignment

In a brief essay, analyze the effect of the point of view in "An Occurrence at Owl Creek Bridge" (page 431). Include a discussion of some of the inferences the point of view requires you to make.

Background

Making Inferences

An **inference** is a conclusion based on observation or known information. An inference is not a fact, but an educated guess. One of the most famous "inferrers" is Sherlock Holmes, who solves mysteries using his amazing powers of deduction. Here is an example of his method:

> I took the tattered object in my hands and turned it over rather ruefully. It was a very ordinary black hat of the usual round shape, hard and much the worse for wear. The lining had been of red silk, but was a good deal discolored. There was no maker's name; but, as Holmes had remarked, the initials "H.B." were scrawled upon one side. It was pierced in the brim for a hat-securer, but the elastic was missing. For the rest, it was cracked, exceedingly dusty, and spotted in several places, although there seemed to have been some attempt to hide the discolored patches by smearing them with ink.
>
> "I can see nothing," said I, handing it back to my friend.
>
> "On the contrary, Watson, you can see everything. You fail, however, to reason from what you see. You are too timid in drawing your inferences."
>
> "Then, pray tell me what it is that you can infer from this hat?"
>
> He picked it up and gazed at it in the peculiar introspective fashion which was characteristic of him.
>
> "It is perhaps less suggestive than it might have been," he remarked, "and yet there are a few inferences which are very distinct, and a few others which represent at least a strong balance of probability. That the man was highly intellectual is of course obvious upon the face of it, and also that he was fairly well-to-do within the last three years, although he has now fallen upon evil days. He had foresight, but has less now than formerly, pointing to a moral retrogression, which, when taken with the decline of his fortunes, seems to indicate some evil influence, probably drink, at work upon him. This may account also for the obvious fact that his wife has ceased to love him."
>
> "My dear Holmes!"
>
> "He has, however, retained some degree of self-respect," he continued, disregarding my remonstrance. "He is a man who leads a sedentary life, goes out little, is out of training entirely, is middle-aged, has grizzled hair which he has had cut within the last few days, and which he anoints with lime-cream. These are the more patent facts which are to be deduced from his hat. Also, by the way, that it is extremely improbable that he has gas laid on in his house.
>
> "You are certainly joking, Holmes."
>
> "Not in the least. Is it possible that even now, when I give you these results, you are unable to see how they are attained?"
>
> —from "The Adventure of the Blue Carbuncle,"
> Sir Arthur Conan Doyle

Part of the pleasure in reading fiction comes from being able to make guesses. Since writers don't tell us everything directly, most reading involves a constant process of inferring. We often have to infer some of the most important aspects of a story, such as:

1. **Characters' motivation.** (The narrator's questions to the raven in Poe's poem seem designed for self-torture.)
2. **Characters' traits.** (Rip Van Winkle is so passive that most of the townspeople sympathize with him.)
3. **Theme.** (Although Huck thinks of himself as a bad boy, Twain is suggesting that virtue has nothing to do with conventional forms of behavior.)

Analyzing Point of View

The **point of view** from which a story is told will determine the kind and the amount of information a reader will get. Keep in mind the four basic points of view:

Revising Essays As students revise their essays, refer them to **Grammar, Usage, and Mechanics: A Reference Guide** at the back of their books.

Exercises in Critical Thinking and Writing/*cont.*

1. **First-person.** The narrator, who is a main character in the story, supplies all the information. The narrator's thoughts are the only ones the reader can be sure of. This first-person narrator can be unreliable.
2. **Omniscient.** The word means "all-knowing," and it refers to a narrator who enters into the minds of all the major characters. With this point of view, the narrator may include judgments and evaluations of characters and events. This narrator is not in the story.
3. **Limited third person.** This narrator, who is not in the story either, focuses on the thoughts and responses of one character. Everyone, including the main character, is referred to by the third-person pronoun (as is the case with the omniscient point of view). With this point of view, we feel we are experiencing everything in just the way one character is experiencing it.
4. **Objective or dramatic.** Like a movie camera, this narrator records only speeches and actions, with absolutely no comments on the characters or events. The only things the reader knows directly are those that are spoken about or acted out.

Prewriting

Look over "An Occurrence at Owl Creek Bridge." As you read, take notes with the following questions in mind.

Part I

1. Why is the man being hanged? Who is he?

Part II

2. Why does the Union scout pretend to be a Confederate soldier? Why does he try to get the planter to sabotage the bridge?
3. Exactly what did the planter do? Why did he do it?

Part III

4. The condemned man's escape is described realistically and in great detail. If he really dies of a broken neck while being hanged, why does Bierce include the whole episode of his escape?
5. How is the story structured? What function does each of the three parts have? Why do you think Bierce arranged the parts in this sequence?
6. What point of view does Bierce use? Is the point of view consistent, or does it change?
7. What information does Bierce withhold from the reader? What is the effect of withholding this information?
8. What different points of view might Bierce have used? How would the story and our perception of it have changed if he had used a different point of view? Would it have been more or less effective? Why?

Writing

Use your prewriting notes to write an essay of at least four paragraphs. You may want to follow this plan:

Paragraph 1: Mention the writer and the story title; identify the point of view; tell whether you think the point of view is effective.
Paragraph 2: Discuss alternate points of view and how they might have changed the impact of the story.
Paragraph 3: Discuss some of the inferences you must make; discuss the effect of the author's withholding certain information.
Paragraph 4: Summarize your responses to the point of view used in the story.

Revising and Proofreading

Use the guidelines in the section at the back of this book, called **Writing About Literature,** to revise and proofread your essay.

THE MODERNS
THE AMERICAN VOICE IN FICTION

Buildings Abstraction, Lancaster 1931 by Charles Demuth. Oil on panel.

The Detroit Institute of Arts, Detroit, Michigan. Founders Society purchase, General Membership Fund.

UNIT SEVEN

Humanities Connection: Responding To The Fine Art

Charles Demuth (1883–1935) was born in Lancaster, Pennsylvania, a city whose buildings he made familiar to many viewers of his paintings. Demuth found a stark beauty in the industrial landscape of America. In representing it, he borrowed from the cubists—painters like Braque and Picasso—who, while trying to show what the eye sees, also attempted to represent the essential underlying forms of the observed objects. As its title suggests, *Buildings Abstraction* reflects the artist's desire to represent objects not just as they appear to the eye but as they essentially are.

? Which elements in this painting seem realistic—as they would be in a photograph? Which details seem to stress the form of the buildings, details that might appear in an architect's drawing? Why do you suppose that this work was chosen to illustrate the opening of "The Moderns" unit?

Teaching The Moderns

The event that forms the far boundary for the era of writers in this unit is World War I. Although America emerged victorious from that war, and—at least in comparison with the European combatants—virtually unscathed, the experience wrought great changes in people's thinking.

In the literature of the nineteenth century, a cluster of ideas and values, now collectively known as the American dream, played an important role. One element of the dream was the vision of America as a new Eden—innocent, beautiful, rewarding. Another was the optimistic belief that the future held boundless opportunity. A third element was the importance of the individual. All of these ideals were to be challenged and questioned in the light of new philosophies and political movements in the post-war world.

The ideal of the Edenic land is stated by the old man in "The Leader of the People" (page 565), but scorned by his son-in-law as no longer applicable to modern life. The optimism that was essential to the American dream is satirized in Babbitt's soulless activities and, more sympathetically, in Anderson's "The Egg." Yet Thomas Wolfe reaffirms the dream of America as bountiful provider; and F. Scott Fitzgerald plays upon the ideal of material success in "Winter Dreams."

Of the original elements of the American dream, the importance of the individual alone remains a serious concern of the writers in this unit. But this idea has changed also. Instead of Emerson's "single man . . . indomitable on his instincts" to whom, in time, "the huge world will come around," Hemingway's twentieth-century hero relies on his pride in his competence, his will to go on, and his ability to exhibit "grace under pressure." Anderson's hero probes patiently but blindly for meaning in his life; Willa Cather's, William Faulkner's, and Eudora Welty's heroes and heroines are able to prevail because they are "capable of compassion and sacrifice and endurance," as Faulkner puts it in his Nobel acceptance address (page 601). Modern American writers have explored the predicament of the individual in many ways, but despite differences, certain common features can be discerned: works are less concerned with plot than with theme; experimenting is done to find ways of representing the thoughts and feelings of characters without authorial intervention; and a distinctive intensity and singleness of emotion figure as key elements in character.

Objectives Of The Moderns Unit

1. To improve reading proficiency and expand vocabulary
2. To gain exposure to notable authors and their works
3. To identify and define major elements in fiction
4. To identify and define significant literary techniques
5. To express and explain responses to fiction
6. To provide practice in the following critical thinking and writing skills
   a. Analyzing character and conflict
   b. Inferring the writer's attitude
   c. Comparing and contrasting works
   d. Responding to a theme and a study
   e. Analyzing a story

Supplementary Support Materials: Unit Seven

1. Unit Introduction Test (*CCB*)
2. American Language Test (*CCB*)
3. Word Analogies Test (*CCB*)
4. Unit Review Test (*CCB*)
5. Critical Thinking and Writing Test (*CCB*)
6. Study Guide to *The Great Gatsby*
7. Instructional Overhead Transparencies

A. Discussing the Quotation Sherwood Anderson was in his early thirties when World War I ended. The ideas he had grown up with—that America was a new Eden, innocent and infinitely promising, and that the future offered boundless opportunity—had, as he writes his son, been blown up by the war. Willa Cather, another American writer a few years older than Anderson, expressed the same sense of irreversible change saying, "The world broke in two in 1922 or thereabout."

You might want to direct students to look as they read the stories in this unit for the consequences of losing the optimism of the prewar years.

THE MODERNS THE AMERICAN VOICE IN FICTION

by **John Leggett**

A

I had a world, and it slipped away from me. The War blew up more than the bodies of men. . . . It blew ideas away—

—Sherwood Anderson, in a letter to his son, November 1929

War, Depression, and a Rejection of Tradition

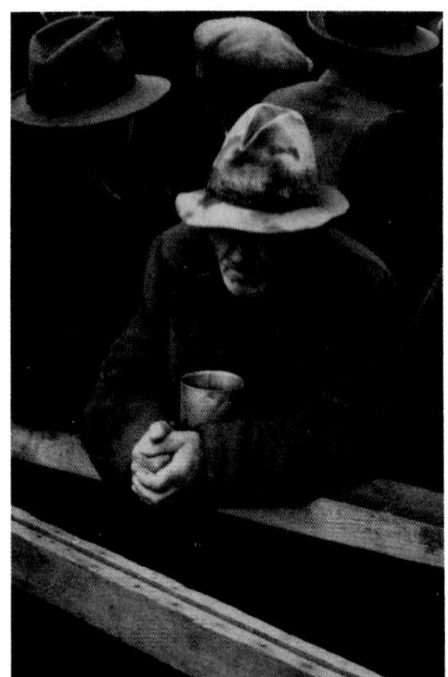

"American fiction had spoken in a young voice: it was brash, somewhat derivative, and as uncertain as an adolescent's."

The so-called Great War (1914–1918) was one of the events that changed the American voice in fiction. Prior to that clash of armies from the old and new worlds, American fiction had spoken in a young voice: it was brash, somewhat derivative, and as uncertain as an adolescent's. Then in 1917 America entered "Mr. Wilson's war," the war which was fought under the bright banners of humanity and righteousness, but which, in fact, became a bloodbath. Nearly a million soldiers were killed in the single battle of Verdun alone.

One of the landmark books about the Great War is American writer Paul Fussell's *The Great War and Modern Memory* (1975), which explores the war's reflection in literature. In the paragraph that follows, Fussell wants the reader to feel what it might have been like to endure the physical hardships, the emotional strain, and the daily fear of life in the trenches.

> To be in the trenches was to experience an unreal, unforgettable enclosure and constraint, as well as a sense of being unoriented and lost. One saw two things only: the walls of an unlocalized, undifferentiated earth and the sky above. Fourteen years after the war J. R. Ackerley was wandering through an unfrequented part of a town in India. "The streets became narrower and narrower as I turned and turned," he writes, "until I felt I was back in the trenches, the houses upon either side being so much of the same color and substance as the rough ground between." That lost feeling is what struck Major Frank Isherwood, who wrote his wife in December, 1914: "The trenches are a labyrinth, I have already lost myself repeatedly. . . . you can't get out of them and walk about the country or see anything at all but two muddy walls on each side of you." What a survivor of the Salient remembers fifty years later are the walls of dirt and the ceiling of sky, and his eloquent optative [wishful] cry rises as if he were still imprisoned there: "To be out of this present, everpresent, eternally present misery, this stinking world of sticky, trickling earth ceilinged by a strip of threatening sky." As the only visible theater of variety, the sky becomes all-important. It was the sight of the sky, almost alone, that had the power to persuade a man that he was not already lost in a common grave.
>
> —from *The Great War and Modern Memory,* Paul Fussell

Alhough America emerged from the war as a victor nation, something was beginning to change. The country seemed to have lost its innocence. Idealism was turning into cynicism, and a few American voices in fiction began to question the authority and tradition which had seemed our bedrock. The war introduced new moral codes, as well as short skirts, bobbed hair, and even new slang expressions. The Americans' sense of a connection to their past seemed to be deteriorating.

There were other reasons for this change in outlook. In 1929, the New York Stock Market crashed. The decade of economic depression that followed brought sufferings to millions of Americans—to those same hard-working people who had put their faith in the boundless capacity of America to provide them with jobs and their children with brighter futures.

American writers, like their European counterparts, were also being profoundly affected by the **modernist** movement. This movement, swept along by disillusionment with traditions that seemed to have become spiritually empty, called for bold experimentation and a sweeping rejection of all traditional themes and styles.

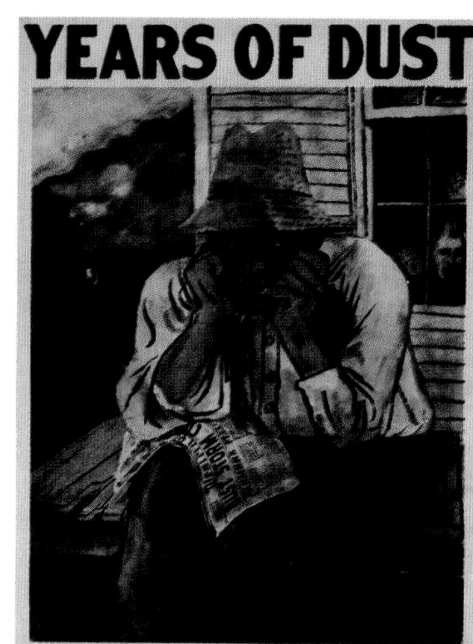

Years of Dust by Ben Shahn (1937). Lithograph printed in color, 38″ × 24¾″.

Collection, The Museum of Modern Art, New York. Gift of the designer.

A

A. Humanities Connection: Discussing the Fine Art
Ben Shahn (1898–1969) was an American painter who dealt mainly with social and political themes. In 1935, Shahn was hired by the Farm Security Administration to depict in photographs the plight of poverty-stricken farmers in the South and Midwest. This poster, created during this period, shows the artist's compassion as well as brilliant graphic sense. Another Shahn painting is reproduced on page 503.

The American Dream

A national voice speaks out of a collective consciousness, or the fabric of beliefs, values, ideals, instincts, and particularly myths which a whole society shares. It does not matter if many of these shared beliefs and values and myths are not *true;* what matters is how firmly the nation believes in them.

If we try to identify our particularly American beliefs—the elements of the American dream—we find three central ideas.

First, there is the idea of America as a new Eden: a beautiful, bountiful, and rewarding land. This idea is expressed in one of the greatest of American novels, *The Great Gatsby,* published in 1925, seven years after the war ended. The novel came out when Prohibition had encouraged the rise of gangsters and when great wealth and the pursuit of pleasure had become ends in themselves for many people. Written by F. Scott Fitzgerald, this novel dealt memorably with both the promise and the disappointment of the "American dream." B

> **"Idealism was turning into cynicism, and a few American voices in fiction began to question the authority and tradition which had seemed our bedrock."**

B. Responding
? What is the first element in the American dream? (The idea of America as a new Eden) Do we still have a belief in the American dream today? If so, how would you describe it? (Most students will agree that we still believe in the American dream, although the future no longer seems to hold boundless opportunities.)

The title character, Gatsby, is a self-made man whose wealth has mysterious and clearly illegal origins. Gatsby moves into a pretentious mansion on Long Island near New York City and tries to woo both society and the woman he loves with a series of lavish parties. His extravagant gestures are in pursuit of a dream. Unfortunately, Gatsby's capacity for dreaming is far greater than any opportunity offered by the Roaring Twenties, and he meets a grotesquely violent end. But Gatsby's greatness is bound up with his tragedy: he believed in an America that had virtually disappeared under the degradations of modern life.

It is left to Nick Carraway, the narrator, to reflect at the end of the novel on the original promise of the "American dream" that lay under all the vulgarities of modern life:

A. Responding
? What are the other two elements of the American dream? (Optimism about the future and a belief in the individual) How important do you think these beliefs are to Americans today? (Answers will vary. Some students may not express optimism about the future due to recessionary economic times in the post-Cold War era and the fierce competition we face in the international marketplace with such industrialized nations as Japan. Most students, however, will say that Americans still hold fast to their belief in the triumph of the individual.)

B. Connections
At this point, you might want students to re-read the selection from Emerson's "Self-Reliance" (page 194) and to discuss Emerson's "defining the American dream."

. . . gradually I became aware of the old island here that flowered once for Dutch sailors' eyes—a fresh, green breast of the new world. Its vanished trees, the trees that had made way for Gatsby's house, had once pandered in whispers to the last and greatest of all human dreams; for a transitory enchanted moment man must have held his breath in the presence of this continent, compelled into an aesthetic contemplation he neither understood nor desired, face to face for the last time in history with something commensurate to his capacity for wonder.

—from *The Great Gatsby,*
F. Scott Fitzgerald

A mansion in Newport, Rhode Island.

A The second element in the American dream is optimism, justified by the ever-expanding opportunity and abundance that we have come to see as our birthright. Most of the time, we Americans have believed in progress—in the fact that our lives are getting better. We tend to view history as a narrative, with a beginning and an end. We conceive of ourselves as moving toward perfection, toward an era of prosperity, justice, and joy that always seems just around the corner.

The third important element in the American dream, and an enduring subject of the American voice, has been a belief in the importance and ultimate triumph of the individual—the independent, self-reliant person.

B We can find all three of these elements reflected in American literature from its beginning, especially in the writings of Ralph Waldo Emerson (see page 187), who is given most credit for defining the essence of the American dream. Emerson did not leave the kind of literary monument left by his contemporaries Walt Whitman and Herman Melville; but some of the essays and speeches he produced in the early nineteenth century are arrows in the eye of the target. Emerson championed the individual. Trust the universe and trust yourself, he wrote. "If the single man plant himself indomitable on his instincts and there abide, the huge world will come around to him." Emerson found God in nature, and he radiated a persuasive optimism. He could find "no calamity which nature cannot repair."

"We Americans have believed in progress—in the fact that our lives are getting better."

The Breakdown of Beliefs and Traditions

It was these inherited ideas of an Edenic land, an optimism in the future, and a faith in individualism that were most heavily damaged by the cannonades of World War I and by the economic crash that followed a decade later. Post-war writers became skeptical of the New England Puritan tradition and the gentility which had been central to the literary ideal. In fact, the center of American literary life now shifted away from New England, which had been the native region of America's most brilliant writers during the nineteenth century. Significantly, the writers you will read in this unit were born in the South, the Midwest, or the West.

For Further Reading
For The Teacher
Nostalgia: Spotlight on the Twenties by Michael Angelo (Universal Books, 1976) provides interesting photographs and trivia from the 1920's. The fact that this is a British publication accounts for the international point of view. However, such American phenomena as jazz and gangsters are well represented.

As traditional beliefs and values were bombarded by the powerful new philosophies and movements in this post-war period, Americans witnessed something of a breakdown in traditional morality and values. Two of these new "movements" were Marxism and psychoanalysis. In Russia, a Marxist revolution had toppled and even murdered an anointed ruler, the Czar. The socialistic beliefs of Karl Marx that had powered the revolution in Russia were in direct opposition to the American system of capitalism and free enterprise. It didn't help that Russia was so far away; Marxists threatened to export their revolution everywhere. From Moscow, the American writer John Reed sent back the alarming message: "I have seen the future and it works."

A

In Vienna, there was another unsettling movement. There, the founder of psychoanalysis, Sigmund Freud, had opened the workings of the unconscious mind to general scrutiny and called for a new understanding of human sexuality and the role it plays in our unconscious thoughts. Throughout America, there was a growing interest in this new field of psychology, and a resultant anxiety about the amount of freedom an individual really had. If our actions were influenced by our subconscious, and if we had no control over our subconscious, there seemed to be little room left for "free will."

One literary result of this interest in the psyche was the narrative technique called **stream of consciousness**. This was a writing style that abandoned chronology and attempted to imitate the moment-by-moment flow of a character's perceptions and memories. Irish writer James Joyce radically changed the very concept of the novel itself by using stream of consciousness in *Ulysses* (1922), his monumental "odyssey" set in Dublin. William Faulkner and Katherine Anne Porter used the stream-of-consciousness technique somewhat later in America. (See page 638.)

Meanwhile, alcohol was singled out as a central social evil. In 1919 the Constitution was amended to prohibit the manufacture and sale of alcoholic beverages. But far from shoring up traditional values, Prohibition ushered in an age that was characterized by the bootlegger, the speakeasy, the cocktail, the short-skirted flapper, the Charleston, the new syncopation of jazz, and the dangerous but lucrative profession of the gangster. Recording the 1920's, and making the era a vivid chapter in our history, F. Scott Fitzgerald gave it its name: the Jazz Age.

Fitzgerald was only one of many American writers and artists who abandoned their own shores after the war for the expatriate life in France. After the war, the dollar was the dominant currency abroad. Living was not only cheap in Paris and on the sunny French Riviera; it was also somehow better there, more exotic, more filled with grace and luxury—and there was no need to go down a cellar stairway to get a drink.

Clearly, something had gone wrong with the American dream—with the idea that America was Eden, with the notion of our inherent virtue, with the conviction that America was a land of heroes. The critic H. L. Mencken scoffed at what he saw as the sheep-like quality of most Americans. Their willingness to follow

"Prohibition ushered in an age that was characterized by the bootlegger, the speakeasy, the cocktail, the short-skirted flapper, the Charleston, the new syncopation of jazz, and the dangerous but lucrative profession of the gangster."

B

"Teaching an old dog new tricks" by John Held. Lithograph.

Cover of LIFE Magazine, February 18, 1926. The New York Public Library.

A. Responding
? Why do you suppose Marxism and psychoanalysis were so unsettling to Americans? (Answers will vary, but both movements were directly opposed to American beliefs and values. An avowed purpose of Marxism was spreading the revolution. Psychoanalysis seemed to do away with "free will.")

B. Humanities Connection: Discussing the Fine Art
This magazine cover by John Held (1889–1958), a famous illustrator for *The New Yorker* and other magazines, depicts the idea of the "flapper," which he did much to establish. This young woman typically has bobbed hair, wears a short dress, and dances with abandon. Held's cover girl could be a caricature of one of the young women attending Jay Gatsby's opulent parties in *The Great Gatsby* (see page 1144).

A. Discussing the Time Line
The division between the past and the present that Anderson, Cather, and other authors in this section saw so clearly occurs about the end of the first line on this chart. Of course, ideas and events that were to shape the future—the theories of Einstein and Freud, the Russian revolution, and America's entry into a European war—were already realities.

The second line of the chart outlines the history of the Twenties—a time of rapid change in social values, business practices, and political views, which culminated in the Great Depression in 1929.

The last line of the chart outlines the history of a very different decade—a time of recovery from economic depression followed by entry into war. The Nobel and Pulitzer prize choices of the 1930's—*The Good Earth* by Pearl Buck and *The Grapes of Wrath* by John Steinbeck—reflect a compassion and social conscience not prevalent in the self-centered 1920's.

As a class project, you might want students to find other events of political, economic, social, scientific, or artistic significance and place them on the time line.

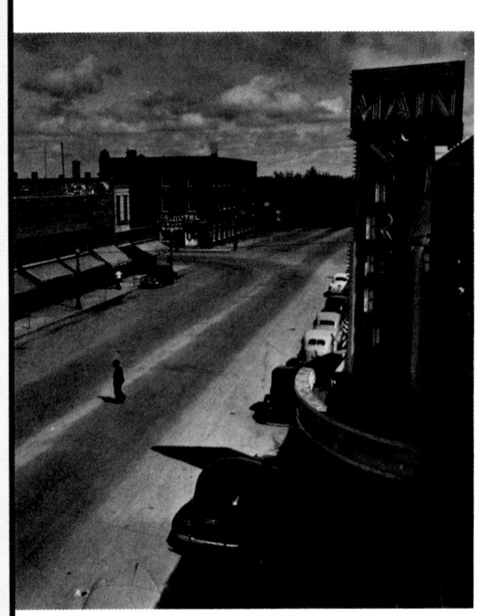

Main Street in Sauk Centre, Minnesota, the setting of Sinclair Lewis's novel.

traditional ways without questioning led him to coin a word to describe the army of consumers that he saw as the American public: "the booboisie" (a take-off on the French word for the middle class, *bourgeoisie*). Mencken's pen seemed to have been dipped in acid.

Disillusionment was a major theme in the fiction of the time. In 1920, Sinclair Lewis (see page 510) lashed out satirically at the parochialism of small-town life in his immensely popular novel, *Main Street.* For Lewis, the widely sentimentalized life of our small towns was actually a narrow-minded, cultural void. In *Babbitt* (1922), Lewis portrayed a middle-class American businessman as profit-driven and small-minded.

In 1925 Theodore Dreiser produced a literary landmark with his prototype of the realistic novel, *An American Tragedy.* The "tragedy" involves the ambitious but luckless Clyde Griffiths, who takes a path that leads him not to the success he seeks, but to the execution chamber. Dreiser sees this path to destruction as an inevitable one, for Clyde does not even question the values American society has thrust upon him. Like the Romantics of an earlier generation, ironically enough, Dreiser placed the seeds of Clyde's destruction in the urban world. Dreiser's story opens and closes within the tall walls of the commercial heart of an American city. *An American Tragedy*—set in a land whose wide-open spaces were once a cause for wonder—is a tragedy of a world enclosed.

1895	1896–1905	1909	1911–1912
Crane publishes *The Red Badge of Courage*, 1895 Final volume of Karl Marx's *Das Kapital* published, 1895	**Dunbar's poetry published, 1896** **Jack London publishes *The Call of the Wild*, 1903** Einstein formulates his theory of relativity, 1905	**William Carlos Williams's first collection of poems published, 1909** Freud lectures on psychoanalysis in U.S., 1909	**Edith Wharton publishes *Ethan Frome*, 1911** *Titanic* sinks, killing 1,513 people, 1912 **Ezra Pound founds Imagist Movement, 1912**

A

1920	1920–1922	1922	1923
Women win the right to vote, 1920 ***Beyond the Horizon* opens and wins Eugene O'Neill the first of four Pulitzer Prizes, 1920**	Prohibition of "intoxicating liquors" begins in U.S., 1920 **Robinson's *Collected Poems* published, 1922**	Stock market boom begins in U.S., 1922 Mussolini seizes power in Italy, 1922 **Millay wins the Pulitzer Prize for Poetry, 1922**	George Gershwin's "Rhapsody in Blue" performed, 1923 **Frost wins the first of four Pulitzer Prizes for Poetry, 1923**

1936–1937	1938–1939	1938–1939	1941
Eugene O'Neill wins Nobel Prize for Literature, 1936 **Steinbeck publishes *Of Mice and Men*, 1937**	**Pearl Buck wins the Nobel Prize for Literature, 1938** ***The Grapes of Wrath* is published in 1939 and wins the Pulitzer Prize**	***Our Town* opens and wins Pulitzer Prize, 1938** Germany invades Poland, September 1, 1939	Pearl Harbor bombed, December 7, 1941 America enters the war in Europe, December 11, 1941

A New American Style and "Hero" in Fiction

The most influential of all these post-World War I writers was Ernest Hemingway (see page 553). It was Hemingway who called himself and his generation "the lost generation." (He borrowed the phrase from his friend Gertrude Stein, but then she in turn was reputed to have heard it from her garage mechanic in Paris.) Hemingway is perhaps most famous for his literary style, which affected the style of American prose fiction for several generations. Much in the fashion of the Puritan writers who strove for a "plain style," Hemingway reduced the flamboyance of literary language to a minimum, to the bones of the truth it must express. He is also well remembered for adding a new kind of hero to American fiction, a character many readers embraced as a protagonist and a role model. This Hemingway hero was a man of action, a man of war, and a tough competitor; he had a code of honor, courage, and endurance. He shows, in Hemingway's words, "grace under pressure."

He is Nick Adams of *In Our Times,* Frederick Henry of *A Farewell to Arms,* Jake Barnes of *The Sun Also Rises,* Robert Jordan of *For Whom the Bell Tolls,* and Santiago of *The Old Man and the Sea.* But the most important thing about this Hemingway hero is that he is thoroughly disillusioned, a quality that reflected Hemingway's own outlook.

For Further Reading For The Teacher
Alfred Kazin's *On Native Grounds* (Harcourt Brace Jovanovich, 1942, 1983) presents a perceptive and balanced view of the authors in this unit and is particularly helpful in interpreting their political and social context.

1913–1915	1915–1916	1917	1917–1920
Frost publishes first book of poetry, 1913 World War I, 1914–1918 **Masters publishes *Spoon River Anthology,* 1915**	British liner *Lusitania* sunk by German U-boats, May 7, 1915 **Sandburg publishes "Chicago," 1916**	**Eliot publishes "The Love Song of J. Alfred Prufrock," 1917** Revolution in Russia topples Czar and establishes socialist government, 1917	U.S. declares war on Germany, April 16, 1917 **Anderson publishes *Winesburg, Ohio,* 1919** Harlem Renaissance begins, 1920

1925–1926	1926–1927	1929–1930	1932–1933
Fitzgerald's *The Great Gatsby* published, 1925 Fascist youth organizations formed in Italy and Germany, 1926	**Wolfe publishes *Look Homeward, Angel,* 1926** Charles Lindbergh makes first solo transatlantic flight, 1927.	U.S. stock market crash, October 24, 1929. Great Depression begins. **Sinclair Lewis wins Nobel Prize for Literature, 1930**	12 million Americans unemployed, 1932 Roosevelt's New Deal begins, 1933 Adolf Hitler appointed German Chancellor, 1933

READING CHECK TEST

1. The three central elements of the American dream are America, the new Eden; optimism about the future; and belief in (a) states' rights (b) the importance of the individual (c) education *(b)*
2. In 1919, the Constitution was amended to (a) give women equal rights (b) limit presidents to two terms (c) prohibit the sale of liquor *(c)*
3. During the Twenties, many American writers led expatriate lives in (a) France (b) North Africa (c) Mexico *(a)*
4. The writer who coined the word *booboisie* was (a) Sinclair Lewis (b) H. L. Mencken (c) F. Scott Fitzgerald *(b)*
5. One of the qualities of the Hemingway hero is the ability to show (a) compassion for the downtrodden (b) grace under pressure (c) how honesty pays *(b)*

A. Responding

? What was Hemingway's answer to the collapse of faith? (A belief in the self and in such "heroic" qualities as decency and bravery. He also believed in recognizing and enjoying life's good moments.)

Hemingway feared, a little like Melville, that at the inscrutable center of creation lay nothing at all.

Nearly a century earlier, Emerson had also sensed a collapse of faith and had told the Class of 1838 at the Harvard Divinity School that the church's hold on people was weakening. Emerson was appalled.

> What greater calamity can fall upon a nation than the lack of worship? Genius leaves the temple to haunt the senate or the market. Literature becomes frivolous. Science is cold. The eye of the youth is not lighted by the hope of other worlds and age is without honor. Society lives to trifles and when men die we do not mention them.
>
> —Ralph Waldo Emerson

A Hemingway found his own "answer" in a belief in the self and in such qualities of decency, bravery, competence, and skill as one can summon. He clung to this belief in spite of what he saw as the absolutely unbeatable odds ranged against us all. A further part of the Hemingway code was the importance of recognizing and snatching up the rare, good, rich moments that life offers, before those moments elude us.

Even though Hemingway rejected Emerson's optimism, a belief in self-reliance still persists in Hemingway's work, as the old idea of America as Eden. Hemingway is really telling us about Eden in his *Up in Michigan* stories, where he describes the lakes and streams and woods he knew as a boy and where he extols the restorative power of nature in a way that Emerson might have recognized. This is the same Edenic America that has come down to us through Mark Twain's Mississippi, through Faulkner's Yoknapatawpha County, and through John Steinbeck's Salinas Valley (see page 620).

"Who are we? Where are we going? And what values should guide us on that search for our human identity?"

As we explore this period of American writing—in some respects, the richest period since the flowering of New England in the first half of the nineteenth century—we stand at the threshold of our own time. Though this part of our own century has seen a major change in American attitudes, you'll recognize many concerns that are consistent with concerns of the past. These writers—some of the best that America has produced—experimented boldly with forms and subject matter. But they were also still trying to find the answers to the basic human questions: Who are we? Where are we going? And what values should guide us on that search for our human identity?

Sherwood Anderson (1876–1941)

When the first stories of Sherwood Anderson were published, they were the subjects of heated debate. *Winesburg, Ohio*, Anderson's series of short stories about the people in a small mid-western town, is now an American classic. But when it first appeared, it was called "unclean, filthy," even by Theodore Dreiser, the popular realistic novelist who had helped Anderson bring his first works to the public.

Sherwood Anderson was born on September 13, 1876, in southern Ohio, the third of seven children. His father was a harness-maker, and his trade was being rendered obsolete by mass production. An easygoing man, the elder Anderson was given to telling tall tales and to heavy drinking.

Since Sherwood often had to help out at home, his schooling was spotty. His mother died when he was fourteen, his father drifted out and away from the family forever, and Anderson's formal education virtually came to an end.

Anderson eventually became an advertising copywriter, and in the spirit of the new century and the "new age," he extolled the world of business in his copy. Married and a family man, he bought a paint factory and continued to write copy ennobling the life he had chosen, even though he felt trapped in it. He was, he later said, following an adage often repeated to him: "Get money. Money makes the mare go."

On November 27, 1912, at the age of thirty-seven, Anderson had had enough. On that day, he walked out on his job and on his whole life. He left the factory muttering, leaving his co-workers with the idea that he had lost his mind.

In 1919, Anderson published *Winesburg, Ohio*. The structure and focus of this collection of stories were inspired by Edgar Lee Masters's collection of poems called *Spoon River Anthology* (page 656). Anderson was concerned not with well-crafted plots in the traditional sense, but with revealing the secret needs and longings of twenty-two people from one small town. The stories are unified by their characters, by their setting, and by Anderson's theory of the "grotesque."

According to the introduction to *Winesburg, Ohio*, a *grotesque* is someone who seizes a single truth out of life and lives by that truth alone. Tragically, these single-minded pursuits drive the characters into isolation. The only person the Winesburg "grotesques" can communicate with is George Willard, a writer. Anderson thus uses Willard to dramatize the function of the artist: That function is, as Anderson sees it, to absorb other people's lives and to "become" them.

What made the stories in *Winesburg* shocking was that Anderson also explored the intimate thoughts of his characters. The result was a series of portraits that were honest, unflinching—and, at the time, painful for many to deal with.

Because there are few dramatic events in the Winesburg stories, many readers dismissed them as "non-stories." One member of the Chicago Group felt that the stories were so formless that Anderson should throw them away. The major complaint from readers, however, dealt with the unconventional subject matter, especially with the themes of sexuality and repression. One woman, who had attended a dinner party with Anderson, sent him a letter saying, ". . . having sat beside you and having read your stories, I feel that I should never be clean again."

In his criticism of industry and of the American dream that money will bring happiness, Anderson proposed his own dream of love as happiness. He once wrote:

A. Responding

What is Anderson's theory of the "grotesque"? (A "grotesque" is someone who seizes a single truth out of life and lives by that truth alone.) Why is this "grotesque" person generally isolated ? (Because of the single-minded pursuit) Given this definition, do you believe that "grotesques" exist in society today? Give examples. (Students might mention scientists, artists, or even entrepreneurs who are driven by a vision that others do not share.)

B. Responding

What does Anderson believe the function of an artist to be? (To absorb other people's lives and to "become" them)

SUPPLEMENTARY SUPPORT MATERIALS
1. Vocabulary Activity Worksheet (*CCB*)
2. Review and Response Worksheet: Symbols (*CCB*)
3. Language Skills Worksheet: Varying Sentence Length (*CCB*)
4. Selection Test (*CCB*)

DEVELOPING VOCABULARY
The following words from the story are tested in the Selection Test. (See also Vocabulary Activity Worksheet.)

unversed grotesque
disillusioned shrilly
vermin prenatal

PREPARATION
ESTABLISHING A PURPOSE. Before they start reading "The Egg," refer students to Question 8 on page 509. Ask them to keep this question in mind as they read the story.

A. Characterization
? What early clues do you have about the character of the narrator's father? (He is described as someone whom nature intended to be a "cheerful, kindly man." He was sociable and happy with his lot in life.)

B. Plot
? At what point did the narrator's father become ambitious? (When he married and became a father)

I began to gather these impressions. There was a thing called happiness toward which men were striving. They never got to it. All of life was amazingly accidental. Love, moments of tenderness and despair, came to the poor and the miserable as to the rich and successful.

It began to seem to me that what was most wanted by all people was love, understanding. Our writers, our storytellers, in wrapping life up into neat little packages, were only betraying life.

As for himself, Anderson kept "escaping" for the rest of his life. Attractive to women, he married four times and traveled as far as Paris, where he met the writer Gertrude Stein who had an important influence on his work. He also met, in Chicago, a young writer who impressed him. It was Anderson who sent the young man—whose name was Ernest Hemingway (page 566)—to Paris with a letter of introduction to Gertrude Stein.

During the Depression and the New Deal that followed it, Anderson's stories became oddly dated and irrelevant. Today, however, a few of Anderson's stories have taken their places as American classics. These include such later stories as "The Egg" from *The Triumph of the Egg* (1921) and "Death in the Woods" and "Brother Death" from *Death in the Woods* (1933).

THE EGG

This story provides a good illustration of Anderson's ability to attack the human condition without attacking the people living in that condition. As you read, keep in mind Anderson's well-known definition of the word *grotesque* (see page 525), which is used in this story in a different sense. Look for clues about how the narrator of the story feels toward his parents.

A My father was, I am sure, intended by nature to be a cheerful, kindly man. Until he was thirty-four years old he worked as a farmhand for a man named Thomas Butterworth whose place lay near the town of Bidwell, Ohio. He had then a horse of his own and on Saturday evenings drove into town to spend a few hours in social intercourse with other farmhands. In town he drank several glasses of beer and stood about in Ben Head's saloon—crowded on Saturday evenings with visiting farmhands. Songs were sung and glasses thumped on the bar. At ten o'clock father drove home along a lonely country road, made his horse comfortable for the night and himself went to bed, quite happy in his position in life. He had at that time no notion of trying to rise in the world.

It was in the spring of his thirty-fifth year that father married my mother, then a country schoolteacher, and in the following spring I came wriggling and crying into the world. Something happened to the two people. They became ambitious. The American passion for getting up in the world took possession of them. B

It may have been that mother was responsible. Being a schoolteacher she had no doubt read books and magazines. She had, I presume, read of how Garfield, Lincoln, and other Americans rose from poverty to fame and greatness and as I lay beside her—in the days of her lying-in[1]—she may have dreamed that I would some day rule men and cities. At any rate she induced father to give up his place as a farmhand, sell his horse and embark on an independent enterprise of his own. She was a tall silent woman with a long nose and troubled gray eyes. For herself she wanted nothing. For father and myself she was incurably ambitious.

The first venture into which the two people went turned out badly. They rented ten acres of

1. **days of her lying-in:** her time spent in bed after giving birth.

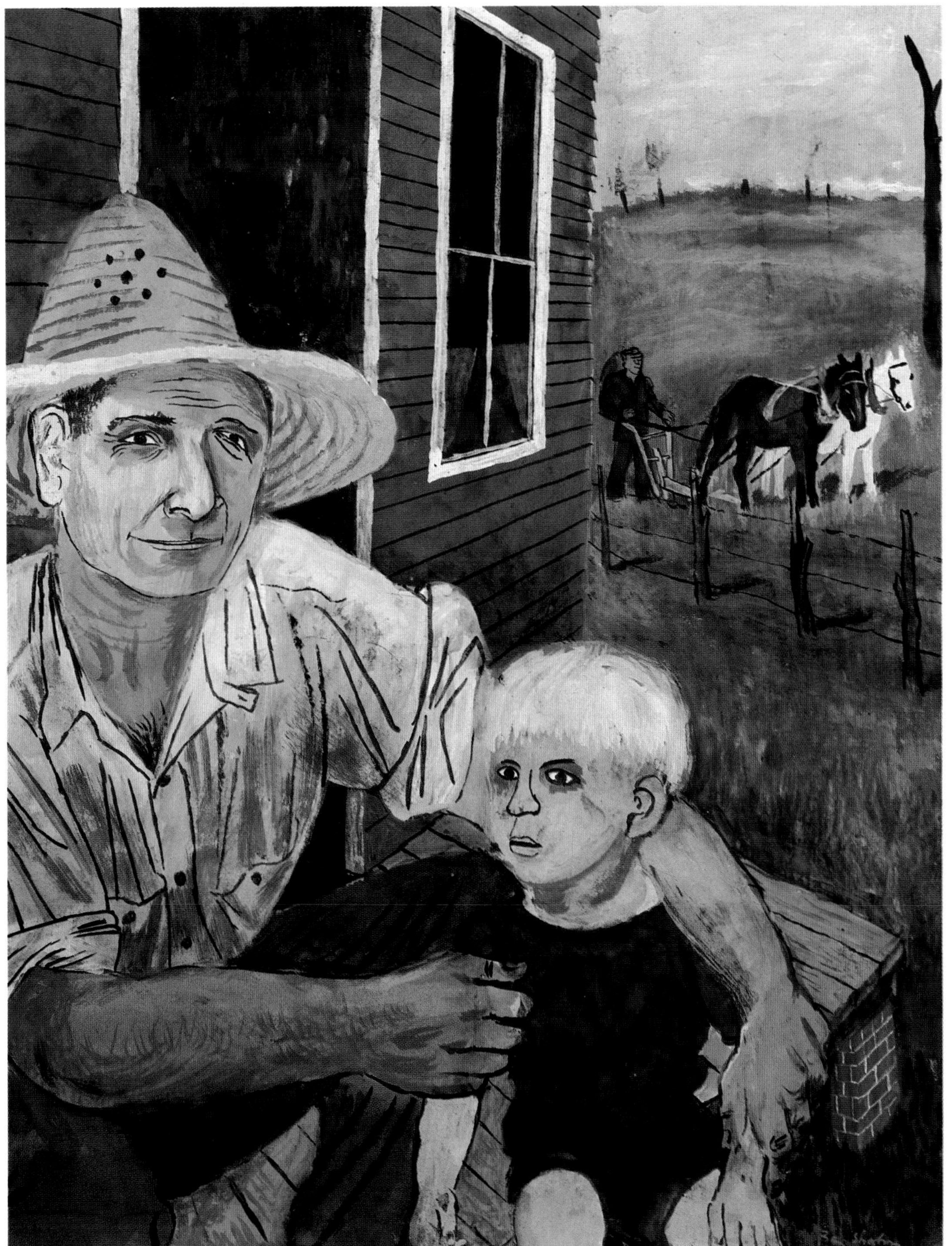

The Farmer and His Son by Ben Shahn. Oil.

Hirshhorn Museum and Sculpture Garden, Smithsonian Institution, Washington, D.C.

Humanities Connection: Discussing the Fine Art
Like the poster on page 495, this painting by Ben Shahn (1898–1969) shows this artist's ability to produce powerful, compassionate images of ordinary people.

Literature and Language: Using Verbal Irony
Students use verbal irony (saying the opposite of what they mean) all the time. "Oh great!" they might say when they run out of gas on a highway. "That's just terrific!" might be a response to a test question they haven't the slightest idea how to answer. Ask them to find examples of verbal irony in the passage from "The Egg" in the bottom left column of page 504, with the sentence that begins "In later life. . . ."

Review other kinds of irony by having students read the definition of *irony* in the Handbook of Literary Terms (page 1175) and the section on irony in "The Four 'Modes' of Fiction" (page 612). Encourage students to discuss the different kinds of irony they see in Anderson's "The Egg." (The tone is ironic. *Dramatic irony*: The narrator and his family seem trapped and doomed to failure. *Situational irony:* The father's attempts to be cheerful and entertain his customers make him appear mad; he frightens and attacks the customer he's trying to entertain.)

A. Hyperbole
This paragraph—a long digression on the misfortunes of chicken farming—is an example of *hyperbole* (hī·pur′ bə lē), obvious exaggeration for comic effect, that is not meant to be taken seriously.

B. Description
? What does the description of the family as they move to Bidwell say about the narrator's first ten years of life? (The fact that the family has only a few, "cheap" possessions and that they move in a borrowed wagon indicates that his first ten years were not easy ones for the narrator. The fact that his father was "habitually silent and discouraged" suggests that the narrator's relationship with his father may have been lacking.)

poor stony land on Griggs's Road, eight miles from Bidwell, and launched into chicken raising. I grew into boyhood on the place and got my first impressions of life there. From the beginning they were impressions of disaster and if, in my turn, I am a gloomy man inclined to see the darker side of life, I attribute it to the fact that what should have been for me the happy joyous days of childhood were spent on a chicken farm.

One unversed in such matters can have no notion of the many and tragic things that can happen to a chicken. It is born out of an egg, lives for a few weeks as a tiny fluffy thing such as you will see pictured on Easter cards, then becomes hideously naked, eats quantities of corn and meal bought by the sweat of your father's brow, gets diseases called pip, cholera, and other names, stands looking with stupid eyes at the sun, becomes sick and dies. A few hens and now and then a rooster, intended to serve God's mysterious ends, struggle through to maturity. The hens lay eggs out of which come other chickens and the dreadful cycle is thus made complete. It is all unbelievably complex. Most philosophers must have been raised on chicken farms. One hopes for so much from a chicken and is so dreadfully disillusioned. Small chickens, just setting out on the journey of life, look so bright and alert and they are in fact so dreadfully stupid. They are so much like people they mix one up in one's judgments of life. If disease does not kill them they wait until your expectations are thoroughly aroused and then walk under the wheels of a wagon—to go squashed and dead back to their maker. Vermin infest their youth, and fortunes must be spent for curative powders. In later life I have seen how a literature has been built up on the subject of fortunes to be made out of the raising of chickens. It is intended to be read by the gods who have just eaten of the tree of the knowledge of good and evil.[2] It is a hopeful literature and declares that much may be done by simple ambitious people who own a few hens. Do not be led astray by it. It was not written for you. Go hunt for gold on the frozen hills of Alaska, put your faith in the honesty of a politician, believe if you will that the world is daily growing better and that good will triumph over evil, but do not read and believe the literature that is written concerning the hen. It was not written for you.

I, however, digress. My tale does not primarily concern itself with the hen. If correctly told it will center on the egg. For ten years my father and mother struggled to make our chicken farm pay and then they gave up that struggle and began another. They moved into the town of Bidwell, Ohio, and embarked in the restaurant business. After ten years of worry with incubators that did not hatch, and with tiny—and in their own way lovely—balls of fluff that passed on into seminaked pullethood and from that into dead henhood, we threw all aside and packing our belongings on a wagon drove down Griggs's Road toward Bidwell, a tiny caravan of hope looking for a new place from which to start on our upward journey through life.

We must have been a sad-looking lot, not, I fancy, unlike refugees fleeing from a battlefield. Mother and I walked in the road. The wagon that contained our goods had been borrowed for the day from Mr. Albert Griggs, a neighbor. Out of its sides stuck the legs of cheap chairs and at the back of the pile of beds, tables, and boxes filled with kitchen utensils was a crate of live chickens, and on top of that the baby carriage in which I had been wheeled about in my infancy. Why we stuck to the baby carriage I don't know. It was unlikely other children would be born and the wheels were broken. People who have few possessions cling tightly to those they have. That is one of the facts that make life so discouraging.

Father rode on top of the wagon. He was then a bald-headed man of forty-five, a little fat and from long association with mother and the chickens he had become habitually silent and discouraged. All during our ten years on the chicken farm he had worked as a laborer on neighboring farms and most of the money he had earned had been spent for remedies to cure chicken diseases, on Wilmer's White Wonder Cholera Cure or Professor Bidlow's Egg Producer or some other preparations that mother found advertised in the poultry papers. There were two little patches of hair on father's head just above his ears. I remember that as a child I used to sit looking at him when he had gone to sleep in a chair before the stove on Sunday afternoons in the winter. I had at that time already begun to read books and have notions of my own and the bald path that led over the top of his head was, I fancied, something like a broad road, such

2. **tree of the knowledge of good and evil:** an allusion to the third chapter of Genesis, and to the tree in Eden that bore the forbidden fruit.

a road as Caesar might have made on which to lead his legions out of Rome and into the wonders of an unknown world. The tufts of hair that grew above father's ears were, I thought, like forests. I fell into a half-sleeping, half-waking state and dreamed I was a tiny thing going along the road into a far beautiful place where there were no chicken farms and where life was a happy eggless affair.

One might write a book concerning our flight from the chicken farm into town. Mother and I walked the entire eight miles—she to be sure that nothing fell from the wagon and I to see the wonders of the world. On the seat of the wagon beside father was his greatest treasure. I will tell you of that.

A On a chicken farm where hundreds and even thousands of chickens come out of eggs surprising things sometimes happen. Grotesques are born out of eggs as out of people. The accident does not often occur—perhaps once in a thousand births. A chicken is, you see, born that has four legs, two pairs of wings, two heads or whatnot. The things do not live. They go quickly back to the hand of their maker that has for a moment trembled. The fact that the poor little things could not live was one of the tragedies of life to father. He had some sort of notion that if he could but bring into henhood or roosterhood a five-legged hen or a two-headed rooster his fortune would be made. He dreamed of taking the wonder about to country fairs and of growing rich by exhibiting it to other farmhands.

At any rate he saved all the little monstrous things that had been born on our chicken farm. They were preserved in alcohol and put each in its own glass bottle. These he had carefully put into a box and on our journey into town it was carried on the wagon seat beside him. He drove the horses with one hand and with the other clung to the box. When we got to our destination the box was taken down at once and the bottles removed. All during our days as keepers of a restaurant in the town of Bidwell, Ohio, the grotesques in their little glass bottles sat on a shelf back of the counter. Mother sometimes protested but father was a rock on the subject of his treasure. The grotesques were, he declared, valuable. People, he said, liked to look at strange and wonderful things.

Did I say that we embarked in the restaurant business in the town of Bidwell, Ohio? I exaggerated a little. The town itself lay at the foot of a low hill and on the shore of a small river. The railroad did not run through the town and the station was a mile away to the north at a place called Pickleville. There had been a cider mill and pickle factory at the station, but before the time of our coming they had both gone out of business. In the morning and in the evening buses came down to the station along a road called Turner's Pike from the hotel on the main street of Bidwell. Our going to the out-of-the-way place to embark in the restaurant business was mother's idea. She talked of it for a year and then one day went off and rented an empty store building opposite the railroad station. It was her idea that the restaurant would be profitable. Traveling men, she said, would be always waiting around to take trains out of town and town people would come to the station to await incoming trains. They would come to the restaurant to buy pieces of pie and drink coffee. Now that I am older I know that she had another motive in going. She was ambitious for me. She wanted me to rise in the world, to get into a town school and become a man of the towns.

At Pickleville father and mother worked hard as they always had done. At first there was the necessity of putting our place into shape to be a restaurant. That took a month. Father built a shelf on which he put tins of vegetables. He painted a sign on which he put his name in large red letters. Below his name was the sharp command—"EAT HERE"—that was so seldom obeyed. A showcase was bought and filled with cigars and tobacco. Mother scrubbed the floor and the walls of the room. I went to school in the town and was glad to be away from the farm and from the presence of the discouraged, sad-looking chickens. Still I was not very joyous. In the evening I walked home from school along Turner's Pike and remembered the children I had seen playing in the town schoolyard. A troop of little girls had gone hopping about and singing. I tried that. Down along the frozen road I went hopping solemnly on one leg. "Hippity Hop to the Barber Shop," I sang shrilly. Then I stopped and looked doubtfully about. I was afraid of being seen in my gay mood. B It must have seemed to me that I was doing a thing that should not be done by one who, like myself, had been raised on a chicken farm where death was a daily visitor.

Mother decided that our restaurant should re-

A. Theme
In this story as a whole, Anderson ironically draws a parallel between the dismal life of a chicken and that of human beings. In this passage he implicitly comments on the human beings he calls "grotesques" as he describes the malformed chicks that the narrator's father prizes so highly.

B. Characterization
The detail of the narrator's feeling guilty about his "gay mood" clearly suggests the baleful effect that chicken farming has had on his life.

A. Foreshadowing
This mention of Father's wanting to save his entertainment for "a young man or woman from Bidwell" sets the stage for his disastrous debut when Joe Kane is his audience.

B. Point of View
Anderson's choice of first-person point of view to tell this story presents a problem in representing the key scene between Father and Joe Kane, at which the narrator is not present. Anderson solves this problem by enveloping this scene between the two parts of the bedroom scene, where the narrator and his mother learn of the debacle in the restaurant. Anderson is then able to use what is essentially an omniscient narrator's point of view in presenting the scene in the restaurant.

main open at night. At ten in the evening a passenger train went north past our door followed by a local freight. The freight crew had switching to do in Pickleville and when the work was done they came to our restaurant for hot coffee and food. Sometimes one of them ordered a fried egg. In the morning at four they returned northbound and again visited us. A little trade began to grow up. Mother slept at night and during the day tended the restaurant and fed our boarders while father slept. He slept in the same bed mother had occupied during the night and I went off to the town of Bidwell and to school. During the long nights, while mother and I slept, father cooked meats that were to go into sandwiches for the lunch baskets of our boarders. Then an idea in regard to getting up in the world came into his head. The American spirit took hold of him. He also became ambitious.

In the long nights when there was little to do father had time to think. That was his undoing. He decided that he had in the past been an unsuccessful man because he had not been cheerful enough and that in the future he would adopt a cheerful outlook on life. In the early morning he came upstairs and got into bed with mother. She woke and the two talked. From my bed in the corner I listened.

It was father's idea that both he and mother should try to entertain the people who came to eat at our restaurant. I cannot now remember his words, but he gave the impression of one about to become in some obscure way a kind of public entertainer. When people, particularly young people from the town of Bidwell, came into our place, as on very rare occasions they did, bright entertaining conversation was to be made. From father's words I gathered that something of the jolly innkeeper effect was to be sought. Mother must have been doubtful from the first, but she said nothing discouraging. It was father's notion that a passion for the company of himself and mother would spring up in the breasts of the younger people of the town of Bidwell. In the evening bright happy groups would come singing down Turner's Pike. They would troop shouting with joy and laughter into our place. There would be song and festivity. I do not mean to give the impression that father spoke so elaborately of the matter. He was as I have said an uncommunicative man. "They want some place to go. I tell you they want some place to go," he said over and over. That was as far as he got. My own imagination has filled in the blanks.

For two or three weeks this notion of father's invaded our house. We did not talk much, but in our daily lives tried earnestly to make smiles take the place of glum looks. Mother smiled at the boarders and I, catching the infection, smiled at our cat. Father became a little feverish in his anxiety to please. There was no doubt, lurking somewhere in him, a touch of the spirit of the showman. He did not waste much of his ammunition on the railroad men he served at night but seemed to be waiting for a young man or woman from Bidwell to come in to show what he could do. (A) On the counter in the restaurant there was a wire basket kept always filled with eggs, and it must have been before his eyes when the idea of being entertaining was born in his brain. There was something prenatal about the way eggs kept themselves connected with the development of his idea. At any rate an egg ruined his new impulse in life. Late one night I was awakened by a roar of anger coming from father's throat. Both mother and I sat upright on our beds. With trembling hands she lighted a lamp that stood on a table by her head. Downstairs the front door of our restaurant went shut with a bang and in a few minutes father tramped up the stairs. He held an egg in his hand and his hand trembled as though he was having a chill. There was a half-insane light in his eyes. As he stood glaring at us I was sure he intended throwing the egg at either mother or me. Then he laid it gently on the table beside the lamp and dropped on his knees beside mother's bed. He began to cry like a boy and I, carried away by his grief, cried with him. The two of us filled the little upstairs room with our wailing voices. It is ridiculous, but of the picture we made I can remember only the fact that mother's hand continually stroked the bald path that ran across the top of his head. I have forgotten what mother said to him and how she induced him to tell her of what had happened downstairs. His explanation also has gone out of my mind. I remember only my own grief and fright and the shiny path over father's head glowing in the lamplight as he knelt by the bed.

As to what happened downstairs. For some unexplainable reason I know the story as well as though I had been a witness to my father's discomfiture. One in time gets to know many unexplainable things. (B) On that evening young Joe Kane,

Reading Check Test

1. The narrator's family's first business venture is a chicken farm. *True*
2. The father and mother pool their savings to buy the farm. *False*
3. The narrator's father has a full head of bushy, unruly hair. *False*
4. The father's greatest treasure is a collection of deformed chicks. *True*
5. The father briefly succeeds in making an egg stand on end. *True*

son of a merchant of Bidwell, came to Pickleville to meet his father, who was expected on the ten o'clock evening train from the South. The train was three hours late and Joe came into our place to loaf about and to wait for its arrival. The local freight train came in and the freight crew were fed. Joe was left alone in the restaurant with father.

From the moment he came into our place the Bidwell young man must have been puzzled by my father's actions. It was his notion that father was angry at him for hanging around. He noticed that the restaurant keeper was apparently disturbed by his presence and he thought of going out. However, it began to rain and he did not fancy the long walk to town and back. He bought a five-cent cigar and ordered a cup of coffee. He had a newspaper in his pocket and took it out and began to read. "I'm waiting for the evening train. It's late," he said apologetically.

For a long time father, whom Joe Kane had never seen before, remained silently gazing at his visitor. He was no doubt suffering from an attack of stage fright. As so often happens in life he had thought so much and so often of the situation that now confronted him that he was somewhat nervous in its presence.

For one thing, he did not know what to do with his hands. He thrust one of them nervously over the counter and shook hands with Joe Kane. "How-de-do," he said. Joe Kane put his newspaper down and stared at him. Father's eye lighted on the basket of eggs that sat on the counter and he began to talk. "Well," he began hesitatingly, "well, you have heard of Christopher Columbus, eh?" He seemed to be angry. "That Christopher Columbus was a cheat," he declared emphatically. "He talked of making an egg stand on its end. He talked, he did, and then he went and broke the end of the egg."

My father seemed to his visitor to be beside himself at the duplicity of Christopher Columbus. He muttered and swore. He declared it was wrong to teach children that Christopher Columbus was a great man when, after all, he cheated at the critical moment. He had declared he would make an egg stand on end and then when his bluff had been called he had done a trick. Still grumbling at Columbus, father took an egg from the basket on the counter and began to walk up and down. He rolled the egg between the palms of his hands. He smiled genially. He began to mumble words regarding the effect to be produced on an egg by the electricity that comes out of the human body. He declared that without breaking its shell and by virtue of rolling it back and forth in his hands he could stand the egg on its end. He explained that the warmth of his hands and the gentle rolling movement he gave the egg created a new center of gravity, and Joe Kane was mildly interested. "I have handled thousands of eggs," father said. "No one knows more about eggs than I do."

He stood the egg on the counter and it fell on its side. He tried the trick again and again, each time rolling the egg between the palms of his hands and saying the words regarding the wonders of electricity and the laws of gravity. When after a half hour's effort he did succeed in making the egg stand for a moment he looked up to find that his visitor was no longer watching. By the time he had succeeded in calling Joe Kane's attention to the success of his effort the egg had again rolled over and lay on its side. A

Afire with the showman's passion and at the same time a good deal disconcerted by the failure of his first effort, father now took the bottles containing the poultry monstrosities down from their place on the shelf and began to show them to his visitor. "How would you like to have seven legs and two heads like this fellow?" he asked, exhibiting the most remarkable of his treasures. A cheerful smile played over his face. He reached over the counter and tried to slap Joe Kane on the shoulder as he had seen men do in Ben Head's saloon when he was a young farmhand and drove to town on Saturday evenings. His visitor was made a little ill by the sight of the body of the terribly deformed bird floating in the alcohol in the bottle and got up to go. Coming from behind the counter father took hold of the young man's arm and led him back to his seat. He grew a little angry and for a moment had to turn his face away and force himself to smile. Then he put the bottles back on the shelf. B In an outburst of generosity he fairly compelled Joe Kane to have a fresh cup of coffee and another cigar at his expense. Then he took a pan and, filling it with vinegar taken from a jug that sat beneath the counter, he declared himself about to do a new trick. "I will heat this egg in this pan of vinegar," he said. "Then I will put it through the neck of a bottle without breaking the shell. When the egg is inside the bottle it will resume its normal shape and the shell will become hard again. Then I will give the bottle with the egg

A. Irony
What is ironic about the father's success in standing the egg on end? (At the moment he succeeds, Joe Kane is no longer looking. When Kane looks again, the egg has rolled over on its side.)

B. Characterization
? What does the detail of Father's having to "turn his face away and force himself to smile" show about Father's suitability for his chosen role as entertainer? (It shows that Father is ill-suited for the role.)

Analyzing the Story

Identifying Facts

1. The narrator's parents became more ambitious: the American passion of "getting up in the world" took hold of them.

2. Chickens are often attacked by disease. A few of them survive into maturity, when the hens lay eggs and the whole gloomy cycle is repeated.

3. The narrator's parents plan to start a restaurant near the train station.

4. The "grotesques" are malformed chickens born with hideous defects. The narrator's father preserves them in alcohol and carries them with him in jars, because he is convinced that they will prove valuable.

He finds them disgusting.

5. He decides to become an entertainer of sorts.

He dreams that the restaurant will become successful as a social center for the townspeople, particularly the young people.

6. The father tries to perform several "tricks" with an egg for Joe Kane's amusement. First he attempts to stand the egg on its end, and then he heats it in vinegar so that the shell will soften and the egg will fit into a bottle. But the father

Closure

Remind students that the story they have just finished is from a collection of Anderson's stories entitled *The Triumph of the Egg*. Ask volunteers to explain that title. What does the triumph of the egg represent? (Intractable reality defeating a brave but ineffectual man)

For Further Reading For Teachers and Students

The Portable Sherwood Anderson, edited by Horace Gregory (Viking, 1977), provides a thorough introduction to Anderson's work, including many short stories, a complete novel (*Poor White*), and selected letters. The introduction by Gregory is helpful in placing Anderson in the context of modern American writing.

in it to you. You can take it about with you wherever you go. People will want to know how you got the egg in the bottle. Don't tell them. Keep them guessing. That is the way to have fun with this trick."

Father grinned and winked at his visitor. Joe Kane decided that the man who confronted him was mildly insane but harmless. He drank the cup of coffee that had been given him and began to read his paper again. When the egg had been heated in vinegar father carried it on a spoon to the counter and going into a back room got an empty bottle. He was angry because his visitor did not watch him as he began to do his trick, but nevertheless went cheerfully to work. For a long time he struggled, trying to get the egg to go through the neck of the bottle. He put the pan of vinegar back on the stove, intending to reheat the egg, then picked it up and burned his fingers. After a second bath in the hot vinegar the shell of the egg had been softened a little but not enough for his purpose. He worked and worked and a spirit of desperate determination took possession of him. When he thought that at last the trick was about to be consummated the delayed train came in at the station and Joe Kane started to go nonchalantly out at the door. Father made a last desperate effort to conquer the egg and make it do the thing that would establish his reputation as one who knew how to entertain guests who came into his restaurant. He worried the egg. He attempted to be somewhat rough with it. He swore and the sweat stood out on his forehead. The egg broke under his hand. When the contents spurted over his clothes, Joe Kane, who had stopped at the door, turned and laughed.

A roar of anger rose from my father's throat. He danced and shouted a string of inarticulate words. Grabbing another egg from the basket on the counter, he threw it, just missing the head of the young man as he dodged through the door and escaped.

Father came upstairs to mother and me with an egg in his hand. I do not know what he intended to do. I imagine he had some idea of destroying it, of destroying all eggs, and that he intended to let mother and me see him begin. When, however, he got into the presence of mother something happened to him. He laid the egg gently on the table and dropped on his knees by the bed as I have already explained. He later decided to close the restaurant for the night and to come upstairs and get into bed. When he did so he blew out the light and after much muttered conversation both he and mother went to sleep. I suppose I went to sleep also, but my sleep was troubled. I awoke at dawn and for a long time looked at the egg that lay on the table. I wondered why eggs had to be and why from the egg came the hen who again laid the egg. The question got into my blood. It has stayed there, I imagine, because I am the son of my father. At any rate, the problem remains unsolved in my mind. And that, I conclude, is but another evidence of the complete and final triumph of the egg—at least as far as my family is concerned.

Responding to the Story

Analyzing the Story

Identifying Facts

1. What change took place in the attitude of his parents shortly after the narrator was born? What does he suggest as a cause of this change?
2. What tragic facts about chickens caused the narrator to become "a gloomy man inclined to see the darker side of life"?
3. Why does the family move to Pickleville?
4. What are the "grotesques"? Why are they regarded as the family's greatest treasure? What does Joe Kane seem to think of them?
5. What means does the father decide on to increase business at his restaurant? What dreams does the father have about the restaurant and its effect on the townspeople?
6. Describe what happens when the father puts his ideas into practice with Joe Kane.

Interpreting Meanings

7. A **symbol** is something used to stand for itself and also for an idea or a force other than itself. A lamb, for example, often symbolizes innocence, and a serpent often symbolizes evil or duplicity. In the hands of a skillful writer, a symbol can have several layers

is nervous and clumsy, and Joe Kane, who is waiting for a train, is easily distracted. When Joe pays no attention, the father becomes angry; when Joe laughs, the father throws the egg at him.

Interpreting Meanings

7. Eggs have often served as symbols of rebirth and fertility: consider, for example, the folk custom of linking Easter with eggs. In Anderson's story, the symbolism of the protective cover perhaps applies to the father, whose obsession with the restaurant may be a kind of protective mechanism, psychologically insulating him from reality. The fact that the shell is easily broken may symbolize the father's disillusionment, when he fails to "entertain" Joe Kane. The egg symbolism perhaps applies to the story on a more general level: the narrator implicitly draws a parallel between the gloomy life cycle of chickens and the life cycle of humanity in general.

8. The "triumph of the egg" may refer to the narrator's disillusionment with his father's life and with his own.

One statement of the story's theme might be as follows: It is inevitable that one generation of human beings will follow another, but it is also inevitable that human beings are doomed to exist in a hard, troubled world.

9. The narrator seems skeptical about this passion for "getting ahead"; materialism, he seems to feel, is a dead end.

A Romantic writer would probably feel favorably about the father's dream, and in a Romantic version of the story the dream might have been successful.

10. The narrator tells us that the father was self-satisfied and content with his life. The evidence revealing his unambitious nature hints that the restaurant venture is doomed.

Student answers will vary. Certainly the father seems to share some traits with Rip Van Winkle.

11. Most students will agree that the father does fit the definition, since he has a single-minded obsession.

12. Most students will agree that the story is both pathetic and comical.

of meaning because its several characteristics can stand for several ideas. A bird, for example, could symbolize freedom because it can fly; fragility because it can be easily destroyed by larger animals; and beauty because of its song. What does the egg symbolize in this story? Describe the layers of symbolism you can find in these characteristics of an egg: Life hatches from eggs; the shell is a protective cover; the shell is easily broken.

8. Why does Anderson refer to "the triumph of the egg" at the story's end? How would you state the story's **theme,** considering this phrase and the egg's symbolism?
9. The narrator says of his parents: "The American passion for getting up in the world took possession of them." How does the narrator feel about this passion? How would a Romantic writer feel about the father's dream of getting ahead, and what would probably become of that dream?
10. Think of what you know about the narrator's father before the family moves to Pickleville. What evidence is there that his scheme to increase his business is bound to fail? Does the father remind you of a common character "type" in American literature? Explain.
11. Does the narrator's father fit Anderson's definition of the word *grotesque* (page 501)? Explain.
12. Do you think this story, especially its final scene, is pathetic or comical, or a combination of both? Why?

Writing About the Story

A Creative Response

1. **Using Another Point of View.** Although she is a powerful force in the family, the narrator's mother plays a minor role in this story. Select one section of the story and imagine the mother's thoughts about it. Then write a passage narrating the events of that part of the story from the mother's vantage point. You can use either the first-person point of view or the limited third person.

A Critical Response

2. **Analyzing Conflict.** If conflict is basic to every story, what is the nature of the conflict in this story? Is it external, internal, or both? Write your analysis of the story's conflict in a three-paragraph essay. Be sure to tell how the conflict is resolved.

Primary Sources

"They were not nice little packages . . ."

On August 27, 1938, Anderson wrote this in a letter to George Freitag, who was corresponding with Anderson about the problems of young writers.

"It is so difficult for most of us to realize how fully and completely commercialism enters into the arts. For example, how are you to know that really the opinion of the publisher or the magazine editor in regard to your work, what is a story and what isn't, means nothing? Some of my own stories, for example, that have now become almost American classics, that are put before students in our schools and colleges as examples of good storytelling, were, when first written, when submitted to editors, and when seen by some of the so-called outstanding American critics, declared not stories at all.

"It is true they were not nice little packages, wrapped and labeled in the O. Henry manner. They were obviously written by one who did not know the answers. They were simple little tales of happenings, things observed and felt. There were no cowboys or daring wild game hunters. None of the people in the tales got lost in burning deserts or went seeking the North Pole. In my stories I simply stayed at home, among my own people, wherever I happened to be, people in my own street. I think I must, very early, have realized that this was my milieu, that is to say, common everyday American lives. The ordinary beliefs of the people about me, that love lasted indefinitely, that success meant happiness, simply did not seem true to me."

—Sherwood Anderson

A. Responding

? Why do you think that the American reading public was "bowled over" by the publication of *Main Street?* (Americans had traditionally associated small towns with positive values and *Main Street* presented small-town life as an "academy of narrow conformity.")

B. Responding

? Why did Lewis reject the Pulitzer Prize for his novel *Arrowsmith?* (Because his novels *Main Street* and *Babbitt* had not won the award)

Sinclair Lewis (1885–1951)

Sinclair Lewis, who was known to his friends as "Hal" or "Red," was a man of immense energy, much of which he channeled directly into writing. He produced scores of novels, stories, plays, and poetry. A great deal of this work was hastily composed, shoddy, and forgettable. But during the golden decade of his life, the 1920's, Lewis wrote half a dozen novels which touched a tender nerve in the American consciousness, shocking and delighting an army of readers by his ridicule of primary American values. As a result of their incisive satire, these works have become fixtures of our literature.

Lewis was born in Sauk Centre, Minnesota, the son of Edwin Lewis, a doctor whose disciplined life set an impressive standard for his son. Lewis was only six when his mother died, and while his stepmother treated him kindly, he grew up feeling he was a disappointment to his father. He was an eager reader, but otherwise a dreamy, difficult boy who did not stand out in any way.

In 1903 he entered Yale and did little better there. A skin disease had left him with a pitted complexion, and he felt unattractive. Although he later compensated for this with charm and an outgoing manner, Lewis was not a popular undergraduate; he did not do well either in his studies or in sports.

His first novel was a boy's adventure story, *Hike and the Aeroplane,* written under a pseudonym for his employer, a publisher, in exchange for two months' salary. His second, *Our Mr. Wrenn,* was rejected by several publishers before Harper accepted it. Despite some good reviews, the book sold poorly. This was also true of *The Trail of the Hawk, The Job, The Innocents,* and *Free Air,* traditional novels which Lewis produced over the next five years, along with stories for the *Saturday Evening Post.*

All of these works were written in the optimistic, "genteel" tradition. But Lewis had also begun to conceive a different kind of novel, one which looked back at the complacent village of A his childhood with a critical eye. This novel became *Main Street.* The village Lewis depicted was the one he recalled so vividly from a painful childhood as an academy of narrow conformity, materialistic in its values and restrictive of every creative impulse.

The American reading public, which held the "small town" to be a stronghold of virtue, generosity, and the homely joys, was bowled over by Harcourt Brace's publication of *Main Street* in 1920. The book became a huge success, eventually selling millions of copies in the biggest publishing event in American history, and making Lewis a wealthy, international celebrity.

Another triumph followed in 1922 with *Babbitt,* in which Lewis portrayed that traditional hero, the American businessman, as a spiritually impoverished, pathetic figure. The novel provoked a furor over the nation's values.

Lewis next turned his pen upon the medical profession. The publication of *Arrowsmith* in 1925 ignited controversy among doctors and medical associations, further stimulating book sales. In that year, Lewis rejected the Pulitzer Prize for *Arrowsmith* on the grounds that the B judges had withheld the honor from *Main Street*

SUPPLEMENTARY SUPPORT MATERIALS

1. Vocabulary Activity Worksheet (*CCB*)
2. Review and Response Worksheet: Satire (*CCB*)
3. Language Skills Worksheet: Transitional Expressions (*CCB*)
4. Selection Test (*CCB*)

DEVELOPING VOCABULARY

The following words from the novel are tested in the Selection Test. (See also Vocabulary Activity Worksheet.)

oratory	canniest
to inebriate	tenet
impromptu	jape
amity	caboodle
to behoove	statuary

PREPARATION

ESTABLISHING A PURPOSE. In this selection Lewis satirizes the reporter who covers Babbitt's speech as well as Babbitt himself. Since the news story's first paragraph exhibits many of Lewis's favorite satiric devices, you may wish to analyze it with students as an introduction to Lewis's method, discussing some or all of the techniques outlined below.

1. *Naming places and events for comic effect* ("annual Get-Together Fest" and "Venetian Ball Room")
2. *Putting hackneyed colloquialisms in the mouths of characters* (*livest* for "liveliest"; *pulled off* for "brought about" or "accomplished")
3. *Mocking genteelism* (the archaic pronoun in "mine host"; *plates* for "dishes prepared in particular ways")
4. *Using misquotation* ("the cup that inspired but did not inebriate" for Cowper's "cups that cheer but not inebriate")
5. *Poking fun at awkwardness of expression* ("those *assembled* feasted on . . . such an *assemblage* of plates"; "plenteous feed"; "the cup . . . in the shape of cider")
6. *Mocking chauvinism* ("as could be rivaled nowhere west of New York, if there")

and *Babbitt*. However, after the publication of *Elmer Gantry* (1927), Lewis's unflattering portrayal of an evangelist clergyman, and of *Dodsworth* (1929), a more sympathetic portrait of a businessman, he became in 1930 the first American to receive the greatest of literary accolades, the Nobel Prize.

Ironically, the prize marked the end of an era in which it seemed that Lewis could do no wrong. His personal life was deteriorating; he divorced his wife to marry Dorothy Thompson, a famous political columnist, only to have this marriage end in divorce as well. He was also drinking heavily, and he was restless, forever on the move.

Nevertheless, he continued to publish. After 1930 he produced nine more novels. Lewis broached important issues in these works: the role of women in social reform, the dangers of fascism, and the evil of race prejudice. But he had lost his satiric bite. Lewis was becoming sentimental, praising some of the traditional values he had once mocked. After a lifetime of exuberance, Lewis became increasingly melancholy—sailing off for Italy in the end, where he died of heart failure in 1951.

BABBITT'S AFTER-DINNER SPEECH

Lewis's "non-hero," George F. Babbitt, has given his name not only to the title of the novel *Babbitt*, but to our language as well. A dictionary might define a "babbitt" as a member of the business class whose unquestioning conformity to its ideals has made him narrow-minded and self-satisfied. "Boosterism," another Lewis coinage, is a hidden form of moneymaking, and it is clearly Babbitt's preoccupation. Babbitt finds comfort in every sort of conformity—dress, work, and recreation; he is wary of diverse opinions and of imagination and freedom.

Here, in Chapter XIV of *Babbitt*, Babbitt delivers a speech to the Real Estate Board in his growing hometown of Zenith. Notice how Babbitt, in his emphasis on pep and enthusiasm, seems to yearn for genuine emotion, and how he pretends to find it in his highly conventional life.

His reputation for oratory established, at the dinner of the Zenith Real Estate Board he made the Annual Address. The *Advocate-Times* reported this speech with unusual fullness:

"One of the livest banquets that has recently been pulled off occurred last night in the annual Get-Together Fest of the Zenith Real Estate Board, held in the Venetian Ball Room of the O'Hearn House. Mine host Gil O'Hearn had as usual done himself proud and those assembled feasted on such an assemblage of plates as could be rivaled nowhere west of New York, if there, and washed down the plenteous feed with the cup which inspired but did not inebriate in the shape of cider from the farm of Chandler Mott, president of the board and who acted as witty and efficient chairman.

"As Mr. Mott was suffering from slight infection and sore throat, G. F. Babbitt made the principal talk. Besides outlining the progress of Torrensing real estate titles, Mr. Babbitt spoke in part as follows:

" 'In rising to address you, with my impromptu speech carefully tucked into my vest pocket, I am reminded of the story of the two Irishmen, Mike and Pat, who were riding on the Pullman. Both of them, I forgot to say, were sailors in the Navy. It seems Mike had the lower berth and by and by he heard a terrible racket from the upper, and when he yelled up to find out what the trouble was, Pat answered, "Shure an' bedad an' how can I ever get a night's sleep at all, at all? I been trying to get into this darned little hammock ever since eight bells!"

" 'Now, gentlemen, standing up here before

A. Responding

? If you were updating Babbitt's account of the way "Our Ideal Citizen" spends his evening, which details would you change or add? Which details would be the same now as then? (Answers will vary, but some students may certainly suggest adding such material goods of the computer era as music cassettes and compact discs as well as home computers.)

B. Characterization

? Based on this first part of his speech, how would you characterize Babbitt? (Answers will vary. Students should take into account Babbitt's "boosterism," his speaking in clichés such as "busier than a bird dog," his opinion of culture as represented by "our number of photographs," and his condemnation of other cultures where artists are "shabby bums living in attics and feeding on booze and spaghetti.")

you, I feel a good deal like Pat, and maybe after I've spieled[1] along for a while, I may feel so darn small that I'll be able to crawl into a Pullman hammock with no trouble at all, at all!

" 'Gentlemen, it strikes me that each year at this annual occasion when friend and foe get together and lay down the battle-ax and let the waves of good-fellowship waft them up the flowery slopes of amity, it behooves us, standing together eye to eye and shoulder to shoulder as fellow-citizens of the best city in the world, to consider where we are both as regards ourselves and the common weal.

" 'It is true that even with our 361,000, or practically 362,000, population, there are, by the last census, almost a score of larger cities in the United States. But, gentlemen, if by the next census we do not stand at least tenth, then I'll be the first to request any knocker to remove my shirt and to eat the same, with the compliments of G. F. Babbitt, Esquire! It may be true that New York, Chicago, and Philadelphia will continue to keep ahead of us in size. But aside from these three cities, which are notoriously so overgrown that no decent white man, nobody who loves his wife and kiddies and God's good out-o'-doors and likes to shake the hand of his neighbor in greeting, would want to live in them—and let me tell you right here and now, I wouldn't trade a high-class Zenith acreage development for the whole length and breadth of Broadway or State Street!—aside from these three, it's evident to any one with a head for facts that Zenith is the finest example of American life and prosperity to be found anywhere.

" 'I don't mean to say we're perfect. We've got a lot to do in the way of extending the paving of motor boulevards, for, believe me, it's the fellow with four to ten thousand a year,[2] say, and an automobile and a nice little family in a bungalow on the edge of town, that makes the wheels of progress go round!

" 'That's the type of fellow that's ruling America today; in fact, it's the ideal type to which the entire world must tend, if there's to be a decent, well-balanced, Christian, go-ahead future for this little old planet! Once in a while I just naturally sit back and size up this Solid American Citizen, with a whale of a lot of satisfaction.

" 'Our Ideal Citizen—I picture him first and foremost as being busier than a bird-dog, not wasting a lot of good time in daydreaming or going to sassiety[3] teas or kicking about things that are none of his business, but putting the zip into some store or profession or art. At night he lights up a good cigar, and climbs into the little old bus, and maybe cusses the carburetor, and shoots out home. He mows the lawn, or sneaks in some practice putting, and then he's ready for dinner. After dinner he tells the kiddies a story, or takes the family to the movies, or plays a few fists of bridge, or reads the evening paper, and a chapter or two of some good lively Western novel if he has a taste for literature, and maybe the folks next door drop in and they sit and visit about their friends and the topics of the day. Then he goes happily to bed, his conscience clear, having contributed his mite to the prosperity of the city and to his own bank account. A

" 'In politics and religion this Sane Citizen is the canniest man on earth; and in the arts he invariably has a natural taste which makes him pick out the best, every time. In no country in the world will you find so many reproductions of the Old Masters and of well-known paintings on parlor walls as in these United States. No country has anything like our number of phonographs, with not only dance records and comic but also the best operas, such as Verdi, rendered by the world's highest-paid singers.

" 'In other countries, art and literature are left to a lot of shabby bums living in attics and feeding on booze and spaghetti, but in America the successful writer or picture-painter is indistinguishable from any other decent business man; and I, for one, am only too glad that the man who has the rare skill to season his message with interesting reading matter and who shows both purpose and pep in handling his literary wares has a chance to drag down his fifty thousand bucks a year, to mingle with the biggest executives on terms of perfect equality, and to show as big a house and as swell a car as any Captain of Industry! But, mind you, it's the appreciation of the Regular Guy who I have been depicting which has made this possible, and you got to hand as much credit to him as to the authors themselves.

" 'Finally, but most important, our Standardized Citizen, even if he is a bachelor, is a lover of

1. **spieled:** talked.
2. Remember that *Babbit* was written in 1922.

3. **sassiety:** satirical pronunciation of "society."

B

Salesmen at a meeting, 1925.

A

the Little Ones, a supporter of the hearthstone which is the basic foundation of our civilization, first, last, and all the time, and the thing that most distinguishes us from the decayed nations of Europe.

B " 'I have never yet toured Europe—and as a matter of fact, I don't know that I care to such an awful lot, as long as there's our own mighty cities and mountains to be seen—but, the way I figure it out, there must be a good many of our own sort of folks abroad. Indeed, one of the most enthusiastic Rotarians I ever met boosted the tenets of one hundred percent pep in a burr[4] that smacked o'bonny Scutlond and all ye bonny braes o' Bobby Burns. But same time, one thing that distinguishes us from our good brothers, the hustlers over there, is that they're willing to take a lot off the snobs and journalists and politicians, while the modern American business man knows how to talk right up for himself, knows how to make it good and plenty clear that he intends to run the works. He doesn't have to call in some highbrow hired man when it's necessary for him to answer the crooked critics of the sane and efficient life. He's not dumb, like the old-fashioned merchant. He's got a vocabulary and a punch.

" 'With all modesty, I want to stand up here as a representative business man and gently whisper, "Here's our kind of folks! Here's the specifications of the Standardized American Citizen!

4. **burr:** Scottish accent.

A. Humanities Connection: Discussing the Photograph
This photograph depicts a group of men whom Babbitt would call "Solid American Citizens." Note the inspirational messages on the posters and the self-serving motto "Help others and they help you." Call students' attention to the similarity in dress of the salesmen and the carnation that sets the sales manager apart from the rest.

B. Characterization
? What does Babbitt reveal about himself in his statement that he doesn't care to visit Europe "such an awful lot"? (Answers will vary. Babbitt does reveal a somewhat limited mind in that he has settled on a certain way of life and evinces no curiosity at all about how others live.)

CLOSURE

Have students discuss whether or not many Americans today share Babbitt's values and attitudes.

READING CHECK TEST

1. Babbitt already enjoys a reputation as an orator before he delivers the Annual Address. *True*
2. Babbitt envies New York's cultural diversity, derived from the many foreign immigrants living there. *False*
3. According to Babbitt, the Second National Tower is the tallest building outside of New York. *False*
4. One of the major products manufactured in Zenith is paper boxes. *True*
5. Babbitt defends the right of professors at the State University to say what they believe. *False*

A. Responding

Has the trend toward standardization that Babbitt praises here continued? How important a feature of American life today is standardization? (Answers will vary, but most students will agree that there is a certain amount of standardization today of clothes and architecture.)

B. Expansion

The model for Chum Frink, the poet Babbitt so admires, is Edgar A. Guest (1881–1959). Guest, who was popular in the twenties and thirties, is probably best known for the line "It takes a heap o' livin' in a house t' make it home."

C. Responding

Why do you suppose Babbitt is so taken with Chum Frink's piece? (Chum Frink is much like Babbitt, an optimist who hands out samples of "sweet sunshine" and who is a booster of standardized values.)

Here's the new generation of Americans: fellows with hair on their chests and smiles in their eyes and adding machines in their offices. We're not doing any boasting, but we like ourselves first-rate, and if you don't like us, look out—better get under cover before the cyclone hits town!"

" 'So! In my clumsy way I have tried to sketch the Real He-man, the fellow with Zip and Bang. And it's because Zenith has so large a proportion of such men that it's the most stable, the greatest of our cities. New York also has its thousands of Real Folks, but New York is cursed with unnumbered foreigners. So are Chicago and San Francisco. Oh, we have a golden roster of cities—Detroit and Cleveland with their renowned factories, Cincinnati with its great machine-tool and soap products, Pittsburgh and Birmingham with their steel, Kansas City and Minneapolis and Omaha that open their bountiful gates on the bosom of the oceanlike wheatlands, and countless other magnificent sister-cities, for, by the last census, there were no less than sixty-eight glorious American burgs[5] with a population of over one hundred thousand! And all these cities stand together for power and purity, and against foreign ideas and communism—Atlanta with Hartford, Rochester with Denver, Milwaukee with Indianapolis, Los Angeles with Scranton, Portland, Maine, with Portland, Oregon. A good live wire from Baltimore or Seattle or Duluth is the twin-brother of every like fellow booster from Buffalo or Akron, Fort Worth or Oskaloosa!

" 'But it's here in Zenith, the home for manly men and womanly women and bright kids, that you find the largest proportion of these Regular Guys, and that's what sets it in a class by itself; that's why Zenith will be remembered in history as having set the pace for a civilization that shall endure when the old time-killing ways are gone forever and the day of earnest efficient endeavor shall have dawned all round the world!

" 'Some time I hope folks will quit handing all the credit to a lot of moth-eaten, mildewed, out-of-date, old European dumps, and give proper credit to the famous Zenith spirit, that clean fighting determination to win Success that has made the little old Zip City celebrated in every land and clime, wherever condensed milk and pasteboard cartons are known! Believe me, the world has fallen too long for these worn-out countries that aren't producing anything but bootblacks and scenery and booze, that haven't got one bathroom per hundred people, and that don't know a loose-leaf ledger from a slipcover; and it's just about time for some Zenithite to get his back up and holler for a showdown!

" 'I tell you, Zenith and her sister-cities are producing a new type of civilization. There are many resemblances between Zenith and these other burgs, and I'm darn glad of it! The extraordinary, growing, and sane standardization of stores, offices, streets, hotels, clothes, and newspapers throughout the United States shows how strong and enduring a type is ours. A

" 'I always like to remember a piece that Chum Frink wrote for the newspapers about his lecture-tours. It is doubtless familiar to many of you, but if you will permit me, I'll take a chance and read it. It's one of the classic poems, like "If" by Kipling, or Ella Wheeler Wilcox's "The Man Worth While"; and I always carry this clipping of it in my note-book: B

C

When I am out upon the road, a poet with a peddler's load, I mostly sing a hearty song, and take a chew and hike along, a-handing out my samples fine of Cheero Brand of sweet sunshine, and peddling optimistic pokes and stable lines of japes and jokes to Lyceums and other folks, to Rotarys, Kiwanis' Clubs, and feel I ain't like other dubs. And then old Major Silas Satan, a brainy cuss who's always waitin', he gives his tail a lively quirk, and gets in quick his dirty work. He fills me up with mullygrubs; my hair the backward way he rubs; he makes me lonelier than a hound, on Sunday when the folks ain't round. And then b' gosh, I would prefer to never be a lecturer, a-ridin' round in classy cars and smoking fifty-cent cigars, and never more I want to roam; I simply want to be back home, a-eatin' flapjacks, hash, and ham, with folks who savvy whom I am!

But when I get that lonely spell, I simply seek the best hotel, no matter in what town I be—St. Paul, Toledo, or K.C., in Washington, Schenectady, in Louisville or Albany. And at that inn it hits my dome that I again am right at home. If I should stand a lengthy spell in front of that first-class hotel, that to the drummers[6] *loves to cater, across from some big film theayter; if I should look around and buzz, and wonder in what town*

5. **burgs:** towns.

6. **drummers:** traveling salesmen.

ANALYZING THE SPEECH

Identifying Facts

1. Zenith will have to plan more paved roads. The "perfect" city, according to Babbitt, is inhabited by ideal citizens who make four to ten thousand a year, drive cars, and live in nice little bungalows.

2. The ideal citizen is busy and energetic, family-oriented, and prosperous. He has judgment in politics and taste in art. Babbitt also calls him the "Sane Citizen," the "Regular Guy," and—most tellingly—the "Standardized Citizen." Babbitt pays no attention at all to considering women in his speech.

3. Babbitt generally regards Europe as corrupt and decadent. He is generally suspicious of foreigners, considering them inferior.

See the response to question 6.

Art and literature are praised by Babbitt, but superficially.

4. Students should be able to supply many details.

Interpreting Meanings

5. The groups include foreigners, non-Christians, and non-whites. It is also evident that Babbitt distrusts liberals and *(Answers continue on next page.)*

I was, I swear that I could never tell! For all the crowd would be so swell, in just the same fine sort of jeans they wear at home, and all the queens with spiffy bonnets on their beans, and all the fellows standing round a-talkin' always, I'll be bound, the same good jolly kind of guff, 'bout autos, politics and stuff and baseball players of renown that Nice Guys talk in my home town!

Then when I entered that hotel, I'd look around and say, "Well, well!" For there would be the same newsstand, same magazines and candies grand, same smokes of famous standard brand, I'd find at home, I'll tell! And when I saw the jolly bunch come waltzing in for eats at lunch, and squaring up in natty duds to platters large of French Fried spuds, why then I'd stand right up and bawl, "I've never left my home at all!" And all replete I'd sit me down beside some guy in derby brown upon a lobby chair of plush, and murmur to him in a rush, "Hello, Bill, tell me, good old scout, how is your stock a-holdin' out?" Then we'd be off, two solid pals, a-chatterin' like giddy gals of flivvers,[7] weather, home, and wives, lodge-brothers then for all our lives! So when Sam Satan makes you blue, good friend, that's what I'd up and do, for in these States where'er you roam, you never leave your home sweet home.

" 'Yes, sir, these other burgs are our true partners in the great game of vital living. But let's not have any mistake about this. I claim that Zenith is the best partner and the fastest-growing partner of the whole caboodle. I trust I may be pardoned if I give a few statistics to back up my claims. If they are old stuff to any of you, yet the tidings of prosperity, like the good news of the Bible, never become tedious to the ears of a real hustler, no matter how oft the sweet story is told! Every intelligent person knows that Zenith manufactures more condensed milk and evaporated cream, more paper boxes, and more lighting fixtures, than any other city in the United States, if not in the world. But it is not so universally known that we also stand second in the manufacture of package butter, sixth in the giant realm of motors and automobiles, and somewhere about third in cheese, leather findings, tar roofing, breakfast food, and overalls!

" 'Our greatness, however, lies not alone in punchful prosperity but equally in that public spirit, that forward-looking idealism and brotherhood, which has marked Zenith ever since its foundation by the Fathers. We have a right, indeed we have a duty toward our fair city, to announce broadcast[8] the facts about our high schools, characterized by their complete plants and the finest school-ventilating systems in the country, bar none; our magnificent new hotels and banks and the paintings and carved marble in their lobbies; and the Second National Tower, the second highest business building in any inland city in the entire country. When I add that we have an unparalleled number of miles of paved streets, bathrooms, vacuum cleaners, and all the other signs of civilization; that our library and art museum are well supported and housed in convenient and roomy buildings; that our park system is more than up to par, with its handsome driveways adorned with grass, shrubs, and statuary, then I give but a hint of the all-round unlimited greatness of Zenith!

" 'I believe, however, in keeping the best to the last. When I remind you that we have one motor car for every five and seven-eighths persons in the city, then I give a rock-ribbed practical indication of the kind of progress and braininess which is synonymous with the name Zenith!

" 'But the way of the righteous is not all roses. Before I close I must call your attention to a problem we have to face this coming year. The worst menace to sound government is not the avowed socialists but a lot of cowards who work under cover—the long-haired gentry who call themselves "liberals" and "radicals" and "non-partisan" and "intelligentsia" and God only knows how many other trick names! Irresponsible teachers and professors constitute the worst of this whole gang, and I am ashamed to say that several of them are on the faculty of our great State University! The U. is my own Alma Mater, and I am proud to be known as an alumni, but there are certain instructors there who seem to think we ought to turn the conduct of the nation over to hoboes and roustabouts.

" 'Those profs are the snakes to be scotched—they and all their milk-and-water ilk! The American businessman is generous to a fault, but one thing he does demand of all teachers and lecturers and journalists: if we're going to pay them our good money, they've got to help us by selling

7. **flivvers:** cars.

8. **broadcast:** used here to mean *publicly.*

A. Irony

? What is ironic about Babbitt's praise of Zenith's high schools, hotels, and banks? (Of all the important aspects of a high school—quality of teaching, curriculum, and so forth—Babbitt mentions their physical plants and ventilating systems. Of the hotels and banks, he praises the external trappings—the paintings and marble of the lobbies.)

B. Expansion

You may wish to explain that *intelligentsia* (in·tel'ə·jent'sē·ə), meaning "class of intellectuals," came into English from Russian, which got it from Latin. (The Russian pronunciation, which keeps the hard *g* of Latin, is sometimes used in English: in·tel'ə·*gent'*sē·ə. The word is usually used derisively, as Babbitt does here, to mean "those who regard themselves as educated and intelligent."

(Continued from previous page.)
people and what he calls "cranks": anyone, in other words, who might dare to differ from "standard" American values.
6. Satire pokes fun at the vices and follies of people and institutions in order to reform them. The portrait of Babbitt is to some extent a caricature. Babbitt consistently exposes himself as an advocate of mediocrity, of blindly rigid adherence to conventional dogmas, and of the exaltation of machines and half-formed doctrines above people. Although he ostensibly believes in family, patriotism, justice, and industry, his picture of the perfect life relies to a great extent on prejudice and jingoism. He consistently emphasizes material objects and ignores the people who own or use them. When he discusses education, for example, he talks about the fine ventilating systems in American high schools, neglecting to mention the teachers, the curriculum, and the students. Babbitt manages to satirize Babbitt, and the system to which he so unthinkingly clings, through the words that come from his own mouth.

Zenith means the highest point. The town's name is ironic because the
(Answers continue in left-hand column.)

(Continued from top.)
achievements that Babbitt takes so seriously point, rather, toward conformity and mediocrity.
7. Student answers will vary. Some students may point out that Babbitt has a vague longing for emotion in his comments on art, literature, and music. But, since he obviously possesses little first-hand exposure to these things, he remains, for the most part, mired in materialism.
8. Student answers will vary. Perhaps Babbitt's fears of anyone or anything "different" spring from deep-seated insecurities.

efficiency and whooping it up for rational prosperity! And when it comes to these blab-mouth, fault-finding, pessimistic, cynical University teachers, let me tell you that during this golden coming year it's just as much our duty to bring influence to have those cusses fired as it is to sell all the real estate and gather in all the good shekels[9] we can.

" 'Not till that is done will our sons and daughters see that the ideal of American manhood and culture isn't a lot of cranks sitting around chewing the rag about their Rights and their Wrongs, but a God-fearing, hustling, successful, two-fisted Regular Guy, who belongs to some church with pep and piety to it, who belongs to the Boosters or the Rotarians or the Kiwanis, to the Elks or Moose or Red Men or Knights of Columbus or any one of a score of organizations of good, jolly, kidding, laughing, sweating, upstanding, lend-a-handing Royal Good Fellows, who plays hard and works hard, and whose answer to his critics is a square-toed boot that'll teach the grouches and smart alecks to respect the He-man and get out and root for Uncle Samuel, U.S.A.!' "

9. **shekels:** used here as slang for "money."

Responding to the Speech

Analyzing the Speech

Identifying Facts

1. According to Babbitt's description of what Zenith has to accomplish in order to become "perfect," how would he define a "perfect" city?
2. List the phrases Babbitt uses to describe his ideal citizen. What is his attitude toward women?
3. How would you describe Babbitt's attitude toward European civilization? Toward foreigners? Toward higher education? Toward art and literature?
4. Find details in the speech that reveal Babbitt's overriding concern with conformity.

Interpreting Meanings

5. Although Babbitt pays lip service to friendship and harmony, he reveals a great amount of prejudice and hostility toward certain groups. Who are these groups? Where does Babbitt reveal his bias? Why would a person like Babbitt dislike or distrust these groups?
6. Babbitt delivers this speech sincerely. But Lewis has written it so that we, as readers, feel his mockery of Babbitt. Tell how Babbitt's speech fits the requirements of **satire** (the use of irony or derision to expose folly). In light of the definition of *zenith,* how is the town's name **ironic?**
7. The headnote says that Babbitt really yearns for emotion. Do you agree? Do you find any evidence of this in his speech? Explain.
8. How would you account for Babbitt's values? Why do you think he needs conformity and fears what is "different"? What are your own responses to Babbitt as you read this speech?

Writing About the Speech

A Creative Response

1. **Answering Babbitt.** Suppose Babbitt were running for public office and this were his stock campaign speech. Write a speech prepared by Babbitt's opponent challenging Babbitt's values and visions.
2. **Updating Babbitt.** Maybe you think Babbitt has made some valid points. Update his speech, to show where it might be delivered today.

A Critical Response

3. **Comparing and Contrasting the Speech with "Self-Reliance."** In his essay "Self-Reliance" (page 194), Ralph Waldo Emerson defines the essence of individualism. In an essay, compare and contrast Babbitt's Regular Guy with Emerson's individual. Is Babbitt's hero an extension or a distortion of Emerson's self-reliant individual? Pay particular attention to what Emerson and Babbitt say or suggest about conformity.

Analyzing Language and Style

Clichés

Clichés are stock expressions that have been used so often we hardly think any more about what they really mean. People who accept clichés instead of more complex ideas can be easily manipulated. Find at least five clichés about American ideals or small-town life used here by Babbitt. What stock responses does Babbitt want to elicit from his audience?

Willa Cather (1873–1947)

Willa Cather was born in rural Virginia, the first of seven children. When she was nine, her father uprooted the family and headed for the untried
A lands of the West, settling in Webster County, Nebraska. She would later recall that this first encounter with the prairie was so striking that she "felt an erasure of personality."

Nevertheless, Cather had a strong curiosity about life and an ambition to make the most of it. She was stimulated by the hard life of the soil she saw around her, and she absorbed the stories of the immigrant families who were her neighbors. Her grandmother read to her from the Bible and John Bunyan's *Pilgrim's Progress;* she herself also read widely, and she became an outstanding student at the Red Cloud, Nebraska, school. In her boyish clothes and haircut, Willa was an unusual figure, and her teachers recognized in her an adolescent nonconformist, already determined on a career in science.

While a freshman at the University of Nebraska, Cather wrote an essay on Thomas Carlyle, the British philosopher and social critic. She dealt with the artist's commitment, which often requires the sacrifice of love and marriage. (Cather herself never married.) When this piece appeared in a Lincoln newspaper, her own ambitions had already turned toward writing. She became a regular contributor to the newspaper and began to write poetry and stories.

By the time Cather graduated from college in 1895, she had won a statewide reputation for brash, bright reviews. She continued to work as a journalist, moving to Pittsburgh for a decade as editor and reviewer for the *Daily Leader.* In 1903, she published her first book, a collection of verse entitled *April Twilights.* She followed it with *The Troll Garden,* a group of stories.

In 1906, the publisher S. S. McClure persuaded her to move to New York and join the staff of his dynamic, muckraking magazine, *McClure's.* For six years she served as a writer and editor, immersed in the social and political currents of the time; in 1912 she resigned from the magazine to give herself completely to writing fiction.

Cather had met the Maine writer Sarah Orne Jewett in 1908 and had been encouraged by her to write about the themes and settings she knew best: the moral values of the hard-working immigrant families on the Midwestern prairie. It was Cather's view that these pioneers, who had sought to bring the wild, new land under cultivation, were heroic and that their era was the heart of the American dream. She saw these immigrant settlers as contributing a cultural richness and an earthy love of life that were lacking in the pale, self-satisfied native-born Americans who clung to the seaboard cities.

O Pioneers!, a novel whose title Cather borrowed from Walt Whitman, appeared in 1913. The work revealed Cather's love for the Nebraska of her childhood; it also praised the men and women she recalled as survivors of their encounter with the stubborn prairie. When Alexandra Bergson, the novel's Scandinavian heroine, looks out upon the land's glorious expanse, she weeps at the very sight of it.

My Ántonia, appearing in 1918, presents a heroine who struggles to find a fulfilling life on the farm. The narrator of this novel is clearly nostalgic, seeing Ántonia as a fortunate exception to the social currents of her time.

As Cather witnessed the decline of the agrarian ideal, her work became increasingly elegiac about the past and disillusioned with the present. *One of Ours* (1922), which was far from Cather's

A. Expansion
This early experience of Cather's was a formative one, for the reaction of a person to his or her environment is the central concern of most of her fiction. In this story, as in *O Pioneers!* (1913) and *My Ántonia* (1918), the environment is the vast plains of Nebraska; in *Death Comes for the Archbishop* (1927), it is the mesas of New Mexico. In most of Cather's work, the natural background for personal emotions and conflicts plays an important role. Her characters generally feel less at home in the cities so dear to Babbitt's heart. As "A Wagner Matinée" suggests, the cultural resources of cities are obtained at the price of discomfort and confusion. Her citified characters usually seem ineffectual in comparison with those whose lives are lived close to nature.

Supplementary Support Materials
1. Vocabulary Activity Worksheet (*CCB*)
2. Review and Response Worksheet: Point of View (*CCB*)
3. Language Skills Worksheet: Participles and Participial Phrases (*CCB*)
4. Selection Test (*CCB*)

Developing Vocabulary
The following words from the story are tested in the Selection Test. (See also Vocabulary Activity Worksheet.)

callow	obliquely
sordid	excruciatingly
trepidation	jocularity

Preparation
1. **Building On Prior Knowledge.** Ask students to share impressions they may have formed of pioneer life on the prairies through reading or viewing the *Little House* stories of Laura Ingalls Wilder or other stories dealing with this setting and period. Elicit both desirable and undesirable features of pioneer life.
(Continued in left-hand column.)

(Continued from top.)
2. **Establishing A Purpose.** Before students start reading, have them read and react to question 6 (Interpreting Meanings) page 524. To help them establish a purpose for reading suggest that they look for reasons why Georgiana, the main character of the story, should be so pessimistic.

A. Music Connection
Richard Wagner's operas (which he called "music dramas") expanded the music world's conception of opera. Wagner rejected the traditional Italian pattern of set arias separated by passages of recitative (res′ə·tə·tēv′), declaimed speechlike passages for exposition and advancing the plot. He substituted "endless melody"—that is, melody molded to the words of the libretto. Wagner also originated the *Leitmotif* (līt′mō·tēf′)—a recurring musical phrase that symbolizes a character, emotion, or event in the musical drama.

best novel but which won her the Pulitzer Prize, features as its hero a young farmer who reflects the author's dissatisfaction with the new men and machines who were betraying the pioneer ideal. The protagonist escapes them only through the Great War in Europe.

In later life and later novels, Cather became ever more nostalgic, ever more estranged from her own times. "The world broke in two in 1922 or thereabout," she said, explaining that no one born in the twentieth century could grasp her own vision of America. She had seen her beloved Nebraska devastated by the machine, and she lamented the end of her epic vision of a noble society. She made no secret of her skepticism toward progress. As an Indian character says in *Death Comes for the Archbishop* (1927), her novel about religious missionaries in New Mexico: "Men travel faster now, but I do not know if they go to better things."

It is often observed that social progress is inevitable, and that the changes which each generation brings do not necessarily destroy old values. Nevertheless, we may want to let Cather remind us of the novelist's duty to keep a wary eye on our relation to scientific progress. It was Cather's profound intuition that a science which offers us new comfort, new speed, new security, and longer life will almost surely demand something of our spirit in return.

A WAGNER MATINÉE

As in most of Willa Cather's novels and stories, setting plays a central role in the story that follows. In this case, however, there are really two settings: The rural Nebraska, in which the narrator, like Cather, spent his formative years, is contrasted with the thriving cultural life of Boston, a large city. Although Cather believed that farm life in the Midwest fostered essential values, she was hardly a romantic in underestimating the hardships of that life, or the lost opportunities for some of the people who lived it.

The story's title refers to the German composer Richard Wagner (väg′nər) (1813–1883), the outstanding Romantic operatic composer of the century. A matinée is an afternoon performance of a play or concert. A

Cather herself loved music.

I received one morning a letter, written in pale ink on glossy, blue-lined notepaper, and bearing the postmark of a little Nebraska village. This communication, worn and rubbed, looking as though it had been carried for some days in a coat pocket that was none too clean, was from my Uncle Howard and informed me that his wife had been left a small legacy by a bachelor relative who had recently died, and that it would be necessary for her to go to Boston to attend to the settling of the estate. He requested me to meet her at the station and render her whatever services might be necessary. On examining the date indicated as that of her arrival, I found it no later than tomorrow. He had characteristically delayed writing until, had I been away from home for a day, I must have missed the good woman altogether.

The name of my Aunt Georgiana called up not alone her own figure, at once pathetic and grotesque, but opened before my feet a gulf of recollection so wide and deep, that, as the letter dropped from my hand, I felt suddenly a stranger to all the present conditions of my existence, wholly ill at ease and out of place amid the familiar surroundings of my study. I became, in short, the gangling farmer-boy my aunt had known, scourged with chilblains[1] and bashfulness, my hands cracked and sore from the corn husking. I felt the knuckles of my thumb tentatively, as though they were raw again. I sat again before her parlor organ, fumbling the scales with my stiff,

1. **chilblains:** an inflammation of the hands and feet caused by exposure to cold and moisture.

red hands, while she, beside me, made canvas mittens for the huskers.

The next morning, after preparing my landlady somewhat, I set out for the station. When the train arrived I had some difficulty in finding my aunt. She was the last of the passengers to alight, and it was not until I got her into the carriage that she seemed really to recognize me. She had come all the way in a day coach; her linen duster had become black with soot and her black bonnet gray with dust during the journey. When we arrived at my boardinghouse the landlady put her to bed at once and I did not see her again until the next morning.

Whatever shock Mrs. Springer experienced at my aunt's appearance, she considerately concealed. As for myself, I saw my aunt's misshapen figure with that feeling of awe and respect with which we behold explorers who have left their ears and fingers north of Franz-Joseph-Land,[2] or their health somewhere along the Upper Congo. My Aunt Georgiana had been a music teacher at the Boston Conservatory, somewhere back in the latter sixties. One summer, while visiting in the little village among the Green Mountains where her ancestors had dwelt for generations, she had kindled the callow fancy of the most idle and shiftless of all the village lads, and had conceived for this Howard Carpenter one of those extravagant passions which a handsome country boy of twenty-one sometimes inspires in an angular, spectacled woman of thirty. When she returned to her duties in Boston, Howard followed her, and the upshot of this inexplicable infatuation was that she eloped with him, eluding the reproaches of her family and the criticisms of her friends by going with him to the Nebraska frontier. Carpenter, who, of course, had no money, had taken a homestead in Red Willow County, fifty miles from the railroad. There they had measured off their quarter section themselves by driving across the prairie in a wagon, to the wheel of which they had tied a red cotton handkerchief, and counting off its revolutions. They built a dugout in the red hillside, one of those cave dwellings whose inmates so often reverted to primitive conditions. Their water they got from the lagoons where the buffalo drank, and their slender stock of provisions was always at the mercy of bands of roving Indians. For thirty years my aunt had not been further than fifty miles from the homestead.

But Mrs. Springer knew nothing of all this, and must have been considerably shocked at what was left of my kinswoman. Beneath the soiled linen duster which, on her arrival, was the most conspicuous feature of her costume, she wore a black stuff[3] dress, whose ornamentation showed that she had surrendered herself unquestioningly into the hands of a country dressmaker. My poor aunt's figure, however, would have presented astonishing difficulties to any dressmaker. Originally stooped, her shoulders were now almost bent together over her sunken chest. She wore no stays, and her gown, which trailed unevenly behind, rose in a sort of peak over her abdomen. She wore ill-fitting false teeth, and her skin was as yellow as a Mongolian's from constant exposure to a pitiless wind and to the alkaline water which hardens the most transparent cuticle into a sort of flexible leather.

I owed to this woman most of the good that ever came my way in my boyhood, and had a reverential affection for her. During the years when I was riding herd for my uncle, my aunt, after cooking the three meals—the first of which was ready at six o'clock in the morning—and putting the six children to bed, would often stand until midnight at her ironing board, with me at the kitchen table beside her, hearing me recite Latin declensions and conjugations,[4] gently shaking me when my drowsy head sank down over a page of irregular verbs. It was to her, at her ironing or mending, that I read my first Shakespeare, and her old text book on mythology was the first that ever came into my empty hands. She taught me my scales and exercises, too—on the little parlor organ, which her husband had bought her after fifteen years, during which she had not so much as seen any instrument, but an accordion that belonged to one of the Norwegian farmhands. She would sit beside me by the hour, darning and counting while I struggled with the "Joyous Farmer," but she seldom talked to me about music, and I understood why. She was a pious woman; she had the consolations of religion and, to her at least, her martyrdom was not wholly

2. **Franz-Joseph-Land:** a group of islands in the Arctic Ocean.

3. **stuff:** cloth, usually woolen.

4. **declensions and conjugations:** lists of noun and verb forms, often memorized by beginning students.

A. Exposition
You may wish to call students' attention to the graceful manner in which Cather provides the necessary exposition in the three paragraphs beginning here.

B. Expansion
The Homestead Act, passed by Congress in 1862, provided for the transfer of 160 acres of public land to homesteaders occupying the land for five years. A small fee was charged. Each homestead occupied one-fourth of a section (640 acres), the unit used to measure public land.

C. Music Connection
"The Joyous Farmer," a title often translated as "The Jolly Farmer," is one of a series of children's pieces composed by Robert Schumann (shoo͞′män), 1810–1856. Students who have studied piano may have learned this or other Schumann pieces in the course of their lessons.

A. Humanities Connection: Discussing the Photograph This photograph of a wheat field in winter suggests what a broad, flat landscape in Nebraska looks like, as well as the isolation of the farm families scattered across the plains.

B. Music Connection *Euryanthe* is an opera composed by Carl Maria von Weber (1786–1826), whose work was an early influence on Wagner.

C. Expansion Mention of the fact that Georgiana had spent her youth in Boston and the later reference to her attending a performance of the *Huguenots* in Paris point up the deprivation she has endured on the isolated farm in Nebraska.

A

Landscape No. 34 by Art Sinsabaugh (1962). Photograph.

sordid. Once when I had been doggedly beating out some easy passages from an old score of *Euryanthe* I had found among her music books, she came up to me and, putting her hands over my eyes, gently drew my head back upon her shoulder, saying tremulously, "Don't love it so well, Clark, or it may be taken from you. Oh! dear boy, pray that whatever your sacrifice may be, it be not that."

B

When my aunt appeared on the morning after her arrival, she was still in a semi-somnambulant[5] state. She seemed not to realize that she was in the city where she had spent her youth, the place longed for hungrily half a lifetime. She had been so wretchedly train-sick throughout the journey that she had no recollection of anything but her discomfort, and, to all intents and purposes, there were but a few hours of nightmare between the farm in Red Willow County and my study on Newbury Street. I had planned a little pleasure for her that afternoon, to repay her for some of the glorious moments she had given me when we used to milk together in the straw-thatched cowshed and she, because I was more than usually tired, or because her husband had spoken sharply to me, would tell me of the splendid performance of the *Huguenots*[6] she had seen in Paris, in her youth. At two o'clock the Symphony Orchestra was to give a Wagner program, and I intended to take my aunt; though, as I conversed with her I grew

C

5. **somnambulant:** sleep-walking.

6. ***Huguenots:*** an opera about the French Protestants of the seventeenth century by Giacomo Meyerbeer (1791–1864).

Literature and Language: Using Verb Tenses to Establish a Narrative
Narratives are usually told in chronological order, originating at the beginning and marching straight through to the end. But writers sometimes vary this order with flashbacks, scenes or memories of a past time that interrupt the chronological sequence of events.

In this story, Willa Cather uses several flashbacks, beginning in the second paragraph, page 518. Ask students to find other examples. (See especially the last paragraph of page 519; top left column and last line left column, page 522.) Point out that Cather uses the past perfect tense in these flashbacks to indicate an action completed at an earlier point.

Pair students and have each member of each pair write a narrative sentence on a related subject. Then have partners work together orally to discuss how they might present the sentences to indicate that one took place before the other.

Indiana University Art Museum, Bloomington.

doubtful about her enjoyment of it. Indeed, for her own sake, I could only wish her taste for such things quite dead, and the long struggle mercifully ended at last. I suggested our visiting the Conservatory and the Common before lunch, but she seemed altogether too timid to wish to venture out. She questioned me absently about various changes in the city, but she was chiefly concerned that she had forgotten to leave instructions about feeding half-skimmed milk to a certain weakling calf, "old Maggie's calf, you know, Clark," she explained, evidently having forgotten how long I had been away. She was further troubled because she had neglected to tell her daughter about the
A freshly opened kit of mackerel in the cellar, which would spoil if it were not used directly.

I asked her whether she had ever heard any of the Wagnerian operas, and found that she had not, though she was perfectly familiar with their respective situations, and had once possessed the piano score of *The Flying Dutchman*. I began to think it would have been best to get her back to Red Willow County without waking her, and regretted having suggested the concert. B

From the time we entered the concert hall, however, she was a trifle less passive and inert, and for the first time seemed to perceive her surroundings. I had felt some trepidation lest she might become aware of the absurdities of her attire, or might experience some painful embarrassment at stepping suddenly into the world to which she had been dead for a quarter of a century. But, again, I found how superficially I had judged her. She sat looking about her with eyes as impersonal, almost as stony, as those with which the granite Rameses in a museum watches the froth and fret[7] that ebbs and flows about his pedestal—separated from it by the lonely stretch of centuries. I have seen this same aloofness in old miners who drift into the Brown hotel at Denver, their pockets full of bullion, their linen soiled, their haggard faces unshaven; standing in the thronged corridors as solitary as though they were still in a frozen camp on the Yukon, conscious that certain experiences have isolated them from their fellows by a gulf no haberdasher[8] could bridge.

We sat at the extreme left of the first balcony, facing the arc of our own and the balcony above us, veritable hanging gardens, brilliant as tulip beds. The matinée audience was made up chiefly of women. One lost the contour of faces and figures, indeed any effect of line whatever, and there was only the color of bodices past counting, the shimmer of fabrics soft and firm, silky and sheer; red, mauve, pink, blue, lilac, purple, ecru, rose, yellow, cream, and white, all the colors that an impressionist finds in a sunlit landscape, with here and there the dead shadow of a frock coat. My Aunt Georgiana regarded them as though they had been so many daubs of tube-paint on a palette.

When the musicians came out and took their places, she gave a little stir of anticipation, and looked with quickening interest down over the rail at that invariable grouping, perhaps the first wholly familiar thing that had greeted her eye since she had left old Maggie and her weakling

7. **fret:** agitations or worries.
8. **haberdasher:** someone who sells men's clothing. A men's clothing store used to be called a "haberdashery."

A. Expansion
A *kit* is a small wooden barrel used for storing butter, cheese, or fish.

B. Responding
? Why do you suppose that the narrator begins to regret having suggested the concert to his aunt? (Her concern seems to be for the situation back home. She seems too timid to venture into the city.)

Closure
Have students discuss whether it was intentionally cruel of Clark to give Georgiana a taste of all that she had given up. Have them consider whether the intensity of her pleasure at the concert is worth the pain she feels at the end of the story.

Reading Check Test

1. The narrator's Aunt Georgiana was once a teacher of ______ in Boston. *music*

2. She met her future husband while vacationing in the ______ Mountains of Vermont. *Green*

3. For thirty years, Georgiana has not been farther than fifty miles from the ______. *homestead* or *farm*

4. The concert Clark and Aunt Georgiana attend is scheduled for ______. *afternoon*

5. The audience at the concert is made up mainly of ______. *women*

A. Music Connection
Wagner's opera *Tannhäuser* (tän′hoi·zər) (1843–1844) is based on the adventures of a legendary German poet and minstrel of that name. The conflicting motives referred to are that of the Pilgrims' Chorus, which represents religion and the Church, and the Venusberg theme, which represents the temptations of the flesh, to which Tannhäuser for a time succumbs.

Climax
? At what point in the story does the aunt reveal that she has not lost her intense love of music? (When the narrator turns to his aunt and sees the tears "glistening on her cheeks") What realization does the narrator have at that moment? (That while the soul may wither to the outward eye, it may, given the right circumstances, flourish again)

calf. I could feel how all those details sank into her soul, for I had not forgotten how they had sunk into mine when I came fresh from plowing forever and forever between green aisles of corn, where, as in a treadmill, one might walk from daybreak to dusk without perceiving a shadow of change. The clean profiles of the musicians, the gloss of their linen, the dull black of their coats, the beloved shapes of the instruments, the patches of yellow light thrown by the green shaded lamps on the smooth, varnished bellies of the cellos and the bass viols in the rear, the restless, wind-tossed forest of fiddle necks and bows—I recalled how, in the first orchestra I had ever heard, those long bow strokes seemed to draw the heart out of me, as a conjurer's stick reels out yards of paper ribbon from a hat.

A The first number was the *Tannhauser* overture. When the horns drew out the first strain of the Pilgrims' chorus, my Aunt Georgiana clutched my coat sleeve. Then it was I first realized that for her this broke a silence of thirty years; the inconceivable silence of the plains. With the battle between the two motives, with the frenzy of the Venusberg theme and its ripping of strings, there came to me an overwhelming sense of the waste and wear we are so powerless to combat; and I saw again the tall, naked house on the prairie, black and grim as a wooden fortress; the black pond where I had learned to swim, its margin pitted with sun-dried cattle tracks; the rain-gullied clay banks about the naked house, the four dwarf ash seedlings where the dishcloths were always hung to dry before the kitchen door. The world there was the flat world of the ancients; to the east, a cornfield that stretched to daybreak; to the west, a corral that reached to sunset; between, the conquests of peace, dearer bought than those of war.

The overture closed, my aunt released my coat sleeve, but she said nothing. She sat staring at the orchestra through a dullness of thirty years, through the films made little by little by each of the three hundred and sixty-five days in every one of them. What, I wondered, did she get from it? She had been a good pianist in her day, I knew, and her musical education had been broader than that of most music teachers of a quarter of a century ago. She had often told me of Mozart's operas and Meyerbeer's, and I could remember hearing her sing, years ago, certain melodies of Verdi's. When I had fallen ill with a fever in her house she used to sit by my cot in the evening—when the cool, night wind blew in through the faded mosquito netting tacked over the window and I lay watching a certain bright star that burned red above the cornfield—and sing "Home to our mountains, O, let us return!" in a way fit to break the heart of a Vermont boy near dead of homesickness already.

I watched her closely through the prelude to *Tristan and Isolde,* trying vainly to conjecture what that seething turmoil of strings and winds might mean to her, but she sat mutely staring at the violin bows that drove obliquely downward like the pelting streaks of rain in a summer shower. Had this music any message for her? Had she enough left to at all comprehend this power which had kindled the world since she had left it? I was in a fever of curiosity, but Aunt Georgiana sat silent upon her peak in Darien.[9] She preserved this utter immobility throughout the number from the *Flying Dutchman,* though her fingers worked mechanically upon her black dress, as though, of themselves, they were recalling the piano score they had once played. Poor old hands! They had been stretched and twisted into mere tentacles to hold and lift and knead with; the palm unduly swollen, the fingers bent and knotted—on one of them a thin, worn band that had once been a wedding ring. As I pressed and gently quieted one of those groping hands, I remembered with quivering eyelids their services for me in other days.

Soon after the tenor began the "Prize Song,"[10] I heard a quick drawn breath and turned to my aunt. Her eyes were closed, but the tears were glistening on her cheeks, and I think, in a moment more, they were in my eyes as well. It never really died, then—the soul that can suffer so excruciatingly and so interminably; it withers to the outward eye only; like that strange moss which can lie on a dusty shelf half a century and yet, if placed in water, grows green again. She wept so throughout the development and elaboration of the melody. B

During the intermission before the second half of the concert, I questioned my aunt and found that the "Prize Song" was not new to her. Some

9. **silent upon her peak in Darien:** an allusion to a poem by John Keats (1795–1821), which is about Keats's awe in the presence of a work of art. (The poem is "On First Looking Into Chapman's Homer.")
10. **"Prize Song":** A beautiful aria from the third act of Wagner's opera *Die Meistersinger.*

ANALYZING THE STORY
Identifying Facts
1. The narrator is Clark, Aunt Georgiana's nephew.

The uncle writes Clark that Georgiana has come into a small inheritance and is coming to Boston to attend to matters connected with the estate.

2. The necessary tasks of farm life kept Georgiana busy from early in the morning to late at night. She washed, cleaned, cooked, and cared for many of the animals. Other hardships included living in a dugout, getting water from the lagoons where the buffalo drank, and defending against Indian raids. Georgiana's principal disappointment was her separation from her music, which she loved.

3. He feels he owed her a great debt because she had instilled in him an appreciation for music and literature.

He has bought tickets for a concert by the Symphony Orchestra.

4. At first she seems impassive and out of touch with her surroundings. Little by little, however, she responds to the music, and in the second half of the concert she weeps from emotion.

(Answers continue on next page.)

years before there had drifted to the farm in Red Willow County a young German, a tramp cow
A puncher, who had sung the chorus at Beyruth, when he was a boy, along with other peasant boys and girls. Of a Sunday morning he used to sit on his gingham-sheeted bed in the hands' bedroom which opened off the kitchen, cleaning the leather of his boots and saddle, singing the "Prize Song," while my aunt went about her work in the kitchen. She had hovered about him until she had prevailed upon him to join the country church, though his sole fitness for this step, in so far as I could gather, lay in his boyish face and his possession of this divine melody. Shortly afterward he had gone to town on the Fourth of July, had drunk for several days, lost his money at a faro table, ridden a saddled Texan steer on a bet, and disappeared with a fractured collarbone. All this my aunt told me huskily, wanderingly, as though she were talking in the weak lapses of illness.

"Well, we have come to better things than the old *Trovatore*[11] at any rate, Aunt Georgie?" I queried, with a well-meant effort at jocularity.

Her lip quivered and she hastily put her handkerchief up to her mouth. From behind it she murmured, "And you have been hearing this ever since you left me, Clark?" Her question was the gentlest and saddest of reproaches.

The second half of the program consisted of four numbers from the *Ring*, and closed with Siegfried's funeral march. My aunt wept quietly, but almost continuously, as a shallow vessel overflows in a rainstorm. From time to time her dim eyes looked up at the lights which studded the ceiling, burning softly under their dull glass globes; doubtless they were stars in truth to her. I was still perplexed as to what measure of musical comprehension was left to her, she who had heard nothing but the singing of Gospel Hymns at Methodist services in the square frame schoolhouse on Section Thirteen for so many years. I was wholly unable to gauge how much of it had been dissolved in soapsuds, or worked into bread, or milked into the bottom of a pail.

The deluge of sound poured on and on; I never knew what she found in the shining current of it; I never knew how far it bore her or past what happy islands. From the trembling of her face I could well believe that before the last numbers

11. **Trovatore:** an opera by the Italian composer Giuseppe Verdi (1813–1901).

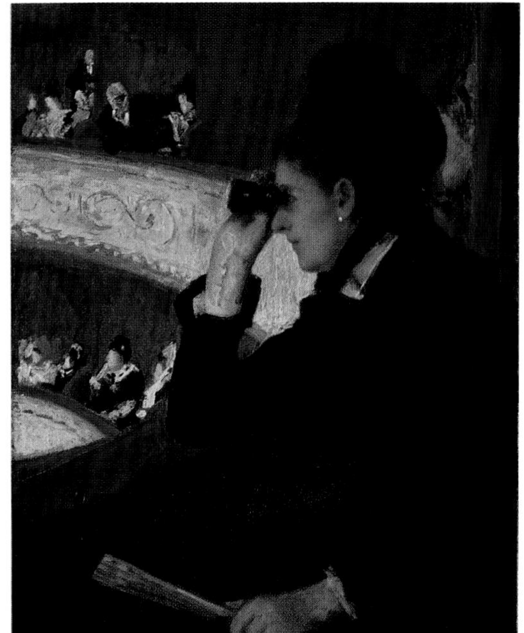

At the Opera by Mary Cassatt (1879). Oil. B

The Hayden Fund, Courtesy,
The Museum of Fine Arts, Boston.

she had been carried out where the myriad graves are, into the gray, nameless burying grounds of the sea; or into some world of death vaster yet, where, from the beginning of the world, hope has lain down with hope and dream with dream and, renouncing, slept.

The concert was over; the people filed out of the hall chattering and laughing, glad to relax and find the living level again, but my kinswoman made no effort to rise. The harpist slipped its green felt cover over his instrument; the flute players shook the water from their mouthpieces; the men of the orchestra went out one by one, leaving the stage to the chairs and music stands, empty as a winter cornfield.

I spoke to my aunt. She burst into tears and sobbed pleadingly. "I don't want to go, Clark, I don't want to go!"

I understood. For her, just outside the door of the concert hall, lay the black pond with the cattle-tracked bluffs; the tall, unpainted house, with weather-curled boards; naked as a tower, the crook-backed ash seedlings where the dishcloths hung to dry; the gaunt, moulting turkeys picking up refuse about the kitchen door.

A. Expansion
The usual spelling is Bayreuth (bī·roit′). Beginning in 1876, an annual festival has been held in this German city, at which the major works of Richard Wagner are performed. The boy Georgiana befriended had apparently been recruited with other young people to sing in the chorus of an early Bayreuth festival.

B. Humanities Connection: Discussing the Fine Art
Mary Cassatt (1845–1926) was a noted American painter and etcher. She lived most of her life in France, where she enjoyed the friendship and esteem of Manet and Degas. An Impressionist from early in her career, Cassatt is noted for her refreshing simplicity and her effective use of color. Note that the man in the upper left of the painting is gazing as intently at the woman in the foreground as she is at the performance on stage.

(Continued from previous page.)
Interpreting Meanings
5. Clark dislikes Howard.

In the first paragraph, Cather hints at this attitude by having the narrator comment that Howard has characteristically delayed writing until the very last minute.

6. Student answers will vary. Most students will agree that her statement reveals a pessimistic attitude.

7. The passages describing Aunt Georgiana's feelings at the concert shift to a third-person omniscient point of view.

Clark may be characterized as sensitive and supportive in the story.

Ask students to discuss the author's choice of a male narrator.

8. Student answers will vary. Students will agree that Clark "understands" that Georgiana clings to the experience of the concert as a symbol of the life she left behind.

9. Students will have various answers. One statement of the theme might be prompted by the narrator's words about the soul (page 522): Even after great hardships, human beings have the capacity to endure and to "flower" again.
(Answers continue in left-hand column.)

(Continued from top.)
Music serves as the catalyst for Georgiana's "reflowering."

10. The passage occurs in the fourth paragraph from the end. Encourage the students to discuss their emotional responses to music.

11. Students will generally agree that the setting is stark and forbidding: note the "tall, naked house . . . black and grim as a wooden fortress," the "black pond . . . its margin pitted with sun-dried cattle tracks," and the "rain-gullied clay banks." Also note the story concludes with an unattractive image of "the gaunt, moulting turkeys picking up refuse about the kitchen door."

12. A Romantic writer might well have idealized Aunt Georgiana's emotions at the concert. Or, possibly, Georgiana would have decided to remain in Boston.

A Romantic writer would probably have idealized the vast, open prairie and minimized the hardships of daily life.

Responding to the Story

Analyzing the Story

Identifying Facts

1. Who is the narrator of the story? What message contained in the uncle's letter sets the action in motion?
2. Numerous **flashbacks** in the story provide information about Aunt Georgiana's life after she moved to Nebraska. Cite some of her hardships and disappointments.
3. Explain why the narrator feels he owed a great debt to Aunt Georgiana. What special treat has he planned for her in Boston?
4. Describe Aunt Georgiana's reactions to the concert.

Interpreting Meanings

5. What seems to be Clark's attitude toward his Uncle Howard? Locate the passage in which Cather hints at this attitude.
6. Georgiana says about music, "Don't love it so well, Clark, or it may be taken from you." How do you feel about this attitude toward life and its joys?
7. As she often does, Cather uses a male narrator to tell her story. Locate passages in which this first-person narrator actually acts as an **omniscient narrator.** How would you characterize Clark? Can you see any reason why Cather didn't use a woman's voice to tell her story?
8. Summarize in your own words what Clark "understands" at the end of the story.
9. The story contrasts the past and present lives of both Aunt Georgiana and her nephew. On the whole, what seems to be Cather's **theme** in the story? How does the central episode of the concert, reflected in the title, contribute to this theme?
10. Willa Cather was an accomplished musician, and the powerful attraction of music is a theme that often recurs in her fiction. Find the passage in which Cather describes the effect the music might have had on Georgiana's imagination and feelings. Does this story convey some of the emotional effects that anyone might experience in listening to music?
11. In contrast to the music and the music hall is the emotional effect of the Nebraska frontier, the **setting** we hear about over and over again in the story. How would you describe the feeling Cather wants us to have for this setting? What specific **images** create this feeling?
12. If this story were told by a Romantic, how would Aunt Georgiana's visit to Boston have turned out? How would a Romantic writer have described the Nebraska farm setting?

Writing About the Story

A Creative Response

1. **Describing a Character.** Write a paragraph describing a person's appearance in a way that reveals something about his or her character. Imitate Cather's techniques in the paragraph on page 519 beginning "But Mrs. Springer knew nothing of all this. . . ." Before you write, decide what characteristics you want to emphasize. Then list some aspects of clothing or appearance that suggest these characteristics.

A Critical Response

2. **Analyzing Imagery.** In a brief essay, contrast the most prominent images Cather uses in this story to describe farm life and city life. Describe the emotional impact of each set of images.
3. **Comparing Responses to Nature.** *Walden,* by Henry David Thoreau (page 207), expresses other feelings about the natural world and its relationship to the human world. In a brief essay, compare and contrast the experience of Cather's heroine with that of Thoreau. How would you account for the different feelings toward the natural world?

Analyzing Language and Style

Figures of Speech

In each figure of speech that follows, identify the two distinct parts of the comparison. Then tell what you think these different things have in common.

1. "We sat at the extreme left of the first balcony, facing the arc of our own and the balcony above us, veritable hanging gardens, brilliant as tulip beds." (Page 521)
2. ". . . the restless, wind-tossed forest of fiddle necks and bows . . ." (Page 522)
3. ". . . I recalled how, in the first orchestra I had ever heard, those long bow strokes seemed to draw the heart out of me, as a conjurer's stick reels out yards of paper ribbon from a hat." (Page 522)
4. ". . . she sat mutely staring at the violin bows that drove obliquely downward like the pelting streaks of rain in a summer shower." (Page 522)
5. "The deluge of sound poured on and on; I never knew what she found in the shining current of it . . ." (Page 523)
6. ". . . the men of the orchestra went out . . . , leaving the stage to the chairs and music stands, empty as a winter cornfield." (Page 523)

Thomas Wolfe (1900–1938)

Thomas Wolfe is probably the most autobiographical of all American writers. Although his novels and short stories are peopled by fictional characters, the fiction actually chronicles the events of his Southern upbringing and his later life in New York and Europe.

Wolfe was born in the Smoky Mountains, in Asheville, North Carolina, the youngest of eight children. Much of his fiction centers on a character named Eugene Gant, the youngest child in a large Southern family, whose life parallels Wolfe's own.

A When Wolfe was eight years old, his parents separated. His mother ran a boardinghouse, which she called My Old Kentucky Home; his father, given to bouts of violent drinking, lived only a few blocks away, behind his stone-cutting shop. The boy, very unhappy with the new situation, lived with his mother. The boardinghouse appears repeatedly in Wolfe's fiction, usually depicted in an unpleasant light.

Wolfe entered college when he was sixteen. At six feet six inches, he dominated any group he was a part of; his extraordinary height was one reason Wolfe was so self-conscious all his life.

After he graduated from the University of North Carolina in 1920, Wolfe studied playwriting at Harvard. In 1924, he moved to New York City, where he taught at New York University while trying unsuccessfully to have his plays produced. That same year, he made the first of seven trips to Europe. The time he spent abroad, like his childhood, became material for his fiction.

During this time, Wolfe became involved with Aline Bernstein, a woman much older than he was. They spent five years together, sometimes in England, sometimes in New York, where Wolfe continued to teach and to work on *Look Homeward, Angel*. Wolfe wrote extensively about this affair later in *The Web and the Rock*.

Look Homeward, Angel, his first and best novel, was completed in 1928. After it was rejected by several publishers, Scribner's showed interest. As a result, Wolfe began what would

become a remarkable association with Maxwell Perkins, the famous editor who persuaded Wolfe to cut three hundred pages from his enormous story and saw the novel through to publication.

By 1935, Perkins felt that Wolfe's second novel, *Of Time and the River*, was ready for publication. This huge, sprawling book continues the story of Eugene Gant, the young Southern writer who moves to a northeastern city.

Wolfe eventually argued with Scribner's, and before his sudden death in 1938, he had signed up with Harper's, another publisher, and delivered to them enormous chunks of a new manuscript. Another editor labored over the mass of material and, after Wolfe's death, published it as several posthumous books, including *You Can't Go Home Again* (1940).

Some readers believe that his editors did not necessarily do Wolfe a service in reducing his manuscripts to manageable novel size. They think that Wolfe wanted to create one huge, epic work of fiction. If this is so, Wolfe's effort was much like Whitman's, though a failure. But, as William Faulkner said, Wolfe's greatness is measured by the magnitude of his failure; he dared what no other American novelist had attempted.

A. Expansion
All of these events figure significantly in Wolfe's fiction. See especially *Look Homeward, Angel.*

SUPPLEMENTARY SUPPORT MATERIALS
1. Vocabulary Activity Worksheet (*CCB*)
2. Review and Response Worksheet: Poetic Prose (*CCB*)
3. Language Skills Worksheet: The Descriptive Paragraph (*CCB*)
4. Selection Test (*CCB*)

DEVELOPING VOCABULARY
The following words from the story are tested in the Selection Test. (See also Vocabulary Activity Worksheet.)

nominal	intermittent
prodigal	luminosity
pungency	opulent
potency	poignancy
languid	surmise

PREPARATION
ESTABLISHING A PURPOSE. Ask students what images come to mind when they think of a circus. (They are not apt to mention food.) Then ask what images come to mind when they think of food and the circus together. (They may mention popcorn, hot dogs, and cotton candy.) Have students read to discover how Wolfe connects these images.

A. Expansion
According to some critics, the "web" of the title symbolizes the South and the boy's mother's people, who are puritanical, hard-bitten, and superstitious. The "rock" is the North (Pennsylvania) and his father's people, who represent liveliness, freedom, and sensuality.

B. Expansion
Earlier in the novel, the boy's father leaves his family to live with another woman. Wolfe once wrote that the search for a father was the controlling theme of all his novels. In this story, the search embraces both an urge to wander and a yearning for home.

C. Sensory Details
Here begins the first catalog (see question 6, page 532). Note that Wolfe doesn't simply name the foods but describes them lavishly. Have students look for other catalogs of sensory details as they read.

HIS FATHER'S EARTH

In the past, when much of the United States was made up of numerous small towns and rural areas, the most exciting event of the year was the circus's coming to town. It began with a parade—colorfully dressed band members, a calliope piping its shrill steam-whistle notes, wild animals roaring in rolling cages, elephants lumbering along in single file, bareback riders on prancing ponies, and a wild array of clowns, acrobats, and jugglers. No wonder that many young observers harbored the secret dream of running away to join the circus.

Not many young dreamers, however, imagined themselves selling tickets, putting up posters, and bartering with farmers for fresh food. But this was Thomas Wolfe's daydream in "His Father's Earth." Just as Napoleon realized the importance of food for his troops ("An army marches on its stomach"), so Wolfe envisioned a circus troupe eating its way through forty states. Wolfe's daydream, an exuberant description of America's geographical features and abundant crops, coincides with the daydream of arriving at his father's house, a place that is not real but fantasy. There, like the happy ending of a fairy tale, he receives one of the warmest welcomes ever described and finds that his entire life is magically put in perspective.

As you read through to the end of the story, ask yourself what "magic congruence" is shared by his "father's earth" and the circus as Wolfe describes it.

Thomas Wolfe liked to get extra mileage from his stories. "His Father's Earth" was published as a short story and also incorporated into his novel *The Web and the Rock*. A

B As the boy stood looking at the circus with his brother, there came to him two images, which had haunted his childhood and the life of every boy who ever lived, but were now for the first time seen together with an instant and magic congruence.[1] And these two images were the images of the circus and his father's earth.

He thought then he had joined a circus and started on the great tour of the nation with it. It was spring: the circus had started in New England and worked westward and then southward as the summer and autumn came on. His nominal duties—for, in his vision, every incident, each face and voice and circumstance were blazing real as life itself—were those of ticket seller, but in this tiny show, everyone did several things: the performers helped put up and take down the tents, load and unload the wagons, and the roustabouts and business people worked wherever they were needed.

The boy sold tickets, but he also posted bills and bartered with tradesmen and farmers in new places for fresh food. He became very shrewd and clever at this work, and loved to do it—some old, sharp, buried talent for shrewd trading, that had come to him from his mountain blood, now aided him. He could get the finest, freshest meats and vegetables at the lowest prices. The circus people were tough and hard, they always had a fierce and ravenous hunger, they would not accept bad food and cooking, they fed stupendously, and they always had the best of everything.

Usually the circus would arrive at a new town very early in the morning, before daybreak. He would go into town immediately: he would go to the markets, or with farmers who had come in for the circus. He felt and saw the purity of first light, he heard the sweet and sudden lutings of first birds, and suddenly he was filled with the earth and morning in new towns, among new men: he walked among the farmers' wagons, and he dealt with them on the spot for the prodigal plenty of their wares—the country melons bedded in sweet hay of wagons, the cool sweet prints of butter wrapped in clean wet cloths, with dew and starlight still on them, the enormous battered cans foaming with fresh milk, the new laid eggs which C

1. **congruence:** harmony.

he bought by the gross and hundred dozens, the tender limy pullets by the score, the rude country wagons laden to the rim with heaped abundancies—with delicate bunches of green scallions, the heavy red ripeness of huge tomatoes, the sweet-leaved lettuces crisp as celery, the fresh podded peas and the succulent young beans, as well as the potatoes spotted with the loamy earth, the powerful winy odor of the apples, the peaches, and the cherries, the juicy corn stacked up in shocks of living green, and the heavy blackened rinds of home-cured hams and bacons.

As the market opened, he would begin to trade and dicker with the butchers for their finest cuts of meat: they would hold great roasts up in their gouted[2] fingers, they would roll up tubs of fresh ground sausage, they would smack with their long palms the flanks of beeves and porks: he would drive back to the circus with a wagon full of meat and vegetables.

At the circus ground the people were already in full activity. He could hear the wonderful timed tattoo of sledges on driven stakes, the shouts of men riding animals down to water, the slow clank and pull of mighty horses, the heavy rumble of the wagons as they rolled down off the circus flat cars. By now the eating table would be erected, and as he arrived, he could see the cooks already busy at their ranges, the long tables set up underneath the canvas with their rows of benches, their tin plates and cups, their strong readiness. There would be the amber indescribable pungency of strong coffee, and the smell of buckwheat batter.

And the circus people would come in for their breakfast: hard and tough, for the most part decent and serious people, the performers, the men and women, the acrobats, the riders, the tumblers, the clowns, the jugglers, the contortionists, and the balancers would come in quietly and eat with a savage and inspired intentness.

The food they ate was as masculine and fragrant as the world they dwelt in: it belonged to the stained world of mellow sun-warmed canvas, the clean and healthful odor of the animals, and the
A mild sweet lyric nature of the land in which they lived as wanderers, and it was there for the asking with a fabulous and stupefying plenty, golden and
B embrowned: they ate stacks of buckwheat cakes, smoking hot, soaked in hunks of yellow butter which they carved at will with a wide free gesture from the piled prints on the table, and which they garnished (if they pleased) with ropes of heavy black molasses, or with the lighter, freer maple syrup.

They ate big steaks for breakfast, hot from the pan and lashed with onions, they ate whole melons, crammed with the ripeness of the deep pink meat, rashers of bacon, and great platters of fried eggs, or eggs scrambled with calves' brains, they helped themselves from pyramids of fruit piled up at intervals on the table—plums, peaches, apples, cherries, grapes, oranges, and bananas—they had great pitchers of thick cream to pour on everything, and they washed their hunger down with pint mugs of strong deep-savored coffee.

For their midday meal they would eat fiercely, hungrily, with wolfish gusts, mightily, with knit brows and convulsive movements of their corded throats. They would eat great roasts of beef with crackled hides, browned in their juices, rare and tender, hot chunks of delicate pork with hems of fragrant fat, delicate young boiled chickens, only a mouthful for these ravenous jaws, twelve-pound pot roasts cooked for hours in an iron pot with new carrots, onions, sprouts, and young potatoes, together with every vegetable that the season yielded: huge roasting ears of corn, smoking hot, stacked like cordwood on two-foot platters, tomatoes cut in slabs with wedges of okra and succotash, and raw onion, mashed potatoes whipped to a creamy smother, boats swimming with pure beef gravy, new carrots, turnips, fresh peas cooked in butter, and fat string beans seasoned with the flavor of big chunks of cooking-pork. In addition, they had every fruit that the place and time afforded: hot crusty apple, peach and cherry pies, encrusted with cinnamon, puddings and cakes of every sort, and blobbering cobblers inches deep.

Thus the circus moved across America, from town to town, from state to state, eating its way from Maine into the great plains of the West, eating its way along the Hudson and the Mississippi rivers, eating its way across the prairies and from the North into the South, eating its way across C
the flat farmlands of the Pennsylvania Dutch colony, the eastern shore of Maryland and back again across the states of Virginia, North Carolina, Tennessee, and Florida—eating all good things that

2. **gouted:** swollen as if suffering from gout, a disease affecting the joints.

A. Expansion
Wolfe linked his writing with that of Walt Whitman, Mark Twain, and Sherwood Anderson—writers with "a poet's vision." Here, the land itself has a lyrical nature.

? In what sense are Wolfe's desciptions highly lyrical? (Students should note the rhythmic cadences and the profusion of sensory details.)

B. Responding

? Which foods particularly appeal to you? What would you list in your own catalog of favorite foods?

C. Connections
Have students compare Wolfe's vision with the Romantic view of America as described on pages 116–121. (Like the Romantics, Wolfe rhapsodizes on the wonders of America—not its scenery or people, but its vast cornucopia of food. Later Wolfe glorifies Nature [see A, next page.])

A. Figurative Language
Ask students to notice the figures of speech in this particularly poetic passage. (Examples: metaphor—"the moon's man"; personification—"stars drown," "birth of light")

B. Conflict
? What words suggest that the circus world is in conflict with the "real world"? ("phantasmal and unreal"; "the enemy") Have students note the physical conflict in the second paragraph, right column.

C. Contrast
? Striking contrasts are a hallmark of Wolfe's style. What dramatic contrasting picture of America does Wolfe present here? (The savage violence contrasts with the earlier picture of a bountifully productive land.)

D. Connections
? In what other selection in the previous unit is nature seen as indifferent? (Crane's "The Open Boat")

this enormous, this inevitably bountiful and abundant cornucopia[3] of a continent yielded.

They ate the cod, bass, mackerel, halibut, clams, and oysters of the New England coast, the terrapin[4] of Maryland, the fat beeves, porks, and cereals of the Middle West, and they had, as well, the heavy juicy peaches, watermelons, cantaloupes of Georgia, the fat sweet shad of the Carolina coasts, and the rounded and exotic citrus fruits of the tropics: the oranges, tangerines, bananas, kumquats, lemons, guavas down in Florida, together with a hundred other fruits and meats—the Vermont turkeys, the mountain trout, the bunched heaviness of the Concord grapes, the red winy bulk of the Oregon apples, as well as the clawed, shelled, and crusted dainties, the crabs, the clams, the pink-meated lobsters that grope their way along the sea floors of America.

A

The boy awoke at morning in three hundred towns with the glimmer of starlight on his face; he was the moon's man; then he saw light quicken in the east, he saw the pale stars drown, he saw the birth of light, he heard the lark's wing, the bird tree, the first liquorous liquefied lutings, the ripe-aired trillings, the plumskinned birdnotes, and he heard the hoof and wheel come down the streets of the nation. He exulted in his work as food-producer for the circus people, and they loved him for it. They said there had never been anyone like him—they banqueted exultantly, with hoarse gulpings and with joy, and they loved him.

Slowly, day by day, the circus worked its way across America, through forty states and through a dozen weathers. It was a little world that moved across the enormous loneliness of the earth, a little world that each day began a new life in new cities, and that left nothing to betray where it had been save a litter of beaten papers, the droppings of the camel and the elephant in Illinois, a patch of trampled grass, and a magical memory.

B

The circus men knew no other earth but this; the earth came to them with the smell of the canvas and the lion's roar. They saw the world behind the lights of the carnival, and everything beyond these lights was phantasmal and unreal to them; it lived for them within the circle of the tent as men and women who sat on benches, as the posts they came to, and sometimes as the enemy.

Their life was filled with the strong joy of food, with the love of traveling, and with danger and hard labor. Always there was the swift violence of change and movement, of putting up and tearing down, and sometimes there was the misery of rain and sleet, and mud above the ankles, of wind that shook their flimsy residence, that ripped the tent stakes from their moorings in the earth and lifted out the great center pole as if it were a match. Now they must wrestle with the wind and hold their dwelling to the earth; now they must fight the weariness of mud and push their heavy wagons through the slime; now, cold and wet and wretched, they must sleep on piles of canvas, upon the flat cars in a driving rain, and sometimes they must fight the enemy—the drunk, the savage, the violent enemy, the bloody man, who dwelt in every place. Sometimes it was the city thug, sometimes the mill hands of the South, sometimes the miners in a Pennsylvania town—the circus people cried, "Hey, Rube!"[5] and fought them with fist and foot, with pike and stake, and the boy saw and knew it all.

When the men in a little town barricaded the street against their parade, they charged the barricade with their animals, and once the sheriff tried to stop the elephant by saying: "Now, damn ye, if you stick your damn trunk another inch, I'll shoot."

C

The circus moved across America foot by foot, mile by mile. He came to know the land. It was rooted in his blood and his brain forever—its food, its fruit, its fields and forests, its deserts, and its mountains, its savage lawlessness. He saw the crimes and the violence of the people with pity, with mercy, and with tenderness: he thought of them as if they were children. They smashed their neighbors' brains out with an ax, they disemboweled one another with knives, they were murderous and lost upon this earth they dwelt upon as strangers.

D

The tongueless blood of the murdered men ran down into the earth, and the earth received it. Upon this enormous and indifferent earth the little trains rattled on over ill-joined rails that loosely bound the sprawling little towns together. Lost and lonely, brief sawings of wood and plaster and cheap brick ugliness, the little towns were scat-

3. **cornucopia:** in Greek mythology, a horn of plenty.
4. **terrapin:** freshwater turtles.

5. **Hey, Rube!** a call for help among circus people when trouble breaks out.

A. Humanities Connection: Responding to the Fine Art
Grant Wood (1892–1942) was a Regionalist painter who depicted the rural settings of his native Iowa. His crisp lines and stylized landscapes reflect an interest in primitives inspired by study and travel in Europe. According to the *Dictionary of American Biography,* Wood, together with fellow Regionalists Thomas Hart Benton and John Steuart Curry, "spoke for the indigenous values and subject matter of the Midwest as embodying the peculiarly American character and spirit."
? Where do you suppose this scene is? (In a rural area, probably in the Midwest) What American values does the painting express? (Values such as the work ethic, earth's bountifulness, and orderliness) What feeling does it convey? (Possible answers include feelings of contentment, stability, and prosperity, among others) Why do you suppose the editors chose this painting to illustrate Wolfe's story? (Basically because the painting captures Wolfe's notion of the spirit of the heartland)

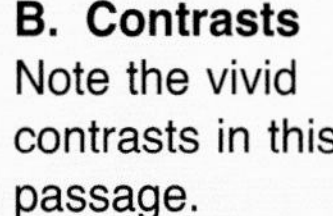

B. Contrasts
Note the vivid contrasts in this passage.

Fall Plowing by Grant Wood (1931). Oil on canvas.

A

From the Deere & Company Art Collection, Moline, Illinois.

tered like encampments through the wilderness. Only the earth remained, which all these people had barely touched, which all these people dwelt upon but could not possess.

B Only the earth remained, the savage and lyrical earth with its rude potency, its thousand vistas, its heights and slopes and levels, with all its violence and delicacy, the terrible fecundity,[6] decay, and growth, its fierce colors, its vital bite and sparkle, its exultancy of space and wandering. And the memory of this earth, the memory of all this universe of sight and sense, was rooted in this boy's heart and brain forever. It fed the hungers of desire and wandering, it breached the walls of his secret and withdrawn spirit. And for every memory of place and continent, of enormous coffee-colored rivers and eight hundred miles of bending wheat, of Atlantic coast and midland prairie, of raw red Piedmont[7] and tropic flatness, there was always the small, fecund, perfect memory of his father's land, the dark side of his soul and his heart's desire, which he had never seen, but which

6. **fecundity:** fertility.

7. **Piedmont:** hilly land east of the Appalachians.

A. Theme

? How can the boy recognize his father's land? (Remember, this is a daydream of wish-fulfillment. His father's land is in the core of his being; it is his heart's desire.)

B. Simile/Conflict

Have students note the powerful similes; there are five in these two sentences.

? What conflict is expressed here? (The conflict between home and wanderlust, between stability and freedom)

C. Theme

? This passage echoes a similar one on pages 529–530. Why do you think Wolfe repeats the idea? (Answers will vary; students may suggest that the passage points to the theme and that it functions as a kind of refrain.)

A he knew with every atom of his life, the strange phantasmal haunting of man's memory. It was a fertile, nobly swelling land, and it was large enough to live in, walled with fulfilled desire.

Abroad in this ocean of earth and vision he thought of his father's land, of its great red barns and nobly swelling earth, its clear familiarity and its haunting strangeness, and its dark and secret heart, its magnificent, its lovely and tragic beauty. He thought of its smell of harbors and its rumors of the seas, the city, and the ships, its wine-red apples and its brown-red soil, its snug weathered houses, and its lyric unutterable ecstacy.

A wonderful thing happened. One morning he awoke suddenly to find himself staring straight up at the pulsing splendor of the stars. At first he did not know where he was, but he knew instantly, even before he looked about him, that he had visited this place before. The circus train had stopped in the heart of the country, for what reason he did not know. He could hear the languid and intermittent breathing of the engine, the strangeness of men's voices in the dark, the casual stamp of the horses in their cars, and all around him the attentive and vital silence of the earth.

Suddenly he raised himself from the pile of canvas on which he slept. It was the moment just before dawn: against the east, the sky had already begun to whiten with the first faint luminosity of day, the invading tides of light crept up the sky, drowning the stars out as they went. The train had halted by a little river which ran swift and deep next to the tracks, and now he knew that what at first had been the sound of silence was the swift and ceaseless music of the river.

There had been rain the night before, and now the river was filled with the sweet clean rain-drenched smell of earthy deposits. He could see the delicate white glimmer of young birch trees leaning from the banks, and on the other side he saw the winding whiteness of the road. Beyond the road, and bordering it, there was an orchard with a wall of lichened stone: a row of apple trees, gnarled and sweet, spread their squat twisted branches out across the road, and in the faint light he saw that they were dense with blossoms: the cool intoxication of their fragrance overpowered him.

As the wan light grew, the earth and all its contours emerged sharply, and he saw again the spare, gaunt loneliness of the earth at dawn, with all its sweet and sudden cries of spring. He saw the worn and ancient design of lichened rocks, the fertile soil of the baked fields, he saw the kept order, the frugal cleanliness, with its springtime overgrowth, the mild tang of opulent greenery. There was an earth with fences, as big as a man's heart, but not so great as his desire, and after his giant wanderings over the prodigal fecundity of the continent, this earth was like a room he once had lived in. He returned to it as a sailor to a small closed harbor, as a man, spent with the hunger of his wandering, comes home. B

Instantly he recognized the scene. He knew that he had come at last into his father's land. It was a magic that he knew but could not speak; he stood upon the lip of time, and all of his life now seemed the mirage of some wizard's spell—the spell of canvas and the circus ring, the spell of the tented world which had possessed him. Here was his home, brought back to him while he slept, like a forgotten dream. Here was the dark side of his soul, his heart's desire, his father's country, the earth his spirit dwelt on as a child. He knew every inch of the landscape, and he knew, past reason, doubt, or argument, that home was not three miles away. C

He got up at once and leaped down to the earth; he knew where he would go. Along the track there was the slow swing and dance of the brakemen's lamps, that moving, mournful, and beautiful cloud of light along the rails of the earth, that he had seen so many times. Already the train was in motion; its bell tolled and its heavy trucks rumbled away from him. He began to walk back along the tracks, for less than a mile away, he knew, where the stream boiled over the lip of a dam, there was a bridge. When he reached the bridge, a deeper light had come: the old red brick of the mill emerged sharply and with the tone and temper of deep joy fell sheer into bright shining waters.

He crossed the bridge and turned left along the road: here it moved away from the river, among fields and through dark woods—dark woods bordered with stark poignancy of fir and pine, with the noble spread of maples, shot with the naked whiteness of birch. Here was the woodland maze: the sweet density of the brake and growth. Sharp thrummings, woodland flitters broke the silence. His steps grew slow, he sat upon a wall, he waited.

Now rose the birdsong in first light, and suddenly he heard each sound the birdsong made.

CLOSURE
Ask students to answer the question posed in the headnote: "What "magic congruence" connects the circus and his father's home? (Both welcome the boy; in both there are images of plentifulness and fulfilled desire. They are "twin images" that haunt him awake and asleep.)

READING CHECK TEST

1. The two images that come to the boy as he stands looking at the circus are ________. *the circus and his father's earth*
2. The boy is nominally a ticket seller, but he spends most of his time ________. *buying or trading for food*
3. The circus people eat food that comes from ________. *all over America*
4. On his travels the boy arrives finally at ________. *his father's house (land)*
5. At the end, the boy is greeted by three people: ________. *his father and his two brothers*

A

Like a flight of shot the sharp fast skaps of sound arose. With chittering bicker, fast-fluttering skirrs of sound, the palmy honeyed bird-cries came. Smooth drops and nuggets of bright gold they were. Now sang the birdtrees filled with lutings in bright air: the thrums, the lark's wing, and tongue-trilling chirrs arose now. The little nameless cries arose and fell with liquorous liquefied lutings, with lirruping chirp, plumbellied smoothness, sweet lucidity.

And now there was the rapid kweet kweet kweet kweet kweet of homing birds and their pwee pwee pwee: others with sharp cricketing stitch, a mosquito buzz with thin metallic tongues, while some with rusty creakings, high shrew's caws, with eerie rasp, with harsh far calls—all birds that are awake in the sweet woodland tangles: and above, there passed the whirr of hidden wings, the strange lost cry of the unknown birds, in full flight now, in which the sweet confusion of their cries was mingled.

Then he got up and went along that road where, he knew, like the prophetic surmise of a dream, the house of his father's blood and kin lay hidden. At length, he came around a bending in the road, he left the wooded land, he passed by hedges and saw the old white house, set in the shoulder of the hill, worn like care and habit in the earth; clean and cool, it sat below the clean dark shelter of its trees: a twist of morning smoke coiled through its chimney.

Then he turned in to the rutted road that led up to the house, and at this moment the enormous figure of a powerful old man appeared around the corner prophetically bearing a smoked ham in one huge hand. And when the boy saw the old man, a cry of greeting burst from his throat, and the old man answered with a roar of welcome that shook the earth.

Then the old man dropped his ham, and waddled forward to meet the boy: they met half down the road, and the old man crushed him in his hug; they tried to speak but could not; they embraced again and in an instant all the years of wandering, the pain of loneliness and the fierce hungers of desire, were scoured away like a scum of frost from a bright glass.

He was a child again, he was a child that had stood upon the lip and leaf of time and heard the quiet tides that move us to our death, and he knew that the child could not be born again, the book of the days could never be turned back, old errors and confusions never righted. And he wept with sorrow for all that was lost and could never be regained, and with joy for all that had been recovered.

B

Suddenly he saw his youth as men on hilltops might look at the whole winding course of rivers to the sea, he saw the blind confusions of his wanderings across the earth, the horror of man's little stricken mote of earth against immensity, and he remembered the proud exultancy of his childhood when all the world lay like a coin between his palms, when he could have touched the horned rim of the moon, when heroes and great actions bent before him.

And he wept, not for himself, but out of love and pity for every youth that ever hoped and wandered and was alone. He had become a man, and he had in him unique glory that belongs to men alone, and that makes them great, and from which they shape their mightiest songs and legends. For out of their pain they utter first a cry for wounded self, then, as their vision deepens, widens, the universe of their marvelous sense leaps out and grips the universe; they feel contempt for gods, respect for men alone, and with the indifference of a selfless passion, enact earth out of a lyric cry.

At this moment, also, two young men burst from the house and came running down the road to greet him. They were powerful and heavy young men, already beginning to show signs of that epic and sensual grossness that distinguished their father. Like their father, they recognized the boy instantly, and in a moment he was engulfed in their mighty energies, borne up among them to the house. And they understood all he wanted to say, but could not speak, and they surrounded him with love and lavish heapings of his plate. And the boy knew the strange miracle of return to the dark land of his heart's desire, the father's land which haunts men like a dream they never knew.

C

Such were the twin images of the circus and his father's land which were to haunt his dreams and waking memory and which now, as he stood there with his brother looking at the circus, fused instantly to a living whole and came to him in a blaze of light.

And in this way, before he had ever set foot upon it, he came for the first time to his father's earth.

A. Language
? What poetic technique dominates this passage? (Onomatopoeia, but note also the alliteration of "liquorous liquefied lutings," repeated from page 528.) What unusual word choices and made-up words does Wolfe use? (*Skirrs, bird trees, lutings, chirrs,* and so on) What is the overall effect of this passage? (It captures the sound and feel of birdsong.) Is this a legitimate use of language in a serious prose piece? (Answers will vary. Students may echo critics' judgments: some revel in Wolfe's language; some criticize it as excessive.)

B. Conflict
? What insight has the boy gained? (Answers will vary. One possibility: The boy sees that his two yearnings—to travel and to find home—are incompatible.)

C. Theme
? What wishes does the boy fulfill in these two fantasies? (A sense of love and belonging, of joy in work, of bounty)

ANALYZING THE STORY
Identifying Facts
1. In paragraph 2, "He thought then" and "in his vision" indicate that the boy is imagining what follows.
2. The story is full of examples, among which are the assonance of the controlling images (circus, earth), the alliteration of "finest, freshest meats" and "sweet and sudden lutings" (paragraphs 3–4), the onomatopoeia of *tattoo* and *clank* and *rumble* (page 527, paragraph 6). Wolfe is especially poetic in his descriptions of bird sounds on pages 528 and 531.

Interpreting Meanings
3. Wolfe describes the food as masculine (page 527) and the land that feeds the circus as fecund. He gives a multitude of examples of the land's bounty, upon which the circus members feed "stupendously."
4. The circus constantly moves on, but his father's earth remains, endures, and prospers. The father represents the fecund earth, and the boy in his fantasy is the one who distributes its bounty.
(Answers continue in left-hand column.)

(Continued from top.)
5. The boy hears the birdsongs when he is with the circus (pages 526, 528), but he hears them in abundant detail when he nears his father's home (page 531). The catalog of birdsongs reminds us of the long lists of food.
6. Answers will vary. Students can work in small groups to analyze the images in different catalogs.
7. The Prodigal Son, when his fortune is depleted, is literally hungry; this boy is hungry for his father and his father's land. In both stories the father welcomes the returning son with food—the fatted calf in the Bible and a ham in this one. One difference is that in the Bible story, the prodigal's brother resents the father's forgiveness; in this story, the brothers also welcome the boy.
8. Answers will vary. Ask students to think of specific images to describe the land or place. (See A Creative Response.)

Responding to the Story

Analyzing the Story

Identifying Facts

1. Which words tell you that Wolfe is describing a fantasy and not reality?
2. What examples of **onomatopoeia, alliteration,** and other **poetic devices** give Wolfe's story the "sound" of poetry?

Interpreting Meaning

3. Wolfe depicts his father as a nurturer—a male version of the "earth mother." What details help create that picture?
4. How does the world of the circus differ from "his father's earth"? What similarities are there in what the boy does and what the father represents?
5. How does Wolfe use the descriptions of birdsong to bring together descriptions of circus life and of home?
6. Wolfe is famous for evocative descriptions, which he presents in a kind of **catalogue** that often sounds like the "catalogues" of Walt Whitman (see page 331). Select one passage of description and tell which **images** appeal to the various senses: sight, taste, smell, hearing, touch.
7. Scenes in this story have uncanny resemblances to some other emotional "reunion" scenes in literature. If you've ever read Homer's *Odyssey,* you might remember Odysseus's reunion, after a twenty-year absence, with his aged father, who is tending his vines. If you know the biblical parable often referred to as the Prodigal Son (Luke 15: 11–32), tell whether you think Wolfe's father-son reunion bears any resemblance to the reunion described there.
8. This story is a powerful description of Wolf's feelings for the land and for home. Describe your own responses to Wolfe's passion. Do you have similar feelings for any land or places?

Writing About the Poem

A Creative Response

1. **Using Accumulation of Detail in a Description.** Write a Wolfe-like description of a place you know well, which includes a wide variety of people or items. Try to pile up (or "accumulate") details that capture the atmosphere of the place. You might describe a sports arena with its teams, cheerleaders, vendors, fans, photographers, broadcasters, umpires, coaches, bench-sitters, etc. Or you might describe a stretch of highway past which travel many different passenger vehicles with all kinds of people on board, and many different trucks with all kinds of cargo.

A Critical Response

2. **Comparing Styles and Techniques.** Reread Walt Whitman's poetry (pages 331–348), especially the verses from "Song of Myself." In a brief essay, compare Whitman's style with that of Wolfe. Before you write, you might gather details in a chart like the following:

	Whitman	Wolfe
1. Use of descriptive catalogues		
2. Celebration of common man		
3. Celebration of America		
4. Emotional effect of writing		

F. Scott Fitzgerald (1896–1940)

If ever there was an author whose life and fiction were one, it was Scott Fitzgerald. The America into which Fitzgerald was born and in which he grew up clung to inherited restraints and proprieties. But it was to change dramatically under the impact of the First World War, when inhibition suddenly was shed for exuberance in the crazy, wonderful, irresponsible era of the 1920's. Scott Fitzgerald—handsome, charming, and uncommonly gifted—was not only part of this time; he thought about it and heard the sound of it and wrote about it in a way that gave it the name "The Jazz Age." He made literary legend of it and, with his lovely wife Zelda, lived it out in all of its excesses. He also almost certainly died of it.

Fitzgerald was born in 1896 in St. Paul, Minnesota, the son of a father with claims to an aristocratic Maryland family. He was named for an ancestor, Francis Scott Key, the composer of the "Star-Spangled Banner." His mother was the daughter of a rich Irish immigrant. The young Scott was a spoiled boy, a failure at school work and—to his own great disappointment—at sports. But he was a success at daydreaming and, while still in his teens, at writing stories and plays.

At Princeton University, which he entered in 1913, he wrote one of the Triangle Club musical shows, contributed to the *Nassau Literary Magazine,* and befriended the serious writers Edmund Wilson and John Peele Bishop. When the United States entered the First World War in 1917, Fitzgerald left college for officers' training school, yearning for heroic adventure on the battlefields of France. He was never sent overseas, but in camp he began work on a novel, *The Romantic Egoist,* which was twice turned down by Scribner's.

While he was stationed at Camp Sheridan in Alabama, romance of a different sort overtook him. He fell deeply in love with Zelda Sayre, a high-spirited and gorgeous woman whose escapades had scandalized her home town of Montgomery. Like Scott, Zelda hungered for new experiences. She was sure of her appeal and felt

it was bound to bring her a full measure of luxury and gaiety. Although Scott courted her persistently, he had not nearly enough money to offer her the kind of marriage she wanted, and at first she turned him down.

Now out of the army, Fitzgerald took a low-paying job he hated; he sent his novel, rewritten and retitled *This Side of Paradise,* off to Scribner's for the third time. In 1919, they agreed to publish it.

"I was an empty bucket," he said of the experience, "so mentally blunted by the summer's writing that I'd taken a job repairing car roofs at the Northern Pacific shops. Then the postman rang, and that day I quit work and ran along the streets stopping automobiles to tell friends and acquaintances about it—my novel *This Side of Paradise* was accepted for publication. That

A. Expansion
By referring to the time line on pages 498 and 499, students can see that the 1920's saw women winning the right to vote (1920), Prohibition beginning (1920), a stock market boom (1922), and the stock market crash (1929).

Since Fitzgerald's work so reflects this period, you may want students to brainstorm to find what additional details they know about the "Jazz Age" from their history courses, their own reading, and television and movies.

A. Expansion
It is an irony of Fitzgerald's life that while condemning the "seductive luxury and heedlessness" of the rich, he sought to emulate their lifestyles, an ambition that eventually was to result in great personal pain.

week the postman rang and rang, and I paid off my terrible small debts, bought a suit and woke up every morning with a world of ineffable toploftiness and promise."

When it was published in March 1920, *This Side of Paradise* was a sensation. The old, prewar world with its Victorian code of behavior had been dumped in favor of a great, gaudy spree of new freedoms. Girls bobbed their hair and shortened their skirts, while boys filled their flasks with bootleg gin. To the wail of saxophones, couples danced the Charleston across the nation's dance floors. In young Fitzgerald's novel, the Jazz Age had found its definition.

Zelda married Scott in April of that year. The newlyweds moved to New York and became the center of a round of parties, while Scott turned out scores of stories. In the first years of the decade, he published two collections of stories, *Flappers and Philosophers* and *Tales of the Jazz Age,* and a second novel, *The Beautiful and Damned.* After a stay in France, the Fitzgeralds returned to St. Paul, where their only child, a daughter named Frances, was born.

Scott announced to Maxwell Perkins, his editor at Scribner's, that he was going to write "something new, something extraordinarily beautiful and simple and intricately patterned." He fulfilled that ambition in *The Great Gatsby,* his nearly flawless masterpiece, which was published in 1925. It tells the story of James Gatz, a poor boy from the Middle West who dreams of success and elegance and finds their incarnation in a Louisville girl named Daisy Fay. When Gatz returns from the war he learns she has become Daisy Buchanan, married to a rich Chicagoan and leading a careless, sumptuous life on Long Island. The hero, now a successful bootlegger known as Jay Gatsby, hopes to win Daisy from what he believes is a loveless, unhappy marriage. The story ends in Gatsby's death, but we can see that it was his dream, his vulnerability and feeling, that are admirable, and that the Buchanans are insulated from life's possibilities by their wealth and self-indulgence.

A The central triumph of *The Great Gatsby* was its revelation of the rich in all their seductive luxury and heedlessness, accompanied by an implicit condemnation of their way of life. It showed wealth as a numbing, dehumanizing force that can destroy the heart. In a remarkably concise work, Fitzgerald probed deeply the ambiguities of the American dream. One of his masterful innovations in this novel—his manipulation of the point of view—matches the ambiguity of the book's theme. The story is told by Nick Carraway, Daisy's cousin. Nick's attitude, both engaged with the events and yet objective toward them, is often singled out as the ideal narrative point of view.

The Great Gatsby won some critical praise, but it was a financial disappointment. Fitzgerald had to work even harder to keep up with the high cost of his and Zelda's international life. He turned out more potboiling short stories (mediocre in quality and written for money) and went to Hollywood to write movie scripts. In 1930, the tenth year of their marriage, Zelda suffered a mental breakdown and was to spend the rest of her life in and out of asylums. Hers was a search for both sanity and identity (her identity which seemed to have been devoured by Scott's productiveness). She aspired to be a dancer and a writer, and in 1932 produced her own novel, *Save Me the Waltz.* This was her thinly disguised account of her troubled marriage.

Scott's novel *Tender Is the Night,* published in 1934, was his rebuttal. Its hero, Dick Diver, is the protector and healer of the mad heroine, Nicole. However, the stock market crash of 1929 had put an end to Fitzgerald's era, and readers had lost interest in the problems of the expatriates like Dick Diver. Still, the book displays Fitzgerald's hard-won experience of life, the commitment to early dreams, the self-destructiveness of charm, and a whole generation's craving for endless youth and irresponsibility. In its despair, *Tender Is the Night* was an epitaph for the Jazz Age.

It was Fitzgerald's epitaph as well. After its publication, he struggled with mounting debts, failing health, drinking, and depression. Zelda was hospitalized, and although Scott suffered under the drudgery of the Hollywood studios, he was bound to them. When he could, he continued to do serious work. Through his love affair with Sheila Graham, a British journalist, he grew interested in the Hollywood producer Irving Thalberg and began work on a novel about him. He was at work on this novel, *The Last Tycoon,* in 1940 when he died of heart failure. *The Last Tycoon* was completed by his friend Edmund Wilson and was published after Fitzgerald's death to wide critical praise.

Supplementary Support Materials
1. Vocabulary Activity Worksheet (*CCB*)
2. Review and Response Worksheet: Tone and Theme (*CCB*)
3. Language Skills Worksheet: Varying Sentence Structure (*CCB*)
4. Selection Test (*CCB*)

Developing Vocabulary
The following words from the story are tested in the Selection Test. (See also Vocabulary Activity Worksheet.)

desolate	to relinquish
furtively	provocative
enormity	indiscretion
to precipitate	somnolent
petulance	plaintive

Preparation
1. **Prereading Journal.** Have students spend a few minutes freewriting about their own ambitions. What do they dream of achieving?

2. **Establishing a Purpose.** Ask volunteers to share some ambitions and dreams. Then tell students to read to discover Dexter Green's dreams and whether they come true for him.

A. Responding
? How does Dexter react to the changing seasons? (To Dexter, spring is dismal; summer is colorful; fall is gorgeous; but winter is melancholy, dreary, and desolate.) Why is it winter that inspires his dreams? (Students should note that despite Dexter's earlier reflections on winter, November raises him to "ecstatic triumph.")

B. Expansion
Fitzgerald once noted that "Winter Dreams" (1922) was the first version of his novel *The Great Gatsby,* published in 1925. Students might enjoy reading the novel (see page 1144) and comparing it to this story.

WINTER DREAMS

Have you ever met someone about whom you thought, "That's the person I want to marry"? If you have, or if you ever do think it, you might find yourself facing the same kinds of problems that Dexter Green does.

"Winter Dreams" opens around 1909. Dexter is fourteen years old, earning pocket money as a caddy for wealthy Minnesota golfers at their private club. As the story ends, nearly eighteen years later, Dexter is a successful businessman in New York City. During that time, Dexter's thoughts and feelings are often focused on Judy Jones, a beautiful young woman with many suitors.

As you read the story, ask yourself how Dexter's two ambitions—achieving material success and winning Judy's hand—are tied together. What is Judy like? Why can't Dexter fully escape from Judy's magnetic charms?

Some of the caddies were poor as sin and lived in one-room houses with a neurasthenic[1] cow in the front yard, but Dexter Green's father owned the second-best grocery store in Black Bear—the best one was "The Hub," patronized by the wealthy people from Sherry Island—and Dexter caddied only for pocket money.

A In the fall when the days became crisp and gray and the long Minnesota winter shut down like the white lid of a box, Dexter's skis moved over the snow that hid the fairways[2] of the golf course. At these times the country gave him a feeling of profound melancholy—it offended him that the links should lie in enforced fallowness, haunted by ragged sparrows for the long season. It was dreary, too, that on the tees where the gay colors fluttered in summer there were now only the desolate sandboxes knee-deep in crusted ice. When he crossed the hills the wind blew cold as misery, and if the sun was out he tramped with his eyes squinted up against the hard dimensionless glare.

In April the winter ceased abruptly. The snow ran down into Black Bear Lake, scarcely tarrying[3] for the early golfers to brave the season with red and black balls. Without elation, without an interval of moist glory, the cold was gone.

Dexter knew that there was something dismal about this Northern spring, just as he knew there was something gorgeous about the fall. Fall made him clinch his hands and tremble and repeat idiotic sentences to himself, and make brisk abrupt gestures of command to imaginary audiences and armies. October filled him with hope which November raised to a sort of ecstatic triumph, and in this mood the fleeting brilliant impressions of the summer at Sherry Island were ready grist to his mill.[4] He became a golf champion and defeated Mr. T. A. Hedrick in a marvelous match played a hundred times over the fairways of his imagination, a match each detail of which he changed about untiringly—sometimes he won with almost laughable ease, sometimes he came up magnificently from behind. Again, stepping from a Pierce-Arrow automobile, like Mr. Mortimer Jones, he strolled frigidly into the lounge of the Sherry Island Golf Club—or perhaps, surrounded by an admiring crowd, he gave an exhibition of fancy diving from the springboard of the club raft. . . . Among those who watched him in open-mouthed wonder was Mr. Mortimer Jones.

And one day it came to pass that Mr. Jones—himself and not his ghost—came up to Dexter with tears in his eyes and said that Dexter was the—best caddy in the club, and wouldn't he decide not to quit if Mr. Jones made it worth his while, because every other—caddy in the club lost one ball a hole for him—regularly—

1. **neurasthenic** (no͞o'ras·thē'nik): as though suffering from a nervous disorder; here, "thin and weak."
2. **fairways:** mowed strips of a golf course. The fairway of each hole starts at the tee and ends at the green.
3. **tarrying:** waiting.
4. **grist to his mill:** something that can be used to advantage.

B

A. Characterization

? What hints does eleven-year-old Judy give of the woman she will become? (The "perceptible spark" and "almost passionate quality of her eyes" suggest that she will be beautiful, tantalizing, passionate, and vital. Her "general ungodliness" suggests that she will be insensitive and perhaps wild.)

"No, sir," said Dexter decisively, "I don't want to caddy anymore." Then, after a pause: "I'm too old."

"You're not more than fourteen. Why the devil did you decide just this morning that you wanted to quit? You promised that next week you'd go over to the state tournament with me."

"I decided I was too old."

Dexter handed in his "A Class" badge, collected what money was due him from the caddymaster, and walked home to Black Bear Village.

"The best——caddy I ever saw," shouted Mr. Mortimer Jones over a drink that afternoon. "Never lost a ball! Willing! Intelligent! Quiet! Honest! Grateful!"

A The little girl who had done this was eleven—beautifully ugly as little girls are apt to be who are destined after a few years to be inexpressibly lovely and bring no end of misery to a great number of men. The spark, however, was perceptible. There was a general ungodliness in the way her lips twisted down at the corners when she smiled, and in the—Heaven help us!—in the almost passionate quality of her eyes. Vitality is born early in such women. It was utterly in evidence now, shining through her thin frame in a sort of glow.

She had come eagerly out on to the course at nine o'clock with a white linen nurse and five small new golf clubs in a white canvas bag which the nurse was carrying. When Dexter first saw her she was standing by the caddy house, rather ill at ease and trying to conceal the fact by engaging her nurse in an obviously unnatural conversation graced by startling and irrelevant grimaces from herself.

"Well, it's certainly a nice day, Hilda," Dexter heard her say. She drew down the corners of her mouth, smiled, and glanced furtively around, her eyes in transit falling for an instant on Dexter.

Then to the nurse:

"Well, I guess there aren't very many people out here this morning, are there?"

The smile again—radiant, blatantly artificial—convincing.

"I don't know what we're supposed to do now," said the nurse, looking nowhere in particular.

"Oh, that's all right. I'll fix it up."

A Dexter stood perfectly still, his mouth slightly ajar. He knew that if he moved forward a step his stare would be in her line of vision—if he moved backward he would lose his full view of her face. For a moment he had not realized how young she was. Now he remembered having seen her several times the year before—in bloomers.

Suddenly, involuntarily, he laughed, a short abrupt laugh—then, startled by himself, he turned and began to walk quickly away.

B "Boy!"

Dexter stopped.

"Boy——"

Beyond question he was addressed. Not only that, but he was treated to that absurd smile, that preposterous smile—the memory of which at least a dozen men were to carry into middle age.

"Boy, do you know where the golf teacher is?"

"He's giving a lesson."

"Well, do you know where the caddy-master is?"

"He isn't here yet this morning."

"Oh." For a moment this baffled her. She stood alternately on her right and left foot.

"We'd like to get a caddy," said the nurse. "Mrs. Mortimer Jones sent us out to play golf, and we don't know how without we get a caddy."

Here she was stopped by an ominous glance

C

The Lucky Caddy by J. F. Kernan (20th c.). Oil on canvas.

Courtesy American Illustrators Gallery/Judy Goffman Fine Arts, New York City.

A. Characterization

? How does Dexter react to the little girl? (He is fascinated by her. When he realizes the spell, he is embarrassed and tries to break it.)

B. Characterization

? How does Dexter feel when Judy calls him "Boy"? (He is astonished by her condescending attitude.)

C. Humanities Connection: Responding to the Fine Art

? Read through to the end of Section I. Why is this a fitting illustration for this part of the story? (It illustrates Dexter's confusion, shock, and frustration.)

A. Responding
? Does Dexter seek only the objects that represent success? Explain your answer. (No. This passage suggests that there is a core of true idealism in Dexter, which is translated into a longing for the beauty of upper-class life.)

B. Expansion
Dexter's life is in some ways a Horatio Alger story. Alger (1834–1899) wrote more than one hundred books for boys, many of which are about bootblacks or newsboys who earn success through hard work, pluck, and virtue. Alger's name has thus become associated with the American dream: overcoming poverty and achieving success through self-reliance and hard work.
? Is achieving wealth and success difficult for Dexter? (No. He is willing to take risks and to work at his business, but success seems to come easily.)

from Miss Jones, followed immediately by the smile.

"There aren't any caddies here except me," said Dexter to the nurse, "and I got to stay here in charge until the caddy-master gets here."

"Oh."

Miss Jones and her retinue now withdrew, and at a proper distance from Dexter became involved in a heated conversation, which was concluded by Miss Jones taking one of the clubs and hitting it on the ground with violence. For further emphasis she raised it again and was about to bring it down smartly upon the nurse's bosom, when the nurse seized the club and twisted it from her hands.

"You damn little mean old *thing!*" cried Miss Jones wildly.

Another argument ensued. Realizing that the elements of the comedy were implied in the scene, Dexter several times began to laugh, but each time restrained the laugh before it reached audibility. He could not resist the monstrous conviction that the little girl was justified in beating the nurse.

The situation was resolved by the fortuitous[5] appearance of the caddy-master, who was appealed to immediately by the nurse.

"Miss Jones is to have a little caddy, and this one says he can't go."

"Mr. McKenna said I was to wait here till you came," said Dexter quickly.

"Well, he's here now." Miss Jones smiled cheerfully at the caddy-master. Then she dropped her bag and set off at a haughty mince toward the first tee.

"Well?" The caddy-master turned to Dexter. "What you standing there like a dummy for? Go pick up the young lady's clubs."

"I don't think I'll go out today," said Dexter.

"You don't——"

"I think I'll quit."

The enormity of his decision frightened him. He was a favorite caddy, and the thirty dollars a month he earned through the summer were not to be made elsewhere around the lake. But he had received a strong emotional shock, and his perturbation required a violent and immediate outlet.

It is not so simple as that, either. As so frequently would be the case in the future, Dexter was unconsciously dictated to by his winter dreams.

5. **fortuitous** (fôr·to͞o′ə·təs): lucky.

II

Now, of course, the quality and the seasonability of these winter dreams varied, but the stuff of them remained. They persuaded Dexter several years later to pass up a business course at the state university—his father, prospering now, would have paid his way—for the precarious[6] advantage of attending an older and more famous university in the East, where he was bothered by his scanty funds. But do not get the impression, because his winter dreams happened to be concerned at first with musings on the rich, that there was anything merely snobbish in the boy. He wanted not association with glittering things and glittering people—he wanted the glittering things themselves. Often he reached out for the best without knowing why he wanted it—and sometimes he ran up against the mysterious denials and prohibitions in which life indulges. It is with one of those denials and not with his career as a whole that this story deals. A

He made money. It was rather amazing. After college he went to the city from which Black Bear Lake draws its wealthy patrons. When he was only twenty-three and had been there not quite two years, there were already people who liked to say: "Now *there's* a boy—" All about him rich men's sons were peddling bonds precariously, or investing patrimonies[7] precariously, or plodding through the two dozen volumes of the "George Washington Commercial Course," but Dexter borrowed a thousand dollars on his college degree and his confident mouth, and bought a partnership in a laundry. B

It was a small laundry when he went into it but Dexter made a specialty of learning how the English washed fine woollen golf stockings without shrinking them, and within a year he was catering to the trade that wore knickerbockers. Men were insisting that their Shetland hose and sweaters go to his laundry just as they had insisted on a caddy who could find golf balls. A little later he was doing their wives' lingerie as well—and running five branches in different parts of the city. Before he was twenty-seven he owned the largest string of laundries in his section of the country. It was then that he sold out and went to New York. But the part of his story that concerns us goes back

6. **precarious** (prē·ker′ē·əs): risky, uncertain.
7. **patrimonies** (pa′trə·mō′nēz): inheritances.

to the days when he was making his first big success.

When he was twenty-three Mr. Hart—one of the gray-haired men who like to say "Now there's a boy"—gave him a guest card to the Sherry Island Golf Club for a weekend. So he signed his name one day on the register, and that afternoon played golf in a foursome with Mr. Hart and Mr. Sandwood and Mr. T. A. Hedrick. He did not consider it necessary to remark that he had once carried Mr. Hart's bag over this same links, and that he knew every trap and gully with his eyes shut—but he found himself glancing at the four caddies who trailed them, trying to catch a gleam or gesture that would remind him of himself, that would lessen the gap which lay between his present and his past.

It was a curious day, slashed abruptly with fleeting, familiar impressions. One minute he had the sense of being a trespasser—in the next he was impressed by the tremendous superiority he felt toward Mr. T. A. Hedrick, who was a bore and not even a good golfer anymore.

Then, because of a ball Mr. Hart lost near the fifteenth green, an enormous thing happened. While they were searching the stiff grasses of the rough there was a clear call of "Fore!"[8] from behind a hill in their rear. And as they all turned abruptly from their search a bright new ball sliced abruptly over the hill and caught Mr. T. A. Hedrick in the abdomen.

"By Gad!" cried Mr. T. A. Hedrick, "they ought to put some of these crazy women off the course. It's getting to be outrageous."

A head and a voice came up together over the hill:

"Do you mind if we go through?"

"You hit me in the stomach!" declared Mr. Hedrick wildly.

"Did I?" The girl approached the group of men. "I'm sorry. I yelled 'Fore!' "

A

Her glance fell casually on each of the men—then scanned the fairway for her ball.

"Did I bounce into the rough?"

It was impossible to determine whether this question was ingenuous[9] or malicious. In a moment, however, she left no doubt, for as her partner came up over the hill she called cheerfully:

"Here I am! I'd have gone on the green except that I hit something."

8. **Fore!** a warning cry given by a golfer before hitting the ball.
9. **ingenuous** (in·jen'yoo·əs): innocent; without guile.

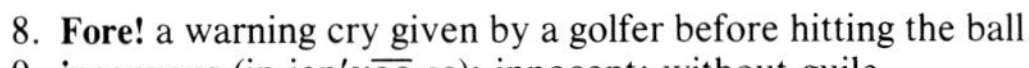

B

Golf or Tennis? by Joseph Christian Leyendecker (1874–1951). Oil on canvas.

Courtesy American Illustrators Gallery/Judy Goffman Fine Arts, New York City.

C

As she took her stance for a short mashie[10] shot, Dexter looked at her closely. She wore a blue gingham dress, rimmed at throat and shoulders with a white edging that accentuated her tan. The quality of exaggeration, of thinness, which had made her passionate eyes and downturning mouth absurd at eleven, was gone now. She was arrestingly beautiful. The color in her cheeks was centered like the color in a picture—it was not a "high" color, but a sort of fluctuating and feverish warmth, so shaded that it seemed at any moment it would recede and disappear. This color and the mobility of her mouth gave a continual impression of flux, of intense life, of passionate vitality—balanced only partially by the sad luxury of her eyes.

10. **mashie:** type of golf club.

A. Characterization

? What does Judy's behavior here suggest about her character? (She is arrogant and self-absorbed yet irresistible in her innocence.)

B. Humanities Connection: About the Fine Art

An annotation on Joseph Christian Leyendecker appears on page 545.

C. Characterization

Compare this description of Judy with that on page 536. Have the youthful hints materialized in the young woman? (Yes. Students should note the similarities between the two descriptions.)

A. Responding

? How do the men evaluate Judy? Why doesn't Dexter voice an opinion? (Mr. Hedrick seems immune to her charms, but Mr. Sandwood finds her very attractive. Dexter is too sharply drawn to her to risk saying something that would betray his emotions.)

B. Expansion

Chin-Chin, The Count of Luxemburg, and *The Chocolate Soldier* were all popular musical shows of the time.

C. Theme

? What kind of mood is Dexter in? (He feels "intense appreciation," in harmony with the world around him.) Is this moment a realization of his winter dreams? (At least partly, yes; he feels himself a part of the beauty and glamour of life.)

She swung her mashie impatiently and without interest, pitching the ball into a sand pit on the other side of the green. With a quick, insincere smile and a careless "Thank you!" she went on after it.

"That Judy Jones!" remarked Mr. Hedrick on the next tee, as they waited—some moments—for her to play on ahead. "All she needs is to be turned up and spanked for six months and then to be married off to an old-fashioned cavalry captain."

"My God, she's good-looking!" said Mr. Sandwood, who was just over thirty.

A "Good-looking!" cried Mr. Hedrick contemptuously, "she always looks as if she wanted to be kissed! Turning those big cow-eyes on every calf in town!"

It was doubtful if Mr. Hedrick intended a reference to the maternal instinct.

"She'd play pretty good golf if she'd try," said Mr. Sandwood.

"She has no form," said Mr. Hedrick solemnly.

"She has a nice figure," said Mr. Sandwood.

"Better thank the Lord she doesn't drive a swifter ball," said Mr. Hart, winking at Dexter.

Later in the afternoon the sun went down with a riotous swirl of gold and varying blues and scarlets, and left the dry, rustling night of Western summer. Dexter watched from the veranda of the Golf Club, watched the even overlap of the waters in the little wind, silver molasses under the harvest moon. Then the moon held a finger to her lips and the lake became a clear pool, pale and quiet. Dexter put on his bathing suit and swam out to the farthest raft, where he stretched dripping on the wet canvas of the springboard.

There was a fish jumping and a star shining and the lights around the lake were gleaming. Over on a dark peninsula a piano was playing the songs of last summer and of summers before that—songs
B from "Chin-Chin" and "The Count of Luxemburg" and "The Chocolate Soldier"—and because the sound of a piano over a stretch of water had always seemed beautiful to Dexter, he lay perfectly quiet and listened.

The tune the piano was playing at that moment had been gay and new five years before when Dexter was a sophomore at college. They had played it at a prom once when he could not afford the luxury of proms, and he had stood outside the gymnasium and listened. The sound of the tune
C precipitated in him a sort of ecstasy and it was with that ecstasy he viewed what happened to him now. It was a mood of intense appreciation, a sense that, for once, he was magnificently attuned to life and that everything about him was radiating a brightness and a glamour he might never know again.

A low, pale oblong detached itself suddenly from the darkness of the island, spitting forth the reverberate sound of a racing motorboat. Two white streamers of cleft water rolled themselves out behind it and almost immediately the boat was beside him, drowning out the hot tinkle of the piano in the drone of its spray. Dexter, raising himself on his arms, was aware of a figure standing at the wheel, of two dark eyes regarding him over the lengthening space of water—then the boat had gone by and was sweeping in an immense and purposeless circle of spray round and round in the middle of the lake. With equal eccentricity one of the circles flattened out and headed back toward the raft.

"Who's that?" she called, shutting off her motor. She was so near now that Dexter could see her bathing suit, which consisted apparently of pink rompers.

The nose of the boat bumped the raft, and as the latter tilted rakishly he was precipitated toward her. With different degrees of interest they recognized each other.

"Aren't you one of those men we played through this afternoon?" she demanded.

He was.

"Well, do you know how to drive a motorboat? Because if you do I wish you'd drive this one so I can ride on the surfboard behind. My name is Judy Jones"—she favored him with an absurd smirk—rather, what tried to be a smirk, for, twist her mouth as she might, it was not grotesque, it was merely beautiful—"and I live in a house over there on the island, and in that house there is a man waiting for me. When he drove up at the door I drove out of the dock because he says I'm his ideal."

There was a fish jumping and a star shining and the lights around the lake were gleaming. Dexter sat beside Judy Jones and she explained how her boat was driven. Then she was in the water, swimming to the floating surfboard with a sinuous[11] crawl. Watching her was without effort to the eye, watching a branch waving or a sea gull flying. Her

11. **sinuous** (sin'yo͞o·əs): curving in and out; snakelike.

Dolphin Bay by William De Leftwich Dodge (c. 1915). Oil on canvas.

Tweed Museum of Art, University of Minnesota, Duluth.

A. Humanities Connection: Responding to the Fine Art
William De Leftwich Dodge (1867–1935) was primarily known as a muralist; his work appears in many important American buildings, including the Library of Congress. When his subject was historical, he researched it meticulously; history and archaeology were two of his lifelong interests. In addition to murals, Dodge also created landscapes, portraits, and book and magazine illustrations, in both watercolor and oil.
? How does this painting mirror Dexter's feelings as Judy swims to him? (Both suggest a promise of romance.)

arms, burned to butternut, moved sinuously among the dull platinum ripples, elbow appearing first, casting the forearm back with a cadence of falling water, then reaching out and down, stabbing a path ahead.

They moved out into the lake; turning, Dexter

A. Characterization
? Compare this passage to paragraph 2 on page 539, where Dexter feels both superior and like a trespasser. What do these passages reveal about his self-image? (He acknowledges his own accomplishments but realizes they are not enough to gain him full entry into the world he yearns for.)

B. Expansion
Fitzgerald extensively mined his own experiences for his fiction, sometimes using actual conversations and passages from letters. He and his wife Zelda, also a writer, fought over who had the "right" to use episodes from their marriage in their writing. Here, Fitzgerald may be recalling his own mother, who often embarrassed him with her odd dress and behavior.

C. Motivation
? Why does Dexter conceal his actual home? (A home in Black Bear Village would emphasize the social distance between himself and the lake residents. Keeble is far enough away to be anonymous.)

D. Characterization
? Is Judy exaggerating, or is she speaking literally? Is she a cruel flirt or simply a youthful romantic? (Answers will vary. Since Fitzgerald's portrait of Judy is sympathetic, most students will see her comments as exaggeration based on her romantic nature.)

saw that she was kneeling on the low rear of the now uptilted surfboard.

"Go faster," she called, "fast as it'll go."

Obediently he jammed the lever forward and the white spray mounted at the bow. When he looked around again the girl was standing up on the rushing board, her arms spread wide, her eyes lifted toward the moon.

"It's awful cold," she shouted. "What's your name?"

He told her.

"Well, why don't you come to dinner tomorrow night?"

His heart turned over like the flywheel of the boat, and, for the second time, her casual whim gave a new direction to his life.

III

Next evening while he waited for her to come downstairs, Dexter peopled the soft deep summer room and the sun porch that opened from it with the men who had already loved Judy Jones. He knew the sort of men they were—the men who when he first went to college had entered from the great prep schools with graceful clothes and the deep tan of healthy summers. He had seen that, in one sense, he was better than these men. He was newer and stronger. Yet in acknowledging to himself that he wished his children to be like them he was admitting that he was but the rough, strong stuff from which they eternally sprang. A

When the time had come for him to wear good clothes, he had known who were the best tailors in America, and the best tailors in America had made him the suit he wore this evening. He had acquired that particular reserve peculiar to his university, that set it off from other universities. He recognized the value to him of such a mannerism and he had adopted it; he knew that to be careless in dress and manner required more confidence than to be careful. But carelessness was for his children. His mother's name had been Krimslich. She was a Bohemian of the peasant class and she had talked broken English to the end of her days. Her son must keep to the set patterns. B

At a little after seven Judy Jones came downstairs. She wore a blue silk afternoon dress, and he was disappointed at first that she had not put on something more elaborate. This feeling was accentuated when, after a brief greeting, she went to the door of a butler's pantry and pushing it open called: "You can serve dinner, Martha." He had rather expected that a butler would announce dinner, that there would be a cocktail. Then he put these thoughts behind him as they sat down side by side on a lounge and looked at each other.

"Father and mother won't be here," she said thoughtfully.

He remembered the last time he had seen her father, and he was glad the parents were not to be here tonight—they might wonder who he was. He had been born in Keeble, a Minnesota village fifty miles farther north, and he always gave Keeble as his home instead of Black Bear Village. Country towns were well enough to come from if they weren't inconveniently in sight and used as footstools by fashionable lakes. C

They talked of his university, which she had visited frequently during the past two years, and of the nearby city which supplied Sherry Island with its patrons, and whither Dexter would return next day to his prospering laundries.

During dinner she slipped into a moody depression, which gave Dexter a feeling of uneasiness. Whatever petulance she uttered in her throaty voice worried him. Whatever she smiled at—at him, at a chicken liver, at nothing—it disturbed him that her smile could have no root in mirth, or even in amusement. When the scarlet corners of her lips curved down, it was less a smile than an invitation to a kiss.

Then, after dinner, she led him out on the dark sun porch and deliberately changed the atmosphere.

"Do you mind if I weep a little?" she said.

"I'm afraid I'm boring you," he responded quickly.

"You're not. I like you. But I've just had a terrible afternoon. There was a man I cared about, and this afternoon he told me out of a clear sky that he was poor as a church mouse. He'd never even hinted it before. Does this sound horribly mundane[12]?"

"Perhaps he was afraid to tell you."

"Suppose he was," she answered. "He didn't start right. You see, if I'd thought of him as poor—well, I've been mad about loads of poor men, and fully intended to marry them all. But in this case, D

12. **mundane** (mun′dān′): everyday, commonplace.

I hadn't thought of him that way, and my interest in him wasn't strong enough to survive the shock. As if a girl calmly informed her fiancé that she was a widow. He might not object to widows, but——

"Let's start right," she interrupted herself suddenly. "Who are you, anyhow?"

For a moment Dexter hesitated. Then:

A "I'm nobody," he announced. "My career is largely a matter of futures."

"Are you poor?"

"No," he said frankly, "I'm probably making more money than any man my age in the Northwest. I know that's an obnoxious remark, but you advised me to start right."

There was a pause. Then she smiled and the corners of her mouth drooped and an almost imperceptible sway brought her closer to him, looking up into his eyes. A lump rose in Dexter's throat, and he waited breathless for the experiment, facing the unpredictable compound that would form mysteriously from the elements of their lips. Then he saw—she communicated her excitement to him, lavishly, deeply, with kisses that were not a promise but a fulfillment. They aroused in him not hunger demanding renewal but surfeit that would demand more surfeit . . . kisses that were like charity, creating want by holding back nothing at all.

It did not take him many hours to decide that he had wanted Judy Jones ever since he was a proud, desirous little boy.

IV

It began like that—and continued, with varying shades of intensity, on such a note right up to the dénouement.[13] Dexter surrendered a part B of himself to the most direct and unprincipled personality with which he had ever come in contact. Whatever Judy wanted, she went after with the full pressure of her charm. There was no divergence of method, no jockeying for position or premeditation of effects—there was a very little mental side to any of her affairs. She simply made men conscious to the highest degree of her physical loveliness. Dexter had no desire to change her. Her deficiencies were knit up with a passionate energy that transcended and justified them.

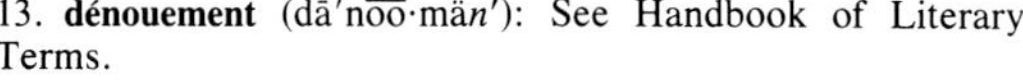

13. **dénouement** (dā′no͞o·män′): See Handbook of Literary Terms.

A. Responding

? What does Dexter mean when he says his career is "a matter of futures"? (He does not work in a family business or have family money, but he has a promising future that he is creating himself.)

B. Characterization

? Here the narrator says outright that Judy is unprincipled. Does this declaration confirm or challenge your own opinion of her? (Answers will vary. This comment will confirm the negative view that some students have of Judy, while others will see it as a challenge to their positive view of her character.) Why doesn't Dexter want to change her? (Judy as she is—lovely and confident, defining her own life without regard to others—is what he sees as glamorous and vital.)

A. Responding
Why does Dexter put up with Judy's behavior? Why do all the other young men do so? (Dexter and the rest of Judy's suitors endure her toying with them because they find her irresistible and hope that she will finally reject the rest of the pack to choose one of them.)

B. Interpretation
What does the narrator mean when he says that Judy says nothing? (Her answers come so glibly that they cannot be taken seriously.)

C. Theme
Have Dexter's dreams changed? (Dexter has by now achieved material success, but the actual fulfillment of his dreams lies with Judy.)

When, as Judy's head lay against his shoulder that first night, she whispered, "I don't know what's the matter with me. Last night I thought I was in love with a man and tonight I think I'm in love with you——"—it seemed to him a beautiful and romantic thing to say. It was the exquisite excitability that for the moment he controlled and owned. But a week later he was compelled to view this same quality in a different light. She took him in her roadster to a picnic supper, and after supper she disappeared, likewise in her roadster, with another man. Dexter became enormously upset and was scarcely able to be decently civil to the other people present. When she assured him that she had not kissed the other man, he knew she was lying—yet he was glad that she had taken the trouble to lie to him.

A He was, as he found before the summer ended, one of a varying dozen who circulated about her. Each of them had at one time been favored above all others—about half of them still basked in the solace of occasional sentimental revivals. Whenever one showed signs of dropping out through long neglect, she granted him a brief honeyed hour, which encouraged him to tag along for a year or so longer. Judy made these forays[14] upon the helpless and defeated without malice, indeed half unconscious that there was anything mischievous in what she did.

When a new man came to town everyone dropped out—dates were automatically canceled.

The helpless part of trying to do anything about it was that she did it all herself. She was not a girl who could be "won" in the kinetic[15] sense—she was proof against cleverness, she was proof against charm; if any of these assailed her too strongly she would immediately resolve the affair to a physical basis, and under the magic of her physical splendor the strong as well as the brilliant played her game and not their own. She was entertained only by the gratification of her desires and by the direct exercise of her own charm. Perhaps from so much youthful love, so many youthful lovers, she had come, in self-defense, to nourish herself wholly from within.

Succeeding Dexter's first exhilaration came restlessness and dissatisfaction. The helpless ecstasy of losing himself in her was opiate[16] rather than tonic. It was fortunate for his work during the winter that those moments of ecstasy came infrequently. Early in their acquaintance it had seemed for a while that there was a deep and spontaneous mutual attraction—that first August, for example—three days of long evenings on her dusky veranda, of strange wan kisses through the late afternoon, in shadowy alcoves or behind the protecting trellises of the garden arbors, of mornings when she was fresh as a dream and almost shy at meeting him in the clarity of the rising day. There was all the ecstasy of an engagement about it, sharpened by his realization that there was no engagement. It was during those three days that, for the first time, he had asked her to marry him. She said "maybe some day," she said "kiss me," she said "I'd like to marry you," she said "I love you"—she said—nothing. B

The three days were interrupted by the arrival of a New York man who visited at her house for half September. To Dexter's agony, rumor engaged them. The man was the son of the president of a great trust company. But at the end of a month it was reported that Judy was yawning. At a dance one night she sat all evening in a motorboat with a local beau, while the New Yorker searched the club for her frantically. She told the local beau that she was bored with her visitor, and two days later he left. She was seen with him at the station, and it was reported that he looked very mournful indeed.

On this note the summer ended. Dexter was twenty-four, and he found himself increasingly in a position to do as he wished. He joined two clubs in the city and lived at one of them. Though he was by no means an integral part of the stag lines[17] at these clubs, he managed to be on hand at dances where Judy Jones was likely to appear. He could have gone out socially as much as he liked—he was an eligible young man, now, and popular with downtown fathers. His confessed devotion to Judy Jones had rather solidified his position. But he had no social aspirations and rather despised the dancing men who were always on tap for the Thursday or Saturday parties and who filled in at dinners with the younger married set. Already he was playing with the idea of going East to New York. He wanted to take Judy Jones with him. No C

14. **forays** (fôr′āz): looting raids.
15. **kinetic** (ki·net′ik): coming about through action or energy.
16. **opiate** (ō′pē·it): having a calming effect.
17. **stag lines:** unaccompanied men at a dance waiting in line for available dance partners.

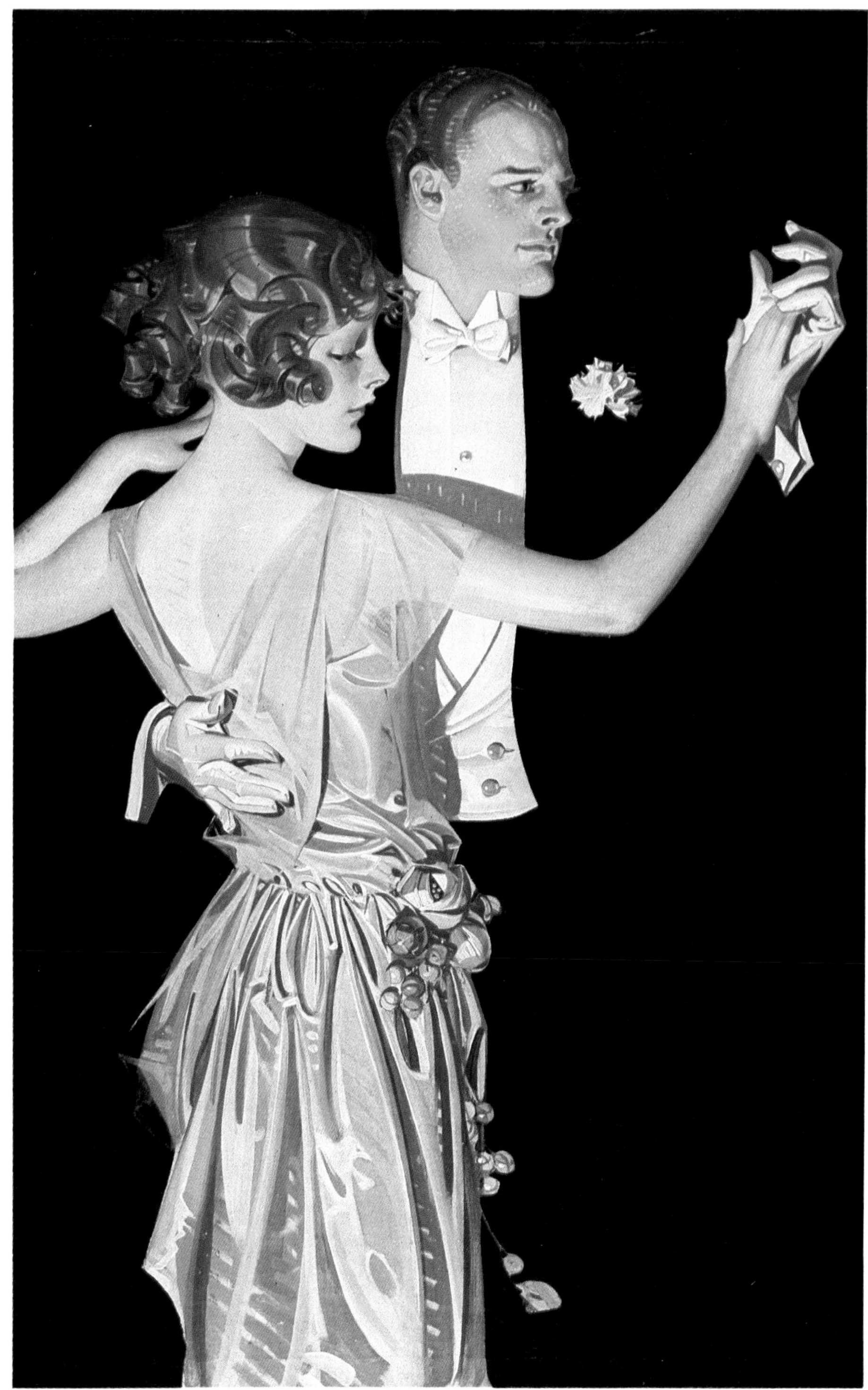

Dancing Couple by Joseph Christian Leyendecker (1913).

Reprinted with the permission of Cluett, Peabody & Co., Inc., manufacturer of Arrow Shirts.

Humanities Connection: Responding to the Fine Art

Joseph Christian Leyendecker (1874–1951), whose family immigrated to America from Germany when he was nine, created a rich lode of Americana in his illustrations for magazine covers, advertising campaigns, and posters. He produced more than three hundred covers for the *Saturday Evening Post,* including a series of cherubic babies immortalized as New Year's symbols. The handsome, immaculately dressed, debonair young man Leyendecker created in his ads for Arrow Shirts became synonymous with the product itself. Leyendecker's distinctive style emphasizes free brushstrokes and strong outlines.

? Does the lifestyle depicted in this picture seem attainable for Dexter? (Yes.)

A. Theme

Is Judy a worthy object of Dexter's idealism? (Students who value Judy's glittering beauty and desirability will see her as worthy. Those who concentrate on her arrogance and erratic behavior will not. Later, students may note that at the end of the story, when Dexter does lose his illusions about Judy, his general disillusionment grows more profound.) Why does the narrator urge us to remember this sentence? (To stress its importance)

B. Responding

In earlier days, access to the "finer things"—books, music, art—differentiated the upper class from the rest of society. Is that still the case? (Some students may argue that the fine arts—especially opera and theater—are still beyond the reach of most Americans. Others may suggest that public television has brought culture to the masses.)

C. Theme

What does Dexter imagine his future with Irene will be like? What will be missing? (He imagines a calm, orderly, contented life, but charm, glamour, and beauty will be missing.) How do the last two sentences of this paragraph hint at what is coming? (Dexter seems to be rebelling at the picture of his future that he has conjured up.)

A disillusion as to the world in which she had grown up could cure his illusion as to her desirability.

Remember that—for only in the light of it can what he did for her be understood.

Eighteen months after he first met Judy Jones he became engaged to another girl. Her name was Irene Scheerer, and her father was one of the men who had always believed in Dexter. Irene was light-haired and sweet and honorable, and a little stout, and she had two suitors whom she pleasantly relinquished when Dexter formally asked her to marry him.

Summer, fall, winter, spring, another summer, another fall—so much he had given of his active life to the incorrigible[18] lips of Judy Jones. She had treated him with interest, with encouragement, with malice, with indifference, with contempt. She had inflicted on him the innumerable little slights and indignities possible in such a case—as if in revenge for having ever cared for him at all. She had beckoned him and yawned at him and beckoned him again and he had responded often with bitterness and narrowed eyes. She had brought him ecstatic happiness and intolerable agony of spirit. She had caused him untold inconvenience and not a little trouble. She had insulted him, and she had ridden over him, and she had played his interest in her against his interest in his work—for fun. She had done everything to him except to criticize him—this she had not done—it seemed to him only because it might have sullied the utter indifference she manifested and sincerely felt toward him.

When autumn had come and gone again it occurred to him that he could not have Judy Jones. He had to beat this into his mind but he convinced himself at last. He lay awake at night for a while and argued it over. He told himself the trouble and the pain she had caused him, he enumerated her glaring deficiencies as a wife. Then he said to himself that he loved her, and after a while he fell asleep. For a week, lest he imagined her husky voice over the telephone or her eyes opposite him at lunch, he worked hard and late, and at night he went to his office and plotted out his years.

At the end of a week he went to a dance and cut in on her once. For almost the first time since they had met he did not ask her to sit out with him or tell her that she was lovely. It hurt him that she did not miss these things—that was all. He was not jealous when he saw that there was a new man tonight. He had been hardened against jealousy long before.

He stayed late at the dance. He sat for an hour with Irene Scheerer and talked about books and about music. He knew very little about either. But he was beginning to be master of his own time now, and he had a rather priggish notion that he—the young and already fabulously successful Dexter Green—should know more about such things. B

That was in October, when he was twenty-five. In January, Dexter and Irene became engaged. It was to be announced in June, and they were to be married three months later.

The Minnesota winter prolonged itself interminably, and it was almost May when the winds came soft and the snow ran down into Black Bear Lake at last. For the first time in over a year Dexter was enjoying a certain tranquillity of spirit. Judy Jones had been in Florida, and afterward in Hot Springs, and somewhere she had been engaged, and somewhere she had broken it off. At first, when Dexter had definitely given her up, it had made him sad that people still linked them together and asked for news of her, but when he began to be placed at dinner next to Irene Scheerer people didn't ask him about her anymore—they told him about her. He ceased to be an authority on her.

May at last. Dexter walked the streets at night when the darkness was damp as rain, wondering that so soon, with so little done, so much of ecstasy had gone from him. May one year back had been marked by Judy's poignant, unforgivable, yet forgiven turbulence—it had been one of those rare times when he fancied she had grown to care for him. That old penny's worth of happiness he had spent for this bushel of content. He knew that Irene would be no more than a curtain spread behind him, a hand moving among gleaming teacups, a voice calling to children . . . fire and loveliness were gone, the magic of nights and the wonder of the varying hours and seasons . . . slender lips, downturning, dropping to his lips and bearing him up into a heaven of eyes. . . . The thing was deep in him. He was too strong and alive for it to die lightly. C

In the middle of May when the weather balanced for a few days on the thin bridge that led to deep summer he turned in one night at Irene's

18. **incorrigible** (in·kôr′ə·jə·bəl): unable to reform.

house. Their engagement was to be announced in a week now—no one would be surprised at it. And tonight they would sit together on the lounge at the University Club and look on for an hour at the dancers. It gave him a sense of solidity to go with her—she was so sturdily popular, so intensely "great."

He mounted the steps of the brownstone house and stepped inside.

"Irene," he called.

Mrs. Scheerer came out of the living room to meet him.

"Dexter," she said, "Irene's gone upstairs with a splitting headache. She wanted to go with you but I made her go to bed."

"Nothing serious, I——"

"Oh, no. She's going to play golf with you in the morning. You can spare her for just one night, can't you, Dexter?"

Her smile was kind. She and Dexter liked each other. In the living room he talked for a moment before he said good night.

Returning to the University Club, where he had rooms, he stood in the doorway for a moment and watched the dancers. He leaned against the door post, nodded at a man or two—yawned.

"Hello, darling."

The familiar voice at his elbow startled him. Judy Jones had left a man and crossed the room to him—Judy Jones, a slender enameled doll in
A cloth of gold: gold in a band at her head, gold in two slipper points at her dress's hem. The fragile glow of her face seemed to blossom as she smiled at him. A breeze of warmth and light blew through the room. His hands in the pockets of his dinner jacket tightened spasmodically. He was filled with a sudden excitement.

"When did you get back?" he asked casually.

"Come here and I'll tell you about it."

She turned and he followed her. She had been away—he could have wept at the wonder of her return. She had passed through enchanted streets, doing things that were like provocative music. All mysterious happenings, all fresh and quickening hopes, had gone away with her, come back with her now.

She turned in the doorway.

"Have you a car here? If you haven't, I have."

"I have a coupé."

In then, with a rustle of golden cloth. He slammed the door. Into so many cars she had stepped—like this—like that—her back against the leather, so—her elbow resting on the door—waiting. She would have been soiled long since had there been anything to soil her—except herself—but this was her own self outpouring.

With an effort he forced himself to start the car and back into the street. This was nothing, he must remember. She had done this before, and he had put her behind him, as he would have crossed a bad account from his books.

He drove slowly downtown and, affecting abstraction, traversed the deserted streets of the business section, peopled here and there where a movie was giving out its crowd or where consumptive[19] or pugilistic youth lounged in front of pool halls. The clink of glasses and the slap of hands on the bars issued from saloons, cloisters of glazed glass and dirty yellow light.

She was watching him closely and the silence was embarrassing, yet in this crisis he could find no casual word with which to profane the hour. At a convenient turning he began to zigzag back toward the University Club.

"Have you missed me?" she asked suddenly.

"Everybody missed you."

He wondered if she knew of Irene Scheerer. She had been back only a day—her absence had been almost contemporaneous with his engagement.

"What a remark!" Judy laughed sadly—without sadness. She looked at him searchingly. He became absorbed in the dashboard.

"You're handsomer than you used to be," she said thoughtfully. "Dexter, you have the most rememberable eyes."

He could have laughed at this, but he did not laugh. It was the sort of thing that was said to sophomores. Yet it stabbed at him.

"I'm awfully tired of everything, darling." She called everyone darling, endowing the endearment with careless, individual comradery. "I wish you'd marry me."

The directness of this confused him. He should have told her now that he was going to marry another girl, but he could not tell her. He could as easily have sworn that he had never loved her.

"I think we'd get along," she continued, on the same note, "unless probably you've forgotten me and fallen in love with another girl."

19. **consumptive** (kən·sump′tiv): wasteful and destructive.

A. Symbol

? Why is Judy pictured all in gold? (The color symbolizes Dexter's dreams, his own Golden Fleece—the wealth he longed for, achieved, and found wanting. It also symbolizes the still-elusive goal of Judy herself and the glamour of life that she represents.)

A. Motivation
? Why does Judy make a renewed play for Dexter? (This comment suggests that she wants to test her power to get Dexter back.)

B. Theme
? When students finish reading, have them come back to this page. Based on the story's ending, what is ironic about Judy's promise here? (She promises Dexter the beauty he longs for—but that is precisely what she will lose. And when she does, Dexter will lose his ideal of beauty.)

C. Characterization
? Does the narrator sympathize with Dexter, or does he consider him a fool for falling for Judy's trick? (The narrator sympathizes with Dexter. Here and elsewhere, he comments on Dexter's essential strength and worth.)

Her confidence was obviously enormous. She had said, in effect, that she found such a thing impossible to believe, that if it were true he had merely committed a childish indiscretion—and probably to show off. She would forgive him, because it was not a matter of any moment but rather something to be brushed aside lightly.

"Of course you could never love anybody but me," she continued. "I like the way you love me. Oh, Dexter, have you forgotten last year?"

"No, I haven't forgotten."

"Neither have I!"

Was she sincerely moved—or was she carried along by the wave of her own acting?

A "I wish we could be like that again," she said, and he forced himself to answer:

"I don't think we can."

"I suppose not. . . . I hear you're giving Irene Scheerer a violent rush."

There was not the faintest emphasis on the name, yet Dexter was suddenly ashamed.

"Oh, take me home," cried Judy suddenly; "I don't want to go back to that idiotic dance—with those children."

Then, as he turned up the street that led to the residence district, Judy began to cry quietly to herself. He had never seen her cry before.

The dark street lightened, the dwellings of the rich loomed up around them, he stopped his coupé in front of the great white bulk of the Mortimer Joneses house, somnolent, gorgeous, drenched with the splendor of the damp moonlight. Its solidity startled him. The strong walls, the steel of the girders, the breadth and beam and pomp of it were there only to bring out the contrast with the young beauty beside him. It was sturdy to accentuate her slightness—as if to show what a breeze could be generated by a butterfly's wing.

He sat perfectly quiet, his nerves in wild clamor, afraid that if he moved he would find her irresistibly in his arms. Two tears had rolled down her wet face and trembled on her upper lip.

B "I'm more beautiful than anybody else," she said brokenly, "why can't I be happy?" Her moist eyes tore at his stability—her mouth turned slowly downward with an exquisite sadness: "I'd like to marry you if you'll have me, Dexter. I suppose you think I'm not worth having, but I'll be so beautiful for you, Dexter."

A million phrases of anger, pride, passion, hatred, tenderness fought on his lips. Then a perfect wave of emotion washed over him, carrying off with it a sediment of wisdom, of convention, of doubt, of honor. This was his girl who was speaking, his own, his beautiful, his pride.

"Won't you come in?" He heard her draw in her breath sharply.

Waiting.

"All right," his voice was trembling, "I'll come in."

V

It was strange that neither when it was over nor a long time afterward did he regret that night. Looking at it from the perspective of ten years, the fact that Judy's flare for him endured just one month seemed of little importance. Nor did it matter that by his yielding he subjected himself to a deeper agony in the end and gave serious hurt to Irene Scheerer and to Irene's parents, who had befriended him. There was nothing sufficiently pictorial about Irene's grief to stamp itself on his mind.

Dexter was at bottom hard-minded. The attitude of the city on his action was of no importance to him, not because he was going to leave the city, but because any outside attitude on the situation seemed superficial. He was completely indifferent to popular opinion. Nor, when he had seen that it was no use, that he did not possess in himself the power to move fundamentally or to hold Judy Jones, did he bear any malice toward her. He loved her, and he would love her until the day he was too old for loving—but he could not have her. So he tasted the deep pain that is reserved only for the strong, just as he had tasted for a little while the deep happiness. C

Even the ultimate falsity of the grounds upon which Judy terminated the engagement that she did not want to "take him away" from Irene—Judy, who had wanted nothing else—did not revolt him. He was beyond any revulsion or any amusement.

He went East in February with the intention of selling out his laundries and settling in New York—but the war came to America in March and changed his plans. He returned to the West, handed over the management of the business to his partner, and went into the first officers' training camp in late April. He was one of those young thousands who greeted the war with a certain amount of relief, welcoming the liberation from webs of tangled emotion.

CLOSURE

Ask students to state the theme of "Winter Dreams" in a sentence or two. Then ask them if they believe this theme applies to the comments they expressed in their prereading journals.

READING CHECK TEST

1. Dexter first sees Judy at **(a)** the lake, **(b)** the golf course, or **(c)** a dance. *b*
2. The business that makes Dexter wealthy is **(a)** stocks and bonds, **(b)** a boat-rental shop, or **(c)** a string of laundries. *c*
3. When he next sees Judy, she is **(a)** in a boat, **(b)** on the golf course, or **(c)** at a dinner. *b*
4. Dexter's courtship of Judy finally ends when **(a)** she drops him, **(b)** he drops her, or **(c)** they get married. *a*
5. When Dexter hears of her again, she is **(a)** playing golf, **(b)** in college, or **(c)** married with children. *c*

VI

This story is not his biography, remember, although things creep into it which have nothing to do with those dreams he had when he was young. We are almost done with them and with him now. There is only one more incident to be related here, and it happens seven years farther on.

It took place in New York, where he had done well—so well that there were no barriers too high for him. He was thirty-two years old, and, except for one flying trip immediately after the war, he had not been West in seven years. A man named Devlin from Detroit came into his office to see him in a business way, and then and there this incident occurred, and closed out, so to speak, this particular side of his life.

A "So you're from the Middle West," said the
man Devlin with careless curiosity. "That's
funny—I thought men like you were probably
B born and raised on Wall Street. You know—wife
of one of my best friends in Detroit came from
your city. I was an usher at the wedding."

Dexter waited with no apprehension of what was coming.

"Judy Simms," said Devlin with no particular interest; "Judy Jones she was once."

"Yes, I knew her." A dull impatience spread over him. He had heard, of course, that she was married—perhaps deliberately he had heard no more.

"Awfully nice girl," brooded Devlin meaninglessly, "I'm sort of sorry for her."

"Why?" Something in Dexter was alert, receptive, at once.

"Oh, Lud Simms has gone to pieces in a way. I don't mean he ill-uses her, but he drinks and runs around——"

"Doesn't she run around?"

"No. Stays at home with her kids."

"Oh."

"She's a little too old for him," said Devlin.

"Too old!" cried Dexter. "Why, man, she's only twenty-seven."

He was possessed with a wild notion of rushing out into the streets and taking a train to Detroit. He rose to his feet spasmodically.

"I guess you're busy," Devlin apologized quickly. "I didn't realize——"

"No, I'm not busy," said Dexter, steadying his voice. "I'm not busy at all. Not busy at all. Did you say she was—twenty-seven? No, I said she was twenty-seven."

Wall Street, New York City.

"Yes, you did," agreed Devlin dryly.

"Go on, then. Go on."

"What do you mean?"

"About Judy Jones."

Devlin looked at him helplessly.

"Well, that's—I told you all there is to it. He treats her like the devil. Oh, they're not going to get divorced or anything. When he's particularly outrageous she forgives him. In fact, I'm inclined to think she loves him. She was a pretty girl when she first came to Detroit."

A. Irony

? What is ironic about Devlin's comment? (Dexter feels himself a trespasser in the world of the rich, yet another outsider sees him as fully part of it.)

B. Expansion

New York City's Wall Street is the home of the stock exchange and thus often associated with the rich and powerful. Tom Wolfe's 1987 novel *The Bonfire of the Vanities* is a biting satire about its corrupting influence.

Connections

In "The Snows of Kilimanjaro," Ernest Hemingway made this reference to his friend Fitzgerald: "He thought they [the very rich] were a special glamorous race and when he found they weren't it wrecked him just as much as any other thing that wrecked him." Ask students to apply this comment to Dexter Green.

ANALYZING THE STORY
Identifying Facts
1. Dexter refuses to caddy for a wealthy, arrogant little girl who wants to play golf.
2. Dexter is playing golf with men he used to caddy for. Still arrogant, Judy plays through.
3. During another chance encounter, Judy says she wants to marry Dexter. He succumbs, putting aside wisdom, doubt, and honor.

The fling lasts only a month, but Dexter does not regret it; even ten years later, his own agony and the hurt suffered by Irene and her family seem unimportant to him.
4. Judy marries Lud Simms, a drinker and an unfaithful husband.

According to a friend of the couple, Judy is a nice girl, but she has lost her looks and seems to devote herself to her husband and children. Devlin doesn't know what Lud sees in Judy but believes she loves him.
5. He has lost his dream, his romantic, youthful ideal.

Interpreting Meanings
6. As a boy Dexter dreams of success. Later he attends a prestigious eastern

A. Characterization
Twenty-seven-year-old Judy is very different from her younger self. What brought about these changes? Are they believable? (The change in her appearance could be the result of disappointment in a sour marriage or natural aging. It seems likely that she would not be as stunningly beautiful as she ages.)

A pretty girl! The phrase struck Dexter as ludicrous.

A "Isn't she—a pretty girl, anymore?"

"Oh, she's all right."

"Look here," said Dexter, sitting down suddenly, "I don't understand. You say she was a 'pretty girl' and now you say she's 'all right.' I don't understand what you mean—Judy Jones wasn't a pretty girl, at all. She was a great beauty. Why, I knew her, I knew her. She was——"

Devlin laughed pleasantly.

"I'm not trying to start a row," he said. "I think Judy's a nice girl and I like her. I can't understand how a man like Lud Simms could fall madly in love with her, but he did." Then he added: "Most of the women like her."

Dexter looked closely at Devlin, thinking wildly that there must be a reason for this, some insensitivity in the man or some private malice.

"Lots of women fade just like *that,*" Devlin snapped his fingers. "You must have seen it happen. Perhaps I've forgotten how pretty she was at her wedding. I've seen her so much since then, you see. She has nice eyes."

A sort of dullness settled down upon Dexter. For the first time in his life he felt like getting very drunk. He knew that he was laughing loudly at something Devlin had said, but he did not know what it was or why it was funny. When, in a few minutes, Devlin went he lay down on his lounge and looked out the window at the New York skyline into which the sun was sinking in dull lovely shades of pink and gold.

He had thought that having nothing else to lose he was invulnerable at last—but he knew that he had just lost something more, as surely as if he had married Judy Jones and seen her fade away before his eyes.

The dream was gone. Something had been taken from him. In a sort of panic he pushed the palms of his hands into his eyes and tried to bring up a picture of the waters lapping on Sherry Island and the moonlit veranda, and gingham on the golf links and the dry sun and the gold color of her neck's soft down. And her mouth damp to his kisses and her eyes plaintive with melancholy and her freshness like new fine linen in the morning. Why, these things were no longer in the world! They had existed and they existed no longer.

For the first time in years the tears were streaming down his face. But they were for himself now. He did not care about mouth and eyes and moving hands. He wanted to care, and he could not care. For he had gone away and he could never go back anymore. The gates were closed, the sun was gone down, and there was no beauty but the gray beauty of steel that withstands all time. Even the grief he could have borne was left behind in the country of illusion, of youth, of the richness of life, where his winter dreams had flourished.

"Long ago," he said, "long ago, there was something in me, but now that thing is gone. Now that thing is gone, that thing is gone. I cannot cry. I cannot care. That thing will come back no more."

Responding to the Story

Analyzing the Story

Identifying Facts

1. What incident leads to Dexter's resignation from his position as a caddy at the golf club?
2. How does Dexter encounter Judy again after nearly a decade?
3. Why does Dexter break his engagement with Irene? Is he sorry later?
4. Whom does Judy end up marrying? What do we learn at the end of the story about her and her marriage?
5. What has Dexter realized he has lost at the end of the story?

Interpreting Meanings

6. What details does Fitzgerald use to persuade the reader that Dexter is an ambitious young man? How do Dexter's actions conform to what the narrator and other characters say about him?
7. In *King Richard III,* Shakespeare refers to "the winter of our discontent." How do Dexter's "winter

university and after graduation is more daring than his contemporaries.

Mr. Jones and Mr. Hart see promise in Dexter; he fulfills their expectations by achieving great success with his laundry business.

7. In winter Dexter dreams of wealth, a "rich man's" athletic skills, and hobnobbing with the wealthy.

Even after he is successful, Dexter feels like a trespasser in the world of the wealthy.

8. Judy represents the beauty and glamour of life and the ease, carelessness, and confidence of the wealthy. Some students may feel Dexter really loves Judy; others may argue that he rather loves what she represents.

9. Answers will vary, but students should deal with Judy's erratic personality and Dexter's reaction to her loss of beauty.

10. The urgency of Dexter's ambitions and his working-class background make him more willing to take risks and to actually involve himself in business.

Dexter wants his children to have what he cannot: an innate sense of belonging to the upper class.

11. Answers will vary, but encourage students to review the discussion of the American Dream on pages 495–496 and the biographical information about Fitzgerald on pages 533–534.

12. Dexter saw Judy as the embodiment of his ideals about the romance and beauty of life. Her loss of beauty signals the irretrievable loss of his youth and "the riches of life." With the death of his idealism, he faces his own mortality.

dreams" reflect his discontent? Does his sense of deprivation subside when he fulfills his ambition to become rich? Explain.

8. When they meet again as adults, Dexter decides that he has "wanted Judy Jones ever since he was a proud, desirous little boy" (page 543). What does Judy represent to Dexter? Explain why you think he really does—or does not—love her.
9. Do you think Dexter would have been happier in the end if Judy had married him? Discuss your responses.
10. What makes Dexter "newer and stronger" (page 542) than the wealthy people he meets? Why, then, does he want his children to be like them?
11. One **theme** of the story is the pursuit of the "American Dream." After reading the story, tell what you think Fitzgerald saw as the "American Dream." Be sure to include Dexter's quest for Judy as part of your answer.
12. Why does Dexter feel a profound sense of loss when he hears about Judy at the end of the story?

Writing About the Story

A Creative Response

1. **Using Another Point of View.** Imagine that you are eleven-year-old Judy Jones and have just met Dexter Green on the golf course for the first time. Write a diary entry describing the encounter. What did he look like? act like? How was he dressed? Did you like him or dislike him? Why?

A Critical Response

2. **Analyzing Characterization.** Sometimes there is evidence within a story that explains a character's personality. At other times, you have to bring to bear your own experience to understand a character's motives. Write an analysis of Judy Jones's character. Before you write, use both the story and your experience to answer these questions: How was Judy a flirt? Was she in love with all her suitors equally, or was she not in love with any of them? To what extent was she trying to control or manipulate her boyfriends? Did she merely want to be the center of attention? Did she enjoy making her boyfriends jealous? How badly were the feelings of her various boyfriends hurt? Did she intend to hurt anyone? Was she selfish in wanting to keep so many boyfriends? Do you think her renewed interest in Dexter was influenced by the fact that he was getting engaged to Irene Scheerer? What behavior, if any, can be attributed to Judy's social status and wealth?
3. **Responding to a Critic.** In a book review of Fitzgerald's stories, novelist Jay McInerney wrote the following:

> . . . the young (poor) boy's quest for the hand of the beautiful, rich princess is undoubtedly Fitzgerald's best plot, the fairy-tale skeleton of his jazz age tales. One supposes that magazine editors preferred the stories in which the quest is successful, but in the better ones, like "Winter Dreams" (1922) and " 'The Sensible Thing' " (1924), the success is qualified or the quest ends in failure.
>
> —Jay McInerney

Write a brief essay in which you analyze the ways in which "Winter Dreams" is like and unlike a fairy tale. Consider the story's **plot, atmosphere,** and evocation of **feeling.** Be sure to cite specifically how it deviates from the fairy-tale formula (aside from the fact that the quest does not succeed).

Analyzing Language and Style

Paradox

A **paradox** is a seemingly contradictory statement which may, upon closer inspection, prove to illuminate a deeper truth. F. Scott Fitzgerald uses paradox frequently in "Winter Dreams," particularly in his descriptions of Judy Jones. For example:

"The smile again—radiant, blatantly artificial—convincing." (page 536)

". . . kisses that were like charity, creating want by holding back nothing at all." (page 543)

Find three more paradoxical descriptions of Judy's behavior. How does this method of phrasing help convey the enigmatic complexity Dexter perceives in her?

551

Primary Sources
A Letter to His Daughter

August 8, 1933
La Paix, Rodgers' Forge,
Towson, Maryland,

"Dear Pie:

"I feel very strongly about you doing duty. Would you give me a little more documentation about your reading in French? I am glad you are happy—but I never believe much in happiness. I never believe in misery either. Those are things you see on the stage or the screen or the printed page, they never really happen to you in life.

"All I believe in in life is the rewards for virtue (according to your talents) and the *punishments* for not fulfilling your duties, which are doubly costly. If there is such a volume in the camp library, will you ask Mrs. Tyson to let you look up a sonnet of Shakespeare's in which the line occurs *Lilies that fester smell far worse than weeds.*

"Have had no thoughts today, life seems composed of getting up a *Saturday Evening Post* story. I think of you, and always pleasantly; but if you call me 'Pappy' again I am going to take the White Cat out and beat his bottom *hard, six times for every time you are impertinent.* Do you react to that?

I will arrange the camp bill.

Half-wit, I will conclude. Things to worry about:

Worry about courage
Worry about cleanliness
Worry about efficiency
Worry about horsemanship . . . .

Things not to worry about:

Don't worry about popular opinion
Don't worry about dolls
Don't worry about the past
Don't worry about the future
Don't worry about growing up
Don't worry about anybody getting ahead of you
Don't worry about triumph
Don't worry about failure unless it comes through your own fault
Don't worry about mosquitoes
Don't worry about flies
Don't worry about insects in general
Don't worry about parents
Don't worry about boys
Don't worry about disappointments
Don't worry about pleasures
Don't worry about satisfactions

Things to think about:

What am I really aiming at?

How good am I really in comparison to my contemporaries in regard to:

(a) Scholarship
(b) Do I really understand about people and am I able to get along with them?
(c) Am I trying to make my body a useful instrument or am I neglecting it?

With dearest love,"

F. Scott Fitzgerald and his daughter, Scotty (1928).

Ernest Hemingway (1898–1961)

Few American authors have offered as powerful a definition of the twentieth-century hero as Ernest Hemingway. Hemingway's fiction presents a strict code of contemporary heroism. It centers on disillusionment with the conventions of an optimistic, patriotic society and a belief that the essence of life is violence, from which there is no refuge. As Hemingway saw it, the only victory that can be won from life lies in a graceful stoicism, a willingness to accept gratefully life's few moments of pleasure. A

Although this image of rugged machismo now seems radically oversimplified, it powerfully affected generations of American readers. Moreover, Hemingway launched a new style of writing, so forceful in its simplicity that it became a measure of excellence around the world.

Like F. Scott Fitzgerald's, Hemingway's own life bore a notable resemblance to the lives of his fictional characters. He was born in the Chicago suburb of Oak Park on July 21, 1899. His father, a doctor, initiated him early into his own love for the Michigan woods and the hunting and fishing that could be found there. Growing up, Ernest boxed and played football devotedly, but he also wrote poetry, short stories, and a column for the school newspaper. Graduating from high school just as America entered World War I, he yearned to enlist, but was rejected by the army because of a boxing injury to his eye. He landed a job as a reporter on the *Kansas City Star.* He reached the war a year later as an ambulance driver for the Italian army; but he had barely joined his unit when he was wounded in the knee, seriously enough to require a dozen operations. This wound was a central episode in both his real and his creative life. During his long convalescence in an Italian hospital, he fell in love with a nurse who became the model for Catherine Barkley, the heroine of his novel *A Farewell to Arms.*

After the armistice in 1918, he returned to Michigan. His experience of coming to terms with the war is reflected in his story "The End of Something." The Nick Adams who sits alone in the woods is escaping the world of men,

trying to restore himself from both a physical and a psychological shattering. He is trying to hold on to his sanity.

In 1921, newly married and with a commission as a roving reporter for the *Toronto Star,* Hemingway set off for Paris. It was the era of the American expatriates, when writers and painters crowded the cafés on the Left Bank of the Seine. Here Hemingway worked at the craft of fiction and met other important writers, among them Scott Fitzgerald, James Joyce, and Ezra Pound (see page 711). But most important, he met Gertrude Stein. She read all of his work and advised him to prune his description and to B

A. Responding
? What did Hemingway see as the only way to gain a victory in this essentially violent life? (Stoicism and acceptance of the few moments of pleasure)

B. Connections
Hemingway wrote of this period in his novel *A Moveable Feast* (Scribner's, 1964, 1981). Students might also be interested in the 1988 film *The Moderns* that portrays the same era in Paris and features Hemingway and Gertrude Stein as somewhat eccentric characters. In one scene, for example, Gertrude Stein, presiding over her famous salon of artists and writers, calls across the crowded room to Hemingway, "Hemingway. The sun also sets."

For Further Reading
For The Teacher

Selected letters exchanged between Maxwell Perkins, the editor who exerted so profound an influence on his distinguished authors, and Fitzgerald, Hemingway, Wolfe, and Anderson appear in *Editor to Author*, edited by John Hall Wheelock (Scribner's, 1950, 1987). The letters illuminate the little-understood relationship between editor and author.

A. Expansion
The famous phrase "the lost generation" generally attributed to Gertrude Stein was in fact not her creation. She heard it applied contemptuously by a Paris garage owner to his young and lackadaisical mechanics.

B. Expansion
When students have completed the Hemingway selection that appears here, you might want them to return to and evaluate this statement of Kazin's, based on their impressions of Hemingway's prose.

"concentrate." Hemingway took her advice and spoke fervently of writing "the truest sentence that you know," and of arriving through straight presentation of unvarnished fact at a "true, simple declarative sentence."

His first book, *Three Stories & Ten Poems,* appeared in 1923 and was followed closely by *In Our Time*. These books, along with *The Torrents of Spring* (1926), a parody of his friend Sherwood Anderson's work, drew scant notice. Then, late in 1926, he published a novel about his Parisian friends transplanted to Pamplona, the Spanish town famous for its running of the bulls. This was *The Sun Also Rises*. The novel brought Hemingway widespread critical attention on both sides of the Atlantic. Gertrude Stein's
A remark, "You are all a lost generation," was the novel's epigraph, and the book did reveal the postwar epoch to itself. Many American readers of Hemingway's age embraced it as a portrait of their shattered lives.

Hemingway was now thirty, and married for the second time. Over the next few years, he went on to write an even more powerful and successful novel, *A Farewell To Arms* (1929). This is the beautifully told, moving story of Frederick Henry, a wounded ambulance driver. While recuperating in an Italian hospital, Henry falls in love with an English nurse, Catherine Barkley. Returned to the front, Henry is disillusioned with the war, makes his famous "separate peace," and deserts. He flees to Switzerland with Catherine, who is now pregnant with his child. Frederick's farewell to Catherine just before her death is one of the most famous passages in American fiction, juxtaposing the writer's cynicism about the human experience with the characters' romantic love.

After the major success of *A Farewell to Arms,* Hemingway established himself as a worldwide adventurer, as though a heroic style was as important to his life as to his fiction. He fished and hunted wherever new seas and continents beckoned. And he regularly resumed his role as war correspondent, most notably during the Spanish Civil War (1936–1939).

During the early 1930's he brought out two books of nonfiction. *Death in the Afternoon* (1932) revealed his fascination with bullfighting; *Green Hills of Africa* (1935) did the same for big game hunting. Significantly, both books centered on the art of killing. His next novel, *To Have and Have Not* (1937), was dismissed by critics as unskillful. It was followed by a disappointing play, *The Fifth Column*. But in 1940, just as the literary world was writing Hemingway off as a has-been, he presented it with another triumph, the novel *For Whom The Bell Tolls*. Although it is a lesser masterpiece than *A Farewell To Arms,* its hero has progressed to the discovery of values worth dying for.

The outbreak of World War II drew Hemingway back into uniform. Although officially a correspondent, he gathered around himself a small army of adventurers. During one battle, a First Army commander reported that Hemingway's band was sixty miles in front of the Americans' advancing line. When the Allies at last reached Paris in 1944, they found that Hemingway had preceded them and had already "liberated" the bar at the Ritz Hotel.

In 1952, Hemingway's celebrated literary accomplishments and his continuous pursuit of excitement and danger had made him as famous as any film star. In spite of his flamboyant exploits, he produced yet another widely acclaimed novel in that year, *The Old Man and the Sea*. It tells of Santiago, a Cuban fisherman, old and down on his luck, who ventures far out in the Gulf Stream and hooks a giant marlin. Santiago battles the fish for two days and nights, and he is towed ever farther out to sea. Although he finally succeeds in subduing the great fish and lashing it to the side of his boat, the sharks tear at the carcass until he is left with only its skeleton. The tale has been interpreted as Hemingway's metaphor for life: a vision of the hero, weighed down by the years, but still able to use his skill to taunt fate and so win a kind of victory from it.

In 1954, Hemingway won the Nobel Prize. He now divided his time between the house he had built in Ketcham, Idaho, and his restless travels all over the world: to Cuba, Venice, Spain, and Africa. His health deteriorated, and periods of elation alternated with episodes of severe depression. After a visit to the Mayo Clinic for treatment, he returned to Idaho. On July 2, 1961, he rose early and with two charges of a double-barreled shotgun, he killed himself.

"He put life back on the page," said critic Alfred Kazin, "made us see, feel, and taste the gift of life . . . . To read Hemingway was always to feel more alive." B

SUPPLEMENTARY SUPPORT MATERIALS
1. Vocabulary Activity Worksheet (*CCB*)
2. Review and Response Worksheet: Characterization (*CCB*)
3. Selection Test (*CCB*)

DEVELOPING VOCABULARY
The following words from the story are tested in the Selection Test. (See also Vocabulary Activity Worksheet.)

pavilion	detached
to lurch	to jostle
fencer	invalided

PREPARATION
ESTABLISHING A PURPOSE. Ask students to try to determine as they read what the word *country* in the title of the story might mean in addition to the literal meaning of "a political entity."

IN ANOTHER COUNTRY

This short story is set in Italy during World War I. The narrator is a soldier who, like Hemingway, had signed up to fight with the Italian army. This soldier has been wounded and is in a hospital in Milan, a large industrial city in the north of Italy. As you read, think about all the "countries" the title might refer to—countries of the mind, as well as actual political entities.

A In the fall the war was always there, but we did not go to it any more. It was cold in the fall in Milan and the dark came very early. Then the electric lights came on, and it was pleasant along the streets looking in the windows. There was much game hanging outside the shops, and the snow powdered in the fur of the foxes and the wind blew their tails. The deer hung stiff and heavy and empty, and small birds blew in the wind and the wind turned their feathers. It was a cold fall and the wind came down from the mountains.

We were all at the hospital every afternoon, and there were different ways of walking across the town through the dusk to the hospital. Two of the ways were alongside canals, but they were long. Always, though, you crossed a bridge across a canal to enter the hospital. There was a choice of three bridges. On one of them a woman sold roasted chestnuts. It was warm, standing in front of her charcoal fire, and the chestnuts were warm afterward in your pocket. The hospital was very old and very beautiful, and you entered through a gate and walked across a courtyard and out a gate on the other side. There were usually funerals starting out from the courtyard. Beyond the old hospital were the new brick pavilions, and there we met every afternoon and were all very polite and interested in what was the matter, and sat in the machines that were to make so much difference.

The doctor came up to the machine where I was sitting and said: "What did you like best to do before the war? Did you practice a sport?"

I said: "Yes, football."

"Good," he said. "You will be able to play football again better than ever."

My knee did not bend and the leg dropped straight from the knee to the ankle without a calf, and the machine was to bend the knee and make it move as in riding a tricycle. But it did not bend yet, and instead the machine lurched when it came to the bending part. The doctor said: "That will all pass. You are a fortunate young man. You will play football again like a champion."

In the next machine was a major who had a little hand like a baby's. He winked at me when the doctor examined his hand, which was between two leather straps that bounced up and down and flapped the stiff fingers, and said: "And will I too play football, captain-doctor?" He had been a very great fencer, and before the war the greatest fencer in Italy.

The doctor went to his office in a back room and brought a photograph which showed a hand that had been withered almost as much as the major's, before it had taken a machine course, and after was a little larger. The major held the photograph with his good hand and looked at it very carefully. "A wound?" he asked.

"An industrial accident," the doctor said.

"Very interesting, very interesting," the major said, and handed it back to the doctor.

"You have confidence?"

"No," said the major.

There were three boys who came each day who were about the same age I was. They were all three from Milan, and one of them was to be a lawyer, and one was to be a painter, and one had intended to be a soldier, and after we were finished with the machines, sometimes we walked back together to the Café Cova, which was next door to the Scala.[1] We walked the short way through the communist quarter because we were four together. The people hated us because we were officers, and from a wine-shop someone would call out, "A basso gli ufficiali!"[2] as we passed. An-

1. **Scala:** La Scala, Milan's renowned opera house.
2. **"A basso gli ufficiali!":** "Down with the officers!"

A. Responding
? What does the sentence "In the fall the war was always there, but we did not go to it any more" make you think of? (The wounded soldiers in the hospital are isolated from the war.) Why does the narrator say that they don't *go* to the war any more? (The expression suggests that the war is something obligatory for those involved in it—like school or church. The narrator and his companions are, however, now "excused" from attending.)

CLOSURE

Point out that the narrator, his four young friends, and the major seem to be set apart by their wounds from the doctors and the citizens of Milan.

? What, if anything, does this isolation of the characters have to do with the title of the story? (In this instance, those who have suffered loss and disillusion make up "another country" from those who are well and whole.)

READING CHECK TEST

1. The hospital in the story is located in ______. *Milan*
2. The doctor who treats the narrator and the other soldiers is particularly proud of ______. *machines*
3. Before the war, the major had been a great ______. *fencer*
4. The narrator's problems with learning Italian involve its ______. *grammar*
5. The major's wife dies of ______. *pneumonia*

A. Irony
There are several layers of irony here. One target is the vanity of an old family, which prizes so highly the distinctive shape of a hereditary nose. The other target is the hospital staff—encouraging, optimistic, but mainly ineffectual.

B. Irony
The suggestion that time spent at the front, not the action a soldier was involved in, determined the medal(s) awarded is ironic.

C. Metaphor
The narrator uses the hawk metaphor to distinguish the three soldiers he regards as fearless and warlike from himself and the boy who wore the handkerchief.

other boy who walked with us sometimes and made us five wore a black silk handkerchief across his face because he had no nose then and his face was to be rebuilt. He had gone out to the front from the military academy and been wounded within an hour after he had gone into the front line for the first time. They rebuilt his face, but he came from a very old family and they could never get the nose exactly right. He went to South America and worked in a bank. But this was a long time ago, and then we did not any of us know how it was going to be afterward. We only knew then that there was always the war, but that we were not going to it any more.

We all had the same medals, except the boy with the black silk bandage across his face, and he had not been at the front long enough to get any medals. The tall boy with a very pale face who was to be a lawyer had been a lieutenant of Arditi[3] and had three medals of the sort we each had only one of. He had lived a very long time with death and was a little detached. We were all a little detached, and there was nothing that held us together except that we met every afternoon at the hospital. Although, as we walked to the Cova through the tough part of town, walking in the dark, with light and singing coming out of the wine-shops, and sometimes having to walk into the street when the men and women would crowd together on the sidewalk so that we would have had to jostle them to get by, we felt held together by there being something that had happened that they, the people who disliked us, did not understand.

We ourselves all understood the Cova, where it was rich and warm and not too brightly lighted, and noisy and smoky at certain hours, and there were always girls at the tables and the illustrated papers on a rack on the wall. The girls at the Cova were very patriotic, and I found that the most patriotic people in Italy were the café girls—and I believe they are still patriotic.

The boys at first were very polite about my medals and asked me what I had done to get them. I showed them the papers, which were written in very beautiful language and full of *fratellanza* and *abnegazione*,[4] but which really said, with the adjectives removed, that I had been given the medals because I was an American. After that their manner changed a little toward me, although I was their friend against outsiders. I was a friend, but I was never really one of them after they had read the citations, because it had been different with them and they had done very different things to get their medals. I had been wounded, it was true; but we all knew that being wounded, after all, was really an accident. I was never ashamed of the ribbons, though, and sometimes, after the cocktail hour, I would imagine myself having done all the things they had done to get their medals; but walking home at night through the empty streets with the cold wind and all the shops closed, trying to keep near the street lights, I knew that I would never have done such things, and I was very much afraid to die, and often lay in bed at night by myself, afraid to die and wondering how I would be when I went back to the front again.

The three with the medals were like hunting-hawks; and I was not a hawk, although I might seem a hawk to those who had never hunted; they, the three, knew better and so we drifted apart. But I stayed good friends with the boy who had been wounded his first day at the front, because he would never know now how he would have turned out; so he could never be accepted either, and I liked him because I thought perhaps he would not have turned out to be a hawk either.

The major, who had been the great fencer, did not believe in bravery, and spent much time while we sat in the machines correcting my grammar. He had complimented me on how I spoke Italian, and we talked together very easily. One day I had said that Italian seemed such an easy language to me that I could not take a great interest in it; everything was so easy to say. "Ah, yes," the major said. "Why, then, do you not take up the use of grammar?" So we took up the use of grammar, and soon Italian was such a difficult language that I was afraid to talk to him until I had the grammar straight in my mind.

The major came very regularly to the hospital. I do not think he ever missed a day, although I am sure he did not believe in the machines. There was a time when none of us believed in the machines, and one day the major said it was all nonsense. The machines were new then and it was we who were to prove them. It was an idiotic idea, he said, "a theory, like another." I had not learned my grammar, and he said I was a stupid impossible disgrace, and he was a fool to have

3. **Arditi:** commandos.
4. ***fratellanza abnegazione:*** brotherhood and self-sacrifice.

ANALYZING THE STORY
Identifying Facts
1. The story is set in Milan in northern Italy during World War I, in the fall. The narrator, a wounded American soldier, tells of a doctor, an Italian major with an injured hand, three young army veterans, and a youth who wore a black handkerchief across his face because his nose had been smashed.
2. The major, who has been a great fencer, has suffered a serious injury to one of his hands. The army veterans have all been wounded in various ways. The narrator has sustained a wound in the knee. The youth with a black handkerchief has had his nose smashed.
3. They hated them because the patients had been officers.
The description of the walks to the hospital, when the four young men would have to jostle people to get by, suggests that the soldiers are isolated from the real life of the Cova district.
4. The narrator feels that the three young men have thoroughly deserved their medals and that his own medals were awarded to him only because he was an American.
(Answers continue on next page.)

bothered with me. He was a small man and he sat straight up in his chair with his right hand thrust into the machine and looked straight ahead at the wall while the straps thumped up and down with his fingers in them.

"What will you do when the war is over if it is over?" he asked me. "Speak grammatically!"

"I will go the States."

"Are you married?"

"No, but I hope to be."

"The more of a fool you are," he said. He seemed very angry. "A man must not marry."

"Why, Signor Maggiore?"

"Don't call me 'Signor Maggiore.' "

"Why must not a man marry?"

"He cannot marry. He cannot marry," he said angrily. "If he is to lose everything, he should not place himself in a position to lose that. He should not place himself in a position to lose. He should find things he cannot lose."

He spoke very angrily and bitterly, and looked straight ahead while he talked.

"But why should he necessarily lose it?"

"He'll lose it," the major said. He was looking at the wall. Then he looked down at the machine and jerked his little hand out from between the straps and slapped it hard against his thigh. "He'll lose it," he almost shouted. "Don't argue with me!" Then he called to the attendant who ran the machines. "Come and turn this damned thing off."

He went back into the other room for the light treatment and the massage. Then I heard him ask the doctor if he might use his telephone and he shut the door. When he came back into the room, I was sitting in another machine. He was wearing his cape and had his cap on, and he came directly toward my machine and put his arm on my shoulder.

"I am so sorry," he said, and patted me on the shoulder with his good hand. "I would not be rude. My wife has just died. You must forgive me." A

"Oh—" I said, feeling sick for him. "I am *so* sorry."

He stood there biting his lower lip. "It is very difficult," he said. "I cannot resign myself."

He looked straight past me and out through the window. Then he began to cry. "I am utterly unable to resign myself," he said and choked. And then crying, his head up looking at nothing, carrying himself straight and soldierly, with tears on both his cheeks and biting his lips, he walked past the machines and out the door.

The doctor told me that the major's wife, who was very young and whom he had not married until he was definitely invalided out of the war, had died of pneumonia. She had been sick only a few days. No one expected her to die. The major did not come to the hospital for three days. Then he came at the usual hour, wearing a black band on the sleeve of his uniform. When he came back, there were large framed photographs around the wall, of all sorts of wounds before and after they had been cured by the machines. In front of the machine the major used were three photographs of hands like his that were completely restored. I do not know where the doctor got them. I always understood we were the first to use the machines. The photographs did not make much difference to the major because he only looked out of the window.

A. Responding
? The major has just learned of his wife's death, yet he speaks very politely to the narrator. How do you account for his rudeness a short time before? (The major has been filled with anxiety at the thought of losing his young wife. Now that he has learned of her death, he tries stoically to accept it and resumes his former politeness.)

Responding to the Story

Analyzing the Story

Identifying Facts

1. Who are the main **characters** in this story, and where is the story **set** (time, place, and season)?
2. Describe what has happened to each of the characters. What "wounds" has each suffered in the war?
3. The patients are the wounded heroes of a nation at war. But why did the people in the wine shops hate them? What details suggest that the young soldiers are isolated from the real life of the Cova district?
4. Within the fraternity of the war-wounded, there seem to be two grades of heroism. How is the narrator different from his companions on the level of heroism? Why does he say "I was not a hawk"?
5. The major with the small hand is at first sympathetic and kindly, but his nature turns to bitterness with his loss. What is his loss? How does he hope to protect himself from this kind of loss?

(Continued from previous page.)

He says, "I was not a hawk" because he secretly doubts that he would have been as brave as the other soldiers.

5. His young wife has died suddenly of pneumonia.

The major cannot resign himself to his grief. He tells the narrator never to get married.

Interpreting Meanings

6. Apparently, the machines are exercise machines that are supposed to strengthen gradually the atrophied muscles of the wounded.

They represent the hopes of the wounded soldiers to return to normal life.

7. The new photos depicting all sorts of wounds before patients had been "cured" by the machines, are supposed to give the major some renewed hope.

8. By repeatedly quoting the doctor and by telling us that the machines are new and evidently improved, the narrator implies a skeptical attitude.

9. The characters have all lost, at least temporarily, their physical health and vigor. In addition, the major has lost his wife to pneumonia. On an emotional level, it

(Answers continue in left-hand column.)

(Continued from top.)

is implied that the characters have lost their sense of optimism and their feeling of "belonging" to a social community.

The opening description of the cold and the darkness, featuring the images of the dead foxes and deer, emphasizes the sense of loss and death.

10. The word *country* in the title literally refers to the narrator's position as an American in a foreign country. But perhaps the word could also refer to a psychological "country"—a state of mind of hopelessness and disillusionment, brought about by the destructive effects of war.

11. Answers will vary. But the theme of the story centers on human loneliness in the face of overwhelming odds: the destruction of war, social conflict, and the loss of those we love and trust.

Interpreting Meanings

6. The machines keep appearing in this story. What are these machines that are to make "all the difference"? How are the machines a reflection of people's attempts to recover what they have lost?
7. What is the significance of the new photos in front of the major's machine at the story's end?
8. What do you think the narrator's **attitude** is toward these machines?
9. How many things can you name that these characters have lost? How does the opening description of the **setting** reinforce this sense of loss and death?
10. What different meanings can you attach to the word *country* in the title? What does it literally mean? What other country or countries could it refer to?
11. How would you state the **theme** of "In Another Country"? What is Hemingway saying about patriotism, heroism, and the trust one should put in love for another human being?

Writing About the Story

A Creative Response

1. **Describing a Setting.** Using Hemingway's opening paragraph as a model, write a description of a setting that gives the impression of either life and hope or death and loss. What season will you describe? What specific words will you use to suggest the feelings you want to convey? What images will you use to reinforce these feelings?

A Critical Response

2. **Responding to Theme.** What is your opinion of Hemingway's theme in "In Another Country"? In an essay, cite the story's theme as you see it and explain your response to that theme.

Primary Sources

Nobel Prize Acceptance Speech, 1954

"Members of the Swedish Academy, Ladies and Gentlemen: Having no facility for speechmaking nor any domination of rhetoric, I wish to thank the administrators of the generosity of Alfred Nobel for this prize. No writer who knows the great writers who did not receive the prize can accept it other than with humility. There is no need to list these writers. Everyone here may make his own list according to his knowledge and his conscience. It would be impossible for me to ask the Ambassador of my country to read a speech in which a writer said all of the things which are in his heart. Things may not be immediately discernible in what a man writes, and in this sometimes he is fortunate; but eventually they are quite clear and by these and the degree of alchemy that he possesses he will endure or be forgotten. Writing, at its best, is a lonely life. Organizations for writers palliate the writer's loneliness but I doubt if they improve his writing. He grows in public stature as he sheds his loneliness and often his work deteriorates. For he does his work alone and if he is a good enough writer he must face eternity, or the lack of it, each day. For a true writer each book should be a new beginning where he tries again for something that is beyond attainment. He should always try for something that has never been done or that others have tried and failed. Then sometimes, with great luck, he will succeed. How simple the writing of literature would be if it were only necessary to write in another way what has been well written. It is because we have had such great writers in the past that a writer is driven far out past where he can go, out to where no one can help him. I have spoken too long for a writer. A writer should write what he has to say and not speak it. Again I thank you."

—Ernest Hemingway

Zora Neale Hurston (1891–1960)

Zora Neale Hurston was born in the all-black town of Eatonville, Florida, in 1891, the fifth of eight children. Her father was an occasional preacher and her mother had taught some country school. Early on, Zora's mother, Lucy Hurston, urged her talented daughter to "jump at the sun." By the age of nine, Zora was an orphan.

As a child, Hurston recalls in her autobiography, "I used to climb to the top of one of the huge chinaberry trees which guarded our front gate and look out over the world. The most interesting thing that I saw was the horizon. . . . It grew upon me that I ought to walk out to the horizon and see what the end of the world was like."

Zora Hurston did just this, and it was no easy journey. From the time she was thirteen, she had to fend for herself, working hard and getting to school so irregularly that she was twenty-seven before she got to Howard University in Washington, D.C. It was there that she began to write.

Hurston published her first story when she was thirty, and immediately she set out for New York. She arrived in the big city with only a dollar and a half in her pocket that was also bulging with talent, confidence, and ambition. The year was 1925 and the black cultural movement known as the Harlem Renaissance was at high tide. A

Hurston was soon in its midst, writing stories and plays that celebrated her blackness. Zora, who liked to wear big hats and turbans and dance and give parties, sometimes shocked other emerging African American artists, especially male writers like Countee Cullen (see page 694), James Weldon Johnson (see page 680), W. E. B. DuBois, and Langston Hughes (see page 688).

Enrolling at prestigious Barnard College, Hurston met the great anthropologist Franz Boas, who believed that Zora's interest was really in his field, the study of human social and cultural behavior. Indeed, Hurston, who became his protégé, did eventually become known as much as a folklorist as a writer of fiction.

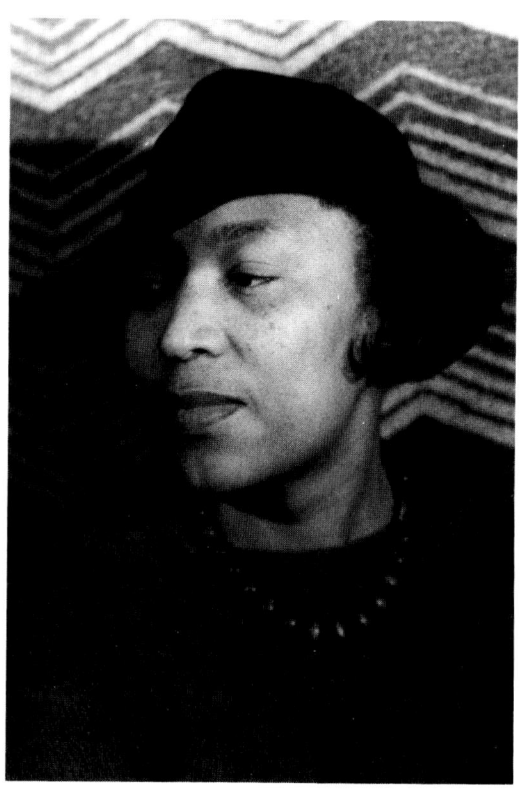

Her musical reviews portraying black folk-culture brought her initial success, but it was *Story* magazine's publication of her short story "The Gilded Six Bits" that launched her literary career. When the Philadelphia publisher J. B. Lippincott asked if she had a novel, Hurston promptly sat down and wrote one. It was published in 1934 as *Jonah's Gourd Vine*.

Mules and Men was published in 1935. Hurston, who traveled through Alabama, Florida, and Louisiana to gather her material, said that she "needed the spy-glass of anthropology" to see clearly those stories she had known since the "rocking of my cradle." Alice Walker says that the stories in *Mules and Men* gave back to her own relatives in the South all the stories they'd forgotten or grown ashamed of.

In 1937, when she was forty-six, Hurston published her best novel, *Their Eyes Were Watching God*. It is the story of a young African American woman, Janie Crawford, who strikes out, much as Hurston herself had done, for the horizon, for a life beyond her expectations of a conventional marriage and household.

A. Expansion
Most of the writers of the Harlem Renaissance were educated African Americans who drew their subject matter from urban life. Few besides Zora Neale Hurston were interested in the rich traditions of the rural South. Hurston is generally considered a major voice in promoting racial heritage—in all its forms—among writers of the Harlem Renaissance.

Hurston's use of dialect has long been a matter of discussion. Some feel that she was merely reproducing a dialect that had come to be considered controversial at the time. But most contemporary critics, including Harold Bloom and Henry Louis Gates, have written extensive analyses of Hurston's expert rendition of the African American vernacular.

SUPPLEMENTARY SUPPORT MATERIALS
1. Review and Response Worksheet: The Tall Tale (*CCB*)
2. Language Skills Worksheet: Punctuating Dialogue (*CCB*)
3. Selection Test (*CCB*)

PREPARATION
1. **BUILDING ON PRIOR KNOWLEDGE.** Ask students what kinds of stories a subjugated (segregated) people would tell.

2. **ESTABLISHING A PURPOSE.** Tell students to read the story to discover the kind of hero the storytellers admire. (The tale *must* be read aloud.)

A. Expansion
An earlier collection of African American folktales was called *Uncle Remus, His Sayings and His Songs.* These materials were recorded in 1880 by Joel Chandler Harris, a white writer. The Uncle Remus stories are now available in a new collection, retold by Julius Lester—*The Tales of Uncle Remus.*

Throughout the last twenty years of her life, Hurston continued to produce fiction and nonfiction and wrote her autobiography. Much of the work was published and favorably received. Some of it was criticized in the African American community for celebrating the life of black people in America rather than confronting the white community for its discrimination.

In any case, Zora Neale Hurston began to have difficulty finding a market for her work, and in 1948 she left New York and returned to Florida. There she worked at odd jobs, moved into a one-room cabin, and became poorer and poorer.

In January of 1960, Zora Neale Hurston died, broke, in Florida, in the Saint Lucie welfare home. A collection had to be taken up to pay for her funeral. Ironically, in the years since her death, much of her work has been brought back into print, and Hurston is now recognized as the forerunner of such celebrated contemporary writers as Toni Morrison and Alice Walker.

But to those who read her, Hurston is a storyteller of great spirit and imagination in her own right. Energetic, funny, unconventional, Zora was a true original, who might have summed up her life in the words of the song, "I did it *my* way."

HOW THE LION MET THE KING OF THE WORLD

A **This charming folktale, from a collection called *Mules and Men,* contains a truth about human nature told in a wonderful, funny, down-home country voice. As with all folktales, there is a childlike quality to the story, to the manner of its telling, and to its characters. These are mostly animals, but fortunately for us, they speak English. And fortunately, like modern cartoon characters, they are never *really* hurt by any violence.**

The story's theme is related to childhood's game of "Who's king of the castle?" Or, you might prefer to compare it to teenage turf wars, or to the high-noon confrontations of law and outlaw in the West.

But the humor is what's all-important, and much of that depends on the animal voices, the Bear and Lion telling us in so many words that we too are animals. When it's a matter of such importance as "Who's boss around here?" we behave pretty much the way the "lower orders" do.

The rest of the comedy comes from the narrative voice, the wholly expressive vernacular of the back-country South. That voice is so expertly portrayed here that once you read the story aloud, you can't mistake its meaning and its playfulness. It's as vivid and full of life as a basket of new pups.

John, the hero of this story, is the great popular hero in African American tales. He is often pitted against formidable adversaries, such as Old Massa (master) and even the Devil.

The stories are told within a "frame," in which a group of men argue about details in the stories they're telling. In this case, two men named Sack Daddy and Dad Boykin are the storytellers. They've been exchanging animal stories.

Y'all been tellin' and lyin' 'bout all dese varmints but you ain't yet spoke about de high chief boss of all de world which is de lion," Sack Daddy commented.

"He's de King of de Beasts, but he ain't no King of de World, now Sack," Dad Boykin spoke up. "He thought *he was de King till John give him a straightenin'."*

"Don't put dat lie out!" Sack Daddy contended. "De lion won't stand no straightenin'."

"Course I 'gree wid you dat everybody can't show de lion no deep point, but John showed it to

Ghana cloth.

him. Oh, yeah, John not only straightened him out, he showed dat ole lion where in."

"When did he do all of dis, Dad? Ah ain't never heard tell of it." Dad spoke up:

Oh, dis was way befo' yo' time. Ah don't recolleck myself. De old folks told me about John and de lion. Well, John was ridin' long one day straddle of his horse when de grizzly bear come pranchin' out in de middle of de road and hollered: "Hold on a minute! They tell me you goin' 'round strowin' it dat youse de King of de World."

John stopped his horse: "Whoa! Yeah, Ah'm de King of de World, don't you b'lieve it?" John told him.

"Naw, you ain't no King. Ah'm de King of de World. You can't be no King till you whip me. Git down and fight."

John hit de ground and de fight started. First, John grabbed him a rough-dried brick and started to work de fat offa de bear's head. De bear just fumbled 'round till he got a good holt, then he begin to squeeze and squeeze. John knowed he couldn't stand dat much longer, do he'd be jus' another man wid his breath done give out. So he reached into his pocket and got out his razor and slipped it between dat bear's ribs. De bear turnt loose and reeled on over in de bushes to lay down. He had enough of dat fight.

John got back on his horse and rode on off.

De lion smelt de bear's blood and come runnin' to where de grizzly was layin' and started to lappin' his blood.

De bear was skeered de lion was gointer eat him while he was all cut and bleedin' nearly to death, so he hollered and said: "*Please* don't touch me, Brer Lion. Ah done met de King of de World and he done cut me all up."

De lion got his bristles all up and clashed down at de bear: "Don't you lay there and tell me you done met de King of de World and not be talkin' 'bout me! Ah'll tear you to pieces!"

"Oh, don't tetch me, Brer Lion! Please lemme alone so Ah kin git well."

"Well, don't you call nobody no King of de World but me."

"But Brer Lion, Ah done *met* de King sho' nuff. Wait till you see him and you'll say Ah'm right."

"Naw, Ah won't, neither. Show him to me and Ah'll show you how much King he is."

"All right, Brer Lion, you jus' have a seat right behind dese bushes. He'll be by here befo' long."

A. Humanities Connection: Responding to the Fine Art
Art has always been an important part of African life, closely tied with everyday activities. ? How are all the animals and other figures and designs on this cloth unified? (All use the same strong colors.)

Why do you think a human face is included near the center of the piece? (Answers will vary. Perhaps all the items on the cloth represent things important for human survival in this culture.)

B. Expansion
Compare John's exploits to Davy Crockett's. Crockett (1786–1836) was a frontiersman, a member of Congress, and a hero of the Alamo, where he died. He became a folk hero. He could lie prodigiously, speak the language of animals, ride the lightning, and whip his weight in wildcats. The same character type appears in Twain's story "The Raftsman" (page 404).

Reading Check Test

1. The story begins when John stops the grizzly bear and challenges him to a fight. *False*
2. John defeats the bear by cutting him with a razor. *True*
3. As the lion and the bear wait for John, first an old man and then a young boy come along. *True*
4. John defeats the lion by lassoing him with a rope. *False*
5. The end of the story leaves the lion as King of the Beasts and leaves John as King of the World. *True*

Analyzing The Story

Interpreting Meanings

1. John rules by might but is aided by weapons.

Like Superman or a Western hero, he performs amazing feats in his encounters with the bear and the lion, and he is fast with a gun.

2. Some students might think that the story does *not* say that might makes

A. Metaphor/ Rhyme
Notice the comparisons of the lion's tail to a bull-whip and torpedoes. Notice, too, that John's answer to the lion is in rhyme.

B. Allusion
The singing of the "mornin' stars" refers to the time of the Creation. The expression comes from the book of Job, where God describes many of the wonders of nature to Job.

C. Rhyme
Here the storyteller uses rhyme again.

Closure
Call on students to explain why these African Americans would appreciate and admire a hero like John.

Lion squatted down by de bear and waited. Fust person he saw goin' up de road was a old man. Lion jumped up and ast de bear, "Is dat him?"

Bear say, "Naw, dat's Uncle Yistiddy, he's a useter-be!"

After while a li'l boy passed down de road. De lion seen him and jumped up agin. "Is dat him?" he ast de bear.

Bear told him, "Naw, dat's li'l tomorrow, he's a gointer-be, you jus' lay quiet. Ah'll let you know when he gits here."

Sho nuff after while here come John on his horse but he had done got his gun. Lion jumped up agin and ast, "Is dat him?"

Bear say: "Yeah, dat's him! Dat's de King of de World."

A Lion reared up and cracked his tail back and forwards like a bull-whip. He 'lowed, "You wait till Ah git thru wid him and you won't be callin' him no King no mo'."

He took and galloped out in de middle of de road right in front of John's horse and laid his years back. His tail was crackin' like torpedoes.

"Stop!" de lion hollered at John. "They tell me you goes for de King of de World!"

John looked him dead in de ball of his eye and told him, "Yeah, Ah'm de King. Don't you like it, don't you take it. Here's mah collar, come and shake it!"

De lion and John eye-balled one another for a minute or two, den de lion sprung on John.

B Talk about fightin'! Man, you ain't seen no sich fightin' and wrasslin' since de mornin' stars sung together. De lion clawed and bit John and John bit him right back.

C Way after while John got to his rifle and he up wid de muzzle right in ole lion's face and pulled de trigger. Long, slim black feller, snatch 'er back and hear 'er beller! Dog damn! Dat was too much for de lion. He turnt go of John and wheeled to run to de woods. John levelled down on him agin and let him have another load, right in his hindquarters.

Dat ole lion give John de book; de bookity book.[1] He hauled de fast mail back into de woods where de bear was laid up.

"Move over," he told de bear. "Ah wanta lay down too."

'How come?" de bear ast him.

"Ah done met de King of de World, and he done ruint me."

"Brer Lion, how you know you done met de King?"

" 'Cause he made lightnin' in my face and thunder in my hips. Ah know Ah done met de King, move over."

1. **bookity book:** a sound word meaning "running."

Responding to the Story

Analyzing the Story

Interpreting Meanings

1. John turns out to be the real king. How does he rule the world in this story? (By might or by wit?) How does he compare with Superman, or with the cowboy hero in American Westerns?
2. If the **message** of this story is that might makes right, would you agree with it? How could you change the story to send a different message? What would that message be?
3. Do you see any **irony** in the fact that the African American slaves made up a folktale about a black man who was "King of the World"? Do you think there are other subtle messages behind this tale?
4. What human **character types** can you detect in the portrayals of the Lion and the Bear?
5. A **colloquialism** is a local peculiarity of speech. Colloquialisms are as plentiful in this story as raisins in a cake. Which expressions are your three favorites? Where does the storyteller add **rhyme** and **figures of speech** to the story?

Writing About the Folktale

A Creative Response

1. **Writing a Folktale.** Choose and name an animal—Sis Snail, Coz Penguin, Brer Armadillo, Brer Cottonmouth, Sister Squirrel—and write a short folktale in which the animal is matched against a natural or

right; others will argue that force does not ensure morality or respect.

If John conquered the lion by his wits, without a violent confrontation, the message would be that people do not need violence to succeed against bullies.

3. The irony is that the storytellers were oppressed.

If there is a subtle message, it is one of defiance—to be "king," one must be willing to stand up to bullies.

4. Both are boastful, like children playing King of the Castle, gang leaders defending their turf, or outlaws daring the world to stop them.

5. Students might cite such colloquialisms as "a useter-be," "gointer-be," and "bookity book." The storyteller adds rhyme in John's challenge to the lion and in the description of the rifle. Among the figures of speech are similes in the description of the lion's tail, hyperbole in the description of the fight, and metaphor in the lion's report and the rifle's effect.

technological enemy. For example, Brer Penguin might face global warming; Brer Armadillo might face the peril of the automobile. Pretend your tale is in the oral tradition and use some funny rhymes and alliteration.

A Critical Response

2. **Comparing Tall Tales.** Tall tales have always been a part of the American tradition. Read Mark Twain's story from *Life on the Mississippi* (page 404) and write a brief essay in which you compare the challenge match in Twain's story with the one in Hurston's tale. Before you write, fill out a chart like the following to organize your points of comparison:

	Twain	Hurston
1. Boasts		
2. Exaggeration		
3. Colorful language		

Performing the Story

A Group Activity

Perhaps because of their broad characterizations and use of a lot of physical action, folktales are often successfully dramatized for the stage, particularly for children's theater. Working with a group, prepare this folktale for performance. You will have to make the following assignments:

1. Scriptwriters
2. A director
3. Actors
4. Costume designer
5. Set designer

Before you begin, you should discuss these questions:

1. Will you use a narrator to tell the parts of the story that are not told directly in dialogue?
2. How much pantomime will you use?
3. Will you use music? (Rock? Folk? Jazz?)

Primary Sources
Collecting Folktales

In her autobiography, *Dust Tracks on a Road*, Zora Neale Hurston tells of her passion, as a child, in Eatonville, Florida, for hearing stories:

"For me, the store porch was the most interesting place that I could think of. I was not allowed to sit around there, naturally. But, I could and did drag my feet going in and out, whenever I was sent there for something, to allow whatever was being said to hang in my ear. I would hear an occasional scrap of gossip in what to me was adult double talk, but which I understood at times. . . .

"But what I really loved to hear was the menfolks holding a 'lying' session. That is, straining against each other in telling folks tales. God, Devil, Brer Rabbit, Brer Fox, Sis Cat, Brer Bear, Lion, Tiger, Buzzard, and all the wood folk walked and talked like natural men. The wives of the storytellers might yell from backyards for them to come and tote some water, or chop wood for the cook stove, and never get a move out of the men. The usual rejoinder was, 'Oh, she's got enough to go on. No matter how much wood you chop, a woman will burn it all up to get a meal. If she got a couple of pieces, she will make it do. If you chop up a whole boxful, she will burn every stick of it. Pay her no mind.' So the storytelling would go right on."

Later on in her autobiography, Hurston, now studying anthropology at Barnard College in New York City, tells how she went out among the people to gather their folktales. She did not succeed at first. Like the Lion in her story, she first had to get a "straightenin'."

"Research is formalized curiosity. It is poking and prying with a purpose. It is a seeking that he who wishes may know the cosmic secrets of the world and they that dwell therein. . . .

"My first six months were disappointing. I found out later that it was not because I had no talents for research, but because I did not have the right approach. The glamor of Barnard College was still upon me. I dwelt in marble halls. I knew where the material was all right. But, I went about asking, in carefully accented Barnardese, 'Pardon me, but do you know any folktales or folksongs?' The men and women who had whole treasuries of material just seeping through their pores looked at me and shook their heads. No, they had never heard of anything like that around there. Maybe it was over in the next county. Why didn't I try over there? I did, and got the selfsame answer. Oh, I got a few little items. But compared with what I did later, not enough to make a flea a waltzing jacket." A

—Zora Neale Hurston

A. Expansion Hurston won praise from fellow writer Langston Hughes, who noted in *The Big Sea* that Miss Hurston was a clever student "who didn't let college give her a broad *a* and who had great scorn for all pretensions, academic or otherwise. That is why she was such a fine folklore collector, able to go among the people and never act as if she had been to school at all."

John Steinbeck (1902–1968)

Most writers would probably agree that fiction which delivers a political message may be effective propaganda, but it is unlikely to be art. John Steinbeck would *not* have agreed with this precept, and he is a notable exception to it.

During the 1930's, the Great Depression cost millions of people their jobs and shook their faith in the American promise. Big business and the corporate farm seemed untouched by hard times. They were angrily perceived by many as impersonal and indifferent to human hardship.

Many novelists of the time were moved by this sense of injustice and turned their pens to a by-product of the Depression known as "the protest novel." Among these writers, John Steinbeck was the most widely praised and successful.

Steinbeck was born in California's Salinas Valley in 1902, the son of a county treasurer and a schoolteacher. Although he graduated from high school and spent some time at Stanford University, he took more pride in the many jobs he held as a young man than in his formal education. He worked as a hod carrier, fruit picker, apprentice painter, laboratory assistant, caretaker, surveyor, and writer. He wrote seventeen novels in all, in addition to stories, plays, filmscripts, and a great deal of journalism.

Steinbeck's first major success came in 1937 with *Of Mice and Men,* a short, best-selling novel which Steinbeck himself adapted into a Broadway play. It is a tale of two itinerant farmhands, George and the powerful but mentally handicapped Lennie. Steinbeck changed a pathetic situation into an affirmative acceptance of life's brutal conflicts, along with its possibilities for fellowship and courage.

He followed this success by joining some Oklahoma farmers—known as "Okies"—who were embarking with great hope to California. Steinbeck lived and worked with them over the next two years, experiencing first-hand the disappointment and injustice they encountered.

The result was his strongest and most enduring novel, *The Grapes of Wrath* (1939). It tells of the Joad family and their forced migration from the Dust Bowl of Oklahoma to California, the region that promised work at decent wages and a chance to buy land. Once arrived, however, the Joads find only the exploitation and poverty of labor camps. Gradually they learn the real meaning of the term "Okies"—people who never even had a chance.

The Grapes of Wrath was an angry book that spoke out on behalf of the migrant workers. Steinbeck sharply criticized a system that bankrupted thousands of farmers and turned them from their own land, making them into paid help for the big growers. When the novel appeared, it was greeted with outbursts of praise and condemnation, and it became the most widely read of all the protest novels of the 1930's.

The Grapes of Wrath won the Pulitzer Prize in 1940. After this major success, however, Steinbeck's eminence waned. Toward the end of his life, Steinbeck achieved a gratifying success with the award of the Nobel Prize in 1962, and with the publication in that year of *Travels with Charley,* a nostalgic account of a trip across America with his aged poodle Charley. But his reputation is grounded on those earlier novels which portray California as the real and symbolic land of American promise.

Supplementary Support Materials
1. Vocabulary Activity Worksheet (*CCB*)
2. Review and Response Worksheet: Characterization (*CCB*)
3. Language Skills Worksheet: Verbs (*CCB*)
4. Selection Test (*CCB*)

Developing Vocabulary
The following words from the story are tested in the Selection Test. (See also Vocabulary Activity Worksheet.)

to belie	centipede
contemptuously	to marshal
judiciously	gopher
unseemly	to retract
staunchness	disconsolately

Preparation
1. Building on Prior Knowledge. Ask volunteers to share their knowledge of the Westward Movement. Elicit details about wagon trains, routes west, hardships, and hazards. If students are rather hazy about the details, assign several to find relevant information in their history books or in encyclopedias.

2. Establishing a Purpose. Tell students that they will encounter several different kinds of conflict in "The Leader of the People." Ask them, as they read, to note these conflicts and try to determine which one is most important to the story.

A. Point of View
In telling this story, Steinbeck employs the third-person limited point of view. Events are viewed through the eyes of Jody, the young farm boy, and the reader is able to share Jody's thoughts and feelings.

B. Conflict
? What is there in this conversation between Jody and Billy that hints at a conflict between Jody and his father? (Jody slumps against the fence post and responds that his father doesn't care about the mice. Also, the word *ominously* hints at a problem between them.)

THE LEADER OF THE PEOPLE

This story appears as the fourth and final part of Steinbeck's novel *The Red Pony* (1945). Each part of this "novel" was published as a complete short story. The stories, all connected by their characters and settings, are called "The Gift," "The Great Mountains," "The Promise," and "The Leader of the People." By far, the most famous of these stories are the first one and the last.

In the following story, a small number of characters are involved in several different conflicts. The first conflict—between a boy and his father—is hinted at in a line of dialogue before the father even makes an appearance. Watch for the development of the other conflicts—including the conflict between dream and reality that might be the heart of the story, and, in many ways, the heart of much American fiction.

On Saturday afternoon Billy Buck, the ranch hand, raked together the last of the old year's haystack and pitched small forkfuls over the wire fence to a few mildly interested cattle. High in the air small clouds like puffs of cannon smoke were driven eastward by the March wind. The wind could be heard whishing in the brush on the ridge crests, but no breath of it penetrated down into the ranch cup.

A The little boy, Jody, emerged from the house eating a thick piece of buttered bread. He saw Billy working on the last of the haystack. Jody tramped down scuffing his shoes in a way he had been told was destructive to good shoe leather. A flock of white pigeons flew out of the black cypress tree as Jody passed, and circled the tree and landed again. A half-grown tortoise-shell cat leaped from the bunkhouse porch, galloped on stiff legs across the road, whirled and galloped back again. Jody picked up a stone to help the game along, but he was too late, for the cat was under the porch before the stone could be discharged. He threw the stone into the cypress tree and started the white pigeons on another whirling flight.

Arriving at the used-up haystack, the boy leaned against the barbed wire fence. "Will that be all of it, do you think?" he asked.

The middle-aged ranch hand stopped his careful raking and stuck his fork into the ground. He took off his black hat and smoothed down his hair. "Nothing left of it that isn't soggy from ground moisture," he said. He replaced his hat and rubbed his dry leathery hands together.

"Ought to be plenty mice," Jody suggested.

"Lousy with them," said Billy. "Just crawling with mice."

"Well, maybe, when you get all through, I could call the dogs and hunt the mice."

"Sure, I guess you could," said Billy Buck. He lifted a forkful of the damp ground hay and threw it into the air. Instantly three mice leaped out and burrowed frantically under the hay again.

Jody sighed with satisfaction. Those plump, sleek, arrogant mice were doomed. For eight months they had lived and multiplied in the haystack. They had been immune from cats, from traps, from poison and from Jody. They had grown smug in their security, overbearing and fat. Now the time of disaster had come; they would not survive another day.

Billy looked up at the top of the hills that surrounded the ranch. "Maybe you better ask your father before you do it," he suggested.

"Well, where is he? I'll ask him now."

"He rode up to the ridge ranch after dinner. He'll be back pretty soon." B

Jody slumped against the fence post. "I don't think he'd care."

As Billy went back to his work he said ominously, "You'd better ask him anyway. You know how he is."

Jody did know. His father, Carl Tiflin, insisted upon giving permission for anything that was done on the ranch, whether it was important or not. Jody sagged farther against the post until he was

A. Point of View

? Does the last part of this sentence (". . . and he dug with an earnestness . . .") sound like something Jody would say or think? What happened to the third-person limited point of view? (Steinbeck momentarily drops into the omniscient point of view to make an observation about dogs, characteristic of him, but one not likely to occur to Jody. Steinbeck resumes the limited point of view in the next paragraph.)

B. Dialogue

? How is the dialogue Steinbeck writes here different from that of Hemingway in "In Another Country"? (Here and elsewhere Steinbeck makes frequent use of adverbs to indicate the manner in which a speaker says something; Hemingway by contrast, rarely supplies such tag lines.)

sitting on the ground. He looked up at the little puffs of wind-driven cloud. "Is it like to rain, Billy?"

"It might. The wind's good for it, but not strong enough."

"Well, I hope it don't rain until after I kill those damn mice." He looked over his shoulder to see whether Billy had noticed the mature profanity. Billy worked on without comment.

Jody turned back and looked at the side hill where the road from the outside world came down. The hill was washed with lean March sunshine. Silver thistles, blue lupins[1] and a few poppies bloomed among the sage bushes. Halfway up the hill Jody could see Doubletree Mutt, the black dog, digging in a squirrel hole. He paddled for a while and then paused to kick bursts of dirt out between his hind legs, and he dug with an earnestness which belied the knowledge he must have had that no dog had ever caught a squirrel by digging in a hole. A

Suddenly, while Jody watched, the black dog stiffened, and backed out of the hole and looked up the hill toward the cleft in the ridge where the road came through. Jody looked up too. For a moment Carl Tiflin on horseback stood out against the pale sky and then he moved down the road toward the house. He carried something white in his hand.

The boy started to his feet. "He's got a letter," Jody cried. He trotted away toward the ranch house, for the letter would probably be read aloud and he wanted to be there. He reached the house before his father did, and ran in. He heard Carl dismount from his creaking saddle and slap the horse on the side to send it to the barn where Billy would unsaddle it and turn it out.

Jody ran into the kitchen. "We got a letter!" he cried.

His mother looked up from a pan of beans. "Who has?"

"Father has. I saw it in his hand."

Carl strode into the kitchen then, and Jody's mother asked, "Who's the letter from, Carl?"

He frowned quickly. "How did you know there was a letter?"

She nodded her head in the boy's direction. "Big-Britches Jody told me."

Jody was embarrassed.

His father looked down at him contemptuously.

1. **lupins:** plants of the bean family, with blue or purple flowers.

"He *is* getting to be a Big-Britches," Carl said. "He's minding everybody's business but his own. Got his big nose into everything."

Mrs. Tiflin relented a little. "Well, he hasn't enough to keep him busy. Who's the letter from?"

Carl still frowned on Jody. "I'll keep him busy if he isn't careful." He held out a sealed letter. "I guess it's from your father."

Mrs. Tiflin took a hairpin from her head and slit open the flap. Her lips pursed judiciously. Jody saw her eyes snap back and forth over the lines. "He says," she translated, "he says he's going to drive out Saturday to stay for a little while. Why, this is Saturday. The letter must have been delayed." She looked at the postmark. "This was mailed day before yesterday. It should have been here yesterday." She looked up questioningly at her husband, and then her face darkened angrily. "Now what have you got that look on you for? He doesn't come often."

Carl turned his eyes away from her anger. He could be stern with her most of the time, but when occasionally her temper arose, he could not combat it.

"What's the matter with you?" she demanded again.

In his explanation there was a tone of apology Jody himself might have used. "It's just that he talks," Carl said lamely. "Just talks."

"Well, what of it? You talk yourself."

"Sure I do. But your father only talks about one thing." B

"Indians!" Jody broke in excitedly. "Indians and crossing the plains!"

Carl turned fiercely on him. "You get out, Mr. Big-Britches! Go on, now! Get out!"

Jody went miserably out the back door and closed the screen with elaborate quietness. Under the kitchen window his shamed, downcast eyes fell upon a curiously shaped stone of such fascination that he squatted down and picked it up and turned it over in his hands.

The voices came clearly to him through the open kitchen window. "Jody's damn well right," he heard his father say. "Just Indians and crossing the plains. I've heard that story about how the horses got driven off about a thousand times. He just goes on and on, and he never changes a word in the things he tells."

When Mrs. Tiflin answered her tone was so changed that Jody, outside the window, looked up from his study of the stone. Her voice had become soft and explanatory. Jody knew how her face would have changed to match the tone. She said quietly, "Look at it this way, Carl. That was the big thing in my father's life. He led a wagon train clear across the plains to the coast, and when it was finished, his life was done. It was a big thing to do, but it didn't last long enough. Look!" she continued, "it's as though he was born to do that, and after he finished it, there wasn't anything more for him to do but think about it and talk about it. If there'd been any farther west to go, he'd have gone. He's told me so himself. But at last there was the ocean. He lives right by the ocean where he had to stop."

A She had caught Carl, caught him and entangled him in her soft tone.

"I've seen him," he agreed quietly. "He goes down and stares off west over the ocean." His voice sharpened a little. "And then he goes up to the Horseshoe Club in Pacific Grove, and he tells people how the Indians drove off the horses."

She tried to catch him again. "Well, it's everything to him. You might be patient with him and pretend to listen."

Carl turned impatiently away. "Well, if it gets too bad, I can always go down to the bunkhouse and sit with Billy," he said irritably. He walked through the house and slammed the front door after him.

Jody ran to his chores. He dumped the grain to the chickens without chasing any of them. He gathered the eggs from the nests. He trotted into the house with the wood and interlaced it so carefully in the wood box that two armloads seemed to fill it to overflowing.

His mother had finished the beans by now. She stirred up the fire and brushed off the stove top with a turkey wing. Jody peered cautiously at her to see whether any rancor toward him remained. "Is he coming today?" Jody asked.

"That's what his letter said."

"Maybe I better walk up the road to meet him."

Mrs. Tiflin clanged the stove lid shut. "That would be nice," she said. "He'd probably like to be met."

"I guess I'll just do it then."

B Outside, Jody whistled shrilly to the dogs. "Come on up the hill," he commanded. The two dogs waved their tails and ran ahead. Along the roadside the sage had tender new tips. Jody tore off some pieces and rubbed them on his hands until the air was filled with the sharp wild smell. With a rush the dogs leaped from the road and yapped into the brush after a rabbit. That was the last Jody saw of them, for when they failed to catch the rabbit, they went back home.

Jody plodded on up the hill toward the ridge top. When he reached the little cleft where the road came through, the afternoon wind struck him and blew up his hair and ruffled his shirt. He looked down on the little hills and ridges below and then out at the huge green Salinas Valley. He could see the white town of Salinas far out in the flat and the flash of its windows under the waning sun. Directly below him, in an oak tree, a crow congress had convened. The tree was black with crows all cawing at once.

Then Jody's eyes followed the wagon road down from the ridge where he stood, and lost it behind a hill, and picked it up again on the other side. On that distant stretch he saw a cart slowly pulled by a bay horse. It disappeared behind the hill. Jody sat down on the ground and watched the place where the cart would reappear again. The wind sang on the hilltops and the puff-ball clouds hurried eastward.

Then the cart came into sight and stopped. A man dressed in black dismounted from the seat and walked to the horse's head. Although it was so far away, Jody knew he had unhooked the check rein, for the horse's head dropped forward. The horse moved on, and the man walked slowly up the hill beside it. Jody gave a glad cry and ran down the road toward them. The squirrels bumped along off the road, and a road runner flirted its tail C and raced over the edge of the hill and sailed out like a glider.

Jody tried to leap into the middle of his shadow at every step. A stone rolled under his foot and he went down. Around a little bend he raced, and there, a short distance ahead, were his grandfather and the cart. The boy dropped from his unseemly running and approached at a dignified walk.

The horse plodded stumble-footedly up the hill and the old man walked beside it. In the lowering sun their giant shadows flickered darkly behind them. The grandfather was dressed in a black broadcloth suit and he wore kid congress gaiters[2] and a black tie on a short, hard collar. He carried his black slouch hat in his hand. His white beard was cropped close and his white eyebrows overhung his eyes like mustaches. The blue eyes were

2. **kid congress gaiters:** goatskin coverings for the feet.

A. Responding
? What does Steinbeck mean when he says that Jody's mother "had caught Carl, caught and entangled him in her soft voice"? (Her soft, gentle manner defuses Carl's anger.)

B. Setting
? This paragraph and the two short ones that follow contain a number of details about the setting. How many different senses does Steinbeck appeal to in these paragraphs? (Four: *smell*—rubbing the sage buds; *hearing*—yapping of the dogs, the wind singing on the hilltops; *sight*—the white town of Salinas in the green valley, the tree black with crows; *touch*—wind striking Jody, ruffling his shirt and blowing his hair.)

C. Expansion
flirted (*v.t.*): moved in a rapid and jerky manner

A. Theme
? How does Jody's grandfather react to the idea of the mouse hunt? (He doesn't think much of it.) What do you begin to learn about the grandfather's relationships to the "people of this generation"? (He doesn't have much respect for them; it is difficult for him to relate to them.)

B. Expansion
Billy's father had been a mule packer—that is, one who transports goods and supplies by mule.

sternly merry. About the whole face and figure there was a granite dignity, so that every motion seemed an impossible thing. Once at rest, it seemed the old man would be stone, would never move again. His steps were slow and certain. Once made, no step could ever be retraced; once headed in a direction, the path would never bend nor the pace increase nor slow.

When Jody appeared around the bend, Grandfather waved his hat slowly in welcome, and he called, "Why, Jody! Come down to meet me, have you?"

Jody sidled near and turned and matched his step to the old man's step and stiffened his body and dragged his heels a little. "Yes, sir," he said. "We got your letter only today."

"Should have been here yesterday," said Grandfather. "It certainly should. How are all the folks?"

"They're fine, sir." He hesitated and then suggested shyly, "Would you like to come on a mouse hunt tomorrow, sir?"

A "Mouse hunt, Jody?" Grandfather chuckled. "Have the people of this generation come down to hunting mice? They aren't very strong, the new people, but I hardly thought mice would be game for them."

"No, sir. It's just play. The haystack's gone. I'm going to drive out the mice to the dogs. And you can watch, or even beat the hay a little."

The stern, merry eyes turned down on him. "I see. You don't eat them, then. You haven't come to that yet."

Jody explained, "The dogs eat them, sir. It wouldn't be much like hunting Indians, I guess."

"No, not much—but then later, when the troops were hunting Indians and shooting children and burning teepees, it wasn't much different from your mouse hunt."

They topped the rise and started down into the ranch cup, and they lost the sun from their shoulders. "You've grown," Grandfather said. "Nearly an inch, I should say."

"More," Jody boasted. "Where they mark me on the door, I'm up more than an inch since Thanksgiving even."

Grandfather's rich throaty voice said, "Maybe you're getting too much water and turning to pith and stalk. Wait until you head out, and then we'll see."

Jody looked quickly into the old man's face to see whether his feelings should be hurt, but there was no will to injure, no punishing nor putting-in-your-place light in the keen blue eyes. "We might kill a pig," Jody suggested.

"Oh, no! I couldn't let you do that. You're just humoring me. It isn't the time and you know it."

"You know Riley, the big boar, sir?"

"Yes. I remember Riley well."

"Well, Riley ate a hole into that same haystack, and it fell down on him and smothered him."

"Pigs do that when they can," said Grandfather.

"Riley was a nice pig, for a boar, sir. I rode him sometimes, and he didn't mind."

A door slammed at the house below them, and they saw Jody's mother standing on the porch waving her apron in welcome. And they saw Carl Tiflin walking up from the barn to be at the house for the arrival.

The sun had disappeared from the hills by now. The blue smoke from the house chimney hung in flat layers in the purpling ranch cup. The puff-ball clouds, dropped by the falling wind, hung listlessly in the sky.

Billy Buck came out of the bunkhouse and flung a wash basin of soapy water on the ground. He had been shaving in midweek, for Billy held Grandfather in reverence, and Grandfather said that Billy was one of the few men of the new generation who had not gone soft. Although Billy was in middle age, Grandfather considered him a boy. Now Billy was hurrying toward the house too.

When Jody and Grandfather arrived, the three were waiting for them in front of the yard gate.

Carl said, "Hello, sir. We've been looking for you."

Mrs. Tiflin kissed Grandfather on the side of his beard, and stood still while his big hand patted her shoulder. Billy shook hands solemnly, grinning under his straw mustache. "I'll put up your horse," said Billy, and he led the rig away.

Grandfather watched him go, and then, turning back to the group, he said as he had said a hundred times before. "There's a good boy. I knew his father, old Mule-tail Buck. I never knew why they called him Mule-tail except he packed mules." B

Mrs. Tiflin turned and led the way into the house. "How long are you going to stay, Father? Your letter didn't say."

"Well, I don't know. I thought I'd stay about two weeks. But I never stay as long as I think I'm going to."

In a short while they were sitting at the white oilcloth table eating their supper. The lamp with the tin reflector hung over the table. Outside the dining room windows the big moths battered softly against the glass.

Grandfather cut his steak into tiny pieces and chewed slowly. "I'm hungry," he said. "Driving out here got my appetite up. It's like when we were crossing. We all got so hungry every night we could hardly wait to let the meat get done. I could eat about five pounds of buffalo meat every night."

"It's moving around does it," said Billy. "My father was a government packer. I helped him when I was a kid. Just the two of us could about clean up a deer's ham."

"I knew your father, Billy," said Grandfather. "A fine man he was. They called him Mule-tail Buck. I don't know why except he packed mules."

"That was it," Billy agreed. "He packed mules."

A Grandfather put down his knife and fork and looked around the table. "I remember one time we ran out of meat—" His voice dropped to a curious low singsong, dropped into a tonal groove the story had worn for itself. "There was no buffalo, no antelope, not even rabbits. The hunters couldn't even shoot a coyote. That was the time for the leader to be on the watch. I was the leader, and I kept my eyes open. Know why? Well, just the minute the people began to get hungry they'd start slaughtering the team oxen. Do you believe that? I've heard of parties that just ate up their draft cattle. Started from the middle and worked toward the ends. Finally they'd eat the lead pair, and then the wheelers. The leader of a party had to keep them from doing that."

In some manner a big moth got into the room and circled the hanging kerosene lamp. Billy got up and tried to clap it between his hands. Carl struck with a cupped palm and caught the moth and broke it. He walked to the window and dropped it out.

"As I was saying," Grandfather began again, but Carl interrupted him. "You'd better eat some more meat. All the rest of us are ready for our pudding."

Jody saw a flash of anger in his mother's eyes. Grandfatner picked up his knife and fork. "I'm pretty hungry, all right," he said. "I'll tell you about that later."

When supper was over, when the family and Billy Buck sat in front of the fireplace in the other room, Jody anxiously watched Grandfather. He saw the signs he knew. The bearded head leaned forward; the eyes lost their sternness and looked wonderingly into the fire; the big lean fingers laced themselves on the black knees. "I wonder," he began, "I just wonder whether I ever told you how those thieving Piutes drove off thirty-five of our horses."

"I think you did," Carl interrupted. "Wasn't it just before you went up into the Tahoe country?"

Grandfather turned quickly toward his son-in-law.

"That's right. I guess I must have told you that story."

"Lots of times," Carl said cruelly, and he avoided his wife's eyes. But he felt the angry eyes on him, and he said, "'Course I'd like to hear it again."

Grandfather looked back at the fire. His fingers unlaced and laced again. Jody knew how he felt, how his insides were collapsed and empty. Hadn't Jody been called a Big-Britches that very afternoon? He arose to heroism and opened himself to the term Big-Britches again. "Tell about Indians," he said softly.

Grandfather's eyes grew stern again. "Boys always want to hear about Indians. It was a job for men, but boys want to hear about it. Well, let's see. Did I ever tell you how I wanted each wagon to carry a long iron plate?"

Everyone but Jody remained silent. Jody said, "No. You didn't."

"Well, when the Indians attacked, we always put the wagons in a circle and fought from between the wheels. I thought that if every wagon carried a long plate with rifle holes, the men could stand the plates on the outside of the wheels when the wagons were in the circle and they would be protected. It would save lives and that would make up for the extra weight of the iron. But of course the party wouldn't do it. No party had done it before and they couldn't see why they should go to the expense. They lived to regret it, too."

Jody looked at his mother, and knew from her expression that she was not listening at all. Carl picked at a callus on his thumb and Billy Buck watched a spider crawling up the wall.

Grandfather's tone dropped into its narrative groove again. Jody knew in advance exactly what words would fall. The story droned on, speeded up for the attack, grew sad over the wounds,

A. Theme
Here the grandfather reveals his importance as a "leader of a party." Much of his dissatisfaction with life in the present is probably from the lack of a significant role.

? Do people in our society today still react like Jody's grandfather when they are deprived of a significant role because of age and perhaps technological developments? (Student answers will vary. Most students will agree that the grandfather's need to relive the old days is understandable.)

Humanities Connection: Discussing the Fine Art
This lithograph is one of many that the highly successful partnership of Nathaniel Currier (1813–1888) and James Merritt Ives (1824–1895) marketed in the years from 1857 to nearly the end of the century. The partners had a shrewd sense of subjects the American public would be attracted to, and they employed a large number of artists to produce picturesque landscapes, sentimental domestic scenes, heroic scenes of frontier life, and a great variety of other pictures appealing to the tastes of the young nation.

This scene, with its romantic landscape, peaceful Indians, and sturdy migrants is comparable to Jody's grandfather's idealized memories of "westering."

The Rocky Mountain Emigrants Crossing the Plains (1866). Lithograph by Currier and Ives.

struck a dirge at the burials on the great plains. Jody sat quietly watching Grandfather. The stern blue eyes were detached. He looked as though he were not very interested in the story himself. A

When it was finished, when the pause had been politely respected as the frontier of the story, Billy Buck stood up and stretched and hitched his trousers. "I guess I'll turn in," he said. Then he faced Grandfather. "I've got an old powder horn and a cap and ball pistol down to the bunkhouse. Did I ever show them to you?"

Grandfather nodded slowly. "Yes, I think you did, Billy. Reminds me of a pistol I had when I was leading the people across." Billy stood politely until the little story was done, and then he said, "Good night," and went out of the house.

Carl Tiflin tried to turn the conversation then. "How's the country between here and Monterey? I've heard it's pretty dry."

"It is dry," said Grandfather. "There's not a drop of water in the Laguna Seca. But it's a long pull from '87. The whole country was powder then, and in '61 I believe all the coyotes starved to death. We had fifteen inches of rain this year."

"Yes, but it all came too early. We could do with some now." Carl's eye fell on Jody. "Hadn't you better be getting to bed?"

Jody stood up obediently. "Can I kill the mice in the old haystack, sir?"

"Mice? Oh! Sure, kill them all off. Billy said there isn't any good hay left."

Jody exchanged a secret and satisfying look with Grandfather. "I'll kill every one tomorrow," he promised.

Jody lay in his bed and thought of the impossible world of Indians and buffaloes, a world that had ceased to be forever. He wished he could have been living in the heroic time, but he knew he was not of heroic timber. No one living now, save possibly Billy Buck, was worthy to do the things that had been done. A race of giants had lived then, fearless men, men of a staunchness unknown in this day. B Jody thought of the wide plains and of the wagons moving across like centipedes. He thought of Grandfather on a huge white horse, marshaling the people. Across his mind marched the great phantoms, and they marched off the earth and they were gone.

He came back to the ranch for a moment, then. He heard the dull rushing sound that space and silence make. He heard one of the dogs, out in the doghouse, scratching a flea and bumping his

A. Responding

? If Jody's grandfather isn't interested in the stories himself, why does he tell them? (Perhaps because he feels his world in the present is so limited that he has nothing else to contribute, or perhaps because he needs to remind himself and others of what he once was)

B. Responding

? What does the fact that Jody considers no one living in his day, except possibly Billy, capable of heroic deeds suggest about Jody's opinion of his father? (Jody doesn't consider Carl the heroic figure that his grandfather was.)

CLOSURE
Have students discuss the conflicts they have recognized in the course of the story (e.g., between Carl and Jody's mother, between Carl and Jody, between Carl and the grandfather).

Elicit the idea that there is another, more significant conflict—between the hunger of the human spirit of heroism and achievement and the prosaic realities of modern life.

READING CHECK TEST

1. As a younger man, Jody's grandfather was the leader of a ________. *wagon train*

2. Jody is looking forward to killing the ________ that live under the haystack. *mice*

3. Billy Buck is the name of a ________ on Jody's father's ranch. *ranch hand* or *hand*

4. The people in the wagon train used steel plates as protection against ________. *Indians*

5. Jody's grandfather overhears ________ saying that nobody wants to hear his stories over and over again. *Carl* or *Jody's father*

A. Responding
? In what tone of voice do you think Carl makes this remark about his father-in-law? (In a sarcastic tone)

B. Responding
? Why do you suppose Carl becomes so angry toward the grandfather? (Answers will vary. However, for Carl, the world of reality is one of grueling sunrise-to-sunset labor on a farm. It may be that he resents the grandfather's dreams.)

C. Characterization
? What does Carl's apology to the grandfather reveal about Carl as a character? (That he is not intrinsically cruel; that he can acknowledge that he has made a mistake)

elbow against the floor with every stroke. Then the wind arose again and the black cypress groaned and Jody went to sleep.

He was up half an hour before the triangle sounded for breakfast. His mother was rattling the stove to make the flames roar when Jody went through the kitchen. "You're up early," she said. "Where are you going?"

"Out to get a good stick. We're going to kill the mice today."

"Who is 'we'?"

"Why, Grandfather and I."

"So you've got him in it. You always like to have someone in with you in case there's blame to share."

"I'll be right back," said Jody. "I just want to have a good stick ready for after breakfast."

He closed the screen door after him and went out into the cool blue morning. The birds were noisy in the dawn and the ranch cats came down from the hill like blunt snakes. They had been hunting gophers in the dark, and although the four cats were full of gopher meat, they sat in a semicircle at the back door and mewed piteously for milk. Doubletree Mutt and Smasher moved sniffing along the edge of the brush, performing the duty with rigid ceremony, but when Jody whistled, their heads jerked up and their tails waved. They plunged down to him, wriggling their skins and yawning. Jody patted their heads seriously, and moved on to the weathered scrap pile. He selected an old broom handle and a short piece of inch-square scrap wood. From his pocket he took a shoelace and tied the ends of the sticks loosely together to make a flail. He whistled his new weapon through the air and struck the ground experimentally, while the dogs leaped aside and whined with apprehension.

Jody turned and started down past the house toward the old haystack ground to look over the field of slaughter, but Billy Buck, sitting patiently on the back steps, called to him, "You better come back. It's only a couple of minutes till breakfast."

Jody changed his course and moved toward the house. He leaned his flail against the steps. "That's to drive the mice out," he said. "I'll bet they're fat. I'll bet they don't know what's going to happen to them today."

"No, nor you either," Billy remarked philosophically, "nor me, nor anyone."

Jody was staggered by this thought. He knew it was true. His imagination twitched away from the mouse hunt. Then his mother came out on the back porch and struck the triangle, and all thoughts fell in a heap.

Grandfather hadn't appeared at the table when they sat down. Billy nodded at his empty chair. "He's all right? He isn't sick?"

"He takes a long time to dress," said Mrs. Tiflin. "He combs his whiskers and rubs up his shoes and brushes his clothes."

Carl scattered sugar on his mush. "A man that's led a wagon train across the plains has got to be pretty careful how he dresses." **A**

Mrs. Tiflin turned on him. "Don't do that, Carl! Please don't!" There was more of threat than of request in her tone. And the threat irritated Carl.

"Well, how many times do I have to listen to the story of the iron plates, and the thirty-five horses? That time's done. Why can't he forget it, now it's done?" He grew angrier while he talked, and his voice rose. "Why does he have to tell them over and over? He came across the plains. All right! Now it's finished. Nobody wants to hear about it over and over." **B**

The door into the kitchen closed softly. The four at the table sat frozen. Carl laid his mush spoon on the table and touched his chin with his fingers.

Then the kitchen door opened and Grandfather walked in. His mouth smiled tightly, and his eyes were squinted. "Good morning," he said, and he sat down and looked at his mush dish.

Carl could not leave it there. "Did—did you hear what I said?"

Grandfather jerked a little nod.

"I don't know what got into me, sir. I didn't mean it. I was just being funny." **C**

Jody glanced in shame at his mother, and he saw that she was looking at Carl, and that she wasn't breathing. It was an awful thing that he was doing. He was tearing himself to pieces to talk like that. It was a terrible thing to him to retract a word, but to retract it in shame was infinitely worse.

Grandfather looked sidewise. "I'm trying to get right side up," he said gently. "I'm not being mad. I don't mind what you said, but it might be true, and I would mind that."

"It isn't true," said Carl. "I'm not feeling well this morning. I'm sorry I said it."

Analyzing The Story

Identifying Facts

1. Jody seems to enjoy his grandfather's company, and he looks forward to hearing again Grandfather's exciting stories about Indians and crossing the plains.

Jody's parents are not nearly so excited as the little boy about Grandfather's arrival.

2. She says that it is the only exciting thing he has ever done in his life.

3. Grandfather tells about leading a wagon train across the plains to the West Coast.

Grandfather was entrusted by the other settlers with overall responsibility for the crossing. Steinbeck indirectly suggests that Grandfather was also a leader in a metaphorical sense—as an aspiring, daring young man, he had participated in a heroic age of the American past, an age which now seems ended forever.

4. Carl insults Grandfather by saying that he should forget his stories; no one wants to hear them told over and over.

Carl's subsequent apology to Grandfather makes Jody feel ashamed.

Interpreting Meanings

5. In Grandfather's mind, westering seems symbolic of the frontier dream—and, in a larger sense, of an aspiring state of mind among Americans. Both he and Jody, in contrast to Carl, have the intuition that such aspirations were linked with heroism.

6. Student answers will vary. Carl is presented as narrow-minded, unimaginative, and slightly tyrannical. Perhaps his intolerance of his father-in-law stems from an unconscious comparison of Grandfather's moment of glory with his own dull routine.

7. The child is portrayed as imaginative and romantic; Grandfather's stories appeal to him because of his ambition for some sort of heroism.

8. Grandfather says that Billy Buck is one of the few men of the new generation who haven't "gone soft." All the characters, including Carl, seem to like Billy Buck; he is responsible, respectful, and solid.

Their actions with the moth reveal a streak of cruelty in both characters.

(Answers continue on next page.)

"Don't be sorry, Carl. An old man doesn't see things sometimes. Maybe you're right. The crossing is finished. Maybe it should be forgotten, now it's done."

Carl got up from the table. "I've had enough to eat. I'm going to work. Take your time, Billy!" He walked quickly out of the dining room. Billy gulped the rest of his food and followed soon after. But Jody could not leave his chair.

"Won't you tell any more stories?" Jody asked.

"Why, sure I'll tell them, but only when—I'm sure people want to hear them."

"I like to hear them, sir."

"Oh! Of course you do, but you're a little boy. It was a job for men, but only little boys like to hear about it."

Jody got up from his place. "I'll wait outside for you, sir. I've got a good stick for those mice."

He waited by the gate until the old man came out on the porch. "Let's go down and kill the mice now," Jody called.

"I think I'll just sit in the sun, Jody. You go kill the mice."

"You can use my stick if you like."

"No, I'll just sit here a while."

Jody turned disconsolately away, and walked down toward the old haystack. He tried to whip up his enthusiasm with thoughts of the fat juicy mice. He beat the ground with his flail. The dogs coaxed and whined about him, but he could not go. Back at the house he could see Grandfather sitting on the porch, looking small and thin and black.

Jody gave up and went to sit on the steps at the old man's feet.

"Back already? Did you kill the mice?"

"No, sir. I'll kill them some other day."

The morning flies buzzed close to the ground and the ants dashed about in front of the steps. The heavy smell of sage slipped down the hill. The porch boards grew warm in the sunshine.

Jody hardly knew when Grandfather started to talk. "I shouldn't stay here, feeling the way I do." He examined his strong old hands. "I feel as though the crossing wasn't worth doing." His eyes moved up the sidehill and stopped on a motionless hawk perched on a dead limb. "I tell those old stories, but they're not what I want to tell. I only know how I want people to feel when I tell them."

"It wasn't Indians that were important, nor adventures, nor even getting out here. It was a whole bunch of people made into one big crawling beast. And I was the head. It was westering and westering. Every man wanted something for himself, but the big beast that was all of them wanted only westering. I was the leader, but if I hadn't been there, someone else would have been the head. The thing had to have a head.

"Under the little bushes the shadows were black at white noonday. When we saw the mountains at last, we cried—all of us. But it wasn't getting here that mattered, it was movement and westering.

"We carried life out here and set it down the way those ants carry eggs. And I was the leader. The westering was as big as God, and the slow steps that made the movement piled up and piled up until the continent was crossed.

"Then we came down to the sea, and it was done." He stopped and wiped his eyes until the rims were red. "That's what I should be telling instead of stories."

When Jody spoke, Grandfather started and looked down at him. "Maybe I could lead the people some day," Jody said.

The old man smiled. "There's no place to go. There's the ocean to stop you. There's a line of old men along the shore hating the ocean because it stopped them."

"In boats I might, sir."

"No place to go, Jody. Every place is taken. But that's not the worst—no, not the worst. Westering has died out of the people. Westering isn't a hunger anymore. It's all done. Your father is right. It is finished." He laced his fingers on his knee and looked at them.

Jody felt very said. "If you'd like a glass of lemonade I could make it for you."

Grandfather was about to refuse, and then he saw Jody's face. "That would be nice," he said. "Yes, it would be nice to drink a lemonade."

Jody ran into the kitchen where his mother was wiping the last of the breakfast dishes. "Can I have a lemon to make a lemonade for Grandfather?"

His mother mimicked—"And another lemon to make a lemonade for you."

"No, ma'am. I don't want one."

"Jody! You're sick!" Then she stopped suddenly. "Take a lemon out of the cooler," she said softly. "Here, I'll reach the squeezer down to you."

(Continued from previous page.)
9. Jody picks up a stone to throw at the cat. He also seems obsessed with chasing and killing the mice.

Jody feels that paying attention to his grandfather, who has been insulted by Carl, is more important than pursuing the mice hunt.
10. Steinbeck has Grandfather imply the softness and puniness of the modern age by making him say, "Have the people of this generation come down to hunting mice?" (page 568).
11. The source of the conflict between Carl and his wife is Grandfather's visit. Although Mrs. Tiflin does not pay attention any more to her father's stories, she insists that her husband show the old man some respect. The source of the conflict between Jody and his father is Carl's determination to control his son and to keep him in his place. Jody's evident pleasure in Grandfather's visit and in his stories also annoys Carl. The source of the conflict between Carl and Grandfather is that Carl is bored and annoyed by Grandfather's obsession with the past.

Student interests in the conflicts will *(Answers continue in left-hand column.)*

(Continued from top.)
vary. Have students give reasons for their responses.

A case may be made for either of the two story focuses or for both.
12. One statement of the theme of the story might run as follows: The imaginative hunger of the human spirit for heroism and great achievement must inevitably clash with harsh, almost brutal realities. Students will differ in their opinions on whether or not any more frontiers exist for young Americans.

Responding to the Story

Analyzing the Story

Identifying Facts

1. Explain why Jody looks forward to his grandfather's visit. In contrast, how do his father and mother feel?
2. According to Mrs. Tiflin, why does her father still talk about leading the wagon train west?
3. What is the subject of Grandfather's stories? In what way was he the "leader of the people"?
4. Steinbeck uses an old fictional device when he has Grandfather overhear something that he was not intended to hear. How does Carl insult the old man, and how does this exchange between the two older men affect Jody?

Interpreting Meanings

5. What seems to have been the true significance of "the crossing" for Jody's grandfather?
6. Carl Tiflin is strongly intolerant of his father-in-law's oft-told stories. Do you think it is just boredom that provokes Carl's anger? Or could he be taking the stories as some reflection on his own life? What might that be?
7. Jody is the one character who can't get enough of his grandfather's old stories. Why does he have the appetite for them?
8. Given what he says and does and given the way other characters respond to him, how would you **characterize** Billy Buck? What do their actions with the moth (page 569) reveal about the characters of Billy and Carl?
9. How does Jody in the early part of the story show a streak of cruelty, perhaps like his father's? What is the significance of his decision to give up the mice hunt?
10. The story is full of **ironies.** How does Steinbeck ironically characterize the modern age by the use of the mice hunt?
11. There are several **conflicts** in "The Leader of the People,"—between Carl Tiflin and his wife, between Jody and his father, and between Jody's father and his grandfather. Describe the source of each conflict. Which interests you the most? Would you say this story is more about family relationships, or more about the changing attitudes of each new generation?
12. What would you say is the **theme** of this story? Do you believe, as Jody's grandfather does, that there are no longer any frontiers for young Americans? If you disagree, where would you look for modern frontiers?

Writing About the Story

A Creative Response

1. **Using Another Point of View.** What has Jody learned from his experience with Grandfather and his father? In a paragraph, write out Jody's thoughts as he looks back on this day ten years later. Write in the first person, using Jody's own voice.

A Critical Response

2. **Comparing and Contrasting Characters.** In an essay, compare and contrast the characters of Grandfather and Carl Tiflin. Consider what you are told about how the characters look, what they say, how they behave, and how other people feel about them. In your essay, use three adjectives to characterize each man.
3. **Comparing Themes.** In an essay, explain how at least two of the stories you have read in this unit touch on the theme of lost opportunities for heroism.

Analyzing Language and Style

Figures of Speech

Scholars have defined three hundred or more figures of speech, but most people are familiar with five types: (1) the **simile,** in which two dissimilar things are compared with the use of specific comparison words (such as *like, as, resembles*); (2) the **metaphor,** in which two dissimilar things are identified without the use of the specific comparison words; (3) **personification,** a type of metaphor in which something inanimate is described as if it is human or alive; (4) **oxymoron,** a combination of two words that seem to contradict each other (wise fool, death in life, sweet sorrow); and (5) **hyperbole,** in which exaggeration is used for special effect.

Following are some figures of speech from "The Leader of the People." See if you can identify the type of figure of speech being used; then paraphrase the figure of speech in your own words.

1. "lean March sunshine" (page 566)
2. "entangled him in her soft tone" (page 567)
3. "wind sang on the hilltops" (page 567)
4. "blue eyes were sternly merry" (page 567)
5. "a granite dignity" (page 568)
6. "how his insides were collapsed and empty" (page 569)
7. "wagons moving across like centipedes" (page 571)
8. "a whole bunch of people made into one big crawling beast" (page 573)

Primary Sources

Nobel Prize Acceptance Speech, 1962

"I thank the Swedish Academy for finding my work worthy of this highest honor. In my heart there may be doubt that I deserve the Nobel Award over other men of letters whom I hold in respect and reverence—but there is no question of my pleasure and pride in having it for myself.

"It is customary for the recipient of this award to offer scholarly or personal comment on the nature and the direction of literature. However, I think it would be well at this particular time to consider the high duties and the responsibilities of the makers of literature.

"Such is the prestige of the Nobel Award and of this place where I stand that I am impelled, not to squeak like a grateful and apologetic mouse, but to roar like a lion out of pride in my profession and in the great and good men who have practiced it through the ages.

"Literature was not promulgated by a pale and emasculated critical priesthood singing their litanies in empty churches—nor is it a game for the cloistered elect, the tinhorn mendicants of low-calorie despair.

A "Literature is as old as speech. It grew out of human need for it and it has not changed except to become more needed. The skalds, the bards, the writers are not separate and exclusive. From the beginning, their functions, their duties, their responsibilities have been decreed by our species.

"Humanity has been passing through a gray and desolate time of confusion. My great predecessor, William Faulkner, speaking here, referred to it as a tragedy of universal physical fear, so long sustained that there were no longer problems of the spirit, so that only the human heart in conflict with itself seemed worth writing about. Faulkner, more than most men, was aware of human strength as well as of human weakness. He knew that the understanding and the resolution of fear are a large part of the writer's reason for being.

B "This is not new. The ancient commission of the writer has not changed. He is charged with exposing our many grievous faults and failures, with dredging up to the light our dark and dangerous dreams for the purpose of improvement.

"Furthermore, the writer is delegated to declare and to celebrate man's proven capacity for greatness of heart and spirit—for gallantry in defeat, for courage, compassion and love. In the endless war against weakness and despair, these are the bright rally flags of hope and emulation. I hold that a writer who does not passionately believe in the perfectability of man has no dedication nor any membership in literature.

"The present universal fear has been the result of a forward surge in our knowledge and manipulation of certain dangerous factors in the physical world. It is true that other phases of understanding have not yet caught up with this great step, but there is no reason to presume that they cannot or will not draw abreast. Indeed, it is a part of the writer's responsibility to make sure that they do. With humanity's long, proud history of standing firm against all of its natural enemies, sometimes in the face of almost certain defeat and extinction, we would be cowardly and stupid to leave the field on the eve of our greatest potential victory.

"Understandably, I have been reading the life of Alfred Nobel; a solitary man, the books say, a thoughtful man. He perfected the release of explosive forces capable of creative good or of destructive evil, but lacking choice, ungoverned by conscience or judgment. C

"Nobel saw some of the cruel and bloody misuses of his inventions. He may even have foreseen the end result of his probing—access to ultimate violence, to final destruction. Some say that he became cynical, but I do not believe this. I think he strove to invent a control—a safety valve. I think he found it finally only in the human mind and the human spirit.

"To me, his thinking is clearly indicated in the categories of these awards. They are offered for increased and continuing knowledge of man and of his world—for *understanding* and *communication,* which are the functions of literature. And they are offered for demonstrations of the capacity for peace—the culmination of all the others.

"Less than fifty years after his death, the door of nature was unlocked and we were offered the dreadful burden of choice. We have usurped many of the powers we once ascribed to God. Fearful and unprepared, we have assumed lordship over the life and death of the whole world of all living things. The danger and the glory and the choice rest finally in man. The test of his perfectibility is at hand.

"Having taken God-like power, we must seek in ourselves for the responsibility and the wisdom we once prayed some deity might have. Man himself has become our greatest hazard and our only hope. So that today, Saint John the Apostle may well be paraphrased: In the end is the *word,* and the word is *man,* and the word is *with* man."

—John Steinbeck

A. Responding
? Steinbeck says that literature "grew out of a human need for it." Why do you think that humans need literature? (Answers will vary. They may include the need for knowledge, self-questioning or enlightenment—as well as the need to tell a story, to instruct or to entertain.)

B. Responding
? What are the writer's responsibilities? (To expose "our many grievous faults and failures" and "our dark and dangerous dreams" and to celebrate our "capacity for greatness of heart and spirit")

C. Responding
? What are the "explosive forces" of which Steinbeck speaks? (Nuclear energy)

A. Satire
? How does Thurber satirize the typical author's biography? (Thurber begins typically with "was born in Columbus, Ohio," but instead of a list of sterling accomplishments, he writes about some of the "awful things that happened to him." Instead of the usual description of the sensitive characteristics of a writer, Thurber mentions that he is so hard to quiet that "people often just go away." He also mentions such dubious accomplishments as winning a canary bird.)

B. Expansion
You may want students to look now at the cartoons on pages 578, 579, and 580 and to discuss Thurber's attitude toward women as it is revealed there.

James Thurber (1894–1961)

James Thurber is generally acknowledged to be the foremost American humorist of the twentieth century. He was a supremely gifted cartoonist and a writer of essays, sketches, and stories. For a 1956 collection of fables, he made fun of the puffery that characterizes biographies of literary figures and presented this self-portrait:

A

> James Thurber was born in Columbus, Ohio, where so many awful things happened to him, on 8 December 1894. He was unable to keep anything on his stomach until he was seven years old, but grew to six feet one and a half inches tall and to weigh a hundred and fifty-four pounds fully dressed for winter. He began to write when he was ten years old and to draw when he was fourteen. Quick to arouse, he is very hard to quiet and people often just go away. At Buckeye Lake, Ohio, in 1923, he won a canary bird throwing baseballs at dolls. He has never been taken at fan-tan.[1] He uses the Thurber overbidding convention and even the most skilled partners have no chance with him. He never listens when anybody else is talking, preferring to keep his mind a blank until they get through, so he can talk. His favorite book is *The Great Gatsby.* His favorite author is Henry James. He wears excellent clothes very badly and can never find his hat. He is Sagittarius with the moon in Aries and gets along fine with persons born between the 20th and the 24th of August.

Thurber did grow up in Columbus, Ohio, where he attended Ohio State University. He then worked as a reporter for the *Columbus Dispatch* and the *Chicago Tribune* for a number of years, before coming to New York City. In 1927, he went to work for *The New Yorker* magazine and remained a member of its staff for the rest of his life. In addition to many collections of stories, essays, and children's books, Thurber collaborated on a successful Broadway play called *The Male Animal* (1940).

His humor often turned on the chaos of contemporary American life. Thurber focused on the "little man," who cannot quite assert himself in a confusing world where women seem surer of their way. Thus, Walter Mitty, the anti-hero of Thurber's most famous story, seeks release in fantasy from a wife who overwhelms him.

While Thurber claimed to welcome the feminist movement, hoping it would seize power and prevent men from blowing the world to bits, he viewed women with a certain ambivalence—as intimidating to their mates, and as mother-figures rather than as partners. (Thurber's attitude toward women is comically revealed in his cartoons that illustrate Mitty's story.) B

Thurber defined humor as "a kind of emotional chaos told about calmly and quietly in retrospect." But humor is not subject to rational explanation. Perhaps this was in the mind of Thurber's friend, the writer Mark Van Doren, when he said of Thurber: "He was an extraordinary man . . . with so many quick changes: gentle and fierce, fascinating and boring, sophisticated and boorish, kind and cruel, broadminded and parochial. You can't explain Thurber."

1. **fan-tan:** a card game.

SUPPLEMENTARY SUPPORT MATERIALS

1. Vocabulary Activity Worksheet (*CCB*)
2. Review and Response Worksheet: Parody (*CCB*)
3. Selection Test (*CCB*)

DEVELOPING VOCABULARY

The following words from the story are tested in the Selection Test. (See also Vocabulary Activity Worksheet.)

craven	rending
insinuatingly	derisive
pandemonium	inscrutable

PREPARATION

1. ESTABLISHING A PURPOSE. Tell your students that the story they are about to read is funny but has something in common with "The Leader of the People." Suggest that as they read they try to identify this common element.

2. PREREADING JOURNAL. Have students write a brief description of an adventure fantasy they have acted out imaginatively—as a nurse, a sports star, or other dramatic figure. Ask them to name the special effects that were important in making their fantasy seem real.

THE SECRET LIFE OF WALTER MITTY

The name Walter Mitty has entered our language as the epitome of the "little guy" who is dominated by an assertive wife. You might recognize both Mitty and the formidable Mrs. Mitty—they are character types that form the basis of many American situation comedies. Mitty is based on a stereotype of the henpecked husband, but Mitty himself is an original. Read the first paragraph and stop. Based on this paragraph, what does it seem as if this story is going to be about?

"We're going through!" The Commander's voice was like thin ice breaking. He wore his full-dress uniform, with the heavily braided white cap pulled down rakishly over one cold gray eye. "We can't make it, sir. It's spoiling for a hurricane, if you ask me." "I'm not asking you, Lieutenant Berg," said the Commander. "Throw on the power lights! Rev her up to 8,500! We're going through!" The pounding of the cylinders increased: ta-pocketa-pocketa-pocketa-*pocketa-pocketa*. The commander stared at the ice forming on the pilot window. He walked over and twisted a row of complicated dials. "Switch on No. 8 auxiliary!" he shouted. "Switch on No. 8 auxiliary!" repeated Lieutenant Berg. "Full strength in No. 3 turret!" shouted the Commander. "Full strength in No. 3 turret!" The crew, bending to their various tasks in the huge, hurtling eight-engined Navy hydroplane, looked at each other and grinned. "The Old Man'll get us through," they said to one another. "The Old Man ain't afraid of Hell!" . . .

"Not so fast! You're driving too fast!" said Mrs. Mitty. "What are you driving so fast for?"

"Hmm?" said Walter Mitty. He looked at his wife, in the seat beside him, with shocked astonishment. She seemed grossly unfamiliar, like a strange woman who had yelled at him in a crowd. "You were up to fifty-five," she said. "You know I don't like to go more than forty. You were up to fifty-five." Walter Mitty drove on toward Waterbury in silence, the roaring of the SN202 through the worst storm in twenty years of Navy flying fading in the remote, intimate airways of his mind. "You're tensed up again," said Mrs. Mitty. "It's one of your days. I wish you'd let Dr. Renshaw look you over."

Walter Mitty stopped the car in front of the building where his wife went to have her hair done. "Remember to get those overshoes while I'm having my hair done," she said. "I don't need overshoes," said Mitty. She put her mirror back into her bag. "We've been all through that," she said, getting out of the car. "You're not a young man any longer." He raced the engine a little. "Why don't you wear your gloves? Have you lost your gloves?" Walter Mitty reached in a pocket and brought out the gloves. He put them on, but after she had turned and gone into the building and he had driven on to a red light, he took them off again. "Pick it up, brother!" snapped a cop as the light changed, and Mitty hastily pulled on his gloves and lurched ahead. He drove around the streets aimlessly for a time, and then he drove past the hospital on his way to the parking lot. A

. . . "It's the millionaire banker, Wellington McMillan," said the pretty nurse. "Yes?" said Walter Mitty, removing his gloves slowly. "Who has the case?" "Dr. Renshaw and Dr. Benbow, but there are two specialists here, Dr. Remington from New York and Mr. Pritchard-Mitford from London. He flew over." A door opened down a long, cool corridor and Dr. Renshaw came out. He looked distraught and haggard. "Hello, Mitty," he said. "We're having the devil's own time with McMillan, the millionaire banker and close personal friend of Roosevelt. Obstreosis of the ductal tract. Tertiary. Wish you'd take a look at him." "Glad to," said Mitty. B

In the operating room there were whispered introductions: "Dr. Remington, Dr. Mitty. Mr. Pritchard-Mitford, Dr. Mitty." "I've read your book on streptothricosis," said Pritchard-Mitford, shaking hands. "A brilliant performance, sir."

A. Responding

? Why does Mitty put his gloves back on when the traffic cop yells at him? (Momentarily flustered, he thinks the policeman is reprimanding him for not following his wife's orders about wearing the gloves.)

B. Responding

? What bits of reality does Mitty incorporate in his hospital fantasy? (Gloves; Dr. Renshaw, his family physician; Roosevelt, who was then President) What stimulus brings on Mitty's great surgeon fantasy? (Driving past the hospital)

A. Responding

? How does Mitty's performance in his operating room fantasy contrast with his real performance in the parking lot? ("Dr. Mitty" repairs a complicated machine and takes over delicate surgery from "two great specialists." In the parking lot, Mitty almost hits another car. The attendant has to park his car.)

B. Responding

? What elements from real life send Mitty into the courtroom fantasy? (The idea of wearing his right arm in a sling so the mechanic won't grin at him; the newsboy shouting about a Waterbury trial; the fact that he has forgotten an item on his wife's shopping list, which gives rise to "Perhaps this will refresh your memory," a cliché of courtroom dramas) What association makes Mitty remember that he is supposed to buy puppy biscuits? (Calling the District Attorney a "miserable cur" in his fantasy)

A ''Thank you,'' said Walter Mitty. ''Didn't know you were in the States, Mitty,'' grumbled Remington. ''Coals to Newcastle,[1] bringing Mitford and me up here for a tertiary.'' ''You are very kind,'' said Mitty. A huge, complicated machine, connected to the operating table, with many tubes and wires, began at this moment to go pocketa-pocketa-pocketa. ''The new anesthetizer is giving way!'' shouted an intern. ''There is no one in the East who knows how to fix it!'' ''Quiet, man!'' said Mitty, in a low, cool voice. He sprang to the machine, which was now going pocketa-pocketa-queep-pocketa-queep. He began fingering delicately a row of glistening dials. ''Give me a fountain pen!'' he snapped. Someone handed him a fountain pen. He pulled a faulty piston out of the machine and inserted the pen in its place. ''That will hold for ten minutes,'' he said. ''Get on with the operation.'' A nurse hurried over and whispered to Renshaw, and Mitty saw the man turn pale. ''Coreopsis has set in,'' said Renshaw nervously. ''If you would take over, Mitty?'' Mitty looked at him and at the craven figure of Benbow, who drank, and at the grave, uncertain faces of the two great specialists. ''If you wish,'' he said. They slipped a white gown on him; he adjusted a mask and drew on thin gloves; nurses handed him shining . . .

''Back it up, Mac! Look out for that Buick!'' Walter Mitty jammed on the brakes. ''Wrong lane, Mac,'' said the parking lot attendant, looking at Mitty closely. ''Gee. Yeh,'' muttered Mitty. He began cautiously to back out of the lane marked ''Exit Only.'' ''Leave her sit there,'' said the attendant. ''I'll put her away.'' Mitty got out of the car. ''Hey, better leave the key.'' ''Oh,'' said Mitty, handing the man the ignition key. The attendant vaulted into the car, backed it up with insolent skill, and put it where it belonged.

They're so damn cocky, thought Walter Mitty, walking along Main Street; they think they know everything. Once he had tried to take his chains off, outside New Milford, and he had got them wound around the axles. A man had had to come out in a wrecking car and unwind them, a young, grinning garageman. Since then Mrs. Mitty always made him drive to a garage to have the chains taken off. The next time, he thought, I'll wear my
B right arm in a sling; they won't grin at me then.

1. **Coals to Newcastle:** a proverbial expression referring to unnecessary effort. Newcastle, in England, produced coal itself.

''House and Woman.''

Cartoon by James Thurber from *The Thurber Carnival* (1957).

I'll have my right arm in a sling and they'll see I couldn't possibly take the chains off myself. He kicked at the slush on the sidewalk. ''Overshoes,'' he said to himself, and he began looking for a shoe store.

When he came out into the street again, with the overshoes in a box under his arm, Walter Mitty began to wonder what the other thing was his wife had told him to get. She had told him, twice, before they set out from their house for Waterbury. In a way he hated these weekly trips to town—he was always getting something wrong. Kleenex, he thought, Squibb's, razor blades? No. Toothpaste, toothbrush, bicarbonate, carborundum, initiative and referendum? He gave it up. But she would remember it. ''Where's the what's-its-name?'' she would ask. ''Don't tell me you forgot the what's-its-name.'' A newsboy went by shouting something about the Waterbury trial.

. . . ''Perhaps this will refresh your memory.'' The District Attorney suddenly thrust a heavy automatic at the quiet figure on the witness stand. ''Have you ever seen this before?'' Walter Mitty took the gun and examined it expertly. ''This is my Webley-Vickers 50.80,'' he said calmly. An excited buzz ran around the courtroom. The Judge rapped for order. ''You are a crack shot with any sort of firearms, I believe?'' said the District Attorney, insinuatingly. ''Objection!'' shouted Mitty's attorney. ''We have shown that the defendant could not have fired the shot. We have shown that

Closure
Ask students to discuss what similarities, if any, they can see between this story and "A Leader of the People." (In both, a hunger for heroic achievement conflicts with humdrum reality.)

Reading Check Test
1. Mrs. Mitty reminds Walter to buy a snow shovel. *False*
2. As Dr. Mitty, Walter repairs the anesthetizer with a metal coat hanger. *False*
3. One item on Walter's shopping list is puppy biscuits. *True*
4. One of the roles Walter imagines himself in is that of a crusading district attorney. *False*
5. An article about German air power triggers Mitty's fantasy about being a World War I ace. *True*

he wore his right arm in a sling on the night of the fourteenth of July." Walter Mitty raised his hand briefly and the bickering attorneys were stilled. "With any known make of gun," he said evenly, "I could have killed Gregory Fitzhurst at three hundred feet *with my left hand.*" Pandemonium broke loose in the courtroom. A woman's scream rose above the bedlam and suddenly a lovely, dark-haired girl was in Walter Mitty's arms. The District Attorney struck at her savagely. Without rising from his chair, Mitty let the man have it on the point of the chin. "You miserable cur!" . . .

"Puppy biscuit," said Walter Mitty. He stopped walking and the buildings of Waterbury rose up out of the misty courtroom and surrounded him again. A woman who was passing laughed. "He said 'Puppy biscuit,' " she said to her companion. "That man said 'Puppy biscuit' to himself." Walter Mitty hurried on. He went into an A. & P., not the first one he came to but a smaller one farther up the street "I want some biscuit for small, young dogs," he said to the clerk. "Any special brand, sir?" The greatest pistol shot in the world thought a moment. "It says 'Puppies Bark for It' on the box," said Walter Mitty.

His wife would be through at the hairdresser's in fifteen minutes, Mitty saw in looking at his watch, unless they had trouble drying it; sometimes they had trouble drying it. She didn't like to get to the hotel first; she would want him to be there waiting for her as usual. He found a big leather chair in the lobby, facing a window, and he put the overshoes and the puppy biscuit on the floor beside it. He picked up an old copy of *Liberty*

A

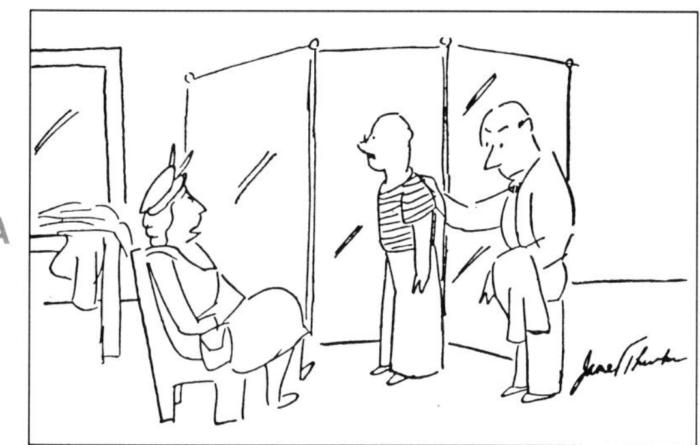

"I don't want him to be comfortable."

Cartoon by James Thurber from *The Thurber Carnival* (1957).

and sank down into the chair. "Can Germany Conquer the World Through the Air?" Walter Mitty looked at the pictures of bombing planes and of ruined streets.

. . . "The cannonading has got the wind up in young Raleigh, sir," said the sergeant. Captain Mitty looked up at him through tousled hair. "Get him to bed," he said wearily. "With the others. I'll fly alone." "But you can't, sir," said the sergeant anxiously. "It takes two men to handle that bomber and the Archies[2] are pounding hell out of the air. Von Richtman's circus[3] is between here and Saulier." "Somebody's got to get that ammunition dump," said Mitty. "I'm going over. Spot of brandy?" He poured a drink for the sergeant and one for himself. War thundered and whined around the dugout and battered at the door. There was a rending of wood and splinters flew through the room. "A bit of a near thing," said Captain Mitty carelessly. "The box barrage is closing in," said the sergeant. "We only live once, Sergeant," said Mitty, with his faint, fleeting smile. "Or do we?" He poured another brandy and tossed it off. "I never see a man could hold his brandy like you, sir," said the sergeant. "Begging your pardon, sir." Captain Mitty stood up and strapped on his huge Webley-Vickers automatic. "It's forty kilometers through hell, sir," said the sergeant. Mitty finished one last brandy. "After all," he said softly, "what isn't?" The pounding of the cannon increased; there was the rat-tat-tatting of machine guns, and from somewhere came the menacing pocketa-pocketa-pocketa of the new flamethrowers. Walter Mitty walked to the door of the dugout humming "Auprès de Ma Blonde."[4] He turned and waved to the sergeant. "Cheerio!" he said. . . .

Something struck his shoulder. "I've been looking all over this hotel for you," said Mrs. Mitty. "Why do you have to hide in this old chair? How did you expect me to find you?" "Things close in," said Walter Mitty vaguely. "What?" Mrs. Mitty said. "Did you get the what's-its-name? The puppy biscuit? What's in that box?" "Overshoes," said Mitty. "Couldn't you have put them on in the store?" "I was thinking," said Walter Mitty. "Does it ever occur to you that I am sometimes thinking?" She looked at him. "I'm

2. **Archies:** German antiaircraft gunners.
3. **circus:** a squadron of planes.
4. **"Auprès de Ma Blonde":** a French song whose title means "Near My Blonde."

A. Humanities Connection: Discussing the Cartoon
The cartoons in this selection illustrate a favorite theme of Thurber's—the battle of the sexes. As these drawings suggest, the struggle is an uneven one, between the uncertain and slightly confused male and the surer and somewhat intimidating female. The cartoon on page 580 shows the male in an uncharacteristic counterattack. Thurber's cartoons appeared regularly in *The New Yorker.*

For Further Reading For The Student
My World—and Welcome to It (Harcourt Brace Jovanovich, 1970) contains a delightful collection of Thurber's cartoons, stories, and essays.

ANALYZING THE STORY
Identifying Facts
1. Walter Mitty leads a routine, dull existence in suburban Connecticut.

Mitty imagines himself as a heroic figure in a variety of romantic daydreams.

2. His errands include getting some overshoes and buying puppy biscuit.

He commands a war plane, performs a tricky surgical operation, testifies at a murder trial, and executes a critical wartime mission.

3. The notion of speed at the opening of the story connects Mitty's fantasy of the Navy plane with Mrs. Mitty's unheroic reproach, "Not so fast! You're driving too fast!" The mention of gloves is associated with "Dr. Mitty's" surgical gloves in the episode of the operating room. This episode ends with the parking lot attendant jarring Mitty back to reality. Mitty's remark to himself that he will wear his right arm in a sling is interwoven with a detail in the courtroom episode. The insult at the end of that fantasy, "You miserable cur!", leads directly into Mitty remembering (in real life) that he needs to buy puppy biscuit. As Mitty leafs through a magazine in the hotel lobby, he sees an article about the German air force; the

going to take your temperature when I get you home,'' she said.

They went out through the revolving doors that made a faintly derisive whistling sound when you pushed them. It was two blocks to the parking lot. At the drugstore on the corner she said, ''Wait here for me. I forgot something. I won't be a minute.'' She was more than a minute. Walter Mitty lighted a cigarette. It began to rain, rain with sleet in it. He stood up against the wall of the drugstore, smoking. . . . He put his shoulders back and his heels together. ''To hell with the handkerchief,'' said Walter Mitty scornfully. He took one last drag on his cigarette and snapped it away. Then, with that faint, fleeting smile playing about his lips, he faced the firing squad; erect and motionless, proud and disdainful, Walter Mitty the Undefeated, inscrutable to the last.

''Well, who made the magic go out? . . .''

Cartoon by James Thurber from *The Thurber Carnival* (1957).

Responding to the Story

Analyzing the Story

Identifying Facts

1. Describe the **setting** of Walter Mitty's everyday life. In contrast, what are the settings of his secret life?
2. What errands is Mitty on in his real life? What deeds does he perform in his secret life?
3. Thurber makes use of a psychological technique known as **free association,** in which words and sounds from real life become associated with elements of Mitty's daydreams. How does each daydream begin, and what sends Mitty into it? What decidedly unheroic events snap Mitty out of his reveries?

Interpreting Meanings

4. What is the central **irony** of Mitty's life? Is this irony humorous, serious, or partly both? Explain.
5. **Parody** is the satirical imitation of someone's speech, manners, or ideas. Where does Thurber use parody in this story? Who or what are the targets of the satire? (Look at the **jargon** bandied about in the daydreams.)
6. Walter Mitty could be seen as one of a line of archetypal American characters that begins with Ben Franklin's ''self-made man.'' What does Mitty's life reveal about the opportunities offered for heroism today? What is your opinion of Thurber's message here?
7. Could Mitty be a disappointed romantic? Explain.

Writing About the Story

A Critical Response

1. **Analyzing Characters.** Walter Mitty and the formidable Mrs. Mitty have by now become stock American character types. In an essay, analyze the characters of Walter and his spouse. In your analysis, tell how the character types of ''Mrs. Mitty'' and ''Walter Mitty'' are found in popular movies and TV shows today.
2. **Comparing Stories.** James Thurber has been accused of being ''tough'' on women, a criticism that has also been leveled against Washington Irving for his portrait of Dame Van Winkle (page 125). In an essay, compare and contrast these two American couples—Rip and his wife, and Walter and Mrs. Mitty. Consider the characters' strengths and weaknesses, the source of their conflicts, the way their conflicts are resolved, the relationships between husband and wife, and the tone of each story.

headline leads into his fantasy about piloting a bomber to destroy an enemy ammunition dump.

Interpreting Meanings

4. The central irony stems from the extreme gulf separating Mitty's real world from his fantasy world. Student interpretations of the tone of the irony will differ.

On the surface, the story is humorous, but there is an element of pathos in the portrait of Mitty's escape from reality.

5. Most obviously, Thurber parodies technical jargon, as with the phrase "obstreosis of the ductal tract" in the hospital fantasy. But we should also notice that Mitty's fantasies themselves are broad parodies of stereotyped situations and characters: the intrepid flight commander leading his anxious crew through a storm, for example.

6. Mitty's life reveals that there are few opportunities offered for heroism today. Thurber implies that heroism exists primarily in the realm of fantasy. Students will differ in their opinions of Thurber's message.

7. Most students will agree that Mitty could be regarded as a disappointed romantic.

Primary Sources

The New Yorker*'s Farewell*

Thurber's long-time associate on *The New Yorker,* E. B. White, wrote this parting tribute to his friend on November 11, 1961.

"I am one of the lucky ones; I knew him before blindness hit him, before fame hit him, and I tend always to think of him as a young artist in a small office in a big city, with all the world still ahead. It was a fine thing to be young and at work in New York for a new magazine when Thurber was young and at work, and I will always be glad that this happened to me.

"It was fortunate that we got on well; the office we shared was the size of a hall bedroom. There was just room enough for two men, two typewriters, and a stack of copy paper. The copy paper disappeared at a scandalous rate—not because our production was high (although it was) but because Thurber used copy paper as the natural receptacle for discarded sorrows, immediate joys, stale dreams, golden prophecies, and messages of good cheer to the outside world and to fellow workers. His mind was never at rest, and his pencil was connected to his mind by the best conductive tissue I have ever seen in action. The whole world knows what a funny man he was, but you had to sit next to him day after day to understand the extravagance of his clowning, the wildness and subtlety of his thinking, and the intensity of his interest in others and his sympathy for their dilemmas—dilemmas that he instantly enlarged, put in focus, and made immortal, just as he enlarged and made immortal the strange goings-on in the Ohio home of his boyhood. His waking dreams and his sleeping dreams commingled shamelessly and uproariously. Ohio was never far from his thoughts, and when he received a medal from his home state in 1953, he wrote, 'The clocks that strike in my dreams are often the clocks of Columbus.' It is a beautiful sentence and a revealing one.

"He was both a practitioner of humor and a defender of it. The day he died, I came on a letter from him, dictated to a secretary and signed in pencil with his sightless and enormous 'Jim.' 'Every time is a time for humor,' he wrote. 'I write humor the way a surgeon operates, because it is a livelihood, because I have a great urge to do it, because many interesting challenges are

A self-portrait of James Thurber and dog.

set up, and because I have the hope it may do some good.' Once, I remember, he heard someone say that humor is a shield, not a sword, and it made him mad. He wasn't going to have anyone beating his sword into a shield. That 'surgeon,' incidentally, is pure Mitty. During his happiest years, Thurber did not write the way a surgeon operates, he wrote the way a child skips rope, the way a mouse waltzes.

"Although he is best known for 'Walter Mitty' and *The Male Animal,* the book of his I like best is *The Last Flower.* In it you will find his faith in the renewal of life, his feeling for the beauty and fragility of life on earth. Like all good writers, he fashioned his own best obituary notice. Nobody else can add to the record, much as he might like to. And of all the flowers, real and figurative, that will find their way to Thurber's last resting place, the one that will remain fresh and wiltproof is the little flower he himself drew, on the last page of that lovely book."

—E. B. White

Katherine Anne Porter (1890–1980)

Katherine Anne Porter was born in a Texas log cabin in 1890, a distant cousin of the American short-story writer William Sidney Porter (better known as O. Henry). She was raised, mostly by her grandmother, as a member of a sprawling family on close terms with hardship and deprivation. Her schooling was fragmentary. In later life she tended to embroider these plain origins with a certain romantic opulence, as though her past could be revised like a novel-in-progress.

The first of her four marriages took place when she was sixteen. She was consistently impatient with lasting marital relationships, and yet she disliked being alone. Her early years were a struggle to define herself as an individual, as a Southern woman, as the beauty which she was, and as the writer which, so very slowly, she was becoming.

After her Texas youth, Porter traveled widely, living at various times in the West, in New York City's Greenwich Village, in New England, Washington, Mexico, Paris, and Berlin. She supported herself as a newspaper reporter and editor and as a translator of French and Spanish literature.

As a creative writer, she was largely self-taught. She became well-read and she had a natural talent for clear, flowing language. She could tell an effortless story in which a searching intelligence was interwoven with honesty, sound psychology, a flawless memory, and a vivid sense of scene. The grace of her objective style concealed the labor that went into it. Porter worked slowly and painstakingly, and she did not begin publishing until she was over thirty.

She produced her first book, *Flowering Judas,* in 1930. This collection of early stories won her a critical reputation as a stylist. The book grew out of Porter's recollections of her Mexican experience immediately after World War I. *Hacienda* (1934) was also set in Mexico, while *Noon Wine* (1937) presented a powerful tale of violence on a Texas farm.

Much of Porter's work presents Southern women characters caught up in a web of custom and obligation. Her main themes include the burden of past evil and the strain with which that evil holds us captive in the present. Miranda, the clearly autobiographical central figure of so many of her stories, is forever trying to separate the fictions of family legend from objective truth. She knows that people do not always tell the truth, and she is skeptical of the romance with which they disguise the realities of poverty and sexuality.

With the publication of her finest story collection, *Pale Horse, Pale Rider* (1939), Porter's growing audience eagerly awaited a promised novel. She began that novel in 1941. It told of the passage of the steamer *Vera* from Mexico to Germany in the summer of 1931, during the early days of Adolf Hitler's rise to power. The passengers are escaping their loneliness and are in search of fantasy, rather than friendship or love. The novel, entitled *Ship of Fools,* is really about the seeds of World War II—a bitter portrait of the Nazi state and the human race's capacity for cruelty. It did not appear until 1962, by which time many of her readers had abandoned hope for it. *Ship of Fools* enjoyed a wide popular success, and it led to the many tributes (including the National Book Award and the Pulitzer Prize) which embellished the final years of Porter's long life.

SUPPLEMENTARY SUPPORT MATERIALS

1. Vocabulary Activity Worksheet (*CCB*)
2. Review and Response Worksheet: Stream of Consciousness and Flashback (*CCB*)
3. Language Skills Worksheet: The Apostrophe (*CCB*)
4. Selection Test (*CCB*)

DEVELOPING VOCABULARY

The following words from the story are tested in the Selection Test. (See also Vocabulary Activity Worksheet.)

tactful	crucifix
whirligig	frippery
hypodermic	nimbus
piety	dyspepsia

PREPARATION

ESTABLISHING A PURPOSE. After students have read the headnote, tell them to keep the title of this story in mind as they read and try to determine what that long-ago event was and how it affects the present.

A. Expansion

Porter said she had several strong elderly people in mind when she wrote this story. One may have been her father-in-law, who summoned his children and daughter-in-law to his deathbed. Another model was undoubtedly Porter's own grandmother, a hardworking woman and a vital force within the family.

B. Responding

? What does the name "Weatherall" suggest to you? (It suggests someone who has weathered a great deal, who has endured and survived.)

THE JILTING OF GRANNY WEATHERALL

Most of the people we know and come across in the course of a day are looking ahead. Even for those in middle or old age, much of life seems to lie before them. What's the weather going to be next Sunday? Where to go on vacation?

A **That's not so with Ellen Weatherall, heroine of this story by Katherine Anne Porter. Ellen is eighty years old and she has absolutely no interest in the future, which she knows is over for her—but the past! Now *there's* something to think about.**

It is said that the memory of an old person is poor for recent events, but the memory of events from long ago are as vivid as the present. That is surely true of eighty-year-old Granny Weatherall. As she lies on her sickbed sifting through what's important to her, she thinks of her children as youngsters, even though they by now are also well along in age. In one lovely image of her daughter Hapsy, Granny herself becomes Hapsy, then the baby in Hapsy's arms, as though they are really all one continuous woman.

And the point of this very perceptive story is what Granny recalls most vividly of all. It happened sixty years ago, Granny Weatherall tells us, and it still hurts.

Although the story uses some dialogue, it mostly employs a narrative technique called *stream of consciousness* or *interior monologue*. This technique allows the reader to overhear Granny's thoughts and memories. These occur to her in no special order, her mind switching back and forth from what is going on around her to what happened long ago, including the central episode of the story.

You will need to be good detectives as you sift clues to learn who all the people in Granny's mind are. As you meet them, ask yourselves what their relationship to Granny is and whether they are living or dead.

Here are some suggestions. Pay careful attention to tenses of verbs since they help distinguish past from present. Also pay attention to the use of quotation marks. They enclose words actually spoken as opposed to unspoken thoughts. Finally, be patient. If a character is mentioned but not immediately identified, wait until more clues are given.

She flicked her wrist neatly out of Doctor Harry's pudgy careful fingers and pulled the sheet up to her chin. The brat ought to be in knee breeches. Doctoring around the country with spectacles on his nose! "Get along now, take your schoolbooks and go. There's nothing wrong with me."

Doctor Harry spread a warm paw like a cushion on her forehead where the forked green vein danced and made her eyelids twitch. "Now, now, be a good girl, and we'll have you up in no time."

"That's no way to speak to a woman nearly eighty years old just because she's down. I'd have you respect your elders, young man."

"Well, Missy, excuse me." Doctor Harry patted her cheek. "But I've got to warn you, haven't I? You're a marvel, but you must be careful or you're going to be good and sorry."

"Don't tell me what I'm going to be. I'm on my feet now, morally speaking. It's Cornelia. I had to go to bed to get rid of her."

Her bones felt loose, and floated around in her skin, and Doctor Harry floated like a balloon around the foot of the bed. He floated and pulled down his waistcoat and swung his glasses on a cord. "Well, stay where you are, it certainly can't hurt you."

"Get along and doctor your sick," said Granny Weatherall. "Leave a well woman alone. I'll call for you when I want you. . . . Where were you forty years ago when I pulled through milk-leg[1] and double pneumonia? You weren't even born. B

1. **milk-leg:** a painful swelling of the leg, a complication of pregnancy.

A. Responding

? Does Granny really resent Cornelia's attention? (Students may suggest that people who seem too good can sometimes bring out the worst in others.)

B. Characterization

? What does this description reveal about Granny's character? (She prefers order in her life; she kept a meticulous house.)

C. Theme

? Why does Granny want to destroy the letters from John and George? What do you think those letters say? (That the letters reveal how "silly" Granny had once been suggest that they concern love. Granny does not want to reveal her passion to her children.)

D. Responding

? What complaint does Granny raise against Cornelia? (Granny believes that Cornelia treats her like a child and just humors her and that Cornelia talks about her as if she weren't there.)

Don't let Cornelia lead you on," she shouted, because Doctor Harry appeared to float up to the ceiling and out. "I pay my own bills, and I don't throw my money away on nonsense!"

She meant to wave good-by, but it was too much trouble. Her eyes closed of themselves, it was like a dark curtain drawn around the bed. The pillow rose and floated under her, pleasant as a hammock in a light wind. She listened to the leaves rustling outside the window. No, somebody was swishing newspapers: no, Cornelia and Doctor Harry were whispering together. She leaped broad awake, thinking they whispered in her ear.

"She was never like this, *never* like this!" "Well, what can we expect?" "Yes, eighty years old. . . ."

A

Well, and what if she was? She still had ears. It was like Cornelia to whisper around doors. She always kept things secret in such a public way. She was always being tactful and kind. Cornelia was dutiful; that was the trouble with her. Dutiful and good: "So good and dutiful," said Granny, "that I'd like to spank her." She saw herself spanking Cornelia and making a fine job of it.

"What'd you say, Mother?"

Granny felt her face tying up in hard knots.

"Can't a body think, I'd like to know?"

"I thought you might want something."

"I do. I want a lot of things. First off, go away and don't whisper."

She lay and drowsed, hoping in her sleep that the children would keep out and let her rest a minute. It had been a long day. Not that she was tired. It was always pleasant to snatch a minute now and then. There was always so much to be done, let me see: tomorrow.

Tomorrow was far away and there was nothing to trouble about. Things were finished somehow when the time came; thank God there was always a little margin over for peace: then a person could spread out the plan of life and tuck in the edges orderly. It was good to have everything clean and folded away, with the hair brushes and tonic bottles sitting straight on the white embroidered linen: the day started without fuss and the pantry shelves laid out with rows of jelly glasses and brown jugs and white stone-china jars with blue whirligigs and words painted on them: coffee, tea, sugar, ginger, cinnamon, allspice: and the bronze clock with the lion on top nicely dusted off. The dust that lion could collect in twenty-four hours! The box in the attic with all those letters tied up, well, she'd have to go through that tomorrow. All those letters—George's letters and John's letters and her letters to them both—lying around for the children to find afterwards made her uneasy. Yes, that would be tomorrow's business. No use to let them know how silly she had been once.

B

C

While she was rummaging around she found death in her mind and it felt clammy and unfamiliar. She had spent so much time preparing for death there was no need for bringing it up again. Let it take care of itself now. When she was sixty she had felt very old, finished, and went around making farewell trips to see her children and grandchildren, with a secret in her mind: This is the very last of your mother, children! Then she made her will and came down with a long fever. That was all just a notion like a lot of other things, but it was lucky too, for she had once for all got over the idea of dying for a long time. Now she couldn't be worried. She hoped she had better sense now. Her father had lived to be one hundred and two years old and had drunk a noggin of strong hot toddy on his last birthday. He told the reporters it was his daily habit, and he owed his long life to that. He had made quite a scandal and was very pleased about it. She believed she'd just plague Cornelia a little.

"Cornelia! Cornelia!" No footsteps, but a sudden hand on her cheek. "Bless you, where have you been?"

"Here, Mother."

"Well, Cornelia, I want a noggin of hot toddy."

"Are you cold, darling?"

"I'm chilly, Cornelia. Lying in bed stops the circulation. I must have told you that a thousand times."

Well, she could just hear Cornelia telling her husband that Mother was getting a little childish and they'd have to humor her. The thing that most annoyed her was that Cornelia thought she was deaf, dumb, and blind. Little hasty glances and tiny gestures tossed around her and over her head saying, "Don't cross her, let her have her way, she's eighty years old," and she sitting there as if she lived in a thin glass cage. Sometimes Granny almost made up her mind to pack up and move back to her own house where nobody could remind her every minute that she was old. Wait, wait, Cornelia, till your own children whisper behind your back!

D

Rest by Frederick Carl Frieseke. Oil on canvas (26″ × 32″).

Maier Museum of Art, Randolph-Macon Woman's College, Lynchburg, Virginia.

In her day she had kept a better house and had got more work done. She wasn't too old yet for Lydia to be driving eighty miles for advice when one of the children jumped the track, and Jimmy still dropped in and talked things over: "Now, Mammy, you've a good business head, I want to know what you think of this? . . ." Old. Cornelia couldn't change the furniture around without asking. Little things, little things! They had been so sweet when they were little. Granny wished the old days were back again with the children young and everything to be done over. It had been a hard pull, but not too much for her. When she thought of all the food she had cooked, and all the clothes she had cut and sewed, and all the gardens she had made—well, the children showed it. There they were, made out of her, and they couldn't get away from that. Sometimes she wanted to see John again and point to them and say, Well, I didn't do so badly, did I? But that would have to wait. That was for tomorrow. She used to think of him as a man, but now all the children were older than their father, and he would be a child beside her if she saw him now. It seemed strange and there was something wrong in the idea. Why, he couldn't possibly recognize her. She had fenced in a hundred acres once, digging the post holes herself and clamping the wires with just a negro boy to help. That changed a woman. John would be looking for a young woman with the peaked

A

B

C

A. Humanities Connection: Responding to the Fine Art Frederick Carl Frieseke (1874–1939) was a famous American impressionist. After the early 1930's, though, Depression-era viewers began to see his work as too sentimental.

Frieseke is noted for his rich use of color and patterns of light.

? What is the mood of the picture, and how does it compare with that of the story? (Answers will vary. Most students will agree that, like the story, the mood of the picture seems sad, reflective, and hopeless.)

B. Characterization

? What do Granny's memories reveal about her character? (She worked extremely hard all her life and is proud of that fact.)

C. Plot

? Why did she have to do even the hard physical work? (Her husband John died young, leaving her to care for the farm and the children.)

A. Responding

? What does Granny mean? (Granny might be alluding to how quickly time has passed, blurring all her accomplishments.) Is she questioning the value of all her work? (Whether or not Granny questions her work, she retains pride in her strength.)

B. Responding

? What do Granny's comments mean on the surface? (She is talking about the harvest.) How do her comments apply to her own life? (Granny doesn't believe in wasting time and certainly her family "used"—benefited from—her work. The warning about losing things may relate to the mysterious missing something referred to on page 587.)

C. Theme

? What two things are associated in Granny's mind? (Hell and the man who jilted her) Why does Granny worry about losing her soul? (Perhaps her rage is so deep that she fears damnation.)

Spanish comb in her hair and the painted fan. Digging post holes changed a woman. Riding country roads in the winter when women had their babies was another thing: sitting up nights with sick horses and sick negroes and sick children and hardly ever losing one. John, I hardly ever lost one of them! John would see that in a minute, that would be something he could understand, she wouldn't have to explain anything!

It made her feel like rolling up her sleeves and putting the whole place to rights again. No matter if Cornelia was determined to be everywhere at once, there were a great many things left undone on this place. She would start tomorrow and do them. It was good to be strong enough for everything, even if all you made melted and changed and slipped under your hands, so that by the time you finished you almost forgot what you were working for. What was it I set out to do? she asked herself intently, but she could not remember. A fog rose over the valley, she saw it marching across the creek swallowing the trees and moving up the hill like an army of ghosts. Soon it would be at the near edge of the orchard, and then it was time to go in and light the lamps. Come in, children, don't stay out in the night air.

Lighting the lamps had been beautiful. The children huddled up to her and breathed like little calves waiting at the bars in the twilight. Their eyes followed the match and watched the flame rise and settle in a blue curve, then they moved away from her. The lamp was lit, they didn't have to be scared and hang on to mother any more. Never, never, never more. God, for all my life I thank Thee. Without Thee, my God, I could never have done it. Hail, Mary, full of grace.

I want you to pick all the fruit this year and see that nothing is wasted. There's always someone who can use it. Don't let good things rot for want of using. You waste life when you waste good food. Don't let things get lost. It's bitter to lose things. Now, don't let me get to thinking, not when I am tired and taking a little nap before supper. . . .

The pillow rose about her shoulders and pressed against her heart and the memory was being squeezed out of it: oh, push down the pillow, somebody: it would smother her if she tried to hold it. Such a fresh breeze blowing and such a green day with no threats in it. But he had not come, just the same. What does a woman do when she has put on the white veil and set out the white cake for a man and he doesn't come? She tried to remember. No, I swear he never harmed me but in that. He never harmed me but in that . . . and what if he did? There was the day, the day, but a whirl of dark smoke rose and covered it, crept up and over into the bright field where everything was planted so carefully in orderly rows. That was hell, she knew hell when she saw it. For sixty years she had prayed against remembering him and against losing her soul in the deep pit of hell, and now the two things were mingled in one and the thought of him was a smoky cloud from hell that moved and crept in her head when she had just got rid of Doctor Harry and was trying to rest a minute. Wounded vanity, Ellen, said a sharp voice in the top of her mind. Don't let your wounded vanity get the upper hand of you. Plenty of girls get jilted. You were jilted, weren't you? Then stand up to it. Her eyelids wavered and let in streamers of blue-gray light like tissue paper over her eyes. She must get up and pull the shades down or she'd never sleep. She was in bed again and the shades were not down. How could that happen? Better turn over, hide from the light, sleeping in the light gave you nightmares. "Mother, how do you feel now?" and a stinging wetness on her forehead. But I don't like having my face washed in cold water!

Hapsy? George? Lydia? Jimmy? No, Cornelia, and her features were swollen and full of little puddles. "They're coming, darling, they'll all be here soon." Go wash your face, child, you look funny.

Instead of obeying, Cornelia knelt down and put her head on the pillow. She seemed to be talking but there was no sound. "Well, are you tongue-tied? Whose birthday is it? Are you going to give a party?"

Cornelia's mouth moved urgently in strange shapes. "Don't do that, you bother me, daughter."

"Oh, no, Mother. Oh, no. . . ."

Nonsense. It was strange about children. They disputed your every word. "No what, Cornelia?"

"Here's Doctor Harry."

"I won't see that boy again. He just left five minutes ago."

"That was this morning, Mother. It's night now. Here's the nurse."

"This is Doctor Harry, Mrs. Weatherall. I never saw you look so young and happy!"

"Ah, I'll never be young again—but I'd be

happy if they'd let me lie in peace and get rested."

She thought she spoke up loudly, but no one answered. A warm weight on her forehead, a warm bracelet on her wrist, and a breeze went on whispering, trying to tell her something. A shuffle of leaves in the everlasting hand of God, He blew on them and they danced and rattled. "Mother, don't mind, we're going to give you a little hypodermic." "Look here, daughter, how do ants get in this bed? I saw sugar ants yesterday." Did you send for Hapsy too?

It was Hapsy she really wanted. She had to go a long way back through a great many rooms to find Hapsy standing with a baby on her arm. She seemed to herself to be Hapsy also, and the baby on Hapsy's arm was Hapsy and himself and herself, all at once, and there was no surprise in the meeting. Then Hapsy melted from within and turned flimsy as gray gauze and the baby was a gauzy shadow, and Hapsy came up close and said, "I thought you'd never come," and looked at her very searchingly and said, "You haven't changed a bit!" They leaned forward to kiss, when Cornelia began whispering from a long way off, "Oh, is there anything you want to tell me? Is there anything I can do for you?"

A

Yes, she had changed her mind after sixty years and she would like to see George. I want you to find George. Find him and be sure to tell him I forgot him. I want him to know I had my husband just the same and my children and my house like any other woman. A good house too and a good husband that I loved and fine children out of him. Better than I hoped for even. Tell him I was given back everything he took away and more. Oh, no, oh, God, no, there was something else besides the house and the man and the children. Oh, surely they were not all? What was it? Something not given back. . . . Her breath crowded down under her ribs and grew into a monstrous frightening shape with cutting edges; it bored up into her head, and the agony was unbelievable: Yes, John, get the Doctor now, no more talk, my time has come.

When this one was born it should be the last. The last. It should have been born first, for it was the one she had truly wanted. Everything came in good time. Nothing left out, left over. She was strong, in three days she would be as well as ever. Better. A woman needed milk in her to have her full health.

B

"Mother, do you hear me?"

"I've been telling you—"

"Mother, Father Connolly's here."

"I went to Holy Communion only last week. Tell him I'm not so sinful as all that."

"Father just wants to speak to you."

He could speak as much as he pleased. It was like him to drop in and inquire about her soul as if it were a teething baby, and then stay on for a cup of tea and a round of cards and gossip. He always had a funny story of some sort, usually about an Irishman who made his little mistakes and confessed them, and the point lay in some absurd thing he would blurt out in the confessional showing his struggles between native piety and original sin. Granny felt easy about her soul. Cornelia, where are your manners? Give Father Connolly a chair. She had her secret comfortable understanding with a few favorite saints who cleared a straight road to God for her. All as surely signed and sealed as the papers for the new Forty Acres. Forever . . . heirs and assigns forever. Since the day the wedding cake was not cut, but thrown out and wasted. The whole bottom dropped out of the world, and there she was blind and sweating with nothing under her feet and the walls falling away. His hand had caught her under the breast, she had not fallen, there was the freshly polished floor with the green rug on it, just as before. He had cursed like a sailor's parrot and said, "I'll kill him for you." Don't lay a hand on him, for my sake leave something to God. "Now, Ellen, you must believe what I tell you. . . ."

C

So there was nothing, nothing to worry about any more, except sometimes in the night one of the children screamed in a nightmare, and they both hustled out shaking and hunting for the matches and calling, "There, wait a minute, here we are!" John, get the doctor now, Hapsy's time has come. But there was Hapsy standing by the bed in a white cap. "Cornelia, tell Hapsy to take off her cap. I can't see her plain."

Her eyes opened very wide and the room stood out like a picture she had seen somewhere. Dark colors with the shadows rising towards the ceiling in long angles. The tall black dresser gleamed with nothing on it but John's picture, enlarged from a little one, with John's eyes very black when they should have been blue. You never saw him, so how do you know how he looked? But the man insisted the copy was perfect, it was very rich and handsome. For a picture, yes, but it's not my husband. The table by the bed had a linen cover

D

A. Responding
? Who is Hapsy? What might her name represent? (Perhaps she is another of Granny's children. But she may not be real at all. Her name suggests *happenstance* or *happy* or both; she may represent what is missing in Granny's life.)

B. Responding
? What confusion has entered Granny's mind? (Granny confuses her pain with that of childbirth.)

C. Responding
? Does this "comfortable understanding" contradict Granny's worry about her soul? (Granny is trying to convince herself that heaven is guaranteed. She believes that it is as sure as the Forty Acres, but on page 588 she worries about those acres.)

D. Responding
? Whom is Granny addressing? (If she is addressing Hapsy, her comment is another clue that Hapsy is not real.)

587

Closure

Have students write a brief paragraph explaining what effect the jilting had on Granny's life.

Reading Check Test

1. The author gives us the viewpoint and thoughts of (a) Dr. Harry, (b) Granny Weatherall, or (c) Cornelia. *(b)*
2. The occasion of the story is a (a) wedding, (b) birth, or (c) death. *(c)*
3. The person responsible for the jilting was (a) John, (b) George, or (c) Hapsy. *(b)*
4. Granny Weatherall's religion is (a) Roman Catholic, (b) Protestant, or (c) Jewish. *(a)*
5. The man that Granny Weatherall had married was (a) John, (b) George, or (c) Dr. Harry. *(a)*

A. Expansion
Porter's metaphor of death as a horse-drawn carriage echoes Emily Dickinson's famous 1863 poem, number 712. (See page 364.)

B. Responding
? What regrets does Granny express? (She regrets the things she hasn't gotten around to doing.)

C. Expansion
The reference is to Matthew 25:1–13, the parable of the wise and foolish virgins. Like the wise virgins, Granny has her candle lit; ironically, however, no bridegroom comes for her.

and a candle and a crucifix. The light was blue from Cornelia's silk lampshades. No sort of light at all, just frippery. You had to live forty years with kerosene lamps to appreciate honest electricity. She felt very strong and she saw Doctor Harry with a rosy nimbus around him.

"You look like a saint, Doctor Harry, and I vow that's as near as you'll ever come to it."

'She's saying something."

"I heard you, Cornelia. What's all this carrying-on?"

"Father Connolly's saying—"

Cornelia's voice staggered and bumped like a cart in a bad road. It rounded corners and turned back again and arrived nowhere. Granny stepped up in the cart very lightly and reached for the reins, but a man sat beside her and she knew him by his hands, driving the cart. She did not look in his face, for she knew without seeing, but looked instead down the road where the trees leaned over and bowed to each other and a thousand birds were singing a Mass. She felt like singing too, but she put her hand in the bosom of her dress and pulled out a rosary, and Father Connolly murmured Latin in a very solemn voice and tickled her feet.[2] My God, will you stop that nonsense? I'm a married woman. What if he did run away and leave me to face the priest by myself? I found another a whole world better. I wouldn't have exchanged my husband for anybody except St. Michael[3] himself, and you may tell him that for me with a thank you in the bargain.

Light flashed on her closed eyelids, and a deep roaring shook her. Cornelia, is that lightning? I hear thunder. There's going to be a storm. Close all the windows. Call the children in. . . . "Mother, here we are, all of us." "Is that you, Hapsy?" "Oh, no, I'm Lydia. We drove as fast as we could." Their faces drifted above her, drifted away. The rosary fell out of her hands and Lydia put it back. Jimmy tried to help, their hands fumbled together, and Granny closed two fingers around Jimmy's thumb. Beads wouldn't do, it must be something alive. She was so amazed her thoughts ran round and round. So, my dear Lord, this is my death and I wasn't even thinking about it. My children have come to see me die. But I can't, it's not time. Oh, I always hated surprises. I wanted to give Cornelia the amethyst set—Cornelia, you're to have the amethyst set, but Hapsy's to wear it when she wants, and, Doctor Harry, do shut up. Nobody sent for you. Oh, my dear Lord, do wait a minute. I meant to do something about the Forty Acres, Jimmy doesn't need it and Lydia will later on, with that worthless husband of hers. I meant to finish the altar cloth and send six bottles of wine to Sister Borgia for her dyspepsia. I want to send six bottles of wine to Sister Borgia, Father Connolly, now don't let me forget.

Cornelia's voice made short turns and tilted over and crashed. "Oh, Mother, oh, Mother, oh, Mother. . . ."

"I'm not going, Cornelia. I'm taken by surprise. I can't go."

You'll see Hapsy again. What about her? "I thought you'd never come." Granny made a long journey outward, looking for Hapsy. What if I don't find her? What then? Her heart sank down and down, there was no bottom to death, she couldn't come to the end of it. The blue light from Cornelia's lampshade drew into a tiny point in the center of her brain, it flickered and winked like an eye, quietly it fluttered and dwindled. Granny lay curled down within herself, amazed and watchful, staring at the point of light that was herself; her body was now only a deeper mass of shadow in an endless darkness and this darkness would curl around the light and swallow it up. God, give a sign!

For the second time there was no sign. Again no bridegroom and the priest in the house. She could not remember any other sorrow because this grief wiped them all away. Oh, no, there's nothing more cruel than this—I'll never forgive it. She stretched herself with a deep breath and blew out the light.

2. **murmured Latin . . . feet:** The priest is performing the last rites of the Roman Catholic Church, which include anointing the feet.
3. **St. Michael:** the prince of all angels. In art he is usually depicted as a handsome knight in white armor.

ANALYZING THE STORY

Identifying Facts

1. Granny is staying at her daughter Cornelia's house. Dr. Harry and Cornelia are with her.

2. Granny's children are Hapsy, Lydia, Jimmy, and Cornelia. Hapsy, her favorite, is dead or imaginary.

3. The title refers to Granny being jilted by George on her wedding day.

Interpreting Meanings

4. Granny is expecting Jesus, the heavenly bridegroom; but when He does not appear, Granny feels even more cruelly betrayed.

5. Granny blows out the candle which had been lit for the last rites (symbolically, to welcome the bridegroom), but she also blows out her own life.

6. It's ironic because Granny clearly remembers George well. George's betrayal has rankled Granny all her life.

7. Answers will vary, but some possibilities are her trust in people, her dream of what her life would be, or some special quality that would have given her life meaning.

8. Granny felt the torment of hell on the day she was jilted.

Granny hopes her place in heaven is assured because of her hard work and prayers.

9. Ellen Weatherall has certainly lived a long, rich life, but the story is not upbeat. The memory of the early betrayal cast a pall over her whole life, and the final betrayal makes her death a terrible one.

10. The point of view is limited omniscient.

Answers will vary, but students should see that more would be lost than gained by a change in the point of view.

Responding to the Story

Analyzing the Story

Identifying Facts

1. Describe the story's opening situation. Who is with Granny?
2. What are the names of Granny's children? Which child was her favorite and apparently no longer alive (if she ever existed at all)?
3. What key event in Granny's long life does the **title** refer to?

Interpreting Meanings

4. The end of the story suggests that Granny, at the moment of her death, is jilted yet another time. Who jilts her in her last moments? How does Granny feel at the moment of this **epiphany**, or revelation?
5. What is the significance of the light that Granny blows out at the end?
6. In recalling George, her vanished fiancé, Granny thinks: "Find him and be sure to tell him I forgot him." What is **ironic** in Granny's thought? How did George really affect her life?
7. There are some **ambiguities** in this story—that is, incidents that could be interpreted in several ways. Probably the most puzzling ambiguity has to do with George. Granny feels she was "given back everything" that was taken away by the jilting. She married and raised a family. Yet then she says that something was "not given back." What might that "something" be?
8. What does it mean when Granny thinks (page 586) "That was hell. She knew hell when she saw it"? How does she feel about heaven?
9. Do you think this is a positive, upbeat story about a woman who lived a long, rich life? Or is it underneath a dark story of loss and betrayal? Explain.
10. The story is a brilliant example of the use of **point of view.** Is the point of view: (a) omniscient, (b) limited omniscient, or (c) first person? How would the effect of the story change if another point of view is used?

Writing About the Story

A Creative Response

1. **Writing a Monologue.** Imagine that you are George, now eighty years old, and have returned just in time to talk to Ellen at her bedside. You know she can hear you but cannot respond. Write a brief monologue in which you reproduce George's thoughts as he looks at the old woman he jilted sixty years ago. Let George think about what happened on that day long ago and what he's been doing since. How does he feel at this moment? Let your monologue reflect George's changing feelings and show how one thought leads, sometimes untidily and irrationally, to another.

A Critical Response

2. **Comparing a Story and a Poem.** Granny Weatherall and Lucinda Matlock (in Edgar Lee Masters's poem on page 640) have certain "family" resemblances. In a brief essay, tell how the two women are similar and, more important, how they are different. You might want to organize your details in a chart like this one:

	Granny	Lucinda
1. Kind of life she led.		
2. Attitude toward people with weakness and complaints.		
3. Attitude toward husband.		
4. Tragedies in her life.		
5. Values.		
6. Feelings about death.		
7. Could both women be called "Weatherall"?		

Analyzing Language and Style

Interior Monologue

Interior monologue is a literary technique that records a character's nonverbalized flow of thoughts, memories, and ideas. It is sometimes referred to as stream of consciousness, but they are not the same. **Stream of consciousness** usually presents bits of the unconscious mind that float up to the surface in the form of fragments, free associations, and dreamlike images. Interior monologue more closely resembles thought—it is more structured, and usually conforms to normal patterns of English syntax. Granny's reminiscences are interior monologues.

As Granny's mind wanders back through the past, her thoughts often seem random or disconnected. But often there is a connection between what is happening in the present and what is coming back to her from the past.

Find at least three places in the story where Granny's mind shifts away from the present and returns to the past. What details in the present trigger her memory in these instances?

William Faulkner (1897–1962)

Yoknapatawpha County, Mississippi, is surely the hardest of American literary place names to pronounce. Still, it is wise to learn how (yäk′-nə·pə·tô′fə), for it is famous as the imagined world of William Faulkner, the scene of his most celebrated novels and stories. Debate will always rage about the position of figures in our literary pantheon, but critics are now unanimous in their opinion that Faulkner is one of the greatest of all American novelists.

Imaginary Yoknapatawpha is similar in many ways to the actual impoverished farmland, with its red clay hills, that rings Oxford, Mississippi, home of the state's university. It was there that William's father, Murray Falkner (William added the "u" to the family name), ran a livery stable and later became the university's business manager. William Faulkner lived and wrote there throughout most of his life.

Faulkner was a mediocre student and quit high school in the tenth grade, but he read widely, and he wrote poetry. At the outbreak of World War I, the U.S. Army rejected him because he failed to meet their height and weight requirements. However, he enlisted in the Canadian Air Force and trained for flight duty, only to see the war end before he was commissioned. Returning to Oxford after the war, he took some courses at the university and did poorly in English. With neither profession nor skill, and a marked distaste for regular employment, he seemed a moody and puzzling young man to his neighbors.

Faulkner took several short-lived jobs, among them that of postmaster for the university. Resigning from this job, he wrote, "I will be damned if I propose to be at the beck and call of every itinerant scoundrel who has two cents to invest in a postage stamp."

In 1924, he left Oxford for New Orleans, where he met Sherwood Anderson (page 501), who had attracted much attention with the publication of *Winesburg, Ohio* (1919), his study of small-town life. Impressed and encouraged by Anderson, Faulkner tried his hand at fiction. In six weeks he completed a first novel, *Soldiers' Pay,* a self-conscious story about the lost generation. Thereafter Faulkner wrote with a tireless energy.

Within the next three years, Faulkner found his great theme: the American South as a microcosm for the universal themes of time, the passions of the human heart, and the destruction of the wilderness. Faulkner saw the South as a nation unto itself, with a strong sense of its noble past and an array of myths by which it clung to its pride, despite the humiliating defeat of the Civil War and the acceptance of the distasteful values of an industrial North. Faulkner started to explore these themes in 1929 with the publication of *Sartoris* and *The Sound and the Fury,* two novels published within months of each other. While *Sartoris* was a fairly conventional novel, it is notable because it was the first story set in mythical Yoknapatawpha, Faulkner's own "little postage stamp of native soil." *The Sound and the Fury* was a milestone in American literature, due to Faulkner's bold manipulation of point of view and of its stream-of-consciousness narrative technique.

In the decade which followed, Faulkner produced a succession of dazzling books: *As I Lay Dying* (1930), *Sanctuary* (1931), *Light in August* (1932), *Absalom! Absalom!* (1936)—considered by many readers to be his finest work—*The Unvanquished* (1938), and *The Hamlet* (1940). These works reveal Faulkner as equally skillful in the tragic and the comic modes. He portrayed the South accurately, perceptively, and with a poignant ambivalence—on the one hand affectionate, on the other critical. He once said of the South, "Well, I love it and I hate it."

Faulkner described his South through fictional families who often reappear from novel to novel. They resemble trees, attaining grandeur, casting much shade, and then growing old and dry, crumbling as the scrub of social change grows up around their fallen limbs and stumps.

There are the aristocratic Sartorises, who resemble Faulkner's own ancestors. Colonel Bayard Sartoris, for example, was patterned after Faulkner's great-grandfather, who rose from rural poverty to command the Second Mississippi Regiment, built a railroad, wrote a best-selling novel, and was murdered on the street by his business partner.

There are also the Compsons, who incorporate some characteristics of the author's immediate family. They form the centerpiece of *The Sound and the Fury,* which records the decline of a once great clan, and with it, the passing of a traditionally Southern world.

As I Lay Dying tells of the poor-white Bundren family and its efforts to bring the body of its matriarch, Addie, back to the town of Jefferson for burial. The novel reveals these humble people as more enduring than their social betters. *Light in August* also concerns the Burden family and explores the problem of racism through the character of the protagonist, Joe Christmas. Although he can pass as white, Joe is regarded as a mulatto; his failure to find a place in either white or black society leads to his murder.

And finally, there are the Snopeses—Faulkner's unforgettable portrayal of a sprawling clan of irresponsible, depraved, socially ambitious varmints, who rise from the dust and cheat their way to respectability and wealth, destroying the old values of aristocracy and peasantry alike.

Faulkner is admittedly a difficult writer, with uncommon methods of handling chronology and point of view. He often forces the reader to piece together events from a seemingly random and fragmentary series of impressions experienced by a variety of narrators. Faulkner's style often strains conventional syntax; he might pile up clause upon clause in an effort to capture the complexity of thought. In *The Sound and the Fury,* for example, he entrusts part of the narrative to the chaotic intelligence of the mentally handicapped son, Benjy Compson. But the efforts of patient readers are richly repaid, as they discover in book after book a mythical universe in which the moral dilemmas are the perennial mysteries of human existence.

By the time he received the Nobel Prize for literature in 1950, Faulkner's best work was behind him. After his richly productive period (1929–1942), he wrote many more stories and novels, including *Intruder in the Dust* (1948), *Requiem for a Nun* (1951), *A Fable* (1954), *The Town* (1957), *The Mansion* (1959), and *The Reivers* (1962). All these works displayed his characteristic virtuosity and willingness to experiment, but his powers were clearly diminished. His critics noted this and tended to underestimate his lasting importance.

Faulkner's writing surely diverged from that of his realist contemporaries—notably Ernest Hemingway, whom he put at the bottom of his own list of the best American contemporary writers. "Wolfe, Hemingway, Dos Passos, and myself," he once chose for his ladder of literary accomplishment. He then explained further: "I rated Wolfe first, myself second. I put Hemingway last. I said we were all failures. All of us had failed to match the dream of perfection. . . . I rated Hemingway last because he stayed within what he knew. He did it fine, but he didn't try for the impossible." A

Of the novel itself, Faulkner said: "The only mistake with any novel is if it fails to create pleasure. That it is not true is irrelevant; a novel is to be enjoyed. A book that fails to create enjoyment is not a good one." B

But there is no argument over William Faulkner's preeminence among Southern writers. As Flannery O'Connor once put it: "The presence alone of Faulkner in our midst makes a great difference in what the writer can and cannot permit himself to do. Nobody wants his mule and wagon stalled on the same track the Dixie Limited is roaring down."

A. Responding
? Based on what you know about Faulkner from this biography and about Wolfe's writing, why do you suppose that Faulkner ranks Wolfe first on the "ladder of literary accomplishment"? (Probably because of the vast, epic nature of Wolfe's writing and the great themes he explored. Hemingway "didn't try for the impossible," while Wolfe did.)

B. Responding
Students might enjoy discussing Faulkner's statement that "the only mistake with any novel is if it fails to create pleasure." ? Is Faulkner condoning the "good read" novels, books of escapism and romance? Or should this statement be considered in the context of novels that try "to match the dream of perfection"? (Encourage students to defend their responses.)

SUPPLEMENTARY SUPPORT MATERIALS
1. Vocabulary Activity Worksheet (*CCB*)
2. Review and Response Worksheet: Characterization and Suspense (*CCB*)
3. Language Skills Worksheet: Sentence Combining with Appositives and Appositive Phrases (*CCB*)
4. Selection Test (*CCB*)

DEVELOPING VOCABULARY
The following words from the story are tested in the Selection Test. (See also Vocabulary Activity Worksheet.)

august	condolence
calligraphy	to circumvent
pallid	virulent
to vanquish	impervious
to vindicate	sibilant

PREPARATION
ESTABLISHING A PURPOSE. Tell students to establish a time line as they read and to place events in Miss Emily's young womanhood, middle years, and old age.

A. Expansion
A gothic story is characterized by romance (often dark or thwarted), mystery, and horror. It is often set in a gloomy, decaying mansion or castle. Horace Walpole's *The Castle of Otranto* (1764) was the first of the genre. Since then, many writers, including Hawthorne and Poe, have used this form.

B. Setting/Expansion
The town is Jefferson, the county seat of Yoknapatawpha County in northern Mississippi—2,400 square miles, 15,611 residents—the fictional world explored by Faulkner in all of his novels and most of his stories.

C. Responding
? What does the narrator mean by referring to Miss Emily in this way? (The townspeople treasure Miss Emily as a representative of the Old Guard. They know that she cannot adapt to the new social order, so they feel obliged to let her live her illusions.)

A ROSE FOR EMILY

The core of this story is a lurid tale, as sensational as any you will see headlined in those scandal sheets displayed at a supermarket's checkout counters. But what turns this account of outrageous human behavior into literature is the relation between the event and its setting. As the story of one eccentric old woman unfolds, we learn some important truths about the rest of her community.

A **William Faulkner is the master of this kind of Southern gothic tale. He knows at first hand the American South and all its powerful social traditions. He understands not only that the South is a major source of the national tradition, but also that it is full of possibilities for great fiction.**

It is all here in "A Rose for Emily"—the social castes, the changes in a society's values, the reverence for the past, the politeness with which people go about the routine of life, and the struggle they undergo to find joy in it.

And when we reflect on the character of Miss Emily, we realize that she is more than merely mad. Perhaps her bizarre behavior is an extension of qualities that are admired in her community—and in many others: a loyalty to family and the past, pride, faith in the old values, a fierce independence, and a scorn for all that is new and widely accepted. And, of course, Miss Emily also has that quality we all share to some degree: a tendency to retreat from reality we don't like, into an unreality where we can have things all our own way.

If parts of the story give off an offensive odor, it comes only in part from Miss Emily's house and her horrible deed. It comes also from the racial slurs used by some of the characters. Such language is offensive to us today, but we must remember that Faulkner has used it to portray as realistically as possible a bygone age in a racially segregated town of the rural South.

I

B When Miss Emily Grierson died, our whole town went to her funeral: the men through a sort of respectful affection for a fallen monument, the women mostly out of curiosity to see the inside of her house, which no one save an old manservant—a combined gardener and cook—had seen in at least ten years.

It was a big, squarish frame house that had once been white, decorated with cupolas[1] and spires and scrolled balconies in the heavily lightsome style of the seventies,[2] set on what had once been our most select street. But garages and cotton gins had encroached and obliterated even the august names of that neighborhood; only Miss Emily's house was left, lifting its stubborn and coquettish decay above the cotton wagons and the gasoline pumps—an eyesore among eyesores. And now Miss Emily had gone to join the representatives of those august names where they lay in the cedar-bemused cemetery among the ranked and anonymous graves of Union and Confederate soldiers who fell at the battle of Jefferson.

Alive, Miss Emily had been a tradition, a duty, and a care; a sort of hereditary obligation upon the town, dating from that day in 1894 when Colo- C nel Sartoris, the mayor—he who fathered the edict that no Negro woman should appear on the streets without an apron—remitted[3] her taxes, the dispensation dating from the death of her father on into perpetuity. Not that Miss Emily would have accepted charity. Colonel Sartoris invented an involved tale to the effect that Miss Emily's father had loaned money to the town, which the town, as a matter of business, preferred this way of repaying. Only a man of Colonel Sartoris' generation and thought could have invented it, and only a woman could have believed it.

1. **cupolas** (kyo͞o′pə·ləz): small domes on a roof.
2. **the seventies:** the 1870's.
3. **remitted:** refrained from enforcing payment of.

That Which I Should Have Done I Did Not Do
by Ivan Le Lorraine Albright (1931–1941). Oil on canvas (97″ × 36″).

The Art Institute of Chicago,
Mary and Leigh B. Block Charitable Fund,
1955.645. Photograph © 1991
The Art Institute of Chicago.

Humanities Connection: Responding to the Fine Art
Ivan L. Albright (1897–1983), born in Chicago, produced very few paintings in his lifetime. What he did produce is very detailed and realistic. This painting took some ten years to complete.

? What is the mood of the painting? (It is dark and gloomy, with a strong sense of mystery and decay or death.) What details in the painting contribute to this atmosphere? (The hand on the door adds to the mystery; the subdued colors and faded roses add to the sense of gloom and decay.) How does the title of the painting relate to its content? (Answers will vary. Perhaps there is a dead person inside the room, and perhaps the title reflects the thoughts of the deceased about his or her life.)

A. Description

? What overall impression is created by this description of the house and Miss Emily herself? (They create a picture of decay.) What words help create this impression? (Students may suggest *dim, dust, disuse, dank, tarnished,* and *cracked,* for example. Perceptive students might note the repetition of the words *tarnished* and *rose.*)

B. Characterization

? Does Miss Emily really believe she owes no taxes, or is she deliberately manipulating the authorities to avoid paying what she owes? (The decay of her house and life suggests that Miss Emily is unable to deal with reality and so would be completely unconcerned with the real tax situation.)

C. Conflict

? What conflicts does this passage suggest? (The town envies the Griersons and so is not unhappy when something happens to bring them down a peg.)

When the next generation, with its more modern ideas, became mayors and aldermen, this arrangement created some little dissatisfaction. On the first of the year they mailed her a tax notice. February came, and there was no reply. They wrote her a formal letter, asking her to call at the sheriff's office at her convenience. A week later the mayor wrote her himself, offering to call or to send his car for her, and received in reply a note on paper of an archaic shape, in a thin, flowing calligraphy in faded ink, to the effect that she no longer went out at all. The tax notice was also enclosed, without comment.

They called a special meeting of the Board of Aldermen. A deputation waited upon her, knocked at the door through which no visitor had passed since she ceased giving china-painting lessons eight or ten years earlier. They were admitted by the old Negro into a dim hall from which a stairway mounted into still more shadow. It smelled of dust and disuse—a close, dank smell. The Negro led them into the parlor. It was furnished in heavy, leather-covered furniture. When the Negro opened the blinds of one window, they could see that the leather was cracked; and when they sat down, a faint dust rose sluggishly about their thighs, spinning with slow motes in the single sun-ray. On a tarnished gilt easel before the fireplace stood a crayon portrait of Miss Emily's father.

A

They rose when she entered—a small, fat woman in black, with a thin gold chain descending to her waist and vanishing into her belt, leaning on an ebony cane with a tarnished gold head. Her skeleton was small and spare; perhaps that was why what would have been merely plumpness in another was obesity in her. She looked bloated, like a body long submerged in motionless water, and of that pallid hue. Her eyes, lost in the fatty ridges of her face, looked like two small pieces of coal pressed into a lump of dough as they moved from one face to another while the visitors stated their errand.

She did not ask them to sit. She just stood in the door and listened quietly until the spokesman came to a stumbling halt. Then they could hear the invisible watch ticking at the end of the gold chain.

Her voice was dry and cold. "I have no taxes in Jefferson. Colonel Sartoris explained it to me. Perhaps one of you can gain access to the city records and satisfy yourselves."

"But we have. We are the city authorities, Miss Emily. Didn't you get a notice from the sheriff, signed by him?"

"I received a paper, yes," Miss Emily said. "Perhaps he considers himself the sheriff . . . I have no taxes in Jefferson."

"But there is nothing on the books to show that, you see. We must go by the—"

"See Colonel Sartoris. I have no taxes in Jefferson." B

"But, Miss Emily—"

"See Colonel Sartoris." (Colonel Sartoris had been dead almost ten years.) "I have no taxes in Jefferson. Tobe!" The Negro appeared. "Show these gentlemen out."

II

So she vanquished them, horse and foot, just as she had vanquished their fathers thirty years before about the smell. That was two years after her father's death and a short time after her sweetheart—the one we believed would marry her—had deserted her. After her father's death she went out very little; after her sweetheart went away, people hardly saw her at all. A few of the ladies had the temerity[4] to call, but were not received, and the only sign of life about the place was the Negro man—a young man then—going in and out with a market basket.

"Just as if a man—any man—could keep a kitchen properly," the ladies said; so they were not surprised when the smell developed. It was another link between the gross, teeming world and the high and mighty Griersons. C

A neighbor, a woman, complained to the mayor, Judge Stevens, eighty years old.

"But what will you have me do about it, madam?" he said.

"Why, send her word to stop it," the woman said. "Isn't there a law?"

"I'm sure that won't be necessary," Judge Stevens said. "It's probably just a snake or a rat that nigger of hers killed in the yard. I'll speak to him about it."

The next day he received two more complaints, one from a man who came in diffident deprecation.[5] "We really must do something about it,

4. **temerity:** rashness.
5. **diffident deprecation:** timid disapproval.

Judge. I'd be the last one in the world to bother Miss Emily, but we've got to do something." That night the Board of Aldermen met—three graybeards and one younger man, a member of the rising generation.

"It's simple enough," he said. "Send her word to have her place cleaned up. Give her a certain time to do it in, and if she don't . . ."

"Dammit, sir," Judge Stevens said, "will you accuse a lady to her face of smelling bad?"

So the next night, after midnight, four men crossed Miss Emily's lawn and slunk about the house like burglars, sniffing along the base of the brickwork and at the cellar openings while one of them performed a regular sowing motion with his hand out of a sack slung from his shoulder. They broke open the cellar door and sprinkled lime there, and in all the outbuildings. As they recrossed the lawn, a window that had been dark was lighted and Miss Emily sat in it, the light behind her, and her upright torso motionless as that of an idol. They crept quietly across the lawn and into the shadow of the locusts that lined the street. After a week or two the smell went away.

That was when people had begun to feel really sorry for her. People in our town, remembering how old lady Wyatt, her great-aunt, had gone completely crazy at last, believed that the Griersons held themselves a little too high for what they really were. None of the young men were quite good enough for Miss Emily and such. We had long thought of them as a tableau, Miss Emily a slender figure in white in the background, her father a spraddled silhouette in the foreground, his back to her and clutching a horsewhip, the two of them framed by the back-flung front door. So when she got to be thirty and was still single, we were not pleased exactly, but vindicated; even with insanity in the family she wouldn't have turned down all of her chances if they had really materialized.

A When her father died, it got about that the house was all that was left to her; and in a way, people were glad. At last they could pity Miss Emily. Being left alone, and a pauper, she had become humanized. Now she too would know the old thrill and the old despair of a penny more or less.

The day after his death all the ladies prepared to call at the house and offer condolence and aid, as is our custom. Miss Emily met them at the door, dressed as usual and with no trace of grief on her face. She told them that her father was not dead. She did that for three days, with the ministers calling on her, and the doctors, trying to persuade her to let them dispose of the body. Just as they were about to resort to law and force, she broke down, and they buried her father quickly.

We did not say she was crazy then. We believed she had to do that. We remembered all the young men her father had driven away, and we knew that B with nothing left, she would have to cling to that which had robbed her, as people will.

III

She was sick for a long time. When we saw her again, her hair was cut short, making her look like a girl, with a vague resemblance to those angels in colored church windows—sort of tragic and serene.

The town had just let the contracts for paving the sidewalks, and in the summer after her father's death they began the work. The construction company came with niggers and mules and machinery, and a foreman named Homer Barron, a Yankee—a big, dark, ready man, with a big voice and eyes lighter than his face. The little boys would follow in groups to hear him cuss the niggers, and the niggers singing in time to the rise and fall of picks. Pretty soon he knew everybody in town. Whenever you heard a lot of laughing anywhere about the square, Homer Barron would be in the center of the group. Presently we began to see him and Miss Emily on Sunday afternoons driving in the yellow-wheeled buggy and the matched team of bays from the livery stable.

At first we were glad that Miss Emily would have an interest, because the ladies all said, "Of course a Grierson would not think seriously of a Northerner, a day laborer." But there were still others, older people, who said that even grief could not cause a real lady to forget *noblesse oblige*[6]—without calling it *noblesse oblige*. They C just said, "Poor Emily. Her kinsfolk should come to her." She had some kin in Alabama; but years ago her father had fallen out with them over the estate of old lady Wyatt, the crazy woman, and there was no communication between the two families. They had not even been represented at the funeral.

---

6. **noblesse oblige** (nō·bles′ ō·blēzh′): the obligation of the upper classes to act kindly toward the lower classes.

A. Conflict
? How might the death of her father change Miss Emily's life? (The townspeople feel compassion for her situation and are willing to befriend her.) Why doesn't Miss Emily accept their offer? (Answers will vary. She might see their kindness as charity and be too proud to accept it.)

B. Responding
? Why did Mr. Grierson drive away all Miss Emily's suitors? (Answers will vary. Perhaps he thought none were good enough for her; perhaps he selfishly wanted to keep her to himself.) Why does Miss Emily deny her father's death? (Answers will vary. She might still be grieving, or getting revenge for his selfishness. She might be clinging to the past—or slipping into madness.)

C. Characterization
? Why does Miss Emily go out with Homer Barron? (She might be lonely.)

A. Characterization
Why are the townspeople shocked? (They are beginning to believe Miss Emily is seriously interested in Homer, a man they see as socially inferior to her.) What does Miss Emily's reaction reveal about her? (She retains her pride. She might believe that one in her position can do whatever she pleases.)

B. Point of View
This is the only time the narrator shows us Miss Emily by herself, apart from what townspeople can actually see. Why does he do so? (He may be underscoring Miss Emily's motive for murdering Homer: She has found him to be a "rat," in the colloquial sense.)

C. Conflict
Why are the townspeople pleased about Miss Emily's supposed marriage? (They are gleefully aware that such a marriage would utterly humiliate Miss Emily's cousins, who are even more "superior" than Miss Emily.)

A

And as soon as the old people said, "Poor Emily," the whispering began. "Do you suppose it's really so?" they said to one another. "Of course it is. What else could . . ." This behind their hands; rustling of craned[7] silk and satin behind jalousies[8] closed upon the sun of Sunday afternoon as the thin, swift clop-clop-clop of the matched team passed: "Poor Emily."

She carried her head high enough—even when we believed that she was fallen. It was as if she demanded more than ever the recognition of her dignity as the last Grierson; as if it had wanted that touch of earthiness to reaffirm her imperviousness. Like when she bought the rat poison, the arsenic. That was over a year after they had begun to say "Poor Emily," and while the two female cousins were visiting her.

"I want some poison," she said to the druggist. She was over thirty then, still a slight woman, though thinner than usual, with cold, haughty black eyes in a face the flesh of which was strained across the temples and about the eyesockets as you imagine a lighthouse-keeper's face ought to look. "I want some poison," she said.

"Yes, Miss Emily. What kind? For rats and such? I'd recom—"

"I want the best you have. I don't care what kind."

The druggist named several. "They'll kill anything up to an elephant. But what you want is—"

"Arsenic," Miss Emily said. "Is that a good one?"

"Is . . . arsenic? Yes, ma'am. But what you want—"

"I want arsenic."

The druggist looked down at her. She looked back at him, erect, her face like a strained flag. "Why, of course," the druggist said. "If that's what you want. But the law requires you to tell what you are going to use it for."

Miss Emily just stared at him, her head tilted back in order to look him eye for eye, until he looked away and went and got the arsenic and wrapped it up. The Negro delivery boy brought her the package; the druggist didn't come back. When she opened the package at home there was written on the box, under the skull and bones: "For rats."

B

IV

So the next day we all said, "She will kill herself"; and we said it would be the best thing. When she had first begun to be seen with Homer Barron, we had said, "She will marry him." Then we said, "She will persuade him yet," because Homer himself had remarked—he liked men, and it was known that he drank with the younger men in the Elks' Club—that he was not a marrying man. Later we said, "Poor Emily" behind the jalousies as they passed on Sunday afternoon in the glittering buggy, Miss Emily with her head high and Homer Barron with his hat cocked and a cigar in his teeth, reins and whip in a yellow glove.

Then some of the ladies began to say that it was a disgrace to the town and a bad example to the young people. The men did not want to interfere, but at last the ladies forced the Baptist minister—Miss Emily's people were Episcopal—to call upon her. He would never divulge what happened during that interview, but he refused to go back again. The next Sunday they again drove about the streets, and the following day the minister's wife wrote to Miss Emily's relations in Alabama.

So she had blood-kin under her roof again and we sat back to watch developments. At first nothing happened. Then we were sure that they were to be married. We learned that Miss Emily had been to the jeweler's and ordered a man's toilet set[9] in silver, with the letters H. B. on each piece. Two days later we learned that she had bought a complete outfit of men's clothing, including a nightshirt, and we said, "They are married." We were really glad. We were glad because the two female cousins were even more Grierson than Miss Emily had ever been.

C

So we were not surprised when Homer Barron—the streets had been finished some time since—was gone. We were a little disappointed that there was not a public blowing-off, but we believed that he had gone on to prepare for Miss

7. **craned:** stretched. (The silk dresses are tight.)

8. **jalousies** (jal′ə·sēz): doors or windows covered with adjustable slats.

9. **toilet set:** set of grooming aids (hairbrush, comb, etc.).

Virginia Museum of Fine Arts, Richmond. Collection of Mr. and Mrs. Paul Mellon.

The Artist's Mother in Her Apartment, Rue de Calais, Paris—Morning by Edouard Vuillard (c. 1922). Oil on millboard.

Humanities Connection: Responding to the Fine Art

Edouard Vuillard (1868–1940) was a French artist famous for his paintings of gardens and interiors. His work often portrays his own private world—a view from a window, corners of his studio, or, as in this work, his mother's apartment.

? Compare and contrast this painting to Faulkner's "painting" of Emily and her home. (Both women are overweight and dressed in black, but Faulkner's Emily is more grotesque. The room in the painting is fairly clean and pleasant, but Faulkner describes a dusty, gloomy house that has not been cleaned in decades.)

From this painting, what kind of a place do you think Vuillard's mother's apartment was? (Answers will vary. Some will see it as a place of quiet and rest; others, as a disturbing, lonely place.)

A. Responding
? What do the townspeople assume has happened? (They believe Homer broke off with Miss Emily and left town.) How do they interpret her staying in her house? (They believe the same pride that motivated her father's actions prevents her from acknowledging her pain.)

B. Setting
? Why do the daughters and granddaughters of the older generation take china-painting lessons from Miss Emily? (They are sent to help Miss Emily without seeming to be giving her charity.) Why does the newer generation not send pupils to her? (The newer generation is less concerned about Miss Emily.)

C. Irony
? This passage suggests the central irony of the story. What is that irony? (The town continues to envy and admire Miss Emily when she actually is living a life of loneliness, desperation, and madness.)

D. Responding
? Why has Tobe stayed with Miss Emily? (Answers will vary. He might feel a sense of duty to her.)

E. Theme
? Why is it fitting that Mr. Grierson's portrait be placed above Miss Emily's casket? (The values that he represents and that Miss Emily clung to are what destroyed her.)

Emily's coming, or to give her a chance to get rid of the cousins. (By that time it was a cabal,[10] and we were all Miss Emily's allies to help circumvent the cousins.) Sure enough, after another week they departed. And, as we had expected all along, within three days Homer Barron was back in town. A neighbor saw the Negro man admit him at the kitchen door at dusk one evening.

A And that was the last we saw of Homer Barron. And of Miss Emily for some time. The Negro man went in and out with the market basket, but the front door remained closed. Now and then we would see her at a window for a moment, as the men did that night when they sprinkled the lime, but for almost six months she did not appear on the streets. Then we knew that this was to be expected too; as if that quality of her father which had thwarted her woman's life so many times had been too virulent and too furious to die.

When we next saw Miss Emily, she had grown fat and her hair was turning gray. During the next few years it grew grayer and grayer until it attained an even pepper-and-salt iron-gray, when it ceased turning. Up to the day of her death at seventy-four it was still that vigorous iron-gray, like the hair of an active man.

From that time on her front door remained closed, save for a period of six or seven years, B when she was about forty, during which she gave lessons in china-painting. She fitted up a studio in one of the downstairs rooms, where the daughters and granddaughters of Colonel Sartoris' contemporaries were sent to her with the same regularity and in the same spirit that they were sent to church on Sundays with a twenty-five-cent piece for the collection plate. Meanwhile her taxes had been remitted.

Then the newer generation became the backbone and the spirit of the town, and the painting pupils grew up and fell away and did not send their children to her with boxes of color and tedious brushes and pictures cut from the ladies' magazines. The front door closed upon the last one and remained closed for good. When the town got free postal delivery, Miss Emily alone refused to let them fasten the metal numbers above her door and attach a mailbox to it. She would not listen to them.

Daily, monthly, yearly we watched the Negro grow grayer and more stooped, going in and out with the market basket. Each December we sent her a tax notice, which would be returned by the post office a week later, unclaimed. C Now and then we would see her in one of the downstairs windows—she had evidently shut up the top floor of the house—like the carven torso of an idol in a niche, looking or not looking at us, we could never tell which. Thus she passed from generation to generation—dear, inescapable, impervious, tranquil, and perverse.

And so she died. Fell ill in the house filled with dust and shadows, with only a doddering Negro man to wait on her. We did not even know she was sick; we had long since given up trying to get any information from the Negro. He talked to no one, probably not even to her, for his voice had grown harsh and rusty, as if from disuse.

She died in one of the downstairs rooms, in a heavy walnut bed with a curtain, her gray head propped on a pillow yellow and moldy with age and lack of sunlight.

V

D The Negro met the first of the ladies at the front door and let them in, with their hushed, sibilant voices and their quick, curious glances, and then he disappeared. He walked right through the house and out the back and was not seen again.

The two female cousins came at once. They held the funeral on the second day, with the town coming to look at Miss Emily beneath a mass of E bought flowers, with the crayon face of her father musing profoundly above the bier and the ladies sibilant and macabre; and the very old men—some in their brushed Confederate uniforms—on the porch and the lawn, talking of Miss Emily as if she had been a contemporary of theirs, believing that they had danced with her and courted her perhaps, confusing time with its mathematical progression, as the old do, to whom all the past is not a diminishing road but, instead, a huge meadow which no winter ever quite touches, divided from them now by the narrow bottleneck of the most recent decade of years.

Already we knew that there was one room in that region above stairs which no one had seen in forty years, and which would have to be forced. They waited until Miss Emily was decently in the ground before they opened it.

10. **cabal** (kə·bal'): small group involved in a plot.

Closure
Have students read "A Comment on the Story" and then discuss how the key points mentioned—inheritance from the past and isolation from the community—destroy Miss Emily.

Reading Check Test
1. Miss Emily refuses to tell the local druggist why she wants to purchase arsenic. *True*
2. When Homer Barron comes calling, Miss Emily's father sends him away. *False*
3. By the time she becomes overweight, Miss Emily's hair has become iron-gray. *True*
4. Townsmen find Miss Emily's body behind a locked door that has had to be forced open. *False*
5. Miss Emily asks the druggist to sprinkle lime around her house because of an offensive smell. *False*

The violence of breaking down the door seemed to fill this room with pervading dust. A thin, acrid pall as of the tomb seemed to lie everywhere upon this room decked and furnished as for a bridal: upon the valance curtains of faded rose color, upon the rose-shaded lights, upon the dressing table, upon the delicate array of crystal and the man's toilet things backed with tarnished silver, silver so tarnished that the monogram was obscured. Among them lay a collar and tie, as if they had just been removed, which, lifted, left upon the surface a pale crescent in the dust. Upon a chair hung the suit, carefully folded; beneath it the two mute shoes and the discarded socks.

The man himself lay in the bed.

For a long while we just stood there, looking down at the profound and fleshless grin. The body had apparently once lain in the attitude of an embrace, but now the long sleep that outlasts love, that conquers even the grimace of love, had cuckolded[11] him. What was left of him, rotted beneath what was left of the nightshirt, had become inextricable from the bed in which he lay; and upon him and upon the pillow beside him lay that even coating of the patient and biding dust.

Then we noticed that in the second pillow was the indentation of a head. One of us lifted something from it, and leaning forward, that faint and invisible dust dry and acrid in the nostrils, we saw a long strand of iron-gray hair.

---

11. **cuckolded:** betrayed (in the sense of a husband who has been deceived by his wife).

A Comment on the Story

The community is nearly everywhere in Faulkner's work as an important force and, diffused and anonymous though it be, it becomes one of the most important elements in the story. A clear illustration of the importance of the community is to be found in "A Rose for Emily." Miss Emily Grierson is one of the numerous characters in Faulkner's work who are warped by their inheritance from the past and who are cut off from the community—sometimes by their own will—to their detriment.

The story of the life and death of Miss Emily is related by a member of the community who, though nameless, thinks of himself as representative of the townsfolk. The first sentence strikes this note: "When Miss Emily Grierson died, our whole town went to her funeral. . . ." The narrator goes on to tell us that "Alive, Miss Emily had been a tradition, a duty, and a care; a sort of hereditary obligation upon the town. . . ." And throughout the story he keeps using such locutions as "At first we were glad. . . ." "So the next day we all said. . . ." "We were glad because the two female cousins. . . ." The nameless narrator suggests what Miss Emily's history of madness and murder meant to the community, though he never puts that meaning into a definition.

Miss Emily's isolation is a fact of consequence: her face is compared to that of a lighthouse keeper—a person who necessarily lives in isolation from the people whom he protects and whose vessels he warns off the rocks and shoals. Moreover, though Miss Emily is mad, perhaps clinically so, her madness, as is nearly always true of Faulkner's mad and obsessed people, has meaning for the sane, for it is an exaggeration or an aberration of traits which all of us have. Miss Emily's madness is in part a consequence of the injury done her by the fact of isolation, but it is also related to certain real virtues—her pride, her aristocratic independence, her unwillingness to try to keep up with the Joneses or even heed what the Joneses are saying. To read "A Rose for Emily" as merely a piece of cheap Southern Gothicism, an attempt to shock and horrify, would be to miss the point. A

—Cleanth Brooks, R. W. B. Lewis, and Robert Penn Warren

Additional Writing Assignment
We see this story only from the townspeople's point of view; we never see Miss Emily's side. Choose any time in Miss Emily's life and write a diary entry that reveals her feelings.

Connections
Both Miss Emily and Ellen Weatherall (in "The Jilting of Granny Weatherall," page 583) are thwarted in love. Have students compare how each deals with the experience. Then have students compare the effects of the different points of view: Miss Emily's story is told from the outside; Granny Weatherall's, from the inside.

A. Expansion
In the introduction to *The Portable Faulkner* (Viking, 1974), critic Malcolm Cowley offers one possible point. Faulkner, he said, wrote of a time of "moral confusion and social decay. He is continually seeking . . . for violent images to convey his sense of outrage."

ANALYZING THE STORY

Identifying Facts

1. They assume it is probably just a dead rat or snake.

Later they realize that the smell came from Homer Barron's corpse.

2. Emily says that her father is still alive and refuses to let his body be buried.

This foreshadows the end of the story, when the townspeople discover Homer's body lying in the upstairs bed, having been there for forty years!

3. Homer Barron, the Yankee foreman of a construction company, was Miss Emily's lover and murder victim. The townspeople found him tough and sociable.

Miss Emily poisoned him with arsenic.

Interpreting Meanings

4. It seems that she had slept next to the body for forty years.

5. The emphasis on Miss Emily's hair color foreshadows the discovery of the gray hair on the pillow.

Her hair begins to turn gray right after the murder.

6. Miss Emily was dominated by her father, who thought none of the young men were good enough for her. Her father "clutching a horsewhip" implies that he

Responding to the Story

Analyzing the Story

Identifying Facts

1. What do the townspeople at first think is causing the smell at Miss Emily's house? Much later, what do they (and you) learn caused the odor?
2. When Miss Emily's father dies, what bizarre behavior does she exhibit? How does her behavior **foreshadow** the end of the story?
3. Who is Homer Barron and how did the community feel about him? What was the cause of his death?

Interpreting Meanings

4. What significance do you see in the strand of iron-gray hair on the second pillow?
5. On page 598, Faulkner emphasizes the way in which Miss Emily's hair turned gray. Why does he go into such detail about it? What is significant about the time she started to go gray?
6. The narrator says on page 595, of Emily and her father, that the townspeople "had long thought of them as a tableau," which is a kind of dramatic picture or scene. This tableau suggests a **conflict.** What do you think the tableau reveals about Emily's relationship with her father? (For whom or what was that horsewhip intended?)
7. How is Colonel Sartoris's white lie to Miss Emily about her taxes an attempt to spare her any embarrassment? One generation later, what does Judge Stevens do to avoid embarrassing her? How do the changes in attitude toward Miss Emily's taxes reflect wider social and economic changes in the South?
8. There are historical details in this story that reveal a great deal about its **setting**. What does the townspeople's attitude toward the African Americans who live in Jefferson tell you about the times? What part do you think Tobe plays in Miss Emily's history?
9. What sort of person do you think the **narrator** of this story is? Is it a man or a woman? Does the narrator pity Miss Emily? Admire her? Hold her in contempt?
10. Faulkner once explained the title "A Rose for Emily" this way:

> "Oh, it's simply the poor woman had no life at all. Her father had kept her more or less locked up and then she had a lover who was about to quit her; she had to murder him. It was just 'A Rose for Emily'—that's all."

Faulkner's answer is not very helpful. What explanations for the title can you think of? Before you answer, reread paragraphs 2 and 4 of Part V. What do roses usually **symbolize?**

Writing About the Story

A Creative Response

1. **Writing a Horror Story.** Write a short-short story (no more than 1200 words) about a solitary, mysterious person, real or imaginary, who lives in your neighborhood. Since the story is so short, you will have to fit vivid descriptive details of the person and information about the community neatly into the narrative. A shocking secret should lie hidden in this person's past. Save the startling truth for the last sentence, as Faulkner does in "A Rose for Emily." Have your narrator speak for the townspeople or neighbors as "we."

A Critical Response

2. **Analyzing a Character.** In a brief essay, write an analysis of Miss Emily's character. Before you write, review all the places in the story where the narrator directly describes what the townspeople thought of Miss Emily. For example, in Part IV he says they thought of her as "dear, inescapable, impervious, tranquil, and perverse." Gather your details into some sort of chart before you start to write, perhaps something like this:

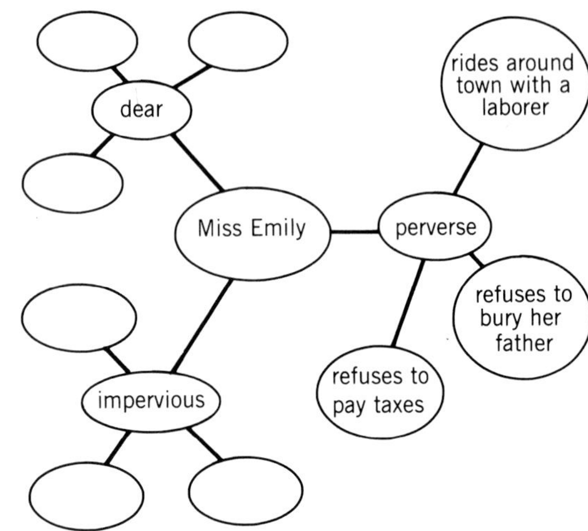

was ready to fend off suitors with force, if necessary. At the same time, his protectiveness must have convinced Emily that she was a person to whom ordinary rules of conduct did not apply.

7. Miss Emily would never accept outright charity, but she could accept that the town owed her something.

Judge Stevens avoids embarrassment by organizing a secret nighttime lime-spreading expedition to deodorize Miss Emily's foul-smelling house.

The changes reflect the decline of "gentility" and the "aristocratic" class of the South, as well as its replacement with a business class concerned with money and progress rather than with the courtesy due to certain persons.

8. The town regards African Americans as second-class citizens, subject to public humiliation by whites and fit only for menial jobs.

Tobe had to know about the corpse in the upstairs room; but being a loyal servant in those repressive days, he said nothing for forty years.

9. The narrator is the voice of the community. As such, the narrator is male and female, rich and poor, old and young.

The narrator regards Miss Emily with pity, admiration, and respect.

10. The most obvious possibility is their association with romantic love, especially a wedding: Note the rose tints in the room where Homer lies, which is "furnished as for a bridal." Used as a symbol of health and vitality, roses provide a macabre contrast with Miss Emily's pallid skin and diseased mind. But roses are also associated with death and funerals—a rose to lie on Miss Emily's casket.

A. Responding

? In this speech Faulkner urges writers to explore "the old universal truths." How does "A Rose for Emily" exhibit his concern for any or all of these? (Students may suggest that the town authorities treat Emily with honor and compassion and that she shows endurance in her lonely pride.)

For your essay, choose only three or four of the most striking characteristics of Miss Emily to discuss. Be sure to cite details from the story that illustrate those unusual traits.

At the end of your essay, explain how you feel about Miss Emily and her crime. What do you think was her **motive?**

3. **Analyzing Plot Sequence.** To analyze the events in this story's plot, make a chart. On the left-hand side list the following events in chronological order. On the right-hand side list the events in the order in which they are disclosed in the story:

> Homer's arriving in town, the visit of the aldermen, Emily's buying the poison, Colonel Sartoris's deciding not to tax Emily, the death of Emily's father, the stench coming from the house, the arrival of Emily's relatives, Homer's disappearance.

Research and Discussion Projects

A Group Activity

In small groups, argue the answers to one of the following questions. Before you debate, you will have to do research in this book or in a library.

1. Is Miss Emily's house, as described in paragraphs 2 and 5 of Part I and in paragraph 4 of Part V, like Roderick Usher's house in Edgar Allan Poe's story "The Fall of the House of Usher" (page 234)?
2. Are Richard Cory (page 634) and Miss Emily both victims of their extreme isolation from their communities?
3. Is Miss Emily's room, as it is finally discovered after her death, like Miss Havisham's apartment in Charles Dickens's novel *Great Expectations?*

Primary Sources

Nobel Prize Acceptance Speech, 1950

"I feel that this award was not made to me as a man but to my work—a life's work in the agony and sweat of the human spirit, not for glory and least of all for profit, but to create out of the materials of the human spirit something which did not exist before. So this award is only mine in trust. It will not be difficult to find a dedication for the money part of it commensurate with the purpose and significance of its origin. But I would like to do the same with the acclaim too, by using this moment as a pinnacle from which I might be listened to by the young men and women already dedicated to the same anguish and travail, among whom is already that one who will someday stand here where I am standing.

"Our tragedy today is a general and universal physical fear so long sustained by now that we can even bear it. There are no longer problems of the spirit. There is only the question: When will I be blown up? Because of this, the young man or woman writing today has forgotten the problems of the human heart in conflict with itself which alone can make good writing because only that is worth writing about, worth the agony and the sweat.

A "He must learn them again. He must teach himself that the basest of all things is to be afraid; and, teaching himself that, forget it forever, leaving no room in his workshop for anything but the old verities and truths of the heart, the old universal truths lacking which any story is ephemeral and doomed—love and honor and pity and pride and compassion and sacrifice. Until he does so he labors under a curse. He writes not of love but of lust, of defeats in which nobody loses anything of value, of victories without hope and worst of all without pity and compassion. His griefs grieve on no universal bones, leaving no scars. He writes not of the heart but of the glands.

"Until he relearns these things he will write as though he stood among and watched the end of man. I decline to accept the end of man. It is easy enough to say that man is immortal simply because he will endure; that when the last ding-dong of doom has clanged and faded from the last worthless rock hanging tideless in the last red and dying evening, that even then there will still be one more sound: that of his puny inexhaustible voice, still talking. I refuse to accept this. I believe that man will not merely endure: he will prevail. He is immortal, not because he alone among creatures has an inexhaustible voice, but because he has a soul, a spirit capable of compassion and sacrifice and endurance. The poet's, the writer's, duty is to write about these things. It is his privilege to help man endure by lifting his heart, by reminding him of the courage and honor and hope and pride and compassion and pity and sacrifice which have been the glory of his past. The poet's voice need not merely be the record of man, it can be one of the props, the pillars to help him endure and prevail."

—William Faulkner

For Further Reading For The Teacher

The letters of Flannery O'Connor (see excerpts, page 611) provide fascinating insights into the mind of this complex personality. The collected letters appear under the title *Habit of Being* (Farrar, Straus & Giroux, 1979).

A. Responding

? What do you suppose Flannery O'Connor meant by her statements that "in a sense sickness is a place, more instructive than a long trip to Europe" and that "sickness before death is a very appropriate thing"? (Sick people may contemplate and assess their past lives. They have time to think about their death.)

B. Expansion

You might want to discuss O'Connor's method of writing and have students compare it with their own. What did she gain by sitting for two hours every day, even when she did not feel inspired? Why does she say that the time had not been wasted when she threw away months of work? (It kept her creative juices flowing.)

C. Expansion

Once students have read "The Life You Save May Be Your Own," you may want to return to this statement and discuss how O'Connor applies the "show, not say" philosophy of writing in her own work.

Flannery O'Connor (1925–1964)

Flannery O'Connor was born in Savannah, Georgia, in 1925 and spent her short life almost entirely in nearby Milledgeville, where her family had lived since before the Civil War. Although she limited herself to a rural, southern literary terrain and the body of her work was small, her place in twentieth-century American literature is secure.

She wrote steadily from 1948 until her death in 1964. For fourteen of those sixteen years she was plagued by lupus, a painful, wasting disease that she had inherited from her father and that kept her ever more confined and immobile. "I have never been anywhere but sick," she wrote. A "In a sense sickness is a place, more instructive than a long trip to Europe, and it's always a place where there's no company, where nobody can follow. Sickness before death is a very appropriate thing and I think those who don't have it miss one of God's great mercies."

She graduated from the Women's College of Georgia in 1945. She then went off to the Writers' Workshop at the University of Iowa. Her first novel, *Wise Blood,* was published in 1952. She followed that novel with a short story collection, *A Good Man Is Hard to Find* (1953), a second novel, *The Violent Bear It Away* (1955), and a second collection of stories, *Everything That Rises Must Converge* (1965).

B Always disciplined as a writer, O'Connor forced herself to sit at her desk without conscious distraction of any sort at the same time every day for two hours, even if no inspiration came. "Sometimes I work for months and have to throw everything away," she commented, "but I don't think any of that time was wasted. Something goes on that makes it easier when it does come well." While her central concern in her fiction was the abstract idea of good and evil, she felt compelled to confine herself to the concrete. "The peculiar problem of the short-story writer," she noted, "is how to make the action he describes reveal as much of the mystery of existence as possible. He has only a short space to do it in and he can't do it by C statement. He has to do it by showing, not by saying, and by showing the concrete—so that his problem is how to make the concrete work double time for him."

From the first, she was recognized as a satirist of astonishing originality and vigor, whose targets were smugness, optimism, and self-righteousness. However, the essential element of Flannery O' Connor's life and work was that she was born a Roman Catholic and that she remained one without the slightest wavering of faith throughout her thirty-nine years. A thunder-and-lightning Christian belief pervades every story and novel she ever wrote. Her attraction to the grotesque and the violent puts off many critics and readers. They fail to appreciate that the violent motifs in her fiction grow from her passionate, Christian vision of our secular times.

What she wanted to tell us, in a voice that could not be ignored, was that in our rationality we had lost the one essential—a spiritual center for our lives. "Redemption is meaningless," O'Connor wrote, "unless there is cause for it in the actual life we live, and for the last few centuries there has been operating in our culture the secular belief that there is no such cause."

The title story of *A Good Man Is Hard to Find,* for example, concerns a family of six, all of whom are killed by an escaped convict, the Misfit. When the grandmother pleads with the Misfit to pray to Jesus for help, he replies: "I don't need no hep. I'm doing all right by myself." O'Connor seems to be saying that we have become so accustomed to the lack of God in our

Supplementary Support Materials
1. Vocabulary Activity Worksheet (*CCB*)
2. Review and Response Worksheet: Tone and Theme (*CCB*)
3. Selection Test (*CCB*)
4. Audiocassette recording

Developing Vocabulary
The following words from the story are tested in the Selection Test. (See also Vocabulary Activity Worksheet.)

to list	to tinker
rooting	crabbed
ravenous	to rue

Preparation
Establishing a Purpose. Ask students to try to determine as they read what the author's attitude toward Shiftlet is.

lives that a writer must use violent means to communicate the point. Her method is rather like that of the expert mule-trainer, who begins a school by smiting the animal on the head with a two-by-four, explaining "First you have to get their attention."

With all their peculiarities, O'Connor's characters are disturbingly familiar. They are homespun figures, worldly as any Georgia barnyard or roadside café, drawn with a kind of humor that balances on the edge of terror. Just as we are made to feel comfortable, enjoying the carnival show, the comedy is miraculously transcended, and we realize that the situation has a philosophical meaning. All the freaks and clowns have taken on God's meaning. God is here, and the devil is too. They are wholly in charge—the devil is tempting away, and, without waiting for the Day of Judgment, God is dishing out a terrible punishment to the wicked.

THE LIFE YOU SAVE MAY BE YOUR OWN

You won't have to read very far to discover that this story is both disturbing and funny. Pay special attention to the way the characters talk. Don't let the casual, down-home voice fool you, however. "The Life You Save May Be Your Own" is an exquisite piece of storytelling. There are three vivid characters here, each one a masterful portrait from the rural South. They find themselves in a situation that is both tragic and comic, and they act out a classic theme—that of innocence beset by evil.

You don't believe that by the story's end Mr. Shiftlet will avoid his punishment, do you? That's no ordinary, passing cloud in his path . . . is it?

The old woman and her daughter were sitting on their porch when Mr. Shiftlet came up their road for the first time. The old woman slid to the edge of her chair and leaned forward, shading her eyes from the piercing sunset with her hand. The daughter could not see far in front of her and continued to play with her fingers. Although the old woman lived in this desolate spot with only her daughter and she had never seen Mr. Shiftlet before, she could tell, even from a distance, that he was a tramp and no one to be afraid of. His left coat sleeve was folded up to show there was only half an arm in it and his gaunt figure listed slightly to the side as if the breeze were pushing him. He had on a black town suit and a brown felt hat that was turned up in the front and down in the back and he carried a tin tool box by a handle. He came on, at an amble, up her road, his face turned toward the sun which appeared to be balancing itself on the peak of a small mountain.

The old woman didn't change her position until he was almost into her yard; then she rose with one hand fisted on her hip. The daughter, a large girl in a short blue organdy dress, saw him all at once and jumped up and began to stamp and point and make excited speechless sounds.

Mr. Shiftlet stopped just inside the yard and set his box on the ground and tipped his hat at her as if she were not in the least afflicted; then he turned toward the old woman and swung the hat all the way off. He had long black slick hair that hung flat from a part in the middle to beyond the tips of his ears on either side. His face descended in forehead for more than half its length and ended suddenly with his features just balanced over a jutting steel-trap jaw. He seemed to be a young man but he had a look of composed dissatisfaction as if he understood life thoroughly. A

"Good evening," the old woman said. She was about the size of a cedar fence post and she had a man's gray hat pulled down low over her head. B

A. Irony
? What makes this sentence about Mr. Shiftlet ironic? (The suggestion that to understand life thoroughly would necessarily result in dissatisfaction is a wry commentary on Shiftlet's sober and pompous manner.)

B. Description
Call attention to the economy with which O'Connor enables the reader to visualize her characters. The old woman is "about the size of a cedar fence post"; later in the paragraph, her daughter is described as having "fat, helpless hands hanging at the wrists" and "eyes as blue as a peacock's neck."

Humanities Connection: Responding to the Photograph

? This photograph was taken during the Depression. What details of people and place indicate the poverty of that time? (Details of people: the idle men sitting on the porch; the thin young girls with their haunting looks, their ill-fitting clothes and clumsy shoes. Details of place: the wood building with its rough-hewn pillars and stained concrete steps; the dirt yard; the firewood stacked under the porch, obviously for heating.)

You may want to have students make predictions about the setting and the characters in the story based on this photograph. Also, you may want students to return to the photograph once they have read the story and discuss how details here reflect those in the story.

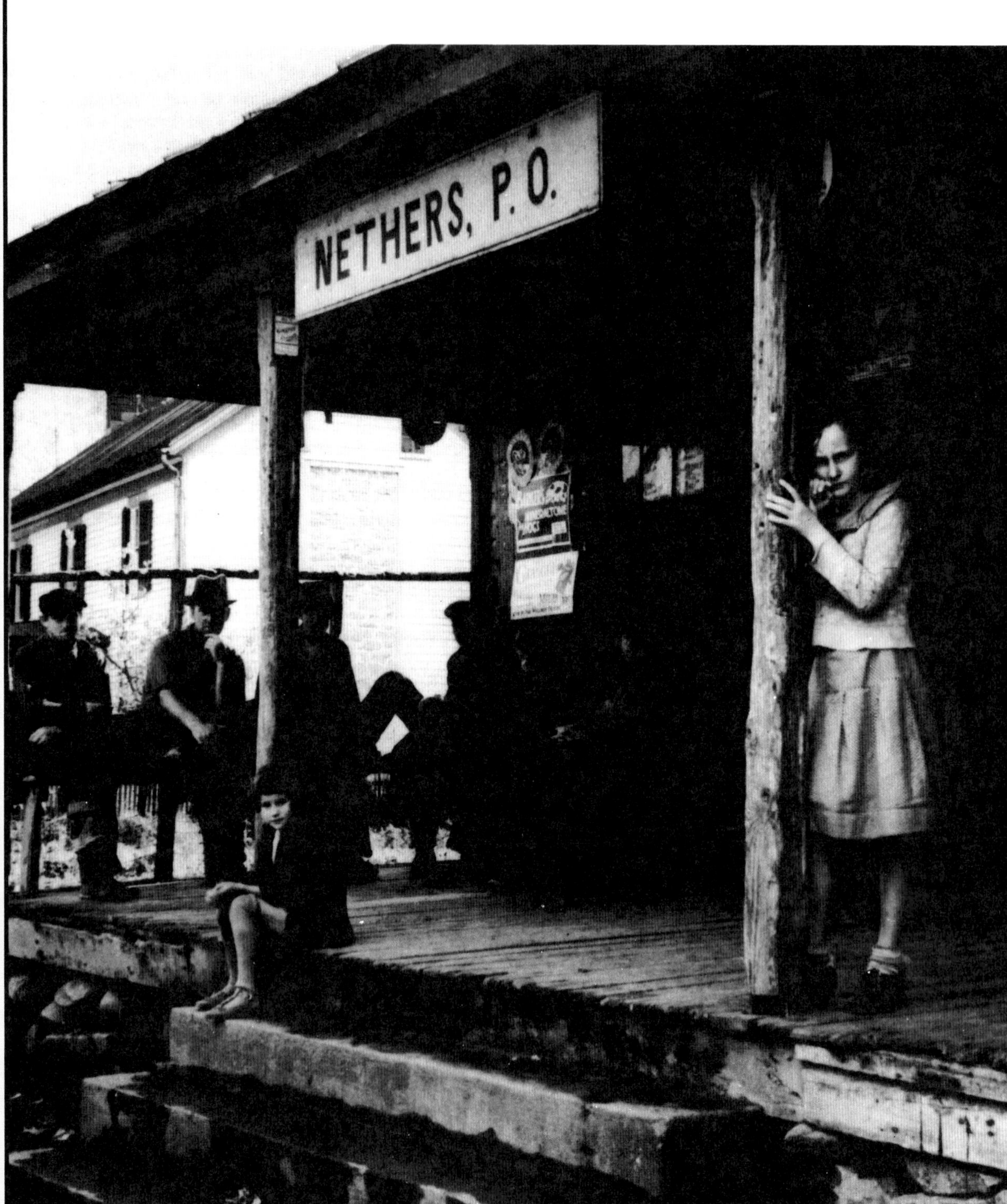

Post office in Nethers, Virginia (1935). Photograph by Arthur Rothstein.

The tramp stood looking at her and didn't answer. He turned his back and faced the sunset. He swung both his whole and his short arm up slowly so that they indicated an expanse of sky and his figure formed a crooked cross. The old woman watched him with her arms folded across her chest as if she were the owner of the sun, and the daughter watched, her head thrust forward and her fat helpless hands hanging at the wrists. She had long pink-gold hair and eyes as blue as a peacock's neck.

He held the pose for almost fifty seconds and then he picked up his box and came on to the porch and dropped down on the bottom step. "Lady," he said in a firm nasal voice, "I'd give a fortune to live where I could see me a sun do that every evening."

"Does it every evening," the old woman said and sat back down. The daughter sat down too and watched him with a cautious sly look as if he were a bird that had come up very close. He leaned to one side, rooting in his pants pocket, and in a second he brought out a package of chewing gum and offered her a piece. She took it and unpeeled it and began to chew without taking her eyes off him. He offered the old woman a piece but she only raised her upper lip to indicate she had no teeth.

Mr. Shiftlet's pale sharp glance had already passed over everything in the yard—the pump near the corner of the house and the big fig tree that three or four chickens were preparing to roost in—and had moved to a shed where he saw the square rusted back of an automobile. "You ladies drive?" he asked.

"That car ain't run in fifteen year," the old woman said. "The day my husband died, it quit running."

"Nothing is like it used to be, lady," he said. "The world is almost rotten."

"That's right," the old woman said. "You from around here?"

"Name Tom T. Shiftlet," he murmured, looking at the tires.

"I'm pleased to meet you," the old woman said. "Name Lucynell Crater and daughter Lucynell Crater. What you doing around here, Mr. Shiftlet?"

He judged the car to be about a 1928 or '29 Ford. "Lady," he said, and turned and gave her his full attention, "lemme tell you something. There's one of these doctors in Atlanta that's taken a knife and cut the human heart—the human heart," he repeated, leaning forward, "out of a man's chest and held it in his hand," and he held his hand out, palm up, as if it were slightly weighted with the human heart, "and studied it like it was a day-old chicken, and lady," he said, allowing a long significant pause in which his head slid forward and his clay-colored eyes brightened, "he don't know no more about it than you or me."

"That's right," the old woman said.

"Why, if he was to take that knife and cut into every corner of it, he still wouldn't know no more than you or me. What you want to bet?"

"Nothing," the old woman said wisely. "Where you come from, Mr. Shiftlet?"

He didn't answer. He reached into his pocket and brought out a sack of tobacco and a package of cigarette papers and rolled himself a cigarette, expertly with one hand, and attached it in a hanging position to his upper lip. Then he took a box of wooden matches from his pocket and struck one on his shoe. He held the burning match as if he were studying the mystery of flame while it traveled dangerously toward his skin. The daughter began to make loud noises and to point to his hand and shake her finger at him, but when the flame was just before touching him, he leaned down with his hand cupped over it as if he were going to set fire to his nose and lit the cigarette.

He flipped away the dead match and blew a stream of gray into the evening. A sly look came over his face. "Lady," he said, "nowadays, people'll do anything anyways. I can tell you my name is Tom T. Shiftlet and I come from Tarwater, Tennessee, but you never have seen me before: how you know I ain't lying? How you know my name ain't Aaron Sparks, lady, and I come from Singleberry, Georgia, or how you know it's not George Speeds and I come from Lucy, Alabama, or how you know I ain't Thompson Bright from Toolafalls, Mississippi?"

"I don't know nothing about you," the old woman muttered, irked.

"Lady," he said, "people don't care how they lie. Maybe the best I can tell you is, I'm a man; but listen lady," he said and paused and made his tone more ominous still, "what is a man?"

The old woman began to gum a seed. "What you carry in that tin box, Mr. Shiftlet?" she asked.

"Tools," he said, put back. "I'm a carpenter."

"Well, if you come out here to work, I'll be able to feed you and give you a place to sleep but

A. Symbolism
Have students note the reference to the "crooked cross" here.

B. Point of View
? How would you describe the point of view from which this story is told—first person, limited third person, or omniscient? (Omniscient; here we are told what Shiftlet is thinking about—the car's age—and elsewhere we are told what the old lady is thinking.)

C. Characterization
? What have you learned about Tom T. Shiftlet so far? (The name "Shiftlet" is appropriate for the tramp who says that he is a carpenter but who apparently has no possessions. At first meeting, Shiftlet appears to be a clever con man. He flatters the old woman by praising her sunset and by equating his and her knowledge with that of a doctor. He quickly spots the old automobile and seems to size up the situation, including Lucynell's retardation.)

A. Responding

? Do you believe Shiftlet when he tells about his "varied life"? (Answers will vary, but students should note that Shiftlet mispronounces "Armed Services" and that although he continues to say things like "he hadn't been raised thataway," Shiftlet's con artistry is already apparent.)

B. Responding

? What does Shiftlet mean when he says he has "a moral intelligence"? How can Shiftlet's statement be an "impossible truth"? (A "moral intelligence" is an understanding of the rightness or wrongness of something. While it is true that such awareness exists, it is an impossibility for Shiftlet.)

C. Irony

? What is ironic about the old woman's response to Shiftlet's comment about monks sleeping in their coffins? (It is ironic that someone would consider sleeping in an old car to be "advanced.")

I can't pay. I'll tell you that before you begin,'' she said.

There was no answer at once and no particular expression on his face. He leaned back against the two-by-four that helped support the porch roof. ''Lady,'' he said slowly, ''there's some men that some things mean more to them than money.'' The old woman rocked without comment and the daughter watched the trigger that moved up and down in his neck. He told the old woman then that all most people were interested in was money, but he asked what a man was made for. He asked her if a man was made for money, or what. He asked her what she thought she was made for but she didn't answer, she only sat rocking and wondered if a one-armed man could put a new roof on her garden house. He asked a lot of questions that she didn't answer. He told her that he was twenty-eight years old and had lived a varied life. He had been a gospel singer, a foreman on the railroad, an assistant in an undertaking parlor, and he come over the radio for three months with Uncle Roy and his Red Creek Wranglers. He said he had fought and bled in the Arm Service of his country and visited every foreign land and that everywhere he had seen people that didn't care if they did a thing one way or another. He said he hadn't been raised thataway. [A]

A fat yellow moon appeared in the branches of the fig tree as if it were going to roost there with the chickens. He said that a man had to escape to the country to see the world whole and that he wished he lived in a desolate place like this where he could see the sun go down every evening like God made it to do.

''Are you married or are you single?'' the old woman asked.

There was a long silence. ''Lady,'' he asked finally, ''where would you find you an innocent woman today? I wouldn't have any of this trash I could just pick up.''

The daughter was leaning very far down, hanging her head almost between her knees watching him through a triangular door she had made in her overturned hair; and she suddenly fell in a heap on the floor and began to whimper. Mr. Shiftlet straightened her out and helped her get back in the chair.

''Is she your baby girl?'' he asked.

''My only,'' the old woman said ''and she's the sweetest girl in the world. I would give her up for nothing on earth. She's smart too. She can sweep the floor, cook, wash, feed the chickens, and hoe. I wouldn't give her up for a casket of jewels.''

''No,'' he said kindly, ''don't ever let any man take her away from you.''

''Any man come after her,'' the old woman said, ''I'll have to stay around the place.''

Mr. Shiftlet's eye in the darkness was focused on a part of the automobile bumper that glittered in the distance. ''Lady,'' he said, jerking his short arm up as if he could point with it to her house and yard and pump, ''there ain't a broken thing on this plantation that I couldn't fix for you, one-arm jackleg or not. I'm a man,'' he said with a sullen dignity, ''even if I ain't a whole one. I got,'' he said, tapping his knuckles on the floor to emphasize the immensity of what he was going to say, ''a moral intelligence!'' and his face pierced out of the darkness into a shaft of doorlight and he stared at her as if he were astonished himself at this impossible truth. [B]

The old woman was not impressed with the phrase. ''I told you you could hang around and work for food,'' she said, ''if you don't mind sleeping in that car yonder.''

''Why listen, lady,'' he said with a grin of delight, ''the monks of old slept in their coffins!''

''They wasn't as advanced as we are,'' the old woman said. [C]

The next morning he began on the roof of the garden house while Lucynell, the daughter, sat on a rock and watched him work. He had not been around a week before the change he had made in the place was apparent. He had patched the front and back steps, built a new hog pen, restored a fence, and taught Lucynell, who was completely deaf and had never said a word in her life, to say the word ''bird.'' The big rosy-faced girl followed him everywhere, saying ''Burrttddt ddbirrrttdt,'' and clapping her hands. The old woman watched from a distance, secretly pleased. She was ravenous for a son-in-law.

Mr. Shiftlet slept on the hard narrow back seat of the car with his feet out the side window. He had his razor and a can of water on a crate that served him as a bedside table and he put up a piece of mirror against the back glass and kept his coat neatly on a hanger that he hung over one of the windows.

In the evenings he sat on the steps and talked while the old woman and Lucynell rocked violently in their chairs on either side of him. The old woman's three mountains were black against the dark blue sky and were visited off and on by various planets and by the moon after it had left the chickens. Mr. Shiftlet pointed out that the reason he had improved this plantation was because he had taken a personal interest in it. He said he was even going to make the automobile run.

He had raised the hood and studied the mechanism and he said he could tell that the car had been built in the days when cars were really built. You take now, he said, one man puts in one bolt and another man puts in another bolt and another man puts in another bolt so that it's a man for a bolt. That's why you have to pay so much for a car: you're paying all those men. Now if you didn't have to pay but one man, you could get you a cheaper car and one that had had a personal interest taken in it, and it would be a better car. The old woman agreed with him that this was so.

Mr. Shiftlet said that the trouble with the world was that nobody cared, or stopped and took any trouble. He said he never would have been able to teach Lucynell to say a word if he hadn't cared and stopped long enough.

"Teach her to say something else," the old woman said.

"What you want her to say next?" Mr. Shiftlet asked.

A The old woman's smile was broad and toothless and suggestive. "Teach her to say 'sugarpie,'" she said.

Mr. Shiftlet already knew what was on her mind.

The next day he began to tinker with the automobile and that evening he told her that if she would buy a fan belt, he would be able to make the car run.

The old woman said she would give him the money. "You see that girl yonder?" she asked, pointing to Lucynell who was sitting on the floor a foot away, watching him, her eyes blue even in the dark. "If it was ever a man wanted to take her away, I would say, 'No man on earth is going to take that sweet girl of mine away from me!' but if he was to say, 'Lady, I don't want to take her away, I want her right here,' I would say, 'Mister, I don't blame you none. I wouldn't pass up a chance to live in a permanent place and get the sweetest girl in the world myself. You ain't no fool,' I would say."

"How old is she?" Mr. Shiftlet asked casually.

"Fifteen, sixteen," the old woman said. The girl was nearly thirty but because of her innocence it was impossible to guess. B

"It would be a good idea to paint it too," Mr. Shiftlet remarked. "You don't want it to rust out."

"We'll see about that later," the old woman said.

The next day he walked into town and returned with the parts he needed and a can of gasoline. Late in the afternoon, terrible noises issued from the shed and the old woman rushed out of the house, thinking Lucynell was somewhere having a fit. Lucynell was sitting on a chicken crate, stamping her feet and screaming, "Burrddttt! bddurrddtttt!" but her fuss was drowned out by the car. With a volley of blasts it emerged from the shed, moving in a fierce and stately way. Mr. Shiftlet was in the driver's seat, sitting very erect. He had an expression of serious modesty on his face as if he had just raised the dead.

That night, rocking on the porch, the old woman began her business, at once. "You want you an innocent woman, don't you?" she asked sympathetically. "You don't want none of this trash."

"No'm, I don't," Mr. Shiftlet said.

"One that can't talk," she continued, "can't sass you back or use foul language. That's the kind for you to have. Right there," and she pointed to Lucynell sitting cross-legged in her chair, holding both feet in her hands.

"That's right," he admitted. "She wouldn't give me any trouble."

"Saturday," the old woman said, "you and her and me can drive into town and get married."

Mr. Shiftlet eased his position on the steps.

"I can't get married right now," he said. "Everything you want to do takes money and I ain't got any."

"What you need with money?" she asked.

"It takes money," he said. "Some people'll do anything anyhow these days, but the way I think, I wouldn't marry no woman that I couldn't take on a trip like she was somebody. I mean take her to a hotel and treat her. I wouldn't marry the Duchesser Windsor," he said firmly, "unless I could take her to a hotel and giver something good to eat.

"I was raised thataway and there ain't a thing I can do about it. My old mother taught me how to do."

"Lucynell don't even know what a hotel is,"

A. Responding

? Why does the old woman suggest that Shiftlet teach Lucynell to say "Sugarpie"? (She hopes that having Lucynell master this term of endearment will help her to realize her scheme of getting Shiftlet to marry her daughter.)

B. Responding

? Explain the irony in describing Lucynell's simplicity as "innocence." (Lucynell is an idiot, capable of speaking only one word. Describing her condition as "innocence" is an ironic understatement.)

Closure
Refer students to question 9, page 610, and ask volunteers to explain how the title relates to the theme of the story. (The appeal to self-interest, which this roadside sign makes, ironically highlights the single-minded self-interest that has motivated both the old woman and Shiftlet and made young Lucynell their hapless victim.)

Reading Check Test
1. Tom Shiftlet is interested in the Crater car from the beginning. *True*
2. Lucynell, the daughter, is just over sixteen years old. *False*
3. Shiftlet claims to have been a gospel singer at one time. *True*
4. The first word that young Lucynell learns to say is "sugarpie." *False*
5. Shiftlet tells Mrs. Crater that he needs money to buy a suit to get married in. *False*

A. Irony
? What is ironic about Shiftlet's "body/spirit" philosophy? (Shiftlet's purpose is to repair the automobile so that his body can move on. Shiftlet's spirit, on the other hand, is static.)

B. Simile
? What does O'Connor's use of the simile "like a weary snake" tell you about Shiftlet? (Answers will vary. Students should consider connotations of the word "snake"—deceit, treachery, evil, and so on.)

the old woman muttered. "Listen here, Mr. Shiftlet," she said, sliding forward in her chair, "you'd be getting a permanent house and a deep well and the most innocent girl in the world. You don't need no money. Lemme tell you something: there ain't any place in the world for a poor disabled friendless drifting man."

The ugly words settled in Mr. Shiftlet's head like a group of buzzards in the top of a tree. He didn't answer at once. He rolled himself a cigarette and lit it and then he said in an even voice, "Lady, a man is divided into two parts, body and spirit."

The old woman clamped her gums together.

A "A body and a spirit," he repeated. "The body, lady, is like a house: it don't go anywhere; but the spirit, lady, is like an automobile: always on the move, always . . ."

"Listen, Mr. Shiftlet," she said, "my well never goes dry and my house is always warm in the winter and there's no mortgage on a thing about this place. You can go to the courthouse and see for yourself. And yonder under that shed is a fine automobile." She laid the bait carefully. "You can have it painted by Saturday. I'll pay for the paint."

B In the darkness, Mr. Shiftlet's smile stretched like a weary snake waking up by a fire. After a second he recalled himself and said, "I'm only saying a man's spirit means more to him than anything else. I would have to take my wife off for the weekend without no regards at all for cost. I got to follow where my spirit says to go."

"I'll give you fifteen dollars for a weekend trip," the old woman said in a crabbed voice. "That's the best I can do."

"That wouldn't hardly pay for more than the gas and the hotel," he said. "It wouldn't feed her."

"Seventeen-fifty," the old woman said. "That's all I got so it isn't any use you trying to milk me. You can take a lunch."

Mr. Shiftlet was deeply hurt by the word "milk." He didn't doubt that she had more money sewed up in her mattress but he had already told her he was not interested in her money. "I'll make that do," he said and rose and walked off without treating with her further.

On Saturday the three of them drove into town in the car that the paint had barely dried on and Mr. Shiftlet and Lucynell were married in the Ordinary's office while the old woman witnessed. As they came out of the courthouse, Mr. Shiftlet began twisting his neck in his collar. He looked morose and bitter as if he had been insulted while someone held him. "That didn't satisfy me none," he said. "That was just something a woman in an office did, nothing but paper work and blood tests. What do they know about my blood? If they was to take my heart and cut it out," he said, "they wouldn't know a thing about me. It didn't satisfy me at all."

"It satisfied the law," the old woman said sharply.

"The law," Mr. Shiftlet said and spit. "It's the law that don't satisfy me."

He had painted the car dark green with a yellow band around it just under the windows. The three of them climbed in the front seat and the old woman said, "Don't Lucynell look pretty? Looks like a baby doll." Lucynell was dressed up in a white dress that her mother had uprooted from a trunk and there was a Panama hat on her head with a bunch of red wooden cherries on the brim. Every now and then her placid expression was changed by a sly isolated little thought like a shoot of green in the desert. "You got a prize!" the old woman said.

Mr. Shiftlet didn't even look at her.

They drove back to the house to let the old woman off and pick up the lunch. When they were ready to leave, she stood staring in the window of the car, with her fingers clenched around the glass. Tears began to seep sideways out of her eyes and run along the dirty creases in her face. "I ain't ever been parted with her for two days before," she said.

Mr. Shiftlet started the motor.

"And I wouldn't let no man have her but you because I seen you would do right. Goodbye, Sugarbaby," she said, clutching at the sleeve of the white dress. Lucynell looked straight at her and didn't seem to see her there at all. Mr. Shiftlet eased the car forward so that she had to move her hands.

The early afternoon was clear and open and surrounded by pale blue sky. Although the car would go only thirty miles an hour, Mr. Shiftlet imagined a terrific climb and dip and swerve that went entirely to his head so that he forgot his morning bitterness. He had always wanted an automobile but he had never been able to afford one before. He drove very fast because he wanted to make Mobile by nightfall.

ANALYZING THE STORY
Identifying Facts
1. Shiftlet fixes the roof of the garden house and repairs the front and back steps; he builds a new hog pen and restores a fence; he teaches Lucynell to say the word "bird"; and he begins to repair the automobile.
2. Shiftlet's continual interest in the car foreshadows the end of the story, when he abandons Lucynell and drives to Mobile. He succeeds in getting old Lucynell to pay for the new parts for the car, and he manages to persuade her to give some money for the wedding trip.

Old Lucynell sees in Shiftlet a solution to her problem in marrying off her innocent, speechless daughter.
3. Shiftlet, who has married Lucynell, abandons her while she is asleep at The Hot Spot and drives off to Mobile.

Interpreting Meanings
4. Among the details students may mention are the following. *Setting:* the sunset is described as "piercing"; the old woman and her daughter live alone in a "desolate spot"; the sun appears precariously balanced on the peak of a small
(Answers continue on next page.)

Occasionally he stopped his thoughts long enough to look at Lucynell in the seat beside him. She had eaten the lunch as soon as they were out of the yard and now she was pulling the cherries off the hat one by one and throwing them out the window. He became depressed in spite of the car. He had driven about a hundred miles when he decided that she must be hungry again and at the next small town they came to, he stopped in front of an aluminum-painted eating place called The Hot Spot and took her in and ordered her a plate of ham and grits. The ride had made her sleepy and as soon as she got up on the stool, she rested her head on the counter and shut her eyes. There was no one in The Hot Spot but Mr. Shiftlet and the boy behind the counter, a pale youth with a greasy rag hung over his shoulder. Before he could dish the food, she was snoring gently.

"Give it to her when she wakes up," Mr. Shiftlet said. "I'll pay for it now."

The boy bent over her and stared at the long pink-gold hair and the half-shut sleeping eyes. Then he looked up and and stared at Mr. Shiftlet. "She looks like an angel of Gawd," he murmured.

A "Hitchhiker," Mr. Shiftlet explained. "I can't wait. I got to make Tuscaloosa."

The boy bent over again and very carefully touched his finger to a strand of the golden hair and Mr. Shiftlet left.

He was more depressed than ever as he drove on by himself. The late afternoon had grown hot and sultry and the country had flattened out. Deep in the sky a storm was preparing very slowly and without thunder as if it meant to drain every drop of air from the earth before it broke. There were times when Mr. Shiftlet preferred not to be alone. B He felt too that a man with a car had a responsibility to others and he kept his eye out for a hitchhiker. Occasionally he saw a sign that warned: "Drive carefully. The life you save may be your own."

The narrow road dropped off on either side into dry fields and here and there a shack or a filling station stood in a clearing. The sun began to set directly in front of the automobile. It was a reddening ball that through his windshield was slightly flat on the bottom and top. He saw a boy in overalls and a gray hat standing on the edge of the road and he slowed the car down and stopped in front of him. The boy didn't have his hand raised to thumb the ride, he was only standing there, but he had a small cardboard suitcase and his hat was set on his head in a way to indicate that he had left somewhere for good. "Son," Mr. Shiftlet said, "I see you want a ride."

The boy didn't say he did or he didn't but he opened the door of the car and got in, and Mr. Shiftlet started driving again. The child held the suitcase on his lap and folded his arms on top of it. He turned his head and looked out the window away from Mr. Shiftlet. Mr. Shiftlet felt oppressed. "Son," he said after a minute, "I got the best old mother in the world so I reckon you only got the second best."

The boy gave him a quick dark glance and then turned his face back out the window.

"It's nothing so sweet," Mr. Shiftlet continued, "as a boy's mother. She taught him his first prayers at her knee, she give him love when no other would, she told him what was right and what wasn't, and she seen that he done the right thing. Son," he said, "I never rued a day in my life like the one I rued when I left that old mother of mine."

The boy shifted in his seat but he didn't look at Mr. Shiftlet. He unfolded his arms and put one hand on the door handle.

"My mother was a angel of Gawd," Mr. Shiftlet C said in a very strained voice. "He took her from heaven and giver to me and I left her." His eyes were instantly clouded over with a mist of tears. The car was barely moving.

The boy turned angrily in the seat. "You go to the devil!" he cried. "My old woman is a fleabag and yours is a stinking polecat!" and with that he flung the door open and jumped out with his suitcase into the ditch.

Mr. Shiftlet was so shocked that for about a hundred feet he drove along slowly with the door still open. A cloud, the exact color of the boy's hat and shaped like a turnip, had descended over the sun, and another, worse looking, crouched behind the car. Mr. Shiftlet felt that the rottenness of the world was about to engulf him. He raised his arm and let it fall again to his breast. "Oh Lord!" he prayed. "Break forth and wash the slime from this earth!"

The turnip continued slowly to descend. After a few minutes there was a guffawing peal of thunder from behind and fantastic raindrops, like tin-can tops, crashed over the rear of Mr. Shiftlet's car. Very quickly he stepped on the gas and with his stump sticking out the window he raced the galloping shower into Mobile.

A. Responding
? Do you think Shiftlet planned to desert Lucynell when he stopped at the Hot Spot, or do you think the idea occurs to him when she falls asleep at the counter? (Answers will vary. Shiftlet probably had not planned on a specific moment for abandoning Lucynell.)

B. Irony
? What makes this statement ironic? (Shiftlet's feeling of "responsibility to others" does not prevent him from abandoning his idiot wife shortly before.)

C. Responding
? Who has just been described as "looking like an angel of Gawd"? (Lucynell asleep at the diner) What is the difference in the purposes of the two similar descriptions? (The young man's description of Lucynell highlights her innocence; Shiftlet's description of his mother is for effect.)

(Continued from previous page.) mountain. *Physical description of the characters:* the strange behavior of young Lucynell; the characterization of Shiftlet as a tramp; old Lucynell rising "with one hand fisted on her hip"; Shiftlet's "long black slick hair" and his "steel-trap jaw"; his look of "composed dissatisfaction" and his peculiar pose against the sky so that his figure forms "a crooked cross"; Shiftlet's "pale sharp glance" and his frequent notice of the automobile; his actions with the burning match; the mention of "the trigger that moved up and down in his neck" (suggesting part of a gun.) *Dialogue:* evasion by both Shiftlet and old Lucynell; Shiftlet's mention of surgery on the human heart in Atlanta; his statements that "the world is almost rotten," "people'll do anything anyways," and "people don't care how they lie."

5. In general, the boy's insults form an abrupt counterpoint to Mr. Shiftlet's mawkishly sentimental statement about his mother.

Mr. Shiftlet is able to see rottenness in others, but not in himself. His melodramatic observations about other people's dishonesty and materialism clash with *(Answers continue in left-hand column.)*

(Continued from top.) the fact that he has just behaved badly by abandoning Lucynell and stealing the automobile.

6. Encourage students to defend their opinions about this complex character. Most students will agree that O'Connor intends for us to be repelled by Shiftlet: some students may observe that his name slyly suggests "shifty" or "shiftless." On the other hand, O'Connor paints a complex portrait. When Mr. Shiftlet declares, for example, that he possesses a "moral intelligence," is he totally wrong? Or is it simply that his deeds in the story (and probably in his past life, as well) do not measure up to the ideals that he so slickly invokes? The description, early in the story, of his figure as a crooked cross against the evening sky seems both symbolic and ambivalent. O'Connor may have meant that Shiftlet is both Christ-like and deeply flawed—perhaps *(Answers continue on next page.)*

Responding to the Story

Analyzing the Story

Identifying Facts

1. Describe the improvements Mr. Shiftlet makes in the Craters' place during his first week there.
2. Explain how Mr. Shiftlet seems to want to exploit the Craters. How does the older Lucynell want to exploit Mr. Shiftlet?
3. What has become of young Lucynell and Mr. Shiftlet by the story's end?

Interpreting Meanings

4. In the opening pages of the story, what details of **setting,** of **characterization,** and of **dialogue** carry potentially ominous or menacing undertones?
5. What is the significance of the remarks made by the hitchhhiker just before he leaps from the moving car? What are we to make of the fact that Mr. Shiftlet feels that "the rottenness of the world" is about to engulf him? What **irony** do you sense in Mr. Shiftlet's realization?
6. The ending of the story focuses on Mr. Shiftlet, rather than on the two Lucynells. Explain how you think the writer means us to regard him. Is he a prophet or a demon? Consider why O'Connor points out, early in the story, that Shiftlet's "figure formed a crooked cross" (page 605).
7. What is the significance of the peculiar clouds and the storm pursuing Mr. Shiftlet toward Mobile at the end of the story?
8. How would the story's **theme** and **effect** have changed if Mr. Shiftlet had returned to the café for Lucynell? How did you feel about the way the story ended?
9. Do you sense **irony** in the story's title? How would you state the story's **theme,** using the warning expressed in the title?
10. Are there any heroes in this story? Do you think it is a story about innocence vs. evil? Or do you think it is a story about a world in which everyone is a rogue? Explain.
11. Think of this story in relation to other stories you have read. What is your response to O'Connor's characters and theme? What do you think of her **tone?**

Writing About the Story

A Creative Response

1. **Extending the Story.** What becomes of Lucynell, asleep in the Hot Spot? Write an ending to the story in which you account for Lucynell.

A Critical Response

2. **Expressing an Opinion.** Read O'Connor's comments about this story under "Primary Sources" (which follows). In a brief essay, tell (a) why you think the TV producers would change the story, (b) whether you think the story would be popular if it were dramatized on TV today, or made into a movie, and (c) why a textbook would omit the last paragraph.
3. **Analyzing the Story.** In an essay, state whether you think the story is an **ironic parody** of a **romance.** (See page 612.) If so, account for these ironic reversals of the typical romance story:
   a. The nurturing mother
   b. The beautiful, innocent young woman
   c. The charming prince who is the rescuer
   d. The romance setting in a fairy-tale kingdom

Analyzing Language and Style

Connotations

In addition to its literal meaning, a word may have **connotative** meanings—that is, associations and emotional overtones that have come to be attached to the word. In this story, O'Connor uses words with strong connotations to reveal an attitude toward the character of Mr. Shiftlet.

1. Skim the story to find four **figures of speech** used to describe Mr. Shiftlet's appearance or actions. What do you associate with each figure of speech? What feelings do the descriptive words arouse in you?
2. Find two words used to describe the cloud and thunder that pursue Mr. Shiftlet toward Mobile.
3. Taken all together, what do you think these six words or phrases reveal about Mr. Shiftlet and the way we are to regard him?
4. For the words *steel-trap, clay-colored, trigger, snake, turnips,* and *guffawed,* substitute words with completely different connotations. What happens to our view of the character of Mr. Shiftlet?

he is an emblem of all those flawed human beings who know the good but somehow lack the faith or character to practice it.

7. Possibly that Shiftlet will be punished.

8. It would have been out of character. The ending is inevitable.

9. Students should first identify the context of the title phrase's occurrence within the story: Mr. Shiftlet sees the words on a road sign immediately after he leaves young Lucynell at The Hot Spot and before he picks up the hitchhiker. The irony of the title may be variously explained. If students examine closely the familiar roadside warning, they may note an almost casual selfishness. (Why not say, for example, that you might save *another* person's life if you drive safely?) This selfishness mingles with an ostensibly public-spirited concern for highway safety. Encourage students to discuss parallels with the character of Shiftlet, as it is presented in the story.

One statement of O'Connor's theme might run as follows: Most people, whatever they say to the contrary, are really preoccupied with their own self-interest.

10. Student answers will vary. It seems to be a deeply ironic story in which everyone is either a victim (Lucynell) or a rogue.

11. Students should be encouraged to analyze the tone of the story carefully. Ask students to discuss how O'Connor mingles irony, broad humor, and pathos with the grotesque. Then encourage students to apply their conclusions to an evaluation of O'Connor's characters and theme.

Primary Sources

The Adventures of Mr. Shiftlet

The following comments are from O'Connor's collection of letters called *The Habit of Being.*

"I am going to New York on the 30th to be, if you please, interviewed by Mr. Harvey Breit (on the 31st) on a program he is starting up over at NBC-TV [*Galley-Proof*]. They are also going to dramatize the opening scene from 'The Life You Save' etc. Do you reckon this is going to corrupt me? I already feel like a combination of Msgr. Sheen and Gorgeous George [a wrestler]. Everybody who has read *Wise Blood* thinks I'm a hillbilly nihilist, whereas I would like to create the impression over the television that I'm a hillbilly Thomist,[1] but I will probably not be able to think of anything to say to Mr. Harvey Breit but 'Huh?' and 'Ah dunno.' When I come back I'll probably have to spend three months day and night in the chicken pen to counteract these evil influences.

. . .

"I have just sold the television rights to 'The Life You Save May Be Your Own' to what I understand is called the General Electric Playhouse. All I know about television is hearsay but somebody told me that this was a production conducted by Ronald Regan (?). I don't know if this means RR will be Mr. Shiftlet or not. A staggering thought. Mr. Shiftlet and the idiot daughter will no doubt go off in a Chrysler and live happily ever after. Anyway, on account of this, I am buying my mother a new refrigerator. While they make hash out of my story, she and me will make ice in the new refrigerator.

. . .

"I have just learned via one of those gossip columns that the story I sold for a TV play is going to be put on in the spring and that a *tap-dancer* by the name of Gene Kelly is going to make his television debut in it. The punishment always fits the crime. They must be going to make a musical out of it.

. . .

". . . A letter from my agent today announces that 'The Life You Save' will be presented February 1 on the Schlitz Playhouse at 9:30 New York time. My eager beaver friend in NY keeps sending me clippings of gossip columns, one announcing that Kelly will star in Flannery O'Connor's 'backwoods love story.' Another saying Kelly says 'It's a kind of hillbilly thing in which I play a guy who *befriends* a deaf-mute girl in the hills of Kentucky. It gives me a great chance to do some straight acting, something I really have no opportunity to do in movies.' See? He ain't had the opportunity before. There'll be no singing & dancing, Kelly says. I think it's channel 5 and people tell me you can't get it very good here, so I hope you will absolutely be in front of your set this time at the correct hour, as I must have some representative there to give Kelly a good leer every now and then for me. I don't know who his leading lady will be, but doubtless my NY friend will be providing that information before long. She thinks this is all hilariously funny and keeps writing me, 'Has dignity no value for you?' etc. It will probably be appropriate to smoke a corncob pipe while watching this. All my kinfolks are going to think that it is a great improvement over the original story.

. . .

"Someone has just called my attention to the fact that this . . . text which has 'The Life You Save' in it has it with the last paragraph omitted. I would be much obliged if you would call Harcourt [her publisher] and tell them. I think some kind of protest ought to be lodged. I suppose there is nothing that can be done about it now but I certainly don't like the idea of my story being in a textbook and the last paragraph omitted. . . ."

—Flannery O'Connor

1. **Thomist:** someone who follows the thinking of the thirteenth-century philosopher Thomas Aquinas.

Elements of Literature

THE FOUR "MODES" OF FICTION

According to some critics, all narrative literature can be more or less described in terms of four basic "modes," or story patterns. These modes are romance, tragedy, irony, and comedy. Tragedy and comedy are opposites, and so are romance and irony.

In the typical **romance** story, a hero or heroine undertakes a quest and is usually successful. In such a story (and we are all familiar with them from the fairy tales of our childhoods), beauty, innocence, and goodness prevail over evil, often with the help of magic or supernatural intervention.

In a typical **tragedy,** on the other hand, the hero or heroine is a noble, admirable character who falls from a position of some prominence to disaster or even death. This tragic hero is overcome by evil, but in the course of the struggle, he or she has also gained self-knowledge and wisdom. Our response to tragedy is often a kind of exhilaration. We have seen the best that human beings are capable of, especially in the face of overwhelming adversity.

Opposite to romance is **irony.** In the world of irony, there are no heroes and no triumphs. There are certainly no fairy godmothers and no magic wands. In some ironic stories, the world is a place where injustice, crime, and general foolishness are taken for granted. The characters who triumph in such a world are often crafty rascals and even con artists—people who learn how to manipulate the world for their own gain. In other forms of irony, the characters are ordinary human beings like ourselves, who are caught in a world that offers little opportunity for heroism. Unlike the great tragic heroes, these characters are all too human. Walter Mitty is an example of this type of character, one who longs for heroism but is limited to shopping for puppy biscuits in Waterbury, Connecticut. The characters in ironic fiction often find themselves in settings that are confining, that offer no opportunities for free choice. Such fiction is often actually set in prisons, totalitarian societies, or even madhouses.

Opposite to tragedy is **comedy.** In a comedy, the central characters are often two lovers who want to marry despite parental and societal obstacles. By the end of a comedy, the young lovers have triumphed over the forces blocking them and are to be married. At the end of many comedies, we even have a wedding, suggesting the renewal of life and love. Other comedies are about characters who triumph over the forces of tradition that are blocking their freedom in some way. At the end of such comedies, the characters are embarked on a new life, unhampered by the bonds that had blocked them earlier.

These are extremely simple descriptions of the complex modes used in narrative literature. You can see from the description of irony that O'Connor's story—and many of the other stories in this unit—can be seen as examples of the ironic mode.

What modes do you think the other stories in this unit are written in?

Eudora Welty (1909–   )

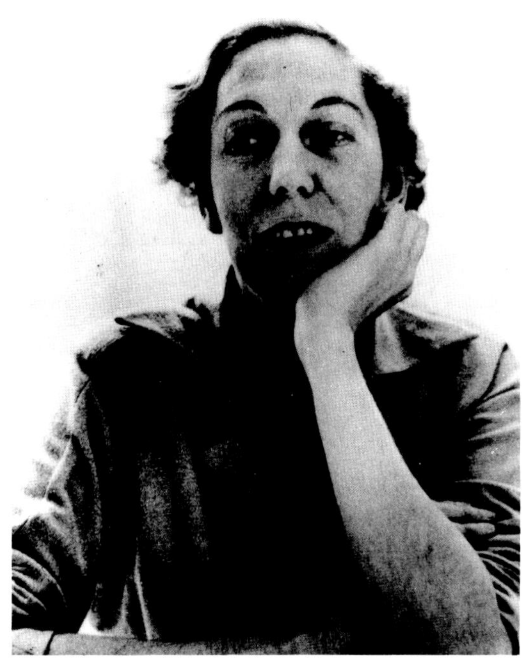

Eudora Welty was born in the quintessentially Southern city of Jackson, Mississippi, and she has lived in Jackson almost her whole life. As the daughter of an insurance man and a schoolteacher, she enjoyed a conventional girlhood. She recalls pleading with her brothers to teach her golf, sharing their enthusiasm for baseball, and bicycling to the library in *two* petticoats to forestall the librarian's caustic remark, "I can see straight through you."

Welty attended Mississippi State College for Women, graduated from the University of Wisconsin, and did graduate work at Columbia University, anticipating a career in advertising. However, the depression sent her home to Jackson with a belief, which did not fail her, that she would succeed as a writer of fiction.

Welty's widely recognized triumph is a painstaking accuracy in colloquial speech. The exactly right word always matters to her. She has always been fascinated by words, by the *way* people say things, by snatches of overheard dialogue. She was once delighted to hear a country woman confess to "a gnawing and a craving" for something. Telling a friend about it, Welty added, "Wasn't that a wonderful way of putting it? A gnawing and a craving!"

She greatly admires the work of Katherine Anne Porter (see page 582), who befriended her when she was sending out stories and getting back rejection slips. It was the literary agent Diarmuid Russell who shared Welty's belief in an ultimate success. He not only took her on as a client, but said of a certain Welty story that if the editor didn't accept it, "he ought to be horsewhipped." (The editor in question bought the story.)

Welty's first collections of stories, *A Curtain of Green* and *The Wide Net,* appeared in the 1940's. These were followed by *The Golden Apples* (1949), one of her best-known volumes of short stories. Then came a novella, *The Ponder Heart* (1954), which was made into a Broadway play. *Losing Battles,* Welty's fine comic novel about a family reunion in the rural South, was published in 1970. Two years later, Welty produced *The Optimist's Daughter,* a poignant short novel about family conflicts; this book won her the Pulitzer Prize. An autobiographical memoir entitled *One Writer's Beginnings,* based on lectures Welty gave at Harvard University, was published in 1983 to wide critical acclaim.

Welty admits to being blessed with a visual mind, and she says that this gift makes for "the best shorthand a writer can have." She once wrote, "To watch everything about me, I regarded grimly and possessively as a *need.*" Clearly, that need became an enviable, artistic vision. A

A. Expansion
On page 619, Eudora Welty describes how the sight of an old woman like Phoenix was the inspiration for "A Worn Path." You might want to discuss how sensitivity to one's environment is crucial for a writer. Students might recall instances in their own writing when some sensory stimulus triggered an idea for a piece of writing.

SUPPLEMENTARY SUPPORT MATERIALS
1. Vocabulary Activity Worksheet (*CCB*)
2. Review and Response Worksheet: Theme (*CCB*)
3. Language Skills Worksheet: Varying Sentence Beginnings (*CCB*)
4. Selection Test (*CCB*)

DEVELOPING VOCABULARY
The following words from the story are tested in the Selection Test. (See also Vocabulary Activity Worksheet.)

phoenix	furrow
meditative	maze
limber	pullet
rouse	lolling
buzzard	lye

ADDITIONAL WRITING ASSIGNMENT
Tell students that from earliest times, writers have used journeys as a metaphor for life. (The most famous of all is Ulysses' long journey home in *The Odyssey.*) Ask them to think about journeys and then write in a few sentences why they make a good metaphor for life.

A. Characterization
? How would you describe Phoenix's relationship with the natural world? (She seems to feel a close kinship to the trees, animals, and even the thorn bush in which she catches her dress.)

A WORN PATH

The major character in this story is named Phoenix Jackson. Before you begin reading, look up the word *phoenix* in a dictionary. As you read, think about why Welty chose this name for her traveler. Phoenix makes her journey in rural Mississippi, late in the Depression era.

It was December—a bright frozen day in the early morning. Far out in the country there was an old Negro woman with her head tied in a red rag, coming along a path through the pinewoods. Her name was Phoenix Jackson. She was very old and small and she walked slowly in the dark pine shadows, moving a little from side to side in her steps, with the balanced heaviness and lightness of a pendulum in a grandfather clock. She carried a thin, small cane made from an umbrella, and with this she kept tapping the frozen earth in front of her. This made a grave and persistent noise in the still air, that seemed meditative like the chirping of a solitary little bird.

She wore a dark striped dress reaching down to her shoe tops, and an equally long apron of bleached sugar sacks, with a full pocket: all neat and tidy, but every time she took a step she might have fallen over her shoelaces, which dragged from her unlaced shoes. She looked straight ahead. Her eyes were blue with age. Her skin had a pattern all its own of numberless branching wrinkles and as though a whole little tree stood in the middle of her forehead, but a golden color ran underneath, and the two knobs of her cheeks were illumined by a yellow burning under the dark. Under the red rag her hair came down on her neck in the frailest of ringlets, still black, and with an odor like copper.

Now and then there was a quivering in the thicket. Old Phoenix said, "Out of my way, all you foxes, owls, beetles, jack rabbits, coons and wild animals! . . . Keep out from under these feet, little bobwhites. . . . Keep the big wild hogs out of my path. Don't let none of those come running my direction. I got a long way." Under her small black-freckled hand her cane, limber as a buggy whip, would switch at the brush as if to rouse up any hiding things.

On she went. The woods were deep and still. The sun made the pine needles almost too bright to look at, up where the wind rocked. The cones dropped as light as feathers. Down in the hollow was the mourning dove—it was not too late for him.

The path ran up a hill. "Seem like there is chains about my feet, time I get this far," she said, in the voice of argument old people keep to use with themselves. "Something always take a hold of me on this hill—pleads I should stay."

After she got to the top she turned and gave a full, severe look behind her where she had come. "Up through pines," she said at length. "Now down through oaks."

Her eyes opened their widest, and she started down gently. But before she got to the bottom of the hill a bush caught her dress.

Her fingers were busy and intent, but her skirts were full and long, so that before she could pull them free in one place they were caught in another. It was not possible to allow the dress to tear. "I in the thorny bush," she said. "Thorns, you doing your appointed work. Never want to let folks pass, no sir. Old eyes thought you was a pretty little *green* bush." A

Finally, trembling all over, she stood free, and after a moment dared to stoop for her cane.

"Sun so high!" she cried, leaning back and looking, while the thick tears went over her eyes. "The time getting all gone here."

At the foot of this hill was a place where a log was laid across the creek.

"Now comes the trial," said Phoenix.

Putting her right foot out, she mounted the log and shut her eyes. Lifting her skirt, leveling her cane fiercely before her, like a festival figure in some parade, she began to march across. Then she opened her eyes and she was safe on the other side.

"I wasn't as old as I thought," she said.

But she sat down to rest. She spread her skirts on the bank around her and folded her hands over

Preparation

Establishing a Purpose. Before students start reading, tell them that "A Worn Path" is about an old woman who undertakes a long and difficult journey. Finding out what motivates her to travel so far can be their purpose for reading.

A. Humanities Connection: Responding to the Photograph

? What details in the photograph accurately reflect what you have read so far in the story? (The landscape, including the path, the fence, and the woods generally reflects details of the story's setting. The woman, however, appears to be larger than Phoenix, who is described in the story as very small. The woman is also not dressed like Phoenix and her cane is larger than Phoenix's.)

Students who are not familiar with the South may not respond to certain details in the photograph, such as the palmetto plants and the gas tank that supplies fuel for cooking and heating.

B. Expansion

Students should note the difficult obstacles Phoenix has to overcome on her journey.

A

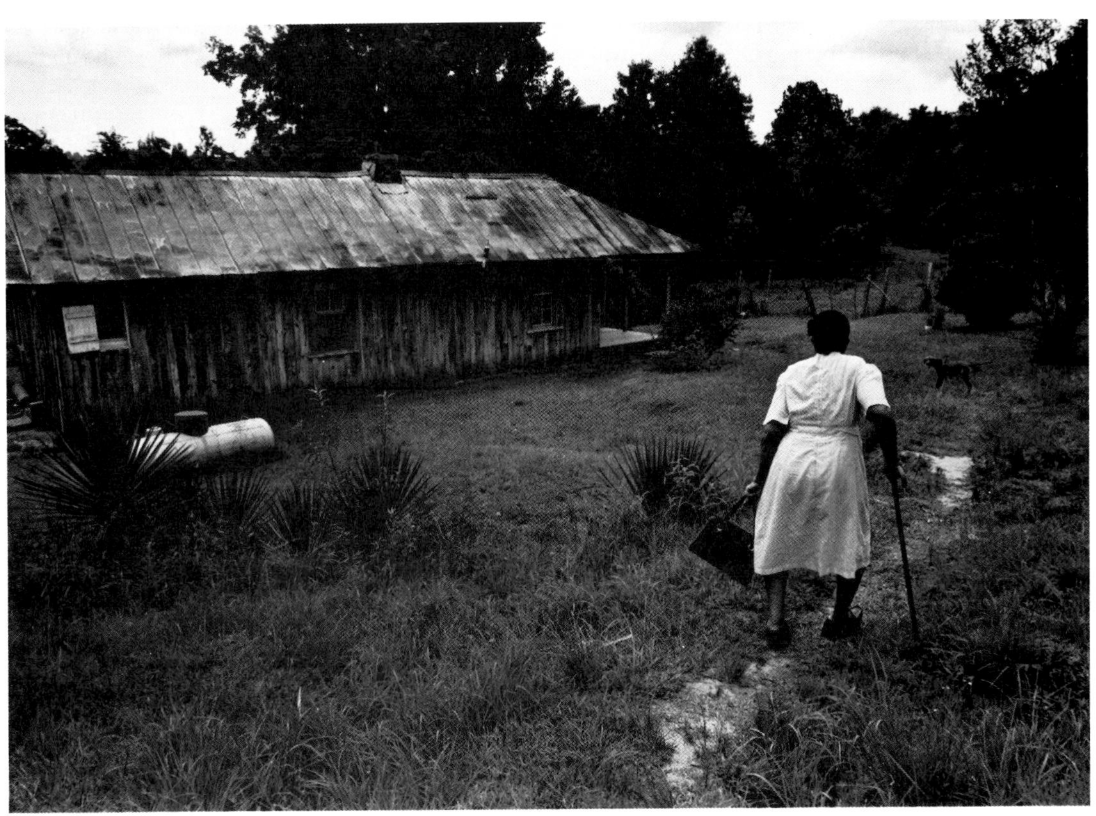

her knees. Up above her was a tree in a pearly cloud of mistletoe. She did not dare to close her eyes, and when a little boy brought her a plate with a slice of marble cake on it she spoke to him. "That would be acceptable," she said. But when she went to take it there was just her own hand in the air.

B So she left that tree, and had to go through a barbed-wire fence. There she had to creep and crawl, spreading her knees and stretching her fingers like a baby trying to climb the steps. But she talked loudly to herself: she could not let her dress be torn now, so late in the day, and she could not pay for having her arm or her leg sawed off if she got caught fast where she was.

At last she was safe through the fence and risen up out in the clearing. Big dead trees, like black men with one arm, were standing in the purple stalks of the withered cotton field. There sat a buzzard.

"Who you watching?"

In the furrow she made her way along.

"Glad this not the season for bulls," she said, looking sideways, "and the good Lord made his snakes to curl up and sleep in the winter. A pleasure I don't see no two-headed snake coming around that tree, where it come once. It took a while to get by him, back in the summer."

She passed through the old cotton and went into a field of dead corn. It whispered and shook and was taller than her head. "Through the maze now," she said, for there was no path.

Then there was something tall, black, and skinny there, moving before her.

At first she took it for a man. It could have been a man dancing in the field. But she stood still and listened, and it did not make a sound. It was as silent as a ghost.

"Ghost," she said sharply, "who be you the ghost of? For I have heard of nary death close by."

But there was no answer—only the ragged dancing in the wind.

She shut her eyes, reached out her hand, and touched a sleeve. She found a coat and inside that an emptiness, cold as ice.

CLOSURE

Ask students to read question 12, page 619. Have them discuss whether or not Phoenix has led a fulfilled life.

READING CHECK TEST

1. The story takes place in winter. *True*
2. Phoenix often talks to herself as she walks along. *True*
3. Her destination is a general store in a nearby town. *False*
4. A hunter gives Phoenix some money. *False*
5. Her grandson suffers from a throat ailment. *True*

A. Irony

The young hunter's condescending notion that Phoenix would make the arduous trip to see Santa Claus becomes very ironic when the reader learns the real reason for her journey.

B. Responding

? Why does Phoenix clap her hands and call attention to the black dog? (She hopes to divert the hunter's attention so that she will have a chance to pick up the nickel.)

"You scarecrow," she said. Her face lighted. "I ought to be shut up for good," she said with laughter. "My senses is gone. I too old. I the oldest people I ever know. Dance, old scarecrow," she said, "while I dancing with you."

She kicked her foot over the furrow, and with mouth drawn down, shook her head once or twice in a little strutting way. Some husks blew down and whirled in streamers about her skirts.

Then she went on, parting her way from side to side with the cane, through the whispering field. At last she came to the end, to a wagon track where the silver grass blew between the red ruts. The quail were walking around like pullets, seeming all dainty and unseen.

"Walk pretty," she said. "This the easy place. This the easy going."

She followed the track, swaying through the quiet bare fields, through the little strings of trees silver in their dead leaves, past cabins silver from weather, with the doors and windows boarded shut, all like old women under a spell sitting there. "I walking in their sleep," she said, nodding her head vigorously.

In a ravine she went where a spring was silently flowing through a hollow log. Old Phoenix bent and drank. "Sweet gum makes the water sweet," she said, and drank more. "Nobody know who made this well, for it was here when I was born."

The track crossed a swampy part where the moss hung as white as lace from every limb. "Sleep on, alligators, and blow your bubbles." Then the track went into the road.

Deep, deep the road went down between the high green-colored banks. Overhead the live oaks met, and it was as dark as a cave.

A black dog with a lolling tongue came up out of the weeds by the ditch. She was meditating, and not ready, and when he came at her she only hit him a little with her cane. Over she went in the ditch, like a little puff of milkweed.

Down there, her senses drifted away. A dream visited her, and she reached her hand up, but nothing reached down and gave her a pull. So she lay there and presently went to talking. "Old woman," she said to herself, "that black dog come up out of the weeds to stall you off, and now there he sitting on his fine tail, smiling at you."

A white man finally came along and found her—a hunter, a young man, with his dog on a chain.

"Well, Granny!" he laughed. "What are you doing there?"

"Lying on my back like a June bug waiting to be turned over, mister," she said, reaching up her hand.

He lifted her up, gave her a swing in the air, and set her down. "Anything broken, Granny?"

"No, sir, them old dead weeds is springy enough," said Phoenix, when she had got her breath. "I thank you for your trouble."

"Where do you live, Granny?" he asked, while the two dogs were growling at each other.

"Away back yonder, sir, behind the ridge. You can't even see it from here."

"On your way home?"

"No sir, I going to town."

"Why, that's too far! That's as far as I walk when I come out myself, and I get something for my trouble." He patted the stuffed bag he carried, and there hung down a little closed claw. It was one of the bobwhites, with its beak hooked bitterly to show it was dead. "Now you go on home, Granny!"

"I bound to go to town, mister," said Phoenix. "The time come around."

He gave another laugh, filling the whole landscape. "I know you old colored people! Wouldn't miss going to town to see Santa Claus!" A

But something held old Phoenix very still. The deep lines in her face went into a fierce and different radiation. Without warning, she had seen with her own eyes a flashing nickel fall out of the man's pocket onto the ground.

"How old are you, Granny?" he was saying.

"There is no telling, mister," she said, "no telling."

Then she gave a little cry and clapped her hands and said, "Git on away from here, dog! Look! Look at that dog!" She laughed as if in admiration. B "He ain't scared of nobody. He a big black dog." She whispered. "Sic him!"

"Watch me get rid of that cur," said the man. "Sic him, Pete! Sic him!"

Phoenix heard the dogs fighting, and heard the man running and throwing sticks. She even heard a gunshot. But she was slowly bending forward by that time, further and further forward, the lids stretched down over her eyes, as if she were doing this in her sleep. Her chin was lowered almost to her knees. The yellow palm of her hand came out from the fold of her apron. Her fingers slid down and along the ground under the piece of money with the grace and care they would have in lifting an egg from under a setting hen. Then she slowly

ANALYZING THE STORY

Identifying Facts

1. Phoenix travels from her home, far out in the country, into the town of Natchez to collect medicine for her grandson, who suffers chronic throat trouble because he has swallowed lye.

Because she is so old, Phoenix must face obstacles of the terrain: walking uphill, crossing a creek on a log, getting through a barbed wire fence, and trying to fend off a dog.

2. Phoenix retrieves one of the nickels when the man she meets on the road drops it. The doctor's attendant gives her the other nickel. She intends to buy a paper windmill for her grandson.

3. The result is successful, in that Phoenix receives the medicine and prepares to buy her grandson a gift.

Interpreting Meanings

4. Numerous personifications of animals and features of the landscape during Phoenix's journey help to identify the old woman with nature. She is identified with time because of her great age: she tells the hunter that there is "no telling" how old she is. By comparing the wrinkles of Phoenix's forehead to a small tree, the

(Answers continue on next page.)

straightened up, she stood erect, and the nickel was in her apron pocket. A bird flew by. Her lips moved. "God watching me the whole time. I come to stealing."

The man came back, and his own dog panted about them. "Well, I scared him off that time," he said, and then he laughed and lifted his gun and pointed it at Phoenix.

She stood straight and faced him.

"Doesn't the gun scare you?" he said, still pointing it.

"No, sir, I seen plenty go off closer by, in my day, and for less than what I done," she said, holding utterly still.

He smiled, and shouldered the gun. "Well, Granny," he said, "you must be a hundred years old, and scared of nothing. I'd give you a dime if I had any money with me. But you take my advice and stay home, and nothing will happen to you."

"I bound to go on my way, mister," said Phoenix. She inclined her head in the red rag. Then they went in different directions, but she could hear the gun shooting again and again over the hill.

She walked on. The shadows hung from the oak trees to the road like curtains. Then she smelled wood smoke, and smelled the river, and she saw a steeple and the cabins on their steep steps. Dozens of little black children whirled around her. There ahead was Natchez shining. Bells were ringing. She walked on.

A In the paved city it was Christmas time. There were red and green electric lights strung and crisscrossed everywhere, and all turned on in the daytime. Old Phoenix would have been lost if she had not distrusted her eyesight and depended on her feet to know where to take her.

She paused quietly on the sidewalk where people were passing by. A lady came along in the crowd, carrying an armful of red-, green- and silver-wrapped presents; she gave off perfume like the red roses in hot summer, and Phoenix stopped her.

"Please, missy, will you lace up my shoe?" She held up her foot.

"What do you want, Grandma?"

"See my shoe," said Phoenix. "Do all right for out in the country, but wouldn't look right to go in a big building."

B "Stand still then, Grandma," said the lady. She put her packages down on the sidewalk beside her and laced and tied both shoes tightly.

"Can't lace 'em with a cane," said Phoenix. "Thank you, missy. I doesn't mind asking a nice lady to tie up my shoe, when I gets out on the street."

Moving slowly and from side to side, she went into the big building, and into a tower of steps, where she walked up and around and around until her feet knew to stop.

She entered a door, and there she saw nailed up on the wall the document that had been stamped with the gold seal and framed in the gold frame, which matched the dream that was hung up in her head.

"Here I be," she said. There was a fixed and ceremonial stiffness over her body.

"A charity case, I suppose," said an attendant who sat at the desk before her.

But Phoenix only looked above her head. There was sweat on her face, the wrinkles in her skin shone like a bright net.

"Speak up, Grandma," the woman said. "What's your name? We must have your history, you know. Have you been here before? What seems to be the trouble with you?"

Old Phoenix only gave a twitch to her face as if a fly were bothering her.

"Are you deaf?" cried the attendant.

But then the nurse came in.

"Oh, that's just old Aunt Phoenix," she said. "She doesn't come for herself—she has a little grandson. She makes these trips just as regular as clockwork. She lives away back off the Old Natchez Trace." She bent down. "Well, Aunt Phoenix, why don't you just take a seat? We won't keep you standing after your long trip." She pointed.

The old woman sat down, bolt upright in the chair.

"Now, how is the boy?" asked the nurse. C

Old Phoenix did not speak.

"I said, how is the boy?"

But Phoenix only waited and stared straight ahead, her face very solemn and withdrawn into rigidity.

"Is his throat any better?" asked the nurse. "Aunt Phoenix, don't you hear me? Is your grandson's throat any better since the last time you came for the medicine?"

With her hands on her knees, the old woman waited, silent, erect and motionless, just as if she were in armor.

"You mustn't take up our time this way, Aunt

A. Setting

? Why do you suppose the author chose to set this story at Christmas time? (Christians celebrate the birth of Christ then, and it is generally believed to be a time of spiritual fulfillment and rebirth. The fact that Phoenix makes her journey at this time adds a spiritual dimension to it—it is through such journeys that we find spiritual fulfillment.)

B. Responding

? How does this young woman's attitude toward Phoenix compare with the hunter's? (This woman helps Phoenix at her request without condescension.)

C. Responding

? Why do you suppose the reason for Phoenix's journey isn't revealed earlier in the story? (Without a specific reason for the journey, it seems more a journey of "Everyman," a journey through life that we all share.)

(Continued from previous page.)
author suggests flourishing, natural growth; this impression is reinforced when Welty speaks of the "golden color."
5. The imagined encounter with the little boy offering marble cake shows that Phoenix is polite and gracious. The question she asks the buzzard ("Who you watching?") indicates that she is imaginative, and perhaps a bit superstitious. The encounter with the scarecrow, when Phoenix tries to dance, shows that she has a sense of humor. The encounter with the bramblebush, in which Phoenix says that she thought "you was a pretty little *green* bush," perhaps suggests that Phoenix is inclined to be optimistic and to look on the bright side of things. Finally, her encounter with the hunter shows that Phoenix is courageous and dignified—perhaps also a bit sly, since she creates a diversion so that she can pick up the nickel the hunter has dropped.
6. Student answers will differ. Most students will agree that Phoenix is heroic in her courage, persistence, dignity, and steadfast love.
7. Perhaps the hunter was having a "joke" at the old woman's expense.
Perhaps the hunter does not even re-

A. Expansion
Phoenix's momentary loss of recent memory is not uncommon in people of her age. She has not forgotten her grandson; she has momentarily forgotten what brought her to these relatively strange surroundings.

B. Expansion
The plight of Phoenix's grandson is made poignantly clear here—he is totally dependent on Phoenix, who is old and has not too firm a grip on life.

For Further Reading For The Student
Students interested in getting better acquainted with this distinguished American writer should be encouraged to read the stories in *A Curtain of Green and Other Stories* (a 50th anniversary edition of which was published by Harcourt Brace Jovanovich in 1991).

Phoenix," the nurse said. "Tell us quickly about your grandson, and get it over. He isn't dead, is he?"

At last there came a flicker and then a flame of comprehension across her face, and she spoke.

"My grandson. It was my memory had left me. There I sat and forgot why I made my long trip."

"Forgot?" The nurse frowned. "After you came so far?"

A Then Phoenix was like an old woman begging a dignified forgiveness for waking up frightened in the night. "I never did go to school, I was too old at the Surrender," she said in a soft voice. "I'm an old woman without an education. It was my memory fail me. My little grandson, he is just the same, and I forgot it in the coming."

"Throat never heals, does it?" said the nurse, speaking in a loud, sure voice to old Phoenix. By now she had a card with something written on it, a little list. "Yes. Swallowed lye. When was it?—January—two-three years ago—"

Phoenix spoke unasked now. "No, missy, he not dead, he just the same. Every little while his throat begin to close up again, and he not able to swallow. He not get his breath. He not able to help himself. So the time come around, and I go on another trip for the soothing medicine."

"All right. The doctor said as long as you came to get it, you could have it," said the nurse. "But it's an obstinate case."

B "My little grandson, he sit up there in the house all wrapped up, waiting by himself," Phoenix went on. "We is the only two left in the world. He suffer and it don't seem to put him back at all. He got a sweet look. He going to last. He wear a little patch quilt and peep out holding his mouth open like a little bird. I remembers so plain now. I not going to forget him again, no, the whole enduring time. I could tell him from all the others in creation."

"All right." The nurse was trying to hush her now. She brought her a bottle of medicine. "Charity," she said, making a check mark in a book.

Old Phoenix held the bottle close to her eyes, and then carefully put it into her pocket.

"I thank you," she said.

"It's Christmas time, Grandma," said the attendant. "Could I give you a few pennies out of my purse?"

"Five pennies is a nickel," said Phoenix stiffly.

"Here's a nickel," said the attendant.

Phoenix rose carefully and held out her hand. She received the nickel and then fished the other nickel out of her pocket and laid it beside the new one. She stared at her palm closely, with her head on one side.

Then she gave a tap with her cane on the floor.

"This is what come to me to do," she said. "I going to the store and buy my child a little windmill they sells, made out of paper. He going to find it hard to believe there such a thing in the world. I'll march myself back where he waiting, holding it straight up in this hand."

She lifted her free hand, gave a little nod, turned around, and walked out of the doctor's office. Then her slow step began on the stairs, going down.

Responding to the Story

Analyzing the Story

Identifying Facts

1. Describe the purpose of Phoenix Jackson's journey. On her way to Natchez, what obstacles does she overcome?
2. Explain how Phoenix acquires the two nickels. How does she intend to spend them?
3. What is the result of Phoenix's long and perilous journey through the woods? Does she get what she wants? Explain.

Interpreting Meanings

4. Phoenix Jackson, the central figure of this story, is surely memorable. How do Welty's descriptions of her **appearance, speech,** and **behavior** identify her with the world of nature and with time itself?
5. Describe what her encounters with the little boy offering marble cake, with the buzzard, with the scarecrow, with the bramblebush, and finally with the hunter tell us about Phoenix's **character.**
6. Would you describe Phoenix as a heroine, in the traditional sense of the word? Why?

alize he has dropped the nickel; for him, in contrast to Phoenix, a nickel may have been a negligible amount of money.

8. It is ironic that the hunter suggests that Phoenix is going to town to see Santa Claus because, in reality, Phoenix is on an errand of love. By bringing the medicine and a present to her grandson, she *becomes* the spirit of love and charity, symbolically represented by Santa Claus at Christmas.

The hunter and the nurses at the hospital treat Phoenix condescendingly because she is old, poor, and black.

9. The phoenix is a mythical bird which was said to be periodically reborn from its own ashes: it is thus a symbol of renewal and regeneration. Within the context of the story, it is an appropriate name for the old woman who travels to town, since she is associated with love and healing.

10. By setting the story at Christmastime, Welty provides a religious resonance for her theme of love and rebirth.

The nurses' detached, condescending attitude ironically clashes with the true, loving spirit of Christmas.

11. Phoenix's act of charity is performed at great sacrifice, whereas the nurse seems to treat "charity" in an offhand and impersonal fashion.

12. Most students will agree that Phoenix, in her harmony with nature and her great love for her grandson, is shown to lead a fulfilled, rather than a tragic, life.

13. The title perhaps suggests that Phoenix has made the journey to town many times over; the path from her home to the doctor's office is thus "well worn." Metaphorically, the title may also suggest the habitual "path" of love in Phoenix's mind and heart. This, in turn, suggests Welty's theme: that the path of love—"worn" because it entails sacrifice and needs to be trodden again and again—is open to us all.

7. What do you suppose possessed the hunter to point his gun at the old woman? Do you think the hunter deliberately lies about not having any money? Or is there another explanation?
8. What is **ironic** about the reason the hunter suggests for Phoenix's long journey? Do many people treat Phoenix condescendingly? Why?
9. Explain the significance of Phoenix's name. Why is it an appropriate name for her?
10. Describe the story's seasonal **setting,** and explain its significance. Does Welty use the setting to make us feel **irony** in the nurses' attitude? Explain.
11. When the nurse gives Phoenix the medicine, she says, "Charity," and makes a check mark in her book. Given the character of Phoenix, what is **ironic** about the nurse's statement and action?
12. When you grasped the purpose of Phoenix's long journey to Natchez, what did you discover about her life? Is it a fulfilled one? Is it tragic? Explain.
13. What do you think is Welty's **theme** in "A Worn Path"? Put another way, what "worn path" is open to us all?

Writing About the Story

A Creative Response

1. **Extending the Story.** Read the essay by Welty that follows below. Then write your own ending for Phoenix's story.

A Critical Response

2. **Analyzing the Journey.** In her comment on the story that follows, Welty summarizes the purposes of the adventures she invented for her character. In an essay, identify the specific parts of the journey that could be categorized as:

   a. dreams
   b. harassments
   c. small triumphs
   d. some jolts to the traveler's pride
   e. some flights of fancy to console the traveler
   f. encounters to scare the traveler
   g. cause to be ashamed
   h. a moment to dance and preen

   In your essay, explain how Phoenix's journey takes on mythic significance—how is it like the quests taken by heroes like Odysseus?
3. **Responding to a Comment.** Welty says of her story, "The only certain thing at all is the worn path," and she identifies the path as a metaphor for the habit of love. In a paragraph, explain what Welty might mean by the "habit of love" and tell why this habit might be compared with a worn path (and not with a new road, or the shining path of a rocket, or a crystal stairway).
4. **Analyzing Character.** Does Phoenix change as a result of her experiences? Or is she essentially timeless? In an essay present your answers to these questions.

Primary Sources

"Is Phoenix Jackson's Grandson Really Dead?"

"A story writer is more than happy to be read by students; the fact that these serious readers think and feel something in response to his work he finds life-giving. At the same time he may not always be able to reply to their specific questions in kind. I wondered if it might clarify something, for both the questioners and myself, if I set down a general reply to the question that comes to me most often in the mail, from both students and their teachers, after some classroom discussion. The unrivaled favorite is this: 'Is Phoenix Jackson's grandson really *dead?*'

"It refers to a short story I wrote years ago called 'A Worn Path,' which tells of a day's journey an old woman makes on foot from deep in the country into town and into a doctor's office on behalf of her little grandson; he is at home, periodically ill, and periodically she comes for his medicine; they give it to her as usual, she receives it and starts the journey back.

"I had not meant to mystify readers by withholding any fact; it is not a writer's business to tease. The story is told through Phoenix's mind as she undertakes her errand. As the author at one with the character as I tell it, I must assume that the boy is alive. As the reader, you are free to think as you like, of course: the story invites you to believe that no matter what happens, Phoenix for as long as she is able to walk and can hold to her purpose will make her journey. The *possibility* that she would keep on even if he were dead is there in her devotion and its single-minded, single-track errand. Certainly the *artistic* truth, which should be good enough for the fact, lies in Phoenix's own answer to that question. When the nurse asks, 'He isn't dead, is he?' she speaks for herself: 'He still the same. He going to last.'

"The grandchild is the incentive. But it is the journey, the going of the errand, that is the story, and the question is not whether the grandchild is in reality alive or dead.

A. Expansion
Students who are sometimes conditioned to search for the one "right" meaning may have difficulty dealing with the notion of ambiguity, a concept that becomes especially significant in interpreting the work of more contemporary writers.

B. Expansion
? At this point you may want students to discuss these questions: What difference does it make whether or not Phoenix's grandson is alive? How would the story have been affected if Welty had added a final part where Phoenix arrives home and finds her grandson waiting for her? (The grandson himself is important only in providing Phoenix with a motive for her journey and as the object of her love. We do not need to see him.)

C. Expansion
Here the author discusses the universality of Phoenix as a character and of her journey.

It doesn't affect the outcome of the story or its meaning from start to finish. But it is not the question itself that has struck me as much as the idea, almost without exception implied in the asking, that for Phoenix's grandson to be dead would somehow make the story 'better.'

"It's *all right,* I want to say to the students who write to me, for things to be what they appear to be, and for words to mean what they say. It's all right, too, for words and appearances to mean more than one thing—ambiguity is a fact of life. A fiction writer's responsibility covers not only what he presents as the facts of a given story but what he chooses to stir up as their implications; in the end, these implications, too, become facts, in the larger, fictional sense. But it is not all right, not in good faith, for things *not* to mean what they say.

"The grandson's plight was real and it made the truth of the story, which is the story of an errand of love carried out. If the child no longer lived, the truth would persist in the 'wornness' of the path. But his being dead can't increase the truth of the story, can't affect it one way or the other. I think I signal this, because the end of the story has been reached before old Phoenix gets home again: she simply starts back. To the question 'Is the grandson really dead?' I could reply that it doesn't make any difference. I could also say that I did not make him up in order to let him play a trick on Phoenix. But my best answer would be: '*Phoenix* is alive.'

"The origin of a story is sometimes a trustworthy clue to the author—or can provide him with the clue—to its key image; maybe in this case it will do the same for the reader. One day I saw a solitary old woman like Phoenix. She was walking; I saw her, at middle distance, in a winter country landscape, and watched her slowly make her way across my line of vision. That sight of her made me write the story. I invented an errand for her, but that only seemed a living part of the figure she was herself: what errand other than for someone else could be making her go? And her going was the first thing, her persisting in her landscape was the real thing, and the first and the real were what I wanted and worked to keep. I brought her up close enough, by imagination, to describe her face, make her present to the eyes, but the full-length figure moving across the winter fields was the indelible one and the image to keep, and the perspective extending into the vanishing distance the true one to hold in mind.

"I invented for my character, as I wrote, some passing adventures—some dreams and harassments and a small triumph or two, some jolts to her pride, some flights of fancy to console her, one or two encounters to scare her, a moment that gave her cause to feel ashamed, a moment to dance and preen—for it had to be a *journey,* and all these things belonged to that, parts of life's uncertainty.

"A narrative line is in its deeper sense, of course, the tracing out of a meaning and the real continuity of a story lies in this probing forward. The real dramatic force of a story depends on the strength of the emotion that has set it going. The emotional value is the measure of the reach of the story. What gives any such content to 'A Worn Path' is not its circumstances but its *subject:* the deep-grained habit of love.

"What I hoped would come clear was that in the whole surround of this story, the world it threads through, the only certain thing at all is the worn path. The habit of love cuts through confusion and stumbles or contrives its way out of difficulty, it remembers the way even when it forgets, for a dumbfounded moment, its reason for being. The path is the thing that matters.

"*Her* victory—old Phoenix's—is when she sees the diploma in the doctor's office, when she finds 'nailed up on the wall the document that had been stamped with the gold seal and framed in the gold frame, which matched the dream that was hung up in her head.' The return with the medicine is just a matter of retracing her own footsteps. It is the part of the journey, and of the story, that can now go without saying.

"In the matter of function, old Phoenix's way might even do as a sort of parallel to your way of work if you are a writer of stories. The way to get there is the all-important, all-absorbing problem, and this problem is your reason for undertaking the story. Your only guide, too, is your sureness about your subject, about what this subject is. Like Phoenix, you work all your life to find your way, through all the obstructions and the false appearances and the upsets you may have brought on yourself, to reach a meaning—using inventions of your imagination, perhaps helped out by your dreams and bits of good luck. And finally too, like Phoenix, you have to assume that what you are working in aid of is life, not death.

"But you would make the trip anyway—wouldn't you?—just on hope."

—Eudora Welty

THE AMERICAN LANGUAGE
by Gary Q. Arpin

Most people think of slang as a kind of corrupt English, the product of ignorance and laziness. They see slang as a sort of linguistic disease that flourishes in the poorest and worst-maintained neighborhoods of the language. Slang, they feel, should be stamped out for the health and well-being of the general public.

But slang or its equivalent is as old as language itself. In fact, many words that at one time were considered slang or were unacceptable later entered the language and are now used by all speakers.

Before the middle of the eighteenth century, the words for slang as we know it today were *cant* and *argot. Cant* referred to the specialized language of thieves and beggars. *Argot* referred to the specialized language of other occupations (sailors and farmers, for examples). Gradually, the word *slang* came to refer to any informal, nonstandard, specialized language. Slang today especially refers to a kind of colorful, lively language that quickly becomes popular and that often just as quickly drops out of use.

Slang has always been popular among the young. When writer Russell Baker explained why he was slow catching up with the word *wimp,* he expressed an age-old adult complaint: "By the time I learned what the latest kid-saying was," he wrote, "kids had stopped saying it."

Why Do We Use Slang?

Why do people use slang? Not usually out of ignorance, despite popular misconceptions. Most slang terms are substitutes for fairly common words or phrases. A waitress who calls in the order "Adam and Eve on a raft—wreck 'em," knows how to say "two scrambled eggs on toast." Looked at from this point of view, using slang is actually a lot of work. One has to learn new, usually unnecessary words, as well as the rules for using them. Moreover, since slang very often goes out of style quickly, this process has to be continually repeated. A lot of work, and to what end?

A We ordinarily think of language as a means of communication. But anthropologists point out that it has a more subtle function as well—marking kinship. Members of a family or tribe reinforce their relatedness by their language. If you think about it for a moment, you will probably realize that your family does the same thing, through the use of some key words or particular "comic" pronunciations. This is the most important function of slang: it marks members of a group and asserts the group's relatedness. Slang is a group's playful, inventive, deliberately informal use of language; it helps to define the members of a group and keep them together.

American Slang

B

"Failure to do your homework on proper grammatical usage will result in a final grade of zero, zip, zilch . . ."

"A waitress who calls in the order 'Adam and Eve on a raft —wreck 'em,' also knows how to say 'two scrambled eggs on toast.' "

A. Responding

? How does slang fulfill the "social kinship" function of language? (Slang is generally used by members of a group to show that they belong.)

B. Humanities Connection: Responding to the Cartoon

? Incongruity is one of the basic elements of humor. What is incongruous about this cartoon? (It is incongruous that a teacher such as the one depicted here would use slang. Also, the first part of the teacher's statement, in standard English, is incongruous with the slang words at the end.)

A. Humanities Connection: Responding to the Cartoon

? What is the incongruity in this cartoon? (The use of slang by these conventionally dressed people in what is obviously some sort of formal business setting)

B. Responding

? What do you suppose Whitman meant by his claim that slang produced poetry and poets? (Poets have a great interest in language and consequently might involve themselves with slang, which is constantly being created and is constantly changing.)

> **"Walt Whitman claimed that slang produced poets and poetry."**

A

"I said all those in favor say 'Aye.'"

Drawing by H. Martin.

"The group" can be of any size and come from any social class. It can be a single family or a large and widespread profession. Teen-agers, athletes, actors, truck drivers, doctors, criminals, movie makers, and soldiers all have their own slang. People outside the group who try to use its slang almost always appear ridiculous. Think of how embarrassing it is to hear middle-aged parents try to use their teen-aged children's slang.

B

Various other theories have attempted to explain slang and its origins. Walt Whitman claimed that slang produced poets and poetry. This is an exaggeration, but it might point to another explanation for the persistence of slang. Slang may be used for the sheer pleasure of making sounds. It may also be a way to create new metaphors, sometimes just for the fun of it, sometimes to capture attention. Perhaps slang is used because as humans we have an impulse to be "word makers." If we look at *The American Thesaurus of Slang* (1953) we can see that people have persisted in making up new slang terms for concepts that already have more than enough terms to name them. Even over thirty years ago, we had 180 slang terms for "having no money"; 400 slang terms for "failing"; 200 slang terms for "getting angry." By now, who can tell how many new slang terms have been added to those lists?

The response to slang on the part of those who do not speak it is often highly critical. This is because some slang is vulgar, or is a pointless corruption of standard speech with no justification other than novelty. Slang can also be imprecise, and some people who use a great deal of popular slang have limited vocabularies. In fact, most slang disappears very quickly. The group being marked by a slang term is also apt to be fluid and hard to define, as the 1920's "flappers" and the later "valley girls" proved to be.

The Origins of American Slang

America has always been a fertile ground for the development of slang, especially since the 1830's, when informality was considered an almost essential aspect of democracy. The country's cowboys, railroad workers, politicians, and members of hundreds of new occupations introduced many slang terms, often to name things for which there were no existing words. The newspaper industry helped to popularize these terms; more recently, television, radio, and movies have done the same thing.

Slang words and phrases develop in exactly the same ways as additions to standard English.

1. Existing words may be given a new meaning. *Sack,* during World War II, became the almost universal slang word for "bed," and it helped to create countless new phrases for "sleep": *hit the sack, sack out, sack time, sack duty,* and *sack drill. Flaky* is a more recent example of a word that has been given a novel slang meaning.

2. Two or more words may be combined to form a new expression. Americans' love affair with cars, for example, gave us the marvelously inventive *rattletrap* and the more recent *gas-guzzler.* One witty compound word, *rubberneck,* was once said to be the best slang word ever coined. The current computer craze has given us *user-friendly,* a personification that describes a program that is kind about your mistakes.

3. A word may be "clipped" to form a shortened word. The word *Jeep* was born in 1941, from "G.P.," or *general purpose vehicle. Fan,* as in *baseball fan,* was clipped from the word *fanatic.*

4. Words may also be borrowed from other languages. During the westward expansion, *bronco* was borrowed from the Spanish for "rough" and *mustang* from the Spanish for "stray." *Boob tube,* a recent slang example, borrows from the Spanish word *bobo,* "fool."

5. Some slang words are simply invented. Among American backwoodsmen of the nineteenth century, the wilder the invention, the better. If you had the *peedoodles,* you were nervous; if you were *puckerstoppled,* you were embarrassed; confusion was *conbobberation;* and a heavy blow, in a fight or from the weather, was a *sockdologer.* Those words have disappeared, but other inventions have remained. *Blizzard,* for example, was first invented to refer to a big windstorm, perhaps from the German word *blitz,* for "lightning." When *blizzard* was used in 1870 by an Iowa newspaper to describe a violent snowstorm, it was found to be so useful that it soon became standard English. A

Nowadays, slang terms are spread by being printed, but in the past, informal language did not see print until it was well established. Vulgar slang terms were never printed. Thus, many slang terms lived and died unrecorded. One of the earliest recorders of American slang was Benjamin Franklin, who published a dictionary of slang terms referring to drunkenness in 1737 (as a warning about its dangers). He found 228 of them, all, as he wrote, "gathered . . . from the modern tavern conversations of tipplers." Almost all of them have disappeared today, including colorful phrases like *been to Barbados, got a brass eye,* and *as stiff as a ring bolt.* Two of them, though, *oiled* and *stewed,* are in current usage. (In 1960, *The Dictionary of American Slang* listed 327 slang synonyms for the same condition.)

B

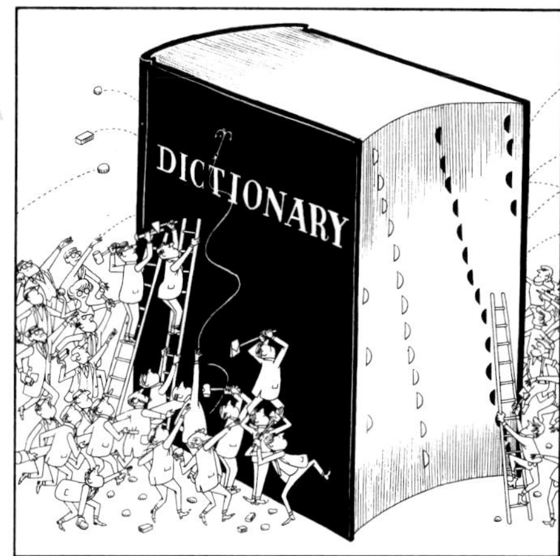

"High Talk" by Roy Doty.

From Slang to Standard English

Most slang terms die quickly. There is a constant turnover, especially among "in" words. *Lounge lizard, hootchie-kootchie,* and *goo-goo eyes* came and went as fast as *cool cat, squaresville, rap,* and *hep.* (*Hep's* offspring, *hip,* is still with us, however.) Terms which fill a need in standard English sometimes make the transition from slang to standard. *Plunder, fix, all right,* and *roughneck* all started as slang and were once condemned by one *highbrow* or another.

Who decides what is slang and what is standard usage? The easiest answer to this is that we all do. Native speakers of a language have a finely tuned sense of the distinction between formal and informal language. As some slang words achieve wide

> **"*Lounge lizard, hootchie-kootchie,* and *goo-goo eyes* came and went as fast as *cool cat, squaresville, rap,* and *hep.*"**

A. Expansion
The acceptance of the slang word *blizzard* into normal English illustrates the process of continuous change that a living language such as English undergoes.

B. Humanities Connection: Responding to the Cartoon
? What point about the English language and language-users is illustrated in this cartoon? (The dictionary represents language as it exists at any one time. That language is constantly being stormed, or assailed, by the language-users.)

Reading Check Test

1. A famous American who collected a dictionary of slang terms was (a) Noah Webster (b) Benjamin Franklin (c) Thomas Jefferson. (*b*)
2. People use slang because they (a) don't know the standard English equivalent (b) want to use the shortest possible expression (c) want to belong. (*c*)
3. Many new slang terms are coined for concepts that (a) already have plenty of words to name them (b) are new to the culture (c) have only technical names. (*a*)
4. Most slang words (a) become part of Standard English (b) die quickly (c) have a long life as slang. (*b*)
5. Dictionary-makers are most likely to label a word *slang* if (a) they are trying to describe how language is used (b) they want to appeal to young people (c) they want to dictate usage. (*c*)

For Further Reading For The Teacher

If you wish to supplement the discussion of slang with current examples and scholarly but accesible commentary, consult *The New Dictionary of American Slang,* edited by Robert L. Chapman (Harper & Row, 1986).

popular usage, though, that distinction may blur. For example, which of these words would you say are slang, and which are standard: *corny, scrumptious, pinhead?* You might say, "Look it up in the dictionary." But the answer depends on which dictionary you use. Dictionaries whose primary purpose is to *describe* the language are apt to provide fewer usage distinctions than dictionaries prepared by lexicographers who feel that it is important to *dictate* usage. Here are the verdicts of three popular American dictionaries on whether or not our three test words are slang:

	Corny	*Scrumptious*	*Pinhead*
Webster's Second International	No	Yes	No
Webster's Third International	No	No	No
American Heritage Dictionary	Yes	Yes	Yes

Obviously, lexicographers disagree on when a word becomes widely enough used to qualify as "standard." Some words, in fact, never make the jump at all. Terms which fill a real informal need often remain as slang for generations. Terms like *rubberneck, to squeal, baloney,* and *nifty* have endured, although regarded as slang for years. These words seem so informal that they resist incorporation into standard English, but they survive to remind us of our capacity for making poetry out of the commonplace.

> "erms like *rubberneck, to squeal, baloney,* and *nifty* have endured, although regarded as slang for years. They survive to remind us of our capacity for making poetry out of the commonplace."

Analyzing Language

1. We have said that *The American Thesaurus of Slang* lists hundreds of slang terms for common experiences or things. How many slang terms can you list for (a) *a car;* (b) *failing;* (c) *getting angry;* (d) *going to sleep?* Once you have your list, discuss the metaphors on which the slang terms are based.

2. Slang is often created by the same processes that create poetry. Slang uses **figurative language,** such as **metaphor** and **simile** (striking comparisons between two things that are dissimilar in most ways) and **hyperbole** (exaggeration). Identify the form of figurative language each of the following words or phrases is based on, and explain the comparisons used. Then provide another example of slang using the same kind of figure of speech.

chicken	to talk someone's ear off
stuffed shirt	tenderfoot
hit the ceiling	rubberneck
out like a light	to put on ice

3. Here are some clipped forms of words in current use. Use a dictionary to identify their full forms.

ad lib	flu	pep
bus	gas	prom
cello	gym	prop

4. Today's slang words might be tomorrow's standard English. All of the following standard words were once considered slang. Check the etymology of each one in a dictionary. Can you propose reasons why each word developed its current meanings?

bleachers	freshman	kidnap
bore	glib	tidy
club	handsome	trip

5. The American genius for creating new words or using old words in creative ways is displayed to advantage in the sports sections of our newspapers. Explain in plain English each of the italicized examples of "sports argot."

   a. Maryland Is 10–2 After *Winning Streak* Is *Snapped* (headline)
   b. Houston used five *fast-break* baskets to take a 17–7 lead.
   c. Susan Brown, *benched* her last game for the first time in three years, scored 25 points and *hauled down* a conference record 27 rebounds.
   d. Carl Furillo *popped out* to shortstop.
   e. Army *punched* its way to Notre Dame's one-yard line.

A. Expansion
In addition to having enough instances on which to base a generalization, it is important to explain any seemingly negative instances. For example, if a play written entirely in verse were to be attributed by some scholars to Shakespeare, one would have to adduce critical opinion to the effect that the play was not part of the Shakespeare canon for the generalization above to be valid.

Exercises in Critical Thinking and Writing

MAKING GENERALIZATIONS

Writing Assignment

Write a brief essay in which you discuss the theme of either William Faulkner's "A Rose for Emily" (page 592) or Flannery O'Connor's "The Life You Save May Be Your Own" (page 603). In your essay, tell how you responded to the theme and to the story as a whole.

Background

What Is a Generalization?

A **generalization** is a statement about every member of a group. Most generalizations include a word such as *all, every, always, no, none,* or *never.* When you use a generalization in writing or speaking, stop to think of how much proof you have for it. The following generalization, for example, would be easy to prove:

> All of Shakespeare's plays are written in both prose and poetry.

That generalization happens to be true. You can prove it by examining all 38 of Shakespeare's plays. A generalization that is proven true is a **valid** generalization.

Other generalizations are not so easy to prove. Consider this one, for example:

> No playwright has created as many different characters as Shakespeare.

In order to prove this generalization, you would have to examine the works of every playwright who ever lived. If you cannot do this, the generalization is an invalid one.

Both of the generalizations you have just read are statements of fact: They can be proven to be true or false. Generalizations, however, often deal with opinions. Here are two examples:

1. All of Faulkner's characters are odd.
2. Flannery O'Connor never created an unbelievable character.

When you use a generalization to state an opinion, you should ask yourself two questions. First, are you familiar with *all* the members of the "group" you are generalizing about? Second, do you have enough examples to support your opinion?

If you can't answer *yes* to the first question, you should avoid using a generalization. Your sentence should include a qualifying word such as *many, most, often,* or *sometimes.*

Even if you can answer *yes* to the first question, think carefully about your supporting evidence. Do you have any doubt about being able to support an all-inclusive statement? If so, use a qualifying word and avoid being caught in error. A

Tell whether each of the following generalizations is a statement of fact or opinion. Then explain what would be necessary to prove each statement. (Don't concern yourself with whether the statement is true or false.)

1. Twentieth-century poetry is easier to understand than eighteenth-century poetry.
2. More women than men write poetry.
3. Ernest Hemingway is the best American writer of the twentieth century.
4. Ernest Hemingway is the most popular American writer of the twentieth century.
5. Modern writers use symbols more frequently than writers of previous centuries did.

Theme as a Generalization

A story's **theme** is the central insight about life that the writer wants to communicate; it's the story's "meaning," its "controlling idea." Usually, the theme is not directly stated; it is left for you to figure out. This is not always an easy job, but if you enjoy thinking, it's an enormously pleasurable one.

The theme of a story is stated as a **generalization,** a statement that applies not just to the specific events and characters in the story, but to life in general or to a whole group of people. Remember that your statement of theme will differ from another reader's. Remember also that the theme is always a statement and always a generalization. That makes it different from the story's **subject** or from a **plot summary.** Compare the following statements about "The Leader of the People" by John Steinbeck (page 565).

Subject of the Story:
How old people feel and how they are treated; the end of the frontier; the loss of the heroic past.

Plot Summary of the Story:
After Jody's father hurts Grandfather's feelings by com-

A. Expansion
You may wish to suggest that students add the following questions to this list:
1. What attitude does the author seem to take toward his or her characters?
2. What is the tone of the story—humorous, ironic, serious, nostalgic, or something else?

Revising Essays
As students revise their essays, refer them to **Grammar, Usage, and Mechanics: A Reference Guide** at the back of their books.

Exercises in Critical Thinking and Writing/*cont.*

plaining about his endless storytelling, Jody goes out of his way to be kind to his grandfather. But at the climax of the story, grandfather learns the truth about how Carl feels about his stories, and he admits that "Westering," and his own usefulness, is over.

Theme of the Story:
Many old people dwell on the past because they feel they have outlived their usefulness. To them, the past often seems more heroic, more exciting, more meaningful than the present. This can result in a clash of generations which can cause pain in a family; often it is only the very youngest members of a family who are patient with the old. At the same time, the story reveals another truth: that life is continually changing; that even as people grow old and change, so do countries and the people in them change. Just as the "leader of the people" of yesterday is merely today's garrulous "old man," so is the frontier of yesterday merely today's beach at Malibu.

Guidelines for Stating a Theme

1. Before you settle on a statement of theme, write out several possible statements. Then test each one on the story as a whole. If a statement of theme doesn't seem to cover all the important parts of a story, then you'll have to go back and revise it. Keep revising your statement of theme until you feel it adequately covers the story as a whole.
2. State the theme as a generalization, but be careful about using universal terms like *every, always,* and *all.* Most thematic statements should include qualifying words, such as *often, may,* and *sometimes.*
3. A theme can sometimes be stated in a single sentence, but this is rare. Avoid reducing the theme to a common saying or to a moral lesson. "It's hard to be old," for example, isn't an adequate statement of the theme of "The Leader of the People." You may need a paragraph or even a whole essay to state the theme of a complex story. A long story or a novel may have more than one theme.
4. Don't agonize over getting it exactly right. There's no single, correct way of stating a story's theme.
5. You don't have to agree with the writer's theme. Based on your own experiences and observations, you may decide that the story's theme just isn't "true."

Prewriting

This isn't an easy assignment; the stories are complex, and they deal with unusual characters. Look back over both stories, and decide which one you have the strongest feelings about. Then reread the story carefully. Take the time to write out the answers to each of the following questions. A

1. What is the story's **subject**?
2. How can the **plot** be summarized in three or four sentences?
3. Who is the main **character** in the story? Does the character change? What does the main character learn as a result of the story's events?
4. Identify the scenes or passages in the story that you think are **key passages.** What makes these passages stand out from the rest of the story?
5. What does the story seem to reveal about human nature or human relationships? What does the story reveal about such things as innocence, evil, responsibility, love?
6. How did the story make you feel as you read it? How did you feel as you thought about it later?

Writing

Use your Prewriting notes to plan your essay. You might follow an organization like this one:

Paragraph 1: Cite the story's title, author, and subject. Summarize the plot in three or four sentences.
Paragraphs 2–3 (or as many paragraphs as you need): State the story's theme as precisely as you can. Cite specific details, characters, and events from the story to support your statement of theme.
Paragraph 4: Tell how you responded to the story and its theme. Tell whether you think the story's theme is valid or significant, or is it trite and overdone?

Revising and Proofreading

Use the guidelines in the section at the back of this book, called **Writing About Literature,** to revise and proofread your essay.

POETRY
VOICES OF AMERICAN CHARACTER

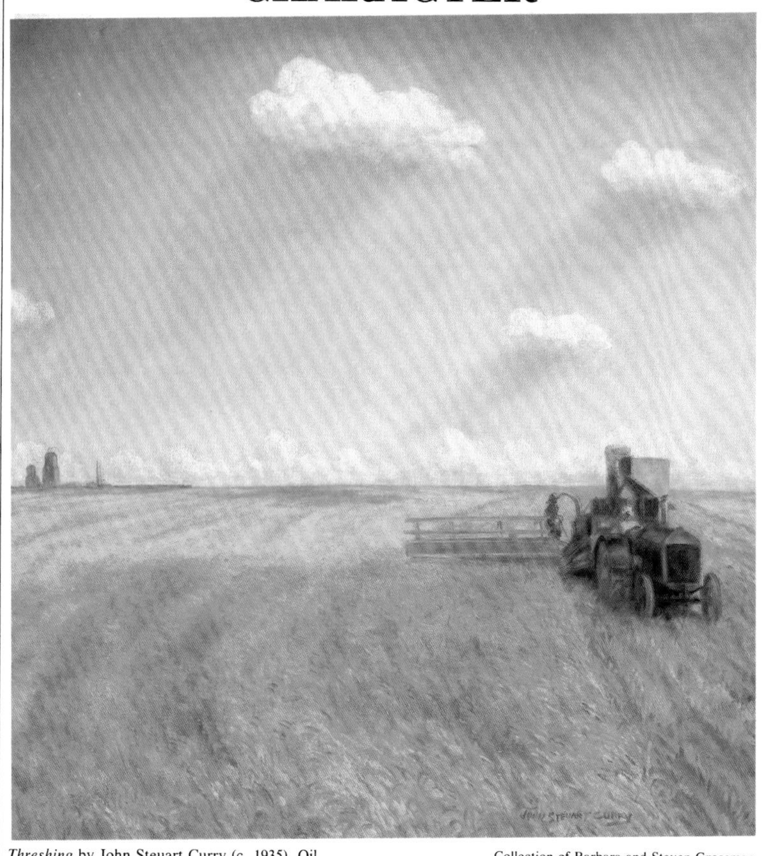

Threshing by John Steuart Curry (c. 1935). Oil. Collection of Barbara and Steven Grossman.

UNIT EIGHT

HUMANITIES CONNECTION: RESPONDING TO THE FINE ART

John Steuart Curry (1897–1946) was one of the leaders, along with Grant Wood (see page 637), of American Scene painting, a movement of the period between the world wars that sought its subject matter in the "real" American environment. Specializing in the rural Midwest, Curry felt that art should grow out of experience and lead to a warm understanding of people and the world.

? Based on this American Scene painting, what do you suppose American Scene poetry, the poetry that you will read in this unit, will be like? (Perhaps realistic poems that deal with ordinary people and ordinary problems)

TEACHING THE POETRY UNIT

The strength and the limitation of the poets in this unit is that they wrote realistically about the lives of ordinary Americans. Their poems tend to be vignettes or anecdotes, comparable in power and intent to good short stories.

The contrast with the American poetry that comes afterward is stark. From the 1920's on, the best American poetry has been concerned with advancing the art form itself, and the subject matter has consisted largely of introspection about the poet's most subtle feelings. This change is equivalent to the change that occurred in the visual arts at the same time.

With the exception of Frost, these poets may not seem so challenging or so impressive as Pound, Eliot, and Stevens. The poets in this unit represent, to many critics, a fallow period before a period of tremendous growth. Paradoxically, however, this makes them readily accessible to the high-school-age reader. In many respects you can approach the poems in this unit almost as though they were works of prose fiction: Analyses of a character and of social message are of primary importance, and even the analyses of language will involve discussions of characters' voices, in the main, rather than of linguistic innovations.

These qualities also create a resemblance between the poems in this unit and the lyrics of songs. The best contemporary rock lyricists, such as Bruce Springsteen, Suzanne Vega, Paul Simon, and Robbie Robertson, tend to write verse vignettes that are strong character studies of American lives.

Several of the poets in this unit had careers that were artificially stunted by the social conditions of their day. African American poets such as Dunbar, Johnson, and Cullen were highly gifted, yet their careers were filled with frustration. Even when they achieved some success, they found themselves in a kind of artistic ghetto, pressured to produce work that would not be threatening to the white intelligentsia: either stereotypical dialect poems or verses in conventional schemes of rhyme and meter that tamed the anger and pain in their message.

All the poets in this unit did, however, produce some moving, lyrical expressions of the human condition. The characters they created and their wisdom still impress.

OBJECTIVES OF THE POETRY UNIT

1. To improve reading proficiency and expand vocabulary
2. To gain exposure to notable poets and their works
3. To define and identify the elements of poetry
4. To define and identify significant literary techniques
5. To respond to poetry orally and in writing
6. To practice the following critical thinking and writing techniques
   a. Analyzing a poem
   b. Comparing and contrasting poems
   c. Analyzing imagery
   d. Responding to a poem's theme and to critics
   e. Comparing authors' attitudes
   f. Comparing sermons

SUPPLEMENTARY SUPPORT MATERIALS: UNIT EIGHT

1. Unit Introduction Test (*CCB*)
2. American Language Test (*CCB*)
3. Word Analogies Test (*CCB*)
4. Unit Review Test (*CCB*)
5. Critical Thinking and Writing Test (*CCB*)
6. Instructional Overhead Transparencies

A. Discussing the Quotation
As your students read the passage, notice that it is a statement about the diversity of America itself, which parallels—indeed causes—the diversity of its art. Frost might be saying that the real America is neither the soil nor the city, the native nor the immigrant, but all of these.

B. Humanities Connection: Discussing the Fine Art
The photograph shows a modernist sculpture by Spanish artist Joan Miró (1893–1983), and a young critic. ? What does this image suggest about modern art? (It is often puzzling; it is often witty; it often appeals to the child's sense of wonder and play in all of us.) Note also how this statue resembles a figure that might have been carved by a "primitive" artist.

POETRY
VOICES OF AMERICAN CHARACTER

by **John Malcolm Brinnin**

A *One cannot say that the real American poetry is the poetry of the soil. One cannot say it is the poetry of the city. One cannot say it is the poetry of the native as one cannot say it is the poetry of the alien. Tell me what America is and I'll tell you what its poetry is.*

–Robert Frost

American Poetry: 1890–1910

B

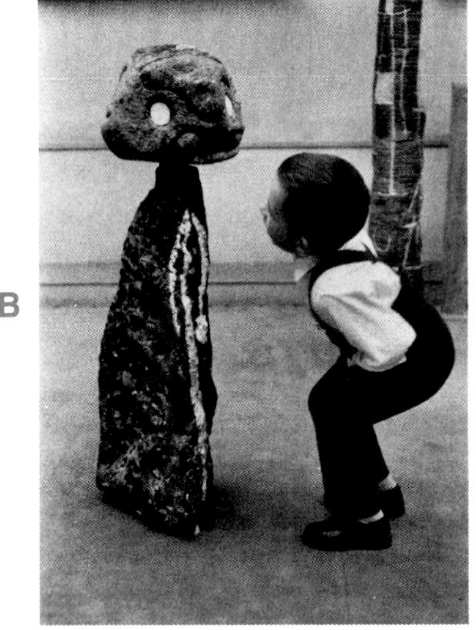

When Walt Whitman died in 1892, he was the nation's famous "good gray poet," but his true genius was as yet unrecognized. Whitman's great contemporary, Emily Dickinson, was still unpublished and unknown. In fact, her work would have been lost to the world were it not for the many packets of handwritten poems she had wrapped up and put away, with no thought that they would ever be published. By 1892, Dickinson had already been dead for six years—"an island in dishonored grass" on the green slopes of a little cemetery in Massachusetts. The magnitude of Whitman's and Dickinson's contributions to poetry would not be clear for years. But these two poets had indeed joined Poe, Melville, Hawthorne, Twain, and Henry James as writers unmistakably American in character and universal in appeal.

After the deaths of Whitman and Dickinson, American poetry went into a decline. But time would show that the comparatively uneventful period between 1890 and 1910 was but the trough of a wave that was about to break. The force of this wave, when it arrived, would be strong enough to wash away the last traces of British influence on American poetry and to carry our poets into their most dazzling period of variety and experimentation.

This period of experimentation began when droves of American poets began to explore the artistic life of Europe. This home-grown talent was invigorated by European influences, especially in Paris, where writers, artists, and composers from all over the world were absorbing the lessons of great painters like Pablo Picasso, Georges Braque, and Henri Matisse. These artists were exploring new ways of seeing and representing reality. The generation of writers that kept pace with them would produce not simply poetry, as the world had always understood it, but "modern poetry." Modernism would become the prevailing international style in poetry until midway into the twentieth century. (See Unit Nine.)

But a few individuals with American accents and American habits of looking at the world provided a powerful counterbalance to the cosmopolitan tendencies of some of their contemporaries. These were the poets of native character, those who ignored or defied the revolutionary new developments that led to modernism. Figuratively speaking, these writers stayed "at home," while almost all the artists they knew were actually on their way to Paris or felt themselves to be living spiritually in its surroundings.

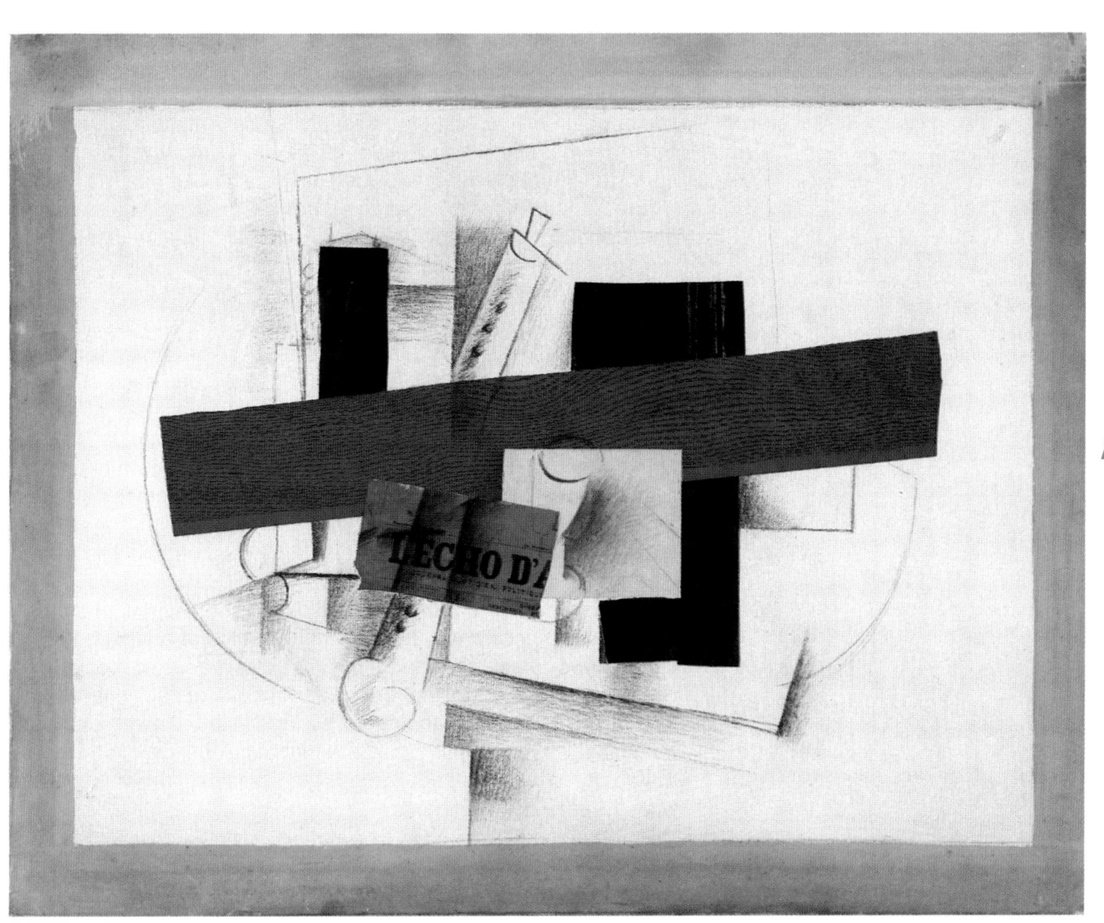

Still Life with Tenora by Georges Braque (1913). Pasted papers, charcoal, chalk and oil on canvas. $37\frac{1}{2} \times 47\frac{3}{8}''$.

Collection, The Museum of Modern Art, New York. Nelson A. Rockefeller Bequest.

A. Humanities Connection: Discussing the Fine Art Georges Braque (1882–1963) was the cofounder of Cubism during the 1910's, along with Picasso. Together they simplified the subject of the painting into nonrepresentational, geometric elements, but recomplicated it with collage elements (such as the scrap of newspaper in this picture) and spatial relationships that are hard to "read."

These poets did not enlist in the reverse emigration that took many grandsons and granddaughters of Europeans back to Europe. Instead, they said what they had to say in plain American speech and without concern for their place in the modernist movement. Their poetry gave expression to voices of the American character.

B. Responding ? Why is this unit subtitled "Voices of American Character"? (Because rather than reflecting the ideas and speech of Europe, the poetry of this period took its voice and its subject matter from America.)

Voices of New England

The greatest among the voices of American character was Robert Frost (page 652). Frost was a poet whose independence was grounded in his ability to handle ordinary New England speech and in his surprising skill in appropriating the most conventional poetic forms and giving them a twist all his own. In an era when "good" was equated with "new," the only new thing about Robert Frost was old: individual poetic genius. Using this gift to impose his own personality on the iambic line in verse, Frost created a poetic voice that was unique and impossible to imitate.

"The only new thing about Robert Frost was old: individual poetic genius."

This Frostian "character" spoke folk wisdom with the serious-

A. Responding

A typical page of a literary manuscript. Note the heavy crossing-over and rewriting. This is a good place to emphasize the fact that virtually everything that is written and published has been thoroughly reworked and revised. Even the most natural-sounding flights of lyrical poetry are probably the results of diligent work. Nor is rewriting confined to a single draft: the poet, after making hand corrections on a sheet of paper, will usually copy it afresh and make hand corrections on the new draft, as often as is required to "get it right."

? How does your own writing process compare with that of this writer? Do you usually revise? How many drafts do you usually go through? Had you realized before that even poets usually revise heavily?

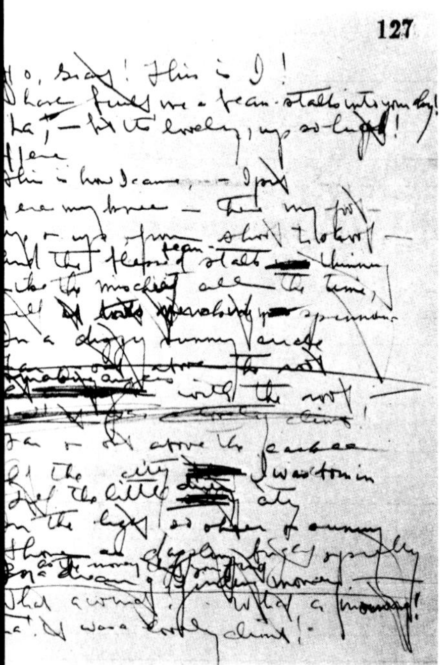

127

A draft of Edna St. Vincent Millay's poem "The Bean-Stalk."

The Library of Congress, Manuscript Division.

A

ness of a philosopher and philosophy with the simple eloquence of a New England farmer. His view of the world was dark because he found darkness in the workings of nature; yet this was the same world of nature which at times presented him with objects of beauty. Frost spent a great part of his life examining nature with curiosity and tenderness and recording his discoveries.

Before Robert Frost had arrived in New England to make it his home and poetic territory, another writer had already established himself as the region's unofficial poetic voice. Edwin Arlington Robinson (page 633) dealt with the daily life of his "Down East home"—Gardiner, Maine—by lightly disguising the place in his poems as Tilbury Town. In the citizens of Gardiner, he found characters like Miniver Cheevy and Richard Cory, each of whom represented an American "type." These characters came into his poems larger than life, and their fates were manifestations of their characters. Like Frost, Robinson tended to regard nature more as a threat than a comfort. He felt that it was our common lot to live in "the black and awful chaos of the night," looking for signs of order and promises of immortality, but seldom finding anything to justify our expectations.

Robinson chose to work in traditional forms. Yet, unlike Frost, he did not impose upon these forms the voice of a single personality. The voices we hear in Robinson's lyrics are varied: sometimes conversational and folksy, but more often touched with a high degree of literacy and controlled by emotional reserve. The most familiar voice in Robinson's work is that of an observer who absorbs everything in sight without disclosing his personal involvement with what he sees and reports.

Another poet with New England roots was Edna St. Vincent Millay (page 647), the child prodigy from a little town on the Maine coast. As an adult in New York City, she became the symbol of the liberated woman of her day. "Vincent," as she was known to her friends, created this role for herself by publishing poems in which women held the social, intellectual, and romantic prerogatives society had previously reserved for men. And once Millay had created this bold, carefree figure of a female Casanova, she was forced to live up to the expectations of her audience.

> "Millay was both the happy recipient of fame and its victim."

A national celebrity while she was still in her twenties, Millay was both the happy recipient of fame and its victim. The fame was based partly on her personal notoriety and partly on her finely crafted verse. She managed to persuade the reading public that her lyrics were cut from the same cloth as those of Shakespeare, Donne, and Keats. But while Millay could imitate these poets, she could not equal them. She was unable to find a modern equivalent for the imagination and craft that had made them great, not merely in their own time, but for all time.

At her best, however, Millay wrote highly emotional, sometimes ecstatic celebrations of nature and of the joy of being alive and young. Her romantic boldness and extravagance of spirit offered a refreshing change from the needlepoint prettiness of familiar "ladies' verse," and she charmed a generation with the unapologetic love of pleasure in her sonnets and quatrains.

A. Responding
? Why was Edgar Lee Masters's *Spoon River Anthology* so shocking to the American public? (Because it presented such a different view of small-town life from that usually held by Americans)

B. Humanities Connection: Discussing the Photograph
James Van Der Zee (1886–1983) was a documentary photographer of Harlem life and a studio portraitist of affluent African Americans in that community. He worked as a professional, self-employed photographer throughout his life, but, like most commercial photographers, could only pursue photography as individual art during spare moments. Additionally, commercial photographic avenues such as advertising and fashion were closed to blacks before World War II. Van Der Zee was discovered as a photographic artist in 1967, by a photographer doing research for the Metropolitan Museum of Art's "Harlem on My Mind" exhibit.

C. Expansion
Depending on your students' backgrounds, they may or may not need an introduction to Harlem, the community in uptown Manhattan that has been a center of African American culture for decades. During the 1920's it was a fashionable address for prominent African American artists and professionals, and a center of artistic development in the field of jazz as well as writing. You might have a group of students prepare a report on the Harlem Renaissance and on Harlem generally.

Voices of the Middle West

Each of these New England poets of the early years of the century was a highly skilled composer of traditional verse. Their fellow poets in the Middle West were more adventuresome. They had begun to produce loose, colloquial lines and rough-hewn stanzas that would bring to the American heartland its own poetic identity.

A One of these Middle Western poets put together a sort of mass biography that told the hidden story of the citizens of a small town. His name was Edgar Lee Masters (page 638), and his book was *Spoon River Anthology* (1915). Along with the stories by Sherwood Anderson (page 501) in *Winesburg, Ohio* (1919), this volume of portraits in verse broke new ground that would be explored by American writers for years to come. At a time when calendar artists were depicting American life as a perpetually sunny adventure, and when some writers were sentimentalizing everything from the good old summertime to the old mill stream, Masters offered a shocking view of small-town life. When he took the lid—the coffin lid, to be exact—off Spoon River and allowed the dead to speak for themselves, they uttered a litany of greed, frustration, and spiritual deprivation. The diction of his talking skeletons was plain, and they made their confessions in the colloquial cadences of free verse. Masters's best-selling collection received the same kind of interest Americans were beginning to give to Freudian case histories.

> **"Geographically, the center of that movement was Harlem. Its spiritual center, however, was not a place on the map but a place in the consciousness of a people whose gifts had long been ignored."**

Voices of the Black Experience

In poetry, black culture found expression in two different ways. Most quickly accepted by white readers were the works of black poets who wrote in conventional forms. These metrically regular and rhymed verse forms made even the most urgent and desperate of black concerns seem undisturbing. The second form of black expression was poetry that based its rhythms on spirituals and jazz, its lyrics on songs known as the blues, and its diction on the street talk of the black ghettos. The conflict that all of this posed for gifted black poets of the nineteenth century can be most clearly seen in the frustrated career of Paul Laurence Dunbar (Page 644).

Foremost among the lyricists were James Weldon Johnson (page 680), Claude McKay (page 686), Langston Hughes (page 688), and Countee Cullen (page 694). These poets brought literary distinction to the broad movement of artists known as the Harlem Renaissance. C Geographically, the center of that movement was Harlem, the section of New York City that stands above 110th Street in Manhattan. Its spiritual center, however, was not a place on the map but a place in the consciousness of a people whose gifts had long been ignored, patronized as "quaint," or otherwise relegated to the margins of American art. But when, hand in hand with the music echoing from New Orleans, Memphis, and Chicago, black poetry became part of the Jazz Age, it was responsible for a new appreciation of the role of black talent in American culture.

B

Group Portrait in the Dark Tower by James Van Der Zee. Photograph.

The Dark Tower was a famous salon in a townhouse on West 136th Street in Harlem. Poems by Hughes and Cullen were painted on the walls.

READING CHECK TEST

1. The early years of this century in Europe saw the development of a vital new artistic movement called ______________. *Modernism*
2. The greatest among the "voices of American character" was ______________. *Robert Frost*
3. Another poet with New England roots was ______________. *E. A. Robinson or Edna St. Vincent Millay*
4. The flowering of African American literature early in this century is called the ______________. *Harlem Renaissance*
5. A notable poetic voice from California during this era was ______________. *Robinson Jeffers*

A. Responding

? Suppose that you are a regional American poet at the beginning of this century, trying to write something true to the experience of the people in your present community or some community where you lived in the past. What would you write about? What ideas and feelings do you want to communicate about the people and places you have known?

B. Expansion (Challenging)

Several of the poets in this unit—Frost, Millay, Robinson, Masters, and Jeffers—became popular successes in a way that very few American poets have since. Not only Masters's *Spoon River Anthology,* but also Robinson's difficult, book-length *Tristram* actually reached the best-seller lists, and Millay and Jeffers became the foci for groups of fans. Your more advanced students, especially, may be interested in discussing the reasons for the decline of this phenomenon.

"American voices reflect our freedom to criticize, to oppose, or to sing proudly of America's richness—from the smoky jazz clubs of Harlem to the spumy ledges of Big Sur in California."

Voices of the West

The most distinctive voice heard during the years when modernism was overtaking traditionalism in poetry was that of Robinson Jeffers (page 676). Jeffers steered a wavering course that kept him neither bound by convention nor committed to experiment. Working sometimes in meter and rhyme, more often in long and sinuous lines of free verse, Jeffers was less notable for his craftsmanship than for his unorthodox attitudes toward progress, religion, and the nature of humanity.

While his contemporaries were celebrating democracy and the rise of the common man, Jeffers took a very dim view of both. He looked at the scientific and political developments of the new century with a godlike remoteness and distaste. Isolating himself on the rocky shore of California's Monterey peninsula, he created metaphors of what he saw from the windows of the stone tower in which he wrote. Although Jeffers did nothing to promote himself or to rally converts to his dissident beliefs, his poetry gained a wide audience during his lifetime. After his death, his poems became an inspiration to the scene inhabited by the Beats and other West Coast literary groups of the 1960's.

Voices of the South

Most American poets of the early twentieth century were characterized by earnestness, sentiment, and simple, unadorned language. One exception was John Crowe Ransom (page 672). Ransom stood for wit, intellectual subtlety, and the mannerisms of another century. Genteel and courtly, he was the product both of the aristocratic Old South and of a classical education, begun at Vanderbilt University in Tennessee and continued as a Rhodes Scholar at Oxford in England. Going against the grain of the typical poetry of his generation, Ransom looked back to seventeenth-century England. The marks of poetic art at that time were formal grace and philosophical playfulness; the role of the poet was to provide witty entertainment for highly educated readers. Like his long-dead models, Ransom could deal with tragic matters without spilling a tear; he could deal with the comic aspects of life without forgetting that laughter and grief eventually join hands. His classical tone was intimidating to some readers. But others saw that his aristocratic genius was only a thin disguise for a gentle, generous nature and a passionate concern for the beauty and elegance of the English language.

A If the American character is defined collectively by the voices that express it, we must conclude that "the American character" is an abstraction. But if we listen to individual voices as they speak for themselves, we become aware that American poetry reflects our national life in all its diversity. In this unit, you'll find American voices that reflect our freedom to criticize, to oppose, or to sing proudly of America's richness—from the smoky jazz clubs of Harlem to the spumy ledges of Big Sur in California.

B

A. Expansion
While some poets can combine their artistic vocation with some other profession (compare with William Carlos Williams, page 717, or Wallace Stevens, page 750), Robinson felt that his only serious work could be writing. This belief caused him hardship and sorrow throughout his life. "I could never have done *anything* but write poetry," he told a friend.

B. Expansion
Poet James Dickey said, "No one ever understood loneliness . . . better than Robinson." His subject was, in Robinson's own words, "the slow tragedy of haunted men." In addition, his verse does not benefit from a vibrant imagistic gift, and he tends to work his way laboriously, in his longer poems, through every conceivable subtlety of a psychological situation, leaving its outcome deliberately ambiguous. Given these traits—which are not the kind that generally attract readers—it is a tribute to his genius that Robinson was popular in his own day and is still read today.

Edwin Arlington Robinson (1869–1935)

By the 1890's, the vitality of the century seemed exhausted and the gathering forces of modernism were still scattered and obscure. Many poets between 1890 and 1910 were churning out the same old rhymes and meters of Romanticism. But in those two decades, one voice spoke with an authentic, contemporary American accent: that of Edwin Arlington Robinson.

The strengths that distinguish Robinson are his native voice and his wise and ironic view of human behavior. Robinson's bedrock realism informs even the most formal of his carefully wrought poems. In some of his poetic portraits of individuals, he anticipates by a decade the more loosely drawn portraits found in Edgar Lee Masters's *Spoon River Anthology*; and in his skill with meter, Robinson foreshadows Robert Frost's gift for bending the strictly counted line to accommodate the ease and flow of vernacular speech.

Robinson was a Yankee from the rocky coast of Maine. Born at Head Tide in 1869, he lived for the next twenty-seven years—except for the two years when he attended Harvard as a special student—in the town of Gardiner. Gardiner became the Tilbury Town of his poems, the home of some of his most famous characters. When he was in his late twenties, Robinson moved to New York City and published his first book. There he supported himself at menial jobs, including one as a timekeeper at the construction site of the new subway system. [A]

After a year of this work, Robinson's fortunes took a surprising turn for the better. Among the young poet's readers was none other than the President of the United States, Theodore Roosevelt. When Roosevelt learned that the poet he

admired was barely scraping by on a laborer's salary, he arranged to have him hired as a clerk by the New York Custom House, a position Robinson held for five years. Another form of assistance came in an invitation to the famous MacDowell Colony in Peterboro, New Hampshire. This was a center for composers, artists, and writers established by the widow of the American composer Edward MacDowell. There Robinson spent long working summers for the greater part of his life. Though he was a loner by temperament, he became a popular poet. [B] Even in an increasingly modernist age, Robinson's poetry, which was traditional in form, continued to be read and admired, and he was awarded the Pulitzer Prize three times. At the time of his death, his reputation had survived the tide of modernism that had once threatened to wash it away.

633

Supplementary Support Materials

1. Vocabulary Activity Worksheet (*CCB*)
2. Review and Response Worksheet: Irony (*CCB*)
3. Selection Test (*CCB*)

Developing Vocabulary

The following words from the poem are tested in the Selection Test. (See also Vocabulary Activity Worksheet.)

sole	pulse
imperially	schooled

Preparation

Establishing a Purpose. Have students read to answer these questions: What happens to Richard Cory? Why does it happen?

A. Imagery

? Who are the "people on the pavement"? How does this image contrast with that of Richard Cory? (The "people on the pavement" are the common people. Richard Cory, on the other hand, through use of the words *crown* and *imperially,* is associated with royalty.)

B. Responding

? *Glittered* here may mean "dispensing light." How does use of the word here contrast with the word *light* in line 13? (Richard Cory gives off *light,* the word perhaps symbolizing success, by walking. The townspeople, on the other hand, must struggle for this light.)

C. Responding

? Why is Richard Cory's death so shocking? (Answers will vary. Students should note that, from the point of view of the townspeople, Cory seemed to have everything.)

Closure

Have students write one-sentence statements explaining the lesson to be found in the poem.

One of the persistent themes of early twentieth-century American poetry is that the conventions of small-town life are a façade which often obscures unpleasant realities. In this famous poem, an unidentified speaker tells what happened to his fellow-citizen Richard Cory. Does the harsh surprise ending hint that the real story is the one that remains untold?

Richard Cory

Whenever Richard Cory went downtown,
A [We people on the pavement looked at him:
He was a gentleman from sole to crown,
Clean favored, and imperially slim.

And he was always quietly arrayed,
And he was always human when he talked;
But still he fluttered pulses when he said,
B ["Good morning," and he glittered when he walked.

And he was rich—yes, richer than a king—
And admirably schooled in every grace:
In fine, we thought that he was everything
To make us wish that we were in his place.

So on we worked, and waited for the light,
And went without the meat, and cursed the bread;
And Richard Cory, one calm summer night,
C [Went home and put a bullet through his head.

Responding to the Poem

Analyzing the Poem

Identifying Details

1. What advantages does Richard Cory have that make the townspeople envy him?
2. What contrasting picture of their own lives is presented in the fourth stanza?
3. List all the details in the poem revealing that the townspeople regarded Richard Cory with awe and a sense of inferiority. How would you define the word *human* in line 6?

Interpreting Meanings

4. What is **ironic** in the fact that Richard Cory took his own life? What irony is there in the fact that the night was calm?
5. What aspects of Richard Cory's life are *not* mentioned? How might these hidden or overlooked areas account for his fate?
6. How would you describe the speaker's **tone**? Does the contrast between the tone of the speaker and the tragic nature of the story heighten the poem's emotional effect? Explain why or why not.
7. What **moral** or lesson might be found in the tale of Richard Cory? Do the poem and its moral have relevance to our experience today?
8. Read Robinson's own comments on "Richard Cory" on the opposite page. What do you think he means when he says there's a lot of "humanity" in the poem? Why do you think it made his correspondent feel "cold"? How do you respond to the poem?

Analyzing The Poem

Identifying Details

1. Richard Cory is rich, graceful, handsome, and polite.

2. Most of the townspeople are poor.

3. Among such words and phrases are the following: "imperially slim" (line 4), "fluttered pulses" (line 7), "he glittered when he walked" (line 8), "richer than a king" (line 9), "admirably schooled in every grace" (line 10), and lines 11–12.

Student definitions might include "humane," "compassionate," "genuinely interested in others."

Interpreting Meanings

4. The irony consists in the speaker's (and our) reversal of expectation: Whereas Richard Cory seemed to enjoy every blessing, he was inwardly so unhappy that he committed suicide.

The irony proceeds from the contrast between the tranquil night and the sudden violence of Cory's self-inflicted death.

5. Nothing is said about Richard Cory's family or friends.

No one really knew him, so his motive for killing himself remains hidden.

6. Most students will agree that the tone of the speaker is admiring toward Richard Cory.

7. Student answers may vary. The poem suggests that appearances may often be deceptive.

Most students will agree that the moral is relevant, especially in a culture which discourages displays of emotion or hints of weakness.

8. Student answers will vary. Many students will suggest that Robinson means that the underlying situation of the poem—the contrast between appearance and reality—is more a part of the human condition than people might at first suspect.

The correspondent was probably shocked by Richard Cory's violent, sudden death.

Answers will vary; encourage students to defend their responses.

Portrait of Jacques Emile Blanche Rouen by John Singer Sargent (late 19th century). Oil.

Musèe des Beaux Arts, Rouen, France.

Analyzing Language and Style

Connotations

Robinson never says it outright, but he implies that his townspeople see Richard Cory as a king. Robinson achieves this effect by using words with connotations of royalty. How do words get such **connotations,** or emotional overtones and associations? In general, connotations come from shared usage.

It would be hard, for example, for a writer to call a character a "lamb" without someone familiar with English making an immediate association with innocence and docility. This would be true even for readers who had never seen a lamb; they would only have to be familiar with the Bible or with nursery rhymes to recognize this archetypal use of the image of the lamb. On the other hand, what do you associate with the word *wolf*? With the word *lion*? Where do you think those associations come from?

1. Find at least five words or phrases in "Richard Cory" that suggest kingliness or royalty.
2. Replace each of these words with a neutral word—one that, in your opinion, has no strong connotations at all. How is the effect of the poem different?
3. What meanings can you suggest for the word *gentleman* in line 3? What associations do you make with that word?
4. Why is *downtown* (line 1) a better word than *uptown* in this poem?

Primary Sources

Robinson on "Richard Cory"

"I've written a nice little thing called 'Richard Cory'—'Whenever Richard Cory went downtown, we people on the pavement looked at him . . . And Richard Cory, one calm summer night, went home and put a bullet through his head.' There isn't any idealism in it, but there's lots of something else—humanity, maybe."

. . .

"Why don't you like 'Richard Cory?' You say it makes you feel cold, but that statement doesn't seem to agree with my impression of your character. It can't be you are squeamish after all. If you are, don't read 'Reuben Bright' or he will knock you down. I used to read about clearness, force, and elegance in the rhetoric books, but I'm afraid I go in chiefly for force. So you will not be offended if I'm not always elegant. There are too many elegant men in the world just now, and they seem to be increasing."

. . .

"I don't have trances, furors, or ecstasies. My poetic spells are of the most prosaic sort. I just sit down and grind it out and use a trifle more tobacco than is good for me."

. . .

"You may call me anything you like—anything but Eddie. I had an aunt who called me Eddie and now she doesn't call me at all."

—from *Letters to Edith Brower,*
Edwin Arlington Robinson

635

SUPPLEMENTARY SUPPORT MATERIALS
1. Vocabulary Activity Worksheet (*CCB*)
2. Review and Response Worksheet: Tone and Theme (*CCB*)
3. Selection Test (*CCB*)

DEVELOPING VOCABULARY
The following words from the poem are tested in the Selection Test. (See also Vocabulary Activity Worksheet.)

assailed — commonplace
steeds — khaki
incessantly — medieval

PREPARATION
ESTABLISHING A PURPOSE. You might have students read this poem to learn why Miniver Cheevy is so unhappy and to decide how they feel about Cheevy and his attitude toward life.

A. Rhyme and Meter/ Interpretation
? Would you describe the rhyme and meter as regular or irregular? (Very regular) How does this singsong quality affect your expectations of the poem? (Elicit from students that such poems are usually comic, rather than tragic.) Based on your reading of "Richard Cory," would you think that this poet is likely to compose a comic poem? (No. The poet is likely to have something in store for us.)
Line 2: "Assailed the seasons" means "cursed the passage of time."

B. Responding
? Why do you suppose that the poet reveals Cheevy's drinking only in the final stanza? (Probably to increase the effect on the reader of his drinking to cope with his lot in life)

CLOSURE
Have individual students paraphrase the poem orally.

The title of this poem is simply a man's name, yet it contains a clue to the poem's meaning. "Miniver" is the white fur trim, sometimes ermine, seen on the costumes of nobility in medieval and Renaissance portraits. The subjects of such portraits included rich and wicked members of the Medici family of Renaissance Italy.

Other references in the poem evoke heroic eras of the past. Camelot was the place where King Arthur presided over the Knights of the Round Table; Thebes was a city famous in the history of ancient Greece; and "Priam's neighbors" were those who lived near Troy, ruled by King Priam during the Trojan War.

Read the poem aloud. From its sound, would you expect it to be comic or tragic?

Miniver Cheevy

A

Miniver Cheevy, child of scorn,
Grew lean while he assailed the seasons;
He wept that he was ever born,
And he had reasons.

Miniver loved the days of old
When swords were bright and steeds were prancing:
The vision of a warrior bold
Would set him dancing.

Miniver sighed for what was not,
And dreamed, and rested from his labors;
He dreamed of Thebes and Camelot,
And Priam's neighbors.

Miniver mourned the ripe renown
That made so many a name so fragrant;
He mourned Romance, now on the town,°
And Art, a vagrant.

Miniver loved the Medici,
Albeit he had never seen one;
He would have sinned incessantly
Could he have been one.

Miniver cursed the commonplace
And eyed a khaki suit with loathing;
He missed the medieval grace
Of iron clothing.

Miniver scorned the gold he sought,
But sore annoyed was he without it;
Miniver thought, and thought, and thought,
And thought about it.

Miniver Cheevy, born too late,
Scratched his head and kept on thinking;
Miniver coughed, and called it fate,
And kept on drinking.

B

15. **on the town:** on welfare.

Responding to the Poem

Analyzing the Poem

Identifying Details

1. Briefly summarize Miniver Cheevy's reasons for weeping that he was ever born.
2. "Romance" and "Art" are **personified** in the fourth stanza. According to Miniver, what has happened to Romance and Art in his own time?
3. How does the disappointed Miniver cope with his lot in life?

Interpreting Meanings

4. What does "child of scorn" mean?
5. Do Miniver's problems really stem from his having been "born too late"? Explain.
6. What is the effect of the abbreviated rhythm in the fourth line of each stanza?
7. Point out three details in the poem that make Miniver appear ridiculous. How would you describe the change in **tone** in the last stanza, and how does this change affect the poem's meaning?

Analyzing the Poem

Identifying Details

1. Miniver wishes that he had been born in one of the more graceful, "civilized" eras of the past. He regards the present era as vulgar and uncultured. There is a hint in lines 25–26 that he affects a scornful attitude toward money; yet he resents being without it.

2. He thinks that Romance and Art have been neglected: Romance is now "on the town" (that is, it depends on public charity), and Art is a "vagrant."

3. He sighs, makes money, and drinks too much.

Interpreting Meanings

4. Perhaps that his parents were bitter too.

5. Most will say no.

6. Student answers may vary. In general, however, the shorter rhythm of each fourth line produces a clipped, ironic effect.

7. Among the details that make Miniver appear slightly ridiculous are the following: "Dancing" at the dream of a "warrior bold" (lines 7–8), sinning "incessantly" as a member of the Medici family (lines 19–20), missing the "medieval grace of iron clothing," or suits of armor (lines 23–24.)

It is only in the last stanza that we learn that Miniver's health is deteriorating: His unhappiness and alienation have led to coughing and constant drinking. Robinson thus combines the irony of the previous stanzas with a note of sympathy in the final four lines.

8. Most students will probably agree that "Miniver Cheevys" are as common in the contemporary world as in any other period. Discuss aspects of the past that people mourn for today.

9. Students should have little trouble participating in a lively discussion. Both men are failed romantics. Although both characters are dreamers, it is clear that they have quite different personalities.

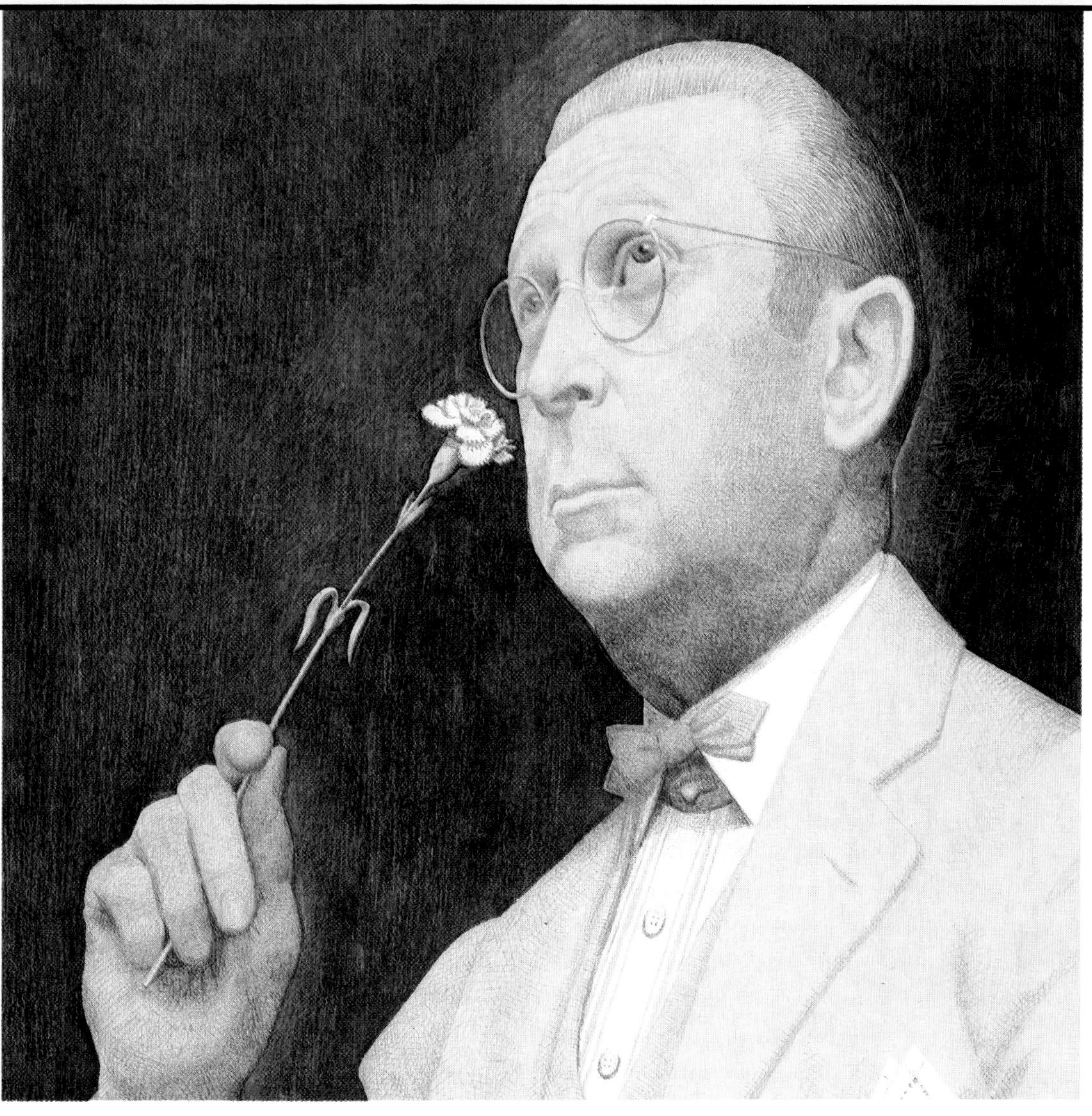

The Sentimental Yearner by Grant Wood (1936). Pencil and colored paper on tan paper.

8. Do you think "Miniver Cheevys" are found in contemporary life? What sorts of worlds do they mourn for?
9. Compare Walter Mitty (page 577) to Miniver Cheevy.

Writing About the Poems

A Creative Response

1. **Using Another Point of View.** Let Richard Cory tell his own story, in either prose or verse. Use the first person "I" and be sure to record what Cory thinks of the people who look up to him.
2. **Answering a Speaker.** Write a letter to Miniver Cheevy giving him advice on how to free himself from his nostalgic thoughts.

A Critical Response

3. **Responding to the Poems.** In a brief essay, tell how you responded to these two poems, and cite specific reasons for your response. You might respond to (a) the characterizations, (b) tone, (c) verse forms, (d) use of irony, or (e) view of life and human nature. Quote from the poems in explaining your response.
4. **Comparing Characters.** In a brief essay, compare and contrast the characters of Richard Cory and Miniver Cheevy. As the focus of your composition, quote a line from either Emerson (pages 187–203) or Thoreau (pages 204–225). Tell specifically how Robinson's characters are distortions of the ideals proposed by the two earlier writers.

A. Expansion
As a class project, you might want to have your students write their own anthology, inventing a fictitious town—doubtless modeled on their own—and writing verse portraits of the people in it. Each student can contribute one poem; you can then copy, staple, and distribute the finished work.

B. Expansion
As a light-hearted imaginative exercise, ask your students to guess the occupation of the man in the picture, assuming they do not know he was a poet. Poetry and poets come in many forms.

Edgar Lee Masters (1869–1950)

Edgar Lee Masters was born in Garnett, Kansas. Like his contemporary Carl Sandburg (page 729), he was a product of that part of the Middle West known as the "corn belt" or "Bible belt." Also like Sandburg, he found his own voice in the free verse that characterized the second decade of the twentieth century. But while Sandburg soon developed his own particular mode of expression and built a career upon it, Masters produced just one book in a spare style that served his homely subject matter. Then he reverted to a more conventionally "poetic" style: pretty, romantic, and wordy.

Yet this one book, *Spoon River Anthology* (1915), was a landmark in American literature, and it made Masters famous. It is a collection of more than two hundred epitaphs spoken by the inhabitants of a cemetery in the fictional town of Spoon River: drunkards, bankers, judges, poets, atheists, preachers, gamblers, druggists, and housewives.

The dramatic device of having the epitaphs spoken by the deceased subjects themselves served Masters brilliantly. Drawing upon his memories of Petersburg and Lewistown—the Illinois towns he knew during his first twenty years—he used the epitaphs to show the hidden underside of American life. Its victims, freed by death to talk without fear of consequences, tell their stories and, bit by bit, fill in a picture of small-town life vastly different from the magazine cover images. Against the sentimentality and folksiness of these images, Masters's voices from the grave made a heartfelt protest that hundreds of thousands of readers recognized as buried truth brought into the daylight.

Spoon River Anthology became one of the most widely read books in an age that was fascinated by psychology. Better than any scientific study, it revealed how the conventions of society warred with the real needs and beliefs of its members. By turning "case histories" into lyrics, Masters gave speech to the inarticulate and, at the same time, brought a new kind of realism to poetry.

SUPPLEMENTARY SUPPORT MATERIALS
1. Vocabulary Activity Worksheet (*CCB*)
2. Review and Response Worksheet: Narration and Theme (*CCB*)
3. Selection Test (*CCB*)

DEVELOPING VOCABULARY
The following words from the poem are tested in the Selection Test. (See also Vocabulary Activity Worksheet.)
epitaph chronicle

PREPARATION
ESTABLISHING A PURPOSE. Have students read the poem to decide what universal message it offers to readers.

Richard Bone, like many other departed citizens of the town, is troubled by his conscience. Bone confesses hypocrisy in quietly accepting false appearances. The name Masters gives this speaker is itself a clue to his profession and his nature. As a stonecutter in life, he engraved words that would identify skeletons; as a spokesman for his own conscience, he speaks words that "cut to the bone." Read the poem aloud to hear how it imitates real speech.

Richard Bone

When I first came to Spoon River
I did not know whether what they told me
Was true or false.
They would bring me the epitaph
And stand around the shop while I worked
And say "He was so kind," "He was wonderful,"
"She was the sweetest woman," "He was a consistent Christian."
And I chiseled for them whatever they wished,
All in ignorance of its truth.
But later, as I lived among the people here,
I knew how near to the life
Were the epitaphs that were ordered for them as they died.
But still I chiseled whatever they paid me to chisel
And made myself party to the false chronicles
Of the stones,
Even as the historian does who writes
Without knowing the truth,
Or because he is influenced to hide it.

Responding to the Poem

Analyzing the Poem

Identifying Details

1. What does Richard Bone come to realize about the town of Spoon River? Explain why he keeps on carving false sentiments.
2. What **analogy,** or comparison, does the speaker draw in the poem's last three lines?

Interpreting Meanings

3. In line 11, the speaker says he knew "how near to the life" were his epitaphs. How do you know he means "how *far* from the life"? Would the latter choice of words have been as effective? Why or why not?
4. What does Bone mean when he says he made himself "party to" the false chronicles of the stones?
5. Is Richard Bone making too much of his job? Or is there a more universal message in this poem? Explain.

Writing About the Poem

A Creative Response

Inventing Names for Characters. Aside from hinting at the character's profession, the name Masters gave to Richard Bone suggests something about his personality. The same can be said about such characters as Miniver Cheevy (see page 636) and Willy Loman in Arthur Miller's play *Death of a Salesman.* Willy has no clout in the business world and few inner resources to fall back upon, and could thus be considered a *low man* in his society. With this in mind, invent a name for each of the fictional characters described below:

1. Someone with serious doubts about his or her abilities
2. Someone other people naturally follow
3. Someone who is very patriotic
4. Someone with no sense of humor

ANALYZING THE POEM
Identifying Details
1. That the pious epitaphs he carved on the tombstones of his clients were very often far from the truth.
Bone's living depended on his clients' goodwill.
2. Bone compares himself to a historian who is either ignorant of the truth or corrupt.

Interpreting Meanings
3. The choice of words "how near to the life" ironically emphasizes the gap between illusion and reality represented by the idealized epitaphs. The more predictable phrase "how far from the life" would probably not have been as effective, since it would not underline Bone's sudden realization.
4. That Bone thinks of himself as an accomplice in some sort of crime.
5. The universal truth is that people should not believe all the history they read.

SUPPLEMENTARY SUPPORT MATERIALS
1. Vocabulary Activity Worksheet (*CCB*)
2. Review and Response Worksheet: Narration (*CCB*)
3. Selection Test (*CCB*)

DEVELOPING VOCABULARY
The following word from the poem is tested in the Selection Test. (See also Vocabulary Activity Worksheet.)
medicinal

PREPARATION
ESTABLISHING A PURPOSE. Have students read this poem to learn about Lucinda Matlock and her philosophy of life.

A. Characterization
? Based on her name, what guesses would you make about Lucinda Matlock? (It suggests strength.) Masters sometimes used names to suggest clues to personalities: Voltaire, Chicken, Dement, Marsh, Hookey, Gray, Sparks, etc.

B. Responding
? What kind of married life has Lucinda Matlock had? (Although she worked hard, she seems to have had a simple but pleasurable life with her husband of seventy years. She did know hardship, however, losing eight of her twelve children.)

C. Responding
? How do you respond to Lucinda Matlock's criticism of "degenerate sons and daughters"? What do you think she would say to the younger generation today? (She might say that they take no pride in accomplishments and therefore lack a positive energetic spirit.)

CLOSURE
Have students give brief oral statements of the theme of the poem.

Among the many voices from the dead that echo through the pages of *Spoon River Anthology*, Lucinda Matlock's is unique in that it seems both to scold and to boast. The scolding is explicit. It is directed at "sons and daughters" whose lax attitudes toward the serious business of life are regarded as "degenerate." The boasting is implicit. It is something we pick up by reading between the lines. Do you agree that the speaker feels she is entitled to a kind of praise because, over a span of ninety-six years, she met the challenges of life in the raw Middle West and overcame them? (Masters based Lucinda Matlock on his grandmother, Lucinda Masters.)

A Lucinda Matlock

I went to dances at Chandlerville,
And played snap-out at Winchester.
One time we changed partners,
Driving home in the moonlight of middle June,
And then I found Davis.
We were married and lived together for seventy years,
Enjoying, working, raising the twelve children,
Eight of whom we lost
B Ere I had reached the age of sixty.
I spun, I wove, I kept the house, I nursed the sick,
I made the garden, and for holiday
Rambled over the fields where sang the larks,
And by Spoon River gathering many a shell,
And many a flower and medicinal weed—
Shouting to the wooded hills, singing to the green valleys.
At ninety-six I had lived enough, that is all,
And passed to a sweet repose.
What is this I hear of sorrow and weariness,
Anger, discontent, and drooping hopes?
Degenerate sons and daughters,
C Life is too strong for you—
It takes life to love Life.

Responding to the Poem

Analyzing the Poem

Identifying Details

1. List the simple pleasures and pastimes the speaker mentions in describing her life. What hardships has she experienced?

Interpreting Meanings

2. Explain why the speaker feels that the younger generation is "degenerate." Is it fair for her to imply that their own lives could be as happy as hers? Or has she simply been lucky in the circumstances of her life?
3. The poem's **theme** is summed up in the last line. Explain the meaning of this final statement. What two meanings do you give to the word *life*?
4. What do you feel is Masters's own attitude toward Lucinda Matlock? Does he regard her as a judgmental old lady, or as a voice of wisdom? Give evidence from the poem to support your view.
5. If it were possible to ask the "sons and daughters" to speak in their own defense, what might they say?

Analyzing the Poem

Identifying Details

1. She mentions dances, games, moonlit drives, gathering shells and flowers, and rambles and singing in the fields.

She has raised twelve children and seen eight of them die before she was sixty years old; she has performed all the household chores and worked in the garden; she has nursed the sick.

Interpreting Meanings

2. She accuses the younger generation of complaining too much and of yielding to sorrow, anger, and discontent.

Student answers will vary. Encourage students to express and defend their opinions. Obviously, to some extent, Lucinda Matlock has been lucky; but she has also had a considerable share of hardship and pain.

3. Lucinda Matlock seems to mean that life cannot be loved and enjoyed unless we fully "live it": that is, plunge ourselves into its mixture of pleasures and hardships.

The first meaning might be "vitality" or "energy"; the second meaning is the root meaning, "human existence."

4. Student answers will vary. In general, Masters seems to admire Lucinda Matlock's joyful acceptance of simple pleasures and her stoic endurance of hardships. Her view is that both happiness and sadness are inevitably part of life. It does no good to give way to anger and to let hopes droop if we are discontented; the road to a full enjoyment of life is, quite simply, the living of it.

5. Students might note that life was simpler in those days. The pressures of modern life overwhelm many people, who then seek refuge in escape and in self-centered behavior.

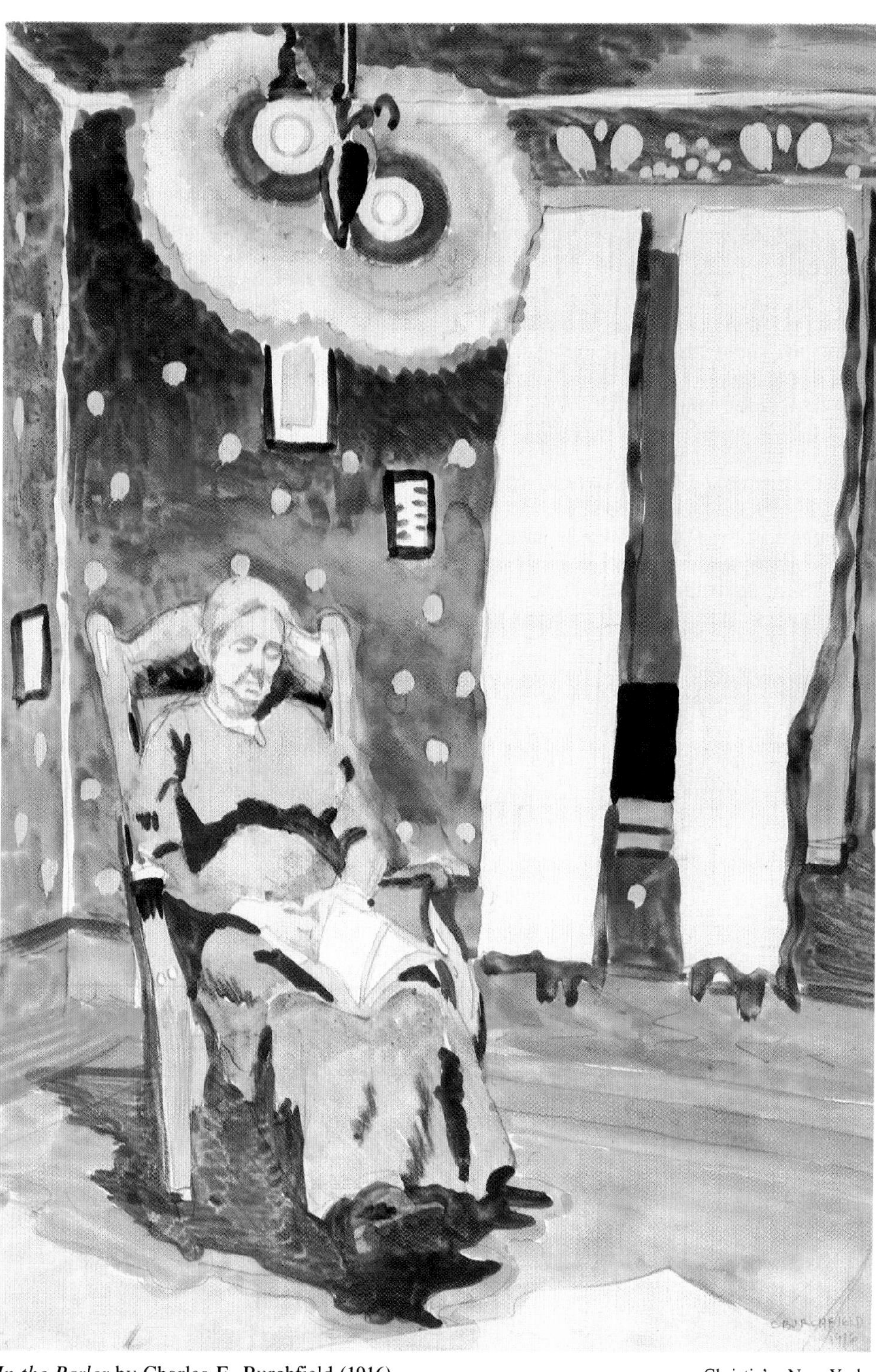

In the Parlor by Charles E. Burchfield (1916). Watercolor and pencil on paper. Christie's, New York.

SUPPLEMENTARY SUPPORT MATERIALS

1. Vocabulary Activity Worksheet (*CCB*)
2. Review and Response Worksheet: Tone and Theme (*CCB*)
3. Selection Test (*CCB*)

DEVELOPING VOCABULARY

The following words from the poem are tested in the Selection Test. (See also Vocabulary Activity Worksheet.)

canning rickety
to solder

PREPARATION

ESTABLISHING A PURPOSE. As students read, suggest that they try to form a mental image of Butch's accident and Butch as he is at the time of the trial.

A. Responding

? What kind of person do you suppose Butch was before he "got religion" and "steadied down"? (From the headnote, we know that Butch drank, and he probably also gambled and had numerous female relationships.)

B. Responding

? How does the news of Butch's accident make you feel? (Angry, bitter)

C. Irony

"I didn't know him at all" is crucial and ironic. Try to elicit from students the idea that it contains an oblique comment on the impersonality of fate. This is a common theme in works about war, such as *Hiroshima* (page 1049) and *Dispatches* (page 1059). Death and disfigurement are always upsetting; what is there additionally about a feeling of impersonality, or undeservedness, that makes them more so? (Without clear responsibility, there is often no clear motive. This makes the victim's suffering meaningless.)

Many of the stories told in *Spoon River Anthology* are interlocking. The villain of the whole book is Deacon Thomas Rhodes, who "ran the church as well as the store and the bank." We hear about Rhodes from a number of victims, including Butch Weldy.

Butch also refers to Jack the Fiddler, a blind man who is buried in the Spoon River cemetery. Jack was killed when Butch, who had been drinking, drove a carriage into a ditch. Read the first line of Butch's epitaph and think about what it implies about the speaker's life.

"Butch" Weldy

A After I got religion and steadied down
They gave me a job in the canning works,
And every morning I had to fill
The tank in the yard with gasoline,
That fed the blowfires in the sheds
To heat the soldering irons.
And I mounted a rickety ladder to do it,
Carrying buckets full of the stuff.
One morning, as I stood there pouring,
The air grew still and seemed to heave,
B And I shot up as the tank exploded,
And down I came with both legs broken,
And my eyes burned crisp as a couple
  of eggs
For someone left a blowfire going,
And something sucked the flame into
  the tank.
The Circuit Judge said whoever did it
Was a fellow-servant of mine, and so
Old Rhodes' son didn't have to pay me.
And I sat on the witness stand as blind
As Jack the Fiddler, saying over and over,
"I didn't know him at all." C

Analyzing the Poem
Identifying Details
1. While filling the tank at the canning factory with gasoline, Butch was the victim of an explosion, ignited by a blowfire which someone had left going. The explosion resulted in two broken legs and permanent blindness.
2. He compares his burnt eyes to a couple of eggs (line 13).
3. The judge reasoned that the explosion was caused by a fellow laborer; Rhodes's son was therefore not responsible.

Interpreting Meanings
4. Perhaps he implies that he formerly led a rather wild life.

The irony results from a reversal of expectation. Whereas such an accident might have been predictable if Butch were living an unruly life, it was surprising in the context of a "steady" life with a regular job and good habits.
5. Student answers will vary. As the speaker in the poem, Butch seems stoic; but the sharply edged vignette at the end of the poem of him repeating, "I didn't know him at all," betrays his emotion.
6. Some students may argue that Masters, as well as Butch, seems bitter: Hints in the poem suggest, for example, that Butch received no compensation because of influence-peddling.
7. Most students will agree that, no matter how well protected the modern workplace is, industrial accidents may always happen. Encourage the students to find and describe specific examples.

Butch would probably be awarded workman's compensation, and possibly a handsome negligence settlement. Ask the students to defend their opinions.

Responding to the Poem

Analyzing the Poem

Identifying Details

1. Describe Butch Weldy's accident.
2. When Butch talks about what happened to him, he produces a horrifying **simile.** What is it?
3. Explain why the Circuit Judge decided that Old Rhodes's son didn't have to compensate Butch for the accident.

Interpreting Meanings

4. When a person says that he has "steadied down," what is he implying about his former way of life? What **irony** do you feel when you consider that this horrible accident took place *after* Butch settled down?
5. How do you think Butch feels about the accident that ruined his life?
6. Do you think Masters shares Butch's feelings about the accident and about the decision made by the judge? Describe what you think Masters's own **tone** is in this poem.
7. *Spoon River Anthology* was published in 1915. Could something like Butch's accident happen today? What do you think a contemporary court of law would do for a victim like Butch?

Writing About the Poem

A Critical Response

Comparing and Contrasting Poems. In a paragraph, compare and contrast "Butch" Weldy with this poem:

Mrs. George Reece

To this generation I would say:
Memorize some bit of verse of truth or beauty.
It may serve a turn in your life.
My husband had nothing to do
With the fall of the bank—he was only cashier.
The wreck was due to the president, Thomas Rhodes.
And his vain, unscrupulous son.
Yet my husband was sent to prison,
And I was left with the children,
To feed and clothe and school them.
And I did it, and sent them forth
Into the world all clean and strong,
And all through the wisdom of Pope, the poet:
"Act well your part, there all the honor lies."

—Edgar Lee Masters

Primary Sources

The Genesis of Spoon River

[1914]

"About the 20th of May my mother came to visit us, and we had many long talks. . . . In our talks now we went over the whole past of Lewistown and Petersburg, bringing up characters and events that had passed from my mind. We traced these persons to their final fates, to the positions in life that they were then in. We had many sessions at this recalling of old days. . . .

"The psychological experience of this was truly wonderful. Finally on the morning she was leaving for Springfield we had a last and rather sobering talk. It was Sunday, too, and after putting her on the train at 53rd Street I walked back home full of strange pensiveness. The little church bell was ringing, but spring was in the air. I went to my room and immediately wrote 'The Hill,' and two or three of the portraits of *Spoon River Anthology.* Almost at once the idea came to me: Why not make this book the book I had thought about in 1906, in which I should draw the macrocosm by portraying the microcosm? Why not put side by side the stories of two characters interlocked in fate, thus giving both misunderstood souls a chance to be justly weighed? . . .

"People ask me over and over where the town of Spoon River is located. As there is no such town, I have to answer that there is only a river. And what a river! What a small stream winding its way through flatlands, amid hills that only distance lifts into any beauty, through jungles of weeds and thickets and melancholy cottonwoods. It goes by little towns as ugly and lonely as the tin-roofed hamlets of Kansas. Yet this is the town, or one of the towns, and this is the river and the country from which I extracted whatever beauty there is in that part of *Spoon River Anthology* which relates to a village depiction, and is not concerned with a world view."

—from *Across Spoon River: An Autobiography,* Edgar Lee Masters

A. Expansion Throughout American history, African American writers have had to face the problem of whether to adopt white literary forms, such as traditional rhyme and meter, or whether to create their own variations that would be truer to their experience. This problem has been compounded by the fact that since the American audience is mostly white, African American writers have felt compelled to write acceptably for this audience in order to gain wide exposure or, in fact, any significant degree of commercial success. Especially if you have many African American students, you might want to discuss the question of whether African American poets ought to write in "white" forms and, if not, what they should strive for in developing new forms of their own.

Paul Laurence Dunbar (1872–1906)

Published black poets were rare in nineteenth-century America, for compelling, obvious reasons. The idea of a poet writing at that time who was not only black, but whose books were also popular and widely praised, might sound far-fetched. Nevertheless, Paul Laurence Dunbar was just such a poet. His brief career should remind us that the vigor of poetry by twentieth-century black writers is not without deep roots in American life. Like other poets of their times, America's earliest black poets adapted the English lyrical tradition to their own purposes and, in turn, made striking contributions to it.

Dunbar was born in Dayton, Ohio, in the midst of the Reconstruction era after the Civil War. Before he was twenty, he had written poems both in dialect and in conventional English which caught the attention of Eastern critics. When his *Lyrics of Lowly Life* (with an introduction by the famous novelist and editor William Dean Howells) was published in 1896, Dunbar found the event a mixed blessing. What made his book popular was its humorous and sentimental portrayal of black life, written in dialect. White readers of the day found these dialect poems "acceptable"—that is, unthreatening to their ideas about black life in America. Those notions included the fantasy that blacks cheerfully accepted their poverty and their isolation from mainstream American life. Consequently, Dunbar's nondialect lyrics, skillful and moving as they were, were largely overlooked by an audience that thoughtlessly stereotyped both the writer and his work. [A]

Dunbar was dismayed by the public's preference for the dialect poems over his serious lyrics. He nevertheless continued to write poetry, novels, and short stories, and he became a popular lecturer in England and America. But he never managed to escape the image that he had created by his skill with dialect; no matter how hard he tried, in the minds of most readers, he continued to be thought of as a kind of entertainer for white readers. When he died, a disappointed man at the early age of thirty-four, he was unaware that the dialect poems celebrated in his own day would soon be a'' but forgotten, while the lyrics that meant most to him would also mean the most to later generations.

Supplementary Support Materials

1. Vocabulary Activity Worksheet (*CCB*)
2. Review and Response Worksheet: Rhythm, Rhyme, and Tone (*CCB*)
3. Selection Test (*CCB*)

Developing Vocabulary

The following words from the poem are tested in the Selection Test. (See also Vocabulary Activity Worksheet.)

pray	smote
sap	nigh
to gurgle	throe
sore	guise
fast	mortal

Preparation

Establishing a Purpose. Have students read to answer the questions, Who are the speakers in this poem? What happens to the second speaker? Why does it happen?

"The Haunted Oak" is a reflection on one of the most shameful periods in American history. The poem recalls the years of "lynch law," when gangs of murderous men meted out their own brand of "justice" to blacks whom they suspected of threatening white supremacy. Read the first two stanzas and stop to be sure you can identify the change in speakers.

The Haunted Oak

Pray why are you so bare, so bare,
 Oh, bough of the old oak tree;
And why, when I go through the shade you throw,
 Runs a shudder over me?

My leaves were green as the best, I trow°
 And sap ran free in my veins,
But I saw in the moonlight dim and weird
 A guiltless victim's pains.

I bent me down to hear his sigh;
 I shook with his gurgling moan,
And I trembled sore when they rode away,
 And left him here alone.

They'd charged him with the old, old crime,
 And set him fast in jail:
Oh, why does the dog howl all night long,
 And why does the night wind wail?

He prayed his prayer and he swore his oath,
 And he raised his hand to the sky;
But the beat of hoofs smote on his ear,
 And the steady tread drew nigh.

I feel the rope against my bark,
 And the weight of him in my grain,
I feel in the throe of his final woe
 The touch of my own last pain.

And never more shall leaves come forth
 On a bough that bears the ban;
I am burned with dread, I am dried and dead,
 From the curse of a guiltless man.

And ever the judge rides by, rides by,
 And goes to hunt the deer,
And ever another rides his soul
 In the guise of a mortal fear.

And ever the man he rides me hard,
 And never a night stays he;
For I feel his curse as a haunted bough,
 On the trunk of a haunted tree.

5. **trow:** believe.

Responding to the Poem

Analyzing the Poem

Identifying Details

1. What characteristics of the tree have prompted the opening questions?
2. What causes the "gurgling moan" in line 10? Who is the "judge" in line 29, and what punishment is visited upon him?
3. In your own words, what is the answer to the question asked in the first stanza?

Interpreting Meanings

4. What does the first stanza contribute to the dramatic thrust of the poem? What would be lost if the poem were to begin with stanza 2? How would the words spoken by the tree be affected?
5. In the final stanza, what larger **symbolic** meaning do the oak tree and its leafless bough assume? What symbolic meanings do the words "curse" (line 28) and "haunted" take on in the context of the final stanza?

Analyzing the Poem

Identifying Details

1. The tree is bare; as the speaker passes beneath it, a shudder runs through him.

2. The moan comes from the victim who is hanged from the tree.

The "judge" may have been the leader of the lynching party. He is punished throughout his life by a terrible sense of guilt for his crime.

3. Student answers will vary. One possibility might be: "My bough will never blossom with leaves because it is cursed by the hanging of an innocent victim."

Interpreting Meanings

4. The first stanza establishes a dramatic dialogue between the questioner and the tree; it also contributes to the poem's setting and to a sense of foreboding and suspense. If the poem had begun with the second stanza, these elements would have been lost.

(Answers continue on next page.)

(Continued from previous page.)

These words would lack a dramatic context.

5. The last stanza implies that it is not only the tree, but also the speaker and (by extension) all humanity that must feel the dreadful responsibility for the murder of an innocent victim by lynching.

In this context, "curse" and "haunted" assume a more general, symbolic meaning. If the oak tree is regarded as a symbol of nature as a whole, including human life, the "curse" on the bough symbolizes a terrible violation of nature. Humanity must always be "haunted" by shame for the heinous persecution by white men of innocent black victims.

6. The meter and rhyme of the poem are those of the traditional ballad stanza; the rhyme scheme is *abcb*, with four strong beats in the second and fourth lines. Repetition is especially marked in the final two stanzas ("And ever . . . And ever . . . ," "rides by, rides by," "haunted"). The form is appropriate because the poem—like many ballads—combines a narrative of a violent act, committed some time in the past, with motifs of the supernatural (a speaking tree, a haunted

(Answers continue in left-hand column.)

(Continued from top.)

bough). Dunbar uses these devices to underline a profound, moral lesson.

7. Students may suggest that the tone is a combination of grief and indignation.

Answers will vary; students may suggest that the tone would be more bitter if the speaker in the poem had been the hanged man.

6. Explain how Dunbar's use of **meter, rhyme,** and **repetition** give his poem the effect of a traditional ballad. Why is this form especially appropriate, given the poem's content?
7. How would you describe the **tone** of the oak tree's story? Given the nature of the story, would you have expected a more bitter tone? Explain.

Writing About the Poem

A Creative Response

1. **Setting the Poem to Music.** If you are so inclined, try setting Dunbar's poem to music. Will you use a plaintive "ballad" sound, or something else?

A Critical Response

2. **Analyzing Imagery.** In a paragraph, discuss the use of concrete imagery in "The Haunted Oak." Give specific examples of imagery appealing to the senses of sight, hearing, and touch.

Analyzing Language and Style

Archaic Diction

Dictionaries describe *archaic* words as terms, or meanings of terms, that occur in older writings but are rarely used today. Sometimes writers deliberately use archaic diction to give their texts a certain old-fashioned flavor. Use a dictionary to check your answers to these questions about Dunbar's diction. You may have to go to the library for a large dictionary.

1. Find six words in the poem that are used in their archaic senses. Look especially at lines 1, 5, 11, 19, 20, and 23.
2. Are any of these words still used today in other senses? If so, use each word in a sentence to show its current meaning (or one of its meanings).
3. Substitute modern terms for each of the archaic words you have found. (You'll have to rewrite some lines to do so.) How do the new words change the poem's effect?

Primary Sources

Dunbar and Dialect Poetry

James Weldon Johnson (page 680) talked with Dunbar about the problem of dialect poetry. Dunbar was unwilling to continue writing in that style:

"We talked again and again about poetry. I told him my doubts regarding the further possibilities of stereotyped dialect. He was hardly less dubious than I. He said, 'You know, of course, that I didn't start as a dialect poet. I simply came to the conclusion that I could write it as well, if not better, than anybody else I knew of, and that by doing so I should gain a hearing, and now they don't want me to write anything but dialect.' There was a tone of self-reproach in what he said; and five years later, in his fatal illness, he sounded that same tone more deeply when he said to me, 'I've kept on doing the same things, and doing them no better. I have never gotten to the things I really wanted to do.' "

—James Weldon Johnson

Edna St. Vincent Millay (1892–1950)

Like Edwin Arlington Robinson, Edna St. Vincent Millay was born on the granite coast of Maine and established her poetic reputation in New York. Also like Robinson, she lived to see the day when, despite many honors and the devotion of a wide audience, she had to realize that her reputation had barely withstood the onslaught of modernism. Millay had much in common with exponents of modernism such as Pound, Eliot, and Hart Crane—except, ironically, a philosophy of poetry.

Millay achieved fame even before she graduated from Vassar College, with the publication of her first collection of verse, *Renascence and Other Poems* (1917). After World War I, she moved to Greenwich Village. This was an era when that section of New York City was not only a haven for artists, but also a place where women were as free as men to speak their minds, to live by their own rules, and to pursue careers—activities that most Americans still considered improper for women. Taking advantage of this liberated atmosphere, Millay became one of its leading voices—a free spirit who wrote saucy and slightly scandalous lyrics in a style that occasionally evoked Elizabethan verse. Millay's philosophy might best be described in her own words:

First Fig

My candle burns at both ends;
  It will not last the night;
But ah, my foes, and oh, my friends—
  It gives a lovely light!

Millay also became caught up in the radical dissent of the time, and she worked passionately, if vainly, to save the anarchists Sacco and Vanzetti, who were executed in Massachusetts in 1927 after a celebrated trial.

"Vincent," as she was familiarly known, was a skilled actress and speaker with the flair of a seasoned performer. Like Vachel Lindsay, she gave recitals during long, nationwide tours in

which she won a degree of celebrity seldom associated with poets.

Both shocking and fascinating to her audiences, Millay grew in popularity even as her poetic achievements began to decline. Her most productive period was between the two World Wars, when she published seven collections of poetry, as well as a series of dramas written for the Provincetown Players in New York. In 1923, she became the first woman to win the Pulitzer Prize for poetry, for *The Ballad of the Harp-Weaver.*

During World War II, Millay determined to write "public" poetry to contribute to the Allied cause. She produced scores of poems which, although widely read, proved that outrage and passion could not substitute for the verbal artistry that poetry demands. The lyricist had been overtaken by the propagandist.

One of the brightest literary stars of a generation was all but faded from sight when, in her fifty-eighth year, Edna St. Vincent Millay died alone at her home, Steepletop.

Comment From A Critic

Poet and critic Babette Deutsch says that Millay was "wanting in depth and complexity," but that she was "the author of a handful of touching songs on the transience of love and the shortness of life." (After students have read Millay's two poems on the following pages, you may want to return to this statement and have students discuss whether or not they agree with it.) Millay's own life turned unhappy in middle age: Her husband and a number of her close friends died in quick succession in the forties, and she suffered from emotional problems and excessive drinking.

Supplementary Support Materials

1. Vocabulary Activity Worksheet (*CCB*)
2. Review and Response Worksheet: Metaphor and Mood (*CCB*)
3. Selection Test (*CCB*)
4. Audiocassette recording

Developing Vocabulary

The following words from the poem are tested in the Selection Test. (See also Vocabulary Activity Worksheet.)

ferry   shawl
wan   fare
to hail

Preparation

Establishing a Purpose. As the headnote indicates, this poem primarily evokes feelings associated with a memory. Ask students to be able to describe those feelings when they have completed the poem.

A. Imagery

? How literally is the imagery in lines 3–6 meant to be interpreted? Describe the scene of the ferry. (The ferry is obviously not a luxury ship—it has few amenities and an earthy smell. The ferry is lighted up in the night and sounds its whistles frequently to warn other ships of its approach. These details are literal, but the "fire" into which the couple look is the brightness they find in each other, and the "hill-top" probably refers to the ferry itself.)

B. Tone

? How would you describe the tone of the poem? Can you find words and phrases that help achieve this tone? How do you feel about the young couple in the poem? Would you like to be them? (It is a happy poem; *merry, bare and bright, bucketful of gold*; the lovers share their joy with the woman.)

The title of the poem is a Spanish word meaning "remembrance" or "souvenir." The poet evokes a happy memory of youth: a carefree night spent riding one of the several ferry boats that once connected the island of Manhattan with its neighbors. Do you recognize the feeling described in the first line?

Recuerdo

We were very tired, we were very merry—
We had gone back and forth all night on the ferry.
It was bare and bright, and smelled like a stable—
But we looked into a fire, we leaned across a table,
We lay on a hill-top underneath the moon;
And the whistles kept blowing, and the dawn came soon.

We were very tired, we were very merry—
We had gone back and forth all night on the ferry;
And you ate an apple, and I ate a pear,
From a dozen of each we had bought somewhere;
And the sky went wan, and the wind came cold,
And the sun rose dripping, a bucketful of gold.

We were very tired, we were very merry,
We had gone back and forth all night on the ferry.
We hailed, "Good morrow, mother!" to a shawl-covered head,
And bought a morning paper, which neither of us read;
And she wept, "God bless you!" for the apples and pears,
And we gave her all our money but our subway fares.

Responding to the Poem

Analyzing the Poem

Identifying Details

1. What details describe what the speaker and her friend did this night?

Interpreting Meanings

2. Who do you think the "we" in the poem are? What do lines 4–5 suggest about their feelings for one another?
3. Why do you think they gave all their money to the "shawl-covered head"? What does this action say about the power of love?
4. Identify the **metaphor** in line 12. Describe what this image reveals about the speaker's feelings.
5. Read the poem aloud, using the tone and pacing of natural speech. Then describe the poem's **meter** and **rhyme scheme.** What use of repetition contributes to the poem's **mood**?

Analyzing Language and Style

Imagery and Feelings

Poetic imagery is not merely decorative; used skillfully, it can help the poet control the reader's responses and feelings. Imagery depends a great deal on the suggestive power of words—on their **connotations.** For example, the image in line 3 ("smelled like a stable") might, for someone who happened to despise the odor of stables, create

CLOSURE

Have individual students suggest adjectives that convey the mood of this poem. Then have students list images in the poem that contribute to that mood.

ANALYZING THE POEM

Identifying Details

1. Line 2 describes an all-night trip on a ferry boat. The couple watched the sunrise (lines 11–12). At the end of their trip, they met a shawl-covered woman (line 15), to whom they gave the apples and the pears they had bought (line 17), as well as all the money they had on them.

Interpreting Meanings

2. The speaker never identifies the other person in the poem, but the context suggests that he is a man with whom she is romantically involved.

The lines have romantic connotations: They give us a picture of two lovers looking into a fire, leaning toward each other across a table, and lying in the moonlight on a hilltop.

3. Students' answers will vary. Most students will agree that the couple are in a happy, carefree, generous mood. It implies that love can inspire sympathy and generosity. It also shows that one part of being in love is the need to share that love with someone else, even if it be a stranger.

4. The sun is compared to a bucket that rises slowly from the sea, containing "gold" rather than water. The image contributes to a portrait of the speaker as romantic and highly emotional; her feelings seem to be almost ecstatic.

5. Students will have various responses. Be sure that the students are able to identify the rocking, lilting rhythm of the poem. They also may note the dominance of iambs and anapests. The rhyme scheme of "Recuerdo" is *aabbcc aaddee aaffgg* (or *aaffdd*).

Band Playing on the Hudson by Reginald Marsh (1932). Watercolor.

a feeling of distaste for this night on the ferry. But for many readers, the odor of a stable suggests something pleasant—earthiness, the warmth of animals, the coziness of a place protected from the out-of-doors.

If the poet had said that the ferry "smelled of manure," we'd have a different image and probably different feelings about the experience.

1. Think of at least one verb that could replace "blowing" (line 6) in order to create a negative or unpleasant feeling.
2. Think of at least three things other than a bucketful of gold to which the poet might have compared the rising sun (line 12) to suggest unpleasant connotations.
3. Think of the image suggested by the phrase "shawl-covered head." How might the poet have described the old woman to suggest something unpleasant or even threatening?
4. In what other ways might Millay have made the woman unpleasant?

SUPPLEMENTARY SUPPORT MATERIALS

1. Vocabulary Activity Worksheet (*CCB*)
2. Review and Response Worksheet: Tone (*CCB*)
3. Selection Test (*CCB*)

DEVELOPING VOCABULARY

The following words from the poem are tested in the Selection Test. (See also Vocabulary Activity Worksheet.)

laurel | formula
indiscriminate | keen
fragment

PREPARATION

ESTABLISHING A PURPOSE. Have students read this dirge to learn what it is that is lost through death and what the poet's attitude toward death is.

A. Interpretation

? What does the poet mean by "indiscriminate dust"? (This phrase is based on the fact that the body decays after death and mingles with the "dust" of the earth. Eventually, all life, "the wise and the lovely" and the unwise and the unlovely, are as one.)

B. Interpretation

? What does the poet mean by "A formula, a phrase remains—but the best is lost"? (Perhaps that something we have said or done may live after us in the minds of others but that the essence of us—all those things that we are when alive—is lost at death.)

In this dirge, or lament, the poet sets up the expectation that the speaker will eventually make some sort of peace with death and destiny. But that expectation is never fulfilled: The speaker maintains a note of stark, unqualified grief right to the end. Do you think Millay is questioning conventional attitudes toward death and loss? Is she perhaps defying the sentiments expressed by other poets and elegists throughout the centuries?

Dirge Without Music

I am not resigned to the shutting away of loving hearts in the hard
ground.
So it is, and so it will be, for so it has been, time out of mind:
Into the darkness they go, the wise and the lovely. Crowned
With lilies and with laurel they go; but I am not resigned.

Lovers and thinkers, into the earth with you.
A Be one with the dull, the indiscriminate dust.
A fragment of what you felt, of what you knew,
B A formula, a phrase remains,—but the best is lost.

The answers quick and keen, the honest look, the laughter, the love,—
They are gone. They are gone to feed the roses. Elegant and curled
Is the blossom. Fragrant is the blossom. I know. But I do not approve.
More precious was the light in your eyes than all the roses in the world.

Down, down, down into the darkness of the grave
Gently they go, the beautiful, the tender, the kind;
Quietly they go, the intelligent, the witty, the brave.
I know. But I do not approve. And I am not resigned.

Responding to the Poem

Analyzing the Poem

Identifying Details

1. In the first stanza, the speaker mourns the loss of "the wise and the lovely." Whose loss does she mourn in stanza 2? Stanza 4?

Interpreting Meanings

2. What phrase best expresses the speaker's attitude toward death?
3. Explain what the speaker means by the statement in line 8 that "the best" is lost after death. What is "the best," in her opinion? Do you agree that "the best is lost" in death?
4. What comparison does the speaker make in lines 10–12? Explain her point here. How does the beauty and delicacy of the flower image help to drive home this point?
5. The last line almost echoes the sentiment of the first, except that the speaker adds another note when she states, "I do not approve." How does this new sentiment affect the **tone** and meaning of the poem?
6. Although this poem contains certain patterns of **rhythm** and **rhyme,** Millay tries not to allow these sound effects to create "music" for her dirge, or "lament."

ANALYZING THE POEM
Identifying Details
1. In the second stanza the speaker mourns the loss of lovers and thinkers. In the fourth, she mourns the beautiful, the tender, and the kind; and also, the intelligent, the witty, and the brave.

Interpreting Meanings
2. Students will have various answers. Many students will suggest that the defiance expressed in the penultimate phrase, "I do not approve," best expresses the speaker's attitude. Others may suggest the phrase "I am not resigned" (lines 4 and 16).
3. In the speaker's opinion, the best is the living, breathing presence in the world of lovers and thinkers.
Students will find it hard to disagree.
4. The remains of the dead fertilize the ground and "help to feed the roses." The speaker compares the light in the eyes of a lost loved one to the elegance and fragrance of these flowers, saying that she values the eyes of her love more than all the roses in the world.
The delicacy of the image emphasizes the elusive, precious, and fragile character of human life.
5. This sentiment injects a further note of bitterness, as if the speaker had been asked to "approve" of death and had politely, but firmly, declined. The sentiment stems from a strongly assertive, individualistic personality, who refuses to conform to fate or to traditional precepts of resignation and acceptance.
6. Millay uses slant rhymes, internal rhymes, and long, irregularly syncopated phrases to emphasize the speaker's anguished quarrel with death. The jerky interruptions of the rhythm in stanza 3 are especially effective, as are the three brief, complete sentences that occupy the poem's last line.
7. Students may suggest that the loss of a loved one would be the most likely occasion for the poem.
8. No one wants to lose a loved one.

Do you think she avoids creating a lilting, musical effect? Explain what you think *is* the effect of the poem's sound.
7. Describe what might have prompted Millay to write this poem.
8. Are this speaker's feelings about death widely shared? Explain.

Writing About the Poems

A Creative Response

1. **Writing a Conversation.** Write a conversation between the speakers in "Recuerdo" and "Dirge Without Music." Have the speakers discuss a topic that allows you to show their attitudes toward life.

A Critical Response

2. **Responding to the Poem.** In protesting against a natural process such as death, Millay risks sounding like someone who has not grown up (although she was in her fifties when she wrote this poem). In a brief essay, explain whether you feel that "Dirge Without Music" expresses an immature attitude toward death, or displays a wise and mature—if unexpected—view. Give reasons for your opinion.
3. **Comparing and Contrasting Poems.** In a brief essay, compare and contrast "Dirge" with "Thanatopsis" by William Cullen Bryant (page 142). Before you write, gather data for your essay by filling out a chart like the following one.

	Millay	Bryant
Speaker		
Subject		
Message		
Tone		
Rhythm		
Rhyme		

Primary Sources

"The brawny male sends his picture"

In 1912, one of the judges for a poetry contest remarked that "Renascence," the poem submitted by E. St. Vincent Millay, Esq., must surely be the work of a forty-five-year-old brawny male. When she heard of this remark, Edna St. Vincent Millay sent this letter.

[December 5, 1912]

"To Mr. Ficke and Mr. Bynner:

"Mr. Earle has acquainted me with your wild surmises. Gentlemen: I must convince you of your error; my reputation is at stake. I simply will not be a 'brawny male.' Not that I have an aversion to brawny males; *au contraire, au contraire.* But I cling to my femininity!

"Is it that you consider brain and brawn so inseparable? I have thought otherwise. Still, that is all a matter of personal opinion. But, gentlemen: When a woman insists that she is twenty, you must not, must not call her forty-five. That is more than wicked; it is indiscreet.

"Mr. Ficke, you are a lawyer. I am very much afraid of lawyers. Spare me, kind sir! Take into consideration my youth—for I am indeed but twenty—and my fragility—for 'I do protest I am a maid'—and—sleuth me no sleuths!

"Seriously: I thank you also for the compliment you have unwittingly given me. For tho I do not yet aspire to be forty-five and brawny, if my verse so represents me, I am more gratified than I can say. When I was a little girl, this is what I thought and wrote:

Let me not shout into the world's great ear
Ere I have something for the world to hear.
Then let my message like an arrow dart
And pierce a way into the world's great heart.

"You cannot know how much I appreciate what you have said about my 'Renascence.'

"If you should care to look up the April, 1907, number of *Current Literature,* you would find a review of my *Land of Romance* (near a review of Mr. Bynner's *Fair of My Fancy*). And you might be interested in Mr. Edward Wheeler's comment: 'The poem which follows (by E. St. Vincent Millay) seems to me to be phenomenal. The author, whether boy or girl we do not know, is just fourteen years of age.'

E. St. V. M.

"P.S. The brawny male sends his picture. I *have* to laugh."

A. Connections
Wallace Stevens (page 750) was at Harvard at the same time as Frost, and E. A. Robinson (page 633) had been there a decade earlier. Of the three famous loners, Frost was the least gregarious. Stevens and Robinson socialized in literary circles at Harvard, but Frost did not.

B. Expansion
During his years of greatest fame, Frost was viewed by the public as a lovable old man, a homespun Yankee sage. After his death, Lawrence Thompson and R. H. Winnick's three-volume official biography overturned this innocent conception, and revealed Frost as a man who was often ill-tempered, manipulative of his loved ones, and jealous of his competitors. Frost was an extremely contradictory person who doubtless had all these elements in him, and who admitted that he liked to play hide-and-seek with the public.

Closure
Have individual students summarize what they think is the poet's attitude toward death. Then have other students explain how the tone of his work reinforces this attitude.

Robert Frost (1874–1963)

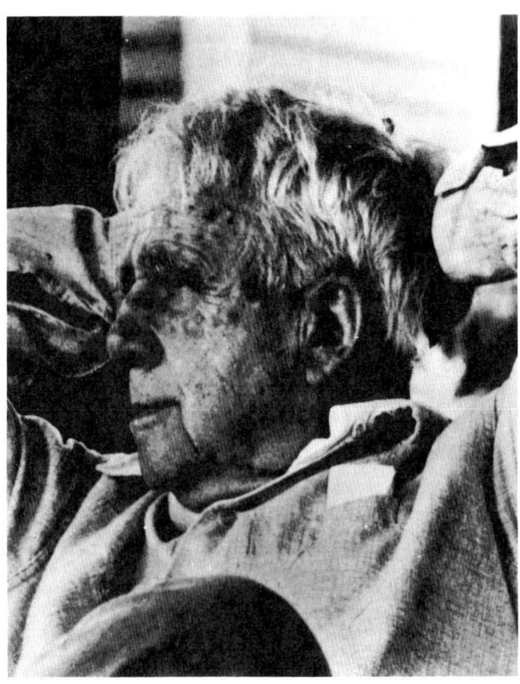

Although Robert Frost is the poet whom Americans most closely identify with New England, he was born in San Francisco, California. He was ten years old before he first saw the New England landscapes and knew the changing seasons that he would later describe with the familiarity of a native son. The boy's move across the country was the result of his father's early death and his mother's decision to settle in the industrial town of Lawrence, Massachusetts. After high school there, Frost entered Dartmouth College in New Hampshire. He decided after a few months that he was not yet ready for higher education, and he returned to Lawrence to work in the cotton mills and to write. His verses, however, found little favor with magazine editors.

In his early twenties, married and with a growing family, Frost finally began to feel the need for a more formal education than his random reading could provide. He took his family to Cambridge, Massachusetts, where he entered Harvard and stayed for only two years. He later wrote of his decision to leave: "Harvard had taken me away from the question of whether I could write or not." A

Frost earned a living as a schoolteacher and as an editor before deciding to try farming. For ten years, Frost tilled the stony New Hampshire soil on thirty acres which his grandfather had bought for him. But he decided that the concentration demanded by writing poetry did not mix with the round-the-clock physical effort of working the land. Discouraged, he returned to teaching for a few years; then in 1912 he sought a complete change of scene by taking his family to England.

The move turned out to be a wise one. Stimulated by meeting English poets, Frost continued to write poetry, though he found his subjects in New England. In the three years he spent abroad, he completed the two volumes that would make him famous—*A Boy's Will* (1913) and *North of Boston* (1914). These collections included several poems that would stand among Frost's best-known works: "The Tuft of Flowers," "In Hardwood Groves," "Mending Wall," "The Death of the Hired Man," and "After Apple-Picking." These poems were marked by a flinty realism and an impressive mastery of iambic rhythm, narrative dialogue, and the dramatic monologue.

When Frost came back to New Hampshire in 1915, he was no longer an obscure scribbler intent on turning New England folkways into poetry; he was an accomplished writer who had already extended the scope and character of American literature into the twentieth century. B In 1916, the publication of *Mountain Interval*—a collection that included such favorites as "The Road Not Taken," "Birches," and " 'Out, Out—' "—solidified his fame. Rewarded with many prizes (including four Pulitzer Prizes and a Congressional medal), numerous honorary degrees, and the faithful attention of a wide readership, Frost spent the rest of his life as a lecturer at a number of colleges, and as a public performer who, as he put it, liked to "say" rather than to recite his poetry.

On stage, Frost in his later years became a character of his own creation—a lovable, fumbling old gent who could nevertheless pierce the minds and hearts of those able to see beyond his play-acting. In private, he was apt to put aside this guileless character and become a sometimes wicked commentator on the pretensions of rival poets; and he could be just as cutting to gushing devotees, who were unaware that he held in contempt the very flattery he demanded.

On Inaugural Day, 1961, standing bareheaded in a bright, cold wind beside President John F. Kennedy on the Capitol steps in Washington, D.C., Frost recited "The Gift Outright." His art with words had brought him not only the friendship of a president (who was half his age) but, by means of radio and television, the largest single audience in history for a poet.

In a period when poetry was being changed by verbal experiment and by exotic influences from abroad, Frost remained devoted to traditional forms and firmly rooted in American soil. If, at the time of his death, he seemed to belong more to the past than to the present, his reputation today is secure. Neither the cranky realism nor the homely philosophy of self-reliance and spiritual independence that mark his work has been forgotten. He was an artist who developed his talents with stubborn persistence, and he found a unique voice that remained unaffected by the clamor of modernism.

Robert Frost reading a poem at the inauguration of John F. Kennedy, January 20, 1961. Four American Presidents are shown in this photograph.

A. Expansion
Frost's friendship with Kennedy led him to take a trip to Russia in September 1962 along with Secretary of the Interior Stewart Udall. There Frost spoke at length with Khrushchev, just a month before the Cuban missile crisis. The two men, who both thought of themselves as men of the soil, got along well, and Frost proposed a "noble rivalry" between the two nations that would be based on spurring each other to achieve their best rather than on mutual destruction. Frost was soon disillusioned about the impact poetry can have on the actions of governments.

B. Humanities Connection: Discussing the Photograph
Flanking Frost on both sides are four Presidents: Eisenhower, Kennedy, Johnson (who is shielding Frost's page from glare with his hat) and Nixon. Ask students if they can find them.

SUPPLEMENTARY SUPPORT MATERIALS

1. Vocabulary Activity Worksheet (*CCB*)
2. Review and Response Worksheet: The Sonnet (*CCB*)
3. Selection Test (*CCB*)
4. Audiocassette recording

DEVELOPING VOCABULARY

The following word from the poem is tested in the Selection Test. (See also Vocabulary Activity Worksheet.)
blight

PREPARATION

ESTABLISHING A PURPOSE. Have students read to understand what Frost observes in the octave about the spider, the flower, and the moth. Then have students read the sestet to understand the questions he poses about them.

A. Title
The title may have a double meaning: it is *about* design, but as a well-made sonnet, it also *is* a design.

B. Interpretation
Note the word *kindred.*
? What is Frost saying? (Literally, he means that the spider and moth are somewhat related forms of life. More broadly, he probably means that all forms of life are somewhat related and yet involved in a pattern of preying upon each other.)

COMMENTS FROM TWO CRITICS
Poet and critic Randall Jarrell cited this poem as one that would help the public see Frost's work as less "sugary." Critic Lionel Trilling, apparently influenced by Jarrell, later mentioned this poem during a speech on Frost's eighty-fifth birthday, during which he saluted Frost for showing a "terrifying universe."

Frost was particularly proud of his sonnets, and he often expressed regret that more of them were not reprinted in the hundreds of anthologies in which his work appeared. "Design" reveals how densely packed with ideas his sonnets can be. Based on the very first line of the poem, what would you predict its tone is going to be? What words make you feel that way?

A Design

I found a dimpled spider, fat and white,
On a white heal-all,° holding up a moth
Like a white piece of rigid satin cloth—
Assorted characters of death and blight
Mixed ready to begin the morning right,
Like the ingredients of a witches' broth—
A snowdrop spider, a flower like a froth,
And dead wings carried like a paper kite.

What had that flower to do with being white,
The wayside blue and innocent heal-all?
B What brought the kindred spider to that height,
Then steered the white moth thither in the night?
What but design of darkness to appall?
If design govern in a thing so small.

2. **heal-all:** a flowering plant believed to have curative powers.

ANALYZING THE POEM
Identifying Details
1. A spider, a moth, and a flowering plant called the heal-all.

Each character is white.

The moth is trapped and killed by the spider on the heal-all.

2. The moth is compared to a "white piece of rigid satin cloth" (line 3). The combination of the three characters is compared to the "ingredients of a witches' broth" (line 6). The flower is "like a froth." The wings of the dead moth are compared to a paper kite (line 8).

3. He wonders what sinister "design" brought the moth to its death on the flower.

Interpreting Meanings
4. The meanings that Frost might be applying may include: a distinctive mark, a personage in a drama, a genetic attribute, and—most generally—a sign.

Have the students apply each definition in turn to the context.

5. The question of line 13 suggests that it is some sinister plan of nature.

6. The final question hints at the possibility that the moth's death is simply a random event.

The phrase might be defined as a "sinister plan of nature."

7. The last line introduces a chilling note of doubt: that the "small" events of nature simply play themselves out in a random fashion.

8. The rhyme scheme is as follows: *abba, abba, aca, acc.* The limited number of rhymes focuses the reader's attention on the color "white."

9. A Puritan writer might have agreed with Frost that the playing out of death in nature could represent an allegory for man, but no Puritan writer would have felt that the universe was randomly governed.

Most students would agree that the Rationalists would have accepted the phenomenon as purely scientific.

10. Encourage students to review the relevant sections of *Moby-Dick* before they launch a class discussion.

Responding to the Poem

Analyzing the Poem

Identifying Details

1. Identify the three "characters" discussed in the poem. What color is each one? What is happening to the three characters?
2. Identify each of the **similes** in the **octave** (first eight lines) of the sonnet.
3. Briefly stated, tell what questions the poet asks in the **sestet** (last six lines) of the sonnet.

Interpreting Meanings

4. Look up the word *character* in a dictionary. Which definitions of the word might Frost be applying in line 4? How does each definition affect the meaning of the line? What justifies the poet's description of these things as "characters of death and blight"?
5. In line 13, the poet answers his own questions with another question. In your own words, explain how this question answers the previous one.
6. In line 14, Frost qualifies his answer with a reservation, beginning with a crucial "if." What final question remains in his mind? How would you define a "design of darkness"?
7. How does the last line affect the whole **tone** and meaning of the poem?
8. Describe the **rhyme scheme** of the poem. In your view, how does Frost's use of a very limited number of rhymes affect the poem's **tone**?
9. How would a Puritan writer from Unit One have answered the questions Frost asks in the poem? How would the Rationalists from Unit Two, or a scientist, answer them?
10. Do you see any similarities between Frost's use of the color white in this poem and Melville's use of white in *Moby-Dick*? (See page 297.) Why do you think each writer chose this color?

Writing About the Poem

A Critical Response

1. **Responding to a Critic.** Laurence Perrine has made this comment about "Design":

> Frost's brief poem, like the wayside blue or white heal-all, seems from the outside innocent enough. But within its fourteen innocent-seeming lines, Frost chillingly poses the problem of evil.
>
> —Laurence Perrine

In an essay, explain your response to this comment on the poem. If you agree with it, give reasons why. If you disagree, be sure to state what *you* think is the central issue in the poem.

2. **Contrasting Three Selections.** In a brief essay, explain how these three writers use the image of a spider: Edward Taylor in "Upon a Spider Catching a Fly" (page 46); Jonathan Edwards in "Sinners in the Hands of an Angry God" (page 37); and Robert Frost in "Design." Remember that often the differences in the use of images and symbols are as interesting and important as the similarities.
3. **Comparing Poems.** In a brief essay, compare "Design" with one of the following poems:

   a. "To a Waterfowl" by William Cullen Bryant (page 139)
   b. "Upon a Spider Catching a Fly" by Edward Taylor (page 46)
   c. "The Rhodora" by Ralph Waldo Emerson (page 198)
   d. "On the Beach at Night" by Walt Whitman (page 343)
   e. "Apparently with no surprise" by Emily Dickinson (page 368)

Before you write, gather your data in a chart like the following one:

	"Design"	Other Poem
Rhyme		
Rhythm		
Figures of speech		
Tone		
Message of poem		

SUPPLEMENTARY SUPPORT MATERIALS

1. Review and Response Worksheet: Symbolism (*CCB*)
2. Selection Test (*CCB*)
3. Audiocassette recording

PREPARATION

1. **BUILDING ON PRIOR KNOWLEDGE.** Many of your students will have been around an ocean at some time, and have probably seen people sitting and gazing out into the water. Ask them why people look out into the water, even when there is seemingly nothing to see? Would it seem strange if a person constantly looked toward the water?

2. **ESTABLISHING A PURPOSE.** Have students read to understand what is symbolized by the sea and the land.

A. Responding

? Given the context of the poem, do you think that the poet means the fact that people "turn their back on the land" to be a value judgment? (Answers will vary.)

B. Interpretation

? What do "out far" and "in deep" mean in these lines? (Literally, that people cannot see a great distance out to the water or down into the water. Symbolically, the words probably refer to the little insight that we have into the complexity of existence.)

C. Responding

? How does this poem make you feel? (Some students may feel rather chilled by its deadpan mockery.) Do you feel Frost's dim view of humanity in this poem is justified, or not? (Students will agree that some people's vision is limited. They may disagree whether or not those people are in the majority.)

Before you read this poem, make a guess as to the meaning of Frost's puzzling title.

Neither Out Far nor In Deep

The people along the sand
All turn and look one way.
A [They turn their back on the land.
They look at the sea all day.

As long as it takes to pass
A ship keeps raising its hull;
The wetter ground like glass
Reflects a standing gull.

The land may vary more;
But wherever the truth may be—
The water comes ashore,
And the people look at the sea.

They cannot look out far.
They cannot look in deep.] B
But when was that ever a bar
To any watch they keep?

C

Responding to the Poem

Analyzing the Poem

Identifying Details

1. What phenomenon of human behavior does the poet observe in the first stanza? According to line 9, why does this behavior seem surprising?
2. What is the one **simile** that gives an imaginative lift to the stark, flat landscape and seascape the poem depicts?

Interpreting Meanings

3. In what way are lines 11–12 tinged with **irony**?
4. On a literal level, why is it that the people in the poem can look neither "out far" nor "in deep"? What more general human limitations might be **symbolized** by our inability to probe the distance and depth of the sea?
5. What might the sea and the land **symbolize** in this poem? What larger meaning might the "watch" (line 16) take on?
6. Comment on the poet's **tone** in the last line. Does he admire the watchers for keeping their vigil in spite of all obstacles? Does he feel scorn or pity for their failure to recognize their limitations? Do you have some other interpretation? Explain.

Writing About the Poem

A Creative Response

1. **Revising the Poem.** Suppose Frost had used the pronoun *you* instead of *they* in the poem. How might the **tone** have differed? Rewrite the first or last stanza, changing *they* to *you.* Include any other changes you think should be made for the sake of consistency. Then write a paragraph explaining how your stanza differs from Frost's.
2. If you have musical talent, invent a melody for the poem.

A Critical Response

3. **Comparing Literary Works.** In a paragraph, compare Frost's message in this poem with Ishmael's reflections on the human response to the sea in the passage from Melville's *Moby-Dick* beginning on page 298. What does each passage suggest about its author's outlook?
4. **Comparing Poems.** In a paragraph, compare "Neither Out Far nor In Deep" with Whitman's "On the Beach at Night Alone" (page 343). Consider the message in each poem, the form it is stated in, and the overall effect of the poem.

CLOSURE

Have students write two or three sentences explaining why Frost chose to include the words *out far* and *in deep* in the title of this poem. What symbolic significance do these words have?

ANALYZING THE POEM

Identifying Details

1. The poet describes people on the beach who turn their backs to the land and gaze out at the water.

The behavior is surprising because, although the variety of the land might be expected to capture the people's interest, they persist in looking out over the sea all day.

2. The simile occurs in lines 7 and 8, where the puddles of water at the shore line are said to reflect the figure of a standing gull "like glass."

Interpreting Meanings

3. The speaker in the poem notes that the land may seem to be more interesting than the sea—but that, "whatever the truth may be," people insist on looking at the water, because it "comes ashore." Ironically, people seem more fascinated by the monotonous lapping of the shore by the waves than in the land itself.

4. They cannot penetrate the opacity of the water by the shoreline, and they cannot distinguish the water clearly when it meets the horizon, far out to sea.

5. Student answers may vary. But the sea could be understood as a symbol for the future in humanity's collective experience and in the particular experience of every individual; the land could symbolize the more familiar territory of the past and the present.

In the symbolic context suggested above, the "watch" might be a figure of speech for every individual's monitoring of his or her own life as it wends toward death.

6. Student answers will vary. In general, Frost's tone seems detached and neutral: His poem is a commentary on the human tendency to regard the future with uncertainty.

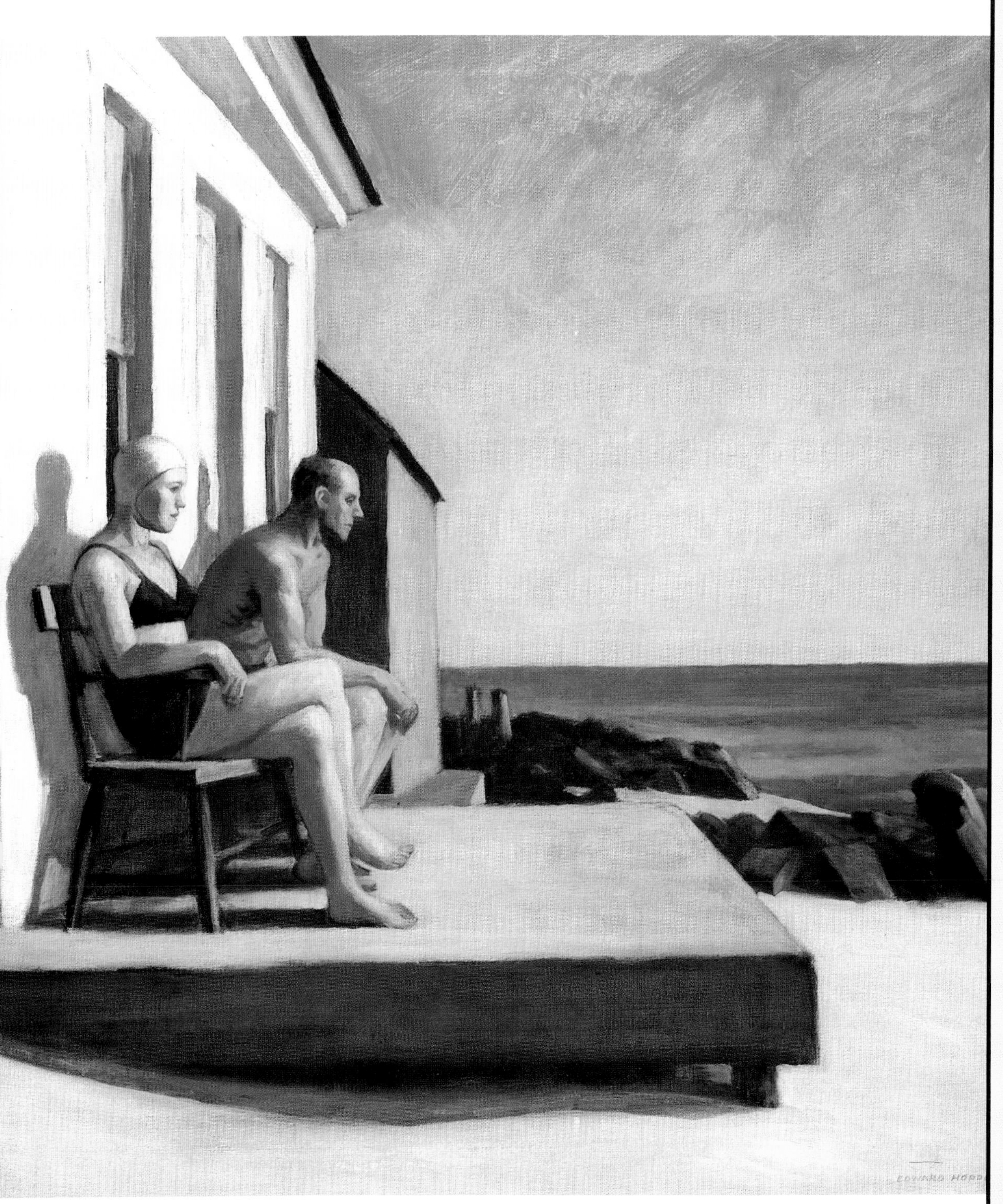

Sea Watchers by Edward Hopper (1952). Oil. Private collection.

SUPPLEMENTARY SUPPORT MATERIALS

1. Vocabulary Activity Worksheet (*CCB*)
2. Review and Response Worksheet: Blank Verse (*CCB*)
3. Selection Test (*CCB*)

DEVELOPING VOCABULARY

The following word from the poem is tested in the Selection Test. (See also Vocabulary Activity Worksheet.)

to subdue

PREPARATION

ESTABLISHING A PURPOSE. The headnote indicates that his poem is a parable. Have students read to learn Frost's message.

A. Interpretation

? How do boys "swing" on birch trees? What might swinging symbolize? (Because the trees are so thin, a boy could climb to the top branches of a young birch, bending the branches downward, and then fling himself outward, letting the branches go as his feet touched the ground. Because the boys are soaring above the earth, one possible symbolic meaning of "swinging" is exercising one's imagination.)

B. Expansion

Bracken is a kind of fern.

C. Symbolism

Is Frost implying something symbolic in the trees' inability to right themselves? (Perhaps Frost feels that exercise is beneficial for both people and trees but that prolonged restraint or tension deforms.)

CLOSURE

Have students write brief summaries, to be shared in class, of the parable in this poem.

As spindly and awkward as a giraffe's legs, the birch trees of Robert Frost's New England have white bark ringed with black. Their trunks are remarkably pliable—a fact which gives this poem its realistic base.

To tell his parable about birch-swinging and to communicate his message, Frost chose blank verse—unrhymed iambic pentameter. The success of the poem depends on how well the poet can maintain the strict beat and, at the same time, sound as if there were no rules to obey but the rhythms of ordinary conversation.

Birches

When I see birches bend to left and right
Across the lines of straighter darker trees,
I like to think some boy's been swinging them.
A But swinging doesn't bend them down to stay
As ice storms do. Often you must have seen them
Loaded with ice a sunny winter morning
After a rain. They click upon themselves
As the breeze rises, and turn many-colored
As the stir cracks and crazes their enamel.
Soon the sun's warmth makes them shed crystal shells
Shattering and avalanching on the snow crust—
Such heaps of broken glass to sweep away
You'd think the inner dome of heaven had fallen.
B They are dragged to the withered bracken by the load,
And they seem not to break; though once they are bowed
C So low for long, they never right themselves:
You may see their trunks arching in the woods
Years afterwards, trailing their leaves on the ground
Like girls on hands and knees that throw their hair
Before them over their heads to dry in the sun.
But I was going to say when Truth broke in
With all her matter of fact about the ice storm,
I should prefer to have some boy bend them
As he went out and in to fetch the cows—
Some boy too far from town to learn baseball,
Whose only play was what he found himself,
Summer or winter, and could play alone.
One by one he subdued his father's trees
By riding them down over and over again
Until he took the stiffness out of them,
And not one but hung limp, not one was left
For him to conquer. He learned all there was
To learn about not launching out too soon
And so not carrying the tree away
Clear to the ground. He always kept his poise
To the top branches, climbing carefully
With the same pains you use to fill a cup
Up to the brim, and even above the brim.
Then he flung outward, feet first, with a swish,

Analyzing the Poem

Identifying Details

1. When he sees the birch trees bend in a wind, the speaker likes to imagine that some boy has been swinging on them.

He realizes that, whereas the trees may bend back after someone swings on them, an ice storm bends them down permanently.

The matter of fact is the realistic description of an actual ice storm.

2. Get away from earth for a while, and then return to it.

Swinging on the birch tree is a metaphor for a temporary absence from the ground (the earth) and then a return to it.

Interpreting Meanings

3. Examples of metaphor: the trees clicking upon themselves (line 7), the stir crazing the tree's enamel (line 9), and the trees shedding crystal shells (line 10). Examples of onomatopoeia include: "stir cracks and crazes" (line 9); "crystal shells" (line 10), "shattering and avalanching on the snow crust" (line 11).

4. At lines 19–20, the bent trunks of the birch trees are compared to girls on their hands and knees, who fling their wet hair over their heads to let it dry in the sun.

At lines 44–47, the speaker compares life to a "pathless wood," and he speaks metaphorically of life's troubles as cobwebs which "burn" and "tickle" in the face.

5. In the exhilaration of physically reaching toward heaven and returning again to earth, the speaker sees a metaphor for his own spiritual needs.

6. Perhaps that we can periodically be refreshed by "breaking away" from routine and reality.

7. On the one hand, the speaker affirms his commitment to life in lines 50–53: He says he does not wish to escape the earth permanently, since it is "the right place for love." But the speaker is sensitive to the bruises and hurts of life, from which we all need occasional escape.

Kicking his way down through the air to the ground.
So was I once myself a swinger of birches.
And so I dream of going back to be.
It's when I'm weary of considerations,
And life is too much like a pathless wood
Where your face burns and tickles with the cobwebs
Broken across it, and one eye is weeping
From a twig's having lashed across it open.
I'd like to get away from earth awhile
And then come back to it and begin over.
May no fate willfully misunderstand me
And half grant what I wish and snatch me away
Not to return. Earth's the right place for love:
I don't know where it's likely to go better.
I'd like to go by climbing a birch tree,
And climb black branches up a snow-white trunk
Toward heaven, till the tree could bear no more,
But dipped its top and set me down again.
That would be good both going and coming back.
One could do worse than be a swinger of birches.

Responding to the Poem

Analyzing the Poem

Identifying Details

1. Describe the scenario that the speaker imagines when he sees birch trees. What realistic objection to his idea does he recognize in lines 4–5? What "matter of fact" does "Truth" break in with in lines 5–20?
2. In lines 48–49, what does the speaker say he would like to do? How does he relate this wish to swinging a birch tree?

Interpreting Meanings

3. Find at least three examples of **metaphor** and **onomatopoeia** in the poem.
4. Two strong **similes** give the poem a richness that is both imaginative and the result of close observation. What are these similes?
5. What does the playful activity of swinging birches seem to **symbolize** in the poem?
6. A **parable** is a short story in which an ordinary event from everyday life is used to teach a much wider moral or religious lesson. Summarize in your own words what you think the moral or message of Frost's parable is.
7. Describe the complex, conflicting attitudes toward life revealed through this parable about birch-swinging.

Writing About the Poem

A Creative Response

1. **Reading Nature.** Write a paragraph or a short poem in which you use an everyday sight or event to comment on a much larger subject.

A Critical Response

2. **Comparing Writings.** You have read how the Puritans and later the Romantics "read" lessons into nature. In a paragraph, tell whether or not you think Frost's poems "Design" and "Birches" are part of this same tradition. Explain why you believe Frost is more like the Puritans or the Romantics in his attitude.
3. **Comparing Attitudes.** Suppose a Puritan writer were to come upon the bent birches. What response might he or she have to the natural scene? Write out that response in a paragraph.
4. **Responding to the Poem.** In a famous remark about the nature of poetry, Frost once said that a poem "begins in delight and ends in wisdom." In a brief essay, show how this applies to "Birches." If you do *not* think it applies, give your reasons. Whichever point of view you take, be sure you define what you think *delight* and *wisdom* mean.

SUPPLEMENTARY SUPPORT MATERIALS
1. Vocabulary Activity Worksheet (*CCB*)
2. Review and Response Worksheet: Visual Imagery in Poetry (*CCB*)
3. Selection Test (*CCB*)

DEVELOPING VOCABULARY
The following words from the poem are tested in the Selection Test. (See also Vocabulary Activity Worksheet.)

boulder	to yelp
abreast	elves

PREPARATION
ESTABLISHING A PURPOSE. There are two seemingly opposite statements in this poem: "Something there is that doesn't love a wall" and "Good fences make good neighbors." Have students read in order to reconcile the two statements in their minds.

A. Title
The title contains a double meaning: the poem is about mending a wall, and the wall itself is something that mends the relationship between neighbors. Elicit the perception, while students look at the photograph on page 661, that a wall is a kind of stitch or seam that looks as if it were repairing a wound in the earth.

B. Responding
? What is it that doesn't love a wall? (The processes of nature damage the wall. Also, the human urge for fellowship dislikes the idea of separation.)

C. Expansion
"On a day" means "one day."

D. Connections
Lines 16–22 show these grown farmers as boyishly playful. Elicit a comparison with the speaker's wish to be a boy in "Birches." (The boy in "Birches" rides them and kicks his way down through the air. The farmers here think of stones as balls.)

New Englanders and other people who live in cold climates are familiar with the way the ground heaves when it freezes. This annual occurrence dislocates stone walls and fences, cracks pavements, and squeezes underground stones and boulders out onto the landscape. This natural phenomenon is caused by the expansion of freezing water in the soil. Frost uses it as the starting point for "Mending Wall." Stop after you've read the first four lines of the poem; think about those lines, and describe the visual subject of the poem up to that point.

Mending Wall

Something there is that doesn't love a wall,
That sends the frozen-ground-swell under it
And spills the upper boulders in the sun,
And makes gaps even two can pass abreast.
The work of hunters is another thing:
I have come after them and made repair
Where they have left not one stone on a stone,
But they would have the rabbit out of hiding,
To please the yelping dogs. The gaps I mean,
No one has seen them made or heard them made,
But at spring mending time we find them there.
I let my neighbor know beyond the hill;
And on a day we meet to walk the line
And set the wall between us once again.
We keep the wall between us as we go.
To each the boulders that have fallen to each.
And some are loaves and some so nearly balls
We have to use a spell to make them balance:
"Stay where you are until our backs are turned!"
We wear our fingers rough with handling them.
Oh, just another kind of outdoor game,
One on a side. It comes to little more:
There where it is we do not need the wall:
He is all pine and I am apple orchard.
My apple trees will never get across
And eat the cones under his pines, I tell him.
He only says, "Good fences make good neighbors."
Spring is the mischief in me, and I wonder
If I could put a notion in his head:
"*Why* do they make good neighbors? Isn't it
Where there are cows? But here there are no cows.
Before I built a wall I'd ask to know
What I was walling in or walling out,
And to whom I was like to give offense.
Something there is that doesn't love a wall,
That wants it down." I could say "Elves" to him,
But it's not elves exactly, and I'd rather

Closure

Have students write two or three sentences, to be shared in class, in which they summarize the symbolism of the wall.

Analyzing the Poem

Identifying Details

1. The speaker observes nature's tendency to force up roots and boulders to disturb the walls that human beings construct on their land. Symbolically, the speaker may be referring to the human tendency to resent or minimize the importance of barriers between people.

The speaker says that hunters often destroy walls.

2. The speaker and his neighbor each walk down their respective sides of the wall, picking up and restoring the boulders that have fallen on their property.

The speaker does not take the wall's rebuilding seriously because he sees no need for a physical barrier between his property and that of his neighbor; the neighbor raises the pine trees, while the *(Answers continue on next page.)*

A

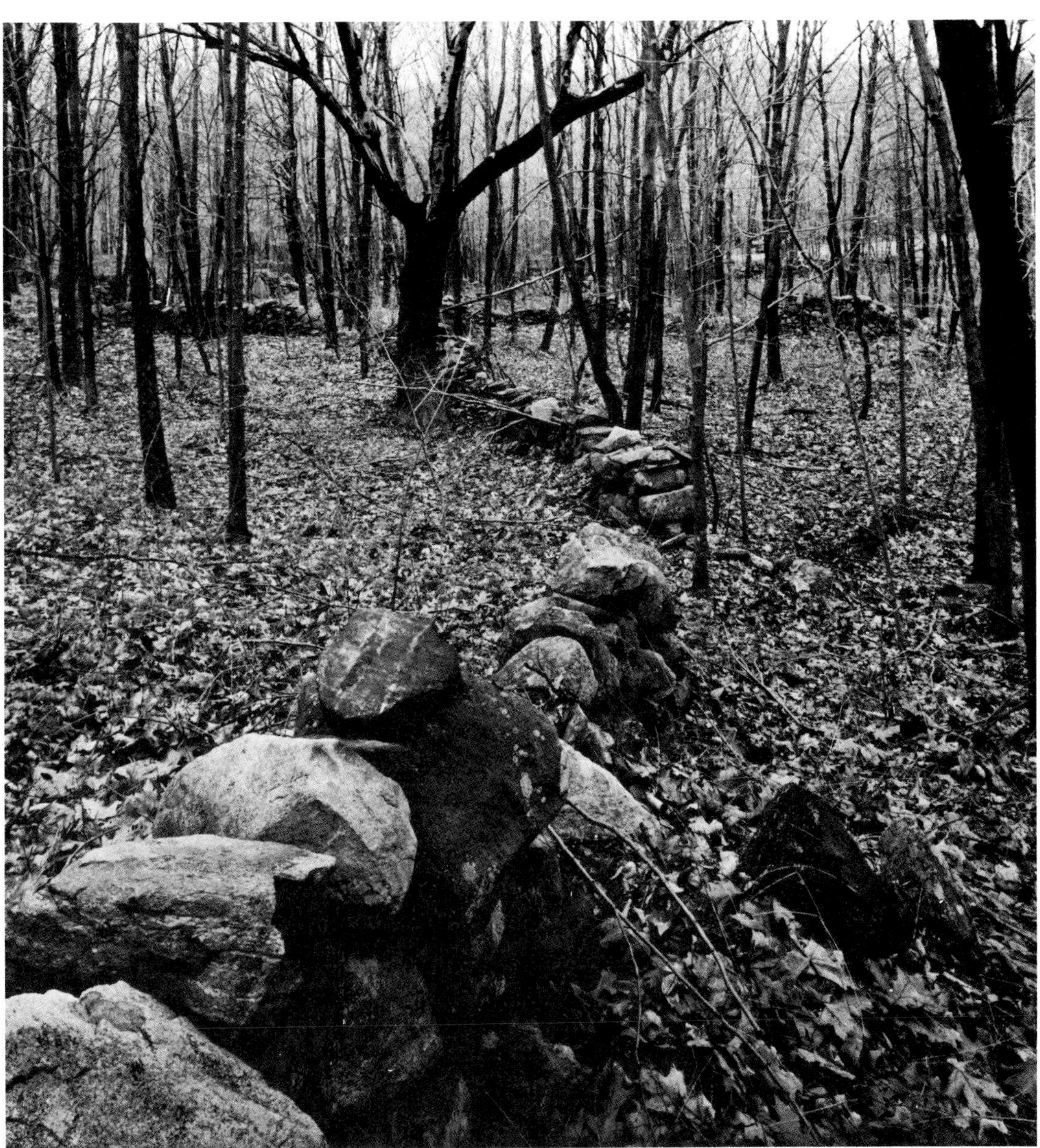

He said it for himself. I see him there,
Bringing a stone grasped firmly by the top
B In each hand, like an old-stone savage armed.
He moves in darkness as it seems to me,
Not of woods only and the shade of trees.
He will not go behind his father's saying,
C And he likes having thought of it so well
He says again, "Good fences make good neighbors."

A. Humanities Connection: Responding to the Photograph
Note the size of the stones: it was not an easy task to move them.

? What kind of feeling does this kind of landscape with its sinuous wall, evoke in us, as opposed to other landscapes—say, an open range with a barbed wire fence, or an urban lot with a chain-link fence, or a suburban tract with straight wooden fences? (Students may suggest that it seems primitive—more relevant to basic human feelings.)

B. Expansion
An "old-stone savage" is a Paleolithic human being.

C. Characterization
Discuss the characterization in these lines. Note the irony that the man is incapable of going past his father's teaching yet is as delighted with it as if it were his own.

(*Continued from previous page.*)
speaker owns an apple orchard. Even without a wall, the two different species of trees will never interfere with each other.
3. The speaker says that, before he built a wall, he would like to know what he was walling in and walling out, and to whom he was likely to give offense.
4. The reference to the mischievous sprites of mythology suits the speaker's quizzical sense of humor.
5. The saying came from the neighbor's father.

Interpreting Meanings

6. The speaker seems open, curious, and playful. His neighbor seems taciturn, reserved, and conservative.
7. The speaker seems to long for emotional common ground with his neighbor: He would like the neighbor to share his own sense of humor.
8. The speaker only hints at the answer, but the comparison mentioning an "old-stone savage armed" in line 40 suggests that the speaker thinks of his neighbor as narrow-minded and primitive. Perhaps he refers to a spiritual or emotional "dark-
(*Answers continue in left-hand column.*)

(*Continued from top.*)
ness," which may have blinded his neighbor to the virtues and pleasures of friendship.
9. The wall may symbolize the barriers which human beings erect between themselves and their fellows.
10. Perhaps he uses the wall-mending as an excuse to find companionship with his neighbor.
11. Student answers will vary. Many students will suggest that the speaker is in greater harmony with nature, since he seems sympathetic and observant.
12. Students may support either of these alternatives. The poet seems intentionally to have left the meaning of this repetition ambiguous.
13. Some students will say that fences separate people. Others will say that establishing property lines prevents arguments.

Responding to the Poem

Analyzing the Poem

Identifying Details

1. What makes the speaker say that "something" doesn't love a wall? Besides this "something," who else sometimes knocks down walls?
2. Describe what is happening in lines 13–16. According to the speaker, why is rebuilding the wall merely a game (lines 23–26)?
3. What question does the speaker think should be settled before building a wall, according to lines 32–34?
4. Why would the speaker say "Elves" (line 36)?
5. From whom did the neighbor get his saying "Good fences make good neighbors"?

Interpreting Meanings

6. In lines 23–27, what two different personality types or temperaments might be dramatized?
7. Why do you think the speaker would rather his neighbor said "Elves" (lines 37–38)?
8. The speaker says in lines 41–42 that the neighboring farmer moves in a "darkness" that is "not of woods only and the shade of trees." What else might this darkness be? Explain the significance of the **simile** in line 40.
9. What might the wall **symbolize**? In your view, what philosophies about human social relations does the poem explore?
10. How do you explain the fact that the man who doesn't see the need for a wall is the one who, every spring, is the first to call upon his neighbor and so make sure the wall is rebuilt? Might he want something more from his neighbor than merely a hand with repair work?
11. Which of these two men is in greater harmony with nature, in your opinion? Why do you think so?
12. When the speaker repeats his neighbor's statement in the poem's last line, does he mean to emphasize his neighbor's stubbornness? Or does he somewhat reluctantly mean to recognize that there's wisdom in the statement?
13. Do *you* believe that "good fences make good neighbors"? Why or why not?

Writing About the Poem

A Creative Response

1. **Changing the Poem's Voice.** Let the neighbor give his answer to this speaker's musings on the purpose of the wall.

A Critical Response

2. **Comparing Poems.** Do you think this poem has anything in common with Dickinson's "The soul selects her own society" (page 357)? Answer this question in a paragraph.

SUPPLEMENTARY SUPPORT MATERIALS

1. Review and Response Worksheet: Personification and Theme in Poetry (*CCB*)
2. Selection Test (*CCB*)
3. Audiocassette recording

PREPARATION

ESTABLISHING A PURPOSE. As the headnote indicates, this poem is the poet's vision of an event that is the opposite of creation. As students read, have them look for images that describe this event.

CLOSURE

Have individual students list the images that create the chilling effect of the poem.

ANALYZING THE POEM

Identifying Details

1. Waves looking over others in line 2, waves thinking in lines 3–4, clouds like locks of hair on a person's head in lines 5–6.

In the Bible, when God creates the world, He says "Let there be light." And after each stage of creation, we read "and God saw that it was good."

Keep these ideas in mind as you read Frost's vision of an event that is the opposite of creation.

Once by the Pacific

The shattered water made a misty din.
Great waves looked over others coming in,
And thought of doing something to the shore
That water never did to land before.
The clouds were low and hairy in the skies,
Like locks blown forward in the gleam of eyes.
You could not tell, and yet it looked as if
The shore was lucky in being backed by cliff,
The cliff in being backed by continent;
It looked as if a night of dark intent
Was coming, and not only a night, an age.
Someone had better be prepared for rage.
There would be more than ocean water broken
Before God's last *Put out the Light* was spoken.

Responding to the Poem

Analyzing the Poem

Identifying Details

1. Identify at least three examples of **personification** in the poem.

Interpreting Meanings

2. What does the scene remind the speaker of?
3. Explain what you think the speaker means by "a night of dark intent . . . not only a night, an age" (lines 10–11). Whose "intent" is he referring to?
4. Who do you think is the "someone" who "had better be prepared for rage" (line 12)? Whose "rage"?
5. Besides ocean water, what else might be "broken" during that rage?
6. *"Put out the light"* is something anyone might say on an ordinary evening at home. How does the use of this casual, domestic phrase make the poem's message even more chilling? What would you say that message is?
7. The poem's **title** suggests that Frost is describing a scene he once saw as he gazed at the Pacific Ocean. What larger "moment" might this scene **symbolize**?
8. Do you view this poem as a warning? Or do you think Frost is just expressing a certain philosophy of life? Explain what the warning might be, or discuss the philosophy.

Writing About the Poem

A Critical Response

Comparing Poems. In a brief essay, compare "Once by the Pacific" to Whitman's poem called "On the Beach at Night" (see page 343). Before you write, gather your data in a chart like the one following. Your essay does not have to include all the items in the chart.

	Whitman	Frost
Message in poem		
Use of symbols		
Tone		
Use of rhymes and rhythms		
Use of imagery		

Interpreting Meanings

2. Some future disaster or calamity.
3. These phrases seem to portend the advent of some dreadful calamity.
   Perhaps the speaker is referring to nature or to God.
4. Perhaps the speaker means "mankind" in general.
   Perhaps a metaphorical rage of natural forces.
5. Homes, lives, cities, the human species itself.
6. The informality of the phrase contrasts with the poetic context.
   Possibly the extinction of humanity and the world.
7. Perhaps the end of the world.
8. The "rage" might be God's or it might be the rage of people.

Supplementary Support Materials
1. Vocabulary Activity Worksheet (*CCB*)
2. Review and Response Worksheet: The Dramatic Lyric (*CCB*)
3. Selection Test (*CCB*)

Developing Vocabulary
The following words from the poem are tested in the Selection Test. (See also Vocabulary Activity Worksheet.)

beholden   pasture
to coax   to pique

Preparation
Establishing a Purpose. Have students read to learn the personalities of the hired man, the husband, and the wife. Since the hired man does not speak in the poem, students should be alert to what the husband and wife say about him.

A. Humanities Connection: Responding to the Fine Art
Andrew Wyeth (b. 1917) is probably the most famous in the three-generation family of artists that also includes N. C. Wyeth (pages 127 and 205) and Jamie Wyeth (page 989). Andrew Wyeth's work also appears on page 179 of this text.
? Look at the man in the painting and try to imagine what he is thinking about and what his life has been like. Do you think that we can tell anything about a person's character or experiences by looking at his or her face? (Very often a person's habitual expression will reveal a sad or contented nature.)

This poem is a dramatic lyric—dramatic because it presents characters who speak in voices assigned to them by the poet, lyric because it is less concerned with describing events and actions than it is with revealing feelings. Most of the poem is a dialogue in blank verse. Its main character never speaks for himself, yet his presence dominates the poem. By the last line, we have heard as much about him as we need in order to understand his background, habits, and attitudes. And in gradually coming to know the "hired man," we also come to know the personalities of the husband and wife whose dialogue carries the drama.

Embedded in the poem is one of Frost's most famous sayings, one often quoted by many people who probably have no idea where it comes from:

> **"Home is the place where, when you have to go there,**
> **They have to take you in."**

The Death of the Hired Man

A

Oil Lamp by Andrew Wyeth (1945). Oil.

Mary sat musing on the lamp flame at the table,
Waiting for Warren. When she heard his step,
She ran on tiptoe down the darkened passage
To meet him in the doorway with the news
And put him on his guard. "Silas is back."
A She pushed him outward with her through the door
And shut it after her. "Be kind," she said.
She took the market things from Warren's arms
And set them on the porch, then drew him down
To sit beside her on the wooden steps.

B "When was I ever anything but kind to him?
But I'll not have the fellow back," he said.
"I told him so last haying, didn't I?
If he left then, I said, that ended it.
What good is he? Who else will harbor him
At his age for the little he can do?
What help he is there's no depending on.
Off he goes always when I need him most.
He thinks he ought to earn a little pay,
Enough at least to buy tobacco with,
So he won't have to beg and be beholden.
'All right,' I say, 'I can't afford to pay
Any fixed wages, though I wish I could.'
'Someone else can.' 'Then someone else will have to.'
I shouldn't mind his bettering himself
If that was what it was. You can be certain,
When he begins like that, there's someone at him
Trying to coax him off with pocket money—
In haying time, when any help is scarce.
In winter he comes back to us. I'm done."

"Sh! not so loud: He'll hear you," Mary said.

"I want him to: He'll have to soon or late."

"He's worn out. He's asleep beside the stove.
When I came up from Rowe's I found him here,
Huddled against the barn door fast asleep,
A miserable sight, and frightening, too—
You needn't smile—I didn't recognize him—
I wasn't looking for him—and he's changed.
Wait till you see."

C "Where did you say he'd been?"

"He didn't say. I dragged him to the house,
And gave him tea and tried to make him smoke.
I tried to make him talk about his travels.
Nothing would do: He just kept nodding off."

A. Characterization/Blank Verse After the first ten lines, you might stop and ask, Who are Mary and Warren? Who is Silas? At this point the identities remain somewhat mysterious—thus enhancing the drama—but they can be guessed from context clues such as the poem's title.

See Analyzing Language and Style, page 669, question 1.

B. Responding ? Do Mary and Warren seem to have two different definitions of *kindness?* What are they? (Mary offers to take care of Silas; Warren offers him work, but without regular pay.)

C. Responding ? What are your feelings about Mary and Warren so far? (She seems warmer and softer.)

A. Tone
How would you describe Warren's tone in this speech? (Cynical, skeptical, knowing)

B. Characterization
The anecdote about Harold Wilson, who had worked at the farm four summers previously and gone on to college and teaching, shows that Silas has lost touch with reality.

C. Responding
How does this speech of Mary's make you feel? (It is likely to arouse sympathy both for Silas and for Mary.)
What does the speech reveal about Silas's ability to communicate in the modern world? (The fact that Silas cannot understand that someone would study Latin for enjoyment and the fact that Silas believes in finding water with a "hazel prong" indicate that he is not at home in the modern world.)

"What did he say? Did he say anything?"

"But little."

"Anything? Mary, confess
A He said he'd come to ditch the meadow for me."

"Warren!"

"But did he? I just want to know."

"Of course he did. What would you have him say?
Surely you wouldn't grudge the poor old man
Some humble way to save his self-respect.
He added, if you really care to know,
He meant to clear the upper pasture, too.
That sounds like something you have heard before?
Warren, I wish you could have heard the way
He jumbled everything. I stopped to look
Two or three times—he made me feel so queer—
To see if he was talking in his sleep.
He ran on Harold Wilson—you remember—
B The boy you had in haying four years since.
He's finished school, and teaching in his college.
Silas declares you'll have to get him back.
He says they two will make a team for work:
Between them they will lay this farm as smooth!
The way he mixed that in with other things.
He thinks young Wilson a likely lad, though daft
On education—you know how they fought
All through July under the blazing sun,
Silas up on the cart to build the load,
Harold along beside to pitch it on."

"Yes, I took care to keep well out of earshot."

"Well, those days trouble Silas like a dream.
You wouldn't think they would. How some things linger!
Harold's young college-boy's assurance piqued him.
After so many years he still keeps finding
Good arguments he sees he might have used.
I sympathize. I know just how he feels
To think of the right thing to say too late.
Harold's associated in his mind with Latin.
C He asked me what I thought of Harold's saying
He studied Latin, like the violin,
Because he liked it—that an argument!
He said he couldn't make the boy believe
He could find water with a hazel prong—
Which showed how much good school had ever done him.
He wanted to go over that. But most of all
He thinks if he could have another chance
To teach him how to build a load of hay——"

Literature and Language: Punctuating Dialogue
Almost all of this poem is a dialogue between Mary and Warren. Ask students to notice how little is not (lines 1–10, 103–110, 121–123, 162–165).

Frost uses only a few dialogue tags to identify the speakers. Ask students how they can keep track of who is talking. Have them find examples of each of the following:

1. A line of space when the speaker changes
2. Direct address, mentioning the name of the person being spoken to (as in lines 45 and 47)
3. A direct response to the other speaker (as in line 32)

Frost also uses punctuation to help us follow who is talking. Each speaker's words are enclosed in quotation marks, and a final quotation mark signals the end of one person's speech.

Have students use **Grammar, Usage, and Mechanics: A Reference Guide** to review the rules for punctuating dialogue. Then ask them to work in small groups to write and punctuate some lines of dialogue related to the poem. They may try the dialogue Mary had with Silas when she found him asleep by the barn.

A
"I know, that's Silas' one accomplishment.
He bundles every forkful in its place,
And tags and numbers it for future reference,
So he can find and easily dislodge it
In the unloading. Silas does that well.
He takes it out in bunches like big birds' nests.
You never see him standing on the hay
He's trying to lift, straining to lift himself."

"He thinks if he could teach him that, he'd be
Some good perhaps to someone in the world.
He hates to see a boy the fool of books.
Poor Silas, so concerned for other folk,
And nothing to look backward to with pride,
And nothing to look forward to with hope,
So now and never any different."

Part of a moon was falling down the west,
Dragging the whole sky with it to the hills.
Its light poured softly in her lap. She saw it
And spread her apron to it. She put out her hand
Among the harplike morning-glory strings,
Taut with the dew from garden bed to eaves,
As if she played unheard some tenderness
That wrought on him beside her in the night.
"Warren," she said, "he has come home to die:
You needn't be afraid he'll leave you this time."

"Home," he mocked gently.

"Yes, what else but home?
It all depends on what you mean by home.
Of course he's nothing to us, anymore
Than was the hound that came a stranger to us
Out of the woods, worn out upon the trail."

B
"Home is the place where, when you have to go there,
They have to take you in."

"I should have called it
Something you somehow haven't to deserve."

Warren leaned out and took a step or two,
Picked up a little stick, and brought it back
And broke it in his hand and tossed it by.
"Silas has better claim on us you think
Than on his brother? Thirteen little miles
As the road winds would bring him to his door.
Silas has walked that far no doubt today.
Why doesn't he go there? His brother's rich,
A somebody—director in the bank."

A. Expansion
Elicit the response that there is something genuinely admirable, but also pathetic, in Silas's sole lifelong accomplishment: neat hay-loading.

Comment From A Critic
Lines 103–110 are a particularly lovely description. Critic William H. Pritchard points out that even in his most simple farm narratives, like "The Death of the Hired Man," Frost has passages of more elevated, lyrical style, possibly to relieve the monotony of being entirely colloquial.

B. Expansion
Lines 118–120 contain the two famous definitions of "home." (See Analyzing the Poem, question 8, page 669.) Aside from the duty-mercy dichotomy, what other dichotomies might the two definitions represent? (Conservative-liberal and male-female were two that Frost himself thought of, according to Lawrance Thompson, his biographer.)

Analyzing The Poem
Identifying Details

1. The basic problem facing the three characters is what to do with Silas, now that he wants to return to work.

2. Warren is reluctant to hire him because, last haying season, Silas asked for fixed wages and then left Warren unexpectedly, just when Warren needed him the most.

3. Silas is piqued that the lad is so wrapped up in education. Harold Wilson studies Latin and is the "fool of books," in Silas's opinion. Silas regrets that he never succeeded in convincing Harold that he could find water with a hazel prong.

Silas wishes he could show Harold how to build a load of hay, so that the boy could "be some good perhaps to someone in the world."

4. Mary suggests that Silas is too proud to call on his brother for help.

5. Remarks that indicate Mary's tenderness for Silas occur in line 7 ("Be kind"), line 31 ("Sh! not so loud: he'll hear you"), lines 49–50 ("Surely you wouldn't grudge the poor old man / Some humble way to save his self-respect"), line 76 ("I sympathize"), line 99 ("Poor Silas, so con-

A. Expansion (Less Challenging) At this point you might ask the class to paraphrase the reasons why Silas hasn't gone to his brother for help.

B. Predicting an Outcome
? What do you think will happen when Warren looks in on Silas? (If students have read the poem at home, ask whether they felt suspense at this point.)

C. Attitude
? What attitude does the poet himself seem to take toward Mary in these lines? (Affection, possibly tinged with condescension)

D. Responding
? Did you like the characters? Did you like the poem? To what extent do you think these two likings depend on each other? What do you think happens next? Describe a possible sequel to this poem.

Closure
Have students suggest words and phrases that characterize the hired man, Mary, and Warren.

"He never told us that."

"We know it, though."

"I think his brother ought to help, of course.
I'll see to that if there is need. He ought of right
To take him in, and might be willing to—
He may be better than appearances.
But have some pity on Silas. Do you think
If he had any pride in claiming kin
Or anything he looked for from his brother,
He'd keep so still about him all this time?"

"I wonder what's between them."
"I can tell you.
Silas is what he is—we wouldn't mind him—
But just the kind that kinsfolk can't abide.
He never did a thing so very bad.
He don't know why he isn't quite as good
As anybody. Worthless though he is,
He won't be made ashamed to please his brother."

"*I* can't think Si ever hurt anyone."

"No, but he hurt my heart the way he lay
And rolled his old head on that sharp-edged chairback.
He wouldn't let me put him on the lounge.
You must go in and see what you can do.
I made the bed up for him there tonight.
You'll be surprised at him—how much he's broken.
His working days are done; I'm sure of it."

"I'd not be in a hurry to say that."

"I haven't been. Go, look, see for yourself.
But, Warren, please remember how it is:
He's come to help you ditch the meadow.
He has a plan. You mustn't laugh at him.
He may not speak of it, and then he may.
I'll sit and see if that small sailing cloud
Will hit or miss the moon."

It hit the moon.
Then there were three there, making a dim row,
The moon, the little silver cloud, and she.

Warren returned—too soon, it seemed to her—
Slipped to her side, caught up her hand and waited.

"Warren?" she questioned.

"Dead," was all he answered.

cerned for other folk"), and line 158 ("You mustn't laugh at him").

Interpreting Meanings

6. Whereas Mary sees Silas as a human being who has "come home to die," Warren at first regards him as an embarrassing nuisance. But as the dialogue continues, Warren is forced to admit that Silas has never harmed anyone.

On the other hand, Warren regards Silas as eccentric and undependable, and he seems put off by Mary's insistence that he take the old man in. On the other hand, Warren admits that Silas is skilled at his job and is basically harmless.

7. These lines describe the setting moon, whose light falls on Mary's apron in her lap. Mary extends her hand to the morning glories, as if she plays on a stringed instrument of "tenderness" as she tries to persuade her husband to be kind to Silas.

The passage shows Mary's innate qualities of pity, understanding, tenderness, and tact.

8. At line 118, Warren defines "home" in a limited, rather negative way—as the place where, "when you have to go there, they have to take you in." In the following lines, Mary defines the concept of "home" in a more positive, giving fashion—as "something you somehow haven't to deserve." Warren implies that Silas's relatives have a duty to accept him. Mary asserts that duty and merit should be irrelevant to Silas's treatment at home, where he should be accepted out of love, with no implications that his comparative failure in life has brought him shame. Most students will agree with the critic's observation.

9. Student answers will vary.

Most students will agree that either of these answers would have been anticlimactic.

10. Students who accept this idea would also have to consider whether or not Silas is ultimately free since he has come back for help.

11. Perhaps the need to respect and feel compassion for others. See also the important comment in question 10.

12. Students' answers will vary.

Responding to the Poem

Analyzing the Poem

Identifying Details

1. Describe the basic problem facing Warren, Mary, and Silas.
2. Why is Warren reluctant to hire Silas?
3. What is Silas's attitude toward Harold Wilson, the college boy about whom he reminisces? What does he wish he could teach the boy, and why?
4. What explanation does Mary suggest for the fact that Silas never talks about his brother?
5. Identify four remarks that reveal Mary's tenderness for Silas.

Interpreting Meanings

6. Describe how Warren's attitude toward Silas differs from Mary's. Do you think Warren's feelings about Silas are mixed? Give evidence from the poem to support your opinion.
7. After a quick narrative introduction, dialogue carries the story until it is more than half told. The narrator reenters in line 103. Identify the details in lines 103–110 that create a vivid **image** of the **setting.** Besides contributing to atmosphere, what does this passage tell us about Mary's **character**?
8. Find the two definitions of "home" offered in the poem. One critic has said that one definition is based on law and duty, the other on mercy. Which is which, and do you agree with the critic's observation? Which definition do you favor?
9. When the conclusion of a play, story, or poem seems to be "inevitable," we take a kind of satisfaction in knowing that no other ending would do. Does the conclusion of this poem strike you as inevitable? Why or why not? What would your feelings have been if, instead of "Dead" in answer to Mary's question, Warren had answered "Asleep," or "Sharpening his scythe"?
10. Consider this possible **irony** in the poem: Warren and Mary, able to hire Silas and to become controlling factors in his life, are here themselves controlled by Silas's independence. Do you think the poet is pointing out that, in the long run, it is the free spirit who has the power to dominate those who "live by the rules"? Do you think this idea is true or false? Explain your answer.
11. State in your own words the poem's **message.** Do you think this message has any particular importance in today's world?
12. How did you feel about each of the three characters in this poem?

Writing About the Poem

A Creative Response

1. **Extending the Poem.** This poem is set in a rural area many years ago. In a paragraph, explain how the basic story told in this poem could be set in contemporary surroundings, with modern characters. You might tell how it could be set in a city, in a rural area, in a suburb, on a modern-day farm, in a migrant-worker camp. Cover these elements of the story: characters, setting, conflict, and resolution.

A Critical Response

2. **Analyzing Characters.** In a three-paragraph essay, analyze the characters of Silas, Mary, and Warren. Consider these elements of characterization: the character's **values**; the character's **conflict,** and the way he or she handles it; the **effect** the character has on others; and any **changes** the character undergoes.

Analyzing Language and Style

Blank Verse

"The poet goes in like a rope skipper to make the most of his opportunities," said Frost in an essay called "The Constant Symbol." "If he trips himself he stops the rope. He is of our stock and has been brought up by ear to choice of two meters, strict iambic and loose iambic (not to count varieties of the latter)." "The Death of the Hired Man" is written in **blank verse,** which is unrhymed iambic pentameter. It is called *blank verse* because the lines do not have end rhymes. *Iambic pentameter* means that there are five iambs to each line; an *iamb* is an unaccented syllable followed by an accented syllable: da DUM; da DUM.

1. Scan the first ten lines and recite them aloud to hear the meter.
2. Look over the poem and find examples of strict iambic and loose iambic meter.
3. Do you think Frost has ever "tripped" himself in this poem?
4. Take ten lines from this poem and rewrite them in the free-verse style of Walt Whitman. (See page 326.) Where will you break the lines? What rearrangement of words will have to be made to break the iambic meter?
5. Look at Frost's comments on free verse in the extract from an interview that follows under "Primary Sources" (page 671). What is *your* opinion of Frost's ideas?

A. Expansion
To understand this poem, students must know that Adam and Eve's expulsion from the Garden of Eden and their loss of innocence symbolically represent the loss of innocence of all humankind, and the individual loss of innocence as one passes from childhood.

The ancient Greeks and Romans also had an image of Paradise, the Golden Age, a time of innocent happiness and beauty. Before the Titan Cronus (Saturn in Roman mythology), who reigned over the other Titans, was dethroned by Zeus, he had reigned in a land in which there was no sickness or sorrow, no labor or war, and everything existed in great abundance. The loss of this Golden Age, too, has come to represent the loss of innocence. This equating of "gold" or "golden" with innocence is echoed in Dylan Thomas's poem "Fern Hill," when the young speaker describes himself in his innocent youth as "golden."

SUPPLEMENTARY SUPPORT MATERIALS
1. Review and Response Worksheet: Sound Effects (*CCB*)
2. Selection Test (*CCB*)
3. Audiocassette recording

PREPARATION
ESTABLISHING A PURPOSE. As students read, ask them to determine what "Eden" and "gold" symbolize.

To understand this little lyric, be sure you know two important accounts: that of the loss of Eden in Genesis, and, in Greek mythology, that of the loss of the Golden Age. When you first read the title of the poem, what do you think it's going to be about?

A Nothing Gold Can Stay

Nature's first green is gold,
Her hardest hue to hold.
Her early leaf's a flower;
But only so an hour.
Then leaf subsides to leaf.
So Eden sank to grief,
So dawn goes down to day.
Nothing gold can stay.

Responding to the Poem

Analyzing the Poem

Identifying Details

1. Identify four specific things in the poem that cannot, or did not, "stay."

Interpreting Meanings

2. Think of what the very first buds of leaves look like in spring, and explain what line 1 means.
3. Explain the natural process described in line 5.
4. What Biblical event is **alluded** to in line 6? What state of mind or situation might "Eden" **symbolize** here?
5. "Gold' as used here is not the precious metal, but an idea. What different ideas might "gold" **symbolize**? Why can't "gold" stay—or do you disagree?
6. Show how its **rhymes** and **rhythm** contribute to this poem's compactness and completeness. How do **alliteration, slant rhyme,** and other **sound echoes** also contribute to the poem's tightly woven effect?
7. How would you describe the speaker's **tone**?

Writing About the Poem

A Creative Response

1. **Paraphrasing.** This poem is composed of only forty words. Try to paraphrase it as briefly as possible. Then read your paraphrase to see if you have left out anything important. Can you paraphrase it in fewer than forty words and still account for every idea?

A Critical Response

2. **Comparing Poems.** In a paragraph, tell how this poem is similar to or different from "Eldorado" by Edgar Allan Poe (page 248) or "Miniver Cheevy" by Edwin Arlington Robinson (page 636). Consider these elements of the poem:

   a. Use of gold as an image and symbol
   b. Message
   c. Tone
   d. Poetic form and technique

Closure
Have students paraphrase the poem orally.

Analyzing the Poem
Identifying Details
1. They are: nature's "first green" (line 1), the flower of nature's "early leaf" (line 3), the paradise of Eden (line 6), and the golden dawn (line 7).

Interpreting Meanings
2. The first buds of leaves in spring often have a gold tinge: the first line means that the "green" of the leaves starts in "gold" buds.
3. The first few leaves of spring give way to a profusion of leaves in summer.
4. Line 6 refers to the Biblical account of humanity's loss of Eden through Adam and Eve's sins of disobedience.

Eden may symbolize a blissful, untroubled, "golden" existence.
5. Among the different ideas that students may suggest are preciousness, perfection, value, nature's beauty, and wealth (both in its material and spiritual aspects).

The speaker of the poem implies that "gold"—as an idea—is transient due to the nature of things. The seasons wax and wane; humans lost the paradise of Eden; day is followed by night.

Students should be encouraged to discuss the main idea of the poem, and to state whether or not they agree, and why.
6. Examples of alliteration include: "green is gold" (line 1), "her hardest hue to hold" (line 2), "dawn goes down to day" (line 7). Slant rhyme: "dawn" and "down" (line 7). Other sound echoes: "only so" (line 4), "Eden . . . grief" (line 6).
7. The tone seems bittersweet or melancholy. Encourage students to defend their responses.

A. Connections
You may want students to look back at the explanatory material on free verse (page 333).

Primary Sources

"I must have the pulse beat of rhythm . . ."

These comments are from an interview held on October 21, 1923, with *New York Times* reporter Rose C. Feld. A month after the interview, Frost won his first Pulitzer Prize. Here, Frost has been talking about American poetry.

". . . We're still a bit afraid. America, for instance, was afraid to accept Walt Whitman when he first sang the songs of democracy. His influence on American poetry began to be felt only after the French had hailed him as a great writer, a literary revolutionist. Our own poet had to be imported from France before we were sure of his strength.

"Today almost every man who writes poetry confesses his debt to Whitman. Many have gone very much further than Whitman would have traveled with them. They are the people who believe in wide straddling.

"I, myself, as I said before, don't like it for myself. I do not write free verse; I write blank verse. I must have the pulse beat of rhythm, I like to hear it beating under the things I write.

"That doesn't mean I do not like to read a bit of free verse occasionally. I do. It sometimes succeeds in painting a picture that is very clear and startling. It's as good as something created momentarily for its sudden startling effect; it hasn't the qualities, however, of something lastingly beautiful. A

"And sometimes my objection to it is that it's a pose. It's not honest. When a man sets out consciously to tear up forms and rhythms and measures, then he is not interested in giving you poetry. He just wants to perform; he wants to show you his tricks. He will get an effect; nobody will deny that, but it is not a harmonious effect.

"Sometimes it strikes me that the free-verse people got their idea from incorrect proof sheets. I have had stuff come from the printers with lines half left out or positions changed about. I read the poems as they stood, distorted and half finished, and I confess I get a rather pleasant sensation from them. They make a sort of nightmarish half-sense."

—Robert Frost

A. Connections
Robert Frost was a manuscript reader for Henry Holt and Company, Frost's own publisher, when Ransom sent his first book of poems there. Frost read it and recommended it for publication, and it was accepted. Ransom's early work shows the influence of Frost in its use of simple, conversational language intensified by rhythm and rhyme. In fact, one of these early poems, "Grace," is about the death of a hired man.

John Crowe Ransom (1888–1974)

John Crowe Ransom, the most influential and intellectually elegant conservative among twentieth-century American poets, was born of Scots-Irish parents in Pulaski, Tennessee. The son of a minister, he attended Vanderbilt University, then became a Rhodes Scholar at Oxford University in England. He returned to Tennessee, and began an illustrious teaching career at Vanderbilt that lasted for more than twenty years. During this stage of his life, his most notable contribution to American writing, aside from his poetry, was his success in bringing together a group of Southern writers. This group was determined to assert Southern cultural values, and it idealized a genteel, agrarian way of life which seemed to offer a more stable environment than Northern industrialism.

The group came to be called the "Fugitives," after the title of a literary magazine that Ransom edited. Its members, who included Allen Tate, Robert Penn Warren, and Donald Davidson, were talented and technically proficient. Their poetry was noted for its combination of intellectual wit and the fatalism associated with Greek tragedy; for a time, their works were a prominent part of the literary scene.

In 1937, Ransom resigned from Vanderbilt to teach at Kenyon College in Ohio. There he founded one of the most famous of all literary magazines, *The Kenyon Review.* By this time, the Fugitives were no longer together as a group, and the philosophy they supported had come to seem reactionary, partly as a result of the growing power of fascism abroad.

Nevertheless, the Fugitives had left an important legacy to critics and poets. They believed that poetry was less a means of self-expression than a rigorous craft to be learned and perfected; the poet should strive for the creation of artfully balanced structures, which readers might contemplate in the same way that art connoisseurs might study a vase or a painting.

The influence of Fugitive doctrine led to the literary development known as the New Criticism, whose main exemplars were Robert Penn Warren, Cleanth Brooks, Yvor Winters, Kenneth Burke, R. P. Blackmur, and Ransom himself. Assistance abroad came from T. S. Eliot (page 740), who, though never a member of the group, was sympathetic for a time to its aims.

The New Critics had an immense influence on the teaching and appreciation of literature in the 1940's and 1950's. They held that each literary work was a world unto itself; it should be analyzed for its technical conventions and use of imagery, without regard for the "fallacies" of biographical criticism. Although the New Critics' focus on language was praiseworthy, their rejection of the importance of biographical and psychological factors to an author's work has come to be regarded as too extreme.

During Ransom's years at Kenyon, scores of poets, many of whom would become well-known, benefited from his scholarship as well as from the wit and wisdom that mark both his poetry and his criticism. Among Ransom's students were Robert Lowell, Randall Jarrell, and James Wright. All of these poets would find larger audiences than their teacher, as changing times made Ransom's work seem like the antique echo of another age. But, in a period when writing was subject to every kind of barbarous incursion, no one man did more than Ransom to keep alive the delicacy, beauty, and endless resources of the English language.

SUPPLEMENTARY SUPPORT MATERIALS

1. Vocabulary Activity Worksheet (*CCB*)
2. Review and Response Worksheet: Tone and Theme (*CCB*)
3. Selection Test (*CCB*)

DEVELOPING VOCABULARY

The following words from the poem are tested in the Selection Test. (See also Vocabulary Activity Worksheet.)

to harry   to vex
to scuttle   primly

PREPARATION

ESTABLISHING A PURPOSE. Have students read to answer the questions, What was the little girl like? What are the bells ringing for? Why is the little girl referred to as "John Whiteside's daughter"?

CLOSURE

Have students suggest words and phrases that describe the little girl in life and in death.

At what times in a person's life might bells be rung? Read the first stanza of the poem. Then stop and see if you can tell what kind of bell this title refers to.

Bells for John Whiteside's Daughter

There was such speed in her little body,
And such lightness in her footfall,
It is no wonder her brown study°
Astonishes us all.

Her wars were bruited° in our high window.
We looked among orchard trees and beyond
Where she took arms against her shadow,
Or harried unto the pond

The lazy geese, like a snow cloud
Dripping their snow on the green grass,
Tricking and stopping, sleepy and proud,
Who cried in goose, Alas,

For the tireless heart within the little
Lady with rod that made them rise
From their noon apple-dreams and scuttle
Goose-fashion under the skies!

But now go the bells, and we are ready,
In one house we are sternly stopped
To say we are vexed at her brown study,
Lying so primly propped.

3. **brown study:** state of being lost in deep thought.

5. **bruited** (bro͞ot′əd): reported.

Responding to the Poem

Analyzing the Poem

Identifying Details

1. What characteristics of John Whiteside's daughter make the speaker astonished at her present "brown study"?

Interpreting Meanings

2. What kinds of "wars" might the little girl have carried on? When you "take arms" against your own shadow, what do you do?
3. Identify the **simile** that describes the geese in the third stanza. What is meant by their "snow"?
4. What action of the little girl caused the geese to cry, "Alas"? What additional overtones does this cry take on, given the poem's subject?
5. What *is* the child's "brown study"? What details in the last stanza make clear what has happened to her?
6. In the last stanza, what word does the speaker use to describe people's emotions at the little girl's "brown study"? Why is this word a surprising choice?
7. Point out other words and details that give the poem an almost light **tone.** Do you think this tone suggests a lack of feeling, or does it, in an unsentimental way, convey the speaker's affection and sadness? Give reasons for your opinion.
8. What are the bells ringing for in the last stanza?

ANALYZING THE POEM

Identifying Details

1. Her speed and lightness.

Interpreting Meanings

2. She played with the geese and may also have carried on playful "wars" with siblings or friends.
You chase your shadow.
3. The geese are compared to a cloud.
Their white feathers.
4. She chased them with a rod.
The cry becomes associated with the little girl's death.
5. Her "brown study" is her appearance in death. Details in the last stanza include the funeral bells.
6. The word "vexed" (line 19).
Because a reader might expect a stronger word.
7. Details include: "lightness in her footfall" (line 2) and the bruiting of "wars" (line 5).
8. The child's funeral service.

SUPPLEMENTARY SUPPORT MATERIALS

1. Vocabulary Activity Worksheet (*CCB*)
2. Review and Response Worksheet: Conflict and Theme (*CCB*)
3. Selection Test (*CCB*)

DEVELOPING VOCABULARY

The following words from the poem are tested in the Selection Test. (See also Vocabulary Activity Worksheet.)

sequel	vaunting
venomous	stoical
leering	lintel

PREPARATION

ESTABLISHING A PURPOSE. Have students read to follow the part of a story that the poem presents. As students read, ask them to imagine what happened to cause the parting.

CLOSURE

Have individual students give brief oral paraphrases of the poem.

A. Title

? What does the title tell you about the lovers' future? (They will not reunite.)

B. Responding

? How would a woman in this situation really feel? (Elicit perceptions of the ambivalence implicit in the description.)

C. Expansion

Her actual age is not stated. (See Writing About the Poem, page 675, number 2.)

COMMENT FROM A CRITIC

Critic Louis D. Rubin, Jr., says that Ransom's poems usually center on a division or duality, and that this division is usually between the head and the heart.

Can you find divisions between the head and the heart in these two Ransom poems?

D. Humanities Connection: Responding to the Fine Art

Eastman Johnson (1824–1906), born in Augusta, Maine, was a fashionable society portraitist.

? What "story" is suggested by this painting?

This poem presents the very last part of a story. We will never know that story, yet we can tell that something has gone wrong; that things weren't supposed to end this way; that even as she dispatches her farewell letter, the woman in the case is ambivalent about what she has done. Except that this woman once had a father whose advice she listened to, we know nothing of what might have been a romance—or no more than a courtship.

Parting, Without a Sequel

She has finished and sealed the letter
At last, which he so richly has deserved,
With characters venomous and hatefully
  curved,
And nothing could be better.

But even as she gave it,
Saying to the blue-capped functioner of
  doom,
"Into his hands," she hoped the leering
  groom
Might somewhere lose and leave it.

Then all the blood
Forsook the face. She was too pale for
  tears,
Observing the ruin of her younger years.
She went and stood

Under her father's vaunting oak
Who kept his peace in wind and sun, and
  glistened
Stoical in the rain; to whom she listened
If he spoke.

And now the agitation of the rain
Rasped his sere° leaves, and he talked low
  and gentle,
Reproaching the wan daughter by the lintel;
Ceasing, and beginning again.

Away went the messenger's bicycle,
His serpent's track went up the hill forever.
And all the time she stood there hot as
  fever
And cold as any icicle.

18. **sere:** dry

Day Dreams by Eastman Johnson (1877). Oil on paper board.

Private collection.

ANALYZING THE POEM
Identifying Details
1. She has sent a letter to her sweetheart to break off their relationship.
2. Details revealing the woman's anger include the following: the fact that the man has "richly deserved" the letter (line 2) and the woman's paleness and the mention of the "ruin of her younger years" in the third stanza.

In the second stanza, she hopes that the messenger may lose the letter; in the fourth stanza, she seeks advice from her father's oak tree; in the last stanza, the reference to her as both hot and cold exposes her ambivalence.

Interpreting Meanings
3. He is the messenger who will deliver the letter.

The fact that the messenger "leers" at the woman emphasizes her distaste for both the man and his errand.
4. This hope reflects her conflict: Even as she sends the letter, part of her wishes that she had never written it, or that it might be lost.
5. The tree speaks "low and gentle" (line 18). It reproaches the young woman for her decision.

An oak tree is generally large, sturdy, and shady, making it an apt symbol for the woman's father.
6. The phrase "serpent's track" may connote the venomous hatred of the woman's letter, carried by the messenger on the bicycle.

Students will have various opinions. In one sense, the track goes on "forever" because the decision expressed in the letter is definitive and complete.
7. The heat suggests the intensity of the woman's emotion, whereas the coldness suggests her feelings of apprehension. The two phrases combine to evoke the woman's conflict.
8. The poem ends with the quixotic rhyme of "bicycle" and "icicle."

Student responses will vary. The ingenious, amusing rhyme creates a note of detachment.
9. Student responses will vary. In popular fiction and sentimental poetry there usually is.

Responding to the Poem

Analyzing the Poem

Identifying Details

1. What decisive action has the poem's main character just taken?
2. The driving force in this poem is a **conflict** within the main character herself. What details reveal her anger? What evidence reveals that she has mixed feelings about her decision?

Interpreting Meanings

3. Identify the "blue-capped functioner of doom" in line 6. Why do you think he is described as "leering"?
4. Why do you think the main character hopes this person might lose her letter?
5. In what fashion does the oak tree "speak" to the daughter in the fifth stanza, and what message does the tree convey? What qualities associated with an oak tree might make it an appropriate **symbol** for the woman's father?
6. Why do you think the messenger's track is described as a "serpent's track" in line 22 instead of, for example, a snail's track or just a wheel track? In what sense does the track go on "forever"?
7. How could someone be "hot as fever" and "cold as any icicle" at the same time? What does this suggest the letter writer is feeling?
8. While **rhyme** can add music to poetry, it can also create wry humor. What ingenious and funny three-syllable rhyme ends the poem? Do you think the poet is making a comment by ending this serious, unhappy story on a slightly ridiculous note?
9. What is the significance of the poem's title? Do you think there usually *is* a "sequel" to stories of unrequited love?

Writing About the Poem

A Critical Response

1. **Comparing Poems.** Write a brief essay comparing "Bells for John Whiteside's Daughter" and James Russell Lowell's "She Came and Went" (page 168). What emotions does each speaker express? What view of death does each poem reveal? Support your comparisons with specific references to the poems.
2. **Filling In Meanings.** Who is the letter writer in "Parting, Without a Sequel"? Is it a young girl who has fallen in love for the first time and been rejected? Or is it an older woman whose lover has rejected her, leaving her to contemplate a lonely old age? Does the main character really talk to the oak tree? Or is it her father who speaks? Is the poet sympathetic to his letter writer? Or is his tone slightly mocking and comical? Answer these questions in a brief essay, using details from the poem to support your interpretations. Then compare your answers in class. Do others agree or disagree, and why?
3. **Comparing Poems.** Compare "Parting, Without a Sequel" to Emily Dickinson's "Heart! We will forget him!" (page 355). Consider these elements of the poems:

   a. Messages **c.** Tones
   b. Speakers **d.** Imagery

4. **Responding to a Critic.** One critic wrote that Ransom's poems emphasized such themes as

> mortality and the fleetingness of youthful vigor and grace . . . and the disparity between the world as man would have it and as it actually is, between what people want and need emotionally and what is available for them . . .
>
> —Thomas Daniel Young

Show how this comment is or is not supported by either or both of the poems you have just read. Support your opinion with references to the poems.

Analyzing Language and Style

Multiple Meanings of Words

1. *Characters* is a word that can mean (a) letters of the alphabet, (b) personal qualities, (c) reputations, (d) persons. Which meaning does the word have in line 3? Do you think Ransom is also suggesting something about his letter writer's feelings or even her character?
2. List the meanings the word *groom* can have. Which meaning specifically applies to line 7? Given the situation in the poem, do you think another meaning is echoed here?
3. Surprisingly, the archaic meaning of the word *wan* is "gloomy or dark." What is the common meaning of the word today? Which meaning does Ransom intend in line 19?
4. The word *sere* in line 18 sounds like *seer.* What does *seer* mean? Do you think Ransom is punning on the word?
5. What does the word *vaunting* mean here? Do you think the use of this word could suggest a slight mockery of the tree's wise advice?

A. Responding Jeffers's life circumstances gave him the luxury of almost complete freedom to live where he wanted, as he wanted. He chose to live in isolation in a beautiful landscape and to be a poet. Many people would agree that his was a wise choice of adaptation to ideal circumstances; many would not. ? If you could choose to live exactly as you wanted, what would you choose? What is your response to Jeffers's choice? (Students should discuss the advantages and disadvantages of the reclusive life.)

Robinson Jeffers (1887–1962)

Robinson Jeffers was born in Pittsburgh, the son of a theology teacher. Since his parents moved from place to place, by the time he was fifteen, he had already spent several years in Europe before the family settled in California. There Jeffers earned a degree from Occidental College and went on to do postgraduate work, including a term at medical school. But Jeffers did not pursue any of the careers he studied for. Fascinated with poetry, he found he could make no serious commitment to anything else.

A In 1912, he inherited money from an uncle. This allowed him the freedom to live on his own terms and to provide for his wife and two sons without ever holding a job. Asserting his sudden independence, Jeffers bought property in the coastal village of Carmel, California. With his own hands he built a stone tower that would serve for the rest of his life as retreat and working studio. As in the case of the Irish poet William Butler Yeats, the tower became symbolic for Jeffers of his world view and his way of life; he lived a monk-like existence apart from neighborly society and the literary world, marked by a lonely devotion to nature.

A man against the American grain, Jeffers had small confidence in the virtues of religion or democracy; he also kept a skeptical eye fixed on scientific progress and social advances. His philosophical outlook, combining fatalism with pessimism, was closer to that of the ancient Greeks than to that of the common American. For wayward humankind, aware of everything but its insignificance, he had little hope. He regarded awareness itself as a kind of disease to which natural forces are immune.

Much of Jeffers's poetic inspiration came from nature's power to endure and silently witness the black comedy of civilization. Jeffers's particular emblems were rocks and the sea, hawks in the wind, and the sea creatures that reproduce themselves on the sea-washed ledges of the Pacific shore.

Although humorless, grandly isolated, and nourished by disgust, Jeffers was able to attract readers who were impressed by the integrity of his single-minded convictions and by his dark vision of the limited life of human beings. His principal collections of poetry include *Tamar and Other Poems* (1924); *The Women at Point Sur* (1927); and *Solstice, and Other Poems* (1935). The title poem of the last volume, Jeffers's dramatic retelling of Euripides' tragedy *Medea,* was successfully produced on Broadway.

"The beauty of things was born before eyes and sufficient to itself," Jeffers wrote; "the heart-breaking beauty / Will remain when there is no heart to break for it."

SUPPLEMENTARY SUPPORT MATERIALS
1. Vocabulary Activity Worksheet (*CCB*)
2. Review and Response Worksheet: Attitude (*CCB*)
3. Selection Test (*CCB*)

DEVELOPING VOCABULARY
The following words from the poem are tested in the Selection Test. (See also Vocabulary Activity Worksheet.)

republic	decadence
empire	compulsory
molten	insufferable
exultance	

PREPARATION
ESTABLISHING A PURPOSE. You might suggest that students read this poem in order to understand how its themes are reflected in the title.

CLOSURE
Have students write two or three sentences, to be shared in class, explaining the title of the poem.

This poem was written in the Big Sur region in California, where great mountains emerge like dripping shoulders out of the Pacific Ocean. The circumstance is that of a remote homestead, built with the speaker's own hands. The speaker is a father determined to live apart from civilization and to have his children learn the lessons of nature rather than those of schoolbooks.

Shine, Perishing Republic

While this America settles in the mold of its vulgarity,
heavily thickening to empire,
And protest, only a bubble in the molten mass, pops and
sighs out, and the mass hardens,

I sadly smiling remember that the flower fades to make
fruit, the fruit rots to make earth.
Out of the mother; and through the spring exultances,
ripeness and decadence; and home to the mother.

You making haste, haste on decay: not blameworthy; life
is good, be it stubbornly long or suddenly
A mortal splendor: meteors are not needed less than
mountains: shine, perishing republic.

But for my children, I would have them keep their distance
from the thickening center; corruption
Never has been compulsory, when the cities lie at the
monster's feet there are left the mountains.

And boys, be in nothing so moderate as in love of man, a
clever servant, insufferable master.
There is the trap that catches noblest spirits, that caught—
they say—God, when he walked on earth.

Responding to the Poem

Analyzing the Poem

Identifying Details

1. To whom is the poem addressed? Which line tells you?
2. In stanza 4, the speaker suggests that his children, and by extension all children, need not surrender to corruption. What alternative does he say is open to them?
3. In contrast to the familiar exhortation to "love thy neighbor," the fifth stanza offers quite different advice. What reason does the speaker give in this stanza for warning his listeners to "be in nothing so moderate as in love of man"?

Interpreting Meanings

4. The first stanza contains an **implied metaphor.** What is America compared to? What does "vulgarity" mean? Why is it so bad that the republic thickens to *empire*?
5. What attitude toward America does the second stanza express?
6. If you were to read the poem aloud, in what **tone** would you read the words "shine, perishing republic"?
7. What is the speaker's attitude in the last stanza? Do you think he really means what he says in line 9?
8. What does the speaker seem to think is the cause of the republic's condition?
9. How would you respond to the poet's message?

ANALYZING THE POEM
Identifying Details
1. To the speaker's children.
Lines 7 and 9.
2. They can go to the "mountains" rather than to the "cities."
3. "Man," he says, is "a clever servant, insufferable master."

Interpreting Meanings
4. America is compared to a "molten mass" in a mold.
"Vulgarity" probably refers to undesirable choices of the majority.
Perhaps because the nation loses its positive qualities such as idealism.
5. That America's decadence is part of a natural cycle.
6. In an ironic, sarcastic tone.
7. A cynical, pessimistic attitude. Some might detect sadness.
Student answers will vary.
8. Conformity, massiveness, power, and intolerance.
9. Be sure they realize that such bitterness can conceal deep love and disappointed idealism.

SUPPLEMENTARY SUPPORT MATERIALS
1. Vocabulary Activity Worksheet (*CCB*)
2. Review and Response Worksheet: Symbolism and Theme (*CCB*)
3. Selection Test (*CCB*)
4. Instructional Overhead Transparency

DEVELOPING VOCABULARY
The following words from the poem are tested in the Selection Test. (See also Vocabulary Activity Worksheet.)
brittle   to glint
ruffled

PREPARATION
ESTABLISHING A PURPOSE. Have students read to understand the complaint made by the speaker in the first four lines and to understand the extended metaphor in the sestet.

A. Metaphor
"Cracked and twilight mirrors" is a metaphor for the poet's verses.

B. Metaphor
Here Jeffers expands his hunting metaphor to include lions as well as swans.

C. Expansion
Here begins Jeffers's reply to his own statements of the first eight lines.

D. Interpretation
? What does Jeffers mean when he says we should love our eyes and minds, even though we may hate ourselves? (We should love the beauty of the world without being excessively introspective about it—without imposing ourselves as a barrier to the world's beauty. As part of the natural world, we too are part of the beauty that deserves to be loved.)

Here is a sonnet in the form of an argument—a poet's argument with himself. In the course of the argument, he condemns his own inadequate efforts to write poetry, becomes content to settle for the simple powers of observation, and, ironically, ends up with a fine poem. What feelings does the image of a wild swan evoke for you?

Love the Wild Swan

"I hate my verses, every line, every word,
Oh pale and brittle pencils ever to try
One grass blade's curve, or the throat of one bird
That clings to twig, ruffled against white sky.
A Oh cracked and twilight mirrors ever to catch
One color, one glinting flash, of the splendor of things.
Unlucky hunter, Oh bullets of wax,
B The lion beauty, the wild-swan wings, the storm of the wings."
C —This wild swan of a world is no hunter's game.
Better bullets than yours would miss the white breast,
Better mirrors than yours would crack in the flame.
Does it matter whether you hate your . . . self? At least
D Love your eyes that can see, your mind that can
Hear the music, the thunder of the wings. Love the wild swan.

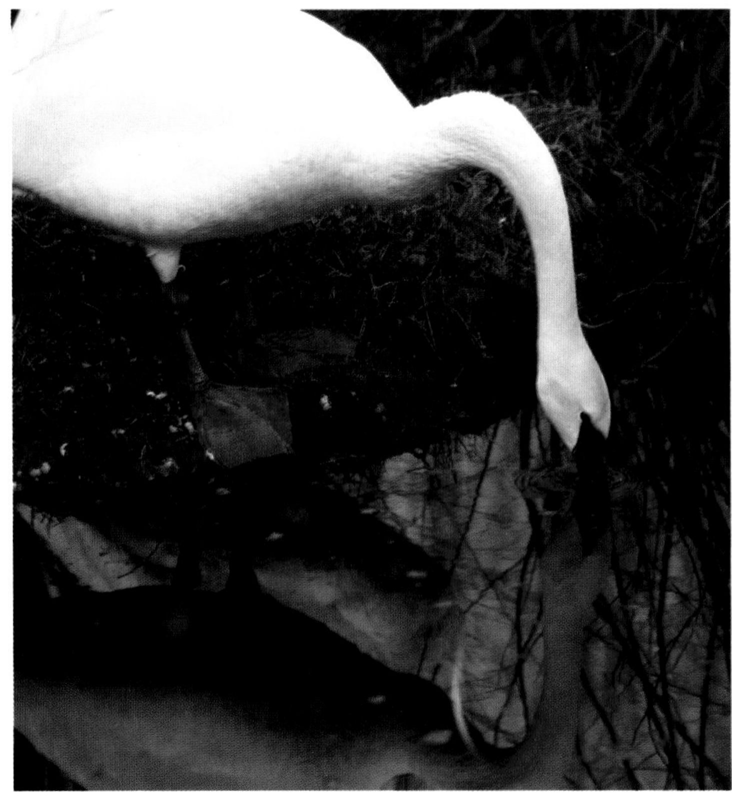

CLOSURE

Have individual students explain the meaning of the first eight lines of the poem. Then have other students explain the meaning of the last six lines.

ANALYZING THE POEM

Identifying Details

1. He feels that his verses are inadequate to capture the splendor of nature.

2. Adjectives that capture this feeling include: "pale," "brittle," "cracked," "twilight," and "unlucky."

3. Another voice consoles the speaker, telling him that the fault is not within himself: No poetry can capture the range and magnificence of nature. The speaker should at least be grateful that his senses can apprehend the "wild swan" of the world.

Interpreting Meanings

4. Mirrors that are "cracked" and "twilight" cannot reflect objects clearly; in a symbolic sense, the poet's perceptions are flawed and fuzzy, or unclear.

The unlucky hunter represents the poet in search of nature, and his bullets of wax are ineffective weapons.

5. Details that extend the metaphor include: the "white breast" of the swan (line 10), the "flame" of the bird's brilliance (line 11), the "music" of the swan's song (line 14).

The comparison suggests an attitude of wonder at the elusive range, beauty, and variety of the natural world.

6. The flame in line 11 may suggest the vitality and brilliance of the natural world, as symbolized by the wild swan. The fact that "better mirrors" might crack in it may indicate that, however sharp a poet's skills may be, he or she can never fully reflect the beauty of nature.

7. Perhaps "verses" or "poetry."

Responding to the Poem

Analyzing the Poem

Identifying Details

1. What complaint does the speaker make in the poem's first four lines?
2. What adjectives in lines 1–8 emphasize the speaker's feeling of weakness and failure?
3. What response is made to the speaker's complaint in the **sestet,** the last six lines of the sonnet?

Interpreting Meanings

4. What might "cracked and twilight mirrors" **symbolize** in line 5? Who is the "unlucky hunter," and what are his "bullets of wax"?
5. This sonnet's **sestet** presents an **extended metaphor** in which the world is compared to a wild swan. What details extend this metaphor? What attitude toward the world does this comparison suggest?
6. What might the "flame" in line 11 be? Why might "better mirrors" crack in it?
7. Why does the speaker hesitate in the middle of line 12? What other word than "self" might he be reaching for?

Writing About the Poems

A Creative Response

1. **Rephrasing a Poem.** Rewrite "Love the Wild Swan" in the form of a dialogue between two people. Include a brief description of each character.

A Critical Response

2. **Responding to the Poem.** "Shine, Perishing Republic" was published in 1930. In a brief essay, explain why you think Jeffers's view of the American condition is or is not still valid. First, summarize the view expressed in the poem. Then tell whether or not you think this view applies to contemporary America. Support your position with specific references to the poem and to contemporary life.

Analyzing Language and Style

Rhymes

Many words in the English language look as if they should rhyme, but don't (*dough/through/bough*). (Such words are called "eye rhymes.") Many other words look as if they don't rhyme, but they do (*dough/go/sew/blow*). **Exact rhymes** are rhymes that consist of the repetition of the accented vowel sound and all succeeding sounds in words (*bicycle/icicle*). **Slant rhymes** (also called **approximate** or **imperfect rhymes**) are sounds that are similar but not exactly the same (*blue/bled; yellow/willow*).

In "Love the Wild Swan," find examples of:

1. Two pairs of end rhymes that look as if they should rhyme exactly, but are actually slant rhymes
2. Two other end rhymes that look as if they should not rhyme at all, but that contain slant rhymes
3. Two other end rhymes that look as if they should not rhyme, but are actually perfect rhymes

A. Expansion
The Autobiography of an Ex-Colored Man is, according to critic Edward Margolies, the best novel by an African American writer before the 1920's. It takes a very light-skinned black youth through a variety of experiences, from the rural South to New York honky-tonks to leisured Europe, before he bitterly decides to pass as white. The narrative voice was so convincing to readers that many assumed it was a genuine autobiography. Johnson later wrote his real autobiography partly to rebut this belief.

THE HARLEM RENAISSANCE

James Weldon Johnson (1871–1938)

James Weldon Johnson—poet, teacher, and lawyer—was born in Jacksonville, Florida. He was educated at Atlanta University in Georgia and Columbia University in New York City. Throughout his career, Johnson was an energetic exponent of civil rights, and in his writing he constantly sought recognition for the contributions that blacks had made to American culture.

After serving as U.S. Consul to Nicaragua and Venezuela (1906–1913), Johnson became a field secretary of the National Association for the Advancement of Colored People (NAACP), and was later named the organization's executive secretary. In 1930, he became a professor at Fisk University. Eight years later, he died in an automobile accident.

Although some of Johnson's early poems are in dialect, he soon abandoned that style for standard English, which he felt was capable of greater variety and power. His principal theme was black pride, which he celebrated in such poems as "Fifty Years," written on the fiftieth anniversary of the Emancipation Proclamation, and "O Black and Unknown Bards," a tribute to the anonymous authors of Negro spirituals. With his brother, the composer John Rosamond Johnson, he wrote a number of songs and light operas, and the brothers collaborated in editing two collections of Negro spirituals.

Johnson was an important leader of the first phase of the Harlem Renaissance. His anthology, *The Book of American Negro Poetry* (1922) was one of the earliest and most significant collections of poems by blacks. In addition to poetry, he wrote fiction (most notably *The Autobiography of an Ex-Colored Man,* published in 1912), A nonfiction studies of black life, and an autobiography, *Along This Way* (1933).

Portrait of James W. Johnson by Winold Reiss (1925). Pastel.

Supplementary Support Materials

1. Vocabulary Activity Worksheet (*CCB*)
2. Review and Response Worksheet: Simile and Implied Metaphor (*CCB*)
3. Selection Test (*CCB*)
4. Audiocassette recording

Developing Vocabulary

The following words from the poem are tested in the Selection Test. (See also Vocabulary Activity Worksheet.)

bosom	to clamp
clap	spur
vineyard	comet
to loose	glittering
reins	furrow

Preparation

Establishing a Purpose. Have students note the subhead of the poem, "A Funeral Sermon." Then have students read the poem as they would a sermon—to learn the poet's message about God, death, and life.

This poem is one of eight "sermons" written by Johnson in the style of the old-time black preachers. He collected the sermons in a book called *God's Trombones*—the trombone being the preacher's voice, "the instrument possessing above all others the power to express the wide and varied range of emotions encompassed by the human voice." Johnson tells us that the man delivering this sermon would intone, moan, plead, blare, crash, and thunder. You should listen to the poem read aloud.

Go Down Death

A Funeral Sermon

Weep not, weep not,
She is not dead;
She's resting in the bosom of Jesus.
A Heart-broken husband—weep no more;
Grief-stricken son—weep no more;
Left-lonesome daughter—weep no more;
She's only just gone home.

Day before yesterday morning,
God was looking down from his great, high heaven,
Looking down on all his children,
B And his eye fell on Sister Caroline,
Tossing on her bed of pain.
And God's big heart was touched with pity,
With the everlasting pity.

And God sat back on his throne,
And he commanded that tall, bright angel standing at his
right hand:
Call me Death!
And that tall, bright angel cried in a voice
That broke like a clap of thunder:
Call Death! Call Death!
And the echo sounded down the streets of heaven
Till it reached away back to that shadowy place,
C Where Death waits with his pale, white horses.

And Death heard the summons,
And he leaped on his fastest horse,
Pale as a sheet in the moonlight.
Up the golden street Death galloped,
And the hoofs of his horse struck fire from the gold,
But they didn't make no sound.
Up Death rode to the Great White Throne,
And waited for God's command.

And God said: Go down, Death, go down,
Go down to Savannah, Georgia,
Down in Yamacraw,

A. Responding

? Who has died? (A woman who was both a wife and mother)

B. Flashback

? A flashback begins here. What is the time and the situation? (The time is the day before yesterday. The woman, named Caroline, is obviously suffering from a disease that causes her great pain.)

C. Allusion

John Milton, in *Paradise Lost*, Book X, line 588, refers to "Death . . . on his pale horse." An earlier reference is that of Revelation 6:8: "Behold a pale horse: and his name that sat on him was Death, and Hell followed with him." Students might discuss why Death and the pale horse are associated in these references, why Death in the poem is associated with "pale, white horses," and why Death himself would be "pale as a sheet in the moonlight."

Literature and Language: Using Colons and Semicolons
Most students are insecure about colons and semicolons. They confuse the two and use them incorrectly, or not at all, in their writing. This poem gives students a chance to see both punctuation marks in action.

Have students look at lines 2, 4, 5, and 6 while you remind them that a semicolon is like a more emphatic comma (note the comma built into its bottom half) and that it marks a pause between parts that already have commas.

Then direct students to lines 16 and 59 and review the rules for using colons. (See **Grammar, Usage, and Mechanics: A Reference Guide**.) How are colons used in this poem? (To set off a quotation, instead of quotation marks.) Have students find other examples (lines 19, 32, 75).

Ask each student to write four sentences containing colons and semicolons. Have students exchange papers to check that they've used these punctuation marks correctly.

Humanities Connection: Discussing the Fine Art
The painting, which was done the same year *God's Trombones* was published, shows Death riding down to earth on his horse (lines 41–51). Aaron Douglas (1898–1979) was an important figure in the Harlem Renaissance, though originally from Kansas. He was known for the geometrical and symbolic qualities of his works, which combined African and Art Deco elements. He painted murals for Fisk University and for the New York Public Library.

Students with artistic talent may want to illustrate some other passage from the funeral sermon.

Go Down Death by Aaron Douglas (1927). Oil on masonite.

Collection of Professor and Mrs. David Driskell, Hyattsville, Maryland.

CLOSURE
Have students list words and phrases that characterize God and Jesus, and then Death, as he is first seen in the poem and then as he is seen by Sister Caroline.

A. Interpretation
? What does the phrase "Go down, Death" mean here? What additional meaning might it have in the title? (Here it refers to God's commandment to Death to go to earth for Sister Caroline. In the title, it might also mean the subjugation of death through the knowledge and acceptance of life after death, as it does in John Donne's "Death Be Not Proud" [1633]: "And Death shall be no more; Death, thou shalt die.")

And find Sister Caroline.
She's borne the burden and heat of the day,
She's labored long in my vineyard,
And she's tired—
She's weary—
A Go down, Death, and bring her to me.

And Death didn't say a word,
B But he loosed the reins on his pale, white horse,
And he clamped the spurs to his bloodless sides,
And out and down he rode,
Through heaven's pearly gates,
Past suns and moons and stars;
On Death rode,
And the foam from his horse was like a comet in the sky;
On Death rode,
Leaving the lightning's flash behind;
Straight on down he came.

While we were watching round her bed,
She turned her eyes and looked away,
She saw what we couldn't see;
She saw Old Death. She saw Old Death
Coming like a falling star.
But Death didn't frighten Sister Caroline;
He looked to her like a welcome friend.
And she whispered to us: I'm going home,
And she smiled and closed her eyes.

And Death took her up like a baby,
And she lay in his icy arms,
But she didn't feel no chill.
And Death began to ride again—
Up beyond the evening star,
Out beyond the morning star,
Into the glittering light of glory,
On to the Great White Throne.

And there he laid Sister Caroline
On the loving breast of Jesus.
And Jesus took his own hand and wiped away her tears,
And he smoothed the furrows from her face,
And the angels sang a little song,
And Jesus rocked her in his arms,
And kept a-saying: Take your rest,
Take your rest, take your rest.

Weep not—weep not,
She is not dead;
She's resting in the bosom of Jesus.

C

B. Word Choice
The words "white," "pale," and "bright" are repeated several times in this poem. Discuss their possible meaning for a largely African American audience in 1927. Analyze the contexts in which these words appear—usually, the context of God and Death.

C. Responding
? What is this poem's attitude toward Sister Caroline? (Respect for her long, productive life) What is its attitude toward death and toward God? (Death is not to be feared, for it brings the soul to rest in heaven, in the arms of a loving God.) Does Hughes make you share those attitudes? (Answers will vary, though many students may find the funeral sermon uplifting or otherwise appealing.)

ANALYZING THE POEM

Identifying Details

1. God is in heaven, and death is in a "shadowy place" (line 22), waiting with his pale, white horses.

Sister Caroline lies on a bed of pain in Savannah, Georgia.

2. She greets Death calmly and like a "welcome friend" who comes to take her home.

3. The similes include the comparison of the angel's voice to a clap of thunder (line 18), the comparison of the foam from Death's horse to a comet (line 48), and the comparison of Death himself to a falling star (line 56).

Interpreting Meanings

4. Most students will agree that the portrait of God and Jesus stresses mercy and gentleness. Details supporting this interpretation include the pity that touches God's heart (lines 13–14), God's compassion for Sister Caroline's weariness (lines 36–39), the mention of the "loving breast" of Jesus (line 69), and the portrait of Jesus rocking Sister Caroline in his arms (lines 70–75).

5. Death is depicted as God's speedy and obedient servant. It is clear in the

Responding to the Poem

Analyzing the Poem

Identifying Details

1. Where is God in stanza 2, and where is Death in stanza 3? According to stanza 5, where is Sister Caroline?
2. How does Sister Caroline respond to Death's arrival in stanza 7?
3. Point out at least three **similes** that help to suggest the power and magnificence of the workings of heaven.

Interpreting Meanings

4. Does the speaker portray God and Jesus as distant, forbidding figures, or as familiar, gentle ones? Point out at least four details that support your interpretation.
5. Death riding a pale horse is a legendary figure in literature and art. Sometimes referred to as the Grim Reaper, he is often pictured as a skeleton on horseback carrying a scythe (a tool used to cut down hay and grass). While most of these traditional representations of death are fearful, the one in this poem is not. How does the poet transform this conventionally horrifying image into an almost comforting one?
6. Johnson was a highly sophisticated writer. Why do you think he uses the informal language of folk tradition for this poem?
7. Why do you think Death rides a "pale" or white horse? Where else have you seen the color white used in a similar **symbolic** way?

Writing About the Poem

A Creative Response

1. **Extending the Poem.** Think about the character of Death as it is drawn in the poem. Write a speech that Death might make to the people addressed in the poem.

A Critical Response

2. **Comparing Sermons.** Extracts from another famous sermon in American literature are on page 37—Jonathan Edwards's "Sinners in the Hands of an Angry God." In a brief essay, compare and contrast Johnson's sermon with Edwards's. Consider these elements of each sermon:

   a. Imagery
   b. Figures of speech
   c. Message
   d. Tone
   e. Audience
   f. Purpose

3. **Comparing and Contrasting Poems.** Compare and contrast the attitudes toward death expressed in "Go Down Death" and Millay's "Dirge Without Music" (page 650). What emotions in the face of death does each speaker convey? What aspects of life—the pleasures or the hardships—does each speaker stress? What view does each take of what happens to human beings after death?

Analyzing Language and Style

Free Verse and the Orator's Style

Johnson and Paul Laurence Dunbar (page 646) had several discussions about poetry. Dunbar was essentially conservative in style, but Johnson was interested in experimenting. When Johnson was working on the poems that would eventually become *God's Trombones,* he talked with Dunbar:

> I showed Paul the things I had done under the sudden influence of Whitman. He read them through and, looking at me with a queer smile, said "I don't like them, and I don't see what you are driving at." He may have been justified, but I was taken aback. I got out my copy of *Leaves of Grass* and read him some of the things I admired most. There was, at least, some personal consolation in the fact that his verdict was the same on Whitman himself.
>
> —James Weldon Johnson

Examine "Go Down Death" and see if you can identify the influence of Whitman (page 326). Look for these elements of Whitman's style:

1. Repetition and parallel structure to create rhythm
2. The language of everyday conversation, including slang
3. Variation of lines, from very long to very short

poem that his function is to release Sister Caroline from hardships, weariness, and illness, and to reunite her with God and with Jesus. Thus, Sister Caroline greets Death as a friend, rather than as a dreaded enemy. The description of Death's journey in the sixth stanza contains no suspenseful foreboding; rather, the poet employs striking imagery to emphasize the heavens' beauty. Finally, it is said in the eighth stanza that Death handles Sister Caroline gently: He "took her up like a baby," and she felt no chill in his icy arms.

6. Student answers will vary. Some will suggest that Johnson uses folk tradition as a means to "humanize" the Bible's teachings about everlasting life. Others may point out that the syntax and diction of folk tradition possess a simple, quiet dignity that is entirely appropriate to Johnson's subject in the poem.

7. Student answers will vary. Remind the students of the use of the color white by Herman Melville in *Moby-Dick* and by Robert Frost in "Design" (page 654).

Primary Sources

God's Trombones

In the preface to *God's Trombones,* Johnson describes the genesis of his poems.

"The old-time preacher was generally a man far above the average in intelligence; he was, not infrequently, a man of positive genius. The earliest of these preachers must have virtually committed many parts of the Bible to memory through hearing the scriptures read or preached from in the white churches which the slaves attended. They were the first of the slaves to learn to read, and their reading was confined to the Bible, and specifically to the more dramatic passages of the Old Testament. A text served mainly as a starting point and often had no relation to the development of the sermon. Nor would the old-time preacher balk at any text within the lids of the Bible. There is the story of one who after reading a rather cryptic passage took off his spectacles, closed the Bible with a bang and by way of preface said, 'Brothers and sisters, this morning—I intend to explain the unexplainable—find out the undefinable—ponder over the imponderable—and unscrew the inscrutable.' "

. . .

"The old-time Negro preacher of parts was above all an orator, and in good measure an actor. He knew the secret of oratory, that at bottom it is a progression of rhythmic words more than it is anything else. Indeed, I have witnessed congregations moved to ecstasy by the rhythmic intoning of sheer incoherencies. He was a master of all the modes of eloquence. He often possessed a voice that was a marvelous instrument, a voice he could modulate from a sepulchral whisper to a crashing thunder clap. His discourse was generally kept at a high pitch of fervency, but occasionally he dropped into colloquialisms and, less often, into humor. He preached a personal and anthropomorphic God, a sure-enough heaven and a red-hot hell. His imagination was bold and unfettered. He had the power to sweep his hearers before him; and so himself was often swept away. At such times his language was not prose but poetry. It was from memories of such preachers there grew the idea of this book of poems."

—James Weldon Johnson

Black preacher at the Fourth Street Church of Christ in Natchez, Mississippi.

Photograph by Eve Arnold (1983).

A. Expansion
McKay looked back on Jamaica as a lost Eden, and throughout his life he sought a simple, earthy kind of existence which he was never able successfully to recapture. He deliberately adopted the image of a vagabond bohemian poet, but felt barred by his intellectualism from being truly accepted by the folk communities he admired. When *Home to Harlem* appeared, it was condemned by some of the older African American intellectuals, such as W. E. B. Du Bois, for the "licentiousness" of its subject matter, but Langston Hughes (page 688) called it "vividly alive" and "the first real flower of the Harlem Renaissance."

B. Humanities Connection: Discussing the Photograph
Carl Van Vechten (1880–1964) was a white novelist and critic who was strongly interested in African American life and in the Harlem Renaissance.

Claude McKay (1890–1948)

Claude McKay was one of the most influential members of the Harlem Renaissance of the A 1920's. He was born and raised on the Caribbean island of Jamaica, the child of poor farm workers. When he was six, he went to live with an older brother who was a schoolteacher, and his early education came chiefly from his brother's library. At nineteen, McKay became a policeman in Kingston, but he was also writing poetry in the Jamaican dialect. In 1912, two volumes of this poetry, *Songs of Jamaica* and *Constab Ballads,* appeared. These popular volumes brought him praise as the Robert Burns of Jamaica, and they won their author a prize which enabled him to travel to the United States. He studied here for two years, first at Tuskegee Institute in Alabama and then at Kansas State College. In 1914 he moved to Harlem, the center of black culture in the United States.

In Harlem, McKay supported himself with a variety of jobs, from longshoreman to handyman to waiter, while he continued to perfect his craft and to publish poetry in periodicals. In 1920, his third book, *Spring in New Hampshire,* was published. His most important book of poetry, *Harlem Shadows,* appeared in 1922.

By this time, McKay was a major figure in the Harlem Renaissance. He had served for a time as an editor of the radical newspapers *The Liberator* and *The Masses*. Like many writers of the time, he was attracted to what was then thought of as the "noble experiment" of communism in the Soviet Union. In 1922 he went to Russia with one of the driving spirits of the American radical movement, Max Eastman. Together, they toured the country and met the architects of Russian communism, including Lenin and Trotsky.

For the next ten years, McKay lived abroad, principally in France. He wrote four novels, including the best-selling *Home to Harlem* (1928), an award-winning work about a black soldier's return from World War I.

 B

Portrait of Claude McKay by Carl Van Vechten (1941).

Courtesy the Eakins Press Foundation and the Estate of Carl Van Vechten.

In the early 1930's, McKay became disillusioned with communism, and, his productive years over, he wrote very little from then on. In 1942, he converted to Roman Catholicism and returned to the United States, where he spent the remainder of his life as a teacher in Catholic schools in Chicago.

Despite the use of Jamaican dialect early in his career, most of McKay's poetry is firmly traditional in form and style. His many sonnets were largely influenced by the English Romantic poets, especially Wordsworth, Keats, and Shelley. In subject matter, however, those sonnets were far from traditional; they express McKay's ambivalent and often defiant feelings about black life in America.

SUPPLEMENTARY SUPPORT MATERIALS
1. Vocabulary Activity Worksheet (*CCB*)
2. Review and Response Worksheet: Imagery and Theme (*CCB*)
3. Selection Test (*CCB*)

DEVELOPING VOCABULARY
The following words from the poem are tested in the Selection Test. (See also Vocabulary Activity Worksheet.)

cultured	to front
vigor	malice
erect	to jeer
to sweep	unerring

PREPARATION
ESTABLISHING A PURPOSE. Suggest that students read the poem to understand the feelings toward his country of a man who had "ambivalent and often defiant feelings about black life in America."

Read the first two lines of this poem. What attitude is the poem likely to express? What do you think is the significance of the first word of the poem?

America

Although she feeds me bread of bitterness,
And sinks into my throat her tiger's tooth,
Stealing my breath of life, I will confess
I love this cultured hell that tests my
  youth!
Her vigor flows like tides into my blood,
Giving me strength erect against her hate.
Her bigness sweeps my being like a flood.
Yet as a rebel fronts a king in state,
I stand within her walls with not a shred
Of terror, malice, not a word of jeer.
Darkly I gaze into the days ahead,
And see her might and granite wonders
  there,
Beneath the touch of Time's unerring hand,
Like priceless treasures sinking in the sand.

Responding to the Poem

Analyzing the Poem

Identifying Details

1. In lines 1–3, what treatment does the poet say he receives from America?
2. What qualities of America cause the speaker to love her anyway?

Interpreting Meanings

3. America is **personified** in this poem as an entity both cruel and powerful. What **images** suggest America's cruelty and injustice? What images convey her power?
4. A rebel with "not a shred / Of terror, malice, not a word of jeer" might seem to be a rebel without a rebellion. How does the poem resolve this **paradox** or apparent contradiction?
5. What does the speaker see happening to America as he gazes into "the days ahead"? How would you explain this projected fate?
6. How does this speaker's attitude toward America compare with that of the speaker of "Shine, Perishing Republic" (page 677)?

Writing About the Poem

A Creative Response

1. **Capturing the Poet's Feelings.** Design a poster or write a bumper sticker that the speaker in this poem might display. Try to capture in a phrase or two the main idea expressed in the poem.

A Critical Response

2. **Comparing and Contrasting Poems.** The title of the following poem is the name of the Egyptian pharaoh Rameses II, who ruled in the thirteenth century B.C., and who left many monuments to himself. The poem is a comment on passing glory. Compare this poem, published in 1817 in England, to "America." Discuss the poems' similarities and differences in form, subject, point of view, and emotion.

Ozymandias

I met a traveler from an antique land
Who said: Two vast and trunkless legs of stone
Stand in the desert . . . Near them, on the sand,
Half sunk, a shattered visage lies, whose frown,
And wrinkled lip, and sneer of cold command,
Tell that its sculptor well those passions read
Which yet survive, stamped on these lifeless
  things,
The hand that mocked them, and the heart that
  fed:
And on the pedestal these words appear:
"My name is Ozymandias, king of kings:
Look on my works, ye Mighty, and despair!"
Nothing beside remains. Round the decay
Of that colossal wreck, boundless and bare
The lone and level sands stretch far away.

—Percy Bysshe Shelley

CLOSURE
Have students write a sentence, to be shared in class, in which they summarize the feelings of the poet toward his country.

ANALYZING THE POEM
Identifying Details
1. That America threatens to strangle him.
2. America's vigor, strength, and bigness.

Interpreting Meanings
3. Such images include "tiger's tooth" (line 2) and the mention of "hate" (line 6).
"Tides" of vigor (line 5) and America's "bigness" sweeping "like a flood" (line 7).
4. The speaker is a philosophical rebel who combines nonviolence with protest against injustice and cruelty.
5. He sees America being destroyed by Time.
Students should note that the earlier part of the poem depicts America as a land of bitterness, victimization, and hatred.
6. This speaker is defiant and admiring. The other is bitter.

Comment From A Critic
Hughes was the most famous of the Harlem Renaissance writers during his own lifetime. Critic Edward Margolies says, "He speaks with directness, honesty, and understanding . . . he writes really of the triumph of the human spirit over adversity."

Hughes's work is remarkable for its sheer readability and for the ever-present sense that one is hearing an authentic human voice.

Langston Hughes (1902–1967)

One evening in 1926, the poet Vachel Lindsay was eating dinner in the Wardman Park Hotel in Washington, D.C. The busboy, a shy twenty-four-year-old black man, left three or four poems near Lindsay's plate. Lindsay liked the poems so much that he read them in his performance that night. The next morning, Washington newspapers carried enthusiastic stories about "The Busboy Poet," and the young writer, Langston Hughes, found that he had been "discovered" overnight. The publicity and Lindsay's encouragement helped Hughes to publish his first volume of poems, *The Weary Blues,* and won him a scholarship to Lincoln University. By the time he graduated from college in 1929, the energetic young author had published a second volume of poetry and a novel.

The busboy who had so shyly approached Lindsay was no beginner. By 1926, Hughes had already published poems in the prestigious black magazine *Crisis* and had been included in an anthology of the Harlem Renaissance, *The New Negro*. He spoke German and Spanish; had lived in Mexico, France, and Italy; and had worked his way to Africa and back as a crew member on a ship. He was ambitious and energetic, and he had learned early to rely on himself. During the career that followed his "overnight" success, Hughes wrote fifteen volumes of verse, six novels, three books of short stories, eleven plays, and a variety of nonfiction works.

Hughes was born in Joplin, Missouri. His parents were well educated and ambitious. They separated when Langston was young, and for a number of years he lived with his maternal grandmother. When he was twelve, he moved with his mother and stepfather to Cleveland, where he attended high school. Here he read the great twentieth-century Midwestern poets—Edgar Lee Masters, Carl Sandburg, and Vachel Lindsay—and started writing poetry under their influence.

When Hughes graduated from high school in 1920, he went to Mexico to live with his father, a successful businessman. His father, Hughes later said, "had great contempt for poor people," and for this and other reasons the two men did not get along. When his father insisted that Langston study to become an engineer, he chose to go to Columbia University in New York, in order to see Harlem. But the attractions of Harlem did not compensate for Hughes's dislike of engineering; he dropped out of school and began to travel. Four years later, he was a busboy in that Washington hotel.

The most important early influence on Hughes's poetry was Carl Sandburg (page 729), who sought to express the voice of the people in free verse, unrestrained by the formal restrictions or stylistic demands of the past. Encouraged by Sandburg's example, Hughes tried to reproduce the voice of black people, especially the blacks of Harlem, the poor people for whom his father had so little sympathy.

Hughes often used jazz rhythms and the repetitive structure of the blues in his poems; toward the end of his career, he wrote poems specifically for jazz accompaniment. He was also responsible for the founding of several black theater companies, and he wrote and translated a number of dramatic works. His work, he said, was an attempt to "explain and illuminate the Negro condition in America." It succeeded in doing that with both vigor and compassion.

SUPPLEMENTARY SUPPORT MATERIALS

1. Review and Response Worksheet: Tone and Theme (*CCB*)
2. Selection Test (*CCB*)

PREPARATION

ESTABLISHING A PURPOSE. Have students read the poem to form a mental image of Harlem.

CLOSURE

Have students list words and phrases that describe Harlem as it is depicted in the poem.

Hughes wrote several poems called "Harlem." In this one, look for signs of the speaker's emotional state. Is he angry, amused, baffled? Can he be described by more than one of these adjectives?

Harlem

Here on the edge of hell
Stands Harlem—
Remembering the old lies,
The old kicks in the back,
The old "Be patient"
They told us before.

Sure, we remember.
Now when the man at the corner store
Says sugar's gone up another two cents,
And bread one,
And there's a new tax on cigarettes—
We remember the job we never had,
Never could get,
And can't have now
Because we're colored.

So we stand here
On the edge of hell
In Harlem
And look out on the world
And wonder
What we're gonna do
In the face of what
We remember.

The Block (detail) by Romare Bearden (1971). Cut and pasted papers on masonite.

The Metropolitan Museum of Art, New York. Gift of Mr. and Mrs. Samuel Shore, 1978. Estate of Romare Bearden.

Responding to the Poem

Analyzing the Poem

Identifying Details

1. Name the specific hardships and injustices that the people of Harlem remember, according to the speaker in the poem.

Interpreting Meanings

2. What ideas about Harlem does the speaker suggest when he says that it is "on the edge of hell"?
3. Do you interpret the poem's final stanza as an expression of powerlessness, or as a threat? Defend your opinion.

Writing About the Poem

A Creative Response

1. **Writing a News Report.** Write the opening paragraph for a newspaper article or TV news special about the Harlem described in the poem. Include at least one of the points made by Hughes.

A Critical Response

2. **Comparing Poems.** Hughes's "Harlem" and McKay's "America" are poetic responses to oppression. In a brief essay, compare the two responses. Which poem do you find more effective as protest, and why?

ANALYZING THE POEM

Identifying Details

1. The people remember lies that they were told, physical abuse, poverty, and their inability to get a job because of their race.

Interpreting Meanings

2. Student answers will vary. Some will note that the image suggests misery and torment, with no relief or escape. Others may suggest the image contains a warning: In its misery, and in the boiling resentment of its citizens, Harlem is close to a violent destruction or flare-up, which might resemble "hell."

3. Students may have various opinions. Remind them that Hughes may have intended both interpretations.

SUPPLEMENTARY SUPPORT MATERIALS

1. Review and Response Worksheet: Tone and Theme (*CCB*)
2. Selection Test (*CCB*)
3. Instructional Overhead Transparency

PREPARATION

ESTABLISHING A PURPOSE. Have students decide the tone of this poem as they read. What pain has this poet felt?

CLOSURE

Have individual students state, in their own words, the message about racism that is contained in this poem.

ANALYZING THE POEM

Identifying Details

1. To eat in the kitchen.
   He will be at the table then.

Interpreting Meanings

2. "They" refers to white people.
   The speaker predicts that white people will eventually grow to recognize the speaker's "beauty"—for he, too, is "America."
3. The central image of a family at the dinner table, the references to the kitchen and to "the dark brother."
4. The poet has substituted the word "am" for the word "sing."
   The identification of the speaker with America highlights the meaning that all citizens, of all colors, are a part of the national "family."
   The poem would lose much of its force.
5. Student answers will vary. You should discuss the Civil Rights Act of 1964 and the Voting Rights Act of 1965.

"My country, tis of thee/Sweet land of liberty/ Of thee I sing." Millions of schoolchildren have sung this song. Here is a comment on that song. Why does this speaker feel excluded from America?

I, Too

I, too, sing America.

I am the darker brother.
They send me to eat in the kitchen
When company comes,
But I laugh,
And eat well,
And grow strong.

Tomorrow,
I'll be at the table
When company comes.
Nobody'll dare
Say to me,
"Eat in the kitchen,"
Then.

Besides,
They'll see how beautiful I am
And be ashamed—

I, too, am America.

Responding to the Poem

Analyzing the Poem

Identifying Details

1. Where does the speaker say he is sent "when company comes"? What does he say his place will be "tomorrow"?

Interpreting Meanings

2. Who are "they" in line 3? What realization does the speaker predict will eventually cause "them" to feel shame?
3. This poem clearly describes the effects of racism, yet there is optimism and forgiveness in the speaker's **tone.** What details in the poem suggest a view of America as one family that will eventually realize the injustice of discrimination?
4. The poem's last line is almost an echo of its first. What change has been made in the last line? What message is highlighted by this change? How would the poem have been affected if these two lines were reversed?
5. Do you think the prophecy in this poem (written in 1922) has in any way come true? In what ways has it not come true?

The Builders-Family by Jacob Lawrence (1974). Oil.

Humanities Connection: Responding to the Fine Art
Jacob Lawrence (b. 1917) was among the first African American artists recognized by the white world. He is thought to represent most consistently the African American experience among the artists of his generation. He has devoted series of paintings to such heroes as Harriet Tubman and Frederick Douglass, and to Harlem.
? Compare this painting by Lawrence with Bearden's paintings on pages 689 and 693. Which artist's work is stronger as a human document? Which is stronger in pictorial terms? Lawrence's picture is stronger as a human document; Bearden's is stronger in pictorial terms.)

Supplementary Support Materials
1. Vocabulary Activity Worksheet (*CCB*)
2. Review and Response Worksheet: Mood (*CCB*)
3. Selection Test (*CCB*)
4. Audiocassette recording

Developing Vocabulary
The following words from the poem are tested in the Selection Test. (See also Vocabulary Activity Worksheet.)

to drone	ebony
croon	rickety
pallor	melancholy

Preparation
Establishing a Purpose. As the headnote indicates, this poem attempts to capture some of the rhythms of blues music. Have students look for sound effects the poet uses to create those rhythms.

A. Expansion
The word *fool* is used affectionately.

B. Dialect
Note that the song-within-the-poem is in stereotyped dialect while the bulk of the poem is in standard English. Students should note, also, the traditional blues themes, like isolation and wish for death, that are expressed in this song.

This might be a good place to discuss the similarities and differences between poems and song lyrics. You might ask students to point out which lines in "The Weary Blues" are like song lyrics and which are more like written poetry.

Among the great contributions of American culture to the world is the music produced by blacks: blues, ragtime, jazz, and all the musical expressions still developing out of them. Here Hughes tries both to report the experience of a "sad raggy tune" and to capture some of its rhythms in words.

The Weary Blues

Droning a drowsy syncopated tune,°
Rocking back and forth to a mellow croon,
  I heard a Negro play.
Down on Lenox Avenue° the other night
By the pale dull pallor of an old gas light
  He did a lazy sway . . .
  He did a lazy sway . . .
To the tune o' those Weary Blues.
With his ebony hands on each ivory key
He made that poor piano moan with melody.
  O Blues!
Swaying to and fro on his rickety stool
A He played that sad raggy tune like a musical fool.
  Sweet Blues!
Coming from a black man's soul.
  O Blues!
In a deep song voice with a melancholy tone
I heard that Negro sing, that old piano moan—
  "Ain't got nobody in all this world,
  Ain't got nobody but ma salf.
  I's gwine to quit ma frownin'
  And put ma troubles on the shelf."
Thump, thump, thump, went his foot on the floor.
B He played a few chords then he sang some more—
  "I got the Weary Blues
  And I can't be satisfied.
  Got the Weary Blues
  And can't be satisfied—
  I ain't happy no mo'
  And I wish that I had died."
And far into the night he crooned that tune.
The stars went out and so did the moon.
The singer stopped playing and went to bed
While the Weary Blues echoed through his head.
He slept like a rock or a man that's dead.

1. **syncopated tune:** a melody in which normally unaccented beats are accented.

4. **Lenox Avenue:** a principal street in Harlem.

CLOSURE

Have individual students suggest a word that doesn't appear in the poem and that captures its mood.

ANALYZING THE POEM

Identifying Details

1. Such words include "droning" and "drowsy" (line 1), "rocking" and "mellow" (line 2), "pale dull pallor" (line 5), "lazy sway" (line 6), "Weary Blues" (line 8), "moan" (lines 10 and 18), "melancholy" (line 17), "troubles" (line 22).

Interpreting Meanings

2. The first verse stresses individualism and optimism; although he is alone, the speaker says he is going to "quit his frowning" and "put his troubles on the shelf." But in the second verse, the singer gives way to sadness, saying he is no longer happy and wishes that he were dead.

3. Students will have various answers. The repetition of words and phrases and the syncopation of longer lines with shorter ones contribute to this effect. Examples include "droning a drowsy" (line 1), "pale dull pallor of an old gas light" (line 5), "lazy sway" (line 6), "poor piano moan with melody" (line 10), "sad raggy tune like a musical fool" (line 13), "thump, thump, thump" (line 23).

4. The effect is ominous and foreboding; the extinction of the stars and the moon seems to hint that the singer dies, either literally or figuratively.

5. The speaker says that the singer sleeps "like a rock" or like "a man that's dead."

The final five words imply that the singer, although he makes a living by entertaining others, has himself given up hope; his spirit is dead.

Jazz Musicians by Romare Bearden. Oil.

Estate of Romare Bearden.

Responding to the Poem

Analyzing the Poem

Identifying Details

1. What are some of the words in the poem that help to create a slow, weary, melancholy **mood**?

Interpreting Meanings

2. How does the message of the blues singer's first verse contrast with that of his second?
3. Describe how the poem's structure suggests the rhythms of blues music. Point out examples of **alliteration** and **onomatopoeia** that also add to the poem's wailing, musical effect.
4. How would you describe the emotional effect of the **image** in line 32?
5. What **similes** in the poem's last line describe how the singer sleeps? What do you think are the implications of the last five words?

Writing About the Poems

A Creative Response

1. **Creating Music for a Poem.** If you are musically inclined, choose any passage in "The Weary Blues" and set it to music. If you can't write music, you might make up a melody for the passage by singing it.

A Critical Response

2. **Comparing the Voices in Two Poems.** Write a brief essay analyzing the attitudes of the speakers in "Harlem" and "I, Too." In what ways are the speakers similar? In what ways are they different?
3. **Comparing Poems.** Years earlier, Walt Whitman had written "I hear America singing" (page 331). He also wrote "I celebrate myself and sing myself" (page 332). In a brief essay, comment on how Hughes's poem echoes these lines and comments on them.

A. Connections
One of Cullen's pupils at a Harlem junior high school was James Baldwin (page 1021.)

B. Humanities Connection: Discussing the Fine Art
Winold Reiss also did the portrait of James Weldon Johnson on page 680. Note the stylistic consistencies between the two portraits.

Countee Cullen (1903–1946)

Countee Cullen grew up in New York City, the adopted son of a Methodist minister. He was a brilliant student, and during high school he was already writing accomplished poems in traditional forms. He graduated *magna cum laude* from New York University in 1925. In his senior year in college, Cullen won the Witter Bynner Award for poetry; that same year, *Color,* his first volume of verse, was published. This collection won a Harmon Gold award and established the young poet's reputation.

After receiving his Master's degree from Harvard in 1926, Cullen worked as an assistant editor of the important black magazine *Opportunity.* His poems were published in such influential periodicals as *Harper's, Poetry,* and *Crisis.* In 1927, he published *Copper Sun,* a collection of verse, and *Caroling Dusk,* an anthology of black poetry. *Caroling Dusk* was a significant contribution to the Harlem Renaissance, but the introduction Cullen wrote for the book was controversial. He called for black poets to write traditional verse and to avoid the restrictions of solely racial themes.

At the peak of his career, in 1928, Cullen married the daughter of the famous black writer W. E. B. Du Bois and published a third collection of poems, *The Ballad of the Brown Girl.* The following year he published a fourth volume, *The Black Christ.* Although he continued to write prose until the end of his life, this was his last collection of poetry. Like some of the Romantic poets he so much admired, Cullen spent his lyric talents early in his life. During the A Great Depression of the 1930's, unable to make a living solely from writing, he began teaching in Harlem public schools, a job that he held until his early death.

Portrait of Countee Cullen by Winold Reiss (1925). Pastel. B

Cullen's verse was most heavily influenced by the poetry of the English Romantics, especially John Keats. He thought of himself primarily as a lyric poet in the Romantic tradition, not as a black poet writing about social and racial themes. Nevertheless, Cullen found himself repeatedly drawn to such themes. He was aware of this conflict and described it in a poem called "Uncle Jim." In the beginning of that poem, the young poet sneers at his uncle, whose heart is "walled up with bitterness" at white people. The poet would prefer to live in a Romantic world with a friend "Who drinks my joy as tipplers drain / Deep goblets filled with wine." But despite his efforts to achieve this ideal state, he finds himself brought back to the problems his uncle represents. "I wonder why," the poem concludes, "My mind should stray . . . / To muse on Uncle Jim."

Supplementary Support Materials

1. Vocabulary Activity Worksheet (*CCB*)
2. Review and Response Worksheet: Theme (*CCB*)
3. Selection Test (*CCB*)

Developing Vocabulary

The following words from the poem are tested in the Selection Test. (See also Vocabulary Activity Worksheet.)

tableau	indignant
splendor	unison
sable	oblivious

Preparation

Establishing a Purpose. As students read, ask them to form a mental image of the tableau presented in the poem.

Closure

Have students write one or two sentences, to be shared in class, explaining the theme of the poem.

Usually, "tableau" means a scene or an action stopped cold, like a still picture in a reel of film. Here we have a "tableau vivant"; that is, a little scene in which figures live and move, a moment caught and preserved.

Tableau

(For Donald Duff)

Locked arm in arm they cross the way,
The black boy and the white,
The golden splendor of the day,
The sable pride of night.

From lowered blinds the dark folk stare,
And here the fair folk talk,
Indignant that these two should dare
In unison to walk.

Oblivious to look and word
They pass, and see no wonder
That lightning brilliant as a sword
Should blaze the path of thunder.

Responding to the Poem

Analyzing the Poem

Identifying Details

1. What **metaphors** describe the two boys in stanza 1?
2. How do the "dark folk" and "fair folk" feel about what the boys are doing?
3. How do the boys respond?

Interpreting Meanings

4. In stanza 3, who or what is the "lightning brilliant as a sword"? Who or what is the "path of thunder"?
5. Why should such a modest and commonplace thing as the friendship between two boys evoke such a dramatic statement? What larger topic is the poem really about?

Analyzing the Poem

Identifying Details

1. The white boy is indirectly compared to the "golden splendor of the day" (line 3), while the black boy is called "the sable pride of night" (line 4).
2. They are "indignant" (line 7).
3. They are "oblivious"; they pay the critics no mind.

Interpreting Meanings

4. The lightning refers to the boys' unexpected courage in risking an interracial friendship; the poet indirectly compares their boldness to the brilliance of a lightning bolt.

The "path of thunder" also refers to the example of the boys' friendship. Their boldness clearly runs the risk of upsetting established conventions—and such boldness, although salutary, may be ominous.

5. Student answers will vary. The larger topic, of course, is racial relations in the country as a whole.

Humanities Connection: Discussing the Fine Art
Raphael Soyer (1899–1988), who was born in Tombov, Russia and who immigrated to the United States in 1912, was the most prominent of three brothers who were all successful painters: the others were his identical twin Moses and their younger brother Isaac. They sustained into modern times the warm, realistic portrait tradition of Rembrandt. Raphael Soyer was known for his urban scenes, interiors, self-portraits, and pictures of quiet moments in the lives of bohemians, artists, and ordinary people. The passengers in this painting are on the New York City subway.

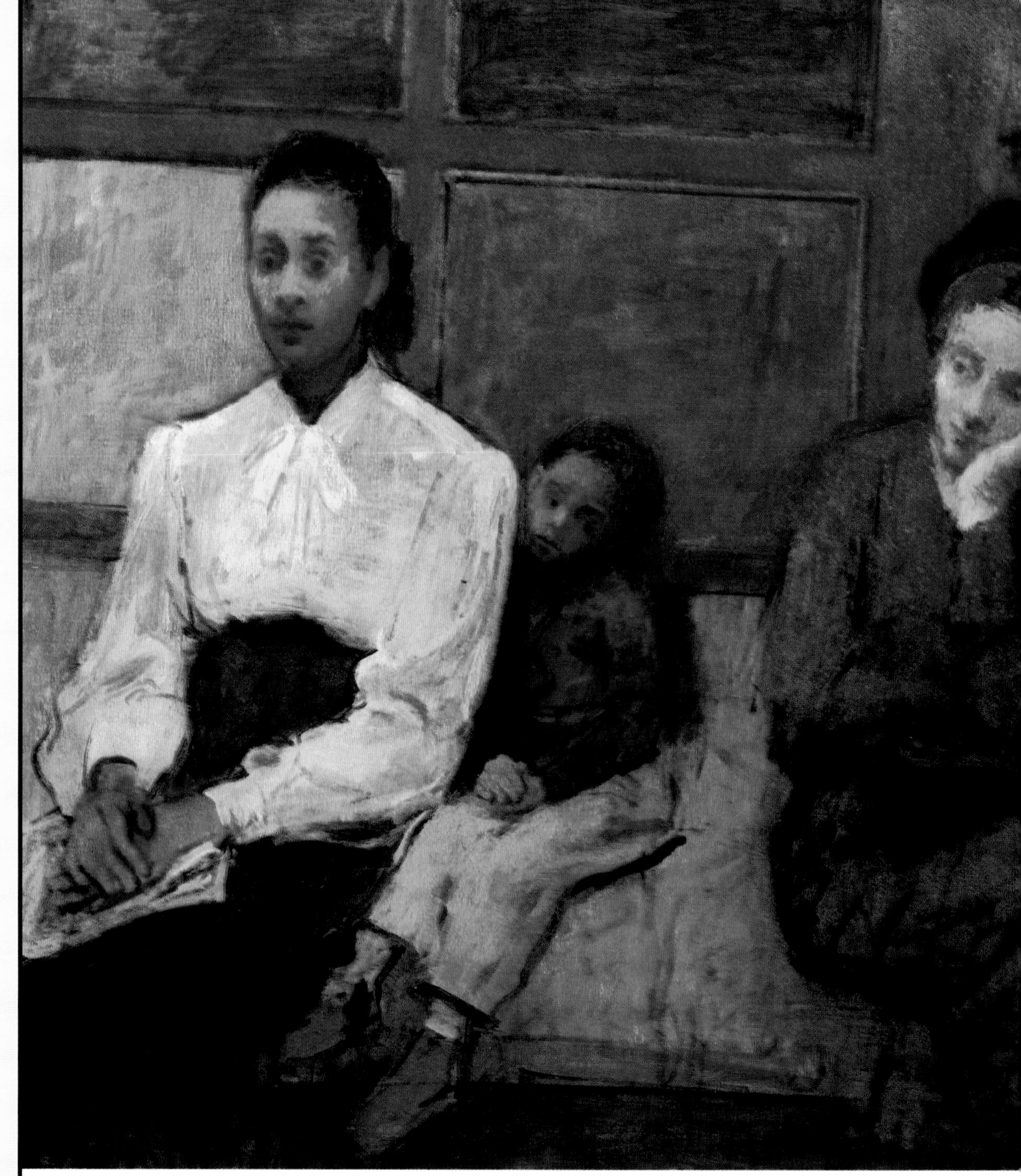

Passengers by Raphael Soyer (1953). Oil.

Collection of Mr. and Mrs. L. D. Johnson.

Supplementary Support Materials

1. Review and Response Worksheet: Theme (*CCB*)
2. Selection Test (*CCB*)

Preparation

Establishing a Purpose. Have students, as they read, imagine the thoughts and feelings of the eight-year-old child at the time this incident happens.

Closure

Have students write their own short version of the incident and how it affects the child.

Think about the title of this poem. Does it suggest something serious, or something relatively minor?

You might be disturbed by one word in this poem—imagine how it affected a child.

Incident

Once, riding in old Baltimore,
  Heart-filled, head-filled with glee,
I saw a Baltimorean
  Keep looking straight at me.

Now I was eight and very small,
  And he was no whit bigger,
And so I smiled, but he poked out
  His tongue, and called me "Nigger."

I saw the whole of Baltimore
  From May until December;
Of all the things that happened there
  That's all that I remember.

Responding to the Poem

Analyzing the Poem

Identifying Details

1. Which line reveals the speaker's mood at the beginning of the incident?
2. How many people are involved in the incident? Who are they?
3. What is the incident?

Interpreting Meanings

4. What might lead an eight-year-old boy to insult another child in the way described here? In what way might a child's prejudice be even more disturbing than an adult's?
5. What **ironic overtones** does the title have? Is this really only an "incident"?
6. The speaker never directly states his emotional response to the experience. How does the last stanza indirectly make clear the impression the event had on him?
7. How did the incident affect you?

Writing About the Poem

A Creative Response

1. **Writing Dialogue.** Write a conversation between the two boys who appear in "Tableau." Have them discuss what happens in "Incident."
2. **Planning a Screenplay.** Suppose you were going to do a short film based on the poem "Incident." Write a list of camera shots, in the order in which they would appear on the screen.
3. **Setting the Poem to Music.** If you can write music, create a melody for "Incident."

A Critical Response

4. **Comparing Poems.** Compare the diction and sentence structure in "Tableau" and "Incident." In a brief essay, show how the poet uses language to create two different effects in poems that are about very similar subjects.

Analyzing the Poem

Identifying Details

1. Line 2.
2. Two people: the eight-year-old narrator and another boy of about his own age.
3. The incident is the racial insult that the other boy gives the narrator.

Interpreting Meanings

4. Parental example, peer pressure, etc.

A child's prejudice suggests the never-ending cycle of prejudice, handed down through generations.

5. To call it a mere "incident" is thus an ironic characterization—since such a title understates the trauma that the speaker suffered.
6. By telling us that this incident was the only thing he could remember about Baltimore in his seven months there, the speaker indirectly emphasizes his profound sense of injury.
7. Students' answers will vary. Most students will empathize with the boy—some more strongly than others.

A. Expansion
According to H. L. Mencken in *The American Language,* all the early writers on American speech noted the absence of dialects, but this was only in comparison with Britain, where a large number of speech variations were found in a small geographical area.

THE AMERICAN LANGUAGE

by Gary Q. Arpin

American Dialects

A James Fenimore Cooper, writing to a British audience in 1828, boasted about the absence of American dialects: "In America, while there are provincial or state peculiarities, in tone, and even in pronunciation and use of certain words, there is no patois [dialect]. An American may distinguish between the Georgian and the New England man, but you cannot." Americans, Cooper claimed, were too active and mobile for dialects to establish themselves—a point with which many other observers agreed.

Yet a little over fifty years later, another American writer claimed to be using no less than *seven* dialects from a fairly small region in a single novel, *Huckleberry Finn* (page 414). "In this book," Mark Twain wrote in an explanatory note, "a number of dialects are used, to wit: the Missouri Negro dialect; the extremest form of the backwoods South-Western dialect; the ordinary 'Pike-County' dialect; and four modified varieties of this last."

Unity or Variety?

Quite a bit had changed in America in that fifty years, but not enough to create a wholesale explosion of dialects where none had existed before. Even if Twain was exaggerating about his "four modified varieties" of the "Pike County dialect," *Huckleberry Finn* depends for part of its effect on its use of dialect. Who was right about American dialects—Cooper or Twain?

Cooper was looking at an America that he was contrasting with England—a young, unified, mobile, democratic country, in which, if there were differences, they were kept within the family. ("An American may distinguish . . . but you cannot.") Moreover, Cooper saw the country evolving toward even greater unity. "The distinctions in speech," he wrote in the same essay, "were far greater twenty years ago than they are now."

Twain was looking very closely at a particular region of America and at distinctions of race, education, upbringing, and geography, all of which had small but significant effects on speech. Moreover, he was looking at a country whose recent Civil War had underscored the disunity of its people.

What we might call the Cooper and the Twain views toward American dialects, then, really represent two ways of looking at America and American speech. The Cooper view saw America as a unified nation marked principally by its distinctness from England. Twain saw the nation in terms of regional distinctions.

> **"The Cooper view saw America as a unified nation marked principally by its distinctness from England. Twain saw the nation in terms of regional distinctions."**

The Cooper view was shared by people like Noah Webster. Webster's dream was to stamp out local dialects and further unify the country (page 173). He stated this attitude in this comparison between American and British language: "We are less infected with various dialects, the remains of the different conquerers of the English nation, than the inhabitants of England." A dialect in Webster's view was a weakness, an infection to be cured by education and spelling reform.

But Twain and other regional writers saw the local speech as one of the best ways of describing the inhabitants of a region. Dialect stories and poems, in fact, were very popular in the late nineteenth and early twentieth centuries. They were usually comic, and much of the humor derived from the funny pronunciations and peculiar local words. At the same time these stories and poems in regional dialect illustrated the wisdom of the common man.

A New Englander called Hosea Bigelow was a famous "common-sense" character created by James Russell Lowell in his *Bigelow Papers.* Here Hosea's New England speech patterns are shown, as he addresses recruiting officers for the Mexican War—a conflict which Hosea, in his common sense, strongly disapproved of.

> Ez fer war, I call it murder—
> There you hev it plain an' flat;
> I don't want to go no furder
> Than my Testyment fer that;
> God hez sed so plump an' fairly,
> It's ez long ez it is broad,
> An' you've gut to git up airly
> Ef you want to take in God.
>
> —from *Bigelow Papers,*
> James Russell Lowell

"Twain and other regional writers saw the local speech as one of the best ways of describing the inhabitants of a region."

What Is a Dialect?

In his novel *The Grapes of Wrath,* John Steinbeck records a conversation between migrant workers from different parts of the country. Here the Joads, from Oklahoma, meet Ivy Wilson, from Kansas:

> "We're Joads," said Pa. "We come from right near Sallisaw."
>
> "Well, we're proud to meet you folks," said Ivy Wilson. "Sairy, these is Joads."
>
> "I knowed you wasn't Oklahomy folks. You talk queer kinda—that ain't no blame, you understan'."
>
> "Ever'body says words different," said Ivy. "Arkansas folks says 'em different, and Oklahomy folks says 'em different. And we seen a lady from Massachusetts, an' she said 'em differentest of all. Couldn't hardly make out what she was sayin'."
>
> —from *The Grapes of Wrath,*
> John Steinbeck

The "queer" talk that makes these Americans so different in speech is, of course, what linguists call dialect. A **dialect** can be defined as the characteristic language habits of a particular speech community. A speech community can be looked at in a very broad

A *"There wuz Maw and me, surrounded by screamin' Frenchmen, our Michelin-book lost and our faithful Cook's tour-guide nowhar in sight! . . ."*

A. Expansion
Mencken says that all American dialects are mutually intelligible with the possible exception of Gullah, a dialect spoken on some islands off the southeastern United States coast. Robert Hendrickson, in *American Talk,* devotes a chapter to Boontling, which was a secret language invented by the residents of Boonville, California. It thrived from about 1890 to 1930 and had a lexicon of 1200 words, such as *chipmunk* for "to hoard" and *earth* for "truth."

A. Expansion
It's generally agreed that the dialectal diversity of America is decreasing because of the influence of television and other mass media and of faster transportation, which have homogenized not only the speech but also the culture of the nation. (See the excerpt from *Blue Highways*, page 1071, for commentary on this phenomenon.)

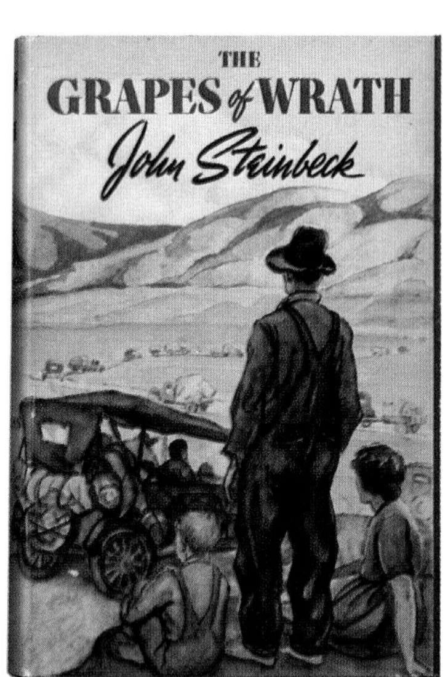

sense (as "American" versus "British"), or it can be subdivided almost endlessly. In fact, since no two people speak in exactly the same way, we might even say that each person speaks in his or her own dialect; linguists even have a term—*idiolect*—for the speech peculiar to one individual at one specific period of his or her life. But though there are differences in the way the Joads, the Wilsons, and the puzzling lady from Massachusetts speak, they all are still clearly "American."

Dialects are distinguished from standard English and from each other in three principal ways:

1. In pronunciation: Pa Joad says "Oklahomy," drops the final "d" in *understand,* and says "kinda" for *kind of.*

2. In vocabulary: Pa Joad uses an expression typical of his region when he says they come from "right near" Sallisaw.

3. In grammar: Pa says "knowed" instead of *knew,* "you wasn't" instead of *you weren't,* and "that ain't no blame."

The grammar of a language is its most profound element—like the skeleton of an animal. Grammar is likely to be changed only superficially in a dialect. There can be an English dialect in which a person can say, "Them was good peaches," but not one in which a person can say, "Peaches good was them." When fundamental grammar rules are violated, the language becomes incoherent. Differences in vocabulary between dialects are more common, and most common are differences in pronunciation.

A A number of factors contribute to the formation of dialects. The most important of these in America have been (1) settlement patterns (who settled in a region, where they came from, and how long they stayed there); (2) distance from a major cultural center; (3) influence of new immigrants; and (4) migration patterns.

America was settled first in the East, and the greatest profusion of dialects still exists there. As settlers moved westward, they brought their own speech patterns with them, but as people from different dialect areas mixed together in the new communities in the West, their dialects became less and less pronounced.

Three Major Dialect Regions

Scholars have divided American speech into three basic types: Northern, Midland, and Southern. Within these three general classifications, there are large and small areas with their own linguistic peculiarities. Western states, in general, have blended these dialects, since their settlers came from all three areas.

As a rule, regional differences in pronunciation and vocabulary are the easiest to pinpoint. If you take a *pail of swill* out to feed the hogs, you're probably a Northern farmer. If you take out a *bucket of slops,* you're probably from the South. If you pronounce *greasy* to rhyme with *we see,* you're probably from the North. If you pronounce it to rhyme with *easy,* you're probably from the Midland or South. Speakers in the Midland will usually sound the *r* in words like *barn* and *horse,* while older speakers in the Northern

"If you pronounce *greasy* to rhyme with *we see,* you're probably from the North. If you pronounce it to rhyme with *easy,* you're probably from the Midland or South."

and Southern regions will tend to eliminate it. Bostonians, as we all know, "pahk the cah." Southerners will say something like "pawk the caw." Sometimes Bostonians add *r*'s to the ends of words, as President John F. Kennedy did when he spoke of "Cubar." Midlanders will usually make no distinction between the pronunciations of *horse* and *hoarse* and *mourning* and *morning.* Older Northerners and Southerners will usually say something like "hawss" and "hohse" and "mawnin' " and "mohnin'." Southerners pronounce the *u* sound in words like *duty* and *news* as "you": "dyuty" and "nyews." Most Northern and Midland speakers will say "dooty" and "nooz."

Dialects and Characterization

As we have seen from the speech of Hosea Bigelow, the accurate portrayal of regional speech is an excellent way of creating both an individual character and a member of a class. The South, with its rich oral culture, is the region where dialect has been most effectively used in literature. Southern writers from William Gilmore Simms and Mark Twain to William Faulkner, Flannery O'Connor, and more recently Bobbie Ann Mason, have made it clear that speech patterns are an essential aspect of both our character and our environment. Here, Georgia writer Flannery O'Connor creates two distinct characters through use of two distinct Southern dialects:

> "Where did that little girl go to, boy?" he asked.
> "I ain't seen nair little girl," the boy said.
> The old man irritably fished in his pocket and handed him a nickel and said, "A pretty little girl in a yeller cotton dress."
> "If you speakin about a stout chile look lak you," the boy said, "she gone off in a truck with a white man."
> "What kind of a truck, what kind of a white man?" he yelled.
> "It were a green pick-up truck," the boy said smacking his lips, "and a white man she call 'daddy.' They gone thataway some time ago."
>
> —from "A View of the Woods,"
> Flannery O'Connor

Kentucky-born Bobbie Ann Mason records this conversation between two women:

> "Law, I wouldn't want to be cremated the way some of them are doing now," says Edda. "To save space."
> "Me neither," says Clausie with a whoop. "Did y'all see one of them Russians on television while back? At his funeral there was this horse and buggy pulling the body, and instead of a casket there was this little-bitty vase propped up there. It was real odd looking."
>
> —from "The Rookers,"
> Bobbie Ann Mason

"The South, with its rich oral culture, is the region where dialect has been most effectively used in literature."

READING CHECK TEST

1. The characteristic language habits of a particular speech community are called a ________. *dialect*

2. James Fenimore Cooper and Mark Twain disagreed about whether ________. *dialects exist in America*

3. The three major American dialect regions are ________. *Northern, Midland, and Southern*

4. The American region in which dialect fiction has been most effectively used is ________. *the South*

5. Dialectal differences in vocabulary and pronunciation show up much more often than differences in ________. *grammar*

Analyzing Language

1. One of the characteristics of a dialect is its use of a particular vocabulary. The objects or activities named by the words in each group below are all the same, but people in different regions of the country give them different names. Which word do you use? Do all of your classmates agree?

   a. *Porch* or *veranda*?
   b. *Pail* or *bucket*?
   c. *Faucet, spigot,* or *tap*?
   d. *Sidewalk* or *pavement*?
   e. *Quarter to four, quarter till four,* or *quarter of four*?
   f. *Graduated college* or *graduated from college*?
   g. *Hero sandwich, hoagie, wedge,* or *submarine*?
   h. *Soda* or *pop*?
   i. *Spider, skillet,* or *frying pan*?
   j. *Stand in line* or *on line*?
   k. *Swimsuit* or *bathing suit*?
   l. *Neaten, tidy,* or *ready up a room*?

2. Read the following passages, which reproduce several American dialects. Then answer the questions that follow.

Missouri, 1840's

"I've done considerable in the doctoring way in my time. Layin' on o' hands is my best holt—for cancer, and paralysis, and sich things; and I k'n tell a fortune pretty good, when I've got somebody along to find out the facts for me. Preachin's my line, too; and workin' camp-meetin's; and missionaryin around."

—from *The Adventures of Huckleberry Finn,*
Mark Twain

Midwest, 1920's

Whoever had been settin' in that chair, why they'd get up when Jim come in and give it to him.

You'd of thought it was a reserved seat like they have sometimes in a theayter. Hod would generally always stand or walk up and down, or some Saturdays, of course, he'd be settin' in this chair part of the time, gettin' a haircut.

Well, Jim would set there a w'ile without openin' his mouth only to spit, and then finally he'd say to me, "Whitey"—my right name, that is, my right first name, is Dick, but everybody round here calls me Whitey—Jim would say, "Whitey, your nose looks like a rosebud tonight. You must of been drinkin' some of your aw de cologne."

—from "Haircut,"
Ring Lardner

African American, New York City, 1980's

"I'm axin you all a simple question. You keep talkin bout what's proper for a woman my age. How old am I anyhow?" And Joe Lee slams his eyes shut and squinches up his face to figure. And Task run a hand over his ear and stare into his glass like the ice cubes goin calculate for him. And Elo just starin at the top of my head like she goin rip the wig off any minute now.

—from "My Man Bovane,"
Toni Cade Bambara

Interstate Truckers, 1980's

"This is that Alabama Rebel, this is that Alabama Rebel, do I have a copy?"

"Ahh, 10–4 on that, Alabama Rebel."

"This is that Alabama Rebel westbound on 80, ah, what's your handle, buddy, and where you comin from?"

"This is that, ah, Toby Trucker, eastbound for that big O town, round about the 445 marker."

"I copy you clear, Toby Trucker. How's about that Smokey Bear situation up by that Lincoln town?"

"Ah, you'll have to hold her back a little through there. Alabama Rebel, ah, place is crawling with Smokies like usual. Saw three of em's lights up on the overpass just after the airport here."

—from "I-80 Nebraska,"
John Sayles

   a. What variations from standard pronunciation do the spellings indicate?
   b. Is each writer consistent in his or her spelling variations? Can you propose reasons for any inconsistencies?
   c. What nonstandard or slang words and phrases are used by each speaker? What do these words mean?
   d. Are the speakers ungrammatical at any points?
   e. Do you find any examples of "eye-dialect"—a word spelled the way it is sounded in standard pronunciation? (An example would be *sez* for *says.*) Can you suggest any reasons why a writer would use eye-dialect?
   f. Which passage reproduces the dialect of a group, not of a region?

Exercises in Critical Thinking and Writing

INTERPRETING AND RESPONDING TO A POEM

Writing Assignment

Write a brief essay interpreting "Only the Polished Skeleton," by Countee Cullen. Include a discussion of the poem's meaning and of the feelings the poem evoked in you.

Background

When you **paraphrase** a work, you restate it in your own words, usually in simpler language. When you **interpret** a work, you explain what you think it means, and you tell how you reached that conclusion. In most cases, an essay of interpretation will include at least some paraphrasing.

The experience of reading a poem leaves us with two basic responses: we understand the poem's meaning and we feel an emotional reaction.

1. The **sense** or **meaning** of a poem is the idea the poet wants to convey. It is similar to the theme of a work of fiction. The meaning of a poem is rarely stated directly. It usually must be inferred by the reader.
2. Emotion is an important element in most poems. Poets evoke feelings in several ways, but you might concentrate on **connotations** and **imagery.**

   a. The **connotations** of a word are the emotions and associations attached to it, in addition to its strict dictionary definitions. The adjectives *determined* and *stubborn,* for example, have similar dictionary definitions, or denotations. Their connotations, however, are very different. Words with strong connotations are sometimes called "loaded words."

   In "The Haunted Oak" (page 645), for example, Dunbar uses connotations to arouse our emotions. What are the connotations of such loaded words as *dread, dried, weird,* and *pain*? What other words and phrases in the poem are loaded with connotations that are likely to create an emotional response?

   b. **Imagery** is the use of concrete, sensual details that appeal to our senses. Since imagery is an essential part of most poetry, your interpretation of a poem will almost certainly include a discussion of images. In "The Haunted Oak," the image of the oak tree is central to the meaning of the poem. What feelings do you associate with Dunbar's image?

Prewriting

Read the following poem several times. (One reading is never enough when you are going to write about a poem.) Try to read it aloud at least once, in order to appreciate its sound effects.

Only the Polished Skeleton

The heart has need of some deceit
  To make its pistons rise and fall;
For less than this it would not beat,
  Nor flush the sluggish vein at all.

With subterfuge and fraud the mind
  Must fend and parry thrust for thrust,
With logic brutal and unkind
  Beat off the onslaughts of the dust.

Only the polished skeleton
  Of flesh relieved and pauperized,
Can rest at ease and think upon
  The worth of all it so despised.

—Countee Cullen

A

Apply the following guidelines to the poem, and take notes on your answers. For questions that ask for examples, jot down examples (line numbers, words, and phrases).

Guidelines for Interpreting a Poem

1. What is the poem's **subject**? Does the poem describe an object or scene, an experience, or a character? Does the poet comment directly on the subject?
2. What **main idea** or meaning is the poet trying to convey? What lines or phrases give clues to the poem's meaning?
3. What would you say is the poem's **tone**—the poet's attitude toward the subject? How does the tone contribute to the total effect of the poem?
4. What **feeling** did you have after reading the poem? What specifically in the poem caused you to feel this way? (How did the imagery, connotations, figurative language, and sound effects affect the way the poem made you feel?)

A. Expansion
For some students the poem will prove less accessible than a somewhat more concrete poem. For these students, you might point out that many critics see racial overtones in the poem. According to these critics Cullen expresses racial bitterness in his statement of what is necessary for the body ("heat") and mind to survive and that only upon death can the individual "rest at ease." Help students to understand the contrast in the poem by pointing out the word *only* at the beginning of the last stanza.

Revising Essays
As students revise their essays, refer them to **Grammar, Usage, and Mechanics: A Reference Guide** at the back of their books.

Exercises in Critical Thinking and Writing/*cont.*

Writing

You might follow this plan for organizing your paper:

Paragraph 1: Cite the title, author, and subject of the poem. Briefly paraphrase the poem.
Paragraph 2: Interpret the poem's meaning, or main idea. Tell how you arrived at this interpretation.
Paragraph 3: Discuss your emotional response to the poem—how did the poem make you feel? Tell what elements in the poem (imagery, word connotation, figurative language, etc.) evoked this response, referring to specific lines and phrases.
Paragraph 4: Summarize your response to the poem as a whole—whether you liked it or not, and why.

Here is an essay of interpretation and response for "The Haunted Oak" by Paul Laurence Dunbar.

In "The Haunted Oak" Paul Laurence Dunbar recalls the era in which lynch mobs seized men and hanged them. The poem uses an unusual point of view to tell about one lynching. The first stanza introduces the speaker in the poem. He asks an old oak tree's withered bough why it is bare. In the rest of the poem, the oak tree tells the story of the lynching, of the tree's sympathy for the victim, and of the effects of the victim's curses.

Cites title, author, subject of poem.
Points out unusual feature—point of view.
Briefly paraphrases poem.

In this poem, Dunbar expresses feelings about the injustice of the lynch mobs, who executed victims and escaped punishment for their crimes. Although he does not mention the victim's race, I know that historically most of the lynch victims were black.

Interprets poem and poet's purpose.

In ironic contrast to the people in the poem, Nature is personified and shown to be in sympathy with the victim. The tree bent "down to hear his sigh" (1. 9) and "trembled sore when they rode away" (1. 11). In the fourth stanza, a dog howls and the night wind moans—as if grieving for the victim.

Points out irony.
Cites lines and phrases from poem to support a point.

But all who are guilty escape punishment for their crime, except for the judge who apparently allowed the lynching to take place and did not prosecute the lynchers. Even as he hunts an innocent deer, the judge is hunted by the guiltless victim, who "rides his soul/In the guise of a mortal fear" (11. 26-27). The victim's curses have other lasting effects: The ghost haunts the oak tree and withers the life from the bough on which he was hanged.

Infers details about the judge.

I felt sadness and anger at the murder of so many guiltless victims, and I felt horror at the way in which they were killed. I also felt a kind of spooky feeling from the images of the "weird" moonlight, the wailing wind, the howling dog, the ghost, and the tree.

Discusses reader's emotional response.
Cites specific images.

Dunbar's tone is very restrained. We know how angry he must be, but he never comments directly on what happened. This makes the effect of the poem even more powerful.

Discusses poet's tone.

I liked "The Haunted Oak" very much. I think the unusual point of view, the mournful and spooky imagery, and the poet's tone all work together to create a powerful poem.

Summarizes reader's response.

Revising and Proofreading

Use the guidelines in the section at the back of this book, called **Writing About Literature,** to revise and proofread your essay.

IMAGISM AND SYMBOLISM

The Chrysler Building Under Construction by Earl Horter (1931). Ink and watercolor on paper.

The Whitney Museum of American Art, New York City. Gift of Mrs. William A. Marstellar

UNIT NINE

Humanities Connection: Responding To The Fine Art

Earl Horter (1881–1940), an artist and illustrator, is best known for his etchings of big-city scenes, including *Smelters—Pittsburgh* and *Ole Creole Quarters, New Orleans.* In *The Chrysler Building Under Construction,* Horter's use of long thin forms and straight lines echoes the art deco style of the Chrysler Building itself. This building, at Lexington Avenue and East 42nd Street, New York City, was erected in 1929, just prior to the Great Depression. For a brief period, it was the world's tallest building.

? Most of the poets in this unit began writing early in the twentieth century. Why do you suppose this art was chosen to represent this period in American literature? (Answers will vary, but students should remember that the United States at this time was becoming a highly industrialized country and a world leader. The world's tallest building, then, is an appropriate symbol. Also, as students will learn from their study of Symbolism and Imagism, the lines of the painting reflect the type of poetry being written.)

Teaching The Imagism And Symbolism Unit

The Imagist movement, proclaimed by Ezra Pound, lasted less than ten years, from 1909 to 1917, but it had significant consequences. Imagism expanded the subject matter of poetry, emphasized the exact word, and helped to make free verse respectable. Imagism was part of a broader movement, Symbolism, which had started in France in the late nineteenth century and which began to influence American poetry in the early decades of the twentieth century. Symbolists stressed the importance of the sound, or music, of verse and, like the Imagists, believed that any subject matter is suitable for poetry.

Since the poems are so often cryptic or ambiguous, Imagism and Symbolism make real demands on the reader. To students in search of the one right answer for every question, such poetry can be a revelation (if multiple interpretations are accepted) or an ordeal (if hard-and-fast answers are demanded). During the study of this unit, your students may be comforted to learn that some critics have called Imagism "the cult of unintelligibility" and Symbolism a haven for the "rimed rebus." For this reason, the text material—the unit introduction, author biographies, and special features—are important to an understanding of the poetry. A brief review of Romanticism and Realism—students can review the introductions to Units Three and Six—can also help remind students of what poets in the early twentieth century were reacting to and rebelling against.

In this unit, students should gain a working knowledge of the meanings of the terms *imagism* and *symbolism,* but they should also keep in mind that poets and poems are more important than labels. Each poet is a creative individual, not just representative of a particular *-ism.* Since great poets can seldom be slotted into neat categories for analysis, students will find more diversity than uniformity in the seven poets who appear here.

Objectives Of The Imagism And Symbolism Unit

1. To improve reading proficiency and expand vocabulary
2. To gain exposure to notable poets and their works
3. To define and identify elements of poetry
4. To define and identify significant literary techniques
5. To respond to poetry orally and in writing
6. To practice the following critical thinking and writing skills:
   - **a.** Explaining poetic images
   - **b.** Comparing a poem with a prose text
   - **c.** Comparing and contrasting poems
   - **d.** Evaluating a character
   - **e.** Comparing characters
   - **f.** Responding to a critic
   - **g.** Interpreting a poem
   - **h.** Analyzing a poem

SUPPLEMENTARY SUPPORT MATERIALS: UNIT NINE

1. Unit Introduction Test (*CCB*)
2. Word Analogies Test (*CCB*)
3. Unit Review Test (*CCB*)
4. Critical Thinking and Writing Test (*CCB*)
5. Critical Thinking and Writing Test (*CCB*)
6. Instructional Overhead Transparencies

A. Responding to the Quotation
? Why "Make it new"? Why might a poet regard newness as essential? (A comment from a biographer of Ezra Pound may spark the discussion: "He [Pound] saw the education of a poet as necessarily a long process, in which the literature of the past must first be learned, and then escaped." Just as language changes constantly, so must poetry change. Have students express their opinions of that viewpoint.)

B. Connections
Students should note the great, though indirect, influence of Edgar Allan Poe on twentieth-century American poetry. A discussion can relate the Poe poems your students have read to this introductory description of them. A classroom comparison of the poetry of Poe (pages 248–259) and Whitman (pages 331–348) will illustrate the contrast.

IMAGISM AND SYMBOLISM

by **John Malcolm Brinnin**

A

Make it new! Art is a joyous thing.

—Ezra Pound

Sometime in the early twentieth century, Americans awoke to a sense that their own national culture had come of age. This was true in poetry and in painting, in jazz music and in modern dance, even in the new architecture of the skyscraper. In all these fields, Americans could point to their own contributions to the art of the Western world.

Up to this point, American poets (except for Whitman and Dickinson, who were still barely recognized) had shown little success in breaking free of their British ties. Ironically, when the liberation came, American poets found their new inspiration in an unexpected place—the "exotic" atmosphere of Paris.

This is not to say that the new poets failed to reflect a sense of the promise and wonder of their own nation. Their work was, for the most part, deeply rooted in the American grain. But, inspired by the revolutionary literary movement in France, they were able to transcend the narrow aspects of their creative lives. Learning from the French poets, the Americans were able to produce a new type of poetry through which the true American genius could speak.

The Influence of Poe

B

This international adventure of modern American poetry began through the influence of a poet who was born in Boston and never set foot in France—Edgar Allan Poe (page 226). In 1847, the French poet Charles Baudelaire (1821–1867) discovered Poe's verse and his critical theories. Baudelaire was impressed to find that Poe was unlike most American poets of the time in one important respect: Poe had no patience with poetry as a sermon or as an argument for some cause. What most excited Baudelaire was Poe's conviction that poetry should be concerned with the revelation of beauty, both physical and spiritual.

Poe was a paradox. Although he lived in the century of expansion, he did not look to the vast geographical frontiers that lighted the imagination of many American writers. He was unlike Walt Whitman, whose broad vision ranged like the sun across the continent and who translated himself into the whole concept of "America." Instead, Poe looked inward for inspiration, to the frontiers of the human mind. There he heard voices that spoke sometimes in angelic tones and sometimes in demonic whispers. Where Whitman celebrated the daylight enterprise and variety of America, Poe dwelt in a twilight zone, where figures from the real world mingled with figures from dreams.

Poe's poems expressed a hidden side of America. They spoke for the America that struggled with the spiritual effects of a culture that was becoming increasingly urban and capitalistic, in which the life of the soul was being eroded by greed and the lust for power.

"Poe dwelt in a twilight zone, where figures from the real world mingled with figures from dreams."

A. Responding (Challenging)

? If a Symbolist poem allows the imagination to discover its own truths within the poem, what effect would that have on the interpretation of the poem? (It would make interpretation a personal, individual matter. The poem could not be "explained" in the way that a more traditional poem, such as Holmes's "The Chambered Nautilus" [page 164] or Emerson's "Concord Hymn" [page 196] could be.)

B. Connections

You may wish to review briefly the literature of Romanticism. Have students look back at the table of contents (pages i–x) to refresh their memories of some of the major authors and works in the Romantic tradition.

Poe's concerns were beauty and human psychology, and his work is filled with settings and objects intended to arouse the feelings of his readers. In these respects, he was a forerunner of the movement in France known as Symbolism. This movement was itself strongly influenced by the works of Poe's French admirer, Charles Baudelaire.

Symbolism: The Search for a New Reality

In France, Symbolism dominated literature roughly from 1875 to 1895, but its influence was not fully felt in America until the second decade of the twentieth century.

Symbolism is a form of expression in which the world of appearances is violently rearranged by artists who seek a different and more truthful version of reality. The Symbolist poets do not merely describe objects; instead, they try to portray the emotional effects that objects produce.

Don't be misled by the term *symbolism.* It does not deal with the religious, national, or psychological symbols we are all familiar with. In fact, the Symbolist movement was concerned with getting rid of such symbols. The first Symbolists believed that these symbols had been overused, to the point where they were so dull that they no longer had any value in poetry.

A key word in symbolism is **revelation.** The Symbolists tried to create poems that would allow the imagination to discover truths. A Imagination is more reliable than reason, the Symbolists said, and just as precise. They insisted with almost religious fervor that mystery exists; that a part of our experience will always remain unexplained by logic and science; and that the task of the imagination is the penetration of the nonrational part of our makeup.

The Flatiron Building in New York City, under construction (1901–1902). The triangular building was designed by D. H. Burnham and Company, and for years was the world's most famous skyscraper.

C

C. Humanities Connection: Discussing the Photograph

The skyscraper, an architectural form that originated in the United States, is an apt symbol for the new era in American life and culture that began just after the turn of the century. Although the first skyscrapers were in Chicago, New York's unusual Flatiron Building emerged as the familiar early example of these buildings.

The appeal of skyscrapers was aesthetic as well as practical. In 1906 Edward Steichen (1879–1973) produced a photographic print in which the Flatiron Building is the central image. Hauntingly evocative, it is a pivotal picture in the transformation of photography into an art form. See John A. Kouwenhoven's *The Columbia Historical Portrait of New York* (New York: Harper & Row, 1953, 1972).

Symbolism vs. Romanticism

Symbolism was a new manifestation of the Romanticism that had swept over Europe and America in the nineteenth century. (See Units Three and Four.) B

The Romantics had stressed the primacy of feeling and the independence of the individual, and they had made a great stand against the mechanization of human life. They respected science as a form of knowledge, but were suspicious of the ways science was being put to use. The Romantics did not celebrate the technological advances of an age of steam power and iron construction, of factories and planned cities. Instead, they found hope for the human race in a return to nature. In the natural world, the Romantics found messages that spoke to the soul and gave it strength.

Now, decades later, the pace of industrialization and mechanization had increased, but the natural world—the haven of the Romantics—had been stripped of much of its mystery. Nature itself had become the object of scientific classification and reinterpretation.

A. Humanities Connection: Responding to the Fine Art
You will want to defer discussing this painting until your students read William Carlos Williams's "The Great Figure," page 719. The third and fourth lines of Williams's poem are "I saw the figure 5/ in gold."

At the time your students read "The Great Figure," you might have them list all the details they notice in the painting. They should find three references to the poet ("Bill," "Carlo," and "W.C.W.") **?** What else in the painting relates to the poem? What does not seem to relate to the poem? To what extent—if at all—does the painting illustrate the poem? (In general, Demuth's paintings were freely developed and were not intended as direct illustrations of the literary works that inspired them.) Have students share their responses in class.

I Saw the Figure 5 in Gold by Charles Demuth (1928). Oil on composition board.

The Metropolitan Museum of Art, New York City. Alfred Steiglitz Collection, 1949.

"The symbolist poets tried to reconstitute the sense of what it meant to be a human in a time when materialism was rapidly replacing religion."

After the publication of Charles Darwin's *The Origin of Species* (1859), the individual who wandered in nature could no longer behave as its divinely ordained master. In fact, according to Darwin's investigations, the human species seemed to have evolved in the same way that the animals had: through survival of the fittest. In short, what faced the artist as the twentieth century opened was the onslaught of the modern world, with its combined victory of science and technology, with its spiritual debasement, and its wholesale impoverishment of masses of people. The Symbolist poets faced this world with a distaste amounting to outrage. They could not, as poets, transform or erase it, so their revolt was spiritual. They tried to reconstitute the sense of what it meant to be human in a time when materialism was rapidly replacing religion and when individualism was succumbing to the power of mass culture.

The result was a pessimism that strongly contrasted with the optimism of most Romantics. The Romantics believed that people and the world could become perfect. The Symbolists had little faith that a true change in social conditions could come about until people recovered the dignity that science and technology had taken away from them.

A. Expansion
Make sure students understand that "In a Station of the Metro" is a complete poem, not an excerpt. Pound said about it, "In a poem of this sort one is trying to record the precise instant when a thing outward and objective transforms itself, or darts into a thing inward and subjective." Pound is trying to convey the complexity of his perception in language of extreme simplicity. Ask students whether they feel he succeeds.

B. Expansion
Guillaume Apollinaire's "It's Raining" is an example of what the poet called his "Calligrammes." Although Apollinaire was greatly influenced by the symbolist poets of the previous generation, "It's Raining" is more nearly a concrete poem—that is, a poem in which the visual effect of the typography is as important as, or more important than, the words themselves. Have students compare "It's Raining" to the Apollinaire poem "Heart, Crown, and Mirror" on page 710. Some students may enjoy trying to create poems of this kind. Point out to them that frequently words alone (without syntax but with the same words repeated many times) are used to form concrete poems.

For Further Research
Amy Lowell and Hilda Doolittle (H.D.) were significant poets in the Imagist movement. You might want to ask volunteers to find additional information about each of these poets and present it orally in class.

Americans and Symbolism

The two Americans who first came into close contact with Symbolism were Ezra Pound (page 711) and T. S. Eliot (page 740). Finding themselves in Europe at the outbreak of World War I, these two poets remained abroad for nearly all of their lives. But their physical absence from America did not diminish their influence. By their poetic practice and their critical writings, they brought the meanings and techniques of the French Symbolist movement into American poetry.

Imagism: "The Exact Word"

The most important single aspect of Symbolism that changed the texture of American poetry was a concern for the purification of language. With the help of several British poets, a group of Americans led by Pound founded a school perhaps better known and understood in America than Symbolism itself. This was the movement known as Imagism, dating from the years 1909–1917.

The **Imagists** were related to the Symbolists only in their conviction that poetry can be made purer by concentration on the precise, clear, unqualified image. Imagery alone, the Imagists believed, could carry a poem's emotion and message. It could do this almost instantly, without all the elaborate metrics and stanza patterns that were part of poetry's traditional mode. The Imagists—including Pound, Hilda Doolittle, and Amy Lowell—took on the role of reformers. They would rid poetry of its prettiness, sentimentality, and artificiality. They would concentrate on the raw power of the image to communicate feeling and thought.

The Imagists issued a "manifesto," or public declaration, proposing "to use the language of common speech," but to use "always the *exact* word, not merely the decorative word." In the same spirit, they called for poetry "hard and clear, never blurred or indefinite."

Aware that images are mostly associated with pictorial art, the Imagists declared: "We are not a school of painters, but we believe that poetry should render particulars exactly and not deal in vague generalities, however magnificent and sonorous." Some of the Imagists' inspiration was drawn from Eastern art forms, particularly the strict Japanese verse form known as **haiku.** In seventeen syllables a haiku juxtaposes two distinct images, and the reader is supposed to experience a moment of enlightenment on seeing how these images are related.

Pound defined an **image** as "that which presents an intellectual and emotional complex in an instant of time." Here is a famous Imagist poem that illustrates this concept:

In a Station of the Metro

The apparition of these faces in the crowd;
Petals on a wet, black bough.

—Ezra Pound

A

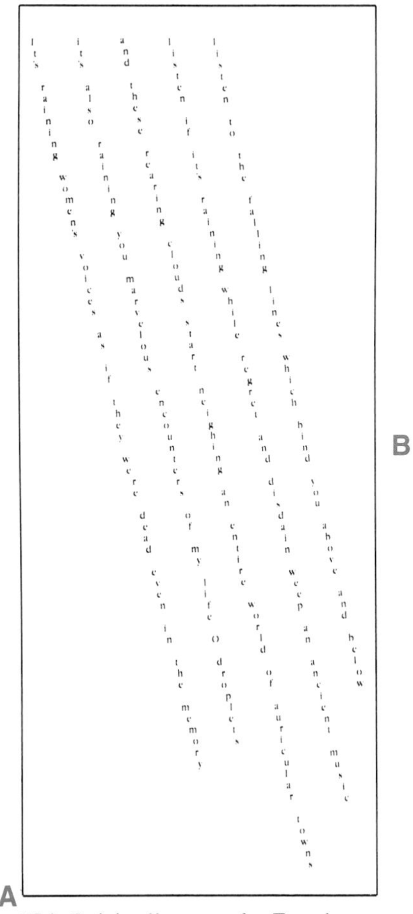

B

"It's Raining," a poem by French Symbolist Guillaume Apollinaire (1880–1918).

Reading Check Test

1. Charles Baudelaire, the French Symbolist poet, admired the verse and critical theories of (a) Walt Whitman (b) Ralph Waldo Emerson (c) T.S. Eliot (d) Edgar Allan Poe. *(d)*

2. Symbolism differed from Romanticism in its (a) use of rhythm (b) pessimism (c) dislike of science (d) verse forms. *(b)*

3. The leading figure in the Imagist movement was (a) Ezra Pound (b) Emily Dickinson (c) Charles Darwin (d) Hilda Doolittle. *(a)*

4. Imagism was inspired in part by (a) ballads (b) haiku (c) science (d) fables. *(b)*

5. Tradition-minded poets were especially bothered by the Imagists' use of (a) symbols (b) rhyme (c) free verse (d) figures of speech. *(c)*

N F L
W A Y H
O M E M E
D A
E R
D T
I L
S I
P K
U E
N
A

W
T K H H D
HE INGS O AVE IED
ONE BY ONE
ARE REBORN IN POETS' HEARTS

IN
IONS THIS
FLECT MIR
RE ROR
THE I
LIKE AM
NOT Guillaume Apollinaire EN
AND CLOSED
GELS A
AN LIVE
GINE AND
MA REAL
I AS
YOU

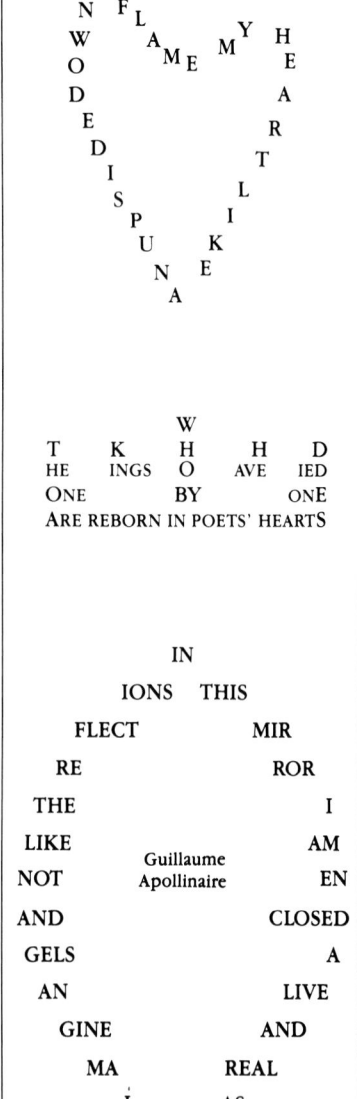

"Heart, Crown, and Mirror," a poem by French Symbolist Guillaume Apollinaire (1880–1918).

In this brief lyric, the "instant of time" is the moment the poet sees the faces in a crowd in a Paris subway station. Suddenly, the faces remind the observer of petals hanging from the wet bough of a tree. The "intellectual and emotional complex" is the moment when we realize that these faces are as fragile as the petals, soon to fall from the black tree.

Today, poems with this sort of imagistic technique are commonplace. But at the time the Imagists published their manifesto on poetry's nature and function, their theory created a great stir. It was disturbing partly because it insisted that the range of poetic subject matter might include the kitchen sink as well as the rising of the moon, the trash can as well as the Chinese porcelain vase.

But the strongest opposition to the Imagists was caused by their proposal "to create new rhythms—as the expression of new moods. . . . We do believe that the individuality of a poet may often be better expressed in free verse than in conventional forms." To tradition-minded poets, this **free verse** was deplorable. It meant a loosening of poetic standards and an assault on the very craft of poetry. The history of poetry in the following decades would prove that these poets were mistaken in their fears about the decline of poetic standards. They did not yet realize that successful free verse was at least as difficult to create as verse written in traditional forms.

While Imagism never became an important movement in itself, it gave rise to some of our finest talents. The reputations of some of the movement's early leaders have faded with time. But others in the forefront of Imagism went beyond the movement's limitations and expanded its insights. Besides Pound and Eliot, these included William Carlos Williams (page 717), Marianne Moore (page 724), E. E. Cummings (page 735), and Wallace Stevens (page 750).

Imagism came to stand for a whole new order of poetry in the United States. Most Americans became acquainted with the movement mainly as the school of "free verse." By this they meant simply poetry without regular rhyming and metrical patterns. But the Imagist program was not only a call for a new method of organizing lines and stanzas; it was an invitation to a new way of seeing the world.

As practiced by its masters, Imagism had much in common with the new art of film. Instead of following normal rules of logic, syntax, and grammar in presenting a subject, Imagists startled their readers. They used closeups, flashbacks, and montage—the film device of showing two or three images at once. Readers could no longer simply sit back and gradually take in a poem as it unrolled, because the connections provided by conventional poets were often omitted by the Imagists. Readers had to grasp on their own the logic of the back-to-back images. In other words, readers now had to participate in a poem in order to understand it. Those unwilling or unable to do this were quick to belittle the products of Imagism and to dismiss the movement as a fad. But modern American poetry, conceived in France by the Symbolist movement and nurtured in the cradle of Imagism, was here to stay.

Comment From A Critic

T.S. Eliot, who received early encouragement from Ezra Pound, acknowledged a personal debt to him in an essay published in 1946:

"No one could have been kinder to younger men, or to writers who, whether younger or not, seemed to him worthy and unrecognized. No poet, furthermore, was, without self-depreciation, more unassuming about his own achievement in poetry. The arrogance which some people have found in him is really something else; and whatever it is, it has not expressed itself in an undue emphasis on the value of his own poems. He liked to be the impresario for younger men, as well as the animator of artistic activity in any milieu in which he found himself. In this role he would go to any lengths of generosity and kindness. . . ."

After reading the biography of Ezra Pound, students might be asked to speculate as to why so kind and generous a man as this would embrace a vicious ideology like fascism. (A brief, persuasive explanation can be found in Christine Froula's *A Guide to Ezra Pound's Selected Poems* [New Directions, 1983], pages 10–12.)

A. Expansion

In addition to Imagism, Pound is often associated with Vorticism (from the word *vortex*), a very short-lived artistic and literary movement (1912–1915) related to futurism and cubism in art.

Ezra Pound (1885–1972)

Ezra Pound is remembered by many people as the man who was charged with treason during World War II and who spent many years in a mental institution. This notoriety, acquired toward the end of his life, has tended to obscure Pound's impact on American poetry. But his healthy influence is still apparent everywhere; the generations of poets who have come after him have confirmed it. They have kept alive a happier memory of a man whose career wavered between brilliance and episodic madness.

Pound was born in Hailey, Idaho, and grew up in Pennsylvania. After graduating from Hamilton College in Clinton, New York, he took the first steps toward a teaching career, first at the University of Pennsylvania and then at Wabash College in Indiana. Even as a young man, however, Pound was too unconventional in his thinking and behavior to fit into a conservative academic community.

In search of greater personal freedom and of contacts with European poets, Pound settled in London in 1908. There he became a leading spokesman for the new poetic movement known as Imagism. He also became a self-exiled critic of American life and torchbearer for any art that challenged the complacent middle class.

Pound—whose slogan was "Make it new!"—was a born teacher whose advice was sought by the most brilliant young writers of the period. T. S. Eliot (page 740) acknowledged Pound's valuable advice when he dedicated his great poem *The Waste Land* (1922) to Pound. For a time, Pound served as an unpaid secretary and mentor to the great Irish poet William Butler Yeats.

After World War I, Pound felt the need for even broader horizons than London offered him. He moved to Paris in 1920, the same year that he published *Hugh Selwyn Mauberley,* one of his most important poems. He spent time with artists from many countries whose innovations put them in the forefront of modernism. Pound also mingled with the American expatriate community—writers who had voluntarily left home to live and write in the headier atmosphere of France. These included Ernest Hemingway (page 553), Gertrude Stein, E. E. Cummings (page 735), and Archibald MacLeish.

In 1924, Pound moved to the town of Rapallo, Italy, overlooking the Tyrrhenian Sea. There he continued to write poetry and criticism. And now came a tragic turning point in Pound's life. His interest in economics and social theory led him to support Benito Mussolini, the Fascist dictator of Italy.

When World War II broke out, Mussolini's government allied itself with Hitler and became an enemy of the United States. Pound stayed in Italy, and in a terrible lapse of judgment turned propagandist for Mussolini's policies. In his radio broadcasts from Italy, Pound denounced the struggle of Great Britain, France, the United States, and the Soviet Union against Germany, Italy, and Japan. Some of these broadcasts were vicious with anti-Semitism.

When the American army advanced northward up the Italian peninsula in 1945, Pound, the notorious propagandist, was taken prisoner. He was confined to a cage on an airstrip near Pisa and eventually returned to the United States to be tried for treason. But psychiatrists judged him to be mentally incompetent, and the poet was committed to St. Elizabeth's, a hospital for the criminally insane, in Washington, D.C.

Twelve years later, he was released through the intercession of poets Archibald MacLeish and Robert Frost, who argued that his literary contributions outweighed his disastrous lack of judgment and his notorious bigotry. Pound lived out the ten years left to him in Rapallo and in Venice. He was a sad old man who rarely spoke. In his rare interviews, he seemed to try to penetrate the meanings of his own life, though he remained assertive and opinionated about poetry, economics, and the state of the world to the end.

During these years of exile, a reporter once asked Pound where he was living. "In hell," the old man answered. "Which hell?" the reporter asked. "Here," said Pound, pressing his heart. "Here."

When he died in Venice, Pound left behind a body of work extending from the delicate lyrics he wrote at the turn of the century to *The Cantos,* an enormous epic he did not complete until well over fifty years later. He also left a public record which still uncomfortably involves scholars and historians in that mystery known as "The Case of Ezra Pound."

SUPPLEMENTARY SUPPORT MATERIALS

1. Vocabulary Activity Worksheet (*CCB*)
2. Review and Response Worksheet: Imagism (*CCB*)
3. Language Skills Worksheet: Diction (*CCB*)
4. Selection Test (*CCB*)
5. Audiocassette recording

DEVELOPING VOCABULARY

The following words from the poem are tested in the Selection Test. (See also Vocabulary Activity Worksheet.)

eddy narrows

PREPARATION

ESTABLISHING A PURPOSE. Have students read Pound's "rules" for writing Imagistic poetry on page 714. Then have students read to determine whether this poem adheres to the guidelines.

A. Imagery

? What images in this stanza identify the speaker and her future husband as children? (The way the speaker's hair is cut and the fact that both are playing identify the two as children.)

B. Humanities Connection: Responding to the Fine Art

The painting by Ch'ien Hsuan (1235–1300), one of China's greatest artists, provides an ideal companion piece to Pound's "The River Merchant's Wife: A Letter," a poem based on the notes of a Chinese scholar.

? What do you see in the painting? What kind of structure does Wang Hsi-chih seem to be standing on? How can you tell (even without the Chinese seals and symbols) that this is an Oriental painting? (Have students share their reactions to the painting.)

Pound pays tribute with this poem to Li T'ai Po, the most famous of ancient Chinese poets. (Li died in 762.) Pound adapts the Chinese poet's tone and some of his style to compose a poem in the form of a letter. After you read the first seven lines, stop and identify the speaker.

The River-Merchant's Wife: A Letter

Li T'ai Po

A

While my hair was still cut straight across my forehead
Played I about the front gate, pulling flowers.
You came by on bamboo stilts, playing horse,
You walked about my seat, playing with blue plums.
And we went on living in the village of Chokan:
Two small people, without dislike or suspicion.

At fourteen I married My Lord you.
I never laughed, being bashful.
Lowering my head, I looked at the wall.
Called to, a thousand times, I never looked back.

B

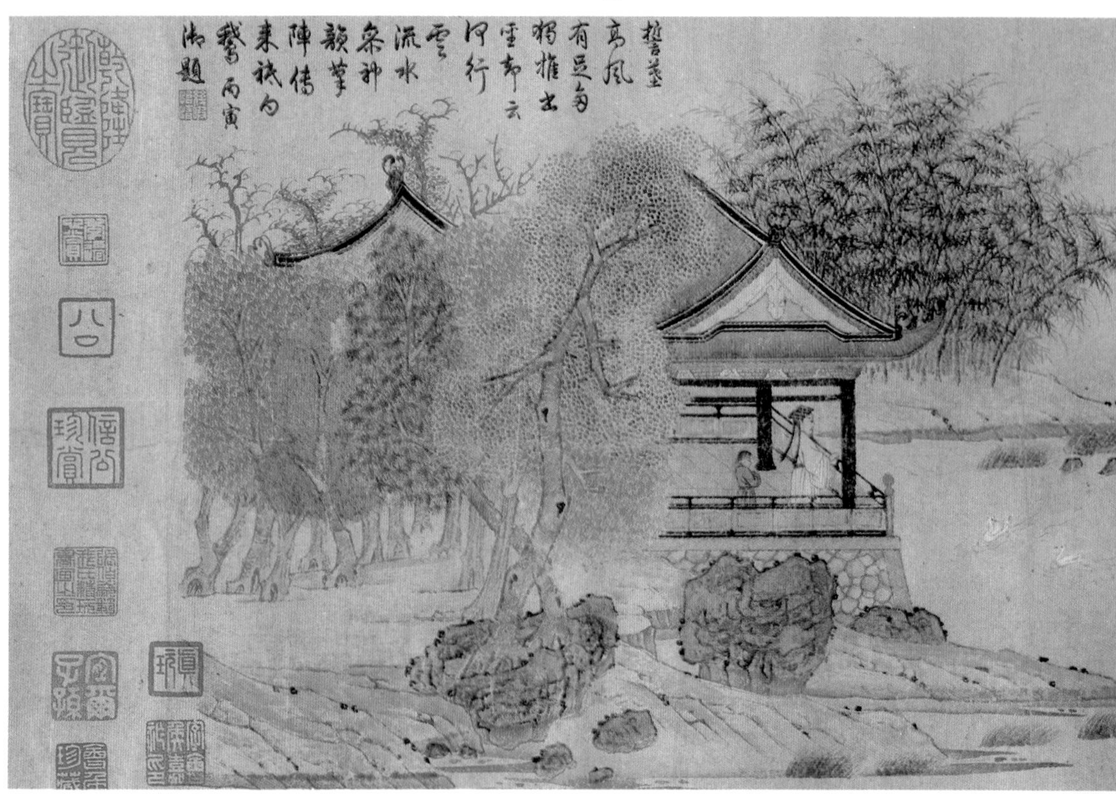

Wang Hsi-chih Watching Geese by Ch'ien Hsuan (detail) (1235–1300). Handscroll, ink color and gold on paper.

COMMENT FROM A CRITIC
Christine Froula's *A Guide to Ezra Pound's Selected Poems* (New Directions, 1983) explains the difficulty Pound had with the first line of this poem. The Chinese scholar, from whose notes Pound was working, had translated Li T'ai Po's line: "My hair was at first covering my brows (child's method of wearing hair)." Pound tried the American *bangs.* His wife suggested the English *fringe.* Amy Lowell and Florence Ayscough translated the line: "When the hair of your unworthy one first began to cover the forehead." A comparison between these suggestions and line 1 in the poem shows how effectively Pound solved his difficulty.

CLOSURE
Have students write a sentence stating what they believe to be the single most vivid image in the poem. Survey the class to learn the various choices.

At fifteen I stopped scowling,
I desired my dust to be mingled with yours
Forever and forever and forever.
Why should I climb the lookout?

At sixteen you departed,
A You went into far Ku-to-yen, by the river of swirling eddies,
And you have been gone five months.
The monkeys make sorrowful noise overhead.

You dragged your feet when you went out.
By the gate now, the moss is grown, the different mosses,
Too deep to clear them away!
The leaves fall early this autumn, in wind.
The paired butterflies are already yellow with August
B Over the grass in the West garden;
They hurt me. I grow older.
If you are coming down through the narrows of the river Kiang,
Please let me know beforehand,
And I will come out to meet you
As far as Cho-fu-Sa.
C

The Metropolitan Museum of Art, New York. Gift of the Dillon Fund, 1973.

A. Setting
? References such as Ku-to-yen and noisy monkeys overhead are unfamiliar to American readers. Why do you suppose Pound chose to set his poem in China, rather than in the United States? (Answers will vary. Students might note that the custom of China in the time this poem is set—that of marrying young children—allowed Pound to develop the theme of slowly growing love.)

B. Imagery
Have students identify at least four striking images in the last stanza. (Lines 19, 21, 23, and 24, for example)

C. Responding
? What thoughts or memories does the poem call to mind? What emotion does it arouse? (Thoughts of love; nostalgia, longing, pain)

ANALYZING THE POEM
Identifying Details
1. In stanza 1, the girl (speaker) and boy play together as children. In stanza 2, bashful at age fourteen, she marries the boy. In stanza 3, at age fifteen, she "stopped scowling." In stanza 4, a year later, her husband leaves on a long river voyage.
2. If her husband will send advance news of his return, she will come to meet him at Cho-fu-Sa.

Interpreting Meanings
3. The speaker's outlook on her marriage changes from shy silence to deep commitment. In line 14, to "climb the lookout" might imply being on watch for her husband's return, or it might be symbolic of her anxiety about the future.
4. That he dragged his feet when he left.
5. Autumn seems right for the speaker's melancholy mood.
6. The "paired butterflies" that remind her of her own separation. To her, five months of separation must seem like a much longer time; it makes her conscious of aging.
(Answers continue in left-hand column.)

(Continued from top.)
7. Perhaps some business affair took longer to settle than he planned.
8. Yes, because of her request at the end of the poem. No, her request is wishful thinking.
Answers will vary.

A. Expansion
Your students may be interested to know that not all the Imagists agreed with Pound's rules or with his leadership. Amy Lowell, a relative newcomer, began publishing Imagist anthologies in the United States. Her publisher pronounced Lowell "the foremost member of the Imagists." Pound, irritated by her presumption and unimpressed by some of the so-called Imagist poems, began calling the movement "Amygism."

Responding to the Poem

Analyzing the Poem

Identifying Details

1. What events are referred to in stanzas 1–4?
2. In the last stanza, what does the wife promise to do?

Interpreting Meanings

3. How is the third stanza a turning point in the poem? In line 14, what is the wife indirectly expressing?
4. What **image** suggests that the husband was reluctant to leave home?
5. How is the season of the year appropriate to the **mood** of the poem?
6. What "hurts" the young wife in line 25, and why? Why does she say, after only five months, that she grows "older" (line 25)?
7. Why do you think the husband left? Do you think he is ever going to return? What may have delayed him?
8. Do you think this letter was ever sent?

Primary Sources

"A Few Don'ts by an Imagist"

A Ezra Pound wrote the following "rules" for poets in an article in the March 1913 issue of *Poetry* magazine. Many of them are useful to all writers.

"It is better to present one Image in a lifetime than to produce voluminous words. . . .

"Pay no attention to the criticism of men who have never themselves written a notable work. Consider the discrepancies between the actual writing of the Greek poets and dramatists, and the theories of the Greco-Roman grammarians, concocted to explain their meters.

Language

"Use no superfluous word, no adjective, which does not reveal something.

"Don't use such an expression as 'dim lands of peace.' It dulls the image. It mixes an abstraction with the concrete. It comes from the writer's not realizing that the natural object is always the *adequate* symbol.

"Go in fear of abstractions. Don't retell in mediocre verse what has already been done in good prose. Don't think any intelligent person is going to be deceived when you try to shirk all the difficulties of the unspeakably difficult art of good prose by chopping your composition into line lengths. . . .

"Don't imagine that the art of poetry is any simpler than the art of music, or that you can please the expert before you have spent at least as much effort on the art of verse as the average piano teacher spends on the art of music.

"Be influenced by as many great artists as you can, but have the decency either to acknowledge the debt outright, or to try to conceal it.

Rhythm and Rhyme

"Let the neophyte know assonance and alliteration, rhyme immediate and delayed, simple and polyphonic, as a musician would expect to know harmony and counterpoint and all the minutiae of his craft. No time is too great to give to these matters or to any one of them, even if the artist seldom has need of them. . . .

"Consider the way of the scientists rather than the way of an advertising agent for a new soap.

"The scientist does not expect to be acclaimed as a great scientist until he has *discovered* something. He begins by learning what has been discovered already. He goes from that point onward. He does not bank on being a charming fellow personally. He does not expect his friends to applaud the results of his freshman class work. Freshmen in poetry are unfortunately not confined to a definite and recognizable classroom. They are 'all over the shop.' Is it any wonder 'the public is indifferent to poetry'?

"Don't chop your stuff into separate iambs. Don't make each line stop dead at the end, and then begin every next line with a heave. Let the beginning of the next line catch the rise of the rhythm wave, unless you want a definite longish pause. . . .

"If you are using a symmetrical form, don't put in what you want to say and then fill up the remaining vacuums with slush. . . ."

—Ezra Pound

THE OBJECTIVE CORRELATIVE

Throughout the poem on pages 712–713, the letter writer's feelings are expressed more often by references to objects and activities than by direct statements. This is a method often practiced by Pound and identified by T. S. Eliot in a famous definition. Eliot said that the only valid way to express emotion in art is to find an **objective correlative.** He defined this term as "a set of objects, a situation, a chain of events which shall be the formula of that *particular* emotion."

The term "objective correlative" soon became a permanent part of the vocabulary of poetic analysis. Seven years earlier, however, Pound had anticipated the essence of the term, when he had referred to poetry as "a sort of inspired mathematics" that gives us "equations for the human emotions."

Eliot's definition became much more widely known. However, both men were getting at the same idea. Poetry, they believed, is a means of expressing emotion *indirectly* but precisely. Poetry does this by finding the images and actions that best embody a feeling.

This position led to a kind of poetic shorthand that eliminated everything but part of the equation (the objective correlative). In this shorthand, a reader would not find the connections that usually join the parts of an argument, a story, or even most poems. Readers are forced to supply these connections by themselves. In doing so, they will discover the logic of the poem. This kind of reading can be hard work, but many people also find it very satisfying.

"The River-Merchant's Wife" is a good example of this kind of poem. How many objective correlatives can you find? In other words, how many examples can you find in the poem where emotions are embodied in objects or actions, instead of being expressed directly?

Begin by concentrating on the ways in which the bride makes her courtship vivid. Then notice how her shy, modest character is established. Continue by finding the concrete equivalents of particular emotions. Think about the "lookout" in line 14 and the "river of swirling eddies" in line 16.

A note of caution: Not every poem deals in objective correlatives. Most poems, including many modern ones, have a logical or narrative sequence that is easy to recognize. But other poems will make no logical sense until *you* supply the connecting links. They are organized, not by a *logical* sequence, but by a *psychological* one. These are the poems that can be analyzed according to Eliot's definition of *objective correlative.*

Ezra Pound in the garden of his Paris studio (1923).

COMMENT FROM A CRITIC

In critiquing Ezra Pound's "The Garden" (page 716), James F. Knapp writes, "Perhaps the greatest misunderstanding of Imagism, by readers as well as by poets who quickly began to imitate it, was that it demanded visual images to the virtual exclusion of everything else"—that objective correlatives were essential. Knapp argues that Pound's "doctrine was far more flexible and subtle than some of his imitators understood." He cites the final stanza of "The Garden" as an example. After your students have read the poem, you might ask them to discuss how the last stanza of the poem illustrates a "flexible and subtle" interpretation of Imagism. Have students identify the objective correlatives, if any, in the poem.

PREPARATION

ESTABLISHING A PURPOSE. Before beginning the poem, be sure students have read the headnote. Then have students read the poem to find the "true subject."

SUPPLEMENTARY SUPPORT MATERIALS

1. Vocabulary Activity Worksheet (*CCB*)
2. Review and Response Worksheet: Imagism (*CCB*)
3. Language Skills Worksheet: Diction (*CCB*)
4. Selection Test (*CCB*)

DEVELOPING VOCABULARY

The following words from the poem are tested in the Selection Test. (See also Vocabulary Activity Worksheet.)

skein	breeding
piecemeal	exquisite
anemia	excessive
rabble	indiscretion

ANALYZING THE POEM

Identifying Details

1. "Like a skein of loose silk blown against a wall."
2. That of the woman's elegance and fragility with the vitality and durability in the "infants of the very poor."

Interpreting Meanings

3. Inability or unwillingness to feel or express emotions.
4. It is an ironic reference to the "meek," for the infants are energetic and strong.
5. "Ancestry"; "proper manners"; "propagation of the species."
6. Answers will vary. She might be put off by his audacity.
7. Answers will vary. Pound's true subject may have to do with the contrast in social classes. Or it may have to do with the barriers to communication we erect.
8. Consider the homeless in our affluent cities.

CLOSURE

Ask students to suggest a word or words to describe the tone of this poem. Discuss the tone in class.

En robe de parade is a quotation from the nineteenth-century French poet Albert Samain. The quotation establishes an ironic tone for the poem. The phrase means "dressed for show"; a military translation might be "in full regalia." The poem seems to be about the woman who is described in the simile in the first stanza, but its true subject is something else.

The Garden

En robe de parade.
—Samain

Like a skein of loose silk blown against a wall
She walks by the railing of a path in Kensington Gardens,°
And she is dying piecemeal
        of a sort of emotional anemia.

And round about there is a rabble
Of the filthy, sturdy, unkillable infants of the very poor.
They shall inherit the earth.

In her is the end of breeding.
Her boredom is exquisite and excessive.
She would like someone to speak to her,
and is almost afraid that I
        will commit that indiscretion.

2. **Kensington Gardens:** a park in London, frequented by people of various social classes.

Responding to the Poem

Analyzing the Poem

Identifying Details

1. What **simile** describes the woman in the first stanza?
2. What contrast is set up in the first two stanzas?

Interpreting Meanings

3. How would you explain "emotional anemia"? How would that cause someone to die "piecemeal"?
4. The phrase "They shall inherit the earth" comes from the New Testament of the Bible (Matthew 5:5). What does the phrase mean in this context?
5. Use a dictionary to find several meanings for *breeding*. Then identify the **pun** in line 8.
6. Why do you think the speaker says he would be committing an *indiscretion* if he engages the woman in conversation?
7. This is a poem about individuals, but it is also about something broader. What is Pound's true subject?
8. Think about the contrast in the first two stanzas. What similar contrast can you think of from your own experience?

Writing About the Poems

A Creative Response

1. **Creating an Image.** Choose a topic you feel strongly about. Then think of a single concrete image that suggests these feelings. In a sentence or phrase, describe that image in a way that communicates your feelings. *Don't express your feeling directly.*

A Critical Response

2. **Explaining Images.** Choose at least three images from one of the poems by Pound, and in a paragraph, explain how each image is used as an objective correlative to convey emotion indirectly.

William Carlos Williams (1883–1963)

William Carlos Williams was born in Rutherford, New Jersey, where he lived and practiced medicine as a pediatrician and obstetrician for most of his adult life. While studying medicine at the University of Pennsylvania, he came in contact with Ezra Pound. Pound's theories of Imagism had a considerable influence on Williams's early verse, which was published in *Poems* (1909) and *The Tempers* (1913). During the next two decades, however, Williams went on to evolve his own distinctive poetic style, which he called Objectivism. Williams defined the source of his poetry as "the local," by which he meant a strict focus on the reality of individual life and its surroundings. Williams looked for a return to the barest essentials in poetry. In this respect, he opposed such contemporaries as Eliot and, to a certain extent, Pound himself, in their frequent use of allusions to art, history, religion, and foreign cultures. (Williams and Eliot, in fact, made no secret of their dislike for each other's work.)

In addition to poetry, Williams produced novels, plays, essays, and several autobiographical memoirs. His influence on twentieth-century American poetry, especially since World War II, has been considerable, and he was awarded the Pulitzer Prize in 1963. His masterpiece is the long epic *Paterson,* a poem which appeared in five volumes over a twelve-year span (1946–1958). In this partly autobiographical epic, a poet wanders the neighborhoods of Paterson, New Jersey, an industrial town near Williams's home, and meditates on the variegated experiences of urban life.

In his insistence on local topics and colloquial speech, Williams allied himself with the kind of poetic revolution championed by the English Romantics a century earlier. William Wordsworth, in his preface to *Lyrical Ballads* (1798), had written that poetry should treat "incidents and situations from common life . . . [in a] selection of language really spoken by men."

Williams deliberately wrote in a spare, detached style about commonplace subjects, the very opposite of what many nineteenth-century American writers had thought of as "poetic material." Using as his slogan "No ideas but in things," Williams wrote of such sights and events as animals at the zoo, schoolgirls walking down a street, a piece of paper blowing down a street, or a raid on the refrigerator. As Marianne Moore, an admirer, pointed out, Williams's topics are "American"—crowds at the movies, turkey nests, mushrooms among the fir trees, mist rising from the duck pond, the ball game.

A. Expansion
William Carlos Williams is one of a number of modern poets whose livelihood was not directly related to writing. Williams was a medical doctor; Wallace Stevens (page 750) was an insurance executive; and in recent years many poets have been college English professors. Ask students what effects, if any, might follow from poets' spending their working lives pursuing other careers.

Additional Writing Assignment
Go over the last paragraph of the Williams biography in class. Then ask students to write at least three sentences suggesting three to five additional topics that Williams might find appropriate for poems.

PREPARATION

ESTABLISHING A PURPOSE. Before students read any of the four poems by William Carlos Williams, review briefly the principles of Imagism. Point out that Williams became disenchanted with Imagism fairly early and pursued what he called Objectivism. Ask students if they see any movement away from Imagism in the four poems as they read them.

SUPPLEMENTARY SUPPORT MATERIALS

1. Review and Response Worksheet: Metaphor and Imagery (*CCB*)
2. Selection Test (*CCB*)
3. Instructional Overhead Transparency

COMMENT FROM A CRITIC

According to Jerome Mazzaro, Williams had a great affection for an old ex-fisherman in whose backyard he saw "the red wheelbarrow surrounded by the white chickens." Many readers overlook the possibility that the opening—"so much depends"—might refer to the owner's (the ex-fisherman's) well-being rather than the poet's or the audience's.

A. Responding/ Diction

? Do you know of any other serious poem that is as short as this one? If so, give its title and author. (Students who have read the unit introduction should remember Ezra Pound's "In a Station of the Metro" [page 709], which contains fourteen words as against Williams's sixteen in "The Red Wheelbarrow," counting the line-divided wheel/barrow as two words. Some students may remember other poems from earlier grades.)

In a poem this short, diction becomes especially important.

? Which words are crucial to the imagery? (All of them, of course, but critics often focus on the color words, *red* and *white,* and the words *glazed* and *beside.*)

The Red Wheelbarrow

so much depends
upon

a red wheel
barrow

glazed with rain
water

beside the white
chickens.

A

A Comment on the Poem

This little poem at first glance seems to be very slight. But it has proved to have the leverage power that Archimedes spoke of when he said "Give me a place to stand, and I will move the world." Where William Carlos Williams stood was a place where ordinary things were *not* used as symbols or metaphors; they were simply ordinary things. The world he moved was the world of poetry, which, before him, saw things not as things in themselves, but objects to be used (to be compared, to be endowed with alien meaning, or to be played with); in themselves, things meant nothing.

How do we talk about this poem? When we consider analyzing it as a poem, where do we begin? Trying to answer these questions leads only to frustration. And that's exactly what Williams had in mind: a composition of words so complete and simple that it would deny all attempts to treat it as a poem.

And yet, there is the temptation to ask what happens in the brief course of the poem that has made it so durable. It was, after all, *composed* and not a typographical accident, so it can be talked about. But our talk must be concerned with the modest premises of the poem; we must not attempt to give it meanings that it does not claim.

The first line contains a vague but enormously suggestive phrase that leads the reader to expect an answer. (*What* depends on *what?*) But, except for the metaphorical lift of the word *glazed,* what the reader gets is only bare, flat reality—a moment captured as permanently as if it had been photographed. If the poem can be said to have some movement, some progress, from its first word to its last, it would be in what we call "reverse action." Our yearning toward what might be implicit in "so much depends" is quietly checked by the homely beauty of what *is.*

In many other poems like this one, Williams brought a realistic new dimension into American poetry. Williams showed us a way of recording the visible world without filtering it through the imagination.

Do you like or dislike this poem? Why?

PREPARATION

ESTABLISHING A PURPOSE. Before students have looked at this poem, ask them to guess what the subject matter of a poem entitled "The Great Figure" would be. Then have them read the poem.

SUPPLEMENTARY SUPPORT MATERIALS

1. Review and Response Worksheet: Metaphor and Imagery (*CCB*)

2. Selection Test (*CCB*)

CLOSURE

Have students write two or three sentences telling what the speaker saw in "the dark city."

The Great Figure

Among the rain
and lights
I saw the figure 5
in gold
on a red
fire truck
moving
tense
unheeded
to gong clangs
siren howls
and wheels rumbling
through the dark city.

A

Responding to the Poem

Analyzing the Poem

Interpreting Meanings

1. What one word is used **metaphorically** to describe the fire truck as if it's a person?
2. Which **images** recreate specific sights and sounds?
3. Did you think the "great figure" was going to be the number 5 on an ordinary old fire truck? What did you expect it to be? What is suggested by the term "great figure"?
4. How do you think the speaker feels about this brief scene?

A. Responding/ Imagery

? One critic has said this poem "lacks the reverberation" of the best Imagist poetry. Do you agree? Explain.

? This is almost a pure Imagist poem—even purer than "The Red Wheelbarrow." Why? (It renders the object, the fire truck, without comment. "The Red Wheelbarrow" injects the author's "so much depends upon" into the imagery.)

ANALYZING THE POEM

Interpreting Meanings

1. The word is *tense.*

2. The images are: lines 1–2—rain and lights; 3–6—the gold figure 5 and red truck; 10—the gong clangs; 11—the siren howls; 13—the dark city.

3. Most students will admit to a sense of surprise, since the term would ordinarily mean a human being—say, a celebrity.

4. He may not have a feeling. He may only want to describe it.

PREPARATION

ESTABLISHING A PURPOSE. The class as a whole should read and discuss the headnote before reading the poem. Point out that a tract, as Williams uses the word, appears in print, whereas a sermon (such as Jonathan Edwards's "Sinners in the Hands of an Angry God," page 37) is given orally.

SUPPLEMENTARY SUPPORT MATERIALS

1. Vocabulary Activity Worksheet (*CCB*)
2. Review and Response Worksheet: Theme (*CCB*)
3. Selection Test (*CCB*)

DEVELOPING VOCABULARY

The following words from the poem are tested in the Selection Test. (See also Vocabulary Activity Worksheet.)

to scour	memento
gilt	unceremoniously
dray	inconspicuous

A. Tone

How would you describe the tone of the speaker toward the townspeople? (The tone is one of irritation or mild contempt; the speaker cannot understand why the townspeople can have been conducting such ostentatious funerals.)

B. Connotation

Context often determines connotation. A word that is neutral in one context may be favorable in another and unfavorable in a third.

What are the connotations of *polished, glass, silk hat, curtains?* (In the context of "Tract," these words all have unfavorable connotations because they are ostentatious.)

A tract is a religious or political message aimed at converting its readers. In this verse tract, Williams describes the way a funeral should be conducted. And yet, by the time he has finished, we realize that "a funeral" is only his apparent subject. He is really talking about the conduct of life, and perhaps even about poetry.

"Tract" was first published in 1917, when horses were still used to draw milk wagons, bread wagons, and ornately decorated hearses. But the poet's comments on horse-drawn hearses could just as easily be applied to the limousines used in funerals today.

Tract

A I will teach you my townspeople
how to perform a funeral—
for you have it over a troop
of artists—
unless one should scour the world—
you have the ground sense necessary.

See! the hearse leads.
I begin with a design for a hearse.
For Christ's sake not black—
nor white either—and not polished!
Let it be weathered—like a farm wagon—
with gilt wheels (this could be
applied fresh at small expense)
or no wheels at all:
a rough dray to drag over the ground.

Knock the glass out!
My God—glass, my townspeople!
For what purpose? Is it for the dead
to look out or for us to see
how well he is housed or to see
the flowers or the lack of them—
or what?
To keep the rain and snow from him?
He will have a heavier rain soon:
pebbles and dirt and what not.
Let there be no glass—
and no upholstery! phew!
and no little brass rollers
and small easy wheels on the bottom—
my townspeople what are you thinking of!

A rough plain hearse then
with gilt wheels and no top at all.
On this the coffin lies
by its own weight.
No wreaths please—
especially no hothouse flowers.
Some common memento is better,
something he prized and is known by:
his old clothes—a few books perhaps—
God knows what! You realize
how we are about these things,
my townspeople—
something will be found—anything—
even flowers if he had come to that.
So much for the hearse.

For heaven's sake though see to the driver!
Take off the silk hat! In fact
that's no place at all for him
up there unceremoniously
dragging our friend out to his own dignity!
Bring him down—bring him down!
Low and inconspicuous! I'd not have him ride
on the wagon at all—damn him—
the undertaker's understrapper!
Let him hold the reins
and walk at the side
and inconspicuously too!

Then briefly as to yourselves:
Walk behind—as they do in France,
seventh class,° or if you ride
Hell take curtains! Go with some show
of inconvenience; sit openly—
to the weather as to grief.
Or do you think you can shut grief in?
What—from us? We who have perhaps
nothing to lose? Share with us
share with us—it will be money
in your pockets.
Go now
I think you are ready.

B

59. **seventh class:** an exaggerated reference to first-, second-, and third-class travel on European trains and buses.

CLOSURE
Have students write a few sentences explaining how the message in "Tract" could apply to Williams's own work as a poet.

ANALYZING THE POEM
Identifying Details
1. To simplify the look of the hearse, the driver, and themselves.

Interpreting Meanings
2. The speaker does not seem really inconsistent, since he remarks that fresh gilt could be applied "at small expense." Perhaps the gilt wheels would emphasize the transitional nature of a funeral—going from this life to the next.
3. The rain in line 23 is literal rain; the rain in line 24 is metaphorical for the pebbles and dirt that will "rain" on the coffin. The speaker does not exhibit cruelty toward the dead. His concern is for the proper reactions of the living at a funeral. The speaker believes that a funeral should honor or at least emphasize the deceased, not merely make the survivors feel good.
4. If the funeral symbolizes poetry, then poetry is dying because people pay more attention to the style than the content.
5. Answers will vary, depending on whether the word *money* is taken literally or metaphorically. Williams may mean only that sharing enriches those who share.
6. The speaker believes that poetry, like funerals, should be plain. The poet's personality, like the driver's, should remain in the background. Poetry, like a funeral, is too important to be overlaid with conventional symbolism and irrelevant show.
7. Answers will vary.

Funeral by Clementine Hunter (1956). House paint on cardboard.

Collection of Siri von Reis.

Humanities Connection: Responding to the Fine Art
This charming example of folk art is the work of Clementine Hunter (b. 1883), born on a Louisiana plantation, who began painting in 1946 after finding a discarded paintbrush. **?** How do you think the speaker in "Tract" would view the funeral in Hunter's painting?

Responding to the Poem

Analyzing the Poem

Identifying Details

1. Name all the different aspects of a funeral mentioned by the speaker. What does he advise the townspeople to do about each aspect of the ritual?

Interpreting Meanings

2. When the speaker calls for "gilt wheels" in line 12 is he being inconsistent? What might such prominent wheels contribute to the funeral scene the speaker is describing?
3. What two kinds of rain is the speaker talking about in lines 23 and 24? In making his suggestions for a funeral, is the speaker exhibiting cruelty or disrespect toward the dead? What is his purpose in calling for all this plainness, and even pain and discomfort for the participants?
4. Assume that the speaker is talking about much more than funerals. What might the "rough plain hearse" represent? What might the driver in lines 45–56 represent? Why would the speaker get so angry when he's talking about the driver?
5. Throughout the poem, the speaker talks of simplicity and honest grief. Then he closes by saying, "share with us—it will be money in your pockets." Do you think this seemingly hard-boiled promise reflects cynicism on the part of the speaker? Or can the promise of "money in your pockets" be interpreted in more than one way?
6. Summarize this speaker's **main idea** about art, even about the way poetry should be written. Assuming that the poem is about poetry as well as about funerals, do you think Williams follows his own directions?
7. What do you think about this "tract"? Do you agree with its advice on ritual and art, or do you prefer richness rather than plainness?

PREPARATION

ESTABLISHING A PURPOSE. Advise students to read the headnote before beginning to read the poem. Have them think about the similarities and differences among the four William Carlos Williams poems in the book.

SUPPLEMENTARY SUPPORT MATERIALS

1. Vocabulary Activity Worksheet (*CCB*)
2. Review and Response Worksheet: Imagism (*CCB*)
3. Selection Test (*CCB*)

DEVELOPING VOCABULARY

The following words from the poem are tested in the Selection Test. (See also Vocabulary Activity Worksheet.)

surge forked
mottled stark

A. Personification

? What words does the poet use to personify spring? To personify the new vegetation? (The words *sluggish* and *dazed* personify spring. The words *naked, uncertain, grip down,* and arguably others, personify the new vegetation.)

B. Connections

? How does "Spring and All" differ in purpose from "The Red Wheelbarrow" and "The Great Figure"? ("Spring and All" deals with a process; the others portray scenes.)

C. Humanities Connection: Responding to the Photograph

? How does the photograph capture the mood of the poem? (The landscape in the photograph is a "waste of brown, muddy fields," but the sunrise offers a promise of new life.)

Like many other poems by Williams, this one is about a process—a development, a transformation, or a condition at the point of change. Here the subject is the coming of spring, examined as if seen under a magnifying glass. The poet also examines the *feeling* of spring, in which changes in nature are reflected in someone who observes them. As you read, try to form mental images of the scene in the poem.

Spring and All

By the road to the contagious hospital°
under the surge of the blue
mottled clouds driven from the
northeast—a cold wind. Beyond, the
waste of broad, muddy fields
brown with dried weeds, standing and fallen

patches of standing water
the scattering of tall trees

All along the road the reddish
purplish, forked, upstanding, twiggy
stuff of bushes and small trees
with dead, brown leaves under them
leafless vines—

Lifeless in appearance, sluggish
dazed spring approaches— A

They enter the new world naked,
cold, uncertain of all
save that they enter. All about them
the cold, familiar wind—

Now the grass, tomorrow
the stiff curl of wildcarrot leaf
One by one objects are defined—
It quickens: clarity, outline of leaf

But now the stark dignity of
entrance—Still, the profound change
has come upon them: rooted, they
grip down and begin to awaken

B

1. **contagious hospital:** for people with contagious diseases.

C

CLOSURE
Ask students to identify and discuss which one of the four Williams poems they like best, and why.

ANALYZING THE POEM
Identifying Details
1. The speaker sees "blue mottled clouds"; "broad muddy fields, brown with dried weeds"; "patches of standing water"; "bushes and small trees with dead leaves"; and "leafless vines." He feels a cold wind.

Interpreting Meanings
2. Its being a "contagious hospital" opens the poem on a melancholy note. Contagion, like death, is an inevitable part of life for the speaker; but so, too, is the "rooting," gripping down," and "awakening" of new life in springtime. These associations would be absent in "by the road to the library."
3. The word *they* might also mean human beings in infancy, since the speaker refers to them as entering the "new world naked" and characterizes them as uncertain in line 17.
4. The word *still* could mean "nevertheless" or it could mean "motionless." With the meaning "motionless," Williams draws our attention to the paradox that things that are apparently "still" may yet be in the process of profound change.
5. Specific references include the description of them entering the world naked (line 16) and the beginning of awakening (line 27). We might even associate the word *rooted* (line 26) with a newborn infant's connection to its mother by the umbilical cord.
6. Williams emphasizes the apparent bleakness of the landscape in early spring. A typical Romantic poem would emphasize the warmth, flowers, and bright colors of late spring.
7. Answers will vary. It might suggest the entrance of a major character and attendants on stage.

Responding to the Poem

Analyzing the Poem

Identifying Details

1. Describe the specific **images** the speaker sees by the road in the first three stanzas.

Interpreting Meanings

2. Is "the contagious hospital" merely incidental in the poem, since the poet would have gone there in the course of his daily rounds? Or does the reference contribute something important to the poem? What would have been lost if the poet had said "by the road to the library," for example?
3. The first three stanzas are about plants. The pronoun in line 16, however, may refer to more than plants. What broader meaning might the word *they* have?
4. Reread the last stanza. Which two meanings of the word *still* makes line 25 a **paradox?**
5. In the course of his career, Williams delivered thousands of babies. Can you see any connection between that fact and the last three stanzas of the poem? What specific references would apply equally to the coming of spring and the birth of an infant?
6. In its treatment of spring, how does this poem differ from a typical Romantic poem?
7. What is the significance of the full title of the poem?

Writing About the Poems

A Creative Response

1. **Retitling Poems.** "The Red Wheelbarrow" and "The Great Figure" have titles that refer to concrete objects. Make up similar titles for "Tract" and "Spring and All." In each case, base your title on a concrete object that suggests the meaning of the poem.

A Critical Response

2. **Analyzing a Poem.** Select any one of the poems you have just read by Williams. In a brief essay, show how he uses concrete objects to make statements about people, art, or life in general.

Primary Sources
Williams Talks About Poetry

"I'll never forget the dream I had a few days after he [Williams's father] died, after a wasting illness, on Christmas Day, 1918. I saw him coming down a peculiar flight of exposed steps, steps I have since identified as those before the dais of Pontius Pilate in some well-known painting. But this was in a New York office building, Pop's office. He was bare-headed and had some business letters in his hand on which he was concentrating as he descended. I noticed him and with joy cried out, 'Pop! So, you're *not* dead!' But he only looked up at me over his right shoulder and commented severely, 'You know all that poetry you're writing. Well, it's no good.' I was left speechless and woke trembling.

. . .

"What were we seeking? No one knew consistently enough to formulate a 'movement.' We were restless and constrained, closely allied with the painters. Impressionism, dadaism, surrealism applied to both painting and the poem. What a battle we made of it merely getting rid of capitals at the beginning of every line! The immediate image, which was impressionistic, sure enough, fascinated us all. We had followed Pound's instructions, his famous 'Don'ts,' eschewing inversions of the phrase. . . . Literary allusions, save in very attenuated form, were unknown to us. Few had the necessary reading.

"We were looked at askance by scholars and those who turned to scholarship for their norm. To my mind the thing that gave us most a semblance of a cause was not Imagism, as some thought, but the line: the poetic line and our hopes for its recovery from stodginess. I say recovery in the sense that one recovers a salt from solution by chemical action. We were destroyers, vulgarians, obscurantists to most who read; though occasionally a witty line, an unusual reference, or a wrench of the simile to force it into approximation with experience rather than reading—bringing a whole proximate 'material' into view—found some response from the alert."

—from *The Autobiography,*
William Carlos Williams

A. Expansion
Marianne Moore, a slight, reserved woman, seemed fated to live in close proximity to others who became famous. As a young child in Kirkwood, Missouri, she lived not far from the one-year-younger T.S. Eliot. A biographer, Donald Hall, remarks, "It seems uncanny that two of the best American poets of this century should have been born and lived within a few miles of one another." At Bryn Mawr she met Hilda Doolittle (H.D.), a day student whose later fame as a poet would rival her own. When Moore taught at the Indian School in Carlisle, Pennsylvania, one of her students was Jim Thorpe, considered by many to be the greatest male athlete in U.S. history. Moving on to Greenwich Village, New York City, she arrived at a time of great artistic ferment. Edna St. Vincent Millay and E.E. Cummings lived there. William Carlos Williams and Wallace Stevens often visited the Village. At parties and eventually as editor of the *Dial,* she came to know them all.

Comment From A Critic
T.S. Eliot wrote of Moore's poetry: "She seems to have saturated her mind in the perfections of prose, in its precision rather than its purple; and to have found her rhythm, her poetry, her appreciation of the individual word, for herself." You might want to ask students to keep Eliot's observation in mind as they read "The Steeple-Jack" and to explain Eliot's meaning in their own words.

Marianne Moore (1887–1972)

A Marianne Moore is remembered by many people as the woman who wrote a poem in 1955 celebrating the only World Series the Brooklyn Dodgers ever won. Moore spent more than half her life in Brooklyn, where she became one of the most famous supporters of the local baseball team.

She was born in Kirkwood, a suburb of St. Louis, Missouri. She became a schoolteacher, a librarian, the editor of *The Dial* (a magazine that encouraged young writers), and one of the outstanding poets of her time.

Moore was a graduate of Bryn Mawr at a time when that college was still known as a school for "bluestockings" (highly educated and well-read women). She spent a good part of her life caring for her brother and mother. When her mother died, Moore lost her best friend—and her toughest critic. In 1929, she moved to Brooklyn. Among the literary celebrities in New York, she was easily identifiable by her antique capes and other eighteenth-century touches in costume.

Behind the costume, however, Moore was a quiet, conventional woman. Mixing with the *literati* did not mean that she endorsed their tolerance in matters of personal behavior or their embrace of anything in the arts that seemed new, or bold, or simply amusing.

The only thing "modern" about Moore was her poetry. Like a bird building a nest, she would carefully piece together in her poetry material gathered from her reading in social and natural history. It has been said of her that no one was ever more indebted to other writers for material and, at the same time, more original. Her poetry reflects some of the influence of the Imagists, and it also makes constant use of the concrete in the tradition of William Carlos Williams. Like the graphic artists of the twentieth century, Moore was able to join apparently unrelated elements of what she observed and bring them into a "picture" with a single focus.

Portrait of Marianne Moore by George Platt Lynes.

In some of her poems, such as "The Steeple-Jack," Moore works like a painter whose nervous strokes and jagged edges capture a hundred details in one moment stopped in time. What she says in this poem might apply to readers approaching her work in general: "It is a privilege to see so much confusion."

PREPARATION

ESTABLISHING A PURPOSE. As students read, have them look for the "little particular details" (see headnote) that make the poem so visual. They should also look for the playful aspects—the fantastic, almost fairy-tale touches.

SUPPLEMENTARY SUPPORT MATERIALS

1. Vocabulary Activity Worksheet (*CCB*)
2. Review and Response Worksheet: Tone and Theme (*CCB*)
3. Selection Test (*CCB*)

DEVELOPING VOCABULARY

The following words from the poem are tested in the Selection Test. (See also Vocabulary Activity Worksheet.)

steeple-jack — bravado
to etch — to interlace
azure — spire
gourd — portico
lichen — waif

A. Metaphor/Simile

? In the first stanza, how does the poet combine a metaphor and a simile? (The metaphor is "water etched/with waves"; etching, literally, is a printing process. The metaphor is then extended with a simile—"waves as formal as the scales/on a fish.")

B. Metaphor

? To what is the storm compared in line 19? (A fife and drum)

C. Noting Details

Be sure students notice the accumulation of details—the list of flowers—in lines 26–35. Students may wish to discuss whether there are *too* many specifics here.

An essentially visual poem, this one also has many thoughtful and playful moments. As Moore carefully paints a portrait of a coastal town, she emphasizes the little particular details and renders them with the same exactness that we find in the paintings and engravings of Albrecht Dürer, the great German artist of the late fifteenth century. Each detail is important to the portrait of the town; some of them also indicate the character of the mind which so meticulously records them.

The Steeple-Jack

Dürer would have seen a reason for living
in a town like this, with eight stranded whales
to look at; with the sweet sea air coming into your house
A on a fine day, from water etched
with waves as formal as the scales
on a fish.

One by one in two's and three's, the seagulls keep
flying back and forth over the town clock,
or sailing around the lighthouse without moving their wings—
rising steadily with a slight
quiver of the body—or flock
mewing where

a sea the purple of the peacock's neck is
paled to greenish azure as Dürer changed
the pine green of the Tyrol to peacock blue and guinea
gray. You can see a twenty-five-
pound lobster; and fish nets arranged
to dry. The

B whirlwind fife-and-drum of the storm bends the salt
marsh grass, disturbs stars in the sky and the
star on the steeple; it is a privilege to see so
much confusion. Disguised by what
might seem the opposite, the seaside flowers and

trees are favored by the fog so that you have
the tropics at first hand: the trumpet vine,
foxglove, giant snapdragon, a salpiglossis that has
spots and stripes; morning-glories, gourds,
or moon-vines trained on fishing twine
at the back door:

C cattails, flags, blueberries and spiderwort,
striped grass, lichens, sunflowers, asters, daisies—
yellow and crab-claw ragged sailors with green bracts—toadplant,
petunias, ferns; pink lilies, blue
ones, tigers; poppies; black sweet peas.
The climate

Literature and Language: Writing Description

In this poem Moore uses the whole battery of descriptive devices: sensory details, images, precise nouns and verbs, and figurative language, even allusion (to the work of the 15th-century artist Albrecht Dürer).

Refer students to the chart of descriptive language on page 1162; then have them chart the sensory details in Moore's poem. (Students should find that visual details predominate, though there are details of touch, smell, and sound.)

Point out that Moore's poem is not just a picture-postcard description of a small town. What does Moore add to the description? (She adds her attitude—approval of the town—and her vision of the way of life in the town.)

A. Line and Stanza Breaks

? Why are the line and stanza breaks so unusual, as in lines 54–55, for example, where *church* and *spire* are divided by both a line and a stanza break? (See question 1, page 728.)

B. Humor

This poem contains both fantasy ("eight stranded whales") and lighthearted humor.

? What line or lines do you find amusing? (Answers will vary. Lines 65–67 present one good example.)

is not right for the banyan, frangipani, or
   jack-fruit trees; or for exotic serpent
life. Ring lizard and snakesskin for the foot, if you see fit;
but here they've cats, not cobras, to
   keep down the rats. The diffident
little newt

with white pin-dots on black horizontal spaced-
   out bands lives here; yet there is nothing that
ambition can buy or take away. The college student
named Ambrose sits on the hillside
   with his not-native books and hat
and sees boats

at sea progress white and rigid as if in
   a groove. Liking an elegance of which
the source is not bravado, he knows by heart the antique
sugar-bowl shaped summerhouse of
   interlacing slats, and the pitch
of the church

A

spire, not true, from which a man in scarlet lets
   down a rope as a spider spins a thread;
he might be part of a novel, but on the sidewalk a
sign says C. J. Poole, Steeple-Jack,
   in black and white; and one in red
and white says

Danger. The church portico has four fluted
   columns, each a single piece of stone, made
modester by whitewash. This would be a fit haven for
waifs, children, animals, prisoners,
   and presidents who have repaid
sin-driven

B

senators by not thinking about them. The
   place has a schoolhouse, a post office in a
   store, fishhouses, henhouses, a three-masted
   schooner on the stocks. The hero, the student,
   the steeple-jack, each in his way,
is at home.

It could not be dangerous to be living
   in a town like this, of simple people,
who have a steeple-jack placing danger signs by the church
while he is gilding the solid-
   pointed star, which on a steeple
stands for hope.

Humanities Connection: Responding to the Photograph
Marianne Moore has created so vivid, specific, and detailed a word picture of the steeple-jack's town that no photograph could possibly match it exactly. ❓ Compare the poem with the photograph. What details are the same or similar? What details are different? (Ask students to be specific, just as Moore is.) What can be found in the poem but not in the photo, and vice versa? Does the photograph convey the same mood as the description of the town in the poem? Similar details include water, seagulls, church spire, boats. Moore's details include specific vegetation, eight stranded whales, Ambrose, church portico.

CLOSURE
Ask students to write one or two sentences telling what it is that makes Moore's poetry unique.

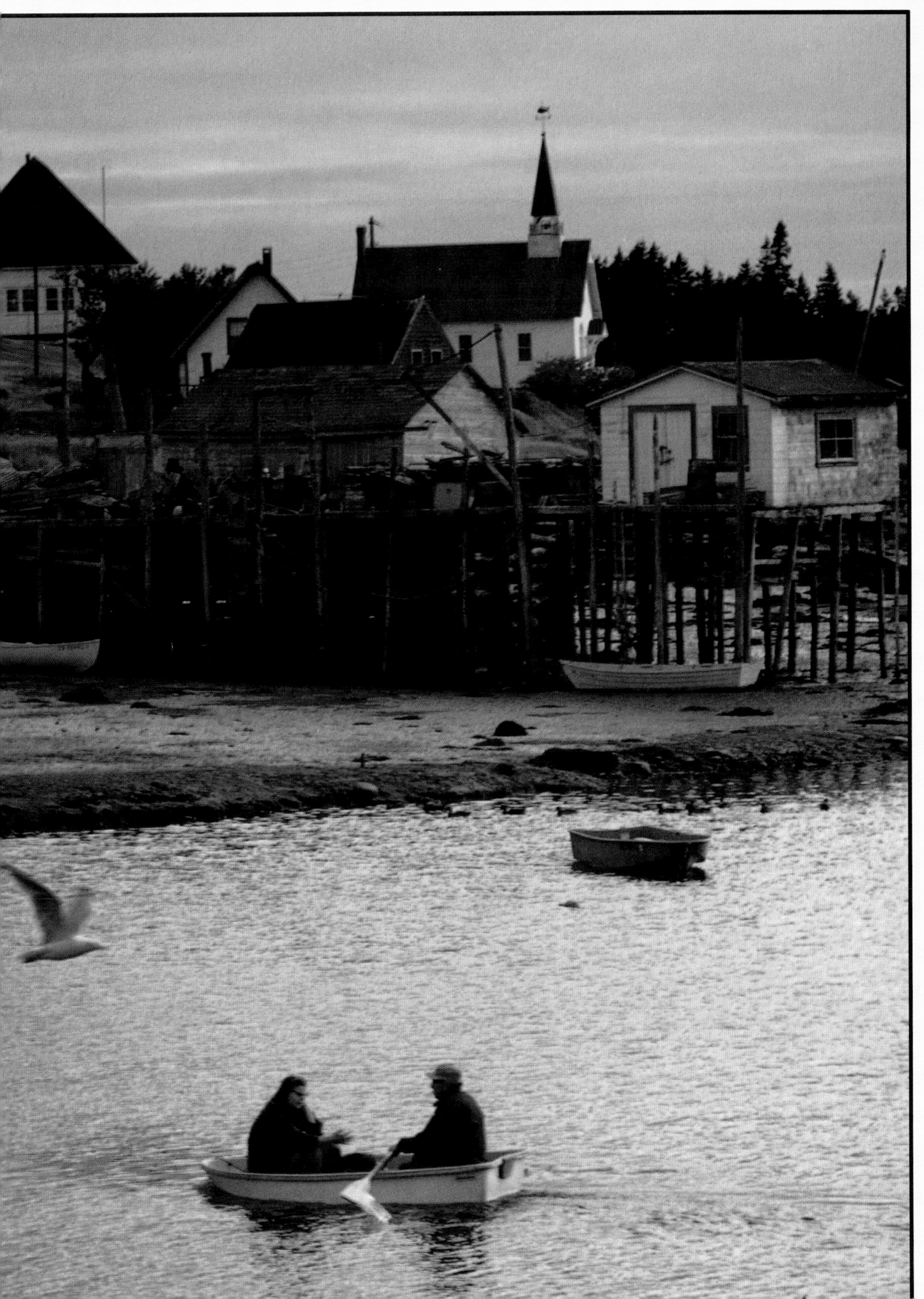

COMMENT FROM A CRITIC
Donald Hall in *Marianne Moore: The Cage and the Animal* (Pegasus, 1970) states that the scene in the poem "might have come straight out of Hans Christian Andersen. It is a storybook town in all its painted primary–color exactness." Ask students to react to that statement. Do they agree? Have them support their opinions with evidence from the poem.

Analyzing The Poem
Identifying Details
1. The repeated pattern is this: 11 syllables in the first line of each stanza, 10 in the second, 14 in the third, 8 in the fourth, 8 in the fifth, and 3 in the sixth. In the fourth and fifth stanzas, the sixth line has 4 syllables.
2. The rhyme scheme is *abcdbe.*
3. Many details suggest a coastal town, among them "eight stranded whales" (line 2), "sweet sea air" (line 3), and sea waves (lines 4–6). Students can name details of color, plant life, animals, and so on. A northern climate (line 36) and a prominent church steeple suggest New England.
4. Some images: "sweet sea air" (line 3), color of the sea (line 13), lobster and fish nets (line 17). See how long a list of images students can make.
5. The speaker approves of the town.

Interpreting Meanings
6. The college student Ambrose is introduced in line 45 as an appreciative observer of town life. Perhaps this use of a relatively young observer suggests the continuing understated beauty of the
(Answers continue in left-hand column.)

(Continued from top.)
town and its simple people.
7. Moore apparently wants to establish the setting precisely and vividly before she presents human characters.
8. The "confusion" apparently stems from the welter of sense impressions of the town taken in by the speaker-observer.
9. Three people of differing backgrounds can call the town home because of the tolerance that exists there.
10. The star symbolizes hope—hope for the town and for humankind.
11. Answers will vary. The tone seems pleasant and comforting. Most students will have a favorable impression of the town.
12. Students should note the difference between the critical, destructive people in Robinson's poems and the "simple people" and their star that "stands for hope" in Moore's poem.

Responding to the Poem

Analyzing the Poem

Identifying Details

1. In "The Steeple-Jack" (as in many of Moore's poems), conventional poetic meter and free verse are replaced by the strict count of **syllables.** Count the number of syllables in each line of the first stanza. Then do the same with the following stanzas. Is the pattern repeated? In which stanza does Moore introduce a new pattern of syllables?
2. The poem is unified by an unusual **rhyme scheme.** To discover what it is, find the two lines that rhyme in the first stanza. Then examine the following stanzas to see if you can find a pattern of rhyme.
3. What details in the poem suggest the location of the town?
4. List as many **images** as you can find that help you see, hear, and smell the town.
5. What does the speaker think of this town?

Interpreting Meanings

6. What role does Ambrose play in the poem?
7. Considering the poem's title, why would Moore take so long to bring in C. J. Poole? Why do you think the poem is named for him?
8. What is the nature of the confusion referred to in the fourth stanza? Why does Moore consider it a privilege to view this confusion?
9. Explain the significance of the fact that the hero, the student, and the steeple-jack are all "at home."
10. Explain what you think is the significance of the star at the poem's end.
11. How would you describe the **tone** of this poem? How did it make you feel about this town?
12. How does Moore's view of a small Maine town contrast with Edwin Arlington Robinson's character studies of people who live in another Maine town? (See pages 634 and 636.)

Writing About the Poem

A Creative Response

1. **Imitating the Poet's Technique.** Imitating Moore's technique of meticulously cataloging the town's sights, sounds, and smells, describe a place you know well and have some feeling for. Select images that will reveal your feelings for this scene. Try to use specific images. For example, Moore does not just say, "There were plants there"; she names twenty-two of them.

A Critical Response

2. **Comparing the Poem to a Prose Text.** How does Moore's vision of the ideal town contrast with Babbitt's view of what makes a perfect "burg"? (See page 511.) Write a paragraph in which you cite the differences between the two visions.

Analyzing Language and Style

Precise Meanings

Like most poets, Marianne Moore loved words and she knew a great number of them. Use a dictionary to be sure you know the precise meanings of *Tyrol, salpiglossis, lichens, bracts, banyan, portico, fluted.*

Primary Sources

Animals and Athletes

"Why an inordinate interest in animals and athletes? They are subjects of art and exemplars of it, are they not? minding their own business. Pangolins, hornbills, pitchers, catchers, do not pry or prey—or prolong the conversation; do not make us self-conscious; look their best when caring least; although in a Frank Buck documentary I saw a leopard insult a crocodile (basking on a river bank—head only visible on the bank), bat the animal on the nose and continue on its way without so much as a look back. Perhaps I really don't know. I do know that I don't know how to account for a person who could be indifferent to miracles of dexterity, a certain feat by Don Zimmer—a Dodger at the time—making a backhand catch, of a ball coming hard from behind on the left, fast enough to take his hand off."

—from *A Marianne Moore Reader*

Comment From The Poet
Carl Sandburg in "Notes for a Preface" in his *Complete Poems* attempts to define poetry. He concludes that any definition has to reside in the work itself: "A poet explains for us what for him is poetry by what he presents to us in his poems. A painter makes definitions of what for him is art by the kind of paintings his brush puts on canvas. . . . The novelist explains his theory of creative literature by the stories and people in his books. There is no escape. There stands the man, the woman, who wrought it. We go to it, read it, look at it, perhaps go back to it many a time and it is for each of us what we make of it. The creator of it can say it means this or that—or it means for you whatever you take it to mean. He can say it happened, it came into being and now it exists apart from him and nothing can be done about it."

Ask students to comment on this quotation. Is Sandburg taking an "anything goes" position on artistic creation? Is he suggesting that anyone who proclaims himself or herself a poet *is* a poet? The discussion should probably touch on the roles of critics and publishers in determining what is accepted as poetry.

Carl Sandburg (1878–1967)

When he died in his ninetieth year, Carl Sandburg was already an American myth. Sandburg's deeply lined, leathery face and his boyish shock of hair had been familiar to his compatriots for more than five decades. As the author of two of the most famous poems of the century—"Chicago" (1914) and "Fog" (1916)—and of a six-volume biography of Abraham Lincoln (1926–1939), Sandburg had carved a place for himself in modern literature. As a poetic spokesman for the American worker in the toils of industrialization, he had become part of the folklore from which he drew his inspiration. While he seemed on the page to be the roughest of American poets, Sandburg was actually a gentle and contemplative man. He found his most characteristic voice in the vernacular—in slang, street talk, and common speech full of clichés and plain expressions.

A descendant of Swedes who had settled in Galesburg, Illinois, where he was born, Sandburg was not so much schooled in a classroom as in the proverbial "school of hard knocks." Before he was twenty, he had ranged the Middle West from Illinois to Nebraska, supporting himself with odd jobs. He thus came in contact with laborers in the fields and the factories that would one day provide his own poetic landscape. Sandburg volunteered to fight in the Spanish-American War that broke out in 1898, more from restlessness than patriotism, and he served in the first Puerto Rican campaign. When the war ended, he was finally ready to go back to school. He graduated from Lombard College in his hometown, where he was captain of the basketball team and editor of the college newspaper. It was at Lombard that Sandburg began to think of himself as a writer, particularly as a poet. But his first professional writing was in advertising, politics, and journalism.

Carl Sandburg photographed by Edward Steichen.

After a succession of jobs, Sandburg finally became known as a poet at the age of thirty-six when the influential magazine *Poetry* published some of his shorter poems, including "Chicago." Sandburg's audacious use of colloquialism and free verse (reflecting to some degree the influence of Walt Whitman) involved him in critical controversy and established his reputation as a major literary figure. The poet's affirmation of American democracy and of the inherent nobility of labor and the working person culminated in one of his best-known collections of poems *The People, Yes* (1936), a Whitmanesque panorama of America that expressed its author's profound social faith. Besides his poetry and the monumental biography of Lincoln, Sandburg composed folk songs and ballads, autobiographical memoirs, and children's books. A

A. Expansion
One of Sandburg's many enterprises was collecting folk songs and ballads from cowboys, convicts, and common people all across America. This activity led to the publication in 1927 of *The American Songbag,* a classic compilation of American folk music.

Humanities Connection: Discussing the Fine Art

Many of the paintings of Louis Lozowick (1892–1973) are cityscapes that emphasize the stark structural lines of buildings, bridges, and factories. His early work often has overtones of cubism. Born in Russia, Lozowick came to the United States at the age of thirteen. As a WPA artist during the Depression, he painted a mural in New York City's main post office. His work has been widely exhibited and has won numerous awards. Lozowick is the author of *Modern Russian Art,* published in 1925.

You might want to have students discuss this painting after they have read Sandburg's poem on the facing page. You can then ask them to write three or four sentences in their journal in which they compare and contrast Lozowick's *Chicago* and Sandburg's "Chicago." (The most striking similarity is that both works have the same title and subject, and each one presents its creator's vision of the city. The most striking difference is that Lozowick's Chicago has no people at all, whereas Sandburg's teems with people and images of people.)

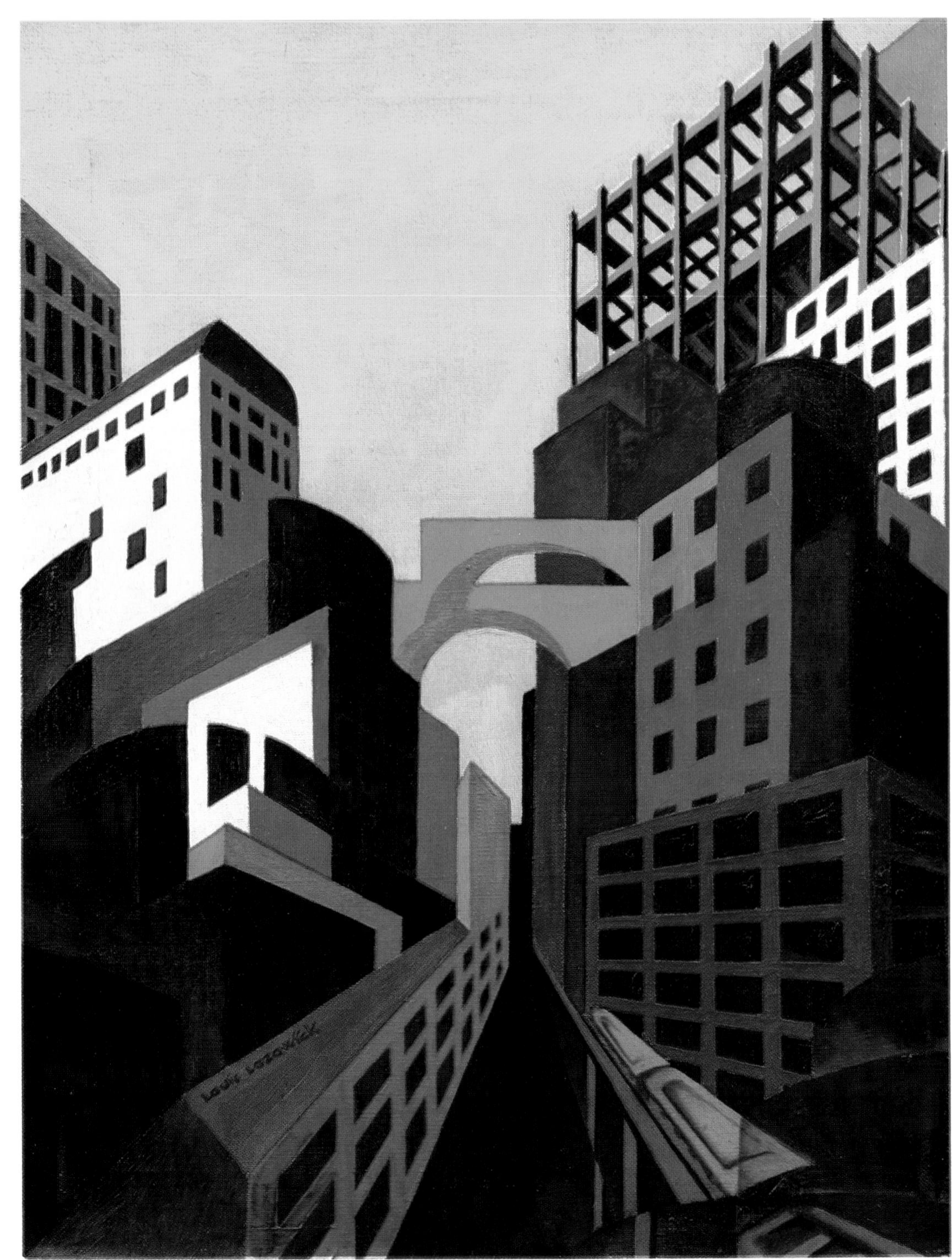

Chicago by Louis Lozowick (1923). Oil. Private Collection, Washington, D.C.

PREPARATION

1. BUILDING ON PRIOR KNOWLEDGE. Before students begin to read, ask them to discuss their impressions of Chicago.

2. ESTABLISHING A PURPOSE. Suggest to students that they look for the poem's central image as they are reading. (See question 3, page 732.)

SUPPLEMENTARY SUPPORT MATERIALS

1. Review and Response Worksheet: Parallelism (*CCB*)
2. Language Skills Worksheet: Subject-Verb Agreement (*CCB*)
3. Selection Test (*CCB*)

Free verse with a ring of oratory in its cadences is characteristic of Sandburg's poetry, and so is the extensive use of apostrophe. Both are combined here as the poet addresses an entire city as though it were a kind of intelligent being, capable of understanding what he says.

Chicago

A Hog Butcher for the World,
Tool Maker, Stacker of Wheat,
Player with Railroads and the Nation's Freight Handler;
Stormy, husky, brawling,
City of the Big Shoulders:

They tell me you are wicked and I believe them, for I
B have seen your painted women under the gas lamps luring the farm boys.
And they tell me you are crooked and I answer: Yes, it is true I have seen the gunman kill and go free to kill again.
And they tell me you are brutal and my reply is: On the faces of women and children I have seen the marks of wanton hunger.
And having answered so I turn once more to those who sneer at this my city, and I give them back the sneer and say to them:
Come and show me another city with lifted head singing so proud to be alive and coarse and strong and cunning.
Flinging magnetic curses amid the toil of piling job on job,
C here is a tall bold slugger set vivid against the little soft cities;
Fierce as a dog with tongue lapping for action, cunning as a savage pitted against the wilderness,
Bareheaded,
Shoveling,
Wrecking,
Planning,
Building, breaking, rebuilding.
Under the smoke, dust all over his mouth, laughing with white teeth,
Under the terrible burden of destiny laughing as a young man laughs,
Laughing even as an ignorant fighter laughs who has never lost a battle,
Bragging and laughing that under his wrist is the pulse, and under his ribs the heart of the people,
Laughing!
Laughing the stormy, husky, brawling laughter of Youth, half-naked, sweating, proud to be Hog Butcher, Tool Maker, Stacker of Wheat, Player with Railroads and Freight Handler to the Nation.

A. Epithets

? What common epithet or epithets for Chicago does the poem not include? (Windy City, Second City, Toddlin' Town)

B. Context Clues

It is sometimes possible to tell approximately when a poem was written by using context clues. From the biography of Sandburg, students know that "Chicago" appeared in 1914. ? What context clue or clues give you some idea of when the poem was written? (The most obvious clue is "gas lamps," an old-fashioned kind of street lighting. See question 7, page 732.)

C. Simile

? To what two things does the poet compare "the bold slugger" (i.e., Chicago) in a pair of similes? (A dog and a savage, line 12)

CLOSURE

Have students write a brief prose statement summarizing Sandburg's opinion of Chicago.

ANALYZING THE POEM
Identifying Details
1. "Hog Butcher"=meat-packing center; "Tool Maker"=manufacturing, heavy industry; "Stacker of Wheat"=grain processing; "Player with Railroads" and "Nation's Freight Handler"=rail hub.
2. People say the city is wicked, crooked, and brutal. The speaker agrees, mentioning prostitutes, murders by gunmen who are then freed, and the hunger of women and children.

Interpreting Meanings
3. The central image is that of a lusty young man. It is introduced in the opening apostrophes and extended with the city/man "Flinging magnetic curses," "Bareheaded," and so on. Youth is emphasized in similes and metaphors. The conclusion refers to the "brawling laughter of youth."
4. The city's main strengths seem to be vitality, industry, pride, and endurance. The city's main weaknesses include wickedness, crime, brutality, and perhaps dirt. On the poet's attitude, answers will vary. Sandburg emphasizes vitality and pride.
(Answers continue in left-hand column.)

(Continued from top.)
5. The last line repeats the apostrophes of lines 1–3.
6. Examples of parallelism include the repetition of apostrophes in lines 1–5; the repeated structure of "they tell me" in lines 6–8; the succession of participles in lines 13–17; the repetition of *under* in lines 18, 19, and 21. Parallelism contributes to the declamatory rhythm of the poem, as if the speaker were formally addressing the city.
7. Answers will vary. The stockyards are now an industrial park. Financing and wholesaling are more important now than then. Heavy industry is less so. The gas lamps are gone. The city is still the world's greatest railhead and a leading manufacturing center. Many of the details about jobs are still valid. Like most big cities, Chicago has its share of "painted women," gangsters, and hunger.
8. Answers will vary.

Responding to the Poem

Analyzing the Poem

Identifying Details

1. Sandburg opens with a litany of **epithets,** or descriptive phrases, about Chicago. What does each of these epithets reveal about the city and the various activities that make up its economy?
2. What do people tell the speaker about Chicago? What is the speaker's answer to each of these comments about the city?

Interpreting Meanings

3. Many different images contribute to this portrait of Chicago, but its central **image** is never named. To what is Chicago really being compared? How is this image introduced and extended?
4. What are the city's main strengths and main weaknesses, according to Sandburg? On balance, what seems to be his attitude toward the city: Does he think it is boastful? Defensive? One-sided? Naive? Proud? Which attitude do you think the poet would most want to emphasize?
5. How does the long list in the last line help to unify the poem?
6. Find at least four examples of **parallelism** in the poem. How does this use of parallelism affect the poem's rhythm?
7. Which features of Chicago do you think have changed since this poem was written in 1914? Which features mentioned in the poem might still be part of the life of the city?
8. What would you say to those critics who have claimed that Sandburg's poetry is full of bluster and proclamations at the expense of thought?

Writing About the Poem

A Creative Response

1. **Writing an Apostrophe.** Think about the epithets Sandburg uses in addressing Chicago in his opening stanza. Then choose a city, town, or other area you know well. Write at least five epithets addressing the place you have chosen, using Sandburg's style as a model.

A Critical Response

2. **Comparing and Contrasting Poems.** Sandburg was one of the poets who followed Walt Whitman's lead toward a less formal mode of expression in poetry. Reread Whitman's "I Hear America Singing" (page 331). Then write a brief essay in which you compare and contrast that poem with Sandburg's "Chicago." Pay specific attention to the two poets' techniques and to their attitudes toward their subjects. Before you write, gather your data in a chart like the following one.

	Whitman	Sandburg
Subject		
Imagery		
Figures of speech		
Rhythm		
Catalogs of details		
Slang and colloquial language		
Tone		

PREPARATION

ESTABLISHING A PURPOSE. The class as a whole should go over the headnote before reading the poem. You may want to point out that poets frequently make use of dual or even multiple meanings of words, thus investing their poems with more complex or more varied meanings. Have students look for words other than *limited* that have such meanings.

SUPPLEMENTARY SUPPORT MATERIALS

1. Review and Response Worksheet: Irony and Theme (*CCB*)
2. Selection Test (*CCB*)

In the time when railroad travel was common, a *limited* run was one that made fewer stops and charged a higher fare than other trains traveling the same route. A limited was therefore usually preferred by busy people who could afford the higher cost. As you read, look for one other meaning of the word *limited*.

Limited

I am riding on a limited express, one of the crack trains of the nation.
Hurtling across the prairie into blue haze and dark air go fifteen all-steel coaches holding a thousand people.
(All the coaches shall be scrap and rust and all the men and women laughing in the diners and sleepers shall pass to ashes.)
I ask a man in the smoker where he is going and he answers: "Omaha."

As "Centuries" Pass in the Night by William Foster (early 20th century). Oil.

Edaville Railroad Collection, South Carver, Massachusetts.

A. Responding
? What is the significance of the fact that the coaches are "all-steel"? (The implication is that they are sturdy and lasting. In the next line, however, the poet notes that they "shall be scrap and rust.")

B. Noting Details
? Why do you suppose the man in the smoker is not named? (The generic *man* makes the experience seem more universal.)

C. Humanities Connection: Discussing the Fine Art
This painting was commissioned by the New York Central Railroad for use in its advertising and promotion. The "Centuries" that are passing are two Twentieth Century Limited express trains. The Twentieth Century Limited provided luxury passenger service.

CLOSURE
Have students write a brief paraphrase of the poem.

ANALYZING THE POEM
Identifying Details
1. The speaker is crossing the prairie of the American Midwest in a fast train.
2. The speaker says that both the passengers and the coaches will one day be scrap, rust, and ashes.

Interpreting Meanings
3. The word means "fine" or "excellent."
4. The paradoxical phrase "limited express" prepares the reader for the self-contradiction underlying the whole poem.
5. The express train is not merely *limited* in limiting the number of stops and number of passengers; it also has a limited lifespan—as do its passengers.
6. The irony in the passenger's answer arises from the speaker's parenthetical thought. A reader almost expects a philosophical answer ("Heaven," perhaps) rather than the factual "Omaha."
7. Answers will vary. Transience is the central theme of both poems.
8. Perhaps the traveler could be pictured on a supersonic aircraft.

ADDITIONAL WRITING ASSIGNMENT
Point out to students that Carl Sandburg has been compared with other poets besides Walt Whitman—among them Edwin Arlington Robinson, Vachel Lindsay, Edgar Lee Masters, and Robert Frost. Ask students to write an essay in which they compare and contrast Sandburg with any one of those four poets. (Brief comparisons to all four can be found in North Callahan's *Carl Sandburg: Lincoln of our Literature* [New York University Press, 1970.])

Responding to the Poem

Analyzing the Poem

Identifying Details

1. Where is the speaker of the poem?
2. What does the speaker predict will happen to the train and its passengers?

Interpreting Meanings

3. What does the word *crack* mean in line 1?
4. What phrase in line 1 prepares the reader for the **paradox,** or self-contradiction, that underlies the whole poem?
5. In your own words state the **main idea** in this poem, using the word *limited.*
6. Do you think there is a double meaning in the speaker's question in line 4? If so, what **irony** do you sense in the other passenger's answer: "Omaha"? (Where is he, and all "riders," really going?)
7. What connections can you see between this poem and Robert Frost's "Nothing Gold Can Stay" on page 670?
8. How could the poem's details be updated?

Primary Sources

"Rhymes are iron fetters"

In his Notes for a Preface to *Complete Poems,* Carl Sandburg quoted another great American poet on rhyme:

"Oliver Wendell Holmes, skilled rhymester, told a young poet: 'When you write in prose you say what you mean. When you write in verse you say what you must.' Having said this to the young man, Holmes bethought himself and then wrote, 'I was thinking more especially of rhymed verse. Rhythm alone is a tether, and not a very long one. But rhymes are iron fetters; it is dragging a chain and ball to march under their incumbrance; it is a clog-dance you are figuring in when you execute your metrical *pas seul.*[1] . . . You want to say something about the heavenly bodies, and you have a beautiful line ending with the word stars. . . . You cannot make any use of cars, I will suppose; you have no occasion to talk about scars; 'the red planet Mars' has been used already; Dibdin has said enough about the gallant tars; what is there left for you but bars? So you give up your trains of thought, capitulate to necessity, and manage to lug in some kind of allusion, in place or out of place, which will allow you to make use of bars. Can there be imagined a more certain process for breaking up all continuity of thought, than this miserable subjugation of intellect to the clink of well or ill matched syllables?'

"The fact is ironic. A proficient and sometimes exquisite performer in rhymed verse goes out of his way to register the point that the more rhyme there is in poetry the more danger of its tricking the writer into something other than the urge in the beginning."

—Carl Sandburg

1. ***pas seul*** (pä söl): French for a solo dance.

COMMENT FROM THE AUTHOR
Students are usually encouraged to keep their audience in mind when writing. Cummings's comment on the subject (found in *The Magic Maker: E. E. Cummings* by Charles Norman) may spark a useful discussion: "The relation of an artist to his audience is neither positive nor negative. It's at right angles. I'm not writing 'difficult' so that simple people won't understand me. I'm not writing 'difficult' for difficult people to understand. Insofar as I have any conception of my audience, it inhibits me. An audience directs things its own way." (You will want to remind students that a teacher's or textbook's advice about the writer's audience typically concerns expository writing. Cummings is speaking of the audience for poetry. How important is the distinction?)

E. E. Cummings (1894–1962)

E. E. Cummings (the initials stand for Edward Estlin) was born in Cambridge, Massachusetts, the son of a Unitarian minister. After a childhood spent within walking distance of Harvard, he attended the university at a time when aspiring writers were beginning to feel the impact of the two developments that would shape the character of American poetry for half a century. These new influences, sources of both inspiration and imitation, were French Symbolism and free verse. Like other poets, Cummings found in the Imagist manifesto guidelines that allowed him to break old rules and to try verbal experiments which would define his style.

If there is such a thing as "rugged individualism" in poetry, Cummings may be its prime example. All by himself, he altered conventional English syntax and made typography and the division of words part of the shape and meaning of a poem. And—in the age of celebration of the common man—he went against the grain by championing the virtues of elitism. "So far as I am concerned," he wrote, "poetry and every other art was and is and forever will be strictly and distinctly a question of individuality . . . poetry is being, not doing. If you wish to follow, even at a distance, the poet's calling . . . you've got to come out of the measurable doing universe into the immeasurable house of being. . . . Nobody else can be alive for you; nor can you be alive for anybody else."

Graduating from college in the midst of World War I, Cummings became part of the conflict well before American soldiers appeared on European battlefields in 1917. He volunteered for an ambulance corps privately financed by Americans and staffed by young men like himself. Crossing to Bordeaux on a French troop ship threatened by German U-Boats, Cummings had hardly begun his duties when a French censor, intercepting one of his typographically odd letters, imprisoned him on suspicion of espionage. Released within three months, and little the worse for wear, Cummings drew upon the experience to produce his first important book of prose, *The Enormous Room* (1922).

After World War I, Cummings returned to France. He was one of the American literary expatriates who found in Paris the freedom and inspiration they felt were denied them by the restrictive Puritanism of their own country. During this period, Cummings refined the eccentric shifts of syntax and typography that would become his trademark. In 1923, he published his first collection of verse, *Tulips and Chimneys,* which was followed by *&* (1925), *XLI Poems* (1925), and *is 5* (1926). His poetry is often marked by jubilant lyricism, as he celebrates love, nature's beauty, and an almost Transcendentalist affirmation of the individual. He reserved his mischievous wit for the satire of the "unman," by which he meant the unthinking, unfeeling temperament of urban "humans."

Cummings split his time between an apartment in Greenwich Village in New York City and a house in Silver Lake, New Hampshire. He died still believing that "when skies are hanged and oceans drowned, / the single secret will still be man."

A. Expansion
Cummings's unusual typography may appear arbitrary to some students, just as it did to some early critics. But in fact the "perverse punctuation," as one reviewer called it, was intentional, precise, and exceedingly important to Cummings. It was a typesetter's nightmare, because Cummings (and later his widow) insisted on exact spacing and placement of words, letters, and punctuation marks. Cummings called many of his poems "picture poems," and these, in particular, had to be properly "framed" on the printed page. There is little question that Cummings's lifelong pursuit of painting influenced his view of poetry. The old saw that "poems are meant to be read aloud" does not apply to all of Cummings's poems, although the lyrical beauty of many of them is breathtaking.

PREPARATION

ESTABLISHING A PURPOSE. After reading the headnote in class, you may want to ask students to discuss examples of black humor with which they are familiar.

SUPPLEMENTARY SUPPORT MATERIALS

1. Vocabulary Activity Worksheet (*CCB*)
2. Review and Response Worksheet: Irony (*CCB*)
3. Selection Test (*CCB*)

DEVELOPING VOCABULARY

The following words from the poem are tested in the Selection Test. (See also Vocabulary Activity Worksheet.)

vaudeville — scrumptious
to indulge — to lurch
auspicious

A. Responding

Why does the speaker refer to farming as "that possibly most inexcusable/of all . . . luxuries"? (As a city dweller, the speaker perhaps regards farm life as an avoidance of real work [farmers know better] and a venture unlikely to succeed.)

B. Humanities Connection: Responding to the Fine Art

May Stevens (b. 1924) is a contemporary artist whose earliest works were ones of social protest. *Prime Time,* painted at the height of the Vietnam war, is a portrait of her father, whom she loved but whom she also saw as epitomizing the psychology that led to Vietnam. **?** What do the man's posture, clothing, and folded arms reveal about him? What is the significance of the blank television behind him? Why do you think the painting is called *Prime Time?* (His head, like the screen, is empty. The man is not in his prime. Prime-time TV is often called mindless.)

So-called "black humor" is a kind of grotesque, irreverent comedy that plays with life's most serious subjects and makes fun of things that are not really funny at all. In this example, Cummings announces his reasonably sober theme at the outset, and then confirms its ironic truth by telling the frustrating and ultimately grisly story of "Uncle Sol." Since the only punctuation marks are the parentheses enclosing the last four lines, we have to find our way through the poem by supplying punctuation dictated by the poem's sense. Watch for the emphases suggested by the words themselves, and the pauses or breaks that echo the rhythms of normal speech.

nobody loses all the time

nobody loses all the time

i had an uncle named
Sol who was a born failure and
nearly everybody said he should have gone
into vaudeville perhaps because my Uncle Sol could
sing McCann He Was A Diver on Xmas Eve like Hell Itself which
may or may not account for the fact that my Uncle

Sol indulged in that possibly most inexcusable
of all to use a highfalootin phrase
luxuries that is or to
wit farming and be
it needlessly
added

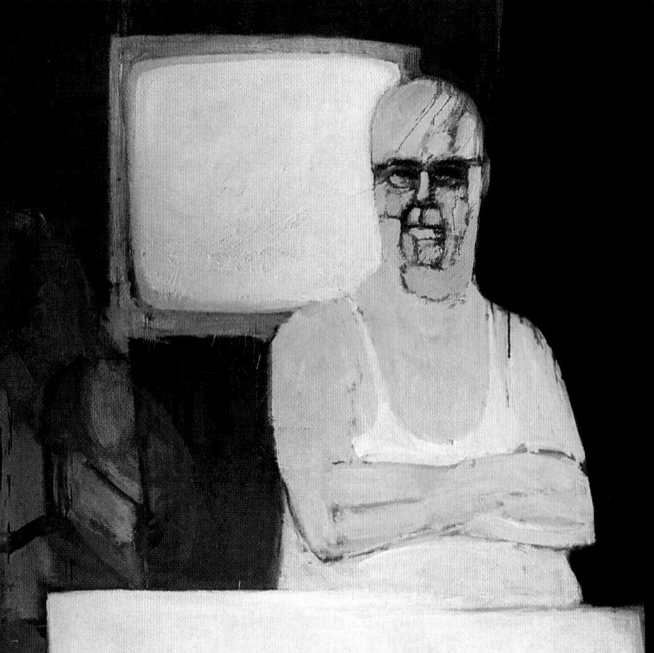

Prime Time by May Stevens (1967). Oil.

The Wichita State University Endowment Association Art Collection, Wichita, Kansas.

CLOSURE

Ask students to write two or three sentences in which they identify some of the words and phrases that show this poem to be humorous. See if there is general agreement in class on the words and phrases chosen.

ANALYZING THE POEM

Interpreting Meanings

1. Even born failures like Uncle Sol attain some success, even if only by the law of averages, and even if the success is not what they would have liked.

2. Answers will vary. The speaker is a kind of breathless narrator of Sol's life. He seems to come from the city, is something of a cynic, and appears keenly aware of the irony of the story.

3. Answers will vary. Some students may say that the poem uses black humor to mock our often euphemistic outlook on death. Urge students to discuss their ideas about the poem. What, besides the opinion of "everybody," shows that Sol wasted his life? Is the speaker something of a smart aleck, passing an unfair judgment on Sol? Does the description of Sol's funeral satirize hypocrisy?

4. Most students will agree that there is a hint of cruelty. Perhaps Cummings intended to shock us and shake up our perceptions of failure, death, and grief. The speaker's tongue-in-cheek tone throughout the poem makes us laugh even at Sol's death and funeral.

my Uncle Sol's farm
failed because the chickens
ate the vegetables so
my Uncle Sol had a
chicken farm till the
skunks ate the chickens when

my Uncle Sol
had a skunk farm but
the skunks caught cold and
died and so
my Uncle Sol imitated the
skunks in a subtle manner

or by drowning himself in the watertank
but somebody who'd given my Uncle Sol a Victor
Victrola and records while he lived presented to
A him upon the auspicious occasion of his decease a
scrumptious not to mention splendiferous funeral with
tall boys in black gloves and flowers and everything and

B i remember we all cried like the Missouri
when my Uncle Sol's coffin lurched because
somebody pressed a button
(and down went
my Uncle
Sol

and started a worm farm)

Responding to the Poem

Analyzing the Poem

Interpreting Meanings

1. What does the title mean? Do you see any significance in the fact that the sun is often called "old sol"?
2. When we read Cummings's collected works, we realize that he used many different borrowed or imitated voices to reveal the characters of the speakers in his poems. From what you hear, and overhear, in this monologue, what sort of person would you say we are listening to? Is he or she aware of the **irony** that runs through the story? When does the irony become clear?
3. This poem is about the career of a "born failure." What else is it about?
4. Do you find a hint of cruelty in the poem? Do you think it is intentional, or that it is incidental? Why do we laugh at the last line, when we should shudder at it?

Writing About the Poem

A Creative Response

1. **Writing in Cummings's Style.** First, write a paragraph of at least ten lines about something interesting that has happened to you or to someone you know. Then rewrite the paragraph without any punctuation. Separate the material into lines: Break the lines to indicate "thought groupings." In addition to eliminating punctuation, you might also experiment with eliminating or changing capitalization.

A Critical Response

2. **Comparing and Contrasting Poems.** In a paragraph, compare and contrast Cummings's poem with Robinson's poem "Richard Cory" (page 634). Discuss how the poems differ in the use of rhyme, meter, and tone.

A. Colloquialisms

? What are three colloquial words or expressions in the poem? (Probably the most obvious are *highfalootin* [line 9], *scrumptious,* and *splendiferous* [line 30]. There is also a cliché in the poem: "auspicious occasion" [line 29]. See Analyzing Language and Style, page 739.)

B. Hyperbole

? What example of hyperbole in the form of a simile do you find near the end of the poem? (The mourners "all cried like the Missouri.")

PREPARATION

ESTABLISHING A PURPOSE. The headnote suggests a method for reading this poem. As with most selections, students will find it helpful to scan the accompanying questions and assignments before beginning to read. By doing so, they will have a clearer idea of what to look for in their reading.

SUPPLEMENTARY SUPPORT MATERIALS

1. Vocabulary Activity Worksheet (*CCB*)
2. Review and Response Worksheet: Diction (*CCB*)
3. Selection Test (*CCB*)
4. Audiocassette recording

DEVELOPING VOCABULARY

The following words from the poem are tested in the Selection Test. (See also Vocabulary Activity Worksheet.)

awry — to flay
fiend — to stifle
keen

A. Syntax
The syntax—the way in which words are put together to form phrases, clauses, or sentences—is unusual in this poem. Words are used in unfamiliar ways—verbs are used as nouns, for example. Ask students to find specific examples.

B. Responding
? The best poetry becomes more enjoyable and revealing with each rereading. Did you find yourself understanding this poem better each time you read it? Explain. (Answers will vary.)

C. Humanities Connection: Responding to the Fine Art
Charles Burchfield (1893–1967), an American painter, is noted for his scenic watercolors, some of which are tinged with surrealism.
? How well do you think this painting goes with the Cummings poem—that is, why was it chosen? (It shows a wild nature.)

Although this poem deals with destruction, it is an optimistic statement about people and the possibilities facing the human race. The syntax here is more difficult than that of the previous poem. Read it through once or twice to get a general idea of what it is saying. Then read it carefully, line by line, noting where sentences and "thought groups" begin and end.

what if a much of a which of a wind

A what if a much of a which of a wind
gives the truth to summer's lie;
bloodies with dizzying leaves the sun
and yanks immortal stars awry?
Blow king to beggar and queen to seem
(blow friend to fiend:blow space to time)
—when skies are hanged and oceans drowned,
the single secret will still be man

what if a keen of a lean wind flays
screaming hills with sleet and snow:
strangles valleys by ropes of thing
and stifles forests in white ago?
Blow hope to terror; blow seeing to blind
(blow pity to envy and soul to mind)
—whose hearts are mountains,roots are trees,
it's they shall cry hello to the spring

what if a dawn of a doom of a dream
bites this universe in two,
peels forever out of his grave
and sprinkles nowhere with me and you?
Blow soon to never and never to twice
(blow life to isn't:blow death to was)
—all nothing's only our hugest home;
the most who die, the more we live

B

Pink Locusts and Windy Moon
by Charles Burchfield (1959). Watercolor.

Collection of the Chase Manhattan Bank, N.A.
Photograph by D. James Dee.

CLOSURE

Ask one student in class to define *slant rhyme* and *internal rhyme.* Have two or more other students give examples of each kind. The examples can be from this poem, or made up, or from memory. (See question 5 below.)

ANALYZING THE POEM

Identifying Details

1. Even if the world is blown away, the secret of human existence will remain.
2. People "whose hearts are mountains, roots are trees" will survive to greet the spring.
3. Even if the universe is blown up, the human spirit will remain.
4. In line 2, "summer's lie" is revealed by the winds of late summer or autumn (lines 1–3). In lines 9–10, the setting seems to be winter, with "lean wind" that "flays/screaming hills with sleet and snow." In line 16, the end of winter is greeted by those who "cry hello to the spring." Whereas the first two stanzas concentrate on the cycle of the seasons, the third stanza focuses on eternity ("dawn of a doom"), using such words as *forever* and *nowhere.*
5. The rhyme scheme of each stanza is *abcbd-dac.* Slant rhyme is used in lines 3 and 8 *(sun* and *man),* lines 5 and 6 (*seem* and *time),* lines 1 and 7 *(wind* and *drowned),* lines 9 and 15 *(flays* and *trees),* lines 19 and 24 *(grave* and *live),* and lines 17 and 25 *(dream* and *home).* Cummings also uses internal rhyme and assonance.

Interpreting Meanings

6. Fears of disappointment, loss, death, oblivion.
7. It makes the poem personal and immediate.
8. Everyone dies. The more souls in eternity, perhaps the greater joy. He is celebrating life.

A. Responding

? Can you think of a reason why Cummings has run together the words *mostpeople* and *Squarerootofminus-one?* (Answers will vary, but the words are logical units.)

Responding to the Poem

Analyzing the Poem

Identifying Details

1. If the world is blown away, what will still survive?
2. Who "shall cry hello to the spring" if the world freezes over?
3. What will happen if the universe is blown up?
4. What **images** describe the seasons of the year in the first two stanzas? How does the third stanza deal with time on a different scale?
5. Describe the **rhyme scheme** of the poem. How does Cummings make use of **slant rhyme?**

Interpreting Meanings

6. What common human fears does Cummings refer to in the first six lines of each stanza? How does he comment on those fears in the last two lines of each stanza?
7. What is the effect of the direct reference to "me and you" in line 20?
8. What do you think Cummings means by the last two lines? Is he celebrating life or death? Explain.

Writing About the Poem

A Critical Response

1. **Comparing Poems.** In a paragraph, compare this poem to Whitman's "On the Beach at Night" on page 343. Consider the theme or message, imagery, tone, form, and structure of the poems before you write.
2. **Comparing the Poems to a Statement.** In the quotation that follows under "Primary Sources," from the introduction to his collection called *New Poems,* Cummings makes several statements about poetry and his audience, and at the same time reveals an attitude toward life itself. In a brief essay, tell whether you find any of these statements related to the messages in his poems. Use specific lines from the poems to support your opinions.

Analyzing Language and Style

Diction

In "nobody loses all the time," Cummings uses two words that would not be found in poetry of an earlier generation.

1. *Highfalootin* is listed in one dictionary as an Americanism—that is, a word that originated in America, or that is peculiar to American English. What does it mean?
2. *Splendiferous* is listed as colloquial, meaning that it would not be used in formal written English. What does it mean?
3. What words might a more conservative writer from a past era have used in place of each of these words?
4. What would be a more elegant and formal way of saying "we all cried like the Missouri"?
5. What does the diction of this poem reveal about its speaker? How does it help set the poem's tone?
6. In "what if a much of a which of a wind," Cummings uses verbs, adjectives, and adverbs as nouns. Find five examples. In each case, what does the word mean as a noun?

Primary Sources

"Miracles are to come"

"The poems to come are for you and for me and are not for mostpeople—it's no use trying to pretend that mostpeople and ourselves are alike. Mostpeople have less in common with ourselves than the squarerootofminusone. You and I are human beings;mostpeople are snobs. . . .

"you and I are not snobs. We can never be born enough. We are human beings;for whom birth is a supremely welcome mystery,the mystery of growing:the mystery which happens only and whenever we are faithful to ourselves. You and I wear the dangerous looseness of doom and find it becoming. Life,for eternal us,is now; and now is much too busy being a little more than everything to seem anything,catastrophic included. . . .

"Miracles are to come. With you I leave a remembrance of miracles:they are by somebody who can love and who shall be continually reborn,a human being;somebody who said to those near him,when his fingers would not hold a brush 'tie it into my hand'—"

—E. E. Cummings

COMMENT FROM A CRITIC/BIOGRAPHER T.S. Eliot wrote a few of his most famous poems while he was a student at Harvard, including "The Love Song of J. Alfred Prufrock." Stephen Spender—poet, critic, and biographer—has written about Eliot's Harvard years:

"When, in early 1914, Bertrand Russell [the famous philosopher] went to Harvard and gave a seminar on symbolic logic, he was much impressed by Eliot, one of his best students. In a letter to Lady Ottoline Morrell he referred to him as 'ultra-civilized' and 'with manners of the finest Etonian type.' 'He knows his classics very well . . . and is altogether impeccable in his taste but has no vigour or life—or enthusiasm. He is going to Oxford where I expect he will be very happy.' "

After your students have read the Eliot biography and "The Love Song of J. Alfred Prufrock," you may want to ask them to discuss (a) how accurate Bertrand Russell's observations seem to have been and (b) how autobiographical the poem seems to be.

COMMENT FROM AN EDITOR Robert Giroux, an editor and a friend of Eliot, witnessed a meeting at Harcourt Brace, the publishing house, between Eliot and Carl Sandburg. Neither cared much for the other's poetry, and the editors tried to arrange to keep the poets apart. At one point, however, Sandburg saw Eliot in Giroux's office and immediately went in. When Giroux returned (he writes), "Sandburg had already drawn up a chair and was moodily gazing across my desk into Eliot's eyes. 'Just look at him!' Sandburg said to me, pointing at Eliot. 'Look at that man's face—the suffering, and the pain.' By this time Eliot was wearing a great big grin. 'You can't hold *him* responsible for the poets and critics who ride on his coat-tails!' With that, he walked out of the office and I realized that one of the great literary encounters of our time had occurred, and as far as I knew Eliot had not uttered a single word."

T. S. Eliot (1888–1965)

At the time when he was regarded as America's most eminent living poet, T. S. Eliot announced that he was an "Anglo-Catholic in religion, a royalist in politics, and a classicist in literature." In 1927, Eliot gave up his American citizenship and became a subject of the King of England. The same year he was received into the Church of England. (By a kind of poetic justice, this loss to America was later to be made up for: W. H. Auden, the leading British poet of his time, became a naturalized American citizen in 1946.) But residence in an adopted country does not necessarily change the philosophy or the style of a poet. Eliot continued to speak in a voice first heard in the Puritan pulpits of Massachusetts. And Auden retained a British sense of language unaffected by the in-roads of American speech.

T. S. Eliot's family was rooted in New England, yet he was born in St. Louis, Missouri, where his father was the chancellor of Washington University. Eliot's childhood awareness of his native city would show itself in his poetry, but only after he had moved far away from St. Louis. He graduated from Harvard and went on to postgraduate work at the Sorbonne in Paris.

Just before the outbreak of World War I, Eliot took up residence in London, the city that would become his home for the rest of his life. There he worked for a time in a bank, suffered a nervous breakdown, married an emotionally troubled Englishwoman, and finally took up the business of literature. He became active as a publisher in the outstanding firm of Faber & Faber, and, on his own, edited *The Criterion,* a literary magazine. As a critic, he was responsible for reviving interest in many neglected poets, notably the seventeenth-century poet John Donne.

Long before he decided to live abroad permanently, Eliot had developed a taste for classical literature. He was as familiar with European and Eastern writings as he was with the masterpieces of English. But the most crucial influence upon his early work came from the late-nineteenth-century French poets who, as a group, came to be known as the Symbolists. When he was nineteen, Eliot came upon a book by the British critic Arthur Symons entitled *The Symbolist Movement in Literature*. "I myself owe Mr. Symons a great debt," wrote Eliot. "But for having read his book I should not . . . have heard of Laforgue and Rimbaud; I should probably not have begun to read Verlaine; and but for reading Verlaine, I should not have heard of Corbière. So the Symons book is one of those which have affected the course of my life."

The poets Eliot mentions were men of distinctly different talents. Yet they all believed in poetry as an art of suggestion rather than statement. They saw poetry as an art of recreating states of mind and feeling, as opposed to reporting or confessing them. These beliefs became the basis of Eliot's own poetic methods. When people complained that this poetic method of suggestion was complex and difficult to understand, Eliot retorted that poetry had to be complex to express the complexities of modern life. More or less ignoring the still undervalued contribution of Walt Whitman, Eliot and other American poets also believed that, divorced from British antecedents, they would once and for all bring the peculiar rhythms of their native speech into the mainstream of world literature. Eliot and these other poets are often referred to as Modernists.

COMMENT FROM THE POET
Although poetry is preeminently the domain of the right word, that does not necessarily mean the most "beautiful" word. In a speech in 1942 at the University of Glasgow, Scotland, Eliot explored the matter of "beautiful words":

"[A] poem is not made only out of 'beautiful words.' I doubt whether, from the point of view of *sound* alone, any word is more or less beautiful than another. . . . The ugly words are the words not fitted for the company in which they find themselves; there are words which are ugly because of rawness or because of antiquation; there are words which are ugly because of foreignness or ill-breeding (e.g., *television*): but I do not believe that any word well-established in its own language is either beautiful or ugly. The music of a word . . . arises from . . . its context."

You might ask students to react to Eliot's remarks and to express their own thoughts on the subject of "beautiful words."

Eliot had an austere view of poetic creativity; he disagreed with those who regarded a poem as a means of self-expression, as a source of comfort, or as a kind of spiritual pep talk. Practicing what he preached, Eliot startled his contemporaries in 1917 with "The Love Song of J. Alfred Prufrock" and "Portrait of a Lady." Then, in 1922, with the editorial advice and encouragement of Ezra Pound, Eliot published *The Waste Land,* a long work which would become the most significant poem of the early twentieth century. The poem was so influential that the word *wasteland* entered common usage from Eliot's work. The word suggests a civilization that is spiritually empty and paralyzed by indecision and anxiety.

Assembled in the manner of a painter's collage or a movie-maker's montage, *The Waste Land* proved that it was possible to write an epic poem of classical scope in the space of 434 lines. Critics pored over the poem's complex structure and its dense network of allusions to world literature, Oriental religion, and anthropology. A few years after *The Waste Land* appeared, Eliot published a series of notes identifying many of his key references. (He was dismayed to find that some of his more ardent admirers were more interested in the notes than in the poem itself.)

In 1925, Eliot published a kind of lyrical postscript to *The Waste Land* called *The Hollow Men,* which predicted in its somber conclusion that the world would not end with a bang but with a whimper. In *The Hollow Men,* Eliot repeats and expands some of the themes of his longer poem and arrives at that point of despair beyond which lie but two alternatives: renewal or annihilation.

For critics surveying Eliot's career, it has become commonplace to say that, after the spiritual dead-end of *The Hollow Men,* Eliot chose hope over despair, and faith over the world-weary cynicism that marked his early years. But there is much evidence in his later poems to indicate that, for Eliot, hope and faith were not conscious choices. Instead, they were the consequences of a submission, even a surrender, to that "peace which passeth understanding" referred to in the last line of *The Waste Land.*

His later poems include *Ash Wednesday* (1930), with its deeply religious spiritual explorations, and *Four Quartets,* which contain the philosophical conclusions of a lifetime (though always tentative).

Eliot spent the remainder of his poetic career in an extended meditation upon the limits of individual will and the limitless power of faith in the presence of grace.

Cited for his work as "a trail-blazing pioneer of modern poetry," Eliot was awarded the Nobel Prize for literature in 1948. In the decades that followed, he came frequently to the United States to lecture and to read his poems, sometimes to audiences so large he had to appear in football stadiums. Some of those who fought to buy tickets on the fifty-yard line were probably unaware of the irony in all of this: that a man once regarded as the most difficult and obscure poet of his era had achieved the drawing power of a rock star.

Ezra Pound (who called Eliot "Possum") wrote a few final words on the death of his old friend, ending with this passage:

"Am I to write 'about' the poet Thomas Stearns Eliot? Or my friend 'the Possum'? Let him rest in peace, I can only repeat, but with the urgency of fifty years ago: READ HIM."

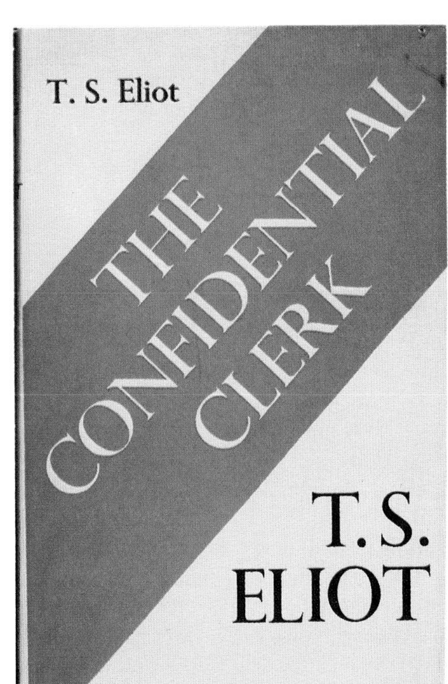

B

A. Responding
? Do you agree with Eliot's "austere view of poetic creativity"? Why or why not? (Many students may feel that the most meaningful poetry *is* personal.)

B. Humanities Connection: Discussing the Illustration
This is the dust jacket of the first edition of Eliot's *The Confidential Clerk* (1954), a verse play about faith and the quest for a personal identity.

Eliot loved writing for the theater, though few of his plays were popular successes. Perhaps his best-known play is *Murder in the Cathedral* (1935), about the assassination of Thomas à Becket in Canterbury Cathedral in 1170. Other verse plays include *The Family Reunion* (1939), *The Cocktail Party* (1950), and *The Elder Statesman* (1958).

PREPARATION

ESTABLISHING A PURPOSE. The class as a whole might read and discuss the headnote before beginning the poem. Advise students to watch for Eliot's figures of speech, some of which are very well known.

SUPPLEMENTARY SUPPORT MATERIALS

1. Vocabulary Activity Worksheet (*CCB*)
2. Review and Response Worksheet: Metaphors and Extended Metaphors (*CCB*)
3. Selection Test (*CCB*)
4. Audiocassette recording

DEVELOPING VOCABULARY

The following words from the poem are tested in the Selection Test. (See also Vocabulary Activity Worksheet.)

etherized, tedious, insidious, formulated, to digress, to scuttle, deferential, politic, meticulous, obtuse

Answers to Marginal Questions

3. The evening is like a person under ether, lying on a table.

7. The speaker wants to take his companion through certain half-deserted streets, past cheap hotels and sawdust restaurants.

22. Pools stand in drains; soot falls from chimneys. The house has a terrace. The season is autumn.

A. Point of View

As line 1 indicates, the point of view of the poem is first person. Yet the position of the speaker seems to shift from inside to outside and back again, while the "I" seems to shift from participant to observer.

? What accounts for this apparent disconnectedness? (The poem is an interior monologue; thoughts are seldom sequential in such writing.)

This poem is written as an interior monologue; it is all going on inside the head of a man named Prufrock. Sometimes Prufrock's line of reasoning is interrupted by an unexpected thought. You will often have to supply the missing connections in the speaker's stream of thoughts and associations.

The poem was published in 1917. As you read, think of how it reflects these ideas about Eliot's own time, and perhaps about ours as well:

1. **The idea that people are spiritually empty.**
2. **The idea that contemporary life is unromantic and unheroic.**

Read the poem through twice. Read it aloud, or listen to it being read aloud, at least once. Then answer the questions in the side-notes.

The Love Song of J. Alfred Prufrock

S'io credesse che mia risposta fosse
A persona che mai tornasse al mondo,
Questa fiamma staria senza piu scosse.
Ma perciocche giammai di questo fondo
Non torno vivo alcun, s'i'odo il vero,
Senza tema d'infamia ti rispondo.°

Epigraph: This quotation is from Dante's great epic poem *The Divine Comedy.* Guido da Montefeltro, a man consigned to Hell for dispensing evil advice, speaks from a flame shaped like a tongue: "If I believed my answer were being made to someone who could return to the world, this flame would shake no more. But since (if what I hear is true) no one has ever returned alive from these depths, I will answer you without fear of disgrace." Think of Prufrock as speaking from another kind of hell—a hell of his own feelings.

A Let us go then, you and I,
When the evening is spread out against the sky
Like a patient etherized upon a table;
Let us go, through certain half-deserted streets,
The muttering retreats
Of restless nights in one-night cheap hotels
And sawdust restaurants with oyster shells:
Streets that follow like a tedious argument
Of insidious intent
To lead you to an overwhelming question . . .
Oh, do not ask, "What is it?"
Let us go and make our visit.

? **3.** *What is the evening compared with?*

? **7.** *List the facts you know about where the speaker wants to take his companion.*

In the room the women come and go
Talking of Michelangelo.°

14. Michelangelo: the great artist of the Italian Renaissance.

The yellow fog that rubs its back upon the window
    panes,
The yellow smoke that rubs its muzzle on the window
    panes
Licked its tongue into the corners of the evening,
Lingered upon the pools that stand in drains,
Let fall upon its back the soot that falls from chimneys,
Slipped by the terrace, made a sudden leap,
And seeing that it was a soft October night,
Curled once about the house, and fell asleep.

? **22.** *What details are you given about this setting? What season is it?*

And indeed there will be time
For the yellow smoke that slides along the street,
Rubbing its back upon the window panes;

Comment From The Poet

Students who are having difficulty with Eliot's language may be interested to know that Eliot himself has something to say on the subject. In "The Three Voices of Poetry," he writes:

"If you complain that a poet is obscure, and apparently ignoring you, the reader, or that he is speaking to a limited circle of initiates from which you are excluded—remember that what he may have been trying to do, was to put something into words which could not be said in any other way, and therefore in a language which may be worth the trouble of learning."

Ask students to comment on Eliot's assertion about the special language or languages of poetry. Do they agree with Eliot that a reader should be prepared to learn an unfamiliar language in order to understand what seems to be obscure poetry?

There will be time, there will be time
To prepare a face to meet the faces that you meet;
There will be time to murder and create,
And time for all the works and days of hands
That lift and drop a question on your plate;
Time for you and time for me,
And time yet for a hundred indecisions,
And for a hundred visions and revisions,
Before the taking of a toast and tea.

In the room the women come and go
Talking of Michelangelo.

And indeed there will be time
To wonder, "Do I dare?" and, "Do I dare?"
Time to turn back and descend the stair,
With a bald spot in the middle of my hair—
[They will say: "How his hair is growing thin!"]
My morning coat, my collar mounting firmly to the chin,
My necktie rich and modest, but asserted by a simple pin—
[They will say: "But how his arms and legs are thin!"]
Do I dare
Disturb the universe?
In a minute there is time
For decisions and revisions which a minute will reverse.

For I have known them all already, known them all—
Have known the evenings, mornings, afternoons,
I have measured out my life with coffee spoons;
I know the voices dying with a dying fall°
Beneath the music from a farther room.
So how should I presume?

And I have known the eyes already, known them all—
The eyes that fix you in a formulated phrase,
And when I am formulated, sprawling on a pin,
When I am pinned and wriggling on the wall,
Then how should I begin
To spit out all the butt-ends of my days and ways?
And how should I presume?

And I have known the arms already, known them all—
Arms that are braceleted and white and bare
[But in the lamplight, downed with light brown hair!]
Is it perfume from a dress
That makes me so digress?
Arms that lie along a table, or wrap about a shawl.
And should I then presume?
And how should I begin?

? **27.** *What does this line mean?*

? **34.** *What words are repeated over and over in this stanza?*

? **38.** *What could he want to dare to do?*

? **41.** *Who are "they"?*

? **42.** *What does Prufrock look like? Is he young, middle-aged, or old?*

? **48.** *Up to this point what do you think Prufrock's chief problem is?*

? **51.** *Has a life that is measured in coffee spoons been very exciting or heroic?*

52. dying fall: in music, notes that fade away.

? **58.** *What do you see here?*

? **60.** *What are his days compared to? Is this a positive or sad image?*

Answers to Marginal Questions

27. Prufrock is acutely aware of how he looks to others. He feels a need to "prepare a face" to meet them.

34. The word *time* appears eight times in the stanza. Four lines begin with the word *And.*

38. He evidently wants to interact with other people, but he lacks the courage.

41. "They" are all those people who in Prufrock's mind are observing him closely and distastefully.

42. He is well-dressed but has a bald spot and thin arms and legs. His age is uncertain.

48. He seems timid and indecisive.

51. The implication is that he sees his life as being dull.

58. The image is that of a mounted but still living specimen, perhaps a worm or an insect.

60. His days are like smoked cigarettes ready to be stubbed out. The image is both unpleasant and sad.

COMMENT FROM A CRITIC

Cleanth Brooks, a noted American critic, made the following remarks in a lecture:

"Eliot once remarked that prose has to do with ideals; poetry, with reality. The statement has proved puzzling to many a reader who has been brought up on just the opposite set of notions, but Eliot's observation seems to me profoundly true. Discursive prose is the medium for carrying on arguments, drawing conclusions, offering solutions. Poetry is the medium *par excellence* for rendering a total situation—for letting us know what it feels like to take a particular action or hold a particular belief or simply to look at something with imaginative sympathy."

You might ask your students to discuss Eliot's observation and Brooks's reaction to it.

Answers to Marginal Questions

72. He has walked through the streets of a lower-class neighborhood.
74. He is comparing himself to a crab.
77. The evening is sleeping, possibly because of feigned sickness. At the beginning of the poem, the evening is compared to an anesthetized patient.
80. He seems to want to establish a relationship with one of the women mentioned earlier.
85. Prufrock lacks confidence; even the "eternal Footman" snickers at him.
94. Like Guido in *The Divine Comedy,* Prufrock is in hell, although Prufrock's is mental and spiritual. If he could rise like Lazarus, he could leave his personal hell and "tell you all."
98. Even if he tells them "all," he expects to be misunderstood and rejected.

. . . . .

Shall I say, I have gone at dusk through narrow streets
And watched the smoke that rises from the pipes
Of lonely men in shirt-sleeves, leaning out of windows? . . .

I should have been a pair of ragged claws
Scuttling across the floors of silent seas.

. . . . .

And the afternoon, the evening, sleeps so peacefully!
Smoothed by long fingers,
Asleep . . . tired . . . or it malingers,°
Stretched on the floor, here beside you and me.
Should I, after tea and cakes and ices,
Have the strength to force the moment to its crisis?
But though I have wept and fasted, wept and prayed,
Though I have seen my head [grown slightly bald] brought in upon a platter,°
I am no prophet—and here's no great matter;
I have seen the moment of my greatness flicker,
And I have seen the eternal Footman hold my coat, and snicker,
And in short, I was afraid.

And would it have been worth it, after all,
After the cups, the marmalade, the tea,
Among the porcelain, among some talk of you and me,
Would it have been worthwhile,
To have bitten off the matter with a smile,
To have squeezed the universe into a ball
To roll it toward some overwhelming question,
To say: "I am Lazarus, come from the dead,
Come back to tell you all, I shall tell you all"—
If one, settling a pillow by her head,
Should say: "That is not what I meant at all,
That is not it, at all."

And would it have been worth it, after all,
Would it have been worthwhile,
After the sunsets and the dooryards and the sprinkled streets,
After the novels, after the teacups, after the skirts that trail along the floor—
And this, and so much more?—
It is impossible to say just what I mean!
But as if a magic lantern° threw the nerves in patterns on a screen:
Would it have been worthwhile
If one, settling a pillow or throwing off a shawl,

72. *What has Prufrock done at night?*

74. *What is the speaker comparing himself to here?*

77. Malingers *means "pretends to be sick." How is this image of the evening connected to the opening one?*

80. *Do you know yet what he is forcing to a crisis? What could it be?*

82. "My head . . . brought in upon a platter": a reference to the Biblical account of Salome, whose dancing so pleased Herod, the ancient King of Judea, that he offered to reward her with her heart's desire (Matthew 14:1–12). Goaded by her spiteful mother, Salome asked for the head of John the Baptist. True to his word, Herod granted her gruesome request and had John's head brought to her on a serving dish. In the many paintings of the subject, the head is notable for its rich and flowing locks.

85. *A footman is a servant. What does this line tell you about Prufrock's confidence?*

94. *Lazarus is the man Christ raised from the dead. How do these lines connect with the opening quote from Dante?*

98. *What is he afraid will happen if he tells them "all"?*

105. magic lantern: something like our modern slide projector.

CLOSURE

Have students make brief oral statements summarizing Prufrock's personality and condition in life.

COMMENT FROM A CRITIC

Stephen Spender does not condone Prufrock for his inaction: "His [Prufrock's] failure, for which he despises himself, is failure to relate either with another person or with the Absolute. He is isolated, he cannot communicate. Although the fact that he is *conditioned* by the society in which he lives may account for his spiritual and sexual enervation, this does not excuse his moral cowardice. The fact that he is able to see his character as the projection of circumstances is still no excuse for his inertia." You might ask students to discuss the issue that Spender raises: To what extent should a person be expected to rise above the circumstances of birth, upbringing, and environment?

And turning toward the window, should say:
  "That is not it at all,
  That is not what I meant, at all."

. . . . .

No! I am not Prince Hamlet, nor was meant to be;
Am an attendant lord, one that will do
To swell a progress,° start a scene or two,
Advise the prince; no doubt, an easy tool,
Deferential, glad to be of use,
Politic, cautious, and meticulous;
Full of high sentence,° but a bit obtuse;
At times, indeed, almost ridiculous—
Almost, at times, the Fool.

  I grow old . . . I grow old . . .
I shall wear the bottoms of my trousers rolled.

  Shall I part my hair behind? Do I dare to eat a peach?
I shall wear white flannel trousers, and walk upon the
    beach.
I have heard the mermaids singing, each to each.

  I do not think that they will sing to me.

  I have seen them riding seaward on the waves
Combing the white hair of the waves blown back
When the wind blows the water white and black.

  We have lingered in the chambers of the sea
By sea-girls wreathed with seaweed red and brown
Till human voices wake us, and we drown.

? **110.** *Who do you think might say this to Prufrock?*

? **111.** *Hamlet is the Prince of Denmark and the hero of Shakespeare's play of that name. What is Prufrock saying "No!" to?*

113. To swell a progress: to fill out a scene in a play, or a pageant; an "extra."

117. Full of high sentence: full of pompous talk.

? **119.** *How does Prufrock feel about himself?*

? **121.** *This was the style of the time, in trousers worn by fashionable young men. What is Prufrock hoping for here?*

? **125.** *If he can't "hear" the mermaids, what will he miss in life?*

? **128.** *What does he see here?*

? **131.** *What breaks the romantic spell cast by the sight of mermaids? What could "drown" mean here?*

Answers to Marginal Questions

110. One of the women to whom Prufrock is attracted might say this if he told "all."

111. Prufrock is saying that he is not a prince (like Hamlet) but like Polonius, the king's ineffectual adviser.

119. He has a very low opinion of himself.

121. By wearing the bottoms of his trousers rolled, Prufrock would be trying to stay in fashion. (Trouser cuffs were just coming into fashion.)

125. If he cannot hear the mermaids, he will presumably spend his life without love.

128. He has seen mermaids on the sea while the wind was forming whitecaps.

131. The romantic spell is broken by human voices. To "drown" is perhaps to lose the hope of love as the mermaids vanish.

A Comment on the Poem

Of all the love songs ever written, this must be one of the oddest and most pathetic. The man who "sings" it has feelings but no one to share them with, and ideas that are realized nowhere but in his own mind. Sensitive emotions and sophisticated thoughts do nothing to help him come to grips with the real world of the streets. He knows that life is "out there," but he also knows that he will never join it, and so he takes refuge in self-dramatization and heroic fantasy. Yet the man himself is not pitiful. He has sufficient knowledge of himself to control his longings and enough of a sense of humor to portray himself as a victim without being victimized.

"I am not Prince Hamlet," he says; and yet, he shares with Hamlet a breadth of vision to see two sides or more of every issue and the inability to act decisively upon any of his insights. If, in the jargon of today, we'd ask, "What's his problem?" the answer would have to be "Self-consciousness—the egocentric trap that keeps an extraordinarily sophisticated man from enjoying the pleasures of this world that simpler men and women pursue and embrace without a thought."

One way to read the poem is to think of it as a movie—scenes follow one another immediately and without the connections or transitions that a conventional writer

ANALYZING THE POEM
Interpreting Meanings
1. "Prude" suggests shyness, insecurity. "Prudence" implies caution, timidity. "Frock" might suggest effeminacy or, in a religious garment, monkishness.
2. Sunset is often associated with fire. The simile suggests that Prufrock may regard himself as an invalid, as someone who has been numbed by anxiety or indecision.
3. The speaker is proposing to the reader (or someone else—even himself) a journey through city streets on some kind of visit. The destination is unclear. It seems they are going to travel through a rundown quarter of a large city—"one-night cheap hotels," restaurants with sawdust on the floor. Comparing half-deserted streets to a "tedious argument" may suggest a mental as well as a physical journey.
4. "Michelangelo" connotes cultivated and refined (perhaps overrefined) conversation.
5. Yellow fog and smoke are being compared to an animal, probably a cat. Details: line 15—"rubs its back"; 16—"rubs its muzzle"; 17—licks its tongue; 19—
(Answers continue in left-hand column.)

(Continued from top.)
lets soot "fall upon its back"; 20—makes "a sudden leap"; 21—sees the softness of the night; 22—curls around the house and falls asleep.
6. We recognize an urban setting, probably London, on an October night. Autumn suggests Prufrock's gloom, his anxiety about the passage of time, and his own mortality. Spring, suggesting hope and rebirth, would be inappropriate.
7. When you "prepare a face" to meet people, you are probably anxious or self-conscious about how they will perceive or judge you. Line 27 reveals that Prufrock is timid and insecure.
8. His physical appearance bothers him, especially as he grows older. He mentions thinning hair and thin legs.
9. Perhaps he has spent much time in coffeehouses or at salons. He may live alone and be bored and lonely.
(Answers continue on next page.)

would provide. When there are connections to be made, the reader must make them. Consequently, the poem is demanding. What it demands is that, in the absence of logical connections, the reader must make the *psychological* connections that underly the poem's structure and content.

"Let us go then," says the speaker, and so invites us (or someone) to join him on a "visit." But, instead of going wherever it is he has in mind, we soon find ourselves observers in the course of the man's search. Our companion seems to be looking for answers to the meaning of life and the nature of romantic love. He tries, without success, to find some place for himself even in the world he knows well. In line 10, we read that he has an "overwhelming question." But he impatiently brushes us aside before we can ask what it is.

Quick as a flash, quick as a shot in a movie that instantly replaces another shot, and before we've taken even one step with our hero, we're confronted with something unexpected: women passing back and forth in a room and discussing Michelangelo, one of the greatest artists of all time. This little glimpse from the corner of the eye, so to speak, introduces an aspect of Prufrock's character that we'll find illustrated time and again. Focusing on one thing, he can't help thinking of something else. Everything actual has its counterpart in an image or a metaphor or a situation, by means of which Eliot can dramatize the dilemma of a man suffering a kind of emotional paralysis. As for the women who "come and go," they may be in an art gallery or in a museum or at a party or someplace else. The importance of their early and sudden appearance is to prepare us for the *method* of the poem. It is made up of a sequence of disjointed scenes that are psychologically related to the speaker's half-formed thoughts.

Time is a motif that recurs throughout the poem. Prufrock is conscious of time, and toward the end of his "love song," he makes his preoccupation clear: "I grow old . . . I grow old. . . ." Oppressed by time, he makes fun of his own obsession with it when he says, "There will be time . . . for a hundred visions." This statement might make us think of a religious revelation and the promise of salvation. But only for a moment. Prufrock soon drops us back into reality by the workaday word *revisions*—as if he is suggesting that the grandeur of imagination could be edited with a blue pencil, and that this would all take place before tea time.

Responding to the Poem

Analyzing the Poem

Interpreting Meanings

1. The very name "J. Alfred Prufrock" gives us clues to the character of our "hero." Think of "prude" and "prudence." Think of what you associate with a "frock"—in terms of costume, in terms of religion. What hints to the man's personality might these details supply?
2. How could the famous **simile** in lines 2–3 reveal that the speaker's mind or will is paralyzed? (What kinds of things are the evening sky and sunset usually compared with?)
3. What is the speaker inviting someone to do in lines 1–12? What kind of place are they going to travel through? How could some of these **images** aiso suggest a journey through someone's *mind*, as well as a physical journey?
4. Think about what the name Michelangelo contributes to the transitional passage in lines 13–14. What would be the effect if, for instance, the women were "talking of Joe DiMaggio" or "discussing detergents"?
5. In lines 15–22 we have one of the most famous **extended metaphors** in modern poetry. What is being directly compared with what? How many details extend the metaphor?
6. While the **setting** of this poem is more a state of mind than a place, certain stanzas and passages provide clues to where we are. This stanza (lines 15–22) is one of them. What does it reveal about time and place? What is the significance, for the poem, of the time of year it names? Why would another time of year (say, spring) be less appropriate for Prufrock's journey?
7. Psychologically speaking, what do you do when you "prepare a face to meet the faces that you meet"? (Think of all the people in the range of your acquaintance. Do you prepare a new face for each of them?) What might line 27 reveal about Prufrock's ego, or sense of self?
8. The self-consciousness of the speaker is nowhere more evident than in lines 37–44. What is he self-conscious and worried about in these lines?
9. In line 51, Prufrock says "I have measured out my life with coffee spoons." What does this imply about

(*Continued from previous page.*)
10. The speaker compares himself to an insect pinned on a wall for display or analysis. Students may consider all the words appropriate. Ask them to make and defend a single choice.
11. Lines 13–14, 35–36 offer a vignette of society women discussing art. Line 75—the speaker sees himself having tea with a woman—a scene that continues through 110. Line 124—the speaker refers to mermaids.
12. In contrast to the upper-class settings familiar to Prufrock, these details suggest a working-class neighborhood. Perhaps Prufrock is always alienated and cannot feel at home anywhere.
13. The metaphor is a striking expression of Prufrock's self-consciousness, timidity, and alienation.
14. The concluding statement, "I was afraid" (line 86) best explains Prufrock's emotional difficulty.
15. Answers will vary. Apparently Prufrock would like to confide his hopes and fears but remains silent out of fear that others might misunderstand him or see him as weak.
16. Prufrock seems to have led a dull, lonely, alienated life. He feels that other people ignore him or dismiss him.
17. The metaphor compares his inner thoughts and emotions, or "nerves," to patterns illuminated by a magic lantern on a screen. Prufrock is afraid that people will respond by ignoring or dismissing his sensitivities.
18. The speaker calls himself an actor playing a minor role in a Shakespearean drama. The tone seems self-mocking.
19. Prufrock, aging, resolves to wear the bottoms of his trousers rolled; but he still has more questions than answers about how to act. He seems not to have overcome his doubts, only to have changed their context.
20. Students are likely to agree that such a person comes across as being elderly and timid.
21. Mermaids carry associations of mysterious, mythical beauty. Prufrock thinks they will not sing for him because he is old and unattractive.
(*Answers continue on next page.*)

the way he has lived? (To answer this question, take into account the fact that "coffeehouses" have long been an important feature of life in England and on the continent of Europe.) What other "measuring devices" would suggest a more exciting life?

10. Lines 56–60 contain another **extended metaphor.** To what does the speaker compare himself? Which of the following words would best describe his self-characterization here: Trapped? Victimized? Humiliated? Exposed?
11. In line 62 Prufrock begins to think about women. What other references does he make to women in the poem? How do you think he feels about women and his attractiveness to them?
12. The setting and people described in lines 70–72 (in the form of a question) are considerably different from the settings and people familiar to Prufrock. How is this place different? What might this experience with another segment of city life tell us about Prufrock?
13. In lines 73–74, we have a critical point in the poem. The speaker reaches for a **metaphor** that will most pointedly dramatize his sense of alienation. The one he chooses is extreme and bizarre. Yet, by this time we know him so well we are not surprised by his attempts to express his remoteness from the rest of the world. Can you explain why Prufrock thinks he should have been a crab at the bottom of the sea?
14. Which statement in the stanza beginning "And the afternoon" (line 75) best explains Prufrock's emotional difficulty?
15. Lines 87–98 echo the widely heard complaint that a "lack of communication" between people is the cause of misunderstanding. What do you think Prufrock would like to tell people? Do you think part of the problem lies in the contrast between the grandeur of Prufrock's expectations and the triviality of people's response to them?
16. In lines 99–104, Prufrock summarizes his life and reaches a point of exasperation that seems close to surrender: "It is impossible to say just what I mean!" What sort of life does he seem to have led?
17. Then, **ironically**—in a poem loaded with irony—he does exactly what he believes is "impossible" by stating what he means in a brilliant visual **metaphor** that exposes him, body and soul, with the force of an X-ray. What is the metaphor? How is he afraid people will respond to his exposure?
18. In lines 111–119, how does the speaker characterize himself? Is he sincere, or is he mocking himself?
19. After all his questions and speculations, the speaker finally arrives at decisiveness in line 121. Explain how he sees his role in life. Do you think he has overcome his doubts, or is he now just ignoring them?
20. In line 122, the speaker asks two questions. How would you characterize someone who worries about the part in his hair and about what he should dare to eat?
21. What do you associate with mermaids (lines 124–125)? What could they represent for the speaker? Why does he believe they will not sing for him?
22. In lines 125–128, the speaker thinks that the mermaids are indifferent to him; and yet he is held by the romantic vision they embody. From what we know of our hero by this time, can you say why he is so fascinated by the sound and sight of such mythological creatures?
23. By means of **paraphrase,** can you restate the meaning of lines 129–131? When "human voices wake us," what do we "drown" in?
24. Think about the poem as a journey, a quest that begins with an invitation to join the man who makes it. What has the journey finally led us to? Can you formulate an answer in a single statement? Or do you think it's possible that the point of the poem is not so much an answer arrived at as an experience lived?
25. Why do you think Eliot called this a "love song"? How is it different from the usual love song?
26. This is one of the most famous poems of the twentieth century. Explain why it has been described as a reflection of spiritual emptiness and emotional paralysis. Do you think its depiction of modern life is accurate?

Writing About the Poem

A Creative Response

1. **Writing a Dialogue.** Write a dialogue between Prufrock and another person. Include in your dialogue some references to the topics in the poem that concern Prufrock. If you are feeling especially inventive, you might imagine the conversation as being with Ralph Waldo Emerson (see page 187), with reference to Emerson's advice in the essay "Self-Reliance."
2. **Imitating Eliot's Style.** Write an interior monologue spoken by someone who wants to invite another person to do something. Let your monologue reflect the random process of the speaker's thoughts. Try to find images that suggest your speaker's feelings and state of mind. Open with Eliot's words: "Let us go then, you and I. . . ."

A Critical Response

3. **Evaluating a Character.** The poem includes often conflicting examples of (a) how Prufrock sees himself, (b) how he thinks others see him, and (c) how he wants others to see him. Write a brief essay describing

(Continued from previous page.)

22. Students may suggest that even though Prufrock seems alienated and disillusioned, he *wants* to believe in romance—if only as an escape.

23. A paraphrase might be: We have nurtured illusions for a long time, until reality has awakened us from our dream.

24. The poem suggests death by drowning for everyone. In the end Prufrock accepts old age and his timorous nature. This is a portrait of "Everyman," whose failure to experience real feeling is the true subject.

25. Eliot's title is almost certainly ironic. This is no usual love song. Rather than being a romantic serenade, the poem expresses indecisiveness and alienation. Prufrock is unable to love.

26. Students should be able to point to examples in the poem that suggest spiritual emptiness and emotional paralysis. Ask students to defend their judgments about its applicability to modern life.

these three views of Prufrock. Conclude your essay by telling whether you do or do not sympathize with him.

4. **Comparing Characters.** Is J. Alfred Prufrock like Walter Mitty in James Thurber's story on page 577? In a brief essay, explain why Prufrock can or cannot be seen as a type of Walter Mitty. Before you write, list all the ways the two characters are alike, and all the ways they differ. Which list is more persuasive?
5. **Responding to a Critic.** Ezra Pound made the following comment about Prufrock in a letter to Harriet Monroe, the editor of *Poetry* magazine. Monroe must have mentioned that Prufrock ends in some kind of triumph (that he "goes off at the end"):

> Now as to Eliot: "Mr. Prufrock" does not "go off at the end." It is a portrait of failure, or of a character which fails, and it would be false art to make it end on a note of triumph. I dislike the paragraph about Hamlet, but it is an early and cherished bit and T. E. won't give it up, and as it is the only portion of the poem that most readers will like at first reading, I don't see that it will do much harm.
>
> —Ezra Pound

In a brief essay, respond to Pound's comments on Prufrock. Do you think it is possible to interpret the poem as ending on a note of triumph? What do *you* think of the paragraph about Hamlet?

6. How old do you think Prufrock is? Write an essay citing evidence from the poem to show that he might be sixty, forty, or twenty years old.

Analyzing Language and Style

Rhythms, Rhymes, Metaphors, and Allusions

"No verse is *libre* for the man who wants to do a good job," Eliot once remarked. Though Eliot's poem is supposedly written in "free verse," it makes use of rhythm, rhyme, and, of course, figurative language.

1. Take the first stanza and identify the lines that conform to a particular meter.
2. How does repetition in the first thirty-four lines help create rhythm in the poem?
3. How many end rhymes can you find in the poem? How many internal rhymes?
4. Make a list of at least five figures of speech in the poem that you think are particularly original and memorable.
5. Note the terms of comparison in the figures of speech. Has Eliot based his comparisons on "things" from modern life? Or has he used comparisons based mostly on elements in the world of nature?

It is characteristic of many poets who are highly educated and intimately aware of the history of their art to make use of allusions. Eliot expects that, just at a glance, his readers will identify his references and see their relationship to the poem. Here is a list of some of the allusions in "Prufrock." Do you know what each one means in the context of the poem?

1. Dante's *Inferno,* a section of *The Divine Comedy* (opening quotation)
2. Michelangelo (line 14)
3. The Greek poet Hesiod and his poem *Works and Days* (line 29)
4. Salome and John the Baptist (line 82)
5. Andrew Marvell's love poem "To His Coy Mistress": "Let us roll all our strength and all / Our sweetness up into one ball . . ." (line 92)
6. The raising of Lazarus from the dead in the Bible (line 94)
7. Hamlet, Prince of Denmark, in Shakespeare's play (line 111)
8. Chaucer's description of an Oxford scholar in the Prologue to *The Canterbury Tales:* "full of high sentence" (line 117)

Drawing by C. Barnotti. © 1987 The New Yorker Magazine, Inc.

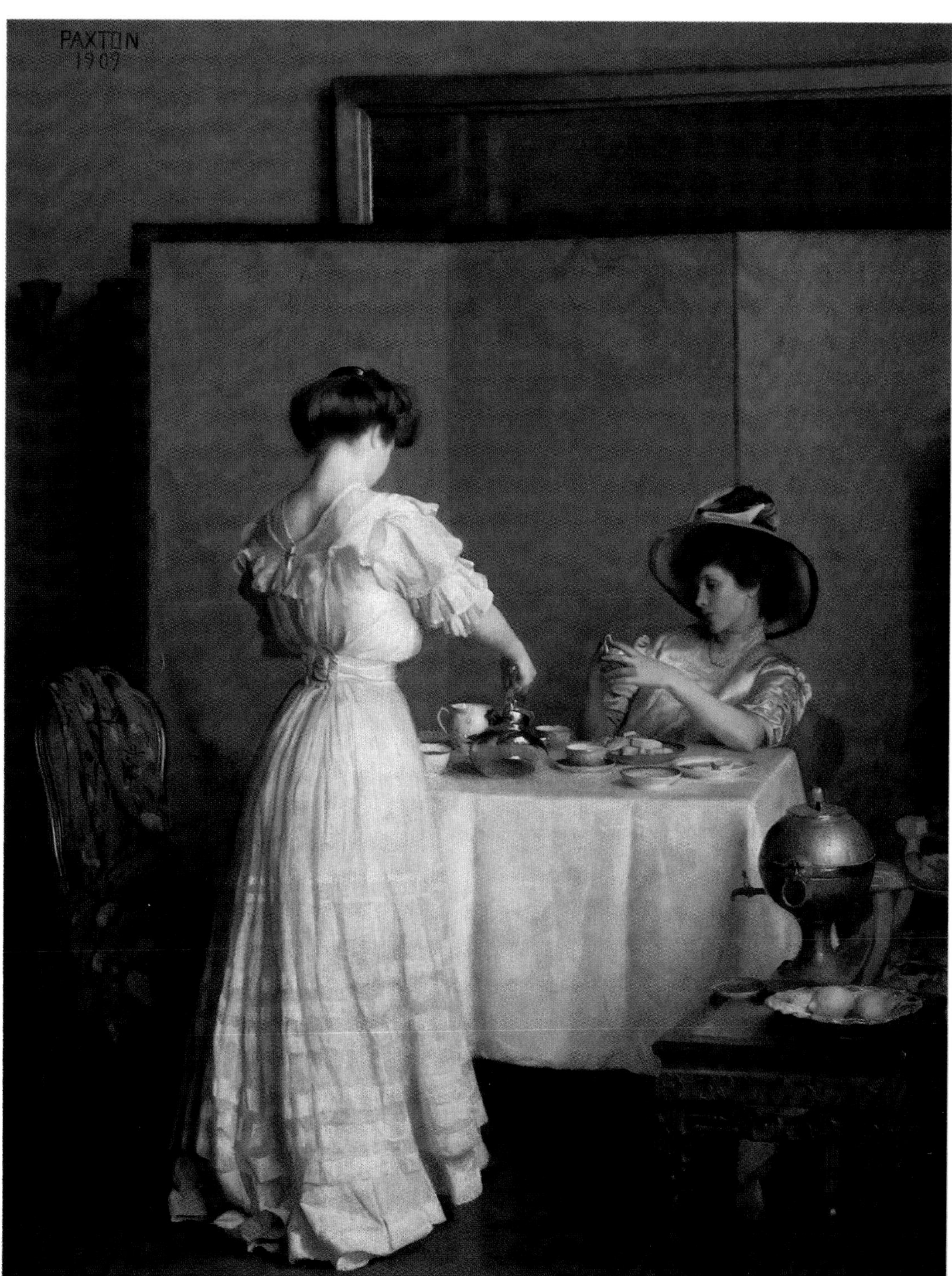

Tea Leaves by William Paxton (1909). Oil.

The Metropolitan Museum of Art, New York.
Gift of George A. Hearn, 1910

Humanities Connection: Discussing the Fine Art

Tea Leaves by William Paxton (1869–1941) is a realistic painting by a contemporary of T.S. Eliot. Paxton was born in Baltimore, studied at the Ecole des Beaux-Arts, Paris, and spent most of his working life in Boston. From 1906 to 1913 he taught at the Boston Museum of Fine Arts School. Paxton's paintings are exhibited at many of America's major art museums, including the Cincinnati Art Museum, the Detroit Institute of Arts, the Wadsworth Atheneum in Hartford, and the Metropolitan Museum of Art in New York City.

COMMENT FROM THE POET
At the age of twenty-six, Wallace Stevens made an entry in his journal commenting on his love for maxims and aphorisms: ". . . How true they all are! I should like to have a library of such things!" Eventually, he did assemble a small library of books containing aphoristic statements. Stevens also wrote original aphorisms, which he kept in two unpublished notebooks, *Adagia* and *Adagia II.* Here are a few of his aphorisms, which your students may wish to discuss:

- Poets confer their identity on the reader. They cannot do this if they intrude personally.
- In poetry, you must love the words, the ideas, the images, and the rhymes with all your capacity to love anything at all.
- All of our ideas come from the natural world. Trees=umbrellas.
- Poetry is metaphor.
- If the answer is frivolous, the question was frivolous.
- Poetry is great only as it exploits great ideas or what is often the same thing, great feelings.

COMMENT FROM THE POET
In 1936 Wallace Stevens delivered a lecture at Harvard, "The Irrational Element in Poetry," that offers insights not only into his own poetry but into the creative process in general. According to Stevens, a poet selects a subject as much by chance as by choice. Development hinges in part on fortuitous and unbidden thoughts. The character of the poet determines the nature of the poetry. Stevens went so far as to say, "A man has no choice about his style." The irrational is involuntary, he said, and becomes virtually the inevitable. You might ask your students to discuss this deterministic view of artistic creation.

Wallace Stevens (1879–1955)

Americans are often surprised to learn that one of their greatest poets was a businessman who walked to his downtown office, sat on boards of directors, served as a vice-president of a major insurance company, and became one of the pillars of a local society dedicated to the collection, investment, and distribution of money. Wallace Stevens was all of these and, almost incidentally, a genius of such magnitude that his place in American literature is still being reassessed and the depth of his vision ever more closely examined. Yet Stevens's life was almost as reclusive and undramatic as was Emily Dickinson's.

Stevens was born into a Pennsylvania Dutch family in Reading, Pennsylvania. His younger life encompassed a well-to-do and carefree childhood and attendance at Harvard College and the New York University Law School. Married early (to the woman whose face you may see on the dime in your pocket), he had one child, Holly, who after his death would assume the editorship of his letters and other posthumously published works.

Stevens lived in New York City for several years; when he was thirty-six he moved to Hartford, Connecticut, where he entered the world of insurance. He kept his creative life completely apart from his preoccupations as a businessman. He maintained his literary friendships almost exclusively by correspondence. Happy with routine, a connoisseur of wines and French painting and a lover of music, Stevens traveled to Cuba and often to Key West, before the range of his outings was reduced to little more than annual attendance at the Harvard-Yale football game. Unlike most of his equally eminent contemporaries, he refused all invitations (until the last years of his life) to give interviews or to recite his poetry in public.

Almost forty-four when he published his first book of verse, *Harmonium* (1923)—a volume that sold a meager few hundred copies—Stevens came late and very quietly onto a scene already occupied by two quite different kinds of poetic expression: the "native" rhythms and down-to-earth concerns of Carl Sandburg and Edgar Lee Masters, and the erudite annotations of experience exemplified by Ezra Pound and T. S. Eliot. Temperamentally, Stevens shared the aspirations of both poetic movements; yet he made his own way along a path that avoided the more extreme practices of either. His sense of place and American character kept him firmly rooted on native ground. But his grasp of metaphysical precision and the resonant power of the image allowed him to soar into realms of "pure" poetry. Stevens went beyond where any other American poet had ever gone before.

While Stevens was deeply influenced by the French poets of the late nineteenth century and by the French Impressionist painters, he also admired the work of American poets with whom he would seem to have little in common. Long before critics or the reading public were aware of the power of William Carlos Williams's common speech and of his flat, almost casual renderings of everyday experience, Stevens knew exactly what his friend was up to. His affection

COMMENT FROM A CRITIC/BIOGRAPHER After graduation from Harvard in 1900, Stevens became a reporter for the *New York Tribune.* He found journalism a harsh and unrewarding field. Milton J. Bates, a biographer, describes his work on the *Tribune:*

". . . Stevens often found himself staying up until four o'clock in the morning to file pieces on the political campaigns of 1900, the Jennie Bosscheiter murder trial, and Stephen Crane's rather shabby funeral. If he had ever thought journalism as glamorous as Richard Harding Davis [a journalist who wrote books about his experiences] made it seem, that illusion was soon laid to rest. Its epitaph might have been the one Stevens penned for Crane, himself a Davis admirer: 'There are few hero-worshippers. Therefore, few heroes.' "

In the fall of 1901, Stevens entered New York University Law School, having decided that his pursuit of writing would have to accompany a career that provided a steady, substantial income.

for Marianne Moore, his beloved "Marianna," was lifelong, as was his admiration for the delicately intricate structures that were the hallmark of her poetry. Toward Robert Frost, his attitude was one of friendly rivalry. "The trouble with you, Robert," Stevens once remarked in the course of one of their meetings, "is that all of your poems have *subjects.*"

That statement, perhaps, contains a clue to how they viewed the function of poetry and to the essential difference between the two men: Frost draws a moral or creates a resonant metaphor from objects in the visible world. Stevens deals in effects, colors, and emotions in such a way as to make objects important only as touchstones for the play of imagination.

In 1955 Wallace Stevens's *Collected Poems* won the Pulitzer Prize for poetry. In a poem called "Of Modern Poetry," Stevens said this of his craft:

It has to be living, to learn the speech of the
 place.
It has to face the men of the time and to meet
The women of the time. It has to think about
 war
And it has to find what will suffice. It has
To construct a new stage.

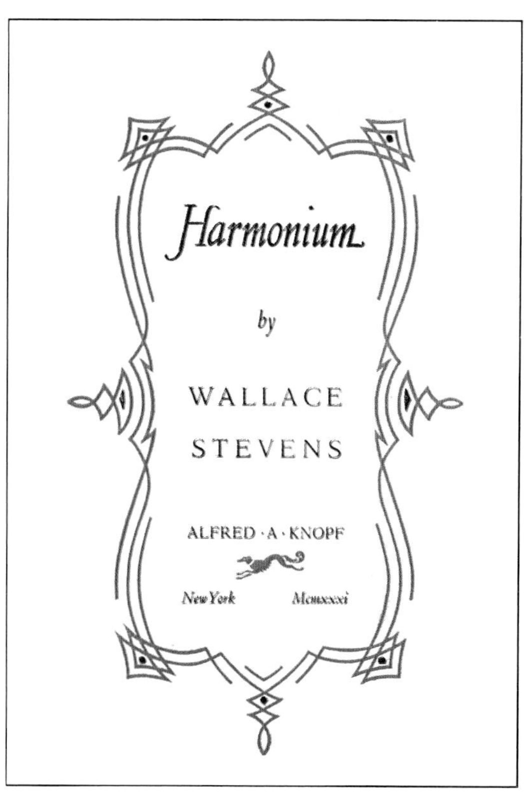

B

A. Responding
? Is Stevens's criticism of Robert Frost—"The trouble with you, Robert, is that all your poems have *subjects*"—a legitimate complaint, or is it simply a good-natured remark? Explain. (Students may feel that Stevens is making a good-natured remark to acknowledge the differences in their views of poetry.)

B. Humanities Connection: Discussing the Illustrations
Stevens's *The Necessary Angel,* published by Alfred A. Knopf, appeared in 1951. *Harmonium,* his first collection of poems, was published in 1923.

Supplementary Support Materials
1. Vocabulary Activity Worksheet (*CCB*)
2. Review and Response Worksheet: Theme (*CCB*)
3. Selection Test (*CCB*)

Developing Vocabulary
The following words from the poem are tested in the Selection Test. (See also Vocabulary Activity Worksheet.)

to contract
personage
to impose
absolute
memorial

Closure
Have students paraphrase the poem orally.

Analyzing The Poem
Identifying Details
1. Life grows shorter, and death is expected.
2. Perhaps a military "three-day [weekend] pass"; or the three days between Christ's death and the resurrection.
3. Answers will vary. Generals or heroes might require pomp—elaborate funeral services—but this soldier does not. He may be the "Unknown Soldier" as an abstract ideal.
4. The clouds pass through the sky in the direction they were going, even though the wind stops.

Interpreting Meanings
5. Like the shortening days in autumn, life can be said to "contract," or become briefer.
6. Possibly the continuation of life even though one person dies, or indifference of the world to the central self.
7. Answers may vary. The poem seems to fit the definition of an elegy. Perhaps consolation comes from the speaker's sympathy with the fallen soldier.

To read Stevens correctly, we have to accept his tendency to combine what is real with what is abstract. In this poem, the soldier is an actual man who "falls." He is also an abstract figure without a name, a rank, "dog-tag," or a nationality—a figure whose death in relation to the elements is little different from any other death. He may be that "Unknown Soldier" for whom nations build monuments—not to house a body, but to enshrine an idea. The poem was written during World War I.

The Death of a Soldier

Life contracts and death is expected,
As in a season of autumn.
The soldier falls.

He does not become a three-days personage,
Imposing his separation,
Calling for pomp.

Death is absolute and without memorial,
As in a season of autumn,
When the wind stops,

When the wind stops and, over the heavens,
The clouds go, nevertheless,
In their direction.

Responding to the Poem

Analyzing the Poem

Identifying Details

1. According to the first two lines, what happens in the season of autumn?
2. What is "a three-days personage" (line 4)?
3. This soldier does not impose his "separation" on the world and does not call for "pomp." What other "soldiers" might do so?
4. According to lines 8–12, what happens in autumn?

Interpreting Meanings

5. How, in a "season of autumn," can life be considered to contract?
6. What do you think the clouds might **symbolize?**
7. Stevens seems to present a human death as no more than an anonymous incident in relation to death's "absolute" force and the indifference of nature. In what sense may "The Death of a Soldier" be considered an **elegy?** Do you think the poem provides the solace and affirmation that most elegies offer?

PREPARATION

ESTABLISHING A PURPOSE. Advise students that they should consider the possible meanings of symbols in this poem—principally those of the jar and the wilderness.

SUPPLEMENTARY SUPPORT MATERIALS

1. Vocabulary Activity Worksheet (*CCB*)
2. Review and Response Worksheet: Theme (*CCB*)
3. Selection Test (*CCB*)
4. Instructional Overhead Transparency

DEVELOPING VOCABULARY

The following words from the poem are tested in the Selection Test. (See also Vocabulary Activity Worksheet.)

slovenly	to sprawl
wilderness	dominion

An anecdote is a brief story, usually one that illustrates an odd or amusing example of human behavior. This anecdote, in contrast, tells a big story. The poet invites us to supply the details that lift it out of the ordinary. As you read, think about the contrast between the scenes described in the first two stanzas.

Anecdote of the Jar

I placed a jar in Tennessee,
And round it was, upon a hill.
It made the slovenly wilderness
Surround that hill.

The wilderness rose up to it,
And sprawled around, no longer wild.
The jar was round upon the ground
And tall and of a port in air.

It took dominion everywhere.
The jar was gray and bare.
It did not give of bird or bush,
Like nothing else in Tennessee.

A

CLOSURE

Ask students to write a two- or three-sentence critical commentary on this poem and share their opinions orally.

A. Humanities Connection: Discussing the Illustration

Literary symbolism poses a problem for the illustrator. Should the illustrator show the object itself—in this case a jar (or jars)? Should the object (the jar) actually be placed in a wilderness—or, as here, in isolation?

? What other suggestions would you have for illustrating this poem?

COMMENT FROM A CRITIC

In 1918 Stevens wrote his wife, "I have always been of two minds about Tennessee." Applying that comment to "Anecdote of the Jar," Richard Ellmann, a critic, observes: "Here pleasure in the vegetable profusion of Tennessee is cynically countered by suspicion of its artistic unkemptness, while delight in the jar's perfection is tinged with cynical regret at its un-Tennessean aridity."

ANALYZING THE POEM
Identifying Details
1. The speaker places a jar on a hill in Tennessee. The adjective he uses is *round.* The speaker says the wilderness is "slovenly."
2. It civilizes or tames the wilderness.
3. The jar takes "dominion everywhere"—it rules its environment. It does not give "of bird or bush"—it has no connection with the untamed wilderness.

Interpreting Meanings
4. Answers will vary. One possible paraphrase: The jar, unlike anything else in the environment, has no connection with its natural surroundings.
5. Answers will vary. The jar, wholly dominant, seems to be a civilizing force; but it poses a constant threat to the world of nature. A symbol of human ingenuity and progress, the jar may also seem sterile and unappealing when compared to the wilderness.
6. Various interpretations are possible. The symbols in the poem can only be interpreted, never finally explained.
7. The wilderness may symbolize nature in its raw, untamed state.
(Answers continue in left-hand column.)

(Continued from top.)
The wilderness might be something as abstract as "chaos."
8. Answers will vary.

A. Expansion
It may be difficult for students to understand that "it is not possible to tell what one's own poems mean, or were intended to mean." Modern critics, such as Northrop Frye, believe that we share a system of archetypes, universal experiences, that exist in our "collective unconscious" and that spill over into our poetry through symbolism. Robert Frost, for example, may not have consciously meant for "Stopping by Woods on a Snowy Evening" to be a poem about death, but a reader may interpret it as such because the symbolism is there.

Responding to the Poem

Analyzing the Poem

Identifying Details

1. Describe what the speaker does in the first stanza. What adjective does the speaker use to describe the jar? How does he describe the wilderness in which he places the jar?
2. In the second stanza, what effect does the jar have on the wilderness?
3. What does the jar "take" in stanza 3? What does it *not* give?

Interpreting Meanings

4. How would you paraphrase lines 11–12?
5. The "jar" is, on one level, a ceramic or clay vessel, designed by human ingenuity, and shaped by human hands. By extension, it might **symbolize** anything made or devised by humans. The jar contrasts with what simply arises out of the vast abundance of nature. The "slovenly wilderness," for example, is nature in its raw state, untamed by efforts to turn it into pastures or farmlands, or even parking lots to serve the customers of supermarkets. What, in your view, is the meaning of the jar's "dominion" over the wilderness (line 9)?
6. Could the jar symbolize poetry, religion, law, and other human endeavors? Explain your answer with references to details in the poem.
7. What might the "wilderness" **symbolize?**
8. Do any details in this poem still puzzle you? If so, tell what they are. Considering what you now know about the poem, explain why these details still puzzle you.

Writing About the Poems

A Critical Response

1. **Comparing Poems.** In a brief essay, summarize what Stevens and Herman Melville, in the poem "Art" (page 319), have to say about the creative process and the power of art.
2. **Analyzing the Poem's Message.** Some people think the jar symbolizes the way art gives order and meaning to "slovenly" nature. Others think the jar symbolizes human interference with nature. Which view do you agree with? Explain your response in a paragraph.

Analyzing Language and Style

Precise Meanings

Like all poets, Stevens was careful about his **diction,** or word choice, frequently making changes in an attempt to find the word that most precisely expresses his meaning.

1. What does the word *contracts* in line 1 of "The Death of a Soldier" mean here? How is "life contracts" different from "life is extinguished"?
2. Suggest at least three other nouns that the poet might have used instead of *jar* in "Anecdote of the Jar." Do you think he chose *jar* because he wanted to suggest a double meaning?
3. Use a dictionary to find out the precise meaning of *slovenly.* Is wild nature usually called "slovenly"? Do you think this word is used to personify nature as a kind of person?
4. What meanings could the word *port* have in line 8?

Primary Sources

Poetry and Meaning

The following statements are from letters Stevens wrote in the 1930's and 1940's.

"Poetry is like anything else; it cannot be made suddenly to drop all its rags and stand out naked, fully disclosed. Everything is complicated; if that were not so, life and poetry and everything else would be a bore."

. . .

A "Obviously, it is not possible to tell one what one's own poems mean, or were intended to mean. On the other hand, it is not the simplest thing in the world to explain a poem. I thought of it this way this morning: A poem is like a man walking on the bank of a river, whose shadow is reflected in the water. If you explain a poem, you are quite likely to do it either in terms of the man or in terms of the shadow, but you have to explain it in terms of the whole. When I said recently that a poem was what was on a page, it seems to me now that I was wrong because that is explaining in terms of the man. But the thing and its double always go together."

—Wallace Stevens

Exercises in Critical Thinking and Writing

ANALYZING A POEM

Writing Assignment

In an essay, analyze either "Disillusionment of Ten O'Clock" by Wallace Stevens or "Poetry" by Marianne Moore. Include a discussion of all the elements that contribute to the poem's meaning. At the end of your analysis, comment on your response to the poem.

Background

When you **analyze,** you focus on the parts that make up a whole. In analyzing a poem, you should focus on such elements as imagery, figurative language, symbolism, tone, structure, and sound effects. After you have discussed each element separately, you should show how they all work together to create the poem's meaning.

As you read through this unit, you were asked frequently to analyze Imagist and Symbolist poems. This writing assignment asks you to apply your skills in analysis to a new poem.

Prewriting

Read both poems and choose one to write about. (It's best to choose one that you have some strong response to.) Before you begin writing, read the poem you have chosen several times. Read it aloud at least once. Look up any unfamiliar words. Then answer the following questions.

Guidelines for Analyzing a Poem

1. What is the poem about? (State the poem's **subject,** and **paraphrase** the poem very briefly.)
2. What is the speaker's (or the poet's) attitude toward the subject of the poem? In other words, what is the poem's **tone?**
3. What **images** does the poet use? What is the emotional effect of these images?
4. What **figures of speech** does the poem contain? What is the significance of the figures of speech?
5. Does the poem contain any **symbols?** If so, what are they, and what do they represent?
6. What **feelings** does the poem evoke?
7. What use does the poet make of **rhyme, meter,** and other **sound effects?** How does the poem's sound affect its sense?
8. Which elements are most important in the poem? Which seem to contribute least to the poem's effectiveness?
9. What does the poem's **title** mean?
10. What does the poem mean, and how have you **responded** to it? Does it remind you of any feeling you have had? Does it tell you something you always knew, but never knew you knew it?

Disillusionment of Ten O'Clock

The houses are haunted
By white nightgowns.
None are green,
Or purple with green rings,
Or green with yellow rings,
Or yellow with blue rings.
None of them are strange,
With socks of lace
And beaded ceintures. A
People are not going
To dream of baboons and periwinkles.
Only, here and there, an old sailor,
Drunk and asleep in his boots,
Catches tigers
In red weather.

—Wallace Stevens

Poetry

I, too, dislike it: there are things that are important
beyond all this fiddle.
Reading it, however, with a perfect contempt for it,
one discovers in
it after all, a place for the genuine.
Hands that can grasp, eyes
that can dilate, hair that can rise
if it must, these things are important not B
because a

high-sounding interpretation can be put upon them
but because they are
useful. When they become so derivative as to
become unintelligible,
the same thing may be said for all of us, that we
do not admire what

A. Expansion
You may want to begin by discussing with students how this poem is a typical Imagist poem, an activity that should help students' comprehension of the poem. Students should understand that the images of the third through the seventh lines describe colorful types of nightgowns contrasted with the stark nightgown image of the second line. And the image of unimaginative dreaming in the tenth and eleventh lines is contrasted with the rich imaginings of the drunken sailor in the last four lines.

B. Expansion
Students might have difficulty understanding what it is about "Poetry" that qualifies it as a poem. If so, have students write a prose paraphrase of the poem. They can then compare their paraphrase with the original for condensation of meaning, metaphor, imagery, and so on.

Revising Essays
As students revise their essays, refer them to **Grammar, Usage, and Mechanics: A Reference Guide** at the back of their books.

Exercises in Critical Thinking and Writing/*cont.*

we cannot understand: the bat
holding on upside down or in quest of something to
eat, elephants pushing, a wild horse taking a roll, a tireless wolf under
a tree, the immovable critic twitching his skin like a horse that feels a flea, the baseball fan, the statistician—
nor is it valid
to discriminate against "business documents and
school-books"; all these phenomena are important. One must make a distinction
however: when dragged into prominence by half poets, the result is not poetry,
nor till the poets among us can be
"literalists of
the imagination"—above
insolence and triviality and can present
for inspection, imaginary gardens with real toads in them, shall we have
it. In the meantime, if you demand on the one hand,
the raw material of poetry in
all its rawness and
that which is on the other hand
genuine, you are interested in poetry.

—Marianne Moore

Writing

The following two paragraphs are from one reader's analysis of "what if a much of a which of a wind" by E. E. Cummings (page 738). Notice how the writer gives a brief paraphrase of the poem, stanza by stanza, and then moves on to talk about form.

The poem "what if a much of a which of a wind" by E. E. Cummings at first seems as confusing as its first-line title. The speaker in the poem seems to be wondering about the possibilities of doom that might befall the human race. In the first stanza the speaker thinks about the winds of autumn that give "the truth to summer's lie" (line 2) and might blow the immortal stars out of their places. The second stanza is about the winds of winter that could possibly bring back the ice age ("and stifles forests in white ago," line 12). In the last stanza, the speaker wonders about "a dawn of a doom of a dream" that destroys the universe, maybe nuclear weapons ("bites this universe in two," line 18). In each stanza, the speaker envisions a time when human life is utterly changed, when all is terror and nothingness. But still, the last two lines in each stanza offer a very positive affirmation of life. Human life, Cummings seems to be saying, will endure the worst catastrophes that humans or nature can devise.

One of the things I noticed about the poem is that, despite its eccentric punctuation, it does have a strict form. The stanzas repeat a complicated pattern. Each stanza begins with a four-line question about the wind, beginning with the words "what if." The fifth and sixth lines of each stanza tell what the wind blows, and most of the things blown are abstract. In each stanza, lines 7–8 offer a two-line resolution, or answer to the question at the beginning of the stanza. . . .

In succeeding paragraphs, this writer should talk about the other elements in the poem and how they contribute to its meaning. The last paragraph, following the instructions, should discuss the writer's response.

Revising and Proofreading

Use the guidelines in the section at the back of this book, called **Writing About Literature,** to revise and proofread your essay.

AMERICAN DRAMA

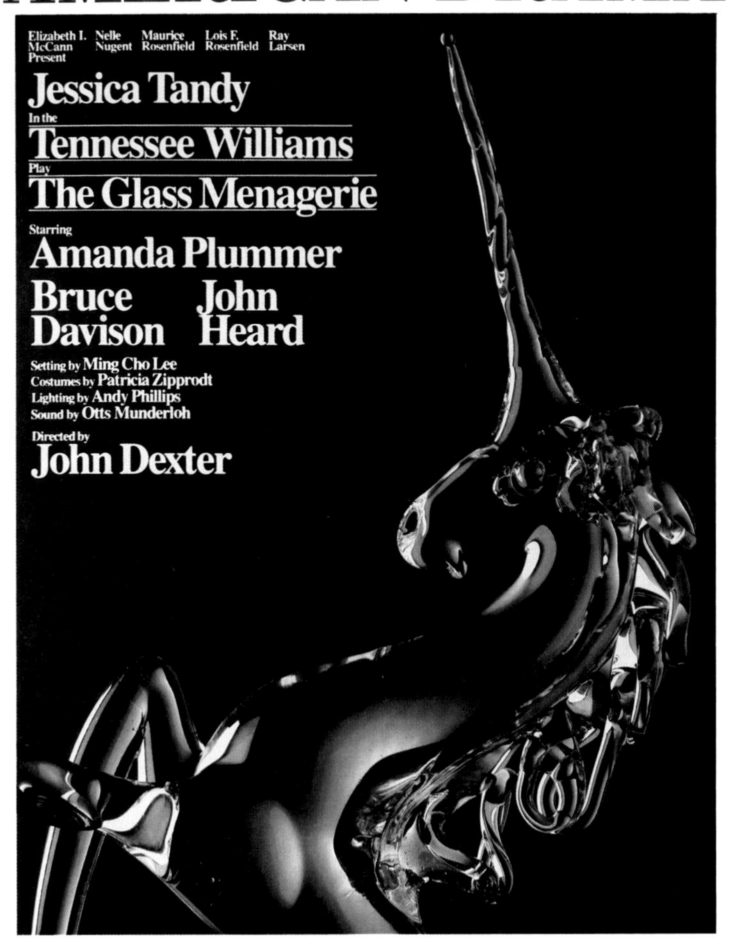

Elizabeth I. McCann Nelle Nugent Maurice Rosenfield Lois F. Rosenfield Ray Larsen Present
Jessica Tandy
In the
Tennessee Williams
Play
The Glass Menagerie
Starring
Amanda Plummer
Bruce Davison John Heard
Setting by Ming Cho Lee
Costumes by Patricia Zipprodt
Lighting by Andy Phillips
Sound by Otts Munderloh
Directed by
John Dexter

UNIT TEN

HUMANITIES CONNECTION: RESPONDING TO THE ILLUSTRATION

The playbill's listing of Jessica Tandy suggests the caliber of players who have enacted the many productions of Tennessee Williams's *The Glass Menagerie* since its 1944 debut. For the purposes of this unit, however, you may wish rather to have students focus on the glass unicorn.

? How might a glass unicorn figure in any play? (It could be a prop.) Why does it seem particularly right for a play titled *The Glass Menagerie?* (It could be one of several animals in a "menagerie" made of glass.) Can you imagine a way in which this exotic object could symbolize a person? (Answers will vary. It could stand for a fragile or unusual person.)

TEACHING THE AMERICAN DRAMA UNIT

In reading the introduction, students should note the following points:

(1) Playwriting differs from other genres of writing in that a play is not finished until the words and gestures the playwright has imagined come to life onstage.

(2) Good plays make dramatic use of conflict. Conflict may be external or internal.

(3) The route to Broadway is difficult. Involved are the playwright, his or her agent, a producer's ability to raise half a million dollars or more to finance the play, a director, actors, and tryouts of the play off Broadway.

(4) Eugene O'Neill (1888–1953) is considered the first important American playwright. Before, American drama consisted of entertainments, often presented by touring companies.

(5) "Drama travels in the caboose of literature" (Robert Sherwood): that is, it is slow to adopt new attitudes and methods, perhaps because it is a social art. People may stalk out of a theater when presented with something they would read—even enjoy—in private.

(6) European drama, which greatly influenced American drama, matured earlier. The Norwegian Henrik Ibsen (1828–1906) tackled subjects like guilt, sexuality, and mental illness; the Swede August Strindberg (1849–1912) brought psychological complexity to his characters; and the Russian Anton Chekhov (1860–1904) focused on the inner emotions and concerns of daily life.

(7) Early twentieth-century American drama was dominated by realism: the illusion that watching a play is looking at life through a missing "fourth wall."

(8) The dominant American dramatists since World War II have been Arthur Miller (born 1915) and Tennessee Williams (1911–1983), both of whom combine realism with poetic expression.

(9) There is currently a swing back to theatricalism, which emphasizes stage effects and imaginative settings. Expressionist (Theater of the Absurd) playwrights aimed not so much to tell a story as to reveal their characters' inner consciousness. They include Samuel Beckett and Eugene Ionesco of Europe, and the American Edward Albee (born 1928).

OBJECTIVES OF THE AMERICAN DRAMA UNIT

1. To improve reading proficiency and expand vocabulary
2. To gain exposure to notable playwrights and their plays
3. To define and identify the elements of drama
4. To define and identify significant literary techniques
5. To interpret and respond to drama, orally and in writing, through analysis of its elements
6. To practice the following critical thinking and writing skills:
   a. Responding to conflict
   b. Responding to "biographical criticism"
   c. Evaluating versions of a play
   d. Analyzing the use of light
   e. Comparing a play with memoirs
   f. Predicting a character's development
   g. Evaluating a play

A. Responding to the Quotation

? Put the second sentence of the quotation into your own words. (Answers will vary.) "Theater" includes movies and television films as well as stage plays. Can you recall a time when *seeing* a story helped you to identify with a character more than you had been able to do from hearing or reading the story? (Answers will vary.)

B. Humanities Connection: Discussing the Illustration

The action in *Our Town*, a Pulitzer Prize play by Thornton Wilder (1897–1975), occurs in the New Hampshire town of Grover's Corners. The Stage Manager, a garrulous Yankee, sits at the side of a very nearly bare stage (on the stool in this sketch), talking with the audience as the play unfolds. This sketch is for Act II, "Love and Marriage"; Act I is "Daily Life" and Act III is "Death." The theatricalism of the play allowed Wilder to build an informal, intimate, and compellingly human story that leads one to treasure ordinary life.

SUPPLEMENTARY SUPPORT MATERIALS: UNIT TEN

1. Unit Introduction Test (*CCB*)
2. Word Analogies Test (*CCB*)
3. Unit Review Test (*CCB*)
4. Critical Thinking and Writing Test (*CCB*)
5. Instructional Overhead Transparencies

AMERICAN DRAMA

by **Robert Anderson**

The Elements of Drama

A

Theater is one of the most emotionally satisfying experiences imaginable. It touches our inner core, and gives insight into who we are.

—Theodore Mann

Drama is probably the most difficult form of writing; it certainly seems to take the longest to learn. According to a saying, young poets are eighteen, young novelists are twenty-four, and young playwrights are thirty.

George S. Kaufman, a noted American writer of comedies during the 1930's and 1940's, said that writing plays was not an art, but a trick. Art or trick, it is difficult, possibly because when a play is written, it is not finished in the same way that a poem or novel is. There remains the painful and pleasurable process of bringing the play to life on stage, with the help of a director, actors, set designer, costume designer, stagehands, musicians, electricians—and a responsive audience. Producing a play is a team effort, and much can go wrong. A beautifully written and acted scene, for example, can be ruined if the electrician dims the lights too rapidly.

Another difference between drama and other literary forms is that movement and gesture are essential elements in drama. Some of the high points in a play may even be nonverbal. In *The Diary of Anne Frank,* for example, Mr. Frank realizes that the Nazis are downstairs and that the family's hiding place is about to be discovered. He turns to his family and friends and spreads his hands in resignation. This heartbreaking moment is conceived by the playwright; but its achievement on the stage—the exact gesture—requires the close and creative cooperation of actor and director.

Young writers are often drawn to the stage by the theatrical trappings: the gestures, the colorful sets, and the magical effects that drama can achieve. But playwrights soon learn that theatrical effects are rarely enough in themselves. The effects and gestures are there only to serve a story, and it must be a story that engages the passions of the collaborators—the director, actors, and dozens of others who work to produce a play. Stage technicians may dazzle our senses with intricate and fascinating effects; but if a play doesn't have a significant story, we find nothing "moving" in the end, because our emotions have not been touched.

B

Costume design for *Our Town* (detail) by Patricia Zipprodt.

Museum of the City of New York. The Theatre Collection.

The Basic Principles of Drama

When a play goes wrong, it is almost always because the writer has failed to conceive the story in dramatic terms. There are, of course, some plays (such as Thornton Wilder's *Our Town*) that "work" in the theater even though they ignore the usual principles of drama. But over the centuries certain principles have developed, and they are usually observed by playwrights who want to catch, hold, and reward the attention of an audience.

A. Humanities Connection: Discussing the Photograph
Long a residential street, Broadway became the main business thoroughfare of New York City in the mid-nineteenth century. Today the street's name evokes its famous theatrical district at Times Square. Some three dozen theaters cluster on Broadway and in side streets in an area bounded by Broadway, Eighth Avenue, 44th Street, and 53rd Street. An average of 70 new productions open annually in this midtown district, collectively called "Broadway." A nickname, "the Great White Way," comes from the title of a 1901 play by A. B. Paine and refers to the area's blazing lights. Also featured are expensive restaurants and clubs where the rich and famous come to be seen, adding to the glitter. *Evita* (see the marquee in the photograph) is a musical by Andrew Lloyd Webber and Tim Rice, based on the life of the former First Lady of Argentina, Eva (Evita) Duarte de Peron (1919–1952). She was a fiery, popular orator who died young, of cancer. *Evita* won the New York Drama Critics' Circle Award as best musical for 1979–1980.

A

The analogy is slightly oversimplified, but we respond to a play in very much the way we respond to a sports event. Let's assume that one summer evening you go to a professional baseball game. For some reason, you take a liking to one of the pitchers. Then someone sitting next to you says that the pitcher has been out with an injured elbow for several weeks and is trying to make a comeback. If he fails in this game, he is finished. You start rooting for him. He gets some bad calls from the plate umpire, and you boo or whistle. Then your neighbor tells you that the pitcher is not pitching his best. Unless he stops protecting his injured elbow and starts putting more speed in his pitches, he will not win.

Most plays have more psychological complexity than this situation does. With a little imagination, however, we can add to the pitcher's problems. Suppose, for instance, that the pitcher's wife is afraid that if he throws too hard, he will ruin his elbow and be unable to play. She tells him that if he damages his elbow further, she will leave him; but, to him, the glory of winning transcends practical matters. To his wife, he is a ball-playing "boy," careless and immature. And so forth. . . .

What has happened in this scenario is what happens in almost every play. Early on, the playwright organizes our emotions behind some character or group of characters: We are "for" them. The playwright has placed these characters in a situation involving **conflict,** and then has made us understand that it is not just any conflict: The character or characters have something vital at stake.

> "We respond to a play in very much the way we respond to a sports event."

A. Humanities Connection: Discussing the Illustration
At first the viewer may wonder what is funny about the sight of an audience enjoying itself. Then the viewer realizes the Mona Lisa is part of the audience.

B. Expansion
The Pulitzer Prizes, endowed by journalist Joseph Pulitzer (1847–1911), are annual awards in American journalism and letters (literature) made by the trustees of New York City's Columbia University. One category of letters is drama. These are a few of the past award-winners and some of our most distinguished plays:
1928 *Strange Interlude*, Eugene O'Neill
1933 *Both Your Houses,* Maxwell Anderson
1938 *Our Town,* Thornton Wilder
1943 *The Skin of Our Teeth,* Thornton Wilder
1948 *A Streetcar Named Desire,* Tennessee Williams
1949 *Death of a Salesman,* Arthur Miller
1953 *Picnic,* William Inge
1955 *Cat on a Hot Tin Roof,* Tennessee Williams
1957 *Long Day's Journey into Night,* Eugene O'Neill
1965 *The Subject Was Roses,* Frank D. Gilroy
1975 *Seascape,* Edward Albee
1981 *Crimes of the Heart,* Beth Henley

Drawing by Chas. Addams.
© 1950 The New Yorker Magazine, Inc.

A

They want to win, and they need to win in order to survive. In the baseball game, the situation is made difficult for the pitcher, who is the **protagonist** (the major character who wants something and who drives the action forward). The pitcher struggles against both **external conflict** (the opposing side) and **internal conflict** (his fears of damaging his arm, his feelings about the pressure from his wife). The fan sitting next to you has given us the background information, or **exposition** (who the pitcher is, what he wants to do, and what he has at stake). The story of a character who, against odds, wants something meaningful has been set in motion. The tension mounts as the innings pass; and we are witnessing, or participating in and enjoying, a drama.

The word *participation* is important. We have all heard ball players say how encouraged they are by the response of the spectators. Actors too may say as they come offstage after a scene, "That's a wonderful audience out there tonight!" And because of the audience, performances often rise to a higher level. It has often been said that a play exists halfway between the stage and the audience. What an audience gets from a performance is directly related to what it brings to the performance, not only in the way of understanding and feeling, but also in enthusiasm. In successful dramatic performances, a note is sounded onstage, and a chord of recognition or responsiveness echoes back from the audience. A play performed in an empty theater is not a play.

How a Play Is Produced

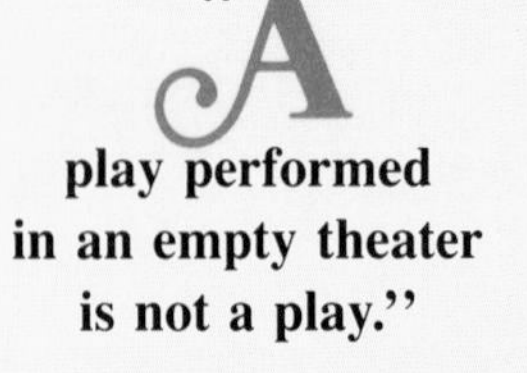
"A
play performed
in an empty theater
is not a play."

The English plays of the late Middle Ages were called miracle plays because they often dealt with stories of miracles from the Bible or the lives of the saints. Any modern-day American play might also be called a miracle play, because it is a miracle that it was written and even more of a miracle that it was produced. In the United States today, drama is dependent on money. Only a few institutional theaters are able to present plays with little or no regard to profit. Most of the plays that are produced (and that therefore stand a chance of becoming part of our dramatic literature) are put on with the idea that they will make money.

To produce a new play by any writer on Broadway costs a minimum of half a million dollars (at this writing). The **producers** (people who advance the money) willing to take such a risk are rare, although such risks *are* taken every season. Even though it operates in a very costly manner, the professional Broadway theater, to its credit, has been the launching pad for most of the distinguished plays in American dramatic literature. B

Recently, regional theaters throughout the country have been presenting new plays by both new and established playwrights. The Broadway producers often visit, look, and take whatever they want for production. For the most part, only a successful Broadway production gives a playwright enough income to plunge in and take the years necessary to write the next play. For that reason, Broadway remains the goal of most playwrights.

There are many stops on the way to New York, some of which become full stops. Over ten thousand plays are copyrighted every year; this probably represents only half of the plays that are actually written. Perhaps several hundred new plays are produced onstage *somewhere* around the country; maybe ten appear on Broadway.

Producers could not hope to cope with reading thousands and thousands of plays, so playwrights must generally find an **agent** who will handle their work. The agent is the producer's first line of defense. Knowing their various tastes, the agent submits a play to likely producers, who may take three months to a year to read it. They may admire the play but still be unwilling to do it. One playwright used to say, "If they take you to lunch, they're not going to invest in your play." A good lunch is a consolation prize, and many playwrights have eaten very well off plays that were never produced.

But if the producer should decide to finance the play, he or she then sits down with the playwright to go over changes suggested for the script, or ideas for directors and actors. Authors maintain control over their scripts, and the playwright is very much involved in the selection of the director and the actors. Of course, since theater is a collaborative medium, the playwright tries to get along with the producer. But if the playwright and producer discover during these preliminary talks that they have incompatible ideas, they can shake hands and part.

The director becomes the playwright's surrogate at rehearsals. In a sense, the director takes the play away from the playwright, and, finally, the actors take it away from both of them.

Rehearsals can involve both pleasure and tension. Many temperaments must mesh as the actors move forward to the climactic moment of opening night. (Note that all the elements of drama itself are present at play rehearsals: striving for a goal, having something at stake, dealing with internal and external conflicts, etc.)

The play opens for a tryout run in a smaller city, or in New York for previews. Sometimes all goes well, and the production needs only some refining and sharpening. More often, the play "needs work"—rewriting, new sets, new costumes, sometimes a new director or a new star. Chaos reigns until opening night, when all the cast will suddenly come down with laryngitis, intestinal upsets, sinus trouble, or splitting headaches. Somehow, the curtain rises, and the show goes on.

The day after the opening, there may or may not be a line of eager theater-goers at the box office. If there is, the playwright has created what may later be called "an American classic," which will be performed around the world and will find its way into the anthologies you study in school. If there isn't a line, the playwright will quickly look around for a way to make a living while writing the next play—if he or she has the courage. The second instance is the more usual. The theater has been called the "fabulous invalid," always teetering on the edge of extinction. If so, playwrights themselves might be called the walking wounded—working, barely surviving, but finally enduring to try once again.

"Chaos reigns until opening night, when all the cast will suddenly come down with laryngitis, intestinal upsets, sinus trouble, or splitting headaches."

Dick Van Dyke in *The Music Man*.

A

A. Humanities Connection: Discussing the Photograph
Actor Dick Van Dyke perfectly embodies Meredith Willson's exuberant traveling "music man," Professor Harold Hill. Stranded in a turn-of-the-century midwestern town, River City, Hill sells band instruments to the town and woos Marion the librarian. The score of *The Music Man* includes the well-known "Seventy-Six Trombones." Willson based his play on his boyhood memories of Mason City, Iowa, in 1912. The musical won the New York Drama Critics' Circle Award as best musical of 1957–1958.

A. Expansion
(See also page 764, American Realism and Eugene O'Neill.) O'Neill's grim and moving psychological plays marked a radical departure from the romantic convention of theater as entertainment. With no uniquely American tradition to guide him, O'Neill introduced many techniques that have become staples to be drawn upon at will: repetition of actions or phrases to underscore dramatic intent, use of symbolic masks or costumes, use of archetypal themes from classical religion and myth, and revival of the Elizabethan devices of soliloquy and aside to reveal a character's inner state. Like Whitman and Twain, O'Neill gained material from the many odd jobs he worked around the country before he began to write. Although several American novelists have won the Nobel Prize in Literature, O'Neill is the only American playwright to have done so, in 1936.

B. Humanities Connection: Discussing the Photograph
Today mostly residential, East Haddam lies between the Connecticut River and steeply rising land to the west. In earlier times the town was a shipping center and boasted a booming salmon industry. The Goodspeed Opera House, a tourist attraction, was built by William Goodspeed in the heyday of river steamboats. Its programs drew people from all over Connecticut; they were housed in the resort hotels then flourishing along the river bank. The elegant Opera House was restored by local citizens and now offers a mixed program of plays, musicals, and films.

The History of American Drama

A

Eugene O'Neill (1888–1953) is generally considered the first important figure in American drama. It is significant that several decades after the 1920 production of his first full-length play, *Beyond the Horizon,* he is still regarded as the most important playwright America has produced.

American drama before O'Neill consisted mostly of shows and entertainments. These wildly theatrical spectacles often featured such delights as chariot races and burning cities, staged by means of special effects that dazzled audiences. Melodramas and farces were also written for famous actors, much as television shows today are created to display the personalities and talents of popular performers. In fact, O'Neill's own father, James, spent the better part of his life touring in a spectacular melodrama based on Alexander Dumas's *The Count of Monte Cristo.*

There was great theatrical activity in nineteenth-century America, a time when there were no movies, radio, or television. Every town of any size had its theater or "opera house" in which touring companies performed. Given the hunger for entertainment, one may wonder why no significant American drama was written in the century that produced, among others, Melville, Emerson, Whitman, Dickinson, and Twain.

B

Goodspeed Opera House in East Haddam, Connecticut. Photograph by Inge Morath.

A. Expansion
Robert Sherwood (1896–1955), wounded in World War I, resolved to do all he could to stop future wars—an attitude evident in his first Broadway play, *The Road to Rome* (1927), and in his Pulitzer Prize play *Idiot's Delight* (1936). He won another Pulitzer in 1940 for *There Shall Be No Light,* a play about the Russian invasion of Finland. Extremely vocal in warning of the dangers of European totalitarianism, Sherwood also served at various times as a special assistant in the War Department (today the Department of Defense), and helped write speeches for President Franklin D. Roosevelt.

B. Expansion
Notable plays: Ibsen: *Peer Gynt* (1867), *A Doll's House* (1879), and *The Master Builder* (1892); Strindberg: *The Father* (1887), *The Dance of Death* (1901), and *A Dream Play* (1902); Chekhov: *The Seagull* (1896), *Uncle Vanya* (1899), *The Three Sisters* (1901), and *The Cherry Orchard* (1904)

Theater as a Social Art

One explanation for this is that theater has usually followed the other arts, rather than pointing the way toward new directions. Robert Sherwood, one of the group of notable American playwrights between 1920 and 1940, once said: "Drama travels in the caboose of literature." The theater seems to take up new attitudes, subject matter, and forms only after they have been explored in the other arts. For the most part, theater tends to dramatize accepted attitudes and values. A

The reason for this is that theater is a social art, one we attend as part of a large group; we seem to respond to something new much more slowly as a group than we do as individuals. When you laugh or cry in the theater, your response is noticed. You are, in a sense, giving your approval, and this approval may be subject to criticism or condemnation by those sitting around you who are not laughing or crying. You may not be shocked to *read* about your secret thoughts, dreams, and desires; but when you *see* them shown on stage as you sit among a thousand people, you may refuse to respond, refuse to acknowledge them. You may even rise up and stalk out of the theater

Thus, the novel and to some extent the poetry of the nineteenth and early twentieth centuries were more daring than the theater in giving us a "record of experience," in showing us life as it *is* lived, not as it *should be* lived. During this period before O'Neill, American drama tended to be mild and sentimental, rarely questioning the life and attitudes it depicted, almost never challenging the accepted traditions of its times.

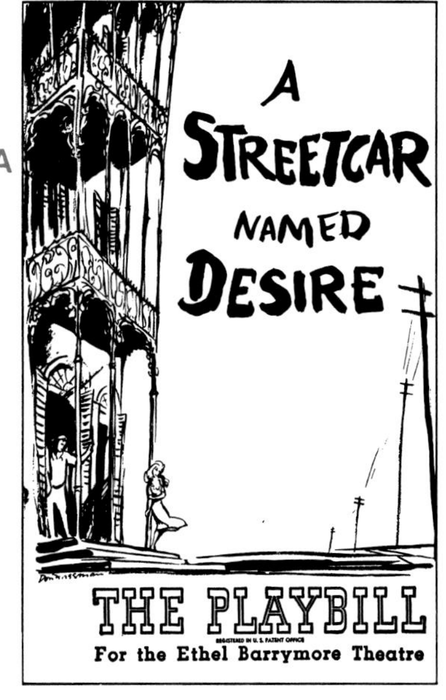

A
STREETCAR
NAMED
DESIRE
THE PLAYBILL
For the Ethel Barrymore Theatre

C

C. Humanities Connection: Discussing the Illustration
Directed by Elia Kazan, Tennessee Williams's *A Streetcar Named Desire* opened on December 3, 1947, at the Ethel Barrymore Theatre in New York. Previewed in New Haven, Boston, and Philadelphia, it starred Jessica Tandy as Blanche DuBois, Marlon Brando as the animalistic Stanley Kowalski, and Kim Hunter and Karl Malden as Stella and Harold. At the Barrymore on opening night, an enormous crowd applauded for a full half hour, Williams was called to the stage, and the critics hailed the play's brilliance. Representative of their reaction is that of Howard Barnes of the *New York Herald-Tribune*, who wrote, "Williams is certainly the Eugene O'Neill of the present period," and his play is "an arresting tragedy . . . a work of rare discernment and craftsmanship."

The Influence of Ibsen, Strindberg, and Chekhov

European drama, which was to influence modern American drama profoundly, "matured" in the last third of the nineteenth century with the achievements of three playwrights: the Norwegian Henrik Ibsen (1828–1906), the Swede August Strindberg (1849–1912), and the Russian Anton Chekhov (1860–1904). Ibsen deliberately tackled subjects such as guilt, sexuality, and mental illness—subjects which had never before been so realistically and disturbingly portrayed on stage. Strindberg brought to his characterizations an unprecedented level of psychological complexity. And Chekhov, along with Ibsen and Strindberg, shifted the subject matter of drama from wildly theatrical displays of external action to inner action and emotions and the concerns of everyday life. Chekhov once remarked, "People don't go to the North Pole and fall off icebergs. They go to the office and quarrel with their wives and eat cabbage soup." B

These three great playwrights bequeathed to their American heirs plays about life as it is actually lived. They presented characters and situations more or less realistically, in what has been called the "slice of life" dramatic technique.

"Chekhov once remarked, 'People don't go to the North Pole and fall off icebergs. They go to the office and quarrel with their wives and eat cabbage soup.'"

A. Humanities Connection: Discussing the Illustration
Strange Interlude (1928), a tremendously long play (nine acts) by Eugene O'Neill, caused a sensation by its revival of the soliloquy and the aside to create a stream of consciousness technique. The protagonist, Nina Leeds, pursues several successive relationships with men, each neurotically affected by her relationship with her father. Nina's bitter conclusion at the end of the many conflicts of the play is that human lives are "merely strange dark interludes in the electrical display of God the Father."

B. Expansion
The Provincetown Players were a group of actors, producers, and playwrights organized in Provincetown, Mass., who moved the next year to New York City, where they worked until 1929. Eugene O'Neill was the Players' most important discovery, but they eventually produced almost 100 plays by many playwrights of the period.

The Washington Square Players was a shorter-lived group, several of whose members founded the Theatre Guild in 1918. The Guild specialized in contemporary productions, particularly the plays of O'Neill and of Irish dramatist George Bernard Shaw (1856–1950). The Guild also helped develop musical theater; for example, by producing Gershwin's *Porgy and Bess* (1935) and by bringing together Richard Rodgers and Oscar Hammerstein II for *Oklahoma!* (1943).

A

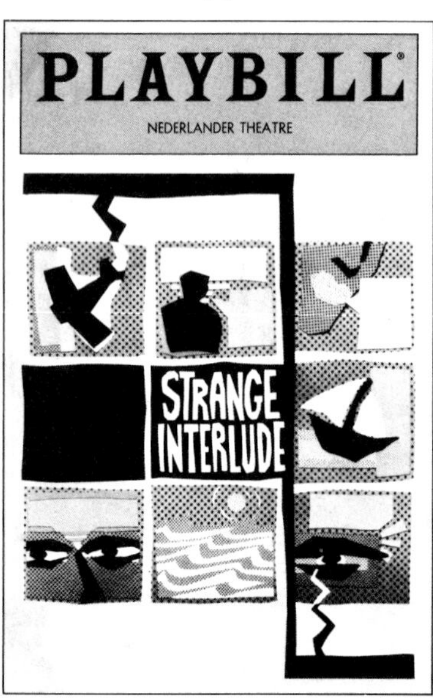

American Realism and Eugene O'Neill

Realistic drama is based on the illusion that when we watch a play, we are looking at life through a "fourth wall" that has been removed so that we can see the action. Soon after the beginning of the twentieth century, realism became the dominant mode of American drama. As with all theatrical revolutions, the movement toward realism began apart from the commercial theater. But very soon after the new drama succeeded in the little theaters off Broadway (about 1916), the commercial theater adopted realism, too.

B In 1916 and 1917, two small theater groups in New York—the Provincetown Players and the Washington Square Players—began to produce new European plays. They also provided a congenial home for new American playwrights. Most notable among these was Eugene O'Neill, whose first one-act plays about the sea were produced by the Provincetown Players in Greenwich Village in 1916. (New movements in the theater have often begun with one-act plays. In addition to O'Neill, Tennessee Williams, Clifford Odets, and Edward Albee all were to start with short plays.)

These theater groups seemed to have no program. They were not sure what they were for, but they were sure what they were against: the established commercial theater. They would produce any play in any style which commercial theater would not touch.

O'Neill gravitated there naturally. Well aware of Sigmund Freud and his new theories about the complex self, O'Neill tried especially hard to reveal more than realism could normally reveal. "The old realism," he wrote, "no longer applies. We have taken too many snapshots of each other in every graceless position; we have endured too much from the banality of surfaces."

In *The Great God Brown* (1926), O'Neill experimented with using masks to differentiate between two sides of a personality. In *Days Without End* (1934), he had two actors play one character to achieve the same end. And in *Strange Interlude* (1928), characters spoke in asides to the audience, revealing thoughts and feelings that could not be expressed in dialogue. With his experimental flair, his enormous output, and his high aspirations for the theater, O'Neill dominated American drama in his generation; he can be said to have "put it on the map." His plays were widely produced abroad, and he was awarded the Nobel Prize for Literature in 1936.

Arthur Miller and Tennessee Williams

The post-World War II years brought two important figures to prominence in American drama: Arthur Miller (born 1915) and Tennessee Williams (1911–1983). Although other playwrights, such as William Inge (1913–1973), have contributed striking and effective plays, Miller and Williams remain the dominant figures of the second half of the century. Miller and Williams represent the two principal movements in modern American drama: realism, and realism combined with an attempt at something more imaginative. From the beginning, American playwrights have tried to break away

A

from realism or to blend it with more poetic expression, as in Miller's *Death of a Salesman* (1949), Williams's *The Glass Menagerie* (1944), and Thornton Wilder's *Our Town* (1938) and *The Skin of Our Teeth* (1942).

Arthur Miller's best work, *Death of a Salesman,* is one of the most successful in fusing the realistic and the imaginative; in all of his other plays, however, Miller is the master of realism. He is a true disciple of Henrik Ibsen, not only in his realistic technique, but in his concern about society's impact on his characters' lives.

In Miller's plays, the course of the action and the development of character depend not only on the characters' psychological makeup, but also on the social, philosophical, and economic atmosphere of their times. Miller's most notable character, Willy Loman in *Death of a Salesman,* is a self-deluded man; but he is also a product of the American dream of success and a victim of

"Miller's most notable character, Willy Loman in *Death of a Salesman,* is a self-deluded man; but he is also a product of the American dream of success and a victim of the American business machine, which disposes of him when he has outlived his usefulness."

A. Humanities Connection: Discussing the Photograph
Shown is the influential but unprepossessing Provincetown Playhouse (see paragraph two of American Realism and Eugene O'Neill and annotation B on page 764). The placard in the door announces a Pulitzer Prize play by Paul Green (1894–1981), *In Abraham's Bosom* (1927). Green, a native of North Carolina, focused on the lives of African Americans and poor whites in the South. *In Abraham's Bosom* concerns the efforts of Abraham McCranie, a mulatto, to found a school for plantation Negroes. He is ultimately killed by a mob as he shouts a defiant prophecy of freedom. Green also wrote *The Lost Colony* (1937), a historical pageant about the early settlement on Roanoke Island, and *Native Son* (1941), a stage adaptation with Richard Wright (page 1004) of Wright's novel of the same title.

A. Humanities Connection: Discussing the Illustration
Arthur Miller notes in his autobiography, *Timebends* (Grove Press, 1987), that the death of his character Willy Loman deeply moved the first people with whom he shared the manuscript of *Death of a Salesman.* The same thing happened at the first performances. In Philadelphia, the curtain fell to silence. People simply sat, lost in thought; many wept. When someone did rouse enough to clap, the applause seemed endless. Opening night at the Morosco in New York—February 10, 1949—created a similar spell. Elia Kazan directed these performances, Jo Mielziner designed the setting and lights, and the major roles were played by Lee J. Cobb (Willy Loman), Mildred Dunnock (Linda), Arthur Kennedy (Biff), and Cameron Mitchell (Happy).

A

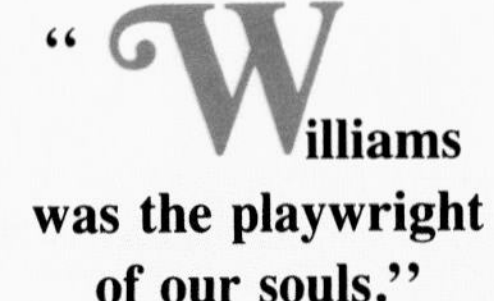

the American business machine, which disposes of him when he has outlived his usefulness.

Miller is a writer of high moral seriousness, whether he is dealing with personal versus social responsibility, as in *All My Sons* (1947), or with witch hunts past and present, as in *The Crucible* (1953). Miller writes a plain and muscular prose that under the force of emotion often becomes eloquent, as in Linda Loman's famous speech in *Death of a Salesman,* where she talks to her two sons about their father:

> I don't say he's a great man. Willy Loman never made a lot of money. His name was never in the paper. He's not the finest character that ever lived. But he's a human being, and a terrible thing is happening to him. So attention must be paid. He's not to be allowed to fall into his grave like an old dog. Attention, attention must finally be paid to such a person.
>
> —from *Death of a Salesman,* Arthur Miller

Although Tennessee Williams was Miller's contemporary, his concern was not with social matters, but with personal ones. If Miller is often the playwright of our social conscience, then Williams was the playwright of our souls. In play after play, he probed the psychological complexities of his characters, especially of his women: Amanda and Laura in *The Glass Menagerie* (1944), Blanche in *A Streetcar Named Desire* (1947), and Alma in *Summer and Smoke* (1948).

In contrast to Miller's spare, plain language, Williams's writing is delicate and sensuous; it is often colored with lush imagery and evocative rhythms. Miller's characters are, by and large, ordinary people with whom we identify because they are caught up in the social tensions of our times. Williams's characters are often women who are "lost ladies," drowning in their own neuroses, but somehow mirroring a part of our own complex psychological selves.

The actual scenes in Williams's plays are usually purely realistic, even though these scenes may deal with colorful and "extreme" characters. But Williams usually theatricalized the realism with "music in the wings" or symbolic props, such as Laura's unicorn in *The Glass Menagerie* or the looming statue of Eternity in *Summer and Smoke.* He always conceived his plays in visually arresting, colorful, theatrical environments—an effort in which he was aided by the imaginative designer Jo Mielziner, who designed the sets for many of his plays.

The Revolt Against Realism

In the mid-nineteenth century, realism in drama was conceived as a revolt against crude theatricalism. Currently, there is a revolt against realism itself in American drama. Naturally, the movement is toward theatricalism again, with its emphasis on stage effects and imaginative settings. This revolt does not confine itself to a

READING CHECK TEST

1. Conflict is of little importance in drama. *False*
2. Eugene O'Neill is considered the first major American playwright. *True*
3. European drama matured earlier than American drama. *True*
4. "Theatricalism" is another name for "realism." *False*
5. Expressionist or absurdist drama focuses on characters' inner consciousness. *True*

A. Humanities Connection: Discussing the Illustration

Happy Days (1961) was written in English—an exception for Samuel Beckett, Irish-born dramatist who settled in Paris in 1937 and began writing in French in 1939. He wrote the works on which his reputation as an absurdist rests between 1947 and 1957. *Waiting for Godot* (1952) is a tragicomedy in which two tramps, continually aware of cold, hunger, and pain, keep waiting for someone named Godot. Meanwhile they quarrel, contemplate suicide and departure, and interact with a passing rich man and his servant. The play is bleak and despairing, yet richly humorous in its assertion of the human will to live despite everything. *Happy Days* continues similar themes and techniques. Overall, Beckett's characters generally advance through worsening stages of decrepitude, in a meaningless world where language is the only weapon against chaos. Yet even language is revealed as incapable of conveying true meaning. Beckett was awarded the Nobel Prize in 1969.

particular manner of staging; instead, it extends to the texture of language and plot in the scripts themselves.

The moral and religious certainties that once bound people together exert little or no force on many modern audiences. Some people believe that survival itself depends on a willingness to accept life as formless or meaningless.

Some American playwrights found this new outlook on life impossible to express in the orderly "beginning, middle, end" format of realism. They borrowed, again from Europe, a theater of fragmentation, impressions, and stream of consciousness that was called "expressionist." **Expressionist drama** aimed at the revelation of characters' interior consciousness without reference to a logical sequence of surface actions. Many writers who used expressionist techniques in drama came to be called playwrights of the Theater of the Absurd.

Samuel Beckett (born 1906) and Eugene Ionesco (born 1912) were among the founders of the Theater of the Absurd. The drama critic Martin Esslin has written this about the Absurdists:

> The action of a play of the Theater of the Absurd is not intended to tell a story but to communicate a pattern of poetic images. To give but one example: Things happen in [Samuel Beckett's] *Waiting for Godot* [1953], but these things do not constitute a plot or a story; they are an image of Beckett's intuition that *nothing really ever happens* in man's existence.
>
> —Martin Esslin

The trouble with a static play that mirrors a static life is that it is static. It is an image, a picture; and a picture can absorb our interest for only so long because it lacks the progression and development of a dramatic story. We can observe a situation without development for about the length of a one-act play. Perhaps this is why so many of the so-called absurdist plays *are* only one act, such as Beckett's *Krapp's Last Tape* and Ionesco's *The Bald Soprano.*

The most significant Absurdist in America has been Edward Albee (born 1928). Albee is not a pure Absurdist, since, like all innovative playwrights, he experiments with many forms. From 1960 to 1970, Albee produced a play a year. These works ranged from his startling, one-act debut, *The Zoo Story* (1960), through the absurdist play *The American Dream* (1961) and the savage and electrifying domestic drama *Who's Afraid of Virginia Woolf?* (1962), which made Albee world-famous.

Experimental drama has increased the options that are open to playwrights. Dramatists now have the freedom to express their deepest feelings in almost any form they choose—provided that their approach can be made comprehensible to an audience and touch their emotions. There are practically no conventions in the theater anymore; there is simply a stage and an audience. Playwrights are free to load the stage with scenery, lights, and special effects; but they are equally free—as the playwright was in the age of Shakespeare—to have an actor gesture toward one side of an utterly bare stage and say, "This is the Forest of Arden."

"There are practically no conventions in the theater anymore; there is simply a stage and an audience."

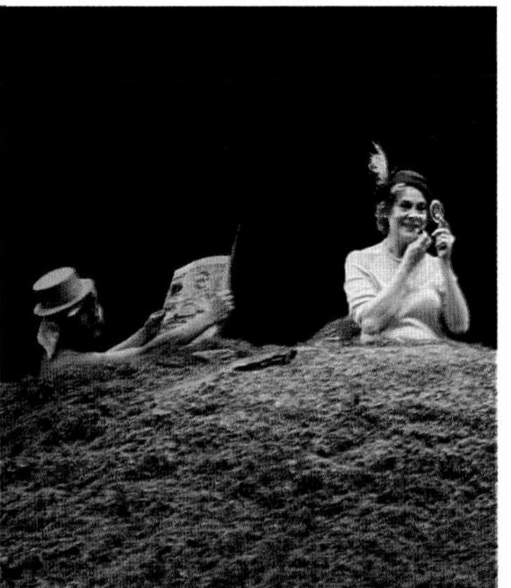

A

Scene from *Happy Days* by Samuel Beckett. The two characters speak all their lines while buried in sand.

A. Humanities Connection: Discussing the Photograph
The photograph is from approximately the same time as the play, the mid-1940's. Accustomed to seeing older portraits of famous writers, students may be surprised that someone so young-looking wrote what has become an American classic. Williams was 33 at the time. Prior to *The Glass Menagerie,* Williams's plays were less mature and more limited in their success, as illustrated by a story told of the flamboyant, outspoken actress Tallulah Bankhead (1903–1968). Unimpressed with a performance of *Orpheus Descending* (a 1957 revision of a play Williams first completed in 1940), she later told Williams, "Darling, they've absolutely ruined your perfectly dreadful play."

Tennessee Williams (1911–1983)

The Glass Menagerie has become an American classic. When it opened on Broadway in the spring of 1945, Mississippi-born Tennessee Williams was practically unknown; almost overnight, he became an international success.

Though Williams became known principally for his colorful women characters—Blanche in *A Streetcar Named Desire* (1947), Alma in *Summer and Smoke* (1948), Maggie in *Cat on a Hot Tin Roof* (1955)—he also created some great male characters, among them Stanley Kowalski in *A Streetcar Named Desire.* Marlon Brando's portrayal of Stanley in the original production, and in the movie, established a kind of mumbling, torn-Tee-shirt technique of acting that was to become popular with many of the younger male actors of the next decade.

The Glass Menagerie is a mixture of straightforward, realistic play construction and "poetic," highly imaginative conception and language. Williams used this combination for most of his works. The structure of his plays is basically conventional; his vision, his "voice," is imaginative and sensitive.

Because *The Glass Menagerie* is a memory play, its images are hazy. In production, when the curtain goes up, we see the apartment and the alley through a transparent gauze curtain called a "scrim." The narrator speaks in a kind of poetic prose, and when the scrim rises, we see the set lit, but with pools of light and shadow.

The characters, too, are poetically conceived and removed from the daily life of the Great Depression of the 1930's. In a few lines in the opening narration, Williams sets the social background of the period; but he is not really interested in the larger society. In all his plays, what interests him most is the psychological makeup of his characters. Laura Wingfield passes her life listening to phonograph records and rearranging her collection of glass animals. Tom wants to be a writer and to escape to the sea. Amanda lives in the past glories of being a Southern belle. In contrast to the Wingfield family, the gentleman caller is not poetic. He is from the real world,

A

and it is the touching confrontation of this real man with the withdrawn Laura that provides the climax of the play.

In December 1944, *The Glass Menagerie* was tried out in Chicago. It was "dying" until the influential drama critic Claudia Cassidy came to its rescue and demanded that people see the play. When it moved on to New York in the spring of 1945, it was an instant success.

Williams had two extraordinary collaborators. Amanda was originally played by one of the great actresses of the American stage, Laurette Taylor. She had been in retirement for some years for many reasons, one of which was that she had developed a drinking problem. She was lured out of retirement by Williams's play, and the natural drama of opening night was increased by the tension generated by the question, "Would Laurette Taylor make it?" She did make it. It was her greatest and her last performance in the theater.

Williams's other great collaborator was Jo Mielziner, the foremost stage designer of his day. Williams was only a young playwright, but he brought both these collaborators a play with a passionate and poetic expression of his feelings for his own sister (see page 811), and with a brilliantly conceived dramatic structure. All of Tennessee Williams's collaborators rose to new heights when they helped him realize on stage this small gem of a play.

PREPARATION

1. ESTABLISHING A PURPOSE. Discuss with students the qualities that, based on the unit introduction, they expect to find in the play. (Realism mixed with delicate or poetic language, "lost" women or other extreme characters, a symbolic glass unicorn) Then have students read the play to answer such questions as the following ones: What elements of realism are found in this play? What are some passages with especially poetic language? What purposes do these passages serve? What are the characters like? If they seem "lost" or extreme in some way, what is the cause of their alienation from society? What does the glass unicorn symbolize?

2. PREREADING JOURNAL. Have students free associate or brainstorm a list of problems they think ordinary people would have had during the Great Depression of the early 1930's, and write about them in their journals. What would people have to do without? How important would it be for every family member to work, and not spend all day listening to records or playing with glass animals?

THE GLASS MENAGERIE

Nobody, not even the rain, has such small hands.

—E. E. Cummings

A

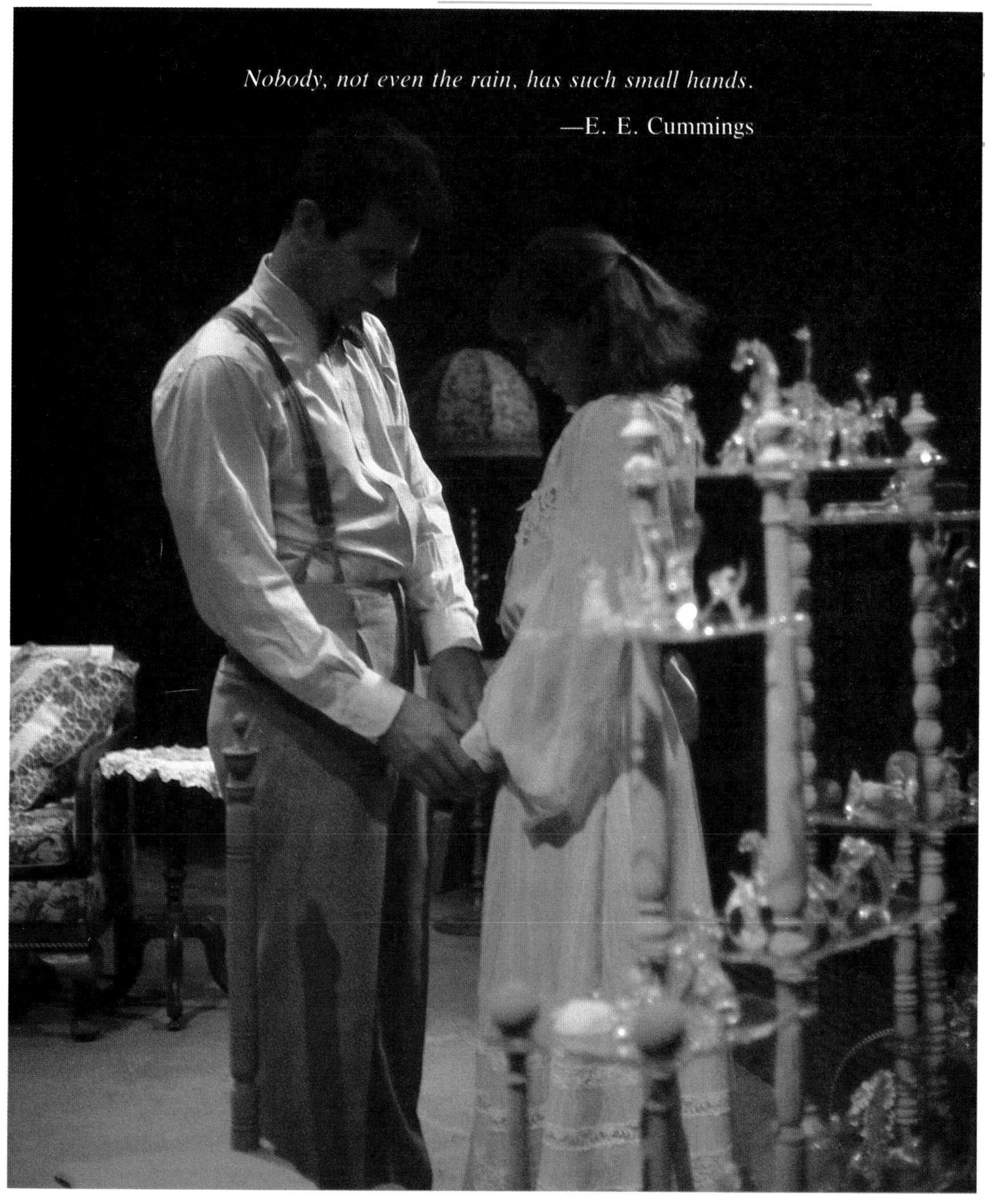

The photographs that illustrate the play are from the Long Wharf Theater Production, in New Haven, Connecticut, 1986.

A. Responding to the Quotation

The words from E. E. Cummings appear on the page after the title page of Williams's play.

? How does the scene appear to illustrate the line from Cummings? (The young man seems to speak it to the young woman.) In what sense does rain have "small hands"? (Its drops are like tiny hands.) How is the line meant to be taken? (As a compliment)

Supplementary Support Materials
1. Vocabulary Activity Worksheet (*CCB*)
2. Review and Response Worksheet: Exposition and Character Development (*CCB*)
3. Language Skills Worksheet: Revision Worksheet 4 (*CCB*)
4. Selection Test (*CCB*)

Developing Vocabulary
The following words from the play are tested in the Selection Test. (See also Vocabulary Activity Worksheet.)

menagerie	to matriculate
paranoiac	emissary
implacable	to masticate
proscenium	nimble
quaint	vivacity

Reading the Play
You may wish to read the entire play aloud. Ahead of time, assign roles to your better readers. Add a fifth student to read all stage directions, and have a sixth student—if possible, one with experience in art or drama—present to the class a drawing of the scene described in the first set of stage directions. Students should follow in their books as the scenes are read, mainly to enable them later to locate specific passages. Read a scene in its entirety before stopping for questions and comments. Response questions follow Scenes 2, 4, 6, and 7 on pages 777, 785, 796, 809–810.

The Characters

Amanda Wingfield (*the mother*)
A little woman of great but confused vitality clinging frantically to another time and place. Her characterization must be carefully created, not copied from type. She is not paranoiac, but her life is paranoia.[1] There is much to admire in Amanda, and as much to love and pity as there is to laugh at. Certainly she has endurance and a kind of heroism, and though her foolishness makes her unwittingly cruel at times, there is tenderness in her slight person.

Laura Wingfield (*her daughter*)
Amanda, having failed to establish contact with reality, continues to live vitally in her illusions, but Laura's situation is even graver. A childhood illness has left her crippled, one leg slightly shorter than the other, and held in a brace. This defect need not be more than suggested on the stage. Stemming from this, Laura's separation increases till she is like a piece of her own glass collection, too exquisitely fragile to move from the shelf.

Tom Wingfield (*her son*)
And the narrator of the play. A poet with a job in a warehouse. His nature is not remorseless, but to escape from a trap he has to act without pity.

Jim O'Connor (*the gentleman caller*)
A nice, ordinary, young man.

Scene 1

The Wingfield apartment is in the rear of the building, one of those vast hive-like conglomerations of cellular living-units that flower at warty growths in overcrowded urban centers of lower middle-class population and are symptomatic of the impulse of this largest and fundamentally enslaved section of American society to avoid fluidity and differentiation and to exist and function as one interfused mass of automatism.

The apartment faces an alley and is entered by a fire escape, a structure whose name is a touch of accidental poetic truth, for all of these huge buildings are always burning with the slow and implacable fires of human desperation. The fire escape is part of what we see—that is, the landing of it and steps descending from it.

The scene is memory and is therefore nonrealistic. Memory takes a lot of poetic license. It omits some details; others are exaggerated, according to the emotional value of the articles it touches, for memory is seated predominantly in the heart. The interior is therefore rather dim and poetic.

At the rise of the curtain, the audience is faced with the dark, grim rear wall of the Wingfield tenement. This building is flanked on both sides by dark, narrow alleys which run into murky canyons of tangled clotheslines, garbage cans, and the sinister latticework of neighboring fire escapes. It is up and down these side alleys that exterior entrances and exits are made during the play. At the end of TOM'S *opening commentary, the dark tenement[2] wall slowly becomes transparent and reveals the interior of the ground-floor Wingfield apartment.*

Nearest the audience is the living room, which also serves as a sleeping room for LAURA, *the sofa unfolding to make her bed. Just beyond, separated from the living room by a wide arch or second proscenium with transparent faded portieres[3] (or second curtain), is the dining room. In an old-fashioned whatnot[4] in the living room are seen scores of transparent glass animals. A blown-up photograph of the father hangs on the wall of the living room, to the left of the archway. It is the face of a very handsome young man in a doughboy's First World War cap. He is gallantly smiling, ineluctably smiling, as if to say "I will be smiling forever."*

Also hanging on the wall, near the photograph, are a typewriter keyboard chart and a Gregg shorthand diagram. An upright typewriter on a small table stands beneath the charts.

1. **paranoia** (par'ə·noi'ə): behavior characterized by delusions, especially of being persecuted.

2. **tenement:** an apartment house in a poor neighborhood.
3. **portieres** (pôr·tyerz'): curtains covering a doorway, used instead of a door.
4. **whatnot**: open shelves for holding small objects ("whatnots").

SCENE 1 SUMMARY: Tom Wingfield, the narrator, sets the scene of this "memory play" and explains who the characters are. Amanda nags Tom, her son, about the way he eats, and urges her daughter, Laura, to stay fresh and pretty for gentleman callers. Laura says she is not expecting anyone. Amanda rehashes old stories about her own popularity as a girl in Mississippi, then sends Laura off to practice her secretarial skills and to stay pretty for supposed callers.

A. Humanities Connection
Discussing the Photograph
The photograph on this page and those on pages 769, 776, 780, 784, 794–795, 802, and 805 are from a 1986 production of the play at the Long Wharf Theatre in New Haven.

Together, the entire set of photographs can be used to review the entire play later. During the reading of the play, the photographs may remind students that plays are not truly alive until acted, and can serve as discussion starters on matters of staging, props, and so on.

The audience hears and sees the opening scene in the dining room through both the transparent fourth wall of the building and the transparent gauze portieres of the dining-room arch. It is during this revealing scene that the fourth wall slowly ascends, out of sight. This transparent exterior wall is not brought down again until the very end of the play, during TOM*'s final speech.*

The narrator is an undisguised convention of the play. He takes whatever license with dramatic convention is convenient to his purposes.

[TOM *enters, dressed as a merchant sailor, and strolls across to the fire escape. There he stops and lights a cigarette. He addresses the audience.*]

Tom. Yes, I have tricks in my pocket, I have things up my sleeve. But I am the opposite of a stage magician. He gives you illusion that has the appearance of truth. I give you truth in the pleasant disguise of illusion.

To begin with, I turn back time. I reverse it to that quaint period, the thirties, when the huge middle class of America was matriculating in a school for the blind. Their eyes had failed them, or they had failed their eyes, and so they were having their fingers pressed forcibly down on the fiery Braille alphabet of a dissolving economy.

In Spain there was revolution. Here there was only shouting and confusion. In Spain there was Guernica. Here there were disturbances of labor, sometimes pretty violent, in otherwise peaceful cities such as Chicago, Cleveland, Saint Louis . . . This is the social background of the play.

[*Music begins to play.*]

The play is memory. Being a memory play, it is dimly lighted, it is sentimental, it is not realistic. In memory everything seems to happen to music. That explains the fiddle in the wings.

I am the narrator of the play, and also a character in it. The other characters are my mother, Amanda, my sister, Laura, and a gentleman caller who appears in the final scenes. He is the most

A

"I give you truth in the pleasant guise of illusion."

A. Allusion
The phrase popular in the era of the play was "to trip the light fantastic"—to dance, to have a good time. The words come from much farther back, lines written by English poet John Milton (1608–1674) in *L'Allegro* (1632): "Come, and trip it, as you go,/On the light fantastic toe."

B. Expansion
Although the screen device was not used in the original acting version of the play, Williams retained it for the published script. The screen was to be a section of wall between the front room and dining room areas, and the images and legends were to be projected from behind. Williams's intention was to "strengthen the effect of what is merely allusion in the writing and allow the primary point to be made more simply . . . than if the entire responsibility were on the spoken lines." After a number of references to the screen have occurred, you may wish to have students comment on the effect they think the technique would have.

realistic character in the play, being an emissary from a world of reality that we were somehow set apart from. But since I have a poet's weakness for symbols, I am using this character also as a symbol; he is the long delayed but always expected something that we live for.

There is a fifth character in the play who doesn't appear except in this larger-than-life-size photograph over the mantel. This is our father who left us a long time ago. He was a telephone man who fell in love with long distances; he gave up his job with the telephone company and A skipped the light fantastic out of town . . .

The last we heard of him was a picture postcard from Mazatlan, on the Pacific coast of Mexico, containing a message of two words: "Hello—Goodbye!" and no address.

I think the rest of the play will explain itself. . . .

[AMANDA*'s voice becomes audible through the portieres.*]

B [*Legend on screen:* "Ou sont les neiges?"[5]]

[TOM *divides the portieres and enters the dining room.* AMANDA *and* LAURA *are seated at a drop-leaf table. Eating is indicated by gestures without food or utensils.* AMANDA *faces the audience.* TOM *and* LAURA *are seated in profile. The interior has lit up softly and through the scrim we see* AMANDA *and* LAURA *seated at the table.*]

Amanda *(calling).* Tom?
Tom. Yes, Mother.
Amanda. We can't say grace until you come to the table!
Tom. Coming, Mother. *(He bows slightly and withdraws, reappearing a few moments later in his place at the table.)*
Amanda *(to her son).* Honey, don't *push* with your *fingers.* If you have to push with something, the thing to push with is a crust of bread. And chew—chew! Animals have secretions in their stomachs which enable them to digest food without mastication, but human beings are supposed to chew their food before they swallow it down. Eat food leisurely, son, and really enjoy it. A well-cooked meal has lots of delicate flavors that have to be held in the mouth for appreciation. So chew your food and give your salivary glands a chance to function!

[TOM *deliberately lays his imaginary fork down and pushes his chair back from the table.*]

Tom. I haven't enjoyed one bite of this dinner because of your constant directions on how to eat it. It's you that make me rush through meals with your hawk-like attention to every bite I take. Sickening—spoils my appetite—all this discussion of—animals' secretion—salivary glands—mastication!
Amanda *(lightly).* Temperament like a Metropolitan star!

[TOM *rises and walks toward the living room.*]

You're not excused from the table.
Tom. I'm getting a cigarette.
Amanda. You smoke too much.

[LAURA *rises.*]

Laura. I'll bring in the blanc mange.[6]

[TOM *remains standing with his cigarette by the portieres.*]

Amanda *(rising).* No, sister—you be the lady this time and I'll be the servant.
Laura. I'm already up.
Amanda. Resume your seat, little sister—I want you to stay fresh and pretty—for gentlemen callers!
Laura *(sitting down).* I'm not expecting any gentlemen callers.
Amanda *(crossing out to the kitchenette, airily).* Sometimes they come when they are least expected! Why, I remember one Sunday afternoon in Blue Mountain—

[*She enters the kitchenette.*]

Tom. I know what's coming!
Laura. Yes. But let her tell it.
Tom. Again?
Laura. She loves to tell it.

[AMANDA *returns with a bowl of dessert.*]

Amanda. One Sunday afternoon in Blue Mountain—your mother received—*seventeen*—gentle-

5. **"Ou sont les neiges"**: French, for "Where are the snows?" This is a reference to a famous line by the fifteenth-century French poet, François Villon. The complete line is a sad question about the passing of time: "But where are the snows of yesteryear?"

6. **blanc mange** (blə·mänj′): a dessert shaped in a mold.

A. Allusion
Midas was a legendary king of Phrygia in Asia Minor. In return for his hospitality to Silenus (a Greek forest god with some features of the horse), Midas was granted his wish that everything he touched might turn to gold. When even his food turned to gold, however, he begged to have the gift removed from him. This was done by his bathing in the Patroclus River, where gold was thereafter found. "To have the Midas touch" is to be very successful in business, as is made clear by Amanda's calling Fitzhugh "the Wolf of Wall Street."

B. Characterization
? Amanda Wingfield was described on page 770 as "clinging frantically to another place and time." How does this scene illustrate that description? (She tells an obviously often-told story about the gentleman callers of her youth.) What do you deduce about behavior expected of young men and women of the earlier time period she recalls? (It sounds as though dating was formal, genteel, and very innocent. Girls had to be able to converse; young men could be somewhat "wild.") Does Amanda seem completely in touch with present reality? (Answers may vary, but since Laura has said she expects no callers, most students will see Amanda as out of touch.)

? So far, do any of the characters remind you of anyone you know? (Answers will vary. Many students know adults who tell "When I was your age" stories.) Do you feel sorry for anyone? (Answers will vary.) Can you identify with anyone to even a small degree? (Answers will vary, but most students have been nagged about some aspect of their behavior and may therefore identify with Tom or Laura.)

men callers! Why, sometimes there weren't chairs enough to accommodate them all. We had to send the servant over to bring in folding chairs from the parish house.
Tom *(remaining at the portieres).* How did you entertain those gentlemen callers?
Amanda. I understood the art of conversation!
Tom. I bet you could talk.
Amanda. Girls in those days *knew* how to talk, I can tell you.
Tom. Yes?

[*Image on screen:* AMANDA *as a girl on a porch, greeting callers.*]

Amanda. They knew how to entertain their gentlemen callers. It wasn't enough for a girl to be possessed of a pretty face and a graceful figure—although I wasn't slighted in either respect. She also needed to have a nimble wit and a tongue to meet all occasions.
Tom. What did you talk about?
Amanda. Things of importance going on in the world! Never anything coarse or common or vulgar.

[*She addresses* TOM *as though he were seated in the vacant chair at the table though he remains by the portieres. He plays this scene as though reading from a script.*]

My callers were gentlemen—all! Among my callers were some of the most prominent young planters of the Mississippi Delta—planters and sons of planters!

[TOM *motions for music and a spot of light on* AMANDA. *Her eyes lift, her face glows, her voice becomes rich and elegiac.*]

[*Screen legend:* "Ou sont les neiges d'antan?"]

There was young Champ Laughlin who later became vice-president of the Delta Planters Bank. Hadley Stevenson who was drowned in Moon Lake and left his widow one hundred and fifty thousand in Government bonds. There were the Cutrere brothers, Wesly and Bates. Bates was one of my bright particular beaux! He got in a quarrel with that wild Wainwright boy. They shot it out on the floor of Moon Lake Casino. Bates was shot through the stomach. Died in the ambulance on his way to Memphis. His widow was also well provided-for, came into eight or ten thousand acres, that's all. She married him on the rebound—never loved her—carried my picture on him the night he died! And there was that boy that every girl in the Delta had set her cap for! That beautiful, brilliant young Fitzhugh boy from Greene County!
Tom. What did he leave his widow?
Amanda. He never married! Gracious, you talk as though all of my old admirers had turned up their toes to the daisies!
Tom. Isn't this the first you've mentioned that still survives?
Amanda. That Fitzhugh boy went North and made a fortune—came to be known as the Wolf of Wall Street! He had the Midas touch, whatever he touched turned to gold! And I could have been Mrs. Duncan J. Fitzhugh, mind you! But—I picked your *father!* A
Laura *(rising).* Mother, let me clear the table.
Amanda. No, dear, you go in front and study your typewriter chart. Or practice your shorthand a little. Stay fresh and pretty!—It's almost time for your gentlemen callers to start arriving. [*She flounces girlishly toward the kitchenette.*] How many do you supppose we're going to entertain this afternoon?

[TOM *throws down the paper and jumps up with a groan.*]

Laura *(alone in the dining room).* I don't believe we're going to receive any, Mother.
Amanda *(reappearing, airily).* What? No one—not one? You must be joking!

[LAURA *nervously echoes her laugh. She slips in a fugitive manner through the half-open portieres and draws them gently behind her. A shaft of very clear light is thrown on her face against the faded tapestry of the curtains. Faintly the music of "The Glass Menagerie" is heard as she continues lightly:*]

Not one gentleman caller? It can't be true! There must be a flood, there must have been a tornado!
Laura. It isn't a flood, it's not a tornado, Mother. I'm just not popular like you were in Blue Mountain. . . .

[TOM *utters another groan.* LAURA *glances at him with a faint, apologetic smile. Her voice catches a little:*]

Mother's afraid I'm going to be an old maid.

[*The scene dims out with "The Glass Menagerie" music.*]

B

SCENE 2 SUMMARY: Amanda discovers that Laura dropped out of business school weeks earlier and has been spending the cold days in parks, museums, and especially the tropical greenhouse at the zoo. Amanda despairs of Laura's finding a man, although Laura, who walks with a limp, reveals that she once had a crush on a boy named Jim O'Connor. He was in her chorus class in high school and called Laura "Blue Roses" after she had been sick with pleurosis and he mistook the word.

Scene 2

On the dark stage the screen is lighted with the image of blue roses. Gradually LAURA'*s figure becomes apparent and the screen goes out. The music subsides.*

LAURA *is seated in the delicate ivory chair at the small claw-foot table. She wears a dress of soft violet material for a kimono—her hair is tied back from her forehead with a ribbon. She is washing and polishing her collection of glass.* AMANDA *appears on the fire escape steps. At the sound of her ascent,* LAURA *catches her breath, thrusts the bowl of ornaments away, and seats herself stiffly before the diagram of the typewriter keyboard as though it held her spellbound. Something has happened to* AMANDA. *It is written in her face as she climbs to the landing: a look that is grim and hopeless and a little absurd. She has on one of those cheap or imitation velvety-looking cloth coats with imitation fur collar. Her hat, is five or six years old, one of those dreadful cloche*[1] *hats that were worn in the late Twenties, and she is clutching an enormous black patent-leather pocketbook with nickel clasps and initials. This is her full-dress outfit, the one she usually wears to the D.A.R.*[2] *Before entering she looks through the door. She purses her lips, opens her eyes very wide, rolls them upward and shakes her head. Then she slowly lets herself in the door. Seeing her mother's expression* LAURA *touches her lips with a nervous gesture.*

Laura. Hello, Mother, I was— *(She makes a nervous gesture toward the chart on the wall.* AMANDA *leans against the shut door and stares at* LAURA *with a martyred look.)*
Amanda. Deception? Deception? *(She slowly removes her hat and gloves, continuing the sweet suffering stare. She lets the hat and gloves fall on the floor—a bit of acting.)*
Laura *(shakily).* How was the D.A.R. meeting?

[AMANDA *slowly opens her purse and removes a dainty white handkerchief which she shakes out delicately and delicately touches to her lips and nostrils.*]

Didn't you go to the D.A.R. meeting, Mother?
Amanda *(faintly, almost inaudibly).* —No.—No. *(then more forcibly:)* I did not have the strength—to go to the D.A.R. In fact, I did not have the courage! I wanted to find a hole in the ground and hide myself in it forever! *(She crosses slowly to the wall and removes the diagram of the typewriter keyboard. She holds it in front of her for a second, staring at it sweetly and sorrowfully—then bites her lips and tears it in two pieces.)*
Laura *(faintly).* Why did you do that, Mother?

[AMANDA *repeats the same procedure with the chart of the Gregg Alphabet.*]

Why are you—
Amanda. Why? Why? How old are you, Laura?
Laura. Mother, you know my age.
Amanda. I thought that you were an adult; it seems that I was mistaken. *(She crosses slowly to the sofa and sinks down and stares at* LAURA.*)*
Laura. Please don't stare at me, Mother.

[AMANDA *closes her eyes and lowers her head. There is a ten-second pause.*]

Amanda. What are we going to do, what is going to become of us, what is the future?

[*There is another pause.*]

Laura. Has something happened, Mother?

[AMANDA *draws a long breath, takes out the handkerchief again, goes through the dabbing process.*]

Mother, has—something happened?
Amanda. I'll be all right in a minute. I'm just bewildered—*(She hesitates.)*—by life. . . .
Laura. Mother, I wish that you would tell me what's happened!
Amanda. As you know, I was supposed to be inducted into my office at the D.A.R. this afternoon.

[*Screen image:* A swarm of typewriters.]

But I stopped off at Rubicam's Business College to speak to your teachers about your having a cold and ask them what progress they thought you were making down there.
Laura. Oh. . . .
Amanda. I went to the typing instructor and introduced myself as your mother. She didn't know who you were. "Wingfield," she said, "We don't have any such student enrolled at the school!" I

---

1. **cloche**: a close-fitting hat.
2. **D.A.R.**: Daughters of the American Revolution, a patriotic organization made up of descendants of those colonists who fought with the American patriots during the Revolutionary War.

Reading Check Test: Scenes 1–2

1. Tom and Laura's father will be home soon. *False*
2. Amanda delights in talking about her popularity in her youth. *True*
3. Laura is doing well in typing and shorthand. *False*
4. The nickname "Blue Roses" comes from "pleurosis." *True*
5. Laura is crippled and sensitive about it. *True*

assured her she did, that you had been going to classes since early in January. "I wonder," she said, "If you could be talking about that terribly shy little girl who dropped out of school after only a few days' attendance?" "No," I said, "Laura, my daughter, has been going to school every day for the past six weeks!" "Excuse me," she said. She took the attendance book out and there was your name, unmistakably printed, and all the dates you were absent until they decided that you had dropped out of school. I still said, "No, there must have been some mistake! There must have been some mix-up in the records!" And she said, "No—I remember her perfectly now. Her hands shook so that she couldn't hit the right keys! The first time we gave a speed test, she broke down completely—was sick at the stomach and almost had to be carried into the wash room! After that morning she never showed up any more. We phoned the house but never got any answer"—While I was working at Famous-Barr, I suppose, demonstrating those—

[*She indicates a brassiere with her hands.*]

Oh! I felt so weak I could barely keep on my feet! I had to sit down while they got me a glass of water! Fifty dollars' tuition, all of our plans—my hopes and ambitions for you—just gone up the spout, just gone up the spout like that.

[LAURA *draws a long breath and gets awkwardly to her feet. She crosses to the victrola*[3] *and winds it up.*]

What are you doing?

Laura. Oh! *(She releases the handle and returns to her seat.)*

Amanda. Laura, where have you been going when you've gone out pretending that you were going to business college?

Laura. I've just been going out walking.

Amanda. That's not true.

Laura. It is. I just went walking.

Amanda. Walking? Walking? In winter? Deliberately courting pneumonia in that light coat? Where did you walk to, Laura?

Laura. All sorts of places—mostly in the park.

Amanda. Even after you'd started catching that cold?

Laura. It was the lesser of two evils, Mother.

[*Screen image:* Winter scene in a park.]

I couldn't go back there. I—threw up—on the floor!

Amanda. From half past seven till after five every day you mean to tell me you walked around in the park, because you wanted to make me think that you were still going to Rubicam's Business College?

Laura. It wasn't as bad as it sounds. I went inside places to get warmed up.

Amanda. Inside where?

Laura. I went in the art museum and the bird houses at the Zoo. I visited the penguins every day! Sometimes I did without lunch and went to the movies. Lately I've been spending most of my afternoons in the Jewel Box, that big glass house where they raise the tropical flowers.

Amanda. You did all this to deceive me, just for deception?

[LAURA *looks down.*] Why?

Laura. Mother, when you're disappointed, you get that awful suffering look on your face, like the picture of Jesus' mother in the museum!

Amanda. Hush!

Laura. I couldn't face it.

[*There is a pause. A whisper of strings is heard. Legend on screen:* "The Crust of Humility."]

Amanda *(hopelessly fingering the huge pocketbook).* So what are we going to do the rest of our lives? Stay home and watch the parades go by? Amuse ourselves with the glass menagerie, darling? Eternally play those worn-out phonograph records your father left as a painful reminder of him? We won't have a business career—we've given that up because it gave us nervous indigestion! *(She laughs wearily.)* What is there left but dependency all our lives? I know so well what becomes of unmarried women who aren't prepared to occupy a position. I've seen such pitiful cases in the South—barely tolerated spinsters living upon the grudging patronage of sister's husband or brother's wife—stuck away in some little mousetrap of a room—encouraged by one in-law to visit another—little birdlike women without any nest—eating the crust of humility all their life!

Is that the future that we've mapped out for ourselves? I swear it's the only alternative I can think of! *(She pauses.)* It isn't a very pleasant alternative, is it? *(She pauses again.)* Of course—some girls *do marry.*

3. **victrola:** record player.

A. Exposition
Each scene of a play contains exposition (revelation of background information), action (events advancing the plot), and foreshadowing (hints of things to come). Call to students' attention the exposition provided here, and reasonable inferences one can draw.
? What does Amanda's reference to her job at Famous-Barr suggest about the family's financial situation? (Demonstrating sounds like a temporary position. Perhaps Tom's wages need supplementing; perhaps Amanda often takes short-term jobs.) What kinds of work would someone with Amanda's background and attitudes be able to get *and* willing to accept? (Her choices would be limited to things like sales or a position as receptionist in a large office. She appears to have neither the secretarial skills she urges on Laura nor education for any profession.)

Analyzing Scenes 1 and 2
Identifying Facts
1. Tom tells us that his family is "set apart" from the real world; that the gentleman caller who appears in the final scenes is an "emissary" from the real world; that his father abandoned his family a long time ago. Tom says that the play is a memory play, that it is sentimental and not realistic.
2. Amanda is the cause of the tension. She nags Tom, criticizing the way he eats and the fact that he smokes too much; she tells her son that he is "not excused from this table." Amanda glorifies and romanticizes her youth in a way that irritates Tom, for she has told the same stories dozens of times. She keeps talking about Laura's gentleman callers as if they were a reality, when she knows that no callers are coming—and we can guess that this must upset her daughter.
3. Amanda discovers that Laura has not been attending her classes at the business school. The opening situation is upset because in it Amanda believes that Laura will be able to get a job and to take care of herself in the future. Because Amanda realizes that this is no longer likely, she vows to find a nice

A. Allusion
The fourteen comic operas of Sir William Gilbert (1836–1911) and Sir Arthur Sullivan (1842–1900) were written for the opera company of Richard D'Oyly Carte (1844–1901). Among the most famous Gilbert and Sullivan comic operas are *H.M.S. Pinafore* (1878), *The Pirates of Penzance* (1879), and *The Mikado* (1885). Highly satiric, the operas poke fun at everything in contemporary Victorian England from bureaucracy to navy life.
? What can you deduce about Jim O'Connor on the basis of the screen image and his having participated in a musical play? (Answers will vary from comments on the personalities of prize-winning students to more solid inferences such as the idea that Jim must have had several talents, including a decent singing voice.)

"He used to call me—Blue Roses."

[LAURA *twists her hands nervously.*]

Haven't you ever liked some boy?
Laura. Yes. I liked one once. *(She rises.)* I came across his picture a while ago.
Amanda *(with some interest).* He gave you his picture?
Laura. No, it's in the yearbook.
Amanda *(disappointed).* Oh—a high school boy.

[*Screen image:* Jim as the high school hero bearing a silver cup.]

Laura. Yes. His name was Jim. *(She lifts the heavy annual from the claw-foot table.)* Here he is in *The Pirates of Penzance.*[4]
Amanda *(absently).* The what?

4. ***The Pirates of Penzance***: a comic operetta by Gilbert and Sullivan.

young man for Laura to marry, and it is this search for the gentleman caller that sets the action in motion.

4. Laura is painfully shy, so much so that she throws up on her first day at business school and never returns. She escapes the real world by spending her days in the art museum, at the zoo, at the movies, and at the tropical flower house.

5. "Blue Roses" is the nickname Jim gave to Laura when they were in high school.

Interpreting Meanings

6. Students may feel that Amanda is strong because she is a survivor in a world that has changed. She is also weak, for she clings to fantasy. She is sympathetic, for she tries to find a way for Laura to survive. At the same time, however, she is demanding.

7. Laura keeps her yearbook with Jim's picture underneath her glass menagerie, which is her most precious possession, and she speaks warmly of Jim and his accomplishments. Laura's talk about Jim, in fact, shows her at her liveliest thus far in the play.

Amanda loses interest in Jim when she finds out that he was only a slight acquaintance of Laura's and that he is not a potential gentleman caller.

8. The scenes are dimly lighted; the picture of the father on the living room wall is referred to and spotlighted. Laura plays old records on the phonograph and escapes to the glass menagerie; the typing table, the typewriter, and the typewriter chart represent Amanda's goal for Laura—a goal that Laura rejects.

The screen image of "blue roses," which we find out was Jim's misunderstanding of "pleurosis," is both poignant and humorous.

9. Student answers will vary. But most students will agree that Laura's shyness makes her easy to identify with, since most people have experienced shyness at one point or another in their lives.

Laura. The operetta the senior class put on. He had a wonderful voice and we sat across the aisle from each other Mondays, Wednesdays, and Fridays in the Aud. Here he is with the silver cup for debating! See his grin?

Amanda *(absently).* He must have a jolly disposition.

Laura. He used to call me—Blue Roses.

[*Screen image:* Blue Roses.]

Amanda. Why did he call you such a name as that?

Laura. When I had that attack of pleurosis[5]—he asked me what was the matter when I came back. I said pleurosis—he thought that I said Blue Roses! So that's what he always called me after that. Whenever he saw me, he'd holler, "Hello, Blue Roses!" I didn't care for the girl that he went out with. Emily Meisenbach. Emily was the best-dressed girl at Soldan. She never struck me, though, as being sincere . . . It says in the Personal Section—they're engaged. That's—six years ago! They must be married by now.

Amanda. Girls that aren't cut out for business careers usually wind up married to some nice man. *(She gets up with a spark of revival.)* Sister, that's what you'll do!

[LAURA *utters a startled, doubtful laugh. She reaches quickly for a piece of glass.*]

Laura. But, Mother—

Amanda. Yes? *(She goes over to the photograph.)*

Laura *(in a tone of frightened apology).* I'm—crippled!

Amanda. Nonsense! Laura, I've told you never, never to use that word. Why, you're not crippled, you just have a little defect—hardly noticeable, even! When people have some slight disadvantage like that, they cultivate other things to make up for it—develop charm—and vivacity—and—*charm!* That's all you have to do! *(She turns again to the photograph.)* One thing your father had *plenty* of—was *charm!*

[*The scene fades out with music.*]

5. **pleurosis:** Laura means pleurisy, a lung infection.

Responding to the Play

Analyzing Scenes 1 and 2

Identifying Facts

1. Tom's opening speech sketches the social background of the play and introduces the main characters. What basic information does Tom provide in this speech about his family? About the gentleman caller? About the nature of the play itself?
2. In Scene 1, how do we know that there is tension among the family members? Who seems to cause the tension?
3. A play is put in motion by some element that upsets the situation at the beginning of the story. The new element here arrives in Scene 2. What is it? How does it upset the opening situation, and how does it set the play in motion?
4. In Scene 2, what does Laura say and do to reveal that she is "set apart" from the real world?
5. What is the significance of the "blue roses" that appear on the screen at the start of Scene 2?

Interpreting Meanings

6. At this point in the play, does Amanda seem to be a weak or a strong character? Does she arouse your sympathy, or do you think Williams wants you to dislike her? Explain.
7. How do we know that the boy in the yearbook was important to Laura? Why doesn't Amanda seem particularly interested in this young man?
8. In *The Glass Menagerie,* Tennessee Williams has created "theater poetry" by using various arts besides language. For example, he uses the two transparencies at the beginning of the play to enhance the idea that this is a memory play. Check through the stage directions and dialogue to find other uses of visual and sound effects which, combined with words, help to create "theater poetry." Do any of these effects add a touch of humor to the play?
9. Few people have Laura's specific physical handicap. Do you think most people can identify with her? Why or why not?

Supplementary Support Materials
1. Vocabulary Activity Worksheet (*CCB*)
2. Review and Response Worksheet: Symbolism (*CCB*)
3. Selection Test (*CCB*)

Developing Vocabulary
The following words from the play are tested in the Selection Test. (See also Vocabulary Activity Worksheet.)

fiasco	aghast
allusion	pinion
to precipitate	motley
to gesticulate	endowment
to jeopardize	importunately

Scene 3
Summary: In her campaign to improve Laura's chances at marriage, Amanda begins selling magazine subscriptions for extra income. Amanda and Tom quarrel violently over his reading habits and nightly movies. Tom hates his job at a shoe company warehouse and appears to want to write. The quarrel ends when he accidentally breaks some of Laura's glass animals.

Scene 3

Legend on screen: "After the fiasco—"

TOM *speaks from the fire escape landing.*

Tom. After the fiasco at Rubicam's Business College, the idea of getting a gentleman caller for Laura began to play a more and more important part in Mother's calculations. It became an obsession. Like some archetype of the universal unconscious,[1] the image of the gentleman caller haunted our small apartment. . . .

[*Screen image:* A young man at the door of a house with flowers.]

An evening at home rarely passed without some allusion to this image, this specter, this hope. . . . Even when he wasn't mentioned, his presence hung in Mother's preoccupied look and in my sister's frightened, apologetic manner—hung like a sentence passed upon the Wingfields!

Mother was a woman of action as well as words. She began to take logical steps in the planned direction. Late that winter and in the early spring—realizing that extra money would be needed to properly feather the nest and plume the bird—she conducted a vigorous campaign on the telephone, roping in subscribers to one of those magazines for matrons called *The Homemaker's Companion,* the type of journal that features the serialized sublimations of ladies of letters who think in terms of delicate cuplike breasts, slim, tapering waists, rich, creamy thighs, eyes like wood smoke in autumn, fingers that soothe and caress like strains of music, bodies as powerful as Etruscan sculpture.

[*Screen image:* The cover of a glamor magazine.]

[AMANDA *enters with the telephone on a long extension cord. She is spotlighted in the dim stage.*]

Amanda. Ida Scott? This is Amanda Wingfield! We *missed* you at the D.A.R. last Monday! I said to myself: She's probably suffering with that sinus condition! How is that sinus condition? Horrors! Heaven have a mercy!—You're a Christian martyr, yes, that's what you are, a Christian martyr! Well, I just now happened to notice that your subscription to the *Companion*'s about to expire! Yes, it expires with the next issue, honey!—just when that wonderful new serial by Bessie Mae Hopper is getting off to such an exciting start. Oh, honey, it's something that you can't miss! You remember how *Gone with the Wind* took everybody by storm? You simply couldn't go out if you hadn't read it. All everybody *talked* was Scarlett O'Hara. Well, this is a book that critics already compare to *Gone with the Wind.* It's the *Gone with the Wind* of the post-World-War generation!—What?—Burning?—Oh, honey, don't let them burn, go take a look in the oven and I'll hold the wire! Heavens—I think she's hung up!

[*The scene dims out.*]

[*Legend on screen:* "You think I'm in love with Continental Shoemakers?"]

[*Before the lights come up again, the violent voices of* TOM *and* AMANDA *are heard. They are quarreling behind the portieres. In front of them stands* LAURA *with clenched hands and panicky expression. A clear pool of light is on her figure throughout this scene.*]

Tom. What in hell am I—
Amanda *(shrilly).* Don't you use that—
Tom. —supposed to do!
Amanda. —expression! Not in my—
Tom. Ohhh!
Amanda. —presence! Have you gone out of your senses?
Tom. I have, that's true, *driven* out!
Amanda. What is the matter with you, you—big—big—IDIOT!
Tom. Look!—I've got *no thing,* no single thing—
Amanda. Lower your voice!
Tom. —in my life here that I can call my OWN! Everything is—
Amanda. Stop that shouting!
Tom. Yesterday you confiscated my books! You had the nerve to—
Amanda. I took that horrible novel back to the library—yes! That hideous book by that insane Mr. Lawrence.[2]

1. **archetype of the universal unconscious**: an image common to all people, one that has persisted in the human unconscious down through the ages.

2. **Mr. Lawrence**: D. H. Lawrence (1885–1930), an English novelist and poet, whose writing was once considered shockingly sexual.

A. Stage Directions

? On the basis of Tom's reading habits and these stage directions, what career does Tom seem to dream of? (He may want to be a writer.) Does he appear to do much writing at home? (The stage directions specify many manuscripts, but the conversation suggests that he spends his nights as well as his working hours out of the house.)

B. Symbols

At the beginning of the scene, Tom explained that the image of the gentleman caller had begun to haunt the apartment. Here Tom points to his father's picture, a prop since the beginning of the play.

? How could the right "gentleman caller" make possible the dreams of all three Wingfields? (Security for Amanda, acceptance for Laura, freedom for Tom) What, then, does "the image of the gentleman caller" stand for? (Happiness, comfort, freedom) Does the picture of Tom and Laura's father also carry symbolic meaning? (For Tom it seems to symbolize freedom from a duty-bound existence. For Amanda it symbolizes desertion. It is not clear whether the picture carries symbolic meaning for Laura.)

C. Responding

? Why does Tom set off on such an elaborate, false tale? (Amanda accuses him of bad behavior, and having had all he can take, he deliberately exaggerates her suspicions, an oratorical technique known as *reductio ad absurdum*, extending an idea to ridiculous limits.)

[TOM *laughs wildly.*]

I cannot control the output of diseased minds or people who cater to them—

[TOM *laughs still more wildly.*]

BUT I WON'T ALLOW SUCH FILTH BROUGHT INTO MY HOUSE! No, no, no, no, no!

Tom. House, house! Who pays rent on it, who makes a slave of himself to—

Amanda *(fairly screeching).* Don't you DARE to—

Tom. No, no, *I* mustn't say things! *I've* got to just—

Amanda. Let me tell you—

Tom. I don't want to hear any more!

[*He tears the portieres open. The dining-room area is lit with a turgid smoky red glow. Now we see* AMANDA; *her hair is in metal curlers and she is wearing a very old bathrobe, much too large for her slight figure, a relic of the faithless* MR. WINGFIELD. *The upright typewriter now stands on the drop-leaf table, along with a wild disarray of manuscripts. The quarrel was probably precipitated by* AMANDA*'s interruption of* TOM*'s creative labor. A chair lies overthrown on the floor. Their gesticulating shadows are cast on the ceiling by the fiery glow.*] A

Amanda. You *will* hear more, you—

Tom. No, I won't hear more, I'm going out!

Amanda. You come right back in—

Tom. Out, out, out! Because I'm—

Amanda. Come back here, Tom Wingfield! I'm not through talking to you!

Tom. Oh, go—

Laura *(desperately).* Tom!

Amanda. You're going to listen, and no more insolence from you! I'm at the end of my patience!

[*He comes back toward her.*]

Tom. What do you think I'm at? Aren't I supposed to have any patience to reach the end of, Mother? I know, I know. It seems unimportant to you, what I'm *doing*—what I *want* to do—having a little *difference* between them! You don't think that—

Amanda. I think you've been doing things that you're ashamed of. That's why you act like this. I don't believe that you go every night to the movies. Nobody goes to the movies night after night. Nobody in their right minds goes to the movies as often as you pretend to. People don't go to the movies at nearly midnight, and movies don't let out at two A.M. Come in stumbling. Muttering to yourself like a maniac! You get three hours' sleep and then go to work. Oh, I can picture the way you're doing down there. Moping, doping, because you're in no condition.

Tom *(wildly).* No, I'm in no condition!

Amanda. What right have you got to jeopardize your job? Jeopardize the security of us all? How do you think we'd manage if you were—

Tom. Listen! You think I'm crazy about the *warehouse? (He bends fiercely toward her slight figure.)* You think I'm in love with the Continental Shoemakers? You think I want to spend fifty-five *years* down there in that—*celotex interior!* with—*fluorescent—tubes!* Look! I'd rather somebody picked up a crowbar and battered out my brains—than go back mornings! I *go!* Every time you come in yelling that damn *"Rise and Shine!" "Rise and Shine!"* I say to myself, "How *lucky dead* people are!" But I get up. I *go!* For sixty-five dollars a month I give up all that I dream of doing and being *ever!* and you say self—*self's* all I ever think of. Why, listen, if self is what I thought of, Mother, I'd be where he is—GONE! *(He points to his father's picture.)* As far as the system of transportation reaches! *(He starts past her. She grabs his arm.)* Don't grab at me, Mother! B

Amanda. Where are you going?

Tom. I'm going to the *movies!*

Amanda. I don't believe that lie!

[TOM *crouches toward her, overtowering her tiny figure. She backs away, gasping.*]

Tom. I'm going to opium dens! Yes, opium dens, dens of vice and criminals' hangouts, Mother. I've joined the Hogan Gang, I'm a hired assassin, I carry a tommy gun in a violin case! I run a string of cat houses in the Valley! They call me Killer, Killer Wingfield, I'm leading a double-life, a simple, honest warehouse worker by day, by night a dynamic *czar* of the *underworld, Mother.* I go to gambling casinos, I spin away fortunes on the roulette table! I wear a patch over one eye and a false mustache, sometimes I put on green whiskers. On those occasions they call me—*El Diablo!* Oh, I could tell you many things to make you sleepless! My enemies plan to dynamite this place. They're going to blow us all sky-high some night! I'll be glad, very happy, and so will you! You'll C

A. Characterization

? Why do Laura's glass animals mean so much to her? (Answers will vary. Perhaps they are the only thing she personally owns, she may simply love their beauty, or she may see in their fragility a symbol of her own.) How do her reactions show that she in some way identifies with her glass animals? (She "cries out as if wounded" and hides her face.) How can you tell that Tom would never deliberately harm Laura or her collection? (The shock of breaking her glass brings him to a halt. He has no glib comment as he drops to his knees to start picking up the pieces.)

go up, up on a broomstick, over Blue Mountain with seventeen gentlemen callers! You ugly—babbling old—*witch. . . . (He goes through a series of violent, clumsy movements, seizing his overcoat, lunging to the door, pulling it fiercely open. The women watch him,* *aghast. His arm catches in the sleeve of the coat as he struggles to pull it on. For a moment he is* *pinioned* *by the bulky garment. With an outraged groan he tears the coat off again, splitting the shoulder of it, and* A *hurls it across the room. It strikes against the shelf of Laura's glass collection, and there is a tinkle of shattering glass. Laura cries out as if wounded.)*

[*Music.*]

[*Screen legend:* "The Glass Menagerie."]

Laura *(shrilly). My glass!*—menagerie. . . . *(She covers her face and turns away.)*

[*But* AMANDA *is still stunned and stupefied by the "ugly witch" so that she barely notices this occurrence. Now she recovers her speech.*]

Amanda *(in an awful voice).* I won't speak to you—until you apologize!

[*She crosses through the portieres and draws them together behind her.* TOM *is left with* LAURA. LAURA *clings weakly to the mantel with her face averted.* TOM *stares at her stupidly for a moment. Then he crosses to the shelf. He drops awkwardly on his knees to collect the fallen glass, glancing at* LAURA *as if he would speak but couldn't.*]

["The Glass Menagerie" music steals in as the scene dims out.]

"You ugly—babbling old—witch . . ."

Scene 4 Summary: Laura waits up for Tom, who tells her about the movies and a magic show. The next morning, Tom apologizes to Amanda because Laura asks him to do so. Amanda again nags Tom about his "selfishness," reveals that she knows he is corresponding with the Merchant Marine, and asks him to find a gentleman caller for Laura. Tom reluctantly agrees.

Scene 4

The interior of the apartment is dark. There is a faint light in the alley. A deep-voiced bell in a church is tolling the hour of five.

TOM *appears at the top of the alley. After each solemn boom of the bell in the tower, he shakes a little noisemaker or rattle as if to express the tiny spasm of man in contrast to the sustained power and dignity of the Almighty. This and the unsteadiness of his advance make it evident that he has been drinking. As he climbs the few steps to the fire escape landing light steals up inside.* LAURA *appears in the front room in a nightdress. She notices that* TOM*'s bed is empty.* TOM *fishes in his pockets for his door key, removes a motley assortment of articles in the search, including a shower of movie ticket stubs and an empty bottle. At last he finds the key, but just as he is about to insert it, it slips from his fingers. He strikes a match and crouches below the door.*

Tom *(bitterly).* One crack—and it falls through!

[LAURA *opens the door.*]

Laura. Tom! Tom, what are you doing?
Tom. Looking for a door key.
Laura. Where have you been all this time?
Tom. I have been to the movies.
Laura. All this time at the movies?
Tom. There was a very long program. There was a Garbo picture and a Mickey Mouse and a travelogue and a newsreel and a preview of coming attractions. And there was an organ solo and a collection for the Milk Fund—simultaneously—which ended up in a terrible fight between a fat lady and an usher!
Laura *(innocently).* Did you have to stay through everything?
Tom. Of course! And, oh, I forgot! There was a big stage show! The headliner on this stage show was Malvolio the Magician. He performed wonderful tricks, many of them, such as pouring water back and forth between pitchers. First it turned to wine and then it turned to beer and then it turned to whisky. I know it was whisky it finally turned into because he needed somebody to come up out of the audience to help him, and I came up—both shows! It was Kentucky Straight Bourbon. A very generous fellow, he gave souvenirs. *(He pulls from his back pocket a shimmering rainbow-colored scarf.)* He gave me this. This is his magic scarf. You can have it, Laura. You wave it over a canary cage and you get a bowl of goldfish. You wave it over the goldfish bowl and they fly away canaries. . . . But the wonderfullest trick of all was the coffin trick. We nailed him into a coffin and he got out of the coffin without removing one nail. *(He has come inside.)* There is a trick that would come in handy for me—get me out of this two-by-four situation! *(He flops onto the bed and starts removing his shoes.)*
Laura. Tom—shhh!
Tom. What're you shushing me for?
Laura. You'll wake up Mother.
Tom. Goody, goody! Pay 'er back for all those "Rise an' Shines." *(He lies down, groaning.)* You know it don't take much intelligence to get yourself into a nailed-up coffin, Laura. But who ever got himself out of one without removing one nail?

(As if in answer, the father's grinning photograph lights up. The scene dims out.)

B

[*Immediately following, the church bell is heard striking six. At the sixth stroke the alarm clock goes off in* AMANDA*'s room, and after a few moments we hear her calling: "Rise and Shine! Rise and Shine!* LAURA*, go tell your brother to rise and shine!"*]

Tom *(sitting up slowly).* I'll rise—but I won't shine.

[*The light increases.*]

Amanda. Laura, tell your brother his coffee is ready.

[LAURA *slips into the front room.*]

Laura. Tom!—It's nearly seven. Don't make Mother nervous.

[*He stares at her stupidly.*]

(Beseechingly). Tom, speak to Mother this morning. Make up with her, apologize, speak to her!
Tom. She won't to me. It's her that started not speaking.
Laura. If you just say you're sorry she'll start speaking.
Tom. Her not speaking—is that such a tragedy?
Laura. Please—please!
Amanda *(calling from the kitchenette).* Laura, are you going to do what I asked you to do, or do I have to get dressed and go out myself?

A. Characterization

Do you take Tom's entire description of his evening as literal fact, or do you think he invents some of it to entertain Laura? What internal clues suggest that he may have been barhopping during the evening? Back up your overall opinion with facts or inferences from this and earlier scenes of the play. (Opinions will vary. A clue in this scene is an apparent need to account for liquor on his breath.)

B. Analogy

Explain the analogy Tom sees between his life and "the wonderfullest trick of all," the coffin trick. What is Tom's coffin? (His dutiful job and life, perhaps even the apartment itself) What are the nails? (Answers will vary—duty, guilt, love for his mother and sister.) Who is the magician, and how can the trick be done? (The magician will have to be Tom himself; his father's method—desertion—may be the method that occurs to him.)

READING CHECK TEST: SCENES 3–4

1. Amanda sells magazine subscriptions by telephone. *True*
2. Tom escapes his troubles by going to the movies. *True*
3. Amanda angrily breaks Laura's glass ornaments. *False*
4. Amanda nags Tom to provide for Laura's future. *True*
5. Amanda praises Tom for his totally unselfish concern for her needs and Laura's. *False*

A. Responding
Read aloud the stage directions from Laura's exit on the dangerous fire escape to Tom's words, "Mother, I—I apologize, Mother." If possible, have two students role-play the scene, getting into the feel of it by imagining a time when they needed to make up after having shouted harmful things in the heat of an argument.

? How do the movements and actions of Tom and Amanda serve to convey emotion to the viewer? What is Tom feeling? What is Amanda feeling? Is Tom doing the right thing by apologizing? Explain. Do you think things will be better between Tom and Amanda after this, worse, or about the same? Why? (Students may note that Tom is the only person Amanda can rely on. She depends on him and resents that. Tom feels trapped. He wants to help his mother but he also wants his life. The situation will probably not change.)

Laura. Going, going—soon as I get on my coat!

[*She pulls on a shapeless felt hat with a nervous, jerky movement, pleadingly glancing at* TOM. *She rushes awkwardly for her coat. The coat is one of* AMANDA'*s, inaccurately made-over, the sleeves too short for* LAURA.]

Butter and what else?
Amanda *(entering from the kitchenette).* Just butter. Tell them to charge it.
Laura. Mother, they make such faces when I do that.
Amanda. Sticks and stones can break our bones, but the expression on Mr. Garfinkel's face won't harm us! Tell your brother his coffee is getting cold.
Laura *(at the door).* Do what I asked you, will you, will you, Tom?

[*He looks sullenly away.*]

Amanda. Laura, go now or just don't go at all!
Laura *(rushing out).* Going—going!

[*A second later she cries out.* TOM *springs up and crosses to the door.* TOM *opens the door.*]

Tom. Laura?
Laura. I'm all right. I slipped, but I'm all right.
Amanda *(peering anxiously after her).* If anyone breaks a leg on those fire-escape steps, the landlord ought to be sued for every cent he possesses! *(She shuts the door. Now she remembers she isn't speaking to* TOM *and returns to the other room.)*

[*As* TOM *comes listlessly for his coffee, she turns her back to him and stands rigidly facing the window on the gloomy gray vault of the areaway. Its light on her face with its aged but childish features is cruelly sharp, satirical as a Daumier*[1] *print.*]

[*The music of "Ave Maria," is heard softly.*]

A [TOM *glances sheepishly but sullenly at her averted figure and slumps at the table. The coffee is scalding hot; he sips it and gasps and spits it back in the cup. At his gasp,* AMANDA *catches her breath and half turns. Then she catches herself and turns back to the window.* TOM *blows on his coffee, glancing sidewise at his mother. She clears her throat.* TOM *clears his. He starts to rise, sinks back down again, scratches his head, clears his throat again.* AMANDA *coughs.* TOM *raises his cup in both hands to blow on it, his eyes staring over the rim of it at his mother for several moments. Then he slowly sets the cup down and awkwardly and hesitantly rises from the chair.*]

Tom *(hoarsely).* Mother. I—I apologize, Mother.

[AMANDA *draws a quick, shuddering breath. Her face works grotesquely. She breaks into childlike tears.*]

I'm sorry for what I said, for everything that I said, I didn't mean it.
Amanda *(sobbingly).* My devotion has made me a witch and so I make myself hateful to my children!
Tom. *No,* you *don't.*
Amanda. I worry so much, don't sleep, it makes me nervous!
Tom *(gently).* I understand that.
Amanda. I've had to put up a solitary battle all these years. But you're my right-hand bower![2] Don't fall down, don't fail!
Tom *(gently).* I try, Mother.
Amanda *(with great enthusiasm).* Try and you will *succeed!* (*The notion makes her breathless.)* Why, you—you're just *full* of natural endowments! Both of my children—they're *unusual* children! Don't you think I know it? I'm so—*proud!* Happy and—feel I've—so much to be thankful for but—promise me one thing, son!
Tom. What, Mother?
Amanda. Promise, son, you'll—never be a drunkard!
Tom *(turns to her grinning).* I will never be a drunkard, Mother.
Amanda. That's what frightened me so, that you'd be drinking! Eat a bowl of Purina!
Tom. Just coffee, Mother.
Amanda. Shredded wheat biscuit?
Tom. No. No, Mother, just coffee.
Amanda. You can't put in a day's work on an empty stomach. You've got ten minutes—don't gulp! Drinking too-hot liquids makes cancer of the stomach. . . . Put cream in.
Tom. No, thank you.
Amanda. To cool it.
Tom. No! No, thank you, I want it black.
Amanda. I know, but it's not good for you. We have to do all that we can to build ourselves up.

1. **Daumier** (dō·myā'): Honoré Daumier (1809–1879), a French artist and caricaturist.

2. **bower**: in certain card games, the two highest cards. The jack of trumps is the right bower, therefore the main support.

ANALYZING SCENES 3 AND 4
Identifying Facts
1. The conflict is between Amanda and Tom.

Amanda begins nagging Tom about the lighting and about sitting up straight. Just as in the scene at the dinner table, she chides Tom as if he were a child. Despite repeated reminders from Tom and from Laura that Tom is trying to write, nothing stops Amanda. Tom explodes in anger, accuses her of confiscating his library books, and ends by calling her an "ugly babbling old witch." Amanda accuses Tom of being impudent, of jeopardizing his job and their security by getting too little sleep, and of lying about where he goes at night.

2. Laura escapes by polishing her glass menagerie, by listening to old phonograph records, and by visiting the zoo, the art museum, and the plant house.

Tom uses movies and drinking as his means of escape. Presumably, he also escapes through his writing, but so far we have no indication of how serious a writer he is, or of how much time he spends writing.

3. Laura has only two lines in this scene *(Answers continue on next page.)*

A. Responding
? Analyze pages 782–784 carefully. On what points can you agree with or sympathize with Amanda? (Perhaps her genuine concern for Laura, her assertion that these days everyone has to sacrifice, her fear that Tom may hurt her as his father did, and her gutsiness at getting back on the telephone day after day to sell magazines people do not seem to want) Where do you sympathize with Tom? (Perhaps at his being misunderstood, at his need for relief from a hated job, or at his humorous sarcasm when pushed too much, as in "I like a lot of adventure" or his tale of involvement in the criminal underworld) What new information is revealed about Laura? (She is two years older than Tom, making her shyness seem more unnatural, even neurotic.) What new information is revealed about Tom? (He is corresponding with the Merchant Marine.)

In these trying times we live in, all that we have to cling to is—each other. . . . That's why it's so important to—Tom, I—I sent out your sister so I could discuss something with you. If you hadn't spoken I would have spoken to you. (*She sits down.*)
Tom (*gently*). What is it, Mother, that you want to discuss?
Amanda. *Laura!*

[TOM *puts his cup down slowly.*]

[*Legend on screen:* "Laura." *Music: "The Glass Menagerie."*]

Tom. —Oh.—Laura . . .
Amanda (*touching his sleeve*). You know how Laura is. So quiet but—still water runs deep! She notices things and I think she—broods about them.

[TOM *looks up.*]

A few days ago I came in and she was crying.
Tom. What about?
Amanda. You.
Tom. Me?
Amanda. She has an idea that you're not happy here.
Tom. What gave her that idea?
Amanda. What gives her any idea? However, you do act strangely. I—I'm not criticizing, understand *that!* I know your ambitions do not lie in the warehouse, that like everybody in the whole wide world—you've had to—make sacrifices, but—Tom—Tom—life's not easy, it calls for—Spartan endurance! There's so many things in my heart that I cannot describe to you! I've never told you but I—*loved* your father. . . .
Tom (*gently*). I know that, Mother.
Amanda. And you—when I see you taking after his ways! Staying out late—and—well, you *had* been drinking the night you were in that—terrifying condition! Laura says that you hate the apartment and that you go out nights to get away from it! Is that true, Tom?
Tom. No. You say there's so much in your heart that you can't describe to me. That's true of me, too. There's so much in my heart that I can't describe to *you!* So let's respect each other's—
Amanda. But, why—*why,* Tom—are you always so *restless?* Where do you *go* to, nights?
Tom. I—go to the movies.
Amanda. Why do you go to the movies so much, Tom?
Tom. I go to the movies because—I like adventure. Adventure is something I don't have much of at work, so I go to the movies.
Amanda. But, Tom, you go to the movies *entirely* too *much!*
Tom. I like a lot of adventure.

[AMANDA *looks baffled, then hurt. As the familiar inquisition resumes,* TOM *becomes hard and impatient again.* AMANDA *slips back into her querulous attitude toward him.*]

[*Image on screen:* A sailing vessel with Jolly Roger.]

Amanda. Most young men find adventure in their careers.
Tom. Then most young men are not employed in a warehouse.
Amanda. The world is full of young men employed in warehouses and offices and factories.
Tom. Do all of them find adventure in their careers?
Amanda. They do or they do without it! Not everybody has a craze for adventure.
Tom. Man is by instinct a lover, a hunter, a fighter, and none of those instincts are given much play at the warehouse!
Amanda. Man is by instinct! Don't quote instinct to me! Instinct is something that people have got away from! It belongs to animals! Christian adults don't want it!
Tom. What do Christian adults want, then, Mother?
Amanda. Superior things! Things of the mind and the spirit! Only animals have to satisfy instincts! Surely your aims are somewhat higher than theirs! Than monkeys—pigs—
Tom. I reckon they're not.
Amanda. You're joking. However, that isn't what I wanted to discuss.
Tom (*rising*). I haven't much time.
Amanda (*pushing his shoulders*). Sit down.
Tom. You want me to punch in red at the warehouse, Mother?
Amanda. You have five minutes. I want to talk about Laura.

[*Screen legend:* "Plans and Provisions."]

Tom. All right! What about Laura?
Amanda. We have to be making some plans and provisions for her. She's older than you, two years, and nothing has happened. She just drifts

A

(Continued from previous page.)
and plays no part in the argument. Her first line occurs at the beginning of the scene when she cautions Amanda not to bother Tom because he is trying to write. Her second line, at the end of the scene, expresses her grief at the breaking of the glass animals.
4. Amanda asks Tom to find a nice young man for Laura.

Interpreting Meanings
5. Most students will agree that our sympathies are with Tom. Amanda is offensive in treating Tom like a small child, and she is annoyingly intrusive when he is trying to write. Even when Tom asks her politely to stop interrupting, she does not let up. We cannot, however, feel that Amanda is evil or despicable, since she does her best to cope with her difficult life and has obviously succeeded in raising her children to adulthood. Also, her nagging of Tom and the plans she makes for Laura are motivated by a desire for her children's well-being.
6. Laura is at ease with Tom, and not afraid of what he will say or do. Unlike Amanda, Laura trusts Tom and believes his stories about where he has been. Also, she seems considerate of Tom's

"Down at the warehouse, aren't there some—nice young men?"

along doing nothing. It frightens me terribly how she just drifts along.
Tom. I guess she's the type that people call home girls.
Amanda. There's no such type, and if there is, it's a pity! That is unless the home is hers, with a husband!
Tom. What?
Amanda. Oh, I can see the handwriting on the wall as plain as I see the nose in front of my face! It's terrifying! More and more you remind me of your father! He was out all hours without explanation—Then *left! Goodbye!* And me with the bag to hold. I saw that letter you got from the Merchant Marine. I know what you're dreaming of. I'm not standing here blindfolded. *(She pauses.)* Very well, then. Then *do* it! But not till there's somebody to take your place.
Tom. What do you mean?
Amanda. I mean that as soon as Laura has got somebody to take care of her, married, a home of her own, independent—why, then you'll be free to go wherever you please, on land, on sea, whichever way the wind blows you! But until that time you've got to look out for your sister. I don't say me because I'm old and don't matter! I say for your sister because she's young and dependent.

I put her in business college—a dismal failure! Frightened her so it made her sick at the stomach. I took her over to the Young People's League at the church. Another fiasco. She spoke to nobody, nobody spoke to her. Now all she does is fool with needs (cautioning Amanda that he is trying to write), and she is not harshly judgmental of his actions. Toward Amanda, on the other hand, Laura seems dependent and fearful.

The moment at the end of Scene 3, when Tom accidently smashes Laura's glass collection, reveals Tom's depth of feeling for Laura.

7. To Amanda, the photo is a constant reminder of the wrong choice she made for a husband—when she might have had so many other successful men. The photo reminds Amanda, as well, of the reason for her finding herself in such difficult circumstances—her husband abandoned her and the children. Tom is surely angry at his father, because if the father had not abandoned the family, Tom would not be trapped as he is. The photo is also a constant reminder to Tom of what seems to be the only way out of his "trap": abandoning the family.

The possibility of Tom's leaving—just like his father—constitutes a threat to the survival of Amanda and Laura, for the family barely survives with Tom's salary.

8. In Scene 1, the bickering between Tom and Amanda has prepared us for conflict and tension between them, although in the opening scene this tension is on a low emotional level. Scene 1 also shows us Amanda treating Tom as if he were a child, which she does at the beginning of Scene 3. Scene 2 also helps us to understand Amanda's anxiety about the future—her worries about who will provide for Laura and for her.

those pieces of glass and play those worn-out records. What kind of a life is that for a girl to lead?

Tom. What can I do about it?

Amanda. Overcome selfishness! Self, self, self is all that you ever think of!

[TOM *springs up and crosses to get his coat. It is ugly and bulky. He pulls on a cap with earmuffs.*]

Where is your muffler? Put your wool muffler on!

[*He snatches it angrily from the closet, tosses it around his neck and pulls both ends tight.*]

Tom! I haven't said what I had in mind to ask you.

Tom. I'm too late to—

Amanda *(catching his arm—very importunately; then shyly).* Down at the warehouse, aren't there some—nice young men?

Tom. No!

Amanda. There *must* be—*some* . . .

Tom. Mother—*(He gestures.)*

Amanda. Find out one that's clean-living—doesn't drink and ask him out for sister!

Tom. What?

Amanda. For *sister!* To *meet!* Get *acquainted!*

Tom *(stamping to the door).* Oh, my *go-osh!*

Amanda. Will you?

[*He opens the door. She says, imploringly:*]

Will you?

[*He starts down the fire escape.*]

Will you? *Will* you dear?

Tom *(calling back).* Yes!

[AMANDA *closes the door hesitantly and with a troubled but faintly hopeful expression.*]

[*Screen image:* The cover of a glamor magazine.]

[*The spotlight picks up* AMANDA *at the phone.*]

Amanda. Ella Cartwright? This is Amanda Wingfield! How are you, honey? How is that kidney condition?

[*There is a five-second pause.*]

Horrors!

[*There is another pause.*]

You're a Christian martyr, yes, honey, that's what you are, a Christian martyr! Well, I just now happened to notice in my little red book that your subscription to the *Companion* has just run out! I knew that you wouldn't want to miss out on the wonderful serial starting in this new issue. It's by Bessie Mae Hopper, the first thing she's written since *Honeymoon for Three*. Wasn't that a strange and interesting story? Well, this one is even lovelier, I believe. It has a sophisticated, society background. It's all about the horsey set on Long Island!

[*The light fades out.*] A

A. Predicting Outcomes

? Suppose that Tom does invite a male friend home. How will Laura act? How will Amanda act? Will the caller be aware of the expectations aroused by his coming? What problems may arise? (Laura will be shy and silent. Amanda will be talkative. The male friend might feel uncomfortable and pressured.)

Responding to the Play

Analyzing Scenes 3 and 4

Identifying Facts

1. In Scene 2, we saw that Amanda was in **conflict** with Laura. Who is in conflict in Scene 3? What starts the conflict, and what is it about?
2. Each of the Wingfields ecapes from unpleasant reality into a comforting, private world. In Scene 1, Amanda escapes from her present circumstances by remembering and talking about her past youth, her beauty, and her romantic successes. How does Laura escape the real world? What does Tom do to escape from his unhappiness?
3. What part does Laura play in the angry argument between Tom and Amanda?
4. What does Amanda ask Tom to do?

Interpreting Meanings

5. In the conflict between Tom and Amanda in Scene 3, which character do you sympathize with, and why? What does Williams want us to feel about Amanda?
6. How is Laura's relationship with Tom different from her relationship with Amanda? How can we tell that Tom is truly fond of Laura?
7. Amanda often refers to her absent husband, and his grinning picture is highlighted at various points during the play. What does the photograph represent to Amanda? To Tom? How is the photo a constant threat to Amanda and Laura's survival?
8. The outburst of anger that ends Scene 3 marks the emotional peak of the play so far. How has the playwright prepared us for Tom's anger and Amanda's accusations?

SUPPLEMENTARY SUPPORT MATERIALS
1. Vocabulary Activity Worksheet (*CCB*)
2. Review and Response Worksheet: Suspense (*CCB*)
3. Selection Test (*CCB*)

DEVELOPING VOCABULARY
The following words from the play are tested in the Selection Test. (See also Vocabulary Activity Worksheet.)

annunciation, unobtrusive, imminent, incandescent, supercilious, tribulations

A. Symbolism
? What other uses of the fire escape do you recall? (Amanda enters from it in Scene 2, page 774. In Scene 4 Tom uses it for his entrance, page 781; and in Scene 4 Laura trips on it, page 782.) What does this clumsy manner of access suggest about the apartment? (It is located in a poorly planned building, probably not in the best part of town.) How does the fire escape also function as a symbol of being trapped, or of escape? (For Tom it is a route to the outer world. For Laura it is an escape *from* the world; she trips on it when she must use it to go out.)

B. Setting
Tennessee Williams briefly attended Washington University in St. Louis, Missouri, but as one assumes to be true also of his character, Tom Wingfield, Williams preferred to put a greater distance between himself and his family.

Scene 5

Legend on the screen: "Annunciation."

Music is heard as the light slowly comes on.

It is early dusk of a spring evening. Supper has just been finished in the Wingfield apartment. AMANDA *and* LAURA, *in light-colored dresses, are removing dishes from the table in the dining room, which is shadowy, their movements formalized almost as a dance or ritual, their moving forms as* A *pale and silent as moths.* TOM, *in white shirt and trousers, rises from the table and crosses toward the fire escape.*

Amanda *(as he passes her).* Son, will you do me a favor?
Tom. What?
Amanda. Comb your hair! You look so pretty when your hair is combed!

[TOM *slouches on the sofa with the evening paper. Its enormous headline reads: "Franco*[1] *Triumphs."*]

There is only one respect in which I would like you to emulate your father.
Tom. What respect is that?
Amanda. The care he always took of his appearance. He never allowed himself to look untidy.

[*He throws down the paper and crosses to the fire escape.*]

Where are you going?
Tom. I'm going out to smoke.
Amanda. You smoke too much. A pack a day at fifteen cents a pack. How much would that amount to in a month? Thirty times fifteen is how much, Tom? Figure it out and you will be as- B tounded at what you could save. Enough to give you a night-school course in accounting at Washington U.! Just think what a wonderful thing that would be for you, son!

[TOM *is unmoved by the thought.*]

Tom. I'd rather smoke. *(He steps out on the landing, letting the screen door slam.)*
Amanda *(sharply).* I know! That's the tragedy of it. . . . *(Alone, she turns to look at her husband's picture.)*

[*Dance music: "The World Is Waiting for the Sunrise!"*]

Tom *(to the audience).* Across the alley from us was the Paradise Dance Hall. On evenings in Spring the windows and doors were open and the music came outdoors. Sometimes the lights were turned out except for a large glass sphere that hung from the ceiling. It would turn slowly about and filter the dusk with delicate rainbow colors. Then the orchestra played a waltz or a tango, something that had a slow and sensuous rhythm. Couples would come outside, to the relative privacy of the alley. You could see them kissing behind ash pits and telephone poles. This was the compensation for lives that passed like mine, without any change or adventure. Adventure and change were imminent in this year. They were waiting around the corner for all these kids. Suspended in the mist over Berchtesgaden, caught in the folds of Chamberlain's umbrella.[2] In Spain there was Guernica![3] But here there was only hot swing music and liquor, dance halls, bars, and movies, and sex that hung in the gloom like a chandelier and flooded the world with brief, deceptive rainbows. . . . All the world was waiting for bombardments!

[AMANDA *turns from the picture and comes outside.*]

Amanda *(sighing).* A fire escape landing's a poor excuse for a porch. *(She spreads a newspaper on a step and sits down, gracefully and demurely as if she were settling into a swing on a Mississippi veranda.)* What are you looking at?
Tom. The moon.
Amanda. Is there a moon this evening?
Tom. It's rising over Garfinkel's Delicatessen.
Amanda. So it is! A little silver slipper of a moon. Have you made a wish on it yet?
Tom. Um-hum.

1. **Franco:** General Francisco Franco, who led the rebel army in the Spanish Civil War and later became Fascist dictator of Spain.

2. **Berchtesgaden . . . Chamberlain's umbrella:** Neville Chamberlain, Britain's Prime Minister, always carried a large, black umbrella. He visited Adolf Hitler at his mountain retreat at Berchtesgaden, Germany, in 1938. At this meeting, the two statesmen agreed that Hitler would be given Czechoslovakia in exchange for a promise not to invade any more countries in Europe—a pledge that Hitler did not keep.
3. **Guernica** (ger·nē′kə): a small town in northern Spain which was fire-bombed by the Fascists during the Spanish Civil War.

Scene 5 Summary: Tom tells Amanda that James D. O'Connor, a clerk at the warehouse, is coming for dinner the following night. Amanda draws multiple inferences from these facts and from the man's name. In her imagination, she already has him marrying Laura. Tom goes out; Amanda calls Laura to wish upon the moon for happiness.

Amanda. What did you wish for?
Tom. That's a secret.
Amanda. A secret, huh? Well, I won't tell mine either. I will be just as mysterious as you.
Tom. I bet I can guess what yours is.
Amanda. Is my head so transparent?
Tom. You're not a sphinx.
Amanda. No, I don't have secrets. I'll tell you what I wished for on the moon. Success and happiness for my precious children! I wish for that whenever there's a moon, and when there isn't a moon, I wish for it, too.
Tom. I thought perhaps you wished for a gentleman caller.
Amanda. Why do you say that?
Tom. Don't you remember asking me to fetch one?
Amanda. I remember suggesting that it would be nice for your sister if you brought home some nice young man from the warehouse. I think that I've made that suggestion more than once.
Tom. Yes, you have made it repeatedly.
Amanda. Well?
Tom. We are going to have one.
Amanda. *What?*
Tom. A gentleman caller!

[*The annunciation is celebrated with music.*]

[AMANDA *rises.*]

[*Image on screen:* A caller with a bouquet.]

Amanda. You mean you have asked some nice young man to come over?
Tom. Yep. I've asked him to dinner.
Amanda. You really did?
Tom. I did!
Amanda. You did, and did he—*accept?*
Tom. He did!
Amanda. Well, well—well, well! That's—lovely!
Tom. I thought that you would be pleased.
Amanda. It's definite then?
Tom. Very definite.
Amanda. Soon?
Tom. Very soon.
Amanda. For heaven's sake, stop putting on and tell me some things, will you?
Tom. What things do you want me to tell you?
Amanda. *Naturally* I would like to know when he's *coming!*
Tom. He's coming tomorrow.
Amanda. *Tomorrow?*
Tom. Yep. Tomorrow.
Amanda. But, Tom!
Tom. Yes, Mother?
Amanda. Tomorrow gives me no time!
Tom. Time for what?
Amanda. Preparations! Why didn't you phone me at once, as soon as you asked him, the minute that he accepted? Then, don't you see, I could have been getting ready!
Tom. You don't have to make any fuss.
Amanda. Oh, Tom, Tom, Tom, of course I have to make a fuss! I want things nice, not sloppy! Not thrown together. I'll certainly have to do some fast thinking, won't I?
Tom. I don't see why you have to think at all.
Amanda. You just don't know. We can't have a gentleman caller in a pigsty! All my wedding silver has to be polished, the monogrammed table linen ought to be laundered! The windows have to be washed and fresh curtains put up. And how about clothes? We have to *wear* something, don't we?
Tom. Mother, this boy is no one to make a fuss over!
Amanda. Do you realize he's the first young man we've introduced to your sister? It's terrible, dreadful, disgraceful that poor little sister has never received a single gentleman caller! Tom, come inside! *(She opens the screen door.)*
Tom. What for?
Amanda. I want to ask you some things.
Tom. If you're going to make such a fuss, I'll call it off, I'll tell him not to come!
Amanda. You certainly won't do anything of the kind. Nothing offends people worse than broken engagements. It simply means I'll have to work like a Turk! We won't be brilliant, but we will pass inspection. Come on inside.

[TOM *follows her inside, groaning.*]

Sit down.
Tom. Any particular place you would like me to sit?
Amanda. Thank heavens I've got that new sofa! I'm also making payments on a floor lamp I'll have sent out! And put the chintz covers on, they'll brighten things up! Of course I'd hoped to have these walls re-papered. . . . What is the young man's name?
Tom. His name is O'Connor.
Amanda. That, of course, means fish—tomorrow is Friday! I'll have that salmon loaf—with Durkee's dressing! What does he do? He works at the warehouse? A

A. Allusion
Amanda assumes that an Irish name means the caller is Roman Catholic. Until many changes in church regulations in the 1960's, Roman Catholics were required to abstain from meat every Friday.

A. Irony

? What is ironic about Amanda's telling Tom to "talk sensibly"? (She is the one who has mapped out an entire future based on unrealistic views.)

B. Responding

? Where did you see these words earlier? (As a screen legend at the bottom of page 783 in Scene 4, just before Amanda harried Tom into agreeing to bring a young man home) How do they relate to this scene? (The scene is full of wildly extrapolated plans for the future as well as practical provisions for a dinner party.)

Tom. Of course! How else would I—

Amanda. Tom, he—doesn't drink?

Tom. Why do you ask me that?

Amanda. Your father *did!*

Tom. Don't get started on that!

Amanda. He *does* drink, then?

Tom. Not that I know of!

Amanda. Make sure, be certain! The last thing I want for my daughter's a boy who drinks!

Tom. Aren't you being a little bit premature? Mr. O'Connor has not yet appeared on the scene!

Amanda. But will tomorrow. To meet your sister, and what do I know about his character? Nothing! Old maids are better off than wives of drunkards!

Tom. Oh, my God!

Amanda. Be still!

Tom *(leaning forward to whisper).* Lots of fellows meet girls whom they don't marry!

A **Amanda.** Oh, talk sensibly, Tom—and don't be sarcastic! *(She has gotten a hairbrush.)*

Tom. What are you doing?

Amanda. I'm brushing that cowlick down! *(She attacks his hair with the brush.)* What is this young man's position at the warehouse?

Tom *(submitting grimly to the brush and the interrogation).* This young man's position is that of a shipping clerk, Mother.

Amanda. Sounds to me like a fairly responsible job, the sort of a job *you* would be in if you just had more *get-up.* What is his salary? Have you any idea?

Tom. I would judge it to be approximately eighty-five dollars a month.

Amanda. Well—not princely, but—

Tom. Twenty more than I make.

Amanda. Yes, how well I know! But for a family man, eighty-five dollars a month is not much more than you can just get by on. . . .

Tom. Yes, but Mr. O'Connor is not a family man.

Amanda. He might be, mightn't he? Some time in the future?

B **Tom.** I see. Plans and provisions.

Amanda. You are the only young man that I know of who ignores the fact that the future becomes the present, the present the past, and the past turns into everlasting regret if you don't plan for it!

Tom. I will think that over and see what I can make of it.

Amanda. Don't be supercilious with your mother! Tell me some more about this—what do you call him?

Tom. James D. O'Connor. The D. is for Delaney.

Amanda. Irish on *both* sides! *Gracious!* And doesn't drink?

Tom. Shall I call him up and ask him right this minute?

Amanda. The only way to find out about those things is to make discreet inquiries at the proper moment. When I was a girl in Blue Mountain and it was suspected that a young man drank, the girl whose attentions he had been receiving, if any girl *was,* would sometimes speak to the minister of his church, or rather her father would if her father was living, and sort of feel him out on the young man's character. That is the way such things are discreetly handled to keep a young woman from making a tragic mistake!

Tom. Then how did you happen to make a tragic mistake?

Amanda. That innocent look of your father's had everyone fooled! He *smiled*—the world was *enchanted!* No girl can do worse than put herself at the mercy of a handsome appearance! I hope that Mr. O'Connor is not too good-looking.

Tom. No, he's not too good-looking. He's covered with freckles and hasn't too much of a nose.

Amanda. He's not right-down homely, though?

Tom. Not right-down homely. Just medium homely, I'd say.

Amanda. Character's what to look for in a man.

Tom. That's what I've always said, Mother.

Amanda. You've never said anything of the kind and I suspect you would never give it a thought.

Tom. Don't be so suspicious of me.

Amanda. At least I hope he's the type that's up and coming.

Tom. I think he really goes in for self-improvement.

Amanda. What reason have you to think so?

Tom. He goes to night school.

Amanda *(beaming).* Splendid! What does he do, I mean study?

Tom. Radio engineering and public speaking!

Amanda. Then he has visions of being advanced in the world! Any young man who studies public speaking is aiming to have an executive job some day! And radio engineering? A thing for the future! Both of these facts are very illuminating. Those are the sort of things that a mother should know concerning any young man who comes to call on her daughter. Seriously or—not.

Tom. One little warning. He doesn't know about Laura. I didn't let on that we had dark ulterior

Scene 6 Summary: Amanda pretties up her daughter and the apartment. When Laura learns that the caller may be the Jim O'Connor she knew in high school, she becomes ill. Jim arrives with Tom; he is the same O'Connor. He is a cheerful young man who plans to progress in business. When he warns Tom that his job is in danger, Tom says it doesn't matter because he has joined the Union of Merchant Seamen. Called to the table for dinner, Laura must be excused because she really is sick with distress.

motives. I just said, why don't you come and have dinner with us? He said okay and that was the whole conversation.

Amanda. I bet it was! You're eloquent as an oyster. However, he'll know about Laura when he gets here. When he sees how lovely and sweet and pretty she is, he'll thank his lucky stars he was asked to dinner.

Tom. Mother, you mustn't expect too much of Laura.

Amanda. What do you mean?

Tom. Laura seems all those things to you and me because she's ours and we love her. We don't even notice she's crippled any more.

Amanda. Don't say crippled! You know that I never allow that word to be used!

Tom. But face facts, Mother. She is and—that's not all—

Amanda. What do you mean "not all?"

Tom. Laura is very different from other girls.

Amanda. I think the difference is all to her advantage.

Tom. Not quite all—in the eyes of others—strangers—she's terribly shy and lives in a world of her own and those things make her seem a little peculiar to people outside the house.

Amanda. Don't say peculiar.

Tom. Face the facts. She is.

[*The dance hall music changes to a tango that has a minor and somewhat ominous tone.*]

Amanda. In what way is she peculiar—may I ask?

Tom *(gently)*. She lives in a world of her own—a world of little glass ornaments, Mother. . . .

[*He gets up.* AMANDA *remains holding the brush, looking at him, troubled.*]

She plays old phonograph records and—that's about all—

[*He glances at himself in the mirror and crosses to the door.*]

Amanda *(sharply)*. Where are you going?

Tom. I'm going to the movies. *(He goes out the screen door.)*

Amanda. Not to the movies, every night to the movies! *(She follows quickly to the screen door.)* I don't believe you always go to the movies!

[*He is gone.* AMANDA *looks worriedly after him for a moment. Then vitality and optimism return and she turns from the door, crossing to the portieres.*]

Laura! Laura!

[LAURA *answers from the kitchenette.*]

Laura. Yes, Mother.

Amanda. Let those dishes go and come in front!

[LAURA *appears with a dish towel.* AMANDA *speaks to her gaily.*]

Laura, come here and make a wish on the moon!

[*Screen image:* The Moon.]

Laura *(entering)*. Moon—moon?

Amanda. A little silver slipper of a moon. Look over your left shoulder, Laura, and make a wish!

[LAURA *looks faintly puzzled as if called out of sleep.* AMANDA *seizes her shoulders and turns her at an angle by the door.*]

Now! Now, darling, *wish!*

Laura. What shall I wish for, Mother?

Amanda *(her voice trembling and her eyes suddenly filling with tears)*. Happiness! Good fortune!

[*The sound of the violin rises and the stage dims out.*]

Scene 6

The light comes up on the fire escape landing. TOM *is leaning against the grill, smoking.*

[*Screen image:* The high school hero.]

Tom. And so the following evening I brought Jim home to dinner. I had known Jim slightly in high school. In high school Jim was a hero. He had tremendous Irish good nature and vitality with the scrubbed and polished look of white chinaware. He seemed to move in a continual spotlight. He was a star in basketball, captain of the debating club, president of the senior class and the glee club and he sang the male lead in the annual light operas. He was always running or bounding, never just walking. He seemed always at the point of defeating the law of gravity. He was shooting with such velocity through his adolescence that you would logically expect him to arrive at nothing short of the White House by the time he was thirty. But Jim apparently ran into more interference after his graduation from Soldan. His speed A

A. Connections
In *The Great Gatsby* (1925) twenty years before Williams's play, F. Scott Fitzgerald (page 533) created a character psychologically similar to Jim. Fitzgerald's Tom Buchanan is "one of those men who reach such an acute limited excellence [in college] that everything afterwards savors of anticlimax" (Chapter 1, *The Great Gatsby*).

A. Titles

Williams titled his first drafts of the play *The Gentleman Caller*. Even though the caller does not appear until Scene 6, to what extent has the idea of the caller affected earlier scenes? (The idea has been discussed since the beginning of the play and causes some of the action. See scene summaries.) To what extent has Laura's glass menagerie been an important element of the play? (We have seen her preoccupation with it, and Tom's breaking some pieces may foreshadow more "breakage," of one kind or another, to come.) So far, which title do you prefer? Why?

B. Stage Directions

Notice the comparison of Laura with the glass.

Can you picture the effect the stage directions refer to? How does the comment again connect Laura with her glass menagerie? (A feeling of both beauty and fragility is evoked.)

had definitely slowed. Six years after he left high school he was holding a job that wasn't much better than mine.

[*Screen image:* The Clerk.]

He was the only one at the warehouse with whom I was on friendly terms. I was valuable to him as someone who could remember his former glory, who had seen him win basketball games and the silver cup in debating. He knew of my secret practice of retiring to a cabinet of the washroom to work on poems when business was slack in the warehouse. He called me Shakespeare. And while the other boys in the warehouse regarded me with suspicious hostility, Jim took a humorous attitude toward me. Gradually his attitude affected the others, their hostility wore off and they also began to smile at me as people smile at an oddly fashioned dog who trots across their path at some distance.

I knew that Jim and Laura had known each other at Soldan, and I had heard Laura speak of his voice. I didn't know if Jim remembered her or not. In high school Laura had been as unobtrusive as Jim had been astonishing. If he did remember Laura, it was not as my sister; for when I asked him to dinner, he grinned and said, "You know, Shakespeare, I never thought of you as having folks!"

He was about to discover that I did. . . .

[*Legend on screen:* "The accent of a coming foot."]

[*The light dims out on* TOM *and comes up in the Wingfield living room—a delicate lemony light. It is about five on a Friday evening of late spring which comes "scattering poems in the sky."*]

A [AMANDA *has worked in preparation for the gentleman caller. The results are astonishing. The new floor lamp with its rose silk shade is in place, a colored paper lantern conceals the broken light fixture in the ceiling, new billowing white curtains are at the windows, chintz covers are on the chairs and sofa, a pair of new sofa pillows make their initial appearance. Open boxes and tissue paper are scattered on the floor.*]

[LAURA *stands in the middle of the room with lifted arms while* AMANDA *crouches before her, adjusting the hem of a new dress, devout and ritualistic. The dress is colored and designed by memory. The arrangement of* LAURA*'s hair is changed; it is softer and more becoming. A fragile unearthly prettiness has come out in* LAURA*; she is like a piece of translucent glass touched by light, given a momentary radiance, not actual, not lasting.*]

Amanda *(impatiently).* Why are you trembling?
Laura. Mother, you've made me so nervous!
Amanda. How have I made you nervous?
Laura. By all this fuss! You make it seem so important!
Amanda. I don't understand you, Laura. You couldn't be satisfied with just sitting home, and yet whenever I try to arrange something for you, you seem to resist it. *(She gets up.)* Now take a look at yourself. No, wait! Wait just a moment—I have an idea!
Laura. What is it now?

[AMANDA *produces two powder puffs which she wraps in handkerchiefs and stuffs in* LAURA*'s bosom.*]

Laura. Mother, what are you doing?
Amanda. They call them "Gay Deceivers"!
Laura. I won't wear them!
Amanda. You will!
Laura. Why should I?
Amanda. Because, to be painfully honest, your chest is flat.
Laura. You make it seem like we were setting a trap.
Amanda. All pretty girls are a trap, a pretty trap, and men expect them to be.

[*Legend on screen:* "A pretty trap."]

Now look at yourself, young lady. This is the prettiest you will ever be! *(She stands back to admire* LAURA.*)* I've got to fix myself now! You're going to be surprised by your mother's appearance!

[AMANDA *crosses through the portieres, humming gaily.* LAURA *moves slowly to the long mirror and stares solemnly at herself. A wind blows the white curtains inward in a slow, graceful motion and with a faint, sorrowful sighing.*]

Amanda *(from somewhere behind the portieres).* It isn't dark enough yet.

[LAURA *turns slowly before the mirror with a troubled look.*]

[*Legend on screen:* "This is my sister: Celebrate her with strings!" *Music plays.*]

Amanda *(laughing, still not visible).* I'm going to show you something. I'm going to make a spectacular appearance!
Laura. What is it, Mother?
Amanda. Possess your soul in patience—you will see! Something I've resurrected from that old trunk! Styles haven't changed so terribly much after all. . . . *(She parts the portieres.)* Now just look at your mother! *(She wears a girlish frock of yellowed voile with a blue silk sash. She carries a bunch of jonquils—the legend of her youth is nearly revived. Now she speaks feverishly:)* This is the dress in which I led the cotillion. Won the cakewalk twice at Sunset Hill, wore one spring to the Governor's Ball in Jackson! See how I sashayed around the ballroom, Laura? *(She raises her skirt and does a mincing step around the room.)* I wore it on Sundays for my gentlemen callers! I had it on the day I met your father. . . . I had malaria fever all that spring. The change of climate from East Tennessee to the Delta—weakened resistance. I had a little temperature all the time—not enough to be serious—just enough to make me restless and giddy! Invitations poured in—parties all over the Delta! "Stay in bed," said Mother, "You have fever!"—but I just wouldn't. I took quinine but kept on going, going! Evenings, dances! Afternoons, long, long rides! Picnics—lovely! So lovely, that country in May—all lacy with dogwood, literally flooded with jonquils! That was the Spring I had the craze for jonquils. Jonquils became an absolute obsession. Mother said, "Honey, there's no more room for jonquils." And still I kept on bringing in more jonquils. Whenever, wherever I saw them, I'd say, "Stop! Stop! I see jonquils!" I made the young men help me gather the jonquils! It was a joke, Amanda and her jonquils. Finally there were no more vases to hold them, every available space was filled with jonquils. No vases to hold them? All right, I'll hold them myself! And then I—*(She stops in front of the picture. Music plays.)* met your father! Malaria fever and jonquils and then—this—boy. . . . *(She switches on the rose-colored lamp.)* I hope they get here before it starts to rain. *(She crosses the room and places the jonquils in a bowl on the table.)* I gave your brother a little extra change so he and Mr. O'Connor could take the service car home.

Laura *(with an altered look).* What did you say his name was?
Amanda. O'Connor.
Laura. What is his first name?
Amanda. I don't remember. Oh, yes, I do. It was—Jim!

[LAURA *sways slightly and catches hold of a chair.*]

[*Legend on screen:* "Not Jim!"]

Laura *(faintly).* Not—Jim!

B

Amanda. Yes, that was it, it was Jim! I've never known a Jim that wasn't nice!

[*The music becomes ominous.*]

Laura. Are you sure his name is Jim O'Connor?
Amanda. Yes. Why?
Laura. Is he the one that Tom used to know in high school?
Amanda. He didn't say so. I think he just got to know him at the warehouse.
Laura. There was a Jim O'Connor we both knew in high school—*(then, with effort)* If that is the one that Tom is bringing to dinner—you'll have to excuse me, I won't come to the table.
Amanda. What sort of nonsense is this?
Laura. You asked me once if I'd ever liked a boy. Don't you remember I showed you this boy's picture?
Amanda. You mean the boy you showed me in the yearbook?
Laura. Yes, that boy.
Amanda. Laura, Laura, were you in love with that boy?
Laura. I don't know, Mother. All I know is I couldn't sit at the table if it was him!
Amanda. It won't be him! It isn't the least bit likely. But whether it is or not, you will come to the table. You will not be excused.
Laura. I'll have to be, Mother.
Amanda. I don't intend to humor your silliness, Laura. I've had too much from you and your brother, both! So just sit down and compose yourself till they come. Tom has forgotten his key so you'll have to let them in, when they arrive.
Laura *(panicky).* Oh, Mother—*you* answer the door!
Amanda *(lightly).* I'll be in the kitchen—busy!
Laura. Oh, Mother, please answer the door, don't make me do it!

A. Responding
? As Amanda emerges in the clothes of her youth, what is your reaction? Is there humor in the scene? Do you pity her? (Answers will vary. Her costume is ludicrous, yet somehow she is not.)

B. Plot
? Explain the effect on Laura of the revelation that the caller's name is Jim O'Connor. (He could be the boy she had a crush on in high school.) Does Laura's extreme reaction suggest anything about the duration of her crush? (Answers will vary, but her earlier calm and her panic now suggest that while just any gentleman caller is less important to her than to Amanda, Jim is different. She may therefore have been fantasizing about him for years. Having him come could destroy what has sustained her.)

Literature and Language: Using Sentence Fragments

Although sentence fragments are considered an error in student writing, they have a respectable role in drama. In actuality, people often speak in fragments, expressing enough of their thoughts to communicate an idea effectively. In an attempt to make dialogue sound natural, playwrights frequently use fragments.

Ask students to find ten sentence fragments somewhere near each other in the play (see, for example, Amanda's second speech on this page and Laura's second speech). Have students rewrite each fragment, adding whatever words are necessary to make a complete sentence. Then ask them to plug their rewritten, complete sentences into Williams's dialogue and read the dialogue aloud to themselves or to a small group. Evaluate the dialogue. Which sounds more like real people talking: Williams's fragments, or the revised complete sentences?

Amanda *(crossing into the kitchenette).* I've got to fix the dressing for the salmon. Fuss, fuss—silliness!—over a gentleman caller!

[*The door swings shut.* LAURA *is left alone.*]

[*Legend on screen:* "Terror!"]

[*She utters a low moan and turns off the lamp—sits stiffly on the edge of the sofa, knotting her fingers together.*]

[*Legend on screen:* "The Opening of a Door!"]

[TOM *and* JIM *appear on the fire escape steps and climb to the landing. Hearing their approach,* LAURA *rises with a panicky gesture. She retreats to the portieres. The doorbell rings.* LAURA *catches her breath and touches her throat. Low drums sound.*]

Amanda *(calling).* Laura, sweetheart! The door!

[LAURA *stares at it without moving.*]

Jim. I think we just beat the rain.
Tom. Uh-huh. *(He rings again, nervously.* JIM *whistles and fishes for a cigarette.)*
Amanda *(very, very gaily).* Laura, that is your brother and Mr. O'Connor! Will you let them in, darling?

[LAURA *crosses toward the kitchenette door.*]

Laura *(breathlessly).* Mother—you go to the door!

[AMANDA *steps out of the kitchenette and stares furiously at* LAURA. *She points imperiously at the door.*]

Laura. Please, please!
Amanda *(in a fierce whisper).* What is the matter with you, you silly thing?
Laura *(desperately).* Please, you answer it, *please!*
Amanda. I told you I wasn't going to humor you, Laura. Why have you chosen this moment to lose your mind?
Laura. Please, please, please, you go!
Amanda. You'll have to go to the door because I can't!
Laura *(despairingly).* I can't either!
Amanda. *Why?*
Laura. I'm *sick!*
Amanda. I'm sick too—of your nonsense! Why can't you and your brother be normal people? Fantastic whims and behavior!

[TOM *gives a long ring.*]

Preposterous goings on! Can you give me one reason—*(She calls out lyrically.) Coming! Just one second!*—why you should be afraid to open a door? Now you answer it, Laura!
Laura. Oh, oh, oh . . . *(She returns through the portieres, darts to the victrola, winds it frantically and turns it on.)*
Amanda. Laura Wingfield, you march right to that door!
Laura. *Yes—yes, Mother!*

[*A faraway, scratchy rendition of "Dardanella" softens the air and gives her strength to move through it. She slips to the door and draws it cautiously open.* TOM *enters with the caller,* JIM O'CONNOR.]

Tom. Laura, this is Jim. Jim, this is my sister, Laura.
Jim *(stepping inside).* I didn't know that Shakespeare had a sister!
Laura *(retreating, stiff and trembling, from the door).* How—how do you do?
Jim *(heartily, extending his hand).* Okay!

[LAURA *touches it hesitantly with hers.*]

Jim. Your hand's *cold,* Laura!
Laura. Yes, well—I've been playing the victrola.
Jim. Must have been playing classical music on it! You ought to play a little hot swing music to warm you up!
Laura. Excuse me—I haven't finished playing the victrola. . . . *(She turns awkwardly and hurries into the front room. She pauses a second by the victrola. Then she catches her breath and darts through the portieres like a frightened deer.)*
Jim *(grinning).* What was the matter?
Tom. Oh—with Laura? Laura is—terribly shy.
Jim. Shy, huh? It's unusual to meet a shy girl nowadays. I don't believe you ever mentioned you had a sister.
Tom. Well, now you know. I have one. Here is the *Post Dispatch.* You want a piece of it?
Jim. Uh-huh.
Tom. What piece? The comics?
Jim. Sports! *(He glances at it.)* Ole Dizzy Dean[4] is on his bad behavior.
Tom *(uninterested).* Yeah? *(He lights a cigarette and goes over to the fire escape door.)*

---

4. **Dizzy Dean:** major league pitcher (1932–1941) with the St. Louis Cardinals and the Chicago Cubs.

Jim. Where are *you* going?
Tom. I'm going out on the terrace.
Jim *(going after him).* You know, Shakespeare—I'm going to sell you a bill of goods!
Tom. What goods?
Jim. A course I'm taking.
Tom. Huh?
Jim. In public speaking! You and me, we're not the warehouse type.
Tom. Thanks—that's good news. But what has public speaking got to do with it?
Jim. It fits you for—executive positions!
Tom. Awww.
Jim. I tell you it's done a helluva lot for me.

[*Image on screen:* Executive at his desk.]

Tom. In what respect?
Jim. In every! Ask yourself what is the difference between you an' me and men in the office down front? Brains?—No!—Ability?—No! Then what? Just one little thing—
Tom. What is that one little thing?
Jim. Primarily it amounts to—social poise! Being able to square up to people and hold your own on any social level!
Amanda *(from the kitchenette).* Tom?
Tom. Yes, Mother?
Amanda. Is that you and Mr. O'Connor?
Tom. Yes, Mother.
Amanda. Well, you just make yourselves comfortable in there.
Tom. Yes. Mother.
Amanda. Ask Mr. O'Connor if he would like to wash his hands.
Jim. Aw, no—no—thank you—I took care of that at the warehouse. Tom—
Tom. Yes?
Jim. Mr. Mendoza was speaking to me about you.
Tom. Favorably?
Jim. What do you think?
Tom. Well—
A **Jim.** You're going to be out of a job if you don't wake up.
Tom. I am waking up—
Jim. You show no signs.
Tom. The signs are interior.

[*Image on screen:* The sailing vessel with the Jolly Roger again.]

Tom. I'm planning to change. *(He leans over the fire escape rail, speaking with quiet exhilaration. The incandescent marquees and signs of the first-run movie houses light his face from across the alley. He looks like a voyager.)* I'm right at the point of committing myself to a future that doesn't include the warehouse and Mr. Mendoza or even a night-school course in public speaking.
Jim. What are you gassing about?
Tom. I'm tired of the movies.
Jim. Movies!
Tom. Yes, movies! Look at them— *(A wave toward the marvels of Grand Avenue.)* All of these glamorous people—having adventures—hogging it all, gobbling the whole thing up! You know what happens? People go to the *movies* instead of *moving!* Hollywood characters are supposed to have all the adventures for everybody in America, while everybody in America sits in a dark room and watches them have them! Yes, until there's a war. That's when adventure becomes available to the masses! *Everyone's* dish, not only Gable's! Then the people in the dark room come out of the dark room to have some adventures themselves—goody, goody! It's our turn now, to go to the South Sea Island—to make a safari—to be exotic, far-off! But I'm not patient. I don't want to wait till then. I'm tired of the *movies* and I am *about* to *move!*
Jim *(incredulously).* Move?
Tom. Yes.
Jim. When?
Tom. Soon!
Jim. Where? Where?

[*The music seems to answer the question, while* TOM *thinks it over. He searches in his pockets.*]

Tom. I'm starting to boil inside. I know I seem dreamy, but inside—well, I'm boiling! Whenever I pick up a shoe, I shudder a little thinking how short life is and what I am doing! Whatever that means, I know it doesn't mean shoes—except as something to wear on a traveler's feet! *(He finds what he has been searching for in his pockets and holds out a paper to* JIM.*)* Look—
Jim. What?
Tom. I'm a member.
Jim *(reading).* The Union of Merchant Seamen.
Tom. I paid my dues this month, instead of the light bill.
Jim. You will regret it when they turn the lights off.
Tom. I won't be here.
Jim. How about your mother?
Tom. I'm like my father. . . . Did you notice how

A. Plot
? What does Jim warn Tom about? (Tom is in danger of losing his job.) What step does Tom tell Jim he has taken toward his "escape" from the warehouse? (He joined the Union of Merchant Seamen, using as dues the money for the light bill.)

B. Characterization
? Describe the personalities of Jim O'Connor and Tom Wingfield. How do they contrast with one another? Who would relate better to Sinclair Lewis's Babbitt (page 511)? Why? (Answers may vary. Most students will see Jim as more likely to go for Babbitt-style boosterism. Tom has a poetic, sensitive nature. He could never be happy as a businessman, because he does not want responsibility of any kind.)

Reading Check Test: Scenes 5–6

1. Tom realizes that Laura lives in a world of her own. *True*
2. Amanda tells Laura to wish upon the moon for a job. *False*
3. Jim O'Connor has not achieved the greatness that his high school achievements seemed to promise. *True*
4. Tom thanks Jim for his warning and promises to buckle down and take his job seriously. *False*
5. Laura is too nervous and sick to eat dinner. *True*

A. Speech Patterns
Notice Jim's use of the slang phrase "you drip" and use of the phrase "thrown off the beam" in the stage directions. (You might ask students for contemporary equivalents.) The right slang adds to the authenticity of a work, but a writer must avoid choices that later may become obscure in meaning.
? As Amanda gets going, what happens to her accent? (It becomes more Southern.) How does Williams convey this effect in print? (He omits consonants, as in "fo' this time," "an' light food," "ou' selves.") Is there anything in the content of Amanda's speech that indicates she caught Tom's and Jim's startled reaction to the dress she is wearing? (She jokingly mocks the dress as "Historical almost!" and goes on to offer another reason for wearing it.)

he's grinning in his picture in there? And he's been absent going on sixteen years!

A **Jim.** You're just talking, you drip. How does your mother feel about it?

Tom. Shhh! Here comes Mother! Mother is not acquainted with my plans!

Amanda *(coming through the portieres).* Where are you all?

Tom. On the terrace, Mother.

[*They start inside. She advances to them.* TOM *is distinctly shocked at her appearance. Even* JIM *blinks a little. He is making his first contact with girlish Southern vivacity and in spite of the night-school course in public speaking is somewhat thrown off the beam by the unexpected outlay of social charm. Certain responses are attempted by* JIM *but are swept aside by* AMANDA*'s gay laughter and chatter.* TOM *is embarrassed but after the first shock* JIM *reacts very warmly. He grins and chuckles, is altogether won over.*]

[*Image on screen:* Amanda as a girl.]

Amanda *(coyly smiling, shaking her girlish ringlets).* Well, well, well, so this is Mr. O'Connor. Introductions entirely unnecessary. I've heard so much about you from my boy. I finally said to him, Tom—good gracious!—why don't you bring this paragon[1] to supper? I'd like to meet this nice young man at the warehouse!—instead of just hearing him sing your praises so much! I don't know why my son is so stand-offish—that's not Southern behavior!

Let's sit down and—I think we could stand a little more air in here! Tom, leave the door open. I felt a nice fresh breeze a moment ago. Where has it gone to? Mmm, so warm already! And not quite summer, even. We're going to burn up when summer really gets started. However, we're having—we're having a very light supper. I think light things are better fo' this time of year. The same as light clothes are. Light clothes an' light food are what warm weather calls fo'. You know our blood gets so thick during th' winter—it takes a while fo' us to *adjust* ou'selves!—when the season changes . . . It's come so quick this year. I wasn't prepared. All of a sudden—heavens! Already summer! I ran to the trunk an' pulled out this light dress—terribly old! Historical almost! But feels so good—so good an' co-ol, y' know. . . .

Tom. Mother—

Amanda. Yes, honey?

Tom. How about—supper?

Amanda. Honey, you go ask Sister if supper is ready! You know that Sister is in full charge of supper! Tell her you hungry boys are waiting for it. *(To* JIM*)* Have you met Laura?

Jim. She—

Amanda. Let you in? Oh, good, you've met already! It's rare for a girl as sweet an' pretty as Laura to be domestic! But Laura is, thank heavens, not only pretty but also very domestic. I'm not at all. I never was a bit. I never could make a thing but angel-food cake. Well, in the South we had so many servants. Gone, gone, gone. All vestige of gracious living! Gone completely! I wasn't prepared for what the future brought me. All of my gentlemen callers were sons of planters and

1. **paragon** (par'ə·gän'): a model of excellence or perfection.

ANALYZING SCENES 4, 5 AND 6
Identifying Facts
1. Tom is sympathetic and patient. The stage directions instruct him to speak gently at the beginning of the scene, and he shows patience in response to the same type of nagging that he found so annoying in Scenes 1 and 3.

Amanda tries to show approval: "You just keep on trying and you're bound to succeed"; "Both my children are—they're very precious children and I've got a lot to be thankful for."
2. She asks him to bring home from the warehouse a clean-living gentleman caller for Laura.
3. He is a shipping clerk at Tom's warehouse and earns about eighty-five dollars a month. His name is James D. O'Connor, and he goes to night school to study public speaking and radio engineering. He is not especially handsome, according to Tom.

She is excited but also upset that the gentleman caller is coming so soon.
4. Tom tells Amanda that a lot of boys meet girls whom they don't marry. He also reminds Amanda that Laura is crippled and very different from other girls—even peculiar. Amanda does not even respond to Tom's first warning, and she completely denies that Laura is peculiar.
5. Amanda transforms herself with a ball dress, resurrected from the days of her youth.

Amanda joyfully, but somewhat unrealistically, looks forward to the gentleman caller's visit as the start of a campaign to get Laura married. Laura is nervous and shy.
6. She is acutely embarrassed and says she will not come to the table.

Amanda reacts sternly, saying that Laura will not be excused.

Interpreting Meanings
7. Amanda cannot seem to stop her nagging—about going to the movies—and her criticism of Tom. Amanda means to ask Tom to bring home a friend for dinner (a gentleman caller); but before she gets to that, she accuses Tom of selfishness, and he becomes very angry. The reader and the audience have the feeling that Amanda's accusations *(Answers continue on next page.)*

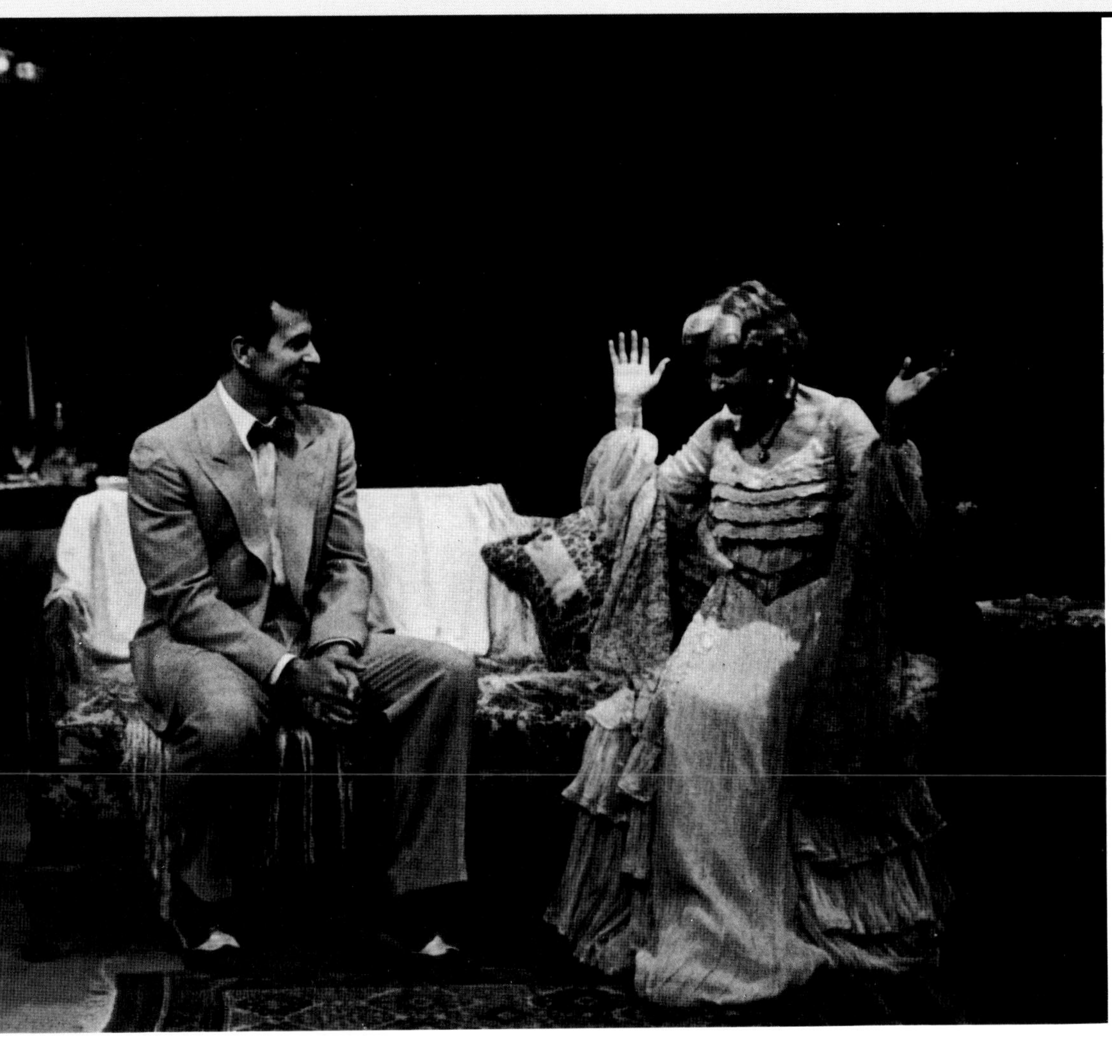

"I married no planter! I married . . . a telephone man who—fell in love with long-distance!"

so of course I assumed that I would be married to one and raise my family on a large piece of land with plenty of servants. But man proposes—and woman accepts the proposal! To vary that old, old saying a little bit[2]—I married no planter! I married a man who worked for the telephone company! That gallantly smiling gentleman over there! *(She points to the picture.)* A telephone man who—fell in love with long-distance! Now he travels and I don't even know where! But what am I going on for about my—tribulations? Tell me yours—I hope you don't have any! Tom?
Tom *(returning).* Yes, Mother?
Amanda. Is supper nearly ready?
Tom. It looks to me like supper is on the table.

2. **But man proposes . . . a bit**: Amanda is referring to the saying, "Man proposes, but God disposes."

Amanda. Let me look— *(She rises prettily and looks through the portieres.)* Oh, lovely! But where is Sister?
Tom. Laura is not feeling well and she says that she thinks she'd better not come to the table.
Amanda. What? Nonsense! Laura? Oh, Laura!
Laura *(from the kitchenette, faintly).* Yes, Mother.
Amanda. You really must come to the table. We won't be seated until you come to the table! Come in, Mr. O'Connor. You sit over there, and I'll. . . . Laura? Laura Wingfield! You're keeping us waiting, honey! We can't say grace until you come to the table!

[*The kitchenette door is pushed weakly open and* LAURA *comes in: She is obviously quite faint, her lips trembling, her eyes wide and staring. She moves unsteadily toward the table.*]

(Continued from previous page.)
have been repeated many times before.
8. Amanda feels desperate because Laura cannot take care of herself, and she realizes that Tom wants to leave them to join the Merchant Marine. Without Tom's salary, she and Laura will not be able to survive, so Amanda takes steps to get Laura married. Tom is equally desperate—to leave the family and his job at the warehouse. He wants adventure, but so far the only step he has taken to achieve his desire is to receive a letter from the Merchant Marine. Laura does not seem desperate; she only wants to be left alone.
9. Williams uses suspense as he carefully, almost logically, prepares us for the arrival of the gentleman caller. This motif is first referred to in Tom's opening speech as a narrator. Scene 1 (Amanda's reminiscences of seventeen gentleman callers), Scene 2 (Amanda's conclusion that only marriage will do for Laura), Tom's speech as the narrator at the opening of Scene 3, and his angry reference to Amanda's gentleman callers at the end of that scene—all of these keep the theme or motif of the gentleman call-
(Answers continue in left-hand column.)

(Continued from top.)
er constantly before us. Although we know that a gentleman caller will arrive, we don't know who he will be, what he'll be like, why he will come or what will happen between him and Laura. All of these still unanswered questions create suspense.
10. Amanda seems sympathetic in this scene. When she figures out that Tom could save $4.50 a month by not smoking, she graciously admits that that "wouldn't be very much." In this scene, Amanda also seems to show a sincere wish for her children's happiness. She is probably more likable here than at any other time so far in the play.
11. The gentleman caller may be surprised to find himself in a more intense situation than he imagined. Tom has done his best to satisfy his mother.

[*Screen legend:* "Terror!"]

[*Outside a summer storm is coming on abruptly. The white curtains billow inward at the windows and there is a sorrowful murmur from the deep blue dusk.*]

[LAURA *suddenly stumbles; she catches at a chair with a faint moan.*]

Tom. Laura!
Amanda. Laura!

[*There is a clap of thunder.*]

[*Screen legend:* "Ah!"]

(Despairingly) Why, Laura, you *are* ill, darling! Tom, help your sister into the living room, dear! Sit in the living room, Laura—rest on the sofa. Well! *(to* JIM *as* TOM *helps his sister to the sofa in the living room)* Standing over the hot stove made her ill! I told her that it was just too warm this evening, but—

[TOM *comes back to the table.*]

Is Laura all right now?
Tom. Yes.
Amanda. What *is* that? Rain? A nice cool rain has come up! *(She gives* JIM *a frightened look.)* I think we may—have grace—now . . .

(TOM *looks at her stupidly.)* Tom, honey—you say grace!
Tom. Oh . . . "For these and all thy mercies—"

[*They bow their heads,* AMANDA *stealing a nervous glance at* JIM. *In the living room* LAURA, *stretched on the sofa, clenches her hand to her lips, to hold back a shuddering sob.*]

God's Holy Name be praised—

[*The scene dims out.*]

Responding to the Play

Analyzing Scenes 4, 5, and 6

Identifying Facts

1. In Scenes 4 and 5, Tom displays an attitude toward his mother that we have not seen before. Describe that attitude, and find the lines of dialogue that reveal it. Cite two lines of dialogue that show that Amanda is also trying to behave differently toward Tom.
2. What had Amanda asked Tom to do at the end of Scene 4?
3. In Scene 5, we hear that the much-talked-about gentleman caller is finally about to arrive. Before we meet him, what information does Tom give us about him? How does Amanda react to this new information about the gentleman caller?
4. In Scene 5, Tom gives his mother two realistic warnings to counter Amanda's pleasant fantasy of the gentleman caller. What are these warnings? How does Amanda react to them?
5. How does Amanda transform herself for the gentleman caller? How is her attitude about their guest different from Laura's?
6. What is Laura's reaction when she learns the identity of the gentleman caller? How does Amanda respond to this reaction?

Interpreting Meanings

7. At the beginning of Scene 4, both Tom and Amanda try to make peace. Why do they begin to argue again?
8. The basic **dramatic situation** from which a play can grow involves a person or persons whom we care about, who are in more or less desperate situations with a great deal at stake. Such characters decide to act and then actually take steps to achieve their "wants." Discuss how these dramatic elements are used up to this point in *The Glass Menagerie.*
9. In most plays, suspense is preferable to surprise. If we reach the top of a hill and look down to see two trains at the moment they crash, it is a **surprise** and it is shocking. But dramatically, it would be more effective if, as we neared the top of the hill, we saw the trains approaching each other on the same track from perhaps a mile apart. This would be **suspense:** we are very anxious about what will happen next. How has Tennessee Williams used suspense in the play up to now?
10. We have seen that Amanda is a complex **character**—not easily described as either "good" or "bad." What aspect of her character do we see in Scenes 5 and 6? Do you feel sympathetic toward her? Explain.
11. What are your feelings for the gentleman caller at this point in the play? How do you feel about Tom?

Supplementary Support Materials
1. Vocabulary Activity Worksheet (*CCB*)
2. Review and Response Worksheet: Progression (*CCB*)
3. Selection Test (*CCB*)

Developing Vocabulary
The following words from the play are tested in the Selection Test. (See also Vocabulary Activity Worksheet.)

luminous	to beleaguer
candelabrum	unicorn
to intimate	abashed
exposition	tumultuously
pleurosis	decorously

Scene 7

It is half an hour later. Dinner is just being finished in the dining room, LAURA *is still huddled upon the sofa, her feet drawn under, her head resting on a pale blue pillow, her eyes wide and mysteriously watchful. The new floor lamp with its shade of rose-colored silk gives a soft, becoming light to her face, bringing out the fragile, unearthly prettiness which usually escapes attention. From outside there is a steady murmur of rain, but it is slackening and soon stops; the air outside becomes pale and luminous as the moon breaks through the clouds. A moment after the curtain rises, the lights in both rooms flicker and go out.*

Jim. Hey, there, Mr. Light Bulb!

[AMANDA *laughs nervously.*]

[*Legend on screen:* "Suspension of a public service."]

Amanda. Where was Moses when the lights went out? Ha-ha. Do you know the answer to that one, Mr. O'Connor?
Jim. No, Ma'am, what's the answer?
Amanda. In the dark!

[JIM *laughs appreciatively.*]

Everybody sit still. I'll light the candles. Isn't it lucky we have them on the table? Where's a match? Which of you gentlemen can provide a match?
Jim. Here.
Amanda. Thank you, Sir.
Jim. Not at all, Ma'am!
Amanda *(as she lights the candles).* I guess the fuse has burnt out. Mr. O'Connor, can you tell a burnt-out fuse? I know I can't and Tom is a total loss when it comes to mechanics.

[*They rise from the table and go into the kitchenette, from where their voices are heard.*]

Oh, be careful you don't bump into something. We don't want our gentleman caller to break his neck. Now wouldn't that be a fine howdy-do?
Jim. Ha-ha! Where is the fuse-box?
Amanda. Right here next to the stove. Can you see anything?
Jim. Just a minute.
Amanda. Isn't electricity a mysterious thing? Wasn't it Benjamin Franklin who tied a key to a kite? We live in such a mysterious universe, don't we? Some people say that science clears up all the mysteries for us. In my opinion it only creates more! Have you found it yet?
Jim. No, Ma'am. All these fuses look okay to me.
Amanda. Tom!
Tom. Yes, Mother?
Amanda. That light bill I gave you several days ago. The one I told you we got the notices about?

[*Legend on screen:* "Ha!"]

Tom. Oh—yeah.
Amanda. You didn't neglect to pay it by any chance?
Tom. Why, I—
Amanda. Didn't! I might have known it!
Jim. Shakespeare probably wrote a poem on that light bill, Mrs. Wingfield.
Amanda. I might have known better than to trust him with it! There's such a high price for negligence in this world!
Jim. Maybe the poem will win a ten-dollar prize.
Amanda. We'll just have to spend the remainder of the evening in the nineteenth century, before Mr. Edison made the Mazda lamp!
Jim. Candlelight is my favorite kind of light.
Amanda. That shows you're romantic! But that's no excuse for Tom. Well, we got through dinner. Very considerate of them to let us get through dinner before they plunged us into everlasting darkness, wasn't it, Mr. O'Connor?
Jim. Ha-ha!
Amanda. Tom, as a penalty for your carelessness you can help me with the dishes.
Jim. Let me give you a hand.
Amanda. Indeed you will not!
Jim. I ought to be good for something.
Amanda. Good for something? *(Her tone is rhapsodic.) You?* Why, Mr. O'Connor, nobody, *nobody's* given me this much entertainment in years—as you have!
Jim. Aw, now, Mrs. Wingfield!
Amanda. I'm not exaggerating, not one bit! But Sister is all by her lonesome. You go keep her company in the parlor! I'll give you this lovely old candelabrum that used to be on the altar at the Church of the Heavenly Rest. It was melted a little out of shape when the church burnt down. Lightning struck it one Spring. Gypsy Jones was holding a revival at the time and he intimated that church was destroyed because the Episcopalians gave card parties. A
Jim. Ha-ha.

Scene 7 Summary:
The lights go out. Amanda and Tom clean up the kitchen. Jim goes in to Laura with a candelabrum. He does recall her from high school, as "Blue Roses." Jim treats Laura with such sensitivity that she opens up enough to try to waltz. She gives Jim the glass unicorn which is accidentally broken in their clumsy dance; Jim apologizes for kissing her and for being unable to come again because he is engaged. As soon as Jim has gone, Amanda furiously accuses Tom of deliberately choosing an ineligible caller. Tom leaves home for the Merchant Marine, always to remember his sister's uncertain future.

A. Humor
? Is Amanda fully aware of the humor of her remarks? (Answers may vary. She told a joke about Moses and seems to believe that her next remark, about an evangelist named Gypsy Jones, is funny.)

A. Allusion
World's fairs, or international expositions as we know them, began at the Crystal Palace exhibition in London in 1851. Important for their emphasis on scientific and technological innovation, "expo's" have also promoted understanding among participating nations. Famous expositions include the one in Paris in 1889, for which the Eiffel Tower was built; the fair of 1939–1940 in San Francisco, celebrating the new Golden Gate Bridge and the Oakland Bay Bridge; and the 1962 exposition in Seattle with its 600-foot "space needle" celebrating the theme "Man in Space." Jim's allusion is to the 1933–1934 exposition held in Chicago to coincide with the city's 100th anniversary.

Amanda. And how about you coaxing Sister to drink a little wine? I think it would be good for her! Can you carry both at once?
Jim. Sure. I'm Superman!
Amanda. Now, Thomas, get into this apron!

[JIM *comes into the dining room, carrying the candelabrum, its candles lighted, in one hand and a glass of wine in the other. The door of the kitchenette swings closed on* AMANDA'*s gay laughter; the flickering light approaches the portieres.* LAURA *sits up nervously as* JIM *enters. She can hardly speak from the almost intolerable strain of being alone with a stranger.*]

[*Screen legend:* "I don't suppose you remember me at all!"]

[*At first, before* JIM'*s warmth overcomes her paralyzing shyness,* LAURA'*s voice is thin and breathless, as though she had just run up a steep flight of stairs.* JIM'*s attitude is gently humorous. While the incident is apparently unimportant, it is to* LAURA *the climax of her secret life.*]

Jim. Hello there, Laura.
Laura *(faintly)*. Hello.

[*She clears her throat.*]

Jim. How are you feeling now? Better?
Laura. Yes. Yes, thank you.
Jim. This is for you. A little dandelion wine. *(He extends the glass toward her with extravagant gallantry.)*
Laura. Thank you.
Jim. Drink it—but don't get drunk!

[*He laughs heartily.* LAURA *takes the glass uncertainly; she laughs shyly.*]

Where shall I set the candles?
Laura. Oh—oh, anywhere . . .
Jim. How about here on the floor? Any objections?
Laura. No.
Jim. I'll spread a newspaper under to catch the drippings. I like to sit on the floor. Mind if I do?
Laura. Oh, no.
Jim. Give me a pillow?
Laura. What?
Jim. A pillow!
Laura. Oh . . . *(She hands him one quickly.)*
Jim. How about you? Don't you like to sit on the floor?
Laura. Oh—yes.
Jim. Why don't you, then?
Laura. I—will.
Jim. Take a pillow!

(LAURA *does. She sits on the floor on the other side of the candelabrum.* JIM *crosses his legs and smiles engagingly at her.)* I can't hardly see you sitting way over there.

Laura. I can—see you.
Jim. I know, but that's not fair, I'm in the limelight.

[LAURA *moves her pillow closer.*]

Good! Now I can see you! Comfortable?
Laura. Yes.
Jim. So am I. Comfortable as a cow! Will you have some gum?
Laura. No, thank you.
Jim. I think that I will indulge, with your permission. *(He musingly unwraps a stick of gum and holds it up.)* Think of the fortune made by the guy that invented the first piece of chewing gum. Amazing, huh? The Wrigley Building is one of the sights of Chicago—I saw it when I went up to the Century of Progress. Did you take in the Century of Progress?
Laura. No, I didn't.
Jim. Well, it was quite a wonderful exposition. What impressed me most was the Hall of Science. Gives you an idea of what the future will be in America, even more wonderful than the present time is! *(There is a pause.* JIM *smiles at her.)* Your brother tells me you're shy. Is that right, Laura?
Laura. I—don't know.
Jim. I judge you to be an old-fashioned type of girl. Well, I think that's a pretty good type to be. Hope you don't think I'm being too personal—do you?
Laura *(hastily, out of embarrassment)*. I believe I *will* take a piece of gum, if you—don't mind. *(clearing her throat)* Mr. O'Connor, have you—kept up with your singing?
Jim. Singing? Me?
Laura. Yes. I remember what a beautiful voice you had.
Jim. When did you hear me sing?

[LAURA *does not answer, and in the long pause which follows a man's voice is heard singing offstage.*]

VOICE:

O blow, ye winds, heigh-ho,
A-roving I will go!
I'm off to my love
With a boxing glove—
Ten thousand miles away!

Jim. You say you've heard me sing?

Laura. Oh, yes! Yes, very often . . . I don't suppose—you remember me—at all?

Jim *(smiling doubtfully).* You know I have an idea I've seen you before. I had that idea soon as you opened the door. It seemed almost like I was about to remember your name. But the name that I started to call you—wasn't a name! And so I stopped myself before I said it.

Laura. Wasn't it—Blue Roses?

Jim *(springing up, grinning).* Blue Roses! My gosh, yes—Blue Roses! That's what I had on my tongue when you opened the door! Isn't it funny what tricks your memory plays? I didn't connect you with high school somehow or other. But that's where it was; it was high school. I didn't even know you were Shakespeare's sister! Gosh, I'm sorry.

Laura. I didn't expect you to. You—barely knew me!

Jim. But we did have a speaking acquaintance, huh?

Laura. Yes, we—spoke to each other.

Jim. When did you recognize me?

Laura. Oh, right away!

Jim. Soon as I came in the door?

Laura. When I heard your name I thought it was probably you. I knew that Tom used to know you a little in high school. So when you came in the door—well, then I was—sure.

Jim. Why didn't you *say* something, then?

Laura *(breathlessly).* I didn't know what to say, I was—too surprised!

Jim. For goodness' sakes! You know, this sure is funny!

Laura. Yes! Yes, isn't it, though . . .

Jim. Didn't we have a class in something together?

Laura. Yes, we did.

Jim. What class was that?

Laura. It was—singing—chorus!

Jim. Aw!

Laura. I sat across the aisle from you in the Aud.

Jim. Aw.

Laura. Mondays, Wednesdays, and Fridays.

Jim. Now I remember—you always came in late.

Laura. Yes, it was so hard for me, getting upstairs. I had that brace on my leg—it clumped so loud!

Jim. I never heard any clumping.

Laura *(wincing at the recollection).* To me it sounded like—thunder!

Jim. Well, well, well, I never even noticed.

Laura. And everybody was seated before I came in. I had to walk in front of all those people. My seat was in the back row. I had to go clumping all the way up the aisle with everyone watching!

Jim. You shouldn't have been self-conscious.

Laura. I know, but I was. It was always such a relief when the singing started.

Jim. Aw, yes, I've placed you now! I used to call you Blue Roses. How was it that I got started calling you that?

Laura. I was out of school a little while with pleurosis. When I came back you asked me what was the matter. I said I had pleurosis—you thought I said *Blue Roses.* That's what you always called me after that!

Jim. I hope you didn't mind.

Laura. Oh, no—I liked it. You see, I wasn't acquainted with many—people. . . .

Jim. As I remember you sort of stuck by yourself.

Laura. I—I—never have had much luck at—making friends.

Jim. I don't see why you wouldn't.

Laura. Well, I—started out badly.

Jim. You mean being—

Laura. Yes, it sort of—stood between me—

Jim. You shouldn't have let it!

Laura. I know, but it did, and—

Jim. You were shy with people!

Laura. I tried not to be but never could—

Jim. Overcome it?

Laura. No, I—I never could!

Jim. I guess being shy is something you have to work out of kind of gradually.

Laura *(sorrowfully).* Yes—I guess it—

Jim. Takes time!

Laura. Yes—

Jim. People are not so dreadful when you know them. That's what you have to remember! And everybody has problems, not just you, but practically everybody has got some problems. You think of yourself as having the only problems, as being the only one who is disappointed. But just look around you and you will see lots of people as disappointed as you are. For instance, I hoped when I was going to high school that I would be further along at this time, six years later, than I

A. Expansion
The lines are from the refrain of "A Capital Ship," a rollicking song about a ship named the *Walloping Window Blind.* The verses are by American nonsense poet Charles Edward Carryl (1842–1920). In this context the refrain is reminiscent of the lilting silliness of a Gilbert and Sullivan operetta, such as *Pirates of Penzance* in which Jim sang and acted. As a sailing song, it can also be taken to foreshadow Tom's departure.

B. Responding
? Everyday wisdom says that you should not compare your "insides" with other people's "outsides." How are this idea and Jim's words related? (Both say that everyone has problems; it's just that other people's problems are less obvious than one's own.)

A. Responding
In this scene Jim and Laura discuss high-school predictions that have not come true in the six years since high school.
? Apply Jim's and Laura's experience to yourself. If the custom were observed, what prediction would you like to see next to your name in your high-school yearbook? Realistically, how far do you think you will have progressed toward that goal six or seven years from now?

A am now. You remember that wonderful write-up I had in *The Torch?*
Laura. Yes! *(She rises and crosses to the table.)*
Jim. It said I was bound to succeed in anything I went into!

[LAURA *returns with the high school year book.*]

Holy Jeez! *The Torch!*

[*He accepts it reverently. They smile across the book with mutual wonder.* LAURA *crouches beside him and they begin to turn the pages.* LAURA*'s shyness is dissolving in his warmth.*]

Laura. Here you are in *The Pirates of Penzance!*
Jim *(wistfully).* I sang the baritone lead in that operetta.
Laura *(raptly).* So—*beautifully!*
Jim *(protesting).* Aw—
Laura. Yes, yes—beautifully—beautifully!
Jim. You heard me?
Laura. All three times!
Jim. No!
Laura. Yes!
Jim. All three performances?
Laura *(looking down).* Yes.
Jim. Why?
Laura. I—wanted to ask you to—autograph my program. *(She takes the program from the back of the year book and shows it to him.)*
Jim. Why didn't you ask me to?
Laura. You were always surrounded by your own friends so much that I never had a chance to.
Jim. You should have just—
Laura. Well, I—thought you might think I was—
Jim. Thought I might think you was—what?
Laura. Oh—
Jim *(with reflective relish).* I was beleaguered by females in those days.
Laura. You were terribly popular!
Jim. Yeah—
Laura. You had such a—friendly way—
Jim. I was spoiled in high school.
Laura. Everybody—liked you!
Jim. Including you?
Laura. I—yes, I—did, too— *(She gently closes the book in her lap.)*
Jim. Well, well, well! Give me that program, Laura.

[*She hands it to him. He signs it with a flourish.*]

There you are—better late than never!
Laura. Oh, I—what a—surprise!
Jim. My signature isn't worth very much right now. But some day—maybe—it will increase in value! Being disappointed is one thing and being discouraged is something else. I am disappointed but I am not discouraged. I'm twenty-three years old. How old are you?
Laura. I'll be twenty-four in June.
Jim. That's not old age!
Laura. No, but—
Jim. You finished high school?
Laura *(with difficulty).* I didn't go back.
Jim. You mean you dropped out?
Laura. I made bad grades in my final examinations. *(She rises and replaces the book and the program on the table. Her voice is strained.)* How is—Emily Meisenbach getting along?
Jim. Oh, that kraut-head!
Laura. Why do you call her that?
Jim. That's what she was.
Laura. You're not still—going with her?
Jim. I never see her.
Laura. It said in the "Personal" section that you were—engaged!
Jim. I know, but I wasn't impressed by that—propaganda!
Laura. It wasn't—the truth?
Jim. Only in Emily's optimistic opinion!
Laura. Oh—

[*Legend:* "What have you done since high school?"]

[JIM *lights a cigarette and leans indolently back on his elbows smiling at* LAURA *with a warmth and charm which lights her inwardly with altar candles. She remains by the table, picks up a piece from the glass menagerie collection, and turns it in her hands to cover her tumult.*]

Jim *(after several reflective puffs on his cigarette).* What have you done since high school?

[*She seems not to hear him.*]

Huh?

[LAURA *looks up.*]

I said what have you done since high school, Laura?
Laura. Nothing much.
Jim. You must have been doing something these six long years.
Laura. Yes.
Jim. Well, then, such as what?

Laura. I took a business course at business college—

Jim. How did that work out?

Laura. Well, not very—well—I had to drop out, it gave me—indigestion—

[JIM *laughs gently.*]

Jim. What are you doing now?

Laura. I don't do anything—much. Oh, please don't think I sit around doing nothing! My glass collection takes up a good deal of time. Glass is something you have to take good care of.

Jim. What did you say—about glass?

Laura. Collection I said—I have one— *(She clears her throat and turns away again, acutely shy.)*

Jim *(abruptly).* You know what I judge to be the trouble with you? Inferiority complex! Know what that is? That's what they call it when someone low-rates himself! I understand it because I had it, too. Although my case was not so aggravated as yours seems to be. I had it until I took up public speaking, developed my voice, and learned that I had an aptitude for science. Before that time I never thought of myself as being outstanding in any way whatsoever! Now I've never made a regular study of it, but I have a friend who says I can analyze people better than doctors that make a profession of it. I don't claim that to be necessarily true, but I can sure guess a person's psychology, Laura! *(He takes out his gum.)* Excuse me, Laura. I always take it out when the flavor is gone. I'll use this scrap of paper to wrap it in. I know how it is to get it stuck on a shoe. *(He wraps the gum in paper and puts it in his pocket.)* Yep—that's what I judge to be your principal trouble. A lack of confidence in yourself as a person. You don't have the proper amount of faith in yourself. I'm basing that fact on a number of your remarks and also on certain observations I've made. For instance that clumping you thought was so awful in high school. You say that you even dreaded to walk into class. You see what you did? You dropped out of school, you gave up an education because of a clump, which as far as I know was practically non-existent! A little physical defect is what you have. Hardly noticeable even! Magnified thousands of times by imagination! You know what my strong advice to you is? Think of yourself as *superior* in some way!

Laura. In what way would I think?

Jim. Why, man alive, Laura! Just look about you a little, what do you see? A world full of common people! All of 'em born and all of 'em going to die! Which of them has one-tenth of your good points! Or mine! Or anyone else's, as far as that goes—gosh! Everybody excels in some one thing. Some in many! *(He unconsciously glances at himself in the mirror.)* All you've got to do is discover in *what!* Take me, for instance. *(He adjusts his tie at the mirror.)* My interest happens to lie in electro-dynamics. I'm taking a course in radio engineering at night school, Laura, on top of a fairly responsible job at the warehouse. I'm taking that course and studying public speaking.

Laura. Ohhhh.

Jim. Because I believe in the future of television! *(Turning his back to her.)* I wish to be ready to go up right along with it. Therefore I'm planning to get in on the ground floor. In fact I've already made the right connections and all that remains is for the industry itself to get under way! Full steam—*(His eyes are starry.) Knowledge*—Zzzzzp! *Money*—Zzzzzzp!—*Power!* That's the cycle democracy is built on!

[*His attitude is convincingly dynamic.* LAURA *stares at him, even her shyness eclipsed in her absolute wonder. He suddenly grins.*]

I guess you think I think a lot of myself!

Laura. No—o-o-o, I—

Jim. Now how about you? Isn't there something you take more interest in than anything else?

Laura. Well, I do—as I said—have my—glass collection—

[*A peal of girlish laughter rings from the kitchenette.*]

Jim. I'm not sure I know what you're talking about. What kind of glass is it?

Laura. Little articles of it, they're ornaments mostly! Most of them are little animals made out of glass, the tiniest little animals in the world. Mother calls them a glass menagerie! Here's an example of one, if you'd like to see it! This one is one of the oldest. It's nearly thirteen.

[*Music:* "The Glass Menagerie."]

[*He stretches out his hand.*]

Oh, be careful—if you breathe, it breaks!

Jim. I'd better not take it. I'm pretty clumsy with things.

Laura. Go on, I trust you with him! *(She places the piece in his palm.)* There now—you're holding

A

A. Symbolism

? In what way is Laura placing her life in Jim's hands? (She shows her trust by sharing her most precious possession and in so doing displays her vulnerability.)

Humanities Connection: Responding to the Photograph The photograph can be used to illustrate the portion of Scene 7 running from the bottom of page 801 through the first half of column 1 on page 803.

? What does the photograph add to your mental picture of the scene? Does it increase or decrease your awareness of the fragility of the unicorn—and of Laura? (Answers will vary.) Why is it appropriate that a unicorn should be Laura's favorite? (The unicorn is a mythical creature with no place in the modern world. Laura, too, is out of place in a world that frightens her.)

"Unicorns—aren't they extinct in the modern world?"

him gently! Hold him over the light, he loves the light! You see how the light shines through him?
Jim. It sure does shine!
Laura. I shouldn't be partial, but he is my favorite one.
Jim. What kind of a thing is this one supposed to be?
Laura. Haven't you noticed the single horn on his forehead?
Jim. A unicorn, huh?
Laura. Mmmm-hmmm!
Jim. Unicorns—aren't they extinct in the modern world?
Laura. I know!
Jim. Poor little fellow, he must feel sort of lonesome.
Laura *(smiling).* Well, if he does, he doesn't complain about it. He stays on a shelf with some horses that don't have horns and all of them seem to get along nicely together.
Jim. How do you know?
Laura *(lightly).* I haven't heard any arguments among them!
Jim *(grinning).* No arguments, huh? Well, that's a pretty good sign! Where shall I set him?
Laura. Put him on the table. They all like a change of scenery once in a while!
Jim. Well, well, well, well—*(He places the glass piece on the table, then raises his arms and stretches.)* Look how big my shadow is when I stretch!
Laura. Oh, oh, yes—it stretches across the ceiling!
Jim *(crossing to the door).* I think it's stopped raining. *(He opens the fire-escape door and the background music changes to a dance tune.)* Where does the music come from?
Laura. From the Paradise Dance Hall across the alley.
Jim. How about cutting the rug a little, Miss Wingfield?
Laura. Oh, I—
Jim. Or is your program filled up? Let me have a look at it. *(He grasps an imaginary card.)* Why, every dance is taken! I'll just have to scratch some out.

[*Waltz music:* "La Golondrina."]

Ahhh, a waltz! *(He executes some sweeping turns by himself, then holds his arms toward* LAURA.*)*
Laura *(breathlessly).* I—can't dance!
Jim. There you go, that inferiority stuff!
Laura. I've never danced in my life!
Jim. Come on, try!
Laura. Oh, but I'd step on you!
Jim. I'm not made out of glass. A
Laura. How—how—how do we start?
Jim. Just leave it to me. You hold your arms out a little.
Laura. Like this?
Jim *(taking her in his arms).* A little bit higher. Right. Now don't tighten up, that's the main thing about it—relax.
Laura *(laughing breathlessly).* It's hard not to.
Jim. Okay.
Laura. I'm afraid you can't budge me.
Jim. What do you bet I can't? *(He swings her into motion.)*
Laura. Goodness, yes, you can!
Jim. Let yourself go, now, Laura, just let yourself go.
Laura. I'm—
Jim. Come on!
Laura. —trying!
Jim. Not so stiff—easy does it!
Laura. I know but I'm—
Jim. Loosen th' backbone! There now, that's a lot better.
Laura. Am I?
Jim. Lots, lots better! *(He moves her about the room in a clumsy waltz.)*
Laura. Oh, my!
Jim. Ha-ha!
Laura. Oh, my goodness!
Jim. Ha-ha-ha!

[*They suddenly bump into the table, and the glass piece on it falls to the floor.* JIM *stops the dance.*]

What did we hit on?
Laura. Table.
Jim. Did something fall off it? I think—
Laura. Yes.
Jim. I hope that it wasn't the little glass horse with the horn!
Laura. Yes. *(She stoops to pick it up.)*
Jim. Aw, aw, aw. Is it broken?
Laura. Now it is just like all the other horses.
Jim. It's lost its—
Laura. Horn! It doesn't matter. Maybe it's a blessing in disguise.
Jim. You'll never forgive me. I bet that that was your favorite piece of glass.
Laura. I don't have favorites much. It's no tragedy, Freckles. Glass breaks so easily. No matter B

A. Characterization
Explore the contrasts between Jim and Laura, using the image of being made out of glass or not. (Responses should center on Jim's ambitious but down-to-earth plans; he is very much a solid person, not made of glass. Laura is fragile, "breakable," and disconnected from the outer world. She *is* "made out of glass.")

B. Responding
Is Laura aware that she has called Jim by an affectionate nickname? (She seems focused on the broken unicorn. Jim misses "Freckles," too; it seems to have slipped in from the fantasy we have inferred that Laura has had.) Is the breaking of the unicorn truly "no tragedy"? What could it foreshadow? (It is a major disruption in the life of someone as sheltered as Laura. It could foreshadow her disappointment if Jim does not continue to be her gentleman caller after this evening.)

A. Responding

Laura is trying to make Jim feel better by this comment. It also offers insight into what is happening in the scene.

? The audience may find Jim a fairly ordinary young man, but how does Laura see him? (She finds him exceptional.) How do Laura's comments on the unicorn relate to the way Jim has been able to make her feel? (He has made her feel like a valuable, interesting, unique person, not a freak.)

B. Responding

? How often has Laura previously been kissed by anyone other than family? (Most likely, never) Is she offended? (She is thrilled.) Why might Jim think she is upset? (She is speechless.) Although he kissed Laura on the lips, does Jim think of her as a potential girlfriend? (No; he speaks of her as a sister.) At this point, what future do you predict for Jim and Laura? (If students have not read ahead, some may predict an all-out courtship; others may predict a good, steady friendship that helps Laura come out of herself.)

how careful you are. The traffic jars the shelves and things fall off them.

Jim. Still I'm awfully sorry that I was the cause.

Laura *(smiling).* I'll just imagine he had an operation. The horn was removed to make him feel less—freakish!

[*They both laugh.*]

Now he will feel more at home with the other horses, the ones that don't have horns. . . .

Jim. Ha-ha, that's very funny! *(Suddenly he is serious.)* I'm glad to see that you have a sense of humor. You know—you're—well—very different! Surprisingly different from anyone else I know! *(His voice becomes soft and hesitant with a genuine feeling.)* Do you mind me telling you that?

[LAURA *is abashed beyond speech.*]

I mean it in a nice way—

[LAURA *nods shyly, looking away.*]

You make me feel sort of—I don't know how to put it! I'm usually pretty good at expressing things, but—this is something that I don't know how to say!

[LAURA *touches her throat and clears it—turns the broken unicorn in her hands. His voice becomes softer.*]

Has anyone ever told you that you were pretty?

[*There is a pause, and the music rises slightly.* LAURA *looks up slowly, with wonder, and shakes her head.*]

Well, you are! In a very different way from anyone else. And all the nicer because of the difference, too.

[*His voice becomes low and husky.* LAURA *turns away, nearly faint with the novelty of her emotions.*]

I wish that you were my sister. I'd teach you to have some confidence in yourself. The different people are not like other people, but being different is nothing to be ashamed of. Because other people are not such wonderful people. They're one hundred times one thousand. You're one times one! They walk all over the earth. You just stay here. They're common as—weeds, but—you—well, you're—*Blue Roses!*

[*Image on screen:* Blue Roses.]

[*The music changes.*]

Laura. I blue is wrong for—roses. . . .

Jim. It's right for you! You're—pretty!

Laura. In what respect am I pretty?

Jim. In all respects—believe me! Your eyes—your hair—are pretty! Your hands are pretty! *(He catches hold of her hand.)* You think I'm making this up because I'm invited to dinner and have to be nice. Oh, I could do that! I could put on an act for you, Laura, and say lots of things without being very sincere. But this time I am. I'm talking to you sincerely. I happened to notice you had this inferiority complex that keeps you from feeling comfortable with people. Somebody needs to build your confidence up and make you proud, instead of shy and turning away and—blushing. Somebody—ought to—*kiss* you, Laura!

[*His hand slips slowly up her arm to her shoulder as the music swells tumultuously. He suddenly turns her about and kisses her on the lips. When he releases her,* LAURA *sinks on the sofa with a bright, dazed look.* JIM *backs away and fishes in his pocket for a cigarette.*]

[*Legend on screen:* "A souvenir."]

Stumblejohn!

[*He lights the cigarette, avoiding her look. There is a peal of girlish laughter from* AMANDA *in the kitchenette.* LAURA *slowly raises and opens her hand. It still contains the little broken glass animal. She looks at it with a tender, bewildered expression.*]

Stumblejohn! I shouldn't have done that—that was way off the beam. You don't smoke, do you?

[*She looks up, smiling, not hearing the question. He sits beside her rather gingerly. She looks at him speechlessly—waiting. He coughs decorously and moves a little farther aside as he considers the situation and senses her feelings, dimly, with perturbation. He speaks gently.*]

Would you—care for a—mint?

[*She doesn't seem to hear him but her look grows brighter even.*]

Peppermint? Life Saver? My pocket's a regular drug store—wherever I go. . . . *(He pops a mint in his mouth. Then he gulps and decides to make a clean breast of it. He speaks slowly and gingerly.)* Laura, you know, if I had a sister like you,

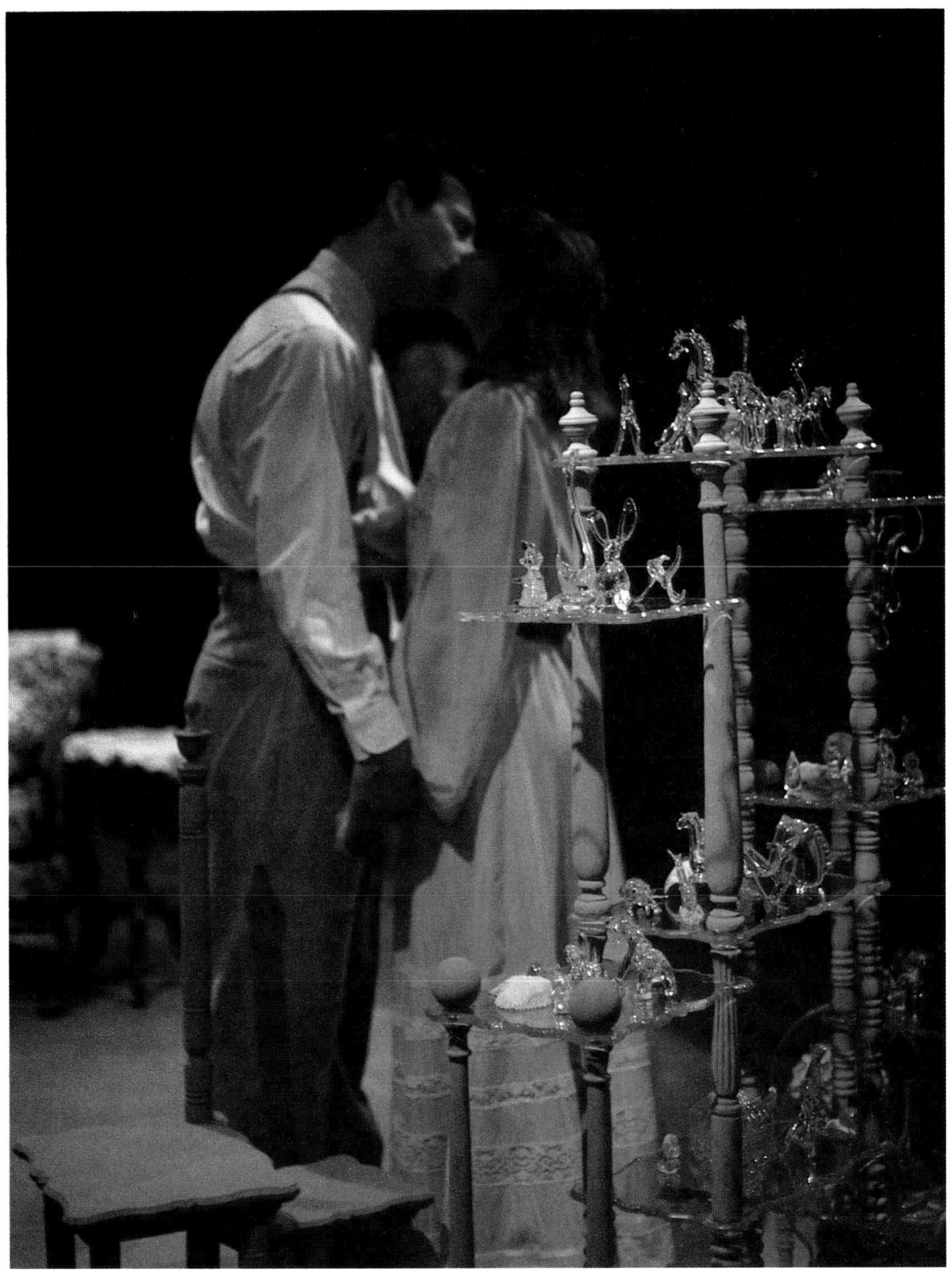

*"Somebody—ought to—*kiss *you, Laura!"*

Humanities Connection: Responding to the Photograph

? How does the photograph enhance your idea of the beauty and fragility of Laura's collection of glass animals? What kinds of care would this collection need? How could rearranging them lead to long periods of time playing with them? (Answers will vary.) Why is the use of blue lighting especially appropriate? (It brings out the beauty of the glass and connects with Jim's nickname for Laura, "Blue Roses.")

A. Irony
Jim says the words, but it is Laura whose entire world has just changed. The man she loves has treated her gently and kindly and kindled her hopes. Jim has no idea of his own importance to Laura, or the fact that his announcement of his engagement shatters a future Laura has just begun to enter.

B. Responding
? Why is it appropriate for Laura to give Jim the hornless unicorn? (Laura is still unique, but the unicorn is not. Now it is just an ordinary "horse," just as Jim is an ordinary person.)

C. Plot
? What new development is Amanda completely unaware of as she enters? (That Jim is engaged and will not be coming back) What conversational snags do you predict for the rest of the scene? What will Amanda think about Tom when she finds out that Jim is engaged? (Answers will vary. Amanda may think Tom was deliberately cruel.)

I'd do the same thing as Tom. I'd bring out fellows and—introduce her to them. The right type of boys—of a type to—appreciate her. Only—well—he made a mistake about me. Maybe I've got no call to be saying this. That may not have been the idea in having me over. But what if it was? There's nothing wrong about that. The only trouble is that in my case—I'm not in a situation to—do the right thing. I can't take down your number and say I'll phone. I can't call up next week and—ask for a date. I thought I had better explain the situation in case you—misunderstood it and—I hurt your feelings. . . .

[*There is a pause. Slowly, very slowly.* LAURA*'s look changes, her eyes returning slowly from his to the glass figure in her palm.* AMANDA *utters another gay laugh in the kitchenette.*]

Laura *(faintly).* You—won't—call again?
Jim. No, Laura, I can't. *(He rises from the sofa.)* As I was just explaining, I've—got strings on me. Laura, I've—been going steady! I go out all the time with a girl named Betty. She's a home-girl like you, and Catholic, and Irish, and in a great many ways we—get along fine. I met her last summer on a moonlight boat trip up the river to Alton, on the *Majestic*. Well—right away from the start it was—love!

[*Legend:* Love!]

[LAURA *sways slightly forward and grips the arm of the sofa. He fails to notice, now enrapt in his own comfortable being.*]

Being in love has made a new man of me!

[*Leaning stiffly forward, clutching the arm of the sofa,* LAURA *struggles visibly with her storm. But* JIM *is oblivious; she is a long way off.*]

A The power of love is really pretty tremendous! Love is something that—changes the whole world, Laura!

[*The storm abates a little and* LAURA *leans back. He notices her again.*]

It happened that Betty's aunt took sick, she got a wire and had to go to Centralia. So Tom—when he asked me to dinner—I naturally just accepted the invitation, not knowing that you—that he—that I— *(He stops awkwardly.)* Huh—I'm a stumblejohn!

[*He flops back on the sofa. The holy candles on the altar of* LAURA*'s face have been snuffed out. There is a look of almost infinite desolation.* JIM *glances at her uneasily.*]

I wish that you would—say something.

[*She bites her lip which was trembling and then bravely smiles. She opens her hand again on the broken glass figure. Then she gently takes his hand and raises it level with her own. She carefully places the unicorn in the palm of his hand, then pushes his fingers closed upon it.*]

What are you—doing that for? You want me to have him? Laura?

[*She nods.*]

What for?
Laura. A—souvenir. . . .

[*She rises unsteadily and crouches beside the victrola to wind it up.*]

[*Legend on screen:* "Things have a way of turning out so badly!" *Or image:* "Gentleman caller waving goodbye—gaily."]

[*At this moment* AMANDA *rushes brightly back into the living room. She bears a pitcher of fruit punch in an old-fashioned cut-glass pitcher, and a plate of macaroons. The plate has a gold border and poppies painted on it.*]

Amanda. Well, well, well! Isn't the air delightful after the shower? I've made you children a little liquid refreshment.

(She turns gaily to JIM.*)* Jim, do you know that song about lemonade?

"Lemonade, lemonade
Made in the shade and stirred with a spade—
Good enough for any old maid!"

Jim *(uneasily).* Ha-ha! No—I never heard it.
Amanda. Why, Laura! You look so serious!
Jim. We were having a serious conversation.
Amanda. Good! Now you're better acquainted!
Jim *(uncertainly).* Ha-ha! Yes.
Amanda. You modern young people are much more serious-minded than my generation. I was so gay as a girl!
Jim. You haven't changed, Mrs. Wingfield.
Amanda. Tonight I'm rejuvenated! The gaiety of the occasion, Mr. O'Connor! *(She tosses her head with a peal of laughter, spilling some lemonade.)* Oooo! I'm baptizing myself!

Closure
Have students choose one of these activities: (1) In class discussion, apply to the people of this play Henry David Thoreau's observation, "The mass of men lead lives of quiet desperation" (*Walden*, "Economy"); (2) With several classmates in a small group, reach a consensus on a probable future for Laura, Amanda, and Tom.

Reading Check Test: Scene 7

1. The reason Amanda first lights a candle is that she finds candles more romantic than electric lights. *False*
2. Jim treats Laura with kindness and consideration. *True*
3. Attempting to dance, Jim and Laura knock down a shelf of Laura's glass ornaments. *False*
4. Jim kisses Laura but apologizes for doing so. *True*
5. Amanda accuses Tom of deliberately tricking her by bringing home an engaged man. *True*

Jim. Here—let me—
Amanda *(setting the pitcher down)*. There now. I discovered we had some maraschino cherries. I dumped them in, juice and all!
Jim. You shouldn't have gone to that trouble, Mrs. Wingfield.
Amanda. Trouble, trouble? Why, it was loads of fun! Didn't you hear me cutting up in the kitchen? I bet your ears were burning! I told Tom how outdone with him I was for keeping you to himself so long a time! He should have brought you over much, much sooner! Well, now that you've found your way, I want you to be a very frequent caller! Not just occasional but all the time. Oh, we're going to have a lot of gay times together! I see them coming! Mmm, just breathe that air! So fresh, and the moon's so pretty! I'll skip back out—I know where my place is when young folks are having a—serious conversation!
Jim. Oh, don't go out, Mrs. Wingfield. The fact of the matter is I've got to be going.
Amanda. Going, now? You're joking! Why, it's only the shank of the evening,[1] Mr. O'Connor!
Jim. Well, you know how it is.
Amanda. You mean you're a young workingman and have to keep workingmen's hours. We'll let you off early tonight. But only on the condition that next time you stay later. What's the best night for you? Isn't Saturday night the best night for you workingmen?
Jim. I have a couple of time-clocks to punch, Mrs. Wingfield. One at morning, another one at night!
Amanda. My, but you *are* ambitious! You work at night, too?
Jim. No, Ma'am, not work but—Betty!

[*He crosses deliberately to pick up his hat. The band at the Paradise Dance Hall goes into a tender waltz.*]

Amanda. Betty? Betty? Who's—Betty?

[*There is an ominous cracking sound in the sky.*]

Jim. Oh, just a girl. The girl I go steady with!

[*He smiles charmingly. The sky falls.*]

[*Legend:* "The Sky Falls."]

Amanda *(a long-drawn exhalation)*. Ohhhh . . . Is it a serious romance, Mr. O'Connor?
Jim. We're going to be married the second Sunday in June.

1. **the shank of the evening**: early in the evening.

Amanda. Ohhhh—how nice! Tom didn't mention that you were engaged to be married.
Jim. The cat's not out of the bag at the warehouse yet. You know how they are. They call you Romeo and stuff like that. *(He stops at the oval mirror to put on his hat. He carefully shapes the brim and the crown to give a discreetly dashing effect.)* It's been a wonderful evening, Mrs. Wingfield. I guess this is what they mean by Southern hospitality. A
Amanda. It really wasn't anything at all.
Jim. I hope it don't seem like I'm rushing off. But I promised Betty I'd pick her up at the Wabash depot, an' by the time I get my jalopy down there her train'll be in. Some women are pretty upset if you keep 'em waiting.
Amanda. Yes, I know—the tyranny of women! *(She extends her hand.)* Goodbye, Mr. O'Connor. I wish you luck—and happiness—and success! All three of them, and so does Laura! Don't you, Laura? B
Laura. Yes!
Jim *(taking Laura's hand)*. Goodbye, Laura. I'm certainly going to treasure that souvenir. And don't you forget the good advice I gave you. *(He raises his voice to a cheery shout.)* So long, Shakespeare! Thanks again, ladies. Good night!

[*He grins and ducks jauntily out. Still bravely grimacing,* AMANDA *closes the door on the gentleman caller. Then she turns back to the room with a puzzled expression. She and* LAURA *don't dare to face each other.* LAURA *crouches beside the victrola to wind it.*]

Amanda *(faintly)*. Things have a way of turning out so badly. I don't believe that I would play the victrola. Well, well—well! Our gentleman caller was engaged to be married! *(She raises her voice.)* Tom!
Tom *(from the kitchenette)*. Yes, Mother?
Amanda. Come in here a minute. I want to tell you something awfully funny.
Tom *(entering with a macaroon and a glass of the lemonade)*. Has the gentleman caller gotten away already?
Amanda. The gentleman caller has made an early departure. What a wonderful joke you played on us!
Tom. How do you mean?
Amanda. You didn't mention that he was engaged to be married.
Tom. Jim? Engaged? C

A. Responding
Does Jim have the slightest awareness of what his news has done not only to Laura, but also to Amanda? Explain. (No. They had built up expectations he knew nothing about. He thought he was just invited for a nice dinner at a friend's house, nothing more.)

B. Character
How does Amanda's lifelong concern with etiquette and the social niceties help her here? (She rises to the occasion, acting hospitably despite the blow to her expectations. She really does know how to treat a guest.)

C. Interpretation
Did Tom know that Jim was engaged? What evidence supports your answer? (He did not know. He acts genuinely surprised, and Jim himself said he had not yet announced the news at work.)

ANALYZING SCENE 7
Identifying Facts

1. The lights go out at the beginning of Scene 7, so that the long scene with the gentleman caller is acted by candlelight. This gives a mysterious, romantic air to the scene, and it also creates the opportunity for a powerful ending for the play—as Laura blows the candles out, perhaps symbolically suggesting the end to a very special day (like a birthday), or perhaps hinting at the extinction of any hopes Tom (and we) may have cherished for Laura's happiness.

2. Jim is charming and honest with Laura. He seems to understand her feelings and not think of her as "peculiar." He gets Laura to relax and to talk. They dance and kiss, and it seems for a moment as if a romance might be possible. Jim tells Laura and Amanda about his engagement to Betty; then he says that he can never come back again.

Interpreting Meanings

3. At the beginning of Scene 7, Laura is lying on the daybed, sick with nervousness. She is shy and apprehensive as Jim brings her the glass of wine, but she begins to relax as she talks to him, even

A. Analyzing

? Pick out the word in Amanda's speech that reveals most strongly the degree to which her fantasy world has been destroyed. (Answers may include *fools* or *deserted*, but *crippled* is stronger. Amanda has refused to speak the word or let others use it, yet now she refers flatly to "an unmarried sister who's crippled." The fantasy is over.)

Amanda. That's what he just informed us.
Tom. I'll be jiggered! I didn't know about that.
Amanda. That seems very peculiar.
Tom. What's peculiar about it?
Amanda. Didn't you call him your best friend down at the warehouse?
Tom. He is, but how did I know?
Amanda. It seems extremely peculiar that you wouldn't know your best friend was going to be married!
Tom. The warehouse is where I work, not where I know things about people!
Amanda. You don't know things anywhere! You live in a dream; you manufacture illusions!

[*He crosses to the door.*]

Where are you going?
Tom. I'm going to the movies.
A **Amanda.** That's right, now that you've had us make such fools of ourselves. The effort, the preparations, all the expense! The new floor lamp, the rug, the clothes for Laura! All for what? To entertain some other girl's fiancé! Go to the movies, go! Don't think about us, a mother deserted, an unmarried sister who's crippled and has no job! Don't let anything interfere with your selfish pleasure! Just go, go, go—to the movies!
Tom. All right, I will! The more you shout about my selfishness to me the quicker I'll go, and I won't go to the movies!
Amanda. Go, then! Go to the moon—you selfish dreamer!

[TOM *smashes his glass on the floor. He plunges out on the fire escape, slamming the door.* LAURA *screams in fright. The dance-hall music becomes louder.* TOM *stands on the fire escape, gripping the rail. The moon breaks through the storm clouds, illuminating his face.*]

[*Legend on screen:* "And so goodbye . . ."]

[TOM*'s closing speech is timed with what is happening inside the house. We see, as though through soundproof glass, that* AMANDA *appears to be making a comforting speech to* LAURA, *who is huddled upon the sofa. Now that we cannot hear the mother's speech, her silliness is gone and she has dignity and tragic beauty.* LAURA*'s hair hides her face until, at the end of the speech, she lifts her head to smile at her mother.* AMANDA*'s gestures are slow and graceful, almost dance-like, as she comforts her daughter. At the end of her speech she glances a moment at the father's picture—then withdraws through the portieres. At the close of* TOM*'s speech,* LAURA *blows out the candles, ending the play.*]

Tom. I didn't go to the moon, I went much further—for time is the longest distance between two places. Not long after that I was fired for writing a poem on the lid of a shoe box. I left Saint Louis. I descended the steps of this fire escape for a last time and followed, from then on, in my father's footsteps, attempting to find in motion what was lost in space. I traveled around a great deal. The cities swept about me like dead leaves, leaves that were brightly colored but torn away from branches. I would have stopped, but I was pursued by something. It always came upon me unawares, taking me altogether by surprise. Perhaps it was a familiar bit of music. Perhaps it was only a piece of transparent glass. Perhaps I am walking along a street at night, in some strange city, before I have found companions. I pass the lighted window of a shop where perfume is sold. The window is filled with pieces of colored glass, tiny transparent bottles in delicate colors, like bits of a shattered rainbow. Then all at once my sister touches my shoulder. I turn around and look into her eyes. Oh, Laura, Laura, I tried to leave you behind me, but I am more faithful than I intended to be! I reach for a cigarette, I cross the street, I run into the movies or a bar, I buy a drink, I speak to the nearest stranger—anything that can blow your candles out!

[LAURA *bends over the candles.*]

For nowadays the world is lit by lightning! Blow out your candles, Laura—and so goodbye. . . .

[*She blows the candles out.*]

telling him of her admiration for him in high school. Laura accepts a stick of gum, shares some painful memories, and listens to his advice. Most of all, she remains—she does not run away. She dances, they kiss: our hopes are at their highest. Suddenly, there is a reversal when Jim announces his engagement to Betty. Laura is disappointed, gives Jim the unicorn, and retreats to her menagerie. Amanda is told the bad news, and Jim leaves. In anger, Amanda lashes out at Tom for playing such a trick on them, and Tom leaves. Things have, indeed, turned out badly.

4. Laura is shy and apprehensive when Jim arrives, but little by little his charm succeeds in thawing her reserve. She shares memories with him and listens to his advice. We can see that she is romantically attracted to him when they dance. But Jim's announcement of his engagement shatters our (and Laura's) hopes.

5. Student answers will vary.

6. In this statement, perhaps Laura is speculating that the loss of the horn, which differentiated the unicorn from the other animals, has made the creature more "normal"—symbolizing, in turn, Laura's own hopes to become less painfully shy and more like other people.

7. The statement is ambiguous: It might refer to the end of a special day, or it might signal the end of Laura's hopes for a normal life.

The Play As A Whole

1. She resembles the glass animals in that she is shy, fragile, and easily hurt; she is transformed into a pretty young woman. The stage directions say that she ". . . is like a piece of translucent glass touched by light, given a momentary radiance, not actual, not lasting." This description suggestively foreshadows the outcome of the play.

Like Laura, the unicorn is different from all the others around it. Laura tells Jim that the unicorn is her favorite animal—thus implying an awareness on her own part that she is "set apart" from the rest of the world. Like Laura herself, the unicorn is a fantasy animal, living in a fan-

(Answers continue on next page.)

A Comment on the Play

When he began to write *The Glass Menagerie,* Tennessee Williams had already written a number of one-act plays. This play is a natural extension for a writer skilled in the one-act form because it has no long, sustained sixty-minute acts. Instead, we have a series of short scenes held together by a simple and appealing story: Amanda tries to find a gentleman caller for Laura.

The play begins with a brief, lively scene of exposition. The first scene introduces us to the family, and we know them instantly. The long-suffering mother lives in the past and manages her son and daughter as if they were still children. The artistic son labors at a menial and unappealing job. The daughter is frail and painfully shy, and she walks with a severe limp. In the first scene, we do not yet know where our primary interest will lie; but at the end of this scene, there is a signpost when Laura says, "Mother is afraid I'm going to be an old maid." Our sympathies are aroused.

With the beginning of Scene 2, a new element enters the story. It upsets the opening situation and moves the story to Amanda's desperate question: "What are we going to do?" The family has to find a way to survive. The mother decides to find a husband for Laura, and the story is underway. Major dramatic questions are posed: Will they find a gentleman caller for Laura? Will he fall in love with her and marry her (and support them)? Almost everything in the rest of the play advances the story toward the answers to these questions, which come in the memorable last scene.

Thus, by the end of Scene 2, we have met the people we care about, people who are in a desperate situation. They have conflicting desires: Tom wants to escape, to go to sea; Laura wants only to be left alone; Amanda wants to find a bridegroom for her daughter. Tom's story is tied into the gentleman caller story because Tom will feel free to leave only when he has found someone to marry his sister and take the responsibility for the family. It is, of course, Amanda's desire that prevails and moves the action forward.

We know from Tom's opening speech that the gentleman caller is going to arrive. We also know from Tom's costume in that opening narration that he does manage to get away to the Merchant Marine. Our suspense, our interest, then, is not in *if* these events are going to happen, but in *how* they are going to happen. In addition, we wonder *what* is going to happen when Laura meets the gentleman caller.

The last scene plays itself out as one of the most beautiful and touching scenes in all of American drama. And Tom escapes with his guilts and his loving memory of his sister, which will haunt him all the days of his life.

Responding to the Play

Analyzing Scene 7

Identifying Facts

1. What does Williams achieve in the way of "theater poetry" by having Tom neglect to pay the light bill?
2. What happens to make us think at first that Jim O'Connor's visit may work out as Amanda hopes? Explain how the evening ends in disappointment for Laura and Amanda.

Interpreting Meanings

3. The gentleman-caller scene is a perfect little play within a play. Tell how the **basic dramatic elements** are used in this scene: characters we care about, placed in a situation where much is at stake, taking steps to get what they want.
4. One of the basic elements of drama is **progression,** or change. Trace the progression of the relationship between Jim and Laura in this scene.
5. How did you feel about Jim O'Connor in this scene?
6. Why does Laura say about the broken horn on the unicorn: "Maybe it's a blessing in disguise"?
7. What does Tom mean at the end when he talks about Laura blowing out her candles?

The Play as a Whole

1. Williams has written of his own sister's collection of glass animals:

> By poetic association they came to represent, in my memory, all the softest emotions that belong to recollection of things past. They stood for all the small and tender things that relieve the austere pattern of life and make it endurable to the sensitive.
>
> —Tennessee Williams

(Continued from previous page.)
tasy world. But once the unicorn's horn is broken, it becomes like all the other animals. Paradoxically, Laura does not grieve at Jim's accidental breaking of the horn; she seems to recognize that Jim may have been the means of restoring her (and the unicorn) to "normalcy." By giving the unicorn to Jim as a souvenir, Laura implicitly entrusts him with her favorite possession, as well as—symbolically—with herself.

2. The movies symbolize escape from painful reality for Tom.

The fire escape is also an escape for Tom: this is where he goes to smoke.

The Paradise Music Hall symbolizes romance and adventure for Tom, as he recalls hearing the music from across the alley and seeing young couples kiss.

Laura's leg brace is a visible reminder of her physical handicap and, therefore, of her "difference" from others.

3. The epigraph from Cummings underlines the pathos and fragility of Laura's world.

4. Students should agree that Scene 7 marks the play's climax. We have two reasons to hope that Jim will fall in love
(Answers continue in left-hand column.)

(Continued from top.)
with Laura. One is Amanda's intense wish to have Laura married to a "nice young man." The other, quite separate wish is Laura's own. Jim is the only man she has ever cared about, and she has never before expressed her feelings to him. She does so in this scene, and he seems to respond—with a dance, a kiss—until suddenly our hopes, and Laura's, are dashed with the announcement of his engagement.

5. We sympathize with Amanda, above all, because she wants her children to be happy. She wants Laura to have a normal life and wants Tom to have ambition and a better life. Amanda also fears that Tom will take to drink as an escape, and she doesn't want that. Because of her own experiences, Amanda knows about life's difficult realities. It is her fear of poverty, alcoholism, and de-
(Answers continue on next page.)

Discuss the **symbolism** of the glass menagerie in relation to Laura. How, for example, does Laura resemble the glass animals? What does the unicorn represent at first, and what does it represent once its horn has been broken?

2. Discuss the way Williams uses the following motifs or props in the play as **symbols.** What does each one represent? How do they relate to the play's theme?

The movies	The fire escape
The Paradise Music Hall	Laura's leg brace

3. Why do you think Williams chose the line from Cummings's poem to open his play?
4. The **climax** of a play is the high point of the story—its most intensely emotional moment. What scene do you think marks the climax of *The Glass Menagerie?*
5. In any story, complexity makes for interesting characters. In good drama, we rarely find a "good guy" pitted against a "bad guy"; the best drama often occurs when both people in a conflict are right. Do you sympathize with Amanda, even though she causes her children to suffer? Do you think Tom and Laura are both wrong and right? Explain.
6. One critic has said that *The Glass Menagerie* shows us a series of contrasts between (a) the dreamer and the doer, (b) the past and the present, (c) fantasy and reality, (d) psychological and physical handicaps, and (e) the desire for escape and the awareness of responsibilities. Choose one of these contrasts, and trace the way it's developed in the play.
7. Williams keeps indicating that music called "The Glass Menagerie" is heard. Locate the places in the play when the music is called for. Discuss in a group the kind of music you think should be provided. If there are musicians in your class, they might compose "The Glass Menagerie" music.

Writing About the Play

A Creative Response

1. **Extending the Play.** We never learn what happens to Laura and Amanda after Tom leaves. The Wingfield household has been barely managing on Tom's meager salary. Write a letter that Laura might have written to Tom two years after her brother's departure.

A Critical Response

2. **Responding to the Play.** *The Glass Menagerie* touches on the **conflict** between an individual's "right to be happy" and the individual's responsibility to others—a very real and frequent personal conflict. In an essay, tell what you think about this conflict. Which should come first—happiness or responsibility? Under what circumstances would your opinion change? Do you think Tom was right or wrong in leaving home?
3. **Commenting on "Biographical Criticism."** The drama critic Brendan Gill wrote this about a 1983 revival of Williams's play:

> *The Glass Menagerie* was sufficiently touching when it burst upon Broadway in 1945, and not least because it seemed to hold strong hints of hope as well as despair: Tom Wingfield's dreams of a future happiness were transparently autobiographical, and would surely be realized by the charming young man who set them down. The play is all the more touching now, in the shadow of the playwright's so often anguished life and grotesque and unnecessary death; how hard he worked and how many superb plays and short stories he gave us, and yet how little happiness he ever knew!
>
> —Brendan Gill

Are biographical facts about the author's life necessary or even helpful to a full understanding and appreciation of the play? Or can *The Glass Menagerie* (or, for that matter, any other work of art) stand on its own without our having to know anything about the author's life? Discuss these questions in a brief essay. Begin by clearly stating your opinion on the necessity or helpfulness of such "biographical criticism." You may refer to other plays, stories, novels, and authors if you wish.

4. **Evaluating Different Versions of the Play.** In the film version of *The Glass Menagerie,* the story has an altogether different ending, with Laura happily and confidently preparing for the arrival of another gentleman caller. In the 1973 television production, the narrator's speeches (those with Tom in his Merchant Marine uniform) were almost entirely omitted from the play. In an essay, tell what you think of both of these changes. How would the changes affect the **theme** and **mood** of the play?
5. **Describing the Use of Lights.** Williams goes to a great deal of trouble to describe the use of lights in his "memory play." In an essay, analyze the way light is used in the play to create mood and to contribute to the play's theme of illusion versus reality. Cite specific passages of the play.
6. **Comparing the Play to the Memoirs.** In a brief essay, compare this play to the information provided in Williams's memoirs, which follow. Before you write, gather your information in a chart like the one that follows:

	Memoirs	Play
Characters		
Setting		
Conflict		

pendence that causes her to establish goals for her children that are not theirs. Amanda manages to save enough money for Laura's business course, and we admire her for her ability to cope and survive. At the end of the play, Williams says that Amanda has "dignity and tragic beauty," and that is why we sympathize with her.

Tom wants to write and to see the world—goals that are understandable and perfectly acceptable. But he is "wrong" because in order to achieve his goals he must abandon his mother and his sister. Laura wants peace in the household, and she also wants to be left alone. For a brief moment at the end of the play, she also appears to want a relationship with Jim. But she is "wrong" because she has not taken responsibility for her own life.

6. Answers will vary.

7. The line is ambiguous. He might mean "Don't light up my memory of you anymore" or "Accept the harsh light of reality."

Primary Sources

The Model for Laura

"The story of my sister Rose's tragedy begins a few years before I commenced my three-year break from college to work for the Continental Shoemakers branch of the International Shoe Company.

"I have mentioned that Rose suffered for several years from mysterious stomach trouble. She was several times hospitalized for this digestive trouble but no ulcer, no physical cause for the illness, could be determined. At last it was recommended that she have 'an exploratory operation.'

"Luckily our family doctor, a brilliant physician, intervened at this point and told my mother, much to her dismay, that it was his (quite accurate) opinion that Rose needed psychiatric attention, the mysterious digestive upset being due, he thought, to psychic or psychosomatic reasons that could be determined only through the course of analysis.

"You can imagine how this struck Miss Edwina. I am afraid that dear Mother has at times seemed to me to have been a moderately controlled hysteric all her life—and in her family tree (on both sides of it, Dakins and Ottes) have been alarming incidences of mental and nervous breakdowns. . . .

"In her early twenties Rose was sent to Knoxville with a few inexpensive party dresses to 'make her debut.' A formal debutante party had been planned by Aunt Belle, but the death of her husband's mother intervened and the debut was 'informal.' A party was given at the Knoxville Country Club, for Rose's informal presentation to society. Aunt Belle had to buy Rose quite a few more dresses during this debut season: Even so the debut was not exactly a howling success. I think Miss Rose fell in love with a young man who did not altogether respond in kind; and Rose was never quite the same. A shadow had fallen over her that was to deepen steadily through the next four or five years.

"When Rose returned from her Knoxville debut, I said, 'How was your visit, Rose?'

"She said, 'Aunt Ella and Aunt Belle only like charming people and I'm not charming.' . . .

"There were years when I was in the shoe company and summers when I was a student at the State University of Missouri when my sister and I spent nearly all our evenings together aside from those which I spent with Hazel.

"What did we do those evenings, Rose and I? Well, we strolled about the business streets of University City. It was a sort of ritual with a pathos that I assure you was never caught in *Menagerie* nor in my story "Portrait of Girl in Glass," on which *Menagerie* was based.

"I think it was Delmar—that long, long street which probably began near the Mississippi River in downtown St. Louis and continued through University City and on out into the country—that Rose and I strolled along in the evenings. There was a root-beer stand at which we always stopped. Rose was inordinately fond of root-beer, especially on warm summer evenings. And before and after our root-beer stop, we would window-shop. Rose's passion . . . was clothes. And all along that part of Delmar that cut through University City were little shops with lighted windows at night in which were displayed dresses and accessories for women. Rose did not have much of a wardrobe and so her window-shopping on Delmar was like a hungry child's gazing through the window-fronts of restaurants. Her taste in clothes was excellent.

" 'How about *that* dress, Rose?'

" 'Oh no, that's tacky. But this one here's very nice.'

"The evening excursions lasted about an hour and a half, and I'd usually follow her into her bedroom when we came home, to continue our warmly desultory chats. I felt most at home in that room, which was furnished with the white ivory bedroom set that had been acquired with the family's 'furnished apartment' on Westminster Place when we first moved to St. Louis in 1918.

"It was the only attractive room in the apartment—or did it seem so because it was my sister's?

"Dad had subleased our first real residence in St. Louis, a very charming two-story Georgian house in the suburb of Clayton, only a block or two from Washington University. . . . Miss Rose's mind again began to slip. Not violently but gradually.

"I remember a drive in the country with young friends. We started, the young friends and I, to laugh at the outrageous behavior of an acquaintance who was losing his mind. Miss Rose turned very grave and stiff in the back seat of the car.

" 'You must never make fun of insanity,' she reproved us. 'It's worse than death.' "

—from *Memoirs,*
Tennessee Williams

A. Humanities Connection: Responding to the Photograph Hansberry was 29 when this play achieved resounding success; she lived to age 34. ? Judging by her picture, what kind of personality would you expect Hansberry to have? Would she be pessimistic? (Her radiant smile is a possible clue that she might have a sense of humor and a positive outlook on life.) Read the biographical introduction to her play on this page to check the accuracy of your perceptions.

ADDITIONAL WRITING ASSIGNMENT This introduction comments that *A Raisin in the Sun*, like *The Glass Menagerie*, concerns a poor family in a desperate situation, with the dreams of different family members coming into conflict. Have students write about how the dreams of an African American family in the 1950's might differ. What potential for conflict do students see?

Lorraine Hansberry (1930–1965)

Lorraine Hansberry grew up in Chicago's Southside, the youngest of four children. Her father was a successful businessman, and her family was relatively wealthy by neighborhood standards.When she was eight, Hansberry's family moved into a hostile white neighborhood because her father, in conjunction with the NAACP, was protesting against the "restrictive covenants" that segregated housing.

Hansberry was educated in Chicago's public schools and showed an early talent for both writing and drawing. She wrote plays and short stories while she was in high school and when she later attended the University of Wisconsin and the Art Institute of New York.

When *A Raisin in the Sun* opened in 1959, it was an instant success. This play marked the beginning of a vigorous black theater movement, which became one of the most vital forces in the modern American theater.

> How to describe the effect *A Raisin in the Sun* had on most of us when it opened in 1959! There I was in Detroit's Cass Theater, a young man who had never seen anywhere a black man express all the things I felt but never had the courage to express. . . . The power of the play had made us all aware of our uniqueness as blacks and had encouraged us to pursue our dreams. Indeed, the play had confirmed that our dreams were possible.
>
> —Woodie King, Jr.

Lloyd Richards directed a superb cast, which included Sidney Poitier, Claudia McNeil, Diana Sands, Ruby Dee, and Louis Gossett. The play was translated into thirty languages and won the New York Drama Critics Award. At twenty-nine, Lorraine Hansberry became the youngest person—and the first black playwright—ever to win this award.

A Raisin in the Sun is in the tradition of the family play. Eugene O'Neill once said that a play should focus on the most intense and basic human relationships, and playwrights throughout the ages have found that stories about families do just that. In some ways, *A Raisin in the Sun* resembles *The Glass Menagerie*. Both plays are about poor families in desperate situations, and in both plays family members struggle to realize a dream that conflicts with the hopes and dreams of other family members. But while Williams is interested mostly in the psychology of his characters, Hansberry is interested as well in the larger sociological picture. Her characters' problems are not only personal; they also stem from the fact that the characters are black and living in America in the mid-twentieth century.

After the success of *A Raisin in the Sun,* Lorraine Hansberry continued to write plays. Her second Broadway play, *The Sign in Sidney Brustein's Window,* opened just three weeks before she died of cancer, at the age of 34. *To Be Young, Gifted, and Black,* a collection of letters, journal entries, speeches, and play excerpts, was published in 1969.

In 1959, just two weeks before *A Raisin in the Sun* opened, someone asked Hansberry why she was so sure that human life should go on:

> I wish to live because life has within it that which is good, that which is beautiful, and that which is love. Therefore, since I have known all of these things, I have found them to be reason enough and—I wish to live. Moreover, because this is so, I wish others to live for generations and generations and generations. . . .

Preparation

Establishing a Purpose. Instead of waiting until after the play, you may wish to begin with reading and discussion of A Comment on the Play, page 865.

? What expectations does this article arouse? (Expectations of realistic action, use of foreshadowing, family conflicts, and a resolution to the conflicts) What other questions does the comment arouse? (Answers will vary. Perhaps, What is each character's dream? Why can't all the dreams be realized? Does someone have to sacrifice a dream?)

A RAISIN IN THE SUN

What happens to a dream deferred?
Does it dry up
Like a raisin in the sun?
Or fester like a sore—
And then run?
Does it stink like rotten meat?
Or crust and sugar over—
Like a syrupy sweet?

Maybe it just sags
Like a heavy load.

Or does it explode?

—Langston Hughes

A. Responding to the Poem

Hughes's poem provided Hansberry with a succinct statement of a theme of her play, as well as its title.

? What does Hughes mean by "dream"? (Hope, goal, ambition) What kinds of dreams are often meant by the phrase "the American dream"? (A family of one's own, a nice home and car, financial success, "bettering" oneself, happiness) Are these dreams limited to any one ethnic group in the United States? (No. They are common to people of different origins.)

SUPPLEMENTARY SUPPORT MATERIALS: ACT ONE
1. Vocabulary Activity Worksheet (*CCB*)
2. Review and Response Worksheet: Characterization and Theme (*CCB*)
3. Language Skills Worksheet: Revision Worksheet 5 (*CCB*)
4. Selection Test (*CCB*)

DEVELOPING VOCABULARY
The following words from Act One are tested in the Selection Test. (See also Vocabulary Activity Worksheet.)

covenant	erratic
sociological	indifferently
to defer	graphically
to fester	to permeate
pretense	heathenism

A Raisin in the Sun was first presented by Philip Rose and David J. Cogan at the Ethel Barrymore Theatre, New York City, March 11, 1959, with the following cast:

(In order of appearance)

Ruth Younger	Ruby Dee
Travis Younger	Glynn Turman
Walter Lee Younger (Brother)	Sidney Poitier
Beneatha Younger	Diana Sands
Lena Younger (Mama)	Claudia McNeil
Joseph Asagai	Ivan Dixon
George Murchison	Louis Gossett
Karl Lindner	John Fiedler
Bobo	Lonne Elder III
Moving Men	Ed Hall, Douglas Turner

Directed by Lloyd Richards

Designed and lighted by Ralph Alswang

Costumes by Virginia Volland

The photographs illustrating the play are from this production (Ossie Davis replaces Sidney Poitier).

The action of the play is set in Chicago's Southside, sometime between World War II and the present.

Act One

Scene 1. Friday morning.
Scene 2. The following morning.

Act Two

Scene 1. Later, the same day.
Scene 2. Friday night, a few weeks later.
Scene 3. Moving day, one week later.

Act Three

An hour later.

Act One

Scene 1

The YOUNGER *living room would be a comfortable and well-ordered room if it were not for a number of indestructible contradictions to this state of being. Its furnishings are typical and undistinguished and their primary feature now is that they have clearly had to accommodate the living of too many people for too many years—and they are tired. Still, we can see that at some time, a time probably no longer remembered by the family (except perhaps for* MAMA*) the furnishings of this room were actually selected with care and love and even hope—and brought to this apartment and arranged with taste and pride.*

That was a long time ago. Now the once loved pattern of the couch upholstery has to fight to show itself from under acres of crocheted doilies and couch covers which have themselves finally come to be more important than the upholstery. And here a table or a chair has been moved to disguise the worn places in the carpet; but the carpet has fought back by showing its weariness, with depressing uniformity, elsewhere on its surface.

Weariness has, in fact, won in this room. Everything has been polished, washed, sat on, used, scrubbed too often. All pretenses but living itself have long since vanished from the very atmosphere of this room.

Moreover, a section of this room, for it is not really a room unto itself, though the landlord's lease would make it seem so, slopes backward to provide a small kitchen area, where the family prepares the meals that are eaten in the living room proper, which must also serve as dining room. The single window that has been provided for these "two" rooms is located in this kitchen area. The sole natural light the family may enjoy in the course of a day is only that which fights its way through this little window.

At left, a door leads to a bedroom which is shared by MAMA *and her daughter,* BENEATHA*. At right, opposite, is a second room (which in the beginning of the life of this apartment was probably a breakfast room) which serves as a bedroom for* WALTER *and his wife,* RUTH.

Time: Sometime between World War II and the present.

Place: Chicago's Southside.

At Rise: It is morning dark in the living room. TRAVIS *is asleep on the make-down bed at center. An alarm clock sounds from within the bedroom at right, and presently* RUTH *enters from that room and closes the door behind her. She crosses sleepily toward the window. As she passes her sleeping son she reaches down and shakes him a little. At the window she raises the shade and a*

ACT ONE SUMMARY: Each member of the Younger family has a different dream of change to come from use of a ten-thousand dollar life insurance check Lena Younger (Mama) is to receive the next day. Walter wants to invest in a liquor store; Beneatha, his sister, wants to go to medical school. She refuses to settle for marriage to a rich man who is courting her. Ruth, Walter's wife, appears to want a better life for their son, Travis. It is uncertain how she will deal with a pregnancy confirmed by the end of this act. Mama wants to improve the family's living conditions.

dusky Southside morning light comes in feebly. She fills a pot with water and puts it on to boil. She calls to the boy, between yawns, in a slightly muffled voice.

RUTH *is about thirty. We can see that she was a pretty girl, even exceptionally so, but now it is apparent that life has been little that she expected, and disappointment has already begun to hang in her face. In a few years, before thirty-five even, she will be known among her people as a "settled woman."*

She crosses to her son and gives him a good, final, rousing shake.

Ruth. Come on now, boy, it's seven thirty! *(Her son sits up at last, in a stupor of sleepiness.)* I say hurry up, Travis! You ain't the only person in the world got to use a bathroom! *(The child, a sturdy, handsome little boy of ten or eleven, drags himself out of the bed and almost blindly takes his towels and "today's clothes" from drawers and a closet and goes out to the bathroom, which is in an outside hall and which is shared by another family or families on the same floor.* RUTH *crosses to the bedroom door at right and opens it and calls in to her husband.)* Walter Lee! . . . It's after seven thirty! Lemme see you do some waking up in their now! *(She waits.)* You better get up from there, man! It's after seven thirty I tell you. *(She waits again.)* All right, you just go ahead and lay there and next thing you know Travis be finished and Mr. Johnson'll be in there and you'll be fussing and cussing round here like a mad man! And be late too! *(She waits, at the end of patience.)* Walter Lee—it's time for you to get up!

[*She waits another second and then starts to go into the bedroom, but is apparently satisfied that her husband has begun to get up. She stops, pulls the door to, and returns to the kitchen area. She wipes her face with a moist cloth and runs her fingers through her sleep-disheveled hair in a vain effort and ties an apron around her housecoat. The bedroom door at right opens and her husband stands in the doorway in his pajamas, which are rumpled and mismated. He is a lean, intense young man in his middle thirties, inclined to quick nervous movements and erratic speech habits—and always in his voice there is a quality of indictment.*[1]]

1. **indictment** (in·dīt′mənt): accusation.

Walter. Is he out yet?

Ruth. What you mean *out?* He ain't hardly got in there good yet.

Walter *(wandering in, still more oriented to sleep than to a new day).* Well, what was you doing all that yelling for if I can't even get in there yet? *(stopping and thinking)* Check coming today? A

A. Foreshadowing

? Anticipation is immediately aroused by Walter's question. What makes it obvious that the check is an important one? (He is barely awake, yet he is already thinking about the check.)

Ruth. They *said* Saturday and this is just Friday and I hopes to God you ain't going to get up here first thing this morning and start talking to me 'bout no money—'cause I 'bout don't want to hear it.

Walter. Something the matter with you this morning?

Ruth. No—I'm just sleepy as the devil. What kind of eggs you want?

Walter. Not scrambled. *(*RUTH *starts to scramble eggs.)* Paper come? *(*RUTH *points impatiently to the rolled up* Tribune *on the table, and he gets it and spreads it out and vaguely reads the front page.)* Set off another bomb yesterday.

Ruth *(maximum indifference).* Did they?

Walter *(looking up).* What's the matter with you?

Ruth. Ain't nothing the matter with me. And don't keep asking me that this morning.

Walter. Ain't nobody bothering you. *(reading the news of the day absently again)* Say Colonel McCormick[2] is sick.

Ruth *(affecting tea-party interest).* Is he now? Poor thing.

Walter *(sighing and looking at his watch).* Oh, me. *(He waits.)* Now what is that boy doing in that bathroom all this time? He just going to have to start getting up earlier. I can't be being late to work on account of him fooling around in there.

Ruth *(turning on him).* Oh, no he ain't going to be getting up no earlier no such thing! It ain't his fault that he can't get to bed no earlier nights 'cause he got a bunch of crazy good-for-nothing clowns sitting up running their mouths in what is supposed to be his bedroom after ten o'clock at night . . .

Walter. That's what you mad about, ain't it? The things I want to talk about with my friends just couldn't be important in your mind, could they?

[*He rises and finds a cigarette in her handbag on the table and crosses to the little window and looks out, smoking and deeply enjoying this first one.*]

2. **Colonel McCormick:** Robert R. McCormick (1880–1955), publisher of the *Chicago Tribune*.

Literature and Language: Putting Adverbs to Work in Drama
Students already know that playwrights often provide stage directions that indicate how an actor's voice should sound when speaking the dialogue. These stage directions are in italics and enclosed in either parentheses or brackets. Note that these stage directions often take the form of adverbs, modifying the understood verb *says* or *speaks*.

Have students find examples of some of the adverbs Hansberry uses in Act One, Scene 1. Encourage volunteers to try reading lines aloud in the tone of voice or manner the adverb specifies. It's more fun if each line is read by several different students.

Alternatively, ask students to suggest adverbs for dialogue for which Hansberry has *not* specified stage directions. They can work together in small groups on different sections of the play—perhaps a scene for each group. Students should think of adverbs for stage directions, practice reading the lines aloud, and then perform their scene for the class.

A. Conflict
? On page 816, what aspects of Walter's behavior create conflict between him and his wife, Ruth? (Smoking as soon as he gets up; keeping Travis up too late)

B. Interpretation
? Whose thoughts is Ruth speaking? (She speaks as if she were Travis.) What shows that she reads Travis correctly? (He turns around and rolls his eyes at her. As the passage continues, it becomes obvious that this is a regular game.)

A **Ruth** *(almost matter of factly, a complaint too automatic to deserve emphasis).* Why you always got to smoke before you eat in the morning?
Walter *(at the window).* Just look at 'em down there . . . Running and racing to work . . . *(He turns and faces his wife and watches her a moment at the stove, and then, suddenly.)* You look young this morning, baby.
Ruth *(indifferently).* Yeah?
Walter. Just for a second—stirring them eggs. It's gone now—just for a second it was—you looked real young again. *(Then, drily)* It's gone now—you look like yourself again.
Ruth. Man, if you don't shut up and leave me alone.
Walter *(looking out to the street again).* First thing a man ought to learn in life is not talk love to no colored woman first thing in the morning. You all some evil people at eight o'clock in the morning.

[TRAVIS *appears in the hall doorway, almost fully dressed and quite wide awake now, his towels and pajamas across his shoulders. He opens the door and signals for his father to make the bathroom in a hurry.*]

Travis *(watching the bathroom).* Daddy, come on!

[WALTER *gets his bathroom utensils and flies out to the bathroom.*]

Ruth. Sit down and have your breakfast, Travis.
Travis. Mama, this is Friday. *(Gleefully)* Check coming tomorrow, huh?
Ruth. You get your mind off money and eat your breakfast.
Travis *(eating).* This is the morning we supposed to bring the fifty cents to school.
Ruth. Well, I ain't got no fifty cents this morning.
Travis. Teacher say we have to.
Ruth. I don't care what teacher say. I ain't got it. Eat your breakfast, Travis.
Travis. I *am* eating.
Ruth. Hush up now and just eat!

[*The boy gives her an exasperated look for her lack of understanding, and eats grudgingly.*]

Travis. You think Grandmama would have it?
Ruth. No! And I want you to stop asking your grandmother for money, you hear me?
Travis *(outraged).* Gaaaleee! I don't ask her, she just gimme it sometimes!
Ruth. Travis Willard Younger—I got too much on me this morning to be—
Travis. Maybe Daddy—
Ruth. *Travis!*

[*The boy hushes abruptly. They are both quiet and tense for several seconds.*]

Travis *(presently).* Could I maybe go carry some groceries in front of the supermarket for a little while after school then?
Ruth. Just hush, I said. (TRAVIS *jabs his spoon into his cereal bowl viciously, and rests his head in anger upon his fists.)* If you through eating, you can get over there and make up your bed.

[*The boy obeys stiffly and crosses the room, almost mechanically, to the bed and more or less carefully folds the covering. He carries the bedding into his mother's room and returns with his books and cap.*]

Travis *(sulking and standing apart from her unnaturally).* I'm gone.
Ruth *(looking up from the stove to inspect him automatically).* Come here. *(He crosses to her and she studies his head.)* If you don't take this comb and fix this here head, you better! (TRAVIS *puts down his books with a great sign of oppression, and crosses to the mirror. His mother mutters under her breath about his "slubbornness.")* 'Bout to march out of here with that head looking just like chickens slept in it! I just don't know where you get your stubborn ways . . . And get your jacket, too. Looks chilly out this morning.
Travis *(with conspicuously brushed hair and jacket).* I'm gone.
Ruth. Get carfare and milk money—*(waving one finger)*—and not a single penny for no caps, you hear me?
Travis *(with sullen politeness).* Yes'm.

[*He turns in outrage to leave. His mother watches after him as in his frustration he approaches the door almost comically. When she speaks to him, her voice has become a very gentle tease.*]

Ruth *(mocking; as she thinks he would say it).* Oh, Mama makes me so mad sometimes, I don't know what to do! *(She waits and continues to his back as he stands stock-still in front of the door.)* I wouldn't kiss that woman goodbye for nothing in this world this morning! *(The boy finally turns around and rolls his eyes at her, knowing the mood has changed and he is vindicated; he does* *not, however, move toward her yet.)* Not for nothing in this world! *(She finally laughs aloud at him and holds out her arms to him and we see that it is a way between them, very old and practiced. He crosses to her and allows her to embrace him warmly but keeps his face fixed with masculine rigidity. She holds him back from her presently and looks at him and runs her fingers over the features of his face. With utter gentleness—)* Now—whose little old angry man are you?

Travis *(The masculinity and gruffness start to fade at last.).* Aw gaalee—Mama . . .

Ruth *(mimicking).* Aw—gaaaaalleeeee, Mama! *(She pushes him, with rough playfulness and finality, toward the door.)* Get on out of here or you going to be late.

Travis *(in the face of love, new aggressiveness).* Mama, could I *please* go carry groceries?

Ruth. Honey, it's starting to get so cold evenings.

Walter *(coming in from the bathroom and drawing a make-believe gun from a make-believe holster and shooting at his son).* What is it he wants to do?

Ruth. Go carry groceries after school at the supermarket.

Walter. Well, let him go . . .

Travis *(quickly, to the ally).* I *have* to—she won't gimme the fifty cents . . .

Walter *(to his wife only).* Why not?

Ruth *(simply, and with flavor).* 'Cause we don't have it.

Walter *(to* RUTH *only).* What you tell the boy things like that for? *(Reaching down into his pants with a rather important gesture)* Here, son—

[*He hands the boy the coin, but his eyes are directed to his wife's.* TRAVIS *takes the money happily.*]

Travis. Thanks, Daddy.

[*He starts out.* RUTH *watches both of them with murder in her eyes.* WALTER *stands and stares back at her with defiance, and suddenly reaches into his pocket again on an afterthought.*]

Walter *(without even looking at his son, still staring hard at his wife).* In fact, here's another fifty cents . . . Buy yourself some fruit today—or take a taxicab to school or something!

Travis. Whoopee—

[*He leaps up and clasps his father around the middle with his legs, and they face each other in mutual appreciation; slowly* WALTER LEE *peeks around the boy to catch the violent rays from his wife's eyes and draws his head back as if shot.*]

Walter. You better get down now—and get to school, man.

Travis *(at the door).* O.K. Goodbye. *(He exits.)*

Walter *(after him, pointing with pride).* That's *my* boy. *(She looks at him in disgust and turns back to her work.)* You know what I was thinking 'bout in the bathroom this morning?

Ruth. No.

Walter. How come you always try to be so pleasant!

Ruth. What is there to be pleasant 'bout!

Walter. You want to know what I was thinking 'bout in the bathroom or not!

Ruth. I know what you thinking 'bout.

Walter *(ignoring her).* 'Bout what me and Willy Harris was talking about last night.

Ruth *(immediately—a refrain).* Willy Harris is a good-for-nothing loud mouth.

Walter. Anybody who talks to me has got to be a good-for-nothing loud mouth, ain't he? And what you know about who is just a good-for-nothing loud mouth? Charlie Atkins was just a "good-for-nothing loud mouth" too, wasn't he! When he wanted me to go in the dry-cleaning business with him. And now—he's grossing a hundred thousand a year. A hundred thousand dollars a year! You still call *him* a loud mouth!

Ruth *(bitterly).* Oh, Walter Lee . . .

[*She folds her head on her arms over the table.*]

Walter *(rising and coming to her and standing over her).* You tired, ain't you? Tired of everything. Me, the boy, the way we live—this beat-up hole—everything. Ain't you? *(She doesn't look up, doesn't answer.)* So tired—moaning and groaning all the time, but you wouldn't do nothing to help, would you? You couldn't be on my side that long for nothing, could you?

Ruth. Walter, please leave me alone.

Walter. A man needs for a woman to back him up . . .

Ruth. Walter—

Walter. Mama would listen to you. You know she listen to you more than she do me and Bennie. She think more of you. All you have to do is just sit down with her when you drinking your coffee one morning and talking 'bout things like you do and—*(He sits down beside her and demonstrates*

A

A. Conflict
? What further conflicts do you discover on this page between Walter and Ruth? (He subverts what she has told Travis by giving him two half-dollars; he finds Ruth "unpleasant"; she dislikes his friend Willy Harris in particular; he feels that she does not support his dreams.)

A. Plot

? What plan for use of the insurance check does Walter want Ruth to urge upon his mother? (Investment in a liquor store with Walter's friends, Willy and Bobo) Whose money is it? (Walter's mother's) What do you think of Walter's plan? (Opinions will vary, but students should comment on Ruth's reminder that the money is Mama's and should consider Ruth's distrust of Walter's proposed business partners.)

graphically what he thinks her methods and tone should be.)—you just sip your coffee, see, and say easy like that you been thinking 'bout that deal Walter Lee is so interested in, 'bout the store and all, and sip some more coffee, like what you saying ain't really that important to you— And the next thing you know, she be listening good and asking you questions and when I come home—I can tell her the details. This ain't no fly-by-night proposition, baby. I mean we figured it out, me and Willy and Bobo.

Ruth *(with a frown).* Bobo?

A **Walter.** Yeah. You see, this little liquor store we got in mind cost seventy-five thousand and we figured the initial investment on the place be 'bout thirty-thousand, see. That be ten thousand each. Course, there's a couple of hundred you got to pay so's you don't spend your life just waiting for them clowns to let your license get approved—

Ruth. You mean graft?

Walter *(frowning impatiently).* Don't call it that. See there, that just goes to show you what women understand about the world. Baby, don't *nothing* happen for you in this world 'less you pay *somebody* off!

Ruth. Walter, leave me alone! *(She raises her head and stares at him vigorously—then says, more quietly.)* Eat your eggs, they gonna be cold.

Walter *(straightening up from her and looking off).* That's it. There you are. Man say to his woman: I got me a dream. His woman say: Eat your eggs. *(Sadly, but gaining in power)* Man say: I got to take hold of this here world, baby! And a woman will say: Eat your eggs and go to work. *(Passionately now)* Man say: I got to change my life, I'm choking to death, baby! And his woman say—*(in utter anguish as he brings his fists down on his thighs)*—Your eggs is getting cold!

Ruth *(softly).* Walter, that ain't none of our money.

Walter *(not listening at all or even looking at her).* This morning, I was lookin' in the mirror and thinking about it . . . I'm thirty-five years old; I been married eleven years and I got a boy who sleeps in the living room—*(very, very quietly)*—and all I got to give him is stories about how rich white people live . . .

Ruth. Eat your eggs, Walter.

Walter. *Damn my eggs . . . damn all the eggs that ever was!*

Ruth. Then go to work.

Walter *(looking up at her).* See—I'm trying to talk to you 'bout myself—*(shaking his head with the repetition)*—and all you can say is eat them eggs and go to work.

Ruth *(wearily).* Honey, you never say nothing new. I listen to you every day, every night and every morning, and you never say nothing new. *(Shrugging)* So you would rather *be* Mr. Arnold than be his chauffeur. So—I would *rather* be living in Buckingham Palace.

Walter. That is just what is wrong with the colored woman in this world . . . Don't understand about building their men up and making 'em feel like they somebody. Like they can do something.

Ruth *(drily, but to hurt).* There *are* colored men who do things.

Walter. No thanks to the colored woman.

Ruth. Well, being a colored woman, I guess I can't help myself none.

[She rises and gets the ironing board and sets it up and attacks a huge pile of rough-dried clothes, sprinkling them in preparation for the ironing and then rolling them into tight fat balls.]

Walter *(mumbling).* We one group of men tied to a race of women with small minds.

[His sister BENEATHA *enters. She is about twenty, as slim and intense as her brother. She is not as pretty as her sister-in-law, but her lean, almost intellectual face has a handsomeness of its own. She wears a bright-red flannel nightie, and her thick hair stands wildly about her head. Her speech is a mixture of many things; it is different from the rest of the family's insofar as education has permeated her sense of English—and perhaps the Midwest rather than the South has finally—at last—won out in her inflection; but not altogether, because over all of it is a soft slurring and transformed use of vowels which is the decided influence of the Southside. She passes through the room without looking at either* RUTH *or* WALTER *and goes to the outside door and looks, a little blindly, out to the bathroom. She sees that it has been lost to the Johnsons. She closes the door with a sleepy vengeance and crosses to the table and sits down a little defeated.]*

Beneatha. I am going to start timing those people.

Walter. You should get up earlier.

Beneatha *(her face in her hands. She is still fighting the urge to go back to bed.).* Really— would you suggest dawn? Where's the paper?

Walter *(pushing the paper across the table to her as he studies her almost clinically, as though he*

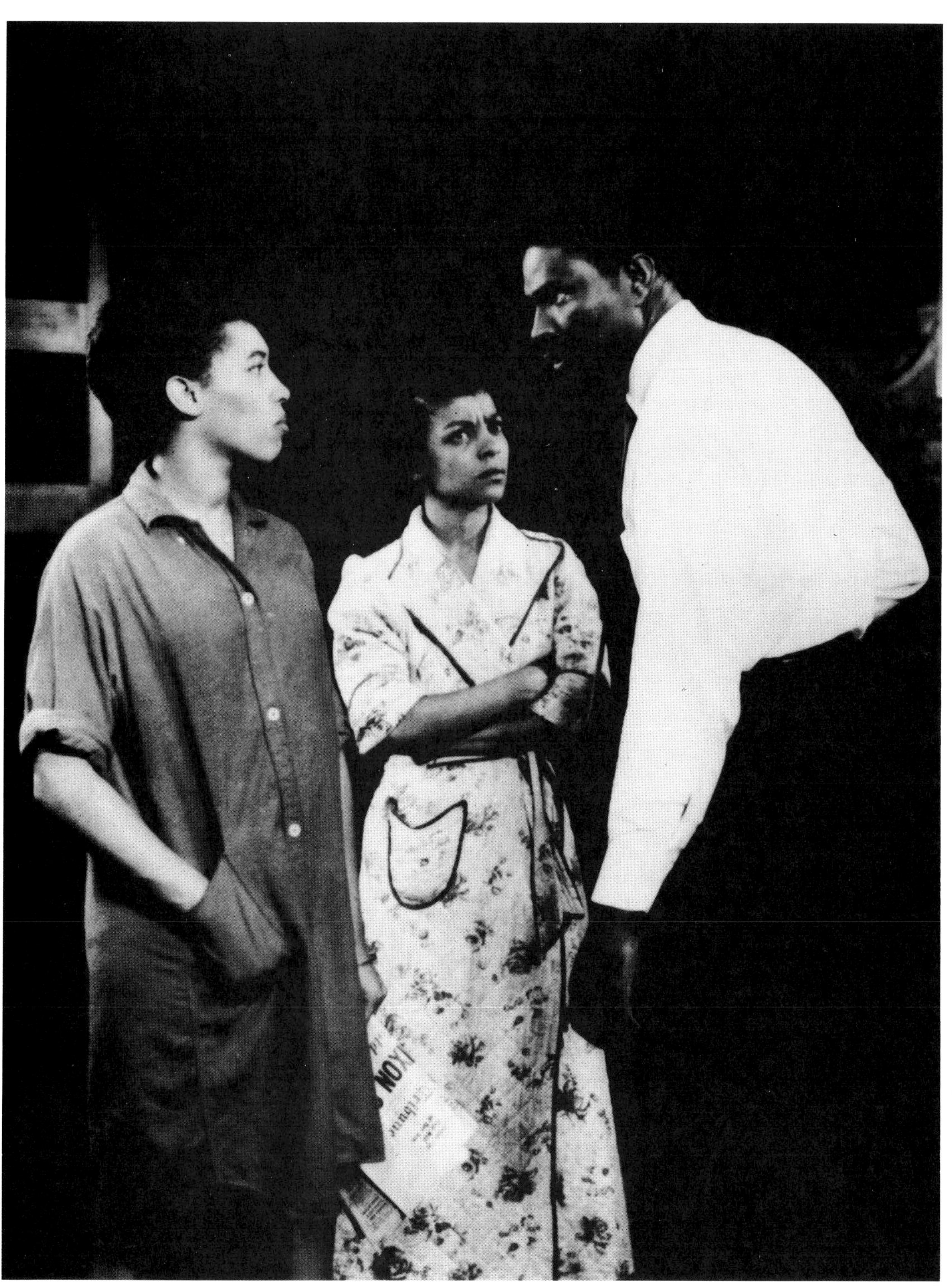

"You know that check is coming tomorrow."

Humanities Connection: Responding to the Photograph

Since Walter is described as a lean and intense young man, it will be helpful if you can share with students some photographs of Sidney Poitier in the role of Walter, Poitier representing that physical type more closely than Ossie Davis. The words below the picture on this occur about halfway down column 1 on page 820.

? Identify the characters in this scene. (From left to right, Beneatha, Ruth, and Walter) How were you able to identify them? (Some students will simply have recognized one or more of the actors. Clues from the play are Ruth's wearing "a housecoat," stage directions, page 815, and the ages given for Beneatha and Ruth—"about 20" and "about 30," respectively.)

A. Characterization

? What new information is revealed about Ruth on this page? (She helped out her sister-in-law by working in people's kitchens.) What do you learn about Beneatha's ambitions? (She wants to be a doctor.) What attitude toward the insurance check is shared by Ruth and Beneatha? (That the money is Mama's, not theirs) What old-fashioned attitudes toward women does Walter express? (Beneatha should become a nurse, not a doctor, or just get married and let a man support her.) Judging by clues so far, do you expect Mama to have her own ideas about use of the money, or to give in easily to Walter? (Considering Walter's having been unsuccessful in previous attempts to sway her, she must be a strong-minded person. Furthermore, she has apparently held this family together despite the tensions created by their cramped living conditions.)

has never seen her before). You a horrible-looking chick at this hour.

Beneatha *(drily).* Good morning, everybody.

Walter *(senselessly).* How is school coming?

Beneatha *(in the same spirit).* Lovely. Lovely. And you know, biology is the greatest. *(Looking up at him)* I dissected something that looked like you yesterday.

Walter. I just wondered if you've made up your mind and everything.

Beneatha *(gaining in sharpness and impatience).* And what did I answer yesterday morning—and the day before that?

Ruth *(from the ironing board, like someone disinterested and old).* Don't be so nasty, Bennie.

Beneatha *(still to her brother).* And the day before that and the day before that!

Walter *(defensively).* I'm interested in you. Something wrong with that? Ain't many girls who decide—

Walter *and* **Beneatha** *(in unison).* —"to be a doctor." *(Silence)*

Walter. Have we figured out yet just exactly how much medical school is going to cost?

Ruth. Walter Lee, why don't you leave that girl alone and get out of here to work?

Beneatha *(exits to the bathroom and bangs on the door).* Come on out of there, please!

[*She comes back into the room.*]

Walter *(looking at his sister intently).* You know the check is coming tomorrow.

Beneatha *(turning on him with a sharpness all her own).* That money belongs to Mama, Walter, and it's for her to decide how she wants to use it. I don't care if she wants to buy a house or a rocket ship or just nail it up somewhere and look at it. It's hers. Not ours—*hers.*

Walter *(bitterly).* Now ain't that fine! You just got your mother's interest at heart, ain't you, girl? You such a nice girl—but if Mama got that money she can always take a few thousand and help you through school too—can't she?

Beneatha. I have never asked anyone around here to do anything for me!

Walter. No! And the line between asking and just accepting when the time comes is big and wide—aint' it!

Beneatha *(with fury).* What do you want from me, Brother—that I quit school or just drop dead, which!

Walter. I don't want nothing but for you to stop acting holy 'round here. Me and Ruth done made some sacrifices for you—why can't you do something for the family?

Ruth. Walter, don't be dragging me in it.

Walter. You are in it— Don't you get up and go work in somebody's kitchen for the last three years to help put clothes on her back?

Ruth. Oh, Walter—that's not fair . . .

Walter. It ain't that nobody expects you to get on your knees and say thank you, Brother; thank you, Ruth; thank you, Mama—and thank you, Travis, for wearing the same pair of shoes for two semesters—

Beneatha *(dropping to her knees).* Well—I *do*—all right?—thank everybody . . . and forgive me for ever wanting to be anything at all . . . forgive me, forgive me!

Ruth. Please stop it! Your mama'll hear you.

Walter. What fool told you you had to be a doctor? If you so crazy 'bout messing 'round with sick people—then go be a nurse like other women—or just get married and be quiet . . .

Beneatha. Well—you finally got it said . . . It took you three years but you finally got it said. Walter, give up; leave me alone—it's Mama's money.

Walter. *He was my father, too!*

Beneatha. So what? He was mine, too—and Travis's grandfather—but the insurance money belongs to Mama. Picking on me is not going to make her give it to you to invest in any liquor stores—*(underbreath, dropping into a chair)*—and I for one say, God bless Mama for that!

Walter *(to* RUTH*).* See—did you hear? Did you hear!

Ruth. Honey, please go to work.

Walter. Nobody in this house is ever going to understand me.

Beneatha. Because you're a nut.

Walter. Who's a nut?

Beneatha. You—you are a nut. Thee is mad, boy.

Walter *(looking at his wife and his sister from the door, very sadly).* The world's most backward race of people, and that's a fact.

Beneatha *(turning slowly in her chair).* And then there are all those prophets who would lead us out of the wilderness—*(*WALTER *slams out of the house.)*—into the swamps!

Ruth. Bennie, why you always gotta be pickin' on your brother? Can't you be a little sweeter sometimes? *(Door opens.* WALTER *walks in.)*

Walter *(to* RUTH*).* I need some money for carfare.

A

A. Characterization
The stage directions introduce Lena Younger, Mama. Pause to have students pick out the traits that most strongly suggest to them the kind of person she will prove to be. (Answers will vary, but should take into account her erect carriage, lively eyes, and soft voice—qualities suggesting a quiet strength different from her son Walter's bombast.)

Ruth *(looks at him, then warms; teasing, but tenderly).* Fifty cents? *(She goes to her bag and gets money.)* Here, take a taxi.

[WALTER *exits.* MAMA *enters. She is a woman in her early sixties, full-bodied and strong. She is one of those women of a certain grace and beauty who wear it so unobtrusively that it takes a while to notice. Her dark-brown face is surrounded by the total whiteness of her hair, and, being a woman who has adjusted to many things in life and overcome many more, her face is full of strength. She has, we can see, wit and faith of a kind that keep her eyes lit and full of interest and expectancy. She is, in a word, a beautiful woman. Her bearing is perhaps most like the noble bearing of the women of the Hereros of Southwest Africa—rather as if she imagines that as she walks she still bears a basket or a vessel upon her head. Her speech, on the other hand, is as careless as her carriage is precise—she is inclined to slur everything—but her voice is perhaps not so much quiet as simply soft.*]

Mama. Who that 'round here slamming doors at this hour?

[*She crosses through the room, goes to the window, opens it, and brings in a feeble little plant growing doggedly in a small pot on the window sill. She feels the dirt and puts it back out.*]

Ruth. That was Walter Lee. He and Bennie was at it again.
Mama. My children and they tempers. Lord, if this little old plant don't get more sun than it's been getting it ain't never going to see spring again. *(She turns from the window.)* What's the matter with you this morning, Ruth? You looks right peaked. You aiming to iron all them things? Leave some for me. I'll get to 'em this afternoon. Bennie honey, it's too drafty honey for you to be sitting 'round half dressed. Where's your robe?
Beneatha. In the cleaners.
Mama. Well, go get mine and put it on.
Beneatha. I'm not cold, Mama, honest.
Mama. I know—but you so thin . . .
Beneatha *(irritably).* Mama, I'm not cold.
Mama *(seeing the make-down bed as* TRAVIS *has left it).* Lord have mercy, look at that poor bed. Bless his heart—he tries, don't he?

[*She moves to the bed* TRAVIS *has sloppily made up.*]

Ruth. No—he don't half try at all 'cause he knows you going to come along behind him and fix everything. That's just how come he don't know how to do nothing right now—you done spoiled that boy so.
Mama. Well—he's a little boy. Ain't supposed to know 'bout housekeeping. My baby, that's what he is. What you fix for his breakfast this morning?
Ruth *(angrily).* I feed my son, Lena!
Mama. I ain't meddling—*(Underbreath; busybodyish)* I just noticed all last week he had cold cereal, and when it starts getting this chilly in the fall a child ought to have some hot grits or something when he goes out in the cold—
Ruth *(furious).* I gave him hot oats—is that all right!
Mama. I ain't meddling. *(Pause)* Put a lot of nice butter on it? *(*RUTH *shoots her an angry look and does not reply.)* He likes lots of butter.
Ruth *(exasperated).* Lena—
Mama *(to* BENEATHA. MAMA *is inclined to wander conversationally sometimes.).* What was you and your brother fussing 'bout this morning?
Beneatha. It's not important, Mama.

[*She gets up and goes to look out at the bathroom, which is apparently free, and she picks up her towels and rushes out.*]

Mama. What was they fighting about?
Ruth. Now you know as well as I do.
Mama *(shaking her head).* Brother still worrying hisself sick about that money?
Ruth. You know he is.
Mama. You had breakfast?
Ruth. Some coffee.
Mama. Girl, you better start eating and looking after yourself better. You almost as thin as Travis.
Ruth. Lena—
Mama. Un-hunh?
Ruth. What are you going to do with it?
Mama. Now don't you start, child. It's too early in the morning to be talking about money. It ain't Christian.
Ruth. It's just that he got his heart set on that store—
Mama. You mean that liquor store that Willy Harris want him to invest in?
Ruth. Yes—
Mama. We ain't no business people, Ruth. We just plain working folks.
Ruth. Ain't nobody business people till they go into business. Walter Lee say colored people ain't

C

B. Symbol
The importance of the plant as a prop will develop as the play continues. For now, call it to students' attention with a simple question.
? How might a "doggedly growing" plant symbolize the people in this play? (The family shows strength and determination; everyone works to combat poverty; they have not abandoned hope for a better life.)

C. Plot
? Are you surprised that Ruth suggests Walter's idea to his mother? (Answers will vary.) What do you deduce about Ruth's feelings for Walter? (She loves him and is willing to support him even when she does not fully agree with his ideas.)

A. Imagery

? What does Mama mean by her "ledger"? (The word evokes the image of a "recording angel" listing in a book the good deeds and bad deeds of her life.) What does the image suggest about Mama's attitude toward religion? (Religious beliefs may be of importance to her.)

B. Characterization

? Mama is here referring to what stereotypical beliefs some white people have about African Americans? (That they lead crime-prone, barely civilized lives) Why do such stereotypes already seem ludicrous in relation to the Younger family? (They are clearly hard-working people whose lives do not differ substantially from the lives of people of any color in the same economic position. They are just *people*.)

C. Humanities Connection: Responding to the Photograph

Mama quotes her husband, Big Walter.

? Examine the details of the picture. What is suggested about Mama by the cross and the apron she wears and by the plant she holds? (She is religious, hard-working, and interested in growing and nurturing things.)

never going to start getting ahead till they start gambling on some different kinds of things in the world—investments and things.

Mama. What done got into you, girl? Walter Lee done finally sold you on investing.

Ruth. No. Mama, something is happening between Walter and me. I don't know what it is—but he needs something—something I can't give him any more. He needs this chance, Lena.

Mama *(frowning deeply)*. But liquor, honey—

Ruth. Well—like Walter say—I spec people going to always be drinking themselves some liquor.

Mama. Well—whether they drinks it or not ain't none of my business. But whether I go into business selling it to 'em *is,* and I don't want that on my ledger this late in life. *(Stopping suddenly and studying her daughter-in-law)* Ruth Younger, what's the matter with you today? You look like you could fall over right there.

A

Ruth. I'm tired.

Mama. Then you better stay home from work today.

Ruth. I can't stay home. She'd be calling up the agency and screaming at them, "My girl didn't come in today—send me somebody! My girl didn't come in!" Oh, she just have a fit . . .

Mama. Well, let her have it. I'll just call her up and say you got the flu—

Ruth *(laughing)*. Why the flu?

Mama. 'Cause it sounds respectable to 'em. Something white people get, too. They know 'bout the flu. Otherwise they think you been cut up or something when you tell 'em you sick.

Ruth. I got to go in. We need the money.

"Seem like God didn't see fit to give the black man nothing but dreams—but He did give us children to make them dreams worthwhile."

Mama. Somebody would of thought my children done all but starved to death the way they talk about money here late. Child, we got a great big old check coming tomorrow.

Ruth *(sincerely, but also self-righteously)*. Now that's your money. It ain't got nothing to do with me. We all feel like that—Walter and Bennie and me—even Travis.

Mama *(thoughtfully, and suddenly very far away)*. Ten thousand dollars—

Ruth. Sure is wonderful.

Mama. Ten thousand dollars.

Ruth. You know what you should do, Miss Lena? You should take yourself a trip somewhere. To Europe or South America or someplace—

Mama *(throwing up her hands at the thought)*. Oh, child!

Ruth. I'm serious. Just pack up and leave! Go on away and enjoy yourself some. Forget about the family and have yourself a ball for once in your life—

Mama *(drily)*. You sound like I'm just about ready to die. Who'd go with me? What I look like wandering 'round Europe by myself?

Ruth. Shoot—these here rich white women do it all the time. They don't think nothing of packing up they suitcases and piling on one of them big steamships and—swoosh!—they gone, child.

Mama. Something always told me I wasn't no rich white woman.

Ruth. Well—what are you going to do with it then?

Mama. I ain't rightly decided. *(Thinking. She speaks now with emphasis.)* Some of it got to be put away for Beneatha and her schoolin'—and ain't nothing going to touch that part of it. Nothing. *(She waits several seconds, trying to make up her mind about something, and looks at* RUTH *a little tentatively before going on.)* Been thinking that we maybe could meet the notes on a little old two-story somewhere, with a yard where Travis could play in the summertime, if we use part of the insurance for a down payment and everybody kind of pitch in. I could maybe take on a little day work again, few days a week—

Ruth *(studying her mother-in-law furtively and concentrating on her ironing, anxious to encourage without seeming to)*. Well, Lord knows, we've put enough rent into this here rat trap to pay for four houses by now . . .

Mama *(looking up at the words "rat trap" and then looking around and leaning back and sighing—in a suddenly reflective mood—)*. "Rat trap"—yes, that's all it is. *(Smiling)* I remember just as well the day me and Big Walter moved in here. Hadn't been married but two weeks and wasn't planning on living here no more than a year. *(She shakes her head at the dissolved dream.)* We was going to set away, little by little, don't you know, and buy a little place out in Morgan Park. We had even picked out the house. *(Chuckling a little)* Looks right dumpy today. But Lord, child, you should know all the dreams I had 'bout buying that house and fixing it up and making me a little garden in the back—*(She waits and stops smiling.)* And didn't none of it happen. *(Dropping her hands in a futile gesture)*

Ruth *(keeps her head down, ironing)*. Yes, life can be a barrel of disappointments, sometimes.

Mama. Honey, Big Walter would come in here some nights back then and slump down on that couch there and just look at the rug, and look at me and look at the rug and then back at me—and I'd know he was down then . . . really down. *(After a second very long and thoughtful pause; she is seeing back to times that only she can see.)* And then, Lord, when I lost that baby—little Claude—I almost thought I was going to lose Big Walter too. Oh, that man grieved hisself! He was one man to love his children.

Ruth. Ain't nothin' can tear at you like losin' your baby.

Mama. I guess that's how come that man finally worked hisself to death like he done. Like he was fighting his own war with this here world that took his baby from him.

Ruth. He sure was a fine man, all right. I always liked Mr. Younger.

Mama. Crazy 'bout his children! God knows there was plenty wrong with Walter Younger—hard-headed, mean, kind of wild with women—plenty wrong with him. But he sure loved his children. Always wanted to have something—be something. That's where Brother gets all these notions, I reckon. Big Walter used to say, he'd get right wet in the eyes sometimes, lean his head back with the water standing in his eyes and say, "Seem like God didn't see fit to give the black man nothing but dreams—but He did give us children to make them dreams seem worthwhile." *(She smiles.)* He could talk like that, don't you know. A

Ruth. Yes, he sure could. He was a good man, Mr. Younger.

Mama. Yes, a fine man—just couldn't never catch up with his dreams, that's all.

A. Characterization

? In commenting on her husband, what does Lena Younger reveal about her own character? (She can love someone whose ways are not her own; she is tolerant and loyal.) Comment on what the line she quotes from Big Walter reveals about his and her priorities. (Family comes first.)

A. Characterization

? When Beneatha says she wants to express herself, why do Mama and Ruth smile? (Beneatha's way of expressing herself keeps changing—it was play-acting, riding, photography, and now it's guitar.) What generation gap exists even between Ruth and Beneatha, when it comes to marrying a man with money? (Ruth may be joking, but seems to think it would be worth marrying a nice rich man even if he were shallow; Beneatha disagrees.) Explain what you think Beneatha means by "shallow." (Answers will vary. Some students may say it means "lacking in depth of ideas, values, or feelings.") On what issue do Beneatha and Mama especially come into conflict? (The role of God in the world) In what ways do you sympathize with Beneatha? Where do you sympathize with Ruth and Mama? (The personal convictions of all three women warrant sympathy.)

[BENEATHA *comes in, brushing her hair and looking up to the ceiling, where the sound of a vacuum cleaner has started up.*]

Beneatha. What could be so dirty on that woman's rugs that she has to vacuum them every single day?

Ruth. I wish certain young women 'round here who I could name would take inspiration about certain rugs in a certain apartment I could also mention.

Beneatha *(shrugging)*. Well, good God, how much cleaning can a house need.

Mama *(not liking the Lord's name used thus)*. Bennie!

Ruth. Just listen to her—just listen!

Beneatha. Oh, . . .

Mama. If you use the Lord's name just one more time—

Beneatha *(a bit of a whine)*. Oh, Mama—

Ruth. Fresh—just fresh as salt, this girl!

Beneatha *(drily)*. Well—if the salt loses its savor[3]—

Mama. Now that will do. I just ain't going to have you 'round here reciting the scriptures in vain—you hear me?

Beneatha. How did I manage to get on everybody's wrong side by just walking into a room?

Ruth. If you weren't so fresh—

Beneatha. Ruth, I'm twenty years old.

Mama. What time you be home from school today?

Beneatha. Kind of late. *(With enthusiasm)* Madeline is going to start my guitar lessons today.

[MAMA *and* RUTH *look up with the same expressions.*]

Mama. Your *what* kind of lessons?

Beneatha. Guitar.

Ruth. Oh, Father!

Mama. How come you done taken it in your mind to learn to play the guitar?

Beneatha. I just want to, that's all.

Mama *(smiling)*. Lord, child, don't you know what to do with yourself? How long it going to be before you get tired of this now—like you got tired of that little play-acting group you joined last year? *(looking at* RUTH*)* And what was it the year before that?

Ruth. The horseback-riding club for which she bought that fifty-five-dollar riding habit that's been hanging in the closet ever since!

Mama *(to* BENEATHA*)*. Why you got to flit so from one thing to another, baby?

Beneatha *(sharply)*. I just want to learn to play the guitar. Is there anything wrong with that?

Mama. Ain't nobody trying to stop you. I just wonders sometimes why you has to flit so from one thing to another all the time. You ain't never done nothing with all that camera equipment you brought home—

Beneatha. I don't flit! I—I experiment with different forms of expression—

Ruth. Like riding a horse?

Beneatha. —People have to express themselves one way or another.

Mama. What is it you want to express?

Beneatha *(angrily)*. Me! *(*MAMA *and* RUTH *look at each other and burst into raucous laughter.)* Don't worry—I don't expect you to understand.

Mama *(to change the subject)*. Who you going out with tomorrow night?

Beneatha *(with displeasure)*. George Murchison again.

Mama *(pleased)*. Oh—you getting a little sweet on him?

Ruth. You ask me, this child ain't sweet on nobody but herself—*(Underbreath)* Express herself!

[*They laugh.*]

Beneatha. Oh—I like George all right, Mama. I mean I like him enough to go out with him and stuff, but—

Ruth *(for devilment)*. What does *and stuff* mean?

Beneatha. Mind your own business.

Mama. Stop picking at her now, Ruth. *(A thoughtful pause, and then a suspicious sudden look at her daughter as she turns in her chair for emphasis.)* What *does* it mean?

Beneatha *(wearily)*. Oh, I just mean I couldn't ever really be serious about George. He's—he's so shallow.

Ruth. Shallow—what do you mean he's shallow? He's *rich!*

Mama. Hush, Ruth.

Beneatha. I know he's rich. He knows he's rich, too.

Ruth. Well—what other qualities a man got to have to satisfy you, little girl?

---

3. **salt . . . savor:** Matthew 5:13: ". . . if the salt has lost its savor . . . it is thenceforth good for nothing, but to cast out. . . ."

Beneatha. You wouldn't even begin to understand. Anybody who married Walter could not possibly understand.
Mama *(outraged).* What kind of way is that to talk about your brother?
Beneatha. Brother is a flip—let's face it.
Mama *(to* RUTH, *helplessly).* What's a flip?
Ruth *(glad to add kindling).* She's saying he's crazy.
Beneatha. Not crazy. Brother isn't really crazy yet—he—he's an elaborate neurotic.
Mama. Hush your mouth!
Beneatha. As for George. Well. George looks good—he's got a beautiful car and he takes me to nice places and, as my sister-in-law says, he is probably the richest boy I will ever get to know and I even like him sometimes—but if the Youngers are sitting around waiting to see if their little Bennie is going to tie up the family with the Murchisons, they are wasting their time.
Ruth. You mean you wouldn't marry George Murchison if he asked you someday? That pretty, rich thing? Honey, I knew you was odd—
Beneatha. No I would not marry him if all I felt for him was what I feel now. Besides, George's family wouldn't really like it.
Mama. Why not?
Beneatha. Oh, Mama—The Murchisons are honest-to-God-real-*live*-rich colored people, and the only people in the world who are more snobbish than rich white people are rich colored people. I thought everybody knew that. I've met Mrs. Murchison. She's a scene!
Mama. You must not dislike people 'cause they well off, honey.
Beneatha. Why not? It makes just as much sense as disliking people 'cause they are poor, and lots of people do that.
Ruth *(a wisdom-of-the-ages manner; to* MAMA*).* Well, she'll get over some of this—
Beneatha. Get over it? What are you talking about, Ruth? Listen, I'm going to be a doctor. I'm not worried about who I'm going to marry yet—if I ever get married.
Mama and Ruth. *If!*
Mama. Now, Bennie—
Beneatha. Oh, I probably will . . . but first I'm going to be a doctor, and George, for one, still thinks that's pretty funny. I couldn't be bothered with that. I am going to be a doctor and everybody around here better understand that!
Mama *(kindly).* 'Course you going to be a doctor, honey, God willing.
Beneatha *(drily).* God hasn't got a thing to do with it.
Mama. Beneatha—that just wasn't necessary.
Beneatha. Well— I get sick of hearing about God.
Mama. Beneatha!
Beneatha. I mean it! I'm just tired of hearing about God all the time. What has He got to do with anything? Does he pay tuition?
Mama. You 'bout to get your fresh little jaw slapped!
Ruth. That's just what she needs, all right!
Beneatha. Why? Why can't I say what I want to around here, like everybody else?
Mama. It don't sound nice for a young girl to say things like that—you wasn't brought up that way. Me and your father went to trouble to get you and Brother to church every Sunday.
Beneatha. Mama, you don't understand. It's all a matter of ideas, and that is just one idea I don't accept. It's not important. I am not going out and be immoral or commit crimes because I don't believe in God. I don't even think about it. It's just that I get tired of Him getting credit for all the things the human race achieves through its own stubborn effort. There simply is no God in heaven—there is only man and it is he who makes miracles! A

[MAMA *absorbs this speech, studies her daughter and rises slowly and crosses to* BENEATHA *and slaps her powerfully across the face. After, there is only silence and the daughter drops her eyes from her mother's face, and* MAMA *is very tall before her.*]

Mama. Now—you say after me, in my mother's house there is still God. *(There is a long pause and* BENEATHA *stares at the floor wordlessly.* MAMA *repeats the phrase with precision and cool emotion.)* In my mother's house there is still God.
Beneatha. In my mother's house there is still God. *(A long pause)*
Mama *(walking away from* BENEATHA, *too disturbed for triumphant posture; stopping and turning back to her daughter).* There are some ideas we ain't going to have in this house. Not long as I am at the head of this family.
Beneatha. Yes, ma'am.

[MAMA *walks out of the room.*]

A. Responding
? What are your reactions to the argument between Mama and Beneatha on religious issues? Consider especially Beneatha's speech. Do you agree with everything she says, some of it, or none of it? (Student answers will vary.)

A. Symbol

? What does the plant symbolize to Mama? (Her own children) What comparison does Mama make? (The plant has never "had enough sunshine or nothing," just as her children have never had all the things they needed.)

B. Foreshadowing

? What other clues have there been that Ruth is not feeling well? (Mama has asked her before, as at the top of page 822.) What do you think the problem may be? (Answers will vary.)

Ruth *(almost gently, with profound understanding).* You think you a woman, Bennie—but you still a little girl. What you did was childish—so you got treated like a child.

Beneatha. I see. *(Quietly)* I also see that everybody thinks it's all right for Mama to be a tyrant. But all the tyranny in the world will never make her right!

[*She picks up her books and goes out.*]

Ruth *(goes to* MAMA*'s door).* She said she was sorry.

Mama *(coming out, going to her plant).* They frightens me, Ruth. My children.

Ruth. You got good children, Lena. They just a little off sometimes—but they're good.

Mama. No—there's something come down between me and them that don't let us understand each other and I don't know what it is. One done almost lost his mind thinking 'bout money all the time and the other done commence to talk about things I can't seem to understand in no form or fashion. What is it that's changing, Ruth?

Ruth *(soothingly, older than her years).* Now . . . you taking it all too seriously. You just got strong-willed children and it takes a strong woman like you to keep 'em in hand.

A **Mama** *(looking at her plant and sprinkling a little water on it).* They spirited all right, my children. Got to admit they got spirit—Bennie and Walter. Like this little old plant that ain't never had enough sunshine or nothing—and look at it . . .

B [*She has her back to* RUTH, *who has had to stop ironing and lean against something and put the back of her hand to her forehead.*]

Ruth *(trying to keep* MAMA *from noticing). You* . . . sure . . . loves that little old thing, don't you? . . .

Mama. Well, I always wanted me a garden like I used to see sometimes at the back of the houses down home. This plant is close as I ever got to having one. *(She looks out of the window as she replaces the plant.)* Lord, ain't nothing as dreary as the view from this window on a dreary day, is there? Why ain't you singing this morning, Ruth? Sing that "No Ways Tired." That song always lifts me up so—*(She turns at last to see that* RUTH *has slipped quietly into a chair, in a state of semiconsciousness.)* Ruth! Ruth honey—what's the matter with you . . . Ruth!

Curtain

Scene 2

It is the following morning; a Saturday morning, and house cleaning is in progress at the YOUNGERS. *Furniture has been shoved hither and yon and* MAMA *is giving the kitchen-area walls a washing down.* BENEATHA, *in dungarees, with a handkerchief tied around her face, is spraying insecticide into the cracks in the walls. As they work, the radio is on and a Southside disk-jockey program is inappropriately filling the house with a rather exotic saxophone blues.* TRAVIS, *the sole idle one, is leaning on his arms, looking out of the window.*

Travis. Grandmama, that stuff Bennie is using smells awful. Can I go downstairs, please?

Mama. Did you get all them chores done already? I ain't seen you doing much.

Travis. Yes'm—finished early. Where did Mama go this morning?

Mama *(looking at* BENEATHA*).* She had to go on a little errand.

Travis. Where?

Mama. To tend to her business.

Travis. Can I go outside then?

Mama. Oh, I guess so. You better stay right in front of the house, though . . . and keep a good lookout for the postman.

Travis. Yes'm. *(He starts out and decides to give his* AUNT BENEATHA *a good swat on the legs as he passes her.)* Leave them poor little old cockroaches alone, they ain't bothering you none.

[*He runs as she swings the spray gun at him both viciously and playfully.* WALTER *enters from the bedroom and goes to the phone.*]

Mama. Look out there, girl, before you be spilling some of that stuff on the child!

Travis *(teasing).* That's right—look out now! *(He exits.)*

Beneatha *(drily).* I can't imagine that it would hurt him—it has never hurt the roaches.

Mama. Well, little boys' hides ain't as tough as Southside roaches.

Walter *(into phone).* Hello—Let me talk to Willy Harris.

Mama. You better get over there behind the bureau. I seen one marching out of there like Napoleon yesterday.

Walter. Hello, Willy? It ain't come yet. It'll be here in a few minutes. Did the lawyer give you the papers?

Beneatha. There's really only one way to get rid of them, Mama—

Mama. How?

Beneatha. Set fire to this building.

Walter. Good. Good. I'll be right over.

Beneatha. Where did Ruth go, Walter?

Walter. I don't know *(He exits abruptly.)*

Beneatha. Mama, where did Ruth go?

Mama *(looking at her with meaning).* To the doctor, I think.

Beneatha. The doctor? What's the matter? *(They exchange glances.)* You don't think—

Mama *(with her sense of drama).* Now I ain't saying what I think. But I ain't never been wrong 'bout a woman neither.

[*The phone rings.*]

Beneatha *(at the phone).* Hay-lo . . . *(Pause, and a moment of recognition)* Well—when did you get back! . . . And how was it? . . . Of course I've missed you—in my way . . . This morning? No . . . house cleaning and all that and Mama hates it if I let people come over when the house is like this . . . You *have?* Well, that's different . . . What is it— Oh, what the heck, come on over . . . Right, see you then. *(She hangs up.)*

Mama *(who has listened vigorously, as is her habit).* Who is that you inviting over here with this house looking like this? You ain't got the pride you was born with!

Beneatha. Asagai doesn't care how houses look, Mama—he's an intellectual.

Mama. *Who?*

Beneatha. Asagai—Joseph Asagai. He's an African boy I met on campus. He's been studying in Canada all summer.

Mama. What's his name?

Beneatha. Asagai, Joseph. Ah-sah-guy . . . He's from Nigeria.[1]

Mama. Oh, that's the little country that was founded by slaves way back . . .

Beneatha. No, Mama—that's Liberia.[2]

Mama. I don't think I never met no African before.

Beneatha. Well, do me a favor and don't ask him a whole lot of ignorant questions about Africans. I mean, do they wear clothes and all that—

Mama. Well, now, I guess if you think we so ignorant 'round here maybe you shouldn't bring your friends here—

Beneatha. It's just that people ask such crazy things. All anyone seems to know about when it comes to Africa is Tarzan—

Mama *(indignantly).* Why should I know anything about Africa?

Beneatha. Why do you give money at church for the missionary work?

Mama. Well, that's to help save people.

Beneatha. You mean save them from *heathenism*—

Mama *(innocently).* Yes.

Beneatha. I'm afraid they need more salvation from the British and the French.

[RUTH *comes in forlornly and pulls off her coat with dejection. They both turn to look at her.*]

Ruth *(dispiritedly).* Well, I guess from all the happy faces—everybody knows.

Beneatha. You pregnant?

Mama. Lord have mercy, I sure hope it's a little old girl. Travis ought to have a sister.

[BENEATHA *and* RUTH *give her a hopeless look for this grandmotherly enthusiasm.*]

Beneatha. How far along are you?

Ruth. Two months.

Beneatha. Did you mean to? I mean did you plan it or was it an accident?

Mama. What do you know about planning or not planning?

Beneatha. Oh, Mama.

Ruth *(wearily).* She's twenty years old, Lena.

Beneatha. Did you plan it, Ruth?

Ruth. Mind your own business.

Beneatha. It is my business—where is he going to live, on the *roof? (There is silence following the remark as the three women react to the sense of it.)* Gee—I didn't mean that, Ruth, honest. Gee, I don't feel like that at all. I—I think it is wonderful.

Ruth *(dully).* Wonderful.

Beneatha. Yes—really.

Mama *(looking at* RUTH, *worried).* Doctor say everything going to be all right?

Ruth *(far away).* Yes—she says everything is going to be fine . . .

Mama *(immediately suspicious).* "She"— What doctor you went to?

[RUTH *folds over, near hysteria.*]

1. **Nigeria:** largest and most populous country on the western coast of Africa. Nigeria was a British protectorate when this play opened, but gained its independence in 1960.
2. **Liberia:** nation on the west coast of Africa, established as a republic in 1847 by freed American slaves.

A. Responding
Beneatha's Nigerian friend, Joseph Asagai, is introduced on this page. Asagai acts as a foil, clarifying differences in attitudes between African and American blacks. Notice that Asagai speaks an almost stilted variety of standard English (for instance, "it is," not "it's"). Students should also know that in the 1950's it was still the fashion for African Americans to straighten their hair by a variety of chemical and ironing means. **?** How do you account for Asagai's perfect English? (He would have learned standard English as a second language.) How else does Asagai differ from American blacks, as represented by the Youngers? (Answers will vary, but may include these differences: Asagai is more worldly; he is proud of his heritage and his physical features, particularly his naturally coarse hair.) What does he find difficult to understand? (Assimilationism; "mutilating" one's hair; the concept of friendship only between men and women) How serious is he about Beneatha? (He sounds ready to propose marriage.) How serious is she about him? (She is not serious about him.)

Mama *(worriedly hovering over* RUTH*).* Ruth honey—what's the matter with you—you sick?

[RUTH *has her fists clenched on her thighs and is fighting hard to suppress a scream that seems to be rising in her.*]

Beneatha. What's the matter with her, Mama?
Mama *(working her fingers in* RUTH*'s shoulder to relax her).* She be all right. Women gets right depressed sometimes when they get her way. *(Speaking softly, expertly, rapidly)* Now you just relax. That's right . . . just lean back, don't think 'bout nothing at all . . . nothing at all—
Ruth. I'm all right . . .

[*The glassy-eyed look melts and then she collapses into a fit of heavy sobbing. The bell rings.*]

Beneatha. Oh, . . . that must be Asagai.
Mama *(to* RUTH*).* Come on now, honey. You need to lie down and rest awhile . . . then have some nice hot food.

[*They exit,* RUTH*'s weight on her mother-in-law.* BENEATHA, *herself profoundly disturbed, opens the door to admit a rather dramatic-looking young man with a large package.*]

A **Asagai.** Hello, Alaiyo—
Beneatha *(holding the door open and regarding him with pleasure).* Hello . . . *(Long pause)* Well—come in. And please excuse everything. My mother was very upset about my letting anyone come here with the place like this.
Asagai *(coming into the room).* You look disturbed too . . . Is something wrong?
Beneatha *(still at the door, absently).* Yes . . . we've all got acute ghetto-itus. *(She smiles and comes toward him, finding a cigarette and sitting.)* So—sit down! How was Canada?
Asagai *(a sophisticate).* Canadian.
Beneatha *(looking at him).* I've very glad you are back.
Asagai *(looking back at her in turn).* Are you really?
Beneatha. Yes—very.
Asagai. Why—you were quite glad when I went away. What happened?
Beneatha. You went away.
Asagai. Ahhhhhhhh.
Beneatha. Before—you wanted to be so serious before there was time.
Asagai. How much time must there be before one knows what one feels?
Beneatha *(stalling this particular conversation; her hands pressed together, in a deliberately childish gesture).* What did you bring me?
Asagai *(handing her the package).* Open it and see.
Beneatha *(eagerly opening the package and drawing out some records and the colorful robes of a Nigerian woman).* Oh, Asagai! . . . You got them for me! . . . How beautiful . . . and the records too! *(She lifts out the robes and runs to the mirror with them and holds the drapery up in front of herself.)*
Asagai *(coming to her at the mirror).* I shall have to teach you how to drape it properly. *(He flings the material about her for the moment and stands back to look at her.)* Ah—*Oh-pay-gay-day, oh-gbah-mu-shay. (a Yoruba*[3] *exclamation for admiration)* You wear it well . . . very well . . . mutilated hair and all.
Beneatha *(turning suddenly).* My hair—what's wrong with my hair?
Asagai *(shrugging).* Were you born with it like that?
Beneatha *(reaching up to touch it).* No . . . of course not.

[*She looks back to the mirror, disturbed.*]

Asagai *(smiling).* How then?
Beneatha. You know perfectly well how . . . as crinkly as yours . . . that's how.
Asagai. And it is ugly to you that way?
Beneatha *(quickly).* Oh, no—not ugly . . . *(More slowly, apologetically)* But it's so hard to manage when it's, well—raw.
Asagai. And so to accommodate that—you mutilate it every week?
Beneatha. It's not mutilation!
Asagai *(laughing aloud at her seriousness).* Oh . . . please! I am only teasing you because you are so very serious about these things. *(He stands back from her and folds his arms across his chest as he watches her pulling at her hair and frowning in the mirror.)* Do you remember the first time you met me at school? . . . *(He laughs.)* You came up to me and you said—and I thought you were the most serious little thing I had ever seen—you said: *(He imitates her.)* "Mr. Asagai—I want very much to talk with you. About Africa. You see, Mr. Asagai, I am looking for my *identity!*" *(He laughs.)*

3. **Yoruba:** a tribe living in southwestern Nigeria, and the language they speak.

A. Responding

? Where did Mama get these comments? (From Beneatha; see page 827, top of the second column) At what point in subsequent lines does she relax into her own natural way of dealing with a guest? (When she questions him about his distance from home and moves on to "decent home-cooked meals")

B. Expansion

The Yoruba are a people of Southwest Nigeria, unusual in the history of Africa for their tendency to form urban communities. The old Yoruba kingdom of Oyo was traditionally one of the largest states of West Africa, but after 1700 its power waned. At the beginning of the nineteenth century, invasions, slave raids, and increased contact with Europeans divided the Yoruba into a number of smaller states. In the second half of the nineteenth century they fell increasingly under British control; they were under direct British administration from 1893 to 1960. Vestiges of Yoruba culture are also found in Brazil and Cuba, where Yoruba were imported as slaves.

Beneatha *(turning to him, not laughing).* Yes— *(Her face is quizzical, profoundly disturbed.)*

Asagai *(still teasing and reaching out and taking her face in his hands and turning her profile to him).* Well . . . it is true that this is not so much a profile of a Hollywood queen as perhaps a queen of the Nile—*(A mock dismissal of the importance of the question)* But what does it matter? Assimilationism[4] is so popular in your country.

Beneatha *(wheeling, passionately, sharply).* I am not an assimilationist!

Asagai *(The protest hangs in the room for a moment and* ASAGAI *studies her, his laughter fading).* Such a serious one. *(There is a pause.)* So—you like the robes? You must take excellent care of them—they are from my sister's personal wardrobe.

Beneatha *(with incredulity).* You—you sent all the way home—for me?

Asagai *(with charm).* For you—I would do much more . . . Well, that is what I came for. I must go.

Beneatha. Will you call me Monday?

Asagai. Yes . . . We have a great deal to talk about. I mean about identity and time and all that.

Beneatha. Time?

Asagai. Yes. About how much time one needs to know what one feels.

Beneatha. You never understood that there is more than one kind of feeling which can exist between a man and a woman—or, at least, there should be.

Asagai *(shaking his head negatively but gently).* No. Between a man and a woman there need be only one kind of feeling. I have that for you . . . Now even . . . right this moment . . .

Beneatha. I know—and by itself—it won't do. I can find that anywhere.

Asagai. For a woman it should be enough.

Beneatha. I know—because that's what it says in all the novels that men write. But it isn't. Go ahead and laugh—but I'm not interested in being someone's little episode in America or—*(with feminine vengeance)*—one of them! *(*ASAGAI *has burst into laughter again.)* That's funny . . . , huh!

Asagai. It's just that every American girl I have known has said that to me. White—black—in this you are all the same. And the same speech, too!

Beneatha *(angrily).* Yuk, yuk, yuk!

Asagai. It's how you can be sure that the world's most liberated women are not liberated at all. You all talk about it too much!

[MAMA *enters and is immediately all social charm because of the presence of a guest.*]

Beneatha. Oh—Mama—this is Mr. Asagai.

Mama. How do you do?

Asagai *(total politeness to an elder).* How do you do, Mrs. Younger. Please forgive me for coming at such an outrageous hour on a Saturday.

Mama. Well, you are quite welcome. I just hope you understand that our house don't always look like this. *(Chatterish)* You must come again. I would love to hear all about—*(not sure of the name)*—your country. I think it's so sad the way our American Negroes don't know anything about Africa 'cept Tarzan and all that. And all that money they pour into these churches when they ought to be helping you people over there drive out them French and Englishmen done taken away your land. A

[*The mother flashes a slightly superior look at her daughter upon completion of the recitation.*]

Asagai *(taken aback by this sudden and acutely unrelated expression of sympathy).* Yes . . . yes . . .

Mama *(smiling at him suddenly and relaxing and looking him over).* How many miles is it from here to where you come from?

Asagai. Many thousands.

Mama *(looking at him as she would* WALTER*).* I bet you don't half look after yourself, being away from your mama either. I spec you better come 'round here from time to time and get yourself some decent home-cooked meals . . .

Asagai *(moved).* Thank you. Thank you very much. *(They are all quiet, then—)* Well . . . I must go. I will call you Monday, Alaiyo.

Mama. What's that he call you?

Asagai. Oh—"Alaiyo." I hope you don't mind. It is what you would call a nickname, I think. It is a Yoruba word. I am a Yoruba. B

Mama *(looking at* BENEATHA*).* I—I thought he was from—

Asagai *(understanding).* Nigeria is my country. Yoruba is my tribal origin—

Beneatha. You didn't tell us what Alaiyo means . . . for all I know, you might be calling me Little Idiot or something . . .

4. **Assimilationism** (ə·sim′ə lā′shəniz′m): the belief that minority groups should drop their ethnic, racial, and religious identities and be absorbed into the mainstream majority culture.

A. Characterization

? Why does Beneatha breathe a soft "thank you" when she finds out what "Alaiyo" means? (Asagai understands her better than she thought; the name means "One for Whom Bread—Food—Is Not Enough." It is exactly right.) How similar are Beneatha and her brother, Walter? Could a masculine form of the same name apply to him? Explain. (Answers will vary. Some students may agree that Beneatha and Walter are alike in their ambitions to be successful but that the two are unalike in how they choose to attain their goals.)

B. Responding

? What is your guess as to Beneatha's destination? Why? (Judging by her actions and the words "To become a queen of the Nile," she is going out to have her hair restored to its natural state.)

Asagai. Well . . . let me see . . . I do not know how just to explain it . . . The sense of a thing can be so different when it changes languages.

Beneatha. You're evading.

A **Asagai.** No—really it is difficult . . . *(Thinking)* It means . . . it means One for Whom Bread—Food—Is Not Enough. *(He looks at her.)* Is that all right?

Beneatha *(understanding, softly).* Thank you.

Mama *(looking from one to the other and not understanding any of it).* Well . . . that's nice . . . You must come see us again—Mr.—

Asagai. Ah-sah-guy . . .

Mama. Yes . . . Do come again.

Asagai. Goodbye. *(He exits.)*

Mama *(after him).* Lord, that's a pretty thing just went out here! *(Insinuatingly, to her daughter)* Yes, I guess I see why we done commence to get so interested in Africa 'round here. Missionaries my aunt Jenny! *(She exits.)*

Beneatha. Oh, Mama! . . .

[*She picks up the Nigerian dress and holds it up to her in front of the mirror again. She sets the headdress on haphazardly and then notices her hair again and clutches at it and then replaces the headdress and frowns at herself. Then she starts to wriggle in front of the mirror as she thinks a Nigerian woman might.* TRAVIS *enters and regards her.*]

Travis. You cracking up?

Beneatha. Shut up.

[*She pulls the headdress off and looks at herself in the mirror and clutches at her hair again and squinches her eyes as if trying to imagine something. Then, suddenly, she gets her raincoat and kerchief and hurriedly prepares for going out.*]

B **Mama** *(coming back into the room).* She's resting now. Travis, baby, run next door and ask Miss Johnson to please let me have a little kitchen cleanser. This here can is empty as Jacob's kettle.

Travis. I just came in.

Mama. Do as you told. *(He exits and she looks at her daughter.)* Where you going?

Beneatha *(halting at the door).* To become a queen of the Nile!

[*She exits in a breathless blaze of glory.* RUTH *appears in the bedroom doorway.*]

Mama. Who told you to get up?

Ruth. Ain't nothing wrong with me to be lying in no bed for. Where did Bennie go?

Mama *(drumming her fingers).* Far as I could make out—to Egypt. *(*RUTH *just looks at her.)* What time is it getting to?

Ruth. Ten twenty. And the mailman going to ring that bell this morning just like he done every morning for the last umpteen years.

[TRAVIS *comes in with the cleanser can.*]

Travis. She say to tell you that she don't have much.

Mama *(angrily).* Lord, some people I could name sure is tight-fisted! *(Directing her grandson)* Mark two cans of cleanser down on the list there. If she that hard up for kitchen cleanser, I sure don't want to forget to get her none!

Ruth. Lena—maybe the woman is just short on cleanser—

Mama *(not listening).* —Much baking powder as she done borrowed from me all these years, she could of done gone into the baking business!

[*The bell sounds suddenly and sharply and all three are stunned—serious and silent—mid-speech. In spite of all the other conversations and distractions of the morning, this is what they have been waiting for, even* TRAVIS, *who looks helplessly from his mother to his grandmother.* RUTH *is first to come to life again.*]

Ruth *(to* TRAVIS*). Get down them steps, boy!*

[TRAVIS *snaps to life and flies out to get the mail.*]

Mama *(her eyes wide, her hand to her breast).* You mean it done really come?

Ruth *(excited).* Oh, Miss Lena!

Mama *(collecting herself).* Well . . . I don't know what we all so excited about 'round here for. We known it was coming for months.

Ruth. That's a whole lot different from having it come and being able to hold it in your hands . . . a piece of paper worth ten thousand dollars . . . *(*TRAVIS *bursts back into the room. He holds the envelope high above his head, like a little dancer, his face is radiant and he is breathless. He moves to his grandmother with sudden slow ceremony and puts the envelope into her hands. She accepts it, and then merely holds it and looks at it.)* Come on! Open it . . . Lord have mercy, I wish Walter Lee was here!

Travis. Open it, Grandmama!

READING CHECK TEST: ACT ONE

1. What is the amount of the insurance check Mama expects to receive? *$10,000*
2. What does Walter want to invest the money in? *A liquor store*
3. What does Beneatha want to become? *A doctor*
4. What does Mama want to use the money for? *Beneatha's education and a house*
5. What news about Ruth stuns Walter? *She is pregnant.*

Humanities Connection: Responding to the Photograph Mama's question appears in the middle of column 2 on text page 829. ? How does the photograph enhance your appreciation of the phrase "pretty thing" as applied to a man? (Here "pretty thing" means someone who is handsome or appealing to the eye.) What message is conveyed by the way Beneatha looks at Asagai? By Mama's posture? (Answers will vary, but most students will agree that Beneatha and Mama react fondly or admiringly toward Asagai.)

"How many miles is it from here to where you come from?"

Analyzing Act One
Identifying Details

1. Our curiosity is first aroused when Walter asks if the check is coming, and Ruth tells him that it is due tomorrow and not to talk to her about money. It is clear that the Youngers do not have much money, although we do not yet know what type of check Walter is expecting. Then Travis enters and mentions the check. In the following dialogue, Ruth refuses to give him fifty cents for school (she says they haven't got money), and tells Travis not to ask Mama for it. But Walter, much to Ruth's annoyance, gives his son a dollar. Then Walter reveals his "investment" plan to Ruth, and urges her to try to persuade Mama. When Beneatha enters, the check is again mentioned: Beneatha says the money will belong to Mama, while Walter accuses her of accepting money to finance her education. In this scene, we learn that Mama will receive the money from an insurance policy, following the death of her husband. When Mama enters, she and Ruth discuss the money and Mama declares that she will not help Walter to finance a liquor store, because that sort of business goes against her convictions. Mama

A. Plot
The long-awaited event occurs; the check arrives and the amount is verified.
? Why is Mama sad? What does she mean by "Ten thousand dollars they give you. Ten thousand dollars"? (Her husband was worth far more than any amount of money.)

B. Predicting an Outcome
? Why does Mama want Walter to talk to Ruth? (So that he can be told about her pregnancy) How do you think he will react when he finds out? (He will probably be upset because a new baby would add to his financial problems.)

C. Plot
? Mama rejects Walter's plan. Can you predict anything that might change her mind? What reactions on Walter's part do you predict as a result? (Most students will predict that Walter would do something drastic.)

Mama *(staring at it).* Now you all be quiet. It's just a check.
Ruth. Open it . . .
Mama *(still staring at it).* Now don't act silly . . . We ain't never been no people to act silly 'bout no money—
Ruth *(swiftly).* We ain't never had none before—*open it!*

[MAMA *finally makes a good strong tear and pulls out the thin blue slice of paper and inspects it closely. The boy and his mother study it raptly over* MAMA'S *shoulders.*]

Mama. *Travis! (She is counting off with doubt.)* Is that the right number of zeros?
Travis. Yes'm . . . ten thousand dollars. Gaalee, Grandmama, you rich.
A **Mama** *(She holds the check away from her, still looking at it. Slowly her face sobers into a mask of unhappiness.).* Ten thousand dollars. *(She hands it to* RUTH.*)* Put it away somewhere, Ruth. *(She does not look at* RUTH; *her eyes seem to be seeing something somewhere very far off.)* Ten thousand dollars they give you. Ten thousand dollars.
Travis *(to his mother, sincerely).* What's the matter with Grandmama—don't she want to be rich?
Ruth *(distractedly).* You go on out and play now, baby. *(*TRAVIS *exits.* MAMA *starts wiping dishes absently, humming intently to herself.* RUTH *turns to her, with kind exasperation.)* You've gone and got yourself upset.
Mama *(not looking at her).* I spec if it wasn't for you all . . . I would just put that money away or give it to the church or something.
Ruth. Now what kind of talk is that. Mr. Younger would just be plain mad if he could hear you talking foolish like that.
Mama *(stopping and staring off).* Yes . . . he sure would. *(Sighing)* We got enough to do with that money, all right. *(She halts then, and turns and looks at her daughter-in-law hard;* RUTH *avoids her eyes and* MAMA *wipes her hands with finality and starts to speak firmly to* RUTH.*)* Where did you go today, girl?
Ruth. To the doctor.
Mama *(impatiently).* Now, Ruth . . . you know better than that. Old Doctor Jones is strange enough in his way but there ain't nothing 'bout him make somebody slip and call him "she"—like you done this morning.
Ruth. Well, that's what happened—my tongue slipped.
Mama. You went to see that woman, didn't you?
Ruth *(defensively, giving herself away).* What woman you talking about?
Mama *(angrily).* That woman who—

[WALTER *enters in great excitement.*]

Walter. Did it come?
Mama *(quietly).* Can't you give people a Christian greeting before you start asking about money?
Walter *(to* RUTH*).* Did it come? *(*RUTH *unfolds the check and lays it quietly before him, watching him intently with thoughts of her own.* WALTER *sits down and grasps it close and counts off the zeros.)* Ten thousand dollars—*(He turns suddenly, frantically to his mother and draws some papers out of his breast pocket.)* Mama—look. Old Willy Harris put everything on paper—
Mama. Son—I think you ought to talk to your wife . . . I'll go on out and leave you alone if you want—
Walter. I can talk to her later—Mama, look—
Mama. Son—
Walter. WILL SOMEBODY PLEASE LISTEN TO ME TODAY!
Mama *(quietly).* I don't 'low no yellin' in this house, Walter Lee, and you know it—*(*WALTER *stares at them in frustration and starts to speak several times.)* And there ain't going to be no investing in no liquor stores. I don't aim to have to speak on that again.

[*A long pause*]

Walter. Oh—so you don't aim to have to speak on that again? So *you* have decided . . . *(Crumpling his papers)* Well, *you* tell that to my boy tonight when you put him to sleep on the living-room couch . . . *(Turning to* MAMA *and speaking directly to her)* Yeah—and tell it to my wife, Mama, tomorrow when she has to go out of here to look after somebody else's kids. And tell it to *me,* Mama, every time we need a new pair of curtains and I have to watch *you* go out and work in somebody's kitchen. Yeah, you tell me then!

[WALTER *starts out.*]

Ruth. Where are you going?
Walter. I'm going out!
Ruth. Where?
Walter. Just out of this house somewhere—

also says that she will put away part of the ten thousand dollars for Beneatha's education; she rejects the idea of taking a trip herself; and she introduces the plan of buying a small house and moving from the apartment—a plan which Ruth subtly encourages. In Scene 2, Walter refers to the check when he talks to Willy Harris on the telephone. The whole family is eagerly awaiting the mailman's arrival. Later in the scene, Travis enters excitedly with the check, and Mama opens the envelope.

2. Walter argues with Ruth over the length of time Travis stays in the bathroom. They then have a small argument over Walter's smoking in the morning. Ruth and Travis argue over the fifty cents which Travis wants to take to school, but mother and son then make up. Walter and Ruth argue over the "investment" plan in the liquor store, and Walter accuses Ruth of not supporting him. When Beneatha enters, she and Walter argue over the use of the insurance money, with Walter accusing Beneatha of being selfish.

3. He wants to invest in a liquor store together with several friends.

Beneatha wants to be a doctor, and she needs money for her education.

4. Mama calls Walter a disgrace to his father's memory because he will not pay attention to his wife, who is pregnant and thinking of an abortion.

Interpreting Meanings

5. Most students will agree that the action is believable.

6. Arguments can be made for both Beneatha and Walter—that they ought to have a chance to achieve their dreams; or for Mama, who is trying to keep the family together; or for the patient, wise, and pregnant Ruth.

7. We are told that Mama is about to receive the check; Walter implies that Mama will listen more to Ruth than she will to Walter himself, and that it is prudent to approach her indirectly; Ruth tells Travis not to bother his grandmother for the fifty cents that he wants; Ruth cautions Walter and Beneatha not to argue because their mother will hear them.

(Answers continue on next page.)

Ruth *(getting her coat).* I'll come too.
Walter. I don't want you to come!
Ruth. I got something to talk to you about, Walter.
Walter. That's too bad.
Mama *(still quietly).* Walter Lee—*(She waits and he finally turns and looks at her.)* Sit down.
Walter. I'm a grown man, Mama.
Mama. Ain't nobody said you wasn't grown. But you still in my house and my presence. And as long as you are—you'll talk to your wife civil. Now sit down.
Ruth *(suddenly).* Oh, let him go out and drink himself to death! He makes me sick to my stomach! *(She flings her coat against him.)*
Walter *(violently).* And you turn mine too, baby! *(RUTH goes into their bedroom and slams the door behind her.)* That was my greatest mistake—
Mama *(still quietly).* Walter, what is the matter with you?
Walter. Matter with me? Ain't nothing the matter with *me!*
Mama. Yes there is. Something eating you up like a crazy man. Something more than me not giving you this money. The past few years I been watching it happen to you. You get all nervous acting and kind of wild in the eyes—*(WALTER jumps up impatiently at her words.)* I said sit there now, I'm talking to you!
Walter. Mama—I don't need no nagging at me today.
Mama. Seem like you getting to a place where you always tied up in some kind of knot about something. But if anybody ask you 'bout it you just yell at 'em and bust out the house and go out and drink somewheres. Walter Lee, people can't live like that. Ruth's a good, patient girl in her way—but you getting to be too much. Boy, don't make the mistake of driving that girl away from you.
Walter. Why—what she do for me?
Mama. She loves you.
Walter. Mama—I'm going out. I want to go off somewhere and be by myself for a while.
Mama. I'm sorry 'bout your liquor store, son. It just wasn't the thing for us to do. That's what I want to tell you about—
Walter. I got to go out, Mama— *(He rises.)*
Mama. It's dangerous, son.
Walter. What's dangerous?
Mama. When a man goes outside his home to look for peace.
Walter *(beseechingly).* Then why can't there never be no peace in this house then?
Mama. You done found it in some other house?
Walter. No—there ain't no woman! Why do women always think there's a woman somewhere when a man gets restless. *(Coming to her)* Mama—Mama—I want so many things . . .
Mama. Yes, son—
Walter. I want so many things that they are driving me kind of crazy . . . Mama—look at me.
Mama. I'm looking at you. You a good-looking boy. You got a job, a nice wife, a fine boy and—
Walter. A job. *(Looks at her)* Mama, a job? I open and close car doors all day long. I drive a man around in his limousine and I say, "Yes, sir; no, sir; very good, sir; shall I take the Drive, sir?" Mama, that ain't no kind of job . . . that ain't nothing at all. *(Very quietly)* Mama, I don't know if I can make you understand.
Mama. Understand what, baby?
Walter *(quietly).* Sometimes it's like I can see the future stretched out in front of me—just plain as day. The future, Mama. Hanging over there at the edge of my days. Just waiting for me—a big, looming blank space—full of *nothing.* Just waiting for me. *(Pause)* Mama—sometimes when I'm downtown and I pass them cool, quiet-looking restaurants where them white boys are sitting back and talking 'bout things . . . sitting there turning deals worth millions of dollars . . . sometimes I see guys don't look much older than me—
Mama. Son—how come you talk so much 'bout money?
Walter *(with immense passion).* Because it is life, Mama!
Mama *(quietly).* Oh—*(Very quietly)* So now its life. Money is life. Once upon a time freedom used to be life—now its money. I guess the world really do change . . .
Walter. No—it was always money, Mama. We just didn't know about it.
Mama. No . . . something has changed. *(She looks at him.)* You something new, boy. In my time we was worried about not being lynched and getting to the North if we could and how to stay alive and still have a pinch of dignity too . . . Now here come you and Beneatha—talking 'bout things we ain't never even thought about hardly, me and your daddy. You ain't satisfied or proud of nothing we done. I mean that you had a home; that we kept you out of trouble till you was grown; that you don't have to ride to work on the back of nobody's streetcar— You my children—but how different we done become.

(Continued from previous page.)
Mama enters with great dignity in her bearing. Her features express nobility and strength, and the stage directions suggest that she is heroic. Her voice is soft. In her first line, she expresses concern about the "slamming doors" that must have been the sign of an argument. In her second speech, she shows that she is indeed a concerned, loving mother: she tells Ruth that she looks peaked and offers to iron some of the clothes, and she reminds Beneatha to put on her robe so that she will not catch cold. She even expresses solicitude about her "old plant." When she sees Travis's messy bed, she emphasizes that he is a little boy, her "baby," who tries.
8. We are shown the strength of Mama's religious beliefs in the scene with Beneatha. When her daughter claims that she doesn't accept the idea of the existence of God, Mama firmly reminds her that—while she remains in Mama's house—Beneatha will acknowledge God.
9. Asagai represents a different, more international viewpoint on the African American experience. He is a Nigerian student in Chicago—well-traveled, liberal,
(Answers continue in left-hand column.)

(Continued from top.)
and passionately convinced that the true roots and identity of American blacks are to be found in Africa. Asagai believes that American blacks should not yield to "assimilationism."

Whereas Asagai opposes assimilationism, George, who is the child of wealthy and successful black parents, seems to have given up his roots and joined the "mainstream" of conventional American society.
10. Among the dramatic questions the playwright raises are: How will the conflict over the insurance money be resolved? What will Ruth do about her pregnancy? Will Mama succeed in her efforts to keep the family together? Students will have various possible answers for each question.

Walter. You just don't understand, Mama, you just don't understand.
Mama. Son—do you know your wife is expecting another baby? *(*WALTER *stands, stunned, and absorbs what his mother has said.)* That's what she wanted to talk to you about. *(*WALTER *sinks down into a chair.)* This ain't for me to be telling—but you ought to know. *(She waits.)* I think Ruth is thinking bout doing something to that child.
Walter *(slowly understanding)*. No— no— Ruth wouldn't—
Mama. When the world gets ugly enough—a woman will do anything for her family. *The part that's already living.*
Walter. You don't know Ruth, Mama, if you think she would—

[RUTH *opens the bedroom door and stands there a little limp.*]

Ruth *(beaten)*. Yes I would too, Walter. *(Pause)* . . .

[*There is total silence as the man stares at his wife and the mother stares at her son.*]

Mama *(presently)*. Well— *(Tightly)* Well—son, I'm waiting to hear you say something . . . I'm waiting to hear how you be your father's son. Be the man he was . . . *(Pause)* Your wife say she don't want your child. And I'm waiting to hear you talk like him and say we a people who give children life, not destroys them—*(She rises.)* I'm waiting to see you stand up and look like your daddy and say we done give up one baby to poverty and that we ain't going to give up nary another one . . . I'm waiting.
Walter. Ruth—
Mama. If you a son of mine, tell her! *(*WALTER *turns, looks at her and can say nothing. She continues, bitterly.)* You . . . you are a disgrace to your father's memory. Somebody get me my hat.

Curtain

Responding to the Play

Analyzing Act One

Identifying Details

1. In the fourth speech of the play, the line "Check coming today?" arouses our interest and curiosity. Trace the development of the check in this act as it moves from something that arouses our curiosity to something that becomes the central plot issue of the play.
2. In a play, our attention is held by people in **conflict.** Look carefully at the opening scene through Walter's exit (page 821). Point out the number of subjects, large and small, over which the characters argue.
3. Walter expresses his "dream" in Scene 1. What does he want to do with Mama's money? How does his dream **conflict** with Beneatha's ambition?
4. At the end of Scene 2, why is Mama so angry with Walter?

Interpreting Meanings

5. It has been said that to enjoy a play we must believe what is happening and care about the characters. Is the action of the play believable so far? Explain your answer.
6. At the end of Act I, which character are you "rooting" for most, and why?
7. There has been a considerable build-up for Mama's entrance, which occurs late in Scene 1. What are we told about Mama before she appears? In a play, showing is better than telling. When she makes her entrance, Mama immediately shows us in small ways what kind of woman and mother she is. What does she do, and what do her actions reveal about her **character**?
8. It is important that we know the strength of Mama's religious beliefs because it is these beliefs that influence her decision not to give Walter the money. How does the playwright show us how strong Mama's beliefs are?
9. The character of Asagai, introduced in Scene 2, gives us a different perspective on life in the Younger household. What does Asagai represent? How is he contrasted with George Murchison, Beneatha's other admirer?
10. What dramatic questions have been posed in this first act? What possible answers could each question have?

SUPPLEMENTARY SUPPORT MATERIALS: ACT TWO

1. Vocabulary Activity Worksheet (*CCB*)
2. Review and Response Worksheet: Stage Directions (*CCB*)
3. Selection Test (*CCB*)

DEVELOPING VOCABULARY

The following words from Act Two are tested in the Selection Test. (See also Vocabulary Activity Worksheet.)

coquettishly	burlesque
ornate	orientation
heritage	dumbfounded
exuberant	facetiousness
strident	ludicrous

A. Music Connection
Black African music varies from culture to culture, but some generalizations can be made. The distinguishing feature is rhythmic complexity achieved by handclaps, xylophones, rattles, and a variety of tuned and untuned drums. Polyphony exists in overlapping solo and choral parts, and occasional simultaneous melodies. Besides the human voice, wind and string instruments are used, including bamboo flutes, ivory trumpets, and the one-string ground bow, which uses a hole in the ground as a resonator. Music is highly functional to tribal life, much of it designed to accompany birth, marriage, and hunting rituals, but some of it purely for entertainment.

Act Two

Scene 1

Time: Later the same day.

At rise: RUTH *is ironing again. She has the radio going. Presently* BENEATHA*'s bedroom door opens and* RUTH*'s mouth falls and she puts down the iron in fascination.*

Ruth. What have we got on tonight!

Beneatha *(emerging grandly from the doorway so that we can see her thoroughly robed in the costume* ASAGAI *brought).* You are looking at what a well-dressed Nigerian woman wears—*(She parades for* RUTH, *her hair completely hidden by the headdress; she is coquettishly fanning herself with an ornate oriental fan, mistakenly more like Butterfly*[1] *than any Nigerian that ever was.)* Isn't it beautiful? *(She promenades to the radio and, with an arrogant flourish, turns off the good loud blues that is playing.)* Enough of this assimilationist junk! *(*RUTH *follows her with her eyes as she goes to the phonograph and puts on a record and turns and waits ceremoniously for the music to come up. Then, with a shout—)* OCOMOGOSIAY![2]

[RUTH *jumps. The music comes up, a lovely Nigerian melody.* BENEATHA *listens, enraptured, her eyes far away—"back to the past." She begins to dance.* RUTH *is dumfounded.*]

Ruth. What kind of dance is that?

Beneatha. A folk dance.

Ruth *(Pearl Bailey*[3]*).* What kind of folks do that, honey?

Beneatha. It's from Nigeria. It's a dance of welcome.

Ruth. Who you welcoming?

Beneatha. The men back to the village.

Ruth. Where they been?

Beneatha. How should I know—out hunting or something. Anyway, they are coming back now . . .

Ruth. Well, that's good.

Beneatha *(with the record).*

Alundi, alundi
Alundi alunya
Jop pu a jeepua
Ang gu soooooooooo

Ai yai yae . . .
Ayehaye—alundi . . .[4]

[WALTER *comes in during this performance; he has obviously been drinking. He leans against the door heavily and watches his sister, at first with distaste. Then his eyes look off—"back to the past"—as he lifts both his fists to the roof, screaming.*]

Walter. YEAH . . . AND ETHIOPIA STRETCH FORTH HER HANDS AGAIN! . . .

Ruth *(drily, looking at him).* Yes—and Africa sure is claiming her own tonight. *(She gives them both up and starts ironing again.)*

Walter *(all in a drunken, dramatic shout).* Shut up! . . . I'm digging them drums . . . them drums move me! . . . *(He makes his weaving way to his wife's face and leans in close to her.)* In my *heart of hearts—(He thumps his chest.)*—I am much warrior!

Ruth *(without even looking up).* In your heart of hearts you are much drunkard.

Walter *(coming away from her and starting to wander around the room, shouting).* Me and Jomo[5] . . . *(Intently, in his sister's face. She has stopped dancing to watch him in this unknown mood.)* That's my man, Kenyatta. *(Shouting and thumping his chest)* FLAMING SPEAR! . . . *(He is suddenly in possession of an imaginary spear and actively spearing enemies all over the room.) OCOMOGOSIAY* . . . THE LION IS WAKING . . . OWIMOWEH![6] *(He pulls his shirt open and leaps up on a table and gestures with his spear. The bell rings.* RUTH *goes to answer.)*

Beneatha *(to encourage* WALTER, *thoroughly caught up with this side of him). OCOMOGOSIAY,* FLAMING SPEAR!

Walter *(on the table, very far gone, his eyes pure glass sheets. He sees what we cannot, that he is a leader of his people, a great chief, a descendant*

1. **Butterfly:** Madama Butterfly, the heroine in the opera by Giacomo Puccini.
2. **Ocomogosiay:** a shout of triumph in battle. It is a coined word, combining syllables from the Yoruba, Swahili, and Zulu languages.
3. **Pearl Bailey:** an American entertainer, singer, and actress. Ruth is imitating her.
4. **alundi . . . alundi:** a Yoruba harvest festival song. *Alundi* means "Happy holiday."
5. **Jomo:** Jomo Kenyatta (1894?–1978), leader and president of Kenya. *Jomo* means "flaming spear."
6. **Owimoweh:** variation of a Zulu word meaning "lion."

ACT TWO SUMMARY
Scene 1: Ruth looks on with amused tolerance as Beneatha and Walter carry on to African music but is embarrassed when George Murchison arrives to take Beneatha to the theater. While she changes, Walter quarrels with Murchison. Walter and Ruth talk until Mama returns: she has put $3500 down on a house in Clybourne Park, a white suburb.
Scene 2: A few weeks later the family is packing to move. Walter has been spending his time people-watching and in bars, not working. To build his confidence Mama gives him the remaining $6500, asking him to set aside $3000 for Beneatha's education and to take charge of the rest. Walter tells Travis his dad is going to do something great.
Scene 3: One week later it is moving day. Karl Lindner, a white man, comes with an offer from the white community to buy out the Youngers. Walter, Ruth, and Beneatha refuse the offer; they enjoy telling Mama about the call and giving her a gift of gardening tools (Travis gives her a gardening hat). The mood changes drastically when Bobo comes to report that Willy has run off with the money that Mama had entrusted to Walter.

Humanities Connection: Responding to the Photograph
Relate the scene shown to the action on pages 835–837.
? Who is seated at the left? (Ruth) What is different about the way Beneatha is dressed? (She is wearing an African dress and headdress.) What elements of the scene did you particularly enjoy? (Answers will vary.) Is there a serious aspect to the scene as well? (Their diverse reactions and motivations symbolize the family split—a serious undercurrent throughout the play.) Why is Ruth unable to join Beneatha and Walter in their play-acting? (Perhaps because the very notion of taking pride in one's roots may be too new for her to embrace; or because she is too absorbed in her own problems to be able to appreciate her African heritage; or because she finds Beneatha too frivolous to take seriously)

"OH, DO YOU HEAR, MY BLACK BROTHERS?"

of Chaka,[7] *and that the hour to march has come).* Listen, my black brothers—

Beneatha. OCOMOGOSIAY!

Walter. —Do you hear the waters rushing against the shores of the coastlands—

Beneatha. OCOMOGOSIAY!

Walter. —Do you hear the screeching of the cocks in yonder hills beyond where the chiefs meet in council for the coming of the mighty war—

Beneatha. OCOMOGOSIAY!

Walter. —Do you hear the beating of the wings of the birds flying low over the mountains and the low places of our land—

[RUTH *opens the door.* GEORGE MURCHISON *enters.*]

Beneatha. OCOMOGOSIAY!

Walter. —Do you hear the singing of the women, singing the war songs of our fathers to the babies in the great houses . . . singing the sweet war songs? OH, DO YOU HEAR, MY BLACK BROTHERS!

Beneatha *(completely gone).* We hear you, Flaming Spear—

Walter. Telling us to prepare for the greatness of the time—*(to* GEORGE*)* Black Brother!

[*He extends his hand for the fraternal clasp.*]

George. Black Brother, your Mother!

Ruth *(having had enough, and embarrassed for the family).* Beneatha, you got company—what's the matter with you? Walter Lee Younger, get down off that table and stop acting like a fool . . .

[WALTER *comes down off the table suddenly and makes a quick exit to the bathroom.*]

Ruth. He's had a little to drink . . . I don't know what her excuse is.

George *(to* BENEATHA*).* Look honey, we're going to the theater—we're not going to be *in* it . . . so go change, huh?

Ruth. You expect this boy to go out with you looking like that?

Beneatha *(looking at* GEORGE*).* That's up to George. If he's ashamed of his heritage—

George. Oh, don't be so proud of yourself, Bennie—just because you look eccentric.

Beneatha. How can something that's natural be eccentric?

George. That's what being eccentric means—being natural. Get dressed.

Beneatha. I don't like that, George.

Ruth. Why must you and your brother make an argument out of everything people say?

Beneatha. Because I hate assimilationist Negroes!

Ruth. Will somebody please tell me what assimila-whoever means!

George. Oh, it's just a college girl's way of calling people Uncle Toms—but that isn't what it means at all.

Ruth. Well, what does it mean?

Beneatha *(cutting* GEORGE *off and staring at him as she replies to* RUTH*).* It means someone who is willing to give up his own culture and submerge himself completely in the dominant, and in this case, *oppressive* culture!

George. Oh, dear, dear, dear! Here we go! A lecture on the African past! On our Great West African Heritage! In one second we will hear all about the great Ashanti[8] empires; the great Songhay[9] civilizations; and the great sculpture of Bénin[10]—and then some poetry in the Bantu[11]—and the whole monologue will end with the word *heritage! (Nastily)* Let's face it, baby, your heritage is nothing but a bunch of raggedy . . . spirituals and some grass huts!

Beneatha. *Grass huts! (*RUTH *crosses to her and forcibly pushes her toward the bedroom.)* See there . . . you are standing there in your splendid ignorance talking about people who were the first to smelt iron on the face of the earth! *(*RUTH *is pushing her through the door.)* The Ashanti were performing surgical operations when the English—*(*RUTH *pulls the door to, with* BENEATHA *on the other side, and smiles graciously at* GEORGE. BENEATHA *opens the door and shouts the end of the sentence defiantly at* GEORGE.*)*—

7. **Chaka:** Zulu chief and military leader (1787?–1828).

8. **Ashanti:** people in west Africa who had a powerful empire in the eighteenth and nineteenth centuries. Ashanti was once a British protectorate, and is now primarily in Ghana.

9. **Songhay:** west African empire in the sixteenth century.

10. **Bénin:** west African kingdom (c. 1400–1700) known for its beautiful sculpture, metalwork, and carved ivory.

11. **Bantu:** family of languages spoken in central and southern Africa, including Zulu and Swahili.

A. Expansion

The footnotes on page 835 and on this page guide students to the major events and peoples of Africa alluded to by Beneatha and Walter. Many of these could serve as topics for further research.

Additionally, the issue of assimilationism, raised by Joseph Asagai in Act One, is now addressed by Beneatha. It is the subject of the second writing assignment on page 866 at the end of the play. It also is of great relevance—not only to African American students but also to any of your students who are recent immigrants and perhaps to any others who feel they know too little about their own ethnic or cultural heritage.

A

A. Characterization

? What is happening to Walter since Mama's refusal to fund his liquor store plan? Is his character undergoing deterioration? (He is drunk; he lies for no reason of any importance; he has grandiose plans, which Murchison greets with boredom.) What makes his remark to George Murchison, "I know you a busy little boy," an insult? (It is demeaning; it suggests that George's father is a real man, but George is not.) If you were George Murchison, how would you have acted and spoken during this scene with Walter (pages 838–839)—as George did, or in some other way? Would Walter's views affect your view of yourself, or would you pity him, and pity Beneatha for having such a brother? Explain. (Answers will vary.)

were still tatooing themselves with blue dragons . . . *(She goes back inside.)*

Ruth. Have a seat, George. *(They both sit.* RUTH *folds her hands rather primly on her lap, determined to demonstrate the civilization of the family.)* Warm, ain't it? I mean for September. *(Pause)* Just like they always say about Chicago weather: If it's too hot or cold for you, just wait a minute and it'll change. *(She smiles happily at this cliché of clichés.)* Everybody say its got to do with them bombs and things they keep setting off. *(Pause)* Would you like a nice cold beer?

George. No, thank you. I don't care for beer. *(He looks at his watch.)* I hope she hurries up.

Ruth. What time is the show?

George. It's an eight-thirty curtain. That's just Chicago, though. In New York standard curtain time is eight forty.

[*He is rather proud of this knowledge.*]

Ruth *(properly appreciating it).* You get to New York a lot?

George *(offhand).* Few times a year.

Ruth. Oh—that's nice. I've never been to New York.

[WALTER *enters. We feel he has relieved himself, but the edge of unreality is still with him.*]

Walter. New York ain't got nothing Chicago ain't. Just a bunch of hustling people all squeezed up together—being "Eastern."

[*He turns his face into a screw of displeasure.*]

George. Oh—you've been?

Walter. *Plenty* of times.

Ruth *(shocked at the lie).* Walter Lee Younger!

Walter *(staring her down).* Plenty! *(Pause)* What we got to drink in this house? Why don't you offer this man some refreshment. *(To* GEORGE*)* They don't know how to entertain people in this house, man.

George. Thank you—I don't really care for anything.

Walter *(feeling his head; sobriety coming).* Where's Mama?

Ruth. She ain't come back yet.

Walter *(looking* MURCHISON *over from head to toe, scrutinizing his carefully casual tweed sports jacket over cashmere V-neck sweater over soft eyelet shirt and tie, and soft slacks, finished off with white buckskin shoes).* Why all you college boys wear them funny-looking white shoes?

Ruth. Walter Lee!

[GEORGE MURCHISON *ignores the remark.*]

Walter *(to* RUTH*).* Well, they look crazy—white shoes, cold as it is.

Ruth *(crushed).* You have to excuse him—

Walter. No he don't! Excuse me for what? What you always excusing me for! I'll excuse myself when I needs to be excused! *(A pause)* They look as funny as them black knee socks Beneatha wears out of here all the time.

Ruth. It's the college *style,* Walter.

Walter. Style?!—She looks like she got burnt legs or something!

Ruth. Oh, Walter—

Walter *(an irritable mimic).* Oh, Walter! Oh, Walter! *(to* MURCHISON*)* How's your old man making out? I understand you all going to buy that big hotel on the Drive? *(He finds a beer in the refrigerator, wanders over to* MURCHISON, *sipping and wiping his lips with the back of his hand, and straddling a chair backwards to talk to the other man.)* Shrewd move. Your old man is all right, man. *(Tapping his head and half winking for emphasis)* I mean he knows how to operate. I mean he thinks *big,* you know what I mean, I mean for a *home,* you know? But I think he's kind of running out of ideas now. I'd like to talk to him. Listen, man, I got some plans that could turn this city upside down. I mean I think like he does. *Big.* Invest big, gamble big, shoot, lose *big* if you have to, you know what I mean. It's hard to find a man on this whole Southside who understands my kind of thinking—you dig? *(He scrutinizes* MURCHISON *again, drinks his beer, squints his eyes and leans in close, confidential, man to man.)* Me and you ought to sit down and talk sometimes, man. Man, I got me some ideas . . .

Murchison *(with boredom).* Yeah—sometimes we'll have to do that, Walter.

Walter *(understanding the indifference, and offended).* Yeah—well, when you get the time, man. I know you a busy little boy.

Ruth. Walter, please—

Walter *(bitterly, hurt).* I know ain't nothing in this world as busy as you colored college boys with your fraternity pins and white shoes . . .

Ruth *(covering her face with humiliation).* Oh, Walter Lee—

Walter. I see you all all the time—with the books tucked under your arms—going to your *(British A—a mimic)* "clahsses." And for what! What in

COMMENT FROM A CRITIC
In his laudatory review of *A Raisin in the Sun* on its opening at the Ethel Barrymore Theatre in 1959, critic Brooks Atkinson wrote that the play is "about human beings who want, on the one hand, to preserve their family pride and, on the other hand, to break out of the poverty that seems to be their fate." Atkinson saw the situations of the play as ranging from "hilarious" to "painful in the extreme." Hansberry made her points, he said, by showing "how character is controlled by environment."

? Think about Atkinson's remarks. Where in the play so far do you see the Younger family striving both to maintain pride and to break out of poverty? (Mama and Ruth try to maintain principles, dignity, and order in the house; Ruth constantly takes outside jobs for extra income; Walter dreams of having his own business; Beneatha aims for a medical education; even Travis wants to work at the supermarket.) What scenes or situations have made you laugh? What scenes or situations have been painful? (Answers will vary.)

the world you learning over there? Filling up your heads—*(counting off on his fingers)*—with the sociology and the psychology—but they teaching you how to be a man? How to take over and run the world? They teaching you how to run a rubber plantation or a steel mill? Naw—just to talk proper and read books and wear white shoes . . .
George *(looking at him with distaste, a little above it all).* You're all wacked up with bitterness, man.
Walter *(intently, almost quietly, between the teeth, glaring at the boy).* And you—ain't you bitter, man? Ain't you just about had it yet? Don't you see no stars gleaming that you can't reach out and grab? You happy? You contented turkey—you happy? You got it made? Bitter? Man, I'm a volcano. Bitter? Here I am a giant—surrounded by ants! Ants who can't even understand what it is the giant is talking about.
Ruth *(passionately and suddenly).* Oh, Walter—ain't you with nobody!
Walter *(violently).* No! 'Cause ain't nobody with me! Not even my own mother!
Ruth. Walter, that's a terrible thing to say!

[BENEATHA *enters, dressed for the evening in a cocktail dress and earrings.*]

George. Well—hey, you look great.
Beneatha. Let's go, George. See you all later.
Ruth. Have a nice time.
George. Thanks. Good night. *(To* WALTER, *sarcastically)* Good night, *Prometheus.*[12]

[BENEATHA *and* GEORGE *exit.*]

Walter *(to* RUTH*).* Who is Prometheus?
Ruth. I don't know. Don't worry about it.
Walter *(in fury, pointing after* GEORGE*).* See there—they get to a point where they can't insult you man to man—they got to go talk about something ain't nobody never heard of!
Ruth. How do you know it was an insult? *(to humor him)* Maybe Prometheus is a nice fellow.
Walter. Prometheus! I bet there ain't even no such thing! I bet that simple-minded clown—
Ruth. Walter— *(She stops what she is doing and looks at him.)*

12. **Prometheus:** in Greek mythology, a Titan (giant) who stole fire from the gods and gave it to humans. Zeus, king of the gods, punished Prometheus by chaining him to a mountain, where each day a vulture ate out his liver. Each night, Zeus caused the liver to be renewed so that the torture was excruciating and endless. Prometheus was finally freed by Hercules.

Walter *(yelling).* Don't start!
Ruth. Start what?
Walter. Your nagging! Where was I? Who was I with? How much money did I spend?
Ruth *(plaintively).* Walter Lee—why don't we just try to talk about it . . .
Walter *(not listening).* I been out talking with people who understand me. People who care about the things I got on my mind.
Ruth *(wearily).* I guess that means people like Willy Harris.
Walter. Yes, people like Willy Harris.
Ruth *(with a sudden flash of impatience).* Why don't you all just hurry up and go into the banking business and stop talking about it!
Walter. Why? You want to know why? 'Cause we all tied up in a race of people that don't know how to do nothing but moan, pray and have babies!

[*The line is too bitter even for him and he looks at her and sits down.*]

A

Ruth. Oh, Walter . . . *(Softly)* Honey, why can't you stop fighting me?
Walter *(without thinking).* Who's fighting you? Who even cares about you?

[*This line begins the retardation of his mood.*]

Ruth. Well—*(She waits a long time, and then with resignation starts to put away her things.)* I guess I might as well go on to bed . . . *(More or less to herself)* I don't know where we lost it . . . but we have . . . *(Then, to him)* I—I'm sorry about this new baby, Walter. . . . I guess I just didn't realize how bad things was with us . . . I guess I just didn't really realize—*(She starts out to the bedroom and stops.)* You want some hot milk?
Walter. Hot milk?
Ruth. Yes—hot milk.
Walter. Why hot milk?
Ruth. 'Cause after all that liquor you come home with you ought to have something hot in your stomach.
Walter. I don't want no milk.
Ruth. You want some coffee then?
Walter. No, I don't want no coffee. I don't want nothing hot to drink. *(Almost plaintively)* Why you always trying to give me something to eat?
Ruth *(standing and looking at him helplessly).* What else can I give you, Walter Lee Younger?

[*She stands and looks at him and presently turns to go out again. He lifts his head and watches her*

A. Dramatic Intensity
At this point Ruth's and Walter's pain and conflicts come to a head, and it looks as though the two may reach an understanding.

? Why does the line ending "have babies" strike even Walter as "too bitter"? (He must suddenly have recalled that his own wife is pregnant.) Why does the line "Who even cares about you?" begin a change in Walter's mood? (Perhaps he realizes he does care about Ruth.) In the lines that follow, Ruth apologizes to Walter for her pregnancy. How do you feel about that? (Answers will vary. Most students will see Walter as equally responsible.) At this point in the play, do you feel equal sympathy for Ruth and Walter, or do you empathize more with one of them? Explain. (Answers will vary. Encourage students to give reasons to back up their responses.)

A. Suspense

? Explain how all of the following contribute to the suspense of the scene on this page: (a) the interruption in Ruth's and Walter's conversation (You want to know where it was going); (b) Travis's late return home (You wonder if he has been in trouble, or perhaps working at the supermarket); (c) Mama's return from a long, unexplained absence (You wonder what she has been doing with the insurance money); (d) Mama's initial ignoring of Walter's "where have you been?" (It delays revelation of her actions); (e) Mama's interference with Ruth's discipline of Travis (It increases tension between Ruth and Mama, who ordinarily get along very well); (f) Mama's choosing to give the news of the new house to Travis. (Mama manipulates the scene: by speaking to Travis, she prevents both Walter and Ruth from saying anything judgmental in his presence.)

going away from him in a new mood which began to emerge when he asked her "Who cares about you?"]

Walter. It's been rough, ain't it, baby? *(She hears and stops but does not turn around he continues to her back.)* I guess between two people there ain't never as much understood as folks generally thinks there is. I mean like between me and you— *(She turns to face him.)* How we gets to the place where we scared to talk softness to each other. *(He waits, thinking hard himself.)* Why you think it got to be like that? *(He is thoughtful, almost as a child would be.)* Ruth, what is it gets into people ought to be close?
Ruth. I don't know, honey. I think about it a lot.
Walter. On account of you and me, you mean? The way things are with us. The way something done come down between us.
Ruth. There ain't so much between us, Walter . . . Not when you come to me and try to talk to me. Try to be with me . . . a little even.
Walter *(total honesty).* Sometimes . . . sometimes . . . I don't even know how to try.
Ruth. Walter—
Walter. Yes?
Ruth *(coming to him, gently and with misgiving, but coming to him).* Honey . . . life don't have to be like this. I mean sometimes people can do things so that things are better . . . You remember how we used to talk when Travis was born . . . about the way we were going to live . . . the kind of house . . . *(She is stroking his head.)* Well, it's all starting to slip away from us . . .

[MAMA *enters, and* WALTER *jumps and shouts at her.*]

Walter. Mama, where have you been?
Mama. My—them steps is longer than they used to be. Whew! *(She sits down and ignores him.)* How you feeling this evening, Ruth?

[RUTH *shrugs, disturbed some at having been prematurely interrupted and watching her husband knowingly.*]

Walter. Mama, where have you been all day?
Mama *(still ignoring him and leaning on the table and changing to more comfortable shoes).* Where's Travis?
Ruth. I let him go out earlier and he ain't come back yet. Boy, is he going to get it!

Walter. Mama!
Mama *(as if she has heard him for the first time).* Yes, son?
Walter. Where did you go this afternoon?
Mama. I went downtown to tend to some business that I had to tend to.
Walter. What kind of business?
Mama. You know better than to question me like a child, Brother.
Walter *(rising and bending over the table).* Where were you Mama? *(Bringing his fists down and shouting)* Mama, you didn't go do something with that insurance money, something crazy?

[*The front door opens slowly, interrupting him, and* TRAVIS *peeks his head in, less than hopefully.*]

Travis *(to his mother).* Mama, I—
Ruth. "Mama I" nothing! You're going to get it, boy! Get on in that bedroom and get yourself ready!
Travis. But I—
Mama. Why don't you all never let the child explain hisself.
Ruth. Keep out of it now, Lena.

[MAMA *clamps her lips together, and* RUTH *advances toward her son menacingly.*]

Ruth. A thousand times I have told you not to go off like that—
Mama *(holding out her arms to her grandson).* Well—at least let me tell him something. I want him to be the first one to hear . . . Come here, Travis. *(The boy obeys, gladly.)* Travis—*(She takes him by the shoulder and looks into his face.)*—you know that money we got in the mail this morning?
Travis. Yes'm—
Mama. Well—what you think your grandmama gone and done with that money?
Travis. I don't know, Grandmama.
Mama *(putting her finger on her nose for emphasis).* She went out and she bought you a house! *(The explosion comes from* WALTER *at the end of the revelation and he jumps up and turns away from all of them in a fury.* MAMA *continues, to* TRAVIS.*)* You glad about the house? It's going to be yours when you get to be a man.
Travis. Yeah—I always wanted to live in a house.
Mama. All right, gimme some sugar then— *(*TRAVIS *puts his arms around her neck as she watches her son over the boy's shoulder. Then, to* TRAVIS, *after the embrace.)* Now when you say

A

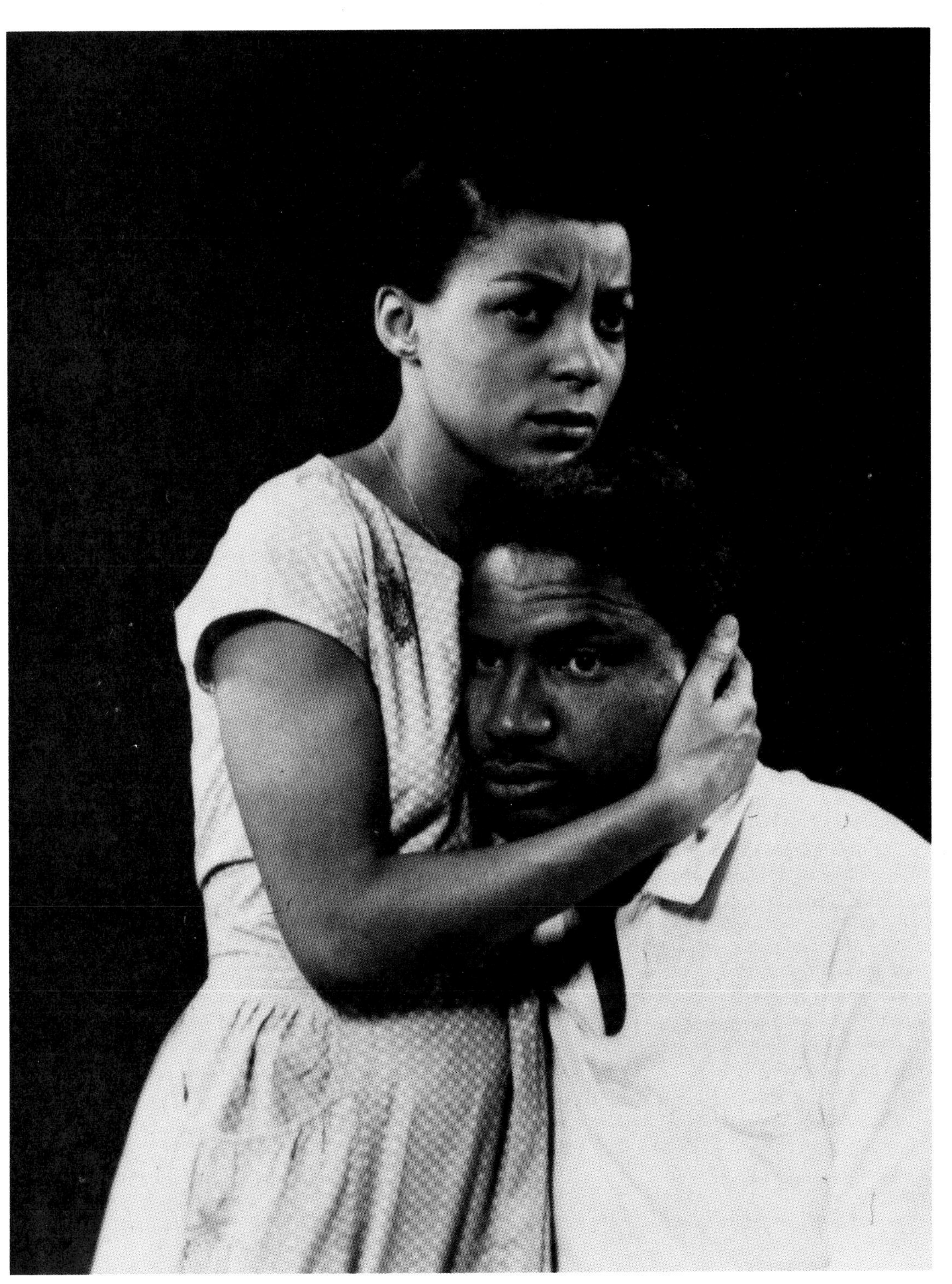

". . . it's all starting to slip away from us . . ."

Humanities Connection: Responding to the Photograph
The photograph illustrates the near rapprochement of Ruth and Walter, interrupted by the return of Mama and Travis. The line is Ruth's, about two thirds down the first column on page 840.

? If you could make Ruth alone responsible for the use of the insurance money, what do you believe she would do with it? Would she buy a house, like Mama, or give the money to Walter? Support your opinion with details from the play. (Answers will vary. There have been many clues that Ruth supports Mama's desire for better living conditions, but we have also seen her proposing Walter's idea to his mother.) If Ruth and Walter had not been interrupted, where might their conversation have led? What hopes or plans for the future might they have agreed on? (Answers will vary.)

A. Expansion Suburban building had exploded after World War II, many builders following the example of housebuilders Levitt & Sons, who introduced the near assembly-line production of row upon row of identical houses in Long Island. Levitt houses, snapped up at prices ranging from $6990 to $7990, featured four rooms, radiant heat, electric kitchens, and a basement that the buyer could finish off. Levitt imitators cut corners more and more, eliminating such "frills" as porches and garages and often doing shoddy work. Even in the late 1950's Mama would have had to shop carefully to get the best value and to find a house in which basic construction had been done properly.

your prayers tonight, you thank God and your grandfather—'cause it was him who give you the house—in his way.

Ruth *(taking the boy from* MAMA *and pushing him toward the bedroom).* Now you get out of here and get ready for your beating.

Travis. Aw, Mama—

Ruth. Get on in there—*(Closing the door behind him and turning radiantly to her mother-in-law)* So you went and did it!

Mama *(quietly, looking at her son with pain).* Yes, I did.

Ruth *(raising both arms classically). Praise God! (Looks at* WALTER *a moment who says nothing. She crosses rapidly to her husband.)* Please, honey—let me be glad . . . you be glad too. *(She has laid her hands on his shoulders, but he shakes himself free of her roughly, without turning to face her.)* Oh, Walter . . . a home . . . *a home. (She comes back to* MAMA.*)* Well—where is it? How big is it? How much it going to cost?

Mama. Well—

Ruth. When we moving?

Mama *(smiling at her).* First of the month.

Ruth *(throwing back her head with jubilance). Praise God!*

Mama *(tentatively, still looking at her son's back turned against her and* RUTH*).* It's—it's a nice house too . . . *(She cannot help speaking directly to him. An imploring quality in her voice, her manner, makes her almost like a girl now.)* Three bedrooms—nice big one for you and Ruth . . . Me and Beneatha still have to share our room, but Travis have one of his own—and *(with difficulty)* I figure if the—new baby—is a boy, we could get one of them double-decker outfits . . . And there's a yard with a little patch of dirt where I could maybe get to grow me a few flowers . . . And a nice big basement . . .

Ruth. Walter honey, be glad—

A **Mama** *(still to his back, fingering things on the table).* 'Course I don't want to make it sound fancier than it is . . . It's just a plain little old house—but it's made good and solid—and it will be *ours*. Walter Lee—it makes a difference in a man when he can walk on floors that belong to *him* . . .

Ruth. Where is it?

Mama *(frightened at this telling).* Well—well—it's out there in Clybourne Park—

[RUTH*'s radiance fades abruptly, and* WALTER *finally turns slowly to face his mother with incredulity and hostility.*]

Ruth. Where?

Mama *(matter-of-factly).* Four o six Clybourne Street, Clybourne Park.

Ruth. Clybourne Park? Mama, there ain't no colored people living in Clybourne Park.

Mama *(almost idiotically).* Well, I guess there's going to be some now.

Walter *(bitterly).* So that's the peace and comfort you went out and bought for us today!

Mama *(raising her eyes to meet his finally).* Son—I just tried to find the nicest place for the least amount of money for my family.

Ruth *(trying to recover from the shock).* Well—well—'course I ain't one never been 'fraid of no crackers, mind you—but—well, wasn't there no other houses nowhere?

Mama. Them houses they put up for colored in them areas way out all seem to cost twice as much as other houses. I did the best I could.

Ruth *(Struck senseless with the news, in its various degrees of goodness and trouble, she sits a moment, her fists propping her chin in thought, and then she starts to rise, bringing her fists down with vigor, the radiance spreading from cheek to cheek again).* Well—well!—All I can say is—if this is my time in life—*my time*—to say goodbye—*(and she builds with momentum as she starts to circle the room with an exuberant, almost tearfully happy release)*—to these . . . cracking walls!—*(She pounds the walls.)*—and these marching roaches!—*(She wipes at an imaginary army of marching roaches.)*—and this cramped little closet which ain't now or never was no kitchen! . . . then I say it loud and good, *Hallelujah! and goodbye misery . . . I don't never want to see your ugly face again! (She laughs joyously, having practically destroyed the apartment, and flings her arms up and lets them come down happily, slowly, reflectively, over her abdomen, aware for the first time perhaps that the life therein pulses with happiness and not despair.)* Lena?

Mama *(moved, watching her happiness).* Yes, honey?

Ruth *(looking off).* Is there—is there a whole lot of sunlight?

Mama *(understanding).* Yes, child, there's a whole lot of sunlight.

[*Long pause*]

Ruth *(collecting herself and going to the door of the room* TRAVIS *is in).* Well—I guess I better see 'bout Travis. *(to* MAMA*)* Lord, I sure don't feel like whipping nobody today! *(She exits.)*

Mama *(The mother and son are left alone now and the mother waits a long time, considering deeply, before she speaks.).* Son—you—you understand what I done, don't you? *(*WALTER *is silent and sullen.)* I—I just seen my family falling apart today . . . just falling to pieces in front of my eyes . . . We couldn't of gone on like we was today. We was going backwards 'stead of forwards—talking 'bout not wanting babies and wishing each other was dead . . . When it gets like that in life—you just got to do something different, push on out and do something bigger . . . *(She waits.)* I wish you say something, son . . . I wish you'd say how deep inside you think I done the right thing—

Walter *(crossing slowly to his bedroom door and finally turning there and speaking measuredly).* What you need me to say you done right for? *You* the head of this family. You run our lives like you want to. It was your money and you did what you wanted with it. So what you need for me to say it was all right for? *(Bitterly, to hurt her as deeply as he knows is possible)* So you butchered up a dream of mine—you—who always talking 'bout your children's dreams . . .

Mama. Walter Lee—

[*He just closes the door behind him.* MAMA *sits alone, thinking heavily.*]

Curtain

Scene 2

Time: Friday night. A few weeks later.

At rise: Packing crates mark the intention of the family to move. BENEATHA *and* GEORGE *come in, presumably from an evening out again.*

George. O.K. . . . O.K., whatever you say . . . *(They both sit on the couch. He tries to kiss her. She moves away.)* Look, we've had a nice evening; let's not spoil it, huh? . . .

[*He again turns her head and tries to nuzzle in and she turns away from him, not with distaste but with momentary lack of interest; in a mood to pursue what they were talking about.*]

Beneatha. I'm *trying* to talk to you.

George. We always talk.

Beneatha. Yes—and I love to talk.

George *(exasperated; rising).* I know it and I don't mind it sometimes . . . I want you to cut it out, see—The moody stuff, I mean. I don't like it. You're a nice-looking girl . . . all over. That's all you need, honey, forget the atmosphere. Guys aren't going to go for the atmosphere—they're going to go for what they see. Be glad for that. Drop the Garbo[1] routine. It doesn't go with you. As for myself, I want a nice—*(groping)*—simple *(thoughtfully)*—sophisticated girl . . . not a poet—O.K.?

[*She rebuffs him again and he starts to leave.*]

Beneatha. Why are you angry?

George. Because this is stupid! I don't go out with you to discuss the nature of "quiet desperation"[2] or to hear all about your thoughts—because the world will go on thinking what it thinks regardless—

Beneatha. Then why read books? Why go to school?

George *(with artificial patience, counting on his fingers).* It's simple. You read books—to learn facts—to get grades—to pass the course—to get a degree. That's all—it has nothing to do with thoughts.

[*A long pause*]

Beneatha. I see. *(A longer pause as she looks at him)* Good night, George.

B

[GEORGE *looks at her a little oddly, and starts to exit. He meets* MAMA *coming in.*]

George. Oh—hello, Mrs. Younger.

Mama. Hello, George, how you feeling?

George. Fine—fine, how are you?

Mama. Oh, a little tired. You know them steps can get you after a day's work. You all have a nice time tonight?

George. Yes—a fine time. Well, good night.

Mama. Good night. *(He exits.* MAMA *closes the door behind her.)* Hello, honey. What you sitting like that for?

Beneatha. I'm just sitting.

---

1. **Garbo:** Greta Garbo (1905–1990), Swedish star of American films, who was famous for her moodiness and for the line "I want to be alone."

2. **"quiet desperation":** George is referring to a line from Henry David Thoreau's *Walden* (see page 207): "The mass of men lead lives of quiet desperation."

A. Setting

In the stage directions, note the passage of time and evidence that moving day is near.

B. Characterization

? Contrast the attitudes of Beneatha and George Murchison toward books. (Beneatha wants to be stimulated to think and to learn; George reads only for grades.) What do you read into Beneatha's "Good night, George"? (It has the sound of "Goodbye, George.")

A. Conflict
? How have things improved between Mama and Beneatha? What details in this passage suggest change on both Beneatha's and Mama's part in order to resolve earlier conflicts? (Beneatha does not argue, and Mama, after checking to be sure Beneatha is serious, simply accepts her daughter's judgment. Beneatha's final, quiet remark underscores the change.)

B. Plot
? What is revealed about Walter's behavior? (He has been leaving the house but not going to work.) What consequences may result? (He may lose his job, and the family still needs his income for house payments and other living expenses.)

Mama. Didn't you have a nice time?
Beneatha. No.
Mama. No? What's the matter?
A
Beneatha. Mama, George is a fool—honest. *(She rises.)*
Mama *(Hustling around unloading the packages she has entered with. She stops).* Is he, baby?
Beneatha. Yes.

[BENEATHA *makes up* TRAVIS'S *bed as she talks.*]

Mama. You sure?
Beneatha. Yes.
Mama. Well—I guess you better not waste your time with no fools.

[BENEATHA *looks up at her mother, watching her put groceries in the refrigerator. Finally she gathers up her things and starts into the bedroom. At the door she stops and looks back at her mother.*]

Beneatha. Mama—
Mama. Yes, baby—
Beneatha. Thank you.
Mama. For what?
Beneatha. For understanding me this time.

[*She exits quickly and the mother stands, smiling a little, looking at the place where* BENEATHA *just stood.* RUTH *enters.*]

Ruth. Now don't you fool with any of this stuff, Lena—
Mama. Oh, I just thought I'd sort a few things out.

B
[*The phone rings.* RUTH *answers.*]

Ruth *(at the phone).* Hello—just a minute. *(Goes to door)* Walter, it's Mrs. Arnold. *(Waits. Goes back to the phone. Tense)* Hello. Yes, this is his wife speaking . . . He's lying down now. Yes . . . well, he'll be in tomorrow. He's been very sick. Yes—I know we should have called, but we were so sure he'd be able to come in today. Yes—yes, I'm very sorry. Yes . . . Thank you very much. *(She hangs up.* WALTER *is standing in the doorway of the bedroom behind her.)* That was Mrs. Arnold.
Walter *(indifferently).* Was it?
Ruth. She said if you don't come in tomorrow that they are getting a new man . . .
Walter. Ain't that sad—ain't that crying sad.
Ruth. She said Mr. Arnold has had to take a cab for three days . . . Walter, you ain't been to work for three days! *(This is a revelation to her.)* Where you been, Walter Lee Younger? *(*WALTER *looks at her and starts to laugh.)* You're going to lose your job.
Walter. That's right . . .
Ruth. Oh, Walter, and with your mother working like a dog every day—
Walter. That's sad too— Everything is sad.
Mama. What you been doing for these three days, son?
Walter. Mama—you don't know all the things a man what got leisure can find to do in this city . . . What's this—Friday night? Well—Wednesday I borrowed Willy Harris's car and I went for a drive . . . just me and myself and I drove and drove . . . Way out . . . way past South Chicago, and I parked the car and I sat and looked at the steel mills all day long. I just sat in the car and looked at them big black chimneys for hours. Then I drove back and I went to the Green Hat. *(Pause)* And Thursday—Thursday I borrowed the car again and I got in it and I pointed it the other way and I drove the other way—for hours—way, way up to Wisconsin, and I looked at the farms. I just drove and looked at the farms. Then I drove back and I went to the Green Hat. *(Pause)* And today—today I didn't get the car. Today I just walked. All over the Southside. And I looked at the Negroes and they looked at me and finally I just sat down on the curb at Thirty-ninth and South Parkway and I just sat there and watched the Negroes go by. And then I went to the Green Hat. You all sad? You all depressed? And you know where I am going right now—

[RUTH *goes out quietly.*]

Mama. Oh, Big Walter, is this the harvest of our days?
Walter. You know what I like about the Green Hat? *(He turns the radio on and a steamy, deep blues pours into the room.)* I like this little cat they got there who blows a sax . . . He blows. He talks to me. He ain't but 'bout five feet tall and he's got a conked[3] head and his eyes is always closed and he's all music—
Mama *(rising and getting some papers out of her handbag).* Walter—
Walter. And there's this other guy who plays the piano . . . and they got a sound. I mean they can work on some music . . . They got the best little

3. **conked:** a style in which the hair is straightened and smoothed flat.

combo in the world in the Green Hat . . . You can just sit there and drink and listen to them three men play and you realize that don't nothing matter in this whole world, but just being there—

Mama. I've helped do it to you, haven't I, son? Walter, I been wrong.

Walter. Naw—you ain't never been wrong about nothing, Mama.

Mama. Listen to me, now. I say I been wrong, son. That I been doing to you what the rest of the world been doing to you. *(She stops and he looks up slowly at her and she meets his eyes pleadingly.)* Walter—what you ain't never understood is that I ain't got nothing, don't own nothing, ain't never really wanted nothing that wasn't for you. There ain't nothing as precious to me . . . There ain't nothing worth holding on to, money, dreams, nothing else—if it means—if it means it's going to destroy my boy. *(She puts her papers in front of him and he watches her without speaking or moving.)* I paid the man thirty-five hundred dollars down on the house. That leaves sixty-five hundred dollars. Monday morning I want you to take this money and take three thousand dollars and put it in a savings account for Beneatha's medical schooling. The rest you put in a checking account—with your name on it. And from now on any penny that come out of it or that go in it is for you to look after. For you to decide. *(She drops her hands a little helplessly.)* It ain't much, but it's all I got in the world and I'm putting it in your hands. I'm telling you to be the head of this family from now on like you supposed to be.

Walter *(stares at the money).* You trust me like that, Mama?

Mama. I ain't never stop trusting you. Like I ain't never stop loving you.

[*She goes out, and* WALTER *sits looking at the money on the table as the music continues in its idiom, pulsing in the room. Finally, in a decisive gesture, he gets up, and, in mingled joy and desperation, picks up the money. At the same moment,* TRAVIS *enters for bed.*]

Travis. What's the mater, Daddy? You drunk?

Walter *(sweetly, more sweetly than we have ever known him).* No, Daddy ain't drunk. Daddy ain't going to never be drunk again . . .

Travis. Well, good night, Daddy.

[*The* FATHER *has come from behind the couch and leans over, embracing his son.*]

Walter. Son, I feel like talking to you tonight.

Travis. About what?

Walter. Oh, about a lot of things. About you and what kind of man you going to be when you grow up. . . . Son—son, what do you want to be when you grow up?

Travis. A bus driver.

Walter *(laughing a little).* A what? Man, that ain't nothing to want to be!

Travis. Why not?

Walter. 'Cause, man—it ain't big enough—you know what I mean.

Travis. I don't know then. I can't make up my mind. Sometimes Mama asks me that too. And sometimes when I tell her I just want to be like you—she says she don't want me to be like that and sometimes she says she does . . .

Walter *(gathering him up in his arms).* You know what, Travis? In seven years you going to be seventeen years old. And things is going to be very different with us in seven years, Travis. . . . One day when you are seventeen I'll come home—home from my office downtown somewhere—

Travis. You don't work in no office, Daddy.

Walter. No—but after tonight. After what your daddy gonna do tonight, there's going to be offices—a whole lot of offices. . . .

Travis. What you gonna do tonight, Daddy?

Walter. You wouldn't understand yet, son, but your daddy's gonna make a transaction . . . a business transaction that's going to change our lives. . . . That's how come one day when you 'bout seventeen years old I'll come home and I'll be pretty tired, you know what I mean, after a day of conferences and secretaries getting things wrong the way they do . . . 'cause an executive's life is hard, man—*(The more he talks the farther away he gets.)* And I'll pull the car up on the driveway . . . just a plain black Chrysler, I think, with white walls—no—black tires. More elegant. Rich people don't have to be flashy . . . though I'll have to get something sportier for Ruth—maybe a Cadillac convertible to do her shopping in. . . . And I'll come up the steps to the house and the gardener will be clipping away at the hedges and he'll say, "Good evening, Mr. Younger." And I'll say, "Hello, Jefferson, how are you this evening?" And I'll go inside and Ruth will come downstairs and meet me at the door and we'll kiss each other and she'll take my arm and we'll go up to your room to see you sitting on the floor with the catalogues of all the great schools

A. Plot

? Explain why Mama hands the $6500 over to Walter. (It is a desperate effort to show that she does believe in him.) What does she ask him to do with the money? (To set aside $3000 for Beneatha's medical education and then to take charge of the remaining $3500 himself.) Judging by what you know of Walter's dreams and character, and by his rambling remarks to Travis, what do you predict Walter will do with the money? How will he explain his actions to the family? (Answers will vary. Those who predict that he will put all of the money into a liquor store partnership will need to offer some ideas on how he will justify this both to Beneatha and to Mama.)

A. Stage Directions
Scene 3 begins exuberantly; it is moving day, and Ruth's singing sets the tone. Students will recall the poignant sadness of spirituals such as "Go Down, Moses" but in this and later scenes should be aware also of the joy expressed in spirituals such as "Joshua Fit de Battle ob Jericho," "My Lord, What a Morning," and "All God's Chillun." These can be found in collections of folk songs and/or spirituals.

B. Humanities Connection: Discussing the Photograph
The photograph illustrates, specifically, Walter's exuberant monologue to Travis after Mama entrusts him with the $6500, but its spirit matches well the action that opens Scene 3 of Act Two, on the facing page.

in America around you. . . . All the great schools in the world! And—and I'll say, all right son—it's your seventeenth birthday, what is it you've decided? . . . Just tell me where you want to go to school and you'll *go*. Just tell me what it is you want to be—and you'll *be* it. . . . Whatever you want to be—Yessir! *(He holds his arms open for* TRAVIS.*)* You just name it, son . . . *(*TRAVIS *leaps into them.)* and I hand you the world!

[WALTER*'s voice has risen in pitch and hysterical promise and on the last line he lifts* TRAVIS *high.*]

Blackout

Scene 3

Time: Saturday, moving day, one week later.

Before the curtain rises, RUTH*'s voice, a strident, dramatic church alto, cuts through the silence.*

It is, in the darkness, a triumphant surge, a penetrating statement of expectation: "Oh, Lord, I don't feel no ways tired! Children, oh, glory hallelujah!"

As the curtain rises we see that RUTH *is alone in the living room, finishing up the family's packing. It is moving day. She is nailing crates and tying cartons.* BENEATHA *enters, carrying a guitar case, and watches her exuberant sister-in-law.*

B

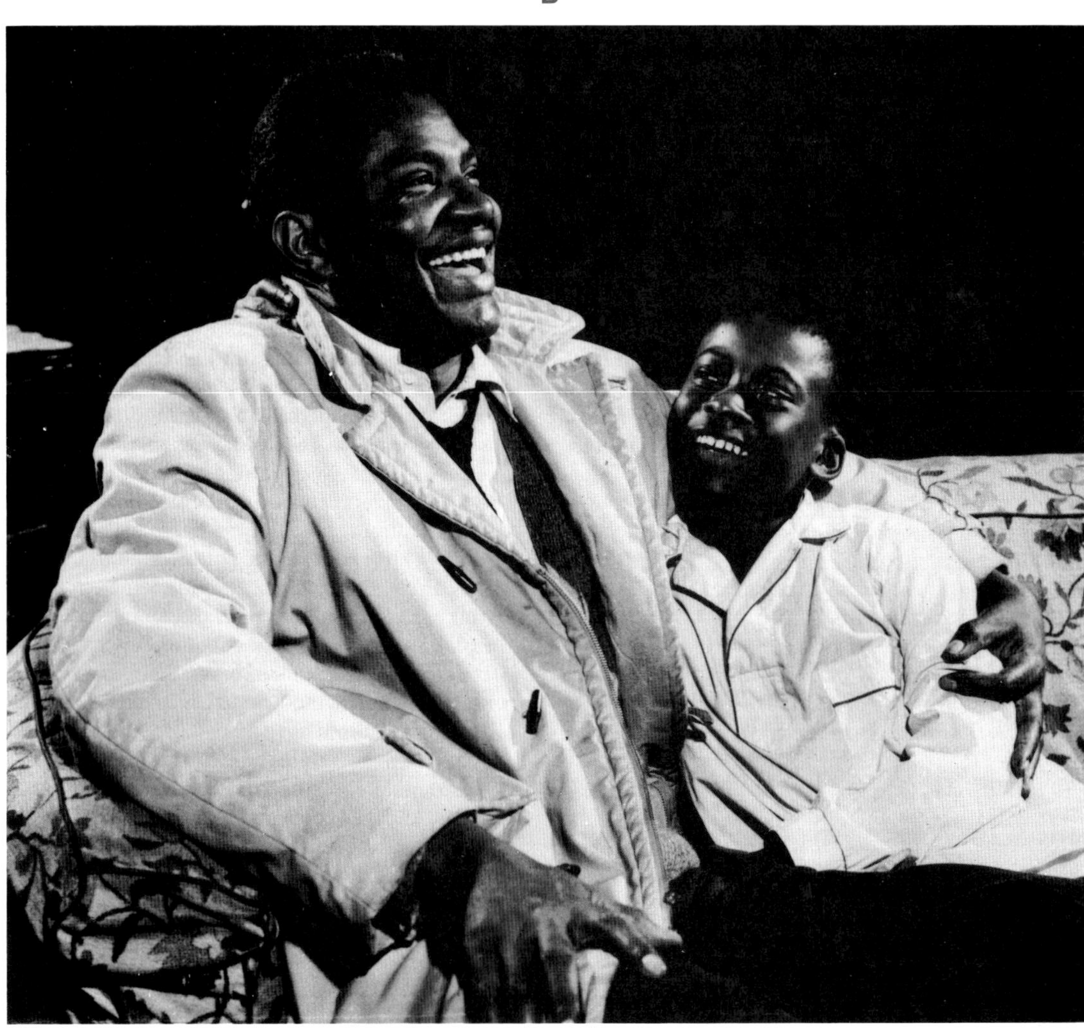

"Just tell me what it is you want to be—and you'll be *it . . ."*

Ruth. Hey!

Beneatha *(putting away the case).* Hi.

Ruth *(pointing at a package).* Honey—look in that package there and see what I found on sale this morning at the South Center. *(*RUTH *gets up and moves to the package and draws out some curtains.)* Lookahere—hand-turned hems!

Beneatha. How do you know the window size out there?

Ruth *(who hadn't thought of that).* Oh— Well, they bound to fit something in the whole house. Anyhow, they was too good a bargain to pass up. *(*RUTH *taps her head, suddenly remembering something.)* Oh, Bennie—I meant to put a special note on that carton over there. That's your mama's good china and she wants 'em to be very careful with it.

Beneatha. I'll do it.

[BENEATHA *finds a piece of paper and starts to draw large letters on it.*]

Ruth. You know what I'm going to do soon as I get in that new house?

Beneatha. What?

Ruth. Honey—I'm going to run me a tub of water up to here . . . *(With her fingers practially up to her nostrils)* And I'm going to get in it—and I am going to sit . . . and sit . . . and sit in that hot water and the first person who knocks to tell *me* to hurry up and come out—

Beneatha. Gets shot at sunrise.

Ruth *(laughing happily).* You said it, sister! *(Noticing how large* BENEATHA *is absent-mindedly making the note)* Honey, they ain't going to read that from no airplane.

Beneatha *(laughing herself).* I guess I always think things have more emphasis if they are big, somehow.

Ruth *(looking up at her and smiling).* You and your brother seem to have that as a philosophy of life. Lord, that man—done changed so 'round here. You know—you know what we did last night? Me and Walter Lee?

Beneatha. What?

Ruth *(smiling to herself).* We went to the movies. *(Looking at* BENEATHA *to see if she understands)* We went to the movies. You know the last time me and Walter went to the movies together?

Beneatha. No.

Ruth. Me neither. That's how long it been. *(Smiling again)* But we went last night. The picture wasn't much good, but that didn't seem to matter. We went—and we held hands.

Beneatha. Oh, Lord!

Ruth. We held hands—and you know what?

Beneatha. What?

Ruth. When we come out of the show it was late and dark and all the stores and things was closed up . . . and it was kind of chilly and there wasn't many people on the streets . . . and we was still holding hands, me and Walter.

Beneatha. You're killing me.

[WALTER *enters with a large package. His happiness is deep in him; he cannot keep still with his new-found exuberance. He is singing and wiggling and snapping his fingers. He puts his package in a corner and puts a phonograph record, which he has brought in with him, on the record player. As the music comes up he dances over to* RUTH *and tries to get her to dance with him. She gives in at last to his raunchiness and in a fit of giggling allows herself to be drawn into his mood and together they deliberately burlesque an old social dance of their youth.*]

Beneatha *(Regarding them a long time as they dance, then drawing in her breath for a deeply exaggerated comment which she does not particularly mean.).* Talk about—olddddddddd-fashionedddddd—Negroes!

Walter *(stopping momentarily).* What kind of Negroes? *(He says this in fun. He is not angry with her today, nor with anyone. He starts to dance with his wife again.)*

Beneatha. Old-fashioned.

Walter *(as he dances with* RUTH*).* You know, when these *New Negroes* have their convention—*(pointing at his sister)*—that is going to be the chairman of the Committee on Unending Agitation. *(He goes on dancing, then stops.)* Race, race, race! . . . Girl, I do believe you are the first person in the history of the entire human race to successfully brainwash yourself. *(*BENEATHA *breaks up and he goes on dancing. He stops again, enjoying his tease.)* Shoot, even the N double A C P takes a holiday sometimes! *(*BENEATHA *and* RUTH *laugh. He dances with* RUTH *some more and starts to laugh and stops and pantomimes someone over an operating table.)* I can just see that chick someday looking down at some poor cat on an operating table before she starts to slice him, saying . . . *(pulling his sleeves back maliciously)* "By the way, what are your views on

A. Responding

? Comment on Ruth's observation that both Beneatha and Walter seem to have as their philosophy of life "things have more emphasis if they are big." Is she right? (Ruth is right. Both Walter and Beneatha are dramatic people in everyday life, and both have big dreams: Beneatha to become a doctor, Walter to become a successful businessman.)

B. Responding

The National Association for the Advancement of Colored People (NAACP), established in 1910 to work for the end of racial discrimination and segregation, was formed following the 1908 lynching of two African Americans in Springfield, Illinois. As early as 1915 the NAACP was able to organize a partially successful boycott of an offensive movie, but early efforts were directed, successfully, against lynchings. By the 1950's, with this worst example of racism under control, the NAACP could turn to other civil rights issues.

A. Suspense

? Suspense builds on this page, the first part of the scene with Lindner. When he says that he is from the Clybourne Park Improvement Association, what kind of message did you immediately think he was going to deliver? (Answers will vary. Some will think he planned to threaten the Youngers.) Which of the three, Walter, Beneatha, or Ruth, is most suspicious of Lindner? (Beneatha) How is this shown? (Through her actions—"Beneatha is watching the man carefully"—and her questions) What double meanings are suggested by Lindner's use of "Improvement Association," "New Neighbors Orientation Committee," "give them the lowdown on the way we do things," and "special community problems"? (Answers will vary but should focus on the fact that the meanings shift when the terms are used in a race-relations context.)

civil rights down there? . . ." *(He laughs at her again and starts to dance happily. The bell sounds.)*

Beneatha. Sticks and stones may break my bones, but . . . words will never hurt me!

[BENEATHA *goes to the door and opens it as* WALTER *and* RUTH *go on with the clowning.* BENEATHA *is somewhat surprised to see a quiet-looking middle-aged white man in a business suit holding his hat and a briefcase in his hand and consulting a small piece of paper.*]

Man. Uh—how do you do, miss. I am looking for a Mrs.—*(He looks at the slip of paper.)* Mrs. Lena Younger?

Beneatha *(smoothing her hair with slight embarrassment).* Oh—yes, that's my mother. Excuse me *(She closes the door and turns to quiet the other two.)* Ruth! Brother! Somebody's here. *(Then she opens the door. The man casts a curious quick glance at all of them.)* Uh—come in please.

Man *(coming in).* Thank you.

Beneatha. My mother isn't here just now. Is it business?

Man. Yes . . . well, of a sort.

Walter *(freely, the Man of the House).* Have a seat, I'm Mrs. Younger's son. I look after most of her business matters.

[RUTH *and* BENEATHA *exchange amused glances.*]

Man *(regarding* WALTER, *and sitting).* Well— My name is Karl Lindner . . .

Walter *(stretching out his hand).* Walter Younger. This is my wife—*(*RUTH *nods politely.)*—and my sister.

Lindner. How do you do.

Walter *(amiably, as he sits himself easily on a chair, leaning with interest forward on his knees and looking expectantly into the newcomer's face).* What can we do for you, Mr. Lindner!

A **Lindner** *(some minor shuffling of the hat and briefcase on his knees).* Well—I am a representative of the Clybourne Park Improvement Association—

Walter *(pointing).* Why don't you sit your things on the floor?

Lindner. Oh—yes. Thank you. *(He slides the briefcase and hat under the chair.)* And as I was saying—I am from the Clybourne Park Improvement Association and we have had it brought to our attention at the last meeting that you people—or at least your mother—has bought a piece of residential property at—*(He digs for the slip of paper again.)*—four o six Clybourne Street . . .

Walter. That's right. Care for something to drink? Ruth, get Mr. Lindner a beer.

Lindner *(upset for some reason).* Oh—no, really. I mean thank you very much, but no thank you.

Ruth *(innocently).* Some coffee?

Lindner. Thank you, nothing at all.

[BENEATHA *is watching the man carefully.*]

Lindner. Well, I don't know how much you folks know about our organization. *(He is a gentle man; thoughtful and somewhat labored in his manner.)* It is one of these community organizations set up to look after—oh, you know, things like block upkeep and special projects and we also have what we call our New Neighbors Orientation Committee . . .

Beneatha *(drily).* Yes—and what do they do?

Lindner *(Turning a little to her and then returning the main force to* WALTER.*).* Well—it's what you might call a sort of welcoming committee, I guess. I mean they, we, I'm the chairman of the committee—go around and see the new people who move into the neighborhood and sort of give them the lowdown on the way we do things out in Clybourne Park.

Beneatha *(with appreciation of the two meanings, which escape* RUTH *and* WALTER*).* Un-huh.

Lindner. And we also have the category of what the association calls—*(He looks elsewhere.)*—uh—special community problems . . .

Beneatha. Yes—and what are some of those?

Walter. Girl, let the man talk.

Lindner *(with understated relief).* Thank you. I would sort of like to explain this thing in my own way. I mean I want to explain to you in a certain way.

Walter. Go ahead.

Lindner. Yes. Well. I'm going to try to get right to the point. I'm sure we'll all appreciate that in the long run.

Beneatha. Yes.

Walter. Be still now!

Lindner. Well—

Ruth *(still innocently).* Would you like another chair—you don't look comfortable.

Lindner *(more frustrated than annoyed).* No, thank you very much. Please. Well—to get right to the point I—*(a great breath, and he is off at last)* I am sure you people must be aware of some of the incidents which have happened in various

A. Humanities Connection: Responding to the Photograph
After you have read the entire scene with Mr. Lindner, come back to this picture and examine the posture and expressions of the people present. How does Beneatha, behind Mr. Lindner, convey her distrust? How is Ruth beginning to feel? Has Walter yet caught on that there is any problem associated with Mr. Lindner's visit? (Answers will vary. Most students will agree the picture shows that Beneatha, with lips pursed and hands behind her back, appears distrustful and skeptical of him; Ruth, looking away from him, appears to be upset at what he is saying; Walter, leaning forward, appears to be listening intently, not having caught on yet to Lindner's true intentions.) Consider Mr. Lindner's character and personality. How does he view himself? (As a decent, fair-minded man who would never resort to violence) How do you view him? (Answers will vary. Most students will recognize the man's hidden bigotry but may nonetheless feel some sympathy for him. It took some courage to be the one to come to the Youngers' home.)

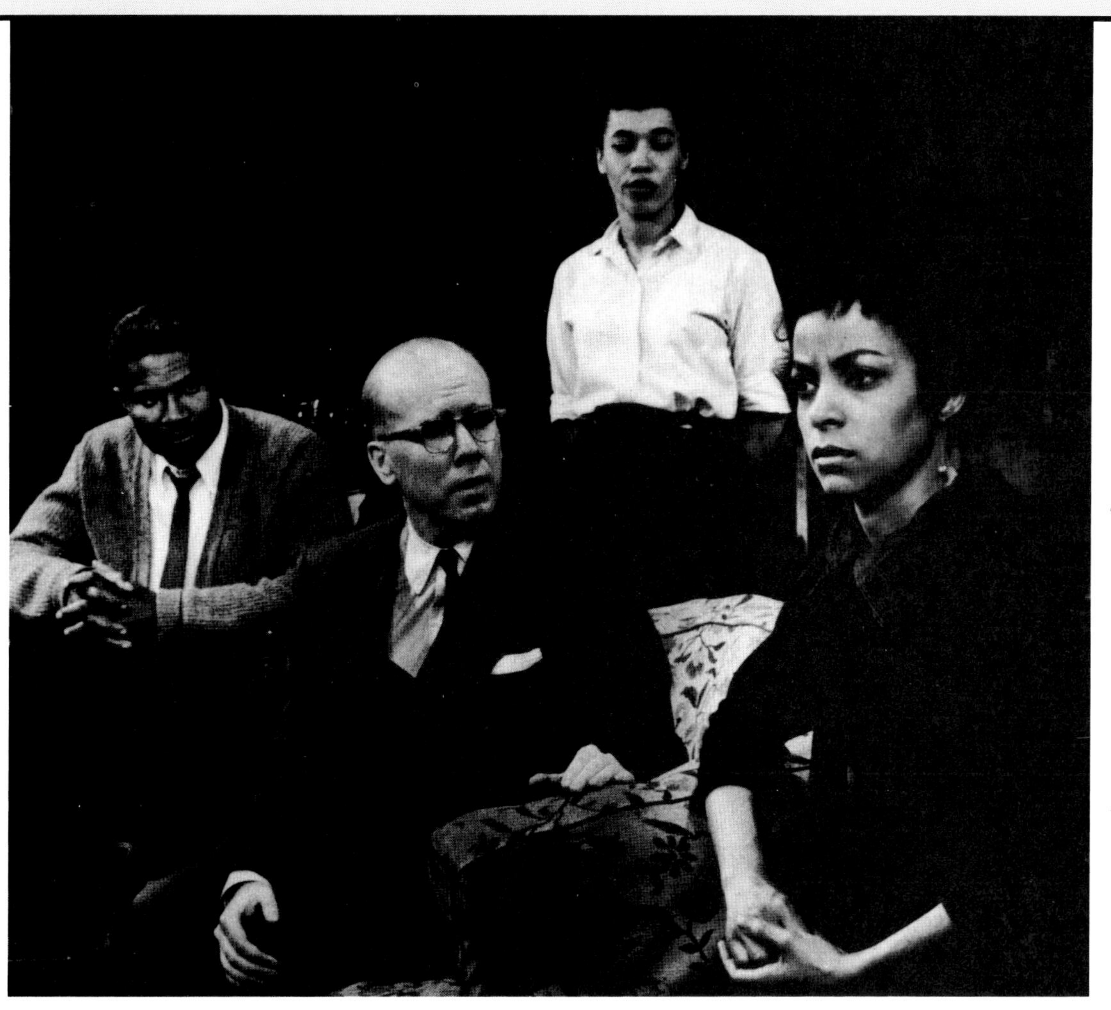

"Today everybody knows what it means to be on the outside of something.*"*

A

B. Word Connotations
In addition to their literal meanings, words carry strong associations, implications, and emotional overtones. Lindner remarks, "Anybody can see that you are a nice family of folks, hard working and honest I'm sure." How do connotations make these words insulting? (Most students will see the thinly veiled racial prejudice and stereotyping, and the "I'm *not* sure" insinuated in the "I'm sure.")

parts of the city when colored people have moved into certain areas—(BENEATHA *exhales heavily and starts tossing a piece of fruit up and down in the air.)* Well—because we have what I think is going to be a unique type of organization in American community life—not only do we deplore that kind of thing—but we are trying to do something about it. (BENEATHA *stops tossing and turns with a new and quizzical interest to the man.)* We feel—*(gaining confidence in his mission because of the interest in the faces of the people he is talking to)*—we feel that most of the trouble in this world, when you come right down to it—*(He hits his knee for emphasis.)*—most of the trouble exists because people just don't sit down and talk to each other.

Ruth *(nodding as she might in church, pleased with the remark).* You can say that again, mister.

Lindner *(more encouraged by such affirmation).* That we don't try hard enough in this world to understand the other fellow's problem. The other guy's point of view.

Ruth. Now that's right.

[BENEATHA *and* WALTER *merely watch and listen with genuine interest.*]

Lindner. Yes—that's the way we feel out in Clybourne Park. And that's why I was elected to come here this afternoon and talk to you people. Friendly like, you know, the way people should talk to each other and see if we couldn't find some way to work this thing out. As I say, the whole business is a matter of *caring* about the other fellow. Anybody can see that you are a nice family of folks, hard working and honest I'm sure. (BENEATHA *frowns slightly, quizzically, her head tilted regarding him.)* Today everybody knows what it means to be on the outside of *something.* And of course, there is always somebody who is B

A. Plot

? What is the actual offer made by Lindner on behalf of the association? (To buy the house from the Youngers for more than they paid for it) Besides the argument of money itself, what other arguments does he use? (Negro families are happier in their own communities; they have nothing to gain by moving in where they are not wanted.) What is the closest Lindner comes to threatening the Youngers? (He says that "people can get awfully worked up when they feel that their whole way of life and everything they've ever worked for is threatened.") Were you surprised by Walter's "Get out"? Why or why not? (Answers will vary. Some students may have thought Walter would go for the money.)

out to take the advantage of people who don't always understand.

Walter. What do you mean?

A **Lindner.** Well—you see our community is made up of people who've worked hard as the dickens for years to build up that little community. They're not rich and fancy people; just hard-working, honest people who don't really have much but those little homes and a dream of the kind of community they want to raise their children in. Now, I don't say we are perfect and there is a lot wrong in some of the things they want. But you've got to admit that a man, right or wrong, has the right to want to have the neighborhood he lives in a certain kind of way. And at the moment the overwhelming majority of our people out there feel that people get along better, take more of a common interest in the life of the community, when they share a common background. I want you to believe me when I tell you that race prejudice simply doesn't enter into it. It is a matter of the people of Clybourne Park believing, rightly or wrongly, as I say, that for the happiness of all concerned that our Negro families are happier when they live in their *own* communities.

Beneatha *(with a grand and bitter gesture).* This, friends, is the Welcoming Committee!

Walter *(dumfounded, looking at* LINDNER*).* Is this what you came marching all the way over here to tell us?

Lindner. Well, now we've been having a fine conversation. I hope you'll hear me all the way through.

Walter *(tightly).* Go ahead, man.

Lindner. You see—in the face of all things I have said, we are prepared to make your family a very generous offer . . .

Beneatha. Thirty pieces and not a coin less![1]

Walter. Yeah?

Lindner *(putting on his glasses and drawing a form out of the briefcase).* Our association is prepared, through the collective effort or our people, to buy the house from you at a financial gain to your family.

Ruth. Lord have mercy, ain't this the living gall!

Walter. All right, you through?

Lindner. Well, I want to give you the exact terms of the financial arrangement—

Walter. We don't want to hear no exact terms of no arrangements. I want to know if you got any more to tell us 'bout getting together?

Lindner *(taking off his glasses).* Well—I don't suppose that you feel . . .

Walter. Never mind how I feel—you got any more to say 'bout how people ought to sit down and talk to each other? . . . Get out of my house, man. *(He turns his back and walks to the door.)*

Lindner *(looking around at the hostile faces and reaching and assembling his hat and briefcase).* Well—I don't understand why you people are reacting this way. What do you think you are going to gain by moving into a neighborhood where you just aren't wanted and where some elements—well—people can get awful worked up when they feel that their whole way of life and everything they've ever worked for is threatened.

Walter. Get out.

Lindner *(at the door, holding a small card).* Well—I'm sorry it went like this.

Walter. Get out.

Lindner *(almost sadly regarding* WALTER*).* You just can't force people to change their hearts, son.

[*He turns and puts his card on a table and exits.* WALTER *pushes the door to with stinging hatred, and stands looking at it.* RUTH *just sits and* BENEATHA *just stands. They say nothing.* MAMA *and* TRAVIS *enter.*]

Mama. Well—this all the packing got done since I left out of here this morning. I testify before God that my children got all the energy of the dead. What time the moving men due?

Beneatha. Four o'clock. You had a caller, Mama. *(She is smiling, teasingly.)*

Mama. Sure enough—who?

Beneatha *(her arms folded saucily).* The Welcoming Committee.

[WALTER *and* RUTH *giggle.*]

Mama *(innocently).* Who?

Beneatha. The Welcoming Committee. They said they're sure going to be glad to see you when you get there.

Walter *(devilishly).* Yeah, they said they can't hardly wait to see your face.

[*Laughter*]

Mama *(sensing their facetiousness).* What's the matter with you all?

1. **Thirty . . . less:** a reference to the thirty pieces of silver Judas Iscariot received for betraying Jesus.

Walter. Ain't nothing the matter with us. We just telling you 'bout the gentleman who came to see you this afternoon. From the Clybourne Park Improvement Association.
Mama. What he want?
Ruth *(in the same mood as* BENEATHA *and* WALTER*)*. To welcome you, honey.
Walter. He said they can't hardly wait. He said the one thing they don't have, that they just *dying* to have out there is a fine family of colored people! *(to* RUTH *and* BENEATHA*)* Ain't that right!
Ruth and Beneatha *(mockingly)*. Yeah! He left his card in case—

[*They indicate the card, and* MAMA *picks it up and throws it on the floor—understanding and looking off as she draws her chair up to the table on which she has put her plant and some sticks and some cord.*]

Mama. Father, give us strength. *(Knowingly—and without fun)* Did he threaten us?
Beneatha. Oh—Mama—they don't do it like that anymore. He talked Brotherhood. He said everybody ought to learn how to sit down and hate each other with good Christian fellowship.

[*She and* WALTER *shake hands to ridicule the remark.*]

Mama *(sadly)*. Lord, protect us . . .
Ruth. You should hear the money those folks raised to buy the house from us. All we paid and then some.
Beneatha. What they think we going to do—eat 'em?
Ruth. No honey, marry 'em.
Mama *(shaking her head)*. Lord, Lord, Lord . . .
Ruth. Well—that's the way the crackers crumble. Joke.
Beneatha *(laughingly noticing what her mother is doing)*. Mama, what are you doing?
Mama. Fixing my plant so it won't get hurt none on the way . . .
Beneatha. Mama, you going to take *that* to the new house?
Mama. Un-huh—
Beneatha. That raggedy-looking old thing?
Mama *(stopping and looking at her)*. It expresses *me*.
Ruth *(with delight, to* BENEATHA*)*. So there, Miss Thing!

[WALTER *comes to* MAMA *suddenly and bends down behind her and squeezes her in his arms with all his strength. She is overwhelmed by the suddenness of it and, though delighted, her manner is like that of* RUTH *and* TRAVIS.]

Mama. Look out now, boy! You make me mess up my thing here!
Walter *(his face lit, he slips down on his knees beside her, his arms still around her)*. Mama . . . you know what it means to climb up in the chariot?
Mama *(gruffly, very happy)*. Get on away from me now . . .
Ruth *(near the gift-wrapped package, trying to catch* WALTER*'s eye)*. Psst—
Walter. What the old song say, Mama . . .
Ruth. Walter— Now? *(She is pointing at the package.)*
Walter *(speaking the lines, sweetly, playfully, in his mother's face)*.

I got wings . . . you got wings . . .
All God's Children got wings . . .

Mama. Boy—get out of my face and do some work . . .
Walter.

When I get to heaven gonna put on my wings,
Gonna fly all over God's heaven . . .

Beneatha *(teasingly, from across the room)*. Everybody talking 'bout heaven ain't going there! C
Walter *(to* RUTH, *who is carrying the box across to them)*. I don't know, you think we ought to give her that . . . Seems to me she ain't been very appreciative around here.
Mama *(eyeing the box, which is obviously a gift)*. What is that?
Walter *(taking it from* RUTH *and putting it on the table in front of* MAMA*)*. Well—what you all think? Should we give it to her?
Ruth. Oh—she was pretty good today.
Mama. I'll good you— *(She turns her eyes to the box again.)*
Beneatha. Open it, Mama.

[*She stands up, looks at it, turns and looks at all of them, and then presses her hands together and does not open the package.*]

Walter *(sweetly)*. Open it, Mama. It's for you. *(*MAMA *looks in his eyes. It is the first present in her life without its being Christmas. Slowly she opens her package and lifts out, one by one, a brand-new sparkling set of gardening tools.* WAL-

A. Responding
? Comment on Beneatha's remark. How does it catch, precisely, the hypocrisy of the association's offer? (Explanations will vary but should include the surface civility and so-called generosity disguising the racism of those who made the offer.)

B. Humor
? What is both comical and exactly right about Mama's line about her plant? (She picks up Beneatha's words from earlier in the play, and the plant *is* a good symbol of her own doggedness and hope for the future.)

C. Allusion
Beneatha's line continues the words of the song Walter has begun.

Reading Check Test: Act Two

1. George Murchison enjoys and approves of Walter's and Beneatha's African act. *False*
2. Mama has put a down payment on a house in a white area called Clybourne Park. *True*
3. Mama says Walter can do anything he wants with the remaining $6500. *False*
4. Walter and Beneatha accept Mr. Lindner's offer for the house. *False*
5. One of Walter's partner's runs off with the money Walter entrusted to him. *True*

Humanities Connection: Responding to the Photograph

? Identify the point in Act Two illustrated by the photograph, and explain what action immediately preceded the scene. (The photograph illustrates the gift giving, mostly contained in the first column on page 853. It immediately follows the family's unanimous rejection of Mr. Lindner's offer.) Why is it especially touching to see the family united in this way? (It is the first time all of them want the same thing and are happy at the same time.) Do you trust the happiness, or do you think something could mar it? What loose ends remain? (What became of the money entrusted to Walter? Will the Clybourne Park Improvement Association back off?)

"To our own Mrs. Miniver . . ."

Analyzing Act Two
Identifying Details
1. Walter, who has had too much to drink, at first seems sarcastic in his reaction to Beneatha's music and her costume. But in his exaggerated routine, which imitates African political rhetoric, Walter soon seems more African than American.

George seems mystified; he is unable to understand either Walter's behavior or Beneatha's costume, and he urges her to change her clothes so that they can go to the theater.
2. Ruth is ecstatically happy that Mama has made a down payment on a house.

In Act One, we have seen that Ruth subtly tried to encourage Mama when Mama speculated that it might be possible for the Youngers to move out of the dreary apartment.
3. Walter is furious that Mama has refused to back him in his investment plan.

The new house is in an overwhelmingly white neighborhood, where the residents are known to be racist.
4. Mama tells Walter that she has been mistaken in not backing him more, but she explains to him that she has never had any money to give him because of the family's poverty. She tells him that she has always felt that there was nothing as precious to her as her children. Therefore, she gives Walter the $6500 that is left over after the down payment. She tells him to deposit $3000 of this money in the bank for Beneatha's medical education; with the rest of the money, he is to start an account in his own name. Mama tells Walter that she trusts him to spend the money as he decides since he should now be the head of the family.

Walter enters in a happy mood, singing and snapping his fingers. He plays music on the phonograph and dances with Ruth, and his first speeches seem to indicate that he has gotten over his bitterness on the question of race. He carries a large box, which—as we later find out—is a present for Mama.
5. The ostensible purpose is to welcome the Youngers to the neighborhood. But it gradually becomes clear that Lindner has another, more *(Answers continue on next page.)*

TER *continues, prodding.)* Ruth made up the note—read it . . .
Mama *(picking up the card and adjusting her glasses).* "To our own Mrs. Miniver[2]—Love from Brother, Ruth, and Beneatha." Ain't that lovely . . .
Travis *(tugging at his father's sleeve).* Daddy, can I give her mine now?
Walter. All right, son. *(*TRAVIS *flies to get his gift.)* Travis didn't want to go in with the rest of us, Mama. He got his own. *(Somewhat amused)* We don't know what it is . . .
Travis *(racing back in the room with a large hatbox and putting it in front of his grandmother).* Here!
Mama. Lord have mercy, baby. You done gone and bought your grandmother a hat?
Travis *(very proud).* Open it!

[*She does and lifts out an elaborate, but very elaborate, wide gardening hat, and all the adults break up at the sight of it.*]

Ruth. Travis, honey, what is that?
Travis *(who thinks it is beautiful and appropriate).* It's a gardening hat! Like the ladies always have on in the magazines when they work in their gardens.
Beneatha *(giggling fiercely).* Travis—we were trying to make Mama Mrs. Miniver—not Scarlett O'Hara![3]
Mama *(indignantly).* What's the matter with you all! This here is a beautiful hat! *(Absurdly)* I always wanted me one just like it!

[*She pops it on her head to prove it to her grandson, and the hat is ludicrous and considerably oversized.*]

Ruth. Hot dog! Go, Mama!
Walter *(doubled over with laughter).* I'm sorry, Mama—but you look like you ready to go out and chop you some cotton sure enough!

[*They all laugh except* MAMA, *out of deference to* TRAVIS*'s feelings.*]

Mama *(gathering the boy up to her).* Bless your heart—this is the prettiest hat I ever owned—*(*WALTER, RUTH, *and* BENEATHA *chime in—noisily, festively, and insincerely congratulating* TRAVIS *on his gift.)* What are we all standing around here for? We ain't finished packin' yet. Bennie, you ain't packed one book.

[*The bell rings.*]

Beneatha. That couldn't be the movers . . . it's not hardly two good yet—

[BENEATHA *goes into her room.* MAMA *starts for door.*]

Walter *(turning, stiffening).* Wait—wait—I'll get it. *(He stands and looks at the door.)*
Mama. You expecting company, son?
Walter *(just looking at the door).* Yeah—yeah . . .

[MAMA *looks at* RUTH, *and they exchange innocent and unfrightened glances.*]

Mama *(not understanding).* Well, let them in, son.
Beneatha *(from her room).* We need some more string.
Mama. Travis—you run to the hardware and get me some string cord.

[MAMA *goes out and* WALTER *turns and looks at* RUTH. TRAVIS *goes to a dish for money.*]

Ruth. Why don't you answer the door, man?
Walter *(suddenly bounding across the floor to her).* 'Cause sometimes it hard to let the future begin! *(Stooping down in her face)*

I got wings! You got wings!
All God's children got wings!

[*He crosses to the door and throws it open. Standing there is a very slight little man in a not too prosperous business suit and with haunted frightened eyes and a hat pulled down tightly, brim up, around his forehead.* TRAVIS *passes between the men and exits.* WALTER *leans deep in the man's face, still in his jubilance.*]

When I get to heaven gonna put on my wings,
Gonna fly all over God's heaven . . .

[*The little man just stares at him.*]

Heaven—

(Suddenly he stops and looks past the little man into the empty hallway.) Where's Willy, man?
Bobo. He ain't with me.
Walter *(not disturbed).* Oh—come on in. You know my wife.

2. **Mrs. Miniver:** a genteel English heroine of a movie by that name, played by Greer Garson.
3. **Scarlett O'Hara:** flamboyant heroine of *Gone With the Wind,* a novel about the South and the Civil War.

(Continued from previous page.) ominous purpose in mind. He reveals that the folks of Clybourne Park do not want blacks to move into the neighborhood and are willing to offer the Youngers a substantial sum to buy them out.

Walter angrily rejects Lindner's proposal and tells him to get out.

6. Bobo fearfully tells Walter that their supposed friend and partner, Willy Harris, has absconded with all their money.

Interpreting Meanings

7. Since Prometheus was the mythical Greek hero who defied the gods and suffered torture as a result, George implies that Walter's rantings are proud, vain, and wrongheaded.

8. Student answers will vary. But the basic conflict between Walter and Ruth—the conflict that is the seed of their growing apart—is the result of Walter's materialistic ambition, which has almost completely overwhelmed his duties and sense of tenderness as a father and as a husband.

9. Beneatha's ambition to become a doctor is serious, and the audience will probably sympathize with her. But it is also clear that Beneatha is immature,

Bobo *(dumbly, taking off his hat).* Yes—h'you, Miss Ruth.

Ruth *(quietly, a mood apart from her husband already, seeing* BOBO*).* Hello, Bobo.

Walter. You right on time today . . . Right on time. That's the way! *(He slaps* BOBO *on his back.)* Sit down . . . lemme hear.

[RUTH *stands stiffly and quietly in back of them, as though somehow she senses death, her eyes fixed on her husband.*]

Bobo *(his frightened eyes on the floor, his hat in his hands).* Could I please get a drink of water, before I tell you about it, Walter Lee?

[WALTER *does not take his eyes off the man.* RUTH *goes blindly to the tap and gets a glass of water and brings it to* BOBO.]

Walter. There ain't nothing wrong, is there?

Bobo. Lemme tell you—

Walter. Man—didn't nothing go wrong?

Bobo. Lemme tell you—Walter Lee. *(Looking at* RUTH *and talking to her more than to* WALTER*)* You know how it was. I got to tell you how it was. I mean first I got to tell you how it was all the way . . . I mean about the money I put in, Walter Lee . . .

Walter *(with taut agitation now).* What about the money you put in?

Bobo. Well—it wasn't much as we told you—me and Willy—*(He stops.)* I'm sorry, Walter. I got a bad feeling about it. I got a real bad feeling about it . . .

Walter. Man, what you telling me about all this for? . . . Tell me what happened in Springfield . . .

Bobo. Springfield.

Ruth *(like a dead woman).* What was supposed to happen in Springfield?

Bobo *(to her).* This deal that me and Walter went into with Willy— Me and Willy was going to go down to Springfield and spread some money 'round so's we wouldn't have to wait so long for the liquor license . . . That's what we were going to do. Everybody said that was the way you had to do, you understand, Miss Ruth?

Walter. Man—what happened down there?

Bobo *(a pitiful man, near tears).* I'm trying to tell you, Walter.

Walter *(screaming at him suddenly).* THEN TELL ME . . . DAMMIT . . . WHAT'S THE MATTER WITH YOU?

Bobo. Man . . . I didn't go to no Springfield, yesterday.

Walter *(halted, life hanging in the moment).* Why not?

Bobo *(the long way, the hard way to tell).* 'Cause I didn't have no reasons to . . .

Walter. Man, what are you talking about!

Bobo. I'm talking about the fact that when I got to the train station yesterday morning—eight o'clock like we planned . . . Man—*Willy didn't never show up.*

Walter. Why . . . where was he . . . where is he?

Bobo. That's what I'm trying to tell you . . . I don't know . . . I waited six hours . . . I called his house . . . and I waited . . . six hours . . . I waited in that train station six hours . . . *(Breaking into tears)* That was all the extra money I had in the world . . . *(Looking up at* WALTER *with the tears running down his face)* Man, *Willy is gone.*

Walter. Gone, what you mean Willy is gone? Gone where? You mean he went by himself. You mean he went off to Springfield by himself—to take care of getting the license—*(Turns and looks anxiously at* RUTH*)* You mean maybe he didn't want too many people in on the business down there? *(Looks to* RUTH *again, as before)* You know Willy got his own ways. *(Looks back to* BOBO*)* Maybe you was late yesterday and he just went on down there without you. Maybe—maybe—he's been callin' you at home tryin' to tell you what happened or something. Maybe—maybe—he just got sick. He's somewhere—he's got to be somewhere. We just got to find him—me and you got to find him. *(Grabs* BOBO *senselessly by the collar and starts to shake him)* We got to!

Bobo *(in sudden angry, frightened agony).* What's the matter with you, Walter! *When a cat take off with your money he don't leave you no maps!*

Walter *(turning madly, as though he is looking for* WILLY *in the very room).* Willy! . . . Willy . . . don't do it . . . Please don't do it . . . Man, not with that money . . . Man, please, not with that money . . . Oh, God, . . . Don't let it be true . . . *(He is wandering around, crying out for* WILLY *and looking for him or perhaps for help from God.)* Man . . . I trusted you . . . Man, I put my life in your hands . . . *(He starts to crumple down on the floor as* RUTH *just covers her face in horror.* MAMA *opens the door and comes into the room, with* BENEATHA *behind her.)* Man . . . *(He starts to pound the floor with his fists, sobbing wildly.) That money is made out of my father's flesh . . .*

allowing herself to become passionately involved in various passing fancies. For example, in Act One we are told that her guitar lessons are likely to be just a fad. In her eagerness to learn about her African heritage, Beneatha's posturing in native costume and her rigidity in "talking down" to the rest of the family seem more than a bit comic. Most students will agree that the relatively complex portrayal of Beneatha prevents her from being merely a stereotype.

10. Mama first reveals her news to Travis, her grandson. Her reason appears to be linked with one of her major goals: the stability and continuity of family life. She tells Travis that one day the house will be his.

11. The first major reversal occurs in connection with Lindner's visit. Whereas it first appears that Lindner's purpose is to welcome the Youngers to their new neighborhood, it turns out that his true goal is to propose a "buyout" of their new house, since they are not welcome in Clybourne Park. When informed of this development, Mama is at first disturbed, but her consternation is followed by pleasure and joy when Walter, Ruth, Beneatha, and Travis give her their presents. This light moment, however, is soon shattered when Bobo enters with the terrible news that Willy Harris has stolen the money that Bobo and Walter had entrusted to him to use in Springfield. Walter, practically speechless, admits to Mama that he never deposited Beneatha's school money in the bank; Mama beats Walter. Remembering her dead husband, Mama prays to God for strength and then crumples on the floor.

At the beginning of the scene, the mood is joyful and expectant. At the end, all seems to have been lost.

12. Student answers will vary. Encourage the students to support their responses with specific references to the play.

Bobo *(standing over him helplessly).* I'm sorry, Walter . . . *(Only* WALTER*'s sobs reply.* BOBO *puts on his hat.)* I had my life staked on this deal, too . . . *(He exits.)*
Mama *(to* WALTER*).* Son—*(She goes to him, bends down to him, talks to his bent head.)* Son . . . Is it gone? Son, I give you sixty-five hundred dollars. Is it gone? All of it? Beneatha's money too?
Walter *(lifting his head slowly).* Mama . . . I never . . . went to the bank at all . . .
Mama *(not wanting to believe him).* You mean . . . your sister's school money . . . you used that too . . . Walter? . . .
Walter. Yessss! . . . All of it . . . It's all gone . . .

[*There is total silence.* RUTH *stands with her face covered with her hands;* BENEATHA *leans forlornly against a wall, fingering a piece of red ribbon from the mother's gift.* MAMA *stops and looks at her son without recognition and then, quite without thinking about it, starts to beat him senselessly in the face.* BENEATHA *goes to them and stops it.*]

Beneatha. Mama!

[MAMA *stops and looks at both of her children and rises slowly and wanders vaguely, aimlessly away from them*]

Mama. I seen . . . him . . . night after night . . . come in . . . and look at the rug . . . and then look at me . . . the red showing in his eyes . . . the veins moving in his head . . . I seen him grow thin and old before he was forty . . . working and working and working like somebody's old horse . . . killing himself . . . and you—you give it all away in a day . . .
Beneatha. Mama—
Mama. Oh, God . . . *(She looks up to Him.)* Look down here—and show me the strength.
Beneatha. Mama—
Mama *(folding over).* Strength . . .
Beneatha *(plaintively).* Mama . . .
Mama. Strength!

Curtain

Responding to the Play

Analyzing Act Two

Identifying Details

1. In Scene 1, how does Walter react to Beneatha's version of an African dance and chant? How does George Murchison react to both Walter and Beneatha?
2. At the end of Scene 1, we find out what Mama has done with the insurance money. What is Ruth's reaction to Mama's news? What hints have we had earlier that this is what Ruth wanted all along?
3. How does Walter react to Mama's announcement? What is the problem with the new house?
4. In Scene 2, what does Mama say and do that makes Walter feel differently about his future? In Scene 3, what are we told and shown that convinces us that Walter has changed?
5. What is the purpose of Mr. Lindner's visit to the Younger family? How does Walter react when he realizes what Mr. Lindner really wants?
6. What bad news does Bobo bring to the family at the end of Scene 3?

Interpreting Meanings

7. In Scene 1, why does George address Walter as "Prometheus"?
8. Walter asks Ruth, "What is it gets into people ought to be close?" When they try to talk about why they are having such problems, they reach no conclusion. What do you think the playwright wants us to understand as the cause of their problems?
9. Beneatha is a serious character, but she also becomes comic through her excesses. Discuss how she can be seen as a comic **character.** Is she a convincing character, or a stereotype? Explain.
10. To which character does Mama first reveal her news in Scene 1? Why?
11. Scene 3 is full of **reversals,** in which sudden shifts take place in the fortunes of the main characters. Discuss the reversals in this scene. What is the mood at the beginning of this scene and at the end?
12. How do you feel about the various characters at this point in the play? Are you rooting for any particular character? Have your sympathies switched from one character to another? Explain.

Supplementary Support Materials: Act Three
1. Vocabulary Activity Worksheet (*CCB*)
2. Review and Response Worksheet: Static and Dynamic Characters (*CCB*)
3. Selection Test (*CCB*)
4. Audiocassette recording

Developing Vocabulary
The following words from Act Three are tested in the Selection Test. (See also Vocabulary Activity Worksheet.)

to replenish	gait
entrepreneur	trek
to elude	raucously

A. Characterization
Previously, how seriously did you take Beneatha's intention to become a doctor? Why? (Some may have thought it another whim like taking up the guitar or horseback riding.) How does her story about "a kid named Rufus" affect your evaluation of her seriousness? (The story and her comments on it show that her desire to become a doctor is much deeper than her other interests.) What line on this page suggests that Asagai understands? ("Children see things very well sometimes . . . ")

Act Three

An hour later.

At curtain, there is a sullen light of gloom in the living room, gray light not unlike that which began the first scene of Act One. At left we can see WALTER *within his room, alone with himself. He is stretched out on the bed, his shirt out and open, his arms under his head. He does not smoke, he does not cry out, he merely lies there, looking up at the ceiling, much as if he were alone in the world.*

In the living room BENEATHA *sits at the table, still surrounded by the now almost ominous packing crates. She sits looking off. We feel that this is a mood struck perhaps an hour before, and it lingers now, full of the empty sound of profound disappointment. We see on a line from her brother's bedroom the sameness of their attitudes. Presently the bell rings and* BENEATHA *rises without ambition or interest in answering. It is* ASAGAI, *smiling broadly, striding into the room with energy and happy expectation and conversation.*

Asagai. I came over . . . I had some free time. I thought I might help with the packing. Ah, I like the look of packing crates! A household in preparation for a journey! It depresses some people . . . but for me . . . it is another feeling. Something full of the flow of life, do you understand? Movement, progress . . . It makes me think of Africa.
Beneatha. Africa!
Asagai. What kind of a mood is this? Have I told you how deeply you move me?
Beneatha. He gave away the money, Asagai . . .
Asagai. Who gave away what money?
Beneatha. The insurance money. My brother gave it away.
Asagai. Gave it away?
Beneatha. He made an investment! With a man even Travis wouldn't have trusted.
Asagai. And it's gone?
Beneatha. Gone!
Asagai. I'm very sorry . . . And you, now?
Beneatha. Me? . . . Me? . . . Me I'm nothing . . . Me. When I was very small . . . we used to take our sleds out in the wintertime and the only hills we had were the ice-covered stone steps of some houses down the street. And we used to fill them in with snow and make them smooth and slide down them all day . . . and it was very dangerous you know . . . far too steep . . . and sure enough one day a kid named Rufus came down too fast and hit the sidewalk . . . and we saw his face just split open right there in front of us . . . And I remember standing there looking at his bloody open face thinking that was the end of Rufus. But the ambulance came and they took him to the hospital and they fixed the broken bones and they sewed it all up . . . and the next time I saw Rufus he just had a little line down the middle of his face . . . I never got over that . . .

[WALTER *sits up, listening on the bed. Throughout this scene it is important that we feel his reaction at all times, that he visibly respond to the words of his sister and* ASAGAI.]

Asagai. What?
Beneatha. That that was what one person could do for another, fix him up—sew up the problem, make him all right again. That was the most marvelous thing in the world . . . I wanted to do that. I always thought it was the one concrete thing in the world that a human being could do. Fix up the sick, you know—and make them whole again. This was truly being God . . .
Asagai. You wanted to be God?
Beneatha. No—I wanted to cure. It used to be so important to me. I wanted to cure. It used to matter. I used to care. I mean about people and how their bodies hurt . . .
Asagai. And you've stopped caring?
Beneatha. Yes—I think so.
Asagai. Why?

[WALTER *rises, goes to the door of his room and is about to open it, then stops and stands listening, leaning on the door jamb.*]

Beneatha. Because it doesn't seem deep enough, close enough to what ails mankind—I mean this thing of sewing up bodies or administering drugs. Don't you understand? It was a child's reaction to the world. I thought that doctors had the secret to all the hurts. . . . That's the way a child sees things—or an idealist.
Asagai. Children see things very well sometimes—and idealists even better.
Beneatha. I know that's what you think. Because you are still where I left off—you still care. This is what you see for the world, for Africa. You with the dreams of the future will patch up all Africa—you are going to cure the Great Sore of colonialism with Independence——
Asagai. Yes!

Act Three Summary: Asagai, hearing about the loss, proposes that Beneatha return to Nigeria with him as his wife. In despair, Walter calls Mr. Lindner for another meeting and tells the family they should accept the offer. Mama, however, successfully challenges Walter's pride, and he formally refuses the offer. The move to the new house begins.

A. Responding
? The words differ, and Beneatha uses a metaphor—independence as penicillin—but how does her "then what?" pick up on the issue of money as a goal, discussed by Walter and Mama in Act One (last half of the second column, page 833)? (In that passage Mama speaks of freedom, survival, dignity, nonsegregated streetcars, and a decent life. Walter says the basic issue—the "then what"—is and always has been money.) What is your answer to "then what"? (Answers will vary.)

Beneatha. Yes—and you think that one word is the penicillin of the human spirit: "Independence!" But then what?

Asagai. That will be the problem for another time. First we must get there.

Beneatha. And where does it end?

Asagai. End? Who even spoke of an end? To life? To living?

Beneatha. An end to misery!

Asagai *(smiling).* You sound like a French intellectual.

Beneatha. No! I sound like a human being who just had her future taken right out of her hands! While I was sleeping in my bed in there, things were happening in this world that directly concerned me—and nobody asked me, consulted me—they just went out and did things—and changed my life. Don't you see there isn't any real progress, Asagai, there is only one large circle that we march in, around and around, each of us with our own little picture—in front of us—our own little mirage that we think is the future.

Asagai. That is the mistake.

Beneatha. What?

Asagai. What you just said—about the circle. It isn't a circle—it is simply a long line—as in geometry, you know, one that reaches into infinity. And because we cannot see the end—we also cannot see how it changes. And it is very odd but those who see the changes are called "idealists"—and those who cannot, or refuse to think, they are the "realists." It is very strange, and amusing too, I think.

Beneatha. You—you are almost religious.

Asagai. Yes . . . I think I have the religion of doing what is necessary in the world—and of worshiping man—because he is so marvelous, you see.

Beneatha. Man is foul! And the human race deserves its misery!

Asagai. You see: *you* have become the religious one in the old sense. Already, and after such a small defeat, you are worshiping despair.

Beneatha. From now on, I worship the truth—and the truth is that people are puny, small, and selfish. . . .

Asagai. Truth? Why is it that you despairing ones always think that only you have the truth? I never thought to see *you* like that. You! Your brother made a stupid, childish mistake—and you are grateful to him. So that now you can give up the ailing human race on account of it. You talk about what good is struggle; what good is anything? Where are we all going? And why are we bothering?

Beneatha. *And you cannot answer it!* All your talk and dreams about Africa and Independence. Independence and then what? What about all the crooks and petty thieves and just plain idiots who will come into power to steal and plunder the same as before—only now they will be black and do it in the name of the new Independence— You cannot answer that.

Asagai *(shouting over her). I live the answer! (Pause)* In my village at home it is the exceptional man who can even read a newspaper . . . or who ever *sees* a book at all. I will go home and much of what I will have to say will seem strange to the people of my village . . . But I will teach and work and things will happen, slowly and swiftly. At times it will seem that nothing changes at all . . . and then again . . . the sudden dramatic events which make history leap into the future. And then quiet again. Retrogression even. Guns, murder, revolution. And I even will have moments when I wonder if the quiet was not better than all that death and hatred. But I will look about my village at the illiteracy and disease and ignorance and I will not wonder long. And perhaps . . . perhaps I will be a great man . . . I mean perhaps I will hold on to the substance of truth and find my way always with the right course . . . and perhaps for it I will be butchered in my bed some night by the servants of empire . . .

Beneatha. *The martyr!*

Asagai. . . . or perhaps I shall live to be a very old man, respected and esteemed in my new nation . . . And perhaps I shall hold office and this is what I'm trying to tell you, Alaiyo; perhaps the things I believe now for my country will be wrong and outmoded, and I will not understand and do terrible things to have things my way or merely to keep my power. Don't you see that there will be young men and women, not British soldiers then, but my own black countrymen . . . to step out of the shadows some evening and slit my then useless throat? Don't you see they have always been there . . . that they always will be. And that such a thing as my own death will be an advance? They who might kill me even . . . actually replenish me!

Beneatha. Oh, Asagai, I know all that.

Asagai. Good! Then stop moaning and groaning and tell me what you plan to do.

Beneatha. Do?

B. Naturalism
? How does Beneatha's speech summarize the philosophy of naturalism? (See page 383, the second paragraph under Frank Norris and Naturalism.) (Beneatha extrapolates from the fact that Walter has determined things directly affecting her future to a general idea that human beings have no control of their lives.) Does Asagai accept this philosophy of life? (He rejects it, asserting that idealists are more correct than so-called realists.)

C. Responding
? Do you agree with Asagai, in the discussion on the rest of the page, that Beneatha (Alaiyo) is giving up too easily? Is her life over because of the loss of the money, as she seems to feel? What advice would you give her? (Though Beneatha feels hopeless, most students will feel that she still can become a doctor. Some would advise her to work hard to attain her goal.)

C

A. Plot

Do you think Beneatha will accept Asagai's proposal? Why or why not? (Answers will vary. Those who say that Beneatha will reject Asagai's proposal will cite the couple's different interests, goals, and priorities.) During Beneatha's speech at the top of column 2, Walter hunts frantically for some object. What is it? (Lindner's card) What do you think he plans to do with it? (The logical guess is that he is going to contact Mr. Lindner, perhaps with the hope of accepting the offer so that the family can still have a house and a little more cash besides.)

B. Responding

What is the first object Mama looks at? (The plant) Why do you think she sets it outside? (Answers will vary. Some will think it means the family is not moving; others, that she has abandoned the plant, meaning that the family is moving.)

Asagai. I have a bit of a suggestion.
Beneatha. What?
Asagai *(rather quietly for him)*. That when it is all over—that you come home with me—
Beneatha *(slapping herself on the forehead with exasperation born of misunderstanding)*. Oh—Asagai—at this moment you decide to be romantic!
A **Asagai** *(quickly understanding the misunderstanding)*. My dear, young creature of the New World—I do not mean across the city—I mean across the ocean; home—to Africa.
Beneatha *(slowly understanding and turning to him with murmured amazement)*. To—to Nigeria?
Asagai. Yes! . . . *(Smiling and lifting his arms playfully)* Three hundred years later the African Prince rose up out of the seas and swept the maiden back across the middle passage over which her ancestors had come—
Beneatha *(unable to play)*. Nigeria?
Asagai. Nigeria. Home. *(Coming to her with genuine romantic flippancy)* I will show you our mountains and our stars; and give you cool drinks from gourds and teach you the old songs and the ways of our people—and, in time, we will pretend that—*(very softly)*—you have only been away for a day—

[She turns her back to him, thinking. He swings her around and takes her full in his arms in a long embrace which proceeds to passion.]

Beneatha *(pulling away)*. You're getting me all mixed up—
Asagai. Why?
Beneatha. Too many things—too many things have happened today. I must sit down and think. I don't know what I feel about anything right this minute.

[She promptly sits down and props her chin on her fist.]

Asagai *(charmed)*. All right, I shall leave you. No—don't get up. *(Touching her, gently, sweetly)* Just sit awhile and think . . . Never be afraid to sit awhile and think. *(He goes to door and looks at her.)* How often I have looked at you and said, "Ah—so this is what the New World hath finally wrought . . ."

[He exits. BENEATHA *sits on alone. Presently* WALTER *enters from his room and starts to rummage through things, feverishly looking for something. She looks up and turns in her seat.]*

Beneatha *(hissingly)*. Yes—just look at what the New World hath wrought! . . . Just look! *(She gestures with bitter disgust.)* There he is! *Monsieur le petit bourgeois noir*[1]—himself! There he is—Symbol of a Rising Class! Entrepreneur! Titan[2] of the system! *(*WALTER *ignores her completely and continues frantically and destructively looking for something and hurling things to floor and tearing things out of their place in his search.* BENEATHA *ignores the eccentricity of his actions and goes on with the monologue of insult.)* Did you dream of yachts on Lake Michigan, Brother? Did you see yourself on that Great Day sitting down at the Conference Table, surrounded by all the mighty bald-headed men in America? All halted, waiting, breathless, waiting for your pronouncements on industry? Waiting for you—Chairman of the Board? *(*WALTER *finds what he is looking for—a small piece of white paper—and pushes it in his pocket and puts on his coat and rushes out without ever having looked at her. She shouts after him.)* I look at you and I see the final triumph of stupidity in the world!

[The door slams and she returns to just sitting again. RUTH *comes quickly out of* MAMA*'s room.]*

Ruth. Who was that?
Beneatha. Your husband.
Ruth. Where did he go?
Beneatha. Who knows—maybe he has an appointment at U.S. Steel.
Ruth *(anxiously, with frightened eyes)*. You didn't say nothing bad to him, did you?
Beneatha. Bad? Say anything bad to him? No—I told him he was a sweet boy and full of dreams and everything is strictly peachy keen, as the ofay kids say!

*[*MAMA *enters from her bedroom. She is lost, vague, trying to catch hold, to make some sense of her former command of the world, but it still eludes her. A sense of waste overwhelms her gait; a measure of apology rides on her shoulders. She goes to her plant, which has remained on the table, looks at it, picks it up and takes it to the window sill and sits it outside, and she stands and looks at it a long moment. Then she closes the*

1. **Monsieur le petit bourgeois noir:** "Mister black lower middle class." The *petit bourgeois* are owners of shops and small businesses.
2. **Titan:** In Greek mythology, the Titans were a race of giants.

A. Characterization

? In her second speech on this page, Mama quotes what people used to say about her: "Lena Eggleston, you aims too high all the time." How does this information help explain the dreams of Walter and Beneatha? (Without their or her realizing it, they may have learned from their mother to dream.)

window, straightens her body with effort and turns around to her children.]

Mama. Well—ain't it a mess in here, though? *(A false cheerfulness, a beginning of something)* I guess we all better stop moping around and get some work done. All this unpacking and everything we got to do. (RUTH *raises her head slowly in response to the sense of the line; and* BENEATHA *in similar manner turns very slowly to look at her mother.)* One of you all better call the moving people and tell 'em not to come.

Ruth. Tell 'em not to come?

Mama. Of course, baby. Ain't no need in 'em coming all the way here and having to go back. They charges for that too. *(She sits down, fingers to her brow, thinking.)* Lord, ever since I was a little girl, I always remembers people saying, "Lena—Lena Eggleston, you aims too high all the time. You needs to slow down and see life a little more like it is. Just slow down some." That's what they always used to say down home—"Lord, that Lena Eggleston is a high-minded thing. She'll get her due one day!"

Ruth. No, Lena . . .

Mama. Me and Big Walter just didn't never learn right.

Ruth. Lena, no! We gotta go. Bennie—tell her . . . *(She rises and crosses to* BENEATHA *with her arms outstretched.* BENEATHA *doesn't respond.)* Tell her we can still move . . . the notes ain't but a hundred and twenty-five a month. We got four grown people in this house—we can work . . .

Mama *(to herself)*. Just aimed too high all the time—

Ruth *(turning and going to* MAMA *fast—the words pouring out with urgency and desperation)*. Lena—I'll work . . . I'll work twenty hours a day in all the kitchens in Chicago . . . I'll strap my baby on my back if I have to and scrub all the floors in America and wash all the sheets in America if I have to—but we got to move . . . We got to get out of here . . .

[MAMA *reaches out absently and pats* RUTH'*s hand.*]

Mama. No—I sees things differently now. Been thinking 'bout some of the things we could do to fix this place up some. I seen a secondhand bureau over on Maxwell Street just the other day that could fit right there. *(She points to where the new furniture might go.* RUTH *wanders away from her.)* Would need some new handles on it and then a little varnish and then it look like something brand-new. And—we can put up them new curtains in the kitchen . . . Why this place be looking fine. Cheer us all up so that we forget trouble ever came . . . *(To* RUTH*)* And you could get some nice screens to put up in your room round the baby's bassinet . . . *(She looks at both of them, pleadingly.)* Sometimes you just got to know when to give up some things . . . and hold on to what you got.

[WALTER *enters from the outside, looking spent and leaning against the door, his coat hanging from him.*]

Mama. Where you been, son?

Walter *(breathing hard)*. Made a call.

Mama. To who, son?

Walter. To The Man.

Mama. What man, baby?

Walter. The Man, Mama. Don't you know who The Man is?

Ruth. Walter Lee?

Walter. *The Man.* Like the guys in the streets say—The Man. Captain Boss—Mistuh Charley . . . Old Captain Please Mr. Bossman . . .

Beneatha *(suddenly)*. Lindner!

Walter. That's right! That's good. I told him to come right over.

Beneatha *(fiercely, understanding)*. For what? What do you want to see him for!

Walter *(looking at his sister)*. We going to do business with him. C

Mama. What you talking 'bout, son?

Walter. Talking 'bout life, Mama. You all always telling me to see life like it is. Well—I laid in there on my back today . . . and I figured it out. Life just like it is. Who gets and who don't get. *(He sits down with his coat on and laughs.)* Mama, you know it's all divided up. Life is. Sure enough. Between the takers and the "tooken." *(He laughs.)* I've figured it out finally. *(He looks around at them.)* Yeah. Some of us always getting "tooken." *(He laughs.)* People like Willy Harris, they don't never get "tooken." And you know why the rest of us do? 'Cause we all mixed up. Mixed up bad. We get to looking 'round for the right and the wrong; and we worry about it and cry about it and stay up nights trying to figure out 'bout the wrong and the right of things all the time . . . And all the time, man, them takers is out there operating, just taking and taking. Willy Har-

B. Plot

? What decision has Mama made about the new house? (The move is off.) Why do you think Mama made this decision? (Ruth's protest about how she will help earn the monthly payments of $125 makes it clear that the Younger household does not have the money to meet the payments.)

C. Plot

? What "business" does Walter want to do with Mr. Lindner? (Sell the house) What is the obvious advantage? (To make money) Do you think Mama will agree to this? Support your answer with details from the play. (Most students will cite instances showing that Mama would be unwilling to take money that involves a basic insult, the implication that her family is no good.) What is your advice to the Younger family—should they swallow their pride and take the money, move in and enjoy the house until they fail to keep up the payments, or take some other course of action?

A. Connections
? How is Willy Harris's function in this play similar to that of Tom Wingfield's father in *The Glass Menagerie?* (Each of them leaves others in the lurch yet paradoxically serves as a symbol of freedom or success to a young man who feels trapped by the circumstances of his life.)

B. Responding
? Why is Beneatha horrified by Walter's plan? What does she mean by "the real honest-to-God bottom"? (If students have no answer at the moment, query again after Mama speaks. Most students will agree that Beneatha feels that Walter has fallen to a new all-time low in terms of his integrity, when he shamelessly says that he is willing to sell the house back to Lindner.)

C. Responding
? How do Mama's words further explain Beneatha's reactions? (The issue is human dignity, not money.)

D. Responding
? Do you believe Walter? Will he feel "Fine! . . . a man . . ."? How does his taking on the dialectal patterns of a slave contribute to your answer? (Most students will see that Walter's current bitterness and anguish will only deepen if he follows through and demeans himself as he proposes.)

A ris? Shoot—Willy Harris don't even count. He don't even count in the big scheme of things. But I'll say one thing for old Willy Harris . . . he's taught me something. He's taught me to keep my eye on what counts in this world. Yeah—*(Shouting out a little)* Thanks, Willy!

Ruth. What did you call that man for, Walter Lee?

Walter. Called him to tell him to come on over to the show. Gonna put on a show for the man. Just what he wants to see. You see, Mama, the man came here today and he told us that them people out there where you want us to move—well they so upset they willing to pay us not to move out there. *(He laughs again.)* And—and oh, Mama—you would of been proud of the way me and Ruth and Bennie acted. We told him to get out . . . Lord have mercy! We told the man to get out. Oh, we was some proud folks this afternoon, yeah. *(He lights a cigarette.)* We were still full of that old-time stuff . . .

Ruth *(coming toward him slowly).* You talking 'bout taking them people's money to keep us from moving in that house?

Walter. I ain't just talking 'bout it, baby—I'm telling you that's what's going to happen.

B **Beneatha.** Oh, God! Where is the bottom! Where is the real honest-to-God bottom so he can't go any farther!

Walter. See—that's the old stuff. You and that boy that was here today. You all want everybody to carry a flag and a spear and sing some marching songs, huh? You wanna spend your life looking into things and trying to find the right and the wrong part, huh? Yeah. You know what's going to happen to that body someday—he'll find himself sitting in a dungeon, locked in forever—and the takers will have the key! Forget it, baby! There ain't no causes—there ain't nothing but taking in this world, and he who takes most is smartest—and it don't make a bit of difference *how.*

Mama. You making something inside me cry, son. Some awful pain inside me.

Walter. Don't cry, Mama. Understand. That white man is going to walk in that door able to write checks for more money than we ever had. It's important to him and I'm going to help him . . . I'm going to put on the show, Mama.

C **Mama.** Son—I come from five generations of people who was slaves and sharecroppers—but ain't nobody in my family never let nobody pay 'em no money that was a way of telling us we wasn't fit to walk the earth. We ain't never been that poor. *(Raising her eyes and looking at him)* We ain't never been that dead inside.

Beneatha. Well—we are dead now. All the talk about dreams and sunlight that goes on in this house. All dead.

Walter. What's the matter with you all! I didn't make this world! It was given to me this way! Lord, yes, I want me some yachts someday! Yes, I want to hang some real pearls 'round my wife's neck. Ain't she supposed to wear no pearls? Somebody tell me—tell me, who decides which woman is suppose to wear pearls in this world. I tell you I am a *man*—and I think my wife should wear some pearls in this world!

[*This last line hangs a good while and* WALTER *begins to move about the room. The word "Man" has penetrated his consciousness; he mumbles it to himself repeatedly between strange agitated pauses as he moves about.*]

Mama. Baby, how you going to feel on the inside?

D **Walter.** Fine! . . . Going to feel fine . . . a man . . .

Mama. You won't have nothing left then, Walter Lee.

Walter *(coming to her).* I'm going to feel fine, Mama. I'm going to look that man in the eyes and say—*(He falters.)*—and say, "All right, Mr. Lindner—*(He falters even more.)*—that's your neighborhood out there. You got the right to keep it like you want. You got the right to have it like you want. Just write the check and—the house is yours." And, and I am going to say—*(His voice almost breaks.)* And you—you people just put the money in my hand and you won't have to live next to this bunch of stinking . . . *(He straightens up and moves away from his mother, walking around the room.)* Maybe—maybe I'll just get down on my black knees . . . *(He does so;* RUTH *and* BENNIE *and* MAMA *watch him in frozen horror.)* Captain, Mistuh, Bossman. *(He starts crying.)* A-hee-hee-hee! *(Wringing his hands in profoundly anguished imitation)* Yasssssuh! Great White Father, just gi' ussen de money, fo' God's sake, and we's ain't gwine come out deh and dirty up yo' white folks neighborhood . . .

[*He breaks down completely, then gets up and goes into the bedroom.*]

Beneatha. That is not a man. That is nothing but a toothless rat.

Mama. Yes—death done come in this here house. *(She is nodding, slowly, reflectively.)* Done come walking in my house. On the lips of my children. You what supposed to be my beginning again. You—what supposed to be my harvest. *(To* BENEATHA*)* You—you mourning your brother?
Beneatha. He's no brother of mine.
Mama. What you say?
Beneatha. I said that that individual in that room is no brother of mine.
Mama. That's what I thought you said. You feeling like you better than he is today? *(*BENEATHA *does not answer.)* Yes? What you tell him a minute ago? That he wasn't a man? Yes? You give him up for me? You done wrote his epitaph too—like the rest of the world? Well, who give you the privilege?
Beneatha. Be on my side for once! You saw what he just did, Mama! You saw him—down on his knees. Wasn't it you who taught me—to despise any man who would do that. Do what he's going to do.
Mama. Yes—I taught you that. Me and your daddy. But I thought I taught you something else too . . . I thought I taught you to love him.
Beneatha. Love him? There is nothing left to love.
Mama. There is always something left to love. And if you ain't learned that, you ain't learned nothing. *(Looking at her)* Have you cried for that boy today? I don't mean for yourself and for the family 'cause we lost the money. I mean for him; what he been through and what it done to him. Child, when do you think is the time to love somebody the most; when they done good and made things easy for everybody? Well then, you ain't through learning—because that ain't the time at all. It's when he's at his lowest and can't believe in hisself 'cause the world done whipped him so. When you starts measuring somebody, measure him right, child, measure him right. Make sure you done taken into account what hills and valleys he come through before he got to wherever he is.

[TRAVIS *bursts into the room at the end of the speech, leaving the door open.*]

Travis. Grandmama—the moving men are downstairs! The truck just pulled up.
Mama *(turning and looking at him).* Are they, baby? They downstairs?

[*She sighs and sits.* LINDNER *appears in the doorway. He peers in and knocks lightly, to gain attention, and comes in. All turn to look at him.*]

Lindner *(hat and briefcase in hand).* Uh—hello . . . *(*RUTH *crosses mechanically to the bedroom door and opens it and lets it swing open freely and slowly as the lights come up on* WALTER *within, still in his coat, sitting at the far corner of the room. He looks up and out through the room to* LINDNER.*)*
Ruth. He's here.

[*A long minute passes and* WALTER *slowly gets up.*]

Lindner *(coming to the table with efficiency, putting his briefcase on the table and starting to unfold papers and unscrew fountain pens).* Well, I certainly was glad to hear from you people. *(*WALTER *has begun the trek out of the room, slowly and awkwardly, rather like a small boy, passing the back of his sleeve across his mouth from time to time.)* Life can really be so much simpler than people let it be most of the time. Well—with whom do I negotiate? You, Mrs. Younger, or your son here? *(*MAMA *sits with her hands folded on her lap and her eyes closed as* WALTER *advances.* TRAVIS *goes close to* LINDNER *and looks at the papers curiously.)* Just some official papers, sonny.
Ruth. Travis, you go downstairs.
Mama *(opening her eyes and looking into* WALTER'*s).* No. Travis, you stay right here. And you make him understand what you doing, Walter Lee. You teach him good. Like Willy Harris taught you. You show where our five generations done come to. Go ahead, son— A
Walter *(looks down into his boy's eyes.* TRAVIS *grins at him merrily and* WALTER *draws him beside him with his arm lightly around his shoulders.).* Well, Mr. Lindner. *(*BENEATHA *turns away.)* We called you—*(There is a profound, simple groping quality in his speech.)*—because, well, me and my family *(He looks around and shifts from one foot to the other.)* Well—we are very plain people . . .
Lindner. Yes—
Walter. I mean—I have worked as a chauffeur most of my life—and my wife here, she does domestic work in people's kitchens. So does my mother. I mean—we are plain people . . .
Lindner. Yes, Mr. Younger—
Walter *(really like a small boy, looking down at his shoes and then up at the man).* And—uh—well, my father, well, he was a laborer most of his life.

A. Plot
The movers and Lindner arrive simultaneously; a decision must be made immediately. **?** How does Mama hit upon the one approach that may affect what Walter says to Lindner? (She appeals to him to make Travis understand what he is doing.) Is it immediately evident whether Walter will accept Lindner's offer or reject it? (Not immediately)

Humanities Connection: Discussing the Photograph
The photograph illustrates the scene on the audiocassette. It clarifies the seriousness and intensity of the entire family as they wait to hear what Walter will say to Mr. Lindner.

The picture also shows more of the stage set than do the other photographs. Theater critic Brooks Atkinson said of it in his opening night review, "Ralph Alswang's set . . . depicts both the poverty and the taste of the family. Like the play, it is 'honest.'"

". . . this is—this is my son, who makes the sixth generation of our family in this country . . ."

CLOSURE

In class discussion have students consider the reaction of one white man who, having attended the stage production of *A Raisin in the Sun,* was astonished to discover that the characters were just plain *people*. How does *A Raisin in the Sun* go beyond political rhetoric to foster understanding among people of different ethnic groups?

READING CHECK TEST: ACT THREE

1. Asagai thinks Beneatha has given up her dreams too easily. *False*
2. Asagai invites Beneatha to come to Africa with him. *True*
3. Walter asks Mr. Lindner to come to the apartment. *True*
4. Mama is proud of the manner in which Walter plans to accept Mr. Lindner's offer. *False*
5. Walter accepts the money from Mr. Lindner. *False*

Lindner *(absolutely confused).* Uh, yes—

Walter *(looking down at his toes once again).* My father almost beat a man to death once because this man called him a bad name or something, you know what I mean?

Lindner. No, I'm afraid I don't.

Walter *(finally straightening up).* Well, what I mean is that we come from people who had a lot of pride. I mean—we are very proud people. And that's my sister over there and she's going to be a doctor—and we are very proud—

Lindner. Well—I am sure that is very nice, but—

Walter *(starting to cry and facing the man eye to eye).* What I am telling you is that we called you over here to tell you that we are very proud and that this is—this is my son, who makes the sixth generation of our family in this country, and that we have all thought about your offer and we have decided to move into our house because my father—my father—he earned it. *(MAMA has her eyes closed and is rocking back and forth as though she were in church, with her head nodding the amen yes.)* We don't want to make no trouble for nobody or fight no causes—but we will try to be good neighbors. That's all we got to say. *(He looks the man absolutely in the eyes.)* We don't want your money. *(He turns and walks away from the man.)*

Lindner *(looking around at all of them).* I take it then that you have decided to occupy.

Beneatha. That's what the man said.

Lindner *(to MAMA in her reverie).* Then I would like to appeal to you, Mrs. Younger. You are older and wiser and understand things better I am sure . . .

Mama *(rising).* I am afraid you don't understand. My son said we was going to move and there ain't nothing left for me to say. *(Shaking her head with double meaning)* You know how these young folks is nowadays, mister. Can't do a thing with 'em. Goodbye. A

Lindner *(folding up his materials).* Well—if you are that final about it . . . There is nothing left for me to say. *(He finishes. He is almost ignored by the family, who are concentrating on WALTER LEE. At the door LINDNER halts and looks around.)* I sure hope you people know what you're doing. *(He shakes his head and exits.)*

Ruth *(looking around and coming to life).* Well, for God's sake—if the moving men are here—LET'S GET THIS BLESSED FAMILY OUT OF HERE!

A. Humor/ Connections

? What is the delightful double meaning in Mama's response to Mr. Lindner? (The notion that she, of all people, can't do a thing with the young people in her household, when she has just taken exactly the right approach to help her son, Walter, do exactly what she hoped he would do)

Students may wish to focus on Lena Younger, Mama, as the unifying force in the Younger family, and compare her with Ma Joad in John Steinbeck's *The Grapes of Wrath* (Viking, 1939). Even without having read Steinbeck's work, you might ask them to apply to this play Ma Joad's words after the family has endured tragedy upon tragedy, "Hush. Don' worry. We'll figger somepin out" (Chapter Thirty).

ANALYZING ACT THREE
Identifying Details
1. Asagai says that his role is to lead his people out of ignorance and to aid their progress.

He asks Beneatha to return to Nigeria with him as his wife.

2. At this point, Walter plans to recoup the stolen money by accepting Lindner's proposal for a buyout of the new house.

They object to his plan because it involves a complete surrender of human dignity.

3. Walter finally stands up for his own dignity and that of his family. He turns away from material ambition and asserts his essential humanity by telling Lindner that the Youngers will not accept his proposal.

4. By having Mama look around at the walls of the apartment, the playwright suggests that she is nostalgic about the past and her many years of married life with Big Walter. As the heaving rises in her and she puts her fist in her mouth, her actions may suggest that she is fearful of the future, of the unknown. But she pulls on her coat, pats her hat, and makes her exit toward new surroundings. As she re-enters for a moment to collect

Mama *(into action).* Ain't it the truth! Look at all this here mess. Ruth, put Travis's good jacket on him . . . Walter Lee, fix your tie and tuck your shirt in, you look like somebody's hoodlum. Lord have mercy, where is my plant? *(She flies to get it amid the general bustling of the family, who are deliberately trying to ignore the nobility of the past moment.)* You all start on down . . . Travis child, don't go empty-handed . . . Ruth, where did I put that box with my skillets in it? I want to be in charge of it myself . . . I'm going to make us the biggest dinner we ever ate tonight . . . Beneatha, what's the matter with them stockings? Pull them things up, girl . . .

[*The family starts to file out as two moving men appear and begin to carry out the heavier pieces of furniture, bumping into the family as they move about.*]

Beneatha. Mama, Asagai—asked me to marry him today and go to Africa—
Mama *(in the middle of her getting-ready activity).* He did? You ain't old enough to marry nobody— *(Seeing the moving men lifting one of her chairs precariously)* Darling, that ain't no bale of cotton, please handle it so we can sit in it again. I had that chair twenty-five years . . .

[*The movers sigh with exasperation and go on with their work.*]

Beneatha *(girlishly and unreasonably trying to pursue the conversation).* To go to Africa, Mama—be a doctor in Africa . . .
Mama *(distracted).* Yes, baby—
Walter. Africa! What he want you to go to Africa for?
Beneatha. To practice there . . .
Walter. Girl, if you don't get all them silly ideas out of your head! You better marry yourself a man with some loot . . .

Beneatha *(angrily, precisely as in the first scene of the play).* What have you got to do with who I marry!
Walter. Plenty. Now I think George Murchison—

[*He and* BENEATHA *go out yelling at each other vigorously;* BENEATHA *is heard saying that she would not marry* GEORGE MURCHISON *if he were Adam and she were Eve, etc. The anger is loud and real till their voices diminish.* RUTH *stands at the door and turns to* MAMA *and smiles knowingly.*]

Mama *(fixing her hat at last).* Yeah—they something all right, my children . . .
Ruth. Yeah—they're something. Let's go, Lena.
Mama *(stalling, starting to look around at the house).* Yes—I'm coming. Ruth—
Ruth. Yes?
Mama *(quietly, woman to woman).* He finally come into his manhood today, didn't he? Kind of like a rainbow after the rain . . .
Ruth *(biting her lip lest her own pride explode in front of* MAMA*).* Yes, Lena.

[WALTER*'s voice calls for them raucously.*]

Mama *(waving* RUTH *out vaguely).* All right, honey—go on down. I be down directly.

[RUTH *hesitates, then exits.* MAMA *stands, at last alone in the living room, her plant on the table before her as the lights start to come down. She looks around at all the walls and ceilings and suddenly, despite herself, while the children call below, a great heaving thing rises in her and she puts her fist to her mouth, takes a final desperate look, pulls her coat about her, pats her hat and goes out. The lights dim down. The door opens and she comes back in, grabs her plant, and goes out for the last time.*]

Curtain

her plant, we are reminded of her nurturing qualities—over and over, during the play, she has displayed tenderness toward the plant, a small growing thing that she has "mothered."

Interpreting Meanings

5. The prop is Mama's plant, which is a symbol for the constant, loving tenderness with which Mama nourishes all who surround her.

6. Student answers may vary, but they should agree that both Mama and Walter are dynamic characters. Mama learns to understand Walter's torment, and she changes as she trusts and supports him more vigorously. Walter learns that, in order to "be a man," he must stand up for his own dignity and must pay more attention to the needs of his wife and children.

Students will probably agree that the minor characters in the play—Asagai, Travis, George, Bobo, and Lindner—are all static characters. Students may give various opinions about Ruth and Beneatha.

7. The poem by Langston Hughes implies that a dream which is too long "deferred" may be the cause of torment, suffering, or violence. The poem most obviously relates to the suffering of Walter in the play. But the play's major theme—that the values of dignity and of love are enduring and triumphant—is somewhat different from the theme of the poem, which ends on an ominous, menacing tone.

Most of the characters in the play have had their dreams deferred in one way or another. Walter has long dreamed of material success and social status. Mama and Ruth dream of holding the family together. Asagai dreams of leading his people toward progress in Africa, and Beneatha dreams of becoming a doctor. By the end of the play, none of these characters has fully achieved his or her dream. But it is strongly implied that the dreams of Mama and Ruth are about to be fulfilled.

8. Three essential values for Mama are religion, love, and human dignity. She reveals the depth of her religious beliefs in Act One, when she firmly reprimands Beneatha for saying that God does

(Answers continue on next page.)

A Comment on the Play

In her play, Lorraine Hansberry deals with the age-old problem of human beings' inhumanity to one another. But, like every artist, she achieves the universal through specific circumstances and characters with which she was very familiar.

Although the characters voice the many attitudes held by blacks at the time the play was written, they are complex characters in their own right. They may be recognizable types, but they are not stereotypes. Mama is the loving, dominating matriarch, steeped in her religion, learning that she must let her son grow up in his own way. Walter, her prime opponent, feels disenfranchised by being black and refuses to accept his "place." Instead, he dreams a dream (like Willy Loman in Arthur Miller's *Death of a Salesman*) that is shaped by the superficial standards he has picked up from the rich white people he serves. In this play, Walter learns to become a man. Beneatha is a serious, liberated "intellectual"; but she is amusing because of her pretensions and her efforts to "express" herself. All these characters are treated with both seriousness and sympathetic humor.

The play's content and attitude derive from the school of Henrik Ibsen, Clifford Odets, and Arthur Miller. Sometimes plays of this genre are accused of being didactic or preachy. All good plays teach or reveal something significant about the human condition, but they usually do so subtly; the point, or "message," arises naturally from the characters and the action. The theme of *A Raisin in the Sun* is that the courage and strength of good people can triumph over adversity, over their own failings, and over the cruelty of society. Goodness shines forth from all of Hansberry's people, and they come through adversity morally improved by their experience.

Like its content and attitudes, the structure of the play derives from the school of classic realism. From the opening scene, the play progresses in a straight line from foreshadowed conflicts to the conflicts themselves, to changes and intensifications of the conflicts, and finally to a resolution.

Mama is going to receive ten thousand dollars in insurance money, and everyone in the family wants to spend it differently, according to his or her "dream deferred." (Note the derivation of Hansberry's title from the famous Langston Hughes poem used as the play's epigraph.) Each character has something important at stake. Each wants to escape the ghetto, but in a different way. And if any one of them realizes his or her dream, it stands to ruin the dream of the others. The conflict is perfect: no compromise or resolution seems possible. In the end, Mama "learns" and changes, and Walter "learns" and changes, making a resolution possible.

Responding to the Play

Analyzing Act Three

Identifying Details

1. In their long scene at the beginning of this act, Beneatha and Asagai discuss his vision of Africa's future. How does Asagai view his role in Africa? What does he ask Beneatha to do?
2. Why does Walter call Mr. Lindner? Why do Ruth, Mama, and Beneatha object to his plan?
3. The scene with Mr. Lindner is the **climax** of the play. What happens during this scene that ends our doubts and worries about the Younger family's future?
4. What do the closing stage directions suggest about Mama's frame of mind just before the final curtain?

Interpreting Meanings

5. A movable object on stage is called a *prop* (short for *property*). We have seen in *The Glass Menagerie* that a prop, such as the glass unicorn, may serve as a **symbol** that stands for much more than the object itself. There is a similar prop in this play. What is it, and what does it symbolize?
6. In a play, certain characters change and grow as a result of their experiences. These are **dynamic** characters. **Static** characters remain essentially the same throughout the play; they do not change in any important way. Which characters in this play are dynamic? Which are static?

(Continued from previous page.)
not exist. In Act Three, she tells Walter that her family, which came from five generations of slaves and sharecroppers, have never allowed anyone to rob them of their dignity with a bribe. And finally, a little later in Act Three, Mama defends Walter to Beneatha, reminding her that 'there is always something left to love."
9. We fear that Walter will "sell out" by making the deal with Lindner.

At first we do not know Walter's plan; we only see him as he listens to the conversation between Asagai and Beneatha and then frantically searches for the piece of paper with Lindner's telephone number. When Walter reveals his plan to Mama and Beneatha, his excitement rises to a fever pitch as he bitterly parodies the actions of a defeated black man, begging a white master for mercy.

As he breaks down and retires to the bedroom, we are almost convinced that Walter is unbalanced, and that he will not heed Mama's words about human dignity. Then the moving men arrive, almost simultaneously with Lindner, and the suspense is intensified since a decision must be made. Mama orders Travis to remain in the room, as Walter has to confront
(Answers continue in left-hand column.)

(Continued from top.)
Lindner. Walter starts out with an apologetic, almost humble tone—but then asserts the pride of the family and finally rejects Lindner's offer.
10. For Walter, the element that rescues him from defeat is a basic realization of his own dignity and pride. Mama, in turn, has made this realization possible when she objects to his plan to debase himself and his family by making the deal with Lindner. Although Mama herself seems broken and defeated, her strong sense of love and support for her children rescues her: this is most visible in the short scene with Beneatha, as she tells her daughter that "there is always something left to love."

7. How are the play's title and the poem by Langston Hughes (page 813) related to the play's **theme?** Which characters in the play have had their "dreams deferred"? Which characters have dreams that come true?
8. During the course of the play, we learn that Mama believes there are several absolutely essential things in life. What would you say Mama's values are? Find passages in the play to support your answer.
9. Discuss the playwright's use of **suspense** in Act Three. What is it that we fear will happen? How does the playwright draw out the action so that our suspense will be heightened?
10. Both Mama and Walter seem "defeated" for a while in Act Three. However, we know from the play's general tone that it cannot end in defeat for these good people. In a way, we "enjoy" their defeat and despair because we sense that the playwright is preparing us for another **reversal.** What is it that rouses each character from defeat to the joyful, triumphant note on which the play ends?

Writing About the Play

A Creative Response

1. **Extending the Play.** At the end of the play, Walter has "become a man" in the eyes of his family and has, in denouncing Mr. Lindner's offer, risen to a noble moment. But has he rid himself of his dream of success, of his anger and bitterness and frustration? In several paragraphs, tell what you think will happen to Walter after the family moves to Clybourne Park.

A Critical Response

2. **Responding to the Characters.** In the characters of Beneatha and Asagai, Hansberry deals with the relationship of American blacks to their African heritage. What did you think of these characters and their feelings about heritage? How important do you think it is for a person to know about his or her cultural, ethnic, racial, or religious background? Is pride in one's heritage necessary for a person to have identity and self-esteem? Or should assimilation be our goal as Americans? In a brief essay, tell what you think about these questions, and give reasons to support your answers.
3. **Evaluating the Play.** Hansberry has said this about playwriting:

> . . . I believe that one of the most sound ideas in dramatic writing is that in order to create the universal, you must pay very great attention to the specific.
>
> —Lorraine Hansberry

Do you think that *A Raisin in the Sun* says something universal about human beings? If so, what? Or do you think that the play focuses in such realistic detail on a specific family living at a particular time on the Southside of Chicago that it fails in its attempt to say something universal about human beings? Discuss these questions in a brief essay.

Primary Sources

A Letter from the Playwright

Lorraine Hansberry wrote the following letter to her mother on January 19, 1959, just before *A Raisin in the Sun* opened in New Haven, Connecticut.

"Dear Mother,

Well—here we are. I am sitting alone in a nice hotel room in New Haven, Conn. Downstairs, next door in the Shubert Theater, technicians are putting the finishing touches on a living room that is supposed to be a Chicago living room. Wednesday the curtain goes up at 8 P.M. The next day the New Haven papers will say what they think about our efforts. A great deal of money has been spent and a lot of people have done some hard, hard work, and it may be the beginning of many different careers.

"The actors are very good and the director is a very talented man—so if it is a poor show I won't be able to blame a soul but your youngest daughter.

"Mama, it is a play that tells the truth about people, Negroes, and life and I think it will help a lot of people to understand how we are just as complicated as they are—and just as mixed up—but above all, that we have among our miserable and downtrodden ranks people who are the very essence of human dignity. That is what, after all the laughter and tears, the play is supposed to say. I hope it will make you very proud. See you soon. Love to all."

EVALUATING A PLAY

Writing Assignment

You are a drama critic sitting in a darkened theater. You watch the characters onstage move and speak as the play unfolds before you. Is it a good play or a bad play? If it's a good play, is it a great play? How can you tell? Write an essay in which you analyze and evaluate one of the plays in this unit.

Background

This assignment involves two critical thinking skills you've already practiced: analyzing and evaluating. When you **analyze** a play, you take the play apart and look at each element separately. You think about how each element functions in the play and about how the elements work together to produce the total effect.

Evaluating requires a judgment about how good or bad, effective or noneffective, something is. For this assignment, you'll evaluate how effectively the playwright has used plot, character, and setting. Then you'll evaluate the play as a whole, answering the question, "How good a play is it?"

Your subjective response to a play is different from an objective evaluation. **Subjective responses** are based entirely on your own feelings and experiences; you either like or dislike a play; it either moves you or it doesn't. But an **objective evaluation** is based on agreed-upon standards, or **criteria.** These criteria are accepted by experts such as drama critics, playwrights, and directors. Here are some of the criteria that are commonly applied to plays.

Guidelines for Evaluating a Play

1. **Characters**
   - **a.** The characters seem real and believable.
   - **b.** The major characters are complex—not flat or stereo typed.
   - **c.** The characters' **motivations**—why they act and speak as they do—are understandable.
   - **d.** The characters' speech is believable and natural.
   - **e.** All of the characters are in some way necessary to the play.
2. **Plot**
   - **a.** The **conflict** or conflicts are clear.
   - **b.** The plot creates **suspense**—an increasing excitement and interest in the outcome of the play.
   - **c.** The play is **unified** and **coherent.** Every action contributes to the meaning of the play.
   - **d.** The events lead to a final **climax**—a decisive scene in which a crucial event occurs that resolves the conflict at last.
   - **e.** The resolution is believable and satisfying. It flows logically from the events that precede it.
   - **f.** The play's **subplots** support or complement the main plot.
3. **Theme**
   - **a.** The play conveys an idea or message about life and human nature, or about the playwright's idea of what the world is like.
   - **b.** The play's message is universal, or nearly so. That is, it can be appreciated by people everywhere, and its message is not "dated."
   - **c.** The play's message is not trite and stereotyped; it is profound and true.
4. **Setting**
   - **a.** The setting helps to reveal something about the characters, the conflict, or the theme.
   - **b.** The setting helps to create a **mood.**

You may be able to think of other criteria for judging whether a play is good or bad. If so, add them to this list.

Prewriting

1. Decide which play in this unit you think is best. Reread the play carefully.
2. Before you can judge how good or bad a play is, you'll need to identify—and **analyze**—some of the play's basic elements. Fill out a chart such as the following:

Play: ________________	
Conflict	
Climax	
Characters	
Motivation	
Theme	
Setting and mood	

Revising Essays As students revise their essays, refer them to **Grammar, Usage, and Mechanics: A Reference Guide** at the back of their books.

Exercises in Critical Thinking and Writing/*cont.*

3. Now you can move on to **evaluating** each element. Don't be timid about making your judgments; trust your instincts. Pretend you're reviewing the play for people who are eager to know your opinion.

Measure the play against each of the criteria listed under **Guidelines.** You might measure each criterion on a scale of 1 to 10 or 0 to 4 stars. Or you can rate each criterion on a scale like this one:

VERY POOR WEAK FAIR AVERAGE GOOD GREAT

4. Next, look over your evaluation of each element and come to some evaluation of the play as a whole. Do you think it's a good play? A great play? Do you think it will still be meaningful a hundred or two hundred years from now? Write a **thesis statement** that expresses your overall evaluation of the play.
5. Now organize your ideas, and decide what you'll include in your essay. Think of the body of your essay as providing support or evidence to back up the opinion that you've expressed in your thesis statement. You probably won't be able to discuss all of the criteria we have suggested; include the ones that give the strongest support to your thesis statement.
6. Find specific examples (incidents, quotations, characters) to support what you plan to say about the play. Jot down scene numbers, page numbers, line numbers, quotations, etc.

Writing

You might use the following plan for organizing your essay. Before you begin writing, make a rough outline of what you'll include in Paragraphs 2-6:

Paragraph 1: Introduction, thesis statement, overall evaluation of play.
Paragraph 2: Evaluation of the play's **characters.**
Paragraph 3: Evaluation of the **plot.**
Paragraph 4: Evaluation of the **theme.** Discuss whether or not you agree with the playwright's "message."
Paragraph 5: Evaluation of the **setting.**
Paragraph 7: Concluding paragraph, giving your subjective response to the play and reasons for that response.

Revising and Proofreading

Use the guidelines in the section at the back of this book, called **Writing About Literature,** to revise and proofread your essay.

Additional Writing Assignment

Pretend you are a TV or movie critic writing for your school newspaper. Write an evaluation of a television drama or series or a movie you have seen recently. Use the criteria here to discuss the elements of the drama or movie. Write at least three paragraphs.

FICTION
1945 TO THE PRESENT

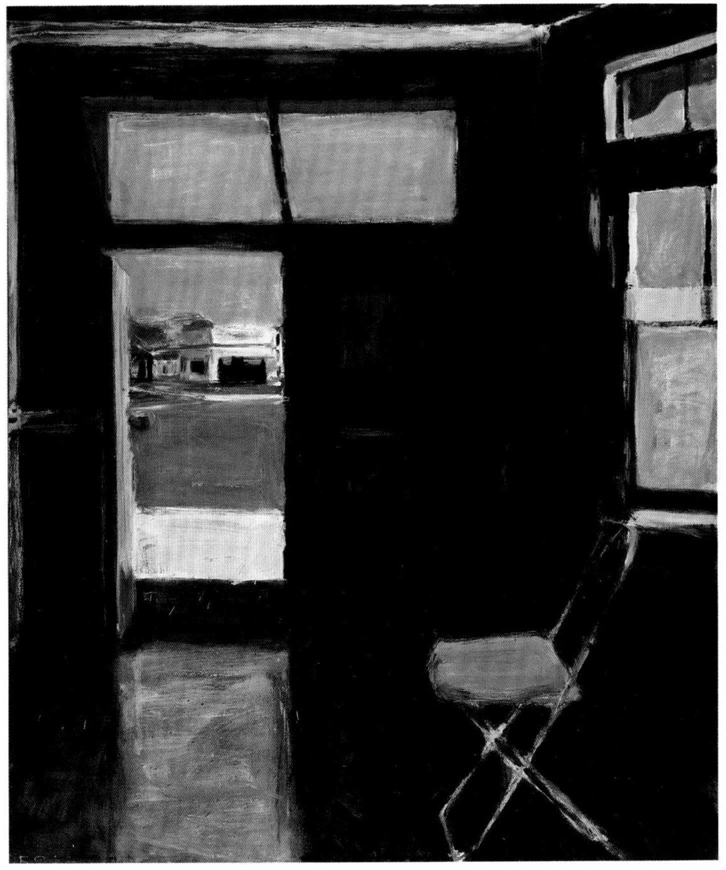

Interior with Doorway by Richard Diebenkorn (1962). Oil. The Pennsylvania Academy of the Fine Arts, Philadelphia. Henry Gilpin Fund.

UNIT ELEVEN

HUMANITIES CONNECTION: DISCUSSING THE FINE ART

Richard Diebenkorn (b. 1922) distills from his own experience the essence of the western American scene. Born in Portland, Oregon, he studied art in California and has maintained a studio in Santa Monica for many years. One art critic describes Diebenkorn's work as "characterized by slapdash brushstrokes, sensuous color and a generally rough and lush atmosphere."

You might ask students to discuss their interpretations of this scene. What kind of building might the artist be in? What kind of building is visible through the doorway? Why might the artist have chosen this scene to paint?

TEACHING THE FICTION UNIT

The stories in this unit are most notable for their diversity. Reading them will give your students a good idea of alternative modes of narrative.

Among these postwar trends are "metafiction" and "magic realism." Metafiction is a style of experimental fiction in which narrative form is itself part of the subject matter of the story. A metafictional story comments not only upon its ostensible subject matter, but also upon the art of fiction itself. Donald Barthelme's story in this unit, "Game" (page 920), does not make an explicit metafictional statement, but it continues Barthelme's investigation of the absurdity of modern life, the fragmenting of personality, and the breakdown of old belief systems.

Where metafiction is directly descended from the modernistic experiments of writers such as Joyce, Stein, and Beckett, magic realism tries to infuse new vigor into storytelling by using the age-old devices of fable, fairy tale, and legend. Works of magic realism are usually set in a recognizably "realistic" setting rendered in skillful detail, but within which the laws of realism are occasionally suspended to create a dreamlike effect. Isaac Bashevis Singer's story "The Key," Mark Helprin's "Tamar," and Bernard Malamud's "The Magic Barrel" are examples.

Other writers in this unit deal with a more straightforward kind of reality, and in their works we find a variety of American ethnic experiences. John Updike's "Son" shows us three generations of white Protestant males, transmitting love from one to the other while experiencing conflict. Though the story is realistic, it makes use of metafiction devices in its shifting time scheme and somewhat ambiguous way of identifying characters. Julia Alvarez's "Daughter of Invention" portrays a family from the Dominican Republic; Amy Tan's "Rules of the Game" is about Chinese Americans. Anne Tyler's "Your Place Is Empty" is about culture clash between an American woman and her Middle Eastern mother-in-law. James Alan McPherson contrasts the attitudes of Northern and Southern African Americans in the past, while Andrea Lee's "New African" is about a middle-class African American family in Pennsylvania.

OBJECTIVES OF THE FICTION UNIT

1. To expand vocabulary and increase reading proficiency
2. To gain exposure to notable authors and their works
3. To define and identify elements of fiction
4. To define and identify significant literary techniques
5. To respond, orally and in writing, to fiction through analysis of its elements
6. To practice the following critical thinking and writing skills:
   - a. Analyzing theme and the writer's method
   - b. Comparing and contrasting literary works
   - c. Responding to literary criticism and to a title
   - d. Analyzing humor
   - e. Analyzing and forming generalizations
   - f. Evaluating a story's ending

Supplementary Support Materials: Unit Eleven

1. Unit Introduction Test (*CCB*)
2. American Language Test (*CCB*)
3. Word Analogies Test (*CCB*)
4. Unit Review Test (*CCB*)
5. Critical Thinking and Writing Test (*CCB*)
6. Instructional Overhead Transparencies

A. Responding to the Quotation

? What landmark events in history besides the dropping of the first atomic bomb have made historical collapse and rise stand out in sharp relief? (Some obvious ones are the Black Death of the Middle Ages, the American Revolution, and the Great Depression of the 1930's.)

B. Expansion

You may want to mention that a second atomic bomb was dropped three days later on the Japanese city of Nagasaki. Despite the subsequent proliferation of nuclear bombs and the ever-present threat of their use, those two World War II atomic bombs are the only ones dropped so far in wartime.

FICTION 1945 TO THE PRESENT

by **John Leggett**

A

At all times, an old world is collapsing and a new world arising; we have better eyes for the collapse than the rise, for the old one is the world we know. The artist, in focusing on his own creation, finds, and offers, relief from the tension and sadness of being burdened not just with consciousness but with historical consciousness. . . .

—from *Hugging the Shore,* John Updike

Literature in the Atomic Age

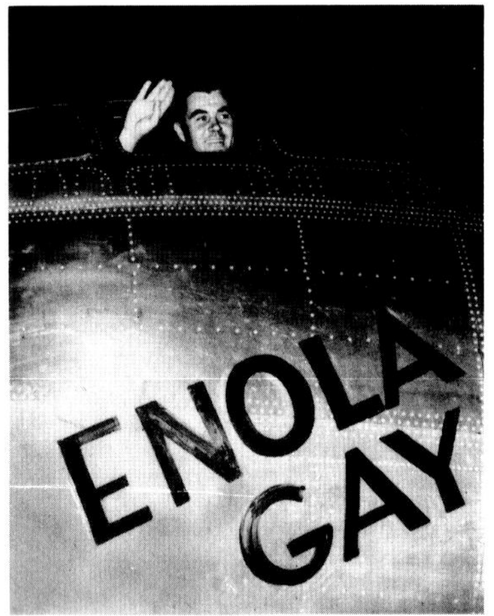

Enola Gay, the airplane that dropped the atomic bomb on Hiroshima.

B

On August 6, 1945, at 8:15 A.M., an atomic bomb was dropped upon the Japanese city of Hiroshima from the U.S. Air Force plane *Enola Gay*. Within seconds, the center of Hiroshima had disappeared. Though the bomb in effect ended World War II, its mushroom cloud has cast a shadow over each generation since.

The bomb is the dramatic symbol of the last half of the twentieth century. Its infamous mushroom cloud represents the proliferation of science and technology, the purpose of which was, ironically enough, to benefit humankind, to make life richer and easier for all of us.

In many ways, science and technology have fulfilled their promise. They have increased our life spans and fed and housed us better. They have moved us faster from place to place—even allowing a few of us to stroll on the surface of the moon.

But at the same time, science and technology have standardized and "assembly-lined" our lives. They have diminished Emerson's rugged individual. Now people often feel they are only a number on a computer disk or credit card. Even their thoughts seem to be shaped or controlled by mass advertising, mass journalism, and mass entertainment. Some people even predict that our new technologies threaten to deliver the planet itself back to lower organisms—to the cockroaches and turtles, perhaps—who may survive the nuclear holocaust which might one day engulf us.

Although many Americans disapproved of the use of the atomic bomb to end World War II, most Americans agreed with the purpose of the war itself. They were fighting against tyranny, against regimes that would destroy the American way of life. Only twenty years later, however, the United States became deeply involved in another overseas war—this time in Vietnam—that would sharply divide the nation. Many Americans could see no purpose in this war, and began to protest American involvement. Perhaps it was this atmosphere of rebellion, or maybe just a sense of the increasing precariousness of existence, that produced the "Sixties generation." Some of these young people used drugs to escape from the real world's uncertainties. Others began to challenge the accepted ideas of American society. Demonstrations, both peaceful and violent, became commonplace.

A. Humanities Connection: Discussing the Fine Art
Ask students for their interpretations of the title (and subject matter) of this painting by Roger Brown (b. 1941). You may want to point out that Nassau County, New York, is a suburban county on Long Island. In 1947, just after World War II, William J. Levitt built Levittown in Nassau County as a private, low-cost housing development for veterans and their families. The community, with a population today of approximately sixty thousand, has often been mentioned (and photographed) as an example of the early postwar suburbs—street after street of look-alike houses. Levittown, incidentally, is in central Long Island; it is not on the water. Students should be aware of that when they interpret the painting.

Roger Brown, a native of Hamilton, Alabama, now lives in Chicago. His paintings have been exhibited in one-person shows in London, New York, Houston, Los Angeles, and other cities.

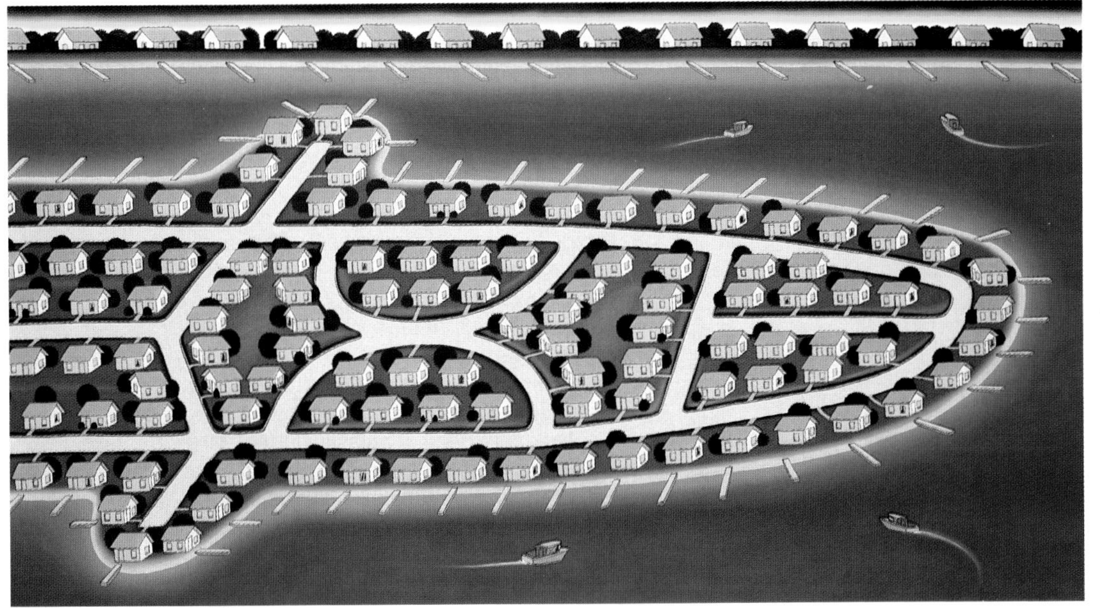

A

Nassau County: A Time-Photo Alteration by Roger Brown (1973). Oil.

Private collection.

The New Voices in Fiction

To some writers, such as Kurt Vonnegut, the madness of the world was an inescapable condition of modern life, and the only appropriate response was hard-edged laughter at life's tragic ironies. The term "black humor" was coined to describe his work, as well as that of Joseph Heller, Terry Southern, and others. Heller's novel *Catch-22* (1962) is set in World War II, but the absurdities it describes belong to post-War life. In *Catch-22,* madness and war are inextricably mixed, not because madness is a result of war but because war is a result of our madness. The novel's protagonist, Yossarian, is a pilot who wants to get out of flying any more combat missions: B

> It was a horrible joke, but Doc Daneeka didn't laugh until Yossarian came to him one mission later and pleaded again, without any real expectation of success, to be grounded. Doc Daneeka snickered once and was soon immersed in problems of his own, which included Chief White Halfoat, who had been challenging him all that morning to Indian wrestle, and Yossarian, who decided right then and there to go crazy.
>
> "You're wasting your time," Doc Daneeka was forced to tell him.
>
> "Can't you ground someone who's crazy?"
>
> "Oh, sure. I have to. There's a rule saying I have to ground anyone who's crazy."
>
> "Then why don't you ground me? I'm crazy. Ask Clevinger."
>
> "Clevinger? Where *is* Clevinger? You find Clevinger and I'll ask him."

"To some writers, the madness of the world was an inescapable condition of modern life."

B. Expansion
Joseph Heller (b. 1923) has sometimes been dismissed as a one-book author. Although that one book, *Catch-22,* is an acknowledged masterpiece, critics have generally not been enthusiastic about his other works. *Catch-22* is a rollicking story, a joy to read, but his second novel, *Something Happened,* is "astonishingly depressing," in Kurt Vonnegut's words. Focusing on one thoroughly dislikable character, Bob Slocum, the novel portrays the "unrelieved misery" of this gray-flannel exemplar of the "good life" in the period after World War II.

Heller himself considers *Something Happened* to be superior to *Catch-22,* but most critics continue to rank his first novel as his best.

Comment From A Critic

"Rare is the first novel successful enough to make its author's reputation. Rarer still is a work of fiction that actually adds a term to the language. Joseph Heller's *Catch-22,* published in 1961, did both."

So begins Stephen W. Potts's *From Here to Absurdity: The Moral Battlefields of Joseph Heller* (The Borgo Press, 1982). *Catch-22* is a novel, writes Potts, filled with apparent direct contradictions, or oxymorons, as in this conversation about sanity and combat duty between Yossarian and Doc Daneeka. Potts uses an oxymoron himself when he refers to *Catch-22* as a novel about "the courageous cowardice of its antihero Yossarian."

"'Sure there's a catch,' Doc Daneeka replied. 'Catch-22. Anyone who wants to get out of combat duty isn't really crazy.' " (Joseph Heller)

"Then ask any of the others. They'll tell you how crazy I am."

"They're crazy."

"Then why don't you ground them?"

"Why don't they ask me to ground them?"

"Because they're crazy, that's why."

"Of course they're crazy," Doc Daneeka replied. "I just told you they're crazy, didn't I? And you can't let crazy people decide whether you're crazy or not, can you?"

Yossarian looked at him soberly and tried another approach. "Is Orr crazy?"

"He sure is," Doc Daneeka said.

"Can you ground him?"

"I sure can. But first he has to ask me to. That's part of the rule."

"Then why doesn't he ask you to?"

"Because he's crazy," Doc Daneeka said. "He has to be crazy to keep flying combat missions after all the close calls he's had. Sure, I can ground Orr. But first he has to ask me to."

"That's all he has to do to be grounded?"

"That's all. Let him ask me."

"And then you can ground him?" Yossarian asked.

"No. Then I can't ground him."

"You mean there's a catch?"

"Sure there's a catch," Doc Daneeka replied. "Catch-22. Anyone who wants to get out of combat duty isn't really crazy."

There was only one catch and that was Catch-22, which specified that a concern for one's own safety in the face of dangers that were real and immediate was the process of a rational mind. Orr was crazy and could be grounded. All he had to do was ask; and as soon as he did, he would no longer be crazy and would have to fly more missions. Orr would be crazy to fly more missions and sane if he didn't, but if he was sane he had to fly them. If he flew them he was crazy and didn't have to; but if he didn't want to he was sane and had to. Yossarian was moved very deeply by the absolute simplicity of this clause of Catch-22 and let out a respectful whistle.

"That's some catch, that Catch-22," he observed.

"It's the best there is," Doc Daneeka agreed.

Yossarian saw it clearly in all its spinning reasonableness. There was an elliptical precision about its perfect pairs of parts that was graceful and shocking, like good modern art, and at times Yossarian wasn't quite sure that he saw it all, just the way he was never quite sure about good modern art or about the flies Orr saw in Appleby's eyes. He had Orr's word to take for the flies in Appleby's eyes.

"Oh, they're there, all right," Orr had assured him about the flies in Appleby's eyes after Yossarian's fist fight with Appleby in the officers' club, "although he probably doesn't

A. Humanities Connection: Discussing the Fine Art
Students should realize that *Grandmother and Grandfather* are free-standing sculptures, not paintings. You might ask why the figures are identified as grandparents rather than younger people. (The radios and TV sets comprising their bodies are relatively old models.) Students will probably enjoy identifying the radio and TV parts that make up the facial features, torsos, arms, and legs of the figures.

Nam June Paik (b. 1932), born in Seoul, South Korea, and educated at the University of Tokyo, pursues an occupation that could scarcely have existed prior to World War II. He is a video artist—a sculptor and painter whose subject matter involves television. He has lived in the United States for many years. In 1969 Paik was artist-in-residence at WGBH-TV, Boston, a major public television station. This artist's works have been widely exhibited throughout the United States and Europe.

even know it. That's why he can't see things as they really are."

"How come he doesn't know it?" inquired Yossarian.

"Because he's got flies in his eyes," Orr explained with exaggerated patience. "How can he see he's got flies in his eyes if he's got flies in his eyes?"

It made as much sense as anything else. . . .

—from *Catch-22*,
Joseph Heller

Here, nonconformity—deciding to go crazy—is the only real sanity, while conformity—continuing to fly combat missions—is true madness. Few felt this way during World War II, when Americans were united against a common enemy, but Yossarian's plight struck a common chord in the less-stable Sixties.

If previous literary eras were dominated by white, Anglo-Saxon, Protestant males, this era has opened up to voices from the neglected sectors of society. Ralph Ellison's novel *Invisible Man* (1952) set a model for an outpouring of fiction about the black experience in America. Similarly, I. B. Singer, Saul Bellow, and Bernard Malamud moved the current of urban Jewish writing into the mainstream of American fiction. Such fiction not only energized but also dominated contemporary literature throughout the fifties and sixties. More recently, from the *barrios* of American cities has come fiction by the newest wave of one of the oldest groups in North America—the Mexicans, Puerto Ricans, Cubans, and Dominicans.

The fiction that captures a wide audience often does so by offering a fresh voice and a new attitude, as though these are the powerful needs of each new generation. J. D. Salinger's novel *Catcher in the Rye* did just that in 1951, giving us, in teen-ager Holden Caulfield's disillusioned view of the "phoniness" of the adult world, a voice that questioned the materialism and hypocrisy that Salinger saw as central to our very values as a society.

Bernard Malamud writing.

Photograph © 1988 by Jill Krementz.

"'How can he see he's got flies in his eyes if he's got flies in his eyes?'"
—Joseph Heller

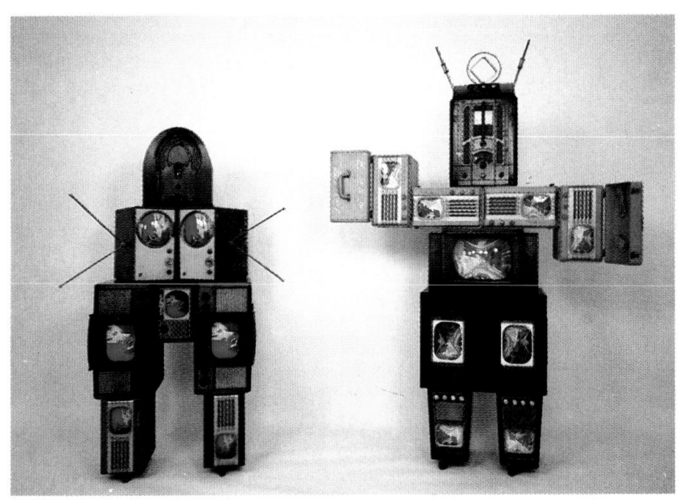

A

Family of Robot: Grandmother (left) and Grandfather (right) by Nam June Paik (1986). Video sculpture.

Carl Solway Gallery, Cincinnati, Ohio.

A. Discussing the Time Line
Since so many of the time-line entries involve the Nobel Prize for Literature and the Pulitzer Prize, you might discuss these two prizes briefly so as to differentiate them.
Nobel Prize: The Nobel Prize for Literature is an international award based on outstanding achievement for the writer's lifetime work, not just for a single book. The award, dating back to 1901, was established by Alfred Nobel, the inventor of dynamite, and is presented in Stockholm, Sweden, on December 10 of each year. Other Nobel prizes are awarded for peace, chemistry, physics, physiology/medicine, and economics.
Pulitzer Prize: Pulitzer Prizes are annual awards for achievements in literature, journalism, and music. In literature, prizes are given in fiction, drama, history, biography, and poetry. Works with American themes are preferred. The award, first given in 1917, was established by newspaper publisher Joseph Pulitzer.

John Updike

THE CENTAUR

"Heaven is the creation inconceivable to man, earth the creation conceivable to him. He himself is the creature on the boundary between heaven and earth."
KARL BARTH

Alfred A. Knopf New York
1963

The Search for Transcendence

The English novel has from its beginnings concerned itself with the depiction of social life, but American fiction has often dealt with larger questions, such as the nature of good and evil and the search for transcendent spiritual values in the natural world. These are principal themes of our greatest nineteenth-century writers, of thinkers like Emerson and Thoreau and of writers of fiction like Melville, Hawthorne, and Poe. And much of the best fiction since World War II—including the work of such varied authors as Saul Bellow, Norman Mailer, Joan Didion, and John Updike—has dealt with these same themes.

Updike's characters, for example, seek spiritual revelations in ordinary life. "The invariable mark of wisdom," Emerson wrote, "is to find the miraculous in the common." This is the wisdom Updike's characters are searching for. Harry "Rabbit" Angstrom, for example, the protagonist of *Rabbit, Run* (1960), is burdened by what he sees as the "fraud" of modern life. Rabbit tries to deal with his many problems—a dead-end job, an unhappy marriage to an alcoholic wife, and the feeling that his best years are long over—by running from them. Yet despite these evasions, he continues to search for some higher meaning. Driving with a minister one day, for example, Rabbit describes his spiritual feelings: " 'Well, I don't know all this about theology, but I'll tell you. I *do*

1942–1945	1945	1945	1947–1948
Physicist Enrico Fermi succeeds in splitting the atom, 1942 6 million Jews murdered in concentration camps in Europe, 1939–1945	War ends in Europe May 8, 1945 Atomic bomb dropped over Hiroshima, August 6, 1945	**Hersey wins the Pulitzer Prize for *A Bell for Adano*, 1945** **Wright publishes *Black Boy*, 1945**	**Robert Lowell wins the Pulitzer Prize for Poetry, 1947** **Eliot receives Nobel Prize for Literature, 1948**
1953	**1954**	**1954–1955**	**1957–1958**
A Joseph McCarthy investigates Communist influence in the government, 1953–1955 **James Baldwin publishes *The Fire Next Time*, 1953**	Segregation of races in public schools declared illegal, 1954 **Hemingway wins the Nobel Prize for Literature, 1954**	**Roethke wins the Pulitzer Prize for Poetry, 1954** **Wallace Stevens wins the Pulitzer Prize for Poetry, 1955**	**Wilbur wins the Pulitzer Prize for Poetry, 1957** **Hansberry's *A Raisin in the Sun* opens on Broadway, 1958**
1969	**1973**	**1976–1977**	**1978**
Momaday wins the Pulitzer Prize for Fiction, 1969 American astronauts land on moon, 1969	**Welty wins the Pulitzer Prize for Fiction, 1973** Watergate Investigation begins in Washington, 1973 Vietnam ceasefire, 1973	U.S. celebrates its Bicentennial, 1976 **James Merrill wins the Pulitzer Prize for Poetry, 1977**	**James McPherson wins the Pulitzer Prize for Nonfiction, 1978** **Isaac Bashevis Singer receives Nobel Prize for Literature, 1978**

Reading Check Test

1. An event in 1945 that changed the shape of the future was the (a) beginning of World War II (b) dropping of an atomic bomb on Hiroshima (c) death of President John F. Kennedy (d) publication of *The Catcher in the Rye (b)*
2. Joseph Heller's *Catch-22* is a novel of (a) realism (b) despair (c) social manners (d) black humor *(d)*
3. All of the following contributed to urban Jewish writing except (a) Ralph Ellison (b) I. B. Singer (c) Bernard Malamud (d) Saul Bellow *(a)*
4. The best fiction since World War II has shown the influence of (a) transcendentalism (b) French symbolism (c) regionalism (d) classicism *(a)*
5. The characters in John Updike's works are often seeking (a) money (b) death (c) escape from suburbia (d) spiritual revelation *(d)*

feel, I guess, that somewhere behind all this'—he gestures outward at the scenery; they are passing the housing development this side of the golf course, half-wood half-brick and one-and-a-half stories in little flat bulldozed yards with tricycles and spindly three-year-old trees, the un-grandest landscape in the world—'there's something that wants me to find it.' "

It is more difficult to find transcendent spiritual values in the cheap clutter of modern life than it was in the woods around Emerson's Concord, but Updike's characters continue the search. "I find myself circling back to man's religious nature," Updike has written of his own work, "and the real loss to man and art alike when that nature has nowhere to plug itself in. . . ." These words could serve to describe the work of a great variety of recent writers whose intellectual roots can be traced to the Transcendentalists of the nineteenth century, and even further back to those hardy, practical Puritans who braved a two-month voyage in a tiny wooden boat in order to find an outlet for their own religious natures.

"It is more difficult to find transcendent spiritual values in the cheap clutter of modern life than it was in the woods around Emerson's Concord."

1949	1950	1951–1952	1952–1960
Faulkner receives Nobel Prize for Literature, 1949 Mao Tse-tung's Communists conquer China, 1949	**Gwendolyn Brooks wins the Pulitzer Prize for Poetry, 1950** U.N. forces enter Korean Conflict, 1950–1953	**J.D. Salinger publishes *The Catcher in the Rye,* 1951** **Ralph Ellison publishes *The Invisible Man,* 1952**	**Marianne Moore wins the Pulitzer Prize for Poetry, 1952** The Eisenhower Years, 1953–1960

1961–1962	1962–1963	1963–1965	1967–1968
Soviet Union (1961) and U.S. (1962) resume nuclear tests, 1961 First troops sent into Vietnam, 1962	**Saul Bellow receives Nobel Prize for Literature, 1962** **William Carlos Williams wins the Pulitzer Prize for Poetry, 1963**	President John F. Kennedy assassinated, 1963 Civil Rights Act prohibits discrimination, 1964 **Berryman wins the Pulitzer Prize for Poetry, 1965**	**Sexton wins the Pulitzer Prize for Poetry, 1967** **Malamud wins the Pulitzer Prize for Fiction, 1967** Martin Luther King, Jr., murdered, April 14, 1968

1979	1982	1983
Russell Baker wins the Pulitzer Prize for Commentary, 1979 Mob in Iran seizes U.S. Embassy and takes 53 hostages, 1979	**Updike wins the Pulitzer Prize for Fiction, 1982** **Plath wins the Pulitzer Prize for Poetry, 1982**	**Baker wins the Pulitzer Prize for Autobiography, 1983** **Walker wins the Pulitzer Prize for Fiction, 1983**

COMMENT FROM THE AUTHOR
In an interview with Richard Burgin, an editor, Isaac Bashevis Singer stressed the realism in his stories: ". . . [W]hile I may write a completely supernatural story, I try to make it as realistic as possible. This adds power to the mystical story, because even a mystical story should have realism. . . . If I read about a man who sees a burning bush [as in the Bible story of Moses] and the fire went sideways instead of up, it would distort the reality of the fire and weaken the mysticism of the story. The more you give a story realistic power, the more you enhance its mystical power, too."

Tell students to keep these comments by Singer in mind as they read "The Key."

Isaac Bashevis Singer (1904–1991)

To say that Isaac Bashevis Singer was the greatest modern writer in Yiddish is no exaggeration. Yiddish is a language derived from Medieval German but written in the Hebrew alphabet. It was once common in New York City, but as the old generation of European immigrants dies out, their language dies out as well.

Despite the small Yiddish-speaking audience, Singer has reached many readers through translation. He has been praised in the most prestigious literary circles, and in 1978 he was awarded the Nobel Prize for Literature.

Singer was born in Poland, the son and grandson of rabbis. He was intended for the rabbinate himself, but he decided that the religious life was too confining. "I began to doubt not the power of God, but all the traditions and dogmas," he has said. Secular writing did appeal to him. "I often met situations which baffled me and from the moment I knew there was such a thing as literature I thought how wonderful it would be to describe such things."

Alarmed by the rise of anti-Semitism and the Nazis in Europe, Singer left for America in 1935, joining his older brother, who was also a writer. In New York, he went to work for the city's Yiddish newspaper, *The Jewish Daily Forward*. Soon, besides newspaper articles, he was publishing his first fiction pieces.

Singer's style is spare, almost Biblical in its apparent simplicity. "When I tell a story, I tell a story," he said. "I don't try to discuss, criticize, or analyze my characters." However, his explicitness seems to be a cloak for the real power of his storytelling, which lies in the poetry of his language and in the mystical quality of his themes. Beneath the surface of the most ordinary circumstances in his stories, supernatural forces—both divine and demonic—are at work.

"I really believe there are spirits in this world," Singer has said, "and that man has a soul and that the soul is not the only spiritual entity in the world. . . . I find it very easy to believe in reincarnation, possession by devils, and other such things. We have many proofs that such things exist."

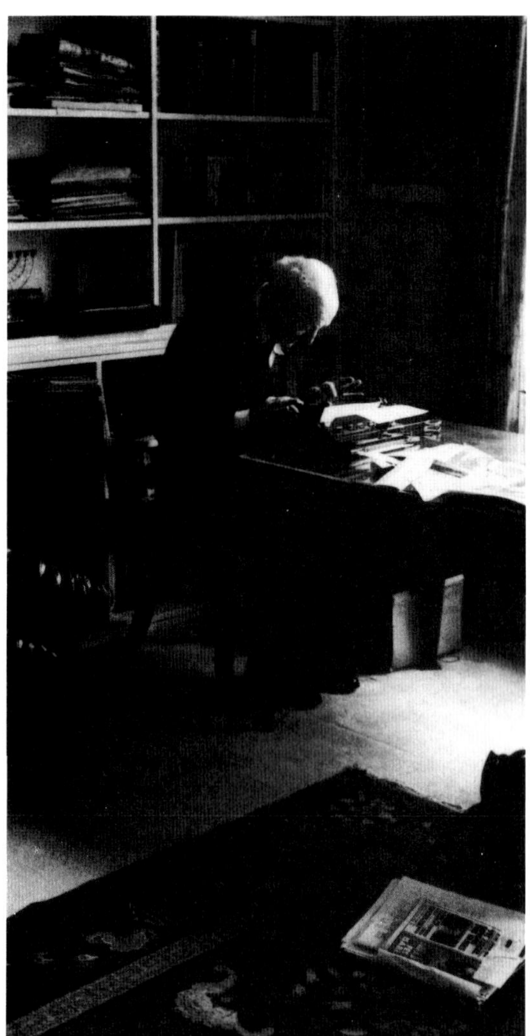

Photograph © 1988 by Jill Krementz.

In 1978 Singer was awarded the Nobel Prize for Literature. Among his best-known works are his novel *The Family Moskat* (1950) and his short-story collections *Gimpel the Fool* (1957), *The Spinoza of Market Street* (1961), *Enemies* (1970), and *A Crown of Feathers* (1973). He has also written volumes of memoirs and books for children. In 1982, his *Collected Stories* was published.

For all his success, Singer lived simply and spoke humbly. "When I began to write I was fifteen and I never heard of anybody making a living from writing. I am still surprised every time I get a check for a story."

SUPPLEMENTARY SUPPORT MATERIALS

1. Vocabulary Activity Worksheet (*CCB*)
2. Review and Response Worksheet: Setting and Conflict (*CCB*)
3. Language Skills Worksheet: Active and Passive Voice (*CCB*)
4. Selection Test (*CCB*)

DEVELOPING VOCABULARY

The following words from the story are tested in the Selection Test. (See also Vocabulary Activity Worksheet.)

rancid	to liquidate
degenerate	constricted
to evict	to obliterate

PREPARATION

ESTABLISHING A PURPOSE. After students have read the headnote and learned the setting of the story, suggest that they concentrate on the conflict in the story as they read it.

A. Character

? Is Bessie Insane? (Students' opinions will vary. Certainly, her fears are excessive, but whether she is actually insane is an open question.)

B. Conflict

? What seems to be the basic conflict in this story? (It seems to be between Bessie and her environment. See question 2, page 883.)

THE KEY

This story is set in the Upper West Side of New York City—a neighborhood that Singer himself had lived in for many years. Many people like Bessie can be seen there today—old people who live alone in a city that seems to ignore them. But Singer was a writer who was interested in redemption. He was also a writer who did not limit himself to realism. Watch what happens to Bessie.

1.

At about three o'clock in the afternoon, Bessie Popkin began to prepare to go down to the street. Going out was connected with many difficulties, especially on a hot summer day: first, forcing her fat body into a corset, squeezing her swollen feet into shoes, and combing her hair, which Bessie dyed at home and which grew wild and was streaked in all colors—yellow, black, gray, red; then making sure that while she was out her neighbors would not break into her apartment and steal linen, clothes, documents, or just disarrange things and make them disappear.

A

Besides human tormentors, Bessie suffered from demons, imps, Evil Powers. She hid her eyeglasses in the night table and found them in a slipper. She placed her bottle of hair dye in the medicine chest; days later she discovered it under the pillow. Once, she left a pot of borsch[1] in the refrigerator, but the Unseen took it from there and after long searching Bessie came upon it in her clothes closet. On its surface was a thick layer of fat that gave off the smell of rancid tallow.

What she went through, how many tricks were played on her and how much she had to wrangle in order not to perish or fall into insanity, only God knew. She had given up the telephone because racketeers and degenerates called her day and night, trying to get secrets out of her. . . . The errand boy from the grocery store attempted to burn her belongings with a cigarette. To evict her from the rent-controlled apartment where she had lived for thirty-five years, the company and the superintendent infested her rooms with rats, mice, cockroaches.

1. **borsch** (bôrsh): (also spelled *borscht*) a Russian beet soup, eaten hot or cold.

B

Bessie had long ago realized that no means were adequate against those determined to be spiteful—not the metal door, the special lock, her letters to the police, the mayor, the FBI, and even the President in Washington. But while one breathed one had to eat. It all took time: checking the windows, the gas vents, securing the drawers. Her paper money she kept in volumes of the encyclopedia, in back copies of the *National Geographic*, and in Sam Popkin's old ledgers. Her stocks and bonds Bessie had hidden among the logs in the fireplace, which was never used, as well as under the seats of the easy chairs. Her jewels she had sewn into the mattress. There was a time when Bessie had safe-deposit boxes at the bank, but she long ago convinced herself that the guards there had passkeys.

At about five o'clock, Bessie was ready to go out. She gave a last look at herself in the mirror—small, broad, with a narrow forehead, a flat nose, and eyes slanting and half closed, like a Chinaman's. Her chin sprouted a little white beard. She wore a faded dress in a flowered print, a misshapen straw hat trimmed with wooden cherries and grapes, and shabby shoes. Before she left, she made a final inspection of the three rooms and the kitchen. Everywhere there were clothes, shoes, and piles of letters that Bessie had not opened. Her husband, Sam Popkin, who had died almost twenty years ago, had liquidated his real estate business before his death, because he was about to retire to Florida. He left her stocks, bonds, and a number of passbooks from savings banks, as well as some mortgages. To this day, firms wrote to Bessie, sent her reports, checks. The Internal Revenue Service claimed taxes from her. Every few weeks she received announcements from a funeral company that sold plots in an "airy cemetery." In former years, Bessie used to answer

Comment From The Author

Singer tells how he created his characters: "I contemplate the people whom I have met in my life who would fit into this story. I sometimes combine two characters and from them make one. . . . I don't invent characters because the Almighty has already invented millions and billions of them."

For Further Reading For The Teacher

For a great many comments by Singer on the craft of writing, see Isaac Bashevis Singer and Richard Burgin's *Conversations with Isaac Bashevis Singer* (Doubleday & Company, Inc., 1985).

A. Point of View

The reader observes the world only through the eyes of Bessie Popkin, yet there is no *I*-narrator.

? Is the point of view of the story first-person or third-person? (It is third-person limited. Singer focuses on the thoughts and feelings of Bessie—no one else. The reader never sees Bessie through the eyes of the Irish super, for example, which could occur with an omniscient viewpoint.)

B. Setting

Because the setting is viewed through Bessie's eyes, nearly every part of it is viewed negatively.

? What are five things about the neighborhood that Bessie dislikes? (She dislikes the noise, the filth, the half-naked urchins, the Spanish-speaking men and women, the dogs barking, the cats meowing, the supermarkets, and much more.)

letters, deposit her checks, keep track of her income and expenses. Lately she had neglected it all. She even stopped buying the newspaper and reading the financial section.

A In the corridor, Bessie tucked cards with signs on them that only she could recognize between the door and the door frame. The keyhole she stuffed with putty. What else could she do—a widow without children, relatives, or friends? There was a time when the neighbors used to open their doors, look out, and laugh at her exaggerated care; others teased her. That had long passed. Bessie spoke to no one. She didn't see well, either. The glasses she had worn for years were of no use. To go to an eye doctor and be fitted for new ones was too much of an effort. Everything was difficult—even entering and leaving the elevator, whose door always closed with a slam.

B Bessie seldom went farther than two blocks from her building. The street between Broadway and Riverside Drive became noisier and filthier from day to day. Hordes of urchins ran around half naked. Dark men with curly hair and wild eyes quarreled in Spanish with little women whose bellies were always swollen in pregnancy. They talked back in rattling voices. Dogs barked, cats meowed. Fires broke out and fire engines, ambulances, and police cars drove up. On Broadway, the old groceries had been replaced by supermarkets, where food must be picked out and put in a wagon and one had to stand in line before the cashier.

God in heaven, since Sam died, New York, America—perhaps the whole world—was falling apart. All the decent people had left the neighborhood and it was overrun by a mob of thieves, robbers, whores. Three times Bessie's pocketbook had been stolen. When she reported it to the police, they just laughed. Every time one crossed the street, one risked one's life. Bessie took a step and stopped. Someone had advised her to use a cane, but she was far from considering herself an old woman or a cripple. Every few weeks she painted her nails red. At times, when the rheumatism left her in peace, she took clothes she used to wear from the closets, tried them on, and studied herself in the mirror.

Opening the door of the supermarket was impossible. She had to wait till someone held it for her. The supermarket itself was a place that only the Devil could have invented. The lamps burned with a glaring light. People pushing wagons were likely to knock down anyone in their path. The shelves were either too high or too low. The noise was deafening, and the contrast between the heat outside and the freezing temperature inside! It was a miracle that she didn't get pneumonia. More than anything else, Bessie was tortured by indecision. She picked up each item with a trembling hand and read the label. This was not the greed of youth but the uncertainty of age. According to Bessie's figuring, today's shopping should not have taken longer than three quarters of an hour, but two hours passed and Bessie was still not finished. When she finally brought the wagon to the cashier, it occurred to her that she had forgotten the box of oatmeal. She went back and a woman took her place in line. Later, when she paid, there was new trouble. Bessie had put the bill in the right side of her bag, but it was not there. After long rummaging, she found it in a small change purse on the opposite side. Yes, who could believe that such things were possible? If she told someone, he would think she was ready for the madhouse.

When Bessie went into the supermarket, the day was still bright; now it was drawing to a close. The sun, yellow and golden, was sinking toward the Hudson, to the hazy hills of New Jersey. The buildings on Broadway radiated the heat they had absorbed. From under gratings where the subway trains rumbled, evil-smelling fumes arose. Bessie held the heavy bag of food in one hand, and in the other she grasped her pocketbook tightly. Never had Broadway seemed to her so wild, so dirty. It stank of softened asphalt, gasoline, rotten fruit, the excrement of dogs. On the sidewalk, among torn newspapers and the butts of cigarettes, pigeons hopped about. It was difficult to understand how these creatures avoided being stepped on in the crush of passers-by. From the blazing sky a golden dust was falling. Before a storefront hung with artificial grass, men in sweated shirts poured papaya juice and pineapple juice into themselves with haste, as if trying to extinguish a fire that consumed their insides. Above their heads hung coconuts carved in the shapes of Indians. On a side street, black and white children had opened a hydrant and were splashing naked in the gutter. In the midst of that heat wave, a truck with microphones drove around blaring out shrill songs and deafening

Humanities Connection
Responding to the Fine Art

Larry Rivers (b. 1922) has had a varied career. He was a saxophonist with jazz bands in New York City in the early 1940's, then made the transition to painter in the 1950's. He has created Broadway set and costume designs, sculpted, and worked with film and video. He was a key figure in the transitional period between Abstract Expressionism and Pop Art.

? What kind of feeling do you get from this picture? What are the women doing? Is the picture a happy or a sad one? (The women appear to have been eating. They look out at us as if waiting for an answer. Their expressions seem serious, but this is balanced by the lightness and brightness of the scene. The picture seems neither happy nor sad, but some tentative state between the two.)

What connection might exist between the painting and the protagonist of Singer's "The Key"? (The women may resemble Bessie slightly, but the main connection may exist between the sketchy style and the incompleteness of Bessie's life.) Encourage students to compare the women. Are they related? (Call attention to the title, which suggests that they are the same person.)

A critic said of Rivers's paintings that they look "as if the artist were unable to focus on the actual subject for very long at a time." Do you agree? (Rivers appears to focus on those elements that are most essential to the composition and the feeling of the scene. Rather than flitting, as the critic implies, he seems to be stripping away irrelevant details in order to reach the essence of the scene.)

The Sitter by Larry Rivers (1956). Oil.

The Metropolitan Museum of Art, New York City. Gift of Hugo Kastor, 1956.

A. Complication
? What complication does Bessie's breaking the key introduce into the plot? (Bessie has no place to turn; she trusts no one. Yet if she is to get into her apartment, she will have to find help somewhere.)

B. Responding
? Why does Bessie revert to Yiddish, "that half-forgotten tongue," when she realizes her predicament? (Aristophanes, the Greek playwright, wrote that "old age is but a second childhood." Bessie, in her despair, says, "O dear Momma," as if longing for the security of childhood.)

C. Foreshadowing
Direct students' attention to the murmur that Bessie hears from her locked apartment. Undoubtedly it foreshadows something—but what? Does it come from the "demons, imps, Evil Powers" with which Bessie has to contend? (See question 7, page 883.)

D. Irony
? By now readers understand that Bessie will perceive any act of courtesy or kindness as one of her enemies' "sly tricks." What kind of irony is this? What does it tell you about Bessie's actual situation? (It is dramatic irony—the reader knows something a character does not. Very possibly there are kind, helpful people in Bessie's neighborhood.)

E. Simile
? To what is the impact of the heat of Broadway compared? (The heat slaps her "like a sheet of tin." Point out that the verb *slapped* is metaphorical [a dead metaphor, perhaps]; the image suggests a conscious intent to strike Bessie.)

blasts about a candidate for political office. From the rear of the truck, a girl with hair that stood up like wires threw out leaflets.

It was all beyond Bessie's strength—crossing the street, waiting for the elevator, and then getting out on the fifth floor before the door slammed. Bessie put the groceries down at the threshold and searched for her keys. She used her nail file to dig the putty out of the keyhole. She put in the key and turned it. But woe, the key broke. Only the handle remained in her hand. Bessie fully grasped the catastrophe. The other people in the building had copies of their keys hanging in the superintendent's apartment, but she trusted no one—some time ago, she had ordered a new combination lock, which she was sure no master key could open. She had a duplicate key somewhere in a drawer, but with her she carried only this one. "Well, this is the end," Bessie said aloud.

There was nobody to turn to for help. The neighbors were her blood enemies. The super only waited for her downfall. Bessie's throat was so constricted that she could not even cry. She looked around, expecting to see the fiend who had delivered this latest blow. Bessie had long since made peace with death, but to die on the steps or in the streets was too harsh. And who knows how long such agony could last? She began to ponder. Was there still open somewhere a store where they fitted keys? Even if there were, what could the locksmith copy from? He would have to come up here with his tools. For that, one needed a mechanic associated with the firm which produced these special locks. If at least she had money with her. But she never carried more than she needed to spend. The cashier in the supermarket had given her back only some twenty-odd cents. "O dear Momma, I don't want to live anymore!" Bessie spoke Yiddish, amazed that she suddenly reverted to that half-forgotten tongue.

After many hesitations, Bessie decided to go back down to the street. Perhaps a hardware store or one of those tiny shops that specialize in keys was still open. She remembered that there used to be such a key stand in the neighborhood. After all, other people's keys must get broken. But what should she do with the food? It was too heavy to carry with her. There was no choice. She would have to leave the bag at the door. "They steal anyhow," Bessie said to herself. Who knows, perhaps the neighbors intentionally manipulated her lock so that she would not be able to enter the apartment while they robbed her or vandalized her belongings.

Before Bessie went down to the street, she put her ear to the door. She heard nothing except a murmur that never stopped, the cause and origin of which Bessie could not figure out. Sometimes it ticked like a clock; other times it buzzed, or groaned—an entity imprisoned in the walls or the water pipes. In her mind Bessie said goodbye to the food, which should have been in the refrigerator, not standing here in the heat. The butter would melt, the milk would turn sour. "It's a punishment! I am cursed, cursed," Bessie muttered. A neighbor was about to go down in the elevator and Bessie signaled to him to hold the door for her. Perhaps he was one of the thieves. He might try to hold her up, assault her. The elevator went down and the man opened the door for her. She wanted to thank him, but remained silent. Why thank her enemies? These were all sly tricks.

When Bessie stepped out into the street, night had fallen. The gutter was flooded with water. The street lamps were reflected in the black pool as in a lake. Again there was a fire in the neighborhood. She heard the wailing of a siren, the clang of fire engines. Her shoes were wet. She came out on Broadway, and the heat slapped her like a sheet of tin. She had difficulty seeing in daytime; at night she was almost blind. There was light in the stores, but what they displayed Bessie could not make out. Passers-by bumped into her, and Bessie regretted that she didn't have a cane. Nevertheless, she began to walk along, close to the windows. She passed a drugstore, a bakery, a shop of rugs, a funeral parlor, but nowhere was there a sign of a hardware store. Bessie continued on her way. Her strength was ebbing, but she was determined not to give up. What should a person do when her key has broken off—die? Perhaps apply to the police. There might be some institution that took care of such cases. But where?

There must have been an accident. The sidewalk was crowded with spectators. Police cars and an ambulance blocked the street. Someone sprayed the asphalt with a hose, probably cleaning away the blood. It occurred to Bessie that the eyes of the onlookers gleamed with an uncanny satisfaction. They enjoy other people's misfortunes, she thought. It is their only comfort in this miserable city. No, she wouldn't find anybody to help her.

Reading Check Test

1. Bessie Popkin keeps her stocks and bonds (a) in a safe-deposit box (b) among the logs in the fireplace (c) in a closet *(b)*
2. Bessie loses her place in line at a supermarket because (a) she has forgotten oatmeal (b) she has misplaced her purse (c) a man pushes ahead of her *(a)*
3. After Bessie's key breaks, she (a) returns the groceries (b) takes the groceries to the super (c) leaves the groceries near her door *(c)*
4. During her night on the church steps, Bessie sees (a) a white butterfly (b) a black cat (c) a policeman *(a)*
5. While Bessie is away, a woman in a nearby apartment (a) steals her groceries (b) reports her missing (c) refrigerates the butter and milk *(c)*

She had come to a church. A few steps led to the closed door, which was protected by an overhang and darkened by shadows. Bessie was barely able to sit down. Her knees wobbled. Her shoes had begun to pinch in the toes and above the heels. A bone in her corset broke and cut into her flesh. "Well, all the Powers of Evil are upon me tonight." Hunger mixed with nausea gnawed at her. An acid fluid came up to her mouth. "Father in heaven, it's my end." She remembered the Yiddish proverb "If one lives without a reckoning, one dies without confession." She had even neglected to write her will.

2.

Bessie must have dozed off, because when she opened her eyes there was a late-night stillness, the street half empty and darkened. Store windows were no longer lit. The heat had evaporated and she felt chilly under her dress. For a moment she thought that her pocketbook had been stolen, but it lay on a step below her, where it had probably slipped. Bessie tried to stretch out her hand for it; her arm was numb. Her head, which rested against the wall, felt as heavy as a stone. Her legs had become wooden. Her ears seemed to be filled with water. She lifted one of her eyelids and saw the moon. It hovered low in the sky over a flat roof, and near it twinkled a greenish star. Bessie gaped. She had almost forgotten that there was a sky, a moon, stars. Years had passed and she never looked up—always down. Her windows were hung with draperies so that the spies across the street could not see her. Well, if there was a sky, perhaps there was also a God, angels, Paradise. Where else did the souls of her parents rest? And where was Sam now?

She, Bessie, had abandoned all her duties. She never visited Sam's grave in the cemetery. She didn't even light a candle on the anniversary of his death. She was so steeped in wrangling with the lower powers that she did not remember the higher ones. For the first time in years, Bessie felt the need to recite a prayer. The Almighty would have mercy on her even though she did not deserve it. Father and Mother might intercede for her on high. Some Hebrew words hung on the tip of her tongue, but she could not recall them. Then she remembered. "Hear, O Israel." But what followed? "God forgive me," Bessie said. "I deserve everything that falls on me."

It became even quieter and cooler. Traffic lights changed from red to green, but a car rarely passed. From somewhere a Negro appeared. He staggered. He stopped not far from Bessie and turned his eyes to her. Then he walked on. Bessie knew that her bag was full of important documents, but for the first time she did not care about her property. Sam had left a fortune; it all had gone for naught. She continued to save for her old age as if she were still young. "How old am I?" Bessie asked herself. "What have I accomplished in all these years? Why didn't I go somewhere, enjoy my money, help somebody?" Something in her laughed. "I was possessed, completely not myself. How else can it be explained?" Bessie was astounded. She felt as if she had awakened from a long sleep. The broken key had opened a door in her brain that had shut when Sam died.

The moon had shifted to the other side of the roof—unusually large, red, its face obliterated. It was almost cold now. Bessie shivered. She realized that she could easily get pneumonia, but the fear of death was gone, along with her fear of being homeless. Fresh breezes drifted from the Hudson River. New stars appeared in the sky. A black cat approached from the other side of the street. For a while, it stood on the edge of the sidewalk and its green eyes looked straight at Bessie. Then slowly and cautiously it drew near. For years Bessie had hated all animals—dogs, cats, pigeons, even sparrows. They carried sicknesses. They made everything filthy. Bessie believed that there was a demon in every cat. She especially dreaded an encounter with a black cat, which was always an omen of evil. But now Bessie felt love for this creature that had no home, no possessions, no doors or keys, and lived on God's bounty. Before the cat neared Bessie, it smelled her bag. Then it began to rub its back on her leg, lifting up its tail and meowing. The poor thing is hungry. I wish I could give her something. How can one hate a creature like this, Bessie wondered. A O Mother of mine, I was bewitched, bewitched. I'll begin a new life. A treacherous thought ran through her mind: perhaps remarry?

The night did not pass without adventure. Once, Bessie saw a white butterfly in the air. It hovered for a while over a parked car and then took off. Bessie knew it was a soul of a newborn baby, since real butterflies do not fly after dark. B

Closure

Have students write two or three sentences explaining their understanding of the cause of Bessie's redemption. Ask them to share their responses in class.

A. Responding

? Why does Bessie's attitude toward cats appear to change? (Bessie feels differently about the homeless, hungry black cat than about cats in general. Considering herself in the same position as the cat, she sympathizes with it.)

B. Symbol

? What does the white butterfly symbolize to Bessie? How does it differ from an ordinary symbol? (The white butterfly symbolizes "the soul of a newborn baby." It differs from an ordinary symbol in that [in Bessie's view] it is not a "real" butterfly at all—it *is* the baby's soul.)

ANALYZING THE STORY

Identifying Facts

1. Bessie is almost paranoid in her fear and suspicion of those around her. She has had her purse stolen three times by muggers, and she lives in constant fear, not only of her neighbors and people on the street, but also of the supernatural—"demons, imps, Evil Powers."

She suspects her neighbors of entering her apartment when she is not there, in order to steal or disarrange her belongings. She no longer uses the telephone because of the disturbing calls she used to receive. The errand boy from the grocery store tried to burn her belongings with a cigarette. The superintendent has infested her apartment with rats and cockroaches in an effort to evict her. Bessie hides her money and valuables in various places. She fortifies her apartment as if against an armed assault. She regards the people on the street suspiciously. She is afraid of the dogs and cats, the street traffic, and the noise. The city seems to her hot, dirty, and menacing.

2. Bessie's basic conflicts arise from fear and mistrust of those around her. She is in conflict with her environment. She is

A. Character
Although Bessie has changed, she may still harbor some suspicions. What may the "depleted" grocery bag suggest to her? (She may assume a thief has taken the items. She may not be concerned. It is unlikely that she guesses the truth.)

B. Responding
? How might Bessie have completed her sentence, "I didn't know that. . . "? (Answers may vary, but most students will say, in effect, that Bessie didn't know that she could turn to her neighbors for help.)

C. Resolution
? Why does Sam appear at the end of the story? (Sam's death had changed Bessie's world, making her frightened and suspicious. Sam's reappearance brings back the good days [even though apparently in death] when happiness and security required no elaborate defenses against others.)

Another time, she wakened to see a ball of fire, a kind of lit-up soap bubble, soar from one roof to another and sink behind it. She was aware that what she saw was the spirit of someone who had just died.

Bessie had fallen asleep. She woke up with a start. It was daybreak. From the side of Central Park the sun rose. Bessie could not see it from here, but on Broadway the sky became pink and reddish. On the building to the left, flames kindled in the windows; the panes ran and blinked like the portholes of a ship. A pigeon landed nearby. It hopped on its little red feet and pecked into something that might have been a dirty piece of stale bread or dried mud. Bessie was baffled. How do these birds live? Where do they sleep at night? And how can they survive the rains, the cold, the snow? I will go home, Bessie decided. People will not leave me in the streets.

Getting up was a torment. Her body seemed glued to the step on which she sat. Her back ached and her legs tingled. Nevertheless, she began to walk slowly toward home. She inhaled the moist morning air. It smelled of grass and coffee. She was no longer alone. From the side streets men and women emerged. They were going to work. They bought newspapers at the stand and went down into the subway. They were silent and strangely peaceful, as if they, too, had gone through a night of soul-searching and come out of it cleansed. When do they get up if they are already on their way to work now, Bessie marveled. No, not all in this neighborhood were gangsters and murderers. One young man even nodded good morning to Bessie. She tried to smile at him, realizing she had forgotten that feminine gesture she knew so well in her youth; it was almost the first lesson her mother had taught her.

She reached her building, and outside stood the Irish super, her deadly enemy. He was talking to the garbage collectors. He was a giant of a man, with a short nose, a long upper lip, sunken cheeks, and a pointed chin. His yellow hair covered a bald spot. He gave Bessie a startled look. "What's the matter, Grandma?"

Stuttering, Bessie told him what had happened to her. She showed him the handle of the key she had clutched in her hand all night.

"Mother of God!" he called out.

"What shall I do?" Bessie asked.

"I will open your door."

"But you don't have a passkey."

"We have to be able to open all doors in case of fire."

The super disappeared into his own apartment for a few mintues, then he came out with some tools and a bunch of keys on a large ring. He went up in the elevator with Bessie. The bag of food still stood on the threshold, but it looked depleted. The super busied himself at the lock. He asked, "What are these cards?"

Bessie did not answer.

"Why didn't you come to me and tell me what happened? To be roaming around all night at your age—my God!" As he poked with his tools, a door opened and a little woman in a housecoat and slippers, her hair bleached and done up in curlers, came out. She said, "What happened to you? Every time I opened the door, I saw this bag. I took out your butter and milk and put them in my refrigerator."

Bessie could barely restrain her tears. "Oh, my good people," she said. "I didn't know that . . ."

The super pulled out the other half of Bessie's key. He worked a little longer. He turned a key and the door opened. The cards fell down. He entered the hallway with Bessie and she sensed the musty odor of an apartment that has not been lived in for a long time. The super said, "Next time, if something like this happens call me. That's what I'm here for."

Bessie wanted to give him a tip, but her hands were too weak to open her bag. The neighbor woman brought in the milk and butter. Bessie went into her bedroom and lay down on the bed. There was a pressure on her breast and she felt like vomiting. Something heavy vibrated up from her feet to her chest. Bessie listened to it without alarm, only curious about the whims of the body; the super and the neighbor talked, and Bessie could not make out what they were saying. The same thing had happened to her over thirty years ago when she had been given anesthesia in the hospital before an operation—the doctor and the nurse were talking but their voices seemed to come from far away in a strange language.

Soon there was silence, and Sam appeared. It was neither day nor night—a strange twilight. In her dream, Bessie knew that Sam was dead but that in some clandestine way he had managed to get away from the grave and visit her. He was feeble and embarrassed. He could not speak. They wandered through a space without a sky, without

obsessed by the suspicion that she will be exploited or victimized.
3. When the key breaks in the lock, Bessie realizes that her chances of getting into her own apartment are slim. Because of her suspicions, she has ordered a new combination lock, which she is sure no master key will open. The neighbors and the superintendent will not help her, she thinks, because they are her enemies. She has no money to pay a locksmith, because she never carries any more money than she needs. Bessie is now forced to leave her food in the corridor, descend to the street, and wander all night, until she is so tired that she falls asleep on the steps of a church.
4. She sees a white butterfly, which she interprets as the soul of a newborn baby. She also sees a "ball of fire," a kind of soap bubble floating in the air, which she thinks is the soul of someone who has just died.
5. Bessie is sympathetic with the pigeon she sees, wondering how it can survive the rain, cold, and snow. She is confident that she can go home and that people will not leave her in the streets. She no longer feels alone. As she watches people going to work, they seem to her "silent and strangely peaceful, as if they, too, had gone through a night of soul-searching and come out of it cleansed." She admires the fact that they have risen so early to go to work, and she is forced to admit that not everyone in the neighborhood is a gangster or a murderer. Bessie tries to smile in response to a young man who nods good morning to her.
6. She experiences great weakness and a kind of seizure, as if she has been put under anesthesia. Then she has a vision of her dead husband, Sam, who walks with her. She hears the words she had heard on the night of her honeymoon, words about not needing a key. The storyteller implies that she dies and goes to heaven.

Interpreting Meanings
7. Perhaps her own soul.
The sound at this point foreshadows Bessie's encounter with the (*Answers continue on next page.*)

earth, a tunnel full of debris—the wreckage of a nameless structure—a corridor dark and winding, yet somehow familiar. They came to a region where two mountains met, and the passage between shone like sunset or sunrise. They stood there hesitating and even a little ashamed. It was like that night of their honeymoon when they went to Ellenville in the Catskills and were let by the hotel owner into their bridal suite. She heard the same words he had said to them then, in the same voice and intonation: "You don't need no key here. Just enter—and *mazel tov*."[2]

—Translated by the author and Evelyn Torton Beck

2. ***mazel tov*** (mä′zəl·tōv): Yiddish for "good luck."

Responding to the Story

Analyzing the Story

Identifying Facts

1. Describe the ways in which Bessie Popkin has isolated herself from her neighbors. Find the details that reveal that Bessie sees her **setting** as hostile and inhuman.
2. Describe Bessie's **conflicts.**
3. The key to the turning point of the story is an actual key. Explain how Bessie's suspicions shut her out of even her own home. What is she now forced to do?
4. Describe the miraculous signs from another world that Bessie sees during the night.
5. As Bessie goes home in the morning, how does the storyteller let us know that she is "cleansed," that she now sees the world in a new light?
6. What happens to Bessie at the end of the story?

Interpreting Meanings

7. As Bessie puts her head to the door on page 880, she hears a murmur. What is the sound? How does this **foreshadow** the ending?
8. As part 2 opens, Bessie awakens on the church steps. The first sign of a figurative "awakening" occurs when we read that she "gaped [because] she had almost forgotten that there was a sky, a moon, stars. Years had passed and she never looked up—always down." What does this last statement mean literally? Given what you know of Bessie, explain what it means **figuratively.**
9. We generally think of **comedies** as stories with happy endings. But comedy can also encompass many other kinds of plots. One critic, Northrop Frye, says that the theme of comedy is the integration of society: By the end of most comedies, a character is incorporated into a community. Given this theory, do you think Singer's story qualifies as an example of comedy? Explain why or why not.
10. How does Singer seem to feel about his characters—would you say he is sympathetic to them, or does he view them with irony and amusement? How do you feel about the people in "The Key"?

Writing About the Story

A Creative Response

1. **Adopting Another Point of View.** Although this story is told by an **omniscient narrator**, the **point of view** is limited to that of a single character. What observations might some of the other characters make about Bessie and her problems? (Include animals as characters in the story.) Write two or three paragraphs in which you relate specific incidents from the story, using the first-person point of view of another character.

A Critical Response

2. **Analyzing the Theme.** When Bessie sits on the steps, she remembers the Yiddish proverb, "If one lives without a reckoning, one dies without confession." Write an essay explaining what you think the proverb means and how it supports the main **theme** of Singer's story. Before you write, think about the following questions: What is a reckoning? In what way has Bessie lived without one? What is the symbolic meaning of the story's title? What confession does Bessie make?
3. **Relating the Speech to the Story.** In a brief essay, cite at least three points in Singer's Nobel lecture (see "Primary Sources," page 884) that relate to "The Key."
4. **Comparing Stories.** In a paragraph, explain how this story is like Eudora Welty's story "A Worn Path" (page 614) in at least two ways. Before you write, consider how each story uses these elements:

   a. Character
   b. A perilous journey
   c. A triumphant resolution
   d. A theme involving love

(Continued from previous page.)
supernatural at the end of the story, when, at the moment of her death, she has a vision of her husband Sam.

8. The literal meaning is that Bessie had been watching only earthbound things—the people and events in the city.

She'd been preoccupied with fear and suspicion. She'd rejected hope and love.

9. It seems to fulfill Frye's criterion. Bessie is reintegrated into society and even welcomed into heaven.

10. All three viewpoints can be found in the story: sympathy, irony, and amusement.

Analyzing Language and Style

Imagery

To help us imagine Bessie's urban setting, Singer uses many **images**—words or combinations of words that appeal to our senses of sight, smell, hearing, taste, or touch.

1. Look at the passage beginning "Never had Broadway seemed to her so wild, so dirty," on page 878. Read the rest of this passage, and list the images according to their sensory connection: sight, smell, hearing, taste, or touch.
2. Imagery is not merely decoration for a story; imagery can help a writer control the reader's feelings. After reading this passage, what feeling do you have for Bessie's setting?
3. In this story, the imagery is especially interesting because it reflects what the main character, Bessie, thinks of her setting. How would you describe Bessie's feelings about her neighborhood? Does the writer necessarily share these feelings?

Primary Sources

Nobel Prize Acceptance Speech, 1978

"The storyteller and poet of our time, as in any other time, must be an entertainer of the spirit in the full sense of the word, not just a preacher of social or political ideals. There is no paradise for bored readers and no excuse for tedious literature that does not intrigue the reader, uplift his spirit, give him the joy and the escape that true art always grants. Nevertheless, it is also true that the serious writer of our time must be deeply concerned about the problems of his generation. He cannot but see that the power of religion, especially belief in revelation, is weaker today than it was in any other epoch in human history. More and more children grow up without faith in God, without belief in reward and punishment, in the immortality of the soul, and even in the validity of ethics. The genuine writer cannot ignore the fact that the family is losing its spiritual foundation. All the dismal prophecies of Oswald Spengler have become realities since the Second World War. No technological achievements can mitigate the disappointment of modern man, his loneliness, his feeling of inferiority, and his fear of war, revolution, and terror. Not only has our generation lost faith in Providence, but also in man himself, in his institutions, and often in those who are nearest to him.

"In their despair a number of those who no longer have confidence in the leadership of our society look up to the writer, the master of words. They hope against hope that the man of talent and sensitivity can perhaps rescue civilization. Maybe there is a spark of the prophet in the artist after all.

"As the son of a people who received the worst blows that human madness can inflict, I have many times resigned myself to never finding a true way out. But a new hope always emerges, telling me that it is not yet too late for all of us to take stock and make a decision. I was brought up to believe in free will. Although I came to doubt all revelation, I can never accept the idea that the universe is a physical or chemical accident, a result of blind evolution. Even though I learned to recognize the lies, the cliches, and the idolatries of the human mind, I still cling to some truths which I think all of us might accept someday. There must be a way for man to attain all possible pleasures, all the powers and knowledge that nature can grant him, and still serve God—a God who speaks in deeds, not in words, and whose vocabulary is the universe.

"I am not ashamed to admit that I belong to those who fantasize that literature is capable of bringing new horizons and new perspectives—philosophical, religious, esthetical, and even social. In the history of old Jewish literature there was never any basic difference between the poet and the prophet. Our ancient poetry often became law and a way of life.

"Some of my cronies in the cafeteria near the *Jewish Daily Forward* in New York call me a pessimist and a decadent, but there is always a background of faith behind resignation. I found comfort in such pessimists and decadents as Baudelaire, Verlaine, Edgar Allan Poe, and Strindberg. My interest in psychic research made me find solace in such mystics as your Swedenborg and in our own Rabbi Nachman Bratzlaver, as well as in a great poet of my time, my friend Aaron Zeitlin, who died a few years ago and left a spiritual inheritance of high quality, most of it in Yiddish.

"The pessimism of the creative person is not decadence, but a mighty passion for the redemption of man. While the poet entertains he continues to search for eternal truths, for the essence of being. In his own fashion he tries to solve the riddle of time and change, to find an answer to suffering, to reveal love in the very abyss of cruelty and injustice. Strange as these words may sound, I often play with the idea that when all the social theories collapse and wars and revolutions leave humanity in utter gloom, the poet—whom Plato banned from his Republic—may rise up to save us all."

—Isaac Bashevis Singer

COMMENT FROM A CRITIC

Mark Shechner, reviewing *The Stories of Bernard Malamud* (1983), emphasizes Malamud's attention to the "sad music of humanity":

"It is a commonplace of criticism that [Malamud's characters] are ruined by circumstance, but it is less often observed that those circumstances are helped along by their own narrowness and rigidity.

"So deeply ingrained is this woe that it seems virtually biological. . . . But in the first postwar decade, it had the full sanction of the times and was well-nigh universal among Jewish writers and intellectuals. The sorrow that penetrates to the bone in Malamud was the mood of a generation of Jewish writers who had been raised in immigrant poverty and worldwide depression and brought abruptly to adulthood by the holocaust. Low spirits came as naturally to them as hunger or ambition or breath.

"But for some of those writers sorrow was a transient mood and a burden, and they were glad to be relieved of it in the 1950's when the prevailing conditions of life would no longer sustain the Dostoevskian migraines . . . [however], Malamud stood aside from the cavalcade of cheerfulness and let it pass unapplauded."

As students read "The Magic Barrel," see whether they agree with Shechner's belief that Malamud consistently sounds "the note of mourning" in his stories.

Bernard Malamud (1914–1986)

Bernard Malamud was one of the principal figures in the group of Jewish writers whose work has enriched American literature in the second half of the twentieth century. Yet Malamud preferred not to be so easily pigeon-holed. He did indeed write *about* Jews, but he wrote *for* all people.

Malamud's characters are usually discovered at some barren level of bare subsistence. Though we may feel compassion for them, they themselves do not display the least self-pity. If their plight is sad, it is also triumphant, because they are surviving in heroic fashion against the odds all humans face.

"As you are grooved, so you are grieved," Malamud once wrote as preamble to an account of his own bleak upbringing. He was the older of two sons of a Russian immigrant storekeeper. His mother died when he was fourteen. He grew up in Brooklyn in a household without books, music, or pictures on the wall. During the Great Depression, he worked at the census office and at a yarn factory to help support his family, but he felt these youthful deprivations were important to him as a writer. Getting down to essential needs and "turning inward," Malamud believed, are the best preparation for a career of making fiction.

It was the suffering of European Jews during World War II that convinced Malamud he had something to say as a writer. "I for one believe that not enough has been made of the tragedy of the destruction of six million Jews," he has said. "Somebody has to cry—even if it's a writer, twenty years later."

Malamud's unique drama is spun out of the commonplace, the tragicomedy of survival in a brutal world. But his stories are always informed by love and, indeed, his characters are largely redeemed by human love.

When he received the 1958 National Book Award for his collection of short stories called *The Magic Barrel*, Malamud spoke up for the contemporary individual: "I am quite tired of the colossally deceitful devaluation of man in this day. . . . Whatever the reason, his fall from

Photograph © 1988 by Jill Krementz.

grace in his eyes is betrayed by the words he has invented to describe himself as he is now: fragmented, abbreviated, other-directed, organizational. . . . The devaluation exists because he accepts it without protest."

Malamud taught English in New York City high schools and fiction at Oregon State University and Bennington College in Vermont. His first novel, *The Natural* (1952), whose central character is a baseball player, was made into a popular film in 1984. His other well-known books are *The Assistant* (1957), which some critics consider his best work, *The Fixer* (1966), and *The Tenants* (1971). He won, over the course of his career, the Pulitzer Prize and National Book Awards.

Malamud was a firm believer in the power of story and plot. "Writers who can't invent stories," he once said, "often pursue other strategies, even substituting style for narrative. I feel that story is the basic element of fiction, though that ideal is not popular with disciples of the 'new novel.' They remind me of the painter who couldn't paint people, so he painted chairs. The story will be with us as long as man is. You know that, in part, because of its effect on children. It's through story that they learn that mystery won't kill them. Through story they learn they have a future."

885

SUPPLEMENTARY SUPPORT MATERIALS

1. Vocabulary Activity Worksheet (*CCB*)
2. Review and Response Worksheet: Paradox (*CCB*)
3. Language Skills Worksheet: Adjective Clauses (*CCB*)
4. Selection Test (*CCB*)

DEVELOPING VOCABULARY

The following words from the story are tested in the Selection Test. (See also Vocabulary Activity Worksheet.)

broker	to avow
to guffaw	nuptial
to upbraid	enamored
clientele	profusion
protestation	machination

PREPARATION

ESTABLISHING A PURPOSE. As they read, students should pay close attention to the characters of Leo Finkle and Pinye Salzman, noticing how each of these men's lives is altered by the matchmaking encounter.

A. Humanities Connection: Responding to the Fine Art

Birthday by Marc Chagall (1887–1985) conveys the air of festive gaiety that the Russian-born artist felt about his approaching marriage to Bella, the woman in the picture. "I had only to open my bedroom window," wrote Chagall, "and blue air, love, and flowers entered with her." He regarded this painting as symbolic of the happiness that awaited the couple.

? Art critics in 1915 generally objected to the simplifications and distortions of anatomy with which Chagall's *Birthday* forms are rendered. What is your reaction to the painting? Do you find the figures crude and childish? Or do you agree with most modern critics, who find them charming, naive, and lyrical? (Answers will vary.)

THE MAGIC BARREL

Within the community of this story, a young person (or even an old person) wanting to marry might ask for the help of a matchmaker. For a fee, the matchmaker would produce a suitable mate. As you read the story, notice how Malamud helps you to picture these characters and their urban setting, and to hear the particular quality of their speech.

A

Birthday by Marc Chagall (1915). Oil on cardboard, 31¾″ × 39¼″. Collection, The Museum of Modern Art, New York. Acquired through the Lillie P. Bliss Bequest.

Not long ago there lived in uptown New York, in a small, almost meager room, though crowded with books, Leo Finkle, a rabbinical student in the Yeshiva University. Finkle, after six years of study, was to be ordained in June and had been advised by an acquaintance that he might find it easier to win himself a congregation if he were married. Since he had no present prospects of marriage, after two tormented days of turning it over in his mind, he called in Pinye Salzman, a marriage broker whose two-line advertisement he had read in the *Forward*.[1]

The matchmaker appeared one night out of the dark fourth-floor hallway of the graystone rooming house where Finkle lived, grasping a black, strapped portfolio that had been worn thin with use. Salzman, who had been long in the business, was of slight but dignified build, wearing an old hat, and an overcoat too short and tight for him. He smelled frankly of fish, which he loved to eat, and although he was missing a few teeth, his presence was not displeasing, because of an amiable manner curiously contrasted with mournful eyes. His voice, his lips, his wisp of beard, his bony fingers were animated, but give him a moment of repose and his mud blue eyes revealed a depth of sadness, a characteristic that put Leo a little at ease although the situation, for him, was inherently tense.

He at once informed Salzman why he had asked him to come, explaining that his home was in Cleveland, and that but for his parents, who had married comparatively late in life, he was alone in the world. He had for six years devoted himself almost entirely to his studies, as a result of which, understandably, he had found himself without time for a social life and the company of young women. Therefore he thought it the better part of trial and error—of embarrassing fumbling—to call in an experienced person to advise him on these matters. He remarked in passing that the function of the marriage broker was ancient and honorable, highly approved in the Jewish community, because it made practical the necessary without hindering joy. Moreover, his own parents had been brought together by a matchmaker. They had made, if not a financially profitable marriage—since neither had possessed any worldly goods to speak of—at least a successful one in the sense of their everlasting devotion to each other. Salzman listened in embarrassed surprise, sensing a sort of apology. Later, however, he experienced a glow of pride in his work, an emotion that had left him years ago, and he heartily approved of Finkle. C

The two went to their business. Leo had led Salzman to the only clear place in the room, a table near a window that overlooked the lamp-lit city. He seated himself at the matchmaker's side but facing him, attempting by an act of will to suppress the unpleasant tickle in his throat. Salzman eagerly unstrapped his portfolio and removed a loose rubber band from a thin packet of much-handled cards. As he flipped through them, a gesture and sound that physically hurt Leo, the student pretended not to see and gazed steadfastly out the window. Although it was still February, winter was on its last legs, signs of which he had for the first time in years begun to notice. He now observed the round white moon, moving high in the sky through a cloud menagerie, and watched with half-open mouth as it penetrated a huge hen, and dropped out of her like an egg laying itself. Salzman, though pretending through eyeglasses he had just slipped on, to be engaged in scanning the writing on the cards, stole occasional glances at the young man's distinguished face, noting with pleasure the long, severe scholar's nose, brown eyes heavy with learning, sensitive yet ascetic lips, and a certain, almost hollow quality of the dark cheeks. He gazed around at shelves upon shelves of books and let out a soft, contented sigh.

When Leo's eyes fell upon the cards, he counted six spread out in Salzman's hand.

"So few?" he asked in disappointment.

"You wouldn't believe me how much cards I got in my office," Salzman replied. "The drawers are already filled to the top, so I keep them now in a barrel, but is every girl good for a new rabbi?"

Leo blushed at this, regretting all he had revealed of himself in a curriculum vitae[2] he had sent to Salzman. He had thought it best to acquaint him with his strict standards and specifications, but in having done so, felt he had told the marriage broker more than was absolutely necessary.

1. ***Forward:*** the *Jewish Daily Forward*, a Yiddish newspaper in New York City.

2. **curriculum vitae** (vīt' ē): a résumé.

A. Exposition
Modern short stories typically begin with action or dialogue, but this one starts with exposition—information about the protagonist (Leo Finkle) and his problem.

B. Characterization
? What details about Salzman suggest that he is not prospering in his business? (His portfolio is worn thin with use. His hat is old; his clothes don't fit. He smells of fish and is missing a few teeth.)

C. Interpretation
? Why does Salzman heartily approve of Finkle? (Finkle is a rabbinical student, which is undoubtedly a plus in Salzman's eyes. Also, Finkle makes it a point to praise the function of matchmaker.)

A. Interpretation
Salzman tries to present each prospective bride in the best possible light.
? Why does he withhold information about the schoolteacher's age? What else that he included about the widow does he not mention for the school teacher? (No doubt he suspects that Leo will want a younger bride. Perceptive students may also note that Salzman was honest and direct in mentioning the widowhood of the 24-year-old woman, and that honesty caused the widow to be rejected. Salzman adjusts his presentation as he learns more about his client. For the schoolteacher there is no mention of a dowry.)

B. Characterization
Malamud's dialogue helps to characterize Leo Finkle.
? From the dialogue so far, what kind of woman does Leo seem to want? (He seems to want a young, attractive, never-married woman. The status and income of the prospective bride's family seem less important than her age and physical appearance. See question 3, page 896.)

He hesitantly inquired, "Do you keep photographs of your clients on file?"

"First comes family, amount of dowry, also what kind promises," Salzman replied, unbuttoning his tight coat and settling himself in the chair. "After comes pictures, rabbi."

"Call me Mr. Finkle. I'm not yet a rabbi."

Salzman said he would, but instead called him doctor, which he changed to rabbi when Leo was not listening too attentively.

Salzman adjusted his horn-rimmed spectacles, gently cleared his throat and read in an eager voice the contents of the top card:

"Sophie P. Twenty-four year. Widow one year. No children. Educated high school and two years college. Father promises eight thousand dollars. Has wonderful wholesale business. Also real estate. On the mother's side comes teachers, also one actor. Well known on Second Avenue."

Leo gazed up in surprise. "Did you say a widow?"

"A widow don't mean spoiled, rabbi. She lived with her husband maybe four months. He was a sick boy she made a mistake to marry him."

"Marrying a widow has never entered my mind."

"This is because you have no experience. A widow, especially if she is young and healthy like this girl, is a wonderful person to marry. She will be thankful to you the rest of her life. Believe me, if I was looking now for a bride, I would marry a widow."

Leo reflected, then shook his head.

Salzman hunched his shoulders in an almost imperceptible gesture of disappointment. He placed the card down on the wooden table and began to read another:

"Lily H. High school teacher. Regular. Not a substitute. Has savings and new Dodge car. Lived in Paris one year. Father is successful dentist thirty-five years. Interested in professional man. Well Americanized family. Wonderful opportunity.

"I knew her personally," said Salzman. "I wish you could see this girl. She is a doll. Also very intelligent. All day you could talk to her about books and theyater and what not. She also knows current events."

A ["I don't believe you mentioned her age?"

"Her age?" Salzman said, raising his brows. "Her age is thirty-two years."

Leo said after a while, "I'm afraid that seems a little too old."

Salzman let out a laugh. "So how old are you, rabbi?"

"Twenty-seven."

"So what is the difference, tell me, between twenty-seven and thirty-two? My own wife is seven years older than me. So what did I suffer? Nothing. If Rothschild's[3] daughter wants to marry you, would you say on account her age, no?"

"Yes," Leo said drily.

Salzman shook off the no in the yes. "Five years don't mean a thing. I give you my word that when you will live with her for one week you will forget her age. What does it mean five years—that she lived more and knows more than somebody who is younger? On this girl, God bless her, years are not wasted. Each one that it comes makes better the bargain."

"What subject does she teach in high school?"

"Languages. If you heard the way she speaks French, you will think it is music. I am in the business twenty-five years, and I recommend her with my whole heart. Believe me, I know what I'm talking, rabbi."

"What's on the next card?" Leo said abruptly.

Salzman reluctantly turned up the third card:

"Ruth K. Nineteen years. Honor student. Father offers thirteen thousand cash to the right bridegroom. He is a medical doctor. Stomach specialist with marvelous practice. Brother-in-law owns own garment business. Particular people."

Salzman looked as if he had read his trump card.

"Did you say nineteen?" Leo asked with interest.

"On the dot."

"Is she attractive?" He blushed. "Pretty?"] B

Salzman kissed his finger tips. "A little doll. On this I give you my word. Let me call the father tonight and you will see what means pretty."

But Leo was troubled. "You're sure she's that young?"

"This I am positive. The father will show you the birth certificate."

"Are you positive there isn't something wrong with her?" Leo insisted.

"Who says there is wrong?"

"I don't understand why an American girl her age should go to a marriage broker."

A smile spread over Salzman's face.

"So for the same reason you went, she comes."

3. **Rothschild:** name of a wealthy banking family.

Literature and Language: Describing with Adjectives
Malamud provides a wealth of details to help us picture Finkle, his room, Salzman, and the bridal candidates. Many of the details are provided by adjectives.

Ask students to tell what they "see" when they picture a room. Because the noun *room* is so general, some vastly different images will arise; the room may be small, large, sunny, gloomy, empty, cluttered, clean, or messy, for example. Explain that adjectives sharpen our mental picture by giving additional information about the general noun.

Also note that a participle is an adjective because it modifies a noun or pronoun:

Finkle was a *graduating* rabbi.
Salzman carried a *worn* portfolio.

Have students turn to the descriptions of the main characters (Finkle, Salzman, and Stella) and think of some additional adjectives, including participles, that Malamud might have used.

Leo flushed. "I am pressed for time."

Salzman, realizing he had been tactless, quickly explained. "The father came, not her. He wants she should have the best, so he looks around himself. When we will locate the right boy he will introduce him and encourage. This makes a better marriage than if a young girl without experience takes for herself. I don't have to tell you this."

"But don't you think this young girl believes in love?" Leo spoke uneasily.

Salzman was about to guffaw but caught himself and said soberly, "Love comes with the right person, not before."

Leo parted dry lips but did not speak. Noticing that Salzman had snatched a glance at the next card, he cleverly asked, "How is her health?"

"Perfect," Salzman said, breathing with difficulty. "Of course, she is a little lame on her right foot from an auto accident that it happened to her when she was twelve years, but nobody notices on account she is so brilliant and also beautiful."

Leo got up heavily and went to the window. He felt curiously bitter and upbraided himself for having called in the marriage broker. Finally, he shook his head.

"Why not?" Salzman persisted, the pitch of his voice rising.

"Because I detest stomach specialists."

"So what do you care what is his business? After you marry her do you need him? Who says he must come every Friday night in your house?"

Ashamed of the way the talk was going, Leo dismissed Salzman, who went home with heavy, melancholy eyes.

Though he had felt only relief at the marriage broker's departure, Leo was in low spirits the next day. He explained it as arising from Salzman's failure to produce a suitable bride for him. He did not care for his type of clientele. But when Leo found himself hesitating whether to seek out another matchmaker, one more polished than Pinye, he wondered if it could be—his protestations to the contrary, and although he honored his father and mother—that he did not, in essence, care for the matchmaking institution? This thought he quickly put out of mind yet found himself still upset. All day he ran around in the woods—missed an important appointment, forgot to give out his laundry, walked out of a Broadway cafeteria without paying and had to run back with the ticket in his hand; had even not recognized his landlady in the street when she passed with a friend and courteously called out, "A good evening to you, Doctor Finkle." By nightfall, however, he had regained sufficient calm to sink his nose into a book and there found peace from his thoughts.

Almost at once there came a knock on the door. Before Leo could say enter, Salzman, commercial cupid, was standing in the room. His face was gray and meager, his expression hungry, and he looked as if he would expire on his feet. Yet the marriage broker managed, by some trick of the muscles, to display a broad smile.

"So good evening. I am invited?"

Leo nodded, disturbed to see him again, yet unwilling to ask the man to leave.

Beaming still, Salzman laid his portfolio on the table. "Rabbi, I got for you tonight good news."

"I've asked you not to call me rabbi. I'm still a student."

"Your worries are finished. I have for you a first-class bride."

"Leave me in peace concerning this subject." Leo pretended lack of interest.

"The world will dance at your wedding."

"Please, Mr. Salzman, no more."

"But first must come back my strength," Salzman said weakly. He fumbled with the portfolio straps and took out of the leather case an oily paper bag, from which he extracted a hard, seeded roll and a small, smoked white fish. With a quick motion of his hand he stripped the fish out of its skin and began ravenously to chew. "All day in a rush," he muttered.

Leo watched him eat.

"A sliced tomato you have maybe?" Salzman hesitantly inquired.

"No."

The marriage broker shut his eyes and ate. When he had finished he carefully cleaned up the crumbs and rolled up the remains of the fish, in the paper bag. His spectacled eyes roamed the room until he discovered, amid some piles of books, a one-burner gas stove. Lifting his hat he humbly asked, "A glass tea you got, rabbi?"

Conscience-stricken, Leo rose and brewed the tea. He served it with a chunk of lemon and two cubes of lump sugar, delighting Salzman.

After he had drunk his tea, Salzman's strength and good spirits were restored.

B

"So tell me, rabbi," he said amiably, "you considered some more the three clients I mentioned yesterday?"

A. Plot Complication
Everything cannot go smoothly in a story; there have to be complications. Finkle's search for a bride is sure to lead to complications. When "Leo got up heavily and went to the window," the reader senses a complication.

? What is the complication? (Leo, dissatisfied with Salzman's prospective brides, sees his marriage-broker plan is not working out.)

B. Characterization
Malamud is famous for his schlemiels. A *schlemiel* is a habitual bungler, a dolt, a person who is always saying or doing the wrong thing.

? Is Salzman a schlemiel, and, if so, why? (Salzman would seem to qualify as a schlemiel. His eating a whitefish bag lunch in Leo's apartment and asking for a sliced tomato and tea are a couple of the typically inappropriate acts of a schlemiel.)

A. Dialogue

? In addition to reducing Lily's age by three years, Salzman evidently says something that whets Leo's interest in the schoolteacher. What might it be? (The most likely answer is that she "talks on all subjects." On the date, Leo notes her conversation approvingly, finding her "surprisingly sound.")

B. Exaggeration

Leo has become convinced that Salzman is so concerned with his marriage prospects that he may be "hiding perhaps high in a tree" observing Leo's date with Lily. He even pictures Salzman as "a cloven-hoofed Pan" bent on forcing a wedding. These exaggerated imaginings are funny; they also foreshadow the story's final scene.

"There was no need to consider."

"Why not?"

"None of them suits me."

"What then suits you?"

Leo let it pass because he could give only a confused answer.

Without waiting for a reply, Salzman asked, "You remember this girl I talked to you—the high school teacher?"

"Age thirty-two?"

But, surprisingly, Salzman's face lit in a smile. "Age twenty-nine."

Leo shot him a look. "Reduced from thirty-two?"

"A mistake," Salzman avowed. "I talked today with the dentist. He took me to his safety deposit box and showed me the birth certificate. She was twenty-nine years last August. They made her a party in the mountains where she went for her vacation. When her father spoke to me the first time I forgot to write the age and I told you thirty-two, but now I remember this was a different client, a widow."

"The same one you told me about? I thought she was twenty-four?"

"A different. Am I responsible that the world is filled with widows?"

"No, but I'm not interested in them, nor for that matter, in school teachers."

Salzman pulled his clasped hands to his breast. Looking at the ceiling he devoutly exclaimed, "Yiddishe kinder,[4] what can I say to somebody that he is not interested in high school teachers? So what then you are interested?"

Leo flushed but controlled himself.

A "In what else will you be interested," Salzman went on, "if you not interested in this fine girl that she speaks four languages and has personally in the bank ten thousand dollars? Also her father guarantees further twelve thousand. Also she has a new car, wonderful clothes, talks on all subjects, and she will give you a first-class home and children. How near do we come in our life to paradise?"

"If she's so wonderful, why wasn't she married ten years ago?"

"Why?" said Salzman with a heavy laugh. "Why? Because she is *partikiler*. This is why. She wants the *best*."

Leo was silent, amused at how he had entangled himself. But Salzman had aroused his interest in Lily H., and he began seriously to consider calling on her. When the marriage broker observed how intently Leo's mind was at work on the facts he had supplied, he felt certain they would soon come to an agreement.

Late Saturday afternoon, conscious of Salzman, Leo Finkle walked with Lily Hirschorn along Riverside Drive. He walked briskly and erectly, wearing with distinction the black fedora[5] he had that morning taken with trepidation out of the dusty hat box on his closet shelf, and the heavy black Saturday coat he had thoroughly whisked clean. Leo also owned a walking stick, a present from a distant relative, but quickly put temptation aside and did not use it. Lily, petite and not unpretty, had on something signifying the approach of spring. She was au courant,[6] animatedly, with all sorts of subjects, and he weighed her words and found her surprisingly sound—score another for Salzman, whom he uneasily sensed to be somewhere around, hiding perhaps high in a tree along the street, flashing the lady signals with a pocket mirror; or perhaps a cloven-hoofed Pan,[7] piping nuptial ditties as he danced his invisible way before them, strewing wild buds on the walk and purple grapes in their path, symbolizing fruit of a union, though there was of course still none.

Lily startled Leo by remarking, "I was thinking of Mr. Salzman, a curious figure, wouldn't you say?"

Not certain what to answer, he nodded.

She bravely went on, blushing, "I for one am grateful for his introducing us. Aren't you?"

He courteously replied, "I am."

"I mean," she said with a little laugh—and it was all in good taste, or at least gave the effect of being not in bad—"do you mind that we came together so?"

He was not displeased with her honesty, recognizing that she meant to set the relationship aright, and understanding that it took a certain amount of experience in life, and courage, to want

4. **Yiddishe kinder:** Yiddish for "Jewish child."

5. **fedora:** a soft hat, usually made of felt, with a curved brim.

6. **au courant** (ō·k$\overline{oo}$·rôh(n)′): a French expression, meaning "knowledgeable" or "abreast of current events."

7. **Pan:** in ancient Greek mythology, a god of the woodlands who was associated with music and weddings.

to do it quite that way. One had to have some sort of past to make that kind of beginning.

He said that he did not mind. Salzman's function was traditional and honorable—valuable for what it might achieve, which, he pointed out, was frequently nothing.

Lily agreed with a sigh. They walked on for a while and she said after a long silence, again with a nervous laugh, "Would you mind if I asked you something a little bit personal? Frankly, I find the subject fascinating." Although Leo shrugged, she went on half embarrassedly, "How was it that you came to your calling? I mean was it a sudden passionate inspiration?"

Leo, after a time, slowly replied, "I was always interested in the Law."

"You saw revealed in it the presence of the Highest?"

He nodded and changed the subject. "I understand that you spent a little time in Paris, Miss Hirschorn?"

"Oh, did Mr. Salzman tell you, Rabbi Finkle?" Leo winced but she went on, "It was ages ago and almost forgotten. I remember I had to return for my sister's wedding."

And Lily would not be put off. "When," she asked in a trembly voice, "did you become enamored of God?"

He stared at her. Then it came to him that she was talking not about Leo Finkle, but of a total stranger, some mystical figure, perhaps even passionate prophet that Salzman had dreamed up for her—no relation to the living or dead. Leo trembled with rage and weakness. The trickster had obviously sold her a bill of goods, just as he had him, who'd expected to become acquainted with a young lady of twenty-nine, only to behold, the moment he laid eyes upon her strained and anxious face, a woman past thirty-five and aging rapidly. Only his self-control had kept him this long in her presence.

"I am not," he said gravely, "a talented religious person," and in seeking words to go on, found himself possessed by shame and fear. "I think," he said in a strained manner, "that I came to God not because I loved Him, but because I did not."

This confession he spoke harshly because its unexpectedness shook him.

Lily wilted. Leo saw a profusion of loaves of bread go flying like ducks high over his head, not unlike the winged loaves by which he had counted himself to sleep last night. Mercifully, then, it snowed, which he would not put past Salzman's machinations.

He was infuriated with the marriage broker and swore he would throw him out of the room the minute he reappeared. But Salzman did not come that night, and when Leo's anger had subsided, an unaccountable despair grew in its place. At first he thought this was caused by his disappointment in Lily, but before long it became evident that he had involved himself with Salzman without a true knowledge of his own intent. He gradually realized—with an emptiness that seized him with six hands—that he had called in the broker to find him a bride because he was incapable of doing it himself. This terrifying insight he had as a result of his meeting and conversation with Lily Hirschorn. Her probing questions had somehow irritated him into revealing—to himself more than her—the true nature of his relationship to God, and from that it had come upon him, with shocking force, that apart from his parents, he had never loved anyone. Or perhaps it went the other way, that he did not love God so well as he might, because he had not loved man. It seemed to Leo that his whole life stood starkly revealed and he saw himself for the first time as he truly was—unloved and loveless. This bitter but somehow not fully unexpected revelation brought him to a point of panic, controlled only by extraordinary effort. He covered his face with his hands and cried.

The week that followed was the worst in his life. He did not eat and lost weight. His beard darkened and grew ragged. He stopped attending seminars and almost never opened a book. He seriously considered leaving the Yeshiva, although he was deeply troubled at the thought of the loss of all his years of study—saw them like pages torn from a book, strewn over the city—and at the devastating effect of this decision upon his parents. But he had lived without knowledge of himself, and never in the Five Books[8] and all the Commentaries—mea culpa[9]—had the truth been revealed to him. He did not know where to turn, and in all this desolating loneliness there was no *to whom*, although he often thought of Lily but not once could bring himself to go downstairs and

B

8. **Five Books:** the Torah, or the first five books of the Bible, revered by Jews as the holiest of the scriptures.
9. **mea culpa:** Latin for "my own fault."

A. Conflict
A story may have many conflicts. At this point in the story, the conflict is between what Leo and Lily consider important.
? What does Lily want to talk about? What does Leo want to talk about? (Lily wants to talk about Leo's "calling," his supposed love of God. Leo wants to talk about Paris—that is, about things of the world.)

B. Point of View
? Why do you think Malamud chose a third-person point of view in this story rather than first person, even though everything is seen through the eyes of Leo Finkle? (Students may have differing opinions. In general, a third-person limited point of view distances the author from the protagonist to some extent, whereas first-person narration inevitably sounds autobiographical.)

A. Metaphor
What makes "the world snowed on him" an effective metaphor in this situation? (Salzman, a schlemiel, is always encountering disasters. The image of his being struck by a snowstorm that turns his face white—that is, being accused of lying by his "rabbi" client—is very effective.)

B. Interpretation
Why does Salzman hurry away after leaving the manila envelope? (He knows that Leo wants nothing more to do with him, but he hopes that by leaving the envelope, Leo will reconsider.)

make the call. He became touchy and irritable, especially with his landlady, who asked him all manner of personal questions; on the other hand, sensing his own disagreeableness, he waylaid her on the stairs and apologized abjectly, until mortified, she ran from him. Out of this, however, he drew the consolation that he was a Jew and that a Jew suffered. But gradually, as the long and terrible week drew to a close, he regained his composure and some idea of purpose in life: to go on as planned. Although he was imperfect, the ideal was not. As for his quest of a bride, the thought of continuing afflicted him with anxiety and heartburn, yet perhaps with this new knowledge of himself he would be more successful than in the past. Perhaps love would now come to him and a bride to that love. And for this sanctified seeking who needed a Salzman?

The marriage broker, a skeleton with haunted eyes, returned that very night. He looked, withal, the picture of frustrated expectancy—as if he had steadfastly waited the week at Miss Lily Hirschorn's side for a telephone call that never came.

Casually coughing, Salzman came immediately to the point: "So how did you like her?"

Leo's anger rose and he could not refrain from chiding the matchmaker: "Why did you lie to me, Salzman?"

A Salzman's pale face went dead white, the world had snowed on him.

"Did you not state that she was twenty-nine?" Leo insisted.

"I give you my word—"

"She was thirty-five, if a day. *At least* thirty-five."

"Of this don't be too sure. Her father told me—"

"Never mind. The worst of it was that you lied to her."

"How did I lie to her, tell me?"

"You told her things about me that weren't true. You made me out to be more, consequently less than I am. She had in mind a totally different person, a sort of semi-mystical Wonder Rabbi."

"All I said, you was a religious man."

"I can imagine."

Salzman sighed. "This is my weakness that I have," he confessed. "My wife says to me I shouldn't be a salesman, but when I have two fine people that they would be wonderful to be married, I am so happy that I talk too much." He smiled wanly. "This is why Salzman is a poor man."

Leo's anger left him. "Well, Salzman, I'm afraid that's all."

The marriage broker fastened hungry eyes on him.

"You don't want anymore a bride?"

"I do," said Leo, "but I have decided to seek her in a different way. I am no longer interested in an arranged marriage. To be frank, I now admit the necessity of premarital love. That is, I want to be in love with the one I marry."

"Love?" said Salzman, astounded. After a moment he remarked, "For us, our love is our life, not for the ladies. In the ghetto they—"

"I know, I know," said Leo. "I've thought of it often. Love, I have said to myself, should be a by-product of living and worship rather than its own end. Yet for myself I find it necessary to establish the level of my need and fulfill it."

Salzman shrugged but answered, "Listen, rabbi, if you want love, this I can find for you also. I have such beautiful clients that you will love them the minute your eyes will see them."

Leo smiled unhappily. "I'm afraid you don't understand."

But Salzman hastily unstrapped his portfolio and withdrew a manila packet from it.

"Pictures," he said, quickly laying the envelope on the table.

Leo called after him to take the pictures away, but as if on the wings of the wind, Salzman had disappeared. B

March came. Leo had returned to his regular routine. Although he felt not quite himself yet—lacked energy—he was making plans for a more active social life. Of course it would cost something, but he was an expert in cutting corners; and when there were no corners left he would make circles rounder. All the while Salzman's pictures had lain on the table, gathering dust. Occasionally as Leo sat studying, or enjoying a cup of tea, his eyes fell on the manila envelope, but he never opened it.

The days went by and no social life to speak of developed with a member of the opposite sex—it was difficult, given the circumstances of his situation. One morning Leo toiled up the stairs of his room and stared out the window at the city. Although the day was bright his view of it was dark. For some time he watched the people in the street below hurrying along and then turned with a heavy heart to his little room. On the table was the packet. With a sudden relentless gesture he tore it open. For a half-hour he stood by the table in a state of excitement, examining the photographs of the ladies Salzman had included. Finally, with a deep sigh he put them down. There were six, of varying degrees of attractiveness, but look at them long enough and they all became Lily Hirschorn: all past their prime, all starved behind bright smiles, not a true personality in the lot. Life, despite their frantic yoohooings, had passed them by; they were pictures in a brief case that stank of fish. After a while, however, as Leo attempted to return the photographs into the envelope, he found in it another, a snapshot of the type taken by a machine for a quarter. He gazed at it a moment and let out a cry.

Her face deeply moved him. Why, he could at first not say. It gave him the impression of youth—spring flowers, yet age—a sense of having been used to the bone, wasted; this came from the eyes, which were hauntingly familiar, yet absolutely strange. He had a vivid impression that he had met her before, but try as he might he could not place her although he could almost recall her name, as if he had read it in her own handwriting. No, this couldn't be; he would have remembered her. It was not, he affirmed, that she had an extraordinary beauty—no, though her face was attractive enough; it was that *something* about her moved him. Feature for feature, even some of the ladies of the photographs could do better; but she leaped forth to his heart—had *lived*, or wanted to—more than just wanted, perhaps regretted how she had lived—had somehow deeply suffered: It could be seen in the depths of those reluctant eyes, and from the way the light enclosed and shone from her, and within her, opening realms of possibility: This was her own. Her he desired. His head ached and eyes narrowed with the intensity of his gazing, then as if an obscure fog had blown up in the mind, he experienced fear of her and was aware that he had received an impression, somehow, of evil. He shuddered, saying softly, it is thus with us all. Leo brewed some tea in a small pot and sat sipping it without sugar, to calm himself. But before he had finished drinking, again with excitement he examined the face and found it good: good for Leo Finkle. Only such a one could understand him and help him seek whatever he was seeking. She might, perhaps, love him. How she had happened to be among the discards in Salzman's barrel he could never guess, but he knew he must urgently go find her.

Leo rushed downstairs, grabbed up the Bronx telephone book, and searched for Salzman's home address. He was not listed, nor was his office. Neither was he in the Manhattan book. But Leo remembered having written down the address on a slip of paper after he had read Salzman's advertisement in the "personals" column of the *Forward*. He ran up to his room and tore through his papers, without luck. It was exasperating. Just when he needed the matchmaker he was nowhere to be found. Fortunately Leo remembered to look in his wallet. There on a card he found his name written and a Bronx address. No phone number was listed, the reason—Leo now recalled—he had originally communicated with Salzman by letter. He got on his coat, put a hat on over his skull cap and hurried to the subway station. All the way to the far end of the Bronx he sat on the edge of his seat. He was more than once tempted to take out the picture and see if the girl's face was as he remembered it, but he refrained, allowing the snapshot to remain in his inside coat pocket, content to have her so close. When the train pulled into the station he was waiting at the door and bolted out. He quickly located the street Salzman had advertised. B

The building he sought was less than a block from the subway, but it was not an office building, nor even a loft, nor a store in which one could rent office space. It was a very old tenement house. Leo found Salzman's name in pencil on a soiled tag under the bell and climbed three dark flights to his apartment. When he knocked, the door was opened by a thin, asthmatic, gray-haired woman, in felt slippers.

"Yes?" she said, expecting nothing. She listened without listening. He could have sworn he had seen her, too, before but knew it was an illusion. C

"Salzman—does he live here? Pinye Salzman," he said, "the matchmaker?"

She stared at him a long minute. "Of course."

He felt embarrassed. "Is he in?"

"No." Her mouth, though left open, offered nothing more.

"The matter is urgent. Can you tell me where his office is?"

A. Foreshadowing
Leo has a vivid impression that he has seen the woman in the photograph before, but at the same time he is sure he hasn't. As in many cases of foreshadowing, only a perceptive reader will draw the correct conclusion from this clue. See question 4, page 896.

B. Setting
? What do Salzman's lack of a telephone number and the very old tenement in which he lives tell the reader about his matchmaking business? (It isn't prospering.)

C. Foreshadowing
The reader learns that Leo thinks he has seen Mrs. Salzman somewhere before—in addition to having seen the woman in the photograph. Leo concludes that this is "an illusion," but a shrewd reader should suspect otherwise.

CLOSURE

Ask students to write two or three sentences describing the character of Salzman's daughter, as they understand it. Discuss these opinions about Stella in class.

READING CHECK TEST

1. The favorite food of Pinye Salzman, the matchmaker, is ______. *fish*

2. Leo wants Pinye to call him "Mr. Finkle," because he has not yet become ______. *a rabbi*

3. At first Leo is not interested in "Lily H.," the high school teacher, saying that she is ______. *too old*

4. In response to Lily's questions, Leo says that he decided to study at Yeshiva because he was *not* enamored of ______. *God*

5. At the very end of the story, Pinye Salzman is chanting prayers for ______. *the dead*

A. Title
Salzman told Finkle earlier that he keeps his files in a barrel whose magic assures happiness. Now Leo finds that there is no such barrel. You may want to have your students discuss why Malamud titled his story "The Magic Barrel." See question 10, page 896.

B. Interpretation
? What does Salzman mean by, "For her to be poor was a sin. This is why to me she is dead now"? (Salzman is a poor man. His daughter could not accept the family's poverty. To escape, she has become "wild, without shame." Presumably—although it is not made explicit—she has become some kind of sexual adventuress. In any case, her transgression is serious enough that she is now "dead" to Salzman—he has nothing to do with her any longer.)

"In the air." She pointed upward.

"You mean he has no office?" Leo asked.

"In his socks."

He peered into the apartment. It was sunless and dingy, one large room divided by a half-open curtain, beyond which he could see a sagging metal bed. The near side of the room was crowded with rickety chairs, old bureaus, a three-legged table, racks of cooking utensils, and all the apparatus of a kitchen. But there was no sign of Salzman or his magic barrel, probably also a figment of the imagination. An odor of frying fish made Leo weak to the knees.

"Where is he?" he insisted. "I've got to see your husband."

At length she answered, "So who knows where he is? Everytime he thinks a new thought he runs to a different place. Go home, he will find you."

"Tell him Leo Finkle."

She gave no sign she had heard.

He walked downstairs, depressed.

But Salzman, breathless, stood waiting at his door.

Leo was astounded and overjoyed. "How did you get here before me?"

"I rushed."

"Come inside."

They entered. Leo fixed tea, and a sardine sandwich for Salzman. As they were drinking he reached behind him for the packet of pictures and handed them to the marriage broker.

Salzman put down his glass and said expectantly, "You found somebody you like?"

"Not among these."

The marriage broker turned away.

"Here is the one I want." Leo held forth the snapshot.

Salzman slipped on his glasses and took the picture into his trembling hand. He turned ghastly and let out a groan.

"What's the matter?" cried Leo.

"Excuse me. Was an accident this picture. She isn't for you."

Salzman frantically shoved the manila packet into his portfolio. He thrust the snapshot into his pocket and fled down the stairs.

Leo, after momentary paralysis, gave chase and cornered the marriage broker in the vestibule. The landlady made hysterical outcries but neither of them listened.

"Give me back the picture, Salzman."

"No." The pain in his eyes was terrible.

"Tell me who she is then."

"This I can't tell you. Excuse me."

He made to depart, but Leo, forgetting himself, seized the matchmaker by his tight coat and shook him frenziedly.

"Please," sighed Salzman. *"Please."*

Leo ashamedly let him go. "Tell me who she is," he begged. "It's very important for me to know."

"She is not for you. She is a wild one—wild, without shame. This is not a bride for a rabbi."

"What do you mean wild?"

"Like an animal. Like a dog. For her to be poor was a sin. This is why to me she is dead now."

"In God's name, what do you mean?"

"Her I can't introduce to you," Salzman cried.

"Why are you so excited?"

"Why, he asks," Salzman said, bursting into tears. "This is my baby, my Stella, she should burn in hell."

Leo hurried up to bed and hid under the covers. Under the covers he thought this life through. Although he soon fell asleep he could not sleep her out of his mind. He woke, beating his breast. Though he prayed to be rid of her, his prayers went unanswered. Through days of torment he endlessly struggled not to love her; fearing success, he escaped it. He then concluded to convert her to goodness, himself to God. The idea alternately nauseated and exalted him.

He perhaps did not know that he had come to a final decision until he encountered Salzman in a Broadway cafeteria. He was sitting alone at a rear table, sucking the bony remains of a fish. The marriage broker appeared haggard, and transparent to the point of vanishing.

Salzman looked up at first without recognizing him. Leo had grown a pointed beard and his eyes were weighted with wisdom.

"Salzman," he said, "love has at last come to my heart."

"Who can love from a picture?" mocked the marriage broker.

"It is not impossible."

"If you can love her, then you can love anybody. Let me show you some new clients that they just sent me their photographs. One is a little doll."

Analyzing The Story

Identifying Facts

1. The protagonist is a young rabbinical student named Leo Finkle, who lives in New York City. About to be ordained, he thinks it will be easier to find employment with a congregation if he is married. After two days of thinking about the matter, he answers the advertisement of a marriage broker named Pinye Salzman in the *Jewish Daily Forward.*

2. Salzman appears one night "out of the dark," perhaps implying adverse circumstances or a tragic past. His coat is old and his overcoat fits badly. He smells of fish, and his eyes are mournful, reflecting a "depth of sadness."

3. Leo does not want to marry a widow, nor does he want a woman who is "too old," namely older than himself. He wants a young and pretty woman who believes in romantic love. Because of his suspicions and insecurity, however, Leo wonders why even the most eligible of Salzman's clients would have consulted a marriage broker in the first place.

Leo discovers a truth about himself when he tells Lily that he is not a "talented religious person." He admits that he came to God because he did *not* love Him. Leo also realizes with horror that, besides not loving God, he has never loved anyone, apart from his parents. He has called in the marriage broker to find him a bride because he is incapable of finding one on his own. He seems to be loveless and unloved.

4. The woman gives him an impression of youth and spring flowers. It seems to Leo that this woman, like him, has somehow suffered deeply. He has an impression of evil, but feels only this woman might understand and possibly even love him.

Leo notices that the woman's eyes are "hauntingly familiar, yet absolutely strange." He has the impression that he has met her before. He even thinks that he might recall her name. These clues hint that she is related to Salzman.

Interpreting Meanings

5. Answers will vary. Somehow Stella has brought *(Answers continue on next page.)*

"Just her I want," Leo murmured.

"Don't be a fool, doctor. Don't bother with her."

"Put me in touch with her. Salzman," Leo said humbly. "Perhaps I can be of service."

Salzman had stopped eating and Leo understood with emotion that it was now arranged.

Leaving the cafeteria, he was, however, afflicted by a tormenting suspicion that Salzman had planned it all to happen this way.

Leo was informed by letter that she would meet him on a certain corner, and she was there one spring night, waiting under a street lamp. He appeared, carrying a small bouquet of violets and rosebuds. Stella stood by the lamp post, smoking. She wore white with red shoes, which fitted his expectations, although in a troubled moment he had imagined the dress red, and only the shoes white. She waited uneasily and shyly. From afar he saw that her eyes—clearly her father's—were filled with desperate innocence. He pictured, in her, his own redemption. Violins and lit candles revolved in the sky. Leo ran forward with flowers outthrust.

Around the corner, Salzman, leaning against a wall, chanted prayers for the dead.

Raffiner by Marc Chagall (undated). Oil.

Museo di Belle Arti, Basilla.

A Comment on the Story

At the opening of this story, a lonely young rabbinical student decides to contact a marriage broker through a newspaper ad. Leo Finkle has been immersed in his studies for six years, he is painfully shy, and he can think of no other way to meet suitable young women. (If the custom seems strange, think of the millions of people today who use computerized dating services.)

Finkle's attitudes have been shaped by years of study and theological debate. It is not surprising that he has had very little time to think about his social life. The tradition of the marriage broker, seemingly exotic in America, was familiar to European Jews of the last century. Brokers fulfilled a genuine social function by negotiating among families and easing embarrassment. It was inevitable that in some of these arranged marriages, the chief feature was not the partners' mutual devotion but the financial or social advantages to the families involved.

Finkle is portrayed as wavering between two worlds. In the old world of his parents (who owed their marriage to a broker), social criteria for marriage were more important than love. Leo himself is originally impelled to look for a wife by an acquaintance's suggestion that "he might find it easier to win himself a congregation if he were married." In his first conversations with Salzman, Finkle is preoccupied by external, superficial criteria. But a profound change is at work in Leo, and he reaches a turning point when he suddenly finds himself admitting to the pleasant, but superficial Lily that "I came to God not because I loved Him, but because I did not." The story then shows him dramatically, even transcendentally caught up in love at first sight. As you think about the story, consider the possibility that Malamud's real interest is not in the probability—or even the future consequences—of Leo's change of heart. Perhaps the writer wants us to witness Leo Finkle's process of self-discovery: his initiation into a new world, where he can exist as an authentic person, capable of love.

(Continued from previous page.) "disgrace" on her family by perhaps running off with a man or even having an illegitimate child.

6. Answers will vary. Salzman may be saying that he is trying to atone for his sins by undertaking his studies or that some divine grace attracted him to the service of God.

The theme of the story involves the power of love and the onset of maturity. To love sincerely, one must first be honest about what one loves or does not love. Finkle's confession provides him with sudden answers to unasked questions about his relation to God and his relation to women. His new maturity resulting from this self-knowledge leads him to opt for romantic love rather than a matchmaker-arranged marriage.

7. Answers will vary. Perhaps he sees in Stella the possibility of love, of good coming from evil. Perhaps he wants to be redeemed from loneliness, alienation.

8. Answers will vary. Some students may argue that Salzman is still sincere in his opposition to their meeting; others may cite Salzman's speedy arrival at Finkle's apartment and his excuse that his *(Answers continue in left-hand column.)*

(Continued from top.) daughter's picture was included "accidentally" as evidence that he intended for the couple to marry all along.

9. The story opens in winter and closes in spring.

This combination of settings suggests a parallel in nature for the progress of the story's plot from suffering to happiness, from loneliness to romantic love, from symbolic "death" to symbolic "rebirth."

10. The title of the story, "The Magic Barrel," refers literally to the barrel (perhaps nonexistent) in which Salzman, the marriage broker, says he keeps his files of eligible women. In a broader sense, the title symbolizes the strange way in which chance (or Salzman's cleverness) has brought Leo Finkle and Stella together.

Responding to the Story

Analyzing the Story

Identifying Facts

1. Almost like an old folk tale, this story opens with a paragraph that summarizes the problem. According to this paragraph, who is the story's protagonist, what does he want, and what steps does he take to get what he wants?
2. Another character—Pinye Salzman—is introduced in the second paragraph. Find the descriptive details that seem to hint that there is something tragic in Salzman's past.
3. From his reactions to Salzman's clients, what do you discover about the kind of woman Finkle wants to marry? Explain what Finkle discovers about himself after the experience with Lily.
4. Explain why Finkle falls in love with the woman in the photograph. What clues hint at her identity?

Interpreting Meanings

5. What do you think caused Stella's father to regard her as dead?
6. Finkle confesses to Lily, "I came to God not because I loved Him, but because I did not." How would you explain this **paradox,** or seeming contradiction? How does Finkle's confession support the **theme** of the story as a whole?
7. Why do you think Finkle pictures in Stella his own redemption? What does he want to be redeemed *from*?
8. What do you think of the last scene in the story? Do you think Salzman arranged a marriage for Finkle after all? Explain.
9. What seasons open and close the story? In terms of the story's **plot,** what significance can you see in these seasonal settings?
10. Explain the story's title.

Writing About the Story

A Creative Response

1. **Extending the Story.** In a paragraph, describe what the characters in this story are doing twenty years after the story ends. Are Leo and Stella in love? Whether they are in love or not, are they still together? Has Salzman forgiven his daughter?

A Critical Response

2. **Comparing Two Stories.** Write an essay comparing "The Magic Barrel" to Singer's "The Key" (page 877). Base your comparison on at least two of the elements listed below:
   a. A comic plot that ends with the character uniting with someone.
   b. The use of visions and dreams
   c. An isolated character who is redeemed by love
   d. A setting that is transformed by love
3. **Responding to a Critic.** Select one of the following comments about Malamud's fiction and write a paragraph responding to it. Tell whether or not the comment has to do with the plot, characters, or theme of "The Magic Barrel."
   a. "Malamud has always had a fondness for telling tales arranged for the purpose of a specific moral lesson." (Alan Lelchuk)
   b. "What it is to be human, and to be humane, is his deepest concern." (Philip Roth)

John Updike (1932–   )

John Updike grew up in the small town of Shillington in rural Pennsylvania. Gifted with what seems a total recall of what it is like to grow up in the American middle class, Updike also displays a skill with language that can evoke our responses to even the most ordinary and familiar events. In short, his talent is for taking our common daily experience and endowing it with both substance and importance.

In his boyhood memoir, *The Dogwood Tree*, Updike portrays his youthful ambition as artistic: ". . . riding a thin pencil line out of Shillington, out of time altogether, into an infinity of unseen and even unborn hearts." He describes returning to Shillington as a mature, successful writer and confronting a picture of himself as this ambitious boy. He senses disappointment: "Like some phantom conjured by this child from a glue bottle, I have executed his commands; acquired pencils, paper, and an office. Now I wait apprehensively for his next command, or at least a nod of appreciation, and he smiles through me as if I am already transparent with failure."

Graduating *summa cum laude* from Harvard College in 1954, Updike studied drawing in England for a year, and on his return to the United States went to work for *The New Yorker*. After two years there, he made the courageous decision to support his young family entirely by writing. He left New York for Massachusetts, and he has since produced a shelf full of impressive novels, stories, poems, and critical essays.

From the first, Updike's stories had a freshness and honesty that brought them regularly into *The New Yorker's* pages. They have since been collected under such titles as *Pigeon Feathers* (1962) and *The Music School* (1966). His novels have brought Updike further acclaim. Among the most successful have been the three tales in the Rabbit series: *Rabbit, Run* (1960), *Rabbit Redux* (1971), and *Rabbit Is Rich* (1981), for which Updike was awarded a Pulitzer Prize.

These novels chronicle the life of Harry "Rabbit" Angstrom, who lives, as his creator might have, an outwardly conventional life in a small Pennsylvania town. In revealing Rabbit's

yearnings and disappointments, the uncertain course of his heart, and the dismaying fluctuations of his relationships with family and friends, Updike gives us a remarkably accurate portrait of the 1960's and 1970's in the United States. Here are Americans like ourselves, reacting to changing attitudes about national, social, and moral behavior. As always with an Updike novel, readers enjoy the feel of life—the sights, smells, and sounds that bring life into focus.

Two of Updike's other widely read novels are *The Centaur* (1963) and *A Month of Sundays* (1975). Of *The Centaur*, Updike notes that it is the only place he could ever say he loved his father. The second novel Updike calls *The Scarlet Letter* in modern dress. Besides his prose and poetry, Updike's essays rank with some of the most perceptive criticism of our day. Several of his critical essays have been collected in a volume entitled *Hugging the Shore* (1983).

In accepting the American Book Award in 1982, Updike said to young writers: "Have faith. May you surround yourselves with parents, editors, mates, and children as supportive as mine have been. But the essential support and encouragement of course come from within, arising out of the mad notion that your society needs to know what only you can tell it."

COMMENT FROM A CRITIC

John Updike's short stories are affirmations of life. According to critic Rachel C. Burchard, the "goodness of man is supported in Updike's short stories by [the following] theme [among others]: Life is good in little things. There are moments of joy, beauty, and insight which, even though fleeting, are as valuable in time's vast spaces as are diamonds caught here and there in the voluminous earth. A few of the critics notice Updike's tendency to dwell on the commonplace events and the small moments of life but fail to realize the significance of this emphasis. Stanley J. Rowland, Jr., says that John Updike devotes his energies to the small scene, but he does not recognize what seems obvious—that to Updike the small scene is the key to life's greatest values."

SUPPLEMENTARY SUPPORT MATERIALS
1. Vocabulary Activity Worksheet (*CCB*)
2. Review and Response Worksheet: Narration (*CCB*)
3. Language Skills Worksheet: Varying Sentence Structure (*CCB*)
4. Selection Test (*CCB*)

DEVELOPING VOCABULARY
The following words from the story are tested in the Selection Test. (See also Vocabulary Activity Worksheet.)

convolution	seminary
mincingly	jaunty
anarchy	claxon

PREPARATION
ESTABLISHING A PURPOSE. The class as a whole should read and discuss the headnote before reading the story. You may want to tell students that Updike writes what one critic has called "lyrical meditations rather than conventional short fictions."

A. Point of View
Identifying the narrator—and keeping that identification clearly in mind—will promote students' understanding and appreciation of the story.
? Who is the narrator in the first section? (He is the father of a fifteen-year-old son. The year is 1973—the date is important for identifying fathers and sons in later sections. See question 1, page 901.)

B. Allusion
The song that the student writer is parodying is "That Lucky Old Sun," popularized by singer Frankie Laine in 1949.

C. Word Choice
? What are some of the words that help to characterize Marion's husband as a submissive person? (Some of them are *charade, fears, cringing, maternally kind, victimized,* and *mincingly*.)

SON

This story deals with several different generations in the same family, so the title has more meanings than you might at first expect. As you begin each section, read slowly to make sure you know which "son" the narrator is talking about. In view of the subject of the story, it might be of interest to know that Updike's older son has become a writer too; like those of his father, David Updike's stories are also appearing in *The New Yorker*. They give yet another perspective on some of the same family situations that have served his father as subject matter.

He is often upstairs, when he has to be home. He prefers to be elsewhere. He is almost sixteen, though beardless still, a man's mind indignantly captive in the frame of a child. I love touching him, but don't often dare. The other day, he had the flu, and a fever, and I gave him a back rub, marveling at the symmetrical knit of muscle, the organic tension. He is high-strung. Yet his sleep is so solid he sweats like a stone in the wall of a well. He wishes for perfection. He would like to destroy us, for we are, variously, too fat, too jocular, too sloppy, too affectionate, too grotesque and heedless in our ways. His mother smokes too much. His younger brother chews with his mouth open. His older sister leaves unbuttoned the top button of her blouses. His younger sister tussles with the dogs, getting them overexcited, avoiding doing her homework. Everyone in the house talks nonsense. He would be a better father than his father. But time has tricked him, has made him a son. After a quarrel, if he cannot go outside and kick a ball, he retreats to a corner of the house and reclines on the beanbag chair in an attitude of strange, infantile or leonine, torpor.[1] We exhaust him, without meaning to. He takes an interest in the newspaper now, the front page as well as the sports, in this tiring year of 1973.

He is upstairs, writing a musical comedy. It is a Sunday in 1949. Somehow, he has volunteered to prepare a high school assembly program; people will sing. Songs of the time go through his head, as he scribbles new words. *Up in de mornin', down at de school, work like a debil for my grades.* Below him, irksome voices grind on, like machines working their way through tunnels. His parents each want something from the other. "Marion, you don't understand that man like I do; he has a heart of gold." This father's charade is very complex: The world, which he fears, is used as a flail[2] on his wife. But from his cringing attitude he would seem to an outsider the one being flailed. With burning red face, the woman accepts the role of aggressor as penance for the fact, the incessant shameful fact, that *he* has to wrestle with the world while she hides here, in solitude, on this farm. This is normal, but does not seem to them to be so. Only by convolution have they arrived at the dominant submissive relationship society has assigned them. For the man is maternally kind and with a smile hugs to himself his jewel, his certainty of being victimized; it is the mother whose tongue is sharp, who sometimes strikes. "Well, he gets you out of the house, and I guess that's gold to you." His answer is "Duty calls," pronounced mincingly. "The social contract is a balance of compromises." This will infuriate her, the son knows; as his heart thickens, the downstairs overflows with her hot voice. *"Don't* wear that smile at me! And *take* your hands off your hips; you look like a sissy!" Their son tries not to listen. When he does, visual details of the downstairs flood his mind: the two antagonists, circling with their coffee cups; the shabby mismatched furniture; the hopeful books; the docile framed photographs of the dead, docile and still as cowed students. This matrix of pain that bore him—he

1. **torpor** (tôr′pôr): sluggishness; apathy.

2. **flail:** a tool used to thresh grain; here, used metaphorically to mean a whip.

A. Expansion
Not many students will be able to identify the model for these two parodic lines, a popular song of 1949 that begins: "Across the alley from the Alamo/Lived a pinto pony and a Navajo."

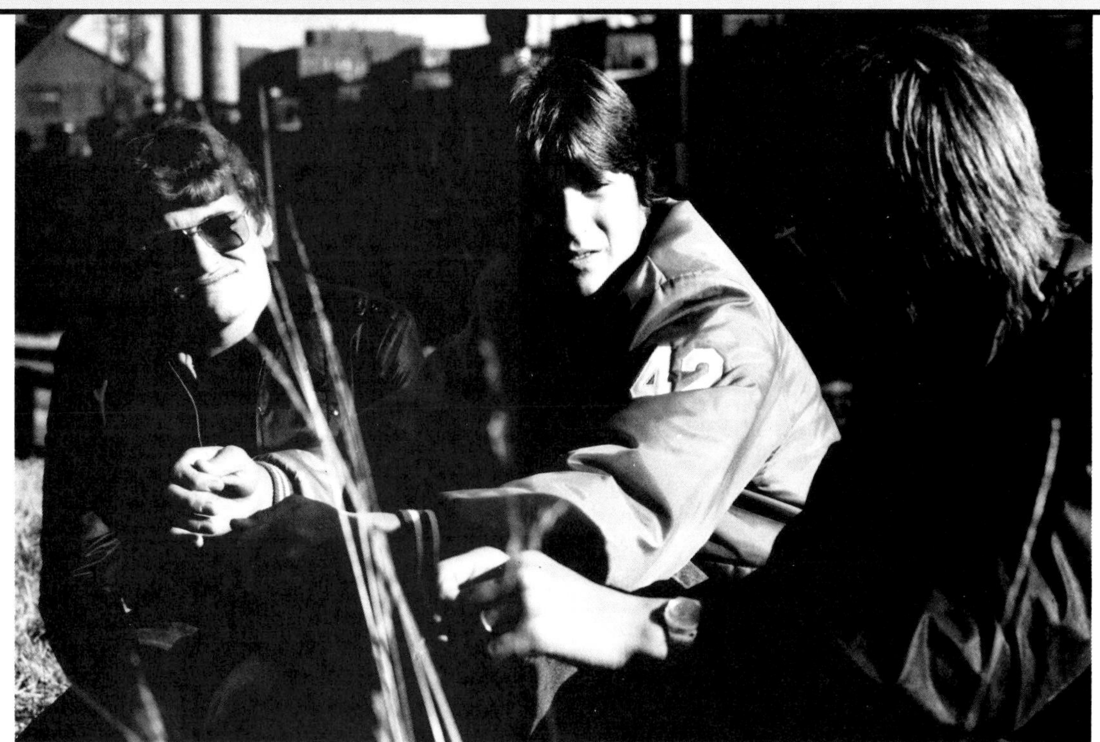

B. Responding
The narrator as a boy yearns for "the cloud that will carry him away, out of this, out."
? Do each of the other sons/fathers have similar yearnings? Explain. (Yes, they seem to. The narrator's son, rebellious, "prefers to be elsewhere." The narrator's father feels trapped as a paperboy and later in his teaching position. The grandfather, unhappy at his Missouri seminary, knows he is preparing for the wrong vocation.) Are such yearnings and dissatisfactions a normal part of life? (Opinions will differ. Most students are likely to agree that occasional feelings of "the grass being greener on the other side of the street" are inevitable and normal.)

feels he is floating above it, sprawled on the bed as on a cloud, stealing songs as they come into his head (*Across the hallway from the guidance room/Lives a French instructor called Mrs. Blum*), contemplating the brown meadow from the upstairs window (last summer's burdock[3] stalks like the beginnings of an alphabet, an apple tree holding three rotten apples as if pondering why they failed to fall), yearning for Monday, for the ride to school with his father, for the bell that calls him to homeroom, for the excitements of class, for Broadway, for fame, for the cloud that will carry him away, out of this, out.

He returns from his paper-delivery route and finds a few Christmas presents for him on the kitchen table. I must guess at the year. 1913? Without opening them, he knocks them to the floor, puts his head on the table, and falls asleep. He must have been consciously dramatizing his plight: His father was sick, money was scarce, he had to work, to win food for the family when he was still a child. In his dismissal of Christmas, he touched a nerve: his love of anarchy, his distrust of the social contract. He treasured this moment of proclamation; else why remember it, hoard a memory so bitter, and confide it to his son many Christmases later? He had a teaching instinct, though he claimed that life miscast him as a schoolteacher. I suffered in his classes, feeling the confusion as a persecution of him, but now wonder if his rebellious heart did not court confusion, not as Communists do, to intrude their own order, but, more radical still, as an end pleasurable in itself, as truth's very body. Yet his handwriting (an old pink permission slip recently fluttered from a book where it had been marking a page for twenty years) was always considerately legible, and he was sitting up doing arithmetic the morning of the day he died.

And letters survive from that yet prior son, written in brown ink, in a tidy tame hand, home to his mother from the Missouri seminary where he was preparing for his vocation. The dates are 1887, 1888, 1889. Nothing much happened: He missed New Jersey, and was teased at a church social for escorting a widow. He wanted to do the right thing, but the little sheets of faded penscript exhale a dispirited calm, as if his heart already knew he would not make a successful minister, or live to be old. His son, my father, when old, drove hundreds of miles out of the way to visit the Missouri town from which those letters had been sent. Strangely, the town had not changed; it looked

3. **burdock:** a coarse, hairy weed with large leaves, prickley, and purple flowers.

READING CHECK TEST

1. The narrator's son is at odds with his father and mother, but he gets along well with his sisters and brother. *False*
2. The narrator's father is less aggressive and sharp-tongued than his mother. *True*
3. When the narrator's father was a boy, he was bitter at having to work to help support the family. *True*
4. The narrator's son is an eager but not very talented soccer player. *False*
5. When the narrator enforces justice on his son, the son at first smiles, and then becomes angry. *True*

ANALYZING THE STORY

Identifying Facts

1. (1) 1973—narrator, a father, talks about his adolescent son; (2) 1949—narrator is seen as a high-school-age son himself; (3) 1913—narrator's father appears as a young paperboy; (4) 1880's—narrator's grandfather's letters are introduced; (5) 1973—narrator, as in section 1, talks about his son; (6) 1960's

CLOSURE

Ask students to describe in class what sets Updike's short story apart stylistically from the other stories they have read.

A. Interpretation

? Why is the narrator's father so depressed by his visit to the seminary town of his father? (Opinions will vary. Perhaps by visiting the scene of his father's unhappiness, he is forcibly reminded of what he considers to be his own failure in life.)

B. Simile

Be sure students notice the simile "referees exotic as zebras." Have them talk about the reasons for its effectiveness.

C. Responding

This is an especially tricky section to decipher. Students must pay close attention to the quotation marks.

? Who is the *I* in the section? Who never "received the call"? (The *I* is the narrator's father; the person who failed to receive the call is the narrator's grandfather.)

just as he had imagined, from his father's descriptions: tall wooden houses, rain-soaked, stacked on a bluff. The town was a sepia[4] postcard mailed homesick home and preserved in an attic. A My father cursed: His father's old sorrow bore him down into depression, into hatred of life. My mother claims his decline in health began at that moment.

He is wonderful to watch, playing soccer. Smaller than the others, my son leaps, heads, dribbles, feints, passes. When a big boy knocks him down, he tumbles on the mud, in his green and black school uniform, in an ecstasy of falling. I am envious. Never for me the jaunty pride of the school uniform, the solemn ritual of the coach's pep talk, the camaraderie of shook hands and slapped backsides, the shadow-striped hush of late afternoon and last quarter, the solemn vaulted universe of official combat, with its cheering mothers and B referees exotic as zebras and the bespectacled timekeeper alert with his claxon. When the boy scores a goal, he runs into the arms of his teammates with upraised arms and his face alight as if blinded by triumph. They lift him from the earth in a union of muddy hugs. What spirit! What valor! What skill! His father, watching from the sidelines, inwardly registers only one complaint: He feels the boy, with his talent, should be more aggressive.

They drove across the state of Pennsylvania to hear their son read in Pittsburgh. But when their presence was announced to the audience, they did not stand; the applause groped for them and died. My mother said afterward she was afraid she might fall into the next row if she tried to stand in the dark. Next morning was sunny, and the three of us searched for the house where once they had lived. They had been happy there; I imagined, indeed, that I had been conceived there, just before the slope of the Depression steepened and fear gripped my family. We found the library where she used to read Turgenev,[5] and the little park where the bums slept close as paving stones in the summer night; but their street kept eluding us, though we circled in the car. On foot, my mother found the tree. She claimed she recognized it, the sooty linden she would gaze into from their apartment windows. The branches, though thicker, had held their pattern. But the house itself, and the entire block, were gone. Stray bricks and rods of iron in the grass suggested that the demolition had been recent. We stood on the empty spot and laughed. They knew it was right, because the railroad tracks were the right distance away. In confirmation, a long freight train pulled itself east around the curve, its great weight gliding as if on a river current; then a silver passenger train came gliding as effortlessly in the other direction. The curve of the tracks tipped the cars slightly toward us. The Golden Triangle,[6] gray and hazed, was off to our left, beyond a forest of bridges. We stood on the grassy rubble that morning, where something once had been, beside the tree still there, and were intensely happy. Why? We knew.

" 'No,' Dad said to me, 'the Christian ministry isn't a job you choose, it's a vocation for which you got to receive a call.' I could tell he wanted me to ask him. We never talked much, but we understood each other, we were both scared devils, not like you and the kid. I asked him, Had he ever received the call? He said No. He said No, he never had. Received the call. That was a terrible thing, for him to admit. And I was the one he told. As far as I knew he never admitted it to anybody, but he admitted it to me. He felt like hell about it, I could tell. That was all we ever said about it. That was enough." C

He has made his younger brother cry, and justice must be done. A father enforces justice. I corner the rat in our bedroom; he is holding a cardboard mailing tube like a sword. The challenge flares white-hot; I roll my weight toward him like a rock down a mountain, and knock the weapon from his hand. He smiles. Smiles! Because my facial expression is silly? Because he is glad that he can still be overpowered, and hence is still protected? Why? I do not hit him. We stand a second, father and son, and then as nimbly as on the soccer field he steps around me and out the door. He slams

4. **sepia** (sē′pē·ə): a brownish color, characteristic of old photographs.
5. **Turgenev** (tōōr·gān′yəf): Ivan Turgenev (1818–1883), Russian novelist and short-story writer.
6. **Golden Triangle:** in Pittsburgh, the junction of the Allegheny and Monongahela rivers to form the Ohio River.

or 70's—narrator's parents hear him speak in Pittsburgh; (7) 1900's or 10's—narrator's father and grandfather converse; (8) 1973—narrator, as in sections 1 and 5, talks about his son.
2. Students may identify such passages throughout the story.
3. When the narrator must punish his son, he has to face the boy's defiant rebellion.

The son smiles, then rushes from the room, slamming the door and shouting obscenities. Later, in his room, he plays his guitar in defiance.

Interpreting Meanings
4. In general, the theme seems to be the ambivalent relationship between fathers and sons.
5. The narrator wishes he and his son could get along better. As a youngster, the narrator wanted his parents not to bicker. The narrator recalls his father being depressed by his minister-father's lack of the "call." The narrator admires his son's accomplishments. The narrator's parents show their pride in his success by driving to Pittsburgh to hear him read.
6. On page 898, col. 2, it is defined as "a balance of compromises." On page 899, col. 1, it suggests a safeguard against anarchy. In the first sense it certainly seems to be observed by fathers and sons, but answers will vary.
7. A "visitor"—the son will move away in time. A "prisoner"—as a child at home, the son lacks certain liberties and has some restraints.
8. Answers will vary. Ask students to explain what might be gained (or lost) with such a title.
9. Possible answers are *bittersweet, nostalgic, paradoxical.*
10. Answers will vary. Some students may suggest that the story will affect parents differently from the way it affects sons or daughters. If so, ask students to explain their opinions.

the door. He shouts obscenities in the hall, slams all the doors he can find on the way to his room. Our moment of smilingly shared silence was the moment of compression; now the explosion. The whole house rocks with it. Downstairs, his siblings and mother come to me and offer advice and psychological analysis. I was too aggressive. He is spoiled. What they can never know, my grief alone to treasure, was that lucid many-sided second of his smiling and my relenting, before the world's wrathful pantomime of power resumed.

As we huddle whispering about him, my son takes his revenge. In his room, he plays his guitar. He has greatly improved this winter; his hands getting bigger is the least of it. He has found in the guitar an escape. He plays the Romanza[7] wherein repeated notes, with a sliding like the heart's valves, let themselves fall along the scale: The notes fall, so gently he bombs us, drops feathery notes down upon us, our visitor, our prisoner.

7. **Romanza** (rō·män′zə): a romantic musical composition.

Responding to the Story

Analyzing the Story

Identifying Facts

1. This story consists of eight related sections. Identify the time period of each section, and the son or family the narrator is talking about.
2. Find passages in each section where the narrator reveals the private thoughts of his characters.
3. What test faces the father-narrator in the last section of the story? How does his son respond to the father's discipline?

Interpreting Meanings

4. This story includes a variety of incidents that range over many different periods. What **thematic** thread unifies the story?
5. Hope is a recurring subject in this story. In what ways are the various characters' hopes for each other disappointed? How are they fulfilled?
6. Updike uses the phrase "the social contract" several times in the course of this story. What do you think he means by this phrase, within the context of the story? Would he probably say that this contract is or is not honored between fathers and sons?
7. At the end of the story, why does the narrator refer to his own son as "our visitor, our prisoner"? How does this phrase relate to the **theme** of the story?
8. Do you think this story could be entitled "Fathers"? Explain why or why not.
9. How would you describe the narrator's **tone** in telling this story? How does he feel about the people in this family?
10. Did you find Updike's portrayal of the relationships between parents and children believable? Did you sympathize with these characters? Do you think the story affects every reader the same way?

Writing About the Story

A Creative Response

1. **Imitating the Story's Structure.** Write at least three episodes for a story called "Daughters." Imitate Updike's style, and let your narrator reveal the private thoughts and feelings of three generations.

A Critical Response

2. **Analyzing the Writer's Method.** In a brief essay, explain whether you believe Updike is being sentimental or realistic in the way he writes about parent-child relationships. Include references to at least two different parent-child relationships from the story.

Analyzing Language and Style

A "Pictorial" Style

1. Updike has said that his writing is pictorial, that he gropes for visual precision. Review "Son" and find at least two passages that capture:

   a. The appearance of a person
   b. The quality of a setting
   c. The quality of a particular feeling

2. What is the **simile** in this passage? What words **personify** the apple tree?

   ". . . he is . . . contemplating the brown meadow from the upstairs window (last summer's burdock stalks like the beginnings of an alphabet, an apple tree holding three rotten apples as if pondering why they failed to fall). . . ."

3. Reread the section beginning, "They drove across the state of Pennsylvania." Rewrite part of it as a poem.

A. Expansion
How the Garcia Girls Lost Their Accents is not a traditional novel; rather, it is a series of interrelated short stories ("Daughter of Invention" being one of them). The stories are told in reverse chronological order, beginning with the three sisters as young women in America and moving backward in time to their childhood in the Dominican Republic.

In the *Library Journal* of May 1, 1991, reviewer Ann H. Fisher called Alvarez a gifted and promising storyteller and *How the Garcia Girls Lost Their Accents* a highly original first novel.

Julia Alvarez (1950–)

Julia (pronounced "hoolia") Alvarez spent her early childhood in the Dominican Republic before moving to the United States. Learning English was only part of her difficulties in adjusting to her new life. She also had to learn to compromise, finding conflicts between American customs and her parents' more traditional, old-fashioned views. This theme is at the heart of her fiction—her short stories as well as her
A novel *How the Garcia Girls Lost Their Accents* (1991).

Before writing fiction, Alvarez wrote poetry and taught poetry courses for twelve years in schools in Kentucky, California, Vermont, Illinois, and Washington, D.C. Her first book of poetry, *Homecoming* (1984), contains "How I Learned to Sweep" (see page 1133).

The recipient of many literary awards, including the American Academy of Poetry Prize, Alvarez is now teaching at Middlebury College in Vermont, her alma mater.

SUPPLEMENTARY SUPPORT MATERIALS
1. Vocabulary Activity Worksheet (*CCB*)
2. Review and Response Worksheet: Characterization (*CCB*)
3. Selection Test (*CCB*)

DEVELOPING VOCABULARY
The following words from the story are tested in the Selection Test. (See also Vocabulary Activity Worksheet.)

disembodied	florid
cursory	expurgated
poignantly	interim
mortified	ultimatum
noncommittal	to reconcile

PREPARATION

1. **BUILDING ON PRIOR KNOWLEDGE.** Ask students who were born in another country to describe the problems they faced in adjusting to American culture.

2. **ESTABLISHING A PURPOSE.** Have students look at the chart on page 910 and then watch for these conflicts as they read, noting how they are developed.

DAUGHTER OF INVENTION

Do you doubt that a story runs on conflict? Here is a splendid one that takes its strength and much of its fun from the clash between the anxious values of Latin American parents and the liberated ones of their New York-raised daughter.

It is fascinating to see how the three characters here have adapted so differently to the liberty the family enjoys in its new country. Each one draws our understanding and affection. While "Cukita" (as her mother calls her) is both narrator and the one we're most likely to identify with, her mother is the most interesting and delightful, and you may decide *she* is the central figure. After all, the title could refer to either, couldn't it?

In any case the mother has become a passionate citizen of her recently adopted country, and what a joy she is with her late-night inventing for the gadget market and her even more imaginative refashioning of the English language's dustiest maxims.

"Daughter of Invention" is a very literary story too, since it turns on Cukita's discovery of the great North American poet and champion of the boastful self, Walt Whitman.

She wanted to invent something, my mother. There was a period after we arrived in this country, until five or so years later, when my mother was inventing. They were never pressing, global needs she was addressing with her pencil and pad. She would have said that was for men to do, rockets and engines that ran on gasoline and turned the wheels of the world. She was just fussing with little house things, don't mind her.

She always invented at night, after settling her house down. On his side of the bed my father would be conked out for an hour already, his Spanish newspaper draped over his chest, his glasses, propped up on his bedside table, looking out eerily at the darkened room like a disembodied guard. But in her lighted corner, like some devoted scholar burning the midnight oil, my mother was inventing, sheets pulled to her lap, pillows propped up behind her, her reading glasses riding the bridge of her nose like a schoolmarm's. On her lap lay one of those innumerable pads of paper my father always brought home from his office, compliments of some pharmaceutical company, advertising tranquilizers or antibiotics or skin cream; in her other hand, my mother held a pencil that looked like a pen with a little cylinder of lead inside. She would work on a sketch of something familiar, but drawn at such close range so she could attach a special nozzle or handier handle, the thing looked peculiar. Once, I mistook the spiral of a corkscrew for a nautilus shell, but it could just as well have been a galaxy forming.

It was the only time all day we'd catch her sitting down, for she herself was living proof of the *perpetuum mobile*[1] machine so many inventors had sought over the ages. [B] My sisters and I would seek her out now when she seemed to have a moment to talk to us: We were having trouble at school or we wanted her to persuade my father to give us permission to go into the city or to a shopping mall or a movie—in broad daylight! My mother would wave us out of her room. "The problem with you girls . . ." [C] I can tell you right now what the problem always boiled down to: We wanted to become Americans and my father—and my mother, at first—would have none of it.

"You girls are going to drive me crazy!" She always threatened if we kept nagging. "When I end up in Bellevue,[2] you'll be safely sorry!"

She spoke in English when she argued with us, even though, in a matter of months, her daughters were the fluent ones. Her English was much better than my father's, but it was still a mishmash of mixed-up idioms and sayings that showed she was "green behind the ears," as she called it. [D]

If my sisters and I tried to get her to talk in Spanish, she'd snap, "When in Rome, do unto the Romans . . ."

1. ***perpetuum mobile*** (pər·pech′o͞o·əm mō′bə·lē): Latin for "perpetual motion."
2. **Bellevue:** a large New York City hospital known for its psychiatric department.

A. Responding
? What do you think of Mami's ideas about the division of labor for men and women? (In Mami's traditional views, men are concerned with the outside world and women with the home. Students may find Mami's views outdated. Encourage them to discuss their ideas about men's and women's roles.)

B. Expansion
Many inventors have tried to create perpetual-motion machines. None has succeeded, even though some inventors have been granted patents.

C. Conflict
? What conflicts does this passage reveal? (Generational and cultural conflicts appear. At this point the girls want to be more American than their parents want them to be.)

D. Language
These are the first of a series of Mami's mangled sayings (see question 2, page 910). Have students look for others.

A. Responding

Note the narrator's explanation of the difference between "Mami" and "Mom." Which role do you think is more important to being a good parent? Why? (Answers will vary, but many will say the traditional parent—"Mami"—role is more essential.)

B. Conflict

What conflict does this passage reveal? (Generational; the narrator sees her mother as an intruder on the narrator's space and time.)

C. Characterization

Why doesn't Mami pursue her inventions seriously? (Lack of encouragement, self-confidence, and knowledge of what to do next)

D. Motivation/Conflict

Why do you think second- and third-generation immigrants tend to turn on new arrivals? (Perhaps older immigrants feel threatened economically by newer immigrants' willingness to work for lower wages.)

I had become the spokesman for my sisters, and I would stand my ground in that bedroom. "We're not going to that school anymore, Mami!"

"You have to." Her eyes would widen with worry. "In this country, it is against the law not to go to school. You want us to get thrown out?"

"You want us to get killed? Those kids were throwing stones today!"

"Sticks and stones don't break bones . . ." she chanted. I could tell, though, by the look on her face, it was as if one of those stones the kids had aimed at us had hit her. But she always pretended we were at fault. "What did you do to provoke them? It takes two to tangle, you know."

A "Thanks, thanks a lot, Mom!" I'd storm out of that room and into mine. I never called her *Mom* except when I wanted her to feel how much she had failed us in this country. She was a good enough Mami, fussing and scolding and giving advice, but a terrible girlfriend parent, a real failure of a Mom.

Back she'd go to her pencil and pad, scribbling and tsking and tearing off paper, finally giving up, and taking up her *New York Times*. Some nights, though, she'd get a good idea, and she'd rush into my room, a flushed look on her face, her tablet of paper in her hand, a cursory knock on the door she'd just thrown open: "Do I have something to show you, Cukita!"

B This was my time to myself, after I'd finished my homework, while my sisters were still downstairs watching TV in the basement. Hunched over my small desk, the overhead light turned off, my lamp shining poignantly on my paper, the rest of the room in warm, soft, uncreated darkness, I wrote my secret poems in my new language.

"You're going to ruin your eyes!" My mother would storm into my room, turning on the overly bright overhead light, scaring off whatever shy passion I had just begun coaxing out of a labyrinth of feelings with the blue thread of my writing.

"Oh Mami!" I'd cry out, my eyes blinking up at her. "I'm writing."

"Ay, Cukita." That was her communal pet name for whoever was in her favor. "Cukita, when I make a million, I'll buy you your very own typewriter." (I'd been nagging my mother for one just like the one father had bought her to do his order forms at home.) "Gravy on the turkey" was what she called it when someone was buttering her up. She'd butter and pour. "I'll hire you your very own typist."

C Down she'd plop on my bed and hold out her pad to me. "Take a guess, Cukita?" I'd study her rough sketch a moment: soap sprayed from the nozzle head of a shower when you turned the knob a certain way? Coffee with creamer already mixed in? Time-released water capsules for your plants when you were away? A key chain with a timer that would go off when your parking meter was about to expire? (The ticking would help you find your keys easily if you mislaid them.) The famous one, famous only in hindsight, was the stick person dragging a square by a rope—a suitcase with wheels? "Oh, of course," we'd humor her. "What every household needs: a shower like a car wash, keys ticking like a bomb, luggage on a leash!" By now, as you can see, it'd become something of a family joke, our Thomas Edison Mami, our Benjamin Franklin Mom.

Her face would fall. "Come on now! Use your head." One more wrong guess, and she'd tell me, pressing with her pencil point the different highlights of this incredible new wonder. "Remember that time we took the car to Bear Mountain, and we re-ah-lized that we had forgotten to pack an opener with our pick-a-nick?" (We kept correcting her, but she insisted this is how it should be said.) "When we were ready to eat we didn't have any way to open the refreshments cans?" (This before fliptop lids, which she claimed had crossed her mind.) "You know what this is now?" A shake of my head. "Is a car bumper, but see this part is a removable can opener. So simple and yet so necessary, no?"

"Yeah, Mami. You should patent it." I'd shrug. She'd tear off the scratch paper and fold it, carefully, corner to corner, as if she were going to save it. But then, she'd toss it in the wastebasket on her way out of the room and give a little laugh like a disclaimer.[3] "It's half of one or two dozen of another . . ."

I suppose none of her daughters was very encouraging. We resented her spending time on those dumb inventions. D Here, we were trying to fit in America among Americans; we needed help figuring out who we were, why these Irish kids whose grandparents were micks two generations ago, why they were calling us spics. Why had we come to the country in the first place? Important, crucial, final things, you see, and here was our

3. **disclaimer:** a renouncing of responsibility for something.

own mother, who didn't have a second to help us puzzle any of this out, inventing gadgets to make life easier for American moms. Why, it seemed as if she were arming our own enemy against us!

One time, she did have a moment of triumph. Every night, she liked to read *The New York Times* in bed before turning off her light, to see what the Americans were up to. One night, she let out a yelp to wake up my father beside her. He sat bolt upright, reaching for his glasses which, in his haste, he knocked across the room. *"Que pasa? Que pasa?"* What is wrong? There was terror in his voice, fear she'd seen in his eyes in the Dominican Republic before we left. We were being watched there; he was being followed; he and mother had often exchanged those looks. They could not talk, of course, though they must have whispered to each other in fear at night in the dark bed. Now in America, he was safe, a success even; his Centro Medico in Brooklyn was thronged with the sick and the homesick. But in dreams, he went back to those awful days and long nights, and my mother's screams confirmed his secret fear: we had not gotten away after all; they had come for us at last.

"Ay, Papi, I'm sorry. Go back to sleep, Cukito. It's nothing, nothing really." My mother held up the *Times* for him to squint at the small print, back page headline, one hand tapping all over the top of the bedside table for his glasses, the other rubbing his eyes to wakefulness.

"Remember, remember how I showed you that suitcase with little wheels so we would not have to carry those heavy bags when we traveled? Someone stole my idea and made a million!" She shook the paper in his face. She shook the paper in all our faces that night. "See! See! This man was no *bobo*! He didn't put all his pokers on a back burner. I kept telling you, one of these days my ship would pass me by in the night!" She wagged her finger at my sisters and my father and me, laughing all the while, one of those eerie laughs crazy people in movies laugh. We had congregated in her room to hear the good news she'd been yelling down the stairs, and now we eyed her and each other. I suppose we were all thinking the same thing: Wouldn't it be weird and sad if Mami did end up in Bellevue as she'd always threatened she might?

"*Ya, ya!* Enough!" She waved us out of her room at last. "There is no use trying to drink spilt milk, that's for sure."

It was the suitcase rollers that stopped my mother's hand; she had weather vaned a minor brainstorm. She would have to start taking herself seriously. That blocked the free play of her ingenuity. Besides, she had also begun working at my father's office, and at night, she was too tired and busy filling in columns with how much money they had made that day to be fooling with gadgets! B

She did take up her pencil and pad one last time to help me out. In ninth grade, I was chosen by my English teacher, Sister Mary Joseph, to deliver the teacher's day address at the school assembly. Back in the Dominican Republic, I was a terrible student. No one could ever get me to sit down to a book. But in New York, I needed to settle somewhere, and the natives were unfriendly, the country inhospitable, so I took root in the language. By high school, the nuns were reading my stories and compositions out loud to my classmates as examples of imagination at work.

This time my imagination jammed. At first I didn't want and then I couldn't seem to write that speech. I suppose I should have thought of it as a "great honor," as my father called it. But I was mortified. I still had a pronounced lilt to my accent, and I did not like to speak in public, subjecting myself to my classmates' ridicule. Recently, they had begun to warm toward my sisters and me, and it took no great figuring to see that to deliver a eulogy[4] for a convent full of crazy, old overweight nuns was no way to endear myself to the members of my class. C

But I didn't know how to get out of it. Week after week, I'd sit down, hoping to polish off some quick, noncommittal little speech. I couldn't get anything down.

The weekend before our Monday morning assembly I went into a panic. My mother would just have to call in and say I was in the hospital, in a coma. I was in the Dominican Republic. Yeah, that was it! Recently, my father had been talking about going back home to live.

My mother tried to calm me down. "Just remember how Mister Lincoln couldn't think of anything to say at the Gettysburg, but then, Bang! 'Four score and once upon a time ago,' " she began reciting. Her version of history was half invention and half truths and whatever else she needed to prove a point. "Something is going to

4. **eulogy** (yo͞o'lə·jē): a public speech of praise.

A. Conflict
? What haunts Papi? (Though he is safe now, memories of terror-filled days in the Dominican Republic haunt him.)

B. Characterization
? Why do you think Mami's discovery stifles her imagination rather than inspires her? (Students may suggest that her inventions were an entertaining hobby; now, seeing she was right about the luggage wheels, she becomes frightened and intimidated. She would have to pursue all her ideas instead of throwing them away.)

C. Conflict
? What conflict does the narrator's worry reveal? (Cultural; she wants to fit in but fears that the speech will alienate her classmates.)

A. Humanities Connection: Responding to the Fine Art
Milton Avery (1893–1965) is regarded as an outstanding colorist and one of the most important American painters of the 20th century. His most frequent subjects were landscapes and seascapes, but he also depicted family life, often with his daughter as his model. Avery's scenes are recognizable, but his simple lines and shapes give them an abstract quality. The effect is one of gentleness and lyrical peace.
? What do you think is the relationship between the two figures in the painting? (They look like mother and daughter or older and younger sisters.) What is the mood of the painting? (Students may suggest peaceful, quiet, sad.)

B. Theme
? What is the actual saying? ("Necessity is the mother of invention.") What does it mean? (Having to do something will force you to find a way to do it.)

A

Two Figures at Desk by Milton Avery (1944). Oil on canvas.

Collection of Neuberger Museum, State University of New York at Purchase. Gift of Roy E. Neuberger. Photograph by Jim Frank.

B

come if you just relax. You'll see, like the Americans say, 'Necessity is the daughter of invention.' I'll help you."

All weekend, she kept coming into my room with help. "Please, Mami, just leave me alone, please," I pleaded with her. But I'd get rid of the goose only to have to contend with the gander. My father kept poking his head in the door just to see if I had "fulfilled my obligations," a phrase he'd used when we were a little younger, and he'd check to see whether we had gone to the bathroom before a car trip. Several times that weekend around the supper table, he'd recite his valedictorian speech from when he graduated from high school. He'd give me pointers on delivery, on the great orators and their tricks. (Humbleness and praise and falling silent with great emotion were his favorities.)

My mother sat across the table, the only one who seemed to be listening to him. My sisters and I were forgetting a lot of our Spanish, and my father's formal, florid diction was even harder to understand. But my mother smiled softly to herself, and turned the Lazy Susan at the center of the table around and around as if it were the prime mover, the first gear of attention.

That Sunday evening, I was reading some poetry to get myself inspired: Whitman in an old book with an engraved cover my father had picked up in a thrift shop next to his office a few weeks back. "I celebrate myself, and sing myself . . ." "He most honors my style who learns under it to destroy the teacher." The poet's words shocked and thrilled me. I had gotten used to the nuns, a literature of appropriate sentiments, poems with a message, expurgated texts. But here was a flesh and blood man, belching and laughing and sweating in poems. "Who touches this book touches a man."

That night, at last, I started to write, recklessly, three, five pages, looking up once only to see my father passing by the hall on tiptoe. When I was done, I read over my words, and my eyes filled. I finally sounded like myself in English!

As soon as I had finished that first draft, I called my mother to my room. She listened attentively, as she had to my father's speech, and in the end, her eyes were glistening too. Her face was soft and warm and proud. "That is a beautiful, beautiful speech, Cukita. I want for your father to hear it before he goes to sleep. Then I will type it for you, all right?"

Down the hall we went, the two of us, faces flushed with accomplishment. Into the master bedroom where my father was propped up on his pillows, still awake, reading the Dominican papers, already days old. He had become interested in his country's fate again. The dictatorship had been toppled. The interim government was going to hold the first free elections in thirty years. There was still some question in his mind whether or not we might want to move back. History was in the making, freedom and hope were in the air again! But my mother had gotten used to the life here. She did not want to go back to the old country where she was only a wife and a mother (and a failed one at that, since she had never had the required son). She did not come straight out and disagree with my father's plans. Instead, she fussed with him about reading the papers in bed, soiling those sheets with those poorly printed, foreign tabloids. "*The Times* is not that bad!" she'd claim if my father tried to humor her by saying they shared the same dirty habit.

The minute my father saw my mother and me, filing in, he put his paper down, and his face brightened as if at long last his wife had delivered a son, and that was the news we were bringing him. His teeth were already grinning from the glass of water next to his bedside lamp, so he lisped when he said, "Eh-speech, eh-speech!"

"It is so beautiful, Papi," my mother previewed him, turning the sound off on his TV. She sat down at the foot of the bed. I stood before both of them, blocking their view of the soldiers in helicopters landing amid silenced gun reports and explosions. A few weeks ago it had been the shores of the Dominican Republic. Now it was the jungles of Southeast Asia they were saving. My mother gave me the nod to begin reading.

I didn't need much encouragement. I put my nose to the fire, as my mother would have said, and read from start to finish without looking up. When I was done, I was a little embarrassed at my pride in my own words. I pretended to quibble with a phrase or two I was sure I'd be talked out of changing. I looked questioningly to my mother. Her face was radiant. She turned to share her pride with my father.

But the expression on his face shocked us both. His toothless mouth had collapsed into a dark zero. His eyes glared at me, then shifted to my mother, accusingly. In barely audible Spanish, as if secret microphones or informers were all about, he whispered, "You will permit her to read *that*?"

My mother's eyebrows shot up, her mouth fell open. In the old country, any whisper of a challenge to authority could bring the secret police in their black V.W.'s. But this was America. People could say what they thought. "What is wrong with her speech?" my mother questioned him.

"What ees wrrrong with her eh-speech?" My father wagged his head at her. His anger was always more frightening in his broken English. As if he had mutilated the language in his fury—and now there was nothing to stand between us and his raw, dumb anger. "What is wrong? I will tell you what is wrong. It shows no gratitude. It is boastful. 'I celebrate myself'? 'The best student learns to destroy the teacher'?" He mocked my plagiarized words. "That is insubordinate. It is improper. It is disrespecting of her teachers—" In his anger he had forgotten his fear of lurking spies: Each wrong he voiced was a decibel higher than the last outrage. Finally, he was yelling at me, "As your father, I forbid you to say that eh-speech!"

My mother leapt to her feet, a sign always that she was about to make a speech or deliver an ultimatum. She was a small woman, and she spoke all her pronouncements standing up, either for more protection or as a carry-over from her girlhood in convent schools where one asked for, and

A. Connections The narrator is reading from Walt Whitman's long poem "Song of Myself" (see excerpts beginning on page 332). The first quotation comes from Section 1 and the second from Section 47.

B. Interpretation ? What does the narrator mean? (The speech has come from her heart, and she has been able to express herself in natural-sounding English.)

C. Conflict ? Why is Papi considering a return to the Dominican Republic, and why is Mami opposed? (Papi has retained greater interest in his native land, reads the Dominican newspapers, and thinks that he might like to be part of the reform effort. Mami, on the other hand, reads the *New York Times,* learns English faster than Papi, and has no desire to go back. She enjoys the greater freedom women have in America.)

Reading Check Test

1. The mother in the story uses her free time to think up ______. *inventions*
2. The mother and father are delighted, but the narrator is dismayed, when she is chosen to give a ______ at school. *speech*
3. Inspired by the poems of ______, the narrator writes a speech that she is pleased with. *Walt Whitman*
4. When her father destroys the girl's speech, ______ helps her invent another. *her mother*
5. At the end of the story, the father shows his remorse by bringing his daughter a new ______. *typewriter*

Closure

Have students look again at the chart on page 910 and briefly discuss the people involved and the outcome of each conflict.

A. Conflict/Irony

? What is ironic about Papi's reaction to the speech? (He is more political than his wife, yet he cannot escape his old habits of fear and submission to authority.)

B. Expansion

One of the most cruel dictators in Latin American history, Trujillo (Rafael Leonides Trujillo Molina) seized power in the Dominican Republic in 1930 during a period of political and economic crises.

Trujillo's regime brought political stability and economic growth to the country; but corruption was rampant, and absolutely no opposition was tolerated. No citizen was safe from arrest, questioning, torture, and execution by the secret police. In 1961 Trujillo was assassinated by members of the army.

C. Interpreting

? How do you imagine the narrator feels about the speech and her success? (She probably hated the speech but was pleased with its success.)

literally took, the floor in order to speak. She stood by my side, shoulder to shoulder; we looked down at my father. "That is no tone of voice, Eduardo—" she began.

A By now, my father was truly furious. I suppose it was bad enough I was rebelling, but here was my mother joining forces with me. Soon he would be surrounded by a house full of independent American women. He too leapt from his bed, throwing off his covers. The Spanish newspapers flew across the room. He snatched my speech out of my hands, held it before my panicked eyes, a vengeful, mad look in his own, and then once, twice, three, four, countless times, he tore my prize into shreds.

"Are you crazy?" My mother lunged at him. "Have you gone mad? That is her speech for tomorrow you have torn up!"

"Have *you* gone mad?" He shook her away. "You were going to let her read that . . . that insult to her teachers?"

"Insult to her teachers!" My mother's face had crumpled up like a piece of paper. On it was written a love note to my father. Ever since they had come to this country, their life together was a constant war. "This is America, Papi, America!" she reminded him now. "You are not in a savage country any more!"

I was on my knees, weeping wildly, collecting all the little pieces of my speech, hoping that I could put it back together before the assembly tomorrow morning. But not even a sibyl[5] could have made sense of all those scattered pieces of paper. All hope was lost. "He broke it, he broke it," I moaned as I picked up a handful of pieces.

Probably, if I had thought a moment about it, I B would not have done what I did next. I would have realized my father had lost brothers and comrades to the dictator Trujillo. For the rest of his life, he would be haunted by blood in the streets and late night disappearances. Even after he had been in the states for years, he jumped if a black Volkswagen passed him on the street. He feared anyone in uniform: the meter maid giving out parking tickets, a museum guard approaching to tell him not to touch his favorite Goya at the Metropolitan.

I took a handful of the scraps I had gathered, stood up, and hurled them in his face. "Chapita!" I said in a low, ugly whisper. "You're just another Chapita!"

It took my father only a moment to register the hated nickname of our dictator, and he was after me. Down the halls we raced, but I was quicker than he and made it to my room just in time to lock the door as my father threw his weight against it. He called down curses on my head, ordered me on his authority as my father to open that door this very instant! He throttled that doorknob, but all to no avail. My mother's love of gadgets saved my hide that night. She had hired a locksmith to install good locks on all the bedroom doors after our house had been broken into while we were away the previous summer. In case burglars broke in again, and we were in the house, they'd have a second round of locks to contend with before they got to us.

"Eduardo," she tried to calm him down. "Don't you ruin my new locks."

He finally did calm down, his anger spent. I heard their footsteps retreating down the hall. I heard their door close, the clicking of their lock. Then, muffled voices, my mother's peaking in anger, in persuasion, my father's deep murmurs of explanation and of self-defense. At last, the house fell silent, before I heard, far off, the gun blasts and explosions, the serious, self-important voices of newscasters reporting their TV war.

A little while later, there was a quiet knock at my door, followed by a tentative attempt at the doorknob. "Cukita?" my mother whispered. "Open up, Cukita."

"Go away," I wailed, but we both knew I was glad she was there, and I needed only a moment's protest to save face before opening that door.

What we ended up doing that night was putting together a speech at the last moment. Two brief pages of stale compliments and the polite commonplaces on teachers, wrought by necessity without much invention by mother for daughter late into the night in the basement on the pad of paper and with the same pencil she had once used for her own inventions, for I was too upset to compose the speech myself. After it was drafted, she typed it up while I stood by, correcting her misnomers and mis-sayings.

She was so very proud of herself when I came home the next day with the success story of the assembly. The nuns had been flattered, the audience had stood up and given "our devoted teach-

5. **sibyl** (sib′əl): a woman, in ancient Greece or Rome, who foretold the future to those who consulted her.

Analyzing the Story

Identifying Facts

1. Mami sketched luggage with wheels before it was commercially available.

Her daughters think she spends more time and energy on her inventions than on helping them with their problems adjusting to this new country.

2. There are many more than four. Early ones include corruptions of "wet behind the ears," "When in Rome, do as the Romans do," "Do unto others as you would have them do unto you," "Sticks and stones may break my bones, but names will never hurt me," and "It takes two to tango."

3. Her fellow students and America itself are unfriendly to her, so she seeks comfort and refuge in reading and writing.

4. He thinks it is ungrateful, boastful, and disrespectful, an insult to her teachers.

5. She throws scraps of the speech in his face and calls him the nickname of the hated dictator Trujillo.

(Answers continue on next page.)

The Brown Hat by Milton Avery (1941). Oil on canvas.

Private Collection.

A

ers a standing ovation," what my mother had suggested they do at the end of my speech.

She clapped her hands together as I recreated the moment for her. "I stole that from your father's speech, remember? Remember how he put that in at the end?" She quoted him in Spanish, then translated for me into English.

That night, I watched him from the upstairs hall window where I'd retreated the minute I heard his car pull up in front of our house. Slowly, my father came up the driveway, a grim expression on his face as he grappled with a large, heavy cardboard box. At the front door, he set the package down carefully and patted all his pockets for his house keys—precisely why my mother had invented her ticking key chain. I heard the snapping open of the locks downstairs. Heard as he struggled to maneuver the box through the narrow doorway. Then, he called my name several times. But I would not answer him.

"My daughter, your father, he love you very much," he explained from the bottom of the stairs. "He just want to protect you." Finally, my mother came up and pleaded with me to go down and reconcile with him. "Your father did not mean to harm. You must pardon him. Always it is better to let bygones be forgotten, no?"

I guess she was right. Downstairs, I found him setting up a brand new electric typewriter on the kitchen table. It was even better than the one I'd been begging to get like my mother's. My father had outdone himself with all the extra features: a plastic carrying case with my initials, in decals, below the handle, a brace to lift the paper upright

B

A. Humanities Connection: Responding to the Fine Art

For information about Milton Avery, see page 906.

? Why do you think Avery called this "The Brown Hat" rather than "The Reading Girl"? (The hat is the thing your eyes are drawn to first because of its size and dark color.) Where do your eyes move after they rest on the hat? (Answers will vary. Probably to the girl's eyes and then down to the paper she is reading.)

What do you think this girl is thinking about? (Answers will vary.)

B. Theme/ Conflict

? How have the relationships between husband and wife, and father and daughter changed? (In buying the deluxe typewriter, the father is apologizing to his daughter and, in effect, relinquishing some of his authority by admitting that his wife was right about the speech.)

(Continued from previous page.)

Interpreting Meanings

6. Papi believes the words are revolutionary, challenging his daughter's teachers and expressing contempt for them.

Whitman is saying that students who challenge established ideas honor their teachers. A good teacher gives students the skills needed to think on their own.

7. (a) Mami mangles another saying when she calls necessity the daughter of invention.

(b) This experience frees her to invent her own life, to find her own voice.

(c) Mami's last invention is a successful speech that leads to a reconciliation among the three characters.

8. The narrator uses "Mami" for the woman who acts like a traditional mother, concerned and watchful. She uses the name "Mom" for the woman who tries to be a friend to her daughters.

This line speaks metaphorically of the love visible on Mami's face. There may be war between her and Papi, and real war in their past and on TV, but Mami's love endures.

9. Answers will vary. Students should take into account both his adherence to

(Answers continue in left-hand column.)

(Continued from top.)

traditional values and Papi's gut-level fear for his daughter, caused by his own experiences in the Dominican Republic.

10. The narrator's comments about the nuns and her textbooks—and the nuns' pleasure at her banal speech—indicate that they would not have been pleased. The speech might have been a disaster.

while I typed, an erase cartridge, an automatic margin tab, a plastic hood like a toaster cover to keep the dust away. Not even my mother, I think, could have invented such a machine!

But her inventing days were over just as mine were starting up with my schoolwide success. That's why I've always thought of that speech my mother wrote for me as her last invention rather than the suitcase rollers everyone else in the family remembers. It was as if she had passed on to me her pencil and pad and said, "Okay, Cukita, here's the buck. You give it a shot."

Responding to the Story

Analyzing the Story

Identifying Facts

1. Nobody in the family takes the mother's inventions seriously. But one invention becomes a huge success—for somebody else. Which one is it? Why did the daughters resent the time she spent on inventions?
2. The narrator's mother is fond of English **aphorisms**—that is, brief wise sayings—but she always seems to get them slightly wrong. List at least four of her mangled sayings and write them correctly.
3. Why did the girl narrating the story take "root in the language" of her new country?
4. Explain why the narrator's father objects to her Whitman-inspired speech.
5. How does the daughter insult her father, after he destroys her speech?

Interpreting Meanings

6. The girl wants to use Whitman's words: "He most honors my style who learns under it to destroy the teacher." What does the girl's father interpret the words to mean? Do you think this is what Whitman really meant by them?
7. A good **title** often has what might be termed "resonance." That is, it echoes with meaning. Explain how Alvarez's title touches on (a) a humorous detail of the story, (b) the **theme** of the story, and (c) the **climax** of the story.
8. The girl's mother is a memorable **character,** though her daughters do not always think so. What does the narrator mean on page 904 when she says "She was a good enough Mami, fussing and scolding and giving advice, but a terrible girlfriend parent, a real failure of a Mom"? What does she mean on page 908 by describing her mother's face: "On it was written a love note to my father"?
9. The **characterization** of the narrator's father is sketchy compared to that of her mother. Yet the father plays a vital role in the plot. Can you understand why the father, given his background, did not want his daughter to challenge authority?
10. How do you think the narrator's "recklessly" composed speech, which so impressed her mother, would have gone over with the nuns?

Writing About the Story

A Creative Response

1. **Writing a Character's Speech.** The narrator's original speech, inspired by Walt Whitman's poetry, ends up as little pieces of paper on the floor. It was apparently a moving speech. Reread the Walt Whitman selections in this book, beginning on page 331. Then write the first page (approximately 250 words) of the speech you think the narrator might have written. You can use the Whitman lines she used or any other Whitman lines you feel are appropriate. Compare a few of the speech openings in class to see how they are similar and how they are different.

A Critical Response

2. **Analyzing Confict.** This story is full of conflicts, some of which are personal and some of which are political. In a brief essay, name and describe at least five conflicts in this story. Before you write, fill out a chart like the following to gather your details:

Conflict	People involved and outcome (if known)
1. Generational conflict	
2. Cultural conflict	
3. Husband-wife conflict	
4. Political conflict within one country	
5. Conflict caused by larger, faraway war	

Amy Tan (1952–   )

Amy Tan's parents fled Communist China and came to the United States shortly before Amy was born. Her mother was originally from Shanghai; her father, an engineer and a Baptist minister, came from Beijing. Amy was born in Oakland, California, where, in spite of her family's strong cultural traditions, she grew up wholly American and in something of a mutiny against the submissiveness expected of Chinese daughters.

When her father and young brother both died of brain tumors (Amy was just fifteen), her mother took her away from the "diseased" house to Switzerland, where she finished high school. Her mother expected her talented daughter to become a neurosurgeon, as well as a pianist in her spare time. When they returned to the United States, Tan enrolled as a pre-med student at Linfield College, a Baptist school in Oregon, which was selected by her mother. But she defied her mother by leaving Linfield to join her boyfriend at San Jose State University, where she changed her major from pre-med to English.

Tan's mother took this defiance as a sort of death between them, and they did not speak for six months. Both mother and daughter mourned their loss of love.

Tan was well aware of her mother's narrative gift (she says her mother can talk for three hours straight), and perhaps it was this which prompted her own desire to write. She began a career as a technical writer for businesses, and was thirty-three when she wrote her first story. Called "Endgame" and written for the Squaw Valley Writers' Conference, it was the first of many stories that would explore the powerful relationship between daughters and their mothers.

These stories were later collected into one volume, which became the now widely known bestseller *The Joy Luck Club*. In it are stories

about Chinese American daughters, interwoven with stories of their four Chinese mothers, who are members of a mah-jongg club in San Francisco.

Amy Tan's mother has become reconciled to her daughter's independence, and now she takes pride in her daughter's success as a writer. But, according to her now-famous daughter, she is still not entirely satisfied with Amy's accomplishment in a land where *all* things are possible. Interestingly, her mother does not see *The Joy Luck Club* as autobiographical.

A subsequent novel by Tan, *The Kitchen God's Wife* (1991), is from a mother's point of view. In it, Winnie Louie tells her grown daughter what her life was like in China during World War II.

A. Expansion
The title *Joy Luck Club* refers to a club first started in war-torn China by one of the mothers. Four women gathered to eat, laugh, tell stories, and play mah-jongg, each week hoping to be lucky—the hope that was their only joy.

Tan wrote the book as a collection of stories, not as a novel, and sold it based on three chapters and brief descriptions of the remaining chapters. "I just went with the story that seemed to want to be told next, and it seemed to alternate between mother and daughter," said Tan in an interview in *Poets and Writers Magazine.* "I'd write a mother's story, and then I'd hear the daughter saying, 'Well, let me tell my side of it.' "

PREPARATION

1. ESTABLISHING A PURPOSE. As suggested in the headnote, have students write down what they think the title means. Encourage students to watch for various types of rules as they read.

2. PREREADING JOURNAL. Have students do some freewriting about the unwritten "rules" of life.

SUPPLEMENTARY SUPPORT MATERIALS

1. Vocabulary Activity Worksheet (*CCB*)
2. Review and Response Worksheet: Plot and Theme (*CCB*)
3. Language Skills Worksheet: Irregular Verbs (*CCB*)
4. Selection Test (*CCB*)

DEVELOPING VOCABULARY

The following words from the story are tested in the Selection Test. (See also Vocabulary Activity Worksheet.)

intricate	retort
benefactor	to tout
adversary	malodorous
foresight	concession
benevolently	to careen

A. Expansion
Tan's first version of "Rules of the Game" was thirteen pages long and took Waverly from age five to age thirty-five. A fellow writer at a workshop pointed out that the draft formed the core of about a dozen stories, told in several different voices. Tan revised that story and succeeding ones many times. Even today, Tan usually revises each page twelve to twenty times, she says, often reading the work aloud to check its rhythmic quality.

B. Expansion
Chess is an ancient game, dating to about 500 A.D. It is the offspring of a Hindu game that originated in Pakistan but spread to Persia (present-day Iran), where it gained its name (from the Persian word *shah,* "king") and its victory call of *checkmate* (from *shah mat,* "the king is dead"). By the 16th century the game had assumed its current form. Benjamin Franklin, who both played chess and wrote about it, popularized it in America.

RULES OF THE GAME

At first, this story appears to be about a Chinese-American girl who stumbles her way into the forbidding world of championship chess and becomes an absolute whiz at it. But presently we come to understand that the story is about a matter far more familiar to us. It is about that clash between a mother's authority over her children and her ambition for them, and a daughter's need to find her own way.

A **This is a theme which Amy Tan explores so tellingly in her stories about Chinese-American families in San Francisco. In this story, "Rules of the Game," we are particularly fascinated by the accurate detail—just how the beat-up chess set arrived in the Jong family, how Waverly became interested in the game while her brothers played, and how her interest grew as theirs waned. It's as if we become Waverly's rooters during her apprenticeship and rapid rise through the tournament, so we are quite unprepared to discover what's really going on in that final match with her true adversary and coach.**

Before you read, write down what you think the title could mean. (Might it have two meanings?)

B My older brother Vincent was the one who actually got the chess set. We had gone to the annual Christmas party held at the First Chinese Baptist Church at the end of the alley. The missionary ladies had put together a Santa bag of gifts donated by members of another church. None of the gifts had names on them. There were separate sacks for boys and girls of different ages.

One of the Chinese parishioners had donned a Santa Claus costume and a stiff paper beard with cotton balls glued to it. I think the only children who thought he was the real thing were too young to know that Santa Claus was not Chinese. When my turn came up, the Santa man asked me how old I was. I thought it was a trick question; I was seven according to the American formula and eight by the Chinese calendar. I said I was born on March 17, 1951. That seemed to satisfy him. He then solemnly asked if I had been a very, very good girl this year and did I believe in Jesus Christ and obey my parents. I knew the only answer to that. I nodded back with equal solemnity.

Having watched the other children opening their gifts, I already knew that the big gifts were not necessarily the nicest ones. One girl my age got a large coloring book of biblical characters, while a less greedy girl who selected a smaller box received a glass vial of lavender toilet water. The sound of the box was also important. A ten-year-old boy had chosen a box that jangled when he shook it. It was a tin globe of the world with a slit for inserting money. He must have thought it was full of dimes and nickels, because when he saw that it had just ten pennies, his face fell with such undisguised disappointment that his mother slapped the side of his head and led him out of the church hall, apologizing to the crowd for her son who had such bad manners he couldn't appreciate such a fine gift.

As I peered into the sack, I quickly fingered the remaining presents, testing their weight, imagining what they contained. I chose a heavy, compact one that was wrapped in shiny silver foil and a red satin ribbon. It was a twelve-pack of Life Savers and I spent the rest of the party arranging and rearranging the candy tubes in the order of my favorites. My brother Winston chose wisely as well. His present turned out to be a box of intricate plastic parts; the instructions on the box proclaimed that when they were properly assembled he would have an authentic miniature replica of a World War II submarine.

Vincent got the chess set, which would have been a very decent present to get at a church Christmas party, except it was obviously used and, as we discovered later, it was missing a black pawn and a white knight. My mother graciously thanked the unknown benefactor, saying, "Too good. Cost too much." At which point, an old lady with fine white, wispy hair nodded toward our family and said with a whistling whisper, "Merry, merry Christmas."

When we got home, my mother told Vincent to throw the chess set away. "She not want it. We not want it," she said, tossing her head stiffly to the side with a tight, proud smile. My brothers had deaf ears. They were already lining up the chess pieces and reading from the dog-eared instruction book.

I watched Vincent and Winston play during Christmas week. The chessboard seemed to hold elaborate secrets waiting to be untangled. The chessmen were more powerful than Old Li's magic herbs that cured ancestral curses. And my brothers wore such serious faces that I was sure something was at stake that was greater than avoiding the tradesmen's door to Hong Sing's.

"Let me! Let me!" I begged between games when one brother or the other would sit back with a deep sigh of relief and victory, the other annoyed, unable to let go of the outcome. Vincent at first refused to let me play, but when I offered my Life Savers as replacements for the buttons that filled in for the missing pieces, he relented. He chose the flavors: wild cherry for the black pawn and peppermint for the white knight. Winner could eat both.

As our mother sprinkled flour and rolled out small doughy circles for the steamed dumplings that would be our dinner that night, Vincent explained the rules, pointing to each piece. "You have sixteen pieces and so do I. One king and queen, two bishops, two knights, two castles, and eight pawns. The pawns can only move forward one step, except on the first move. Then they can move two. But they can only take men by moving crossways like this, except in the beginning, when you can move ahead and take another pawn."

"Why?" I asked as I moved my pawn. "Why can't they move more steps?"

"Because they're pawns," he said.

"But why do they go crossways to take other men. Why aren't there any women and children?"

"Why is the sky blue? Why must you always ask stupid questions?" asked Vincent. "This is a game. These are the rules. I didn't make them up. See. Here. In the book." He jabbed a page with a pawn in his hand. "Pawn. P-A-W-N. Pawn. Read it yourself."

My mother patted the flour off her hands. "Let me see book," she said quietly. She scanned the pages quickly, not reading the foreign English symbols, seeming to search deliberately for nothing in particular. A

"This American rules," she concluded at last. "Every time people come out from foreign country, must know rules. You not know, judge say, Too bad, go back. They not telling you why so you can use their way go forward. They say, Don't know why, you find out yourself. But they knowing all the time. Better you take it, find out why yourself." She tossed her head back with a satisfied smile.

I found out about all the whys later. I read the rules and looked up all the big words in a dictionary. I borrowed books from the Chinatown library. I studied each chess piece, trying to absorb the power each contained.

I learned about opening moves and why it's important to control the center early on: the shortest distance between two points is straight down the middle. I learned about the middle game and why tactics between two adversaries are like clashing ideas; the one who plays better has the clearest plans for both attacking and getting out of traps. I learned why it is essential in the endgame to have foresight, a mathematical understanding of all possible moves, and patience; all weaknesses and advantages become evident to a strong adversary and are obscured to a tiring opponent. I discovered that for the whole game one must gather invisible strengths and see the endgame before the game begins.

I also found out why I should never reveal "why" to others. A little knowledge withheld is a great advantage one should store for future use. That is the power of chess. It is a game of secrets in which one must show and never tell.

I loved the secrets I found within the sixty-four black and white squares. I carefully drew a handmade chessboard and pinned it to the wall next to my bed, where at night I would stare for hours at imaginary battles. Soon I no longer lost any games or Life Savers, but I lost my adversaries. Winston and Vincent decided they were more interested in roaming the streets after school in their Hopalong Cassidy cowboy hats.

On a cold spring afternoon, while walking home from school, I detoured through the playground

A. Conflict
? Why does the narrator emphasize the pawn's play? What does the word *pawn* mean when applied to a person? (A pawn is a person used to advance someone else's purposes. The narrator is being used by her brothers to supply Life Savers for the missing chess pieces.) As students read the story, have them decide if Waverly is using her family as pawns, or whether her mother is using her.

B. Expansion
The original title of this story was "Endgame." After students read the story, ask them which title they prefer and why.

C. Interpretation
? What do the narrator's comments here mean in terms of chess? (She is talking about game strategy: One can make moves that will puzzle the opponent if one knows their end result.) Do her comments apply to other situations in life? (Answers will vary; encourage specific examples.)

A. Interpretation ? How does Lau Po regard his new opponent? (He believes her to be a silly little girl.) What does Waverly mean when she says that she "displayed her retort"? (She doesn't answer him in words; instead she shows him her skill.) What earlier comment about chess does her response echo? (Chess is a game of showing, not telling.)

at the end of our alley. I saw a group of old men, two seated across a folding table playing a game of chess, others smoking pipes, eating peanuts, and watching. I ran home and grabbed Vincent's chess set, which was bound in a cardboard box with rubber bands. I also carefully selected two prized rolls of Life Savers. I came back to the park and approached a man who was observing the game.

"Want to play?" I asked him. His face widened with surprise and he grinned as he looked at the box under my arm.

"Little sister, been a long time since I play with dolls," he said, smiling benevolently. I quickly put the box down next to him on the bench and displayed my retort.

Lau Po, as he allowed me to call him, turned out to be a much better player than my brothers. I lost many games and many Life Savers. But over the weeks, with each diminishing roll of candies, I added new secrets. Lau Po gave me the names. The Double Attack from the East and West

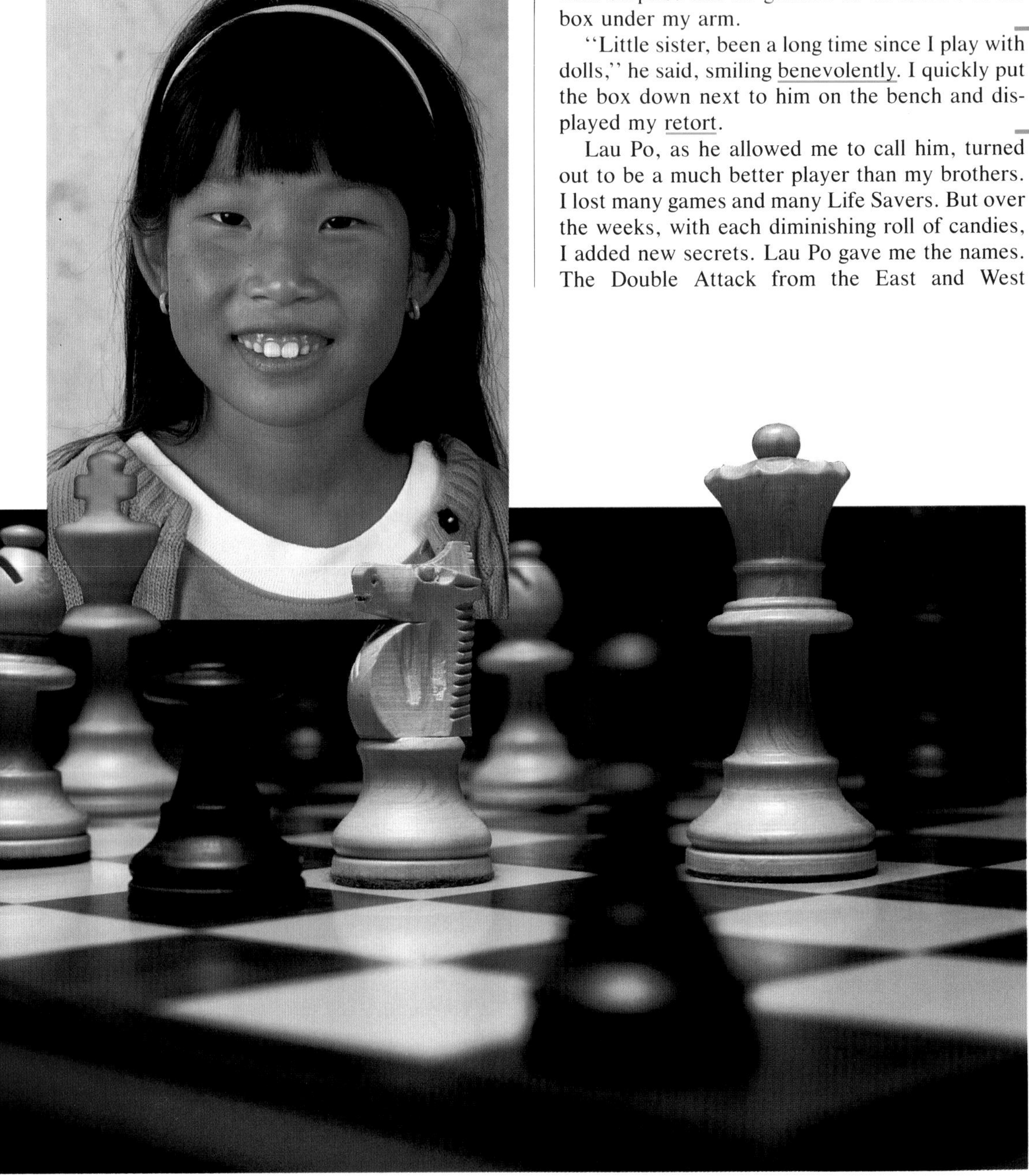

Reading Check Test

1. Waverly's brother receives a chess set at **(a)** a birthday party, **(b)** a Christmas party, or **(c)** an awards ceremony. *(b)*
2. Waverly learns how to play chess from **(a)** her mother, **(b)** a book, or **(c)** an old man. *(b)*
3. Waverly's mother takes pride in her when she **(a)** starts to win tournaments, **(b)** runs away, or **(c)** beats her brothers at chess. *(a)*
4. On market day Waverly runs away when she is **(a)** embarrassed by her mother, **(b)** photographed for a magazine, or **(c)** defeated in a game of chess. *(a)*
5. Waverly eventually realizes that her most persistent adversary is **(a)** Lau Po, **(b)** her mother, or **(c)** the man in the black suit. *(b)*

Shores. Throwing Stones on the Drowning Man. The Sudden Meeting of the Clan. The Surprise from the Sleeping Guard. The Humble Servant Who Kills the King. Sand in the Eyes of Advancing Forces. A Double Killing Without Blood.

There were also the fine points of chess etiquette. Keep captured men in neat rows, as well-tended prisoners. Never announce "Check" with vanity, lest someone with an unseen sword slit your throat. Never hurl pieces into the sandbox after you have lost a game, because then you must find them again, by yourself, after apologizing to all around you. By the end of the summer, Lau Po had taught me all he knew, and I had become a better chess player.

A small weekend crowd of Chinese people and tourists would gather as I played and defeated my opponents one by one. My mother would join the crowds during these outdoor exhibition games. She sat proudly on the bench, telling my admirers with proper Chinese humility, "Is luck."

A man who watched me play in the park suggested that my mother allow me to play in local chess tournaments. My mother smiled graciously, an answer that meant nothing. I desperately wanted to go, but I bit back my tongue. I knew she would not let me play among strangers. So as we walked home I said in a small voice that I didn't want to play in the local tournament. They would have American rules. If I lost, I would bring shame on my family.

"Is shame you fall down nobody push you," said my mother.

During my first tournament, my mother sat with me in the front row as I waited for my turn. I frequently bounced my legs to unstick them from the cold metal seat of the folding chair. When my name was called, I leapt up. My mother unwrapped something in her lap. It was her *chang*, a small tablet of red jade which held the sun's fire. "Is luck," she whispered, and tucked it into my dress pocket. I turned to my opponent, a fifteen-year-old boy from Oakland. He looked at me, wrinkling his nose.

As I began to play, the boy disappeared, the color ran out of the room, and I saw only my white pieces and his black ones waiting on the other side. A light wind began blowing past my ears. It whispered secrets only I could hear.

"Blow from the South," it murmured. "The wind leaves no trail." I saw a clear path, the traps to avoid. The crowd rustled. "Shhh! Shhh!" said the corners of the room. The wind blew stronger. "Throw sand from the East to distract him." The knight came forward ready for the sacrifice. The wind hissed, louder and louder. "Blow, blow, blow. He cannot see. He is blind now. Make him lean away from the wind so he is easier to knock down."

"Check," I said, as the wind roared with laughter. The wind died down to little puffs, my own breath.

My mother placed my first trophy next to a new plastic chess set that the neighborhood Tao society had given to me. As she wiped each piece with a soft cloth, she said, "Next time win more, lose less."

"Ma, it's not how many pieces you lose," I said. "Sometimes you need to lose pieces to get ahead."

"Better to lose less, see if you really need."

At the next tournament, I won again, but it was my mother who wore the triumphant grin.

"Lost eight piece this time. Last time was eleven. What I tell you? Better off lose less!" I was annoyed, but I couldn't say anything.

I attended more tournaments, each one farther away from home. I won all games, in all divisions. The Chinese bakery downstairs from our flat displayed my growing collection of trophies in its window, amidst the dust-covered cakes that were never picked up. The day after I won an important regional tournament, the window encased a fresh sheet cake with whipped-cream frosting and red script saying, "Congratulations, Waverly Jong, Chinatown Chess Champion." Soon after that, a flower shop, headstone engraver, and funeral parlor offered to sponsor me in national tournaments. That's when my mother decided I no longer had to do the dishes. Winston and Vincent had to do my chores.

"Why does she get to play and we do all the work," complained Vincent.

"Is new American rules," said my mother. "Meimei[1] play, squeeze all her brains out for win chess. You play, worth squeeze towel."

C

By my ninth birthday, I was a national chess champion. I was still some 429 points away from

1. **Meimei** (mā′mā): Chinese for "little sister."

A. Conflict

? How does Waverly get her mother to let her play in the tournament? (She uses reverse psychology, pretending a fear of failure.) What does her mother's answer mean? (It's more shameful to give up without trying than to fail.)

B. Figurative Language

The narrator associates wind with her thoughts about strategy here, in her confrontation with her mother on the street, and at the story's end. ? What does the wind represent to Waverly? (Her knowledge of strategy) How does the wind's advice echo Waverly's earlier comments about chess? (She is keeping the boy guessing, avoiding his traps and distracting him into hers.)

C. Conflict

? Why does Waverly's mother free her from household chores? (Her mother wants Waverly to devote her time to chess.) How would that make Waverly and her brothers feel? (Answers will vary.)

CLOSURE

Have students identify the central conflict of the story and describe how that conflict is dealt with by the end of the story. (The ending is something of a cliff-hanger; we expect the conflict between Waverly and her mother to continue.)

A. Expansion

Bobby Fischer (b. 1943) was also a child prodigy, the youngest chess player ever ranked as an international grand master. He won the first of many U. S. championships in 1958. The match that won him the world championship in 1972 generated enormous worldwide interest in chess.

B. Interpretation

? What "game" is Waverly playing here? To what purpose? (She is deliberately creating an image of a sweet little girl. This strategy again conceals her "invisible strengths," enabling her to confuse her opponent with the incongruity of her appearance and her skill.) Does Waverly enjoy this game as much as she enjoys chess? (Answers will vary.)

C. Conflict

? Are Waverly's complaints serious ones? Why do her parents give in to her? How would their doing so make Waverly feel? How would her brothers feel? (Answers will vary.)

grand-master status,[2] but I was touted as the Great American Hope, a child prodigy and a girl to boot. A They ran a photo of me in *Life* magazine next to a quote in which Bobby Fischer said, "There will never be a woman grand master." "Your move, Bobby," said the caption.

The day they took the magazine picture I wore neatly plaited braids clipped with plastic barrettes trimmed with rhinestones. I was playing in a large high school auditorium that echoed with phlegmy coughs and the squeaky rubber knobs of chair legs sliding across freshly waxed wooden floors. Seated across from me was an American man, about the same age as Lau Po, maybe fifty. I remember that his sweaty brow seemed to weep at my every move. He wore a dark, malodorous suit. One of his pockets was stuffed with a great white kerchief on which he wiped his palm before sweeping his hand over the chosen chess piece with great flourish.

B In my crisp pink-and-white dress with scratchy lace at the neck, one of two my mother had sewn for these special occasions, I would clasp my hands under my chin, the delicate points of my elbows poised lightly on the table in the manner my mother had shown me for posing for the press. I would swing my patent leather shoes back and forth like an impatient child riding on a school bus. Then I would pause, suck in my lips, twirl my chosen piece in midair as if undecided, and then firmly plant it in its new threatening place, with a triumphant smile thrown back at my opponent for good measure.

I no longer played in the alley of Waverly Place. I never visited the playground where the pigeons and old men gathered. I went to school, then directly home to learn new chess secrets, cleverly concealed advantages, more escape routes.

But I found it difficult to concentrate at home. My mother had a habit of standing over me while I plotted out my games. I think she thought of herself as my protective ally. Her lips would be sealed tight, and after each move I made, a soft "Hmmmmph" would escape from her nose.

"Ma, I can't practice when you stand there like that," I said one day. She retreated to the kitchen and made loud noises with the pots and pans. When the crashing stopped, I could see out of the corner of my eye that she was standing in the doorway. "Hmmmph!" Only this one came out of her tight throat.

C My parents made many concessions to allow me to practice. One time I complained that the bedroom I shared was so noisy that I couldn't think. Thereafter, my brothers slept in a bed in the living room facing the street. I said I couldn't finish my rice; my head didn't work right when my stomach was too full. I left the table with half-finished bowls and nobody complained. But there was one duty I couldn't avoid. I had to accompany my mother on Saturday market days when I had no tournament to play. My mother would proudly walk with me, visiting many shops, buying very little. "This my daughter Wave-ly Jong," she said to whoever looked her way.

One day, after we left a shop I said under my breath, "I wish you wouldn't do that, telling everybody I'm your daughter." My mother stopped walking. Crowds of people with heavy bags pushed past us on the sidewalk, bumping into first one shoulder, then another.

"Aiii-ya. So shame be with mother?" She grasped my hand even tighter as she glared at me.

I looked down. "It's not that, it's just so obvious. It's just so embarrassing."

"Embarrass you be my daughter?" Her voice was cracking with anger.

"That's not what I meant. That's not what I said."

"What you say?"

I knew it was a mistake to say anything more, but I heard my voice speaking. "Why do you have to use me to show off? If you want to show off, then why don't you learn to play chess."

My mother's eyes turned into dangerous black slits. She had no words for me, just sharp silence.

I felt the wind rushing around my hot ears. I jerked my hand out of my mother's tight grasp and spun around, knocking into an old woman. Her bag of groceries spilled to the ground.

"Aii-ya! Stupid girl!" my mother and the woman cried. Oranges and tin cans careened down the sidewalk. As my mother stooped to help the old woman pick up the escaping food, I took off.

I raced down the street, dashing between people, not looking back as my mother screamed shrilly, "Meimei! Meimei!" I fled down an alley,

---

2. **grand-master status:** an expert ranking in international chess competition.

A. Interpretation

? How would you rephrase the mother's comment? ("Since she doesn't care about us, we don't care about her.") Has the mother won a victory? How? (Answers will vary. Students may suggest that her victory is hollow and may be only temporary.)

Analyzing The Story

Identifying Facts

1. Vincent received it as a gift at a church Christmas party.

The boys let Waverly play when she offers Life Savers as replacements for two missing pieces.

2. She shows her ambition for Waverly when she advises Waverly to lose fewer pieces, relieves Waverly from chores so Waverly can practice, hovers while Waverly practices, and gives in to Waverly's complaints. She shows her pride by attending Waverly's games, sewing dresses for Waverly, and introducing Waverly to passersby.

(Answers continue on next page.)

past dark curtained shops and merchants washing the grime off their windows. I sped into the sunlight, into a large street crowded with tourists examining trinkets and souvenirs. I ducked into another dark alley, down another street, up another alley. I ran until it hurt and I realized I had nowhere to go, that I was not running from anything. The alleys contained no escape routes.

My breath came out like angry smoke. It was cold. I sat down on an upturned plastic pail next to a stack of empty boxes, cupping my chin with my hands, thinking hard. I imagined my mother, first walking briskly down one street or another looking for me, then giving up and returning home to await my arrival. After two hours, I stood up on creaking legs and slowly walked home.

The alley was quiet and I could see the yellow lights shining from our flat like two tiger's eyes in the night. I climbed the sixteen steps to the door, advancing quietly up each so as not to make any warning sounds. I turned the knob; the door was locked. I heard a chair moving, quick steps, the locks turning—click! click! click!—and then the door opened.

"About time you got home," said Vincent. "Boy, are you in trouble."

He slid back to the dinner table. On a platter were the remains of a large fish, its fleshy head still connected to bones swimming upstream in vain escape. Standing there waiting for my punishment, I heard my mother speak in a dry voice.

"We not concerning this girl. This girl not have concerning for us."

Nobody looked at me. Bone chopsticks clicked against the insides of bowls being emptied into hungry mouths.

I walked into my room, closed the door, and lay down on my bed. The room was dark, the ceiling filled with shadows from the dinnertime lights of neighboring flats.

In my head, I saw a chessboard with sixty-four black and white squares. Opposite me was my opponent, two angry black slits. She wore a triumphant smile. "Strongest wind cannot be seen," she said.

Her black men advanced across the plane, slowly marching to each successive level as a single unit. My white pieces screamed as they scurried and fell off the board one by one. As her men drew closer to my edge, I felt myself growing light. I rose up into the air and flew out the window. Higher and higher, above the alley, over the tops of tiled roofs, where I was gathered up by the wind and pushed up toward the night sky until everything below me disappeared and I was alone.

I closed my eyes and pondered my next move.

B

Responding to the Story

C

Analyzing the Story

Identifying Facts

1. How did the Jong family get their first chess set? Explain how young Waverly came to be allowed to play with her brothers.
2. "Show, don't tell" is an important rule of **characterization.** Point out some of the ways in which Waverly's mother shows she is ambitious for her daughter. How does she show that she is proud of Waverly's accomplishments?
3. As a result of Waverly's success at chess, what **conflicts** arise between her and her mother?

Interpreting Meanings

4. Think about what it is in Waverly's nature that draws her to the intricate game of chess. What does Waverly learn is the "power of chess"? How does this discovery relate to the relationship between Waverly and her mother?
5. What does Waverly's mother mean when she says on page 913, "She not want it. We not want it"? How do the boys' actions following this remark show the cultural and generational **conflicts** between the mother and her children?
6. Why does Waverly resent having her mother "show her off"? What do you think is her mother's **motive?**

(Continued from previous page.)
3. Waverly sees chess as her game, but her mother seems to want to be part of it. Waverly believes that her mother is using her to show off.

Interpreting Meanings
4. Waverly's curiosity and competitiveness seem to draw her to chess, but students may suggest other characteristics. She learns that the "power of chess" lies in keeping secrets and using your secret strategy to manipulate your opponent.

Waverly applies this principle when she gets her mother to let her play in a tournament but forgets it when she confronts her mother on the street.
5. Waverly's mother does not want to accept someone else's castoff, but the boys have no such scruples.
6. Answers will vary. Perhaps Waverly feels that her mother is taking credit for her own accomplishments.

Her mother's motives probably center on pride in her daughter and a desire to share in her victories.
7. The wind that blows in Waverly's mind during her first tournament echoes that statement: "The wind leaves no trail."
(Answers continue in left-hand column.)

(Continued from top.)
Answers should refer to what the narrator calls "invisible strengths."
8. Waverly studies escape routes in chess, soft noises escape from her mother, food escapes on the street, and Waverly and the supper fish vainly seek escape routes. Answers should note that Waverly is trying to escape from her mother's dominance.
9. Waverly's fantasy suggests that escape is possible.

Answers about her next move will vary. (In a later chapter in the book, Waverly at first resolves to give up chess; but when she does return, she finds she has lost her gift. She quits for good when she is fourteen.)
10. Many rules figure in the story: how to talk to Santa Claus, how to play chess, how to make one's way in a new culture, how to use reverse psychology to get one's way, how family chores are distributed. The title refers to both chess and mother-daughter relationships.

7. Waverly's imaginary opponent has the last word when she says on page 917, "Strongest wind cannot be seen." Where else in the story is that statement used? Explain what you think it means.
8. Find passages toward the end of the story which talk about "escapes" of various sorts. Do you think Waverly is trying to escape anything in this story? Explain.
9. What do you think is the significance of Waverly's fantasy at the story's end? Given what you've learned about her character, what do you predict will be her "next move"?
10. Think about the story's **title.** Find passages in the story where "rules" of various sorts are talked about. Might the title have two meanings? What could they be?

Writing About the Story

A Critical Response

1. **Responding to a Critic.** In a review of *The Joy Luck Club* that appeared in *The Washington Post*, one critic made this observation:

> These women from China find trying to talk to their daughters like trying to plug a foreign appliance into an American outlet. The current won't work. Impulses collide and nothing flows through the wires except anger and exasperation. When one daughter remarks, "I'm my own person," the mother thinks, "How can she be her own person? When did I give her up?"
>
> —Susan Dooley

In a brief essay tell whether or not you think this quotation applies to "Rules of the Game." Does it fit? Is the communication between mother and daughter as negative as this passage implies? Use quotations from both Susan Dooley and Amy Tan in your response. State your opinion about the relevance of the critic's quote in your first or last sentence.

2. **Putting the Characters in Different Stories.** Although Waverly Jong is much younger than Julia Alvarez's "Cukita" (page 903), both girls have ideas or desires that conflict with those of their parents. In a brief essay, tell what you imagine would happen if Mrs. Jong and Cukita's mother entered each other's story. If Mrs. Jong could be brought into Julia Alvarez's story, whose side would she take, that of Cukita's mother or that of her father? (You might quote speeches from "Rules of the Game" to support your opinion.) If Cukita's mother could be introduced to Mrs. Jong, what advice would she give her? (Make up dialogue, if you wish.)

Analyzing Language and Style

The "Language" of Games (A Group Activity)

Choose a sport or game familiar to you and your classmates. Working in groups, prepare reports on the "etiquette" of the game, its unwritten rules, and the colorful terms used to describe its special maneuvers or plays. Before you begin, review Tan's discussion of the "language" of chess on pages 914–915.

Primary Sources

An Interview with Amy Tan

In a magazine interview, Amy Tan answered questions about her stories of mothers and daughters in *The Joy Luck Club*. Here are some of her responses:

Q: Do you have advice to offer aspiring novelists?
A: You have to develop a discipline, and you have to learn that you can't always wait for inspiration. Also, I think young writers try to imitate the people they admire, and that's dangerous. No matter how well you imitate Tama Janowitz or Jay McInerney, it doesn't work. You have to find your own voice.

Q: How do Chinese Americans like your book?
A: My feelings were so personal, I didn't think anyone else felt that way. The surprise is how many Chinese people have said, "Your stories are so much like my family." They thought I had been eavesdropping in their living rooms.

Q: How does your mother feel about your success?
A: The day the book was number four on the New York *Times* Best-Seller list, I showed the list to my mother. She looked at it, laid her finger across the line, and asked, "Who's number three? And two? And one?" She's very proud, but none of this impresses her too much, and she doesn't think that I should be impressed either. But she was also saying, "I think you should be number one."

Donald Barthelme (1931–1989)

Donald Barthelme was an experimenter in fiction, a true member of the avant-garde, sometimes known as a "post-modernist." He is widely regarded as one of the ablest and most versatile American stylists—witty, adventurous, and profound.

In broadest terms, Barthelme's premise was that while literature of the past functioned to revitalize the imagination, storytelling has largely lost the power to inspire, persuade, or even entertain us. He felt that our language has gone bankrupt. Since words no longer effectively communicate feelings, he said, they have lost the power to move us. Like the promotional and professional jargon that bombards us, contemporary language is thick with sludge and stuffing. Its use of clichés and its verbosity often obscure truth rather than reveal it. As Snow White, the title character of Barthelme's 1967 novel, says, "Oh I wish there were some words in the world that were not the words I always hear!"

But it was not the corruption of our language alone that troubled Barthelme. He saw the problems with language as a reflection of a contemporary society so dehumanized, so lacking in quality, that it can no longer sustain the kind of myths that once gave us our identity. Thus, he felt, the whole point of storytelling is lost.

In his fiction, Barthelme deliberately set out to create a banal world that fails to make distinctions of quality in people, things, and ideas. Then, since he felt it was no longer possible to write about real life or the real world, he took writing itself for his subject—the art of making art out of language. Barthelme used language distinctively. As his interest lay in the form and sound of language, he tended to play with words, to make art out of fragments, much as contemporary painters make art out of everyday junk and pop artists make art out of cartoons.

Barthelme's plots are also unconventional. They are episodic, a clutter of styles, absurdities, and slapstick. "The only forms I trust," he said, "are fragments." His characters are types, two-dimensional parodies of themselves, rather than fully developed individuals.

Photograph © 1988 by Jill Krementz.

In Barthelme's hands, a myth is likely to turn into realism, and realism into absurdity; readers can lose their way in Barthelme's fiction, trying to identify with the proceedings and wondering about the writer's point. Barthelme explained to those who are puzzled by his work: "Art is not difficult because it wishes to be difficult, rather because it wishes to be art. However much the writer might long to be, in his work, simple, honest, straightforward, these virtues are no longer available to him. He discovers that in being simple, honest, straightforward, nothing much happens . . . we are looking for the as yet unspeakable, the as yet unspoken."

Barthelme was born in Philadelphia and raised and educated in Texas. After serving with the U.S. Army in the Orient, he worked as a reporter on the *Houston Post,* as a museum director, as the editor of an art and literature review, as a professor of English at the City University of New York, and, most recently, as a teacher of creative writing at the University of Texas at Houston. He was a regular contributor to *The New Yorker.* Collections of his stories include *Come Back, Dr. Caligari* (1964), *Unspeakable Practices, Unnatural Acts* (1968), from which "Game" is taken, and *Overnight to Many Distant Cities* (1983).

Comment From A Critic
Richard Gilman has written that Barthelme is "one of a handful of American writers who are working to replenish and extend the art of fiction instead of trying to add to the stock of entertainments, visions and humanist documents that fiction keeps piling up."

SUPPLEMENTARY SUPPORT MATERIALS
1. Vocabulary Activity Worksheet (*CCB*)
2. Review and Response Worksheet: Experimental Fiction (*CCB*)
3. Language Skills Worksheet: Pronoun Antecedent Agreement (*CCB*)
4. Selection Test (*CCB*)

DEVELOPING VOCABULARY
The following words from the story are tested in the Selection Test. (See also Vocabulary Activity Worksheet.)

console	exemplary
to sate	acrimoniously
scrupulously	nether

PREPARATION
ESTABLISHING A PURPOSE. The headnote suggests that students focus on the various meanings of the word *game* as they read this story. Additionally, you might want to have them look for examples of repetition, a device the author uses extensively and effectively.

A. Euphemism
A euphemism, or pleasant expression for something that is unpleasant, can be metaphorical. The narrator's "the bird flies" is both a euphemism and a metaphor.
? Explain what "the bird" is. (A nuclear missile) How much do Shotwell and the narrator know about the bird's mission? (They know very little. Near the end of the story, the narrator seems to know that the bird is aimed at a city, but he doesn't know what city. See question 4, page 923.)

B. Humor
The theme of this story is serious, but there are touches of humor throughout.
? What is amusing in the narrator's comment about Shotwell's .25 caliber Beretta? (The narrator describes the gun and its location but says he does not know about it.)

C. Parody
What is Barthelme parodying in these lines? (He is parodying military/bureaucratic procedures and prose.)

GAME

How many distinct meanings can you think of for the word *game*? What does it mean to a child? To a professional athlete? To a hunter? Keep these various meanings of the word in mind as you read the story. Remember what Barthelme has said about art being difficult. Read the story slowly, and don't expect everything to be immediately understandable.

Shotwell keeps the jacks and the rubber ball in his attaché case and will not allow me to play with them. He plays with them, alone, sitting on the floor near the console hour after hour, chanting "onesies, twosies, threesies, foursies" in a precise, well-modulated voice, not so loud as to be annoying, not so soft as to allow me to forget. I point out to Shotwell that two can derive more enjoyment from playing jacks than one, but he is not interested. I have asked repeatedly to be allowed to play by myself, but he simply shakes his head. "Why?" I ask. "They're mine," he says. And when he has finished, when he has sated himself, back they go into the attaché case.

It is unfair but there is nothing I can do about it, I am aching to get my hands on them.

Shotwell and I watch the console. Shotwell and I live under the ground and watch the console. If certain events take place upon the console, we are to insert our keys in the appropriate locks and turn our keys. Shotwell has a key and I have a key. If we turn our keys simultaneously the bird flies, certain switches are activated and the bird flies. But the bird never flies. In one hundred thirty-three days the bird has not flown. Meanwhile Shotwell and I watch each other. We each wear a .45 and if Shotwell behaves strangely I am supposed to shoot him. If I behave strangely Shotwell is supposed to shoot me. We watch the console and think about shooting each other and think about the bird. Shotwell's behavior with the jacks is strange. Is it strange? I do not know. Perhaps he is merely selfish . . ., perhaps his character is flawed, perhaps his childhood was twisted. I do not know.

Each of us wears a .45 and each of us is supposed to shoot the other if the other is behaving strangely. How strangely is strangely? I do not know. In addition to the .45 I have a .38 which Shotwell does not know about concealed in my attaché case, and Shotwell has a .25 caliber Beretta which I do not know about strapped to his right calf. Sometimes instead of watching the console I pointedly watch Shotwell's .45, but this is simply a ruse, simply a maneuver, in reality I am watching his hand when it dangles in the vicinity of his right calf. If he decides I am behaving strangely he will shoot me not with the .45 but with the Beretta. Similarly Shotwell pretends to watch my .45 but he is really watching my hand resting idly atop my attaché case, my hand resting idly atop my attaché case, my hand. My hand resting idly atop my attaché case.

In the beginning I took care to behave normally. So did Shotwell. Our behavior was painfully normal. Norms of politeness, consideration, speech, and personal habits were scrupulously observed. But then it became apparent that an error had been made, that our relief was not going to arrive. Owing to an oversight. Owing to an oversight we have been here for one hundred thirty-three days. When it became clear that an error had been made, that we were not to be relieved, the norms were relaxed. Definitions of normality were redrawn in the agreement of January 1, called by us, The Agreement. Uniform regulations were relaxed, and mealtimes are no longer rigorously scheduled. We eat when we are hungry and sleep when we are tired. Considerations of rank and precedence were temporarily put aside, a handsome concession on the part of Shotwell, who is a captain, whereas I am only a first lieutenant. One of us watches the console at all times rather than two of us watching the console at all times, except when we are both on our feet. One of us watches the console at all times and if the bird flies then that one wakes the other and we turn our keys in the locks simultaneously and the bird flies. Our system involves a delay of perhaps twelve seconds but I do not care because I am not well, and Shotwell does not care because he is not himself. After the agreement was signed Shotwell produced the jacks and the rubber ball from his attaché case, and I began to write a series of descriptions of forms occurring in nature, such as a shell, a leaf, a stone, an animal. On the walls.

Shotwell plays jacks and I write descriptions of natural forms on the walls.

Shotwell is enrolled in a USAFI[1] course which leads to a master's degree in business administration from the University of Wisconsin (although we are not in Wisconsin, we are in Utah, Montana, or Idaho). When we went down it was in either Utah, Montana, or Idaho, I don't remember. We have been here for one hundred thirty-three days owing to an oversight. The pale green reinforced concrete walls sweat and the air conditioning zips on and off erratically and Shotwell reads *Introduction to Marketing* by Lassiter and Munk, making notes with a blue ballpoint pen. Shotwell is not himself but I do not know it, he presents a calm aspect and reads *Introduction to Marketing* and makes his exemplary notes with a blue ballpoint pen, meanwhile controlling the .38 in my attaché case with one-third of his attention. I am not well.

We have been here one hundred thirty-three days owing to an oversight. Although now we are not sure what is oversight, what is plan. Perhaps the plan is for us to stay here permanently, or if not permanently at least for a year, for three hundred sixty-five days. Or if not for a year for some number of days known to them and not known to us, such as two hundred days. Or perhaps they are observing our behavior in some way, sensors of some kind, perhaps our behavior determines the number of days. It may be that they are pleased with us, with our behavior, not in every detail but in sum. Perhaps the whole thing is very successful, perhaps the whole thing is an experiment and the experiment is very successful. I do not know. But I suspect that the only way they can persuade sun-loving creatures into their pale green sweating reinforced concrete rooms under the ground is to say that the system is twelve hours on, twelve hours off. And then lock us below for some number of days known to them and not known to us. We eat well although the frozen enchiladas are damp when defrosted and the frozen devil's food cake is sour and untasty. We sleep uneasily and acrimoniously. I hear Shotwell shouting in his sleep, objecting, denouncing, cursing sometimes, weeping sometimes, in his sleep. When Shotwell sleeps I try to pick the lock on his attaché case, so as to get at the jacks. Thus far I have been unsuccessful. Nor has Shotwell been successful in picking the locks on my attaché case so as to get the .38. I have seen the marks on the shiny surface. I laughed, in the latrine, pale green walls sweating and the air conditioning whispering, in the latrine.

I write descriptions of natural forms on the walls, scratching them on the tile surface with a diamond. The diamond is a two and one-half carat solitaire I had in my attaché case when we went down. It was for Lucy. The south wall of the room containing the console is already covered. I have described a shell, a leaf, a stone, animals, a baseball bat. I am aware that the baseball bat is not a natural form. Yet I described it "The baseball bat," I said, "is typically made of wood. It is typically one meter in length or a little longer, fat at one end, tapering to afford a comfortable grip at the other. The end with the handhold typically offers a slight rim, or lip, at the nether extremity, to prevent slippage." My description of the baseball bat ran to 4500 words, all scratched with a diamond on the south wall. Does Shotwell read what I have written? I do not know. I am aware that Shotwell regards my writing-behavior as a little strange. Yet it is no stranger than his jacks-behavior, or the day he appeared in black bathing trunks with the .25 caliber Beretta strapped to his right calf and stood over the console, trying to span with his two arms outstretched the distance between the locks. He could not do it, I had already tried, standing over the console with my two arms outstretched, the distance is too great. I was moved to comment but did not comment, comment would have provoked counter-comment, comment would have led God knows where. They had in their infinite patience, in their infinite foresight, in their infinite wisdom already imagined a man standing over the console with his two arms outstretched, trying to span with his two arms outstretched the distance between the locks.

Shotwell is not himself. He has made certain overtures. The burden of his message is not clear. It has something to do with the keys, with the

B

1. **USAFI:** United States Armed Forces Information, an organization that supervises courses taken by service members.

A. Repetition
The narrator says he does not care about the twelve-second delay in launching the bird, "because I am not well." Have students notice how many times the narrator claims he is not well.
? Does he mean he is physically ill? Mentally ill? (There is no evidence of physical illness, but many signs that both he and Shotwell are on the edge of mental collapse.)

B. Humor
? Since a baseball bat is not a "natural form," why does the narrator include it? (The apparent answer is for its humor—the narrator may "naturally" consider the baseball bat one of civilization's great inventions.)

CLOSURE

Have students write a two- or three-sentence resolution to the plot. Responses should be shared orally in class.

READING CHECK TEST

1. The narrator has no interest in Shotwell's jacks and wishes Shotwell would not play with them. *False*
2. In the 133 days the two men have spent underground, the bird has not flown. *True*
3. By the agreement of January 1, Shotwell, although a colonel, has agreed to put aside considerations of rank. *False*
4. Shotwell successfully picks the lock on the narrator's attaché case and gains possession of the .38. *False*
5. The narrator does not know what city the bird is targeted to hit. *True*

A. Interpretation

The narrator makes it appear that he cannot understand what Shotwell has in mind concerning the keys and locks. This seems strange because the keys have only one function—to make the bird fly. **?** Why might the narrator be confused about Shotwell's intentions? (A possible answer is that the narrator regards nuclear war as unimaginable. Now, faced with the prospect of touching it off himself, his mind refuses to accept the obvious.)

B. Resolution

The story lacks a resolution. Although not exactly a lady-or-tiger ending, it is ambiguous. The reader never learns how the conflicts are resolved. See question 2, page 923.

locks. Shotwell is a strange person. He appears to be less affected by our situation than I. He goes about his business stolidly, watching the console, studying *Introduction to Marketing*, bouncing his rubber ball on the floor in a steady, rhythmical, conscientious manner. He appears to be less affected by our situation than I am. He is stolid. He says nothing. But he has made certain overtures, certain overtures have been made. I am not sure that I understand them. They have something to do with the keys, with the locks. Shotwell has something in mind. Stolidly he shucks the shiny silver paper from the frozen enchiladas, stolidly he stuffs them into the electric oven. But he has something in mind. But there must be a quid pro quo.[2] I insist on a quid pro quo. I have something in mind.

A

I am not well. I do not know our target. They do not tell us for which city the bird is targeted. I do not know. That is planning. That is not my responsibility. My responsibility is to watch the console and when certain events take place upon the console, turn my key in the lock. Shotwell bounces the rubber ball on the floor in a steady, stolid, rhythmical manner. I am aching to get my hands on the ball, on the jacks. We have been here one hundred thirty-three days owing to an oversight. I write on the walls. Shotwell chants "onesies, twosies, threesies, foursies" in a precise, well-modulated voice. Now he cups the jacks and the rubber ball in his hands and rattles them suggestively. I do not know for which city the bird is targeted. Shotwell is not himself.

Sometimes I cannot sleep. Sometimes Shotwell cannot sleep. Sometimes when Shotwell cradles me in his arms and rocks me to sleep, singing Brahms' "Guten abend, gut Nacht,"[3] or I cradle Shotwell in my arms and rock him to sleep, singing, I understand what it is Shotwell wishes me to do. At such moments we are very close. But only if he will give me the jacks. That is fair. There is something he wants me to do with my key, while he does something with his key. But only if he will give me my turn. That is fair. I am not well.

2. **quid pro quo:** a Latin expression meaning "an even exchange."

3. **"Guten . . . Nacht":** German for "Good evening, good night," the opening words of Brahms' *Lullaby*.

A Comment on the Story

Almost every element of Barthelme's story contributes to its satirical, absurdist tone. As in the plays of the theater of the absurd composed by writers like Samuel Beckett and Eugene Ionesco, statements either do not follow each other logically, or they are connected by pseudo-logic. The narrator's constant repetition suggests the mind of someone on the brink of a precipice, desperately trying to hold on to words as symbols of reality and sanity.

The two characters, Shotwell and the unnamed narrator, are confined underground for an indefinite period. We never learn the exact details of the mission they may be called upon to carry out, but it clearly involves nuclear warfare and so could result in world destruction.

The first-person narration underscores the horror as we know only what the speaker can tell us about his own situation. Both he and Shotwell have been reduced to infantilism as they wait for the terrible contingency on the console: Childlike pastimes alternate with petty jealousies and disturbing nightmares. The two men's gradual dehumanization is relieved only when they "rock each other to sleep." The men's eccentric behavior is portrayed as a desperate attempt to blot out the horror of their circumstances, but the story makes it clear that they are on the edge of madness: Note that Shotwell seems determined to destroy them by singlehandedly activating the two locks that will launch a holocaust.

As you read Barthelme's vignette of life in the nuclear age, it may be easy to dismiss the particulars of his vision as exaggerated or surrealistic. But consider that a serious theme may underlie this apparently absurdist story. Our modern methods of warfare, Barthelme seems to be suggesting, are horrible not only because of their potential for physical destruction, but also because of the way their very existence corrodes the collective conscience of humanity.

Analyzing The Story

Identifying Facts

1. The narrator is a military officer, assigned to duty at a missile launch site. His external conflict stems from his enforced confinement and Shotwell's bizarre behavior. His internal conflict arises from his own anxiety.

2. No; by the end of the story the narrator seems as unnerved as ever.

Interpreting Meanings

3. Shotwell and the narrator are assigned to watch a console and be ready to initiate a missile attack. The monotony of their duty has apparently affected their stability—Shotwell plays with jacks and a rubber ball, repeats childish phrases, and will not share his "toys." Both show signs of extreme stress. They are no longer able to think clearly and have relaxed the rules governing their behavior. Unconsciously and desperately, they seek some change in their situation. What happened before the story begins is speculative.

4. It is never stated directly, but the bird seems to be a missile, probably armed with a nuclear warhead.

5. Answers will vary; the men who were supposed to relieve Shotwell and the narrator have not arrived.

6. Shotwell's attempt to span the distance between the two locks with his outstretched arms implies that he may intend to start a nuclear war by firing the "bird" on his own.

7. Repeated phrases include these: "Owing to an oversight," "I am not well," "He has something in mind," "Shotwell is not himself."

The repetition underlines the numbness and horror of the situation, suggesting the characters' slowly disintegrating mental states.

8. The implication is that these drawings are like the primitive paintings of early humans on the walls of caves. Should a nuclear war occur, the writing might serve to give future beings some idea of our culture. The ironic implication is that two men have regressed to a primitive state.

9. Barthelme's theme is the terrifying nature of nuclear war. The title "Game" underscores this danger from its association with "war games."

Responding to the Story

Analyzing the Story

Identifying Facts

1. Despite his experimentation, Barthelme still uses the essential elements of fiction. Who is the **narrator** of this story? What is the **setting**? What is the narrator's problem, or **conflict**?
2. Is there a **resolution** to the conflict?

Interpreting Meanings

3. Which details in the first three paragraphs suggest the state of Shotwell's and the narrator's minds? How would you explain the men's strange behavior? What do you think has happened before the story begins?
4. What is the "bird"?
5. What might be the oversight that has led to the men's confinement?
6. The narrator is apprehensive that Shotwell has "something in mind." Does the story offer a clue as to what that "something" might be? Explain.
7. The writer uses a great deal of **repetition** in this story. What phrases are most often repeated? How does this repetition contribute to the characterization?
8. What "repetition" of history is suggested by the narrator's drawings on the walls?
9. What would you say is Barthelme's **theme** in this story? How does the **title** suggest the theme?

Writing About the Story

A Creative Response

1. **Writing the Beginning.** In a paragraph or two, summarize what has happened above ground while the narrator and Shotwell have been below ground. If you feel that "Game" is basically absurd, you can continue the absurdity.
2. **Extending the Story.** In another paragraph, describe what the narrator and Shotwell are doing five years later. You can continue the narration in the first-person, or you can switch to an omniscient narrator.

A Critical Response

3. **Comparing the Story to a Poem.** In the following poem—one of the most famous of the century—W. H. Auden describes a citizen of the modern world. In an essay, tell whether you think Barthelme's characters and Auden's citizen all live in the same world. Have they all lost their freedom? Do they all live in a society that has ignored their humanity? Cite passages from the story and poem to support your opinion.

The Unknown Citizen

(To JS/07/M/378
This Marble Monument
Is Erected by the State)

He was found by the Bureau of Statistics to be
One against whom there was no official complaint,
And all the reports on his conduct agree
That, in the modern sense of an old-fashioned word, he was a saint,
For in everything he did he served the Greater Community.
Except for the War till the day he retired
He worked in a factory and never got fired,
But satisfied his employers, Fudge Motors Inc.
Yet he wasn't a scab or odd in his views,
For his Union reports that he paid his dues
(Our report on his Union shows it was sound)
And our Social Psychology workers found
That he was popular with his mates and liked a drink.
The Press are convinced that he bought a paper every day
And that his reactions to advertisements were normal in every way.
Policies taken out in his name prove that he was fully insured,
And his Health card shows he was once in hospital but left it cured.
Both Producers Research and High-Grade Living declare
He was fully sensible to the advantages of the Installment Plan
And had everything necessary to the Modern Man,
A phonograph, a radio, a car, and a frigidaire.
Our researchers into Public Opinion are content
That he held the proper opinions for the time of year;
When there was peace, he was for peace; when there was war, he went.
He was married and added five children to the population,
Which our Eugenist says was the right number for a parent of his generation,
And our teachers report that he never interfered with their education.
Was he free? Was he happy? The question is absurd:
Had anything been wrong, we should certainly have heard.

—W. H. Auden

A. Expansion
The object of satire can be a philosophical system. Voltaire's *Candide,* for instance, is a biting satire on the cheery optimism of Leibniz and his followers. Satire can also be aimed at a political system, as is George Orwell's *Animal Farm,* a witty fantasy on the failure of Soviet communism. Occasionally, the object of satire is one person, as in John Dryden's *Mac Flecknoe,* a personal attack on the poet Thomas Shadwell, and one of the most famous verse satires in English.

B. Humanities Connection: Discussing the Illustration
John Tenniel (1820–1914), an English painter, illustrator, and caricaturist, is best known for his illustrations of Lewis Carroll's *Alice's Adventures in Wonderland* (1865) and *Alice Through the Looking-Glass* (1872). Of course, Tenniel did far more than illustrate *Alice.* During his long and distinguished career, he contributed regularly to the British humor magazine *Punch* and exhibited often at the Royal Academy.

The Elements of Literature

SATIRE

A **Satire**—ridiculing human foolishness or wrongdoing—is ultimately moral. The sting of satire is meant to cure the human race of its pretensions and blindness. While a realistic, ironic writer wants us to come to terms with the world as it is, the satirist wants to reform that world. The satirist's premise is that when an unacceptable situation is exposed to ridicule and laughter, it cannot last very long.

Satire requires two things to be successful: (1) wit, or humor based on fantasy, or humor based on a sense of the absurd, and (2) a target.

The humor of the satirist almost always involves some use of **irony,** that is, it involves a discrepancy between what we *expect* or think is *appropriate* and what actually *is.* Satirists also use **hyperbole,** or exaggeration, for effect, and **incongruity,** a kind of irony that brings together two ideas (or events or people) which do not belong together (*incongruous* means "not fitting together").

One of the great satirists of all time was the Irish-born writer Jonathan Swift (1667–1745). In *Gulliver's Travels* (1726), Swift took as his target the narrow-minded, hypocritical, and cruel British society of his time. Swift mocked his fellow citizens' pretensions to superiority by describing, among other wonders, a race of noble horses who are unquestionably superior to the British in intellect and in morals. In 1729 Swift published a satiric essay called "A Modest Proposal," in which his fictional narrator suggested that the British could solve their vexing Irish problem (and also their food shortages) by serving poor Irish children up as food for the rich landlords, "who, as they have already devoured most of the parents, seem to have best title to their children."

One of the great weapons of a certain type of satire is **fantasy,** the creation of a world where common sense has collapsed. Two of the most famous fantasies in the English language are Lewis Carroll's *Alice's Adventures in Wonderland* (1865) and *Through the Looking-Glass* (1871). In these books, the whole world is turned on its head. Even language itself no longer means what we think it means. "When *I* use a word," proclaims Humpty Dumpty, "it means what I choose it to mean—neither more nor less." This world of satiric fantasy is also found in *Gulliver's Travels.* There, for only one example, the horses not only speak, but also govern themselves in a way far superior to human governments.

At times a satirist's fantasy will turn to the absurd or grotesque, and we get what is known as "gallows humor," an Americanism which means morbid or cynical humor (literally, humor when facing the hangman). Swift's "A Modest Proposal" becomes grotesque when the narrator dares to suggest cannibalism as a solution to an economic problem.

B

An illustration by John Tenniel for *Alice in Wonderland.*

Satire has a long history in American literature. The shrewd counsels of prudence we hear from Franklin's Poor Richard (see page 81) are a kind of satire, in which the writer suggests practical ways to succeed in a world that is less than ideal. Mark Twain was more of a satirist than he generally receives credit for; his raftsmen on page 404 are part of a long line of boasters and rogues in literature who use wit and verbal exuberance to survive in a world full of crime and foolishness. Sinclair Lewis (see page 511) used the techniques of satire to puncture the smugness of a small-town (or small-minded) businessman. James Thurber created in Walter Mitty (see page 577) an American version of the man bullied by a woman, an archetypal character popular in satire at least from the days of ancient Rome.

What absurd ideas do you find in Barthelme's satire? Do the narrator and Shotwell respond to their limited world in the way that Twain's raftsmen do, or are they more the Walter Mitty type?

Mark Helprin (1947–   )

Mark Helprin grew up in New York City and in nearby Ossining. He graduated from Harvard and has a master's degree from Harvard in Middle Eastern studies. When he was twenty-five, he enlisted in the Israeli army and served for a year in its infantry and air force. He also worked for a time in the British merchant navy.

Helprin's fiction is highly readable, marked by a lyrical grace of language and a delight in the extravagant and in the fabulous. Many of his short stories have appeared in *The New Yorker*. His first book, published in 1975, was a collection called *A Dove of the East and Other Stories*. A second volume, *Ellis Island and Other Stories*, followed in 1980. "Tamar" is from that collection.

His first novel, *Refiner's Fire*, published in 1977, is a picaresque tale about a soldier of fortune whose many adventures include a memorable participation in the battle for the Golan Heights on the border of Israel and Syria. A second novel, *Winter's Tale*, appeared in 1983. A romantic fantasy, *Winter's Tale* is set just before the year 2000 and tells of the adventures of a burglar-hero who leads a group of people across the snowdrifts of time in search of the Promised Land of Justice, which they have to discover by December 1999. One of the novel's unusual features is a flying white horse, a fugitive from a Brooklyn milk wagon. Both of Helprin's novels were widely reviewed and discussed, and *Winter's Tale* was a major popular success.

Photograph © 1988 by Jill Krementz.

Comment From The Author

Leslie Hanscom, a columnist, interviewed Mark Helprin in 1984 after the remarkable popular success of Helprin's novel *Winter's Tale.*

" 'I always feel in writing [Helprin said] as if I'm riding a cannon shell and it's pulling me. I find that what I do mainly in writing is put [a story] within rails of iron. I strengthen it and compress it, discipline it.'

"Nonetheless, many critics charge that he overwrites. He protests.

" 'People have this Hemingway feeling that everything has to be restrained, and you're not supposed to make too many metaphors,' he said. 'But Hemingway is not my model. My models are *The Divine Comedy* and the Bible and Shakespeare—where they use language to the fullest.' "

SUPPLEMENTARY SUPPORT MATERIALS

1. Vocabulary Activity Worksheet (*CCB*)
2. Review and Response Worksheet: Point of View (*CCB*)
3. Language Skills Worksheet: Adverb Clauses (*CCB*)
4. Selection Test (*CCB*)

DEVELOPING VOCABULARY

The following words from the story are tested in the Selection Test. (See also Vocabulary Activity Worksheet.)

superficial	hierarchy
intricacy	to parry
leaden	to embolden

PREPARATION

ESTABLISHING A PURPOSE. Be sure that students read the headnote and also that they know enough about the Holocaust to appreciate the theme of the story. Have students notice the author's diction: not only the figurative language but also Helprin's word choice in general.

A. Humanities Connection: Responding to the Illustration

? Define the word *refugee*. (A person who flees for safety, especially one who flees to a foreign country to escape danger or persecution) Who might the two refugees in the photograph be? From where might they be fleeing? How urgent is their flight? (Tell students to use visual clues, such as the woman's wristwatch, in reaching their conclusions.)

TAMAR

This story takes place in London, just before the outbreak of World War II. The story presumes that the reader is aware of the Holocaust—the killing of six million Jewish men, women, and children by the Nazis during World War II. Helprin's narrative here is slow and roundabout. The character named in the title doesn't even appear until halfway through the story. Be patient. Helprin has a reason for telling the story the way he does.

A

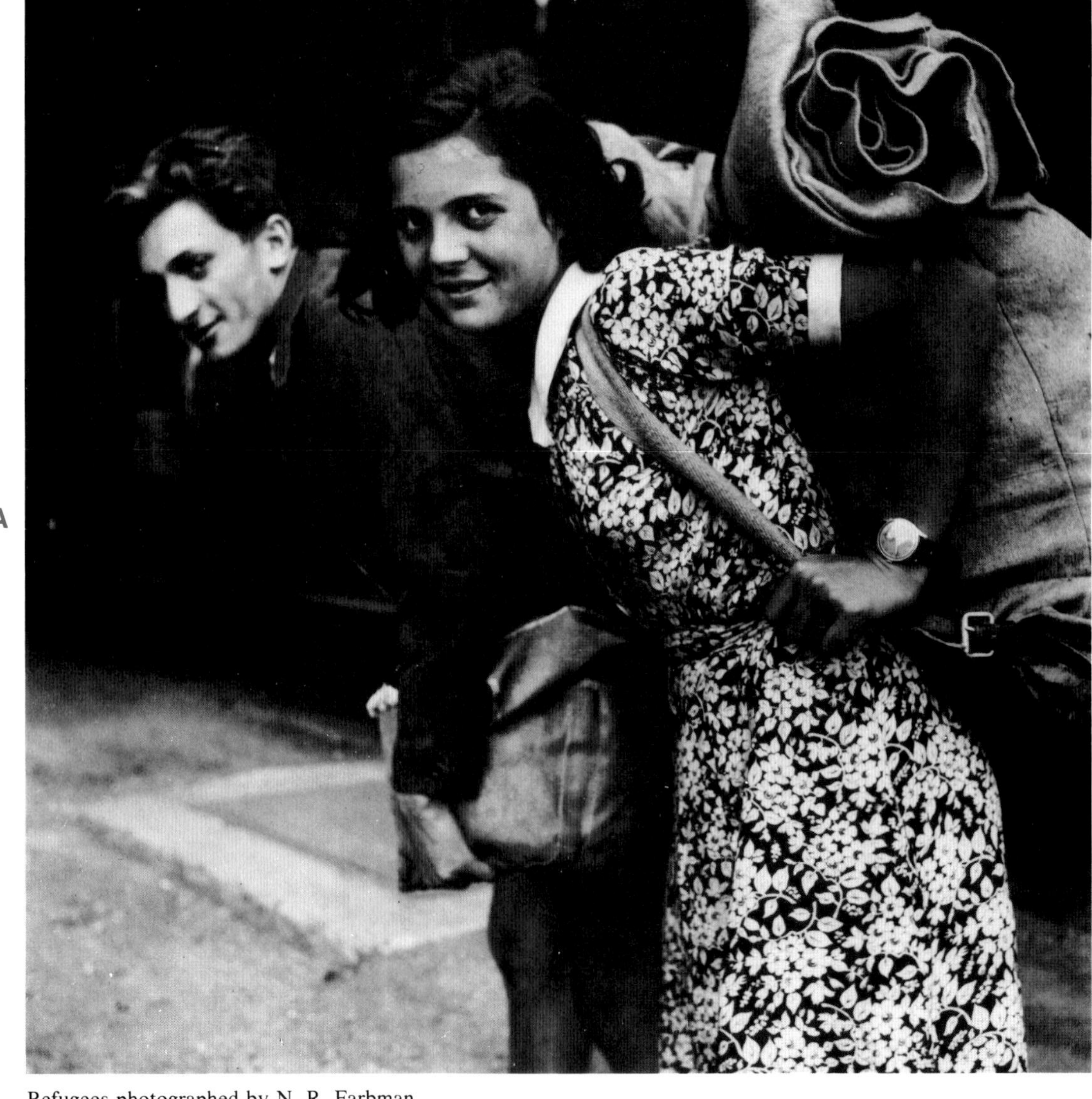

Refugees photographed by N. R. Farbman.

A. Expansion
"Before the War"—that is, World War II—means before September 1, 1939, when Hitler invaded Poland, and Britain and France declared war on Germany. (Before World War II officially began, Hitler had already annexed the Saar, 1935; the Rhineland, 1936; Austria, 1938; and Czechoslovakia, 1938.

B. Characterization
? What does the narrator mean by "I have since forgiven myself"? (He means that when he was younger he overrated his ability to save European Jews through the art scheme. Now he realizes the futility of his efforts.)

C. Simile/Metaphor
Have students identify the simile and metaphor and explain the power of the simile. (The simile is "green pine valleys as sharp as chevrons." The metaphor is "silent white ribbons of wood smoke." The simile is particularly powerful because of its ominous military overtones.)

D. Setting
The author introduces his London setting gradually, picturing it as bright and enlivening.
? What made London seem so appealing to him? (He was suddenly meeting a great many well-to-do people at social events. He found the contrast with the grim situation in Eastern Europe striking.)

Before the War, in London, I was trying to arrange a system whereby the Jews of Germany and Austria could sell their paintings and other works of art without depressing demand. It was very serious business, for our primary aim was to require that twenty-five percent of each sale go into an escape fund to provide transport for those who could not make it on their own. We thought that we could exact this price if we managed to keep market values steady. But all of Europe was on edge about the political situation, and no one was in the mood to buy anything. And then, after *Kristallnacht*,[1] every Jew in Germany came forward, wanting to sell precious objects.

At the time of our greatest hope, my job was to set up fronts for selling what we expected would be a flood of art coming from Middle Europe. If it had appeared that English collectors were opening their storerooms to take advantage of a favorable market, the excitement might well have pushed values upward. So we tried to get the cooperation of those prominent collectors who had the foresight to see what was about to happen on the Continent and were in sympathy with our cause. Excepting a very few, these were Jews. The others simply were not interested, and, anyway, we did not want to divulge the plan in too many places.

Soon I found myself deeply involved in the high society of Jews in London and in their great houses throughout the countryside. My conviction was then, as it is now, that it is not possible for Jews to be in "society" but that their efforts to be so are (except when immoderate or in bad taste) courageous, for the mechanisms of high social status are encouragements of vulnerability, safe only for those who can afford to lose themselves in pursuits superficial and deep and not fear that their fundamental positions will drop out from under them as a result of their inattention. My attitudes toward the Jewish peers and the Jewish upper class in general was mixed, and had complex roots. I admired their bravery while occasionally chafing at their blindness. I knew that, in spite of their learning and culture, they were isolated in such a way as to make me—a young man of thirty-two—far better a judge of certain things than were they. I had been in the ghetto in Warsaw not a month before, and the people there had confided to me that they felt the end was near. They said, "Tell them, in England, that in Poland they are killing Jews." I had been in Berlin, Munich, Vienna, and Prague. I had passed through Jewish villages from Riga to Bucharest,[2] where I had seen a temple about to fall. How misty and beautiful it was, that autumn. I cannot describe the quiet. It was as if the nineteenth century—indeed, all the past—were in hiding and feared to give itself away. The whole world of the Jews in Central Europe looked outward with the saddest eyes. What could *I* do? I tried my best. I was working for the Jewish Agency, and had just come from two years in Palestine, in the desert, and thought that my responsibility was to save the Jews of Europe. Like all young men, I was full of speeches that I could not deliver. Somehow, I imagined that the art scheme would be everything. I have since forgiven myself. B

Visions of the Jews in the forests, in green pine valleys as sharp as chevrons,[3] in villages marked by silent white ribbons of wood smoke, never left me as I undertook to master the intricacies of the London social season. I cannot remember when I have enjoyed myself more. C Sometimes I became as lost and trusting as my hosts, and, even when I did not, the contrast between the Eastern European *Heimat*[4] and the drawing rooms of modern London was incalculably enlivening. I was suspended between two dream-worlds.

Just before Christmas, that time in all capitals when the city flares most brightly, I was oppressed with invitations. I had a blue pad upon which I listed my engagements, and one terrible, lovely week it had sixteen entries. I met so many dukes, duchesses, M.P.s,[5] industrialists, and academics that my eyes began to cross. But we had begun to succeed in hammering out a network for art sales, and I was confident and happy. D

Then a magical power in the Jewish Agency must have decided that these several score dinners had made me into a diplomat, for I received an invitation to a dinner party on the twenty-first at the house of the most eminent Jew in all the Brit-

1. ***Kristallnacht*** (kris·täl′näkht): German for "night of broken windows." On the night of November 9, 1938, Nazi forces brutally attacked the Jews and their places of business throughout Germany and Austria. After Kristallnacht, there could be little doubt as to the fate in store for European Jews.

2. **Riga . . . Bucharest:** the capitals of Latvia and Rumania, respectively.
3. **chevrons:** a military insignia, consisting of a V-shaped bar.
4. ***Heimat:*** German for "homeland."
5. **M.P.s:** in Britain, Members of Parliament.

A. Metaphor
This sentence consists of an elaborate metaphor. Ask students to explain the metaphor in their own words. (The narrator—who has "ballooned with pride"—compares his pomposity, or vanity, to an ugly, overweight man. This man, or "monster," is so huge that the "entire seventeenth century" [hyperbole]—a century noted for frilly, elegant dress—could not have clothed him.) Point out to students that this metaphor, with its image of clothing a monster, leads directly into the narrator's buying a "beautiful three-piece suit."

B. Complication
The narrator's grand plan to "save the Jews of Europe" is sidetracked by his late arrival at the dinner party and his consequent placement at the children's table.

ish Empire. Only that summer, I had scrubbed pots, guarded at night, and lived in a tent, in a collective settlement in the Negev.[6] Now I ballooned with pride. The entire seventeenth century could not have produced enough frills to clothe the heavy monster of my pomposity. Sure that all my troubles were over forever, I spent every bit of my money on the most beautiful three-piece suit in London. When the tailor—who was himself a knight—heard where I was going, he set his men to work, and they finished it in three days. London became, for me, the set of a joyous light opera.

On the night of the twentieth, just twenty-four hours before what I assumed would be my apotheosis[7] (it was said that the Prime Minister would be there, and I imagined myself declaring to him a leaden diplomatic précis along the lines of the Magna Carta or the Treaty of Vienna[8]), I had yet another engagement, this one at the house of a Jewish art dealer whom I had recently regarded as a big fish. I was so overconfident that I left my hotel without his address, thinking that I would manage to find it anyway, since I knew its approximate location in Chelsea.[9]

I was due at six-thirty. For an hour and a half I rushed through Chelsea in this direction and that, trying to find the house. Everyone, it seemed, was having a dinner party, and all the buildings looked alike. When, finally, I arrived at the right square, I stood in a little park and stared at the house. It was five stories tall and it was lit like a theater. Through the sparkling windows came firelight, candlelight, and glimpses of enormous chandeliers—while the snow fell as if in time to sad and troubling music. Red and disheveled from running about, I stood in my splendid suit, frightened to go in. In that square, the coal smoke was coiling about like a great menagerie of airborne snakes, and occasionally it caught me and choked me in its unbearable fumes. But I remember it with fondness, because it was the smell of Europe in the winter; and, though it was devilish and foul, it seemed to say that, underneath everything, another world was at work, that the last century was alive in its clumsiness and warmth, signaling that all was well and that great contexts remained unbroken.

I was afraid to go in, because I was so late and because I knew what a fool I had been in judging these people according to the hierarchy in which they believed, and thus underrating them in comparison to the plutocrats[10] of the next night. But I took hold of myself and rang their bell. I heard conversation stop. A servant came to the door. Each of his steps shot through the wood like an X-ray. I was taken upstairs to a magnificent room in which were five tables of well-dressed people completely motionless and silent, like a group of deer surprised by a hunter. Every eye was upon me. Though frightened of fainting, I remained upright and seemingly composed. My host stood to greet me. Then he took me about like a roast, and introduced me to each and every guest, all of whom had a particular smile that can be described only as simultaneously benevolent, sadistic, and amused. I don't know why, but I broke into German, though my German was not the best. They must have been thinking, Who is this strange red-faced German who does not speak his own language well? Or perhaps they thought that I was confused as to my whereabouts. I suppose I was.

Then Herr Dennis, as I called him, took me by the arm and explained that, since they had readjusted the seating in my absence, I (who, the next day, would be waltzing with the Prime Minister) would have to sit at the children's table. It was a very great blow, especially since the poor children were bunched up all by themselves in a little ell of the room that led to the kitchen. I was in no position to protest; in fact, I was, by that time, quite numb.

As he led me, in a daze, toward the children's table, I imagined myself sitting with five or ten infants in bibs, staring down at them as if from a high tower, eating sullenly like a god exiled from Olympus. But when we rounded the corner of the ell, I discovered that the children were adolescents; and their charm arose to envelop me. First, there were four red-headed girl cousins, all in

6. **Negev:** a desert region in southern Israel.
7. **apotheosis** (a·po·thē·ō′sis): glorification; utmost happiness.
8. **Magna Carta . . . Vienna:** the Magna Carta was the great charter guaranteeing English liberties, signed by King John and the English barons in 1215; the Treaty of Vienna concluded the Napoleonic wars in 1815.
9. **Chelsea:** a district of London.

10. **plutocrats:** people whose wealth gives them power.

Literature and Language: Analyzing Tone
When they've finished reading the story, ask students to discuss what they think is the writer's or narrator's attitude toward the characters and events. Have students begin by reading the entry for *tone* in the **Handbook of Literary Terms** (page 1182). Tone, according to the definition there, is a result of diction (word choice) and style. *Style* (see page 1181) is even harder to define, more elusive than tone.

Students will probably agree that the story's tone is mournful and serious but not quite tragic, though they may suggest other words to describe it. Some may suggest that the tone is a bit sentimental, in the narrator's memory of lost opportunities for love.

Challenge students to try to pin down what exactly in the text creates the tone. This is a difficult task, one that may interest advanced students or volunteers.

white. They were from thirteen to sixteen; they had between them several hundred million freckles; and they were so disturbed by my sudden arrival that they spent the next half hour swallowing, darting their eyes about, clearing their throats, and adjusting fallen locks of hair. They spoke as seriously as very old theologians, but ever so much more delicately; they pieced together their sentences with great care, the way new skaters skate, and when they finished they breathed in relief, not unlike students of a difficult Oriental language, who must recite in class. At the end of these ordeals, they looked at each other with the split-second glances common to people who are very familiar. Then, there was a boy with dark woolly hair and the peculiarly adolescent animal-lost-out-on-the-heath expression common to young men whose abilities greatly exceed their experience. At my appearance, he lowered his horns, knowing that he was going to spend the rest of the evening bashing himself against a castle wall. I admired his courage; I liked him; I remembered. Next to him was a fat boy who wanted to be an opera singer. He was only fourteen, and when he saw that the threat presented by the woolly-haired boy was neutralized, he went wild with excitement, blooming at the four cousins with a gregariousness of which he had probably never been aware.

I liked these children. They seemed somewhat effete,[11] and sheltered, but I knew that this was because I was used to the adolescents of our collective, who were much older than their years, and that these young people were the products of an ultra-refined system of schooling. I knew that, if protected during this vulnerability, they might emerge with unmatched strength. I had been through the same system, and had seen my schoolmates undergo miraculous transformations. I knew as well that they were destined for a long and terrible war, but, then again, so were we all. Yes, I liked these children, and I enjoyed the fact that I had left those years behind.

I have not described everyone at that table. One remains. She was the daughter of my host, the eldest, the tallest, the most beautiful. Her name was Tamar, and as I had turned the corner she had seemed to rise in the air to meet me, while the others were lost in the dark. Tamar and I had faced one another in a moment of silence that I will not ever forget. Sometimes, on a windy day, crosscurrented waves in the shallows near a beach will spread about, trapped in a caldron of bars and brakes, until two run together face to face and then fall back in shocked tranquillity. So it was with Tamar. It was as if I had run right into her. I was breathless, and I believe that she was, too.

I immediately took command of myself, and did not look at her. In fact, I studied every face before I studied hers—black eyes; black hair; her mouth and eyes showing her youth and strength in the way they were set, in the way they moved, not ever having been tried or defeated or abused. She wore a rich white silk blouse that was wonderfully open at the top, and a string of matched pearls. For a moment, I was convinced that she was in her twenties, but when she smiled I saw a touching thin silver wire across her upper teeth, and I knew that she was probably no more than seventeen. She *was* seventeen, soon to be eighteen, soon to take off the wire, soon (in fact) to become a nurse with the Eighth Army in Egypt. But at that time she was just on the verge of becoming a woman, and she virtually glowed with the fact.

As soon as I saw the wire, I felt as if I could talk with her in a way that could be managed, and I did. Unlike the four red-headed cousins, she was fearless and direct. She laughed out loud without the slightest self-consciousness, and I felt as if in our conversation we were not speaking but dancing. Perhaps it was because she was so clear of voice, so alert, and so straightforward. She was old enough to parry, and she did, extraordinarily well. B

"Tamar is going to Brussels next year," volunteered one of the red-haired girls, in the manner of a handmaiden at court, "to study at the Royal Laboratory for Underzek and Verpen."

"No, no, no," said Tamar. "What you're thinking of, Hannah, is called the Koninklijk Laboratorium voor Onderzoek van Voorwerpen van Kunst en Wetenschap, and it's in The Hague." She glided over the minefield of Dutch words without hesitation and in a perfect accent.

"Does Tamar speak Dutch?" I asked, looking right at her.

"Yes," she answered, "Tamar speaks Dutch, because she learnt it at her Dutch grandmother's knee—Daddy's mother. But," she continued, shaking a finger gently at Hannah, though really speaking to me, "I'm going to Brussels, to study

11. **effete** (ə·fēt′): overrefined and delicate.

A. Description
The physical description of Tamar appears in the next paragraph. Here the narrator is describing the effect that his first sight of Tamar had on him.
? What was that effect? (it was love at first sight.)

B. Noting Details
Have students notice the narrator's reaction to the thin silver wire across Tamar's upper teeth. It marks Tamar as an adolescent, putting the narrator more at ease. See question 3, page 932.

Closure
Have students discuss the last paragraph of the story in class, analyzing Helprin's thoughts sentence by sentence.

A. Humor
Be sure your students understand this *ba-bob-Richard* sequence. When the narrator corrects *shiski ba* to *shiski bob,* the fat boy, mistakenly thinking the narrator is addressing him by name (Bob), corrects the *Bob* to *Richard.* This causes the four cousins to burst into hysterical laughter.

restoration at the Institut Central des Beaux-Arts, or, if Fascism flies out the window in Italy between now and next year, to the Istituto Nazionale per il Restauro, in Rome."

When she realized that her recitation of the names of these formidable institutes, each in its own language, might have seemed ostentatious, she blushed.

Emboldened nearly to giddiness, the fat boy interjected, "We went to Rome. We ate shiski ba there, and the streets are made of water."

"That's *Venice, stupid,*" said one of the red-haired girls. "And what is shiski ba?"

A "Shiski ba," answered the fat boy, guilelessly, "is roasted meat on a stick. The Turks sell it in the park."

"Bob,"[12] I offered, by way of instruction. A silence followed, during which the poor boy looked at me blankly.

"Richard," he said, sending the four cousins (who knew him well) into a fit of hysteria. Tamar tried not to laugh, because she knew that he hung on her every gesture and word.

To change the subject, I challenged Tamar. "Do you really think," I said, "that you will be able to study on the Continent?"

She shrugged her shoulders and smiled in a way that belied her age. "I'll do the best I can," she answered. "Even if there is a war, it will have an end. I'll still be young, and I'll start again."

My eyes opened at this. I don't know exactly why; perhaps it was that I imagined her in the future and became entranced with the possibility that I might encounter her then—in some faraway place where affection could run unrestrained. But I wanted to steer things away from art, war, and love.

So, while constantly fending off the quixotic[13] charges of the woolly-haired boy (without ever really looking at him), I told a long story about Palestine. Because they were children, more or less, I told them anything I wanted to tell them. Until long after the adults had left for the living room, I spoke of impossible battles between Jews and Bedouins,[14] of feats of endurance which made me reel merely in imagining them, of horses that flew, and golden shafts of light, pillars of fire,

A Nazi squadron rounds up Jewish survivors of the Warsaw Ghetto, April 1943.

miracles here and there, the wonders of spoken Hebrew, and the lions that guarded the banks and post offices of Jerusalem—in short, anything which seemed as if it might be believed.

Tamar alternated between belief and disbelief with the satisfying rhythm of a blade turning back and forth over a whetstone.[15] She was weaving soft acceptance and sparkling disdain together in a tapestry which I feared she would throw right over my head. She did this in a most delicate cross-examination, the object of which was to

12. **Bob:** the narrator corrects the boy's pronunciation of *shish kebab.*
13. **quixotic:** idealistic to an impractical degree (like Don Quixote in Cervantes's novel).
14. **Bedouins:** nomadic tribes of Arabs who roam the desert.

15. **whetstone:** stone used for sharpening tools.

READING CHECK TEST

1. The narrator hopes to use part of the money from the sale of art owned by Jews to (a) oppose Hitler's policies (b) help finance the state of Israel (c) help Jews escape from Central Europe *(c)*

2. In anticipation of meeting "the most eminent Jew in all the British empire," the narrator (a) goes to the opera (b) buys a new suit (c) cancels an appointment *(b)*

3. The narrator arrives late at the art dealer's house because he has (a) missed his bus (b) lost his invitation (c) left his hotel without the address *(c)*

4. Tamar is all of the following *except* (a) the host's daughter (b) eighteen years old (c) Jewish *(b)*

5. The narrator believes he might not have known Tamar so well except for (a) the woolly-haired boy (b) Erika, the opera singer (c) a slim bit of wire *(c)*

A. Humanities Connection: Discussing the Photograph
Although your students should already be aware of the fate of European Jews between 1939 and 1945, you may wish to review the Holocaust briefly. In more than thirty concentration camps in Germany and Eastern Europe—Buchenwald, Auschwitz, Belsen, Dachau, and others—the Nazis systematically slaughtered civilian men, women, and children who belonged to what Hitler regarded as "inferior races." The victims included Poles, Czechs, Russians, and others, but the greatest number were Jews. Some six million European Jews perished in Nazi Germany's program of genocide, most of them in gas chambers.

Centre de Documentation Contemporaine, Paris

A

draw out more of the tale for the sake of the children, to satisfy her own curiosity, to mock me gently, and to continue—by entrapment and release—the feeling we had that, though we were still, we were dancing.

"Why," she asked, "did you not get water from the Bedouins that you captured, if you had already gone without it for ten days?"

"Ah!" I said, holding up my finger in the same way she had done with Hannah. "I was only able to capture them because they themselves had run out of water, and were thirstier than I was. And I did not capture them with a gun but by giving a graphic dissertation on European fountains; they were especially taken with my description of the Diana fountain in Bushy Park, and I believe that they would have followed me anywhere after I told them what goes on in the Place de la Concorde."[16]

"What is it like to be a British Jew in Palestine?" asked Hannah, earnestly, and with such *Weltschmerz*[17] that it was as if an alpine storm cloud had rolled over the table.

"What is it like? It's like being an Italian Negro in Ethiopia, or"—I looked at Tamar—"like living in a continuous production of 'Romeo and Juliet.' " I had meant the allusion to "Romeo and Juliet" to be purely illustrative, but with a life of

16. **Place de la Concorde:** one of the principal squares in Paris.
17. ***Weltschmerz*** (velt' shmerts): a German expression meaning "sentimental melancholy over the state of the world."

ANALYZING THE STORY
Identifying Details
1. The narrator is in London in 1938 to organize a network for the sale of art belonging to German and Austrian Jews. Part of the proceeds will go toward an escape fund for Jews fleeing persecution.
2. The narrator evidently enjoys London society. He believes he understands the Jewish upper classes in England. He admires their courage, but feels that they have failed to understand the Nazi threat.
3. Tamar is a black-haired, black-eyed girl of seventeen, although she looks older. She wears a white silk blouse and a string of matched pearls. She dreams of studying art restoration in Brussels.

The thin silver wire that Tamar wears to straighten her teeth shows the narrator that the girl is an adolescent. He feels more comfortable with her, and decides he can talk to her.

Interpreting Meanings
4. Tamar's beauty and poise make a deep impression on the narrator. He finds her romantically captivating. The blush at the reference to *Romeo and Juliet* connotes embarrassment at the notion of first love.

its own it turned Tamar as red as a throbbing coal, and I, a generation apart, nearly followed suit. I was caught in my own springe,[18] enchanted—yet never really in danger, for not only did her father come to fetch me back into the world of adults but I had run those rapids before, and knew the still and deep water at their end.

I recall exactly how the children were sitting when I left them, poised to explode in gossip as soon as I had disappeared—it is likely that in my absence I was cut to ribbons by the woolly-haired boy, and perhaps deservedly so. As Tamar's father and I climbed a broad staircase to the library, where we would discuss business, I remembered the opera singer with whom I had once fallen in love. Her voice was like liquid or a jewel. I have not since heard such a beautiful voice. But she was, oddly enough, almost unknown. I went to Covent Garden[19] to find out in what productions she would sing. Her name was Erika, and when I inquired of the old man at the ticket office I found that he, too, was in love with her.

"I'm too old," he said, "and you're too young." I knew that this was true, and I must have looked pained, because he grabbed me through the ticket window and said, "Don't you see, it's much better that way!"

"I see nothing," I said. "If that's better, then I'm sorry to be alive."

"Wait," he said, and laughed. "You'll see. It's sweeter, much sweeter."

I went to the opera that season two dozen times just to see and hear Erika of the liquid voice. I wanted, despite the fact that I was fifteen, to marry her immediately, to run away to Brazil or Argentina, to take her with me to the South Seas, etc., etc., etc. It had been unspeakable torture to watch her on a brilliantly lighted stage, singing in a way that fired up all my emotions.

But by the time I met Tamar, I knew that a lighted stage is often best left untouched, and I knew, further, that all connections are temporary, and, therefore, can be enjoyed in their fullness even after the most insubstantial touch—if only one knows how. I was, that night, in a dream within a dream. I was young again in a room of bright colors and laughter; and all the time the dark image of a smoky continent called me away and threatened to tear me apart. I did not know then that there is no contradiction in such contradictions; they are made for one another; without them, we would have nothing to lose and nothing to love.

Tamar was the most lovely girl—and had it not been for that delicate and slim bit of silver wire, I might not have known her as well as I did. Her father agreed to the scheme, but then the scheme collapsed, and the world collapsed soon after. Six years of war. Most of the Jews did not survive. Most of the paintings did. In six years of war, there was probably not a day when I did not think of the time when I had had to sit at the children's table, in a world of vulnerable beauty. Perhaps things are most beautiful when they are not quite real; when you look upon a scene as an outsider, and come to possess it in its entirety and forever; when you live the present with the lucidity and feeling of memory; when, for want of connection, the world deepens and becomes art.

18. **springe:** a snare, often used to catch birds.
19. **Covent Garden:** London's principal opera house.

Responding to the Story

Analyzing the Story

Identifying Facts

1. Explain why the narrator is in London at the beginning of the story, and what he is hoping to do.
2. Find passages that reveal his attitude toward the well-to-do Jews in London society. What does he think they have failed to understand?
3. What do you learn about Tamar's appearance, her age, and her dreams? What effect does the thin silver wire have on the narrator?

Interpreting Meanings

4. How would you explain Tamar's attraction to the narrator? What can we infer when Tamar blushes at the reference to Romeo and Juliet?

5. The narrator fell in love with Erika from afar at the age of fifteen. He wanted to run away with her. The episode shows the narrator's romantic sensibility.
6. Opinions will vary. The narrator's meeting with Tamar and his ignorance of her fate are poignant because of his knowledge (and ours) of the coming Holocaust. The ironic reminders occur in the third and last paragraphs.
7. Opinions will vary. The narrator's comment about the Jewish upper classes' "bravery" and "blindness" suggests that Dennis and his family are symbolic of many Jews who failed to heed the warning signs of persecution in Europe.

The children's table reminds the narrator of the young people's vulnerability and—perhaps—of his own youth.

8. The narrator says that all connections are temporary, "and, therefore, can be enjoyed in their fullness even after the most insubstantial touch." He is aware of the contradiction between the luxury and beauty of his surroundings on that night and the horror of Europe on the verge of war—the "dark image of a smoky continent." Thinking of the "vulnerable beauty" of Tamar's world, the narrator speculates that "perhaps things are most beautiful when they are not quite real."
9. Answers will vary. In general, the narrator seems to use the beautiful memory of Tamar as an idealistic, stylized counterpart to the ensuing war; Tamar becomes associated with art, which expands and enriches the cold, hard facts of reality.
10. Answers will vary. Urge the students to support their answers with specific references to the text.

5. What does Erika, the opera singer, have to do with the story of Tamar?
6. What effect does Helprin achieve by wrapping the story of Tamar inside an account of the Nazis and the war? What passages of the story remind us, ironically, of what is about to happen in Europe?
7. What larger group of people might be represented by Herr Dennis and his family and friends? What do you think the children's table itself stands for in the narrator's memory?
8. The narrator uses a number of **paradoxes,** or apparent contradictions to sum up the story in the last two paragraphs. Identify each paradox.
9. What does "the world deepens and becomes art" mean? Explain the outlook on life that the narrator seems to be describing in the last passage. What is your response to what he says here?
10. Is this a romantic love story? Or is it a story about the redemptive power of beauty and art? Explain.

Writing About the Story

A Creative Response

1. **Writing a Journal Entry.** Imagine that Tamar kept a journal. Write an entry she might have recorded on the day she met the narrator at the dinner party.

A Critical Response

2. **Explaining a Statement.** On page 927, at the end of a paragraph describing how he felt about the Jews of London and Europe, and explaining how he came to be doing what he was doing, the narrator says, "I have since forgiven myself." In a paragraph, explain what you think this statement means. Before you write, look for other passages in the story that reveal how the narrator feels about that time in London.
3. **Responding to a Title.** In a brief essay, explain why Helprin chose the title "Tamar" for this story. In your essay, include your response to the title: Do you think it's a good one? Before you write, decide how the character of Tamar might be central to the point of Helprin's story.

Analyzing Language and Style

Figurative Language

Helprin's writings are distinguished by a style that is rich in descriptive detail and figurative language—the language of metaphors, similes, and personification.

1. "Visions of the Jews in the forests, in green pine valleys as sharp as chevrons. . . ."
   a. Describe the image created by this **simile**.
   b. What is significant about the choice of the word *chevron* in this particular context?
2. "The entire seventeenth century could not have produced enough frills to clothe the heavy monster of my pomposity."
   a. What is *pomposity*?
   b. How is it **personified** here?
   c. What does this image reveal about the narrator's feelings about himself?
3. "London became, for me, the set of a joyous light opera."
   a. What does this **metaphor** reveal about the narrator's feelings for London?
   b. Why is this image **ironic,** considering the narrator's purpose in London?
4. "It [the house] was five stories tall and it was lit like a theater."
   a. What does the comparison with a theater suggest, beyond an image of a brightly lit place?
   b. How would the effect have been different if the house had been compared with "a church full of candles" or with "a brightly lit palace"?
5. ". . . the snow fell as if in time to sad and troubling music." (Page 928)
   a. What is the emotional effect of this **simile**?
   b. Think of at least two other ways the snowfall might have been described to suggest other moods.
6. ". . . the coal smoke was coiling about like a great menagerie of airborne snakes. . . ." (Page 928)
   a. What is the emotional effect of this **simile**?
   b. In "The Love Song of J. Alfred Prufrock" (page 742), what is the same smoke compared with, and to what effect?
7. ". . . well-dressed people completely motionless and silent, like a group of deer surprised by a hunter." (Page 928) In light of what we know is going to happen to the Jews of Europe, why is this **simile** tragically appropriate?
8. "Then he took me about like a roast. . . ." (Page 928)
   a. Describe the picture this **simile** puts in your mind.
   b. What does the choice of comparison reveal about the narrator's attitude toward himself?
9. Find three comparisons describing the cousins at the children's table on page 928. What feeling for the children is revealed in each comparison?
10. The most significant figure of speech in the story might be the long extended **simile** describing the narrator's meeting with Tamar. Find the simile and explain in your own words what it reveals about the significance of this encounter.

COMMENT FROM THE AUTHOR
In Tim O'Brien's *Going After Cacciato,* Paul Berlin (who is also the protagonist of "Speaking of Courage") ponders the question of courage: "The issue, of course, was courage. How to behave. The issue was not fearlessness. The issue was how to act wisely in spite of fear."

Ask students to compare Berlin's observation with Henry Fleming's thoughts and actions in Stephen Crane's "A Mystery of Heroism" (page 457). You might first have them make their comparisons on the basis of this brief quote, then discuss the question again after they have read "Speaking of Courage."

Tim O'Brien (1946–)

Tim O'Brien was born in Austin, Minnesota, and graduated from Macalester College. In 1968, he was drafted and served with the U.S. Army in Vietnam, where he attained the rank of sergeant. Returning from the war, he went to Harvard for graduate work in English. A summer internship on the *Washington Post* led to a job as national affairs reporter for that newspaper.

O'Brien had been writing stories since childhood, and even in the midst of his academic work, he knew he wanted to write full-time. It was his military experience in Vietnam that provided the material for his fiction and personal narratives. *If I Die in a Combat Zone, Box Me Up and Ship Me Home* (1973) is a collection of anecdotes and observations of his duty in Vietnam. The book drew widespread approval, particularly from veterans, as an authentic re-creation of the footsoldiers' experience in an unpopular war.

"I started writing fiction," O'Brien has said, "to get away from the whole idea of aping reality. I was tired of echoing what reality is and I was more interested in questions of what might be, what might have happened, what could have happened."

O'Brien's first novel, *Northern Lights*, appeared in 1974 and dealt with a veteran returned to civilian life. A second novel, *Going After Cacciato*, followed in 1978. This novel returned to the jungle war to give a soldier's fantasy of quitting the battle and walking off across the mountains to find Paris. *Cacciato* was acclaimed as one of the few novels to have captured the essence of the Vietnam experience, and it won the National Book Award in 1979.

"*Cacciato* was an imagined novel," O'Brien has said. "It was a novel of psychology. I didn't want to tell the events of Vietnam again. I'd already done that once. I didn't want to say here's what it's like to get shot, and see people shot. I wanted to get into the head of a human being, a character, and write about terror and questions of courage and obligation to duty, and conscience."

SUPPLEMENTARY SUPPORT MATERIALS
1. Vocabulary Activity Worksheet (*CCB*)
2. Review and Response Worksheet: Conflict (*CCB*)
3. Language Skills Worksheet: Commas (*CCB*)
4. Selection Test (*CCB*)

DEVELOPING VOCABULARY
The following words from the story are tested in the Selection Test. (See also Vocabulary Activity Worksheet.)

tepid	insignia
circumference	platoon
electron	mole
causeway	tactile
valor	to electrocute

PREPARATION
BUILDING ON PRIOR KNOWLEDGE. You will probably want to precede the reading of this story with some discussion of the Vietnam War. Of particular relevance is the way Vietnam veterans were regarded—that is, not very favorably—immediately after the war.

SPEAKING OF COURAGE

Before he published the full novel about Cacciato, O'Brien published portions of it as short stories in various magazines. This story, which appeared in a different form in the novel, was named one of the O. Henry Prize Stories of 1978.

The novel about Cacciato is told through the eyes and sensibilities of a young soldier from Iowa named Paul Berlin. In this story, Paul has recently returned from battle duty in Vietnam. Like many veterans of that war, he is confused over the meaning of his experience. He is also vaguely dissatisfied with his performance.

The war was over, and there was no place in particular to go. Paul Berlin followed the tar road in its seven-mile loop around the lake, then he started all over again, driving slowly, feeling safe inside his father's big Chevy, now and again looking out onto the lake to watch the boats and waterskiers and scenery. It was Sunday and it was summer, and things seemed pretty much the same. The lake was the same. The houses were the same, all low-slung and split level and modern, porches and picture windows facing the water. The lots were spacious. On the lake side of the road, the houses were handsome and set deep in, well-kept and painted, with docks jutting out into the lake, and boats moored and covered with canvas, and gardens, and sometimes even gardeners, and stone patios with barbecue spits and grills, and wooden shingles saying who lived where. On the other side of the road, to his left, the houses were also handsome, though less expensive and on a smaller scale and with no docks or boats or wooden shingles. The road was a sort of boundary between the affluent and the almost affluent, and to live on the lake side of the road was one of the few natural privileges in a town of the prairie—the difference between watching the sun set over cornfields or over the lake.

It was a good-sized lake. In high school he'd driven round and round and round with his friends and pretty girls, talking about urgent matters, worrying eagerly about the existence of God and theories of causation, or wondering whether Sally Hankins, who lived on the lake side of the road, would want to pull into the shelter of Sunset Park. Then, there had been a war. But there had always been the lake. It had been dug out by the southernmost advance of the Wisconsin glacier. Fed by neither springs nor streams, it was a tepid, algaed lake that depended on fickle prarie rains for replenishment. Still, it was the town's only lake, the only one in twenty-six miles, and at night the moon made a white swath across its waters, and on sunny days it was nice to look at, and that evening it would dazzle with the reflections of fireworks, and it was the center of things from the very start, always there to be driven around, still mesmerizing and quieting and a good audience for silence, a seven-mile flat circumference that could be traveled by slow car in twenty-five minutes. It was not such a good lake for swimming. After college, he'd caught an ear infection that had almost kept him out of the war. And the lake had drowned Max Arnold, keeping him out of the war entirely. Max had been one who liked to talk about the existence of God. "No, I'm not saying *that*," he would say carefully against the drone of the engine. "I'm saying it is possible as an idea, even necessary as an idea, a final cause in the whole structure of causation." Now he knew, perhaps. Before the war, they'd driven around the lake as friends, but now Max was dead and most of the others were living in Des Moines or Sioux City, or going to school somewhere, or holding down jobs. None of the girls was left. Sally Hankins was married. His father would not talk. His father had been in another war, so he knew the truth already, and he would not talk about it, and there was no one left to talk with.

He turned on the radio. The car's big engine fired machinery that blew cold air all over him. Clockwise, like an electron spinning forever around its nucleus, the big Chevy circled the lake, and he had little to do but sit in the air conditioning, both hands on the wheel, letting the car carry

A. Style
Many critics have commented on O'Brien's stylistic debt to Ernest Hemingway.
? What in this paragraph seems to echo Hemingway's writing? (The most notable feature may be the straightforward declarative style: "The war was over. . . . It was Sunday and it was summer. . . . The lake was the same. The houses were the same.")

B. Figures of Speech
Have students notice the figurative phrase about the lake being "a good audience for silence." That single phrase has aspects of metaphor (comparison of unlike objects), personification (nonhuman object talked about as if human), and oxymoron (contradictory terms: *audience, silence*).

For Further Reading For Students And Teachers
A book that tells the story of the Memorial and contains a complete alphabetical list of names (on the wall they are chronological by date of death) is Jan C. Scruggs and Joel L. Swerdlow's *To Heal a Nation: The Vietnam Veterans Memorial* (Harper & Row, 1985).

Humanities Connection: Discussing the Photograph
The story of how the Vietnam Veterans Memorial came to be is an inspiring one. The idea for it came to Jan Scruggs, a former rifleman with the U.S. Army 199th Light Infantry Brigade, after watching the movie *The Deer Hunter.* Scruggs told his wife, "I'm going to build a memorial to all the guys who served in Vietnam. It'll have the name of everyone killed." His wife thought he was having delusions, but Scruggs was serious. Three and a half years later, following a design competition won by 21-year-old Maya Ying Lin, the 493-foot-long monument stood near the Lincoln Memorial. Today it attracts thousands of visitors a day, many of them relatives or friends of those whose names appear on the wall.

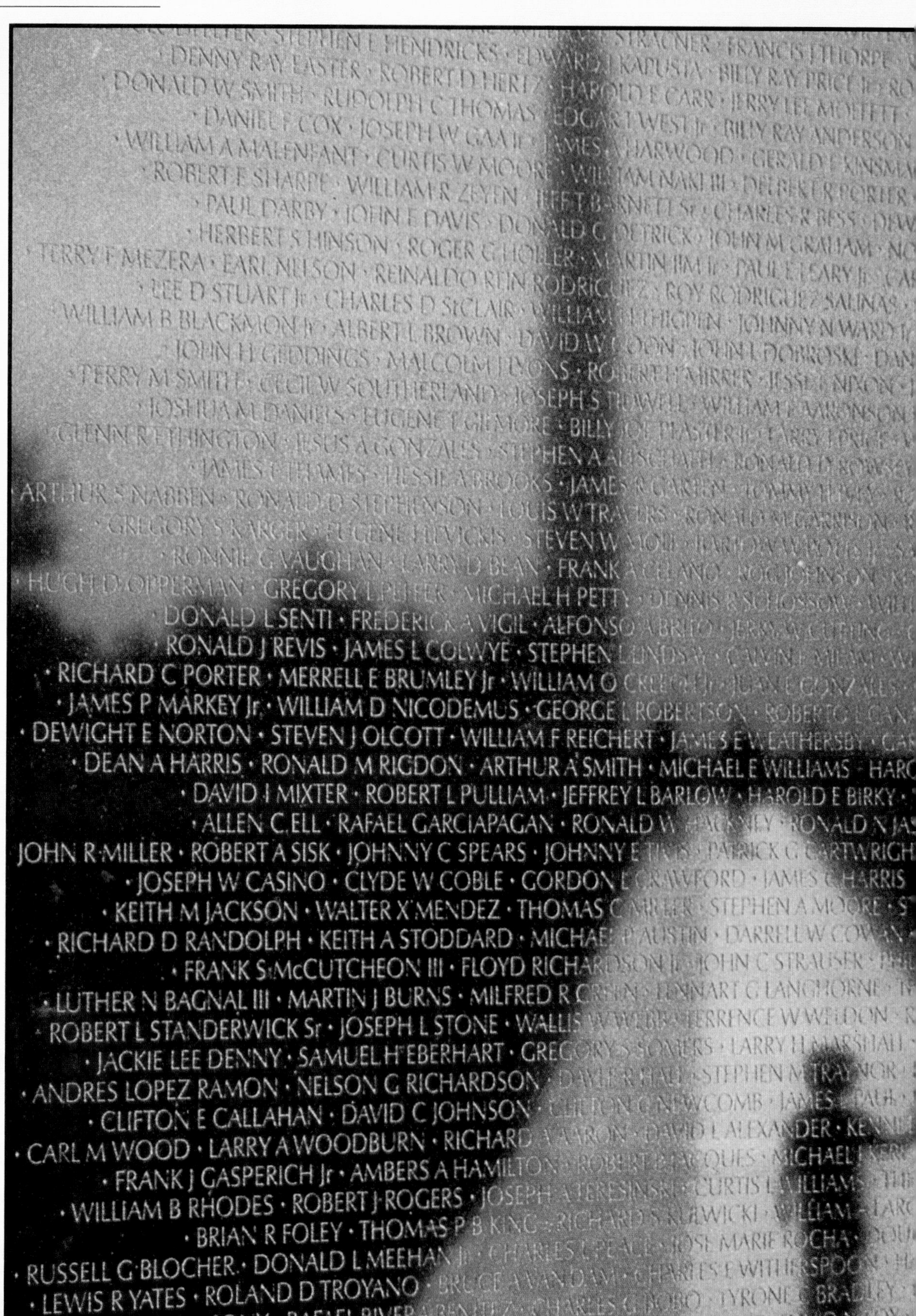

him in orbit. It was a lazy Sunday. The town was small. Out on the lake, a man's motorboat had stalled, and the fellow was bent over the silver motor with a wrench and a frown, and beyond him there were waterskiers and smooth July waters and two mud hens.

The road curved west. The sun was low in front of him, and he figured it was close to five o'clock. Twenty after, he guessed. The war had taught him to figure time. Even without the sun, waking from sleep, he could usually place it within fifteen minutes either way. He wished his father were there beside him, so he could say, "Well, looks about five-twenty," and his father would look at his watch and say, "Hey! How'd you do that?" "One of those things you learn in the war," he would say. "I know exactly what you mean," his father would then say, and the ice would be broken, and then they would be able to talk about it as they circled the lake.

He drove past Slater Park and across the causeway and past Sunset Park. The radio announcer sounded tired. He said it was five-thirty. The temperature in Des Moines was eighty-one degrees, and "All you on the road, drive carefully now, you hear, on this fine Fourth of July." Along the road, kicking stones in front of them, two young boys were hiking with knapsacks and toy rifles and canteens. He honked going by, but neither boy looked up. Already he'd passed them six times, forty-two miles, nearly three hours. He watched the boys recede in his rearview mirror. They turned purply colored, like clotted blood, before finally disappearing.

"How many medals did you win?" his father might have asked.

"Seven," he would have said, "though none of them were for valor."

"That's all right," his father would have answered, knowing full well that many brave men did not win medals for their bravery, and that others won medals for doing nothing. "What are the medals you won?"

And he would have listed them, as a kind of starting place for talking about the war: the Combat Infantryman's Badge, the Air Medal, the Bronze Star (without a V-device for valor), the Army Commendation Medal, the Vietnam Campaign Medal, the Good Conduct Medal, and the Purple Heart, though it wasn't much of a wound, and there was no scar, and it didn't hurt and never had. While none of them was for valor, the decorations still looked good on the uniform in his closet, and if anyone were to ask, he would have explained what each signified, and eventually he would have talked about the medals he did not win, and why he did not win them, and how afraid he had been.

"Well," his father might have said, "that's an impressive list of medals, all right."

"But none were for valor."

"I understand."

And that would have been the time for telling his father that he'd almost won the Silver Star, or maybe even the Medal of Honor.

"I almost won the Silver Star," he would have said.

"How's that?"

"Oh, it's just a war story."

"What's wrong with war stories?" his father would have said.

"Nothing, except I guess nobody wants to hear them."

"Tell me," his father would have said.

And then, circling the lake, he would have started the story by saying what a crazy hot day it had been when Frenchie Tucker crawled like a snake into the clay tunnel and got shot in the neck, going on with the story in great detail, telling how it smelled and what the sounds had been, everything, then going on to say how he'd almost won the Silver Star for valor.

"Well," his father would have said, "that's not a very pretty story."

"I wasn't very brave."

"You have seven medals."

"True, true," he would have said, "but I might have had eight," but even so, seven medals was pretty good, hinting at courage with their bright colors and heavy metals. "But I wasn't brave," he would have admitted.

"You weren't a coward, either," his father would have said.

"I might have been a hero."

"But you weren't a coward," his father would have insisted.

"No," Paul Berlin would have said, holding the wheel slightly right of center to produce the constant clockwise motion, "no, I wasn't a coward, and I wasn't brave, but I had the chance." He would have explained, if anyone were there to listen, that his most precious medal, except for the one he did not win, was the Combat Infantryman's Badge. While not strictly speaking a genu-

B

A. Interpretation

? Why is this conversation presented as one that only might have been—"might have asked," "would have said"? (Paul's father will not talk with him about the war. See question 2, page 941.)

B. Dialogue

Dialogue can reveal character and advance the plot. This dialogue that Paul is imagining shows something about Paul's feelings toward his father.

? How does Paul feel toward his father? (He seems to like and respect him, but wishes his father would talk to him.)

A. Repetition
Paul has "no place in particular to go." That phrase repeats the wording of the first sentence of the story. **?** How does the author's repetition of words and phrases emphasize Paul's aimlessness? (Verbal repetition, like the physical repetition of Paul's circling the lake, underscores the fact that he has nothing meaningful to do—his old friends are gone, and the war seems to have sapped his desire for involvement in his community.)

B. Symbol
? What is symbolic about the sprinkler that Paul observes? (The rotating sprinkler symbolizes futility. Its circular motion is comparable to Paul's circling the lake. Moreover, because the grass is so dry, the sprinkling is "hopeless." Likewise, Paul's activity is getting him nowhere.)

ine medal—more an insignia of soldierdom—the CIB meant that he had seen the war as a real soldier, on the ground. It meant he'd had the opportunity to be brave, it meant that. It meant, too, that he'd seen Frenchie Tucker crawl into the tunnel so that just his feet were left showing, and heard the sound when he got shot in the neck. With its crossed rifles and silver and blue colors, the CIB was really not such a bad decoration, not as good as the Silver Star or Medal of Honor, but still evidence that he'd once been there with the chance to be very brave. "I wasn't brave," he would have said, "but I might have been."

The road descended into the outskirts of town, turning northwest past the junior college and tennis courts, then past the city park where tables were spread with sheets of colored plastic as picnickers listened to the high school band, then past the municipal docks where a fat woman stood in pedal-pushers and white socks, fishing for bullheads.[1] There were no other fish in the lake, excepting some perch and a few worthless carp. It was a bad lake for swimming and fishing both.

He was in no great hurry. There was no place in particular to go. The day was very hot, but inside the Chevy the air was cold and oily and secure, and he liked the sound of the big engine and the radio and the air conditioning. Through the windows, as though seen through one-way glass, the town shined like a stop-motion photograph, or a memory. The town could not talk, and it would not listen, and it was really a very small town anyway. "How'd you like to hear about the time I almost won the Silver Star for valor?" he might have said. The Chevy seemed to know its way around the lake.

It was late afternoon. Along an unused railway spur, four men were erecting steel launchers for the evening fireworks. They were dressed alike in khaki trousers, work shirts, visored caps, and black boots. They were sweating. Two of them were unloading crates of explosives from a city truck, stacking the crates near the steel launchers. They were talking. One of them was laughing. "How'd you like to hear about it?" he might have murmured, but the men did not look up. Later they would blow color into the sky. The lake would be like a mirror, and the picnickers would sigh. The colors would open wide. "Well, it was this crazy hot day," he would have said to anyone who asked, "and Frenchie Tucker took off his helmet and pack and crawled into the tunnel with a forty-five and a knife, and the whole platoon stood in a circle around the mouth of the tunnel to watch him go down. 'Don't get blowed away,' said Stink Harris, but Frenchie was already inside and he didn't hear. You could see his feet wiggling, and you could smell the dirt and clay, and then, when he got shot through the neck, you could smell the gunpowder and you could see Frenchie's feet jerk, and that was the day I could have won the Silver Star for valor."

The Chevy rolled smoothly across the old railroad spur. To his right, there was only the open lake. To his left, the lawns were scorched dry like October corn. Hopelessly, round and round, a rotating sprinkler scattered water into Doctor Mason's vegetable garden. In August it would get worse. The lake would turn green, thick with bacteria and decay, and the golf course would dry up, and dragonflies would crack open for lack of good water. The summer seemed permanent.

The big Chevy curled past the A&W and Centennial Beach, and he started his seventh revolution around the lake.

He followed the road past the handsome low-slung houses. Back to Slater Park, across the causeway, around to Sunset Park, as though riding on tracks.

Out on the lake, the man with the stalled motorboat was still fiddling with the engine.

The two boys were still trudging on their hike. They did not look up when he honked.

The pair of mud hens floated like wooden decoys. The waterskiers looked tan and happy, and the spray behind them looked clean.

It was all distant and pretty.

Facing the sun again, he figured it was nearly six o'clock. Not much later the tired announcer in Des Moines confirmed it, his voice seeming to rock itself into a Sunday afternoon snooze.

Too bad, he thought. If Max were there, he would say something meaningful about the announcer's fatigue, and relate it to the sun low and red now over the lake, and the war, and courage. Too bad that all the girls had gone away. And his father, who already knew the difficulties of being brave, and who preferred silence.

Circling the lake, with time to talk, he would have told the truth. He would not have faked it. Starting with the admission that he had not been

1. **bullheads:** a type of freshwater fish with a spiny head and wide mouth.

Literature and Language: Using Simple Sentences
Review with students that a simple sentence may have a compound subject and verb (or both) as well as modifiers and phrases. What distinguishes simple sentences from all other sentences is that simple sentences are made up of only one independent clause. Compound sentences have two or more independent clauses; complex sentences have at least one subordinate clause. Encourage students to refer to **Grammar, Usage, and Mechanics: A Reference Guide** for more information.

Students should notice O'Brien's effective use of short, simple sentences in this story. Have them look, for example, at the first paragraph in the right column on this page that begins, "He passed . . ." How many simple sentences can they find? (They should find seven; one sentence is compound.)

Have students discuss why O'Brien might have included so many simple sentences. (The young soldier, profoundly affected by the war, thinks ploddingly. He can only handle one thought at a time.)

truly brave, he would have next said he hadn't been a coward, either. "I almost won the Silver Star for valor," he would have said, and, even so, he'd learned many important things in the war. Like telling time without a watch. He had learned to step lightly. He knew, just by the sound, the difference between friendly and enemy mortars, and with time to talk and with an audience, he could explain the difference in great detail. He could tell people that the enemy fired 82-millimeter mortar rounds, while we fired 81's, and that this was a real advantage to the enemy since they could steal our rounds and shoot them from their own weapons. He knew many lies. Simple, unprofound things. He knew it is a lie that only stupid men are brave. He knew that a man can die of fright, literally, because it had happened just that way to Billy Boy Watkins after his foot had been blown off. Billy Boy had been scared to death. Dead of a heart attack caused by fright, according to Doc Peret, who would know. He knew, too, that it is a lie, the old saying that you never hear the shot that gets you, because Frenchie Tucker was shot in the neck, and after they dragged him out of the tunnel he lay there and told everyone his great discovery; he'd heard it coming the whole way, he said excitedly; and then he raised his thumb and bled through his mouth, grinning at the great discovery. So the old saying was surely a lie, or else Frenchie Tucker was lying himself, which under the circumstances was hard to believe. He knew a lot of things. They were not new or profound, but they were true. He knew that he might have won a Silver Star, like Frenchie, if he'd been able to finish what Frenchie started in the foul tunnel. He knew many war stories, a thousand details, smells and the confusion of the senses, but nobody was there to listen, A [and nobody knew a damn about the war because nobody believed it was really a war at all.] It was not a war for war stories, or talk of valor, and nobody asked questions about the details, such as how afraid you can be, or what the particular sounds were, or whether it hurts to be shot, or what you think about and hear and see on ambush, or whether you can really tell in a firefight which way to shoot, which you can't, or how you become brave enough to win the Silver Star, or how it smells of sulfur against your cheek after firing eighteen fast rounds, or how you crawl on hands and knees without knowing direction, and how, after crawling into the red-mouthed tunnel, you close your eyes like a mole and follow the tunnel walls and smell Frenchie's fresh blood and know a bullet cannot miss in there, and how there is nowhere to go but forward or backward, eyes closed, and how you can't go forward, and lose all sense, and are dragged out by the heels, losing the Silver Star. All the details, without profundity, simple and age old, but nobody wants to hear war stories because they are age old and not new and not profound, and because everyone knows already that it hadn't been a war like other wars. If Max or his father were ever to ask, or anybody, he would say. "Well, first off, it was a war the same as any war," which would not sound profound at all, but which would be the truth. Then he would explain what he meant in great detail, explaining that, right or wrong or win or lose, at root it had been a real war, regardless of corruption in high places or politics or sociology or the existence of God. His father knew it already, though. Which was why he didn't ask. And Max could not ask. It was a small town, but it wasn't the town's fault, either.

He passed the sprawling ranch-style homes. He lit a cigarette. He had learned to smoke in the war. He opened the window a crack but kept the air conditioner going full, and again he circled the lake. His thoughts were the same. Out on the lake, the man was frantically yanking the cord to his stalled outboard motor. Along the causeway, the two boys marched on. The pair of mud hens sought sludge at the bottom of the lake, heads under water and tails bobbing.

Six-thirty, he thought. The lake had divided into two halves. One half still glistened. The other was caught in shadow. Soon it would be dark. The crew of workers would shoot the sky full of color, for the war was over, and the town would celebrate independence. He passed Sunset Park once again, and more houses, and the junior college and tennis courts, and the picnickers and the high school band, and the municipal docks where the fat woman patiently waited for fish.

Already, though it wasn't quite dusk, the A&W was awash in neon lights.

He maneuvered his father's Chevy into one of the parking slots, let the engine idle, and waited. The place was doing a good holiday business. Mostly kids in their fathers' cars, a few farmers in for the day, a few faces he thought he remembered, but no names. He sat still. With the sound of the engine and air conditioning and radio, he

A. Expansion
Students need some understanding of history to understand why "nobody believed it was really a war at all." First, like the Korean War of the early 1950's, the Vietnam War was undeclared. In addition, it was an unpopular war. Some Americans felt that the U.S. presence in South Vietnam only served to continue the corrupt government left over from the country's former colonial status under the French. Finally, when U.S. troops withdrew and North and South Vietnam were unified under Communist rule, many Americans preferred to forget the war.

CLOSURE

Have students discuss the possible reasons for Paul's seeming aimlessness. In other words, what do they think may be responsible for his internal conflicts.

READING CHECK TEST

1. Most of the houses along the lake are old, rather shabby, and in need of paint. *False*
2. Paul Berlin received seven medals in the war, but none of them was for valor. *True*
3. The day Berlin could have won his Silver Star was the day Frenchie Tucker was shot through the neck. *True*
4. In Vietnam, Berlin learned that a man can die from fright. *True*
5. The man whose motorboat stalls finally gets the engine going. *False.*

A. Dialogue
Be sure students notice the pseudo-military nature of this talk on the intercom. (See question 9 on page 941).

B. Responding
? How do you feel about the end of the story? Are you satisfied? Is it an effective ending? Does it suggest that anything in Paul's life will change? (Have students point to specific story details to support their responses.)

could not hear the kids laughing, or the cars coming and going and burning rubber. But it didn't matter, it seemed proper, and he sat patiently and watched while mosquitoes and June bugs swarmed off the lake to attack the orange-colored lighting. A slim, hipless, deft young blonde delivered trays of food, passing him by as if the big Chevy were invisible, but he waited. The tired announcer in Des Moines gave the time, seven o'clock. He could trace the fall of dusk in the orange lights which grew brighter and sharper. It was a bad war for medals. But the Silver Star would have been nice. Nice to have been brave. The tactile, certain substance of the Silver Star, and how he could have rubbed his fingers over it, remembering the tunnel and the smell of clay in his nose, going forward and not backward in simple bravery. He waited patiently. The mosquitoes were electrocuting themselves against a Pest-Rid machine. The slim young carhop ignored him, chatting with four boys in a Firebird, her legs in nylons even in mid-summer.

He honked once, a little embarrassed, but she did not turn. The four boys were laughing. He could not hear them, or the joke, but he could see their bright eyes and the way their heads moved. She patted the cheek of the driver.

He honked again, twice. He could not hear the sound. The girl did not hear, either.

He honked again, this time leaning on the horn. His ears buzzed. The air conditioning shot cold air into his lap. The girl turned slowly, as though hearing something very distant, not at all sure. She said something to the boys, and they laughed, then she moved reluctantly toward him. EAT MAMA BURGERS said the orange and brown button on her chest. "How'd you like to hear about the war," he whispered, feeling vengeful. "The time I almost won the Silver Star."

She stood at the window, straight up so he could not see her face, only the button that said, EAT MAMA BURGERS. "Papa Burger, root beer, and french fries," he said, but the girl did not move or answer. She rapped on the window.

"Papa Burger, root beer, and french fries," he said, rolling it down.

She leaned down. She shook her head dumbly. Her eyes were as lovely and fuzzy as cotton candy.

"Papa Burger, root beer, and french fries," he said slowly, pronouncing the words separately and distinctly for her.

She stared at him with her strange eyes. "You blind?" she chirped suddenly. She gestured toward an intercom attached to a steel post. "You blind or something?"

"Papa Burger, root beer, and french fries."

"Push the button," she said, "and place your order." Then, first punching the button for him, she returned to her friends in the Firebird.

"Order," commanded a tinny voice.

"Papa Burger, root beer, and french fries."

"Roger-dodger," the voice said. "Repeat: one Papa, one beer, one fries. Stand by. That's it?"

"Roger," said Paul Berlin.

"Out," said the voice, and the intercom squeaked and went dead.

"Out," said Paul Berlin.

When the slim carhop brought him his tray, he ate quickly, without looking up, then punched the intercom button.

"Order," said the tinny voice.

"I'm done."

"That's it?"

"Yes, all done."

"Roger-dodger, over n' out," said the voice.

"Out."

On his ninth revolution around the lake he passed the hiking boys for the last time. The man with the stalled motorboat was paddling toward shore. The mud hens were gone. The fat woman was reeling in her line. The sun had left a smudge of watercolor on the horizon, and the bandshell was empty, and Doctor Mason's sprinkler went round and round.

On his tenth revolution, he switched off the air conditioning, cranked open a window and rested his elbow comfortably on the sill, driving with one hand. He could trace the contours of the tunnel. He could talk about the scrambling sense of being lost, though he could not describe it even in his thoughts. He could talk about the terror, but he could not describe it or even feel it anymore. He could talk about emerging to see sunlight, but he could not feel the warmth, or see the faces of the men who looked away, or talk about his shame. There was no one to talk to, and nothing to say.

On his eleventh revolution, the sky went crazy with color.

He pulled into Sunset Park and stopped in the shadow of a picnic shelter. After a time, he got out and walked down to the beach and stood with his arms folded and watched the fireworks. For a small town, it was a pretty good show.

ANALYZING THE STORY

Identifying Facts

1. The story takes place on a summer Sunday near a lake in Paul Berlin's home town in Iowa, some time after Paul has returned from his tour of duty in Vietnam.

Paul remembers the sounds from the mortars, the smell of sulfur, and the sight of the wall of a tunnel.

2. Paul wishes that his father would talk openly with him about the war.

3. He learned how to tell time without a watch; he learned to step lightly; he learned the difference between friendly and enemy mortars; he learned to smoke. He also learned that a man can die of fright, and that it is a lie that only stupid men are brave.

People don't want to hear about the war because nobody believes that it was a war like other wars.

4. Frenchie crawled into a clay tunnel, where he was shot in the neck, earning him a Silver Star.

5. He wishes that he had been a hero and won medals for valor.

He wants to tell his father war stories.

Interpreting Meanings

6. Paul's father may actually be disappointed with him—or may have self-doubts about his own wartime conduct. Both know that courage is a complex phenomenon.

The father knows the grim facts of war already, having served in "another war," probably World War II.

7. The circular action underlines Paul's aimlessness. His awareness of time contrasts with his lack of ambition to use it productively.

8. Independence Day is a day of national pride, but war can take a terrible, invisible toll on those who fight.

9. A trivial scene echoes a combat situation.

10. In the second paragraph; their purpose is a matter of opinion.

11. It does not seem to be resolved.

12. Answers will vary, but most will agree that, on balance, Paul is courageous.

13. Answers will vary, but the fear of death is the same in any war. One difference in Vietnam was not knowing who the enemy was: Guerilla forces were indistinguishable from civilians.

Responding to the Story

Analyzing the Story

Identifying Facts

1. Describe the story's **setting**. In contrast, what sights, sounds, and smells does Paul remember from his time in Vietnam?
2. What does Paul wish his father would do?
3. List the things Paul has learned as a result of the war. According to Paul, why don't people want to hear about the war?
4. Explain what Frenchie Tucker did in Vietnam. What happened to him as a result?
5. What does Paul wish he had done in Vietnam? What does he want to tell his father?

Interpreting Meanings

6. Why do you think it is so difficult for Paul and his father to talk? What does Paul mean when he says that his father "knew the truth already"? What *truth* does his father know? How does he know it?
7. Discuss the **symbolic** meaning of the repeated circular action in the story, and of the repeated references to time.
8. What is the **symbolic** meaning of the date in the story's context?
9. Given his experiences, what is **ironic** about the military language in Paul's conversation with the disembodied voice on the drive-in's intercom system?
10. Find the passages where Paul mentions conversations about God. What purpose do you think these passages serve?
11. Do you think Paul's **internal conflict** has been resolved by the end of the story? Explain.
12. Do you think Paul is or is not a courageous person? Explain your answer.
13. Could Paul's feelings be the same for any soldier, in any war? Or do you think the Vietnam war was different? Explain.

Writing About the Story

A Creative Response

1. **Inventing an Interview.** Imagine that a TV reporter approaches Paul Berlin for an interview about Vietnam for that night's July 4 newscast. Write a dialogue made up of the reporter's questions and Berlin's answers.

A Critical Response

2. **Comparing Stories.** Both "Speaking of Courage" and Mark Helprin's "Tamar" (page 926) deal indirectly with the trauma of warfare. In a brief essay, explain how both stories use **contrast** to deal with their themes on this subject. In planning your essay, consider how contrast is evident in each story's setting, characterization, and tone of voice.

James Alan McPherson (1943–)

Born in Savannah, Georgia, James Alan McPherson recalls growing up in a lower-class black neighborhood, going to segregated schools, and knowing no white people socially. Looking back on his early years, he sees himself as the beneficiary of a series of contracts between the United States government and various institutions of society. One of these contracts helped him to enroll at Morris Brown College in Atlanta. Another contract helped him get a part-time job as a dining-car waiter for the Great Northern Railway.

A creative writing contest sponsored by the *Reader's Digest* started him writing fiction, and he sold his first story to *The Atlantic Monthly* in 1965. He continued to write while attending Harvard Law School and working as a janitor in a Cambridge apartment house. This job, he said later, gave him the solitude to write, and thus was probably the best contract he ever made.

McPherson's first collection of stories, *Hue and Cry*, appeared in 1969 and was widely praised for transcending stereotypes in both black and white characters. McPherson believes Americans need to find a basis other than race (which tends to erect walls between people) to deal with complex relationships in a society that is becoming more democratic and more offended by racial stereotypes.

"Those of us who are black," McPherson says, "and who have had to defend our humanity, should be obliged to continue defending it, on higher and higher levels, not of power, which is a kind of tragic trap, but on higher levels of consciousness."

In *Elbow Room,* a second collection of stories published in 1977, McPherson was aiming to present his hope for an America in which each citizen would contain the diversity of all, "carry the mainstream of the culture inside himself. As an American, . . . he would be a synthesis of high and low, black and white, city and country, provincial and universal. If he could live with these contradictions he would be simply a representative American." *Elbow Room* won the Pulitzer Prize in 1978.

McPherson has been a professor at the Writers' Workshop of the University of Iowa. He has also taught at the University of Virginia, Morgan State University, the University of California at Santa Cruz, and Harvard.

"Why I Like Country Music" first appeared in *The Harvard Advocate*.

Supplementary Support Materials
1. Vocabulary Activity Worksheet (*CCB*)
2. Review and Response Worksheet: Tone (*CCB*)
3. Language Skills Worksheet: Noun Clauses (*CCB*)
4. Selection Test (*CCB*)

Developing Vocabulary
The following words from the story are tested in the Selection Test. (See also Vocabulary Activity Worksheet.)

flux	plaited
to capitulate	condescension
castigation	cryptic

Preparation
Establishing a Purpose. Have students read the headnote, which suggests that when they read the story they pay special attention to its tone. Question 9, page 952, will help give them direction as they pursue this purpose.

A. Point of View
? From what point of view is the story told? (The point of view is first person.)

B. Simile
? Why is the Ibo and Yoruba comparison an especially apt one? (Two divergent black cultures in Africa are being compared to two divergent black cultures [New York City and small town South Carolina] in the United States.)

WHY I LIKE COUNTRY MUSIC

Despite its title, this story is more about an important childhood experience than about country music. The music, however, plays a major role in the experience. As you read, pay careful attention to the tone of voice in which the story is told. Try to imagine that you are listening to the narrator as he talks aloud. You should be able to hear a very distinctive voice, similar to that of a subtle comedian beguiling an audience with a tale based on real life.

No one will believe that I like country music. Even my wife scoffs when told such a possibility exists. "Go on!" Gloria tells me. "I can see blues, bebop, maybe even a little buckdancing. But not bluegrass." Gloria says, "Hillbilly stuff is not just music. It's like the New York Stock Exchange. The minute you see a sharp rise in it, you better watch out."

I tend to argue the point, but quietly, and mostly to myself. Gloria was born and raised in New York; she has come to believe in the stock exchange as the only index of economic health. My perceptions were shaped in South Carolina; and long ago I learned there, as a waiter in private clubs, to gauge economic flux by the tips people gave. We tend to disagree on other matters too, but the thing that gives me most frustration is trying to make her understand why I like country music. Perhaps it is because she hates the South and has capitulated emotionally to the horror stories told by refugees from down home. Perhaps it is because Gloria is third generation Northern-born. I do not know. What I do know is that, while the two of us are black, the distance between us is sometimes as great as that between Ibo and Yoruba.[1] And I do know that, despite her protestations, I like country music.

"You are crazy," Gloria tells me.

I tend to argue the point, but quietly, and mostly to myself.

Of course I do not like all country stuff; just pieces that make the right connections. I like banjo because sometimes I hear ancestors in the strumming. I like the fiddle-like refrain in "Dixie" for the very same reason. But most of all I like square dancing—the interplay between fiddle and caller, the stomping, the swishing of dresses, the strutting, the proud turnings, the laughter. Most of all I like the laughter. In recent months I have wondered why I like this music and this dance. I have drawn no general conclusions, but from time to time I suspect it is because the square dance is the only dance form I ever mastered.

"I wouldn't say that in public," Gloria warns me.

I agree with her, but still affirm the truth of it, although quietly, and mostly to myself.

Dear Gloria: This is the truth of how it was:

In my youth in that distant country, while others learned to strut, I grew stiff as a winter cornstalk. When my playmates harmonized their rhythms, I stood on the sidelines in atonic[2] detachment. While they shimmied, I merely jerked in lackluster imitation. I relate these facts here, not in remorse or self-castigation, but as a true confession of my circumstances. In those days, down in our small corner of South Carolina, proficiency in dance was a form of storytelling. A boy could say, "I traveled here and there, saw this and fought that, conquered him and made love to her, lied to them, told a few others the truth, just so I could come back here and let you know what things out there are really like." He could communicate all this with smooth, graceful jiggles of

1. **Ibo and Yoruba** (ē'bō; yō'rōō·bä): two separate and distinct West African tribes in Nigeria.

2. **atonic:** weak; languid.

A. Setting
The setting of the story is described partially in terms of conflict.

? Why do you think people from the "far Northern places" were admired and envied by those who were born and raised in this "small corner of South Carolina"? (The text gives many reasons. They boil down to "nothing new ever happens here that doesn't come from the North.")

B. Interpretation

? What does the narrator mean when he says that Gweneth was "from the South Carolina section of Brooklyn"? (When they moved from the South into Northern cities, African Americans tended to settle in neighborhoods where others from the same region already lived. Immigrants from overseas have generally done the same thing.)

his round bottom, synchronized with intricately coordinated sweeps of his arms and small, unexcited movements of his legs. Little girls could communicate much more.

A But sadly, I could do none of it. Development of these skills depended on the ministrations of family and neighbors. My family did not dance; our closest neighbor was a true-believing Seventh Day Adventist. Moreover, most new dances came from up North, brought to town usually by people returning to riff[3] on the good life said to exist in those far Northern places. They prowled our dirt streets in rented Cadillacs; paraded our brick sidewalks exhibiting styles abstracted from the fullness of life in Harlem, South Philadelphia, Roxbury, Baltimore, and the South Side of Chicago. They confronted our provincial clothes merchants with the arrogant reminder, "But people ain't wearin' this in New Yo*kkk!*" Each of their movements, as well as their world-weary smoothness, told us locals meaningful tales of what was missing in our lives. Unfortunately, those of us under strict parental supervision, or those of us without Northern connections, could only stand at a distance and worship these envoys of culture. We stood on the sidelines—styleless, gestureless, danceless, doing nothing more than an improvised one-butt shuffle—hoping for one of them to touch our lives. It was my good fortune, during my tenth year on the sidelines, to have one of these Northerners introduce me to the square dance.

My dear, dear Gloria, her name was Gweneth Lawson:

She was a pretty, chocolate brown little girl with dark brown eyes and two long black braids. After all these years, the image of these two braids evokes in me all there is to remember about Gweneth Lawson. They were plaited across the top of her head and hung to a point just above the back of her Peter Pan collar. Sometimes she wore two bows, one red and one blue, and these tended to sway lazily near the place on her neck where the smooth brown of her skin and the white of her collar met the ink-bottle black of her hair. Even when I cannot remember her face, I remember the rainbow of deep, rich colors in which she lived. This is so because I watched them, every weekday, from my desk directly behind hers in our fourth-grade class. And she wore the most magical perfume, or lotion, smelling just slightly of fresh-cut lemons, that wafted back to me whenever she made the slightest movement at her desk. Now I must tell you this much more, dear Gloria: Whenever I smell fresh lemons, whether in the market or at home, I look around me—not for Gweneth Lawson, but for some quiet corner where I can revive in private certain memories of her. And in pursuing these memories across such lemony bridges, I rediscover that I loved her.

Gweneth was from the South Carolina section of Brooklyn. Her parents had sent her south to live with her uncle, Mr. Richard Lawson, the brick mason, for an unspecified period of time. Just why they did this I do not know, unless it was their plan to have her absorb more of South Carolina folkways than conditions in Brooklyn would allow. She was a gentle, soft-spoken girl; I recall no condescension in her manner. This was all the more admirable because our unrestrained awe of a Northern-born black person usually induced in him some grand sense of his own importance. You must know that in those days older folks would point to someone and say, "He's from the North," and the statement would be sufficient in itself. Mothers made their children behave by advising that, if they led exemplary lives and attended church regularly, when they died they would go to New York. Only someone who understands what London meant to Dick Whittington, or how California and the suburbs function in the national mind, could appreciate the mythical dimensions of this Northlore.

But Gweneth Lawson was above regional idealization. Though I might have loved her partly because she was a Northerner, I loved her more because of the world of colors that seemed to be suspended about her head. I loved her glowing forehead and I loved her bright, dark brown eyes; I loved the black braids, the red and blue and sometimes yellow and pink ribbons; I loved the way the deep, rich brown of her neck melted into the pink or white cloth of her Peter Pan collar; I loved the lemony vapor on which she floated and from which on occasion, she seemed to be inviting me to be buoyed up, up, up into her happy world; I loved the way she caused my heart to tumble whenever, during a restless moment, she seemed about to turn her head in my direction; I loved her more, though torturously, on the many occasions when she did not turn. Because I was a shy

3. **riff:** improvise, as a jazz musician does.

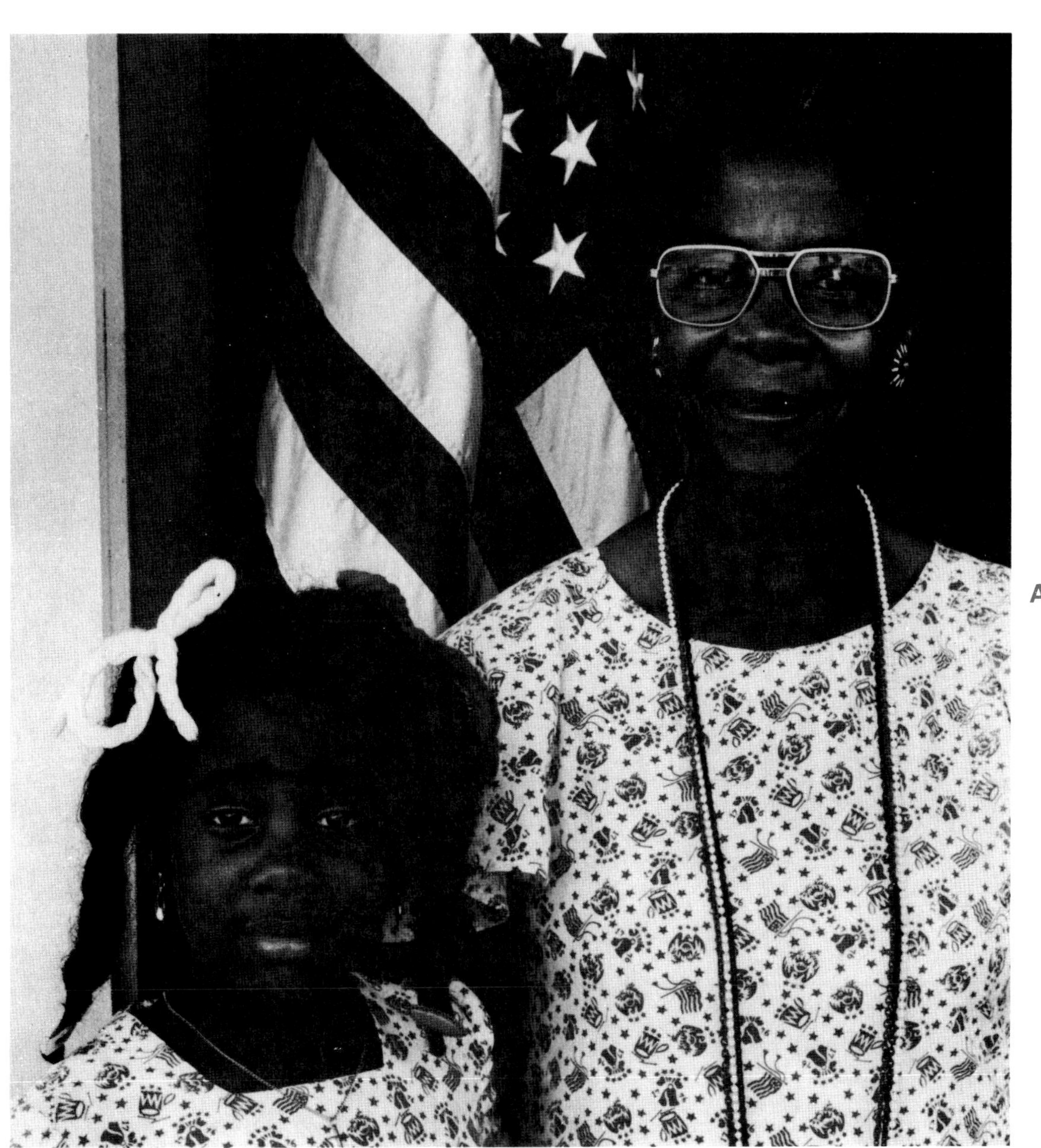

boy, I loved the way I could love her silently, at least six hours a day, without ever having to disclose my love.

My platonic[4] state of mind might have stretched onward into a blissful infinity had not Mrs. Esther Clay Boswell, our teacher, made it her business to pry into the affair. Although she prided herself on being a strict disciplinarian, Mrs. Boswell was not without a sense of humor. A round, full-breasted woman in her early forties, she liked to amuse herself, and sometimes the class as well, by calling the attention of all eyes to whoever of

4. **platonic** (plə·ton′ik): not sensual, but purely spiritual.

A. Humanities Connection: Responding to the Photograph

? Compare the descriptions of Gweneth Lawson and Mrs. Esther Clay Boswell in the story with the girl and woman in the photograph. Are there any similarities? Any differences? (Gweneth had braids, too; this girl appears to be wearing two braids with bows of different colors. Mrs. Boswell was a "round" woman.) Do the girl and woman appear to be student and teacher? (The American flag could suggest a classroom setting, but the identical fabric in the two dresses hints at a family relationship.)

A. Characterization
An effective method of characterization is to let the character speak. **?** What does Mrs. Boswell's speech tell the reader about her personality and expectations as a teacher? (Answers will vary, but all will agree that Mrs. Boswell won't put up with any nonsense.)

B. Responding
? Is Mrs. Boswell being cruel in using Clarence Buford as the "helpmeet in this exercise" to exemplify the error ("meekness and indecision" in certain students) so as to correct the error? (Opinions will differ. Students should note that her method seems to work—later in the story the ordinarily shy narrator responds to a crisis by acting boldly and decisively.)

us violated the structure she imposed on classroom activities. She was particularly hard on people like me who could not contain an impulse to daydream, or those who allowed their eyes to wander too far away from lessons printed on the blackboard. A black and white sign posted under the electric clock next to the door summed up her attitude toward this kind of truancy: NOTICE TO ALL CLOCKWATCHERS, it read, TIME PASSES, WILL YOU? Nor did she abide timidity in her students.

A

Her voice booming, "Speak up, boy!" was more than enough to cause the more emotional among us, including me, to break into convenient flows of warm tears. But by doing this we violated yet another rule, one on which depended our very survival in Mrs. Esther Clay Boswell's class. She would spell out this rule for us as she paced before her desk, slapping a thick, homemade ruler against the flat of her brown palm. "There ain't no *babies* in here," she would recite. *Thaap!* "Anybody thinks he's still a *baby* . . ." *Thaap!* ". . . should crawl back home to his mama. . . ." *Thaap!* "You little bunnies shed your *last water* . . ." *Thaap!* ". . . the minute you left home to come in here." *Thaap!* "From now on, you g'on do all your *cryin'* . . ." *Thaap!* ". . . *in church!*" *Thaap!* Whenever one of us compelled her to make this speech it would seem to me that her eyes paused overlong on my face. She would seem to be daring me, as if suspicious that, in addition to my secret passion for Gweneth Lawson, which she might excuse, I was also in the habit of throwing fits of temper.

She had read me right. I was the product of too much attention from my father. He favored me, paraded me around on his shoulder, inflated my ego constantly. . . . This, along with my father's generous attentions, made me selfish and used to having my own way. I *expected* to have my own way in most things, and when I could not, I tended to throw tantrums calculated to break through any barrier raised against me.

Mrs. Boswell was also perceptive in assessing the extent of my infatuation with Gweneth Lawson. Despite my stealth in telegraphing emissions of affection into the back part of Gweneth's brain, I could not help but observe, occasionally, Mrs. Boswell's cool glance pausing on the two of us. But she never said a word. Instead, she would settle her eyes momentarily on Gweneth's face and then pass quickly to mine. But in that instant she seemed to be saying, "Don't look back now, girl, but I *know* that bald-headed boy behind you has you on his mind." She seemed to watch me daily, with a combination of amusement and absolute detachment in her brown eyes. And when she stared, it was not at me but at the normal focus on my attention: the end of Gweneth Lawson's black braids. Whenever I sensed Mrs. Boswell watching I would look away quickly, either down at my brown desktop or across the room to the blackboard. But her eyes could not be eluded this easily. Without looking at anyone in particular, she could make a specific point to one person in a manner so general that only long afterward did the real object of her attention realize it had been intended for him.

"Now you little brown bunnies," she might say, "and you black buck rabbits and you few cottontails mixed in. . . ." And here, it sometimes seemed to me, she allowed her eyes to pause casually on me before resuming their sweep of the entire room. "Now I know your mamas already made you think life is a bed of roses, but in *my* classroom you got to know the footpaths through the *sticky* parts of the rosebed." It was her custom during this ritual to prod and goad those of us who were developing reputations for meekness and indecision; yet her method was Socratic[5] in that she compelled us, indirectly, to supply our own answers by exploiting one person as the walking symbol of the error she intended to correct. Clarence Buford, for example, an oversized but good-natured boy from a very poor family, served often as the helpmeet in this exercise.

"Buford," she might begin, slapping the ruler against her palm, "how does a tongue-tied country boy like you expect to get a wife?"

"I don't want no wife," Buford might grumble softly.

Of course the class would laugh.

"Oh yes you do," Mrs. Boswell would respond. "All you buck rabbits want wives." *Thaap!* "So how do you let a girl know you not just a bump on a log?"

"I know! I know!" a high voice might call from a seat across from mine. This, of course, would be Leon Pugh. A peanut-brown boy with curly hair, he seemed to know everything. Moreover, he seemed to take pride in being the only one who knew answers to life questions and would wave

5. **Socratic** (sō·kra′tik): referring to the Greek philosopher Socrates (469–399 B.C.), whose method of teaching involved asking questions that would lead to the correct answer.

Literature and Language: Using Subordinate Clauses
Remind students that subordinate clauses provide information, answer questions, and generally help us to explain ourselves better. The title "Why I Like Country Music" is a subordinate clause. Ask students to find at least four more on page 947. Tell them that subordinate clauses begin with words like *that, which, because, when, what, while,* and *how* but that the word sometimes is understood rather than stated directly.

Remind students that subordinate clauses can't stand alone. "Why I Like Country Music," for example, isn't a complete sentence; it's a fragment. A subordinate clause must be attached to an independent clause to make a complete sentence. When you're sure that students understand what a subordinate clause is, ask them to write sentences with subordinate clauses about each of these topics:

1. The author
2. The narrator
3. His wife
4. Gweneth Lawson
5. Mrs. Esther Clay Boswell
6. Leon Pugh

his arms excitedly whenever our attentions were focused on such matters. It seemed to me his voice would be extra loud and his arms waved more strenuously whenever he was certain that Gweneth Lawson, seated across from him, was interested in an answer to Mrs. Esther Clay Boswell's question. His eager arms, it seemed to me, would be reaching out to grasp Gweneth instead of the question asked.

"Buford, you twisted-tongue, bunion-toed country boy," Mrs. Boswell might say, ignoring Leon Pugh's hysterical arm-waving, "you gonna let a cottontail like Leon get a girlfriend before you?"

"I don't want no girlfriend," Clarence Buford would almost sob. "I don't like no girls."

The class would laugh again while Leon Pugh manipulated his arms like a flight navigator under battle conditions. "I know! I know! I swear to *God* I know!"

When at last Mrs. Boswell would turn in his direction, I might sense that she was tempted momentarily to ask me for an answer. But as in most such exercises, it was the worldly-wise Leon Pugh who supplied this. "What do *you* think Leon?" she would ask inevitably, but with a rather lifeless slap of the ruler against her palm.

"My daddy told me . . ." Leon would shout, turning slyly to beam at Gweneth, ". . . my daddy and my big brother from the Bronx New York told me that to git *anythin'* in this world you gotta learn how to blow your own horn."

"Why, Leon?" Mrs. Boswell might ask in a bored voice.

"Because," the little boy would recite, puffing out his chest, "because if you don't blow your own horn ain't nobody else g'on blow it for you. That's what my daddy said."

"What do you think about that, Buford?" Mrs. Boswell would ask.

"I don't want no girlfriend anyhow," the puzzled Clarence Buford might say.

And then the cryptic lesson would suddenly be dropped.

This was Mrs. Esther Clay Boswell's method of teaching. More than anything written on the blackboard, her questions were calculated to make us turn around in our chairs and inquire in guarded whispers of each other, and especially of the wise and confident Leon Pugh, "What does she mean?" But none of us, besides Pugh, seemed able to comprehend what it was we ought to know but did not know. And Mrs. Boswell, plump brown fox that she was, never volunteered any more in the way of confirmation than was necessary to keep us interested. Instead, she paraded around us, methodically slapping the homemade ruler against her palm, suggesting by her silence more depth to her question, indeed, more implications in Leon's answer, than we were then able to perceive. And during such moments, whether inspired by selfishness or by the peculiar way Mrs. Boswell looked at me, I felt that finding answers to such questions was a task she had set for me, of all the members of the class.

Of course Leon Pugh, among other lesser lights, was my chief rival for the affections of Gweneth Lawson. All during the school year, from September through the winter rains, he bested me in my attempts to look directly into her eyes and say a simple, heartfelt, "hey." This was my ambition, but I never seemed able to get close enough to her attention. At Thanksgiving I helped draw a bounteous yellow cornucopia[6] on the blackboard, with fruits and flowers matching the colors that floated around Gweneth's head; Leon Pugh made one by himself, a masterwork of silver paper and multicolored crepe, which he hung on the door. Its silver tail curled upward to a point just below the face of Mrs. Boswell's clock. At Christmas, when we drew names out of a hat for the exchange of gifts, I drew the name of Queen Rose Phipps, a fairly unattractive squash-yellow girl of absolutely no interest to me. Pugh, whether through collusion with the boy who handled the lottery or through pure luck, pulled forth from the hat the magic name of Gweneth Lawson. He gave her a set of deep purple bows for her braids and a basket of pecans from his father's tree. Uninterested now in the spirit of the occasion, I delivered to Queen Rose Phipps a pair of white socks. Each time Gweneth wore the purple bows she would glance over at Leon and smile. Each time Queen Rose wore my white socks I would turn away in embarrassment, lest I should see them pulling down into her shoes and exposing her skinny ankles.

After class, on wet winter days, I would trail along behind Gweneth to the bus stop, pause near the steps while she entered, and follow her down the aisle until she chose a seat. Usually, however, in clear violation of the code of conduct to which

6. **cornucopia** (kôr·no͞o·kō′pē·ə): a horn of plenty.

B

A. Foreshadowing
? What does Leon's "turning slyly to beam at Gweneth" imply? Is there earlier foreshadowing of the same kind? (It appears that Leon, like the narrator, is interested in Gweneth. Earlier Leon waved his arms as if "to grasp Gweneth" instead of simply signaling his willingness to answer a question.)

B. Conflict
? The personal conflict between the narrator and Leon Pugh is now clear. Does this conflict have anything to do with the broader North-South conflict in the story? Explain. (It does in the sense that Leon, with this "Bronx New York" brother, seems to represent Northern attitudes, while the narrator is a provincial Southerner.)

A. Plot
One reviewer of *Elbow Room,* the book in which this story appears, observed, "Elbow room is what virtually every character in these stories seeks: each wants room enough to break free from his own stereotyped life, his hollow role, his own restraining sensibility."
? Does the reviewer's comment reflect the wishes of the characters in this story? Explain. (Both the narrator and Leon wish to clear the field in their pursuit of Gweneth.)

B. Complication
Both the narrator and Leon Pugh are separated from Gweneth by Mrs. Boswell's assignments.
? What does the narrator do to try to overcome this complication? What happens? (He asks to be reassigned to the Maypole plaiters because he cannot "dance a lick." Mrs. Boswell tells him that "you don't have to *dance* to do the square dance.")

all gentlemen were expected to adhere, Leon Pugh would already be on the bus and shouting to passers-by, "Move off! Get away! This here seat by me is reserved for the girl from Brooklyn New York." Discouraged but not defeated, I would swing into the seat next nearest her and cast calf-eyed glances of wounded affection at the back of her head or at the brown, rainbow profile of her face. And at her stop, some eight or nine blocks from mine, I would disembark behind her along with a crowd of other love-struck boys. There would then follow a well-rehearsed scene in which all of us, save Leon Pugh, pretended to have gotten off the bus either too late or too soon to wend our proper paths homeward. And at slight cost to ourselves we enjoyed the advantage of being able to walk close by her as she glided toward her uncle's green-frame house. There, after pausing on the wooden steps and smiling radiantly around the crowd like a spring sun in that cold winter rain, she would sing, "Bye, y'all," and disappear into the structure with the mystery of a goddess.

A

Afterward I would walk away, but slowly, much slower than the other boys, warmed by the music and light in her voice against the sharp, wet winds of the February afternoon.

I loved her, dear Gloria, and I danced with her and smelled the lemony youth of her and told her that I loved her, all this in a way you would never believe:

You would not know or remember, as I do, that in those days, in our area of the country, we enjoyed a pleasingly ironic mixture of Yankee and Confederate folkways. Our meals and manners, our speech, our attitudes toward certain ambiguous areas of history, even our acceptance of tragedy as the normal course of life—these things and more defined us as Southern. Yet the stern morality of our parents, their toughness and penny-pinching and attitudes toward work, their covert allegiance toward certain ideals, even the directions toward which they turned our faces, made us more Yankee than Cavalier. Moreover, some of our schools were named for Confederate men of distinction, but others were named for the stern-faced believers who had swept down from the North to save a people back, back long ago, in those long forgotten days of once upon a time. Still, our schoolbooks, our required classroom songs, our flags, our very relation to the statues and monuments in public parks, negated the story that these dreamers from the North had ever come. We sang the state song, memorized the verses of homegrown poets, honored in our books the names and dates of historical events both before and after that Historical Event which, in our region, supplanted even the division of the millennia introduced by the followers of Jesus Christ. Given the silent circumstances of our cultural environment, it was ironic, and perhaps just, that we maintained a synthesis of two traditions no longer supportive of each other. Thus it became traditional at our school to celebrate the arrival of spring on May first by both the ritual plaiting of the Maypole and square dancing.

On that day, as on a few others, the Superintendent of Schools and several officials were likely to visit our schoolyard and stand next to the rusty metal swings, watching the fourth, fifth, and sixth graders bob up and down and behind and before each other, around the gaily painted Maypoles. These happy children would pull and twist long runs of billowy crepe paper into wondrous, multicolored plaits. Afterward, on the edges of thunderous applause from teachers, parents and visiting dignitaries, a wave of elaborately costumed children would rush out onto the grounds in groups of eight and proceed with the square dance. "Dog*gone!*" the Superintendent of Schools was heard to exclaim on one occasion. "Y'all do it so good it just makes your *bones* set up and take notice."

Such was the schedule two weeks prior to May first, when Mrs. Boswell announced to our class that as fourth graders we were now eligible to participate in the festivities. The class was divided into two general sections of sixteen each, one group preparing to plait the pole and a second group, containing an equal number of boys and girls, practicing turns for our part in the square dance. I was chosen to square dance; so was Leon Pugh. Gweneth Lawson was placed with the pole plaiters. I was depressed until I remembered, happily, that I could not dance a lick. I reported this fact to Mrs. Boswell just after drawing, during recess, saying that my lack of skill would only result in our class making a poor showing. I asked to be reassigned to the group of Maypole plaiters. Mrs. B. looked me over with considerable amusement tugging at the corners of her mouth. "Oh, you don't have to *dance* to do the square dance," she said. "That's a dance that was made up to mock folks that couldn't dance." She paused a second before adding thoughtfully: "The worse

A. Allusions

? In Leon Pugh's nonsense song, to what does "Ezekiel's wheel" refer? (In the Bible's book of Ezekiel, the prophet Ezekiel sees in the sky (10:15) four cherubim, each with four faces. Beside each cherub is a terrifying, whirling wheel that moves like a castor and is full of eyes. Leon would also know Ezekiel from the spiritual "Ezekiel Saw de Wheel.")

? Who are Jack Johnson and Jim Jeffries, as referred to in the song? (On July 4, 1910, in Reno, Nevada, African American heavyweight boxing champion Jack Johnson knocked out the previously undefeated Jim Jeffries, a white boxer who came out of retirement for the bout.)

B. Complication

Most of this page involves a further complication for the narrator, who for a few happy moments had thought he would be a part of Gweneth's team.

? What is Mrs. Boswell's purpose in making these various reassignments? Is she trying to frustrate the narrator's plan to be with Gweneth? (Opinions may vary, but since Mrs. Boswell's first act is to move Gweneth to the square dance team—rather than moving a boy—it does appear that she recognizes the narrator's intent and wishes to thwart it.)

you are at dancing, the better you can square dance. It's just about the best dance in the world for a stiff little bunny like you."

"I want to plait the Maypole," I said.

"You'll square dance or I'll grease your little butt," Mrs. Esther Clay Boswell said.

"I ain't gonna do *nothin'!*" I muttered. But I said this quietly, and mostly to myself, while walking away from her desk. For the rest of the day she watched me closely, as if she knew what I was thinking.

The next morning I brought a note from my father. "Dear Mrs. Boswell:" I had watched him write earlier that morning, "My boy does not square dance. Please excuse him as I am afraid he will break down and cry and mess up the show. Yours truly . . ."

Mrs. Boswell said nothing after she had read the note. She merely waved me to my seat. But in the early afternoon, when she read aloud the lists of those assigned to dancing and Maypole plaiting, she paused as my name rolled off her tongue. "You don't have to stay on the square dance team," she called to me. "You go on out in the yard with the Maypole team."

I was ecstatic. I hurried to my place in line some three warm bodies behind Gweneth Lawson. We prepared to march out.

"Wait a minute," Mrs. Boswell called. "Now it looks like we got seventeen bunnies on the Maypole team and fifteen on the square dance. We have to even things up." She made a thorough examination of both lists, scratching her head. Then she looked carefully up and down the line of stomping Maypoleites. "Miss Gweneth Lawson, you cute little cottontail you, it looks like you gonna have to go over to the square dance team. That'll give us eight sets of partners for the square dance . . . but now we have another problem." She made a great display of counting the members of the two squads of square dancers. "Now there's sixteen square dancers all right, but when we pair them off we got a problem of higher mathematics. With nine girls and only seven *boys*, looks like we gotta switch a girl from square dancing to Maypole and a boy from Maypole to square dancing."

I waited hopefully for Gweneth Lawson to volunteer. But just at that moment the clever Leon Pugh grabbed her hand and began jitterbugging as though he could hardly wait for the record player to be turned on and the dancing to begin.

"What a cute couple," Mrs. Boswell observed absently. "Now which one of you other girls wants to join up with the Maypole team?"

Following Pugh's example, the seven remaining boys grabbed the girls they wanted as partners. Only skinny Queen Rose Phipps and shy Beverly Hankins remained unclaimed. Queen Rose giggled nervously.

"Queen Rose," Mrs. B. called, "I know you don't mind plaiting the Maypole." She waved her ruler in a gesture of casual dismissal. Queen Rose raced across the room and squeezed into line.

"*Now*," Mrs. Boswell said, "I need a boy to come across to the square dancers."

I was not unmindful of the free interchange of partners involved in square dancing, even though Leon Pugh had beat me in claiming the partner of my choice. All I really wanted was one moment swinging Gweneth Lawson in my arms. I raised my hand slowly.

"Oh, not *you*, little bunny," Mrs. Boswell said. "You and your daddy claim you don't like to square dance." She slapped her ruler against her palm. *Thaap! Thaap!* Then she said, "Clarence Buford, I *know* a big-footed country boy like you can square dance better than anybody. Come on over here and kiss cute little Miss Beverly Hankins."

"I don't like no girls *noway*," Buford mumbled. But he went over and stood next to the giggling Beverly Hankins.

"Now!" said Mrs. B. "March on out in that yard and give that pole a good plaiting!"

We started to march out. Over my shoulder, as I reached the door, I glimpsed the overjoyed Leon Pugh whirling lightly on his toes. He sang in a confident tone:

"I saw the Lord give Moses a pocketful of
roses.
I skid Ezekiel's wheel on a ripe banana peel.
I rowed the Nile, flew over a stile,
Saw Jack Johnson pick his teeth
With toenails from Jim Jeffries' feets . . ."

A

"Grab your partners!" Mrs. Esther Clay Boswell was saying as the oak door slammed behind us.

I had been undone. For almost two weeks I was obliged to stand on the sidelines and watch Leon Pugh allemande[7] left and do-si-do my be-

7. **allemande** (al·lə·mônd′): a dance step in a square dance.

B

A. Characterization

? What kind of person is Leon Pugh? Is the reader supposed to dislike him? (Leon Pugh is a brash, talented youngster whom the other boys envy. The reader, empathizing with the shy narrator, hopes to see Leon bested, but most students will probably not truly dislike him.)

B. Dialogue

? What does the quoted remark of the white Superintendent of Schools (along with his remark on page 948) reveal about the level of his education? (The immediate assumption is that he lacks education. However, it is possible that he is talking down to his listeners.)

loved Gweneth. Worse, she seemed to be enjoying it. But I must give Leon proper credit: He was a dancing fool. In a matter of days he had mastered, and then improved on, the various turns and bows and gestures of the square dance. He leaped while the others plodded, whirled each girl through his arms with lightness and finesse, chattered playfully at the other boys when they tumbled over their own feet. Mrs. Boswell stood by the record player calling, "Put some *strut* in it, Buford, you big potato sack. Watch Leon and see how *he* does it." I leaned against the classroom wall and watched the dancers, my own group having already exhausted the limited variations possible in matters of Maypole plaiting.

At home each night I begged my father to send another note to Mrs. Boswell, this time stating that I had no interest in the Maypole. But he resisted my entreaties and even threatened me with a whipping if I did not participate and make him proud of me. The real cause of his irritation was the considerable investment he had already made in purchasing an outfit for me. Mrs. Boswell had required all her students, square dancers and Maypole plaiters alike, to report on May first in outfits suitable for square dancing. My father had bought a new pair of dungarees, a blue shirt, a red and white polka-dot bandanna and a cowboy hat. He was in no mood to bend under the emotional weight of my demands. As a matter of fact, early in the morning of May first he stood beside my bed with the bandanna in his left hand and his leather belt in his right hand, just in case I developed a sudden fever.

I dragged myself heavily through the warm, blue spring morning toward school, dressed like a carnival cowboy. When I entered the classroom I sulked against the wall, being content to watch the other children. And what happy buzzings and jumping and excitement they made as they compared costumes. Clarence Buford wore a Tom Mix hat and a brown vest over a green shirt with red sixshooter patterns embossed on its collar. Another boy, Paul Carter, was dressed entirely in black, with a fluffy white handkerchief puffing from his neck. But Leon Pugh caught the attention of all eyes. He wore a red and white checkered shirt, a loose green bandanna clasped at his throat by a shining silver buffalo head, brown chaps sewed onto his dungarees, and shiny brown cowboy boots with silver spurs that clanked each time he moved. In his hand he carried a carefully creased brown cowboy hat. He announced his fear that it would lose its shape and planned to put it on only when the dancing started. He would allow no one to touch it. Instead, he stood around clanking his feet and smoothing the crease in his fabulous hat and saying loudly, "My daddy says it pays to look good no matter what you put on."

The girls seemed prettier and much older than their ages. Even Queen Rose Phipps wore rouge on her cheeks that complemented her pale color. Shy Beverly Hankins had come dressed in a blue and white checkered bonnet and a crisp blue apron; she looked like a frontier mother. But Gweneth Lawson, my Gweneth Lawson, dominated the group of girls. She wore a long red dress with sheaves and sheaves of sparkling white crinoline belling it outward so it seemed she was floating. On her honey-brown wrists golden bracelets sparkled. A deep blue bandanna enclosed her head with the wonder of a summer sky. Black patent leather shoes glistened like half-hidden stars beneath the red and white of her hemline. She stood smiling before us and we marveled. At that moment I would have given the world to have been able to lead her about on my arm.

Mrs. Boswell watched us approvingly from behind her desk. Finally, at noon, she called, "Let's go on out!" Thirty-two living rainbows cascaded toward the door. Pole plaiters formed one line. Square dancers formed another. Mrs. Boswell strolled officiously past us in review. It seemed to me she almost paused while passing the spot where I stood on line. But she brushed past me, straightening an apron here, applying spittle and a rub to a rouge cheek there, waving a wary finger at an over-anxious boy. Then she whacked her ruler against her palm and led us out into the yard. The fifth and sixth graders had already assembled. On one end of the playground were a dozen or so tall painted poles with long, thin wisps of green and blue and yellow and rust-brown crepe floating lazily on the sweet spring breezes.

"Maypole teams *up!*" called Mr. Henry Lucas, our principal, from his platform by the swings. Beside him stood the white Superintendent of Schools (who said later of the square dance, it was reported to all the classes, "Lord y'all square dance so *good* it makes me plumb *ashamed* us white folks ain't takin' better care of our art stuff."). "Maypole teams up!" Mr. Henry Lucas shouted again. Some fifty of us, screaming shrilly, rushed to grasp our favorite color crepe. Then, to

READING CHECK TEST

1. The only dance form the narrator ever mastered is (a) the jitterbug (b) the square dance (c) the hustle *(b)*

2. Gweneth Lawson's perfume or lotion has the odor of (a) lemons (b) roses (c) a pine forest *(a)*

3. Leon Pugh has a big brother from (a) South Philadelphia (b) Jamaica (c) the Bronx *(c)*

4. To join the Maypole team with Gweneth, the narrator enlists the aid of (a) his father (b) Queen Rose Phipps (c) Mrs. Boswell *(a)*

5. The narrator gets to dance with Gweneth because Leon Pugh (a) is sick (b) wears spurs (c) argues with Mrs. Boswell *(b)*

the music of "Sing Praise for All the Brightness and the Joy of Spring," we pulled and plaited in teams of six or seven until every pole was twisted as tight and as colorfully as the braids on Gweneth Lawson's head. Then, to the applause of proud teachers and parents and the whistles of the Superintendent of Schools, we scattered happily back under the wings of our respective teachers. I stood next to Mrs. Boswell, winded and trembling but confident I had done my best. She glanced down at me and said in a quiet voice, "I do believe you are learning the rhythm of the thing."

I did not respond.

"Let's *go!*" Leon Pugh shouted to the other kids, grabbing Gweneth Lawson's arm and taking a few clanking steps forward.

"Wait a minute, Leon," Mrs. Boswell hissed."Mr. Lucas has to change the record."

Leon sighed. "But if we don't git out there first, all them other teams will take the best spots."

"Wait!" Mrs. Boswell ordered.

Leon sulked. He inched closer to Gweneth. I watched him swing her hand impatiently. He stamped his feet and his silver spurs jangled.

Mrs. Boswell looked down at his feet. "Why, Leon," she said, "you can't go out there with razors on your shoes."

"These ain't razors," Leon muttered. "These here are spurs my brother in Bronx New York sent me just for this here dance."

"You have to take them off," Mrs. Boswell said.

Leon growled. But he reached down quickly and attempted to jerk the silver spurs from the heels of his boots. They did not come off. "No time!" he called, standing suddenly. "Mr. Lucas done put the record on."

"Leon, you might *cut* somebody with those things," Mrs. Boswell said. "Miss Gweneth Lawson's pretty red dress could get caught in those things and then she'll fall as surely as I'm standin' here."

"I'll just go out with my boots off," Leon replied.

But Mrs. Boswell shook her head firmly. "You just run on to the lunchroom and ask cook for some butter or mayo. That'll help 'em slip off." She paused, looking out over the black dirt playground. "And if you miss the first dance, why there'll be a second and maybe even a third. We'll get a Maypole plaiter to sub for you."

My heart leaped. Leon sensed it and stared at me. His hand tightened on Gweneth's as she stood radiant and smiling in the loving spring sunlight. Leon let her hand drop and bent quickly, pulling at the spurs with the fury of a Samson.

"Square dancers *up!*" Mr. Henry Lucas called. . . .

The fifth and sixth graders were screaming and rushing toward the center of the yard. Already the record was scratching out the high, slick voice of the caller. . . . Leon moaned.

Mrs. Boswell looked directly at Gweneth, standing alone and abandoned next to Leon. "Miss Gweneth Lawson," Mrs. Boswell said in a cool voice, "it's a cryin' shame there ain't no prince to take you to that ball out there."

I do not remember moving, but I know I stood with Gweneth at the center of the yard. What I did there I do not know, but I remember watching the movements of others and doing what they did just after they had done it. Still, I cannot remember just when I looked into my partner's face or what I saw there. The scratchy voice of the caller bellowed directions and I obeyed:

"Allemande left with your left hand
Right to your partner with a right and left grand . . ."

Although I was told later that I made an allemande right instead of left, I have no memory of the mistake.

"When you get to your partner pass her by
And pick up the next girl on the sly . . ."

Nor can I remember picking up any other girl. I only remember that during many turns and do-si-dos I found myself looking into the warm brown eyes of Gweneth Lawson. I recall that she smiled at me. I recall that she laughed on another turn. I recall that I laughed with her an eternity later.

". . . promenade that dear old thing
Throw your head right back and sing be-*cause,*
just be-*cause . . ."*

I do remember quite well that during the final promenade before the record ended, Gweneth stood beside me and I said to her in a voice much louder than that of the caller, "When I get up to Brooklyn I hope I see you." But I do not remember what she said in response. I want to remember that she smiled.

I know I smiled, dear Gloria. I smiled with the

CLOSURE
Ask students to write three or four sentences in which they explain why the narrator likes country music. Have them share their responses in class.

A. Climax
McPherson's story is a structurally traditional one. A series of complications are followed by the climax, beginning with, "Why, Leon," she [Mrs. Boswell] said, "you can't go out there with razors on your shoes." This climax, like the other elements in the story, grows out of the situation.

? Why are these spurs of Leon's a particularly fitting instrument of his downfall? (Leon is always on top of things, and these spurs from "my brother in Bronx New York" are his pride.)

ANALYZING THE STORY
Identifying Facts
1. Country music reminds the narrator of his school days, when he was infatuated with his fourth-grade classmate Gweneth Lawson and square-danced with her.
2. He remembers her prettiness, her braids, the colors of the clothes she wore, and the lemony smell of her perfume or lotion.

His worldly-wise classmate, Leon Pugh, is also interested in Gweneth.
3. Mrs. Boswell is a stern disciplinarian who employs a Socratic method with her students, asking them questions that often mystify them.

She thwarts the narrator by shifting the teams for the Maypole celebration.
4. He wants to attract Gweneth.

He asks to be excused from square dancing and to join the Maypole team.

Mrs. Boswell sends Leon off to have his spurs removed, and the narrator takes Leon's place.
5. The narrator grew up in South Carolina; his wife was reared in the North. Gweneth Lawson was also from the *(Answers continue in left-hand column.)*

(Continued from top.)
North; she appeared exotic to the narrator when he was a child. Numerous details about habits, attitudes, and clothes supplement the conflict, or contrast, between North and South in the story.
6. Country music reminds him of a childhood love.

Interpreting Meanings
7. It may be a lightly ironic metaphor that emphasizes how important his memories of Gweneth are.
8. Most students will probably agree that the story is comic. The shy narrator achieves his dream.
9. The narrator addresses the story to his wife. The effect is ironic.
10. It has elements of both. On the one hand, it illustrates the narrator's romantic sensibility; on the other, it is a vividly realistic evocation of childhood.
11. Most students will agree that McPherson handles both very well.

lemonness of her and the loving of her pressed deep into those saving places of my private self. It was my plan to savor these, and I did savor them. But when I reached New York, many years later, I did not think of Brooklyn. I followed the old, beaten, steady paths into uptown Manhattan. By then I had learned to dance to many other kinds of music. And I had forgotten the savory smell of lemon. But I think sometimes of Gweneth now when I hear country music. And although it is difficult to explain to you, I still maintain that I am no mere arithmetician in the art of the square dance. I am into the calculus of it.

"Go on!" you will tell me, backing into your Northern mythology. "I can see the hustle, the hump, maybe even the Ibo highlife. But no hillbilly."

These days I am firm about arguing the point, but, as always, quietly, and mostly to myself.

Responding to the Story

Analyzing the Story

Identifying Facts

1. Explain why the narrator has such positive feelings about country music, even though his wife and most of his friends and acquaintances don't care for it.
2. What does the narrator remember best about Gweneth Lawson? Who is his rival for Gweneth's attentions?
3. Describe Mrs. Boswell's teaching method. How does this method affect the action of the story?
4. What does the main character want? What actions does he take to get what he wants? What twist of fate helps him?
5. Describe the broader **conflict** in this story—the one that exists between North and South, "country" and New York.
6. What is the answer to the "Why" in the title?

Interpreting Meanings

7. How would you interpret the narrator's statement at the story's end: that he is no mere arithmetician in the art of square dancing—that he is into the "calculus" of it?
8. Would you classify the story as a **comedy?** Remember that a comedy often deals with a character who ends up being accepted into a community, and that it may or may not be overwhelmingly funny.
9. To whom is the story addressed? What effect does this audience have on the **tone** of the story?
10. Does the story tend to be romantic or realistic? Cite specific elements in the story to support your opinion.
11. Children and dialect are both difficult to portray realistically and convincingly. How would you rate McPherson's characterizations and dialogue?

Writing About the Story

A Creative Response

1. **Writing a Characterization.** In a brief essay, characterize someone who has made a vivid impression on you. Develop your character by telling an anecdote that reveals something specific about his or her personality. Try to reproduce your character's speech.

A Critical Response

2. **Analyzing a Character.** Take one of the characters in the story—Mrs. Boswell, Leon Pugh, the narrator, or Gweneth Lawson, and analyze his or her personality. Before you write, consider these methods of characterization: by appearance; by speech; by actions; by responses of other characters. Look also for any direct comments made by the writer. At the end of your essay, describe your own response to the character, including your assessment of his or her credibility.
3. **Analyzing Humor.** Humor is very difficult to analyze; perhaps we hesitate to "tear apart" something that is funny because the nature of humor makes analysis seem slightly pompous. Nevertheless, humor *can* be analyzed. In a brief essay, analyze the sources of humor in McPherson's story. Consider these elements of humor before you start writing:

   a. Exaggeration for effect
   b. Self-mockery
   c. Comic irony
   d. Incongruity
   e. Comic descriptions
   f. Understatement

Anne Tyler (1941–   )

Anne Tyler remembers feeling as a child that what happened in books was far more reasonable and interesting than what happened in life. As a result, she spent her childhood reading and waiting to become an adult.

In the course of this wait she became a writer. She feels her attraction to writing stemmed from her sense of being set apart from others—a sense that came, in turn, from growing up in a wilderness Quaker community. Tyler is a private person, happiest when the world does not intrude upon her.

As an adolescent, Tyler was charmed by a Eudora Welty story which revealed to her that it was possible to write interestingly about the most ordinary people. "People have always seemed funny and strange to me, and touching in unexpected ways," she says. "It's not a matter of choice; it just seems to me that even the most ordinary person, in real life, will turn out to have something unusual at his center."

Tyler is a mother and the wife of a psychiatrist (an Iranian, like the husband in the following story), who is also a writer, and she has thought a great deal about the necessary divisions in the life of a writer with other responsibilities. "I have spent so long erecting partitions around the part of me that writes, learning how to close the door on it when ordinary life intervenes, how to close the door on ordinary life when it's time to start writing again—that I'm not sure I could fit the two parts of me back together now."

Tyler likens the connection between the world of her family and the world of her writing to a string. "When the children come home I drop the string. I close the study door and that's the end of it. It doesn't always work perfectly, of course. There are times when it doesn't work at all; if a child is sick, for instance, I can't possibly drop the children's end of the string, and I've learned not to try. It's easier just to stop writing for a while."

"It seems to me," she says, "that since I've had children, I've grown richer and deeper. They may have slowed down my writing for a while, but when I did write I had more of a self to speak from. After all, who else in the world do you *have* to love, no matter what?"

She tells of a friend, another mother, who once asked, "Have you found work yet? Or are you still just writing?" Tyler did not take offense because she often shares the feeling that writing is insubstantial. She can recall thinking, "Any day now I will have said all I have to say; I'll have used up all my characters, and then I'll be free to get on with my real life."

She has never reached that point. "Even when I feel I have no ideas at all, and can't possibly start the next chapter, I have a sense of something still bottled in me, trying to get out."

Born in Minnesota in 1941, Tyler studied writing at Duke University, from which she graduated in 1961. Her stories have appeared in *The New Yorker, The Antioch Review,* and *The Southern Review.* She has written ten novels, including *Searching for Caleb* (1976), *Earthly Possessions* (1977), *Morgan's Passing* (1980), *Dinner at the Homesick Restaurant* (1982), and *The Accidental Tourist* (1985). "Your Place Is Empty," which first appeared in *The New Yorker*, was selected for inclusion in *The Best American Short Stories of 1977.*

COMMENT FROM A CRITIC
Of Anne Tyler's *Dinner at the Homesick Restaurant,* John Updike writes: the "paradoxes of the family . . . include love that must for survival flee its object, and daily communication that masks silence—that deep resentful silence of those who live together. . . . The family, that institution meant to shelter our frailty, in fact serves as a theater for intimate cruelties. . . ."

After students have read "Your Place Is Empty," you might ask them to discuss this comment in relation to the story.

SUPPLEMENTARY SUPPORT MATERIALS

1. Vocabulary Activity Worksheet (*CCB*)
2. Review and Response Worksheet: Shifting Points of View (*CCB*)
3. Language Skills Worksheet: End Marks (*CCB*)
4. Selection Test (*CCB*)
5. Audiocassette recording

DEVELOPING VOCABULARY

The following words from the story are tested in the Selection Test. (See also Vocabulary Activity Worksheet.)

steadfastly, intuition, brocade, to implore, swathe, perpetual, chintz, paisley, taint, currant

A. Foreshadowing Elizabeth, Hassan, and Mrs. Ardavi each has a different idea about the length of Mrs. Ardavi's visit.

? Why is this almost certain to lead to trouble? (See A Comment on the Story, page 965.)

B. Point of View After starting with an omniscient viewpoint, the story now changes its point of view to third-person limited.

YOUR PLACE IS EMPTY

This story deals with a common situation among young married couples—the strain resulting from an extended visit by a parent. In this case, the situation also involves a clash of cultures, since it is an Iranian mother who is staying with her son and his American wife. The story is told in the third person, and the opening section sets the scene. Once the mother is introduced, everything is revealed from her point of view.

A Early in October, Hassan Ardavi invited his mother to come from Iran for a visit. His mother accepted immediately. It wasn't clear how long the visit was to last. Hassan's wife thought three months would be a good length of time. Hassan himself had planned on six months, and said so in his letter of invitation. But his mother felt that after such a long trip six months would be too short, and she was counting on staying a year. Hassan's little girl, who wasn't yet two, had no idea of time at all. She was told that her grandmother was coming but she soon forgot about it.

Hassan's wife was named Elizabeth, not an easy word for Iranians to pronounce. She would have been recognized as American the world over—a blond, pretty girl with long bones and an ungraceful way of walking. One of her strong points was an ability to pick up foreign languages, and before her mother-in-law's arrival she bought a textbook and taught herself Persian. "*Salaam aleikum*,"[1] she told the mirror every morning. Her daughter watched, startled, from her place on the potty-chair. Elizabeth ran through possible situations in her mind and looked up the words for them. "Would you like more tea? Do you take sugar?" At suppertime she spoke Persian to her husband, who looked amused at the new tone she gave his language, with her flat, factual American voice. He wrote his mother and told her Elizabeth had a surprise for her.

Their house was a three-story Colonial, but only the first two stories were in use. Now they cleared the third of its trunks and china barrels and *National Geographics*, and they moved in a few pieces of furniture. Elizabeth sewed flowered curtains for the window. She was unusually careful with them; to a foreign mother-in-law, fine seams might matter. Also, Hassan bought a pocket compass, which he placed in the top dresser drawer. "For her prayers," he said. "She'll want to face Mecca.[2] She prays three times a day."

"But which direction is Mecca from here?" Elizabeth asked.

Hassan only shrugged. He had never said the prayers himself, not even as a child. His earliest memory was of tickling the soles of his mother's feet while she prayed steadfastly on; everyone knew it was forbidden to pause once you'd started.

B Mrs. Ardavi felt nervous about the descent from the plane. She inched down the staircase sideways, one hand tight on the railing, the other clutching her shawl. It was night, and cold. The air seemed curiously opaque. She arrived on solid ground and stood collecting herself—a small, stocky woman in black, with a kerchief over her smooth gray hair. She held her back very straight, as if she had just had her feelings hurt. In picturing this moment she had always thought Hassan would be waiting beside the plane, but there was no sign of him. Blue lights dotted the darkness behind her, an angular terminal loomed ahead, and an official was herding the passengers toward a plate-glass door. She followed, entangled in a web of meaningless sounds such as those you might hear in a fever dream.

Immigration. Baggage Claims. Customs. To all she spread her hands and beamed and shrugged,

1. ***Salaam aleikum:*** Persian for "Peace be with you."

2. **Mecca:** the holiest shrine of Islam, located in modern Saudi Arabia. Moslems throughout the world turn to face the direction of Mecca when they pray.

PREPARATION

ESTABLISHING A PURPOSE. Through characterization, flashbacks, and tone, the author shows an increasingly bitter clash between cultures, generations, and personalities. Advise students to observe how each of the three literary elements helps to underscore the conflicts.

A. Humanities Connection: Responding to the Fine Art

Barbara Kassel (b. 1952), like Anne Tyler, lives in Baltimore, Maryland. She has been an instructor and professor of art at Colby College, the Maryland Art Institute, and Goucher College. Her oil and watercolor paintings have been exhibited in the United States and Italy.

? (This question should be asked after students finish the story.) How would Mrs. Ardavi react to *Dagney's Room?* Would she find it more pleasant than Elizabeth's house? If she lived in this room, how might she decorate it? (The spare geometry of this room would probably make her feel very unhappy. There is a description of Mrs. Ardavi's room in column one, page 963.)

B. Foreshadowing

? What may the two religious medals on chains suggest about the development of the story? (It seems likely that Mrs. Ardavi will try, perhaps subtly, to press her religion on the family.)

C. Responding

How will Elizabeth probably react to these gifts of native food, especially the yogurt curd "stuck with bits of sheep hair and manure"? (She probably will not appreciate them.)

Dagney's Room by Barbara Kassel (1984). Oil. A

Collection of Laura Skoler, Maplewood, New Jersey.

showing she spoke no English. Meanwhile her fellow-passengers waved to a blur of faces beyond a glass wall. It seemed they all knew people here; she was the only one who didn't. She had issued from the plane like a newborn baby, speechless and friendless. And the customs official didn't seem pleased with her. She had brought too many gifts. She had stuffed her bags with them, discarding all but the most necessary pieces of her clothing so that she would have more room. There were silver tea sets and gold jewelry for her daughter-in-law, and for her granddaughter a doll dressed in the complicated costume of a nomad tribe, an embroidered sheepskin vest, and two religious medals on chains—one a disc inscribed with the name of Allah, the other a tiny gold Koran,[3] with a very effective prayer for long life folded up within it. B The customs official sifted gold through his fingers like sand and frowned at the Koran. "Have I done something wrong?" she asked. But of course he didn't understand her. Though you'd think, really, that if he would just *listen* hard enough, just meet her eyes once . . . it was a very simple language, there was no reason why it shouldn't come through to him.

For Hassan, she'd brought food. She had gathered all his favorite foods and put them in a drawstring bag embroidered with peacocks. When the official opened the bag he said something under his breath and called another man over. Together they unwrapped tiny newspaper packets and sniffed at various herbs. "Sumac," she told them. "Powder of lemons. Shambahleh." They gazed at her blankly. They untied a small cloth sack and rummaged through the kashk she had brought for soup. It rolled beneath their fingers and across the counter—hard white balls of yogurt curd, stuck with bits of sheep hair and manure. C Some peasant had labored for hours to make that kashk. Mrs. Ardavi picked up one piece and replaced it firmly in the sack. Maybe the official understood her meaning: She was running out of patience. He threw up his hands. He slid her belongings down the counter. She was free to go.

Free to go where?

Dazed and stumbling, a pyramid of knobby parcels and bags, scraps of velvet and brocade and tapestry, she made her way to the glass wall. A

3. **Allah . . . Koran:** Allah is God, the supreme deity of Islam. The Koran is the Islamic holy book, consisting of visions and regulations recorded by the prophet Mohammed.

A. Characterization
What is revealed by the fact that Mrs. Ardavi thinks Hassan will die on the way to the airport or else is already dead? (She is fearful and superstitious.) What makes her finally recognize him? (She recalls a "pleasantly bitter herblike smell" from his boyhood.)

B. Title
What does "your place is empty" mean in the context of these letters from Mrs. Ardavi to Hassan? (It means that in Iran no one is sitting at his place at the table, or perhaps that no one occupies the room that used to be his. See question 8, page 966.)

C. Interpretation
Why do Mrs. Ardavi and Hassan not talk on the drive to the house? (Opinions will vary. Hassan has already put in a long day at work, and he may feel that there will be plenty of time to talk during her visit. Or he may want to keep his mind on his driving. The important point is that she thinks she is being ignored and thus decides to say nothing herself.)

D. Conflict
Have students notice that Mrs. Ardavi views her son as being "on the other side of the fence, the American side."
If Mrs. Ardavi has been anticipating any conflict, whom might she have placed on each side? (However unrealistically, she may have expected herself and her son Hassan to be allied against Elizabeth.)

door opened out of nowhere and a stranger blocked her path. "Khanoum Jun," he said. It was a name that only her children would use, but she passed him blindly and he had to touch her arm before she would look up.

He had put on weight. She didn't know him. The last time she'd seen him he was a thin, stoop-shouldered medical student disappearing into an Air France jet without a backward glance. "Khanoum Jun, it's me," this stranger said, but she went on searching his face with cloudy eyes. No doubt he was a bearer of bad news. Was that it? A recurrent dream had warned her that she would never see her son again—that he would die on his way to the airport, or had already been dead for months but no one wanted to break the news; some second or third cousin in America had continued signing Hassan's name to his cheerful, anonymous letters. Now here was this man with graying hair and a thick mustache, his clothes American but his face Iranian, his eyes sadly familiar, as if they belonged to someone else. "Don't you believe me?" he said. He kissed her on both cheeks. It was his smell she recognized first—a pleasantly bitter, herblike smell that brought her the image of Hassan as a child, reaching thin arms around her neck. "It's you, Hassan," she said, and then she started crying against his gray tweed shoulder.

They were quiet during the long drive home. Once she reached over to touch his face, having wanted to do so for miles. None of the out-of-focus snapshots he'd sent had prepared her for the way he had aged. "How long has it been?" she asked. "Twelve years?" But both of them knew to the day how long it had been. All those letters of hers: "My dear Hassan, ten years now and still your place is empty." "Eleven years and still . . .'

Hassan squinted through the windshield at the oncoming headlights. His mother started fretting over her kerchief, which she knew she ought not to have worn. She'd been told so by her youngest sister, who had been to America twice. "It marks you," her sister had said. But that square of silk was the last, shrunken reminder of the veil she used to hide beneath, before the previous Shah[4] had banished such things. At her age, how could she expose herself? And then her teeth; her teeth were a problem too. Her youngest sister had said, "You ought to get dentures made, I'm sure there aren't three whole teeth in your head." But Mrs. Ardavi was scared of dentists. Now she covered her mouth with one hand and looked sideways at Hassan, though so far he hadn't seemed to notice. He was busy maneuvering his car into the right-hand lane.

This silence was the last thing she had expected. For weeks she'd been saving up stray bits of gossip, weaving together the family stories she would tell him. There were three hundred people in her family—most of them related to each other in three or four different ways, all leading intricate and scandalous lives she had planned to discuss in detail, but instead she stared sadly out the window. You'd think Hassan would ask. You'd think they could have a better conversation than this, after such a long time. Disappointment made her cross, and now she stubbornly refused to speak even when she saw something she wanted to comment on, some imposing building or unfamiliar brand of car sliding past her into the darkness.

By the time they arrived it was nearly midnight. None of the houses were lit but Hassan's—worn brick, older than she would have expected. "Here we are," said Hassan. The competence with which he parked the car, fitting it neatly into a small space by the curb, put him firmly on the other side of the fence, the American side. She would have to face her daughter-in-law alone. As they climbed the front steps she whispered, "How do you say it again?"

"Say what?" Hassan asked.

"Her name. Lizabet?"

"Elizabeth. Like Elizabeth Taylor. *You* know."

"Yes, yes, of course," said his mother. Then she lifted her chin, holding tight to the straps of her purse.

Elizabeth was wearing blue jeans and a pair of fluffy slippers. Her hair was blond as corn silk, cut short and straight, and her face had the grave, sleepy look of a child's. As soon as she had opened the door she said, "*Salaam aleikum.*" Mrs. Ardavi, overcome with relief at the Persian greeting, threw her arms around her and kissed both cheeks. Then they led her into the living room, which looked comfortable but a little too plain. The furniture was straight-edged, the rugs uninteresting, though the curtains had a nice figured pattern that caught her eye. In one corner sat a shiny red kiddie car complete with license plates. "Is that the child's?" she asked.

4. **Shah:** before the Iranian revolution, the ruler of Iran.

"Hilary's?" She hesitated over the name. "Could I see her?"

"*Now?*" said Hassan.

But Elizabeth told him, "That's all right." (Women understood these things.) She beckoned to her mother-in-law. They climbed the stairs together, up to the second floor, into a little room that smelled of milk and rubber and talcum powder, smells she would know anywhere. Even in the half-light from the hallway, she could tell that Hilary was beautiful. She had black, tumbling hair, long black lashes, and skin of a tone they called wheat-colored, lighter than Hassan's. "There," said Elizabeth. "Thank you," said Mrs. Ardavi. Her voice was formal, but this was her first grandchild and it took her a moment to recover herself. Then they stepped back into the hallway. "I brought her some medals," she whispered. "I hope you don't mind."

"Medals?" said Elizabeth. She repeated the word anxiously, mispronouncing it.

"Only an Allah and a Koran, both very tiny. You'll hardly know they're there. I'm not used to seeing a child without a medal. It worries me."

Automatically her fingers traced a chain around her neck, ending in the hollow of her collarbone. Elizabeth nodded, looking relieved. "*Oh* yes. Medals," she said.

"Is that all right?"

"Yes, of course."

Mrs. Ardavi took heart. "Hassan laughs," she said. "He doesn't believe in these things. But when he left I put a prayer in his suitcase pocket, and you see he's been protected. Now if Hilary wore a medal, I could sleep nights."

"Of course," Elizabeth said again.

When they re-entered the living room, Mrs. Ardavi was smiling, and she kissed Hassan on the top of his head before she sat down.

American days were tightly scheduled, divided not into morning and afternoon but into 9:00, 9:30, and so forth, each half hour possessing its own set activity. It was marvelous. Mrs. Ardavi wrote her sisters: "They're more organized here. My daughter-in-law never wastes a minute." How terrible, her sisters wrote back. They were all in Teheran, drinking cup after cup of tea and idly guessing who might come and visit. "No, you misunderstand," Mrs. Ardavi protested. "I like it this way. I'm fitting in wonderfully." And to her youngest sister she wrote, "You'd think I was American. No one guesses otherwise." This wasn't true, of course, but she hoped it would be true in the future.

Hassan was a doctor. He worked long hours, from six in the morning until six at night. While she was still washing for her morning prayers she could hear him tiptoe down the stairs and out the front door. His car would start up, a distant rumble far below her, and from her bathroom window she could watch it swing out from beneath a tatter of red leaves and round the corner and disappear. Then she would sigh and return to her sink. Before prayers she had to wash her face, her hands, and the soles of her feet. She had to draw her wet fingers down the part in her hair. After that she returned to her room, where she swathed herself tightly in her long black veil and knelt on a beaded velvet prayer mat. East was where the window was, curtained by chintz and misted over. On the east wall she hung a lithograph of the Caliph Ali and a color snapshot of her third son, Babak, whose marriage she had arranged just a few months before this visit. If Babak hadn't married, she never could have come. He was the youngest, spoiled by being the only son at home. It had taken her three years to find a wife for him. (One was too modern, one too lazy, one so perfect she had been suspicious.) But finally the proper girl had turned up, modest and well-mannered and sufficiently wide of hip, and Mrs. Ardavi and the bridal couple had settled in a fine new house on the outskirts of Teheran. Now every time she prayed, she added a word of thanks that at last she had a home for her old age. After that, she unwound her veil and laid it carefully in a drawer. From another drawer she took thick cotton stockings and elastic garters; she stuffed her swollen feet into open-toed vinyl sandals. Unless she was going out, she wore a housecoat. It amazed her how wasteful Americans were with their clothing.

Downstairs, Elizabeth would have started her tea and buttered a piece of toast for her. Elizabeth and Hilary ate bacon and eggs, but bacon of course was unclean and Mrs. Ardavi never accepted any.[5] Nor had it even been offered to her, except once, jokingly, by Hassan. The distinctive, smoky smell rose to meet her as she descended the stairs. "What does it taste like?" she always asked. She was dying to know. But Elizabeth's vocabulary didn't cover the taste of bacon; she

5. The Koran forbids Moslems to eat pork.

A. Complication

Why might Elizabeth's acceptance of the medals create future problems? (In her heart, Mrs. Ardavi is unwilling to accept the Americanization of Hassan and Hilary. The gift of medals appears to be an opening wedge to impose customs or beliefs on them that Hassan has already rejected.)

B. Irony

When Mrs. Ardavi says, "I'm fitting in wonderfully," there is a discrepancy between what she says and what is literally true. This incongruity is a mix of verbal irony (for Mrs. Ardavi realizes she's not being truthful) and dramatic irony (for the reader knows better than she just how far from the truth her words are).

A. Flashback
Point out to students that this is one of a number of flashbacks that provide information about Mrs. Ardavi's life in Iran.

B. Interpretation
Hearing the words *telephone*, *television*, and *radio* leads Mrs. Ardavi to think that American conversations are "largely technical."

? What mistake does she make in interpreting these conversations? (She seems to think the women are talking about the mechanical devices rather than about the communication and entertainment provided by the devices.)

only said it was salty and then laughed and gave up. They had learned very early to travel a well-worn conversational path, avoiding the dead ends caused by unfamiliar words. "Did you sleep well?" Elizabeth always asked in her funny, childish accent, and Mrs. Ardavi answered, "So-so." Then they would turn and watch Hilary, who sat on a booster seat eating scrambled eggs, a thin chain of Persian gold crossing the back of her neck. Conversation was easier, or even unnecessary, as long as Hilary was there.

In the mornings Elizabeth cleaned house. Mrs. Ardavi used that time for letter writing. She had dozens of letters to write, to all her aunts and uncles and her thirteen sisters. (Her father had had three wives, and a surprising number of children even for that day and age.) Then there was Babak. His wife was in her second month of pregnancy, so Mrs. Ardavi wrote long accounts of the American child-rearing methods. "There are some things I don't agree with," she wrote. "They let Hilary play outdoors by herself, with not even a servant to keep an eye on her." Then she would trail off and gaze thoughtfully at Hilary, who sat on the floor watching a television program called "Captain Kangaroo."

A

Mrs. Ardavi's own childhood had been murky and grim. From the age of nine she was wrapped in a veil, one corner of it clenched in her teeth to hide her face whenever she appeared on the streets. Her father, a respected man high up in public life, used to chase servant girls through the halls and trap them, giggling, in vacant bedrooms. At the age of ten she was forced to watch her mother bleed to death in childbirth, and when she screamed the midwife had struck her across the face and held her down till she had properly kissed her mother goodbye. There seemed no connection at all between her and this little overalled American. At times, when Hilary had one of her temper tantrums, Mrs. Ardavi waited in horror for Elizabeth to slap her and then, when no slap came, felt a mixture of relief and anger. "In Iran—" she would begin, and if Hassan was there he always said, "But this is not Iran, remember?"

After lunch Hilary took a nap, and Mrs. Ardavi went upstairs to say her noontime prayers and take a nap as well. Then she might do a little laundry in her bathtub. Laundry was a problem here. Although she liked Elizabeth, the fact was that the girl was a Christian, and therefore unclean; it would never do to have a Christian wash a Moslem's clothes. The automatic dryer was also unclean, having contained, at some point, a Christian's underwear. So she had to ask Hassan to buy her a drying rack. It came unassembled. Elizabeth put it together for her, stick by stick, and then Mrs. Ardavi held it under her shower and rinsed it off, hoping that would be enough to remove any taint. The Koran didn't cover this sort of situation.

When Hilary was up from her nap they walked her to the park—Elizabeth in her eternal blue jeans and Mrs. Ardavi in her kerchief and shawl, taking short painful steps in small shoes that bulged over her bunions. They still hadn't seen to her teeth, although by now Hassan had noticed them. She was hoping he might forget about the dentist, but then she saw him remembering every time she laughed and revealed her five brown teeth set wide apart.

At the park she laughed a great deal. It was her only way of communicating with the other women. They sat on the benches ringing the playground, and while Elizabeth translated their questions Mrs. Ardavi laughed and nodded at them over and over. "They want to know if you like it here," Elizabeth said. Mrs. Ardavi answered at length, but Elizabeth's translation was very short. Then gradually the other women forgot her, and conversation rattled on while she sat silent and watched each speaker's lips. The few recognizable words—"telephone," "television," "radio"—gave her the impression that American conversations were largely technical, even among women. Their gestures were wide and slow, disproving her youngest sister's statement that in America everyone was in a hurry. On the contrary, these women were dreamlike, moving singly or in twos across wide flat spaces beneath white November skies when they departed.

Later, at home, Mrs. Ardavi would say, "The red-haired girl, is she pregnant? She looked it, I thought. Is the fat girl happy in her marriage?" She asked with some urgency, plucking Elizabeth's sleeve when she was slow to answer. People's private lives fascinated her. On Saturday trips to the supermarket she liked to single out some interesting stranger. "What's the matter with that *jerky*-moving man? That girl, is she one of your dark-skinned people?" Elizabeth answered too softly, and never seemed to follow Mrs. Ardavi's pointing finger.

Supper was difficult; Mrs. Ardavi didn't like American food. Even when Elizabeth made some-

Literature and Language: Establishing Meaning Through Verb Tenses
To help readers keep track of when things happen, writers are careful to use verb tenses correctly. Use pages 1193–1194 to review with students the forms and uses of the six verb tenses: present, past, future, present perfect, past perfect, future perfect. Then ask students to choose the tense of the verb in parentheses that fits the meaning of the sentence and the story.

1. Mrs. Ardavi's husband (*die*) six years after they were married. (*died* or *had died*)
2. Her youngest son Barak (*marry*) only a few months before she (*arrive*) in America. (*had married*, *arrived*)
3. Twelve years (*pass*) since Mrs. Ardavi (*see*) Hassan. (*had passed*, *had seen*)
4. In America he (*become*) a doctor and (*marry*) Elizabeth. (*had become* or *became*; *had married* or *married*)
5. When Mrs. Ardavi (*return*) to Iran, she probably (*live*) with Barak. (*returns* or *returned*; *will live* or *lived*)

A. Noting Details
You may want to point out to students how the author uses incidents rather than exposition to show what is happening. Instead of telling the reader that Elizabeth and Hassan are ignoring Mrs. Ardavi, Elizabeth is shown "finishing one book and reaching for the next without even glancing up" while Hassan chews a thumbnail and watches a senator.

thing Iranian, it had an American taste to it—the vegetables still faintly crisp, the onions transparent rather than nicely blackened. "Vegetables not thoroughly cooked retain a certain acidity," Mrs. Ardavi said, laying down her fork. "This is a cause of constipation and stomachaches. At night I often have heartburn. It's been three full days since I moved my bowels." Elizabeth merely bent over her plate, offering no symptoms of her own in return. Hassan said, "At the table, Khanoum? At the table?"

Eventually she decided to cook supper herself. Over Elizabeth's protests she began at three every afternoon, filling the house with the smell of dillweed and arranging pots on counters and cabinets and finally, when there was no more space, on the floor. She squatted on the floor with her skirt tucked between her knees and stirred great bowls of minced greens while behind her, on the gas range, four different pots of food bubbled and steamed. The kitchen was becoming more homelike, she thought. A bowl of yogurt brewed beside the stove, a kettle of rice soaked in the sink, and the top of the dishwasher was curlicued with the yellow dye from saffron. In one corner sat the pudding pan, black on the bottom from the times she had cooked down sugar to make a sweet for her intestines. "Now, this is your rest period," she always told Elizabeth. "Come to the table in three hours and be surprised." But Elizabeth only hovered around the kitchen, disturbing the serene, steam-filled air with clatter and slams as she put away pots, or pacing between stove and sink, her arms folded across her chest. At supper she ate little; Mrs. Ardavi wondered how Americans got so tall on such small suppers. Hassan, on the other hand, had second and third helpings. "I must be gaining five pounds a week," he said. "None of my clothes fit."

"That's good to hear," said his mother. And Elizabeth added something but in English, which Hassan answered in English also. Often now they broke into English for paragraphs at a time—Elizabeth speaking softly, looking at her plate, and Hassan answering at length and sometimes reaching across the table to cover her hand.

At night, after her evening prayers, Mrs. Ardavi watched television on the living room couch. She brought her veil downstairs and wrapped it around her to keep the drafts away. Her shoes lay on the rug beneath her, and scattered down the length of the couch were her knitting bag, her sack of burned sugar, her magnifying glass, and *My First Golden Dictionary*. Elizabeth read novels in an easy chair, and Hassan watched TV so that he could translate the difficult parts of the plot. Not that Mrs. Ardavi had much trouble. American plots were easy to guess at, particularly the Westerns. And when the program was boring—a documentary or a special news feature—she could pass the time by talking to Hassan. "Your cousin Farah wrote," she said. "Do you remember her? A homely girl, too dark. She's getting a divorce and in my opinion it's fortunate; he's from a lower class. Do you remember Farah?"

Hassan only grunted, his eyes on the screen. He was interested in American politics. So was she, for that matter. She had wept for President Kennedy, and carried Jackie's picture in her purse. But these news programs were long and dry, and if Hassan wouldn't talk she was forced to turn at last to her *Golden Dictionary.*

In her childhood, she had been taught by expensive foreign tutors. Her mind was her great gift, the compensation for a large, plain face and a stocky figure. But now what she had learned seemed lost, forgotten utterly or fogged by years, so that Hassan gave a snort whenever she told him some fact that she had dredged up from her memory. It seemed that everything she studied now had to penetrate through a great thick layer before it reached her mind. "Tonk you," she practiced. "Tonk you. Tonk you." "Thank you," Hassan corrected her. He pointed out useful words in her dictionary—grocery store words, household words—but she grew impatient with their woodenness. What she wanted was the language to display her personality, her famous courtesy, and her magical intuition about the inside lives of other people. Nightly she learned "salt," "bread," "spoon," but with an inner sense of dullness, and every morning when she woke her English was once again confined to "thank you" and "NBC."

Elizabeth, meanwhile, read on, finishing one book and reaching for the next without even glancing up. Hassan chewed a thumbnail and watched a senator. He shouldn't be disturbed, of course, **A** but time after time his mother felt the silence and the whispery turning of pages stretching her nerves until she had to speak. "Hassan?"

"Hmm."

"My chest seems tight. I'm sure a cold is coming on. Don't you have a tonic?"

"No," said Hassan.

A. Dialogue
This exchange between Mrs. Ardavi and Hassan points up the conflict between mother and son.

? Why does she persist in asking for a remedy when common sense tells her to stop? (Opinions will vary. Mrs. Ardavi seems to like to provoke confrontations. Perhaps the best student responses will be anecdotal, since Mrs. Ardavi's personality trait is not uncommon, although the motive underlying it is seldom clear.)

B. Flashback

? Does this picture of Mrs. Ardavi's relationship with her husband make her a more appealing or a less appealing figure? How might the relationship cause her to view marriage in general? (These are matters of opinion. Any reasonable answers should be accepted.)

He dispensed medicines all day; he listened to complaints. Common sense told her to stop, but she persisted, encouraged by some demon that wouldn't let her tongue lie still. "Don't you have some syrup? What about that liquid you gave me for constipation? Would that help?"

A "No, it wouldn't," said Hassan.

He drove her on, somehow. The less he gave, the more she had to ask. "Well, aspirin? Vitamins?" Until Hassan said, "Will you just let me *watch?*" Then she could lapse into silence again, or even gather up the clutter of her belongings and bid the two of them good night.

She slept badly. Often she lay awake for hours, fingering the edge of the sheet and staring at the ceiling. Memories crowded in on her, old grievances and fears, injustices that had never been righted. For the first time in years she thought of her husband, a gentle, weak man given to surprising outbursts of temper. She hadn't loved him when she married him, and at his death from a liver ailment six years later her main feeling had been resentment. Was it fair to be widowed so young, while other women were supported and protected? She had moved from her husband's home back to the old family estate, where five of her sisters still lived. There she had stayed till

B Babak's wedding, drinking tea all day with her sisters and pulling the string by which the rest of the family was attached. Marriages were arranged, funerals attended, childbirth discussed in fine detail; servants' disputes were settled, and feuds patched up and then restarted. Her husband's face had quickly faded, leaving only a vacant spot in her mind. But now she could see him so clearly—a wasted figure on his deathbed, beard untrimmed, turban coming loose, eyes imploring her for something more than an absent-minded pat on the cheek as she passed through his room on her way to check the children.

She saw the thin faces of her three small boys as they sat on the rug eating rice. Hassan was the stubborn, mischievous one, with perpetual scabs on his knees. Babak was the cuddly one. Ali was the oldest, who had caused so much worry—weak, like his father, demanding, but capable of turning suddenly charming. Four years ago he had died of a brain hemorrhage, slumping over a dinner table in faraway Shīrāz,[6] where he'd gone to be free of his wife, who was also his double first cousin. Ever since he was born he had disturbed his mother's sleep, first because she worried over what he would amount to and now, after his death, because she lay awake listing all she had done wrong with him. She had been too lenient. No, too harsh. There was no telling. Mistakes she had made floated on the ceiling like ghosts—allowances she'd made when she knew she shouldn't have, protections he had not deserved, blows which perhaps he had not deserved either.

She would have liked to talk to Hassan about it, but anytime she tried he changed the subject. Maybe he was angry about the way he had heard of Ali's death. It was customary to break such news gradually. She had started a series of tactful letters, beginning by saying that Ali was seriously ill when in truth he was already buried. Something in the letter had given her away—perhaps her plans for a rest cure by the seaside, which she never would have considered if she'd had an ailing son at home. Hassan had telephoned overseas, taking three nights to reach her. "Tell me what's wrong," he said. "I know there's something." When her tears kept her from answering, he asked, "Is he dead?" His voice sounded angry, but that might have been due to a poor connection. And when he hung up, cutting her off before she could say all she wanted, she thought, I should have told him straight out. I had forgotten that about him. Now when she spoke of Ali he listened politely, with his face frozen. She would have told him anything, all about the death and burial and

6. **Shīrāz:** city in southwestern Iran.

that witch of a wife throwing herself, too late, into the grave; but Hassan never asked.

Death was moving in on her. Oh, not on her personally (the women in her family lived a century or longer, burying the men one by one) but on everybody around her, all the cousins and uncles and brothers-in-law. No sooner had she laid away her mourning clothes than it was time to bring them out again. Recently she had begun to feel she would outlive her two other sons as well, and she fought off sleep because of the dreams it brought—Babak lying stiff and cold in his grave, Hassan crumpled over in some dark American alley. Terrifying images would zoom at her out of the night. In the end she had to wrap herself in her veil and sleep instead on the Persian rug, which had the dusty smell of home and was, anyway, more comfortable than her unsteady foreign mattress.

At Christmas time, Hassan and Elizabeth gave Mrs. Ardavi a brightly colored American dress with short sleeves. She wore it to an Iranian party, even leaving off her kerchief in a sudden fit of daring. Everyone commented on how nice she looked. "Really you fit right in," a girl told her. "May I write to my mother about you? She was over here for a year and a half and never once stepped out of the house without her kerchief." Mrs. Ardavi beamed. It was true she would never have associated with these people at home—children of civil servants and bank clerks, newly rich now they'd finished medical school. The wives called their husbands "Doctor" even in direct address. But still it felt good to be speaking so much Persian; her tongue nearly ran away with her. "I see you're expecting a baby," she said to one of the wives. "Is it your first? I could tell by your eyes. Now don't be nervous. I had three myself; my mother had seven and never felt a pain in her life. She would squat down to serve my father's breakfast and 'Eh?' she would say. 'Aga Jun, it's the baby!' and there it would be on the floor between her feet, waiting for her to cut the cord and finish pouring the tea." She neglected to mention how her mother had died. All her natural tact came back to her, her gift with words and her knowledge of how to hold an audience. She bubbled and sparkled like a girl, and her face fell when it was time to go home.

After the party, she spent two or three days noticing more keenly than ever the loss of her language, and talking more feverishly when Hassan came home in the evening. This business of being a foreigner was something changeable. Boundaries kept shifting, and sometimes it was she who was the foreigner but other times Elizabeth, or even Hassan. (Wasn't it true, she often wondered, that there was a greater distance between men and women than between Americans and Iranians, or even *Eskimos* and Iranians?) Hassan was the foreigner when she and Elizabeth conspired to hide a miniature Koran in his glove compartment; he would have laughed at them. "You see," she told Elizabeth, "I know there's nothing to it, but it makes me feel better. When my sons were born I took them all to the bath attendant to have their blood let. People say it brings long life. I know that's superstition, but whenever afterward I saw those ridges down their backs I felt safe. Don't you understand?" And Elizabeth said, "Of course." She smuggled the Koran into the car herself, and hid it beneath the Texaco maps. Hassan saw nothing.

Hilary was a foreigner forever. She dodged her grandmother's yearning hands, and when the grown-ups spoke Persian she fretted and misbehaved and pulled on Elizabeth's sleeve. Mrs. Ardavi had to remind herself constantly not to kiss the child too much, not to reach out for a hug, not to offer her lap. In this country people kept more separate. They kept so separate that at times she felt hurt. They tried to be so subtle, so undemonstrative. She would never understand this place.

In January they took her to a dentist, who made clucking noises when he looked in her mouth. "What does he say?" she asked. "Tell me the worst." But Hassan was talking in a low voice to Elizabeth, and he waved her aside. They seemed to be having a misunderstanding of some sort. "What does he *say*, Hassan?"

"Just a minute."

She craned around in the high-backed chair, fighting off the dentist's little mirror. "I have to know," she told Hassan.

"He says your teeth are terrible. They have to be extracted and the gums surgically smoothed. He wants to know if you'll be here for another few months; he can't schedule you till later."

A cold lump of fear swelled in her stomach. Unfortunately she *would* be here; it had only been three months so far and she was planning to stay a year. So she had to watch numbly while her life

A. Irony

? What is ironic about the Iranian girl's remark "You fit right in"? (The observation is ironic because, on a day-to-day basis, Mrs. Ardavi does *not* fit in. Her dress is a Christmas present from Hassan and Elizabeth. She has left off her kerchief only "in a sudden fit of daring." The main reason she likes the party is that she is "speaking so much Persian." This party is an anomaly; Mrs. Ardavi fits right in not because it is an American party but because it is an Iranian party in America.)

A. Dialogue
? How does the dialogue show the deteriorating situation between Mrs. Ardavi and Elizabeth? (Although Elizabeth has "followed a well-worn conversational path" during the entire visit, she is now curt and antagonistic in answering questions of which she disapproves.)

B. Interpretation
? Why is Elizabeth doing all this cleaning out of bureaus and closets? (Opinions will differ. Evidently, she wants to do something that will keep her busy and at the same time keep her away from Mrs. Ardavi.)

was signed away, whole strings of appointments made, and little white cards filled out. And Hassan didn't even look sympathetic. He was still involved in whatever this argument was with Elizabeth. The two of them failed to notice how her hands were shaking.

It snowed all of January, the worst snow they had had in years. When she came downstairs in the mornings she found the kitchen icy cold, crisscrossed by drafts. "The sort of cold enters your bones," she told Elizabeth. "I'm sure to fall sick." Elizabeth only nodded. Some mornings now her face was pale and puffy, as if she had a secret worry, but Mrs. Ardavi had learned that it was better not to ask about it.

Early in February there was a sudden warm spell. Snow melted and all the trees dripped in the sunshine. "We're going for a walk," Elizabeth said, and Mrs. Ardavi said, "I'll come too." In spite of the warmth, she toiled upstairs for her woolen shawl. She didn't like to take chances. And she worried over Hilary's bare ears. "Won't she catch cold?" she asked. "I think we should cover her head."

"She'll be all right," said Elizabeth, and then shut her face in a certain stubborn way she had.

In the park, Elizabeth and Hilary made snowballs from the last of the snow and threw them at each other, narrowly missing Mrs. Ardavi, who stood watching with her arms folded and her hands tucked in her sleeves.

The next morning, something was wrong with Hilary. She sat at the breakfast table and cried steadily, refusing all food. "Now, now," her grandmother said, "won't you tell old Ka Jun what's wrong?" But when she came close Hilary screamed louder. By noon she was worse. Elizabeth called Hassan, and he came home immediately and laid a hand on Hilary's forehead and said she should go to the pediatrician. He drove them there himself. "It's her ears, I'm sure of it," Mrs. Ardavi said in the waiting room. For some reason Hassan grew angry. "Do you always know better than the experts?" he asked her. "What are we coming to the doctor for? We could have talked to you and saved the trip." His mother lowered her eyes and examined her purse straps. She understood that he was anxious, but all the same her feelings were hurt and when they rose to go into the office she stayed behind.

Later Hassan came back and sat down again. "There's an infection in her middle ear," he told her. "The doctor's going to give her a shot of penicillin." Her mother nodded, careful not to annoy him by reminding him she had thought as much. Then Hilary started crying. She must be getting her shot now. Mrs. Ardavi herself was terrified of needles, and she sat gripping her purse until her fingers turned white, staring around the waiting room, which seemed pathetically cheerful, with its worn wooden toys and nursery-school paintings. Her own ear ached in sympathy. She thought of a time when she had boxed Ali's ears too hard and he had wept all that day and gone to sleep sucking his thumb.

While Hassan was there she was careful not to say anything, but the following morning at breakfast she said, "Elizabeth dear, do you remember that walk we took day before yesterday?"

"Yes," said Elizabeth. She was squeezing oranges for Hilary, who'd grown cheerful again and was eating a huge breakfast.

"Remember I said Hilary should wear a hat? Now you see you should have been more careful. Because of you she fell sick; she could have died. Do you see that now?"

"No," said Elizabeth.

Was her Persian that scanty? Lately it seemed to have shrunk and hardened, like a stale piece of bread. Mrs. Ardavi sighed and tried again. "Without a hat, you see—" she began. But Elizabeth had set down her orange, picked up Hilary, and walked out of the room. Mrs. Ardavi stared after her, wondering if she'd said something wrong.

For the rest of the day, Elizabeth was busy in her room. She was cleaning out bureaus and closets. A couple of times Mrs. Ardavi advanced as far as the doorway, where she stood awkwardly watching. Hilary sat on the floor playing with a discarded perfume bottle. Everything, it seemed, was about to be thrown away—buttonless blouses and stretched-out sweaters, stockings and combs and empty lipstick tubes. "Could I be of any help?" Mrs. Ardavi asked, but Elizabeth said, "Oh, no. Thank you very much." Her voice was cheerful. Yet when Hassan came home he went upstairs and stayed a long time, and the door remained shut behind him.

Supper that night was an especially fine stew, Hassan's favorite ever since childhood, but he didn't say a word about it. He hardly spoke at all,

A. Description

? What does Mrs. Ardavi's room decoration suggest about her "fitting right in"? (She is trying to create a homelike setting—an Iranian atmosphere—in her room. Except for the orange and aqua plastic pots, she does not care much for American decoration. She is "fitting right in" by clinging to reminders of her life in Iran.)

B. Characterization

Students should note that Mrs. Ardavi's problems run deeper than American culture and Hassan's Christian wife. Babak's Iranian wife, approved of by Mrs. Ardavi in an arranged marriage, has already become "disrespectful." Babak was about to ask his mother to move when the trip to America occurred.

C. Interpretation

Why is Elizabeth so apparently cruel toward Mrs. Ardavi, and why is Hassan so solicitous? (It is unclear whether Elizabeth is actually being cruel. Mrs. Ardavi says, "It's mainly my heart," suggesting that the tooth-pulling may have been routine. Routine or not, Elizabeth has few tender feelings left for Mrs. Ardavi and might not sympathize even with genuine suffering. Hassan is solicitous because he thinks she is having a hard time and probably because he recognizes that Elizabeth, in her present state of mind, will not pay much attention to her mother-in-law's complaints, legitimate or not.)

in fact. Then later, when Elizabeth was upstairs putting Hilary to bed, he said, "Khanoum Jun, I want to talk to you."

"Yes, Hassan," she said, laying aside her knitting. She was frightened by his seriousness, the black weight of his mustache, and her own father's deep black eyes. But what had she done? She knotted her hands and looked up at him, swallowing.

"I understand you've been interfering," he said.

"I, Hassan?"

"Elizabeth isn't the kind you can do that with. And she's raising the child just fine on her own."

"Well, of course she is," said his mother. "Did I ever say otherwise?"

"Show it, then. Don't offer criticisms."

"Very well," she said. She picked up her knitting and began counting stitches, as if she'd forgotten the conversation entirely. But that evening she was unusually quiet, and at nine o'clock she excused herself to go to bed. "So early?" Hassan asked.

"I'm tired," she told him, and left with her back very straight.

Her room surrounded her like a nest. She had built up layers of herself on every surface—tapestries and bits of lace and lengths of paisley. The bureau was covered with gilt-framed pictures of the saints, and snapshots of her sisters at family gatherings. On the windowsill were little plants in orange and aqua plastic pots—her favorite American colors. Her bedside table held bottles of medicine, ivory prayer beads, and a tiny brick of holy earth. The rest of the house was bare and shiny, impersonal; this room was as comforting as her shawl.

Still, she didn't sleep well. Ghosts rose up again, tugging at her thoughts. Why did things turn out so badly for her? Her father had preferred her brothers, a fact that crushed her even after all these years. Her husband had had three children by her and then complained that she was cold. And what comfort were children? If she had stayed in Iran any longer Babak would have asked her to move; she'd seen it coming. There'd been some disrespect creeping into his bride's behavior, some unwillingness to take advice, which Babak had overlooked even when his mother pointed it out to him. And Hassan was worse—always so stubborn, much too independent. She had offered him anything if he would just stay in Iran but he had said no; he was set on leaving her. And he had flatly refused to take along his cousin Shora as his wife, though everyone pointed out how lonely he would be. He was so anxious to break away, to get *going*, to come to this hardhearted country and take up with a Christian girl. Oh, she should have laughed when he left, and saved her tears for someone more deserving. She never should have come here, she never should have asked anything of him again. When finally she went to sleep it seemed that her eyes remained open, burning large and dry beneath her lids.

In the morning she had a toothache. She could hardly walk for the pain. It was only Friday (the first of her dental appointments was for Monday), but the dentist made time for her during the afternoon and pulled the tooth. Elizabeth said it wouldn't hurt, but it did. Elizabeth treated it as something insignificant, merely a small break in her schedule, which required the hiring of a babysitter. She wouldn't even call Hassan home from work. "What could he do?" she asked.

So when Hassan returned that evening it was all a surprise to him—the sight of his mother with a bloody cotton cylinder hanging out over her lower lip like a long tooth. "What *happened* to you?" he asked. To make it worse, Hilary was screaming and had been all afternoon. Mrs. Ardavi put her hands over her ears, wincing. "Will you make that child hush?" Hassan told Elizabeth. "I think we should get my mother to bed." He guided her toward the stairs, and she allowed herself to lean on him. "It's mainly my heart," she said. "You know how scared I am of dentists." When he had folded back her bedspread and helped her to lie down she closed her eyes gratefully, resting one arm across her forehead. Even the comfort of hot tea was denied her; she had to stay on cold foods for twelve hours. Hassan fixed her a glass of ice water. He was very considerate, she thought. He seemed as shaken at the sight of her as Hilary had been. All during the evening he kept coming to check on her, and twice in the night she heard him climbing the stairs to listen at her door. When she moaned he called, "Are you awake?"

"Of course," she said.

"Can I get you anything?"

"No, no."

C

CLOSURE
Have students write two or three sentences telling whether they think culture, generational differences, or personality contributed most to the breakdown in relations between Elizabeth and Mrs. Ardavi.

READING CHECK TEST
1. When Mrs. Ardavi first sees Hilary, she wants to place ______ around her neck. *a medal* or *medals*
2. Mrs. Ardavi will not eat ______, although she is intrigued by its smell. *bacon*
3. Hassan was annoyed when his mother withheld the truth about the ______ of his brother Ali. *death*
4. When Hilary gets an ear infection, Mrs. Ardavi says it was because she did not ______. *wear a hat*
5. Hassan tells his mother it is the American custom for guests to stay in the host's home for only ______. *three months*

A. Climax
This cloud of insects from the tin confectioner's box that Mrs. Ardavi had brought from Iran decides the outcome. For Elizabeth, it is the last straw.

B. Resolution
Custom, which has created so many misunderstandings, is now brought into play (with some guile) to get Mrs. Ardavi to leave. The supposed American custom of "three months for house guests," followed by their living in an apartment nearby, persuades her to return to Iran.

C. Reprise
You may want to note that Hassan, as on the opening trip from the airport, has very little to say to his mother.

In the morning she descended the stairs with slow, groping feet, keeping a tight hold on the railing. "It was a very hard night," she said. "At four my gum started throbbing. Is that normal? I think these American pain pills are constipating. Maybe a little prune juice would restore my regularity."

"I'll get it," Hassan said. "You sit down. Did you take the milk of magnesia?"

"Oh, yes, but I'm afraid it wasn't enough," she said.

Elizabeth handed Hassan a platter of bacon, not looking at him.

After breakfast, while Hassan and his mother were still sitting over their tea, Elizabeth started cleaning the kitchen. She made quite a bit of noise. She sorted the silverware and then went through a tangle of utensils, discarding bent spatulas and rusty tongs. "May I help?" asked Mrs. Ardavi. Elizabeth shook her head. She seemed to have these fits of throwing things away. Now she was standing on the counter to take everything from the upper cabinets—crackers, cereals, half-empty bottles of spices. On the very top shelf was a flowered tin confectioner's box with Persian lettering on it, forgotten since the day Mrs. Ardavi had brought it. "My!" said Mrs. Ardavi. "Won't Hilary be surprised!" Elizabeth pried the lid off. Out flew a cloud of insects, grayish-brown with V-shaped wings. They brushed past Elizabeth's face and fluttered through her hair and swarmed toward the ceiling, where they dimmed the light fixture. Elizabeth flung the box as far from her as possible and climbed down from the counter. "Goodness!" said Mrs. Ardavi. "Why, *we* have those at home!" Hassan lowered his teacup. Mixed nuts and dried currants rolled every which way on the floor; more insects swung toward the ceiling. Elizabeth sat on the nearest chair and buried her head in her hands. "Elizabeth?" said Hassan. A

But she wouldn't look at him. In the end she simply rose and went upstairs, shutting the bedroom door with a gentle, definite click, which they heard all the way down in the kitchen because they were listening so hard.

"Excuse me," Hassan said to his mother.

She nodded and stared into her tea.

After he was gone she went to find Hilary, and she set her on her knee, babbling various folk rhymes to her while straining her ears toward the silence overhead. But Hilary squirmed off her lap and went to play with a truck. Then Hassan came downstairs again. He didn't say a word about Elizabeth.

On the following day, when Mrs. Ardavi's tooth was better, she and Hassan had a little talk upstairs in her room. They were very polite with each other. Hassan asked his mother how long they could hope for her to stay. His mother said she hadn't really thought about it. Hassan said that in America it was the custom to have house guests for three months only. After that they moved to a separate apartment nearby, which he'd be glad to provide for her as soon as he could find one, maybe next week. "Ah, an apartment," said his mother, looking impressed. But she had never lived alone a day in her life, and so after a suitable pause she said that she would hate to put him to so much expense. "Especially," she said, "when I'm going in such a short time anyway, since I'm homesick for my sisters."

"Well, then," said Hassan.

At supper that night, Hassan announced that his mother was missing her sisters and would like to leave. Elizabeth lowered her glass. "Leave?" she said.

Mrs. Ardavi said, "And Babak's wife, of course, will be asking for me when the baby arrives."

"Well . . . but what about the dentist? You were supposed to start your appointments on Monday."

"It's not important," Mrs. Ardavi said.

"But we set up all those—"

"There are plenty of dentists she can see at home," Hassan told Elizabeth. "We have dentists in Iran, for God's sake. Do you imagine we're barbarians?"

"No," Elizabeth said.

On the evening of the third of March, Hassan drove his mother to the airport. He was worrying about the road, which was slippery after a snowfall. He couldn't find much to say to his mother. And once they had arrived, he deliberately kept the conversation to trivia—the verifying of tickets, checking of departure times, weighing of baggage. Her baggage was fourteen pounds overweight. It didn't make sense; all she had were her clothes and a few small gifts for her sisters. "Why is it so heavy?" Hassan asked. "What have you got in there?" But his mother only said, "I don't know," and straightened her shawl, looking elsewhere.

Analyzing The Story
Identifying Facts

1. Mrs. Ardavi is so confused and frustrated that she does not recognize her son: he has aged and put on weight, and his clothes are unfamiliar and American. It is only when she smells him that she really believes that this is the son she has not seen in twelve years.

Mrs. Ardavi is embarrassed by her kerchief and her bad teeth. She is disappointed that her son Hassan is not eager to talk while driving.

2. She wants to see Hilary, her grandchild, who is asleep.

3. She is frustrated by the language barrier and seems too old to absorb the English words she learns. She cannot understand television programs. She objects to the food. She finds Americans undemonstrative. She sleeps badly, worrying about the past and future.

4. Flashbacks reveal that Mrs. Ardavi's childhood was scarred by tragedy: her father was a womanizer, and her mother died in childbirth when Mrs. Ardavi was ten. She grew up in a strict household. Her father evidently preferred her brothers. Mrs. Ardavi resents the early death of her husband, whom she had not loved during their six years of marriage. Mrs. Ardavi worries whether she was too harsh with her unhappily married eldest son, Ali, who died four years ago of a brain hemorrhage. She also regrets not having told Hassan directly of his brother's death. She wonders whether or not she will be able to continue living with her youngest son, Babak, and his wife. All of these flashbacks contribute to a complex portrait of Mrs. Ardavi.

5. Mrs. Ardavi interferes with the preparation of food and with Elizabeth's care of Hilary. Even though she apparently means well, she becomes a classic "meddling mother-in-law."

Mrs. Ardavi is obviously not as aware as the reader is of these signs.

Elizabeth becomes gradually more and more angry. The end result is that Hassan must indirectly ask his mother to leave.

(Answers continue on next page.)

Hassan bent to open a tooled-leather suitcase. Inside he found three empty urn-shaped wine bottles, the permanent-press sheets from her bed, and a sample box of detergent that had come in yesterday's mail. "Listen," said Hassan, "do you know how much I'd have to pay to fly these things over? What's the matter with you?"

"I wanted to show my sisters," his mother said.

"Well, forget it. Now, what else have you got?"

But something about her—the vague, childlike eyes set upon some faraway object—made him give in. He opened no more bags. He even regretted his sharpness, and when her flight was announced he hugged her closely and kissed the top of her head. "Go with God," he said.

"Goodbye, Hassan."

She set off down the corridor by herself, straggling behind a line of businessmen. They all wore hats. His mother wore her scarf, and of all the travelers she alone, securely kerchiefed and shawled, setting her small shoes resolutely on the gleaming tiles, seemed undeniably a foreigner.

A Comment on the Story

The title of this story underlines one of its major themes: a failure to communicate. Tyler is not the only twentieth-century writer to explore this theme, but she gives it special resonance here by establishing a context of two very different cultures, American and Iranian, in conflict within a single family.

Before the violent Iranian Revolution in 1978, when the Shah was overthrown, Iran and the United States had enjoyed fairly close relations. Young upper-class Iranians, such as Hassan Ardavi, were often sent to college in the West, and it was relatively common for them to remain there, pursuing professional careers in their adopted country. In Tyler's story, Hassan is portrayed as completely assimilated into American ways: He has married an American, has bought a house in a suburb, and has abandoned traditional Islamic religious attitudes. When we learn in the first paragraph that his mother plans "on staying a year" with Hassan and his family, we are immediately alerted to a potential clash.

Despite all of the characters' good intentions, the visit is doomed almost from the beginning. The description of Mrs. Ardavi at the airport, "entangled in a web of meaningless sounds such as those you might hear in a fever dream," foreshadows the story's poignant and sometimes humorous course. Tyler repeatedly invites us to consider the obstacles that confront Mrs. Ardavi, and through flashbacks we learn some of the roots of the considerable anxieties that haunt her. But we are also asked to ponder her inflexibility, her lack of tact, and her self-pity.

Mrs. Ardavi comes to America naively eager to fit in. But it is soon clear that, at her age, the tug of the old ways is too strong. Whereas her son has found a place in his new country, she does not. And, as the story hints, she may no longer even have a place back in Iran. As you discuss the story, consider whether the author is suggesting that the feeling of uprootedness is a particularly twentieth-century phenomenon—the inevitable result, perhaps, of modern technological progress. Ironically enough, it is at an airport—one of the great symbols of an age of technology and communications—that Tyler twice shows us most starkly the alienation of Mrs. Ardavi.

Responding to the Story

Analyzing the Story

Identifying Facts

1. Describe the reunion of Hassan and his mother at the airport. Explain why Mrs. Ardavi is embarrassed and disappointed on the way to her son's home.
2. What is the first thing Mrs. Ardavi wants to do when she arrives at Hassan's house?
3. In what specific ways does Mrs. Ardavi find it hard to adapt to life in America?
4. What facts do you learn about Mrs. Ardavi in the various **flashbacks**?
5. List the signs of tension that develop between Mrs. Ardavi and Elizabeth. Is Mrs. Ardavi as aware of these signs as the reader is? What is the eventual outcome of this **conflict** between the two women?

(Continued from previous page.)
Interpreting Meanings
6. The conflict in the story arises in great part because Mrs. Ardavi, set in her ways, cannot adjust to American culture. Although Elizabeth makes an effort to welcome Mrs. Ardavi, she is unable to adjust to some Iranian ways.

The conflict is also generational: Mrs. Ardavi's inability to understand that her son Hassan has chosen a new way of life, and Hassan's inability, or refusal, to compromise that way of life in order to humor his mother.

7. The tone at the beginning is light, even comic. At the end, the tone is dark, almost tragic.

Students will have various responses. Most will agree that the contrast suggests that Mrs. Ardavi's visit was a failure. She is unable to adjust to American ways, and her actions alienate her son and daughter-in-law. However, even though Mrs. Ardavi is inflexible and "difficult," the author creates sympathy for her by emphasizing her loneliness.

8. Literally, the phrase probably means that Hassan's place at the family table is empty, since he is absent. The implica-
(Answers continue in left-hand column.)

(Continued from top.)
tion is that she is urging him to return home.

At the end of the story, as Mrs. Ardavi makes her lonely departure, it appears that Hassan's place will be forever "empty" in Iran.

9. Answers will vary. The relationship is flawed by an inability to communicate. Mrs. Ardavi refuses to understand and accept the fact that her son has adopted the ways of a different culture.

Students may sympathize with any of the characters.

Whether the writer "stacks the deck" is a matter of opinion. Ask students to back up opinions with specific references.

10. The theme seems to be that the passage of time, geographical separation, and a conflict of cultures may drive a wedge between even a mother and son. Most students will agree that the theme is universal.

Interpreting Meanings

6. In what ways is the **conflict** in this story the result of a clash of cultures? In what ways is it a clash of generations?
7. Describe the difference in **tone** between the beginning of the story and its end. How does this contrast comment on Mrs. Ardavi's visit?
8. What does Mrs. Ardavi mean when she writes to her son, "Your place is empty"? What additional meaning does this take on as the story ends?
9. How would you describe the relationship between Hassan and his mother? Which character do you feel most sympathy for in this story? Do you think the writer "stacks the deck" for or against any of the characters? Explain.
10. What would you say is the **theme** of this story? Is the story about a universal human experience, or is it only about people at this time, and in this place? Explain.

Writing About the Story

A Creative Response

1. **Taking Another Point of View.** Narrate the events of one incident in the story from Elizabeth's point of view. The incident should happen exactly as it is narrated in the story now; but shift the point of view from the limited third-person with its focus on Mrs. Ardavi, to the limited third-person with its focus on Elizabeth.

A Critical Response

2. **Comparing Two Stories.** Write a brief essay comparing this story with Updike's "Son" (page 898). What parent-child tensions do both stories deal with?
3. **Responding to the Story.** Can you see some advantages to Mrs. Ardavi's ways over the ways of her Americanized son and his wife? In a brief essay, discuss the differences in cultures revealed in this story, and how you respond to them.

Primary Sources
"Still Just Writing"

"I was standing in the schoolyard waiting for a child when another mother came up to me. 'Have you found work yet?' she asked. 'Or are you still just writing?'

"Now, how am I supposed to answer that?

"I could take offense, come to think of it. Maybe the reason I didn't is that I halfway share her attitude. They're *paying* me for this? For just writing down untruthful stories? I'd better look around for more permanent employment. For I do consider writing to be a finite job. I expect that any day now, I will have said all I have to say; I'll have used up all my characters, and then I'll be free to get on with my real life. When I make a note of new ideas on index cards, I imagine I'm clearing out my head, and that soon it will be empty and spacious. I file the cards in a little blue box, and I can picture myself using the final card one day—ah! through at last!—and throwing the blue box away. I'm like a dentist who continually fights tooth decay, working toward the time when he's conquered it altogether and done himself out of a job. But my head keeps loading up again; the little blue box stays crowded and messy. Even when I feel I have no ideas at all, and can't possibly start the next chapter, I have a sense of something still bottled in me, trying to get out. . . .

"I spent my adolescence planning to be an artist, not a writer. After all, books had to be about major events, and none had ever happened to me. All I knew were tobacco workers, stringing the leaves I handed them and talking up a storm. Then I found a book of Eudora Welty's short stories in the high school library. She was writing about Edna Earle, who was so slow-witted she could sit all day just pondering how the tail of the *C* got through the loop of the *L* on the Coca-Cola sign. Why, I knew Edna Earle. You mean you could *write* about such people? I have always meant to send Eudora Welty a thank-you note, but I imagine she would find it a little strange."

—from "Still Just Writing,"
Anne Tyler

Andrea Lee (1953–)

A Andrea Lee grew up in Yeadon, a prosperous Philadelphia suburb favored by black professionals. It was a place where grounds were well kept, children were sent off to good schools, and prejudice was something you learned about from books and television.

"Yeadon was as solid a repository of American virtues and American flaws as any other close-knit suburban community," she has said. "It had, and still has, its own peculiar flavor—a lively mixture of materialism, idealism, and ironic humor that prevents the minds of its children from stagnating."

In 1978, Lee went to Russia with her husband, a graduate student in Russian history, for eight months' study at Moscow State University and for another two months in Leningrad. The young Americans stood in lines and rode the subways with ordinary Russians. This year-long trip resulted in a series of articles which were collected in her much-praised book *Russian Journal*.

Lee's first novel was published in 1984. The heroine, Sarah Phillips, shares with Lee a prosperous upbringing and a Harvard education. Sarah is the daughter of a black minister who combines old-fashioned Baptist charisma with a contemporary dedication to the civil rights movement.

Photograph © 1988 by Jill Krementz.

Lee is now a staff writer for *The New Yorker* and currently lives in Rome.

A. Expansion
Lee's quiet, affluent upbringing forms the background of her first novel, *Sarah Phillips,* whose heroine observes that the old-fashioned black middle class "has carried on with cautious pomp for years in eastern cities and suburbs, using its considerable fund to attempt poignant imitations of high society. . . ."

In *Sarah Phillips,* the heroine's father is a prosperous Baptist minister and her mother a prim ex-schoolteacher. The minister, according to one critic, "can throw an occasional member of his mostly female flock 'into fits of rapturous shrieks' " whether he is preaching fire and brimstone sermons or advocating civil-rights causes. Sarah's mother, although a strong believer in thrift, "vacations in Europe and shops at Saks."

SUPPLEMENTARY SUPPORT MATERIALS

1. Vocabulary Activity Worksheet (*CCB*)
2. Review and Response Worksheet: Conflict and Resolution (*CCB*)
3. Language Skills Worksheet: Appositives and Appositive Phrases (*CCB*)
4. Selection Test (*CCB*)

DEVELOPING VOCABULARY

The following words from the story are tested in the Selection Test. (See also Vocabulary Activity Worksheet.)

miasma	efficacy
lassitude	wistfulness
domain	to insinuate
sanctified	incantatory
fervor	archaic

PREPARATION

ESTABLISHING A PURPOSE. Have students think about the theme of this story as they are reading it. The theme grows out of the conflict and its resolution.

A. Setting

? How does the narrator contrast her home with the place she goes to church? (The dusty leaves, the shade, the wind, and the rhythm of cicadas contrast with the rattling trolleys and packed congregation of church. The narrator lives in the suburbs and goes to church in the city.)

B. Characterization

? What does the ladies' "weakness for elegant footwear and French perfume" suggest about their economic status? (The ladies are well-to-do.)

NEW AFRICAN

Before reading this story, you might review the section on Puritan beliefs in Unit One (page 6). This story, set in Philadelphia in 1963, deals with a Baptist church whose members believe that baptism should be given only to those people who ask for it after receiving a special call from God.

On a hot Sunday morning in the summer of 1963, I was sitting with my mother, my brother Matthew, and my Aunts Lily, Emma, and May in a central pew of the New African Baptist Church. It was mid-August, and the hum of the big electric fans at the back of the church was almost enough to muffle my father's voice from the pulpit; behind me I could hear Mrs. Gordon, a stout, feeble old woman who always complained of dizziness, remark sharply to her daughter that at the rate the air-conditioning fund was growing it might as well be for the next century. Facing the congregation, my father—who was Reverend Ashley to the rest of the world—mopped his brow with a handkerchief and drank glasses of ice water from the heavy old-fashioned pitcher on the table by his side. He was still reading the text. Next, he'd do the sermon, then the baptism, and it would be an hour, maybe two, before the service was over. I rubbed my chin and then idly began to snap the elastic band that held my red straw hat in place over two stiff shoulder-length braids.

A What I really wanted to do, I decided, was to go home, put on my shorts, and climb up into the tree house I'd built the day before with Matthew. We'd nailed an old bushel basket high in the branches of the big maple tree that stretched above the sidewalk in front of the house; it made a crow's nest where you could sit comfortably, except for a few splinters, and read or peer through the dusty leaves at the cars that passed down the quiet suburban road. There was shade and wind and a feeling of adventure in a treetop, where the air seemed to vibrate with the dry rhythm of the cicadas; it was as different as possible from church, where trolleys[1] passing in the city street outside set the stained-glass windows rattling and the packed congregation sat in a near-visible miasma of emotion and cologne.

I slouched between Mama and Aunt Lily and felt myself going limp with lassitude and boredom, as if the heat had melted my bones; the only thing about me with any character seemed to be my firmly starched eyelet dress. Below the scalloped hem, my legs were skinny and wiry, the legs of a ten-year-old amazon,[2] scarred from violent adventures with bicycles and skates. A fingernail tapped my wrist; it was Aunt Emma, reaching across Aunt Lily to press a piece of butterscotch into my hand. When I slipped the candy into my mouth, it tasted faintly of Arpège;[3] my mother and her three sisters were monumental women, ample of bust and slim of ankle, with a weakness for elegant footwear and French perfume. As they leaned back and forth to exchange discreet bits of gossip, they fanned themselves and me with fans from the Byron J. Wiggins Funeral Parlor. The fans, which were fluttering throughout the church, bore a depiction of the Good Shepherd: a hollow-eyed blond Christ holding three fat pink-cheeked children. This Christ resembled the Christ who stood among apostles on the stained-glass windows of the church. Deacon Wiggins, a thoughtful man, had also provided New African with a few dozen fans bearing the picture of a black child praying, but I rarely saw these in use.

There was little that was new or very African about the New African Baptist Church: The original congregation had been formed in 1813 by three young men from Philadelphia's large community of free blacks, and before many generations had passed it had become spiritual home to

1. **trolleys:** mass-transit vehicles that run along tracks set into the street. Trolleys used to be a common sight in American cities.

2. **amazon:** term for a strong, athletic woman, from the Amazons of Greek mythology, who were a race of female warriors.
3. **Arpège:** a brand of perfume.

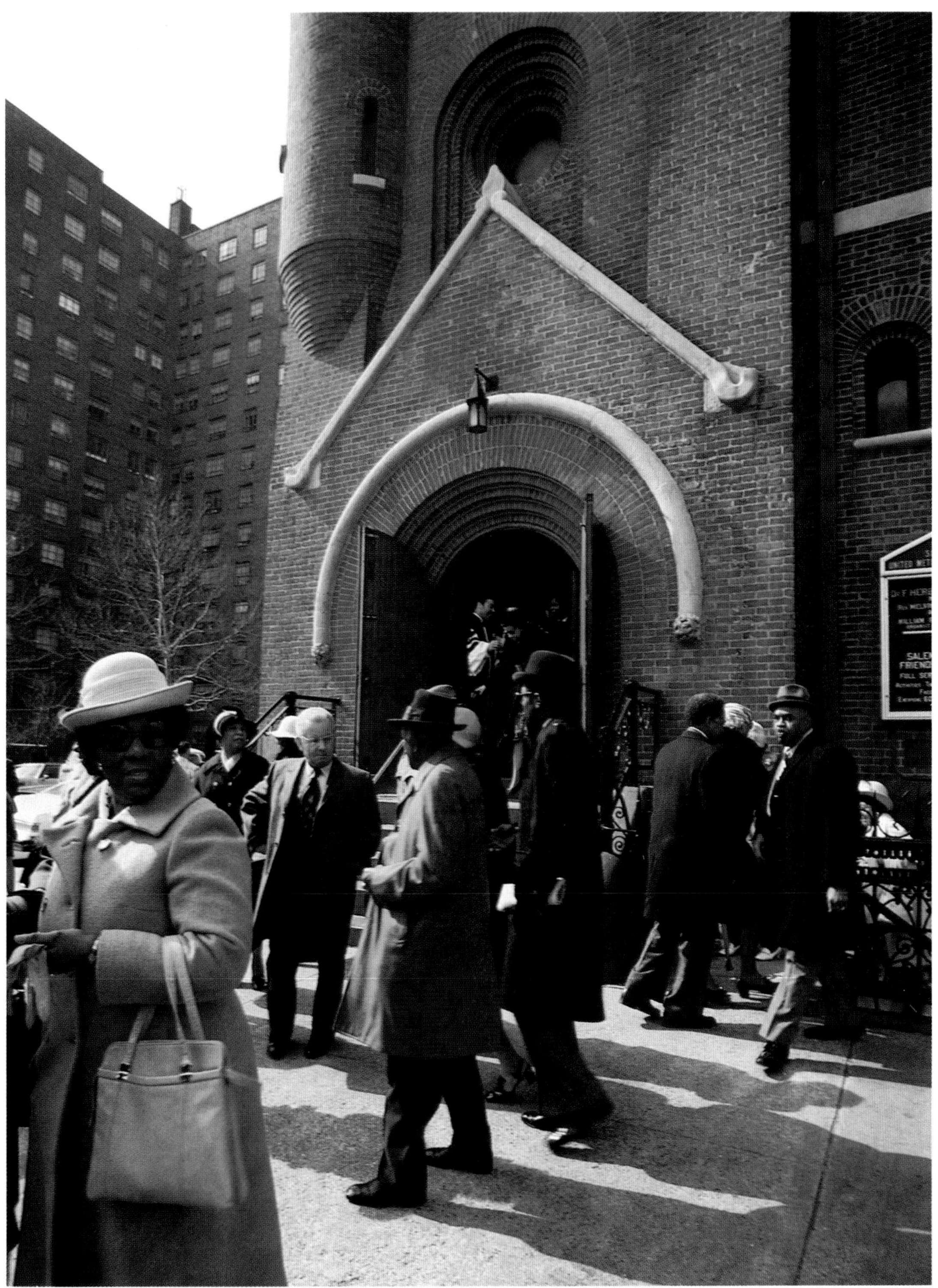

Humanities Connection: Responding to the Photograph

? Compare the church in the photograph with the New African Baptist Church described in the story. (See page 970.) What are the similarities? What are the differences? (Similarities are that the church in the photo is attended by prosperous blacks and is located in a city. Differences are that the church in the photo is built of red brick, whereas the New African is "a gray Gothic structure." The pictured church [United Methodist] has high-rise apartments near it; the New African [Baptist] is "isolated" in a "run-down" area marked by "bottles and papers and loungers.")

A. Fiction/ Nonfiction
The line between fiction and nonfiction is not always clear. "New African" appeared in *The New Yorker* as a short story. It also comprises a chapter in the novel *Sarah Phillips.* Yet reviewers of the novel questioned whether they were reading fiction. One wrote, "Whatever the degree of imaginative embroidery, the basic fictionality of what we are being told is in doubt. One feels this without any knowledge of the author. It is the writing itself that requires such a view." Another critic wrote that Andrea Lee's writing is "intensely autobiographical" and that "straightforward autobiography is more useful to her than fiction."

Students may find it helpful to discuss the dividing line between fiction and nonfiction. Sometimes, as in this story, it can be hazy.

a collection of prosperous, conservative, generally light-skinned parishioners. The church was a gray Gothic structure, set on the corner of a run-down street in South Philadelphia a dozen blocks below Rittenhouse Square and a few blocks west of the spare, clannish Italian neighborhoods that produced Frankie Avalon and Frank Rizzo.[4] At the turn of the century, the neighborhood had been a tidy collection of brick houses with scrubbed marble steps—the homes of a group of solid citizens whom Booker T. Washington,[5] in a centennial address to the church, described as "the ablest Negro businessmen of our generation." Here my father had grown up aspiring to preach to the congregation of New African—an ambition encouraged by my grandmother Ashley, a formidable churchwoman; here, too, my mother and her sisters had walked with linked arms to Sunday services, exchanging affected little catch phrases of Latin and French they had learned at Girls' High.

A In the nineteen-fifties, many of the parishioners, seized by the national urge toward the suburbs, moved to newly integrated towns outside the city, leaving the streets around New African to fill with bottles and papers and loungers. The big church stood suddenly isolated. It had not been abandoned—on Sundays the front steps overflowed with members who had driven in—but there was a tentative feeling in the atmosphere of those Sunday mornings, as if through the muddle of social change the future of New African had become unclear. Matthew and I, suburban children, felt a mixture of pride and animosity toward the church. On the one hand, it was a marvelous private domain, a richly decorated and infinitely suggestive playground where we were petted by a congregation that adored our father; on the other hand, it seemed a bit like a dreadful old relative in the city, one who forced us into tedious visits and who linked us to a past that came to seem embarrassingly primitive as we grew older.

I slid down in my seat, let my head roll back, and looked up at the blue arches of the church ceiling. Lower than these, in back of the altar, was an enormous gilded cross. Still lower, in a semicircle around the pulpit, sat the choir, flanked by two tall golden files of organ pipes, and below the choir was a somber crescent of dark-suited deacons. In front, at the center of everything, his bald head gleaming under the lights, was Daddy. On summer Sundays he wore white robes, and when he raised his arms the heavy material fell in curving folds, like the ridged petals of an Easter lily. Usually when I came through the crowd to kiss him after the service, his cheek beneath my lips felt wet and gravelly with sweat and a new growth of beard sprouted since morning. Today, however, was a baptismal Sunday, and I wouldn't have a chance to kiss him until he was freshly shaven and cool from the shower he took after the ceremony. The baptismal pool was in an alcove to the left of the altar; it had mirrored walls and red velvet curtains, and above it, swaying on a string, hung a stuffed white dove.

Daddy paused in the invocation and asked the choir to pray. The choir began to sing softly:

Blessed assurance,
Jesus is mine!
O what a foretaste
Of glory divine!

In the middle of the hymn, I edged my head around my mother's muscular arm (she swam every day of the summer) and peered at Matthew. He sat bolt upright in his navy blue summer suit, holding a hymnal and a pencil, his long legs planted in front of him, his freckled twelve-year-old face that was so like my father's wearing not the demonic grin it bore when we played alone but a maddeningly composed, attentive expression. "Two hours!" I mouthed at him, and pulled back at a warning pressure from my mother. Then I joined in the singing, feeling disappointed: Matthew had returned me a look of scorn. Just lately, he had started acting very superior and tolerant about tedious Sunday mornings. A month before, he'd been baptized, marching up to the pool in a line of white-robed children, as the congregation murmured happily about Reverend Ashley's son. Afterward, Mrs. Pinkston, a tiny yellow-skinned old woman with a blind left eye, had come up and given me a painful hug, whispering that she was praying night and day for the pastor's daughter to hear the call.

Whenever I thought about baptism, I bit my fingernails; the subject brought out a deep-rooted balkiness in me. Ever since I could remember, Matthew and I had made a game of dispelling the

4. **Avalon . . . Rizzo:** Frankie Avalon was a popular singer; Frank Rizzo was a mayor of Philadelphia.
5. **Booker T. Washington** (1856–1915): noted black American author and educator.

mysteries of worship with a gleeful secular eye: We knew how the bread and wine were prepared for Communion, and where Daddy bought his robes (Ekhardt Brothers, in north Philadelphia, makers also of robes for choirs, academicians, and judges). Yet there was an unassailable magic about an act as public and dramatic as baptism. I felt toward it the slightly exasperated awe a stagehand may feel on realizing that although he can identify with professional exactitude the minutest components of a show, there is still something indefinable in the power that makes it a cohesive whole. Though I could not put it into words, I believed that the decision to make a frightening and embarrassing backward plunge into a pool of sanctified water meant that you had received a summons to Christianity as unmistakable as the blare of an automobile horn. I believed this with the same fervor with which, already, I believed in the power of romance, especially in the miraculous efficacy of a lover's first kiss. I had never been kissed by a lover, nor had I heard the call to baptism.

For a Baptist minister and his wife, my father and mother were unusually relaxed about religion: Matthew and I had never been required to read the Bible, and my father's sermons had been criticized by some older church members for omitting the word "sin." Mama and Daddy never tried to push me toward baptism, but a number of other people did. On holidays, when I would retreat from the noise of the family dinner table and try to read in my favorite place, the window seat in Matthew's room, with the curtains drawn to form a tent, Aunt Lily would come and find me. She was the youngest of my mother's sisters, a kindergarten teacher with the fatally overdeveloped air of quaintness that is one mark of an old maid. Aunt Lily hoped and hoped again with various suitors, but even I knew she would never find a husband. I respected her because she gave me wonderful books of fairy tales, inscribed in her neat, loopy writing; when she talked about religion, however, she assumed an anxious, flirtatious air that made me cringe. "Well, Miss Sarah, what are you scared of?" she would ask, and tug gently on one of my braids, bringing her plump face so close to mine that I could see her powder, which was, in accordance with the custom of fashionable colored ladies, several shades lighter than her olive skin. "God isn't anyone to be afraid of," she'd continue, as I looked at her with my best deadpan expression. "He's someone nice, just as nice as your daddy"—I had always suspected Aunt Lily of having a crush on my father—"and he loves you, in the same way your daddy does."

"You would make us all so happy!" I was told at different times by Aunt Lily, Aunt Emma, and Aunt May. The only people who said nothing at all were Mama and Daddy, but I sensed in them a thoughtful suppressed wistfulness that maddened me.

After the hymn, Daddy read aloud a few verses from the third chapter of Luke—verses I recognized in the almost instinctive way in which I was familiar with all of the well-traveled parts of the Old and New Testaments. "Prepare ye the way of the Lord, make his paths straight," he read, in a mild voice. "Every valley shall be filled, and every mountain and hill shall be brought low; and the crooked shall be made straight, and the rough ways shall be made smooth; And all flesh shall see the salvation of God."

He had a habit of pausing to fix his gaze on part of the congregation as he read, and that Sunday he seemed to be talking to a small group of strangers who sat in the front row. These visitors were young white men and women, students from Philadelphia colleges, who for the past year had been coming to hear him talk. It was hard to tell them apart: All the men seemed to have beards, and the women wore their hair long and straight. Their informal clothes stood out in that elaborate assembly, and church members whispered angrily that the young women didn't wear hats. I found the students appealing and rather romantic, with their earnest eyes and timid air of being perpetually sorry about something. It was clear that they had good intentions, and I could not understand why so many of the adults in the congregation seemed to dislike them. After services, they would hover around Daddy. "Never a more beautiful sermon," they would say in low, fervent voices, and sometimes they seemed to have tears in their eyes.

I wasn't impressed by their praise of my father; it was only what everyone said. People called him a champion of civil rights; he gave speeches on the radio, and occasionally he appeared on television. (The first time I'd seen him on Channel 5, I'd been gravely disappointed by the way he looked: The bright lights exaggerated the furrows that ran between his nose and mouth, and his narrow eyes gave him a sinister air; he looked like an Oriental villain in a Saturday-afternoon

A. Diction
Critics have been generous in their praise for Andrea Lee's diction, or word choice. Remind your students that outstanding diction is more than simply figurative language; it can be superb literal language as well. Lee's statement about Aunt Lily and her "fatally overdeveloped air of quaintness" is an example of noteworthy diction. Ask students to identify at least one other example from this paragraph. (Two examples are: "inscribed in her neat, loopy writing" and "an anxious flirtatious air that made me cringe." Students may suggest other suitable examples.)

A. Irony
At age ten, the narrator thought that her father's going to jail in Alabama was a disgrace, but the young white student churchgoers saw it as a mark of distinction. **?** Why do the students view going to jail in Alabama, ironically, as "almost miraculous"? (Reverend Ashley was a nonviolent protester of segregation in the 1960's, one who adhered to the precepts of the Reverend Martin Luther King, Jr. Protesters at the time expected to go to jail; it was part of their plan, and no stigma was attached to being arrested.)

B. Characterization
Reverend Ashley is carefully and lovingly sketched. You might want to ask students to characterize him briefly in their own words. (See question 6, page 976.)

C. Conflict
Although Sarah's father never insists that she be baptized, he clearly would like to have her "listen to" Jesus, heed the call, and trust "the Son of God to set you straight." **?** Why does he not simply require that she be baptized? (Opinions may vary, but perhaps the most reasonable answer is that he truly believes she must hear the call. If she does not hear it, he will not force her to pretend.)

thriller.) During the past year, he'd organized a boycott that integrated the staff of a huge food plant in Philadelphia, and he'd been away several times to attend marches and meetings in the South. I was privately embarrassed to have a parent who freely admitted going to jail in Alabama, but the students who visited New African seemed to think it almost miraculous. Their conversations with my father were peppered with references to places I had never seen, towns I imagined as being swathed in a mist of darkness visible: Selma, Macon, Birmingham, Biloxi.

A

Matthew and I had long ago observed that what Daddy generally did in his sermons was to speak very softly and then surprise everyone with a shout. Of course, I knew that there was more to it than that: Even in those days, I recognized a genius of personality in my father. He loved crowds, handling them with the expert good humor of a man entirely in his element. At church banquets, at the vast annual picnic that was held at a lake in New Jersey, or at any gathering in the back yards and living rooms of the town where we lived, the sound I heard most often was the booming of Daddy's voice followed by shouts of laughter from the people around him. He had a passion for oratory; at home he infuriated Matthew and me by staging absurd debates at the dinner table, verbal melees[6] that he won quite selfishly, with a loud crow of delight at his own virtuosity. "Is a fruit a vegetable?" he would demand. "Is a zipper a machine?" Matthew and I would plead with him to be quiet as we strained to get our points across, but it was no use. When the last word had resounded and we sat looking at him in irritated silence, he would clear his throat, settle his collar, and resume eating, his face still glowing with an irrepressible glee.

B

When he preached, he showed the same private delight: A look of rapt pleasure seemed to broaden and brighten the contours of his angular face until it actually appeared to give off light as he spoke. He could preach in two very different ways. One was the delicate, sonorous idiom of formal oratory, with which he must have won the prizes he held from his seminary days. The second was a hectoring,[7] insinuating, incantatory tone, full of the rhythms of the South he had never lived in, linking him to generations of thunderous Baptist preachers. When he used this tone, as he was doing now, affectionate laughter rippled through the pews.

"I know," he said, looking out over the congregation and blinking his eyes rapidly, "that there are certain people in this room—oh, I don't have to name names or point a finger—who have ignored that small true voice, the voice that is the voice of Jesus calling out in the shadowy depths of the soul. And while you all are looking around and wondering just who those 'certain people' are, I want to tell you a secret: They are you and me and your brother-in-law, and every man, woman, and child here this morning. All of us listen to our bellies when they tell us it is time to eat, we pay attention to our eyes when they grow heavy from wanting sleep, but when it comes to the sacred knowledge our hearts can offer, we are deaf, dumb, blind, and senseless. Throw away that blindness, that deafness, that sulky indifference. When all the world lies to you, Jesus will tell you what is right. Listen to him. Call on him. In these times of confusion, when there are a dozen different ways to turn, and Mama and Papa can't help you, trust Jesus to set you straight. Listen to him. The Son of God has the answers. Call on him. Call on him. Call on him."

The sermon was punctuated with an occasional loud "Amen!" from Miss Middleton, an excitable old lady whose eyes flashed defiantly at the reproving faces of those around her. New African was not the kind of Baptist church where shouting was a normal part of the service; I sometimes heard my father mock the staid congregation by calling it Saint African. Whenever Miss Middleton loosed her tongue (sometimes she went off into fits of rapturous shrieks and had to be helped outside by the church nurse), my mother and aunts exchanged grimaces and shrugged, as if confronted by incomprehensibly barbarous behavior.

When Daddy had spoken the final words of the sermon, he drank a glass of water and vanished through the set of red velvet curtains to the right of the altar. At the same time, the choir began what was described in the church bulletin as a "selection." Selections were arenas for the running dispute between the choir and the choirmaster. Jordan Grimes, the choirmaster, was a Curtis[8]

6. **melees** (mā′lāz): disputes, battles.
7. **hectoring:** bullying.
8. **Curtis:** the Curtis School of Music.

A. Simile

? What makes this simile—"like carvings on a scarab"—especially appropriate? (The narrator says that the creases on Deacon West's brow look deliberate; a carving is deliberate. An Egyptian scarab is very old; Deacon West is very old. Finally, [a fact students are unlikely to know] the Egyptian scarab is a symbol of resurrection, or rebirth, which fits the theme of this story very well.)

B. Interpretation

The narrator says that the prelude to the ceremony of baptism "fascinated and disturbed me more than anything else at church."

? Why might the narrator be so affected by this event? (Opinions will vary. For one thing, she takes baptism very seriously. It awes her, as it does the other children ["they all had solemn expressions of terror on their faces"]. The lights have been dimmed and closed draperies will be drawn back, creating an atmosphere of anticipation and mystery.)

graduate who was partial to Handel, but the choir preferred artistic spirituals performed in the lush, heroic style of Paul Robeson.[9] Grimes had triumphed that Sunday. As the choir gave a spirited but unwilling rendition of Agnus Dei,[10] I saw old Deacon West smile in approval. A veteran of the Spanish-American War, he admitted to being ninety-four but was said to be older; his round yellowish face, otherwise unlined, bore three deliberate-looking horizontal creases on the brow, like carvings on a scarab.[11] "That old man is as flirtatious as a boy of twenty!" my mother often said, watching his stiff, courtly movements among the ladies of the church. Sometimes he gave me a dry kiss and a piece of peppermint after the service; I liked his crackling white collars and smell of bay rum.

The selection ended; Jordan Grimes struck two deep chords on the organ, and the lights in the church went low. A subtle stir ran through the congregation, and I moved closer to my mother. This was the moment that fascinated and disturbed me more than anything else at church: the prelude to the ceremony of baptism. Deacon West rose and drew open the draperies that had been closed around the baptismal pool, and there stood my father in water to his waist.

The choir began to sing:

> We're marching to Zion,
> Beautiful, beautiful Zion;
> We're marching upward to Zion
> The beautiful city of God.

Down the aisle, guided by two church mothers, came a procession of eight children and adolescents. They wore white robes, the girls with white ribbons in their hair, and they all had solemn expressions of terror on their faces. I knew each one of them. There was Billy Price, a big slow-moving boy of thirteen, the son of Deacon Price. There were the Duckery twins. There was Caroline Piggee, whom I hated because of her long black curls, her dimpled pink face, and her lisp that ravished grown-ups. There was Georgie Battis and Sue Anne Ivory, and Wendell and Mabel Cullen.

My mother gave me a nudge. "Run up to the side of the pool!" she whispered. It was the custom for unbaptized children to watch the ceremony from the front of the church. They sat on the knees of the deacons and church mothers, and it was not unusual for a child to volunteer then and there for next month's baptism. I made my way quickly down the dark aisle, feeling the carpet slip under the smooth soles of my patent leather shoes.

When I reached the front pew, I sat down in the bony lap of Bessie Gray, an old woman who often took care of Matthew and me when our parents were away; we called her Aunt Bessie. She was a fanatically devout Christian whose strict ideas on child-rearing had evolved over decades of domestic service to a rich white family in Delaware; the link between us, a mixture of hostility and grudging affection, had been forged in hours of pitched battles over bedtimes and proper behavior. Her worshipful respect for my father, whom she called "the Rev," was only exceeded by her pride—the malice-tinged pride of an omniscient family servant—in her "white children," to whom she often unflatteringly compared Matthew and me. It was easy to see why my mother and her circle of fashionable matrons described Bessie Gray as "archaic"—you had only to look at her black straw hat attached with three enormous old-fashioned pins to her knot of frizzy white hair. Her lean brown-skinned face was dominated by a hawk nose inherited from some Indian ancestor and punctuated by an enormous black mole; her eyes were small, shrewd, and baleful. She talked in ways that were already passing into history and parody, and she wore a thick orange face powder that smelled like dead leaves.

I leaned against her spare bosom and watched the other children clustered near the pool, their bonnets and hair ribbons and round heads outlined in the dim light. For a minute it was very still. Somewhere in the hot, darkened church a baby gave a fretful murmur; from outside came the sound of cars passing in the street. The candidates for baptism, looking stiff and self-conscious, stood lined up on the short stairway leading to the pool, Sue Anne Ivory fiddled with her hair ribbon, and then put her fingers in her mouth.

Daddy spoke the opening phrases of the ceremony: "In the Baptist Church, we do not baptize infants, but believe that a person must choose salvation for himself."

9. **Paul Robeson** (1898–1976): black American actor and singer.
10. **Agnus Dei:** Latin for "Lamb of God." It is sung as part of the Catholic mass and of many Protestant church services.
11. **scarab:** a beetle-shaped religious symbol of the ancient Egyptians.

C. Expansion

The age of the person to be baptized as well as the method of baptism is important to an understanding of this story. In many Christian churches, the narrator would have been baptized as an infant by being sprinkled with a small amount of water. In a Baptist church, on the other hand, the person to be baptized usually is at least an adolescent and may be an adult. Moreover, the Baptists require "total immersion"—that is, the person's entire body must be briefly under water. A large baptismal pool—or, in rural regions, a river or creek—is thus necessary.

A. Allusion
You might want to ask students to explain what they know about John the Baptist. (John the Baptist, a cousin of Jesus, was a notable preacher, famous for baptizing his followers in the Jordan River, in the water of regeneration. John also baptized Jesus. In later years, John the Baptist angered Herodias, the wife of Herod, and at the direct request of Herodias's daughter Salome, John was beheaded.)

B. Symbol
The stuffed dove hanging over the pool has been mentioned before. ? What does it symbolize? (It symbolizes "the Spirit of God," Matthew 3:16, or "the Holy Ghost," Luke 3:22. In the context of this story, it probably does not symbolize peace, since a dove is expressly associated in the Biblical passages above with the baptism of Jesus.)

I didn't listen to the words; what I noticed was the music of the whole—how the big voice darkened and lightened in tone, and how the grand architecture of the Biblical sentences ennobled the voice. The story, of course, was about Jesus, and John the Baptist. One phrase struck me newly each time: "This is my beloved son, in whom I am well pleased!" Daddy sang out those words in a clear, triumphant voice, and the choir echoed him. Ever since I could understand it, this phrase had made me feel melancholy; it seemed to expose a hard knot of disobedience that had always lain within me. When I heard it, I thought enviously of Matthew, for whom life always seemed to be a sedate and ordered affair; he, not I, was a child in whom a father could be well pleased.

Daddy beckoned to Billy Price, the first baptismal candidate in line, and Billy, ungainly in his white robe, descended the flight of steps into the pool. In soft, slow voices, the choir began to sing:

> Wade in the water,
> Wade in the water, children,
> Wade in the water, children.
> God gonna trouble
> The water.

In spite of Jordan Grimes's efforts, the choir swayed like a gospel chorus as it sang this spiritual; the result was to add an eerie jazz beat to the minor chords. The music gave me gooseflesh. Daddy had told me that this was the same song that the slaves had sung long ago in the South, when they gathered to be baptized in rivers and streams. Although I cared little about history, and found it hard to picture the slaves as being any ancestors of mine, I could clearly imagine them coming together beside a broad muddy river that wound away between trees drooping with strange vegetation. They walked silently in lines, their faces very black against their white clothes, leading their children; the whole scene was bathed in the heavy golden light that meant age and solemnity, the same light that seemed to weigh down the Israelites in illustrated volumes of Bible stories, and that shone now from the baptismal pool, giving the ceremony the air of a spectacle staged in a dream.

All attention in the darkened auditorium was now focused on the pool, where between the red curtains my father stood holding Billy Price by the shoulders. Daddy stared into Billy's face, and the boy stared back, his lips set and trembling. "And now, by the power invested in me," said Daddy, "I baptize you in the name of the Father, the Son, and the Holy Ghost." As he pronounced these words, he conveyed a tenderness as efficient and impersonal as a physician's professional manner; beneath it, however, I could see a strong private gladness, the same delight that transformed the contours of his face when he preached a sermon. He paused to flick a drop of water off his forehead, and then, with a single smooth, powerful motion of his arms, he laid Billy Price back into the water as if he were putting an infant to bed. I caught my breath as the boy went backward. When he came up, sputtering, two church mothers helped him out of the pool and through a doorway into a room where he would be dried and dressed. Daddy shook the water from his hands and gave a slight smile as another child entered the pool.

One by one, the baptismal candidates descended the stairs. Sue Anne Ivory began to cry, and had to be comforted. Caroline Piggee blushed and looked up at my father with such a coquettish air that I jealously wondered how he could stand it. After a few baptisms, my attention wandered, and I began to gnaw the edge of my thumb and to peer at the pale faces of the visiting college students. Then I thought about Matthew, who had punched me in the arm that morning and had shouted, "No punchbacks!" I also thought about a collection of horse chestnuts I meant to assemble in the fall, and about two books, one whose subject was adults and divorces, and another, by E. Nesbit, that continued the adventures of the Bastable children.

After Wendell Cullen had left the water (glancing uneasily back at the wet robe trailing behind him), Daddy stood alone among the curtains and the mirrors. The moving reflections from the pool made the stuffed dove hanging over him seem to flutter on its string. "Dear Lord," said Daddy, as Jordan Grimes struck a chord. "Bless these children who have chosen to be baptized in accordance with your teaching, and who have been reborn to carry out your work. In each of them, surely, you are well pleased." He paused, staring out into the darkened auditorium. "And if there is anyone out there—man, woman, child—who wishes to accept Christ today, and to be baptized next month, let him come forward now." He

Closure

Ask students to write two or three sentences explaining how the main conflict in the story is resolved. Encourage them to share their responses with the class.

Reading Check Test

1. The New African Baptist Church is located in a rundown area of New York City. *False*
2. Sarah feels that a person needs only a slight nudge toward religion in order to be baptized. *False*
3. Reverend Ashley directs his sermon toward the white college students in the congregation, but he clearly dislikes the way they dress. *False*
4. Sarah observes the baptism from the front pew of the church. *True*
5. Aunt Bessie relents when Sarah makes it clear that she does not want to be baptized. *False*

glanced around eagerly. "Oh, do come forward and give Christ your heart and give me your hand!"

Just then, Aunt Bessie gave me a little shake and whispered sharply, "Go on up and accept Jesus!"

I stiffened, and dug my bitten fingernails into my palms. The last clash of wills I had had with Aunt Bessie had been when she, crazily set in her old Southern attitudes, had tried to make me wear an enormous straw hat, as her "white children" did, when I played outside in the sun; the old woman had driven me to madness, and I had ended up spanked and sullen, crouching moodily under the dining room table. But this was different, outrageous, none of her business. I shook my head violently, and she took advantage of the darkness in the church to seize both of my shoulders and jounce me with considerable roughness, whispering, "Now, listen, young lady! Your daddy up there is calling you to Christ. Your big brother has already given his soul to the Lord. Now Daddy wants his little girl to step forward."

"No he doesn't." I glanced at the baptismal pool, where my father was clasping the hand of a strange man who had come up to him. I hoped that this would distract Aunt Bessie, but she was tireless.

"Your mama and your Aunt Lily and your Aunt May all want you to answer the call. You're hurting them when you say no to Jesus."

"No I'm not!" I spoke out loud, and I saw the people nearby turn to look at me. At the sound of my voice, Daddy, who was a few yards away, faltered for a minute in what he was saying and glanced over in my direction.

Just then, Aunt Bessie seemed to lose her head. She stood up, pulling me with her, and while I was still frozen in a dreadful paralysis tried to drag me down the aisle toward my father. The two of us began a brief struggle that could not have lasted more than a few seconds but that seemed an endless mortal conflict—my slippery patent leather shoes braced against the floor, my straw hat sliding cockeyed and lodging against one ear, my right arm twisting and twisting in the iron circle of the old woman's grip, my nostrils full of the dead-leaf smell of her powder and black skirts. In an instant, I had wrenched my arm free and darted up the aisle toward Mama, my aunts, and Matthew. As I slipped past the darkened pews, I imagined that I could feel eyes on me and hear whispers. "What'd you do, dummy?" whispered Matthew, tugging on my sash as I reached our pew, but I pushed past him without answering. Although it was hot in the church, my teeth were chattering: It was the first time I had won a battle with a grown-up, and the earth seemed to be about to cave in beneath me. I squeezed in between Mama and Aunt Lily just as the lights came back on in the church. In the baptismal pool, Daddy raised his arms for the last time. "The Lord bless you and keep you," came his big voice. "The Lord be gracious unto you, and give you peace."

What was curious was how uncannily subdued my parents were when they heard of my skirmish with Aunt Bessie. Normally, they were swift to punish Matthew and me for misbehavior in church and breaches in politeness toward adults; this episode combined the two, and smacked of sacrilege besides. Yet once I had made an unwilling apology to the old woman (as I kissed her she shot me such a vengeful look that I realized that forever after it was to be war to the death between the two of us), I was permitted, after we had driven home, to climb up into the green shade of the big maple tree. In those days, more than now, I fell away into a remote dimension whenever I opened a book; that afternoon, as I sat with rings of sunlight and shadow moving over my arms and legs, and winged yellow seeds plopping down onto the pages of "The Story of the Treasure Seekers," I felt a vague uneasiness—a sense of having misplaced something, of being myself misplaced. I was holding myself quite aloof from considering what had happened, as I did with most drastic events, but through the adventures of the Bastables I kept remembering the way my father had looked when he'd heard what happened. He had looked not severe or angry but merely puzzled, and he had regarded me with the same puzzled expression, as if he'd just discovered that I existed and didn't know what to do with me. "What happened, Sairy?" he asked, using an old baby nickname, and I said, "I didn't want to go up there." I hadn't cried at all, and that was another curious thing.

After that Sunday, all pressure on me to accept baptism ceased. I turned twelve, fifteen, then eighteen without being baptized, a fact that scandalized some of the congregation, but my parents, C

A. Climax

What brings about the climax of the story? (When Aunt Bessie says, "Go on up and accept Jesus," she sets off a clash of wills with the narrator. The struggle ends when the narrator breaks away from Aunt Bessie's grip and races to rejoin her family.)

B. Responding

Does this story awaken any memories—of people, places, events, sounds, sights, smells, attitudes? Explain.

C. Resolution

What is the resolution, or denouement, of the story? (All efforts to get the narrator to accept baptism cease. Her parents had not put pressure on her, and after the episode with Aunt Bessie they never say a word about it. Later in her life, the narrator is pleased, because she feels that her father granted her a "peculiar gift of freedom" through his forbearance.)

ANALYZING THE STORY

Identifying Facts

1. It is a hot summer day in 1963 in the New African Baptist Church in Philadelphia.

Students may mention the electric fans, Rev. Ashley's mopping his brow and drinking ice water, and the narrator's wish to put on shorts.

2. She thinks Matthew has a superior attitude now that he has been baptized. She may envy his appearing "proper" in the eyes of the congregation.

3. Sarah is bored and wants to go play in her tree house. She feels claustrophobic in church, and she slouches in the pew. All the same, she clearly admires her father, the pastor.

She refuses because she does not feel the call.

Interpreting Meanings

4. Most students will agree that there is a resolution. She is grateful that her father did not force her to form her religious beliefs when she was a child.

5. She is objecting to having a religion chosen for her.

She feels disoriented because her parents do nothing to punish her for her *(Answers continue in left-hand column.)*

(Continued from top.) "misconduct" in church.

6. He is an inspiring preacher, a social activist, a gifted debater. An extrovert, he is remarkably patient and restrained with his daughter.

7. Among the conflicts are: children *vs.* parents, traditional attitudes *vs.* questioning and independence, and old Southern *vs.* modern urban.

8. The "new" African in the story seems to be the narrator, who challenges many traditional expectations.

9. Sarah feels that pride of place is given to males—her brother Matthew, for example. Aunt Bessie's praise of rich white people and their manners makes Sarah uncomfortable, and she resents the pressure of her relatives to be baptized. Students may suggest that the story is really about a young person's struggle to be loved and to fit in without compromising her integrity.

who openly discussed everything else, never said a word to me. The issue, and the episode that had illuminated it, was surrounded by a clear ring of silence that, for our garrulous[12] family, was something close to supernatural. I continued to go to New African—in fact, continued longer than Matthew, who dropped out abruptly after his freshman year in college. The ambiguousness in my relations with the old church gave me at times an inflated sense of privilege (I saw myself as a romantically isolated religious heroine, a sort of self-made Baptist martyr) and at other times a feeling of loss that I was too proud ever to acknowledge. I never went up to take my father's hand, and he never commented upon this fact to me. It was an odd pact, one that I could never consider in the light of day. It was only much later, after he died, and I left New African forever, that I began to examine the peculiar gift of freedom my father—whose entire soul was in the church, and in his exuberant, bewitching tongue—had granted me through his silence.

12. **garrulous** (gar′ə·ləs): talkative.

Responding to the Story

Analyzing the Story

Identifying Facts

1. Describe the **setting** as it is presented in the opening of the story. What details in the first three paragraphs help you feel the summer heat of the city?
2. In what ways does Sarah feel her brother growing away from her? What passages show that she regards him as more "acceptable" than she is?
3. Find the passages throughout the story that reveal Sarah's conflicting feelings about the church. Why has she refused to go for baptism?

Interpreting Meanings

4. Is there a **resolution** to Sarah's **conflict** by the story's end? Explain.
5. In refusing to be baptized, what do you think Sarah is really objecting to? How would you explain the feeling of being "misplaced," which she experiences at the story's end?
6. From what Sarah says about him, how would you **characterize** her father? What does Sarah mean in the tribute she pays to her father in the story's last sentence?
7. What **conflicts** between generations and cultures do you infer from the story?
8. How does the **title** of the story relate to these conflicts? Who is really the "new" African in the story?
9. This story is presented as a memoir of childhood. Do you think the writer's main purpose is to present a realistic record of a single experience in 1963? Or does she evoke a more profound set of **themes** about being a young black female in 1963? Support your answer with specific references to the story.

Writing About the Story

A Creative Response

1. **Imitating the Writer's Style.** In a paragraph, describe a young person (who might or might not be yourself) who is a member of a large audience attending some function. Imitating Lee's style in the opening paragraphs of this story, tell what this person is wearing, and identify his or her setting. Then tell what this person sees, hears, smells, and what he or she thinks about the setting and audience. Write from the first-person point of view. Before you write, decide what **tone** your narrator will take toward the situation.

A Critical Response

2. **Analyzing Character.** In a brief essay, analyze the character of either Sarah or her father. Consider how character can be revealed by these methods:

   a. By describing appearance
   b. By describing actions
   c. By quoting the character's words and speeches
   d. By showing people's response to the character
   e. By revealing private thoughts and feelings
   f. By direct comment from the writer

3. **Making Generalizations About the Stories.** Think about the stories you have read in this unit and write an essay in which you make some generalizations about the **themes** they reveal and the **subjects** they are based on. Before you write, consider these points:

   a. The use of the family as a subject
   b. The use of generational or cultural conflicts
   c. The use of love as part of the theme

THE AMERICAN LANGUAGE

by Gary Q. Arpin

One day in 1837, Captain Frederick Marryat, a British naval officer visiting the United States, was escorting a young lady in Niagara Falls, New York. She slipped and grazed her shin, and Marryat asked, "Did you hurt your leg much?" What he said seemed to offend her.

"She turned from me," Marryat wrote, "evidently much shocked." Puzzled, he asked her what he had done wrong. The word *leg*, she told him, was never used in the presence of ladies. What word was used for "such articles," the captain asked her. "Her reply," he wrote, "was that the word *limb* was used."

Later, Marryat visited a girls' school, where he saw a piano. He jokingly described it as having four limbs. "However," he went on, "that the ladies who visited their daughters might feel in its full force the extreme delicacy of the mistress of the establishment . . . she had dressed all these four limbs in modest little trousers."

Marryat may have invented those trousers, but he did not invent the delicacy that had caused a leg to become a limb. The year 1837 marked the beginning of the 63-year reign of Queen Victoria in England. One of the meanings of the adjective formed from her name—*Victorian*—is "having excessively severe standards of respectability." The Victorian Age became known for its prudery, an attitude that was as common in some American social circles as it was in England.

During this period in America, the only polite word for women's stockings was *hose*, and undergarments were referred to as *unmentionables*. Even the word *woman* was considered vulgar; *female* and *lady* became its acceptable substitutes.

Victorians were so offended by the names of body parts that they developed a new vocabulary for meals. A chicken or turkey leg became a *drumstick* or a *first joint*; the thigh became the *second joint*; chicken or turkey breast came to be called simply *white meat*.

Euphemisms for Taboo Words

A word or phrase that is substituted for one that is considered offensive or upsetting is called a **euphemism.** (The word comes from two Greek words that mean "good saying.") People use euphemisms in an attempt to hide a reality that they find unpleasant.

Why do certain words become "taboo," or forbidden, while other words with the same meaning are acceptable? There is no simple answer to that, because the role that language plays in our lives is so complex. A

Euphemisms

Drawing by Dana Froden.

"Victorians were so offended by the names of body parts that they developed a new vocabulary for meals. A chicken or turkey leg became a *drumstick* or a *first joint.*"

A. Expansion
Sometimes words that once seemed perfectly acceptable become unpopular almost overnight. When the United States entered World War I in 1917, for example, German words and German place names suddenly seemed unpatriotic. *Sauerkraut* became *liberty cabbage. Brandenburg,* Texas, became *Old Glory. Thalheim,* California, was translated into *Valley Home.* But Germans form a large immigrant group in the United States, and many German names stayed the same. *Kindergarten* and *hamburger* remained, as did *Berlin,* New Hampshire, and *Bismarck,* North Dakota.

A. Words as Symbols

You may want to stress the symbolic nature of language in discussing taboo words. As the text points out, there is nothing inherently good or bad about any word. The relationship of words to things is an arbitrary one. Although this may appear to be an obvious truth, people forget it, and young children do not understand it. A child, when asked if the *moon* could have been called the *sun* and vice versa, may answer, "No, because the sun makes it warm and the moon gives light." Once a word becomes established, emotions attach to it. For example, there are people who avoid using the word *cancer.* They may say "the big C." Although these people realize that *cancer* could have been called *zingdot* or *renster* or *blivery,* in fact it was not, and they wish to avoid speaking of the thing, the affliction, that the word *cancer* represents. So they use a euphemism.

A

One thing is certain, though. There is nothing inherent in any word that makes it good or bad. Words become acceptable or offensive only because people give them those qualities. For example, people learning a foreign language often want to know the forbidden words of that language. They are almost always disappointed when they learn a few of them. To a new speaker of a language, individual words have no "reputation" at all. They are only collections of sounds. They lack the illicit flavor they have for people who have been forbidden to use them.

"Some words become taboo because they refer to experiences we find psychologically overwhelming."

Some words become taboo because they refer to experiences we find psychologically overwhelming. The more terrifying the experience, the more euphemisms we are likely to devise for it. For example, we have dozens of ways of talking about death without using that word. Some of our euphemisms for death are respectful, such as *departed, breathed her last, went to her final reward,* and *met his Maker.* Some are neutral, like *passed on, passed away,* and *deceased.* Others are humorous: *Kicked the bucket, went West,* and *cashed in his chips* are flip ways of reducing the awfulness of death.

Euphemisms and "Civilized Behavior"

"'The essentially English word *bull,*' William Bartlett wrote, 'is refined beyond the mountains . . . into *cow-creature, male-cow,* and even *gentleman-cow!*' "

In some cultures, vulgar language is no more worthy of comment than well-worn clothing. But Americans have been especially prone to euphemisms for a number of reasons. The Puritan founders of the country were concerned with purifying language as well as religious practices. While they did not completely eradicate profanity, they certainly created an atmosphere that was hostile to vulgar speech. The Americans who moved westward, on the other hand, were a profane lot, and the exuberance of frontier speech was often pretty raw. Oddly enough, it was in the pioneer communities that linguistic delicacy was strongest. "The essentially English word *bull,*" William Bartlett wrote, "is refined beyond the mountains . . . into *cow-creature, male-cow,* and even *gentleman-cow*! A friend who resided many years in the West has told me of an incident where a gray-headed man of sixty doffed his hat reverently and apologized to a clergyman for having used inadvertently in his hearing the plain Saxon term [bull]."

The physical frontier was thus also a linguistic frontier of sorts, the place where the vulgar met the civilized. On the one hand, there was the language of those who subdued the land—exuberant, exaggerated, profane. On the other hand, there was the language of delicacy that paid homage to civilization—especially when civilization was represented by preachers and women. With no history to speak of, no centuries of aristocracy to provide standards of behavior, Americans were faced with the task of creating standards at virtually the same time that they were wrestling to create towns and farms out of the wilderness. And at times Americans went overboard as much in the direction of gentility as they did in the direction of exuberance. The result was often an odd mixture of the profane and the overly delicate.

A. Responding
Ask students to look at a map of their state (or of the United States) and find at least five place names that they consider to be examples of anticipatory naming. For example, Columbia Cross Roads, a tiny community in northern Pennsylvania, did not become the hub of the nation that its name suggests.

"The Language of Anticipation"

Another aspect of the need to provide a kind of instant civilization is what historian Daniel Boorstin has called "the language of anticipation." This form of "good speaking" described things as they were to be in the future, rather than as they were at the time. Wealthy City, Kansas, which never fulfilled the promise of its name and dwindled into extinction, is an example of this kind of positive thinking. This linguistic optimism was a common phenomenon in a country where someone confronting a muddy, stump-filled plain might imagine a prosperous farm. As Boorstin points out, even the country's name "the United States of America," which appears in the Constitution, was anticipatory. "It expressed hope that the new nation be *united*, that the components be *states*, and that somehow they could be identified with the whole of *America*." (*State*, until that time, referred only to sovereign nations.)

Examples of this kind of "anticipatory" euphemism abound in American history. Americans needed to talk "big." For instance, *city* was preferred over the more modest (if more accurate) *town*. Many cities boasted an *opera house*, even if it was only a tiny auditorium that presented troupes of traveling jugglers. "The elegant *hotel*," Boorstin writes, "was widely applied to ramshackle, flea-bitten inns and taverns. Americans thought they were not exaggerating but only anticipating—describing things which had not quite yet 'gone through the formality of taking place.' "

It is in this spirit that Pittsburgh described itself in 1817 as "the Birmingham of America." (Birmingham was the center of heavy industry in England.) An English visitor that year wrote that he "expected to have been enveloped in clouds of smoke issuing from a thousand furnaces, and stunned with the din of ten thousand hammers." What he found was a sleepy western town with very big dreams.

> **"Americans needed to talk 'big.' Many cities boasted an 'opera house,' even if it was only a tiny auditorium."**

Euphemisms and Democracy

A love of inflated descriptive terms has a long history in America. Relentlessly democratic, we declared every man a "gentleman," while the British restricted the term to men of a particular social standing. Proud of being a nation with no inherited titles, we almost immediately began to generate countless acquired titles.

A British traveler in New York in 1744 remarked on the great many colonels he encountered. "It is a common saying here," he wrote, "that a man has no right to that dignity unless he has killed a rattlesnake." Governors of states were empowered to bestow that title (along with captain and major) on virtually anyone they wished, and many did so with great zeal.

Americans applied a similar principle to occupations. The word *servant*, with its unpleasant connotations of a class-ridden society, was replaced early in our history by the euphemistic *help* (or *hired help*). Any occupation that was in danger of falling below a certain level of acceptability was usually yanked up by its linguistic boot-

Drawing by Jo Teodorescu.

B. Responding
Point out to your students that builders and developers often try to choose fine-sounding names for their projects. Miller's Swamp becomes Fairview Acres. Apartment buildings take names such as Royal Palm Court and Barchester Arms. Ordinary streets are elevated to boulevards or parkways.
? What are some places in your community whose names are euphemistic in that they are pleasant- or impressive-sounding designations for fairly ordinary sites. Where, for example, do your "sanitation workers" take your "refuse"?

C. Responding
? What are some of the inherited titles in Great Britain? (King, queen, prince, princess, duke, duchess, marquess, earl, viscount, viscountess, baron, baroness)

A. Responding

? What is a shorter, easier word for each of the following Latinate words? Check the dictionary to see if the shorter word is Anglo-Saxon (OE). Some possible answers are shown.

acrimonious (bitter—OE)
homicide (murder—OE)
iniquitous (evil—OE)
velocity (speed—OE)
veracity (truth—OE)

straps. This principle has led to a kind of relentless linguistic upgrading of occupations, especially in the twentieth century. At times, this process is very subtle; at other times, very obvious.

What is the difference, for example, between a *teacher* and an *educator?* Most people would agree that *educator* has a slightly more prestigious ring to it. This can be accounted for by taking a look at where English words came from.

> **"Most people would agree that *educator* has a slightly more prestigious ring to it than *teacher.*"**

Latinate Words and Anglo-Saxon Words

English is composed primarily of Anglo-Saxon and Latin-based words. Historically, the Anglo-Saxon words have been the property of the common people, while the Latinate words have filtered down from the upper classes. This was especially the case after the Norman conquest of England (1066). After that invasion, French was the official language of England for generations. Most people in England, however, continued to speak their own Anglo-Saxon language. During this bilingual period, the language was further enriched with synonyms. In most cases, the Latinate or French word became the genteel word, while the Anglo-Saxon word became the common word. Thus came the difference between the Anglo-Saxon *taecan* (teacher) and the Latin *educare* (educator).

A Latinate words usually have more syllables than Anglo-Saxon words; a greater number of syllables often indicates a slide up the scale of acceptability. A *profession* (Latinate) is somehow more important than a *job* (Anglo-Saxon). American job titles (or "career designations") have undergone frequent upgradings as a result of this tendency toward linguistic respectability. The history of the word *mortician* is an excellent example of this tendency. The first recorded use of *mortician* was in 1895, when the *Embalmer's Monthly* suggested it as a replacement for the less dignified, Anglo-Saxon *undertaker.* (*Undertaker* means "one who undertakes, or contracts, to perform a funeral." It has been in use since the seventeenth century.) Undertakers, seeking a more professional term, linked the Latin word for death, *mors*, to the dignified suffix *-cian* (*physician*) and the new word caught on.

> **"A greater number of syllables often indicates a slide up the scale of respectability."**

Another Latinate word, *professor*, has been applied to a great variety of occupations in America. Every male teacher was called a professor in the nineteenth century, as were band leaders and dancing masters. Professor Harold Hill in the musical comedy *The Music Man* assumed the title in his capacity as a traveling salesman who peddled musical instruments. Of course, the term was also used humorously, especially by journalists, to refer to almost any occupation, from bartenders to baseball players.

Euphemism and Distortion

Euphemisms can demonstrate sensitivity to the feelings of others. But euphemisms can also obscure meaning. Language can provide a veil to hide behind.

A A boss would rather "terminate" an employee than "fire" him, not because it makes the employee feel any better but because it makes the boss feel better. Governments also can hide behind euphemistic language. A government does not like to think of itself as "invading" another country, for example. It will make an *incursion*, or *liberate* the country instead. It is wrong to be the aggressor in a war, and *invasion* is a very aggressive word.

Many people have attacked the bureaucratic tendency to use long Latinate words wherever a short Anglo-Saxon word would serve just as well. One of the most memorable of these attacks is an essay called "Politics and the English Language," written in 1946 by George Orwell. Orwell pointed out that "where there is a gap between one's real and one's declared aims, one turns as it were instinctively to long words and exhausted idioms, like a cuttlefish squirting out ink."

Orwell's examples included words like *pacification* (for attacking defenseless villages), and *elimination of unreliable elements* (for the imprisonment or murder of political opponents). In these kinds of euphemisms, Orwell wrote, "a mass of Latin words falls upon the facts like soft snow, blurring the outlines and covering up all the details."

To parody this tendency, Orwell rewrote a famous passage from the Bible as a modern bureaucrat might phrase it.

> Objective considerations of contemporary phenomena compels the conclusion that success or failure in competitive activities exhibits no tendency to be commensurate with innate capacity, but that a considerable element of the unpredictable must invariably be taken into account.

Here is the original, from Ecclesiastes:

> I returned and saw under the sun, that the race is not to the swift, nor the battle to the strong, neither yet bread to the wise, nor yet riches to men of understanding, nor yet favor to men of skill; but time and chance happeneth to them all.

Drawing by Tom Bloom.

Analyzing Language

1. Look through your local Yellow Pages or some other business directory. Find at least three examples of euphemistic titles for occupations or businesses. What ordinary word is each example replacing?
2. Invent an "upgraded" word or phrase for each of the following: *student, automobile, baby sitter, apartment house.*
3. Write the column titles *Plain* and *Fancy* on your paper. Decide which word in each of the following pairs belongs in each column. Then find each one in a dictionary. Write *L* next to the word if it comes from Latin. Write *AS* if it comes from Anglo-Saxon.

eat/dine	spit/expectorate
love/cherish	cheap/inexpensive
achieve/win	beef/cow
pig/pork	work/career
veal/calf	father/parent

4. Write your own definition of each of the following bureaucratic euphemisms:
   a. armed conflict
   b. unlawful deprivation of life
   c. dependent upon distilled spirits
   d. a controlled-substance abuser

A. Expansion
Some years ago, William H. Whyte, Jr., an editor at *Fortune* Magazine, wrote an article called "The Language of Business." In it he took business executives to task for what he called "businessese"—a uniform, wordy, jargon-filled prose that he accused them of writing. "A businessman," he wrote, "who castigates government bureaucrats, for example, is at the same time apt to be activating, expediting, implementing, effectuating, optimizing, minimizing, maximizing, and finalizing—and at all levels and echelons within the framework of broad policy areas." He concluded that people in business needed "an *awareness* of good English" more than they needed formulas or prescriptions for writing.

Revising Essays
As students revise their essays, refer them to **Grammar, Usage, and Mechanics: A Reference Guide** at the back of their books.

A. Expansion
This assignment asks students to evaluate the ending of one of the ten stories in the unit. It is important that students note a major point given in Background—a writer may deliberately choose not to provide closure on all conflicts, but to leave some of them unresolved. To help students choose a story, you might list the ten stories on the board or give students a list of the authors and titles with spaces left for students to briefly recall and jot down the ending of each story. After choosing the story that most interests them, students can then continue, individually or in small groups, with the notetaking questions in the second column and the directions for organizing the essay.

Exercises in Critical Thinking and Writing

EVALUATING A STORY'S ENDING

Writing Assignment

A Write an essay in which you analyze the ending of one story in this unit. Discuss the various elements that make the story and its ending either effective or not effective, in your opinion.

Background

When you read a story, your mind often jumps ahead of what you are reading, as you try to guess what will happen next. **Predicting outcomes** provides some of the pleasure in reading fiction. The more you read, the more skilled you become at spotting clues worked into the narrative. One reason you continue reading a story is to feel the satisfaction of learning how close you came to predicting the right outcome.

Many modern stories, including some in this unit, do not end with a climax or resolution which gives you a sense of closure. Instead, they end with one or more conflicts unresolved, one or more questions unanswered, or one or more loose ends still untied.

In evaluating a short story, you have to balance your own expectations with the intent of the writer. If a story does not end with a neat, compact solution, it is possible that the writer wanted to leave you with more questions than answers.

Bernard Malamud and O. Henry, for example, both wrote short stories. But the two writers did not have the same view of the world, and their stories reflect the differences. O. Henry's typical surprise endings might cause you to smile as you instantly perceive the "lesson" of his story. Malamud is more likely to leave you with many unanswered questions, as you wonder whether there are any lessons at all to be learned from human experience.

Prewriting

Reread the story you have chosen to write about. As you read the story, try to answer each of the following questions. Write your answers in the form of notes, which you will use later for your essay.

Questions for Evaluating the Ending of a Short Story

1. The first time you read the story, what did you think was going to happen? Were you correct?
2. What was your original response to the ending of the story? Did you find it satisfying or not? Can you explain why?
3. Do you feel the writer cheated you out of a scene he or she had led you to expect?
4. Were there clues in the story that **foreshadowed** its end? Were the clues consistent with the outcome of the story? Did the writer drop any false clues?
5. Does the ending seem logical, given the nature of the characters? Does it seem inevitable? Can you imagine other endings that would be consistent with the rest of the story?
6. How did the ending contribute to the theme of the story? What is that theme?

Writing

Using your notes, prepare your essay. You might follow this plan:

Paragraph 1: Mention the title, the author, and the subject of the story; summarize the story's ending.
Paragraph 2: Explain why you think the ending was or was not logical and inevitable. Did the writer foreshadow the outcome of the story?
Paragraph 3: Evaluate the ending in terms of the theme and characterization. Discuss one or more alternative endings and explain why they would have been more or less satisfying.
Paragraph 4: Discuss your emotional response to the ending of the story.

Revising and Proofreading

To revise and proofread your essay, refer to the guidelines in the section at the back of the book called **Writing About Literature.**

MODERN NONFICTION

A Lawn Sprinkler by David Hockney (1967). Acrylic on canvas. © David Hockney.

UNIT TWELVE

Humanities Connection: Discussing The Fine Art

David Hockney (b. 1937) is a modern British painter who commonly uses the sun-drenched lawns and pools of suburban California as his subjects. As in *A Lawn Sprinkler,* Hockney frequently combines photo-realistic details with nonrealistic elements, such as distortions in perspective or fanciful treatment of selected objects. In this painting, the sprinkler itself receives the special treatment, with the low arcs of water forming complex patterns and larger sheets of water patterned by brush strokes to resemble the wings of a butterfly.

Teaching The Modern Nonfiction Unit

Nonfiction thrived in the United States before there was much fiction to speak of. This unit, coming near the end of the year's work, might be a good place to cast a brief backward glance at some of the earlier nonfiction, to help prepare your students for what is to come. The rich vein of autobiographical writings in American literature proceeds—despite the differences in subject matter—from Benjamin Franklin to Richard Wright. N. Scott Momaday's observations on Native American culture can be compared and contrasted with the observations of white writers of the Colonial period. Michael Herr's reportage from Vietnam is descended from a long and honorable line of wartime writing not only in nonfiction like Whitman's *Specimen Days*, but also in fiction such as Crane's *Red Badge of Courage*. Contemporary essayists who write personally about the natural world, such as Annie Dillard and Lewis Thomas, are the direct literary descendants of Henry David Thoreau.

In the nonfiction of recent decades, there is a brash willingness to place the individual writer's consciousness at the heart of the work, rather than maintaining a stance of objectivity. There is a willingness to try new forms—to mix fiction and nonfiction as Maxine Hong Kingston does, or expository prose and lyrical prose-poems as in the book-length version of *The Way to Rainy Mountain*. In the journalism of Hersey and Herr, there is a strong quality which the earlier writers, at the beginning of a new nation's history, had not had time yet to develop: disillusionment with war. And in the personal odyssey of William Least Heat Moon, we find another quality which, by definition, cannot be found in the infancy of a republic: nostalgia.

Because the contemporary essay is such a personal form, and because it doesn't require the imposition of an artificial structure—a plot—upon its material, it is particularly adaptable to student writing assignments. Then, too, some of your students may already have had experience writing articles for the school newspaper; all of them have had experience writing expository essays. In this unit, more than in other units, they'll have the feeling that in writing about the selections, they are practicing the same skills as the writers themselves: observing, evaluating, criticizing, explaining, and stating their views.

Objectives Of The Modern Nonfiction Unit

1. To expand vocabulary and increase reading proficiency
2. To gain exposure to notable authors and their works
3. To define and identify elements of nonfiction
4. To define and identify significant literary techniques
5. To interpret and respond to nonfiction, orally and in writing, through analysis of its elements
6. To practice the following critical thinking and writing skills
   a. Analyzing an essay
   b. Analyzing style, atmosphere, character, and suspense
   c. Comparing and contrasting two works of literature
   d. Responding to a critical statement
   e. Imitating a writer's technique
   f. Evaluating fact and opinion in nonfiction

SUPPLEMENTARY SUPPORT MATERIALS: UNIT TWELVE

1. Unit Introduction Test (*CCB*)
2. American Language Test (*CCB*)
3. Word Analogies Test (*CCB*)
4. Unit Review Test (*CCB*)
5. Critical Thinking and Writing Test (*CCB*)
6. Instructional Overhead Transparencies

A. Discussing the Quotation
William Zinsser (1922–1979), who pronounced his name zin′zər, was himself a noted writer of nonfiction. Once a staff member of the now-defunct *New York Herald Tribune*, Zinsser later contributed regularly to magazines.

Perhaps one reason writers and teachers of writing feel that they should prefer fiction to nonfiction is that the former is often thought of as "creative" and the latter (by implication, anyway) as "noncreative." As the selections in this unit will show, there can be plenty of creativity in a piece of nonfiction.

You may wish to call students' attention to the curious shifting of metaphors in the quotation, as Zinsser shifts from the image of a royal palace to a temple and back to a palace again.

MODERN NONFICTION

by **Susan Allen Toth** A

. . . nonfiction is the place where much of the best writing of the day is being done. Yet many writers and teachers of writing continue to feel vaguely guilty if they prefer it to fiction—nonfiction is the slightly disreputable younger brother in the royal house of literature. No such guilt is necessary. While the keepers of the temple weren't looking, nonfiction crept in and occupied the throne.

—William Zinsser

Nonfiction's Coming of Age

Until fairly recently, "nonfiction" had a negative connotation. It meant whatever was *not* fiction—suggesting that "nonfiction" was a nonliterary form and a non-art. Nonfiction writers were often lumped together with journalists, who were in turn defined as non-literary folk whose work was quickly done, quickly read, and quickly discarded. Scholars and critics tended to concentrate on the search for the elusive Great American Novel, which was thought to be more important than anything a nonfiction writer could produce. A few literature anthologies included essays; but generations grew up thinking that essayists were dull indeed, for as young schoolchildren they had been forced to study only examples from past centuries whose language and culture they barely understood.

In the last twenty years, however, nonfiction has come into its own. Major front-page reviews now discuss the art (not just the factual content) of books on computers, architecture, geography, history, movies, and other subjects. Bestseller lists, which have always included self-help books, cookbooks, and exercise manuals, now also regularly feature memoirs, biographies, histories, and the same books that fascinate major critics. In the selections that follow, you will read award-winning examples of some of these works.

"Critics are still uncertain about the terminology they should apply to nonfiction."

Nonfiction's Critical Terminology

Critics are still uncertain about the terminology they should apply to nonfiction. For instance, when discussing fiction, we can talk about character, plot, theme, and setting; in more complex fiction, we can analyze different points of view, irony, metaphors, symbols, and levels of meaning. Some of these traditional literary terms can be used with nonfiction, but not consistently.

More troubling is the problem of ascertaining "facts" or "accuracy." No one expects a novel to be "true," although it may be based on verifiable facts. But truth or "accuracy" is often a test applied to nonfiction, with frequently unsatisfactory results. A class in contemporary American literature recently read Peter Matthiessen's *The Snow Leopard*, a travel memoir dealing with, among other things, wildlife in the Himalayas, the writer's understanding of Zen Buddhism, and his search for the meaning of life. The class praised the book for its penetrating observations, its philosophical depth, and its narrative technique. They were then asked if they would like it just as much if they learned that it was fiction, that in fact Matthiessen had never left his New York apartment, that he had done extensive library research but had never gone to the Himalayas at all. (This was, of course, *not* the case.) No, many students said, they would not like the book as well. It would no longer be *true*. Wasn't truth what distinguished nonfiction from fiction?

"Wasn't truth what distinguished nonfiction from fiction?"

The "New Journalism"

This kind of question was often raised in the 1960's when "new journalism" began to appear. Writers like Truman Capote (*In Cold Blood*, 1966); Tom Wolfe (*The Kandy-Kolored Tangerine-Flake Streamline Baby*, 1965; *The Pump House Gang*, 1968; and *The Electric Kool-Aid Acid Test*, 1968); Joan Didion (*Slouching Toward Bethlehem*, 1968); Norman Mailer (*The Armies of the Night,* 1968), and others attracted attention by describing contemporary culture and actual events in strongly individual voices and with many of the devices of fiction: character development, suspense, setting, point of view, symbol, irony, and even "plot." A

No longer did a "new journalist" need to keep personal opinion and his or her presence rigorously out of the writing; in fact, presence and participation were often critical. Joan Didion bought a dress for a defendant in the Charles Manson trial she was covering as a journalist; Truman Capote befriended the murderers he was writing about in a book he called "a nonfiction novel." Readers *wanted* to know just what the writer was thinking or feeling about the subject, and so the *tone* of a book became as important as its facts. When Mary McCarthy wrote *Memories of a Catholic Girlhood* in 1965, she cheerfully admitted that she even sometimes altered or invented facts: "I arranged actual events so as to make a good story out of them," she wrote.

Nonfiction: A Popular Form

If "facts" do not distinguish nonfiction from fiction, what does? No one is exactly sure. What readers *are* sure about is their interest in the growing number of nonfiction books that use the traditional attractions of accomplished fiction writers: people to care about, suspense, compelling use of language. Many readers are disappointed in modern novels. The modern novel has increasingly focused on elaborate stylistic techniques, intellectual games, and absurdist humor. It is understandable that some readers, eager for literature that will illuminate their lives, enrich their knowledge, or provide them with entertainment, have turned to nonfiction instead.

"If 'facts' do not distinguish nonfiction from fiction, what does? No one is exactly sure."

In the world of nonfiction, they find many exciting writers. Some, like Truman Capote, Norman Mailer, Joan Didion, James

A. Expansion
Capote's *In Cold Blood* first appeared in installments in *The New Yorker*, as did *The Snow Leopard* (1978) and *Memories of a Catholic Girlhood*. That magazine devoted an entire issue (August 31, 1946) to *Hiroshima*, John Hersey's account of the bombing of that city and its aftermath. *The New Yorker* consistently publishes nonfiction (as well as fiction and poetry) of the highest quality.

READING CHECK TEST

1. Until recently, nonfiction (a) was unheard of (b) had a negative connotation (c) was highly regarded. *(b)*
2. One problem with nonfiction is (a) ascertaining facts (b) technical language (c) holding the reader's interest. *(a)*
3. Peter Matthiessen wrote a travel book about Tibet (a) without leaving New York (b) that contains philosophical reflections (c) that angered the Chinese government. *(b)*
4. The murderers whose story is told in *In Cold Blood* were (a) captured by Capote (b) helped to escape by Capote (c) befriended by Capote. *(c)*
5. Many readers have turned to nonfiction because (a) they are disappointed in modern novels (b) they want to excel at trivia games (c) truth is stranger than fiction. *(a)*

A. Humanities Connection: Discussing the Photograph
This photograph of E. B. White by Jill Krementz, the highly successful portrait photographer, is a conscious imitation of the paintings of Andrew Wyeth—the open window looking out on the sea, the spare furnishings, and the reflection in the raised windowpane recall features of that artist's work.

B. Responding
? Why do you suppose the nonfiction writing Howard admires differs from that in news magazines? (One possibility is that the nonfiction she admires analyzes facts and events and presents a coherent point of view toward them.)

E. B. White in Maine.

Photograph © 1988 by Jill Krementz.
A

Baldwin, Mary McCarthy, and John Hersey, are also well known as novelists. Others have built reputations primarily with their nonfiction.

One example is E. B. White (see page 987). Many critics and writers consider White one of the finest writers this century has produced. Although he is beloved for his children's stories, he is praised mainly for his mastery of the personal essay.

Within the individual forms of nonfiction, standards of evaluation are evolving, and they are often very high. Reviewing Barry Lopez's book on Arctic landscape and wildlife, *Arctic Dreams* (1986), a critic in the *New York Times Book Review* cited the admirable qualities of other nature writers.

> Conveying this . . . allegiance to life . . . [is] at the heart of nature writing, whether by scientists like Loren Eiseley and Aldo Leopold or rhapsodists like Mr. Lopez and John Muir. It infuses the fine angry essays of Edward Abbey and the lilting meditations of Annie Dillard, the rage of Farley Mowat, and the elegance of E. B. White.
>
> —*The New York Times*

In her introduction to a collection of contemporary American essays, novelist and memoirist Maureen Howard writes:

B

> If I must declare a thesis at all, it is that during a time when the social sciences have dealt us a surfeit of information on our society and ourselves with no solutions, during a time when we have over-dosed on visual images accompanied by meager undernourished texts—the news magazines, the nightly roundup—many of our best American writers have been drawn to the imaginative possibilities of short nonfiction.
>
> —Maureen Howard

William Zinsser agrees:

> My roster of the new literature, in short, would include all the writers who come bearing knowledge and presenting it clearly and making an arrangement of it that constitutes a thoughtful act of writing. In an age when survival is tenuous and events so often outrun our ability to make sense of them, these are important writers.
>
> —William Zinsser

These nonfiction writers are also fun to read. Some you will like better than others, depending on your preference in style and your interest in certain subjects. But any form that encompasses Russell Baker's satirical jabs at modern education (page 1003) and Michael Herr's wildly offbeat but serious reporting of the war in Vietnam (page 1059) has something for the curious and thoughtful reader. The following selections show some of the different and tempting directions in which twentieth-century American nonfiction can take you. You may never catch up with all of it, but you will embark on a fascinating lifetime journey.

E. B. White (1899–1985)

For most of his adult life, E. B. White wrote for the country's most prestigious magazine, *The New Yorker*; he also enchanted several generations with his classic children's books. In spite of these accomplishments, White effectively stayed out of the public eye. When critic Scott Elledge published a biography of White in 1984, one grumpy reviewer commented that White's life was so uninteresting—no scandals, no lurid adventures, no seamy love life—that Elledge had wasted his time.

True, the facts of White's life seem fairly simple. He grew up in a comfortable home in Mount Vernon, New York, attended Cornell University, joined *The New Yorker* in its early days, married Katharine S. Angell, an editor there, and formed an important friendship with humorist James Thurber (see page 594), who also wrote for the magazine. Together, Thurber and White helped to give *The New Yorker* its distinctive tone; they also collaborated on a gentle spoof, *Is Sex Necessary? Or Why You Feel the Way You Do* (1929).

Eventually, the Whites moved permanently to a salt-water farm in Allen Cove, Maine. From this retreat, which forms the background for some of his best work, White continued to write, producing a series of essays for *Harper's* later published under the title *One Man's Meat* (1942), and others collected in *Quo Vadimus* (1939), *The Second Tree from the Corner* (1954), *The Points of My Compass* (1962), and *The Essays of E. B. White* (1977). His letters—themselves witty and stylish essays—were gathered in *The Letters of E. B. White* in 1976 and in *Poems and Sketches* in 1981.

Children, of course, continue to read *Stuart Little* (1945) (Stuart is a mouse), *Charlotte's Web* (1952) (Charlotte is a spider), and *The Trumpet of the Swan* (1970). Students and aspiring writers of all ages create a continuing demand for White's pungent, humorous writing handbook, *The Elements of Style*, which was written by White's teacher, William Strunk, Jr., and edited and revised by White himself. (By 1982, "Strunk and White," as teachers sometimes call it, had sold more than five and a half million copies.)

During his long life, White suffered from a variety of physical and nervous ailments. He disliked public appearances, and in his letters he often mentions his health as a reason for avoiding them. He answered inquiries of all sorts pleasantly and thoughtfully, but he kept some of his deepest fears and feelings to himself. Elledge's biography is respectful and does not attempt to probe those private matters.

The critic who thought White's life "uninteresting" missed the spirit of White's work. He is a dramatist of the commonplace. With an easy, conversational, and luminous style so free of artifice that it defies imitation, White explored the meaning of small details that form the texture of everyday reality. His observation is remarkably acute, and his powers of simple description are awesome. Those observed and reported details, apparently trivial at first, gradually build into issues and themes of deep importance: the meaning of life, beauty, impermanence, fear of death, the power of affection.

All his life, White was concerned about the fate of the earth and the often misguided people who live on it. In 1971, accepting the National Medal for Literature, he wrote:

> Only hope can carry us aloft, can keep us afloat. Only hope, and a certain faith that the incredible structure that has been fashioned by this most strange and ingenious of all the mammals cannot end in ruin and disaster. This faith is a writer's faith, for writing itself is an act of faith, nothing else. And it must be the writer, above all others, who keeps it alive—choked with laughter, or with pain.

Laughter was, in fact, White's steadying companion. His humor, like Thurber's, was grounded in a deep sense of human absurdity, fired by the offbeat surprises and implausibilities in everyday encounters. His humor was also endearing. Because White knew how to laugh—at himself more than at anyone else—his readers feel at home with him and soon find themselves sharing his other emotions as well.

No nonfiction writer who cares about style can afford to ignore E. B. White. He has been praised by contemporary writers as diverse as John Updike and Eudora Welty. Noted critic Benjamin De Mott once wrote:

For Further Reading For The Teacher
E. B. White's letters, further enriched by the commentary of their author and notes by the editor, appear in *The Letters of E. B. White* (Harper & Row, 1971). A photograph of Fred, the officious dachshund, is included.

Supplementary Support Materials
1. Vocabulary Activity Worksheet (*CCB*)
2. Review and Response Worksheet: Style (*CCB*)
3. Language Skills Worksheet: Clauses (*CCB*)
4. Selection Test (*CCB*)

Developing Vocabulary
The following words from the essay are tested in the Selection Test. (See also Vocabulary Activity Worksheet.)

to premeditate	vicariously
farcical	transitory
desultory	to snuffle
corrugated	to feign
ruse	penitence

Preparation
1. **Establishing a Purpose.** Before they begin to read, ask students to read question 5, page 993. Finding out the answer will be their purpose for reading the essay.
2. **Prereading Journal.** Have students write a paragraph describing a time when they or a character in a book or movie took care of an ailing animal. They should describe the special feeling that develops between the "nurse" and the "patient."

A. Hyperbole
? Does White use hyperbole in this paragraph? (Yes. Comparing the raising and butchering of a pig to tragedy is an instance of hyperbole.)

B. Responding
? What is the significance of White's statement that "the loss we felt was not the loss of ham but the loss of pig"? (In the course of nursing the pig, White develops a bond with it, so that he feels an emotional loss at its death.)

What is beyond criticism in a White essay is the music. The man knows all the tunes, all the limited lovely music that a plain English sentence can play. . . . On nearly every page, there are subtleties of rhythm and pace, interweavings of the sonorous and racy rare in most contemporary writing.

—Benjamin De Mott

Readers who claim they "hate essays" have bought White's books, read his letters, and come to feel they have made a friend—and important discoveries about themselves. Perhaps no other twentieth-century writer has done as much to make the essay form accessible, entertaining, and challenging.

DEATH OF A PIG

At the beginning of this essay, White says he "feels driven to account" for the stretch of time when a pig sickened and died on his farm. Something in his tone suggests that more than the death of a farm animal is on his mind. As you read the essay, try to identify the larger topic White is really writing about.

I spent several days and nights in mid-September with an ailing pig, and I feel driven to account for this stretch of time, more particularly since the pig died at last, and I lived, and things might easily have gone the other way round and none left to do the accounting. Even now, so close to the event, I cannot recall the hours sharply and am not ready to say whether death came on the third night or the fourth night. This uncertainty afflicts me with a sense of personal deterioration; if I were in decent health I would know how many nights I had sat up with a pig.

A The scheme of buying a spring pig in blossomtime, feeding it through summer and fall, and butchering it when the solid cold weather arrives is a familiar scheme to me and follows an antique pattern. It is a tragedy enacted on most farms with perfect fidelity to the original script. The murder, being premeditated, is in the first degree but is quick and skillful, and the smoked bacon and ham provide a ceremonial ending whose fitness is seldom questioned.

Once in a while something slips—one of the actors goes up in his lines and the whole performance stumbles and halts. My pig simply failed to show up for a meal. The alarm spread rapidly. The classic outline of the tragedy was lost. I found myself cast suddenly in the role of pig's friend and physician—a farcical character with an enema bag for a prop. I had a presentiment,[1] the very first afternoon, that the play would never regain its balance and that my sympathies were now wholly with the pig. This was slapstick—the sort of dramatic treatment that instantly appealed to my old dachshund, Fred, who joined the vigil, held the bag, and, when all was over, presided at the interment.[2] When we slid the body into the grave, we both were shaken to the core. The loss we felt was not the loss of ham but the loss of pig. He had evidently become precious to me, not that he represented a distant nourishment in a hungry time, but that he had suffered in a suffering world. But I'm running ahead of my story and shall have to go back.

My pigpen is at the bottom of an old orchard below the house. The pigs I have raised have lived in a faded building that once was an icehouse. There is a pleasant yard to move about in, shaded by an apple tree that overhangs the low rail fence. A pig couldn't ask for anything better—or none has, at any rate. The sawdust in the icehouse makes a comfortable bottom in which to root, and a warm bed. This sawdust, however, came under

1. **presentiment:** premonition, foreboding.
2. **interment:** burial.

Portrait of a Pig by Jamie Wyeth (c. 1970). Oil. The Brandywine River Museum, Chadds Ford, Pennsylvania.

suspicion when the pig took sick. One of my neighbors said he thought the pig would have done better on new ground—the same principle that applies in planting potatoes. He said there might be something unhealthy about that sawdust, that he never thought well of sawdust.

It was about four o'clock in the afternoon when I first noticed that there was something wrong with the pig. He failed to appear at the trough for his supper, and when a pig (or a child) refuses supper a chill wave of fear runs through any household, or ice-household. After examining my pig, who was stretched out in the sawdust inside the building, I went to the phone and cranked it four times. Mr. Dameron answered. "What's good for a sick pig?" I asked. (There is never any identification needed on a country phone; the person on the other end knows who is talking by the sound of the voice and by the character of the question.)

"I don't know, I never had a sick pig," said Mr. Dameron, "but I can find out quick enough. You hang up and I'll call Henry."

Mr. Dameron was back on the line again in five minutes. "Henry says roll him over on his back and give him two ounces of castor oil or sweet oil, and if that doesn't do the trick give him an injection of soapy water. He says he's almost sure the pig's plugged up, and even if he's wrong, it can't do any harm."

I thanked Mr. Dameron. I didn't go right down to the pig, though. I sank into a chair and sat still for a few minutes to think about my troubles, and then I got up and went to the barn, catching up on some odds and ends that needed tending to. Unconsciously I held off, for an hour, the deed by which I would officially recognize the collapse of the performance of raising a pig; I wanted no interruption in the regularity of feeding, the steadiness of growth, the even succession of days. I wanted no interruption, wanted no oil, no deviation. I just wanted to keep on raising a pig, full meal after full meal, spring into summer into fall. I didn't even know whether there were two ounces of castor oil on the place. B

A. Responding
? What is the effect of adding "or a child" in parentheses? (The mock-heroic tone of the sentence is emphasized by including this seeming afterthought. If White had written ". . . when a child refuses supper. . .," the sentence would have had no comic effect, save for the word play at the end—*ice-household.*)

B. Expansion
Bringing the philosophical reflections of the three previous sentences to an abrupt halt with this matter-of-fact observation is a typical device of White's.

For Further Reading For The Teacher

Here at The New Yorker by Brendan Gill (Random House, 1975) is a charming account of life on the staff of this distinguished magazine and contains insightful portraits of E. B. White, Thurber, and others.

A. Responding

? Does White really attribute these human thoughts and emotions to the pig? (No. He avoids this through the use of "as though" and "seeming," which have the effect of showing that White is imagining the pig thinking these things as he scratches it.)

B. Expansion

scaling: rising; ascending

C. Theme

Elicit from students that the last clause in this long sentence is a fairly explicit statement of the theme of this essay.

D. Responding

? What is the purpose of bringing Fred, the dachshund, into the essay? (The description of Fred's behavior provides a note of comic relief in what otherwise might have become a lugubrious account.)

Shortly after five o'clock I remembered that we had been invited out to dinner that night and realized that if I were to dose a pig there was no time to lose. The dinner date seemed a familiar conflict: I move in a desultory society and often a week or two will roll by without my going to anybody's house to dinner or anyone's coming to mine, but when an occasion does arise, and I am summoned, something usually turns up (an hour or two in advance) to make all human intercourse seem vastly inappropriate. I have come to believe that there is in hostesses a special power of divination, and that they deliberately arrange dinners to coincide with pig failure or some other sort of failure. At any rate, it was after five o'clock and I knew I could put off no longer the evil hour.

When my son and I arrived at the pigyard, armed with a small bottle of castor oil and a length of clothesline, the pig had emerged from his house and was standing in the middle of his yard, listlessly. He gave us a slim greeting. I could see that he felt uncomfortable and uncertain. I had brought the clothesline thinking I'd have to tie him (the pig weighed more than a hundred pounds), but we never used it. My son reached down, grabbed both front legs, upset him quickly, and when he opened his mouth to scream I turned the oil into his throat—a pink, corrugated area I had never seen before. I had just time to read the label while the neck of the bottle was in his mouth. It said Puretest. The screams, slightly muffled by oil, were pitched in the hysterically high range of pig-sound, as though torture were being carried out, but they didn't last long: It was all over rather suddenly, and, his legs released, the pig righted himself.

In the upset position the corners of his mouth had been turned down, giving him a frowning expression. Back on his feet again, he regained the set smile that a pig wears even in sickness. He stood his ground, sucking slightly at the residue of oil; a few drops leaked out of his lips while his wicked eyes, shaded by their coy little lashes, turned on me in disgust and hatred. I scratched him gently with oily fingers and he remained quiet, as though trying to recall the satisfaction of being scratched when in health, and seeming to rehearse in his mind the indignity to which he had just been subjected. I noticed, as I stood there, four or five small dark spots on his back near the tail end, reddish brown in color, each about the size of a housefly. I could not make out what they were. They did not look troublesome but at the same time they did not look like mere surface bruises or chafe marks. Rather they seemed blemishes of internal origin. His stiff white bristles almost completely hid them and I had to part the bristles with my fingers to get a good look.

Several hours later, a few mintues before midnight, having dined well and at someone else's expense, I returned to the pighouse with a flashlight. The patient was asleep. Kneeling, I felt his ears (as you might put your hand on the forehead of a child) and they seemed cool, and then with the light made a careful examination of the yard and the house for sign that the oil had worked. I found none and went to bed.

We had been having an unseasonable spell of weather—hot, close days, with the fog shutting in every night, scaling for a few hours in midday, then creeping back again at dark, drifting in first over the trees on the point, then suddenly blowing across the fields, blotting out the world and taking possession of houses, men, and animals. Everyone kept hoping for a break, but the break failed to come. Next day was another hot one. I visited the pig before breakfast and tried to tempt him with a little milk in his trough. He just stared at it, while I made a sucking sound through my teeth to remind him of past pleasures of the feast. With very small, timid pigs, weanlings, this ruse is often quite successful and will encourage them to eat; but with a large, sick pig the ruse is senseless and the sound I made must have made him feel, if anything, more miserable. He not only did not crave food, he felt a positive revulsion to it. I found a place under the apple tree where he had vomited in the night.

At this point, although a depression had settled over me, I didn't suppose that I was going to lose my pig. From the lustiness of a healthy pig a man derives a feeling of personal lustiness; the stuff that goes into the trough and is received with such enthusiasm is an earnest[3] of some later feast of his own, and when this suddenly comes to an end and the food lies stale and untouched, souring in the sun, the pig's imbalance becomes the man's, vicariously, and life seems insecure, displaced, transitory.

As my own spirits declined, along with the pig's, the spirits of my vile old dachshund rose. The frequency of our trips down the footpath through

3. **earnest:** a proof, or a sign.

CLOSURE

Direct students' attention to question 5, page 993, once again. Ask volunteers to state the theme and purpose of the essay in their own words.

READING CHECK TEST

1. White's dog Fred held the enema bag. *True*

2. White says he will never forget the third night of the vigil, when the pig died. *False*

3. White was worried about catching a skin disease from the pig. *True*

4. The veterinarian gave the pig an injection to end his misery. *False*

5. The pig's death later became a subject of jokes among White's neighbors. *False*

the orchard to the pigyard delighted him, although he suffers greatly from arthritis, moves with difficulty, and would be bedridden if he could find anyone willing to serve him meals on a tray.

He never missed a chance to visit the pig with me, and he made many professional calls on his own. You could see him down there at all hours, his white face parting the grass along the fence as he wobbled and stumbled about, his stethoscope dangling—a happy quack, writing his villainous prescriptions and grinning his corrosive grin. When the enema bag appeared, and the bucket of warm suds, his happiness was complete, and he managed to squeeze his enormous body between the two lowest rails of the yard and then assumed full charge of the irrigation. Once, when I lowered the bag to check the flow, he reached in and hurriedly drank a few mouthfuls of the suds to test their potency. I have noticed that Fred will feverishly consume any substance that is associated with trouble—the bitter flavor is to his liking. When the bag was above reach, he concentrated on the pig and was everywhere at once, a tower of strength and inconvenience. The pig, curiously enough, stood rather quietly through this colonic[4] carnival, and the enema, though ineffective, was not as difficult as I had anticipated.

I discovered, though, that once having given a pig an enema there is no turning back, no chance of resuming one of life's more stereotyped roles. The pig's lot and mine were inextricably bound now, as though the rubber tube were the silver cord. From then until the time of his death I held the pig steadily in the bowl of my mind; the task of trying to deliver him from his misery became a strong obsession. His suffering soon became the embodiment of all earthly wretchedness. Along toward the end of the afternoon, defeated in physicking, I phoned the veterinary twenty miles away and placed the case formally in his hands. He was full of questions, and when I casually mentioned the dark spots on the pig's back, his voice changed its tone.

"I don't want to scare you," he said, "but when there are spots, erysipelas[5] has to be considered."

Together we considered erysipelas, with frequent interruptions from the telephone operator, who wasn't sure the connection had been established.

"If a pig has erysipelas can he give it to a person?" I asked.

"Yes, he can," replied the vet.

"Have they answered?" asked the operator.

"Yes, they have," I said. Then I addressed the vet again. "You better come over here and examine this pig right away."

"I can't come myself," said the vet, "but McFarland can come this evening if that's all right. Mac knows more about pigs than I do anyway. You needn't worry too much about the spots. To indicate erysipelas they would have to be deep hemorrhagic infarcts."

"Deep hemorrhagic what?" I asked.

"Infarcts," said the vet.

"Have they answered?" asked the operator.

"Well," I said, "I don't know what you'd call these spots, except they're about the size of a housefly. If the pig has erysipelas I guess I have it, too, by this time, because we've been very close lately."

"McFarland will be over," said the vet.

I hung up. My throat felt dry and I went to the cupboard and got a bottle of whiskey. Deep hemorrhagic infarcts—the phrase began fastening its hooks in my head. I had assumed that there could be nothing much wrong with a pig during the months it was being groomed for murder; my confidence in the essential health and endurance of pigs had been strong and deep, particularly in the health of pigs that belonged to me and that were part of my proud scheme. The awakening had been violent, and I minded it all the more because I knew that what could be true of my pig could be true also of the rest of my tidy world. I tried to put this distasteful idea from me, but it kept recurring. I took a short drink of the whiskey and then, although I wanted to go down to the yard and look for fresh signs, I was scared to. I was certain I had erysipelas.

It was long after dark and the supper dishes had been put away when a car drove in and McFarland got out. He had a girl with him. I could just make her out in the darkness—she seemed young and pretty. "This is Miss Owen," he said. "We've been having a picnic supper on the shore, that's why I'm late."

McFarland stood in the driveway and stripped off his jacket, then his shirt. His stocky arms and capable hands showed up in my flashlight's gleam as I helped him find his coverall and get zipped up. The rear seat of his car contained an astonish-

4. **colonic:** having to do with the colon.
5. **erysipelas:** an acute infectious disease of the skin.

A. Metaphor/ Allusion
"Silver cord" is an allusion to Ecclesiastes 12:6 ("Or the silver cord be loosed, or the golden bowl be broken"), where the bowl suspended by the silver cord is a metaphor for life. Here White makes the metaphor do double duty by suggesting that it connects him with the pig, as an umbilical cord connects mother and child. (Notice that the Ecclesiastes metaphor seems to echo in White's mind, as he refers in the next sentence to "the bowl of my mind.")

B. Theme
? Why does White find this illness of the pig so disturbing? (It reminds him that many of the things one takes for granted, including one's own health and life, are uncertain.)

Analyzing the Essay

Identifying Facts

1. White says that things might easily have turned out differently: he might have died and the pig might have lived, and then there would be no one left to write about the story. He also says that he sympathized with the pig, since it suffered in a "suffering world."

White compares the process to a play (a tragedy) with actors—a well-recognized and approved script, in which each participant has his own motives and actions.

2. The narrator suddenly comes to see himself as "cast" in the role of the pig's suffering, and he dreads its death.

White identifies with the pig when he tries to feed it supper and it won't eat; when he sees its pink throat and it screams in pain; when he scratches the pig and feels its ears; when he tends the pig like an ill human patient. The narrator cries when the pig dies and says that he will visit its grave on "flagless memorial days."

Interpreting Meanings

3. Fred is present at the treatments and at the burial of the pig.

A. Concrete Detail

Call students' attention to the way in which this concrete detail creates a vivid image of the sick pig.

B. Responding

? Why does White say he cried "in-tears"? (This coinage alludes to the veterinarian's use of the term "deep hemorrhagic infarct" (which means heavy bleeding affecting an area of tissue that is dead or dying). "Hemorrhagic in-tears" is another instance of hyperbole.)

C. Allusion

The allusion is to *Devotion XVII* of John Donne: ". . . therefore never send to know for whom the bell tolls; it tolls for thee."

ing amount of paraphernalia, which he soon overhauled, selecting a chain, a syringe, a bottle of oil, a rubber tube, and some other things I couldn't identify. Miss Owen said she'd go along with us and see the pig. I led the way down the warm slope of the orchard, my light picking out the path for them, and we all three climbed the fence, entered the pighouse, and squatted by the pig while McFarland took a rectal reading. My flashlight picked up the glitter of an engagement ring on the girl's hand.

"No elevation," said McFarland, twisting the thermometer in the light. "You needn't worry about erysipelas." He ran his hand slowly over the pig's stomach and at one point the pig cried out in pain.

"Poor piggledy-wiggledy!" said Miss Owen.

The treatment I had been giving the pig for two days was then repeated, somewhat more expertly, by the doctor, Miss Owen and I handing him things as he needed them—holding the chain that he had looped around the pig's upper jaw, holding the syringe, holding the bottle stopper, the end of the tube, all of us working in darkness and in comfort, working with the instinctive teamwork induced by emergency conditions, the pig unprotesting, the house shadowy, protecting, intimate. I went to bed tired but with a feeling of relief that I had turned over part of the responsibility of the case to a licensed doctor. I was beginning to think, though, that the pig was not going to live.

He died twenty-four hours later, or it might have been forty-eight—there is a blur in time here, and I may have lost or picked up a day in the telling and the pig one in the dying. At intervals during the last day I took cool fresh water down to him, and at such times as he found the strength to get to his feet he would stand with head in the pail and snuffle his snout around. He drank a few sips but no more; yet it seemed to comfort him to dip his nose in water and bobble it about, sucking in and blowing out through his teeth. Much of the time, now, he lay indoors half buried in sawdust. Once, near the last, while I was attending him I saw him try to make a bed for himself but he lacked the strength, and when he set his snout into the dust he was unable to plow even the little furrow he needed to lie down in.

He came out of the house to die. When I went down, before going to bed, he lay stretched in the yard a few feet from the door. I knelt, saw that he was dead, and left him there: His face had a mild look, expressive neither of deep peace nor of deep suffering, although I think he had suffered a good deal. I went back up to the house and to bed, and cried internally—deep hemorrhagic intears. I didn't wake till nearly eight the next morning, and when I looked out the open window the grave was already being dug, down beyond the dump under a wild apple. I could hear the spade strike against the small rocks that blocked the way. Never send to know for whom the grave is dug, I said to myself, it's dug for thee. Fred, I well knew, was supervising the work of digging, so I ate breakfast slowly.

It was a Saturday morning. The thicket in which I found the gravediggers at work was dark and warm, the sky overcast. Here, among alders and young hackmatacks, at the foot of the apple tree, Lennie had dug a beautiful hole, five feet long, three feet wide, three feet deep. He was standing in it, removing the last spadefuls of earth while Fred patrolled the brink in simple but impressive circles, disturbing the loose earth of the mound so that it trickled back in. There had been no rain in weeks and the soil, even three feet down, was dry and powdery. As I stood and stared, an enormous earthworm which had been partially exposed by the spade at the bottom dug itself deeper and made a slow withdrawal, seeking even remoter moistures at even lonelier depths. And just as Lennie stepped out and rested his spade against the tree and lit a cigarette, a small green apple separated itself from a branch overhead and fell into the hole. Everything about this last scene seemed overwritten—the dismal sky, the shabby woods, the imminence of rain, the worm (legendary bedfellow of the dead), the apple (conventional garnish of a pig).

But even so, there was a directness and dispatch[6] about animal burial, I thought, that made it a more decent affair than human burial: There was no stopover in the undertaker's foul parlor, no wreath nor spray; and when we hitched a line to the pig's hind legs and dragged him swiftly from his yard, throwing our weight into the harness and leaving a wake of crushed grass and smoothed rubble over the dump, ours was a businesslike procession, with Fred, the dishonorable pallbearer, staggering along in the rear, his perverse

6. **dispatch:** speed.

Fred becomes a figure of black humor in the essay—a sort of disturbing, lugubrious presence which contrasts with the sympathetic narrator. Some students may offer the opinion that the rather grotesque portrayal of Fred prevents the essay from becoming mawkish or sentimental.

4. Among such passages are the introduction of Fred as "vile," the description of the dog as making "professional calls," the mention of Fred "supervising" the digging of the grave, the reference to him at the pig's funeral as the "dishonorable pallbearer." At the end of the essay, Fred is said to be able to direct mourners to the pig's grave.

Students will probably agree that White does not really hate his dog. He is amused by the dog's nosiness and curiosity, and a bit annoyed at Fred's evident lack of sympathy for the pig.

5. He seems shaken because the pig's illness and death come to seem like a symbol of unforeseen suffering and death in the human lot.

White calls the incident a "tragedy." He says he mourned the pig's death with "deep hemorrhagic in-tears."

6. Student answers will vary. They might remember the pig. They may learn some things about themselves.

7. White explains his purpose in the first three paragraphs. His purpose might be explained as follows: he wants to record the death of his pig because its circumstances led him to reflect on life in a "suffering world."

8. Students may point to the third paragraph, where White mentions the fact that the pig had become precious to him because it suffered.

9. Student answers will vary. Ask them to defend their responses with logical reasoning and with specific references to the text of the essay.

bereavement showing in every seam in his face; and the post mortem performed handily and swiftly right at the edge of the grave, so that the inwards that had caused the pig's death preceded him into the ground and he lay at last resting squarely on the cause of his own undoing.

I threw in the first shovelful, and then we worked rapidly and without talk, until the job was complete. I picked up the rope, made it fast to Fred's collar (he is a notorious ghoul), and we all three filed back up the path to the house, Fred bringing up the rear and holding back every inch of the way, feigning unusual stiffness. I noticed that although he weighed far less than the pig, he was harder to drag, being possessed of the vital spark.

The news of the death of my pig traveled fast and far, and I received many expressions of sympathy from friends and neighbors, for no one took the event lightly and the premature expiration of a pig is, I soon discovered, a departure which the community marks solemnly on its calendar, a sorrow in which it feels fully involved. I have written this account in penitence and in grief, as a man who failed to raise his pig, and to explain my deviation from the classic course of so many raised pigs. The grave in the woods is unmarked, but Fred can direct the mourner to it unerringly and with immense good will, and I know he and I shall often revisit it, singly and together, in seasons of reflection and despair, on flagless memorial days of our own choosing.

Responding to the Essay

Analyzing the Essay

Identifying Facts

1. Why does the narrator want to write about the pig? In the second paragraph, what comparison does he use to describe the process of raising a pig?
2. How does the narrator come to regard the pig's suffering and death? Find the passage where he identifies with the pig.

Interpreting Meanings

3. How often does Fred the dachshund appear? What is Fred's importance in the essay?
4. Find the passages where Fred is described as if he were human. White refers to his pet as a "vile" dachshund. Does White really dislike Fred? How would you describe his feelings toward his nosy dog?
5. Why were White's feelings about life—its sorrows and uncertainties—shaken by the death of his pig? What examples of **hyperbole** (exaggeration) does he use to illustrate his shaken feelings?
6. Why do you think White and Fred will visit the grave? What will they learn there?
7. Where does White explain his **purpose** in writing this essay? How would you explain this statement of purpose?
8. What passage or sentences would you say are key to this essay and its **theme**?
9. How did you respond to the essay—to its animal and its human characters?

Writing About the Essay

A Creative Response

1. **Imitating White's Technique.** Write a real or imagined recollection of an animal. Give the animal a human personality.

A Critical Response

2. **Analyzing Style.** In an essay, analyze White's essay to show how he creates humor. Before you write, consider how White uses these elements of humor:

   a. Comic metaphors
   b. Comic images
   c. Irony
   d. Exaggeration
   e. Puns

3. **Describing a Character.** In a brief essay, describe the character of Fred the dachshund as White creates it. Describe Fred's appearance, interests, and responses to the pig's problems.
4. **Explaining Allusion.** When, on page 992, White says "Never send to know for whom the grave is dug, . . . it's dug for thee," he is alluding to Meditation 17, written in 1623 by the English poet John Donne. (It is sometimes printed in part and called "No Man Is an Island.") Locate Donne's poem, and in an essay explain (a) why White uses the line at this point in his essay, and (b) what it adds to the essay's themes.

A. Expansion
You may wish to define these "catchwords" for your students.

black hole: a collapsed star, so condensed that neither light nor matter can escape from its gravitational field
quasar: a star-like object extremely distant from earth that emits great amounts of light, radio waves, or both
DNA: basic material in the nucleus of a cell that contains and transmits the genetic code that determines heredity
gene-splicing: deliberate alteration of a piece of DNA to establish a new heredity pattern—a technique of genetic engineering
$E = mc^2$: the mass-energy equation deduced by Einstein. It predicts the amount of energy (E) released when a mass (m) is annihilated. (The *c* stands for the speed of light in empty space.) This theory predicts the conversion of matter to energy that occurs in nuclear reactions.

Lewis Thomas (1913–   )

Scientists and imaginative writers—poets, dramatists, storytellers—were not always thought of as belonging to different groups. For hundreds of years, educated people assumed that they could and *should* master the fundamentals of both the arts and the sciences. Those who studied the "liberal arts" assumed that they could easily learn to grasp the basic principles of how the world was put together. But in the twentieth century, science no longer seems so accessible to even the college-educated reader; as a result, writers have been reluctant to discuss theories their audiences can only dimly understand. How many of us can state, clearly and succinctly, the current state of knowledge in biology? Physics?
A Astronomy? At best, most people may recognize familiar catchwords, such as black hole, quasar, DNA, gene-splicing, $E = mc^2$; but they would be hard-pressed to explain their meaning.

As writers have moved away in ignorance and frustration from discussing science and what its theories imply, they have retreated into the private sphere of life: families, personal relationships, individual careers and problems. In an essay called "Poetry in a Discouraging Time," critic Christopher Clausen discusses what has happened to the art of poetry. "Nearly everyone agrees," he writes, "that poetry in the twentieth century—at least in English-speaking countries—is not so highly honored nor widely read as it once was. Few doubt that the rise of science has had something to do with displacing it as a publicly important vehicle for those truths that people accept as being centrally important."

The separation of science from art has worried scientists as well. C. P. Snow, a British scientist and novelist, described this division of intellectuals into two distinct communities in a famous lecture, "The Two Cultures and the Scientific Revolution," delivered in 1959 at Cambridge University in England. Decrying the increasing gulf separating the two cultures, he proposed educational reforms that might bridge the gap. Snow began a debate that still continues, and variations of his ideas still haunt college and university administrators.

Snow was a rarity in being a scientist who could write for a general audience. If an average reader picks up a professional scientific journal, he or she is unlikely to find it either comprehensible or illuminating, let alone entertaining. Yet many readers hunger to be told something about advances in science; they want to share the excitement they can sense happening there. And as more people realize that technological advances are transforming their lives—and perhaps threatening their existence as a species—they need to know how and why things happen. Otherwise, how can ordinary citizens make informed decisions about the space program, nuclear weapons, pollution control, or genetic engineering?

So when a scientist appears who can write not only clearly, but wittily and profoundly, he or she is eagerly welcomed. It is a select company: Stephen Jay Gould, Roger B. Swain, Isaac Asimov, Carl Sagan, Loren Eiseley, among others. In a slightly different company are a handful of doctors who have written skillfully and movingly about their professional experiences, like surgeons William Nolen and Richard Selzer. Among these scientists who see themselves also as hu-

SUPPLEMENTARY SUPPORT MATERIALS

1. Vocabulary Activity Worksheet (*CCB*)
2. Review and Response Worksheet: Tone (*CCB*)
3. Language Skills Worksheet: Semicolons and Colons (*CCB*)
4. Selection Test (*CCB*)

DEVELOPING VOCABULARY

The following words from the essay are tested in the Selection Test. (See also Vocabulary Activity Worksheet.)

plausible	concave
acronym	to animate
interstellar	to sprout
finite	sentient
suffused	amenities

PREPARATION

ESTABLISHING A PURPOSE. Ask students to consider what we would have to say to intelligent creatures on another planet, if we suddenly discovered their existence. Suggest that they keep this question in mind as they read Thomas's essay about such a possibility.

manists, physician Lewis Thomas has won a pre-eminent place.

Born in New York and educated at Princeton and Harvard, Thomas became a research pathologist. He served as a professor of pediatric research at the University of Minnesota, as dean at New York University-Bellevue Medical Center and at the Yale Medical School, and as president and then chancellor at Memorial Sloan-Kettering Cancer Center in New York.

Thomas's first book, *The Lives of a Cell* (1974), a collection of essays originally published in *The New England Journal of Medicine*, won the National Book Award. Two other collections followed: *The Medusa and the Snail* (1979) and *Late Night Thoughts on Listening to Mahler's Ninth Symphony* (1983). He also published a memoir of his life as a doctor, *The Youngest Science* (1983).

His interest is not merely technical. Thomas is deeply concerned with whether the human race will survive, although he continues to feel hope and optimism. Novelist John Updike wrote that Thomas's "willingness to see possibility where others see only doom is tonic and welcome."

Thomas has written, "There is a deeper need to teach science to those who will be needed for thinking about it, and this means pretty nearly everyone else. . . . And the poets, on whose shoulders the future rests, might, late nights, thinking things over, begin to see some meanings that elude the rest of us." Thomas finds scientific mysteries both exciting and heartening.

A. Expansion
Sciences are sometimes informally classified as "hard" or "soft" on the basis of the degree of precision or accuracy of statements made in them; thus, radioastronomy would be the "hardest" science, and biology relatively less hard. The social sciences are regarded as "soft" sciences.

CETI

Thomas's essays typically combine detailed scientific fact, wit, and a humane theme. In "Ceti," Thomas begins with the relatively common speculation that there may be life on other worlds. His uncommon approach to this possibility is that we ought to consider carefully what our first messages to such life would be. Specialized scientific words are footnoted, but you should examine content clues and word structures to see if you can figure out what these words (and others) mean.

Tau Ceti is a relatively nearby star that sufficiently resembles our sun to make its solar system a plausible candidate for the existence of life. We are, it appears, ready to begin getting in touch with Ceti, and with any other interested celestial body in more remote places, out to the edge. CETI is also, by intention, the acronym of the First International Conference on Communication with Extraterrestrial Intelligence, held in 1972 in Soviet Armenia under the joint sponsorship of the National Academy of Sciences of the United States and the Soviet Academy which involved eminent physicists and astronomers from various countries, most of whom are convinced that the odds for the existence of life elsewhere are very high, with a reasonable probability that there are civilizations, one place or another, with technologic mastery matching or exceeding ours.

On this assumption, the conferees thought it likely that radioastronomy would be the generally accepted mode of interstellar communication, on grounds of speed and economy. They made a formal recommendation that we organize an international cooperative program, with new and immense radio telescopes, to probe the reaches of deep space for electromagnetic signals making sense. Eventually, we would plan to send out messages on our own and receive answers, but at the outset it seems more practical to begin by catching snatches of conversation between others.

So, the highest of all our complex technologies in the hardest of our sciences will soon be engaged, full scale, in what is essentially biologic research—and with some aspects of social science, at that. A

The earth has become, just in the last decade, too small a place. We have the feeling of being

Reading Check Test

1. Scientists are interested in the nearby star Tau Ceti because ______. *it is a plausible candidate for the existence of life*

2. First contact with extraterrestrial species is likely to be made through the medium of ______. *radioastronomy*

3. Two-way conversation with extraterrestrials would be made difficult because ______. *there would be very long pauses between messages*

4. Thomas says that the safest and most attractive message for earthlings to send would be ______. *music*

5. Thomas says that if we sent messages to extraterrestrials about our current affairs, they would become ______ by the time we received a reply. *out of date / embarrassing*

A. Expansion
B. F. Skinner, the noted behaviorist, was famous for his experiments with pigeons. Among other feats, he managed to teach pigeons to knock a Ping-Pong ball back and forth by rewarding and reinforcing those random movements of the pigeons that were conducive to the desired action. The comparison suggests how slow the process is and how much trial and error is involved.

Closure
Have students discuss what the most important things are that we would want to learn about extraterrestrial life.

For Further Reading For Students And Teachers
The Lives of a Cell, the collection of essays from which CETI is taken, provides a fascinating and surprisingly optimistic view of nature and mankind. A paperback edition is available from Bantam (1974).

confined—shut in; it is something like outgrowing a small town in a small county. The views of the dark, pocked surface of Mars, still lifeless to judge from the latest photographs, do not seem to have extended our reach; instead, they bring closer, too close, another unsatisfactory feature of our local environment. The blue noonday sky, cloudless, has lost its old look of immensity. The word is out that the sky is not limitless; it is finite. It is, in truth, only a kind of local roof, a membrane under which we live, luminous but confusingly refractile[1] when suffused with sunlight; we can sense its concave surface a few miles over our heads. We know that it is tough and thick enough so that when hard objects strike it from the outside they burst into flames. The color photographs of the earth are more amazing than anything outside: We live inside a blue chamber, a bubble of air blown by ourselves. The other sky beyond, absolutely black and appalling, is wide-open country, irresistible for exploration.

Here we go, then. An extraterrestrial embryologist, having a close look at us from time to time, would probably conclude that the morphogenesis[2] of the earth is coming along well, with the beginnings of a nervous system and fair-sized ganglions[3] in the form of cities, and now with specialized, dish-shaped sensory organs, miles across, ready to receive stimuli. He may well wonder, however, how we will go about responding. We are evolving
A into the situation of a Skinner pigeon in a Skinner box,[4] peering about in all directions, trying to make connections, probing.

When the first word comes in from outer space, finally, we will probably be used to the idea. We can already provide a quite good explanation for the origin of life, here or elsewhere. Given a moist planet with methane, formaldehyde, ammonia, and some usable minerals, all of which abound, exposed to lightning or ultraviolet irradiation at the right temperature, life might start off almost anywhere. The tricky, unsolved thing is how to get the polymers[5] to arrange in membranes and invent replication.[6] The rest is clear going. If they follow our protocol, it will be anaerobic[7] life at first, then photosynthesis and the first exhalation of oxygen, then respiring life and the great burst of variation, then speciation[8] and, finally, some kind of consciousness. It is easy, in the telling.

I suspect that when we have recovered from the first easy acceptance of signs of life from elsewhere, and finished nodding at each other, and finished smiling, we will be in for shock. We have had it our way, relatively speaking, being unique all these years, and it will be hard to deal with the thought that the whole, infinitely huge, spinning, clocklike apparatus around us is itself animate, and can sprout life whenever the conditions are right. We will respond, beyond doubt, by making connections after the fashion of established life, floating out our filaments, extending pili,[9] but we will end up feeling smaller than ever, as small as a single cell, with a quite new sense of continuity. It will take some getting used to.

The immediate problem, however, is a much more practical, down-to-earth matter, and must be giving insomnia to the CETI participants. Let us assume that there is, indeed, sentient life in one or another part of remote space, and that we will be successful in getting in touch with it. What on earth are we going to talk about? If, as seems likely, it is a hundred or more light years away, there are going to be some very long pauses. The barest amenities, on which we rely for opening conversations—Hello, are you there? from us, followed by Yes, hello, from them—will take two hundred years at least. By the time we have our party we may have forgotten what we had in mind.

We could begin by gambling on the rightness of our technology and just send out news of ourselves, like a mimeographed Christmas letter, but we would have to choose our items carefully, with durability of meaning in mind. Whatever information we provide must still make sense to us two centuries later, and must still seem important, or the conversation will be an embarrassment to all concerned. In two hundred years it is, as we have found, easy to lose the thread.

1. **refractile:** appearing to be or capable of being bent.
2. **morphogenesis:** development of an organism.
3. **ganglions:** masses of nerve cells.
4. **Skinner box:** an enclosure in which small animals are conditioned to obey certain stimuli. The box is named for its inventor, the American psychologist B. F. Skinner.
5. **polymers:** compounds of the same chemical elements.
6. **replication:** duplication; reproduction.
7. **anaerobic:** able to live without air or oxygen.
8. **speciation:** formation of new and different biological species.
9. **pili:** hairlike structures.

ANALYZING THE ESSAY
Identifying Facts
1. CETI is an acronym, referring to a conference on the Communication with Extraterrestrial Intelligence, held in 1972.
2. Participants at an international conference have proposed that radioastronomy offers the best chance of communicating with any life that may exist outside the solar system.
3. Since the target for communication, the relatively nearby star Tau Ceti, is one hundred light years from Earth, answers to the messages sent from Earth will not be received for two centuries after the messages are sent. The time lag will thus make meaningful communication difficult.
4. The author suggests that it would be best to send nonverbal messages at first: he suggests (if technology permits) that the best thing to do would be to beam the music of Bach into space.

Interpreting Meanings
5. Although the essay largely depends on the "assumption" that intelligent life exists outside the solar system, and that such beings would be able to respond to messages from Earth, at the very end Thomas stops us short by suggesting that if we did in fact receive an answer ("Yes, hello"), we might "want to stop there and think . . . for quite a long time." The implication is that such a discovery would deliver a major shock to our sense of uniqueness as the only intelligent, living beings in the universe. The tone is humorous and whimsical.
6. Thomas amplifies his meaning when he says, a little later on, "We could tell the harder truths later." He implies that, although the music of Bach was one of humanity's most glorious creations, there have been others in which we can take considerably less pride.
7. Answers will vary. In general, Thomas points to the fact that humans are fallible and vulnerable.
8. Students will probably agree that it is relatively difficult to categorize the essay, since it contains both rationalist and Romantic elements.
9. Student answers will vary.

Perhaps the safest thing to do at the outset, if technology permits, is to send music. This language may be the best we have for explaining what we are like to others in space, with least ambiguity. I would vote for Bach, all of Bach, streamed out into space, over and over again. We would be bragging, of course, but it is surely excusable for us to put the best possible face on at the beginning of such an acquaintance. We can tell the harder truths later. And, to do ourselves justice, music would give a fairer picture of what we are really like than some of the other things we might be sending, like *Time*, say, or a history of the UN or Presidential speeches. We could send out our science, of course, but just think of the wincing at this end when the polite comments arrive two hundred years from now. Whatever we offer as today's items of liveliest interest are bound to be out of date and irrelevant, maybe even ridiculous. I think we should stick to music.

Perhaps, if the technology can be adapted to it, we should send some paintings. Nothing would better describe what this place is like, to an outsider, than the Cézanne[10] demonstrations that an apple is really part fruit, part earth.

What kinds of questions should we ask? The choices will be hard, and everyone will want his special question first. What are your smallest particles? Did you think yourselves unique? Do you have colds? Have you anything quicker than light? Do you always tell the truth? Do you cry? There is no end to the list.

Perhaps we should wait a while, until we are sure we know what we want to know, before we get down to detailed questions. After all, the main question will be the opener: Hello, are you there? If the reply should turn out to be Yes, hello, we might want to stop there and think about that, for quite a long time.

10. **Cézanne:** Paul Cézanne (1839–1906), French post-Impressionist painter.

Responding to the Essay

Analyzing the Essay

Identifying Facts

1. What does the essay's title refer to?
2. What technique has recently been proposed for human communication with life outside the solar system?
3. What practical problem will have to be faced by the CETI participants in such communication?
4. How does Thomas suggest that this problem could be solved?

Interpreting Meanings

5. In what kind of **tone** does Thomas close the essay?
6. When Thomas says we should beam Bach into outer space, he adds, "We would be bragging, of course." What does he mean?
7. What different aspects of our humanity does Thomas suggest in the questions he thinks we might ask, such as "Do you always tell the truth? Do you cry?" What do these questions reveal about our nature?
8. Think of the other essayists you have read: Franklin, Emerson, and Thoreau, for example. Would you describe Thomas as a rationalist, like Franklin, or as a Romantic idealist, like Emerson and Thoreau? Or is it impossible to categorize this essay?
9. Would you take issue with any of Thomas's points in this essay?

Writing About the Essay

A Creative Response

1. **Expressing Your Point of View.** Suppose you had to formulate the questions we might ask of sentient life in another part of remote space. In one paragraph, write out the questions you would ask. In a second paragraph, explain what "news of ourselves" you would send: Music? Newspapers? Technological contraptions? Art? In a third paragraph, tell what "harder truths" we might have to tell these beings later.

A Critical Response

2. **Evaluating the Essay.** Suppose this were a chapter in a high-school science textbook. How would you evaluate it? What is its main topic? What does it "teach"? Write out your evaluation in a paragraph.

For Further Reading For Students And Teachers
Growing Up (Signet, 1984) Baker's autobiography, reveals a sensitivity and emotional depth not evident from his columns alone. If time permits, you may wish to read aloud to your class a sample from this touching and funny book. Chapter 2, in which Baker recounts his failures as a magazine salesman and his decision to escape the world of work by becoming a writer is short and provides a charming supplement to the short pieces in this unit. It is included in *Elements of Literature, Fourth Course*.

Russell Baker (1925–)

Russell Baker is usually classified as a "humorist," but such a label is far too limiting. In his regular column written for the *New York Times* since 1962, Baker has commented on human foibles and follies, sometimes lightly, sometimes with seriousness, but almost always with a wit that provides a lesson. In "School vs. Education," reprinted here, Baker's attack on the American educational system is sharpened, rather than softened, by the humor of his exaggerations. "Little Red Riding Hood Revisited," has an entirely different target—the deterioration of the English language. Yet Baker can write a column with equal zest about the quality of the food he and his wife find at a truckstop. He observes whatever is going on around him, and American eating habits sometimes interest him as much as the philosophical basis of education.

Writing a column for more than twenty-five years requires not only stamina, but also irrepressible curiosity and unflagging interest in the details and happenings of daily life. Henry James once remarked that a writer should be someone "on whom nothing is lost." He probably meant that a writer watches, listens, picks up vibrations, sees the significance of small details, and interprets the meaning of events no one else notices. Russell Baker has these gifts. Critic R. Z. Sheppard has described how he uses them: "At his best, Baker fills his allotted space opposite the editorial page with bizarre, often bleak fantasies about human foolishness. At his second best, he holds a funhouse mirror up to the nature of the consumer state."

Baker has told the story of his childhood during the Great Depression in a best-selling autobiography, *Growing Up*. The book is a poignant, sometimes ambivalent tribute to the resilience and toughness of his mother, who was widowed when Russell was only five.

Baker casually describes his seventh-grade decision to become a writer. After he failed dismally as a magazine salesman, his mother saw an "A" on his seventh-grade composition on "my summer vacation." She immediately suggested that perhaps he could be a writer:

> I clasped the idea to my heart. I had never met a writer, had shown no previous urge to write, and hadn't a notion of how to become a writer, but I loved stories and thought that making up stories must surely be almost as much fun as reading them. Best of all, though, and what really gladdened my heart, was the ease of a writer's life. Writers did not have to trudge through the town peddling from canvas bags, defending themselves against angry dogs, being rejected by surly strangers. Writers did not have to ring doorbells. So far as I could make out, what writers did couldn't even be classified as work.

Born in Virginia, Baker remained an Easterner. He graduated from Johns Hopkins University in Baltimore in 1947, joined the staff of the *Baltimore Sun*, and for the first two years covered a news beat. He didn't write a word himself, but phoned in his information to "rewrite" editors. He says:

> I spent those years prowling the slums of Baltimore, studying the psychology of cops, watching people's homes burn, deciphering semiliterate police reports of dented fenders and suicides, and hanging around accident wards listening to people die. One night, sit-

Supplementary Support Materials
1. Vocabulary Activity Worksheet (*CCB*)
2. Review and Response Worksheet: Satire (*CCB*)
3. Selection Test (*CCB*)

Developing Vocabulary
The following words from the essay are tested in the Selection Test. (See also Vocabulary Activity Worksheet.)

accessible	to masticate
indeterminate	propriety
incursion	aperture
to ascertain	

Preparation
Establishing a Purpose. Tell students that in this piece Russell Baker pokes fun at a number of different users of jargon. Have them try to identify these various targets as they read the selection.

ting in a West Baltimore police station, patiently hating a skinny little clerk but forcing a smile nevertheless as he described for the hundredth time the pleasures he derived from attending hangings, I saw a cop come in with his ear in one hand and the man who had bitten it off gripped firmly in the other.

Baker is seldom grim or intense for long, however. He turns his phrases so that recognition arrives with laughter, and sometimes he writes a column that sounds as if he is simply enjoying his own exuberance. This essentially good-tempered point of view may be necessary for the sanity and long-term success of a newspaper columnist.

Not all humorists share that attitude, of course. Essayist Fran Leibowitz, whose sharp, biting humor has won her an admiring following, was once quoted as saying that all humor is basically abrasive and negative. But, she continued, if you disparage the mass audience, you have no readers, so that's one of the reasons there's not much good humor on the market today. The other reason for the lack of humor in books today, according to the ascerbic Leibowitz, is that "people are morons."

As his essay "Little Red Riding Hood Revisited" shows, Baker is not afraid to "disparage" a mass audience. Nor does he believe, as "School vs. Education" shows, that people are morons.

LITTLE RED RIDING HOOD REVISITED

As the British writer George Orwell pointed out in a famous essay he wrote in the 1940's, the use of language to confuse or suppress critical thinking has emerged as one of the fundamental dangers of our century. Orwell drew his examples from politics. Here, Russell Baker uses a familiar folk tale to satirize jargon, overinflated rhetoric, and other abuses of language in our time. See how many different types of abuses you can recognize in "the modern American language," as Baker presents it. What tone does Baker set in his very first sentence?

In an effort to make the classics accessible to contemporary readers, I am translating them into the modern American language. Here is the translation of *Little Red Riding Hood:*

Once upon a point in time, a small person named Little Red Riding Hood initiated plans for the preparation, delivery, and transportation of foodstuffs to her grandmother, a senior citizen residing at a place of residence in a wooded area of indeterminate dimension.

In the process of implementing this program, her incursion into the area was in mid-transportation process when it attained interface with an alleged perpetrator. This individual, a wolf, made inquiry as to the whereabouts of Little Red Riding Hood's goal, as well as inferring that he was desirous of ascertaining the contents of Little Red Riding Hood's foodstuffs basket, and all that.

"It would be inappropriate to lie to me," the wolf said, displaying his huge jaw capability. Sensing that he was a mass of repressed hostility intertwined with acute alienation, she indicated. C

"I see you indicating," the wolf said, "but what I don't see is whatever it is you're indicating at, you dig?"

Little Red Riding Hood indicated more fully, making one thing perfectly clear—to wit, that it was to her grandmother's residence and with a consignment of foodstuffs that her mission consisted of taking her to and with.

At this point in time the wolf moderated his rhetoric and proceeded to grandmother's resi-

A. Jargon
? At whom is Baker poking fun in this paragraph? Who says "point in time" when *time* alone would do? (Bureaucrats and politicians; the expression "point in time" became famous during the Watergate hearings of 1973.)

B. Jargon
? Bureaucratese continues in this paragraph, but what group of people are most likely to say "alleged perpetrator"? (Journalists)

C. Jargon
? What group do you think is most likely to talk about "hostility" and "alienation"? (Psychiatrists and psychologists)

CLOSURE

Using question 5 on page 1001 as a guide, have volunteers identify passages satirizing the jargon of each of these fields.

READING CHECK TEST

1. The wolf is "a mass of repressed hostility intertwined with acute alienation." *True*
2. Little Red Riding Hood carries "a consignment of foodstuffs." *True*
3. Little Red Riding Hood says, "Grandmother, your ocular implements are of an extraordinary order of magnitude." *True*
4. Grandma is put in a television commercial for a headache remedy. *False*
5. The ingestion of one grandmother exceeds the wolf's recommended cholesterol intake. *True*

A. Humanities Connection: Discussing the Engraving
Gustave Doré (1832–1883) was a highly successful French illustrator, engraver, and painter. He excelled at depicting weird or highly dramatic scenes like this one. Note the attention to such minute details as the snuff falling from the box, the shadow made by the falling eyeglasses, and the intricate patterns of the wolf's pelt. Doré's most famous illustrations are probably those for Dante's *Divine Comedy* and the Bible.

B. Euphemism
? What is this sentence really saying? (That the grandmother was eaten up)

C. Expansion
Then-President Jimmy Carter made the expression "national malaise" familiar in a speech in 1978.

A

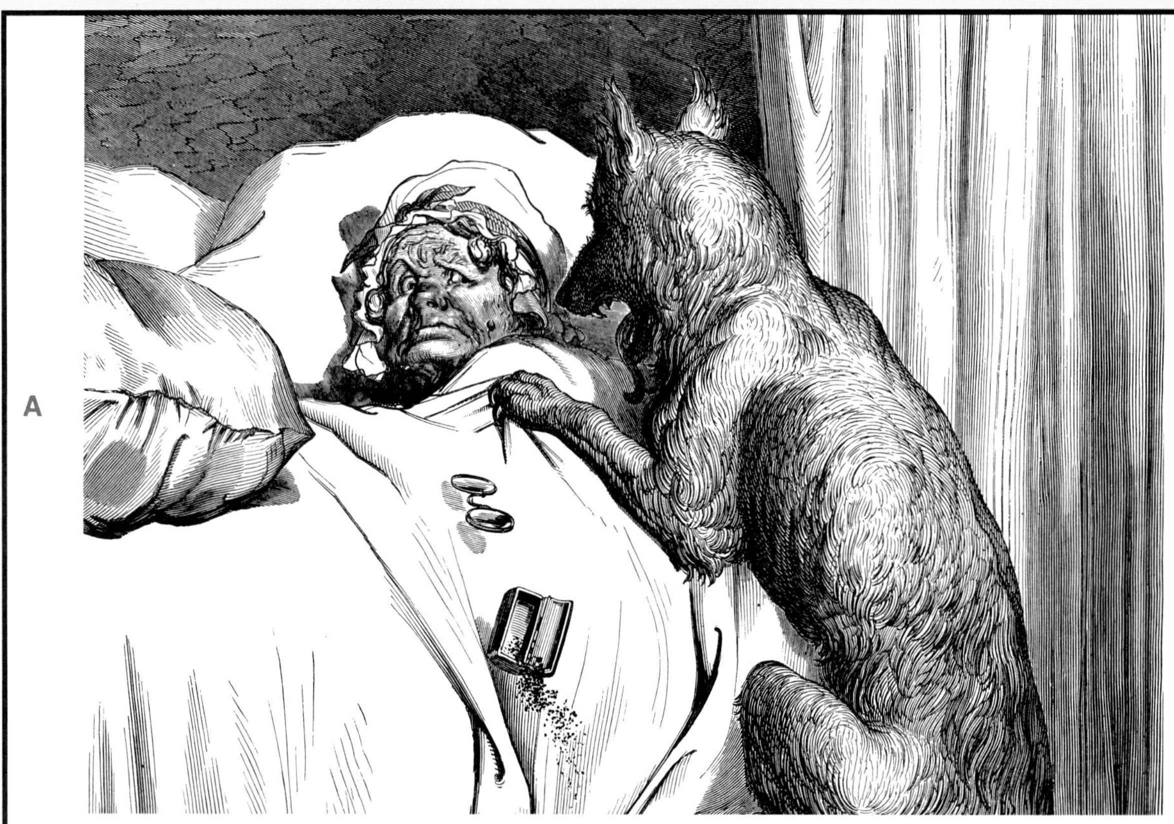

Little Red Riding Hood by Gustave Doré (late 19th century). Engraving.

B dence. The elderly person was then subjected to the disadvantages of total consumption and transferred to residence in the perpetrator's stomach.

"That will raise the old woman's consciousness," the wolf said to himself. He was not a bad wolf, but only a victim of an oppressive society, a society that not only denied wolves' rights, but actually boasted of its capacity for keeping the wolf from the door. An interior malaise made itself manifest inside the wolf.

C "Is that the national malaise I sense within my digestive tract?" wondered the wolf. "Or is it the old person seeking to retaliate for her consumption by telling wolf jokes to my duodenum?" It was time to make a judgment. The time was now, the hour had struck, the body lupine cried out for decision. The wolf was up to the challenge. He took two stomach powders right away and got into bed.

The wolf had adopted the abdominal distress recovery posture when Little Red Riding Hood achieved his presence.

"Grandmother," she said, "your ocular implements are of an extraordinary order of magnitude."

"The purpose of this enlarged viewing capability," said the wolf, "is to enable your image to register a more precise impression upon my sight systems."

"In reference to your ears," said Little Red Riding Hood, "it is noted with the deepest respect that far from being underprivileged, their elongation and enlargement appear to qualify you for unparalleled distinction."

"I hear you loud and clear, kid," said the wolf, "but what about these new choppers?"

"If it is not inappropriate," said Little Red Riding Hood, "it might be observed that with your new miracle masticating products you may even be able to chew taffy again."

This observation was followed by the adoption of an aggressive posture on the part of the wolf and the assertion that it was also possible for him, due to the high efficiency ratio of his jaw, to consume little persons, plus, as he stated, his firm determination to do so at once without delay and with all due process and propriety, not withstanding the fact that the ingestion of one entire grandmother had already provided twice his daily recommended cholesterol intake.

ANALYZING THE ESSAY
Identifying Facts
1. He says that he is making the classics more accessible to modern readers by translating them into contemporary language.

Interpreting Meanings
2. Students may claim they recognized the irony as early as Baker's first sentence, with the use of the words "translating" and "modern American language." For most students, the irony will have been apparent by the end of the second paragraph.
3. Students will have various answers. Examples of slang include "you dig," "I hear you loud and clear, kid," "new choppers." Examples of jargon include: "daily recommended cholesterol intake," "attained interface with an alleged perpetrator," "a mass of repressed hostility intertwined with acute alienation," "sight systems," "miracle masticating products." Examples of pleonasm: "residing at a place of residence," "and all that," "her mission consisted of taking her to and with," "the time was now, the hour had struck." Students will have various opinions on the inappropriateness of each example. In general, by deliberately including these misuses of language, Baker violates the principles of clarity and coherence in writing, and he amusingly combines levels of language that are ordinarily kept separate.
4. Among the euphemisms students may mention in the essay are the following: "senior citizen" (for "old woman"), "alleged perpetrator" (for "criminal"), "repressed hostility" (for "hatred"), and "stomach discontent" (for "indigestion").
5. He takes aim at anyone in any field who uses gobbledegook instead of lucid English. Unfortunately, the list is long. The students should be able to illustrate barbs at each of the fields mentioned with numerous phrases in the essay.

There ensued flight by Little Red Riding Hood accompanied by pursuit in respect to the wolf and a subsequent intervention on the part of a third party, heretofore unnoted in the record.

Due to the firmness of the intervention, the wolf's stomach underwent ax-assisted aperture with the result that Little Red Riding Hood's grandmother was enabled to be removed with only minor discomfort.

The wolf's indigestion was immediately alleviated with such effectiveness that he signed a contract with the intervening third party to perform with grandmother in a television commercial demonstrating the swiftness of this dramatic relief for stomach discontent.

"I'm going to be on television," cried grandmother.

And they all joined her happily in crying, "What a phenomena!"

Responding to the Essay

Analyzing the Essay

Identifying Facts

1. In the first paragraph, how does the writer state his purpose?

Interpreting Meanings

2. When was it first clear to you that the statement of purpose was **ironic**?
3. Baker finds several *kinds* of language misuse to mock in this updated fairy tale. Identify at least one example each of word error, **slang, jargon,** and **pleonasm** (redundancy, or the use of more words than is necessary for the expression of an idea). How could each passage be stated in plain speech?
4. The "modern American language" that Baker mocks here is often guilty of using words to obscure unpleasant reality. This use of a word or phrase that is less offensive than another is called **euphemism;** an example is the use of the phrase *passed away* instead of the more straightforward verb *died*. What euphemisms can you find in this story? What unpleasant reality is each attempting to hide?
5. Who or what are Baker's real targets in this **satire**? (Can you find barbs aimed at the fields of politics, sociology, medicine, law, and psychology?)

Writing About the Essay

A Creative Response

Imitating Baker's Technique. Continue Baker's put-down of contemporary slang, jargon, verbosity, and euphemism by retelling another fairy tale in the "modern American language."

Analyzing Language and Style

Jargon

The abuse of language that Baker satirizes most vehemently in "Little Red Riding Hood Revisited" is jargon.

The term **jargon** has several meanings. On the one hand, it is the specialized, technical language used by people who work in a particular field or share a common interest. Computer users, for example, use the term *bytes* to refer to quantities of information that have been encoded electronically; sailors use the terms *port* and *starboard* to refer to left and right; basketball players talk of *picks* and *sky hooks*. There is nothing wrong with this kind of jargon used in its place: It serves as a useful shorthand among people who share technical knowledge.

The other kind of **jargon** is cumbersome, verbose language (often including **clichés**) which obscures, rather than clarifies, meaning. It is this second kind of jargon that Baker attacks. If you have ever had to "translate" the directions for setting a digital watch, or for filling out a tax return, or for completing an application for employment, you might have encountered this kind of jargon. Here is the first sentence of Baker's third paragraph. Note the phrases in italics:

"In the process of *implementing this program*, her *incursion into the area* was in *mid-transportation process* when it *attained interface* with an *alleged perpetrator*."

We could label these phrases as jargon used in politics, military, communications, computer science, and law enforcement. In a folk tale intended for an audience of young children they become laughable.

1. Rewrite three paragraphs of Baker's "translation" of this folk tale, eliminating the jargon. Make the paragraphs read as simply and naturally as you can.
2. In a dictionary, look up the derivation of the word *jargon*. How is the origin of the word appropriate?

Supplementary Support Materials

1. Vocabulary Activity Worksheet (*CCB*)
2. Review and Response Worksheet: Hyperbole (*CCB*)
3. Language Skills Worksheet: Parallel Structure (*CCB*)
4. Selection Test (*CCB*)

Developing Vocabulary

The following words from the essay are tested in the Selection Test. (See also Vocabulary Activity Worksheet.)

cohesion incentive
pigmentation

Preparation

Establishing A Purpose. Before they start to read, have students reflect on the possible meanings of the title. Suggest that as they read, they try to determine Baker's single most important criticism of modern education from kindergarten through twelfth grade.

A. Responding

? Baker uses hyperbole, or exaggeration, in discussing what children learn from television.

Do you believe that television is a bad influence on young children? on adults? (Urge students to answer without referring to "educational" shows.)

B. Responding

? Baker seems to believe that the threat of being kept back would motivate children to try harder. Do you agree, or is this an instance of oversimplification?

Closure

Point out that Baker raises serious problems—excessive reliance on testing, labeling students as slow or smart, and overemphasis on getting into college. He oversimplifies greatly for comic effect. Have students discuss whether this oversimplification helps people to understand a problem or makes them want to try to solve it. (Students, as the afflicted group, may favor Baker's approach and may be more moved to action than adults.)

SCHOOL VS. EDUCATION

Baker often begins his humorous essays with a premise, or assumption, that seems perfectly serious. In the first paragraph of "School vs. Education," for example, it seems as if he is promising us a serious survey of the skills that children have mastered at the age of six. But the second paragraph begins to make clear that Baker has used the word "skills" ironically. Before you read, discuss the title: Is there a difference between "school" and "education"?

By the age of six the average child will have completed the basic American education and be ready to enter school. If the child has been attentive in these preschool years, he or she will already have mastered many skills.

A From television, the child will have learned how to pick a lock, commit a fairly elaborate bank holdup, prevent wetness all day long, get the laundry twice as white, and kill people with a variety of sophisticated armaments.

From watching his parents, the child, in many cases, will already know how to smoke, how much soda to mix with whiskey, what kind of language to use when angry, and how to violate the speed laws without being caught.

At this point, the child is ready for the second stage of education, which occurs in school. There, a variety of lessons may be learned in the very first days.

The teacher may illustrate the economic importance of belonging to a strong union by closing down the school before the child arrives. Fathers and mothers may demonstrate to the child the social cohesion that can be built on shared hatred by demonstrating their dislike for children whose pigmentation displeases them. In the latter event, the child may receive visual instruction in techniques of stoning buses, cracking skulls with a nightstick, and subduing mobs with tear gas. Formal education has begun.

During formal education, the child learns that life is for testing. This stage lasts twelve years, a period during which the child learns that success comes from telling testers what they want to hear.

Early in this stage, the child learns that he is either dumb or smart. If the teacher puts intelligent demands upon the child, the child learns he is smart. If the teacher expects little of the child, the child learns he is dumb and soon quits bothering to tell the testers what they want to hear.

At this point, education becomes more subtle. The child taught by school that he is dumb observes that neither he, she, nor any of the many children who are even dumber, ever fails to be promoted to the next grade. From this, the child learns that while everybody talks a lot about the virtue of being smart, there is very little incentive to stop being dumb.

What is the point of school, besides attendance? the child wonders. As the end of the first formal stage of education approaches, school answers this question. The point is to equip the child to enter college.

Children who have been taught they are smart have no difficulty. They have been happily telling testers what they want to hear for twelve years. Being artists at telling testers what they want to hear, they are admitted to college joyously, where they promptly learn that they are the hope of America.

Children whose education has been limited to adjusting themselves to their schools' low estimates of them are admitted to less joyous colleges which, in some cases, may teach them to read.

At this stage of education, a fresh question arises for everyone. If the point of lower education was to get into college, what is the point of college? The answer is soon learned. The point of college is to prepare the student—no longer a child now—to get into graduate school. In college, the student learns that it is no longer enough simply to tell the testers what they want to hear. Many are tested for graduate school; few are admitted.

Those excluded may be denied valuable certificates to prosper in medicine, at the bar, in the corporate boardroom. The student learns that the

READING CHECK TEST

1. During the first six years of life a child learns most from ______. *watching its parents / watching television*
2. During formal education a student learns that life is for ______. *testing*
3. The point of school is to equip the child for ______. *college*
4. The point of college is to equip the student for ______. *graduate school*
5. After the former students have attained worldly success, they may one day have the leisure and inclination to ______. *read books*

ANALYZING THE ESSAY
Identifying Facts
1. To equip children to enter college.
To enter graduate school.
Graduate school provides students with "valuable certificates to prosper in medicine, at the bar, and in the corporate boardroom."

race is to the cunning and often, alas, to the unprincipled.

Thus, the student learns the importance of destroying competitors and emerges richly prepared to play his role in the great simmering melodrama of American life.

Afterward, the former student's destiny fulfilled, his life rich with Oriental carpets, rare porcelain, and full bank accounts, he may one day find himself with the leisure and the inclination to open a book with a curious mind, and start to become educated.

Interpreting Meanings
2. Skills include picking a lock, robbing a bank, getting the laundry twice as white, and waging war.
He implies that our society is violent and overly commercial.
Answers will vary. Encourage students to support their opinions.
3. For examples see the opening paragraphs on the "skills" learned by preschoolers.
Answers will vary. These points *have* been made in more serious essays. Baker's essay may be remembered longer.
4. The title implies that school and education are antithetical concepts.
The message is that schools are bureaucracies that exist more for the sake of existing than for teaching.
5. To open a book with a curious mind.
Answers will vary. Encourage students to support their opinions.

Responding to the Essay

Analyzing the Essay

Identifying Facts

1. What does Baker claim is "the point" of lower education in America? Of higher education? Of graduate school?

Interpreting Meanings

2. Baker remarks **satirically** on the so-called "skills" a preschooler receives. What are these skills, and what do they say about the society in which the child is growing up? Do you agree with Baker's points? Why or why not?
3. Much of Baker's humor derives from his gift for **hyperbole**, or exaggeration for effect. What are some examples of comic hyperbole in this essay? Do you think these points would be more effectively made in a serious essay? Why or why not?
4. What is the significance of the essay's title? How would you state Baker's main **theme**, or message?
5. According to Baker, what do American schoolchildren *not* learn during their formal education? Do you agree with him? Why or why not?

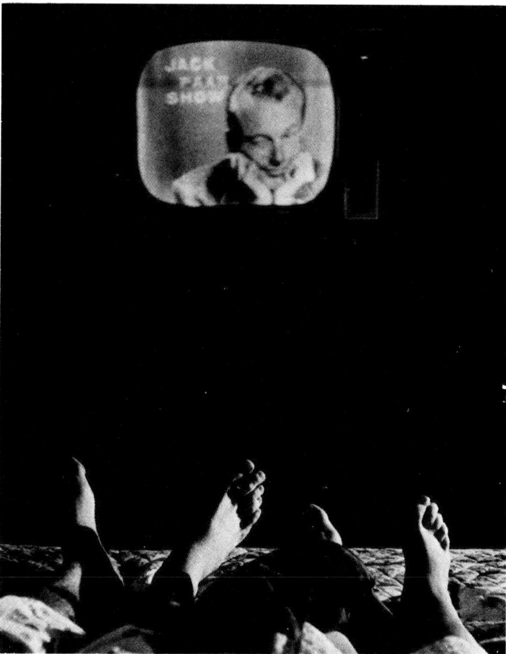

The Jack Paar Show. Photograph taken by Cornell Capa, 1959.

Writing About the Essay

A Creative Response

1. **Answering the Writer.** This essay originally appeared in a newspaper column. Write a letter to the editor telling what you think of it.

A Critical Response

2. **Supporting an Assertion with Examples.** Take one or more of the main points in "School vs. Education" and give some supporting examples from your experience. If you disagree with Baker's main points, give examples from your own experiences to refute them.

Analyzing Language and Style

Irony

1. What is ironic (or unexpected and inappropriate) about what the child learns from his or her parents?
2. What is ironic about what Baker calls "formal education" in paragraph 5?
3. What is ironic about what the child learns about success on tests?

Richard Wright (1908–1960)

Richard Wright was a writer with a gift for making people intensely uncomfortable—which is one measure of his power. He is typically described as the first black writer to expose American racism to a large white audience. But this cool academic assessment fails to capture the angry, relentless drive of his most famous novel, *Native Son* (1940), or of his autobiography, *Black Boy* (1945).

A Black writers who followed Wright have had to emerge from his shadow; one of the most eloquent, James Baldwin (page 1027), even wrote an essay that repudiated Wright's influence, arguing that Wright had ignored some of the strengths of black life and had absorbed too completely white fantasies about black revenge. (But in a bow toward Wright, Baldwin called his own first book of essays *Notes of a Native Son*.)

In explaining Wright, critics have had to deal with his temporary membership in the Communist Party and with his eventual self-exile in Paris, where he lived for the last thirteen years of his life. Full of contradictions, Wright is hard to label. His early death at fifty-two cut off any connection to the generation of black writers who came of age in the 1960's and 1970's. These black writers—Baldwin, Ralph Ellison, Eldridge Cleaver, Toni Morrison, Maya Angelou, Alice Walker—have almost eclipsed Wright, just as his naturalistic style might sound out-of-date in a literary world that increasingly values elaborately intellectual technique, intricate narrative structures, and bleakly objective voices.

But Wright has not been forgotten. When the University of Mississippi organized a symposium on Wright and his work in 1985, it was front-page news in the *New York Times*. Part of the poignancy of such posthumous recognition comes from the fact that Wright had remembered his home state of Mississippi with "ambivalence." It is interesting to speculate on how he might have reacted to an authority on Southern culture who told the *Times*: "Faulkner is considered the top Mississippi writer, but I would put Wright with Eudora Welty and Tennessee Williams in their international reputation."

Wright's life began in poverty. His father, a sharecropper on a Mississippi farm, abandoned his family when Wright was five; when the boy was twelve, his mother could no longer support the family. Raised by various relatives, Wright early learned the bitter lessons of survival on ghetto streets. He remembers becoming familiar with alcohol at the age of six, working in a disreputable hotel while still a child, living with "the sustained expectation of violence." By borrowing a white man's library card, he was finally able to gain access to books. He wrote later that "it had been only through books—at best, no more than vicarious cultural transfusions—that I had managed to keep myself alive."

At seventeen, he fled the South forever, moving to Chicago and then to New York. In Chicago he found encouragement to continue his self-education and to write. He joined the WPA Writers Project, a Depression-era government organization that provided livelihood for many unemployed writers. He began to explore Marxism and eventually joined the Communist Party, at a time when many people thought it offered hope for a more equitable reorganization of society (and before the horrors of the Stalinist purges became public knowledge). Eventually disillusioned, Wright left the Party in 1942.

A. Expansion
Some critics objected that the depiction of Bigger Thomas, the protagonist of *Native Son*, as a sullen resentful adolescent who was the brutalized product of the slum ghetto, is oversimplified. They point out that Wright himself was able to transcend a similar environment. Responding, Wright insisted that he had known people like Bigger all of his life and that if they did not commit murder, as Bigger does, it was only because they did not have murder in their hearts.

B. Expansion
The account of Wright's early years is a grim one. Because of his family's frequent moves, he remained in no one school for a whole academic year until he was in the eighth grade. An alcoholic at six, involved in petty theft as an adolescent, Wright in his early years showed little promise of the career he was to have.

Supplementary Support Materials
1. Vocabulary Activity Worksheet (*CCB*)
2. Review and Response Worksheet: Characterization (*CCB*)
3. Language Skills Worksheet: Coordinating Conjunctions (*CCB*)
4. Selection Test (*CCB*)

Developing Vocabulary
These words from the autobiography are tested in the Selection Test. (See also Vocabulary Activity Worksheet.)

solace	copiously
to flay	jauntily
ardently	mulatto
guise	vindictive
to gall	void

A. Dialogue
Wright had a good ear for the rhythms of speech, and he uses dialogue effectively throughout this autobiography to involve the reader in whatever scene he is depicting.

B. Expansion
This is the one agreeable experience involving his father that Wright mentions in this selection.

Wright achieved his first real recognition in 1940 with *Native Son*, a violent tale of a victimized black man, Bigger Thomas, who accidentally kills once, then murders again to avoid betrayal.

Black Boy secured Wright's fame. Some readers regard it as Wright's masterpiece; as one commented, "the truly 'created' self in an autobiography is more rare than the successful character in fiction." *Black Boy* became a best-seller, topping all the lists. But in the fifteen years following its publication, Wright, then living abroad, never wrote a book that equaled its success. He tried to understand the historical and cultural place of black people in modern life, visiting Africa and recording his observations in books like *Black Power* (1954) and *White Man, Listen!* (1957). But he felt as much an alien in Africa as anywhere else. He died in Paris, where he had found as much of a home as he could.

FROM BLACK BOY

In this excerpt from the early part of Wright's autobiography, the images of "home" are mainly those of physical and emotional hunger. The prose is spare and bitter, as if it reflected the gaunt look of a ghost that the boy feels standing by his bed at night. Yet after his memories of his irresponsible and uncaring father, Wright arrives at a final view of the old man that is rich in detail and emotional complexity.

One day my mother told me that we were going to Memphis on a boat, the *Kate Adams*, and my eagerness thereafter made the days seem endless. Each night I went to bed hoping that the next morning would be the day of departure.

[A] "How big is the boat?" I asked my mother.

"As big as a mountain," she said.

"Has it got a whistle?"

"Yes."

"Does the whistle blow?"

"Yes."

"When?"

"When the captain wants it to blow."

"Why do they call it the *Kate Adams*?"

"Because that's the boat's name."

"What color is the boat?"

"White."

"How long will we be on the boat?"

"All day and all night."

"Will we sleep on the boat?"

"Yes, when we get sleepy, we'll sleep. Now, hush."

For days I had dreamed about a huge white boat floating on a vast body of water, but when my mother took me down to the levee on the day of leaving, I saw a tiny, dirty boat that was not at all like the boat I had imagined. I was disappointed and when time came to go on board I cried and my mother thought that I did not want to go with her to Memphis, and I could not tell her what the trouble was. Solace came when I wandered about the boat and gazed at Negroes throwing dice, drinking whiskey, playing cards, lolling on boxes, eating, talking, and singing. My father took me down into the engine room and the throbbing machines enthralled me for hours. [B]

In Memphis we lived in a one-story brick tenement. The stone buildings and the concrete pavements looked bleak and hostile to me. The absence of green, growing things made the city seem dead. Living space for the four of us—my mother, my brother, my father, and me—was a kitchen and a bedroom. In the front and rear were paved areas in which my brother and I could play, but for days I was afraid to go into the strange city streets alone.

It was in this tenement that the personality of

PREPARATION

ESTABLISHING A PURPOSE. Tell students that a central concern in the selection they are about to read is Richard's attitude toward his father. Suggest that they look for clues to Richard's feelings about his father when they first move to Memphis, after the father has deserted the family, and at Richard's meeting with his father twenty-five years later.

A. Expansion
Explain to your students that when Wright was a young child, there was no welfare, food-stamp program, or public day care to mitigate the suffering caused by poverty.

B. Responding
What image of Richard's father does this new image displace? (That of an alien, remote lawgiver)

my father first came fully into the orbit of my concern. He worked as a night porter in a Beale Street drugstore and he became important and forbidding to me only when I learned that I could not make noise when he was asleep in the daytime. He was the lawgiver in our family and I never laughed in his presence. I used to lurk timidly in the kitchen doorway and watch his huge body sitting slumped at the table. I stared at him with awe as he gulped his beer from a tin bucket, as he ate long and heavily, sighed, belched, closed his eyes to nod on a stuffed belly. He was quite fat and his bloated stomach always lapped over his belt. He was always a stranger to me, always somehow alien and remote. . . .

Hunger stole upon me so slowly that at first I was not aware of what hunger really meant. Hunger had always been more or less at my elbow when I played, but now I began to wake up at night to find hunger standing at my bedside, staring at me gauntly. The hunger I had known before this had been no grim, hostile stranger; it had been a normal hunger that had made me beg constantly for bread, and when I ate a crust or two I was satisfied. But this new hunger baffled me, scared me, made me angry and insistent. Whenever I begged for food now my mother would pour me a cup of tea which would still the clamor in my stomach for a moment or two; but a little later I would feel hunger nudging my ribs, twisting my empty guts until they ached. I would grow dizzy and my vision would dim. I became less active in my play, and for the first time in my life I had to pause and think of what was happening to me.

"Mama, I'm hungry," I complained one afternoon.

"Jump up and catch a kungry," she said, trying to make me laugh and forget.

"What's a *kungry*?"

"It's what little boys eat when they get hungry," she said.

"What does it taste like?"

"I don't know."

"Then why do you tell me to catch one?"

"Because you said that you were hungry," she said, smiling.

I sensed that she was teasing me and it made me angry.

"But I'm hungry. I want to eat."

"You'll have to wait."

"But I want to eat now."

"But there's nothing to eat," she told me.

"Why?"

"Just because there's none," she explained.

"But I want to eat," I said, beginning to cry.

"You'll just have to wait," she said again.

"But why?"

"For God to send some food."

"When is He going to send it?"

"I don't know."

"But I'm hungry!"

She was ironing and she paused and looked at me with tears in her eyes.

"Where's your father?" she asked me.

I stared in bewilderment. Yes, it was true that my father had not come home to sleep for many days now and I could make as much noise as I wanted. Though I had not known why he was absent, I had been glad that he was not there to shout his restrictions at me. But it had never occurred to me that his absence would mean that there would be no food.

"I don't know," I said.

"Who brings food into the house?" my mother asked me.

"Papa," I said. "He always brought food."

"Well, your father isn't here now," she said.

"Where is he?"

"I don't know," she said.

"But I'm hungry," I whimpered, stomping my feet.

"You'll have to wait until I get a job and buy food," she said.

As the days slid past the image of my father became associated with my pangs of hunger, and whenever I felt hunger I thought of him with a deep biological bitterness.

My mother finally went to work as a cook and left me and my brother alone in the flat each day with a loaf of bread and a pot of tea. When she returned at evening she would be tired and dispirited and would cry a lot. Sometimes, when she was in despair, she would call us to her and talk to us for hours, telling us that we now had no father, that our lives would be different from those of other children, that we must learn as soon as possible to take care of ourselves, to dress ourselves, to prepare our own food; that we must take upon ourselves the responsibility of the flat while she worked. Half frightened, we would promise solemnly. We did not understand what

Literature and Language: Varying Sentence Structure
If every sentence were the same length and had the same structure, readers would fall promptly asleep. To keep readers alert, writers change tempo by varying sentence length and using a variety of sentence structures and beginnings.

Ask students to focus on the paragraph that begins, "She slammed . . ." in the middle of the right-hand column, below. Have them look carefully at sentence lengths, noticing how several short sentences provide contrast with longer sentences. Next, have them examine sentence structure to locate examples of simple, compound, complex, and compound-complex sentences. (Review the definitions and examples on pages 1187–1188.) Finally, have students focus on sentence beginnings. Which sentence begins with a subordinate clause? (Sixth) How do all but one of the other sentences begin? (With the subject *I*)

Have students analyze sentence variety in several other paragraphs.

A. Responding
? This famous scene, in which Richard returns to best the gang of boys, makes exciting reading. Do you think his mother was right to force him to face them? (Encourage students to defend their responses and to suggest other options.)

had happened between our father and our mother and the most that these long talks did to us was to make us feel a vague dread. Whenever we asked why father had left, she would tell us that we were too young to know.

One evening my mother told me that thereafter I would have to do the shopping for food. She took me to the corner store to show me the way. I was proud; I felt like a grown-up. The next afternoon I looped the basket over my arm and went down the pavement toward the store. When I reached the corner, a gang of boys grabbed me, knocked me down, snatched the basket, took the money, and sent me running home in panic. That evening I told my mother what had happened, but she made no comment; she sat down at once, wrote another note, gave me more money, and sent me out to the grocery again. I crept down the steps and saw the same gang of boys playing down the street. I ran back in to the house.

"What's the matter?" my mother asked.

"It's those same boys," I said. "They'll beat me."

"You've got to get over that," she said. "Now, go on."

"I'm scared," I said.

"Go on and don't pay any attention to them," she said.

I went out of the door and walked briskly down the sidewalk, praying that the gang would not molest me. But when I came abreast of them someone shouted.

"There he is!"

They came toward me and I broke into a wild run toward home. They overtook me and flung me to the pavement. I yelled, pleaded, kicked, but they wrenched the money out of my hand. They yanked me to my feet, gave me a few slaps, and sent me home sobbing. My mother met me at the door.

"They b-beat m-me," I gasped. "They t-t-took the m-money."

I started up the steps, seeking the shelter of the house.

"Don't you come in here," my mother warned me.

I froze in my tracks and stared at her.

"But they're coming after me," I said.

"You just stay right where you are," she said in a deadly tone. "I'm going to teach you this night to stand up and fight for yourself."

She went into the house and I waited, terrified, wondering what she was about. Presently she returned with more money and another note; she also had a long heavy stick.

"Take this money, this note, and this stick," she said. "Go to the store and buy those groceries. If those boys bother you, then fight."

I was baffled. My mother was telling me to fight, a thing that she had never done before.

"But I'm scared," I said.

"Don't you come into this house until you've gotten those groceries," she said.

"They'll beat me; they'll beat me," I said.

"Then stay in the streets; don't come back here!"

I ran up the steps and tried to force my way past her into the house. A stinging slap came on my jaw. I stood on the sidewalk, crying.

"Please, let me wait until tomorrow," I begged.

"No," she said. "Go now! If you come back into this house without those groceries, I'll whip you!"

She slammed the door and I heard the key turn in the lock. I shook with fright. I was alone upon the dark, hostile streets and gangs were after me. **A** I had the choice of being beaten at home or away from home. I clutched the stick, crying, trying to reason. If I were beaten at home, there was absolutely nothing that I could do about it; but if I were beaten in the streets, I had a chance to fight and defend myself. I walked slowly down the sidewalk, coming closer to the gang of boys, holding the stick tightly. I was so full of fear that I could scarcely breathe. I was almost upon them now.

"There he is again!" the cry went up.

They surrounded me quickly and began to grab for my hand.

"I'll kill you!" I threatened.

They closed in. In blind fear I let the stick fly, feeling it crack against a boy's skull. I swung again, lamming another skull, then another. Realizing that they would retaliate if I let up for but a second, I fought to lay them low, to knock them cold, to kill them so that they could not strike back at me. I flayed with tears in my eyes, teeth clenched, stark fear making me throw every ounce of my strength behind each blow. I hit again and again, dropping the money and the grocery list. The boys scattered, yelling, nursing their heads, staring at me in utter disbelief. They had never seen such frenzy. I stood panting, egging

A. Responding
? At times, because of anger or fear, Richard is unable to speak or move. Is this seeming paralysis understandable? Have you ever felt like that in an extremely emotional situation?

them on, taunting them to come on and fight. When they refused, I ran after them and they tore out for their homes, screaming. The parents of the boys rushed into the streets and threatened me, and for the first time in my life I shouted at grown-ups, telling them that I would give them the same if they bothered me. I finally found my grocery list and the money and went to the store. On my way back I kept my stick poised for instant use, but there was not a single boy in sight. That night I won the right to the streets of Memphis. . . .

After my father's desertion, my mother's ardently religious disposition dominated the household and I was often taken to Sunday school where I met God's representative in the guise of a tall, black preacher. One Sunday my mother invited the tall, black preacher to a dinner of fried chicken. I was happy, not because the preacher was coming but because of the chicken. One or two neighbors also were invited. But no sooner had the preacher arrived than I began to resent him, for I learned at once that he, like my father, was used to having his own way. The hour for dinner came and I was wedged at the table between talking and laughing adults. In the center of the table was a huge platter of golden-brown fried chicken. I compared the bowl of soup that sat before me with the crispy chicken and decided in favor of the chicken. The others began to eat their soup, but I could not touch mine.

"Eat your soup," my mother said.

"I don't want any," I said.

"You won't get anything else until you've eaten your soup," she said.

The preacher had finished his soup and had asked that the platter of chicken be passed to him. It galled me. He smiled, cocked his head this way and that, picking out choice pieces. I forced a spoonful of soup down my throat and looked to see if my speed matched that of the preacher. It did not. There were already bare chicken bones on his plate, and he was reaching for more. I tried eating my soup faster, but it was no use; the other people were now serving themselves chicken and the platter was more than half empty. I gave up and sat staring in despair at the vanishing pieces of fried chicken.

"Eat your soup or you won't get anything," my mother warned.

A I looked at her appealingly and could not answer. As piece after piece of chicken was eaten, I was unable to eat my soup at all. I grew hot with anger. The preacher was laughing and joking and the grown-ups were hanging on his words. My growing hate of the preacher finally became more important than God or religion and I could no longer contain myself. I leaped up from the table, knowing that I should be ashamed of what I was doing, but unable to stop, and screamed, running blindly from the room.

"That preacher's going to eat *all* the chicken!" I bawled.

The preacher tossed back his head and roared with laughter, but my mother was angry and told me that I was to have no dinner because of my bad manners.

When I awakened one morning my mother told me that we were going to see a judge who would make my father support me and my brother. An hour later all three of us were sitting in a huge crowded room. I was overwhelmed by the many faces and the voices which I could not understand. High above me was a white face which my mother told me was the face of the judge. Across the huge room sat my father, smiling confidently, looking at us. My mother warned me not to be fooled by my father's friendly manner; she told me that the judge might ask me questions, and if he did I must tell him the truth. I agreed, yet I hoped that the judge would not ask me anything.

For some reason the entire thing struck me as being useless; I felt that if my father were going to feed me, then he would have done so regardless of what a judge said to him. And I did not want my father to feed me; I was hungry, but my thoughts of food did not now center about him. I waited, growing restless, hungry. My mother gave me a dry sandwich and I munched and stared, longing to go home. Finally I heard my mother's name called; she rose and began weeping so copiously that she could not talk for a few moments; at last she managed to say that her husband had deserted her and two children, that her children were hungry, that they stayed hungry, that she worked, that she was trying to raise them alone. Then my father was called; he came forward jauntily, smiling. He tried to kiss my mother, but she turned away from him. I only heard one sentence of what he said.

"I'm doing all I can, Your Honor," he mumbled, grinning.

It had been painful to sit and watch my mother

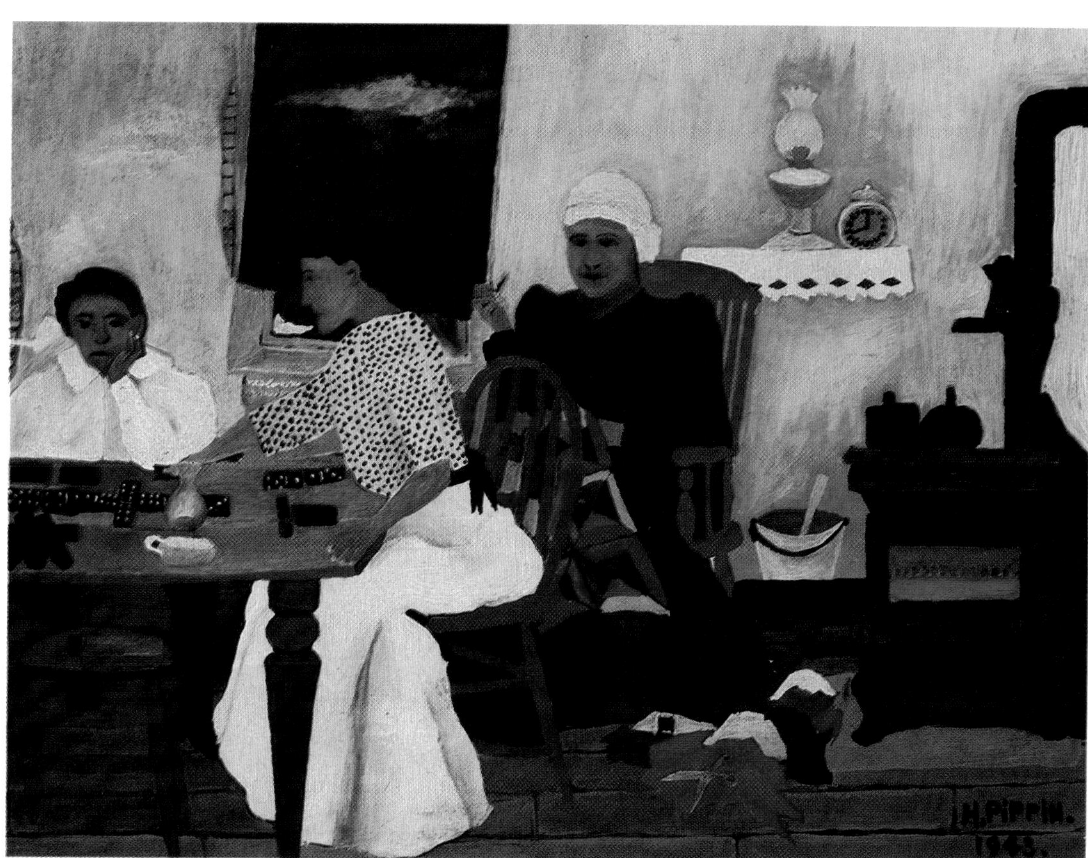

Domino Players (detail) by Horace Pippin (1943). Oil on composition board.

A

The Phillips Collection, Washington, D.C.

crying and my father laughing and I was glad when we were outside in the sunny streets. Back at home my mother wept again and talked complainingly about the unfairness of the judge who had accepted my father's word. After the court scene, I tried to forget my father; I did not hate him; I simply did not want to think of him. Often when we were hungry my mother would beg me to go to my father's job and ask him for a dollar, a dime, a nickel . . . But I would never consent to go. I did not want to see him.

My mother fell ill and the problem of food became an acute, daily agony. Hunger was with us always. Sometimes the neighbors would feed us or a dollar bill would come in the mail from my grandmother. It was winter and I would buy a dime's worth of coal each morning from the corner coalyard and lug it home in paper bags. For a time I remained out of school to wait upon my mother, then Granny came to visit us and I returned to school.

At night there were long, halting discussions about our going to live with Granny, but nothing came of it. Perhaps there was not enough money for railroad fare. Angered by having been hauled into court, my father now spurned us completely. I heard long, angrily whispered conversations between my mother and grandmother to the effect that "that woman ought to be killed for breaking up a home." What irked me was the ceaseless talk and no action. If someone had suggested that my father be killed, I would perhaps have become interested; if someone had suggested that his name never be mentioned, I would no doubt have agreed; if someone had suggested that we move to another city, I would have been glad. But there was only endless talk that led nowhere and I began to keep away from home as much as possible,

A. Humanities Connection: Discussing the Fine Art
Horace Pippin (1888–1946) was an important American painter of primitives—that is, paintings that reflect a lack of formal training. Severely wounded in World War I, Pippin worked as a porter and warehouseman before gaining recognition for his painting in the 1930's. This conventional interior scene has the charm of simple naturalness. The muted pastel colors of dusty brown, whitish gray, and olive green with accents of red produce an effect of warmth and harmony. The quiet dignity of the figures contrasts with the symbols of poverty—the cracked plaster and the simple furnishings. Note the lack of perspective in representing the dominoes and other objects on the table—a common characteristic of primitive painting.

A. Expansion
Point out that advances in social welfare since Wright's childhood make the sending of a child to an orphanage so that the mother can work seem outlandish. However, in 1912, when this incident takes place, there were few other options for Wright's mother.

B. Connections
This scene of the children pulling up tufts of grass has a Dickensian grimness.

preferring the simplicity of the streets to the worried, futile talk at home.

Finally we could no longer pay the rent for our dingy flat; the few dollars that Granny had left us before she went home were gone. Half sick and in despair, my mother made the rounds of the charitable institutions, seeking help. She found an orphan home that agreed to assume the guidance of me and my brother provided my mother worked and made small payments. My mother hated to be separated from us, but she had no choice.

The orphan home was a two-story frame building set amid trees in a wide, green field. My mother ushered me and my brother one morning into the building and into the presence of a tall, gaunt, mulatto woman who called herself Miss Simon. At once she took a fancy to me and I was frightened speechless; I was afraid of her the moment I saw her and my fear lasted during my entire stay in the home.

The house was crowded with children and there was always a storm of noise. The daily routine was blurred to me and I never quite grasped it. The most abiding feeling I had each day was hunger and fear. The meals were skimpy and there were only two of them. Just before we went to bed each night we were given a slice of bread smeared with molasses. The children were silent, hostile, vindictive, continuously complaining of hunger. There was an overall atmosphere of nervousness and intrigue, of children telling tales upon others, of children being deprived of food to punish them.

The home did not have the money to check the growth of the wide stretches of grass by having it mown, so it had to be pulled by hand. Each morning after we had eaten a breakfast that seemed like no breakfast at all, an older child would lead a herd of us to the vast lawn and we would get on our knees and wrench the grass loose from the dirt with our fingers. At intervals Miss Simon would make a tour of inspection, examining the pile of pulled grass beside each child, scolding or praising according to the size of the pile. Many mornings I was too weak from hunger to pull the grass; I would grow dizzy and my mind would become blank and I would find myself, after an interval of unconsciousness, upon my hands and knees, my head whirling, my eyes staring in bleak astonishment at the green grass, wondering where I was, feeling that I was emerging from a dream . . .

During the first days my mother came each night to visit me and my brother, then her visits stopped. I began to wonder if she, too, like my father, had disappeared into the unknown. I was rapidly learning to distrust everything and everybody. When my mother did come, I asked her why had she remained away so long and she told me that Miss Simon had forbidden her to visit us, that Miss Simon had said that she was spoiling us with too much attention. I begged my mother to take me away; she wept and told me to wait, that soon she would take us to Arkansas. She left and my heart sank.

Miss Simon tried to win my confidence; she asked me if I would like to be adopted by her if my mother consented and I said no. She would take me into her apartment and talk to me, but her words had no effect. Dread and distrust had already become a daily part of my being and my memory grew sharp, my senses more impressionable; I began to be aware of myself as a distinct personality striving against others. I held myself in, afraid to act or speak until I was sure of my surroundings, feeling most of the time that I was suspended over a void. My imagination soared; I dreamed of running away. Each morning I vowed that I would leave the next morning, but the next morning always found me afraid.

One day Miss Simon told me that thereafter I was to help her in the office. I ate lunch with her and, strangely, when I sat facing her at the table, my hunger vanished. The woman killed something in me. Next she called me to her desk where she sat addressing envelopes.

"Step up close to the desk," she said. "Don't be afraid."

I went and stood at her elbow. There was a wart on her chin and I stared at it.

"Now, take a blotter from over there and blot each envelope after I'm through writing on it," she instructed me, pointing to a blotter that stood about a foot from my hand.

I stared and did not move or answer.

"Take the blotter," she said.

I wanted to reach for the blotter and succeeded only in twitching my arm.

"Here," she said sharply, reaching for the blotter and shoving it into my fingers.

She wrote in ink on an envelope and pushed it toward me. Holding the blotter in my hand, I stared at the envelope and could not move.

"Blot it," she said.

For Further Reading For The Teacher
The Art of Richard Wright by Edward Margolies (Southern Illinois University Press, 1969) provides an informative discussion of Wright's work, both fiction and nonfiction. Chapter 2 ("The Fractured Personality") offers valuable background material relating to *Black Boy*.

For Further Reading For the Student
Interested students should be encouraged to read all of *Black Boy: A Record of Childhood and Youth* (Harper and Brothers, 1945).

I could not lift my hand. I knew what she had said; I knew what she wanted me to do; and I had heard her correctly. I wanted to look at her and say something, tell her why I could not move; but my eyes were fixed upon the floor. I could not summon enough courage while she sat there looking at me to reach over the yawning space of twelve inches and blot the wet ink on the envelope.

''Blot it!'' she spoke sharply.

Still I could not move or answer.

''Look at me!''

I could not lift my eyes. She reached her hand to my face and I twisted away.

''What's wrong with you?'' she demanded.

I began to cry and she drove me from the room. I decided that as soon as night came I would run away. The dinner bell rang and I did not go to the table, but hid in a corner of the hallway. When I heard the dishes rattling at the table, I opened the door and ran down the walk to the street. Dusk was falling. Doubt made me stop. Ought I go back? No; hunger was back there, and fear. I went on, coming to concrete sidewalks. People passed me. Where was I going? I did not know. The farther I walked the more frantic I became. In a confused and vague way I knew that I was doing more running *away* from than running *toward* something. I stopped. The streets seemed dangerous. The buildings were massive and dark. The moon shone and the trees loomed frighteningly. No, I could not go on. I would go back. But I had walked so far and had turned too many corners and had not kept track of the direction. Which way led back to the orphan home? I did not know. I was lost.

I stood in the middle of the sidewalk and cried. A ''white'' policeman came to me and I wondered if he was going to beat me. He asked me what was the matter and I told him that I was trying to find my mother. His ''white'' face created a new fear in me. I was remembering the tale of the ''white'' man who had beaten the ''black'' boy. A crowd gathered and I was urged to tell where I lived. Curiously, I was too full of fear to cry now. I wanted to tell the ''white'' face that I had run off from an orphan home and that Miss Simon ran it, but I was afraid. Finally I was taken to the police station where I was fed. I felt better. I sat in a big chair where I was surrounded by ''white'' policemen, but they seemed to ignore me. Through the window I could see that night had completely fallen and that lights now gleamed in the streets. I grew sleepy and dozed. My shoulder was shaken gently and I opened my eyes and looked into a ''white'' face of another policeman who was sitting beside me. He asked me questions in a quiet, confidential tone, and quite before I knew it he was not ''white'' anymore. I told him that I had run away from an orphan home and that Miss Simon ran it. A

It was but a matter of minutes before I was walking alongside a policeman, heading toward the home. The policeman led me to the front gate and I saw Miss Simon waiting for me on the steps. She identified me and I was left in her charge. I begged her not to beat me, but she yanked me upstairs into an empty room and lashed me thoroughly. Sobbing, I slunk off to bed, resolved to run away again. But I was watched closely after that.

My mother was informed upon her next visit that I had tried to run away and she was terribly upset.

''Why did you do it?'' she asked.

''I don't want to stay here,'' I told her.

''But you must,'' she said. ''How can I work if I'm to worry about you? You must remember that you have no father. I'm doing all I can.''

''I don't want to stay here,'' I repeated.

''Then, if I take you to your father . . .''

''I don't want to stay with him either,'' I said.

''But I want you to ask him for enough money for us to go to my sister's in Arkansas,'' she said.

Again I was faced with choices I did not like, but I finally agreed. After all, my hate for my father was not so great and urgent as my hate for the orphan home. My mother held to her idea and one night a week or so later I found myself standing in a room in a frame house. My father and a strange woman were sitting before a bright fire that blazed in a grate. My mother and I were standing about six feet away, as though we were afraid to approach them any closer.

''It's not for me,'' my mother was saying. ''It's for your children that I'm asking you for money.''

''I ain't got nothing,'' my father said, laughing.

''Come here, boy,'' the strange woman called to me.

I looked at her and did not move.

''Give him a nickel,'' the woman said. ''He's cute.''

''Come here, Richard,'' my father said, stretching out his hand.

A. Responding
? What is the point of the repeated use of *white* in quotation marks in this paragraph? (At first, Richard sees the policemen only as whites and is afraid. The sympathetic officer gains his confidence and makes him forget the difference in race.)

Reading Check Test

1. This selection takes place in Atlanta, Georgia. *False*
2. Richard's mother wouldn't let him back in the house until he faced down the bullies. *True*
3. The judge made Richard's father contribute money to his family's support. *False*
4. As a bedtime snack, the orphanage children were given bread and molasses. *True*
5. Richard's mother told him not to take the nickel his father offered him. *True*

Analyzing The Autobiography

Identifying Facts

1. Among the other important pictures that Wright creates are the description of himself as a hungry boy, the incident with the gang, the picture of dinner with the preacher, the pictures of the father and the strange woman, and Wright's meeting with his sharecropper father twenty-five years later.

A. Characterization

? What impression is created by the fact that Richard's father laughs continually throughout this serious confrontation? (He appears weak, irresponsible, and unfeeling.)

B. Symbolism

? Is Wright talking only about his father here? (No. He sees his father as a symbol for rural blacks whose folk culture, built up from plantation days, is ill-suited to urban life.)

Closure

Ask volunteers to explain the different effects the city has had on the lives of Richard and his father. Have them also explain how the realization of their differences leads Richard to forgive his father.

I backed away, shaking my head, keeping my eyes on the fire.

"He is a cute child," the strange woman said.

"You ought to be ashamed," my mother said to the strange woman. "You're starving my children."

"Now, don't you-all fight," my father said, laughing.

"I'll take that poker and hit you!" I blurted at my father.

He looked at my mother and laughed louder.

"You told him to say that," he said.

"Don't say such things, Richard," my mother said.

"You ought to be dead," I said to the strange woman.

The woman laughed and threw her arms about my father's neck. I grew ashamed and wanted to leave.

"How can you starve your children?" my mother asked.

"Let Richard stay with me," my father said.

"Do you want to stay with your father, Richard?" my mother asked.

"No," I said.

"You'll get plenty to eat," he said.

"I'm hungry now," I told him. "But I won't stay with you."

"Aw, give the boy a nickel," the woman said.

My father ran his hand into his pocket and pulled out a nickel.

"Here, Richard," he said.

"Don't take it," my mother said.

"Don't teach him to be a fool," my father said. "Here, Richard, take it."

I looked at my mother, at the strange woman, at my father, then into the fire. I wanted to take the nickel, but I did not want to take it from my father.

"You ought to be ashamed," my mother said, weeping. "Giving your son a nickel when he's hungry. If there's a God, He'll pay you back."

A "That's all I got," my father said, laughing again and returning the nickel to his pocket.

We left. I had the feeling that I had had to do with something unclean. Many times in the years after that the image of my father and the strange woman, their faces lit by the dancing flames, would surge up in my imagination so vivid and strong that I felt I could reach out and touch it; I would stare at it, feeling that it possessed some vital meaning which always eluded me.

A quarter of a century was to elapse between the time when I saw my father sitting with the strange woman and the time when I was to see him again, standing alone upon the red clay of a Mississippi plantation, a sharecropper, clad in ragged overalls, holding a muddy hoe in his gnarled, veined hands—a quarter of a century during which my mind and consciousness had become so greatly and violently altered that when I tried to talk to him I realized that, though ties of blood made us kin, though I could see a shadow of my face in his face, though there was an echo of my voice in his voice, we were forever strangers, speaking a different language, living on vastly distant planes of reality. That day a quarter of a century later when I visited him on the plantation—he was standing against the sky, smiling toothlessly, his hair whitened, his body bent, his eyes glazed with dim recollection, his fearsome aspect of twenty-five years ago gone forever from him—I was overwhelmed to realize that he could never understand me or the scalding experiences that had swept me beyond his life and into an area of living that he could never know. I stood before him, poised, my mind aching as it embraced the simple nakedness of his life, feeling how completely his soul was imprisoned by the slow flow of the seasons, by wind and rain and sun, how fastened were his memories to a crude and raw past, how chained were his actions and emotions to the direct, animalistic impulses of his withering body . .

From the white landowners above him there had not been handed to him a chance to learn the meaning of loyalty, of sentiment, of tradition. Joy was as unknown to him as was despair. As a creature of the earth, he endured, hearty, whole, seemingly indestructible, with no regrets and no hope. He asked easy, drawing questions about me, his other son, his wife, and he laughed, amused, when I informed him of their destinies. I forgave him and pitied him as my eyes looked past him to the unpainted wooden shack. From far beyond the horizons that bound this bleak plantation there had come to me through my living the knowledge that my father was a black peasant who had gone to the city seeking life, but who had failed in the city; a black peasant whose life had been hopelessly snarled in the city, and who had at last fled the city—that same city which had lifted me in its burning arms and borne me toward alien and undreamed-of shores of knowing. B

2. He mentions his waking up at night, the clamor in his stomach, his dizziness and listlessness.
3. He concluded that his father's frequent absences from home were associated with the family's poverty and hunger.
4. He fought back with a stick against the other boys in the gang.
5. The father is strict with the boy and is lazy; he also drinks too much. Richard is afraid of him.

In the courtroom scene and in the later confrontation with Wright, his mother, and the strange woman, the father behaves in an offhand, irresponsible fashion. He seems indifferent to the family's plight.
6. He realizes that he and his father are "forever strangers" and that his father could never understand him.

Whereas his father failed there, the city has borne the narrator "toward alien and undreamed-of shores of knowing."

Interpreting Meanings
7. She is trying to teach him that, to grow up, he needs to be able to take care of and defend himself.

Answers will vary. Ask students to support their responses.
8. The boy cannot eat because he resents the preacher's greed and selfishness.

The detail reveals that Richard can be angry, righteous, and stubborn.
9. Richard's father deserted the family. His mother ran out of money and could not afford to pay the rent on their dingy flat.

Answers will vary. It is possible that the family could have gone on some sort of public assistance program.
10. Answers will vary. Most students will agree that the image is so powerful by itself that it is more effective without any comment from the narrator.
11. He probably means that he realized subconsciously that his father had forsaken the family forever.

Responding to the Autobiography

Analyzing the Autobiography

Identifying Facts

1. In most of this excerpt, Wright works in swift strokes to draw sharp **images** or pictures of his life. One such picture, for example, shows the boy and his mother confronting his father in court. Another shows the boy standing by Miss Simon's desk in the orphanage. What other important pictures are created in these extracts from the autobiography?
2. What details does Wright use to make the reader feel the hunger he experienced as a boy?
3. Why did Richard associate his father with his pangs of hunger?
4. How did Richard win the right to the streets of Memphis?
5. Wright speaks of how "the personality of my father first came fully into the orbit of my concern" (page 1005). What *is* that personality? How does his father behave in the courtroom scene and in the later confrontation with Richard, his mother, and the strange woman?
6. What does Wright realize about his father in the last passage? How was the city's effect on his father different from its effect on Wright himself?

Interpreting Meanings

7. When his mother gives Richard a heavy stick and sends him back to confront the street bullies, what lesson is she trying to teach him? Do you think she was right? Was there anything else she could have done instead?
8. Why can't Richard eat his soup when the preacher is devouring the fried chicken? What does this detail reveal about the boy's **character**?
9. What sad events finally forced Richard's mother to send her sons to an orphanage? If Wright had been living in a contemporary city, what might have happened to him and his family?
10. One of the most painful **images** in this excerpt is the one of the young boy pulling grass at the orphanage. Wright makes no direct comment on this scene, except to describe his physical sensations. What might he have said? Do you wish he had said it, or do you think it wasn't necessary? What feelings does this scene evoke in you?
11. Remembering his father and the strange woman, "their faces lit by the dancing flames," Wright says that he felt that in later life this scene "possessed some vital meaning which always eluded me." What do you think he means?

Writing About the Autobiography

A Creative Response

1. **Experimenting with Point of View.** Write a monologue from Richard's mother's point of view, in which she tells her feelings and memories about the time she sent Richard back to the streets with a stick. Or, write a series of paragraphs in which all the different characters "remember" Richard Wright from their own perspective: Miss Simon, the policeman, the judge, the strange woman, the father, the mother.

A Critical Response

2. **Comparing and Contrasting Two Writers.** In a short essay, compare the **style** and the **themes** of Wright's story with those in Mark Twain's *The Adventures of Huckleberry Finn* (page 414) or in Susan Toth's *Ivy Days* (page 1034). In your comments on style, consider sentence structure, dialogue, the use of detail, and tone of voice. How did each piece of writing affect you?

Analyzing Language and Style

Dialogue

We often think of **dialogue**, or the directly quoted words of conversation between two or more people, as the property of drama or fiction. But dialogue can also play a significant role in nonfiction. In this excerpt from Wright's autobiography, for example, almost every scene is dramatized through dialogue.

Wright might easily have chosen a different approach. For instance, instead of quoting the conversation between himself and his mother in the first scene, he might have simply described his eagerness to see the *Kate Adams*, his speculations about the boat's size, its whistle, and its name. But by recalling and presenting his conversation with his mother, Wright *shows*, rather than describes, his feelings. At the same time, he creates a vivid and touching character portrait of his mother.

Select one scene from this excerpt that includes dialogue, and examine the conversation carefully. Then write a paragraph in which you describe what the situation would be like *without* the use of dialogue. Answer these questions in your paragraphs.

1. What specific contributions do you think the dialogue makes to the scene's total effect and to Wright's characterizations?
2. Would the scene have been as effective if the dialogue had been omitted?

For Further Reading For Students And Teachers

Dee Brown's *Bury My Heart at Wounded Knee* (Holt, Rinehart & Winston, 1970) is a unique and disturbing history of the West from the Native American point of view. The title alludes to the burial at Wounded Knee, South Dakota, of the heart and bones of the great Sioux warrior, Crazy Horse, after he was killed while an army captive in 1877.

A. Expansion

The Kiowa's migration southward proved to be a highly favorable development for the tribe. Learning from the Crows, they quickly adopted horses and firearms as central parts of their culture. They acquired great wealth and power, mainly through attacks on settlements. The Kiowa united with the Comanche and other tribes to resist the westward push of the white settlers. Because of their skillful horsemanship, the Kiowa were instrumental in winning many engagements against the whites before they were overcome by sheer numbers.

N. Scott Momaday (1934–)

Among the voices of the American past, one of the most poignant and powerful to make itself heard at last has been that of the Native American, or the American Indian. In the past, the American Indian appeared in literature and the other arts in the baldest of stereotypes, either as a noble, primitive warrior or as a fearsome, ignorant savage. One has only to look at Western movies from the 1940's or 1950's to see how blatant these stereotypes were. Even in American history, textbooks seldom questioned the popular view that the white settlers' gradual "winning of the West" was a virtuous struggle against the unwarranted resistance of the Indians. Few Americans gave much thought either to the moral basis on which the United States expanded, or to the history of Native Americans.

When the civil rights movement of the late 1950's brought the plight of American blacks to the public, other minority groups began to demand their fair share of attention, too. Native Americans spoke loudly and clearly of loss, injustice, and prejudice. Among many books telling their story have been popular historian Dee Brown's *Bury My Heart at Wounded Knee* (1970), Vine Deloria's novel *Custer Died for Your Sins* (1969), Lynn Andrews's novel *Medicine Woman* (1983), Louise Erdrich's novel *Love Medicine* (1984), and the works of N. Scott Momaday.

Momaday was born in Lawton, Oklahoma, of Kiowa ancestry on his father's side, and part Cherokee on his mother's. After receiving a B.A. degree from New Mexico State University, Momaday studied creative writing at Stanford University, where he received his Ph.D. in 1963. He taught at the University of California at Santa Barbara for several years, then at Berkeley and at New Mexico State.

But Momaday broke loose from the standard academic mold with two works grounded in his knowledge of American Indian life: a Pulitzer-Prize-winning novel, *House Made of Dawn* (1968), and two memoirs, *The Way to Rainy Mountain* (1969) and *The Names* (1976). *The Way to Rainy Mountain* is part legend, part history, and part poetry, with an unusual artistic addition of striking illustrations by Momaday's father. Following the introduction, Momaday describes the Kiowas' history in a form that is associative and imagistic; it works on the reader's imagination in subtle ways that do not depend on a straightforward narrative. On one page, he sets down a Kiowa legend; on the facing page, he places a short excerpt from a traditional history and then a personal memory of his own. The inner truth blends with the outer; emotion mixes with fact.

The Kiowas' journey to Rainy Mountain begins in the hidden mists of time, when a tribe of unknown origin descends from the headwaters of the Yellowstone River eastward to the Black Hills (now in South Dakota) and south to the Wichita Mountains. It ends in a cemetery where many of Momaday's Kiowa kinfolk are buried. A Momaday says that "the journey is an evocation of three things in particular: a landscape that is incomparable, a time that is gone forever, and the human spirit, which endures."

The incomparable landscape is the Great Plains, wind-swept and lonely, in turn brilliant with summer sun and buried in winter snows. Momaday's love of the land where he grew up suffuses everything he writes. He reminds us of both the spiritual richness and the rigors of living close to the land, under a wide, open sky, in harmony with the changing seasons. In his work, Momaday has looked at his own particular landscape from so many angles that his pictures often shimmer like a prism.

SUPPLEMENTARY SUPPORT MATERIALS

1. Vocabulary Activity Worksheet (*CCB*)
2. Review and Response Worksheet: Imagery (*CCB*)
3. Language Skills Worksheet: Adjectives (*CCB*)
4. Selection Test (*CCB*)
5. Audiocassette recording

DEVELOPING VOCABULARY

The following words from the essay are tested in the Selection Test. (See also Vocabulary Activity Worksheet.)

linear	to consummate
to pillage	deicide
luxuriant	opaque
solstice	enmity
to engender	to hie

PREPARATION

1. ESTABLISHING A PURPOSE. Before beginning the selection, have students read question 1, page 1019, which will help them focus on a purpose for reading.

2. PREREADING JOURNAL. Have students write about a grandparent or other older relative who has exerted a strong influence on their lives.

FROM THE WAY TO RAINY MOUNTAIN

An American Portrait by Fritz Scholder (1979). Oil. Courtesy The Anschutz Collection, Denver, Colorado.

Humanities Connection: Discussing the Fine Art

Fritz Scholder (b. 1937), himself one-quarter Native American, turned to Native American subject matter in 1964 after experimenting in pop art and expressionism. Rejecting the folkloric style of portraying Native Americans, Scholder uses a dramatic expressionist approach. *An American Portrait,* with its seemingly blood-smeared face and with its figure partly in native garb and partly draped with an American flag, suggests the complex and often tragic relationship of Native and white Americans.

A. Expansion
Students may be interested to know that although horses originated in North America, the species became extinct here in prehistoric times. The Spanish settlers reintroduced the horse to America, and Native Americans acquired horses from them.

This essay is not a simple narrative. Momaday uses frequent flashbacks to earlier times, and often omits transitional passages. The essay will make more sense if you approach it as a kind of poem in which the narrator traces, in his imagination, the heroic and ultimately tragic history of his people, the Kiowa. (Refer to the map on page 1018 to find the places Momaday is about to re-create.) As you read, think about this comment from the end of *Rainy Mountain:* "Once in his life a man ought to concentrate his mind upon the remembered earth . . . ."

A single knoll rises out of the plain in Oklahoma north and west of the Wichita Range. For my people, the Kiowas, it is an old landmark, and they gave it the name Rainy Mountain. The hardest weather in the world is there. Winter brings blizzards, hot tornadic winds arise in the spring, and in summer the prairie is an anvil's edge. The grass turns brittle and brown, and it cracks beneath your feet. There are green belts along the rivers and creeks, linear groves of hickory and pecan, willow and witch hazel. At a distance in July or August the steaming foliage seems almost to writhe in fire. Great green and yellow grasshoppers are everywhere in the tall grass, popping up like corn to sting the flesh, and tortoises crawl about on the red earth, going nowhere in the plenty of time. Loneliness is an aspect of the land. All things in the plain are isolate; there is no confusion of objects in the eye, but *one* hill or *one* tree or *one* man. To look upon that landscape in the early morning, with the sun at your back, is to lose the sense of proportion. Your imagination comes to life, and this, you think, is where Creation was begun.

I returned to Rainy Mountain in July. My grandmother had died in the spring, and I wanted to be at her grave. She had lived to be very old and at last infirm. Her only living daughter was with her when she died, and I was told that in death her face was that of a child.

I like to think of her as a child. When she was born, the Kiowas were living that last great moment of their history. For more than a hundred years they had controlled the open range from the Smoky Hill River to the Red, from the headwaters of the Canadian to the fork of the Arkansas and Cimarron. In alliance with the Comanches, they had ruled the whole of the southern Plains. War was their sacred business, and they were among the finest horsemen the world has ever known. But warfare for the Kiowas was pre-eminently a matter of disposition rather than of survival, and they never understood the grim, unrelenting advance of the U.S. Cavalry. When at last, divided and ill-provisioned, they were driven onto the Staked Plains in the cold rains of autumn, they fell into panic. In Palo Duro Canyon they abandoned their crucial stores to pillage and had nothing then but their lives. In order to save themselves, they surrendered to the soldiers at Fort Sill and were imprisoned in the old stone corral that now stands as a military museum. My grandmother was spared the humiliation of those high gray walls by eight or ten years, but she must have known from birth the affliction of defeat, the dark brooding of old warriors.

Her name was Aho, and she belonged to the last culture to evolve in North America. Her forebears came down from the high country in western Montana nearly three centuries ago. They were a mountain people, a mysterious tribe of hunters whose language has never been positively classified in any major group. In the late seventeenth century they began a long migration to the south and east. It was a journey toward the dawn, and it led to a golden age. Along the way the Kiowas were befriended by the Crows, who gave them the culture and religion of the Plains. They acquired horses, and their ancient nomadic spirit was suddenly free of the ground. They acquired Tai-me, the sacred Sun Dance doll, from that moment the object and symbol of their worship, and so shared in the divinity of the sun. Not least, they acquired the sense of destiny, therefore courage and pride. When they entered upon the southern Plains they had been transformed. No longer were they slaves to the simple necessity of survival; they were a lordly and dangerous society of fighters and thieves, hunters and priests of the sun. According to their origin myth, they entered the world through a hollow log. From one point of view, their migration was the fruit of an old prophecy, for indeed they emerged from a sunless world.

Although my grandmother lived out her long life in the shadow of Rainy Mountain, the immense landscape of the continental interior lay like memory in her blood. She could tell of the Crows, whom she had never seen, and of the

A

Literature and Language: Combining Sentences with Appositives

An appositive is a noun or pronoun that explains or identifies the noun or pronoun right next to it. Appositives often have modifiers and are set off by commas, as in these examples.

Aho, *Momaday's grandmother,* saw the Sun Dances when she was a child.

The Crows, *a Plains tribe,* befriended the Kiowa.

Appositives not only pack more information into a sentence; they also can be used to combine two short sentences.

Ask students to find an appositive in the essay's second sentence and another in the first sentence of the Big Dipper legend (top right column, page 1017). Have them combine the following sentences by changing each first sentence into an appositive.

1. Tai-me is the Sun Dance doll. It is sacred to the Kiowa.

2. Devils Tower is a strange formation in the Black Hills. It is the setting of the movie *Close Encounters of the Third Kind.*

3. *House Made of Dawn* is a novel by N. Scott Momaday. It won the Pulitzer Prize in 1968.

Black Hills, where she had never been. I wanted to see in reality what she had seen more perfectly in the mind's eye, and traveled fifteen hundred miles to begin my pilgrimage.

Yellowstone, it seemed to me, was the top of the world, a region of deep lakes and dark timber, canyons and waterfalls. But, beautiful as it is, one might have the sense of confinement there. The skyline in all directions is close at hand, the high wall of the woods and deep cleavages of shade. There is a perfect freedom in the mountains, but it belongs to the eagle and the elk, the badger and the bear. The Kiowas reckoned their stature by the distance they could see, and they were bent and blind in the wilderness.

Descending eastward, the highland meadows are a stairway to the plain. In July the inland slope of the Rockies is luxuriant with flax and buckwheat, stonecrop and larkspur. The earth unfolds and the limit of the land recedes. Clusters of trees, and animals grazing far in the distance, cause the vision to reach away and wonder to build upon the mind. The sun follows a longer course in the day, and the sky is immense beyond all comparison. The great billowing clouds that sail upon it are shadows that move upon the grain like water, dividing light. Farther down, in the land of the Crows and Blackfeet, the plain is yellow. Sweet clover takes hold of the hills and bends upon itself to cover and seal the soil. There the Kiowas paused on their way; they had come to the place where they must change their lives. The sun is at home on the plains. Precisely there does it have the certain character of a god. When the Kiowas came to the land of the Crows, they could see the dark lees of the hills at dawn across the Bighorn River, the profusion of light on the grain shelves, the oldest deity ranging after the solstices. Not yet would they veer southward to the caldron of the land that lay below; they must wean their blood from the northern winter and hold the mountains a while longer in their view. They bore Tai-me in procession to the east.

A dark mist lay over the Black Hills, and the land was like iron. At the top of a ridge I caught A sight of Devils Tower upthrust against the gray sky as if in the birth of time the core of the earth had broken through its crust and the motion of the world was begun. There are things in nature that engender an awful quiet in the heart of man; Devil's Tower is one of them. Two centuries ago, because they could not do otherwise, the Kiowas made a legend at the base of the rock. My grandmother said:

> *Eight children were there at play, seven sisters and their brother. Suddenly the boy was struck dumb; he trembled and began to run upon his hands and feet. His fingers became claws, and his body was covered with fur. Directly there was a bear where the boy had been. The sisters were terrified; they ran, and the bear after them. They came to the stump of a great tree, and the tree spoke to them. It bade them climb upon it, and as they did so it began to rise into the air. The bear came to kill them, but they were just beyond its reach. It reared against the tree and scored the bark all around with its claws. The seven sisters were borne into the sky, and they became the stars of the Big Dipper.*

From that moment, and so long as the legend lives, the Kiowas have kinsmen in the night sky. Whatever they were in the mountains, they could be no more. However tenuous their well-being, however much they had suffered and would suffer again, they had found a way out of the wilderness.

My grandmother had a reverence for the sun, a holy regard that now is all but gone out of mankind. There was a wariness in her, and an ancient awe. She was a Christian in her later years, but she had come a long way about, and she never forgot her birthright. As a child she had been to B the Sun Dances; she had taken part in those annual rites, and by them she had learned the restoration of her people in the presence of Tai-me. She was about seven when the last Kiowa Sun Dance was held in 1887 on the Washita River above Rainy Mountain Creek. The buffalo were gone. In order to consummate the ancient sacrifice—to impale the head of a buffalo bull upon the medicine tree—a delegation of old men journeyed into Texas, there to beg and barter for an animal from the Goodnight herd. She was ten when the Kiowas came together for the last time as a living Sun Dance culture. They could find no buffalo; they had to hang an old hide from the sacred tree. Before the dance could begin, a company of soldiers rode out from Fort Sill under orders to disperse the tribe. Forbidden without cause the essential act of their faith, having seen the wild herds slaughtered and left to rot upon the ground, the Kiowas backed away forever from the medicine tree. That was July 20, 1890, at the great

A. Expansion

As is noted in question 4, page 1019, Devils Tower figures as a key element in the movie *Close Encounters of the Third Kind.* Encourage students who may remember the movie or others who have visited the Black Hills to describe the rock tower.

B. Responding

What is Momaday saying about his grandmother's religious life? (That she combined elements of her native religion with the Christianity she later adopted)

CLOSURE
Have students discuss how Momaday is able to describe the life of the Kiowa tribe by describing the life of his grandmother. Elicit specific examples.

READING CHECK TEST
1. The climate near Rainy Mountain is mild. *False*
2. Before they migrated to the plains, the Kiowa were hunters in the mountains of Montana. *True*
3. According to Kiowa legend, the seven stars of the Big Dipper originated as seven brothers. *False*
4. The sacred dance of the Kiowa is called the Sun Dance. *True*
5. The Kiowa ruled the southern plains in alliance with the Comanche. *True*

A. Details
How does Momaday develop the image "Houses are like sentinels . . . keepers of the weather watch"? (The details of what happens to the house—wood, nails, windows—all reflect the effects of the severe weather in the plains.)

B. Responding
Why do "you approach [the houses] for a longer time than you expect"? (Because distance is deceptive on the plains, and a distant object appears to be closer to the viewer than it really is)

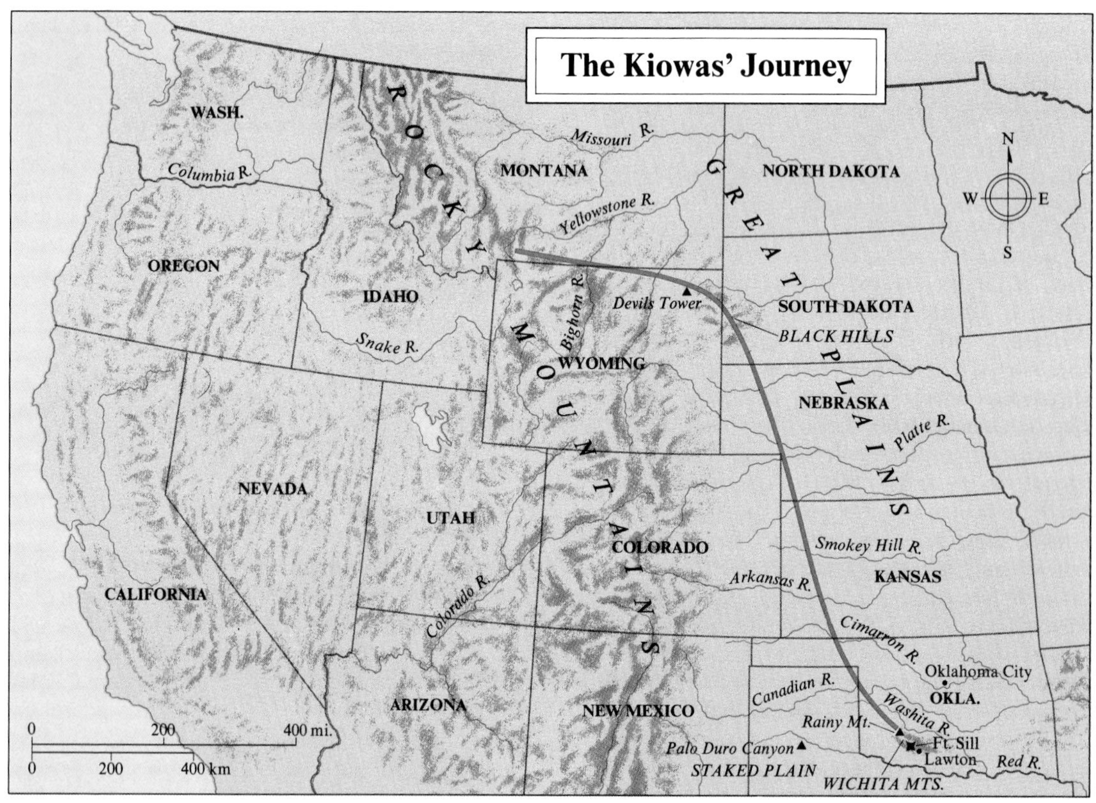

bend of the Washita. My grandmother was there. Without bitterness, and for as long as she lived, she bore a vision of deicide.

Now that I can have her only in memory, I see my grandmother in the several postures that were peculiar to her: standing at the wood stove on a winter morning and turning meat in a great iron skillet; sitting at the south window, bent above her beadwork, and afterwards, when her vision failed, looking down for a long time into the fold of her hands; going out upon a cane, very slowly as she did when the weight of age came upon her; praying. I remember her most often at prayer. She made long, rambling prayers out of suffering and hope, having seen many things. I was never sure that I had the right to hear, so exclusive were they of all mere custom and company. The last time I saw her she prayed standing by the side of her bed at night, naked to the waist, the light of a kerosene lamp moving upon her dark skin. Her long, black hair, always drawn and braided in the day, lay upon her shoulders and against her breasts like a shawl. I do not speak Kiowa, and I never understood her prayers, but there was something inherently sad in the sound, some merest hesitation upon the syllables of sorrow. She began in a high and descending pitch, exhausting her breath to silence; then again and again—and always the same intensity of effort, of something that is, and is not, like urgency in the human voice. Transported so in the dancing light among the shadows of her room, she seemed beyond the reach of time. But that was illusion; I think I knew then that I should not see her again.

Houses are like sentinels in the plain, old keepers of the weather watch. There, in a very little while, wood takes on the appearance of great age. All colors wear soon away in the wind and rain, and then the wood is burned gray and the grain appears and the nails turn red with rust. The windowpanes are black and opaque; you imagine there is nothing within, and indeed there are many ghosts, bones given up to the land. They stand here and there against the sky, and you approach them for a longer time than you expect. They belong in the distance; it is their domain. A B

Analyzing The Essay

Identifying Facts

1. His grandmother died in the spring, and he wants to go to a sacred landmark of the Kiowa to visit her grave.

2. Answers will vary, but may include: the eagle and the elk; flax and buckwheat; pecan and willow.

3. Answers will vary. Students should mention that the sun was a divinity and that the Kiowa rites included Sun Dances.

4. Seven sisters ran from their brother when he was magically transformed into a bear. They climbed a tree and were lifted into the sky, where they became the stars of the Big Dipper.

The rock appears once to have been the tree that bore the seven sisters to the sky.

5. They were dispersed, and their religion died out.

Interpreting Meanings

6. Momaday seems to imply that the migration was a "journey toward the dawn" because it led to a "golden age" for the Kiowa before their eventual dispersal toward the end of the nineteenth century.

7. Momaday uses this phrase as a figure of speech for the fact that Aho witnessed the death of the Sun Dance religion in 1890, when the Kiowa were dispersed.

Students will probably agree that the Kiowa religious feeling survived in both Aho and her grandson.

8. Student answers will vary, but from the references connecting the Kiowa with celestial kinsmen in the night sky, the cricket might be interpreted as symbolic of the Kiowa themselves—or of the scattered descendants of a dispersed tribe, who might be said to resemble a cricket in their fragility, and also a fossil in the age of their heritage.

9. Some of the images Momaday uses to convey strong feelings of light and life are the bright sun of the plains, the Sun Dance, and dawn. Images of darkness and death include the dark mist over the Black Hills, the darkness of night, and the dark stones of the cemetery.

(Answers continue on next page.)

Once there was a lot of sound in my grandmother's house, a lot of coming and going, feasting and talk. The summers there were full of excitement and reunion. The Kiowas are a summer people; they abide the cold and keep to themselves, but when the season turns and the land becomes warm and vital they cannot hold still; an old love of going returns upon them. The aged visitors who came to my grandmother's house when I was a child were made of lean and leather, and they bore themselves upright. They wore great black hats and bright ample shirts that shook in the wind. They rubbed fat upon their hair and wound their braids with strips of colored cloth. Some of them painted their faces and carried the scars of old and cherished enmities. They were an old council of warlords, come to remind and be reminded of who they were. Their wives and daughters served them well. The women might indulge themselves; gossip was at once the mark and compensation of their servitude. They made loud and elaborate talk among themselves, full of jest and gesture, fright and false alarm. They went abroad in fringed and flowered shawls, bright beadwork and German silver. They were at home in the kitchen, and they prepared meals that were banquets.

There were frequent prayer meetings, and great nocturnal feasts. When I was a child I played with my cousins outside, where the lamplight fell upon the ground and the singing of the old people rose up around us and carried away into the darkness. There were a lot of good things to eat, a lot of laughter and surprise. And afterwards, when the quiet returned, I lay down with my grandmother and could hear the frogs away by the river and feel the motion of the air.

Now there is a funeral silence in the rooms, the endless wake of some final word. The walls have closed in upon my grandmother's house. When I returned to it in mourning, I saw for the first time in my life how small it was. It was late at night, and there was a white moon, nearly full. I sat for a long time on the stone steps by the kitchen door. From there I could see out across the land; I could see the long row of trees by the creek, the low light upon the rolling plains, and the stars of the Big Dipper. Once I looked at the moon and caught sight of a strange thing. A cricket had perched upon the handrail, only a few inches away from me. My line of vision was such that the creature filled the moon like a fossil. It had gone there, I thought, to live and die, for there, of all places, was its small definition made whole and eternal. A warm wind rose up and purled[1] like the longing within me.

The next morning I awoke at dawn and went out on the dirt road to Rainy Mountain. It was already hot, and the grasshoppers began to fill the air. Still, it was early in the morning, and the birds sang out of the shadows. The long yellow grass on the mountain shone in the bright light, and a scissortail hied above the land. There, where it ought to be, at the end of a long and legendary way, was my grandmother's grave. Here and there on the dark stones were ancestral names. Looking back once, I saw the mountain and came away.

1. **purled:** moved in ripples or eddies.

Responding to the Essay

Analyzing the Essay

Identifying Facts

1. Explain why the narrator returns to Rainy Mountain. What "pilgrimage" does he make, and why?
2. Momaday takes pains to describe the land the Kiowas traveled through on their journey, mentioning not only the large features of the landscape—plains and mountains—but also creatures, crops, and trees that flourish there. List some of these details that help you feel as if you know what the Great Plains are like.
3. What did you learn from this essay about the Kiowa religion and the role of the sun in their rituals?
4. What was the origin of the Big Dipper, according to Kiowa legend? How does this myth also explain the peculiar formation called Devils Tower? (This rock outcropping, by the way, played a key role in the movie *Close Encounters of the Third Kind*.)
5. What eventually happened to the Kiowa?

(Continued from previous page.)

In general, most students will probably agree that the images of darkness predominate in the essay.

The mood of the essay is meditative and elegiac—dark, but not despairing.

10. Momaday praises the Kiowas' ability to survive their migration, their fine horsemanship warfare, their piety in religion, and their sense of freedom. He mourns their defeat by the U.S. Cavalry, the forced disintegration of their religion, and the passing of such customs and traditions as the feasts and the nocturnal prayer meetings that he remembers as a child.

11. Most students will probably agree that the Kiowa resemble the Puritans and the Romantic writers in that they "read lessons" in nature. The only example we have here, however, is the legend they created at Devils Tower. Where the Puritans found proof of their idea of God in nature, the Kiowa appear to have used nature to expand their idea of religion. This explanation of the Tower and the Big Dipper adds eight figures to their pantheon. Ask students to defend their opinions.

COMMENT FROM A CRITIC

Read the following comment by Vernow E. Lattin to your class, and ask volunteers to relate Momaday's vision of the land to those of earlier American writers.

"[Momaday has] created a new romanticism, with a reverence for the land, a transcendent optimism, and a sense of mythic wholeness. His reverence for the land can be compared to the pastoral vision found in most mainstream American literature. . . ."

FOR FURTHER READING FOR THE TEACHER

Momaday's Pulitzer-prize-winning novel, *House Made of Dawn* (Harper & Row, 1977), centers on the protagonist's finding his religious and racial bearings through an ancestor—in this case, his grandfather.

Interpreting Meanings

6. Momaday says about the Kiowa's long migration to the south and east, "It was a journey toward the dawn . . ." (page 1016). How would you interpret this statement?
7. What does Momaday mean on page 1018 when he says his grandmother "bore a vision of deicide"? Do you think the Kiowa religious feeling survived in Aho? In her grandson?
8. Toward the end of this essay, Momaday tells of seeing a cricket in such a way that "the creature filled the moon like a fossil." It is an important **image**, one that his father chose to illustrate with a picture. Momaday comments: "It had gone there, I thought, to live and die, for there, of all places, was its small definition made whole and eternal." How do you interpret this comment? Do you think the cricket has any value as a **symbol**?
9. List the **images** that Momaday uses to convey strong contrasting feelings of light and life, darkness and death. Which set of images seems to you to be dominant? In your opinion, is the overall **mood** of this essay light or dark? Explain your answer.
10. The book *The Way to Rainy Mountain* is in part an **elegy**. Strictly speaking, an elegy is a funeral song or a poem praising a dead person. What does Momaday praise about the Kiowa? What does he mourn?
11. Do you think Momaday and the Kiowa, like the earlier Puritan and Romantic writers, "read lessons" in nature? Explain.

Writing About the Essay

A Creative Response

1. **Writing a Description.** Momaday's essay is filled with nostalgia, or a longing for the past. For him, the land around Rainy Mountain is associated with childhood and ancestral memories. Try to think of a place you associate with your own childhood—an attic, a field, a house, a store. Write a description using images to describe what it looked like and to suggest what it meant to you.

A Critical Response

2. **Analyzing Atmosphere.** Write a short essay in which you identify and evaluate the ways Momaday uses **setting** to create mood and atmosphere in this excerpt. Before you write, list all the images in the essay that help establish its setting. Then, generalizing from these images, write a sentence describing the mood they suggest.
3. **Responding to a Statement.** "There are things in nature that engender an awful quiet in the heart of man." In a paragraph, write your response to this statement from page 1017.

Analyzing Language and Style

Poetic Prose

N. Scott Momaday, who considers himself chiefly a poet, writes his memoirs in gracefully evocative **poetic prose**. These questions all relate to the paragraph on page 1017 beginning "Descending eastward. . . ."

1. "Descending eastward, the highland meadows are a stairway to the plain."
   a. What **figure of speech** does Momaday use in this sentence?
   b. Explain the terms of the comparison and describe the **image** it creates.
2. "The earth unfolds and the limit of the land recedes."
   a. What **comparison** is implicit in the word *unfolds*?
   b. Describe the **image** created in the sentence.
3. "The great billowing clouds that sail upon it [the sky] are shadows that move upon the grain like water, dividing light."
   a. Identify the **metaphor** in this sentence.
   b. Identify the **simile**.
   c. How would you explain the meaning of the last phrase, "dividing light"?
4. "The sun is at home on the plains. Precisely there does it have the certain character of a god."
   a. How is the sun **personified** in the first sentence?
   b. Why do you think the writer uses inverted word order in the second sentence?
5. "Not yet would they [the Kiowa] veer southward to the caldron of the land that lay below; they must wean their blood from the northern winter and hold the mountains a while longer in their view."
   a. What **figures of speech** can you identify in this sentence?
   b. Rewrite the sentence using straightforward prose style, and compare your version with the original. What has been lost?

James Baldwin (1924–1987)

James Baldwin, one of the most controversial, stirring writers of the twentieth century, was born in the Harlem section of New York City. At the age of twenty-four, Baldwin won a fellowship that allowed him to travel to Europe, and he completed his first novel, *Go Tell It on the Mountain* (1953), while living in Paris. But it was *Notes of a Native Son*, his collection of autobiographical essays published two years later in 1955, that gained Baldwin his reputation as an American writer of the first rank.

As Baldwin himself said, he was compelled to write about being black because "it was the gate I had to unlock before I could write about anything else." His essays, often bitterly ironic, flow from his conviction that the writer's duty is "to examine attitudes, to go beneath the surface, to tap the source."

In the decade that witnessed the beginnings of the American civil rights movement, Baldwin's audacious, searing scrutiny of racial injustice played a major role in forcing leaders, black and white, to come to terms with the nation's most anguishing problem: the treatment of black Americans.

In the early sixties, Baldwin's reputation grew with the publication of two more collections of essays: *Nobody Knows My Name* (1961) and *The Fire Next Time* (1963), a ground-breaking book and perhaps Baldwin's best. He later published several novels, participated in television documentaries, and remained a prominent, humane, and intelligent spokesman for racial justice in American life. He died in France.

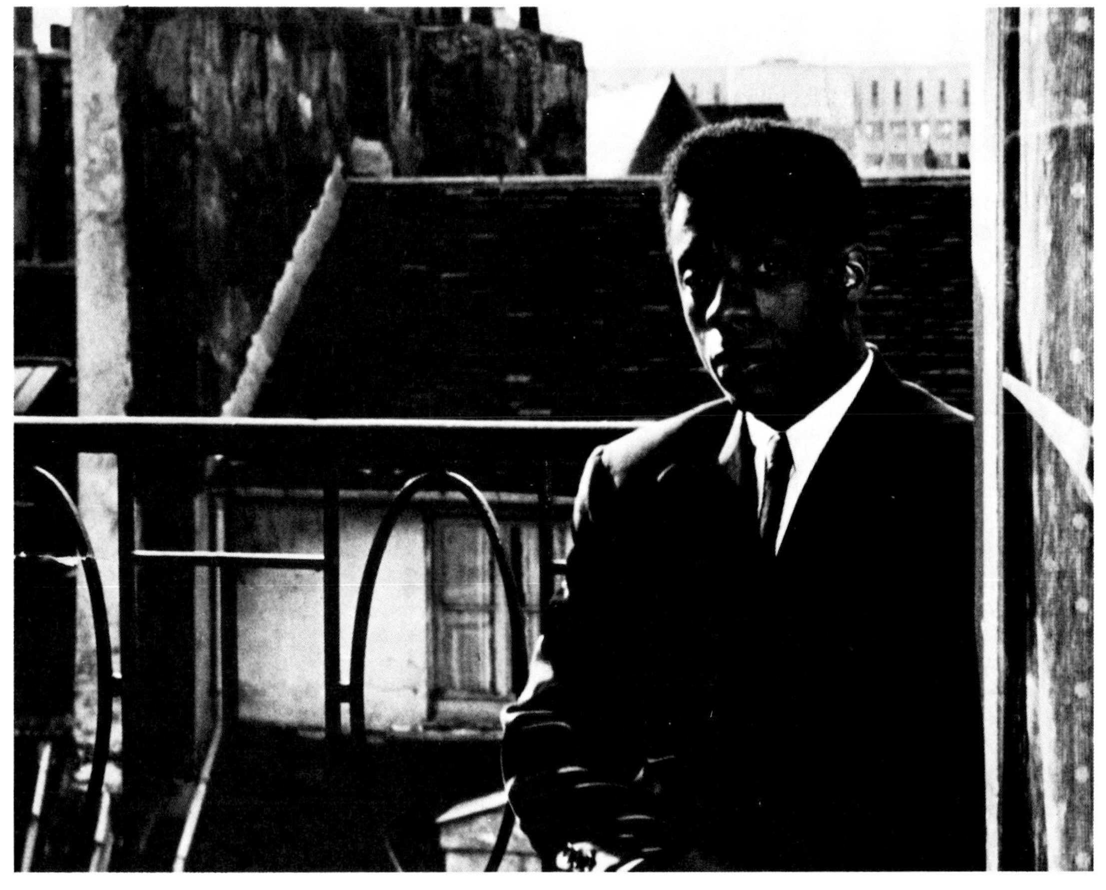

A. Expansion
After graduating from De Witt Clinton High School in 1942, Baldwin moved to New York's Greenwich Village, where he supported himself by working as a handyman, office boy, and waiter until he was able to publish book reviews in national magazines. He was befriended by Richard Wright (page 1004), who later helped him obtain a writing fellowship.

SUPPLEMENTARY SUPPORT MATERIALS
1. Vocabulary Activity Worksheet (*CCB*)
2. Review and Response Worksheet: Tone (*CCB*)
3. Language Skills Worksheet: Repetition and Wordiness (*CCB*)
4. Selection Test (*CCB*)

DEVELOPING VOCABULARY
The following words from the essay are tested in the Selection Test. (See also Vocabulary Activity Worksheet.)

bleak	interloper
to censor	limbo
to hazard	pallid
articulate	ambiguity
coherent	to pulverize

A. Expansion
The Eugene F. Saxton Memorial Trust Award is intended to encourage young writers who have a work in progress.

B. Irony
? At whom is this ironic remark aimed? (At the publishers who assigned the book reviews in particular and at whites in general)

AUTOBIOGRAPHICAL NOTES

Baldwin begins this essay with a factual account of his youth, adolescence, and young manhood. But he soon lives up to his statement that "part of the business of the writer is to examine attitudes," by probing his own outlook more deeply. The essay was published in 1955.

I was born in Harlem thirty-one years ago. I began plotting novels at about the time I learned to read. The story of my childhood is the usual bleak fantasy, and we can dismiss it with the restrained observation that I certainly would not consider living it again. In those days my mother was given to the exasperating and mysterious habit of having babies. As they were born, I took them over with one hand and held a book with the other. The children probably suffered, though they have since been kind enough to deny it, and in this way I read *Uncle Tom's Cabin* and *A Tale of Two Cities* over and over and over again; in this way, in fact, I read just about everything I could get my hands on—except the Bible, probably because it was the only book I was encouraged to read. I must also confess that I wrote—a great deal—and my first professional triumph, in any case, the first effort of mine to be seen in print, occurred at the age of twelve or thereabouts, when a short story I had written about the Spanish revolution won some sort of prize in an extremely short-lived church newspaper. I remember the story was censored by the lady editor, though I don't remember why, and I was outraged.

Also wrote plays, and songs, for one of which I received a letter of congratulations from Mayor La Guardia,[1] and poetry, about which the less said, the better. My mother was delighted by all these goings-on, but my father wasn't; he wanted me to be a preacher. When I was fourteen I became a preacher, and when I was seventeen I stopped. Very shortly thereafter I left home. For God knows how long I struggled with the world of commerce and industry—I guess they would say they struggled with *me*—and when I was about twenty-one I had enough done of a novel to get a Saxton Fellowship. When I was twenty-two the fellowship was over, the novel turned out to be unsalable, and I started waiting on tables in a Village[2] restaurant and writing book reviews—mostly, as it turned out, about the Negro problem, concerning which the color of my skin made me automatically an expert. Did another book, in company with photographer Theodore Pelatowski, about the storefront churches in Harlem. This book met exactly the same fate as my first—fellowship, but no sale (It was a Rosenwald Fellowship.) By the time I was twenty-four I had decided to stop reviewing books about the Negro problem—which, by this time, was only slightly less horrible in print than it was in life—and I packed my bags and went to France, where I finished, God knows how, *Go Tell It on the Mountain*.

Any writer, I suppose, feels that the world into which he was born is nothing less than a conspiracy against the cultivation of his talent—which attitude certainly has a great deal to support it. On the other hand, it is only because the world looks on his talent with such a frightening indifference that the artist is compelled to make his talent important. So that any writer, looking back over even so short a span of time as I am here forced to assess, finds that the things which hurt him and the things which helped him cannot be divorced from each other; he could be helped in a certain way only because he was hurt in a certain way; and his help is simply to be enabled to move from one conundrum[3] to the next—one is tempted

1. **Mayor La Guardia:** Fiorello La Guardia (1882–1947), mayor of New York City, 1934–1945.

2. **Village:** Greenwich Village, a district of Manhattan.
3. **conundrum** (kə·nun′drəm): riddle; puzzling problem.

PREPARATION

ESTABLISHING A PURPOSE. Before they begin reading, ask students to pay special attention to Baldwin's tone as an expression of his attitude toward his problem as an African American writer.

CLOSURE

Ask students to discuss what the tone of this selection mainly reflects—Baldwin's attitude toward the reader, toward the problem of being an African American writer, or toward the art of writing.

to say that he moves from one disaster to the next. When one begins looking for influences one finds them by the score. I haven't thought much about my own, not enough anyway; I hazard that the King James Bible, the rhetoric of the storefront church, something ironic and violent and perpetually understated in Negro speech—and something of Dickens' love for bravura[4]—have something to do with me today; but I wouldn't stake my life on it. Likewise, innumerable people have helped me in many ways; but finally, I suppose, the most difficult (and most rewarding) thing in my life has been the fact that I was born a Negro and was forced, therefore, to effect some kind of truce with this reality. (Truce, by the way, is the best one can hope for.)

One of the difficulties about being a Negro writer (and this is not special pleading, since I don't mean to suggest that he has it worse than anybody else) is that the Negro problem is written about so widely. The bookshelves groan under the weight of information, and everyone therefore considers himself informed. And this information, furthermore, operates usually (generally, popularly) to reinforce traditional attitudes. Of traditional attitudes there are only two—For or Against—and I, personally, find it difficult to say which attitude has caused me the most pain. I am speaking as a writer; from a social point of view I am perfectly aware that the change from ill will to good will, however motivated, however imperfect, however expressed, is better than no change at all.

But it is part of the business of the writer—as I see it—to examine attitudes, to go beneath the surface, to tap the source. From this point of view the Negro problem is nearly inaccessible. It is not only written about so widely; it is written about so badly. It is quite possible to say that the price a Negro pays for becoming articulate is to find himself, at length, with nothing to be articulate about. ("You taught me language," says Caliban to Prospero, "and my profit on't is I know how to curse.")[5] Consider: The tremendous social activity that this problem generates imposes on whites and Negroes alike the necessity of looking forward, of working to bring about a better day. This is fine, it keeps the waters troubled; it is all, indeed, that has made possible the Negro's progress. Nevertheless, social affairs are not generally speaking the writer's prime concern, whether they ought to be or not; it is absolutely necessary that he establish between himself and these affairs a distance which will allow, at least, for clarity, so that before he can look forward in any meaningful sense, he must first be allowed to take a long look back. In the context of the Negro problem neither whites nor blacks, for excellent reasons of their own, have the faintest desire to look back; but I think that the past is all that makes the present coherent, and further, that the past will remain horrible for exactly as long as we refuse to assess it honestly.

I know, in any case, that the most crucial time in my own development came when I was forced to recognize that I was a kind of bastard of the West; when I followed the line of my past I did not find myself in Europe but in Africa. And this meant that in some subtle way, in a really profound way, I brought to Shakespeare, Bach, Rembrandt, to the stones of Paris, to the cathedral at Chartres, and to the Empire State Building, a special attitude. These were not really my creations, they did not contain my history; I might search in them in vain forever for any reflection of myself. I was an interloper; this was not my heritage. At the same time I had no other heritage which I could possibly hope to use—I had certainly been unfitted for the jungle or the tribe. I would have to appropriate these white centuries, I would have to make them mine—I would have to accept my special attitude, my special place in this scheme—otherwise I would have no place in *any* scheme. What was the most difficult was the fact that I was forced to admit something I had always hidden from myself, which the American Negro has had to hide from himself as the price of his public progress; that I hated and feared white people. This did not mean that I loved black people; on the contrary, I despised them, possibly because they failed to produce Rembrandt. In effect, I hated and feared the world. And this meant, not only that I thus gave the world an altogether murderous power over me, but also that in such a self-destroying limbo I could never hope to write.

One writes out of one thing only—one's own experience. Everything depends on how relentlessly one forces from this experience the last drop, sweet or bitter, it can possibly give. This is

4. **bravura** (brə·voor′ə): daring; a dashing display.

5. Caliban is a rough creature of nature whom Prospero tries to civilize. See *The Tempest* by William Shakespeare, Act I, Scene 2, line 363.

A. Responding

? Explain what Baldwin means by the two "traditional attitudes." (He refers to those prejudiced against African Americans and those who want to help them.)

B. Responding

? Explain in your own words what the special attitude was that Baldwin brought to these people and things? (He felt that he was alien to the culture that had produced these artists or works.)

C. Expansion

You may wish to remind students of the passage from *Black Boy* in which Richard at first sees the policemen only as "white" and fears them (page 1011).

Reading Check Test

1. James Baldwin is the youngest in a family of many children. *False*
2. His parents encourage him to read the Bible. *True*
3. As a young man, Baldwin lives for a while in Mexico. *False*
4. Baldwin accuses both blacks and whites of dwelling too much on their past conflicts. *False*
5. Baldwin says that he loves above all the bohemian life. *False*

Analyzing The Essay

Identifying Facts

1. Baldwin says that the most crucial time in his development was when he realized that he was "a kind of bastard of the West": he approached the masterpieces of Western culture with an African perspective. He says that he hated and feared the world.

(Answers continue in left-hand column.)

(Continued from top.)

2. Baldwin says that the business of the writer is going beneath surfaces and examining attitudes. He writes that the "Negro problem" is inaccessible, because, although it is written about widely, it is analyzed badly. Although an honest assessment of the past may be painful for members of both races, such an assessment is vital, nevertheless.
3. He says that his ambition is to last and to get his work done. He wants to be an honest man and a good writer.

Interpreting Meanings

4. Student answers will vary. Ask the students if they are acquainted with any of Ellison's works, especially his landmark novel, *Invisible Man*.
5. Some possibilities include "serious," "retrospective," and "personal."
6. Student answers will vary. Ask students to support and defend their opinions.

the only real concern of the artist, to recreate out of the disorder of life that order which is art. The difficulty then, for me, of being a Negro writer was the fact that I was, in effect, prohibited from examining my own experience too closely by the tremendous demands and the very real dangers of my social situation.

I don't think the dilemma outlined above is uncommon. I do think, since writers work in the disastrously explicit medium of language, that it goes a little way toward explaining why, out of the enormous resources of Negro speech and life, and despite the example of Negro music, prose written by Negroes has been generally speaking so pallid and so harsh. I have not written about being a Negro at such length because I expect that to be my only subject, but only because it was the gate I had to unlock before I could hope to write about anything else. I don't think that the Negro problem in America can be even discussed coherently without bearing in mind its context; its context being the history, traditions, customs, the moral assumptions and preoccupations of the country; in short, the general social fabric. Appearances to the contrary, no one in America escapes its effects and everyone in America bears some responsibility for it. I believe this the more firmly because it is the overwhelming tendency to speak of this problem as though it were a thing apart. But in the work of Faulkner, in the general attitude and certain specific passages in Robert Penn Warren, and, most significantly, in the advent of Ralph Ellison, one sees the beginnings—at least—of a more genuinely penetrating search. Mr. Ellison, by the way, is the first Negro novelist I have ever read to utilize in language, and brilliantly, some of the ambiguity and irony of Negro life.

About my interests: I don't know if I have any, unless the morbid desire to own a sixteen-millimeter camera and make experimental movies can be so classified. Otherwise, I love to eat and drink—it's my melancholy conviction that I've scarcely ever had enough to eat (this is because it's *impossible* to eat enough if you're worried about the next meal)—and I love to argue with people who do not disagree with me too profoundly, and I love to laugh. I do *not* like bohemia,[6] or bohemians, I do not like people whose principal aim is pleasure, and I do not like people who are *earnest* about anything. I don't like people who like me because I'm a Negro; neither do I like people who find in the same accident grounds for contempt. I love America more than any other country in the world, and, exactly for this reason, I insist on the right to criticize her perpetually. I think all theories are suspect, that the finest principles may have to be modified, or may even be pulverized by the demands of life, and that one must find, therefore, one's own moral center and move through the world hoping that this center will guide one aright. I consider that I have many responsibilities, but none greater than this: to last, as Hemingway says, and get my work done.

I want to be an honest man and a good writer.

6. **bohemia** (bō·hē′mē·ə): any unconventional, nonconformist community, often made up of artists.

Responding to the Essay

Analyzing the Essay

Identifying Facts

1. What was the "most crucial time" in Baldwin's own development? What did he learn about himself then?
2. How does Baldwin describe the "business of the writer," and what does this have to do with what he calls "the Negro problem"?
3. What does Baldwin say is his greatest responsibility?

Interpreting Meanings

4. Baldwin says that Ralph Ellison was the first black novelist to express brilliantly "some of the ambiguity and irony of Negro life." What do you think he means?
5. How would you describe Baldwin's **tone**?
6. Could any of Baldwin's points be challenged today?

Writing About the Essay

A Creative Response

Writing a Response. Write a brief essay in which you respond to Baldwin's points in these autobiographical notes. You might call your essay "Notes to a Native Son, _____ Years Later."

Maxine Hong Kingston (1940–   )

No anthology of American literature can be completely comprehensive, representing every kind of writer and every kind of writing. But today, most anthologies try to suggest some of the remarkable diversity in our culture and literature. However, only a few decades ago, a typical anthology would have given its readers the impression that most significant American writers and their subjects were white, male, and middle-class. Women, Native Americans, blacks, other ethnic groups, blue-collar workers, and the poor were romanticized or stereotyped; they did not often have the chance to tell their stories directly. Maxine Hong Kingston, born in California of Chinese immigrant parents, speaks for some of these long-stifled voices.

The form of Kingston's writing—how she chooses to tell her story—is innovative as well. Her first book, *The Woman Warrior: Memoirs of a Girlhood Among Ghosts* (1976), is a mixture of autobiography, myth, poetic meditation, and fiction. It conveys Kingston's memories and feelings about what it was like to grow up in a strange world (America) populated by what she and her family thought of as white-skinned "ghosts."

The book received immediate acclaim. William McPherson of the *Washington Post* wrote: "*The Woman Warrior* is a strange, sometimes savagely terrifying and, in the literal sense, wonderful story about growing up caught between two highly sophisticated and utterly alien cultures, both vivid, often menacing, and equally mysterious." Paul Gray said in *Time*: "Exiles and refugees tell sad stories of the life they left behind. Even sadder, sometimes, is the muteness of their children. They are likely to find the old ways and old language excess baggage, especially if their adopted homeland is the U.S., where the race is to the swift and the adaptable. Thus a heritage of centuries can die in a generation of embarrassed silence. *The Woman Warrior* gives that silence a voice."

When *The Woman Warrior* won the National Book Critics Circle Award for general nonfiction in 1976, Kingston emerged from relative ano-

nymity into national attention. The suddenness of her appearance as an important literary figure was startling. Critic John Leonard wrote that fall in *The New York Times* that he heard the rumbles of "the big guns of autumn lining up, the howitzers of Vonnegut and Updike and Cheever and Mailer" [all famous novelists]; "but listen," he went on, "this week a remarkable book has been quietly published; it is one of the best I've read in years."

Where had Kingston been until the age of 36? Like many writers, especially women, who are often absorbed by family responsibilities or income-producing jobs for years, she did not publish her first major work until middle age. (Although some writers become famous when they are quite young, it is not true that you have failed as a writer if you have not been published before you are thirty.)

Named for an American woman in the gambling house where her father worked for a time, Maxine Hong grew up in the Chinatown of Stockton, California. She earned a B.A. from the University of California at Berkeley in 1962 and taught high-school English and mathematics. In 1962 she married actor Earl Kingston. After

SUPPLEMENTARY SUPPORT MATERIALS
1. Vocabulary Activity Worksheet (*CCB*)
2. Review and Response Worksheet: First-Person Narration (*CCB*)
3. Language Skills Worksheet: Prepositions and Prepositional Phrases (*CCB*)
4. Selection Test (*CCB*)

DEVELOPING VOCABULARY
The following words from the memoir are tested in the Selection Test. (See also Vocabulary Activity Worksheet.)

faltering	pastel
to loiter	to blurt
spigot	embroidery
to pad	to embed
nape	recluse

PREPARATION
1. ESTABLISHING A PURPOSE. Explain to students before they start to read that the narrator of this selection dislikes a classmate intensely and is cruel to her. Ask them to try to determine, as they read, the reason for her hostility.

A. Expansion
The narrator has ambivalent feelings about the goal of becoming "American-feminine." Finding the right way to talk (not too loud, as the narrator feels Chinese women speak) led to the invention of the American-feminine speaking personality.

B. Expansion
Apparently both sisters started school later than most of their classmates—the younger one a year and the older two years late.

C. Responding
? To whom does the pronoun *we* refer to? (To the narrator and the quiet girl)

their son was born, the Kingstons moved to Hawaii; critic Susan Currier finds it significant that Kingston "continues to reside in Hawaii, halfway between the two cultures which have rent her spirit and inspired her art."

In 1980, Kingston published a companion piece to *The Woman Warrior*, a kind of ancestral history called *China Men*. Currier has described this book as "a sort of vindication of all the Chinese who helped build America but who were rewarded with abuse and neglect." In recent years, Kingston has been working on a novel which will reportedly *not* center on her own Chinese family and ancestors.

Despite the attention given to her first two books, Kingston has remained relatively private. She seldom gives interviews or appears at public readings. In her two memoirs, she does not always answer some of the personal questions raised by her writing. In the passage that follows, even a careful reader will not be able to decide what is truth, what is fiction, and what is simply left unsaid. This ambiguity gives Kingston's work much of its haunting quality.

THE GIRL WHO WOULDN'T TALK

The Chinese-American family in this extract from *The Woman Warrior* lives in Stockton, California. Just before this episode starts, the narrator has been talking about speech and Chinese voices, which Kingston says are louder than American voices. Describing her own voice, the narrator says: "You could hear splinters in my voice, bones running jagged against one another. I was loud, though. I was glad I didn't whisper."

The heart of this story has to do with childhood cruelty, a problem that knows no cultural or linguistic barriers.

The "ghosts" mentioned by the narrator are the white Americans, who seemed so strange to the Chinese.

Normal Chinese women's voices are strong and bossy. We American-Chinese girls had to whisper to make ourselves American-feminine. Apparently we whispered even more softly than the Americans. Once a year the teachers referred my sister and me to speech therapy, but our voices would straighten out, unpredictably normal, for the therapists. Some of us gave up, shook our heads, and said nothing, not one word. Some of us could not even shake our heads. At times shaking my head no is more self-assertion than I can manage. Most of us eventually found [A] some voice, however faltering. We invented an American-feminine speaking personality, except for that one girl who could not speak up even in Chinese school.

She was a year older than I and was in my class for twelve years. During all those years she read aloud but would not talk. Her older sister was usually beside her; their parents kept the older daughter back to protect the younger one. [B] They were six and seven years old when they began school. Although I had flunked kindergarten, I was the same age as most other students in our class; my parents had probably lied about my age, so I had had a head start and came out even. My younger sister was in the class below me; we were normal ages and normally separated. The parents of the quiet girl, on the other hand, protected both daughters. When it sprinkled, they kept them home from school. The girls did not work for a living the way we did. But in other ways we were the same.

We were similar in sports. [C] We held the bat on our shoulders until we walked to first base. (You got a strike only when you actually struck at the

A. Characterization
? What does the way the quiet girl places the bat on home plate tell you about her? (She is very neat, a quality that the narrator dislikes in her.)

B. Responding
? What clues does the narrator provide here as to the reasons for her animosity toward the quiet girl? (The narrator recognizes similarities between herself and the girl: she also sees in her aspects of the "Chinese feminine" personality that she wishes to suppress in herself.)

C. Responding
? Why did the narrator feel arrogant in the sixth grade? (Probably because sixth graders were the oldest students in the school, moving on to a junior high school the next year)

D. Expansion
The top of the newspaper map was red to mark North Korean territory. The red portion went up and down, reflecting the rapid changes in the fortunes of that war: At first the North Koreans occupied most of South Korea; then they were driven back almost to the Chinese border; then Chinese soldiers entered the fighting on the North Korean side, and the South Koreans and Americans were pushed back down again.

ball.) Sometimes the pitcher wouldn't bother to throw to us. "Automatic walk," the other children would call, sending us on our way. By fourth or fifth grade, though, some of us would try to hit the ball. "Easy out," the other kids would say. I hit the ball a couple of times. Baseball was nice in that there was a definite spot to run to after hitting the ball. Basketball confused me because when I caught the ball I didn't know whom to throw it to. "Me. Me," the kids would be yelling. "Over here." Suddenly it would occur to me I hadn't memorized which ghosts were on my team and which were on the other. When the kids said, "Automatic walk," the girl who was quieter than I kneeled with one end of the bat in each hand and placed it carefully on the plate. Then she dusted her hands as she walked to first base, where she rubbed her hands softly, fingers spread. She always got tagged out before second base. She would whisper-read but not talk. Her whisper was as soft as if she had no muscles. She seemed to be breathing from a distance. I heard no anger or tension.

I joined in at lunchtime when the other students, the Chinese too, talked about whether or not she was mute, although obviously she was not if she could read aloud. People told how *they* had tried *their* best to be friendly. *They* said hello, but if she refused to answer, well, they didn't see why they had to say hello anymore. She had no friends of her own but followed her sister everywhere, although people and she herself probably thought I was her friend. I also followed her sister about, who was fairly normal. She was almost two years older and read more than anyone else.

I hated the younger sister, the quiet one. I hated her when she was the last chosen for her team and I, the last chosen for my team. I hated her for her China doll hair cut. I hated her at music time for the wheezes that came out of her plastic flute.

One afternoon in the sixth grade (that year I was arrogant with talk, not knowing there were going to be high school dances and college seminars to set me back), I and my little sister and the quiet girl and her big sister stayed late after school for some reason. The cement was cooling, and the tetherball poles made shadows across the gravel. The hooks at the rope ends were clinking against the poles. We shouldn't have been so late; there was laundry work to do and Chinese school to get to by 5:00. The last time we had stayed late, my mother had phoned the police and told them we had been kidnaped by bandits. The radio stations broadcast our descriptions. I had to get home before she did that again. But sometimes if you loitered long enough in the schoolyard, the other children would have gone home and you could play with the equipment before the office took it away. We were chasing one another through the playground and in and out of the basement, where the playroom and lavatory were. During air raid drills (it was during the Korean War, which you knew about because every day the front page of the newspaper printed a map of Korea with the top part red and going up and down like a window shade), we curled up in this basement. Now everyone was gone. The playroom was army green and had nothing in it but a long trough with drinking spigots in rows. Pipes across the ceiling led to the drinking fountains and to the toilets in the next room. When someone flushed you could hear the water and other matter, which the children named, running inside the big pipe above the drinking spigots. There was one playroom for girls next to the girls' lavatory and one playroom for boys next to the boys' lavatory. The stalls were open and the toilets had no lids, by which we knew that ghosts have no sense of shame or privacy.

Inside the playroom the light bulbs in cages had already been turned off. Daylight came in x-patterns through the caging at the windows. I looked out and, seeing no one in the schoolyard, ran outside to climb the fire escape upside down, hanging on to the metal stairs with fingers and toes.

I did a flip off the fire escape and ran across the schoolyard. The day was a great eye, and it was not paying much attention to me now. I could disappear with the sun; I could turn quickly sideways and slip into a different world. It seemed I could run faster at this time, and by evening I would be able to fly. As the afternoon wore on we could run into the forbidden places—the boys' big yard, the boys' playroom. We could go into the boys' lavatory and look at the urinals. The only time during school hours I had crossed the boys' yard was when a flatbed truck with a giant thing covered with canvas and tied down with ropes had parked across the street. The children had told one another that it was a gorilla in captivity; we couldn't decide whether the sign said "Trail of the Gorilla" or "Trial of the Gorilla." The thing was as big as a house. The teachers couldn't stop us from hysterically rushing to the fence and cling-

Humanities Connection: Responding to the Photograph
The Asian girl and the American flag she carries are sharply defined against out-of-focus banners that provide an almost abstract background.

? Does this girl look the way the narrator in the selection would like to look, or does she represent the kind of Chinese femininity the narrator dislikes? (The girl in the picture has the look the narrator admires.)

Labor Day parade. Photograph taken by Eve Arnold, 1983.

Literature and Language: Using Adjective Clauses
Point out that the title "The Girl Who Wouldn't Talk" contains an adjective clause—a subordinate clause that modifies a noun or pronoun. Remind students that adjective clauses often begin with the words *that, which, who,* or *whom*. Then ask them to identify the adjective clause in the title and the noun it modifies. (*Who Wouldn't Talk* modifies *Girl.*)

Sometimes adjective clauses provide more information about the noun or pronoun they modify (nonessential clauses); at other times they pin down a specific person or object (essential clauses). In this case we ask, Which girl? Not just any girl, but the one who wouldn't talk. The clause is essential.

Most people are insecure about punctuating an adjective clause. Should it be set off with commas, or not? If you want to deal with this rather elite punctuation problem, have students turn to page 1214, rule 3. Then have students write three sentences that contain adjective clauses, adding commas where necessary.

ing to the wire mesh. Now I ran across the boys' yard clear to the Cyclone fence and thought about the hair that I had seen sticking out of the canvas. It was going to be summer soon, so you could feel that freedom coming on too.

I ran back into the girls' yard, and there was the quiet sister all by herself. I ran past her, and she followed me into the girls' lavatory. My footsteps rang hard against cement and tile because of the taps I had nailed into my shoes. Her footsteps were soft, padding after me. There was no one in the lavatory but the two of us. I ran all around the rows of twenty-five open stalls to make sure of that. No sisters. I think we must have been playing hide-and-go-seek. She was not good at hiding by herself and usually followed her sister; they'd hide in the same place. They must have gotten separated. In this growing twilight, a child could hide and never be found.

I stopped abruptly in front of the sinks, and she came running toward me before she could stop herself, so that she almost collided with me. I walked closer. She backed away, puzzlement, then alarm in her eyes.

"You're going to talk," I said, my voice steady and normal, as it is when talking to the familiar, the weak, and the small. "I am going to make you talk, you sissy-girl." She stopped backing away and stood fixed.

I looked into her face so I could hate it close up. She wore black bangs, and her cheeks were pink and white. She was baby-soft. I thought that I could put my thumb on her nose and push it bonelessly in, indent her face. I could poke dimples into her cheeks. I could work her face around like dough. She stood still, and I did not want to look at her face anymore; I hated fragility. I walked around her, looked her up and down the way the Mexican and Negro girls did when they fought, so tough. I hated her weak neck, the way it did not support her head but let it droop; her head would fall backward. I stared at the curve of her nape. I wished I was able to see what my own neck looked like from the back and sides. I hoped it did not look like hers; I wanted a stout neck. I grew my hair long to hide it in case it was a flower-stem neck. I walked around to the front of her to hate her face some more.

I reached up and took the fatty part of her cheek, not dough, but meat, between my thumb and finger. This close, and I saw no pores. "Talk," I said. "Are you going to talk?" Her skin was fleshy, like squid out of which the glassy blades of bones had been pulled. I wanted tough skin, hard brown skin. I had callused my hands; I had scratched dirt to blacken the nails, which I cut straight across to make stubby fingers. I gave her face a squeeze. "Talk." When I let go, the pink rushed back into my white thumbprint on her skin. I walked around to her side. "Talk!" I shouted into the side of her head. Her straight hair hung, the same all these years, no ringlets or braids or permanents. I squeezed her other cheek. "Are you? Huh? Are you going to talk?" She tried to shake her head, but I had hold of her face. She had no muscles to jerk away. Her skin seemed to stretch. I let go in horror. What if it came away in my hand? "No, huh?" I said, rubbing the touch of her off my fingers. "Say 'No,' then," I said. I gave her another pinch and a twist. "Say 'No.' " She shook her head, her straight hair turning with her head, not swinging side to side like the pretty girls'. She was so neat. Her neatness bothered me. I hated the way she folded the wax paper from her lunch; she did not wad her brown paper bag and her school papers. I hated her clothes—the blue pastel cardigan, the white blouse with the collar that lay flat over the cardigan, the home-made flat, cotton skirt she wore when everybody else was wearing flared skirts. I hated pastels; I would wear black always. I squeezed again, harder, even though her cheek had a weak rubbery feeling I did not like. I squeezed one cheek, then the other, back and forth until the tears ran out of her eyes as if I had pulled them out. "Stop crying," I said, but although she habitually followed me around, she did not obey. Her eyes dripped; her nose dripped. She wiped her eyes with her papery fingers. The skin on her hands and arms seemed powdery-dry, like tracing paper, onion paper. I hated her fingers. I could snap them like breadsticks. I pushed her hands down. "Say 'Hi,' " I said. " 'Hi'. Like that. Say your name. Go ahead. Say it. Or are you stupid? You're so stupid, you don't know your own name, is that it? When I say, 'What's your name?' you just blurt it out, O.K.? What's your name?" Last year the whole class had laughed at a boy who couldn't fill out a form because he didn't know his father's name. The teacher sighed, exasperated and was very sarcastic, "Don't you notice things? What does your mother call him?" she said. The class laughed at how dumb he was not to notice things. "She calls him father of me," he said. Even we

A. Responding
? Why does the narrator check all the toilet stalls? (She has already decided that she is going to make the quiet girl speak.)

B. Responding
? What does the narrator admire about the Mexican and black girls she has seen fighting? (They seem very tough, in contrast to the quiet girl who has so many of the passive, gentle qualities that she would like to suppress in herself.)

C. Characterization
? The narrator is tormented by possible similarities between herself and the quiet girl. Why? (The quiet girl embodies many qualities of Chinese femininity that the narrator despises but fears she shares.)

A. Figurative Language
The narrator uses a number of unpleasant similes to describe the quiet girl to suggest how repulsive she found her.
? List at least three of these unflattering similes that appear in this long paragraph that begins on page 1029. ("Her skin was fleshy, like squid out of which the glassy blades of bones had been pulled"; "The skin on her . . . arms seemed powdery-dry, like tracing paper"; ". . . her little white ears, like white cutworms")

B. Responding
? What is it that particularly startles the quiet girl? (The narrator's saying that she has heard the quiet girl speak)

C. Responding
? What makes the narrator think of "little bound feet, the toes twisted under the balls"? (As she attacks the quiet girl, she is attacking her own Chinese heritage—a former feature of which was the binding of the feet of girl children.)

D. Concrete Details
Call students' attention to the way the detail of the visible tear ducts helps the reader to see the crying child.

laughed although we knew that his mother did not call his father by name, and a son does not know his father's name. We laughed and were relieved that our parents had had the foresight to tell us some names we could give the teachers. "If you're not stupid," I said to the quiet girl, "what's your name?" She shook her head, and some hair caught in the tears; wet black hair stuck to the side of the pink and white face. I reached up (she was taller than I) and took a strand of hair. I pulled it. "Well, then, let's honk your hair," I said. "Honk. Honk." Then I pulled the other side—"ho-o-n-nk"—a long pull; "ho-o-n-n-nk"—a longer pull. I could see her little white ears, like white cutworms curled underneath the hair. "Talk!" I yelled into each cutworm.

I looked right at her. "I know you talk," I said. "I've heard you." Her eyebrows flew up. Something in those black eyes was startled, and I pursued it. "I was walking past your house when you didn't know I was there. I heard you yell in English and in Chinese. You weren't just talking. You were shouting. I heard you shout. You were saying, 'Where are you?' Say that again. Go ahead, just the way you did at home." I yanked harder on the hair, but steadily, not jerking. I did not want to pull it out. "Go ahead. Say, 'Where are you?' Say it loud enough for your sister to come. Call her. Make her come help you. Call her name. I'll stop if she comes. So call. Go ahead."

She shook her head, her mouth curved down, crying. I could see her tiny white teeth, baby teeth. I wanted to grow big strong yellow teeth. "You do have a tongue," I said. "So use it." I pulled the hair at her temples, pulled the tears out of her eyes. "Say, 'Ow' " I said. "Just 'Ow.' Say, 'Let go.' Go ahead. Say it. I'll honk you again if you don't say, 'Let me alone.' Say, 'Leave me alone,' and I'll let you go. I will. I'll let go if you say it. You can stop this anytime you want to, you know. All you have to do is tell me to stop. Just say, 'Stop.' You're just asking for it, aren't you? You're just asking for another honk. Well then, I'll have to give you another honk. Say, 'Stop.' " But she didn't. I had to pull again and again.

Sounds did come out of her mouth, sobs, chokes, noises that were almost words. Snot ran out of her nose. She tried to wipe it on her hands, but there was too much of it. She used her sleeve. "You're disgusting," I told her. "Look at you, snot streaming down your nose, and you won't say a word to stop it. You're such a nothing." I moved behind her and pulled the hair growing out of her weak neck. I let go. I stood silent for a long time. Then I screamed, "Talk!" I would scare the words out of her. If she had had little bound feet, the toes twisted under the balls, I would have jumped up and landed on them—crunch!—stomped on them with my iron shoes. She cried hard, sobbing aloud. "Cry, 'Mama,' " I said. "Come on. Cry, 'Mama.' Say, 'Stop it.' "

I put my finger on her pointed chin. "I don't like you. I don't like the weak little toots you make on your flute. Wheeze. Wheeze. I don't like the way you don't swing at the ball. I don't like the way you're the last one chosen. I don't like the way you can't make a fist for tetherball. Why don't you make a fist? Come on. Get tough. Come on. Throw fists." I pushed at her long hands; they swung limply at her sides. Her fingers were so long, I thought maybe they had an extra joint. They couldn't possibly make fists like other people's. "Make a fist," I said. "Come on. Just fold those fingers up; fingers on the inside, thumbs on the outside. Say something. Honk me back. You're so tall, and you let me pick on you.

"Would you like a hanky? I can't get you one with embroidery on it or crocheting along the edges, but I'll get you some toilet paper if you tell me to. Go ahead. Ask me. I'll get it for you if you ask." She did not stop crying. "Why don't you scream, 'Help'?" I suggested. "Say, 'Help.' Go ahead." She cried on. "O.K. O.K. Don't talk. Just scream, and I'll let you go. Won't that feel good? Go ahead. Like this." I screamed not too loudly. My voice hit the tile and rang it as if I had thrown a rock at it. The stalls opened wider and the toilets wider and darker. Shadows leaned at angles I had not seen before. It was very late. Maybe a janitor had locked me in with this girl for the night. Her black eyes blinked and stared, blinked and stared. I felt dizzy from hunger. We had been in this lavatory together forever. My mother would call the police again if I didn't bring my sister home soon. "I'll let you go if you say just one word," I said. "You can even say 'a' or 'the,' and I'll let you go. Come on. Please." She didn't shake her head anymore, only cried steadily, so much water coming out of her. I could see the two duct holes where the tears welled out. Quarts of tears but no words. I grabbed her by the shoulder. I could feel bones. The light was coming in queerly through the frosted glass with the chicken wire embedded in it. Her crying was like an animal's—a seal's—

Closure

Have students discuss how the families of the narrator and the quiet girl reflect two different immigrant attitudes toward life in their new country.

Reading Check Test

1. The girl who wouldn't talk does use her voice when she reads aloud. *True*
2. The quiet girl and Maxine are different in every way. *False*
3. One day Maxine catches the quiet girl in the school lavatory. *True*
4. Maxine torments the quiet girl by pinching her and trying to make her talk. *True*
5. Soon after the incident with Maxine, the quiet girl becomes ill with a mysterious paralysis. *False*

and it echoed around the basement. "Do you want to stay here all night?" I asked. "Your mother is wondering what happened to her baby. You wouldn't want to have her mad at you. You'd better say something." I shook her shoulder. I pulled her hair again. I squeezed her face. "Come on! Talk! Talk! Talk!" She didn't seem to feel it anymore when I pulled her hair. "There's nobody here but you and me. This isn't a classroom or a playground or a crowd. I'm just one person. You can talk in front of one person. Don't make me pull harder and harder until you talk." But her hair seemed to stretch; she did not say a word. "I'm going to pull harder. Don't make me pull anymore, or your hair will come out and you're going to be bald. Do you want to be bald? You don't want to be bald, do you?"

Far away, coming from the edge of town, I heard whistles blow. The cannery was changing shifts, letting out the afternoon people, and still we were here at school. It was a sad sound—work done. The air was lonelier after the sound died.

"Why won't you talk?" I started to cry. What if I couldn't stop, and everyone would want to know what happened? "Now look what you've done," I scolded. "You're going to pay for this. I want to know why. And you're going to tell me why. You don't see I'm trying to help you out, do you? Do you want to be like this, dumb (do you know what dumb means?), your whole life? Don't you ever want to be a cheerleader? Or a pompon girl? What are you going to do for a living? Yeah, you're going to have to work because you can't be a housewife. Somebody has to marry you before you can be a housewife. And you, you are a plant. Do you know that? That's all you are if you don't talk. If you don't talk, you can't have a personality. You'll have no personality and no hair. You've got to let people know you have a personality and a brain. You think somebody is going to take care of you all your stupid life? You think you'll always have your big sister? You think somebody's going to marry you, is that it? Well, you're not the type that gets dates, let alone gets married. Nobody's going to notice you. And you have to talk for interviews, speak right up in front of the boss. Don't you know that? You're so dumb. Why do I waste my time on you?" Sniffling and snorting. I couldn't stop crying and talking at the same time. I kept wiping my nose on my arm, my sweater lost somewhere (probably not worn because my mother said to wear a sweater). It seemed as if I had spent my life in that basement, doing the worst thing I had yet done to another person. "I'm doing this for your own good," I said. "Don't you dare tell anyone I've been bad to you. Talk. Please talk."

I was getting dizzy from the air I was gulping. Her sobs and my sobs were bouncing wildly off the tile, sometimes together, sometimes alternating. "I don't understand why you won't say just one word," I cried, clenching my teeth. My knees were shaking, and I hung on to her hair to stand up. Another time I'd stayed too late, I had had to walk around two Negro kids who were bonking each other's head on the concrete. I went back later to see if the concrete had cracks in it. "Look. I'll give you something if you talk. I'll give you my pencil box. I'll buy you some candy. O.K.? What do you want? Tell me. Just say it, and I'll give it to you. Just say, 'yes,' or, 'O.K.,' or, 'Baby Ruth.' " But she didn't want anything.

I had stopped pinching her cheek because I did not like the feel of her skin. I would go crazy if it came away in my hands. "I skinned her," I would have to confess.

Suddenly I heard footsteps hurrying through the basement, and her sister ran into the lavatory calling her name. "Oh, there you are," I said. "We've been waiting for you. I was only trying to teach her to talk. She wouldn't cooperate, though." Her sister went into one of the stalls and got handfuls of toilet paper and wiped her off. Then we found my sister, and we walked home together. "Your family really ought to force her to speak," I advised all the way home. "You mustn't pamper her."

The world is sometimes just, and I spent the next eighteen months sick in bed with a mysterious illness. There was no pain and no symptoms, though the middle line in my left palm broke in two. Instead of starting junior high school, I lived like the Victorian recluses I read about. I had a rented hospital bed in the living room, where I watched soap operas on TV, and my family cranked me up and down. I saw no one but my family, who took good care of me. I could have no visitors, no other relatives, no villagers. My bed was against the west window, and I watched the seasons change the peach tree. I had a bell to ring for help. I used a bedpan. It was the best year and a half of my life. Nothing happened.

But one day my mother, the doctor, said, "You're ready to get up today. It's time to get up

Analyzing The Memoir

Identifying Facts

1. The narrator hates the younger sister because she regards her as passive, weak, soft, fragile, delicate, neat, privileged, and too "Chinese."

2. Maxine uses a variety of physical and psychological torments. She pushes, pinches, and shakes her, and she pulls her hair. She taunts her by calling her a sissy; she shouts at her and orders her to stop crying; she calls her stupid, and mockingly orders her to call her sister for help; she calls her disgusting, and she tells her that she will never be married because she is a "plant" with no personality.

She is puzzled and alarmed, but she endures the narrator's torments without ever speaking.

3. The narrator falls ill and is forced to spend a year and a half at home in bed.

(Answers continue on next page.)

(Continued from previous page.)

Interpreting Meanings

4. Students will have various opinions. For the narrator, the girl seems to represent the delicate, traditional Chinese image of femininity and submission—an image that the narrator, at this stage of her life, has firmly rejected. She thus hates the girl as representative of the aspects of her own heritage that she would prefer to suppress.

Student answers will vary.

5. Student answers will vary. The narrator seems angry at her own family, at the "ghosts" of American society, at herself, and at the conflicts posed by loyalty to her own family and community on the one hand, and the pressures to become assimilated to the "ghost" society on the other.

6. Student answers will vary. Obviously, the girl is characterized as habitually silent. In these circumstances, she may have been so shocked and petrified with fear that she could not possibly have uttered a word, even if she had wanted to speak.

7. Kingston herself provides a cryptic explanation in the next line when she says *(Answers continue in left-hand column.)*

(Continued from top.)

that during this period "nothing happened." Perhaps she means that her seclusion at home temporarily spared her the tension and conflicts of growing up "between two cultures."

Student answers will vary. Some students may suggest that the illness was a psychosomatic reaction—the narrator's sense of guilt for having treated the younger sister so cruelly.

8. Student answers will vary. Note that the narrator refers to the "weak little toots" that the silent girl makes on her flute. Perhaps part of the narrator's motivation in writing the essay is as belated atonement for her cruelty to the silent girl.

and go to school." I walked about outside to get my legs working, leaning on a staff I cut from the peach tree. The sky and trees, the sun were immense—no longer framed by a window, no longer grayed with a fly screen. I sat down on the sidewalk in amazement—the night, the stars. But at school I had to figure out again how to talk. I met again the poor girl I had tormented. She had not changed. She wore the same clothes, haircut, and manner as when we were in elementary school, no make-up on the pink and white face, while the other Asian girls were starting to tape their eyelids. She continued to be able to read aloud. But there was hardly any reading aloud anymore, less and less as we got into high school.

I was wrong about nobody taking care of her. Her sister became a clerk-typist and stayed unmarried. They lived with her mother and father. She did not have to leave the house except to go to the movies. She was supported. She was protected by her family, as they would normally have done in China if they could have afforded it, not sent off to school with strangers, ghosts, boys.

Responding to the Memoir

Analyzing the Memoir

Identifying Facts

1. What are the reasons the narrator hates the younger sister, despite the fact that the girls were alike in so many ways?
2. How does the narrator try to make the silent girl talk? (Note the psychological and physical torments she applies.) What is the girl's response?
3. What happens to the narrator after this incident that makes her say that "the world is sometimes just"?

Interpreting Meanings

4. Why do you think the narrator cares so intensely about making the silent girl talk? Do her feelings strike you as credible—have you experienced feelings like this yourself, or observed them in others?
5. Underlying this passage is a deep undercurrent of anger, which at first seems directed simply at the silent girl. What else could the narrator be angry about?
6. The silent girl was obviously able to speak. Why do you think she did *not* speak?
7. What implication do you draw from the fact that Kingston says that her time in bed "was the best year and a half of my life"? Do you think the illness really had anything to do with her treatment of the silent girl?
8. This episode comes from a chapter called "A Song for a Barbarian Reed Pipe." What could be the significance of the title, and how is this story of the silent girl related to it?

Writing About the Memoir

A Critical Response

Analyzing a Character. In a paragraph, discuss the character of the narrator as it is presented in this extract. Consider these basic elements of characterization. Which elements does Kingston use?

1. Appearance
2. Speech
3. Actions
4. Private thoughts and feelings
5. Responses of other people to the character

Conclude your essay by discussing your response to the way Kingston characterizes herself.

Analyzing Language and Style

Imagery and Feelings

At times, Kingston's images can evoke powerful responses from us and can reveal the narrator's strong feelings as well.

1. What are the implications of the term *ghosts* used to describe the white society that, for the narrator, exists beyond and outside her own world?
2. Find the images describing the silent girl's skin; her fingers; the skin on her hands and arms; her ears; and her crying. What feelings about the girl do these images reveal? How do they make *you* respond to the girl and to her tormentor, the narrator?

Susan Allen Toth (1940–   )

As editor of this section of the textbook, I have the odd task of writing about myself. Of course, I could pretend that someone else was doing it, or write an impersonal narrative, as if I were observing my life from afar. But as a writer and a teacher of writing, I have long felt that too many of us are frightened of using the first-person voice. We have been taught that somehow it is wrong to say *I*. Instead, we learn a dull, vague bureaucratese, filled with passive constructions such as "It can be seen by many readers . . . ," "It can easily be understood that . . . ," or "In conclusion, it can be pointed out that. . . ." We are not fooling anyone—the reader knows it is the individual writer's judgment—but we are pretending that we are part of some impressive institution. We think that *I* doesn't sound important enough. It is also rather scary to write *I*; we don't have anyone else to hide behind.

As a memoirist (someone who writes directly about all or part of her personal experience), I have written two books with an *I*. The first, *Blooming: A Small-Town Girlhood* (1981), is about my childhood and adolescence in Ames, Iowa, in the 1940's and 1950's. The second, *Ivy Days: Making My Way Out East* (1984) (which is excerpted here), is a kind of sequel, describing my experiences as a Midwestern girl at an Eastern Ivy League women's college. In both books, I try to see my life as clearly as I can, remembering both pain and pleasure, which were often mixed. I am glad when readers find my writing humorous; but I am more deeply pleased by those who also sense my disappointments, fears, and continuing uncertainties, experiences and feelings that were part of my (and most people's) growing up.

The biographical facts of my life are short and don't say much about personality, family, fate, or luck, among other determinants of who you are and what you do. I was born in 1940 in Ames, Iowa, where I lived until I went to Smith College in 1957. After graduating from Smith, I traveled west to Berkeley for a master's degree in English. In 1963 I married and began teaching at San Francisco State. A year later, I moved to Minnesota. In 1969 I finished my Ph.D. at the University of Minnesota and joined the faculty of Macalester College in St. Paul, where I am now firmly and fondly attached. In 1971 my daughter Jennifer was born; in 1974 I was divorced; in 1978 I published my first short story in a national magazine and began thinking I might be able to write a book about growing up in a vanished time. In 1985 I married architect James Stageberg and, after twenty years in St. Paul, moved across the Mississippi to Minneapolis, where I now live in a modernist house that overlooks a city lake. How can mere facts convey the deep tremors of any of these events?

I began publishing fiction and essays rather late in life, although I had been writing in one form or another, from journalism to scholarly research, as long as I can remember. Most of my work since 1978 has been nonfiction, from personal essays to reviews, as well as memoir, in such different periodicals as *Harper's, Redbook, McCalls,* and *The New York Times.*

Since I have always been a willing prey to the web and texture of life, I have a passion for detail. Perhaps that is why I so much admire E. B. White. Like Sarah Orne Jewett, the nineteenth-century New England writer who is the other main influence on my style, White has an eye for the small but crucial detail that conveys atmosphere and feeling. I am sometimes asked if I kept a journal when I was growing up; unlike many writers, I didn't. My mind seems to be like a grandmother's attic; it accumulates scenes and characters, bits of dialogue and lots of stage properties. I write partly to clean out the attic. And also I like to sort through the piles and see what, among the junk and mess, has value. A

A. Expansion
Sarah Orne Jewett (1849–1909) wrote perceptive and sympathetic stories of the people of her native Maine. A precise stylist, she was greatly influenced by Flaubert. Jewett's work, in turn, exerted a strong influence on Willa Cather (see page 517).

SUPPLEMENTARY SUPPORT MATERIALS
1. Vocabulary Activity Worksheet (*CCB*)
2. Review and Response Worksheet: Objectivity *vs.* Subjectivity (*CCB*)
3. Language Skills Worksheet: Spelling Demons (*CCB*)
4. Selection Test (*CCB*)

DEVELOPING VOCABULARY
The following words from the memoir are tested in the Selection Test. (See also Vocabulary Activity Worksheet.)

percale	disparate
sarong	truncated
fabrication	tulle
sheaf	savvy
transcendent	schizophrenia

PREPARATION
ESTABLISHING A PURPOSE. Tell students that this selection describes the experience of a Midwestern girl beginning her college career at an Eastern school. Suggest that they read to learn how she manages this big adjustment.

A. Concrete Detail
? What details help to make this daunting experience vividly clear to the reader? (The blinding spotlights; the cold tiles underfoot; the heat of the lights; the matter-of-fact manner of the photographer and gym teacher)

B. Expansion
At the time the writer was attending Smith College in Northampton, Amherst College in nearby Amherst, Massachusetts, was a men's college. Amherst is now co-ed.

OUT EAST

This chapter from *Ivy Days* begins after the narrator, Sue Allen, has arrived at Smith College. Like almost all freshmen far from home for the first time, Sue Allen is still homesick, still surprised by college customs, and, most important, still trying to fit in.

A "All right, Allen, drop the sheet," said a brisk voice. Though blinded by two glowing spotlights, I tried to meet for a reassuring moment the matter-of-fact eyes of the gym teacher who stood next to the photographer. I blinked, couldn't focus, and gave up. Taking a deep breath, I sucked in my stomach, straightened stiffly, and dropped the white percale sheet I'd modestly wound like a disinfected sarong around my nude body. Though my feet tingled with cold from the tile floor, the heat of the lights assaulted my bare skin. Behind the camera the photographer pressed a button with a loud click. "Turn sideways, please," she said, sounding bored. Another click. "All right. That's all. That will do it. Pick up your sheet. Out the door on your left." The gym teacher strode toward the other door, where a long line of girls, anonymously white-sheeted, waited. "Next, please. Hurry up, please. Name?" she called, not waiting to see if I had yet made my exit. Hurriedly wrapping the sheet around me again, its ends flapping and dragging, I scurried out of the small stuffy room toward the lockers. Now I could get dressed and go back to the House. I hadn't yet learned to call it home.

Posture Pictures were a mesmerizing highlight of Smith's Orientation Week. All freshmen were required to take Basic Motor Skills, where they would learn proper body movement, and these pictures were a diagnostic tool. Each girl's body, carefully studied in black-and-white by the physical education staff, its flaws, faults, and misalignments noted, was graded A to F. In an individual conference, a phys-ed instructor would inform a freshman of her possibilities for improving this grade. You could not graduate from Smith until your body was at least a C, and many seniors, we were warned, spent a humiliating spring semester

trying to expand their chests and tuck in their tailbones.

Although Posture Pictures were taken within the first few days, I knew none of us freshmen would see them for several weeks. Meanwhile rumors flourished, most of which, my Big Sister, Dulie, comforted me, were total fabrications. No, no, it wasn't true that Amherst men sometimes B broke into the gym offices, raided the files, and stole the whole sheaf of pictures. And then posted

A. Humanities Connection: Responding to the Photograph
This photograph of a group dance at a high school prom illustrates the kind of formals girls wore to these events in the forties and fifties, which Toth describes at the top of page 1037 (left-hand column). Cornell Capa (b. 1918), the photographer, also represented by a picture on page 1003, is notable for his ability to capture the essential quality of human experiences in candid shots.

? Assuming these young people were high school seniors when this picture was taken in 1954, how old must they be now?

B. Expansion
Bobby socks—short white socks worn with one or two rolls—were so universally worn by adolescent girls in the forties and fifties that they became symbols of conformity to teenage fads.

? What items of clothing are enjoying a fad this year? For girls? For boys?

A

Bunny hop in Michigan City, Indiana. Photograph taken by Cornell Capa for *Life* magazine, 1954.

them on telephone poles with names attached. At least, she'd heard it maybe had happened *once*, but only once, and that was a long time ago. Don't worry, Sue, don't worry.

Somehow I had not expected to be so cleanly stripped in my first week at Smith. Whenever I thought of entering life in the East, opening the door that stood invisibly somewhere in eastern Pennsylvania, and stepping into a world of old ivy-covered brick buildings, white Colonial houses, and rock-strewn farms, I saw myself as suitably clothed. When I passed through that door, I would be transformed, a <u>transcendent</u> hope like that in Handel's *Messiah*[1] when the bass triumphantly trumpets forth, "And we shall be changed." No longer swathed in white triple-rolled socks and billowing crinolined skirts, I would suddenly be B

1. ***Messiah:*** an oratorio by George Frederic Handel (1685–1759).

A. Allusion
The reference is to "First Fig," a short poem by Millay: My candle burns at both ends;/It will not last the night;/ But, ah, my foes, and, oh, my friends—/It gives a lovely light.

B. Responding
How realistic a picture of everyday life in high school or college would you be able to form from pictures in magazines? (Not very. The scenes, activities, and clothing are likely to be idealized, not typical.)

adorned in whatever sleek, sophisticated robes they were currently wearing "out East." Some days, when I felt more confident, I called it "back East." Though my Erickson ancestors had come from the Old Country, the Allen side proudly traced itself back to Ethan Allen, the Green Mountain Boys, and Vermont. Back East. "Out East," though, felt more accurate: a far-off land, unknown, frightening.

My idea of the East was drawn from many disparate images. Some had sunk visually into my mind from years of staring at the large Currier & Ives calendars the Travelers' Insurance agent, from whom we never bought insurance, hopefully sent my mother each December: horse-drawn carriages dashing through snow, hunters shouldering newly shot turkeys, fields tidied by stone walls and villages crowned by white steeples. Others had filtered through poetry and prose in high school American literature class: Hawthorne, Melville, Whittier, Longfellow, Amy Lowell, Sarah Teasdale, and a touch of Edna St.Vincent Millay. From Hawthorne I envisioned crumbling manses, dark gloomy rooms, lurking Puritans; from Whittier, happy snowbound families that nonetheless had shipwrecks in their background.

New England men wrote about sin, sorrow, and the sea; the few women, about love and music. Sara Teasdale promised life had loveliness to sell: that sounded more like life in the East than in Iowa. I knew Amy Lowell was a "bluestocking,"[2] an image which had little to do with legs in my mind, but rather with short, cropped hair (there was a picture of Amy in our book) and a mannish, aggressive attitude toward life. Women in the East were obviously individualists. Edna St. Vincent Millay climbed rocks at dawn, lay stretched out listening to the surf just as I listened to the waves
A on the shore at Lake Carlos, and burned her candle, illogically but wonderfully, at both ends.

I wasn't exactly sure how Edna St. Vincent Millay, whom I admired so furiously I always accorded her the dignity of her full name, dressed. I wanted to know because, wondering what people were like out East, I thought I would find them less foreign if I knew what they wore. Clothes were a language I understood. I knew what Eastern college girls looked like. I had seen them all in the August issue of *Mademoiselle*. During high school, I studied that bulging catalog of fashions, "The College Issue," as if I were a medical student poring over Gray's *Anatomy*, memorizing each twist of sinew or articulation of bone. Since I had never visited any Eastern college campus, I searched for clues to manners and mores[3] in the backgrounds of pictures as well as in the foreground models. I could never differentiate among the brick administration buildings, ivy-covered dormitories, and sidewalks crowded with bicycles. The University of Pennsylvania, as displayed in *Mademoiselle*, did not stand out from Simmons, or Vassar, or Middlebury. Even Agnes Scott (down South) and Stanford (out West) seemed discouragingly similar to the hallowed halls back East. And the girls, to my surprise, all looked much the same, no matter where they were from: slender figures, glossy caps of hair, triumphant smiles.

The Eastern look, I eventually decided, was meant to accommodate the two main Eastern activities, sports and parties. Girls in Ames didn't have many athletic opportunities: We swam, played volleyball at picnics, hit badminton birds in each other's back yards, and occasionally bowled a few lines. Two or three girls whose parents belonged to the Country Club golfed, though not seriously. But if the pictures in my magazines and college catalogs told the truth, Eastern girls played lots of sports: They canoed, wielded field hockey sticks, skiied in nearby mountains. They had swim meets and tennis ladders, outing clubs and crew teams, horseback riding and lacrosse. For all these activities, they had special costumes, white tennis skirts, riding jodhpurs, ski sweaters. Even their everyday clothes seemed sporty to me—brisk, crisp, and no-nonsense; blazers, knee socks, kilts, and Bermuda shorts all had a kind of truncated efficiency. B

When Eastern girls weren't racing across an athletic field or tennis court, they were liable, I gathered, to be at parties. Ames only had two kinds of parties when I was in high school: casual "record hops," at school or at someone's house, where one wore one's best skirt and sweater; or "formals," the big social events like the Junior-Senior Prom or the Christmas Dance, which one

2. **"bluestocking":** a learned, bookish woman (from the blue worsted stockings worn by the leading figures at literary meetings in eighteenth-century London).

3. **mores** (mōr′āz): customs.

CLOSURE

Have students discuss what Toth's most satisfying accomplishment was in her four years at Smith. (Having achieved an authentic look—one not exactly like everyone else's but nevertheless "shoe")

READING CHECK TEST

1. The selection takes place during the late 1950's. *True*

2. Each Smith girl's body receives a grade before the girl is allowed to graduate. *True*

3. Sue's literary idol at the time is Emily Dickinson. *False*

4. Before going to Smith, Sue had never been to a cocktail party. *True*

5. Sue solves her wardrobe problem by buying a rumpled trenchcoat on sale. *True*

attended in strapless bodice and layers of tulle. But social life in the East looked much more complicated. Catalogs and brochures showed varying glimpses of "mixers," football games, house dances, fraternity costume parties, and informal "dates" that seemed to involve standing around outside, and smiling broadly, under a large tree or on the banks of a small pond.

The kind of party that worried me most, though, was the "cocktail party," which everyone I knew in Ames agreed was liable to take a lot of my time in the East. Since I didn't drink yet, except an occasional sip of sherry, I was uneasy at this idea. But primarily I wasn't sure what I would be supposed to wear. No one in Ames High had any use for a "cocktail dress," and I did considerable research, pondering racks of what we called "party dresses," as well as magazine layouts, before I decided what a cocktail dress was. Girls in my Eastern pictures definitely wore them a lot: tight black dresses, with perhaps a knee-high slit in the back, three-quarter sleeves, a V-neckline in front. When the time arrived for me to make my fateful purchase—I could only afford one—I faltered, fearing bulges, and chose a conservative, high-neck, princess-style dress, double-breasted with shiny buttons. Though the dress was expensive, I reassured myself that I could wear it "other places"—maybe to a fancy restaurant or funerals, of neither of which at age seventeen I had much experience. A

After agonies of observation, conclusions, and final selection, I arrived with trunk and suitcases at Smith only to find that I was both overprepared and still, inexplicably, shut out of Eastern fashion. When I got off the train in Northampton, hot and sweaty in my homemade tweed suit and little hat, I could see immediately that the older girls, the real "Smithies" who met us freshmen at the station, as well as some more savvy newcomers, were not dressed quite as *Mademoiselle* had promised me. No spiffy knickers, linen jackets, certainly no suits. At first the "Smithies" looked sloppy: button-down shirts with tails hanging out over jeans or slacks, faded madras Bermuda shorts, sweaters and plaid skirts whose colors didn't always match. But soon I found how hard it was to emulate this look, not only because I didn't own most of those items, but also because, when I tried them, they just did not feel right. B Wool crew-neck sweaters itched at the back of my neck; knee socks slowly crept to my ankles and collapsed; pleated skirts pulled over my hips. They didn't belong to me. The girls I envied obviously did not *think* about their clothes; they simply got up in the morning, pulled on what they'd been comfortable in for years, and headed out to face the day. C

Although I tried to revise my expectations, and achieve the faded, woolly look I saw around me, I was seldom satisfied. Because I had little spending money left for clothes, I shopped the sale racks. As a result, I ended up with a plaid skirt that wasn't really a kilt; an Orlon sweater rather than wool; a corduroy vest instead of a tweed blazer. After only a few days on campus, I knew where to look for the genuine articles, but I quickly found I couldn't afford them. All along Green Street, a commercial block just a few feet from Lawrence House, small, exclusive shops offered tempting window displays of skirts, sweaters, Bermudas, blazers, ribbon belts, and chintz knitting bags. One store, I discovered, didn't even have much stock inside. Instead, with a rack of only a few choice coats and suits, the management subtly suggested that a serious shopper, one worthy of their attention, would sit in one of the velvet-upholstered, gilt-backed chairs and let Madame Laletti bring an appropriate selection from the back room. Once I mistakenly wandered inside; caught, I pretended I was "just browsing," fingering intently the two or three available coats before escaping.

The presence of Green Street, its shops glittering with gold circle pins and flowering with Liberty of London blouses, was a constant reminder of a kind of schizophrenia I dimly sensed at Smith. On the one hand, much to my surprise, dress was very democratic. During the week everyone was casual, sloppy, even determinedly grubby. Many of us wore jeans, safety-pinned skirts, old baggy sweaters, and sometimes spent all day in our gym outfits, coarse cotton tunics over matching bright jersey bloomers. Without closely examining the original fabric on which the dirt flourished, one couldn't distinguish a DuPont or Rockefeller in a smudged pair of slacks from Mary O'Connor, Jane Doe, or Sue Allen from Ames, Iowa. No one tried to impress anyone else. Until, at least, the weekend. On Friday, as hordes of girls left the campus for weekend dates, they blossomed in pea jackets, tams, cashmere polo coats, and even short, snappy Peck and Peck suits, and they carried suitcases whose bulging sides suggested outfits

A. Irony
This sentence offers a good example of the writer's gently ironic humor. To rationalize the expensive purchase, the narrator thinks of occasions for wearing the dress that are mainly outside her experience.

B. Responding
Have you ever tried to emulate a particular look that is fashionable and found it difficult, as the writer did?

C. Responding
Do you think the girls Toth envied really did not think about their clothes? (Answers will vary. The author does, however, provide a sound example to back up her statement when she says that the girls she envied had been comfortable in their clothes for years.)

ANALYZING THE MEMOIR

Identifying Facts

1. She says that she drew her ideas about the East from "many disparate images": Currier & Ives calendar pictures, New England writers she had read in high school literature class (including Melville, Whittier, Longfellow, Edna St. Vincent Millay, and Hawthorne), and issues of *Mademoiselle*.

2. She thought that the "Eastern look" consisted of sports and party clothes: blazers, tennis skirts, ski sweaters, riding costumes, and cocktail dresses.

3. The dirty, rumpled look is described as involving a trenchcoat that Sue bought on sale—worn with jeans, a sweatshirt, and gray, soiled "tennies," or tennis sneakers. The "Green Street" look was traditional and affluent: skirts, blazers, sweaters, and chintz knitting bags.

Interpreting Meanings

4. Student answers will vary. Considering that the whole piece focuses so much on clothes, it is ironic that the first image we have of the college freshmen is in gym class, stripped for "posture pictures." The emotional effect perhaps conveys some of the nervousness and

A. Responding

? Why is "Studying this weekend" in quotation marks? (This was a standard explanation used by students who had no date or special plans for the weekend.)

B. Responding

? What word currently means "with it" in your school?

Mademoiselle would have approved. Although dates appeared on Fridays through Sundays, popping up on lawns, porches, and living room carpets like rare and short-lived jack-in-the-pulpits, those of us left on campus pretended not to notice. A "Studying this weekend," we determinedly remained as we were, wrinkled and defiantly grundgy in our everyday skirts and stained cardigans.

Although in my four years at Smith, I never really felt I had the right wardrobe—or was sure I could successfully wear it if I did—I was eventually able to achieve the rumpled, dirty look that I thought was my only alternative to Green Street. Late in my junior year, I found a trench coat on sale in downtown Northampton. Although it was not just like everyone else's in style and color—too creamy white, no epaulets—it was my first trench coat, and I loved it. Soon it acquired a patina of smudges, smears, and studied neglect. With it I wore my "tennies,"[4] also gradually soiled to a satisfactory gray.

4. **"tennies":** slang for tennis sneakers.

On the sunny spring morning of my senior year when I knew I might receive an award at honors chapel—I had read about one for which I was a logical candidate—I deliberately dressed in jeans, sweatshirt, gray tennies, and my battered trench coat. Hands jammed casually in my pockets, belt looped around my waist, collar turned up, I strode happily up the stage stairs to accept the certificate for the Victoria Louise Schrager Prize from the outstretched hand of President Mendenhall. It was for a senior who had made an outstanding contribution in academics and extracurricular activities, and it meant to me that at last I had made it. Yet I was almost as proud of how I looked: not beautiful, not striking, but absolutely authentic. I remember wiggling my bare toes in my threadbare sneakers, secure in the knowledge that my stark ankles (though rubbed rawish red at the back) looked much more sophisticated than if I'd worn socks. For a brief while at Smith we had a word, plain but oddly transformed, that meant "with it," "cool," or "neat." That low-keyed and powerful word was "shoe." For those moments on the stage, I felt "shoe." Finally I was dressed right. B

Responding to the Memoir

Analyzing the Memoir

Identifying Details

1. Before she came to Massachusetts, where had Sue Allen gotten her ideas about the East?
2. What did she think was the "Eastern look"?
3. The writer says she finally achieved a "dirty, rumpled look" that she felt was her only alternative to "Green Street." What details describe these two alternatives?

Interpreting Meanings

4. Why does this section (the first chapter in the book) begin with a description of Posture Pictures? What is the emotional effect of the opening paragraph?
5. Although the writer talks about clothes, she is trying to convey some of her feelings about her first days at college. What were these feelings? Do you think they are fairly universal?
6. Why was it so important to Sue Allen that she look like the "Eastern girls"? What does this reveal about her **character** at this stage of her life?
7. Groups have different ways of identifying who belongs, who is "in" and who is "out." What are some of the different groups you see in your school, and how are they identified?
8. This passage also talks about **stereotypes**—fixed ideas about people and events that allow for no individuality. Stereotypes are often based on racial or religious prejudice. What are these stereotypes? What pictures do you have about areas of the United States you have never seen—the East, West, North, or South? For example, what do you see in your mind's eye when someone talks about Nashville? New York? San Francisco? New Orleans? Gary, Indiana? Where do you think such stereotypes come from?
9. Do you think the memoir is about something important, or do you think clothing is essentially a trivial subject? (Is clothing the real topic of the memoir?)

anxiety of a freshman in her first days away from home at college.

5. Sue Allen lacked confidence and was eager to fit in with those around her.

Students probably agree that these feelings are universal.

6. She was self-conscious and wanted to fit in with the other girls who were strangers to her. Her attitude reveals that she was relatively insecure and nervous about other people's acceptance at the time.

7. Student answers will vary. Encourage them to identify as many different groups as they can, and to be as specific as possible about details of clothing, posture, language, and so on.

8. The essay refers to stereotypes of fashion and maturity, of self-assurance, attractiveness, and sophistication.

Student answers will vary. Encourage students to offer specific responses and to defend their opinions.

9. Whatever their opinions about the importance of clothing, most students will agree that clothing is only the superficial subject of the memoir. The memoir is really about the narrator's feelings as she confronts a new, adult world.

Writing About the Memoir

A Creative Response

1. **Imitating Toth's Technique.** Belonging, or not belonging, is a painful subject. But much good writing comes from examining pain. (Philip Roth, a celebrated American novelist, once said, "We writers are lucky: Nothing truly bad can happen to us. It's all material.") If you can stand it, write a description of a time when you desperately wanted to belong to something—and couldn't.
2. **Changing the Point of View.** Select an incident from this memoir and rewrite it from another point of view. How might the **tone** of the account change as the interpretation of events changes?

A Critical Response

3. **Developing a Statement.** "Clothes were a language I understood." Write a short essay explaining what this sentence means and whether you think most people would agree with it.
4. **Evaluating Objectivity.** In the extract from an article that follows (under "Primary Sources"), Susan Toth talks about the accuracy of memory. In a brief essay, evaluate her memoir in terms of its objectivity. Do you think the writer has been honest? Do you think she has reported facts in an unbiased way? Do you think that someone else reporting on some of these same events might view them differently?

Primary Sources
"The Importance of Being Remembered"

Several years after the publication of her two memoirs, Susan Allen Toth wrote an article about the responses she had received to her books.

"The importance of feeling remembered—of having one's everyday life, pleasures and sorrows set down in the semipermanence of print—came home poignantly at another book-signing gathering. My former high school drama coach, whom I had respected and loved, appeared with an urgent question. I had written in *Blooming* about the death of his small daughter and its effect on me 23 years before. I had changed names and a few identifying facts, as I did with anyone easily recognizable. Although her real name was Susie—like mine, so I had never forgotten it—I had called her Mary. After grasping my hand and congratulating me on my book, he paused. Looking intently into my eyes, his face strained and shadowed by that old and terrible loss, he said, 'I have to know one thing. You called her Mary in the book. Did you remember her real name?' I assured him I had, and his face eased.

"Not all my audience was convinced that I *did* remember my facts correctly. 'Weren't you making up the Mystery Farm of the Week?' more than one person at public readings asked suspiciously, referring to a popular newspaper feature I'd mentioned. Some who had grown up in small towns, with the confidence of those who have detasseled corn or cheered at a high school basketball tournament, rose indignantly to my defense on this and other matters. Young people—meaning those under 40—often could not believe the innocence I claimed for those of us

who grew up in the 1950's in that Iowa town or a little later in Northampton, Massachusetts. 'Could *anyone* have been that naïve?' they asked. I could only attest that I had told the truth as scrupulously as I could."

—Susan Allen Toth

Supplementary Support Materials
1. Vocabulary Activity Worksheet (*CCB*)
2. Review and Response Worksheet: Tone and Symbol (*CCB*)
3. Language Skills Worksheet: Subordinate Clauses (*CCB*)
4. Selection Test (*CCB*)

Developing Vocabulary
The following words from the essay are tested in the Selection Test. (See also Vocabulary Activity Worksheet.)
dispossession heritage
sensibility ephemeral
to disinherit

Alice Walker (1944–)

"Black women are called, in the folklore that so aptly identifies one's status in society, 'the *mule* of the world,' " Alice Walker has written, "because we have been handed the burdens that everyone else—*everyone* else—refused to carry." In her poetry, essays, and novels, Walker has celebrated the endurance, the strength, and the creativity of these women through the ages.

Alice Walker was born in Eatonton, Georgia, and grew up on a succession of farms in the area. Her father was a sharecropper, and her mother "labored beside—not behind" him in the fields, cared for their eight children, and still never failed, wherever they were living, to have a large and beautiful flower garden. This spirit of hard work and determination to enrich her life has served as an inspiration to Walker throughout her career.

Walker attended Spelman College in Atlanta and Sarah Lawrence College in Bronxville, New York, where she studied with poet Muriel Rukeyser. During this time she was also active in the Civil Rights Movement in Georgia and Mississippi, and she traveled in Africa. The poems in her first volume of poetry, many of them inspired by these activities, were written in a week-long frenzy of creativity at Sarah Lawrence. "Each morning," she later wrote, "the poems finished during the night were stuffed under Muriel Rukeyser's door—her classroom was an old gardener's cottage in the middle of the campus. Then I would hurry back to my room to write some more. I didn't care what she did with the poems. I only knew I wanted someone to read them as if they were new leaves sprouting from an old tree. The same energy that impelled me to write them carried them to her door." What Rukeyser did was to give the poems to her agent, and *Once* was published by Harcourt Brace Jovanovich a few years later.

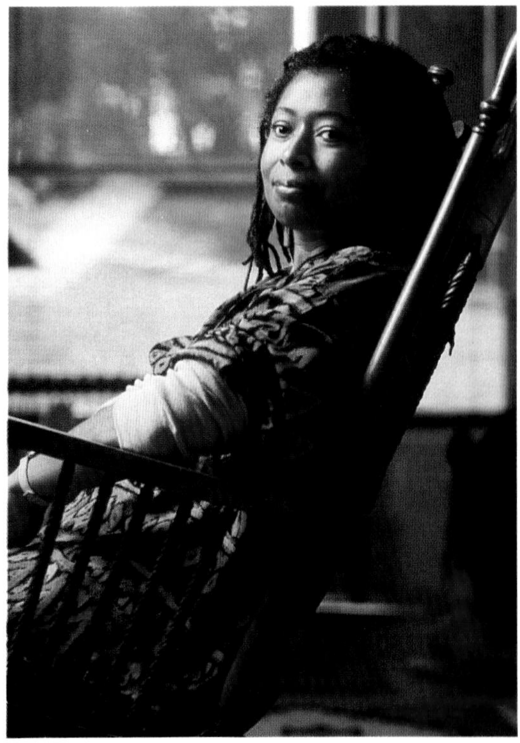

After graduating from college, Walker began a career of teaching and writing. She pioneered the teaching of university courses in black women writers and has worked tirelessly to bring an understanding of their work to a wider audience. Her collection of Zora Neale Hurston's writings, *I Love Myself When I Am Laughing*, appeared in 1979. In addition to poetry, Walker is the author of a number of critically acclaimed novels, including *Meridian* (1976), the Pulitzer Prize winner *The Color Purple* (1982), and *The Temple of My Familiar* (1989). A collection of essays, *In Search of Our Mothers' Gardens*, appeared in 1983. In the title essay, she celebrates not just the few black women who managed, against all odds, to become recognized as artists, but the unknown and unsung thousands, like her own mother, whose creativity flowered in their everyday lives.

PREPARATION

1. BUILDING ON PRIOR KNOWLEDGE. Ask students what they know of Martin Luther King, Jr. (1929–1968), who advocated and practiced nonviolent resistance to segregation. During the 1950's and 1960's, King led numerous demonstrations and voter registration drives, including the massive March on Washington in 1963. For his work, King was awarded the Nobel Peace Prize in 1964, and in his honor the third Monday in January is a federal holiday.

2. ESTABLISHING A PURPOSE. As suggested in the headnote, have students note the setting and audience for this tribute. Then tell students to think about how these two elements affect the meaning and tone of speech.

FOR FURTHER READING FOR STUDENTS AND TEACHERS

A Testament of Hope: The Essential Writings of Martin Luther King, Jr., edited by James M. Washington (Harper, 1985), collects King's most important writings and speeches, arranged by topic and presented with detailed commentaries.

CHOICE: A TRIBUTE TO DR. MARTIN LUTHER KING, JR.

With eloquence and style, Dr. Martin Luther King, Jr., brought the message of civil rights to a world television audience. His voice sounded a clarion call for the elimination of racism in the United States through nonviolent resistance. To a generation of African Americans, he became a symbol of the struggle to fulfill at last the century-old promise of emancipation.

As you read, be aware of the setting and the audience for Walker's tribute to Dr. King, who was killed by an assassin on April 4, 1968, as he stood on a motel balcony in Memphis, Tennessee.

[This address was made in 1972 at a Jackson, Mississippi, restaurant that refused to serve people of color until forced to do so by the Civil Rights Movement a few years before.]

. . .

My great-great-great-grandmother walked as a slave from Virginia to Eatonton, Georgia—which passes for the Walker ancestral home—with two babies on her hips. She lived to be a hundred and twenty-five years old and my own father knew her as a boy. (It is in memory of this walk that I choose to keep and to embrace my "maiden" name, Walker.)

There is a cemetery near our family church where she is buried; but because her marker was made of wood and rotted years ago, it is impossible to tell exactly where her body lies. In the same cemetery are most of my mother's people, who have lived in Georgia for so long nobody even remembers when they came. And all of my great-aunts and -uncles are there, and my grandfather and grandmother, and, very recently, my own father.

If it is true that land does not belong to anyone until they have buried a body in it, then the land of my birthplace belongs to me, dozens of times over. Yet the history of my family, like that of all black Southerners, is a history of dispossession. We loved the land and worked the land, but we never owned it; and even if we bought land, as my great-grandfather did after the Civil War, it was always in danger of being taken away, as his was, during the period following Reconstruction.

My father inherited nothing of material value from his father, and when I came of age in the early sixties I awoke to the bitter knowledge that in order just to continue to love the land of my birth, I was expected to leave it. For black people—including my parents—had learned a long time ago that to stay willingly in a beloved but brutal place is to risk losing the love and being forced to acknowledge only the brutality. A

It is a part of the black Southern sensibility that we treasure memories; for such a long time, that is all of our homeland those of us who at one time or another were forced away from it have been allowed to have.

I watched my brothers, one by one, leave our home and leave the South. I watched my sisters do the same. This was not unusual; abandonment, except for memories, was the common thing, except for those who "could not do any better," or those whose strength or stubbornness was so colossal they took the risk that others could not bear.

In 1960, my mother bought a television set, and each day after school I watched Hamilton Holmes and Charlayne Hunter as they struggled to integrate—fair-skinned as they were—the University of Georgia. And then, one day, there appeared the face of Dr. Martin Luther King, Jr. What a funny name, I thought. At the moment I first saw him, he was being handcuffed and shoved into a police

A. Connections

Compare Walker's two themes—deep love of the land and acknowledgment of brutality—to the picture painted by Thomas Wolfe in "His Father's Earth" (page 526). How are the two authors' feelings similar? (Both express the importance of ties to the land and a feeling of "homelessness.") How do the assumptions and expectations of the boy in Wolfe's story differ from the historical ones cited by Walker? (The boy has left of his own free will; he was not made to feel unwanted.)

Writing Assignment
Ask students to write their own brief tributes to Martin Luther King, Jr., based on their prior knowledge and Walker's essay.

CLOSURE
Ask students to summarize Walker's tribute to Martin Luther King. Then ask them to analyze how their tributes are similar to and different from Walker's speech.

READING CHECK TEST
1. Walker tells how before Dr. King, African American Southerners were usually forced away from their birthplace. *True*
2. Walker first saw Dr. King when he was preaching a sermon. *False*
3. Because of King, Walker vowed not to leave her home without a struggle. *True*
4. Dr. King's philosophy and teachings were easy for people to follow. *False*
5. Walker says King's greatest accomplishment was to give back to his people a sense of community. *True*

A. Humanities Connection: About the Fine Art
Romare Bearden (1914–1988) is of immense importance in modern African American art, both because of his own work and because of his support of other African American artists and art history. Bearden used stylized realism in some works and abstract techniques in others. Soft, muted washes of color seem to make his shapes float on the canvas. Much of his work is filled with the symbols, myths, and memories of the African American experience. (Two other Bearden paintings appear on pages 689 and 693.)

The Garden by Romare Bearden (1978). Watercolor.

Private Collection, courtesy Sheldon Ross Gallery, Birmingham, Michigan.

truck. He had dared to claim his rights as a native son, and had been arrested. He displayed no fear, but seemed calm and serene, unaware of his own extraordinary courage. His whole body, like his conscience, was at peace.

At the moment I saw his resistance I knew I would never be able to live in this country without resisting everything that sought to disinherit me, and I would never be forced away from the land of my birth without a fight.

He was The One, The Hero, The One Fearless Person for whom we had waited. I hadn't even realized before that we *had* been waiting for Martin Luther King, Jr., but we had. And I knew it for sure when my mother added his name to the list of people she prayed for every night.

I sometimes think that it was literally the prayers of people like my mother and father, who had bowed down in the struggle for such a long time, that kept Dr. King alive until five years ago. For years we went to bed praying for his life, and awoke with the question "Is the 'Lord' still here?"

The public acts of Dr. King you know. They are visible all around you. His voice you would recognize sooner than any other voice you have heard in this century—this in spite of the fact that certain municipal libraries, like the one in down-

ANALYZING THE ESSAY

Identifying Facts

1. She gave the speech in 1972 in a restaurant in Jackson, Mississippi, which had until a few years before refused to serve blacks.

That the restaurant is open to all, says Walker, is largely due to King's efforts.

2. They often were dispossessed by the threat of brutality.

3. She watched a news account of his arrest.

King became a hero to her; she resolved to fight for her birthright, too.

Interpreting Meanings

4. African Americans "owned" land in the South by virtue of being buried in it, working it, and buying it. Paradoxically, they were not allowed to stay on it and call it home.

5. King delivered his people from acceptance of the status quo and to their heritage and home.

Answers will vary.

6. They now can be secure in the land of their birth. They are free to own the land and to move upon it as they wish.

Students may suggest that *home* refers to a sense of full participation in America—a sense of safety, no matter where one lives.

7. She means that these groups were denied what was their right by virtue of being human and American—freedom, choice, and their heritage.

8. Because of King's efforts, all people can now choose to enter this restaurant or stay away, and to stay on the land or go elsewhere.

9. By personalizing the story, Walker universalizes it. She invites listeners to identify with her experiences and, by extension, with the experiences of all the dispossessed.

Without this section, the speech would be less effective and might fail to reveal King's immense effect on the nation's psyche.

town Jackson, do not carry recordings of his speeches, and the librarians chuckle cruelly when asked why they do not.

You know, if you have read his books, that his is a complex and revolutionary philosophy that few people are capable of understanding fully or have the patience to embody in themselves. Which is our weakness, which is our loss.

And if you know anything about good Baptist preaching, you can imagine what you missed if you never had a chance to hear Martin Luther King, Jr., preach at Ebeneezer Baptist Church.

You know of the prizes and awards that he tended to think very little of. And you know of his concern for the disinherited: the American Indian, the Mexican American, and the poor American white—for whom he cared much.

You know that this very room, in this very restaurant, was closed to people of color not more than five years ago. And that we eat here together tonight largely through his efforts and his blood. We accept the common pleasures of life, assuredly, in his name.

But add to all of these things the one thing that seems to me second to none in importance: He gave us back our heritage. He gave us back our homeland; the bones and dust of our ancestors, who may now sleep within our caring *and* our hearing. He gave us the blueness of the Georgia sky in autumn as in summer; the colors of the Southern winter as well as glimpses of the green of vacation-time spring. Those of our relatives we used to invite for a visit we now can ask to stay. . . . He gave us full-time use of our own woods, and restored our memories to those of us who were forced to run away, as realities we might each day enjoy and leave for our children.

He gave us continuity of place, without which community is ephemeral. He gave us home.

Responding to the Essay

Analyzing the Essay

Identifying Facts

1. When and where did Alice Walker give this speech? What is the significance of the location?
2. According to Walker, why did African American people once have to leave the South?
3. Under what circumstances did Walker first learn about Dr. Martin Luther King, Jr.? How did he affect her life?

Interpreting Meanings

4. A **paradox** is a seeming contradiction; if someone grew up on a ship but never learned to swim, that would be a paradox. What paradox does Walker describe here, in the paragraph beginning "If it is true that land . . ."?
5. Although heroism is never easy to define, few Americans would deny that Dr. King is an authentic hero. In literature heroes are often portrayed as deliverers of their people. How does Dr. King qualify as a "deliverer"? What other people in history do you think of as "deliverers"?
6. In 1940, a noted white Southern writer named Thomas Wolfe (see page 525) wrote a novel called *You Can't Go Home Again.* Alice Walker, speaking in 1972, maintains that—at long last—Southern black Americans *can* go home again. Why can they now go home (or, if they wish to, stay home)? What larger meaning do you read into the word *home* in the last sentence?
7. Alice Walker writes that Dr. King was concerned for the "disinherited" of all ethnic backgrounds. What do you think she means by *disinherited?*
8. Explain the significance of the word *choice* in the title of the essay.
9. In the first eight paragraphs, Alice Walker talks about her own family. What emotions do these personal anecdotes appeal to? What would be lost if the speech began with paragraph number nine?

An Oral Presentation

Be ready to give Alice Walker's speech in front of your class. Decide ahead of time what words you will emphasize, what tone you will adopt, what gestures you will use. When you are part of the audience listening to a classmate's presentation, take notes so that you can make helpful suggestions. You should also be able to explain what the speaker did that was effective.

FOR FURTHER READING
FOR THE STUDENT
The House on Mango Street, published by Arte Publico (Houston, 1986) will appeal to many students. Episodes are included in *Elements of Literature, Fourth Course*.

Sandra Cisneros (1954–)

The youngest writer represented in this book, Sandra Cisneros was born in Chicago to Mexican-American parents.

Cisneros remembers her childhood as solitary, even though, she says, her parents would be hard-pressed to remember it that way, since the nine members of the family were living in cramped apartments where the only room with any privacy was the bathroom. But the solitude proved important. If she had had a sister or a friend, Cisneros thinks, she would not have needed to bury herself in books as she did. She read voraciously—the lives of the saints, Horatio Alger's office-boy-makes-good stories, the Doctor Doolittle books, *Alice in Wonderland*, and fairy tales. (She imagined herself as the lone sister in "Six Swans." "Was it no coincidence," she later asked, "my family name translated is 'keeper of swans'?")

Cisneros went to college in Chicago and then, in a significant move, went on to the Writer's Workshop at the University of Iowa for a Master of Fine Arts. There she found her subjects in the matter of her own life, and began writing in earnest. Her first book of poetry is called *Bad Boys* (1980); her first novel, *The House on Mango Street* (1984), was awarded the Before Columbus American Book Award. Her latest book of poetry is *My Wicked Wicked Ways* (1987), an allusion to the title of an autobiography by Errol Flynn, a 1940's movie star. As the following essay tells you, she has lived in many places; she has taught creative writing in high school; and she has taught at California State University at Chico.

It is appropriate that the youngest writer in this book has drawn sustenance from one of the older ones.

When I was growing up in Chicago, and going to college in Chicago, and not traveling anywhere except on CTA buses and subway trains but desperately wanting to break loose, I liked to think of my favorite American poet, Emily Dickinson, who lived during the last century in a little town called Amherst and hardly traveled beyond. I liked to think of

that extraordinary woman who in her later life never even strayed beyond the house and its gardens, but who wrote in her lifetime 1,775 poems. No one knew she was a poet until after she died, and then when they discovered those poems handwritten on sheets of paper folded and stitched together, the world rang like a bell.

I used to think of her and she gave me inspiration and hope all the years in high school and the first two in college when I was too busy being in love to write. Inside, some part of me secretly clung to the dream of becoming a writer. But what I didn't realize about Emily Dickinson until many years later was that she had a few essentials going for her: (1) an education, (2) a room of her own in a house of her own that she shared with her sister Lavinia, and (3) money—inherited along with the house after her father died. She even had a maid, an Irish housekeeper who did, I suspect, most of the household chores. It's true Emily Dickinson baked and sewed for her sister Lavinia and her beloved brother Austin, but she baked and sewed because she wanted to, not because she *had* to. I wonder if Emily Dickinson's Irish housekeeper wrote poetry or if she ever had the secret desire to study and be anything besides a housekeeper.

SUPPLEMENTARY SUPPORT MATERIALS
1. Vocabulary Activity Worksheet (*CCB*)
2. Review and Response Worksheet: Figurative Language (*CCB*)
3. Language Skills Worksheet: Weak Words and Clichés (*CCB*)
4. Selection Test (*CCB*)

DEVELOPING VOCABULARY
The following words from the essay are tested in the Selection Test. (See also Vocabulary Activity Worksheet.)

to subsist	to document
tortilla	promenader
nomadic	residency

PREPARATION
1. BUILDING ON PRIOR KNOWLEDGE. Ask volunteers to retell the tale of *Rumplestiltskin.* Elicit the fact that the miller's daughter is set this impossible task because of the boasting of her father. (Rumplestiltskin then appears to do the work of spinning straw into gold and later reappears to claim his reward.)

2. ESTABLISHING A PURPOSE. Inform students that the writer of this selection uses the metaphor of spinning straw into gold in two ways. Have them read to find out the meanings this metaphor has in this selection.

STRAW INTO GOLD
THE METAMORPHOSIS OF THE EVERYDAY

It is a characteristic of American writers that they inevitably turn to their childhoods for their subjects—at least for their early works. In this essay, which was written initially as a speech, a young writer tells an old story: of her metamorphosis into a storyteller, a poet, a writer. Before you read, see if you know what old fairy tale the words "straw into gold" allude to.

When I was living in an artists' colony in the south of France, some fellow Latin-Americans who taught at the university in Aix-en-Provence invited me to share a home-cooked meal with them. I had been living abroad almost a year then on an NEA grant, subsisting mainly on French bread and lentils while in France so that my money could last longer. So when the invitation to dinner arrived, I accepted without hesitation. Especially since they had promised Mexican food.

What I didn't realize when they made this invitation was that I was supposed to be involved in preparing this meal. I guess they assumed I knew how to cook Mexican food because I was Mexican. They wanted specifically tortillas, though I'd never made a tortilla in my life.

It's true I had witnessed my mother rolling the little armies of dough into perfect circles, but my mother's family is from Guanajuato, *provinciales,* country folk. They only know how to make flour tortillas. My father's family, on the other hand, is *chilango,* from Mexico City. We ate corn tortillas but we didn't make them. Someone was sent to the corner tortilleria to buy some. I'd never seen anybody make corn tortillas. Ever.

Well, somehow my Latino hosts had gotten a hold of a packet of corn flour, and this is what they tossed my way with orders to produce tortillas. *Asi como sea.* Any ol' way, they said and went back to their cooking.

Why did I feel like the woman in the fairy tale who was locked in a room and ordered to spin straw into gold? I had the same sick feeling when I was required to write my critical essay for my MFA[1] exam—the only piece of noncreative writing necessary in order to get my graduate degree. How was I to start? There were rules involved here, unlike writing a poem or story, which I did intuitively. There was a step-by-step process needed and I had better know it. I felt as if making tortillas, or writing a critical paper for that matter, were tasks so impossible I wanted to break down into tears.

Somehow though, I managed to make those tortillas—crooked and burnt, but edible nonetheless. My hosts were absolutely ignorant when it came to Mexican food; they thought my tortillas were delicious. (I'm glad my mama wasn't there.) A Thinking back and looking at that photograph documenting the three of us consuming those lopsided circles I am amazed. Just as I am amazed I could finish my MFA exam (lopsided and crooked, but finished all the same). Didn't think I could do it. But I did.

I've managed to do a lot of things in my life I didn't think I was capable of and which many others didn't think me capable of either. Especially because I am a woman, a Latina, an only daughter in a family of six men. My father would've liked to have seen me married long ago. In our culture, men and women don't leave their father's house except by way of marriage. I crossed my father's threshold with nothing carrying me but my own two feet. A woman whom no one came for and no one chased away.

To make matters worse, I had left before any of my six brothers had ventured away from home. I had broken a terrible taboo. Somehow, looking back at photos of myself as a child, I wonder if I was aware of having begun already my own quiet war. B

I like to think that somehow my family, my Mexicanness, my poverty all had something to do

1. **MFA:** Master of Fine Arts.

A. Responding
? This essay was originally a speech. What are some features of the writing that sound more like a speech than a piece of expository writing? (Idiomatic shortening of sentences: "Didn't think I could do it"; parenthetical asides: "I'm glad my mama wasn't there"; loose, largely unsubordinated sentence structure; occasional sentence fragments: "An amazing woman who . . . can sing an opera")

B. Characterization
? What does this sentence suggest about Sandra's character as a young girl? (Answers will vary. Some possibilities: that she was already independent-minded and not one to be bound by tradition)

CLOSURE

Have students discuss the two meanings of the straw-to-gold metaphor. Elicit ideas as to how the two ideas are different and how they are similar. (See the answer to question 7, page 1047.)

READING CHECK TEST

1. While living in Mexico, the writer is asked to make tortillas. *True*

2. Cisneros's most satisfying accomplishment is writing a critical essay for her MFA degree. *False*

3. Cisneros is an only daughter in a family of six men. *True*

4. Cisneros was not an especially bright student and did not like school. *True*

5. As an adult, Cisneros does many things that she does not think she can do. *True*

A. Word Choice

? What does *sappy* usually mean? (Foolish; silly) What does the word mean as the writer uses it here? (Sentimental; easily moved to tears)

B. Responding

? What does the expression "Odd man out" mean? (A method of singling out one of three persons by matching coins) What makes Sandra "odd woman out"? (On the return of her oldest brother, Kiki transfers his allegiance from her to him.)

C. Connections

? How does Sandra's school experience compare with that of the narrator of "The Girl Who Wouldn't Talk"? (Both characters face the problem of minority children adjusting.) Which character in that story does Sandra's description of her school days remind you of? (Answers will vary. Many students will name the quiet girl.)

with shaping me into a writer. I like to think my parents were preparing me all along for my life as an artist even though they didn't know it. From my father I inherited a love of wandering. He was born in Mexico City but as a young man he traveled into the U.S. vagabonding. He eventually was drafted and thus became a citizen. Some of the stories he has told about his first months in the U.S. with little or no English surface in my stories in *The House on Mango Street* as well as others I have in mind to write in the future. From A him I inherited a sappy heart. (He still cries when he watches the Mexican soaps—especially if they deal with children who have forsaken their parents.)

My mother was born like me—in Chicago but of Mexican descent. It would be her tough, streetwise voice that would haunt all my stories and poems. An amazing woman who loves to draw and read books and can sing an opera. A smart cookie.

When I was a little girl we traveled to Mexico City so much I thought my grandparents' house on La Fortuna, Number 12, was home. It was the only constant in our nomadic ramblings from one Chicago flat to another. The house on Destiny Street, Number 12, in the colonia Tepeyac, would be perhaps the only home I knew, and that nostalgia for a home would be a theme that would obsess me.

My brothers also figured greatly in my art. Especially the oldest two; I grew up in their shadows. Henry, the second oldest and my favorite, appears often in poems I have written and in stories which at times only borrow his nickname, Kiki. He played a major role in my childhood. We were bunkbed mates. We were co-conspirators. We were pals. Until my oldest brother came back B from studying in Mexico and left me odd-woman-out for always.

What would my teachers say if they knew I was a writer? Who would've guessed it? I wasn't a very bright student. I didn't much like school because we moved so much and I was always new and funny-looking. In my fifth-grade report card, I have nothing but an avalanche of C's and D's, but I don't remember being that stupid. I was good at art and I read plenty of library books and Kiki C laughed at all my jokes. At home I was fine, but at school I never opened my mouth except when the teacher called on me, the first time I'd speak all day.

When I think how I see myself, it would have to be at age eleven. I know I'm thirty-two on the outside, but inside I'm eleven. I'm the girl in the picture with skinny arms and a crumpled shirt and crooked hair. I didn't like school because all they saw was the outside me. School was lots of rules and sitting with your hands folded and being very afraid all the time. I liked looking out the window and thinking. I liked staring at the girl across the way writing her name over and over again in red ink. I wondered why the boy with the dirty collar in front of me didn't have a mama who took better care of him.

I think my mama and papa did the best they could to keep us warm and clean and never hungry. We had birthday and graduation parties and things like that, but there was another hunger that had to be fed. There was a hunger I didn't even have a name for. Was this when I began writing?

In 1966 we moved into a house, a real one, our first real home. This meant we didn't have to change schools and be the new kids on the block every couple of years. We could make friends and not be afraid we'd have to say goodbye to them and start all over. My brothers and the flock of boys they brought home would become important characters eventually for my stories—Louie and his cousins, Meme Ortiz and his dog with two names, one in English and one in Spanish.

My mother flourished in her own home. She took books out of the library and taught herself to garden, producing flowers so envied we had to put a lock on the gate to keep out the midnight flower thieves. My mother is still gardening to this day.

This was the period in my life, that slippery age when you are both child and woman and neither, I was to record in *The House on Mango Street*. I was still shy. I was a girl who couldn't come out of her shell.

How was I to know I would be recording and documenting the women who sat their sadness on an elbow and stared out a window? It would be the city streets of Chicago I would later record, but from a child's eyes.

I've done all kinds of things I didn't think I could do since then. I've gone to a prestigious university, studied with famous writers, and taken away an MFA degree. I've taught poetry in the schools in Illinois and Texas. I've gotten an NEA[2]

2. **NEA:** National Education Association, an organization of teachers and school administrators.

Analyzing The Essay
Identifying Facts
1. To the writer, making tortillas is a step-by-step process that must be followed. Unlike creative writing, which Cisneros says that she does intuitively, the critical essay for the MFA exam also is a step-by-step process.
2. From her father, she inherited a love for traveling and for storytelling and, evidently, a certain amount of sentimentality. From her mother, Cisneros inherited a "street smart" voice that is reflected in her writing.
3. As a child, Cisneros was taken so often to her grandparents' home in Mexico City that it seemed like home to her. The nostalgia was for this home in Mexico that was the only constant home she had until her early teen years.

Interpreting Meanings
4. Although responses will vary somewhat, answers should be consistent with the meaning of the word *metamorphosis* ("change of form or substance") and with Cisneros's allusion to the Rumplestiltskin story, in which straw is miraculously transformed into gold.
5. For many of these women, daily life was filled with the sadness of unfulfilled dreams, and it was this sadness that was propped on an elbow to stare out the window.
6. The images and figures of speech Cisneros uses in her descriptions of places to which she has traveled reveal her poetic ability, as do the descriptions of herself as an eleven-year-old schoolgirl and of the women who stare out the window.
7. Cisneros uses the Rumplestiltskin tale in two ways. The feelings of the woman facing the overwhelming task of spinning straw into gold are a metaphor to describe Cisneros's feelings when she was faced with a "step-by-step" task. The actual transformation of the straw into gold is used as a metaphor to describe the writer's belief that the experiences of life can be the raw material for art.

grant and run away with it as far as my courage would take me. I've seen the bleached and bitter mountains of the Peloponnesus. I've lived on a Greek island. I've been to Venice twice. In Rapallo, I met Ilona once and forever and took her sad heart with me across the south of France and into Spain.

I've lived in Yugoslavia. I've been to the famous Nice flower market behind the opera house. I've lived in a village in the pre-Alps and witnessed the daily parade of promenaders.

I've moved since Europe to the strange and wonderful country of Texas, land of polaroid-blue skies and big bugs. I met a mayor with my last name. I met famous Chicana/o artists and writers and *politicos*.

Texas is another chapter in my life. It brought with it the Dobie-Paisano Fellowship, a six-month residency on a 265-acre ranch. But most important Texas brought Mexico back to me.

Sitting at my favorite people-watching spot, the snaky Woolworth's counter across the street from the Alamo, I can't think of anything else I'd rather be than a writer. I've traveled and lectured from Cape Cod to San Francisco, to Spain, Yugoslavia, Greece, Mexico, France, Italy, and finally today to Seguin, Texas. Along the way there is straw for the taking. With a little imagination, it can be spun into gold.

Responding to the Essay

Analyzing the Essay

Identifying Facts

1. How do the writer's feelings about making the tortillas connect to her feelings about writing the MFA essay?
2. Exactly how did her family help shape her into a writer?
3. Why does she think nostalgia for a home is a theme that obsesses her?

Interpreting Meanings

4. How would you interpret the subtitle "The Metamorphosis of the Everyday"?
5. What do you think Cisneros means when she says she documented the women "who sat their sadness on an elbow and stared out a window"?
6. What **images** and **figures of speech** in this essay reveal that the writer is also a poet?
7. How does Cisneros use the fairy tale of Rumplestiltskin as a **metaphor** for her writing? What do you think of the metaphor?

Writing About the Essay

A Critical Response

Identifying the Main Idea. This essay was delivered as a speech at Texas Lutheran College. What do you think is the writer's major **purpose**? What would you say is her **main idea**? If you were a member of her audience, how would this speech have affected you? Answer these questions in a paragraph.

Primary Sources

Discovering a Voice

"As a young writer in college I was aware I had to find my voice, but how was I to know it would be the voice I used at home, the one I acquired as a result of one English-speaking mother and one Spanish-speaking father? My mother's English was learned in the Mexican/Italian neighborhood she grew up in on Chicago's near South Side, an English learned from playmates and school since her own parents spoke Spanish exclusively. My father, on the other hand, spoke to us in a Spanish of grandmothers and children, a language embroidered with the diminutive. To give you an example:

My mother: 'Good lucky I raised you kids right so you wouldn't hang around with the punks and floozies on the corner and wind up no good to nobody.'

My father (translated more or less from the Spanish): 'Eat a little bit more, my heaven, before leaving the table and fill your tum-tum up good.'

"These two voices at odds with each other—my mother's punch-you-in-the-nose English and my father's powdered-sugar Spanish—curiously are the voices that surface in my writing. What I'm especially aware of of late is how the Spanish syntax and word choice occurs in my work even though I write in English."

—from "Ghosts and Voices,"
Sandra Cisneros

For Further Reading For The Student

As timely now as it was in 1946, *Hiroshima* (Knopf, 1946) is sure to have great impact and meaning for thoughtful high school students.

A. Expansion

A British critic writing in the *Times Literary Supplement* complained that Hersey's decision to focus on six who survived tends to play down the horror of the bombing.

B. Responding

? How would you react, as a reader of *The New Yorker*, if you picked up a copy and found no cartoons, no advertisements, none of the usual contents, but one long piece of reporting about the destruction of a city by an atom bomb?

John Hersey (1914–)

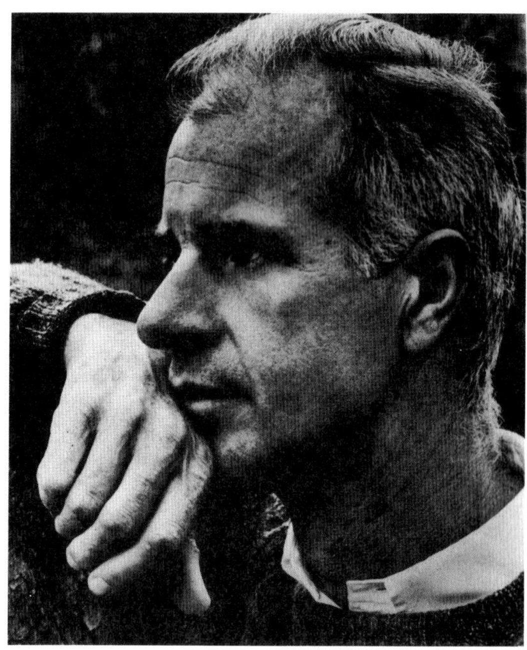

John Hersey was born in China, where he lived until he was eleven. He graduated from Yale and studied at Cambridge University in England, served as private secretary to the novelist Sinclair Lewis, and reported from the South Pacific and the Mediterranean during World War II for *Time* and *Life* magazines.

But "journalism" (if that means objective factual reporting) could not contain Hersey's passionate concern about contemporary events. In 1945 he won the Pulitzer Prize for his novel *A Bell for Adano*, based on what he had seen of American military government in Italy. Some critics saw this novel as a troubling examination of democracy, its ideals, and the difficulties of putting it into practice. A year later, Hersey followed this success with *Hiroshima*. Combining the techniques of a novel and the factual air of journalism to describe a real event, *Hiroshima* began what some critics call the genre of the "nonfiction novel." Hersey took an almost incomprehensible fact, the dropping of an atomic A bomb on a civilian population, and showed how it affected the lives of six survivors. Through their eyes, Americans could experience this catastrophe as if it were happening to them and to their friends and neighbors. Through Hersey's vivid narrative and his gift for characterization, the unimaginable became horrifyingly real.

Hiroshima became a national event, a precursor of the kind of "celebrity" status best-sellers often enjoy today, with attention paid to the authors on talk shows and in interviews in magazines and newspapers. B *Hiroshima* first appeared in *The New Yorker*, which devoted its entire issue to the book—a startling commitment for a magazine. Critic Sam Girgus reported that Albert Einstein ordered one thousand copies of it, the American Broadcasting Company had the book read aloud on its radio stations, and the Book-of-the-Month Club distributed free copies, on the grounds that nothing else in print "could be of more importance at this moment to the human race." *Hiroshima* has been called the most significant piece of reportage of modern times.

After *Hiroshima*, Hersey became famous as a writer who could make history understandable. He continued to dramatize issues and events, dealing with the Holocaust, racism, fascism, narrow utilitarian education, and other evils of modern life. He called his type of fiction "the novel of contemporary history" and wrote that "this kind of novel should make anyone who reads it better able to meet life in his generation—whenever that generation may be." He has produced books at markedly steady intervals from the 1940's to the 1980's. These include the highly acclaimed novel *The Wall* (1950), about the annihilation of Polish Jews in the Warsaw ghetto, and *Blues* (1987), a brilliant "meditation" on Hersey's favorite sport, fishing (which, of course, turns out to be about much more than fly-casting and trolling).

However, none of Hersey's work in the past three decades has had the impact of *Hiroshima*. Whether *Hiroshima*'s impact was "literary" or "social," whether it has lasting significance or whether it will not be read fifty years from now, no one can say for sure. There is no doubt, however, that the book still continues to force readers to face the horrifying realities of nuclear war. In almost half a century, no book on nuclear warfare has come close to *Hiroshima*'s impact on our moral and ethical sensibilities.

Supplementary Support Materials

1. Vocabulary Activity Worksheet (*CCB*)
2. Review and Response Worksheet: Subjective *vs.* Objective Reporting (*CCB*)
3. Language Skills Worksheet: Infinitives and Infinitive Phrases (*CCB*)
4. Selection Test (*CCB*)

Developing Vocabulary

The following words from the history are tested in the Selection Test. (See also Vocabulary Activity Worksheet.)

volition	incessant
rendezvous	convivial
abstinence	to buffet
estuarial	repugnant
hedonistic	terminus

Preparation

1. Building On Prior Knowledge. Most students should have at last a vague knowledge of the events leading to the end of World War II; however, this selection will become more meaningful if this prior knowledge is refreshed and reinforced. You may wish to have all students read a brief encyclopedia account of World War II; alternatively, you might ask several students to research the events of the last year of the war in their American history book, encyclopedias, and other sources and report to the class.

2. Establishing A Purpose. Before they begin reading, have students read question 10, page 1057. It will help them focus on a central purpose for reading the selection.

Humanities Connection: Discussing the Photograph

Without the caption, who could believe that this photograph had been taken of a section of a city where a quarter of a million people once lived? The forlorn figure in the foreground, his possessions bundled together on the handlebars of his bicycle, deepens the sense of desolation.

A NOISELESS FLASH

Hiroshima after the atomic blast.

A. Responding
? What one thing do the six people described in this paragraph have in common? (By chance, they were among the survivors when a hundred thousand of their fellow citizens were killed.)
(Hiroshima: hir′ə·shē′mə *or* hi·rō′shi·mə)

As you read John Hersey's re-creation of the frightening dawn of the atomic age (from the first chapter of *Hiroshima*), notice how he piles up precise, factual details to give his account authenticity. Hersey's narrative technique is also worth watching: he repeatedly builds up suspense about each of his characters' lives just before the bomb explodes.

A At exactly fifteen minutes past eight in the morning, on August 6, 1945, Japanese time, at the moment when the atomic bomb flashed above Hiroshima, Miss Toshiko Sasaki, a clerk in the personnel department of the East Asia Tin works, had just sat down at her place in the plant office and was turning her head to speak to the girl at the next desk. At that same moment, Dr. Masakazu Fujii was settling down cross-legged to read the Osaka *Asahi* on the porch of his private hospital, overhanging one of the seven deltaic rivers which divide Hiroshima; Mrs. Hatsuyo Nakamura, a tailor's widow, stood by the window of her kitchen, watching a neighbor tearing down his house because it lay in the path of an air-raid-defense fire lane; Father Wilhelm Kleinsorge, a German priest of the Society of Jesus, reclined in his underwear on a cot on the top floor of his order's three-story mission house, reading a Jesuit magazine, *Stimmen der Zeit;*[1] Dr. Terufumi Sasaki, a young member of the surgical staff of the city's large, modern Red Cross Hospital, walked along one of the hospital corridors with a blood specimen for a Wassermann test[2] in his hand; and the Reverend Mr. Kiyoshi Tanimoto, pastor of the Hiroshima Methodist Church, paused at the door of a rich man's house in Koi, the city's western suburb, and prepared to unload a handcart full of things he had evacuated from town in fear of the massive B-29 raid which everyone expected Hiroshima to suffer. A hundred thousand people were killed by the atomic bomb, and these six were among the survivors. They still wonder why they lived when so many others died. Each of them counts many small items of chance or volition—a step taken in time, a decision to go indoors, catching one streetcar instead of the next—that spared him. And now each knows that in the act of survival he lived a dozen lives and saw more death than he ever thought he would see. At the time, none of them knew anything.

The Reverend Mr. Tanimoto got up at five o'clock that morning. He was alone in the parsonage, because for some time his wife had been commuting with their year-old baby to spend nights with a friend in Ushida, a suburb to the north. Of all the important cities of Japan, only two, Kyoto and Hiroshima, had not been visited in strength by *B-san*, or Mr. B, as the Japanese, with a mixture of respect and unhappy familiarity, called the B-29; and Mr. Tanimoto, like all his neighbors and friends, was almost sick with anxiety. He had heard uncomfortably detailed accounts of mass raids on Kure, Iwakuni, Tokuyama, and other nearby towns; he was sure Hiroshima's turn would come soon. He had slept badly the night before, because there had been several air raid warnings. Hiroshima had been getting such warnings almost every night for weeks, for at that time the B-29s were using Lake Biwa, northeast of Hiroshima, as a rendezvous point, and no matter what city the Americans planned to hit, the Superfortresses streamed in over the coast near Hiroshima. The frequency of the warnings and the continued abstinence of Mr. B with respect to Hiroshima had made its citizens jittery; a rumor was going around that the Americans were saving something special for the city.

Mr. Tanimoto is a small man, quick to talk, laugh, and cry. He wears his black hair parted in the middle and rather long; the prominence of the frontal bones just above his eyebrows and the smallness of his mustache, mouth, and chin give him a strange, old-young look, boyish and yet wise, weak and yet fiery. He moves nervously and fast, but with a restraint which suggests that he is a cautious, thoughtful man. He showed, indeed, just those qualities in the uneasy days before the bomb fell. Besides having his wife spend the nights in Ushida, Mr. Tanimoto had been carrying all the portable things from his church, in the close-packed residential district called Nagaragawa, to a house that belonged to a rayon manufacturer in Koi, two miles from the center of town. The rayon man, a Mr. Matsui, had opened his then unoccupied estate to a large number of his friends and acquaintances, so that they might evacuate

1. ***Stimmen der Zeit*** (shtim′ən der tsīt): German for "Voices of the Time."
2. **Wassermann test:** a test used to identify syphilis.

A. Foreign Words
Hersey sprinkles Japanese words throughout this selection to provide an authentic Japanese flavor.
? How does Hersey let the reader know the meaning of the foreign words? (He uses restatement—giving the English equivalent right after the Japanese word or expression.)

B. Responding
The calmness with which the people react to the air raid warning indicates how quickly the dangerous becomes routine in wartime.
? Were the people of Hiroshima right in thinking the alarm only signaled the approach of an American weather plane? (No. The warning signaled the approach of the plane carrying the atom bomb.)

C. Irony
? Why is it ironic that the all-clear was sounded? (Because moments later the atom bomb exploded)
? Why did the radar operators assume the three planes comprised a reconnaissance? (Because bombing raids were usually carried out by large numbers of B-29's)

D. Expansion
The wooden construction of Japanese houses accounts for the extreme precautions against fire referred to on page 1053, left-hand column.

E. Imagery
This is the first of a series of striking images suggesting the visual effect of the bomb explosion. Compare Mrs. Nakamura's impression (page 1053, right-hand column) and that of Dr. Sasaki (page 1056, left-hand column).

whatever they wished to a safe distance from the probable target area. Mr. Tanimoto had had no difficulty in moving chairs, hymnals, Bibles, altar gear, and church records by pushcart himself, but the organ console and an upright piano required some aid. A friend of his named Matsuo had, the day before, helped him get the piano out to Koi; in return, he had promised this day to assist Mr. Matsuo in hauling out a daughter's belongings. That is why he had risen so early.

Mr. Tanimoto cooked his own breakfast. He felt awfully tired. The effort of moving the piano the day before, a sleepless night, weeks of worry and unbalanced diet, the cares of his parish—all combined to make him feel hardly adequate to the new day's work. There was another thing, too: Mr. Tanimoto had studied theology at Emory College, in Atlanta, Georgia; he had graduated in 1940; he spoke excellent English; he dressed in American clothes; he had corresponded with many American friends right up to the time the war began; and among a people obsessed with a fear of being spied upon—perhaps almost obsessed himself—he found himself growing increasingly uneasy. The police had questioned him several times, and just a few days before, he had heard that an influential acquaintance, a Mr. Tanaka, a retired officer of the Toyo Kisen Kaisha steamship line, an anti-Christian, a man famous in Hiroshima for his showy philanthropies and notorious for his personal tyrannies, had been telling people that Tanimoto should not be trusted. In compensation, to show himself publicly a good Japanese, Mr. Tanimoto had taken on the chairmanship of his local *tonarigumi*, or Neighborhood Association, and to his other duties and concerns this position had added the business of organizing air raid defense for about twenty families. A

Before six o'clock that morning, Mr. Tanimoto started for Mr. Matsuo's house. There he found that their burden was to be a *tansu*, a large Japanese cabinet, full of clothing and household goods. The two men set out. The morning was perfectly clear and so warm that the day promised to be uncomfortable. A few minutes after they started, the air raid siren went off—a minute-long blast that warned of approaching planes but indicated to the people of Hiroshima only a slight degree of danger, since it sounded every morning at this time, when an American weather plane came over. B The two men pulled and pushed the handcart through the city streets. Hiroshima was a fan-shaped city, lying mostly on the six islands formed by the seven estuarial rivers that branch out from the Ota River; its main commercial and residential districts, covering about four square miles in the center of the city, contained three-quarters of its population, which had been reduced by several evacuation programs from a wartime peak of 380,000 to about 245,000. Factories and other residential districts, or suburbs, lay compactly around the edges of the city. To the south were the docks, an airport, and the island-studded Inland Sea. A rim of mountains runs around the other three sides of the delta. Mr. Tanimoto and Mr. Matsuo took their way through the shopping center, already full of people, and across two of the rivers to the sloping streets of Koi, and up them to the outskirts and foothills. As they started up a valley away from the tight-ranked houses, the all-clear sounded. (The Japanese radar operators, detecting only three planes, supposed that they comprised a reconnaissance.[3]) C Pushing the handcart up to the rayon man's house was tiring, and the men, after they had maneuvered their load into the driveway and to the front steps, paused to rest awhile. They stood with a wing of the house between them and the city. Like most homes in this part of Japan, the house consisted of a wooden frame and wooden walls supporting a heavy tile roof. D Its front hall, packed with rolls of bedding and clothing, looked like a cool cave full of fat cushions. Opposite the house, to the right of the front door, there was a large, finicky rock garden. There was no sound of planes. The morning was still; the place was cool and pleasant.

Then a tremendous flash of light cut across the sky. Mr. Tanimoto has a distinct recollection that it traveled from east to west, from the city toward the hills. It seemed a sheet of sun. E Both he and Mr. Matsuo reacted in terror—and both had time to react (for they were 3,500 yards, or two miles, from the center of the explosion). Mr. Matsuo dashed up the front steps into the house and dived among the bedrolls and buried himself there. Mr. Tanimoto took four or five steps and threw himself between two big rocks in the garden. He bellied up very hard against one of them. As his face was against the stone, he did not see what happened. He felt a sudden pressure, and then splinters and pieces of board and fragments of tile fell on him. He heard no roar. (Almost no one in Hiroshima

3. **reconnaissance** (ri·kän′ə·zənts): an exploratory mission.

A. Responding
What is significant about these dugouts? (They suggest that the Japanese were ready to resist invasion to the last person. This fact is often used to explain why the United States used the atom bomb.)

B. Responding
What is it that Mr. Tanimoto mistakes for a local dust cloud? (Radioactive fallout from the bomb)

C. Irony
Why does Hersey put "safe areas" in quotation marks? (In the actual event, there were no safe areas in the whole city.)

D. Humanities Connection: Discussing the Photograph
This photograph graphically shows the makeshift provision that was all that could be managed to care for the wounded in the devastated city. The well couple are providing the patient with the care and familial sympathy without which (as Hersey explains on page 1054) the patient "would be miserable indeed."

recalls hearing any noise of the bomb. But a fisherman in his sampan[4] on the Inland Sea near Tsuzu, the man with whom Mr. Tanimoto's mother-in-law and sister-in-law were living, saw the flash and heard a tremendous explosion; he was nearly twenty miles from Hiroshima, but the thunder was greater than when the B-29s hit Iwakuni, only five miles away.)

When he dared, Mr. Tanimoto raised his head and saw that the rayon man's house had collapsed. He thought a bomb had fallen directly on it. Such clouds of dust had risen that there was a sort of twilight around. In panic, not thinking for the moment of Mr. Matsuo under the ruins, he dashed out into the street. He noticed as he ran that the concrete wall of the estate had fallen over—toward the house rather than away from it. In the street, the first thing he saw was a squad of soldiers who had been burrowing into the hillside A opposite, making one of the thousands of dugouts in which the Japanese apparently intended to resist invasion, hill by hill, life for life; the soldiers were coming out of the hole, where they should have been safe, and blood was running from their heads, chests, and backs. They were silent and dazed.

Under what seemed to be a local dust cloud, the day grew darker and darker. B

At nearly midnight, the night before the bomb was dropped, an announcer on the city's radio station said that about two hundred B-29s were approaching southern Honshu[5] and advised the population of Hiroshima to evacuate to their designated "safe areas." C Mrs. Hatsuyo Nakamura, the tailor's widow, who lived in the section called Noboricho and who had long had a habit of doing as she was told, got her three children—a ten-year-old boy, Toshio, an eight-year-old girl, Yaeko, and a five-year-old girl, Myeko—out of bed and dressed

4. **sampan:** a small, flat-bottomed boat.

5. **Honshu:** the largest island of Japan.

Hiroshima injured.

D

them and walked with them to the military area known as the East Parade Ground, on the northeast edge of the city. There she unrolled some mats and the children lay down on them. They slept until about two, when they were awakened by the roar of the planes going over Hiroshima.

As soon as the planes had passed, Mrs. Nakamura started back with her children. They reached home a little after two-thirty and she immediately turned on the radio, which, to her distress, was just then broadcasting a fresh warning. When she looked at the children and saw how tired they were, and when she thought of the number of trips they had made in past weeks, all to no purpose, to the East Parade Ground, she decided that in spite of the instructions on the radio, she simply could not face starting out all over again. She put the children in their bedrolls on the floor, lay down herself at three o'clock, and fell asleep at once, so soundly that when the planes passed over later, she did not waken to their sound.

The siren jarred her awake at about seven. She arose, dressed quickly, and hurried to the house of Mr. Nakamoto, the head of her Neighborhood Association, and asked him what she should do. He said that she should remain at home unless an urgent warning—a series of intermittent blasts of the siren—was sounded. She returned home, lit the stove in the kitchen, set some rice to cook, and sat down to read that morning's Hiroshima *Chugoku*. To her relief, the all-clear sounded at eight o'clock. She heard the children stirring, so she went and gave each of them a handful of peanuts and told them to stay on their bedrolls, because they were tired from the night's walk. She had hoped that they would go back to sleep, but the man in the house directly to the south began to make a terrible hullabaloo of hammering, wedging, ripping, and splitting. The prefectural government, convinced, as everyone in Hiroshima was, that the city would be attacked soon, had begun to press with threats and warnings for the completion of wide fire lanes, which, it was hoped, might act in conjunction with the rivers to localize any fires started by an incendiary raid; and the neighbor was reluctantly sacrificing his home to the city's safety. Just the day before, the prefecture had ordered all able-bodied girls from the secondary schools to spend a few days helping to clear these lanes, and they started work soon after the all-clear sounded.

Mrs. Nakamura went back to the kitchen, looked at the rice, and began watching the man next door. At first, she was annoyed with him for making so much noise, but then she was moved almost to tears by pity. Her emotion was specifically directed toward her neighbor, tearing down his home, board by board, at a time when there was so much unavoidable destruction, but undoubtedly she also felt a generalized, community pity, to say nothing of self-pity. She had not had an easy time. Her husband, Isawa, had gone into the Army just after Myeko was born, and she had heard nothing from or of him for a long time, until, on March 5, 1942, she received a seven-word telegram: "Isawa died an honorable death at Singapore." She learned later that he had died on February 15th, the day Singapore fell, and that he had been a corporal. Isawa had been a not particularly prosperous tailor, and his only capital was a Sankoku sewing machine. After his death, when his allotments stopped coming, Mrs. Nakamura got out the machine and began to take in piecework herself, and since then had supported the children, but poorly, by sewing.

As Mrs. Nakamura stood watching her neighbor, everything flashed whiter than any white she had ever seen. She did not notice what happened to the man next door; the reflex of a mother set her in motion toward her children. She had taken a single step (the house was 1,350 yards, or three-quarters of a mile, from the center of the explosion) when something picked her up and she seemed to fly into the next room over the raised sleeping platform, pursued by parts of her house. B

Timbers fell around her as she landed, and a shower of tiles pommelled her; everything became dark, for she was buried. The debris did not cover her deeply. She rose up and freed herself. She heard a child cry, "Mother, help me!," and saw her youngest—Myeko, the five-year-old—buried up to her breast and unable to move. As Mrs. Nakamura started frantically to claw her way toward the baby, she could see or hear nothing of her other children.

In the days right before the bombing, Dr. Masakazu Fujii, being prosperous, hedonistic, and at the time not too busy, had been allowing himself the luxury of sleeping until nine or nine-thirty, but fortunately he had to get up early the morning the bomb was dropped to see a house guest off on a train. He rose at six, and half an hour later walked with his friend to the station, not far away, across

A. Responding

? Why would the rivers of Hiroshima help to localize fires? (The seven estuarial rivers divided the city into six islands; these plus the wide fire lanes would, it was hoped, keep fires from spreading.)

B. Responding

? How is it that Mrs. Nakamura is able to take a step before the force of the explosion hurls her into the next room? (The light from the explosion traveled faster than the concussion from it.)

A. Expansion
This family solicitude for a sick member is touchingly evident in the photograph of the makeshift hospital on page 1052.

B. Responding
? Why is the direction in which Dr. Fujii's porch faced important? (The fact that it faced away from the center of the city probably saved his life.)

C. Imagery
The image is vivid and particularly appropriate for a Japanese, who commonly eats with chopsticks.

D. Expansion
You may wish to remind students that Germany had surrendered three months before the bomb fell on Hiroshima.

two of the rivers. He was back home by seven, just as the siren sounded its sustained warning. He ate breakfast and then, because the morning was already hot, undressed down to his underwear and went out on the porch to read the paper. This porch—in fact, the whole building—was curiously constructed. Dr. Fujii was the proprietor of a peculiarly Japanese institution: a private, single-doctor hospital. This building, perched beside and over the water of the Kyo River, and next to the bridge of the same name, contained thirty rooms for thirty patients and their kinfolk—for, according to Japanese custom, when a person falls sick and goes to a hospital, one or more members of his family go and live there with him, to cook for him, bathe, massage, and read to him, and to offer incessant familial sympathy, without which a Japanese patient would be miserable indeed. Dr. Fujii had no beds—only straw mats—for his patients. He did, however, have all sorts of modern equipment: an x-ray machine, diathermy[6] apparatus, and a fine tiled laboratory. The structure rested two-thirds on the land, one-third on piles over the tidal waters of the Kyo. This overhang, the part of the building where Dr. Fujii lived, was queer-looking, but it was cool in summer and from the porch, which faced away from the center of the city, the prospect of the river, with pleasure boats drifting up and down it, was always refreshing. Dr. Fujii had occasionally had anxious moments when the Ota and its mouth branches rose to flood, but the piling was apparently firm enough and the house had always held.

Dr. Fujii had been relatively idle for about a month because in July, as the number of untouched cities in Japan dwindled and as Hiroshima seemed more and more inevitably a target, he began turning patients away, on the ground that in case of a fire raid he would not be able to evacuate them. Now he had only two patients left—a woman from Yano, injured in the shoulder, and a young man of twenty-five recovering from burns he had suffered when the steel factory near Hiroshima in which he worked had been hit. Dr. Fujii had six nurses to tend his patients. His wife and children were safe; his wife and one son were living outside Osaka, and another son and two daughters were in the country on Kyushu.[7] A niece was living with him, and a maid and a manservant. He had little to do and did not mind, for he had saved some money. At fifty, he was healthy, convivial, and calm, and he was pleased to pass the evenings drinking whiskey with friends, always sensibly and for the sake of conversation. Before the war, he had affected brands imported from Scotland and America; now he was perfectly satisfied with the best Japanese brand, Suntory.

Dr. Fujii sat down cross-legged in his underwear on the spotless matting of the porch, put on his glasses, and started reading the Osaka *Asahi*. He liked to read the Osaka news because his wife was there. He saw the flash. To him—faced away from the center and looking at his paper—it seemed a brilliant yellow. Startled, he began to rise to his feet. In that moment (he was 1,550 yards from the center), the hospital leaned behind his rising and, with a terrible ripping noise, toppled into the river. The Doctor, still in the act of getting to his feet, was thrown forward and around and over; he was buffeted and gripped; he lost track of everything, because things were so speeded up; he felt the water.

Dr. Fujii hardly had time to think that he was dying before he realized that he was alive, squeezed tightly by two long timbers in a V across his chest, like a morsel suspended between two huge chopsticks—held upright, so that he could not move, with his head miraculously above water and his torso and legs in it. The remains of his hospital were all around him in a mad assortment of splintered lumber and materials for the relief of pain. His left shoulder hurt terribly. His glasses were gone.

Father Wilhelm Kleinsorge, of the Society of Jesus, was, on the morning of the explosion, in rather frail condition. The Japanese wartime diet had not sustained him, and he felt the strain of being a foreigner in an increasingly xenophobic[8] Japan; even a German, since the defeat of the Fatherland, was unpopular. Father Kleinsorge had, at thirty-eight, the look of a boy growing too fast—thin in the face, with a prominent Adam's apple, a hollow chest, dangling hands, big feet. He walked clumsily, leaning forward a little. He was tired all the time. To make matters worse, he had suffered for two days, along with Father Cies-

6. **diathermy:** heat treatment.
7. **Kyushu:** the southernmost of the principal islands of Japan.
8. **xenophobic** (zen·ə·fō'bik): disliking or fearing foreigners.

Closure
Have students discuss how the effect of this account, which views the bombing of Hiroshima through the eyes of six survivors, is different from what that of a straight expository account would be.

Reading Check Test
1. The two characters named Sasaki are brother and sister. *False*
2. Hiroshima is left relatively unharmed before the atomic blast. *True*
3. Mrs. Nakamura hears only one of her three children after the blast. *True*
4. The Japanese call B-29's "the big guys." *False*
5. Dr. Sasaki is the only doctor in his hospital who is unhurt. *True*

lik, a fellow-priest, from a rather painful and urgent diarrhea, which they blamed on the beans and black ration bread they were obliged to eat. Two other priests then living in the mission compound, which was in the Noboricho section—Father Superior LaSalle and Father Schiffer—had happily escaped this affliction.

Father Kleinsorge woke up about six the morning the bomb was dropped, and half an hour later—he was a bit tardy because of his sickness—he began to read Mass in the mission chapel, a small Japanese-style wooden building which was without pews, since its worshipers knelt on the usual Japanese matted floor, facing an altar graced with splendid silks, brass, silver, and heavy embroideries. This morning, a Monday, the only worshipers were Mr. Takemoto, a theological student living in the mission house; Mr. Fukai, the secretary of the diocese; Mrs. Murata, the mission's devoutly Christian housekeeper; and his fellow-priests. After Mass, while Father Kleinsorge was reading the Prayers of Thanksgiving, the siren sounded. He stopped the service and the missionaries retired across the compound to the bigger building. There, in his room on the ground floor, to the right of the front door, Father Kleinsorge changed into a military uniform which he had acquired when he was teaching at the Rokko Middle School in Kobe and which he wore during air raid alerts.

After an alarm, Father Kleinsorge always went out and scanned the sky, and in this instance, when he stepped outside, he was glad to see only the single weather plane that flew over Hiroshima each day about this time. Satisfied that nothing would happen, he went in and breakfasted with the other Fathers on substitute coffee and ration bread, which, under the circumstances, was especially repugnant to him. The Fathers sat and talked a while, until, at eight, they heard the all-clear. They went then to various parts of the building. Father Schiffer retired to his room to do some writing. Father Cieslik sat in his room in a straight chair with a pillow over his stomach to ease his pain, and read. Father Superior LaSalle stood at the window of his room, thinking. Father Kleinsorge went up to a room on the third floor, took off all his clothes except his underwear, and stretched out on his right side on a cot and began reading his *Stimmen der Zeit*.

After the terrible flash—which, Father Kleinsorge later realized, reminded him of something he had read as a boy about a large meteor colliding with the earth—he had time (since he was 1,400 yards from the center) for one thought: A bomb has fallen directly on us. Then, for a few seconds or minutes, he went out of his mind.

Father Kleinsorge never knew how he got out of the house. The next things he was conscious of were that he was wandering around in the mission's vegetable garden in his underwear, bleeding slightly from small cuts along his left flank; that all the buildings round about had fallen down except the Jesuits' mission house, which had long before been braced and double-braced by a priest named Groppe, who was terrified of earthquakes; that the day had turned dark; and that Murata-*san*, the housekeeper, was nearby, crying over and over, "*Shu Jesusu, awaremi tamia!* Our Lord Jesus, have pity on us!" A

On the train on the way into Hiroshima from the country, where he lived with his mother, Dr. Terufumi Sasaki, the Red Cross Hospital surgeon, thought over an unpleasant nightmare he had had the night before. His mother's home was in Mukaihara, thirty miles from the city, and it took him two hours by train and tram to reach the hospital. He had slept uneasily all night and had wakened an hour earlier than usual, and, feeling sluggish and slightly feverish, had debated whether to go to the hospital at all; his sense of duty finally forced him to go, and he had started out on an earlier train than he took most mornings. The dream had particularly frightened him because it was so closely associated, on the surface at least, with a disturbing actuality. He was only twenty-five years old and had just completed his training at the Eastern Medical University, in Tsingtao, China. B He was something of an idealist and was much distressed by the inadequacy of medical facilities in the country town where his mother lived. Quite on his own, and without a permit, he had begun visiting a few sick people out there in the evenings, after his eight hours at the hospital and four hours' commuting. He had recently learned that the penalty for practicing without a permit was severe; a fellow-doctor whom he had asked about it had given him a serious scolding. Nevertheless, he had continued to practice. In his dream, he had been at the bedside of a country patient when the police and the doctor he had consulted burst into the room, seized him, dragged him outside, and beat him up

A. Responding
? What happens to Father Kleinsorge immediately after he thinks a bomb has fallen directly on the compound? (The force of the explosion levels the buildings and throws him out into the garden.)

B. Expansion
Tsingtao (ching·dou′), now spelled Qingdao, is a large city on the Yellow River, which was occupied by Japan at the time Dr. Terufumi trained there.

ANALYZING THE HISTORY

Identifying Facts

1. They are all fairly ordinary people: a clerk, a private doctor, a priest, a widow, a young surgeon, and a minister. Each of them attributes his or her survival to "small items of chance or volition."

2. Mr. Tanimoto remembers the flash as a "sheet of sun" that traveled across the sky. Mrs. Nakamura recalls the flash as "whiter than any white she had ever seen." Dr. Fujii, looking away from the sky, remembered a brilliant yellow. Father Kleinsorge thought of a meteor colliding with the earth. Dr. Sasaki saw the light reflected, like a gigantic photographic flash. Finally, the office of Miss Sasaki was filled with a "blinding light."

3. Students may choose among many such details. For example, in the first paragraph Dr. Fujii is sitting on the porch of his hospital to read the morning newspaper; Father Kleinsorge is in his underwear reading a magazine; and Mr. Tanimoto is helping a friend move.

4. The Japanese radio operators, who detected only three planes, thought the mission was a reconnaissance.

5. Hersey does not offer any reasons for the dropping of the bomb in this section.

A. Imagery Another vivid image suggests the effect of the explosion on those who witnessed it.

B. Responding ? Why does Hersey say "as only a Japanese would" in describing Dr. Sasaki's behavior? (The Japanese set great store by their honor, which Dr. Sasaki would feel to be jeopardized by cowardly behavior, even though no one was there to witness it.)

C. Irony ? Why is the fact that the patient had been dreadfully afraid of having syphilis ironic? (While the man dreaded one calamity, another, worse one, overtook him.)

cruelly. On the train, he just about decided to give up the work in Mukaihara, since he felt it would be impossible to get a permit, because the authorities would hold that it would conflict with his duties at the Red Cross Hospital.

At the terminus, he caught a streetcar at once. (He later calculated that if he had taken his customary train that morning, and if he had had to wait a few minutes for the streetcar, as often happened, he would have been close to the center at the time of the explosion and would surely have perished.) He arrived at the hospital at seven-forty and reported to the chief surgeon. A few minutes later, he went to a room on the first floor and drew blood from the arm of a man in order to perform a Wassermann test. The laboratory containing the incubators for the test was on the third floor. With the blood specimen in his left hand, walking in a kind of distraction he had felt all morning, probably because of the dream and his restless night, he started along the main corridor on his way toward the stairs. He was one step beyond an open window when the light of the bomb was
A reflected, like a gigantic photograph flash, in the corridor. He ducked down on one knee and said
B to himself, as only a Japanese would, "Sasaki, *gambare!* Be brave!" Just then (the building was 1,650 yards from the center), the blast ripped through the hospital. The glasses he was wearing flew off his face; the bottle of blood crashed against one wall, his Japanese slippers zipped out from under his feet—but otherwise, thanks to where he stood, he was untouched.

Dr. Sasaki shouted the name of the chief surgeon and rushed around to the man's office and found him terribly cut by glass. The hospital was in horrible confusion: heavy partitions and ceilings had fallen on patients, beds had overturned, windows had blown in and cut people, blood was spattered on the walls and floors, instruments were everywhere, many of the patients were running about screaming, many more lay dead. (A colleague working in the laboratory to which Dr.
C Sasaki had been walking was dead; Dr. Sasaki's patient, whom he had just left and who a few moments before had been dreadfully afraid of syphilis, was also dead.) Dr. Sasaki found himself the only doctor in the hospital who was unhurt.

Dr. Sasaki, who believed that the enemy had hit only the building he was in, got bandages and began to bind the wounds of those inside the hospital; while outside, all over Hiroshima, maimed and dying citizens turned their unsteady steps toward the Red Cross Hospital to begin an invasion that was to make Dr. Sasaki forget his private nightmare for a long, long time.

Miss Toshiko Sasaki, the East Asia Tin Works clerk, who is not related to Dr. Sasaki, got up at three o'clock in the morning on the day the bomb fell. There was extra housework to do. Her eleven-month-old brother, Akio, had come down the day before with a serious stomach upset; her mother had taken him to the Tamura Pediatric Hospital and was staying there with him. Miss Sasaki, who was about twenty, had to cook breakfast for her father, a brother, a sister, and herself, and—since the hospital, because of the war, was unable to provide food—to prepare a whole day's meals for her mother and the baby, in time for her father, who worked in a factory making rubber earplugs for artillery crews, to take the food by on his way to the plant. When she had finished and had cleaned and put away the cooking things, it was nearly seven. The family lived in Koi, and she had a forty-five-minute trip to the tin works, in the section of town called Kannonmachi. She was in charge of the personnel records in the factory. She left Koi at seven, and as soon as she reached the plant, she went with some of the other girls from the personnel department to the factory auditorium. A prominent local Navy man, a former employee, had committed suicide the day before by throwing himself under a train—a death considered honorable enough to warrant a memorial service, which was to be held at the tin works at ten o'clock that morning. In the large hall, Miss Sasaki and the others made suitable preparations for the meeting. This work took about twenty minutes.

Miss Sasaki went back to her office and sat down at her desk. She was quite far from the windows, which were off to her left, and behind her were a couple of tall bookcases containing all the books of the factory library, which the personnel department had organized. She settled herself at her desk, put some things in a drawer, and shifted papers. She thought that before she began to make entries in her lists of new employees, discharges, and departures for the Army, she would chat for a moment with the girl at her right. Just as she turned her head away from the windows, the room was filled with a blinding light. She was paralyzed by fear, fixed still in her chair

He focuses instead on the reactions of ordinary, everyday people.

Interpreting Meanings

6. Irony is inherent in each story, for the daily routines of each character are sharply reversed by the violent reality of the bombs being dropped. In the last image it is especially ironic that books, which are symbols of civilization, seriously injure Miss Sasaki.

7. We feel the horror of war because he reports its effects on ordinary people.

Hersey seems humane and sympathetic toward both nationalities.

8. Most students will be free of preconceptions, even though they know that the Japanese opposed the United States in World War II. They may agree that Hersey treats the Japanese in this selection as ordinary people, affected by war just as Americans might be affected by it. Some will say that the piece evokes sympathy for the victims of the bomb. Encourage students to discuss this question within the bounds of Hersey's piece; urge them to note that he deliberately downplays political and military matters, confining his attention to an objective description of what typical citizens of Hiroshima were doing at the moment of the bombing.

Students may readily imagine that the reception of *Hiroshima* was more controversial in 1946, the year after the atomic bomb was dropped. You may want to encourage them to discuss the role of time's passage in our perspectives on history. How, for example, do they regard the 1980's today? How would their views contrast with those of students five years ago?

9. Historians or journalists might have given, for example, a drily objective description of the bare facts of the incident, together with a few quotations from some of the eyewitnesses who survived.

10. For one thing, it was the first use of a weapon and a technology that could destroy the world.

for a long moment (the plant was 1,600 yards from the center).

Everything fell, and Miss Sasaki lost consciousness. The ceiling dropped suddenly and the wooden floor above collapsed in splinters and the people up there came down and the roof above them gave way; but principally and first of all, the bookcases right behind her swooped forward and the contents threw her down, with her left leg horribly twisted and breaking underneath her. There, in the tin factory, in the first moment of the atomic age, a human being was crushed by books.

Responding to the History

Analyzing the History

Identifying Facts

1. Who are the six survivors presented in this section, and what do they have in common?
2. What simple **images** does Hersey use to help us imagine the actual physical impact of the bomb? For example, how does he describe the flash as seen by each character?
3. What small, commonplace **human interest** details does Hersey give about his **characters** so that they come alive and seem like people we might know?
4. How does Hersey explain the **ironic** fact that an all-clear signal sounded just before the bomb was dropped?
5. Does Hersey give any details in this section to suggest the reasons the bomb was dropped? Explain.

Interpreting Meanings

6. What **ironies** can you find in each character's story—including the irony of the last image?
7. In this selection, Hersey refrains from moralizing. Nevertheless, he does communicate an **attitude** toward war. How does he accomplish that? How would you describe his attitude toward the Japanese? Toward the Americans?
8. During World War II, most Americans felt that the Japanese, like the Germans, were enemies and aggressors to be destroyed no matter what the cost. How do you respond to Hersey's treatment of the Japanese in this piece? How do you think readers in 1946—one year after the war ended—would have responded?
9. What other methods might a historian or journalist have used to tell this story? What do you think of Hersey's method?
10. From what you have read here, and from what you know of history, can you explain why in human and political terms, the explosion at Hiroshima was a central event in the twentieth century?

Writing About the History

A Critical Response

1. **Analyzing Suspense.** Readers of Hersey's *Hiroshima* know what the "plot" is before they open the book. In a brief essay, show how, in this extract, Hersey manages, nevertheless, to create suspense. What questions does he plant in your mind? When does he answer them?
2. **Classifying a Literary Work.** Define what you think "literature" is, and then discuss in a brief essay whether or not *Hiroshima* fulfills the requirements of literature.
3. **Evaluating the Report.** In **subjective** reporting, the writer expresses personal emotions and attitudes toward the events and characters he or she is writing about. In **objective** reporting, the writer presents only observable, verifiable facts and keeps his or her own feelings at a distance. At times, the only way we can infer how such a writer feels about an event is to examine the details specifically chosen for inclusion or omission. In an essay, evaluate Hersey's report in terms of its objectivity and subjectivity. Cite specific passages to support your opinion.

Analyzing Language and Style

Japanese Terms

John Hersey creates a particular tone for his report when he notes (page 1050) that the Japanese had a nickname for the B-29 bomber planes that regularly damaged their cities: "*B-san*, or Mr. B." This appositive (which is a context clue that directly defines the word) also gives us an idea of what the word *-san,* might mean when attached to a noun. Often Hersey's use of Japanese terms like *B-san* helps to establish the authenticity of his report. Notice, however, that Hersey almost always helps his readers by including a definition or an appositive phrase that provides the meaning of the terms. Find seven Japanese terms defined within the context of this report.

For Further Reading
For The Teacher
Michael Herr's *Dispatches* (Knopf, 1977), from which this selection has been taken, reflects impressions he formed as a correspondent for *Esquire* beginning in 1967. *Dispatches* was widely praised when it appeared in 1977; C. D. B. Bryan, himself a distinguished reporter of the war, called it "the best book to have been written about the Vietnam War."

Michael Herr (1940–)

In a preface to *Dispatches* (1977), based on his experiences as a war correspondent in Vietnam, Michael Herr acknowledges permission to quote lyrics from a long list of songs. The songs are not at all like tunes from the two world wars, boisterous marching songs like "As the Caissons Go Rolling Along" or mournful love lyrics like "Lili Marlene." What Herr recalls from Vietnam are the pounding rhythms of rock and roll, country music, hard rock, the Beatles, Mick Jagger, Keith Richards, and Bob Dylan. Those voices are often harsh, dissonant, bitter, and accusatory. They insist on making themselves heard. That is the same tone in which Herr reports on the war.

For several years after the formal fighting ended in Vietnam, no major books appeared about America's longest and most unpopular war. It was also a war America had not won, and one which many Americans had vehemently opposed. No one seemed to want to talk about what had gone wrong and why. Many Americans preferred to forget it.

But in the late 1970's, the silence ended. Just as insistently as the voices in the songs Herr remembers, novelists, poets, dramatists, screenwriters, and journalists have begun to try to capture some sense from a seemingly senseless war. Important nonfiction books have included Ronald Glasser's *365 Days*; Philip Caputo's *A Rumor of War* (1977); Ron Kovic's *Born on the Fourth of July* (1976); Frances Fitzgerald's *Fire in the Lake*; Tim O'Brien's *If I Die in a Combat Zone, Box Me Up and Ship Me Home* (1973). In 1978, O'Brien (see page 884), a veteran of Vietnam, won the National Book Award for his novel *Going After Cacciato*, a complicated and powerful tale of a soldier fleeing the Vietnam battlefield. Other significant novels are Robert Stone's *Dog Soldiers* (1973), Steven Smith's *American Boys* (1975), and James Webb's *Fields of Fire* (1978).

What may strike a reader of the following excerpt from Herr's *Dispatches* is how different it seems in tone and intent from John Hersey's third-person narrative in *Hiroshima* (page 1048). Herr's voice is intensely personal, with sudden sharp emphasis, angry asides, and moments of black humor. Herr himself is very much present in these dispatches, which are news bulletins from the front; we see him as one of his own characters, jumping in and out of "choppers," interviewing a colonel, eating in a mess hall with the soldiers. Spewing out information in a breathless rush, he hurries through his story, sometimes flashing forward to new scenes, sometimes backward to old ones, tossing in images and song lyrics, introducing characters and anecdotes with the speed of snapshots, and then moving on. The effect is compelling: Herr catches the prose rhythm of a war that has no center, no beginning, and no end.

Other writers about Vietnam have admired Herr's work. Playwright David Rabe (*Streamers, The Basic Training of Pavlo Hummel, Sticks and Bones*) commented:

> Michael Herr is the only writer I've read who has written in the mad-pop-poetic / bureaucratically camouflaged language in which Vietnam was lived. The trees take up attack postures, sanity defoliates before your eyes, and the generals spin out theories like Macbeth's witches. He gets very close to taking you all the way over.
>
> —David Rabe

SUPPLEMENTARY SUPPORT MATERIALS
1. Vocabulary Activity Worksheet (*CCB*)
2. Review and Response Worksheet: Anecdotal Narrative (*CCB*)
3. Selection Test (*CCB*)

DEVELOPING VOCABULARY
The following words from the reports are tested in the Selection Test. (See also Vocabulary Activity Worksheet.)

aborigine	connoisseur
recalcitrance	nonchalant
to interdict	dispersion

PREPARATION
1. BUILDING ON PRIOR KNOWLEDGE. Ask volunteers to give a brief account of American involvement in the Vietnam War. (You may wish to assign several of the volunteers to read accounts of the war in their history books and report their findings.)

2. ESTABLISHING A PURPOSE. Tell students that the anecdotes that make up this selection may seem disjointed fragments. Suggest that as they read they try to relate these separate pieces into a unified impression.

FROM DISPATCHES

Just as the terrain of the Vietnam Highlands possessed a nightmarish, disorienting quality, so the experiences and memories of the war that Herr describes seem fragmented, jagged, discontinuous. To mirror this theme, the author structures his narrative around a series of anecdotes, rather than in a conventional chronological framework. It is up to you, the reader, to interpret these anecdotes as you would interpret a mosaic, judging for yourself what each fragment contributes to the whole picture.

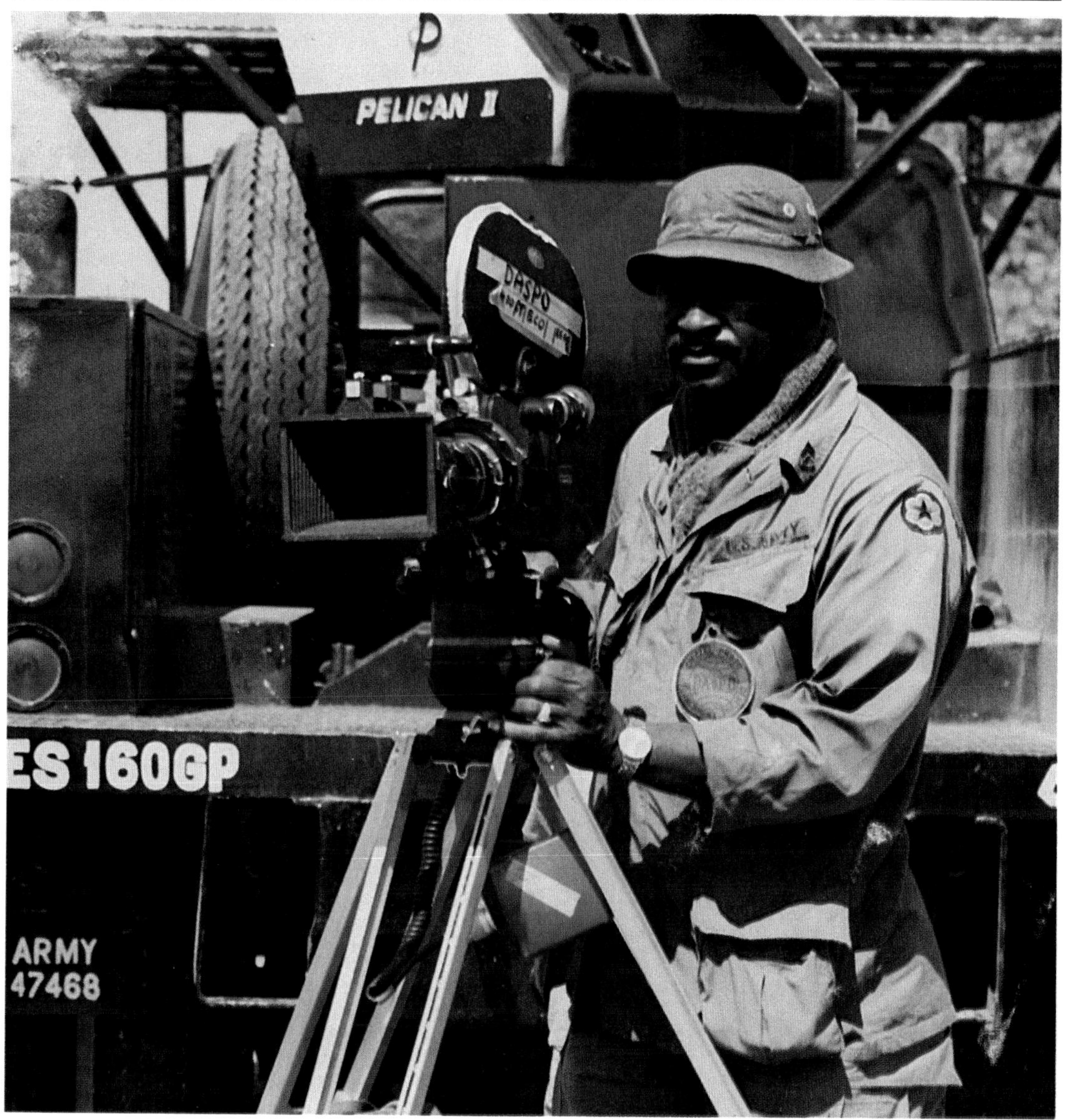

A

A. Humanities Connection: Discussing the Photograph
The cameraman who is the subject of this photograph is a curious symbol of the Vietnam War. Other wars have been photographed, beginning with Mathew B. Brady's stunning visual record of the Civil War; however, no war before this one had been recorded in such detail on film, which was then projected nightly onto millions of American television screens. Discuss with students how the repulsion that so many Americans came to feel toward this war may have been, in part, the result of their being eyewitnesses to it by way of the television screen.

A. Irony
? Explain the irony in this sentence. (Herr says we admired the restless spirits of the Montagnards. But because we had destroyed their crops and villages, they in fact had no choice but to move on nomadically.)

B. Responding
? What general impression of the Vietnam Highlands does Herr convey in this long first paragraph? (That the country is weird, sinister, baffling)

The Highlands

The Highlands of Vietnam are spooky, unbearably spooky, spooky beyond belief. They are a run of erratic mountain ranges, gnarled valleys, jungled ravines and abrupt plains where Montagnard villages cluster, thin, and disappear as the terrain steepens. The Montagnards in all of their tribal components make up the most primitive and mysterious portion of the Vietnamese population, a population that has always confused Americans even in its most Westernized segments. Strictly speaking, the Montagnards are not really Vietnamese at all, certainly not *South* Vietnamese, but a kind of upgraded, demi-enlightened Annamese[1] aborigine, often living in nakedness and brooding silence in their villages. Most Vietnamese and most Montagnards consider each other inferior, and while many Montagnards hired out as mercenaries to the American Special Forces, that older, racially based enmity often slowed down the Allied effort. Many Americans considered them to be nomadic, but the war had had more to do with that than anything in their temperament. A We napalmed[2] off their crops and flattened their villages, and then admired the restlessness in their spirit. Their nakedness, their painted bodies, their recalcitrance, their silent composure before strangers, their benign savagery, and the sheer, awesome ugliness of them combined to make most Americans who were forced to associate with them a little uncomfortable over the long run. It would seem fitting, ordained, that they should live in the Highlands, among triple canopies, where sudden, contrary mists offered sinister bafflement, where the daily heat and the nighttime cold kept you perpetually, increasingly, on edge, where the silences were interrupted only by the sighing of cattle or the rotor-thud of a helicopter, the one sound I know that is both sharp and dull at the same time. The Puritan belief that Satan dwelt in Nature could have been born here, where even on the coldest, freshest mountaintops you could smell jungle and that tension between rot and genesis that all jungles give off. B It is ghost story country, and for Americans it had been the scene of some of the war's vilest surprises. The Ia Drang battles of late 1965 constituted the first and worst of these surprises. They marked the first wholesale appearance of North Vietnamese regulars in the South, and no one who was around then can ever forget the horror of it or, to this day, get over the confidence and sophistication with which entire battalions came to engage Americans in a war. A few correspondents, a few soldiers back for second and third tours still shuddered uncontrollably at what they remembered: impromptu positions held to the last man and then overrun; Americans and North Vietnamese stiff in one another's death embrace, the eyes wide open, their teeth bared or sunk deep into enemy flesh; the number of helicopters shot down (relief mission after relief mission after relief mission . . .); the NVA[3] equipment hauls which included the first AK-47 assault rifles, the first RPG-7 rockets, the hundreds of aluminum grave markers. No, a lot of the ones who saw that, the toughest of them, didn't even like to talk about it. The very best of our divisions, the 1st Air Cavalry, was blooded in the Ia Drang that autumn, and while the official number of dead was released at around three hundred, I never met anyone who had been there, including officers of the Cav, who would settle for less than three or even four times that figure.

There is a point of view that says that the United States got involved in the Vietnam War, commitments and interests aside, simply because we thought it would be easy. But after the Ia Drang, that first arrogance sat less and less well about the shoulders of the Command; it never vanished. There was never again a real guerrilla war after Ia Drang, except in the Delta, and the old Giap[4] stratagem of interdicting the South through the Highlands, cutting the country in two, came to be taken seriously, even obsessively, by many influential Americans.

Oh, that terrain! The bloody, maddening uncanniness of it! When the hideous Battle of Dak To ended at the top of Hill 875, we announced that four thousand of them had been killed; it had been the purest slaughter, our losses were bad, but clearly it was another American victory. But when the top of the hill was reached, the number of NVA found was four. Four. Of course more dead, hundreds more, but the corpses kicked and

1. **Annamese:** referring to Annam, a district of Vietnam.
2. **napalmed:** *napalm* was a petroleum product used in flamethrowers.
3. **NVA:** the North Vietnamese army.
4. **Giap:** Vietnamese general who opposed the French in 1954.

COMMENT FROM A CRITIC
Concluding his review of *Dispatches*, Paul Gray observed: "Herr dared to travel to that irrational place and to come back with the worst imaginable news: war thrives because men still love it."
Read this comment to your students and ask them to react to it on the basis of their reading of this selection.

counted and photographed and buried numbered four. Where, Colonel? And how, and why? Spooky. Everything up there was spooky, and it would have been that way even if there had been no war. You were there in a place where you didn't belong, where things were glimpsed for which you would have to pay and where things went unglimpsed for which you would also have to pay, a place where they didn't play with the mystery but killed you straight off for trespassing. The towns had names that laid a quick, chilly touch on your bones: Kontum, Dak Mat Lop, Dak Roman Peng, Poli Klang, Buon Blech, Pleiku, Pleime, Plei Vi Drin. Just moving through those towns or being based somewhere above them spaced you out, and every time I'd have that vision of myself lying dead somewhere, it was always up there, in the Highlands. It was enough to make an American commander sink to his knees and plead, "O God! Just *once*, let it be our way. We have the strength, give us the terms!" Not even the Cav, with their style and courage and mobility, were able to penetrate that abiding Highland face. They killed a lot of Communists, but that was all they did, because the number of Communist dead meant nothing, changed nothing.

Sean Flynn, photographer and connoisseur of the Vietnam War, told me that he once stood on the vantage of a firebase up there with a battalion commander. It was at dusk, those ghastly mists were fuming out of the valley floor, ingesting light. The colonel squinted at the distance for a long time. Then he swept his hand very slowly along the line of the jungle, across the hills and ridges running into Cambodia (the Sanctuary!). "Flynn," he said. "Somewhere out there . . . is the *entire First NVA Division*."

O dear God, just once!

"Tell My Folks . . ."

There was a spec 4[5] in the Special Forces at Can Tho, a shy Indian boy from Chinle, Arizona, with large wet eyes the color of ripe olives and a quiet way of speaking, a really nice way of putting things, kind to everyone without ever being stupid or soft about it. On the night that the compound and the airstrip were hit, he came and asked me if there was a chaplain anywhere around. He wasn't very religious, he said, but he was worried about tonight. He'd just volunteered for a "suicide squad," two jeeps that were going to drive across the airstrip with mortars and a recoilless rifle. It looked bad, I had to admit it; there were so few of us in the compound that they'd had to put me on the reaction force. It might be bad. He just had a feeling about it, he'd seen what always happened to guys whenever they got that feeling, at least he *thought* it was that feeling, a bad one, the worst he'd ever had.

I told him that the only chaplains I could think of would be in the town, and we both knew that the town was cut off.

"Oh," he said "Look, then. If I get it tonight . . ."

"It'll be okay."

"Listen, though. If it happens . . . I think it's going to . . . will you make sure the colonel tells my folks I was looking for a chaplain anyway?"

I promised, and the jeeps loaded and drove off. I heard later that there had been a brief firefight, but that no one had been hurt. They didn't have to use the recoilless. They all drove back into the compound two hours later. The next morning at breakfast he sat at another table, saying a lot of loud, brutal things about the gooks,[6] and he wouldn't look at me. But at noon he came over and squeezed my arm and smiled, his eyes fixed somewhere just to the right of my own.

The Wounded

For two days now, ever since the Tet Offensive[7] had begun, they had been coming by the hundreds to the province hospital at Can Tho. They were usually either very young or very old or women, and their wounds were often horrible. The more lightly wounded were being treated quickly in the hospital yard, and the more serious cases were simply placed in one of the corridors to die. There were just too many of them to treat, the doctors had worked without a break, and now, on the second afternoon, the Viet Cong began shelling the hospital.

5. **spec 4:** the rank of specialist, fourth class, in the Special Forces, or Green Berets.

6. **gooks:** pejorative American slang for the enemy.

7. **Tet Offensive:** the major North Vietnamese offensive that began with Tet, the lunar new year holiday, in January, 1968.

A. Responding
? To what extent, do you think, Herr means that all of Vietnam—not just the Highlands—was a place where Americans "didn't belong"? (Answers will vary. The forbidding description of the Highlands is no doubt intended in part at least to apply to the whole country.)

B. Responding
? Explain "O dear God, just once!" (The reference is to the words of the American commander, quoted in the long paragraph at the top of this column, who wishes that for once the war could be fought in the manner to which American soldiers were accustomed.)

C. Characterization
? Explain the young man's behavior at breakfast the morning after his dangerous mission. (He says brutal things to appear tough; he is unable to look Herr in the eye because he is ashamed of being afraid on the night before.)

CLOSURE

Ask students to compare the impressions they have formed from this selection with those received from the *M*A*S*H* or *China Beach* series and other television programs or movies about war that they may have seen. Have them say which accounts seemed more real and moving and explain why.

READING CHECK TEST

1 Most Vietnamese and Montagnards consider each other inferior. *True*

2. The Green Beret in "Tell My Folks" refuses to speak to Herr. *False*

3. The Army surgeon in "The Wounded" can't hold his beer can because his hands are slippery with oil from repairing the machinery. *False*

4. Herr writes, "They were always telling you that you mustn't forget the dead." *True*

5. Herr watches helicopters drop into the sea as their Vietnamese pilots jump clear. *True*

A. Connections

? How is this hospital scene like those you have seen on television, and how is it different? (The overworked doctor and the informality of the correspondent bringing in beer are similar; the ugly details of the amputation and the surgeon's hands slippery from blood would have been toned down, only briefly shown, or merely implied.)

B. Irony

? Why are these sentence fragments run together? (All of the sentence parts are conventional sentiments that the old correspondent is used to stringing together.)

C. Irony

The ex-medic gives the blind man's message an ironic twist by making *darker* mean "more gloomy or hopeless" instead of "more without light."

A

One of the Vietnamese nurses handed me a cold can of beer and asked me to take it down the hall where one of the Army surgeons was operating. The door of the room was ajar, and I walked right in. I probably should have looked first. A little girl was laying on the table, looking with wide dry eyes at the wall. Her left leg was gone, and a sharp piece of bone about six inches long extended from the exposed stump. The leg itself was on the floor, half wrapped in a piece of paper. The doctor was a major, and he'd been working alone. He could not have looked worse if he'd lain all night in a trough of blood. His hands were so slippery that I had to hold the can to his mouth for him and tip it up as his head went back. I couldn't look at the girl.

"Is it all right?" he said quietly.

"It's okay now. I expect I'll be sick as hell later on."

He placed his hand on the girl's forehead and said, "Hello, little darling." He thanked me for bringing the beer. He probably thought that he was smiling, but nothing changed anywhere in his face. He'd been working this way for nearly twenty hours.

The Correspondents

B

There's a candle end burning in a corner of the bunker, held to the top of a steel helmet by melted wax, the light guttering over a battered typewriter, and the Old Guy is getting one off: "Tat-tat-tat, tatta-tatta-tat like your kid or your brother or your sweetheart maybe never wanted much for himself never asked for anything except for what he knew to be his some men have a name for it and they call it Courage when the great guns are still at last across Europe what will it matter maybe after all that this one boy from Cleveland Ohio won't be coming back-a-tat-tat." You can hear shellfire landing just outside, a little gravel falls into the typewriter, but the candle burns on, throwing its faint light over the bowed head and the few remaining wisps of white hair. Two men, the Colonel and the Kid, stand by the door watching. "Why, Sir?" the Kid asks. "What makes him do it? He could be sitting safe in London right now." "I don't know, son," the Colonel says. "Maybe he figures he's got a job to do, too. Maybe it's because he's somebody who really cares. . . ."

Back Home

During my first month back I woke up one night and knew that my living room was full of dead Marines. It actually happened three or four times, after a dream I was having those nights (the kind of dream one never had in Vietnam), and that first time it wasn't just some holding dread left by the dream, I knew they were there, so that after I'd turned on the light by my bed and smoked a cigarette I lay there for a moment thinking that I'd have to go out soon and cover them. I don't want to make anything out of this and I certainly don't want sympathy; going to that place was my idea to begin with, I could have left anytime, and as those things go, I paid little enough, almost nothing. Some guys come back and see their nightmares break in the streets in daylight, some become inhabited and stay that way, all kinds of things can trail after you, and besides, after a while my thing went away almost completely, the dream, too. I know a guy who had been a combat medic in the Central Highlands, and two years later he was still sleeping with all the lights on. We were walking across 57th Street one afternoon and passed a blind man carrying a sign that read, MY DAYS ARE DARKER THAN YOUR NIGHTS. "Don't bet on it, man," the ex-medic said. C

Remembering the Dead

. . . You'd see people walking around whom you'd watched die in aid stations and helicopters. The boy with the huge Adam's apple and the wire-rimmed glasses sitting by himself at a table on the Continental terrace[8] had seemed much more nonchalant as a dead Marine two weeks before at the Rockpile than he did now, wearing the red 1st Division patch, trying to order a Coke from the waiter while a couple of margouilla lizards chased each other up and down the white column behind his head. I thought for a second that I was going to faint when I saw him. After a fast second look I knew that he wasn't a ghost or even a double, there actually wasn't much resemblance at all, but by then my breath was gummed up in my throat and my face was cold and white, shake shake shake. "Nothing to worry about boy," Page said.

8. **the Continental terrace:** the terrace of a hotel in Saigon, then the capital of South Vietnam.

Analyzing The Reports

Identifying Facts

1. Among the details that students may mention are the following: the gnarled valleys and jungled ravines, the description of the mysterious Montagnards, the sudden mists, the extremes of heat by day and cold at night, and the smell of the jungle.

2. The ex-medic rejects the notion that his own nights are "dark"; in fact, nightmares about the war disturb his sleep and he never turns the lights off when he goes to bed.

3. Herr cannot shake the memories of those who have been killed, even though he knows that it is a mistake to become too morbid.

Interpreting Meanings

4. Student answers will vary. Ask the students to cite specific images from the extract.

5. He doesn't solve the puzzle because he wants to leave hanging the implication that there was something deceptive about "official" tallies of war casualties.

6. The effect is both poignant and ironic. The soldier was probably ashamed of the premonitions he had about his own death.

7. Student answers will vary. Have students consider whether Herr seems to imply that the Old Guy is there to generate sympathy for the soldiers, to support the war effort, to follow his own mercenary ends—or a combination of these motives.

8. Student interpretations of the passage will vary. In general, Herr seems to be saying that the Americans in Vietnam had the deck stacked against them; they were completely out of their element, in a mysterious land where no conventional rules of warfare were relevant to their situation.

"Just your nineteenth nervous breakdown."

They were always telling you that you mustn't forget the dead, and they were always telling you that you shouldn't let yourself think about them too much. You couldn't remain effective as a soldier or a reporter if you got all hung up on the dead, fell into patterns of morbid sensitivity, entered perpetual mourning. "You'll get used to it," people would say, but I never did, actually it got personal and went the other way.

The War Ends

The war ended, and then it really ended, the cities "fell," I watched the choppers I'd loved dropping into the South China Sea as their Vietnamese pilots jumped clear, and one last chopper revved it up, lifted off, and flew out of my chest.

I saw a picture of a North Vietnamese soldier sitting in the same spot on the Danang River where the press center had been, where we'd sat smoking and joking and going, "Too much!" and "Far out!" and "Oh my God it gets so freaky out there!" He looked so unbelievably peaceful, I knew that somewhere that night and every night there'd be people sitting together over there talking about the bad old days of jubilee and that one of them would remember and say, Yes, never mind, there were some nice ones, too. And no moves left for me at all but to write down some few last words and make the dispersion, Vietnam Vietnam Vietnam, we've all been there.

Responding to the Reports

Analyzing the Reports

Identifying Facts

1. Herr says that the Vietnam Highlands are "spooky," and that the "Puritan belief that Satan dwelt in Nature could have been born here." What details support his characterization?
2. Why does the ex-medic say "Don't bet on it, man," to the blind man's sign on 57th Street?
3. How does Herr remember the dead?

Interpreting Meanings

4. What visual **images** from these excerpts make you feel the horror of war most acutely?
5. Herr tells us that in the Battle of Dak To, the American command announced that they had killed four thousand. "But when the top of the hill was reached, the number of NVA found was four." What does Herr imply here? Why doesn't he solve the puzzle for us?
6. What is the effect of the anecdote about the soldier who is sure he will be killed on a suicide mission? Why do you think the soldier wouldn't look at Herr after he came back from the mission unharmed?
7. Does Herr's picture of "The Correspondent" conform to the stereotyped picture most people have of war correspondents? How does Herr want you to feel about this correspondent?
8. Herr writes, "You were there in a place where you didn't belong, where things were glimpsed for which you would have to pay and where things went unglimpsed for which you would also have to pay, a place where they didn't play with the mystery but killed you straight off for trespassing." What do you think this passage means?

Writing About the Reports

A Creative Response

1. **Assessing the Impact of an Essay.** Write a short essay describing why Herr's piece affected—or did *not* affect—your feelings and attitudes about war.

A Critical Response

2. **Comparing and Contrasting Two Writers.** Compare and contrast John Hersey's report (page 1048) with Michael Herr's. Consider the following points:
   a. Method of reporting
   b. Objectivity vs. subjectivity
   c. Attitude toward war
   d. Use of imagery for shock value
3. **Analyzing a Writer's Personality.** Despite writing in the first person, Herr does not tell us much directly about himself. Write a short essay telling what you think you know about him.
4. **Analyzing Women's Roles.** What part do women play in Hersey's and Herr's reports? Write a short essay about the role of women in war.

Supplementary Support Materials
1. Vocabulary Activity Worksheet (*CCB*)
2. Review and Response Worksheet: Satire and Irony (*CCB*)
3. Language Skills Worksheet: The Descriptive Paragraph (*CCB*)
4. Selection Test (*CCB*)

Developing Vocabulary
The following words from the essay are tested in the Selection Test. (See also Vocabulary Activity Worksheet.)

to disembark	exploitation
dilapidated	domination
latrine	notorious
ingenuity	boutique

A. Responding
After students have read the essay, have them apply these historical facts and Kincaid's comments to the essay.

? What does it mean to wear sackcloth and ashes? (In Biblical times, penitents wore coarse, rough garments, usually made of goats' hair, and sprinkled ashes on their heads. Now the term is used metaphorically to represent mourning or penitence.) Do you agree that the British should atone for past injustices? Should tourists? How do you think this essay will affect your perception of places you visit?

Jamaica Kincaid (1949–)

Jamaica Kincaid was born Elaine Potter Richardson on the West Indian island of Antigua. The social conditions on this tiny island (only twelve miles long by nine miles wide) were a strong formative influence on her. During Kincaid's childhood and youth, Antigua was a British dependency (it is now an independent nation and a member of the British Commonwealth), and to a young black girl growing up there, the contrasts between British and native, rich and poor, masters and servants, were uncomfortably strong. The white British community, for the most part, lived isolated and privileged lives of leisure, while the black islanders, who had originally been brought there as slaves, worked in trades, or as fishermen, farmers, or servants. Most of Kincaid's friends, family, and teachers accepted these contrasts as the order of things, and admired the British and tried to emulate them. "In my generation," she has said, "the height of being a civilized person was to be English and to love English things." Her own response, though, was to come to despise the English and the colonial system that created such injustices. "The English . . . don't seem to know that this empire business was all wrong," she writes in *A Small Place,* "and they should, at least, be wearing sackcloth and ashes in token penance of the wrongs committed. . . ." [A]

In her formal education at government schools, she was seen as a troublemaker, sullen and quick to talk back. "I was always being accused of being rude," she said, "because I gave some back chat. I moved very slowly. I was never where I should be. I wasn't really angry yet. I was just incredibly unhappy."

A major source of that unhappiness, in addition to the social conditions on the island, was her own strained relationship with her mother, who gradually withdrew her affection from the little girl, at first in tending to her younger brothers, and then in apparent disappointment at her daughter's increasingly troubled behavior. "I was a good child, and then eventually I couldn't be a good child anymore. But I didn't know how to tell her that I was another kind of child, so I would just lie. And it became clear to her that I was a liar." Ironically, Kincaid's sharp tongue and her elaborate lying would become the strengths of her work as a writer—her verbal facility and her rich imagination. The social injustice of the island and the personal injustice of her mother's treatment of her became central themes in her later work.

When she was seventeen, Kincaid came to the United States to work as an *au pair* and to continue her education. She was not to return to Antigua—or to communicate with her mother—for nineteen years. She studied first at Westchester Community College in New York, and later, after working for several years, at Franconia College in New Hampshire. In the early 1970's, she began writing magazine articles, and it was then that she changed her name to Jamaica Kincaid. The change of name was a form of liberation for her (as it has been for many other writers). It was "a way for me to do things without being the same person who couldn't do them—the same person who had all these weights." She contributed some items to the *New Yorker* and soon became one of their staff writers. In 1978, her first piece of fiction, "Girl," was published in the *New Yorker*. Since

PREPARATION

1. BUILDING ON PRIOR KNOWLEDGE. Ask students what images come to mind when they think of a Caribbean island. Are any of these images promoted by television commercials or magazine ads aimed at tourists? Now ask students what they imagine everyday life is like for residents of these islands. If there are students in your class from the Caribbean, invite volunteers to comment. You might have them locate Antigua on a map to see why the essay is about "a *small* place."

2. ESTABLISHING A PURPOSE. After students have read the headnote, suggest that they read to discover why the writer is angry.

then, she has published a collection of stories, *At the Bottom of the River* (1983); a novel, *Annie John* (1985); and a nonfiction book about Antigua, *A Small Place* (1988). She lives in Vermont with her husband and two children.

Kincaid's stories are characterized by a deceptively simple, but highly poetic style, which often relies on incantation and incremental repetition for its effects, as in this passage from "Girl": "Wash the white clothes on Monday and put them on the stone heap; wash the color clothes on Tuesday and put them on the clothesline to dry." Narrative is less important than effect, and in some stories the plot is hardly evident at all. Mothers and daughters are frequently subjects of her stories, and aspects of everyday life often take on a dreamlike, magical quality. The effect of Kincaid's unusual style is to reveal to the reader the mystery, the pain, and the beauty of our lives.

FROM A SMALL PLACE

Suppose you are looking for a tropical island paradise where you can spend your vacation. Browsing through various travel brochures, you choose Antigua, a Caribbean island in the West Indies. What glorious sunshine! What inviting, clear, warm ocean water! What tempting stretches of clean sandy beaches! And while you are basking in the sun or enjoying your meals at a luxurious hotel, you might even learn some of the island's history. It's no secret that Antigua was formerly a British colony, that it still has close ties to England, and that its predominantly black population descended from former slaves brought from Africa. However, you might leave the island in blissful ignorance, knowing no more than these few historical facts.

But what do the black citizens of Antigua think of their island home? What kind of government services do they get from the schools and hospitals? Who is growing rich at others' expense? Where does the corruption lie hidden? And what do the citizens think of the tourists who come and go, fueling the economy?

Jamaica Kincaid, who grew up in Antigua, directly addresses you, the reader and potential island visitor, in her book *A Small Place*, as she takes you on a highly revealing guided tour. You might not like what the author shows you, for her satiric tone forces you to confront not only the ugly side of paradise but also your own failings and blind spots.

If you go to Antigua as a tourist, this is what you will see. If you come by airplane, you will land at the V. C. Bird International Airport. Vere Cornwall (V. C.) Bird is the Prime Minister of Antigua. You may be the sort of tourist who would wonder why a Prime Minister would want an airport named after him—why not a school, why not a hospital, why not some great public monument? You are a tourist and you have not yet seen a school in Antigua, you have not yet seen the hospital in Antigua, you have not yet seen a public monument in Antigua. As your plane descends to land, you might say, What a beautiful island Antigua is—more beautiful than any of the other islands you have seen, and they were very beautiful, in their way, but they were much too green, much too lush with vegetation, which indicated to you, the tourist, that they got quite a bit of rainfall, and rain is the very thing that you, just now, do not want, for you are thinking of the hard and cold and dark and long days you spent working in North America (or, worse, Europe), earning some money so that you could stay in this place (Antigua) where the sun always shines and where the climate is deliciously hot and dry for the four to ten days you are going to be staying

A. Responding

? Do tourists generally see any of these things? (No.) Kincaid is implying that they should; at this point, do you agree with her?

A. Irony
? What is ironic about the way Kincaid ends this paragraph? (Since she is telling readers what must never cross their minds, she must, in fact, want them to think about it.)

B. Theme
? What is Kincaid contrasting in this passage? (She contrasts the carefree tourists laden with luggage to Antiguans returning with food and clothes for their relatives.) What is the implication of this contrast? (That islanders cannot afford these necessities at home)

C. Irony
? Why would tourists find bad roads marvelous? (Tourists would see them as quaint and exotic.)

D. Responding
? This is the only time Kincaid says directly that tourists are wrong not to think about something. Why does she break her pattern here? (Other evils she discusses do not affect tourists directly, but poor hospitals definitely could.)

A there; and since you are on your holiday, since you are a tourist, the thought of what it might be like for someone who had to live day in, day out in a place that suffers constantly from drought, and so has to watch carefully every drop of fresh water used (while at the same time surrounded by a sea and an ocean—the Caribbean Sea on one side, the Atlantic Ocean on the other), must never cross your mind.

B You disembark from your plane. You go through customs. Since you are a tourist, a North American or European—to be frank, white—and not an Antiguan black returning to Antigua from Europe or North America with cardboard boxes of much needed cheap clothes and food for relatives, you move through customs swiftly, you move through customs with ease. Your bags are not searched. You emerge from customs into the hot, clean air: immediately you feel cleansed, immediately you feel blessed (which is to say special); you feel free. You see a man, a taxi driver; you ask him to take you to your destination; he quotes you a price. You immediately think that the price is in the local currency, for you are a tourist and you are familiar with these things (rates of exchange) and you feel even more free, for things seem so cheap, but then your driver ends by saying, "In U.S. currency." You may say, "Hmmmm, do you have a formal sheet that lists official prices and destinations?" Your driver obeys the law and shows you the sheet, and he apologizes for the incredible mistake he has made in quoting you a price off the top of his head which is so vastly different (favoring him) from the one listed. You are driven to your hotel by this taxi driver in his taxi, a brand-new Japanese-made vehicle. C The road on which you are traveling is a very bad road, very much in need of repair. You are feeling wonderful, so you say, "Oh, what a marvelous change these bad roads are from the splendid highways I am used to in North America." (Or, worse, Europe.) Your driver is reckless; he is a dangerous man who drives in the middle of the road when he thinks no other cars are coming in the opposite direction, passes other cars on blind curves that run uphill, drives at sixty miles an hour on narrow, curving roads when the road sign, a rusting, beat-up thing left over from colonial days, says 40 MPH. This might frighten you (you are on your holiday; you are a tourist); this might excite you (you are on your holiday; you are a tourist), though if you are from New York and take taxis you are used to this style of driving: most of the taxi drivers in New York are from places in the world like this. You are looking out the window (because you want to get your money's worth); you notice that all the cars you see are brand-new, or almost brand-new, and that they are all Japanese-made. There are no American cars in Antigua—no new ones, at any rate; none that were manufactured in the last ten years. You continue to look at the cars and you say to yourself, Why, they look brand-new, but they have an awful sound, like an old car—a very old, dilapidated car. How to account for that? Well, possibly it's because they use leaded gasoline in these brand-new cars whose engines were built to use nonleaded gasoline, but you mustn't ask the person driving the car if this is so, because he or she has never heard of unleaded gasoline. You look closely at the car; you see that it's a model of a Japanese car that you might hesitate to buy; it's a model that's very expensive; it's a model that's quite impractical for a person who has to work as hard as you do and who watches every penny you earn so that you can afford this holiday you are on. How do they afford such a car? And do they live in a luxurious house to match such a car? Well, no. You will be surprised, then, to see that most likely the person driving this brand-new car filled with the wrong gas lives in a house that, in comparison, is far beneath the status of the car; and if you were to ask why you would be told that the banks are encouraged by the government to make loans available for cars, but loans for houses not so easily available; and if you ask again why, you will be told that the two main car dealerships in Antigua are owned in part or outright by ministers in government. Oh, but you are on holiday and the sight of these brand-new cars driven by people who may or may not have really passed their driving test (there was once a scandal about driving licenses for sale) would not really stir up these thoughts in you. You pass a building sitting in a sea of dust and you think, It's some latrines for people just passing by, but when you look again you see the building has written on it PIGOTT'S SCHOOL. D You pass the hospital, the Holberton Hospital, and how wrong you are not to think about this, for though you are a tourist on your holiday, what if your heart should miss a few beats? What if a blood vessel in your neck should break? What if one of these people driving those brand-new cars filled with the wrong gas fails to

pass safely while going uphill on a curve and you are in the car going in the opposite direction? Will you be comforted to know that the hospital is staffed with doctors that no actual Antiguan trusts; that Antiguans always say about the doctors, "I don't want them near me"; that Antiguans refer to them not as doctors but as "the three men" (there are three of them); that when the Minister of Health himself doesn't feel well he takes the first plane to New York to see a real doctor; that if any one of the ministers in government needs medical care he flies to New York to get it?

It's a good thing that you brought your own books with you, for you couldn't just go to the library and borrow some. Antigua used to have a splendid library, but in The Earthquake (everyone talks about it that way—The Earthquake; we Antiguans, for I am one, have a great sense of things, and the more meaningful the thing, the more meaningless we make it) the library building was damaged. This was in 1974, and soon after that a sign was placed on the front of the building saying, THIS BUILDING WAS DAMAGED IN THE EARTHQUAKE OF 1974. REPAIRS ARE PENDING. The sign hangs there, and hangs there more than a decade later, with its unfulfilled promise of repair, and you might see this as a sort of quaintness on the part of these islanders, these people descended from slaves—what a strange, unusual perception of time they have. REPAIRS ARE PENDING, and here it is many years later, but perhaps in a world that is twelve miles long and nine miles wide (the size of Antigua) twelve years and twelve minutes and twelve days are all the same. The library is one of those splendid old buildings from colonial times, and the sign telling of the repairs is a splendid old sign from colonial times. Not very long after The Earthquake Antigua got its independence from Britain, making Antigua a state in its own right, and Antiguans are so proud of this that each year, to mark the day, they go to church and thank God, a British God, for this. But you should not think of the confusion that must lie in all that and you must not think of the damaged library. You have brought your own books with you, and among them is one of those new books about economic history, one of those books explaining

A. Interpretation

? What does Kincaid mean by the comment in parentheses? (Students might suggest that The Earthquake caused significant damage, but by referring to it in an offhand way, Antiguans play down its importance.)

CLOSURE
Have students briefly state Kincaid's main point and their own response to the point and to the way she makes it.

READING CHECK TEST

1. Antigua is a lush tropical island. *True*
2. According to Kincaid, Antiguans place great faith in their medical facilities. *False*
3. The island's library was closed by the British when they withdrew from Antigua. *False*
4. Many Antiguans drive expensive cars but live in rundown houses. *True*
5. Kincaid says the government of Antigua is known for being ethical and efficient. *False*

A. Interpretation
What do wristwatches have to do with Kincaid's point here? (Kincaid refers to European and American obsession with time, compared to the more relaxed attitude of people in warmer climates. She is continuing her argument that the colonial powers credit their success to their own efficiency, not to native labor.)

B. Irony
Is Kincaid sincere when she says readers needn't let these things bother them? (No. She wants readers to think seriously and feel guilty.)

C. Interpretation
Why do Antiguans hate this merchant family? (Kincaid sees the merchant family as people who used their success to continue the exploitation of Antiguans.)

D. Expansion
Evita's name may be a sly reference to Eva Perón (?1919–1952), the controversial mistress and wife of Juan Perón, dictator of Argentina.

how the West (meaning Europe and North America after its conquest and settlement by Europeans) got rich: the West got rich not from the free (free—in this case meaning got-for-nothing) and then undervalued labor, for generations, of the people like me you see walking around you in Antigua but from the ingenuity of small shopkeepers in Sheffield and Yorkshire and Lancashire, or wherever; and what a great part the invention of the wristwatch played in it, for there was nothing noble-minded men could not do when they discovered they could slap time on their wrists just like that (isn't that the last straw; for not only did we have to suffer the unspeakableness of slavery, but the satisfaction to be had from "We made you bastards rich" is taken away, too), and so you needn't let that slightly funny feeling you have from time to time about exploitation, oppression, domination develop into full-fledged unease, discomfort; you could ruin your holiday. They are not responsible for what you have; you owe them nothing; in fact, you did them a big favor, and you can provide one hundred examples. For here you are now, passing by Government House. And here you are now, passing by the Prime Minister's Office and the Parliament Building, and overlooking these, with a splendid view of St. John's Harbor, the American Embassy. If it were not for you, they would not have Government House, and Prime Minister's Office, and Parliament Building and embassy of powerful country. Now you are passing a mansion, an extraordinary house painted the color of old cow dung, with more aerials and antennas attached to it than you will see even at the American Embassy. The people who live in this house are a merchant family who came to Antigua from the Middle East less than twenty years ago. When this family first came to Antigua, they sold dry goods door to door from suitcases they carried on their backs. Now they own a lot of Antigua; they regularly lend money to the government, they build enormous (for Antigua), ugly (for Antigua), concrete buildings in Antigua's capital, St. John's, which the government then rents for huge sums of money; a member of their family is the Antiguan Ambassador to Syria; Antiguans hate them. Not far from this mansion is another mansion, the home of a drug smuggler. Everybody knows he's a drug smuggler, and if just as you were driving by he stepped out of his door your driver might point him out to you as the notorious person that he is, for this drug smuggler is so rich people say he buys cars in tens—ten of this one, ten of that one—and that he bought a house (another mansion) near Five Islands, contents included, with cash he carried in a suitcase: three hundred and fifty thousand American dollars, and, to the surprise of the seller of the house, lots of American dollars were left over. Overlooking the drug smuggler's mansion is yet another mansion, and leading up to it is the best paved road in all of Antigua—even better than the road that was paved for the Queen's visit in 1985 (when the Queen came, all the roads that she would travel on were paved anew, so that the Queen might have been left with the impression that riding in a car in Antigua was a pleasant experience). In this mansion lives a woman sophisticated people in Antigua call Evita. She is a notorious woman. She's young and beautiful and the girlfriend of somebody very high up in the government. Evita is notorious because her relationship with this high government official has made her the owner of boutiques and property and given her a say in cabinet meetings, and all sorts of other privileges such a relationship would bring a beautiful young woman.

Oh, but by now you are tired of all this looking, and you want to reach your destination—your hotel, your room. You long to refresh yourself; you long to eat some nice lobster, some nice local food. You take a bath, you brush your teeth. You get dressed again; as you get dressed, you look out the window. That water—have you ever seen anything like it? Far out, to the horizon, the color of the water is navy blue; nearer, the water is the color of the North American sky. From there to the shore, the water is pale, silvery, clear, so clear that you can see its pinkish-white sand bottom. Oh, what beauty! Oh, what beauty! You have never seen anything like this. You are so excited. You breathe shallow. You breathe deep. You see a beautiful boy skimming the water, godlike, on a Windsurfer. You see an incredibly unattractive, fat, pastrylike-fleshed woman enjoying a walk on the beautiful sand, with a man, an incredibly unattractive, fat, pastrylike-fleshed man; you see the pleasure they're taking in their surroundings. Still standing, looking out the window, you see yourself lying on the beach, enjoying the amazing sun (a sun so powerful and yet so beautiful, the way it is always overhead as if on permanent guard, ready to stamp out any cloud that dares to darken and so empty rain on you and ruin your holiday;

ANALYZING THE ESSAY

Identifying Facts

1. The cab driver quotes a higher fee than that specified on an official rate sheet but claims he was just talking off the top of his head.

2. In 1974 the library was badly damaged in an earthquake, but it still has not been repaired.

3. The mansions are inhabited by people who have exploited the Antiguans: a Middle Eastern merchant, a drug smuggler, and a government official's mistress.

Interpreting Meanings

4. Government officials, who own the two biggest car dealerships, encourage banks to make car loans.

Presumably, both dealerships handle only Japanese cars.

5. The implied answer is that the official will benefit financially from the tourist trade.

Kincaid suggests that the government is corrupt, its officials more interested in lining their own pockets than in serving the people of Antigua.

6. Kincaid paints tourists as ignorant, insensitive, and exploitative.

She particularly despises the British, who enslaved the Antiguans and demeaned their work.

7. She is being ironic. She really means that tourists must be aware of historical truths and current reality.

8. Answers will vary. No reader could fail to have some response to the essay, whether positive or negative.

9. Students should cite Kincaid's specific criticisms of each of these problems, which suggest the reform she seeks.

10. The repetition of the phrase drives home Kincaid's point—that tourists care only about their own pleasure, not about the reality of life on the island. Kincaid is telling tourists to open their eyes and see the truth.

a sun that is your personal friend). You see yourself taking a walk on that beach, you see yourself meeting new people (only they are new in a very limited way, for they are people just like you). You see yourself eating some delicious, locally grown food. You see yourself, you see yourself . . . You must not wonder what exactly happened to the contents of your lavatory when you flushed it. You must not wonder where your bath-water went when you pulled out the stopper. You must not wonder what happened when you brushed your teeth. Oh, it might all end up in the water you are thinking of taking a swim in; the contents of your lavatory might, just might, graze gently against your ankle as you wade carefree in the water, for you see, in Antigua, there is no proper sewage-disposal system. But the Caribbean Sea is very big and the Atlantic Ocean is even bigger; it would amaze even you to know the number of black slaves this ocean has swallowed up. When you sit down to eat your delicious meal, it's better that you don't know that most of what you are eating came off a plane from Miami. And before it got on a plane in Miami, who knows where it came from? A good guess is that it came from a place like Antigua first, where it was grown dirt-cheap, went to Miami, and came back. There is a world of something in this, but I can't go into it right now.

Responding to the Essay

Analyzing the Essay

Identifying Facts

1. All over the world, tourists are regarded as likely targets for rogues and con artists. What happens to the tourist who takes a taxi from Antigua's airport? How does the taxi driver explain the discrepancy?
2. The library in Antigua is an important detail in Kincaid's book. What happened to the library in 1974? What has happened to it since?
3. According to Kincaid, what sort of people live in all the mansions in Antigua?

Interpreting Meanings

4. Explain the significance of the fact that nearly all the cars in Antigua are new or nearly new. What is significant in the fact that nearly all the cars are Japanese?
5. At the beginning of the essay, Kincaid raises the question of why the Prime Minister wanted an airport rather than a school or hospital named for him. What is the implied answer to the question? What is Kincaid suggesting about the government's priorities?
6. **Tone** refers to the writer's attitude toward his or her subject, or audience. Kincaid never states flatly that she dislikes tourists, but her tone suggests that she does. What specific evidence of dislike and mockery do you find in the essay? How does she regard the British, Antigua's former rulers?
7. Kincaid uses **irony,** one of the devices of **satire.** Is Kincaid being ironic when she says "You must not wonder" about this or that, or when she says "It's better that you don't know" certain things? What does she really mean?
8. In the eighteenth century in England, Jonathan Swift wrote a bitterly satiric essay called "A Modest Proposal," in which the essay's fictional narrator suggested that poor Irish families raise their babies as food for the English to solve Ireland's economic problems. Many readers were outraged by the essay. How did you respond to Kincaid's satiric guide for tourists in Antigua?
9. The purpose of **satire** is to bring about reform. What does Kincaid want to see reformed in Antigua? (Consider such topics as schools, hospitals, roads, water, and sewage disposal.)
10. On page 1069 Kincaid repeats the phrase "You see yourself." Explain how these words express the **theme** of Kincaid's essay.

Writing About the Essay

A Creative Response

Taking Your Readers on a Tour. Write a paragraph in which you address the readers as "you" and take them on a tour of a place you know well. Before you start to write, decide what **tone** you will take toward your reader and the place you are describing. (Will you be satiric? Admiring? Nostalgic? Horrified?)

A. Responding

? Under what letter would you look in your library card catalog to find a book by this author? (Most libraries probably list the writer under *L,* for Least Heat Moon. Since he also uses his English ancestor's name, William Trogdon, his author card may also be found under *T.* The title card for *Blue Highways* appears under B, as one would expect.)

SUPPLEMENTARY SUPPORT MATERIALS

1. Vocabulary Activity Worksheet (*CCB*)
2. Review and Response Worksheet: Imagery (*CCB*)
3. Language Skills Worksheet: Nouns (*CCB*)
4. Selection Test (*CCB*)

DEVELOPING VOCABULARY

The following words from the journal are tested in the Selection Test. (See also Vocabulary Activity Worksheet.)

saturated	effete
infallible	junction
legend	blight
chiropractor	bolster
hue	gallivanting

B. Expansion

The ghost dance was a central ritual of the religion of the Plains Indians. The ritual lasted five nights, and on the last, the dancing continued until dawn. The ghost dance was a kind of prayer for the fulfillment of the religion's central prophecy—that the westward expansion of the white men would stop and the land would be returned to the Indians. The Sioux Indians danced the ghost dance just before the massacre of hundreds of Sioux at Wounded Knee, South Dakota, in 1890.

William Least Heat Moon (1939–   )

The United States is such a huge, sprawling country, with so many diverse people and traditions, that novelists have had a hard time capturing its entirety. Many novelists have struggled to find a story or a history that will somehow explain everything, and that they hope they might turn into "The Great American Novel." That definitive work has never been written. Instead, some of the best insights into Americans and their ways of life have appeared in nonfiction accounts written by travelers.

As early as 1835, Alexis de Tocqueville, a visiting Frenchman, wrote *Democracy in America,* still treasured as a profound philosophical commentary on the American character. Not only did travelers report back to Europe, but Americans soon began to write to one another. Trying to picture or explain different parts of the country, writers turned journals into such nineteenth-century classics as Mark Twain's *Roughing It* (1872) and *Life on the Mississippi* (1883), Henry James's *The American Scene* (1907), Henry David Thoreau's *The Maine Woods* (1864), and Clarence King's *Mountaineering in the Sierra Nevada* (1872). Modern writers have explored America in books like Jack Kerouac's *On the Road* (1957), John Steinbeck's *Travels with Charley* (1962), and Robert Pirsig's *Zen and the Art of Motorcycle Maintenance* (1974).

So, William Least Heat Moon's *Blue Highways: A Journey into America* (1982) follows a strong literary tradition of Americans who have had the urge to "pick up and go" and who have then written about their travels.

William Least Heat Moon is descended mainly from the Sioux people in Missouri. His Christian name, he explains, comes from an immigrant Lancashire ancestor eight generations back, whereas his last name comes from his Sioux father. "My father calls himself Heat Moon"—(the name for the seventh month in the Sioux calendar)—"my elder brother Little Heat Moon. I, coming last, am therefore Least. It has been a long lesson of a name to learn." [A] When Moon was thirty-eight, his marriage and his teaching job both ended, and he left his Missouri home in a converted Ford van, on the theory that "a man who couldn't make things go right could at least go."

The van was both transport and home, a 1975 half-ton Econoline ("your basic plumber's model"), which Least Heat Moon had converted into a six-by-ten bedroom, kitchen, bathroom, and parlor. "It came," he says, "equipped with power nothing and drove like what it was: a truck." He christened the van Ghost Dancing, [B] which is the name the Plains Indians gave to ceremonies in which they prayed for the return of their old life. And in a sense, Least Heat Moon's trip was such a ceremony. "I took to the open road in search of places where change did not mean ruin and where time and men and deeds connected."

Blue Highways, an edited journal of his travels, shows that he found what he sought. He was determined to stick to the back roads of America, the ones printed in blue on old highways maps, as opposed to the main routes, which were printed in red. In spite of temptations, he avoided the interstates. "Life doesn't happen along interstates. It's against the law." On roads sometimes "so crooked they could run for the legislature," his voyage took him east from Missouri to North Carolina, south to Loui-

PREPARATION

1. ESTABLISHING A PURPOSE. Ask students to imagine what kind of encounters they might have if they set out on a journey along backroads without a special destination or purpose. Suggest that this selection will give them an idea of what might happen.

2. PREREADING JOURNAL. Have students jot down a few comical place names they have encountered, and ask them to nominate the one they would be most curious to visit. Encourage students to share their place names.

siana, then west across Texas to New Mexico, north through Utah and California to Washington state, back across the northernmost boundary of the United States all the way to Maine, south again to New Jersey, and finally west back to Missouri. The rough circular trip, he thought, "would give a purpose—to come around again."

Along the "blue highways" Least Heat Moon encountered the astonishing place names of America: Lookingglass and Remote, in Oregon; Tell City, Indiana; Simplicity, Virginia; New Freedom, Pennsylvania; New Hope, Tennessee; Why, Arizona; Whynot, Mississippi; Igo and Ono, California; Stinking Water Branch, Dead Horse Fork, Cutthroat Gulch, Calamity River, and Damnation Creek.

Unlike some contemporary travelers who have everywhere found a sad, petty-minded, and materialistic America, Least Heat Moon usually liked the people he met. He found them as vigorous, imaginative, and astonishing as the names of the places where they lived. His journal is a celebration of these rural people—their struggles, their poverty, their spiritual wealth and dignity. They treated him well, and he admired them. As he quietly notes in the excerpt that follows, "Down along the ridge, I wondered why it's always those who live on little who are the ones to ask you to dinner."

"If you would like to know who and what America is at the center," said N. Scott Momaday (see page 1014), "read this book. This is what we, as a people, are about." It is a heartening thought.

A. Responding

? Why would the number of wall calendars be a measure of a restaurant's quality? (Answers will vary. One possibility: The presence of calendars seems to promise a homey, unsophisticated atmosphere. They wouldn't be found in a slick, fast-food restaurant. Another possibility: The people who work there like to be surrounded by the pretty pictures one finds in calendars. Such people usually take pride in their work and like to make their customers happy.)

FROM BLUE HIGHWAYS

William Least Heat Moon's account of his travels across America is full of compassionate, understated humor. As you read the selection, look for places where the humor establishes a certain atmosphere and tone for the journal.

Had it not been raining hard that morning on the Livingston square, I never would have learned of Nameless, Tennessee. Waiting for the rain to ease, I lay on my bunk and read the atlas to pass time rather than to see where I might go. In Kentucky were towns with fine names like Boreing, Bear Wallow, Decoy, Subtle, Mud Lick, Mummie, Neon; Belcher was just down the road from Mouthcard, and Minnie only ten miles from Mousie.

I looked at Tennessee. Turtletown eight miles from Ducktown. And also: Peavine, Wheel, Milky Way, Love Joy, Dull, Weakly, Fly, Spot, Miser Station, Only, McBurg, Peeled Chestnut, Clouds, Topsy, Isoline. And the best of all, Nameless. The logic! I was heading east, and Nameless lay forty-five miles west. I decided to go anyway.

The rain stopped, but things looked saturated, even bricks. In Gainesboro, a hill town with a square of businesses around the Jackson County Courthouse, I stopped for directions and breakfast. There is one almost infallible way to find honest food at just prices in blue-highway America: Count the wall calendars in a cafe. A

No calendar: Same as an interstate pit stop.

One calendar: Preprocessed food assembled in New Jersey.

Two calendars: Only if fish trophies present.

Three calendars: Can't miss on the farm-boy breakfasts.

Four calendars: Try the ho-made pie too.

Five calendars: Keep it under your hat, or they'll franchise.

One time I found a six-calendar cafe in the Ozarks, which served fried chicken, peach pie, and chocolate malts, that left me searching for another ever since. I've never seen a seven-calendar place. But

A. Humanities Connection: Discussing the Fine Art
This painting, one of five panels of the *Highway Series* by Allan D'Arcangelo, is an example of Pop Art, a movement that began in the 1960's, partly as a reaction against the seriousness of abstract painting. Like many other Pop artists, D'Arcangelo used conventional public images—here the signs for an oil company and a highway—in a simplified composition.

A

U. S. Highway 1 (panel 3) by Allan D'Arcangelo (1963). Acrylic on canvas.

Virginia Museum of Fine Arts, Richmond. Gift of Sydney and Frances Lewis.

old-time travelers—road men in a day when cars had running boards and lunchroom windows said AIR COOLED in blue letters with icicles dripping from the tops—those travelers have told me the golden legends of seven-calendar cafes.

To the rider of back roads, nothing shows the tone, the voice of a small town more quickly than the breakfast grill or the five-thirty tavern. Much of what the people do and believe and share is evident then. The City Cafe in Gainesboro had three calendars that I could see from the walk. Inside were no interstate refugees with full bladders and empty tanks, no wild-eyed children just released from the glassy cell of a station wagon back seat, no long-haul truckers talking in CB numbers.[1] There were only townspeople wearing overalls, or catalog-order suits with five-and-dime ties, or uniforms. That is, here were farmers and mill hands, bank clerks, the dry goods merchant, a policeman, and chiropractor's receptionist. Because it was Saturday, there were also mothers and children.

I ordered my standard on-the-road breakfast: two eggs up, hash browns, tomato juice. The waitress, whose pale, almost translucent skin shifted hue in the gray light like a thin slice of mother of pearl, brought the food. Next to the eggs was a

1. **CB numbers:** Users of citizens' band radios, or CB's, use numbers for simple messages (such as "ten-four" for "message received").

Literature and Language: Using Apostrophes
Apostrophes plague students, who invariably put them in the wrong place, insert them where they're not needed, or leave them out when they are. You can review the two basic uses for apostrophes—in possessives and in contractions—by having students read pages 1219–1221 of **Grammar, Usage, and Mechanics: A Reference Guide.**

Then ask students to find apostrophes in William Least Heat Moon's travel essay and tell what their purpose is. They should find several possessives *(chiropractor's, Wattses', Mother's)* and even more contractions. The apostrophe signals omitted letters in a contraction; it also shows where letter sounds are dropped in words Heat Moon has spelled to show pronunciation. The waitress's conversation, for example, includes words that omit the final *g* sound (*doin', Lookin', goin',* and so on).

Have students review the troublemaker homonyms *(you're, your; it's, its; they're; their)* and the possessive pronouns, which never have apostrophes *(its, yours, ours, his, hers, theirs;* rule 4, page 1220).

biscuit with a little yellow Smiley button stuck in it. She said, "You from the North?"

"I guess I am." A Missourian gets used to Southerners thinking him a Yankee, a Northerner considering him a cracker, a Westerner sneering at his effete Easternness, and the Easterner taking him for a cowhand.

"So whata you doin' in the mountains?"

"Talking to people. Taking some pictures. Looking mostly."

"Lookin' for what?"

"A three-calendar cafe that serves Smiley buttons on the biscuits."

"You needed a smile. Tell me really."

"I don't know. Actually, I'm looking for some jam to put on this biscuit now that you've brought one."

She came back with grape jelly. In a land of quince jelly, apple butter, apricot jam, blueberry preserves, pear conserves, and lemon marmalade, you always get grape jelly.

"Whata you lookin' for?"

Like anyone else, I'm embarrassed to eat in front of a watcher, particularly if I'm getting interviewed. "Why don't you have a cup of coffee?"

"Cain't right now. You gonna tell me?"

"I don't know how to describe it to you. Call it harmony."

She waited for something more. "Is that it?" Someone called her to the kitchen. I had managed almost to finish by the time she came back. She sat on the edge of the booth. "I started out in life not likin' anything, but then it grew on me. Maybe that'll happen to you." She watched me spread the jelly. "Saw your van." She watched me eat the biscuit. "You sleep in there?" I told her I did. "I'd love to do that, but I'd be scared spitless."

"I don't mind being scared spitless. Sometimes."

"I'd love to take off cross country. I like to look at different license plates. But I'd take a dog. You carry a dog?" A

"I don't know if I got directions for where you're goin'," the ambulance driver said. "I *think* there's a Nameless down the Shepardsville Road."

"When I get to Shepardsville, will I have gone too far?"

"Ain't no Shepardsville."

"How will I know when I'm there?"

"Cain't say for certain."

"What's Nameless look like?"

"Don't recollect."

"Is the road paved?"

"It's possible."

Those were the directions. I was looking for an unnumbered road named after a nonexistent town that would take me to a place called Nameless that nobody was sure existed.

Clumps of wild garlic lined the country highway that I hoped was the Shepardsville Road. It scrimmaged with the mountain as it tried to stay on top of the ridges; the hillsides were so steep and thick with oak, I felt as if I were following a trail through the misty treetops. Chickens, doing more work with their necks than legs, ran across the road, and, with a battering of wings, half leapt and half flew into the lower branches of oaks. A vicious pair of mixed-breed German shepherds raced along trying to eat the tires. After miles, I decided I'd missed the town—assuming there truly *was* a Nameless, Tennessee. It wouldn't be the first time I'd qualified for the Ponce de Leon[2] Believe Anything Award.

I stopped beside a big man loading tools in a pickup. "I may be lost."

"Where'd you lose the right road?"

"I don't know. Somewhere around nineteen sixty-five." B

"Highway fifty-six, you mean?"

"I came down fifty-six. I think I should've turned at the last junction."

"Only thing down that road's stumps and huckleberries, and the berries ain't there in March. Where you tryin' to get to?"

"Nameless. If there is such a place."

"You might not know Thurmond Watts, but he's got him a store down the road. That's Nameless at his store. Still there all right, but I might not vouch you that tomorrow." He came up to the van. "In my Army days, I wrote Nameless, Tennessee, for my place of birth on all the papers, even though I lived on this end of the ridge. All these ridges and hollers got names of their own. That's Steam Mill Holler over yonder. Named after the steam engine in the gristmill. Miller had him just one arm but done a good business."

"What business you in?"

"I've always farmed, but I work in Cookeville now in a heatin' element factory. Bad back made

2. **Ponce de Leon:** Spanish explorer (1460–1521) who, according to legend, was looking for the Fountain of Youth.

A. Responding
? Why would the waitress want to "carry a dog" if she drove cross-country like Moon? (For protection)

B. Interpretation
? What does Moon mean by this response? (He is saying, metaphorically, that his life took a wrong turn around 1965—that is, when Moon was about twenty-six.)

A. Expansion
A "briar blade" is a scythe.

B. Responding
? What does Madison Wheeler mean by "a man becomes what he does"? (That a person's work shapes his or her character and outlook on life) What does he find wrong with factory work? (Presumably that it is repetitious and uncreative)

me go to town to work." He pointed to a wooden building not much bigger than his truck. By the slanting porch, a faded Double Cola sign said J M WHEELER STORE. "That used to be my business. That's me—Madison Wheeler. Feller came by one day. From Detroit. He wanted to buy the sign because he carried my name too. But I didn't sell. Want to keep my name up." He gave a cigarette a good slow smoking. "Had a decent business for five years, but too much of it was in credit. Then them supermarkets down in Cookeville opened, and I was buyin' higher than they was sellin'. With these hard roads now, everybody gets out of the hollers to shop or work. Don't stay up in here anymore. This tar road under my shoes done my business in, and it's likely to do Nameless in."

"Do you wish it was still the old way?"

"I got no debts now. I got two boys raised, and they never been in trouble. I got a brick house and some corn and tobacco and a few Hampshire hogs and Herefords. A good bull. Bull's pumpin' better blood than I do. Real generous man in town let me put my cow in with his stud. I couldna paid the fee on that specimen otherwise." He took another long, meditative pull on his filter tip. "If you're satisfied, that's all they are to it. I'll tell you, people from all over the nation—Florida, Mississippi—are comin' in here to retire because it's good country. But our young ones don't stay on. Not much way to make a livin' in here anymore. Take me. I been beatin' on these stumps all my life, tryin' to farm these hills. They don't give much up to you. Fightin' rocks and briars all the time. One of the first things I recollect is A [swingin' a briar blade—filed out of an old saw it was. Now they come in with them crawlers and push out a pasture in a day. Still, it's a grudgin' land—like the gourd. Got to hard cuss gourd seed, they say, to get it up out of the ground."

The whole time, my rig sat in the middle of the right lane while we stood talking next to it and wiped at the mist. No one else came or went. Wheeler said, "Factory work's easier on the back, B [and I don't mind it, understand, but a man becomes what he does. Got to watch that. That's why I keep at farmin', although the crops haven't ever throve. It's the doin' that's important." He looked up suddenly. "My apologies. I didn't ask what you do that gets you into these hollers."

I told him. I'd been gone only six days, but my account of the trip already had taken on some polish.

He nodded. "Satisfaction is doin' what's important to yourself. A man ought to honor other people, but he's got to honor what he believes in too."

As I started the engine, Wheeler said, "If you get back this way, stop in and see me. Always got beans and taters and a little piece of meat."

Down along the ridge, I wondered why it's always those who live on little who are the ones to ask you to dinner.

Nameless, Tennessee, was a town of maybe ninety people if you pushed it, a dozen houses along the road, a couple of barns, same number of churches, a general merchandise store selling Fire Chief gasoline, and a community center with a lighted volleyball court. Behind the center was an open-roof, rusting metal privy with PAINT ME on the door; in the hollow of a nearby oak lay a full pint of Jack Daniel's Black Label. From the houses, the odor of coal smoke.

Next to a red tobacco barn stood the general merchandise with a poster of Senator Albert Gore, Jr., smiling from the window. I knocked. The door opened partway. A tall, thin man said, "Closed up. For good," and started to shut the door.

"Don't want to buy anything. Just a question for Mr. Thurmond Watts."

The man peered through the slight opening. He looked me over. "What question would that be?"

"If this is Nameless, Tennessee, could he tell me how it got that name?"

The man turned back into the store and called out, "Miss Ginny! Somebody here wants to know how Nameless come to be Nameless."

Miss Ginny edged to the door and looked me and my truck over. Clearly, she didn't approve. She said, "You know as well as I do, Thurmond. Don't keep him on the stoop in the damp to tell him." Miss Ginny, I found out, was Mrs. Virginia Watts, Thurmond's wife.

I stepped in and they both began telling the story, adding a detail here, the other correcting a fact there, both smiling at the foolishness of it all. It seems the hilltop settlement went for years without a name. Then one day the Post Office Department told the people if they wanted mail up on the mountain they would have to give the place a name you could properly address a letter to. The community met; there were only a handful, but they commenced debating. Some wanted patriotic names, some names for nature, one man recommended in all seriousness his own name. They couldn't agree, and they ran out of names to argue about. Finally, a fellow tired of the talk; he didn't like the mail he received anyway. "Forget the durn Post Office," he said. "This here's a nameless place if I ever seen one, so leave it be." And that's just what they did.

Watts pointed out the window. "We used to have signs on the road, but the Halloween boys keep tearin' them down."

"You think Nameless is a funny name," Miss Ginny said. "I see it plain in your eyes. Well, you take yourself up north a piece to Difficult or Defeated or Shake Rag. Now them are silly names."

A The old store, lighted only by three fifty-watt bulbs, smelled of coal oil and baking bread. In the middle of the rectangular room, where the oak floor sagged a little, stood an iron stove. To the right was a wooden table with an unfinished game of checkers and a stool made from an apple-tree stump. On shelves around the walls sat earthen jugs with corncob stoppers, a few canned goods, and some of the two thousand old clocks and clockworks Thurmond Watts owned. Only one was ticking; the others he just looked at. I asked how long he'd been in the store.

"Thirty-five years, but we closed the first day of the year. We're hopin' to sell it to a churchly couple. Upright people. No athians."[3]

"Did you build this store?"

"I built this one, but it's the third general store on the ground. I fear it'll be the last. I take no pleasure in that. Once you could come in here for a gallon of paint, a pickle, a pair of shoes, and a can of corn."

"Or horehound candy," Miss Ginny said. "Or corsets and salves. We had cough syrups and all that for the body. In season, we'd buy and sell blackberries and walnuts and chestnuts, before the blight got them. And outside, Thurmond milled corn and sharpened plows. Even shoed a horse sometimes."

"We could fix up a horse or a man or a baby," Watts said.

"Thurmond, tell him we had a doctor on the ridge in them days."

"We had a doctor on the ridge in them days. As good as any doctor alivin'. He'd cut a crooked toenail or deliver a woman. Dead these last years."

3. **athians:** atheists.

"I got some bad ham meat one day," Miss Ginny said, "and took to vomitin'. All day, all night. Hangin' on the drop edge of yonder. I said to Thurmond, 'Thurmond, unless you want shut of me, call the doctor.' "

"I studied on it," Watts said.

"You never did. You got him right now. He come over and put three drops of iodeen in half a glass of well water. I drank it down and the vomitin' stopped with the last swallow. Would you think iodeen could do that?"

"He put Miss Ginny on one teaspoon of spirits of ammonia in well water for her nerves. Ain't nothin' works better for her to this day."

"Calms me like the hand of the Lord."

Hilda, the Wattses' daughter, came out of the back room. "I remember him," she said. "I was just a baby. Y'all were talkin' to him, and he lifted me up on the counter and gave me a stick of Juicy Fruit and a piece of cheese."

"Knew the old medicines," Watts said. "Only drugstore he needed was a good kitchen cabinet. None of them antee-beeotics that hit you worsen your ailment. Forgotten lore now, the old medicines, because they ain't profit in iodeen."

Miss Ginny started back to the side room where she and her sister Marilyn were taking apart a duck-down mattress to make bolsters. She stopped at the window for another look at Ghost Dancing. "How do you sleep in that thing? Ain't you all cramped and cold?"

"How does the clam sleep in his shell?" Watts said in my defense. B

"Thurmond, get the boy a piece of buttermilk pie afore he goes on."

"Hilda, get him some buttermilk pie." He looked at me. "You like good music?" I said I did. He cranked up an old Edison phonograph, the kind with the big morning-glory blossom for a speaker, and put on a wax cylinder. "This will be 'My Mother's Prayer,' " he said.

While I ate buttermilk pie, Watts served as disc jockey of Nameless, Tennessee. "Here's 'Mountain Rose.' " It was one of those moments that you know at the time will stay with you to the grave: the sweet pie, the gaunt man playing the old music, the coals in the stove glowing orange, the scent of kerosene and hot bread. "Here's 'Evening Rhapsody.' " The music was so heavily romantic we both laughed. I thought: It is for this I have come.

Feathered over and giggling, Miss Ginny

A. Concrete Detail
This description creates a vivid impression of the country store in the reader's mind. ? To how many different senses does this description appeal? (Three—sight, smell, hearing)

B. Responding
? In what way is Watts's remark a "defense" of Moon's practice of sleeping in his van? (He is saying that people's ideas of comfort depend on what they are accustomed to.)

READING CHECK TEST

1. The author says that the way to find the best cafes is to (a) count the trucks in the lot (b) count the wall calendars (c) see if the cook is fat or skinny. *(b)*

2. What town is the author trying to find? (a) Nameless, Kentucky (b) Nameless, North Carolina (c) Nameless, Tennessee. *(c)*

3. The author feels that those most likely to invite a traveler to supper are (a) those who have plenty to spare (b) those who are superstitious (c) those who have little. *(c)*

4. Thurmond Watts (a) has just bought his store (b) is trying to sell his store (c) has just sold his store. *(b)*

5. Ginny Watts keeps (a) a birth book (b) a death book (c) a wish book. *(b)*

A. Responding

? What does Miss Ginny record in her *Deathbook*? (The deaths of everyone she knows or whose death she hears reported on the radio)

CLOSURE

Read the last full paragraph on page 1075. Then ask volunteers to explain why Moon thinks "It is for this I have come."

stepped from the side room. She knew she was a sight. "Thurmond, give him some lunch. Still looks hungry."

Hilda pulled food off the woodstove in the back room: home-butchered and canned whole-hog sausage, home-canned June apples, turnip greens, cole slaw, potatoes, stuffing, hot cornbread. All delicious.

Watts and Hilda sat and talked while I ate. "Wish you would join me."

"We've ate," Watts said. "Can't beat a woodstove for flavorful cookin'."

He told me he was raised in a one-hundred-fifty-year-old cabin still standing in one of the hollows. "How many's left," he said, "that grew up in a log cabin? I ain't the last surely, but I must be climbin' on the list."

Hilda cleared the table. "You Watts ladies know how to cook."

"She's in nursin' school at Tennessee Tech. I went over for one of them football games last year there at Coevul." To say *Cookeville*, you let the word collapse in upon itself so that it comes out "Coevul."

"Do you like football?" I asked.

"Don't know. I was so high up in that stadium, I never opened my eyes."

Watts went to the back and returned with a fat spiral notebook that he set on the table. His expression had changed. "Miss Ginny's *Deathbook*."

The thing startled me. Was it something I was supposed to sign? He opened it but said nothing. There were scads of names written in a tidy hand over pages incised to crinkliness by a ballpoint. Chronologically, the names had piled up: wives, grandparents, a stillborn infant, relatives, friends close and distant. Names, names. After each, the
A date of *the* unknown finally known and transcribed. The last entry bore yesterday's date.

"She's wrote out twenty years' worth. Ever day she listens to the hospital report on the radio and puts the names in. Folks come by to check a date. Or they just turn through the books. Read them like a scrapbook."

Hilda said, "Like Saint Peter at the gates inscribin' the names."

Watts took my arm. "Come along." He led me to the fruit cellar under the store. As we went down, he said, "Always take a newborn baby upstairs afore you take him downstairs, otherwise you'll incline him downwards."

The cellar was dry and full of cobwebs and jar after jar of home-canned food, the bottles organized as a shopkeeper would: sausage, pumpkin, sweet pickles, tomatoes, corn relish, blackberries, peppers, squash, jellies. He held a hand out toward the dusty bottles. "Our tomorrows."

Upstairs again, he said, "Hope to sell the store to the right folk. I see now, though, it'll be somebody offen the ridge. I've studied on it, and maybe it's the end of our place." He stirred the coals. "This store could give a comfortable livin', but not likely get you rich. But just gettin' by is dice rollin' to people nowadays. I never did see my day guaranteed."

When it was time to go, Watts said, "If you find anyone along your way wants a good store—on the road to Cordell Hull Lake—tell them about us."

I said I would. Miss Ginny and Hilda and Marilyn came out to say goodbye. It was cold and drizzling again. "Weather to give a man the weary dismals," Watts grumbled. "Where you headed from here?"

"I don't know."

"Can't get lost then."

Miss Ginny looked again at my rig. It had worried her from the first as it had my mother. "I hope you don't get yourself kilt in that durn thing gallivantin' around the country."

"Come back when the hills dry off," Watts said. "We'll go lookin for some of them round rocks all sparkly inside."

I thought a moment. "Geodes?"[4]

"Them's the ones. The country's properly full of them."

4. **Geodes:** stones having cavities lined with colorful crystals.

ANALYZING THE JOURNAL

Identifying Facts

1. He counts the wall calendars.

2. He says he is searching for something that can be called harmony.

The waitress says that she started out in life not liking anything, but that "then it [life] grew on me."

3. The Post Office insisted that the community have a name so that mail could be delivered. When the inhabitants met to name the town, they couldn't agree, so the place went by the name of "Nameless."

Interpreting Meanings

4. See the side note on page 1071 of this book.

5. The generosity of the Wattses in sharing their food with Least Heat Moon shows that they are good people.

6. Students should point to the paragraph beginning, "The old store, lighted only by three fifty-watt bulbs . . ." (page 1075).

Numerous passages indicate that the area is poor.

The Wattses' cheerfulness and generosity, despite their poverty, keep their story from being depressing.

7. Students should point to a variety of examples from the dialogue.

8. He feels that he has found the "harmony" that he was searching for.

9. He is whimsically curious.

Student answers will vary.

10. His whole book is filled with encounters (like this one) that took place in part to counteract loneliness. Solitude also helps one to "socialize" with oneself.

Most students will agree that Least Heat Moon's idea parallels, or echoes, Thoreau's satisfaction in living alone in simple surroundings.

Responding to the Journal

Analyzing the Journal

Identifying Facts

1. What system does Least Heat Moon use to judge the food at small cafes in blue-highway America?
2. According to what he tells the waitress in the cafe, what is Moon searching for? What is the waitress's response?
3. Explain how Nameless, Tennessee, got its name.

Interpreting Meanings

4. The notion that the honesty of the food and the justice of the prices in a cafe can be "infallibly" judged by the number of calendars on the wall is nonsense (a clear indication that "nonfiction" does not always deal in statistical fact). What sort of truth does the idea nevertheless suggest? A common bit of American travel lore has it that the eight-wheelers will be parked outside the best cafe—the logic being that truckers travel enough to discover where the good food is. What sort of logic would lead you to choose wall calendars as a guide?
5. Least Heat Moon knows that food—what it is, how it is served, who shares it—tells a lot about the people who eat it. Where in this excerpt does food tell us about character?
6. What **concrete detail** helps paint a vivid picture of the Watts's home? Of the economic deterioration of the area? What details keep the Watts's story from being a depressing one?
7. The writer lets Madison Wheeler and the Watts family speak for themselves, and though it is highly unlikely that Least Heat Moon has total recall of their words, he captures the flavor of the country in re-creating their dialogue. Find examples of **images, expressions, proverbs,** and uncommon **grammar** that tell us who and what these people are.
8. Least Heat Moon eats buttermilk pie while an old man plays music on a hand-cranked phonograph, and he says, "It is for this I have come." What does he mean?
9. Why does Least Heat Moon want to go to Nameless? What do you think of his reasons?
10. The waitress of the City Cafe insists that she would travel with a dog for company. But Least Heat Moon takes his journey "accompanied" (as he says elsewhere) "only by a small gray spider crawling the dashboard." What evidence supports Moon's contention that "You get sociable traveling alone"? What do you think of this idea? Do you hear echoes of Thoreau here? (See page 204.)

Writing About the Journal

A Creative Response

1. **Writing an Essay.** Part of the pleasure that Least Heat Moon takes in his journey is a love of language, of the wild names that Americans have chosen for their towns, rivers, and mountains. And part of the pleasure of reading him is that he is observant enough to call these names to our attention. Find a detailed map of your state (or of any province or county in the English-speaking world) and write an essay about the place names that please or amuse you. Can you explain why they do so? Can you tell what the names imply about the people in the area or about its history? Can you propose reasons why some of the names were chosen?

A Critical Response

2. **Describing the Writer's Character.** We learn to know Least Heat Moon as much from how people react to him as from what he tells us about himself. Write a short description of Least Heat Moon as a character in his own story.
3. **Comparing and Contrasting Literary Journeys.** The idea of a journey is a common motif, or image, in literature. Compare and contrast Least Heat Moon's journey with N. Scott Momaday's journey in *The Way to Rainy Mountain* (page 1015). What different purposes do the two writers have? What is the effect of each journey?

Analyzing Language and Style

Metaphors

Least Heat Moon has this exchange with "a big man loading tools in a pickup" (page 1073):

> "Where'd you lose the right road?"
> "I don't know. Somewhere around nineteen sixty-five."
> "Highway fifty-six, you mean?"

No, that's not what he means. Least Heat Moon's reply is metaphorical, a **metaphor** being a figure of speech in which one thing is compared to another, as in "the voyage of life," or "the tender bud of youth." In this case, Least Heat Moon takes "the right road" as a metaphor for something else.

1. What *does* he mean by his answer?
2. What is meant by these metaphors:
   a. "Hangin' on the drop edge of yonder" (page 1075)
   b. "How does the clam sleep in his shell?" (page 1075)
   c. "Our tomorrows" (page 1076)

A. Expansion
The railroad, as it is called in the United States, and the railway, as it is known in England, came to both countries at about the same time; and each then found its own names for the new technology. *Caboose* is the British word for a ship's galley, but only Americans use it to name the last car on a freight train. (The English call this the *braking car.*) In this country, goods shipped by rail are called *freight* and the car that carries it a *freight car.* In England, the same car is called a *goods van,* and what it carries is *goods.* Finally, Americans may go to a *depot* to board a train; in England, a depot is only for the storage of freight.

THE AMERICAN LANGUAGE

by Gary Q. Arpin

High Tech's Influence

Before *high tech* there was just plain *technology*. The nineteenth-century British author Richard Burton used the word *technology* in his *Travels* to refer to fairly simple practical arts (such as extracting dye from plants). But, appropriately enough, it was an American who first used the word in its present meaning of "applied science." In 1829, Professor Joel Bigelow published *The Elements of Technology* (subtitled *The Application of the Sciences to the Useful Arts*).

> **"The train gave people something to do—watch the train come in—and it gave rise to a new social designation—'the other side of the tracks.'"**

The Train and New Words

The technology of that time, of course, was chiefly steam, and the steam engine entered people's lives in the form of factories, steamboats, and, most pervasively, the locomotive. The speed and breadth of the railroad's impact on American lives was unprecedented. In 1830, there were seventy-three miles of railroad track in the United States. By 1850, there were 8,879 miles. Ten years after that, there were 30,636 miles. "The world has seen nothing like it before," Daniel Webster wrote. "The progress of the age has almost outstripped human belief."

The railroad was an inescapable aspect of American life. It rolled past Walden Pond and provided Thoreau the opportunity for some of his most valuable meditations. It rolled past Daniel Webster's farmhouse, and, as he wrote, "the thunder of engines and the scream of steam-whistles . . . not a little disturbed the peace and repose of its occupants." It rolled through the centers of thousands of towns, including Amherst, Massachusetts, where, around 1862, Emily Dickinson imagined it to "lap the miles and eat the valleys up." The train gave people something new to do—watch the train come in—and it gave rise to a new social designation—"the other side of the tracks."

The new application of steam technology required a host of new words. Where did these terms come from? The same processes of word formation applied to railroad terms as had applied to Americanisms in general. Some words were invented, like *diesel* (after Rudolph Diesel, the diesel engine's inventor). Many other words and phrases were formed by combining existing words, as in *red cap* and *whistle stop*.

A substantial number of other words pertaining to the new mode of transportation were borrowed from other forms of transportation that had preceded the railroad. (This began a process that continues today, as one technology lends its words to its successor.) A Sailing ships and steamboats provided the railroad with terms like *berth, caboose, crew, gondola,* and *all aboard*. The stage coach provided *car, coach, conductor,* and *station*.

THE IMPERIAL TRAIN OF THE ORLEANS RAILWAY.—THE SALOON OF HONOUR.—SEE SUPPLEMENT, PAGE 186

From Specialized Use to Popular Use

Most technological terms had a well-defined and specific job to do. Other terms, though, found a broader popularity, usually through metaphor, and they entered standard usage. To be *under pressure*, for example, is a phrase borrowed from the steam engine. Most of us use the term only in its metaphoric sense, without thinking where it came from. It is these terms and phrases, which have crossed the tracks from their technological neighborhood to that of general usage, that are of the greatest interest.

The railroad gave us many such terms, from *right-of-way* to *sidetrack*. The metaphoric sense of one railroad term—*sleepers*— A was slightly bent by Thoreau in a well-known passage in *Walden*. The rails of the railroad track were fastened to crossties. Because these beams were laid on their flat sides, between the rails, they became known in America as *sleepers* (a term still used by carpenters to refer to boards laid this way). Thoreau, concerned that the machine was becoming our master rather than our slave, took the word back to its roots and reminded readers of the lives sacrificed to build the railroad. "We do not ride upon the railroad," he wrote; "it rides upon us. Did you ever think what those sleepers are that underlie the railroad? Each one is a man, an Irish man, or a Yankee man. The rails are laid on them, and they are covered with sand, and the cars run smoothly over them. They are sound sleepers, I assure you."

"To be *under pressure*, for example, is a phrase borrowed from the steam engine."

A. Sleepers
"Sleepers," with the meaning "railroad ties," is now more common in England than in the United States, probably because the Americanism *sleeper,* meaning a sleeping car, displaced the earlier meaning.

New Words from *Tele* and *Graph*

At about the same time as the railroad was crisscrossing the American continent, the telegraph was doing it too. The word *telegraph* (coined from two Greek words, *tele*, "afar," and *graphein,* "to write") had been used in England since the eighteenth century to refer to various forms of semaphores (railway signaling apparatus, usually flags or lights). The word *telegraph,* though, became popular only with the invention of the Morse telegraph in the nineteenth century (another example of one technology lending its words to its successor).

William Marconi and his earlier apparatus for telegraphing without wires.

Telegram is a true Americanism, coined in Albany, New York, in 1852. "A friend desires us to give notice," wrote the Albany *Evening Journal,* "that he will ask leave . . . to introduce a new word. It is *telegram,* instead of *telegraphic dispatch."* The word, so politely brought into the world, encountered some vigorous opposition before being accepted. The reason? It was not a proper combination of Greek words. The proper word, purists argued, was *telegrapheme.*

Tele and *graph* have been busy root words since the early nineteenth century. *Photograph* appeared in 1839 (*photo* is Greek for "light"). For a number of years, *photographist* fought it out with the rival *photographer* before disapppearing. Late in the nineteenth century, the *cinematograph* (*kinema* is Greek for "motion") appeared. It was shortened to *cinema* in England, but changed to

A. Expansion
Acronyms are so pervasive a part of our culture that dictionaries of them are in print. One such reference is *The Dictionary of Initials,* published by the Citadel Press in 1981. The editors thoughtfully provide blank space at the end of each alphabetical listing for adding new acronyms.

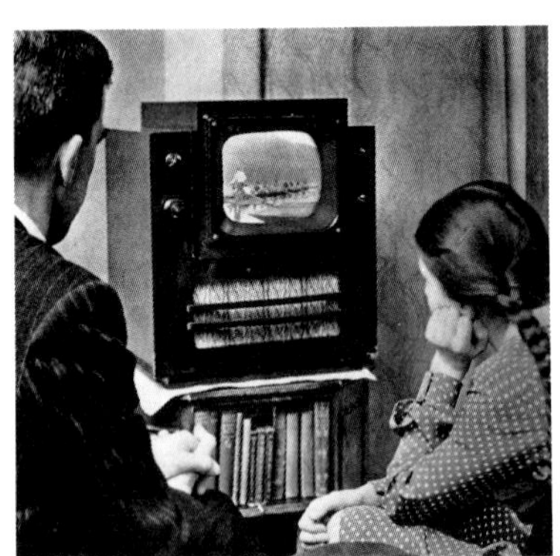

Watching television in the early 1950's.

> "One method of forming new words, now so popular that it threatens to overwhelm us, is the use of acronyms."

moving picture in the United States and later shortened to *movie.* (*Flick,* from the flickering that movies used to be plagued with, is probably a newspaper invention.)

The *telephone* was invented in 1876 and the *phonograph* in 1877 (*phono* is Greek for "voice"). The technology for wireless communication led to the *radiotelegraph* in the late nineteenth century. In 1906 this was shortened to *radio,* although it was not until the 1920's that commercial radio became popular.

The television achieved popular commercial success in the late 1940's. The British shortened *television* to *telly,* while Americans abbreviated it to *TV.* (This was a period, as we shall see, when initials and acronyms were especially popular in the United States.)

Acronyms: Convenient Abbreviations

One method of forming new words, now so popular that it threatens A to overwhelm us, is the use of acronyms. (The word *acronym* is probably an Americanism, although the practice is ancient.) The term comes from the Greek words for "tip" and "name," and refers to a word formed from the combination of the first letters of the words in a phrase. *Radar* was a technological acronym (from "*ra*dio *d*etecting *a*nd *r*anging") and it quickly knocked out the British candidate, *radiolocator. Sonar* ("sound navigation and ranging") followed, as did, much later, *laser* ("light amplification by stimulated emission of radiation").

The acronym device was not the sole property of scientists and technologists. In the twentieth century, wars and bureaucracy have bred many of these conveniently shortened words, from AWOL ("absent without leave"), coined in the First World War, to UNICEF ("United Nations International Children's Emergency Fund"). The Second World War saw the growth of a great many more alphabetical designations, such as POW ("prisoner of war"), and also a great many acronyms, such as WAVE and WAC ("Women Accepted for Volunteer Emergency Service" and "Women's Army Corps"). WAVE is an example of the now common practice of first inventing the acronym and then finding a phrase to justify it. A term like AWOL, on the other hand, grew into an acronym. In its early days the letters were pronounced separately, while now it is common to pronounce it "ay wall." Why do you think the pronunciation of POW didn't make a similar shift?

The Airplane

The airplane had an effect on American culture in the twentieth century similar to the effect of the railroad in the nineteenth. *Aeroplane* originally referred to the plane of the wing, which provides the lift, but the word quickly came to refer to the entire craft. The word had been spelled *airplane* in the United States since the 1870's. When the Wright Brothers patented their flying machine in 1906, the word was already there, waiting for them. The new technology of *aeronautics* borrowed part of its name from sailing technology (*nautes* is Greek for "sailor"), and it borrowed a number of technical terms from sailing as well. *Cockpit, cabin, stewardess, steward, rudder,* and many other terms were adapted from the ocean liners that the airplane was shortly to drive almost to extinction. New words and combinations, like *barnstorm, tailspin,* and *Mayday* (from the French *m'aidez*—"help me"), came into common usage as a result of the airplane.

Nautes, by the way, connects the ancient and the modern worlds in a strikingly direct way. The *Argonauts* sailed with Jason in a ship called the *Argo* in search of the Golden Fleece in Greek mythology. The *astronauts* ("star sailors") sailed to the moon in [A] the twentieth century. (The *Astros* play in Houston, long associated [B] with the space program, and the first artificial turf, *Astroturf*, was developed for their stadium. Thus the stars found their way into the fabric of the national pastime.)

Space and Computer Jargon

The space program brought together experts in several advanced technologies, from military pilots to civil engineers and scientists. Americans heard their jargon on television and adopted some of it. Terms like *countdown, blast-off, malfunction,* and *put on hold* are all familiar to us from the astronauts' jargon. Flyers had long had a number of terms for an unexplained malfunction. The word *gremlin* was common during World War II, to be replaced by *bug*, which is still in use. The word the astronauts probably use most often, though, is *glitch*, a term immediately taken over by computer experts.

The language associated with computers is often highly technical, and much of it will probably never enter standard usage. *RAM, ROM,* and *DOS,* acronyms for "Random Access Memory," "Read Only Memory," and "Disk Operating System," are all familiar to computer users, but they seem to have little application outside their technical uses. Computer people have adapted many standard English words to technical uses, though, and a number of these are edging back into the noncomputer world with slightly different meanings.

The most notable of these are nouns that have been changed to verbs. *Access, format,* and *program* are being used as verbs with some frequency today, although some purists object to such usages as unfamiliar and unattractive. (*Program* has already produced an offspring, *deprogram,* referring to "reverse brainwashing.") *Interface* (both as a noun and a verb) has also had an inhospitable reception from purists and other people who are sensitive to language. It remains to be seen whether *interface* and other terms will enter standard English or fade back into the pages of technical dictionaries. If such terms survive, it will be because they are perceived to fill a real need in the language.

Computer slang is often lively and whimsical. If a programmer interferes with someone else's program, for example, he is said to

"You've learned to respond to verbal commands. Now let's test your computer literacy."

"Computer slang is often lively and whimsical. If a programmer interferes with someone else's program, for example, he is said to *bomb the program.* (Not a nice thing to do.)"

A. Expansion
The Soviet equivalent of *astronauts* is *cosmonauts* (*cosmo-*, "universe," + *naut,* "sailor")

B. Expansion
The *Astros,* like *Astroturf,* were probably named for the Astrodome, the dome structure where both may be found. The stadium dome was originally transparent, like the structures for housing astronomical or navigational instruments it was named after, and real grass grew in it. When baseball players complained that they could not see fly balls against the dome, it was altered to be translucent. Because grass would no longer grow there, Astroturf was developed.

READING CHECK TEST

1. The word *technology* means (a) scientific language (b) applied science (c) jargon. *(b)*

2. The expression *under pressure* is borrowed from (a) Ernest Hemingway (b) electrical technology (c) steam technology. *(c)*

3. The word *telegraph* originally referred to (a) railroad semaphores (b) smoke signals (c) wireless communications. *(a)*

4. A word formed by combining the first letters of words in a phrase is (a) a homonym (b) an acrostic (c) an acronym. *(c)*

5. *Mayday,* from the French *m'aldez,* means (a) Help me! (b) Watch out! (c) A O.K.! *(a)*

A. Responding

? What are some current slang terms that relate to computers and their use? (Students should offer many examples.)

bomb the program. (Not a nice thing to do.) Programs that stop working unexpectedly *hang* or *crash,* sometimes as the result of a *spike,* or a surge in electricity. When personal-computer owners talk about *booting a computer,* nonowners fume, but the new terms are necessary. (*Boot* is a shortening of *bootstrap,* which comes from the familiar expression *to pull yourself up by your bootstraps,* or "to start from nothing").

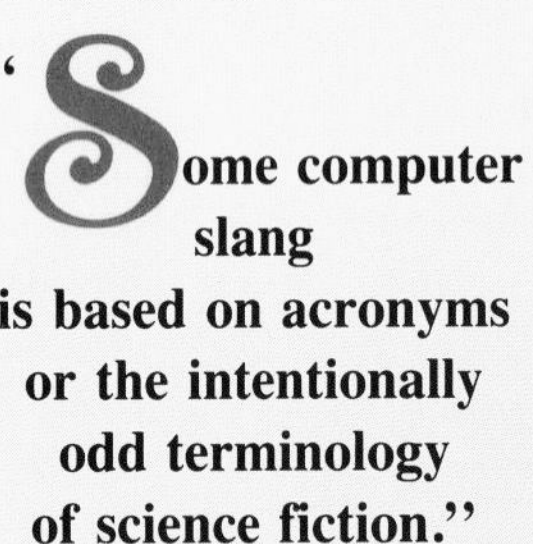
"Some computer slang is based on acronyms or the intentionally odd terminology of science fiction."

Some computer slang is based on acronyms or the intentionally odd terminology of science fiction. *GIGO* (Garbage In, Garbage Out) has achieved some popularity among those who are not *digit heads*—which is not a polite term. Computer buffs prefer to call themselves *hackers*, a term originally referring to someone who is not very good at something. The word is probably derived from the awkward hacking strokes of beginning tennis players and golfers. Its computer use may have come from the term *hacking around*, "doing something of little value."

A When *Time* magazine declared the personal computer the "Machine of the Year" in 1983, they published a number of slang terms, including *gweep*, "an overworked hacker"; *frobnitz*, "thingamajig"; and *glork*, "mild surprise." The sci-fi background of such terms is clear—they are intended to look as little like English words as possible. As a result, they will probably have relatively short lives. They may even be obsolete now.

Analyzing Language

1. The following terms, once associated only with trains, cars, or airplanes, soon entered general usage. Which technology does each term come from? What has the term come to mean in standard usage, and how did it come to take on that meaning? A dictionary may help.

A jerkwater town	A back-seat driver
To sidetrack	A tailspin
A stopover	To bail out
The wrong side of the tracks	A nosedive

2. Many words from medicine and psychology have entered everyday use, but not in their strict clinical sense. What is the clinical meaning of each of the following italicized words, and what does each word mean metaphorically in these sentences?

   a. Stuart is *allergic* to hard work.
   b. Brooklyn was *obsessed* with baseball that season.
   c. Economists predict an *anemic* recovery.
   d. Julia is not *sanguine* about the prospect of a job.
   e. There has been an *epidemic* of burglaries on Sixteenth Street.

3. Using several newspapers or newsmagazines, find five acronyms in current usage. Is the acronym pronounced as a word or as separate letters?
4. List five computer terms or phrases that are in standard (noncomputer) usage, and tell how each is used. List five more computer terms that you think might enter standard usage in the future, and tell what they mean. You should be able to find a dictionary or glossary of computer terms in a library.

Exercises in Critical Thinking and Writing

EVALUATING NONFICTION: FACT AND OPINION

Writing Assignment

Write a brief essay evaluating any one of the nonfiction selections you have read in this unit.

Background

Distinguishing Between Fact and Opinion

A **fact** is a statement that can be verified, or proven to be true or false. An **opinion** is a statement of personal judgment or interpretation. Opinions are not less important than facts, but, without support, an opinion does not have much substance.

Science derives its data from observations of the natural world. The morning paper tells us that sunrise tomorrow will be at 6:02 A.M., and that high tide will occur at 3:53 P.M. We take these statements as fact because we believe that they are based on centuries of observation. For the same reasons, we are inclined to accept as factual Lewis Thomas's statement that communication with intelligent life outside our planet will take 200 years. We assume that Lewis, a scientist, knows the accepted facts (to date, anyway) about distances and the speed of light.

But how do you verify statements that relate to human beings in everyday life or in history? You must have a reliable witness whose ability to observe, understand, and report you can trust, and whose honesty is beyond question. When Russell Baker asserts that there are children who "soon quit bothering to tell the testers what they want to hear," we can accept it as a fact if other reliable witnesses are able to observe the same phenomenon. The same is true of history. For historic facts, we turn to documentation in primary sources—letters, essays, and reports of first-hand observers.

1. Write three statements that you believe are facts. One should be from the realm of science, one from history, and the third from any other source—perhaps even yesterday's newspaper.
2. Decide how you would verify each statement, and then share your statements with the class. A
3. Does everyone agree that your statements are facts? Is there any disagreement on whether or how they can be verified?

Evaluating Nonfiction

Robert Penn Warren called William Least Heat Moon's *Blue Highways* "a masterpiece." What makes one nonfiction selection good and another weak? B Such evaluations should be based on **objective criteria,** or standards—not on **subjective responses** alone. C Thinking about what's good and bad in the writing of others will also help you to improve your own writing style.

Guidelines for Evaluating Nonfiction

1. What is the writer's **purpose** (to entertain, tell a story, explain, inform, persuade, satirize, describe)? How well has the writer achieved that purpose?
2. What is the writer's **audience**? Has the writer manipulated the style of the selection to appeal especially to that audience?
3. What **facts** does the writer include? What are the writer's sources?
   a. **Personal experiences:** direct observation, memories, interviews, or conversations
   b. **Research:** quotations from letters, diaries, memoirs, interviews, essays, other writers' works, accepted facts
4. What **opinions** (conclusions, judgments, interpretations) does the writer offer? What **evidence** (facts, reasons, examples) is included to support these opinions? Do I agree or disagree with the opinions?
5. What is the **tone** of the writing?
6. Does the selection hold my **interest**? Why or why not? What techniques has the writer used to hold my interest?
7. Did the selection stir my **feelings** or make me **think**? Did I learn anything? What?
8. Are the writer's ideas clearly conveyed? How graceful and readable is the writer's style? Has the writer avoided clichés and jargon? What specifically gives the writing its flavor? (Imagery? Figures of speech?)

A. Expansion
Emphasize that the statement of a reliable authority constitutes verification, as in the case of Thomas's earlier statement.

B. Responding
? Why should you take seriously Robert Penn Warren's opinion about *Blue Highways*? (Because Warren was a distinguished critic, a Pulitzer-prize winning novelist and poet, and a former Poet Laureate of the Library of Congress—hence, a reliable witness)

C. Responding
? Explain the difference between *objective criteria* and *subjective response.* (*Objective criteria:* standards for judgment that are widely accepted and do not depend upon the feelings of a particular person; *subjective response:* a reaction based on the feelings or temperament of a particular person)

A. Responding
? Do the credentials of Professor Rutland indicate that his opinions relating to Madison are probably reliable? (Yes)

B. Responding
? What, according to the reviewer, is Rutland's purpose in writing his book on Madison? (To provide a shorter biography than the massive six-volume one by Irving Brant)

Revising Essays
As students revise their essays, refer them to **Grammar, Usage, and Mechanics: A Reference Guide** at the back of their books.

Exercises in Critical Thinking and Writing/*cont.*

Here is a portion of an evaluation of a biography of James Madison, a central figure in the framing of the Constitution and President of the United States from 1809–1817. The review was published in a newspaper.

A Robert Allen Rutland, a professor of history at the University of Tulsa, is an experienced specialist in the history of the American Revolution, the founding of the Republic, and the struggle to maintain the Federal Union during its fragile youth. In *James Madison*, he makes a strong case for Madison as *the* Founding Father, surpassing all others. Opinions on this conclusion may differ, but the author's evidence is impressive.

Mr. Rutland uses voluminous quotations from letters, speeches, and other sources to set forth Madison's views on republicanism, individual liberty, the balance (or division) of power among the branches of government, financial honesty, and slavery. The reader is left in no doubt as to Madison's importance as an effective republican leader at a time when post-Revolution America cried out for organization and leadership. . . .

B In his preface, Mr. Rutland states that his book is for the reader who does not want to face Irving Brant's six-volume biography, also entitled *James Madison* (1941–1961). That is a commendable aim, and this book fulfills the writer's purpose admirably. But the length of a scholarly work is only part of the picture. The manner of the writing is something different, and here Mr. Rutland runs into difficulty. Although there are bright passages in which the reader can almost see the action and sense the atmosphere of the time, there are also many pages filled with quotations from documents (properly footnoted) where the reading is hard slogging.

Madison's life was filled with intellectual dueling, expressed in the roundabout language of his day. He was a man of thought and of ideals, a soft-spoken, low-key intellectual whose life was busy but hardly colorful. So it requires dedication to Madison for the reader to concentrate steadily on this book in order to reap the benefits of the author's considerable scholarship. . . .

—Alden Todd

Prewriting

Choose a selection that you feel strongly about, and reread it carefully with the guidelines in mind. Take notes as you read.

Before you write, jot down your responses to each of the guidelines cited above. Use all these notes as the rough draft of your evaluation.

Be sure you have formulated a thesis statement before you begin writing. Before you write, test your thesis statement: Does it apply to all the points you'll make in your essay? You might find that you have to revise it slightly, or even heavily.

Writing

In your opening paragraph, cite the title and author of the piece you are evaluating. It will help to keep your topic in focus if you state your thesis statement in the first paragraph also.

In each succeeding paragraph, cite evidence from the selection to support your opinions. Open each succeeding paragraph with a topic statement.

In your concluding paragraph, summarize your evaluation.

Revising and Proofreading

Use the guidelines in the section at the back of this book, called **Writing About Literature,** to revise and proofread your essay.

POETRY IN A TIME OF DIVERSITY

Double Talk by Inez Storer (1987). Oil. Rena Bransten Gallery, San Francisco.

UNIT THIRTEEN

HUMANITIES CONNECTION: DISCUSSING THE FINE ART

Inez Storer (b. 1933) was born in Santa Monica, California, and studied at both the University of California at Berkeley and the San Francisco Art Institute. She is known for her sculpture and collages; note that the details in *Double Talk* have the quality of a collage. Point out that the relaxation of form, casual style, and individualized expressionism of recent poetry can also be found in post-World War II painting. Contemporary art is also experiencing a "time of diversity."

TEACHING THE POETRY UNIT

American poetry today is a far cry from the traditional rhythms and rhymes of William Cullen Bryant and Ralph Waldo Emerson. Since World War II, a number of stylistic schools have flourished, and many individual poets have flourished without belonging to any school. No single poet has loomed so large to provide an intimidating example, in contrast to the modernist era, when Pound and Eliot dominated the scene. Instead, more recognition has been given to poetry outside the traditional mainstream.

The formalist view of poems as purely external aesthetic objects, which dominated critical thought to the age of Eliot, has now been replaced by subjectivism. The poet Donald Hall makes a distinction among several kinds of subjective poetry currently being written. Confessional poetry is a direct, colloquial style in which the poet speaks of the most intimate emotional problems, usually in free verse. Confessionalism was at its height in the 1950's and 1960's; later, a new style that Hall calls "expressionism" or "neo-surrealism" became current. It is a poetry of wild imagery, where what is most important is not the technical skill of the poet or the harrowingness of the poet's private life, but the originality of the poet's imagination. Alongside these two movements, African American poetry and the poetry of other ethnic groups has developed in a manner marked by forcefulness, linguistic vigor, and above all, a sense of reality.

During several of the poets' careers, there has been a development from a more formal verse early on to a less restrictive verse form later on. (Robert Lowell is the most obvious such case.) This repeated pattern shows the overall development of American poetry in this period: a loosening of formal bonds and a willingness to take on any subject and reveal any emotion. At the same time, however, standards of craftsmanship have not declined. The average American poem published today, with its subtle uses of internal rhyme, assonance, syllabic stresses, and varying line lengths, is undoubtedly more sophisticated than the rather mechanical rhymed and metered average American poem of a century ago.

OBJECTIVES OF THE POETRY UNIT

1. To improve reading proficiency and expand vocabulary
2. To gain exposure to notable poets and their poems
3. To define and identify elements of poetry
4. To define and identify significant literary techniques
5. To respond to poetry, orally and in writing, through analysis of its elements
6. To practice the following critical thinking and writing skills
   a. Comparing and contrasting poems
   b. Analyzing a poem
   c. Interpreting a poem
   d. Using another point of view
   e. Imitating a poet's technique
   f. Comparing and contrasting poetry and prose
   g. Analyzing an image
   h. Evaluating a poem

A. Responding to the Quotation

? What can be learned from the poetry of a particular time period that may not be revealed in the books and newspapers of the era?

? What poems from previous literary periods revealed something about that age?

Supplementary Support Materials: Unit Thirteen

1. Unit Introduction Test *(CCB)*
2. Word Analogies Test *(CCB)*
3. Unit Review Test *(CCB)*
4. Critical Thinking and Writing Test *(CCB)*

B. Expansion
Hyatt Waggoner states that Modernism is based on three principles: a) the poet records observation; b) the poet's feelings and attitudes must not intervene in the process of recording; and c) the poet is essentially a craftsperson.

C. Connections
Referring to Modernism, Robert Phillips states that the "apotheosis of this dry aesthetic" appears in John Crowe Ransom's poem "Bells for John Whiteside's Daughter" (page 673) where the poet describes death euphemistically as a "brown study" and grief as merely "vexing."

POETRY IN A TIME OF DIVERSITY

by **John Malcolm Brinnin**

A Time of Diversity

A *One judges an age, just as one judges a poet, by its best poems . . .*

—Randall Jarrell

It is difficult to describe the course of American poetry since 1945, because recent trends are still too close to be viewed objectively. Moreover, in recent years, unprecedented numbers of Americans have been writing poetry, so it is a special challenge to determine which poets and which movements will last.

The Decline of Modernism

Nevertheless, there are a number of clear, significant differences between American poetry written before 1945 and the poetry written in the decades since. The twenty years between World War I and World War II marked the flowering and near-monopoly of **modernist poetry.** This was the kind of poetry defined, by and large, by the theory and practice of T. S. Eliot (page 740), Ezra Pound (page 711), and, somewhat later, of W. H. Auden. B

In 1917, Eliot had called for an impersonal, objective poetry that would transcend the subjective emotions of the poet. The poem, said Eliot, should be impersonal, allusive (it should make references, or allusions, to other works), and intellectually challenging. Modernist writers followed Ezra Pound's insistence that the image was all-important and that all unnecessary words should be omitted; but in doing this, they often eliminated material that could have made their poetry more accessible to readers. C

By the early 1950's, though, there was a growing sense that modernism was somehow becoming played out, that it was no longer appropriate for the times. The era itself may have had something to do with the shift away from modernism. A generation had returned from war to a country where conformity and material success were predominant values. The Soviet Union and the atomic bomb worried Americans in the late 1940's and early 1950's; but acquiring a house and a car and making money were generally of more immediate importance. "These are the tranquilized Fifties," Robert Lowell wrote in a poem toward the end of that decade, as he ironically described the complacent scene around him:

> I hog a whole house on Boston's
> "hardly passionate Marlborough Street,"
> where even the man
> scavenging the filth in the back alley trash cans,
> has two children, a beach wagon, a helpmate,
> and is a "young Republican."
>
> —from "Memories of West Street and Lepke," Robert Lowell

"'These are the tranquilized Fifties,' Robert Lowell wrote."

Reading Check Test

1. Modernist poetry declined after World War II. *True*
2. In the 1950's people were concerned with conformity and material success. *True*
3. Young nonconformists objected to Allen Ginsberg's poem "Howl." *False*
4. Ginsberg's concern with social injustice and the power of the imagination influenced other poets. *True*
5. Confessional poets wrote emotional poems about details of their private lives. *True*

The Beat Poets

In 1956, a poem called *Howl* was published by Allen Ginsberg, who could by no stretch of the imagination be described as dull. A cry of outrage against the conformity of the 1950's, *Howl* was as far removed from the "safe" confines of modernism as could be imagined. It began, "I saw the best minds of my generation destroyed by madness, starving hysterical naked," and it continued at the same intense pitch for hundreds of lines.

Together with *On the Road* (1957), Jack Kerouac's novel celebrating the bohemian life, *Howl* quickly became a kind of Bible for young nonconformists known as the Beat Generation. Beat poetry and the Beat life style of poetry readings, jazz, and late-night coffeehouses in San Francisco and New York's Greenwich Village had an immediate impact on popular culture. *Life* magazine even ran illustrated stories about the new bohemians.

Howl provided the first clear alternative to "academic" poetry—intellectual poetry that seemed to be written for analysis in the classroom, not poetry that addressed the real concerns of contemporary life. Many of Ginsberg's concerns—the injustices of modern life, the importance of the imagination—became the principal themes of poetry a decade later.

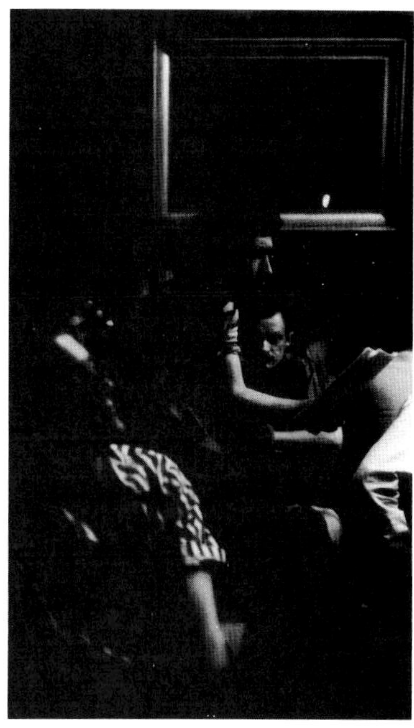

Poetry reading in a coffeehouse in New York City (1959). Photograph by Burt Glinn.

Poetry and Personal Experience

In 1959, Robert Lowell published *Life Studies,* one of the most important and influential volumes of verse to appear since World War II. These poems were about personal experiences that modernist poets had avoided dealing with directly: emotional problems, alcoholism, illness, and depression. In *Life Studies,* Lowell clearly and decisively broke with Eliot's theory that poetry should be impersonal; in doing so, he helped to reunite, both for himself and for other writers, "the man who suffers and the mind which creates."

Shortly after *Life Studies* appeared, a critic described Lowell's poems as "**confessional.**" The label stuck, and the Confessional School of poets, mostly friends or students of Lowell, was officially born. These poets—including Sylvia Plath (page 1119), Anne Sexton (page 1122), and John Berryman (page 1124)—wrote frank, sometimes brutal poems about their private lives. Nothing could have been further from Eliot's model.

By the mid-1970's, many of the first generation of major postwar poets were dead, as were some of the second generation. Williams and Roethke and Plath all died in 1963. The 1970's saw the deaths of Berryman, Sexton, and Lowell. With Lowell's death, the American literary world was again without a major poet to provide it with definition and a common sense of direction.

The young poets who emerged in the 1970's and early 1980's have written in a variety of styles and about a broad spectrum of subjects. Few of them would call poetry impersonal.

"The Confessional School of poets wrote frank, sometimes brutal poems about their private lives."

Comment From A Critic

Stephen Stepanchev credits Jack Kerouac with coining the term "beat" and adds: "In a religious sense, 'beatness' is related to 'beatitude' and suggests the innocence, blessedness, and raptness of the hip angel aspiring to be united with the One. In a musical sense, it implies the keeping of a beat, the jazz beat, and so being in harmony with others in the groove, those who can be turned on to the truth. And, in a sociological and psychological sense, it describes the condition of the outsider, the man who is down and out, who looks at 'square' society from the peripheries and rejects its disciplines, goals, and values."

A. Expansion

In "Elegy for Jane" (page 1089) Roethke's knowledge of what he termed "minimal creatures" provides a sensitive portrait of Jane's spirit and behavior in his writing class. In line 2, her initial wariness and quick smile are like the swift, darting maneuvers of a fish; once "startled into talk," however, she is like a fish leaping out of water "balanced in the delight of her talk" or a wren whose song trembles the small branches. In the next stanza her sadness is like that of a small animal who scrapes its cheek against straw. She is unassuming and meek: like the common sparrow or a fern she leaves a fragile impression. And in stanza 4, like a pigeon she is skittery, or nervous.

Comment From A Critic

In his overview of Roethke's poetry, Stanley Kunitz remarked: "Roethke's imagination is kinesthetic, stimulated by nerve ends and muscles." Other critics have also commented on the motion and physical sensation that appear in Roethke's poetry. "Elegy for Jane" is filled with such kinesthetic images: the limp neckcurls, the leaping fish and singing wren, "tail into the wind"; trembling twigs; a cheek scraping against straw; and a skittery pigeon. In this poem, the tone of tragic loss is heightened by the unstated contrast between these images and the stillness of death.

Theodore Roethke (1908–1963)

Theodore Roethke was born in Saginaw, Michigan, where his father owned the largest greenhouse complex in the state. His childhood was A spent close to nature, nurturing cuttings and small plants and walking in the vast acres of woodlands owned by his family. This childhood world would provide the foundation for much of his poetry, which often looks at the smallest aspects of nature—worms, snails, tiny seedlings—through the eyes of a child. "I have a genuine love of nature," he wrote when he was a sophomore in college. "When I get alone under an open sky where man isn't too evident—then I'm tremendously exalted and a thousand vivid ideas and sweet visions flood my consciousness." Later, he said "Everything that lives is holy: I call upon these holy forms of life."

Roethke studied law and wrote advertising copy for some time after graduating from college, but his desire to become a writer finally led him to graduate school. He began a teaching career at the University of Pennsylvania (where he also coached the tennis team); and from 1947 until his death he taught at the University of Washington. Roethke was a passionate and dedicated teacher who brought the same energy to the classroom that he brought to poetry. He sought in teaching the same rewards he sought in his writing: transcendence and illumination. "Most teaching is visceral," he wrote, "and the general uproar that constitutes a verse class, especially so. It is as ephemeral as the dance. . . . [Teaching] is what is left after all the reading and thinking and reciting: the residue, the illumination."

The search for illumination and ecstasy was a fundamental concern for Roethke in life as well as in poetry. This search brought with it a psychological imbalance that he tried to face openly and employ honestly in his verse. "My heart keeps open house," he wrote in an early poem.

My truths are all foreknown,
This anguish self-revealed.
I'm naked to the bone,
With nakedness my shield.
—from "Open House"

Between 1947 and 1958 Roethke published four volumes and received a number of honors, including the Pulitzer Prize, the National Book Award, and the Bollingen Award. A poet of both pain and joy, the dark and the light, Roethke tried to find in both extremes the same transcendent moment, "a consciousness beyond the mundane," as he once put it, "a purity, a final innocence."

Supplementary Support Materials
1. Review and Response Worksheet: Figures of Speech (*CCB*)
2. Selection Test (*CCB*)

Preparation

Establishing a Purpose. Ask students to look for evidence that Jane was "not just a name on a class list, but a precious human being" to Roethke. (The images in stanzas 1–3 reveal Roethke's awareness of Jane as a unique, vulnerable individual.)

Closure

Before publication of this poem, Roethke was criticized for his inability to portray real people or real emotion. In class discussion, ask students, on the basis of "Elegy for Jane," do you think this criticism is fair or unfair?

In this poem, a sensitive and caring man who is "neither father nor lover" inevitably shares some of the feelings of both. The poet writes an elegy for a young woman who probably never realized that, in the eyes of her teacher, she was not just a name on a class list, but a precious human being.

Elegy for Jane

My Student, Thrown by a Horse

I remember the neckcurls, limp and damp as tendrils,
And her quick look, a sidelong pickerel smile;
And how, once startled into talk, the light syllables leaped for her,
And she balanced in the delight of her thought,
A wren, happy, tail into the wind,
Her song trembling the twigs and small branches.
The shade sang with her;
The leaves, their whispers turned to kissing;
And the mold sang in the bleached valleys under the rose.

Oh, when she was sad, she cast herself down into such a pure depth,
Even a father could not find her:
Scraping her cheek against straw;
Stirring the clearest water.

My sparrow, you are not here,
Waiting like a fern, making a spiny shadow.
The sides of wet stones cannot console me,
Nor the moss, wound with the last light.

If only I could nudge you from this sleep,
A My maimed darling, my skittery pigeon.
Over this damp grave I speak the words of my love:
I, with no rights in this matter,
Neither father nor lover.

Responding to the Poem

Analyzing the Poem

Identifying Details

1. Count the number of times in the poem when the dead girl, or something about her, is compared to a plant or animal.

Interpreting Meanings

2. What do the comparisons to plants and animals tell us about the speaker's personality?
3. What, in your opinion, is the effect of the speaker's saying he has "no rights in this matter" (line 21)?

Writing About the Poem

A Critical Response

Comparing Poems. Compare the treatment of death and mourning in "Elegy for Jane" and John Crowe Ransom's "Bells for John Whiteside's Daughter" (page 673). Consider the poems' **figures of speech** and **tones.**

Analyzing the Poem

Identifying Details

1. References include the suggestion of a plant's tendrils (line 1); a pickerel, or small fish (line 2); a wren (lines 5–6); the implication of a small animal "scraping her cheek against straw" (line 12); "my sparrow" (line 14); a fern (line 15); "skittery pigeon" (line 19).

Interpreting Meanings

2. They suggest tenderness, sympathy, and keen observation.
3. Most students will agree that the phrase heightens the sense of loss by implying that the grief of the speaker, who has "no rights," is only a portion of that felt by family and friends.

A. Irony

Stanza 1 suggests that Roethke "startled," or nudged Jane into voicing her poetic talent. ? What defeat does Roethke face in stanza 4? (He cannot nudge her from this final sleep.)

Comment From The Poet

"There's a tendency today—more than a tendency, it's almost a conspiracy—to delimit poets, to restrict them to the political and the socially or racially conscious. . . . I can't imagine any poet worth his salt today not being aware of social evils, human needs. But I feel I have the right to deal with these matters in my own way, in terms of my own understanding of what a poet is. I resist whatever would force me into a role as politician, sociologist, or yeasayer to current ideologies."

Robert Hayden (1913–1980)

Photograph © 1988 by Jill Krementz.

Born and raised in a slum district of Detroit, Robert Hayden graduated from Wayne State University and received his M.A. from the University of Michigan. There, in Michigan, Hayden formed friendships with young poets of his own age. These friendships were based on shared poetic tastes and upon enthusiastic readings of the American and British writers who were united by anti-Fascist sentiment and by the political optimism that flourished until the outbreak of the Spanish Civil War in 1936. (The Spanish war made it clear that the emergent democracies in Europe would be opposed to the death by the military power of the old regimes.)

His university associations greatly enhanced Hayden's understanding of the poetic techniques developed in the early twentieth century and of the ways in which poetry could serve as the voice of political consciousness. But Hayden was unprepared for the eruption of the loosely joined poetry written by his younger black contemporaries who came to prominence in the racially troubled 1960's.

Hayden was as deeply committed to the same causes and to the same demands for equality and liberation as they were; but he was temperamentally unable to abandon the standards of the art of poetry as he understood them in order to transform his work into what he saw as propaganda, however righteously motivated. He was also reluctant to accept the notion that poetry by blacks should be judged only on the basis of its immediate impact and momentary relevance.

Hayden's career as a college teacher began at Fisk University in Tennessee and was crowned by his acceptance of a distinguished professorship at the University of Michigan—the same institution where, as a poor freshman, he lived in a segregated rooming house. His notable collections of verse include *Heart-Shape in the Dust* (1940); *The Lion and the Archer* (1948); *Figure of Time: Poems* (1955); *Words in the Mourning Time: Poems* (1970); and *The Night-Blooming Cereus* (1972). His style in these collections ranges from the strictly traditional form of the sonnet to the effective use of free verse in dramatic and narrative poems. Hayden was a member of the American Academy and Institute of Arts and Letters. Just before his death, he served as Consultant in Poetry to the Library of Congress, the first black poet ever to hold that position.

SUPPLEMENTARY SUPPORT MATERIALS

1. Review and Response Worksheet: Imagery (*CCB*)

2. Selection Test (*CCB*)

PREPARATION

ESTABLISHING A PURPOSE. If possible, play the song "Summertime" from *Porgy and Bess.* Ask students to consider the tone of the song. (Students will probably note that it is relaxed, even lazy.) Ask students, as they read, to consider the tone of Hayden's poem and to look for clues that reveal the speaker's attitude about his childhood experiences.

The title is part of the first line of a famous song from George Gershwin's and Du Bose Heyward's opera *Porgy and Bess* (1935). To complete the line, we add, "is easy," and so we have the touchstone of the poem—a statement combining irony with simple fact.

The substance of the poem is what "he [the poet] recalls." As a child in Detroit, Hayden lived in a black ghetto: not the Catfish Row of Charleston, South Carolina, the setting of the opera.

"Trees of heaven" (line 6) is a reference to the sumac trees that flourish even in the concrete and asphalt of crowded cities. "Mosaic eyes" (line 20) are the eyes of the Old Testament prophet and deliverer Moses. Jack Johnson (line 29) was the first black heavyweight boxing champion, a man who became rich and lived in the flamboyant high style identified with the "roaring twenties." If his limousine was not literally cut from a diamond, it was flashy enough to make people think of it as a dazzling jewel. "Ethiopia" in line 32 refers to a black homeland famous in history.

"Summertime and the Living . . ."

Nobody planted roses, he recalls,
A but sunflowers gangled° there sometimes,
tough-stalked and bold
and like the vivid children there unplanned.
There circus-poster horses curveted°
in trees of heaven
above the quarrels and shattered glass,
and he was bareback rider of them all.

No roses there in summer—
oh, never roses except when people died—
and no vacations for his elders,
so harshened after each unrelenting day
that they were shouting-angry.
B But summer was, they said, the poor folks' time
of year. And he remembers
how they would sit on broken steps amid

The fevered tossings of the dusk, the dark,
wafting hearsay with funeral-parlor fans
or making evening solemn by
their quietness. Feels their Mosaic eyes
C upon him, though the florist roses
that only sorrow could afford
long since have bidden them Godspeed.

Oh, summer summer summertime—

Then grim street preachers shook
their tambourines and Bibles in the face
of tolerant wickedness;
then Elks parades and big splendiferous
Jack Johnson in his diamond limousine
set the ghetto burgeoning
with fantasies
of Ethiopia spreading her gorgeous wings.

2. **gangled:** gathered, clustered.

5. **curveted:** leaped upward.

A. Imagery
Sunflowers, linked to the "vivid children," are hardy blooms that thrive in adverse conditions. Roses, associated with spiritual values and common in suburban gardens, are valued for their delicacy but are difficult to raise. One implication of the first line may be that the ghetto could not nourish the sensitive or spiritual in its youth—only boldness and toughness.

B. Imagery
? What does the image of folks sitting on "broken steps" suggest? (The image hints at their resignation and acceptance of the limitations of ghetto life.)

C. Metaphor
Moses, who led his people out of slavery in Egypt, never entered the Promised Land himself. ? How are the elders "Mosaic"? (Although they will never attain a "promised land" of equality and opportunity, their wisdom can guide the young.)

CLOSURE

Return to the questions of the poem's tone and the poet's attitude. Have individual students suggest words and phrases that describe the tone of the poem.

ANALYZING THE POEM

Identifying Details

1. Images include the sunflowers; children; the shattered glass; hard-working, quarrelsome adults who never vacation; and folks gossiping on the broken steps.
2. Roses are not planted in the ghetto (line 1); they appear only at funerals (lines 9–10); they can be afforded only in times of sorrow (lines 21–22).
3. He remembers the street preachers, parades, and the limousine.

Interpreting Meanings

4. The preacher's austerity contrasts with Jack Johnson's extravagance.
5. Both have "tough stalks," are "bold" and "unplanned."

(Answers continue in left-hand column.)

(Continued from top.)

6. "Delighted," the boy imagines himself as a bareback rider.

The poster suggests the exotic realm of the imagination, which contrasts with the drab realities of the ghetto.
7. It suggests the fertile power of the "fantasies." Although the ghetto is vastly different from Ethiopia, dreams of power, pomp, and dignity still inspire its residents.
8. Omission of the last words ("is easy") in Gershwin's song emphasizes the gap between the ghetto residents' dreams and reality.
9. The toughness, resilience, and optimism of stanza 1 is echoed by the proud vision of ancient Africa in the last stanza.

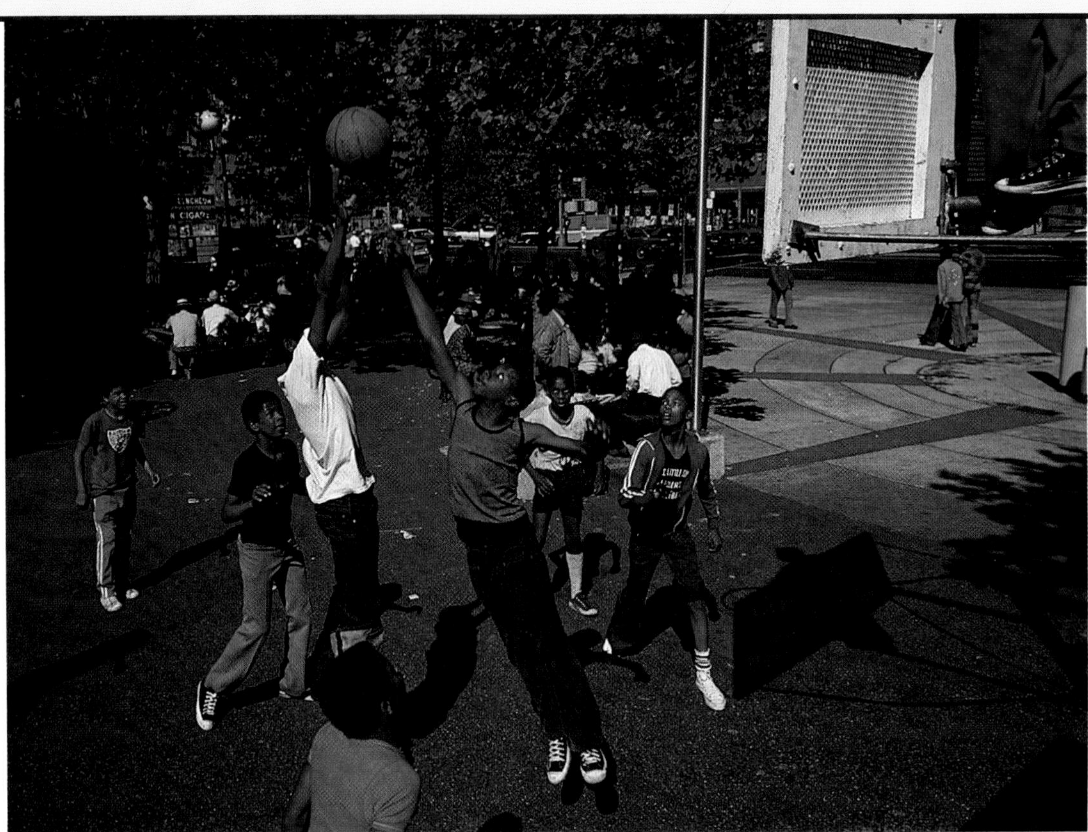

Responding to the Poem

Analyzing the Poem

Identifying Details

1. What **images** does the poet use in the first three stanzas to describe the ghetto of his youth?
2. Roses are mentioned three times in the poem. Identify these contexts, and explain what the speaker connects with roses in each instance.
3. What does the speaker remember in the last stanza?

Interpreting Meanings

4. What is the implied contrast between the "grim street preachers" (line 25) and Jack Johnson?
5. In the first stanza, what do the "sunflowers" (line 2) and the "vivid children" (line 4) have in common?
6. How did the boy react to the circus poster (line 5)? How does the **image** of the circus poster contrast with the boy's all-too-real setting?
7. "Burgeoning" (line 30) means "suddenly growing or developing." What does the use of this word in this context suggest?
8. In what way is the poem's title **ironic**?
9. How does the **tone** of the last five lines echo the tone of the first stanza?

Writing About the Poem

A Creative Response

1. **Giving an Oral Reading.** Find an instrumental recording of "Summertime." (It has been recorded by hundreds of performers.) Listen to it several times as you read Hayden's poem. Then prepare an oral reading for your class, using the recording as background music.

A Critical Response

2. **Analyzing the Poem.** It could be argued that "Summertime and the Living . . ." expresses mixed feelings about the poet's youth. In a brief essay, discuss the use of ambiguity in this poem, paying particular attention to the treatment of material and spiritual values.

A. Expansion
Bishop's early awareness of death and the shock of her mother's sudden lapses into mental illness inevitably affected Bishop's poetry. Helen Vendler finds in Bishop's poems a vibration "between two frequencies—the domestic and the strange." As Vendler points out, the security of the home is most threatened when "death intrudes on the domestic circle"—the situation viewed in "First Death in Nova Scotia" (page 1094) from the child's perspective. The child's attempts to understand the presence of the strange within the familiar may explain the inconsistencies in the poet's use of red as a symbol of domestic warmth and white as a sign of winter and death.

Elizabeth Bishop (1911–1979)

A "poet's poet," Elizabeth Bishop has been the acknowledged master of both the highest art and most meticulous craft for many of the important poets of her time. She has also been an unacknowledged inspiration for many others still trying to solve the mystery of her impenetrable simplicity.

Born in Worcester, Massachusetts, she spent her early years in a Nova Scotia village—a childhood marked by the early death of her father and darkened by the long illness of her mother. These circumstances, in effect, made her an orphan whose upbringing was entrusted to the care of relatives.

At the time of her mother's death in a psychiatric hospital, Bishop was a student at Vassar College. After graduation, she embarked on a career quietly devoted to poetry and, by means of a private income, to travels. During these travels, she discovered two places congenial enough to detain her for years—Key West and Rio de Janeiro. *Questions of Travel,* the title she gave to one of her last books, might serve as an index to the story of a life told in poems that are always "letters from abroad." In these poems, places, near or far, provide merely temporary settings for an endless inquiry into the nature of perception and reality. In 1956 her *Poems: North and South—A Cold Spring* was awarded the Pulitzer Prize.

In the final years of her life, Bishop lived on the Boston waterfront in an apartment on Lewis Wharf and spent her summers on an island off the coast of Maine. These changes of scene came about when her close friend Robert Lowell became ill and Harvard University invited her to take over the classes he had been scheduled to

teach. She continued to teach at Harvard until her death.

A shy woman with a taste for the exotic as well as a love of the ordinary, Bishop surrounded herself with artifacts acquired in the course of her travels. She conducted herself with a scrupulous conventionality much at odds with the audacity and profundity of her imagination. Her poems most truly reveal her character: a combination of the conservatism and moral rectitude associated with "the north" and the casual sensuousness and cheerfully untidy sprawl associated with nature and the everyday outdoor life of "the south." For Elizabeth Bishop, geography was less a matter of maps and place names than of states of mind and areas of feeling. B

B. Expansion
The use of geography and natural events to portray a state of mind is evident in "Little Exercise" (page 1096), which has been interpreted as a symbolic description of the poetic process—the way an idea "storms" the poet's mind. This perspective includes both meanings of "exercise." (See question 3, Analyzing Language and Style, page 1097.) The poem becomes both a "performance" that realistically captures a storm's progress and a symbolic record of the mental "exertion" involved in the creation of a poem. Such an interpretation resolves the poem's alternate images of the storm as violent and refreshing or gentle and the enigmatic final stanza where "someone"—perhaps the reader or an observer unaware of the poet's mental activity—is undisturbed by the storm.

SUPPLEMENTARY SUPPORT MATERIALS
1. Review and Response Worksheet: Tone *(CCB)*
2. Selection Test *(CCB)*

PREPARATION
PREREADING JOURNAL. Ask students to write briefly about something that bewildered them as a child—something adults did not adequately explain. Encourage them to capture all the details of their youthful understanding.

CLOSURE
Have students write two or three sentences, to be shared in class, that describe the effect that confronting death has on the child in this poem.

A. Humanities Connection: Discussing the Fine Art
Peter Blume (b. 1906) was born in Russia but immigrated to Brooklyn, New York, with his family in 1911. *Winter, New Hampshire* reflects a flat, almost one-dimensional quality that emphasizes the loneliness of the farms beneath the looming snowbanks and threatening sky. The lack of detail, skewed perspective, and use of dark against dark contrasted with white heightens the somber tone.

The death here is "first" only because it was the event in Elizabeth Bishop's childhood that first acquainted her with mortality.

If the setting (Nova Scotia) were not named in this poem's title, certain details might be puzzling. The "chromographs," or tinted photographs, of the British royal family indicate Canada's place in the British Empire at that time. "The Maple Leaf (Forever)" refers to the Canadian national anthem and to the image of a maple leaf on the Canadian flag. In a Nova Scotian parlor, a "stuffed loon"—or any other bird from the lakes or shores of the province—was a common decorative item.

In those days, people who had died were "laid out" at home—that is, their coffins were brought into the family parlor or living room, and for one to three days, members of the family and friends came to pay their last respects. Anyone who remembers this ritual from childhood knows that it is an occasion one never forgets.

First Death in Nova Scotia

A

Winter, New Hampshire by Peter Blume. Oil.

Courtesy, Museum of Fine Arts, Boston. Bequest of John Spaulding.

ANALYZING THE POEM

Identifying Details

1. The speaker describes the home funeral of a cousin, little Arthur.
2. The picture of British royalty, the loon, the marble table, the coffin like a cake, and the reference to Jack Frost.
3. The smallest page at court.

Interpreting Meanings

4. Both "I was lifted up" (line 24) and the references to a doll and Jack Frost suggest a child's perspective.
5. The loon is an image of a death as unnecessary and inexplicable as Arthur's.
6. The cold parlor, the frozen lake of marble, the cold breast of the loon, Jack Frost, and the roads deep in snow suggest the icy shock of the speaker.
7. The question underlines the child's muddled understanding of death as the end to life's options.
8. Answers will vary. Certainly the child-like detachment of the poem would give way to a tragic sense of personal loss.

A In the cold, cold parlor
my mother laid out Arthur
beneath the chromographs:
Edward, Prince of Wales,
with Princess Alexandra,
and King George with Queen Mary.
Below them on the table
stood a stuffed loon
shot and stuffed by Uncle
Arthur, Arthur's father.

Since Uncle Arthur fired
a bullet into him,
he hadn't said a word.
B He kept his own counsel
on his white, frozen lake,
the marble-topped table.
His breast was deep and white,
cold and caressable;
his eyes were red glass,
much to be desired.

"Come," said my mother,
"Come and say goodbye
C to your little cousin Arthur."
I was lifted up and given
one lily of the valley
to put in Arthur's hand.
Arthur's coffin was
a little frosted cake,
and the red-eyed loon eyed it
from his white, frozen lake.

Arthur was very small.
He was all white, like a doll
that hadn't been painted yet.
Jack Frost had started to paint him
the way he always painted
the Maple Leaf (Forever).
He had just begun on his hair,
a few red strokes, and then
Jack Frost had dropped the brush
and left him white, forever.

The gracious royal couples
were warm in red and ermine;
their feet were well wrapped up
in the ladies' ermine trains.
They invited Arthur to be
the smallest page at court.
But how could Arthur go,
clutching his tiny lily,
with his eyes shut up so tight
and the roads deep in snow?

A. Interpretation The extreme cold of the parlor introduces the first element of strangeness and of death. **?** Why is the parlor colder than usual? (Since the body was not embalmed, but "laid out" at home, the heat was turned off to prevent deterioration.)

B. Symbol The stuffed loon serves as a symbol of death and "strangeness made domestic." In some cultures, the loon's eerie, nocturnal cry is thought to be an omen of approaching death.

C. Theme **?** What efforts to "domesticate" the strangeness of death appear here? ("Saying goodbye" implies some kind of communication and lessens the finality of death; the aromatic lily and the clothing or coverings that make the coffin "a little frosted" cake disguise the less-appealing aspects of death.)

Responding to the Poem

Analyzing the Poem

Identifying Details

1. Describe the situation in the poem.
2. What **images** help you picture the parlor?
3. What does the speaker imagine the royal family has invited Arthur to be?

Interpreting Meanings

4. How can you tell that this poem is written from the perspective of a child?
5. What do you think the stuffed loon contributes to the meaning of this poem?
6. Find all the **images** in the poem that have to do with cold or snow. Why are they appropriate?
7. The poem ends with a **rhetorical question**—one that does not call for an answer. How does this question affect the emotional content of the poem?
8. Suppose the speaker in the poem were Arthur's mother. How would that change the **tone** of the poem? Are the sentiments in the poem appropriate to the person who is expressing them? Explain.

SUPPLEMENTARY SUPPORT MATERIALS
1. Review and Response Worksheet: Similes *(CCB)*
2. Selection Test *(CCB)*

PREPARATION

BUILDING ON PRIOR KNOWLEDGE. Ask students to define the term "brainstorming." Point out that, literally, this word suggests a storm of mental ideas, and direct students to think of how this image relates to Bishop's poem.

CLOSURE

Discuss the following question: If the storm represents the mental exercise of creating a poem, what does Bishop tell us about that process?

A. Symbol
? If the storm represents the poetic process as it affects the mind, what does the image of the growling dog suggest? (The poet does not choose to create the poem; instead the idea arises, growling and seeking a place to rest.)

B. Rhyme
? What words at the end of later lines rhyme with *keys*? (*Families* [line 6], *trees* [line 10], and *series* [line 16])

C. Interpretation
? How does this image of the refreshing rain relate to the creative process? (The poet may be suggesting that just as the storm relieves the broken sidewalk and refreshes the sea, so, too, the creation of the poem relieves the broken places of the spirit.)

Since the title of this poem gives us no indication as to what its subject is, we have to assume that it calls attention to the poet's method of composing her poem. This method might be described as taking notes and making observations about a thunderstorm. But you'll soon be aware that these are not the sort of eyewitness details we'd expect from a reporter. Instead, they amount to a series of little pictures in the poet's mind, pictures she would like us to think about.

Little Exercise

A Think of the storm roaming the sky uneasily
like a dog looking for a place to sleep in,
listen to it growling.

B Think how they must look now, the mangrove keys°
lying out there unresponsive to the lightning
in dark, coarse-fibered families,

where occasionally a heron may undo his head,
shake up his feathers, make an uncertain comment
when the surrounding water shines.

Think of the boulevard and the little palm trees
all stuck in rows, suddenly revealed
as fistfuls of limp fish-skeletons.

C It is raining here. The boulevard
and its broken sidewalks with weeds in every crack,
are relieved to be wet, the sea to be freshened.

Now the storm goes away again in a series
of small, badly lit battle-scenes,
each in "Another part of the field."°

Think of someone sleeping in the bottom of a rowboat
tied to a mangrove root or the pile of a bridge;
think of him as uninjured, barely disturbed.

4. **mangrove keys:** small islands created by dirt and other matter collecting around the roots of a mangrove tree, which grows in shallow waters.

18. **"Another . . . field":** a stage direction used in battle scenes of Shakespearean plays.

Responding to the Poem

Analyzing the Poem

Identifying Details

1. Geographically, where does the poem occur? Name the clues that support your sense of its locale.
2. The movement of the poem has much in common with that of a documentary movie. A series of quick shots, one after the other, tell a story in pictures. Describe the "shots" you see.
3. In a poem full of comparisons of one thing with another, two are full-fledged **similes.** Where are they?
4. What uses of **personification** can you identify in the poem?

Interpreting Meanings

5. The only human being in this poem is "someone" who does not make an appearance until the very end. Who might this person be? What might the poet want to

ANALYZING THE POEM
Identifying Details
1. Clues that the locale is tropical include the mangrove keys, the heron, and the palm trees; "keys" suggests Florida.
2. The storm gathers (stanza 1); the mangrove keys wait "unresponsive" (stanza 2); a heron shakes his feathers (stanza 3); the branches of palm trees are blown inside out (stanza 4); the rain hits the cracks in the sidewalk (stanza 5); the storm moves on with intermittent lightning and thunder (stanza 6); someone sleeps unaware in a boat (stanza 7).
3. Line 2: "like a dog . . ." and line 12: "as fistfuls of limp fish-skeletons."
4. Line 6: the mangrove keys in "families"; line 8: the heron's "comment"; lines 13–15: the boulevard is "relieved" and the sea is "freshened."

Interpreting Meanings
5. Answers will vary. The person might be the speaker. If the person is not the poet, then the act of creativity leaves him undisturbed.
6. See note B on page 1093 of this book.

A. Humanities Connection: Discussing the Fine Art
Winslow Homer (1836–1910) was the foremost figure of nineteenth-century naturalism. His individualistic style probably resulted from his lack of formal training. In 1883 he built a studio in Prout's Neck, Maine, where he painted his famous seascapes. *In a Florida Jungle* was one of many watercolors Homer produced on a three-month visit to the Tampa area. Philip Beam, a noted critic of Homer's work, comments: "From the very first the tropics made a tremendous impression on Homer. The brilliant sunshine brought out the richness of the vegetation and . . . outlined forms and masses and details with a clarity of definition he had never known before."

A

In a Florida Jungle by Winslow Homer (1886). Watercolor. Worcester Art Museum, Worcester, Massachusetts.

suggest by telling us to think of this person as "uninjured, barely disturbed"?

6. By calling her poem "Little Exercise," Elizabeth Bishop seems to make light of her verse, as though it were no more than a skillful assemblage of observations about a storm. But perhaps her lighthearted approach disguises deeper meanings. What might at least one of these meanings be?

Writing About the Poems

A Creative Response

1. **Imitating the Writer's Technique.** Write a series of notes of your own, or a poem, called "Little Exercise." Concentrate on a scene of action or a setting and write down at least five vivid images that you notice in it. Open with the words "Think of. . . ."

A Critical Response

2. **Comparing Poems.** Like Marianne Moore, Bishop creates her artistry from the accumulation of vivid details. Select one of Bishop's poems, and in a brief essay, compare and contrast her use of details with the method used by Marianne Moore in "The Steeple-Jack" (page 725).

Analyzing Language and Style

Multiple Meanings

Poets sometimes use a word with multiple meanings, intending to make us think about the two (or more) meanings at once.

1. What various meanings can the word *frosted* have? Can it have more than one meaning in line 28 of "First Death in Nova Scotia"?
2. What are the various meanings of *exercise*? Could more than one meaning apply to the title?
3. What meanings can the word *disturbed* have? In what sense or senses is the word used in the last line of "Little Exercise"?

A. Expansion
M. L. Rosenthal identifies one way in which Jarrell's awareness of the distance between "life and myths about life" affects his poetry. Rosenthal notes in many of Jarrell's poems a characteristic pattern: "a static initial state of sadness; then a phase of confusion that lets deeper depression flood into the poem; and then a final bitter thrust." Ask students to note how this pattern appears in "The Death of the Ball Turret Gunner" on the facing page.

B. Expansion
Older and far more aware of the brutalities of war than the young servicemen he trained, Jarrell felt tremendous empathy for their situation. The title of his volume *Little Friend, Little Friend* is based on details from the poem "2nd Air Force": A newspaper article tells of an incident over Germany in which a fighter pilot protecting his homeland radios an Allied bomber and says, "Little Friend, Little Friend. I got two engines on fire. Can you see me?" Aware of the fighter pilot's plea and weary of the senseless waste of war, the bomber disengages and radios back, "Let's go home."

Randall Jarrell (1914–1965)

One of the most careful and erudite readers of contemporary poetry, Randall Jarrell was, at the same time, both an abrasive critic and a generous promoter of the art.

Born in Nashville, Tennessee, Jarrell was brought up in California. His childhood experiences included close observation of the gaudy remnants of the "old" Hollywood, a personal acquaintance with the MGM lion, and an apprehension of the difference between fantasy and fact, between life and myths about life, that would provide him with themes for poetry for years to come. [A]

After graduating from Vanderbilt University in his native city, Jarrell began a career that led to membership in the English departments of many colleges and universities, from Texas to New York. In 1942, he joined the Army Air Corps, served for a time as a pilot and then, for a longer time, as Celestial Navigation Trainer of pilots assigned to fly the famous B-29 bombers of World War II. Out of this experience came two notable books of poetry, *Little Friend, Little Friend* (1945) and *Losses* (1948). In the regard of many critics, these books have not been surpassed as American contributions to the literature of World War II. [B]

A man of extraordinary wit, Jarrell gave full play to his gifts in his often caustic and devastating critical articles and essays, particularly in *A Sad Heart at the Supermarket* (1962). In poetry, however, his faculty for contemptuous criticism is kept under wraps. His wit shows itself only in mellow good humor ("I feel like the

first men who read Wordsworth. / It's so simple I can't understand it.") and in a resigned toleration of the more absurd aspects of American life.

Struck by a car while walking on a North Carolina highway in 1965, Jarrell's tragic death raised some questions. But of his loss to American letters and to the poets who had counted upon him to explain, judge, and celebrate their art, there was no question at all.

SUPPLEMENTARY SUPPORT MATERIALS
1. Review and Response Worksheet: Point of View *(CCB)*
2. Selection Test *(CCB)*

PREPARATION
ESTABLISHING A PURPOSE. Discuss Jarrell's comments under Primary Sources (page 1095) before turning to the poem.

CLOSURE
Ask students, working in small groups, to write a short paraphrase.

A. Interpretation
? What do the contrasting phrases "dream of life" and "nightmare fighters" suggest? (The first phrase suggests the dreamy innocence and stability the young soldier felt at home, "in his mother's sleep"; the second phrase implies a harsh initiation into brutal realities of war: danger, violence, lack of concern for the individual.)

These five lines make up the most famous poem to come out of World War II. Jarrell describes the "ball turret" in his comment at the bottom of the page.

The Death of the Ball Turret Gunner

From my mother's sleep I fell into the State,
And I hunched in its belly till my wet fur froze.
Six miles from earth, loosed from its dream of life,
I woke to black flak and the nightmare fighters.
When I died they washed me out of the turret with a hose.

Responding to the Poem

Analyzing the Poem

Responding to Details

1. What is the temperature like in the ball turret?
2. How far from earth does the bomber ascend? What happens at that altitude?
3. What happens to the gunner?

Interpreting Meanings

4. "Belly" here can be read on two levels. What two bellies could the speaker be talking about? How is the ball turret like a womb?
5. How do you know that the speaker didn't enter the army as a result of a rational decision?
6. What is the speaker's "wet fur"? Why do you think he compares himself to an animal?
7. How does the grisly process described in the final line fit in with the rest of the poem?
8. While the speaker is not around to receive a medal, he *is* a hero. Why do you think he shows no awareness of that fact?
9. What, in the long run, is this poem about? Is it about political dissent? Is it a statement about the way things in the world are regimented and mechanized? Is it about the destruction of the innocent?

Writing About the Poem

A Creative Response

Writing from Another Point of View. Find a newspaper article about someone who has died. Then write a paragraph or a short poem from the imagined point of view of the dead person. Imitate, as closely as you can, the style of "The Death of the Ball Turret Gunner."

Primary Sources
The Ball Turret

"A ball turret was a plexiglass sphere set into the belly of a B-17 or B-24, and inhabited by two .50 caliber machine guns and one man, a short small man. When this gunner tracked with his machine guns a fighter attacking his bomber from below, he revolved with the turret; hunched upsidedown in his little sphere, he looked like the fetus in the womb. The fighters which attacked him were armed with cannon firing explosive shells. The hose was a steam hose."

—Randall Jarrell

ANALYZING THE POEM
Identifying Details
1. It is very cold.
2. It ascends six miles; the gunner's sweat freezes inside his fleece-lined jacket.
3. He is fatally wounded by flak from enemy planes.

Interpreting Meanings
4. It suggests both a part of the plane and a mother's womb—like a womb, the turret surrounds the gunner.
5. "I fell" (line 1) implies he was drafted or blundered into military service.
6. The "wet fur," or the sweat-soaked lining of the pilot's jacket, obliquely indicates the fear, powerlessness, and dependence on instinct of an animal.
7. It reinforces the indifference of the world to an individual death.
8. He is dead; a medal would not bring him back.
9. Answers will vary. Some students may consider it to be about abortion.

A. Expansion
Although it is an early work, "De Witt Williams" (page 1101) reflects the poet's interest in African American speech and culture. In fact, in 1962 when Oscar Brown, Jr., set the poem to music and recorded it as "Elegy for a Plain Black Boy," several radio stations refused to play the song. The ban centered on the phrase "plain black boy," with its echo of a time when all African American adult males were "boys," a pejorative label that denied their manhood. Brook's response to the ban, "A Defense of Elegy," is an eloquent explanation of the poem and defense of the word *black,* which was then seen in as a derogatory variation of *Negro.*

B. Expansion (Less Challenging)
Students will have little difficulty reading the novel *Maud Martha* independently. It is a simple, but touchingly honest portrayal of a young girl's initiation into both adulthood and the prejudiced American society of the 1950's.

Gwendolyn Brooks (1917–)

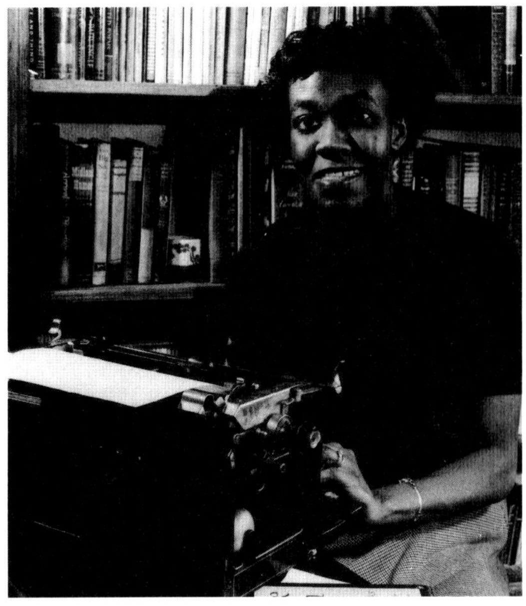

Gwendolyn Brooks established her credentials early, in two volumes of poetry (one of which was awarded the Pulitzer Prize in 1949) that demonstrated her skill in the conventional poetic forms. After this, Brooks began to turn to more open forms and to a more extensive use of common speech. This transition was sparked by two developments. One was the insistence of young black poets that their poetry should not only reflect their own special experience, but that it should also be based in the speech rhythms and the vernacular of urban black culture. The other development was the expansion of black consciousness and black power in the embattled years of the 1950's and 1960's, when the triumphs of the civil rights movement gave new cohesion and pride to the followers of Martin Luther King, Jr.

Kansas-born, Gwendolyn Brooks grew up in Chicago and has been identified with that city and its enormous black community for most of her life. Much honored by her city and her state, she has won an illustrious place in both. Brooks has been honored not only because of her literary achievements, but also because of her efforts in behalf of young black writers, to whom she has given practical advice and encouragement. For many of these young writers, Brooks, in her role as teacher and editor, has opened doors to self-realization and to professional careers.

Brooks's works include the short novel *Maud Martha* (1953), an autobiographical work called *Report from Part One* (1972), and her poetry, collected in books called *Annie Allen* (1949) and *Family Pictures* (1970).

SUPPLEMENTARY SUPPORT MATERIALS
1. Review and Response Worksheet: Irony (*CCB*)
2. Selection Test (*CCB*)

PREPARATION
BUILDING ON PRIOR KNOWLEDGE. Review what students know about "Swing Low, Sweet Chariot" and spirituals in general. The spiritual Brooks uses is based on the prophet Elijah's transport to heaven in a flaming chariot shortly after parting the Jordan River, the boundary of the Promised Land (2 Kings 2:7–11).

CLOSURE
Have students write a sentence or two, to be shared in class, describing De Witt Williams's life.

With borrowings from the spiritual "Swing Low, Sweet Chariot," Gwendolyn Brooks writes a poem that also has the rhythm of a song. Part of this rhythm is due to her use of the trochee—a metrical foot in which an accented syllable is followed by one that is not accented. From the title, we know that De Witt Williams is dead. Although the poem provides few details, we are nevertheless asked to imagine what the life of this "plain black boy" was like. "The L" refers to Chicago's elevated railway. "Forty-seventh Street" and "Northwest Corner, Prairie" are part of the south side. You should read the poem aloud.

Of De Witt Williams on His Way to Lincoln Cemetery

He was born in Alabama.
He was bred in Illinois.

He was nothing but a
Plain black boy.

Swing low swing low sweet sweet chariot.
Nothing but a plain black boy.

Drive him past the Pool Hall.
Drive him past the Show.
Blind within his casket,
But maybe he will know.

Down through Forty-seventh Street:
Underneath the L,
And Northwest Corner, Prairie,
That he loved so well.

Don't forget the Dance Halls—
Warwick and Savoy,
Where he picked his women, where
He drank his liquid joy.

Born in Alabama.
Bred in Illinois.
He was nothing but a
Plain black boy.

Swing low swing low sweet sweet chariot.
Nothing but a plain black boy.

Responding to the Poem

Analyzing the Poem

Interpreting Meanings

1. On the basis of the details given about the route of his funeral procession, how would you characterize De Witt Williams?
2. What is the effect of the word "maybe" in line 10?
3. With a background so humble, why do you think De Witt Williams is important enough to be the inspiration for a poem?
4. "De Witt" and "Lincoln" are both prominent names in American history. Do you think the poet wants us to accept them as merely incidental facts? Or do you think she intends a touch of **irony** here?
5. How would you describe the **tone** of this elegy?

Writing About the Poem

A Creative Response

Preparing a Choral Reading. Get together with two or more classmates. Plan and rehearse a reading of the poem that alternates between single and multiple voices. Then perform the reading for the class. If you were to have background music for the recitation, what music would you choose?

ANALYZING THE POEM
Interpreting Meanings
1. The pool hall, show, dance halls, and references to picking his women and drinking imply that De Witt valued entertainment and pleasure.
2. It might suggest religious faith, or doubt.
3. He's an example of a life wasted in the ghetto.
4. Surely she intends the irony. Lincoln signed the Emancipation Proclamation and De Witt Clinton was an early abolitionist. If anyone doubts the significance of the name, have them try the name John Doe instead. (There's a lot of hope invested in a name like De Witt.)
5. Answers will vary, but should include the perception of sorrow for a wasted life.

For Further Reading For The Student

The short poem "Children of the Light" from *Lord Weary's Castle* (1946) deals with themes similar to those in "For the Union Dead" and would be an appropriate work for class study. An excellent commentary on the poem appears in *Crowell's Handbook of Contemporary American Poetry* by Karl Malkoff (Thomas Crowell Co., 1973).

A. Expansion
New Criticism, which emphasizes close reading and concentration on the text itself rather than historical or biographical factors, took its name from John Crowe Ransom's book *The New Criticism* (1941). Cleanth Brooks and Robert Penn Warren's *Understanding Poetry* (1938) demonstrated the techniques of New Criticism. The movement views literature not as entertainment or propaganda, but as a form of knowledge with a "language" of its own that communicates truths not conveyed by areas such as history, philosophy, or science.

Robert Lowell (1917–1977)

Of all the poets who came to maturity in the years immediately after World War II, none displayed greater ability or exerted more influence than Robert Lowell. From virtually the beginning of his career, Lowell was a central figure in American poetry, earning the admiration of his peers and the recognition of the literary establishment. His first published volume, *Lord Weary's Castle,* won the Pulitzer Prize in 1946; from then until his death more than thirty years later, he was a major figure in modern literature.

Lowell was born into an aristocratic Boston family whose ancestors went back to the *Mayflower.* Among them were well-known ministers, judges, politicians, educators, and literary figures. Nineteenth-century poet James Russell Lowell (page 167) was his great-uncle; Amy Lowell, the poet who helped promote the cause of Imagism (page 706), was his cousin.

This rich heritage was both blessing and burden to Lowell. He grew up with American history in his veins. "In some ways you are the luckiest poet I know!" his friend Elizabeth Bishop once wrote to Lowell, explaining that in writing about his family he was also automatically writing about American history. "All you have to do is put down the names," she said. At the same time, though, his family's conservative, traditional, Beacon Hill background was suffocating to the young poet. Much of Lowell's adolescence and early adulthood consisted of rebellious acts intended to carve out his own identity as an individual and as a poet.

One early act of rebellion against his family was to leave Harvard after two years and transfer to Kenyon College in Ohio, where poet John Crowe Ransom (page 672) was teaching. The summer before he enrolled at Kenyon, Lowell lived in a tent on poet Allen Tate's lawn in Nashville, Tennessee, soaking up all he could learn from Tate about writing poetry. Tate and Ransom were both supporters of what was
A called the New Criticism. They admired (and wrote) densely packed, "formal, difficult poems," as Lowell later put it, and Lowell also began writing in this manner.

He graduated from Kenyon in 1940, married novelist Jean Stafford, and started what would be a distinguished career of teaching and writing. A year later, in what was at least partially another rebellious act against his family's Protestant roots, he converted to Roman Catholicism.

In the early days of World War II, Lowell tried to enlist in the Navy several times, but was rejected for his poor eyesight. By 1943, appalled at the destruction caused by American bombing in Europe, he refused induction into the Army and was sentenced to prison for a year and a day. "I was a fire-breathing Catholic C.O. [conscientious objector]," he later wrote in a poem called "Memories of West Street and Lepke," "and made my manic statement, / telling off the state and president."

The poems that emerged from this period, in volumes like *Land of Unlikeness, Lord Weary's Castle,* and *The Mills of the Kavanaughs,* were tight, formal, and intellectually challenging. They often combined a dark view of American history with symbols drawn from Catholic doctrine, and they usually presented a grim vision of a world about to end. Their complex diction and many-leveled puns sometimes obscured their meaning. When *Lord Weary's Castle* was published, the Boston *Globe* exclaimed that Lowell was the "most promising poet in a hundred years." But his own father was quoted in the same article as saying, "Poets seem to see more in his work than most other people." That was also true.

Lowell had great natural ability, but he also revised and rewrote obsessively, often going through twenty or thirty drafts of a poem before he was happy with it.

In the 1950's, Lowell's style and subject matter gradually changed, although he never gave up his habit of endlessly revising his work. At poetry readings with writers like Allen Ginsberg, whose loose, freewheeling style was instantly communicable to audiences, Lowell began simplifying some of his own poems as he read them. "I'd make little changes just impromptu," he later said. "I began to have a certain disrespect for the tight forms. If you could make it easier just by changing syllables, then why not?" As a result, Lowell began consciously writing a looser, freer verse. Paradoxically, writing more formally was more natural for Lowell, and he would thus often "translate" tight, rhymed couplets into free verse as he revised.

Lowell's subject matter in these poems became more personal than in his earlier work. All of his life, he suffered great bouts of mental instability, and, until medication succeeded in stabilizing his condition, he sometimes had to be hospitalized. In these poems, which were eventually published together with a prose memoir in *Life Studies* (1959), Lowell wrote frankly about his situation as a "Mayflower screwball." His tone was not self-pitying or self-indulgent. Instead, he usually described his suffering with light irony intended to keep things in perspective. "What use is my sense of humor?" he asked in "Waking in the Blue," a poem about a period he spent in a psychiatric hospital. The implicit answer was that his sense of humor helped him to tolerate a painful situation.

Life Studies was one of the most influential works of poetry written after World War II. It helped to make acceptable the highly personal poetry being written by a number of younger poets, many of whom were Lowell's students: Sylvia Plath (page 1119) and Anne Sexton (page 1122). These poets, along with others such as John Berryman (page 1124), are sometimes referred to as "confessional poets" because of the intimate details in their poems.

In the 1960's, Lowell became more and more of a public figure. Like many writers of the time, he expressed opposition to the war in Vietnam in his writing and speeches, and, on one well-publicized occasion, he refused an invitation to participate in a White House Festival of the Arts. His poetry of this period remained personal, and he wrote a great many unrhymed sonnets, first published as *Notebooks* in 1969 and then in revised form as *History* in 1973. In addition to poetry, Lowell wrote a number of well-received dramas during this period, most notably *The Old Glory* (1965), which adapted stories by Herman Melville and Nathaniel Hawthorne.

In 1977, returning to New York from London, he died of a heart attack in a taxi coming from the airport.

Five Pulitzer-Prize winners honor the late Randall Jarrell in 1966 at Yale University. From left: Robert Penn Warren, Robert Lowell, Mrs. Jarrell, John Berryman, Stanley Kunitz, and Richard Wilbur.

A. Expansion
While many of the poems in *Life Studies* have an autobiographical element, Lowell commented: "They're not always factually true. There's a good deal of tinkering with fact. You leave out a lot, and emphasize this and not that. Your actual experience is a complete flux. I've invented facts and changed things. . . . So there's a lot of artistry, I hope, in the poems."

B. Expansion
"For the Union Dead" first appeared in print at the end of the paperback version of *Life Studies* and was originally titled "Colonel Shaw and the Massachusetts' 54th." The 54th was the subject of the movie *Glory* (1989).

C. Connections
Lowell's refusal of a White House dinner invitation from President Johnson and his participation in the march on the Pentagon are recorded in Norman Mailer's fictionalized history *Armies of the Night* (1968).

PREPARATION

ESTABLISHING A PURPOSE. Have students follow the text of the poem as they listen to the reading on the accompanying audiocassette. As they listen a second time, have them compile a list of questions to be answered when they read the poem on their own.

SUPPLEMENTARY SUPPORT MATERIALS

1. Review and Response Worksheet: Metaphor (*CCB*)
2. Selection Test (*CCB*)
3. Audiocassette recording

A. Symbolism
Some critics see the aquarium as a symbol for the Union—our nation in the past.
? How is an aquarium like a political body? (It is a contained space, with boundaries, that allows some freedom. The glass walls and light, like the tenets of free speech and voting, enable observation and evaluation of the inhabitants' behavior.)

B. Interpretation
? What does this metaphor suggest? (The abandoned aquarium, like the Union, is barren—a wasteland of sand.)

C. Symbol
? What is implied by the contrast between fish and dinosaurs? (Fish, one of the oldest forms of life, adapted to change and survived. Dinosaurs, a less-sophisticated form of life, inexplicably became extinct.)

"They gave up everything to serve the Republic," says the Latin inscription preceding this poem. "They" are all the Union soldiers who served during the Civil War. But, more specifically, "they" are the members of the first regiment of black soldiers from a free state, in this case Massachusetts. Under a white commander, Robert Gould Shaw, this regiment stormed Fort Wagner, South Carolina, in an assault resulting in many deaths, including that of the commander himself.

The subject of the poem is not that event, however, but its memorial—the bronze monument by the great sculptor Augustus Saint-Gaudens, which stands in Boston Common, the park directly across from the State House.

Today, Boston has a new aquarium that is a major tourist attraction. In 1959, when "For the Union Dead" was written, an older aquarium in South Boston—empty, deserted, and dilapidated—provided just the right image to set up the relationship between past and present.

Because this is a difficult poem, you should read it at least twice. A comment follows the poem.

For the Union Dead

"Relinquunt Omnia Servare Rem Publicam."

A The old South Boston Aquarium stands
B in a Sahara of snow now. Its broken windows are boarded.
The bronze weathervane cod has lost half its scales.
The airy tanks are dry.

Once my nose crawled like a snail on the glass;
my hand tingled
to burst the bubbles
drifting from the noses of the cowed, compliant fish.

My hand draws back. I often sigh still
for the dark downward and vegetating kingdom
of the fish and reptile. One morning last March,
I pressed against the new barbed and galvanized
C fence on the Boston Common. Behind their cage,
yellow dinosaur steam shovels were grunting
as they cropped up tons of mush and grass
to gouge their underworld garage.

Parking spaces luxuriate like civic
sand piles in the heart of Boston.
A girdle of orange, Puritan-pumpkin colored girders
braces the tingling Statehouse,

shaking over the excavations, as it faces Colonel Shaw
and his bell-cheeked Negro infantry
on St. Gaudens' shaking Civil War relief,
propped by a plank splint against the garage's earthquake.

Two months after marching through Boston,
half the regiment was dead;
at the dedication,
William James could almost hear the bronze Negroes breathe.

CLOSURE

The poem is so rich with implication that closure may be difficult. You might divide the class into groups and ask each to formulate two still unanswered questions. After students have read A Comment on the Poem, page 1106, especially the first paragraph, have them consider the remaining questions in class discussion.

Their monument sticks like a fishbone
in the city's throat.
Its Colonel is as lean
as a compass-needle.

He has an angry wrenlike vigilance,
a greyhound's gentle tautness;
he seems to wince at pleasure,
and suffocate for privacy.

A He is out of bounds now. He rejoices in man's lovely,
peculiar power to choose life and die—
when he leads his black soldiers to death,
he cannot bend his back.

On a thousand small town New England greens,
the old white churches hold their air
B of sparse, sincere rebellion; frayed flags
quilt the graveyards of the Grand Army of the Republic.

C The stone statues of the abstract Union Soldier
grow slimmer and younger each year—
wasp-waisted, they doze over muskets
and muse through their sideburns . . .

Shaw's father wanted no monument
except the ditch,
where his son's body was thrown
and lost with his "niggers."

The ditch is nearer.
There are no statues for the last war° here;
on Boylston Street, a commercial photograph
D shows Hiroshima boiling

over a Mosler Safe, the "Rock of Ages"
that survived the blast. Space is nearer.
When I crouch to my television set,
the drained faces of Negro schoolchildren rise like balloons.

Colonel Shaw
is riding on his bubble,
he waits
for the blessḗd break.

The Aquarium *is* gone. Everywhere,
giant finned cars nose forward like fish;
a savage servility
slides by on grease.

---

54. **the last war:** that is, World War II.

A. Interpretation
? What is the "peculiar power"? (Lowell seems to refer to man's ability to risk death to protect important values.)

B. Word Choice
? What does the word *frayed* suggest? (The values and heroism that shaped the nation are worn-out.)

C. Expansion
These monuments, carved out of the sandstone and limestone used in the nineteenth century, literally did wear away.

D. Symbol/Irony
? What "monument" to World War II does Lowell describe? (An advertisement, or monument to materialism, for Mosler safes.)

ANALYZING THE POEM
Identifying Details

1. The aquarium is said to be standing in a Sahara of snow; it has broken and boarded windows; the airy tanks are dry.

2. The speaker says that he pressed against a barbed and galvanized fence on the Boston Common, where he saw yellow steam shovels that looked like dinosaurs gouging up earth to construct an underground parking garage.

The steam shovels are compared to yellow dinosaurs.

3. The monument is described as "shaking"; it is made of bronze figures.

The colonel is compared with a compass-needle (line 32), an angry wren (line 33), and a taut greyhound (line 34).

4. They remind the speaker of quilts.

5. Half the regiment was dead two months after marching through Boston (lines 25–26): the body of the colonel and the bodies of his troops were thrown into the ditch (lines 50–52).

6. The luxury automobiles that "glide by" are compared to "fish" (line 66), reminding us of the fish in the old aquarium.

A. Humanities Connection: Discussing the Fine Art
Augustus Saint-Gaudens (1848–1907) was the most noted American sculptor of the nineteenth century. He was born in Dublin, Ireland, to French parents who immigrated to the United States when he was an infant. For nearly ten years, he studied in Paris, Florence, and Rome. In addition to the Shaw Memorial, he crafted two memorials to Lincoln. (Other Saint-Gaudens works appear on pages 1 and 356.)

A Comment on the Poem

A good poem can withstand anything said about it, whether it is interpretation or criticism. Understanding "For the Union Dead" depends upon the knowledge the reader brings to it as much as it depends upon what the poem itself offers. After you read this poem, you should try to paraphrase it, in order to clarify some of its references and allusions and to open possibilities of interpretation. When your paraphrase ends, the poem will not. Instead, it will invite you to go back to the first line and, newly equipped, begin an emotional and intellectual adventure. Looking at the ruined aquarium on its desert of snow, the poet remembers how, as a child, he used to press his nose right up against the glass of the great fish tanks; he recalls how his hand itched to get inside the tanks and play with the rising bubbles and all the marvelous sea-creatures that swam in them. But he is no longer a child. He draws back his hand, even though something in his nature still hungers to explore another order of life—that subconscious region where all beings in the "vegetating kingdom" had their beginnings.

The grown man won't press his nose against the glass. Instead, he presses himself against the fence that makes a "cage" in which steam shovels are gouging out space for an underground parking garage. The tremors of excavation work are so thunderous that both the State House and the bronze monument facing it have to be braced for protection. The jeopardy in which "progress" has placed both State House and monument brings the poet's central subject—the black regiment—into focus.

Having paraded through Boston as heroes on their way to the battlefield, half of these soldiers were dead within two months. When the monument to them was dedicated in 1897, the memory of these men was so much alive, and their faces and figures so faithfully rendered in bronze, that the great American psychologist William James felt that they almost breathed.

But now the poet observes that the monument "sticks like a fishbone in the city's throat," meaning that it is an irritant. Ironically, Boston is not only the city where the abolitionist movement was stronger than anywhere else; it is also, like many places in the United States, a place where racism has persisted. The poet compares Colonel Shaw, the regiment's leader, to the needle on a compass; this characterization suggests that Shaw pointed the way, a way in which whites and blacks united might become part of a nation's most honorable history.

Then follows a more detailed description of Colonel Shaw, in which certain features are regarded as evidence of a great character. This makes him "out of bounds" in a time and place where his special kind of vision and integrity are conspicuously lacking.

Then, instantaneously, like a change of scene in a movie, the poet's eye suddenly "pans" over the New England landscape (line 41). Churches on village greens remind him of the Revolutionary War; cemeteries with their "quilt" of ragged flags recall the Civil War; the young soldiers of the Union, "stone statues" all alike, remain young and slim as their nation grows older and fatter.

A

Robert Gould Shaw Memorial by Augustus Saint-Gaudens (1894–1897). Bronze.

Boston Common, Boston, Massachusetts.

Colonel Shaw's father, we learn, felt that the monument to his son was unnecessary; people had only to remember the ditch where the young commander's body was thrown with those of his soldiers. "The ditch," that common boneyard of blacks and whites, "is nearer," says the poet. Why? Because nuclear holocaust threatens a world more preoccupied with sales and profits than with its own survival. The annihilation of the Japanese city of Hiroshima by an atom bomb is used by the manufacturers of Mosler Safes to hustle their product. An advertisement shows the safe's "survival factor," and even compares it with the "Rock of Ages," or the cross of Christ.

The bubbles that rose in the fish tanks of the old aquarium return at the end of the poem. They are now "balloons" which the poet compares to the "drained faces" of black youngsters. They also appear as the buried dream of Colonel Shaw which, like a bubble, may still "break" when idealism explodes into reality.

The old aquarium and everything it stood for in the speaker's childhood imagination no longer exist. "Finned" luxury cars now "slide by," just as the marvelous fish once glided through the bubbly depths of their tanks. To the speaker, the chrome-laden automobiles represent a "savage servility." They move "on grease," the byproduct of the oil that supplies the modern world's energy, and the end-product and sludgy residue of the world's great power.

Interpreting Meanings

7. Lowell seems to mean that only in man is found the reasoning power that can choose either life or death.

8. This reference probably refers to the lengthy crisis sparked by the desegregation of the Boston city schools in the 1950's and 1960's. Similar crises occurred in other American cities.

9. Student answers will vary. The phrase might imply a materialism (symbolized by the luxurious, showy cars) which the speaker regards as savage or barbaric. "Servility" would thus be a reference to the modern world's worship of money. The word "grease" is appropriate in the context of cars and machines—it also may connote flattery and dishonesty as means to achieve wealth, as in "greasing someone's palm" (bribery).

10. Students may point out that *union* could be used as an adjective—the meaning of the title would thus be "the dead who served the Union." But if *union* is used as a noun, and *dead* as an adjective, the meaning changes; read this way, the title implies that our nation, preserved at such price by the likes of Colonel Shaw and his men, had died a spiritual death in the modern world.

11. Student answers will vary. Many students will agree that Lowell's tone is mixed, in that he seems to be ironic, nostalgic, *and* sarcastic about life in his city.

Responding to the Poem

Analyzing the Poem

Identifying Details

1. What **images** describe the old South Boston Aquarium?
2. What **images** describe what the speaker saw on Boston Common? What **metaphor** describes the steam shovels?
3. What **images** describe the St. Gaudens monument? How many things is the colonel compared with?
4. What do the frayed flags in the graveyards remind the speaker of?
5. What details tell you what happened to Colonel Shaw and his men?
6. What **image** in the last stanza reminds us of the scene described in the second stanza?

Interpreting Meanings

7. What does the poet mean by saying Colonel Shaw "rejoices in man's lovely, / peculiar power to choose life and die" (lines 37–38)?
8. What historical events in Boston and other American cities might the poet be referring to with the mention of the "drained faces" of black children on television (line 60)?
9. What do you think is the "savage servility" mentioned in the last stanza?
10. Explain how the title of the poem could have at least two meanings.
11. How does the speaker feel about what he sees in his city? How would you describe the poem's **tone**: Is it ironic, nostalgic, or sarcastic? Explain.

Writing About the Poem

A Creative Response

1. **Writing a Description.** Choose a building, preferably an old one that you have seen often. Write a paragraph or a short poem describing the building as it is now, and as it once was. Does the change in the building reflect a wider change in society, or in your town?

A Critical Response

2. **Comparing and Contrasting Poems.** In 1867, Henry Timrod (1828–1867) wrote the following poem for the commemoration of the graves of the Confederate dead at Magnolia Cemetery in Charleston, South Carolina. In an essay, explain how this poem is like or unlike Lowell's in terms of (a) **theme** or **message,** (b) **tone,** (c) **diction,** and (d) **form.**

Ode on the Confederate Dead

SUNG AT THE OCCASION OF DECORATING THE GRAVES AT MAGNOLIA CEMETERY, CHARLESTON, S.C., 1867

Sleep sweetly in your humble graves,
  Sleep, martyrs of a fallen cause;
Though yet no marble column craves
  The pilgrim here to pause.

In seeds of laurel in the earth
  The blossom of your fame is blown,
And somewhere, waiting for its birth,
  The shaft is in the stone!°

Meanwhile, behalf the tardy years
  Which keep in trust your storied tombs,
Behold! your sisters bring their tears,
  And these memorial blooms.

Small tributes! but your shades will smile
  More proudly on these wreaths today,
Than when some cannon-molded pile
  Shall overlook this bay.

Stoop, angels, hither from the skies!
  There is no holier spot of ground
Than where defeated valor lies,
  By mourning beauty crowned!

---

8. An allusion to the Arthurian legend. Arthur proved he was the rightful king by pulling a sword out of a stone.

Richard Wilbur (1921–   )

New York City was his birthplace, but Richard Wilbur grew up in suburban New Jersey. He attended Amherst College in Massachusetts, served with combat troops in Europe during World War II, and went to graduate school at Harvard. There he prepared for the illustrious teaching career that has taken him to long-term appointments at Wellesley, Wesleyan (Connecticut), and Smith.

From the moment his first book, *The Beautiful Changes* (1947), arrived on the poetic scene, Wilbur was recognized as the most graceful and technically adept poet in the younger generation. His poetry is reminiscent of the meters and natural speech of Robert Frost and of the metaphysical elegance and emotional reticence of Wallace Stevens.

But the influences of Frost and Stevens are merely overtones. Wilbur's poetic character is forged of his own unassertive religious devotion, his political liberalism, and his irrepressible delight in "the things of this world." Wilbur writes at a time when poetry has often been marked by self-exploitation and formlessness, as well as by uneasy borrowings from the paintings of minimalists and surrealists. But Wilbur has continued to write lyrics demanding scrupulous care and skill. His inward vision of delight finds expression in measured speech and indelible metaphor.

Wilbur's famous English translation of Moliere's comedy *The Misanthrope* has been followed in recent years by other translations from the great French playwright.

When Wilbur is not embarked on reading tours that take him across the breadth of the continent, he divides his time between Cummington, Massachusetts, the Berkshire village where he lives within a stone's throw of the homestead of William Cullen Bryant, and Key West, Florida. There his house is almost adjacent to the residences of his fellow poets John Ciardi and James Merrill.

Wilbur's collection *Things of This World* (1956) won the Pulitzer Prize and the National Book Award. In 1987 he was named America's Poet Laureate.

SUPPLEMENTARY SUPPORT MATERIALS
1. Review and Response Worksheet: Imagery (*CCB*)
2. Selection Test (*CCB*)
3. Audiocassette recording

PREPARATION
ESTABLISHING A PURPOSE. Before students read the poem, consider all possible meanings of the title and discuss the use of ambiguity in poetry. (See question 5 below.)

CLOSURE
Have individual students give brief oral paraphrases of the poem.

This title presents us with an ambiguity: Does it mean that our idea of what is beautiful is subject to change? Or does it suggest that the poem is about changes, or with beautiful transformations? As we learn almost at once, the poem erases these distinctions by uniting them: The beautiful *does* change, and changes can be beautiful.

"Queen Anne's Lace" is a common weed. Its flower looks like a crocheted doily with a tiny ruby at its center. "Lucernes" is a reference to the glacier-fed Alpine *Lac Lucerne* in Switzerland.

The Beautiful Changes

One wading a Fall meadow finds on all sides
The Queen Anne's Lace lying like lilies
On water; it glides
So from the walker, it turns
Dry grass to a lake, as the slightest shade of
you
Valleys my mind in fabulous blue Lucernes.

The beautiful changes as a forest is changed
By a chameleon's tuning his skin to it;
As a mantis, arranged
On a green leaf, grows
Into it, makes the leaf leafier, and proves
Any greenness is deeper than anyone knows.

Your hands hold roses always in a way that
says
They are not only yours; the beautiful
changes
In such kind ways,
Wishing ever to sunder
Things and things' selves for a second finding,
to lose
For a moment all that it touches back to
wonder.

Responding to the Poem

Analyzing the Poem

Identifying Details

1. What does the Queen Anne's Lace do to the dry grass? What does the thought of "you" do to the speaker?
2. What do the chameleon and the mantis in stanza 2 have in common?
3. What does the beautiful do in the last stanza?

Interpreting Meanings

4. With great delicacy, the final stanza makes a strong statement. **Paraphrase** that statement.
5. In your own words explain the two meanings expressed by the title. Does the poem as a whole support one meaning or the other, or both?
6. Is this a love poem? Pick out the lines that support your answer.

ANALYZING THE POEM
Identifying Details
1. The weed turns the dry grass into a lake; "you" creates images of fabulous blue lakes.
2. Both blend into and increase the beauty of their environment.
3. It changes in kind ways.

Interpreting Meanings
4. Beautiful things can be appreciated anew; beauty offers a "second finding."
5. (a) The beautiful is always in flux or changing; (b) the changes in nature are beautiful.
Responses will vary.
6. References to "the slightest shade of you" (line 5) and "your hands" (lines 13–14) suggest a love poem, but students may feel that the poem is a more universal comment on "the beautiful."

SUPPLEMENTARY SUPPORT MATERIALS
1. Review and Response Worksheet: Meter and Rhyme (*CCB*)
2. Selection Test (*CCB*)

PREPARATION

ESTABLISHING A PURPOSE. Have students read to answer the following questions: What "clashing ideas" about time appear in the poem, especially in the last line? What arguments and counter-arguments are presented?

CLOSURE

Ask students to write a sentence or two answering this question: Based on the evidence in the poem, is Wilbur criticizing or sympathizing with humanity's attitude toward time?

A. Ambiguity
The critic Donald Hall points out that "settlement" can mean "a coming down of snow through the air, a community, or a final arrangement."

B. Simile
The simile, which compares the leaves to dancers in a spell, can be viewed as a paradigm of the human predicament—like the leaves, we are caught and held by time; we flutter or dance—that is, live and act—downward toward death.

C. Humanities Connection: Discussing the Fine Art
Charles Burchfield (1893–1967) lived most of his life in Gardenville, New York. In the 1930's, influenced by Sherwood Anderson's *Winesburg, Ohio,* he produced stark, realistic scenes of small-town life done in monochromes—shades of either gray or brown that capture the economic struggle and weariness of the Depression. (Other Burchfield works appear on pages 158, 641, and 738.)

Time is the name we give to an idea. "More time, more time," says Richard Wilbur. He speaks for us all in a poem concerned with a moment that includes eternity. The occasion is New Year's Eve, when the bells that tell time are "wrangling" with the snow that marks time, as if there were something uneasy and still unresolved in the relationship of a minute of time to all time.

The first two stanzas give us pictures of time present. In the third and fourth stanzas, time past is made vivid by what has survived: the outlines of million-year-old ferns as they are found pressed into stone; the huge prehistoric beasts called mammoths—some of which, buried in the ice of polar regions, are still visible; and the famous little dog perfectly preserved in the same volcanic ashes that suffocated the great city of Pompeii nearly two thousand years ago.

Year's End

Now winter downs the dying of the year,
A And night is all a settlement of snow;
From the soft street the rooms of houses show
A gathered light, a shapen atmosphere,
Like frozen-over lakes whose ice is thin
And still allows some stirring down within.

I've known the wind by water banks to shake
The late leaves down, which frozen where they fell
B And held in ice as dancers in a spell
Fluttered all winter long into a lake;
Graved on the dark in gestures of descent,
They seemed their own most perfect monument.

C

Six O'Clock by Charles Burchfield (1936). Watercolor.

Everson Museum of Art, Syracuse, New York. Museum purchase with funds from the Jennie Dickson Buck Fund.

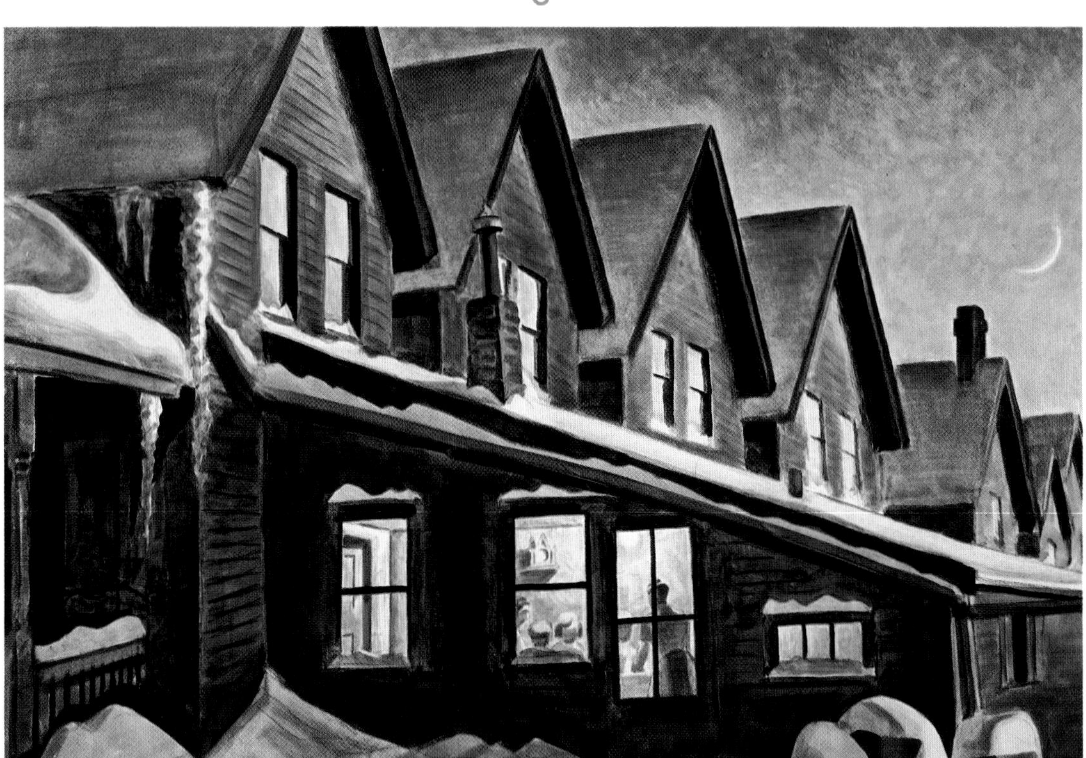

Analyzing The Poem

Identifying Details

1. The time is late on New Year's Eve.
2. (a) "To defeat" or "lay prostrate"; (b) "to line with down or soft feathers."
3. Examples include the fossilized fern, the mammoths preserved in ice, and the small dog preserved in the volcanic ash.
4. The metaphor links human life to threads of yarn or cloth, which fray into the future. The cloth is only "wrought" (completed as a tapestry) in "afterthoughts."

Interpreting Meanings

5. He wants the assurance of living longer, having more time to reach his goals.
6. The sound of the radio is muffled by the snow and its distance from the speaker.
7. The tension is between past, present, and future—human's aspirations and their actual accomplishments.
8. Answers will vary. Have students explain and defend their opinions.

There was perfection in the death of ferns
Which laid their fragile cheeks against the stone
A million years. Great mammoths overthrown
Composedly have made their long sojourns,
A Like palaces of patience, in the gray
And changeless lands of ice. And at Pompeii

The little dog lay curled and did not rise
But slept the deeper as the ashes rose
And found the people incomplete, and froze
The random hands, the loose unready eyes
Of men expecting yet another sun
To do the shapely thing they had not done.

These sudden ends of time must give us pause.
We fray into the future, rarely wrought
Save in the tapestries of afterthought.
B More time, more time. Barrages of applause
Come muffled from a buried radio.
The New-year bells are wrangling with the snow.

A. Responding

? Is our consciousness of time a blessing or a curse? What if we lived in a realm where time did not exist? (The poem is ambivalent. While the nonrational elements of nature are perfect, composed, and patient, this serenity is balanced by references to stone, the "gray and changeless lands of ice," and the ashes of Pompeii. The eradication of time implies both peace and immobility—a frozen stillness.)

B. Theme

? How can lines 28–29 be interpreted? (The applause marking the start of the new year seems an emblem of humanity's optimistic and arbitrary illusion of renewing time. The fact that it's "muffled" and reaches the street from a "buried" radio reminds us of the "settlement" of the snow and time's inevitable victory.)

Responding to the Poem

Analyzing the Poem

Identifying Details

1. At what time of year is the speaker expressing his thoughts?
2. In line 1, what two different meanings of the word *down* are suggested?
3. What examples does the poet use in the third and fourth stanzas to illustrate the "sudden ends of time"?
4. What does the poet compare people to in lines 26 and 27?

Interpreting Meanings

5. Why does the speaker ask for "more time"? (line 28)
6. Why do you think the radio is "buried"? (line 29)
7. What is the **problem,** or tension, that the speaker presents in this poem? How does the **image** in the last line concisely express that tension?
8. Do you agree that we "fray into the future"? Explain.

Writing About the Poems

A Critical Response

Analyzing the Poems. In both "The Beautiful Changes" and "Year's End," Wilbur gently challenges common assumptions about beauty, love, and death. In a brief essay, show how Wilbur attempts to persuade us of an unusual, even **paradoxical** (seemingly contradictory) way of considering these subjects.

Analyzing Language and Style

Sound Effects

Wilbur's poems often have the effect of free verse, but they are written with the most careful attention to metrics and rhyme.

1. What is the **rhyme scheme** of "Year's End"?
2. Can you find any **internal rhymes**?
3. What basic **meter** is the poem written in?
4. What variations does the poet introduce to keep the meter from sounding sing-song and the rhymes from sounding mechanical?
5. How many examples of **alliteration** can you find? Of **assonance**?
6. What sounds in the poem seem to echo the poem's sense, or contribute to its mood?

COMMENT FROM THE POET

In "Sled Burial, Dream Ceremony" (page 1113) the poet questions the nature of death. Dickey states that the poem is about the "death of . . . an American Southerner. Southerners are always mystified by the customs of people who live where there's a lot of snow. Except in travels, I've never seen much snow. Snow is exotic to the Southerner. It seems to me that death is the most foreign thing from what your life has been. In this poem, I made a little drama in which the Southerner, in order to be fully dead, would have to enter into the country of snow where people who were the most foreign to him lived. The poem describes a ritual in which he arrives on a train in his coffin and is taken on a sled by these people, who are wrapped in scarves to keep their heads warm, to a lake where a door is cut in the ice, and he is buried in the lake. The Southerner then knows he is truly dead, because he is in the ultimate foreignness."

James Dickey (1923–)

One of the most robust and resourceful of American poets, James Dickey was born in Atlanta, Georgia, and educated at Vanderbilt University in Nashville, Tennessee. He has exemplified the modern spirit of his native state ever since, at the comparatively late age of thirty-seven, he published his first collection of poems. This volume announced the arrival of a talent independent of poetic "schools," or even of the bookish life styles to which most young poets are drawn. A high-school football player, a fighter pilot in World War II and in the Korean War, as well as an enthusiastic hunter (sometimes with bow and arrow), Dickey comes to poetry as a man of action. His deepest philosophical concerns have to do with conscious man and woman and unconscious nature, and the endless lessons to be learned from their interaction.

At his best, Dickey is a poet of situations gravely posed, of situations dramatized by moral alternatives or made urgent by haunting questions of guilt, regret, and human culpability.

Dickey's story-telling talent is matched by the vigor and skill of his "open" poetic techniques. But though he dispenses with conventional forms, he does not abandon the rigid control they demand. Dickey depends on his own innate sense of balance and spacing to achieve what other poets can achieve only by more formal means.

Photograph © 1988 by Jill Krementz.

Dickey has been much in the public eye since the success of his novel *Deliverance* (1970) and the motion picture based on it (in which he appeared in the role of a sheriff). Dickey is also remembered as the only poet besides Robert Frost whose friendship with a President—in his case, with fellow Georgian Jimmy Carter—has become part of the literary lore of the century.

SUPPLEMENTARY SUPPORT MATERIALS
1. Review and Response Worksheet: Figurative Language (*CCB*)
2. Selection Test (*CCB*)

PREPARATION

ESTABLISHING A PURPOSE. Have students read the poem to determine whether they agree with Dickey's interpretation of the poem in Comment from the Poet, page 1112.

CLOSURE

To review students' understanding of the poem, have them briefly debate the following question: Based on the evidence in the poem, does the poet believe in an afterlife?

As in all dreams, the details are photographically exact, and yet the meaning is elusive. To share his funeral march, the poet asks us to share the dream that he had—at least insofar as he can re-create it in words.

Sled Burial, Dream Ceremony

A

Cross by the Sea, Canada by Georgia O'Keeffe (1932). Oil.

The Currier Gallery of Art, Manchester, New Hampshire. Currier Funds 1960.1.

While the south rains, the north
Is snowing, and the dead southerner
Is taken there. He lies with the top of his casket
B Open, his hair combed, the particles in the air
Changing to other things. The train stops

In a small furry village, and men in flap-eared caps
And others with women's scarves tied around their heads
And business hats over those, unload him,
And one of them reaches inside the coffin and places
The southerner's hand at the center

A. Humanities Connection: Discussing the Fine Art
Georgia O'Keeffe (1888–1986) was born in Wisconsin but spent much of her life on an isolated New Mexico ranch. Critics view her unique, easily recognizable style as enigmatic and difficult to define: a mixture of forms from nature so simplified they approach abstract geometric shapes and precisionistic detail. Often, it is a quality of stark clarity, almost austerity, and the sense of viewing something seen in a dream or vision, that characterizes her work.

B. Imagery
The journey from railroad track to road to rabbit track, and the absence of any path, reinforces the image of death as a "sailing into uncharted territory."

ANALYZING THE POEM

Identifying Details

1. The body travels by train to the far North, is loaded on a sled, and is taken to a lake where a hole is cut in the ice and the body is buried.

2. The corpse is compared to a sailboat.

Interpreting Meanings

3. In line 16 the bushes are compared to an army; in line 35 they are compared to the observers of the burial.

4. The simile is the comparison of the coffin to a boat, which fills its sails and moves off. The image suggests a journey; ancient people often put their dead in boats for the journey to the afterlife.

5. See the poet's comment on page 1112 of this book.

6. Note "army of gunny-sacked bushes" (line 16), "Not fooled that the snow is cotton" (line 22), "The woods fall/ Slowly off all of them" (lines 22–23), "Summoned from village sleep into someone else's dream" (line 36).

7. Opinions will vary. Certainly their manifest content is similar.

A. Interpretation

? Why do the faces on the window shed tears? (The faces appear to cry because the heat inside the houses causes the condensation to run.)

B. Interpretation

? Why do you think Dickey lists three tools? (If ice is viewed as the final boundary between life and death, he may be emphasizing the difficulty involved in breaking through to that realm.)

C. Metaphor

? What literal and symbolic meaning can be attached to this metaphor? (Because they are bundled in heavy clothing, the people literally look like the bushes; if this world is simply a preface to an eternal realm, the people in it are similar to the dormant bushes that will bloom again.)

Of his dead breast. They load him onto a sled,
An old-fashioned sled with high-curled runners,
Drawn by horses with bells, and begin
To walk out of town, past dull red barns
Inching closer to the road as it snows

Harder, past an army of gunny-sacked bushes,
Past horses with flakes in the hollows of their swaybacks,
Past round faces drawn by children
On kitchen windows, all shedding basic-shaped tears.
The coffin top still is wide open;

His dead eyes stare through his lids,
Not fooled that the snow is cotton. The woods fall
Slowly off all of them, until they are walking
Between rigid little houses of ice-fishers
On a plain which is a great plain of water

Until the last rabbit track fails, and they are
At the center. They take axes, shovels, mattocks,
Dig the snow away, and saw the ice in the form
Of his coffin, lifting the slab like a door
Without hinges. The snow creaks under the sled

As they unload him like hay, holding his weight by ropes.
Sensing an unwanted freedom, a fish
Slides by, under the hole leading up through the snow
To nothing, and is gone. The coffin's shadow
Is white, and they stand there, gunny-sacked bushes,

Summoned from village sleep into someone else's dream
Of death, and let him down, still seeing the flakes in the air
At the place they are born of pure shadow
Like his dead eyelids, rocking for a moment like a boat
On utter foreignness, before he fills and sails down.

Responding to the Poem

Analyzing the Poem

Identifying Details

1. Briefly summarize what happens to the southerner.
2. What is the dead person compared to in lines 39–40?

Interpreting Meanings

3. The phrase "gunny-sacked bushes" appears twice. What is compared to the wrapped-up bushes in each **metaphor**?
4. What new **simile** is introduced in the last stanza? Do you think this could suggest that one kind of journey may lead to the beginning of another? If so, what could that other journey be?
5. This is a dream meditation on death. Why do you think the poet chose to make the dead man from the South and to situate his burial spot in the North?
6. What lines in the poem seem appropriate to the perception of events in a dream?
7. Do you think this poem has anything in common with Williams's poem "Tract" (page 720)? Explain.

COMMENT FROM A CRITIC
In her study of Merrill's work, Judith Moffett discusses the need for every poet to "make some sort of provisional peace with the inscrutable nature of what he sees"—that is, with the nature of reality and what can be known. She concludes that Merrill's work "makes it clear that knowing he cannot know has never tormented him. . . . His mature view is that . . . in a tragic world ambiguities are a blessing, and what we don't know can rarely hurt us as much as what we do know." You may want to discuss whether this philosophy underlies "Kite Poem" (page 1116).

James Merrill (1926–)

The most urbane and learned of contemporary American poets, James Merrill was born in New York City, the son of one of the nation's most eminent businessmen. He spent his childhood in New York and on the eastern part of Long Island before he was sent to Lawrenceville Academy in New Jersey. Following in his father's footsteps, Merrill attended Amherst College. After living for extensive periods in Paris and Rome, he took up a semi-permanent residence in Athens, which lasted for more than two decades. But Merrill's life abroad was not one of self-imposed exile or—as in the case of the famous expatriate writers of the 1920's—based on a desire to escape the parochialism of American culture. Merrill returned to his own country often. He held short-term teaching positions at several colleges, gave hundreds of public readings, and maintained many close friendships in the academic and literary communities.

Merrill's talent was full-blown and distinctive by the time he reached the age of twenty—a fact that marks him as a prodigy. He was one of those people—rare among writers, but not among musicians and painters—whose earliest works show signs of precocious mastery. Beginning as a lyricist, Merrill published nine volumes of increasingly impressive work before turning his attention to the slow and artful composition of an epic, *The Changing Light at Sandover.* No doubt the longest poem in recent years, this poem is also regarded by many critics and scholars as one of the greatest works of epic dimension in this century. It was published in three separate books that were, each in its own way, so extraordinarily brilliant that they brought Merrill almost every award and prize that poetry is capable of garnering. *The Changing Light at Sandover* appeared as one volume in 1981. Some reviewers and academics hailed it as one of the supreme products of American genius. But others in literary and academic professions took the poem as an affront. It was a prodigious performance, which disturbed minds with settled views and forced them to consider what they could not comfortably ignore.

Merrill was aware of the controversial reception of his masterpiece, but he was not involved in either its defense or its promotion. Merrill soon returned to lyrics that annotate his engagement with life as it is lived between his permanent home in the seaside village of Stonington, Connecticut, and his winter residence in the historically designated "old town" of Key West, Florida.

COMMENT FROM THE POET
When Merrill was sixteen, his father surprised him by privately publishing a collection of his son's childhood poems. Years later, Merrill commented: "*Jim's Book*, as he titled it, thrilled me for days, then mortified me for a quarter-century. . . . It opened my eyes enough at least to see how much remained to be learned about writing."

SUPPLEMENTARY SUPPORT MATERIALS

1. Review and Response Worksheet: Sound Effects (*CCB*)
2. Selection Test (*CCB*)
3. Audiocassette recording

PREPARATION

ESTABLISHING A PURPOSE. Point out that "Kite Poem" includes two speakers (the parson and the narrator) and a story-within-a-story. Ask students to look for clues to the narrator's attitude.

CLOSURE

Ask students to write two or three sentences in which they cite one piece of evidence from the poem to define the speaker's attitude. Does he agree with the parson or the girls? Is he neutral?

ANALYZING THE POEM

Identifying Details

1. A man who tried to fly by climbing on a kite disappeared; his coat was found two counties away. The story is a lesson to his daughters to behave sensibly.

2. They titter.

3. They secretly meet their suitors.

4. Internal rhyme: *certain / person* (line 1); *port / sport* (lines 3–4); *missing / kissing* (lines 6, 8); *kite / night* (lines 5, 9 and 17–18). Approximate rhyme: *person / parson / lesson* (lines 1, 2, 7); *port / sought / chore* (lines 3–4); *kite / coat* (line 5); *meant / crescent / pheasant* (lines 7, 9, 10).

Examples of alliteration are *person* and *parson* (lines 1–2); "climbing up on a kite" (line 5); and "finishing his pheasant, their father" (line 10).

Interpreting Meanings

5. For the parson's daughters, natural urges (symbolized by the moon) proved more persuasive

(Answers continue on next page.)

Imagine this poem as being set in the nineteenth century. Try to hear the difference between the parson's words and the words of the speaker of the poem.

Kite Poem

"One is reminded of a certain person,"
Continued the parson, settling back in his chair
With a glass of port, "who sought to emulate
The sport of birds (it was something of a chore)
By climbing up on a kite. They found his coat
Two counties away; the man himself was missing."

His daughters tittered: it was meant to be a lesson
To them—they had been caught kissing, or some such nonsense,
The night before, under the crescent moon.
So, finishing his pheasant, their father began
This thirty-minute discourse, ending with
A story improbable from the start. He paused for breath,

Having shown but a few of the dangers. However, the wind
Blew out the candles and the moon wrought changes
Which the daughters felt along their stockings. Then,
Thus persuaded, they fled to their young men
Waiting in the sweet night by the raspberry bed,
And kissed and kissed, as though to escape on a kite.

Responding to the Poem

Analyzing the Poem

Identifying Details

1. What story does the parson tell his daughters? Why does he tell it?
2. How do the daughters react to his instructive tale?
3. What do the daughters do later?
4. How many **internal rhymes,** approximate rhymes, and examples of **alliteration,** can you find in the poem?

Interpreting Meanings

5. The poem begins with a little story containing a moral. When it ends, that moral has been forgotten and replaced by another. What is the moral we are left with?
6. The parson stands for one thing; the moon for another. How would you state the difference?
7. Why does the poet call this "Kite Poem"?

Writing About the Poem

A Creative Response

Taking Another Point of View. Write the daughters' response to the parson. Have them explain the moral they took from his story (which was not the moral he intended).

(Continued from previous page.)
than a sermon.
6. The parson stands for prudence and restraint; the moon for the forces of nature or desire.
7. The kite may symbolize freedom and escape.

Adrienne Rich (1929–)

Adrienne Rich was born in Baltimore, Maryland. She attended Radcliffe College and published her first volume of poems, *A Change of World,* in 1951, the year she graduated. Poet W. H. Auden selected the volume for the prestigious Yale University Press Younger Poets Series. In his introduction, he wrote that Rich's poems "are neatly and modestly dressed, speak quietly but do not mumble, respect their elders but are not cowed by them."

Rich later saw these poems as too heavily influenced by her "elders," especially by British modernist poets like W. B. Yeats and Auden himself. Their tightly constructed forms, she felt, had gotten in the way of the personal and political subject matter she had wanted to deal with but had been unable to write about directly. "Formalism," she wrote of these poems, "was part of the strategy—like asbestos gloves, it allowed me to handle materials I couldn't pick up barehanded."

In her later volumes, especially those published after the mid-1960's, Rich strove to break away from the tight craftsmanship of her early poems, and her work became more feminist and political in content. She had come to see, she later wrote, that "politics was not something 'out there' but something 'in here' and of the essence of my condition." As she examined her own situation as a woman, Rich was also addressing larger questions of personal and political relationships.

Like Robert Lowell (page 1102) and Sylvia Plath (page 1119), Rich presented herself as a representative of her times; the less rigid and less traditional forms that she later adopted allowed her to handle such subject matter "barehanded." Her later poems, collected in such volumes as *The Will to Change* (1971), *Diving into the Wreck* (1973), and *A Wild Patience Has Taken Me This Far* (1981), became somewhat less "neatly and modestly dressed," but they also became more direct and more urgent.

A. Expansion
"Power" (page 1118) reveals Rich's skill in combining personal and political themes. On one level, the poem treats the dark side of personal power—that fame so valued in a competitive patriarchal society. Rich not only shows the cost in suffering that underlies fame, but also hints that the lure of success could lead one to ignore the negative or destructive aspects of new discoveries, such as radium. On another level, the details of stanza 3 (Curie's wounds and the phrase "a test tube or pencil") have personal meaning. The cataracts that cloud the eye reflect both Rich's early attempts to express her talent within the confines of a poetic dictated by men and her blind acceptance of traditional notions of her role as wife and mother. The suppurating fingers and pencil indicate the hardships of writing. Written after Rich achieved recognition (power), the poem seems an acknowledgement of her own pain.

Supplementary Support Materials
1. Review and Response Worksheet: Irony and Theme (*CCB*)
2. Selection Test (*CCB*)
3. Instructional Overhead Transparency

Preparation
Establishing a Purpose. Discuss the statement "Power is a double-edged sword." What does the quote tell us about the nature of power? How does power affect those who possess it?

Closure
Have students, based on the evidence in the poem, discuss the following question: How does Rich view Curie's behavior? Is she critical? Admiring? Sympathetic?

A. Symbol/Irony
Nineteenth-century tonics, given primarily to women by doctors who were usually male, reduced pain but often led to addiction because they contained opium or morphine.
? With this in mind, what is symbolic about the old bottle? (Like Curie's radium, the tonic also helped people counteract the destructive power of nature. Like radium, the tonic could also, ironically, destroy.)

Analyzing the Poem
Identifying Details
1. A backhoe unearths a 100-year-old amber medicine bottle.

Interpreting Meanings
2. The last line sums up the poem's irony: Currie's "wounds" (illness) "came from the same source as her power."
3. Answers will vary. To some, Curie's "wounds" may suggest Christ's wounds.
4. Opinions will vary. Urge students to defend their views with text references.

With the assistance of her husband, Polish-born Marie Curie (1867–1934) discovered radium, the radioactive element that made X-rays, nuclear fission, and nuclear weapons possible. Twice awarded the Nobel Prize, once for physics and once for chemistry, she remains the most honored woman scientist in history. But, like many of the survivors of the atomic bomb dropped on Hiroshima, Marie Curie died of the effects of radiation. In her case, the deadly emanations came not from a bomb dropped from the sky, but from the substances stored in her own laboratory.

Power

Living   in the earth-deposits   of our history

A
Today a backhoe divulged   out of a crumbling flank of earth
one bottle   amber   perfect   a hundred-year-old
cure for fever   or melancholy   a tonic
for living on this earth   in the winters of this climate

Today I was reading about Marie Curie:
she must have known she suffered   from radiation sickness
her body bombarded for years   by the element
she had purified
It seems she denied to the end
the source of the cataracts on her eyes
the cracked and suppurating skin   of her finger-ends
till she could no longer hold   a test-tube or a pencil

She died   a famous woman   denying
her wounds
denying
her wounds   came   from the same source as her power

Responding to the Poem

Analyzing the Poem

Identifying Details

1. What accidental discovery, described in the first stanza, is the occasion for the poem?

Interpreting Meanings

2. How would you state directly the grim **ironies** of this poem?
3. Can you think of other situations in which "wounds" might come from the same source as "power"?
4. Do you think this is a political poem? If so, give your reasons.

Writing About the Poem

A Critical Response

Analyzing the Poem. The poem is concerned with two discoveries. In an essay, tell what you think they have in common, and what is their essential difference.

Sylvia Plath (1932–1963)

Until her tragic death in 1963, Sylvia Plath's existence was, from most appearances, a model of achievement. She was born in Boston and spent her early years in the nearby seaside town of Winthrop. Both her parents were immigrants—her father, a professor of biology at Boston University, from Poland, and her mother, a teacher of secretarial skills, from Austria. A key event in Sylvia's life was the death of her father from diabetes, when she was only eight years old.

Plath started writing stories and poems while she was still in grammar school. Even at the earliest stages of her career, she was persistent: she received forty-five rejection slips from *Seventeen* magazine before finally publishing a story there in 1950. She won a scholarship to Smith College, where she flourished. She was active in campus activities, went off to Yale and Harvard for parties and dances, and continued to write poems and stories. She won a much-coveted fiction prize at *Mademoiselle* magazine in her junior year at Smith, and spent that summer as a guest editor in the magazine's New York office.

The first serious sign of the dangerous turbulence in her emotional life came at the end of that storybook summer, when she was overcome by depression and attempted suicide. After a period of psychiatric treatment and electro-shock therapy—"the agony of slow rebirth and psychic regeneration," as she called it—she returned to college and her promising career. But she was ill with manic depression, years before drug therapy was available.

After graduating *summa cum laude* from Smith, Plath went to Cambridge University in England on a Fulbright fellowship. At Cambridge, she met English poet Ted Hughes, whom she married in 1956. They lived in Boston during the late 1950's, and in early 1960 they moved to London, where Plath's first book of poetry, *The Colossus,* was published. In April of that year, their daughter Frieda was born. A second child, Nicholas, was born in 1962. The following year, Plath's autobiographical novel, *The Bell Jar,* was published.

During 1962 and the first weeks of 1963, in London, Plath wrote poetry at a furious pace—sometimes two or three poems a day. The subject matter and style of these poems, published in a volume called *Ariel* three years after her death, were significantly different from her earlier work. Most of the poems in *The Colossus* were relatively restrained and formal, displaying the influence of a number of poets, from the classicism of John Crowe Ransom (page 690) to the exuberance of Theodore Roethke (page 1084). But the *Ariel* poems, especially the bitter poems about her father and about her own attempts at suicide, showed a violence and a frankness that no reader of her earlier work would have anticipated. As Robert Lowell wrote in his foreword to the book, "These poems are playing Russian roulette with six cartridges in the cylinder, a game of 'chicken,' the wheels of both cars locked and unable to swerve." The poems were, he said, an "appalling and triumphant fulfillment" of her talents, but they came at an unbearably high price. By 1963, Plath was separated from her husband and caring for two babies in an unheated London flat. In February, during the coldest London winter in a hundred and fifty years, Plath's depression returned. She attempted suicide again, and this time she succeeded.

A. Expansion
Students often believe the ability to write well is simply a "gift" and assume all published writers possess a special "genius" that makes writing effortless and recognition immediate. As a result, young writers become discouraged or are unwilling to carry out the time-consuming process of revision. Point out the stubborn determination Plath showed in getting her work published. How many of them, in comparison, would try-out for a sports team or apply for a job forty-five times? You might add that Anne Sexton (page 1122) once commented that she wrote three hundred pages of variations and revisions to create one short poem.

SUPPLEMENTARY SUPPORT MATERIALS

1. Review and Response Worksheet: Symbolism (*CCB*)

2. Selection Test (*CCB*)

PREPARATION

PREREADING JOURNAL. Set the stage for thoughtful discussion by asking students to write, and then share, their thoughts about the negative aspects, even dangers, of romantic love—how it might change or inhibit one's identity or self-esteem, limit freedom, or lead to uncertainty and pain.

CLOSURE

To review the ideas in Plath's poem, you might ask students to compare it with "Kite Poem" (page 1116).

A. Word Choice

What does the word *ceremonious* suggest? (The formal, set procedure of a ceremony, such as a wedding or funeral, contains and directs strong emotions.)

B. Word Choice

What word in this line indicates that the young woman's observations are not objective? (*Judged*)

C. Metaphor

? What does the weather represent? (Her new and motley feelings for the young man) What is irrational and muddled, yet appropriate, in the image of a "barricade" against the "weather"? (The mixed metaphor, implying that a barbed-wire barricade around the house will protect her from the weather, is an illogical but psychologically accurate reflection of the girl's confused thinking.)

The word *spinster* is an uncomplimentary term for a woman, usually an older one, who has never married. In this poem, the psychology of one spinster who chose to remain unmarried is explained in terms of order and disorder, safety and jeopardy, and their counterparts in the actual and symbolic aspects of winter and spring. This poem is from Plath's first collection, *The Colossus*.

Spinster

Now this particular girl
A [During a ceremonious April walk
With her latest suitor
Found herself, of a sudden, intolerably struck
By the birds' irregular babel
And the leaves' litter.

By this tumult afflicted, she
Observed her lover's gestures unbalance the air,
His gait stray uneven
Through a rank wilderness of fern and flower.
B [She judged petals in disarray,
The whole season, sloven.

How she longed for winter then!—
Scrupulously austere in its order
Of white and black
Ice and rock, each sentiment within border,
And heart's frosty discipline
Exact as a snowflake.

But here—a burgeoning
Unruly enough to pitch her five queenly wits
Into vulgar motley—
A treason not to be borne. Let idiots
Reel giddy in bedlam spring:
She withdrew neatly.

C [And round her house she set
Such a barricade of barb and check
Against mutinous weather
As no mere insurgent man could hope to break
With curse, fist, threat
Or love, either.

Analyzing The Poem
Identifying Details
1. On a walk with her suitor, the girl is disturbed by the birds' "babel" and the leaves' "litter."
2. The young man's unbalancing gestures and stray, uneven gait.
3. The "austerity," "order," and "frosty discipline" of winter are opposed to spring's disarray.
4. She withdraws, literally, from the spring weather, and, psychologically, from her suitor's love.

Interpreting Meanings
5. Threatened by love, the girl sees a dangerous correspondence between spring's "unruly burgeoning" and her own emotions.
6. Her barricade of "barb and check" is probably intended to be both literal and symbolic.
7. Answers will vary. It could be about anyone who withdraws from the world. Perhaps it is about a poet. Compare with Dickinson's poem, page 357.

Responding to the Poem

Analyzing the Poem

Identifying Details

1. Describe the situation in the first stanza. What sounds and sights so upset the girl?
2. What increases the girl's sense of affliction in the second stanza?
3. What aspects of winter in the third stanza contrast with the aspects of April that the girl observes on her walk?
4. What does the girl do in the fourth and fifth stanzas? What is she trying to "keep out" in the fifth stanza?

Interpreting Meaning

5. *Bedlam,* in stanza 4, is the archaic word for an insane asylum. It is drawn from the name *Bethlehem,* the name of the famous "madhouse" in the city of London. How can "spring" be regarded as a kind of "bedlam" or "chaos"? Why would anyone "fear" spring?
6. The fifth stanza is about the defenses put up by "this particular girl" once she has withdrawn from April, her suitor, and the normal expectations of society. What are these defenses? Do you think they are actual defenses, or are they more **symbolic**? Explain.
7. How might the poem be read not only as a comment on a particular kind of female psychology, but also as a series of **metaphors** that illuminate a kind of temperament that is not necessarily female?

Analyzing Language and Vocabulary

Multiple Meanings

1. In stanza 4, *burgeoning* means, literally, "to come into flower," as in the case of buds, leaves, and blossoms. *Burgeoning* can also refer to "the sudden manifestation of a feeling or an idea." How, in this stanza, are both meanings of *burgeoning* suggested?
2. "Motley" in stanza 4 refers to a kind of multicolored costume worn by clowns and jesters. Used as an adjective, it can also mean "made up of different elements." When the girl's "five *queenly* wits" (that is, her five senses) are pitched "into *vulgar* motley," what do you picture happening? What—psychologically speaking—is also happening?

A

Emily Dickinson and the Raven by Will Barnet (1980). Oil.

Private Collection.

A. Humanities Connection: Responding to the Fine Art
Will Barnet was born in 1911 in Beverly, Massachusetts and attended art school in Boston. Barnet often completes as many as thirty sketches of a work before he starts to paint.
? In what ways is *Emily Dickinson and the Raven* an appropriate work for Plath's poem? (Students may suggest that the bare simplicity and stark design reflect the spinster's desire for an ordered, unemotional world. The dark figure of Dickinson is apropos because she was a spinster and recluse, one who found personal relationships difficult and seemed to reveal herself only in her poetry. In Poe's "The Raven" a young man, sitting alone with his books, mourns his lost love. The last stanza, especially, denies the possibility of love's continuation in an eternal realm beyond this disordered world.)

SUPPLEMENTARY SUPPORT MATERIALS
1. Review and Response Worksheet: Figurative Language and Theme (*CCB*)
2. Selection Test (*CCB*)

PREPARATION
1. **BUILDING ON PRIOR KNOWLEDGE.** Ask which students have ridden to the top of very tall buildings, such as skyscrapers in major cities. Have these students describe their thoughts as they rose higher and higher and when they reached the top and looked out, down, and up.

2. **ESTABLISHING A PURPOSE.** Tell students to find evidence that explains what the key represents.

CLOSURE
Ask students to state in their own words the connection between an elevator to the sky and a key that opens–something.

A. Expansion
Although it led to her first volume of poetry, Sexton felt tremendous guilt over her breakdown and her inability to care for her daughter. Her early poems often contain references to herself as a rat or a demon.

COMMENT FROM A CRITIC
The critic Robert Boyers states that the reader is never bothered by the self-centered aspect of Sexton's poetry because her "evocation of these problems gives them a resonance which is unmistakably general, universally relevant."

Anne Sexton (1928–1974)

The violent frankness of Sylvia Plath's *Ariel* poems came as a surprise after her earlier work, but the same cannot be said of her friend, Anne Sexton. A Sexton's poetry from the beginning was often concerned with the dark side of a stormy emotional life. The titles of a number of her volumes indicate her preoccupation with her own bouts of illness: *To Bedlam and Part Way Back* (1960), *Live or Die* (1966), *The Death Notebooks* (1974), and *The Awful Rowing Toward God* (1975).

Sexton was born in Newton, Massachusetts, and went to Garland Junior College. She started writing poetry in the mid-1950's, but she made up for her relatively late start with an energy and dedication that produced a stream of poems from 1960 (when her first volume was published) to the early 1970's. She studied with Robert Lowell and was influenced by the work of her friend W. D. Snodgrass, whose volume *Heart's Needle* had traced the emotional consequences of a difficult midlife divorce.

From the beginning, Anne Sexton's poetry was intended to be, as she said, "a shock to the senses." Her second book, *All My Pretty Ones* (1962), contained an epigraph from Franz Kafka: ". . . the books we need are the kind that act upon us like a misfortune, that make us suffer like the death of someone we love more than ourselves . . . a book should serve as the ax for the frozen sea within us."

Although Sexton's work was often intensely personal, it also spoke to a number of wider issues, especially the problems of women and their image in society. Many of her poems are dramatic monologues that portray women in moments of crisis.

Sexton's poetry was received with great enthusiasm by general readers and her fellow poets; she was honored with a number of awards, including the Pulitzer Prize in 1966.

Analyzing the Poem

Identifying Details

1. If there is a fire, guests above the fifth floor cannot count on firefighters or elevators for escape.

Interpreting Meanings

2. Answers will vary. The phrase connotes going beyond one's limitations, extending one's imagination, and even leaving one's senses.

3. Answers will vary. Students might interpret the key as a way of unlocking the door to the ultimate challenge of discovering and coming to terms with the unknown.

4. Answers will vary. Both keys can be seen as positive symbols. Bessie's key opens a revived sense of community, and the key in this poem can lead to something "useful," a key word.

A. Interpretation

? Why do people warn the speaker about "climbing out of yourself"? (Answers will vary. Unrestricted creativity is exhilarating yet emotionally and mentally dangerous.)

B. Interpretation

? How would you interpret these images? Do you see a pattern? (Answers will vary. Ask students to give reasons for their opinions.)

The first ten lines are factual, even prosaic. Then, like the elevator itself, the speaker takes off into a realm of fantasy where familiar things become bizarre, and an ordinary elevator ride turns into a mysterious passage leading to "a very large key, / that opens something—."

What should we make of this key? Might it open the secret of the universe? Or the door to self-understanding? Or could it be just another figment of the imagination of an insecure person who's scared of elevators and fire and has a tendency to see mystery in everything?

Reread the poem as if you were looking for evidence and see what answer to these questions comes closest to the mark.

Riding the Elevator into the Sky

As the fireman said:
Don't book a room over the fifth floor
in any hotel in New York.
They have ladders that will reach further
but no one will climb them.
As the New York *Times* said:
The elevator always seeks out
the floor of the fire
and automatically opens
and won't shut.
A These are the warnings
that you must forget
if you're climbing out of yourself.
If you're going to smash into the sky.

Many times I've gone past
the fifth floor,
cranking upward,
but only once
have I gone all the way up.
Sixtieth floor:
small plants and swans bending
into their grave.
Floor two hundred:
mountains with the patience of a cat,
silence wearing its sneakers.
Floor five hundred:
messages and letters centuries old, B
birds to drink,
a kitchen of clouds.
Floor six thousand:
the stars,
skeletons on fire,
their arms singing.
And a key,
a very large key,
that opens something—
some useful door—
somewhere—
up there.

Responding to the Poem

Analyzing the Poem

Identifying Details

1. In your own words, tell what exactly is the danger of taking a New York hotel room above the fifth floor (lines 1–10).

Interpreting Meanings

2. What might the poet mean in line 13 by "climbing out of yourself"?
3. What might the "very large key" and the "useful door" represent?
4. How might the key be related to the one at the end of Isaac Singer's story "The Key" (page 877)?

Writing About the Poem

A Creative Response

1. **Describing Images.** Imagine that you are a famous nonrealist painter—perhaps Pablo Picasso or Salvador Dali. How would you represent the images in lines 20–35?

A Critical Response

2. **Writing a Comparison.** Read E. E. Cummings's poem "who knows if the moon's." (You should be able to find this poem in the library.) Compare it with Sexton's poem. What similarities and differences do you find?

A. Expansion
Berryman's structured early style is evident in "Winter Landscape" (page 1125), which is one long sentence divided into five stanzas of regular iambic pentameter, or blank verse. As one critic points out, this form encourages the reader to move from line to line, taking in the whole composition without a pause, just as one would view a painting.

B. Connections
The Dream Songs includes elegies for Presidents Eisenhower and Kennedy as well as for many of the writers discussed in this text: Robert Frost, Wallace Stevens, William Carlos Williams, Randall Jarrell, Sylvia Plath, and Theodore Roethke.

C. Expansion
In a 1965 essay Berryman stated that "Winter Landscape" was written shortly after his return from Cambridge and was influenced by his visits to France and Germany, especially the Nazi stronghold of Heidelberg in 1938–1939. He adds that this work led to the discovery that "a poem's force may be pivoted on a missing or misrepresented element in an agreed-upon or imposed design"—in this case, the painting. He terms the work "a war poem of an unusual negative kind. The common title of the picture is 'Hunters in the Snow' and of course the poet knows this. But, he pretends not to, and calls their spears (twice) 'poles,' the governing resultant emotion being a certain stubborn incredulity—as the hunters are loosed while the peace nations plunge again into war."

John Berryman (1914–1972)

A Like his friend Robert Lowell, John Berryman started his career in the 1940's by writing tight, complex poems influenced by the great poets of the early twentieth century. The major influence for Lowell was T. S. Eliot; for Berryman, it was the Irish poet William Butler Yeats. Both Lowell and Berryman changed their styles drastically in the late 1950's and early 1960's. Lowell shifted to the looser, more relaxed verse of *Life Studies*. Berryman moved to a quirky, nervous, eighteen-line form that he used in his long work, *The Dream Songs* (1969), published in segments over a thirteen-year period. One volume of this work won the Pulitzer Prize in 1965.

B In *The Dream Songs,* Berryman created a character he called Henry. Through Henry, the poet dealt with a vast number of subjects, public and private, in an eccentric style that sometimes baffled critics. The book was a personal record of the poet's turbulent life, and his responses to events, especially the deaths of his poet friends.

John Berryman was born John Smith in McAlester, Oklahoma. His father was a banker and his mother was a schoolteacher. When John was ten, the family moved to Tampa, Florida. His parents' marriage was stormy and unstable, and a few months before John's twelfth birthday his father shot himself to death outside the boy's window.

John's mother moved to New York and remarried, and the boy took on his stepfather's name. C He graduated from Columbia University in New York City and spent two years at Cambridge University in England. When he returned to the United States, he began teaching and writing. During his career, he taught at a number of schools, including Harvard, Princeton, and the University of Minnesota.

In 1948, Berryman published his first volume, *The Dispossessed.* Some of these poems dealt indirectly with his father's death, others with World War II. The sense of dispossession, of being "put out of one's own," as Berryman later referred to it, pervades much of his early work. Berryman felt personally dispossessed by the loss of his father, and publicly dispossessed by the actions of governments during the war.

In 1956, Berryman published *Homage to Mistress Bradstreet,* an unusual, book-length poem about the Colonial poet Anne Bradstreet and the alienation he imagined she experienced. Here too, Berryman's sense of loss and dispossession is strong: "Both of our worlds unhanded us," Berryman says to the Colonial poet at one point.

SUPPLEMENTARY SUPPORT MATERIALS
1. Review and Response Worksheet: Rhythm (*CCB*)
2. Selection Test (*CCB*)

PREPARATION

ESTABLISHING A PURPOSE. Since a full understanding of Berryman's poem requires close attention to differences in detail between the painting and the poem, try to find a slide of the painting. Ask students to note what details in the painting the poet includes in the poem and which he omits or misrepresents.

CLOSURE

Have students write briefly on the question, Why didn't Berryman use the painting's title for his poem? (Students who understand the poet's purpose and theme will realize that he consciously refuses to recognize the hunters.)

This poem is partly an interpretation of *Hunters in the Snow*, a painting by the great sixteenth-century Flemish artist Pieter Brueghel (see below). It is also an independent discourse on time, history, and the nature of art. The poem's twenty-five lines make up a single sentence. Notice how skillfully the strict iambic rhythm flows from beginning to end.

Winter Landscape

Hunters in the Snow by Pieter Brueghel the Elder (1565). Oil on wood.

Kunsthistorisches Museum, Vienna.

A

The three men coming down the winter hill
In brown, with tall poles and a pack of hounds
At heel, through the arrangement of the trees,
Past the five figures at the burning straw,
Returning cold and silent to their town,

Returning to the drifted snow, the rink
Lively with children, to the older men,
The long companions they can never reach,
The blue light, men with ladders, by the church
The sledge and shadow in the twilit street,

A. Humanities Connection: Responding to the Fine Art

The Flemish painter Pieter Brueghel the Elder was born about 1525 and died in Brussels in 1569. *Hunters in the Snow,* part of a series of landscapes depicting the months of the year, is distinguished by the clarity of detail and serene arrangement of people and objects.

? Since other works by Brueghel (*The Triumph of Death, The Massacre of the Innocents*) are clearer illustrations of war, why do you think the poet chose to write about this work? (Students may feel the bare trees and black birds are ominous, similar to the atmosphere of Europe in the late 1930's. The villagers' indifference to the hunters about to disrupt the scene also suggests European apathy.)

ANALYZING THE POEM

Identifying Details

1. Three men, followed by hounds, descend a hill past five figures at a fire, toward a town where children skate and men with ladders work near the church. A sledge, the red houses, and a small bridge are also mentioned.

2. "Cold and silent" (line 5), "the long companions they can never reach" (line 8), "these men . . . will keep the scene" (lines 16–17), and "irrecoverably lost" (line 15).

Interpreting Meanings

3. The conscious effort of the painter to balance elements of the picture.

Both have power to re-create nature.

4. Older men stay home in mundane jobs.

They could also be the old masters.

5. *Sandy* could connote treacherous times or an uncertain future; students may be familiar with the expression "the sands of time."

The same evils are perpetuated generation after generation (such as war).

6. *Configuration,* which echoes *arrangement,* implies that the creative artist shapes reality to conform to an imaginative vision.

A. Noting Details/Theme
Note the phrases that foreshadow the approach of war.

B. Interpretation
? Why is the phrase "in brown" repeated? (Perhaps because the Nazis were called "brownshirts")

C. Ambiguity
The critic Gary Arpin notes that the poem leads directly to this question and suggests that the pun on morning (mourning) and the emphasis on the hunters' returning imply a second world war.

D. Theme
Be sure students note that the speaker accurately describes small details of the painting but does not recognize the three figures as hunters (despite the hounds); twice he calls their spears "poles."

Are not aware that in the sandy time
To come, the evil waste of history
A Outstretched, they will be seen upon the brow
Of that same hill: when all their company
Will have been irrecoverably lost,

B These men, this particular three in brown
Witnessed by birds will keep the scene and say
By their configuration with the trees,
The small bridge, the red houses and the fire,
What place, what time, what morning occasion
C
Sent them into the wood, a pack of hounds
D At heel and the tall poles upon their shoulders,
Thence to return as now we see them and
Ankle-deep in snow down the winter hill
Descend, while three birds watch and the fourth flies.

Responding to the Poem

Analyzing the Poem

Identifying Details

1. Describe the scene in the painting that Berryman uses as the basis for the poem.
2. What details emphasize that the scene has been frozen in time?

Interpreting Meanings

3. In stanza 1, what does the word *arrangement* suggest? What are the implications of this word for both a poet and a painter?
4. In the second stanza, the statement about the "older men" in lines 6 and 7 has to do with both life and art. In terms of life, what does this statement suggest? What does it say about art?
5. What are the implications of the word *sandy* in line 11? In what ways might history be considered an "evil waste"?
6. In the fourth stanza, what word echoes *arrangement* in line 3? How does this word remind us that art does not merely record life, but manipulates it?

Writing About the Poem

A Creative Response

Imitating the Poet's Technique. Either continue to write about Brueghel's winter landscape, or take another painting from this book and describe what you think the original scene was like. Describe what will "never happen" in that painting.

A. Expansion
Wright's life offers an opportunity to discuss the painful choices a professional poet may face. Raised in a blue-collar, working-class family, Wright respected the simple, honest dignity of men like his father, who worked in a glass factory for fifty years. In contrast, the post-World War II realm of professional poetry was dominated by academics from privileged upper-class backgrounds; rivalries and competition were often intense. The prevalent style was sophisticated and intellectual, decorative, and symbolic. It is not surprising that Wright felt uneasy and guilty about pursuing a poetic career that offered poor financial rewards in this alien climate. It may be that he sought to preserve what he valued in his Ohio background by retaining a voice the critic Alfred Kazin labeled "flat Ohio . . . obstinately plain" and by sympathetically portraying the migrants, worn factory workers, and farmers he had known.

James Wright (1927–1980)

James Wright, the son of a factory worker, was born in Martins Ferry, Ohio, that part of the country that was once considered the crossroads of the industrial North and the rural South. Early on, Wright came to know the sooty hills and blast furnaces of his hometown. His knowledge of the men and women whose existence was governed by job layoffs and the ups and downs of the economy remained with him all his life and became an important source of his poetry.

While he was attending a vocational high school in Martins Ferry, two of Wright's teachers became aware of his unusual writing ability and encouraged him to develop his talent. He went on to study at Kenyon College in Ohio with John Crowe Ransom (page 672), the eminent poet and teacher. He spent a year in Vienna and returned to do graduate work at the University of Washington. There he came under the good influence of another famous poet-teacher, Theodore Roethke (page 1088). Wright's own distinction as a poet was recognized at once when, at the age of thirty, he published his first book, *The Green Wall* (1957).

For most of his adult life, Wright taught literature and creative writing at the University of Minnesota, at Macalester College in St. Paul, Minnesota, and finally at Hunter College in New York City, where he died at the age of fifty-two.

Wright's lyricism is based on a clear-eyed sense of the gritty realities of a seam of American life that is more often sung about in country music than written about in poetry. His sympathetic concern for the poor and the inarticulate gives his work a strong emotional focus. But he avoids the predictable sentimental pitfalls through the elegance and economy of his style.

Photograph © 1988 by Jill Krementz.

Wright said, toward the end of his life, "I have written about the things I am deeply concerned with—crickets outside my window, cold and hungry old men, ghosts in the twilight, horses in a field, a red-haired child in her mother's arms, a feeling of desolation in the fall, some cities I've known. I try and say how I love my country and how I despise the way it is treated. I try and speak of the beauty and again of the ugliness in the lives of the poor and neglected."

B. Expansion
Like Roethke, Wright sought some spiritual significance in existence. One critic noted that Wright "never lost his belief that there had to be something other, something better—a realm of paradisal happiness from which man came and toward which he might journey. This realm is most clearly perceived in . . . 'A Blessing,' which achieves apotheosis for its speaker in the concluding three lines."

1127

Literature and Language: Using Precise Verbs

James Wright's choice of verbs adds much to our enjoyment of this poem. To appreciate his artful diction, ask students to try these substitutions for the poem on page 1129:

(line 2) Replace *bounds* with *comes*.
(line 4) Replace *Darken with* with *Show*.
(line 9) Replace *ripple* with *move*.
(line 11) Replace *bow* with *go*.

What do Wright's verbs enable the reader to do that these more general verbs do not? (Picture the action clearly)

Ask students to suggest several precise verbs to replace the vague, general verbs in the following sentences. Students can work alone, with a partner, or as part of a small group.

1. Exhausted Daria *sits* on the couch.
2. "Turn that radio down," Mom *said*.
3. Four more people *go* into the already packed subway car.
4. For hours the raging fires *move* from house to house.
5. Travis *walked* through the icy rain.

Humanities Connection: Discussing the Fine Art

Famous for his depiction of the American West, Frederic Remington (1861–1909) was not only a painter but also a sculptor and magazine illustrator. A native of New York, Remington had little formal training in art. At Yale, he dropped an art course to pursue athletics. His art career dates from a trip from Montana to Texas in 1880. A sketch from this trip was accepted by *Harper's Weekly* in 1882. The serenity of *Horses at a Mountain Stream* is somewhat atypical. More often Remington's work has a strong narrative element that captures both the characters and action of the vanishing West in scenes of Indian battles, bronco-busting, and cattle drives.

Horses at a Mountain Stream by Frederic Remington. Oil.

SUPPLEMENTARY SUPPORT MATERIALS
1. Review and Response Worksheet: Metamorphoses (*CCB*)
2. Selection Test (*CCB*)

PREPARATION
PREREADING JOURNAL. Direct students to describe specifically, in less than twelve sentences, a moment when they felt great joy in the natural world.

CLOSURE
Have students write two or three sentences explaining the metamorphosis in the poem.

ANALYZING THE POEM
Identifying Details
1. The progression moves from the highway, over the barbed wire, to physical closeness with the ponies. The poet first observes the animals' affectionate behavior, appearance, and lack of fear. Then, he wants to reach out and hold one—to communicate his feelings. The experience prompts an inner ecstasy—a breaking into blossom.
2. Line 4: the ponies' eyes "darken with kindness"; lines 5–6: they come "gladly" to "welcome" the speaker; line 9: they can "hardly contain their happiness." Additional examples appear in lines 11–13 and 20–21.

Interpreting Meanings
3. The title implies the speaker's gratitude for the unexpected beauty and joy of the encounter; he has been blessed.
4. It could mean that no matter how much two beings love each other, they can never be as close as they wish and they are intensely lonely.
5. The speaker has the feeling his body could break into blossom like a flower. It is an image of great beauty that describes an ecstatic feeling.

A simple everyday incident leads to a moment of transcendence—an experience in which actuality falls away and the spirit is released into a state of being for which most people can find no words. Here a poet describes that state as one in which he feels as though he might "break into blossom."

A Blessing

Just off the highway to Rochester, Minnesota,
Twilight bounds softly forth on the grass.
And the eyes of those two Indian ponies
Darken with kindness.
They have come gladly out of the willows
To welcome my friend and me.
We step over the barbed wire into the pasture
Where they have been grazing all day, alone.
They ripple tensely, they can hardly contain their happiness
That we have come.
They bow shyly as wet swans. They love each other.
There is no loneliness like theirs.
At home once more,
They begin munching the young tufts of spring in the darkness.
I would like to hold the slenderer one in my arms,
For she has walked over to me
And nuzzled my left hand.
She is black and white,
Her mane falls wild on her forehead,
And the light breeze moves me to caress her long ear
That is delicate as the skin over a girl's wrist.
Suddenly I realize
That if I stepped out of my body I would break
Into blossom.

Responding to the Poem

Analyzing the Poem

Identifying Details

1. In one sense, the poem is a progression from a road in Minnesota to a "place" that exists only in the realm of feeling. Trace the steps by which the speaker is led from a spot on the map to a "place" with no physical location.
2. **Anthropomorphism** is a term used to describe the tendency of human beings to read their own feelings into nonhuman objects. In how many places in this poem does the author ascribe human feelings to the ponies?

Interpreting Meanings

3. What is the significance of the poem's title?
4. What do you think the author means by the phrase, "There is no loneliness like theirs" (line 12)?
5. In Greek mythology, human beings often undergo marvelous transformations called **metamorphoses.** What metamorphosis ends this poem? Do you think it is a good one to describe a particular feeling?

Writing About the Poem

Comparing Two Writers. In an essay, identify all the points of comparison you can find between this poem and the prose extract from *Nature* by Emerson on page 191.

For Further Reading For Students And Teachers
When the Legends Die, by Hal Borland (Bantam, 1984), is the sensitive story of a young Ute boy raised in the wilderness but sent to a boarding school after his parents' death. He runs away and becomes a successful rodeo rider but cannot be complete until he returns to the wilderness.
Erdrich's own *Love Medicine* and her husband Michael Dorris's *Yellow Raft in Blue Water* can be recommended to mature students.

Louise Erdrich (1954–)

Louise Erdrich, who is part Chippewa, part German, grew up in North Dakota near the Turtle Mountain Reservation, where her grandfather was tribal chairman. The Indian Affairs Boarding School mentioned in her poem (page 1131) was where she went to school and where both her parents worked. "It was a small-town life," she said, "—lots of kids living on a teacher's salary, and we were a chaotic, pretty typical family." Her parents got her interested in reading and writing early. "My father used to give me a nickel for every story I wrote," she explained.

As a student at Dartmouth College, Erdrich won a number of prizes for her poetry and fiction, and after earning a master's degree, she returned to Dartmouth as a writer in residence. In 1984, forty-four of Erdrich's poems, including "Indian Boarding School—The Runaways," were published in a collection called *Jacklight*. In reviewing that collection, critic Michael Loudon wrote that the language in the poems "again and again sings to its own vision."

In addition to writing poetry, Erdrich has collaborated with her husband, Michael Dorris, in writing four novels: *Love Medicine* (1984), *The Beet Queen* (1986), *Tracks* (1988), and *The Crown of Columbus* (1991). "The language is all Louise's," Michael explained in an interview, "but the writing comes out of our shared experience." Erdrich's short stories have won numerous prizes, including two O. Henry Awards, two National Magazine Fiction Awards, and the Pushcart Prize.

The school referred to in the title is one of many set up by the United States government with the purpose of giving Native American children an education more in line with contemporary American values than with those of the various tribes to which these children belong. In the schools, the training they get is practical and meant to be useful to young people of one culture who must earn their living in another culture and live by the rules of that culture.

But for many children forced to leave their homes, their families, and the surroundings in which they grew up, the supposed advantages offered them are not enough to offset the terrible experience of being uprooted. Dressed, like prisoners, in "regulation clothes" and confined to live among strangers, they sometimes find the routines and disciplines of these schools unbearable and so try to run away—from their temporary and comfortless "home" to the true home they carry in their hearts and recall in their dreams. As the poem makes clear, the chances of finding their way back are thin. The children know this, yet nothing stops them from "hopping a freight" like those other young people in the days of the Great Depression who didn't know where they were going but were convinced that anywhere was better than here.

Supplementary Support Materials
1. Review and Response Worksheet: Imagery and Theme (*CCB*)
2. Selection Test (*CCB*)

Preparation

1. **Prereading Journal.** Have students record their thoughts about the meaning of the word *home.*

2. **Establishing a Purpose.** Tell students to read the poem to discover what the runaways are telling them.

Closure

Ask students how these runaways might define *home*; see how many reasons they can list as to why the place where the runaways have been living cannot be called "home."

Indian Boarding School: The Runaways

Home's the place we head for in our sleep.
Boxcars stumbling north in dreams
don't wait for us. We catch them on the run.
The rails, old lacerations° that we love,
shoot parallel across the face and break
just under Turtle Mountains.° Riding scars
you can't get lost. Home is the place they cross.

The lame guard strikes a match and makes the dark
A less tolerant. We watch through cracks in boards
as the land starts rolling, rolling till it hurts
to be here, cold in regulation clothes.
We know the sheriff's waiting at midrun°
to take us back. His car is dumb and warm.
The highway doesn't rock, it only hums
like a wing of long insults. The worn-down welts
of ancient punishments lead back and forth.

All runaways wear dresses, long green ones,
B the color you would think shame was. We scrub
the sidewalks down because it's shameful work.
Our brushes cut the stone in watered arcs
and in the soak frail outlines shiver clear
a moment, things us kids pressed on the dark
face before it hardened, pale, remembering
delicate old injuries, the spines of names and leaves.

4. **lacerations:** jagged wounds.

6. **Turtle Mountains:** mountains in North Dakota, site of a Chippewa Reservation.

12. **midrun:** the midpoint of the train's route.

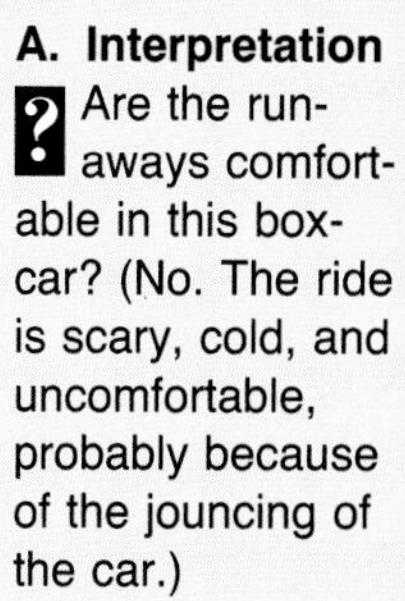

A. Interpretation
Are the runaways comfortable in this boxcar? (No. The ride is scary, cold, and uncomfortable, probably because of the jouncing of the car.)

B. Interpretation
Why do the runaways have to scrub the sidewalks? (Perhaps as punishment for running away. Since the speaker implies that all the children are runaways in their dreams, the scrubbing might also be a routine duty, a demeaning aspect of life at the boarding school.)

Analyzing the Poem

Identifying Details

1. The lame guard is probably a station attendant pausing for a cigarette.

The runaways see him through cracks in the boxcar when the train pulls into a station.

2. The regulation clothes are school uniforms.

The speaker compares the color green to shame.

3. The sheriff is waiting to take them back to the school.

Interpreting Meanings

4. *Dumb* here probably means "unable to speak." (The car can't yell at them.) It might also suggest stupidity, or it might mean that the car does not speak words of comfort to them.

5. The speaker talks of heading for home "in our sleep" and boxcars heading north "in dreams."

6. *Scars* refer to the gashes in the land created by the train tracks, *welts* to the highways, and *injuries* to the impressions left by the children in the wet cement. She repeats these words to emphasize the children's psychic pain.

(Answers continue in left-hand column.)

(Continued from top)

7. The children wrote their names in the wet cement and pressed leaves into it. The words *frail outlines* and *spines* suggest that these are fossil remains of the children.

8. The speaker feels pity and compassion for the children.

Answers will vary. (You might ask what they think is the most important word or phrase in the poem.)

Responding to the Poem

Analyzing the Poem

Identifying Details

1. Who is the "lame guard"? Where are the runaways when they see the guard?
2. What are the "regulation clothes" the runaways are wearing? To what does the poet compare the color green?
3. What happens when the runaways get to midrun?

Interpreting Meanings

4. **Diction** in poetry always demands close attention. What does the word *dumb* mean in the line, "His car is dumb and warm"?
5. The author once admitted, "I never ran away. I was too chicken." What evidence do you find in the first stanza to suggest that the speaker, although portraying runaways, might not be a runaway herself?
6. The **imagery** of scars introduced in line 4 is picked up several times in the poem. What does the poet mean by *scars* (line 6), *welts* (line 15), and *injuries* (line 24)? Why do you think the poet repeats so often these words having to do with pain?
7. In lines 20–24, we see the children scrubbing the sidewalks. What things did they press on the cement before it hardened? What words make these **images** on the sidewalks seem like those fossils that reveal the imprints of ancient leaves and creatures?
8. How does this speaker feel about the runaways? Describe your own response to the poem and to the events in it.

Writing About the Poem

A Critical Response

Responding to a Remark by the Poet. Erdrich, in an interview with poet Joseph Bruchac, says this of the poem "Indian Boarding School: The Runaways":

> This, though, is a particular type of running away. It's running home; it's not running away from home.

In a brief essay, explain what you think the remark means.

Primary Sources

The Wellsprings of Creativity

Perhaps the most common question asked of a writer is "Where do you get your ideas?" It is a legitimate question but a very hard one to answer. Louise Erdrich, the author of "Indian Boarding School: The Runaways," was asked this question in an interview. Here is part of her answer:

"I really don't control the subject matter; it just takes me. I believe that a poet or a fiction writer is something like a medium at a séance who lets the voices speak. Of course, a person has to study and develop technical expertise. But a writer can't control subject and background. If he or she is true to what's happening, the story will take over. It was, in fact, hard for me to do that when stories started being written that had to do with the Chippewa side of the family because I just didn't feel comfortable with it for a long time. I didn't know what to make of it being so strong. It took a while to be comfortable and just say, 'I'm not going to fight it.' 'Runaways' is one of the first poems that came out of letting go and just letting my own background or dreams surface on the page."

—Louise Erdrich

Supplementary Support Materials

1. Review and Response Worksheet: Meter and Rhyme (*CCB*)
2. Selection Test (*CCB*)

Preparation

Establishing a Purpose. Ask students to consider how television has altered American life. What disturbing events or images have they seen on television? Are there some events television should not film?

Closure

Since Alvarez's poems are deceptively simple, you might want to discuss the ambiguity of "sweep"—specifically, its military meaning—and the subtle allusion to the expression "ashes to ashes, dust to dust."

You won't read far in this poem before you discover allusions to the war in Vietnam. Read aloud, to hear how the poet manages to make a poem written with concern for meter and rhyme sound like everyday conversation. (A biography of Julia Alvarez appears on page 902.)

How I Learned to Sweep by Julia Alvarez

My mother never taught me sweeping. . . .
One afternoon she found me watching
TV. She eyed the dusty floor
boldly, and put a broom before
me, and said she'd like to be able
to eat her dinner off that table,
and nodded at my feet, then left.
I knew right off what she expected
and went at it. I stepped and swept;
the TV blared the news; I kept
my mind on what I had to do,
until in minutes, I was through.
Her floor was as immaculate
as a just-washed dinner plate.
I waited for her to return
and turned to watch the President,
live from the White House, talk of war:
in the Far East our soldiers were
landing in their helicopters
into jungles their propellers
swept like weeds seen underwater
while perplexing shots were fired
from those beautiful green gardens
into which these dragonflies
filled with little men descended.
I got up and swept again
as they fell out of the sky.
I swept all the harder when
I watched a dozen of them die . . .
as if their dust fell through the screen
upon the floor I had just cleaned.
She came back and turned the dial;
The screen went dark. *That's beautiful,*
she said, and ran her clean hand through
my hair, and on, over the windowsill, coffee table, rocker, desk,
and held it up—I held my breath—
That's beautiful, she said, impressed,
she hadn't found a speck of death.

Responding to the Poem

Analyzing the Poem

Identifying Details

1. What was on TV the afternoon the speaker learned to sweep?
2. According to the speaker, why was her mother impressed with her work?
3. Where does this poet use **rhymes**? How would you describe the poem's **meter**? Give reasons for your answers.

Interpreting Meanings

4. What are the dragonflies in line 24? Why do you think the speaker sweeps all the harder as they fall out of the sky?
5. What do you think she is trying to clean, in addition to her mother's dusty floor?
6. What is the significance of the last line, in light of what the speaker has seen on TV? Explain.
7. Is this poem about sweeping, or is it really about something else? Explain your opinion.

Writing About the Poem

A Critical Response

1. **Analyzing an Image.** In a brief essay, trace the use of the image of dust in this poem. What do you think the dust might mean in the poem? Why do you think the writer uses the word *dust* instead of the word *dirt* or *grit*?
2. **Comparing Poems.** In a brief essay, compare and contrast the imagery used in Alvarez's and Ginsberg's poems (see page 1135). What aspect of modern life does each poet draw his or her imagery from?

Analyzing the Poem

Identifying Details

1. A news report on the war.
2. She is impressed because the room is immaculately clean.
3. Full or half rhymes end some couplets; she also uses rhymes in groups of four lines.

The meter is a mix of iambic tetrameter and trochaic tetrameter.

Interpreting Meanings

4. They are helicopters. She sweeps harder because she is shocked by images of death on the screen.
5. Perhaps she's trying to "wipe away" the deaths of the soldiers.
6. The line is ironic. Encourage students to relate the dust being cleaned to the "dust" in the funeral "Dust thou art, and unto dust thou shalt return."
7. The poem is really about "how I learned to sweep away the reality of death."

A. Connections
A number of factors also suggest Walt Whitman's (page 326) influence on Ginsberg's poetry: the garrulous voice in Ginsberg's work and his concern with social issues, his discovery of the spiritual in the sensual, his interest in Oriental philosophy, and his "cataloguing" of examples or concrete objects. In "A Supermarket in California," Ginsberg addresses Whitman directly: "In my hungry fatigue, and shopping for images, I went into the neon fruit supermarket, dreaming of your enumerations." (You might ask students to note the presence of some of these elements in "Homework," page 1135.)

B. Expansion
The subtitle of "Homework" is a tribute to the poet Kenneth Koch, a professor at Columbia University, who has published several volumes of poetry and such classic works on the teaching of poetry as *Rose, Where Did You Get That Red?* and *Wishes, Lies, and Dreams.*

C. Expansion
In one decade Allen Ginsberg rose from an aberrant, nonconformist curiosity on the outskirts of the poetic world to become the hero of the popular hippie subculture. In the 1950's even the most daring journals rejected his work; ten years later, one of his poems appeared in *Life* magazine.

Allen Ginsberg (1926–)

The son of Louis Ginsberg, a schoolteacher and poet of conventional tendencies and modest reputation, Allen Ginsberg was born in Newark, New Jersey, and brought up in nearby Paterson. Paterson is the industrial town given literary prominence by William Carlos Williams, the poet who came to be young Ginsberg's spiritual father and poetic master. Like Williams, Ginsberg was at first attracted to the great poets of England. But in what amounted to a hundred and eighty degree turn in his thought and prac- A tice, Ginsberg soon became one of the staunchest promoters of the American idiom and of poetry that echoed the rhythms of American speech.

While still at Columbia College, from which B he graduated in 1948, Ginsberg became associated with the novelist Jack Kerouac and with other young writers who would eventually constitute the literary movement known as the Beat Generation. In footloose travels abroad and "on the road" across the United States, Ginsberg typefied the restless and alienated nature of the C Beat Generation and its sub-culture. When, at the age of thirty, he published his long poem *Howl,* Ginsberg became the Beats' most famous spokesman.

Ginsberg and other members of his Beat Generation eventually joined forces, so to speak, with Lawrence Ferlinghetti, Gary Snyder, and other writers with similar ideologies or techniques and established a group known as the San Francisco Renaissance. Ginsberg's influence broadened, and his role as a kind of literary and philosophical *guru* made him the standard-bearer of dissent in the conduct of life, as well as in the practice of his art.

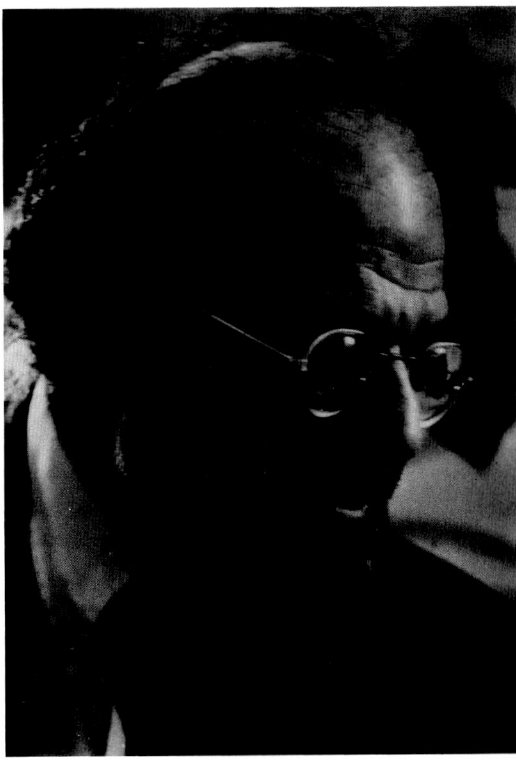
Photograph © 1988 by Jill Krementz.

In the open forms in which he writes, Ginsberg has explored Eastern and Western mysticism from Buddha to William Blake. Even though he has been preoccupied with the human psyche, Ginsberg has also called for realistic action against war, against the abuse of nature, and against all curbs on freedom.

Supplementary Support Materials

1. Review and Response Worksheet: Catalog Poetry (*CCB*)
2. Selection Test (*CCB*)

Preparation

Establishing a Purpose. Ask students individually to list the five most serious problems in today's world. List their responses on the chalkboard and encourage them to note which ones appear in Ginsberg's poem.

Closure

Briefly discuss students' reactions to the poem: Is the laundry metaphor an effective and amusing way to draw attention to the need for reform? Or, does the poem trivialize serious concerns?

This poem has a double meaning (pollution and politics) and a single point of view. The speaker is impatient with those powers that spoil the natural world and with those that contribute to the world's turmoil. Most of its references are the commonplace stuff of newspaper headlines. As you read, you might think of the poem as a series of exaggerated visual cartoons. (Kenneth Koch is a New York City poet.)

Homework

Homage Kenneth Koch

If I were doing my Laundry I'd wash my dirty Iran
I'd throw in my United States, and pour on the Ivory Soap, scrub up Africa, put all the birds and elephants back in the jungle,
I'd wash the Amazon river and clean the oily Carib & Gulf of Mexico,
Rub that smog off the North Pole, wipe up all the pipelines in Alaska,
Rub a dub dub for Rocky Flats and Los Alamos, Flush that sparkly Cesium out of Love Canal
Rinse down the Acid Rain over the Parthenon & Sphinx, Drain the Sludge out of the Mediterranean basin & make it azure again,
Put some blueing back into the sky over the Rhine, bleach the little Clouds so snow return white as snow,
Cleanse the Hudson Thames & Neckar, Drain the Suds out of Lake Erie
Then I'd throw big Asia in one giant Load & wash out the blood & Agent Orange,
Dump the whole mess of Russia and China in the wringer, squeeze out the tattletail Gray of U.S. Central American police state,
& put the planet in the drier & let it sit 20 minutes or an Aeon till it came out clean.

Responding to the Poem

Analyzing the Poem

Identifying Details

1. This poem refers to a number of social and environmental ills in the modern world. Identify as many of these situations as you can.
2. In the last line, how long does the speaker say he will wait for the wash to come "out clean"?
3. List the verbs in the poem that give it a sense of action. Do all the verbs have to do with doing a laundry?

Interpreting Meanings

4. What underlying **metaphor** pervades the poem?
5. Characterize the **tone** of the poem. How does Ginsberg mingle amusing and serious elements?
6. What significances can you identify in the poem's **title**?
7. What is Ginsberg's **main idea**? What do you think of his specific choices for the wash?

Analyzing the Poem

Identifying Details

1. Students may mention the following categories: (1) violent revolution; (2) political oppression; (3) environmental damage; (4) air pollution; and (5) chemical warfare. Rocky Flats and Los Alamos are nuclear waste sites in the Southwest; the village of Love Canal, with its buried toxic wastes, is near Buffalo, NY; Neckar is a polluted river in Germany.
2. He says, humorously, that he will wait either twenty minutes or an "Aeon"—an immensely long span of time.
3. Among the verbs that students may list are the following: *wash* (line 1), *throw* (line 2), *pour* (line 2), *scrub up* (line 2), *clean* (line 3), *rub* (line 4), *wipe* (line 4), *rinse* (line 6), *drain* (line 6), *bleach* (line 7), *cleanse* (line 7), *dump* (line 10), *squeeze* (line 10). Most students will agree that the majority of the verbs have to do with doing laundry. *(Answers continue on next page.)*

(Continued from previous page.)

Interpreting Meanings

4. The underlying metaphor is that of the speaker purifying the world, just as one might stuff one's dirty laundry into a washing machine, clean it with detergent, and then put it in the drier.

5. The whimsy of the underlying metaphor provides the humor. Ginsberg's incidental references to well-known world problems (war, revolution, environmental pollution, political tyranny) provide the serious elements.

6. Students will have different opinions. The title "Homework" ironically suggests that the speaker may be a young student, trying to solve a few problems for the next day's class. This interpretation would deliberately clash with the serious, apparently intractable problems of world affairs referred to in the poem. But perhaps Ginsberg's intention is to suggest that the problems are not really intractable: With good will and serious effort, they may be resolved as quickly and as easily as a child does his or her homework, or as an urban apartment dweller runs his or her laundry through a washing machine. The open-ended conclu-

(Answers continue in left-hand column.)

(Continued from top.)

sion, where the speaker says he will put the planet in the drier and wait for "20 minutes or an Aeon" till it comes out clean, seems to underscore the view that solving world crises may be simply a matter of possessing the necessary determination. The title "Homework" could also be read as more generally prescriptive: perhaps Ginsberg means to imply that working to solve what he sees as evil in the world should be a "homework" assignment—or a daily obligation—for all concerned citizens of the planet.

7. One statement of Ginsberg's main idea is that the world needs to be cleaned up, both physically and morally. Students will have differing opinions about the poet's specific choices for the wash. Ask students to defend their opinions with reasons in class.

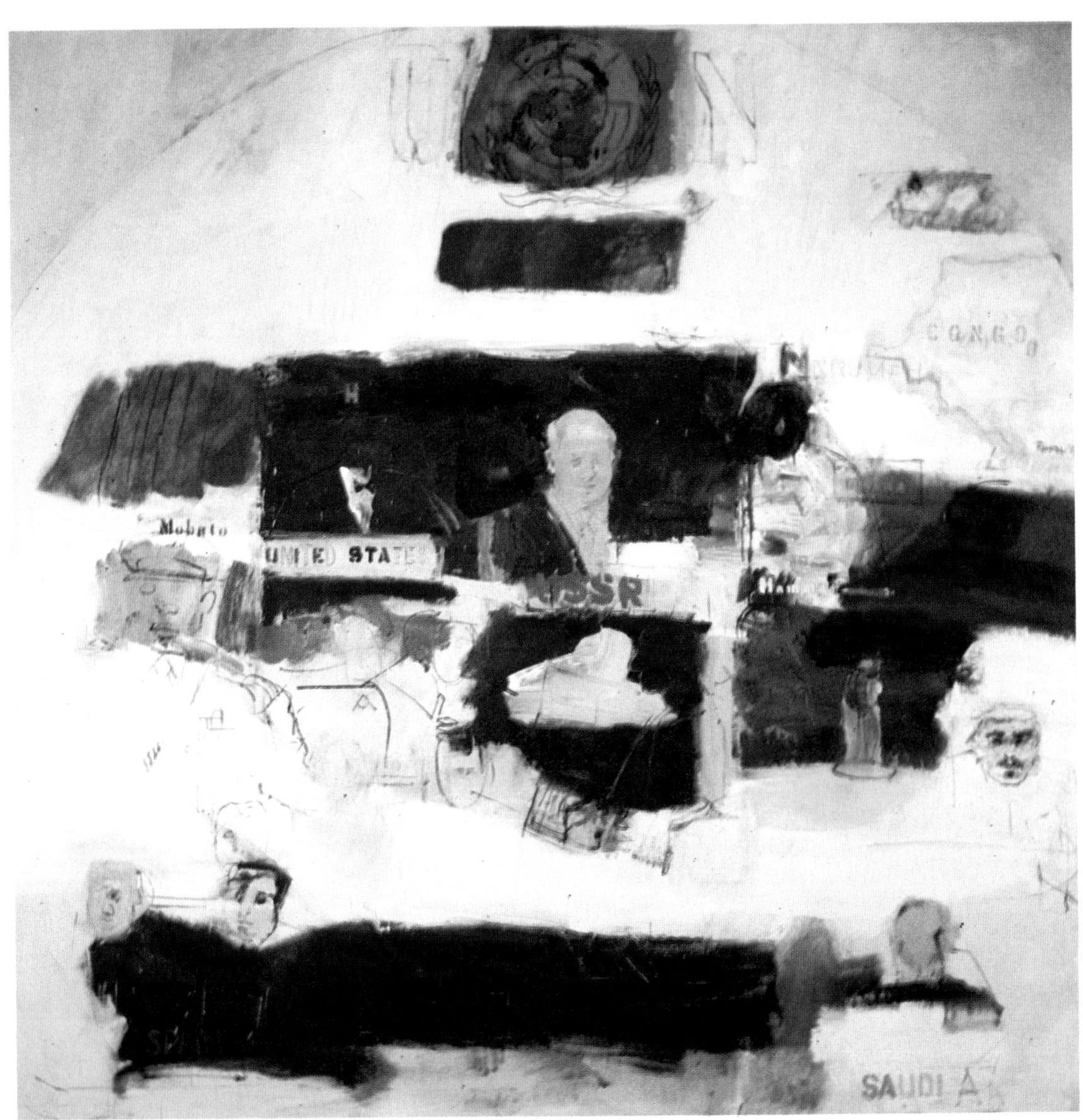

U.N. Painting by Larry Rivers (1959). Oil. Private Collection.

Writing About the Poem

A Creative Response

1. **Imitating the Writer's Technique.** Write a poem in which you describe, as Ginsberg does, what you would "wash" in the world if you could. Open with the line "If I were doing my laundry, I'd wash . . ." Imitate Ginsberg's technique and use proper names.

A Critical Response

2. **Evaluating the Poem.** In a brief essay, explain what elements qualify this piece of writing as a poem. Consider these elements of poetry: **repetition, rhythm, rhyme,** and **figurative language.**

EVALUATING A POEM

Writing Assignment

Write a brief essay in which you analyze and evaluate one of the following poems.

That Gull

That gull, for instance,
a clam in his straw beak
like a growth, or a black snout—
see how he loops it in toward shore
& with a rough
egg-breaking guess, drops it,
then swoops to gargle the soft stuff.

Observe how he leaves
his dishes broken & unwashed,
goes scissoring up & windward
—like the soul on its aëry ladders—
there to tilt & soar.
One more simile aloft, *n'est-ce pas,*°
in the vast metaphor?

—John Malcolm Brinnin

13. **n'est-ce pas** (nes pä'): French for "Right?" or "Isn't that so?"

Washyuma Motor Hotel

Beneath the cement foundations
of the motel, the ancient spirits
of the people conspire sacred tricks.
They tell stories and jokes and laugh
and laugh.

The American passersby
get out of their hot, stuffy cars
at evening, pay their money wordlessly,
and fall asleep without benefit of dreams.
The next morning, they get up,
dress automatically, brush their teeth,
get in their cars and drive away.
They haven't noticed that the cement
foundations of the motor hotel
are crumbling, bit by bit.

The ancient spirits tell stories
and jokes and laugh and laugh.

—Simon J. Ortiz

Background

How can you evaluate the quality of a poem? When you evaluate something, you make judgments based on objective standards, or criteria. You can use the following guidelines to evaluate any poem. (You may want to add a few criteria of your own to this list.)

Guidelines for Evaluating a Poem

1. Do you **respond** in some way to the poem? Does it affect your emotions or make you think? Does it remind you of anything in your own experience?
2. What is the controlling **idea** in the poem? Is it an important idea, or an overworked idea?
3. Is every **word** in the poem necessary? Do the words express ideas precisely, or are they vague and inexact?
4. Does the poem contain fresh **images** and **figures of speech?** Or are they trite and clichéd?
5. Does the poem use **sound** effectively? Does the sound of the poem support the poem's meaning?

1137

Revising Essays As students revise their essays, refer them to **Grammar, Usage, and Mechanics: A Reference Guide** at the back of their books.

Exercises in Critical Thinking and Writing/*cont.*

Prewriting

Before you write, be sure you have read the poem carefully several times. Read it at least once aloud. Be sure you can explain the figures of speech in the poem. (What is compared with what?) Be sure you understand all the words and allusions.

Then use the guidelines to take notes. Use your notes as the raw material for your essay.

Here are a few sample notes taken by a reader who was about to evaluate the poem "Homework" by Allen Ginsberg:

1. **Response:** poem made me laugh and then made me think about the whole idea of renewing the world. It also put very comical images in my head.
2. **Controlling idea:** that sometimes we dream of being so god-like that we could just scrub the world down so that it shines innocent and clean again. (A neat idea and an important one)
3. **Words:** many precise names and precise actions (name some verbs).
4. **Figures of speech:** best part of the poem. (Etc.)

Writing

Now write your evaluation of one of the poems here. Write at least four paragraphs.

Guidelines for Writing an Evaluation

1. In your opening paragraph, include a **thesis statement** that expresses your overall evaluation of the poem. Use the rest of your essay to present "evidence" to support this evaluation.
2. Organize your essay carefully. Present your ideas in the best possible order. You might want to save your most important point for last; or, you might want to start off with it.
3. Express your ideas in the clearest possible way. Get rid of excess wordiness.
4. Support every judgment with one or two examples. Quote phrases from the poem. Be sure to give the line number for each citation.

Revising and Proofreading

Reread your first draft several times. Make changes in wording and organization until you are satisfied. Be sure that you've supported your opinions or generalizations.

Use the guidelines in the section at the back of this book, called **Writing About Literature,** to revise and proofread your essay.

INDEX

1. E. B. White writes
2. Longfellow born
3. Bowdoin College
4. Millay born
5. E. A. Robinson writes
6. J. D. Salinger writes
7. Cummings lives
8. Frost's farm
9. Bradford writes
10. Rowlandson taken captive
11. Edwards's church
12. Bradstreet writes
13. Taylor's church
14. Bryant born
15. Whittier boyhood
16. Holmes born
17. James Russell Lowell born
18. Emerson born
19. Dickinson home
20. Walden Pond
21. Sexton born
22. Robert Lowell and Plath born
23. Algonquian myths and legends
24. Webster writes dictionary
25. Merrill lives
26. Knight travels
27. Stevens lives
28. Whitman writes
29. Melville born
30. Cullen writes
31. Singer writes
32. Hughes writes
33. Hersey writes
34. Herr writes
35. Helprin boyhood
36. Harte born
37. Crane born
38. Paine writes
39. Wilbur boyhood
40. Franklin writes
41. Andrea Lee born
42. Updike born
43. Jeffers born
44. Fitzgerald home
45. Douglass boyhood
46. Rich born
47. Byrd writes
48. Patrick Henry born
49. Jefferson born
50. Poe boyhood
51. Russell Baker born
52. Pearl S. Buck born
53. Thomas Wolfe born
54. O. Henry born
55. Henry Timrod born
56. O'Connor born
57. McPherson born
58. Walker born
59. James Weldon Johnson born
60. Tennessee Williams lives
61. Bishop lives
62. McKay studies (Tuskegee Inst.)
63. Jarrell born
64. Ransom teaches (Vanderbilt)
65. Dickey educated
66. Robert Penn Warren born
67. Dreiser born
68. Dunbar born
69. Bierce born
70. Thurber born
71. Sherwood Anderson's Winesburg
72. James Wright born
73. Roethke born
74. Hayden born
75. Thornton Wilder born
76. Tim O'Brien born
77. Sandburg born
78. Masters's Spoon River
79. Hansberry born
80. Sinclair Lewis born
81. Fitzgerald born
82. Toth girlhood
83. Twain boyhood
84. Eliot born
85. Moore born
86. Least Heat Moon writes
87. Williams's dramas
88. K.A. Porter born
89. Barthelme teaches
90. Berryman born
91. Brooks born
92. Masters born
93. Cather's stories
94. Chippewa and Sioux myths and legends
95. Momaday's Devils Tower
96. K.A. Porter writes
97. Momaday writes
98. Thornton Wilder writes
99. Navaho myths and legends
100. Pound born
101. Hemingway buried
102. Twain stories and sketches
103. Steinbeck stories
104. Frost born
105. Malamud teaches
106. Roethke teaches
107. Cheyenne myths and legends
108. Jack London stories
109. Kingston writes
110. Faulkner stories
111. Welty home
112. Richard Wright born
113. Jeffers writes

1139

The Scarlet Letter by Nathaniel Hawthorne
For a biography of Hawthorne, see text pages 263–264. For further background on the novel, additional activities, and tests, see the separate study guide on *The Scarlet Letter.*

The Novel

STUDY GUIDE

The Scarlet Letter by Nathaniel Hawthorne

The Elements of the Novel

The Themes

The critic Regis Michaud had this to say about the protagonist of *The Scarlet Letter*: "We will remember the tragic story of Hester Prynne, the beautiful Puritan seduced by the Reverend Dimmesdale. Hester gave everything to love. She was put in the stocks and condemned to wear embroidered on her blouse the letter *A*. . . . Note well—Hester Prynne has no shame. . . . The world has condemned her, but she does not cease to love. . . ."

Although the main character of this novel suffers no remorse at first, she does, eventually, suffer the consequences of her choice.

The main theme of *The Scarlet Letter* concerns sin and its effect on the individual. Hawthorne explores this theme by tracing the consequences of different kinds of sin for three different characters. For Hester, Dimmesdale, and Chillingworth, the consequence of sin is alienation; as their sins differ, so do the kinds of alienation that result from them.

Hester's isolation is physical: the townspeople shun her. The scarlet letter keeps them away from her, creating a "magic circle of ignominy." However, the scarlet letter, painful as it is, is the key to Hester's redemption. No reconciliation with God, society, or self is possible, in Hawthorne's view, without confessing one's sin and coming to terms with it. As Hawthorne states the "moral" of his novel: "Be true! Be true! Show freely to the world, if not your worst, yet some trait whereby the worst can be inferred." Hester's pregnancy makes her sin evident to all. She works out her redemption slowly and painfully in the public view. Through her work as a "sister of mercy," she reconciles herself with society, which begins to interpret the meaning of the *A* as standing for *Able*.

For Dimmesdale and Chillingworth, it is otherwise. Both mingle freely in society and enjoy respect. But Dimmesdale suffers agonizing guilt and self-loathing; the admiration his parishioners show him wounds him because of his sense of his unworthiness and alienation from God. His redemption is possible only when he publicly confesses his sins on the scaffold. Chillingworth's sin lies in his single-minded pursuit of vengeance—in violating "in cold blood, the sanctity of a human heart." His obsession transforms him into a fiend; his isolation is represented by the dread his dark face and stooping posture inspire in the children of the town. His secret sin, which finally destroys him, is unpardonable because he himself is unable to forgive.

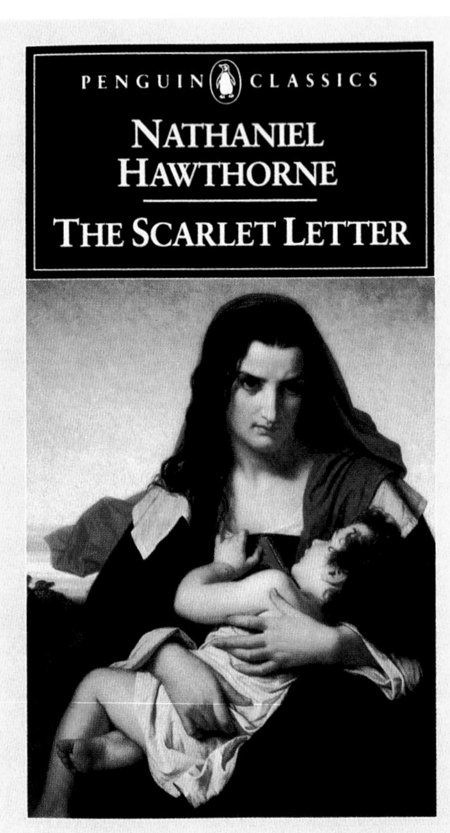

A secondary theme in *The Scarlet Letter* is that sin brings special knowledge or insights to the sinner, as the apple from the forbidden tree brought knowledge to Adam and Eve. The symbolic *A* enables Hester to perceive the hidden sin of others; Dimmesdale's sin also enables him to look into the hearts of his parishioners and makes him a more powerful preacher; Chillingworth gains preternatural insights into his victim's soul; Mistress Hibbins intuitively senses the minister's sin. Pearl, whose birth is the consequence of sin, is precocious and seems intuitively to recognize that Dimmesdale is her father.

In *The Scarlet Letter*, Hawthorne employs situations appropriate to a religious view of sin and expiation, but his interest in sin is primarily in its psychological consequences for the sinner.

The Plot

The basic plot of *The Scarlet Letter* involves the familiar triangle of husband, wife, and lover. Hawthorne, however, does not concern himself with the aspects of this situation that interest most novelists or dramatists—for example, the seduction or the wife's conflict between loyalty and attraction. He begins his story long after the adulterous act has occurred in order to focus on the effects of sin on the three principal characters. The novel opens with the scene of Hester's public humiliation—the first step of her painful path to redemption. But the main psychological movement in the novel derives from Chillingworth's insatiable quest for vengeance against Hester's lover. As Mark Van Doren observes in his book *Nathaniel Hawthorne*, the tragic events of the story follow with inevitability. "There was no other solution for [Hawthorne's] story, given Hester's strength, Dimmesdale's weakness, and Chillingworth's perversion, than the one he found. Rather as we read it, it finds itself."

The Structure of the Novel

To present his story, Hawthorne chose a dramatic method in which characters interact in a relatively few fully developed scenes, much as if they were appearing on stage. This kind of novel, which Henry James later developed so successfully, was an innovation in 1850. Hawthorne had several reasons for seeking a new form. The one long work he had attempted, *Fanshawe: A Tale*, had been a failure and had convinced Hawthorne that the chronicle of events, then the conventional form for the novel, was not his forte. He had instead developed great skill in writing short pieces—both stories and essays. Hawthorne's innovative new form enabled him to perfect separate scenes as though they were his usual short pieces and to avoid an uncongenial way of telling a long story. The result was a series of dramatic scenes with some expository chapters interspersed—these mainly focusing on a single character.

The main scenes in *The Scarlet Letter* are (1) the marketplace, where Hester suffers her public humiliation (Chapters I–III); (2) Hester's prison chamber, where she has her confrontation with Chillingworth (Chapter IV); (3) Governor Bellingham's house, where Hester pleads to retain custody of Pearl (Chapters VII and VIII); (4) the house where Chillingworth and Dimmesdale lodge—the scenes in which the minister resists confessing to Chillingworth and in which the physician finds proof of his suspicions (Chapter X); (5) the scaffold, where the minister stands with Hester and Pearl late at night (Chapter XII); (6) the seashore, where Hester informs Chillingworth that she will no longer keep her vow of secrecy (Chapters XIV and XV); (7) the forest, where Hester and Pearl await Dimmesdale, and Hester and he are momentarily reunited (Chapters XVI–XIX) and (8) the marketplace—the culminating scene in which the minister first preaches his greatest sermon, then publicly confesses his sins and dies in Hester's arms (Chapter XXIII).

Setting the three crucial scenes of the novel (numbered 1, 5, and 8 above) on the scaffold underscores the unity of the action, bringing together the four major characters in their changing circumstances at the beginning, middle, and end of the novel.

The Characters

Of the major characters in *The Scarlet Letter*, Hester is by far the most fully realized. She is also the most sympathetic, for readers readily respond to her strength, dignity, and passion. Hester steadfastly endures her punishment and through her long suffering is absolved; however, Hester never repents in so many words of her love for Dimmesdale (although in his concluding chapter, Hawthorne implies that she is repentant).

Arthur Dimmesdale is a character so weak that only the facts of Hester's love and his extreme suffering lend him any reality. Yet some critics consider him to be the central character—the true tragic figure of the novel.

Chillingworth is a character essential to the theme, but too much the stock villain of melodrama to be completely believable. Yet, Chillingworth does change in the course of the novel from the scholar "thoughtful for others, craving little for himself" to a fiend who tortures Dimmesdale and tries to prevent him from making his saving confession.

Pearl, like Chillingworth, is necessary to the development of the theme. The embodiment of the consequence of sin, she remains mainly a symbol until the climactic scene on the scaffold in which she is humanized by grief.

Irony

Irony permeates *The Scarlet Letter*. Situational irony is central to the action of the novel. Chillingworth, the wronged husband, who might normally claim the reader's sympathy, turns out to be a fiend. A physician, whose mission is to cure, he befriends his patient in order to destroy him. Dimmesdale, agonized by guilt and self-loathing, is nevertheless able to achieve great heights in the pulpit.

Dramatic irony occurs most poignantly on those occasions when Hester and Dimmesdale meet in public and must communicate in ways that onlookers will not understand. A notable example of verbal irony occurs when Hawthorne accounts for the popularity of Hester's needlework among the Puritans as follows: "Vanity, it may be, chose to mortify itself, by putting on . . . the garments that had been wrought by sinful hands."

Symbolism

Hawthorne makes extensive use of symbols in *The Scarlet Letter*. Some objects keep the same symbolic significance throughout—the scaffold, which represents public notice, and weeds and unsightly vegetation, which stand for moral evil. Others—like the forest, which represents both nature and the threatening powers of the mythical Black Man—are ambivalent. The central symbol, the scarlet letter itself, changes in meaning, for the reader as well as for the people of Boston, as Hester steadfastly works out her absolution.

Henry James believed that Hawthorne used symbols to excess, as this passage from his essay indicates:

> In *The Scarlet Letter* there is a great deal of symbolism; there is, I think, too much. It is overdone at times, and becomes mechanical; it ceases to be impressive, and grazes triviality. The idea of the mystic *A* which the young minister finds imprinted upon his breast and eating into his flesh, in sympathy with the embroidered badge that Hester is condemned to wear, appears to me to be a case in point. This suggestion should, I think, have been just made and dropped; to insist upon it, and return to it, is to exaggerate the weak side of the subject. Hawthorne returns to it constantly, plays with it, and seems charmed by it; until at last the reader feels tempted to declare that his employment of it is puerile.
>
> —from "Hawthorne"
> Henry James

Many readers who are willing to accept the letter imprinted on the minister's flesh question Hawthorne's use of the immense letter *A* that lights up the marketplace in Chapter XII. Such misjudgments—if that is what they are—are minor blemishes. Hawthorne's scarlet letter is a powerful symbol that impresses itself on every reader's memory.

Writing About the Novel

A Creative Response

1. **Writing a New Ending.** The ending of *The Scarlet Letter* seems inevitable. But is it? Suppose the ship Hester and Dimmesdale were planning to take to Europe had sailed a few days earlier—before the Election Day sermon. Write a synopsis that sketches what happens to Hester, Pearl, and Dimmesdale after they flee from Boston.
2. **Supplying a Missing Scene.** Boston was a small village in the 1640's. Hester and Dimmesdale must have encountered each other sometimes. Suppose that Hester is leaving the Reverend Mr. Wilson's house, where she has delivered some needlework, and meets Dimmesdale just outside the door. This meeting takes place about two years after her humiliation on the scaffold and before the scene at Governor Bellingham's. Write a short dialogue, with stage directions, which reveals what they say to each other.
3. **Using Another Point of View.** In *The Scarlet Letter*, Hawthorne employs a third-person point of view. He mainly depicts the thoughts of only one character in a chapter. If he is showing what Hester is thinking, he is unlikely to give us a glimpse into the mind of the person she is talking to.

   In Chapter XII, Chillingworth comes upon the scene of Hester, Dimmesdale, and Pearl on the scaffold as the marketplace is suddenly lit up. Describe the scene from his point of view, using the first person. Show what he feels about this surprising sight. End the scene with his suggestion that he accompany the minister home.

A Critical Response

4. **Responding to Criticism.** Not all critics agree on how the events of the novel should be interpreted. Some regard Hester's ill-fated love for Dimmesdale as the result of a tragic flaw in her character. Others view Hester as a tragic heroine who renounces the strict forms of Puritanism and follows her own nature. The tragedy, they believe, results not from flaws in her character, but from the evils of Puritan society. Write a brief persuasive essay stating your opinion on this matter.
5. **Reading a Hawthorne Sketch.** Read Hawthorne's sketch "Endicott and the Red Cross," published in 1837, thirteen years before *The Scarlet Letter*. Compare in detail the author's picture of Puritan Salem with his picture of early Boston in the novel. Cite details of the sketch that Hawthorne used later in *The Scarlet Letter*.
6. **Assessing a Villain.** Many readers consider Chillingworth essential to the plot, but not a believable character. They find him to be too much the villain of melodrama—the kind of drama that oversimplifies characterization and exaggerates emotional content. Comment on this point of view, indicating whether you agree, partly agree, or disagree. Cite evidence from the novel to support your opinion.

Going Beyond the Novel

A Creative Response

1. **Writing an Autobiographical Sketch.** Write an autobiographical sketch by Pearl on her twentieth birthday, thirteen years after the events of *The Scarlet Letter.* Show how she feels about Hester, her own childhood, Dimmesdale, and the events of the story.
2. **Writing in Chillingworth's Journal.** Write a series of journal entries that Chillingworth might have written between the time of the scene at Governor Bellingham's (Chapter VIII) and the confirmation of his suspicion about the minister (Chapter X). Try to suggest both his growing certainty of Dimmesdale's guilt and his growing obsession for revenge.
3. **Presenting the Reverend John Wilson's Account.** John Wilson was an eyewitness to the climactic scene in which Dimmesdale mounts the scaffold with Hester and Pearl, confesses, and dies. Write the account of these events as Wilson might have written it in a letter to a friend in Salem. The account should include what he saw (or didn't see) on the minister's chest and how he explained Chillingworth's behavior on the scaffold.

A Critical Response

4. **Comparing Themes.** A number of themes treated in *The Scarlet Letter* found earlier expression in Hawthorne's stories, such as "Young Goodman Brown," "The Minister's Black Veil," and "Ethan Brand." Read these stories and explain what relation the theme of each has to the theme of *The Scarlet Letter*.
5. **Reporting on Puritanism.** Research and write a report on Puritanism in the Massachusetts Bay Colony. Your report should include descriptions of the American Puritans, religious tolerance in the colony, requirements for citizenship, and form of government.
6. **Analyzing Allegories.** Write a composition discussing Hawthorne as an allegorist—a writer of stories that illustrate religious or moral principles. Base your report on *The Scarlet Letter* and two or more of the following stories: "Young Goodman Brown," "Rappaccini's Daughter," "The Minister's Black Veil," "The Birthmark," and "Ethan Brand."
7. **Comparing the Novel with a Play.** Read the play *The Crucible* by Arthur Miller and compare Miller's picture of Puritan society with Hawthorne's in *The Scarlet Letter*.

1143

***The Great Gatsby* by F. Scott Fitzgerald**

For a biography of F. Scott Fitzgerald, see text pages 533–534. For further background on the novel, additional activities, and tests, see the separate study guide on *The Great Gatsby.*

The Novel

STUDY GUIDE

The Great Gatsby by F. Scott Fitzgerald

Elements of the Novel

The Themes

In a story called "The Rich Boy," F. Scott Fitzgerald wrote, "Let me tell you about the very rich. They are different from you and me. They possess and enjoy early, and it does something to them, makes them soft where we are hard, and cynical where we are trustful." *The Great Gatsby* is Fitzgerald's most thorough and penetrating study of the personalities of the rich, represented by Daisy, Tom, and to some extent, Jordan.

During the novel's various critical moments, these characters retreat into the protective cocoon of their wealth. Although this pattern becomes most obvious after Myrtle's death, it also appears in Daisy's youth. Readers are told that after her night with Jay Gatsby in Louisville, she "vanished into her rich house, into her rich, full life, leaving Gatsby—nothing."

The rich, in Fitzgerald's world, are almost always those who are born rich, not those who earn money, even if it is a great deal of money. Gatsby, for all his wealth, never becomes one of the "rich." Fitzgerald frequently explores the boundaries of social class in his writing, as well as the exclusion of the newly rich from certain well-established circles. His fascination with this issue is at least partly autobiographical, stemming from his initial romantic failure as the poor young man who asked for the hand of Zelda Sayre.

A related theme is love. Modern love in this novel is a matter of violence and egoism rather than tenderness and affection. Tom causes Daisy untold anguish, and yet she cannot bring herself to leave him. If Tom is emotionally brutal toward Daisy, he is both emotionally and physically brutal toward Myrtle. Myrtle herself treats her husband, George, with great scorn. Nick comes close to loving Jordan, but despite the fact that he says that "dishonesty in a woman is a thing you never blame deeply," her character flaws ultimately make it impossible for him to love her. The purest love in the novel is Gatsby's love for Daisy, but Daisy, like Jordan, is too flawed for such an emotion.

The thing that makes Gatsby great is his capacity for dreaming. He creates his very identity, his "Platonic conception of himself," out of his dreams. One of the major conflicts in the novel is between Gatsby's dreams and the material world in which they must find their fulfillment. The object of all his dreaming is Daisy: she is the part of the material world that will fulfill his dream. But

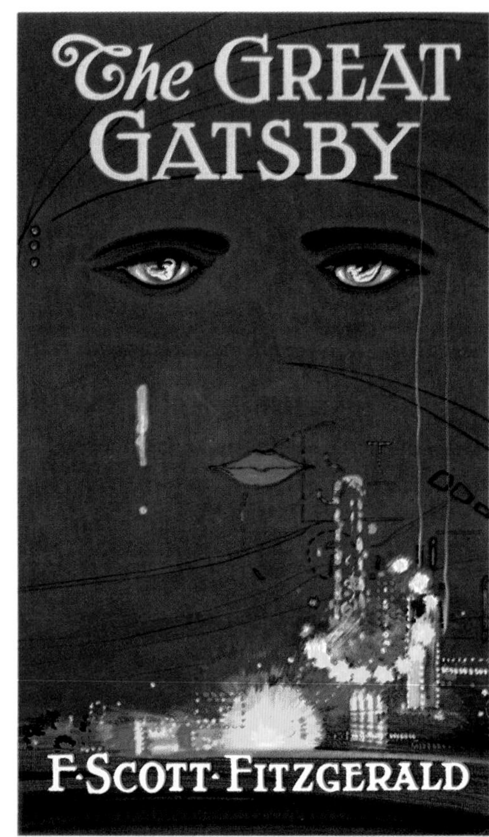

Daisy is shallow, unfaithful, and selfish—she is not really worthy of his devotion.

The great theme in *Gatsby*, the one which brings together all the others, is the American Dream and the way it unfolds in an era of decadence and corruption. The corruption runs through the behavior of almost all the characters: Meyer Wolfsheim fixes the 1919 World Series, Jordan Baker cheats at golf, and most of the guests at Gatsby's parties serve this corruption either directly (by being criminals) or indirectly (by catering to cheap popular tastes). Daisy, the wealthy golden girl, is a symbol of the American Dream, and in pursuing her, Gatsby is pursuing that dream—but Daisy is a corrupt symbol since she stands only for money, not for the ideals behind the dream. A society that produces the valley of the ashes and the corrupt characters mentioned above cannot produce a better goal for Gatsby. The greatness of the dream is present in the intensity of Gatsby's feelings, but it is also present in Nick's descriptions of his Midwest at the end of the book and in his description of how awe-inspiring America must have been when it was unsettled and unspoiled.

Point of View and Style

The story is told in the first person, from Nick Carraway's point of view. Nick is a reliable narrator, and the reader comes to trust him and share his values and attitudes. Nick's admiration for Gatsby, expressed at the very beginning of the book, keeps the reader aware of Gatsby's good points. No matter how foolish or corrupt he may act later on, we know that at core Gatsby is great. Similarly, Nick's increasingly harsh and objective view of Tom and Daisy prevents the reader from overromanticizing the lives of the wealthy. In terms of background and values, Nick is in between Gatsby and the Buchanans. Like Gatsby, he is from the Midwest, and he shares with Gatsby that great formative experience of young men of the period, the war. But he is related to Daisy and went to school with Tom, so he is really a part of both worlds.

This dualism extends to Nick's language, which varies from the lyric to the satiric. At its lyric best (as for example at the end of the novel) Nick's language expresses the rich dreamlike quality of American life. In its satiric mode, Nick's language scornfully rejects the corrupt materialism of modern American life. Nick is a master of deadpan humor, and the novel has a myriad of small comic touches (in the parties, in the byplay between Tom and Daisy, in Gatsby's behavior) which should not be overlooked.

The Setting

Gatsby's story could have taken place in no other setting and no other period. The twenties was a time of extravagant behavior, in business and public life and in private life. The automobile, fast and dangerous, and only just becoming available in great numbers, was practically a symbol of the period. Fitzgerald had lived in Great Neck, Long Island, the model for West Egg, and he had attended parties as lavish as any that Gatsby threw.

Physically, the setting helps to emphasize the novel's dualistic thematic elements (rich/poor, dreams/material reality). East Egg and West Egg face each other across the bay, West Egg being a kind of arrivistes' version of East Egg. Gatsby's house faces the Buchanans' across the bay. He is within sight of the realization of his dream, but will get no closer.

Midway between West Egg and New York lies the "valley of ashes," the poor area where Myrtle lives. Fitzgerald's description of this region makes it clear that it is most important to him (see "Symbolism," below).

Satire

The Great Gatsby provides a clearly satiric portrait of life in the twenties. The behavior of the guests (many of whom were not invited) at Gatsby's parties shows them, mostly in a comical way, to be venal, superficial, egocentered, and dissolute.

The portrait of Meyer Wolfsheim, the gangster who fixed the World Series, who wears cuff links made of human teeth, and who offers Nick a "gonnegtion," satirizes the romantic gangster of the twenties, as common a figure of the period as the speak-easy.

Symbolism

The symbolic elements of *Gatsby* help to give a universal resonance to the story. Gatsby is not just a young man from the Midwest who made a lot of money in questionable ways, and West Egg is not just an affluent suburb. Fitzgerald's use of symbolism helps to make this clear. The green light on Daisy's dock that Gatsby stares at longingly from his beach comes to represent the essence of Gatsby's dreams, "the orgiastic future that year by year recedes before us."

The center of the setting, the valley of ashes with its ash-gray men and impenetrable dust, is a symbolic representation of the setting as a whole, the wasteland of twentieth-century American life. The "dust that floated in the wake of [Gatsby's] dreams" comes from the valley of ashes. At the center of the valley of ashes is the billboard containing the "eyes of Dr. T. J. Eckleburg." This surreal image is for George Wilson a symbol of the eyes of God, and many critics agree.

Note that symbolism does in its way what the satire does in *its*, that is, presents a portrait of a corrupt twentieth-century America. The disparate elements of the novel work together in support of its principal themes.

Historical Context of *The Great Gatsby*

Gatsby is very much a novel of the early 1920's. Reading *The Great Gatsby* should give the reader a good feeling for what it was like to live at the beginning of the flapper era. Much of what is described in the novel is based on fact. Gatsby's parties are based on equally lavish parties that the Fitzgeralds attended while they lived in Great Neck in 1922, the year in which the novel takes place. Bootleggers and stock swindlers, like Gatsby, were making millions of dollars, and when they were arrested, their cases got a great deal of publicity. Fitzgerald followed one particular case in 1922 very closely. Edward Fuller, a stockbroker, was charged with selling stocks that didn't exist—a case that he used when he had Gatsby involved in selling counterfeit stocks.

In 1919, a gambler and gangster named Arnold Rothstein fixed the World Series, causing a scandal that rocked America. Rothstein was protected by New York City's corrupt political machine, and he made millions in gambling and bootlegging until his murder in 1928. Meyer Wolfsheim in *Gatsby* is based on Rothstein, and readers at the time would have recognized him immediately.

Two crucial historical events play an important role in *Gatsby*. The first is World War I, in which Gatsby and Nick both fought. The war, which was protracted and ugly, produced a generation of disillusioned veterans. The second event is of course the Volstead Act of 1919, which ushered in the years of Prohibition. Prohibition, which was one of the most widely ignored laws in United States history, made almost everyone a criminal, at least technically, and contributed to the moral laxity which is evident in *Gatsby*.

Writing About the Novel

A Creative Response

1. **Writing an Additional Chapter.** Fitzgerald said that he thought the biggest fault in *Gatsby* was that he didn't provide a picture of Daisy and Gatsby's relationship after they get together at Nick's house and before the blowup at the Plaza. Write a brief chapter that does this. Use Nick's point of view, and assume that either Daisy or Gatsby (or both) told Nick what the relationship was like.
2. **Using Another Point of View.** Write an account of the meeting with Gatsby at Nick's house and the subsequent tour of Gatsby's house from Daisy's point of view. What did it feel like to see Gatsby again after so many years?
3. **Writing a New Ending.** Assume that George Wilson did not kill Gatsby, and describe Gatsby's life after the end of the novel. Keep your characterization consistent with Gatsby's characterization in the novel.
4. **Casting the Movie.** There have been three movie versions of *The Great Gatsby*, the latest in 1974, starring Robert Redford and Mia Farrow. Like the earlier productions, this movie received mixed reviews. If you were chosen to cast a fourth film version of *Gatsby*, whom would you choose as stars? Write a persuasive essay, in the form of a memo, in which you recommend the performers you think should play Nick Carraway, Jay Gatsby, Daisy Buchanan, Tom Buchanan, Myrtle Wilson, Jordan Baker, George Wilson, and Meyer Wolfsheim. Make your choices as true to Fitzgerald's descriptions as you can.

A Critical Response

5. **Discussing a Theme.** Corruption of people and society is one of the themes in *Gatsby*. What characters may be said to be corrupt, and why? How is corruption related to the setting and to other themes, such as Gatsby's dream?
6. **Analyzing a Character.** Why does Tom behave the way he does? Is he all bad, or a mixture of bad and good?
7. **Responding to a Critic.** Today Fitzgerald's novel is considered a classic, but when it appeared in 1925, many critics dismissed it as inferior. H. L. Mencken, while praising the novel, had these reservations:

   > What ails it, fundamentally, is the plain fact that it is simply a story—that Fitzgerald seems to be far more interested in maintaining its suspense than in getting under the skins of its people. It is not that they are false; it is that they are taken too much for granted. Only Gatsby himself genuinely lives and breathes. The rest are mere marionettes—often astonishingly lifelike, but nevertheless not quite alive.

   Do you agree? Write an essay in which you respond to Mencken's criticism. In supporting or refuting Mencken's remarks, be specific. Cite descriptions, quote dialogue, and make comparisons. Open your essay with a statement that makes your response clear.
8. **Analyzing a Character.** Philosophically, **idealism** places reality not in the material world but in a world of ideas. Discuss Gatsby's idealism, pointing out its origins, its growth, and its loss in the novel.

Going Beyond the Novel

A Creative Response

1. **Writing a New Ending.** Assume that Daisy and Tom divorce a year after Gatsby's death. Write a description (using Nick's point of view) of the life of either of them now that they are separated.
2. **Describing a Character.** Assume that you are Gatsby, the year before the novel takes place. Write a letter to your father describing your accomplishments and aspirations.

3. **Extending the Story.** Assume that Nick has become an old man. Write a diary entry in which he describes how knowing Gatsby has changed his life.
4. **Writing a Feature Article.** You are a newspaper reporter working for the East Egg *Globe*. Your editor has asked you to do a feature article on Dr. T. J. Eckleburg's billboard, an eyesore that is still standing near the highway. The editor wants you to explain who Eckleburg was and why he or she put up the billboard. Make up a catchy headline for your story.

A Critical Response

5. **Researching Historical Background.** Research the Volstead Act and write a paper describing the effects of prohibition on American life in the twenties.
6. **Learning More About the Author.** Using several biographical sources, research Fitzgerald's years in Hollywood, and write a paper discussing his reputation at the time, how he lived and what he wrote.
7. **Reading Other Works by Fitzgerald.** Read the short stories collected in *Babylon Revisited* and compare them to *The Great Gatsby.* How are they related in subject and theme? How are they different?
8. **Researching Historical Background.** Research the importance of the automobile in the twenties. How many were there, what did they cost, how did people feel about them?
9. **Comparing Sources.** Read Zelda Fitzgerald's autobiographical novel *Save Me the Waltz* and F. Scott Fitzgerald's response (considered by many to be his masterpiece), *Tender Is the Night*. Compare and contrast the husband's and the wife's description of their life together.

WRITING ABOUT LITERATURE

Writing Answers to Essay Questions

Most units in this book are followed by Exercises in Critical Thinking and Writing, which include step-by-step instruction in using the writing process for answering questions about literature. These exercises are listed in the index in the back of this book. The following strategies will give you additional help in organizing and writing your essays.

1. **Read the essay question carefully.** Make sure you understand exactly what the question is asking and note how much evidence is required. Look for these *key verbs*:

• **Analyze:** This verb means "to break something down into its elements," so you can see its true nature.

EXAMPLE: *Analyze the character of Rip Van Winkle.*
STRATEGY: Review the ways a writer can create character (see page 1141). Then make a list of what you know about Rip and how you know it. Use your list to make a generalization about Rip's character.

• **Compare:** This means "to point out similarities." **Contrast** means "to point out differences."

EXAMPLE: *Contrast "Annabel Lee" with "Bells for John Whiteside's Daughter."*
STRATEGY: Make a chart listing the differences in the poems. Focus on the elements of poetry: sound effects, form, figures of speech, imagery, tone, and main idea.

• **Describe:** This means you should tell how something looks, sounds, smells, tastes, or feels.

EXAMPLE: *Describe Jay Gatsby, as he is portrayed in "Gatsby's Party."*
STRATEGY: Reread the excerpt and list all the details describing Gatsby's appearance and manner. Look for details telling how Gatsby looks, acts, and speaks, and how he affects other people.

• **Discuss:** This means you should comment in a general way.

EXAMPLE: *Discuss the use of imagery in three poems by William Carlos Williams.*
STRATEGY: Make a list of the images and note where they are drawn from: nature, city, etc. Are the images important to the meaning and tone of the poems? What emotions do they carry?

• **Evaluate:** This means "to judge how effective something is."

EXAMPLE: *Evaluate the play* The Glass Menagerie.
STRATEGY: Think about the elements of drama and evaluate the way they are used in this particular play. Is the plot consistent and logical? Are the characters credible? Is the theme important and not trite? Is the language fresh and original?

• **Illustrate:** You should provide examples to support an idea or statement.

EXAMPLE: *Illustrate the use of dialect in Mark Twain's works.*
STRATEGY: First, define dialect. Then list the examples of dialectical pronunciations, vocabulary, and syntax in Twain's work. In your essay, cite a few examples of dialect that are most interesting, or funny, or convincing.

• **Interpret:** You must explain the meaning or importance of something.

EXAMPLE: *Interpret the theme of Malamud's story "The Magic Barrel."*
STRATEGY: First, reread the story carefully, and then write down several statements that might serve as the story's theme. Review the story to see which statement best covers all the key elements in the story. Cite incidents and key passages that support your statement of theme.

• **Respond:** This asks that you give your personal reactions to a work. (This is a "subjective" assignment.)

EXAMPLE: *Explain your response to Andrea Lee's story "New African."*
STRATEGY: Write down your immediate response: Tell whether you liked or disliked the story, how it made you feel, what it made you think about. Whenever possible, write down reasons for your response. Then review the main elements of the story (plot, character, theme, point of view, setting, tone) and write down your response to the way the writer used each element.

2. **Write a thesis statement stating the main idea of your essay.** Be sure to gather evidence to support your thesis statement. Do a rough outline that includes two or three main points to support the main idea. You may want to write several thesis statements and test each one out. Select the one that best covers all your main points.

3. **Write one paragraph for each point you wish to make.** Include topic sentences; try to express each topic as clearly and simply as you can.

4. **End with a paragraph that summarizes or restates your main points.** Try to conclude your essay with a good "clincher sentence."

Writing and Revising a Research Paper

You may be asked to choose your own topic for a research report about a literary work. This means that your essay should include information from three or more outside sources (sources in addition to the story, poem, play, essay, or novel you are writing about).

Prewriting

1. Choose a limited topic that you can cover adequately. In a report of 500–700 words, for example, you can't possibly cover all of Henry Wadsworth Longfellow's life or discuss all of his poetry. But you can discuss and interpret one poem, or you can compare and contrast two poems.

2. In the library, look for information about your topic, and take notes. You will find information in the card catalogue listed under the author's name. Your librarian will direct you to other reference works available in your particular library. As you take notes, use notecards, and be sure to include the source (title of book or magazine article, author, publisher, and date of copyright) and page reference on each card. You may have several different cards (on different topics) from a single source. For example, from one article about Longfellow's poetry, you might have one notecard on the various themes he wrote about and another separate card with comments on his imagery.

3. Write several thesis statements. Eventually you will select one that best covers your topic.

4. Develop a working outline. List two or three important ideas that will develop or support your thesis statement. To support each of these ideas, use quotations, specific details, and examples from the work you are writing about. (The work you are writing about is known as the *primary source*. You might also refer to other works, letters, and journals by the same writer. The quotations and information from books, articles, and reviews about the work or its writer are known as *secondary sources*.) Once you've arranged your main ideas and quotations in the order that seems most logical to you, you'll have an informal working outline.

Writing

The draft of your essay should include the following parts:

1. Introduction. The first paragraph should catch the audience's interest and tell what the essay will be about. Your thesis statement should begin or end the opening paragraph.

2. Body. The body of your essay should develop your thesis statement. Each paragraph in the body of your essay should include a topic sentence and supporting evidence.

3. Conclusion. The final paragraph may restate the thesis statement, summarize the main ideas, or give your personal response to the work.

Revising

Reread your first draft at least once for content and at least once for style.

1. Content. Check to see that you've supported your thesis statement with enough strong evidence. Make sure you have documented information from three or more sources.

2. Style. To make your essay read smoothly, you may need to combine some choppy sentences or break up long sentences into shorter ones. Cut unnecessary or repetitive words and phrases. Make sure your ideas are clear and easy to follow. You'll find revision is easier if you try to listen to your words, as if you are reading the essay aloud.

Proofreading

Remember that the titles of poems, short stories, and essays should be enclosed in quotation marks. The titles of plays, novels, and other book-length works should be in italics. (In handwriting and typing, italics are indicated by underlining.) Use the following proofreader's symbols to correct errors in spelling and punctuation.

Symbol	Example	Meaning of Symbol
≡	Sarah knight (≡ under k)	Capitalize a lower-case letter.
/	A Farewell To Arms (/ through T)	Change a capital letter to lower case.
∧	The ∧ Gatsby (Great inserted)	Insert a word or phrase.

Symbol	Example	Meaning
∧	High Non (o inserted: High Noon)	Insert a letter.
⊙	F⊙ Scott Fitzgerald	Add a period.
^,^	"I^,^ Too"	Add a comma.
❛❛/❜❜	❛❛Elegy for Jane❜❜	Insert quotation marks.
—	From <u>Black Boy</u>	Set in italics.
∿	An~~en~~ne Tyler	Change the order of the letters.
⌒	Emily Dickins~~s~~on	Delete and close up space.
¶	¶William Faulkner died in 1962.	Begin a new paragraph.

A Model Essay

The following essay is a comment on "Divina Commedia I" by Henry Wadsworth Longfellow. The essay shows revisions that the writer made in the first draft.

Oft have I seen at some cathedral door
  A laborer, pausing in the dust and heat,
  Lay down his burden, and with reverent feet
  Enter, and cross himself, and on the floor
Kneel to repeat his paternoster° o'er;
  Far off the noises of the world retreat;
  The loud vociferations of the street
  Become an undistinguishable roar.
So, as I enter here from day to day,
  And leave my burden at this minster gate,°
  Kneeling in prayer, and not ashamed to pray,
The tumult of the time disconsolate
  To inarticulate murmurs dies away,
  While the eternal ages watch and wait.

—Henry Wadsworth Longfellow

5. **paternoster** (pät'ər nôs'tər): the Lord's Prayer (*pater noster* is "our father" in Latin).

10. **minster gate:** church gate.

"Divina Commedia I" by Henry Wadsworth Longfellow

INTRODUCTORY PARAGRAPH

Catches reader's interest.

You can ~~read~~ understand a poem without knowing anything about ~~it~~ the writer's life, but sometimes, if you don't know the biographical details, you miss a lot. To understand "Divina Commedia I" by Henry Wadsworth Longfellow, you will find it helpful to know some details about Longfellow's life and about his poetry in general.

Thesis statement.

BODY

Topic statement.

The details of Longfellow's life that relate to "Divina Commedia I" are tragic. After his wife's ~~tragic~~ death in 1861, Longfellow used to begin each day translating some of Dante's poem, The Divine Comedy, into English. "Divina Commedia I" is the first of six sonnets that Longfellow wrote ~~to serve~~ as prefaces to Dante's epic. Three years before this particular sonnet was written, Longfellow's wife was burned to death inher home, when some sealing wax fell on the lcloth of her light dress and ignited it. Longfellow himself ~~almost died of the burns he received~~ when he tried to beat out the flames with his bare hands. The "burden" referred to in the sonnet must refer to the burden of sadness the poet carries with him.

Supporting details.

Cites secondary source.

Cites from the poem.

Some pof Longfellow's ~~theories of poetry~~ also helps to illumine this sonnet. According to William Charvat, Longfellow's poems tend to teach austere lessons: "We are to work for work's sake. We are to accept life's labors, deprivals, and sorrows." ~~This~~ sonnet illustrates this ~~lesson~~. For Longfellow, the work of translation helped ~~to accept~~ life's sorrows. This is an optimistic almost Puritantic belief; it seemed to have worked with Longfellow.

Topic statement.

Supporting details.

Cites secondary source.

Aother characgeristic of Longrfellow's poetry ~~helps~~ to the poem. According to Leonard Unger, Longfellow's lyric and meditative poems have a characteristic development. They moving from "image to analogy to statement." This is the pattern of ~~Longfellow's poem.~~ The poem begins with ~~an~~ image of a laborer lying down his burden (probably his tools) and praying in a ~~church~~ (lines 1-8). While he prays, the street noises retreat. With the words "So, I enter . . . ," the speaker makes an analogy between the laborer's act and his own act ~~of lying~~ down his ~~own~~ burden to pray. ~~His~~ burden is ~~not a~~ physical ~~one, but a~~

Topic statement.

Cites secondary source.

Supporting details.

Cites from poem.

Writing About Literature

~~mental burden,~~ but the prayer has the same effect on him that it has on the laborer. For the poet, ~~it connects him~~ prayer is a connection with eternity. "The disconsolate present time dies away, to reveal the waiting ages of eternity."

CONCLUSION

Summarizes topic.

~~Without knowing~~ Before I knew that the poet at the time was mourning ~~over~~ the loss of his wife, I thought the poem ~~would be more~~ was puzzling. Once ~~you~~ I knew ~~the reasons~~ why Longfellow ~~had for seeking~~ sought comfort in prayer, ~~then~~ the poem ~~becomes~~ became a much more powerful and spoke to a feeling I could share.

Documenting Sources

Find out which method of documentation your teacher prefers: parenthetical citations, footnotes, or end notes.

1. **Parenthetical citations** give brief information in parentheses immediately after a quotation or other reference. More detailed information about each source is given in the bibliography. This simplified method of documenting sources is recommended by the MLA (Modern Language Association).

For a quotation from a prose passage by a writer who is identified in the text: *page number.*
In "Rip Van Winkle," Washington Irving explains that Rip has a "foolish and well-oiled disposition" (page 128).
For a quotation by a writer whose name is *not* mentioned in the text: *Author's last name, page number.*
The first arrivals to Cape Cod saw "a hideous and desolate wilderness" (Bradford, 14).
For a quotation from a play: *Act, Scene.*
When she has announced that she has bought a house with the insurance money, Mama tells Walter that the family ". . . couldn't of gone on like we was today. We was going backwards 'stead of forwards. . . ." (Act II, Scene 1).
For a quotation from a poem: *line number.*
Robinson begins his poem by calling Miniver Cheevy a "child of scorn" (line 1).

2. **Footnotes** are placed at the bottom of the page on which the reference appears. A raised number at the end of the reference within the essay indicates a footnote(1). Footnotes are generally numbered consecutively within a work.

[1] Wagenknecht, Edward, *Henry Wadsworth Longfellow* (New York: Oxford University Press, 1966).

[2] Charvat, William, "Henry Wadsworth Longfellow" in *Major Writers of America, Shorter Edition*, edited by Perry Miller *et al.* (New York: Harcourt Brace Jovanovich, 1966).

Check a writing handbook, or ask your teacher for the style for footnoting poems, magazine articles, interviews, and books with more than one author.

3. **End notes** are identical to footnotes except that they are listed on a separate page entitled "Notes" at the end of a paper. End notes are numbered consecutively.

4. A **bibliography** should be included at the end of your essay. This is an alphabetical list of all the sources you consulted in researching your essay, even if they don't appear in your footnotes. Bibliography entries are listed alphabetically by the author's last name. Here is a bibliography that lists the sources for the model essay on Longfellow's "Divina Commedia I."

Bibliography

Charvat, William, "Henry Wadsworth Longfellow" in *Major Writers of America, Shorter Edition*, edited by Perry Miller *et al.* (New York: Harcourt Brace Jovanovich, 1966).

Unger, Leonard, editor-in-chief, *American Writers: A Collection of Literary Biographies* (New York: Charles Scribner's Sons).

Wagenknecht, Edward, *Henry Wadsworth Longfellow* (New York: Oxford University Press, 1966).

Preteaching Note

You can use this lesson in a variety of ways: to help students achieve clarity in their own use of pronouns and antecedents, to help them decipher complicated uses of pronouns and antecedents in their reading, or to help them understand an author's use of point of view. In the selected passage, for example, the author uses "us" to refer to specific people—the narrator and her sister. Sometimes, though, the "we" can expand to mean "people like us." You might discuss the use of "we" with your students before and after they read the Literary Model. What impact does it have on the reader when an author uses the word "we"? Why does it make the reader want to identify with or take sides with the author?

Toni Morrison and *The Bluest Eye*

Pulitzer Prize-winning author Toni Morrison (1931–) has been exploring the issues of African American identity since the publication of her first novel, *The Bluest Eye*, in 1969. This novel charts the growth of the narrator, Claudia, and her sister, Frieda, two African American children growing up in the small industrial town of Lorain, Ohio, in the 1940's. Their classmate, Pecola, fantasizes about having blue eyes, an image of white American status that she thinks will protect her from the brutality within her own family.

Morrison's upbringing gave her a firm belief in the importance of community, which she has described as both restrictive and empowering. She sees her own identity as a writer as having been shaped both by her childhood hometown (again, Lorain, Ohio) and by her heritage as an African American woman. She once said that this identity gave her access to an extremely wide range of emotions and perceptions and that the dual exposure has enlarged her world and her writing.

Literature & Language

Using Pronouns and Antecedents Correctly

Literary Model

In the following passage Toni Morrison recalls her feelings about a new girl in school. Have you experienced a similar situation?

This disrupter of seasons was a new girl in school named Maureen Peal. A high-yellow dream child with long brown hair braided into two lynch ropes that hung down her back. She was rich, at least by our standards, as rich as the richest of the white girls, swaddled in comfort and care. The quality of her clothes threatened to derange Frieda and me. Patent-leather shoes with buckles, a cheaper version of which we got only at Easter and which had disintegrated by the end of May. Fluffy sweaters the color of lemon drops tucked into skirts with pleats so orderly they astounded us. Brightly colored knee socks with white borders, a brown velvet coat trimmed in white rabbit fur, and a matching muff. There was a hint of spring in her sloe green eyes, something summery in her complexion, and a rich autumn ripeness in her walk.

She enchanted the entire school. When teachers called on her, they smiled encouragingly. Black boys didn't trip her in the halls; white boys didn't stone her, white girls didn't suck their teeth when she was assigned to be their work partners; black girls stepped aside when she wanted to use the sink in the girls' toilet, and their eyes genuflected under sliding lids. She never had to search for anybody to eat with in the cafeteria—they flocked to the table of her choice, where she opened fastidious lunches, shaming our jelly-stained bread with egg-salad sandwiches cut into four dainty squares, pink-frosted cupcakes, sticks of celery and carrots, proud, dark apples. She even bought and liked white milk.

Frieda and I were bemused, irritated, and fascinated by her. We looked hard for flaws to restore our equilibrium, but had to be content at first with uglying up her name, changing Maureen Peal to Meringue Pie. Later a minor epiphany was ours when we discovered that she had a dog tooth—a charming one to be sure—but a dog tooth nonetheless. And when we found out that she had been born with six fingers on each hand and that there was a little bump where each extra one had been removed, we smiled. They were small triumphs, but we took what we could get—snickering behind her back and calling her Six-finger-dog-tooth-meringue-pie. But we had to do it alone, for none of the other girls would co-operate with our hostility. They adored her.

When she was assigned a locker next to mine, I could indulge my jealousy four times a day. My sister and I both suspected that we were secretly prepared to be her friend, if she would let us, but I knew it would be a dangerous friendship, for when my eye traced the white border patterns of those Kelly-green knee socks, and felt the pull and slack of my brown stockings, I wanted to kick her. And when I thought of the unearned haughtiness in her eyes, I plotted accidental slammings of locker doors on her hand.

—from *The Bluest Eye,*
Toni Morrison

Grammar Note

Note that the narrator talks about the new girl throughout the passage but gives the girl's name only twice. She mentions her own sister, Frieda, only twice by name, and she never gives the names of her other classmates.

How can the author write about so many people, including herself, and not use names? Morrison uses pronouns instead of names. A **pronoun** is a word that takes the place of a noun, or the name of a person, place, or thing. In the following example, *she* is used in place of *Maureen.*

This disrupter of seasons was a new girl in school named Maureen Peal. . . . *She* was rich. . . .

Here is a list of the **personal pronouns** and their possessive forms.

Examining the Writer's Technique

Pronouns	Antecedents
I	narrator
her	Maureen Peal
We, our	narrator and Frieda
her	Maureen Peal
ours, we	narrator and Frieda
she	Maureen Peal
we	narrator and Frieda
she	Maureen Peal
we, we, we	narrator and Frieda
her, her	Maureen Peal
we, our	narrator and Frieda
it	snickering, calling
They	"the other girls"
her	Maureen Peal

Using Pronouns in Your Writing Encourage students to think of a variety of points of view that Maureen might display. For example, she might indeed display the "unearned haughtiness" that the narrator attributes to her; or she might feel guilty, shy, confused, or simply content with her "superior" status. Since Morrison stresses that Maureen's status comes both from her light skin and from her enviable possessions, you might also encourage students to consider the issues of race and class as they write their responses.

Literature & Language / *cont.*

Personal Pronouns			
I, me you	he, him, she, her	it	they, them we, us
Possessive Forms of Personal Pronouns			
my, mine your, yours	his her, hers	its	their, theirs our, ours

Some other commonly used pronouns are *who, whom, whose, whoever, whomever, which, that, this, what.*

We use pronouns in speech and writing to avoid endless repetition of names and other nouns. Although the use of pronouns is essential to good writing, it is important that they are not used incorrectly or vaguely. It should always be clear to the reader to whom or what the pronoun refers.

> Frieda and Maureen were very talented. *She* loved to dance and sing.

The meaning of these sentences is confusing, because we cannot tell whether *she* refers to Frieda or Maureen.

The word to which a pronoun refers is called its **antecedent**. The antecedents of the italicized pronouns are in bold type in this passage:

> This disrupter of seasons was a new girl in school named **Maureen Peal**. . . . *She* was rich, at least by our standards, as rich as the richest of the white girls, swaddled in comfort and care. The quality of *her* clothes threatened to derange **Frieda and me**. Patent-leather shoes with buckles, a cheaper version of which *we* got only at Easter and which had disintegrated by the end of May.

Note the pronoun *our* in the second sentence. It has no clear antecedent. From the context, however, the reader can infer that the antecedent is "girls like us" or "the rest of us." To avoid the possibility of confusion in your writing, give every pronoun a clear antecedent.

> When the **teacher** called on her, *she* smiled encouragingly. [Unclear]
> When *she* called on Maureen, the **teacher** smiled encouragingly. [Clear]

A common mistake in writing involves the vague use of the pronouns *it, which, that,* and *this.*

> Maureen Peal had a dog tooth and was born with six fingers on each hand **which** had been removed. [Unclear]

> Maureen Peal had a dog tooth and was born with six fingers on each hand. The extra fingers had been removed. [Clear]

Examining the Writer's Technique

With a partner, analyze Morrison's use of pronouns by doing the following activity.

On a chart like the one below, list each pronoun used in paragraph 3. Next to each pronoun, write its antecedent.

Pronouns	Antecedents

Using Pronouns in Your Writing

Writing a Response. Assume you are Maureen Peal, the subject of Toni Morrison's narrative, and you have just read what Morrison wrote. Write a response, in which you explain what your thoughts were at the time these events took place. Tell how you felt about being a new girl in school and how you experienced the students' reactions to you. Write as "I." Be sure you use pronouns correctly. Remember, each pronoun must have a clear antecedent. Your response might begin like this:

> I entered school in the autumn of that year, a new girl who felt out of place immediately . . .

Preteaching Note
This lesson can help students understand how to express their ideas more precisely through combining sentences. It can also help them understand an author's ideas more precisely, as they understand that different ways of combining sentences produce different meanings.

You might introduce the lesson with the following exercise. On the chalkboard, write two sentences, such as *Karen has terrible stage fright* and *She loves acting*. Then invite students to combine and change these sentences in as many logical ways as possible—for example, *Although Karen has terrible stage fright, she loves acting; Karen has terrible stage fright; but she loves acting; Karen, who loves acting, has terrible stage fright;* and so on.

Langston Hughes
One of the most inspiring American writers of the twentieth century is Langston Hughes. His poetry, fiction, essays, and plays helped to promote a tradition of African American literature that drew on both literary and folk sources. Hughes's poetry is notable for its introduction of jazz rhythms into literature. His fiction was among the first to portray poor and working-class African Americans with dignity, humor, and insight. Hughes's life and work inspired later generations of African American writers, writers who have admired both the integrity of his work and his determination to reach a broad American audience.

Literature & Language

Combining Sentences

Literary Model

In this passage a biographer describes a place and a person that had a formative influence on the poet Langston Hughes (see pages 688–693).

He was born near midnight on February 1, 1902, in the city of Joplin, Missouri. The date of his birth he would take on faith, since Missouri did not require the registration of infants, and his birth was never entered officially there. He was named James Langston Hughes. Soon the first name (after his father) was ignored, and he grew up as Langston Hughes. His earliest memory was not of Joplin but of a house of two bedrooms and a side sitting-room at 732 Alabama Street in Lawrence, Kansas. Off to one side was a shed kitchen, and behind the house stood a woodshed, an outhouse, and a pump for drawing water. The neighborhood, quiet and shaded, nestled at the foot of a hill crowned by Kansas University; from the top one could see plains of wheat rolling to the horizon, and the silty green crook of the Kansas River where it bent toward the northern edge of Lawrence before drifting east toward the Missouri. Here, in almost the exact center of the continental United States, Hughes would pass most of the first thirteen years of his life.

Mostly he lived with his maternal grandmother, "a small woman, brown, slightly bent, with very long hair almost to her waist and only slightly gray in places. . . . Her face was very wrinkled like an Indian squaw's." Mary Sampson Patterson Leary Langston was almost seventy years old when Langston was born. He remembered her spending most of her time in an old-fashioned rocking chair; except to attend the weekly meeting of her lodge, Mary Langston generally stayed at home. At night she read a chapter of the Bible, combed out her long hair, rolled it under a white nightcap, and went to bed. "She never shouted or got happy, and at night when she knelt down and prayed, she prayed silently." But she also read to her grandson from Grimms' fairy tales, or from the Bible and whatever magazines and newspapers she could afford. Or she held him in her lap and in a calm, clipped voice related tales of heroism, of slavery and freedom, and especially of brave men and women who had striven to aid the colored race. "Through my grandmother's stories always life moved, moved heroically toward an end," Hughes would recall. But of black folk-ways, so important later to her grandson, she said nothing. "She had been away from the South since her youth so she evidently did not remember any Negro folk-stories. At least, she never told me any."

—from *The Life of Langston Hughes, Vol.1,*
Arnold Rampersad

A Note on Sentence Combining

When children first learn to write, they tend to use very short sentences, which create a choppy rhythm, like the following:

I have a dog. He is brown. His name is Traveler.

As children mature, however, their writing matures also:

I have a brown dog, and his name is Traveler.
I have a brown dog named Traveler.

These sentences flow more smoothly and are easier and more pleasing to read than a string of short, clipped sentences.

As children mature, they also are able to combine ideas in order to show relationships and to make certain ideas more emphatic than others. Read this string of short, simple sentences about Langston Hughes:

He was born near midnight. He was born on February 1, 1902. He was born in the city of Joplin, Missouri. He would take on faith the date of his birth. Missouri did not require the registration of infants. His birth was never entered officially there.

To show cause-and-effect relationships, and to create a smoother rhythmic style, Arnold Rampersad uses longer and more complex sentence constructions:

He was born near midnight on February 1, 1902, in the city of Joplin, Missouri. The date of his birth he would

Examining the Writer's Style
Answers will vary but should resemble the following:
1. A shed kitchen was off to one side. A woodshed, an outhouse, and a pump for drawing water stood behind the house. The neighborhood was quiet and shaded. It nestled at the foot of a hill. The hill was crowned by Kansas University. . . .
2. The third sentence in the paragraph uses a subordinate clause introduced by the word *when*.
3. The fifth sentence could have been written as four simple sentences
4. The two short sentences—the second and the last in the paragraph—convey an air of finality and abruptness that call upon the reader to think more carefully about what has just been said.

Using Sentence Combining in Your Writing
Suggest that students begin by numbering the facts to form a rough outline. Encourage them to develop a thesis sentence that will help them to shape their paragraphs. Remind them that sentence-combining techniques may help them to express their ideas but that the ideas themselves will be shaped by the thesis statement they choose.

When evaluating student work, focus on how students organize their paragraphs to support a central thesis and on how they use sentence-combining techniques to help their sentences flow clearly and smoothly.

Literature & Language/*cont.*

take on faith, since Missouri did not require the registration of infants, and his birth was never entered officially there.

One of the most common ways of combining sentences is to join two simple sentences with a coordinating conjunction, such as *and*, *but*, *or*, *nor*:

Soon the first name was ignored, *and* he grew up as Langston Hughes.

Another way of combining information is to subordinate one idea to another. This is done by joining a subordinate clause to an independent clause, using a subordinating conjunction, such as *although*, *if*, *because*, *since*:

The date of his birth he would take on faith, *since* Missouri did not require the registration of infants.

Writers use a variety of other methods to combine sentences. For example, they can drop words from one sentence and add the remaining words to the other sentence, as in the following example:

Separate: The neighborhood nestled at the foot of a hill crowned by Kansas University. The neighborhood was *quiet and shaded*.
Combined: The neighborhood, *quiet and shaded*, nestled at the foot of a hill crowned by Kansas University.

Examining the Writer's Style

Working with a partner, use the following items to analyze Rampersad's style.

1. In order to appreciate Rampersad's sentence-combining techniques, break down the passage beginning "Off to one side" and ending "first thirteen years of his life" into a series of simple sentences. Compare your sentences with those of your partner to be sure you have reduced Rampersad's sentences to their simplest form.
2. Good writers do not combine sentences randomly or thoughtlessly. The information they combine must be related, and the combination must make this relationship clear. Copy a sentence from the second paragraph of the selection that conveys information about Langston Hughes's grandmother. What construction is used to combine this information?
3. Copy a sentence from paragraph 2 that could have been written as four simple sentences.
4. Though sentence combining can improve the flow of writing, the short sentence is very effective when it is carefully placed. Copy two short sentences from paragraph 2. What impact do you think these short sentences are supposed to have on the reader?

Using Sentence Combining in Your Writing

Writing a Biographical Sketch. Read carefully the following list of facts about the life of Langston Hughes. Use these facts and sentence-combining techniques to write a biographical sketch of Hughes.

born in 1902 in Joplin, Missouri; died 1967 in New York—
attended Columbia University in 1921—
held a variety of odd jobs and traveled by freight all over the world—
wrote poetry, short stories, and autobiographical works—
The Weary Blues (1926) was first collection of poetry—
poetry expresses the tragedy of racism—
work reflects growing demands for social justice—
poetry often written to imitate the rhythms of jazz—
poetry often written in vernacular—
humorous sketches of Harlem life collected in *The Best of Simple* (1961)—
received Spingarn Medal in 1960—
knew such artists as Paul Robeson, Zora Neale Hurston, Carl Van Vechten, and Ernest Hemingway—

Preteaching Note
Through this lesson, students can better understand why sentence fragments are so often confusing. You can also use this lesson to help students understand why writers sometimes use sentence fragments intentionally.

You might introduce the lesson by writing a few sentence fragments on the chalkboard—possibly copying the material from adaptation 1a on page 1158. Encourage students to identify how *My brother and I* differs from the two sentences. Then have them discuss the impact of those words—confusion? Greater emphasis? A sense of mystery?

John Wayne, American Hero
For at least four decades, John Wayne (1907–1979) was not just a movie star; he was the quintessential symbol of American masculinity. "The Duke" symbolized strength, competence, bravery, protectiveness, authority, and the willingness to go it alone in the face of incredible odds. In many of his roles—especially in westerns and military films—he embodied the American virtues of staking out new worlds and preserving lawful behavior.

During the late 1960's and the 1970's, when the antiwar and the women's movements criticized violence and the "macho" mentality, Wayne's symbolism took on more negative aspects. He remained a popular figure with many, however—perhaps for nostalgic reasons—even after he retired from acting. Many fiction and nonfiction writers have noted the contradictory experiences of growing up with the powerful symbol of John Wayne.

Literature & Language

Correcting Sentence Fragments

Literary Model

In this passage, Joan Didion recalls her reaction to a swaggering movie star.

> In the summer of 1943 I was eight, and my father and mother and small brother and I were at Peterson Field in Colorado Springs. A hot wind blew through that summer, blew until it seemed that before August broke, all the dust in Kansas would be in Colorado, would have drifted over the tar-paper barracks and the temporary strip and stopped only when it hit Pikes Peak. There was not much to do, a summer like that: there was the day they brought in the first B-29, an event to remember but scarcely a vacation program. There was an Officers' Club, but no swimming pool; all the Officers' Club had of interest was artificial blue rain behind the bar. The rain interested me a good deal, but I could not spend the summer watching it, and so we went, my brother and I, to the movies.
>
> We went three and four afternoons a week, sat on folding chairs in the darkened Quonset hut which served as a theater, and it was there, that summer of 1943 while the hot wind blew outside, that I first saw John Wayne. Saw the walk, heard the voice. Heard him tell the girl in the picture called *War of the Wildcats* that he would build her a house, "at the bend in the river where the cottonwoods grow." As it happened I did not grow up to be the kind of woman who is the heroine in a Western, and although the men I have known have had many virtues and have taken me to live in many places I have come to love, they have never been John Wayne, and they have never taken me to that bend in the river where the cottonwoods grow. Deep in that part of my heart where the artificial rain forever falls, that is still the line I wait to hear.
>
> —from *Slouching Towards Bethlehem*,
> Joan Didion

Grammar Note

A **sentence** is a group of words containing a subject and a verb and expressing a complete thought. A sentence begins with a capital letter and ends with some appropriate mark of punctuation, usually a period. A **sentence fragment** is a group of words that is punctuated as a sentence but does not express a complete thought. The words in bold type in the following passages are examples of fragments:

> I was eight, and my father and mother and small brother and I were at Peterson Field in Colorado Springs. **In the summer of 1943.**
>
> I enjoy movies with lots of action. **And suspense.** Movies can send chills up your spine or bring tears to your eyes. **Even though you know what you are watching is not real.**

By themselves these word groups in bold type do not make complete sense. Some of them do not have subjects and verbs; they are just phrases. (*In the summer of 1943. And suspense.*) One is a dependent clause and its meaning is complete only when it is part of the preceding sentence. (*Even though you know what you are watching is not real.*) All of these word groups must be combined with other words to express a complete thought.

Fragments are common in speech, and some professional writers use fragments to reflect informal speech patterns in their writing or to create other special stylistic effects. Didion uses sentence fragments twice. In the fragments in bold type below, she has left out the subjects.

> We went three and four afternoons a week, sat on folding chairs in the darkened Quonset hut which served as a theater, and it was there, that summer of 1943 while the hot wind blew outside, that I first saw John Wayne. **Saw the walk, heard the voice. Heard him tell the girl in a picture called *War of the Wildcats* that he would build her a house, "at the bend in the river where the cottonwoods grow."**

Didion is a highly respected published writer and, without worrying that people will accuse her of not knowing the rules of grammar, she can use fragments like this for dramatic effect. Here she imitates the informal patterns of spoken English, especially the "tough guy," clipped fragments allegedly spoken by cowboys—the kinds of characters played by John Wayne.

Examining the Writer's Style
Answers will vary but should resemble the following:
1. a. Although the rain interested me, I could not spend the summer watching it, so my brother and I went to the movies.
b. There was an Officers Club, but it had no swimming pool.
c. As it happened, I did not grow up to be the kind of woman who is the heroine in a Western. Nevertheless, the men I have known have had many virtues and have taken me to live in many places I have come to love.
2. a. I tell you this neither in a spirit of self-revelation nor as an exercise in total recall.
b. When he rode through my childhood—and perhaps through yours—John Wayne determined forever the shape of certain dreams.
c. Because it did not seem possible that such a man could fall ill, that he could carry within him that most inexplicable and ungovernable of diseases, the rumor struck some obscure anxiety.

Avoiding Sentence Fragments in Your Writing
Suggest that students begin by brainstorming everything they can think of about the character and his or her impact on them. Then encourage students to organize their essays around a thesis statement that focuses on this character's impact on them. Evaluate student work based on the choice of details to convey a main idea and on the use of complete sentences to express thoughts clearly.

To correct a fragment, add a subject or verb or do whatever else is necessary to make it a complete thought. If Didion had wanted to change one fragment into a complete sentence, she could have edited her copy like this:

Fragment: Saw the walk, heard the voice.
Sentence: **I** saw the walk, heard the voice.

Sometimes the fragment has to be joined to another sentence that comes before or after it.

Fragment: I was eight, and my father and mother and small brother and I were at Peterson Field in Colorado Springs. **In the summer of 1943.**
Sentence: **In the summer of 1943,** I was eight, and my father and mother and small brother and I were at Peterson Field in Colorado Springs.

Examining the Writer's Style

1. Identify the fragments in the following adaptations of Didion's writing, and edit each passage so you've eliminated the fragment.
   - **a.** The rain interested me a good deal, but I could not spend the summer watching it. And so we went. My brother and I.
   - **b.** There was an Officers Club. But no swimming pool.
   - **c.** As it happened I did not grow up to be the kind of woman who is the heroine in a Western. Although the men I have known have had many virtues and have taken me to live in many places I have come to love.
2. Correct the fragments in these adaptations from another part of this essay.
   - **a.** I tell you this neither in a spirit of self-revelation. Nor as an exercise in total recall.
   - **b.** John Wayne determined forever the shape of certain dreams when he rode through my childhood. And perhaps through yours.
   - **c.** It did not seem possible that such a man could fall ill. Could carry within him that most inexplicable and ungovernable of diseases. The rumor struck some obscure anxiety.

Analyzing Sentence Fragments

Work in small groups to find examples of sentence fragments in the work of professional writers. (Check news magazines and advertising copy, in particular.) Discuss why the writers might have chosen to use fragments in these instances. How do the fragments affect you?

Avoiding Sentence Fragments in Your Writing

Describing a Movie Star or Character. Write an essay about a film star or a character from a movie who made a very big impression on you.

- **a.** Before you begin to write, try to remember someone whom you admire greatly. Can you recall dreaming about meeting that person or wanting to look or act like him or her? Take notes as you relive your feelings through your memories. Focus on the characteristics of the individual as well as on his or her influence on you. You might want to conclude with a statement on whether or not the person's influence continues to affect you.
- **b.** Using your notes, write at least three paragraphs. Be careful to avoid fragments. Ask a classmate to read your paper and tell you if you have made your subject and his or her influence clear.

Preteaching Note
Students may wish to supplement this material with **Grammar, Usage, and Mechanics: A Reference Guide** coverage of comma rules.

It might be helpful to begin the lesson by having volunteers share examples with the class of sentences that require commas. You may wish to prompt students with such questions as "What about when you are writing dialogue?" or "How can commas make a list easier to read?" You might then record student suggestions on the chalkboard, comparing them later with the examples of comma use given in the lesson.

Elie Wiesel and the Holocaust
The period of history in which Nazi Germany persecuted Jews and other "undesirables" is so horrific that it has become known as the "Holocaust," a word that means "great or total destruction of life by fire." Since the main thrust of the Holocaust was to rid Hitler's domain of Jews (along with Gypsies, Slavs, and homosexuals), the word has come to suggest genocide—the attempt to destroy an entire people.

Wiesel was one of the Jews taken by the Nazis in the spring of 1944, when he was only 15 years old. Although he survived, his parents and younger sister did not. He later learned that his older sisters survived as well. This experience became the foundation of Wiesel's many accounts dealing with the Holocaust. However, Wiesel remained silent about this experience for many years, because he didn't believe he could possibly communicate its full horror. Finally, in 1956, he published *Night*, the autobiographical novel that was to be the first of many works bearing witness to the Holocaust.

Literature & Language

Using Commas Correctly

Literary Model

In 1944 Elie Wiesel and his family lived in Sighet, a small village in Transylvania (present-day Romania). In this selection from his memoir *Night*, Wiesel recalls how, as a young boy, he waited for the terrible day that he and his family would be forced from their home by the Hungarian police and Nazis and taken to concentration camps. Elie was the only member of his family to survive.

I was up at dawn. I wanted time to pray before we were expelled.

My father had got up earlier to go and seek information. He came back at about eight o'clock. Good news: it wasn't today that we were leaving the town. We were only to move into the little ghetto. There we would wait for the last transport. We should be the last to leave.

At nine o'clock, Sunday's scenes began all over again. Policemen with truncheons yelling:

"All Jews outside!"

We were ready. I was the first to leave. I did not want to see my parents' faces. I did not want to break into tears. We stayed sitting down in the middle of the road, as the others had done the day before yesterday. There was the same infernal heat. The same thirst. But there was no longer anyone left to bring us water.

I looked at our house, where I had spent so many years in my search for God; in fasting in order to hasten the coming of the Messiah; in imagining what my life would be like. Yet I felt little sorrow. I thought of nothing.

"Get up! Count off!"

Standing. Counting off. Sitting down. Standing up again. On the ground once more. Endlessly. We waited impatiently to be fetched. What were they waiting for? At last the order came:

"Forward march!"

My father wept. It was the first time I had ever seen him weep. I had never imagined that he could. As for my mother, she walked with a set expression on her face, without a word, deep in thought. I looked at my little sister Tzipora, her fair hair well combed, a red coat over her arm, a little girl of seven. The bundle on her back was too heavy for her. She gritted her teeth. She knew by now that it would be useless to complain. The police were striking out with their truncheons. "Faster!" I had no strength left. The journey had only just begun, and I felt so weak. . . .

"Faster! Faster! Get on with you, lazy swine!" yelled the Hungarian police.

It was from that moment that I began to hate them, and my hate is still the only link between us today. They were our first oppressors. They were the first of the faces of hell and death.

We were ordered to run. We advanced in double time. Who would have thought we were so strong? Behind their windows, behind their shutters, our compatriots looked out at us as we passed.

At last we reached our destination. Throwing our bags to the ground, we sank down:

"Oh God, Lord of the Universe, take pity upon us in Thy great mercy. . . ."

— from *Night*,
Elie Wiesel

Grammar Note

The comma is perhaps the most frequently used and misused punctuation mark. Generally, the **comma** signals the reader to pause, as the period signals a full stop. Commas also set off various sentence parts or elements to make reading easier.

One important use of the comma is **to set off independent clauses joined by a coordinating conjunction**, such as *and*, *but*, *or*, *nor*, *for*, *so*. (An **independent clause** is one that makes sense when standing alone.)

> It was from that moment that I began to hate them, and my hate is still the only link between us today.

The exception to this rule applies when two independent clauses are very short. Then the comma may be omitted.

> They were ordered to run and they advanced in double time.

Examining the Writer's Style
Responses may vary but should resemble the following:
1. Sunday's scenes began all over again, as policemen with truncheons were yelling.
2. They had us standing, counting off, sitting down, and standing up again.
3. The bundle on her back was too heavy for her, so she gritted her teeth.
4. At last we reached the destination that they had determined for us.
5. The police were striking out with their truncheons, which they did frequently, and they struck a man standing near me.

Using Commas Correctly in Your Writing
Encourage students to read both versions aloud, carefully noting the rhythms of each. You might wish to have listeners comment on the rhythm of sentences read by others, so that students can pay full attention to listening without being distracted by the experience of reading aloud. Students should notice that short, spare sentences create a sense of horror, whereas longer sentences may convey a more relaxed rhythm.

Literature & Language/*cont.*

Errors occur when writers leave out the coordinating conjunction and try to join the two clauses with a comma and no conjunction. This error is called a **comma splice**.

Comma splice: Elie's father had gotten up earlier to go and seek information, he came back about eight o'clock.
Correct: **Elie's father had gotten up earlier to go and seek information, and he came back about eight o'clock.**

A comma is used **to signal a pause after an introductory element** in a sentence. That element may be a single word, a phrase, or a clause.

Single word: **No,** the secret was well kept.
Phrase: **At nine o'clock,** Sunday's scenes began all over again.
Clause: **As they threw their bags,** they fell to the ground.

Commas are also used **to set off nonrestrictive elements** in a sentence. A **nonrestrictive element** is a word, phrase, or clause that is not essential to the basic meaning of the sentence. To show that such elements are nonrestrictive or nonessential, set them off with commas.

Nonrestrictive clause: *Night,* **which is a personal recollection of the holocaust,** was published in 1960.

Note that a comma is placed both before and after the nonrestrictive element.

When the sentence contains restrictive elements, these are *not* set off by commas. **Restrictive elements** are essential words, phrases, or clauses, which, if taken out, would change the basic meaning of the sentence.

Restrictive clause: The day **that they dreaded for so long** finally came.

The clause in bold type is restrictive because without it the meaning of the sentence would be unclear or incomplete. Note, *no* commas are used with restrictive clauses.

Another common use of the comma is **to separate items in a series**. A **series** consists of three or more words, phrases, or clauses of equal grammatical rank. Typically, commas are placed after each element except the last one. (The word *and* or *or* often appears before the last element in a series.)

Items in a series: . . . They were not taking away any **gold, silver, or other objects** of value.

I looked at my little sister Tzipora, **her fair hair well combed, a red coat over her arm, a little girl of seven**.

Examining the Writer's Style

Rewrite the following sentences, correcting the errors in comma use.

1. Sunday's scenes began all over again, policemen with truncheons were yelling.
2. They had us standing, counting off sitting down and standing up again.
3. The bundle on her back was too heavy for her, she gritted her teeth.
4. At last we reached the destination, that they had determined for us.
5. The police were striking out with their truncheons which they did frequently and they struck a man standing near me.

Using Commas Correctly in Your Writing

Changing Sentence Style. Elie Wiesel's style in this passage is to use frequent series of short, spare sentences. Locate two or three of these series of short sentences. Then turn any two of Wiesel's short, simple sentences into a single, longer sentence that combines two independent clauses. Be sure to punctuate your sentences correctly. Then read Wiesel's original series of sentences and your revision aloud. Is there a difference in effect? How would you describe the impact of Wiesel's sentence style?

Preteaching Note
Students will find this lesson helpful both in appreciating the power of anecdotal writing and in thinking about how to construct their own descriptive and narrative work. You might introduce the lesson by inviting students to read the one-sentence summary that introduces the Literary Model and then having them make predictions about what the tone and content of the piece will be. Encourage student volunteers to share their predictions with the class, perhaps writing their suggestions on the chalkboard. Afterward, you and your class might discuss how accurate the predictions were and what the writer did to confirm or upset the reader's expectations.

Accounts of Favorite Teachers
One of the most popular modes for a memoir is the writer's account of the special teacher that helped him or her to learn an important lesson. The lesson might be related to language, as in Julia Alvarez's *My English* or Ernesto Galarza's *Barrio Boy.* Or the lesson might have to do with valuing oneself and setting goals as in Mark Mathabane's *Kaffir Boy,* an account of growing up in South Africa. One of the most moving accounts of an important teacher is Helen Keller's *The Autobiography of Helen Keller,* in which she relates how her teacher, Annie Sullivan, helped her to understand the meaning of language. Students may enjoy reading and discussing memoirs such as these.

Literature & Language

Using the Descriptive and Narrative Modes

Literary Model

In this passage, a writer describes how a teacher helped her to feel at home with the English language. (A "habit" is the dress worn by Sister Bernadette. At the time this anecdote takes place, nuns wore black habits and head coverings known as "wimples.")

> Sister Bernadette stood at the chalkboard. Her chalk was always snapping in two because she wrote with so much energy, her whole habit shaking with the swing of her arm, her hand tap tap tapping on the board. "Here's a simple sentence: *The snow fell.*" Sister Bernadette pointed with her chalk, her eyebrows lifted, her wimple poked up. Sometimes I could see little bits of gray hair disclosed by her wobbly habit. "But watch what happens if we put an adverb at the beginning and a prepositional phrase at the end: *Gently the snow fell on the bare hills.*" I thought about the snow. I saw how it might fall on the hills, tapping lightly on the bare branches of trees. Softly it would fall on the cold cold fields. On toys children had left out in the cold, and on cars and on little birds and on people out late walking on the streets. Sister Bernadette filled the chalkboard with snowy print, on and on, handling and shaping and moving the language, scribbling all over the board until English, those little bricks of meaning, those little fixed units and counters, became a charged, fluid mass that carried me in its great fluent waves, rolling and moving onward, to deposit me on the shores of the only homeland. I was no longer a foreigner with no ground to stand on. I had landed in language.
>
> I had come into my English.
>
> —from *My English,*
> Julia Alvarez

A Note on the Descriptive and Narrative Modes

Description is the mode of writing that uses language to help us *see* something very clearly. To create a picture, description uses language that appeals to our sense of sight, and also to our senses of smell, touch, hearing, and taste. Notice that Julia Alvarez allows us to "see" and "hear" Sister Bernadette at the chalkboard, energetically writing, with the chalk "snapping in two." When Alvarez describes English words as "little bricks of meaning," we sense the solidity of bricks and understand the feeling of security that learning a new language gave her. Description often creates a **mood** or **emotion**. In this passage, we share the narrator's exhilaration.

It is almost impossible to write a description without conveying a tone. **Tone** is the writer's attitude toward his or her subject, characters, and audience. A writer's tone may be playful, sarcastic, critical, somber, and so on. Alvarez conveys a tone of admiration toward Sister Bernadette. (Imagine the other tones she might have expressed in a description of how she learned grammar!)

Narration is the mode of writing that tells about a series of events that take place in time. Short stories, which are built on a series of related events, are a common form of narrative, but the narrative mode is also used widely in nonfiction (memoirs, biographies, news reports) and even in poetry. Usually a narrative is told in **chronological order**—in the order in which the events occurred in time. For example, Julia Alvarez first presents Sister Bernadette standing at the chalkboard, then writing a simple sentence, and finally adding other words to that sentence.

Examining the Writer's Style

Working with a partner, examine Alvarez's style by completing these activities.

1. Copy the left chart on the next page. Then, in the appropriate columns, fill in the descriptive words and phrases that help you to "see" this classroom and the teacher, and to share the narrator's private thoughts.
2. The word *tapping* is used to describe two different sounds. Explain the difference in the sounds.
3. Why is *snowy* a good descriptive word for the "print" mentioned in the passage?
4. What words and phrases indicate action and movement in time? What has the narrator achieved at the end of the passage?
5. Which word best describes the author's attitude toward learning English: *timid, confused, exuberant?* What words and phrases in the passage help convey that tone?
6. If the passage were to continue in chronological order and with the same tone, what might happen next? What kind of event would change the tone of the passage?

Examining the Writer's Style
Answers will vary but may include the following:
1. Sight: chalk snapping in two, habit shaking, eyebrows lifted, wimple poked up; **Hearing:** hand tap tap tapping, snow tapping lightly; **Touch:** cold cold fields, fluid mass.
2. The chalk's tapping on chalkboard is harsh and sharp; the snow's tapping on branches is soft and gentle.
3. *Snowy* evokes the image of the snow as well as the chalk.
4. *Sometimes, on and on, became, no longer.*
The speaker has come into a new understanding about the English language.
5. The word *exuberant.*
Images of the mass and the great wave reinforce the tone.
6. Answers will vary. The narrator might cross plains and scale mountains next.
Again, answers will vary. The narrator might begin to feel overwhelmed or exhausted, or she might be brought back to reality by being called on—and possibly found unprepared.

Writing in the Descriptive and Narrative Modes
1. Writing a Character Sketch. Encourage students to quickly jot down the words that come to mind as they picture their characters in particular situations. Remind peer reviewers to be positive in their comments, noting strengths as well as weaknesses. Student writing should use specific details to convey events, places, feelings, and possibly a physical picture of the character being described.
2. Changing the Tone. Students may wish to use a thesaurus or dictionary to find words with connotations other than those that Alvarez used. Encourage students to choose words that work together to create a consistent attitude and a realistic picture.

Literature & Language / *cont.*

DESCRIPTIVE LANGUAGE				
Sight	**Hearing**	**Touch**	**Smell**	**Taste**

Writing in the Descriptive and Narrative Modes

1. **Writing a Character Sketch.** Alvarez's little anecdote is at the same time a character sketch of Sister Bernadette and a little story about how the nun taught English. Write a character sketch of your own in which you relate a series of events that reveal something about a particular character you feel strongly about.
   a. To help you think of ideas, you might fill out a chart like the one at the top of the next column.

Person	
Events that took place	
My feeling about the person and events	
Specific descriptive details about the setting and person	

   b. Choose a partner and exchange character sketches. See if your partner can identify the tone you have tried to convey about your character and about the events you are narrating.
   c. If your classmate did not identify the tone you were trying to convey, ask for suggestions on how to make your tone clearer. Then read your character sketch to the class for other reactions.
2. **Changing the Tone.** Imagine that you are a student in the same class as Julia Alvarez but you have had a different attitude toward learning English. Rewrite the snowfall image. Before you begin, list the details Alvarez used to describe a soft, gentle snowfall. Next to those details, write words that might be used to describe a different kind of snowfall, a threatening or blinding one, for example. Then rewrite the passage, choosing different words and details to convey your attitude.

Preteaching Note
You can use this lesson in a variety of ways: to help students get a handle on their own expository and persuasive essays; to aid students' appreciation of other expository and persuasive writers; and to help students distinguish between fact and opinion, exposition and persuasion.

You might begin the lesson by asking students about the ways that they try to convince someone to share their point of view. List student examples or suggestions on the chalkboard. Have them look for persuasive techniques as they read the Literary Model.

Television
Since its beginnings, television has been a controversial form of entertainment. Many trends in television programming seem to support MacNeil's argument. For example, many advertisements have been shortened from one minute to 30 seconds to the current preferred length of 15 seconds. Thus, viewers are bombarded with shorter and shorter bits of information, which some observers believe leads to "sensory overload"—the inability to think rationally about the large amount of information being taken in within a short time.

If students are interested in having their assumptions about television challenged further, they might enjoy reading *The Plug-In Drug* by Marie Winn and *Four Arguments for the Elimination of Television* by Jerry Mander.

Using the Expository and Persuasive Aims

Literary Model

In this passage from an essay, a television newscaster has two aims: He wants to explain what he thinks is wrong with television, and he wants to convince his readers to share his views. (He wants them to turn off the TV!)

It is difficult to escape the influence of television. If you fit the statistical averages, by the age of 20 you will have been exposed to at least 20,000 hours of television. You can add 10,000 hours for each decade you have lived after the age of 20. The only things Americans do more than watch television are work and sleep.

Calculate for a moment what could be done with even a part of those hours. Five thousand hours, I am told, are what a typical college undergraduate spends working on a bachelor's degree. In 10,000 hours you could have learned enough to become an astronomer or engineer. You could have learned several languages fluently. If it appealed to you, you could be reading Homer in the original Greek or Dostoyevsky in Russian. If it didn't, you could have walked around the world and written a book about it.

The trouble with television is that it discourages concentration. Almost anything interesting and rewarding in life requires some constructive, consistently applied effort. The dullest, the least gifted of us can achieve things that seem miraculous to those who never concentrate on anything. But television encourages us to apply no effort. It sells us instant gratification. It diverts us only to divert, to make the time pass without pain.

Television's variety becomes a narcotic, not a stimulus. Its serial, kaleidoscopic exposures force us to follow its lead. The viewer is on a perpetual guided tour: 30 minutes at the museum, 30 at the cathedral, 30 for a drink, then back on the bus to the next attraction—except on television, typically, the spans allotted are on the order of minutes or seconds, and the chosen delights are more often car crashes and people killing one another. In short, a lot of television usurps one of the most precious of all human gifts, the ability to focus your attention yourself, rather than just passively surrender it.

Capturing your attention—and holding it—is the prime motive of most television programming and enhances its role as a profitable advertising vehicle. Programmers live in constant fear of losing anyone's attention—anyone's. The surest way to avoid doing so is to keep everything brief, not to strain the attention of anyone but instead to provide a constant stimulation through variety, novelty, action and movement. Quite simply, television operates on the appeal to the short attention span.

—from "The Trouble with Television,"
Robert MacNeil

A Note on the Expository and Persuasive Aims

The aim of **exposition** is to inform, define, explain, or clarify facts or theories. News stories and encyclopedia articles are examples of writings with an expository aim. Writers of exposition frequently use verifiable facts, statistics, and examples to illustrate and support their main ideas.

The aim of **persuasion** is to influence, persuade, and convince other people to adopt the writer's opinion or to take a particular action. Since **opinions** are attitudes, beliefs, and values that cannot be proved or disproved scientifically, persuasive writers often use appeals to our emotion as well as logical arguments. Political speeches and letters to the editor are examples of writings with a persuasive aim.

Often a writer will want to explain or inform *and* persuade at the same time. Newspaper editorials, opinion columns, and book and movie reviews are examples of writings with both expository and persuasive aims. In his essay, Robert MacNeil aims both to inform his readers about the influence of television and to persuade them that it has harmful effects.

Examining the Writer's Style

Copy the chart on the next page. Working with a partner, use the following questions to help you fill out the chart. You will have to state the main idea of each paragraph and cite the kind of support MacNeil uses to inform or persuade the reader (facts, examples, opinions, etc.)

Examining the Writer's Style
Responses will vary. The chart might be completed as follows:
1. Television is hard to escape—statistics on numbers of televisions.
2. More profitable things could be done with time spent watching TV—examples of alternative activities.
3. Television discourages concentration—compared to other activities.
4. Television is a narcotic—extended analogy of "guided tour."
5. Television appeals to short attention spans—description of programmers' concerns.

Suggested responses to numbered questions are implied above. Suggested response to question 6: Students may find that MacNeil uses such loaded words as *narcotic, chosen delights,* and *precious . . . gifts.*

Writing with Expository and Persuasive Aims
Students may wish to brainstorm in small groups to come up with defenses of television. Encourage them to do some research to locate examples, situations, and arguments that might support a pro-television view. Remind students that they don't have to agree with their own arguments; this is an exercise in drafting a rebuttal. Student writing should include clear, focused thesis statements effectively supported by examples and details.

Main Idea of Paragraph	Support for Main Idea
1	
2	
3	
4	
5	

1. Before giving his opinion on the trouble with television, MacNeil provides information on television's negative impact on Americans. What are the main ideas of the first two paragraphs?
2. How does MacNeil support these main ideas?
3. In which paragraph does MacNeil state his opinon about the trouble with television? What is his opinion? How does he support his opinion?
4. What is the "guided tour analogy," or comparison, intended to accomplish?
5. Of the arguments MacNeil uses to support his opinion, which do you find most effective? Why?
6. Are any of MacNeil's arguments intended to appeal to our emotions? Does he use any "loaded" words to manipulate our feelings so we'll agree with him?

Writing with Expository and Persuasive Aims

Writing a Rebuttal. Suppose you are a television executive or performer who thinks MacNeil has given a misleading or one-sided view of television's influence. Write a letter to MacNeil explaining "What's Good About Television."

1. Before you write, list the positive effects you think television has had on society and on individuals. Consider different types of programming as well as different types of viewers, such as children, shut-ins, and senior citizens. As you write, remember that you are trying to inform *and* persuade your reader about the effects of television. Therefore, you must support your position with logical arguments and/or specific evidence. You might do research to see if there are studies documenting the positive effects of television viewing.
2. Exchange letters with a partner. Identify the positive aspects of television as stated in the letter. Tell the writer which of his or her main ideas—and supporting information—are most effective and which are weakest. Give reasons for your evaluations and suggestions for improvement.
3. Rewrite your own letter, taking into account the comments of your partner. Try to strengthen the points that your partner found weak. Then read your letter aloud to the class.

Preteaching Note
This lesson can help students to become more sensitive to persuasive techniques. Grasping the distinction between intellectual argument and emotional appeal will both aid students in drafting their own work and make them more careful, skeptical, and appreciative readers. You might invite students to use the introductory paragraph as a springboard for making predictions about what types of arguments Tecumseh might use to achieve his goal. You may want to write their predictions on the chalkboard; then, after they have read the selection, students can compare their predictions with Tecumseh's actual presentation.

Tecumseh
Tecumseh (?1768–1813) was the chief and military leader of the Shawnee, a nation that had been concentrated in Ohio by the time Tecumseh was born. From their Ohio base, the Shawnee fought bravely against the encroachment of European Americans onto their land; in 1795, however, they were forced to move to Indiana. There, Tecumseh and his brother established a settlement on the Tippecanoe River. In 1811 William Henry Harrison—later to become President of the United States—disbanded that settlement by means of the treaty to which Tecumseh is reacting in the selection on this page. This treaty effectively ended the independent military movement of the Shawnee nation. Tecumseh, who joined forces with the British in the War of 1812, died in the Battle of the Thames.

Literature & Language

Using the Persuasive Aim

Literary Model

In 1811, a Shawnee Chief named Tecumseh made the following speech condemning a treaty that William Henry Harrison had made with the Native Americans. Tecumseh wanted to unite all the American Indian tribes into a single alliance that could defend their lands against the invasion by white people.

It is true I am a Shawnee. My forefathers were warriors. Their son is a warrior. From them I only take my existence; from my tribe I take nothing. I am the maker of my own fortune; and oh! that I could make that of my red people, and of my country, as great as the conceptions of my mind, when I think of the Spirit that rules the universe. I would not then come to Governor Harrison, to ask him to tear the treaty and to obliterate the landmark; but I would say to him: Sir, you have liberty to return to your own country. The being within, communing with past ages, tells me that once, nor until lately, there was no white man on this continent. That it then all belonged to red men, children of the same parents, placed on it by the Great Spirit that made them, to keep it, to traverse it, to enjoy its productions, and to fill it with the same race. Once a happy race. Since made miserable by the white people, who are never contented, but always encroaching. The way, and the only way, to check and to stop this evil, is for all the red men to unite in claiming a common and equal right in the land, as it was at first, and should be yet; for it never was divided, but belongs to all for the use of each. That no part has a right to sell, even to each other, much less to strangers; those who want all, and will not do with less.

The white people have no right to take the land from the Indians because they had it first; it is theirs. They may sell, but all must join. Any sale not made by all is not valid. The late sale is bad. It was made by a part only. Part do not know how to sell. It requires all to make a bargain for all. All red men have equal rights to the unoccupied land. The right of occupancy is as good in one place as in another. There cannot be two occupations in the same place. The first excludes all others. It is not so in hunting or traveling; for there the same ground will serve many, as they may follow each other all day; but the camp is stationary, and that is occupancy. It belongs to the first who sits down on his blanket or skins which he has thrown upon the ground; and till he leaves it no other has a right.

—Tecumseh

A Note on the Persuasive Aim

Writers and speakers have a **persuasive aim** when their purpose is to move an audience to think or act in a certain way. A coach trying to extract an extra effort from the team, a mother trying to convince a child to take vitamins, or a political candidate trying to get people's votes are examples of speakers with a persuasive aim. Writers of newspaper editorials, of letters to the editor, and of syndicated columns also often aim to persuade readers to adopt their opinion or to take some action.

In the sermon "Sinners in the Hands of an Angry God" (page 37), Jonathan Edwards tries to persuade his congregation to lead more righteous lives. In the pamphlet "The Crisis, No. 1" (page 94), Tom Paine tries to convince American colonists to take up arms against the British. In "Life in the Woods" (page 207), Henry David Thoreau urges readers to simplify their lives.

To achieve their persuasive aim, writers rely on two major techniques: **intellectual argument** and **emotional appeal**. In an intellectual argument, you must support a position with factual evidence and/or logical reasoning. In his speech, Tecumseh reasons that those who occupy land first are its rightful owners.

Appeals to the emotions can be made in many ways. The writer may appeal to people's sense of goodness or fair play, to their fears, to their hopes, or even to their prejudices. Tecumseh makes an emotional appeal to the audience's sense of guilt and compassion when he states that at one time his own people were happy, and now they are miserable.

Examining the Writer's Technique

Work with a partner to complete these activities and the chart that follows.

1. One technique of persuasion is to get the audience on your side at the beginning of the argument. At the very

Examining the Writer's Technique Responses will vary but should resemble the following:
1. His warrior status and heritage.
They want to know that he is no weakling or coward.
2. The introduction comes via a "debate" with Governor Harrison.
It becomes unclear how the Governor would react.
3. He refers to the Great Spirit that made North America.
4. Whites don't own the land, since all Indians were involved in the sale. The Indians also claim squatter's rights because they set up their homes on the land first—and are living on it still.
5. Tecumseh argues both law and the emotional force implicit in human rights.
6. Points and Arguments: Indians own the land—whites came later, encroached, and made Indians miserable. Indians must unite—that's how it has always been. No one Indian has the right to sell—all must agree to any sale. Hunting and traveling can be shared—but a settlement cannot be shared.

Writing with a Persuasive Aim
1. Persuading Others to Your Way of Thinking. Encourage students to outline their points carefully before they begin drafting their essays. When they work with their partners, suggest that the partners offer the best arguments they can think of against the arguments raised in the writing, to challenge students to come up with thoughtful responses. Evaluate student writing based on the presentation of a clear thesis that is supported by two or more effective arguments.
2. Answering Tecumseh Encourage students to draw a line down the middle of their papers. On one side, have them write "Logical Arguments"; on the other side, "Emotional Arguments." Encourage students to brainstorm every argument they can think of before they write. As you evaluate student essays, look for clear, thoughtful arguments that are forcefully presented and supported with details.

least you should try immediately to make your audience receptive to your opinion. To "soften" the audience, many writers and speakers do not immediately state their main points; they start instead with a point the audience is more likely to agree with. What two points does Tecumseh begin with? Why is the audience likely to accept these points?

2. Even when he introduces his main point, Tecumseh does so in a roundabout way. How does he introduce his main topic? How might this wording affect the governor?
3. Persuasive writers and speakers often bring God into their arguments, implying that they have right on their side. Where does Tecumseh use this technique?
4. Tecumseh gives two arguments to support his claim that the treaty should be torn up. What are those arguments?
5. What is the point of the "camp" and "blanket" analogy he makes at the end? Is this an intellectual argument or an emotional appeal? Or both?
6. Fill out this chart to show Tecumseh's main points and the arguments he uses to support them.

Point	Argument

Writing with a Persuasive Aim

1. **Persuading Others to Your Way of Thinking.** Assume that the mayor of your town or city has offered a $1,000 prize to the person who comes up with the most effective plan to solve one of the town's or city's major problems. Write a persuasive essay describing your plan. Your proposal must be intellectually sound, making a strong, logical argument. It must also be emotionally powerful: You want the judges of the proposal to have a positive "gut reaction" to your argument.
   - **a.** Before you write, think about crucial issues facing your town or city. Review your local newspapers not only for issues but also for information on what is being done and said about the problems. Select an issue you have strong feelings about.
   - **b.** Propose one way or two to resolve the problem.
   - **c.** Think of ways you can reach the emotions of your audience. As you write the beginning of your proposal, try to establish a common ground with the audience before making your main point.
   - **d.** Exchange your proposal with a partner's. Evaluate your partner's presentation of the issue and the proposed solution. Is the proposal reasonable? Can it actually be implemented for a sum of money the local government can afford? Does the proposal have emotional appeal? Is the proposed solution fair? (Will any group pay too heavily for it?)
   - **e.** Rewrite your paper, considering the reaction of your partner. Where appropriate, make your points clearer or more persuasive by giving more factual evidence or logical reasons. If necessary, make a stronger appeal to the emotions. You might consider sending your proposal to the local newspaper.
2. **Answering Tecumseh.** Suppose you are Governor Harrison and want to respond to Tecumseh. You do not wish to break the treaty, but you would like to keep the peace and you do not want to offend him. Write a response explaining why you think the treaty is valid and why your people are justified in keeping the disputed land. Include promises that would offer Tecumseh some hope that he and his people will not have to remain "miserable." Remember to use both logical and emotional arguments.

Preteaching Note
The diction in this poem will help awaken in students an appreciation for the power of effective diction. You might begin the lesson by reading the poem aloud or calling on classroom volunteers to do so. After the poem has been read, suggest that students close their eyes and call out images or words that they remember or associate with the experience of hearing the poem. Note their thoughts on the chalkboard as you discuss the poem in class.

Robert Penn Warren
This Pulitzer Prize-winning poet and novelist was born in 1905. His early work was primarily poetry that dealt with mystical and metaphysical subjects. Later work was simpler and more concerned with Warren's native region of the South. Warren's novels include *All the King's Men,* an examination of the Louisiana demagogue Huey "Kingfish" Long. His literature textbooks, which called upon readers and writers to ignore social and topical concerns in order to focus on "universal" images and truths, became an important influence in the 1940's.

Literature & Language

Using Effective Diction

Literary Model

This poem about old age explores the writer's feelings about the effects of time on memory. For another look at a selection with a similar theme, see "The Jilting of Granny Weatherall" on page 583.

Small Eternity

The time comes when you count the names—
    whether
Dim or flaming in the head's dark, or whether
In stone cut, time-crumbling or moss-glutted.
You count the names to reconstruct yourself.

But a face remembered may blur, even as
    you stare
At a headstone. Or sometimes a face, as
    though from air,
Will stare at you with a boyish smile—but, not
Stone-moored, blows away like dandelion
    fuzz.

It is very disturbing. It is as though you were
The idiot boy who ventures out on pond-ice
Too thin, and hears here—hears there—
    the creak
And crackling spread. That is the sound
    Reality

Makes as it gives beneath your metaphysical
Poundage. Memory dies. Or lies. Time
Is a wind that never shifts airt.* Pray only
That, in the midst of selfishness, some

Small act of careless kindness,
    half-unconscious, some
Unwitting smile or brush of lips, may glow
In some other mind's dark that's lost your
    name, but stumbles
Upon that momentary Eternity.

—Robert Penn Warren

***airt:** direction.

Notes on Diction

Diction refers to a writer's choice of words and to the way the writer uses those words. Diction may be described in many ways: formal, informal, colloquial, slang, poetic, ornate, plain, etc. Sandburg's diction in the poem "Chicago" (page 731) is plain:

> Under the smoke, dust all over his mouth, laughing
>   with white teeth
> Under the terrible burden of destiny laughing as a young
>   man laughs, . . .

By contrast, F. Scott Fitzgerald's diction in "Winter Dreams" (page 539) is more ornate and poetic:

> She wore a blue gingham dress, rimmed at throat and shoulders with a white edging that accentuated her tan. The quality of exaggeration, of thinness, which had made her passionate eyes and downturning mouth absurd at eleven, was gone now. She was arrestingly beautiful. The color in her cheeks was centered like the color in a picture. . . .

Several aspects of a writer's diction are worth paying attention to: (1) the writer's use of **precise words** instead of vague general words (Warren says "the brush of lips" instead of the more general "kiss"); (2) the writer's use of **vivid words** (Warren describes the tombstone as "moss-glutted" not merely "mossy"); (3) the writer's use of **metaphor** (in the most vivid metaphor of the poem, Warren identifies the sound of reality with "the creak and crackling spread" of ice breaking on a pond); and (4) the writer's use of words with particular **connotations.**

Connotations are the associations and emotional overtones that have become attached to a word or phrase through usage. For example, *assertive* and *pushy* both mean "taking the initiative," but *assertive* carries a positive connotation and *pushy* a negative one. We tend to think of those who get ahead of us as *pushy,* but we prefer to think of ourselves as *assertive.*

In line 2 of this poem, Warren chooses the word *flaming,* rather than *bright,* to contrast with *dim.* Why? Perhaps because the word *flaming* carries the connotation of wildly bright, more colorful and intense than mere brightness. It also might suggest fire, burning, a

Examining the Writer's Style
Responses will vary. Possible responses include the following:

1. *reconstruct*—to rebuild; change your identity, recover your composure. *stone-moored*—held down by stone; connotes the heavy tombstone and the weight of death. *fuzz*—dandelion seeds; lint, trash, garbage. *glow*—to shine with a gentle light; to "light up" someone's mind with an idea, to inspire or reach. *stumbles*—trips; discovers, falls into knowledge, death, or Eternity.

2. One suggests the heaviness of death; the other suggests the "lightness" and fragility of human life.

3. It suggests pounding, heaviness—again, the weight of death.

4. They evoke the sounds of a closing coffin.

5. Its meaning of "unconscious" suggests the unconsciousness of death.

Using Effective Diction in Your Writing

1. Describing a Feeling. Encourage students to find images and details that are as specific as possible, particularly if they are describing a relatively abstract feeling. Suggest that peer reviewers begin by telling the writer their initial reaction to the writing; that way, writers can see whether they are communicating their ideas effectively. Evaluate student work based on its precise use of language to convey a particular feeling.

2. Describing Faces. Once again, suggest that students focus on specific details. Students may enjoy using similes, metaphors, or other figures of speech to convey the faces they remember. Student descriptions will be successful if they help the reader to picture the faces being described.

beacon of light. By this word choice, the poet suggests layers and layers of meaning that would not be available in the word *bright.*

In the last line, and in the title, Warren uses an **oxymoron**, a combination of words that seem to contradict each other. Eternity by its very nature cannot be momentary, "of short duration." What Warren is suggesting is that the momentary loss of memory is a momentary death, a momentary taste of eternity. He would have made an entirely different point if he had written "*temporary* eternity." Although both words mean "of short duration," *momentary* connotes a moment that is brief but of worth and importance, whereas *temporary* suggests insignificance and lack of true value.

Examining the Writer's Style

With a partner, examine Warren's choice of words by doing the following activities.

1. Complete the chart below, giving the precise meaning and the connotations of each word cited from the poem. (When you think of connotations, think of all the feelings, things, and ideas that you associate with the word.)

Word	Precise Meaning	Connotations
reconstruct (line 4)		
stone-moored (line 8)		
fuzz (line 8)		
glow (line 18)		
stumbles (line 19)		

2. In stanza 2, why are the opposing images "stone-moored" and "blows away like dandelion fuzz" appropriate for the subject of the poem?
3. Why is "poundage" (line 14), a more effective word than "weight" or "body"?
4. Why are "creak" (line 11) and "crackling" (line 12) especially vivid word choices?
5. Based on its dictionary meaning alone, why is "unwitting" (line 18) a good word choice?

Using Effective Diction in Your Writing

1. **Describing a Feeling.** Write a paragraph or short poem describing a particular feeling. Robert Penn Warren describes the sensation of forgetfulness, of the effects time has on memory. You might describe how you feel entering a room full of strangers, or how you feel when you're exercising or playing team sports or falling in love or being rejected.
   - **a.** Before you write, choose a feeling that you know well and can describe pretty accurately. Then freewrite, listing all the words you can think of that describe this feeling. Imagine what the feeling could be compared with. For example, you might try completing this sentence: "[Your feeling] is like. . . ." After you write your paragraph or poem, review it closely, word by word, to be sure your words:
     - **(1)** are precise, not vague and general
     - **(2)** convey vivid images
     - **(3)** use strong metaphors to help your reader share your feeling
     - **(4)** carry the right connotations.
   - **b.** Trade papers with a partner and read your partner's poem or paragraph carefully. Try to understand the feeling your partner is attempting to express. Point to specific words that are particularly effective. Discuss any words that seem vague or weak or imprecise.
   - **c.** Rewrite your own paragraph or poem, using the comments of your partner as an aid. If you are blocked, a dictionary and a thesaurus might help you find the right words.
2. **Describing Faces.** In stanza 2, Warren describes faces from the past that come to mind, some in a blur, some with a smile, before they fade away. Describe the faces of people you have seen in a children's playground, a crowded stadium, an angry mob, in a dream, or in a nightmare. Use words that precisely and vividly describe the faces. Try to find words that connote, or suggest, the feelings the faces arouse in you.

HANDBOOK OF LITERARY TERMS

You will find more information about the terms in this Handbook at the pages given at the ends of the entries. To learn more about **Allegory,** for example, turn to pages 30, 232, and 246 in this book.

Cross-references at the ends of some entries refer to other entries in the Handbook containing related information. For instance, at the end of **Antagonist** you are referred to **Protagonist.**

ALLEGORY A story or poem in which characters, settings, and events stand for other people or events or for abstract ideas or qualities. An allegory can be read on one level for its literal meaning and on a second level for its symbolic, or allegorical, meaning. The most famous allegory in the English language is *The Pilgrim's Progress* (1678) by Puritan writer John Bunyan, in which Pilgrim, in his journey to the Celestial City, meets such personages as Mr. Worldly Wiseman, Hopeful, and Giant Despair and travels to such places as the Slough of Despond, the Valley of Humiliation, and Doubting Castle. All Puritans were trained to see their own lives as allegories of Biblical experiences. Nathaniel Hawthorne's and Edgar Allan Poe's fictions are often called allegorical.

See pages 30, 232, 246.

ALLITERATION The repetition of the same or similar consonant sounds in words that are close together. Alliteration is used to create musical effects and to establish mood. In the following line from "The Tide Rises, the Tide Falls" by Henry Wadsworth Longfellow, the repetition of the "s" sound is an example of alliteration:

The sea, the sea in the darkness calls

See pages 254, 262, 333.

ALLUSION A reference to someone or something that is known from history, literature, religion, politics, sports, science, or some other branch of culture. T. S. Eliot drew on his knowledge of the Bible when he alluded to the raising of Lazarus from the dead in "The Love Song of J. Alfred Prufrock" on page 742. The title of Robert Hayden's poem "Summertime and the Living . . ." on page 1091 is an allusion to a song from the opera *Porgy and Bess*.

You won't understand the following cartoon unless you recognize the fairy tale it alludes to.

"They're offering a deal—you can pay court costs and damages, they drop charges of breaking and entering."

Drawing by Maslin. © 1988 The New Yorker Magazine, Inc.

See pages 30, 91, 160, 170, 232, 254, 319, 392, 670, 749, 993.

AMBIGUITY A technique by which a writer deliberately suggests two or more different, and sometimes conflicting, meanings in a work. Nathaniel Hawthorne's "Rappaccini's Daughter" on page 275 has an ambiguous ending; the title of Richard Wilbur's "The Beautiful Changes" on page 1109 is also deliberately ambiguous.

See page 463.

ANALOGY A comparison made between two things to show how they are alike. In "The Crisis" on page 94 Thomas Paine draws an analogy between a thief breaking into a house and the King of England interfering in the affairs of the American colonies.

See pages 99, 639.

ANAPEST A metrical foot that has two unstressed syllables followed by one stressed syllable. The word *coexist* is an example of an anapest.

ANECDOTE A very brief story, told to illustrate a point or serve as an example of something. In Benjamin Franklin's *Autobiography* (page 74), the account of the speckled ax is an anecdote.

See page 80.

ANTAGONIST The opponent who struggles against or blocks the hero, or protagonist, in a story. In Mark Twain's *The Adventures of Huckleberry Finn*, Miss Watson is one of Huck's many antagonists. In Herman Melville's *Moby-Dick*, the white whale is Ahab's antagonist.

See also *Protagonist*.

ANTHROPOMORPHISM Attributing human characteristics to an animal or inanimate object. E. B. White creates humor by anthropomorphizing his dog Fred in his essay "Death of a Pig" (page 988).

See page 1129.

APHORISM A brief, cleverly worded statement that makes a wise observation about life. Benjamin Franklin's *Poor Richard's Almanack* (page 84) is a book of aphorisms. Ralph Waldo Emerson's style is **aphoristic**—he incorporates many pithy sayings into his essays (which is why he is so quotable).

See page 202.

APOSTROPHE A technique by which a writer addresses an inanimate object, an idea, or a person who is either dead or absent. William Cullen Bryant apostrophizes a bird in "To a Waterfowl" (page 139). Ralph Waldo Emerson apostrophizes a flower in "The Rhodora" (page 198). Oliver Wendell Holmes apostrophizes a shell and his soul in "The Chambered Nautilus" (page 164).

See pages 196, 199.

ARGUMENT A form of persuasion that appeals to reason (instead of emotion) to convince an audience to think or act in a certain way. The *Declaration of Independence* provides some famous examples of argument.

See pages 99, 107.
See also *Persuasion*.

ASSONANCE The repetition of similar vowel sounds followed by different consonant sounds, especially in words that are close together. Notice the repeated sound of "i" in the following lines by Henry Wadsworth Longfellow:

> The tide rises, the tide falls,
> The twilight darkens, the curlew calls

See page 333.
See also *Alliteration, Onomatopoeia, Rhyme.*

AUTOBIOGRAPHY An account of the writer's own life. Benjamin Franklin's autobiography (page 74) is one of the most famous autobiographies in American literature. A selection from Richard Wright's autobiography, *Black Boy*, is on page 1005.

See pages 74, 84, 1005.

BALLAD A song or poem that tells a story. The typical ballad tells a tragic story in the form of a monologue or dialogue. Ballads usually have a simple, steady rhythm, a rhyme pattern, and a refrain, all of which make them easy to memorize. Ballads composed by unknown singers and passed on orally from one generation to the next are called **folk ballads. Literary ballads** are written to imitate the sounds and subjects of folk ballads. A strong tradition of folk ballads and of literary ballads exists in the United States. Country-and-western music, for example, frequently features songs written to imitate the old ballads.

BIOGRAPHY An account of someone's life written by another person. The most famous biography in American literature is Carl Sandburg's multivolume life of Abraham Lincoln.

BLANK VERSE Poetry written in unrhymed iambic pentameter. Blank verse has a long history in English literature. It was used notably by such poets as Shakespeare and Milton in the sixteenth and seventeenth centuries and by Robert Frost in the twentieth.

See pages 144, 669.
See also *Iambic Pentameter.*

CADENCE The natural, rhythmic rise and fall of a language as it is normally spoken. Cadence is different from **meter,** in which the stressed and unstressed syllables of a poetic line are carefully counted to conform to a regular pattern. Walt Whitman was a master at imitating the cadences of spoken American English in his free verse.

See pages 324, 333, 335, 349.
See also *Free Verse, Meter, Rhythm.*

CAESURA A pause or break within a line of poetry. Some pauses are indicated by punctuation; others are suggested by phrasing or meaning. In these lines, the caesuras are marked by double vertical lines. These pauses are indicated by punctuation:

> Announced by all the trumpets of the sky,
> Arrives the snow, ‖ and, ‖ driving o'er the fields,
> Seems nowhere to alight: ‖ the whited air
> Hides hills and woods . . .
>
> —from "The Snow-Storm,"
> Ralph Waldo Emerson

CATALOGUE A list of things, people, or events. Cataloging was a favorite device of Walt Whitman, who included lists throughout *Leaves of Grass*.

See pages 324, 337, 345, 349, 413, 532.

CHARACTER An individual in a story or play. A character always has human traits, even if the character is an animal, as in Aesop's fables, or a god, as in the Greek and Roman myths.

The process by which the writer reveals the personality of a character is called **characterization.** A writer can reveal a character in the following ways:

1. By telling us directly what the character is like: sneaky, generous, mean to pets, and so on.
2. By describing how the character looks and dresses.
3. By letting us hear the character speak.
4. By revealing the character's private thoughts and feelings.
5. By revealing the character's effect on other people—showing how other characters feel or behave toward the character.
6. By showing the character in action.

The first method of revealing a character is called **direct characterization.** When a writer uses this method, we do not have to figure out what a character's personality is like—the writer tells us directly. The other five methods of revealing a character are known as **indirect characterization.** When a writer uses these methods, we have to exercise our own judgment, putting clues together to figure out what a character is like—just as we do in real life when we are getting to know someone.

Characters are often classified as static or dynamic. A **static character** is one who does not change much in the course of a story. A **dynamic character,** on the other hand, changes in some important way as a result of the story's action. Characters can also be classified as flat or round. **Flat characters** have only one or two personality traits. They are one-dimensional, like a piece of cardboard; they can be summed up by a single phrase. In contrast, **round characters** have more dimensions to their personalities—they are complex, just as real people are.

See pages 80, 136, 274, 292, 301, 304, 309, 413, 574, 834, 855, 865.

CLICHÉ A word or phrase, often a figure of speech, that has become lifeless because of overuse. Some examples of clichés are: "green with envy," "quiet as a mouse," and "pretty as a picture." Russell Baker mocks the use of clichés in his essay "Little Red Riding Hood Revisited" (page 999).

See pages 516, 1051.

CLIMAX That point in a plot that creates the greatest intensity, suspense, or interest. The climax is usually the point at which the conflict in the story is resolved.

See pages 232, 292, 810, 865.

COMEDY In general, a story that ends with a happy resolution of the conflicts faced by the main character or characters. In many comedies, the conflict is provided when a young couple that wishes to marry is blocked by adult figures. In many comedies, the main character at the end has moved into a world of greater freedom; this is the kind of comedy we see in Washington Irving's "Rip Van Winkle." Some comedies are humorous; some are not.

See pages 612, 883.

CONCEIT An elaborate metaphor that compares two things that are startlingly different. Often a conceit is also a very lengthy comparison. The poems of Edward Taylor (pages 46 and 49) and of Emily Dickinson (pages 355–369) are known for their conceits. T. S. Eliot, in more recent literary history, also used conceits (see page 742).

See page 48.

CONCRETE POEM A poem in which the words are arranged on a page to suggest a visual representation of the subject. In English poetry in the seventeenth century, poets wrote concrete poems in the shapes of such things as crosses, altars, and wings; today poets write concrete poems in the shapes of waves, hearts, cats, flowers.

See pages 709, 710.

CONFESSIONAL POETRY A twentieth-century term used to describe poetry that uses intimate material from the poet's life. The material is usually painful, disturbing, or sad. In twentieth-century American literature, some of the leading Confessional poets have been Robert Lowell, John Berryman, Anne Sexton, and Sylvia Plath.

See page 1087.

CONFLICT The struggle between opposing forces or characters in a story. A conflict can be **internal,** involving opposing forces within a person's mind. James Thurber's "The Secret Life of Walter Mitty" (page 677), for example, deals with a man who has a comical internal conflict between his desire for heroism and his cowardice in the face of a formidable spouse. **External** conflicts can exist between two people, between a person and nature or a machine, or between a person and a whole society. In "Your Place Is Empty" (page 954), for example, Anne Tyler shows two characters (or two cultures) coming into conflict. Many stories have both types of conflict.

See pages 137, 574, 760, 810, 834, 889, 923, 941, 965, 976.

CONNOTATION The associations and emotional overtones that have become attached to a word or phrase, in addition to its strict dictionary definition. The words *determined, firm, rigid, stubborn,* and *pigheaded* have similar dictionary definitions, but widely varying connotations, or overtones of meaning. *Determined* and *firm* both suggest an admirable kind of resoluteness; *rigid* suggests an inability to bend and a kind of mindless refusal to change. (It calls to mind a rigid board.) *Stubborn* and *pigheaded,* on the other hand, have strongly negative connotations. *Stubborn* has associations with a mule, and *pigheaded* with the pig, which, wrongly or not, is an animal often associated with stupidity. Here are some other words that are more or less synonymous but which have vastly different connotations: *fastidious* and *fussy; day-dreamer* and *escapist; scent, odor,* and *stink*. Words with strong connotations are often called **loaded words.**

See pages 163, 201, 232, 247, 249, 293, 610, 635, 648.

CONSONANCE The repetition of the same or similar final consonant sounds on accented syllables or in important words. The expressions *tick-tock* and *ping-pong* contain examples of consonance. Some modern poets use consonance in place of rhyme.

COUPLET Two consecutive rhyming lines of poetry. If the two rhyming lines express a complete thought, they are called a **closed couplet.** The following lines are from a poem built on a series of closed couplets.

> If ever wife was happy in a man,
> Compare with me, ye women, if you can.
>
> —from "To My Dear and Loving Husband,"
> Anne Bradstreet

See page 44.

DACTYL A metrical foot of three syllables in which the first syllable is stressed and the next two are unstressed. The word téndĕncy̆ is a dactyl.

DENOUEMENT (dā·no͞o·mä*n*′) The conclusion (or resolution) of a story. In French, the word means "unraveling." At this point in a story, all the mysteries are unraveled, the conflicts are resolved, and all the questions raised by the plot are answered. Much modern fiction ends before the denouement, so that the story leaves us with a sense of incompleteness.

DESCRIPTION A form of discourse that uses language to create a mood or emotion. Description does this by the use of words that appeal to our senses: sight, hearing, touch, sound, taste. Walt Whitman gives a wonderful description of a Civil War battlefield in "A Night Battle, Over a Week Since" (page 442).

See page 428.

DIALECT A way of speaking that is characteristic of a certain social group or of the inhabitants of a certain geographical area. Dialects may differ from one another in vocabulary, pronunciation, and grammar. As in most countries, one dialect has become dominant in America, and it is known as Standard English. This is the dialect used most often on national radio and television news broadcasts. Many writers try to capture dialects to give their stories local color, humor, or an air of authenticity. Among the writers in this book who make skilled use of dialect are Mark Twain, Eudora Welty, Flannery O'Connor, William Faulkner, and Langston Hughes.

See pages 404, 413, 611, 646, 698–702.

DICTION A speaker or writer's choice of words. Diction can be formal, informal, colloquial, full of slang, poetic, ornate, plain, abstract, concrete, etc. Diction is dependent on the writer's subject, purpose, and audience. Some words, for example, are suited to informal conversations, but are inappropriate in a formal speech. Diction has a powerful effect on the **tone** of a piece of writing. Russell Baker mocks the diction of Washington bureaucrats in his essay "Little Red Riding Hood Revisited" (page 999).

See pages 58, 349, 371, 646, 739.

DRAMATIC MONOLOGUE A poem in which a character speaks to one or more listeners. The reactions of the listener must be inferred by the reader. From the speaker's words, the reader learns about the setting, the situation, the identity of the other characters, and the personality of the speaker. The outstanding dramatic monologue in American literature is T. S. Eliot's "The Love Song of J. Alfred Prufrock" (page 742). The poems in Edgar Lee Masters's *Spoon River Anthology* are also dramatic monologues.

ELEGY A poem of mourning, usually about someone who has died. Most elegies are written to mark a person's death, but some extend their subject to reflect on life, death, and the fleeting nature of beauty. The elegies in this book include William Cullen Bryant's "Thanatopsis" (page 142), John Crowe Ransom's "Bells for John Whiteside's Daughter" (page 673), and Theodore Roethke's "Elegy for Jane" (page 1089).

See pages 752, 1020.

EPIC A long narrative poem, written in heightened language, which recounts the deeds of a heroic character who

embodies the values of a particular society. Epics in English include *Beowulf* (c. 700) and John Milton's *Paradise Lost* (1667). Some critics view Walt Whitman's *Leaves of Grass* as an American epic, in which the hero is the questing poet.

See page 329.

EPITHET A descriptive word or phrase that is frequently used to characterize a person or thing. The epithet "the father of his country" is often used to characterize George Washington. New York City's popular epithet, "the Big Apple," is frequently used by advertisers. Epics such as Homer's *Odyssey* and *Iliad* frequently use **stock epithets** over and over again to describe certain characters or places: "patient Penelope," "wily Odysseus," "earth-shaker" (for Poseidon).

ESSAY A short piece of nonfiction prose in which the writer discusses some aspect of a subject. The word *essay* comes from the French *essai*, meaning "to try," a derivation that suggests that the essay form is not an exhaustive treatment of a subject. Essays are sometimes classified as formal or informal, or as formal or personal (or familiar). The form has been especially popular in the twentieth century, particularly among American writers. Some famous American essayists of the past include Thomas Paine (page 93), Ralph Waldo Emerson (page 187), and Henry David Thoreau (page 204). More recent essayists include E. B. White (page 987), Lewis Thomas (page 995), Russell Baker (page 998), James Baldwin (page 1021), Joan Didion, Alice Walker, and Edward Abbey.

See Unit Twelve.

EXPOSITION One of the four major forms of discourse, in which something is explained or "set forth." Exposition is most commonly used in nonfiction. The word *exposition* also refers to that part of a plot in which the reader is given important background information on the characters, their setting, and their problems. Such exposition is usually provided at the opening of a story or play. A good example is Tom's opening speech in Tennessee Williams's *The Glass Menagerie* (see page 771).

See page 760.

FABLE A very short story told in prose or poetry that teaches a practical lesson about how to succeed in life. In many fables, the characters are animals that behave like people. The most ancient fabulist is the Greek Aesop; the most famous American fabulist is James Thurber (page 576), who produced two collections: *Fables for Our Time* and *Further Fables for Our Time*.

FARCE A type of comedy in which ridiculous and often stereotyped characters are involved in silly, far-fetched situations. The humor in a farce is often physical and slapstick, with characters being hit in the face with pies or running into open doors. American movies have produced many farces, including those starring Laurel and Hardy, Abbott and Costello, and the Marx brothers.

FIGURE OF SPEECH A word or phrase that describes one thing in terms of another and that is not meant to be taken literally. Figures of speech always involve a comparison of two things that are basically very dissimilar. Hundreds of figures of speech have been identified by scholars; the most common ones are **simile, metaphor, personification,** and **symbol.** Figurative language is also basic to everyday speech. Statements like "She is a tower of strength" and "He is a pain in the neck" use figures of speech.

See pages 40, 148, 195, 293, 304, 359, 428, 524, 574, 1032.
See also *Metaphor, Simile, Personification, Symbol.*

FLASHBACK A scene that interrupts the normal chronological sequence of events in a story to depict something that happened at an earlier time. Although the word was coined to describe a technique used by movie makers, the technique itself is at least as old as ancient Greek literature. Much of Homer's epic poem the *Odyssey* is a flashback. Willa Cather uses frequent flashbacks to reveal the past of her heroine in "A Wagner Matinée" (page 518).

See pages 438, 524.

FOIL A character who acts as a contrast to another character. In Nathaniel Hawthorne's "Rappaccini's Daughter," the sane physician Signor Baglioni is a foil to the mad scientist Rappaccini.

See page 292.

FOOT A metrical unit of poetry. A foot always contains at least one stressed syllable, and, usually, one or more unstressed syllables. An **iamb** is a common foot in English poetry: It consists of an unstressed syllable followed by a stressed syllable (˘ ʹ).

See also *Anapest, Dactyl, Iamb, Spondee, Trochee.*

FORESHADOWING The use of hints and clues to suggest what will happen later in a plot. A writer might use foreshadowing to create suspense or to prefigure later events. In "The Outcasts of Poker Flat," for example, Bret Harte foreshadows the conclusion of his story by placing hints in the dialogue between Mr. Oakhurst and his companions.

See pages 301, 309, 400.

FORMS OF DISCOURSE A system of classifying writing according to purpose. The four main forms of discourse are **description, narration, exposition,** and **persuasion.**

FREE VERSE Poetry that does not conform to a regular meter or rhyme scheme. Poets who write in free verse try to reproduce the natural rhythms of the spoken language. Free verse uses the traditional poetic elements of **imagery, figures of speech, repetition, internal rhyme, alliteration,** and **onomatopoeia.** The first American practitioner of free verse was Walt Whitman (page 326). Some of Whitman's heirs are William Carlos Williams (page 717), Carl Sandburg (page 729), and Allen Ginsberg (page 1134).

See pages 324, 333, 684, 710.

HYPERBOLE A figure of speech that uses an incredible exaggeration, or overstatement, for effect. In *The Adventures of Huckleberry Finn*, Mark Twain has Huck use hyperbole for comic effect, as in this passage, in which Huck explains what he thinks he knows about kings:

> My, you ought to seen old Henry the Eight when he was in bloom. He *was* a blossom. He used to marry a new wife every day, and chop off her head next morning. And he would do it as indifferent as if he was ordering up eggs. "Fetch up Nell Gwynn," he says. They fetch her up. Next morning, "Chop off her head!" And they chop it off. . . . "Ring up fair Rosamun." Fair Rosamun answers the bell. Next morning, "Chop off her head."
>
> —from *The Adventures of Huckleberry Finn*,
> Mark Twain

See pages 413, 574, 983, 1003.

IAMB A metrical foot in poetry that has an unstressed syllable followed by a stressed syllable, as in the word prŏtéct.

See pages 44, 144.

IAMBIC PENTAMETER A line of poetry that contains five iambic feet. The iambic pentameter line is the most common in English and American poetry. Shakespeare and John Milton, among others, used iambic pentameter in their major works. So did such American poets as William Cullen Bryant, Ralph Waldo Emerson, Robert Frost, and Wallace Stevens. Here, for example, are the opening lines of a poem by Emerson:

> In̆ Máy, whĕn séa wĭnds piércéd oŭr sólĭtudés,
> Ĭ foúnd thĕ frésh Rhŏdórā ín thĕ wóods
>
> —from "The Rhodora,"
> Ralph Waldo Emerson

See pages 145, 199.

IMAGERY The use of language to evoke a picture or a concrete sensation of a person, a thing, a place, or an experience. Although most images appeal to the sense of sight, they also sometimes appeal to the senses of taste, smell, hearing, and touch as well.

See pages 40, 51, 99, 145, 151, 160, 166, 168, 193, 232, 246, 260, 316, 335, 340, 344, 356, 357, 359, 413, 428, 648, 1032.

IMAGISM A twentieth-century movement in European and American poetry which advocated the creation of hard, clear images, concisely written in everyday speech. The leading Imagist poets in America were Ezra Pound, Amy Lowell, Hilda Doolittle, and William Carlos Williams.

See page 709.

IMPRESSIONISM A nineteenth-century movement in literature and art which advocated a recording of the artist's personal impressions of the world, rather than a strict representation of reality. Some of the famous American Impressionists in art were Mary Cassatt, Maurice Prendergast, and William Merritt Chase.

INCONGRUITY The deliberate joining of opposites or of elements that are not appropriate to each other. T. S. Eliot's famous opening simile in "The Love Song of J. Alfred Prufrock" joins two incongruous elements: a sunset and a patient knocked out by ether on an operating table. Incongruity can also be used for humor; we laugh at the sight of an elephant dressed in a pink tutu because the two elements are incongruous. Writers also use incongruity for dramatic effect. In Donald Barthelme's "Game" (page 976), the childish actions of the characters are in sharp contrast with the nuclear war they can start by turning a key.

See pages 171, 413.

INTERNAL RHYME Rhyme that occurs within a line of poetry or within consecutive lines. The first line of the following pair includes an internal rhyme.

And so, all the nighttide, I lie down by the side
Of my darling—my darling—my life and my bride
—from "Annabel Lee,"
Edgar Allan Poe

See also *Rhyme*.

INVERSION The reversal of the normal word order in a sentence or phrase. An English sentence normally is built on subject-verb-complement, in that order. An inverted sentence reverses one or more of those elements. In poetry written many years ago, writers often inverted word order as a matter of course, in order to have the words conform to the meter, or to create rhymes. The poetry of Anne Bradstreet (page 42) contains many inversions, as in the first line of the poem on the burning of her house:

In silent night when rest I took

In prose, inversion is often used for emphasis, as when Patrick Henry, in his fiery speech to the Virginia Convention, said "Suffer not yourselves to be betrayed with a kiss" (instead of "Do not suffer [allow] yourselves, etc."

See pages 43, 145, 166, 199.

IRONY In general, a discrepancy between appearances and reality. There are three main types of irony: (1) **Verbal irony** occurs when someone says one thing but really means something else. When Benjamin Franklin refers to the Native Americans as "savages" in his essay on page 81, he is using irony. He really means that their oppressors are savage and that the Native Americans are highly civilized. (2) **Situational irony** takes place when there is a discrepancy between what is expected to happen, or what would be appropriate to happen, and what really does happen. A famous use of situational irony is in Edwin Arlington Robinson's poem "Richard Cory," in which a man in an enviable position, with every advantage, takes his own life. (3) **Dramatic irony** is so called because it is often used on stage. In this kind of irony, a character in the play or story thinks one thing is true, but the audience or reader knows better. When Emily Dickinson writes "Success is counted sweetest by those who ne'er succeed," we sense a kind of dramatic irony: We know, but the poet did not, that she would in fact be counted as enormously successful by later generations.

See pages 163, 292, 318, 362, 365, 384, 401, 516, 574, 610, 612, 619, 634, 737, 1003, 1047.

LOCAL COLOR A term applied to fiction or poetry which tends to place special emphasis on a particular setting, including its customs, clothing, dialect, and landscape. Local color flourished in the United States after the Civil War. The most famous local colorists are Bret Harte (West), Sarah Orne Jewett (Maine), Joel Chandler Harris (Georgia), Kate Chopin (Louisiana), James Whitcomb Riley (Indiana), Hamlin Garland (Middle West), and O. Henry (New York City).

See *Regionalism.*

LYRIC POEM A poem that does not tell a story but expresses the personal feelings or thoughts of a speaker. Lyric poems in this text range from the philosophic "Thanatopsis" by William Cullen Bryant to the satiric "Homework" by Allen Ginsberg.

See Units Five, Eight, Nine, and Thirteen.

METAPHOR A figure of speech that makes a comparison between two unlike things without the use of such specific words of comparison as *like, as, than,* or *resembles*. There are several kinds of metaphor:

1. A **directly stated metaphor** states the comparison explicitly: "Fame is a bee" (Emily Dickinson).
2. An **implied metaphor** does not state explicitly the two terms of the comparison: "I like to see it lap the miles" (Emily Dickinson) is an implied metaphor in which the verb *lap* implies a comparison between "it" (which is a train) and some animal that "laps" up water.
3. An **extended metaphor** is a metaphor that is extended or developed as far as the writer wants to take it. Dickinson's poem beginning "Fame is a bee" is an extended metaphor: The comparison between fame and a bee is extended through four lines. (See also page 766.)
4. A **dead metaphor** is a metaphor that has been used so often that the comparison is no longer vivid: "The head of the house," "the seat of government," "a knotty problem" are all dead metaphors.
5. A **mixed metaphor** is a metaphor that has gotten out of control and mixes its terms so that they are visually or imaginatively incompatible. If you say, "The President is a lame duck who is running out of gas," you've lost control of your metaphor and have produced a statement that is ridiculous (ducks do not run out of gas).

See pages 35, 44, 47, 62, 91, 99, 145, 151, 163, 166, 195, 219, 309, 357, 360, 367, 390, 413, 574, 1077.

METER A pattern of stressed and unstressed syllables in poetry. The meter of a poem is commonly indicated by using the symbol (′) for stressed syllables and the symbol (◡) for unstressed syllables. This is called **scanning** the poem. The following lines from Edward Arlington Robinson's "Richard Cory" are scanned.

Meter is described as **iambic, trochaic, dactylic,** or **an-**

1175

apestic. These lines from "Richard Cory" are iambic because they are built on iambs—an unstressed syllable followed by a stressed syllable.

> And he was always quietly arrayed
> And he was always human when he talked;

See pages 249, 252, 260, 357, 360.

METONYMY A figure of speech in which a person, place, or thing is referred to by something closely associated with it. Referring to a king as "the crown" is an example of metonymy, as is calling a car "wheels."

MODERNISM A term for the bold new experimental styles and forms that swept the arts during the first third of the twentieth century. Modernism called for changes in subject matter, in fictional styles, in poetic forms, and in attitudes. T. S. Eliot and Ezra Pound are associated with the Modernist movement in poetry. Their aim was to rid poetry of its nineteenth-century "prettiness" and sentimentality.

See pages 740, 1086.
See also *Imagism, Symbolism.*

MOTIVATION The reasons for a character's behavior. In order for us to understand why characters act the way they do, their motivation has to be believable, at least in terms of the story. At times, a writer will directly reveal motivation; in subtler fiction, we have to use details from the story to infer motivation.

See also *Character.*

NARRATIVE The form of discourse that tells about a series of events. Narration is used in all kinds of literature: fiction, nonfiction, and poetry. Usually a narrative is told in **chronological order**—in the order in which the events occurred. The other three major forms of discourse are **description, exposition,** and **persuasion.**

NATURALISM A nineteenth-century literary movement that was an extension of realism and that claimed to portray life exactly as it was. The Naturalists relied heavily on the new fields of psychology and sociology, and they tended to dissect human behavior with complete objectivity, the way a scientist would dissect a specimen in the laboratory. The Naturalists were also influenced by Darwinian theories of the survival of the fittest. Naturalists believed that human behavior is determined by heredity and environment; they felt that people have no recourse to supernatural forces and that human beings, like the animals, are subject to laws of nature beyond their control. The outstanding Naturalists among American writers are Theodore Dreiser, Stephen Crane (see page 439), and Frank Norris. Some people consider John Steinbeck's *The Grapes of Wrath* a Naturalistic novel, in which characters are the pawns of economic conditions.

See pages 383, 478.
See also *Realism.*

OBJECTIVE CORRELATIVE An object, a situation, or a chain of events which serves as the formula for a specific emotion. The term was first used by T. S. Eliot in an essay.

See page 715.

OCTAVE An eight-line poem, or the first eight lines of a Petrarchan sonnet.

See also *Sonnet.*

ODE A lyric poem, usually long, on a serious subject and written in dignified language. In ancient Greece and Rome, odes were written to be read in public at ceremonial occasions. In modern literature, odes tend to be more private, informal, and reflective. Robert Lowell's "For the Union Dead" (page 1104) and Henry Timrod's "Ode on the Confederate Dead" (page 1107) are examples of the personal, meditative ode.

ONOMATOPOEIA The use of sounds that echo their sense. The word *buzz*, for example, is an onomatopoeic word because it imitates the sound it names. Onomatopoeia is an important element in most poetry.

See pages 141, 154, 262, 333, 337.

OXYMORON A figure of speech that combines opposite or contradictory terms in a brief phrase. "Sweet sorrow," "deafening silence," and "living death" are common oxymorons. (Some jokesters claim that phrases like "jumbo shrimp," "congressional leadership," and "limited nuclear war" are also oxymorons.)

See page 574.

PARABLE A relatively short story that teaches a moral, or lesson, about how to lead a good life. The most famous parables are those told by Jesus in the Gospels.

See pages 47, 266, 274, 659.

PARADOX A statement that appears self-contradictory, but that reveals a kind of truth. Many writers like to use paradox because it allows them to express the complexity of life by showing how opposing ideas can be both contradictory and true. Emily Dickinson often used paradoxes, as in this line: "I taste a liquor never brewed."

See pages 48, 171, 193, 224, 687, 723, 734.

PARALLEL STRUCTURE (also called parallelism) The repetition of words or phrases that have similar grammatical structures. In his Gettysburg Address, Lincoln used several memorable examples of parallel structure, as when he refers to "government of the people, by the people, for the people."

> Four score and seven years ago our fathers brought forth on this continent a new nation, conceived in liberty, and dedicated to the proposition that all men are created equal.
>
> Now we are engaged in a great civil war, testing whether that nation, or any nation so conceived and so dedicated, can long endure. We are met on a great battlefield of that war. We have come to dedicate a portion of that field as a final resting place for those who here gave their lives that that nation might live. It is altogether fitting and proper that we should do this.
>
> But, in a larger sense, we cannot dedicate—we cannot consecrate—we cannot hallow—this ground. The brave men, living and dead, who struggled here, have consecrated it far above our poor power to add or detract. The world will little note nor long remember what we say here, but it can never forget what they did here. It is for us the living, rather, to be dedicated here to the unfinished work which they who fought here have thus far so nobly advanced. It is rather for us to be here dedicated to the great task remaining before us—that from these honored dead we take increased devotion to that cause for which they gave the last full measure of devotion—that we here highly resolve that these dead shall not have died in vain—that this nation, under God, shall have a new birth of freedom—and that government of the people, by the people, for the people, shall not perish from the earth.
>
> —"The Gettysburg Address,"
> Abraham Lincoln

See pages 107, 333, 337, 732.

PARODY A work that makes fun of another work by imitating some aspect of the writer's style. Parodies often achieve their effects by humorously exaggerating certain features in the original work. Russell Baker's "Little Red Riding Hood Revisited" parodies the jargon of bureaucrats (page 999) by using language that makes the old fairy tale practically incomprehensible.

See pages 309, 580, 610.

PERSONIFICATION A figure of speech in which an object or animal is given human feelings, thoughts, or attitudes. Personification is a type of metaphor in which two dissimilar things are compared. In "To the Fringed Gentian," Bryant personifies a flower by giving it an eye and eyelashes:

> Then doth thy sweet and quiet eye
> Look through its fringes to the sky.

See pages 60–62, 145, 154, 199, 201, 247, 316, 365, 368, 463, 574, 636.
See also *Anthropomorphism, Apostrophe.*

PERSUASION One of the four forms of discourse, which uses reason and emotional appeals to convince a reader to think or act in a certain way. Persuasion is used in the Declaration of Independence (page 101), in Patrick Henry's "Give me liberty or give me death" speech (page 88), and in Thomas Paine's "The Crisis" (page 94). Persuasion is almost exclusively used in nonfiction, particularly in essays and speeches.

See page 92.

PLAIN STYLE A way of writing that stresses simplicity and clarity of expression. The plain style was favored by most Puritan writers, who avoided unnecessary ornamentation in all phases of their lives, including church ritual. In general, the plain style is characterized by simple sentences, by the use of everyday words from common speech, and by clear and direct statements. The plain style eliminates elaborate figures of speech and imagery. One of the chief exponents of the plain style in later American literature was Ernest Hemingway (page 553).

See pages 9, 22, 558.

PLOT The series of related events in a story or play, sometimes called the *storyline.* Most short-story plots contain the following elements: **exposition,** which tells us who the characters are and introduces their conflict; **complications,** which arise as the characters take steps to resolve their conflicts; the **climax,** that exciting or suspenseful moment when the outcome of the conflict is imminent; and a **resolution** or **denouement,** when the story's problems are all resolved, and the story ends.

The plots of dramas and novels are somewhat more complex because of their length. A schematic representation of a typical dramatic plot follows. It is based on a "pyramid" developed by the nineteenth-century German critic Gustav Freitag. The **rising action** refers to all the actions that take place before the **turning point** (sometimes called the **crisis**). This is the point at which the hero or heroine experiences a reversal of fortune: in a comedy, things begin to work out well; in a tragedy they get worse and worse. (In Shakespeare's plays, the turning point takes place in the third act. In *Romeo and Juliet,* for example, after he kills Mercutio in the third act, Romeo experiences one disaster after another.) All the action after the turning point is called **falling action** because it is leading to the final resolution (happy or unhappy) of the conflict. The major **climax** in most plays and novels takes place just before the ending; in Shakespeare's plays, it takes place in the fifth and last act. (In *Romeo and Juliet*, the major climax takes place when the two young people kill themselves.)

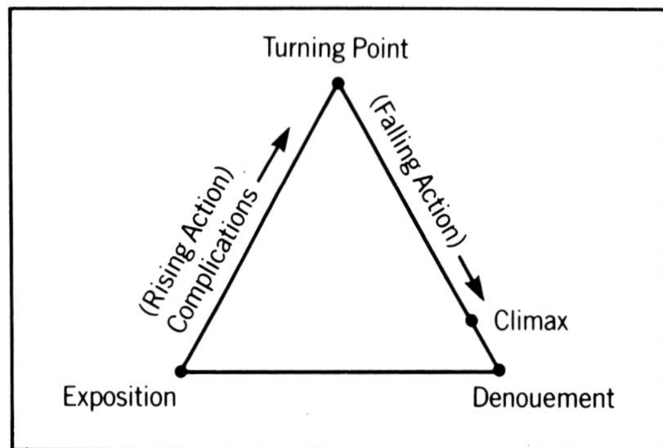

See page 896.

POINT OF VIEW The vantage point from which the writer tells a story. In broad terms, there are four main points of view: **first-person, third-person limited, omniscient,** and **objective.**

1. In the **first-person point of view,** one of the characters in the story tells the story, using first-person pronouns such as *I* and *we*. With this point of view, we can know only what the narrator knows. Mark Twain's novel *The Adventures of Huckleberry Finn* is told from the first-person point of view, by the novel's main character, a boy named Huck Finn. One of the great pleasures of that novel, in fact, is that its point of view allows us to hear Huck's very distinct voice and dialect.

2. In the **third-person limited point of view,** an unknown narrator (usually thought of as the author) tells the story, but this narrator zooms in to focus on the thoughts and feelings of only one character. (This point of view gets its name because the narrator refers to all the characters as *he, she,* and *they*; this narrator does not use the first-person pronoun *I*.) Like the first-person point of view, however, this point of view also limits us to the perceptions of one character, but in this case the narrator can tell us many things about the character, things that the character himself (or herself) might be unaware of. For example, Eudora Welty tells "A Worn Path" (page 614) from the third-person limited point of view of her heroine, an old woman named Phoenix Jackson. At one point, Welty's narrator tells us that Phoenix was "like an old woman begging a dignified forgiveness."

3. In the **omniscient point of view,** an omniscient (or "all-knowing") narrator tells the story, also using the third-person pronouns. However, this narrator, instead of focusing on one character only, often tells us everything about many characters: their motives, weaknesses, hopes, childhoods, and sometimes even their futures. This narrator can also comment directly on the character's actions. Washington Irving's "Rip Van Winkle" (page 125) is told from the omniscient point of view.

4. In the **objective point of view,** a narrator who is totally impersonal and objective tells the story, with no comment on any characters or events. The objective point of view is like the point of view of a movie camera; it is totally impersonal, and what we know is only what the camera might see. This narrator never gives any direct revelation of the characters' thoughts or motives. Ernest Hemingway (page 553) uses this objective point of view, which is why his stories often seem so puzzling to readers. "What happened?" we ask. The *reader* must infer what happens in Hemingway's stories, just as in real life we have to infer the motives, thoughts, and feelings of people we meet.

See pages 246, 301, 309, 438, 478, 524.

PROTAGONIST The central character in a story, the one who initiates or drives the action. The protagonist might or might not be the story's hero; some protagonists are actually the villains in the story.

See page 760.
See also *Antagonist.*

PUN A "play on words" based on the multiple meanings of a single word or on words that sound alike but mean different things. An example of the first type of pun is a singer explaining her claim that she was locked out of an audition because she couldn't find the right key. The second kind of pun can be found in the opening lines of Shakespeare's *Julius Caesar*, where a carpenter claims to be a mender of men's souls. Puns are often used as humor, but some puns are a serious element in poetry.

See pages 368, 716.

QUATRAIN A poem consisting of four lines, or four lines of a poem that can be considered as a unit. The typical ballad stanza, for example, is a quatrain.

RATIONALISM A movement that began in Europe in the seventeenth century, which held that we can arrive at truth by using our reason rather than relying on the authority of the past, on the authority of the Church, or on intuition. The Rationalists believed that all people were born with an innate ethical sense and had the ability to regulate and improve their own lives.

See page 68.

REALISM A style of writing, developed in the nineteenth century, that attempts to depict life accurately without idealizing or romanticizing it. Instead of writing about the long ago or far away, the realists concentrate often on contemporary life and on middle- and lower-class lives in particular. Among the outstanding realistic novelists in America are Stephen Crane (page 455), Willa Cather (page 517), and John Steinbeck (page 564).

See page 384.
See also *Naturalism, Romanticism.*

REFRAIN A word, phrase, line, or group of lines that is repeated, for effect, several times in a poem. Refrains are often used in ballads and other narrative poems. "And the tide rises, the tide falls" is a refrain in Longfellow's lyric (page 152), as is "in this kingdom by the sea" in Poe's "Annabel Lee" (page 250).

See page 168.

REGIONALISM Literature that emphasizes a specific geographic setting and that reproduces the speech, behavior, and attitudes of the people who live in that region. Among the great regional writers of the twentieth century are Sinclair Lewis (Midwest); John Steinbeck (California); and William Faulkner, Flannery O'Connor, and Eudora Welty (the South).

See page 381.

RESOLUTION The conclusion of a story, when all or most of the conflicts have been settled; often called the *dénouement.*

RHETORICAL QUESTION A question asked for an effect, and not actually requiring an answer. In his speech to the Virginia Convention, Patrick Henry asks several rhetorical questions. Such questions presume the audience agrees with the speaker on the answers.

See pages 91, 1095.

RHYME The repetition of vowel sounds in accented syllables and all succeeding syllables. *Listen* and *glisten* rhyme, as do *decay* and *away*. When words within the same line of poetry have repeated sounds, we have an example of **internal rhyme. End rhyme** refers to rhyming words at the ends of lines.

The pattern of rhymes in a poem is called a **rhyme scheme**. Rhyme scheme is commonly indicated with letters of the alphabet, each rhyming sound represented by a different letter of the alphabet. For example, the rhyme scheme of the following lines is *abab.*

Tell me not, in mournful numbers, *a*
Life is but an empty dream!— *b*
For the soul is dead that slumbers, *a*
And things are not what they seem. *b*

—from "A Psalm of Life,"
Henry Wadsworth Longfellow

Approximate rhymes (also called **off-rhymes, half rhymes, imperfect rhymes,** or **slant rhymes**) are words that have some correspondence in sound but not an exact one. Examples of approximate rhymes are often found in Emily Dickinson's poems. *Flash* and *flesh* are approximate rhymes, as are *stream* and *storm,* and *early* and *barley*. Approximate rhyme has the effect of catching the reader off guard: Where you expect a perfect rhyme, you get only an approximation. The emotional effect is something like that of the sound of a sharp or flat note in music.

See pages 47, 252, 254, 260, 262, 360, 679, 730.

RHYTHM A rise and fall of the voice produced by the alternation of stressed and unstressed syllables in language. When rhythm is tightly controlled and the stressed and unstressed syllables fall into a pattern, it is called **meter.**

See pages 340, 371, 671.
See also *Cadence, Meter.*

ROMANCE In general, a story in which an idealized hero or heroine undertakes a quest and is successful. In a romance, beauty, innocence, and goodness usually prevail over evil. In the past, romances were often set in the distant past and they used a great deal of fantasy. The laws of nature are often suspended in a romance, so that the hero or heroine often has supernatural powers, as we see in the adventures of King Arthur and his knights. Stories set in the American West are in the romance mode, except that the supernatural elements are eliminated (though the sheriff-hero usually has a nearly magical skill with his gun). Today we also use the word *romance* to refer to a kind of popular "potboiler" love story, which often takes place in an exotic setting.

See pages 610, 612.

ROMANTICISM A revolt against Rationalism that affected literature and the other arts, beginning in the late eighteenth century and remaining strong throughout most of the nineteenth century. Romanticism is marked by these characteristics: (1) a conviction that intuition, imagination, and emotion are superior to reason; (2) a conviction that poetry is superior to science; (3) a belief that contemplation of the natural world is a means of discovering the truth that lies behind mere reality; (4) a distrust of industry and city life and an idealization of rural life and of the wilderness; (5) an interest in the more "natural" past and in the supernatural. Romanticism affected so many creative people that it was bound to take many different forms; the result is that it is difficult to define the word in a way that includes everyone who might be called a Romantic. In the nineteenth century, for example, Romantics were outspoken in their love of nature and contempt for technology. In this century, however, as nature has been taken over by developers and highways, some writers have taken a romantic view of machines, buildings, and other products of technology.

See pages 118, 707.

SATIRE A type of writing that ridicules the shortcomings of people or institutions in an attempt to bring about a change. Satire can cover a wide range of tones, from gentle spoofing to savage mockery. In "A Fable for Critics," for example, James Russell Lowell pokes good-natured fun at his literary contemporaries (page 170). In *Babbitt's After-Dinner Speech* (page 511), Sinclair Lewis presents a vicious portrait of a small-town businessman. Satire is always intensely moral. Mark Twain, in *The Adventures of Huckleberry Finn* (page 414), satirizes a whole spectrum of American life, but the thrust of the novel is moral: Twain is making us see things that should not be permitted to exist (slavery is one of them).

See pages 136, 170, 516, 1001, 1069.

SCANNING The analysis of a poem to determine its meter. When you scan a poem, you describe the pattern of stressed and unstressed syllables in each line. Stresses or accents are indicated by the symbol (′) and unstressed syllables by the symbol (˘).

To him who in the love of Nature holds
Communion with her visible forms, she speaks
A various language: for his gayer hours
She has a voice of gladness, and a smile

—from "Thanatopsis,"
William Cullen Bryant

See pages 44, 370.
See also *Iambic Pentameter, Meter.*

SESTET Six lines of poetry, especially the last six lines of a Petrarchan sonnet.

See also *Sonnet.*

SETTING The time and location where a story takes place. Setting can have several functions in fiction: (1) Setting is often used to create **conflict.** In the purest and often simplest form of story, a character is in conflict with some element of a setting: The outcasts of Poker Flat in Bret Harte's story on page 394 are in conflict with a blizzard (the blizzard wins). (2) Often the setting helps to create **atmosphere** or **mood,** as does Edgar Allan Poe's setting of a decaying mansion in "The Fall of the House of Usher" (page 234). (3) Setting can also create and delineate **character:** Bessie Popkin's disorderly and locked-up apartment in Singer's story "The Key" (page 877) reflects Bessie's own isolation and emotional chaos.

See pages 136, 246, 292, 349, 438, 524, 558.

SIMILE A figure of speech that makes an explicit comparison between two unlike things, using a word such as *like, as, than,* or *resembles*.

Helen, thy beauty is to me
Like those Nicéan barks of yore

—from "To Helen,"
Edgar Allan Poe

See pages 151, 168, 219, 254, 304, 359, 363, 574, 643.
See also *Figure of Speech, Metaphor.*

SOLILOQUY A long speech made by a character in a play while no other characters are on stage. A soliloquy is different from a monologue in that the speaker appears to be thinking aloud, not addressing a listener. In *The Glass Menagerie* (page 769), Tom's periodic speeches are examples of soliloquies.

SONNET A fourteen-line lyric poem, usually written in iambic pentameter, that has one of two basic structures. The **Petrarchan sonnet,** also called the **Italian sonnet,** is named after the fourteenth-century Italian poet Petrarch. Its first eight lines, called the **octave,** ask a question or pose a problem. These lines have a rhyme scheme of *abba, abba*. The last six lines, called the **sestet,** respond to the question or problem. These lines have a rhyme scheme of *cde, cde*.

The form used to such perfection by William Shakespeare is known as the **English** or **Shakespearean sonnet.** It has three four-line units, or **quatrains,** and it concludes with a **couplet.** The most common rhyme scheme for the Shakespearean sonnet is *abab, cdcd, efef, gg*.

Longfellow, whose sonnet "The Cross of Snow" is on page 147, wrote many sonnets, as did Edna St. Vincent Millay (page 647), Robert Frost (page 652), and E. E. Cummings (page 735).

See pages 148, 655.

1180

SPONDEE A metrical foot consisting of two syllables, both of which are stressed. The words *trueblue* and *nineteen* are made of spondees. When Whitman wrote "Beat! beat! drums" he used spondees. Spondaic feet are rarely used extensively because of their "thump-thump" sound. However, poets sometimes use spondees to provide a brief change from an iambic or trochaic beat, or to provide emphasis.

STEREOTYPE A fixed idea or conception of a character or an idea which does not allow for any individuality, often based on religious, social, or racial prejudices. Some common stereotypes are the unsophisticated farmer, the socially inept honor student, the dumb athlete, and the lazy teen-ager. Stereotypes are often deliberately used in comedies and in melodramas, where they receive instant recognition from the audience and make genuine characterization unnecessary. Babbitt in Sinclair Lewis's novel (page 511) has given rise to a whole range of unfair stereotypes based on the insensitive businessman—though at the time, Babbitt was an original.

See pages 137, 982.

STREAM OF CONSCIOUSNESS A style of writing that portrays the inner (often chaotic) workings of a character's mind. The stream-of-consciousness technique usually consists of a recording of the random flow of ideas, memories, associations, images, and emotions, as they arise spontaneously in a character's mind. William Faulkner, in his great novel *The Sound and the Fury*, used a stream-of-consciousness technique. Two of the other great writers that used a stream-of-consciousness technique are the Irish writer James Joyce and the English writer Virginia Woolf.

See pages 497, 589.

STYLE The distinctive way in which a writer uses language. Styles can be plain, ornate, metaphorical, spare, descriptive, and so on. Style is determined by such factors as sentence length and complexity, syntax, use of figurative language and imagery, and diction.

See *Plain Style, Ornate Style, Stream of Consciousness.*

SURREALISM A movement in art and literature that started in Europe during the 1920's. Surrealists wanted to replace conventional realism with the full expression of the unconscious mind, which they considered to be more real than the "real" world of appearances. Surrealists, influenced by the psychoanalytic theories of Sigmund Freud, tried not to censor the images that came from their dreams or to impose logical connections on these images. This resulted in surprising combinations of "inner" and "outer" reality—a "suprareality." Surrealism affected writers as different as T. S. Eliot (page 740) and Donald Barthelme (page 919). Two famous Surreal artists are Salvador Dali and Marc Chagall. (See pages 886 and 895.)

SUSPENSE A feeling of uncertainty and curiosity about what will happen next in a story. A key element in fiction and drama, suspense is one of the "hooks" a writer uses to keep the readers or audience interested.

See pages 796, 866.

SYMBOL A person, place, thing, or event that has meaning in itself and that also stands for something more than itself. We can distinguish between **public** and **personal symbols.** The dove, for example, is a public symbol of peace—that is, it is widely accepted the world over as such a symbol. Uncle Sam is a public symbol that stands for the United States; a picture of a skull and crossbones is a public symbol of death; two snakes coiled around a staff are a widely accepted symbol of the medical profession.

Most symbols used in literature are personal symbols; even though a symbol may be widely used, a writer will usually adapt it in some imaginative, personal way so that it can suggest not just one, but a myriad of meanings. One of the most commonly used symbols in literature, for example, is the journey, which can stand for a search for truth, for redemption from evil, or for discovery of the self and freedom. The journey of Huck Finn and Jim down the Mississippi River has been interpreted to symbolize all of these concepts, and more.

Many writers, particularly those known as the Symbolists, have tried to find new symbols by which to express the complexities of experience.

See pages 141, 163, 232, 247, 249, 260, 274, 292, 316, 344, 428, 478, 508, 645, 662, 670, 754, 810.

SYMBOLISM A literary movement that originated in late-nineteenth-century France, in which writers rearranged the world of appearances in order to reveal a more truthful version of reality. The Symbolists believed that direct statements of feeling were inadequate; instead they called for new and striking symbols to evoke complexities of meaning and mood. The French Symbolists were influenced by the poetry and critical writings of the American Edgar Allan Poe (page 226). The poetry of Ezra Pound (page 711), T. S. Eliot (page 740), and Wallace Stevens (page 750) is in the Symbolist tradition.

See pages 549, 586, 707.

SYNECDOCHE A figure of speech in which a part represents the whole. The capital city of a nation, for example, is often spoken of as though it were the government: "Washington and Teheran are both claiming popular support for

1181

their positions." In "The Love Song of J. Alfred Prufrock," T. S. Eliot writes, "And I have known the arms already. . . ." In that line, the word *arms* stands for the women he has known.

TALL TALE An outrageously exaggerated, humorous story that is obviously unbelievable. Tall tales are part of the folk literature of many countries, including America. Perhaps the most famous tall tale in American literature is Mark Twain's "The Celebrated Jumping Frog of Calaveras County." The bragging of the raftsmen in Twain's *Life on the Mississippi* (page 404) also provides examples of tall tales.

THEME The insight about human life that is revealed in a literary work. Themes are rarely stated directly in literature. Most often, a reader has to infer the theme of a work after considerable thought. Theme is different from **subject.** A story's subject might be stated as "growing up," "love," "heroism," or "fear." The theme is the statement the writer wants to make about that subject: "For most young people, growing up is a process that involves the pain of achieving self-knowledge." Theme must be stated in at least one sentence; most themes are complex enough to require several sentences, or even an essay.

See pages 136, 141, 232, 274, 368, 401, 479, 509, 524, 558, 574, 610.

TONE The attitude a writer takes toward the subject of a work, the characters in it, or the audience. In speaking, we use voice inflections to show how we feel about what we are saying. Writers manipulate language in an attempt to achieve the same effect. For example, John Hersey takes an objective tone in telling about the nuclear explosion in "A Noiseless Flash" (page 1049). In contrast, Michael Herr's tone toward the Vietnam war in "Dispatches" (page 1059) is subjective, confused, even fearful. Tone is dependent on **diction** and **style**, and we cannot say we have understood any work of literature until we have sensed the writer's tone. Tone can be described in a single word: objective, solemn, playful, ironic, sarcastic, critical, reverent, irreverent, philosophical, cynical, and so on.

See pages 35, 80, 136, 145, 151, 249, 274, 335, 340, 355, 362, 363, 365, 428, 634, 643, 655.

TRAGEDY In general, a story in which a heroic character either dies or comes to some other unhappy end. In most tragedies, the main character is in an enviable, even exalted position when the story begins (in classical tragedies and in Shakespeare, the tragic hero is a king or queen, prince or princess). This character may bring about his or her own downfall because of an error in judgment or because of a personality failure known as a **tragic flaw** (Creon's stubbornness in *Antigone*, Hamlet's indecision). Or, the downfall may result from forces totally outside the character's control (Job in the Bible is the tragic victim of a wager between God and Satan). The tragic character has usually gained wisdom at the end of the story, in spite of suffering defeat, or even death. Our feeling on reading or viewing a tragedy is usually exaltation—despite the unhappy ending—because we have witnessed the best that human beings are capable of.

See page 612.
See also *Comedy*.

TRANSCENDENTALISM A nineteenth-century movement in the Romantic tradition, which held that every individual can reach ultimate truths through spiritual intuition, which transcends reasons and sensory experience. The Transcendental movement was centered in Concord, Massachusetts, the home of its leading exponents, Ralph Waldo Emerson and Henry David Thoreau. The basic tenets of the Transcendentalists were (1) a belief that God is present in every aspect of Nature, including every human being; (2) the conviction that everyone is capable of apprehending God through the use of intuition; (3) the belief that all of nature is symbolic of the spirit. A corollary of these beliefs was an optimistic view of the world as good and evil as nonexistent.

See pages 183, 316.

TROCHEE A metrical foot made up of an accented syllable followed by an unaccented syllable, as in the word *taxi.* A trochee is the opposite of an iamb and is sometimes used to vary the rhythm of an iambic poem.

See pages 151, 262, 333.

UNDERSTATEMENT A statement that says less than what is meant. Understatement, paradoxically, can make us recognize the truth of something by saying that just the opposite is true. If you sit down to a dinner plate that contains only a peanut-butter sandwich and you say, "A feast for a king," you are using understatement to emphasize how little, in fact, is on your plate. Understatement is often used to make an ironic point; it can also be used for humor.

See also *Hyperbole*.

VERNACULAR The language spoken by the people who live in a particular locality.

See also *Dialect*.

A Reference Guide
The ELEMENTS OF LITERATURE program provides three features to help you integrate language study with the study of literature. (1) The first feature is a series of exercises in the student text called **Literature and Language.** (2) The second is a series of **Language Skills Worksheets** that are found in the Core Components Binder. (3) The third is this complete and succinct guide to grammar, usage, and mechanics.

This handbook can be used in several ways. It will be useful to students for whom English is a second language. It will be a convenient reference handbook for all students who need to confirm definitions and the rules of grammar, usage, and mechanics, particularly as they need this help in writing. The guide will also be useful to you, the teacher, when you wish to review terminology and rules.

The guide consists of the following: (1) grammatical terminology and definitions, with examples; (2) rules governing standard English usage, with examples; (3) spelling hints; and (4) occasional boxed "Tips for Writers." If you wish to give students practice in applying their skills to *(Continued on next page.)*

GRAMMAR, USAGE, AND MECHANICS: A REFERENCE GUIDE

NOTE TO STUDENTS
As you write and revise formal essays and papers on topics in literature, you may want to review points of grammar, usage, capitalization, punctuation, and spelling. This reference section provides rules and examples that you will find helpful in your writing.

PARTS OF SPEECH

Nouns

1. **A *noun* is a word used to name a person, place, thing, or idea.**

   EXAMPLES
   child, chemist, Christine, Dr. King [people]
   city, state, California, Mexico [places]
   tool, fruit, Ford, peach [things]
   beauty, wealth, value, freedom [ideas]

2. **A *common noun* names a class or a group of persons, places, or things. A *proper noun* names a particular person, place, or thing.**

   EXAMPLES

Common	*Proper*
author	Elizabeth Bishop
island	Oahu
play	*King Lear*

3. **An *abstract noun* names a quality, a characteristic, or an idea. A *concrete noun* names an object that can be perceived by the senses.**

   EXAMPLES

Abstract	*Concrete*
faith	pepper
integrity	book
health	wallet
hope	town

4. **A *compound noun* is a single noun made up of two or more words. Compound nouns may be common or proper.**

   EXAMPLES
   class ring, know-it-all, gatekeeper, Los Angeles

Pronouns

1. **A *pronoun* is a word used in place of one or more than one noun. The noun the pronoun stands for is called its *antecedent.***

   EXAMPLES
   Allen told **his** mother **he** would be home late. [The pronouns *his* and *he* refer to the antecedent *Allen.*]
   Debbie and Ed called **their** mother to say **they** had arrived safely at camp.

2. **Forms of personal pronouns combined with *-self* or *-selves* may be used reflexively, to refer to the subject, or intensively, for emphasis.**

   EXAMPLES
   myself, yourself, himself, herself, itself; ourselves, yourselves, themselves

3. ***Relative pronouns* are used to introduce subordinate clauses.**

   EXAMPLES
   who, whom, whose, which, that, whoever, whomever, whichever

4. ***Interrogative pronouns* are used in questions.**

   EXAMPLES
   who, whom, whose, which, what

5. ***Demonstrative pronouns* point out a particular person or thing.**

   EXAMPLES
   this child [singular demonstrative pronoun]
   that cat [singular demonstrative pronoun]
   these books [plural demonstrative pronoun]
   those records [plural demonstrative pronoun]

6. ***Indefinite pronouns* refer to persons, places, or things but not to any specific ones.**

   EXAMPLES
   all, another, any, anybody, anyone, both, each, either, everybody, everyone, everything, few, many, more, most, much, neither, nobody, none, no one, several, some, somebody, someone, such

(Continued from previous page.) grammar, usage, and mechanics, we refer you to the Core Components Binder. There you will find the **Language Skills Worksheets** which directly integrate the study of language and its application to specific literary selections in the text. To find these **Language Skills Worksheets,** simply read the lists of Supplementary Support Materials that precede each selection in this Annotated Teacher's Edition.

Adjectives

1. **An *adjective* is a word used to modify a noun or a pronoun. Adjectives answer questions such as *What kind? Which one? How much?* or *How many?***

EXAMPLES
blue sky [What kind?] **that** cat [Which one?]
little help [How much?]
two colors, **few** choices [How many?]

2. ***A, an,* and *the* are special adjectives called *articles.***

3. **A *proper adjective* is an adjective that is formed from a proper noun. Proper adjectives, like proper nouns, are always capitalized.**

EXAMPLES
English history, **Swedish** meatballs, **Norse** mythology

4. **Other parts of speech such as pronouns and nouns may be used as adjectives.**

EXAMPLES
The **Maine** coastline is rocky. [noun as adjective]
Both dogs were terriers. [pronoun as adjective]

Verbs

1. **A *verb* is a word that expresses action or otherwise helps to make a sentence. An *action verb* is a word that expresses a physical or mental action.**

EXAMPLES
wash, knit, sew, climb [physical actions]
think, know, recognize [mental actions]

2. **A *linking verb* is a word that does not express an action. A linking verb helps to make a sentence by joining the subject with a noun or adjective in the predicate.**

EXAMPLES
Whitney Houston is an exciting **singer.** [*Is* links the subject *Whitney Houston* with the noun *singer* in the predicate.]
She sounds **wonderful** on her new album. [*Sounds* links the subject *she* with the adjective *wonderful* in the predicate.]

3. **A one-word verb is called a *main verb.* Sometimes a main verb is accompanied by other verbs called *helping verbs.* The main verb and the helping verb together make up a *verb phrase.***

EXAMPLES
The family doctor **has advised** bed rest. [The verb phrase is *has advised.* The main verb is *advised* and *has* is the helping verb.]
My temperature **has been** normal all day. [The verb phrase is *has been.* The main verb is *been* and *has* is the helping verb.]

Adverbs

1. **An *adverb* is a word used to modify a verb, an adjective, or another adverb. Adverbs usually answer questions such as: *Where? When? How? To what extent?***

EXAMPLES
I put the new videotape machine **upstairs**. [Where?]
Jan and I watched it **yesterday**. [When?]

2. **Some nouns may be used adverbially.**

EXAMPLES
He finally went **home.** [Where?]
It weighed **ten pounds.** [How much?]

Prepositions

1. **A *preposition* is a word used to show the relationship of a noun or a pronoun to some other word in the sentence. Below are common prepositions.**

EXAMPLES

above	behind	for	on
across	below	from	over
after	beside	in	since
amid	between	into	to
among	by	like	through
around	down	near	under
at	during	of	with
before	except	off	within

2. **The noun or pronoun following the preposition is called the *object of the preposition.* Words that modify the object may come between the preposition and the object. Taken together, the preposition, its object, and the modifiers of the object are called a *prepositional phrase.***

EXAMPLES
The student wrote a long poem **about the violent sea.** [In this sentence, the prepositional phrase is *about the violent sea. About* is the preposition, *sea* is the object of the preposition, and the words *the violent* modify *sea.*]

TIPS FOR WRITERS

Use an adverb only after an action verb. Use an adjective after a linking verb to modify a noun or pronoun in the subject of a sentence.

EXAMPLES
The chocolate cake tasted good. [*Good* is an adjective that appears after the linking verb *tasted* and modifies the subject noun *cake.*]
The pastry chef baked well. [*Well* is an adverb that modifies the action verb *baked.*]

Conjunctions

1. **A *conjunction* is a word that joins words or groups of words. *Coordinating conjunctions* join two or more words, phrases, or sentence parts of equal rank. The words *and, but, or, nor, for, so,* and *yet* are called coordinating conjunctions.**

   EXAMPLES
   Guitar **and** violin are my instruments. [The two words *guitar* and *violin* are joined by *and.*]
   I cannot go, **so** you must take my place. [Two sentences are joined by *so.*]

2. ***Correlative conjunctions* are always found in pairs that have other words separating them: *either . . . or, neither . . . nor, both . . . and, not only . . . but also.***

   EXAMPLE
   Both Francine **and** Kevin are taking Russian.

3. ***Subordinating conjunctions* are used to introduce subordinate clauses in complex sentences. Common subordinating conjunctions include *after, as soon as, because, if, so that, until, when,* and *while.*** (See page 1188 for an exploration of complex sentences.)

Interjections

An *interjection* is a word that expresses emotion and that is not related grammatically to other words in the sentence.

EXAMPLES
Gosh! That dance is not easy to do.
Oh, it's not difficult if you practice.

THE SENTENCE

Elements of a Sentence

1. **A *sentence* is a group of words expressing a complete thought. A group of words that does not express a complete thought is a *fragment.***

   FRAGMENTS
   Played the concerto. [We do not know *who* played the concerto.]
   After she played the piece. [We do not know *what happened* after she played the piece.]

   SENTENCES
   Midori played the concerto. [The sentence expresses a complete thought.]
   After she played the piece, Midori gave an encore.

2. **The *subject* of a sentence is the part about which something is being said. The *simple subject* is the main word in a subject. The *complete subject* is the simple subject and all the words that go with it.**

   EXAMPLES
   The orchestra conductor waited in the wings. [*The orchestra conductor* is the complete subject. *Conductor* is the simple subject.]
   On the stage sat **several cellists.** [*Several cellists* is the complete subject. *Cellists* is the simple subject.]

3. **The *predicate* of a sentence is the part that says something about the subject. The *simple predicate,* or *verb,* is the main word in a predicate. The *complete predicate* is the simple predicate and all the words that go with it.**

   EXAMPLES
   The orchestra conductor **waited in the wings.** [*Waited in the wings* is the complete predicate. *Waited* is the simple predicate.]
   On the stage sat several cellists. [*On the stage sat* is the complete predicate. *Sat* is the simple predicate.]

Phrases

1. **A *phrase* is a group of related words that is used as a single part of speech and does not contain a verb and its subject. Three common types of phrases include verb phrases, noun phrases, and prepositional phrases.**

   EXAMPLE
   The puppy was barking at the toy bear. [*The puppy* is a noun phrase, *is barking* is a verb phrase, and *at the toy bear* is a prepositional phrase.]

2. **An *adjective phrase* is a prepositional phrase that modifies a noun or a pronoun.**

   EXAMPLE
   The towel **with the blue stripe** is mine. [The phrase *with the blue stripe* modifies the noun *towel.*]

3. **An *adverb phrase* is a prepositional phrase that modifies a verb, an adjective, or another adverb.**

EXAMPLE
The midday sun disappeared **behind a cloud.** [The phrase *behind a cloud* modifies the verb *disappeared.*]

4. **A *verbal* is a form of a verb used as another part of speech. Verbals may have modifiers and complements. There are three kinds of verbals: participles, gerunds, and infinitives.**

5. **A *participle* is a verb form used as an adjective. Both present participles and past participles can be used as adjectives.**

EXAMPLES
A **floating** bottle attracted our attention. [modifies *bottle*]
The **crumpled** paper inside intrigued us. [modifies *paper*]

6. **A *participial phrase* consists of a participle and any modifiers or complements, all of which act together as an adjective.**

EXAMPLE
Bobbing in the water, the bottle floated past us. [The participial phrase *bobbing in the water* modifies *bottle.*]

7. **A *gerund* is a verb form ending in *-ing* that is used as a noun.**

EXAMPLES
Swimming provides good exercise. [The gerund *swimming* acts as subject of *provides.*]
My sister and I enjoy **biking.** [The gerund *biking* is the direct object of the verb *enjoy.*]

8. **A *gerund phrase* consists of a gerund and any complements or modifiers it may have.**

EXAMPLES
Walking along the seashore is one of my favorite activities. [The gerund phrase *Walking along the seashore* is the complete subject.]
Have I asked you about **joining our club?** [The gerund phrase *joining our club* is the object of the preposition *about.*]

9. **An *infinitive* is a verb form, usually preceded by *to*, that is used as a noun, an adjective, or an adverb.**

EXAMPLES
Bert likes **to dive.** [used as a noun]
The box was difficult **to carry.** [used as an adverb]

10. **An *infinitive phrase* consists of an infinitive and any complements or modifiers it may have.**

EXAMPLE
I want **to win the race.** [*To win the race* acts as direct object of *want.*]

11. **An *appositive* is a noun or pronoun that follows another noun to identify or explain it. An *appositive phrase* is made up of an appositive and its modifiers.**

EXAMPLES
My cousin **Al** is an accomplished singer.
Mr. Allison**, the director of our choir,** is also a singer.

Clauses

1. **A *clause* is a group of words that contains a verb and its subject and is used as part of a sentence. An *independent clause* expresses a complete thought and can stand by itself as a sentence. A *dependent* (or *subordinate*) *clause* does not express a complete thought and cannot stand alone. Subordinate clauses can be used as adjectives, nouns, or adverbs.**

EXAMPLES
Since it was Saturday, **I mowed the lawn.** [independent clause]
I oiled the lawn mower **before I began.** [dependent clause]

2. **An *adjective clause* is a subordinate clause that modifies a noun or pronoun.**

EXAMPLE
The man **who met me at the airport** helped me carry my bags. [adjective clause modifying *man*]

3. **A *noun clause* is a subordinate clause that is used as a noun.**

EXAMPLE
She said **that she enjoyed my novel.** [noun clause used as a direct object]

4. **An *adverb clause* is a subordinate clause that is used as an adverb.**

EXAMPLE
Call me **when you get to the hotel.** [adverb clause modifying *call*]

Kinds of Sentences

1. **A *declarative sentence* makes a statement. It is followed by a period.**

2. **An *interrogative sentence* asks a question. It is followed by a question mark.**

3. **An *imperative sentence* gives a command or request. It is followed by a period. Strong commands are followed by exclamation points.**

4. **An *exclamatory sentence* shows excitement or expresses a strong feeling. It is followed by an exclamation point.**

   EXAMPLES
   The water is calm this morning. [declarative]
   Is there a storm predicted? [interrogative]
   Check the weather report. [imperative]
   Be careful! [imperative]
   What a beautiful beach this is! [exclamatory]

Sentence Complements

1. **A *complement* is a word or phrase that completes the meaning begun by the subject and verb.**

2. **The *direct object* receives the action expressed by the verb or names the result of the action. A direct object answers the question *What?* or *Whom?* after the action verb.**

   EXAMPLES
   The landlord painted the **apartment** for the new tenant. [*Apartment* is the direct object; it receives the action of the verb *painted.*]
   The new tenant signed a five-year **lease.** [*Lease* is the direct object; it receives the action of the verb *signed.*]

3. **The *indirect object* of the verb precedes the direct object and tells *to whom* (or *what*) or *for whom* (or *what*) the action of the verb is done.**

   EXAMPLES
   My sister wrote **me** a long letter. [*Me* is the indirect object because it tells *to whom* my sister wrote a long letter.]
   The clerk gave the **customers** free bars of soap. [*Customers* is the indirect object because it tells *to whom* the clerk gave free bars of soap.]

4. **A *subject complement* is a word that follows a linking verb and refers to (explains or describes) the subject.**

   EXAMPLES
   That dog seems **thirsty.**
   This kitten is her **pet.**

5. **If the subject complement is a noun or pronoun, it is called a *predicate nominative.***

   EXAMPLES
   Next Monday is my **birthday.** [*Birthday* is a predicate nominative. It is a noun that renames the subject *Monday.*]
   The donor was **she.** [*She* is a predicate nominative. It is a pronoun that renames the subject *donor.*]

6. **If the subject complement is an adjective, it is called a *predicate adjective.* A predicate adjective modifies the subject of the sentence.**

   EXAMPLES
   The book is **new.** [*New* is a predicate adjective modifying the subject *book.*]
   The cover looks **attractive.** [*Attractive* is a predicate adjective modifying the subject *cover.*]

7. **An *objective complement* is a complement that refers to the direct object of an action verb. The objective complement may be either a noun or an adjective. Verbs that take objective complements include *make, consider, elect, appoint, name, choose,* and *render.***

   EXAMPLES
   We named our new puppy **Frisky.** [The complement *Frisky* refers to the direct object *puppy* and completes the meaning of the verb *named.*]
   The award made my grandfather **happy.** [The complement *happy* modifies the direct object *grandfather* and completes the meaning of the verb *made.*]

Sentence Structure

1. **A *simple sentence* has one independent clause and no dependent (or subordinate) clauses. A simple sentence may have a compound subject, a compound predicate, or both.**

   EXAMPLES
   The seal scratched its chin. [simple sentence]
   The seal pup and its mother lay on the rocks. [simple sentence with compound subject]
   An old seal crawled up on a rock and went to sleep. [simple sentence with compound predicate]
   A boy and his mother watched the seals and took photographs. [simple sentence with compound subject and compound predicate]

2. **A *compound sentence* has two or more independent clauses but no dependent (or subordinate) clauses.**

EXAMPLES
Len likes directing plays, but his sister prefers building scenery. [This sentence has two independent clauses joined by the conjunction *but.*]
The drama club's first production was *Our Town,* the second was *Take Her, She's mine,* and the third was *Godspell.* [This sentence has three independent clauses, the last two of which are joined by the conjunction *and.*]

3. **A *complex sentence* has one independent clause and at least one dependent (subordinate) clause.**

EXAMPLES
After I saw the the first play, I joined the drama club. [*I joined the drama club* is the independent clause, and *after I saw the first play* is a dependent adverb clause.]
I had a leading role in a new production before I knew it. [*I had a leading role in a new production* is the independent clause, and *before I knew it* is a dependent adverb clause.]

4. **A *compound-complex sentence* has two or more independent clauses and at least one dependent (subordinate) clause.**

EXAMPLE
Len likes plays, but I prefer musicals, which have singing and dancing. [*Len likes plays* and *I prefer musicals* are both independent clauses. *Which have singing and dancing* is a dependent adjective clause.]

TIPS FOR WRITERS

Do not use a comma in a compound subject or predicate in which two elements are joined by a conjunction. Do use commas to separate all the elements in a compound subject or predicate with three or more elements.

EXAMPLES
Julio and Mica have joined the drama club. [Two elements in a compound subject are not separated by a comma.]
Julio, Sebastian, and Mica have joined the drama club. [Three elements in a compound subject are separated by commas.]

PROBLEMS OF AGREEMENT

Agreement of Subject and Verb

1. **A verb should agree with its subject in number. Singular subjects take singular verbs. Plural subjects take plural verbs.**

EXAMPLES
She raises chickens. [The singular verb *raises* agrees with the singular subject *she.*]
They raise chickens. [The plural verb *raise* agrees with the plural subject *they.*]

Like single-word verbs, verb phrases also agree with their subjects. However, in a verb phrase, only the first auxiliary (helping) verb changes its form to agree with a singular or plural subject.

EXAMPLES
A **hen was eating** grain.
Two **hens were eating** grain.

2. **The number of the subject is not changed by a phrase following the subject.**

EXAMPLES
This **collection** of coins **is** valuable. [*Collection* is the subject, not *coins.*]
These **coins** of gold **are** antiques. [*Coins* is the subject, not *gold.*]

3. **Compound prepositions such as *together with, in addition to, as well as,* and *along with* following the subject do not affect the number of the subject.**

EXAMPLE
Ken, together with his brothers, **is entering** the marathon. [The subject of the sentence is singular because it names one person, *Ken.* Therefore, the predicate of the sentence uses the singular auxiliary verb form *is.*]

4. **The following indefinite pronouns are singular: *each, either, neither, one, everyone, everybody, no one, nobody, anyone, anybody, someone, somebody.***

EXAMPLES
Each of the poets **writes** rhymed verse. [*Each one* writes.]
Neither of the poems **is** a sonnet. [*Neither one* is a sonnet.]
Someone was reading the poem aloud. [*One* person was reading.]

5. **The following pronouns are plural: *several, few, both, many.***

EXAMPLES
Several of these poems **are** translations.
Few of the poems **have** metaphors.
Are both of these poems new?

6. **The pronouns *some, all, most, any,* and *none* may be either singular or plural. These pronouns are singular when they refer to a singular word and plural when they refer to a plural word.**

EXAMPLES
Some of the imagery **is** unusual. [*Some* refers to the singular noun *imagery.*]
Some of the images **are** good. [*Some* refers to the plural noun *images.*]

All of the writing **is** witty.
All of the poems **are** in rhyme.

Most of the poetry **reads** well.
Most of the poems **read** well.

7. **Compound subjects joined by the word *and* are usually plural in form and therefore take a plural verb.**

A **compound subject** is a subject that contains two or more nouns or pronouns that are the subject of the same verb.

EXAMPLES
Jiri and **Suni collect** rare books. [Two persons are *collectors.*]
Chaucer, Shakespeare, and **Milton are** the greatest writers in the English language. [Three people are *writers.*]

TIPS FOR WRITERS

The words *any* and *none* may be singular even when they refer to a plural word if the speaker is thinking of each item individually. The words *any* and *none* are plural only if the speaker is thinking of several items as a group.

Any of these books **is** worth reading. [*Any one book* is worth reading.]
None of the books **was** bad. [*Not one book* was bad.]
Any of these books **are** worth reading. [*All the books* are worth reading.]
None of the books **were** bad. [*No books* were bad.]

8. **Compound subjects that name only one person or thing take a singular verb.**

EXAMPLES
My **secretary and receptionist is** James Strongheart. [One person is your secretary and receptionist.]
Ham and eggs is a great breakfast dish.

9. **Singular subjects joined by the words *or* or *nor* take a singular verb.**

EXAMPLE
Either **Rajed** or **Paolo drives** that way. [*Either* Rajed *or* Paolo drives, not both.]

10. **When a singular subject and a plural subject are joined by *or* or *nor,* the verb agrees with the subject nearer the verb.**

ACCEPTABLE
Neither the accountants nor the **business manager was** happy with the report.
Neither the business manager nor the **accountants were** happy with the report.

Other Problems in Subject–Verb Agreement

11. **The contractions *don't* and *doesn't* must agree with their subjects.**

With the subjects *I* and *you* and with plural subjects, use the contraction *don't (do not).*

EXAMPLES

I **don't** care.	They **don't** cry.
You **don't** know.	These **don't** wilt.
We **don't** dare.	Pencils **don't** leak.

With singular subjects, use the singular *doesn't (does not).*

EXAMPLES

He **doesn't** care.	One **doesn't** cry.
She **doesn't** know.	This **doesn't** leak.
It **doesn't** pay.	Donna **doesn't** forget.

12. **Use a plural verb with a singular collective noun when you are referring to the individual parts or members of the group acting separately. Use a singular verb when you refer to the group acting together as a unit. *Collective nouns* are singular in form, but they name a group of persons or things.**

EXAMPLES

army	club	fleet	jury
assembly	committee	flock	panel
audience	faculty	group	swarm
class	family	herd	team

EXAMPLES
The team **have** put their uniforms on. [*Team* is thought of as individuals.]
The team **has** won eight out of its nine games. [*Team* is thought of as a unit.]

Be sure that any pronoun referring to the collective noun has the same number as the noun (*their* in the first example above, *its* in the second).

TIPS FOR WRITERS

When the subject follows the verb, find the subject and make sure that the verb agrees with it. The most common uses of the subject-following-verb form are in sentences beginning with *here* and *there* and in questions.

Here **is** a red **pencil.**	Here **are** two red **pencils.**
There **is** my **notebook.**	There **are** my **notebooks.**

13. A verb agrees with its subject, not with its predicate nominative.

STANDARD
The botanical **exhibits** (S) **are** my main interest (PN).
My main **interest** (S) **is** the botanical exhibits (PN).

14. Contractions such as *here's, where's, how's,* and *what's* include the verb *is.* Do not use one of these contractions unless a singular subject follows it.

NONSTANDARD
There's some details we need to discuss.

STANDARD
There **are** some **details** we need to discuss.

15. A word or a phrase stating a weight, a measurement, or an amount of money or time is usually considered one item and takes a singular verb.

EXAMPLES
Two dollars is quite cheap for a cap like that.
Two thirds of the wheat shipment **was** lost in transit.

Sometimes, however, the amount is thought of as individual pieces or parts. If so, a plural verb is used.

EXAMPLES
Five of the coins **were** fifty-cent pieces.
Three fourths of the students **take** carpentry.

16. The title of a work of art, literature, or music, even when plural in form, takes a singular verb.

EXAMPLES
Raphael's ***School of Athens*** **is** a well-known painting. [one work of art]
"Spotted Horses" is one of my favorite short stories. [one story]

17. *Every* or *many a* before a subject calls for a singular verb.

EXAMPLES
Almost every senior **was** at the meeting.
Many a teacher **was** delighted.

18. A few nouns that look plural in form take singular verbs.

EXAMPLES
The **news** of the landing **was** received with joy.
Linguistics is an interesting subject.

Some nouns that end in *-s* take a plural verb even though they refer to a single item.

EXAMPLES
Tweezers are very handy.
Were the **pants** too tight?

Agreement of Pronoun and Antecedent

1. A pronoun should agree with its antecedent in number and gender.

A pronoun usually refers to a noun or another pronoun that comes before it. The word that a pronoun refers to is called its **antecedent.**

A few singular personal pronouns have forms that indicate the gender of the antecedent. *He, him,* and *his* are masculine; *she, her,* and *hers* are feminine; and *it* and *its* are neuter.

EXAMPLE
Ana sold **her** car last week.
Each **floor** has **its** own laundry room.

1190

2. **When the antecedent of a personal pronoun is another kind of pronoun, look in a phrase following the antecedent to determine gender.**

EXAMPLES
Each of the **girls** makes **her** own clothing.
One of the **boys** grows **his** own vegetables.

3. **When the antecedent may be either masculine or feminine, use both the masculine and the feminine forms.**

EXAMPLES
Every one of the clerks complained about **his or her** work hours.
A **traveler** should plan to carry **his or her** own luggage.

4. **Use a singular pronoun to refer to *each, either, neither, one, everyone, everybody, no one, nobody, anyone, anybody, someone,* or *somebody.***

EXAMPLES
Somebody dropped **his or her** ticket.
One of the ushers has programs in **his** hands.
Everyone in the cast knows **her** role.
Each ticket has **its** own seat number.

When the meaning of *everyone* and *everybody* is clearly plural, use the plural pronoun.

CONFUSING
Everyone wore **his** or **her** name tag.

CLEAR
Everyone wore **their** name tags.

5. **Two or more singular antecedents joined by *or* or *nor* should be referred to by a singular pronoun.**

EXAMPLES
Neither **Mike nor Don** bought **himself** a new jacket.
Flo or Aliki will make **her** presentation tomorrow.

6. **Two or more antecedents joined by *and* should be referred to by a plural pronoun.**

EXAMPLES
Hannah and Mike showed **their** project to the class.
Martina and Tia ran quickly to get to **their** seats.

7. **The number of a relative pronoun is determined by the number of its antecedent.**

EXAMPLES
Everyone who knows him likes him. [*Who* refers to the singular pronoun *everyone* and thus takes the singular verb form *knows.*]
All who know him like him. [*Who* refers to the plural pronoun *all* and thus takes the plural verb form *know.*]

TIPS FOR WRITERS

Sentences with two or more singular antecedents joined by *or* or *nor* can sound awkward if the antecedents are of different genders. If a sentence sounds awkward, revise it to avoid the problem.

AWKWARD
Randy or **Fay** will drive **his** or **her** car.

REVISED
Randy will drive **his** car, or **Fay** will drive **hers**.

USING VERBS CORRECTLY

The Principal Parts of Verbs

1. **The four principal parts of a verb are the *infinitive*, the *present participle*, the *past*, and the *past participle*.**

The principal parts of the verb *ring*, for example, are *ring* (infinitive), *ringing* (present participle), *rang* (past), and *rung* (past participle). These principal parts are used to form all of the verb tenses.

EXAMPLES
The bell **rings** every morning.
The bell is **ringing** now.
The bell **rang** an hour ago.
The bell has **rung** for today.

Regular Verbs

2. **A regular verb forms its past and past participle by adding *-d* or *-ed* to the infinitive.**

INFINITIVE	PRESENT PARTICIPLE	PAST	PAST PARTICIPLE
bake	baking	baked	(have) baked
wish	wishing	wished	(have) wished

The present participle of most regular verbs ending in *-e* drops the *-e* before adding *-ing.*

One common error in the use of the past and the past participle forms is to leave off the *-d* or *-ed* ending.

1191

NONSTANDARD
She use to make her own clothes.

STANDARD
She **used** to make her own clothes.

NONSTANDARD
He was suppose to be here at noon.

STANDARD
He was **supposed** to be here at noon.

Another error is doubling the ending.

NONSTANDARD
The inexperienced swimmer almost drownded.

STANDARD
The inexperienced swimmer almost **drowned.**

A few regular verbs have an alternate past form ending in *-t.* For example, the past form of *leap* may be written *leaped* or *leapt.*

Irregular Verbs

3. An *irregular verb* forms its past and past participle in some other way than by adding *-d* or *-ed.*

Irregular verbs form their past and past participle in one or more of these ways: changing a vowel, changing consonants, adding *-en,* making no change at all.

INFINITIVE	PAST	PAST PARTICIPLE
drink	drank	(have) drunk
hold	held	(have) held
drive	drove	(have) driven
hit	hit	(have) hit
take	took	(have) taken

If you are not sure about the parts of a verb, look in a dictionary, which lists the principal parts of irregular verbs. In the next column, you will find a list of frequently misused irregular verbs.

Irregular Verbs Frequently Misused

INFINITIVE	PRESENT PARTICIPLE	PAST	PAST PARTICIPLE
arise	arising	arose	(have) arisen
begin	beginning	began	(have) begun
bet	betting	bet	(have) bet
bleed	bleeding	bled	(have) bled
blow	blowing	blew	(have) blown
break	breaking	broke	(have) broken
bring	bringing	brought	(have) brought
burst	bursting	burst	(have) burst
choose	choosing	chose	(have) chosen
come	coming	came	(have) come
dig	digging	dug	(have) dug
do	doing	did	(have) done
drink	drinking	drank	(have) drunk
drive	driving	drove	(have) driven
eat	eating	ate	(have) eaten
fall	falling	fell	(have) fallen
fly	flying	flew	(have) flown
freeze	freezing	froze	(have) frozen
give	giving	gave	(have) given
go	going	went	(have) gone
grow	growing	grew	(have) grown
know	knowing	knew	(have) known
leave	leaving	left	(have) ieft
lend	lending	lent	(have) lent
put	putting	put	(have) put
ride	riding	rode	(have) ridden
ring	ringing	rang	(have) rung
run	running	ran	(have) run
see	seeing	saw	(have) seen
seek	seeking	sought	(have) sought
shake	shaking	shook	(have) shaken
shrink	shrinking	shrank	(have) shrunk
sink	sinking	sank	(have) sunk
speak	speaking	spoke	(have) spoken
steal	stealing	stole	(have) stolen
sting	stinging	stung	(have) stung
strike	striking	struck	(have) struck
swear	swearing	swore	(have) sworn
swim	swimming	swam	(have) swum
take	taking	took	(have) taken
tear	tearing	tore	(have) torn
throw	throwing	threw	(have) thrown
wear	wearing	wore	(have) worn
win	winning	won	(have) won
write	writing	wrote	(have) written

4. When the present participle or the past participle is used as a main verb (simple predicate) in a sentence, it always requires a helping verb to form a verb phrase.

MAIN VERB +	HELPING VERB =	VERB PHRASE
taking	am	am taking
going	have been	have been going
walking	was	was walking
taken	have	have taken
gone	had	had gone
walked	has	has walked

5. The time expressed by a verb is called the *tense* of the verb. Every verb in English has six tenses: present, past, future, present perfect, past perfect, future perfect.

The following list shows six tense forms of *take*. Giving all the forms of a verb in this way is called **conjugating** the verb.

Conjugation of *Take*

Present Tense

Singular	*Plural*
I take	we take
you take	you take
he, she, *or* it takes	they take

Past Tense

Singular	*Plural*
I took	we took
you took	you took
he, she, *or* it took	they took

Future Tense

Singular	*Plural*
I will (shall) take	we will (shall) take
you will take	you will take
he, she, *or* it will take	they will take

Present Perfect Tense

Singular	*Plural*
I have taken	we have taken
you have taken	you have taken
he, she, *or* it has taken	they have taken

Past Perfect Tense

Singular	*Plural*
I had taken	we had taken
you had taken	you had taken
he, she, *or* it had taken	they had taken

Future Perfect Tense

Singular	*Plural*
I will (shall) have taken	we will (shall) have taken
you will have taken	you will have taken
he, she, *or* it will have taken	they will have taken

Each of the six tenses has an additional form called the **progressive form**, which expresses continuing action. It consists of a form of the verb *be* plus the present participle of the verb. The progressive is not a separate tense but an additional form of each of the six tenses in the conjugation.

Progressive Forms

Present Progressive: am, are, is taking

Past Progressive: was, were taking

Future Progressive: will (shall) be taking

Present Perfect Progressive: has, have been taking

Past Perfect Progressive: had been taking

Future Perfect Progressive: will (shall) have been taking

6. The present tense is used mainly to convey these ideas:

An action occurring now, at the present time. (The progressive form is used to express continuing action or action in progress.)

EXAMPLES
Selma **looks** pleased.
Abdul **is looking** through the photo album.

Customary or habitual action or state of being.

EXAMPLES
I usually **walk** to school.
She often **rides** her bicycle.

A general truth, something true at all times.

EXAMPLES
History **repeats** itself.
The sum of the angles of a triangle **equals** 180°.

The historical present is used to describe events or characters in a novel way or past events described as if they were happening now.

EXAMPLE
At the beginning of the story, Claire **expects** little from life.

7. The past tense is used mainly to express an action (or to help make a statement about something) that occurred in the past but did not continue into the present.

EXAMPLES
In September she **won** the lottery.
The bell **rang** just as I **was eating** my lunch.

1193

Past action can also be expressed idiomatically.

EXAMPLES
I **used** to dislike spinach.
I **did enjoy** Spain from the very first moment.

8. The future tense is used to express an action that will occur in the future.

EXAMPLES
We **will be flying** directly over Salt Lake City in an hour.
The plane **will land** at 4:00 P.M.
I **will attend** classes at the university during the fall semester.

Future action can also be expressed idiomatically using the present tense.

EXAMPLES
On Monday we **fly** to Mexico.
She **is going to fly** to Mexico on Monday.
Next Monday we **leave** for Mexico.

9. The present perfect tense is used mainly to express an action that has been completed at some indefinite time in the past or an action begun in the past and still going on.

EXAMPLES
She **has finished** the book.
We **have waited** here for forty minutes.
I **have known** him for more than three years.

10. The past perfect tense is used mainly to express an action that was completed in the past and preceded some other past action or event.

EXAMPLES
Suddenly I remembered what the old man **had told** me about patience. [The telling preceded the remembering.]
I **had eaten** all the fruit by the time I arrived at the bus station. [The eating preceded the arriving.]

11. The future perfect tense is used mainly to express an action that wil be completed in the future before some other future action or event takes place.

EXAMPLES
The festival **will have ended** by the time we arrive in Madrid.
By Monday I **will have been** in Spain for ten days.

Consistency of Tenses

12. Do not change needlessly from one tense to another.

NONSTANDARD
Myra took the book and leaves with it. [*Took* is past tense; *leaves* is present tense.]

STANDARD
Myra **took** the book and **left** with it. [*Took* and *left* are past tense.]

The perfect tenses are used to express completed action.

NONSTANDARD
I realized that I left my keys at home. [Since the action of losing was completed before the action of realizing, the verb should be *had left* not *left.*]

STANDARD
I realized that I **had left** my keys at home.

13. Use the present infinitive to express an action that follows another action.

CONFUSING
Angel said that he had hoped to have gone to Paris this year.

CLEAR
Angel said that he had hoped **to go** to Paris this year.

14. Use the perfect infinitive to express an action that occurred before another action.

EXAMPLE
The astronomer claimed to have sighted the new meteor. [The sighting occurred before the claim.]

TIPS FOR WRITERS

Using the correct verb tense can help make your instructions clear by showing whether an action occurs before, after, or at the same time as another action.

BEFORE / AFTER
When you have chopped the ingredients, put them in the frying pan.

SAME TIME
As you chop the ingredients, put them in the frying pan.

Active and Passive Voice

1. **A verb in the active voice expresses an action done *by* its subject. A verb in the passive voice expresses an action done *to* its subject.**

   ACTIVE VOICE
   The clown **amused** the crowd. [The subject, *clown,* performs the action.]

   PASSIVE VOICE
   The crowd **was amused** by the clown. [The subject, *the crowd*, receives the action.]

   In the pair of sentences above, the object of the active sentence becomes the subject of the passive one. The subject of the active sentence is now expressed in a prepositional phrase. In fact, this phrase can often be omitted from the passive sentence.

   PASSIVE
   The crowd **was amused.**

   In a passive sentence, the verb phrase always includes a form of *be* and the past participle of the main verb. Other helping verbs may also be included.

   ACTIVE VOICE
   S O
   Someone **has eaten** the last cookie.

   PASSIVE VOICE
   S
   The last cookie **has been eaten.**

2. **When a verb that takes both a direct and an indirect object is changed from the active voice to the passive voice, either object may be the subject of the passive-voice sentence. The other object becomes the complement of the passive-voice verb. The object is called a *retained object.***

   ACTIVE VOICE
   She gave me a package.
   I received a package.

   PASSIVE VOICE
   I was given a **package.**
   A package was given to **me.**

   The following list shows the conjugation of the verb *drive* in the passive voice. Compare this conjugation with the one on page 1193.

Conjugation of *Drive* in the Passive Voice

Present Tense

Singular	*Plural*
I am driven	we are driven
you are driven	you are driven
he, she, *or* it is driven	they are driven

Past Tense

Singular	*Plural*
I was driven	we were driven
you were driven	you were driven
he, she, *or* it was driven	they were driven

Future Tense

Singular	*Plural*
I will be driven	we will be driven
you will be driven	you will be driven
he, she, *or* it will be driven	they will be driven

Present Perfect Tense

Singular	*Plural*
I have been driven	we have been driven
you have been driven	you have been driven
he, she, *or* it has been driven	they have been driven

Past Perfect Tense

Singular	*Plural*
I had been driven	we had been driven
you had been driven	you had been driven
he, she, *or* it had been driven	they had been driven

Future Perfect Tense

Singular	*Plural*
I will have been driven	we will have been driven
you will have been driven	you will have been driven
he, she, *or* it will have been driven	they will have been driven

3. **Verbs have three moods. The *indicative mood* is used to make statements of fact. The *imperative mood* is used to express a request or command. The *subjunctive mood* is used to express a condition contrary to fact or to express a wish.**

1195

EXAMPLES
I **am** patient. (indicative)
Be patient. (imperative)
If I **were** patient, I would wait for her. (subjunctive)

4. **The subjunctive mood has three tenses: present, past, and perfect**

Conjugation of *Be* in the Subjunctive Mood

Present Tense

Singular	*Plural*
I be	we be
you be	you be
he, she, *or* it be	they be

Past Tense

Singular	*Plural*
I were	we were
you were	you were
he, she, *or* it were	they were

Present Perfect Tense

Singular	*Plural*
I have been	we have been
you have been	you have been
he, she, *or* it have been	they have been

Past Perfect Tense

Singular	*Plural*
I had been	we had been
you had been	you had been
he, she, *or* it had been	they had been

5. **Use the present subjunctive in certain formal constructions.**

EXAMPLES
I move that the meeting **be** adjourned.
It is crucial that Jonas **be** at the meeting.
I told her that she **need** not stay for the entire meeting.

6. **Use the past and perfect subjunctive in contrary-to-fact statements and statements expressing a wish.**

EXAMPLES
If I **were** you, I would reveal the contents of that letter.
If she **had told** us, we would have waited until she arrived.
It seemed as if a flood **were pouring** down from the skies.
I wish my brother **were** here now.

Special Problems with Verbs

Using *Lie* and *Lay* Correctly

1. **The verb *lie* means "to rest" or "recline," "to remain lying in a position." *Lie* never takes an object. The verb *lay* means "to put" or "to place" (something). *Lay* usually takes an object.**

INFINITIVE	PRESENT PARTICIPLE	PAST	PAST PARTICIPLE
lie	lying	lay	(have) lain
lay	laying	laid	(have) laid

EXAMPLES
I sometimes **lie** on the grass in the backyard.
The mail **is lying** on the table.
Those books **have lain** there for years.
Yesterday Raul **lay** in bed all day.
How long **has** the mail **lain** there?
The shovel and the rake should not **be lying** against the wall.

Lay those packages down.
I **am laying** the clean sheets on this chair.
Raul **laid** the foundation for his house.
Have you **laid** your book aside?
Please **lay** your napkin on the table.
Gail **is laying** expensive ceramic tiles on the kitchen floor.

Using *Sit* and *Set* Correctly

2. **The verb *sit* means "to rest in an upright, seated position." *Sit* almost never takes an object. The verb *set* means "to put" or "to place" (something). *Set* usually takes an object. Notice that *set* does not change form in the past or past participle.**

INFINITIVE	PRESENT PARTICIPLE	PAST	PAST PARTICIPLE
sit	sitting	sat	(have) sat
set	setting	set	(have) set

Using *Rise* and *Raise* Correctly

3. **The verb *rise* means "to go in an upward direction." *Rise* never has an object. The verb *raise* means "to move something in an upward direction." *Raise* usually takes an object.**

INFINITIVE	PRESENT PARTICIPLE	PAST	PAST PARTICIPLE
rise	rising	rose	(have) risen
raise	raising	raised	(have) raised

USING PRONOUNS CORRECTLY

Nominative and Objective Uses

Case

1. ***Case* is the form of a noun or pronoun that shows its use in a sentence. In English, there are three cases: *nominative, objective,* and *possessive.***

   Choosing the correct case form for a noun is no problem, because the form remains the same in the nominative and objective cases.

   EXAMPLE
   My biology **teacher** shares her office with another **teacher.**

   Only in the possessive case does a noun change its form, usually by adding an apostrophe and *s.*

   EXAMPLE
   My **teacher's** office is small.

   EXAMPLE
   I [nominative] remembered to bring **my** [possessive] umbrella with **me** [objective] when I went to London last year.

The Case Forms of Personal Pronouns

2. **Here are the case forms of personal pronouns. Notice that all personal pronouns, except *you* and *it,* have different nominative and objective forms.**

PERSONAL PRONOUNS

SINGULAR

Nominative Case	Objective Case	Possessive Case
I	me	my, mine
you	you	your, yours
he, she, it	him, her, it	his, her, hers, its

PLURAL

Nominative Case	Objective Case	Possessive Case
we	us	our, ours
you	you	your, yours
they	them	their, theirs

The Nominative Case

1. **The subject of a verb is in the nominative case.**

   EXAMPLE
   She was pleased that **they** had arrived. [*She* is the subject of *was; they* is the subject of *had arrived.*]

TIPS FOR WRITERS

Sometimes the pronouns *we* and *they* sound awkward when used as parts of a compound subject. In such cases, it is a good idea to revise the sentence.

AWKWARD
We and they plan to have lunch today.

BETTER
We plan to have lunch with **them** today.

2. **A *predicate nominative* is in the nominative case.**

   A *predicate nominative* is a noun or pronoun that follows a linking verb and explains or identifies the subject of the sentence.

   A pronoun used as a predicate nominative always follows a form of the verb *be* or a verb phrase ending in *be* or *been.*

   EXAMPLES
   That is **she.**
   It could be **he.**

The Objective Case

3. **The *direct object* of a verb is in the objective case.**

   A *direct object* is a noun or pronoun that receives the action of the verb or shows the result of the action.

   EXAMPLES
   Rob told **her** about the program last night. [*Rob* is the subject of the verb *told.* Rob told *whom?* The answer is *her.*]
   The report surprised **William** and **me.**

4. **The *indirect object* of the verb is in the objective case.**

   An *indirect object* is a noun or pronoun that tells to whom or for whom something is done. Pronouns used as indirect objects are in the objective case: *me, him, her, us, them.*

   EXAMPLES
   The noise gave **her** a scare.
   Artie gave **me** two compact discs.

Grammar, Usage, and Mechanics

5. **The *object of a preposition* is in the objective case.**

A prepositional phrase begins with a preposition and ends with a noun or pronoun, which is the *object of the preposition.* A pronoun used as an object of a preposition must be in the objective case.

EXAMPLES
Roman walked in front of **us**.

Errors often occur when the object of a preposition is compound. You can usually figure out the correct pronouns by trying each one separately in the prepositional phrase.

NONSTANDARD
Pat stood behind her and I. [*Pat stood behind her* is correct. *Pat stood behind I* is incorrect. The correct forms of the pronouns are *her* and *me.*]

STANDARD
Pat stood behind **her** and **me**.

6. **In an infinitive clause, both the subject and object of the infinitive are in the objective case.**

EXAMPLE
Sam wanted **me to help him.** [*Me* is the subject of *to help. Him* is the object. The entire infinitive clause is the direct object of *wanted.*]

Many people use the incorrect pronoun forms with the preposition *between.* You have probably heard phrases such as *between you and I* and *between you and he.* These phrases are incorrect. The pronouns are objects of a preposition and should be in the objective case. The correct phrases are *between you and me* and *between you and him.*

TIPS FOR WRITERS

Some mistakes in usage are more common than others. In speech, for example, people often incorrectly use the pronoun *me* for *I* in a compound subject.

INCORRECT
Maria and me drove all the way.

CORRECT
Maria and I drove all the way.

Special Pronoun Problems

Using *Who* and *Whom* Correctly

7. ***Who* is used as subject or predicate nominative, and *whom* is used as an object.**

NOMINATIVE	OBJECTIVE
who	whom
whoever	whomever

In spoken English, the use of *whom* is becoming less common. In fact, when you are speaking, you may correctly begin any question with *who,* regardless of the grammar of the sentence. In written English, however, you should make a distinction between *who* and *whom.*

8. **The use of *who* or *whom* in a subordinate clause depends on how the pronoun functions in the clause.**

When you choose between *who(ever)* or *whom(ever)* in a subordinate clause, follow these steps:

STEP 1: Find the subordinate clause.
STEP 2: Decide how the pronoun is used in the clause—as subject, predicate nominative, object of the verb, or object of a preposition.
STEP 3: Determine the case of the pronoun according to the rules of standard English.
STEP 4: Select the correct form of the pronoun.

EXAMPLE
(*Whoever, whomever*) I choose will lead the group.
STEP 1: The subordinate clause is (*whoever, whomever*) *I choose.*
STEP 2: In this clause, the subject is *I,* the verb is *choose,* and the pronoun is the direct object of the verb *choose*: *I choose* (*whoever, whomever*).
STEP 3: The direct object of a verb is in the objective case.
STEP 4: The objective form is *whomever.*
ANSWER: **Whomever** I choose will lead the group.

Remember that no words outside the subordinate clause affect the case of the pronoun. In this example, the entire clause is used as the subject of *will lead,* the verb in the main clause. The pronoun *whomever* is used as the direct object (objective case) within its clause.

Frequently, in subordinate clauses *whom* is omitted (understood).

EXAMPLES
The person [whom] I choose is Ana.
The person [whom] I wrote to is a famous South American sculptor.

9. **Pronouns used as *appositives* are in the same case as the word to which they refer.**

An *appositive* is a noun or pronoun that follows another noun or pronoun to identify or explain it.

EXAMPLES
The singers, **he, she,** and **I,** sang with true feeling. [Since *singers* is the subject of the sentence, the pronouns in apposition with it (*he, she, I*) must be in the nominative case.]

TIPS FOR WRITERS

To figure out the correct form for a pronoun used with an appositive or as an appositive, read the sentence with only the pronoun.

EXAMPLES
Mrs. Kiri asked two swimmers, Pei and (*he, him*), to clean the pool. [Omit the direct object, *swimmers:* Mrs. Kiri asked Pei and him to help.]
(*We, us*) team members offered to help. [Omit the appositive, *team members:* We offered to help.]

10. **Use the possessive case of a noun or pronoun before a gerund. Do not confuse the gerund form with the present participle, also an *-ing* form of the verb.**

EXAMPLES
The audience enjoyed **my singing.** [The gerund *singing* is the object of the verb *enjoyed.* The possessive form *my* modifies the gerund.]
Can you imagine **me singing** a romantic aria before an audience of more than 200 people? [Here the participle *singing* modifies *me,* the object of *imagine.*]

The Pronoun in an Incomplete Construction

11. **After *than* and *as* introducing an incomplete construction, use the form of the pronoun that you would use if the construction were completed.**

Notice how pronouns change the meaning of sentences with incomplete constructions.

EXAMPLES
Erica likes Nico better than **I.**
Erica likes Nico better than **me.**

In the first sentence, the nominative case pronoun *I* is the subject of an understood verb: *Erica likes Nico better than I* [*like Nico*]. In the second sentence, the objective case pronoun *me* is the object of the understood verb: *Erica likes Nico better than* [*Erica likes*] *me.*

EXAMPLES
I speak to you more often than **she** [speaks to you].
I speak to you more often than [I speak to] **her.**

Did she assist Abu as much as **I** [assisted Abu]?
Did she assist Abu as much as [she assisted] **me**?

USING MODIFIERS CORRECTLY

1. **Adjectives and adverbs are modifiers, that is, they state qualities of other parts of speech. Adjectives modify nouns and pronouns. Adverbs modify verbs, adjectives, and other adverbs.**

EXAMPLES
ripe plum **juicy** oranges [adjectives]
sing **softly** run **well** [adverbs]

2. **Use adjectives to compare one noun with another noun that has the same quality.**

EXAMPLES
This plum is **riper** than that one.
That orange is **juicier** than this one.

3. **Use adverbs to make comparisons between verbs.**

EXAMPLE
I ate my meal slowly, but Lena ate hers even **more slowly.**

4. **There are three degrees of comparison: *positive, comparative,* and *superlative.***

POSITIVE	COMPARATIVE	SUPERLATIVE
cool	cooler	coolest
wet	wetter	wettest
tasty	tastier	tastiest
helpful	more helpful	most helpful
slowly	more slowly	most slowly
good	better	best
bad	worse	worst

5. **A one-syllable modifier regularly forms its comparative and superlative degrees by adding *-er* and *-est.***

POSITIVE	COMPARATIVE	SUPERLATIVE
tall	taller	tallest
gray	grayer	grayest
short	shorter	shortest

6. **Some two-syllable modifiers form their comparative and superlative degrees by adding *-er* and *-est.* Other two-syllable modifiers form their comparative and superlative degrees with *more* and *most.***

POSITIVE	COMPARATIVE	SUPERLATIVE
able	abler	ablest
lively	livelier	liveliest
woeful	more woeful	most woeful
scenic	more scenic	most scenic
foolish	more foolish	most foolish

Some two-syllable modifiers may take either *-er, -est* or *more, most: often, oftener, oftenest* or *often, more often, most often.*

If you are unsure of how a two-syllable modifier is compared, look in an unabridged dictionary.

7. **Modifiers that have more than two syllables form their comparative and superlative degrees with *more* and *most.***

POSITIVE	COMPARATIVE	SUPERLATIVE
popular	more popular	most popular
serious	more serious	most serious
voraciously	more voraciously	most voraciously

8. **Modifiers that indicate less of a quality use the word *less* or *least* before the modifier.**

POSITIVE	COMPARATIVE	SUPERLATIVE
neat	less neat	least neat
costly	less costly	least costly
soggy	less soggy	least soggy

Irregular Comparison

9. **Here are some commonly used modifiers which do not follow the regular methods of forming their comparative and superlative degrees.**

POSITIVE	COMPARATIVE	SUPERLATIVE
bad	worse	worst
good	better	best
well	better	best
many	more	most
much	more	most

Do not add the *-er, -est* or *more, most* forms to irregularly compared forms: *worse,* not *worser* or *more worse.*

Use of Comparative and Superlative Forms

10. **Use the comparative degree when comparing two things. Use the superlative degree when comparing more than two.**

COMPARATIVE
I found *Shane* **more enjoyable** than *White Fang.*
Writing a novel seems **more time-consuming** than writing short stories.
I think that William Faulkner is a **better** novelist than Saul Bellow.

SUPERLATIVE
Call of the Wild was the **most enjoyable** novel I read this year.
Père Goriot is the **longest** novel I have ever read in French.
Writing a short story is the **most interesting** assignment I've had so far.

In everyday conversation, people sometimes use the superlative degree in comparing two things: *Put your best foot forward.*

11. **Include the word *other* or *else* when comparing one thing with others that belong in the same group.**

NONSTANDARD
Nana sings better than any member of her family. [Nana is a member of her own family, and she cannot be a better singer than herself. The word *other* should be added.]

STANDARD
Nana sings better than any **other** member of her family.

NONSTANDARD
Bridget runs faster than anyone. [The word *anyone* includes all people, and Bridget is a person. Since she cannot run faster than herself, the word *else* should be added to clarify the meaning.]

STANDARD
Bridget runs faster than anyone **else.**

12. **Avoid double comparisons.**

A **double comparison** is incorrect because it contains both *-er* and *more* or *-est* and *most.*

NONSTANDARD
This vase is more cheaper than that one.

STANDARD
This vase is **cheaper** than that one.

NONSTANDARD
This is the most coldest winter we have had in two decades.

STANDARD
This is the **coldest** winter we have had in two decades.

13. **Be sure your comparisons are clear.**

UNCLEAR
Rain here last summer was as scarce as the Sahara Desert. [This sentence incorrectly compares rain to a desert.]

CLEAR
Rain here last summer was as scarce as it is in the Sahara Desert.

UNCLEAR
The wingspan of an eagle is greater than a barn owl. [This sentence incorrectly compares wingspan of an eagle to a barn owl, not the barn owl's wingspan.]

CLEAR
The wingspan of an eagle is greater than that of a barn owl.

or

The wingspan of an eagle is greater than the wingspan of a barn owl.

Both parts of an incomplete comparison should be stated if there is any chance of misunderstanding.

UNCLEAR
I taught her more than Tamara.

CLEAR
I taught her more than I taught Tamara.

CLEAR
I taught her more than Tamara taught her.

TIPS FOR WRITERS

In writing papers about literary topics, you will often need to compare and contrast two or more literary works or specific aspects of them, such as character, plot, setting, style, imagery, and theme. Comparisons, accurately expressed, can help you to make logical points about different works of literature. For example, you may have occasion to show that a character in a particular play is *less developed* than another character. You might wish to demonstrate that the structure or rhyme scheme of one poem is considerably *more complex* than the structure or rhyme scheme of another poem, or that the setting of two novels are *closely related.* Effective use of comparisons can enliven your writing about literature in surprising ways.

Dangling Modifiers

14. **A modifying phrase or clause that does not clearly and sensibly modify a word in a sentence is a *dangling modifier.***

When a modifying phrase containing a verbal comes at the beginning of a sentence, the phrase is followed by a comma. Immediately after that comma should come the word that the phrase modifies.

UNCLEAR
Walking down the lane, a daffodil popped up out of the ground.

CLEAR
Walking down the lane, **I** saw a daffodil popping up out of the ground.

UNCLEAR
To communicate quickly, a mobile phone helps our sales representatives.

CLEAR
To communicate quickly, our sales representatives use a mobile phone.

UNCLEAR
Tied together in a neat package, Jim discovered a stack of valuable old books in a corner of the musty attic.

CLEAR
Tied together in a neat package, a stack of valuable old books lay in a corner of the musty attic.

15. **To correct a dangling modifier, rearrange the words in the sentence or add words to make the meaning logical and clear.**

DANGLING
To have a beautiful garden, weeds must be pulled.

CORRECTED
To have a beautiful garden, you (a person) must pull weeds.

or

If you want to have a beautiful garden, you must pull weeds.

DANGLING
While washing the dishes, a glass fell on the kitchen floor.

CORRECTED
While washing the dishes, I let a glass fall on the kitchen floor.

or

While washing the dishes, I dropped a glass on the kitchen floor.

Misplaced Modifiers

16. **A misplaced modifier is a phrase or clause that sounds awkward because it modifies the wrong word(s). Modifying phrases should be placed as near as possible to the words they modify.**

MISPLACED
I heard about the terrible train accident on the evening television news.

CORRECTED
On the evening television news, I heard about the terrible train accident.

MISPLACED
I was promoted to an assistant vice president after only three years with the company on Friday.

CORRECTED
On Friday, I was promoted to an assistant vice president after only three years with the company.

MISPLACED
I made muffins for my friends with blueberries in them.

CORRECTED
I made muffins with blueberries in them for my friends.

TIPS FOR WRITERS

A sentence may appear to have a dangling modifier when *you* is the understood subject. In such cases, the modifier is not dangling; it is modifying the understood subject.

EXAMPLE
To learn the latest weather prediction, (you) tune in to the Weather Channel.

MISPLACED
The school chorus gave a concert after rehearsing only six weeks on Sunday afternoon.

CORRECTED
On Sunday afternoon, the school chorus gave a concert, after rehearsing only six weeks.

MISPLACED
The children watched the entertaining clowns with glee.

CORRECTED
With glee, the children watched the entertaining clowns.

Misplaced Clause Modifiers

17. **Place an adjective or adverb clause as near as possible to the word it modifies.**

MISPLACED
I bought a dozen eggs at a farmers' market, which cost $2.00.
I saw an interesting documentary at the film festival, which was three hours long.

CORRECTED
At a farmers' market, I bought a dozen eggs which cost $2.00.
At the film festival, I saw an interesting documentary which was three hours long.

Always place the modifying clause as close as possible to the word it modifies.

MISPLACED
He is building a model airplane for a friend that runs on gasoline.

CORRECTED
For a friend, he is building a model airplane that runs on gasoline.

COMMON USAGE PROBLEMS

a, an

These *indefinite articles* refer to one of a general group. Use *a* before words beginning with a consonant sound; use *an* before words beginning with a vowel sound.

EXAMPLES
We saw **a** Geo and **an** Oldsmobile go by.
A horse has been in the pasture for **an** hour.

In the second example above, *a* is used before *horse* because the *h* in *horse* is pronounced. *An* is used before *hour* because the *h* in *hour* is not pronounced.

accept, except

Accept is a verb that means "to receive." *Except* may be either a verb or a preposition. As a verb, it means "to leave out" or "to omit." As a preposition, *except* means "excluding."

EXAMPLES
I tearfully **accepted** her apology.
All the drummers **except** Tim joined the new jazz group at the school.

affect, effect

Affect is a verb meaning "to influence." *Effect* used as a verb means "to accomplish." Used as a noun, *effect* means "the result of some action."

EXAMPLES
The drought **affects** the water level at the reservoir.
The last rainfall had not **affected** the water level enough to make a difference in the emergency.
The scientists know that only the correct medication will **effect** a cure for the disease.
The talk had a good **effect** on the student's grades.

ain't

Avoid the word *ain't* in speaking or writing. Use of this word is always considered to be nonstandard English.

all the farther, all the faster

This should be "as far as" and "as fast as."

DIALECT
This is all the faster I can run.

STANDARD
This is **as fast as** I can run.

allusion, illusion

An *allusion is* an intentional reference to something. An *illusion* is a false idea or a misleading appearance.

EXAMPLES
The speaker made many **allusions** to classical mythology.
Good stage lighting can create the **illusion** of space.

a lot

Do not write the expression *a lot* as one word. It should always be written as two words.

EXAMPLE
I was carrying **a lot** of books.

alumni, alumnae

Alumni is the plural of *alumnus* (a male graduate). *Alumnae* is the plural of *alumna* (a female graduate).

EXAMPLES
Many of the **alumni** of that college have become professional basketball players.
The **alumnae** were all asked what they thought about admitting men to the school.

among

see **between, among.**

amount, number

Use *amount* to refer to a singular word. Use *number* to refer to a plural word.

EXAMPLES
A small **number** of magazines [plural] arrive.
The **amount** of sugar [singular] in that bowl is surely less than a cup.

and etc.

Etc. is an abbreviation of the Latin phrase *et cetera*, meaning "*and* other things." Thus, do not use *and* with *etc.*

EXAMPLE
My father collects baseball cards, pennants, team booklets, etc. [not *and etc.*]

anywheres, everywheres, nowheres, somewheres

Use these words without the final *s.*

EXAMPLE
I saw the kitten **somewhere** [not *somewheres*].

as, like

See **like, as.**

as if

See **like, as if.**

at

Do not use *at* after *where.*

NONSTANDARD
Is that where you live at?

STANDARD
Is that **where** you live?

bad, badly

Bad is an adjective. *Badly* is an adverb.

EXAMPLES
Your team is performing **badly.**
The prospects for victory look **bad.**

because

In informal English the expression *The reason is* is often completed with a clause introduced by *because.* In formal English use the conjunction *that* to introduce the clause.

INFORMAL
The reason I left **was because** I felt sick.

FORMAL
The reason I left **was that I** felt sick.

being as, being that

Do not use these phrases for *since* or *because.*

NONSTANDARD
Being as it was late, I decided to go home.

STANDARD
Because it was late, I decided to go home.

beside, besides

Beside is a preposition that means "by the side of" someone or something. *Besides* as a preposition means "in addition to." As an adverb, *besides* means "moreover."

EXAMPLES
Set those packages down **beside** the telephone.
Besides baseball cards and team pennants, the box contained several baseball caps.
You'll enjoy the exhibit. **Besides,** you can write an interesting report on it.

between, among

Use *between* when you are referring to two things at a time, even though they may be part of a group consisting of more than two.

EXAMPLES
Place the nickel **between** the penny and the dime.
I could not decide which of the five plants to buy because there was not much difference **between** them. [Although there are more than two plants, each one is being compared with the others separately.]

Use *among* when you are thinking of a group rather than of separate individuals.

EXAMPLES
We divided the fifty dollars **among** the ten of us.
There was much disagreement **among** the members about club dues. [The members are thought of as a group.]

bring, take

Bring means "to come carrying something." *Take* means "to go carrying something." Think of *bring* as related to *come, take* as related to *go.*

EXAMPLES
Bring your own suitcase.
Bill, **take** Meg's suitcase upstairs.

bust, busted

Avoid using these words as verbs. Use a form of either *burst* or *break.*

EXAMPLES
The balloon **burst** [not *busted*] near the cat.
The racing car **broke** [not *busted*] a speed record.

can't hardly, haven't scarcely

The words *hardly* and *scarcely* convey a negative meaning. They should never be used with another negative word.

EXAMPLES
I can [not *can't*] **hardly** hear you.
They **have** [not *haven't*] scarcely enough money to buy food.

can't help but

Avoid this expression in formal English.

INFORMAL
I can't help but notice how quiet that dog is.

FORMAL
I can't help **noticing** how quiet that dog is.
I cannot but **notice** how quiet that dog is.

could of

Do not write *of* with the helping verb *could*. Write *could have*. Also avoid *ought to of, should of, would of, might of,* and *must of.*

EXAMPLE
Louis could **have** [not *of*] baked that apple pie.

discover, invent

Discover means "to be the first to find, see, or learn about something that already exists." *Invent* means "to be the first to do or make something."

EXAMPLES
Barry **discovered** a secret room in the old house.
Cass **invented** a story about a ghost who lives there.

don't, doesn't

Don't is the contraction of *do not*. *Doesn't* is the contraction of *does not*. Use *doesn't*, not *don't*, with *he, she, it, this,* and singular nouns.

EXAMPLE
It **doesn't** [not *don't*] matter.
Chocolate **doesn't** [not *don't*] agree with me.

done

Never use *done* as the past form of *do;* the past form of *do* is *did*. *Done* is the past participle and requires an auxiliary verb.

NONSTANDARD
It done what you asked.

STANDARD
It **did** what you asked.
It **has done** what you asked.

effect

See **affect, effect.**

emigrate, immigrate

Emigrate means "to go away from a country." Immigrate means "to come into a country."

EXAMPLES
A great number of people **emigrated** from Ireland during the nineteenth century.
Many of them **immigrated** to the United States.

everywheres

See **anywheres,** etc.

fewer, less

Fewer is used with plural words. *Less* is used with singular words. *Fewer* tells "how many"; *less* tells "how much."

EXAMPLES
There were **fewer** bushels of potatoes harvested this year than last.
The result is **less** food for the country.

good, well

Good is always an adjective. Never use *good* to modify a verb; use *well,* which is an adverb.

NONSTANDARD
The drummer played good.

STANDARD
The drummer played **well.**

Although it is usually an adverb, *well* is used as an adjective to mean "healthy."

EXAMPLE
I do not feel **well.**

Feel good and *feel well* mean different things. *Feel good* means "to feel happy or pleased." *Feel well* simply means "to feel healthy."

EXAMPLES
The award made him feel **good.**
Gregory didn't feel **well,** so he went downtown to see his doctor.

The use of *good* as an adverb is increasing in conversational English, but it should not be used that way in writing.

had of

See **of.**

had ought, hadn't ought

Unlike other verbs, *ought* is not used with *had*.

NONSTANDARD
Chin had ought to be more careful; he hadn't ought to forget his sister's birthday.

STANDARD
Chin **ought** to be more careful; he **ought not** to forget his sister's birthday.

haven't but, haven't only

In these expressions *but* and *only* convey a negative idea. Avoid using them with *not* in formal writing.

INFORMAL
I haven't but one essay left to write.

FORMAL
I **have but** one essay to write.
I **have only** one essay to write.

he, she, they

Do not use an unnecessary pronoun after a noun. This error is called the **double subject.**

NONSTANDARD
My sister she repairs her own car.

STANDARD
My sister repairs her own car.

immigrate

See **emigrate.**

imply, infer

Imply means "to suggest something." *Infer* means "to interpret or get a certain meaning" from a remark.

EXAMPLES
Vera **implied** that she would vote for me in the election.
I **inferred** that she liked my stand on the issues.

in, into

In means "within." *Into* means "from the outside to the inside."

EXAMPLES
The letter was lying **in** the basket.
I reached **into** the basket and pulled out the letter.

kind, sort, type

The words *this, that, these,* and *those* should always agree in number with the words *kind, sort, type.*

EXAMPLE
This kind of computer has more memory than any of **those** other **kinds.**

lay, lie

See page 1196.

learn, teach

Learn means "to acquire knowledge." *Teach* means "to instruct" or "to show how."

EXAMPLE
A professional coach **teaches** me tennis; I am **learning** to play well.

leave, let

Leave means "to go away" or "to depart from." *Let* means "to allow" or "to permit."

NONSTANDARD
Leave me help you with those packages.

STANDARD
Let me help you with those packages.

STANDARD
Let's **leave** before the last train departs.

less

See **fewer, less.**

like, as

Like is a preposition. In informal English, *like* is often used as a conjunction meaning "as." In formal English, always use *as.*

EXAMPLES
It is not **like** him to be generous. [The preposition *like* introduces the phrase *like him.*]
You should speak to your lawyer **as** your accountant advises. [*Your accountant advises* is a clause and needs the subordinating conjunction *as* to introduce it.]

like, as if

In formal written English, *like* should not be used for the compound conjunctions *as if* or *as though.*

EXAMPLE
The lawn looks **as though** [not *like*] it was cut after the heavy rain.

might of, must of

See **could of.**

no, none, nothing

Do not use these words with another negative.

NONSTANDARD
I don't have no change.

STANDARD
I have **no** change.
I **don't have any** change.

NONSTANDARD
That old automobile won't give you nothing but trouble.

STANDARD
That old car **won't give you anything** but trouble.
That old car **will give you nothing** but trouble.

NONSTANDARD
We looked for four-leaf clovers in the grass, but there weren't none.

STANDARD
We looked for four-leaf clovers in the grass, but there **weren't any.**
We looked for four-leaf clovers in the grass, but there **were none.**

nowheres

See **anywheres,** etc.

number, amount

See **amount, number.**

of

Do not use of with prepositions such as *inside, off,* or *outside.*

EXAMPLES
They stepped **off** [not *off of*] the train.
The rug was **outside** [not *outside of*] the house on the clothesline.
What's **inside** [not *inside of*] that closet?

Of is also unnecessary with *had.*

EXAMPLE
If I **had** [not *had of*] known, I would have called the police.

or, nor

Use *or* with *either*; use *nor* with *neither.*

EXAMPLES
We have a choice of **either** a comedy **or** a mystery.
Neither June **nor** Elliot want to go with us to the art gallery.

ought to of

See **could of.**

respectfully, respectively

Respectfully means "with respect" or "full of respect." *Respectively* means "each in the order indicated."

EXAMPLES
I acknowledged the remark **respectfully**.
The scores for Jim, Hannah, and Emma were 58, 62, and 59, **respectively**.

rise, raise

See page 1196.

shall, will

Some people prefer to use *shall* with first person pronouns and *will* with second and third person pronouns in the future and future perfect tenses. Nowadays, most Americans do not make this distinction. *Will* is acceptable in the first person as well as in the other two.

sit, set

See page 1196.

slow, slowly

Slow is generally used as an adjective. *Slowly* is always used as an adverb.

EXAMPLES
The boat moved **slowly** through the canal.
The statistics suggested a **slow** growth in employment.

so

Avoid using *so* in writing whenever you can.

EXAMPLE
The harbor was fogged in, so the Statue of Liberty was not visible.
Because the harbor was fogged in, the Statue of Liberty was not visible.

some, somewhat

In writing, do not use *some* for *somewhat* as an adverb.

NONSTANDARD
My piano playing has improved some.

STANDARD
My piano playing has improved **somewhat.**

take, bring
See **bring, take.**

than, then
Do not confuse these words. *Than* is a conjunction; it is used to make comparisons. *Then* is an adverb; it tells about time.

EXAMPLES
We loosened the nuts, removed the flat tire, and **then** put on the spare.
This cake is tastier **than** that one.
We cut the cake. **Then** we served each person a piece.
I enjoyed our vacation in the mountains more **than** our trip to the shore.

them
Them should not be used as an adjective. Use *those.*

NONSTANDARD
Do you hear them drumbeats?

STANDARD
Do you hear **those** drumbeats?

this here, that there
The words *here* and *there* are unnecessary after *this* and *that.*

EXAMPLES
Would you rather borrow **this** [not *this here*] book instead of **that** [not *that there*] one?
Why don't we eat at **this** [not *this here*] restaurant rather than **that** [not *that there*] one?

this kind, sort, type
See **kind,** etc.

type, type of
Do not use *type* as an adjective before a noun. *Type* is a noun. Do not omit *of* after type.

EXAMPLE
This **type of** motor is much more powerful for its size than you would think.

way, ways
Use *way,* not *ways,* in referring to a distance.

EXAMPLE
We've traveled a long **way** [not *ways*] since Monday.

when, where
Do not use *when* or *where* incorrectly in writing a definition.

NONSTANDARD
A "square" is when all four sides and angles of a quadrilateral are equal.

STANDARD
A "square" is a quadrilateral with four equal sides and four equal angles.

where
Do not use *where* for *that.*

EXAMPLES
I heard from your mother **that** [not *where*] you had won a scholarship.
He found out this morning **that** [not *where*] he would be quarterback.

which, that, who
The relative pronoun *who* refers to people only; *which* refers to things only; *that* refers to either people or things.

EXAMPLES
The woman **who** spoke at the meeting is our mayor. [person]
Our town, **which** is not large, has many problems. [thing]
Her topic was one **that** interested everyone at the meeting. [thing]
The mayor is a person **that** works for the good of the town. [person]
The film, **which** is quite moving, has several glaring weaknesses. [thing]

who, whom
See pages 1198–1199.

without, unless
Do not use the preposition *without* in place of the conjunction *unless.*

EXAMPLES
I cannot go **unless** [not *without*] I finish my homework.
Unless [not *without*] she receives written permission, he cannot go on the trip.

would of
See **could of.**

THE RULES FOR CAPITALIZATION

First Words

1. **Capitalize the first word in every sentence.**

EXAMPLES
Each section of the garden seemed to have its own color theme. **I**n one corner there were a host of blues—delphiniums, asters, and violets. **I**n yet another we found only orange and yellow flowers.

Traditionally, the first word of a line of poetry is capitalized.

EXAMPLES
Water, water, everywhere,
And all the boards did shrink;
Water, water, everywhere,
Nor any drop to drink.

—from "The Rime of the Ancient Mariner,"
Samuel Taylor Coleridge

Some writers do not follow these practices. When you are quoting, use capital letters exactly as they are used in the source of the quotation.

Pronoun *I* and Interjection *O*

2. **Capitalize the pronoun *I* and the interjection *O*.**

EXAMPLE
Mark and **I** seldom play tennis together on that old court.

Although it is rarely used, *O* is always capitalized. Generally, it is reserved for invocations and is followed by the name of the person or thing being addressed. You will more often use the interjection *oh,* which is not capitalized unless it is the first word in a sentence.

EXAMPLES
"Sing, **O** Muse, of the wrath of Achilles" is the opening line of Homer's *Iliad.*

The bus was late, and **oh**, how glad I was!

Proper Nouns and Proper Adjectives

3. **Capitalize proper nouns and proper adjectives.**
A **common noun** names a class or a group of people, places, or things. A **proper noun** names a particular person, place, or thing. Proper adjectives are formed from proper nouns.

Common nouns are not capitalized unless they begin a sentence or a direct quotation or are included in a title (see pages 1209–1212, 1218). Proper nouns are always capitalized.

COMMON NOUNS
a **p**oet, a **c**ountry, a **s**tatesman, a **r**iver

PROPER NOUNS
Pindar, **F**inland, **T**homas **J**efferson, **A**mazon

PROPER ADJECTIVES
Pindaric ode, **F**innish sauna, **J**effersonian democracy, **A**mazonian jungle

Some proper names consist of more than one word. In these names, short prepositions (generally, fewer than five letters) and articles are not capitalized.

EXAMPLES
Lake **o**f **t**he Woods
People **f**or **t**he Ethical Treatment **o**f Animals
Richard **t**he Lionhearted

Proper nouns and adjectives sometimes lose their capitals through frequent usage.

EXAMPLES
volt **q**uixotic

To find out whether a noun should be capitalized, check in a dictionary. The dictionary will tell you if a word should always be capitalized or if it should be capitalized only in certain uses.

Names of People

4. **Capitalize the names of people.**

EXAMPLES
GIVEN NAMES
Amantha
Ned

SURNAMES
Chin
Marquardt

Geographical Names

5. **Capitalize geographical names.**

TOWNS, CITIES
Seattle, **B**irmingham, **S**ingapore, **S**an **M**ateo, **P**ort-of-**S**pain

Grammar, Usage, and Mechanics

COUNTIES, TOWNSHIPS
Cook **C**ounty, **T**ownship of **T**eaneck

STATES
Alabama, **T**exas, **M**ississippi, **I**ndiana, **N**ew **M**exico

REGIONS
the **E**ast, the **S**outh, the **S**outhwest, the **M**iddle **W**est, **M**aritime **P**rovinces, the **H**ighlands

Words such as *north, west,* and *southeast* are not capitalized when they indicate direction.

EXAMPLES
east of town, traveling **s**outhwest

However, these words are capitalized when they name a particular place.

EXAMPLES
states in the **N**ortheast
driving in the **S**outhwest

COUNTRIES
the **U**nited **S**tates of **A**merica, **C**zechoslovakia, **D**enmark

CONTINENTS
South **A**merica, **A**sia, **A**ntarctica, **A**frica

ISLANDS
Martha's **V**ineyard, **P**olynesia, **I**sle **R**oyale

MOUNTAINS
Andes **M**ountains, **M**ount **E**verest, the **A**lps, **M**ount **A**rarat

BODIES OF WATER
Pacific **O**cean, **B**altic **S**ea, **H**udson **R**iver, **B**ay of **B**engal

PARKS
Denali **N**ational **P**ark, **A**rctic **N**ational **W**ildlife **R**efuge

ROADS, HIGHWAYS, STREETS
Route 41, **I**nterstate 285, **N**ew **J**ersey **T**urnpike, **W**ilmettia **A**venue, **W**est **F**ourth **S**treet

In a hyphenated number, the second word begins with a small letter.

EXAMPLE
Thirty-**t**hird **S**treet

Organizations

6. Capitalize names of organizations, businesses, institutions, and government bodies.

ORGANIZATIONS
American **B**ar **A**ssociation, **N**ational **C**ollegiate **A**thletic **A**ssociation, **A**merican **A**ssociation of **R**etired **P**ersons

The word *party* is usually written without a capital letter when it follows a proper adjective.

EXAMPLES
Republican **p**arty, **D**emocratic **p**arty, **W**hig **p**arty

BUSINESSES
Proctor & **G**amble **C**ompany, **S**outhwestern **B**ell, **F**ord **M**otor **C**ompany

INSTITUTIONS
United **S**tates **A**ir **F**orce, **H**arvard **U**niversity, **S**mith **C**ollege, **N**ew **T**rier **H**igh **S**chool

Do not capitalize words like *hotel, theater, college, high school,* and *post office* unless they are part of a proper name.

EXAMPLES

Knox **C**ollege	a **c**ollege professor
Ambassador **E**ast **H**otel	a **h**otel in Chicago
Helen **H**ayes **T**heater	a **t**heater in New York
Tampa **P**ost **O**ffice	a local **p**ost **o**ffice
Kings **C**ounty **C**ourthouse	the **c**ourthouse steps

GOVERNMENT BODIES
Senate, **C**ensus **B**ureau **S**ervice, **H**ouse of **C**ommons, **D**epartment of the **I**nterior

Historical Events

7. Capitalize the names of historical events and periods, special events, and calendar items.

HISTORICAL EVENTS AND PERIODS
Bloodless **R**evolution, **B**attle of **B**ull **R**un, the **H**undred **Y**ears' **W**ar, **I**ron **A**ge, **C**enozoic **P**eriod

SPECIAL EVENTS
America's **C**up **R**ace, **O**lympic **G**ames, **C**ommencement **D**ay

CALENDAR ITEMS
Wednesday, **A**ugust, **F**lag **D**ay, **N**ew **Y**ear's **D**ay

Nationalities and Races

8. Capitalize the names of nationalities, races, and peoples.

EXAMPLES
Venezuelan, Italian, Yoruba, Asian, Zulu, Sioux, Nordic

Brand Names

9. Capitalize the brand names of business products.

EXAMPLES
Ritz, Dodge, Dynel

Do not capitalize the noun that often follows a brand name: Dynel fabric

TIPS FOR WRITERS

Do not capitalize the names of seasons unless they are personified or are part of the names of special events.

EXAMPLES
"I saw old Autumn in the misty morn." [personification]
We will be on the decorating committee for the annual Winter Carnival. [special event]

Particular Places, Things, Events

10. Capitalize the names of ships, planets, monuments, awards, and any other particular places, things, or events.

SHIPS, TRAINS
the *Pinta*, the ***U.S.S.*** *Missouri*, the *City of New Orleans*, the *Santa Fe Chief*

AIRCRAFT, SPACECRAFT, MISSILES
Spirit of St. Louis, *Friendship 7*, *Luna 9*

PLANETS, STARS
Pluto, Polaris, the Milky Way

Sun, moon and *earth* are not capitalized unless they are listed with other heavenly bodies.

MONUMENTS, MEMORIALS
the Parthenon, Vietnam Veteran's Memorial

BUILDINGS
White House, Pentagon

AWARDS
Navy Cross, Distinguished Service Medal, Purple Heart

Specific Courses, Languages

11. Do *not* capitalize names of school subjects, except for languages and for course names followed by a number.

EXAMPLES
This year I am taking English literature, world history, Stenography I, a foreign language, and American literature, drama, geometry, chemistry, and French IV.

Do *not* capitalize the name of a class (*freshman, sophomore, junior, senior*) unless it is used as part of a proper noun.

EXAMPLE
All freshmen may register next week for the Freshman-Sophomore Debate.

Titles of People

12. Capitalize the title of a person when it comes before a name.

EXAMPLES

President Carter	Mr. Martinez
Dr. Seuss	Ms. Peer
Professor Fisch	Principal Donna Rothstein

Do not capitalize a title used alone or following a person's name, especially if the title is preceded by *a* or *the.*

EXAMPLES
We met the principal at the dinner.
John F. Kennedy was first elected senator from Massachusetts in 1952.
Claudius I was emperor of Rome from A.D. 41–54.
The governor of the state is to be the main speaker at the commencement exercises.

13. Capitalize words showing family relationship when used with a person's name but *not* when preceded by a possessive or article.

EXAMPLES
Bea's grandmother is over eighty years of age.
We had dinner with Aunt Tess and Uncle Fred.
My mother enjoys visiting relatives.
Would Cousin Suzanne like to go sightseeing?
But: My cousin Suzanne is here.

Grammar, Usage, and Mechanics

Titles of Literary and Other Creative Works

14. Capitalize the first and last words and all important words in titles of books, periodicals, poems, stories, historical documents, movies, television programs, works of art, and musical compositions.

Unimportant words in a title are
articles: *a, an, the*
short prepositions (fewer than five letters): *of, to, for, from*
coordinating conjunctions: *and, but, so, nor, or, yet, for*

BOOKS
Of Time and the River, Period of Adjustment, The War of the Worlds, The Pilgrim's Progress, A Journal of the Plague Year

PERIODICALS
the *Atlantic, Better Homes and Gardens, New England Journal of Medicine*

POEMS
"The Rime of the Ancient Mariner," "The Pardoner's Tale," "La Belle Dame Sans Merci"

STORIES
"The Fall of the House of Usher," "The Lady in the Looking Glass: A Reflection," "The Last Leaf"

HISTORICAL DOCUMENTS
Emancipation Proclamation, Magna Carta, Bill of Rights

TELEVISION PROGRAMS
Face the Nation, Sixty Minutes, Mystery, The Bill Cosby Show

WORKS OF ART
Early Sunday Morning, The Violin

MUSICAL COMPOSITIONS
"The Rose of Tralee," *The Barber of Seville*, "Anniversary Waltz,""See You in September," Beethoven's *Moonlight Sonata*

The words *a, an,* and *the* written before a title are capitalized only when they are the first word of a title.

EXAMPLES
A Bell for Adano, The Life of Samuel Johnson, An Essay on Man

Before the names of magazines and newspapers, *a, an,* and *the* are usually not capitalized.

EXAMPLES
Did you happen to see a copy of the *Atlantic Monthly* last month?
I read the *Denver Post.*
My sister subscribes to the *San Francisco Chronicle.*

Religions

15. Capitalize names of religions and their followers, holy celebrations, holy writings, and specific deities.

RELIGIONS AND FOLLOWERS
Judaism, Hinduism, Islam, Mormonism, Muslim, Jainist, Methodist, Quaker, Seventh-Day Adventist, Presbyterian, Catholic

HOLY DAYS AND SEASONS
Advent, Ramadan, Passover, Pentecost, Lent, Day of Atonement

HOLY WRITINGS
the Bible, Koran, Upanishads, Psalms, Acts of the Apostles, the Talmud

SPECIFIC DEITIES
Allah, God, Brahma, Jehovah

The word *god* is not capitalized when it refers to the gods of ancient mythology.

EXAMPLE
The gods of classical mythology were said to live on Mount Olympus.
The ancient Greek poet paid tribute to the goddess Hera.

PUNCTUATION

End Marks

End marks—*periods, question marks,* and *exclamation points*—are used to indicate the purpose of a sentence.

1. **Use a period to end a statement (*or* declarative sentence).**

EXAMPLES
These books are for sale.
Janet questioned who they were.
No one in the class knew the answer.

Notice in the second example that a declarative sentence containing an indirect question is followed by a period.

2. **Use a question mark to end a question (*or* interrogative sentence).**

EXAMPLES
Should we water these plants?
Is this a daffodil?
Who brought that bouquet?

A direct question may have the same word order as a declarative sentence. Since it is a question, however, it is followed by a question mark.

EXAMPLES
We can eat now?
It was a good show?

3. **Use an exclamation point to end an exclamation.**

EXAMPLES
Marvelous! What a display!
Ouch!
Watch out!

TIPS FOR WRITERS

Be sure to distinguish between a declarative sentence that contains an indirect question and an interrogative sentence, which asks a direct question.

INDIRECT QUESTION
Michael asked **where the trowel was.** [declarative]

DIRECT QUESTION
Michael asked, **"Where is the trowel?"** [interrogative]

Sometimes declarative and imperative sentences show such strong feeling that they are more like exclamations than statements or questions. If so, an exclamation point should be used instead of a period or question mark.

EXAMPLES
The pot is overflowing!
Can't you help!
Don't go near that!
This is a disaster!

4. **Use a period or exclamation point to end an imperative sentence.**

When an imperative sentence makes a request, it is generally followed by a period. Imperative sentences, particularly commands, may also show strong feeling. In such cases, an exclamation point should be used.

EXAMPLES
Please don't rush.
Don't rush!

Sometimes, a command or request is stated in the form of a question. Because of the purpose, however, the sentence is really an imperative sentence and is followed by a period or an exclamation point.

EXAMPLES
May I warn you now.
Will you stop!

5. **Use a period after an abbreviation.**

Personal Names: G. B. Shaw, O. Henry
Titles Used with Names: Mr., Ms., Mrs., Dr.
States: Fla., Mo., Pa., Ala.
Time of Day: A.M., P.M.
Years: B.C., A.D.
Addresses: Ave., St., Blvd.,
Organizations and Companies: Assn., Co., Corp., Inc.
Units of Measure: lb., oz., in., ft., yd., mi.

Abbreviations for government agencies and international organizations and some other frequently used abbreviations are written without periods. Abbreviations in the metric system are often written without the periods, especially in science books.

TIPS FOR WRITERS

If an abbreviation comes at the end of a statement, do not use an additional period as an end mark. However, use a question mark or an exclamation point if one is needed.

EXAMPLES
Holly was born in Washington, D.C.
When did she leave Washington, D.C.?

Commas

1. **Use commas to separate two or more adjectives preceding a noun.**

   EXAMPLE
   We ate **hot, crispy, homebaked biscuits.**

   When the last adjective in a series is thought of as part of the noun, the comma before the two adjectives should be separated by a comma:

   EXAMPLES
   The house has a **large sitting room.**
   Have a glass of **cool, tangy orange juice.**

   You can use two tests to determine whether two adjectives should be separated by a comma:

   TEST 1:
   Insert the word *and* between the adjectives. If *and* fits sensibly between the adjectives, use a comma. In the first example sentence, *and* cannot be logically inserted: *large and sitting room.* In the second sentence, *and* sounds logical between the first two adjectives (*cool and tangy*) but not between the second and third (*tangy and orange*).

   TEST 2:
   Change the order of the adjectives. If the order of the adjectives can be reversed sensibly, use a comma. *Tangy, cool orange juice* makes sense, but *orange tangy juice* and *sitting large room* do not.

2. **Use commas before *and, but, or, nor, for, so,* and *yet* when they join independent clauses.**

   Mark turned the switch, and **the screen lit up.**
   The family has a car, yet **they always use the bus.**

   Do not be misled by compound verbs, which often make a sentence look as though it contains two independent clauses.

   COMPOUND SENTENCE
   Ralph cut the patterns, and **Mel sewed the costumes**. [two independent clauses]

   SIMPLE SENTENCE
   Arnie **designed** the sets and **painted** scenery. [one subject with a compound verb]

   In the following correctly punctuated compound sentence, notice that independent clauses appear on both sides of the coordinating conjunction.

   He wrote poetry, and **he loved to act.**

3. **Use commas to set off nonessential clauses and nonessential participial phrases.**

   A *nonessential* (or *nonrestrictive)* clause or participial phrase adds information that is not necessary to the main idea in the sentence. Omitting such a clause or phrase will not change the meaning of the sentence.

   NONESSENTIAL CLAUSES
   John**, who is my best friend,** leaves for college next week.
   My old car**, which I have had for five years,** still runs well.

   NONESSENTIAL PHRASES
   John**, my youngest son,** is tall for his age.
   Ted**, anxious to see the new play,** stood in line for a ticket.
   The Return of the Native, **written by Thomas Hardy,** was published in 1878 and is one of his best novels.

   When a clause or phrase is necessary to the meaning of a sentence—that is, when it tells *which ones*—the clause or phrase is *essential* (or *restrictive),* and commas are *not* used.

   Notice how the meaning of each sentence below changes when the essential clause or phrase is omitted.

   ESSENTIAL CLAUSES
   Only those students **who have taken geometry** may register for this course.
   A poem **that I wrote** was published in that magazine.

   An adjective clause beginning with *that* is usually essential.

1214

TIPS FOR WRITERS

A comma is always used before *for, so,* and *yet* joining two independent clauses. The comma may be omitted, however, before *and, but, or,* or *nor* when the independent clauses are very short and when there is no chance of confusion.

EXAMPLES
I missed my plane, so I took another flight.
I read the book and I found it exciting.

ESSENTIAL PHRASES
A dog **bearing no identification** wandered into our yard.
The most famous student **taught by Aristotle** was Alexander the Great.

4. **Use a comma after introductory words such as *well, yes, no,* and *why* when they begin a sentence.**

EXAMPLES
Yes, those are fresh clams.
Well, we bought them at the fish market.

5. **Use a comma after an introductory participial phrase.**

EXAMPLES
Standing under my umbrella, I was able to keep almost dry.
Amused by the play, the audience could not stop laughing.

6. **Use a comma after a series of introductory prepositional phrases.**

EXAMPLES
From the last row of the balcony, we heard loud applause.
By the end of the long game, many fans had left the stadium.

A short introductory prepositional phrase does not require a comma unless the comma is necessary to make the meaning clear.

EXAMPLES
With my computer I can store data easily.
With my computer, calculations are easy to do. [The comma is necessary to avoid reading *computer calculations.*]

7. **Use a comma after an introductory adverb clause.**

EXAMPLES
As the national anthem was sung, the audience stood respectfully.
When you reach the corner, make a left turn.

8. **Use commas to set off elements that interrupt the sentence.**

EXAMPLES
Your letter, **in fact,** never arrived.
Yvonne**, of course,** won the contest easily.

If an "interrupter" comes at the beginning or at the end of a sentence, only one comma is needed.

EXAMPLES
After all, who knows better than I?
There is one more problem**, however.**

9. **Use commas to set off appositives and appositive phrases.**

EXAMPLES
The dog**, an Irish setter,** was well trained.
Her favorite novelist, **P. G. Wodehouse,** was also a playwright and short-story writer.
Everyone, **even their third cousins,** was there to celebrate their anniversary.

When an appositive has no modifiers and is closely related to the word preceding it, it should not be set off by commas.

EXAMPLES
The American composer **Ives** is his favorite.
We **students** bear a responsibility.

10. **Use commas to set off words used in direct address.**

EXAMPLES
Emma, you are our new vice president.
I practiced that sonatina all week, **Mr. Caligari.**
Your hair, **Gerry,** needs cutting.

11. **Use commas to set off parenthetical expressions.**

EXAMPLES
Strictly speaking, earth is "an oval sphere."
It is, **I believe,** an oblate spheroid.
It is a superb astronomy book, **in fact.**

A contrasting expression introduced by *not* is parenthetical and must be set off by commas.

EXAMPLE
It was the sun**, not the rain,** that did the damage.

12. **Use a comma to separate items in dates and addresses.**

EXAMPLES
My sister left for **Boston, Massachusetts,** on **Friday, September 13, 1991.**
On **December 24, 1991,** my new address will be **305 West Healey Street, Champaign, IL 61820.**

Notice that no comma separates the month and day (December 24) or the house number and street name (305 West Healey Street) because each is considered one item. Also, the ZIP code is not separated from the name of the state by a comma: Champaign, IL 61820.

13. **Use a comma after the salutation of a friendly letter and after the closing of any letter.**

EXAMPLES
Dear Mr. Smith**,**
Sincerely yours**,**
My dear Olga**,**
Yours very truly**,**
Dear Aunt May**,**

14. **Use a comma after a name followed by an abbreviation such as *Jr., Sr.,* and *M.D.***

EXAMPLES
David Wong**, Jr.**
Ens. M. E. Tilley**, U.S.N.**
Karl Enesco**, M.D**
Adam Clayton Powell**, Jr.**
Martin Luther King**, Sr.**

Semicolons

1. **Use a semicolon between independent clauses in a sentence if they are not joined by *and, but, or, nor, for, so,* or *yet.***

Notice in the following examples that the semicolon replaces the comma and the conjunction joining the independent clauses.

EXAMPLES
First I vacuumed the floor**, and** then I began dusting the furniture.
First I vacuumed the floor; then I began dusting the furniture.
Merv will visit Mexico**, but** his brother will go to Brazil.
Merv will visit Mexico; his brother will go to Brazil.

A semicolon can be used between two closely related independent clauses.

EXAMPLE
Zev made the sauce. Then he boiled the pasta.
Zev made the sauce; then he boiled the pasta.

2. **Use a semicolon between independent clauses joined by conjunctive adverbs or transitional expressions.**

EXAMPLES
Anne was late**; however,** the performance began even later.
There were four different salads**; in addition,** there was cold beef and ham.

When conjunctive adverbs and transitional expressions appear *within* one of the clauses and not *between* clauses, they are usually punctuated as interrupters (set off by commas). The two clauses are still separated by a semicolon.

EXAMPLE
A doubleheader was scheduled; **the second game, however,** was halted by rain.

3. **Use a semicolon (rather than a comma) to separate independent clauses joined by a coordinating conjunction when there are commas within the clauses.**

CONFUSING
Cabbage, corn, and kale are vegetables, and figs and dates are fruits.

CLEAR
Cabbage, corn, and kale are vegetables**;** figs and dates are fruits.

CONFUSING
Reaching into her purse and taking out the antique coins, Susan looked at them carefully, scrutinizing each one, but, in spite of her need, she could not bear to sell them.

CLEAR
Reaching into her purse and taking out the antique coins, Susan looked at them carefully, scrutinizing each one**;** but, in spite of her need, she could not bear to sell them.

4. **Use a semicolon between items in a series if the items contain commas.**

EXAMPLES
She has relatives in **Riga, Latvia; St. Petersburg, Russia; Prague, Czechoslovakia; and Paris, France.**
Concerts are scheduled for **Friday, September 20; Monday, September 23; and Thursday, September 26.**

Colons

1. **Use a colon before a list of items, especially after expressions like *the following* and *as follows.***

EXAMPLES
For your term paper you may choose to write on one of **the following plays:** *Candida*, *Pygmalion*, or *Man* and *Superman*.
Other herbs are **as follows:** basil, thyme, sage, and dill.

If a noun is followed by a list of appositives, then the colon is used to make the sentence clear.

EXAMPLES
At the intersection there were three signs: To Madison, To Milwaukee, and To Rockford.
You need to consider three issues: finances, publicity, and voter apathy.

Do *not* use a colon before a list that follows a verb or a preposition.

INCORRECT
Additional courses are: computer science, logic, algebra, and system design.

CORRECT
Additional courses are computer science, logic, algebra, and system design.

2. **Use a colon before a long, formal statement or quotation.**

EXAMPLE
Alfred North Whitehead wrote: "Intelligence is quickness to apprehend as distinct from ability, which is capacity to act wisely on the thing apprehended."

3. **Use a colon between the hour and the minute.**

EXAMPLES
8:15 P.M. 10:00 A.M.

4. **Use a colon between chapter and verse in referring to passages from the Bible.**

EXAMPLES
Psalms 150:1 Genesis 5:7

5. **Use a colon between volume and issue number or between volume and page number of a periodical.**

EXAMPLES
Smithsonian 22:8 [volume and issue number]
Smithsonian 22:54 [volume and page number]

6. **Use a colon after the salutation of a business letter.**

EXAMPLES
Dear Ms. Davila: Dear Dr. Fenton:
Dear Sir: To Whom It May Concern:

Italics

When writing or typing, indicate italics by underlining. If your composition were to be printed, the underlined words would be set in italics. For example, if you type:

Arthur Miller wrote <u>Death of a Salesman</u>.

the sentence would be printed like this:

Arthur Miller wrote *Death of a Salesman.*

If you use a personal computer, you can probably set words in italics yourself.

1. **Use italics (underlining) for titles of books, plays, films, periodicals, works of art, long musical compositions, newspapers, long poems, television programs, ships, aircraft, and so on.**

BOOKS: Through the Looking Glass, The Sound and the Fury
PLAYS: Uncle Vanya, The Two Gentlemen of Verona, The Crucible
FILMS: Gone with the Wind, 101 Dalmatians
PERIODICALS: Newsweek, Chicago Sun-Times
WORKS OF ART: Irises, The Shrimp Girl
LONG MUSICAL COMPOSITIONS: Elijah, Richard Strauss's *Don Juan*
TELEVISION SERIES: The Golden Girls, Major Dad, Perfect Strangers
SHIPS: Normandy, USS Missouri
AIRCRAFT, SPACECRAFT: Hindenburg, Gemini 7, Apollo 11

1217

The words *a, an,* and *the* written before a title are italicized only when they are part of the title. Before the names of newspapers and magazines, however, they are not italicized, even if they are capitalized on the front page of the newspaper or on the cover of the magazine.

EXAMPLES
I bought Henry James's ***The Wings of the Dove.***
In the museum we saw Picasso's ***The Old Guitarist.***
I subscribe to the ***Boston Globe*** and the ***National Geographic.***

Magazine articles, chapter headings, and titles of short poems, short stories, short musical compositions, and individual episodes of TV shows, when referred to in a composition, should be placed in quotation marks, not italicized. See the following section.

2. **Use italics (underlining) for words, letters, and figures referred to as such and for foreign words.**

EXAMPLES
The word ***bungalow*** comes from Hindu.
The word ***assessor*** has four ***s***'s.
The ***6*** on my application looks like an ***8.***
I gave the woman her change, and she said, ***"Danke."***

Quotation Marks

1. **Use quotation marks to enclose a direct quotation—a person's exact words.**

EXAMPLES
Ben asked, **"What time is it?"**
"It's almost noon," I answered.

2. **Begin a direct quotation with a capital letter.**

EXAMPLES
After the performance Jim said, "**T**hat was a beautiful concert."
Felicia said, "**A**t the bottom of page 36." [Although this quotation is not a sentence, it is Felicia's complete remark.]

If the direct quotation is obviously a fragment of the original quotation, it may begin with a small letter.

EXAMPLE
Please take the advice of Shakespeare's Polonius, and "**n**either a borrower nor a lender be." [The quotation is obviously only a phrase from Polonius's sentence.]

3. **When a quoted sentence is divided into two parts by an interrupting expression, begin the second part with a small letter.**

EXAMPLE
"I think," he said, "**t**hat we will arrive by noon."

If the second part of a quotation is a new sentence, a period (not a comma) follows the interrupting expression; and the second part begins with a capital letter.

EXAMPLE
"I tried to buy a ticket," Marissa said. "The performance is sold out, however."

An interrupting expression is not a part of a quotation and therefore should never be inside quotation marks.

INCORRECT
"Don't be late, he said, or you'll miss my solo."

CORRECT
"Don't be late," he said, **"or you'll miss my solo."**

When two or more sentences by the same speaker are quoted together, use only one set of quotation marks.

INCORRECT
Carla said, "The winter is certainly dry." "Why has there been so little snow?"

CORRECT
Carla said, **"**The winter is certainly dry. Why has there been so little snow?**"**

TIPS FOR WRITERS

Do not use quotation marks for *indirect quotations.*

DIRECT QUOTATIONS
Stella said, "I want to see that film."
He asked me, "Have you ever seen so much hail?"

INDIRECT QUOTATION
Stella said that she wanted to see that film.
He asked me if I had ever seen so much hail.

4. **Set off a direct quotation from the rest of the sentence by commas or by a question mark or an exclamation point.**

EXAMPLES
The guide said, "I hope you have enjoyed your tour," as he bid us goodbye.
Miranda said, "Are you still hungry?" as she brought in the cake.

5. **Place commas and periods inside closing quotation marks.**

EXAMPLES
"I haven't heard the opera**,"** remarked Jan, "but I understand it is an interesting piece**."**
He read aloud "Song of Myself**,"** a poem by Walt Whitman.

6. **Place semicolons and colons outside closing quotation marks.**

EXAMPLES
Chaucer once wrote, "Murder will out"**;** I wonder in which poem this appears.
The following foods were offered as "appetizers of the day"**:** fruit cup, artichoke hearts, and zucchini slices.

7. **If the quotation is a question or an exclamation, place question marks and exclamation points inside the closing quotation marks. Otherwise, place them outside.**

EXAMPLES
"Is it snowing?" I asked, looking up from my book.
"We're having a blizzard!" Hal answered.
What is the meaning of **"choler"?**

8. **When you write dialogue (a conversation), begin a new paragraph every time the speaker changes.**

EXAMPLE
"Hello," she said. "Haven't we met before?"
"I don't know," Jason answered. "Should we have?"
"Your're a clever man," she said. "You tell me."

9. **When a quoted passage consists of more than one paragraph, put quotation marks at the beginning of each paragraph and at the end of the entire passage. Do not put quotation marks after any paragraph but the last.**

EXAMPLE
"For four hours," the announcer reported, "no one knew the outcome of the negotiations, because the meeting was held in closed session.
"Finally, the doors opened, and the delegates came out, one by one. The President walked swiftly up to the speaker's stand and spoke to reporters.**"**

10. **Use single quotation marks to enclose a quotation within a quotation.**

EXAMPLES
Perplexed, Tiffany asked, "Which newspaper had as its headline **'All the News That's Fit to Print'**?"
Mr. Mott said, "One of my favorite poems is Walt Whitman's **'When Lilacs Last in the Dooryard Bloom'd.'"**
Caroline asked, "Who said **'Go to Mount Claire'**?"

11. **Use quotation marks to enclose titles of articles, short stories, essays, poems, songs, individual episodes of TV shows, chapters, and other parts of books or periodicals.**

EXAMPLES
Please read Harte's short story **"The Outcasts of Poker Flat."**
The song **"I Think I Chose Right"** was an audience favorite.

Italicize the title of a poem long enough to be published in a separate volume. Such poems are usually divided into titled or numbered sections, such as cantos, parts, or books. Long musical compositions include operas, symphonies, ballets, oratorios, and concertos.

EXAMPLES
In my report on Willa Cather, I plan to quote from *My Ántonia* and from her "A Wagner Matinee."
He sang "Comfort Ye" from the *Messiah*.

Apostrophes

With the Possessive Case

1. **Add an apostrophe and an *s* to form the possessive case of a singular noun. The *possessive* of a noun or pronoun shows ownership or relationship.**

EXAMPLES

a **reviewer's** opinion	a **father's** love
the **secretary's** notes	**Mel's** book
Sarah's wallet	the **dog's** tail

2. **Add only an apostrophe to a proper name ending in an *s*-sound if the name has two or more syllables or if the addition of *'s* makes the name awkward to pronounce.**

EXAMPLES
Sophocles' plays
Mr. Jimenez' class

3. **Add only an apostrophe to form the possessive case of a plural noun ending in *s.***

EXAMPLES
states' budgets
doctors' offices
fifty cents' worth

Although most plural nouns end in *s,* some are irregular. To form the possessive case of a plural noun that does not end in *s,* add an apostrophe and an *s.*

EXAMPLES
geese's honks
men's shirtings

Do not use an apostrophe to form the *plural* of a noun. Remember that the apostrophe shows ownership or relationship.

INCORRECT
Two riders' had loose saddles.

CORRECT
Two **riders** had loose saddles.

CORRECT
Two **riders'** saddles came loose.

4. **Do not use an apostrophe with a possessive personal pronoun.**

My, your, her, its, our, and *their* are used before a noun. *Mine, yours, hers, ours,* and *theirs,* on the other hand, are never used before a noun; they are used as subjects, complements, or objects in sentences. *His* may be used in either way.

EXAMPLES
I borrowed **your** necklace. I borrowed a book of **yours.**
That is **her** new automobile. That new automobile is **hers.**
His cartoon was clever. **His** was a clever cartoon.
Al has **our** car; Rex has **theirs.**
This is **her** earring. This is an earring of **hers.**

The possessive form of *who* is *whose,* not *who's.* Do not write *it's* for *its,* or *they're* for *their.*

5. **Add an apostrophe and an *s* to form the possessive case of an indefinite pronoun.**

EXAMPLES
everybody**'s** question
no one**'s** fault
another**'s** problem
neither**'s** answer

6. **For possessives of compound words, names of organizations and businesses, and words showing joint possession, make only the last word possessive in form.**

COMPOUND WORDS
someone else's suggestion
city council's meeting
brother-in-law's bowling ball

ORGANIZATIONS
American Red Cross's fund
Amnesty International's campaign

BUSINESS
A.T. & T.'s employees

JOINT POSSESSION
Jan and Sally**'s** project [the project belongs to both Jan and Sally] was judged by all who saw it to be the best in the competition.

When one of the words showing joint possession is a pronoun, both words should be possessive in form.

EXAMPLES
Bert's and my model airplanes [not *Bert and my model airplanes*] were entered in the crafts fairs this year.
Mom's and my tennis scores have improved a lot since we began to play three times a week.

7. **When two or more persons possess something individually, make each of their names possessive in form.**

EXAMPLES
Mrs. Roth's and **Mrs. Simpson's** classes [the classes of two different women] meet on alternate Mondays at the same time.
Kate's and **Kim's cats** [individual, not joint, possession] won ribbons at this year's cat show.

With Contractions

8. **Use an apostrophe to show where letters or numbers have been omitted in a contraction.**

   EXAMPLES
   who is . . . who's
   1991 . . . '91
   is not . . . isn't
   he will . . . he'll
   I am . . . I'm
   you are . . . you're
   were not . . . weren't

   EXCEPTIONS
   will not . . . won't
   shall not . . . shan't

9. **To prevent confusion, use an apostrophe and an *s* to form the plurals of lowercase letters, some uppercase letters, numerals, and some words referred to as words.**

   EXAMPLE
   Good writers dot their ***i's*** and cross their ***t's***.

Hyphens

1. **Use a hyphen in some compound nouns.**

   EXAMPLES
   brand-new, great-grandmother, mother-in-law

2. **Use a hyphen to divide a word at the end of a line.**

   EXAMPLE
   One of my favorite words is the noun **anthology**.

   Divide an already hyphenated word only at a hyphen.

   INCORRECT
   Yesterday at the fair he went on the mer-
   ry-go-round.

   CORRECT
   Yesterday at the fair he went on the **merry-
   go-round.**

   Do not divide a word so that one letter stands alone.

   INCORRECT
   The young couple rented a new a-
   partment.

   CORRECT
   The young couple rented a new **apartment.**

3. **Use a hyphen with compound numbers from *twenty-one* to *ninety-nine* and with fractions used as adjectives.**

   EXAMPLES
   twenty-four degrees
   one-third gallon [but *one third* of the paint]

4. **Use a hyphen with the prefixes *ex-*, *self-*, *all-*, and with the suffix *-elect*, and with all prefixes before a proper noun or proper adjective.**

   EXAMPLES
   ex-governor, **mid-**September, **self-**taught, president-**elect**

Dashes

Use a dash to indicate an abrupt break in thought or speech or an unfinished statement or question.

Many words and phrases are used parenthetically: that is, they break into the main thought of a sentence. Most parenthetical elements are set off by commas or parentheses.

EXAMPLES
Radishes**, however,** do not agree with me.
The answer**, she realized,** was incorrect.
The genie**, nevertheless,** granted the wish.

Sometimes these elements demand a stronger emphasis. In such instances, a dash is used.

EXAMPLE
The best scene in the play is—but you should decide that yourself.

Parentheses

Use parentheses to enclose material that is added to a sentence but is not considered of major importance.

EXAMPLES
During World War I **(from 1914 to 1918)**, the airplane came into prominence in military strategy.

Punctuation marks are used within parentheses when the parenthetical matter is a full sentence. However, a punctuation mark is not placed within parentheses if the mark belongs to the sentence as a whole.

EXAMPLE
Mark your answers clearly. (Do not use ink.)

1221

SPELLING

TIPS FOR WRITERS

Here are five tips for improving your spelling.
1. To learn the spelling of a word, pronounce it, study it, and write it.
2. Use a dictionary.
3. Spell by syllables.
4. Proofread for careless spelling errors.
5. Keep a spelling notebook.

Words with *ie* and *ei*

1. Write *ie* when the sound is long *e*, except after *c*.

EXAMPLES

achieve	shield	ceiling	reprieve	receive
chief	thief	siege	fiend	field

2. Write *ei* when the sound is not long *e*.

EXAMPLES

neighbor	weigh	forfeit
deign	heinous	height
freight	sleigh	feign

EXCEPTIONS
friend, mischief, financier, seize

Words with *-cede, -ceed,* and *-sede*

3. Only one English word ends in *-sede: supersede;* only three words end in *-ceed: exceed, proceed,* and *succeed;* all other words with this sound end in *-cede.*

EXAMPLES

precede	recede	secede
intercede	concede	accede

Adding Prefixes

4. When a prefix is added to a word, the spelling of the original word itself remains the same.

EXAMPLES
pre + dispose = **pre**dispose
il + legible = **il**legible
mis + match = **mis**match
re + place = **re**place
im + mature = **im**mature

Adding Prefixes

5. When the suffix *-ness* or *-ly* is added to a word, the spelling of the original word remains the same.

EXAMPLES
definite + ly = definite**ly**
like + ness = like**ness**
dear + ly = dear**ly**

EXCEPTIONS
Words ending in *y* usually change the *y* to *i* before *-ness* and *-ly:*

ready—readiness; clumsy—clumsily

But most one-syllable adjectives ending in *y* follow rule 5: *sly—slyness; dry—dryly*
True, due, and *whole* drop the final *e* before *-ly: truly, duly, wholly*

6. Drop the final silent *e* before adding a suffix that begins with a vowel.

EXAMPLES
pose + ing = posing
decide + able = decidable
desire + ous = desirous
create + ed = created

EXCEPTIONS
1. Keep the final silent *e* in words ending in *ce* or *ge* before a suffix that begins with *a* or *o: manageable, courageous*
2. To avoid confusion with other words, keep the final silent *e* in some words: *dyeing* and *dying, singeing* and *singing.*

7. Keep the final silent *e* before adding a suffix that begins with a consonant.

EXAMPLES

nine + ty = nin**e**ty	bare + ly = bar**e**ly
hope + ful = hop**e**ful	love + less = lov**e**less

EXCEPTIONS
nine + th = ninth
argue + ment = argument

8. When a word ends in *y* preceded by a consonant, change the *y* to *i* before any suffix except one beginning with *i*.

EXAMPLES
dizzy + ness = dizz**i**ness
plenty + ful = plent**i**ful
defy + ed = def**i**ed
modify + ing = modif**y**ing

EXCEPTIONS

1. Some one-syllable words:
   shy + ness = shyness
   sky + ward = skyward
2. *lady* and *baby* with suffixes:
   ladylike ladyship babyhood

9. When a word ends in *y* preceded by a vowel, simply add the suffix.

EXAMPLES
buoy + ant = buoyant
boy + hood = boyhood
replay + ed = replayed
cloy + ing = cloying

EXCEPTIONS
day + ly = daily
say + ed = said
pay + ed = paid

Doubling Final Consonants

10. When a word ends in a consonant, double the final consonant before a suffix that begins with a vowel only if the word: (1) has only one syllable or is accented on the last syllable, and (2) ends in a single consonant preceded by a single vowel.

EXAMPLES
mop + ing = mo**pp**ing
repel + ent = repe**ll**ent
deter + ence = dete**rr**ence
bat + ing = ba**tt**ing
ship + ing = shi**pp**ing

Otherwise, simply add the suffix.

EXAMPLES
link + ed = linked
pack + ing = packing
resist + ance = resistance
treat + ment = treatment

Plurals of Nouns

11. To form the plurals of most English nouns, add *s*.

SINGULAR	PLURAL
sack	sack**s**
mallet	mallet**s**
reel	reel**s**
morning	morning**s**
viola	viola**s**
flower	flower**s**
paint	paint**s**

12. To form the plurals of other nouns, follow these rules.

If the noun ends in *s, x, z, ch,* or *sh,* add *es.*

SINGULAR	PLURAL
pass	pass**es**
box	box**es**
waltz	waltz**es**
watch	watch**es**
mix	mix**es**
sash	sash**es**

If the noun ends in *y* preceded by a consonant, change the *y* to *i* and add *es.*

SINGULAR	PLURAL
fry	fr**ies**
dairy	dair**ies**
jury	jur**ies**
ruby	rub**ies**

EXCEPTION
The plurals of proper nouns: the *Brophy**s***, the *McNulty**s***.

If the noun ends in *y* preceded by a vowel add *s.*

SINGULAR	PLURAL
turkey	turkey**s**
tray	tray**s**
key	key**s**

For some nouns ending in *f* or *fe,* change the *f* to *v* and add *s* or *es.*

Noticing how the plural is pronounced will help you remember whether to change the *f* to *v.*

SINGULAR	PLURAL
gulf	gulf**s**
chief	chief**s**
elf	el**ves**
leaf	lea**ves**
wife	wi**ves**
shelf	shel**ves**

If the noun ends in *o* preceded by a consonant, add *es.*

SINGULAR	PLURAL
echo	echo**es**
hero	hero**es**
tomato	tomato**es**

1223

If the noun ends in *o* preceded by a vowel, add *s*.

SINGULAR	PLURAL
patio	patio**s**
stereo	stereo**s**
tattoo	tattoo**s**
video	video**s**
rodeo	rodeo**s**

EXCEPTIONS

SINGULAR	PLURAL
poncho	ponchos
zoo	zoos
tango	tangos

Nouns for musical terms that end in *o* preceded by a consonant form the plural by adding only *s*.

SINGULAR	PLURAL
soprano	soprano**s**
trio	trio**s**
piano	piano**s**
alto	alto**s**

A number of nouns that end in *o* preceded by a consonant have two plural forms.

SINGULAR	PLURAL
tornado	tornado**s** *or* tornado**es**
mango	mango**s** *or* mango**es**
zero	zero**s** *or* zero**es**
flamingo	flamingo**s** *or* flamingo**es**

The best way to handle plurals of words ending in *o* preceded by a consonant is to check their spelling in a dictionary.

The plurals of some nouns are formed in irregular ways.

SINGULAR	PLURAL
foot	feet
woman	women
louse	lice
child	children
goose	geese

Some nouns have the same form in both the singular and the plural.

SINGULAR AND PLURAL

deer	moose	salmon	Japanese
series	sheep	fowl	krill

Plurals of Compound Nouns

13. If a compound noun is written as one word, form the plural by adding *s* or *es*.

SINGULAR	PLURAL
kneecap	kneecap**s**
cupful	cupful**s**
lockup	lockup**s**
eyelash	eyelash**es**
hookup	hookup**s**
treehouse	treehouse**s**

If a compound noun is hyphenated or written as two words, make the main noun plural. The *main noun* is the noun that is modified.

SINGULAR	PLURAL
brother-in-law	brother**s**-in-law
notary public	notar**ies** public
runner-up	runner**s**-up
passer-by	passer**s**-by

EXCEPTIONS

SINGULAR	PLURAL
mock-up	mock-ups
lean-to	lean-tos
drop-off	drop-offs
close-up	close-ups

Plurals of Latin and Greek Loan Words

14. Some nouns borrowed from Latin and Greek form the plural as in the original language.

SINGULAR	PLURAL
nucleus	nucl**ei**
crisis	cris**es**
datum	dat**a**
basis	bas**es**
vertebra	vertebr**ae**
phenomenon	phenomen**a**

A few Latin and Greek loan words have two plural forms.

SINGULAR	PLURAL
medium	medi**a** *or* medium**s**
vortex	vorti**ces** *or* vorte**xes**
curriculum	curricul**a** *or* curriculum**s**
gymnasium	gymnasi**a** *or* gymnasium**s**

Check a dictionary to find the preferred spelling of such plurals.

Plurals of Numbers, Letters, Symbols, and Words Used as Words

15. To form the plurals of numerals, most capital letters, symbols, and words used as words, add an *s.*

EXAMPLES
Put the **5s** and the **Ms** in this file.
Change the **&s** to **ands.**

To prevent confusion, use an apostrophe and an *s* to form the plurals of lowercase letters, certain capital letters, and some words used as words.

EXAMPLES
Your **b's** look like **h's.**
Ramon got all **B's** last semester.
His constant **you know's** bothered me.
Please watch your **p's** and **q's**.

The plurals of decades and centuries may be formed by adding an *s* or an apostrophe and an *s* (*'s*).

EXAMPLES
My grandparents were married during the **'50s.**
Many new dances were invented during the **1900's** (*or* **1900s**).

Spelling Numbers

16. Always spell out a number that begins a sentence.

EXAMPLE
Four thousand five hundred pounds of concrete were used to build the foundation.

17. Within a sentence, spell out numbers that can be written in one word or two words; use numerals for other numbers.

EXAMPLES
I have only **three** weeks in which to build **two** cabinets.
Over the weekend we hiked **fifty-one** miles.
Mona has a collection of **483** different postage stamps.

18. Spell out numbers used to indicate order.

EXAMPLE
My sister placed **fourth** [not 4th] in the contest.

EXCEPTION
Use numerals for dates when you include the name of the month. Always use numerals for years.

EXAMPLE
Summer school begins on June **3** [not 3rd]. [Writing *the third of June* is also correct.]
World War II ended in **1945.**

Words Often Confused

You can prevent many spelling errors by learning the difference between the words grouped together in this section. Some of them are confusing because they are *homonyms*—that is, they're pronounced alike. Others are confusing because they're spelled the same or nearly the same.

all ready — [pronoun plus adjective] *everyone ready*
By then we were *all ready* to begin our dress rehearsal.

already — [adverb] *previously*
I have *already* purchased my books.

all right — [This is the only acceptable spelling. Although the spelling *alright* appears in some dictionaries, it has not become standard usage.]

altar — *a table or stand at which religious rites are performed*
The *altar* is carved from stone.

alter — *to change*
I have had to *alter* my plans.

all together — *everyone in the same place*
All together now, repeat these words.

altogether — *entirely*
You are *altogether* right in your assessment.

born — *given life*
Professor Robert Wong was *born* in China in 1952.

borne — *carried; endured*
The seeds are *borne* aloft by the wind.
She has *borne* more than her share of physical pain.

brake — *a stopping device*
The *brakes* on our car were not fixed.

break — *to shatter, sever*
This CD will not *break.*

Grammar, Usage, and Mechanics

capital	[noun] *center of government* or *money or property used in business;* [adjective] *punishable by death* or *of major importance* or *excellent* or *uppercase* Salem is the *capital* of Oregon. Funding this organization requires much *capital.* Treason is often a *capital* offense. The *capital* virtue of this area is an abundance of water. The weather was *capital.* This word needs a *capital* letter.
capitol	[noun] *building, statehouse* Our *capitol* building is a beautiful structure.
choose	[verb, used for present and future tense] *select* *Choose* a seat.
chose	[verb, past tense, rhymes with *nose*] I *chose* not to take a vacation this year.
clothes	*garments; wearing apparel* I really prefer old *clothes.*
cloths	*pieces of cloth; fabrics* I always use felt *cloths* to polish silver.
coarse	*rough* or *crude* I prefer a *coarse* grind of coffee. The dialogue was rather *coarse.*
course	*path of action or progress* or *unit of study* or *track or way;* also used with *of* to mean *naturally* or *certainly* The atmospheric disturbance took us somewhat off *course.* I must take a *course* in statistics. The golf *course* is soggy. Of *course,* you and I know better.
complement	[noun] *something that completes or makes perfect;* [verb] *to complete or make perfect* What is the *complement* of this angle? That green hat *complements* your red hair.
compliment	[noun] *a remark that expresses approval, praise, or admiration;* [verb] *to pay a compliment* I thank you for the *compliment.* Let me *compliment* you on that wonderful meal.
consul	*the representative of a foreign country* The Latvian *consul* is now in the city.
council	*a group called together to accomplish a job* The student *council* has not yet had its first meeting.
councilor	*a member of a council* My mother was just elected district *councilor.*
counsel	[noun] *advice*; [verb] *to give advice* I came to seek your *counsel* about my problem. Did you *counsel* her to see a doctor?
counselor	*one who gives advice* I went to see the career *counselor.*
des´ert	[noun] *a dry region* Rain in the *desert* is heavy but infrequent.
desert´	[verb] *to leave* I hope you won't *desert* me in my time of need.
dessert	[noun] *the final course of a meal* *Dessert* was served in the garden.
formally	*properly, according to strict rules* We have not been *formally* introduced.
formerly	*previously, in the past* Our new professor *formerly* taught at Columbia University.
hear	*to receive sounds through the ears* Do you *hear* the birds?
here	*this place* Wait *here* until I return.
ingenious	*clever; resourceful; skillful* What an *ingenious* solution to the problem!
ingenuous	*innocent; trusting; frank* She has an *ingenuous* smile that wins everyone over.
its	[possessive of *it*] Each suite has *its* own balcony.
it's	[contraction of *it is*] *It's* true that I am engaged.
later	*more late; at a subsequent time* I'll meet you *later.*
latter	*the second of two* Almonds or pecans will do, but I prefer the *latter.*

lead	[verb, present tense, pronounced *leed*] *to go first* *Lead* the way to the newly discovered cave.
led	[verb, past tense of *lead*] The waiter *led* us to our table.
lead	[noun, pronounced *led*] *a heavy metal;* also *graphite in a pencil* The Latin word for *lead* is *plumbum.*
loose	[adjective, rhymes with *noose*] *free* or *not close together* Are the horses running *loose* in the pasture? We made a rather *loose* agreement.
lose	[verb, pronounced *looz*] *to suffer loss* Don't *lose* your ticket.
miner	*a worker in a mine* The *miners* emerging from the mine were weary.
minor	*under legal age;* also, *smaller or less important* (as opposed to *major*) *Minors* are not eligible. The other problems we have are relatively *minor* ones.
moral	[adjective] *having to do with good or right;* [noun] *a lesson in conduct* *Moral* issues were discussed. Each of Aesop's fables has a *moral.*
morale	[noun] *mental condition, spirit* The team's *morale* was low.
peace	*absence of conflict* The president welcomed the thought of *peace.*
piece	*a part of something* Examine this *piece* of fabric.
personal	*individual; private* Her *personal view* is that we should not buy the gift.
personnel	*a group of people employed in the same work or service; a staff* Most of the *personnel* working in this office work with computers.
plain	[adjective] *not fancy* or *clear;* [noun] *a flat area of land* We enjoy *plain* food. The purpose seemed quite *plain.* These *plains* were once occupied by buffalo.
plane	[noun] *a flat surface, a level;* also *a tool* or *an airplane* How many geometrical *planes* are there? The lecture occurred on a higher *plane* than I could understand. The carpenter smoothed the surface with his *plane.* Our *plane* was overbooked.
principal	[noun] *head of a school;* [adjective] *main, most important* The *principal* opened the assembly. The *principal* issue was voter apathy.
principle	[noun] *a rule of conduct;* also *a law* or *a main fact* My father was guided by his *principles.* I studied the *principles* of logic.
quiet	*silent, still* The terriers are *quiet* after they've eaten.
quite	*to a great extent or degree, completely* Her voice is *quite* strong. I was *quite* pleased to be invited to visit them.
rout	*disorderly flight; to put to flight* The attack led to a complete *rout* of the enemy troops. We need to *rout* the insects from their nests.
route	*a road; a way to go* The path is the only *route* that will take you to the maple grove.
stationary	*in a fixed position* Are the tiles *stationary?*
stationery	*writing paper* The *stationery* was most expensive.
straight	*not crooked or curved; direct* Use that ruler to draw a *straight* line. This road will take you *straight* into the heart of town.
strait	*channel between two large bodies of water; also (plural) difficulty; distress* The *Strait* of Hormuz joins the Persian Gulf and the Gulf of Oman. We are in difficult economic *straits* now.

1227

than [conjunction, used for comparisons]
I heard more birds *than* dogs.

then [adverb, indicating *at that time* or *next*]
Were you *then* escorted to the front?
I drained the pasta, and *then* I added the sauce.

their [possessive of *they*]
The lawyers gave *their* opinions.

there [noun] *a place* [also an expletive used to begin a sentence]
Can we be *there* by Tuesday?
There were many repairs to be made.

they're [contraction of *they are*]
They're coming from Brazil.

to [preposition; also part of the infinitive form of a verb]
I came *to* a standstill.
She helped us *to* avoid getting lost.

too *also* or *more than enough*
I chose a tuna sandwich, and Bob did, *too.*
These temperatures are *too* hot.

two *the sum of one + one*
He had *two* bouquets for us.

waist [noun] *the middle part of the body*
This skirt is too large in the *waist.*

waste [noun] *unused material;* [verb] *to squander*
The creation of *waste* is a major concern.
Don't *waste* your effort reading that article.

weather *conditions outdoors*
The *weather* is unpredictable.

whether [indicates alternative or doubt]
I wondered *whether* the costumes were handmade.

who's [contraction of *who is, who has*]
I don't know *who's* downstairs.
Who's been to the market?

whose [possessive of who]
Whose copy of *War and Peace* was it?

your [possessive form of *you]*
Give me *your* flashlight.

you're contraction of *you are*
You're the first to arrive.

GLOSSARY

The glossary below is an alphabetical list of words found in the selections in this book. Use this glossary just as you use a dictionary—to find out the meanings of unfamiliar words. (A few technical, foreign, or more obscure words in this book are not listed here but are defined instead for you in the footnotes that accompany each selection.)

Many words in the English language have more than one meaning. This glossary gives the meanings that apply to the words as they are used in the selections in this book. Words closely related in form and meaning are usually listed together in one entry (*delta* and *deltaic*), and the definition is given for the first form.

The following abbreviations are used:

adj., adjective **n.**, noun **v.**, verb
adv., adverb **pl.**, plural form

Unless a word is very simple to pronounce, its pronunciation is given in parentheses. A guide to the pronunciation symbols appears at the bottom of each right-hand glossary page.

For more information about the words in this glossary, or about words not listed here, consult a dictionary.

abate (ə·bāt′) ***v.*** To diminish; lessen.
abeyance (ə·bā′əns) ***n.*** Temporary suspension.
abhor (ab·hôr′) ***v.*** To detest; hate.
abominable (ə·bäm′ə·nə·b′l) ***adj.*** Nasty and disgusting.
abreast (ə·brest′) ***adj.*** Side by side.
absolve (ab·zälv′) ***v.*** To free from guilt or blame.
abyss (ə·bis′) ***n.*** Bottomless gulf or pit; anything too deep for measurement.
acclivity (ə·kliv′ə·tē) ***n.*** An upward slope of ground.
accrue (ə·kro͞o′) ***v.*** To come as a natural growth, advantage, or right to.
acrimonious (ak′rə·mō′nē·əs) ***adj.*** Bitter; harsh.
acronym (ak′rə·nim) ***n.*** A word formed from the first, or the first few, letters of a series of words, such as *radar,* from *ra*dio *d*etecting *a*nd *r*anging.
adversary (ad′vər·ser′ē) ***n.*** Opponent; enemy.
affliction (ə·flik′shən) ***n.*** Anything causing pain, suffering, or distress.
affluent (af′lo͞o·wənt) ***adj.*** Wealthy.
aghast (ə·gast′) ***adj.*** Terrified; feeling great horror.
airs (erz) ***n. pl.*** Melodies.
akimbo (ə·kim′bō) ***adj.*** With hands on hips and elbows bent outward.
alight (ə·līt′) ***v.*** To come down after flight; descend and settle.
allay (a·lā′) ***v.*** To quiet; calm; put (fears) to rest.
aloft (ə·lôft′) ***adv.*** In the air; high up.
amenities (ə·men′ə·tēz) ***n. pl.*** Things that add to one's comfort; conveniences.
anemia (ə·nē′mē·ə) ***n.*** Lack of vigor or vitality; lifelessness.
anguish (aŋ′gwish) ***n.*** Great suffering; agony.
anon (ə·nän′) ***adv.*** Soon.
antagonist (an·tag′ə·nist) ***n.*** Opponent; competitor.
apotheosis (ə·päth′ē·ō′sis) ***n.*** Glorification of a person or thing.
apparition (ap′ə·rish′ən) ***n.*** A strange figure appearing suddenly and thought to be a ghost.
appropriate (ə·prō′prē·āt′) ***v.*** To take for one's own or exclusive use; take improperly, without permission.
arching (är′chiŋ) ***adj.*** Curving or bending.
arduous (är′jo͞o·wəs) ***adj.*** Difficult to do; strenuous.
arrogant (ar′ə·gənt) ***adj.*** Full of pride and self-importance.
articulate (är·tik′yə·lāt′) ***v.*** To express clearly.
assail (ə·sāl′) ***v.*** To attack.
assent (ə·sent′) ***n.*** Agreement; approval.
audacity (ô·das′ə·tē) ***n.*** Shameless boldness; insolence.
auspicious (ôs·pish′əs) ***adj.*** Favorable; suggesting a good future.
automatism (ô·täm′ə·tiz′m) ***n.*** Automaton; an apparatus that automatically performs certain actions without thought or understanding.
avert (ə·vurt′) ***v.*** To prevent; keep from happening.
awry (ə·rī′) ***adv.*** Out of shape or out of normal order.

bedlam (bed′ləm) ***n.*** A situation characterized by noise and confusion.
beholden (bē·hōld′ən) *adj.* Indebted; obliged to feel grateful.
benign (bi·nīn′) ***adj.*** Favorable; beneficial; causing no harm.
bequeath (bē·kwēth′) ***v.*** To leave to someone in a will.

bier (bir) ***n.*** A platform on which a coffin or corpse is placed.
bliss (blis) ***n.*** Great joy or happiness.
blithe (blīth) ***adj.*** Cheerful; carefree.
borne (bôrn) ***v.*** Carried. (Past participle of *bear.*)
brash (brash) ***adj.*** Hasty and reckless; rash.
brittle (brit''l) ***adj.*** Easily broken because it is hard and not flexible.
burgeon (bur'jən) ***v.*** To sprout; expand; flourish.

cadence (kād''ns) ***n.*** Rhythm.
calamity (kə·lam'ə·tē) ***n.*** Extreme misfortune; disaster.
camaraderie (käm'ə·räd'ər·ē) ***n.*** Warm feeling among friends.
cater-cornered (kat'ē·kôr'nərd) ***adj.*** Diagonal.
caterwaul (kat'ər·wôl') ***v.*** To make a shrill, howling sound.
censure (sen'shər) ***n.*** An official expression of disapproval.
chafe (chāf) ***v.*** To irritate or make sore by rubbing.
chromograph (krō'mə·graf') ***n.*** A tinted photograph.
circumspect (sur'kəm·spekt') ***adj.*** Cautious; careful to consider all details before acting or judging.
clamor (klam'ər) ***n.*** A loud, sustained noise.
claxon (klak's'n) ***n.*** An electric horn with a loud, shrill sound. (A variant spelling of *klaxon.*)
cohesion (kō·hē'zhən) ***n.*** The tendency to stick together.
comport (kəm·pôrt') ***v.*** **1.** To agree with. **2.** To behave in a specified manner.
conglomeration (kən·gläm'ə·rā'shən) ***n.*** A mixture or mass of miscellaneous things.
conjecture (kən·jek'chər) ***v.*** To guess.
connubial (kə·nōō'bē·əl) ***adj.*** Having to do with marriage.
conscription (kən·skrip'shən) ***n.*** Compulsory induction into the military.
consign (kən·sīn') ***v.*** To hand over or deliver; put into the care of another.
constrain (kən·strān') ***v.*** To hold back; restrain; confine.
convivial (kən·viv'ē·əl) ***adj.*** Sociable; jovial.
countenance (koun'tə·nəns) ***n.*** Facial features or expressions.
cow (kou) ***v.*** To fill with fear; intimidate.
craven (krā'vən) ***adj.*** Cowardly.
credulous (krej'ōō·ləs) ***adj.*** Easily convinced; tending to believe too readily.
croon (krōōn) ***v.*** To sing or hum in a low, gentle tone.

dauntless (dônt'lis) ***adj.*** Fearless.
dearness (dir'nis) ***n.*** High price; great expense.
decadence (dek'ə·dəns) ***n.*** Deterioration; decay.
decorum (di·kôr'əm) ***n.*** Propriety and good taste in speech, manners, dress, etc.
deferential (def'ə·ren'shəl) ***adj.*** Respectful; extremely courteous.
delirium (di·lir'ē·əm) ***n.*** A temporary state of extreme mental excitement, marked by restlessness, confused speech, and hallucinations.
delta (del'tə) ***n.*** A deposit of sand and soil that forms at the mouth of a river. ***adj.*** **Deltaic.**
descry (di·skrī') ***v.*** To catch sight of.
desiccated (des'i·kāt'ed) ***adj.*** Preserved by drying out.
desultory (des''l·tôr'ē) ***adj.*** Passing from one thing to another in an aimless way; disconnected; not methodical.
diagnostic (dī'əg·näs'tik) ***adj.*** Of or constituting a diagnosis, a decision on the nature of a disease after a careful examination of symptoms.
dilemma (di·lem'ə) ***n.*** A problem that can be solved only by choosing between equally unpleasant alternatives.
din (din) ***n.*** A loud, continuous noise.
dirge (durj) ***n.*** A song, poem, or musical composition that expresses mourning.
discern (di·surn') ***v.*** To perceive or recognize; make out clearly.
discernment (di·surn'mənt) ***n.*** Keen perception or judgment; insight.
disdain (dis·dān') ***n.*** Contempt; scorn.
disjointed (dis·joint'id) ***adj.*** Disconnected; without unity.
dismal (diz'm'l) ***adj.*** Gloomy; bleak; depressing.
disparate (dis'pər·it) ***adj.*** Distinct or different in some essential way.
dissertation (dis'ər·tā'shən) ***n.*** A long, formal written or spoken presentation on some topic.
dissuade (di·swād') ***v.*** To advise or persuade against.
divest (də·vest') ***v.*** To get rid of something unwanted.
divulge (də·vulj') ***v.*** To reveal.
dowry (dou'rē) ***n.*** The money or property that a woman brings to her husband at marriage.
dumbly (dum'lē) ***adv.*** Silently.

eccentric (ik·sen'trik) ***adj.*** Odd; unconventional; out of the ordinary.
eddies (ed'ēz) ***n. pl.*** Currents of air or water that move against the main current and form whirlpools or whirlwinds.
egress (ē'gres) ***n.*** The act of going out; a way out; exit.
eloquence (el'ə·kwəns) ***n.*** Skill in speaking or writing.
elude (i·lōōd') ***v.*** To avoid or escape by means of skill.
emanate (em'ə·nāt') ***v.*** To send forth; emit; issue.
embrasure (im·brā'zhər) ***n.*** An opening, as for a door or window.
eminent (em'ə·nənt) ***adj.*** Outstanding; noteworthy.

emissary (em'ə·ser'ē) ***n.*** An agent sent on a specific mission.
encumbrance (in·kum'brəns) ***n.*** Something that hinders or obstructs; burden.
enfeeble (in·fē'b'l) ***v.*** To weaken.
enmity (en'mə·tē) ***n.*** Hatred.
entreat (in·trēt') ***v.*** To plead with; beg.
epitaph (ep'ə·taf') ***n.*** A short composition written in memory of a dead person; an inscription on a tombstone.
epoch (ep'ək) ***n.*** A period in history considered important because of certain events, developments, or people.
equable (ek'wə·b'l) ***adj.*** Not easily upset; uniform; steady.
erratic (i·rat'ik) ***adj.*** Irregular; random; wandering.
exasperate (ig·zas'pə·rāt') ***v.*** To irritate or annoy.
execrable (ek'si·krə·b'l) ***adj.*** Detestable; hateful.
execration (ek'si·krā'shən) ***n.*** A curse; the act of calling down evil upon.
exemplary (ig·zem'plə·rē) ***adj.*** Worth imitating; serving as a model or example.
expedient (ik·spē'dē·ənt) ***n.*** Something useful or convenient.
expunge (ik·spunj') ***v.*** To erase or remove completely.
extort (ik·stôrt') ***v.*** To take by violence or threats of violence.
extricate (eks'trə·kāt') ***v.*** To disentangle; set free or release.
exultance (ig·zul't'ns) ***n.*** An expression of joy or triumph.

facilitate (fə·sil'ə·tāt') ***v.*** To make easy.
feeble (fē'b'l) ***adj.*** Weak; without force or effectiveness.
fiasco (fē·as'kō) ***n.*** A project that ends in total failure.
fissure (fish'ər) ***n.*** A long, narrow crack or opening; a dividing into parts.
flak (flak) ***n.*** The fire of antiaircraft guns.
fleeting (flēt'iŋ) ***adj.*** Passing swiftly; not lasting.
fluidity (flo͞o·wid'ə·tē) ***n.*** Ease of movement.
forbearance (fôr·ber'əns) ***n.*** Self-control; patient restraint.
formidable (fôr'mə·də·b'l) ***adj.*** Hard to overcome; impressive in size, excellence, etc.
founder (foun'dər) ***v.*** To break down; collapse; fail.
frugality (fro͞o·gal'ə·tē) ***n.*** The quality of being not wasteful; thrift; economy.

gait (gāt) ***n.*** Manner of walking or running.
gaunt (gônt) ***adj.*** Thin and hollow-eyed, as from great hunger or age.
genial (jēn'yəl) ***adj.*** Cheerful, friendly, and sympathetic.
gesticulate (jes·tik'yə·lāt') ***v.*** To gesture with the hands or arms.

harangue (hə·raŋ') ***v.*** To scold repeatedly.
harry (har'ē) ***v.*** To force or push along.
hedonistic (hēd''n·is'tik) ***adj.*** Devoted to the pursuit of pleasure.
heretofore (hir'tə·fôr') ***adv.*** Until now.
hobgoblin (häb'gäb'lin) ***n.*** A frightening hallucination.
hostile (häs't'l) ***adj.*** Not friendly.
hypocrisy (hi·päk'rə·sē) ***n.*** The pretense of feeling what one does not feel or of being what one is not.
hypothesis (hī·päth'ə·sis) ***n.*** An unproved theory temporarily accepted to explain certain facts.

illumine (i·lo͞o'min) ***v.*** To light.
imminence (im'ə·nəns) ***n.*** The quality of being likely to happen without delay; threatening.
impart (im·pärt') ***v.*** To make known; tell; reveal.
impassiveness (im·pas'iv·nis) ***n.*** The quality of not feeling or not showing emotion.
impede (im·pēd') ***v.*** To obstruct; hinder the progress of.
impel (im·pel') ***v.*** To force; push forward.
imperious (im·pir'ē·əs) ***adj.*** **1.** Urgent; imperative. **2.** Acting in a dictatorial manner; overbearing and arrogant.
impertinence (im·pur't'n·əns) ***n.*** Disrespect; insolence.
impervious (im·pur'vē·əs) ***adj.*** Not affected.
impetuous (im·pech'o͞o·wəs) ***adj.*** Acting with little or no thought; rash.
impious (im'pē·əs) ***adj.*** Lacking reverence for God.
implacable (im·plak'ə·b'l) ***adj.*** Relentless; not likely to be appeased or satisfied.
importunity (im'pôr·to͞on'ə·tē) ***n.*** Persistence in making a request or a demand.
impromptu (im·prämp'to͞o) ***adj.*** Without preparation; spur-of-the-moment; unrehearsed.
impropriety (im'prə·prī'ə·tē) ***n.*** The quality of being improper or inappropriate.
inalienable (in·āl'yən·ə·b'l) ***adj.*** Not capable of being taken away or transferred.
incessantly (in·ses''nt·lē) ***adv.*** Without interruption.
inconceivable (in'kən·sē'və·b'l) ***adj.*** Not able to be thought of, understood, imagined, or believed.
indiscreet (in'dis·krēt') ***adj.*** Unwise; without thought or judgment.

fat, āpe, cär; ten, ēven; is, bīte; gō, hôrn, to͞ol, look; oil, out; up, fur; get; joy; yet; chin; she; thin, ***then***; **zh,** leisure; **ŋ,** ring; ə for *a* in *ago, e* in *agent, i* in *sanity, o* in *comply, u* in *focus;* ' as in *able* (ā'b'l).

indiscriminate (in'dis·krim'ə·nit) ***adj.*** Not making careful choices or distinctions.
indolent (in'də·lənt) ***adj.*** Lazy; idle.
indubitably (in·do͞o'bi·tə·blē) ***adv.*** Beyond doubt; unquestionably.
inebriate (in·ē'brē·āt') ***v.*** To make drunk; intoxicate.
inert (in·urt') ***adj.*** Inactive; not moving.
inestimable (in·es'tə·mə·b'l) ***adj.*** Too great or valuable to be properly measured.
inevitable (in·ev'ə·tə·b'l) ***adj.*** Unavoidable.
infallible (in·fal'ə·b'l) ***adj.*** Unable to make an error. ***n.*** **Infallibility.**
infatuation (in·fach'o͞o·wā'shən) ***n.*** State of being carried away by foolish love or affection.
infidel (in'fə·d'l) ***n.*** Someone who does not believe in a particular religion.
ingress (in'gres) ***n.*** The act of going in; a way in; entrance.
iniquity (in·ik'wə·tē) ***n.*** Wickedness; evil; sin.
innuendo (in'yo͞o·wen'dō) ***n.*** An indirect remark or reference that implies something belittling or insulting; an insinuation.
insidious (in·sid'ē·əs) ***adj.*** Characterized by treachery or slyness; more dangerous than seems apparent.
insoluble (in·säl'yo͞o·b'l) ***adj.*** Without a solution.
insular (in'sə·lər) ***adj.*** Having the form of an island.
insuperable (in·so͞o'pər·ə·b'l) ***adj.*** Not able to be overcome or passed by.
insurgent (in·sur'jənt) ***n.*** Someone who rises up against established authority; a rebel.
interfuse (in'tər·fyo͞oz') ***v.*** To combine by mixing, blending, or fusing together.
interminable (in·tur'mi·nə·b'l) ***adj.*** Endless.
intermittent (in'tər·mit''nt) ***adj.*** Stopping and starting at intervals; periodic.
internecine (in'tər·nē'sin) ***adj.*** Mutually destructive or harmful; deadly or harmful to both sides of a conflict.
intimate (in'tə·māt') ***v.*** To make known indirectly; hint or imply.
intuition (in'to͞o·wish'ən) ***n. pl.*** The faculty that enables one to learn without the conscious use of reasoning.
invective (in·vek'tiv) ***n.*** A violent, abusive verbal attack.
iteration (it'ə·rā'shən) ***n.*** Repetition.
itinerant (ī·tin'ər·ənt) ***adj.*** Traveling from place to place.

jargon (jär'gən) ***n.*** **1.** Specialized terminology used by a particular group of people. **2.** Obscure and often pretentious language.
jaunty (jônt'ē) ***adj.*** Sprightly; perky; having an easy confidence.

laborious (lə·bôr'ē·əs) ***adj.*** Involving much hard work; difficult.
lament (lə·ment') ***v.*** To express deep sorrow; mourn.
leonine (lē'ə·nīn') ***adj.*** Like a lion.
loathsome (lōth'səm) ***adj.*** Disgusting; detestable.
loll (läl) ***v.*** **1.** To droop. **2.** To lounge about in a lazy, relaxed manner.
loquacity (lō·kwas'ə·tē) ***n.*** A tendency to talk excessively.
ludicrous (lo͞o'di·krəs) ***adj.*** Laughably ridiculous.

magnitude (mag'nə·to͞od') ***n.*** Greatness in size, extent, or influence.
malodorous (mal·ō'dər·əs) ***adj.*** Bad-smelling.
manifestation (man'ə·fes·tā'shən) ***n.*** Demonstration or expression.
manifold (man'ə·fōld') ***adj.*** Having many forms or parts.
maritime (mar'ə·tīm') ***adj.*** Having to do with the sea.
martial (mär'shəl) ***adj.*** Military; having to do with war.
mean (mēn) ***adj.*** Low in quality, value, or importance.
meditative (med'ə·tāt'iv) ***adj.*** Inclined to reflect upon and think deeply about ideas.
mesmerize (mez'mər·īz') ***v.*** To hypnotize; put in a trance.
mete (mēt) ***v.*** To give out measured portions; distribute.
meticulous (mə·tik'yo͞o·ləs) ***adj.*** Excessively careful about details; finicky.
mirth (murth) ***n.*** Joyfulness; merriment.
motley (mät'lē) ***adj.*** Made up of many different, often clashing, elements.
mottled (mät''ld) ***adj.*** Marked with streaks or blots.
multitudes (mul'tə·to͞odz') ***n. pl.*** Vast numbers.
murky (mur'kē) ***adj.*** Heavy with smoke or mist; dark and gloomy.
myriad (mir'ē·əd) ***adj.*** Of an indefinitely large number; innumerable.

nimble (nim'b'l) ***adj.*** Marked by quick light movement; marked by mental alertness.
nomadic (nō·mad'ik) ***adj.*** Characteristic of a wanderer who has no fixed home.
norms (nôrmz) ***n. pl.*** Standards or models for a group.

oblivious (ə·bliv'ē·əs) ***adj.*** Unmindful of; completely unaffected by.
obnoxious (əb·näk'shəs) ***adj.*** Very unpleasant; objectionable; offensive.
obsequious (əb·sē'kwē·əs) ***adj.*** Much too willing to serve or obey; overly submissive.
obstinancy (äb'stə·nə·sē) ***n.*** Stubbornness.
obtrude (əb·tro͞od') ***v.*** To thrust forward; push out.
occult (ə·kult') ***adj.*** Beyond human understanding; mysterious.
ominous (äm'ə·nəs) ***adj.*** Threatening; sinister; having the character of a prediction of evil.

1232

opulent (äp′yo͞o·lənt) ***adj.*** Rich; luxurious; abundant.
opulent (äp′yə·lənt) ***adj.*** Rich; luxurious; abundant.
orb ***n.*** A sphere.
ordeal (ôr·dēl′) ***n.*** A difficult or painful experience.
oscillate (äs′ə·lāt′) ***v.*** To swing or move regularly back and forth.
ostentatious (äs′tən·tā′shəs) ***adj.*** Characterized by a showy display of wealth, knowledge, etc.

pagan (pā′gən) ***n.*** A person who is not a Christian, a Moslem, or a Jew.
pallid (pal′id) ***adj.*** Pale; faint in color.
pallor (pal′ər) ***n.*** Paleness; lack of color.
paraphernalia (par′ə·fər·nāl′yə) ***n.*** Gear; equipment; any collection of things used in a certain activity.
pedestrian (pə·des′trē·ən) ***adj.*** Ordinary; dull.
pending (pen′diŋ) ***adj.*** Not yet decided or established.
pensive (pen′siv) ***adj.*** Thoughtful.
perturbation (pʉr′tər·bā′shən) ***n.*** Disturbance; great annoyance.
pestilential (pes′tə·len′shəl) ***adj.*** Full of contagious germs.
pickerel (pik′ər·əl) ***n.*** A small freshwater fish.
pigmentation (pig′mən·tā′shən) ***n.*** Coloration in plants or animals.
pique (pēk) ***v.*** To annoy.
placid (plas′id) ***adj.*** Calm; quiet.
plausible (plô′zə·b′l) ***adj.*** Seemingly true; believable.
plunder (plun′dər) ***n.*** Goods taken by force or fraud; loot.
politic (päl′ə·tik) ***adj.*** Having practical wisdom; shrewd; diplomatic.
pompous (päm′pəs) ***adj.*** Pretentious in speech or behavior; self-important.
portfolio (pôrt·fō′lē′ō′) ***n.*** A flat, portable case for carrying loose sheets of paper; a briefcase.
precedence (pres′ə·dəns) ***n.*** Priority; the act or right of preceding in importance.
precept (prē′sept) ***n.*** A rule of action or conduct.
premonitory (pri·män′ə·tôr′ē) ***adj.*** Relating to a feeling that something bad will soon happen.
preoccupied (prē·äk′yo͞o·pīd′) ***adj.*** Wholly absorbed in one's thoughts.
preposterous (prē·päs′tər·əs) ***adj.*** Absurd; ridiculously illogical.
presage (prē·sāj′) ***v.*** To give a warning of future evil.
prevail (prē·vāl′) ***v.*** To gain the advantage or mastery; be victorious; triumph.
prevalent (prev′ə·lənt) ***adj.*** Generally practiced or accepted.
prodigal (präd′i·gəl) ***adj.*** Wasteful.
profane (prō·fān′) ***adj.*** Showing disrespect or contempt for sacred things.
prostrate (präs′trāt) ***adj.*** Lying with the face down, in demonstration of great humility.
protocol (prōt′ə·kôl′) ***n.*** **1.** Any set of rules governing behavior, natural or artificial. **2.** The code of ceremonial rites and courtesies accepted as proper in official dealings.
provoke (prō·vōk′) ***v.*** To anger, irritate, or annoy; stir up.
prudent (pro͞od′nt) ***adj.*** Cautious; capable of sound judgment.
pugilistic (pyo͞o′jil·is′tik) ***adj.*** Inclined to fistfighting.
pulverize (pul′və·rīz′) ***v.*** To crush or grind into a powder or dust.

quail (kwāl) ***v.*** To draw back in fear.
quell (kwel) ***v.*** To quiet; put an end to.
querulous (kwer′ə·ləs) ***adj.*** Inclined to find fault; full of complaint.

rakish (rā′kish) ***adj.*** Dashing, careless.
ravening (rav′′n·iŋ) ***adj.*** Greedily or wildly hungry.
realm (relm) ***n.*** Region or area.
reconnoiter (rē′kə·noit′ər) ***v.*** To make a survey or careful examination of an area.
rectify (rek′tə·fī′) ***v.*** To correct; set right.
remonstrance (ri·män′strəns) ***n.*** A protest or complaint.
remote (ri·mōt′) ***adj.*** Far away; secluded.
rend (rend) ***v.*** To tear or rip.
repose (ri·pōz′) ***n.*** Rest; sleep; freedom from worry.
reprobate (rep′rə·bāt′) ***v.*** To disapprove of strongly; condemn.
repugnant (ri·pug′nənt) ***adj.*** Distasteful; offensive; disagreeable.
retinue (ret′n·yo͞o) ***n.*** Group of attendants.
revere (ri·vir′) ***v.*** To regard with deep respect or love.
revery (rev′ər·ē) ***n.*** Daydream.
robust (rō·bust′) ***adj.*** Strong and healthy.
row (rou) ***n.*** A noisy quarrel or disturbance.
ruse (ro͞oz) ***n.*** A trick meant to deceive someone.

sage (sāj) ***n.*** A wise person respected for experience and judgment.
scoff (skäf) ***v.*** To make fun of by showing contempt or scorn.
scrimmage (skrim′ij) ***n.*** A brief, disorganized battle.
scrupulous (skro͞o′pyə·ləs) ***adj.*** Demanding precision, care, and exactness.

fat, āpe, cär; ten, ēven; is, bīte; gō, hôrn, to͞ol, look; oil, out; up, fʉr; get; joy; yet; chin; she; thin, *th*en; zh, leisure; ŋ, ring; ə for *a* in *ago, e* in *agent, i* in *sanity, o* in *comply, u* in *focus;* ′ as in *able* (ā′b′l).

1233

scuttle (skut′'l) *v.* To run quickly away from danger or trouble.
sentience (sen′shəns) *n.* Capacity for feeling or perceiving; consciousness.
sentinel (sen′ti·n'l) *n.* A guard set to protect a group.
skein (skān) *n.* Thread or yarn wound in a coil.
skulk (skulk) *v.* To move in a sneaky or sinister manner.
slough (slo͞o) *n.* A swamp.
slovenly (sluv′ən·lē) *adj.* Careless in appearance or habits.
smote (smōt) *v.* Hit or struck hard. (Past tense of *smite*.)
solace (säl′is) *n.* An easing of grief, loneliness, or discomfort.
spasm (spaz′m) *n.* A sudden, violent, temporary activity.
speckled (spek′'ld) *adj.* Covered with small marks of contrasting colors.
spy (spī) *v.* To notice.
squabble (skwäb′'l) *n.* A noisy, petty quarrel or dispute.
stanchion (stan′chən) *n.* An upright bar, beam, or post used as a support.
starkly (stärk′lē) *adv.* In an unsoftened or unembellished way.
stoicism (stō′i·siz′m) *n.* Unemotional acceptance of both pleasure and pain.
stolid (stäl′id) *adj.* Having or showing little or no emotion or sensitivity.
submissive (sub·mis′iv) *adj.* Obedient; yielding; tending to give in without resistance.
suffused (sə·fyo͞ozd′) *adj.* Filled with a glow or color.
sundry (sun′drē) *adj.* Various; miscellaneous.
supinely (so͞o·pīn′lē) *adv.* Lying on the back, face upward.
surfeit (sʉr′fit) *n.* Excessive amount.
symmetrical (si·met′ri·k'l) *adj.* Having the same form or arrangement on each side.
symptomatic (simp′tə·mat′ik) *adj.* Showing symptoms or signs of.

tactile (tak′t'l) *adj.* Able to be perceived by the sense of touch.
taunt (tônt) *v.* To tease in scornful or sarcastic language.
tedious (tē′dē·əs) *adj.* Tiresome; boring.
temporal (tem′pər·əl) *adj.* Worldly, not spiritual.
tendrils (ten′drəlz) *n. pl.* Threadlike parts of a climbing plant that coil around an object.
tentatively (ten′tə·tiv·lē) *adv.* Timidly; with hesitation or uncertainty.
tepid (tep′id) *adj.* Lukewarm; lacking warmth of feeling or enthusiasm.
till (til) *v.* To cultivate, in order to raise crops.
transfixed (trans·fikst′) *adj.* Made motionless, as if fastened to a spot.
translucent (trans·lo͞o′s'nt) *adj.* Allowing light to pass through.
travail (trav′āl) *n.* Intense pain; agony.
travesty (trav′is·tē) *v.* To make fun of by doing an exaggerated imitation; ridicule.
trepidation (trep′ə·dā′shən) *n.* Fearful uncertainty; anxiety.
tumultuous (to͞o·mul′cho͞o·wəs) *adj.* Wild and noisy; greatly agitated.
turgid (tʉr′jid) *adj.* Overstated in a self-important way; pompous.
turmoil (tʉr′moil) *n.* Commotion; uproar; confusion.

unseemly (un·sēm′lē) *adj.* Improper; indecent.
upbraid (up·brād′) *v.* To scold severely or bitterly.
utilitarian (yo͞o·til′ə·ter′ē·ən) *adj.* Stressing usefulness over beauty and other values.

vain (vān′) *adj.* **1.** Futile; ineffectual. **2.** Conceited.
vanquish (vaŋ′kwish) *v.* To defeat.
velocity (və·läs′ə·tē) *n.* Speed.
venerable (ven′ər·ə·b'l) *adj.* Worthy of respect or reverence.
venomous (ven′əm·əs) *adj.* Poisonous; intended to harm.
vex (veks) *v.* To annoy; irritate.
vigilance (vij′ə·ləns) *n.* Watchfulness; alertness.
vindictive (vin·dik′tiv) *adj.* Revengeful in spirit; seeking revenge.
vivacity (vi·vas′ə·tē) *n.* Liveliness of spirit; animation.
vivid (viv′id) *adj.* Forming clear or striking mental images; strong; active.
volition (vō·lish′ən) *n.* A conscious or deliberate decision or choice.
vulnerability (vul′nər·ə·bil′ə·tē) *n.* Openness to attack or criticism; a condition of being easily hurt.

wanton (wän′t'n) *adj.* Unprovoked and unjustifiable; deliberately hurtful.
wax (waks) *v.* To become.
waylay (wā′lā′) *v.* To ambush; wait for and attack.
wrench (rench) *v.* To twist, pull, or jerk suddenly and violently.
wrest (rest) *v.* To take by force or violence.

yawp (yôp) *n.* Rough, vigorous language.

zealous (zel′əs) *adj.* Fervent; enthusiastic; devoted to a purpose or mission.

INDEX OF SKILLS

LITERARY SKILLS

LANGUAGE AND STYLE SKILLS

Most of the page numbers listed below refer to discussions that appear in the **Analyzing Language and Style** exercises. Additional page references for some terms may also be found in the Literary Skills index.

SPEAKING AND LISTENING SKILLS

COMPOSITION AND CRITICAL THINKING SKILLS

Writing: A Creative Response

Writing: A Critical Response

CRITICAL THINKING EXERCISES

The following is a list of the two-page exercises that follow each unit, in which critical thinking skills are taught step by step following the stages of the writing process. Additional exercises calling for critical thinking, including the skill of synthesis, are found in the composition assignments indexed on pages 1237–1238. The following exercises are listed in the order in which they appear in the text.

INDEX OF COMMENTARIES

From *Black Boy* by Richard Wright. Copyright 1937, 1942, 1944, 1945 by Richard Wright. ***Harvard University Press and the Trustees of Amherst College:*** "Because I could not stop for Death," "A Bird came down the Walk," "Heart! We Will Forget him!," "I died for Beauty—but was scarce," "I Heard a Fly Buzz—when I died," "I never saw a Moor," "If you were coming in the Fall," from "Success is counted sweetest," "The Soul selects her own Society," and "Tell all the Truth" from *The Poems of Emily Dickinson,* edited by Thomas H. Johnson, Cambridge, Mass.: The Belknap Press of Harvard University Press. Copyright 1951, © 1955, 1979, 1983 by the President and Fellows of Harvard College. ***Hill and Wang, a division of Farrar, Straus and Giroux, Inc.:*** From *Night* by Elie Wiesel, translated by Stella Rodway. English translation copyright © 1960 by MacGibbon and Kee. ***Henry Holt and Company, Inc.:*** From *Israfel: The Life and Times of Edgar Allan Poe* by Hervey Allen. Copyright 1926 by Hervey Allen; copyright renewed 1954 by Ann Andrews Allen. "Indian Boarding School: The Runaways" from *Jacklight: Poems* by Louise Erdrich. Copyright © 1984 by Louise Erdrich. First appeared in *Frontiers* magazine. "The Death of the Hired Man," "Design," "Mending Wall," "Neither Out Far Nor In Deep," "Nothing Gold Can Stay," and "Once by the Pacific" from *The Poetry of Robert Frost,* edited by Edward Connery Lathem. Copyright 1923, 1928, 1930, 1939, © 1969 by Holt, Rinehart and Winston; copyright 1936, 1951, © 1956, 1958 by Robert Frost. From *Across Spoon River: An Autobiography* by Edgar Lee Masters. Copyright 1936 by Edgar Lee Masters. Copyright © 1964 by Ellen Coyne Masters. From *The Bluest Eye* by Toni Morrison. Copyright © 1970 by Toni Morrison. ***Houghton Mifflin Co.:*** "Riding the Elevator into the Sky" from *The Awful Rowing Toward God* by Anne Sexton. Copyright © 1975 by Loring Conant, Jr., Executor of the Estate of Anne Sexton. ***International Creative Management, Inc.:*** "Speaking of Courage" by Tim O'Brien from *The Massachusetts Review,* vol. XVII, no. 2, Summer 1976. Copyright © 1976 by Tim O'Brien. ***Mary Jarrell:*** From "Obscurity of the Poet" from *Poetry and the Age* by Randall Jarrell. Copyright 1951, 1953 by Randall Jarrell. ***Alfred A. Knopf, Inc.:*** From *Dispatches* (Retitled: "The Highlands," "Tell My Folks . . . ," "The Wounded," "The Correspondents," "Back Home," "Remembering the Dead," and "The War Ends") by Michael Herr. Copyright © 1977 by Michael Herr. "A Noiseless Flash" from *Hiroshima* by John Hersey. Copyright renewed 1973 by John Hersey. "Dream Deferred" (Retitled: "Harlem") from *The Panther and the Lash* by Langston Hughes. Copyright 1926 by Alfred A. Knopf, Inc., and renewed 1951 by Langston Hughes. "Harlem," "I, Too," and "The Weary Blues" from *Selected Poems of Langston Hughes.* Copyright 1926, 1948 by Alfred A. Knopf, Inc.; renewed 1954 by Langston Hughes. From "Obscurity of the Poet" from *Poetry and the Age* by Randall Jarrell. Copyright 1951, 1953 by Randall Jarrell. From *An American Procession* by Alfred Kazin. Copyright © 1984 by Alfred Kazin. From *The Woman Warrior* by Maxine Hong Kingston. Copyright © 1975, 1976 by Maxine Hong Kingston. "Spinster" from *The Colossus and Other Poems* by Sylvia Plath. Copyright © 1961 by Sylvia Plath. "Bells for John Whiteside's Daughter" from *Selected Poems, Third Edition, Revised and Enlarged* by John Crowe Ransom. Copyright 1924 by Alfred A. Knopf, Inc., and renewed 1952 by John Crowe Ransom. "Parting Without a Sequel" from *Selected Poems, Third Edition, Revised and Enlarged* by John Crowe Ransom. Copyright 1927 by Alfred A. Knopf, Inc., and renewed 1955 by John Crowe Ransom. "Anecdote of the Jar," "The Death of a Soldier," and "Disillusionment of Ten O'Clock" from *The Collected Poems of Wallace Stevens.* Copyright 1923 and renewed 1951 by Wallace Stevens. From *Letters of Wallace Stevens,* selected and edited by Holly Stevens. Copyright © 1966 by Holly Stevens. From "Of Modern Poetry" from *The Collected Poems of Wallace Stevens.* Copyright 1942 by Wallace Stevens; copyright renewed © 1970 by Holly Stevens. "Son" from *Problems and Other Stories* by John Updike. Copyright © 1973 by John Updike. From "1865: The Better Angels of Our Nature" from *The Civil War: An Illustrated History* by Geoffrey C. Ward, based on a documentary filmscript by Geoffrey C. Ward, Ric Burns, and Ken Burns. Copyright © 1990 by American Documentaries, Inc. ***Rozanne Knudson, Executor of the Literary Estate of May Swenson:*** From the Introduction by May Swenson from *Spoon River Anthology* by Edgar Lee Masters. Published by Macmillan Publishing Company. ***Lescher & Lescher, Ltd.:*** "Huckleberry Finn: The Little Lower Layer" from *Three Bags Full: Essays in American Fiction* by Philip Young. Copyright © 1952, 1972 by Philip Young. ***Little, Brown and Company:*** From *Longfellow: His Life and Work* by Newton Arvin. Copyright © 1963 by Newton Arvin. From "Why I Like Country Music" from *Elbow Room* by James Alan McPherson. Slightly abridged. Copyright © 1974 by James Alan McPherson. From "Out East" from *Ivy Days: Making My Way Out East* by Susan Allen Toth. Copyright © 1984 by Susan Allen Toth. ***Little, Brown and Company, in association with The Atlantic Monthly Press:*** From *Blue Highways: A Journey into America* by William Least Heat Moon. Copyright © 1982 by William Least Heat Moon. ***Liveright Publishing Corporation:*** "what if a much of a which of a wind" and from Introduction to *New Poems* from *Collected Poems, 1913–1962* by E. E. Cummings. Copyright © 1923, 1925, 1931, 1935, 1938, 1939, 1940, 1944, 1945, 1946, 1947, 1948, 1949, 1950, 1951, 1952, 1953, 1954, 1955, 1956, 1957, 1958, 1959, 1960, 1961, 1962 by the Trustees for the E. E. Cummings Trust; copyright © 1961, 1963, 1968 by Marion Morehouse Cummings. "nobody loses all the time" from *IS 5, poems* by E. E. Cummings. Copyright 1926 by Horace Liveright; copyright renewed 1954 by E. E. Cummings. "Summertime and the Living . . ." from *Angle of Ascent, New and Selected Poems* by Robert Hayden. Copyright © 1966, 1970, 1972, 1975 by Robert Hayden. ***Macmillan Publishing Company:*** "Poetry" from *Collected Poems of Marianne Moore.* Copyright 1935 by Marianne Moore; copyright renewed © 1963 by Marianne Moore and T. S. Eliot. ***Robert MacNeil and Reader's Digest:*** From "The Trouble with Television" delivered by Robert MacNeil at The President's Leadership Forum, State University of New York at Purchase, November 13, 1984. Originally appeared in *Reader's Digest,* March 1985. ***Ellen C. Masters:*** "Butch Weldy," "Lucinda Matlock," "Mrs. George Reece," and "Richard Bone" from *Spoon River Anthology* by Edgar Lee Masters. Published by Macmillan Publishing Company. ***McIntosh and Otis, Inc.:*** From John Steinbeck's Acceptance Speech for the Nobel Prize for literature in 1962. Copyright © 1963 by John Steinbeck. Originally published in *Vogue* Magazine, March 1, 1963. ***Merriam-Webster Inc:*** The definition "proud" from *Webster's Third International Dictionary.* Copyright © 1986 by Merriam-Webster Inc., publisher of the Merriam-Webster® dictionaries. ***James Merrill:*** "Kite Poem" from *First Poems* by James Merrill. Copyright 1950 by Alfred A. Knopf, Inc.: copyright renewed © 1978 by James Merrill. ***William Morrow Co.:*** From *Kate Chopin* by Emily Toth. Copyright © 1990 by Emily Toth. ***Ellen Neuwald, Inc.:*** From a quote by David Rabe from *Dispatches* by Michael Herr. ***New Directions Publishing Corporation:*** From "Letters to Francis Scott Fitzgerald" from *The Crack Up* by F. Scott Fitzgerald. Copyright 1945 by New Directions Publishing Corporation. "The Garden," "In a Station of the Metro," "A Pact," and

1239

"The River Merchant's Wife" from *Personae* by Ezra Pound. Copyright 1926 by Ezra Pound. "Letter to Harriet Monroe" by Ezra Pound from *Selected Letters 1907–1941*. Copyright 1950 by Ezra Pound. "The Red Wheelbarrow," "Spring and All," and "Tract" by William Carlos Williams. Copyright 1938 by New Directions Publishing Corporation. From *The Autobiography of William Carlos Williams*. Copyright 1951 by William Carlos Williams. "The Great Figure" from *Collected Poems, Volume 1: 1909–1939* by William Carlos Williams. Copyright 1938 by New Directions Publishing Corporation. ***New World Dictionaries, A division of Simon & Schuster, Inc., New York, NY:*** From *Webster's New World Dictionary of the American Language*, Second College Edition. Copyright © 1986 by Simon & Schuster, Inc. ***The New York Times Company:*** "Little Red Riding Hood Revisited" by Russell Baker from *The New York Times*, January 13, 1980. Copyright © 1980 by The New York Times Company. "School vs. Education" by Russell Baker from *The New York Times*, September 9, 1975. Copyright © 1975 by The New York Times Company. From "Robert Frost Relieves His Mind" by Rose C. Feld, from *The New York Times Book Review*, October 21, 1923. Copyright © 1923 by The New York Times Company. From "Fitzgerald Revisited" by Jay McInerney (review of *The Short Stories of F. Scott Fitzgerald*) from *The New York Times*, Sunday Book Review, August 15, 1991. Copyright © 1991 by The New York Times Company. From "Master Republican" by Alden Todd (review of *James Madison, The Founding Father*) from *The New York Times Book Review*, December 13, 1987. Copyright © 1987 by The New York Times Company. "The Importance of Being Remembered" by Susan Allen Toth from *The New York Times Book Review*, June 28, 1987. Copyright © 1987 by The New York Times Company. ***The New Yorker:*** From "James Thurber" from *The New Yorker*, November 11, 1961. Copyright © 1961 by The New Yorker Magazine, Inc. From "Medicine of Make-Believe" by Brendan Gill from *The New Yorker*, December 12, 1983. Copyright © 1983 by Brendan Gill. ***W. W. Norton:*** "Power" from *The Fact of a Doorframe, Poems Selected and New, 1950–1984* by Adrienne Rich. Copyright © 1975, 1978 by W. W. Norton & Company, Inc.; copyright © 1981, 1984 by Adrienne Rich. Excerpt by Anne Tyler from *The Writer on Her Work*, edited by Janet Sternburg. Copyright © 1980 by Janet Sternburg. ***Harold Ober Associates Incorporated:*** "The Egg" by Sherwood Anderson. Copyright 1921 by B. W. Huebsch, Inc.; copyright renewed 1948 by Eleanor C. Anderson. From *Letters of Sherwood Anderson*, edited by H. M. Jones and Walter Rideout. Copyright 1953 by Eleanor Anderson; copyright renewed © 1981 by Eleanor Copenhaver Anderson. Published by Little, Brown and Company. ***Simon J. Ortiz:*** "Washyuma Motor Hotel" from *Going for the Rain* by Simon J. Ortiz. Copyright © 1976 by Simon J. Ortiz. ***Oxford University Press, Inc.:*** From *The Great War and Modern Memory* by Paul Fussell. Copyright © 1975 by Oxford University Press, Inc. Footnotes omitted. From *The Life of Langston Hughes, Volume 1: 1902–1941* by Arnold Rampersad. Copyright © 1986 by Arnold Rampersad. ***Pantheon Books, a division of Random House, Inc.:*** "Grandmother Spider Steals the Sun" from *American Indian Myths and Legends* by Richard Erdoes and Alfonso Ortiz. Copyright © 1984 by Richard Erdoes and Alfonso Ortiz. ***Prentice Hall:*** From *The Scope of Fiction* by Robert Penn Warren and Cleanth Brooks. Copyright © 1960 by Appleton-Century-Crofts, Inc. ***Publisher's Weekly:*** Quote by E. B. White from *Publisher's Weekly*, December 6, 1971. Copyright © 1971 by Xerox Corporation. Published by R. R. Bowker Company, a Xerox company. ***The Putnam Publishing Group:*** From *The Joy Luck Club* by Amy Tan. Copyright © 1989 by Amy Tan. ***Random House, Inc.:*** "The Unknown Citizen" from *W. H. Auden: Collected Poems* by W. H. Auden, edited by Edward Mendelson. Copyright 1940 and renewed © 1968 by W. H. Auden. From "My Man Bovanne" from *Gorilla, My Love* by Toni Cade Bambara. Copyright © 1972 by Toni Cade Bambara. From *The Americans: The National Experience* by Daniel Boorstin. Copyright © 1965 by Daniel Boorstin. "A Rose for Emily" by William Faulkner from *Collected Stories of William Faulkner*. Copyright 1930 and renewed © 1958 by William Faulkner. From "William Faulkner's Speech of Acceptance upon the award of the Nobel Prize for Literature" from *The Faulkner Reader*. Copyright 1954 by William Faulkner. From *A Raisin in the Sun* by Lorraine Hansberry. Copyright © 1958 by Robert Nemiroff, as an unpublished work. Copyright © 1959, 1966, 1984 by Robert Nemiroff. Slightly adapted. "Love the Wild Swan" from *The Selected Poetry of Robinson Jeffers*. Copyright 1935 and renewed © 1963 by Donnan Jeffers and Garth Jeffers. "Shine, Perishing Republic" from *The Selected Poetry of Robinson Jeffers*. Copyright 1925 and renewed 1953 by Robinson Jeffers. From "New African" from *Sarah Phillips* by Andrea Lee. Copyright © 1984 by Andrea Lee. From *Hugging the Shore* by John Updike. Copyright © 1983 by John Updike. "Small Eternity" from *Rumor Verified: Poems 1979–1980* by Robert Penn Warren. Copyright © 1979, 1980, 1981 by Robert Penn Warren. "Is Phoenix Jackson's Grandson Really Dead?" from *The Eye of the Story: Selected Essays and Reviews* by Eudora Welty. Copyright © 1978 by Eudora Welty. From *The Glass Menagerie* by Tennessee Williams. Copyright 1945 by Tennessee Williams and Edwina D. Williams; copyright renewed © 1973 by Tennessee Williams. ***Russell & Volkening as agents for Anne Tyler:*** "Your Place Is Empty" by Anne Tyler. Copyright © 1976 by Anne Tyler. Originally appeared in *The New Yorker*, November 22, 1976. ***St. Martin's Press, Inc.:*** From *American Literature: The Makers and the Making*, Volume II, edited by Cleanth Brooks, R. W. B. Lewis, and Robert Penn Warren. Copyright © 1973 by St. Martin's Press. From "A Rose for Emily (1930)" from *American Literature: The Makers and the Making*, Volume II, edited by Cleanth Brooks, R. W. B. Lewis, and Robert Penn Warren. Copyright © 1973 by St. Martin's Press, Inc. ***The Saturday Evening Post Society:*** From "I Saw Lee Surrender" by Seth M. Flint from *The Saturday Evening Post*, vol. 248, no. 5, July/August 1976. Copyright © 1976 by The Saturday Evening Post Company. ***John Sayles:*** From "I-80 Nebraska M.490-M.205" by John Sayles from *The Atlantic Monthly*, May 1975. Copyright © 1975 by John Sayles. ***Charles Scribner's Sons, an imprint of Macmillan Publishing Company:*** "Winter Dreams" from *All the Sad Young Men* by F. Scott Fitzgerald. Copyright 1922 by Metropolitan Publications, Inc.; copyright renewed 1950 by Frances Scott Fitzgerald Lanahan. "In Another Country" from *Men Without Women* by Ernest Hemingway. Copyright 1927 by Charles Scribner's Sons; copyright renewed © 1955 by Ernest Hemingway. From "Haircut" from *Haircut and Other Stories* by Ring Lardner. Copyright 1925, 1953 by Ellis A. Lardner. ***Simon & Schuster, Inc.:*** From "Catch-22: The Great American Trap" from *Catch-22* by Joseph Heller. Copyright © 1955, 1961 by Joseph Heller. ***Sunstone Press:*** "Breath of Life" by Frank Hamilton Cushing and "Song of the Sky Loom" from *Songs of the Tewa*, translated by Dr. Herbert Joseph Spinden from *Four Winds: Poems from Indian Rituals* by Gene Meany Hodge. Copyright © 1977 by Gene Meany Hodge. ***Joan Chatfield Taylor:*** From "Cosmo Talks to Amy Tan" from *Cosmopolitan*, November 1989, p. 178. Copyright © 1989 by Hearst Corporation. ***Rosemary Thurber:*** "The Secret Life of Walter Mitty" from *My World—And Welcome to It* by James Thurber. Copyright 1942 by James Thurber; copy-

1240

right © 1970 by Helen W. Thurber and Rosemary T. Sauers. ***Time Warner Inc.:*** From "Book of Changes" by Paul Gray from *Time*, December 6, 1976. Copyright © 1976 by Time Warner Inc. ***Twayne Publishers, a division of G. K. Hall & Co., Boston:*** "America" from *Selected Poems of Claude McKay*. Copyright © 1981 by Twayne Publishers, a division of G. K. Hall & Co. ***Universal Press Syndicate:*** "Coyote Finishes His Work" from *Giving Birth to Thunder, Sleeping with His Daughter: Coyote Builds North America* by Barry Lopez. Copyright © 1977 by Barry Holstun Lopez. ***University of Arizona Press:*** From "Whatever Is Really Yours" from *Survival This Way: Interviews with American Indian Poets* by Joseph Bruchac. Copyright © 1987 by The Arizona Board of Regents. All rights reserved. ***University of New Mexico Press:*** From *The Way to Rainy Mountain* by N. Scott Momaday. Copyright © 1969 by The University of New Mexico Press. First published in *The Reporter*, January 26, 1967. ***Amanda Urban as Agent for Toni Morrison:*** From *The Bluest Eye* by Toni Morrison. Copyright © 1970 by Toni Morrison. ***Viking Penguin, a division of Penguin Books USA Inc.:*** From Introduction from *Penguin Book of Contemporary Essays* by Maureen Howard. Introduction, selection, and compilation copyright © 1984 by Maureen Howard. "Go Down Death—A Funeral Sermon," "Preface" from *God's Trombones* by James Weldon Johnson. Copyright 1927 by The Viking Press, Inc., copyright renewed © 1955 by Grace Nail Johnson. From *Studies in Classic American Literature* by D. H. Lawrence. Copyright 1923 by Thomas Seltzer, Inc.; renewed 1950 by Frieda Lawrence; copyright © 1961 by The Estate of Mrs. Frieda Lawrence. From *Death of a Salesman* by Arthur Miller. Copyright 1949, © 1977 by Arthur Miller. "The Steeple-Jack" from *The Complete Poems of Marianne Moore*. Copyright 1951, © 1970 by Marianne Moore; copyright renewed © 1979 by Lawrence E. Brinn and Louise Cranee, Executors of the Estate of Marianne Moore. "The Leader of the People" from *The Red Pony* by John Steinbeck. Copyright 1933, 1937, 1938, © renewed 1961, 1965, 1966 by John Steinbeck. "Ceti" from *The Lives of a Cell* by Lewis Thomas. Copyright © 1972 by The Massachusetts Medical Society. From *Benjamin Franklin* by Carl Van Doren. Copyright 1938 by Carl Van Doren; renewed © 1966 by Margaret Van Doren Bevans, Anne Van Doren Ross, and Barbara Van Doren Klaw. ***Vintage Press, a division of Random House, Inc.:*** From *The Odyssey* by Homer, translated by Robert Fitzgerald. Copyright © 1963 by Robert Fitzgerald. ***The Washington Post:*** From "Mah-Jongg and the Ladies of the Club" by Susan Dooley from "Book World," page 7, from *The Washington Post*, March 5, 1989. Copyright © 1989 by *The Washington Post*. ***Wesleyan University Press and University Press of New England:*** "Blessing" from *The Branch Will Not Break* by James Wright. Copyright © 1961 by James Wright. "Sled Burial, Dream Ceremony" from *Poems 1957–1967* by James Dickey. Copyright © 1965 by James Dickey. ***Wylie, Aitken & Stone, Inc., as agents for the Estate of Donald Barthelme:*** "Game" from *Unspeakable Practices, Unnatural Acts* by Donald Barthelme. Copyright © 1965, 1968 by Donald Barthelme. Originally published in *The New Yorker*. ***William K. Zinsser:*** From *On Writing Well*, Third Edition, by William Zinsser. Copyright © 1976, 1980, 1985 by William K. Zinsser.

1241

PICTURE CREDITS Table of Contents credits appear at the end of the PICTURE CREDITS. **Unit 1** p. 3 top rt.: Culver Pictures; p. 3 bottom left: Laurie Platt Winfrey, Inc.; p. 9: The Granger Collection, New York; p. 29: The New York Public Library; p. 33: The Granger Collection, New York; p. 36: The Bettmann Archive; p. 48: Frans Lanting/Photo Researchers, Inc.; p. 55: Rare Books and Manuscripts Division, The New York Public Library, Astor, Lenox and Tilden Foundations. p. 59 top rt.: Sun or Moon symbol courtesy of the Museum of Northern Arizona, Flagstaff. **Unit 2** p. 65: Photo: Schoonover Studios, Ltd.; p. 75: The Granger Collection, New York; p. 89: The Granger Collection, New York; p. 93: The Bettmann Archive; p. 100: Independence National Historic Park; p. 109: The Granger Collection, New York. **Unit 3** p. 118: Laurie Platt Winfrey, Inc.; p. 122 top: The Bettmann Archive; p. 122 bottom: Kaari Ward; p. 124: The Max Polster Archive; p. 138: The National Academy of Design; p. 140: Bill Wilson/Photo Researchers; p. 146: The Bettmann Archive; p. 152: The Granger Collection, New York; p. 155: John Lewis Stage/The Image Bank; p. 156: The Granger Collection, New York; p. 161: The Granger Collection, New York; p. 162: Phillip N. Known/Stock, Boston; p. 165: Scott Camazzine/Photo Researchers; p. 167: The Granger Collection, New York; p. 169: Giraudon/Art Resource, New York; p. 171: Omni International; p. 173: Culver Pictures; p. 175: Murray Belsky. **Unit 4** p. 181: Culver Pictures; p. 183: The Bettmann Archive; p. 184: The Bettmann Archive; p. 185: Rebus, Inc.; p. 186: Rebus, Inc.; p. 189: The Bettmann Archive; p. 192: Art Resource; p. 197: Stuart Cohen/Stock, Boston; p. 198: Michael Gadomski, Bruce Coleman Inc.; p. 201: Margaret Durrance/Photo Researchers; p. 203: David E. Scherman; p. 210: Eliot Porter; p. 226: The Bettmann Archive; p. 229: The Granger Collection, New York; p. 235: New York Public Library, Prints Division; p. 249: Lee Boltin; p. 252: Historic New Orleans Collection; p. 253: Nimatallah/Art Resource, New York; p. 256: Photo: Antonio Frasconi; p. 263: The Bettmann Archive; p. 294: Culver Pictures; p. 295: The Lighthouse Museum, Stonington, Connecticut. **Unit 5** p. 324: Rare Books and Manuscripts Division, The New York Public Library, Astor, Lenox and Tilden Foundations; p. 325: Culver Pictures; p. 326: The Granger Collection, New York; p. 329: Culver Pictures; p. 341: © Steven Kaufman/Peter Arnold Inc.; p. 349: The Bettmann Archive; p. 352: Culver Pictures; p. 354: Sotheby's; p. 356: Jerry L. Thompson; p. 359: Sotheby's; p. 361: © S. J. Krasemann/Peter Arnold; p. 365: International Museum of Photography at George Eastman House, Rochester, New York; p. 366: Steven J. Krasemann/Photo Researchers; p. 368: Bill Ivey/Photo Researchers; p. 369: Stephen Dalton/Photo Researchers. **Unit 6** p. 376: The New York Public Library, Rare Book Division; p. 378: The National Archives; p. 379: The Library of Congress; p. 380: International Museum of Photography at George Eastman House, Rochester, New York; p. 381: International Museum of Photography at George Eastman House, Rochester, New York; p. 384: Laurie Platt Winfrey, Inc.; p. 385: Collection of Robert Weinstein; p. 393: Culver Pictures; p. 401: Arizona Pioneer Historical Society; p. 402: The Bettmann Archive; p. 430: The Bettmann Archive; p. 439: (left) Samuel Higginbotham Orange; Photo by Larry Sherer; (right) Massachusetts Historical Society; p. 441: Library of Congress; p. 442: (knife) Museum of the Confederacy, from *The Civil War: Confederate Ordeal.* Photo by Larry Scherer. © 1984 Time-Life Books Inc. (sword) Craig Caba. Photo by Larry Sherer. (cap) Craig Nannos, from *The Civil War: Decoying the Yanks.* Photo by Larry Sherer. © 1984 Time-Life Books Inc.; pp. 442–443: (rifle) Mollus, from *The Civil War: Fight for Chattanooga.* Photo by Larry Sherer. © 1985 Time-Life Books Inc.; p. 443: (canteen) Russ A. Pritchard, from *The Civil War: Confederate Ordeal.* Photo by Larry Sherer. © 1984 Time-Life Books Inc. (shoes) Museum of the Confederacy, from *The Civil War: Confederate Ordeal.* Photo by Larry Sherer. © 1984 Time-Life Books Inc. (cap) Museum of the Confederacy, from *The Civil War: Decoying the Yanks.* Photo by Larry Sherer. © 1984 Time-Life Books Inc. (cartridges) Museum of the Confederacy, from *The Civil War: Master Index.* Photo by Larry Sherer. © 1987 Time-Life Books Inc. (purse) Howard Wert Collection, from *The Civil War: Gettysburg.* Photo by Larry Sherer. © 1985 Time-Life Books Inc. (photo, left) Atlanta Historical Society; (photo, right) Eleanor S. Brockenbrough Library, The Museum of the Confederacy, Richmond. Photo by Katherine Wetzel. (postmark) George Fistrovich; p. 445: Library of Congress; p. 446: (center) Chicago Historical Society; (bottom) Library of Congress; p. 447: Massachusetts Commandery Military Order of the Loyal Legion and the U.S. Army Military History Institute; p. 449: (left) Museum of the Confederacy, from *The Civil War: Tenting Tonight.* Photo by Larry Sherer. © 1984 Time-Life Books Inc. (right) George Fistrovich; p. 451: (left) Historical Picture Services; (right) Library of Congress; pp. 452, 452–453 bottom: Library of Congress; p. 453 top: (detail) The Lincoln Museum, Fort Wayne, Indiana, a part of Lincoln National Corporation; p. 454: (top rt.) Library of Congress; (bottom) Appomattox Court House National Historical Park, National Park Service, U.S. Department of the Interior, from *The Civil War: Pursuit to Appomattox.* Photo by Ronald Jennings. © 1987 Time-Life Books Inc.; p. 455: The Bettmann Archive; p. 456: The University of Virginia Library; pp. 458–459: Antietam Battlefield Park, from *The Civil War: Bloodiest Day.* Photo by Larry Sherer. © 1984 Time-Life Books Inc; p. 480: Missouri Historical Society. **Unit 7** p. 494: Culver Pictures; p. 496: Culver Pictures; p. 497: The New York Public Library; p. 498: David E. Scherman; p. 499: Rebus, Inc.; p. 501: Culver Pictures; p. 503: Joseph Martin/Art Resource, New York; p. 510: The Bettmann Archive; p. 513: Photographic Archives, The University of Louisville; p. 517: The Bettmann Archive; p. 525: Culver Pictures; p. 533: The Bettmann Archive; p. 536: Peter Fiore/The Image Bank; p. 543: © Liberty Collection/The Image Bank; p. 549: © Meryl Rosner/The Image Bank; p. 552: Culver Pictures; p. 553: The Granger Collection, New York; p. 559: The Berg Collection/The New York Public Library; p. 561: Doran H. Ross, Los Angeles; p. 564: Culver Pictures; p. 570: The Granger Collection, New York; p. 575: Culver Pictures; p. 576: Culver Pictures; p. 582: Culver Pictures; p. 590: The Granger Collection, New York; p. 602: AP/Wide World Photos; p. 604: Arthur Rothstein; p. 613: UPI/Bettmann Newsphotos; p. 615: Roland Freeman; p. 621: Harbaugh/Rothco Cartoons. **Unit 8** p. 628: Rapho Agence/Photo Researchers; p. 630: The Library of Congress, Manuscript Division; p. 631: © 1987, Donna Van Der Zee; p. 632: Rebus, Inc.; p. 633: The Bettmann Archive; p. 635: Giraudon/Art Resource New York; p. 638: Culver Pictures; p. 641: Christie's; p. 642: Dennis Stock/Magnum; p. 644: The Granger Collection, New York; p. 647: The Bettmann Archive; p. 649: Sotheby's; p. 652: The Bettmann Archive; p. 653: UPI/Bettmann Newsphotos; p. 654: Ross Jacana/The Image Bank; p. 657: Photo courtesy of The Museum of Fine Arts, Boston; p. 661: The New York Public Library; p. 664: Sotheby's; p. 671: D. P. Hershkowitz/Bruce Coleman, Inc.; p. 672: The Granger Collection, New York; p. 674: Private Collection; p. 676: UPI/Bettmann Newsphotos; p. 678: © Horst Schaefer/Peter Arnold Inc.; p. 680: The Granger Collection, New York; p. 682: Studio Museum, Harlem; p. 685: © 1983 Eve Arnold/Magnum; p. 688: UPI/Bettmann Newsphotos; p. 691: Photo: Chris Eden; p. 694: The Granger Collection, New York; p. 699: Fisher/Punch/Rothco Cartoons: p. 700: Rebus, Inc. **Unit 9** p. 707: Culver Pictures; p. 715: The Bettmann Archive; p. 717: Culver Pictures; p. 718: Gordon R. Gainer/The Stock Market; p. 719: Jeffrey Gove/The Image Bank; p. 721: Photo courtesy of Jay Johnson, America's Folk Heritage Gallery, New York; p. 722: Alvis Upitis/The Image Bank; p. 724: The Bettmann Archive; pp. 726–727: Nicholas DeVore III/Bruce Coleman Inc.; p. 729: The Bettmann Archive; p. 730: The Bettmann Archive; p. 735: AP/Wide World; p. 738: Photo: D. James Dee; p. 740: UPI/Bettmann Newsphotos; p. 741: Bob Rubic/Gotham Book Mart; p. 750: The Bettmann Archive, p. 751: Bob Rubic/Gotham Book Mart; p. 753: Judy Lee Wade/Rebus, Inc. **Unit 10** p. 757: The Triton Gallery; p. 759: Philip Prosen/The Image Bank; p. 762: Inge Morath/Magnum; p. 763: PLAYBILL®, Inc. Used by permission; p. 764: PLAYBILL®, Inc. Used by permission; p. 765: Culver Pictures; p. 766: PLAYBILL®, Inc. Used by permission; p. 767: p. 768: The Bettmann Archive; Martha Swope; pp. 769–805: T. Charles Erickson, The Long Wharf Theater, New Haven, Connecticut; p. 812: The Bettmann Archive; pp. 813–863: Billy Rose Theatre

1242

Collection, The New York Public Library for the Performing Arts, Astor, Lenox and Tilden Foundations. Photos by Bob Rubic. **Unit 11** p. 870: Culver Pictures; p. 871: Photo courtesy of The Phyllis Kind Gallery, Chicago; p. 886: SCALA/Art Resource, New York; p. 895: SCALA/Art Resource Inc.; p. 896: Santi Visalli/The Image Bank; p. 897: The Granger Collection, New York; p. 899: Joan Liftin/Magnum; p. 902: UPI/Bettmann Newsphotos; p. 911: © 1990 Robert Foothorap; p. 914: (top) Maria Taglienti/The Image Bank; (bottom) Whitney Lane/The Image Bank; p. 924: Culver Pictures; p. 926: N. R. Farbman/Life Picture Service; p. 934: Kelly Wise, Alfred A. Knopf; p. 936: Eric Meola/The Image Bank; p. 941: Bob Gelberg/The Image Bank; p. 942: Wide World Photos; p. 945: Roland Freeman; p. 953: Diana Walker, Alfred A. Knopf; p. 960: Alan Reininger/Contact Stock Images/Woodfin Camp; p. 969: Oliver Rebbot/Woodfin Camp. **Unit 12** p. 983: © David Hockney; p. 994: UPI/Bettmann Newsphotos; p. 998: Beverly Hall; p. 1003: Cornell Capa/Magnum; p. 1004: AP/Wide World Photos; p. 1014: Jim Kalett; p. 1015: Photo by James O. Milmoe; p. 1021: Schomburg Center for Research in Black Culture, The New York Public Library; p. 1025: Floyd K. Takeuchi, Alfred A. Knopf; p. 1028: Eve Arnold/Magnum; p. 1035: Cornell Capa, LIFE Magazine © Time-Warner, Inc.; p. 1039: Melissa Matine; p. 1040: © Jeff Reinking/Picture Group; p. 1044: Rubén Guzmán; p. 1048: The Granger Collection, New York; p. 1049: Culver Pictures; p. 1052: Shunkichi/Kikuchi/Magnum; p. 1058: © 1988 Thomas Victor; p. 1059: Leroy Massie; p. 1064: Sigrid Estrada; p. 1067: Melchior DiGiacomo/The Image Bank; p. 1070: Robert Lindholm; p. 1078: Culver Pictures; p. 1079: Culver Pictures; p. 1080: Culver Pictures; p. 1081: Schwadron/Rothco Cartoons. **Unit 13** p. 1087: Burt Glinn/Magnum; p. 1088: Rollie McKenna; p. 1092: LeRoy Woodson, Jr./Wheeler Pictures; p. 1093: Rollie McKenna; p. 1098: UPI/Bettmann Newsphotos; p. 1100: The Granger Collection, New York; p. 1102: The Bettmann Archive; p. 1103: UPI/Bettmann Newsphotos; p. 1106: R. Avery/Stock, Boston; p. 1108: Clemens Kalischer; p. 1109: © Bill O'Conner/Peter Arnold Inc.; p. 1117: Thomas Victor; p. 1119: © Rollie McKenna; p. 1122: UPI/Bettmann Newsphotos; p. 1124: © Rollie McKenna; p. 1125: SCALA/Art Resource, New York; p. 1130: © Christopher Little/Outline Press, p. 1131: © Bruce Hucko.

Table of Contents p. viii: Collection of Dr. William Greenspon. Photo: Whitney Museum of American Art; p. x: Calouste Gulbenkian Museum, Lisbon, Portugal; p. xi: Chicago Historical Society; p. xiii: Bob Gelberg/The Image Bank; p. xv: © Bruce Hucko; p. xvi: Patti McConville/The Image Bank.

1243

INDEX OF AUTHORS AND TITLES

Page numbers in italic type refer to the pages on which author biographies appear.

1245